THE ROUTLEDGE DICTIONARY OF HISTORICAL SLANG

THE ROUTLEDGE DICTIONARY OF HISTORICAL SLANG

ERIC PARTRIDGE

ABRIDGED BY JACQUELINE SIMPSON

ROUTLEDGE & KEGAN PAUL
LONDON

This cloth-bound edition, first published in 1973
by Routledge & Kegan Paul Ltd
Broadway House, 68-74 Carter Lane,
London EC4V 5EL,
is based on A Dictionary of Slang and Unconventional English, *first published by Routledge & Kegan Paul Ltd in 1937. Revised and enlarged editions appeared in 1938, 1949, 1951 and 1961. From the last of these, published in two volumes, this book has been compiled.*

Printed in Great Britain by
Unwin Brothers Limited
The Gresham Press, Old Woking, Surrey, England
A member of the Staples Printing Group

ISBN 0 7100 7761 0

A NOTE ON THIS EDITION

This book is an abridgement of the 1961 edition of Eric Partridge's *A Dictionary of Slang and Unconventional English*, containing only those words and expressions which were already in use before the First World War, and which may therefore be considered as historical, rather than modern, slang. The process of abridgement has also entailed omitting solecisms, malapropisms and grammatical points recorded in the 1961 edition.

ABBREVIATIONS AND SIGNS

abbr.	abbreviation, or shortening; abbreviated, abridged
adj.	adjective
adv.	adverb
after	after the fashion of; on the analogy of
anon.	anonymous
app.	apparently
Apperson	G. L. Apperson, *English Proverbs and Proverbial Phrases*, 1929
A.-S.	Anglo-Saxon
B.	Sidney J. Baker, *Australian Slang*, 1942
B. & L.	Barrère & Leland's *A Dictionary of Slang, Jargon and Cant*, 1889 (A–K)–1890 (L–Z).
B. & P.	Brophy & Partridge, *Songs and Slang of the British Soldier 1914–18*, 3rd ed., 1931
Baumann	Heinrich Baumann's *Londonismen*, 1887
B.E.	B.E.'s *Dictionary of the Canting Crew*, ca 1690. (Better dated 1698–9)
Bee	'Jon Bee', *Dictionary of the Turf*, 1823
Bowen	F. Bowen's *Sea Slang*, 1929
Boxiana	Pierce Egan, *Boxiana*, 4 vols., 1818–24
Brandon	Brandon's Glossary of Cant in 'Ducange Anglicus'
c.	cant, i.e. language of the underworld
C.	century; as C.18, the 18th century
c. and low	cant and low slang
ca	about (the year . . .)
cf.	compare
C.O.D.	*Concise Oxford Dictionary*
Coles	E. Coles, *Dictionary*, 1676
coll	colloquial(ism)
Collinson	W. E. Collinson, *Contemporary English*, 1927
c.p.	a catch-phrase
d.	died
Dawson	L. Dawson's *Nicknames and Pseudonyms*, 1908
dial.	dialect; dialectal(ly)
Dict.	Dictionary
D.N.B.	*Dictionary of National Biography*
'Ducange Anglicus'	his *The Vulgar Tongue*, 1857
ed.	edition
E.D.D.	*The English Dialect Dictionary*, by Joseph Wright, 1896–1905
e.g.	for example
Egan's Grose	See 'Grose' below
Eng.	English
esp.	especially
ex	from; derived from
F. & Gibbons	Fraser & Gibbons, *Soldier and Sailor Words and Phrases*, 1925

F. & H.	Farmer & Henley's *Slang and its Analogues*, 7 vols., 1890–1904
fig.	figurative(ly)
fl.	flourished (*floruit*)
Fr.	French
Franklyn	Julian Franklyn, *Dictionary of Rhyming Slang*, 1960
gen.	general(ly); usual(ly)
Ger.	German
Gr.	Greek
Grose	Grose's *Dictionary of the Vulgar Tongue* (1785, 1788, 1796, 1811, 1823). Hence, Egan's Grose = Egan's ed. of Grose, 1823. Grose, P. = my annotated reprint of the 3rd ed.
G.W.	the Great War, 1914–18
H.	J. C. Hotten, *The Slang Dictionary*, 1859, 1860, etc.
ibid. (ib.)	in the same authority or book
id.	the same
i.e.	that is
imm.	immediately
Irwin	Godfrey Irwin, *American Tramp and Underworld Slang*, 1931
It.	Italian
j.	jargon, i.e. technical(ity)
Jice Doone	Jice Doone, *Timely Tips to New Australians*, 1926
Jon Bee	see 'Bee'
L.	Latin
Lewis	W. J. Lewis, *The Language of Cricket*, 1934
Lex. Bal.	*The Lexicon Balatronicum*, or 4th ed. of Grose, 1811
lit.	literal(ly)
literary	literary English, i.e. unused in ordinary speech
Lyell	T. Lyell's *Slang, Phrase and Idiom in Colloquial English*, 1931
Mayhew	Henry Mayhew, *London Labour and the London Poor*, 3 vols., 1851
M.E.	Middle English
M.L.	Medieval Latin
mod.	modern
Morris	E. E. Morris, *Austral English*, 1898
n.	noun
N.B.	note carefully
Nevinson, 1895	H. W. Nevinson, *Neighbours of Ours*, 1895
ob.	obsolescent; cf. †
occ.	occasional(ly)
O.E.	Old English; i.e. before ca 1150
O.E.D. (Sup.)	*The Oxford English Dictionary* (Supplement)
on	on the analogy of
Onions	C. T. Onions, *A Shakespeare Glossary*, ed. of 1913
opp.	opposite; as opposed to
orig.	original(ly)
Pettman	C. Pettman, *Africanderisms*, 1913
pl.	plural; in the plural

Port.	Portuguese
ppl	participle; participial
p.ppl	past participle
prob.	probable, probably
pron.	pronounced; pronunciation
pub.	published
Pugh	Edwin Pugh, *The Cockney at Home*, 1914
Pugh (2)	Edwin Pugh, *The Spoilers*, 1906
q.v.	which see!
resp.	respective(ly)
s.	slang
sc.	supply!; understand!
S.E.	Standard English
Sessions	*Session Paper of the Central Criminal Court*, 1729–1913
Sinks	Anon., *Sinks of London Laid Open*, 1848
Slang	My *Slang To-Day and Yesterday*, revised ed., 1935
Smart & Crofton	B. C. Smart & H. T. Crofton, *The Dialect of the English Gypsies*, revised ed., 1875
S.O.D.	*The Shorter Oxford Dictionary*
sol.	solecism; solecistic
Sp.	Spanish
Spy	C. E. Westmacott, *The English Spy*, 1825; vol. II, 1826
s.v.	see at
temp.	in or at the time of
Thornton	R. H. Thornton's *American Glossary*, 1912
U.S.	The United States of America; American
v.	verb. Hence, v.i., intransitive; v.t., transitive
Vaux	J. H. Vaux's 'Glossary of Cant, 1812', in his *Memoirs*, 1819
vbl n.	verbal noun
vulg.	vulgar(ism). I.e. a word, in no way slangy, avoided in polite society
W.	Ernest Weekley's *Etymological Dictionary of Modern English*
Ware	J. Redding Ware's *Passing English*, 1909
Weekley	see 'W.' above
Words!	My *Words, Words, Words!*, 1933
Yule & Burnell	Yule & Burnell, *Hobson-Jobson*, revised ed., 1903
— (before a date)	known to exist then and presumably used some years earlier
+ (after a date)	in significant first use then, but still extant
†	obsolete; cf. ob.
=	equal(s); equal to; equivalent to
>	become(s); became
* (before a word)	a cant term

A date, unpreceded by 'ca', signifies that this is the earliest discovered record; it is well to bear in mind, however, that in slang, cant, colloquialism, catch-phrase, and solecism, the first *use* goes back generally a few, occasionally many, years earlier.

The boundary between historical and modern slang, for the purposes of the present work, has been set at 1914.

A NOTE ON ARRANGEMENT

There are two main systems of arranging words in a dictionary. The strictly alphabetical; the 'something before nothing'. No system is wholly satisfactory; the arrangements in the O.E.D., in Webster and, to compare small things with great, the present dictionary are open to severe criticism – severe but unreasonable. No arrangement is, for no arrangement can be, perfect.

Here, the 'something before nothing' system has been adopted – for the simple reason that it is the most suitable to a dictionary of this kind. Thus *A.B.* precedes *abaddon*, but it also precedes *Aaron*. Perhaps an example is more illuminating: *a; A.B.; A.B.C.; ABC, as easy as; a-cockbill; A.D.; a.f.; A from a windmill; A1; Aaron; abaa; abaddon*. Further, all *come* (or *come-*) terms, beginning with *come*, including *come it*, *come out*, *come the . . .*, and ending with *come Yorkshire*, precede *comedy-merchant*. Phrases in which the headword comes last precede those in which it comes first; thus *bell, sound as a* precedes *bell, book and candle*. Phrases in which the headword is in the plural or in the genitive do not immediately follow those where the headword is in the nominative singular, but take their own alphabetical place; thus *bells down* follows *bellowser* (not *bell-rope*), and *bull's eye* follows *bullocky* (not *bull-puncher*). Terms that are spelt both as two words (e.g. *cock-tail*) and as one (*cocktail*) present a difficulty; I give them as, e.g., *cock-tail*, and at, e.g., *cocktail* insert a cross-reference: to scholars, some of these precautions may seem mere foolishness, but there are others to be considered. Cross-references to words included elsewhere in this dictionary are set in small capitals; references in italics are to S.E., dialect, or foreign words, or to modern colloquialisms, etc.

TECHNICAL TERMS

Back-slang. See *Slang*, pp. 276–7. The earliest reference to it which I have seen occurs in G. W. M. Reynolds's *Pickwick Abroad*, 1839, p. 587 (footnote).

Cant is the 'secret' speech of the underworld. This word *cant* dates from ca 1700 – *canting* is much earlier – and was long contemptuous and almost coll, as is the v., which dates from ca 1600; likewise *canter*, *canting*. See my *Slang*; Grose, P.; O.E.D.; F. & H.; and Weekley.

Centre slang, see *Slang*, pp. 277–8.

Grafters' slang is the s. used by those who work a line at fair or market, e.g. as fortune-teller or quack doctor. Some of it is Parlary, some Romany, some Yiddish, some rhyming s.; some of it, too, verges on c. The authority on the subject is Mr Philip Allingham: see his fascinating *Cheapjack*, 1934.

Hobson-Jobson. The deliberate perversion of foreign words into approximately similar-sounding English ones.

'Inevitable' nicknames are of two classes: general; particular. The general denote nationality (FROG (2); IKEY; JOCK; MICK; TAFFY) or a physical trait (BLUEY (4); SNOWY (2); TINY).

The particular, which are the 'inevitable nicknames' *par excellence*, attach themselves to certain surnames; like the general, they are rarely bestowed on women.

They app. arose first in the Navy (see esp. PINCHER (3); cf. NOBBY (2) and TUG (3)) and soon – by 1890 or so – reached the Army. They derive from the commonness of some phrase, as in '*Happy* Day' and '*Hooky* Walker'; from an historical or a vocational association, as in '*Pedlar* Palmer', '*Dusty* Miller', and '*Shoey* Smith'; from a merely semantic suggestion, as in '*Lackery* (or *Timber*) Wood' and '*Shiner* White'; rarely from a neat phrasal connection as in '*Jumper* Cross' (*jump across*); occ. from a well-known trade article or advertisement, as in '*Blanco* White' and '*Johnny* Walker'; from a famous personage, as in '*Pincher* Martin', '*Nobby* Ewart', '*Spiky* Sullivan' – the largest of the ascertained-origin groups; and from some anecdotal cause or incidental (or local) notoriety, as in '*Pills* Holloway', '*Rattler* Morgan'.

F. & H.; Bowen; and personal research. For an article on the subject, see *A Covey of Partridge*, 1937.

Lingua Franca is a mixture of Italian, French, Greek, and Spanish used for intercommunication between traders in the Eastern Mediterranean and Near East.

marrowskying. The transposition of the initials of words (as in *poke a smipe*, smoke a pipe), with variant adj. and n. *marrowsky* or *mowrowsky*: ca 1860–1900. In 1848 described by Albert Smith as *Gower Street dialect* (cf. MEDICAL GREEK), it was affected by students of London University and constitutes *spoonerism* before the letter. Perhaps ex the name of a Polish count, as the O.E.D. suggests. See esp. *Slang* at 'Oddities'.

Mumpers' talk is tramps' c. Thus 'No. 747', *The Autobiography of a Gipsy*, speaks of 'that strange mixture of thieves' Latin and mumpers' talk which has so often done duty for genuine Romnimus' (Romany).

Oxford '*-er*'. At Oxford, it began late in 1875 and came from Rugby School. By this process, the original word is changed and gen. abridged; then *-er* is added. Thus, *memorial* > *memugger*, the *Radcliffe* Camera > *the Radder* (for *the* is prefixed where the original has *the*). Occ. the word is pluralized, where the original ends in *s*: as in *Adders*, Addison's Walk, *Jaggers*, Jesus College. This *-er* has got itself into gen. upper-middle class s. See esp. *Slang*, revised ed. (1935), pp. 208–9.

Parlary. The 'Lingua Franca' – but actually as to 90% of its words, Italianate – vocabulary of C.18–mid-19 actors and mid-C.19–20 costermongers and showmen: (orig. low) coll. (How long the word itself has existed, I do not know: prob. not before ca 1850, when the vocabulary was much enlarged and the principal users changed so radically, though itinerant and inferior actors supply the link.) Ex It. *parlare*, to speak. cf. PALARIE and see *Slang*, *passim*, and at 'Circus Slang,' and P. Allingham's *Cheapjack*, 1934. e.g. DONAH; LETTY; MADZA; MUNGAREE; NANTEE; OMEE; SALTEE; SAY; TRAY (3).

A full account of this Cinderella among languages appears in my book of essays and studies upon language, *Here, There and Everywhere*, 1949.

Parlary is more general than the less serviceable Parlyaree. In late C.19–early 20, *palarey* or *palary* was very common, esp. among music-hall artists. Sydney Lester's title for his glossary, *Vardi the Palary*, means 'Know Parlary'.

pidgin, rarely **pidjun,** often **pigeon**; occ. **pidjin.** Pidgin- or pigeon-English, 'the jargon, consisting chiefly of English words, often corrupted in pronunciation, and arranged according to Chinese idiom, used for intercommunication between Chinese and Europeans at seaports, etc.', S.O.D.: coll abbr. >: from ca 1855. (By itself, *pidgin*, etc., occurs in 1850.) A Chinese corruption of *business*, perhaps via *bidginess*, *bidgin*; *pigeon* is an English 'improvement' on *pidgin*.

Rhyming slang dates from ca 1840; originated among Cockneys, where now still commonest; eschewed by the middle and upper classes, it had its apotheosis in the First World War. e.g. ABRAHAM'S WILLING, a shilling; the second word is often (but by no means always) suppressed, as in ELEPHANT'S (TRUNK), drunk. See my *Slang*, revised ed.

The entire question of rhyming s. has, for the first time, been adequately treated by Julian Franklyn in *Rhyming Slang*, 1960: a history and a study, a glossary and even a 'reverse' glossary. This book covers Great Britain and Ireland, Australia and the U.S.

Romany. The language of the English Gypsies. It contributes many words to c. and to low s., esp. grafters'.

Shelta is 'a kind of cryptic Irish spoken by tinkers and confirmed tramps; a secret jargon composed chiefly of Gaelic words disguised by changes of initial, transposition of letters, back-slanging and similar devices', F. & H. Discovered in 1876 by Leland, who published his account of it in his *Gypsies*, 1882: considerable attention has been paid to it since the Gypsy Lore Society started in 1889, its Journal in 1890. (See, e.g., TOBY.)

'Travelling language' is a C.18 term – it occurs, e.g., in Bampfylde-Moore Carew – for the s. of vagabonds and, to a less degree, of criminals.

Ziph. That ancient linguistic aberration which consists in saying, e.g., *shagall wege gogo* for *shall we go*. See *Slang*, p. 278.

A

A.B. An able-bodied seaman (—1875): coll by 1900. *Chambers's Journal*, No. 627, 1875.

A.B.C. An Aerated Bread Company's tea-shop: from ca 1880; coll. 2. At Christ's Hospital, C.19, ale, bread and cheese on 'going-home night'.

ABC, (as) easy as. Extremely easy or simple to do: C.19–20. Adumbrated in 1595 by Shakespeare's 'then comes answer like an Absey booke'. Always coll.

a-cockbill. Free; dangling free; nautical coll (—1887).

A.D. A drink: male dancers' coll (—1909) inscribed on dance-programmes; ob.

a.f. Having met with (come across) a 'flat' (q.v.), who has, to the speaker's advantage, laid his bets all wrong: the turf (—1823); †by 1870.

A from a windmill or the gable-end, not to know. To be very ignorant, or illiterate: coll: resp. C.15, C.19–20 (ob.). See also B FROM . . .

A1. Excellent, first-class: first of ships (Lloyd's Register); then of persons and things, Dickens, 1837. U.S. form: *A No. 1*. Variants, *A1 copper-bottomed* (Charles Hindley, 1876), now ob.; *A1 at Lloyd's* (from ca 1850); *first-class, letter A, No. 1* (—1860). 2. A commander of 900 men: Fenian coll > j.: ca 1865–90. Erroneously *No. 1*. (A lower officer was known as *B*.)

***Aaron,** in c., a cadger; *the Aaron*, a captain of thieves. ?C.17–19. cf. ABANDANNAD, a pickpocket.

abaa. A non-unionist; hence, adj.: silly. Proletarian (—1903).

***abaddon.** A thief turned informer: c.: late C.19–20; ob. ?a pun on *a bad 'un* and the angel *Abaddon*.

***abandannad.** A thief specializing in BANDANNA handkerchiefs: c. (—1864). There is perhaps a pun on *abandoned*. 2. Hence, any petty thief: c.: late C.19–20; virtually †.

abandoned habits. The riding dresses of demi-mondaines in Hyde Park: ca 1870–1900.

abandonment. Bankruptcy of a railway company: financiers' and brokers': ca 1880–1905.

abber. At Harrow School, an abstract or an absit: from 1890s. Oxford *-er*, see p. 11.

abbess (1782+), **Lady Abbess** (—1785). The keeper of a brothel: late C.18–19. A procuress: C.19. Ex Fr. *abbesse*, a female brothel-keeper. cf. ABBOT and see esp. F. & H. *Peter Pindar*, John Wolcot (d. 1819):

> So an old abbess, for the rattling rakes,
> A tempting dish of human nature makes,
> And dresses up a luscious maid.

abbey lubber. A lazy monk: ca 1538–1750: coll >, by 1600, S.E. 2. A lazy, thriftless person: nautical, ca 1750–1900.

abbot. The husband, or the preferred male, of a brothel-keeper (see ABBESS): C.19. cf. the old S.E. terms, *abbot of misrule*, *abbot of unreason*, a leader in a disorderly festivity.

Abbott's teeth. A ca 1820–40 variant of ELLENBOROUGH'S TEETH. Pierce Egan, *Life in London*, 1821.

abdar. A teetotaller: Anglo-Indian: from ca 1870. Ex Hindustani for a water-carrier.

abel-w(h)ackets, see ABLE-W(H)ACKETS.

Aberdeen cutlet. A dried haddock: from ca 1870. By F. & H. denoted familiar, but definitely s. Ob. cf. BILLINGSGATE PHEASANT; YARMOUTH CAPON.

Abergavenny. A penny: rhyming: since ca 1880.

Abigail. A lady's-maid: from ca 1616, though not recorded fig. till 47 years later: coll >, by 1800, S.E. Ex the Bible. In Beaumont & Fletcher, Fielding, Smollett; coll from ca 1700. Now outmoded literary.

***abishag.** Illegitimate child of a mother seduced by a married man: c.: from ca 1860; slightly ob. Ex Hebrew for 'the mother's error'.

able-w(h)ackets, wrongly *abel-w(h)ackets*. A nautical card-game in which every lost point – or game – entails a whack with a knotted handkerchief: coll: from ca 1780; †by 1883: witness Clark Russell's nautical dictionary.

Abney Park, to have gone to. To be dead: proletarian London (—1909); very ob. Ex Abney Park Cemetery.

abnormality; abnormeth. 'A person of crooked ways, an informer, a deformed or humpbacked person': resp. from ca 1880 and ca 1840–80. By confusion of *abnormal* and *enormity*.

abo; Abo. An aboriginal: Australian coll: mid-C.19–20, orig. journalistic. Jice Doone.

aboard of, fall. To meet (a person): nautical coll (—1887).

abominable. A late C.19–20 sol., or jocular coll, for *abdominal*; esp. in *abominable pains*. 2. Very unpleasant: coll, from ca 1860: the same with the adv. **(-ably)**. cf. the S.E. senses and:

abominate. To dislike 'intensely', i.e. very much: from ca 1875. Coll.

about, the other way. (Fig.) precisely the contrary: gen. in reference to a statement just made. Coll, from ca 1860.

about one, have something. 'To show character or ability'; to be, in some undefined or intangible way, charming or, perhaps because of some mystery, fascinating: coll (and dial.): from ca 1890 (?earlier). E.D.D. (Sup.), 'That fellow has something about him, I must admit.' cf. the analogous use of *there's something to* (a person or a thing).

about proper. An illiterate variant of PROPER, adv.

about right. Correct; adequate. Frank Smedley, 1850. Coll.

about the size of it. Approximately (right): from ca 1870, coll; ?orig. U.S.

above board. Openly; without artifice or dishonesty. Coll verging on, and occ. achieving, S.E. Ex position of hands in card-playing for money. Earliest record, 1608.

above par. In excellent health, spirits, money in hand, mild drunkenness. All from ca 1870, ex stocks and shares at a premium. cf. *below par*.

abrac; Abrac. Learning: ca 1820–50. Corruption of *Arabic* or abbr. of *abracadabra*.

Abraham. 'A clothier's shop of the lowest description': chiefly East End of London and ex the Jewish name; ca 1870–1920. 2. The penis: low: late C.19–20; ob. Whence *Abraham's bosom*, the female pudend.

Abra(ha)m, sham, see ABRA(HA)M-SHAM.

***Abra(ha)m-cove or -man.** A pseudo-madman seeking alms; a genuine lunatic allowed on certain days to leave Bethlehem Hospital (whence *bedlam beggar*) to beg. The term flourished most ca 1550–1700, *A. cove* being, however, unrecorded in C.16; this sense > archaic only ca 1830; ex Luke xvii (Lazarus); described by Awdelay, Harman, Shakespeare, Massinger, B.E., Grose. 2. Also, in late C.18–19, a mendicant pretending to be an old naval rating cast on the streets. cf. ABRAM. 3. (Only **Abram man.**) A thief of pocket-books: c. (—1823); †by 1870.

Abra(ha)m-sham. A feigned illness or destitution: C.19. Ex *sham Abra(ha)m*, to pretend sickness (—1759), in C.19 mainly nautical and often *do Abra(ha)m*; also – see ABRAHAM NEWLAND – to forge banknotes, †by 1840.

***Abraham Grains** (or **g-**). A publican brewing his own beer: c.: late C.19–20.

Abraham Newland. A banknote, ex the Bank of England's chief cashier of 1778–1807: ca 1780–1830; Glascock uses it in 1829. H., 2nd ed. (1860), records the c.p. (?orig. the words of a song), *sham Abraham you may, but you mustn't sham Abraham Newland.*

***Abraham suit, on the.** Engaged in any begging-letter dodge that will arouse sympathy: c.: from ca 1860: ob.

abraham (or abram) work. Any sham or swindle, esp. if commercial: mid-C.19–20; ob. As adj. *abra(ha)m* = spurious, as in c. ABRAHAM SUIT, false pretences or representations: C.19.

Abrahamer. A vagrant: low (—1823); †by 1900. 'Jon Bee', who defines *Abrahamers* as 'a lot, or receptacle full of beggars, half naked, ragged, and dirty': an ambiguous set of words.

Abraham's balsam. Death by hanging: C.18 low. Punning S.E. *Abraham's balm* (tree).

Abraham's willing. A shilling: rhyming s. (—1859).

abram. A malingerer: C.19–20 nautical; ob. 2. As adj., c.: mad, C.16–17; naked, C.17–18, this latter developing ex *auburn* corrupted, for (as in Shakespeare) *abra-(ha)m*, later *abram-coloured*, = auburn, hence fair. cf. the *abrannoi* (naked) of Hungarian Gypsy. 3. For *sham Abram*, see ABRA(HA)M-SHAM.

abram, v. To feign sickness: ?ca 1840–90. *Sinks*, 1848. Perhaps rhyming s.

***abram cove.** 'A Naked or poor Man, also a lusty strong Rogue', B.E.; the latter being of the 17th Order of the Canting Crew: c.: C.17–early 19. cf. ABRAM, 2.

Abram man, see ABRAHAM-MAN. **Abram-sham,** see ABRAHAM-SHAM. **abram work,** see ABRAHAM WORK.

abridgements. Knee-breeches. ?Nonce word: Bulwer Lytton's play, *Money*, 1840.

abroad. In error, wide of the mark (Dickens); earlier (Pierce Egan, 1821), *all abroad*, with additional sense of 'confused';

all abroad is, in the former sense, now ob. From ca 1860; both coll. 2. Also, (of convicts) transported: ca 1810–90. 3. At Winchester College, C.19, (*come*) *abroad* meant to return to work after being ill.

abroaded. Living on the Continent as a defaulter from England: Society, 1860–90. 2. Sent to a penal settlement whether at home or in the Colonies: police, ca 1840–80. cf. ABROAD (2). 3. In c., imprisoned anywhere: ca 1870–1920.

abs. At Winchester College in C.19, now ob.: **abs**ent; to take away; to depart (quickly). ca 1840, *abs a* TOLLY, to put out a candle; late C.19–20; to extinguish a candle demands the 'notion' *dump* it. To *have one's wind absed* is to get a 'breather' or 'winder'.

***abscotchalater,** see ABSQUATULATE.

absence without leave, give (one). To discharge (one) suddenly from employment: from ca 1820; ob.

absent without leave. (Of one) having absconded: from ca 1860. 2. In c., escaped from prison: id.

absent-minded beggar. A soldier: semi-jocular coll: 1899–1902. Ex Kipling's poem.

absentee. A convict: semi-euphemistic coll: ca 1810–60.

absolutely true. Utterly false: Society: ca 1880. Ex title of book.

absquatulate. To depart, gen. hastily or in disgrace. Anglicized ca 1860, ob. by 1900; orig. U.S. (1837). An artificial word: perhaps on *abscond* and *squat*, with a L. ending. Hence *absquatulating*, *-ize*, *-ation*, *-ator*, not very gen.; and **abscotchalater*, one in hiding from the police. 2. v.t., rare: to cause to do so: 1844 (O.E.D.).

Abyssinian medal. A button showing in the fly: military: ca 1896–1914. Ex the Abyssinian War (1893–6).

Ac, the. The Royal Academy: artists': from ca 1870; slightly ob.

academic nudity. 'Appearance in public without cap or gown', Ware: Oxford University (—1909).

academician. A harlot: ca 1760–1820. Ex *academy*, a brothel: c. of late C.17–18. In C.19, *academy* = a thieves' school: cf. Fagin in *Oliver Twist*. But in late C.19–20, *academy* is also a hard-labour prison and (—1823) its inmates are *academicians*.

academics. (University) cap and gown: from ca 1820; ob. Coll rather than s.; the j. would be *academicals*.

Academite. 'A graduate of the old Royal Naval Academy at Portsmouth': nautical coll: from ca 1870; ob. Bowen.

***Academy.** See ACADEMICIAN. 2. A billiard-room: ca 1885–1910. Ware, 'Imported from Paris'.

Academy, the. Platonism and Platonists: from the 1630s: academic s. >, in C.18 university coll >, by 1830, philosophic j. The other four of the chief schools of Greek philosophy are *The Garden* (Epicureanism), *The Lyceum* (Aristotelianism), *The Porch* (Stoicism), and *The Tub* (Cynicism): same period and changes of status. 2. A lunatic asylum: ca 1730–90. Alexander Cruden in a pamphlet of 1754.

acater. A ship chandler: nautical coll C.19–20; ob. A survival of †S.E. *acatur*, a purveyor: ex Fr. *acheteur*, a buyer.

***acceleration.** Starvation; esp. *die of acceleration*: vagrants' c.; from ca 1880; ob. Also **accelerator,** a Union relieving officer: id. Ex refusals 'to give food to the dying outcast'.

accident. An untimely, or accidental, call of nature: coll: 1899.

accident-maker. A report dealing with accidents and disasters: London journalists' (—1887).

accommodation house. A brothel; a disorderly house; from ca 1820, now ob. Coll.

***accommodator.** One who negotiates a compounding of felonies or other crimes: c.: from ca 1870: ob.

according, that's. A coll abbr. of the cautious *that's according to*, i.e. dependent on, *the circumstances*. (Not in the sense, in accordance *with*.)

according to Cocker. Properly, correctly. From ca 1760, ex Edward Cocker (d. 1675). The U.S. phrase (partly acclimatized in England by 1909: Ware) is *according to Gunter*, a famous mathematician: the C.19 nautical, *according to John Norie*, the editor of a much-consulted Navigators' Manual. cf.:

according to Hoyle. Correct; correctly: coll: late C.19–20. Ex Edmond Hoyle's *The Polite Gamester*, 1752; soon titled *Mr Hoyle's Games of Whist . . .*, 12th edition, 1760; then as *Hoyle's Games Improved*, 1786; in C.19, there appeared innumerable re-editings, improvements, enlargements, abridgements. cf. ACCORDING TO COCKER.

account, go on the. To turn pirate, or buccaneer (—1812). Coll, †. Scott.

account for. To kill: from ca 1840

(Thackeray, 1842). Sporting coll >, by 1890, S.E.

accounts, cast up one's. To vomit: C.17–19. A nautical variant, C.19–20: *audit one's accounts at the court of Neptune*. 2. In c., to turn King's evidence: mid-C.19–20; ob.

accumulator. (Racing) a better carrying forward a win to the next event: from ca 1870.

ace, king, queen, jack. A jocular non-Catholic description of the sign of the Cross: late C.19–20.

ace of spades. A widow: C.19. 2. The female pudend: low: mid-C.19–20. F. & H., 'Hence, *to play one's ace and take the Jack = to receive a man*'. 3. A widow: low (—1811); †by 1890. 4. A black-haired woman: proletarian (—1903).

ace of, within an. Almost: C.18–20: coll >, by 1800, S.E. 'Facetious' Tom Brown, 1704. Orig. *ambs-* or *ames-ace*.

acid drop. A rating that's always either arguing or quarrelling or complaining: naval: since ca 1900. Granville.

ack! No! as the refusal of a request: Christ's Hospital, C.19. cf. Romany *ac!*, stuff!

***ackman,** c., is a fresh-water thief: mid-C.18–19. Corruption of ARKMAN. F. & H. adduces also *ack-pirate* and *ack-riff*.

acknowledge the corn, v.i. Admit, acknowledge (Sala, 1883); ob. Ex U.S. (—1840), to admit failure or outwitting.

***acorn, a horse foaled by an.** The gallows; gen. as *ride a horse . . .*, to be hanged: c.: late C.17–mid-19. Motteux, Ainsworth. cf. THREE- or WOODEN-LEGGED MARE.

acquaintance, scrape (an). To make acquaintance. Coll: Farquhar, 1698, 'no scraping acquaintance, for Heaven's sake'.

acre, knave's. A mid-C.16–early 17 variant of WEEPING CROSS. See also BEGGAR'S BUSH for a very pertinent quotation.

Acres, Bob Acres. A coward, esp. if boastful. Ex a character in Sheridan's *Rivals*, 1775. Coll, †.

acrobat. A drinking glass (—1903). Punning *tumbler*.

across, come. To meet with accidentally: mid-C.19–20: coll.

act Charley More. To act honestly; to do the fair thing. Naval: C.19–20. Granville. Charley More was a Maltese publican whose house sign bore the legend 'Charley More, the square thing'.

act of parliament. (Military) small beer perforce supplied free to a soldier: late C.18–early 19.

Acteon. A cuckold: C.17–18. 2. To cuckold: late C.17–early 18. Coll. Ex legend of Diana and Acteon, whose transformation involved horns.

acting dickey. A temporary appointment: naval (—1806); ob. on *acting order*. 2. (often *a. D.*) A man acting in the name of an enrolled solicitor: legal (—1903).

acting lady. An inferior actress: ironic theatrical coll: 1883, *Entr'acte* (February). Mrs Langtry's social-cum-theatrical success in 1882 caused many society women to try their luck on the stage; mostly with deplorable results.

acting the deceitful. (Theatrical.) Acting: C.19. Duncombe.

active citizen. A louse: low (—1811); †by 1890. cf. BOSOM FRIEND.

actor's Bible, the. *The Era*: theatrical coll: ca 1860–1918. A fling at sacred matters prompted by the sensation caused by *Essays and Reviews*.

actual, the. Money, collectively, esp. if in cash: mid-C.19–20. At this word, F. & H. has an admirable essayette on, and list of English and foreign synonyms for, money. In 1890 there were at least 130 English and 50 French synonyms.

ad. An advertisement: printers' coll: 1852 (*Household Words*, v., 5/2). Occ. *advert*, rarely *adver*.

ad lib. A coll abbr. of *ad libitum*, as much as one likes: C.19–20.

adad! An expletive: coll: ca 1660–1770. Prob. ex EGAD!

Adam. A bailiff, a police sergeant: C.16–17. Shakespeare. 2. In mid-C.17–19 c., an accomplice: with TILER following, a pickpocket's assistant. 3. A foreman: workmen's (—1903); ob.

Adam; adam, v. (Gen. in passive.) To marry: c.: 1781, G. Parker, '"What, are you and Moll *adamed*?" "Yes . . . and by a RUM TOM PAT too"'; †by 1850. Ex Adam and Eve.

Adam and Eve. To believe: rhyming s. (—1914). 2. To leave: rhyming s.: late C.19–20.

Adam and Eve's togs. Nudity: proletarian London (—1909); slightly ob. cf. BIRTHDAY SUIT.

Adamizing. A cadet's being lowered naked on to the parade ground at night, he being able to return only by presenting himself to the guard: Sandhurst: ca 1830–55. Mockler-Ferryman, 1900.

Adam, not to know (someone) from. Not to know at all: coll: mid-C.18–20. *Sessions* Feb. 1784 (p. 400).

Adam's ale. Water. Coll. C.17–18; jocular S.E. in C.19–20, but now outworn. Prynne. The Scottish equivalent is *Adam's wine* (—1859).

Adam tiler, see ADAM, n., 2.

add. To come to the correct or wished for total: coll: 1850, Dickens.

added to the list. i.e. of geldings in training; hence, castrated. Racing s. (—1874). Orig. a euphemism.

addel, see ADDLE.

Adders. Addison's Walk: Oxford University: late C.19–20. By the 'Oxford *-er*'.

addition. Paint or rouge or powder for the face: ca 1690–1770. Mrs Centlivre: 'Addition is only paint, madam.' Society s. 2. See RULE OF THREE.

addle; often spelt **addel.** Putrid drinking water: nautical: late C.19–20. Ex *addled.*

addle cove. A fool; a facile dupe: late C.18–19. On *addle-head* or *-pate.*

addle-plot. 'A Martin Mar-all', B.E.; a spoil-sport: coll: late C.17–18.

addlings. 'Pay accumulated on a voyage or during a commission': nautical, esp. naval: late C.19–20. Bowen.

a-deary me! Dear me!: lower-class coll (—1896) and dial. (—1865).

***adept.** A pickpocket; a conjuror: c.: C.18. 2. An alchemist: c.: mid-C.17–18.

adjective-jerker. A journalist: literary: late C.19–20; ob. cf. INK-SLINGER.

adjutant's gig. (Military) a roller, esp. that of the barracks: ca 1870–1914.

***Adkins's Academy.** A certain London house of correction: c. (—1823); †by 1860.

administer (a rebuke or blow). To give, deal: mid-C.19–20: jocular coll >, by 1900, S.E.

admiral, tap the. (Nautical) to drink illicitly: mid-C.19–20; ob. cf. *suck the* MONKEY. The origin of the phrase is ghoulish but interesting. A certain admiral whose name I cannot remember died while in the West Indies and as it was desired to bury him in England his coffin was filled with rum to preserve the body as was not uncommonly done in those days (about 1830–40). A guard was mounted over the coffin during the journey and this guard was frequently found drunk. Nobody could understand where the guard got the liquor until it was found that the admiral had been tapped!

admiral of the blue. A publican; a tapster: ca 1730–1860. (In C.17, the British Fleet was divided into the red, white, and blue squadrons, a division that held until late in C.19.)

admiral of the narrow seas. A drunk man vomiting into another's lap: nautical: mid-C.17–mid-19.

admiral of the red. A wine-bibber: C.19, mainly nautical. cf.:

admiral of the white. A coward: mid-C.19–20; ob. Never very much used.

admirals of the red, white, and blue. Bedizened beadles or bumbles: C.19.

Admiralty ham. Any tinned meat: naval: late C.19–20.

ado, dead for. Dead and done with: C.16–17; coll > S.E.

ado, once for. Once for all: C.17; coll > S.E.

adod! A C.17 oath: coll cf. BEDAD; EGAD.

***Adonee.** God: c.: ?ca 1550–1890; B. & L., vaguely classifying as 'old cant'. Ex Hebrew.

adonis. A kind of wig: ca 1760–1800: coll bordering on S.E. cf. *Adonis* (1765+), a beau. (O.E.D.)

adonize. (Of men) to adorn one's person: C.17–19. Society s. that > Society j.

adore. To like (very much): mid-C.19–20; (mostly Society) coll.

adrift. Harmless (C.17); discharged (C.18–19); temporarily missing or absent without leave (mid-C.19–20); wide of the mark, confused (C.20: coll). Nautical. B.E. has '*I'll turn ye adrift*, a Tar-phrase, I'll prevent ye doing me any harm'; Bowen records the third sense.

'ads. God's: a coll minced oath occurring in combination (*Adsbody, adsheart*): late C.16–early 19. Congreve, Smollett. cf. ODS and UDS.

adventure(s), at (all). At random, wholly at risk: coll >, by 1600, S.E.; late C.15–18. Caxton, Berners, Locke.

advert, see AD.

advertisement conveyancers. Sandwich men: London society: ca 1883–5. Coined by Gladstone and ridiculed by Society.

Adzooks! A coll expletive or oath: mid-C.18–mid-C.19. i.e. *God's hooks* > *'d's hooks* > *adshooks* > *Adzooks*. cf. 'ADS.

aeger. A medical certificate; a degree taken by one excused for illness (1865): coll >, by 1890, j. Ex *aegrotat* (—1794), the same – though always j.

Aetna. 'A small boiler for "brewing"': Winchester: from ca 1860; ob.

afeard. Afraid: C.16–20: S.E. until early C.18, then dial. and coll. Lit., *afeared*, terrified, ex †*afear*. Also *'feard*.

affair. Of things, esp. buildings, machines: coll from ca 1800. Gen. with a preceding adj. or a sequent adj. phrase, e.g. 'The house was a crazy affair of old corrugated iron'. 2. Male or female genitals: C.19–20. If used euphemistically, the term is ineligible; but if used lazily, the term is s.

affair of honour. A duel resulting in an innocent man's death: ca 1800–70. Coll.

affidavit men. Professional witnesses ready to swear to anything: late C.17–18. (cf. KNIGHT OF THE POST.)

affigraphy, see AFFYGRAPHY.

***afflicke,** a thief, is either c. or low: C.17. Rowlands, in *Martin Mark-all.* But see FLICK.

afflicted. Tipsy: coll: mid-C.19–20; ob. Orig. euphemistic.

afflictions. Mourning clothes and accessories: chiefly drapers', mid-C.19–20; ob. Hence, *mitigated afflictions*, half-mourning.

affygraphy, to an. Exactly, precisely. Mid-C.19–20. Sol. Perhaps a confusion of *affidavit* and *autobiography*. Also *in an affygraphy*, immediately: C.19–20. Moe. *The Night Watch* (II, 85), 1828. Perhaps influenced by *(in) half a jiffy*.

afloat; with back teeth well afloat. Drunk: from late 1880s; ob.

afore and **ahind (ahint),** before and behind resp., have, since ca 1880, been either low coll or perhaps rather sol. when they are not dial.

aft, get. To be promoted from the lower deck to the rank of officer: naval coll: C.19–20. Granville, 'the officers' quarters are in the after-part of the ship'.

aft through the hawse-hole. (Of an officer) who has gained his commission by promotion from the lower deck: Navy: mid-C.19–20. Granville. See HAWSE-HOLES.

after-dinner, or **afternoon('s), man.** An afternoon tippler: resp.: C.19–20, C.17–19: coll verging on S.E. Overbury, Earle, Smythe-Palmer.

after four, after twelve. 4–5 p.m., 12–2 p.m.: C.19 Eton; the latter is in Whyte Melville's *Good for Nothing*. Perhaps rather j. than coll.

after you with the push! A London street c.p. addressed with ironic politeness to one who has roughly brushed past: ca 1900–14.

afternoon! Good afternoon!: coll: mid-C.19–20. cf. DAY! and MORNING!

afternoon buyer. One on the look-out for bargains: provincial coll (—1903).

afternoon farmer. A procrastinator: s. only in non-farming uses. Mid-C.19–20, ob.

afternoon man, see AFTER-DINNER MAN.

afternoon tea. Detention after 3 p.m.: Royal High School, Edinburgh (—1903).

afternoonified. Smart: Society, esp. in London: 1897–ca 1914. Ware quotes an anecdote.

against. Against (i.e. for) the time when: low coll when not dial.: mid-C.19–20. J. Greenwood, 'If I don't get the breakfuss ready against Jim comes in'.

against (the) collar. In difficulties; at a disadvantage: ca 1850–1900.

against the grain. Unwilling(ly), unpleasant(ly): mid-C.17–19, coll; in C.20, S.E. Ray, Swift, Dickens.

agardente. 'Fiery spirits . . . smuggled on board in the Mediterranean': naval coll: mid-C.19–20. Bowen. Ex Sp. *agua ardiente*, brandy.

agate. A very small person: late C.16–17; coll > S.E. Ex the tiny figures cut on agate seals.

aggerawator, rarely *agg(e)ravator*; occ. *hagrerwa(i)ter* or *-or*. A well-greased lock of hair twisted spirally, on the temple, towards either the ear or the outer corner of the eye; esp. among costermongers: ca 1830–1910. For a very early mention, see Dickens's *Sketches by Boz.* cf. BOW-CATCHER; NEWGATE KNOCKER.

aggie. A marble made of agate – or of something that, in appearance, resembles agate: children's: since ca 1880. The *Manchester Evening News*, 27 March 1939.

Aggie, see. To visit the w.c.: schools': mid-C.19–20.

aggregate, v.t. To amount, in aggregate, to: 1865 (O.E.D.): coll.

agility, show one's. (Of women) in crossing a stile, in being swung, to show much of the person: ca 1870–1914. Perhaps a pun on *virility*.

agitate, v.t. To ring (a bell): jocular coll; from ca 1830.

agitator. A bell-rope; a knocker: ca 1860–1900. Ex preceding.

agony, pile up (or **on**) **the.** To exaggerate. Ex U.S. (Haliburton, 1835), anglicized ca 1855.

agony column. The personal column in a newspaper's advertisements (first in *The Times*). Laurence Oliphant, in *Piccadilly*, 1870; W. Black, 1873. Coll by 1880.

agony in red. A vermilion costume: London society: ca 1879–81. Ex Aestheticism.

agony-piler. (Theatrical) an actor of sensational parts: ca 1870–1910.

agree like bells. Explained by the fuller form, *a.l.b., they want nothing but hanging*: coll verging on (proverbial) S.E.: 1630, T. Adams; 1732, Fuller; ob. cf. the C.18–20 (ob.) *agree like pickpockets in a fair*.

agreeable ruts of life, the. The female pudend: low 'superior' (—1903); ob.

aground. At a loss; ruined: C.18–20. Coll > in C.19, S.E.

ah, que je can be bete! How stupid I am: 'half-society' (Ware): ca 1899–1912. Macaronic with Fr. *je*, I, and *bête*, stupid.

ahind, ahint, see AFORE.

aidh. Butter: Shelta: C.18–20.

aim. The person that aims: coll: from ca 1880. cf. S.E. *shot*.

ainoch. Thing: Shelta: C.18–20.

ain't it a treat. Street: rhyming s.: from ca 1870.

air, in the. (Of news, rumours) generally known or suspected, but not yet in print: C.19 coll; uncertain, problematic, remote or fanciful: C.19 coll.

air, take the. To go for a walk: coll > S.E.: C.19–20. Also, make oneself scarce: coll; from ca 1880.

***air and exercise.** A flogging at the cart's tail: c.: late C.18–early 19. 2. In C.19 c., penal servitude. 3. Ca 1820–40, 'the pillory, revolving', Bee.

air-hole. 'A small public garden, gen. a dismally converted graveyard': London society: 1885–95. Ware ascribes it to the Metropolitan Public Gardens Association.

air-man-chair. A chairman: music-halls': ca 1880–1900. By transposition of *ch* and the duplication of *air*; a variation on central s.

air one's heels. To loiter, dawdle about: mid-C.19–20: s. >, by 1900, coll.

air one's vocabulary. To talk for the sake of talking or for that of effect: coll: from ca 1820. Ob.

airing. (The turf) a race run with no intention of winning: ca 1870–1914.

airing, give it an. An imperative = take it away!; coll; from ca 1890.

airs, give oneself. To put on SIDE or SWANK: coll in C.18, then S.E. Fielding.

airy-fairy. As light or dainty as a fairy: coll, now verging on S.E.: 1869, W. S. Gilbert. Ex Tennyson's *airy, fairy Lilian*.

Ajax. A jakes, a water-closet: late C.16–18. A spate of cloacal wit was loosed by Harington's tract *The Metamorphosis of Ajax*, 1596.

ak dum. At once: military: late C.19–20. Ex Hindustani *ek dam*.

Akerman's hotel. Newgate prison. 'In 1787,' says Grose, 'a person of that name was the gaoler, or keeper.' †by 1850.

Akeybo. As in 'He beats Akeybo, and Akeybo beats the devil': proletarian (—1874); ob. cf. BANAGHAN; BANAGHER. *Akeybo*, however, remains an etymological puzzle. Is there a connection with Welsh Gypsy *ake tu!*, here thou art! (a toast: cf. HERE'S TO YOU!)?

alacompain. Rain: rhyming s. (—1859); ob. Also *alla-, ali-, eli-*. cf. FRANCE AND SPAIN.

Albany beef. North American sturgeon: nautical: mid-C.19–20. Ex that town.

albert. Abbr. *Albert chain*, a kind of watch-chain: from ca 1884; coll till ca 1901, then S.E. Ex the name of the Prince Consort of Queen Victoria.

Albertine. 'An adroit, calculating, business-like mistress': aristocratic: ca 1860–80. Ware. Ex the character so named in Dumas the Younger's *Le Père Prodigue*.

Albertopolis. Kensington Gore, London: Londoners': the 1860s. Yates, 1864; H., 1874, notes it as †. Ex Albert Prince Consort, intimately associated with this district.

albonized. Whitened: pugilistic, ca 1855–1900. Ex L. *albus*, white. cf. EBONY OPTIC.

***alderman.** A half-crown: c.: from 1830s; ob. Ex its size. 2. A long pipe (= CHURCHWARDEN): ca 1800–50. 3. A turkey, esp. if roasted and garnished with sausages: late C.18–early 20; variant *alderman in chains*. George Parker, ca 1782, says it is c. 4. Late C.19 c., precisely a 'JEMMY': see CITIZEN. *Daily Telegraph*, 14 May 1883. 5. A qualified swimmer: Felsted School: ca 1870–90. Ex the *Alders*, a deep pool in the Chelmer. 6. A prominent belly: from ca 1890. So many aldermen have one.

alderman, vote for the. To indulge in drink: ca 1810–50. cf. LUSHINGTON, and:

alderman in chains, see ALDERMAN, 3.

Alderman Lushington. Intoxicants: Australian, ca 1850–1900. Ex *Alderman* LUSHINGTON IS CONCERNED, he is drunk: a c.p. of ca 1810–50.

aldermanity. The quality of being an alderman; a body of aldermen. From ca 1625; in C.19–20, S.E. *Aldermanship* is the regular form, *aldermanity* a jocular variant, a cultured coll after *humanity*.

alderman's eyes. (House) flies: rhyming s.: since ca 1890; ob.

alderman's pace. A slow and solemn gait: C.17 coll > S.E. Cotgrave; Ray.

Aldgate, a draught or **bill on the pump at.** A bad bill of exchange: late C.18–19 commercial.

ale-draper. An ale-house keeper (implied in 1592): jocular coll >, by 1750, S.E. †by 1850. This jocular term actually occurs in the burial-entry of a Lincolnshire parish register of the C.18.

ale-head wind, beatin(g) up against an. Drunk: nautical: late C.19–20. i.e. 'tacking all over the place', esp. the pavement.

ale-knight. A drunkard; a boon companion (1575): C.16–17: coll > S.E.

ale-spinner. A brewer; a publican. C.19.

ale-stake. A tippler: coll, C.17–18. In S.E. *ale-stake* = *ale-pole*, a pole serving as an ale-house sign.

alecie, alecy. Lunacy; intoxication: Lyly, 1598. Cited as an example of pedantic nonce-words, it may be considered s. because of its derivation, after *lunacy*, from *ale* + *cy*. (N.B.: despite a subconscious belief to the contrary, culture and/or pedantry do not prevent a word from being s. or coll; indeed, culture and pedantry have their own unconventionalisms.)

alemnoch. Milk: Shelta: C.18–20.

ales, in his. In his cups, or rather his tankards of ale (*ale* orig. synonymous with *beer*): C.16–17; coll Shakespeare.

Alexander. To hang (a person): Anglo-Irish coll: ca 1670–1800. Ex the merciless way in which Sir Jerome Alexander, an Irish judge in 1660–74, carried out the duties of his office. F. & H., revised.

Alexandra limp. The limp affected, as a compliment to the Princess of Wales, by Society ca 1865–80. Coll *Chambers's Journal*, 1876. cf. GRECIAN BEND.

Algerine. (Theatrical) one who, when salaries are not paid, reproaches the manager. Also, an impecunious borrower of small sums. ca 1850–1900. Perhaps ex the U.S. sense: a pirate (1844).

Algie, -y. Generic for a young male aristocrat (esp. if English): coll: from ca 1895.

alive, look. (Gen. in imperative.) To make haste: coll: 1858, T. Hughes, '[He] . . . told [them] to look alive and get their job done.'

alive and kicking; all alivo. Very alert and active. Coll: resp. from ca 1850 and ca 1840: see ALL SERENE.

alive or dead. Head: rhyming s.: ? late C.19–20.

aliveo. Lively; sprightly: (low) coll: late C.19–20. Ex ALL ALIVO.

all, and, see AND ALL.

all a-cock. 'Overthrown, vanquished', Ware: proletarian (—1909). Ware thinks that it derives either ex *knocked into a* COCKED HAT or ex cock-fighting.

all a treat. 'Perfection of enjoyment, sometimes used satirically to depict mild catastrophe', Ware: London street coll (—1909).

all abroad, see ABROAD.

all afloat. A coat: rhyming s. (—1859).

all alive. (Tailors') ill-fitting: ca 1850–1910.

all alivo, see ALIVE AND KICKING.

all arms and legs, see ARMS AND LEGS.

all at sea. At a loss; confused: C.19–20; coll from ca 1890. cf. ABROAD.

all brandy. (Of things) excellent, commendable: non-aristocratic: ca 1870–1910.

all bum. A street c.p. applied, ca 1860–1900, to a woman wearing a large bustle.

all callao (or **-io**). Quite happy: nautical: late C.19–20; ob. Perhaps ex *alcohol*.

all cando. All right: naval: late C.19–20. Perhaps from *all white*, rhyming s. for *right*, by pun on L. *cand*idus, white.

all dick(e)y with, see DICKY, adj.

all-fired. Infernal; cursèd. Orig. (1835) U.S.; anglicized ca 1860. Euphemizes *hell-fired*. 2. Hence the adv. *all-firedly*: U.S. (1860), anglicized ca. 1870; ob.

all fours, be or **go on.** To proceed evenly. C.19–20 coll.

***all gay!** The coast is clear: C.19 c. cf. BOB, adj.

***All Hallows.** The 'tolling place' (?scene of robbery), in PRIGGING LAW (lay): c. of ca 1580–1630. Greene, 1592.

all hands and the cook. Everybody on the ship: nautical coll: mid-C.19–20. The cook being called on only in emergency.

all-hands ship. A ship on which all hands are employed continuously: nautical coll: mid-C.19–20.

all hands to the pump. A concentration of effort: C.18–19; ob. by 1890. Coll rather than s.

all harbour light. All right: orig. (1897) and mostly cabbies' rhyming s.; ob.

all his buttons on, have. To be shrewd, alert, and/or active: London proletariat: ca 1880–1915.

all holiday at Peckham. A mid-C.18–19 proverbial saying = no work and no food (pun on *peck*); doomed, ruined.

all-hot. A hot potato: low (—1857); †by 1900.

all in, adj. (Stock Exchange) depressed (of the market): coll: mid-C.19–20; opp. ALL OUT, 5. These are also terms shouted by dealers when prices are, esp., falling or rising.

all in fits. (Of clothes) ill-made: mid-C.19–20: tailors'.

all jaw (like a sheep's head). Excessively talkative; eloquent. From ca 1870; ob. Variant, *all mouth*: ca 1880–1910.

all languages. Bad language: coll: ca 1800–40. *Sessions*, Dec. 1809.

all legs and wings. (Of a sailing vessel) overmasted: nautical: late C.19–20; ob.

all Lombard Street to ninepence, to a china orange. Heavy odds: coll: 1819+, —1880 respectively. The former is †; the latter slightly ob. cf. BET YOU A MILLION TO A BIT OF DIRT!, and see comment at LOMBARD STREET . . .

all manner. All kinds of things, 'things' usually being made specific to suit the context: lower classes coll: from ca 1870.

all my eye (and Betty Martin). Nonsense! '*All my eye* is perhaps the earliest form (Goldsmith has it in 1768), although it is clear that Grose's version' – *that's my eye, Betty Martin* – 'was already familiar in 1785. . . cf. the Fr. *mon œil!*,' Grose, P. The *Betty Martin* part, despite ingenious, too ingenious, hypotheses (esp. that sponsored by 'Jon Bee' and silently borrowed by H.: 'a corruption . . . of . . . *Oh, mihi, beate Martine*'), remains a mystery. It is, however, interesting to note that Moore the poet has, in 1819, *all my eye, Betty*, and Poole, in *Hamlet Travestied*, 1811, has *that's all my eye and Tommy*; this problematic *tommy* recurs in HELL AND TOMMY. In *The Phoenician Origin of Britons, Scots, and Anglo-Saxons*, 1914, Dr L. A. Waddell derives the phrase from *o mihi, Brito Martis*, 'Oh (bring help) to me, Brito Martis'. She was the tutelary goddess of Crete, and her cult was that of, or associated with, the sun-cult of the Phoenicians, who so early traded with the Britons for Cornish tin.

all my eye and (my) elbow. A London elaboration of the preceding: 1882. Ware, 'One can wink with the eye and nudge with the elbow at once'; he also points to the possibility of mere alliteration. cf.:

all my eye and my grandmother. A London variant (—1887) of the preceding; ob. cf. *so's your grandmother!*, which, in late C.19–20, expresses incredulity: gen. throughout England.

all nations. A mixture of drinks from all the unfinished bottles: late C.18–early 19. 2. A coat many-coloured or much-patched: C.19.

all-night man. A body-snatcher: ca 1800–50. See esp. Ramsay, *Reminiscences*, 1861.

all of a heap. Astounded; nonplussed: C.18–20; coll by 1800. In Shakespeare, *all on a heap*.

all of a hough, or huh. Clumsy; unworkmanlike: tailors', ca 1870–1914. 2. Lopsided: ex Somerset dial., from ca 1820. It occurs, as *all of a hoo*, in Glascock, *The Naval Sketch-Book*, II, 1829, and as *all ahoo* in *The Night Watch*, II, 85, 1828.

all of a piece. 'Awkward, without proper distribution or relation of parts': low coll (—1909); slightly ob. Ware.

all one's own. One's own master: London apprentices': ca 1850–1905.

all out. Completely: from C.14; coll > S.E. by ca 1750. 2. Of a big drink, ex *drink all out*, to empty a glass, C.17–19, coll. 3. In error: C.19–20. 4. (The turf) unsuccessful: ca 1870–1900. 5. (Stock Exchange) improving, cf. ALL IN for period and status. 6. Exhausted: athletics, ca 1880–1900; then gen. 7. Exerting every effort; since the early 1890s.

all over, adj. Feeling ill or sore all over the body: coll: 1851, Mayhew, who affords also the earliest English instance of ALL-OVERISH.

all over, be. To be dead: lower classes' coll: 1898, Edwin Pugh, *Tony Drum*.

all over grumble. Inferior; very unsatisfactory: London proletarian: 1886, *Referee*, 28 March: 'It has been a case of all over grumble, but Thursday's show was all over approval'; ob.

all over red. Dangerous: ca 1860–1920. Ex the railway signal.

all-over pattern. A pattern that is either very intricate or non-recurrent or formed of units unseparated by the 'ground': coll from ca 1880.

all over the shop. Ubiquitous (G. R. Sims, 1883); disconcerted (1887).

all over with, it is. (Of persons) ruined; disgraced; fatally ill or mortally wounded: from ca 1860; coll, soon S.E. cf. the L. *actum est de*.

all-overish. Having an indefinite feeling of

general indisposition or unease: from ca 1840: coll. Perhaps ex U.S., where it is recorded as early as 1833.

all-overishness. The state of feeling 'ALL-OVERISH': from ca 1840; coll. Early examples in Harrison Ainsworth (1854) and John Mills (1841).

all plopa. Quite right; correct: pidgin: mid-C.19–20.

all right. Virtuous: coll: late C.19–20. W. B. Maxwell, *Hill Rise*, 1908.

all right! Yes!, agreed!; you needn't worry! C.19–20; coll. As adj. and rare adv., *all right* is S.E.

all right up to now. Serene, smiling: a c.p., mainly women's: 1878–ca 1915. 'Used by Herbert Campbell ... in Covent Garden Theatre Pantomime, 1878', Ware, who adds that it is derived ex '*enceinte* women making the remark as to their condition'.

all round my hat. Indisposed: ca 1850–1900. As an exclamation (1834–ca 1890) = nonsense! (See *all around my* HAT.) Hence, *spicy as all round my hat* (ca 1870–1900), sensational: 1882, *Punch*.

all-rounder. A versatile or adaptable person, esp. at sport (—1887); coll >, by 1910, S.E. 2. A collar of equal height all round and meeting in front (Trollope, 1857), unfashionable by ca 1885, rarely worn after 1890.

all saints, see MOTHER OF ALL SAINTS.

all serene. Correct; safe; favourable: c.p., now ob. *Sessions*, 8 April 1852: policeman *loq.*, 'He said, "It is all serene" – that means calm, square, beautiful.'

all-set. (Of a rogue, a desperate character) 'ready to start upon any kind of robbery, or other mischief', Bee, 1823: low or perhaps c. 2. Ready; arranged in order; comfortable: coll: from ca 1870. Ex the *all set? – ready! – go!* used in starting those athletic races in which the starter does not employ a pistol.

all(-)shapes. Of irregular form: coll: late C.19–20.

all Sir Garnet, see SIR GARNET.

all smoke, gammon and pickles or **spinach.** All nothing, i.e. all nonsense: ca 1870–1900.

all sorts. Tap-droppings ('Jon Bee', 1823); cf. ALLS; ALL NATIONS.

all souls, see MOTHER OF ALL SAINTS.

all spice, all-spice. A grocer: mid-C.19–20; ob. The S.E. sense, aromatic herb, goes back to the early C.17.

all standing, brought up. Unable to deal with a situation: naval coll: C.19–20. Granville.

all-standing, sleep, or, gen., **turn in.** 'To turn in with one's clothes on': nautical coll: from ca 1800.

all t.h. Good; correct. Tailors' A1, *all right*: ca 1860–1910.

all the better for seeing you! A c.p. reply to 'How are you?': late C.19–20.

all the go. Genuine; thoroughly satisfactory; esp. in demand, fashionable (see GO): from ca 1780; ob.

all the way down. Completely suitable or suited: coll, ca 1850–1910. Lit., from top to toe. 2. Hence, as adv.: excellently. A coll of late C.19–20.

all the way there. A variant, ca 1860–90, of ALL THERE.

all the world and his wife, see WIFE, ALL THE ...

all there. Honest, reliable (—1860); ready-witted (1880); sane (late C.19–20). Also applied to 'one with his whole thought directed to the occasion, *totus in illis*, as Horace says, and so at his best' (*Notes and Queries*, 24 April 1937): coll: from ca 1885.

all to pieces. Collapsed, ruined: C.17–20 coll. 2. Out of form or condition: C.19–20, ob. 3. (Of a woman) confined: mid-C.19–20. All three esp. with *go*.

all to smash. Utterly (Cuthbert Bede, 1861); ob. 2. Ruined, bankrupt, mid-C.19–20. H., 1st ed. Perhaps ex Somerset dial.

all U.P., see U.P.

all up (with). Of things, projects: fruitless, ruined: late C.18–20. Of persons: bankrupt, utterly foiled, doomed to die: C.19–20, as in Dickens's 'all up with Squeers'. Rarely *up* alone. The nuance 'utterly exhausted, virtually defeated' – e.g. in boxing – occurs in *Boxiana*, I, 1818. *It's all up* occurs in vol. III, 1821. The sense 'doomed to die' appears in *Sessions*, 3 July 1843.

all very large and fine. A c.p. indicative of ironic approval: coll: 1886; slightly ob. Ex 'the refrain of a song sung by Mr Herbert Campbell' (Ware): cf. ALL RIGHT UP TO NOW.

all white, see ALL CANDO.

all wind and piss. A contemptuous c.p.: (probably) C.19–20. Ex the semi-proverbial C.18–20 *like the* BARBER'S CAT, *all ...*

all wool and a yard wide. Utterly good and honest (person): late C.19–20. Ex drapery.

allacompain, see ALACOMPAIN.

allee samee. Identical with, similar to, like: pidgin (—1883).

alleluia lass. A Salvation Army girl: London proletarian: 1886; ob.

alleviator. A drink. Coined by Mark Lemon in the 1840s. Ob.

all(e)y. A marble of medium size: C.18–20 schoolboys' coll > S.E. Defoe has it. Perhaps ex *alabaster*. 2. A go-between: proletarian (—1909); virtually †. Ware derives ex Fr. *aller*, to go.

alley, (right) up one's. One's concern, applied to what one knows or can do very well: coll: since ca 1905. Deliberate variation of ... STREET. 2. Hence, since ca 1910, applied to something delightful.

allicholly. Melancholy: jocular coll or deliberate s. in Shakespeare's *Two Gentlemen of Verona*: punning *ale* + *melancholy*. cf. LEMONCHOLY.

alligator. See HALLIGATOR. 2. One who, singing, opens his mouth wide: ca 1820–50.

alligator pear. An avocado pear: South African coll (—1892). By corruption.

allo. All; every: pidgin: mid-C.19–20.

allow. Weekly pocket-money: Harrow School, C.19–20; ob.

alls. Short for ALL NATIONS (tap-droppings); ca 1840–1914. 2. Also, ca 1850–1900, a workman's term – the American equivalent is, or used to be, *bens* – for his tools.

Allslops. Allsopp & Sons' ale: not upper-classes': from ca 1900. It had a slump in quality at one time; the name has unjustly stuck.

***ally-beg.** Comfort of a bed; a comfortable bed: c.: C.18–20; ob. Prob. = 'pleasant little bed'.

almanach. The female pudend: low: late C.19–early 20.

almighty. Great(ly), might(il)y. A U.S. coll never properly acclimatized in Great Britain and now ob. De Quincey, 1824: 'Such rubbish, such almighty nonsense (to speak *transatlanticé*) ...' 2. Grand; impressive: proletarian coll verging on sol.: mid-C.19–20. Nevinson, 1895, makes a Shadwellite describe a picture having 'somethink almighty about it'.

almighty dollar, the. Wealth: coll (—1859) ex U.S. (1836). Probably coined by Washington Irving, after Ben Jonson's *almighty gold*, though the first printed record does not occur in Irving's work. In England the phrase is always satirical, nor is it yet S.E.: and frequently it connotes the (supposed) American devotion to and absorption in money-making.

almond. Penis: mostly Cockneys': from ca 1890. An abbr. of *almond rock*, rhyming s. for the same since ca 1880: on COCK.

almond rocks. Socks: rhyming s.: late C.19–20.

aloft. Dead: C.18–20; ob. Also coll is *go aloft*, to die: Dibdin's *Tom Bowling*, 1790, contains the verses:

> Faithful below, Tom did his duty,
> And now he's gone aloft.

At *aloft*, F. & H. has a fascinating synonymy for 'to die'; see too the essay on euphemisms in *Words!* cf. ALOW AND ALOFT.

alone, go. To be experienced, wary, and alert: ca 1800–25.

along, get. An imperative = go away!: coll; C.19–20. Ordinarily, *get along* is S.E. and = get on, move along.

along-shore boys. Landsmen: nautical coll (—1823); †by 1910.

along with. A coll weakening of *with*: late C.19–20.

aloud, used fig., is coll: mid-C.19–20. (The O.E.D. record: 1872.)

alow and aloft. 'Below decks and aloft'; nautical coll: mid-C.19–20. Bowen. 2. Hence, 'dead and alive', i.e. lethargic, dull: nautical: late C.19–20; ob. ibid.

***Alsatia (the Higher).** Whitefriars. **Alsatia the Lower,** the Mint in Southwark, London. c. of ca 1680–1800; afterwards, historical. From early in C.17 until 1697, when both liberties or asylums or sanctuaries were suppressed, these were the haunts of bankrupts, fleeing debtors, gamesters and sharks. In Shadwell's comedy, *The Squire of Alsatia* – the first record of the term – occurs the illuminating: 'Who are these? Some inhabitants of Whitefryers; some bullies of Alsatia.' *Alsatia* = Alsace, a 'debateable ground' province. In C.18–19 *Alsatia* meant any asylum for criminals, any low quarter, while *squire of Alsatia* synonymized a sharper or a SHADY spendthrift. Besides Shadwell's play, consult Scott's *Fortunes of Nigel*, Macaulay's *History* at I, iii, E. Beresford Chancellor's *Annals of Fleet Street*, and M. Melville Balfour's historical novel, *The Long Robe*.

Alsatia phrase. A term in s. or, esp., in c.: Swift, 1704; †by 1750. Coll > very soon S.E.

***Alsatian.** Pertaining to ALSATIA; criminal; debauched: c. of late C.17–18; then historical. Whence the n.

alt, in. Haughty: coll: 1748, Richardson; †by 1820. Ex *altitude*.

alta(or e or u)ma(or e)l(l). All together; altogether (adv.): late C.17–18. N., the total of a bill, an account: C.18. Adj., nautical, esp. of s. and j.: C.18. Since the adv. and the n. are always, so far as I can discover, spelt *alta*(or *e*)*me*(or *a*)*l*(*l*) and F. & H. derives them from Dutch *altemal* (modern Dutch *allemaal*) – Hexham, 1658, 'Al-te-mael, Wholly, or All at once' – and since the O.E.D. derives the adj., always spelt *altumal*, from *altum* (*mare*) + *al*, the two forms and derivations suggest, indeed they almost necessitate, two distinct origins.

altar. 'Master's desk in old Lower Senior Room': Bootham School: late C.19–20. Ex the shape.

alter the jeff's click. To make a garment regardless of the cutter's chalkings or instructions: tailors' (—1903).

***altham,** C.16 c., a wife; a mistress. Whence(?) the c. adj. AUTEM.

altitudes, in the (or **his, my,** etc.). In elevated mood (coll: Jonson, 1630); drunk (ca 1700). Both were †by 1840. cf. ELEVATE.

altocad. An oldish paid member who in the choir takes alto: Winchester College, from ca 1850.

altogether, the. The nude: coll: 1894, Du Maurier. i.e. *the altogether* (wholly) *naked*.

altogethery. Drunk: Society: 1816, Byron. Ex *altogether drunk*.

always in trouble like a Drury Lane whore. A late C.19–20 c.p. 'stigmatizing either self-pity or successive misfortunes to an individual' (Atkinson).

amazingly. Very: coll; from ca 1790. Maria Edgeworth, 'She speaks English amazingly well for a Frenchwoman.'

ambassador. A sailors' trick upon new hands: mid-C.18–19. In a King-Neptune form, *King Arthur*. 2. See:

ambassador of commerce. A commercial traveller: coll: late C.19–20; ob.

Ambassador of Morocco. A shoemaker: ca 1810–30. Punning *morocco* (leather).

ambi, ambitious. 'Zealous, with a view to personal advantage; also foolishly zealous, asking for more work, etc., etc.', John Masefield, in the *Conway*, 1933. Conway Training Ship s., from ca 1880.

ambi(or o)dexter. A double-dealing witness, lawyer or juror: C.16–19; coll; S.E. after 1800. 2. Any double-dealer: from ca 1550, coll; by 1880 S.E.

ambrol. A naval corruption of *admiral*: late C.17–18.

ambs-ace, ames ace. Bad luck: M.E.–C.19. 2. Next to nothing: C.17–18. Lit. the double ace; and soon coll. 3. *Within ambs-ace*, almost: late C.17–early 19, coll in C.18–19.

amen-chapel. 'The service used in Winchester School [*sic*] upon Founder's Commemorations, and certain other occasions, in which the responses and Amens are accompanied on the organ', E.D.D., 1896.

amen-curler. A parish clerk: late C.18–19. A C.18 variant: *amen-clerk*. A mid-C.19–20 variant, *amen-bawler* (Mayhew, 1851). cf. AMEN-WALLAH and:

amen-snorter. A parson. Rare in England, frequent in Australia (ca 1880–1900).

'amen' to everything, say 'yes' and. To agree to everything: coll: late C.18–mid-19. cf. AMENER.

amen-wallah. A chaplain's clerk: C.19–20. cf. AMEN-CURLER.

amener. An assiduous assenter: C.19–20; ob. (*Amen*, the concluding word.)

American shoulders. A coat cut square to give the appearance of broadness. From ca 1870; at first, tailors' j., but s. by 1890.

***American tweezers.** A burglar's instrument for opening doors: from ca 1870; orig. c.

amidships. On the solar plexus; in or on the belly. Nautical: C.18–20.

Aminidab, Aminadab. A Quaker: C.18–early 19; derisive. Ned Ward, 1709; Grose.

ammunition. Toilet paper: C.19–20; ob. cf. BUM-FODDER.

ammunition leg. A wooden leg: military: C.19. (*Ammunition* = munition.)

ammunition wife. (Gen. pl.) A harlot: nautical: ca 1820–70. cf. GUNPOWDER and 'HOT STUFF'.

amorosa. A wanton: ca 1630–1720: Society, mainly. It. word, never acclimatized.

amoroso. A (male) lover: ca 1615–1770; chiefly Society. An It. word never properly anglicized.

amourette. A trifling love affair or, esp., amour: ca 1860–1914: Society coll. Directly ex Fr.; cf. C.17 S.E. *amorets*, dalliance.

amours, in. In love: gen. followed by *with* (some person): ca 1725–1800: Society s. > coll > S.E.

ampersand. The posterior(s). '&' used to

come at the end of nursery-book alphabets: hence the hinder parts. ca 1885–1914.

amputate one's mahogany or **timber.** To CUT (v., 4) *one's stick*, to depart, esp. depart quickly: from the 1850s; ob. There is a rich synonymy for rapid departure; see F. & H., also my *Slang*.

***amuse,** in late C.17–18 c., is to throw dust, pepper, snuff, etc., in the eyes of the person to be robbed; an *amuser* is one who does this.

amy. 'A friendly alien serving in a man-of-war': naval: ca 1800–60. Bowen notes that in the old days there were many foreigners serving in the British Navy. ?a mutilated blend of *enemy man* or simply an adoption of Fr. *ami*, a friend.

anabaptist. A pickpocket who, caught in the act, is ducked in pond or at pump: late C.18–early 19.

analken. To wash: Shelta: C.18–20.

analt. To sweep (with broom): id.

anan. 'What do you say, Sir?' in reply to an order or remark not understood: naval: C.18. Perhaps *anon* corrupted.

anatomy. An extremely emaciated – or skinny – person: late C.16–20. (Low) coll. cf. ATOMY.

anca. A man; a husband or sweetheart: low: C.19. Price Warung, *Tales*, 1897 (p. 58). Ex Greek *anēr*.

anchor, bring one's arse to an. To sit down: nautical: late C.18–mid-19. cf.:

anchor, swallow the. To settle down – above all, to loaf – on shore, esp. if one is still active: nautical: late C.19–20.

anchor (oneself), come to an anchor. To halt; sit down, rest; sojourn. Coll, C.18–20. 2. Hence *anchor*, an abode or a place of residence: C.19–20 coll. At first nautical, both v. and n. soon > gen.

anchor to the windward of the law, let go an. To keep within the letter of the law: nautical: late C.18–mid-19.

ancient mariner. A sea-gull: nautical: C.19–20. Sea-gulls are 'supposed to possess the souls of dead sailormen', Bowen. cf. Coleridge's *Ancient Mariner*.

ancient mariners. At Oxford, an occasionally rowing group or crew of dons; at Cambridge, any graduates who, still associated with the university, continue to row. From ca 1880; ob. Ware quotes the *Daily News* of 7 Nov. 1884.

and all. As well: lower-class coll tag implying a grumble: from ca 1860. cf. S.E. usage.

(and) don't you forget it! A c.p. orig. U.S. (—1888) adopted in England ca 1890. An almost pointless intensive.

and he didn't! A tailors' c.p. implying a discreditable action: ca 1870–1920.

and no error or **mistake!** see MISTAKE, AND NO.

and no flies. And no doubt about it: low c.p. tag: ca 1840–60. Mayhew, I, 1851.

and no mogue! A tailors' implication of slight incredulity = 'that's true?' From ca 1880. Possibly *mogue* represents the Fr. *moquerie*: cf. the synonymous Fr. *moque* (C.15–16). More prob., as Mr H. R. Spencer of Camberley, Surrey, has proposed, ex the German underworld and Gypsies' *mogeln* (long *o*, which would phonetically explain the *-ue*) – coming into Eng. via Yiddish.

and no whistle. Another tailors' implication: that the speaker is actually, though ostensibly not, speaking of himself. ca 1860–1900.

and so he died; and then she died. These Restoration-drama tags verge on c.pp.: See Dryden, ed. Summers, I, 419.

and so she prayed me to tell ye. An almost meaningless c.p. (with slight variations) rounding off a sentence: ca 1670–90. e.g. in Duffett's burlesque, *The Mock-Tempest*, 1675.

and the rest! A sarcastic retort or comment: from ca 1860. The implication is that something has been omitted.

and things, see THINGS, AND.

and welcome! And you're welcome to it; I'm glad (to let you have it, etc.): coll, non-aristocratic: late C.19–20. Manchon.

Andrew. A gentleman's servant: coll > S.E.: 1698, Congreve; †by 1800. Because a very common name. 2. In full, ANDREW MILLAB. A ship, esp. *of war*: rhyming s. (—1864); ob. 3. Hence, a revenue cutter; Australian smugglers': ca 1870–1900. But this, like sense 2, may abbr. *Andrew Miller's* (or *-ar's*) *lugger*, 'a king's ship and vessel', 1813 (sea cant), a phrase †by 1880. 4. Abbr. ANDREW MILLAR, 2; always *the Andrew*.

Andrew Millar. See ANDREW, 2. 2. The Royal Navy: hence, any Government department: naval: mid-C.19–20; ob. Ex 'a notorious Press-gang "tough" who shanghaied so many victims into the Navy that the sailors of the period thought it belonged to him' (Granville).

Andy Cain. Rain: rhyming s.: late C.19–20.

Angel. A harlot plying near the Angel at

Islington: low Cockney (—1909). cf. SLUKER.

angel, flying angel. A ride astride a person's shoulders (James Greenwood, 1880): ca 1860–1900.

angel altogether. A confirmed drunkard. Mainly West Indian: ca 1876–1914.

angel-maker. A baby-farmer: proletarian: 1889; ob. Ware, 'Because so many of the farmed babies die.' Probably ex the Fr. *faiseuse des anges*.

angelic, Angelica. An unmarried girl. The former ca 1810–50, the latter ca 1840–1900. Moncrieff in *Tom and Jerry*, 1821, speaks of 'the angelics at Almack's'.

angel's food. Strong ale: ca 1575–1620. Harrison's *England*, II, viii.

angel's foot-stool. A sail carried over the moon-sail by American clippers: nautical coll: mid-C.19–20; ob.

angel's gear. Women's clothes: nautical: mid-C.19–20; ob.

angel's oil. Money employed in bribery. Variant, *oil of angels*. C.17. Punning *angel*, the small gold coin struck in 1465.

angel's suit. Coat and waistcoat made in one, with trousers buttoned thereto. Tailors', ca 1870–1885. 'Neither garment nor name was extensively adopted,' F. & H.

angel's whisper, see WHISPER, ANGEL'S.

***angler.** A pilferer who, with a hooked stick, steals from open windows and doors: mid-C.16–early 19. cf. AREA SNEAK; HOOKER. 2. A hook: c. of ca 1580–1620. Greene.

Anglican inch. 'The short square whisker . . . so much affected by the Broad Church party': ritualistic clergy's: 1870; very ob.

***angling cove.** A receiver of stolen goods: C.19 c. In C.18–early 19 c., *angling for farthings* is begging, with cap and string, from a prison window.

angry boy. A BLOOD: late C.16–17. Greene; Beaumont & Fletcher.

Anguagela. Language: central s. (—1909); ob., as all central s. is.

angular party. A gathering or social group odd in number: coll, from ca 1870; ob.

Animal. The Elephant and Castle Station: London Railway passengers': ca 1860–1910. 2. **The Animal.** 'A disguised, or flippant, reference amongst boon companions to the tavern, used in common when the sign is zoological . . . but more esp. referring to the Elephant and Castle . . .; until (1882) this place was exceptionally dubbed "Jumbo",' Ware.

animal, go the whole. A U.S. phrase adapted by Dickens as *go the extreme animal*, by Sala as . . . *entire* . . . A C.19 variant on the U.S. GO THE WHOLE HOG.

animal, mere. 'A very silly fellow', B.E.: late C.17–18 coll. Wycherley.

animal spirits. Liveliness of character, (gen. considerable) vivacity of manner and action, a healthy animalism: coll; from ca 1810. Jane Austen.

ankle, have sprained one's. To have been seduced (cf. Fr. *avoir mal aux genoux*): late C.18–20; ob.

ankle-beater. A boy specializing (ca 1820–80) in driving, to the slaughter-yard, the animals purchased by the butcher. To avoid the damaging of flesh, only the beasts' ankles were touched. Also known as a PENNY-BOY.

ankle-bone. A crawfish: nautical: late C.19–20; ob.

***ankle-spring warehouse.** The stocks: Anglo-Irish c.: ca 1780–1830. But cf. SPRING-ANKLE WAREHOUSE.

Ann-chovey, see CHOVEY.

Anna Maria. A fire: rhyming s.: 1892, 'Pomes' Marshall, *Sporting Times*, 29 Oct.

annas of dark blood, have at least two. To be of mixed parentage: Anglo-Indian coll (—1886). cf. COFFEE-COLOUR.

Anne's fan, properly *Queen Anne's fan*. Thumb to nose and fingers outspread; intensified by twiddled fingers or by addition of other hand similarly outspread: late C.18–19. Now COCK SNOOKS at a person.

anno domini. Late middle, or old, age (1885); old ('extremely old' is *B.C.*); the passage of the years (however young one is after early adulthood): from ca 1910. Coll. Ware, 1909, '"He must be very anno domini, mustn't he?" "A.D.? my dear fellow, say B.C."'; *B.C.* is virtually †. cf. *anno domini ship*, an old-fashioned whaler: whaling: from ca 1880; ob.

annual. A holiday taken once a year: coll (—1903).

anodyne necklace. A halter: mid-C.18–early 19. Goldsmith, 1766. (In C.17 simply NECKLACE.) One of numerous synonyms (see HORSE-NIGHTCAP). In C.18 also a supposedly medicinal amulet.

anoint. To beat well, to thrash: C.17–20; ob. Adumbrated in M.E.

anoint a (or the) palm. To bribe: C.16–18. cf. GREASE *the palm*.

anointed. Depraved, worthless, pejoratively ulter: late C.18–19; ?mainly Anglo-Irish. Prob. ex ANOINT.

anonyma. A demi-mondaine, esp. if a high-flyer. ca 1860–79, then less common; rare in C.20. Sala, 1864, 'Bah! There are so many anonymas nowadays.'

another, you're, see YOU ARE ANOTHER.

another acrobat. Another drink: punning *tumbler*: ca 1870–1900.

another guess; another guess sort of man. (A) FLY (man): C.19. Perhaps ex *another gates*, but prob. direct from U.S.

another point(, steward)! Make that drink stronger!: nautical: from ca 1860. *Glasgow Herald*, 9 Nov. 1864. cf. the NORTH drinking-terms.

anser, see GOOSE.

antagonize, v.i. To compete; strive to win: sporting coll (—1887).

Anthony; St Anthony's pig; antony pig. The smallest pig in a litter: late C.16–20; ob. Coll by 1750. St Anthony the hermit was the patron of swineherds.

Ant(h)ony, cuff or **knock.** To knock one's knees together in walking: late C.18–19. Variant, *cuff Jonas*. 2. **Ant(h)ony Cuffin,** a knock-kneed man: C.19.

anti. A person opposed to a given opinion or party; one by nature a rebel, an objector: coll (1889). Ex the adj.

antidote. 'A very homely woman', B.E.: jocular: late C.17–mid 18. Against lust.

antimony. Type: printers' (—1890). F. & H., 'Antimony is a constituent part' of the metal.

antipodean. With everything topsy-turvy: from ca 1850. Orig. jocularly pedantic S.E., then jocularly coll.

Antipodes, the or **her.** The female pudend: late C.19–20. 2. The backside: since ca 1840.

antiquated rogue. An ex-thief; an out-of-date thief: ca 1660–1730. At the angle formed by three linguistic regions: c., j., and S.E. Only in B.E.

Antony, see ANTHONY.

any. At all: s. (and dial.): late C.19–20. Kipling, 1890, 'You don't want bein' made more drunk any.'

any, I'm not taking (—1903) or **having** (from ca 1895). Not for me!; 'not for JOE!': c.p. Hence in ordinary constructions. The earlier form occurs in J. Milne, *Epistles of Atkins*, 1902.

any how, anyhow. Indifferently; badly: coll (—1859).

any racket. A penny faggot: rhyming s., ca 1855–1910.

any road, see ROAD, 3.

anything, as or **like.** Very; much; vigorously. The *as* form, C.16–20; ob.; the *like*, C.18–20. Coll.

anythingarian. A person of no fixed or decided views: from ca 1707, when coined by Swift; whence *anythingarianism*, defined by Kingsley in 1851 as 'modern Neo-Platonism'. Coll, soon S.E.; ob.

anywhere down there! A tailors' c.p. when something is dropped on the floor: ca 1860–1910.

apartments to let. (With *have*) brainless; silly: from early 1860s. 2. In C.18, descriptive of a widow.

ape, make anyone his. To befool: C.17–19 coll. Variant, *put an ape into one's hood* or *cap*.

'apenny bumper. 'A two-farthing omnibus ride': London streets': ca 1870–1900. Ware.

'apenny dip. A ship: rhyming s.: since ca 1860.

'apenny-lot day. 'A bad time for business': costers' (—1909); ob. Ware. Because on such a day the sales total ½d.

apes in hell, lead. To be an old maid: C.16–20; ob. 'Euphues' Lyly was one of the first to record the phrase; Gascoigne was app. the first. Apperson. Whence, *ape-leader*, an old maid: mid-C.17–early 19.

ape's paternoster, say an. To chatter with cold. Recorded by Cotgrave in 1611. For the quaint proverbs and proverbial sayings connected with the ape, see esp. G. L. Apperson's *English Proverbs*, 1929.

apiece. For each person: coll; C.19–20. (S.E. when applied to things.)

apostles. 'The knight-heads, bollards and bitts of a sailing-ship': nautical: mid-C.19–20; ob. Bowen. Why?

apostles, manoeuvre the. To rob Peter to pay Paul: mid-C.18–20; ob.

Apostles, the (Twelve). The last twelve on the degree list: Cambridge University: late C.18–19. Ex *post alios*, after the others, is H.'s suggestion. Variant, *the chosen twelve*.

Apostle's Grove, the. St John's Wood district, London: 1864. Variant, *the Grove of the Evangelist*: H., 5th ed., 1874. Ex the numerous demi-mondaines living there ca 1860–1910. Ob.

apothecaries' Latin. Law Latin, dog Latin: late C.18–early 19 coll.

apothecary, talk like an. To talk nonsense: mid-C.18–early 19: coll.

apothecary's bill. A long bill: mid-C.18–early 19.

app. Apparatus: chemists' (not druggists') and chemical students': from ca 1860.

apple and pip. To urinate: late C.19–20. Rhyming on SIP, back-s. for PISS. (Franklyn, 2nd.)

apple and pears, see APPLES AND PEARS.

apple fritter. A bitter (ale): rhyming s.: late C.19–20.

apple-cart. The human body. Grose, 2nd ed., 1788, has 'down with his apple-cart; knock or throw him down': cf. H., 1st ed., 1859, '"down with his applecart," i.e. upset him. *North*[ern.]' In *upset the apple-cart* there seems to be a merging of two senses: body and, in dialect, plan; originating app. ca 1800, this phrase > coll ca 1850.

apple-cart, upset the old woman's; upset the apple-cart and spill the gooseberries (or **peaches).** Variants, dating from ca 1880, of *upset the apple-cart*: see preceding entry.

apple-dumpling shop. A woman's bosom: late C.18–19. cf. APPLE-MONGER.

apple-monger, apple-squire; apron-squire. A harlot's bully. Coll, respectively C.18, C.16–early 19, late C.16–19. Perhaps ex *apple*, a woman's breast. cf. APPLE-DUMPLING SHOP.

apple-pie bed. A bed short-sheeted: late C.18–20; coll by 1830; S.E. by 1880. Grose, 2nd ed., defines it as 'A bed made apple-pye fashion, like what is termed a turnover apple-pye'.

Apple-Pie Day. That day on which, at Winchester College, six-and-six was, C.19, played. On this day, the Thursday after the first Tuesday in December, apple-pies were served on 'GOMERS', in College, for dinner.

apple-pie order. Perfect order, impeccable precision (Scott, 1813): coll >, by 1900, S.E.

apple-sauce. Impudence: mostly lower middle class: late C.19–20. See SAUCE.

apple-squire. A male bawd: orig. (—1591), c. Greene. See also APPLE-MONGER.

Appleby?, who has any lands in. A c.p. addressed to 'The Man at whose Door the Glass stands Long' (B.E. at *landlord*): late C.17–mid 18. (cf. PARSON MALLUM and PARSON PALMER.) Perhaps orig. of cider.

apples. Testicles: low: C.19–20. cf. NUTMEGS. 2. See APPLES AND PEARS.

apples and pears. Stairs (—1859). 'Ducange Anglicus,' 1st ed., and H., 1st ed., have *apple and pears.* Ware records, for 1882, the abbr. *apples*, which has never > gen.

apples swim! how we. What a good time we have! C.17–20; ob. Clarke, 1639; Ray, 1678; FitzGerald, 1852. In C.19 often tagged with *quoth the horse-turd.* The c.p. is applied to parvenus and pretenders. It has been known in Germany since C.16, both in the Latin *Nos poma natamus* and in the German *Da schwimmen wir Apfel, sagte der Rossapfel und schwamm mit den echten*, Look at us apples swimming, said the ball of horse-dung, swimming with the genuine apples. See HOW WE APPLES SWIM!

appro, on. Coll: abbr. *on approbation* or *approval* (things), from ca 1870; *on approbation* (persons): from ca 1900.

'appy dosser, see DOSSER.

apricock (-) water. Apricock, i.e. apricot, ale: 1728, Anon., *The Quaker's Opera.*

April fools. Tools: rhyming s.: late C.19–20. 2. Stools: mostly public-house rhyming s.: since ca 1910.

April gentleman. A man newly married: coll; C.16–17. Greene. Ex the popularity of marriages in April.

apron-rogue. A labourer, an artisan: C.17 coll. (In C.17 S.E., *apron-man.*)

apron-squire, see APPLE-MONGER.

apron-string hold or **tenure.** An estate held only during a wife's life: late C.17–19 coll. Ray, 1678, 'To hold by the apron-strings, i.e. in right of his wife.'

apron-strings, tied to (or **always at) the** (or **a woman's).** Dangling after a woman, C.18; under petticoat government, C.18–20.

apron-up. Pregnant: lower and lower-middle class coll: C.19–20; ob. Because modest women tend, in pregnancy, to use their aprons as 'disguise'.

apron-washings. Porter: proletarian (—1903); ob. Ex brewers' *porters*' aprons.

aproneer. A shopkeeper: ca 1650–1720; coll. During the Civil War, a Roundhead. On the other hand, *aproner* (ca. 1600–40) = a barman, a waiter.

aqua pompaginis (or **pump-).** Apothecaries' Latin for water from the well: C.18–early 19. Harrison Ainsworth, drawing heavily on Egan's Grose, uses the term several times.

aquarius. 'Controller of evening bath "set"': Bootham School s. (late C.19–20) verging on j.

aquatics. A game of cricket played by the oarsmen; the playing-field used by them: Eton; mid C.19–20.

Arab, city Arab, street Arab. A young vagrant; a poor boy playing much in the streets. Coll >, by 1910, S.E.: respectively —1872, 1848, ca 1855.

Arabs; Arab merchants. 'The Indian merchants and shopkeepers in Natal are locally, but erroneously, known by these designations. They are chiefly Mohammedans and are also known as "Bombay merchants",' Pettman: from early 1890s.

arbor vitae. Lit., the tree of life, i.e. the penis: late C.18–20; ob. Pedantic.

Arbroath! A Scottish sporting c.p. (from 6 Sept. 1885) to anyone boasting. Because on 5 Sept. 1885, Dundee Harp defeated Aberdeen Rovers by 35–0 and sent a telegram to their great rivals Arbroath, 'You can't beat this', to which Arbroath, having the same day defeated Bon Accord, in a Scottish Cup Tie, by 36–0, replied, 'Can't we?'

***arch-cove** or **rogue.** As c., the leader of a gang of thieves: from ca 1600 to 1800. The latter as s., a confirmed rogue, from ca 1650; playfully, C.18–19. In c., *arch* = principal; confirmed; extremely adept. *Arch-doll* or DOXY, however, is the wife of an *arch*-COVE: Grose, 2nd ed.

archdeacon. Merton ale, stronger brew: Oxford University, C.19–20; ob.

archduke. A comical or an eccentric man: late C.17–18. Perhaps suggested by the Duke in *Measure for Measure*.

Archer up! (He, etc., is) safe; or, bound to win: London c.p.: 1881–6. Ex the famous jockey, Fred Archer, who (d. 1886) sprang into fame in 1881.

***ard.** Hot, both of objects and of persons or passions: C.17–early 19 c. Ex Fr. *ardent*.

ardelio(n). A busybody: C.17; coll. Never properly acclimatized. Florio; Burton. Ex L. *ardelio* ex *ardere*, to be zealous.

ardent. Spirituous liquor: Society: 1870. Abbr. *ardent spirits*.

area-sneak. A sneak haunting areas in order to thieve (Vaux, 1812; Dickens, 1838). Coll; S.E. by 1880 at latest. For a lengthy list of English and Continental synonyms for a thief see F. & H.

arer. A Cockney term of ca 1900–15, as in Ware's quotation, 'We *are*, and what's more, we can't be any arer,' i.e. more so.

'arf-and-'arf. Ale and porter mixed equally: Cockney; from ca 1830. cf.:

arfarfanarf. Drunk: Cockney (—1909); ob. Lit., half, half, and half; applied orig. to one who has had many an ARF-AND-ARF.

arg. To argue: low (—1903).

argal; argol-bargol. In Shakespeare, *argal* = therefore: obviously corrupted from *ergo*. *Argol-bargol*, unsound reasoning, cavilling – as v., to bandy words – is of the C.19–20 (ob.) and seems to be echoically rhyming after *willy-nilly*, HOCUS-POCUS, etc. Moreover, *The Times*, in 1863, used *argal* as = quibble, and Galt, forty years earlier, employed the adj. *argol-bargolous*, quarrelsome; *argy-bargy* (—1887) is mostly Scottish. Note, however, that *argle*, to dispute about, dates from ca 1589.

***argot.** 'A term used amongst London thieves for their secret . . . language', H.: c. (—1859). The Fr. *argot*, properly cant, loosely slang. 2. For its misuse as = 'slang', see introductory chapter of *Slang*: 1843, *Quarterly Review*, 'Some modern argot or vulgarism'.

argue the leg off an iron pot. To be, on one occasion or many, extremely argumentative: coll: from ca 1880. Also *argue a dog's tail off*: coll (—1903).

argufy. To signify: mid-C.18–20: low coll and dial. 1726, Trial of Hester Jennings in *Select Trials from 1724 to 1732*, 1735. In *Hodgson's National Songster*, 1832, is an old song entitled 'What Argufies Pride and Ambition?' 2. Hence, to pester with argument: id.: 1771, Smollett; ob. 3. Hence, v.i., to argue, wrangle: id.: 1800, Maria Edgeworth. The commonest sense.

argy-bargy, see ARGAL.

Aristippus. Canary wine: C.17: Middleton, 'rich Aristippus, sparkling sherry'. Ex the hedonistic Greek philosopher.

aristo. An aristocrat: dated by the O.E.D. Sup. at 1864, but perhaps rather from ca 1790 and perhaps influenced by Fr. s.

aristocrat. A SWELL, a TOFF: C.19–20; coll, but at no time at all gen.

aristocratic vein. (Gen. pl.) A blue vein: theatrical coll (—1909); ob. cf. S.E. *blue blood*.

Aristotle. A bottle: rhyming s.: late C.19–20; ob.

***ark,** see ARKMAN. 2. A barrack-room chest: military coll (—1903); ob. A survival ex S.E.

***ark and win(n)s.** A sculler; a row-boat; c.: late C.18–mid 19. See ARKMAN.

ark-floater. An aged actor: C.19. Ex *Noah's ark* + *floats*, the footlights.

***ark-pirate.** A thief 'working' navigable rivers: nautical c. (—1823); †by 1900.

***arkman.** A Thames waterman: C.18–19; c. or low. *Ark*, a boat, is not c. except perhaps ca 1750–1850. Thence *ark-ruff(ian)*, a fresh-water thief: c.; C.18–mid 19.

Arleens. Orleans plums: Cockney coll. Recorded by Baumann, 1887.

arm, as long as one's. Very long: coll; late C.19–20.

arm, chance one's, see CHANCE YOUR ARM!

arm, make a long. To stretch one's arm after something: from ca 1880; coll.

arm, under the. (Of a job) additional: tailors' (—1903).

***arm-pits, work under the.** To avoid being hanged, to commit only petty larcenies: c.: C.19.

arm-props. Crutches: coll: from ca 1820; †by 1910. Moncrieff, 1821.

arm the lead. 'To fill a small cavity with tallow to bring up a sample of the bottom' when sounding the depth: nautical: mid-C.19–20: coll >, by 1900, j. Bowen.

armour, be in. To be pot-valiant: late C.17–18. cf. *Dutch courage* and perhaps the C.17 proverbial *armour is light at table* (Apperson).

armour, fight in. To use a FRENCH LETTER: ca 1780–1840.

arms and legs (, all). Weak beer: without *body*. C.19–20.

arm's length, work at. To work at a disadvantage; clumsily: coll > S.E.; C.19–20; ob.

arms of Murphy, in the. Asleep: low (—1903). i.e. *Morpheus*.

arrah! An Anglo-Irish expletive of emotion, excitement: coll: late C.17–20.

array. To thrash, flog; afflict; disfigure, befoul: ironically or jocularly coll: late C.14–16. cf. DRESS DOWN, DRESSING DOWN.

arri! An exclamation of astonishment or vexation: Midland Districts of South Africa: coll: from early 1880s. Ex Hottentot *are*.

'Arry and 'Arriet. A typical costermonger and his, or any, coster lass; hence, any low-bred and lively (esp. if not old) man and woman. Popularized by Milliken. From ca 1870; coll. Whence *'Arryish*, 'costermongerish', vulgarly jovial: coll; from ca 1880. Also, *'Arry's worrier*, a concertina: Cockney: 1885; ob.

ars musica. The 'musical' ARSE, i.e. the podex: late C.18–19. Punning the L. for musical art.

arse. Posterior; buttocks. Until ca 1660, S.E.; then a vulg. ca 1700–1930, rarely printed in full: even B.E. (1690) on one occasion prints as 'ar—', and Grose often omits the *r*.

arse, v.t. To kick: C.19–20: s.

arse, anchor one's. A C.19–20 variant of ANCHOR, BRING . . .

arse!, ask my. I don't know!: low: mid-C.19–20. See also ASK MINE . . .

arse, grease a fat sow in the, see GREASE . . .

arse, hang an or **the.** To hold or hang back; to hesitate timorously: C.17–20 coll; ob.

arse!, my; my foot! Expressions of marked incredulity; intense negatives: low: since ca 1880, ca 1860, resp.

arse!, so is my (†mine). A low c.p. of incredulity or contempt: C.17–20. Jonson. Also *kiss †mine* or *my arse!*: C.18–20. Swift.

arse about, v.i. In late C.18–19, to turn round: a vulgarism.

arse and shite through his ribs, he would lend his. A c.p. applied to 'anyone who lends his money inconsiderately', Grose, 2nd ed.: ca 1780–1860.

arse-cooler. (Women's dress, C.19) a bustle.

arse-crawl, v.i. To toady: low coll: late C.19–20.

arse-crawler or **-creeper.** A sycophant: low coll: late C.19–20.

arse-foot. A penguin: (nautical) coll (—1598); Florio, Goldsmith; †by 1880. Because its feet are placed so far back.

arse from one's elbow, not to know one's. To be very ignorant: lower classes': late C.19–20.

arse-hole. Anus: a coll vulgarism: C.19 (?18)–20.

arse-hole crawler; often simply CRAWLER. A sycophant: low: late C.19–20.

Arse-hole Square. Boyish and youthful wit in parroted reply to 'Where?': mostly Cockneys': late C.19–20.

arse-hole to breakfast time, from. All the way; all the time: low: late C.19–20.

arse-holes to breakfast time. Upside down: utterly confused: most unsatisfactory: Cockney: late C.19–20. Thus 'Them ahses built all . . .' or 'Take no notice of him – he's always . . .'

arse-holes (to you)! A low contemptuous interjection: late C.19–20. Ex ARSE-HOLE.

arse if it was loose, he would lose his. A c.p. 'said of a careless person', Grose, 2nd ed.: ca 1780–1860; but in a more gen. form C.16. Nowadays we say . . . *head* . . .

arse off. Depart: late C.19–20: s.

arse on . . ., see BANDBOX.

arse over turkey. Head over heels: low: late C.19–20.

arse upwards. In good luck; luckily; coll: C.17–20. Esp. *rise with one's* . . .

arse-worm. 'A little diminutive Fellow', B.E.: late C.17–18.

arsty! Slowly!; slow down!: Regular Army: late C.19–20. Ex Hindustani *ahisti*. Opp. JILDI.

arsy-varsy, adv. Head over heels, esp. with *fall*, C.18–20; adj., preposterous, topsy-turvy, mid-C.17–19. Ex *varsy*, a rhyming addition, properly *versy*, L. *versus* (turned), and coll.

artesian. Beer made in Australia: Australian: ca 1880–1914.

artful dodger. A lodger: rhyming s. (—1857). 2. An expert thief: ca 1864–1900, perhaps ex the character in *Oliver Twist*.

artful fox. A theatre box: music-hall rhyming s.: 1882; †by 1916.

Arthur, King, see AMBASSADOR. Grose, 1st ed.

artichoke, see HEARTY-CHOKE.

artichoke ripe. To smoke a pipe; rhyming s.: ca 1855–80.

article. A girl, a woman: ca 1810–70. 2. Contemptuous of any person: from ca 1856; coll. Ex 'its common use in trade for an item of commodity, as in the phr[ase] "What's the next article?" of the mod. shopkeeper,' E.D.D.

article, the (very). The precise thing; the thing (or person) most needed. Coll. From ca 1850. Trollope.

article of virtue. Virgin: ca 1850–1914. Punning *virtue*, (*objets de*) *vertu*.

articles. Breeches, trousers; C.18–19. 2. In c. of 1780–1830, a suit of clothes.

artilleryman. A drunkard: low (—1903). Ex noisiness.

artist. A person, CHAP, 'fellow': from ca 1905.

arty-and-crafty. Artistic but not notably useful or comfortable: coll: 1902.

— as —. Very —; e.g. *drunk as drunk*, very drunk: coll: mid-C.19–20. Perhaps ex — *as can be*.

as . . . as they make 'em. Utterly; very. Esp. with *bad, drunk, fast, mad*. From ca 1880. Coll.

as ever is. A (mostly lower classes') coll c.p. tag, emphasizing the preceding statement: mid-C.19–20. Edward Lear (d. 1888) once wrote, ca 1873, 'I shall go either to Sardinia, or India, or Jumsibobjigglequack this next winter as ever is.'

as much use as my arse, often preceded by *you're*. A low abusive c.p.: late C.19–20.

as you were. 'Used . . . to one who is going too fast in his assertions' (—1864). Coll. Ex Army.

ash beans and long oats. A thrashing: London streets': C.19. Augustus Mayhew, *Paved with Gold*, 1857, 'Give him with all my might a good feed of "long oats" and "ash beans".'

ash-cat. A fireman in the Merchant Service: nautical, esp. naval: late C.19–20.

ash-plant. A light cane carried by subalterns: military coll: 1870; ob. Ex its material.

Ashes, the. 'The symbolical remains of English cricket taken back to Australia' (S.O.D.): 1882. Also *win, regain* or *recover*, or *lose the Ashes*, to win or lose a series of test matches (from the English point of view): 1883 (W. J. Lewis).

Asia Minor. Kensington and Bayswater (London, W.8 and W.2), ex the large number of retired Indian Civil Servants there resident ca 1860–1910: London: ca 1880–1915.

asinego, occ. **assinego.** A little ass: C.17. 2. A fool: C.17–18. Shakespeare has 'An Asinico may tutor thee; Thou . . . Asse.' Ex Sp.

ask. 'A jockey is said to "ask" . . . a horse when rousing him to greater exertion': turf: from ca 1860. B. & L.

ask another! Don't be silly!: Cockney c.p. addressed to one who asks a stale riddle: 1896; ob.

ask bogy. An evasive reply: nautical mid-C.18–19. Sea-wit, says Grose, for 'ask mine a-se'. cf. BOGY, and GOOSEBERRY-GRINDER.

ask for it. To incur foolishly; be fooled unnecessarily, ludicrously: coll: C.20; the O.E.D. (Sup.) dates it at 1909, but it is at least four years older. cf. BUY IT.

ask me (or my) behind is a mid-C.19–20 variant of *ask my* (or *me*) ARSE.

ask mine, (in C.19–20) my, arse! A low coll evasive reply: mid-C.18–20; orig. nautical.

ask out. To invite to (an) entertainment: coll: from late 1880s.

asker. A beggar: euphemistic s.: 1858, Reade; ob.

***askew.** A cup: c. of ca 1550–1650. ?etymology. Prob. from Fr. *escuelle*, a cup.

asking, not you by your. A c.p. reply (late C.18–early 19) to 'Who owns this?' cf. the late C.19–20 *none the better for your asking* (health).

asking!, that's. i.e. when you shouldn't, or when I shouldn't reply: coll c.p.: late C.19–20.

ass. A compositor: journalists', ca 1850–1900. Variant, DONKEY. 2. A very stupid or ignorant person: formerly S.E.; in C.20, coll. (N.B., *make an ass of* is going the same way.) 3. Arse: dial. and late coll: C.19–20. This is the gen. U.S. pronunciation.

ass about. To fool about: schoolboys' (—1899). cf. ASS, 2.

assassin. An ornamental bow worn on the female breast: ca 1900–14. Very KILLING.

assig. An assignation, an appointment: ca 1680–1830.

assinego, see ASINEGO.

astarrakan. Astrakhan (fur): jocular Cockney: late C.19–20.

aste. Rare c. for money: early C.17. Nares. Ex It. *asta*, auction.

astronomer. A drunkard 'that knocks his head against a post, then looks up at the sky': s. (—1650). 2. A horse that carries its head high: C.19.

at that, see THAT, AT.

at the Inn of the Morning Star. (Sleeping) in the open air: coll, rather literary, verging on S.E.: from ca 1880; ob. Suggested by Fr. *à la belle étoile*.

atcha! All right!: military: from ca 1860. Ex Hindustani *accha*, good.

atfler, see HATFLER.

Athanasian wench. 'A forward girl, ready to oblige every man that shall ask her', Grose. ca 1700–1830. Variant, *quicunque vult* (whosoever desires) – the opening words of the Athanasian Creed.

Athenaeum; gen. **the A.** The penis: cultured (—1903); very ob. Perhaps ex *Athenaeum*, an association of persons meeting for mutual improvement.

Atkins, see TOMMY, 4.

Atlantic ranger. A herring: coll: from ca 1880; ob. Variant, SEA-ROVER.

atomy. A very small, a small thin, a small deformed person: late C.16–19. Coll by 1700; from mid-C.19, S.E.; slightly ob. Ex ANATOMY (variant OTOMY) – confused prob. by *atom*. Shakespeare: 'Thou atomy, thou! . . . you thin thing.' Sala: 'A miserable little atomy, more deformed, more diminutive, more mutilated than any beggar in a bowl.'

atrocious. Very bad; execrable; very noticeable: coll; from ca 1830. 2. adv. in *-ly*: 1831, Alford, 'The letter had an atrociously long sentence in it.'

atrocity. A bad blunder; an offence against good taste, manners, or morals. 1878.

attack. To address oneself to; commence. From ca 1820, coll; after ca 1860, S.E. due to Gallic influence.

attend to. To thrash: coll; from ca 1800. cf. L. *animadvertere*.

attic; occ., not before ca 1850, and now ob., **attic-storey.** The head: pugilistic (—1823). By 1870 (Dean Alford), gen. cf. UPPER STOREY. 2. Esp. (*be*) *queer in the attic*, weak-minded; rarely, mad: from ca 1870. Ex 3. Orig. (—1859), *queer in the attic* = intoxicated: pugilistic; †by 1890. 4. The female pudend (*attic* only): low (—1903); ob.

attorney. A goose or turkey drumstick, grilled and devilled: punning DEVIL, a lawyer working for another: 1829, Griffin, 'I love a plain beef steak before a grilled attorney'; ob. (*Attorney* as a legal title was abolished in England in 1873.) 2. In c., a legal adviser to criminals: late C.19–20, ob.

Attorney-General. A drinker 'so free that he will pledge all comers': —1650: s.

Attorney-General's devil. A barrister doing a K.C.'s heavy work: ca 1860–1920.

au reservoir! *Au revoir*. Orig. U.S., adopted ca 1880.

auctioneer, deliver or **give** or **tip (one) the.** To knock a person down: ca 1860–1930. Sala, 1863 (*deliver*); H., 5th ed. (*tip*). 'Tom Sayers's right hand was known to pugilistic fame as the *auctioneer*' (Sayers, d. 1865, fought from 1849 to 1860, in which latter year he drew, miraculously, with Heenan); Manchon.

audit. Abbr. *audit ale*, a brew peculiar to Trinity College, Cambridge, and several other Cambridge and Oxford colleges; made orig. for drinking on audit days: mid-C.19–20; coll verging on S.E. Ouida, 1872.

audit one's accounts, see ACCOUNTS . . .

Auguste. A minor circus-clown, a 'feed' to the JOEY (3) or Chief Clown: circus: late C.19–20. Prob. from one so named.

Auld Hornie. The devil. Mainly Scottish: C.18–20, ob. Ex his horn. For accounts of the devil's names, see Weekley's *Word and Names*, 1932, and *Words!*, 1933. 2. The penis: Scots (—1903). A pun on HORN, a priapism.

Auld Reekie. Orig. the old-town part of Edinburgh: late C.18–ca 1860. Then the whole city. Lit., 'Old Smoky'; cf. THE GREAT SMOKE, London. Coll from ca 1890.

auly-auly. (Winchester College) a game played ca 1700–1840 in Grass Court after Saturday afternoon chapel. A collective game with an india-rubber ball. Supposedly ex *haul ye, call ye*, but, in view of Winchester's fame in Classics, prob. ex Gr. *αὐλή*, a court or a quadrangle.

aunt. A procuress, a concubine, a prostitute: C.17–ca 1830. *Mine* (or *my*) *aunt*, as in Grose, 1st ed. Shakespeare,

> Summer songs for me and my aunts,
> While we lie tumbling in the hay.

2. Also, at Oxford and Cambridge Universities, a students' name for 'the sister university': C.17–18. Fuller, 1755. 3. A children's coll for a non-related woman (cf. *uncle*): C.19–20. cf. the U.S. usage (an aged Negress as addressed by a child) and see AUNTIE.

aunt, or auntie, go to see one's. To visit the w.c.: euphemistic, mostly women's: from ca 1850. cf. MRS JONES, which is occ. *Aunt Jones*.

aunt, my, see MY AUNT.

aunt!, my. A mild exclamation: coll: from late 1880s.

aunt had been my uncle, if my, see MAN, IF MY AUNT . . .

Aunt Maria. The female pudend: low (—1903).

Aunt Sally. A wicket-keeper: cricketers' jocular coll: 1898.

Aunt's sisters. Ancestors: London middle-class (—1909). By pun.

auntie, aunty. Coll form of *aunt*: from ca 1790. Also, like UNCLE, used by children for a friend of the house: C.19–20. 2. See AUNT, GO TO SEE ONE'S.

Australian flag. A shirt-tail rucked up between trousers and waistcoat: Australian, ca 1870–1910.

***autem,** a church, mid-C.16–18 c., is the parent of many other c. terms, e.g. *autem bawler*, a parson; *autem cackler*, a Dissenter or a married woman; *autem-cackle tub*, a Dissenters' meeting-house or a pulpit; *autem dipper* or *diver*, a Baptist, or a pickpocket specializing in churches; *autem gog(g)ler*, a pretended prophet, or a conjuror; *autem jet*, a parson; *autem prickear*, see *autem cackler*; *autem quaver*, a Quaker; and *autem-quaver tub*, a Quakers' meeting-house or a desk therein. Perhaps essentially 'altar': cf. Fr. *autel*: with *-em* substituted for *-el*. In c. of C.16–18, *-am -em, -om, -um* are common suffixes.

autem, adj. Married, esp. in the two c. terms, *autem cove*, a married man, and *autem mort*, a married woman: C.17–18. Perhaps ex ALTHAM, a wife.

author-baiting. Summoning an unsuccessful dramatist before the curtain: theatrical, ca 1870–1900.

auto. Abbr. *automobile*: 1899; coll; S.E. by 1910 but never gen. Ex Fr.

***autom, autum.** Variants of AUTEM.

autumn. (The season or time of) an execution by hanging: low: mid-C.19–20; ob.

avast! Hold on! Be quiet! Stop! Nautical: C.17–20; coll >, by late C.19, S.E. Prob. ex Dutch *hou'vast*, hold fast.

avaunt, give the. To dismiss (a person): late C.16–early 17. Shakespeare. Ex *avaunt!*, be off! (C.15+).

average man, the. The ordinary person: C.19–20; coll > S.E. cf. the MAN IN THE STREET.

***avering.** A boy's begging naked to arouse compassion: c.: late C.17–early 18. Kennett, 1695, has also *go a-avering*. ?ex *aver*, to declare (it) true.

avoirdupois. Obesity: jocular coll; late C.19–20.

***avoirdupois lay.** The thieving of brass weights from shop counters: late C.18–mid 19 c.

avuncular relation or **relative.** A pawnbroker: facetiously coll, ca 1860–1900. Sala, in 1859, speaks of pawnbroking as *avuncular life*. cf. UNCLE.

awake. To inform, let know: from mid-1850s; ob.

***awaste.** A c. form of *avast* as in BING *avast*.

away. Erroneous for *way*: C.17–18. Hakluyt, Smollett. 2. In imperatives, e.g. *say away*, it gives to the phrase a coll tinge: C.17 (?earlier)–20. 3. To depart: theatrical: ca 1905–14. Ex melodramatic *away!* 4. In prison: low London (—1909). By euphemism.

aweer. Aware: Cockney low coll (—1887).

awful, esp. *a penny awful*. A PENNY

DREADFUL, a blood-and-thunder tale. ca 1860–1900.

awful, adj. A catch-intensive. Apparently C.18 Scottish, then U.S. (see Bartlett), and ca 1840 adopted in England. Lamb, 1834: 'She is indeed, as the Americans would express it, something awful.' Coll, as is the adv. *awful(ly)* = very: mid-C. 19–20. In 1859 occurs *awfully clever*; *Punch* satirized it in 1877 in the phrase, 'it's too awfully nice'.

***awful place, the.** Dartmoor Prison: c. dating from the late 1890s.

awfully, see AWFUL, adj.

'Awkins. A severe man; one not to be trifled with: Cockney: ca 1880–1900. Ex Judge Sir Frederic Hawkins, reputed to be a 'hanging' judge.

awkward. Pregnant: euphemistic: late C. 19–20; ob.

awkward squad. Recruits, esp. a segregated group of recruits, commencing to learn to drill or having their drill improved: naval and military, from ca 1870; coll by 1890.

awls and be gone, pack up one's. To depart for good: (low) coll (—1673). Prob. *awls* is a corruption of *all*, as Manchon suggests.

awry, tread the shoe. To fall from virtue: C.16–20, ob.; coll; then, in C.18–20, S.E. cf. in S.E. *take* or *make a false step*.

axe, where the chicken got the, see CHICKEN GOT ...

axe after the helve, send the. (Better, *send the helve after the hatchet*.) To take a further useless step; send good money after bad. Coll; from C.16; in C.19–20, rare but S.E.

axe in the helve, put the. To solve a doubt. Coll; from C.16; ob. Like the preceding, proverbial.

axe (or axes) to grind. An ulterior motive, gen. selfish. Coll, orig. (—1815) U.S., adopted ca 1840. At first of politics, it soon widened in applicability; by 1850, moreover, it had > S.E.

ax(e)-my-eye, an. A very alert fellow: cheapjacks', ca 1850–1910. Hindley.

axle-grease, see GREASE, n., 5.

B

b. A bug: coll; from ca 1860. Also *b flat*: 1836. Ex the insect's initial letter and appearance. 2. In c., abbr. BLUE. 3. See A1, 2.

b. and s.; B. and S. Brandy and soda: Whyte-Melville, 1868: s. >, ca 1890, coll. The *b* is occ. separable, as in 'Give me some B in my S', Baumann, 1887.

***b.c.** A person bringing a wholly inadequate action for libel: from ca 1870. Ex the *bloody cat* of an actual lawsuit. †.

B.C., see ANNO DOMINI.

B.C. play. A Classical drama: theatrical: 1885; very ob. i.e. before Christ.

b flat, see B, 1.

B-flat homey; B-flat polone (or poloney). A fat man, a fat woman, esp. in a sideshow: partly Parlary, wholly fair-ground: late C.19–20.

B from a battledore, or, rarely, **from a broomstick** or, very gen., **from a bull's foot, not to know.** To be illiterate, extremely ignorant: resp. mid-C.16–17, C.19, C.15–20. A battledore was an alphabet-hornbook. For the first phrase and the third, see esp. Apperson's *English Proverbs and Proverbial Phrases*. Also *not to know great A from a battledore* or *(great) A from a bull's foot*.

B.H. A bank holiday: non-aristocratic coll: 1880; ob.

b.k.'s. 'Military officers in *mufti*, when out on the spree, and not wishing their profession to be known, speak of their barracks as the B.K.'s', H., 3rd ed.: military (—1864); ob.

B.N.C. Brasenose College, Oxford: from ca 1840: coll >, by 1900, j. cf. BRAZEN NOSE COLLEGE, YOU WERE BRED IN.

B.P. The British Public: theatrical (1867) >, by 1910, gen. coll.

b.t.m. A coll domestic euphemism for BOTTOM (posterior): late C.19–20.

ba-ha. Bronchitis: tailors': from the 1890s; slightly ob. By deliberate slurring.

baa-baa. A sheep: nursery coll: C.19–20. Ex the sheep's bleat. cf. BOW-WOW; COCK-A-DOODLE(-DOO); MOO-COW; QUACK-QUACK.

***baa cheat.** A sheep: c.: C.18. Anon., *Street-Robberies Consider'd* (*ba cheat*), 1728. Lit., 'baa' + (CHEAT =) thing.

baa-lamb. A lamb (cf. BAA-BAA): nursery coll: C.19–20.

baas. A master, a manager, a head man of any sort: South African coll: 1785, Sparrman, *A Voyage to the Cape of Good Hope . . . from 1772 to 1776*. Ex Dutch *baas*, master, foreman. 2. The term of address to the skipper of a Dutch ship: nautical coll: C.19–20.

baba. A coll, gen. a child's, variant of PAPA: C.19–20. In late C.16–17, *bab*. 2. In Anglo-Indian coll, a child. Ex Turki *baba* influenced by our *baby*.

babbie, babby, vocative. Baby: coll: late C.19–20. Ex C.16–20 dial.

babe. The latest-elected member of the House of Commons: opp. *father of the house*. Parliamentary coll: from ca 1870.

babe in the wood. A criminal in the stocks or the pillory: late C.18–early 19.

babe of grace. Bee defines the pl as 'sanctified-looking persons, not so': fast society: ca 1820–40.

babes. A gang of disreputables who, at an auction, forbear to bid against the bigger dealers; their reward, drinks and/or cash. From ca 1860 ob. cf. KNOCK-OUT.

Babsky. A wind-swept part of Liverpool: Liverpool: 1886. i.e. *Bay o' Biscay*.

baby. A twopenny bottle of soda-water: public-house: ca 1875–1900. 2. A girl, a sweetheart: fast sporting s.: from ca 1895.

baby, the. A diamond-mining sifting machine: Vaal River coll (—1886); ob. Ex: *Babe*, its American inventor. Pettman, who notes *baby*, to sift ground with this machine: from mid-1880s.

Baby Act, plead the. To excuse oneself as too inexperienced: from ca 1900; ob. Ex: 2. 'To plead minority as voiding a contract': coll: from late 1890s. Ex the plea of *infancy* in its legal sense.

baby and nurse. 'A small bottle of soda-water and two-pennyworth of spirit in it': public-house: ca 1876–1900. Ware. cf. BABY.

baby bunting, see BUNTING.

baby crying, the. The bugle-call to defaulters: military: late C.19–20; ob. cf. WHISPER, ANGEL'S, 1.

baby-farmer, see FARM and FARMER, 3.

baby-maker. The penis: euphemistically jocular: late C.19–20; ob.

baby- or **baby's-pap.** A cap: (mostly underworld) rhyming slang: ca 1855–1900.

baby-pulling. Obstetrics: medical students': since ca 1880.

babylon(it)ish. C.19 Winchester College for a dressing-gown: ex *Babylon(it)ish garment*.

baby's leg. Meat roll; marmalade roll; roly-poly pudding: Regular Army: late C.19–20.

baby's pap, see BABY-PAP.

baby's public-house. The female breast: proletarian: 1884. *Referee*, 5 Oct.

bacca, bacco, baccy. Tobacco: low coll: resp. 1824, 1793, 1828. cf. BACKER.

bacca- or **bacco-chew.** A chewing tobacco: coll: prob. late C.18–20. Ex an unidentified British source, the *Port Folio* of 28 Aug. 1805, quotes an anonymous song, *Dustman Bill*, thus:

> Cries he, 'My Wenches, ever dear,
> Whate'er be your opinions,
> I love ye better both, d'ye hear,
> Than bacco-chew or onions.'

bacca-pipes. Whiskers curled in ringlets (—1880; †by 1890).

baccare!; backare! Go back, retire! ca 1540–1680. Heywood; Udall; Lyly; Shakespeare, 'Baccare! you are marvellous forward'; Howell, 1659. Jocular on *back*: perhaps Latinized or Italianized *back there*.

Bacchus. A set of Latin verses written on Shrove Tuesday at Eton: ?C.18–early 19: coll at Eton College. Ex the verses there written, on that day, in praise or dispraise of Bacchus. Anon., *Etoniana*, 1865.

bacco, baccy, baccy-box, see BACCA.

bach. A bachelor: in U.S. in 1850s; anglicized ca 1900. Ware prefers *bache*. cf.:

bach, occ. **batch,** v. To live by oneself, doing one's own work; orig. like a bachelor. Ex U.S.; anglicized ca 1890. cf. the n.

Bachelor. 'A lean drunkard': —1650: s.

Bachelor of Law. A drinker with 'a purple face, inchac't with Rubies': —1650: s.

bachelor!, then the town bull is a. A semi-proverbial c.p. retort incredulous on a woman's alleged chastity: mid-C.17–18. Ray, 1678; he does not, however, restrict it to either women or chastity.

bachelor's baby. An illegitimate child: coll, mid-C.19–20. Whiteing, 1899, Ray, ca 1670, and Grose, 1788, have *bachelor's* (or *batchelor's*) *son*.

bachelor's fare. Bread, cheese, and kisses: C.18–19. Swift, ca 1708 (published 30 years later): '*Lady*. . . . Some ladies . . . have promised to breakfast with you . . .; what will you give us? *Colonel*. Why, faith, madam, bachelor's fare, bread and cheese and kisses'.

back. A water-closet: domestic: late C.19–20. From the days of backyard privies.

back, on one's. Penniless; utterly puzzled: late C.19–20. Nautically, *on the bones of one's back*.

back, ride on one's. To fool or deceive a person, esp. successfully: coll: C.18–19.

back and belly. All over: C.18–19 familiar coll. *Keep one b. and b.*, C.18–19 coll; adumbrated in C.16.

back and fill, see BACKING AND FILLING.

back-biters, his bosom friends are become his. A punning c.p. (cf. BOSOM FRIEND) of ca 1700–1840. Swift, ca 1708.

back-breaker. A person setting, or a thing being, a task beyond normal endurance: C.18–20 coll. The adj., *back-breaking*, gen. goes with *job* or *work*.

back-breakers. 'Old-fashioned ship's pumps': nautical: late C.19–20. Bowen. A special application of the preceding.

back-chat. A variant of BACK-TALK: 'A slang term applied to saucy or impertinent replies', Pettman: South African (—1901) and (?hence) Australian.

***back-cheat.** A cloak: C.18–early 19: c.

back door, a gentleman or **an usher of the.** A sodomist: mid-C.18–20, ob. Hence *back-door* ▪*work*, sodomy. cf. BACK-GAMMON-PLAYER.

back-door trot. Diarrhoea: from ca 1870; orig. dial. cf. JERRY-GO-NIMBLE.

back-door trumpet. A mid-C.19–20 variant of ARS MUSICA.

back down, often a *square back-down*. An utter collapse; complete surrender of claims: from early 1880s: coll. 2. A severe rebuff: from ca 1890. 3. See SQUARE BACK-DOWN.

back down. To yield, to retire: from ca 1880: coll >, by 1910, S.E. Ex U.S. (1849).

back-ender. 'A horse entered for a race late in the season', F. & H.: racing coll: ca 1889. Ex *back-end*, the last two months of the horse-racing season.

back-hair part. A role 'in which the agony of the performance at one point in the drama admits of the feminine tresses in question floating over the shoulders': theatrical: 1884. Ware.

back-hairing. 'Feminine fighting, in which

the occipital locks suffer severely', Ware: London streets' (—1909).

back-hand. To drink more than one's share: ca 1850–1910. In G. A. Lawrence's best novel, *Guy Livingstone*, 1857, it occurs as a vbl n., *back-handing*.

back-handed. Indirect; unfair: from ca 1815: coll >, by 1880, S.E. Dickens, 1865, has *a back-handed reminder*. cf. BACK-HANDER, 3.

back-handed turn. An unprofitable transaction: Stock Exchange, ca 1870–1914.

back-hander. A drink either additional or out of turn: coll: ca 1850–1900. Ex: 2. A blow with the back of the hand: coll >, by 1870, S.E.: 1836, Marryat; Farrar. 3. Hence, a rebuke: ca 1860–1900 (e.g. in Whyte-Melville): coll >, by 1900, S.E. cf. BACK-HANDED.

back is up, – Sir, I see somebody has offended you, for your. A jeering c.p. addressed to a hump-backed man: ca 1780–1850. See BACK UP, adj.

***back-jump.** To enter (e.g. a house) by a back door or window: c. from ca 1855. Ex: 2. A back window: c. (—1812). Because one jumps from it in escape.

back of, break the, see BREAK THE NECK.

back o' me hand to ye! the. An Anglo-Irish retort: c.p.: late C.19–20. Euphemistic?

back o' the green. Behind the scenes: theatrical and music-halls': ca 1880–1910. Ware, with reference to the green curtain and in imperfect rhyme on *scenes*.

back of the hand down. Bribery: from ca 1890; ob. (J. Milne, *The Epistles of Atkins*, 1902.)

back out. To retreat from a difficulty or unpleasantness: 1818, Scott: coll >, by 1860, S.E. Ex lit. sense.

back-racket. A *tu-quoque*: coll; C.17–18. Ex the S.E. sense, 'the return of a ball in tennis'.

back-row hopper. A sponger affecting taverns haunted by actors: theatrical (—1909): virtually †.

***back scratched, have one's.** To be flogged: c.: from ca 1870. Orig. of the CAT O' NINE TAILS.

back-scratching. (A) flogging: naval: late C.19–early 20. (As sycophantic flattery, it is S.E.)

***back-scuttle.** Same as BACK-SLANG IT: c. of C.19. *Do* or *have a back-scuttle*, to possess a woman *a retro*: low: mid-C.19–20. 2. Hence, v. and n.: (to commit) sodomy: low: late C.19–20.

back-seam, be (down) on one's. To be out of luck, unfortunate. Tailors' (—1887). cf. BACK, ON ONE'S.

back seat, take a. To retire; yield; fail. Orig. (1863) U.S.; anglicized ca 1880: coll.

***back-slang it.** To go out the back way: ca 1810–1910: low; prob. orig. c. cf. BACK SLUM. 2. In Australia, ca 1850–1905, to seek unoffered lodging in the country. Perhaps ex the following sense: 3. To go a circuitous or private way through the streets in order to avoid meeting certain persons: c. of ca 1810–50.

***back slum.** A back room; the back-entrance of a building. 'Thus, we'll *give it* 'em *on the back slum*, means, we'll get in at the back door,' Vaux, 1812: c. >, ca 1870, low. cf. BACK-JUMP and BACK-SLANG IT.

back slums. (—1821) s. for residential area of criminals and near-criminals.

back-staircase. A woman's BUSTLE: ca 1850–1900.

***back-stall.** In C.19–20 ob. c., an accomplice covering a thief. cf. STALL.

back-strapped. (Of a ship or a boat) 'carried back into an awkward position by the tide and held there': nautical coll: mid-C.19–20. Bowen.

back-swap, n. and v. To cry off a bargain; the crying-off: coll verging on s.: 1888, Fothergill, *Leverhouse*, '"Then it's agreed?" . . . "Yes, no back-swaps."' Lit., to go back on a SWAP.

back-talk. Impudence; verbal recalcitrance. Esp. as *no back-talk!* From ca 1870; coll. cf. BACK-CHAT. Ex dial.

back-timber. Clothing: C.17–18: coll.

back-tommy. Cloth covering the stays at the waist: tailors': late C.19–20.

back or **backs to the wall.** Hard pressed: C.19 coll, C.20 S.E. In C.16–18 with *at* for *to*.

back up. To be ready to help, chiefly in games: coll (in C.20, S.E.): from ca 1860. 2. Winchester College, from ca 1870: to call out, e.g. for help.

back up, adj. Annoyed, aroused. *One's back to be up*, to be annoyed, C.18–19 coll; *put* or *set one's back up*, to be, or to make, annoyed, C.18–20 coll: from ca 1800 both phrases tended to be considered as S.E. though not literary. Since ca 1870, *get one's back up*, to become or to make annoyed, is the gen. form: this, however, has always been coll. cf. BACK IS UP.

back-up, or **horn, pills.** Aphrodisiacs: low: since ca 1910.

backare! see BACCARE!

backed. Dead: late C.17–early 19. Perhaps = set on one's back; B.E. and Grose, however, explain as 'on six men's shoulders', i.e. carried to the grave.

backer, back(e)y. Tobacco: low coll: 1848, Dickens (*backer*). cf. BACCA.

backgammon-player. A sodomist: mid-C.18–early 19; cf. *gentleman of the* BACK DOOR.

backgammoner. The same: ca 1820–80.

background. Retiring; modest: coll: 1896, 'A reticent, background kind of lover', O.E.D., i.e. keeping in the background.

backing and filling, vbl n. and adj. Irresolute, dilatory, shifty; shiftiness, irresolution: coll: from ca 1840. Ex nautical j. In Barham's use, 'moving zigzag', the orig. sense lingers. Bowen adds the sense, 'lazy': nautical: ca 1850–1900.

backings-up. The ends of half-burnt faggots: Winchester College, C.19.

backs to the wall, see BACK TO THE WALL.

backsheesh, -shish; baksheesh, ba(c)kshee, see BAKSHEE.

backside. The posteriors: C.16–20. Always S.E., but ca 1870–1914 a vulgarism. See *Slang*, p. 138.

backward, ring the bells. To give the alarm: ca 1500–1890; coll > S.E. Cleveland, Scott. Ex the practice of beginning with the bass when the bells were rung.

backward in coming forward. Shy; modest: jocular coll (semi-c.p.): from mid-C.19.

backward station. 'In the old Coastguard Service one that was considered most undesirable, frequently on account of its distance from a school': coastguardsmen's coll: C.19. Bowen.

backwards, piss. To defecate: low: late C.19–20; ob.

backy. A shop-mate working behind another: tailors', from ca 1870; ob. 2. See BACKER.

***bacon,** see BACON, SAVE ONE'S.

bacon, a good voice to beg. A c.p. derisive of an ill voice: late C.17–18. B.E.

bacon, pull. To put one's fingers derisively to one's nose: mid-C.19–20.

bacon, save one's. To escape narrowly: late C.17–20; coll from ca 1750. A. Behn, 1682, 'I go (to church) to save my bacon as they say, once a month.' Perhaps from the days of heretics burnt at the stake; *A New Canting Dict.* (1725), however, says that in this phrase, *bacon* 'in the Canting Sense, is the Prize, of whatever kind, which Robbers make in their Enterprizes'.

bacon-faced. Full-faced: late C.17–19. Recorded first in Otway.

bacon-fed. Fat; greasy: coll: late C.16–19. Occurring in Shakespeare.

bacon-slicer. A rustic: coll: mid C.17–early 19. Urquhart, 1653.

bacon-tree. A pig: Lancashire jocular coll: 1867, Brierley, *Marlocks*; slightly ob. Because a pig is 'growing bacon', E.D.D.

bad. Difficult; esp. in *bad to beat*, as in Hawley Smart's *Post to Finish*, 1884: coll. Ob.

bad, go to the. To be ruined; become depraved. From ca 1860; coll >, ca 1910, S.E. Early users are Miss Braddon and 'Dagonet' Sims. Ex *to the bad*, in deficit.

bad, not. Rather or (patronizingly) quite good: upper (hence, derivatively, middle) classes' coll: from ca 1860 (Ware); the O.E.D. (Sup.) example at 1835 is prob. isolated and perhaps inoperative.

bad, not half. Fairly good: coll: from late 1890s. cf. NOT HALF.

bad, taken. Taken ill: (low) coll: since ca 1840. On TAKEN SHORT.

bad, to the. In deficit. The O.E.D. quotes an example in 1816. Coll.

bad bargain. A worthless soldier (gen. preceded by *King's* or *Queen's*): C.18–20; coll from 1800. 2. Hence, since ca 1860 (without *King's* or *Queen's*), any worthless person: coll.

bad cess to! Evil befall . . .! Anglo-Irish coll; from ca 1850. Prob. ex *cess* = assessment, levy, rate(s); but perhaps abbr. *success*.

bad egg. A rascal; a scoundrel; worthless fellow. Orig. (1853) U.S.; anglicized ca 1860. Thornton, '. . . The *κὰκου κόρακος κακὸν ᾠὸν* of the Greeks.'

bad form. Vulgar; rude; unaccepted of Society: Society s.: from ca 1860, according to Ware. Ob., *not done* superseding it. In C.20, *b.f.* > coll. *Punch*, 1882 (an Eton boy to his hale old uncle): '. . . Energy's such awful bad form, you know!' Ex horse-racing.

bad ha(lf)penny. A ne'er-do-well: from ca 1850. Ex the c.p., *it is a bad halfpenny*, said by one who, having failed, returns as he went: ca 1810–50.

bad hat. A rascal: from ca 1880. Besant, 1883. In the *Daily Telegraph* of 28 July 1894, G. A. Sala, citing Sir William Fraser's *Words on Wellington*, suggests that the phrase *what a shocking bad hat*, which > a c.p., was coined by the Duke in the 1830s: this rests on hearsay. Sala continues, 'The catchword soon lost its political associations, and after a few years, was merged in the purely imbecile query, "Who's your hatter?"' which was †by 1900. Ware thinks that *bad hat* was, prob., Irish in origin, 'the worst Hibernian characters always wearing bad high hats (caps are not recognized in kingly Ireland)'. cf. BAD LOT and see HAT!, WHAT A SHOCKING BAD.

bad lot. A person of – often worse than – indifferent morals: coll: Thackeray, 1849. Ex auctioneering. cf. BAD EGG; BAD HAT; BAD 'UN.

bad mark, see MARK, BAD or GOOD.

bad match twist. Red hair and black whiskers: hairdresser's, from ca 1870; †.

bad shilling, a. One's last shilling: proletarian (—1909); slightly ob. 2. A remittance man: Australian coll: late C.19–20.

bad shot. A poor guess (—1884; Kinglake in *Eothen*).

bad slang. Spurious curiosities: circus, from ca 1870. Hindley, 1876.

bad 'un. Same as BAD HAT: early C.19–20.

bad young man, see GOOD YOUNG MAN.

Baden-Powell. A trowel: workmen's rhyming s.: late C.19–20.

***badge.** A brand in the hand: C.18 c.

***badge, he has got his.** He has been branded on the hand: c. of ca 1720–1840.

***badge-cove.** A parish-pensioner: C.18–early 19. 2. In C.16–18, a licensed beggar. Both low; prob. c. – at first at any rate.

badger. Nautical (occ. with *-bag*): Neptune in equatorial ceremonies: C.19. 2. Schoolboys': a red-headed person: C.19–20, ob.; at Wellington, late C.19, a 2nd XV Rugby player. 3. In c., a river-thief who, after robbing, murders and throws his victim into the river: ca 1720–1830. Hence perhaps: 4, in C.19 c., a common harlot. 5. A brush: artists': late C.19–20. 6. In Australia often, though ever less, used catachrestically for a bandicoot, rock-wallaby, or, esp. in Tasmania, a wombat: C.19–20.

badger, v. To tease; persecute. Perhaps s. when recorded by Grose in 1785, but very soon coll; S.E. by 1860. Perhaps ex lit. *draw the badger*; cf.:

badger, overdraw the. To overdraw one's banking account: ca 1840–1914. Hood. (?ex †S.E. *overdraw one's banker*.)

badger-bag. 'Neptune and his court in the ceremony of crossing the Line': nautical: mid-C.19–20. It occurs in W. N. Glascock, *The Naval Sketch-Book*, I, 1825, as 'old Badger-bag's track', glossed by Glascock thus: 'A name given by Jack [=sailors] to Neptune, when playing tricks on travellers upon first crossing the Line'. See BADGER, n., 1.

badger-box. A very small dwelling, like an inverted **V** in section: Tasmanian coll: ca 1870–1915. *Proceedings of the Royal Society of Tasmania*, Sept. 1875. Ex badgers' 'dwellings'.

badger-legged. With one leg shorter than the other: coll: from ca 1700; ob. cf. the earlier semi-proverbial *badger-like, one leg shorter than the other* (Howell, 1659). Ex the erroneous belief that a badger has legs of unequal length.

badges and bull's eyes. Badges and medals: military: Oct. 1899; †by 1915. Applied (says the *Daily Telegraph*, 21 Dec. 1899) by General Gatacre to the officers' badges, etc., because they offered so splendid a mark for Boer bullets.

badgy. An enlisted boy; **badgy fiddler,** a boy trumpeter: military: ca 1850–1905. Either because he was a nuisance or because he was bullied or persecuted.

Badian. A Barbadian: ca 1860 + in the West Indies. cf. BIM.

badminton. A cooling drink, esp. a claret-cup: Disraeli (1845), Whyte-Melville (1853), Ouida (1868). Coll >, by 1870, S.E.; ob. 2. In boxing slang, ca 1860–90, blood. cf. CLARET. Ex the Duke of Beaufort's seat of that name. The former sense has suggested the latter.

baffaty. Calico: drapery-trade s. (—1864); ob. Ex S.E. *baft*, *bafta(h)*, *baffeta*.

bag. Milk: Westminster School, C.19–20. 2. See BAGS, 1. 3. A pot of beer: printers' (—1887). cf. BAG, GET ONE'S HEAD IN A. 4. A woman, esp. a middle-aged or elderly slattern ('that old bag'); in certain contexts, a slatternly prostitute or part-time prostitute. I don't recall my having heard it before ca 1924, but suspect that it goes back to the 1890s or even to the 1880s.

bag, v. To obtain for oneself, esp. anything advantageous: Mortimer Collins, 1880, but also for at least a decade earlier. 2. To catch, take, or steal (1818): a common school term, Farrar using it in 1862. 3. To beget or to conceive: C.15–17. All three senses, coll. 4. To dismiss or discharge (a person): 1848, *Chaplain's Report of Preston House of Correction*; 1895, W. Westall, *Sons of Belial*; rather ob. cf. SACK, V.

bag, empty the. To tell everything; close a discussion: coll, C. 18–19.

bag, get or **put one's head in a** or **the.** To drink: printers' and sailors': from middle 1880s. The *Saturday Review*, 14 May 1887. See BAG, n., 3.

bag, give the. To deceive: C.16–17, coll, as are the senses, to give (a master) warning, to abandon (a thing): late C.16–17; in C.18, *give* (one) *the bag* often = to slip away from (a person), while, 2, in late C.18–19 the phrase came to mean dismiss (cf. *give the* SACK). In C.17–18 *receive the bag* = get the sack, be dismissed; coll. But *give the bag to hold* = to engage one's attention with a view to deceive: late C.17–19: coll >, by 1800, S.E.

bag, in the bottom of the. In reserve; as a last resource: mid-C.17–18: coll >, by 1750, S.E.

bag, let the cat out of the. To disclose a secret or a trick: from ca 1750: coll >, by 1840, S.E. Wolcot, Mrs Gaskell.

bag, put one in a. To have the upper hand of: C.17–18 coll. Fuller.

bag, put one's head in a, see BAG, GET ONE'S HEAD . . .

bag and baggage. Entirely; leaving nothing. Esp. of departure. Coll >, by 1800, S.E. C.16–20. Orig. dignified military j.

bag and bottle. Food and drink: mid-C.17–18 coll. Eachard's *Observations*, 1671.

bag and wallet, turn to. To become a beggar: late C.16–17 coll. Hakluyt.

bag o(f) beer. A quart of beer: proletarian (—1909).

bag of bones. A very thin person: Dickens, 1838: coll.

bag o(f) moonshine. Nonsense: C.19–20; ob. Lower-class coll. cf. metaphorical S.E. sense of *moonshine*: unreality.

bag of mystery, see BAGS OF MYSTERY.

bag of nails, squint like a. To squint very badly : late C.18–mid-19. Grose, 2nd ed., 'i.e. his eyes are directed as many ways as the points of a bag of nails.'

bag of tricks, the; or the whole b. of t. Every expedient: C.19–20. Ex the fable of the Fox and the Cat. 2. Penis and testicles: low: mid-C.19–20.

bag on the bowline. To drift off a course: nautical coll: early C.19–20. cf. BAGGY, adj.

***bag-thief,** see BAGGER.

baggage. A saucy young woman: Davenant, 1672; coll by 1700. A worthless man: C.16–17. A harlot or a loose woman: Shakespeare, 1596; coll by 1660; †by 1800. Rubbish, nonsense: C.16, e.g. in Gascoigne.

baggage, heavy. Women and children: late C.18–19; cf. Fr. *pas de bagage en train de plaisir*.

bagged, have one's wind. To be winded: Public Schools': from ca 1880. E. H. Hornung, *Raffles*, 1899, 'Bunny, you've had your wind bagged at footer, I daresay; you know what that's like?' Ex BAG, v., 2.

***bagger, bag-thief.** One who, in stealing rings, seizes the victim's hand: late C.19–early 20 c. Ex Fr. *bague*, a ring.

bagging. Food taken between meals: provincial s. rather than dial., C.18–19. In Lancashire dial., from ca 1880, high tea.

baggy. (Gen. pl.) A rating in the old naval troopers: military: ca 1860–1900. Bowen, 'On account of their uniform trousers.'

baggy, adj. (Of clothes, esp. trousers at the knee) unduly stretched: coll (1858) >, by 1910, S.E.

bagman. A commercial traveller: S.E. in C.18 (—1765) and until ca 1850, when it > pejorative and coll. 2. A bag-fox: sporting (1875). 3. A tramp: Australian coll: late C.19–20.

bagpipe. A long-winded talker: C.17–19; Carlyle has it. Coll. 2. As v., to indulge in a sexual practice that even F. & H. says is 'too indecent for explanation': late C.18–19. Grose, 1st ed., has recorded the synonymous HUFFLE: neither word occurs in later edd.

bags. Trousers: 'Cuthbert Bede', in *Verdant Green*, 1853. A low variant, from ca 1860 but ob., is BUM-BAGS. ca 1870–1910, GO-TO-MEETING *bags*, (a man's) best clothes, and 1850–90, HOWLING *bags*: trousers very LOUD in pattern or colour(s).

bags!; bags I! That's mine! Schoolboys' from ca 1860. cf. FAIN I; PIKE I! On illiterate *says I*. 2. Hence, *I bags first go* (innings): from not later than 1897, likewise schoolboys'.

bags, have the. To be of age; have plenty of money: mid-C.19–20: coll; ob. Variant, *have the bags off*.

bags, take the. To be hare in hare-and-hounds: athletic, coll: from ca 1870.

bags I! see BAGS!

bags off, have the, see BAGS, HAVE THE.

bags of mystery. Sausages and saveloys: from ca 1850, says Ware. Whiteing, *No. 5, John Street*, 1899. Rare in the singular.

bail! see BALE!

bail, to give leg. To run away from: coll:

from ca 1770; ob. Scott in *Guy Mannering*. Occ. varied in C.19 as *take leg bail and give land security*.

bail up. To demand payment, money, or other settlement from: Australian, from ca 1878. Esp. Morris. Ex earlier lit. use: (of a bushranger) to hold up – which (—1864) was, by Cockneys, adopted, in the imperative, to mean 'Stop!'.

bailed man. (Gen. pl.) One who had bribed the Press Gang for his immunity: nautical coll: mid-C.18–mid-19.

bailer. A ball that, on being bowled, hits the bails: cricket; the O.E.D. records it for 1881. Coll >, by 1900, S.E.

bails, the. The milking shed: Australian coll, esp. dairy-farmers': late C.19–20. 'John is not in the house; he must be down at the bails.' Ex the *bail* that holds the head of a cow that is being milked.

baist (properly **baste) a snarl.** To work up a quarrel: tailors': from ca 1860.

bait; esp. *a rousing bait* or *bate*, a great rage (Eton). Anger; rage: from mid-1850s. Mayhew, 1857; Anstey's *Vice Versa*, 1882. University and esp. Public School. Perhaps a back-formation ex *baited*, harassed or tormented. 2. See SCOTCH BAIT, WELSH BAIT.

bait-land. A port where refreshments can be procured: C.18–19, nautical, †by 1867.

bak, see BUCK, n., 11, v., 2.

bake, v. To rest, lie down: Winchester College, C.19. Whence (†by 1890), *bakester*, a sluggard. cf. also BAKER and BAKING-LEAVE.

bake it. To refrain from visiting the w.c. when one should go there to ease the major need: low: late C.19–20.

bake one's bread. To kill (a person): C.14–19; coll > S.E.

baked. (Of persons) exhausted: ca 1790–1910, coll. 2. **only half baked,** half-witted: coll: from ca 1860; ob.

baked and **mashed.** Baked – mashed – potatoes: domestic and (cheap) restaurants' coll: late C.19–20.

***baked dinner.** Bread – which is baked: c.: from ca 1860; virtually †. Ex a joke played on newcomers to prison.

baker. A cushion; any seat. Winchester College, C.19. Whence (†by 1890) *baker-layer*, a fag carrying from hall a prefect's cushion.

baker (or Baker)!, not today. A lower-classes' c.p. addressed to a man paying unwelcome attentions (to a woman): 1885–ca 1915. Ex housewives' reply to a baker and also ex a soldier named Baker paying undesired court to a young lady. cf. NOT TONIGHT, JOSEPHINE!

baker, spell. To attempt something difficult: C.18–19 coll. From old spelling books, where *baker* was gen. the first disyllabic word.

baker-legged, baker-kneed. C.17–18, C.18–19 coll: knock-kneed. 2. Effeminate: C.17–18.

baker's dozen. Thirteen counted as twelve; loosely, fourteen so counted: late C.16–20: coll >, by 1800, S.E. Florio, Fielding, Scott, *et alii*. cf. DEVIL'S DOZEN. 2. 'Grimly used for a family of twelve and another,' Ware: proletarian coll (—1909). ?'another on the way'. 3. A cousin: rhyming s.: late C.19–20.

baker's dozen, give one a. To thrash vigorously: mid-C.19–20; ob. cf. WHAT FOR.

bakester, see BAKE, V.

bakey or **bakie.** A baked potato: low coll: late C.19–20.

baking. Very hot: with *weather* or *day*. Coll: from ca 1850.

baking leave. Permission to sit in another's study: from ca 1885, Winchester College. Prior to this date: permission to rest.

baking place: a sofa. Ex BAKE, V.

baking-spittle. The human tongue: Yorkshire and Lancashire s., not dial.: from ca 1890. Ex *b.-s.*, 'a thin spade-shaped board with a handle, used in baking cakes', E.D.D.

bakshee (C.20 only), **backshee; ba(c)k-sheesh** (most gen. form), **buckshee, buck-sheesh, buckshish.** A tip; gratuity. Near-Eastern and Anglo-Indian; from ca 1750. Popularized by the British Army in India and Egypt, though it was fairly gen. even by 1800. The forms in *-ee* are the more coll. Ex the Persian (thence Arabic, Urdu and Turkish) word for a present. 2. Occ. as v.t. and v.i.: coll: from ca 1880. 3. (Likewise ex sense 1.) adj. and adv., free, costing nothing: late C.19–20: orig. and mainly military.

bala. 'Low, mean, or senseless talk', Bee: rare London: ca 1820–50. cf. Cornish *bal*, loud talking.

balaam. (Journalistic) PADDING (2) kept in standing type: Scott, 1826; slightly ob. A strange perversion of the Biblical Balaam and his ass. cf.:

balaam-basket. (Journalistic) the receptacle for type representing PADDING (2). Also, the basket for rejected contributions

(1827). Both senses are slightly ob. Ex preceding.

balaclava. 'A full beard': ca 1856–70. Ex the beards worn by those soldiers who were lucky enough to return from the Crimea.

Balaclava day. (Military) a pay-day. 'Balaclava, in the Crimean War (1854–6), was the base of supply for the English troops; and, as pay was drawn, the men went . . . to make their purchases,' F. & H.

balance. The remainder: in England, orig. (ca 1864) a sol. ex U.S. (1819: Thornton), but accepted by English businessmen ca 1870 and > very gen. s. by 1880.

Balbus. A Latin prose-composition (book): school coll. From the textbook of Dr Arnold (d. 1842): recorded in 1870.

bald. See BLADDER OF LARD. cf. *bald as a coot*: coll: late C.13–20.

bald-coot. An elderly or old man who, in gambling, is plucked: fast life (—1823); †by 1890. 'Jon Bee', *Dictionary of the Turf*.

bald-faced stag. A bald-headed man: from ca 1860; ob. cf. STAG.

bald-headed. (Of a ship in square-rig) 'with nothing over her top-gallants'; (of a schooner) 'without top-masts': nautical: mid-C.19–20; ob. Bowen.

bald-headed, go (at) it. To be impetuous or whole-hearted in an action. Orig. (—1850) U.S.; anglicized ca 1900. Perhaps a perversion of Dutch *balddadig*, audacious. It is perhaps worth noting that the popularly ascribed origin of the phrase *go bald-headed at it* is the Marquis of Granby's dashing charge at Warburg (1760), 'when his wig fell off and his squadron followed the bald but undaunted head of their noble leader' (*Army Quarterly*, July 1937).

bald-headed butter. Butter without hairs: trade (—1909); ob.

bald-headed hermit. The penis: 'cultured': late C.19–20; ob.

bald-headed prairie. Great treeless and shrubless plains: Canadian coll: since ca 1880.

bald-rib. A thin bony person: jocularly coll; from ca 1620. Ex S.E. sense, 'a joint of pork cut nearer the rump than the spare-rib', S.O.D.

balderdash. A nonsensical farrago of words: from ca 1660; coll by 1700; S.E. by ca 1730. Prob. ex earlier (late C.16–17) sense, 'froth'. 2. As adulterated wine, late C.17–18, the term presumably never rose above coll.

***baldover, baldower.** A leader, a spokesman: C.19–20, ob., c. Ex German c., which has, presumably via Yiddish, taken it ex Hebrew *bal* (=*baal*, master, lord, owner) + *dovor* (word).

balductum. Nonsense; verbal farrago: late C.16–17. Orig. (and S.E.) a posset.

Baldy. Nickname for a bald-headed man: coll: C.19–20.

bale; baal; bail. No!: Australian 'pidgin' (—1870). Ex Aborigine. cf. CABON.

bale up, see BAIL UP.

Bales, a little drive with. Imprisonment, or the going there: London streets': ca 1880–1900. Ex that policeman who at one time superintended the BLACK MARIA.

***ball.** A prison ration of food, esp. the six ounces of meat; also, a drink. Both are mid-C.19–20 c.; the former occurs in Brandon, 1839.

ball, have got the. To have the advantage: tailors': from ca 1860. Ex games.

ball, open the. To begin: from ca 1810: coll; in C.20, S.E. Byron; *Eton Chronicle*, 20 July 1876.

ball, take up the. To take one's due turn in conversation, work, etc.: coll >, by 1900, S.E.; from ca 1840.

ball at one's feet, have the. To have something in one's power: coll >, by 1880, S.E.; from ca 1800. Occ. and earlier, *before one*.

ball before the bound, catch or **take the.** To forestall, anticipate opportunity: coll >, by 1800, S.E.; from ca 1640.

ball is with you, the. It is your turn; it is 'up to' you: coll >, by 1910, S.E.; from ca 1850; slightly ob.

ball-keeper. A fag looking after cricket-, foot-balls: C.19, Winchester College.

ball of fire. A glass of brandy: ca 1820–60. Ex sensation in throat: for semantics, cf. FIRE A SLUG.

ball o(f) wax. A shoemaker: C.19. Ex the wax used in shoemaking.

ball rolling, or **up, keep the.** To keep an activity, a conversation, going: coll >, by 1840, S.E.; from ca 1780. *Set the ball rolling* therefore = to begin, start a thing going: same period. cf. *open the* BALL where however the *ball* = a dance.

ball under the line, strike the. To fail: coll: mid-C.16–17. Ex (royal) tennis.

ballad-basket. A street singer: C.19. In C.19, a street singer sang mostly ballads, which, now, are much less popular; *basket* has perhaps been suggested by the synonymous STREET PITCHER.

ballahou. 'A term of derision applied to an ill-conditioned slovenly ship', *The Cen-*

tury Dict.: nautical: from ca 1885. ?etymology: not impossibly ex BALLYHOOLY. cf. BALLYHOO OF BLAZES.

Ballambangjang, Straits of. Straits as imaginary as they are narrow: nautical coll (—1864); slightly ob.

Ballarat lantern. Candle set in bottle neck: Australian: late C.19–20. Ex mining days.

ballast. Money: from ca 1850, orig. nautical. Whence (—1890; now ob.) *well ballasted*, rich.

ballast-shooting. 'The strictly prohibited sailing-ship practice of dumping ballast overboard at the end of a voyage, to the detriment of the fairway': nautical coll: late C.19–20; ob. Bowen.

balley, see BALLY, V.

ballock; now gen. **bollock.** A testicle; gen. in pl. A very old word, S.E. until ca 1840, then a vulg. cf.:

ballocks. A parson: late C.17–early 19. In 1864 the Officer Commanding the Straits Fleet always referred to his chaplain as Ballocks. Often as *ballocks the rector*. 2. Nonsense: late C.19–20. Now gen. *bollocks*. cf. BALLS, and CODS; very rarely with *all*.

ballocky, adj. Naked: c. and low: from ca 1905.

Ballocky Bill the Sailor. A mythical person commemorated in a late C.19–20 low ballad; he is reputed to have been most generously testicled. Pronounced and occ. spelt *bollicky*. cf., as perhaps partially operative, dial. BALLOCKY, *bollocky*, left-handed, or, hence, clumsy.

balloon. 'A week's enforced idleness from want of work', Ware: tailors' (—1909); ob. Ex Fr. *bilan*.

balloon-juice. Soda-water: 'public-house, 1883', Ware. Ex gaseousness. 2. Whence *balloon-juice lowerer*, a total abstainer: ca 1884–1920.

ballooning. Jockeying of the prices of stocks: Stock Exchange (—1890, ob.).

balls; all balls. Nonsense (—1890). Low coll. For semantics, cf. BALLOCKS, 2, and *boloney* (orig. U.S.).

balls, bring through. To collect footballs to be blown up: Winchester College, from ca 1850.

balls, have (got) someone by the. To have utterly in one's power, esp. of women over men: low: late C.19–20. (G. Kersh, 1944.)

balls of, make (a). To spoil; do wrongly (—1890). Low.

balls on, see DO ONE'S BALLS ON.

balls to you! Rats to you!: low: late C.19–20. (cf. BALLS.)

ballum rancum. A dance at which all the women are harlots; Grose, 2nd ed., adds, 'N.B. The company dance in their birthday suits': from ca 1660, see Dryden's *Kind Keeper*, 1677–8, and cf. *ballers* in Pepys's *Diary*, 30 May 1668; †by 1900. cf. BUFF-BALL. Ex BALL, a testicle.

bally; gen. **balley.** To depart (speedily): London traders' (—1909); virtually †. cf. V., SKIP; WALTZ.

bally, adj. A euphemism for BLOODY: since ca 1840. *Sessions*, April 1851. W., after F. & H. (revised), suggests ex *Ballyhooly truth*; cf. BLIGHTER; BLINKING; BLOOMING. See my *Words!*

bally-rag, see BULLY-RAG.

ballyhoo of blazes. 'The last word of contempt for a slovenly ship': nautical: since ca 1880. Bowen. Perhaps ex *ballahou*, 'a West Indian schooner with foremast raking forward and mainmast aft' (Bowen).

ballyhooly. Copy-writers' or politicians' exaggeration; 'advance publicity of a vulgar or misleading kind' (H. G. Le Mesurier): from ca 1910. Abbr. *Ballyhooly truth*, a ca 1880–85 music-hall tag perhaps ex *whole bloody truth*.

Ballylana, drunk as. Very drunk: Anglo-Irish coll: late C.19–20. Perhaps rather *Ballylannan*.

balm. A lie (—1820; †by 1900). Duncombe. Variant of BAM.

balmedest balm. 'Balm in the extreme', Ware: proletarian London (—1909); virtually †.

balmy. (Always *the b.*) Sleep. Dickens in *The Old Curiosity Shop*, 1840: 'As it's rather late, I'll try and get a wink or two of the balmy.' Prob. suggested by *balmy slumbers* (Shakespeare), *balmy sleep* (Young).

balmy; perhaps more correctly **barmy,** adj.: anything from stolid to manifestly insane; gen., just a little mad. Henry Mayhew, 1851. Whence *balmy* COVE, a weak-minded man. Perhaps ex S.E. *balmy*, soft, but see also BARMY: the latter form prob. suggested the former.

***balsam.** Money: late C.17–18, c.; C.19–early 20, s. B.E.; Grose; Ware, prob. wrong in stating that it was 'orig. confined to dispensing chemists'. Ex its healing properties.

bam; bamb (C.18). A HOAX; an imposition: *Dyche's Dictionary* (5th ed.), 1748. Ex: 2. As v.i., to sham, be in jest (—1754); v.t.

hoax (in print, 1738), a sense that was current as early as 1707. Abbr. BAMBOOZLE.

bamblusterate. Noisily to HOAX or to confuse: rare: C.19. Ex BAM + *bluster*.

bamboo backsheesh. A blow evoked by importunate begging for money: Anglo-Indian: from ca 1850; ob. See BAKSHEE.

bamboozle. To HOAX, deceive, impose upon (both v.t. and v.i.): Cibber, 1703. To mystify (1712). Swift in 1710: 'The third refinement . . . consists in the choice of certain words invented by some pretty fellows, such as banter, bamboozle, country-put, and kidney, some of which are now struggling for the vogue, and others are in possession of it.' In late C.18–mid-19 naval s., it meant 'to deceive an enemy by hoisting false colours' (Bowen). As n., Cibber, 1703; **bamboozling** (1709) is much more frequent and occurs also as adj. (—1731). **bamboozable,** easily deceivable, is a late (1886) development, and so is **bamboozlement** (1855): these two were never s. but have never quite risen to S.E. Etymology still a mystery; prob. ex a c. word of which no record is extant; perhaps ex BANTER corrupted, or rather, perverted; W., however, suggests an interesting alternative.

bamboozler. A hoaxer, an imposer on others (1712).

bambosh. Humbug; a hoax(ing): 1865: rare and ob. Prob. ex BAM + BOSH.

ban. A Lord-Lieutenant of Ireland: Irish: C.18–20; ob. Ware, 'Bedad, one ban or anoder, 'tis the same man.' Perhaps punning *ban*, a curse or edict, and *banshee*, the precursor of sorrow, as Ware suggests.

Banaghan, beat. To tell a (too) marvellous story: orig. and mostly Anglo-Irish coll: late C.18–20.

banagher. To bang. I find no record earlier than F. & H. (1890), which says 'old'. App. †by 1900. Prob. a word heard by Farmer in his youth and possibly a reduction from *beat Banaghan* or, from ca 1840, *Banagher* (or *banagher*): this phrase, however, suggests that *banagher* may be a development of BANG, to strike violently, a view supported by the fact that the most usual form is *this bangs Ban(n)agher*, an Irish proverbial saying, with which cf. *beat* CREATION, for *Banagher* is a village in King's County (W.).

banana!, have a. A low c.p. of contempt: late C.19–20; ob. Ex a popular song. 2. Perhaps ex the popular song, 'I had a banana with Lady Diana', the phrase *to have a banana with* meant, from ca 1905, to coït with (a woman). cf. CARROT.

Bananaland; Bananalander. Queensland; a native of. Australian coll (—1887); slightly ob.

Banbury. A loose woman: low London: 1894, *People*, 4 Feb. By association with hot-cross buns and '(jam-)tarts' (s.v. JAM-TART, 2).

Banbury story (of a cock and bull). 'Silly chat', B.E.: late C.17–early 19. cf. the C.19 dial. *Banbury tale* and see Grose, P.

banchoot, beteechoot. A coarse Anglo-Indian term of abuse: late C.18–20; ob. In Hindustani, *choad* is a male copulator; *ban*, pron. *bahn* (*barn*), is 'sister'; *betee*, 'daughter'. Hence *banchoad*: *beteechoat* = copulator with sister, daughter; hence, a deadly insult. In late C.19–20, gen. BARN-SHOOT.

banco. Evening preparation, superintended by a monitor: Charterhouse: from ca 1832. Tod, *Charterhouse*, 1900, p. 81. cf. TOY-TIME and, for origin, the legal *in banco*.

band-party, the. Members of the Church of England: military: late C.19–20; ob.

band played!, and then the. The fat is in the fire: c.p.; ca 1880–1910. cf. GOOD NIGHT! and Kipling's 'It's "Thank you, Mister Atkins", when the band begins to play' (1892).

bandage-roller. A sick-bay rating: naval: late C.19–20.

bandan(n)a. A silk (in C.20, also cotton) handkerchief, with white or yellow spots left in the coloured base: coll in C.18 India, but there accepted ca 1800, in England in 1854 (Thackeray), as S.E.

bandbox, (orig. that is) my or mine arse on (Bee, in) a! That won't do!: a late C.18–mid-19 c.p. Ex the inadequacy of a bandbox as a seat.

bandboxical. Like, or of the size of, a bandbox: coll: 1787, Beckford, 'Cooped up in a close, bandboxical apartment'; slightly ob. On *paradoxical*.

banded. Hungry: c. or low: 1812, Vaux. cf. *wear the* BANDS. (With band or belt tightened round one's middle.)

bandicoot, poor as a. Extremely poor: Australian coll: late C.19–20.

bando! Make (the rope) fast: coll, Anglo-Indian; whence London docks (—1886). Direct ex Hindustani *bandho*.

bandog. A bailiff or his assistant: late C.17–18. Ex lit. sense, a fierce mastiff watch-dog: ex *band*, a fastening. 2. Also late C.18–early 19, a bandbox: either sol. or jocular.

bandog and Bedlam, speak. To speak in a rage, like a madman: late C.16–17 coll. Dekker. cf. preceding entry, 1.

bandok, see BUNDOOK.

bandore. A widow's head-dress (the Fr. *bandeau* corrupted): ca 1690–1750: orig., perhaps S.E.; by 1785 coll if not s.

***bands, wear the.** To be hungry. C.19: c. or low. cf. BANDED.

bandstand. 'A circular gun-platform on a warship': naval: late C.19–20. Bowen.

bandy. A sixpence: mid-C.19–20 (ob.); c. and low s. Because easily bent: cf. BENDER and CRIPPLE. 2. A bandicoot: Australian.

bandy. To band together: '—1818', says O.E.D.; but B.E. (?1690) has it = 'follow a faction': so that, in C.18, it was probably – until ca 1760, at any rate (for Grose does not give it) – either s. or coll.

bandy chair. A Banbury chair, i.e. a seat formed by two people crossing hands: Cockneys': from ca 1880.

bane, the. Brandy: low: late C.19–20; ob. Pugh (2), '"You give me a drop o' the bane," said Marketer; "an' don't be so 'andy wi' your tongue."' Suggested by BLUE RUIN.

bang. A blow (—1550). If on a thing, S.E.; if on a person, still coll (as in *a bang on the nose*). 2. A sudden movement, (unexpected) impetus, as in C.18–20 *with a bang*. Coll. 3. 'The front hair cut square across the forehead' (1880), ex U.S.: a sense that rapidly > S.E., though the v. (1882) is even yet hardly S.E. 4. A lie: s. (1879, Meredith) >, by 1910, coll; ob.

bang, an intensive, as in 'the whole *bang* lot': mostly Australian: late C.19–20.

bang, v. To strike. If the object is a thing, it is S.E.; if a person, coll (—1550). 2. To outdo: from ca 1805: coll. 3. Loudly or recklessly to offer stock in the open market, with the intention of lowering the price if necessary: Stock Exchange: from ca 1880. Often as vbl n., *banging*.

bang, adv. Noisily and suddenly; suddenly; immediately; also, entirely, utterly: coll: late C.18–late 19. *The Night Watch*, 1828, at II, 117.

bang alley; bangalay. The timber of *Eucalyptus botrioides*: Sydney workmen's: late C.19–20. Aborigine.

bang Banagher, see BANAGHER.

bang-beggar. A constable (—1865): orig. and mainly Scots. E.D.D. Ex Northern dial.

bang goes saxpence! A jocular c.p. applied to any small expense incurred, esp. if on entertainment or with a light heart: from ca 1880. Popularized by Sir Harry Lauder; originated by C. Keene, *Punch*, 5 Dec. 1868. Here, *bang* suggests abruptness.

bang-Mary. A 'bain Marie': kitchen sol. (—1909) verging on coll. cf. BUMMAREE, n., 2.

bang-off. Immediately: coll: C.19–20. Ex detonation.

bang-out, v. To depart hurriedly and noisily: C.19–20, ob. Adv., entirely and suddenly: C.19–20.

bang-pitcher. A drunkard: C.17–18; coll. Clarke, 1639. cf. *toss-pot*.

bang-straw. A thresher: ?orig. and mainly dial.: late C.19–20, ob. Grose, 1785, adds: 'Applied to all the servants of a farmer'.

bang-tail. A harlot: s.: Ned Ward, 1703.

bang-tailed. (Esp. of horse) short-tailed: T. Hughes, 1861. Coll rising to S.E. The n., *bang-tail*, is recorded for 1870 by the O.E.D., which considers it S.E.

bang through the elephant, have been. To be thoroughly experienced in dissipation: low London (—1909); virtually †. Ware refers it to *elephant* = ELEPHANT'S TRUNK, drunk; but cf. rather ELEPHANT, SEE THE, and BANG UP TO THE ELEPHANT.

bang-up. A dandy: in fast life (—1811). 1882 in *Punch*. Ex the adj.: 2. First-rate: *Lex. Bal.*, 1811; Vaux, 1812, implies that it may, slightly earlier, have been (the certainly synonymous) *bang-up to the mark*; the Smiths in *Rejected Addresses*, 1812: †by 1910, except in U.S. cf. SLAP-UP. Prob. echoic; but perhaps, as Ware suggests, influenced by Fr. *bien* used exclamatorily. The form *banged-up* was later and less used. 3. v.t., make smart, as, passively, in the third of William Combe's *Tours*.

bang-up prime. An intensive of BANG-UP, 2: 1811, *Lex. Bal.*; †by 1890.

bang up to the Elephant. 'Perfect, complete, unapproachable', Ware: London: 1882–ca 1910. With reference to the Elephant and Castle Tavern, long the centre of South London public-house life.

bang-word, see BANG, n., 4.

bangalay, see BANG ALLEY. **banged-up,** see BANG-UP.

banged up to the eyes. Drunk: mid-C.19–20, ob.

banger. A notable lie: from ca 1810; †by

1900. cf. THUMPER. 2. One who 'bangs': Stock Exchange (—1895). Ex BANG, v., 3.

bangies, see BANGY. **banging,** see BANG, v., 3.

banging, adj. Great: coll: Grose, 2nd ed. (1788), has *a fine banging boy*, but the O.E.D.'s quotation from Nashe (1596) may be a genuine anticipation of both the 'great' and the 'overwhelming' sense. One of the many percussive adjj. that are coll. cf. THUMPING. 2. In C.19, *a banging lie*. 3. Also, C.19 coll, overwhelming, as in *a banging majority*.

bangle. (Gen. pl.) A hoop round a made mast: nautical: late C.19–20; ob.

bangs Ban(n)agher and Ban(n)agher bangs the world, that. A mid-C.19–20 variant of *this bangs Ban(n)agher*, *beat Banaghan* (etc.): see BANAGHER.

bangster. A braggart: mid-C.16–18 coll verging on S.E. 2. Whence, victor: id.: Scott, 1820; now † except in dial. (mostly Scottish).

bangy. Brown sugar: Winchester College, C.19; ex *Bangalore*. adj., brown, whence *bangies*, brown trousers: both, from ca 1855, Winchester College; *Bangy Gate*, that gate 'by Racquet Court, into Kingsgate Street' and 'a brown gate from Grass Court to Sick House Meads' (F. & H.): id.; ibid.

banian or **banyan.** The skin: nautical: late C.19–20; ob. 2. A lounging-jacket or short dressing-gown: *The Night Watch*, 1828 (II, 57). Ex S.E. sense.

banian- or **banyan-days.** Days on which sailors eat no flesh: nautical: indirectly in Purchas, 1609; directly in Ovington, 1690. In C.19 (now rare), the term > fairly gen., e.g. in Lamb and Thackeray. Ex the Banians, a Hindu caste or class of traders, who eat not of flesh.

banian (or banyan)-party. 'A picnic party from a man-of-war': naval: mid-C.19–20. Bowen. Ex preceding. cf. BANZAI PARTY.

banjo. A bed-pan: ca 1850–1910. Ex the shape.

banjo box. A wooden box for washing alluvial metal: Australian miners': late C.19–20.

banjoey. A banjoist: London society: 1890s. Ex *banjoist* + JOEY n., 3, a clown. Ware, 'Said to be a trouvaille by the Prince of Wales [King Edward VII], who brought banjo orchestras into fashion, being a banjoey himself.'

bank. A lump sum; one's fortune: C.19–20 coll, ob. An extension of C.16–18 S.E. *bank*, a sum or amount of money. 2. **The Bank,** in C.19 c., is Millbank Prison. 3. The issuing of pocket-money: Public Schools: late C.19–20.

***bank,** v. In C.19–20 c.: to purloin; put in a safe place; go equal or fair shares.

bank on. To anticipate as certain: from ca 1880: coll >, by 1910, S.E. To consider as safe as money in the bank: cf. SAFE AS THE BANK OF ENGLAND.

bank up, v.i. and t. To complete, almost to excess: North Country coal districts' coll (—1896). Ex 'building up a huge fire'.

banker. A river running flush – or almost flush – with the top of its banks: Australian (—1888). Coll by 1890 and 'accepted' by 1900 – if not before. 2. See BAWKER.

Banker Chapel Ho. Whitechapel; hence, vulgar language: East London (—1909); virtually †. Ware, 'A ludicrous Italian translation – *Bianca*, white; *cappella*, chapel ... Anglicization entering in, the first word got into "Banker" and the second back into "Chapel", with the addition of the rousing and cheery "oh!"'

bankers. Clumsy boots or shoes: C.19, †by 1890.

bankrupt cart. A one-horse chaise: ca 1785–95 and very sectional. Grose, 2nd ed., 'Said to be so called by a Lord Chief Justice, from their being so frequently used on Sunday jaunts by extravagant shopkeepers and tradesmen.'

bankruptcy list, to be put on the. To be completely knocked out: pugilistic: ca 1820–60. Egan, *Randall's Diary*, 1823.

Bankside ladies. Harlots, esp. of the theatrical quarter: coll: C.17. Randolph, 1638. In 1721, Strype 'explains': 'The Bank-Side where the Stews were'.

bannock. A hard ship's-biscuit: nautical catachresis: late C.19–20.

bant. To follow a special dietary for the reduction of obesity: from 1865; soon coll. Ex *banting*, such a dietary (1863), devised by W. Banting, a London cabinet-maker: a word coll by the next year, S.E. by 1870, but now slightly ob.

banter. Ridicule, esp. if wantonly merry or supposedly humorous. B.E., 1690: 'a pleasant way of prating, which seems in earnest, but is in jest, a sort of ridicule'. In 1688 it was s., but in C.18 it came gradually to mean harmless raillery and by 1800 it attained S.E. Swift (1704) called the word 'Alsatia phrase'. Ex:

banter, v. Ridicule, make fun of (1667,

Pepys); in C.18, prob. ca 1750, it lost both its sting and its s. associations and > S.E. 2. As = to cheat, deceive, impose on, it was current only ca 1685–1820. Etymology problematic; but if – as Swift, in 1710, says – it 'was first borrowed from the bullies in White Friars', then it is perhaps a perversion of † S.E. *ban*, to chide.

banterer, bantering. The agent and action of BANTER, V.

bantling. A bastard, lit. a child conceived on a *bench* and not in the marriage-bed: late C.16–17 and, in this sense, certainly not lower than coll. But = a child, a brat, it was s. in late C.17–18.

banyan, see BANIAN. **banyan-days** and **-party,** see BANIAN-DAYS and -PARTY.

banzai party. Naval men going ashore on a spree. The same as a *hurrah-party*, for *banzai* is Japanese for *hurrah*, 'the phrase dating from the British Navy's enthusiasm for anything Japanese during the Russian war' (1904–5); ob. Bowen.

bapper. A baker: Scottish coll: mid-C.19–20; ob. Pejoratively ex *bap*, a bread-cake.

baptist. 'A pickpocket caught and ducked', Bee: ca 1820–50. Ex ANABAPTIST.

baptize or **-ise.** Esp. of wine, to dilute: C.17–early 19. Healey, *Theophrastus*, 1636. cf. CHRISTEN.

baptized. Drowned: Australian: since ca 1830.

bar. One pound sterling; orig., a sovereign: c.: late C.19–20. Direct ex Romany; the gypsies' *bar* prob. derives ex Romany *bauro*, big or heavy – cf. Gr. *βαρύς*.

bar, over the. Half-drunk, fuddled: nautical: ca 1810–70.

bar-keep. A bar-keeper: coll: late C.19–20. Abbr. *bar-keeper*.

bar-rabble. A pre-arranged FAMINE: Bootham School: late C.19–20.

baragan tailor. A rough-working tailor: tailors', ca 1870–1914. Ex *barragan*, a kind of fustian.

***barb,** v.t. To clip or shave gold. Ben Jonson in *The Alchemist*. C.17 c. Ex *to barber*.

Barbados. To transport to Barbados: coll >, by 1700, S.E.: ca 1650–1850.

barbar. A scholarship candidate from another school: Durham School: late C.19–20. Ex L. *barbarus*, a stranger, a barbarian. cf. SKY.

barber. A thick faggot; any large piece of timber: Winchester College, C.19–20.

barber, v., see BARBERIZE.

barber, that's the. A street saying of ca 1760–1825 signifying approbation.

barber-monger. A fop: coll, C.17–18. Shakespeare. Frequently visiting the barber.

barberize, -ise; also **barber.** Act as a deputy in the writing of (a task or an imposition): University and Public School: ca 1850–80. 'Cuthbert Bede', 1853. Ex tradition of a learned barber so employed.

barber's block, see BLOCK, BARBER'S.

barber's cat. A weak, sickly-looking, esp. if thin, person: from ca 1860; ob. Ware suggests that it is a corruption of BARE BRISKET. 2. A loquacious, gossipy, or tale-bearing person: mostly military: late C. 19–20. Often *like a barber's cat, all wind and piss*: late C.19–20.

barber's chair. A harlot, 'as common as a barber's chair' (Grose). From ca 1570; †by 1890. See e.g. Burton's *Anatomy* and Motteux's translation of *Pantagruel*. (The whole phrase = very common, fit for general use.)

barber's clerk. A person overdressed: from ca 1830 (ob.), esp. among mechanics and artisans. The term occurs in Dickens. cf. BARBER-MONGER. 2. Hence, a well-groomed seaman not much use at his job: nautical: mid-C.19–20; ob.

barber's knife. A razor: C.18–early 19: coll verging on (?achieving) S.E.

barber's knock. 'A double knock, the first hard and the second soft as if by accident', F. & H. revised: ca 1820–60.

barber's music. Harsh, discordant music (—1660); †by 1800. Coll bordering on S.E. (A cittern was provided by the barber for his waiting customers.)

barber's sign. Penis and testicles: low: late C.18–19. Grose, 2nd ed., explains this scabrous pun.

barbly. Babble, noise: pidgin: from ca 1860. cf. BOBBERY.

Barclay (and) Perkins. Stout: Cockney (—1909); virtually †. Ex the brewers, *Barclay, Perkins & Co.*

***bard (or bar'd) dice,** see BARRED DICE.

bare-bone(s). A skinny person: coll; late C.16–early 19.

bare-brisket. The same: proletarian: C.19–20; ob. Suggested by preceding.

bare navy (or N.). The rigid scale of preserved rations, without fresh meat or supplementaries: naval: late C.19–20.

bared, be. To be shaved: low: ca 1860–1910.

bargain, beat a or **the.** To haggle: ca 1660–1700. Coll >, almost imm., S.E. Killigrew, Pepys.

bargain, Dutch, see DUTCH BARGAIN.

bargain, make the best of a bad. To combat a misfortune: from ca 1790; coll till ca 1840, then S.E. Boswell, 'According to the vulgar phrase, "making the best of a bad bargain"', O.E.D. But the phrase is found as early as 1663 (Pepys) with *market* (†by 1850), as 1680 (L'Estrange) with the rarer *game* (†by 1800).

bargain, sell a. To befool; as in Shakespeare and Swift, who, however, uses it of a specific 'sell' practised at Court. †by ca 1750. Coll.

barge. Printers': either a 'case' in which there is a dearth of the most useful letters or a receptacle for 'spaces' if formes are being corrected away from 'case'. Perhaps j. rather than s.: from ca 1870; ob. 2. Little cricket: Sherborne School: late C.19–20. Prob. ex clumsiness of the stump used as a bat. 3. See BARGES. 4. A dispute: low: late C.19–20. Ex BARGE, v., 1.

barge, v. Speak roughly or abusively to: ca 1850–1920. Albert Smith, 1861, 'Whereupon they all began to barge the master at once'. Prob. ex *bargee.* 2. Whence, at Charterhouse and Uppingham, to hustle (a person): late C.19–20. 3. Hence (?), gen. *barge about*: to move, or rush, heavily (about): late C.19–20. Ex a barge's clumsy motion. cf. the next three entries. 4. To push or knock: Public Schools': late C.19–20. P. G. Wodehouse, *Tales of St Austin's*, 1903, 'To him there was something wonderfully entertaining in the process of "bargeing" the end man off the edge of the form into space, and upsetting his books over him.'

barge-arse. A person with a rotund behind: low: ca 1870–1910. Whence *barge-arsed.*

barge into. To collide with: orig. Uppingham School (—1890).

barge-man. (Gen. pl.) A large, black-headed maggot of the kind that formerly infested ship's biscuits: nautical: from ca 1800: ob.

barge-mate. The officer taking command of a ship when notabilities visited it: naval: ca 1880.

barge-pole. The largest stick in a faggot; hence any large piece of wood. Winchester College, from ca 1850; †. cf. BARBER, n.

barge-pole, wouldn't touch with (the end of) a. One person thus indicates that he will have nothing to do with either another person or, it may be, a project: coll: late C.19–20. cf. *not* TOUCH WITH A PAIR OF TONGS.

bargee. A lout; an uncultivated person: Public Schools' coll: 1909, P. G. Wodehouse, *Mike.*

barges. Imitation breasts: proletarian: ca 1884–90. Ware adds: 'Which arrived from France, and prevailed for about four years . . . From their likeness to the wide prow of canal-barges.'

bark. An Irish person: C.19. See BARKS. 2. The human skin: from ca 1750; in C.18, dial. 3. A cough: from ca 1870; coll, as is the vbl n., *barking*, (a fit of) coughing (—1788: see Grose at BARKSHIRE, 2). 4. An objectionable fellow; a very severe one: Cockneys': from ca 1910. Ex *bastard* with allusion to dog's bark or snarl.

bark, v.t. Scrape the skin off: from ca 1850, e.g. in *Tom Brown's Schooldays.* 2. v.i. To cough; from ca 1880. 3. 'To sit up at night to watch the fire when camping out in the open veld,' Pettman: South African: 1873, Boyle, *To the Cape for Diamonds.* Ex a dog's barking.

bark and growl. A trowel: rhyming s.: since ca 1870. (D. W. Barrett, *Navvies*, 1880.)

bark at the moon. To agitate, or to clamour, uselessly: C.17–20. Coll; S.E. in C.19–20. With *against* for *at*, C.15–17; S.E. after 1550, having been coll.

bark off, take the. To reduce in value; as in Dickens, 1849. (Take the skin off.)

bark up the wrong tree. To be at fault in an attempt, an aim, a method; follow a false scent; deal with the wrong person. Orig. U.S. (—1833); anglicized ca 1890, but less in Britain than in Australia and New Zealand. Coll rather than s. Ex a dog hunting a racoon.

barker. A pistol: Scott (1815), Dickens, Charles Kingsley. Variation of c., and earlier, BARKING IRONS. 2. (Nautical) a lower-deck gun on a ship of war: ca 1840–90. 3. One who, standing in front of shops or shows, attracts the attention of passers-by: B.E., 1690; coll by 1800, S.E. by 1850. cf. BOW-WOW SHOP. 4. A noisy brawler: Caxton, 1483; †by 1660 in England, but extant in U.S. in C.19. 5. (University) a noisy, assertive man; also, favourably, a great swell: C.19. 6. A sheepdrover's assistant, deputizing a dog:

Greenwood, *Outcasts of London*, 1879. 7. A person with a nasty cough: from ca 1880. 8. One who 'barks' as at BARK, v., 3: 1873.

barkey, barky. A ship well liked by its crew: sailors': from ca 1810 or earlier. W. N. Glascock, *The Naval Sketch-Book*, II, 1826, 'Jack's fancy phrase for a favourite ship'. 2. A little bark: coll: from ca 1840. Diminutive of Naval *bark* or *barque*.

Barking Creek, have been to. To have a bad cough: a ca 1820–50 variant of BARKSHIRE, 2.

***barking irons.** Pistols: late C.18–early C.19 c.; recorded by Grose, 1785. 2. In the Navy, ca 1830–70, large duelling pistols.

Barkis is willin(g). An indication of a man's willingness to marry; later, to do anything. Coll. Ex the character in *David Copperfield*, 1849–50.

Barks. The Irish: either low or c. To judge by the anon. *No. 747*, in use ca 1845, but prob. much earlier. cf.:

Barkshire. Ireland: C.19. 2. Also, late C.18–19, as in Grose, 2nd ed., 'A member or candidate for Barkshire; said of one troubled with a cough, vulgarly styled barking'; ob.

barley broth. 'Oil of barley', i.e. strong beer: 1785, Grose; †by 1860.

barley-bun gentleman. A rich gentleman eating poorly and otherwise living in a miserly way: coll: C.17. Minsheu.

barley-cap. A tippler: late C.16–17. E. Gilpin, 1598. 2. *Have on*, or *wear*, *a barley-cap*, to be drunk, a drunkard: late C.16–17 coll.

barmy. Very eccentric; mad: mid-C.19–20. Ex *barmy*, full of barm, i.e. yeast. cf. (mainly Yorkshire) proverbial saying, *his brains will work without barm*, Ray, 1670; Burns, 1785, 'My barmish noddle's working fine'; Ware, 1909, notes the variant *barmy in the crumpet*. The E.D.D. remarks, 'frothing like barm [yeast], hence, full of ferment, flighty, empty-headed'. cf. BALMY. 2. Hence, a mad or a very eccentric person: non-cultured: from ca 1880. Also in dial.

barn. A public ball-room: London: ca 1892–1915. Ware derives ex *Highbury Barn*, a 'garden ball-room'; possibly ex *barn dance*. cf. BARNER.

barn, a parson's. 'Never so full but there is still room for more', Grose, 2nd ed.: C.18–early 19 coll whence the C.19 Dorsetshire *big as a parson's barn*.

barn-door. A target too big to be missed; coll: late C.17–20; hence *barn-door practice*, battues in which the game can hardly escape. 2. A batsman who blocks every ball: from ca 1880; ob. cf. STONEWALLER.

barn-door savage. A yokel: ca 1880–1910. Ex dial.

barn-mouse, bitten by a. Tipsy: late C.18–early 19.

barn-stormer. A strolling player: theatrical (—1859). Coll by 1884 (O.E.D.'s date), S.E. by 1900. 2. *barn-storming*, ranting acting, must also have long preceded the earliest O.E.D. record (1884). They frequently performed and stormed in barns: see, e.g., Hugh Walpole's *Rogue Herries*.

Barnaby dance. To move quickly or unevenly: C.18–19 coll. Ex '*Barnaby*, an old dance to a quick movement' (Grose, 2nd ed.) popular in C.17. Barnaby, it seems, was a dancing jester.

barnacle. A too constant attendant; an acquaintance keeping uncomfortably close to one: from ca 1600; coll. 2. One who speaks through his nose: ca 1550–1660. 3, 4, 5, 6. In † c., there are at least four senses: A pickpocket: (?C.18–) C.19; a good job easily got: late C.17–18; a gratuity given, at horse-sales, to grooms: late C.17–18; a decoy swindler: late C.16–early 17: Greene, Dekker. 7. 'A senior officer who hangs on to the job to which his juniors hope to be appointed': naval: late C.19–20. Bowen.

barnacled, adj. Wearing spectacles: from ca 1690; coll.

barnacles. Spectacles: in mid-C.16–17, gen. coloured; in C.18–19, any spectacles: coll. Prob. ex *barnacle*, a powerful bit for horse or ass (as in Wyclif, 1382), for these old spectacles pinched the nose considerably. 2. In c. (late C.17–18) fetters.

***barnard.** The (gen. drunken) man acting as a decoy in BARNARD'S LAW (*Lay*): c.: ca 1530–1630. Anon., *Dice Play*, 1532; Greene; Dekker. Occ. *bernard*.

***barnard's law.** 'A drunken cosinage by cards', Greene: c.: ca 1530–1630.

barndook, see BUNDOOK.

Barner, barner. 'A "roaring" blade, a fast man of North London', Ware, who derives it ex 'Highbury Barn, one of those rustic London gardens which became common casinos': North London: ca 1860–80. cf. BARN.

Barnet. An abbr. of BARNET FAIR: from ca 1880. See quotation at SIR GARNET.

barnet! Nonsense: ca 1800–80, Christ's Hospital. ?cf. BARNEY, n., 3.

Barnet Fair. The hair: rhyming s., orig. (—1857) thieves'.

barney. A jollification, esp. if rowdy; an outing: from late 1850s; ob. ?ex *Barney*, typical of a noisy Irishman (cf. PADDY, anger). 2. ?hence, crowd: low s. or c. (—1859). 3. Humbug, cheating: low (1864). This sense may have a different origin: cf. '*come! come! that's Barney Castle!* . . . an expression often uttered when a person is heard making a bad excuse in a still worse cause', recorded in the *Denham Tracts*, 1846–59, Apperson, whose other two *Barney* proverbs suggest that the ultimate reference is to 'the holding of Barnard Castle by Sir George Bowes during the Rising of the North in 1569', E. M. Wright, *Rustic Speech*, 1913. 4. Hence, an unfair sporting event, esp. a boxing match (—1877); ob. 5. EYE-WASH (1884+).

barney, adj. Unfair, pre-arranged: *Bell's Life*, 3 Jan. 1885, '. . . barney contests have been plentiful'. Ex the n., 4 and 5.

barney, bit of. A scuffle, fight or heated argument; esp. rowdyism in a public-house: late C.19–20.

barney, do a. To prevent a horse from winning: turf: from ca 1870. See BARNEY, n., 4.

Barney's bull, like. Extremely fatigued or (physically) distressed: a low c.p. of late C.19–20, esp. among Australians. Often was added either *bitched, buggered, and bewildered* or *well fucked and far from home*: these two phrases occ. stand by themselves.

barnshoot. 'A corruption of the Hindustani word *bahinchut*. A vile and unforgivable insult in India, this word is a piece of gentle badinage in England,' George Orwell, *Down and Out in Paris and London*, 1933. Earlier BANCHOOT.

Barnwell ague. Venereal disease: ca 1670–1850. Ray, 1678.

Baron George. A stout man: South London: ca 1882–1915. Ware derives it ex 'a Mr George Parkes, a portly theatrical lessee in S. London, who came to be called Baron George; e.g. "He's quite the Baron George!"'

baronet. A sirloin of beef: Fielding, *Tom Jones*, 1749. Ex earlier *baron of beef*, by a pun on *Sir*. This *baronet*, jocular, was never much used; †by 1800.

barrack, see BARRACKING. **Barrack.** Berwick: nautical coll: C.18–20. e.g., a *Barrack master* was the captain of a Berwick smack carrying 'passengers down the East Coast before the days of steam' (Bowen).

barrack-hack. A woman attending garrison balls year after year: from ca 1860; ob. 2. A soldier's trull: from ca 1850; coll. At this word, F. & H. has a long list of English, French, Italian and Spanish synonyms for a prostitute.

barrack-rat. (Gen. pl.) Indian Army, non-officers', from ca 1880, as in Richards, 'Children born in Barracks were referred to as "barrack-rats": it was always a wonder to me how the poor kids survived the heat, and they were washed-out little things.'

barrack-room lawyer. A soldier professing to know military law: Army coll: late C.19–20.

barracking. Banter, chaff; noisy jeering at either visiting or native cricket or football teams that offend the spectators, esp. at Sydney and Melbourne; not, as the S.O.D. says, 'so as to disconcert players', but merely to demonstrate and emphasize the spectators' displeasure; Australian (—1890), coll by 1897. The v., jeer at, interrupt clamorously, appears to have arisen ca 1880 as a football term, which, in its sporting sense, it remained until ca 1896; *barrack for*, however, has always (—1890) meant to support, esp. to support enthusiastically. A *barracker*, noisy interrupter, is not recorded before 1893; as a supporter, not before 1894. The various words were known in England as early as 1900. Either ex Aboriginal BORAK (n., chaff, fun), as the author of *Austral English* and the S.O.D. editors contend, or ex costermonger Cockney *barrakin*, BARRIKIN, gibberish, a jumble of words (—1851), as W. suggests, or else, as I hold, from BARRIKIN influenced by BORAK. Note, however, that the very able journalist, Guy Innes, says, in a private letter of 1 March 1944, 'I have always understood, and indeed believe, that this word originated from the widespread description in Melbourne of the rough teams that used to play football on the vacant land near the Victoria *Barracks* on the St Kilda Road as *barrackers*.'

barracks. The marines' quarters aboard: naval coll: early C.19–20.

barracoota, -couta. An inhabitant of Hobart, Tasmania: Australian nickname

(—1898); ob. Ex the name of an edible fish.

barrakin, see BARRIKIN.

***barred cater tra(y) or trey.** (Gen. pl.) False dice so made that the four (*quatre*) and the three (*trois*) were seldom cast: c. of ca 1600–50. Dekker; Taylor (1630).

***barred dice.** Card-sharpers' tampered dice: late C.16–17 c. Greene (*barddice*).

barrel-fever. Ill health, disease, caused by excessive drinking: late C.18–20; ob. Grose, 3rd ed., 'He died of the barrel fever.'

barrel of treacle. Love: low London: 1883. Ex its sweetness.

barrel the better herring, never a. Nothing to choose between them: coll: from 1530s; slightly ob. Bale, ca 1540; Jonson, 1633; Fielding, 1736; FitzGerald, 1852. Obviously ex the fish-markets.

barrel tinter. Beer: Yorkshire s., not dial: 1851, Tom Treddlehoyle, *Trip ta Lunnan.*

barrener. A cow not calving for a given season, i.e. for a year: farming coll > S.E.: from ca 1870.

***barrer.** To convey (a DRUNK, 2) home on a barrow: either low Cockney or c.: ca 1870–1915.

barres. (Gaming) money lost but not yet paid: C.17–early 19. Ex BAR.

barrikin; occ. **barrakin.** Gibberish; a farrago of words; jargon: Cockney's: Henry Mayhew, 1851; ob. Of the prob. Fr. original (*baragouin*) H., 1st ed., rather aptly remarks that '*Miège* calls it "a sort of stuff",' for Frenchmen still say *Je ne puis rien comprendre à ce baragouin.* cf. BARRACKING.

barring-out. (Schools) the shutting of the door against a master: from ca 1700; coll; S.E. by ca 1840. Notable instances in Swift and Tennyson.

barrister. 'He that brawls or wrangles in his cups': *The English Liberal Science*, 1650.

***barrister's.** A coffee-house affected by thieves: c.: late C.19–early 20. Ex 'a celebrated host of this name', Ware.

barrow-bunter. A female costermonger: coll: mid-C.18–19; ob. by 1890. Smollett, 1771.

barrow-man. A costermonger: C.17–19; S.E. by 1700. 2. A man under sentence of transportation: ca 1810–50. *Lex. Bal.*, 'Alluding to the convicts at Woolwich, who are principally employed in wheeling barrows full of brick or dirt'.

barrow-tram. An ungainly person: C.19. Lit., *b.-t.* = the shaft of a barrow (C.16–19).

barrow wallah. A big man (occ., thing); **chota wallah,** a little man (loosely, thing): Regular Army coll: late C.19–20. Direct ex Hindustani.

bart. A harpoon: C.19. Bowen, 'More used by the sword-fishermen than the whalers'. Perhaps an abbr. of the †Westmorland *bartle*, the large pin in the game of ninepins.

barter. A half-volley at cricket: Winchester College, from ca 1835; there, too, the v. = to swipe (1836) and *hitting barters* (—1890), practice at catching. All, orig. coll, soon > S.E. See F. & H., as well as Mansfield's and Adams's books on the College (1870, 1878 resp.); also W. J. Lewis, who, in his admirable lexicon, *The Language of Cricket*, 1934, derives it from Robert Barter: 'He entered Winchester College in 1803, and held the post of Warden from 1832 till 1861'; 'He was renowned for his half-volley hits.'

Bartholomew baby (or **doll**). A gaudily dressed doll (1670), a tawdrily dressed woman (1682): the former, coll, soon S.E., the latter always s. Both †by 1850 or so.

Bartholomew(-Boar)-Pig. A fat man: late C.16–17. Roasted pigs were a great attraction at Bartholomew Fair (West Smithfield, London, 1133–1855): see esp. Jonson's Rabelaisian comedy, *Bartholomew Fair*, 1614.

Bart's. St Bartholomew's Hospital, London: orig. (from ca 1880) medical students'.

base Trojan. A term of abuse: late C.16–early 17. Shakespeare, *Henry V.*

baseball. 'Small, insignificant. (Orig. and mainly U.S., "1880 on".) Sometimes heard in Liverpool. Suggested by the small size of the ball in question', Ware: as Liverpool s., it dates ca 1890–1915.

bash, to strike with a crushing blow (—1790), is S.E. in the North, only just S.E. – if not, rather, coll – in the South. The same is true of the n. (from ca 1800); certainly neither is dignified. In c., however, it = to beat heavily with the fists only: C.19–20. 2. To flog: since ca 1880. vbl n., *bashing*. The origin is obscure: but prob. it is either echoic or, as W. suggests, a blend of BANG + SMASH, or, again, a thickening of *pash.*

bash the bishop, see BISHOP, FLOG THE.

basher. A prize-fighter: low. Also, but in c., a professional thug. From ca 1860.

2. A tin receptacle holding treacle: naval: ca 1850–1900. 3. The nickname of any pugilist who is a slugger rather than a skilled boxer: mostly sporting: late C.19–20.

***bashing-in; bashing-out.** A flogging at the beginning (*-in*) or at the end (*-out*) of a 'ruffian's term of imprisonment': c.: from ca 1870. Ex BASH, 2. Moreover, *bashing* exists independently.

Bashi-Bazouk. A ruffian; mildly, a rascal: from ca 1870; ob. Orig. a Turkish irregular soldier (from ca 1850). 2. A Royal Marine, 'a name that appears to have been bestowed when Phipps Hornby took the Fleet up the Dardanelles in 1877', Bowen; virtually †.

basil. A fetter on one leg only: c.: late C.16–18. Greene.

Basing, that's. A card-playing c.p., of mid-C.17–18, applied when clubs are turned up trumps. Ex Basing House, captured in the Civil War while the inmates were playing cards. By a pun: 'Clubs were trumps when Basing was taken.' F. & H. revised.

basinite. A hot-water FAG (n., 2): Charterhouse: C.19.

basket! A cry directed, in cock-pits, at persons unable, or unwilling, to pay their debts: C.18. Such persons were suspended in a basket over the cock-pits. 2. Hence *basketed*, left out in the cold, misunderstood, nonplussed: late C.18–19. 3. Stale news: tailors': late C.19–20. Perhaps ex *waste-basket*.

basket, be brought or **go, to the.** To be imprisoned: C.17–18 coll.

basket, left in the. Rejected; abandoned: mid-C.19–20: coll >, by 1890, S.E. Like the worst fruit.

basket, pick of the. The best: from ca 1870; coll >, by 1910, S.E.

basket, pin the. To conclude, settle: mid-C.17–18 coll. Osborn, ca 1659.

***basket, with a kid in the.** Pregnant: c.: C.19.

basket-making. Sexual intercourse: mid-C.18–early 19.

basket of chips, grin like a. To grin broadly: late C.18–mid-19, coll. cf. *smile like . . . chips*, an old Shropshire saying.

basket of oranges. A pretty woman: 'Australian, passing to England', says Ware: late C.19–early 20. Ex *basket of oranges*, 'a discovery of nuggets of gold in the gold fields': Australian miners' coll: late C.19–20; ob.

basket-scrambler. One who lives on charity: C.17–18; coll.

basketed, see BASKET!

basso. A shoal: nautical coll: C.19. Perhaps ex Staffordshire *bassiloe*, the mound of earth at or near the edge of a pit.

bastardly gullion. A bastard's bastard: (Lancashire dial. and) low coll: late C.18–early 19. cf. BELL-BASTARD.

baste. To thrash: from ca 1530. In C.16, coll; thereafter, S.E., though far from dignified.

***Bastile.** A workhouse: low (mostly vagrants'), from ca 1860; esp. in the North. Ex its short-lived S.E. sense (a prison) comes STEEL. 2. Early in C.19, among criminals, *Bastile* was applied as a nickname to Coldbath Fields Prison, demolished ca 1890.

basting. A thrashing: in Shakespeare and till ca 1660, coll; then virtually S.E. Grose records it as *give* (a person) *his basting*(*s*).

bat. A prostitute favouring the night: C.17–early 19. 2. Pace: from ca 1800; dial. >, ca 1870, s. Prob. ex dial. *bat*, a stroke. 3. A spoken language (orig. that of India): military: late C.19–20. Ex Hindustani for speech, word. Only in BOLO or SLING or SPIN THE BAT.

bat, carry (out) – occ. **bring out – one's.** To outlast others; finally to succeed: coll: from ca 1870. Ex a batsman not out at cricket; the lit. sense 'goes back to the less luxurious days when the man "out" left the bat for the next comer', W.

bat, off (rarely **on**) **one's own.** Without assistance; independently: coll >, by 1880, S.E. (Sydney Smith, 1845.) Also ex cricket.

***bat-fowl,** v.t. and i. To swindle; victimize the simple or the inexperienced: from ca 1585. Greene. Very little later were its pure derivatives, *bat-fowler*, a swindler, confidence trickster, and the vbl n., *bat-fowling*. All †by 1840. Ex the nocturnal catching of birds by dazzling them and then batting them with a stick.

bat-mugger. An instrument for rubbing oil into cricket bats: Winchester College, ca 1860–1910.

batch. A dose or bout of liquor: late C.18–early 19. Prob. ex dial.: ?cf. *batch*, a quantity of things (e.g. bottles).

batch, v., see BACH, v. **batchelor's fare,** see BACHELOR'S FARE.

batchy. Silly; mad: military: late C.19–20. Perhaps ex Hindustani.

bate, see BAIT.

***Bate's Farm** or **Garden,** occ. preceded by **Charley.** Coldbath Fields Prison: C.19 c. Partly ex a warder's name. Whence:

***Bates' farm, feed the chickens on Charley.** To be put to the treadmill: c. of ca 1860–90. Ex preceding.

bath, give the order of the. To duck: from ca 1890. Punning; cf. *give the Order of the Boot*, see ORDER . . .

Bath, go to. To become a beggar: mid-C. 17–19. Bath, being fashionable, attracted many vagrants. As, ca 1830–1930, an injunction, often with addition of *and get your head shaved*: stop!, go away!, 'dry up, you're cracked!' In addition to beggars, Bath drew lunatics, who were 'supposed to benefit from the waters' of this noted spa (W.).

bathing machine. A 10-ton brig: sailors', ca 1850–1900. 2. Whence, a four-wheeled cab: London busmen's: ca 1890–1915.

***batner,** see BATTENER.

***bats.** A pair of bad boots: c. or low s.: from ca 1855.

bats in the belfry, have. To be very eccentric; mad, to any degree: late C.19–20.

batt. A battalion: military coll: late C.19–20.

batta, see BATTY, n.

***battalion.** A gang of criminals: C.18 c.

***batt(e)ner.** An ox: mid-C.17–18 c. Beef tending to *batten* (fatten).

batter. Wear and tear: C.19–20 coll. 'He can't stand the batter,' H., 1864. 2. A variant of BUTTER, n., 2. 3. See BATTERS.

batter, (go) on the. (To walk the streets) as a harlot, to be debauched; to be on a riotous SPREE: from late 1830s; ob. H. Rodger, 1839; Whiteing, 1899. Presumably cognate with U.S. *bat* (1848); cf. BAIT.

batter through. To struggle through (e.g. a part): proletarian: C.19–20; ob. Abbr. *batter one's way through*.

battered. Given up to debauchery: from ca 1860: †. cf. BATTER, (GO) ON THE.

battered bully. A late C.17–early 18 term combining two senses of *battered*, thus: 'an old well cudgell'd and bruis'd huffing fellow', B.E.: low coll.

batters. Defective type: printers': 1880: coll >, by 1910, j. Ex *batter*, 'a bruise on the face of printing type'.

Battersea'd. (Of the male member) treated medically for venereal disease: ca 1715–90. *Select Trials at the Old Bailey*, 1743 (Dublin, vol. 2), trial of George White in 1726, 'Mine is best, yours has been Battersea'd.' See SIMPLES, *go to Battersea to* BE CUT FOR THE.

Battle of the Nile. A TILE, a hat: rhyming s. (—1859); ob. Occ. *battle* (—1874).

battle-royal. A vehement quarrel, a vigorous fight: from ca 1690; coll >, by 1840, S.E. Ex medieval jousting between two sides each commanded by a king (S.E.); also cock-pit j.

battle the watch. 'To do one's best against difficulty. To depend on one's own exertions': nautical coll: mid-C.19–20; slightly ob. Bowen.

battledore, see B FROM A BATTLEDORE, NOT TO KNOW. cf. *battledore-boy*, one learning his alphabet: late C.17–mid-18: coll or, rather, S.E. Here, however, *battledore* is abbr. *battle-dore-book*, a horn-book.

***battler.** A gangster handy with his fists and fond of using them: Glasgow c. and low s.: late C.19–20.

battlings. (Public Schools') a weekly allowance of money (—1864). Either coll or j. Mostly at Winchester, where used from before 1859.

***battner,** see BATTENER. (Coles spells it *batner*.)

batty. Wages, perquisites: coll: orig. (Hook, 1824,) *bhatta*, ex Hindustani; in India it properly meant (late C.17–20) subsistence money, extra pay on campaign, then pay for Indian service.

batty-fang. To beat: coll: C.19–20, ob. Also, in C.17–19, *batter-fang*. Prob., to hit and bite; Ware's 'evidently *battre à fin*' is presumably a joke.

baub, see BOB!, S'HELP ME. **baubee,** see BAWBEES.

baubles, see BAWBLES. **baudye,** see BAWDY, etc.

baulk. (Winchester College) a false report: from ca 1850. Hence *sport a baulk*, to circulate one. 2. (Gen.) a mistake: mid-C.19–20, ob. A survival of *balk*, *baulk*, C.15–18 S.E. for a mistake or blunder.

baulk (balk) at. To avoid: coll: W. N. Glascock, *Sailors and Saints*, 1829. Semantics: 'jib at'.

baulk (or balk), in. Checked; at a loss: coll; from ca 1880. Ex billiards.

***baulker.** Frequently spelt BAWKER.

'baw-baw', quoth Bagshaw. You're a liar: semi-proverbial c.p. (—1570); †by 1700. Levins; Nashe. Ex *baw-baw!*, indicating contempt or derision; *Bagshaw*, prob. for the jingle.

bawbard. Larboard: nautical coll: C.18–19. A corruption of *larboard* (Bowen); prob. influenced by Fr. *babord.*

bawbees. Money; cash. C.19–20. In singular, coll for a halfpenny, a COPPER (2): late C.17–20.

bawbles. (Properly but rarely **baubles.**) Human testicles: late C.18–early 19. Earlier, e.g. in Shakespeare, *bauble* = the penis; this is prob. S.E.

bawcock. A fine fellow, gen. derisively: Shakespeare's *Henry V*; †by 1700, though resuscitated by Ainsworth in 1862. Coll; ex Fr. *beau coq.*

bawd. A procurer or – as always after 1700 – a procuress. In C.14–16, S.E.; in C.17–18, coll; in C.19–20, literary. In C.18–19 occ. a female brothel-keeper. Prob. abbr. *bawdstrot.*

bawdy bachelor. A 'confirmed' bachelor: late C.17–19, low coll. (But how hard he falls!)

bawdy banquet. Whoremongering: C.16; not recorded before Harman, 1567. ?c.

***bawdy basket.** In mid-C.16–17, c.; in C.18, ob. s.; †by 1840. A seller – gen. female – of obscene literature, ballads, pins, tape, but living mostly by theft. Ex the bawdy books carried in the basket. 2. A harlot: this rarer sense (late C.16–17) is indubitably s.

bawdy-house bottle. A very small one: late C.17–18: low coll.

***bawdy-ken.** A brothel: c. or low s.: ca 1810–60.

bawd(y) physic. A saucy fellow: ca 1560–90: c. or low. Awdelay.

***bawker.** A cheater at bowls: late C.16–early 17 c. Greene. (=*baulker.*)

bay, the. The sick-bay: naval coll: mid-C.19–20. Hence, *bay man*, a sick-bay attendant: naval coll: late C.19–20.

Bay fever. 'A term of ridicule applied to convicts who sham illness to avoid being sent to Botany Bay,' *Lex. Bal.*: coll: ca 1810–60. cf.:

Bay of Condolence. 'Where we console our friends, if plucked, and left at a nonplus', Egan's Grose, 1823: Oxford University: ca 1820–40.

Bayard of ten toes. One's feet. Esp. *ride B. . . . toes*, to walk. Coll in late C.16–early 18, then dial. (ob.). Breton, Fuller, Grose. Breton's use in *Good and Bad*, 1616, tends to show that the phrase had been current long before that. Ex *Bayard*, a horse famous in medieval romance.

Bayswater captain. A sponger: ca 1879–1910; mostly London. Because so many of these club parasites resided in Bayswater, W.2. cf. TURNPIKE-SAILOR.

baywindow. A belly protuberant through either pregnancy or obesity: mid-C.19–20.

***bazaar.** A shop; a counter: c.: ca 1830–80. Ex (and cf.) S.E. sense ex Hindi – ultimately Persian *bazar*, a market. 2. A public-house bar: rhyming s.: late C.19–20.

bazaar, v.t. To rob; gen. as *bazaar'd*: Society: 1882–ca 1915. Ware derives it ex 'the extortion practised by remorseless, smiling English ladies at bazaars'.

bazaar (or B.), in the. In the (money-) market; to be bought; procurable: Anglo-Indian coll of late C.19–20.

be damned, see DAMNED! . . .

be gorra! see BEGORRA! **be jabers!** see JABERS, BY. **be there,** see THERE, BE.

beach, be or go on the. To be or become a beach-comber: coll: late C.19–20. cf.:

beach, on the. Ashore, whether on leave or having retired from the sea: nautical: mid-C.19–20. Also **be beached,** to be 'put out of employment': naval: late C.19–20.

beach-cadger. A beggar favouring seaside resorts: ca 1860–1910: coll.

beach-comber. A (disreputable) fellow haunting the sea-shore for odd jobs (*Blackwood's Magazine*, 1847). Coll; from ca 1870, S.E.; perhaps, as Thornton implies, orig. U.S. 2. A river boatman: nautical: from ca 1860; ob. 3. A sea-shore thief: ?c.: from ca 1865. 4. 'A yachting tourist', Ware: nautical: ca 1890–1915.

beach-men. 'West African surf men and interpreters': nautical coll verging on S.E.: late C.19–20. Bowen.

beach-tramper. A coastguardsman: nautical: ca 1880–1910.

beached, be, see BEACH, ON THE.

beacon. A red nose: mostly Cockneys': from ca 1890.

bead-counter. A cleric, religious recluse, or worshipper: coll: C.19. Malkin, 1809. Ex the use of the rosary in the Roman Catholic communion.

***beadle.** A blue roquelaure; esp. to *fly* or *sport a beadle*, to wear one: c.: ca 1820–50. Prob. because beadles often wore a blue jacket.

beagle-ball. (Gen. pl.) A meat rissole served in the Royal Naval College, Dartmouth: there: late C.19–20.

***beak.** A magistrate: C.18–20. In C.16–17, the form was *beck*, the meaning a constable (a sense lingering till ca 1860);

also it was c., as *beak* itself was until ca 1850, since when the most frequent use has been *up before the beak*, on trial by a magistrate. Hence, 2, in schools (esp. Eton and Marlborough), from ca 1880, an assista.. master. 3. The nose: Ward, 1715.

***beak,** v. Late C.16–early 17 c. as in Rowlands, 1610, 'What maund doe you beake, what kind of begging use you?' 2. To bring (a malefactor) before a magistrate: low (—1887). Baumann, who rightly implies that it is used mostly in the passive. Ex BEAK, n., 1.

beak, strop one's. (Of the male) to coït: low: late C.19–20; ob.

beak-gander. A judge in the higher courts: from ca 1870; ob. (*Gander* = old man.)

***beaker,** occ. abbr. to **beak.** A fowl. C.19–20 c. as is (—1839: Brandon) the derivative *beak(er)-hunter*, a poultry-yard thief.

***beaksman.** A constable: C.18–19 c. Ex BEAK, 1. cf. BECK, n.

Beaky, n. Nickname for any person, esp. a man, with a big, sharp nose: Cockney: mid-C.19–20.

beam, broad in the. (Of a person) broad-seated: C.19–20; orig. nautical.

beam-ends. The buttocks: Marryat, 1830; *Cuthbert Bede*, 1853. cf.:

beam-ends, on one's. Utterly exhausted: nautical: ca 1800–80. Marryat. 2. In a difficulty (Dickens, 1844); short of money (H. Mayhew). Coll. Ex a vessel in imminent danger of capsizing.

beamy old buss. Any very broad ship: nautical coll: mid-C.19–20. Ex the broad herring buss or smack; cf. *broad in the* BEAM.

bean or **bien.** A guinea coin: prob. c.: ca 1800–40; a sovereign: low: ca 1840–1900. (The guinea coin ceased in 1813 to be struck.) In pl, money, esp. cash: from late 1850s. ?ex Fr. *bien*, something good. 2. The head: late C.19–20. Ex shape (very approximate!). 3. The penis: low: late C.19–20. ?ex the *glans penis*.

bean, not have a. Esp. *I haven't a bean*, I'm penniless: late C.19–20. cf.:

bean, not worth a. Of very little value: from C.13; coll since ca 1400.

bean-belly. A Leicestershire man: mid-C.17–19. Adumbrated in C.15. Leicestershire has for centuries produced an abundance of beans.

bean-cod. 'The Iberian type of small craft with sharp lines and a stream raking aft from the waterline': nautical: C.19–20; virtually †. Bowen. Ex shape.

bean-feast. A jollification: C.20. Orig. (1806) an annual feast given to workmen by their employers. (Tailors as early as 1890 applied *bean-feast* to any good meal.) Hence *bean-feaster*, ca 1883–1900, a participator in such an annual feast.

bean-pole or **-stick.** A tall thin man: coll (?ex dial.) > almost S.E.: from ca 1830.

bean-tosser. The penis: low: late C.19–20; ob.

beaner. A chastisement: proletarian, mostly London (—1909); ob. Ex *give* BEANS.

beano. Orig. (—1898) an annual feast: printers'. 2. From ca 1897 (see Ware), a jollification. Ex BEAN-FEAST, perhaps (via lingua franca) influenced by Sp. *bueno* or It. *buono*, good. cf. BINGO.

beanpea. An effeminate youth: ca 1875–1915. Ex a case of two youths, *B. and P.*, tried by Lord Cockburn (d. 1880).

beans, full of. Vigorous; energetic; in high spirits: from ca 1870. cf. BEANY.

beans, give. To chastise; defeat severely (—1890). Kipling. 2. *get beans*, be chastised. Probably ex ASH BEANS . . .

beans, like. Excellently; forcibly: from ca 1860; ob.

beans in a or **one blue bladder, three blue.** Noisy and empty talk: late C.16–18. Origin obscure: even Nares failed to discover it.

beans make five (white ones), know how many. To be alert: Galt, 1830; adumbrated in Shelton's *know how many numbers are five*, 1612.

beany. Vigorous; spirited: from ca 1850. cf. *full of* BEANS: beans being great energy-makers. 2. Hence, in good humour: from ca 1860.

bear. At first (ca 1700), stock sold in the hope of a fall: either S.E. or j. Then (—1744) the speculator for a fall, as in Foote, Colman, Scott; the term > coll only ca 1900, Peacock having, in 1860, written: 'In Stock Exchange slang, bulls are speculators for a rise, bears for a fall.' See the chapter on commercial slang in my *Slang*. The orig. phrase was prob. *sell the bear-skin*, such bargainers being called *bear-skin jobbers*, in reference to the proverb, 'to sell the bear's skin before one has caught the bear'. Hence, *sell a bear*, to sell what one does not possess: C.18 coll. cf. BULL, 5. 2. The pupil of a private tutor: late C.18–mid-C.19. See BEAR-LEADER.

Also, 3, a very gruff person: C.18–20 coll. Notably used by Lord Chesterfield. 4. 'A matted stone or shot, or a coir mat filled with sand, dragged over the deck to clean it after the fashion of a holystone' (Bowen): nautical coll: mid-C.19–20; ob. Ex ob. S.E. *bear* (*bere*), a pillow-case.

bear, v.i. To speculate for a fall in prices: Stock Exchange, from ca 1840, as is the v.t. sense, to effect or manoeuvre a fall in the price of (a stock or commodity).

bear, it would bite or **have bit you, if it were** or **had been a.** A semi-proverbial c.p. applied, as B.E. phrases it, to 'him that makes a close search after what lies just under his Nose': C.17–18. Draxe, 1633; Swift.

bear, play the. To behave rudely and roughly: late C.16–17: coll >, by 1600, S.E.

bear a bob. To lend a hand: nautical and gen.: C.19–20; ob. Imperative: look alive!: nautical, C.19–20.

bear a fist. To bear a hand, to help: nautical coll (—1806); †by 1890. John Davis, *The Post-Captain*, 1806. (Moe.)

bear fight. A rough and tumble in good part: Society coll: from ca 1880.

bear-garden discourse (or **language**) or **jaw.** 'Rude, vulgar language', Grose, 1st ed.: late C.17–early 19. With *discourse* or *language*, coll; with JAW, s. Ray, 1678, has 'He speaks Bear-garden.'

bear-leader. A travelling tutor in the days of the Grand Tour: Walpole, 1749; Thackeray, 1848. Coll in C.19; †by 1880. He licks 'cubs' into shape.

bear-play. Rough and noisy behaviour: apparently not recorded before 1883. Coll, soon S.E.

bear-up. The act of pursuing a woman: coll: U.S. >, by 1900, Australian; rare. H. Lawson.

bear to the stake, go like a. To '*hang an* ARSE', B.E.: coll: C.15–early 19. Lydgate, ca 1430: Florio; Defoe; Scott.

bear up, v. To support in a SWINDLE (—1828); ob. by 1900. Hence *bearer-up*, such a supporter. Hence, 2, v.i., to 'log-roll' (see LOG-ROLLER): 1883, *Referee*, 2 Dec. 3. Have courage: coll, C.17; S.E. thereafter, though the imperative, *bear up!*, has a coll tang.

bear with, play the. To play the deuce with: dial. (—1881) >, by 1889, coll; ob.

beard, make a man's. To outwit or trick him: coll: C.15–16.

beard, to one's. To a person's face; frankly; openly: coll; from ca 1780.

beard without a razor, make a man's. To behead: coll: ca 1520–1700.

beard-splitter. A frequenter of prostitutes, an enjoyer of women: late C.17–early 18. cf. U.S. low s. or c. *beard-jammer*. 2. Also, the penis: C.18–19. cf. HAIR-DIVIDER.

bearded cad. A College porter conveying luggage from station to school: Winchester College, ca 1850–1910.

beärgered. Drunk: low coll (—1859); ob. by 1910.

bearing, vbl n. Acting as a speculating BEAR: from ca 1860, Stock Exchange.

bearings, bring one to one's. To cause to see reason: late C.18–20 coll, orig. (—1785) nautical.

bearish. Indicative of, natural to, or tending to, a fall in prices: Stock Exchange; from ca 1880.

bears?, are you there with your. There you are again!; so soon? James Howell, 1642; Richardson, 1740; Scott, 1820. †.

bear's paw. A saw: rhyming s., mostly workmen's: late C.19–20.

bearskin-jobber. A seller of BEAR stock (—1726); money market; ob. by 1750.

beast. Anything naturally unpleasant or momentarily displeasing, as *a beast of a day*: coll: from ca 1860. 2. A youth who, having left school, goes to Cambridge to study before entering the University: Cambridge University; from ca 1820; very ob. 3. A bicycle: youths': ca 1870–90.

beast, drink like a. To drink only when thirsty: late C.18–19. Contrast S.E. *drink like a fish*.

beast with two backs. 'A man and woman in the act of copulation', Grose; gen. with *make* (*the*), as in Shakespeare's *Othello*. †by 1830 and prob. never gen. s. Originally, apparently, a translation of Rabelais's *faire la bête à deux dos*.

beastie. A coll and endearing form, orig. Scottish, of *beast*: gen. only since ca 1890.

beastly. Unpleasant; bad (however slightly): coll. From ca 1850, as is the adv., which = very. Anstey, 1882, has *feeling beastly*; *Daily Telegraph*, 1865, 'he was in good health ... looked almost "beastly well"': but adumbrations appear in Barclay, 1509, Dekker in 1611, in Johnson, 1778, and in Dickens, 1844.

beasty, see BHEESTIE.

beat. A normal round (as of prostitute or policeman): G. A. Stevens, 1788; sphere of influence: *Saturday Review*, 1862. In both senses, coll for some forty years, then S.E. but not literary. 2. Hence, one's 'lady friend': naval seamen's: late C.19–20.

beat, adj. Exhausted: from ca 1830. Often DEAD BEAT. 2. Baffled, defeated: coll: from ca 1840.

beat, get a. (Constructed with *on.*) To obtain an advantage (over): from ca 1850; ob. In c., the term implies secret, shady, or illicit means.

beat a carpet, couldn't. Ineffective; weak; or of a very 'poor' boxer: late C.19–20; coll.

beat daddy-mammy. To practise the elements of drum-beating: C.18 military.

beat goose or (nautical) **the booby.** To strike the hands across the chest and under the armpits to warm one's chilled fingers: coll: from ca 1880. Earlier, *cuff* or *beat Jonas*. Jocularly varying *beat oneself*.

***beat it upon the hoof.** To walk; to tramp: c.: ca 1680–1760. Anon., *The Post Boy robbed...*, 1706.

beat one's way through the world. To push oneself ahead: from ca 1860: coll.

beat-out. Exhausted: coll: 1860. †by 1910.

beat the hoof. To walk: late C.17–18. In Anthony Wood's *Athenae Oxonienses*, 1691.

beat the road. To travel by rail without paying: low, mostly U.S. (—1890).

beat the streets. To walk up and down: C.19–20: coll till ca 1890, then S.E.

beat up the quarters of. To visit unexpectedly, very informally: coll: 1741, Richardson; Ware (the shorter form). From ca 1891, gen. just *beat up*. Ex S.E. sense, 'to disturb'.

beaten out. Impoverished: in very severe straits: H. Mayhew, 1851; coll; ob.

***beater.** The decoy in a swindle: c. of ca 1585–1620. Greene. Ex fowling. 2. A foot: low: from ca 1860; ob. Abbr. DEW-BEATERS. cf.:

***beater-cases.** Boots: in late C.18–early 19, c.; then low s. Nearly † in 1859, quite † by 1890. Succeeded, in mid-C.19, by TROTTER-CASES.

***beating the bush.** The inveigling of a prospective victim: c. of ca 1585–95. Greene.

beau-catcher, see BOW-CATCHER.

beau-nasty. 'One finely dressed, but dirty', Grose, 2nd ed.: late C.18–early 19.

beau-trap. A sharper, neatly dressed: late C.17–18. 2. A loose pavement-stone, overlying water: late C.18–early 19. 3. A fop outwardly well dressed but of unclean linen, body, habits: late C.18–early 19.

beautiful. An adj. applied coll by a person to anything that he likes very much: mid-C.19–20. cf. SWEET.

beauty, be a. Gen. *he's a beauty!*, *you're a beauty*, i.e. a person very clumsy or not to be trusted or relied on: coll: from ca 1880. Ex ironic use of lit. sense.

beauty, it was a great. It was a fine sight: coll: ca 1520–1600. Berners, 1523. cf.:

beauty of it, that's – occ. **that was** – **the.** That is the feature affording the greatest pleasure or keenest satisfaction: coll: 1754, Richardson, 'That's the beauty of it; to offend and make up at pleasure'.

beauty sleep. Sleep before midnight, supposedly conducive to good looks and health: Frank Smedley's first notable novel, *Frank Fairleigh*, 1850: coll >, by 1910, S.E.

beaver. A beard. Hence: 2. A bearded man: s.: perhaps as early as 1907. (As a hat, S.E.)

beaver, cock one's. To assume a swaggering air: C.17, as in that strange Cambridge Platonist, Henry More, in 1642. Coll.

beaver, in. In tall hat and non-academical attire: ca 1820–60: university.

beaver-tail. 'A feminine mode of wearing the back-hair ... loose in a ... net ... which fell ... on to the shoulders.' Ex resemblance to 'a beaver's flat and comparatively shapeless tail', Ware, who classifies it as middle-class of ca 1860–70.

bebee; beebee. A lady: Anglo-Indian coll (—1864). By 1886 no longer applied to ladies: in fact, in late C.19–20 military, it = a bed-mate. Ex Hindustani *bibi*, a lady.

becall. To reprimand; abuse; slander: Cockney coll: from ca 1880. Clarence Rook, *passim*.

becalmed, the sail sticks to the mast, – I am. 'My shirt sticks to my back,' Grose, 1st ed., adding: 'A piece of sea wit sported in hot weather': a nautical c.p. of mid-C.18–mid-19.

***beck.** A constable; a beadle: c.: mid-C.16–17. See BEAK, 1.

***beck,** v. To imprison: (?C.18–)C.19 c.; rare. Reade in his greatest novel, 1861.

beckets!, hands out. Hands out of your pockets!: nautical: from ca 1800; ob. A becket is a nautical loop or bracket.

bed, get up on the wrong side of the, see WRONG SIDE. **bed, more belongs to marriage than ...** see LEGS IN A BED ...

bed, go up a ladder to. To be hanged: mid-

C.18–early 19: low s. verging on c. 'In many country places', says Grose, 1st ed., 'persons hanged are made to mount up a ladder, which is afterwards turned round or taken away; whence the term, "turned off".'

bed of guns. A ship over-gunned: jocular naval coll: C.19–20; ob.

bed one has made, lie or **sleep in the.** To abide (patiently) by one's actions: from ca 1750; coll > proverbial >, by 1850, S.E. Hanway, 1753. By fig. extension of *make a bed*, to put it in order.

bed with a mattock, put to, often amplified with *and tucked up with a spade*. Dead and buried: C.18–early 19. From ca 1830, the form was gen. *put to bed with a pickaxe and shovel*, while C.19–20 dial. prefers *put to bed with a shovel*.

bed-fag(g)ot. A hussy; a harlot: coll: C.19–20; ob. (Not a Society term.) Ex *fagot* as part of firewood. cf. WARMING-PAN. But *bed-sister*, *-piece*, and *-presser* may be S.E.

bed-filling. 'Lying down after dinner to rest and digest': Regular Army's: ca 1880–1914.

bed-house. A house of assignation where beds may be had for any period desired: C.19 coll.

bed in one's boots, go to. To be very drunk: low coll: late C.19–20.

bed-launching, n. 'Overturning the bed on the sleeping occupant': Sandhurst coll: from ca 1830.

bed-post, between you and me and the. Between ourselves: coll: 1830; Bulwer Lytton, 1832. Variants with *post*, as in Dickens, 1838 – *door-post*, from ca 1860 – *gate-post*, id.

bed-post or **-staff, in the twinkling of a.** Immediately: resp. from ca 1820 (ob.), and ca 1670–1850 (Shadwell, 1676). Prob. ex its well-known use as a ready and handy weapon.

bed-presser, see BED-FAG(G)OT. 2. A dull, heavy fellow: coll: late C.19–20; ob.

bed-sitter. A bed-sitting room: s. (from ca 1890). Oxford *-er*.

bed-staff, in the twinkling of a, see BED-POST, IN . . .

bed-tick. The American national flag, the Stars and Stripes: nautical: mid-C.19–20. Pejorative of the colour-scheme, and alluding to the coverings of mattresses.

bed-work. Lit., work that can be done in bed; hence, very easy work: coll: late C.16–18. Shakespeare, in *Troilus and Cressida*.

bedad! An Anglo-Irish coll asseveration: 1710, Swift; 1848, Thackeray, '"Bedad it's him," said Mrs O'Dowd.' Lit., *by dad* or (cf. BEGAD) *by God*.

bedaubed all over with lace. A 'vulgar saying of any one dressed in clothes richly laced', Grose, 1st ed.: mid-C.18–mid-19.

bedder. A college servant: Cambridge University; from ca 1870. 2. A bed-room: Oxford University (1897); ob. cf. BED-SITTER.

Bedford go. A rich chuckle: taverns': ca 1835–60. Ex Paul Bedford, the actor.

Bedfordshire. Bed: C.17–20, ob.; coll. Middleton, 1608, 'You come rather out of Bedfordshire; we cannot lie quiet in our beds for you'; Cotton; Swift; Hood. cf. BLANKET FAIR; CLOTH MARKET; *land of* NOD; SHEET-ALLEY. These simple witticisms (cf. GUTTER LANE) are mostly old.

Bedlam, like. Confused, noisy, unreasonable, all to a 'mad' extent: coll; late C.18–20. Ex the famous London lunatic asylum.

bee in one's or **the head** or **bonnet, have a.** To have queer ideas, be eccentric: C.17–20; adumbrated in 1553 (Apperson); ob. A variant: *one's head is full of bees*, C.16–20: this, however, also = one is (very) 'anxious' or 'restless' (Heywood; Franklin, 1745); †by 1900.

bee-line, make or **take a.** To go direct: coll; orig. (—1830) U.S.; anglicized ca 1870.

beebee, see BEBEE.

Beecham's pills: often shortened to *Beecham's*. Rhyming s. for 'testicles', mispronounced *testikills*: late C.19–20. Probably suggested by the synonymous s. *pills*.

beef. Human flesh, as in *put on beef*, put on weight: from ca 1860. Coll. 2. Hence, in pejorative address, e.g. *you great beef, you!*: coll: late C.19–20; ob. 3. Strength; effort: nautical (—1863): whence *beef up!*, try harder – also coll. 4. The male member: C.19–20; ob. 5. Cat's meat: Clare Market, London: ca 1870–1900. 6. A shout; a yell: theatrical: from ca 1880; ob. Ware suggests, as genesis: *bull – bellow – beef*. cf., however, BEEF!

beef, v.t. To shout, yell: theatrical: from ca 1880; ob. cf. BEEF, n., 6, and BEEF! 2. See BEEF IT.

beef! Stop thief: c. >, by 1870, low s.: ca 1810–1910.

beef, be dressed like Christmas. Dressed

in one's best: from ca 1861; ob. Ex a butcher's shop on Christmas Eve. cf. MUTTON DRESSED AS LAMB.

beef, be in a man's. To wound him with a sword: late C.18–early 19. cf.:

beef, be in a woman's. To have intercourse with a woman: late C.18–mid-19. Contrast preceding entry and cf. *do* or *have a bit of beef, take in beef,* low for women *in coïtu*: C.19–20.

***beef** or **hot beef, cry** or **give.** To set up a hue and cry: c.: C.18–20, ob. Occ. WHIDDLE BEEF.

***beef, make.** To decamp: C.19 c. cf. AMPUTATE . . ., and BEEF, CRY.

beef!, more. Work harder: nautical coll: mid-C.19–20. cf. BEEF UP!

beef, take in, see BEEF, BE IN A WOMAN'S.

***beef, whiddle,** see WHIDDLE BEEF.

beef a bravo. To lead the applause: music-halls': from ca 1880; ob. Ex BEEF, v.

beef-bag. A shirt: Australian: since ca 1860. 'Tom Collins', *Such is Life*, 1903.

beef-brained. Dull-witted: C.17, coll. Feltham, 1627. cf. BEEF-WITTED.

beef-head. A blockhead: coll, C.18–early 19. Unrecorded before 1775. Whence *beef-headed* (—1864).

beef-heart. (Gen. pl.) A bean: low: late C.19–20. Rhyming on FART: ex the effect of (peas and) beans.

beef (it), v. To eat heartily: C.19 coll; orig. dial., then East End Cockney.

beef-stick. The bone in a joint of beef: military: ca 1870–1910.

beef to the heels, like a Mullingar heifer. (Of a man) stalwart, (of a woman) 'fine': mostly Anglo-Irish: mid-C.19–20.

beef-tugging. 'Eating cook-shop meat, not too tender, at lunch-time', Ware: City of London, mostly clerks' (—1909); ob.

beef up, see BEEF, n., 3.

beef up! Pull especially hard!, 'put some beef into it': nautical (—1903).

beef-witted. Doltish: coll verging on S.E.: late C.16–20; ob. (cf. BEEF-BRAINED.) As in Shakespeare's *Troilus and Cressida*. Whence *beef-wittedness* (—1863).

beefiness. Solid physique: coll, orig. (—1859) at Oxford. cf. BEEFY.

***beefment, on the.** On the alert: c.: from ca 1880. cf. BEEF!

beefy. Thick, esp. of hands or ankles (—1859); obese, fleshy (—1860); stolid (1859): coll, all three senses. 2. Lucky (—1874).

Beelzebub's Paradise. Hell: C.19–20 literary coll; ob. Ex St Matthew x. 25 and xii. 27. Heywood, in his *Proverbs*, 1546, had used *Beelzebub's bower*.

been and (done). A tautological elaboration, indicative of surprise or annoyance, of the second participle: illiterate coll: 1837, Dickens, 'See what you've been and done.' cf.:

been and gone and done it, I (etc., **have** or **he** (etc.) **has.** A jocularly coll emphasized form of *I have* (etc.) *done it*, with esp. reference to marriage. Ex illiterate speech (*gorn and done it* or as in preceding entry): cf. P. G. Wodehouse, *Tales of St Austin's*, 1903, 'Captain Kettle had, in the expressive language of the man in the street, been and gone and done it.' This elaboration is peculiarly reminiscent of *veni, vidi, vici*, which is a rhetorical amplification of *vici*.

been in the sun, see SUN, HAVE BEEN IN THE.

been there. (Of women) having sexual experience: C.19–20. (Of men) experienced; shrewd: anglicized ca 1900 ex (—1888) U.S. Both senses are coll, and rare except when preceded by *has* or *have*.

***beenship,** see BENESHIP.

beer, v. To drink beer; to become intoxicated: coll; ca 1780–1850, as in *Peter Pindar*.

beer, do a. To take a drink of beer: coll (—1880). See DO A BEER, A BITTER . . .

beer, in. Drunk: C.19–20. A coll that, ca 1880, > S.E. cf. *in liquor*.

beer, on the. On a bout of drinking: lower-class coll (—1909). More gen., *on the* BOOZE.

beer, small, n. and adj. (Something) unimportant, trifling: C.17–20, coll. Shakespeare in *Othello*: 'To suckle fools, and chronicle small beer'. Hence *think no small beer of oneself*, have a good opinion of oneself, as in De Quincey (?earliest record), 1840.

beer and skittles, not all. Not wholly pleasant: coll from ca 1860.

beer-barrel. The human body: C.19–20, coll; ob. cf. BACON, SAVE ONE'S, and:

beer-bottle. 'A stout, red-faced man': London streets' (—1909); ob.

beer-drink. A gathering of aborigines to drink 'Kaffir beer': South African coll: from the 1890s.

beer-eater. A mighty drinker of beer: 1887, *Referee*, 21 Aug.; ob., except in the Army.

beer o(h). A c.p. cry among artisans exacting a fine for some breach or omission: ca 1850–1900.

beer-slinger. A drinker, esp. if frequent, of beer: from ca 1870.

Beer Street (or beer street). The throat: low (—1909); ob. cf. GUTTER LANE.

beerage, see BEEROCRACY. (ca 1880–1900.)

beeriness. Near-intoxication: coll from ca 1865. Ex S.E. *beery* (1859: H., 1st ed.).

beerocracy. Brewers and publicans: coined in either 1880 or 1881. This might be described as pedantic coll; the likewise coll *beerage*, which, esp. as *beerage and peerage*, was much neater and much more viable, had app. > †by 1909 if not, indeed, by 1900 (Ware's testimony being ambiguous).

bees. Money: late C.19–20. Short for BEES AND HONEY.

bees, his head is full of. To be very anxious, fanciful, restless: coll: ca 1540–1850.

bees and honey. Money: rhyming s.: from not later than 1892.

bee's knee, not as big as a. Very small; gen. applied to a tiny piece of anything: late C.18–20: coll (ob.) and dial. verging on S.E.

***bees-wax.** Soft, inferior cheese: c. or low s.: Moncrieff, in *Tom and Jerry*, 1821; ob. 2. Whence (?), a bore: gen. as *old bees-wax*: ca 1850–1900.

bees-waxers. Football-boots: Winchester College, from ca 1840.

bees-wing, old. A nickname for a genial drinker: from ca 1870; gen. in address. Ex the film in long-kept port wine.

beestie, see BHEESTIE.

beetle, as deaf or dull or dumb as a. Extremely deaf, dull, or dumb: coll verging on S.E.: resp. C.18–19, C.16–17, and C.17–18. This may refer to the implement, not the insect.

beetle-case. A large boot or shoe: ca 1850–1900.

beetle-crusher. A large, esp. if flat, foot: from ca 1840 and popularized by Leech in *Punch*. In this sense, no longer gen. after 1880, *beetle-squasher* was an occ. variant. 2. A large boot or shoe (—1869). 3. (Military) an infantryman: from ca 1885; cf. the more usual MUD-CRUSHER.

beetle-crushing. Solid of tread: coll, from ca 1870. Anon., *Anteros*, 1871.

beetle-squasher, see BEETLE-CRUSHER.

beetle-sticker. An entomologist: from ca 1870; perhaps coll rather than s.

beetroot mug. A red face: London streets': ca 1870–1915. Prob. coined by Charles Ross, that creator of Ally Sloper, who was 'a humorist of the more popular kind' (Ware).

before the wind. Well-placed, prospering, fortunate: coll: from ca 1840; orig. nautical.

before-time. Formerly, previously, of old: pidgin: from ca 1860.

beforehand with the world. Having a reserve of money: from ca 1640; coll; in C.19 S.E.

beg (a person) **for a fool, an idiot** or **an innocent.** To consider, set down as a fool; from ca 1580: coll >, ca 1700, S.E.; in C.19–20, archaic.

beg yer pardon. A garden: rhyming s.: late C.19–20.

beg your pudding (or pudden)! I beg your pardon: lower-middle-class jocular: from ca 1890.

begad! An exclamation, gen. in support: coll: 1742, Fielding. Ex *by God!*

begarra! An occ. variant of BEGORRA(H)!

Begats, the (or italicized or 'quoted'). The Book of Genesis: middle-class: since ca 1870.

beggar. A euphemism for BUGGER: whether n. or v. e.g. in *I'll be beggared if . . .!*, I swear I won't . . .: C.19–20. 2. (n. only.) Playfully coll: from ca 1830; cf. SCAMP. 3. A man, chap, fellow: from ca 1850.

beggar boy's ass. Bass (the drink): rhyming s.: late C.19–20. Often abbr. to *beggar boy's*. 2. Money: rhyming s. (on BRASS): late C.19–20.

beggar on the gentleman, put the. To drink beer after spirits: mid-C.19–20, ob. A variant of *put a* CHURL (UP)ON THE GENTLEMAN.

beggar-maker. A publican: late C.18–early 19, coll. Grose, 1st ed., where also *beggar-makers*, an ale-house: an entry that should, I think, read *beggar-maker*, etc., for the singular is all that is necessary.

beggared if, see BEGGAR, 1.

beggarly. Mere: coll; C.19–20. e.g. 'He gave the rescuer a beggarly fiver.'

beggars. Cards of denomination 2 to 10: coll, C.19–20; ob.

beggar's benison. 'May your prick and (your) purse never fail you': low: C.18–early 19. Grose, 1st ed. cf. BEST IN CHRISTENDOM; BOTH ENDS OF THE BUSK.

beggars' bolts or **bullets.** Stones: coll, resp. late C.16–17, late C.18–early 19 (as in Grose, 1st ed.).

beggar's brown. Scotch snuff: coll: C.19–

20; ob. Orig. and mainly Scottish. It is light brown in colour.

beggar's bush, go (home) by. To be ruined: late C.16–19; in 1564, Bullein has a rare variant, thus: 'In the ende thei go home . . . by weepyng cross, by beggers barne, and by knave's acre,' Apperson. Beggars have always, in summer, slept under trees and bushes; in winter, if possible, they naturally seek a barn.

beggar's plush. Corduroy or perhaps cotton velvet: late C.17–18 coll. *London Gazette*, 1688.

beggar's velvet. Downy matter accumulating under furniture: C.19–20. ob.: coll.

begin to, not to. 'Not to (do something)' emphasized; to be in no way; fall short of being or doing: coll: U.S. (1842), anglicized ca 1860. e.g. an ill-disposed person might say, 'This does not begin to be a dictionary.'

begin (up)on. To attack, either physically or verbally: coll: ca 1825, Mrs Sherwood, 'All the company began upon her, and bade her mind her own affairs.'

begorra(h)! By God: Anglo-Irish coll: C.19–20. By corruption. cf. *be* JABERS!

begum. A rich widow: Anglo-Indian: mid-C.19–20; ob. A derivation from the S.E. sense, a lady of royal or other high rank in Hindustan.

behave is short and coll for *behave yourself properly*: since ca 1870. Mostly nursery ('Behave, miss, or I'll smack you') and lower-class.

behind. The posterior; the rear part of a garment. The first record is of 1786. See *Slang*. 2. At Eton and Winchester Colleges, ca 1850–1914, a back at SOCCER: coll > j.

behind chests. 'Dark nooks on the orlop deck': *The Conway*: from ca 1875. Masefield's history of that training-ship.

behind oneself, be. To be late, a long way behind, far from 'up to the minute': non-aristocratic coll: 1896; slightly ob.

behindativeness, have (e.g. a deal of). To have a (big) dress-pannier: Society: 1888–ca 1905.

***Beilby's ball** (*where the sheriff plays the music* is added in Grose, 3rd ed.), **dance at.** To be hanged: late C.18–early 19: prob. orig. c. It is not known who Mr Beilby was; perhaps a notable London sheriff. But *Beilby's* is more prob. a personified and punning perversion of *bilboes*, fetters; F. & H. infers that it implied an Old *Bailey* hanging.

bejan, occ. **baijan.** A freshman at the Universities of Edinburgh (where †by 1880), Aberdeen, St Andrew's. From ca 1640: s. only in C.17, then j. Ex the *bec jaune* of the Sorbonne, where the term was certainly s. An early form of *bec jaune*, an ignorant person, was *béjaune*.

***bel-shangle.** (Perhaps) a buffoon: prob. c.: late C.16–early 17. Kemp, 1600. ?*bell-jangler*.

belay. To speak, esp. if vigorously: nautical: from ca 1790; ob. Dibdin, 'My timbers! what lingo he'd coil and belay.' 2. To stop, gen. *belay that yarn!*, we've had enough of that story: nautical (—1823). cf.:

belay there! Stop! Nautical: from ca 1860.

belaying-pin soup. Rough treatment of seamen by officers, esp. in sailing-ships: nautical: late C.19–20; ob.

belch. Beer, esp. if inferior and therefore apt to cause belching: from ca 1690; ob. One recalls Sir Toby Belch, a jolly blade, but he, I surmise, avoided poor beer. cf. SWIPES.

belch, v.i. To eructate: C.11–20: S.E. until mid-C.19, then a vulgarism.

belcher. A blue handkerchief white- or, occ., yellow-spotted (*The Port Folio*, 1807); from ca 1860 loosely, a handkerchief of any base with spots of another colour. Soon > coll, and from ca 1875 it has been S.E. Ex the boxer Jim Belcher (d. 1811). 2. A (gen. hard) drinker of beer: C. Hindley, 1876, but prob. in use at least twenty years earlier: circus and showmen's s., which is nearer to c. than to s. 3. A thick ring: 1851, Mayhew; ob. c.

belfa. A harlot: s.: Ned Ward, 1703.

belfry, the. The head: see BATS IN THE BELFRY.

believe you, I. Yes! Coll (—1835, when employed by Dickens); ob. cf. the much later c.p., I BELIEVE YOU, MY BOY!

***bell.** A song: C.19 tramps' c. (—1859). Abbr. *bellow*.

bell, v. To run away with (a marble): schoolboys', ca 1850–1910.

bell, ring one's own. To blow one's own trumpet: coll verging on S.E.: C.19–20; ob. cf. *who pulled your chain?*

bell, sound as a. In excellent health, of unimpaired physique: coll, C.19–20.

bell-bastard. The bastard child of a bastard mother: C.19 West Country. Why the *bell*? cf. BASTARDLY GULLION.

bell, book and candle. Jocular coll for the

accessories of a religious ceremony: C.19–20; coll > S.E. Ex a medieval form of excommunication, these nn. occurring in the final sentence.

bell-rope. A man's curl in front of the ear; cf. AGGERAWATOR. Punning *bell* and *belle*. Low (—1868); ob.

bell-shangle, see BEL-SHANGLE.

bell the cat. To undertake something dangerous: from ca 1720, coll; S.E. by 1800.

bell-top. A *membrum virile* unusually large-headed; gen. as adj., *bell-topped*, occ. *-knobbed.* C.19 (?–C.20). F. & H. designate it as 'harlotry'.

bell-topper. A silk hat: Australia and New Zealand, from ca 1850: coll by 1900.

bell-wether. Leader of a mob: C.15–20; coll >, by 1750, S.E. Ex 'a flock of sheep, where the wether has a bell about its neck', Grose. 2. 'A clamorous noisy man', B.E.: s. in C.17–early 19, coll in C.15–16.

beller-croaker. Ravishingly beautiful: non-educated: ca 1860–85. A corruption of Fr. *belle à croquer*, which 'lasted into 1883, in English Society', Ware.

bellering cake. 'Cake in which the plums are so far apart that they have to beller (bellow) when they wish to converse', Ware: schools' (—1909); ob.

bellers, see BELLOWS.

bellier. A punch to the belly: pugilistic coll: ca 1810–1930. *Boxiana*, III, 1821.

bellowdrama. Melodrama: jocular coll: late C.19–20. Rhyming.

bellower. A town crier: late C.18–early 19.

bellows; illiterately, **bellers.** The lungs. Recorded for 1615, but that was a fig. use; as s., C.18–20. cf.:

bellows away!; bellows him well! An adjuration to a boxer not to spare his opponent, i.e. to make him pant for wind: boxing: ca 1820–70.

bellows to mend, have. (Of a horse) to be broken-winded; hence, of a man: mid-C.19–20. 'Cuthbert Bede' in *Verdant Green.*

***bellowsed.** Transported as a convict: ca 1820–60. cf. LAG, v., 4.

bellowser. A blow in 'the wind': boxing, from ca 1810; ob. Hence, 2, a sentence of transportation for life: c. of ca 1810–60. Vaux, *knap* (i.e. nap) *a bellowser.*

bells down. The last peal of chapel-warning: Winchester College, ca 1840–1900. *Bells go single* was the second of the warning-notices. See the works of Mansfield and Adams.

belly, his eye was bigger than his. 'A saying of a person at table, who takes more on his plate than he can eat', Grose, 2nd ed.: mid-C.18–mid-19.

belly-ache. A pain in the bowels. Since ca 1840 it has been considered both coll and low, but orig. (—1552), and until ca 1800, it was S.E.

belly-ache, v. Grumble, complain, esp. querulously or unreasonably: ex U.S. (—1881), anglicized ca 1900: coll, somewhat low.

belly and wipe my eyes with it, I could take up the slack of my. I am very hungry: a nautical c.p., frequent on ships where rations are inadequate: late C.19–20.

belly-bound. Costive: coll: from ca 1660 and gen. of horses.

belly-bumper or **-buster, get a.** To be got with child; whence *belly-bump*, coït. Low: C.19–20. 'In an old collection of dances and tunes in my library, printed about 1703, one of the dances is entitled The Maiden's Blush, or Bump her Belly. It is to be danced "long way, for as many as will". A sort of Roger de Coverley affair, with a romping lilt,' Alexander McQueen, 3 July 1953.

belly-buster. A bad fall = a clumsy dive into water: Australian coll: late C.19–20. 2. Specifically, a dive in which the entire front of the body hits the water at the same time: late C.19–20.

belly-button. Navel: lowish: mid-C.19–20.

belly-can. A tin vessel that, shaped like a saddle, is easily secreted about the body: used for the illicit conveyance of beer and holding about four quarts: political, 1889 +, but ob. by 1900.

***belly-cheat.** An apron: ca 1600–1830: c. or low s. Compounds with CHEAT, earlier *chete*, a thing, an article, are all either low s. or c. 2. Also: food: c.: C.17. Fletcher, 1622. 3. (cf. sense 1.) A pad designed to produce a semblance of pregnancy: c. (—1823); †by 1900.

belly-cheer. Food: late C.16–early 19; slightly earlier (—1549), gratification of the belly. v., to feast heartily or luxuriously: C.16–17. Orig. these terms were S.E., but in the later C.17 the v., in C.18–19 the n., were coll. The vbl n., *belly-cheering*, meant eating and drinking: C.18–19 coll.

belly-flop. A BELLY-BUSTER: coll: since ca 1870.

belly-friend. A hanger-on: C.17–18, coll verging on S.E.

belly-full, bellyful. A thrashing: late

C.16–19; e.g. in Nashe, Chapman, Pepys. In the sense of a sufficiency, the word has, since ca 1840, > coll simply because it is considered coarse. (Of a woman) *have a* – or *have got her* – *bellyful*, to be with child: low: late C.18–mid-19.

belly-furniture. Food: C.17 coll, as in Urquhart's *Rabelais*; cf. BELLY-TIMBER.

belly-go-firster. (Boxing) an initial blow, given – as such a blow was once so often given – in the belly. C.19.

belly-gut. A greedy, lazy person; gen. of a man: coll: C.16–18.

belly-hedge. (Shrewsbury School) a steeplechase obstruction belly-high and therefore easily jumped: from ca 1850.

belly-paunch. A glutton: mid-C.16–17, coll verging on S.E.; cf. BELLY-GUT.

belly-piece. A concubine, a mistress, a harlot: coll: C.17. 2. Also, an apron (cf. BELLY-CHEAT): late C.17–18; coll. It occurs in that lively, slangy play, Shadwell's *Bury Fair*.

belly-plea. An excuse of pregnancy, esp. among female prisoners. C.18–early 19, coll. Defoe, in *Moll Flanders*, 1721: 'My mother pleaded her belly, and being found quick with child, she was respited for about seven months'; Gay, in *The Beggar's Opera*.

belly-ruffian. The penis: ?C.17–19: low (?coll rather than s.).

belly thinks . . ., see THROAT IS CUT, ONE'S BELLY THINKS ONE'S.

belly-timber. Food: from ca 1600. In C.17, S.E.; then coll. In C.19 s.; in C.20, an archaism. Butler's use tended to make it ludicrous.

belly-up, adj. and adv. Of a pregnant woman: C.17–18, low.

belly-vengeance. Sour beer: C.19. Since ca 1870, it is mainly dial. cf.:

belly-wash. Thin liquor, rinsings: coll: late C.19–20.

bellyful, fight for a. i.e. 'without stakes, wager, or payment', Bee: pugilistic: mid-C.18–20; very ob.

belongings. Goods, possessions: coll, from ca 1800. 2. Relatives: Dickens, 1852; coll; ob.

below the belt, adv. and adj. Unfair(ly): from ca 1870; coll.

belswagger. A bully; blustering fellow: coll: Greene, 1592; Dryden, 1680. †by 1830. 2. A womanizer; a pimp: C.18. Ash's Dictionary distinguishes by spelling the former *bellyswagger*, the latter as *belswagger*.

belt. A hit, blow, punch. 'He caught me an awful belt on the ear.' From ca 1895. Ex the v.: cf. BELTING.

belter. A harlot: 'old', says F. & H. (revised): but when? She 'punishes' one's purse. cf. BELTINKER.

belting. A thrashing, whether punitive or pugilistic: mid-C.19–20: coll verging on S.E.

beltinker, n. and v. A thrashing, to thrash. Coll: ?C.19. Perhaps a pun on *belt*, thrash with a belt.

Belvidere. A handsome fellow: Londoners': ca 1880–1905. Ex Apollo Belvidere.

bembow. Variant of BUMBO, 2. 'A Swaker of Bembow a piece,' *Sessions*, 28 June–1 July 1738, trial of Alice Gibson.

bemused (with beer). In C.18–mid-19, S.E., as in its originator, Pope; ca 1860 it > a fashionable phrase and genuinely s.; ob.

ben. A coat, C.19, ex BENJAMIN; a waistcoat (—1846), ex BENJY. Both ob. 2. (Theatrical) a benefit performance: from ca 1850. cf. *stand ben*, to stand treat (—1823); †by 1900. 3. In c., a fool: late C.17–18. ?'a good fellow': see BENE. 4. A TARRADIDDLE: Society: ca 1880–1914. Ware: *ben* ex *Ben* ex *Ben Tro* ex *Ben Trovato* ex *Benjamin Trovato* ex *se non è vero – è Benjamin* (for *ben*) *trovato*, if it isn't true it's nonetheless felicitous. 5. 'The "bens" or lockers' (W. N. Glascock, *Sailors and Saints*, 1829): naval: ca 1805–50. Ex S.E. *ben*, an inner room.

***ben**, adj.; gen. **bene**; often **bien.** Good: c.: mid-C.16–early 19. Ex L. *bene*, well (adv.), or Fr. *bien*. cf. at BENE.

ben, stand, see BEN, n., 2.

***ben-** or **bene-bowsie.** Drunk (esp. with good wine): c.: C.17–18. Jonson. Ex BENE *bowse*.

***ben cull**, C.19; **ben cove**, C.17–18. Both c.: for a friend or a companion. See BEN and BENE, *bene* also being found, in same sense, with COVE and, less often, CULL.

***Ben Flake** or **ben-flake.** A steak: thieves' rhyming s.: from ca 1855. (Rhyming s. may have been invented by criminals.)

Ben Tro and **Ben Trovato**, see BEN, n., 4.

***benar.** Better. **Benat**: best. The former in Coles, but prob. both are C.17–18; c. See BENE.

bench-winner. A dog successful at many dog-shows: Society: 1897, *Daily Telegraph*, 11 Feb.; ob. Ex the exhibits being placed on benches.

bench-points. 'Classified physical advantages': London: ca 1900–15. Ware. Ex show animals. cf. preceding.

bencher. 'He that loves to drink in hugger-mugger': *The English Liberal Science*, 1650.

bend (mid-C.18–20); **bend to** (mid-C.19–20). To drink hard: Scots; ob. Alan Ramsay; lexicographer Jamieson; memoirist Ramsay. O.E.D., 'Perhaps "to pull, strain" in reference to pulling or straining a bow . . .; or "to ply, apply oneself to".'

bend, above one's. Beyond one's ability: coll from ca 1860; ob. Earlier U.S. Perhaps *above one's bent*.

bend down for. To submit to *effeminatio*: euphemistic coll: late C.19–20.

bend, Grecian. The body bent forward in walking: a Society vogue of ca 1872–80. The term long outlasted the craze and is now but moribund.

bend, on a. A-drinking; on a spree: U.S. (1887) anglicized ca 1890. Also *on the bend*; see sense 2 of:

bend, on the. Crooked, underhand: coll from ca 1850; ob. cf. CROOKED. 2. The same as the preceding entry: 1891, Kipling. Prob. ex *on a bender*: see BENDER, 4.

bend, round the, see ROUND THE BEND.

bend o(f) the filbert. A bow, a nod: low London: ca 1860–1900. See FILBERT, 2.

bender. A sixpence: late C.18–20, ob.: c. >, by 1820, low s. Parker, *Life's Painter of Variegated Characters*, 1789; Dickens, 1836; Whyte-Melville, 1869. (Because easily bent.) 'Ducange Anglicus', 1857, defines it as a shilling; prob. in error. 2. The arm: C.19–20, ob.: cf. the C.17–18 medical use of the term for a flexor muscle. 3. Hence, the elbow: late C.19–20; ob. 4. A drinking spree: orig. (1827), U.S.; anglicized ca 1895. cf. *on a* BEND, and Ramsay's and Tannahill's *bender*, a hard drinker. 5. In certain Public Schools, a stroke of the cane administered to a boy bending his back: from ca 1870. 6. General schoolboys', ca 1870–1910: 'the bow-shaped segment of a paper kite'. Blackley, *Hay Fever*, 1873. 7. A TALL story: nautical: late C.19–20. cf. the next two entries.

***bender!** I don't believe it!; as a c.p. tag, I'll do no such thing: c. (—1812); †by 1890. cf.:

bender, over the. Exaggerated, untrue; often as an exclamation of incredulity. cf. *over the* LEFT (shoulder). C.19–20, ob. 2. (Of a partridge) before 1 Sept.; (of a pheasant) before 1 Oct.: poachers' (—1909).

bendigo. A rough fur cap: ca 1845–1900. Ex the Nottingham prize-fighter, Wm Thompson (1811–89), *nom-de-guerre*'d Bendigo, whose first challenge dates 1835 and who afterwards turned evangelist: see Weekley's *Romance of Words*.

***bene, bien.** In c. as n., tongue: C.16–18, prob. by transference ex the adj.: 2. Good, with *benar*, better, and *benat*, best: mid-C.16–early 19. Variant BEN, and even *bien*. e.g. *ben(e) bowse*, BOOZE, etc., excellent liquor.

***bene (or bien), on the.** Well: expeditiously. As in B.E.'s *pike on the bene* (there spelt *bien*), run away quickly. c. of late C.17–18.

***bene darkmans!** Good night! Mid-C.16–18: c. See DARKMANS; contrast LIGHTMANS.

***bene feaker.** A counterfeiter of bills: late C.17–18: c. BENE here = skilful. See FAKER.

***bene feaker of gybes.** A counterfeiter of passes: late C.17–18: c. See GYBE, n.

***bene, or bien, mort.** A fine woman or pretty girl; hence, a hostess. C.16–18: c. Revived by e.g. Scott. See MORT, MOT, a woman, a girl.

benefit, take the. i.e. of the insolvent debtor's Act: coll (—1823); †by 1890.

***ben(e)ship.** Profitable: worshipful: mid-C.16–18 c. 2. Hence adv., *beneshiply*, worshipfully: C.17–18. Ex BENE, 2.

benevolence. 'Ostentation and fear united, with hopes of retaliation in kind *hereafter*', Bee, 1823: Society: ca 1820–40.

***benfeaker.** A variant of BENE FEAKER.

Bengal blanket. The sun; a blue sky: soldiers in India: mid-C.19–20; very ob. cf. BLUE BLANKET.

bengi. An onion: military, from ca 1860. Perhaps cognate with Somerset *benge*, to drink to excess; cf. BINGE.

bengy, see BENJY.

***benish,** occ. **bennish.** Foolish: late C.17–18 c. See BEN, n. 3.

benison, beggar's, see BEGGAR'S BENISON.

benjamin or **Benjamin.** A coat (from ca 1815), whence *upper benjamin* (1817), a greatcoat. Peacock in *Nightmare Abbey*: 'His heart is seen to beat through his upper Benjamin.' Borrow in *Lavengro*: 'The coachman . . . with . . . fashionable Benjamin'. The word may have begun as c.; in C.20, ob. Perhaps, as Brewer suggests, ex the name of a tailor; more prob. on JOSEPH'S COAT. 2. At Winchester College, from ca 1860, a small ruler, i.e. *Benjamin* small in comparison with *Joseph*. 3. A husband: Australian pidgin-English (—1870). Chas. H. Allen, *A Visit to Queensland*, 1870. cf. MARY.

Benjamin Trovato, see BEN, n., 4.

benjo. A riotous holiday: nautical: late C.19–20; ob. Perhaps ex BEANO + BENDER, 4; Ware suggests derivation ex *buen giorno* (?via Lingua Franca).

***benjy.** A waistcoat: c. > low (—1821); ob. Haggart. Ex BENJAMIN, 1. 2. Hence, a waistcoat-maker: tailors': mid-C.19–20. 3. Nautical (perhaps ex dial.), C.19: a straw hat, low-crowned and broad-brimmed.

***benly,** rare adv. Well: c.: ?mid-C.18–early 19. Perhaps abbr. BENESHIP(LY).

bennish, see BENISH.

benny, have a. (Unwittingly) to wet one's bed at night: military (not officers'): from ca 1890. Richards. Origin? Perhaps *benny* = BENJAMIN, a little one; the minor contrasted with the major physical need.

bens. Tools: workmen's: late C.19–20. ?ex BEN, n., 2.

***benship,** see BENESHIP.

bent on a splice, be. To be on the look-out for a wife: nautical: from ca 1860; ob. Perhaps punning SPLICED, married.

beong; occ. **beonck.** (Costers') a shilling: mid-C.19–20. Ex *bianco* (lit. white), a silver coin. It. via Lingua Franca.

***bereavement lurk.** The pretended loss of a wife as a pretext for begging: c. (—1875). Ribton-Turner, *Vagrants and Vagrancy*. See LURK and contrast DEAD LURK.

berge. A spy-glass or telescope: naval: ca 1810–60. Captain Glascock, *Land Sharks and Sea Gulls*, 1838. Ex a proper name?

Berkeley. The *pudendum muliebre*: C.20. Abbr. *Berkeley Hunt*, a CUNT. 2. In the pl, and from ca 1875 – never, obviously, with *Hunt* – it denotes a woman's breasts; F. & H. adduce Romany *berk* (or *burk*), breast, pl *berkia*. cf.:

Berkshire Hunt. The female pudend: rhyming s.: ?mid-C.19–20. Franklyn, *Rhyming*, believes it to form the original of the synonymous BERKELEY *Hunt* and the *Berkeley* form to be accidental.

Bermoothes, see BERMUDAS.

Bermudas, Bermoothes. A London district (cf. ALSATIA) privileged against arrest: certain alleys and passages contiguous to Drury Lane, near Covent Garden, and north of the Strand: Jonson, *The Devil's an Ass* (1616): 'Keeps he still your quarter in the Bermudas.' Grose and Ainsworth are almost certainly in error in referring the term to the Mint in Southwark. In C.17, certain notable debtors fled to the Bermuda Islands, says Nares.

Bermudian. A wet ship: naval coll: C.19. Ex 'the Bermudian-built 3-masted schooners in the Napoleonic wars': they 'went through the waves instead of rising to them' (Bowen).

***bernard,** see BARNARD.

beside the lighter. In a bad condition: late C.17–18. Perhaps the lighter going out to a ship proceeding to the convict plantations. cf. *beside the* BOOK.

besognio. A low, worthless fellow: coll: ca 1620–1840. Pronounced and often spelt *besonio*. Ex It. *bisogna* via S.E. *beso(g)nio*, a raw soldier.

besom, jump the. To go through a mock marriage: ca 1700–1820. Manchon implies its survival into C.20. cf. BROOMSTICK, JUMP THE.

bespeak-night. (Theatrical) a benefit performance: from the mid-1830s; ob. Ex *bespeak*, to choose, arrange, the actor's friends choosing the play. Often abbr. to *bespeak* (as in Ware).

***bess.** A burglar's tool: see BETTY. See BROWN BESS.

Bess o' Bedlam. An insane beggar: C.17–early 19. Scott in *Kenilworth*: 'Why, what Bess of Bedlam is this, would ask to see my lord on such a day as the present?'

best. To worst; get the better of: coll (—1859), as in H., 1st ed., and in Charles Hindley's best-known book, *A Cheap Jack*. 2. Hence, to cheat, as in Hindley, 'His game was besting everybody, whether it was for pounds, shillings, or pence,' 1876. cf. BESTER. 3. Hence as in *best the pistol*, to get away before the pistol is fired: athletics: 1889, *Polytechnic Magazine*, 7 July.

***best, get one's money at the.** 'To live by dishonest or fraudulent practices': c. (—1812); †by 1890. Vaux.

***best, give,** see GIVE BEST.

best, not in the. Not in the best of tempers: coll: from ca 1890.

best bib and tucker, gen. one's, occ. the. (Rarely of children's and only loosely of men's) best clothes: U.S. (1793), anglicized in Lancashire dial. ca 1870, in coll ca 1880; ob.

best foot or leg foremost, put one's. To

try hard: coll >, by 1850, S.E.: *foot* from late C.16, *leg* from late C.15; ob.

best in Christendom, to the. A toast very popular ca 1750–80 (cf. BEGGAR'S BENISON and BOTH ENDS OF THE BUSK). Sc. CUNT.

best leg of three, the. The penis: low: late C.19–20; ob.

best of a bad bargain (etc.), see BARGAIN, BEST ...

best of a Charley, the. 'Upsetting a watchman in his box', Egan's Grose: ca 1820–40.

best part, best thing, etc. The best part, thing, etc.: coll: late C.19–20.

best the pistol, see BEST, 3.

***bester.** A swindler; a 'smart Alec' criminally or illicitly: orig. (—1859), c.; then low. See quotation at CRAWLER.

bet!, you. Certainly: ?orig. (ca 1870) U.S., anglicized ca 1890. 2. *You betcha* (or *betcher*), *you bet your* (e.g. *boots*): U.S. phrases anglicized ca 1905.

bet you a million to a bit of dirt! A sporting c.p. indicative of 'the betting man's Ultima Thule of confidence', Ware: ca 1880–1914. cf. ALL LOMBARD STREET TO A CHINA ORANGE.

bet your boots or **life** or **bottom dollar!** Orig. (resp. 1868, 1852, and 1882) U.S.; anglicized ca 1910, 1880, 1890 resp., largely owing to the writings of Bret Harte and Mark Twain.

betcha, betcher; you betcha (or betcher), see BET, YOU, 2.

beteechoot, see BANCHOOT.

bethel the city. To refrain from keeping a hospitable table; to eat at chop-houses: C.18. Ex Bethel, one of the two Sheriffs of London elected in 1680.

***Bethlehemites.** Christmas carol-singers: late C.18–early 19 c. Ex *Bethlehem*, frequent in carols.

Betsy. The inevitable nickname of anyone surnamed Gay: late C.19–20. Ex the old song. Bowen considers it to have been orig. naval. cf. DUSTY, 3.

better, v. To re-lock a door: c. of ca 1810–50. Ex BETTY, a picklock.

better for your asking, no or **none the;** or **never the better for you.** A c.p.: the 1st, late C.19–20; the 2nd, late C.18–20, but slightly ob. by 1960; the 3rd, late C.17–18, occurring in, e.g., Swift, *Polite Conversation*, 1738.

better half. A wife: coll from ca 1570. In C.16–18, *my better half* and seriously, in C.19–20, *a*, or *anyone's*, *b. h.*, and jocularly.

better never than come in rags! i.e. in poverty (see RAG, a farthing): a c.p. retort to *better late than never*: ca 1820–50.

better than a drowned policeman. (Of a person) very pleasant, attractive, good or expert: c.p.: ca 1900–15.

better than a poke in the eye with a sharp stick. Better than nothing; by meiosis, very much better than nothing or than a setback: mid-C.19–20.

betterish. Somewhat better or superior: coll (—1888); verging on S.E. – but ugly!

bettermost. Best: (somewhat low) coll (—1887).

betting, often corrupted to **getting, round.** The laying of odds on all the likely horses: from ca 1860; ob. Whence *better round*, such a better, as in 'Thormanby', *Famous Racing Men*, 1882.

betting lay, the. Betting on horses: turf (—1887).

betty, occ. bess. A picklock (instrument): mid-C.17–19. Orig. c.; the form *bess* (†by 1880) remained c. For *betty*, much the commoner, see Head's *English Rogue*, Coles, B.E., Ned Ward, Grose, and Henry Mayhew; for *bess*, B.E. and Grose. cf. JEMMY, n., and JENNY, n., and see esp. Grose, P. 2. Also (cf. MOLLY), a man assuming a woman's domestic duties: C.19–20; coll. cf. BETTY, v. 3. Miss, as a title: Bootham School: late C.19–20.

betty, v. Fuss, or potter, *about*: coll: from ca 1850; slightly ob.

***betty!, all.** It's all up! C.19 c.; opp. *it's all bob*, see BOB, adj. 2. (This kind of pun (*Betty* and *Bob*) is not rare in c.)

Betty Martin, see ALL MY EYE (AND BETTY MARTIN).

betwattled. Astounded, bewildered; betrayed: late C.18–early 19.

between the flags. On the actual racecourse: sporting (—1865); ob.

between wind and water, see SHOOT BETWEEN WIND AND WATER. **between you and me (and ...),** see BED-POST ...

betwixt and between. Intermediate(ly); indecisive(ly); neither one thing nor the other: adv. and adj. Coll: from ca 1830. 'A betwixt and between fashionable street', Marryat.

bever; often **beaver;** occ. **bevir,** etc. etc. Orig. S.E. and in C.19–20 mainly dial., but as used at Eton and as *bevers* at Winchester College for afternoon tea – a sense recorded by B.E. – it is s. See in my *Words!* the essay entitled 'The Art of Lightening Work'. Ex L. *bibere*, to drink, in the Old Fr. form, *beivre*, this is one of the most interesting words in the language. cf. BIVVY and BEVERAGE. 2. Hence, as v.: C.17–early 19.

beverage. 'A Garnish, money for any thing', B.E.; Grose adds that it is drink-money – cf. the Fr. *pourboire* – demanded of any person wearing a new suit; in gen., a tip. Coll: late C.17–20; †by ca 1820, except in dial.

bevie, v.; gen. **bevvy.** To drink: Parlary, esp. among grafters: late C.19–20.

bevie, bevvy. A public-house: mid-C.19–20 Parlary. 2. Beer; loosely, any drink: military and theatrical: late C.19–20. Either ex sense 1 or ex *beverage*.

bevie-homey. A drunkard: grafters': mid-C.19–20.

bevir, see BEVER.

bevor. A wedge of bread obtainable between dinner and supper: Charterhouse (school): late C.17–19. Probably cf. BEVER, 1.

beware. Any drinkable: low s., from ca 1840. Mayhew in that mine of Cockney and low s., *London Labour and the London Poor*, 4 vols., 1851–61, says in vol. iii: 'We (strolling actors) call breakfast, dinner, tea, supper, all of them "numyare"; and all beer, brandy, water, or soup, are "beware".' *Numyare* (?a corruption of It. *mangiare*, to eat) and *beware* (cf. BEVER; BEVERAGE; BIVVY) are Lingua Franca words employed in Parlary, the s. of circuses, showmen, and strolling actors: see *Slang*, section on the circus.

***bewer.** A girl: c. (—1845): rare and ob. See *No. 747*, p. 416. Ex Shelta.

bexandebs. Easy-going young Jewesses in the Wentworth Street district: East London: late C.18–20; ob. Ex *Beck* (Rebecca) + *Deb* (Deborah).

Bexley Heath. Teeth: rhyming s.: late C. 19–20. Sometimes shortened to *Bexleys*.

beyond, be (a person). To pass the comprehension of: coll; from ca 1800. Jane Austen.

bheestie, -y. A water-bearer: from ca 1780: Anglo-Indian coll >, by 1850, j. Ex Urdu *bhisti*, but prob. by a pun on Scots *beastie*, a little beast. (In C.18, often spelt *beasty*; in C.19 *beestie*.)

b'hoy. 'A town rowdy; a gay fellow', Thornton: ex U.S. (1846), anglicized – almost wholly in the latter sense – ca 1865. Ex Irish pronunciation.

bianc. A shilling: c. and Parlary: mid-C.19–20. It. *bianco*, white.

Bianca Capella. (Gen. pl.) A 'White Chapeller' (cigar): East London: 1886, *Referee*, 6 June. cf. BANKER CHAPEL HO.

bias, on the. Illicit: dishonourable; dishonest: dressmakers' (—1909). cf. *on the cross* (at CROSS).

***bib, nap a** or **one's.** To weep: c. or low s.; late C.18–20; ob. G. Parker, 1789; Vaux; Egan. Lit., to take one's bib in order to wipe away one's tears.

bib-all-night. A toper: C.17, coll. (*Bib*, to tipple.)

bib and tucker, best, see BEST BIB . . .

bible. Nautical: 'a hand-axe; a small holystone [sandstone employed in the cleaning of decks], so called from seamen using them kneeling': Admiral Smyth in his valuable *Sailors' Word Book*, 1867. C.18–20; ob. The holystones were also named PRAYER-BOOKS. For nautical s. in gen., see *Slang*. 2. Lead wrapped round the body by those who *fly the* BLUE PIGEON; what they stow in their pockets is a *testament*: c.: late C.18–mid-19. G. Parker, 1789. 3. ?hence: in mid-C.19–20 c. (vagrants'), a pedlar's box of pins, needles, laces, etc.

bible, v. Implied in BIBLER, BIBLING.

bible, that's. That's true; that's excellent: C.19–20 (ob.), coll. cf. S.E. *Bible oath*.

Bible-banger. A pious, esp. if ranting person: late C.19–20. cf. BIBLE-POUNDER.

***bible-carrier.** One who sells songs without singing them: c. (vagrants'): ca 1850–1915.

Bible class, been to a. 'With two black eyes, got in a fight': printers' (—1909). Ware. Prob. suggested by the noise and excitement common at printers' *chapels*.

Bible-clerk. (Winchester College) a prefect appointed to full power for one week; he reads the lessons in chapel. From ca 1850: see esp. Mansfield and Adams: coll soon > j. (In S.E., an Oxford term.)

bible (or B.) leaf. (Gen. pl.) A thin strip of blubber ready for the fry-pot: whalers': coll: late C.19–20. Ex leaves preserved by being kept in the family Bible.

Bible-mill. A public-house; esp., noisy talking there: London proletarians': ca 1850–1910. Ware, 'An attack upon Bible classes.'

Bible-pounder. A clergyman, esp. if excitable: coll, C.19–20. cf. BIBLE-BANGER.

Bible-thumper. A pious seaman: nautical coll: mid-C.19–20. cf. BIBLE-BANGER.

bibler, bibling. Six cuts on the back: the

former ca 1830–60, the latter from ca 1860. Winchester College: see Adams, Mansfield, and *Blackwood's Magazine*, 1864, vol. xcv. A *bibler*, later *bibling*, *under nail*: a pillory-process before the cuts were administered. The *bibling-rod*, a handle with four apple-twigs twisted together at the end: invented by Warden Baker in 1454; †by 1890. 2. One's *Bible oath*: low: ca 1815–1900.

biccy or **bikky.** Biscuit: nursery and domestic coll: from ca 1870.

bid stand, bid-stand, bidstand. A highwayman: coll: late C.16–?18. Ben Jonson. For the philology of highwaymen, see *Words!*

biddy. A chicken: coll: late C.16–early 19; then dial. Occ. CHICKABIDDY. 2. A young woman (ex *Bridget*): C.18–early 19, as in Grose, 1st ed. 3. Any woman: C.19, as in O. W. Holmes, *Guardian Angel*, 1869. 4. At Winchester College, see:

bidet or **biddy.** A bath. Also, though this is S.E. as *bidet*, coll as *biddy*, defined thus by Grose: 'A kind of tub, contrived for ladies to wash themselves, for which purpose they bestride it like a little French pony or post horse, called in French bidets', as also is this toilet accessory. 2. See:

biddy-biddy; biddybid. The burr named in Maori *piripiri*: New Zealand coll (—1880). By the process of Hobson-Jobson. 2. Hence, gen. as *biddy*, to rid of burrs: 1880.

'Bidgee, the. The Murrumbidgee River: Australian coll: mid-C.19–20.

***bien,** see BEAN, BEN and BENE.

***bienly.** Excellently: c.: late C.18–early 19. See BENE.

biff. A blow; (?orig. U.S., anglicized) ca 1895. Prob. an abbr. and emaciated form of *buffet*. 2. Slightly earlier as v., gen. v.t.: to hit resoundingly, sharply, abruptly, or crisply. e.g., 'I'll biff him one if he's not careful.' Echoic or as in sense 1.

biffin. An intimate friend: from ca 1840; virtually †. Ex a kind of apple. cf. RIBSTONE and PIPPIN, 2.

big. Great; important: coll; from ca 1570. On the verge of S.E. is this humorous substitute for *great* as in Shakespeare's 'I Pompey am, Pompey surnam'd the big'.

big, look. To attempt an impressive manner: coll, C.16–19. e.g. in Shakespeare's *Winter's Tale*.

big, talk. To boast, talk pretentiously: from ca 1650; coll verging on S.E. Smollett, 1771: 'The squire affected . . . to talk big.'

big as bull-beef, see BULL-BEEF, BIG AS.

big-bellied. Far gone in pregnancy: Addison, 1711. Coll: ob.

Big Ben. The clock in the tower of the Houses of Parliament, Westminster: coll (—1869). Ex Sir Benjamin Hall, under whose Commissionership of Works it was constructed in 1856–7.

big bird, get or **give the.** To be hissed; to hiss. Theatrical; cf. *give the goose* and *be goosed*. From ca 1860. See GOOSE, n., 3 and v., and BIRD, n., 2. 2. Ware, however, notes that ca 1860–1910 the phrase also = 'to be appreciatively hissed for one's performance in the role of villain'.

big bug. An important person: orig. (1830) U.S.; anglicized ca 1880. Prob. ultimately ex C.18 *bug*, a person of considerable importance (?).

big conk, big cock (or **cunt**). A c.p. that – verging upon the status of a proverb – implies that the possession of a large nose entails also that of a large sexual member or part: low: late (?mid-)C.19–20.

big country. Open country: hunting coll (—1890).

big digger. At cards, the ace of spades (cf. DIGGERS, 2): from ca 1850; ob.

big dog. A chucker-out: coll: from ca 1870. 'He was "big-dog" to a disorderly house,' *Good Words*, June 1884.

big drink. The ocean, esp. the Atlantic: Miss Braddon, 1882. (In U.S., from 1846, the Mississippi.)

big, or **long, drink.** Liquor from a long glass: C.19–20, coll.

***big gates, the.** Prison (generic); a prison: c.: late C.19–20.

big gun. A person of note: orig. U.S.; anglicized by 1897.

big head. The morning-after feeling (—1880): coll. *Get a* or *the b.h.*, to become intoxicated: from ca 1870.

big, or **large, house.** The workhouse: among the indigent (—1851). Mayhew. In the U.S., a prison.

big number. (Gen. pl.) A brothel: Parisian Englishmen's: ca 1820–1910. Ex 'the huge size of the number on the swinging door, never shut, never more than two or three inches open', Ware. Possibly in part, also, a pun on *bagnio*.

big one or **un.** A notable person: coll, ca 1800–50; cf. BIG GUN and BIG POT and BIG WIG.

big people. Important people: coll: from ca 1855; slightly ob. Trollope.

big pond. The Atlantic: (prob. ex U.S. and anglicized) ca 1880; cf. BIG DRINK.

big pot. A person of consequence; a don: Oxford, ca 1850–60. Thence, solely the former and in gen. use. Perhaps POT, n., 6, abbr. *potentate*. Ware implies that, ca 1878–82, it had, in the music-halls, the special sense of 'a leader, supreme personage'.

big side. (Rugby and other Public Schools') the bigger boys combining in one game or sport; the ground used therefor. Whence *b.-s. run*, a paper chase in which all houses take part. C.19–20; ob. It derives from the fact that early games of Rugby football were played with sides of any numbers, the whole school often participating.

big smoke (or B.S.), the, see SMOKE, n., 2.

big talk. Pompous, or sesquipedalian, speech: (—1874) coll.

big triangle, the. 'The old sailing-ship tramping route – from U.K. to Australia with general cargo, on to the West Coast of S. America with coal from Newcastle, N.S.W., and then home with nitrates': from ca 1860 (now ob.): nautical coll >, by 1880, j.

big(-)wig. A person of high rank or position or money. It occurs in Ned Ward early in C.18, but it > gen. only ca 1840. Whence *big-wigged*, consequential (Carlyle, 1851), *big-wiggery*, a display of pompousness or importance (Thackeray, 1848), and *big-wiggism*, pomposity, pretentiousness (George Eliot): all three being coll at first, then soon S.E. – though seldom employed. 2. The head of a College: Oxford: ca 1818–60.

big word. A word of many syllables or much pretentiousness: coll (—1879) rising to S.E. In the pl, pomposity: from ca 1850.

bike. Abbr. *bicycle*: from ca 1890.

***bil.** A late C.17–mid-18 c. abbr., recorded by B.E., of BILBOA.

bilayutee pawnee. Soda-water: Anglo-Indian coll (—1886). See PARNEE.

bilbo(a). In C.16–17, S.E.: a sword noted for the excellence of its temper and made orig. at Bilbao in Spain. Hence, in late C.17–18 (in C.19, archaic), coll: the sword of a bully. Congreve in *The Old Bachelor*: 'Tell them . . . he must refund – or bilbo's the word, and slaughter will ensue.'

Bilboy's ball, see BEILBY'S BALL.

bilge. Nonsense, empty talk: Public Schools': from ca 1906.

bilge-cod. Fish served at dinner on Fridays: *Conway* Training Ship s.: from ca 1890. Masefield.

bilge-water. Bad beer: coll: C.19–20. Ex the bad water collecting at the bottom of a ship.

bilk. A statement or a reply devoid of truth or sense: ca 1630–1800. Perhaps a thinned form of *balk*. 2. A HOAX, HUMBUG, or imposition (—1664); ob. Hence, 3. A swindler or a cheat, as in Sheridan, 'Johnny W[i]lks, Johnny W[i]lks, thou greatest of bilks', 1790. Adj., wrong, misleading, senseless: C.18. Ex cribbage and = *balk*.

bilk, v. To deceive, cheat; defraud, fail to pay; elude, evade: all these coll senses (B.E. is prob. wrong in considering the word to be c.) arose in Restoration days and all had > S.E. by 1750. Grose, 1st ed., 'Bilking a coachman, a box keeper, or a poor whore, was formerly among men of the town thought a gallant action.' cf. the n.

***bilk the blues.** To evade the police: c. or low s.: from ca 1845; ob.

bilk the schoolmaster. To gain knowledge – esp. by experience – without paying for it: 1821, Moncrieff's *Tom and Jerry*: coll; ob.

bilker. A cheat(er), swindler: s. (1717) >, ca 1800, coll; now almost S.E. Likewise *bilking*, vbl n. (—1750), was almost S.E. by 1850; *bilker* is now, except in its abbr. form *bilk*, rather ob.

bill. A list of boys due to see the headmaster at noon, as in Brinsley Richards, *Seven Years at Eton*, 1876; also of those excused from 'absence'. At Harrow School, names-calling: from ca 1850. 2. In c., a term of imprisonment: from ca 1830. Always with *long* or *short*. 3. A variant of BIL.

bill at sight, pay a. To be, by nature, apt to enter into sexual intercourse: ca 1820–1910.

Bill Bailey. A jocular c.p. form of address: ca 1900–12.

bill brighter. A small faggot used for lighting coal fires: from ca 1840 ex Bill Bright, a servant, extant at least as late as 1830: Winchester College.

bill in the water, hold one with (his). To keep (him) in suspense: ca 1570–1700. Coll.

bill of sale. Widow's mourning clothes, esp. her hat: late C.17–19 (†by 1890). cf. HOUSE (or TENEMENT) TO LET.

bill on the pump at Aldgate, see ALDGATE . . .

bill up. To confine (a soldier) to barracks: military coll (—1890). Esp. as:

billed up. Confined to barracks: in the Guards' regiments, ca 1860–1915.

biller, billing-boy. A boy distributing advertisements (*bills*): commercial coll (—1887).

billet. A post, a job: from ca 1880; coll. In c., *get a billet* = to get a soft job in prison: late C.19–20.

billet, every bullet has its. Every bullet must land somewhere, and only those die in battle who are marked by fate for such a death. Coll from ca 1695. Wesley in his *Journal*, 6 June 1765, 'He never received one wound. So true is the old saying of King William, that "every bullet has its billet".' The phrase is anticipated by Gascoigne, 1575, 'Every bullet hath a lighting place'; cf. Smollett's 'Every shot has its commission, d'ye see.'

billiard-block. One who, for ulterior motives, suffers fools and other disagreeables with apparent gladness: Mrs Gore, *Mothers and Daughters*, 1831. †Society s.

***billiard slum.** In Australian c. of ca 1870–1910, false pretences. Here, SLUM, n., 4 = trick, dodge, game. *Go on the b.s.*, to practise such trickery. Ex: *give it (to) 'em on the billiard slum*, to impose on them with that swindle which is termed a MACE: c. of ca 1810–70.

billicock, see BILLY-COCK.

billing-boy, see BILLER.

Billingsgate. Foul language; vituperation: Commonwealth period; coll > S.E. by 1800. Gayton, 1654, 'Most bitter Billingsgate rhetorick.' The language used at the Billingsgate fish-market was certainly 'strong'. 2. Whence, a person foul-mouthed or vituperative: ca 1680–1830.

Billingsgate (it). To talk coarsely; to vituperate (a person): (—1678) coll; †by 1850. In C.19–20, *talk Billingsgate*, also coll.

Billingsgate fish-fag, no better than a. Rude; uncouth: C.19–20 coll; ob.

Billingsgate pheasant. A red herring: from ca 1830; ob. cf. ATLANTIC RANGER.

Billio, see BILLY-O.

Bill(y). Shakespeare; esp. SPOUT BILLY: (low) coll (—1887). Ex *William* Shakespeare. 2. **(Billy.)** Abbr. SILLY BILLY: coll: late C.19–20.

billy. A silk pocket-handkerchief: ca 1820–1900: c. (Scottish, says 'Ducange Anglicus', citing Brandon, 1839) or low. Other C.19 styles and fancies in handkerchiefs – several of the terms survive – were the BELCHER; BIRD'S-EYE WIPE; BLOOD-RED FANCY; BLUE BILLY; CREAM FANCY; KINGSMAN; RANDAL'S-MAN; WATERMAN; YELLOW FANCY; YELLOW-MAN. 2. A truncheon (—1874). Ex U.S. 3. In Australia and derivatively, but less, in New Zealand, the can that serves the bushman as both kettle and tea-pot: s. (ca 1850) >, by 1880, coll; *billy-can* (—1892) is rarer and more an urban than a rural term. 4. In c., *billy* is stolen metal: mid-C.19–20. cf. *billy-hunting*. 5. The removal or shifting of a marble: schoolboys': late C.19–20. 6. Abbr. *billycock (hat)*: coll (—1887). 7. See BILLY WITH, PLAY.

billy (or B.), whistling. A locomotive: coll: late C.19–20. cf. PUFFING BILLY.

Billy Barlow. A street clown, a mountebank: from ca 1840. Ex an actual character, the hero of a slang song. Such a clown is also called a *Jim Crow* (by rhyming s. with *saltimbanco*) or a *saltimbanco*.

Billy born drunk. 'A drunkard beyond the memory of his neighbours', Ware: low London: 1895, *People*, 6 Jan.; very ob.

billy-boy. (Sailors') a two-masted vessel resembling a galliot, the fore-mast square-rigged. Coming mostly from Goole, they are also called *Humber keels*. From ca 1850; coll.

billy-button. A journeyman tailor: from ca 1840. 2. In rhyming s., mutton (—1857).

***billy buz(z)man.** A thief specializing in silk pocket- and necker-chiefs: ca 1830–1900 c. See BILLY, 1, and BUZZ, v., 2.

billy-can, see BILLY, 3.

billy-cock. A low-crowned, wide-brimmed felt hat: coll (—1862). In Australia, the hat so named is made of hard, not soft felt, and its brim is turned up: coll (—1880). The word may be a phonetic development from the C.18 *bully-cocked* (Amherst's *Terrae Filius*, 1721); but the hats were, in precisely this style, made first for *Billy Coke*, a Melton Mowbray sportsman, ca 1842 – though admittedly this derivation smacks of folk-etymology.

billy-cock gang, the. The clergy: navvies': ca 1870–1910. Ex their hats.

billy-doo. A *billet-doux*, a love-letter: C.18–20; coll.

***billy-fencer.** A marine-store dealer: c.; from ca 1840; ob. See the two words.

***billy-fencing shop.** A shop receiving stolen precious metal: c. (—1845); ob.

billy-goat. A male goat: coll: 1861, Peacock. 2. Hence (—1882) the s. sense, a tufted beard.

billy-goat in stays. An effeminate officer: naval: ca 1870–85, when many young 'swells' wore stays.

Billy Gorman. A foreman; rhyming s.: since ca 1870. (D. W. Barrett, *Navvies*, 1880.) cf. the later JOE O'GORMAN.

billy-ho, see BILLY-O.

***billy-hunting.** Post-1820, ob. c. for collecting and buying old metal: ex BILLY, 4. Also, going out to steal silk handkerchiefs: same period: ex BILLY, 1.

billy-o (or oh) or occ. **billy-ho, like.** With great vigour or speed: mid-C.19–20. The *Referee*, 9 Aug. 1885, 'It'll rain like *billy-ho*!' Perhaps ex the name used euphemistically for *the devil.*

Billy Puffer or **B.p.** or **b.p.** A name given to the early steamers by seamen: ca 1840. Bowen, 'Compare Puffing Billies on land,' i.e. locomotives.

billy-roller. 'A long stout stick . . . used . . . to beat the little ones employed in the mills when their strength fails', Mrs Trollope, *Michael Armstrong*, 1840. (The O.E.D. records at 1834.) See, too, Ure's *Dict. of the Arts*, vol. iii, 1875. Coll, †. cf. BILLY, 2.

billy stink. A form of cheap Indian wood-alcohol – 'its effect on most drinkers was terrible': Indian Army: from ca 1880.

Billy Turniptop. An agricultural labourer: from ca 1890; virtually †. *Daily Telegraph*, 10 July 1895.

billy with, play. To play the deuce with: coll: late C.19–20. See also BILLY-O.

Bim (or Bimm); Bimshire. A Barbadian (cf. BADIAN); the island of Barbados, which is also (—1890) called LITTLE ENGLAND: coll: mid-C.19–20. Perhaps ex VIM, as suggested in Paton's *Down the Islands*, 1887.

bime-by. By-and-by: dial. (—1839) and Cockney sol. (—1887). Ex U.S., where recorded in 1824.

Bimm, see BIM.

bimph. Toilet paper: Public Schools': late C.19–20. cf. BUMF.

bimster. 'A rope's end used in the training ships for punishment purposes': naval: late C.19–20. Bowen. Perhaps *beamster*, something applied to the 'beam' or rump: but cf. *bim* for BUM (C.20).

binco. A light, a paraffin flare: late C.19–20. A corruption of Fr. *bianco*, white, from the whiteness of the illumination they afford: cf. BIANC.

***binder.** An egg: late C.19–20 c. >, by 1910, low. cf. the † S.E. medical sense of *binder*: anything causing constipation. 2. A drink, as in A. Binstead, *Gal's Gossip*, 1899.

bindle. A notable HOWLER: Dulwich College (—1907). Origin? Perhaps a blend: ?*bungle* + *swindle.*

bing or **byng.** Gen. *bing a-vast.* To go: c. of mid-C.16–early 19. Scott has *b. out*, in *Guy Mannering*, and *b. avast*, in *Nigel.* Perhaps of Romany origin.

binge. A drinking bout: Oxford University (—1889). Perhaps ex BINGO; or ex dial. v. *binge* influenced by *bingo*, the latter being the more prob., for *binge*, a heavy drinking-bout, exists in dial. as early as 1854. 2. See:

binge, have a; haul off and take a binge. To (go away to) get a sleep: nautical: ca 1880–1910.

binge a cask. 'To get the remaining liquor from the wood by rinsing it with water': nautical coll: C.19–20. Bowen. Ex *binge*, to drench: see BINGE. Also BULL THE (or A) BARREL.

bingey or **bingy** (hard *g*). Penis: Anglo-Irish nursery: late C.19–20. Origin?

***bingo.** In late C.17 and in C.18, c.; in C.19 (as in *Tom Brown at Oxford*), s.; ob. Spirituous liquor, esp. brandy. Perhaps *b*, (cf. *b. and s.*) + STINGO, or ex *binge*, to soak, steep, after *stingo* (see Grose, P.). The word occurs notably in *Fighting Attie's Song*, in Lytton's *Paul Clifford.* The O.E.D. dates it at 1861. 2. Whence *bingo boy* and *mort*, male and female dram-drinker: c. of late C.17–early 19.

***bingo club.** 'A set of Rakes, Lovers of that Liquor' (brandy), B.E.: late C.17–18 c.

***bingo mort,** see BINGO, 2.

bingy. Adj. (of butter) bad, ropy. Largely dial. (—1857); as s., ob. 2. See BINGEY.

binnacle word. An affected, a too literary word, which, says Grose (1785), the sailors jeeringly offer to chalk up on the binnacle. †by 1890.

binned, be. To be hanged: London: 1883–ca 1910. Ware, 'Referring to Bartholomew Binns, a hangman appointed in 1883.'

bint. A girl or woman; a prostitute – in which role the female was often called *saïda* [sah-eeda] *bint*, lit. 'a "Good-day!"

daughter': among soldiers in Egypt: late C.19–20. Direct ex Arabic.

biockey. Money: Anglo-Italian, esp. in London: mid-C.19–20. Ex It. *baiocchi*, 'browns'.

bionc. A shilling; Parlary: mid-C.19–20. A variant of BIANC.

birch, n. A room: 1893, P. H. Emerson's *Signor Lippo*. Short for:

birch broom. A room: rhyming s. (—1857).

birch-broom in a fit, like a. (Of a head) rough, tously, tousled: C.19; e.g. in Hindley's *Cheap Jack*, 1876.

Birchen or **Birchin(g) Lane, send one to.** To flog; ex *birch*, to thrash: coll: ?C.17–18. An allusion to Birchin Lane, London. cf.:

birchen salve, anoint with. To cane; thrash: C.16–17 coll. Tyndale.

Bird; always **the Bird.** The Eagle Tavern: theatrical: ca 1840–85. Ware, 'General Booth of the Salvation Army bought it up (1882).'

***bird.** 'The foole that is caught', Greene: c. of ca 1585–1600. 2. As **the bird,** a hissing of an actor: theatrical (1883; ob.); cf. BIG BIRD; GOOSE. Actors used to say 'The bird's there.' Ex the hissing of a goose. 3. A man, a chap; esp. in *old bird* (1853). cf. DOWNY BIRD. 4. A troublesome seaman: nautical: early C.19–20. 5. **(A) bird,** a girl: from ca 1880. A sweetheart: military: from ca 1890. A harlot: from ca 1900. The last two nuances may represent a survival ex early S.E., but more prob. they have arisen independently. 6. See BIRD, GIVE THE.

bird, v. To thieve, steal, seek for plunder: late C.16–17. cf. BLACK-BIRD, V.

bird, big, see BIG BIRD . . .

bird, funny. An occ. variant of BIRD, QUEER: late C.19–20.

bird, give (one) or, hence, **get the.** To dismiss (a person), send him about his business; to be so treated: late C.19–20. Ex the theatre: see BIRD, n., 2.

bird, like a, see the LIKE A . . . entry.

bird, little. An unnamed informant or, rarely, informer: (—1833) coll >, by 1890, S.E. – though far from literary.

bird, old, see BIRD, n., 3.

bird, queer. A strange fellow: C.19–20; coll. See QUEER BIRD.

Bird and Baby, the. A mid-C.18–early 19 facetious version of the Eagle and Child (inn).

bird-cage. (Women's dress) a bustle: ca 1850–1900. 2. A four-wheeled cab: ca 1850–1910. 3. (Racing) The Newmarket race-course paddock where the saddling is done (—1884); ob.

bird-lime. A thief: C.18, e.g. in Vanbrugh. 2. Time: rhyming s. (—1857).

bird-mouthed. Apt to mince matters: from ca 1600; coll > S.E. by 1700; ob.

bird of passage. A person never long in one place: C.19–20: coll.

bird-spit. A rapier: coll: ca 1600–1820.

bird-witted. Wild-headed, inattentive; inconsiderate; gullible: ca 1600–1890; coll till ca 1800, then S.E.

bird's-eye. Baumann, 1887, records it as a variant, from ca 1810, of:

bird's-eye wipe. A silk handkerchief with eye-like spots: from ca 1800; ob. Also *bird's-eye fogle*: low. Adumbrated in Pepys's *Diary* (*bird's-eye hood*); app. first in Egan's Grose, 1823. cf. BILLY.

birds of a feather. Rogues of the same gang: late C.17–18. Ex late C.16–20 S.E. sense, persons of like character, mainly in the proverb *birds of a feather fly* (1578; long †) or *flock* (1607) *together*, as esp. in Apperson.

birds with one stone, kill two. To manage to do two things where one expects, or has a right to expect, to do only one: from ca 1600; coll till ca 1700, when it > S.E.

birk. A house; back s. on CRIB, n., 3. H., 1st ed., 1859.

birthday suit, in one's. Naked. Smollett, *Humphry Clinker*, 1771: 'I went in the morning to a private place, along with the housemaid, and we bathed in our birth-day soot.' Prob. suggested by Swift's *birthday gear*, 1731 – cf. the rare *birthday attire* (1860): both of which are prob. to be accounted as s.

biscuit; occ. a **dog-biscuit.** A brown mattress or palliasse: military: 1909. Ex shape, colour, and hardness.

biscuit, take the, see CAKE, TAKE THE, and TAKE THE BISCUIT.

biscuit and beer. To subject to a *biscuit and beer bet*, a swindling bet of a biscuit against a glass of beer: low London: ca 1850–1910.

bishop. A fly burnt at a candle: late C.16–mid-17. Florio. cf. the v., 1. cf. 2., 'a mushroom growth in the wick of a burning candle': late C.16–19. 3. A warm drink of wine, with sugar and either oranges or lemons: Ned Ward in *The English Spy*, that work which, at the beginning of C.18, held an unflattering but realistically witty mirror up to London. Ob. by 1890 after being coll by 1750, S.E. by 1800. 4. 'One of the largest of Mrs Philips's purses [cundums], used to contain the others', Grose, 1st ed.: low: late C.18–early 19. 5. A chamber-pot: C.19–20, ob. 6. At Winchester College, ca 1820–1900, the sapling that binds a large faggot together; cf. DEAN.

bishop, v. Burn, let burn: coll, C.18–20. Ex the C.16–20 (ob.) proverbial sayings, 'The bishop has put his foot into the pot' or 'The bishop hath played the cook', both recorded in Tyndale. 2. To use deception, esp. the burning of marks into the teeth, to make a horse look young (—1727, R. Bradley, *The Family Dict.*): v.t. ex a man so named, and often as vbl n., *bishoping*. Coll by ca 1780, S.E. by ca 1820. 3. To murder by drowning: from 1836, when one Bishop drowned a boy in order to sell the body for dissecting purposes: the irrepressible Barham, 'I burk'd the papa, now I'll bishop the son.' 4. In printing, *bishop the balls*, to water the balls: 1811, *Lex. Bal.*; ob.

bishop! (rarely); **oh bishop!** A c.p. used in derision on the announcement of stale news: the 1890s: *Conway* Training Ship.

bishop, do a, see DO A BISHOP.

bishop, flog the. (Of men) masturbate: low: late C.19–20. Also *bash the bishop* (esp. Army). Ex resemblance of the *glans penis* to a mitre, or, more probably, to a chess bishop.

bishop hath blessed it!, the. A c.p. of C.16 applied 'when a thing speedeth not well' (Tyndale, 1528).

bishoping. The performing of a bishop's duties: coll: 1857, Trollope. 2. See BISHOP, v., 2.

bishop's finger. A guide-post: C.19. Halliwell. cf. FINGER-POST, a parson.

bishop's sister's son, he is the. He has a big 'pull' (much influence): ecclesiastical c.p.: C.16. Tyndale, 1528.

bishop's wife, as in *what, a bishop's wife? eat and drink in your gloves?* A semi-proverbial c.p. of mid-C.17–early 18. Ray, 1678. 'This is a cryptic saying,' remarks Apperson; prob. it = 'You're quite the fine lady (now)!'

Bismarcker, bismarquer, to. Cheat, esp. at cards or billiards: ca 1866–1900. In 1865–6, Bismarck, the German Chancellor, pursued a foreign policy that rendered indignant a large section of European thought. The *bismarquer* form shows Fr. influence.

bisque, give (someone) **fifteen,** etc., **and a.** To defeat very easily; 'leave standing'. Coll: from ca 1880; ob. Ex tennis.

bit. In C.16–early 19 c., with variant *bite*, money; in C.19 c., *bit* also = a purse. 2. The silver piece of lowest denomination in almost any country: C.18–19. 3. Any small piece of money: coll, C.19–20, ob. 4. A fourpenny-bit (1829): still so called in 1890, though JOEY was much commoner. 5. The smallest coin in Jamaica: Dyche, 1748. 6. A term of imprisonment: c. (—1869) > low. 7. A girl, a young woman, esp. regarded sexually: low coll: C.19–20. cf. PIECE. 8. In such phrases as *a bit of a fool*, rather or somewhat of a fool, the word is coll; from ca 1800. 9. Coll also in the adv. phrases *a bit*, a little or a whit, late C.17–20; *not a bit*, not at all, from ca 1749 (Fielding); and *every bit*, entirely (—1719). 10. Likewise coll when it = a short while, either as *for*, or *in*, *a bit* or simply as *a bit*: from ca 1650. Walton; Wm Godwin, in his best work (*Caleb Williams*), 'I think we may as well stop here a bit.'

***bit,** past ppl of BITE, v., 1: 'Robb'd, Cheated or Out-witted', B.E.

bit, do a, see DO A BIT.

bit, do one's, see DO ONE'S BIT.

bit, have a. (Of a male, whether human or other animal) to copulate: lower-classes: late C.19–20. cf. DO A BIT, 2.

bit by a barn weasel. Drunk: ca 1650.

***bit-faker** or **bit-turner-out.** A coiner of bad money: C.19–20 c.; the latter †. Whence *bit-faking*, vbl n., counterfeiting. See BIT, n., 1.

bit his grannam, see BITE ONE'S GRANNAM.

bit-maker. A counterfeiter (—1857), ob.: low, perhaps even c.

bit o(f) beef. 'A quid of tobacco; less than a pipeful. A ... reference to tobacco-chewing staying hunger', Ware: low: ca 1850–1910.

bit of; bits of. (cf. BIT, n., 8.) When used affectionately or depreciatively, it is a coll, dating from late C.18. Anderson, *Ballads*, 1808, 'Oor bits o' bairns'.

bit of black velvet, see BLACK VELVET.

bit o(f) blink. A drink: tavern rhyming s. (—1909): ob.

bit of blood. A high-spirited or a thorough-bred horse: 1819, Tom Moore; slightly ob.

bit o(f) bull. Beef: C.19. Like the preceding entry, s. verging on coll.

bit of cavalry. A horse: ca 1825–1915. Moncrieff, 1821.

bit o(f) crumb. 'A pretty plump girl – one of the series of words designating woman imm. following the introduction of "jam" as the fashionable term (in unfashionable quarters) for lovely woman', Ware: from ca 1880; ob. cf. CRUMMY, 1, and BIT OF GREASE.

bit of cunt. A girl or woman, regarded sexually: low: from 1870 at the latest.

bit of doing, take a. To be difficult to do: coll: late C.19–20.

bit of ebony. A Negro or a Negress: C.19–20, † coll.

bit of fat. An unexpected advantage, esp. (cf. BUNCE) if pecuniary: C.19–20; cf. FAT, n., l. 2. Whence *have a bit of fat from the eye*, to eat 'the orbits' of a sheep's eyes – a delicacy (Ware, 1909).

bit of fluff. The same as BIT OF MUSLIN: C.20.

***bit of gig.** Fun; a spree: c. (—1823); very ob.

bit o(f) grease. (Not derogatory.) A stout and smiling Hindu woman: Anglo-Indian military (—1909). cf. BIT OF CRUMB.

bit of grey. 'An elderly person at a ball or a marriage ... to give an air of staid dignity': Society: ca 1880–1910. Ware. Ex grey hair.

bit of hard (or **stiff**). A *penis* (*erectus*): low: C.19–20.

bit of haw-haw. A fop; London taverns': ca 1860–1914. Ex *haw! haw!*

bit of hollow, see HOLLOW, n.

bit of it!, not a. No; not at all; you're wrong: coll: late C.19–20.

bit o(f) jam. Something easy; a pretty, esp. if accessible, girl; prob. from ca 1850, though Ware dates it at 1879. cf. TART, JAM, 2; and see BIT OF CRUMB.

***bit of leaf.** Tobacco: mid-C.19–20 c.; ob. J. Greenwood, 1876.

bit of (one's) mind. Gen. with *give*. One's candid, unfavourable opinion: coll; from ca 1860.

bit o(f) muslin. A (young) girl, esp. if a prostitute: T. W. Moncrieff, *Tom and Jerry*, 1821; Whiteing, 1899, 'She's a neat little bit o' muslin, ain't she now?' cf. SKIRT, n., and BIT OF FLUFF.

bit of mutton. A woman; gen. a harlot. C.19–20, ob.; perhaps coll rather than s.

bit of nifty, see NIFTY, n.

bit of parchment. A convict's certificate of freedom: Australian policemen's: ca 1825–70. John Lang, *Botany Bay*, 1859.

bit o(f) pooh. Flattery, 'blarney'; courtship: workmen's (—1909); almost †. Ex *pooh!*, nonsense!

bit o(f) prairie. 'A momentary lull in the traffic at any point in the Strand. . . From the bareness of the road for a mere moment, e.g. "A bit o' prairie – go",' Ware: London: ca 1850–1914. cf. S.E. *island*.

bit o(f) raspberry. An attractive girl: from ca 1880; very ob. Ware. On BIT OF JAM.

bit o(f) red. A soldier: coll: late C.18–19. Ex colour of jacket.

bit of skirt. A girl; a woman: coll: from ca 1900; esp. military, Australian, New Zealand.

bit of snug. The act of kind: low: late C.19–20; ?ob. 2. The penis: id.: id.

bit o(f) soap. A charming girl – though frail: low London: 1883–ca 1914.

bit of sticks. A copse: sporting, from ca 1860; ob.

bit of stiff. Money not *in specie*; a bank or a currency note; a bill of exchange: from ca 1850. Lever. Whence *do a bit of stiff*, to accept a bill of exchange or a post-dated cheque. 2. See BIT OF HARD.

bit o(f) stuff. An overdressed man: low (—1828). 2. A (young) woman; mid-C.19–20; ob. cf. Marryat's *piece of stuff*, 1834, and BIT OF MUSLIN. 3. A boxer: pugilistic: ca 1810–50. *Boxiana*, I, 1818.

bit o(f) tripe. A wife: rhyming (!) s. (—1909); virtually †. cf. TROUBLE AND STRIFE.

bit on, (have) a. (To lay) a stake: racing: 1894, George Moore. 2. As adj., *a bit on* = drunk: low: C.19–20; ob. ?cf. BITE ONE'S GRANNAM.

bit the blow, see BITE A BLOW. **Bit-turner-out,** see BIT-FAKER.

bitch. A lewd woman: S.E. from origin (—1400) to ca 1660, when it > coll; since ca 1837 it has been a vulg. rather than a coll. As coll: e.g. in Arbuthnot's *John Bull* and Fielding's *Tom Jones*. 2. Opprobriously of a man: in C.16, S.E.; in C.17–18, coll, as in Hobbes and Fielding. 3. Tea: Cambridge University, ca 1820–1914. Prob. ex STAND BITCH. 4. The queen in playing-cards, mainly public-house; from ca 1840. cf. BUTCHER, 1.

bitch, v. Go whoring; frequent harlots: from Restoration times to ca 1830: coll. Ex BITCH, n., 1. 2. To yield, cry off, from fear: coll verging on S.E.: C.18–early 19. Ex a bitch's yielding. 3. v.t., to spoil or bungle: from ca 1820: coll. Prob. a thinned form of *botch*.

bitch!, I may be a whore but can't be a. A low London woman's c.p. reply on being called a BITCH: late C.18–mid-19. Grose (1st ed.), who prefaces it with: 'The most offensive appellation that can be given to an English woman, even more provoking than that of whore, as may be gathered from the regular Billingsgate or St Giles answer', etc. cf. the C.18 proverbial saying, *the bitch that I mean is not a dog* (Apperson).

bitch, stand. To preside at tea or perform some other female part: late C.18–early 19.

bitch booby. A rustic lass: mid-C.18–early 19; military. cf. DOG BOOBY.

bitch-party. A party composed of women: from ca 1880. Orig. (ca 1850) a tea-party: Cambridge and Oxford. Ex BITCH, n., 3.

bitch-pie!, go to hell (where you belong) **and help your mother to make a.** A c.p. elaboration of *go to hell!*: mid-C.18–20; ob.

bitch the pot. To pour out the tea: undergraduates': late C.18–mid-19.

bitched, buggered, and bewildered, see BARNEY'S BULL.

bitches' wine. Champagne: from ca 1850. cf. CAT'S WATER.

bitching, adj. A violent pejorative: Australian: mid-C.19–20.

bitching, adv. Another violent pejorative: Australian: mid-C.19–20.

***bite.** The female pudend: (prob.) c.: late C.17–early 19, as in B.E. ('*The Cull wapt the Mort's bite*, i.e. the Fellow enjoyed the Whore briskly') and Grose; perhaps ex A.-S. *byht*, the fork of the legs, a sense recurring in *Sir Gawayn*, vv. 1340, 1349. 2. A deception, from harmless to criminal: Steele, 1711; ob. by 1890, †by 1920. Hence, 3. A sharper; trickster: c. or low s. > gen. s.: late C.17–early 19, as in B.E., Fielding, Smollett. Hence, 4. A hard bargainer: C.19. ?hence, 5. Any person or thing suspected of being different from, not necessarily worse than, what appearances indicate: C.19–20 coll, ob. 6. (cf. sense 4.) A Yorkshireman: from late 1850s, though recorded in Cumberland dialect as early as 1805; ob.; at first, pejorative. 7. In c., C.16–early 19: money; cash. It occurs as late as John Davis's novel, *The Post Captain*, 1805. cf. BIT, 1.

***bite,** v. To steal; rob: late C.17–early 19 c. 2. Deceive, swindle; orig. (—1669) c., but by 1709, when Steele employs it in the *Tatter*, it is clearly s.; except in the passive, †by ca 1870. 3. To 'take the bait': C.17–20 coll. 4. To drive a hard bargain with: C.19–20 coll.

bite! Sold! done! tricked you! Only ca 1700–60. Swift makes a male character, in reply to a young woman's 'I'm sure the gallows groans for you', exclaim, 'Bite, Miss; I was but in jest.' 2. At Charterhouse, C.19–20: CAVE! 3. At the Blue-Coat School: give it to me!: 1887, Baumann.

***bite a blow;** gen. **to have bit the blow.** To have 'accomplish'd the Theft, plaied the Cheat, or done the Feat', B.E.: c. of late C.17–18.

bite in the collar or the cod-piece?, do they. A c.p. of late C.18–early 19. 'Water wit to anglers', says Grose, 3rd ed.

bite (up)on the bit or **the bridle.** To be reduced in circumstances: C.14–20: coll verging on S.E.; in C.19–20, mainly dial. Gower, ca 1390; Latimer; Smollett.

bite one's, or **the, ear.** To borrow money from: since ca 1850. In C.19, c.: in C.20, low.

bite one's grannam, gen. as **to have bit one's grannam.** To be very drunk: mid-C.17–18.

bite one's hips. To regret something: tailors', ca 1850–1910.

bite one's name in. To drink heavily; tipple: low: C.19–20; very ob.

bite one's, or **the, thumb.** To make a contemptuous gesture; v.t. with *at*. Coll: C.16–18. Shakespeare, in *Romeo and Juliet*: 'I will bite my thumb at them: which is a disgrace to them if they bear it.'

***bite the tooth.** To be successful: c.: late C.19–20. Ware, 'Origin unknown'.

bite up, n. A disagreeable altercation: tailors', ca 1840–1920; as is *biting up*, grief, bitter regret.

biteëtite, see BITYTITE.

biter. A sharper; late C.17–18 c. Cotton. 2. A hoaxer: from late C.17 coll passing to S.E.; except in *the biter bit*, †by ca 1870. 3. In mid-C.18–early 19 low s., 'a lascivious, rampant wench', Grose.

bites, when the maggot. At one's own sweet will: coll; from late C.17; very ob. L'Estrange.

biting up, see BITE UP.

bits of, see BIT OF.

***bitt.** A variant of BIT, 1.

bitten, see BITE, V.

bitter. (A glass of) bitter beer: coll: 'Cuthbert Bede', 1856, '. . . to do bitters,

. . . the act of drinking bitter beer'. After ca 1880, coll.

bitter-ender. One who resists or fights to the bitter end: coll: mid-C.19–20.

bitter-gatter. Beer and gin mixed: Cockney and military (not officers'): from ca 1870.

bitter oath, e.g. **take one's.** To swear solemnly: low: ca 1850–1910. Corruption of *better oath* (as, e.g., *by God!* is 'better' than *by hell!, the devil!*, etc.).

bittock. A distance or a period of uncertain length; properly, a little bit. Orig. (—1802), dial.; but from ca 1860, also coll.

***bitty.** A skeleton key: c.: late C.19–20. Ex *bit*, a piece of mechanism.

bitwise. Little by little: coll: from the 1890s; very ob.

bitytite; biteëtite (or bite-etite). Hunger: (low) East London: ca 1890–1915. Ex *bite* on *appetite*. cf. DRINKITITE.

bivvy. Dial. and Cockney (?ex L. *bibere* via Lingua Franca) for: beer, esp. in *shant o(f) bivvy*, a pot or a quart of beer. In Cockney since ca 1840. 2. A bivouac: military: from ca 1900.

biyeghin. Stealing: theft: Shelta: C.18–20.

biz. Business. Orig. (1865) U.S.; anglicized ca 1880: it appears in the *Saturday Review*, 5 Jan. 1884, in Baumann, and in the 'comic strip', *Ally Sloper*, on 17 Aug. 1889. 2. The theatrical profession: late C.19–20.

blab, a; blab, to. An indiscreet talker; to talk indiscreetly, also v.t. C.16–20. Until ca 1660, S.E.; thereafter, the v. is coll, the n. is almost s. Likewise *blabber* and † *blabberer*, in the same senses, were orig. S.E., but from ca 1750 coll. *Blabbing*, tale-telling, indiscreet talk, has always been coll rather than S.E.: from ca 1600.

black. A poacher working with a blackened face: s. or coll: C.18. 2. A BLACKGUARD: fast life: ca 1805–50.

black-a-moor, black Moor. (Gen. unhyphenated.) Recorded in 1547; †in S.E. senses. In C.19–20 used as a nickname and as a playful endearment (cf. *Turk*): essentially coll. Also adj. As in *blackavised*, the *a* is prob. euphonic and to be compared with the nonsensical but metrically useful *-a* in jog-trot verses.

***black and tan.** Porter (or stout) mixed equally with ale: from ca 1850: c. (vagrants') >, by 1900, gen. low s. Ex resp. colours.

***black and white.** Night; to-night: c. rhyming s.: late C.19–20.

black and white, in. Written or printed; hence, binding. Late C.16–20, coll. cf. *black on white*, which, C.19–20, only very rarely applies to writing and tends to denote the printing of illustrations, hence printed illustrations.

black arse. A kettle; a pot: late C.17–early 19. From the proverb, 'the pot calls the kettle black arse', the last word has disappeared (*pudoris causa*).

black art. An undertaker's business: from ca 1850; undertakers'. 2. In late C.16–19 c., lock-picking. 3. The printer's trade: printers' jocular: ? mid-C.19–20.

black as the Earl of Hell's riding-boots or **waistcoat.** (Of a night) pitch-dark: resp. naval and nautical: resp. ca 1900–25 and 1880–1910.

black-bagging. 'Dynamitarding': journalistic coll: 1884–ca 1910. Ex the black bags in which the explosive so often was carried.

black-ball. To exclude (a person) from a club: late C.18–20: coll >, ca 1830, S.E. Ex the black ball indicative of rejection.

black-balling, vbl n. of preceding term. 2. Stealing, pilfering: nautical: ca 1850–1910. It originated on the old Black Ball line of steamers between Liverpool and New York: a line infamous for the cruelty of its officers, the pilfering of its sailors.

black-beetle. In Thames-side s., from ca 1860; thus in Nevinson, 1895, 'At last a perlice boat with two black-beetles and a water-rat, as we calls the Thames perlice and a sergeant, they pick me up.'

black beetles. The lower classes: coll: ca 1810–50. Moncrieff, 1821.

black bird. An African captive aboard a slaver: nautical (—1864): this sense is rare. 2. Gen., a Polynesian indentured labourer, virtually a slave: nautical (—1871); soon coll. See esp. the anon. pamphlet entitled *Narrative of the Vogue of the Brig 'Carl'*, 1871.

black-bird, v. To capture Negroes and esp. Polynesians: nautical (—1885). The term > S.E. soon after this branch of kidnapping ceased. Whence *black-birding*, vbl n., such kidnapping (—1871), and adj. (—1883).

black(-)bird catching. The slave-trade: nautical (—1864). Displaced by *black-birding* (1871).

black-birders. Kidnappers of Polynesians for labour (—1880); quickly coll; by 1900, S.E.

black-birding, see BLACK-BIRD, v., and BLACK-BIRD CATCHING.

black books, in one's. Out of favour. Late C.16–20 coll. In C.19–20 gen. regarded as S.E.

***black box.** A lawyer: either c. or low s.: ca 1690–1860. Duncombe's *Sinks of London*, 1848. Ex the black boxes in which he deposits clients' papers.

black boy. A parson: C.17 until ca 1860. cf. BLACK COAT.

black bracelets. Handcuffs: (?late C.18–19). e.g. in Harrison Ainsworth's *Jack Sheppard*.

black cap, see WHITE SHEEP.

black cattle. Parsons: mid-C.18–20; ob. Whence *black-cattle show*, a gathering of clergymen: C.18–19. 2. Lice: C.19–20; ob.

black coat. A parson: from ca 1860: coll; ob.

black cutter. A service cutter for the use of Dartmouth naval cadets: naval coll verging on j.: late C.19–20.

black diamond. A rough person who is nevertheless very good or very clever: ca 1800–75. Displaced by ROUGH DIAMOND.

black diamonds. Coals: from ca 1810: c. until ca 1840, then s.; by 1870, coll. Various, *Gavarni in London*, 1848.

black dog. A counterfeit silver coin, esp. a shilling: ca 1705–30. (*Black* had long before been applied to base coins.) 2. Ill-humour: coll, from ca 1825; ob. Scott.

black – occ. **blue** (—C.18) – **dog, blush like a.** i.e. not at all: hence, to be shameless: mid-C.16–18; coll. Gosson, Swift.

black dog (sitting) on one's back, have (got) a. To be depressed: coll: late C.19–20; ob. Lyell. cf. POMPEY.

black doll. The sign outside a DOLLY-SHOP. Dickens, *Sketches by Boz*, 1835. Ob. if not †.

black donkey, ride the. To cheat in weight: costers': late C.19–20. 2. To sulk, be ill-humoured or obstinate: mid-C.19–20; ob. Ex a donkey's obstinacy; *black* merely intensifies.

black draught, give (someone) **the.** To administer the *coup-de-grâce* to a sailor dangerously ill: nautical: since ca 1870. Visualized as a black medicine given as a purge. See also Irwin and *Underworld.*

black eye, give a bottle a. To empty a bottle (of spirits): late C.18–mid-19.

***black-faced mob.** A gang of burglars who, blackening their faces as a disguise, trust to violence rather than skill: c. (—1845); ob.

black fly. Pejorative for a clergyman: ca 1780–1850. Esp. in relation to farmers, who, on account of the tithes, dislike clergymen more than they do insect pests.

***black friars!; Blackfriars!** Beware! look out!: mid-C.19–20 c.

Black Friday. A gen. examination: schoolboys': C.17. cf. BLACK MONDAY. 2. 10 May 1886, when Overend, Gurney & Co.'s bank suspended payment; ob.

black gentleman, the. The devil: C.17–mid-19: coll verging on familiar S.E. Dekker. Also *the black man*: mid-C.19–20; ob. Meredith.

black gown. A learned person: C.18; coll.

black guard, later **blackguard.** A scoundrel, esp. if unprincipled: from ca 1730; > coll ca 1770, S.E. ca 1830. At first this was a collective n.: in C.16–17, the scullions of a great house; in late C.16–17, the Devil's body-guard; in C.17, the camp-followers; in C.18, a body of attendants of black dress, race, or character, or the underworld, esp. the shoe-blacking portion thereof.. A collective adumbration of the sense, 'a criminal, a scoundrel', occurs in a MS. of 1683: '. . . of late a sort of vicious, idle, and masterless boys and rogues, commonly called the black-guard . . .' Two notable derivatives are: *blackguard*, v. To act the blackguard (—1786); S.E. by 1800, but long †. Treat as a blackguard, revile (1823+); S.E. by 1850. And: *blackguard*, adj., blackguardly; vile. From ca 1750; S.E. by 1800. Smollett, 1760: 'He is become a blackguard gaol-bird'; Byron, 'I have heard him use language as blackguard as his action.' For this interesting word – the early senses are all coll rather than s., and all became S.E. thirty to fifty years after their birth – see an admirable summary in the S.O.D., a storehouse in the O.E.D., a most informative paragraph in Weekley's *More Words Ancient and Modern*, and a commentary-lexicon in F. & H.

black hat. A new immigrant: Australian: ca 1885–1905. Perhaps ex the bowler so common among Englishmen, so rare among Australians. cf. POMMY.

Black Hole, the. Cheltenham: from ca 1870; ob. Ex the number of former residents of India, esp. officers and civil servants, who go to live there. 2. A place of imprisonment, 1831, whence the famous Black Hole of Calcutta (1757). 3. Whence, a punishment cell or the guard-room: military: recorded in N. Fanning, *The*

Adventures of an American Officer, 1806, in reference to the year 1778.

black house. A business house of long hours and miserable wages: ca 1820–1900, trade.

Black Indies. Newcastle: ca 1690–1830. But in C.19–20 (ob.), among seamen, it means Shields and Sunderland as well.

black is . . ., see BLACK'S HIS EYE.

black jack. A leathern drinking-jug: late C.16–20, ob.; > coll ca 1700, S.E. ca 1800. 2. At Winchester College, C.19, a leathern beer-jug holding two gallons. 3. A (small) black portmanteau: London bag-makers' and -sellers': mid-C.19–early 20. 4. The ace of spades: coll: from ca 1860.

black job. A funeral; also adj.: from ca 1850. cf. BLACK ART, 1.

black joke. The female pudend: early C.18–early 19. A scholarly wit has pertinently asked, 'Something to be cracked?'

black-leg, usually as one word. A turf swindler: Parsons, *Newmarket*, vol. ii, 1771. 'So called perhaps from their appearing generally in boots, or else from game cocks, whose legs are always black', Grose, 1st ed.; W., however, suggests – more pertinently – that it is 'a description of the ROOK' (q.v.). 2. Whence, any sharper: 1774, Colman, *Man of Business*. Perhaps ex *black-leg(s)*, a disease affecting the legs of sheep and cattle (1722, S.O.D.). 3. (Ex 1 and 2.) Pejorative for a workman willing to continue when his companions have gone on strike (1865): S.E. by 1900. 4. Hence, fig., any non-participator (1889).

black-leg, v. (Tailors') to boycott a fellow-tailor: ca 1870–1910. 2. v.i., or as *black-leg it*, to return to work before a strike has been settled: from ca 1885; coll.

black-legged, adj. Swindling: c. of ca 1790–1850. (Anon. ballad, *The Rolling Blossom*, ca 1800.)

black-leggery. Swindling: Maginn, 1832; coll; S.E. by 1850, but never very common.

black man, the. The Devil. See BLACK GENTLEMAN.

black man choke, enough to make a, see CHOKE, ENOUGH TO . . .

***black man's, blackmans.** The dark; night: a C.17–18 c. variant of DARKMANS. Jonson.

***black Maria.** A prison van, for the conveyance of prisoners. From ca 1870: orig. c.; by 1902, s. Occ. *sable Maria*. By personification.

black (or B—) Monday. The Monday on which, after the (esp. summer) holidays, school re-opens: from ca 1730: 'What is called by school-boys Black Monday', Fielding, *Tom Jones*. Contrast BLOODY MONDAY. 2. The Monday – it often was a Monday – on which the death-sentence was executed: from ca 1840.

black mouth. A slanderer: from ca 1640; ob. Coll, passing in C.19–20 to S.E. B.E. has it as the corresponding adj.

black mummer. An actor habitually unkempt and unclean: ca 1820–90.

black muns. Late C.17–18: 'hoods and scarves of alamode lutestring', Grose. B.E. gives as c., which it may be; MUNS = face.

black neb. A person with democratic sympathies, orig. and esp. with France: ca 1790–1800.

black nob. A non-unionist; a blackleg: from ca 1870; ob. Punning BLACK-LEG.

***black ointment.** Pieces of raw meat: c.: from ca 1870. Perhaps ex meat poultice for black eye.

black pope (or B.P.), the. The Superior-General of the Jesuits: Roman Catholics' nickname (—1877).

black pot. A toper: late C.16–19. Ex *black pot*, a beer mug. (The S.O.D. is, I think, wrong to ignore F. & H.'s pre-1818 (= Scott) examples, indecisive though they be.) 2. A Eurasian apothecary in an Army hospital in India: Indian Army (not officers'): from ca 1890.

Black Prince. The devil: ca 1590–1700, coll.

black psalm, sing the. To weep: mid-C.18–early 19. Grose, 1st ed., 'A saying used to children.'

Black Rod. Gentleman Usher of the Black Rod: C.17–20, coll.

black Sal or Suke(y). A kettle: low: mid-C.19–20; ob.

black Saturday. A Saturday on which, because of advances received, there is no wage to take: mid-C.19–20, workmen's. cf. DEAD HORSE.

black shark. An attorney: mostly naval: ca 1820–60.

black sheep. Mild for a scapegrace, a 'bad lot': from ca 1790; coll. Perhaps ex '*Ba! Ba! black sheep*'. 2. A workman refusing to join in a strike: ca 1860–1900. 3. As v., Winchester College, to JOCKEY, get above: C.19.

black ship. One of the 'teak-built ships from Indian yards in the days of the East India Company': nautical: mid-C.18–mid-19. Bowen.

black-silk barge. A stout woman that,

frequenting dances, dresses thus to minimize her amplitude: ball-room (—1909). cf. BARGES.

***black-spice racket.** The stealing of tools, bag and soot from chimney-sweepers: c.: (?C.18–) early C.19.

***black spy.** The devil: late C.17–18 c. and low.

black squad. A stokehold crew: nautical coll: late C.19–20.

black strap. Pejorative for thick, sweet port: coll: late C.18–19; variant, *black stripe*. Ex *strap*, wine, C.16. 2. A task imposed as punishment on soldiers at Gibraltar, late C.18–early 19: military. 3. Molasses: C.19–20 (ob.): naval. Ex sense 1. 4. The hospital in a ship of war: naval: late C.18–mid-19. cf. sense 2. 5. (Gen. pl.) One of 'the specially made strong bags used for removing pilfered cargo from a ship'; nautical (either low or c.): mid-C.19–20. Bowen.

black Sukey, see BLACK SAL.

black teapot. A Negro footman: lower class: C.19–20; ob.

black velvet, a bit of. Coitus with a coloured woman: military: late C.19–20.

black whale. An Antarctic right-whale: nautical coll: mid-C.19–20.

black-work. Funeral-undertaking (1859, G. A. Sala, *Gaslight and Daylight*). cf. BLACK ART, 1, and BLACK JOB.

blackamoor's teeth. Cowrie shells: C.18, coll.

blackberry swagger. A hawker of tapes, shoelaces, etc.: c. or low s.: ca 1850–1910.

blackbird and thrush. To clean (one's boots): rhyming s. (on *brush*): 1880, Barret, *Navvies*.

blackee, blackey, see BLACKY.

Blackford block, swell, -toff. A person (gen. male) well-dressed on occasion: London: ca 1890–1910. 'Blackford's is a well-known ... tailors' and outfitting establishment which also lets out evening and other garments on hire,' F. & H. (revised).

Blackfriars!, see BLACK FRIARS!

blackguard, see BLACK GUARD.

blackleg, see BLACK-LEG.

***blackmans,** see BLACK MAN'S.

black's his, my or **your eye, say.** To accuse; reprimand: C.15–20, ob.; coll. A mid-C.18–19 variant was *say black is the white of your eye*, as in Smollett. Note, however, that *black's the white of my eye* is 'an old-time sea protestation of innocence' (Bowen).

blacksmith's daughter. A key (—1859); esp. in dial. (which has also *blacksmith's wife*), lock and key, padlock.

blacksmith's shop. 'The apron of the unpopular Cunningham's patent reefing topsails in the mid-19th century', Bowen: nautical: at that period.

Blackwall, have been to. To have a black eye: Cockney: ca 1865–85.

Blackwall fashion. (To conduct a sailing-ship) 'with all the smartness and ceremony of the old Blackwall Frigates. On the other hand it was frequently applied to a seaman who did not exert himself unduly': nautical: C.19. Bowen.

blacky; occ. blackey, blackee, blackie. A black man: from ca 1810; coll; occ. as a nickname. Moore, 1815; Thackeray, 1864. cf. DARKY, 3.

bladder. A very talkative, long-winded person: from ca 1578; coll >, by 1800, S.E.; ob. by 1900.

bladder of lard. A bald-headed person (—1864); low. Ex *bladdered lard*. cf. the app. later semi-proverbial *bald as a bladder of lard*.

bladderdash. Nonsense: low: late C.19–20; slightly ob. Corrupted *balderdash*.

blade. A 'good fellow', or simply a man: from ca 1859 (H., 1st ed.). ca 1750–1860, a sharp fellow: coll. Late C.16–early 18, a roisterer, a gallant: S.E. The earliest sense appears in Shakespeare, the second in Goldsmith, and the latest in Dickens. cf. Fr. *une bonne épée*, a noted swordsman.

bladhunk. Prison: Shelta: C.18–20.

blame it! Euphemistic for *damn it!*: coll. cf. *blamenation*, damnation. C.19–20; ob.

blamed. A coll pejorative (=BLINKING, BLANKETY): non-aristocratic: late C.19–20. Ex U.S.

blandander. To tempt blandishingly, to cajole: coll: 1888, Kipling; ob. By rhyming reduplication on the stem of *blandish*.

blandiloquence. Smooth or flattering speech or talk: mid-C.17–20; ob. The O.E.D. considers it S.E.; W., s.; perhaps it is a pedantic coll. Blount, 1656. Ex L. for 'bland speech'.

blank, blanked. Damn; damned. From ca 1850. 'Cuthbert Bede'. Most euphemisms are neither s. nor coll, but *blamenation* and *blank(ed)* are resp. s. and coll; see BLANKETY. 2. See BLINKERS!, BLANK YOUR.

blanker. A discharge-certificate with one corner removed to indicate bad conduct: naval: late C.19–20.

blanket. The coating of blubber in a whale: nautical coll: mid-C.19–20.

blanket, (born) on the wrong side of the. Illegitimate: from ca 1770; coll; from ca 1850, S.E. Smollett.

blanket, lawful. A wife: from ca 1800; coll.

blanket, wet. A spoil-sport: coll (—1830).

Blanket Bay. The nautical form (late C.19–20: Manchon) of BLANKET FAIR. cf.:

blanket-drill. An afternoon siesta: Regular Army: late C.19–20.

blanket fair. Bed: coll: C.19–20, ob. cf. BEDFORDSHIRE; SHEET-ALLEY; CLOTH MARKET.

blanket hornpipe. Sexual intercourse: from ca 1810; ob. cf. the C.17 S.E. *blanket-love*, illicit amours.

blanket show, the. Bed. Esp. to children, 'You're for the blanket show': domestic: late C.19–20.

blanketeer, see HOT BLANKETEER.

blankety; blanky. Damned; accursed: coll (mostly and prob. orig. American): from ca 1880. Ex BLANK, the 'blank' being the dash ('—') beloved of prudes and printers.

blarm me! Blimey!: Cockney (—1887).

blarmed, adj. BLAMED, CONFOUNDED (e.g. thing): Cockney (—1887).

blarney. Honeyed flattery, smooth cajolery (—1819); coll. Grose, 1785, records a sense rather more grave: 'He has licked the Blarney stone; he deals in the wonderful, or tips us the traveller'; ibid. 'To tip the Blarney, is figuratively used for telling a marvellous story, or falsity.' In the 3rd ed. he adds: 'Also sometimes to express flattery.' Ex a stone in the wall of Castle Blarney, Ireland, the kissing of which – 'a gymnastic operation', W. – is reputed to ensure a gift of cajolery and unblushing effrontery. cf.:

blarney, v.i. and v.t. To cajole; flatter grossly: coll, ex the n. Southey in 1803. The vbl n. *blarneying* is fairly common, *blarneyer* much less so.

blarney, tip the. To BLARNEY (v.i.): ca 1810–90.

blarneyfied, adj. Blarneyed: 1830, *Fraser's Magazine*, 'No balderdash of blarneyfied botheration.'

blarsted, see BLASTED.

blasé. Satiated with pleasure. From 1819 until ca 1860, s., but ca 1860–1900 coll; thereafter S.E. Byron uses the term, but its popularity came ca 1840–44, when two versions of the Fr. farce, *L'Homme Blasé*, were played on the London stage.

blashy. Esp. *a blashy day*, wretched weather: nautical coll (—1887) ex dial. *blashy*, gusty, rainy (1788).

blast. To curse and swear (intransitively): coll >, in late C.19, S.E.: from ca 1850, in gen. use (orig. military); foreshadowed in C.17. *The Part Folio*, 16 May 1807, p. 313: 'Mrs Bassett . . . insisted upon some liquor, would not quit the house without it, and began to blow up the hostess and to blast the rose (sign of the Rose).'

blast, at (or in) full. (Hard) at work: coll; from ca 1860; now bordering on S.E. Ex the lit. sense (—1800).

blasted. As a euphemism for BLOODY, it has no place here, but as a low expletive adj., violently coll and = 'execrable', it is in point. From ca 1740. (cf. the ensuing pair of entries.) The spelling *blarsted* is superfluous: nobody except a rustic, i.e. in dial., so draws out the *a* – and even then the spelling should be, not *blarsted* but *blaasted*.

blasted brimstone. A harlot: ca 1780–1830.

blasted fellow. An abandoned rogue: ca 1760–1830; cf. Chesterfield's 'the most notorious blasted rascal in the world', in a letter of 8 Jan. 1750.

***blater.** A sheep: C.18–mid-19 c. Lytton. A corruption of BLEATER, 2. See BLEATING. 2. A calf: c.: mid-C.18–19.

blather, see BLETHER. **blatherskite,** see BLETHERSKATE.

(blaze away and) **blaze away!** Look sharp! Work hard! Later (cf. FIRE AWAY) go ahead! Coll: from ca 1825 in the indicative and from ca 1850 as an adjuration. Ex the rapid firing of cannons and rifles.

blazer. A (light) sports jacket: 1880. Orig. the bright scarlet jacket of the Lady Margaret Boat Club of St John's College, Cambridge. Coll; in C.20, S.E. *Punch* in 1885: 'Harkaway turns up clad in what he calls a blazer, which makes him look like a nigger minstrel out for a holiday.' 2. A bomb-ketch; a mortar-boat: naval: C.19.

blazers. Spectacles: Cockney (—1887); ob. Ex the sun therefrom reflected.

blazes. The bright clothes of flunkeys: ex the episode of Sam Weller and the SWARRY in Dickens's *Pickwick Papers*. Ob. cf.:

blazes! A forcible exclamation: from the 1830s. Ex the flames of hell.

blazes, drunk as. Exceedingly drunk: from ca 1840. Perhaps not from BLAZES! but a folk-etymology corruption of *drunk as blaizers*, ca 1830–60, a phrase arising from a feast held in honour of St Blaize, *blaizers* being the participants.

blazes, go to. To depart hastily; to disappear melodramatically: cf. the adjuration, *go to blazes!* and *to* († *the*) *blazes* (e.g. *with it*)! From the mid-1830s. Also in such phrases as that in 'He consigned me to blazes.' See BLAZES!

blazes?!, how or **what** or **who the.** An intensive coll interrogation; e.g. in Dickens, 1838, 'What the blazes is in the wind now?', and ibid, 1836, 'How the blazes you can stand the head-work you do, is a mystery to me.' See BLAZES!

blazes, like. Vehemently; with ardour. 1818, Alfred Burton, *Johnny Newcome*; coll. As in Disraeli's *Sybil*, 'They ... cheered the red-coats like blazes.' Moreover, *as blazes* – as an intensive – prob. goes back to very early C.19 or even to late C.18. It occurs in, e.g., W. N. Glascock, *Sailors and Saints*, 1829 (p. 184), '... as black as blazes'. (Moe.)

Blazes, Old. The devil: from ca 1845; ob. cf. BLAZES!

blazing. A coll intensive adj. (gen. euphemistic; e.g. for BLOODY), as in *a blazing shame*: from ca 1880.

***bleached mort.** A very fair-complexioned girl: mid-C.18–early 19 c. Prob. ex *the* MORT *lay last night a-bleaching*, 'the wench looks very fair to Day', *A New Canting Dict.*, 1725.

bleacher. A cad: Tonbridge: late C.19–20. Marples. Euphemism? 2. A (reprehensible) girl or woman: ?ca 1790–1860. *The Night Watch*, 1828 (II, 99), 'That she-devil, Sophy, though as worthless a bleecher as ever stepped in shoe-leather ...' and, on p. 104, 'The next was an old bleecher of a woman'. Origin?

blear the eyes of. To hoodwink, deceive, trick: C.14–19; coll > S.E. by C.16. Chaucer, Shakespeare, Scott. cf. *throw dust in the eyes*.

bleat, n. A grumble: naval: late C.19–20. cf.:

bleat, v. To complain, grumble; to lay information: from ca 1560. This pejorative implies either feebleness or cowardice or an unpleasant readiness to blab.

***bleater.** A victim of SHARP or ROOK: c.: C.17–early 19. Dekker. 2. A sheep: c.: C.17–early 19. cf.:

***bleating,** in C.17–early 19 c., is an adj.: sheep; as in *bleating* CULL, a sheep-stealer; *bleating* PRIG or RIG, sheep-stealing; *bleating* CHEAT = a sheep.

bleecher, see BLEACHER, 2.

bleed. Blood, 'as "She'll have his bleed" – usually said of a woman who is rating her husband', Ware: proletarian (mostly London): from ca 1890. cf. BLEEDING. 2. A 'blood', a SWELL: Tonbridge: since ca 1870. i.e. BLOOD, n., 2, thinned.

bleed, v. To extort, overtly or covertly, money from: late C.17–20, coll. 2. v.i. part (freely) with money: from ca 1660, coll in C.19; ob.; little used since ca 1850. Dryden, 1668, 'He is vehement, and bleeds on to fourscore or an hundred; and I, not willing to tempt fortune, come away a moderate winner of two hundred pistoles.' 3. In printing, a book *bleeds* when the margin is so cut away that portions of the printed matter are also removed: from ca 1870: s. > coll > j.

bleed a buoy. 'To let the water out': nautical coll (now verging on j.): mid-C.19–20. Bowen.

bleed the monkey. (Naval) to steal rum from the mess tub or MONKEY. C.19. cf. *suck the* MONKEY, and *tap the* ADMIRAL.

bleeder. A spur: low: C.19–20; ob. 2. A sovereign: C.19–20 sporting, ob. 3. A notable duffer: university s., ca 1870–1910. Hence, gen., = a BLOODY fool, ca 1880–1914. 4. Hence (owing to the influence of *silly bleeder*), a fellow, a man: *Sessions*, 26 April 1887; mainly Cockney. See essay, 'The Word *Bloody*', in *Words!* cf.:

bleeding. A low coll intensive adj. of little meaning: its import is emotional, not mental. (Rarely used as a euphemism for BLOODY.) From ca 1857. Besant & Rice in *Son of Vulcan*, 1877, 'When he isn't up to one dodge he is up to another. You make no bleeding error.' cf. BLEED, n., and BLEEDER.

bleeding, adv. Intensive: approximately 'much' or 'very': since ca 1870. *Sessions*, 8 Jan. 1884, 'If you don't bleeding well let me go.'

***bleeding cully.** An easy victim; a ready parter with money: late C.17–late 19 c. Ex BLEED, V., 2.

bleeding new. Quite new; fresh: mid-18–20, ob.; coll. Ex fish, which do not bleed when stale.

bless my (or **me**) **soul!** see SOUL!, BLESS MY.

bless oneself. Ironical for curse: from ca 1600; coll. After ca 1800, S.E. 'How my

Lord Treasurer did bless himself,' Pepys in his diary, 1 April 1665. Also, *to bless* another: to reprimand, scold, curse, curse at, swear at him: coll > S.E.: C.19–20.

bless oneself with, not a (penny, shilling, etc.) to. Penniless: from ca 1550: coll till ca 1800, then S.E. Dickens has it. 'In allusion to the cross on the silver penny . . . or to the practice of crossing the palm with a piece of silver', S.O.D. In fact a proverbial phrase, recorded in 1540, runs: *not a cross* (coin) *to bless oneself with.*

bless one's stars. To consider oneself lucky: coll (—1845). Hood.

blessed, blest. As euphemism, S.E.; as irony, coll: C.19–20. cf. BLESS ONESELF. But *blessed if I do* = I certainly won't, is 'pure' coll; from ca 1880.

blessing. A small surplus of goods given by a huckster: late C.18–19; coll. Extant in dial. 2. A bottle of whisky given to the pilot as he left a ship: nautical coll: C.19.

blether, occ. blather. Vapid or noisy talk; voluble nonsense: coll from ca 1840. The term is ex Scottish and Northern dial. and was orig. (M.E.) – and still is – a v. *Blather* is the earlier form, but its use in coll English is owing to U.S. influence. Edward Yates, in *Broken to Harness*, 1864: 'There's a letter . . . from Sir Mordaunt . . . promisin' all sorts of things; but I'm sick of him and his blather.' W. Clark Russell, 1884: 'Mrs O'Brien was blathering about the pedigree of the O'Briens.' *Pall Mall Gazette*, 3 May 1886: 'Havelock's florid adjurations to his men, the grim veterans of the 78th, bluntly characterised as blether.' Hence *blethering*, vbl n. and adj., in exactly corresponding senses: dial. >, ca 1860, coll.

bletherskate, occ. blatherskite. The former is the Scottish, the latter the American form: orig. (C.17), Scottish dial.; > popular in U.S. in 1860s and coll in England and Australia ca 1870.

blew. To inform on, expose: mid-C.19–20, ob. cf. BLOW UPON. 2. To cause to disappear; spend, waste: from ca 1850: gen. of money, as in *blew one's screw*, squander one's wages or salary. ?ex idea of sending into the sky (W.). *Sporting Times*, better known as the *Pink Un*, 29 June 1889:

Isabel and Maudie knew the Turf and
all its arts –
They had often blewed a dollar on a
wrong 'un –
And Isabel one evening met a mug from
rural parts,
An attenuated Juggins, and a long 'un.

blew, adj. An † form of BLUE.

***blew it.** To inform to the police: c. (—1839); ob.

blewed, see BLUED.

bliged. Obliged: Cockney coll (—1887).

blighter. A contemptible person (rarely of a woman): from ca 1896. A euphemism (perhaps on BLITHERING) for BUGGER. 2. A 'Jonah' actor: theatrical (1898); ob.

blim(e)y, occ. blymy! Abbr. GORBLIMY (God blind me)!: mostly Cockney: late C.19–20.

blind. The night time: C.19 coll. 2. A pretext: from ca 1660. In C.18, coll; thereafter, S.E. 3. Among printers, from ca 1870, a paragraph mark, ¶: ex the filling-up of the 'eye' of the reversed *P*.

blind, v. To curse: soldiers' > gen.: from the late 1880s. Kipling:

If you're cast for fatigue by a sergeant
unkind,
Don't grouse like a woman, nor crack on,
nor blind.

Ex such curses as *blind your eyes!* 2. To cheat (a person): c. or low: ca 1815–40.

blind, adj. In liquor; tipsy: C.17–18 c.

blind, go (it). To enter uninformed or rashly into an undertaking: U.S. (1848) anglicized ca 1900. Prob. ex poker.

blind, when the devil is. Never: from ca 1650, ob.; coll. Howell, Scott.

blind alley. The *pudendum muliebre*: low: C.19–20.

blind as a brickbat. Lit. and fig., exceedingly blind: coll verging on S.E.: Dickens, 1850. Ex the C.17–20 S.E. *blind as a bat*. cf. the idiomatic *blind as a beetle, as a buzzard, as a mole*.

blind buckler. A wooden plug that, for use with hawse-pipes, has no passage for the cable: nautical coll verging on j.: late C.19–20.

blind cheeks. The posteriors: late C.17–20, ob.; after ca 1800, coll. Recorded first in B.E., who adds '*Kiss my Blind-cheeks*, Kiss my Ar—'; Grose, 2nd ed., has 'Buss blind cheeks; kiss mine a–se.' cf.: *blind Cupid*. The same: low: ca 1810–60.

blind drunk. Very drunk: from late C.18: coll >, ca 1890, S.E. See quotation at NAB THE BIB.

blind eye. The podex: low: C.18–20; ob. cf. BLIND CHEEKS.

blind fart. A noiseless but particularly noisome breaking of wind: low: late C.19–20.

blind guard. A guard-post invisible from the central watch-house (and therefore popular): coastguardsmen's coll: C.19.

***blind harper.** A beggar that, counterfeiting blindness, plays the harp or the fiddle: late C.17–18 c.

blind Hookey. A great risk: non-aristocratic: prob. from early C.19, to judge by *The Night Watch*, 1828 (II, 147), 'the blind-hookey system' (reckless gambling); ob.

blind man (occ. officer, reader). One who deals with 'blind', i.e. imperfectly or indistinctly addressed, letters: from ca 1864. S. > coll > j.

blind man's holiday. Night, darkness: late C.16–17. From 1690, the gloaming: early examples occur in B.E. and Swift. Coll; in late C.19–20, S.E.

blind monkeys to evacuate, lead the. A C.19–20 (ob.) coll, implicative of a person's inability to do any worth-while job. Apparently from ca 1840 and in reference to the Zoological Gardens: see H.

blind roller. A single, unexpected big sea in calm weather: nautical coll: mid-C.19–20.

blind side. The weakest, most assailable side: Chapman, 1606. Coll; S.E. in C.19–20.

blind swiping, see SWIPING.

blinded with science. A c.p. applied to brawn defeated by brains: ex boxing: it arose when the scientific boxers began, ca 1880, to defeat the old bruisers.

***blinder, take a.** To die: mid-C.19–20 c.; ob. i.e. take a blind leap in, or into, the dark.

blindo. A drunken SPREE or bout: low: ca 1860–1910. cf. WIDO.

blindo, v. To die: ca 1860–1910. Military: perhaps on DEKKO, and cf. BLINDER, TAKE A.

***blink.** A light: c. of ca 1820–70. 2. See BIT OF BLINK.

***blink-fencer.** A seller of spectacles: mid-C.19–20 (ob.) c. Ex *blinks* = blinkers; see BLINKS, 1, and FENCE(R).

blinker. The eye (1816, ob.); pl, spectacles: coll > S.E.: from ca 1730. 2. A hard blow in the eye: C.19. 3. A blackened eye: Norwich s. (—1860); †.

blinkers!, blank your. Damn your eyes!: jocularly euphemistic (—1890); ob. See BLINKER, 1.

blinking. A verbal counter, indicating mild reprobation or mere excitement: from ca 1890. 'Prob. for *blanking*, euphemism for *bleeding*, with vowel thinned as in *bilk*', W.

***blinko.** An amateur entertainment – gen. held at a PUB: c.: from ca 1870; ob. Perhaps because it makes one *blink*; in form, cf. BLINDO.

***blinks.** A pair of spectacles: c. (—1845); ob. 2. One who blinks: a coll nickname: C.17–20. 3. Eyes: Cockneys': from ca 1870.

blip-o! A derisive cry at a boat's coxswain colliding with anything: *Worcester* Training Ship: late C.19–20.

blister, v. To punish moderately; to fine: proletarian: from 1890; ob.

blister it, them, etc. Blast it, them!: euphemistic coll: 1840, H. Cockton.

blithering (gen. with **idiot**). Volubly nonsensical; hence merely 'arrant': coll (1889) >, by 1930, S.E. 'Thinned form of ... *blether*, with vowel perhaps suggested by *drivelling*', W.

blizzard. A sharp or stunning blow; an overwhelming argument, a severe reprimand. Coll: orig. (—1830), U.S.; anglicized ca 1875.

blizzard collar. A woman's high stand-up collar: Society: 1897, *Daily Telegraph*, 16 Jan. Ware, 'Suggestive of cold weather'.

***bloak,** see BLOKE.

bloat. 'A drowned body. (2) A drunkard. (3) A contemptuous term applied indiscriminately to anybody', A. H. Dawson: ?error for *bloater*. Late C.19–20.

bloated aristocrat. Any man of rank and wealth: coll; from ca 1850, though adumbrated in 1731. Thackeray, 1861: 'What a bloated aristocrat Thingamy has become since he got his place!'

bloater, my. A vocative to a man's male friend: Cockneys': from ca 1880.

blob. A 'duck's egg' (s. v. DUCK, 6): cricket: coll: 1898, says Ware. 1934, W. J. Lewis, 'From the cipher 0 placed against his name on the score-sheet'; ultimately ex *blob*, a blot, a shapeless mass. 2. Patter or beggars' tales: vagrants' c. (—1861). Mayhew. cf.:

***blob,** v. To talk, esp. if indiscreetly; to PATTER: from ca 1850; c. Same period: *on the blob*, by talking (Mayhew, 1851). Ex BLAB.

blob, get a. To make no score: cricketers' coll: 1905, Norman Gale (W. J. Lewis). Ex the n. Also *make a blob*, 1903; used fig., to make nothing, it is likewise coll: from ca 1905.

blob, on the, see BLOB, v.

block. A person either stupid or hard-hearted: C.16–20; coll until ca 1660, then S.E. Early examples are offered by Udall (in *Ralph Roister Doister*), Shakespeare, Jonson. cf. *deaf, dull,* etc., *as a block.* 2. The head: C.17–20. Shirley, ca 1637. 3. In Scottish c., a policeman: recorded for 1868 (Ware), but prob. from ca 1860.

block, v.t. Have intercourse with a woman: C.20, low. 2. See BLOCK A HAT. 3. (Usually *block a pub.*) To occupy, or remain, long in: non-aristocratic (—1909). Ware, 'Gen. said of a sot'. 4. To stand someone a drink: low: ca 1830–90.

block, a chip of the same or **(same) old.** Of the same character; with inherited characteristics. Coll: C.17–20. In a sermon, Sanderson, 1627: 'Am I not a child of the same Adam, a vessel of the same clay, a chip of the same block with him?'

block, barber's. The head: from ca 1820; in Scott. 2. Also, an over-dressed man (—1876, ob.). Both ex the wooden block on which barbers displayed a wig.

block, do the. To promenade: 1869, Marcus Clarke: Melbourne s. >, by 1890, gen. Australian coll. Ex the fashionable block of buildings in Collins Street between Swanston and Elizabeth Streets. 2. Hence, *on the block,* promenading thus: Australian coll: 1896, *Argus,* 17 July.

block, off one's. Panicky; crazy; occ., angry: late C.19–20. See BLOCK, n., 2.

block a hat. 'To knock a man's hat down over his eyes', H., 3rd ed.: from ca 1860. Perhaps ex BLOCK, 2, the head.

block-house. A prison: ca 1620–1840, but not gen. before late C.18.

block-ornament, blocker. A small piece of inferior meat displayed on a butcher's *block*: coll: from ca 1845; slightly ob. 2. A queer-looking person: from ca 1860; †.

block with a razor, cut a. (Often *blocks* for *a block.*) To try in a futile or incongruous way: coll. Goldsmith, 1774. Ob.

blocker, see BLOCK-ORNAMENT.

***bloke;** in mid-C.19, occ. **bloak.** Occ. contemptuous; occ. a term of address among sailors. A man; a chap, fellow (—1839). Until ca 1860, c.; until ca 1900, low. Pre-1870 examples: Brandon (in 'Ducange Anglicus'), Mayhew, Sala, Kingsley, Ouida, Miss Braddon, James Greenwood. Also, 2. A lover ('Sally and her bloke', Ware): from ca 1880. 3. In cabmen's s., a customer, from ca 1840. 4. In late C.19–early 20 universities', an 'outsider', a book-grubber. Perhaps ex Dutch *blok,* a fool, or (via Romany) ex Hindustani, *loke,* a man; Weekley thinks that it derives ex Shelta (Irish tinkers' c.). Note, however, the slightly earlier *gloak* or GLOACH: though, of course, *gloak* may well derive ex Shelta.

bloke, the. The commander of one's man-of-war: naval: late C.19–20.

***bloke with the jasey, the.** The judge: c. or low s. (—1874). Ex BLOKE, 1.

blokey. A familiar form of BLOKE, 1: ca 1835–90. *A Comic English Grammar,* 1841.

blonked, see BLANKED.

blood. A fast or a foppish man: C.16–early 19, coll. Now literary and archaic. 2. University and Public Schools': a senior held to be a setter of fashion and manners: from ca 1880. 3. Money: coll: C. 18–19. 4. A wall-flower: low, mostly London: late C.19–20; slightly ob. cf. BUG, n., 3: likewise ex the colour. 5. A PENNY DREADFUL: naval (—1909). 6. A third-class shot: military: late C.19–20; ob. 7. A blood orange: fruiterers' and grocers' coll: late C.19–20.

blood, v. Deprive of money: ca 1860–1910. Hawley Smart, 1884. cf. BLEED.

blood, adj. Fashionable; distinguished: Public Schools': late C.19–20. P. G. Wodehouse, *Mike,* 1909, 'You might think it was the blood thing to do to imitate him.' Ex BLOOD, n., 2.

blood, in and **out of.** Vigorous, weak. C.19–20 hunting s. ex hunting j.

blood and entrails (more gen., **guts).** The red ensign: nautical: late C.19–20.

blood and guts alderman. A pompous man; a man with a large CORPORATION: C.19.

blood and 'ouns! i.e. God's blood and wounds: an oath, C.18–19.

blood and thunder. A mixture of port wine and brandy: ca 1860–1910. Ex colour and effect, resp. (The phrase was orig. an oath.)

blood-and-thunder tales. Low-class, sensational, over-adventurous fiction: ?orig. U.S.; in England from ca 1885. Coll. cf. AWFUL; PENNY DREADFUL; SHILLING SHOCKER.

blood ball. 'The butchers' annual hopser [*sic*], a very lusty and fierce-eyed function': London trade: late C.19–20; virtually †. Ware. cf. BUNG, n., bung-ball, s.v. 1.

blood-boat. A tally-boat: naval: late

C.19–20. Ex high prices charged. 2. A particularly hard sailing ship with a brutal afterguard: nautical coll: mid-C.19–20.

blood-curdler or -freezer. A thrilling, esp. a creepy narration or incident: coll, from ca 1870. cf. BLOOD-AND-THUNDER TALES; SHILLING SHOCKER; THRILLER; and BLOOD, n., 5.

blood for blood. In kind: tradesmen's, esp. in purchase and payment; from ca 1780; ob.

blood for breakfast! (, there's). A naval c.p. (late C.19–20) in reference to the admiral's or captain's morning temper if it is bad.

blood-freezer, see BLOOD-CURDLER.

Blood-Hole, the. A Poplar theatre specializing in melodrama: East London: ca 1880–1914.

blood or beer! A London streets' jocular c.p. = fight or pay for such refreshment!: ca 1900–15.

blood-red fancy. A red silk handkerchief (—1839, ob.): boxing world.

blood-sucker. A lazy fellow involving his shipmates in additional work: nautical coll: ca 1800 or earlier.

blood-tub. A theatre 'specializing in the worst forms of blood-and-thunder melodrama, and generally gives two shows a night': Londoners': from ca 1885; extant. Applied orig. to a popular theatre in N.W. London.

blood-worm. A sausage; esp. a black pudding: proletarian London: ca 1850–1910.

bloody, adj. A low coll intensive, orig., and still occ., connoting detestation: from ca 1780, at least. *Sessions*, May 1785 (p. 772), 'The prisoner, Fennell, swore an oath if he had a knife he would cut his bloody fingers off.' *Lex. Bal.*, 1811, 'A favourite word used by the thieves in swearing, as bloody eyes, bloody rascal'; Egan, 1823, added: '*Irish*'.

bloody, adv. (In mid-C.17–18, gen. *bloody drunk*.) Also a low coll intensive; = very. C.17–20, but respectable till ca 1750. In C.17, there was an undertone of violence, in early C.18 (cf. BLOOD, n.) of high but roistering birth: from ca 1750, neutral ethically and socially, but objectionable aesthetically. There is no need for ingenious etymologies: the idea of blood suffices. For both adj. and adv., see F. & H., O.E.D., Weekley's *Adjectives* and his *Words Ancient and Modern*, Robert Graves's *Lars Porsena* in the revised ed., and esp. my *Words!*; the last contains a 2,000-word essay on the subject.

bloody back. A soldier: pejorative: late C.18–early 19. Ex the scarlet uniform.

bloody carpet bags of, make. To mutilate, e.g. with a razor: imported (—1909) into Liverpool from U.S.; ob. Many carpet bags are red.

***bloody end to me!; I wish my bloody eyes may drop out if it is not true!; God strike me blind!** Thieves' oaths recorded in Egan's Grose, 1823.

bloody flag. That single red flag which is the signal for close action: naval: C.19–20; ob.

Bloody Forty (or b.f.), the. A criminal gang infesting the Liverpool Docks in the 1850s: nautical coll. It was 'broken up by Captain Samuels of the *Dreadnought*' (Bowen).

bloody jemmy. An uncooked sheep's head: ca 1810–1914. Also known as a SANGUINARY JAMES and a MOUNTAIN-PECKER.

bloody (or B.) Monday. The first day of vacation, set aside for the detention and punishment of offenders: schoolboys' (orig. Winchester): ca 1670–1770. Contrast BLACK MONDAY.

bloomer. A mistake: Australian and English (—1889). Perhaps a 'blend' of BLOOMING *error*.

bloomeration. Illumination: London illiterate: 1897; ob. and, prob. never gen.

blooming. (Occ. euphemistic – cf. BLEEDING – for BLOODY.) A mild intensive adj. and adv.; cf. BALLY; BLINKING. The S.O.D. dates the earliest instance at 1882; the usage was foreshadowed early in C.18. Its popularity in the 1880s was owing largely to Alfred G. Vance, the comic singer.

***bloss, blowse.** A wench; a low harlot: the former certainly c. always, the latter prob. a c. word at one period. These senses date from late C.17. Prob. ex BLOWSE, 2, but not impossibly abbr. BLOSSOM. cf. BLOWER, 2. 2. 'A Thief or Shop-lift', B.E.: c. of late C.17–early 19. Prob. an extension of sense 1.

blossom. A 'poetic' variant of either BLOSS or BLOWEN. It occurs in the anon. ballad, *The Rolling Blossom*, ca 1800: low: ca 1790–1850.

blossom-faced, bloated; **blossom-nose,** a tippler: lower classes': mid-C.19–20; ob.

***blot the scrip.** To put in writing: mid-C.17–18; prob. c. Hence *blot the scrip and* *jark it*, to stand engaged; be bound for anyone: late C.17–18 c. JARK = a, or to, seal.

blotto. Drunk: from ca 1905. P. G. Wodehouse, of a drunken man, 'He was oiled, boiled, fried, plastered, whiffled, sozzled, and blotto.' Ex the porousness of blotting-paper, possibly suggested or influenced by Romany *motto*, intoxicated.

blouser. 'To cover up, to hide, to render nugatory', to mislead: ca 1880–1914. Ex the Fr. workman's *blouse*. Ware, 'Probably in an anti-Gallican spirit'.

blow. In c., goods, esp. in BITE A BLOW: late C.17–18. 2. A shilling: ca 1870–1910, low. 3. A SPREE, drunken frolic: Oxford and Cambridge, ca 1800–70. 4. A breathing-space: coll, C.19–20. cf. *get a blow*, to get a breath of fresh air, or a considerable exposure to wind: from ca 1890; coll. 5. A harlot: c. or low s. (—1823); †by 1890. Abbr. BLOWEN.

blow, v. To fume, storm, speak angrily: C.16–20, coll. In later C.19–20 the term, in its first two nuances, has, after nearly a century of obsolescence, been revived by contact with Australia and America, where, as 'to boast', it had – and has – a second life. 2. To inform, give information (v.t. absolute, in B.E., but gen. with *up* or *upon*, later *on*): from ca 1570; S.E. till ca 1660, coll till C.19, then s. 'D—n me, if I don't blow . . . I'll tell Tom Neville,' Leigh Hunt. 3. The euphemistic *blow* (*me!*) is also used as a low jocular coll = to curse, swear at (often with past tense *blowed*), v.i. and v.t.: 1825, Glascock, *The Naval Sketch-Book*, I, 113. Occ. *blow me tight!*; *blow me up!*, current ca 1780–1830 (George Parker), *blow it!*: mid-C.19–20 (cf. BLAST *it!*). 4. Spend, lose money: see BLEW. 5. University, occ. as *go on the blow*: to indulge in a spree: C.19. 6. Winchester College, C.19–20: to blush (a corruption or a variant of BLUE). 7. To open (a safe) by the use of powder: c.: late C.19–20. 8. To smoke (a pipe): from ca 1840. Ex:

blow a cloud. To smoke a cigar or a pipe: coll, verging on S.E.: late C.18–19. Tom Moore, 1819. (In late C.17–18, *raise a cloud* = to smoke a pipe.)

blow-along, roll-along tub. A full-lined sailing-ship: clipper-ship sailors' coll: mid-C.19–20: ob.

blow-book. A book containing indelicate pictures: C.18, coll. *Post Man*, 8 June 1708.

blow great guns. To blow a violent gale: from ca 1840; coll. Hugh Miller. Occ. *b.g.g. and small arms*, †.

blow hot and cold. To vacillate; be treacherous: mid-C.16–20; coll till ca 1800, then S.E.

blow (in) a bowl. To be a confirmed drunkard: C.16 (?early 17); coll. Barclay, 1515.

blow in one's pipe. To spend money: low: ca 1870–1920. cf. BLOW, v., 4.

blow it!; blow me (tight)!; blow me up! See BLOW, v., 3; for 1st, see also BLEW IT.

blow off steam. To work, talk, swear, etc., hard, as a 'safety-valve': from ca 1830; coll.

***blow off the loose corns.** 'To Lie now and then with a Woman', B.E.: late C.17–mid-18; c. cf. BLOW THE GROUNDSELS.

blow one's bazoo. To boast, 'show off': ca 1870–1910. Ex Dutch *bazu* = *bazuin*, trumpet.

blow one's hide out. To eat heavily: low coll (–1857); ob.

blow-out. A heavy meal; from ca 1820. Bee, 1823; Scott, 1824. 2. v., *blow oneself out*: Barham, 1837; H., 1874, 'Sometimes the expression is, "*blow out* your bags".' 3. In c., to steal (something): late C.19–20; ob.

blow sky high. To scold, or blame, most vehemently: ?orig. U.S. and anglicized ca 1900.

***blow the gab or gaff.** To reveal a secret: in C.18, c.; then, always with GAFF, low s., as in Marryat.

blow the grampus. (Nautical) to throw cold water on a man asleep on duty: C.19–20; ob.

***blow the groundsels.** To 'lie with' a woman on the floor: C.17–18; c. In B.E. *blow-off on . . .*

blow through. (Of a man) to copulate: low: late C.19–20.

blow together. To make in a slovenly way: tailors': from ca 1850; ob.

blow-up. A discovery, disclosure: coll: late C.18–early 19. 2. A scolding: from ca 1839. More gen. BLOWING-UP. Ex: 3. v., to scold: see passage cited at BLAST, v., 4. A quarrel (temporary): from ca 1830.

blow upon. To betray: C.15–19, coll. To make public: C.17–19. To discredit: C.17–19, coll.

blowed, be. Euphemistic when *blowed* = damned; otherwise, low coll. From ca 1810. 'I am *blowed* if I appeer ageenst him unless I am drogged in': *Sessions*, 1827.

Still earlier in James Henry Lewis, *Lectures on the Art of Writing*, 7th ed., 1816, 'It'll be all dickey wee me, I'm blowed if it won't!'

***blowen; blowin(g).** A woman, esp. a harlot: c.: resp. late C.18–19 and late C.17–early 19. Borrow, in his *Romano Lavo-Lil*, says: 'Signifying a sister in debauchery . . . the Beluñi of the Spanish Gypsies'.

blower. A boaster; a very talkative person. Australian (and U.S.): from ca 1860; ob. 2. In late C.17–18 c., a mistress; a whore, as in Coles, 1676. In C.19 c., a girl: pejoratively opp. to JOMER. A variant of BLOWEN. 3. A pipe: low (—1811); †by 1890.

blower and striker. A hard officer; esp., a BUCKO mate: nautical: late C.19–20.

blowhard. A boaster: Australian: 1880. In U.S. (1855; ob.), an adj., whence prob. the n. 2. Whence, a blustering officer, of no use with his fists: sailing-ship seamen's: from ca 1885.

blowing, vbl n. Boasting: from ca 1860. Trollope in Australia and New Zealand, 1873, 'A fine art much cultivated in the colonies, for which the colonial phrase of "blowing" has been created'. 2. See BLOWEN.

blowing marlin-spikes(, it's). (It is) a full gale: nautical coll: mid-C.19–20. i.e. the gale is strong enough to lift a marlin-spike (or almost).

blowing of a match, in the. In a moment: coll, mostly London (—1887); ob.

blowing-up. A scolding: Sir George Simpson's *Journal of Occurrences in the Athabasca Department, 1820 and 1821*, 'Mr Clarke gave him what is vulgarly called "a good blowing up".'

blowsabella. A country wench: C.18; coll. Suggested by the character in Gay's poem, *The Shepherd's Week*. cf. *blousalinda*, which likewise has a coll savour. 2. Hence, a harlot: low s.: Ned Ward, 1709. cf.:

blowse, blowze. A beggar's trull; a wench: late C.16–18: either c. or low s. Chapman in *All Fools*. cf. BLOSS. cf.: 2. A slatternly woman: C.16–18. 3. A shrewish woman: Ned Ward, 1712.

blub. To weep, esp. of children: mid-C.19–20. Ex *to* BLUBBER. 2. Also, to wet with weeping: coll: 1804, Tarras. Ex equivalent BLUBBER, V.

***blubber.** The mouth: in C.18–early 19, c.; then s. 2. A woman's breasts: low: late C.18–20, esp. in *sport blubber*, to expose the breasts.

blubber, v. To weep effusively, noisily: C.15–20. Until ca 1800, S.E.; then coll. Smollett, Scott. (Gen. pejorative.)

blubber and guts. Obesity: C.19–20, ob.; low. cf.:

blubber-belly. A fat person: C.19–20, low coll; ob. cf. preceding entry.

blubber-boiler. A variant (from ca 1860) of BLUBBER-HUNTER.

blubber-head(ed). (A) foolish (person): C.19–20, ob. Mostly nautical.

blubber-hunter. A whaling-ship: pejorative nautical coll: mid-C.19–20.

blucher. Winchester College: a prefect in half power: ca 1830–1915. Also, a non-privileged cab plying at railway stations: ca 1850–1900. Ex the Prussian field-marshal, who arrived somewhat late at the Battle of Waterloo.

***bludgeon business,** see SWINGING THE STICK.

***bludgeoner.** A harlot's bully; a bawdy-house chucker-out: c. (—1852); ob. Also, in late C.19–20, BLUDGER.

***bludger.** A thief apt to use a bludgeon, i.e. violence: c.; from ca 1850. 2. See BLUDGEONER.

blue. This word, in the S.E., coll, and s. of C.18–20 – it is rare before ca 1700 – plays a protean and almost intangible part, for it expresses a gamut of opinions and emotions. For an excellent gen. introduction on the subject, see F. & H. at *blue*.

blue. The Blue Squadron: from ca 1700; orig. naval and coll; in C.19, gen. and S.E. See the note at ADMIRAL OF THE BLUE. 2. A BLUE STOCKING: 1788, Mme D'Arblay; after ca 1800, coll. Byron, in *Don Juan*: 'The Blues, that tender tribe, who sigh o'er sonnets'; 'Cuthbert Bede': 'Elizabeth, the very Virgin Queen of Blues'. Hence *blue* = female learning; †by 1900: Byron, 'a twilight tinge of blue'. 3. A scholar of Christ's Hospital: abbr. *blue-coat boy*: from ca 1820; †. 4. A policeman: from ca 1835. cf. BLUE BOTTLE and BLUE BOYS, *men in* BLUE, etc. 5. A compromise between the half-pint and the pint pot: public-house, ca 1870–1900. 6. Gen. *get Don's blue*. Fig. for election to an Oxford or Cambridge team in a major inter-university sport or competition: mid-C.19–20: soon coll. The Oxford colours are dark, the Cambridge light, blue. 7. (Gen. p.l) A bluejacket: nautical coll: mid-C.18–20; ob.

blue, v. Blush: early C.18. At Winchester College in C.19. Swift, in the *Tatler*, 'If a Virgin blushes, we no longer cry she blues.' 2. To spend, waste: mid-C.19–20, see BLEW. 3. Pawn, pledge: ca 1850–1920. 4. To miscalculate; bungle; ruin: 1880. 5. In mid-C.19 gen. c., to steal; plunder.

blue, adj. (Of women) learned, literary: from ca 1780; coll. In C.19–20 (ob.), S.E. Lever, in *Harry Lorrequer*, 'She was a . . . very little blue – rather a dabbler in the "ologies" than a real disciple.' 2. Obscene: from late 1830s (cf. BLUENESS): coll by 1900. Perhaps ex the blue dress of harlots (F. & H.), perhaps ex *La Bibliothèque Bleue*, a series of French books (H.), perhaps simply in contrast to *brown* as in BROWN TALK, adj. 3. Gloomy, low-spirited: from ca 1850, coll: cf. BLUE, LOOK; *in a* BLUE FUNK.

blue, a bolt from the. Something (gen. unpleasant) wholly unexpected (—1888); coll.

blue, bit of. 'An obscene or libidinous anecdote' (B. & L.): from ca 1870.

blue, by all that's. Decidedly! Gen., however, a euphemism for 'by God!': coll: from 1820s; ob. ?ex *parbleu* = *par Dieu.*

blue, look. To be confounded, astonished, disappointed: late C.16–20, coll. 2. See BLUE, TILL ALL IS, 2.

blue, make the air. To curse; to use obscene or blasphemous language: mid-C.19–20.

blue, men in. (Singular rare.) The police: coll: from ca 1870; ob.

blue, till all is. To the utmost, the limit; for an indefinite time: perhaps orig. U.S. (1806); ob. Admiral Smyth refers to a ship reaching deep, i.e. blue, water. 2. In drinking: till one becomes drunk, as in Gardner, 1831; *till all look* or *seem blue* is a C.17 (?–18) variant.

blue, true. Faithful(ness): C.17–20, coll. Foreshadowed ca 1500. In C.17, of Scottish Whigs; in C.19–20, of strong Tories.

blue and white, gentleman in. A policeman: coll: ca 1860–1900.

blue-apron. A tradesman: C.18–19, coll > S.E. Amherst, *Terrae Filius*, 1726.

blue as a razor. Extremely blue: late C.18–early 19. Grose, 2nd ed., pertinently suggests *blue as azure*.

blue-back. One of the old privately prepared charts: nautical coll: C.19–20; ob. Contrast:

blue-backs. Orange Free State paper money: ca 1860–1900.

***blue-belly.** A policeman: c. (—1909). cf. BLUE, n., 4.

blue bill. Winchester College: a tradesman's bill sent to the pupil's home: C.19–20, ob. Ex the colour of the envelopes gen. used.

blue billy. A blue handkerchief white-spotted: low: boxing: from the 1830s; ob.

blue blanket. The sky: C.18–20 coll; ob. Defoe in his *History of the Devil*. cf. BENGAL BLANKET. 2. 'A rough overcoat made of coarse pilot cloth', H., 2nd ed.: coll: ca 1860–90.

blue blazes. Hell: from ca 1870. Ex blue flames from brimstone. 2. Spirituous liquors: non-aristocratic: from ca 1875.

blue boar. A venereal chancre: late C.18–19, low. Perhaps ex the Blue Boar Tavern, in the 'Latin Quarter' of the London of ca 1750–1850.

blue boat. (Gen. pl.) A skiff for the use of cadets at Dartmouth: naval coll: late C.19–20. cf. BLACK CUTTER.

blue bottle. A beadle, a policeman: coll: 1597, Shakespeare. Little used in late C.17–18, but repopularized ca 1850. 2. A serving man: coll: C.19. Scott, G. P. R. James. cf. BLUE-APRON.

blue boy. A chancre: C.18–19, low. cf. BLUE BOAR.

blue boys. (Rare in singular.) The police: James Greenwood, 1883. Ob.

blue butter. Mercurial ointment, against parasites: (Cockney) coll: from ca 1870; ob.

Blue Cap. A Scotsman: ca 1590–1800; coll > S.E. cf. the S.E. *blue bonnet*.

blue coat. A blue-coated soldier: C.16–17. In C.19, occ. for a sailor. Coll usages. 2. A policeman: C.17–20, ob. 3. Also, a serving man: C.17–18.

blue dahlia. Something rare or unheard of: coll (—1888) >, almost imm., S.E. cf. Robert Hichens's *The Green Carnation*, 1894, and *blue roses*, 1885 (*Daily News*, 25 June).

blue damn, (I don't care a). A slightly evasive curse: coll (—1909); ob. Ware's semantics are rather far-fetched: prob. ex BLUE, adj., 2.

blue devils. Low spirits: from ca 1780: coll >, by 1850, S.E. Cowper has *Mr Blue Devil*. Ex *blue devil*, a baleful demon. Hence, 2, delirium tremens: from ca 1822: coll >, by 1880, S.E. Scott and Cobbett. cf. BLUES, 3. 3. The police: ca 1845–1905. cf. BLUES, 4.

blue fear. Extreme fright: ca 1870–1900;

coll, rare. R. L. Stevenson. cf. BLUE FUNK.

blue fire, adj. Sensational: from ca 1870; mainly theatrical. Ex a blue light used on the stage to create a weird effect; cf. S.E. *blue light.*

blue flag. A publican: mid-C.18–early 19. Esp. in *hoist the b.f.*, become a publican.

blue funk. Extreme fear (—1856). Thomas Hughes popularized it.

blue-handled rake. 'The railing and steps leading to the platform of a fair-booth stage': late C.19–20. Ware.

***blue it,** see BLEW IT.

blue jack (or **Jack**). Cholera morbus: nautical (—1909). Ex skin colour. On YELLOW JACK.

blue light. A sanctimonious seaman: nautical: early C.19–20. In the Indian Army, a blue light was the symbol of temperance.

blue lights. A naval gunner: naval: late C.19–20.

blue Monday. A Monday spent, away from work, in dissipation: from ca 1880; ob.

blue moon. A rarely recurrent (event or) period: coll. J. Burrows, *Life in St George's Fields*, 1821. 2. A spoon: rhyming s.: late C.19–20. 3. To SPOON: from ca 1890.

blue moon, once in a. Extremely seldom: coll: C.17–20. *Till a blue moon* occurs in 1860, and the phrase is adumbrated as early as 1528 (Roy & Barlowe).

blue murder, cry, see:

blue murder(s). Cries of terror or alarm: a great noise, horrible din: from late 1850s; coll. Gen. as *cry b. m.* cf. the Fr. *morbleu*, which, however, = *mort (de) Dieu.*

Blue Nose. A Nova Scotian: coll; orig. (1830) U.S., anglicized ca 1840. Ex the extreme cold of the Nova Scotian winter.

blue o'clock in the morning, at. 'Pre-dawn, when black sky gives way to purple': London streets': 1886, *Daily News*, 12 Oct.; ob. Rhyming on *two o'clock.*

blue paper, fly, see FLY BLUE PAPER.

blue peter. (Cards) the signal for trumps at whist: coll > j.: ca 1860–1905. 2. Also fig. in its coll use, as in Byron, for immediate departure.

blue pigeon. (Nautical) the sounding-lead, from ca 1820. 2. In mid-C.18–19 c., *blue pigeon* is roofing-lead; hence, *b.-p. flyer* is a stealer of lead from houses and churches. cf.:

***blue pigeon, fly the.** To steal roof-lead and lead pipes from house and church exteriors: mid-C.18–19 c. cf. BLUE PIGEON, 2.

blue pill. A bullet: C.19. cf. the American *blue whistler* and BLUE PLUM. 2. A mercury pill against syphilis: c. (—1887); ob.

***blue plum(b).** A mid-C.18–19 c. term for a bullet. Harrison Ainsworth, 1834. Grose has the following phrases: *surfeited with a blue plumb*, 'wounded with a bullet', and *a sortment* (i.e. an assortment) *of George R—'s* (i.e. Rex's) *blue plumbs*, 'a volley of ball, shot from soldiers' firelocks'.

blue ribbon. Gin: low: mid-C.19–20; ob. cf. SATIN.

blue-ribbon faker. A blatant upholder of abstinence from liquor: London streets': 1882–ca 1914. For semantics see:

blue-ribboner or **-ribbonite.** A teetotaller: coll verging on S.E.: from ca 1880. The blue ribbon worn by certain teetotallers is recorded in 1878 (S.O.D.).

blue ruin. Gin; esp., bad gin: from ca 1810; ob. *Lex. Bal.*, Keats, T. Moore, Lytton, Sala. cf. (its prob. 'offspring') BLUE RIBBON and BLUE TAPE.

blue shirt at the mast-head, (there's) a. (There is) a call for assistance: nautical: late C.19–20. Ex the blue flag then flown.

blue skin. A Presbyterian: C.18–early 19. Blue is the Presbyterian colour; 'Hudibras' Butler speaks of 'Presbyterian true blue'. 2. In the West Indies: a half-breed of black and white: C.19–20, ob. 3. In late C.18–early 19, any 'person begotten on a black woman by a white man', Grose, 2nd ed. cf.:

blue squadron, (belonging to the). (Of) mixed blood, white with Hindu: India, C.19. In late C.18–early 19, of anyone with 'a lick of the tar brush', Grose, 3rd ed. (cf. TAR-BRUSH . . .). See the note appended to ADMIRAL OF THE BLUE.

blue stocking. A literary or a learned lady (—1790). The adj. began to be applied in the 1750s to the frequenters of Montagu House, London, where literary and cognate talk replaced cards. Both n. and adj. were coll by 1810, S.E. by 1820; both are ob. Ex the blue worsted stockings affected by Benjamin Stillingfleet, a near-poet, who was a shining light of the Montagu House assemblies – by Admiral Boscawen dubbed the Blue Stocking Society.

blue stone. Gin or whisky so inferior that it resembles vitriol, which in Scottish and

Northern dial. is called 'blue stone': ca 1850–1900.

blue tape. Gin: ca 1780–1850; perhaps c. cf. BLUE RUIN and SKY BLUE, 1.

blued, occ. **blewed.** Drunk: low: C.19–20; ob. This word perhaps influenced SCREWED and SLEWED. 2. In low spirits: ca 1850–1900. cf. BLUES, 2.

bluely, come off. To have ill success, bad luck: coll; ca 1650–1840. Urquhart.

blueness. Indecency: literary s.; not much used. Carlyle, 1840. Ex BLUE, adj., 2.

blues, the. See BLUE, n., 2 and 7. 2. Despondency; low spirits. Apparently Washington Irving was, in 1807, the first to abbr. BLUE DEVILS. 3. Delirium tremens: from ca 1850 but never very gen. 4. The police: see BLUE, n., 4: from ca1835. 'Sometimes called the Royal Regiment of Foot-guards *Blue*', H., 5th ed.: ca 1870–90.

***bluey.** In mid-C.19–20 c., lead: ex BLUE PIGEON. 2. A bushman's, esp. a sundowner's, bundle, usually wrapped in a blue blanket: Australian (—1888). Esp. in *hump bluey*, to go on the tramp (—1890). cf. SWAG, n., 5. 3. In Tasmania, a 'smock-coat' shirt or blouse worn in wet districts (1891, ob.). 4. A nickname for a red-headed man: from ca 1890, esp. in Australia and New Zealand.

***bluey-cracking.** The stealing of lead from building-exteriors: c. (—1845); ob. cf. BLUE PIGEON, and:

bluey-hunter. A habitual stealer of lead roofing and piping: mid-C.19–20 c. cf. BLUE-PIGEON *flyer*.

bluff. A considerable assurance adopted to impress an opponent: orig. (—1848) U.S., anglicized ca 1870: cf. the v. Coll. 2. In low s., an excuse: a sense firmly grounded in England – see Mayhew's *London Labour* – as early as 1851: this sense may, perhaps, not come from the U.S.

bluff, v.i. and v.t. To impress, intimidate, make an excuse; *bluff off*, to frighten away by bluffing; *bluff out of*, to frighten out of. Orig. (1850) U.S.; anglicized as coll, in the early 1860s or even the late 1850s, for H., 1859, makes no comment on the American origin of either n. or v. The American usage, for both n. and v., perhaps derives from the Restoration senses, *bluff*, to blindfold (as in Ray) and *look bluff*, look big (as in B.E.); but see BLUFFING and W. at *bluff*.

***bluffer.** In c. of mid-C.17–early 19, 'a Host, Inn-keeper or Victualler', B.E.; Coles, 1676. Prob. ex dial. *bluff*, to hoodwink. 2. An imposer who relies on an assumed appearance and speech: from ca 1885; coll. 3. A bosun: nautical: ca 1840–1914.

bluffing, vbl n. 'Imposing on another with a show of force, where no real force exists: a phrase taken from the game of poker', Thornton, who records it for U.S. at 1850. Anglicized, as coll, ca 1880.

bluggy. A jocular, therefore s., not – except among purists or prudes – a euphemistic twisting of BLOODY: 1876. The O.E.D. (Sup.) remarks: '(A) pretended infantile pronunciation of *bloody*'. Hence, *blugginess* (1894: ibid.).

blunderbuss. A stupid, or ignorant, clumsy fellow: from ca 1690; coll verging on, perhaps achieving, S.E.; ob. Ex the weapon's unwieldiness. 2. Also, ca 1680–1800, a noisy and truculent talker: coll. Ex the noise of its report.

blunk. A squall; a period of squally weather: dial. (—1790) >, by 1820, nautical coll. Dial. has a v. *blunk*, which is cognate with *blench*.

***blunt.** Money, esp. cash (—1714); orig. c.; ob., except among tramps as *the blunt*. John Hall, Grose (2nd ed.), Moncrieff, Dickens (in *Oliver Twist*), *Punch* (1882). Etymology doubtful: perhaps, indeed prob., ex the blunt rim of coins; perhaps, however, ex John Blunt, chairman of the South Sea Company; or perhaps, despite its surface improbability, ex the Fr. *blond* (cf. BROWN, a halfpenny), as H. and F. & H. maintain. 2. Whence *in blunt*, *out of blunt*, rich, poor: C.19.

Blunt Magazine. A bank; esp. the Bank of England: low: ca 1820–60. Ex BLUNT, 1.

blunted. In possession of money: rare; ca 1850–90. Gen. *well-blunted*. Ex BLUNT.

blunty. A variant of the preceding. 'Jon Bee', 1823.

blurt! Pooh! A FIG for!: late C.16–(?only early) 17: coll. Lyly. cf. the derisive c.p., *blurt, master constable!*: C.17. Middleton.

blusteration. Bluster; a blustering: dial. (—1803) >, ca 1860, coll.

bly!; bly me. Reduced forms of *God blimey*, GORBLIMEY: low: late C.19–20.

***bly-hunker.** A horse: vagrants' c. (—1845); †. Prob. of Shelta origin.

bo. A common vocative among British seamen in the Napoleonic wars, with or without preceding 'my'. It occurs frequently in W. N. Glascock's works. Prob. ex BOR.

bo or **boo to a goose, say** or **cry;** occ. to **a battledore.** To open one's mouth; to talk, speak: gen. in negative. Coll; from ca 1580.

bo-peep. Sleep: rhyming s.: D. W. Barrett, *Navvies*, 1880–83. 2. The stocks: ca 1760–1850. One's head peeps out.

***bo-peep, play at.** In turn to hide and appear in public; to keep watch: late C.18–early 19. Ex the game.

boa-constrictor. An instructor: naval: late C.19–20; virtually †. Ex his 'fascinating' eye.

board. A sideboard: furniture-dealers' coll: late C.19–20. 2. A railway signal: railwaymen's: from the 1880s. *Tit-Bits*, 1 Nov. 1890, notes the synonymous *stick*.

board, v. To accost: C.16–20. In Surrey and Shakespeare, S.E.; but from ca 1660, coll, as in Vanbrugh's *False Friend*, 'What do you expect from boarding a woman ... already heart and soul engaged to another?' In C.19–20, much more definitely nautical in flavour: before 1800, the Fr. *aborder*, to approach, accost, impressed rather by its Gallicism than by its nauticism. 2. ?hence, to borrow money from (a person): military (—1890); ob.

board, above, see ABOVE BOARD.

board, keep one's name on the. To remain a member of one's College: Cambridge coll: from ca 1850.

board, on the. (Tailoring) enjoying all the privileges and perquisites of a competent workman: ca 1850–1920. Perhaps j. rather than s.

board, sail on another. To behave differently: C.16–early 17; coll.

board, sweep the. To win all the prizes; obtain every honour: coll: from ca 1830. Ex the card-game senses, take all the cards, win all the stakes: S.E., C.17–20.

board, under. Deceptively: C.17–18; coll. cf. ABOVE BOARD.

board in the smoke. (Nautical) to take by surprise: C.19. Ex the lit. usage of boarding a ship under cover of broadside-smoke.

Board-man, see BOARDMAN, 2.

board of green cloth. A card table: C.19–20; a billiard-table: C.18–20. Coll; ob.

board you! Pass the bottle on: nautical (—1890); ob.

board the beef in the smoke. To eat dinner: nautical, esp. naval: ca 1790–1860. Moe has found it in 1806.

board-work, see BOARDMAN, 1.

boarder-bug. A boarder at school: schoolboys': from late C.19 Opp. DAY-BUG, same period.

***boarding house** or **school.** A prison; house of correction: c.; ca 1690–1840. Hence, *boarding scholars*, 'Bridewell-birds', B.E.

***boardman.** A STANDING PATTERER, who often carried a board with coloured pictures: c. (vagrants'): ca 1840–1900. The practice was, by Cockneys, called *board-work*. 2. (Or **Board-man.**) A school-attendance inspector: London coll (—1887); ob.

boards, the. The stage; theatre: from ca 1770: coll till ca 1880, then S.E.

***boat,** always **the boat.** The hulks; or any public works or prison: c.; ca 1810–95. Mayhew. Ex convict-hulks.

***boat,** v. To transport (convicts): ca 1800–60. 2. To sentence to penal servitude: ca 1870–1910. Both are c. In the latter sense, *get the boat* or *be boated* = to receive a severe sentence.

boat, be in the same. i.e. in the same position or circumstance(s): coll, from ca 1850, though anticipated in late C.16.

boat, good. A soldier spending freely among poorer comrades: military: ca 1890–1915.

boat, have an oar in another's or **every.** To meddle, be a busybody: from mid-C.16; ob. Coll till ca 1600, then S.E.

boat, push out the. To pay for a round of drinks: naval: late C.19–20.

boat, put on the. To deport; as adj., deported: low: late C.19–20.

boat, sail in the same. To act together: coll; from late C.16; in C.19–20. S.E.

boatswain-captain. A naval captain thoroughly competent as a seaman: naval coll, contemptuously used by the envious: C.19.

boaty. Fond of, addicted to, boating: coll: 1886. cf. *horsey*.

bob. A man, a fellow: coll: from ca 1700; ob. cf. JACK and TOM, DICK AND HARRY, the commonness of the name giving rise to a generic sense. cf. sense 3, where, however, the idea may be that of *bobbing* in, out, and up; also *dry* and *wet bob* (see BOB, DRY). 2. A shilling: *Sessions*, June 1789. Origin obscure: perhaps abbr. BOBSTICK; Weekley suggests ex ROBERT, 2. cf. JOEY. 3. In c., a shop-lifter's assistant: late C.17–19. cf. sense 1. 4. Gin: C.18. 5. At Winchester College, C.19: a large white beer-jug, holding about a gallon. 6. See BOB, S'HELP ME.

***bob,** v.; occ. as **bob out of.** To cheat, trick. Late C.17–19 c. C.14–16, S.E.; C.17, coll. Ex Old Fr. *bober*, to befool.

bob, adj. Lively, pleasant, 'nice': C.18–20; ob. Cibber, 1721. Coll. 2. In c., safe; esp. in *all is bob*; late C.17–early 19. cf. *all* BETTY!

bob! Stop! Enough!: Society, ca 1880–1900. Ex gen. *bob it!*, drop it! (—1864).

bob!, all is, see BOB, adj., 2.

bob!, bear a. Be quick! Look lively: coll, from ca 1860; ob. Ex *bear a bob* (lit., a refrain), join in the chorus.

bob, dry. Incomplete coïtion: applied to the man: ca 1660–1930. Rochester. Ex *dry bob*, a blow that leaves the skin intact. 2. See:

bob, dry and **wet.** At Eton College, one who concentrates resp. on land games and sports, and on boating, swimming, (recently) water-polo. *Dry bob* occurs in Disraeli's *Coningsby*: the terms would therefore seem to date from ca 1835; they were coll by 1875, S.E. by 1900.

bob, give the. To dismiss: C.17, coll. (In S.E., *give the bob* = to befool, impose on.)

bob, light. A soldier in the light infantry, artillery, etc.; coll; from ca 1840. Here, as in BOB, DRY *and* WET, *bob* abbr. *Robert*, so common a name that it > generic for a man, a fellow; cf. JACK; JOE; DICK, etc.

bob (or in Ware, baub)!, s'help me. As an oath, euphemistic (*bob* = God). It is s. only when, as in 'Jon Bee', 1823, in Barham, 1837, and in James Payn, 1880, it is virtually or actually an asseveration (='you may be sure') made jocularly. 'The word . . . comes from Catholic England, and is "babe" – meaning the infant Saviour,' Ware. Now *s'help*, S'ELP, is often, deliberately or otherwise, pronounced SWELP, and among the middle and upper classes, after ca 1890, it is always spoken in jest.

bob, shift one's. To move, go away: mid-C.18–20; ob. 2. Exchange places: naval: ca 1805–50.

bob, wet, see BOB, DRY.

bob a nob. Almost a c.p.: a shilling a head: ca 1820–1910.

bob around. To go quickly from place to place: coll; from ca 1860. cf. *shift one's* BOB.

***bob cull.** A 'good fellow', pleasant companion: late C.18–19 c. See BOB, adj., and CULL.

Bob, Harry, and Dick. Sick, esp. after drink: rhyming s.: 1868; virtually †.

***bob ken; bowman ken.** 'A good or well Furnished House, full of Booty, worth Robbing; also a House that Harbours Rogues and Thieves', B.E.: c.: late C.17–early 19.

bob (or Bob) my pal. A girl: rhyming s. on GAL. From ca 1855; ob.

bob-tailor. 'A cruiser-sterned merchant ship': nautical: late C.19–20. Bowen.

bob(b)bajee. A cook: Regular Army coll: mid-C.19–20; ob. Ex Hindustani *bawachi*.

bobber. A fellow-workman; mate, chum: dial. (—1860) >, by 1870, coll and by 1885, s. Ex lit. sense. 2. A spurious pl of BOB, shilling, as in *two bobber*, a two-shilling piece, though this (ca 1880–1910) may conceivably be due to the Oxford *-er*.

bobbers. A fringe of pieces of cork or wood worn on a hat to keep the flies away: Australian: late C.19–20.

bobbery. A noise; disturbance; squabble. From ca 1800: Kenney has it in his comedy, *Raising the Wind*, 1803; *Punch* honoured it in 1879. Ex Hindi *Bap re!*, Oh, father: often employed to express grief or surprise. See also BUBBERY.

bobbery-pack. A heterogeneous squadron: naval: ca 1820–90. Bowen, 'Borrowed from the sportsmen ashore'.

bobbin!, that's the end of the. That's the end of it!; that's finished!: non-aristocratic coll c.p. verging on proverbial S.E.: mid-C.19–20; ob. B. & L., '. . . When all the thread is wound off a *bobbin* or spool. . . It rose from the refrain of a song which was popular in 1850.'

bobbish. 'Clever, smart, spruce', Grose, 2nd ed.: ca 1785–1820. Ex *bob*, 'a light, rebounding movement'. 2. Hence, in good health and/or spirits: implied in 1813; ob. except as *pretty bobbish*. Adv., *bobbishly*: 1813, Scott; ob.

bobble. A confused movement of water: nautical coll: from the 1870s. Ex:

bobble, v.i. To move with frequent or continual bobbing: coll: 1812, W. Tennant. A frequentative of BOB.

bobbles. Testicles, gen. a human: sol. for BAWBLES (but cf. BOBBLE): C.19–20; ob.

bobbly. Jerky, jumpy: coll: 1909 (O.E.D. Sup.). Ex BOBBLE, V.

bobby. A policeman: *Sessions*, June 1844. Ex Mr, later Sir, ROBERT Peel (cf. PEELER), mainly responsible for the Metropolitan Police Act of 1828. F. & H. points out that, long before 1828, *Bobby the beadle* = 'a guardian of a public square or other open space'. 2. Hence, at Oxford and Cambridge, ca 1860–90, the proctors were called *bobbies*.

Bobby Atkins. An occ., coll variant of

Tommy Atkins (see at TOMMY, 4): ca 1900–14.

bobby-dazzler. A dazzling person: s.: from ca 1890. Ex dial.; perhaps euphemistic for BLOODY DAZZLER.

***bobby(-)horse.** A chink-backed horse: vagrants' c. (—1845); ob.

***bobby-twister.** A burglar or thief who, on being pursued or seized, uses violence: mid-C.19–20 (ob.): c. Ex BOBBY, a policeman.

bobby's labourer. A special constable: such constables' in 1868. See BOBBY, 1.

Bob's-a-dying. Idling; idling and dozing: nautical: ?ca 1790–1850. Wm N. Glascock, *Sailors and Saints*, 1829 (I, 179), 'Nothing but dining, and dancing, and Bobs-a-dying on deck from daylight till dark'.

Bob's horse, with nobody to pay the reckoning, – off, like. To decamp with all money, furniture and personal effects: nautical: from 1830s; ob. Dana.

Bob's your uncle. Everything is perfect: c.p.: from ca 1890. ?cf. BOB, adj.

bobstay. 'The frenum of a man's yard', Grose, 2nd ed.: mid-C.18–20 (ob.); low coll.

***bobstick.** A shilling's worth (—1789). Orig. c., then low s.; †by 1860. George Parker; Moncrieff, 1821. Whence perhaps BOB, n., 2 – but then what is the origin of *bobstick*?

bobtail, bob-tail, bob tail. A lewd woman, lit. one with a lively pudend: coll: C.17–18. cf. WAG-TAIL. 2. A contemptible fellow: C.17, perhaps coll. cf.: 3. A eunuch; an impotent man: C.17–18; ex *bob* = cut short (cf. *a bobtail horse*) and TAIL = male member. 4. A partridge: vendors of game: late C.18–early 19. Ex its short tail. 5. A dandy wearing a pointed tail-coat: early C.19: mostly proletarian.

bobtail, rag-tag and; or tag-rag and bobtail. The rabble (—1659); coll in C.18, S.E. thereafter: the common herd (of any social class): C.19–20. Pepys has it first, but it was doubtless used earlier.

boco, boko. The nose. Orig. (ca 1820) pugilistic, but gen. by 1873. Prob. ex BEAK; but if COCONUT (also, in U.S., simply *coco* or, erroneously, *cocoa*) existed some years before its earliest record, then perhaps *boco* derives ex BEAK (3) + *coco*. Ware thinks that it may derive ex Grimaldi's tapping his nose and exclaiming *c'est beaucoup*. 2. Nonsense: ca 1870–1910; etymology uncertain. *Punch*, 25 Sept. 1886: 'Lopsided Free Trade is all boko.'

boco-smasher. A rough: low London: late C.19–early 20. Ex BOCO, 1.

Bodder. The Bodleian Library: Oxford University: from the late 1890s. Ex BODLEY: see 'the Oxford *er*', p. 11.

bod(d)eration. An early C.19 form of *botheration* (see BOTHER).

Bodger. The inevitable nickname of all men surnamed Lees: late C.19–20: mostly naval and military.

bodier. (Boxing) a blow on the side; loosely, on breast or belly: ca 1810–1914.

bodies. The king's body-guards. cf.: Major John André's poem, *The Cow Chase*, New York, 1780, London, 1781, with *the Bodies* footnoted thus: 'A cant' – here, fashionable slang – 'appellation given amongst the soldiery to the corps that had the honour to guard his Majesty's person'.

***bodikin.** A contraction of BAWDY-KEN, a brothel: c.: ca 1820–50.

Bodikin(s), see BODY.

bodkin. (Sporting) one who sleeps in a bed only on alternate nights: ca 1850–1900. Ex the next entry. 2. A midshipman's dirk: jocular naval coll: C.19–20; ob.

bodkin, ride or **sit.** C.19–20; adumbrated in Ford, 1638, and occurring in 1798 as to *bodkin* alone; ob. To be wedged between two others when there is, altogether, room for only two. Coll. Ex *bodkin*, to make, as it were, a bodkin of.

Bodley, the. The Oxford University Library: from ca 1870; coll. cf. BODDER.

body appears, from ca 1530, as part of many ancient oaths. e.g. *Bod(i)kin(s)*, a little body.

body. A person: in C.19–20, either a sol. or a facetious coll. In dial., however, its usage is serious and respectable.

body, v. To punch (one's opponent) on the body – i.e. the trunk: pugilistic coll: ca 1805–70. *Boxiana*, II, 1818.

body-bag. A shirt: low: ca 1820–70.

body-binder. A waistcoat, or perhaps a broad belt: ca 1810–40, esp. in boxing circles. The *Plymouth Telegraph*, (?March) 1822, 'Bartlett entered first, and *doffed* the *castor* from his *nob*, his *blue bird's-eye* from his *squeeze*, and his *body-binder* from his *bread-basket*.'

body-lining. Bread: drapers' (—1909). Ex their trade.

body-louse, brag or **brisk** or **busy as a.** Very brisk or busy: coll; resp. late C.16–17, (the gen. form) mid-C.17–20, mid-C.17–19.

body of divinity bound in black calf. A parson: mid-C.18–early 19.

***body-slangs.** Fetters: C.19 c. (See SLANGS.)

body-snatcher. A bailiff: mid-C.18–early 19: perhaps c. 2. A member of a ship's police force: nautical: mid-C.19–20; ob. 3. A policeman: ca 1840–1900, low. 4. A resurrectionist (—1812), ob.: coll; after ca 1850, S.E. Body-snatching > a trade ca 1827. 5. An undertaker: from ca 1820; ob. 6. A cat-stealer (—1859), †by 1900. 7. A cabman: London streets': ca 1840–60. Ex his habits.

bog, often **bogs.** Abbr. BOG-HOUSE, a privy: (—1825): s., orig. Oxford University. 2. In c. (?ever in the singular), the land-reclaiming works at Dartmoor: from ca 1860; ob.

bog, v. To ease oneself, evacuate: from ca 1870: s. Ex preceding or possibly ex:

bog, go to. 'To go to stool', *Lex. Bal.*, 1811: low.

bog-gang. A party of convicts detailed for the work defined at BOG, n., 2.

bog-house. A privy: from ca 1670; low coll. Head in *The English Rogue*. Ex the ca 1550–1660 S.E. *boggard.*

Bog-land. Ireland: late C.17–20, ob. Coll, orig. and mainly jocular. cf.:

Bog-Lander. An Irishman: coll: from ca 1690; ob. Ireland is famous for rain: cf. BOG-TROTTER and URINAL OF THE PLANETS.

bog-Latin. Spurious Latin: late C.18–20, ob.; coll. ?an Irish perversion of DOG-LATIN.

bog-orange. A potato: C.18–20, ob.; coll. So many potatoes come from Ireland.

bog-shop. A ca 1840–1910 low variant of BOG-HOUSE.

bog-trotter. A wild Irishman (cf. BOG-LANDER): coll: from ca 1680. Ex the numerous bogs in Ireland. 2. Earlier, ca 1660–90, 'Scotch or North Country Moss-troopers or High-way Men', B.E. (cf. Camden): coll. 3. From late C.17, however, the term > a nickname for any Irish person whatsoever.

bog-trotting. A pejorative adj. applied to Irishmen, esp. if uncouth: from ca 1750; coll. Employed by Goldsmith and Thackeray.

bogey, see BOGY. 2., see SWEEP, n., 3. 3., see POKE BOGEY.

boggart, be off at, with *Meredith* occ. added. To be, or go, off at full tilt or, fig., impetuously: Midlands: late C.19–20. Ex Midlands dial. (of a horse) *take* (*the*) *boggart*, take fright. A *boggart* is, of course, a bogy or hobgoblin or ghost.

boggle-de-botch, boggledybotch. A bungling; a 'mess': coll (—1834); ob. Maria Edgeworth, 1834. Ex *boggle*, a, or to, bungle, and *botch*, to do, or make, clumsily.

boggy. (Gen. of a child) diarrhoea: schoolboys': late C.19–20. Ex BOG, n., 1.

bogh. To get; hold; make (esp. a person) work: Shelta: C.18–20.

bogie. A bathe: Australian: since ca 1815. Alex. Harris, *The Emigrant Family*, 1849. Ex Aboriginal. 2. Hence, a swimming-hole; a bath: Australian: late C.19–20.

boguer. A clumsy sailing-ship: nautical coll: mid-C.19–20. ?*bogger*.

bogus. Sham; spurious; illicit. Orig. (—1840), U.S. and = counterfeit (ex instrument, thus named, for the uttering of base coin). Acclimatized ca 1860 in England, where it > coll ca 1900. As W. remarks, '*calibogus*, "rum and spruce beer, an American beverage" (Grose (1st ed.)) suggests a parallel to *balderdash*'; but, as F. & H. (revised) remarks, *bogus* may be cognate with BOGY; the editor proposes derivation ex *bogy* on HOCUS-POCUS. cf. SCAMP; SNIDE.

bogy, see ASK BOGY. 2. A landlord: from ca 1860; ob. Perhaps orig. *bogy-man.* Ex BOGY, OLD. 3. See SWEEP, n., 3.

bogy, adj. Sombre of tint or colour: studio s., ca 1870–1910.

Bogy (or Bogey), Old. The devil: from ca 1820. Soon coll. Occ. without *old.* But a comparison with ASK BOGY suggests that this sense, which precedes by thirty years that of a goblin, a person to be dreaded, may be fifty years earlier than 1820. It is true that *bogle*, the presumed and prob. orig. of *bogy*, antedates BOG-HOUSE by 150 years or so, yet the indelicate sense of *ask bogy* provides a not-to-be-ridiculed possibility both of *ask bogy*'s derivation from *bog-house* and even of an esoteric connection between *ask bogy*, *bog-house*, and *Bogy*.

***boil.** To betray: ca 1600–50; ?orig. c. Rowlands; Middleton & Dekker.

boil down. To condense: orig. (—1880) journalistic coll.

boil one's lobster. To leave the Church for the Army: mid-C.18–early 19: military. i.e. exchange black garb for red uniform, as lobsters change colour in cooking.

boil over. To fly into a rage: coll, from ca 1850.

boiled. Boiled beef or mutton: coll, since ca 1840. Dickens, 1848, 'A great piece of cold boiled.'

Boiled Bell (or **b.-b.**). Port Glasgow: nautical, esp. by Greenock men: mid-C.19–20. Bowen, 'The reference is to a traditional bell . . . painted so much that it would not ring'; the paint had to be boiled off.

boiled lobster, see LOBSTER, BOILED.

boiled owl, drunk as a. Extremely drunk: from the early 1880s. Why? Ware thinks that it may be a corruption of *drunk as Abel Boyle*.

boiled stuff. Collectively for harlots: ca 1580–1630; as in Shakespeare's *Cymbeline*. Prob. extremely rare outside of *Cymbeline*.

boiler. Abbr. POT-BOILER. 2. At Winchester College, until ca 1910, a *four and sixpenny boiler* was actually a large, plain coffee-pot used for heating water, from, not the price, but the amount of milk they held; and a *τὸ πᾶν boiler* – lit. a whole-lot boiler – was a large saucepan-like vessel in which water for BIDETS was heated. 3. A hat: Public Schools': ca 1880–1915.

boilers. At the Royal Military Academy, from ca 1880, boiled potatoes. cf. GREASERS.

***boiling.** A discovery, a betrayal: c. of ca 1600–59. Ex BOIL.

boiling, the whole. The whole lot: 1822, 'A Real Paddy', *Real Life in Ireland*. Common also in U.S. (*the boiling*, 1796). Ex *boiling*, a quantity of food boiled at the one time: cf. S.E. *batch*. Also cf. *the whole* SHOOT.

boiling point, at (the). About to fly into a rage: from ca 1880; coll. Adumbrated by Emerson.

***boke.** The nose: a late C.19–20 c. variant of BOCO.

boko, see BOCO. **boko-smasher,** see BOCO-SMASHER.

bold as a miller's shirt. Explained by its frequent appendage, *which every day takes a rogue by the collar*. Coll: C.18–early 19.

bold as brass. Presumptuous; shameless: from ca 1780; coll. George Parker; Thackeray, 1846, 'He came in as bold as brass'. cf. BRASS, 2.

bold boat. A seaworthy ship: nautical coll: mid-C.19–20. Bowen has also a *bold hawse,* 'said of a ship when her hawse pipes are well out of the water'. Both phrases verge on j.

boldrumptious. Presumptuous: late C.19–early 20. Ex *bold* + RUMPUS + the *-tuous* of *presumptuous*.

boler, see BOWLER.

bollicky, see BALLOCKY. **Bollicky Bill,** see BALLOCKY BILL THE SAILOR.

bollocks, see BALLOCK and BALLOCKS, 2.

bolly. At Marlborough College: pudding, esp. if boiled; from ca 1860; ob. cf. the North Country *boily*, gruel. Both, prob. ex Fr. *bouillie*.

bolo, v. To speak; esp. *bolo the* BAT, to speak the language, and therefore = SLING (or *spin*) *the bat*: Regular Army: late C.19–20. Ex Hindustani.

bolster-pudding. A roly-poly pudding: non-aristocratic: late C.19–20. Ex shape.

bolt. The throat: early C.19; mainly Cockney. Moncrieff in *Tom and Jerry*. Perhaps ex †*bo(u)lt*, a flour-sieve. 2. A rupture, gen. incompletely honourable, with a political party: coll: orig. (—1840) U.S.; accepted in England as a coll, ca 1860.

bolt, v. To escape; depart hastily: C.17–20. In C.17 S.E.; ca 1710–80, coll; ca 1780–1870, s.; then coll, then in C.20, again S.E. In Moncrieff and Barham it is wholly s.; the latter having 'Jessy ransack'd the house, popp'd her breeks on, and when so | Disguis'd, bolted off with her beau – one Lorenzo.' 2. v.t., to eat hurriedly, without chewing; gulp down: coll: from ca 1780. Grose, 1785; Wolcot, 1794; Dickens, 1843. With the speed of a bolt. 3. To break with a political party (*bolt from*): orig. (1813) U.S., anglicized ca 1860 as a coll.

bolt, butcher and. A political c.p. applied contemporaneously to the Egyptian policy of 1884–5.

***bolt, get the.** To be sentenced to penal servitude: c.; from ca 1840. Influenced by BOAT, n. and v.

***Bolt-in-Tun, go to the.** To bolt, run away: c.; from ca 1810; †. Ex a famous London inn. A play on the v. BOLT. Also, as c.p., *the Bolt-in-Tun is concerned* (Vaux): †by 1890.

bolt of it, make a shaft or a; gen. a bolt or a shaft. To risk this or that issue; accept a risk: ca 1590–1750; coll >, by 1660, S.E. Shakespeare; Fuller.

Bolt Street, turn the corner of. To run away: low coll: from ca 1880; ob. Ex *make a bolt for it*.

bolt the moon. To depart with one's goods without paying the rent: C.19–20; ob. cf. MOONLIGHT FLIT.

bolt upright. An emphasis-tag: mostly Cockneys': from ca 1880. e.g. 'I'll be damned, bolt upright.'

bolter. In c., one who, for fear of arrest, hides in his own house: C.18. Dyche, 1748. 2. One restive under authority: coll: from ca 1850; ob. cf. Fr. *rouspéteur*. 3. One who leaves his political party: coll: orig. (1812) U.S.; anglicized ca 1870 as a coll.

bolter of the Mint, or of White Friars. One who may peep out but does not, for fear of arrest, venture abroad. Prob. orig. c.: ca 1690–1800.

boltsprit, bowsprit. Late C.17–18, C.19–20 (ob.) resp.: the nose. Until ca 1770, low. Shadwell; B.E., '*He has broke his Boltsprit*, he has lost his Nose with the Pox.'

bolus. An apothecary; a physician: late C.18–20, ob. Ex *bolus*, a large pill.

***boman.** A gallant fellow: c.: C.17–18. See quotation at POP, n., 3. Prob. ex *beau man*. Also as adj.

***boman ken.** A variant of *bowman ken*: see BOB KEN.

***boman prig.** An expert thief: c.: late C.17–early 19.

Bombay duck. That Indian fish which, alive, is called the *bummalo*, whence, by the Law of Hobson-Jobson, the present anomaly (cf. WELSH RABBIT): at first (C.18) coll; by 1890 S.E. Cordiner in his C.18 *Voyage to India*.

Bombay oyster. A glass of milk containing a double dose of castor-oil: training-ships': late C.19–20. Bowen.

Bombay Rock. Bombareck in India: nautical: 1812, Morier.

bombo, see BUMBO.

bom'deer. A bombardier: military coll (—1887).

bona. A girl; a belle: C.19–20, ob.; low, prob. a reminiscence of BONA-ROBA. cf. DONA.

bona, adj. Good; pleasant, agreeable: theatre and circus s., from ca 1850. e.g. in Thomas Frost's *Circus Life*, 1875. cf. BONO.

bona, adv. Very: Parlary: since ca 1860. (P. H. Emerson, *Signor Lippo*, 1893.) Ex the adj.

bona roba, bona-roba. A harlot, esp. a showy one: late C.16–early 19; in C.18–19, archaic and S.E. Shakespeare, Jonson, Cowley, Scott. Ex It. *buona roba*, lit. a fine dress.

bonanza. A stroke of fortune; a prosperous enterprise. Orig. (1847) U.S., a rich mine – perhaps ex an actual Nevada mine. Accepted in England as a coll, ca 1895, and as S.E., ca 1910. Ultimately, via the Sp. *bonanza*, prosperity, ex L. *bonus*, good.

bonce; occ. **bonse.** The head: schoolboys': from ca 1870. Ex *bonce* (—1862), a large marble.

bone. A subscriber's ticket for the Opera: London: C.19; †by 1887. Ex Fr. *abonnement*, subscription. 2. (Always *the bone.*) The thin man: London: 1882–ca 1910. 3. (*The bone.*) The *penis erectus*: Cockneys'; mid-C.19–20.

***bone,** v. To seize, arrest; rob, thieve; make off with. From ca 1690; until ca 1830 (witness B.E., Dyche, Grose (2nd ed.), Vaux), c. As s., it appears in Dickens, 1838, and Miss Braddon, 1861; see *Words!* and cf. MAKE; NAB; WIN. 'Perhaps from the dog making off with the bone', W.

***bone,** adj. Good; excellent: c.; from ca 1850; ob. Mayhew, 1851. Ex Fr. *bon* or It. *buono*. Opp. GAMMY. cf. BONA and BONO.

bone, dry or **hard as a.** Free from moisture: coll (—1833) >, by 1890, S.E.

bone-ache. Venereal disease, esp. in men: late C.16–17; coll verging on S.E. Nashe, Shakespeare.

bone-baster. A staff or cudgel: coll: late C.16–mid-17.

bone-box. The mouth: late C.18–20, low. Grose, 1st ed. Contrast BONE-HOUSE.

bone-breaker. Fever and ague: lower classes': late C.19–20; ob.

bone-cleaner. A servant: late C.19–20; ob. cf. BONE-PICKER, 1.

bone-crusher. A large-calibre rifle: sporting; from ca 1850; ob. Stanley's *Livingstone*, 1872.

bone-grubber. A scavenger and seller of bones from refuse-heaps and -tins: coll; from ca 1850, the word occurring in Henry Mayhew. cf. the C.18 *grubber*. 2. A resurrectionist: ca 1820–60. 3. Hence, anyone having to do with funerals; esp. a mute: from ca 1860; ob.

bone-house. The human body: coll, from ca 1860; ob. 2. A charnel-house: from ca 1820; ob. 3. A coffin: coll: from the 1790s; †by 1890.

bone in any one's hood, put a. To cut off his head: C.16–early 17; facetious coll.

bone in the mouth, carry a. (Of a ship) to make the water foam before her, 'cut a feather': nautical coll: C.19–20; ob. Bowen prefers *bone in her teeth*.

bone in the throat, have a; occ. leg, arm,

etc. C.16–20, coll, the *throat* form (app. †by 1800) occurring in Udall, 1542, the *arm* in Torriano, 1666, the *leg* in Swift, ca 1708 (printed 1738): a humorous excuse; a feigned obstacle.

bone-lazy. Extremely indolent: coll: from 1890s. Ex LAZY-BONES on S.E. *bone-idle*.

bone-picker. A footman: late C.18–19, coll in the latter. Because frequently he has to eat leavings. 2. A collector and seller of bones, rags, and other refuse from the streets and garbage-tins: from ca 1850: coll >, by 1910, S.E. Ruskin, *Crown of Wild Olives*, 1866.

bone-polisher. A CAT-O'-NINE-TAILS (1848); its wielder (1857): nautical.

bone-setter. A horse hard in the riding; a rickety conveyance: mid-C.18–early 19. Ironical pun on *bone-setter*, a surgeon. cf. BONE-SHAKER.

bone-shake. To ride one of the early bicycles: ca 1867–1910.

bone-shaker. The early bicycle: from 1865 or 1866. The first bicycle to be cranked and pedalled was ridden in Paris in 1864; England followed suit most enthusiastically. These old bicycles lacked indiarubber tyres and were very heavy; as late as 1889 a 'safety roadster' weighed 36 pounds, but as early as 1870–71 'the low, long bone-shaker began to fall in public esteem'. cf. BONE-SETTER.

bone-shop. A workhouse: lower classes' (—1909); slightly ob.

bone-sore *or* **-tired.** Very idle: coll, now verging on S.E.: from 1880s. Ex dial. cf. BONE-LAZY.

bone the sweeter the meat, the nearer the, see MEAT, THE NEARER . . .

bone with, pick a. (Occ. *bones.*) To have an unpleasant matter to settle with someone: coll: mid-C.16–20.

bone-yard. A cemetery: Canadian: late C.19–20.

boner. A sharp blow on the spine: Winchester College, mid-C.19–20; ob. 2. See BONERS.

boner nochy! Good night!: Clerkenwell (London), which contains many Italians: late C.19–20. Ex the It. for 'good-night!', though *nochy* more closely resembles Sp. *noche*.

boners. A form of punishment: Charterhouse: †before 1900. A. H. Tod, *Charterhouse*, 1900. cf. BONER, 1.

bones. Dice: C.14–20; coll in C.14–15, thereafter S.E. 2. Bones played castanet-wise (—1590): coll, but very soon S.E. 3. A player of the bones: from ca 1840; coll. 4. The human teeth: C.19–20; ob. 5. A surgeon: C.19; abbr. SAWBONES. 6. Something very good, orig. tasty; almost an adj.: from ca 1880; ob. Coll. Tupper. Prob. = L. *bonus*, good.

bones!, by these ten. A coll asseveration: late C.15–early 17. Shakespeare. An allusion to one's fingers (cf. *by this hand I witness*). cf. the late C.16 exclamation *bones a* (or *of*) *me* (or *you*)*!*

bones, feel a thing in one's. To have an idea; feel sure: coll; 1875 (O.E.D. Sup.); by 1910, S.E. Ex *be in one's bones*, to be felt as certain: itself S.E. verging on coll.

bones, make no. To hesitate not; make no scruple: C.16–20; coll. Udall, Greene, Wycherley, Thackeray. In C.15–16 the more gen. phrase was *find no bones* (*in the matter*): this – along with *without more bones*, without further obstacle, delay, discussion (late C.16–19) – would indicate that the reference is to bones in soup or stew.

bones, sleep on, see SLEEP ON BONES.

bones of, be upon the. To attack: late C.17–18, low. L'Estrange (d. 1704): 'Puss had a month's mind to be upon the bones of him, but was not willing to pick a quarrel.'

***bongy,** drunk, in the anon. *Street-Robberies Consider'd*, 1728, is prob. a misprint for *bousy*, BOOZY.

Boniface. The landlord of an inn or a country tavern: C.18–20, ex the bonny-faced, jovial inn-keeper in Farquhar's lively comedy, *The Beaux' Stratagem*, 1707. The first record, however, of the generic use is not until 1803, and by 1850 the term was considered S.E.

bonk. A short, steep hill: circus s.; from ca 1840; ob. C. Hindley, *Adventures of a Cheap Jack*, 1876. Adopted from dial.

bonner. A bonfire: Oxford undergraduates': from late 1890s. 'Oxford *-er*.' Perhaps in allusion to 'Bishop Bonner, who certainly lit up many bonfires – Smithfield way', Ware.

***bonnet, bonneter.** —1812, —1841 resp., both c. in origin: a gambling cheat or decoy; a decoy at auctions. Possibly 'a reminiscence of Fr. *deux etes dans un bonnet*, hand and glove', W. cf. 2, a pretext or a pretence: Vaux, *Flash Dict.*, 1812; orig. c.; †by 1890. 3. A woman (cf. PETTICOAT; SKIRT): ca 1870–1900; coll.

bonnet, v. Act as a decoy (see the n.); cheat; illicitly puff: C.19–20, low; ob. 2.

To crush a man's hat over his eyes: coll (1837; ob.); Dickens often uses the word; vbl n. not uncommon either. 3. See BONNET FOR.

bonnet, have a bee in one's, see BEE IN . . .

bonnet, have a green. To go bankrupt: C.18–19; coll. Ramsay – in fact it is mainly Scottish. Ex the green cap formerly worn by bankrupts.

bonnet-builder. A milliner: coll (—1839); ob. Jocular.

***bonnet for.** To corroborate the assertions of, put a favourable construction on the actions of: c. of ca 1810–70. cf. BONNET, v., 1.

bonnet-laird. A petty proprietor: Scots coll: ca 1810–60. 'As wearing a bonnet, like humbler folk', F. & H. (revised).

bonnet-man. A Highlander: coll verging on S.E.: C.19. cf. KILTIE.

bonneter. A decoy (see BONNET, n., 1). 2. A crushing blow on the hat: ca 1840–1910.

bonnets so blue. Irish stew: rhyming s. (—1859); ob.

bonny-clabber, -clapper, -clatter, -clab-(b)o(r)e. Sour butter-milk: coll: C.17–18. Jonson, 1630. Ex Irish *baine*, milk + *claba*, thick.

bono, adj. Good: Parlary: from ca 1840. Via Lingua Franca. cf. BONA.

bono-Johnny. An Englishman: London's East End (—1890) and 'pidgin' English (—1909). Ex preceding. As it were 'honest John (Bull)'.

bono (h)omee (or **ommy).** Husband: Parlary: mid-C.19–20. For the elements, see BONO, good, and OMEE: cf. archaic S.E. *goodman*, husband.

bonse, see BONCE.

bonus. An additional dividend (—1808); money received unexpectedly or additionally: from ca 1770. Both senses were orig. money-market s.; by 1830, coll; by 1860, S.E. *Bonus* is mock-Latin for *bonum*, a good thing. cf. BUNCE.

boo to a goose, see BO TO A GOOSE.

boo-boo. The posteriors: children's: late C.19–20.

boobies' hutch. More gen. BOOBY'S HUTCH.

booby, beat the, see BEAT GOOSE.

booby-hutch. In late C.19–early 20 c. or low, a police station, a cell. 2. In C.18-early 19, it meant a one-horse chaise or a buggy. Also a leather bottle.

booby-trap. A practical joke of the jug-of-water-on-top-of-door kind: coll (—1850); after ca 1890, S.E.

booby's hutch. A barracks' drinking-point open after the canteen closes: military: ca 1860–1910. Ware, 'Satire . . . upon the fools who have never had enough'. cf. BOOBY-HUTCH.

boodle. Bribe(ry), illicit spoils, political perquisites, profits quietly appropriated, party funds – all these are *boodle*. Orig. (1858: Thornton) U.S.; anglicized ca 1890; in C.20, coll. Hence, money in general, with no reference to the illicit: coll; orig. (—1888) U.S.; > gen. in England ca 1900, but this sense has remained s. Etymology obscure: W. suggests Dutch *boedel*, estates, effects. 2. A stupid noodle: ca 1860–90. Kingsley, 1862. Perhaps a corruption of NOODLE.

***booget.** An itinerant tinker's basket: c. of ca 1560–1640. Perversion of †S.E. *budget*, a bag or wallet.

boohoo; boo-hoo. To weep noisily: coll: from 1830s. Echoic.

book. (Sporting.) A BOOKMAKER'S arrangement of his bets on a given day's racing or other 'bookmaker-able' competition. (The bookmaker tries so to arrange his bets that he will be unlikely to lose.) Coll: from ca 1830; in *Henrietta Temple*, 1837, Disraeli, 'Am I to be branded because I have made half a million by a good book?' Hence, a betting-book: from ca 1850; coll. Both senses have, since 1900, been j. 2. A libretto: C.18–20, coll; the words of a play: from ca 1850; coll. 3. The first six tricks at whist (—1890), at bridge (—1910): these coll terms soon > j. 4. A bookmaker: Australian. Abbr. BOOKY. 5. A newspaper, a magazine: illiterate coll: since ca 1880.

book, v. Engage (a person) as a guest: coll (1872). 2. To pelt with books: schoolboys' (—1909). 3. To catch (a person) wrong-doing: Public Schools': from ca 1895. P. G. Wodehouse, *The Pothunters*, 1902, 'If he books a chap out of bounds it keeps him happy for a week.' 4. To understand, 'get the hang of': Public Schools': from late 1890s. ibid., 'There's a pane taken clean out. I booked it in a second as I was going past to the track.'

book, beside the. (Utterly) mistaken: from ca 1670; ob. Coll >, by 1700, S.E. Walker, 1672. cf. BESIDE THE LIGHTER.

book, bring to. Cause to show authority, genuineness; investigate; hence, detect: coll, C.19–20. Orig., to ask chapter and verse for a statement.

book, by (the). In set phrases: late C.16–

20; orig. coll but soon S.E. Shakespeare, 'You kisse by th' booke.'

book, drive to the. To make (someone) give sworn evidence: C.15–18: coll soon S.E.

book, know one's. To come to a decision; see one's potential advantage: coll; from ca 1880; ob.

book, let run for the. (Of a bookmaker) not to be against a horse: from ca 1870.

book, out of one's. Mistaken(ly): C.16–17; coll, soon S.E. Latimer.

book, speak like a. To talk excellent sense: informatively, accurately: coll; from ca 1840; prob. from U.S., where '*talk* like a book' occurs as early as 1829.

book, suit one's. To be opportune, very suitable: coll (—1851) >, by 1890, S.E. Prob. ex betting.

book, take a leaf out of a person's. To follow his (gen. his good) example: C.18–20; coll till C.20, when S.E.

book, without. Late C.17–20; occ. *without his book*. Without authority; from memory. Orig. coll, soon S.E.

book-boy. A native 'shipped in certain ships on the West African trade to help the officers tally cargo': nautical coll verging on j.: late C.19–20. Bowen.

book-form. Theoretical form, at first of horses; coll (—1880).

'book!' he says; and can't read a paper yet. A c.p. of ca 1890–1914, addressed to one who has explosively broken wind.

book-holder. A prompter: theatrical (—1864); ob. by 1890.

book-keeper. 'One who never returns borrowed books', Grose (2nd ed.), who speaks feelingly: coll; late C.18–early 19. Punning one who keeps accounts.

book of (the) words. A catalogue: jocular coll: from ca 1880. 2. A libretto: id.: from ca 1890.

book-pad, v.t. and i. To plagiarize: pedantic after FOOT-PAD: ca 1680–1730.

book-work. Oxford and Cambridge: memorizable matter in mathematics: ca 1845–90 as s.; then coll, by 1910 S.E., for any 'SWOTtable' learning.

booka. Hungry: Regular Army: late C.19–20. Ex Hindustani *bhukha*.

booked, ppl adj. Destined; caught; disposed of. Coll (—1839), orig. low. Brandon, Hood, Jas. Payn. cf. BOOK, v.

bookie, see BOOKY.

bookmaker. A professional taker of the odds at races of any sort. (Contrast with the professional PUNTER, 2, who deposits money, i.e. backs a horse, with the bookmaker and who bets only on certain races.) He keeps a book (lays the odds) and operates from a stand on the course or from an office. (—1862) coll; by 1880, S.E. Hence a *bookmaker's pocket* (a sporting coll), a breast-pocket, inside the waistcoat, for notes of high denomination: from ca 1850.

bookmaker's pocket, see BOOKMAKER.

books. A pack of cards: C.18–20. Mrs Centlivre. cf. DEVIL'S BOOKS.

books, get or make. To make the highest score: coll (—1890); slightly ob.

books, in a person's good or **bad.** In favour, or disfavour, with him: coll; C.19–20. In C.16–18, the phrase was *in* or *out of a person's books*: coll > S.E., though Grose has it.

***books, plant the.** 'To place the cards in the pack in an unfair manner', *Lex. Bal.*: c. of ca 1810–70.

books, shut the. To cease from business operations: coll (—1858); ob.

booky, often **bookie.** (In all such words, the *-y* form is preferable.) A BOOKMAKER: sporting s.: 1881, says Ware. See *Slang* at pp. 241–7 for a dialogue in bookies' s. 2. A bouquet: low coll, mostly Cockney (—1887).

booky, adj. Bookish: from ca 1880; coll. Presumably from U.S., where used as early as 1833.

boom. A rush of (esp. commercial) activity; effective launching of any goods or stocks; vigorous support of a person. Orig. (—1875) U.S.; anglicized as a coll ca 1883. 2. 'Pushing, by vigorous publicity, a person, game, or book': from ca 1890: coll till ca 1905, then S.E. There was, e.g., a Trilby boom in 1896–97.

boom, v.i. and t. To go, set, off with a rush, at first of a ship, then in commerce, then in publicity. In its fig. and mod. senses, orig. (1850) U.S.; accepted as coll in England ca 1885, in C.20 S.E. Perhaps ex some such phrase as '*a ship comes booming*, "she comes with all the sail she can make"' (*Sea Dict.*, 1708): W.

boom off, top one's. To start: nautical: prob. from ca 1810. 2. **top your boom!** see TOP . . .

boom-passenger. A convict on board ship: nautical, ca 1830–60. Convicts were chained to, or took exercise on, the booms.

boomer. One who booms an enterprise: coll, from ca 1890. Orig. U.S. (—1885). 2. In Australia, a very large kangaroo, esp. if a male; in its earliest spelling (1830), *boomah*. Soon > coll. Ex BOOM, v. 3. Whence, anything very large: coll: 1885; slightly ob.

booming. Flourishing; successful. Coll, in England from ca 1890; orig. (—1879) U.S. 2. Large: Australian: from ca 1860.

boomlet. A little BOOM: Stock Exchange coll: from mid-1890s; Ware dates it at 1896. cf.:

boomster. One who booms stock: money-market coll (1898). Ex U.S.

boon-companion. A drinking(-bout) companion; 'a good fellow': 1566, Drant: coll >, by C.18, S.E. Whence *boon-companionship*, Nashe, 1592; in C.18–20, S.E.

boord(e), see BORD(E).

boorish, the. Illiterate speech: C.17. Shakespeare.

boose, see BOOZE. **boos(e)y,** see BOOZY.

boost. Vigorous support; 'push up'. Orig. (1825) U.S., anglicized ca 1865. Ex:

boost, v. To support vigorously; 'push' enthusiastically, significantly. Orig. (1825), U.S.; anglicized ca 1860. Origin obscure: ?ex *boot* + *hoist*.

boot. Money; an advance on wages: tailors' and shoemakers'; late C.19–20.

boot, v. To thrash; punish with a strap: military, C.19–20; ob. At first with a jack-boot. 2. To kick, e.g. 'I booted him good and hard': coll: from ca 1880. 3. Hence (gen. *boot out*), to dismiss, get rid of: 1902.

boot, give or **get the.** To dismiss; be dismissed: s. (1888, Rider Haggard).

boot-catch(er). An inn servant who pulls off guests' boots: C.18–early 19. The longer form, the more gen., is in Swift and Grose.

boot-eater. A juror who would rather 'eat his boots' than find a person guilty: 1880; ob. Coll.

boot is on the other leg, the. The case is altered; the responsibility is another's: coll; C.19–20, ob.

boot-jack. A general-utility actor: theatrical (—1895). Ex a boot-jack's usefulness.

boot-joe. Musketry drill: military: mid-C.19–early 20. Why?

boot-lick. To toady (to); undertake 'dirty' work (for): coll. Ex U.S. (1845), anglicized in the 1880s.

boot-licker. A toady; a doer of 'dirty' work: coll (—1890). The U.S. form is *boot-lick*.

boot-neck. A Royal Marine: naval: mid-C.19–20; ob. Bowen; F. & Gibbons, 'From the tab closing the tunic collar'. cf. LEATHER-NECK.

boot out, see BOOT, v., 3.

boot serve for either leg, make one. To speak, rarely to act, ambiguously: C.16–17; coll > S.E.

***booth.** A house, as in HEAVE *a booth*, rob a house: mid-C.16–19 c.

booth-burster. A noisy actor: from ca 1870; ob. cf. BARN-STORMER and:

booth-star. A leading actor (or actress) in a booth or a minor theatre: theatrical coll (—1909); ob.

bootie (or -y). Beautiful: Society girls': ca 1840–80. Diprose's *Book about London*, 1872. cf. nursery *bootiful* or *booful*.

boots. The youngest officer in a mess: military: late C.18–20. 2. A servant, gen. a youth, affected to the cleaning of boots: late C.18–20; from ca 1820, coll; post-1850, S.E. 3. See LAZY- and SLY-BOOTS, where *boots* = a fellow.

boots!, bet your, see BET YOUR BOOTS.

boots, buy old. To marry, or keep, another's cast-off mistress: C.18–19; coll. cf. *ride in a person's old* BOOTS.

boots, go to bed in one's, see BED IN . . .

boots, have one's heart in one's. To be much afraid: C.19–20, coll. In C.17–18, *wish one's heart* . . .

boots, in one's. At work; still working; not in bed. Gen. with *die*. Coll mid-C.19–20. In S.E., *die in one's boots* or *shoes* is to be hanged. 2. Very drunk: late C.19–20; ob.

boots, like old. Vigorously, thoroughgoingly: coll, C.19–20. Lit., like the devil. Variant with *as*: Miss Bridgman, 1870, 'She's as tough as old boots.'

boots!, not in these. Certainly not!: c.p. of ca 1867–1900.

boots, – over shoes, over. adj. and adv.: recklessly persistent: coll, ca 1640–1820.

boots, ride in (a person's) **old.** 'To marry or keep his cast-off mistress', Grose, 2nd ed.: late C.18–mid-19. cf. BOOTS, BUY OLD.

booty. Playing booty: C.17–18. See:

booty, play. To play falsely; covertly to help one's apparent opponent: C.16–19. Until ca 1660, c.; then s. merging into coll; from ca 1790, S.E. As in Dekker, Fielding, Scott, Disraeli.

booty-fellow. A sharer in plunder: see preceding entry. C.17–early 19. Coll.

***booze** (C.18–20), rarely **booz** (late C.17–18); **boose** (C.18–20); **bouze** (C.16–20, as is, also, **bouse**); **bowse** (C.16–20); **bowze** (C.18). (The O.E.D.'s quotation of ca 1300 prob. refers to a drinking vessel.) Drink, liquor: c. (—1567) until C.19, then low s. Ex v., 1. 2. Hence, a draught of liquor:

late C.17–20. 3. (Also ex sense 1.) A drinking-bout: 1786, Burns: low s. >, by ca 1850, gen. s. > by 1900, coll.

***booze,** etc., v. To drink, esp. heavily; tipple: (in C.14, S.E.; it reappears as c. in mid-) C.16–20: status thenceforth as for n. Harman, Nashe, B.E., Colman, Grose, Thackeray. Perhaps ex Dutch *buizen* (low Ger. *busen*) to drink to excess. 2. Hence *booze* (etc.) *it*, mostly C.17, always c., and v.t., C.17–20, e.g. in Harington. 3. v.t. To spend or dissipate in liquor: mid-C.19–20. Often *booze away* (e.g. a fortune).

booze, on the. On a prolonged drinking bout: low (—1889) >, by 1910, coll.

booze-fencer or **-pusher.** A licensed victualler: low London: from ca 1880; ob.

booze one's (or the) jib or **tip;** also **booze up.** (Nautical) to drink heavily; tipple: 1837, Marryat; ob.

booze-out. A meal, esp. a good 'feed': Naval: from ca 1870; ob.

booze-shunter. A beer drinker: orig. (—1870), railwaymen's: from ca 1870, gen. public-house; slightly ob.

booze-up. A drinking bout: low: late C.19–20. *Sessions*, 26 Oct. 1897.

boozed, etc., ppl adj. Drunk: C.19–20, low. P. Crook, in *The War of Hats*, 1850, 'Boozed in their tavern dens, | The scurril press drove all their dirty pens.'

boozed-up. A late C.19 variant of the preceding.

boozer, etc. A drunkard (—1611): low. Cotgrave, Wolcot, Thackeray. 2. A public-house: chiefly Australian and New Zealand (—1914); also (1895) English c. and low s. *People*, 6 Jan. 1895.

boozing, etc., vbl n. Heavy drinking; guzzling: C.16–20, low. Until ca 1660, c. Harman, Nashe, Head, G. Eliot. 2. Also, adj.: C.16–20: same remarks. Addicted to drink.

***boozing cheat.** A bottle: c.; C.17–18 (?earlier). See CHEAT.

***boozing-glass.** A wine-glass; a tumbler: c.; C.17–early 19.

***boozing ken.** A drinking den; an alehouse: c.; mid-C.16–mid-19.

***boozington;** or, in derisive address, **Mr Boozington.** A drunkard: Australian c.; ca 1860–1910. Prob. after LUSHINGTON.

boozy, etc. Drunken, esp. if mildly; showing the marks of drink: C.16–20, ob.; low. Skelton, in his famous poem of the drunken Eleanor, 'Droupy and drowsie, | Scurvy and lousie, | Her face all bowsie'; Dryden, in his *Juvenal*, 'Which in his cups the bowsy poet sings'; Thackeray, in *The Book of Snobs*, 'The boozy unshorn wretch'. (The earliest spellings of the *booze* group are in *-use*, *-uze*; the *-oze* form seems not to occur before C.18.)

bor, gen. in vocative. Mate, friend: on the borders of dial. (Eastern counties of England), Romany (properly *ba*), and provincial s.: C.19–20. cf. Middle High Ger. *bur*.

borachio. A drunkard: coll: late C.17–early 19. Also, perhaps earlier, as noted by B.E., a skin for holding wine: coll. Ex It. or Sp. The Parlary form is *borarco*.

borak, see '2' in:

borak, poke. To impart fictitious news to a credulous person; to jeer. v.t. with *at*. Australian (—1885), ex a New South Wales Aborigine word. 2. **borak,** banter, fun, occurs independently in 1845.

borarco, see BORACHIO.

bord, see BORD(E).

bord you! (Properly, no doubt, *board you*.) C.19. Nautical, in drinking: my turn next!

***bord(e).** In c. of mid-C.16–18, a shilling. Perhaps ex *bord*, a shield. 2. Whence *half borde*, a sixpence.

bordeaux. Blood: boxing, ca 1850–1910. cf. BADMINTON and esp. CLARET.

bordello. A brothel: late C.16–18; coll.

bore. Ennui (1766). 2. A boring thing, an annoyance (1778). Prob. ex next entry. 3. A wearying, an uncongenial, person (—1785): Grose. Until ca 1820, the second and third senses were coll, thereafter S.E.; the first hardly outlived the C.18; the rare sense, 4, a bored, a listless person, arose in 1766 and soon died. Of the third, Grose remarks that it was 'much in fashion about the years 1780 and 1781'; it again > fashionable ca 1810.

bore, v. To weary a person (1768); coll. In C.19–20, S.E. Perhaps ex *bore*, an instrument for boring; cf. A.-S. *borian*, to pierce.

Borealis. Abbr. *Aurora Borealis*: late C.18–20: coll >, by 1850, S.E.

boretto-man. A sodomite: s.: Ned Ward, 1703.

born call. Sound reason: Australian coll (now rare): 1890, Mrs Campbell Praed, *The Romance of a Station*.

born days, in (all) one's. In one's lifetime; ever: coll: 1742, Richardson.

born in a barn?, were you. A c.p. directed at someone who leaves a door open: late C.19–20.

born in a mill. Deaf: coll: ca 1570–1700. Whetstone, 1578; Ray, 1678. i.e. deafened by the noise of a mill working at top speed.

born under a threepenny-halfpenny planet (, never to be worth a groat). Extremely unsuccessful: C.17–19; coll.

born weak. Nautical, of a vessel: weakly built. From ca 1850; ob.

born with a silver spoon in one's mouth, see SILVER SPOON . . .

born with the horn. A coarse c.p., applied to a lecher: late C.19–20. A rhyme on HORN, 4.

born yesterday, not. Esp. 'I wasn't born yesterday' (not a fool): c.p. late C.19–20.

borough-monger. A rabbit: rare Scottish: C.19. Pun on *burrow*.

borrow. To steal: jocularly coll: from ca 1880.

borrow trouble. To seek trouble; to anticipate it unnecessarily or very unwisely: coll: from the 1890s.

***bos-ken.** A farm-house: mid-C.19–20 vagrants' c. Mayhew, 1851. Ex L. *bos*, an ox; *ken*, a place or house. cf.:

***bos-man.** A farmer: mid-C.19–20 c. (vagrants'). Ex Dutch. Etymology disputable, but cf. BOS-KEN.

bose. Abbr. *bo'sun*, itself an eligible slurring of *boatswain*. Both are nautical, the former dating from (?)the late C.19, the latter from (?)the late C.18. The former is often used in addressing that link between officers and deck-hands.

bosh. Trash; nonsense: 1834. Coll after ca 1860. Ex Turkish (for 'empty', 'worthless'); popularized by Morier's *Ayesha* and later novels. 2. Hence, as interjection: nonsense!: 1852; coll after ca 1870. Dickens in *Bleak House*. 3. In vagrants' c., a fiddle: see BOSH-FAKER. 4. Butterine; oleomargarine; similar substitutes for butter: lower official English (—1909); ob. Ex sense 1. 5. An impressive figure, esp. in CUT A BOSH: c.: C.18–early 19.

bosh, v. To spoil; mar: 1870; ob. Ex the n., 1. 2. Hence, to humbug, make fun of (—1883), as in Miss Braddon's *Golden Calf*. 3. Cut a dash: coll; from ca 1709; †. Ex Fr. *ébauche*, via English *bosh*, an outline or rough sketch (—1751); †.

bosh, adj. Inferior; 'wretched' (e.g. *bosh boots*): from ca 1880; ob. Ex n., 1. cf. BOSHY.

bosh lines (the). (The) marionettes: showmen's: from ca 1855. Lit., violin strings.

***bosh-faker.** A violin-player: vagrants' c.; from ca 1850. In Romany, *bosh* is a violin; the use of *faker* as = *maker* is unusual.

boshman. The same as BOSH-FAKER: low or c. (—1865).

boshy, adj. Trashy; nonsensical: coll. (—1882; slightly ob.) Anstey in *Vice Versa*. cf. BOSH, n., 1.

bosken. Incorrect for BOS-KEN, as *bosman* perhaps is for BOS-MAN.

boskiness. Fuddlement; state of intoxication: from ca 1880; ob. Coll. Ex:

bosky. Dazed or fuddled; mildly drunk: 1730, Bailey; ob. Possibly dial., and perhaps ex *bosky*, wooded, bushy; though it 'may be perverted from Sp. *boquiseco*, dry mouthed', W., who, however, acutely adds that 'adjs. expressive of drunkenness seem to be created spontaneously.'

bosom friend. A body-louse: C.18–20. In proverbial form as *no friend like to a bosom friend, as the man said when he pulled out a louse*, Fuller, 1732 (Apperson). cf. BACKBITERS. An alternative form is *bosom chum*: military: late C.19–20.

boss. A fat woman: ca 1575–1650: coll. Lyly. Ex *boss*, a protuberance. 2. A master, owner, manager; leader; a SWELL: in these senses, orig. (1806), U.S.; anglicized ca 1850. In England the term has a jocular undertone; in Australia and New Zealand, it lacks that undertone. Ex Dutch *baas*, master. 3. (Gen. with *political*.) 'The leader of a corrupt following', Thornton: coll, orig. (—1908), U.S. and still applied rarely to politics outside of the U.S. 4. A short-sighted person; one who squints: mid-C.19–20, ob. ?ex Scots *boss*, hollow, powerless. 5. Hence (?), a miss, mistake, blunder: C.19–20, ob. cf. the v., 2.

boss, v. To be the master or the manager of; control, direct. Orig. (1856), U.S.; anglicized ca 1870, as in the *Athenaeum*, 9 March 1872, 'A child wishing to charge his sister with being the aggressor in a quarrel for which he was punished, exclaimed, "I did not boss the job; it was sister."' 2. To miss, v.t. and i.; to bungle; to fail in an examination: schoolboys' s. in the main: from ca 1870. Perhaps ex BOSS-EYED; cf. BOSS, adj., 3.

boss, adj. Chief, principal: orig. (1840), U.S.; anglicized ca 1875. 2. Pleasant; excellent; champion. Orig. (—1888), U.S.; anglicized ca 1895, but never very gen. 3. Short-sighted: Christ's Hospital (—1887). Abbr. BOSS-EYED. cf. BOSS, v., 2.

boss, have a. To have a look: schoolboys': from ca 1899. cf. BOSS-EYE(D).

boss-cockie. A farmer employing labour and himself working: Australian (—1898). Ex and opp. COCKATOO.

boss-eye. One who squints or has an injured eye: from ca 1880; ob. In a broadside ballad of ?1884. cf. BOSS, n., 4. Imm. ex:

boss-eyed, adj. With one eye injured; with a squint: from ca 1860. Baumann, 1887, notes the variant *bos-eyed.* Perhaps on † *boss-backed*, hump-backed.

boss-shot. A bad aim: see BOSS, n. and v., (to) miss. ca 1870–1914; extant in dial. cf. BOSS, n., 4, and BOSS-EYED.

bossers. Spectacles: ca 1870–1910. Prob. ex BOSS-EYED.

bossy, adj. Over-fond of acting as leader or of giving orders: late C.19–20. Ex (—1882) U.S.: cf. BOSS, n., 2, and v., 1.

Boston wait. (Gen. in pl.) A frog: jocular coll (—1769); †by 1850, except in dial. – and even there, now virtually †.

bostruchizer; occ. **-yzer.** A small comb for curling the whiskers: Oxford University: ca 1870–80. Prob. ex Gr. βόστρυχος, a ringlet.

bo'sun, see BOSE.

***botanical excursion.** Transportation, orig. and properly to Botany Bay, Australia: c.; ca 1820–70.

botanize, v.i. To go to Botany Bay as a convict: 1819, Scott, in a letter; †by 1890.

Botany Bay. 1, Worcester College, Oxford (1853); 2, a portion of Trinity College, Dublin (1841). The former in 'Cuthbert Bede', *Verdant Green*, the latter in Lever, *Charles O'Malley*. Because of their distance from (*a*) other colleges, (*b*) the rest of the college, the reference being to Botany Bay in New South Wales – so far from England. 3. In c., penal servitude: ca 1790–1900. Ex the famous penal settlement (1787–1867) at that place. cf. BOTANICAL EXCURSION and next two entries. 4. 'The Rotunda of *the Bank*; the Jobbers and Brokers there being for the most part those who have been absolved from *the house* opposite', Bee: London commercial: ca 1820–50.

Botany Bay, go to. To be transported as a convict: euphemistic coll: ca 1810–60.

Botany Bay fever. Transportation; penal servitude. ca 1815–60.

Botany-beer party. 'A meeting where no intoxicants are drunk': Society: ca 1882–1910. Ware.

botch. A tailor: mid-C.18–19. Grose, 2nd ed. Abbr. *botcher*. cf. SNIP. (In Whitby dial., a cobbler.)

both ends of the busk! A late C.18–early 19 toast. Ex the piece of whalebone stiffening the front of women's stays. cf. BEST IN CHRISTENDOM.

both sheets aft. With both hands in his pockets: nautical: late C.19–20.

bother, v. To bewilder (with noise); confuse, fluster: mostly Anglo-Irish: ca 1715–1850. Perhaps ex *pother*, but perhaps ex Gaelic. 2. Hence, to pester, worry: from ca 1740. v.i., to give trouble, make a fuss: from ca 1770. All senses are coll, as is *botheration* (1800), the act of bothering, a petty annoyance. Both *bother* and *botheration* are used as exclamations. 3. *I'm* or *I'll be bothered* is a disguised form of swearing (see BUGGER, v., 1): coll: prob. from the 1860s.

Botherams (-ums). The nickname of a latter-C.18 convivial society. 2. (Rare in singular.) Yellow marigolds: agricultural (—1909); ob. except in a few localities. They are 'difficult to get rid of'.

botheration, see BOTHER, 2. **botherment.** Variation of *botheration*: coll: early C.19–20; ob.

bothered!, I'm or **I'll be,** see BOTHER, 3.

bots, botts, the. Colic; belly-ache. From ca 1770; coll when not, as usually, dial. Orig., an animal disease caused by maggots.

bottle, on the. (Reared) by means of the feeding-bottle: coll in C.19.

bottle, over a. In a sociable way: from ca 1770: coll; in late C.19–20, S.E.

bottle, turn out no. To fail: sporting: from ca 1870; ob.

bottle-ache. Drunkenness; delirium tremens: mid-C.19–20; ob.

bottle-arse; bottle-arsed. (A person) 'broad in the beam': low coll: late C.19–20; ob. 2. (*bottle-arsed* only.) See:

bottle-arsed, adj. (Printers', concerning type) thicker at one end than at the other: coll: ca 1760–1910; in C.20, of type wider at the bottom than at the top. 2. See preceding.

bottle-boy. An apothecary's assistant; a doctor's page: coll: from ca 1855; slightly ob.

bottle-head, n. and adj. (A) stupid (fellow): the n., ca 1654; the adj. (variant, as in Grose, *bottle-headed*), ca 1690. Coll; in C.19–20, S.E. but archaic.

bottle-holder. A second at a boxing-match (1753; in C.20, ob.): coll. Smollett in *Count Fathom*, 'An old bruiser makes a good bottle-holder.' 2. Hence, a second, backer, supporter, adviser: Scott, *The Antiquary*, 1816: coll. *Punch* in 1851 had a cartoon of Palmerston as the 'judicious bottle-holder', for he gave much help to oppressed states; *bottle-holder* > his nickname. Whence *bottle-holding*: journalistic, ca 1860–1900, for support, backing.

bottle-nose. A person with a large nose: (low) coll: late C.19–20.

bottle of brandy in a glass. A glass of beer: ca 1885–1905. It didn't deserve a longer life.

bottle of smoke, pass the. To countenance a white lie: coll: Dickens, 1855: ob.

bottle of spruce. Twopence: rhyming s. on *deuce*, two. (—1859; ob.) 2. Nothing; almost nothing; (almost) valueless: non-aristocratic: late C.18–mid-19. Ex *spruce beer*, which was inferior.

bottle-screws. Stiff, formal curls: coll, ca 1800–40. Succeeded by CORKSCREWS.

bottle-sucker. Nautical, ca 1850–1914: an able-*b*odied *s*eaman, *b.s.* being humorously expanded.

bottle-tit or **-tom.** The long-tailed tit, from the shape of its nest: coll, from ca 1845.

bottle-up. To keep, hold back: C.17–20, coll; restrain (feelings): C.19–20, also coll. (Military) enclose, shut up: C.19–20; coll, but S.E. in C.20.

bottle-washer. Often *head cook and b.-w.* A factotum: jocular coll: 1876, C. Hindley, 'Fred Jolly being the head-cook and bottle-washer'.

bottled. 'Arrested, stopped, glued in one place': low coll: 1898; ob. Ware, who considers that it partly arises from the bottling-up, in Santiago, of the Spanish fleet by the U.S. squadron.

bottled up, be. To be fully engaged and so unable to accept any further engagements: low (—1887); ob. 2. See BOTTLE-UP.

bottom. The posteriors: 1794, Dr Darwin: coll. See *Slang*, p. 138. Ex lit. sense, as prob. is: 2. Capital, property: C.17, coll. 3. Stamina, GRIT: 1747; ob. Captain Godfrey, in *The Science of Defence*, was apparently the first to use the term in print, thus: '... Bottom, that is, wind and spirit, or heart, or wherever you can fix the residence of courage'. Little used after 1855, PLUCK taking its place. Semantically: that on which a thing rests, or that which is at the base, is dependable. 4. Spirit poured into a glass before water is added: coll; from ca 1850, Trollope having it in 1857, Theodore Martin as a v. in 1854.

bottom, at (the). In reality: coll in C.18, S.E. in C.19–20.

bottom, stand on one's own. To be independent: C.17–20; coll till ca 1800, then S.E.; cf. the proverbial *let every tub stand on its own bottom*: C.17–20.

bottom dollar, see BET YOUR BOOTS.

bottom facts. The precise truth: coll, from ca 1890, but not much used. Orig. (—1877) U.S.

bottom of, be at the. To be the actual, not merely the supposed, author or source of: coll in C.18, S.E. in C.19–20. Steele has the equivalent *be at the bottom on't*.

bottom of a woman's 'tu quoque', the. 'The crown of her head', Grose, 3rd ed.: late C.18–early 19. See TU QUOQUE.

bottom out, tale of a tub with the. 'A sleeveless frivolous Tale', B.E.: coll: late C.17–mid-18. cf. the title of Swift's masterpiece.

bottom out of, knock the. To overcome, defeat; expose (the fallacy of). Orig. (—1900) U.S.; anglicized ca 1905 as a coll.

bottom-wetter, see WET BOTTOM.

bottomer. In drinking, a draught or a gulp that empties the glass or tankard: C.19–20; coll.

bottomless pit. The female pudend: late C.18–early 19. (In S.E., hell: cf. Boccaccio's story about 'putting the devil in hell'.)

botty. An infant's posterior: orig. and mainly nursery. Mid-C.19–20; coll. Ex BOTTOM.

botty, adj. Conceited, swaggering: at first, and still chiefly racing s. (—1860) and dial. Lit., troubled with the botts (parasitic worms).

boughs, up in the. Much excited; in a passion. Coll; late C.17–early 19. B.E., Grose; the former has the variant *a-top of the house*.

***boufer.** A C.18 variant of BUFFER, a dog. C. Hitchin, *The Regulator*, 1718.

boughs, wide in the, see BOWS.

Bouguereau quality. Risky effeminacy: art-world coll (1884) >, by 1910, j.; ob. Ware notes that this Fr. painter (1825–1905) excelled in delicate presentation of the – mostly feminine – nude. Punning on BUGGER and Fr. *bougre*.

boule. 'A conversation in which anyone may join'; Charterhouse: ca 1860–1910. A. H. Tod. Ex Gr. βουλή, a council.

bounce. A boastful lie, a pretentious swagger: coll >, by 1800, S.E. (archaic in

C.20): Steele, 1714, 'This is supposed to be only a bounce.' Ex †*bounce*, the loud noise of an explosion. 2. Hence, an exaggeration: coll (—1765); as in Goldsmith, Whyte-Melville. 3. Impudence: coll; from ca 1850: as in *Blackwood's Magazine*, May 1880, 'The whole heroic adventure was the veriest bounce, the merest bunkum!' Adumbrated in Ned Ward in 1703. Ex senses 1, 2. 4. A boaster, swaggerer: from ca 1690. 5. Hence, a flashily dressed swindler: from ca 1800: low. All these five senses are practically †; the only operative extant one being that wholly C.20 *bounce*, = a bluffer, esp. if constitutional, regular or persistent. 6. Cherry brandy: low: from the 1890s. Prob. ex its exhilarating effect. 7. A big dog-fish: nautical: late C.19–20. Ex its bounding ways.

bounce, v.i. and t. To bluster, hector; boast; bully; scold: C.17–20; ob. Coll; but all except the last > S.E. ca 1750. 2. v.i. and (with *out of*) t., to lie (†), cheat, swindle: from ca 1750. Foote, 1762, 'If it had come to an oath, I don't think he would have bounced.' cf. the n., senses 4, 5. 3. To scold severely: coll (—1888). cf. sense 1 of the n.: semantically, 'blow up'. 4. To bluff (a person): military: late C.19–20. 5. To coït with (a woman): low: late C.19–20.

***bounce, give it to 'em upon the.** To escape from the police, even to extract an apology from them, by assuming an appearance of respectability and importance: c. of ca 1810–60.

bounce, on the. ('In continual spasmodic movement': S.E.: C.18–19. Hence:) Lively: ca 1850–1900; coll. 2. Hence, since ca 1850: as a, by attempting a, bluff; by rushing one.

bounceable, bouncible. Prone to boast; bumptious: ca 1825–1910; coll. Samuel Warren, 1830; 1849, Charles Dickens, who, eleven years earlier, uses the coll adv. *bounceably*. cf. n., 1, and v., 1.

bounceful. Arrogant; domineering: Cockney coll: ca 1850–90. Mayhew. Ex BOUNCE, n., 1, 3.

bouncer. A bully, swaggerer, blusterer: late C.17–19; coll. Ex BOUNCE, v., 1. 2. A cheat, swindler; also (—1839), a thief operating while bargaining with a shopkeeper (Brandon): from ca 1770, †; perhaps orig. c. Extant, however, is the nuance, a professional beggar: Cockneys': 1851, Mayhew; ob. E.D.D. 3. A liar: coll; ca 1755–1900, as in Foote's comedy, *The Liar*. Hence, a lie, esp. a big lie: from ca 1800; coll; ob. 4. Anything large (cf. BOUNCING): coll: late C.16–20; ob. Nashe, 1596, 'My Book will grow such a bouncer, that those which buy it must be faine to hire a porter to carry it after them in a basket.' 5. Naval, ca 1860–1914: a gun that 'kicks' when fired. 6. In c., a harlot's bully: C.19–20, ob. 7. A CHUCKER-OUT: public-house s. (1883, *Daily News*, 26 July) >, by 1910, coll. Perhaps orig. U.S.

bouncible, see BOUNCEABLE.

bouncing, n. A good scolding (—1885): coll. cf. BOUNCE, v., 3.

bouncing, adj. Big rather than elegant; lusty, vigorous; mid-C.16–20; coll, but after ca 1700, S.E. 2. Of a lie: C.19, coll. cf. *a* THUMPING *lie*.

***bouncing ben.** A learned man: c. (—1864).

***bouncing buffer.** A beggar: c. of ca 1820–60. Ainsworth, 1834.

***bouncing cheat.** A bottle: c. of ca 1720–1830. Ex the noise of drawn corks.

bound, I dare or **will be.** I feel certain: certainly: coll; from ca 1530; the *dare* form being rare after ca 1800.

bounder. A four-wheeler cab, a GROWLER: ca 1855–1900. 2. (University) a dog-cart: ca 1840–1900. 3. One whose manners or company are unacceptable: Cambridge University, from ca 1883. Lit., one who bounds 'offensively' about. 4. Hence, a vulgar though well-dressed man, an unwelcome pretender to Society, a vulgarly irrepressible person – gen. a man – within Society: from ca 1885.

***bounetter.** A fortune-telling cheat: C.19 c., mostly vagrants'. Brandon, 1839. Prob. a Gypsy corruption of BONNET(ER).

boung, see BUNG, n., 3. **boung-nipper,** see BUNG-NIPPER.

bous(e), bouz(e); bousy, etc., see BOOZE.

'bout. A coll abbr. of *about*: almost S.E. in C.13–18; but, esp. in words of command, e.g. *'bout turn*, it is mainly naval and military: C.19–20.

bouz. A variant of BOOZY.

bow. (Boating, competitive or otherwise) the rower sitting nearest to the bow: coll: from ca 1830.

bow, by the string rather than by the. By the most direct way: late C.17–18; coll > S.E.

bow, draw the long. To exaggerate; lie; from ca 1820; coll. Byron.

bow, shoot in another's. To practise an art not one's own: C.17–18: coll soon > S.E.

bow, two or many strings to one's. With

more resources than one, with an alternative: coll > S.E.; from ca 1550. In C.19–20, gen. in reference to suitors or sweethearts. Ex archery.

bow and arrow. A sparrow: rhyming s.: late C.19–20.

bow-catcher. A kiss curl: ca 1820–1900. Corruption of *beau-catcher*, which is a variant form.

bow-hand, (wide) on the, adv. and adj. Wide of the mark; inaccurate: C.17–18; coll soon > S.E.

bow up to the ear, draw the. To act with alacrity; exert oneself: coll; from ca 1850; ob.

bow-window. A big belly. From the 1830s. Marryat, 1840. Ex shape.

bow-windowed. Big-bellied: from the 1840s. Thackeray in *Pendennis*. Ex preceding.

bow-wow. A dog: jocular and nursery coll: from ca 1780. 1800, Cowper, 'Your aggrieved bow-wow'. Ex the bark. cf. MOO-COW, etc. 2. A lover, a 'dangler': mainly in India; from ca 1850. Ex his 'yapping'.

bow-wow mutton. Dog's flesh: ca 1780–1890. Grose, 1st ed. Ware, 1909, '(Naval) [Mutton] so bad that it might be dog-flesh'.

bow-wow shop. A salesman's shop in, e.g., Monmouth Street: late C.18–early 19. Grose, 2nd ed., 'So called because the servant (at the door) barks and the master bites'.

bow-wow word. An echoic word: from ca 1860. Academic coll (coined by Max Müller) >, by 1890, S.E. The (always S.E.) *bow-wow theory* is that of human speech imitating animal sounds.

bow-wows, go to the. To go to 'the dogs' (s.v. DOGS...); jocular coll: 1838, Dickens.

bowd-eaten. (Of biscuits) eaten by weevils: dial. (where gen. *boud*) and nautical coll: mid-C.19–20.

***bowl;** gen. **bowl-out.** A discovery, disclosure: c.: C.19. Ex cricket.

bowl a gallon. To do the HAT-TRICK: cricketers' at Eton: ca 1860–90. Thus, the bowler earned a gallon of beer.

bowl (or try) for timber. To propel the ball at the batsmen's legs: cricketers' coll: ca 1890–1914.

bowl off. To die: 1837, Dickens; †by 1900.

bowl out. To overcome, defeat, get the better of: from ca 1810. Ex cricket. 2. In c., gen. in passive, to arrest, try, and convict: C.19–20. 3. For the n., see BOWL.

bowl over. To defeat, worst; dumbfound (—1862). Ex skittles. Another variant (Dickens's) is *bowl down*, 1865.

bowl the hoop. Soup: rhyming s. (—1859); ob.

bowla, but gen. in pl **(bowlas)** or in pl used as singular. A round tart made of sugar, apple, and bread: ca 1820–1900; coll. Mayhew, 1851. ? ex the Anglo-Indian *bowla*, a portmanteau.

bowled. (Winchester College) 'ploughed' (s.v. PLOUGH, v.) in an examination. C.19–20, †. cf. CROPPLED.

bowler (1882); **bowler-hat** (1861); occ. **boler** (—1890). A stiff felt hat; fairly low in the crown and gen. black: coll. In its etymology, it was long regarded as a *bowl*-shaped hat, but it almost certainly derives ex the name of a London hatter.

bowles. Shoes: ca 1850–1910. ?ex *bowl-shaped.*

***bowman.** Excellent, adept; mostly *bowman* PRIG, 'an eminent Thief...; a dexterous Cheat', *A New Canting Dict.*, 1725: c. of ca 1720–1840. ?*beau* (fine). 2. Whence *bowman*, n., a thief: c. (—1823); †by 1890.

bowman, all's. All's safe: c.; from ca 1820; †by 1890. cf. BOB.

***bowman ken,** see BOB KEN.

bows, wide in the. 'With wide hips and posteriors', *Lex. Bal.*, where, as in Egan's Grose, *bows* is spelt *boughs*: nautical coll: ca 1810–70.

bows under(, with). Having too much work to do: nautical coll: late C.19–20. Ex a ship labouring in a heavy sea.

bowse, bowser, bowsy, etc., see BOOZE, etc.; but:

bowse, v. To haul hard, is nautical coll: C.19–20. Perhaps cognate with dial. *bowse*, to rush, as the wind.

bowse, in. In trouble: nautical coll: mid-C.19–20. Perhaps cf. dial. *bowse*, the recoil of a gust of wind against a wall.

bowsprit. The nose: see BOLTSPRIT. *Bowsprit in parenthesis, have one's*, to have one's nose pulled: C.19, orig. nautical (officers'). 2. The penis: low nautical: ca 1820–80.

bowyer. (Lit., a bowman: C.15+.) An exaggerator; a liar: mid-C.18–early 19. cf. *draw the long* BOW.

bowze, etc., see BOOZE, etc.

box. A small drinking-place: late C.17–18: coll. cf. the mod. Fr. *boîte*. 2. In

C.19 c., a prison cell. 3. (*the box.*) A coffin; esp. *put in the box*: military coll: late C.19–20. 4. A safe of the old-fashioned kind: c.: late C.19–20.

box, v. To take possession of, BAG: Winchester School, from ca 1850; ob. 2. Overturn in one's box, in reference to a watchman or a sentry (—1851, ob.); esp. *box a* CHARLEY. 3. To give a Christmas box: coll: from ca 1845; ob. 4. In C.19 racing c., esp. as *box carefully*: (of a bookie) to see that one's betting liabilities do not exceed one's cash in hand. 5. To mix (two flocks or herds): Australian and New Zealand pastoral coll: from ca 1870.

box, be in a. To be cornered; in a fix: coll, C.19–20, ob.

box, bring to, is the active form of *be in a* BOX. In W. N. Glascock, *The Naval Sketch-Book*, I, 1825.

box, in a or **the wrong.** Out of one's element, in a false position, in error. Coll, mid-C.16–20. In C.16, Ridley, Udall (J. not N.); later, Smollett, Marryat. 'The original allusion appears to be lost; was it to the boxes of an apothecary?', O.E.D.

box, on the. On strike and receiving strike pay: workmen's, mainly in North England: ca 1880–1910.

box!, the. Prepare for battle: naval coll (—1823); †by 1870.

box about, box it about. To drink briskly: C.17–18.

box Harry. To take lunch and afternoon-tea together: commercial travellers'; ca 1850–1910. Ex: 2. To do without a meal: from ca 1820.

box-hat. A tall silk hat: lower class s. (—1890) verging on coll.

***box-irons.** Shoes: ca 1780–1830; c.

box-lobby loungers. A FAST (2) London coll of ca 1820–60; thus in Bee, 1823, 'The ante-room at the Theatres is frequented by persons *on the Town* of both sexes, who meet there to make appointments, lounging about.'

box-lobby puppy. A 'cheap' would-be man of fashion, a step above an *upper-box Jackadandy* (see JACK-A-DANDY), who is usually an apprentice or a shop-assistant: described by the *London Chronicle* of 20–23 Nov. 1783: apparently ca 1770–1800.

box of dominoes. The mouth and teeth: pugilistic: C.19–20. It occurs in the *New Monthly Magazine* at some date before Feb. 1822 as 'A blow in the mouth is a mugger; and if in addition to this, an injury should be done to the teeth, it is called a rattling of the box of dominoes'.

box of minutes. A watch; a watchmaker's shop: ca 1860–80.

box off. To fight with one's fists: naval: ca 1805–50. Glascock, *Sketch-Book*, I, 1825.

box the compass. To answer all questions; to adapt oneself to circumstances: orig. and mainly nautical; coll; mid-C.18–20. Smollett, 1751, 'A light, good-humoured, sensible wench, who knows very well how to box her compass'. Ex the nautical feat of naming, in order, backwards, or irregularly, the thirty-two points of the compass.

box the Jesuit and get cockroaches. To masturbate: mid-C.18–19. Grose, 1st ed., 'a sea term'. An unsavoury pun on COCK and a too true criticism of nautical and cloistered life.

box the wine bin. To leave the table after drinking but little: fast life: ca 1815–40. *Spy*, II, 1826.

box-wallah. A native pedlar, gen. itinerant: Anglo-Indian coll; from ca 1820.

boxer. A stiff, low-crowned felt hat: Australian (—1897). 2. A tall hat: ca 1880–1910. cf. BOX-HAT.

boxing-out. A bout of boxing: U.S. >, before 1909, Australian coll.

boy. A hump on a man's back: lower class, from ca 1800. Whence *him and his boy*, a hunchback. 2. In India, hence South Africa and Australia: a native servant: C.17–20; coll. 'Influenced by Telugu *bōyi*, Tamil *bōvi*, a caste who were usually palankeen bearers', W. 3. (Often *the boy.*) Champagne: from ca 1880; ob. *Punch*, 1882, 'Beastly dinner, but very good boy. Had two magnums of it.' 4. See B'HOY. 5. (Also **the boyo.**) Always with **the**: penis: late C.19–20.

boy, my or **old.** A term of address: coll, though sometimes it is, clearly, familiar S.E.: C.17–20. Shakespeare, Richardson.

boy, old (with **the**). One's father: late C.19–20. One's business chief, 'governor': C.20. The devil: C.19–20, jocular. All now coll, though s. at their inception.

boy, yellow, see YELLOW BOY.

boy Jones, the. A secret, or unnamed, informant: a virtual c.p., mostly London: mid-C.19. Ex an inquisitive boy who wormed his way several times into Buckingham Palace.

boy with the boots, the; the nailer; Old Nick. The joker in a pack of cards: Anglo-Irish: late C.19–20. Ex his effectiveness.

boyno! A friendly valediction or, occ.,

greeting: nautical (—1909); slightly ob. Ware. Ex or via Lingua Franca for 'good'.

boyo. (Gen. vocative.) Boy: late C.19–20. This *-o* is an endearment-suffix. Ex Anglo-Irish *boyo*, 'lad, chap, boy'. 2. See **boy,** 5.

boys; always **the boys.** The fraternity of bookmakers and their associates: racing: from ca 1820. 2. The lively young fellows of any locality: from ca 1860; coll. cf. LAD OF THE VILLAGE.

Boys, Angry or **Roaring.** A set of young bloods, noisy-mannered, delighting to commit outrages and enter into quarrels, in late Elizabethan and in Jacobean days. Greene, *Tu Quoque*, 'This is no angry, nor no roaring boy, but a blustering boy.' Coll; since ca 1660, S.E. and merely historical. cf. MOHOCK.

Boys of the Holy Ground. Bands of roughs frequenting the less reputable parts of St Giles, London, ca 1800–25. Moore, *Tom Crib's Memorial*, 1819.

bozzimacoo! Kiss my arse!: low Yorkshire: ca 1850–1910. A corruption of *baisez mon cul*.

brace, face and. To bluster, domineer; be defiant: C.16: coll. Skelton; Latimer, 'Men . . . woulde face it and brace it and make a shewe of upryght dealynge.' cf. *brace* (*up*), *brace oneself*.

brace – or **couple** – **of shakes, in a.** In a moment; almost immediately: from ca 1820. Egan's Grose, 1823, has '(*in a*) *brace of snaps*. Instantly' and classifies it as nautical.

brace tavern, the. Late C.18–early 19 only; low: 'a room in the S.E. corner of the King's Bench, where, for the convenience of prisoners residing thereabouts, beer purchased at the tap-house was retailed at a halfpenny per pot advance. It was kept by two brothers of the name of Partridge, and thence called the *Brace*,' Grose, 2nd ed.

***brace up.** To pawn stolen goods, esp. at a good price: C.19–20 c.; ob. Ware suggests that it may derive from Fr. c. *braser* as in *braser des faffes*, to fabricate false papers.

bracelet. A handcuff: from ca 1660. Always low; in C.17–18, prob. c.; ob.

bracer. A tonic: C.18–19. 'What you need is a bracer.' The medical sense, which was S.E., has long been †; as another word for a strong drink (cf. TONIC, 2), a coll, from ca 1860: ex U.S.

brack. A mackerel: nautical: late C.19–20. Ex Isle of Man dial.

bracket-face(d). Ugly: late C.17–early 19. Whence:

bracket-mug. An ugly face: C.19.

brad-faking. A mid-C.19 corruption of BROAD-FAKING.

brads. Money; copper coins. From ca 1810 (Vaux recording it in 1812); low until ca 1860, by which date the 'copper' sense was †. Prob. ex the shoemakers' rivets so named.

brads, tip the. To be generous with money; hence, be a gentleman: ca 1810–40; low.

bradshaw. A person very good at figures: middle-class coll (—1909). Ex *Bradshaw's Railway Guide*.

brag. A braggart; 'A vapouring, swaggering, bullying Fellow', B.E.: late C.17–20. After ca 1800, S.E. 2. In c., a money-lender; a Jew: C.19–20. Ex his exorbitant demands.

***braggadocia, -io.** Three months' imprisonment to reputed thieves, who prob. boast that they can do it 'on their heads': c.; ca 1850–70. Dickens in *Reprinted Pieces*, 1857.

Brahma. 'Something good. Also a flashily dressed girl': Regular Army: late C.19–20. F. & Gibbons. Ex *Brahma*, the Hindu deity: the idols being often bejewelled. 2. See BRAMAH KNOWS.

brain, bear a. To be cautious; have a brain, i.e. some intelligence: C.16–early 19; coll soon > S.E. Skelton.

brain, have on the. Be obsessed by, crazy about: mid-C.19–20. Coll in C.19, then S.E.

brain-canister. The head: pugilistic: ca 1850–85. On:

brain-pan. The head: C.17–20, ob.; after ca 1730, coll. Skelton, Dekker, Scott.

brains. The paste with which a sub-editor sticks his scissors-cuttings together: printers' (—1887); slightly ob.

brains, beat, break, cudgel one's; drag; busy, puzzle one's. To think hard, in order to understand or to contrive: C.16–20, except *break* (†by 1800): all coll; but all, since ca 1860, S.E.

brains, have some guts in one's. To be knowledgeable: late C.18–early 19: coll.

brains, pick or **suck someone's.** To elicit information, knowledge, 'brain-wave', and utilize it (without permission). Coll (—1838), very soon S.E. Lytton.

brains as guts, if you had as much. (Gen. followed by *what a clever fellow you would* *be!*) A c.p. addressed to a person fat and stupid: ca 1780–1820.

brainy. Clever: coll; late C.19–20. Ex U.S. (—1873).

brake, set one's face in a. To assume a 'poker' face: coll; C.17. Ex *brake*, 'a framework intended to hold anything steady' (O.E.D.). Variants with *looks*, *vizard*, etc. Chapman in that fine, ranting tragedy, *Bussy D'Amboise*, 1607, 'O (like a Strumpet) learn to set thy looks | In an eternal Brake.'

Bramah knows: *I* don't. A euphemism (!) for GOD KNOWS: I DON'T!: ca 1880–1910. More correctly *Brahma*.

bramble. A lawyer: mainly Kentish, hence and partly Cockney, s.: ca 1850–1914. It catches you.

bramble-gelder. An agriculturist: chiefly Suffolk, but occ. heard elsewhere: mid-C.19–20; ob.

bran. A loaf: coll, ca 1830–1910. Dickens in *Oliver Twist*. Ex *bran-loaf*.

bran-faced. Freckled: mid-C.18–early 19: coll. cf. CHRISTENED BY A BAKER.

bran mash, bran-mash. Bread soaked in tea or coffee: military, from ca 1870; ob.

branch cag(g). 'Talking shop': naval: Granville. See CAG.

brandy; brandy coatee. A cloak; raincoat: Anglo-Indian: C.19–20; ob. A hybrid.

brandy, all, see ALL BRANDY.

brandy and Fashoda. Brandy and soda: Society: Oct. 1898–early 99. Ex 'the discovery of the Fr. captain, Marchand, at Fashoda'.

brandy blossom. A red-pimpled nose: coll (—1887). Ex *b.b.*, a pimple that, on the nose, is caused by drink, esp. by brandy.

brandy-face. A drunkard: late C.17–early 19. Cotton, ca 1687, 'You goodman brandy-face'. Whence:

brandy-faced. Red-faced, esp. from liquor: from ca 1700. Grose; Sala, 'brandy-faced viragos'.

brandy is Latin for (a) goose, later fish. The former (ob.), from late C.16; the latter (†), from ca 1850. Coll. Mar-Prelate's *Epitome*, 1588; Swift; Marryat. Brewer has thus neatly stated the semantic equation: '*What is the Latin for goose?* (Answer) *Brandy*. The pun is on the word answer. *Anser* is the Latin for goose, which brandy follows as surely and quickly as an answer follows a question.' Concerning *fish*, Mayhew tells us that the richer kinds of fish produce a queasy stomach, restored only by a drink of brandy. cf.:

brandy is Latin for pig and goose. Halliwell, 1847: 'An apology for drinking a dram after either'. Coll; extremely ob. A variant on the preceding entry.

brandy pawnee (occ. **pahnee**). Brandy and water. India and the Army: coll. From ca 1810. Thackeray, 1848, 'The refreshment of brandy-pawnee which he was forced to take'. See PARNEE.

brandy-shunter. A too frequent imbiber of brandy: non-aristocratic: from ca 1880; ob. On BOOZE-SHUNTER.

brandy ticket, be sent with a. To be sent to hospital with one's bad character set forth on the ticket that accompanies one thither. Naval: ca 1800–60. Captain Glascock, 1838. i.e. *branded* ticket.

brass. Money. In late C.16–17, S.E.; in C.18, coll; thereafter, s. Mrs Gaskell; Miss Braddon, 'Steeve's a little too fond of the brass to murder you for nothing.' H., 5th ed., '"Tin" is also used, and so are most forms of metal.' 2. Impudence; effrontery. Adumbrated by Shakespeare, but popularized by Defoe in *The True Born Englishman*, 'a needful competence of English brass'. Also in Farquhar, North, Goldsmith, T. Moore, Dickens. Coll; in C.19–20, S.E. Prob. suggested by slightly earlier BRAZEN-FACE.

brass-bound and copper-fastened. (Of a lad) dressed in a midshipman's uniform: nautical; mid-C.19–20; ob.

brass-bounder. A midshipman; a premium apprentice: nautical: late C.19–20. Ex preceding.

brass candlestick, (his) face has been rubbed with a. A c.p. applied to an impudent person: from ca 1870. In elaboration of BRASS, 2.

brass-face. An impudent person: coll: ca 1820–60. Ex BRASS, 2.

brass farthing. A farthing – or less. Coll: mid-C.17–20; S.E. after ca 1850.

brass-hat. A high-ranked officer: military: 1893, Kipling. Ex 'gilt ornamentation of his cap'.

***brass-knocker.** Broken victuals: scraps of food: vagrants' c. (—1874); ob. ?ex the hardness, or possibly, via India, ex Hindustani *basi khana*, stale food; it affords an interesting comment on Yule & Burnell's *brass-knocker*.

brass monkey, see MONKEY, COLD ENOUGH . . .

brass-plate merchant. An inferior middleman in coal: ca 1840–1920; mainly London. Mayhew.

brass-rags, see PART BRASS-RAGS.

brasser. A bully: Christ's Hospital, C.19–20; ob. Ex BRASS, 2.

brassy. Impudent; shameless: coll (—1576); S.E. after 1800; in C.20, ob. Wolcot, i.e. *Peter Pindar*, 'Betty was too brassy.' cf. the S.E. usages, and BRASS, 2.

brat. Brother; 'one behaving in a manner not befitting his years': Bootham School: late C.19–20.

bratchet. A little brat: endearing or pejorative coll: from ca 1600; ob. by 1900.

brattery. A nursery: pejorative coll: from ca 1780. Beckford, 1834, 'The apartment above my head proves a squalling brattery.'

brave. A bully; assassin: late C.16–17; coll; thereafter S.E.; ob. by 1850, †by 1890.

bravo. 'A mercenary Murderer, that will kill any body', B.E.; Steele, 'dogged by bravoes'. Late C.16–18, coll; thereafter S.E.

brawn. Strength as opp. to brains: coll, C.19–20.

brayvo, Hicks! Splendid!: music-halls' and minor theatres': from ca 1830; ob. by 1910. Ware, 'In approbation of muscular demonstration. ... From Hicks, a celebrated ... actor ..., more esp. "upon the Surrey side" ... [In late C.19–early 20] applied in S. London widely; e.g. "Brayvo Hicks – into 'er again."'

brazen-face. A brazen-faced person: late C.16–20, ob.; coll till ca 1800, then S.E.

Brazen Nose College, you were bred in. You are impudent: c.p.: C.18. Fuller. A pun on BRAZEN-FACE and Brasenose College, Oxford.

brazil, as hard as. Extremely hard: from ca 1635. Coll till 1700, then S.E.; ob. Either ex *Brazil-wood* or, much less prob., ex *brazil*, iron pyrites.

breach. A breach of promise: 1840, Dickens: coll now verging on S.E.

bread!, as I live by. As true (or sure) as I stand here!: coll: late C.19–20.

bread, in bad. In a disagreeable situation: mid-C.18–mid-19: coll. Here, *bread* = employment. cf.:

bread, out of. Out of work: coll, mid-C.18–early 19.

bread and butter. A livelihood: coll, from ca 1840. Ex U.S. (1820). 2. A gutter: rhyming s.: late C.19–20.

bread-and-butter, adj. Boyish, girlish, esp. schoolgirlish, as in *a bread-and-butter miss*: coll; from ca 1860. 2. See BREAD AND BUTTER WAREHOUSE.

bread and butter letter. A letter thanking one's recent hostess: Society: anglicized, as a coll, ca 1905 ex U.S.

bread and butter of mine, no. No business of mine; no potential profit for me: coll: from ca 1760; ob.

bread and butter squadron (or with capitals). The Mediterranean Squadron: naval: late C.19–20. Because it is 'cushy'.

Bread and Butter Warehouse. The Ranelagh Gardens of C.18–early 19. In reference to their debauchery – cf. Joseph Warton's *Ranelagh House*, 1747 – *bread-and-butter fashion* being a mid-C.18–20 c.p. descriptive of human coition.

bread and butter wicket. A wicket extremely easy for batsmen: cricketers' coll: 1887.

bread and cheese, adj. Ordinary; inferior; stingy: coll: late C.17–19. 2. n., plain fare or living: late C.16–20, coll > S.E. by 1700. 3. n. or v., sneeze: rhyming s.: late C.19–20.

bread and cheese in one's head, have (got). To be drunk: mid-C.17–mid-18; coll and proverbial.

bread and meat. The commissariat: military, from ca 1850.

bread-artist. An artist working merely for a living: art: from 1890s; very ob. A variation of POT-BOILER with a pun on *bred*.

bread-bags. Anyone in the victualling department: Army, Navy: mid-C.19–20; ob.

bread-barge. The distributing tray or basket of biscuits: nautical, C.19–20; ob.

bread-basket. The stomach: from ca 1750. Foote, 1753, 'I let drive ..., made the soup-maigre rumble in his bread-basket, and laid him sprawling.' cf. BREAD-ROOM; DUMPLING-DEPOT; PORRIDGE-BOWL, and VICTUALLING DEPARTMENT: all pugilistic.

bread buttered on both sides. Great or unexpected good fortune: coll; mid-C.17–20. Ray, 1678; Lockhart.

bread is buttered, know on which side one's. To seek one's own advantage: C.16–20: coll; in C.19–20, S.E. Heywood, Cibber, Scott, Vachell.

bread out of one's mouth, take the. To spoil or destroy a person's livelihood; to remove what another is on the point of enjoying. From ca 1700; coll till C.19, then S.E.

bread-picker. A junior's nominal office at Winchester College: C.19. Evidently ex some old fagging-duty connected with bread.

bread-room. The stomach: 1761, Smollett; †by 1860. cf. BREAD-BASKET and VICTUALLING DEPARTMENT.

bread-room Jack. A purser's servant: nautical: mid-C.19–20; ob.

breads. Portions or helpings of bread: coll: ca 1860–1910.

bread-snapper. A child: Glasgow lower-classes' from ca 1880. Suggested by S.E. *bread-winner*.

***break.** Money collected by friends for a prisoner's defence or for his assistance when he leaves prison: c.: from ca 1870; ob. J. W. Horsley. 2. A continuous or an unbroken run or journey: railwaymen's coll: 1898. Prob. ex a break at billiards.

break, v. To CUT (v., 2) (a person): middle-class (—1909).

break a lance with. To enjoy a woman: C.19–20. Coll. Eligible only when jocular, otherwise a mere S.E. euphemism. Ex S.E. sense: to enter the lists against.

break a straw with. To quarrel with: jocular coll: C.17–18. Florio's *Montaigne*.

break-bulk. A captain who appropriates a portion of his cargo: C.17–20, ob.; coll till ca 1700, then S.E. Ex S.E. *to break bulk*, to begin to unload.

break-down. A measure of liquor: Australian, ca 1850–1910. 2. A noisy dance: coll, orig. U.S., anglicized in Edmund Yates, 1864; from ca 1880, also coll, a convivial gathering. Also, from ca 1870, as v., to dance riotously, be boisterously convivial, and adj., riotously dancing, noisily convivial.

break-necker. A ball that, with a very big break, takes a wicket: cricketers': ca 1850–80.

break-o'-day drum. 'A tavern which is open all night' (B. & L.): low: from ca 1860. cf. DRUM, 2.

break one's back. To become bankrupt: coll, C.17–18, as in Shakespeare's *Henry VIII*. To cause to go bankrupt: C.17–20, coll, as in Rowley, 1632; and in H., 3rd ed.; and in Baring-Gould's *The Gamecocks*, 1887.

break one's duck, see DUCK, n., 6.

break one's leg, see BROKEN-LEGGED.

break one's shins against, see COVENT GARDEN RAILS . . .

break out in a fresh place. To commence a new undertaking; assume (lit. or fig.) a different position: ?orig. U.S. and anglicized ca 1905.

break-pulpit. A noisy, vigorous preacher: late C.16–17; coll.

***break shins.** To borrow money: C.17–20; ob. In C.17–18, c. cf. BITE ONE'S EAR.

break square(s). To depart from or to interrupt the usual order; do harm. *It breaks no square*, it does not matter, was proverbial. From ca 1560; coll till ca 1620, then S.E. The proverb is ob., the phrase †.

break-teeth words. Words hard to pronounce: late C.18–early 19: coll. cf. JAW-BREAKER.

break the back of, see BREAK THE NECK OF.

break the balls. To begin: sporting, from ca 1870; ob. In billiards j., the phrase = to commence playing.

break the ice. To begin; get to know a person. From ca 1590. Coll; by 1800, S.E. Nashe, Shirley, Dickens.

break the neck, occ. the back, of. To have almost completed; to accomplish the major, or the most difficult, part of any undertaking. From ca 1860; in C.19, coll.

break up, break-up. (As v., idiomatic S.E.) The end of a school-term, or of any performance. It may be very old; 'the accustomed time of the breaking-up of the school' occurs in Popeson's Rules for Bungay Grammar School, Suffolk, ca 1600. From ca 1840: coll soon > S.E.

breakfast, think about. To be absorbed in thought: coll: late C.19–20; ob.

breakfuss. Breakfast: London low coll: mid-C.19–20. See quotation at AGAINST.

breaking one's neck for a (drink, etc.**), be.** To long for a (drink, etc.): coll: late C.19–20. Perhaps ex *to* (*be willing to*) *break one's neck for the sake of* . . .

***breaking-up of the spell.** 'The nightly termination of performance at the Theatres Royal, which is regularly attended by pick-pockets of the lower order', Vaux: c. of ca 1810–80. Here, *spell* = SPELL-KEN, a theatre.

breaky-leg. A shilling: ca 1835–70. **2.** Strong drink: from ca 1860; ob. Ex its effects.

breast fleet, belong to the. To be a Roman Catholic: late C.18–early 19. Ex the crossing or beating of hands on the breast.

breast of, make a clean. To confess in full. From ca 1750: coll till ca 1800, then S.E.

breathe again. To be and feel relieved in mind: C.19–20, anticipated by Shakespeare; coll > S.E. 'Phew! we breathe again.'

breather. A tropical squall: nautical: late C.19–20.

breech, gen. in passive. To flog, be

flogged on the breech: in C.16–18, coll if not S.E.; in C.19–20, schoolboys' s., ob. Tusser, 'Maides, up I beseech yee | Least Mistres doe breech yee'; Massinger, 'How he looks! like a school-boy that . . . went to be breech'd.'

breech makes buttons, one's, see BUTTONS, ONE'S . . .

***breeched.** Rich; in good case: c.: from ca 1810; ob. Vaux. cf. *have the* BAGS, and Fr. *déculotté*, bankrupt.

breeches. Trousers: coll and jocular (also in dial.): from ca 1850. In S.E., breeches come no farther than just below the knee.

breeches, wear the. (Of women) to usurp a husband's authority, be BOSS (n., 2). From ca 1550, though the idea is clearly indicated in C.15. Coll until ca 1700, when it > S.E. Nashe, 1591, 'Diverse great stormes are this yere to be feared, especially in houses where the wives weare the breeches.'

breeches-part. A role in which an actress wears male attire: theatrical (—1865); ob.

breeching. A flogging: in C.16–18, S.E.; in C.19–20 (ob.), schoolboys' s.

breed-bate. A causer or fomenter of bate, i.e. strife: late C.16–20; ob. Coll >, by 1620, S.E. Shakespeare, 'No tel-tale, nor no breede-bate', 1598.

breeding. Parentage: low coll: ca 1597–1620. Shakespeare. Ex primary S.E. sense.

breeding-cage. A bed: low: ca 1860–1920. W. E. Henley, in an unpublished ballad written in 1875, 'In the breeding cage I cops her, | With her stays off, all a-blowin'! | Three parts sprung . . .'

breef, see BRIEF, 3. **breefs,** see BRIEFS.

breeks. Orig. dial. (esp. Scottish) form of *breeches*. Since ca 1860, coll for trousers, very rarely for breeches.

breeze. A disturbance, ROW, quarrel, tiff: coll from ca 1780. T. Moore. 2. A rumour; a gossipy whisper: coll: 1879, Stevenson; ob.

breeze. To boast: military: mid-C.19–early 20. cf. BLOW in same sense.

breeze in one's breech, have a. To be perturbed: coll: C.17. Beaumont & Fletcher; Ray. A breeze is a gadfly. Whence BREEZE, n., 1.

brek. Breakfast: certain Public Schools: late C.19–20: cf.:

brekker. Breakfast. From late 1880s. By elision of *fast* and collision of *break* and the Oxford *-er*, though – admittedly – it looks rather like a child's slurring of *breakfast*.

brevet-wife. 'A woman who, without being married to a man, lives with him, takes his name, and enjoys all the privileges of a wife', F. & H. Coll: ca 1870–1914.

brew, n. 'Drink made on the spot': Bootham School: late C.19–20. Ex: 2. A study-tea: certain Public Schools': mid-C.19–20. cf.:

brew, v.i. To make afternoon tea: Marlborough and hence other Public Schools: mid-C.19–20, ob. Hence *brewing*, the making thereof. 2. v.i., to have afternoon tea: at certain other Public Schools: late C.19–20.

brewer, fetch the. To become intoxicated: from ca 1840; ob. cf.:

brewer's fizzle. Beer; ale: 1714, Ned Ward, *The Republican Procession*; †by 1800, and never common.

brewer's horse. A drunkard. Late C.16–20; ob. Shakespeare, 1597, Falstaff speaking, 'I am a peppercorn, a brewer's horse'; Halliwell, 1847. In late C.19–20, mainly dial. Often in semi-proverbial form, *one whom (a) brewer's horse hath* (or *has*) *bit*. cf.:

brewery, cop the. To get drunk: low: from ca 1860; ob.

brewising, see BRUISING THE BED.

Brian o'Lynn, occ. o' Linn. Gin: rhyming s. (—1857, ob.).

briar, properly **brier.** A briar-wood pipe: coll, from ca 1870; now virtually S.E.

briar-root. 'A corrugated, badly-shaped nose': proletarian (—1909); ob. Ware. Ex a briar-root pipe.

brick. A loyal, dependable person (orig. only of men); 'a good fellow': 1840: s. >, ca 1890, coll. Barham, 'a regular brick'; Thackeray, 1855, 'a dear little brick'; George Eliot, 1876, 'a fellow like nobody else, and, in fine, a brick'. Prob. ex the solidity of a brick; a fanciful etymology is Aristotle's τετράγωνος ἀνήρ, a man worthy of commemoration on a monumental stone. 2. A misfortune, piece of hard luck: Public Schools': 1909, P. G. Wodehouse, *Mike*. 3. A piece of bread; bread: Charterhouse: late C.19–20. As a loaf of bread: 1848, *Sinks*: low s. †by 1900.

brick, drop a. Make a *faux pas*, esp. of tact or speech. The phrase is said to have arisen at Trinity College, Cambridge, in May 1905, after an incident in which the stentorian orders of the Sergeant-Major of the Trinity College Company of University Volunteers frightened some builders into dropping their bricks. The Sergeant-Major subsequently said that he felt that each time he gave an order he too was going to drop a brick.

brick, like a; like bricks; like a thousand (of) bricks. The second seems to be the oldest form (Dickens, 1836; Barham); the third to have been orig. (1842) U.S. Vigorously, energetically, thoroughly, very quickly, with a good will. Coll >, by 1890, S.E.

brick in the hat, have a. To be intoxicated: non-aristocracy: from ca 1870. Semantics: top-heavy.

brick walls, make. To eat one's food without masticating it: lower classes': late C.19–20.

brickduster. A dust-storm: Sydney (—1880); coll. See BRICKFIELDER.

bricked. Smartly or fashionably dressed: late C.16–mid-17: ?orig. c. Greene.

brickfielder. (Less often BRICKDUSTER; cf. (*southerly*) BUSTER, 6.) A Sydney coll for a cold dust- or sand-storm brought by southerly winds from near-by brickfields and sand-hills: ca 1830–90. But from ca 1860, and predominantly from ca 1890, the word has meant a severe hot wind, with dust or without. The change in meaning was caused largely by the disappearance, ca 1870, of the brickfields themselves. Morris's *Austral English* gives an excellent account of the word.

brickish. Excellent; 'fine', 'jolly': 1856, A. Smith. Ex BRICK, n., 1.

bricklayer. A clergyman. From ca 1850; ob. Perhaps ex the part played by ecclesiastics in architecture. For interesting suppositions, see F. & H.

bricklayer's clerk. A lubberly sailor: nautical: ca 1820–1925. cf. STRAW-YARDER.

bricks. A sort of pudding: Wellington College, from ca 1870; ob. 2. See BRICK, LIKE A.

bricks and mortar. A heavy style of acting: theatrical: prob. since the 1890s.

bricky. A bricklayer or his assistant; coll (1880). 2. Hence, a low fellow: schoolboys': from ca 1895.

bricky, adj. Fearless; adroit; like a BRICK: 1864; perhaps orig. schoolboys'; slightly ob. cf. BRICKISH.

bride and groom. A broom: rhyming s.: late C.19–20.

bridge. (Cards) a cheating trick by which a particular card is located, and made operative in the cut, by previously imparting to it a slight curve; that curve produces an almost imperceptible gap in the resultant pack. From ca 1850; after ca 1870, j. Mayhew, Lever, Yates. vbl n., *bridging*. 2. Hence (?) an absentee from a meeting: printers': from ca 1880; very ob.

***bridge,** v. To betray the confidence of. Variant: THROW OVER THE BRIDGE: c. or low s. (—1812); †by 1900.

bridge, a gold or **a silver.** An easy and attractive means of escape: late C.16–20; ob. Coll > S.E. in C.17.

bridge, beside the. Astray; off the track: C.17–18; coll. Culpepper, 1652.

bridge of anyone's nose, make a. To push the bottle past him, so that he misses a drink. Coll: mid-C.18–early 19; then dial.

bridge-ornament. (Gen. pl) An executive officer: nautical engineers': late C.19–20. Opp. EDUCATED TRIMMER.

bridge-telegraph. A boy standing at the engine-room sky-light and repeating the captain's orders: London river-steamers': ca 1850–1910.

bridges and no grasses. (A meeting, a pact, that is) secret: printers': from ca 1880; ob.

bridges, bridges! 'A cry to arrest a long-winded story': printers': from ca 1880; ob. Ware, 'Prob. corruption of (Fr.) "abrégeons – abrégeons" . . . Anglicized'.

bridgeting. The plausible acquisition of money from Irish servant girls, for political – or allegedly political – purposes: 1866; ob. *Bridget* (*Biddy*), a Christian name very gen. in Ireland.

bridle-cull. A highwayman: low or c.: ca 1740–1800. Fielding. See CULL.

Bridport or **Brydport dagger, stabbed with a.** Hanged. The *Bridport dagger* is a hangman's rope, much hemp being grown round Bridport: mid-C.17–early 19; coll. Fuller; Grose's *Provincial Glossary*; Southey.

brief. A ticket of any kind; a pocket-book: from ca 1850. In C.19, c.; in C.20, low s. (In the late C.19–20 Army, it signifies a discharge certificate.) Ex its shortness. Hence BRIEFLESS, ticketless. 2. In late C.19–20 c., a false reference or recommendation. 3. Often spelt *breef* and always preceded by *the*: a cheating-device at cards: late C.17–18. 4. (cf. sense 2.) A letter: proletarian: mid-C.19–20.

***brief, get one's.** To obtain one's ticket-of-leave: c.: late C.19–20.

***brief-jigger.** A ticket-office, esp. at a railway-station: c. (—1850).

***brief-snatcher.** A pocket-book thief: c.:

mid-C.19–20. See BRIEF, 1. 2. Also, vbl n., *brief-snatching*.

briefless. Ticketless: from ca 1870. Low in C.20; earlier, c.

Briefless, Mr. An advocate without brief: coll, mostly London (—1887); ob.

***briefs.** 'Jockeyed' playing-cards: C.18–20; low, if not indeed c. Occ. *breefs*. cf. BRIEF 3.

brier, see BRIAR.

briers, in the. In trouble: C.16–18; coll. *Briers*, vexation(s), is S.E., C.16–20, ob.

brig, the. Punishment cells: naval, mostly American: mid-C.19–20. Often *in the Dutch brig*. 2. **The Brig.** The pilot-steamer at the mouth of the Hughly: nautical coll: late C.19–20.

brigdie. A basking shark: C.19 nautical coll ex Scots dial. (—1810).

***brigh.** A pocket, esp. a trousers-pocket: c. (—1879); ob. ?ex *breeks*.

Brigham. Inevitable nickname for anyone surnamed Young: late C.19–20. Ex the Mormonite.

bright. A dandy, fop, finical fellow: Society: ca 1760–80. cf. SMART.

bright in the eye. Slightly drunk: from ca 1870: s. till C.20, then coll; ob. (Lyell).

bright specimen, a. A silly, foolish, rash, stupid, bungling person. (Always complementary to the verb *to be*.) Coll (—1888).

bright-work juice. Liquid metal-polish: *Conway* cadets': from ca 1895.

Brighton bitter. A mixture of mild and bitter beer sold as bitter: public-houses' (—1909); ob. cf.:

Brighton tipper. 'The celebrated staggering ale', Dickens, 1843. Coll, ca 1830–70.

brights, clean the. To clean and polish the brass and copper accessories and ornaments, and the silver ornaments: domestic coll: mid-C.19–20.

brilliant is short for the next: 1821, *Boxiana*, III, 'Full of *heavy wet* (q.v.) and Booth's *brilliant*'.

brilliant stark-naked, see STARK-NAKED.

brim. A harlot: late C.17–mid-19. cf. sense 3. 2. A termagant; an angry, violent woman: from ca 1780. 3. In late C.19–20 c., a fearless harlot. Abbr. *brimstone*.

brim, v. (Of a man) to have intercourse; v.t., **with.** C.17–18, sporting. Ex the copulation of boar with sow.

brimmer. A hat with a brim, esp. if big: mid-C.17–early 18; coll at first, then S.E. 2. A variant of BRIM, 1: c. of ca 1820–50.

brimstone. A virago, a spitfire: from ca 1700; coll verging on S.E.; ob. by 1890. '"Oh, madam," said the bishop, "do you know what a brimstone of a wife he had?"', Bishop Burnet, 1712. 2. Also, a harlot: from ca 1690. Both ex *brimstone*, sulphur, which is notably inflammable.

brimstone and treacle. Flowers of sulphur and dark treacle: domestic coll: from ca 1880.

briney or **briny, the.** The sea: coll (1856). Whyte-Melville in *Kate Coventry*. cf. Dick Swiveller's use of *the mazy* and *the* ROSY: W. 2. Hence, *do the briny*, to weep: low: mid-C.19–20; ob. 'Cuthbert Bede'. See MAIN, TURN ON THE.

bring. To steal: ca 1820–60. Bee, who cites a v.i. sense: 'Dogs are said "to *bring* well", when they run off with goods for their masters.'

bring down the house, bring the house down. To be heartily applauded (—1754). Coll until ca 1895, then S.E. 'His apprehension that your statues will bring the house down', the *World*, 1754; 'Why, it would . . . bring down the house,' 'Cuthbert Bede', 1853.

bring-'em near. A telescope: nautical: late C.19–20.

bring in. (Of a jury) to find, e.g. guilty. Coll (—1888). 'The jury brought her in not guilty.'

bring off. (Of a girl) to induce an orgasm in (a man); less often, (of a man) in a girl: coll: probably since C.16.

bring on. To excite sexually: coll: probably since C.16.

bring up, v.i. and t. To vomit: coll; from ca 1830.

briny, the, see BRINEY.

brisk as a bee or as **a bee in a tar-pot.** (C.18–20, latterly dial.), as in Fielding, and *brisk as bottled ale* (C.18), as in Gay. Very lively: coll. cf. BODY-LOUSE.

brisk up (occ. **about**). To enliven or animate: coll: 1864. Dickens.

brisket-beater. A Roman Catholic: late C.18–19. From beating the breast in token of penitence. cf. BREAST FLEET . . ., CRAW (*-thumper*).

brisket-cut. A punch on the breast- or collar-bone: pugilistic: ca 1820–50.

bristles, bristle dice. C.19, C.16–19 resp.; perhaps c. Dice falsified by the insertion of bristles. *Bristles* occurs in Scott's novel of the underworld, *The Fortunes of Nigel*.

Bristol. A visiting-card: Society: ca 1830–1914. Ware, 'From the date when these articles were printed upon Bristol – i.e. cardboard'.

Bristol man. 'The son of an Irish thief and a Welch whore', *Lex. Bal.*: low: ca 1810–50. Because both of those worthies would geographically tend to drift to Bristol.

Bristol milk. Sherry; esp. rich sherry: from ca 1660; coll till ca 1800, then S.E. Prynne, Fuller, Grose, Macaulay. Ex the large quantities of sherry imported, in C.17–18, into England by way of Bristol.

Bristol stone. Sham diamond(s): C.17–18. In S.E., to this day, the term *Bristol diamond* or *gem* or *stone* denotes a transparent rock-crystal found in the limestone at Clifton, that beautiful outer suburb of Bristol.

British champa(i)gne. Porter: ca 1810–40. cf. ENGLISH BURGUNDY.

British constitution, unable to say. Drunk: coll: late C.19–20; ob.

British Museum religion. Anglican ceremonialists advocating the precise following of medieval uses: ecclesiastical pejorative coll: ca 1899–1902.

British roarer. The heraldic lion: non-aristocratic: from ca 1880; ob.

Briton, a. A good fellow; a staunch friend; a loyal, helpful person. Coll: from ca 1890.

broach claret. To draw blood: boxing: from ca 1820; ob.

broad. A 20-shilling piece: low: C.19. Manchon.

broad, adj. Alert; 'knowing': late C.19–20; ob. Suggested by WIDE, 2.

Broad, the. Broad Street, Oxford: Oxford undergraduates': from the 1890s.

broad and shallow, adj. Middle-way: applied to the 'Broad' Church, as opp. to the 'High' and 'Low' Churches: coll: ca 1854; ob. cf. HIGH AND DRY and LOW AND SLOW.

broad-arse(d). (A person) 'broad in the beam': low coll: late C.19–20.

broad as it's long (or long as it's broad), it's as. It makes no difference; it comes to the same thing either way. From the 1670s; in C.19–20, S.E. Ray, 1678; 'Hudibras' Butler.

broad-brim. A Quaker: 1712, ob.; coll. The *Spectator*, Fielding. Ex the Quakers' broad-brimmed hats. 2. ca 1840–90, any quiet, sedate old man. 3. Hence *broad-brimmed*, Quakerish; sedate: from ca 1700; coll; ob.

broad-brimmer. A broad-brimmed hat: coll: ca 1855–1900.

broad-cooper. A brewers' negotiator with publicans; he is an aristocrat among 'commercials'. Brewers, ca 1850–1914.

***broad cove.** A card-sharper (—1821): c. See BROADS.

***broad-faker.** A card-player; esp., a card-sharper: C.19–20 c.

broad-faking. Card-playing, esp. if shady; also three-card trickery: c.; from ca 1855.

***broad-fencer.** A 'correct card' seller at horse-races: c.: from ca 1850.

broad-gauge lady. A large-hipped woman: railway officials' (ca 1880) >, by 1884, gen.; †by 1900.

broad in the beam, see BEAM, BROAD IN THE.

***broad mob, the.** 'Broadsmen' (s.v. BROADSMAN): c.: late C.19–20. David Hume.

***broad-pitcher.** A man with a three-card-trick 'outfit': c.: from the 1860s. B. Hemyng, *Out of the Ring*, 1870.

***broad-player.** An expert card-player, not necessarily a sharper; c. (—1812); ob.

***broads.** Playing cards: c. from ca 1780; ob. George Parker, Vaux, Ainsworth, Charles E. Leach.

***broadsman.** A card-sharper: from ca 1850: c. Charles E. Leach. Ex BROADS.

broady. Cloth: coll, somewhat low: from ca 1850. Mayhew. Ex *broadcloth*. 2. Hence, in c., anything worth stealing: from before 1890.

***broady-worker.** A seller of vile shoddy as excellent and, esp., stolen material: ca 1845–1914; c.

brock. A dirty fellow, a 'skunk': late C.16–19; coll verging on S.E. Ex *brock*, a badger.

brock, v. To bully; tease: Winchester College: mid-C.19–20, ob. Ex: 2. To taunt; to chaff: ibid.: ca 1800–1850. Perhaps ex Ger. *brocken*.

brockster. (Winchester College) a bully: a persistent teaser: mid-C.19–20.

broganeer, broganier. 'One who has a strong Irish pronunciation or accent', Grose, 1st ed.: coll: latish C.18–early 19. Ex *brogue*.

brogues. Breeches: Christ's Hospital, C.19–20; ob. Coll rather than s., for in mid-C.19 S.E. it meant either hose or trousers.

broiler. A very hot day: from ca 1815: in C.20, S.E. cf. ROASTER; SCORCHER.

broke. Bankrupt; very short of money. Often – e.g. in N. Kingsley, 1851 – DEAD or – e.g. in G. R. Sims, 1887 – STONE

BROKE. Coll; from ca 1820. 2. Dismissed from the Service: naval officers' coll: C.19–20.

broken feather in one's wing, have a. To have a stain on one's character: C.19–20, ob.; coll verging on S.E. Mrs Oliphant in *Phoebe*, 1880.

broken her leg at the church-door, she hath. From a hard-working girl she has, on being married, become a slattern: coll and (mainly Cheshire) dial. Contrast the phrases at BROKEN-LEGGED.

broken-kneed. (Of a girl or woman) seduced: C.18–20; ob.; coll. Ex farriery. cf. *have sprained one's* ANKLE and:

broken-legged, ppl adj. Seduced: C.17–20; ob. Coll. More gen. is the semi-proverbial coll form, *she hath broken her leg* (occ. *elbow*) *above the knee*. Beaumont & Fletcher, Cibber, Grose. cf. the C.19–20 Craven dial. *he hath broken his leg*, of 'a dissolute person on whom a child has been filiated', and contrast BROKEN HER LEG . . .

broker. A pedlar or monger: pejorative: late C.14–18; S.E. till C.17, when it > coll. 2. In late C.16–early 17 c., a receiver of stolen goods. Greene in 2nd *Cony-Catching*. 3. **broker**; gen. **dead-broker**; occ. **stony-broker.** A person either ruined or penniless: coll: from ca 1890.

brokered, be. To suffer a visitation by the brokers: lower classes': from 1897; ob. Ware.

brolly. An umbrella: from ca 1873; in C.20, coll. H., 5th ed., 1874; *Punch*, 6 June 1885. F. & H.: 'First used at Winchester, being subsequently adopted at both Oxford and Cambridge Universities'.

bronco-buster. A breaker-in of broncos: coll, U.S. (1880s) anglicized by 1897.

bronze. A cheat, deception, HUMBUG: ca 1815–60. *Blackwood's*, No. 1, 1817. 2. Impudence: 1821, Egan, *Life in London*. cf. BRASS, 2. 3. Also as v.t.: same period.

Brooks of Sheffield. This conveys a warning to be careful as to names: middle classes' c.p.: ca 1850–1910. Ex *David Copperfield*, where David is thus referred to by Mr Murdstone.

broom. A warrant: C.18–19, coll; mainly dial. Also, 2. the *pudenda muliebria*: C.19–20, low; whence *broomstick*, the male member. cf. C.19–20 Scottish *besom*, a low woman.

broom, v. (gen. **broom it).** To depart; run away: low: late C.18–19. Moncrieff, 1821. Suggested by *sweep away*.

broom-squires. Mainly Gypsy squatters that, esp. in the New Forest, earn a living by making brooms out of heath: C.19–20; after ca 1900, S.E.

broom up (at the mast-head), she carries the. She's a whore: a seaport c.p. of ca 1820–90. Ex that broom which, attached to the mast-head, signified that a ship was sold.

broombee, see BRUMBIE.

broomstick. A rough cricket bat, of one piece of wood. Coll; from ca 1870; ob. 2. A worthless bail: C.19 low. 3. See BROOM, n., 2.

broomstick, enough to charm the heart of a. Very charming: ironic coll (—1887); ob.

broomstick, jump (over) the; hop the broom(stick); marry over the broomstick. The first, C.18–20; the second and third, C.19–20: all coll and ob. Though unmarried, to live as man and wife: in reference to the pretence-marriage ceremony performed by both parties jumping over a stick. The ceremony itself = *a broomstick wedding*. cf. *jump the* BESOM and WESTMINSTER WEDDING.

broseley. A pipe, esp. in *cock a broseley*, smoke a pipe. ca 1815–90. Broseley, in Shropshire, is – or was – famous for its CHURCHWARDENS.

brosier, brozier. A boy with no more pocket-money: Eton College: from ca 1830; ob. Ex Cheshire *brozier*, a bankrupt. cf. gen. coll *broziered*, ruined, penniless, bankrupt: late C.18–early 19.

brosier, brozier, v. To clear the table or the larder of: Eton: mid-C.19–20, ob. Rev. W. Rogers, *Reminiscences*, 1888. Ex BROSIER, n.; cf.:

brosier- or brozier-my-dame, v. and n. (To make) a clearance of the housekeeper's larder: Eton College: from ca 1835.

broth. Breath: low: late C.19–20.

broth, in lunatic's. Drunk: 1902, *Daily Telegraph*, 20 June; ob. cf.:

broth, take one's. To drink (liquor): mid-C.18–mid-19 nautical. cf. preceding entry.

broth of a boy, a. A real, an essential boy: coll; Byron in *Don Juan*, 1822. Orig. and mainly Anglo-Irish. Ex the effervescence of broth; or perhaps rather 'the essence of manhood, as broth is the essence of meat', P. W. Joyce.

brother blade. A fellow-soldier; one of the same trade or profession (cf. BROTHER CHIP): C.19–20, ob. 2. In mid-C.17–18, *brother of the blade*, a swordsman, hence a soldier. Coll.

brother bung. A fellow-publican: London taverns': from ca 1880.

brother chip. A fellow-carpenter: C.18. In C.19–20, one of the same calling or trade: as in Clare's *Poems of Rural Life*, 1820. Mainly provincial. Coll.

brother of the angle. A fellow-angler; an angler: from ca 1650; ob. Coll > S.E. Walton.

brother of the blade, see BROTHER BLADE, 2.

brother of the brush. An artist: coll: late C.17–20. 2. A house-painter: C.19–20.

brother of the bung. A brewer; a fellow-brewer. Coll: late C.18–20, ob. cf. BUNG, n., and BROTHER BUNG.

brother of the buskin. A (fellow-)player, actor: late C.18–20 coll, ob.

brother of the coif. A serjeant-at-law: C.18–19 coll. Addison. Ex *coif*, a close-fitting white cap formerly worn by lawyers, esp. serjeants-at-law.

brother of the gusset. A pimp, a procurer, a whoremaster: late C.17–19; coll. cf. PLACKET.

brother of the quill. An author: late C.17–20 coll.

brother of the string. A fiddler; a musician: coll, late C.17–20, ob.

brother of the whip. A coachman: coll, mid-C.18–20. *World*, 1756.

brother smut. Gen. in *ditto, brother* (rarely *sister*) *smut*: the same to you!; you too: mid-C.19–20 coll. cf. *pot calling the kettle* BLACK ARSE.

brother starling. A man sharing another's mistress: late C.17–early 19.

brother-where-art-thou. A drunk man: late C.19–20. Manchon, '... Qui cherche toujours son camarade en lui demandant où es-tu?'

brought up all standing, see ALL STANDING...

brought up with a round turn. To be suddenly or unexpectedly checked: naval coll: C.19–20.

Broughtonian. A boxer: coll: ca 1750–1800. Ex Broughton, the champion of England ca 1730–35.

Broughton's mark, see MARK, n., 5.

brown. A halfpenny; a COPPER (2): from ca 1810; low until ca 1830. Vaux, 1812; Barham, 'The magic effect of ... crowns upon people whose pockets boast nothing but browns'. 2. Porter, whereas *heavy brown* = stout: Corcoran's *The Fancy*, 1820. Both, C.19. 3. The anus: low: mid-C.19–20. Hence 4. An act of sodomy (often *a bit of brown*): ?mid-C.19–20.

brown, v. To do perfectly; hence, to worst: from ca 1870, †. Abbr. *do brown.* 2. Understand: from ca 1830; ob. 3. To fire indiscriminately at: 1873: coll >, by 1910, S.E. Ex BROWN, INTO THE; see sense 2.

brown, adj. Alert (to), familiar (with). From ca 1820; 'J. Bee', *Picture of London*, 1828.

brown, do. To do thoroughly; hence, to worst; to cheat. From ca 1820; gen. as *done brown*, completely swindled. *Boxiana*, IV, 1824, 'He is then said to be "cooked" or "done brown" and "dished".' There is an anticipation in 'Ha! browne done!' in the anon. *John Bon*, ca 1600. In U.S., *do up brown*: see Thornton. 2. *do it brown*, to prolong a frolic or a spree, to exceed sensible bounds: from ca 1850; ob.

brown, do a. To commit sodomy: low: late C.19–20. See BROWN, n., 3.

brown, into the. (Shooting) into the midst of a covey, not at one particular bird: coll (1845) > S.E. by 1910. 2. Hence, fig.: 1885: coll > S.E. by 1910.

brown Bess or **Bessie.** A harlot: C.17, coll. 2. The old regulation flint-lock musket: coll, C.18–19. Recorded first in Grose, 1st ed., but prob. used much earlier; *brown musquet* occurs in 1708. Ex the brown stock, the frequent browning of the barrel, and the soldier's devotion to the weapon. 3. In rhyming s.: yes! (—1859); ob.

brown Bess, hug. To serve as a private soldier: ca 1780–1850; coll. See BROWN BESS, 2.

brown cow. A barrel of beer: C.18–early 19: coll.

brown George. A loaf of coarse brown bread, prob. munition-bread: late C.17–early 19: orig. naval and military s., then gen. coll. 2. Also, a hard, coarse biscuit: late C.18–19: coll. 3. Hence, ca 1780–1850, a brown wig: coll in C.19. 4. Hence also, an earthenware jug, orig. and gen. brown: from ca 1860; soon coll.

brown hat. A cat: rhyming s.: late C.19–20.

brown Janet. A knapsack: nautical: mid-C.19–20, ob. In dial. as early as 1788 (E.D.D.).

brown Joe. Rhyming s. for 'no!' (cf. BROWN BESS, yes!) From ca 1855; ob.

brown madam. (Variant MISS BROWN.)

The MONOSYLLABLE: late C.18–early 19; low.

***brown-paper men.** Low gamblers: c. of ca 1850–1900. They play for pence or 'browns'. See BROWN, n., l.

brown-paper warrant. A warrant for boatswains, carpenters, etc., granted and cancellable by the captain: naval: C.19. Ex colour thereof and in allusion to the uses to which brown paper is put.

brown polish. A mulatto: late C.19–20; ob. cf. DAY AND MARTIN.

brown salve! A term indicative of surprise coupled with understanding: ca 1850–70.

brown shell. (Gen. pl) An onion: proletarian: mid-C.19–20.

brown talk. Very 'proper' conversation: coll, from ca 1700; ob. cf. *brown study*, C.16–20, serious thoughts, in C.20 an idle reverie – B.E., by the way, considered it as either s. or coll for 'a deep Thought or Speculation'. Contrast BLUE, immoral.

brown to, v.t. To understand, to TWIG (4): low (—1909); ob. Ware, 'Prob. from a keen man of this name'; H., 2nd ed., records it as an Americanism.

brownie, browny. The polar bear: nautical: coll: mid-C.19–20. 2. An Australian coll, dating from the 1880s: 'Cake made of flour, fat and sugar, commonly known as "Browny"', E. D. Cleland, *The White Kangaroo*, 1890. 3. A copper coin: ca 1820–1910. Ex BROWN, n., 1. 4. (Gen. pl) A cheap cigarette – three for a BROWN or halfpenny: 'lower London' (Ware): ca 1896–1915.

browse. To idle; take things easily: Marlborough and Royal Military Academy, C.19–20; ob. Whence:

browse, adj. Idle; with little work. Marlborough and R.M.A.; C.19–20; ob.

brozier, see BROSIER.

bruffam. A brougham: Society: ca 1860–1910. A pronunciation-pun, for whereas *brougham* is pronounced *broom*, the surname *Brough* is pronounced *Bruff*.

bruise, v. To fight; box: pugilists', C.19–20, ob. Anticipated in Fletcher, 1625, 'He shall bruise three a month.'

bruise along. To pound along: hunting: from ca 1860. cf. BRUISER, 3.

bruise-water. A broad-bowed ship: nautical coll: mid-C.19–20; ob.

bruiser. A prize-fighter; 1742. In C.19–20, coll, as in S. Warren, 1830, 'a scientific . . . thorough-bred bruiser'. Hence, 2, any person fond of fighting with the fists; a chucker-out: C.19–20, coll. 3. A reckless rider: hunting: 1830; cf. BRUISE ALONG and BRUISING, adj. 4. In c., harlot's FANCY-MAN or bully: mid-C.19. cf. BOUNCER. 5. 'An inferior workman among chasers' (of metal): trade coll (—1788); ob. Ex his rough workmanship.

bruising. Fighting with the fists: C.19–20, coll. Ex C.18–20 (coll after 1800) sense: boxing, as in Smollett, 1751, and Thackeray, 1855, 'bruising . . . a fine manly old English custom'. ca 1800–30, boxing was not only popular but fashionable.

bruising, ppl adj. (Given to) pounding along or reckless riding. Hunting: from ca 1870. Ex BRUISE ALONG. cf. BRUISER, 3.

bruising-match. A boxing-match: from ca 1790; coll till ca 1850, when it > S.E.

bruising or **brewising the bed.** Fouling the bed: low: late C.18–early 19. Grose, 1st ed., 'From *brewes*, or *browes*, oatmeal boiled in the pot with salt beef.'

brum. A counterfeit coin: C.18–20; in late C.17, counterfeit groats. Abbr. BRUMMAGEM. 2. A spur: coll, 1834+ but now †. 3. Almost anything, but esp. jewellery, that is counterfeit or worthless: from ca 1870; e.g. in the *Daily Telegraph*, 9 July 1883. 4. Copper coins minted by Boulton & Watt, at their Birmingham works (—1787); †, except historically. 5. **(Brum.)** A native of BRUMMAGEM, Birmingham: from ca 1870. 6. **(Brum.)** Birmingham itself: from ca 1860.

brum, adj. Not genuine; counterfeit; trashy: from ca 1880; rather rare. Lit., made at *Brum* (n., 6, Birmingham). 2. Hence, at Winchester College: mean; poor; stingy: 1883 (E.D.D.). Ex BRUM(MAGEM), or ex L. *bruma*, winter, or – the traditional College explanation – ex L. *brevissimum*, the shortest (thing). Wrench, however, adduces Kentish dial. *brumpt*, bankrupt, penniless.

brumbie or **brumby**; occ. **broombee, brumbee.** A wild horse: Australian coll. Orig. (ca 1864) in Queensland, but gen. by 1888 as we see by Cassell's *Picturesque Australasia*, of that date. The word appears in Kipling's *Plain Tales from the Hills*. Perhaps ex Aborigine *booramby*, wild. Morris, thus: *Illustrated Tasmanian*, 13 June 1935, however, in a convincing article on 'Wild "Brumbies",' states that the term arose in the second decade of C.19 in New South Wales and that the term derives ex Major Wm Brumby, who, from Richmond, went to Australia early in C.19; he was a keen breeder of horses, and many of his young horses ran more or less, finally quite, wild. (The Brumby family now lives in Tasmania.)

Brummagem. Birmingham: from ca 1860; except as dial., low coll. 2. Base money: in late C.17–early 18, counterfeit groats; C.18–20, any counterfeit money, esp. of copper, as in Martin's Dict., 1754, and in Southey's fascinating farrago-'omnibus', *The Doctor*. Ex the local spelling, which was – and still often is – phonetic of the local pronunciation. *Brummagem* = *Bromwicham* (after *Bromwich*), a corruption of *Brimidgeham*, the old form of *Birmingham*. Faked antiques, etc., are still made at Birmingham. 3. A spur: from ca 1830; ob.

Brummagem, adj. Counterfeit; cheap and pretentious: coll; 1637, 'Bromedgham blades' = inferior swords. ca 1690, B.E., '*Bromigham-conscience*, very bad [one], *Bromigham-protestants*, Dissenters or Whiggs [see the O.E.D.], *Bromigham-wine*, Balderdash, Sophisticate, Taplash.' The C.20 connotation is that of shoddiness or of showy inferiority: as such, it is coll. See then.

Brummagem buttons. Counterfeit coin, esp. of copper (—1836); ob. cf. BRUMMAGEM, n., 2.

brummish. Counterfeit; doubtful; inferior: coll: from ca 1800; slightly ob. cf. BRUM.

brunch. Breakfast and lunch in one: university s.: coined by Guy Beringer in 1895, > coll ca 1905.

brush. A hasty departure: coll: C.18–19; in the latter, coll. Fielding in *Tom Jones*. 2. He who departs hastily: c. (—1748); †by 1850. Dyche. 3. A house-painter: mid-C.19–20; ob. cf. BROTHER OF THE BRUSH. 4. A small dram-drinking glass: public-houses' (—1909); slightly ob. Ex resemblance of its outline to that of a house-painter's brush.

brush, v. To depart hastily; run away. Late C.17–20, ob. In C.17, c. or low; in C.18, s. then coll. Post-1800, coll and then S.E. 'Sergeant Matcham had brush'd with the dibs', Barham. Also *brush along* or *off*: C.19. 2. To flog: Christ's Hospital, C.19–20.

brush, at a or at the first. At first; immediately: coll: C.15–18.

brush, brother of the, see BROTHER OF THE BRUSH.

***brush, buy a.** To run away: c. of ca 1670–1830. Also, C.19–20 (s., not c.), *show one's brush*. cf. BRUSH, n. and v.

***brush and lope.** To depart hastily, to decamp: late C.18–mid-19: c. Lit., to depart and run. See BRUSH, v., 1.

brush one's coat for him. To thrash (cf. DUST ONE'S CASSOCK): coll: ca 1660–1820. Bunyan.

brush up a flat. To flatter, SOFT-SOAP a person: C.19–20, low.

brush with, have a. To fight with a man, lie with a woman: mid-C.18–20, ob.

brusher. A full glass: ca 1690–1830. 2. A schoolmaster: C.19–20. Prob. abbr. BUM-BRUSHER; cf. BRUSH, v., 2.

brusher, give. To depart with debts unpaid; e.g. 'He gave them brusher': Australian-bush s. (—1898). Ex *brusher*, a small and lively wallaby.

brute. One who has not matriculated: Cambridge University, C.19. Prob. ex S.E. *brute*. 2. A term of reprobation: coll, from ca 1660. 'The brute of a cigar required relighting', G. Eliot.

bry or **Bry.** Abbr. BRIAN O' LYNN: 1868.

Bryant & May's chuckaway. (Gen. pl.) A girl working in that firm's match-factory: East London: 1876; ob. by 1910. A *chuckaway* is a lucifer match; such match-making used to be unhealthy.

Bryan o' Lynn, see BRIAN O' LYNN.

Brydport, see BRIDPORT DAGGER.

***bub.** Strong drink, esp. malt liquor: from ca 1670; ob.: c. until ca 1820, then low. Head. Often as *bub and* GRUB, food and (strong) drink. Either echoic or ex L. *bibere*, to drink; Dr Wm Matthews says: abbr. of *bubble*. 2. A brother, rare, C.18; C.19–20, (mostly U.S.) a little boy. Perhaps ex Ger. *bube*, boy (W.). 3. A woman's breast, C.19–20; rare in singular and not very frequent in this abbr. form: see BUBBY. 4. 'One that is cheated; an easy, soft Fellow', B.E.: late C.17–19; c. until ca 1810. Abbr. BUBBLE.

***bub,** v. To drink: C.18–19; c. until ca 1820, then low. Prob. ex BUB, n., 1. 2. To bribe; cheat: C.18–early 19; rare; low, as in D'Urfey, 1719, 'Another makes racing a Trade . . . And many a Crimp match has made, | By bubbing another Man's Groom.' Ex BUBBLE, v. cf. BUB, n., 4.

bub, humming. Strong beer or ale: ca 1820–90. See BUB, n., 1.

***bubber.** A hard drinker; a toper. C.17–late 18: c. in C.17, then low. cf. BUB, n., 1, and v., 1. 2. A drinking-bowl: c.: late C.17–early 19. 3. A stealer of plate from taverns and inns: c. of ca 1670–1830. cf. sense 1.

bubbery. Senseless clamour; 'a wordy noise in the street': low (—1818); †by 1900. A corruption of BOBBERY.

bubbing. Drinking, tippling: ca 1670–1830: low. cf. BUB and BUBBER.

bubble. A dupe; a gullible person: ca 1668–1840. Sedley, Shadwell, Swift ('We are thus become the dupes and bubbles of Europe'), Fielding, George Barrington (who left England 'for his country's good'). Coll >, ca 1800, S.E. cf. and presumably ex:

bubble, v. To cheat, swindle; delude, humbug; overreach: coll, but S.E. after ca 1800: 1664, Etherege; Dryden; Fielding, 'He . . . actually bubbled several of their money'; Sheridan; McCarthy the historian, 1880, 'the French Emperor had bubbled [Cobden]'. Also *bubble* (a person) *of*, *out of*, or *into*: 1675, Wycherley. Perhaps ex *bubble*, 'to cover or spread with bubbles' (O.E.D.); more prob. via 'delude with *bubbles*' or unrealities, as W. proposes. cf. BUBBLE COMPANY.

bubble, bar the. 'To except against the general rule, that he who lays the odds, must always be adjudged the loser; this is restricted to betts laid for liquor', Grose, 2nd ed.: drinking: late C.18–early 19. Punning BUBBLE, a deception, + *bib* (or *bibber*) as a drinking term.

bubble and squeak. Cold meat fried with potatoes and greens, or with cabbage alone. Coll. From ca 1770: Grose, 1st ed., being the first to record it in a dictionary; it occurs, however, in Bridges's *Homer*, 1772. After ca 1830, S.E.; Lytton has it in *My Novel.* Ex the sound emitted by this dish when cooking. 2. A Greek: rhyming s.: from ca 1870. 3. A magistrate: rhyming s. (on BEAK): late C.19–20.

bubble and squeak, v. To speak: rhyming s.: (?)mid-C.19–20.

bubble-bow or **-boy.** A lady's tweezer case: ca 1704–60: s. > coll. Pope. (=beau-befooler.)

bubble buff. A bailiff: C.17. Rowlands.

bubble company. A dishonest firm: coll passing to S.E., C.19–20. Adumbrated in C.18: see Martin's Dict., 2nd ed., 1754: '*Bubble* . . . a name given to certain projects for raising money on imaginary grounds': the South Sea Bubble was semantically responsible.

bubbleable. Gullible: *temp.* Restoration. Rare: coll.

bubbled, ppl adj. Gulled, befooled, deluded. Coll, late C.17–20; ob. Defoe:

Who shall this bubbled nation disabuse,
While they, their own felicities refuse?

bubbler. A swindler: ca 1720–1830: coll > S.E. by 1770. Pope.

bubbling, adj. Cheating: ca 1675–1750. Wycherley. (The n. is late – 1730 – and S.E.)

bubbling squeak. Hot soup: military: mid-C.19–20; ob. cf. BUBBLE AND SQUEAK.

bubbly, often **the bubbly.** Champagne: from ca 1895.

bubbly Jock. A turkey cock. Orig. (—1785) Scottish; but well acclimatized in England by 1840; Thackeray and Besant & Rice use it. Either it is ex the turkey's 'bubbly' cry or it is an early rhyming synonym (see *Slang*, p. 274). 2. Hence, a stupid boaster: C.19. 3. Hence, a conceited, pragmatical fellow; a prig; a cad: from ca 1860; ob. G. A. Sala, 1883.

bubby. A woman's breast. Rare in singular. Late C.17–20; S.E. till late C.18, then dial. and low. D'Urfey, in 1686, 'The Ladies here may without Scandal shew | Face or white Bubbies, to each ogling Beau.' Congreve, in *The Old Bachelor*, 'Did not her eyes twinkle, and her mouth water? Did she not pull up her little bubbies?' Either ex *bub*, to drink, or semantically ex a milk-needing babe's *bu bu!*; for the latter possibility, see the congruous matter in Weekley's delightful baby-talk essay in *Adjectives and Other Words.*

***bube.** Syphilis: late C.17–early 19 c. Ex S.E. *bubo*, which Coles, 1676, perhaps wrongly classifies as c. even though he applies his c. *bubo* to POX, his S.E. *bubo* to 'a large fiery pimple'.

Buck. A nickname for all men surnamed Taylor: orig. nautical: late C.19–20. Prob. ex 'Buck' Taylor, a popular member of Buffalo Bill's cowboy team visiting England in 1887.

buck. A forward, daring woman: rare, perhaps only c.: ca 1720–30. 2. Likewise coll, a man of spirit and gay conduct: ca 1700–1805. Grose, 2nd ed., has *buck of the first head*, 'a blood or choice spirit', a notable debauchee; prob. ex *like a buck of the first head*, which, in Ray, 1678, means little more than pert or brisk. 'A large assembly of young fellows, whom they call bucks', Fielding, 1752. 3. A dandy: from ca 1805, ob. by 1887, now merely archaic: coll > S.E. Thackeray in *Vanity Fair*, 'A most tremendous buck'. cf. DUDE;

MASHER; SWELL. 4. A cuckold: ca 1770–1820. Abbr. BUCK('S) FACE. 5. An unlicensed cab-driver: ca 1850–1905. Also, same period, a sham fare, a hanger-about at omnibus-stands. 6. A sixpence: C.19–20, ob.; gen. with a preceding sum in shillings, as *three and a buck*. Prob. abbr. FYE-BUCK. 7. A large marble: schoolboys', ca 1870–1910. 8. In British Guiana (1869), a native Indian of South America: coll rather than s. 9. Grose, 1st ed., 1785, has '*buck*, a blind horse': this is rare, but hardly disputable: presumably s.: late C.18–early 19. 10. A small dealer in the service of a greater (a 'stock-master'): Cockney (—1887). 11. Conversation: 1895, Mrs Croker. Ex Hindustani *bak*. Also *bukh*.

buck, v. To falsify – an account or balance-sheet: commercial, from ca 1870; ob. cf. COOK. 2. (Also *bukh*, *bukk*; Manchon spells it *bak*.) To chatter; talk with egotistical super-abundance: Anglo-Indian coll: 1880. Ex Hindustani *bakna*. Yule & Burnell. (cf. BUCK, n., 11.) Whence *buck-stick*, a chatterer (—1888). 3. Also, v.i., to object, be reluctant (v.t. with *at*): coll, from ca 1890; mainly Australia and New Zealand.

buck, adj. Handsome: Winchester College; C.19. Ex BUCK, n., 3, a dandy.

buck, go to. A low coll of C.18, as in *A New Canting Dict.*, 1725, '*She wants to go to buck*, . . . of a wanton Woman, who is desirous of Male Conversation.'

buck, old. A term of address: from ca 1830.

buck, run a. To poll an invalid vote: late C.18–early 19; orig. and mainly Anglo-Irish. cf. BUCK, n., 9; perhaps, however, a pun on *run amuck*.

buck a (blessed) hurricane or **a town down.** Resp. —1870, —1881, both ob., Australian coll: (of a horse) to buck furiously. A. C. Grant: *Bush Life in Queensland*, 1881, at I, 131, for both.

buck against. To oppose violently: coll (—1909). Ex U.S. cf. BUCK, v., 3.

***buck bail.** 'Bail given by a sharper for one of the gang', Grose, 2nd ed.: late C.18–early 19; c. and low.

buck-doctor. A Government veterinary surgeon: coll of South African Midlands: late C.19–20. Ex early attention to lung-diseased goats.

buck down. To be sorry; unhappy. Winchester College, from ca 1860; ob. cf. BUCKED, 1.

buck face, buck's face. A cuckold: late C.17–early 19.

buck-fat. Goat-lard: Cape Colony coll (—1902). cf. BUCK-DOCTOR.

buck-fever. The nervous excitement of a young sportsman when out shooting: South African coll: 1892, Nicolls & Eglinton, *The Sportsman in South Africa*.

buck fitch. An old lecher or roué: late C.17–early 19. *Fitch* = *fitchew* = polecat.

buck of the first head, see BUCK, n., 2.

buck one's stumps. To get a move on (lit., stir one's legs): *Conway* Training Ship (—1891).

buck-shot. A settlers' term for granulated lava (always imbedded in a sandy alluvium): New Zealand s. (—1851) > coll.

buck the tiger. To gamble heavily: U.S. (from ca 1862), anglicized before 1909; ob.

buck tooth. A large tooth that projects: from ca 1750; in C.18–19, S.E.; in C.20, coll.

buck up. Orig. (—1854), v.i. and t., to dress up. Ex BUCK, n., 3, a dandy. Then, 2, from ca 1860, to make haste, or – esp. in the imperative – to become energetic, cheerful. Also, 3, from ca 1895, to encourage, cheer up, or refresh ('A spot of b. and s. bucked him up no end'); and as v.i., to be encouraged; esp. in *buck up!*

bucked. Tired: Uppingham, from ca 1860; ob. Contrast BUCK UP. 2. Encouraged, elated; cheered, cheerful: from ca 1905. cf. BUCK UP, 3.

buckeen. A bully: coll, Anglo-Irish: late C.18–early 19. In S.E., 'a younger son'. Ex BUCK after *squireen*.

bucker. A porpoise: nautical: mid-C.19–20. Ex its jumps into the air.

***bucket,** v. To deceive, cheat, swindle, ruin: from ca 1810; until ca 1830, c. or low. Vaux, Scott. 2. To ride (a horse) hard: from ca 1850: coll; in C.20 j. Often as vbl n., *bucketing* (Whyte-Melville, 1856). 3. In rowing: to take the water with a scoop; swing the body; hurry unduly the body's forward swing: from ca 1869; coll.

bucket. A glass of spirits: low Ayrshire: 1870, John Kelso Hunter, *Life Studies of Character*, 'A rest for twa-three minutes, and a bucket the piece wad be acceptable.' Also cheapjacks'; C. Hindley, *The Life of a Cheapjack*, 1876. 2. See BUCKET AFLOAT.

bucket, give the. (With indirect object.) To dismiss from one's employment: coll (—1863). cf. GIVE THE BAG.

bucket, kick the. To die: late C.18–20.

Grose, 1785; Wolcot, 'Pitt has kicked the bucket', 1796. Prob. ex the beam or yoke from which, as in Norfolk, pigs are hung; *bucket* in this sense is C.16–20 S.E.

bucket afloat. A coat: rhyming s. (—1874): †. Often simply *bucket*.

bucket shop. An unauthorized office for the sale of stocks: orig. (?1881) U.S., anglicized ca 1887; Ware prob. errs when he dates its English use as early as 1870. In C.19, coll. Ex *bucket*, 'the vessel in which water is drawn out of a well' (Johnson) or ex BUCKET (v., 1), to swindle, or ex the bucket into which falls the recording-tape or 'ticker'.

***bucketing concern.** The vbl n. of BUCKET, v., 1: c. of ca 1810–80.

buckets. Boots: fast life: ca 1820–50. Pierce Egan, *Finish*, 1828. One 'pours' one's feet into them.

bucketsful, coming down in. Raining heavily: coll: late C.19–20.

buckhorse. A blow, or a smart box, on the ear: coll; from ca 1850, ex Buckhorse, actually John Smith, a celebrated pugilist, who would, for a small sum, allow one to strike him severely on the side of the head. Often as vbl n., *buckhorsing*: see *Blackwood's Magazine*, 1864, vol. II, the Public Schools' Report – Westminster.

buckie. A refractory person: coll, when not, as gen., Scottish: C.18–19; ob., except among tailors, who, in late C.19–20, use it also of a bad tailor or of a shoemaker.

bucking. Washing sails: nautical coll: mid-C.19–20. Ex a technical process in bleaching.

Buckinger's boot. The MONOSYLLABLE: ca 1740–95. Ex Matthew Buckinger, a daft limbless fellow married to 'a tall handsome woman', Grose, 3rd ed.

buckish. Foppish, dandyish: from ca 1780. Until ca 1870, S.E.; then coll; ob. *Mme D'Arblay's Diary*, at 1782; Wolcot; George Parker; Combe; George Eliot.

buckle. A fetter (gen. pl): coll, C.17–early 18. 2. Condition, state, mood: Australian, ca 1850–1910. By confusion of *fettle* with *fetter*? 3. Figure 2 in House (Bingo): late C.19–20. Shortened rhyming s. *buckle-my-shoe*.

buckle, v. To be married: late C.17–19, extant as vbl n., *buckling*. Marry, v.t.: C.18–20. Both are coll; the former in Dryden, 'Is this an age to buckle with a bride?', the latter in, e.g. Scott, 'Dr R., who buckles beggars for a tester and a dram of Geneva.' 2. In c. and low s., v.t., to arrest: mid-C.19–20 (ob.); gen. in past ppl passive.

buckle and bare thong, come (or **be brought) to.** To be stripped of – to lose – everything: coll: ca 1550–1850, though extant in dial.

buckle(-)beggar. A celebrator of prison, hence of irregular, marriages; a hedge priest. Coll. Late C.17–early 19. Orig. and mainly Scottish. cf. COUPLE-BEGGAR.

buckle-bosom. A constable: C.17: coll. Mabbe's translation of *Guzman d'Alfarache*.

buckle down. To settle down: mid-C.19–20: coll. cf. BUCKLE TO.

buckle-hammed. Crooked-legged: C.17: coll. Gaule, 1629, has 'Buckle-hamm'd, Stump-legg'd, Splay-footed'.

buckle-hole (of one's belt), be reduced or **starved to the last.** To be near death by starvation: Cockney coll (—1887).

buckle my shoe, see BUCKLE, n., 3.

buckle of the girdle (or, C.19, **belt), turn the.** To prepare to fight: coll (Cromwell, 1656, 'an homely expression'): late C.16–19; extant in dial. Ex the turning of the buckle to the back, so that the belly be not injured thereby.

buckle to, v.i. Set to with a will, apply oneself energetically (1712). Coll. A development from *buckle*, v.i., to grapple, as in Butler, 'He with the foe began to buckle', 1663. 2. v.t., understand: C.19.

Buckley?, who struck. A c.p. used, in C.19, to irritate Irishmen. Origin obscure – though H., 5th ed., offers a plausible and amusing story.

***Buckley's (chance).** A forlorn hope: Australian. 'Buckley was a declared outlaw whose chance of escape was made hopeless,' Jice Doone. He died in 1856, so prob. from 1856. (There have been many other explanations.)

bucko (pl **-oes).** A swashbuckling, domineering, or blustering man; occ. as term of address; swagger or bluster: nautical (—1909). Ex BUCK, n., 2, +*o*.

buckra. A white man: orig. (1794) in Negro talk; then, after ca 1860, among those Britons who lived in the wilder parts of the British Empire. Coll ex Calabar *backra*, master.

buck's face, see BUCK FACE.

buckshee, see BAKSHEE.

buckshot rule. A political coll for the upholding of government only, or chiefly, by a constabulary armed with rifles. Orig. applied to the Ireland of 1881. *Buck(-)shot* is large shot.

buckskin. An American soldier during the Revolutionary war; also, ca 1820–60, a native American. Ex U.S. sense (1755+): a Virginian.

bucksome. Happy; in good spirits: a C.19 survival, at Winchester College, of C.17–18 '*bucksom*, wanton, merry', B.E. *Bucksome* is from BUCK (UP), and influenced by *buxom*, of which, need I say?, B.E.'s *bucksome* is merely a variant spelling and nowise related to BUCK.

buckstick, see BUCK, v., 2.

bud, nip in the. To check or ruin a project in its beginnings: from ca 1840; coll passing, in late C.19, into S.E. The † *crush in the bud* occurs as early as 1746.

***budge; 'or sneaking budge',** Grose, 1st ed. A sneaking thief: c. or low s.: from ca 1670. Head; Coles, esp. of cloaks; Fielding, in *Amelia*. †by 1850. 2. A thief's accomplice, esp. one who hides in a house to open the door later: c.: C.18. 3. Liquor: c. (—1821); †. A perversion of BUB, n., 1, or BOOZE.

budge, v. To depart: low: mid-C.18–19. Grose, 1st ed. cf. S.E. *budge*, to move however slightly. 2. To inform; SPLIT, 2: low (—1859); ob. by 1890.

***budge, sneaking** or **standing.** A thief's scout or spy: c.: late C.18–19.

***budge a beak(e).** To decamp; to flee from justice: C.17 (early): c. BEAK = a constable.

***budge and snudge.** A housebreaker and his assistant; such burglary: ca 1670–1800; c.

***budge kain.** A public-house: Scottish c. (—1823); †by 1900. cf. BUDGE, n., 3. Presumably *kain* = KEN.

***budger.** A drunkard: C.19 c. Ex BUDGE, n., 3.

budgeree. Good; excellent. Australian, from ca 1800. Recorded as early as 1793 and 'dictionaried' in 1796. Ex Port Jackson Aborigine dial.

budget, open one's. To speak one's mind: C.17–early 18: coll.

***budging ken.** A public-house: C.19 c. Hence, COVE *of the b.-k.*, a publican. Ex BUDGE, n., last sense.

budgy. Drunk: low: from at least the 1830s. The American *Spirit of the Times*, 20 June 1840 (p. 192, col. 3), app. refers to an English source in the quotation, 'What budgy brutes you all are.' Ex BUDGE, n., 3.

budmash. A rascal; a thief: Regular Army: late C.19–20. Ex Hindustani *badmash.*

bufa, see BUFFER, 1.

***bufe.** A dog: mid-C.16–18 c. Ex its bark: cf. BUFFER, 1, and *bugher*, an 'anglicized' representation of the Scottish *bugher* pronounced properly *bu'ha*, loosely *buffer*: cf. the correct pronunciation of Scottish words like *Benachie* (approximately *Ben-a-he*).

***bufe-nabber, -napper.** Mid-C.17–early 19, C.19 c.: a dog-stealer.

***bufe's nob.** A dog's head: c. (—1785); †by 1900.

buff. The bare skin: coll, C.17–20; ob. except in *stripped to the buff* (C.19–20). Chapman, 1654, 'Then for accoutrements you wear the buff.' Ex the colour. 2. A man; a fellow; often as a term of address: coll: ca 1700–1830. Smollett, in *Roderick Random*, 1748. cf. BUFFER, sense 2. 3. A variant of BUFE: C.18. cf. BUFF-(K)NAPPER.

buff, v. To strip oneself, often as *buff it*. From ca 1850; ob. Mayhew. It occurs also in *buff well*, to appear to advantage when (almost) stripped: sporting, esp. boxing: prob. since ca 1810 or even 1800. Ex BUFF, n., 1; perhaps imm. ex BUFFING THE DOG. 2. To maintain a statement; swear to a person's identity (*buff to*); inform on. If absolutely, *buff it*: 'Do you buff it?' From ca 1880. Perhaps ex *to buffet* or *to* BLUFF. 3. To polish with a buff: coll in metal trades from ca 1880. 4. See BUFFING THE DOG.

buff, in. Naked: C.17–20. At first s., then coll. Dekker, 'I go . . . in buff.' Already ob. by 1890. See BUFF, n., 1.

buff, stand. To bear the brunt; endure without flinching. v.t. with *to* or *against*. Coll; from *temp.* Restoration; ob. by 1850, †by 1890. cf. BUFF, v., and S.E. *be a buffer, buffer state*. Butler, in *Hudibras's Epitaph*, ca 1680: 'And for the good old cause stood buff | 'Gainst many a bitter kick and cuff'; Fielding; Dyche's Dict.; Scott.

buff and blue, or **blue and buff.** The Whig party: ca 1690–1830: political coll. Ex its former colours.

***buff-ball.** C.19–20; ob.; c. and low. Greenwood, *In Strange Company*, 1880: 'The most favourite entertainment at this place is known as buff-ball, in which both sexes – innocent of clothing – madly join.' cf. BALLUM RANCUM and BUTTOCK-BALL.

buff-coat. A soldier: ca 1660–1900: coll >, by 1700, S.E.

***buff-(k)napper.** A dog-stealer: c.: C.18–early 19.

buff nor baff, say neither. To say nothing at all: coll: late C.15–17. A C.16–19 variant is *not to say buff to a wolf's shadow*. Here, *buff*, like *baff*, is prob. echoic.

***buff to the stuff.** To claim stolen property: late C.19–20 c. Ware. See BUFF, v., 2.

buffalo. A buffalo-robe: Canadian and U.S. coll: 1856.

buffar. Dog-like: c. (—1688). See BUFE, and:

***buffer.** A dog: in mid-C.16–early 19 c.; after ca 1830, low; ob. The C.16–17, occ. the C.18, spellings are BUFE, *bufa, buffa*. Lover, in *Handy Andy*, 1840: 'It is not every day we get a badger . . . I'll send for my "buffer" . . . spanking sport.' In late C.19–20 circus s., a performing dog: as in: 'Risley kids and slanging buffers, | Lord alone knows how they suffers.' (Risley kids are children used in foot juggling.) 2. In late C.17–18 c., 'a Rogue that kills good sound Horses only for their Skins', B.E. 3. A man, in C.19 often, in C.20 gen., as *old buffer*. Recorded in 1749; Barham; Anstey, 'an old yellow buffer'. Perhaps ex BUFF, the bare skin, but cf. dial. sense, a foolish fellow. 4. One who, for money, takes a false oath: C.19. cf. *to* BUFF, 2. 5. A boxer: mostly Anglo-Irish: ca 1810–50. Tom Moore in *Tom Crib's Memorial*, 1819, 'Sprightly *to the Scratch* both Buffers came.' cf. S.E. *buffet*. 6. A boatswain's mate: naval: mid-C.19–20. It was he who, in the old days, administered the CAT, 2. 7. A pistol: early C.19. Scott, 1824. cf. BARKER. 8. An innkeeper, says Grose, 1st ed. Perhaps an error, perhaps a variant of BLUFFER, 1. If authentic, then it is prob. c. of ca 1780–1830.

***buffer-lurking.** Dog-stealing: C.19 c.

***buffer-nabber.** A dog-stealer: c. (—1823); ob. See BUFFER, n., 1.

***buffer's nab.** A false seal, shaped like a dog's head (*nab* = NOB), to a false pass. Late C.17–18 c. cf. BUFE'S NOB.

buffers. Female breasts: low: late C.19–20.

***buffing the dog.** The practice of killing such stolen dogs as are not advertised for, stripping them of their skins (cf. BUFF, n., 1 and v., 1), which are sold, and giving the flesh to other dogs: c. (—1781): app. †by 1860 or so. Prob. ex BUFF, n., 1.

buffle. A fool: mid-C.16–18; coll >, by 1720, S.E. Ex Fr. *buffle*, a buffalo, and abbr.:

buffle-head. A fool; an ignorant fellow: mid-C.17–18; coll till ca 1700, then S.E. Whence:

buffle-headed. Foolish: stupid: late C.17–19; coll until ca 1750, then S.E.

buffy. Drunk: from ca 1859; ob. Yates, 1866, 'Flexor was fine and buffy when he came home last night.' Perhaps a corruption of BUDGY, or ex BEVIE.

buffy, old. 'Old fellow', *Sessions*, 30 Oct. 1845: low s.: ca 1825–70. Ex BUFFER, 3?

***buft.** Either a decoy (*buffet*) or a bully: late C.16 c. Greene.

bug. Anglo-Irish, mid-C.18–19: an Englishman. Ex bugs, introduced, Irishmen say, into Ireland by Englishmen. 2. In c., a breast-pin: mid-C.19–20; ob. 3. (Gen. pl.) A wall-flower: low London (—1909). cf. BLOOD, n., 4. 4. See BIG BUG.

bug, v. To exchange 'some of the dearest materials of which a hat is made for others of less value', Grose, 1st ed.: late C.18–early 19: hatters'. 2. To bribe: late C.17–19 c.; cf. BUG THE WRIT. Whence vbl n., *bugging*, the police's taking of bribes not to arrest: late C.17–19 c. 3. Also, to give; hand over (*bug over*): c. (—1812): †.

bug-blinding. A bout of whitewashing: military, from ca 1870; ob.

bug-hunter. An upholsterer: late C.18–19. 2. A robber of the dead: mid-C.19–20: c. or low s. 3. One who collects as an entomologist: coll: 1889 (O.E.D.). 4. A robber of drunken men's breast-pins: c.: from ca 1860. Ex BUG, n., 2.

bug in a rug, snug as a, see SNUG AS . . .

bug-juice. 1. Hair-oil. 2. Ginger ale: ca 1870–1910, low.

bug-shooter. A volunteer (soldier): schools' and universities': ca 1898–1914.

***bug the writ.** (Of bailiffs) to refrain from, or postpone, serving a writ, money having passed: c.: late C.18–early 19.

bug-trap. A small vessel; a bunk: nautical: from ca 1890. Because easily overrun with cockroaches.

bug-walk. A bed: low; ca 1850–1930.

***bugaboo.** A sheriff's officer; a weekly creditor: C.19 c. Ex lit. sense.

buggah. A variant, rare in C.20, of sense 2 of:

bugger. In c., a stealer of breast-pins from drunks: C.19. Ex BUG, n., 2. 2. A man: fellow; chap: low coll; 1719, D'Urfey. In S.E. (C.16–20), a sodomite. Ex L. *Bulgarus*, a Bulgarian; Albigensian heretics were often accused of perversion.

bugger, v. To spoil; ruin; check or

change drastically: from ca 1880. The expletive use is recorded at a very much earlier date: *Sessions*, Dec. 1793, p. 86, 'She said, b**st and b-gg-r your eyes, I have got none of your money.' 2. Cheat at cards: c. or low: late C.19–20.

bugger! A strong expletive: latish C.19–20.

bugger all. A low variant of *damn all.*

bugger in the coals. 'A thinnish cake spreckled [*sic*] with currents and baked hastily on the glowing embers', William Kelly, *Life in Victoria*, 1859: Australian: ca 1830–90.

bugger it. A variant of BUGGER!

bugger off. To depart, to decamp: low: late C.19–20. cf. FUCK OFF and PISS OFF.

bugger up. To spoil, ruin; nullify: low: late C.19–20. cf. BUGGER, v., 1.

bugger you! A strong expletive: low (—1887).

buggeranto. A sodomite: s.: Ned Ward, 1703.

buggerlugs. An offensive term of address: mainly nautical: late C.19–20.

buggery, adj. A strong pejorative epithet: low: from ca 1870.

buggery, like. Vigorously, cruelly, vindictively; or, as an expletive, 'certainly not!'. From ca 1890.

***bugher**; occ. as in Coles, 1676, *bughar*. A dog, esp. if a mongrel or given to yelping or barking: ca 1670–1820: orig. c., then low. cf. BUFFER, 1, and see BUFE.

bugs. A dirty seaman: nautical: late C.19–20.

build. (Of clothes) make, cut, tailoring: coll: from ca 1840. 'Cuthbert Bede', *Verdant Green*, 1853; *Punch*, 10 Jan. 1880, in the delightful contribution on *The Spread of Education*. cf. BUILD UP.

build a chapel. To steer badly: nautical: C.19–20, ob.

***build up.** 'To array in good clothes, for trade purposes': c.: late C.19–20. Ware. cf. BUILD.

built by the mile . . . see COTTON-BOX.

built that way. (Gen. in negative.) Like, such a person as, that; of such a nature or character. Orig. (—1890), U.S.; anglicized ca 1900 as a coll.

bukh, see BUCK, n., 11, and v., 2. **bukk,** see BUCK, v., 2.

bukra, adv. Tomorrow: military: since ca 1880. Ex Arabic for 'tomorrow'.

bulchin. Lit., a bull-calf. A term of contempt or endearment to boy, youth, or man: coll, ca 1615–1830. 2. B.E. has it for a chubby boy or lad: coll, C.17–18. Also as *bulkin* (late C.16–17) and, in Grose, *bull chin.*

bulge (on a person), get the. To obtain an advantage: U.S. (1860), partly anglicized ca 1890; ob. Whence:

bulge on, have (got) the. To have the advantage of: E. E. Hornung, *Raffles,* 1889.

bulger, n. and adj. (Anything) large. Coll (—1859); ob.

bulgine. An engine: nautical: mid-C.19–20; ob. An old shanty has: 'Clear the track, let the bulgine run.'

***bulk,** a thief's assistant, late C.17–mid-19, is certainly c., as is *bulk and* FILE (pickpocket and his jostling accomplice): Coles, 1676. 2. *bulker*, the same and of same period, is prob. c.: but *bulker*, a low harlot, if c. in late C.17, > low s. in mid-C.18. Lit., one who sleeps on a *bulk* or heap.

***bulker,** see preceding entry. B.E.

bulkin, see BULCHIN.

***bulky.** A police constable: Northern c. or low: C.19–20; ob. *Edinburgh Magazine*, Aug. 1821.

bulky, adj. Rich, generous; generously rich. Winchester College, C.19–20. Opp. BRUM, adj., 2.

bull. False hair worn by women, ca 1690–1770. 2. Abbr. BULL'S-EYE, a crown piece: c.: late C.18–19. 3. c. also (—1860) is the sense: a ration of beef; and (3, *a*), the C.20 one, ex U.S.: a policeman. 4. In † S.E., a ludicrous jest, a self-contradictory statement. But in C.19–20, a ludicrous inconsistency unnoticed by its perpetrator and often producing an unintentional pun. *Irish* was not added until ca 1850, about which time the coll > S.E. Henry Kingsley, in one of his two best novels, *Geoffrey Hamlyn*, 1859: 'the most outrageous of Irish bulls'. ?suggested by COCK-AND-BULL STORY. 5. In the money market (opp. to BEAR), a speculator for a rise: from ca 1840. Orig. (1714) a speculation for a rise. At first, in either sense, s.; but by 1880, 1740 resp., coll. 6. Coll, lower classes, from ca 1850, 'a "bull" is a teapot with the leaves left in for a second brew', G. R. Sims, in *How the Poor Live*, 1887. 7. At Winchester College, from ca 1873 but now ob., cold beef, esp. at breakfast (cf. sense 3). 8. Abbr. *John Bull*: ca 1825–1900, coll. 9. Abbr. *bull's-eye*, the centre of the target; hence, a hit there. From ca 1870. Military and marksmen's. 10. A broken-winded horse: low:

late C.19–20. **11.** A small keg: nautical: C.19–20.

bull, v. To have intercourse with a woman (cf. the C.17–early 19 proverb, 'who bulls the cow must keep the calf'): low coll, C.18–20. 2. To befool, mock: C.16–17. To cheat: C.17–18. Both nuances coll. 3. (Stock Exchange) v.i. and t., try to raise the price (of): from ca 1840; coll after 1880. 4. See BULL THE BARREL.

bull and cow. A ROW, disturbance: rhyming s. (—1859).

bull at a (five-barred) gate, like a. Furiously; impetuously; clumsily: coll: late C.19–20, coll.

bull-bait. To bully; hector. Dickens in *Great Expectations*, 1860. ?a nonce-word.

bull-beef; occ. bull's-beef. Meat, esp. if beef: C.16–20, ob.; low coll. 2. adj., fierce, haughty, intolerant: C.18, coll.

bull-beef, big as. Stout and hearty; very big; big and grim: coll: late C.17–18; thereafter, dial. W. Robertson, 1681; Motteux, 1712. cf.:

bull-beef, eat. To become strong; fierce, presumptuous: late C.16–19. Gosson, 1579.

bull-beef, like. Big and grim, esp. with *bluster* and *look*. C.17–19; coll. Wolcot. See BULL-BEEF, BIG AS.

bull-beef!, sell yourself for. Often preceded by *go and.* A C.19 coll: run away!; don't be silly!

bull-beef, ugly as. Very ugly indeed. C.18–19 coll. Ex BULL-BEEF, BIG AS.

bull by the tail, trust one as far as one could fling a. i.e. not at all: coll: 1853, Reade; ob.

bull-calf. A big hulking or clumsy fellow: mid-C.18–early 19; coll.

bull chin, see BULCHIN.

bull-dance. A dance with men only: nautical: mid-C.19–20; ob. cf. BULL-PARTY; STAG-DANCE.

bull-dog. A sheriff's officer: late C.17–early 19: coll. Farquhar, 1698. 2. A pistol: late C.17–19: coll. cf. BARKER and BUFFER, 7. Farquhar, 1700, 'He whips out his stiletto, and I whips out my bull-dog'; Scott, 1825. 3. (Naval) a main-deck gun, C.19–20; ob. If housed or covered, it is a *muzzled b.-d.* 4. A sugar-loaf: early C.19; low, perhaps c. 5. A university (Oxford or Cambridge) proctor's assistant: from ca 1810; coll. Lockhart, in 1823, 'Long-forgotten stories of proctors bit and bull-dogs baffled.' See also PROCTOR'S DOGS. 6. A member of Trinity College, Cambridge: C.19; †by 1890.

bull-dose or -doze. A severe flogging, as is *bull-dozing*, which also = violent, esp. if political, coercion. Orig. (—1876), U.S., anglicized ca 1881 as a coll. Ex:

bull-doze, v. To flog severely; hence coerce by violent methods, esp. in politics. Orig. U.S., anglicized ca 1880 as a coll. Hence *bull-dozer*, an applier of violent coercion. Lit., to give a dose strong enough for a bull; W., however, thinks there may be some connection with † Dutch *doesen*, to strike violently and resoundingly.

bull(-)finch. A fool; a stupid fellow: coll, C.17–18. 2. In hunting, a high quickset hedge that, with a ditch on one side, is too – or almost too – difficult for a horse to jump. From ca 1830; by 1890, S.E. G. Lawrence in *Guy Livingstone*, 'an ugly black bull-finch'. Perhaps a perversion of *bull-fence*. Whence:

bull-finch, v.i. To leap a horse *through* such a hedge: from ca 1840; coll. 2. Hence *bull-fincher,* a horseman that does, or is fond of doing, this: coll, from ca 1850. Also, such a hedge: coll (1862).

bull-flesh. Boastfulness; swagger: coll: 1820; †by 1890.

bull-head. A stupid fellow: C.17–18; coll. cf. S.E. *bull-headed*, impetuously.

bull in a china shop, like a. Clumsily: coll (—1841), verging, in C.20, on S.E. Marryat. Perhaps suggested by COW IN A CAGE . . .

***bull in trouble.** A BULL (5) in the pound: c. (—1823); †by 1890.

bull-jine. A locomotive: nautical; from ca 1850; ob. Perhaps ex U.S. Punning *engine*: *hengine*, *hen-gine* or *-jine*. Also BULGINE.

bull money. 'Money extorted from or given by those who in places of public resort have been detected *in flagrante delicto* with a woman, as a bribe to silence', F. & H.; low coll, from ca 1870; ob.

bull-nurse. A male attendant on the sick: nautical: ca 1840–1900. *Graphic*, 4 April 1885, 'Years ago (it may be so still) it was the sailors' phrase . . .'

bull-party. A party of men only: C.19–20; ob. C.19. cf. BULL-DANCE.

bull-puncher. Both a variant of *cow-puncher* and an abbr. of BULLOCK-PUNCHER. Australian: from ca 1870; ob. C. H. Eden, *My Wife and I in Queensland*, 1872.

bull the (or a) barrel or cask. To pour

water into an empty rum cask and, after a sensible interval, to drink the intoxicating resultant: nautical (—1824); ob. If the officers, to keep the wood moist, used salt water, even the ensuing *salt-water bull* was sometimes drunk. One speaks also of *bulling a teapot*; cf. BULL, n., 6.

***bull-tit.** A horse with broken wind: c., mostly vagrants': ca 1830–80. cf. ROARER.

bullet, get and **give the.** To be dismissed and to dismiss, resp. *Get the b.* seems to be the earlier: from ca 1840 and recorded in Savage's *Dict. of Printing*, 1841; *get the instant bullet* is to be discharged on the spot. *Shake the bullet at one* (from ca 1850): to threaten with dismissal. Ex the effectiveness of a bullet.

bullet fever, the. Self-inflicted wound(s): military: ca 1770–1830.

bullet has its billet, every, see BILLET, EVERY BULLET HAS ITS.

bullet-head(ed), n. and adj. Dull or foolish (person): coll: C.17–18. cf. the S.E. and the U.S. senses.

bulletin, false as a. Inaccurate; false: coll, ca 1795–1820, when, according to Carlyle, it was a proverbial saying.

bullfincher, see BULL-FINCH, V.

bullish. (Stock Exchange) aiming at or tending to a rise in prices: from ca 1880; coll. 'Bullish about cotton', 1884 (S.O.D.). Ex BULL, n., 5.

bullock. A cheat at marbles: schoolboys', ca 1840–1910. *Notes and Queries*, 3 Nov. 1855. 2. A Royal Marine artilleryman: ca 1820–90. 3. Hence, any Royal Marine: likewise naval: late C.19–20. 4. A bushman: Australian: ca 1870–1900; very rarely, BULLOCK-PUNCHER, from ca 1870, being much commoner: a bullock-driver.

bullock, v. To bully, intimidate: coll, from ca 1715. M. Davies, 1716; Fielding; Foote; Grose. Since ca 1900, dial. only. 2. See BULLOCK'S HORN.

***bullock-and-file.** A 'buttock-and-file' (see at BUTTOCK AND TONGUE): c.: late C.18–mid-19. Baumann. ?A fusion of *bulk-and-file* (s.v. BULK) and *buttock-and-file*. More prob. Baumann's misreading.

bullock-puncher. A bullock-driver: Australian, from ca 1840; coll. cf. BULL-PUNCHER.

bullock's heart. A fart: rnyming s. (—1890). 2. 'A single . . . order to print, of two hundred and fifty copies only, the lowest paying number in the scale of prices . . . Not a "fat" but a "lean" job, hence the comparison to a bullock's heart, which, unless suffering from "fatty degeneration", is the essence of leanness', Jacobi in Barrère & Leland, 1890: printers': from the 1880s.

bullock's horn. To pawn: rhyming s. (—1874); often abbr. to *bullock*. 2. Also = in pawn, ca 1870–1910; occ. abbr. to *bullocks*, which is extant.

bullock's liver. A river: rhyming s.: late C.19–20.

bullocks' pettitoes. Pigs' trotters: s.: Ned Ward, 1703.

bullocky. A bullock-driver: Australian and New Zealand, from ca 1840 or 1850. At first s., then coll. Also, as in Boldrewood's *Colonial Reformer*, 1890, an adj. cf. BULLOCK, n., 4.

bull's-eye. A crown piece: late C.17–early 19: c. cf. BULL, n., 2. 2. A globular sweetmeat of peppermint: from ca 1820; coll until ca 1850, when it > S.E. Hone's *Every-Day Book*, 1825. 3. A bull's-eye lantern: coll (—1851). 4. (South Africa) a small dark cloud, red-hearted, frequently seen about the Cape of Good Hope and supposed to foretell a storm; the storm so portended. Recorded, the cloud in 1753, the storm in 1849: coll by 1870, S.E. by 1900. 5. A small, thick, old-fashioned watch: C.19. (Smaller than a TURNIP.) 6. See BADGES AND BULL'S-EYES.

bull's-eye villas. The small open tents used by the Volunteers at their annual gathering: ca 1870–1914.

bull's feather, give or get the. To cuckold or be cuckolded: C.17–early 19; coll. Nares quotes a C.17 song entitled *The Bull's Feather*, and Richardson uses it in *Clarissa Harlowe*. cf. the Fr. *se planter des plumes de bœuf* and the C.16–early 19 variant *wear the bull's feather* (as in Grose, 1st ed.).

bull's foot, see B FROM A BATTLEDORE.

bull's noon. Midnight: low: 1839; very ob. and mainly provincial.

bull's-wool. The dry, tenuously fibrous 'inner portion of the covering of the stringy-bark tree', Morris: Australian, esp. Tasmanian (—1898): coll.

bully. A protector and exploiter of prostitutes: from ca 1690; coll until ca 1750, then S.E. Defoe in his *Jure Divino*, 1706, 'Mars the celestial bully they adore, | And Venus for an everlasting whore.' Ex the S.E. C.16–17 sense of sweetheart. 2. Companion, mate: from ca 1820: nautical (and dial.). 3. In Eton football, a scrimmage (cf. Winchester College HOT): recorded in 1865, it has since ca 1890 ranked as a coll and it may now be considered S.E. 4. Abbr. BULLY-BEEF or corruption of Fr. *bouilli*: pickled or tinned beef: 1883: coll in C.19.

bully, adj. First-rate, CHAMPION, splendid: Canada, Australia, and New Zealand, from ca 1860, ex U.S. 'The roof fell in, there was a "bully" blaze', Meade's *New Zealand*, 1870. Ex the late C.17–18 S.E. *bully*, worthy, admirable, applied only to persons.

bully about the muzzle. 'Too thick and large in the mouth', Ware: dog-fanciers': 1883, Miss Braddon.

bully-back. A brothel's bully and chucker-out; a bully supporting another person: C.18–early 19. Amherst, 1726, 'old lecherous bully-backs', and Grose, who describes some of this scoundrel's wiles and duties. Occ. *bully-buck*. Also as v.

bully-beef. (cf. BULLY, n., 4.) In the Navy, boiled salt beef; in the Army, tinned beef. *Bully* may be the earlier form, *bully-beef* an elaboration after BULL-BEEF. From ca 1884. Coll till ca 1900, then S.E.

bully-beggar. A sol. form of †S.E. *bull-beggar*, which may itself be a corruption of *bugbear*. C.18–early 19.

***bully-cock.** One who foments quarrels in order to rob the quarrellers: c. or low s.: late C.18–early 19. 2. A low, round, broad-brimmed hat: see BILLY-COCK.

bully fake. A piece of luck: low London: ca 1882–1915. Ex BULLY, adj. + FAKE, an action.

bully fop. A brainless, silly, talkative fellow, apt to hector: ca 1680–1800. B.E. describes as c., but I very much doubt it.

bully for you!, CAPITAL!, reached England ca 1870 after having, in 1864–6, enjoyed a phenomenal vogue in the U.S.

bully huff-cap. A boasting bully, a hector: coll: C.18. More gen.: *bully-huff*, late C.17–18, as in Cotton and B.E.

bully-rag, occ. **bally-rag.** To intimidate; revile; scold vehemently: from late 1750s, Thomas Warton employing it in his *Oxford Newsman's Verses*, 1760. Coll (and dial.), as is the derivative vbl n., *bully-*, occ. *bally-*, *ragging*, recorded first in 1863 but doubtless used a century earlier. Etymology obscure: perhaps, semantically, to 'make a bully's rag of' (a person).

bully-rock or **-rook.** A boon companion: late C.16–early 18: coll, as in Shakespeare. 2. ca 1650–1720, c., then low s. for a hired ruffian or 'a boisterous, hectoring fellow', Martin's Dict., 1754. The *rock* form is not recorded before 1653 and may be in error for *rook*. B.E. has *-rock*, but B.E. contains a few misprints – some of which have been solemnly reproduced by other writers.

bully ruffian. A highwayman who, in attacking, uses many oaths and imprecations: late C.17–18.

bully-trap. A mild-looking man the match of any ruffian: mid-C.18–early 19. 2. In late C.17–early 18 c., a sharper, a cheat.

bully up. To hurry, gen. in imperative: Uppingham School: mid-C.19–20; ob.

bulrush, seek or **find a knot in a.** To look for – or find – difficulties where there are none: late C.16–18; coll till ca 1700, then S.E.

bum. The posteriors: dating from M.E.; not abbr. BOTTOM, which, in this sense, dates only from C.18; prob. echoic: cf. It. *bum*, the sound of an explosion. Shakespeare, Jonson, Swift. This good English word began to lose caste ca 1790, and ca 1840 it > a vulg. and has been eschewed. 2. Abbr. BUM-BAILIFF: ca 1660–1880 (but extant in Anglo-Irish for a sheriff's assistant): coll. Butler, 1663, 'Sergeant Bum'; Ned Ward, in *The London Spy*, 'The Vermin of the Law, the Bum.' 3. A child's, and a childish word, for a drink: coll, C.16–17. 4. A birching: Public Schools', C.19; cf. the C.17–18 v., to strike, thump. 5. See BUM BALL.

bum, v. To arrest: late C.17–18. Ex BUM, n., 2. 2. To serve with a county-court summons. C.19–20; ob.

bum, adj. Disreputable: London fast or sporting s.: ca 1885–1905.

bum. A coll contraction of *by my*: ca 1570–90. Edwards, 1571, 'Bum broth, but few such roisters come to my years.'

bum, have a bit of. To coït with a woman: lower class: late C.19–20.

bum, toe – occ. **hoof** – **one's.** To kick one's behind; CHUCK OUT. Low coll: from ca 1870.

bum-bags. Trousers: low; from ca 1855. See BAGS. Prob. ex Warwickshire dial. (1840).

bum-bailiff or **baily.** 'A bailiff of the meanest kind', Johnson. Recorded in 1601 (Shakespeare), it was coll in C.17, S.E. in C.18–19; in C.20, archaic. Blackstone considered it a corruption of *bound bailiff*, but prob. the term comes ex the constant and touching proximity of bailiff to victim.

bum ball (1870); less gen. **bum** (1867). A cricketers' catachresis for a *bump(-)ball.*

bum-bass. A violoncello: low coll: late C.18–19. Samuel Pegge in *Anonymiana*, 1809.

bum-baste. To beat hard on the posteriors: mid-C.16–17. In C.18–19 coll, to beat, thrash. From ca 1860, dial. only. cf. BASTE.

bum-beating, vbl n. Jostling: C.17; coll. Beaumont & Fletcher in *Wit without Malice.*

bum-boat. A scavenger's boat: C.17–early 18: coll. 2. A boat carrying provisions or merchandise to ships lying in port or at some distance from the shore: s. (—1769) > coll >, by 1880, S.E.

bum boozer. A desperate drinker: theatrical (—1909); ob.

bum-boy. A catamite: low coll: late (?mid-) C.19–20.

bum-brusher. A schoolmaster; an usher. From ca 1700. Tom Brown, 1704; *New London Magazine*, 1788, '. . . that great nursery of bum-brushers, Appleby School'; *Blackwood's Magazine*, Oct. 1832. cf. FLAYBOTTOMIST.

***bum card.** A marked playing-card: ca 1570–1620: gaming c., revived in C.20. Northbrook, *Treatise against Dicing*, 1577; Rowlands, 1608.

***bum-charter.** Prison bread steeped in hot water: c. of ca 1810–50.

bum clink. Inferior beer: Midland Counties' s., from ca 1830; ob. (*Clink*, a ringing sound.) cf. CLINK, n., 3.

Bum Court. The Ecclesiastical Court: a low nickname: ca 1540–90. Perhaps ex the members' long sessions on their backsides (see BUM, n., 1).

bum-creeper. 'One who walks bent almost double', F. & H. revised: low: late C.19–20.

bum-curtain. (Cambridge University) a very short gown: 1835; †. Esp., until 1835, the Caius College gown; after that date, esp. the St John's gown. See Charles Whibley's delightful *Three Centuries of Cambridge Wit*, 1889.

bum-feag(u)e, -feagle, -feg. To thrash, esp. on the posteriors: jocular coll: late C.16–early 17.

bum-fiddle. The posteriors: late C.17–early 19, low. Cotton, Grose, Southey. For the pun, cf. ARS MUSICA. Fletcher, 1620, has 'bum-fiddled with a bastard', i.e. saddled with one: but *bum-fiddle*, v., is also used to mean: use as toilet paper: and dates from ca 1550. The derivative *bum-fiddler*, ?a fornicator, is C.17 and rare.

bum-fidget. A restless person: C.18–19, low coll.

bum-fighter; -fighting. A whoremonger; coïtion: low coll: C.18. D'Urfey, 1719.

bum-fluff. That unsightly hair which disfigures the faces of pubescent boys; these unfortunate youths are often advised to *smear it with butter and get the cat to lick it off*: Cockneys': late C.19–20.

bum-fodder. Trashy literature: from ca 1650; S.E. till ca 1800, then coll; †by 1890. In 1660 an anon. (Alexander Brome's?) verse satire on the Rump Parliament bears this arresting title: 'Bumm-Fodder; or, Waste-Paper proper to wipe the nation's rump with, or your own'. 2. Toilet paper: from ca 1659. Often, in C.19–20, abbr. to BUMF.

bum-freezer. An Eton jacket: C.19–20, low. cf. BUM-PERISHER.

bum-jerker. A schoolmaster: low: C.19–20; very ob. Malkin, 1809.

bum-perisher and **-shaver.** A short-tailed coat; a jacket. cf. BUM-CURTAIN.

bum-roll. The C.17 coll equivalent of a bustle or dress-improver. Jonson in the *Poetaster*. cf. BIRD-CAGE.

bum-shop. A brothel; the *pudendum muliebre*: low: mid-C.19–20; ob.

bum-suck; often **bumsuck,** v.i., to toady: coll: late C.19–20.

bum-sucker. A toady, lick-spittle; a sponger, hanger-on. C.19–20, low coll.

bum-trap. A bailiff: mid-C.18–early 19. Fielding in *Tom Jones*. Perhaps the origin of TRAP, 2, police. Ex BUM, n., 2.

bumble; bumbler. A blunderer; an idler: resp. late C.18–mid-19, mid-C.19–20. 2. (Only *bumble.*) Hence, a beadle: first in Dickens's *Oliver Twist*, as a person's name, and then, 1856, any beadle: coll, soon S.E., as was *bumbledom*, stupid and pompous officiousness, 1856+.

bumble, v. To fornicate: Restoration period. e.g. in Dryden's *The Kind Keeper*. cf. BUM-SHOP.

bumble-puppy. Family, i.e. inexpert, whist (—1884): coll; ob. 2. Also, ca 1800–80, a public-house version of the ancient game of troule-in-madame: coll.

bumbles. Horses' blinkers: Northern coll, C.19–20.

bumbo; occ. **bombo.** The female pudend: mid-C.18–19, West Indian; orig. a Negroes' word. 2. A drink composed of rum, sugar, water, and nutmeg (*Sessions*, 1738, spelt *bumbow*: earliest record), or of brandy, water, and sugar. A Northern variation was made with gin: coll passing to S.E. cf. It. *bombo*, a child's word for a drink, but prob. ex *bum*, childish for drink, after RUMBO.

bumf. A schoolboys' and soldiers' abbr. of BUM-FODDER, toilet paper: mid-C.19–20. Hence, from ca 1870, paper: hence, the Wellington College *bumf-hunt*, a paper-chase.

bumf, v.i. and t. To crib by copying another's work: Charterhouse: late C.19–20. Ex the n.

bumfer. A boy given to cribbing from another's work: Charterhouse: late C.19–20. Ex BUMF, V.

bumkin. 'A burlesque term for the posteriors.' C.17. Nares, well-read lexicographer. Lit., a little bum: see BUM, n., 1.

bummaree. A Billingsgate fishmarket middle-man (—1786): coll till ca 1800, when it > S.E. Etymology obscure; perhaps ex S.E. *bottomry* (1622): cf. Fr. *bomerie*, bottomry. cf. the v. 2. A *bain-marie*: cooks' (—1909). cf. BANG-MARY.

bummaree, v.i. and t. To retail fish on a large scale: mid-C.19–20, coll >, by 1900, S.E. Hence, vbl n., *bummareeing* (*it*), such retailing: G. A. Sala, 1859. Ex preceding. 2. 'To run up a score at a newly opened public-house': ca 1820–80.

bummer. A BUM-BAILIFF: ca 1670–1810. 2. A severe pecuniary loss: racing: ca 1870–1914. 3. A beggar, a sponger, a loafer: orig. (1856), U.S.; anglicized ca 1870. ?ex Ger. *bummler*, an idler; a tramp.

bumming. A thrashing: schools, esp. Wellington College, C.19–20; ob. 2. vbl n., loafing, sponging: from ca 1895, orig. U.S.

bummy. (cf. BUMMER.) A corruption of BUM-BAILIFF: C.18–19.

bump. A human faculty: coll: from ca 1820. Ex *bump*, a cranial prominence as in phrenology: (1815): likewise coll.

bump-supper. A supper to celebrate a college boat's success in Sloggers or Toggers, Mays or Eights: Cambridge, Oxford. From ca 1860; coll until C.20, then S.E.

bumper. A full glass: from ca 1660: in C.18, coll; thereafter S.E. 2. A crowded house: theatrical (1839, Dickens). 3. Anything very large: coll: from ca 1859. cf. CORKER; THUMPER; WHACKER; WHOPPER. 4. A bumping race: Oxford and Cambridge Universities': 1910. Perhaps ex:

Bumpers, the. The Bumping Races at: Shrewsbury School: late C.19–20. Desmond Coke, *The Bending of a Twig*, 1906. On SLOGGER and TOGGER, 2.

bumping. Large: coll: from ca 1860; somewhat ob. cf. BUMPER, 3.

bumpkin, see BUMKIN.

bumpology, bumposopher. The 'science' of cranial 'bumps'; one learned therein: jocular coll: 1834, 1836.

bumps!, now she; what ho, she bumps! Excellent!; splendid!: coll: resp. ca 1895–1910, from ca 1905. Prob. ex boating.

bumpsie, -sy. Drunk: coll: C.17. *Tarleton's Jests*, 1611 (Halliwell). 'Apt to bump into people' is a possible suggestion as to origin.

bumptious. Self-assertive: coll; from ca 1800. Mme D'Arblay, Dickens. Other senses, S.E.: the same applies to *bumptiousness* (Hughes, 1857) and *bumptiously* (M. Collins, 1871). Prob. ex *bump*, a sudden collision or a dull heavy blow, on some such word as *fractious*.

bumsuck, see BUM-SUCK.

bun. A familiar coll for the squirrel: from late C.16. Perhaps hence, 2, a coll endearment: C.17–19. cf. BUNNY, 3. 3. In C.17–19, the *pudendum muliebre* (cf. Grose, 2nd ed., 'To touch bun for luck; a practice observed among sailors going on a cruize'), ex the Scottish and Northern dial. sense the tail of a hare, hence, in Scottish, the 'tail' of a person. 4. A familiar name for a rabbit: coll: late C.18–20. Abbr. BUNNY. 5. A harlot: (—1889). Prob. ex sense 3.

bun or **cake, take the.** To obtain first honours; 'beat the band'. While CAKE is orig. U.S., anglicized ca 1885, *take the bun* is an English derivative: from the early 1890s. In Australia, ca 1895–1905, *capture the pickled biscuit*. See TAKE THE BISCUIT.

bun-feast or **-fight.** A tea-party: late C.19–20 coll. cf. CRUMPET-SCRAMBLE; MUFFIN-FIGHT.

bun for luck, touch. The C.18–19 (?†) nautical practice of effecting an intimate caress (see BUN, 3) before going on a (long) voyage.

bun-penny. An early Queen Victoria penny showing her with a bun: coll: late C.19–20.

bun-puncher or **-strangler.** A teetotaller: military: late C.19–20; ob. Resp. Frank Richards and F. & Gibbons. Ex preference of buns to beer.

bun-struggle or **-worry.** A tea-party for sailors or soldiers: military and naval: from ca 1870.

bun-wallah. A variant of BUN-PUNCHER. cf. *char-wallah*, a tea-totaller, CHAR, 2.

bunce (the predominant C.19–20 spelling), **bunse, bunt(s).** Money: C.18–early 19. D'Urfey spells it *buns*. In mid-C.19–20 it = (costermongers') perquisites; profit; commission; Mayhew spells it *bunse* and *bunts*, and pertinently proposes derivation ex sham L. BONUS. 2. At Edinburgh High School (—1879), he who, when another finds anything, cries *bunce!* has a traditional, though ob., claim to the half of it: whence *stick up for your bunce* = claim one's share, stand up for oneself.

buncer. A seller on commission: from ca 1860.

bunch of dog's meat. 'A squalling child in arms' (*Sinks*, 1848): low: ca 1825–70.

bunch of fives. The hand; fist: pugilistic: *Boxiana* III, 1821. cf. FIVES.

bunco, see BUNKO. **buncombe,** see BUNKUM.

bund. A dam; a dyke: Anglo-Indian coll; from ca 1810. 2. An embanked (seashore) quay: Anglo-Chinese (—1875). Ex Persian.

bundabust. Preparations; preliminary arrangements: Regular Army: late C.19–20. Ex Hindustani *band-o-bast*, a tying and binding. 2. Revenue settlement (often *bundobust*).

bunder-boat. A boat used either for communicating with ships at anchor or for purely coastal trade: on the Bombay and Madras coast. Anglo-Indian coll (—1825). Ex Hindi *bandar*, a harbour, ex Persian.

bundle-man. A married seaman: lowerdeck: nautical: from ca 1890. Frazer & Gibbons. 'Apparently suggested by the small bundle tied up with a blue handkerchief which married seamen in a Home Port usually take ashore with them when going on leave.'

bundle of ten. Army blankets, because rolled in tens: military: late C.19–20.

bundle off. To send away hurriedly: from ca 1820; coll; from 1880, S.E.

bundle-tail. A short lass either fat or squat: late C.17–18.

bundle up. To attach (someone) in force: low: 1824, J. Wright, *Morning at Bow Street*, 'He was bundled up or enveloped, as it were, in a posse of charleys': †by 1900.

bundook; occ. **bandook** or **barndook;** even, says Manchon, **bundoop.** A rifle; earlier, a musket; earlier still, cross-bow. Ultimately ex the Arabic *banadik*, Venice, where cross-bows were made. (Native Egyptians still call Venice *Bundookia*.) The Regular Army stationed in India used the term as early as C.18.

bundook and spike. A Regular Army term, from ca 1850, for rifle and bayonet. See the preceding entry.

bung. A brewer; a landlord of a PUB, esp. in sporting circles; (nautical) a master's assistant superintending the serving of grog. From ca 1850; all senses ob. Hence, *bung-ball*, the annual dance held by the brewers: London trade (—1909). 2. In c. of mid-C.16–early 19, a purse. cf. A.-S. and Frisian *pung*, a purse. 3. Hence, in c. or low s. of late C.16–17, e.g. in Shakespeare, a cutpurse. Hence *bung-knife*, late C.16, is either a knife for purse-slitting or one kept in a purse. 4. (Also *bung-hole*.) The anus: low: late C.18–20. 5. Only in *tell a bung*, to tell a lie: schoolboys' (—1887); ob. Perhaps the corruption of a noted liar's surname. 6. A blow, a punch: low: late C.19–20.

bung, v. Gen. as *bung up*, to close up the eyes with a blow: C.19–20 coll, esp. among boxers. But in C.16–early 18, S.E., and applicable to mouth, ears, etc., and fig. 2. Often as *bung over*, to pass, hand (over), give; (not before C.20) to send (a person, e.g. into the Navy; or a thing, e.g. a letter to the post): coll. Shakespeare, Beaumont & Fletcher. 3. To throw forcibly: dial. (—1825) >, ca 1890, s. Echoic. 4. To deceive with a lie: C.19. cf. CRAM; STUFF.

bung, adj. Drunk; fuddled: a Scottish low coll: C.18–20; ob. Ramsay. ?'bung-full'.

bung, adv. Heavily; 'smack': coll: late C.19–20. Esp. (*go*, etc.) *bung into*. Kipling.

bung, go. To explode, go to smash: from ca 1860; ob. 2. Hence, mainly in Australia, slightly in New Zealand, to fail, esp. to go bankrupt: from ca 1880: prob. influenced by *go bong* or *bung*, to die, a 'pidgin' phrase (—1881) ex East Australian aborigine adj. *bong*, *bung*, dead: cf. *Humpey*(-) *Bong*, lit. the dead houses, a suburb of Brisbane (see HUMP(E)Y).

bung-ball, see BUNG, n., 1.

bung-eyed. Drunk; fuddled: low: mid-C.19–20, ob. Mayhew. Ex Scottish *bung*, tipsy. 2. Hence, cross-eyed: low: from ca 1860; slightly ob.

bung-hole, see BUNG, n., 4.

***bung-juice.** Beer; porter. C.19–20 (ob.) c. Ex *bung*, a stopper for casks.

***bung-nipper.** A cutpurse. In mid-C.17–18, c.; in C.19 low s. Ex BUNG, n., 2.

bung it! Stow it! Low: late C.19–20.

bung off. To depart: from ca 1905.

bung one's eye. To drink heartily: mid-C.18–early 19. Hence, to drink a dram: late C.18–early 19. i.e. till one's eyes close.

bung-starter. Nautical: (*a*) the captain of the hold; (*b*) an apprentice serving in the hold. Both (—1867) are ob.

bung up and bilge free. Everything aboard in excellent order: nautical: late C.19–20. Ex proper storing of barrels.

bung upwards, adv. On his face; prone: late C.18–19 (orig. brewers'). Suggested by ARSE UPWARDS, or by *bung-hole*, the anus (s.v. BUNG, n., 4).

bungaree or **-rie.** A public-house: low: from ca 1870. Ex BUNG, n., 1.

Bungay!, go to. Go to hell! C.19; mostly dial. Bungay is a township in East Suffolk; it has vestiges of a castle built by that aristocratic family, the *Bigods*. In C.19 there was a Suffolk phrase *go to Bungay for a bottom* (or *to get new-bottomed*) applied to repairs for wherries.

Bungay fair and broke(n) both his legs, he's been to. He's drunk; he got drunk: C.19 coll. cf. preceding entry and BREAKY-LEG, 2.

bunged-up. Damaged, stove in, clogged up: coll: late C.19–20.

bungery. A tavern: mostly London (—1909); ob. cf. BUNG, n., 1. Also BUNGAREE.

bungie-bird. Pejorative for a friar: late C.16–early 17. cf. Greene's Friar Bacon and Friar Bungay.

bungler. 'An unperforming Husband', B.E.: C.17–18; coll.

Bungs. A ship's cooper: mid C.19–20.

buniony. Lumpy in outline: art: 1880; ob. Ex 'a bunion breaking up the "drawing" of a foot'.

bunk. The sisters' sitting-room at the end-entrance to a hospital ward: nurses': late C.19–20.

bunk, v. To decamp: from early 1890s: orig. low; in C.20, near-coll. *Referee*, 16 Feb. 1885. 2. Hence, to absent oneself from: from ca 1890. 3. At Wellington College: to expel; ca 1870–1915. 4. *bunk* (*it*), to sleep in a bunk: coll. Orig. and mainly U.S.: anglicized ca 1886.

bunk, do a. To depart hastily: from ca 1865. cf. BUNK, v., 1. See also DO A BUNK.

bunked, be or get. To be expelled: Shrewsbury School: late C.19–20. Desmond Coke, *The Bending of a Twig*, 1906. Ex BUNK, to depart.

bunker. Beer: ca 1850–1910. ?ex *bona aqua* or ex *coal-bunker*, from which one 'coals up' (see COAL UP, v.). 2. A feast in a low lodging-house: low (—1887). Perhaps ex sense 1.

bunker-cat. A low-class fireman: Canadian nautical: late C.19–20.

bunkered, be. To be in a situation difficult of escape: coll: 1890. Ex golf. cf. *stymied*.

bunko. (Of persons) shifty; disreputable: seaports' (esp. Liverpool), from ca 1905, ex U.S. cf.:

bunko-steerer. A swindler, esp. at cards: orig. (—1876), U.S.; anglicized ca 1895, but never at all gen. Ex *bunko*, occ. *bunco*, a swindling card-game or lottery.

bunkum or **buncombe.** In England from ca 1856; ex U.S. (—1827). In C.19, coll. Talk, empty or TALL; HUMBUG, n., 3; claptrap; insincere eloquence. G. A. Sala, 1859: '. . . "bunkum" (an Americanism I feel constrained to use, as signifying nothingness, ineffably inept and irremediably fire-perforated windbaggery, and sublimated cucumber sunbeams . . .)'. Ex *Buncombe* County, North Carolina.

bunky. Awkward; badly finished: Christ's Hospital, C.19–20; ob.

bunnick (up). To settle; dispose of; thrash: Cockney: ca 1880–1914. *Punch*, 17 July 1886, 'We've bunnicked up Gladsting' (Gladstone). Perhaps cognate with *bunker* (in BUNKERED).

bunny. A rabbit: in C.17 s., then coll. The S.O.D. records at 1606; B.E. has it. 2. In C.20, an occ. variant of *rabbit*, a very poor player of any given game. 3. The female pudend: C.18–20. D'Urfey, 1719. Diminutive of BUN, 3.

bunny-grub. Green vegetables: Cheltenham College: mid-C.19–20. cf. GRASS, n., 3, and:

bunny's meat. The same: nautical: late C.19–20.

buns, bunse, see BUNCE.

bunt. An apron: late C.18–early 19. Grose, 2nd ed. Ex the S.E. *bunt*, the bag- or pouch-shaped part of a net or a sail. 2. See BUNCE; ca 1850–1900. Mayhew.

bunt, v. Knock; butt; 'to run against or jostle', Grose, 2nd ed. Except when used of animals, this (—1788) is coll and dial. Perhaps ex *butt* + *bounce* (or *bunch*), as the O.E.D. suggests.

bunt fair. Before the wind: nautical coll: late C.19–20.

bunter. A low, esp. a low thieving, harlot: from ca 1700. Ned Ward, 1707, 'Punks,

Strolers, Market Dames, and Bunters'; Goldsmith, 1765. In this sense until ca 1900. Perhaps ex BUNT; i.e. a sifter of men, not of meal. 2. Derivatively, ca 1730–1900, any low woman. Attributively in Walpole's *Parish Register*, 1759, 'Here Fielding met his bunter Muse.' 3. (Semantically, cf. sense 1.) A gatherer of rags, bones, etc.: from ca 1745. Dyche's Dict., 1748; Mayhew. 4. A woman who, after a brief sojourn, departs from her lodgings without paying: ca 1830–1900. Mayhew. Too early to be ex BUNK, to depart; cf. senses 1 and 3.

bunter's tea. Strong liquor (?gin): ca 1715–60. Anon., *The Quakers Opera*, 1728. '*Quaker*. . . . What hast thou got? *Poorlean.* Sir, you may have what you please, Wind or right Nanty or South-Sea, or Cock-my-Cap, or Kill-Grief, or Comfort, or White Tape, or Poverty, or Bunter's Tea, or Apricock-Water, or Roll-me-in-the-Kennel, or Diddle or Meat Drink-Washing-and-Lodging, or Kill-Cobler, or in plain English, Geneva.'

bunting. A coll endearment, esp. as *baby bunting*: from ca 1660. Perhaps ex Scottish *buntin.*

bunting time. Late C.17–mid-18, coll: 'when the Grass is high enough to hide the young Men and Maids', B.E. cf. BUNT, V.

***buntling.** (Gen. pl.) A petticoat: late C.17–early 19 c. Ex BUNT, n.

Bunty. The inevitable nickname of any short man: military: late C.19–20. Ex dial. (and U.S.) *bunty*, short and stout.

bunyip. A HUMBUG, an impostor: Australian: since ca 1860. Tom Collins, *Such is Life*, 1903. The bunyip is a fabulous Australian animal.

bup, see:

bupper. Bread and butter: children's, whence lower classes': C.19–20. By 'infantile reduction', says Ware, who notes the occ. abbr. *bup.*

bur, see BURR.

burble. To talk continuously with little pertinence or sense: H. C. Bailey, 1904. cf. the C.16–17 S.E. *burble*, to make a bubbling sound.

***Burdon's Hotel.** Whitecross Street Prison: c. ca 1850–1910. Ex a Governor named Burdon.

burerk, see BURICK.

***Burford bait,** see TAKE A BURFORD BAIT.

burgoo, burgue. Oatmeal porridge: from ca 1740: coll. Ex *burghul*, Turkish for wheat porridge. Whence:

burgoo-eater. A Scottish seaman: nautical: late C.19–20.

***burick,** occ. **burerk.** At first (—1812), a prostitute, a low woman: c. From ca 1850, a lady, esp. if showily dressed: low. Mayhew, 1851. From ca 1890 the word has increasingly meant, chiefly among Cockneys, a wife, 'old woman'. The etymology is obscure; but *burick* may perhaps be found to derive ex the Romany *burk*, a breast, pl *burkaari*, or to be a corruption of Scots *bure*, a loose woman, recorded by E.D.D. for 1807.

burk. To avoid work: New Zealand: from ca 1880. Rhyming with *shirk*?

burke. To dye one's moustaches: military: *Sessions*, 1832. Dyed for uniformity, the semantic key being *burke*, to smother, as did the celebrated criminal executed in 1829. (*Burke*, to hush up, from ca 1840, was at first a coll development from its natural meaning, to strangle or suffocate, which arose in 1829.)

***burn,** in c., = to cheat, swindle: C.17–18. (Extant in dial.) cf. BURN THE KEN. 2. To smoke (tobacco): late C.19–20.

burn, one's ears. To feel that somebody is speaking of one: coll; from ca 1750, but in other forms from C.14 (e.g. Chaucer).

burn (a hole) in one's pocket. Of money and gen. preceded by *money*: to be eager to spend one's money, a definite sum often being mentioned. Coll; 1768, Tucker, concerning children, 'As we say, it [money] burns in their pockets.'

burn-crust. A baker: mid-C.18–20; jocular, coll rather than s.

burn daylight. Lit., have a light burning in the daytime, hence to waste the daylight. At first (ca 1587), coll; soon S.E. Shakespeare, in *Romeo*, 'Come, we burn daylight.'

burn it blue. To act outrageously (?): C.18. Swift in *Stephen and Chloe*.

burn my breeches, like DASH *my wig!*, is a jocular oath. Both are in Moore's *Tom Crib.*

burn one's or the candle at both ends. To work early and late, or to work early and pursue pleasure till late, in the day. From ca 1650. Coll > S.E. by 1800. Ex the Fr. phrase recorded in England as early as Cotgrave. 2. (Only . . . *the* . . .) To be very wasteful: coll: mid-C.18–20. Smollett.

burn one's fingers. To incur harm, damage by meddling. From ca 1700. Coll > S.E.

burn oneself out. To work too hard and die early. C.19–20 coll > S.E. by 1900.

***burn the ken.** To live at an inn or lodging-house without paying one's quarters: C.18–early 19: cf. BURN THE TOWN.

burn the parade. To warn for guard more men than are necessary and then excuse the supernumeraries for money – ostensibly to buy coal and candles for the guard: mid-C.18–early 19, military.

burn the planks. To remain long seated. Coll verging on S.E.: from ca 1840; ob. Carlyle.

burn the Thames. To do something very remarkable: coll: Wolcot, 1787; ob. A jocular variation of *set the Thames on fire.*

burn the town. (Of soldiers and sailors) to leave a place without paying for one's quarters: late C.17–18. cf. BURN THE KEN.

burn the water. To spear salmon by torchlight. From ca 1800; s. > coll by 1850, S.E. by 1890.

burn you! Go to hell!: (low) coll (—1887); ob. Ex dial., where it occurs as early as 1760.

burned, burnt, ppl adj. Infected with venereal disease. Late C.16–20, ob.; coll. Shakespeare's pun in *Lear*, 'No heretics burned, but wenches' suitors'; B.E., 'Poxt, or swingingly Clapt'. cf. the mid-C.18–early 19 sailors' 'be sent out a sacrifice and come home a burnt offering', of catching a venereal disease abroad (Grose, 1st ed.).

***burner.** A card-sharper: C.18 (?earlier) c. Ex BURN. 2. A sharp blow or punch: c.: C.19. Ex the tingle it causes. 3. See:

burner, burning. A venereal disease: the latter (coll > S.E.) from ca 1750; the former (s. > coll) from ca 1810 (*Lex. Bal.*) and ob. cf. BURNED.

burner of navigable rivers, be no. To be a simple or a quite ordinary person: mid-C.18–early 19. cf. BURN THE THAMES.

burning, vbl n. Smoking: training-ships': late C.19–20.

burning shame. 'A lighted candle stuck into the private parts of a woman', Grose, 1st ed.: low: mid-C.18–early 19. Punning the stock phrase. 2. 'Having a watchman placed at the door of a bawdy-house, with a lantern on his staff, in the daytime, to deter persons from going in and out', Egan's Grose: low: ca 1820–40.

burnt, see BURNED.

burnt offering, see BURNED. 2. Food, esp. meat, that has been allowed to burn: jocular coll: late C.19–20.

burp. Esp. of a baby, to eructate; also v.t., to cause (a baby) to belch: late C.19–20 (?very much earlier): coll.

bur(r). A hanger-on, a persistent 'clinger': late C.16–20; until ca 1750 it was coll, then it > S.E.; slightly ob.

bur(r), v. To fight; scrimmage; RAG. Marlborough College: mid-C.19–20, ob.

burr-pump. The old manual bilge-pump: nautical coll: mid-C.19–20; ob. Because it so often 'stuck'.

burra, adj. Great, big; important, as *burra* SAHIB. Chiefly in India: from ca 1800.

burra beebee. A lady claiming, or very apt to claim, precedence at a party: Anglo-Indian: recorded in 1807; ob. In Hindi, lit. great lady.

burra khana. Lit., big dinner, it = a great, gen. a solemn, banquet: Anglo-Indian (—1880).

burra mem. The chief lady at a station: Anglo-Indian (—1903). Lit. *burra*, great, + MEM, white lady. See MEM-SAHIB; cf. BURRA BEEBEE.

burrow. To hide; live secretly or quietly. From ca 1750. Coll in C.18, then S.E. The S.O.D. quotes 'to burrow in mean lodgings', Marryat.

***burst.** A burglary: c. (—1857); ob. 2. A SPREE; a hearty meal. Esp. *on the burst*, on the spree: *Blackwood's*, 1880; Praed, 1881, in *Policy and Passion*. Coll. 3. (Sporting) a spurt (—1862): coll >, by 1900, S.E. 4. Hence (?), the 'outpour of theatrical audiences about [11 p.m.] into the Strand'; London police: 1879; ob. Ware.

burst, v. To drink, v.t. with *pot, cup, bottle*, etc.: coll: from ca 1850; †. 2. To spend extravagantly: from ca 1890. See BUST, v., 3.

burst at the broadside. To break wind: drinkers': ca 1670–1850.

burst him (her, etc.)**!** Confound him: low coll. (—1887); ob.

burst one's crust. To break one's skin: boxers': ca 1800–80.

burst up. To be greatly perturbed, angered, excited: coll; late C.19–20; ob.

bursted. Burst (past tense and ppl): since ca 1800, dial. and, otherwise, sol.

burster. Bread: low (—1848). 2. An exhausting physical effort: coll; rather rare. Recorded in 1851. 3. (Racing) a heavy fall, CROPPER: from ca 1860; ob. 4. (Australia) a violent gale from the south, esp. at Sydney: from ca 1870; coll; rare for (*southerly*) BUSTER (6). 5. See BUSTER.

Burton-on-Trent. The rent one pays: rhyming s.: from ca 1880. Often abbr. to *Burton.*

***bury a moll.** c. and low: to run away from a mistress: from ca 1850. Perhaps suggested by dial. (—1847) *burying-a-wife*, 'a feast given by an apprentice at the expiration of his articles', Halliwell.

bury a Quaker. To defecate, evacuate: orig. and mainly Anglo-Irish: from ca 1800. F. & H., at *bury*, gives a long list of synonyms. cf. QUAKER, 2.

bury the hatchet. (In C.14–18, *hang up the hatchet.*) To swear peace, become friendly again. Ex U.S. (ca 1784), anglicized ca 1790 as a coll that, in C.20, has > S.E.; Wolcot uses it in 1794. Ex a Red Indian custom.

bus. Abbr. *business*: in the theatrical sense. From ca 1850. (Pronounced *biz.*) 2. Abbr. *omnibus*: from 1832. Harriet Martineau, Dickens, Thackeray, Black the novelist. 3. (A) dowdy dress: society: 1881. i.e. a dress suited only to that conveyance. 4. Enough! stop!: Anglo-Indian coll (—1853). Ex Hindi *bas.*

bus, v. Also *bus it*. To go by *bus* (n., 2): coll; 1838.

bus! see BUS, n., 4.

bus-bellied Ben. An alderman: East London: ca 1840–1910. Ex tendency to corpulence.

bus-napper, see BUZZ, v., 2. **bus-napper's kinchin,** see BUZZ-NAPPER'S KINCHIN.

***bush.** Either any or some special so-named tavern where a PIGEON (4) is plucked: c. of ca 1585–95. Greene. 2. The CAT-O'-NINE-TAILS: c.: from ca 1890. 3. Pubic hair: mid-C.19–20: low, after being a literary euphemism.

bush or **bush it.** To camp in the bush: from ca 1885; not much used. 2. *be bushed*, be lost in the bush (—1856); hence, 3, to be lost, at a loss: from ca 1870; all three are Australian coll. Both voices occur in B. L. Farjeon's *In Australian Wilds*, 1889. With sense 3, cf. the early C.19 c. *bushed*, penniless, destitute, and BUSHY PARK, AT.

bush, beat or **go about the.** To go deviously (fig.): coll, from ca 1550; the latter †by 1850.

bush, take to the. To become a bushranger: Australian coll: ca 1835–90.

bush baptist. A person of uncertain religion: Australian and New Zealand (—1910) mostly; but orig. English, it being used by soldiers in the Boer War – witness J. Milne, *The Epistles of Atkins*, 1902.

***bush-cove.** A gypsy: c. (—1823); †by 1900. 'Jon Bee', 1823, says, 'From their lodging under hedges, etc.'

bush lawyer. A layman fancying he knows all about the law – and given to laying it down: Australian coll: from early 1890s. H. G. Turner, 1896. See also LAWYER.

bush-ranger. A convict, later anyone, living on plunder in the Australian bush: recorded in 1806: coll soon > S.E. Now usually *bushranger*.

bush-scrubber. 'A bushman's word for a boor, bumpkin, or slatternly person': Australian coll: 1896. Morris. Ex the *scrub*, whence such a person may be presumed to have come.

bush-whacker. Australian, ex U.S.: an axe-man, feller of trees, opener of new country: C.19.

***bushed,** see BUSH, v., 2.

bushed on, vbl adj. Pleased; delighted with. C.19.

bushel and peck. The neck: rhyming s.: late C.19–20.

bushel bubby. A woman with large, full breasts: low: mid-C.18–19. Ex *bushel*, a large quantity, + *bubby*, a woman's breast.

bushy. A dweller in 'the bush' or remoter country districts: Australian coll: from late 1890s.

Bushy Park. A lark (lit. and fig.): rhyming s. (—1859). 2. The female pubic hair: low: from ca 1860. Hence, *take a turn in Bushy Park*, to possess a woman. But, see:

***Bushy Park, at; in the park.** Poor: c.: from ca 1810; virtually †.

business. Sexual intercourse: C.17–18, coll. Taylor the Water Poet, 1630, 'Laïs . . . asked Demosthenes one hundred crownes for one night's businesse.' 2. (Theatrical) dialogue as opp. to action: S.E., late C.17–early 18; but from ca 1750, as in the *World*, 1753, and Scott, in 1820, it has meant by-play and as such it is coll. 3. A matter in which one may intervene or meddle: late C.17–20; coll. 4. In deliberately vague reference to material objects: coll: 1654, Evelyn; 1847, Leigh Hunt, 'A business of screws and iron wheels'. cf. AFFAIR. 5. A difficult matter: coll; from ca 1840. Carlyle, 'If he had known what a business it was to govern the Abbey . . .', 1843. 6. Defecation, esp. in *do one's business*: nursery coll: mid-C.19–20.

business, do one's (for one), v.i. and t. To

kill; cause death of. From ca 1660; S.E. until ca 1800, then coll.

business, mean. To be in earnest: coll: 1857, Hughes.

business, mind one's own. To abstain from meddling in what does not concern one. Coll. From ca 1860; earlier, S.E.

business, quite a. Something unexpectedly difficult to do, obtain, etc.: coll: late C.19–20.

business, send about one's. To dismiss, send packing, just as *go about one's business* = to depart. In C.17–18, the latter, S.E.; in C.19, both coll; in C.20, both S.E.

business end, the. The commercial part of a firm's activities: coll: late C.19–20. 2. The part that matters: coll: from ca 1890. e.g. the business end of a sword is the point or the blade. Ex:

business end of a tin tack, the. The point of a tack: U.S. (—1882), anglicized in 1883 (*Daily News*, 27 March).

***busk.** To sell obscene songs and books in public-houses; whence *busking*, such occupation, and *busker*, such vendor. Orig. – prob. the 1840s, though not recorded till the '50s – vagrants' and always low. Mayhew, *London Labour and the London Poor*, vols. I and III. Prob. ex C.18–20 S.E. *busk*, cf. nautical *busk*, to cruise as a pirate. 2. Hence, to perform in the street: grafters': from ca 1850.

busk!, both ends of the, see BOTH ENDS ...

***busker.** A man who sings or performs in a public-house: c. (—1859). cf. BUSK. 2. Hence, an itinerant: c. or low s. (—1874).

Busky. A frequent nickname of men surnamed Smith: naval and military: late C.19–20.

busnack; gen. as vbl n. To pry; to interfere unduly, be fussy: naval: late C.19–20; ob. Prob. ex the *buzz* of a fly. Whence *buzz-nagger*.

buss. A variant of BUS, n., 2.

buss. A scholarship or bursary: Aberdeenshire s., not dial.: 1851, Wm Anderson, *Rhymes, Reveries and Reminiscences*. Perhaps because as pleasant as a kiss, or by corruption of Fr. *bourse*.

buss-beggar. A harlot, old and of the lowest: low coll: C.17–19. 2. Specifically, 'an old superannuated fumbler, whom none but' beggar-women 'will suffer to kiss them', Grose, 1st ed.: low coll: C.18–early 19.

bust. Sol. for *burst*, n. and v. Apparently unrecorded in England before 1830, Dickens being one of the earliest sources: *Oliver Twist* (*busting*, adj.); *Nicholas Nickleby*, 'His genius would have busted'; *Martin Chuzzlewit*, 'Keep cool, Jefferson ... don't bust'; *Two Cities*, 'Bust me if I don't think he'd been a drinking!'

bust, n. A frolic, SPREE, drinking-bout: esp. as *go on the bust*, orig. (—1860), U.S., acclimatized ca 1880. cf. BURST. 2. In c., a burglary: ca 1850–1910. See also BURST, n., 1.

bust, v. To bust; explode: sol. except when jocularly deliberate. Dickens, 1838. 2. To put out of breath: from ca 1870. e.g. in *Taking Out the Baby*, a broadside ballad of ca 1880. 3. In c. (occ. as BURST), to rob a house, v.t., rarely v.i.; also, v.i., to inform to the police, whence the vbl n., *busting*. Both C.19–20, the latter ob. 4. To degrade a non-commissioned officer: military coll: late C.19–20.

bust-maker. A womanizer; a seducer. Low coll: C.19. Ex the bosom's enlargement in pregnancy and punning the S.E. sense.

bust me! A mild oath: non-aristocratic: 1859, Dickens. Also *bust it!*, *bust you* (or *yer*)!

bust up. (Or hyphenated.) A great quarrel, ROW, or excitement: 1899, Kipling: coll now on verge of S.E.

busted, or **gone bust.** Ruined: coll: late C.19–20.

buster, burster. A small new loaf; a large bun. Until ca 1850, the form is gen. *burster*; after, *buster*. *Burster* occurs in Moncrieff's *Tom and Jerry*, *buster* in H., 1st ed., and Hindley's *Cheap Jack*. Ob. 2. (*Buster* only.) Anything of superior size or astounding nature: orig. (—1850), U.S., anglicized ca 1859, e.g. in Dickens's *Great Expectations*. 3. In c., a burglar: ca 1845–1910. 4. A spree, rarely except in *in for a buster*, determined on or ready for a spree: orig. U.S.; from ca 1858 in England (cf. BUST, n.); ob. 5. Hence, a dashing fellow: low: from ca 1860; ob. 6. (Australian) a southerly gale with much sand or dust, esp. at Sydney: coll, from ca 1880. Much earlier and more gen. as *southerly buster*. cf. BRICKFIELDER. 7. (Gen. *burster*.) A very successful day or season: grafters': from ca 1880. Ex sense 2.

buster, a, adv. Hollow; utterly: low: ca 1885–1910. See quotation at MOLROWING.

buster, come a. To fall, or be thrown, heavily from a horse: coll: Australian (—1888).

buster, go in or (on) a. To spend regardless of expense: mostly Cockneys': from ca 1885; ob. Anstey, *Voces Populi*, vol. II, 1892.

buster, old, see OLD BUSTER.

bustle. A dress-improver. Recorded in 1788 and presumably coll for a few years before becoming S.E., as in Dickens, Miss Mitford, Trollope. 2. Money: from ca 1810. At first c., but fairly gen., low s. by ca 1860; ob.

bustle, v. To confuse; perplex: coll, from ca 1850. cf. the transitive S.E. senses.

busy as a hen with one chick. Anxious; fussy; ludicrously proud: C.17–20 (ob.); proverbial coll. Shirley, 1632; Grose.

busy as the devil in a high (in mid-C.19–20, often **in a gale of) wind.** In a great flurry: low coll: from ca 1780; ob.

busy-sack. A carpet-bag: coll: from ca 1860; ob. cf. American *grip-sack*.

butch. To be a butcher, act as or like a butcher. In late C.18–early 19, S.E.; thereafter, and still, dial.; but in non-dial. circumstances it is, from ca 1900, coll: so too with the vbl n. *butching*.

butcha. A baby, a young child: Anglo-Indian (—1864). Ex Hindustani.

butcher. The king in playing-cards. Orig., ca 1850, and, though ob., still mainly public-house s. cf. BITCH, n., 4. 2. Stout (the drink): public-houses': from ca 1890. Butchers are often fat. 3. In C.19 c.: a medical officer. 4. A slop-master: artisans': ca 1850–1900. Mayhew.

butcher! Mid-C.18–early 19; nautical and military: a jocular comment (on need of bleeding) when a comrade falls down.

butcher about. To make a din; humbug or fool about. Wellington College: late C.19–20, ob. Perhaps a euphemism for BUGGER *about*.

butcher and bolt, see BOLT, BUTCHER AND.

butchering, adj. and adv. Far; much; great(ly); low: from ca 1870; ob. e.g. 'a butchering sight too forward' (J. Greenwood). cf. BLOODY and other violences.

butcher's, see BUTCHER'S (HOOK). 2. Noon: low (Parlary): 1893, R. H. Emerson, *Signor Lippo*.

butcher's bill. The casualty list of a battle, esp. of those killed: coll (—1881). Occ. for the monetary cost of a war: coll (—1887). If this term, in either sense, is employed sarcastically and indignantly, it is then, for all its cynicism, rather S.E. than coll.

butcher's dog, be or lie like a. To 'lie by the beef without touching it; a simile often applicable to married men', Grose, 2nd ed. Low coll: late C.18–early 19.

butcher's (hook). A look: rhyming s.: late C.19–20.

butcher's horse by his carrying a calf so well, that must have been a. A c.p. jest at the expense of an awkward rider. Ray, in *English Proverbs*, 2nd ed., 1678, gives it in a slightly different form. Coll: C.17–20; ob.

butcher's jelly. Injured meat: lower classes': 1887, *Standard*, 24 Sept.

butcher's meat. Meat had on credit and not yet paid for: late C.18–19 jocular punning the S.E. sense of the phrase.

butcher's mourning. A white hat with a black mourning hat-band: from ca 1860; ob. Apparently ex butchers' distaste for black hats.

butcher's shop, the. The execution shed: prison officers': late C.19–20.

butler's grace. A 'thank-you' but no money: coll: 1609, Melton; †by 1700.

butt. A buttock; also the buttocks: low coll in C.19–20 after being, in C.15–17, S.E. (Also dial. and U.S. coll.)

butt in. To interfere; interrupt: v.i.; v.t., *butt into*, rare. From ca 1895; coll.

butteker. A shop: late C.18–19. Prob. ex Fr. *boutique* or Sp. *bodega*. cf. BUTTIKEN.

butter. An inch of butter: C.18–19 Cambridge. e.g. in pl, 'Send me a roll and two butters.' Grose who, in 2nd ed., corrects the *Oxford* of the 1st. 2. Fulsome flattery, unctuous praise, SOFT SOAP. From ca 1820; coll. *Blackwood's Magazine*, 1823, 'You have been daubed over by the dirty butter of his applause.' cf. the slightly earlier BUTTERING-UP.

butter, v. In c. and low, to increase the stakes at every game or, in dicing, at every throw: ca 1690–1840. 2. Flatter, or praise, unctuously or fulsomely. Coll; from late C.19. Congreve, in *The Way of the World*, 1700: 'The squire that's buttered still is sure to be undone.' Coll; S.E. by 1850. 3. 'To cheat or defraud in a smooth or plausible manner', *A New Canting Dict.*, 1725: c.: C.18. 4. To whip; from ca 1820; ob. Gen. as *buttered*, past ppl passive. 5. To miss (a catch): cricket: 1891. Ex BUTTER-FINGERS.

butter and cheese of, make. To HUMBUG; bewilder: C.17; coll. cf. Gr. τυρεύειν.

butter-and-eggs. 'The feat of butter-and-eggs consists in going down the [frozen] slide on one foot and beating with the heel and toe of the other at short intervals,'

Macmillan's Magazine, Jan. 1862. Coll. cf. *knocking at the* COBBLER'S DOOR. 2. A popular, i.e. (when not sol.) coll, name for flowers of two shades of yellow, esp. toad-flax and narcissus: from ca 1770.

butter-and-eggs trot. A short jig-trot: coll; mid-C.18–early 19. Ex market women's gait.

butter-bag or **-box.** A Dutchman: C.17–early 19. Dekker and B.E. have the latter, Howell the former. ?ex Holland as a formerly important butter-producing country, or rather ex 'the great quantity of butter eaten by people of that country', Grose, 1st ed.

butter-boat, empty the. To lavish compliments; also, to battle. Coll; from early 1860s. A butter-boat is a table vessel in which one serves melted butter.

butter-box. A full-lined coasting brig: nautical coll, orig. (—1840), U.S.; anglicized ca 1850; ob. 2. A Dutch ship or seaman: nautical coll: C.19–20; ob. cf. BUTTER-BAG. 3. A fop: Ned Ward, 1703. 4. A Dutchman: ibid.: 1700.

butter-churn. A turn (on the stage): music-halls' rhyming s. (—1909).

butter-coloured beauties. 'A dozen or so pale yellow motor-cabs' appearing in 1897: London: 1897. Ware. cf. MARGARINE MESS.

butter dear, don't make. A jape addressed to patient anglers: mid-C.18–early 19. The origin of the phrase is (fortunately, I suspect) obscure.

butter-fingered. Apt to let things, esp. (1841) a ball, slip from one's hand: coll. Meredith in *Evan Harrington*. Ex:

butter-fingers. One who lets things, esp. a ball, slip from his grasp. Coll; Dickens, 1837; Hood, 1857, 'He was a slovenly player, and went among the cricket lovers by the sobriquet of butter-fingers.'

butter-flap. A trap, i.e. a light carriage: rhyming s. (—1873). Ob. Also (—1859), but †by 1870, a cap. cf. BABY PAP.

butter in one's eyes, have no. To be clear-sighted, hence alert and shrewd: coll: ca 1810–70. Alfred Burton, *Johnny Newcome*, 1818.

butter-mouth. A Dutchman: pejorative coll: mid-C.16–19. cf. BUTTER-BAG.

Butter-Nut. A soldier in the Southern Army in the American Civil War: 1863 and soon anglicized. Ex the brownish-grey uniform, often dyed with butternut bark.

butter one's bread on both sides. To be wasteful. Coll; from ca 1660.

butter-print. A child, esp. if illegitimate: Fletcher, 1616; †by 1800. cf. BUTTERCUP.

butter-queen and **-whore.** A scolding butter-woman: coll; resp. C.17 (H. More), late C.16–18 (Nashe, T. Brydges).

butter-slide. A very slippery ice-slide: children's coll: late C.19–20. Prob. ex the sense current ca 1850–90, a mischievous trick of Victorian small boys who put a lump of butter down where their elders would tread on it and take a fall.

butter upon bacon. Extravagance; extravagant; domestic coll (—1909).

butter-weight. Good measure: ca 1730–1900. Coll. Swift, 1733, 'Yet why should we be lac'd so strait? | I'll give my monarch butter-weight.' Ex *b.-w.*, formerly 18 (or more) ounces to the pound.

butter when it's hot, it will cut. Of a knife that is blunt. Coll from ca 1860.

butter will stick on his bread, no. He is always unlucky: C.17–19; coll. Scott. With *cleave*: C.16–17.

butter would not melt in one's mouth, (look) as if. (To seem) demure. Coll from the 1530s; Palsgrave, Latimer, Sedley, Swift, Scott, Thackeray. In reference to women, Swift and Grose add: *yet, I warrant you, cheese would not choke her*, the meaning of which must be left to the reader who will look at CHEESE.

buttercup. A child. A pet name: coll. Mrs Lynn Linton, 1877. From ca 1865; ob.

buttered bun(s). A mistress: ca 1670–90, as in W. Cullen, 1679, in reference to Louise de Quérouaille. 2. (In C.19–20 only **buttered bun.**) A harlot submitting sexually to several, or more, men in quick succession: C.17–20; slightly ob. Grose, 1st ed., 'One lying with a woman that has just lain with another man, is said to have a buttered bun.' 3. **(buttered bun.)** 'A Man pretty much in Liquor', *A New Canting Dict.*, 1725: low: ca 1720–60. 4. A country fool: Ned Ward, 1715. Matthews, however, may err in distinguishing it from sense 3.

butterfly. A river barge: nautical; from ca 1870; ob. Ironical. 2. The reins-guard affixed to the top of a hansom cab: cabmen's, from ca 1870; ob. Coll.

butterfly boat. A paddle (esp. if excursion) steamer: nautical: mid-C.19–20. Ex the 'wings'.

buttering-up. Fulsome flattery or praise: coll, ca 1815–60. Tom Moore, 1819, 'This buttering-up against the grain'.

buttery. Addicted to excessive flattery:

from ca 1840; coll passing to S.E. cf. BUTTER, v., 2. 2. The adj. to BUTTER-FINGERS: cricketers' coll: 1864.

buttery Benjie. A Scottish Universities s. synonym for BEJAN: from ca 1840; ob.

***buttiken.** A shop: c. (—1857); †by 1890. While KEN = a place, *butti* prob. = Fr. *boutique*.

butting. An obscure C.16 endearment: coll. Skelton. Perhaps cognate with BUNTING.

***buttock.** A low whore: ca 1660–1830: c.

buttock and tongue. A shrew. C.18–19. ?punning c. *buttock and twang* (late C.17–early 19), a common prostitute but no thief (also a *down buttock and sham file*, Grose, 1st ed.) and perhaps glancing at c. *buttock and file* (late C.17–early 19), a prostitute who is also a pickpocket; if in the latter c. phrase SHAM is inserted before FILE, the sense of the former c. phrase is obtained.

buttock and trimmings, see RUMP AND A DOZEN.

buttock-ball. A dance attended by prostitutes. Low coll: late C.17–early 19. Tom Brown, 1687. cf. BALLUM-RANCUM. See BUTTOCK. 2. Human coïtion: late C.18–early 19. Here the reference is doubly anatomical.

buttock-banqueting. Harlotry: coll: C.16–early 17.

buttock-broker. A procuress; the proprietress or manager of a brothel; a match-maker. Late C.17–early 19; low. In the first two senses, BUTTOCK = a harlot, in the third a cheek of the posteriors.

buttock-mail. A fine imposed for fornication: Scottish pejorative coll: C.16–19. Lyndesay, Scott.

buttocking-shop. A low brothel: low: C.19. Also *buttocking*-KEN: c.: C.19.

***button.** A shilling: good, ca 1840–1900; counterfeit, from ca 1780; orig. c., then low; †. cf. BRUMMAGEM BUTTONS. 2. An illicit decoy of any kind: from ca 1840; c. and low. Mayhew. 3. A baby's penis: low: C.19–20. 4. Clitoris: low: C.19–20.

***button,** v. Decoy, v.t.; v.i., act as an enticer in swindles. From ca 1840; ob.: c. and low. cf. BUTTON, n., 2.

button, have lost a; be a button short. To be slightly crazy: proletarian: late C.19–20; ob.

button, not to care a (brass). Not to care at all. Coll: C.15–20. cf. *not care a* RAP.

button, take by the. To BUTTON-HOLE. C.19–20. Coll, soon S.E.

button-boy. A page: coll; from ca 1875. cf. BUTTONS, BOY IN.

button-bung. A button thief: 'old', says F. & H.; prob. C.17.

button-bu(r)ster. A low comedian: theatrical, from ca 1870; ob. It is the audience that suffers.

button-catcher. A tailor: mostly nautical: from ca 1870; ob. cf. SNIP.

button-hole. Abbr. *button-hole flower(s)* or *bouquet*. Recorded in 1879. Coll. 2. The female pudend: low: mid-C.19–20. Hence *button-hole worker, working*, penis, coïtion, and *button-hole factory*, a brothel, a bed.

button-hole, v. To button-hold, i.e. to catch hold of a person by a button and detain him, unwilling, in conversation. Orig. (—1862) coll.

button-hole, take one down a; occ. take a b.-h. lower. To humiliate; to de-conceit: coll: from late C.16. Shakespeare.

button-holer. A button-hole flower: coll. App. first in *Punch*, 29 Nov. 1884.

button on, have a. To be despondent; temporarily depressed. Tailors', from ca 1860; ob.

button on to. To get hold of (a person), to button-hold (him); to cultivate (his) company: 1904, Charles Turley. Perhaps ex BUTTON-HOLE (v.) + COTTON *on to*.

button-pound. Money, esp. cash: provincial s., ca 1840–1900. Extant in dial., whence prob. it came.

button short, be a, see BUTTON, HAVE LOST A.

button up. To refrain from admitting a loss or disappointment: coll; from ca 1890. Ex U.S. stock-broking (1841).

***buttoner.** A decoy (see BUTTON, v.): c. >, ca 1870, low; from ca 1839. Ob. Brandon; *Blackwood's Magazine*, 1841; *Cornhill Magazine*, 1862.

buttons. A page: coll: 1848, Thackeray. Ex numerous jacket-buttons. cf. BOOTS. 2. The warden or superintendent: workhouses' (—1887).

buttons, boy in. A page: from ca 1855; coll.

buttons!, dash my. A coll and often jocular exclamation of surprise or vexation: ca 1840–1914.

buttons, have a soul above. To be, actually or in presumption only, superior to one's position: coll: C.19–20. Adumbrated in Colman, 1795, luminous in Marryat and Thackeray.

buttons, it is in one's. One is bound to succeed: coll: late C.16–18. Shakespeare, 1598, ''Tis in his buttons, he will carry 't.'

buttons, one's arse or **breech makes.** Also *make buttons* (C.17–19). To look or be sorry, sad, in great fear: coll; mid-C.16–early 19. Gabriel Harvey, captious critic, laborious versifier, and patterning prosateur; playwright Middleton; Grose, 3rd ed., 'His a–se makes buttons,' he is ready to befoul himself through fear; in Ainsworth's *Latin Dict.*, 1808, we find *his tail maketh buttons.* Ex *buttons*, the excreta of sheep.

buttons (on or **on one), not to have all one's.** To be slightly mad; weak-minded. Mid-C.19–20; ob. In dial. the affirmative form, indicative of great shrewdness, is common.

butty. A comrade, a mate; a policeman's assistant (†). Coll and dial.: from ca 1850. Henry Kingsley, 1859. Either from mining, where *butty* = a middleman, or from Romany *booty-pal*, a fellow workman, or, most prob., ex Warwickshire *butty*, a fellow servant or labourer (Rev. A. Macaulay, *History of Claybrook*, 1791). Perhaps cf. U.S. *buddy*. 2. Buttered bread: Liverpool: late C.19–20.

buvare. Any drinkable: Parlary and low: from ca 1840. cf. BEWARE.

buxed. HARD-UP; without money: London schools': ca 1870–95. A perversion of BUSTED: cf. BROKE and SMASHED UP.

buxie. An occ. variant of BAKSHEE.

Buxton bloaters. Fat men and women wheeled in bath-chairs, at Buxton: late C.19–early 20.

Buxton limp. 'The hobbling walk of invalids taking the waters': Society, esp. at Buxton: 1883–ca 1890. Ware. On ALEXANDRA LIMP.

buy, v. To incur, hear, receive, be 'landed with' (something unpleasant) with one's eyes open or very credulously: from ca 1800. cf. ASK FOR IT.

***buy a brush,** see BRUSH, BUY A.

buy a prop! The market is flat (with no support): Stock Exchange, ca 1880–1900.

buy a white horse. To squander money: nautical: late C.19–20. Ex the fleeting splendour of a 'white horse' wave.

buy and sell. To betray for a bribe: coll verging on S.E.: C.18–19.

buy it!, I'll. Tell me the answer or catch: c.p.: from ca 1905. Ex BUY, v.

buy one's boots in Crooked Lane and one's stockings in Bandy-Legged Walk. To have crooked or bandy legs: a mid-C.18–early 19 c.p.

buy one's thirst. To pay for a drink: U.S., anglicized in 1884; virtually †by 1909.

buz(z). A parlour and a public-house game, in which the players count 1, 2, 3, 4, etc., with *buz(z)* substituted for seven and any multiple thereof: coll, then, by 1900, S.E. From ca 1860; ob. Miss Allcott, *Little Women*, 1868. 2. (Gen. *the buzz.*) In c., the picking of pockets: late C.18–early 19. cf. the v., 2. 3. A rumour: naval coll: late C.19–20. Ex ob. S.E. *buzz*, a busy or persistent rumour. 4. The n. corresponding to sense 1 of the v.: mid-C.19–20. 'It's your buzz' = It's time you filled your glass.

buz(z), v.t. Drain (a bottle or decanter) to the last drop. Coll: C.18–19. Anon., *Tyburn's Worthies*, 1722. ?BOOZE, corrupted. See BUZZA. In C.19, to share equally the last of a bottle of wine, when there is not a full glass for each person. 2. v.i. and t., to pick pockets: from ca 1800: c., then – ca 1860 – low. Whence the late C.18–19 c. terms, *buz(z)-man*, *buz(z)-gloak*, *buzz-bloke* or *-cove*, and *buzz-napper*, a pickpocket. 3. To cast forcibly, throw swiftly: coll: 1893, Kipling, 'Dennis buzzed his carbine after him, and it caught him on the back of his head.'

buzz about, or **around, like a blue-arsed fly.** To be – or appear to be – excessively or officiously busy: late C.19–20.

***buz(z)-faking.** Pocket-picking. C.19 c. Ware has *buz-faker*.

***buz(z)-gloak,** see BUZZ, v., 2.

***buz(z)-man,** see BUZZ, v., 2. 2. More gen., however, an informer: c. (—1864). cf. BUZZ, n., 2.

buzz-nagger, *see* BUSNACK.

***buz(z)-nappers' academy.** A school for the training of thieves: late C.18–mid-19 c. George Parker, 1781; see, e.g., *Oliver Twist*.

***buz(z)-napper's kinchin.** A watchman: late C.18–early 19 c.

buzza. An early form of *to* BUZZ, sense 1: late C.18 only. Grose, 1st ed.: 'To *buzza one* is to challenge him to pour out all the wine in the bottle into his glass, undertaking to drink it', i.e. the whole of the wine, 'should it prove more than the glass would hold; commonly said to one who hesitates to drink a bottle that is nearly out'. In the 3rd ed., he adds: 'Some derive it from *bouze all*, i.e. drink it all.'

buzzard. A stupid, ignorant, foolish, gullible person: C.14–19, extant in dial. B.E. gives as s., S.O.D. as S.E.; prob. it wavered between coll and S.E. before it > dial.

Often, in C.18–20, in form *blind buzzard.* Ex *buzzard*, a useless hawk.

buzzer. A whisperer of scandal and gossip: C.17–18; coll. Shakespeare. 2. A pickpocket: from ca 1850; c. and low; ob. cf. *buz-napper*. Ex BUZZ, v., 2. 3. A motor-car: non-aristocratic: 1898 (Ware).

***buzzing.** Pocket-picking: c. (—1812). See BUZZ, v., 2.

buzzy. Crazy: ca 1880–1914. Lit., making one's head buzz.

by and by. Presently; soon. C.16–20; coll, but S.E. (though not dignified) after ca 1700.

by the by(e). Incidentally. In conversation only. C.18–20; coll > S.E. So, too, *by the way*.

by the wind. In difficulties; short of money: C.19–20 (ob.), nautical.

by-blow. A bastard: late C.16–20; coll till ca 1800, then S.E. Robert Browning, 'A drab's brat, a beggar's bye-blow'. cf.:

by-chop. A bastard: C.17–18; coll. Ben Jonson. cf.:

by-scape. A bastard: mid-C.17; coll verging on S.E. cf.:

by-slip. A bastard: late C.17–18; coll soon > S.E. 'Ungracious by-slips', Hacket, 1693, in the *Life of Williams*, one of the great biographies.

bye-bye. A sound made to induce sleep in a child: coll: C.17–20. Hence *go to bye-bye*, orig. an imperative, > go to sleep, fall asleep; go to bed: C.19–20; coll. In C.20, often *go (to) bye-byes*.

bye-bye! Good-bye! C.18–20; coll. Recorded in 1709.

bye-commoner. One who mistakenly thinks he can box: pugilistic: ca 1820–50. Ex COMMONER, 2.

by(e)-drink or **-drinking.** A drink, gen. stronger than tea, at other than meal-times. From ca 1760; coll, but S.E. in C.19–20; ob.

byme-by, see BIME-BY.

byte, see BITE, of which it is a frequent C.17–18 spelling.

C

C.H. A conquering hero: coll: Nov. 1882. Ex the frequent playing, to soldiers returned from the Egyptian War, of 'See the Conquering Hero Comes'.

C.-T., see COCK-CHAFER.

C.T.A. The police: circus and showmen's: from ca 1860. Origin?

ca'-canny, adj., applied to an employee's policy of working slowly, 'going slow'. Coll, recorded in 1896. Ex Scottish; lit., call shrewdly, i.e. go cautiously.

ca sa or **ca-sa,** see CASA, 1.

cab. Abbr. *cavalier* influenced by Sp. *caballero*: ca 1650–1710. Coll. 2. Abbr. *cabriolet*, a public carriage, two- or four-wheeled, seating two or four persons, and drawn by one horse, introduced into England in 1820, the term appearing seven years later, at first s., then soon coll, then by 1860 S.E. Occ., a cab-driver (1850, Thackeray). 3. A brothel: ca 1800–50. *Lex. Bal.*: 'How many tails have you in your cab? i.e. how many girls have you in your bawdy house?' Prob. ex *cabin.* 4. (Universities' and Public Schools') from ca 1850 as in 'Cuthbert Bede', *Verdant Green*, 1853: 'Those who can't afford a coach get a cab' – one of this author's best puns – '*alias* a crib, *alias* a translation'. Ex CABBAGE, n., 5. 5. A cabbage: Shelta: C.18–20.

cab; gen. **cab it,** v. To go by cab: coll; from ca 1830; Dickens has it in *Pickwick Papers*; ob. 2. (Schoolboys') to use a CRIB (n., 7): from ca 1855. Ex CABBAGE, v., 2. 3. To pilfer: schoolboys' (—1891); ob. Perhaps ex Scots: see E.D.D.

cab-moll. A harlot professionally fond of cabs and trains: low; ca 1840–1900. 2. A prostitute in a brothel: low: ca 1840–1910.

cabbage. Pieces of material filched by tailors; small profits in the shape of material. After ca 1660, coll; by 1800, S.E. Randolph, 1638; Dyche, 1748; Cobbett, 1821. Perhaps ex *garbage*: see O.E.D. and F. & H. (but see also KIBOSH ON . . .). cf. HELL. 2. A tailor: late C.17–early 19. 3. A late C.17 mode of dressing the hair similar to the chignon: coll, ca 1680–1720, as in the anon. *Mundus Muliebris*, 'Behind the noddle every baggage | Wears bundle "choux", in English cabbage.' 4. A cigar, esp. if inferior: coll: from ca 1840, ob. *Punch's Almanack*, 12 Aug. 1843, punningly: 'The cigar dealers, objecting to their lands being cribbed, have made us pay for the cabbage ever since.' 5. A translation or CRIB, n., 7: from ca 1850; schoolboys'; ob. 6. The female pudend: C.19–20, ob. cf. CAULIFLOWER (3) and GREENS. 7. (*The Cabbage.*) The *Savoy* Theatre: 1881; slightly ob. 8. A 'chap' or 'fellow': ca 1750–70. Johnson, 1756, in the *Connoisseur*, 'Those who . . . call a man a cabbage, an odd fish, and an unaccountable muskin, should never come into company without an interpreter.' Suggested by the Fr. *mon chou* (as endearment).

cabbage, v. To purloin: orig. and mainly of tailors: from ca 1700; soon coll and by 1800 S.E.; Arbuthnot, in *John Bull*, 1712. 2. (Schoolboys') to CRIB, from ca 1830, recorded 1837: this precedes the n. *cabbage*, whence CAB, a CRIB, n., 7. vbl n., *cabbaging*: pilfering; cribbing: C.19–20; ob.

cabbage-contractor. A tailor: low (perhaps c.): C.19. Ex CABBAGE, n., 1.

cabbage-garden patriot. A coward: political coll: 1848–ca 1910. William Smith O'Brien (1803–64) led, in the summer of 1848, a pitiable insurrection in Ireland; his followers having fled, he successfully hid for several days in a cabbage-patch.

cabbage-gelder. A market gardener; a greengrocer: late C.19–20; ob.

cabbage-head. A fool: coll: from ca 1660. A broadside ballad of ca 1880: 'I ought to call him cabbage-head, | He is so very green.' In F. & H., a synonymy.

cabbage-leaf. An inferior cigar: from ca 1840; ob. cf. CABBAGE, n., 4.

cabbage-looking, see GREEN AS I'M . . .

***cabbage-plant.** An umbrella: c.: ca 1820–60, Egan's Grose, where also *summer cabbage.*

cabbage-stump. A leg: C.19–20; gen. in pl. cf. DRUMSTICK.

cabbage-tree. A hat, large, low-crowned, broad-brimmed, made from cabbage-tree leaves: Australia: from ca 1850; †.

cabbage-tree mob; cabbagites. Roughs: Australian, ca 1850–80. Ex their cabbage-palm hats. This word gave way to LARRI-

KIN(s), Lt-Col. G. C. Mundy's *Our Antipodes*, 1852.

cabbager. A tailor: C.19–20; ob. See CABBAGE, n., 1 and 2.

cabbagites, see CABBAGE-TREE MOB.

cabber. A cab-horse: 1884; coll. *The Times*, 27 Oct. 1884.

cabbie, cabby. A cab-driver: coll; from ca 1850. Smedley, 1852, in *Lewis Arundel*; Yates, in *Broken to Harness*. Ex CAB, n., 2.

cabbing. (vbl n. ex CAB, v., 2.) The use of a crib: esp. at Shrewsbury School. See notably Desmond Coke's wholly admirable school-story, *The Bending of a Twig*, 1906.

cabin-cracker, -cracking. A thief breaking into a ship's cabins; the act or action: nautical (—1887).

cabin-window, through the. (Of an officer obtaining his position) entirely through influence: naval officers': late C.19–20. Opp. HAWSE-HOLES . . .

cable, slip one's, see SLIP ONE'S BREATH.

cable-hanger. An illicit catcher of oysters: C.18–20; coll; ob. Defoe in his *Tour Through Great Britain*.

cable has parted, one's. One dies: nautical coll (—1887).

cabman's rest. A female breast; gen. in pl: rhyming s., from ca 1870.

cabobbled, ppl adj. Perplexed; confused: nautical, C.19–20, ob. Perhaps an intensive of BUBBLE, to deceive; the word occurs also in dial. which has *bobble*, a ground swell of the sea.

cabon. Much: Australian (orig. and mainly Queensland) 'pidgin' (—1872). Chas. H. Allen, *A Visit to Queensland and her Goldfields*, 1872. Ex Aborigine.

caboodle, the whole. The whole lot (persons or things): orig. (1848), U.S., anglicized ca 1895. Prob. via U.S. *the whole kit and boodle* (*kit and* being slurred to *ca*), ex English KIT (2) and U.S. *boodle*, 'a crowd' (Thornton), itself perhaps ex Portuguese *cabedal*, 'a stock, what a man is worth': W.

***caboose.** A kitchen: tramps' c.: mid-C.19–20. Ex *caboose*, a ship's galley. 2. A prison ashore: nautical: late C.19–20; ob.

cacafuego. A spitfire; braggart; bully: C.17–early 19. Until ca 1680, S.E.; ca 1680–1750, coll; then s. Its descent in the wordy world was due to its lit. meaning, shit-fire, for ca 1750 it began to be considered vulgar.

cack, n. and (rare) v. (To void) excrement. Orig. S.E.; in late C.19–20 dial. and low coll. Among children, often as a semi-interjection, *cacky*. Ex L. *cacare*; prob. echoic.

cackle. Idle talk. Without *the* it is S.E.; with inseparable *the*, it is coll, as in *Punch*, 10 Sept. 1887, 'If a feller would tackle | A feminine fair up to Dick, | He 'as got to be dabs at the cackle.' C.19–20. Ex: 2. The patter of clowns: from ca 1840. 3. Hence, the dialogue of a play: from ca 1870. cf. v., 2.

cackle, v.i. To reveal secrets by indiscreet or otherwise foolish talk: late C.17–20 c. and low; ob. 2. The v. corresponding to n., 2 and 3: theatrical: same periods.

cackle!, cut the. SHUT UP!: late C.19–20.

cackle, up to the, see UP TO THE CACKLE.

cackle-berry. (Gen. pl) An egg: Canadian: late C.19–20. Ex U.S.

cackle-chucker. (Theatrical) a prompter: from ca 1860; ob.

cackle-merchant. (Theatrical) a dramatic author: from ca 1860; ob.

***cackle-tub.** A pulpit: c. > low; from ca 1850. Musgrave, *Savage London*, 1888. cf. *tub-thumper*, at TUB, n., 1.

cackler. A blabber: coll, C.18–20. Other senses, S.E. 2. A showman with a speaking part: from ca 1840. In C.20, loosely, an actor. Dickens. 3. A fowl (—1673); orig. c.; by 1730, low; in C.20, almost coll and certainly ob. Hence, *cackler's ken*, a hen-roost; a fowl-house: 1788, Grose, 2nd ed.

***cackling cheat** or **chete.** A fowl: c.: ca 1550–1830.

cackling-cove. An actor: theatrical: from ca 1830. Lit., talking or talkative man. Also called a MUMMERY-COVE.

***cackling fart.** An egg: c.: late C.17–18. *Cackling* here = CACKLER's (sense 3).

cacky. Human excrement: mostly children's and, domestically, women's coll: since ca 1880. Ex CACK.

cacky, adj. Of or like excrement, hence yellowish-brown; hence, filthy, malodorous: coll, mostly children's: late C.19–20. Ex CACK.

cad. At Oxford and certain Public Schools (esp. Eton), from ca 1820, a townsman: pejoratively. Abbr. *caddie*, *cadee* (i.e. cadet). Hence, 2, an ill-bred, esp. if vulgar, fellow: from ca 1820; ob. Since ca 1900, a man devoid of fine instincts or delicate feelings. Coll. Kingsley, Thackeray, Anstey. 3. A passenger taken up by a coachman for his own profit: coll, from ca 1790; †by 1870. 4. An omnibus conductor: coll, ca 1832–70. Hood, Dickens, Mayhew. 5. An inferior assistant or an assistant in a low association: coll, ca 1834–1900. Theodore Hook. 6. A messenger, errand-boy: coll, ca 1835–1914, as in Hood, 'Not to forget that saucy lad | (Ostentation's favourite cad), | The page, who looked so splendidly clad'. 7. A familiar friend; a CHUM: ca 1840–1900; coll.

cad-catcher. A picture 'painted to attract the undiscriminating', *Artist*, 1 Feb. 1882: art s. >, by 1890, coll; ob. cf. POT-BOILER.

cadator. A beggar pretending to be a decayed gentleman: low or c.: late C.17–early 18. Not in O.E.D., but in Ned Ward (who also has *cadator sweetner*, a confidence trickster), and Tom Brown. Ex L. *cadere*, to fall.

cadaver. A bankrupt; a bankruptcy: U.S. (—1900) anglicized, in commerce, ca 1905: coll.

caddee. A thief's assistant or abettor: c. according to Baumann, but S.E. according to O.E.D. – Baumann is prob. right. Note that in 'Jon Bee', *A Living Picture of London*, 1828, we have these two senses: (1) a fellow who hangs about the yards of an inn and, for a shilling or two, procures, for the landlords, 'customers from other inns': inns' and taverns': ca 1820–60; (2) such a hanger-on, who permits himself to pass counterfeit money: c.: ca 1820–80. cf. CADEE SMASHER.

caddie, caddy. 'A bush name for a slouch hat': Australian (—1898). Morris. Perhaps a corruption of CADY.

caddish. Offensively ill-bred: from ca 1860 (recorded, 1868); coll. Shirley Brooks in *Sooner or Later*, Mrs Lynn Linton in *Patricia Kemball*.

***cadee smasher.** A professed tout to inn-keepers, but one who occ. acts as a SMASHER (4): c.: ca 1810–70. Here *cadee* = *cadet*, inferior.

cademy. Academy: lower-class coll: late C.19–20.

cadey, see CADY.

cadge. The act or the practice of begging: low coll, from ca 1810. ?ex *catch*.

cadge, v. To go about begging: from ca 1810. 2. v.t., to beg from (a person): low (—1811). Also, 3, beg, obtain by begging: recorded in 1848. Low coll. n. and v. are recorded in Vaux's *Flash Dict.*, 1812, and since ca 1880 the words have occ. been used jocularly and inoffensively. Perhaps imm. ex Dutch, ultimately ex Fr. *cage*, a wicker basket carried on back of cadger (pedlar) or his pony. For a synonymy, see F. & H.

cadge, do a, see DO A CADGE.

***cadge-cloak** or **-gloak.** A beggar: C.18–early 19. Bamfylde-Moore Carew. See GLOACH.

cadger. A beggar, esp. if whining: from ca 1820; low coll. (But in Scots as early as 1737: see E.D.D.) Egan's Grose, where wrongly classified as c. 2. Whence, a genteel, despicable 'sponger': coll; from ca 1880. A transitional use occurs in James Greenwood's *The Little Ragamuffins*, 1884. For synonymy, see F. & H. 3. 'Slangily applied to cabmen when they are off the rank soliciting fares, or to waiters who hang about and fawn for a gratuity': ca 1870–1910. B. & L.

cadging. Esp. *cadging-bag* and *cadging-face*. vbl n., abject begging; 'sponging'. Coll; recorded in 1839 (Brandon), but prob. much earlier. Henry Kingsley, James Greenwood. 2. Applied esp. to 'cabmen when they are off the ranks, and soliciting a fare': ca 1855–1900.

cadi. An occ. variant of CADY.

cads on castors. Bicyclists: ca 1880–85. *Daily News*, 10 Sept. 1885.

cady; occ. **cadey** or **kadi.** A hat. From ca 1885. (Recorded in Lancashire dial. in 1869: see E.D.D.) Walford's *Antiquarian*, April 1887: 'Sixpence I gave for my cady, | A penny I gave for my stick.' Perhaps ex Yiddish; perhaps, however, a corruption of Romany *stadi*, a hat, itself prob. ex Modern Gr. σκιάδι (Sampson). cf. CADDIE.

Caffre's lightener, see KAFFIR'S LIGHTENER.

cag. A quarrelsome argument; gossip: nautical: from ca 1870, slightly ob.

cag, v. 'To irritate, affront, anger': schoolboys': 1801, Southey (E.D.D.). 2. And as early as 1811 (*Lex. Bal.*) it = to render sulky, ill humoured. Prob. ex dial.

cag, carry the. To be vexed or sullen: low: 1811, *Lex. Bal.* cf. preceding.

cag-mag, see CAGMAG.

cage. In C.16–17, S.E. (as in Shakespeare) and = a prison. In C.17–19, low if not indeed c., for a lock-up. At *cage*, F. & H. has a list of synonyms, English, French, German, Spanish, and Italian, for a prison. 2. A dress-improver: coll; from ca 1850; †. cf. BIRD-CAGE. 3. A bed: ca 1860–1900. Abbr. BREEDING-CAGE. 4. **(The Cage)** the Ladies' Gallery in the House of Commons (—1870). *London Figaro*, 10 June 1870.

cagg, n. and v. reflexive. (A vow) to

abstain from liquor for a certain period: mid-C.18–early 19 military. Perhaps cognate with CAG, v.: thus, to vex or mortify oneself by abstention from liquor.

caggy. Unfit to eat: dial, and low coll, now † as latter: 1848, Marryat. Ex:

cagmag; cag-mag. (Of food, esp. meat) odds and ends, scraps, refuse. From ca 1810; ob. Coll ex dial. Mayhew, *London Labour*, 'Do I ever eat my own game if it's high? No, sir, never, I couldn't stand such cag-mag.' Also as adj., tainted, inferior (—1860); ob. Origin obscure: but prob. the term derives ex *cag(g)-mag(g)*, an old goose (see Grose, 2nd ed.). 2. Hence, gossip, idle talk: Cockney coll: from ca 1880. (Also in dial.)

Cain, raise. To make a disturbance, a din; to quarrel noisily. Orig. (ca 1840), U.S., anglicized ca 1870. App. euphemistic for *raise the devil*. cf. *raise hell and* TOMMY and CANE UPON ABEL.

Cain and Abel. A table: rhyming s. (—1857). 'Ducange Anglicus', 1st ed., classifies it as c., but it very soon > gen. Cockney.

Cainsham smoke. The tears of a wife-beaten husband: C.17–18; coll. Etymology obscure: presumably topographically proverbial.

cairn, add a stone to someone's. To honour a person as much as possible after his death: coll; C.18–19. Ex a Celtic proverbial saying, recorded by traveller Pennant in 1772.

cake, cakey. A fool, gull, or blockhead: late C.18–20, ob. In C.19–20, coll. Grose, 1785; J. R. Planché, 'Your resignation proves that you must be | The greatest cake he in his land could see!'; Mrs Henry Wood. From either the softness of some cakes or the flatness of others: in either case, a pun. 2. At Christ's Hospital (*cake* only), C.19–20, ob., a stroke with a cane.

cake, v. (Christ's Hospital) to cane: C.19–20, ob.

cake, get one's share of the. To succeed: coll, C.17–18. cf.:

cake, take the. To carry off the honours; be the best; (theatrical) FILL THE BILL: coll, from ca 1880. In 1882 or 1883, a lyric declared that, 'For rudeness to the Grand Old Man, Lord Randolph [Churchill] takes the cake.' Ex U.S. 'The allusion is not to a cake walk', as Thornton suggests, for *cake-walk* is later; perhaps 'a jocular allusion to Gr. πυραμοῦς, prize of victory, orig. cake of roasted wheat and honey awarded to person of greatest vigilance in night-watch', W., but see note at TAKE THE BISCUIT. See also *take the* BUN.

cake and has paid (her) a loaf, the devil owed (her) a. A great instead of a small misfortune has befallen her. Coll: C.17–19. B.E.

cake is dough, one's. One's project, or one's business, has failed: mid-C.16–20: coll. Becon, 1559; Shakespeare; B.E.; Hardy. The S.O.D., app. misled by Nares, says †, but this is incorrect, though the phrase may – only *may* – be ob. A Scottish variant (Ramsay, 1737) is *one's meal is dough*.

Cakes, Land of. Scotland: C.18–20; coll.

cakes, like hot. Very quickly, promptly; esp. *sell* or *go like* . . . Orig. U.S., anglicized ca 1888.

cakes and ale. Pleasant food; good living: coll, from ca 1570. Shakespeare, 1601, 'Dost thou think, because thou art vertuous, there shall be no more Cakes and Ale?'

cakey, see CAKE, n., 1.

***cakey-pannum fencer.** A street seller of pastry: C.19 c. See PANNAM.

Cal. Abbr. *Calcraft*, the common hangman: ca 1860–70.

calaboose, n. and (rarely) v. Prison, esp. a common gaol. Nautical ex Spanish via (1797) U.S. Dana, 1840, has the Sp. form, *calabozo*.

calculate, v. Think, believe, expect, suppose; intend. Coll, anglicized ca 1870 ex U.S. (—1812) usage. John Galt in *Lawrie*.

Caleb Quotem. A parish clerk; jack of all trades. Coll, ca 1860–80. From a character in *The Wags of Windsor*.

calf. A meek, harmless, (and occ.) brainless person: C.16–20. S.O.D. gives as S.E., but it is surely coll?! Hamilton Aïdé, *Morals and Mysteries*, 1872, 'She had a girlish fancy for the good-looking young calf.'

calf, slip or **cast the** or **one's.** (Of women) to have a miscarriage; to suffer abortion: C.17–18: facetiously coll. Pepys.

calf-bed. Bovine parturition: jocular after *child-bed*: Southey, 1822. Rare.

calf-clingers. Very close-fitting trousers, i.e. pantaloons: ca 1830–1914. James Greenwood, *The Little Ragamuffins*, 1884.

calf in the cow's belly, eat the. To anticipate unduly: mid-C.17–20 proverbial coll; ob. Fuller; Richardson in *Clarissa Harlowe*.

calf-lolly. An idle simpleton: coll, mid-C.17–18. Urquhart. cf. CALF and LOBLOLLY-BOY.

calf-love. A youthful and romantic attachment: coll; from ca 1820.

***calf-sticking.** The selling of worthless, on the pretence that they are smuggled, goods: c.; ca 1850–1920.

calf-, cow-, and **bull-week.** Coll, ca 1830–80. The 1st, 2nd, and 3rd week before Christmas: among operatives, who, during this period, worked hours increasing in length in each successive week, until in *bull-week* they had extremely little time free. *Echo*, 4 Dec. 1871.

calf's head. A very stupid fellow: late C.16–early 19; coll. 2. 'A white-faced man with a large head': lower classes': from ca 1860.

calfskin, smack. To swear on the Bible: low: mid-C.19–20; ob.

calfskin fiddle. A drum: late C.18–early 19.

calibash. A New South Wales farmers' term (ca 1860–1900), thus in R. D. Barton's *Reminiscences of an Australian Pioneer*, 1917: 'In those days . . . everyone [on the station] was paid by orders, "calibashes" we used to call them, drawn on himself by the person paying. The townships all followed the same system.' Prob. ex some Aborigine word.

calico. Thin, attenuated; wasted. Coll: C.18–20; ob. N. Bailey, *Colloquies of Erasmus*, 1725; Sala, 1861.

calico ball. A cheap public dance: ca 1860–1915; coll. The rare adj. *calico-bally*, derivatively = somewhat fast, occurs in a ca 1890 ballad, *The Flipperty-Flop Young Man*. *Calico hop*, heard occ. in England, is the U.S. version.

calicot. A CAD (2): trade: ca 1885–1910. Ex coll Fr. *calicot*, a counter-jumper.

California or **Californian.** Gen. in (*-ns*) pl. A gold piece: from ca 1860. Ex the gold-fields rush (1849) and wealth of California.

Californian. A red, a hard-dried, herring: from ca 1850; ob. Actually, Scottish herrings, the name coming from the Californian gold-discoveries. cf. ATLANTIC RANGER.

calk. See CAULK. 2. To throw: Eton College, C.19–20, ob.

call, n. The time when the masters do not call 'absence': Eton coll: C.19–20.

call, v. To beg through (e.g. a street): c.: mid-C.18–20. Bamfylde-Moore Carew, 'I called a whole street.' Ex the v.i., *to call*, to call at a house to beg: which is S.E. 2. (Nearly always in passive.) Abbr. *call to the bar*: legal: from ca 1830. Dickens in *Sketches by Boz*. 3. To blame: lower classes' coll: late C.19–20. 'Don't call me, sir, if I'm a bit clumsy at first.' Ex CALL DOWN, or *call names*.

call, have the. To be in the most demand: from ca 1840; coll; by 1880, S.E.

call a go. To change one's stand, alter one's tactics, give in: mid-C.19–20. Low: prob. ex cribbage.

call down. To reprimand: late C.19–20; coll. cf. †S.E. *call down*, to denounce.

call in. (*At* makes it v.t.) To visit a place incidentally: coll: from ca 1700.

call of, within. Near. From ca 1700: coll soon S.E.

call one for everything under the sun. To abuse thoroughly, vilify vigorously: coll: late C.19–20. cf. the C.17–early 19 (then dial.) *call*, to abuse, vilify.

call-out. A summons: coll., esp. Londoners': late C.19–20.

call sir and something else. To address as *sirrah*; hence, to speak contemptuously to: coll: ca 1660–1800.

call upon, have a. To have the first chance of or with. Orig. (—1888), U.S.; anglicized ca 1895, but never very gen. Coll.

Callao painter. An evil-smelling gas arising from sea at that port: nautical coll: late C.19–20.

***calle.** A cloak; a gown: c. of ca 1670–1840.

***calp** (C.19) or **kelp** (C.18–19). A hat: ca 1750–1850. John Poulter. cf. *calpac(k)*, a Turkish and Tartar felt cap (recorded 1813); any oriental or exotic cap.

calves gone to grass. Spindle shanks, meagre calves. Late C.17–20 (ob.); coll. Ray, 1678, 'His calves are gone down to grass.' A late C.18–19 variant is *veal will be cheap, calves fall*.

calves' heads, there are many ways of dressing. i.e. of doing any, but esp. a foolish, thing. C.19–20; ob.

calves' heads are best hot. A jeering apology for one who sits down to eat with his hat on: coll; C.19–20.

calx. (Eton College) the goal line in football. Not recorded before 1864. Ex the L. word.

Cam roads. 'Retreat to Cambridge by way of a change', Egan's Grose: Oxford University: ca 1820–40.

Camberwell Death-trap, the. The Surrey Canal: Camberwell (London): ca 1870–

1900. Ex the number of children who, playing on its crumbling banks, were drowned there.

cambra. A dog: Shelta: C.18–20.

Cambridge fortune. A woman without substance: late C.17–early 19. Like WHITECHAPEL FORTUNE, it is scabrous, Grose defining: 'A wind-mill and a water-mill' (qq.v.). These objects, here indelicately punned, being in the C.18 very common in Cambridgeshire.

Cambridge (occ. **Cambridgeshire) oak.** A willow: mid-C.18–20 coll; ob. Willows abound in the Fen district.

Cambridgeshire camel. A native of, one long resident in, Cambridgeshire: mid-C.17–mid-19. Fuller, 1662; Grose in his *Provincial Glossary*. Ex stilt-walking in the Fens.

Cambridgeshire, or **fen, nightingale.** A frog: C.19–20. Ex the dykes and canals so common in that county. cf. CAPE NIGHTINGALE.

Cambridgeshire oak, see CAMBRIDGE OAK.

Camden Town. A BROWN, i.e. a halfpenny: rhyming s. (—1859).

came up! Come up!: London cabmen to their horses: ca 1890–1915.

camel. A giraffe: South African coll, esp. among hunters: mid-C.19–20.

camel night. Guest night on a warship: naval: late C.19–20. Why? Perhaps because, on that night, one did not 'get the HUMP', for *lucus a non lucendo* etymologies are fairly common in s. cf.:

camel's complaint. The HUMP, low spirits. From ca 1870; ob.

camera obscura. The posterior (—1900): facetious. Perhaps ex U.S.

***camesa, camisa, camiscia, camise, kemesa.** A shirt or a shift: c.; ca 1660–1880. Ex Sp. *camisa*. cf. COMMISSION.

cami. Abbr. *camisole*: from ca 1900; shop and women's. Also *cammy*.

camisa, camiscia, see CAMESA.

***camister.** A clergyman: c. (—1851). Ex L. *camisia*, an alb, after *minister*; cf., however, CANISTER, 3.

camp. To sleep or rest in an unusual place or at an unusual time (—1893): Australian coll. 2. Hence, 'to stop for a rest in the middle of the day', Morris: idem: 1891. Occ. as a n. 3. To prove superior to: Australian: 1886, C. H. Kendall; very ob. Perhaps ex †S.E. *camp*, to contend, and *camping*, warfare.

camp, adj. Addicted to 'actions and gestures of exaggerated emphasis . . . Prob. from the Fr.', Ware; pleasantly ostentatious or, in manner, affected: London streets' (—1909). (Perhaps rather ex the C.19–20 dial. *camp* or *kemp*, uncouth, rough.)

camp, go to. To go to bed; lie down to rest: Australian coll, from ca 1880. Also *have a camp*, to rest for a while. cf. CAMP, v., 2.

camp, take into. To kill. From ca 1880, orig. U.S.; ob. (Mark Twain.)

camp-candlestick. An empty bottle; a bayonet: late C.18–early 19. Military.

camp-stool brigade. The early waiters outside a theatre, etc.: coll, from ca 1880.

campaign coat. A late C.17 mode in men's dress; orig. military and S.E.; then loosely and coll; the word > † ca 1750. 2. In C.18 c., a tattered cloak worn to move compassion.

***Campbell's academy.** The hulks: ca 1770–1820; c., then low. A Mr Campbell was the first director.

campo. A playground or playing field: schools': C.17. Ex *in campo*.

can, the. A reprimand: nautical: late C.19–20. See CARRY THE CAN. 2. A barman: a Lambeth term, from ca 1890. 3. A simpleton: military: from ca 1890.

can back, take the, see TAKE THE CAN BACK, and CAN.

can do. I can (do it); can you (do it)?: 'pidgin': mid-C.19–20. 2. Hence, all right!: military: late C.19–20.

can I help you with that? A non-aristocratic c.p. (1895; ob.) implying 'I'd like some of that.' Ware, 'When said to the fairer sex the import is different.'

can of oil. A boil: rhyming s.: late C.19–20.

can you say uncle to that? A dustmen's c.p. (—1909), in which *say uncle* = 'reply'. Ware notes that the c.p. answer is *yes – I can*. Perhaps there is a pun on dust-bins.

canader. A Canadian canoe: Oxford undergraduates' (—1909); ob. By 'Oxford *-er*'.

canadoe. A drink from a can: rare: C.17 jocular coll. *Histrio-Mastix*, 1610, 'And now, my maisters, in this bravadoe, | I can read no more without Canadoe. | *Omnes*. What ho! some Canadoe quickly!' ?*can* + *d'eau*, macaronic for a can of water, the water being *eau de vie*.

canaller. One who works or lives on a canal-boat (1864); a canal-boat (1887): coll: mostly U.S.

canary; occ. in senses **1–4, canary-bird.**

An arch knavish boy, a young wag: late C.17–18. 2. A gaol-bird: c. and low: mid-C.17–20; ob. Recorded in Australia, 1827–90, of a convict. Peter Cunningham, 1827, says: ex the yellow clothes they wear on landing. 3. A mistress: C.18–early 19, ex c. sense, a harlot. 4. A guinea: C.18–early 19; from ca 1830, a sovereign: ob. Ex its yellow colour: cf. YELLOW BOY. 5. A written promise of a donation or a subscription: Salvation Army: 1882. Coined by General Booth ex the colour of the demand-slips. (The semantics of the senses 1–2: resp. liveliness, cage; nos. 3–5 colour.) 6. Also a sol., orig. malapropistic as in Shakespeare's *Merry Wives of Windsor*, for *quandary*. 7. In c. (—1862), a thief's female assistant. cf. CROW, n., 2. 8. A 'chorus-singer amongst the public – gen. in gallery': music-halls': 1870; ob. Ware. 9. 'An ideal hip-adornment', actually a modified cod-piece: costermongers' dress and term: 1876. Ware notes that it has some connection with the 'nightingale' of Boccaccio's sprightly story.

canary-bird, see preceding, senses 1–4.

cancer, catch or **capture a.** (Rowing, university) CATCH A CRAB. Coll, ca 1850–1900. Hood in *Pen and Pencil Pictures*, 1857. Ex L. *cancer*, a crab.

candidate. To stand as a candidate. (vbl n. and adj., *candidating*.) Coll: from ca 1880. Not common.

candle, not able or **fit to hold a,** followed by **to.** Not fit to be compared with; *not in the same* STREET. From ca 1640; a coll that was S.E. by 1800. Developed from the affirmative form of the phrase (to help as a subordinate): C.15–18 and S.E.

candle, sell or let by inch of. To sell or let, hence to do anything, under fantastic or trivially precise conditions. Coll: from ca 1650; S.E. after ca 1750. Ex an auction at which bids are received only while a small piece of candle remains burning. (Variant: *by the candle*.)

candle, the game is not worth the. Of any activity not worth the cost or the trouble: coll, from ca 1550; in C.18–20, S.E. Ex the playing of cards.

candle at both ends, burn one's or **the,** see BURN ONE'S CANDLE . . .

candle-ends, drink off or **eat.** Lit. and fig., thus to express devotion while drinking a lady's health: ca 1590–1640. The O.E.D. gives as S.E., but this is prob. because its users are Shakespeare, Fletcher, Ben Jonson: orig., it was prob. coll.

candle-keeper. (Winchester College) a privileged senior not a prefect: C.19–20, ob.

candle-shop. 'A Roman Catholic chapel, or Ritualistic church – from the plenitude of lights', Ware; Low Churchmen's (—1909).

candle-stick. A candidate: Winchester College, from ca 1840. Ob. For this and for CANDLE-KEEPER, see Mansfield's and Adams's books on the College. 2. Gen. in pl, a fountain in Trafalgar Square, London, W.C.2: from ca 1840; ob. Mayhew. 3. In pl, bad, small, or untunable bells: 'Hark! how the candlesticks rattle,' Grose, 1st ed.: mid-C.18–early 19.

candle to the devil, hold or **set a.** To be actively evil: C.19–20, coll; the earlier sense (mid-C.15–18), with *before* instead of *to*, is to placate with a candle, i.e. to treat the devil as a saint. The two senses tend to overlap.

candle-waster. One who studies, one who dissipates, late at night: coll: late C.16–20; rare after C.17. Shakespeare in *Much Ado about Nothing*.

candles, see, see SEE STARS.

candy. Drunk: mid-C.18–early 19. Rare outside of Ireland.

candy(-)man. A bailiff, process-server: Northern, from 1844; ob. Ex an 1844 army of ejectors among whom were a few 'candy-men' or hawkers of sweets; the term spread rapidly.

cane upon Abel. A stout stick stoutly laid about a man's shoulders: late C.17–early 19 coll. cf. *raise* CAIN and CAIN AND ABEL.

caniculars. Doggerel verses: jocularly pedantic coll: 1872. Ex L. *canis*, a dog.

canine. A dog: jocular coll: from 1869; ob.

canister. The head: from ca 1790; mainly pugilistic; ob. Moncrieff, 1821, 'I've nobb'd him on the canister.' 2. See CANISTER-CAP. 3. A clergyman; a preacher: London streets' (—1909). Prob. a corruption of CAMISTER.

canister-cap. A hat: from ca 1820. ca 1870 it was abbr. to *canister*.

***cank**; in C.17, occ. *canke*. Dumb: from ca 1670: c. >, in C.18, s.; >, in early C.19, dial.; †by 1885. Extant in dial. is *cank*, to gabble, chatter, gossip.

***cannaken, -kin.** An occ. variant of CANNIKEN, -KIN.

cannibal. C.17–18 coll: 'a cruel rigid Fellow in dealing', B.E. Ex lit. S.E. sense. 2. (Cambridge University) a College's second boat that beats, i.e. 'bumps', its first, or a third that beats its second: from ca 1880. Earlier (—1864), a training boat for freshmen, i.e. a boat racing in SLOGGERS; also its rowers. In the former sense, cannibalism is punned on, while in the latter *cannot-pull* is jocularly corrupted.

***canniken, cannikin.** The plague: c. of ca 1670–1820. ?etymology: perhaps cognate with S.E. *canker*.

cannon. A round beef steak pudding: low (—1909). Ware. Ex resemblance to small cannon ball.

***can(n)on,** adj. Drunk: c. (—1879). ?abbr. **cannoned*, mod. s. 'shot'. cf. Ger. *er ist geschossen*.

cannon ball. A nickname (1852–ca 1880) for an irreconcilable opponent of free trade. Gen. in pl. *Saturday Review*, 30 Oct. 1858. 2. A human testicle: likewise gen. in pl: from ca 1885.

canoe, paddle one's own. To be independent. Orig. (1828), U.S., anglicized ca 1875: coll. Perhaps one might mention the French teacher's GAG (3): *pas d'elle yeux Rhône que nous*. (Such tricks should be collected: cf. ηβπ, to eat a bit of pie!)

canoe it. To travel, or go, in a canoe: coll: from ca 1880 in U.S., soon adopted in England.

canoeuvre. 'A low manoeuvre or essay at deception', Bee: rare London: ca 1820–50.

canoneer. One skilled in *canon* law, i.e. a canonist. ca 1640–1800: jocular coll after *cannoneer*. Baxter, 1659, 'We turn this Canon against the Canoneers.'

canoodle, v.t. and i. Fondle; bill and coo. Coll. Orig. (—1859), U.S., thoroughly anglicized by G. A. Sala in 1864. Perhaps ex *canny*, gentle, on FIRKYTOODLE; but cf. the Somersetshire *canoodle*, a donkey, which may be noodle (fool) intensified. 2. Also as n., though *canoodling* (Sala, 1859) is more gen. 3. To coax: from ca 1870; ob. 4. At Oxford University, ca 1860–70, to propel a canoe. By a pun on *canoe*.

***cant.** In c. (vagrants'), both food (—1860) and (—1839) a gift (see CANT OF TOGS). 2. (Pugilistic) a blow: coll; from ca 1750. Ex S.E. sense: a toss, a throw.

***cant,** v. In c., v.i. and t.: to speak; to talk: mid-C.16–19.

cant a slug into your bread(-)room! Drink a dram! Nautical: mid-C.18–early 19.

can't-keep-still. A treadmill: rhyming s.: ca 1850–90.

***cant of dobbin.** A roll of ribbon: c.: ca 1810–60. See DOBBIN, 2.

***cant of togs.** A gift of clothes: beggars' c. (—1839). Ware shrewdly remarks, 'The mode of begging for clothes affords a word to describe the present or benefit gained by canting.'

can't see a hole in or through a ladder. Of a person very drunk. From ca 1855. Sometimes, and at least as early as 1882, ... *a forty-foot ladder* (Ware).

can't show itself (or oneself) to. To be inferior to: lower classes': 1880; ob.

can't you feel the shrimps? Don't you smell the sea?: Cockney c.p.: 1876; ob.

Cantab. A member of the University of Cambridge: coll, first in Coventry's amusing novel, *Pompey the Little*, 1750. Abbr. *Cantabrigian*.

cantabank. A common or inferior singer of ballads: from ca 1840; coll. Earlier, S.E. for a singer upon a platform. Ex It. *cantambanco*.

cantankerous. Cross-grained, ill-humoured; acridly self-willed; quarrelsome. Coll: ?coined by Goldsmith in *She Stoops to Conquer*, 1772; Sheridan, *The Rivals*. Perhaps, says O.E.D., ex M.E. *contak*, contention, after *cankerous*; H., 3rd ed. suggests a corruption of *contentious*; W. thinks that the word may be of Irish formation (as suggested by O.E.D.). 2. Also, adv. with *-ly*, abstract n. with *-ness*.

canteen. A public-house: South African coll, prob. at first military: from ca 1830. 2. Hence, *canteen-keeper*, the proprietor of one: 1832.

canteen-keeper, see CANTEEN.

canteen medal. A beer stain on one's tunic: military: from ca 1875. 2. A good-conduct medal: military: late C.19–20. Many of those who wore it were hard drinkers – but they had even harder heads.

canteen wallah. A man addicted to beer: military coll: late C.19–20.

canter, see CANTING CREW.

Canterbury. 'A sort of a short or Hand-gallop', B.E.: C.17–18. Abbr. *Canterbury gallop*, cf. *C. pace*, *trot*, *rate*, etc. (Whence *canter*, v. recorded in 1706, n. (an easy gallop) in 1755.)

Canterbury tale or occ. **story.** A story long and tedious: from ca 1540; at first coll, but soon S.E. Latimer, 1549; Turberville, 1579; Grose, 1st ed. Ex the long stories told by pilgrims proceeding to Canterbury.

canticle. A parish clerk: mid-C.18–early 19. The parish clerk led the congregation's singing. cf. AMEN-CURLER.

canting crew, the. Criminals and vagabonds, the *canters* (C.17–18): C.17–19: coll. In B.E.'s title, 1690; Hindley's *James Catnach*, 1878.

canvas or **canvass.** Human skin, pelt: pugilistic: ca 1810–70. *Boxiana*, III, 1821.

canvas, receive the. To be dismissed: C.17, coll. Shirley in *The Brothers*. cf. *get* and *give the* BAG or *the* SACK, n., 2.

canvas-climber. A sailor: coll: late C.16–17. Shakespeare in *Pericles*.

canvas town. A mushroom town: coll, from ca 1850; Dickens, 1853. Hence, 2, the Volunteer Encampment at Wimbledon (not since ca 1905) or Bisley where the National Rifle Association meets.

canvas(s)eens. (Nautical) a sailor's canvas trousers: coll, C.19–20, ob.

cap. The proceeds from an improvised collection (cf. *to send round the cap* or *hat*, C.19–20 coll), esp. for a huntsman on the death of the fox: ca 1850–1914. Abbr. *cap-money*, S.E. and extant. 2. At Westminster School, the amount collected at 'play' and 'election' dinners. 3. (Gen. in pl.) Abbr. *capital letter*: coll, orig. printers' (—1900), then publishers' and authors'. 4. In c., a false cover to a COVER-DOWN or tossing-coin: ca 1840–80. 5. A synonym for c. sense of BONNET, n.: c.: ca 1810–50. 6. (Only in vocative.) Captain: coll: late C.19–20. Ware, 1909, 'Common in America – gaining ground in England'.

cap, v. (University and Public School) to take off one's cap or hat in salutation of: late C.16–20, ob. Coll, S.E. by 1700. '. . . To cap a fellow', *Gradus ad Cantabrigiam*, 1803. 2. In c., to take an oath: late C.17–early 19.

cap, put on one's considering or **thinking.** To think, take time to think: coll, from ca 1650.

cap acquaintance. Persons only slightly acquainted: C.18–early 19; coll.

cap after it, fling or **throw one's.** To do something that is no longer of use, esp. when a project or a business is past hope. Coll: late C.17–19.

cap at, cast one's. 'To show indifference to, give up for lost': C.16–17; coll. In proverbial form: *cast one's cap into the wind*.

cap at, set one's. (Of women only) to try, and keep trying, to gain a man's heart – or hand. Coll, from ca 1770. Goldsmith, Thackeray. Variant: *cock one's cap at*: as in Glascock, *Sailors and Saints*, 1829. Ex navigation: cf. Fr. *mettre le cap sur*.

cap be made of wool, if his or **your.** As sure as his cap is made of wool, i.e. indubitably: C.17–18; coll.

***cap for.** See BONNET FOR: c.: ca 1810–40.

cap on nine hairs, (with his). Jaunty or jovial, the cap being worn at an extreme angle: naval: late C.19–20.

***cap,** or **cast, one's skin.** To strip naked: C.19–20 (ob.) c.

cap set, have one's. Variant: **have (enough) under one's cap.** To be drunk: coll: C.17–18. cf.:

cap-sick. Intoxicated: coll: C.17 (?18). H. Hutton's anatomization of folly, 1619.

cap the quadrangle. C.18 university: (of undergraduates) 'to cross the area of the college cap in hand, in reverence to the Fellows who sometimes walk there', Grose, 2nd ed.

capabarre. 'The looting of naval stores, mentioned in Marryat' (Bowen): naval coll: C.19. Semantics: 'by curtailment'.

cape, v.i. To keep a course: nautical coll: C.19–20.

cape, n. A guard-room: Army s. (—1898). Prob. ex Lat. *capere*, to take.

Cape Cod turkey. Salt fish: ?mainly nautical (—1874). On BOMBAY DUCK.

Cape doctor, the. A strong S.E. wind: Cape Colony coll: C.19–20. 'In the earlier days . . . when the Cape was used by Anglo-Indians as a sanatorium, they were wont to term these winds the *Cape Doctor* and they still retain the name,' Pettman, 1913.

Cape Flyaway. Imaginary land on the horizon: nautical coll: C.19–20.

Cape Horn, double, see DOUBLE CAPE HORN.

Cape Horn fever. Malingering in bad weather: sailing-ship seamen's: mid-C.19–20.

Cape Horn rainwater. Rum: nautical: late C.19–20; slightly ob.

Cape nightingale. A frog: South African coll: from ca 1880. H. A. Bryden, *Kloof and Karoo*, 1889. cf. CAMBRIDGESHIRE NIGHTINGALE.

Cape smoke. 'A brandy manufactured in nearly all the vine-growing districts of the Colony', Pettman: South African coll.: 1848, H. H. Methuen, *Life in the Wilderness*. Described in 1879 as 'a poison calculated to burn the inside of a rhinoceros'. It is of a cloudy colour.

Cape Stiff. Cape Horn: nautical: mid-C.19–20. Because, to a sailing ship, it was stiff work to beat round it.

capella. A coat: theatrical, C.19–20, ob. Direct ex It.

capeovi. Sick, ill: costermongers', from ca 1860; ob. cf. CAPIVVY, CRY.

caper. A DODGE, device, performance: coll, orig. (—1851) low. *London Herald*, 23 March 1867, '"He'll get five years penal for this little caper," said the policeman.' Ex the S.E. senses and cf. *play the giddy goat*, for ultimately *caper* is the L. *caper*, a goat. 2. Whence, a chorister boy; a ballet-girl: low: mid-C.19–20; ob. Mayhew.

caper, v.i. To be hanged: late C.18–mid 19. Wolcot. Prob. ex *cut a* CAPER UPON NOTHING.

caper-corner-ways. Diagonally: nautical coll: C.19–20. Presumably *caper* is a corruption of *cater*, four.

caper-merchant. A dancing master: mid-C.18–19. cf. HOP-MERCHANT.

caper (up)on nothing, cut a; occ. **cut capers . . .** Like **cut caper sauce,** = to be hanged: low coll, C.18–19. Hanging has many synonyms, some much grimmer than these.

caperdewsie, occ. **caperdochy** (as in Heywood, 1600) or **cappadochio.** Stocks; a prison. Low: late C.16–17.

capital. Excellent: coll, from ca 1760; S.E. after ca 1820. Often as exclamation. Ex *capital*, important. cf. the tendency of AWFUL, adj.

capital, work. To commit a capital offence: c. or low; from ca 1830.

capital out of, make. To turn to account. From ca 1850; coll almost imm. S.E.

capitation drugget. Cheap and inferior drugget: coll, late C.17–18. Ex the capitation tax on this clothing-material.

capivvy, cry. To be persecuted to death, or near to it: sporting s., from ca 1840; ob. Orig. a hunting term, as in Surtees, *Handley Cross*, 1843.

capon. A red herring: from ca 1640. Orig. jocular S.E., it > coll ca 1700. cf. YARMOUTH CAPON.

capot me! A coll imprecation: mid-C.18–early 19. Foote. Ex *capot*, to SCORE OFF.

cappadochio, see CAPERDEWSIE.

capped, be. To be checked by strong currents: nautical coll: mid-C.19–20. Bowen.

capper. (Auctioneers') a dummy bidder at an auction: from ca 1870.

capricornified. 'Hornified', cuckolded: mid-C.18–early 19.

caprification. Artificial fertilization: catachrestic: from 1830s.

capron hardy. An impudent fellow: coll; ca 1450–1630.

caps, pull. (Only of women) to wrangle in unseemly fashion: from ca 1750; ob. if not †; coll. Colman, 1763, 'A man that half the women in town would pull caps for'; Scott, 1825, 'Well, dearest Rachel, we will not pull caps about this man.'

capsize, v.t. To overturn, upset: orig. nautical s. (witness use by Dibdin and Grose, 2nd ed.), prob. ex Sp. *cabezar* (—1788); S.E. by 1820.

capstan, the. A punishment whereby the arms were outstretched on a capstan-bar and a weight suspended from the neck: naval coll: C.17–early 18.

capstan-step. The time or beat kept by the old ship's fiddler for capstan work: nautical: C.19.

captain. A familiar and/or jesting term of address: coll; C.17–20. Shakespeare. cf. U.S. *judge*. 2. In C.18, a prosperous highwayman, a gaming- or a bawdy-house bully: both low, the latter perhaps c. 3. Money, esp. in *the captain is not at home*, I have no money: C.18–early 19. 4. A glandered horse: knackers' s., from ca 1830. 5. See CAPTAIN IS AT HOME.

Captain Armstrong. A dishonest jockey: from ca 1860. More gen. in phrase, *come Captain Armstrong*, to 'pull' a horse and thus prevent him from winning: from ca 1850. Turf. *Sporting Life*, 5 Nov. 1864.

***Captain Bates?, been to see.** A 'how-d'ye-do' to one recently released from gaol: c., then Cockney: late C.19–20. 'Captain Bates was a well-known metropolitan prison-governor,' Ware.

Captain Cook; Cooker or **cooker.** Orig. (—1879), a wild pig; hence (—1894), 'a gaunt, ill-shaped, or sorry-looking pig', E. Wakefield: New Zealand; slightly ob. Pigs were introduced into New Zealand by Captain Cook. 2. (*Captain Cook.*) A book: rhyming s.: late C.19–20.

Captain Copperthorn's crew. All officers; a crew in which everyone wishes to be captain: mid-C.18–19; nautical.

Captain Cork. A man slow in passing the bottle: C.19–20, ob.; military.

Captain Crank. The leader of a group of highwaymen: C.18–early 19.

Captain Criterion. A racing SHARP; mostly London theatrical and smart society: ?ca 1880–1905. Ex a music-hall song:

I'm Captain Criterion of London,
Dashing and never afraid.
If ever you find a mug's been well done,
Be sure that it's by our brigade.

The Criterion Theatre and Restaurant (founded in 1874) obtained an injunction against the singer, and the song was suppressed.

Captain Grand. A haughty, blustering man: C.18–19; coll.

Captain Hackum. (Hack 'em.) A fighting, blustering bully: ca 1600–1850.

captain is at home or **come, the.** Menstruation proceeds: late C.18–19; low. Punning *catamenia*; see also *The flag is up*, at FLAG, 3.

Captain Kettle. To settle (vigorously), v.t.: rhyming s. of ca 1899–1950. Ex the famous character of Cutcliffe Hyne's stories.

captain lieutenant. Meat half-way between veal and beef: military: late C.18–19. Ex the brevet officer, who, receiving lieutenant's pay, ranks as a captain. (The rank was abolished before 1893.)

Captain MacFluffer, as in **take C.M. badly.** (To have a bad bout of) loss of memory on the stage: theatrical (—1909); ob. An elaboration of FLUFF, n., 2, and v., 3; the *Mac* may pun the Scottish *mak'*, to make – whence *MacFluffer* is, lit., a 'fluff'-maker.

Captain Podd. An C.18 nickname for a puppet-showman.

Captain Queernabs. An ill-dressed or shabby man: late C.17–early 19. In C.17–mid-18, either c. or low s.

Captain Quiz. A mocker: C.18; coll. Amplifying QUIZ.

Captain Sharp. An arrant cheat; a huffing, sneaking, cowardly bully: late C.17–early 19. 2. Hence, a gamesters' bully: mid-C.18–early 19.

Captain Swosser. A blustering naval officer: non-aristocratic coll (—1882); ob. Ex a character of Marryat's.

Captain Tom. The leader of a mob; the mob itself: late C.17–early 19.

car it. To go by car (of whatever sort the context indicates): coll: from ca 1860.

***caravan.** A dupe; a man swindled: late C.17–18. C. and low. Etherege, in *The Man of Mode*, 'What spruce prig is that? A caravan, lately come from Paris.' Perhaps ex caravans frequently robbed. 2. ?hence, a large sum of money: late C.17–18 c. cf. CARGO, 2. 3. A railway train carrying people to a prize-fight: from ca 1845; boxing. Prob. ex its length: cf., however, Blount, 1674: 'Of late corruptly used with us for a kind of waggon to carry passengers to and from London.'

caravansera. A railway station: ca 1845–1900; boxing. Ex CARAVAN, 3.

carbonado. To cut, hack: late C.16–17. Coll. soon S.E. Shakespeare.

carbuncle face. A red, large-pimpled face: coll: late C.17–18.

card. A device; expedient: from ca 1700 (but cf. CARD, THAT'S A SURE); ob. by 1900. Frances Brooke, in *Lady Julia Mandeville*. 2. A 'character', an odd fellow: from ca 1835. Dickens, 1836; *The Card*, a novel (1911) by Arnold Bennett. 'It may be an extension of the metaphorical *good card*, *sure card*, etc., or . . . an anglicized form of Scottish *caird*, tinker (cf. *artful beggar*, etc.)': W. Often with DOWNY, KNOWING, QUEER. 3. (the card.) The correct number, price, or thing, the TICKET: from ca 1850, coll. Mayhew. Perhaps ex the CORRECT CARD of racing. 4. A troublesome rating: naval: late C.19–20. Ex 2.

card, v. To torture with a loom-card: from ca 1550; coll, passing to S.E. In C.19, an Irish political diversion. *Scots Observer*, 1889, 'to card a woman's hide'. Ob. The n. is *carding*. 2. To fix on a card: trade coll: from ca 1880.

card, a cooling. Anything that cools enthusiasm: ca 1570–1750; coll. Ex an obscure card-game.

card, a leading. An example or precedent: coll; C.17–19.

card, one's best. A last resort; more gen., one's best plan of action. Coll: C.19–20.

card, speak by the. To speak precisely, most accurately. Coll: C.17–20; S.E. in C.19–20. Shakespeare in *Hamlet*, 'We must speak by the card, or equivocation will undo us.'

card, that's a sure. That's a safe device or expedient, or one likely to bring success; also of such a person. C.16–20; coll. *Thersites, an Interlude*, ca 1537.

***card-con(e)y-catching.** Swindling: c.: late C.16. Greene. See CONY-CATCHING.

card of ten, brag or **face it out with a.** To assume a bold front: ca 1540–1700; coll. Ex cards; a card of ten pips being none too high.

cardinal. Mulled red wine: from ca 1860. In *Tom Brown at Oxford*. 2. Gen. in pl, a shoeblack. From ca 1880.

cardinal, adj. Carnal, esp. in *cardinal sin*:

mid-C.16–20 sol. Shakespeare jocularly uses *cardinally* for *carnally*. Vice versa, *carnal* is sol. for cardinal, esp. in *the carnal points*: C.16–20.

cardinal is come, the. A variant of CAPTAIN IS . . .

cards, a house of. An unsafe project or circumstance: from ca 1800; coll soon S.E.

cards, have or go in with good. Reasonably to expect success: late C.16–18: coll, > S.E. in C.17.

cards, on the. Possible; almost probable. Coll >, by 1880, S.E.; gen. from 1849, when popularized by Dickens; in use earlier, being adumbrated by Smollett in 1749. Opp. to *out of the cards*, which lasted only ca 1810–70. Perhaps ex cartomancy.

cards . . ., play one's. With *badly*, *well*, etc. To act clumsily, cleverly, etc. From ca 1640; coll, soon S.E.

cards, show one's. To disclose one's power or plans: from ca 1580; coll, soon S.E.

cards, throw up (or **down) one's.** To abandon a project, a career, etc. From late C.17; coll.

care a pin, farthing, rap, a damn, three damns, a tinker's curse, a fig – not to. These phrases are all coll, resp. —1633, 1709, 1800, 1785, 1760, 1830, 1820. There are others: e.g. . . . *a button*, *a chip*, *a cent* (mostly U.S.).

***care-grinder**, gen. preceded by *vertical*. The treadmill: c.; ca 1860–1900.

care if I . . ., I don't. I am disposed to . . . From ca 1840; coll, now on verge of S.E.

care if I do, I don't. Yes, all right. Orig. (—1870), U.S., anglicized ca 1900. (Gen. in acceptance of a drink.)

careening; careened. Physic-taking; forced to take physic: naval: ca 1820–60. Ex lit. S.E. sense.

careful. Mean in money matters: coll: from ca 1890.

carfindo. A ship's carpenter: naval: C.19. Perhaps a corruption of *carpenter* influenced by dial. *carf*, a notch in wood.

cargo. Contemptuous for a person: C.17; coll. Ben Jonson. Perhaps ex Sp. *cargo*. 2. Money: c. and low, late C.17–18. For semantics, cf. CARAVAN, 2. 3. (Winchester College) a hamper from home: from ca 1840; ob.

cargo (or C.) Bill. A R.N. Reserve officer serving in the Navy: naval: ca 1870–1914. He used to be considered a PASSENGER.

Carmagnole. A French soldier: ca 1790–1800. Burns uses it of Satan. Ex the Fr. revolutionary song.

carmes or **carnes.** Flattery; blandishments: rather low: ca 1860–1910. Ex Romany.

carmine. Blood: sporting (—1860); †by 1900. *Chambers's Journal*, 1860. cf. RUBY and CLARET.

carney, carny. Seductive flattery; suave hypocrisy. *The London Guide*, 1818; coll. (See CARNEYING.) More common as v.t. and i.:

carn(e)y, v. To coax, wheedle insinuatingly: coll (—1811) and dial. ?ex It. *carne*, flesh. cf. the n. and the next two entries.

carneying, ppl adj. Wheedling, coaxing, insinuating, seductively flattering, suavely hypocritical: from ca 1830. Coll. Mayhew; R. L. Stevenson, 1884, 'the female dog, that mass of carneying affectations'. This and its radical prob. come ex L. *caro*, *carnis*, flesh (cf. S.E. *carnal* and c. *carnish*, meat), via It. *carne* and after BLARNEY.

***carnish.** Meat: C.19–20 c. Ex Lingua Franca ex It. Hence *carnish*-KEN, a thieves' eating-house or 'PROG-shop'. North Country.

carny, see CARNEY.

caroon. In low Cockney and Parlary: a crown(piece). ca 1845–1915; surviving in MADZA *caroon*, half a crown. Perhaps ex It. *corona*, perhaps merely *crown* mispronounced; Sampson's note at *kuruna* suggests a Gypsy origin (cf. Romany *koórona*).

carpenter scene. Comic dialogue, in front of the curtain, while elaborate sets are being erected: theatrical: ca 1860–95.

carpet, v. To reprimand: coll: recorded in 1840, H. Cockton's once famous novel, *Valentine Vox*. Ex CARPET, WALK THE.

carpet, bring on the. To bring (a matter) up or forward for discussion: from ca 1720; coll till C.19, when S.E. Lit., bring on the table (before the council, etc.), for carpets 'covered tables and beds before they were used for floors': W.

carpet, walk the. To be reprimanded: from ca 1820; coll. John Galt. Ex 'servants . . . summoned into the "parlour" for a wigging', W.

carpet-bag recruit. (Military) a recruit worth more than what he stands up in: from ca 1875. cf. the U.S. adj., *carpet-bag*, and n., *carpet-bagger*.

carpet-dance. An (informal) drawing-room dance: Society coll (1877); ob.

carpet-knight. Prior to 1800 the stress is on the boudoir; after, on the drawing-room (see CARPET-MAN). A stay-at-home soldier: from ca 1570; coll; in C.19–20, S.E. Etymologically, 'one knighted at court, kneeling on the carpet before the throne, instead of on the battlefield', W.

carpet-man or **-monger.** A frequenter of ladies' boudoirs and carpeted chambers: late C.16–17; coll. The occupation is *carpet-trade*: late C.16–17, coll. 2. (*carpet-man* only.) A naval officer promoted by influence: naval: late C.19–20.

carpet-road. A level, well-kept road: coll: late C.17–18.

carpet-swab. A carpet bag: from ca 1835; coll. Barham in his poem, *Misadventure at Margate.*

carpet tom-cat. An officer often with and very attentive to the ladies: military: ca 1875–1910.

carpeting. A scolding: coll: from ca 1870; ob. Ex CARPET, V.

carriage, Her Majesty's, see QUEEN'S BUS.

carriage-company. People – orig. merchants and tradesmen – having their own carriages: coll > S.E.; from ca 1830; ob. Thackeray, 1855, 'No phrase more elegant ... than ... "seeing a great deal of carriage-company"'.

carried. Married: rhyming s. (—1909); ob.

***carrier,** in (?late C.17–)C.18–early 19 c., is a criminal band's spy or look-out.

carrier pigeon. (Racing) a person running hither and thither with 'commissions'. From ca 1850. 2. In c., a victimizer of lottery-office keepers: mid-C.18–early 19.

carrion. A harlot: C.18–19. 2. The human body: C.19–20; pejoratively indicated in C.17, = low coll. 3. Draught cattle: Australian: since ca 1860. By humorous depreciation, but with a reference to the grim potentialities of drought.

carrion-case. A shirt; a chemise. Low: C.19–20; ob.

carrion-hunter. An undertaker: ca 1780–1850. Grose, 1st ed. *Carrion* = corpse was S.E. of ca 1760–1900. cf. COLD COOK.

carrion-row. A place where inferior meat is sold: ca 1720–1800. Swift.

carrot!, take a. A low and insulting c.p. (—1874); ob. Orig. said to women only and of a scabrous implication: contrast *have a* BANANA!, the C.20 innocent phrase that soon came, in certain circles, to be used obscenely. cf. the ob. French *Et ta sœur, aime-t-elle les radis?*

carrot-pated, see CARROTY.

carrots. Red hair: coll: Wesley *père* seems to have been, in 1685, the first to print the term, as B.E. was the first to record it of a red-haired person; as the latter, a rather uncouth nickname.

carroty. Having red hair: from ca 1740; coll >, by 1880, S.E. Smollett in *Roderick Random*, Thackeray in *The Newcomes*. Mark Lemon, the mid-Victorian humorist, noted of the Greeks that all the Graces were Χάριται. Earlier was *carrot-pated* (B.E.), likewise coll. (Often misspelt *carrotty.*)

carry a (great) stroke. To have, wield much influence: ca 1640–1800; coll > S.E.

carry an M under one's girdle, see GIRDLE, NE'ER AN ...

carry coals. To endure, put up with an insult or an injury: late C.16–17: coll >, by 1620, S.E. Shakespeare, in *Romeo and Juliet*, 'Gregory, o' my word, we'll not carry coals.'

carry corn. To behave well in success: mid-C.19–20, gen. as '... doesn't carry corn well'. Ex the behaviour of corn-fed horses. Doubtless adopted from dial. (E.D.D. records it for 1845) and at first mainly rural.

carry-knave. A low harlot: C.17–18; coll. Taylor the Water Poet.

carry me out and bury me decent(ly)! An exclamation indicative of the auditor's incredulity or, occ., displeasure: coll; from ca 1780. After ca 1870, gen. abbr. to *carry me out!* Post-1850 variants, were *carry me out and leave me in the gutter*, *carry me upstairs*, *carry me home*, and *whoa, carry me out!* cf. LET ME DIE and GOOD NIGHT!

carry milk-pails. 'Presently a gentleman, "carrying milk-pails", as the [London street] boys called it – that is, with a lady on each arm – advanced up the colonnade.' Augustus Mayhew, 1857: ca 1830–80. cf. MILK-SHOP.

carry on. To behave conspicuously; frolic; flirt. Coll: from ca 1850. Whyte-Melville, 1856, 'Lady Carmine's eldest girl is carrying on with young Thriftless.' Prob. nautical in origin: ex *carrying on sail.* See CARRYINGS-ON.

carry on or **carry under.** A c.p. slogan employed by old sailing-ship captains, 'whose creed was to clap on sail regardless of risk' (Bowen): C.19–20.

carry out one's bat, see BAT.

carry-tale. A tale-bearer: ca 1570–1840; coll in C.16, then S.E.

carry the can. To accept the blame for one's own or another's error: services': late C.19–20. Prob. suggested by:

***carry the keg.** A c. pun on *carry the* CAG: 1812, Vaux; †by 1890. Whence DISTILLER, WALKING.

***carry the stick.** Applied to the operation whereby a woman, in conversation, robs a well-dressed elderly, or drunk, man, and her male associate, masquerading as a detective, makes a fuss and enables her to depart. Scottish thieves': ca 1860–1920. The London equivalent, same period, is *to trip up*.

carryings-on. Conspicuous behaviour; frolics; flirtation: from ca 1840; coll. G. A. Sala, 1859. A much earlier coll sense is: questionable proceedings, as in Butler, *Hudibras*, 'Is this the end | To which these Carryings-on did tend?' cf. GOINGS-ON.

***carsey.** A C.19–20 c. variant of CASA, a house, a den, a brothel. 2. A w.c.: low Cockney: from ca 1870. cf. CASE, n., 9. 3. A public-house: Parlary: since ca 1860. (P. H. Emerson, *Signor Lippo*, 1893.)

cart. A race-course: racing-men's: ca 1855–70. ?connected with CORRECT CARD. 2. The upper shell of a crab: coll and dial. (—1850). 3. A bed: Regular Army: mid-C.19–20; ob.

cart, v.t. To defeat, surpass, do better than: Oxford and Cambridge University: from ca 1850. Esp. as *we carted them home*, defeated them badly. cf. the next entry. 2. To hit vigorously at cricket: Public Schools': from ca 1890.

cart, in the. Wrong; in the wrong; in a FIX. Esp. as *put in the cart*, to deceive, trick, embarrass, incommode seriously, as a jockey his owner. Racing and gen. from ca 1865. Occ. as *carted* or as *in the box*. 'Perhaps goes back to the cart in which criminals were taken to execution,' W. 2. In the know: from ca 1870. *Referee*, 1 April 1883. 3. (Occ. as *on the tail-board*), it is applied to the lowest scorer: gaming, mid-C.19–20. cf. sense 1.

cart, walk the. To walk over the course: racing, from ca 1870. In 'Ducange Anglicus', 1857, the form is *traverse the cart*. 2. See TRAVERSE THE CART.

cart away, occ. **off** or **out.** To remove: coll, C.19–20.

cart before the horse, set or **put.** To reverse the usual order, whether of things or of ideas. From ca 1500; a coll that, in C.17, > S.E.

cart-grease. Bad butter, then any butter: from ca 1875. cf. COW-GREASE.

cart out with. As 'He's carting out with Liz' = he's courting her: Cockneys': since ca 1880. Ex, not 'he's carting her out', but 'he's carting himself out with her.'

cart-wheel. Variant COACH-WHEEL. Both gen. abbr. to WHEEL. A crown piece: low: from ca 1855. 2. A broad hint: C.19. 3. turn cart-wheels, to execute a series of lateral somersaults (the arms and legs resembling wheel-spokes): from ca 1860; coll. Earlier (ca 1840–75), *do a* CATHARINE WHEEL.

carts. A pair of shoes: mid-C.19–20; ob. Hotten explains by Norfolk *cart*, a crab's shell; Ware refers it to the noise made by a labourer walking heavily.

carty. Of the build and/or breed of a cart-horse: 1863; coll.

carve-up. A fight, or even a war: mostly Cockneys': since ca 1905.

Carvel's ring. The *pudendum muliebre*: mid-C.18–early 19: low coll. Ex a scabrous anecdote, for which see the (sometimes legally) inimitable Grose (1st ed.)

carver and gilder. A match-maker: from ca 1820; ob.

casa, ca-sa, or **ca. sa.** A writ of *capias ad satisfaciendum*. Legal coll: late C.18–20; ob. 2. casa, case. A house, a brothel, c., C.17–20, leads to C.19–20 c. and low s. *case-house*, a brothel, and late C.18–19 c. and low s. *case vrow*, a harlot attached to a particular bawdy-house. 3. The *case* form, in C.19, also means a water-closet. Ex It. *casa*.

casabianc. The last of anything, esp. of cigarettes: naval and military. Mid-C.19–20. Ex *Casabianca*, the boy hero of Mrs Hemans's poem.

cascade. A trundling and gymnastic performance: theatrical, from ca 1840; ob. 2. Beer: in Tasmania, then slightly on the Australian continent: from ca 1880. Ex the cascade water from which it was made: the firm that, at Hobart, makes it is known as the Cascade Brewery Company.

cascade, v. To vomit: low coll: from the early 1660s. Pepys once 'cascaded' at the theatre.

***case.** A bad crown-piece: c. and low, ca 1835–1900. Hence, the sum of five shillings: C.20 low. Prob. ex Yiddish *caser*. 2. An eccentric person, a CHARACTER, a

CURE. Orig. (—1833), U.S., anglicized ca 1850. 3. The female pudend: C.17 (e.g. in Fletcher's *The Chances*). 4. An unfortunate matter, end, as in 'I fear it's a case with him': from ca 1864. 5. The certainty to fall in love: from ca 1870, as 'it's a case with them.' Miss Braddon, in *To the Bitter End*, 1872. 6. A love-affair: schoolgirls', from ca 1860; ob. 7. A love-affair between two boys: Public Schools': C.20. 8. See CASA, 2. 9. Hence, occ., a water-closet: c. or low s. (—1864).

'case. Abbr. *in case* (=to ensure against the possibility, or the fact, that): coll: from ca 1890.

case-hardened. Tough; of one who is a HARD CASE: both coll, the latter (orig. U.S.) from ca 1860, the former from ca 1700 and S.E. by 1800.

case of crabs. A failure: coll, ca 1870–1920. ?ex CATCH A CRAB.

case of pickles. An incident, esp. if untoward; a break-down, -up. Coll: from ca 1870.

case of stump, a. (e.g. he is) penniless. Coll: ca 1870–1900. cf. STUMP, v., 2.

***case-vrow,** C.18–19; **case-fro,** late C.17–18. See CASA, 2. The *vrow* is Dutch for a woman, the *fro* indicates German influence thereon.

casein(e). 'The correct thing'; punning *the* CHEESE. Rare. †by 1900. Charles Kingsley in a letter of May 1856. (The *-ine* form is incorrect.)

***caser.** A crown piece; the sum of five shillings: c. (—1874). Ex Yiddish.

***casey;** occ. **cassey.** Cheese. C.19–20 c. cf. CASSAM; CASH; CAZ. Ex L. *caseus*.

***cash; cass.** Abbr. CASSAM, *cassan*, cheese: c.: late C.17–19; C.18–19. See also CAZ.

cash, equal to. Of undoubted and indubitable merit. Coll: from ca 1840; orig. (—1835) U.S.

cash, in; out of. Having plenty of: no: money. (*In cash* occurs in Thackeray.) Coll: from ca 1840.

cash a dog, see FLY A KITE.

cash a prescription. To have a prescription made up. Coll: from ca 1880; ob.

cash and carried. Married: rhyming s.: late C.19–20. cf. DOT AND CARRIED.

cash (or hand in, or pass in) one's checks. To die: orig. (—1860), U.S., anglicized ca 1875. *Checks* = counters in the game of poker. cf. PEG OUT.

cash up, v.i. and t. Settle a debt; pay: from ca 1830; ob. Barham; Dickens, in *Martin Chuzzlewit*; Sala, 'They'll never cash up a farthing piece.'

cashier. To deprive of one's cash: late C.16–early 17. Shakespeare – ?elsewhere.

cask. A (small) brougham: ca 1853–1900; Society. Less gen. than PILL-BOX.

cask, bull the, see BULL THE CASK.

***cassam, cassan, cassom, casson, casum.** Cheese: mid-C.16–20 c. The earliest and commonest form is *cassan*; *cash*, an abbr., appears in C.17; *casum* in C.18. See CASEY, CASH, and CAZ. cf. the *cas* of Romany.

cast, at the last. At one's last chance or shift: c. 1450–1750; coll >, by 1600, S.E. Ex dicing.

cast, give a. To assist: waggoners' and estuary-sailors' coll: mid-C.19–20.

cast an optic. To look: sporting (—1909); slightly ob.

cast beyond the moon. To make wild guesses: coll soon > S.E.: from ca 1540; ob. Heywood.

cast(-)me(-)down. Cassidony, i.e. French lavender: sol.: ca 1580–1800. Gerard, in his famous *Herbal* (1597), speaks of the 'simple people' who 'doe call it Castte me downe'.

cast-off. A discarded mistress: coll: from ca 1800. 2. In pl, landsmen's clothes: nautical: C.19–20. 3. Also, any discarded clothes: coll; C.19–20.

cast off. To unbind; to set free: nautical: C.19. *Dublin University Magazine*, March 1834 (p. 252), '"Cast him off!" *. . . . .* Unbind him.'

cast one's skin. To strip oneself to the BUFF: low: ca 1815–80. *Sinks*, 1848. See also CAP ONE'S SKIN.

cast stones against the wind. To work in vain: C.17–18; coll soon > S.E.

cast up one's accounts, see ACCOUNTS.

***castell.** To see, look: early C.17; perhaps c. or coll, its history being problematic. Recorded in Rowlands, *Martin Mark-All*, 1610. ?ex *castle* as a vantage-point.

caster, see CASTOR. 2. A cast-off or rejected person, animal, or thing: from ca 1850; coll. 3. In mid-C.16–18 c., a cloak.

***Castieu's Hotel.** The Melbourne gaol: Australian c. of ca 1880–1910. Ex a man's name.

castle. Abbr. *castle in Spain* or the more gen. and English *castle in the air*: coll, C.19–20.

***Castle, the.** Holloway Prison: c.: late C.19–20.

Castle of St Thomas. 'The Penitentiary in St Thomas's parish, where the frail part of the Oxford belles are sent under surveillance,' Egan's Grose: Oxford University: ca 1820–40.

castle-rag. A FLAG, i.e. a fourpenny piece: rhyming s. (—1859).

castor; occ. caster. A hat, orig. of beaver's fur: in C.17–early 18, S.E.; ca 1760–1810, coll; then s. Entick's *London*, 1640; Martin's Dict., 2nd ed., 1754; Moncrieff's *Tom and Jerry*, 1821.

castor, adj. and exclamation. All right: excellent: Australian: from ca 1905. Suggested by DINKUM *oil.*

castor-oil artist or **merchant.** A surgeon; a physician: military: from ca 1905.

casual. A casual ward in a hospital; an occasional workman, pauper, visitor, etc.: coll; resp. from ca 1850 and from ca 1820. Bee, 1823, notes it of a boarder in a lodging house.

casual, adj. Uncertain, undependable, happy-go-lucky, slightly careless and callous: coll, from ca 1880.

casualty. A casual labourer: Londoners' coll: ca 1850–1910. Mayhew, *London Labour*, II, 'The "casuals" or the "casualties" (always called amongst the men "cazzelties")'. Hence CASUALTY BOY.

casualty, adj. Casual: Londoners' coll: mid-C.19–20; ob. Mayhew, 1851, 'Red herrings, and other cas'alty fish'. Ex the dial. adj. *casualty*, for which see the E.D.D.

casualty boy. 'A boy who hires himself out to a costermonger', E.D.D.: London coll: ca 1850–1910. Mayhew. Often *casalty boy*.

cat. A harlot: C.16–19; in C.19, ob.; by 1910, †. Lyndesay, 1535, in his satire on wantons. This sense of *cat* is due to Dutch influence. 2. Abbr. CAT-O'-NINE-TAILS: apparently first in 1788, in Falconbridge's *African Slave Trade*: coll; by 1820, S.E. 3. In C.20 c., punishment by the 'cat'. 4. Abbr. TAME CAT. 5. The female pudend: coll, C.19–20: otherwise PUSS, cf. Fr. *le chat*. 6. Related is mid-C.19–20 (ob.) c. sense, a lady's muff (see MUFF, n.). Brandon, 1839. 7. Also c. (—1812), a quart pot, a pint pot being a KITTEN. It is implied by Vaux's CAT AND KITTEN RIG. 8. A landlady in lodgings (rooms or boarding house): from ca 1820; ob. Peake in his comedy, *Comfortable Lodgings*, 1827. 9. See CHESHIRE CAT.

cat, v. To vomit: late C.18–20: low coll; in C.20, mainly dial. cf. CAT, SHOOT THE.

cat, do a, see DO A CAT.

***cat, flying,** see FLYING-CAT.

***cat, free a.** To steal a muff: c. (—1864). See CAT, n., 6.

cat, grin like a Cheshire, see CHESHIRE CAT . . .

cat, not room enough to swing a. Cramped for space; very small: coll >, in late C.19, S.E.: from ca 1770. Smollett. i.e. a CAT-O'-NINE-TAILS.

cat, old. 'A cross old woman', Grose, 1st ed.: coll: mid-C.18–20.

cat, pinch the; gen. **be pinching . . .** This proletarian phrase has, from ca 1880, been applied to a man who, hand in pocket, palps his genitals.

cat!, s'elp (or **s'help**) **the.** A variant of BOB!, S'ELP ME: low (—1890); ob. See also SWELP.

cat, shoot the. To vomit: C.19–20; coll. Marryat in *The King's Own*, 1830, 'I'm cursedly inclined to shoot the cat.' A C.17–18 variant, *jerk the cat*; a C.17–20 ob. variant, *whip the cat*, as in Taylor the Water Poet, 1630. 2. 'To sound a refrain in the infantry bugle call to defaulters' drill, which, it is fancied, follows the sound of the words "*Shoot the cat – shoot the cat*",' F. & H.: military: from ca 1880.

cat, sick as a. Vomiting; very sick indeed: coll: mid-C.19–20.

cat, whip the. To indulge in a certain practical joke: C.18–19; coll. In C.17–18, *draw* or *pull* someone *through the water with a cat*, as in Jonson's *Bartholomew Fair*, 1614, in B.E., and in Grose: for an explanation of the origin of the phrases, see Grose. 2. (Orig. of tailors.) To work at private houses: coll; from ca 1785; ob.

cat?, who ate or **stole the.** A c.p. against pilferers: C.19–20, ob.; coll. Perhaps ex an actual incident.

cat?, who shot the. A stock reproach to the Volunteers: from ca 1850.

cat and dog life, lead a. (Of married couples) to be constantly quarrelling: coll, from ca 1560. B.E. has *agree like Dog and Cat.*

cat and I'll kill your dog, you kill my. An exchange of (the lower) social amenities: C.19–20; coll. cf. Scottish *ca' me, ca' thee.*

***cat-and-kitten hunting** or **sneaking.** The stealing of quart and pint pots (see CAT, n., 7): c. (—1859); ob. cf.:

***cat and kitten rig.** The ca 1810–50 form of the preceding.

cat and mouse. A house: rhyming s. (—1857).

cat-faced. Ugly: low coll (North of England): mid-C.19–20. Its original, *cat-face*, a pejorative n., may be dial.

cat-gut scraper, see CATGUT-SCRAPER.

cat-harping fashion. Nautical, late C.18–19: 'Drinking cross ways, and not as usual over the left thumb', Grose, 1st ed. Ex CATHARPIN-FASHION.

cat has kittened in one's mouth, to feel as if a. To 'have a mouth' after being drunk: from ca 1600; coll. Field in his indelicate play, *Amends for Ladies*, 1618. cf. Fr. *avoir la gueule de bois*.

cat-heads. Female breasts: naval, mostly lowerdeck: late C.18–mid-19. *The Night Watch* (II, 89), 1828, but also, much earlier in John Davis, *The Post Captain*. Ex nautical j. In W. N. Glascock, *The Naval Sketch-Book*, II, 1826, it seems to mean 'falsies'.

cat in hell without claws, no more chance than a. A late C.18–mid-19 c.p. applied to 'one who enters into a dispute or quarrel with one greatly above his match', Grose, 3rd ed.

cat in the pan, turn. To change sides, from self-interest; be a turncoat. Coll: from —1384; ob. e.g. in Wyclif; Bacon's *Essays*; an anon. song entitled *The Vicar of Bray* (ca 1720); Scott in *Old Mortality*. Whence *cat in (the) pan*, a turncoat or traitor. Perhaps ex *cake in the pan*, i.e. a pancake: which is often turned.

cat jumps, see, occ. watch, how or which way the. To observe the course of events: coll; from ca 1820. Scott; Lytton. cf. SIT ON THE FENCE.

cat-lap. Thin beverage, esp. tea: coll: from ca 1780. Grose (1st ed.), Scott, Miss Braddon.

cat laugh, enough to – or it would – make a. (It is) extremely funny, droll, ludicrous: coll: 1851, Planché; 1898, Weyman.

cat-market. Many persons all speaking at the one time: coll; C.19–20.

***cat-match.** A bowling match in which a dishonest expert is engaged with bad players: late C.17–18 c.

cat-nap. A short sleep had while sitting: coll; from ca 1850.

cat-o'-nine-tails. A nine-lashed scourge, until 1881 employed in the British army and navy; since, though decreasingly, for criminals. From ca 1670. From ca 1700, coll; from ca 1780, S.E. In Head's *The English Rogue*; Vanbrugh, in *The False Friend*, 'You dread reformers of an impious age, | You awful cat-a-nine-tails to the stage'; Smollett in *Roderick Random*.

cat on hot bricks, see HOT BRICKS.

***cat on testy dodge, a.** 'A ladylike beggar worrying ladies at their houses for money – if only a sixpence (tester)', Ware: c. of ca 1870–1914.

cat out of the bag, let the, see at BAG . . .

cat-party. A party of women only: coll, C.19–20. Also *cats' party*: sporting (—1888); slightly ob. cf. BITCH- and HEN-PARTY, see also STAG-PARTY.

cat-shooter, see SATURDAY SOLDIER.

cat-skin. An inferior make of silk hat: 1857, Hughes; ob. by 1900. cf. and see RABBIT-SKIN.

cat speak (and a wise man dumb), enough or able to make a. Astounding: coll: late C.16–20, ob. D'Urfey, 1719, 'Old Liquor able to make a Cat speak'; Dickens elaborates. The *man* addition appears in 1661, in a form that shows D'Urfey to be repeating a proverb: 'Old liquor able to make a cat speak and a wise man dumb': a proverb implicit in Shakespeare's *Tempest*, I, ii, 'Open your mouth', etc., and in one – perhaps an earlier – Shirburn Ballad, 'Who is it but loves good liquor? 'Twill make a catte speake.'

cat-sticks. Thin legs: late C.18–mid-19: coll. ?ex TRAP-STICKS.

cat up. A variant of CAT, v.: late C.19–20.

cat-witted. Obstinate and spiteful: coll: ca 1660–1930. Contrast the dial. senses: scatterbrained, silly, conceited, whimsical.

catamaran. 'An old scraggy woman', Grose, 3rd ed.: from not later than 1791. Whence the soon prevailing nuance: a cross-grained person, esp. if a woman; a vixenish old woman: coll (—1833). Marryat; Thackeray, in *The Newcomes*, 'What an infernal tartar and catamaran!' ?a corruption of *cat o' mountain* (as in Fletcher's *The Custom of the Country*, 1616), which, in U.S., has, since ca 1830, meant a shrew.

cataract. A black satin scarf worn by 'commercials' for the surface and effect it offers to jewellery: ca 1830–70.

catastrophe. The tail, the end. Late C.16–early 19, jocular coll, as in Shakespeare, (Falstaff): 'I'll tickle your catastrophe.'

catawamp(o)us; occ. **catawamptious.** Avid; fierce, eager; violently destructive: orig. U.S.; almost imm. anglicized by Dickens in *Martin Chuzzlewit*. The adv. (*-ly*) appeared notably in England in Lytton's *My Novel*, 1853. Perhaps, says W., suggested by *catamount*.

catawampus. Vermin and insects, esp. the stingers and biters. From ca 1870; Mortimer Collins, 1880, '. . . catawampuses, as the ladies call them'. Ex preceding.

catch. A person matrimonially desirable: coll; anticipated by Dryden's 'The Gentleman had a great Catch of her, as they say,' and Jane Austen's 'on the catch for a husband', the term > gen. only ca 1830–45. 2. In c., C.17–19, a prize, a booty.

catch, v.i. To become pregnant: coll, mostly lower classes': late C.19–20.

catch (rarely cut) a crab. In rowing, to mull one's stroke, esp. by jamming the oar in the water as if a crab had caught it. Coll: late C.18–20.

catch a Tartar. Unexpectedly to meet one's superior; be hoist by one's own petard. Late C.17–20: coll till ca 1850, then S.E. Dryden, Smollett, Fanny Burney. For semantics, see TARTAR, . . .

catch afire. To set fire to: Cockney coll: mid-C.19–20. Edwin Pugh, *A Street in Suburbia*, 1895, 'It blazed up in the pan an' caught the chimley afire almost.'

catch-bet. A bet made to inveigle the unwary: low coll; from ca 1870.

catch club, a member of the. A bailiff or his assistant: late C.18–early 19: jocular coll.

***catch cocks.** To obtain money on false pretences: military c., late C.19–20; ob. Ware, who notes that the vbl n. is *cock-catching*.

catch cold. 'I told her if she did not give it me again she would *catch cold*, meaning she would repent of it' (rather, get into trouble, be 'for it'): 1775.

catch 'em (all) alive-o! A c.p. of ca 1850–80. Orig. a fisherman's phrase, but by 1853, if not a year or two earlier, it had a tremendous vogue. Its intent was to raise a smile, its meaning almost null. 2. (Gen. without the '-o'.) A fly-paper: from ca 1855; ob. Mayhew; Dickens in *Little Dorrit*. 3. A small comb (cf. LOUSE-TRAP): ca 1860–1910. 4. The female pudend: low: from ca 1864: ob.

catch-fake. The doubling of a rope badly coiled: nautical coll: late C.19–20. i.e. a faked 'catch'.

catch-fart. A footman or a page: late C.17–19. He stands behind his master.

catch it. To be scolded, reprimanded; castigated: coll; from ca 1830. Marryat, *Jacob Faithful*, 1835, 'We all thought Tom was about to catch it.'

catch me!; catch me at it! I'll do no such thing! Coll: from ca 1770. Mrs Cowley, Galt, Dickens ('"Catch you at forgetting anything!" exclaimed Carker').

catch on. Coll: to join on, attach oneself to: coll: from ca 1884. 2. To 'take', be a success: from ca 1886: coll. 3. To understand, grasp the meaning or significance, apprehend: orig. (—1884), U.S., anglicized ca 1888: coll.

catch, occ. get, on the hop. To surprise; find unprepared. From ca 1861: coll. *The Chickaleary Cove*, a popular song – the famous Vance, its singer: 'For to get me on the hop, or on my "tibby" drop, | You must wake up very early in the morning.'

catch one's death (of cold). To get a severe chill: coll, from ca 1870.

catch out. To detect in a mistake or a misdoing: 1815, Jane Austen: coll >, by 1900, S.E. Ex cricket; cf. BOWL OUT.

catch-penny. A penny GAFF (show or exhibition); a broadsheet describing an imaginary murder. Coll: ca 1820–1910. Other senses are S.E.

catch the bird. To have a short sleep: nautical: late C.19–20.

catch the wind of the word. Quickly to apprehend (cf. CATCH ON): orig. Irish. C.19–20; ob.

catch up. To interrupt, 'pull up', correct (a person): from ca 1840; coll till ca 1900, then S.E. Dickens, in *Barnaby Rudge*, 'You catch me up so very short.'

catchee. Pidgin English for *catch*, as *havee* for *have*: C.18–20; also to obtain, find out, hold, win.

catching flies. Gaping: coll: C.19–20.

catching harvest. A dangerous time for a robbery on account of congested roads: coll: C.18–mid-19.

catchpole rap(p)aree. A constable: Ned Ward, 1709.

catchy. Attractive, esp. if vulgarly so: 1831: coll, as orig. were the senses: soon popular (e.g. of a tune), from ca 1880, and tricky (as of examination questions), from ca 1884. But from ca 1890 all three meanings have been S.E. 2. Inclined to take an (esp. undue) advantage: (—)1859. 3. Spasmodic: coll: U.S., 1872; England, 1883. 4. Merry: Scots coll: 1804, Tarras.

caterpillar. An illicit or an illegal liver-by-his-wits: late C.16–17: orig. c., then s., then almost S.E. 2. Whence, a soldier: mid-C.18–early 19. 3. A ladies' school a-walking in line, two by two: Society: 1848. cf. CROCODILE.

caterwaul, v. To make sexual love: late C.16–20 (ob.): coll until ca 1700, then s. The vbl n. *caterwauling* is more gen. Nashe; Congreve; Smollett, concerning the servant-maids in *Humphrey Clinker*, '... junketting and caterwauling with the fellows of the country'.

catever, n. and adj. (A) queer (affair), (a) bad or inferior (thing). Low and Parlary: from ca 1840. The spelling is various. Ex It. *cattivo*, bad.

catgut-scraper. A fiddler: late C.17–20; ob.; coll. Ned Ward, Wolcot, Mayhew.

Catharine or Catherine wheel, do a. To do a lateral somersault, a CART-WHEEL, 3: coll, ca 1850–1900.

catharpin fashion. 'When People in Company Drink cross, and not going about from the Right to the Left', B.E.: drinkers': late C.17–18. Ex Gr. κατὰ + πίνειν, to drink. The early form of CAT-HARPING FASHION.

cathedral. A high hat: Winchester College, C.19–20.

cathedral, adj. Old-fashioned; antique. Coll: late C.17–early 19.

Catherine Hayes. A drink made of claret, sugar, and nutmeg: ca 1858–1890; Australian. Prob. ex the Irish singer so popular in Australia. Frank Fowler, 1859.

Catherine wheel, see CATHARINE WHEEL, DO A.

catolla, catoller. A noisy fellow, either prating or foolish – or both. Early C.19. Pierce Egan used it of a foolish betting man (1825).

cats, fight like Kilkenny. To fight even unto mutual destruction: coll: C.19–20. It is said that Cromwell's soldiers in Ireland used to amuse themselves by tying two cats together by their tails and hanging them over a clothes line. Of course the wretched animals clawed each other to death.

cats and dogs, rain. To rain hard: coll: Swift adumbrated this coll in 1710 and employed it in 1738 (date of printing; written ca 1708); Shelley; Barham. C.19 humorists often added *and pitchforks and shovels*.

cat's foot, see CAT'S PAW.

cat's foot, live under the. To be henpecked: coll: late C.17–19. Ray, 1678; Grose; Spurgeon.

cat's head. The end of a shoulder of mutton: Winchester College, from ca 1830; ob. cf. DISPAR.

cat's meat. The human lungs: low coll: from ca 1820. Ex the 'lights' of animals, a favourite food of cats.

cat's neck, who shall hang the bell about the. Who will take the risk? C.17–18 coll: = BELL THE CAT.

cats of nine tails of all prices, he has. A late C.18–early 19 low c.p. applied to the hangman.

cat's party, see CAT-PARTY.

cat's paw. A dupe: late C.18–20; coll until ca 1820, then S.E. *Cat's foot* was so used a century earlier.

cat's water. Gin: low: mid-C.19–20. cf. BITCHES' *wine* and esp. the semantic determinant, OLD TOM.

catskin, see CAT-SKIN.

catso. The male member: C.17–early 18. Also, same period, a scamp, rogue, cullion. The former sense, recorded in 1702, precedes the other by six years. Also an exclamation with later form GADSO. Ex the It. *cazzo*, the *membrum virile*, the word has, in its different senses, several very English parallels.

catting, vbl n. 'Drawing a Fellow through a Pond with a Cat', B.E.: late C.17–19; coll. cf. *whip the* CAT. 2. A vomiting: C.19–20, low: see *shoot the* CAT. 3. Running after harlots and near-harlots: coll: late C.17–early 19. See CAT, n.

cattle. A pejorative fairly strong in C.16–18, fairly mild (as in *kittle cattle* = women) in C.19–20, applied to human beings: Gosson, 1579, 'Poets, and Pipers, and suche peevishe Cattel'; Shakespeare, in *As You Like It*, of boys and women; Evelyn, '... concubines, and cattell of that sort'; G. R. Sims, in *The Dagonet Ballads*, 'Queer cattle is women to deal with.' Strictly, S.E.; but the contemptuous usage makes the term analogous to coll. It is the etymological kinship with *chattels* which prompted – perhaps rather it determined – the contempt. Note, too, that in the late C.17–early 18 the word was wholly coll in the sense recorded by B.E.: '*Cattle*, Whores. *Sad Cattle*, Impudent Lewd Women', with which cf. Evelyn's phrase, preceded as it is by a reference to 'Nelly', i.e. Nell Gwynn. In C.18–early 19, *sad cattle* also meant gypsies, while in c. *black cattle* = lice; in C.19 low coll, *small cattle* = vermin, lice.

cattle-racket. A system of plunder: Australian coll: ca 1850–1900. Ex a wholesale plunder in cattle in New South Wales, app. in the 1840s.

cattley man. A cattleman: Australian coll: since ca 1880.

catty. Spiteful and sly: gen. of women: from ca 1885: coll >, by 1910, S.E. *Cattish*, S.E. in the same sense, occurs a few years earlier.

caucus as a pejorative was, at first (say 1878–90), so close to being coll as makes no difference. Its other senses, ex the U.S., have always been S.E. For this interesting and significant word see esp. the O.E.D., Thornton, Weekley, S.O.D.

caudge-pawed. Left-handed: coll and dial: mid-C.17–20; ob. cf. *cack-*, *car-* and CAW-HANDED, also LEFTY and MAULEY.

caudle of hemp-seed, or **hempen caudle.** Hanging: jocular coll: late C.16–early 17. The latter in Shakespeare.

caul, be born with a. To be born lucky: coll: C.17–20, ob. Ben Jonson; Dickens. Ex the belief that those born with one were safe from drowning.

cauli. Cauliflower: coll: late C.19–20.

cauliflower. A clerical wig modish *temp.* Queen Anne; hence, v.i. and t., to powder a wig: both soon †. 2. Whence, 'any one who wears powder on his head', Bee: ca 1820–40. 3. The female pudend: C.18–19. See Grose (1st ed.) for a witty, broad, and improbable origin. cf. CABBAGE, 6, and GREENS. 4. The foaming top to (e.g. a tankard of) beer: from ca 1870, ob. Ex Scots, where recorded as early as 1813. Contrast the Fr. *un bock sans faux-col.*

caulk or **caulking.** A (short) sleep: nautical; from very early C.19. Perhaps ex: 2. A dram: nautical; from ca 1800. Semantics: 'something to keep out the wet' or 'the damp'.

caulk, v. To sleep, esp. if surreptitiously: nautical; from ca 1810. cf. n., 1. 2. v.t., to cease, 'shut up': nautical, from ca 1880. W. Clark Russell. Ex the lit. sense. 3. Also nautical: to copulate with: from ca 1840. cf. the M.E. *cauk*, (of birds) to tread: ex L. *calcare.*

caulk my dead-lights! Damnation: nautical (—1887). cf. *damn my eyes!*

caulker; occ. misspelt **cawker.** Nautical: a dram: from ca 1805; e.g. in Charles Kingsley. cf. CAULK, n., 2, and perhaps v., 1. 2. Anything incredible; esp. a lie: from ca 1860. H., 3rd ed.; Clark Russell's *Jack's Courtship*. Perhaps influenced by CORKER. cf. CRAMMER. 3. 'A stranger, a novice' (*Spy*, 1825): Eton: ca 1815–60. *Spy* spells it *cawker.*

cause. 'A particular local organization, enterprise, mission, or church', O.E.D.: religious coll (—1893). Ex *make common cause (with).*

'cause. Because. In mid-C.16–early 17, S.E.; ca 1640–1780, coll; thereafter, sol. (and dial.). See also next entry:

'cause why? or **!** Why; the reason why; the reason. In C.14–16, S.E.; 17–18 coll; 19–20 dial. and, elsewhere, increasingly sol. As for *'cause* alone, the pronunciation, as a sol., varies from *caws* through *coz* and *cuz*, to even *case.*

causey, causy; cawsey, cawsy. Latrines: low: late C.19–20. Ex one or other of the secondary meanings of dial. *causey*, causeway, highway, street, perhaps influenced by c. *carsey.*

caution. A person or a thing wonderful, unusual, or, esp., odd, eccentric: coll: anglicized by Whyte-Melville in 1853 (*Digby Grand*; again in *Good for Nothing*) ex U.S. (—1835). i.e. one with whom caution should be employed. 2. Hence, at Oxford, from 1865, a CURE, a CHARACTER; and this has, in England, been the predominant usage, likewise coll. 3. (Ex sense 1.) A person mildly bad: from ca 1880. e.g. 'Dad's a bit of a caution when he's had too much to drink.'

cautions, the four. A mid-C.18–early 19 c.p., explained thus by Grose, 1st ed.: 'I. Beware of a woman before. II. Beware of a horse behind. III. Beware of a cart sideways. IV. Beware of a priest every way.'

cavalier. To play the cavalier, escort a lady: coll >, by 1890, S.E.: ca 1860–1910.

cavalry curate. A curate who, in a large parish, rides a horse in the discharge of his duties: from early 1890s: coll.

cavaulting, cavolting. Sexual intercourse: c. or low s.: C.17–early 19. Whence *cavaulting-school*, a brothel: late C.17–early 19. Ex Lingua Franca *cavolta*, riding and 'horsing' (s.v. HORSE, v.); ex Low L. *caballus*, a horse. cf. CAVORT.

cave. (Political) a small group of politicians seceding, on some special bill or cause, from their party; the secession: 1866. (cf. *Adullamites.*) Orig. *cave of Adullam* – see 1 *Samuel*, 22, 1–2. 2. Coll abbr. *Cavalier*: ca 1647–81. A. Brome, in *Songs*, 1661.

cave, v.i., see CAVE IN, 1.

cave! Schoolboys'. ?first at Eton College, for 'beware!' Direct ex the L. word. From ca 1750 (?).

cave-dwellers. Brutal atavists: Society coll: 1890; ob. cf. CAVE-MAN.

cave in, v.i. To yield, esp. when further opposition is futile or impossible; occ. *cave*. With *in*, coll; without, s. Anglicized ca 1855 ex U.S. (—1840) ex East Anglian dial., as is the v.t., to break down, smash, BASH in: anglicized ca 1885; but cf. the S.E. *cave* (C.16–20), to hollow (out), and *cave in*, to subside concavely (late C.18–20). 2. (Political) to form a CAVE, a cabal: ca 1880–1900.

cave-man. A HE-MAN, a rough and virile fellow: coll: from ca 1895.

cave of antiquity. 'Depôt of old authors', Egan's Grose: Oxford University: ca 1820–40. More prob., *Cave of Antiquity*, the Bodleian Library.

cave out. (Gen. ppl adj., *caved out*.) To come to an end, be finished: coll anglicized (—1909) ex U.S. 'From the metal casing in a tunnel', Ware.

caves is the Winchester College pronunciation of *calves* (of the legs). Wrench.

cavey, see CAVY.

caviar(e). The obnoxious matter 'blacked out' of foreign periodicals by the Russian Press Censor: from ca 1888. *St James's Gazette*, 25 April 1890, uses *caviar(e)* as a v.t. In Tsarist days, irreligious or socialistic matter; *temp.* Soviet, powerfully religious or insidiously capitalistic opinions. The word, a good example of literary s., is ob.

cavish, see CAVY.

cavolting, see CAVAULTING.

cavort. To prance (of horses); make a horse prance. Hence, to frisk, lit. and fig. Anglicized ca 1900 ex (—1834) U.S. 'Perhaps cowboy perversion of *curvet*', W.

cavy; cavey. A Cavalier: coll: ca 1645–70. Whence adj., *cavish*, 1664.

caw-handed, late C.17–20; **caw-pawed,** late C.18–20; both ob. Awkward. In dial., *caw* is a fool, whence *caw-baby*, an awkward or timid boy. cf. CAUDGE-PAWED.

cawfin. A badly found ship: marine: 1876, the date at which Samuel Plimsoll (d. 1898) finally got 'the Plimsoll line' incorporated in law; ob. A corruption, or rather a Cockney pronunciation, of *coffin*.

cawker, see CAULKER.

cawsey or **cawsy,** see CAUSEY.

caxon, caxton and **Caxton,** (theatrical) a wig, C.19–20, ob., is perhaps a corruption, after Caxton the printer's name, of †*caxon*, which = an old weather-beaten wig, says Grose (1st ed.), but 'a kind of wig', says S.O.D.; the latter gives it as S.E. – as prob. it was.

***caz,** in C.19 c., is cheese. *As good as caz*, easy to do, a 'sure thing'. cf. (*the*) CHEESE. 2. An easy dupe: c.: mid-C.19–20.

caze. The female pudend: C.19–20, ob.

***cedar.** In late C.19–20 c., a pencil. Obviously ex the wood of that tree. cf. East Anglian *cedar-pencil*, a lead pencil. 2. A pair-oared boat, canvasless, in-rigged, easily upset: Eton, C.19–20, ob.

cee. A small quantity of beer: C.17–18, university s. > S.E. cf. CUE.

Celestial. A Chinese: from ca 1860: coll; by 1880, S.E. – if jocular, for otherwise the word is pure journalese, which has been described as 'not the language written by journalists but that spoken by politicians'. 2. A jocular coll applied to a turned-up nose: from ca 1865. It points to heaven. cf. STAR-GAZER. 3. see CELESTIALS.

celestial poultry. Angels: low coll: from ca 1870; virtually †.

celestials. Occupants of the gallery: *Referee*, 5 Oct. 1884; ob. On *the* GODS, 2.

cellar-flap. A dance performed within a very small compass: low coll (—1877); ob.

cellarous. Of, in, belonging or natural to a cellar. The jocular intention of Dickens's word – in *The Uncommercial Traveller*, 1860 – makes it a coll, which, since it has not been seriously adopted, it remains.

cellars. Boots: London streets' (—1909); ob. Ware. Opp. GARRET, the head.

cellier. An unmitigated lie: ca 1681–1710; coll. Ex the impudently mendacious Mrs Elizabeth Cellier of the Meal Tub Plot, 1680. In *The Pope's Harbinger*, 1682, '... a modern and most proper phrase to signifie any Egregious Lye'. See, e.g., the anon. pamphlet *The Tryal and Sentences of Elizabeth Cellier, for Writing ... A Scandalous Libel Called Malice Defeated*, 1680.

'cello. Abbr. *violoncello*: from ca 1880. Coll. >, by 1910, S.E.

cemetery (or C.), the. The Dogger Bank: fishermen's coll: C.19–early 20. So many come to grief there every winter.

cent per cent. A usurer: coll: C.17–19. cf. SIXTY PER CENT.

centipees, see SANK.

centre of bliss. Coll verging on S.E.: from ca 1790: *pudendum muliebre*.

centurion. One who scores 100 or over: cricketers' coll: from ca 1885; ob. *Graphic*, 31 July 1886.

century. £100: the turf: from ca 1860. 2. 100 runs or more: from ca 1880: coll >, by 1900, S.E. *Graphic*, 11 Aug. 1883.

'cept. Except: low, when not childish, coll: C.19–20.

cert. Abbr. *certainty*: from mid-1880s (still mainly sporting): s. Often *a dead cert. Man of the World*, 29 June 1889, 'Pioneer is a cert. for the St James's.'

certain sure, for. Absolutely; with certainty; unhesitatingly: (rather illiterate) coll: mid-C.19–20.

certainty. (Gen. in pl.) A male infant: printers': from ca 1860. cf. UNCERTAINTY.

certainty, a dead. A horse, etc., supposed to be certain to win; a thing sure to happen. Coll: 1859+. cf. the S.E. *moral certainty*.

cess, see BAD CESS TO. 2. In South African coll (from ca 1860), 'an expression of disgust in common use, occasionally elaborated into "pooh-gaciss"', Pettman. Ex Cape Dutch *sis* or *sies* employed in the same way.

***chafe,** v.t. To thrash: from ca 1670; ob. Prob. orig. c. cf. Fr. *chauffer* and (to) WARM.

***chafe-litter.** In mid-C.16–early 17 c., a saucy fellow; cf. BAWDY PHYSIC.

chafer, v. To copulate: low coll: C.19–20, ob. For etymology, cf. CHAUVERING.

chaff. Banter, ridicule; humbug: coll. Clearly in *The Fancy*, vol. I, 1821, but perhaps anticipated in 1648. For etymology, see CHAFF, v. 2. (Christ's Hospital) a small article: from ca 1860. Perhaps ex *chaffer*, haggling, influenced by *chattel*.

chaff, v. To banter, lightly rail at or rally, 'quiz'. S.O.D. dates at 1827, but cf. CHAFFING-CRIB and F. & H.'s extremely significant C.17 example from the anon. ballad entitled *The Downfall of Charing Cross*: like the n., it > gen. only ca 1830. Prob. ex *chafe*, to gall, fret, irritate. 2. cf. the c. sense of ca 1820–50: 'to blow up [i.e. to boast]; to talk aloud', Egan's Grose, 1823. 3. (Christ's Hospital) v.t., to exchange, esp. small articles. From ca 1860. W. H. Blanch, *Blue Coat Boys*, 1877.

chaff, adj. Pleasant; glad: Christ's Hospital, from ca 1865. Occ. *chaffy*.

chaff! Interjection indicative of pleasure, joy. Christ's Hospital, from ca 1865.

***chaff-cutter.** A slanderer: c. of ca 1840–90. Ex: 2. A knowing and plausibly talkative person: c. (—1823); †by 1860. cf. CHAFF, v., 2.

chaffer. A banterer; a joker at the expense of others: coll; *Boxiana*, III, 1821. Mayhew, 'She was . . . the best chaffer on the road; not one of them could stand up against her tongue.' 2. The mouth or throat: *Boxiana*, III, 1821, 'Cool their *chaffer* with a drop of *heavy wet*.' ? etymology. 3. An Arctic whale, an Arctic grampus: nautical coll: mid-C.19–20. Ex Shetlands *chaffer*, the round-lipped whale.

chaffing-crib. A man's DEN; the room where he receives his intimates. Moncrieff in *Tom and Jerry*, 1821. Low coll; †by 1900.

chaffy. Full of banter, ridicule, or badinage: mid-C.19–20: coll >, by 1890, S.E.; rare. 2. See CHAFF, adj. 3. Pleased: Christ's Hospital, ca 1905.

chaft. 'Chafed': see CHAFE.

chai. Tea. In C.17, among merchants and in middle-class society, *cha* was occ. used in England; in C.19, revived among soldiers as *char*, it > s. Ex Chinese. 2. See CHAL.

***chain-gang.** Jewellers; watch-chain makers: c.; from ca 1860; ob.

chain-lightning. Potato-spirit: lower London: 1885, *Daily News*, 22 Dec. In U.S. as early as 1843 of any raw whisky. Ex its effect: 'poisonous to a degree. Smuggled chiefly', Ware.

chair, call a. To appoint a president 'at a tavern-party, when discussion ensues', Bee: public-house: ca 1820–60.

chair, put in the. To fail to pay (a person): cab-drivers', ca 1860–1900. *Social Science Review*, vol. I, 1864.

chair-bottomer. A cane-plaiter of chair-bottoms: proletarian coll (—1887).

chair days. Old age: Society coll: 1898, Sir E. Arnold; virtually †.

chair-marking. To write, not figure, the date in, or heavily to endorse, a cab-driver's licence, as a hint of the holder's undesirability: cab-owners', from ca 1885. *Pall Mall Gazette*, 15 Sept. 1890.

chal. A man, fellow, chap (the feminine is *chai, chie*): Romany; in C.19–20 used occ. in low coll. Its ultimate origin is unknown: see esp. Sampson at *čal*. cf. PAL, much more gen.

chal droch. A knife: Shelta: C.18–20.

C(h)aldee, C(h)aldese. To trick, cheat, impose upon. Butler, 'He . . . Chows'd and Caldes'd you like a blockhead,' *Hudibras*, II. ca 1660–1720; coll. ?ex *Chaldee(s)* = an astrologer.

chalk. A point in one's favour: coll, from ca 1850, ex the S.E. sense of a score chalked up in an ale-house. Edmund Yates, 1864. 2. A scratch, more gen. a scar: nautical, ca 1830–1915. Marryat in *Poor Jack*.

chalk, v. To make (a newcomer) pay his

footing: nautical, ca 1840–1900. 2. In C.18–19 c., to strike or slash, esp. a person's face. cf. CHALKER, 2. 3. See CHALK OFF; CHALK UP.

chalk, adj. Unknown; hence, incompetent. Whence *chalk-jockeys*, jockeys unknown or incompetent or both. Racing: ca 1870–90. Because their names were written up on the telegraph board in chalk only, not painted or printed on it.

chalk, able to walk a. Sober: coll (orig. nautical or military): from ca 1820. Scots, *line for chalk*. See also WALK THE CHALK.

chalk, by a long. By much: from ca 1840; coll. C. Brontë in *The Professor*. Slightly earlier is *by long chalks*, as in Barham, while *by many chalks* appears ca 1880, as in 'the best thing out by many chalks', Grenville Murray, 1883. Often with *beat*, and in C.20 gen. in the negative. Ex 'the use of chalk in scoring points in games', W.

chalk against, n. and v. (To have) 'an unsettled misunderstanding or grudge', Ware: lower classes': mid-C.19–20; ob. Ex chalking a debt against a name.

chalk down, see CHALK OUT.

Chalk Farm. An arm: rhymings. (—1857).

chalk head. A person smart at figures: coll, from ca 1850. *Punch*, 1856. 2. Hence, a waiter, rarely so called outside of London. *Punch*, 1861.

chalk is up, one's. One's credit is exhausted: public-house coll (—1887): ob. Ex *chalk up*.

***chalk off,** v.t. To observe a person attentively so as to remember him: c. (—1857).

chalk out, occ. **down.** To mark out a course of action or conduct: from ca 1570. Coll in C.16, thereafter S.E.

chalk up, occ. **chalk.** To consider in a person's favour: coll, from ca 1890. Ex the S.E. sense, C.16–20, to put to one's account, orig. by chalking the (usually, drinking) score on a wall. cf. CHALLIK IT OOP.

chalk your pull! Hold on!; steady!: printers' (—1887).

chalker. A London milkman: ca 1850–1900. Ex the addition of chalky water to milk. cf. COW-WITH-THE-IRON-TAIL. 2. (Gen. in pl.). One who, at night, slashes the face of innocent citizens: a C.18 Irish practice; cf. MOHOCK. Coll whence *chalking*, 'the amusement [so] described', Grose, 1st ed.

chalking him in. 'The steward's action of drawing a chalk line round any Western Ocean passenger who sits in the captain's chair, the penalty for which is a drink for every steward in the saloon': nautical coll: late C.19–20. Bowen.

chalks. Legs: low: ca 1825–70. *Sinks*, 1848.

chalks, by. An Australian coll variant (ca 1880–1910) of *by a long* CHALK. Boldrewood, 1888, in the best of the bushranging novels. Ex Cumberland dial.

chalks, make. (Often as vbl n., *making chalks*.) To be punished standing on two chalk lines and bending one's back: the Royal Navy School at Greenwich: ca 1840–1900.

chalks, walk or **stump one's.** To move or run away; make one's departure. From ca 1840. cf. CHALKS.

chalks on, give. To be much superior to: late C.19–20.

Chalky. A frequent nickname of men surnamed White: naval and military: late C.19–20. cf. *Blanco*.

challik it oop! Put it to my credit (esp. in a tavern): theatrical c.p. (—1909) introduced, presumably, by some dialectal (?Nottinghamshire) comedian; ob.

cham or **chammy.** Pronounced *sham*: whence many puns. Abbr. *champagne*. *All the Year Round*, 18 Feb. 1871. cf. BUBBLY.

cham, v. To drink champagne: from ca 1875. †.

chamber-day. 'A day at the beginning of each half when "chambers" [the bedrooms of scholars] were open all day for the re-arrangement of their occupants' (E.D.D.): mid-C.19–20: Winchester s. verging on j. N.B., one says *in* (not *in the*) *chambers*.

chamber-music. The sound made by a chamber-pot being used: jocular domestic: late C.19–20.

Chamber of Horrors. The Peeresses' Gallery in the House of Lords (contrast CAGE, 4): Parliamentary, from ca 1870. Ex the room so named at Madame Tussaud's. cf. senses 3, 4. 2. A sausage; gen. in pl. From ca 1880. cf. BAGS OF MYSTERY. 3. 'Room at Lloyd's (Royal Exchange) where are "walled" notices of shipwrecks and casualties at sea', Ware: City of London: late C.19–20. 4. 'The corridor or repository in which Messrs Christie (King Street, St James's) locate the valueless pictures that are sent to them from all parts of the world as supposed genuine old masters', Ware: Society (—1909).

chambers, see CHAMBER-DAY.

chameleon diet. A very meagre diet: hence, nothing to eat: late C.17–18; coll. Adumbrated by Shakespeare in *Hamlet*, III, ii.

chamming. Indulgence in champagne: from ca 1875. Ob.

champ up. To chew (up); eat up: (low) coll (—1887); ob. Ex horses eating.

Champagne Charley. Any noted drinker of champagne; hence, any dissipated man: mostly Londoners': from 1868; ob. B. & L., 'The name of a song which appeared in 1868. . . The original *Charley* was a wine-merchant that was very generous with presents of champagne to his friends.'

champagne shoulders. Sloping shoulders: Society: ca 1860–80. Ware, 'From the likeness to the drooping shoulder of the champagne bottle as distinct from the squarish ditto of the sherry or port bottle'.

champagne weather. Bad weather: ironic Society coll: ca 1860–1910.

champagner. A courtesan: music-halls': ca 1880–1912. Ex the champagne formerly so frequently drunk by these perfect ladies.

Champaigne Country. Dining and wining; champagne drinking: Oxford and buckish: ca 1810–40. Pierce Egan, *Life in London*, 1821.

champion. Excellent; arrant: coll, from the 1890s. Esp. predicatively, as 'that's champion!' Ex such phrases as *champion fighting-cock*, *champion pugilist*. 2. Also adv.: coll: late C.19–20.

champion slump of 1897, the. The motor-car: London, 1897–ca 1910. Ware alludes to the unsuccessful *début* of the motor-car in 1896–7. cf. BUTTER-COLOURED BEAUTIES.

chance, v.t. To risk, take one's chances of or in: coll; from ca 1830. Esp. *chance it*, used absolutely.

chance, main. By itself, *the main chance* occurs as early as 1597 in Shakespeare and notably in 1693, in Dryden's translation of *Persius*: 'Be careful still of the main chance, my son.' *An eye to the main chance* appears first in Jonson's play, *The Case is Altered*, 1609, it is often preceded by *have* (a variant is *stand to the main chance*, 1579), and it may have originated in the game of hazard. Orig. = the most important issue or feature or possibility, it has, in C.19–20, very rarely meant other than the chance of profit or advantage to oneself. Prob. always coll (except in C.20, when it is S.E.), though the O.E.D. hints a c. complexion.

chance, on the, adv., adj. (Acting) on the possibility *of* or *that*. Orig. (ca 1780) coll; by 1830, at latest, S.E.

chance, stand a fair, good, etc. To be likely to do, (with *of*) to get. From ca 1790; still of a coll cast though virtually S.E. since ca 1880.

chance, take a. To risk it, esp. if the chance is a poor one: C.19–20; coll in C.19.

chance, take one's. At first, C.14–19, S.E., to risk it; from ca 1800, to seize one's opportunity: coll till ca 1860, then S.E.

chance child. An illegitimate child: from ca 1838; coll.

chance the ducks, and. Come what may, as in 'I'll do it and chance the ducks.' A pleonastic c.p., from ca 1870; ob. Recorded in H., 5th ed., and Northall's *Folk Phrases*, 1894. cf.:

chance your arm! Chance it!, try it on!: coll, orig. tailors': from ca 1870; ob. Among soldiers, *chance one's arm* meant 'to take a risk in the hope of achieving something worth while', from the late 1890s, the implication being the loss of one's stripes; the phrase, however, prob. arose ex boxing. cf. preceding entry. 2. Hence, make an attempt: late C.19–20: tailors'.

chancellor's egg. A day-old barrister: legal: late C.19–20; ob.

chancer. A liar; also, an incompetent workman, or one too confident of his ability: tailors': from ca 1870: coll.

chancery, in. Fig. from ca 1835: coll. In parlous case, an awkward situation. Lit., pugilistic: the head under an opponent's weaker arm to be punched with his stronger: from ca 1815 and as in Moore's *Tom Crib's Memorial*, 1819.

chancy; occ. **chancey.** (Seldom of persons) unsure, uncertain, untrustworthy: coll: 1860. George Eliot. (In C.16–18 Scottish, lucky.)

***chandler-ken.** A chandler's shop: c. (—1812); †by 1890.

chaney-eyed. One-eyed; rarely and †, glassy-eyed. Low coll: from ca 1860; ob. *Chaney* = *chiney*, China, china, or Chinese, hence with small eyes or eyes like those of a China doll.

change, v.t. and i. To 'turn', curdle (e.g. milk): coll and dial.: from ca 1830. 2. v.i., to change one's clothes: coll; C.17–20.

change, give. To 'pay out', punish: coll: from ca 1860. Gen. v.t., e.g. 'I gave him his change.'

change, give no. Absolute or ('he gave

me no change') v.t.: to give no satisfaction, esp. to reveal nothing. Coll, from ca 1890.

change about or **over,** v.i. To change or be changed in position, circumstances, or post: coll; the former from ca 1840 (Dickens, 1844), the latter from ca 1860.

change about one, have all one's. To be clever, esp. to be quick-witted. Coll, from ca 1880.

change artiste, quick. (Music-halls) one who changes costume for successive songs or scenes: from ca 1870. Coll in C.19, S.E. in C.20.

change bags. Knickerbockers for football, flannel trousers (?orig. grey) for cricket: Eton College, from ca 1855; ob.

change foot. To play the turncoat: coll: ca 1600–1750.

change on, put the. To mislead, deceive. Dryden, 1677, 'By this light, she has put the change upon him!'; Congreve, Scott. Coll, from ca 1660; †by ca 1900.

change one's note or **tune.** The former from ca 1700, the latter from ca 1570: coll. To alter one's behaviour, professed opinion, speech, expression.

change out of, take one's or **the.** To take the equivalent of a thing; be revenged upon a person. Coll: from ca 1825. John Wilson, 1829; Whyte-Melville, 1854; Henry Kingsley, on several occasions. Often exclamatory, to the accompaniment of a blow, a neat retort, a crisply decisive act: *take your change out of that!*

change over, see CHANGE ABOUT.

changes, ring the. To change a better article for a worse (coll), esp., 2, bad money for good (orig. c. >, ca 1830, low s. > by 1869, gen. s. >, ca 1900, coll): from ca 1660, ca 1780 resp. Smollett has 'ringing out the changes on the balance of power'. 3. To muddle a tradesman over the correct change to be received: c.: from ca 1880.

Channel-fever. Homesickness: nautical: mid-C.19–20. i.e. the English Channel.

Channel-groping. Cruising in home waters: naval: late C.19–20.

Channel-money. Subsistence-money paid to sailors waiting on a ship in dry dock: nautical coll: late C.19–20.

***chant.** Any distinguishing mark on personal effects. 2. A person's name or address. 3. A song sung in the street. 4. An advertisement in newspaper or handbill. All ca 1810–90; c. >, except sense 4, low s. ca 1850. For senses 1, 2, 4, the semantics are that these things proclaim a person's identity.

***chant,** v. To talk; sing songs in the street: c. and low, often as *chaunt*: from ca 1840, ob. Mayhew, 'A running patterer [q.v.] . . . who also occasionally chaunts'. 2. To sell (a horse) by fraudulent statements: c. and low: from ca 1810. *English Magazine*, 1816. Prob. 'sing the praises of'. 3. Orig. c., then low, from ca 1800: to mark a person's name, initials, etc., on clothes, plate, etc. †: i.e. to proclaim his identity. cf. CHANT, n., 1, 2, 4. 4. To be advertised for: c. of ca 1810–90. cf. n., 4. 5. v.i., to swear: sporting: 1886–ca 1914.

***chant, tip (one) a queer.** To give a false address to: c. of ca 1810–90. See CHANT, n., 2.

chanter, chaunter; often **horse-cha(u)nter.** A horse-dealer who sells by fraudulent representation: from ca 1817. Moncrieff, Dickens, Thackeray, Henley. 2. In vagrants' c., a street patterer: ca 1830–1900.

***chanter(-)cull.** A contemporaneous c. variant of CHANTER, 2: Ainsworth, 1834.

chant(e)y, see SHANTY.

chanticleer. Penis: literary and cultured: mid-C.19–20. Punning COCK, 1.

chanting, chaunting, vbl n. The dishonest sale of a horse by the concealment of its condition or temper and/or by *bishoping* (see BISHOP, v., 2). From ca 1818. Often *horse-cha(u)nting*. 2. In c., street ballad-singing: ca 1818–1900. cf. CHANTER.

***chanting ken** (or **slum**). A music-hall: late C.19–20 c. KEN = a house or a place.

chap. A 'customer', a fellow. From ca 1715, when Ned Ward uses it as 'friend'; coll. In C.20, rarely (unless prefaced by *old*) of an old or 'oldish' man. (Abbr. *chapman*; ex the C.16–early 18 sense, extant in dial., a buyer, a customer.) Grose, 'an odd chap'; Byron; Scott; Thackeray; Mrs Henry Wood, 'You might give a chap a civil answer.' cf. CUSTOMER; MERCHANT, and the Scottish *callant*. 2. A male sweetheart: non-aristocratic coll (—1887). Doubtless ex dial., where recorded before 1850. 3. A sailor: proletarian coll (—1887).

Chapel; only as **the Chapel.** Whitechapel: Cockneys': mid-C.19–20. cf. DITCH, THE and CHAPEL, adj.

chapel; chapel of ease. A water-closet: from ca 1860. cf. the S.E. meaning and the Fr. *cabinet d'aisance*.

chapel, v. (Of a don, gen. the Dean) to order (an undergraduate) to attend chapel twice daily for a specified period: university, passing to coll and S.E.: from ca 1845.

Chapel, adj. Of Whitechapel (London): Cockneys': mid-C.19–20.

chapel, keep a. To attend once: university, passing to coll and j.: from ca 1850.

chapel-folk. Nonconformists as opp. to Episcopalians (esp. Anglicans): a snobbish coll; from ca 1830.

Chapel cart, see WHITECHAPEL BROUGHAM.

chapel of ease, see CHAPEL, n.

***chapel of little ease.** A police station; detention cell: c. (—1871); ob. cf. CHAPEL, n.

chaperon. 'The cicisbeo, or gentleman usher, to a lady', Grose, 3rd ed.: mid-C.18–early 19 coll.

***chapped, chapt.** Thirsty: from ca 1670. Orig. c.: from ca 1820, low.

chapper. The mouth: low London (—1909).

chapper, v. To drink: low London (—1909).

chappie; occ. chappy. Coll, from ca 1820. At first = little fellow, but from ca 1880 it = *chap*, esp. as a term of address with *old*, *my good* or *dear*, etc., or as = a man about town; G. A. Sala, in the *Illustrated London News*, 24 March 1883, 'Lord Boodle, a rapid chappie always ready to bet on everything with everybody.' As a Society term it flourished in the '80s.

chappow. A raid: Anglo-Indian: from ca 1860. Mayne Reid. Ex a Pushtoo word.

chappy. For the n., see CHAPPIE. 2. Talkative: a late C.17–mid-18 coll. i.e. given to using his chaps, chops, jaws.

chaps me that! (Galt's *chapse* is incorrect.) I claim that: Scottish children's coll: mid-C.19–20. Ex *chap*, to choose, bespeak. cf. BAGS!

chapt, see CHAPPED.

chapter, to the end of the. Always; to the end; until death: coll: from ca 1840.

char. Abbr. *charwoman*: from ca 1875: coll. cf. CHARLADY and S.E. *chore*. 2. In late C.19–20 military: tea. Ex *cha*, a S.E. form (C.16–19).

char, chare, v. To come in to do the cleaning work in a house, shop, office, or institution. The S.O.D. records for 1732; in the C.18, the meaning was simply to do odd jobs. Coleridge, of all people, uses the word in 1810 in its mod. sense. vbl n., *charing* or *charring*, C.19–20.

character. An eccentric or odd person: coll: Goldsmith, 1773, 'A very impudent fellow this! but he's a character, and I'll humour him'; Lamb, who was himself one. From ca 1870, an odd person of much humour or wit: likewise, coll.

***character academy.** 'A resort of servants without characters, which are there concocted', F. & H., revised ed. (at *academy*): c.: late C.19–20.

***charactered.** Branded on the hand; LETTERED: C.18–early 19, low if not indeed at first c.

chare, char(r)ing, see CHAR, v.

charge. A prisoner brought up for trial on a charge or accusation: from late 1850s. Sala.

charge, take. (Of a thing) to get out of control: coll: 1890.

Charing Cross (pron. *Crorse*). A horse: rhyming s. (—1857).

***chariot.** An omnibus: c.; from ca 1850; almost †. Whence *chariot-buzzing* (H., 1st ed.), pocket-picking in an omnibus; cf. the neater Fr. argotic *faire l'omnicroche*.

charity-bob, the. 'The quick, jerky curtsey made by charity school-girls', a curtsy rapidly vanishing as long ago as 1883: coll: ca 1870–1915.

charity sloop. A 10-gun brig: naval coll during Napoleonic wars. Bowen, 'Officially rated as sloops for the benefit of their commanders'.

charlady. Jocularly coll for a charwoman: since the 1890s.

Charles his friend. The young man serving as foil to the *jeune premier*: theatrical: from ca 1870. Ex description in the *dramatis personae*.

Charles James. A theatre box: theatrical: late C.19–20: rhyming on Charles James Fox. 2. A fox: hunting s.: id.

charley, charlie; or with capitals. A night watchman: from ca 1810. Vaux, 1812; Hood, 1845. †by 1900, except historically. Etymology unknown; but prob. ex the very common Christian name. 2. A small, pointed beard: coll: from ca 1830. Hook, 1841. Ex *Charles I*. 3. With capital C, a fox: from ca 1850; coll. Hughes in *Tom Brown's Schooldays*. 4. (Tailors') the nap on glossy cloth: from ca 1865 (ob.); also 5, a round-shouldered figure or person: from ca 1870 (ob.). 6. See CHARLEYS. 7. A gold watch: c.: from ca 1830. By pun ex sense 1. 8. See CHARLEY RONCE.

Charley Freer. Beer: sporting rhyming s. (—1909).

Charley (or Charlie) Hunt; often in C.20 shortened to *Charley* (*Charlie*). The female pudend: rhyming s.: since ca 1890. cf. BERKELEY.

***charley-ken.** A watchman's (post or) box: c.: ca 1810–50. See CHARLEY, 1.

Charley Lancaster. A 'han'kercher' = handkerchief. Rhyming s. (—1857).

charley-man. A variant (ca 1820–40) of CHARLEY, 1.

Charley Mason. A basin: rhyming s.: since ca 1880.

Charley Noble. The galley funnel: naval: mid-C.19–20; ob. Ex a Commander Noble (ca 1840), who insisted that the cowl of the galley funnel be kept bright.

***charley-pitcher.** A prowling sharper: c., from ca 1855. Etymology doubtful; perhaps via *Charley* [*a*] *pitcher*.

Charley Prescot. A waistcoat: rhyming s. (—1857).

Charley Randy. Brandy: navvies' rhyming s.: ca 1860–1910.

Charley (or -ie) Ronce. A souteneur or prostitute's bully: late C.19–20: rhyming s. on PONCE. Often shortened to *Charley* which, derivatively, = very smart, 'one of the boys'.

charley's fiddle. A watchman's rattle: fast life: ca 1815–40. W. T. Moncrieff, *Tom and Jerry*, 1821. See CHARLEY, 1.

Charley Skinner. Dinner: navvies' rhyming s.: ca 1860–1910.

Charley Wag, play the. To play truant: from ca 1865. Charles Hindley, 1876. Henley, in 1887, ellipsed the phrase to *Charley-wag*, but he created no precedent.

charleys or **charlies.** (Always in pl.) The paps of a woman: from ca 1840. ?etymology, unless on analogy of FANNY; if, however, the term was orig. c., it may derive ex Romany *chara* (or *charro*), to touch, meddle with, as in Smart & Crofton. (Ware suggests origin in the opulent charms displayed by the mistresses of Charles II.) Hence occ. *Bobby and Charley*. 2. Thick twine-gloves: Winchester College, ca 1850–80. Introduced by a Mr *Charles* Griffith.

charlie, see CHARLEY.

charming mottle. A bottle: Australian rhyming s.: ca 1880–1910. (Sydney) *Bulletin*, 18 Jan. 1902.

charms. (Always pl.) A woman's breasts: C.18–20. Until ca 1840, S.E.; then coll and, very soon, s. as in 'flashes her charms', displays ... ?ex Fr. *appas*. 2. In singular, late C.16–18 c. for a picklock. Greene; Grose. cf. S.E. *moral suasion*.

charp. A bed: Regular Army: late C.19–20. Jackson, 'From the Hindustani, charpoy'.

charperer; or **charpering omee** (or **omer**). A policeman: Parlary: since ca 1860. P. H. Emerson, *Signor Lippo*, 1893. The shorter prob. derives from the longer term. cf.:

charpering carsey. A police station: Parlary: since ca 1870. In, e.g., P. H. Emerson, 1893. cf. the preceding entry, where OMEE = a man; here, *carsey* = CASA = a house. The dominant element, *charpering* = 'searching': ex It. *cercare*, 'to search (for)'.

charring, see CHAR, v.

charter. To bespeak or hire, esp. a vehicle: from ca 1865: coll. Ex *to charter a ship*.

Charterhouse, sister of the. A great talker, esp. in reply to a husband: C.16 coll. Tyndale, referring to the monks, says in 1528, 'Their silence shall be a satisfaction for her.' The foundation (1384) of this benevolent institution allows for women as well as men – Brothers and Sisters of Charterhouse.

charver (or **charva**). A sexual embrace: theatrical (orig. Parlary): late C.19–20. See CHAUVERING and:

charver, v. To despoil; to interfere with and spoil (one's business): grafters': late C.19–20. Ex the Romany for 'to copulate with (a woman)'. Hence:

charvered, ppl adj. Exhausted, tired out: id.: id. cf. the low FUCKED in the same sense.

chase me, girls! An Edwardian c.p. expressive of high male spirits.

chasing, vbl n. The exceeding of a stated amount, or standard, of production: workmen's, from ca 1880; s. tending to coll. Rae's *Socialism*, 1884.

chass. To chase; to harry: naval cadets': since ca 1880.

chasse. A drink after coffee: 1860, Surtees, *Plain or Ringlets*.

chassé. To dismiss: Society, ca 1845–1900. Thackeray, 1847, 'He was *chasséd* on the spot'; Yates, 1868. Ex Fr. *chasser*, to chase away, though perhaps imm. ex dancing j.

chat. As free-and-easy talk, always S.E., C.16–20. 2. The female pudend: C.19–20, ob. Ex the Fr. word. cf. CAT, 5, and PUSS. 3. The truth; 'the correct thing', the TICKET (?coll): from ca 1815. Moore. 4. The subject under discussion; the point: coll (ob.): 1848, Lover; Trollope, 1862, 'That's the chat as I take it.' 5. In mid-C.19–20 Parlary, a thing, an object; anything. 6. Impudence: ca 1870–1900 (*chat* is extant in dial.): coll. 7. An enterprise, esp. a criminal job: c.: from ca 1870. 8. A seal to a letter: c. of ca 1810–60. Gen. pl. 9. A house: c. (—1879); ob. Ex CHEAT. 10. (Usually in pl *chats.*) A person: circusmen's: late C.19–20. 'Fake the chats' = talk to the crowd to keep them quiet. 11. Also **chate, chatt,** often in pl: the gallows: mid-C.16–18 c. cf. *CHEAT.

chat, v. More frequent as v.i. than as v.t.; more correct spelling, *chatt.* To search for lice: from ca 1850: low and perhaps c. cf. CHATT.

***chat-hole.** A hole made by convicts in a wall so that they can talk: c.: from ca 1870.

***chate,** see CHAT, n., 11, CHATTE, CHEAT.

Chatham rat. A seaman from the Medway depot: naval: late C.19–20. Rats abound there.

Chats. The inevitable nickname of anyone surnamed Harris: lower classes' and naval: late C.19–20.

***chatt.** A louse: late C.17–20. Orig. c., from ca 1830 s. Prob., as Grose suggests, ex *chattels* = LIVE STOCK or *chattels* = movable property. Synonymy in F. & H.; cf. CRABS, n., 2; GENTLEMAN'S COMPANION; GERMAN DUCK, 2. 2. In pl, dice: C.19 low. 3. See CHAT, n., 11.

chatta. An umbrella: Anglo-Indian coll: from ca 1690.

***chatte.** An occ. variant of *chate,* the gallows: see CHAT, n., 11.

chatter-basket. A prattling child: esp. among nurses: orig. dial., coll since ca 1850. Much less gen. are the variants *chatter-bladder* (low), *chatter-bones* (mainly U.S.), *chatter-cart.* cf.:

chatter-box, mod. **chatterbox.** Grose, 1st ed.: 'One whose tongue runs twelve score to the dozen'. Coll till 1880, then S.E. Dickens, *The Old Curiosity Shop.* On the C.16–17 SAUCEBOX.

chatter-broth. Tea: the drink and the party: late C.18–19. cf. SCANDAL BROTH, CHATTERING-BROTH and the jocular S.E. *chatter-water,* which is very ob.

chatter-cart, see CHATTER-BASKET.

chatteration. Persistent or systematic chattering: from 1862. Perhaps rather a pedantic jocularity than a coll.

chatterer. A blow – esp. if on the mouth – that makes the recipient's teeth chatter: pugilistic: from ca 1820. *Boxiana,* IV, 1824.

***chatterers.** The teeth: c.: C.19–20; ob. cf. GRINDERS.

***chattering.** 'A blow given on the mouth', Egan's Grose: c. of ca 1820–60. Ex its effect.

chattering-broth. Tea: provincial (mostly Staffordshire) s., not dial.: from before 1897.

chattermag, n. and v. Chatter: coll: late C.19–20. cf. MAG, v.

***chattery.** Cotton or linen goods or, occ., separate article: c. (—1821); ob. Haggart.

chatting, vbl n. of CHAT, v.

***chattry-feeder.** A spoon: C.19 c. (Orig. and mainly at Millbank Prison.)

chatts, see CHATT.

chatty. A pot – esp. if porous – for water: Anglo-Indian coll: from ca 1780. 2. A filthy man. Abbr. *chatty* DOSSER: ca 1810–80: low. Ex CHATT, a louse. 3. Among sailors, it survives as 'any seaman who is dirty or untidy, or careless in his appearance' (Bowen). 4. (Chatty.) The inevitable nickname of anyone surnamed Mather: nautical and lower classes': late C.19–20. Bowen, 'From a celebrated character in naval fiction ... whether the uncomplimentary meaning applies... or not'.

chatty. Lousy: low: from ca 1810.

chauki, see CHOKEY.

chaunt, see CHANT.

***chaunt the play.** To expose and/or explain the ways and tricks of thieves: ob. c.; from ca 1845.

chaunted, properly **chanted.** Celebrated, hence famous. Lit.: in street ballads. Reynolds in his boxing verses, *The Fancy.* Reynolds (not to be confused with the prolific serial-writer) was the latest-comer of the great 'pugilistic' trio of 1815–30: Tom Moore, Pierce Egan, J. H. Reynolds.

chaunter, see CHANTER.

***chaunter cove.** A newspaper reporter: c. from ca 1840. Contrast CHAUNTING COVE.

***chaunter-cull.** A writer of street ballads, carols, songs, last dying speeches, etc., for *ad hoc* consumption; gen. to be found in a PUB. Not recorded before George Parker, 1781, but prob. existent from ca 1720. c.; ob. by 1890, †by 1900.

***chaunter upon the leer.** c. and low, ca 1830–70: an advertiser. (By itself, *chaunter* is c. for a street singer, C.18–19: see CHANTER.)

***chaunting cove.** A dishonest horse-dealer: c. of ca 1820–90. See CHANTING.

chauvering. Sexual intercourse: Lingua Franca (?) and low: from ca 1840. Whence the low *chauvering* DONA or MOLL, a harlot. cf. CHARVER. Etymology obscure:

but there is perhaps some connection either with Fr. *chauffer*, to heat, with S.E. *chafe*, and with Northern dial. *chauve*, to become heated, to rub together or, more prob., with Romany *charvo* (or *charva*, *-er*), to touch, meddle with.

chav(v)y. A child: Parlary: from ca 1860. Ex Romany *chavo* or *chavi*.

chaw. A yokel: from ca 1850. Thomas Hughes. Abbr. CHAW-BACON. 2. The process of chewing; a mouthful (e.g. a quid of tobacco). From ca 1740: orig. S.E.; from ca 1860, either a low coll or a sol. or – see E.D.D. – dial. for *chew*. 3. A trick, a HOAX: university, ca 1870–1900. cf. BITE, n., 2.

chaw, v. To eat, or chew, noisily: C.16–20. Until ca 1850, S.E., then either low coll or sol. 2. To bite: from ca 1870. Kipling in the *Scots Observer*, 1890 (in a poem called *The Oont*), 'And when we saves his bloomin' life, he chaws our bloomin' arm.' 3. (University) to deceive, HOAX, impose upon: ca 1869–1914. cf. BITE, V. 4. To defeat, overcome: coll (—1887).

chaw-bacon. A yokel: coll; from ca 1810. Whyte-Melville in *General Bounce*.

chaw(-)over. To repeat one's words to satiety: low coll (?ex Yorkshire dial.); from ca 1820.

chaw the fat. A naval variant (late C.19–20) of CHEW THE FAT.

chaw(-)up. To destroy, smash, DO FOR: from ca 1840, mainly U.S. Dickens.

chawer. One who chews, esp. if roughly (—1611): orig. S.E.; in C.19–20, low coll. Cotgrave. Rare. The same applies to the C.16–20 *chawing*, chewing, (fig.) rumination.

chaws. Sexual intercourse: low coll: from ca 1860; ob. cf. CHAUVERING.

cheap, dirt or **dog.** The former from ca 1835 (Dickens in *Oliver Twist*, 1838); the latter from ca 1570 (Holinshed has it) and †by 1840. Coll.

cheap, feel. In ordinary sense, S.E., though not literary. In s., to feel ill after a bout of drinking: from ca 1880; ob. Hence, *cheapness*: late C.19–20.

cheap, on the. Cheaply; economically. Coll; from the late 1850s.

cheap and nasty. Either lit., or = pleasing to the eye, inferior in fact. From ca 1830: coll >, by 1890, S.E. *Athenaeum*, 29 Oct. 1864, '. . . or, in a local form, "cheap and nasty, like Short's in the Strand", a proverb applied to the deceased founder of cheap dinners'; this gibe no longer holds good.

cheap and nasty bargain. An apprentice: nautical officers': late C.19–20. Ex preceding.

cheap as dirt, see CHEAP, DIRT.

cheap beer. 'Beer given by publicans at night-time to officers': policemen's (—1909). Ware.

cheap-tripper. One who goes on cheap trips: coll; from ca 1858. James Payn.

cheapness, see CHEAP, FEEL.

Cheapside, come at it, or **home, by (way of).** To buy a thing cheap: mid-C.18–19; coll. Variant: *get it by way of Cheapside*.

***cheat,** occ. **chate, chete,** etc., is a mid-C.16–19 c. word – gen. = thing, article – appearing in many combinations, e.g. BELLY-CHEAT, an apron, and QUACKING-CHEAT, a duck: in only a very few instances has this term penetrated English proper even to the extent of becoming s. Probably related to *chattle*. The unpreceded pl means the gallows: cf. CHAT, n., 11.

cheat the worms. To recover from a serious illness: proletarian coll (—1887).

cheatee. One who is cheated: coll; from ca 1660, very rare in C.18, revived in C.19.

***cheating law.** Card-sharping: late C.16–early 17; c. Greene.

***cheats.** Sham cuffs or wristbands: c. and low, late C.17–early 19. 2. In Randle Holme's *Armoury*, 1688, a showy, fur-backed waistcoat. (See also note on CHEAT.) 3. See TRINE, v., 2.

check, take. To be offended: coll verging on S.E.: ca 1660–1780. Ex dogs at fault.

check it up or **check up.** To enter a theatre with another person's discarded pass-out check: theatrical and theatre-goers' (—1909); ob.

checks, hand in one's, see CASH ONE'S CHECKS.

chee, adj. Long: 'pidgin': from ca 1870. Abbr. *muchee*.

chee-chee. Of mixed European and Indian parentage. An adj. deriving from a Hindi exclamation = fie! 2. As a n., the minced English of half-breeds; the half-breeds as a class. Both date from ca 1780: best classified as an Anglo-Indian coll. cf. CHI-CHI.

cheechako. A tenderfoot: Canadian (Yukon and N.W.): late C.19–20. Note Robert W. Service, *Ballads of a Cheechako*, 1909. A Chinook jargon word, lit. 'newcomer': *chee*, new; *chako*, to come.

cheek. Insolence to an elder or superior: coll: from ca 1830; recorded in Marryat's *Poor Jack*, 1840, a locus exemplifying *give* *cheek* = TO CHEEK, q.v.; George Moore, *The Mummer's Wife*, 1884, 'If he gives me any of his cheek, I'll knock him down.' cf. LIP. 2. Audacity, effrontery, assurance: coll: from ca 1850. Mayhew, of doctors: 'They'd actually have the cheek to put a blister on a cork leg.' cf. FACE. 3. A share: from ca 1820: low coll. Esp. in 'where's my cheek?' and the set phrase, *to one's own cheek*, all to oneself, as in 'Jon Bee', 1823, and Lever's *Charles O'Malley*, 1841. 4. See CHEEKS.

cheek, v. To address saucily: from ca 1840: coll. Mayhew, Dickens. Occ., though †by 1920, *to cheek up*. Commonest form: *give cheek*; v.t. with *to*.

cheek, have the. To be insolent or audacious enough (to do something): coll: mid-C.19–20. cf. *have the* FACE (or *front*).

cheek-ache, get or **have the.** To be made to blush; to be ashamed of what one has done: artisans' and tailors' from ca 1860; ob.

cheek it. To face it out: coll: 1851, Mayhew; 1887, Baumann (*cheek it out*). Ex CHEEK, V.

cheeker. One who speaks or addresses others impudently: 1840 (O.E.D.): coll. Rare in C.20. Ex CHEEK, V.

cheekiness. Impudence; cool confidence; audacity; tendency to 'give cheek'. Coll, recorded in 1847; Aytoun & Martin; Trollope in *The Three Clerks*. Ex CHEEK, n., 1.

cheekish. Impudent; saucy: coll, ca 1850–1900. Mayhew.

cheeks. The posteriors: coll, from ca 1750. Grose, by implication. cf. BLIND CHEEKS. 2. A jeering, insulting interjection: ca 1860–80. 3. 'Cheeks, an imaginary person; nobody; as in "Who does that belong to? Cheeks!"' (*Sinks*, 1848): low: ca 1780–1870. *Sessions*, Feb. 1791 (p. 203).

cheeks and ears. A fanciful name for a head-dress not long in fashion: coll: C.17. It occurs in *The London Prodigal*, 1605.

cheeks near cunnyborough!, ask. *Ask my* ARSE! Mid-C.18–early 19 low London c.p. used by women only. See CHEEKS; *cunnyborough* = CUNNY = CUNT. Grose, 1st ed.

Cheeks the Marine. Mr Nobody. A character created by Marryat, who conscientiously popularized it: *Peter Simple*, 1833. Fifty years later, Clark Russell, in his nautical glossary, defined the term as 'an imaginary being in a man-of-war'. By 1850 there had arisen the now ob. *tell that to Cheeks the Marine* = *tell that to the* MARINES. Prob. ex CHEEKS, 3.

cheeky. Saucy, impudent, insolent, COOL. 'Ducange Anglicus', 1857; Henry Kingsley, 1859. Ex CHEEK, n., 1, 2.

cheeky new fellow, see NEW FELLOW.

cheer, give (one) **the.** To bid a person welcome: proletarian coll: from ca 1870; ob.

cheerer. 'A glass of grog, or of punch', Bee: public-house coll: ca 1820–80. Ex its effect. (The term occurs in Scots as early as 1790.)

cheery. Cheerful, lively: C.17–20. Also, apt to cheer or enliven: C.18–20, ob. On the borderline between coll and S.E.; Johnson considered it a ludicrous word – it is certainly unnecessary beside *cheerful*.

chees and chaws. The Italianate pronunciation of ecclesiastical Latin: British Catholics': ca 1850–1900.

cheese. An adept; a smart or a clever fellow: Public School and university: ca 1860–1900. Ex CHEESE, THE. 2. See CHEESE, THE. 3. Smegma: low: mid-C.18–20.

cheese, v.t. Very rare except in *cheese it!*, be quiet!: low from ca 1855; previously c. (—1812), when also = run away! Ex *cease*.

cheese, believe or **persuade** or **make believe that the moon is made of.** To believe firmly, or to cause another to believe, something astounding or impossible or absurd; hence, to be a fool, to befool another. Frith, ca 1529; Wilkins the philosopher; Ainsworth the lexicographer. Coll; in C.18–20, S.E.

cheese, hard. In comment or exclamation: bad luck! From ca 1870; coll and dial.

cheese, howling. An overdressed dandy or BLOOD: Cambridge University, ca 1860–95. Prob. ex the next; cf. CHEESE, n., 1, and:

cheese, the. The fashion; the best; 'the correct thing'. Recorded in *The London Guide* in 1818, apparently soon after the birth of this phrase, which seems to have > gen. only ca 1840. Barham; Reade, 1863, a character, concerning marriages, saying 'I've heard Nudity is not the cheese on public occasions.' Prob. ex the Urdu *chiz*, a thing; but see CAZ. cf. the derivative *the* STILTON.

cheese and crust! A proletarian perversion and evasion (—1909) of *Jesus Christ!*

cheese and kisses. Wife: late C.19–20. Rhyming on MISSIS.

cheese-cutter. A prominently aquiline nose: from ca 1870; ob. 2. The large, square peak of a cap: whence *cheese-cutter caps*: ca 1870–1910. 3. A peaked 'full-dress' cap: *Conway* training-ship: from ca 1895; ob. 4. In pl, bandy legs: from ca 1840; ob.

cheese it! See CHEESE, v. 2. Occ. = CAVE!: low: late C.19–20.

cheese-knife. A sword: military; from ca 1870. cf. TOASTING-FORK.

cheese-toaster. A sword: coll: ca 1770–1913: military. Grose, 1st ed.; Thackeray. cf. in Shakespeare, *Henry V*, II, i, 8–11 (Oxford edition). cf. CHEESE-KNIFE and TOASTING-FORK. F. & H. gives the synonymy.

cheeser. An eructation: low coll: C.19–20, ob. 2. 'A strong smelling fart', *Lex. Bal.*, 1811; ob. 3. A chestnut: Cockneys': late C.19–20.

cheeses, make. (Schoolgirls) the making of one's dress and petticoat, after a rapid gyration of the body and a quick sinking to the ground or floor, spread into a cheese-like form. Hence, to curtsy profoundly. Coll; from ca 1855. Thackeray, De Quincey, Besant & Rice. Ex Fr. *faire des fromages*: even Littré records it.

cheesy. Showy, fine (opp. DUSTY): coll; from mid-1850s. Surtees in *Ask Mamma*. Ex CHEESE, THE. 2. Smelly: (low) coll: late C.19–20. Ex the smell of strong cheese.

cheesy-hammy-eggy-topsides. A savoury popular with those who have sailed with Chinese cooks: (nautical) officers': late C.19–20. Cheese and ham with an egg on top.

chello. A variant of *jillo* = JILDI.

Chelsea, get. To obtain the benefit of Chelsea military hospital: military, mid-C.18–early 19.

Chelsea College, see LOMBARD STREET TO A ...

chemozzle. An occ. variant of SHEMOZZLE.

***Chepemans.** Cheapside Market: C.17 c. see -MANS.

cheque, have seen the. To have exact knowledge: coll, from ca 1870; ob.

cheque, little, see LITTLE CHEQUE.

cheri or **Cheri.** A charming woman: Society: ca 1840–60. Ware, 'From Madame Montigny, of the Gymnase, Paris. Her stage name remained Rose Cheri. She was a singularly pure woman, and an angelic actress. Word used by upper class men in society ... to describe the nature of their mistresses.' (?rather *chérie.*)

***cherpin.** A book: c. of ca 1840–1900. Anon., '*No. 747*'. Etymology?

cherrilet, cherrylet. Gen. in pl. A nipple: late C.16–17. Sylvester, 'Those twins ... Curled-purled cherrielets'. On the borderline between coll and S.E.

***cherry.** A young girl: c., latter half of C.19. cf. CHERRY-PIE and CHERRY-RIPE.

cherry-bounce. Cherry-brandy: coll; from ca 1790; but in Robertson's *Phraseologia Generalis*, 1693, as *cherry-bouncer*. cf. the S.E. sense, brandy and sugar.

cherry-colour(ed). Either black or red: in a common card-cheating trick: low coll: from ca 1850. cf. Grose's *cherry-coloured cat*, a black one.

cherry-merry. Merry; convivial; slightly drunk: coll (—1775). Perhaps the same as Middleton's *kerry merry*. ?CHEERY corrupted; but cf. CHIRPING-MERRY. 2. (Anglo-Indian) a present of money: coll: from ca 1850. cf.:

cherry-merry bamboo. A thrashing: Anglo-Indian, from ca 1860; ob. Lit., a present of bamboo: see CHERRY-MERRY, 2.

cherry ogs. A game played with cherry-stones on the pavement: London children's: since ca 1880. See OGG.

cherry pickers. Inferior seamen: nautical: late C.19–20.

cherry-pie. A girl: from ca 1870; ob. cf. c. CHERRY.

cherry-pipe. A woman: low rhyming s. on c. CHERRY-RIPE, a woman. From ca 1880; ob.

cherry-ripe. A Bow Street runner: C.18–early 19. Ex the scarlet waistcoat. 2. A footman dressed in red plush: from ca 1860; ob. 3. A pipe: rhyming s. (—1857). 4. In c., a woman: from ca 1840. cf. CHERRY.

cherry-ripe! A way of calling *ripe cherries!* Coll: from ca 1600. Herrick.

cherub, see CHERUBIMS, 2.

cherubims. Peevish children: late C.18–early 19; coll. Facetiously allusive to 'To Thee cherubim and seraphim continually do cry' in the Te Deum. 2. Chorister, mod. choir, boys: from ca 1850; ob. Also *cherubs*. Perhaps ex the Te Deum verse.

cherubims (or -ins), in the. Unsubstantial; 'in the clouds': C.16–17; coll; rare. Udall.

Cheshire, the. *The* CHEESE, 'the correct thing', perfection: ca 1870–1900.

Cheshire cat; often **cat**. An inhabitant of Cheshire: coll nickname (—1884).

Cheshire cat, grin like a. To laugh, or smile, broadly. Pejorative coll: from ca 1770. Wolcot, 'Lo, like a Cheshire cat our Court will grin!'; Thackeray; 'Lewis Carroll' in *Alice in Wonderland.* In C.19 one often added *eating cheese*, *chewing gravel*, or *evacuating bones*. Origin still a mystery. I surmise but cannot prove *cheeser*, a cat very fond of cheese, *a cheeser* having > *a cheeser cat* > *a Cheshire cat*; hence *grin like a Cheshire cat* would = to be as pleased as a 'cheeser' that has just eaten cheese. Or the development might be *cheeser*: *Cheshire-cheeser*: *Cheshire cat*.

chessy. Characteristic of good play at chess: coll: 1883.

chest, chuck out one's. To pull oneself together; stand firm: coll: from ca 1860; ob.

chest, over the, see GUN, OVER THE.

chest and bedding. A woman's breasts: nautical (—1785); †by 1900.

chest-plaster. A young actor: theatrical: 1883–ca 1890. A satirical description by the older actors: 'From the heart-shaped shirt-front worn with a very open dress-waistcoat, and starched almost into a cuirass . . . (*See* Shape and Shirt.)' Ware.

chestnut. Abbr. *chestnut-coloured horse*: coll: from ca 1840. 2. A stale story or outworn jest. Coll, 1886 +, ex slightly earlier U.S. Perhaps ex 'a special oft-repeated story in which a chestnut-tree is particularly mentioned', W. (cf. O.E.D. quotation for 1888); perhaps ex *roast chestnuts* (cf. *do* BROWN).

chesto!, chest-o! 'Request to anyone to get off a chest lid, so that the chest may be opened', Masefield. *Conway* Training Ship: from ca 1880.

***chete**, see CHEAT.

Chevalier Atkins. A journalistic coll variation, ca 1895–1910, of *Tommy Atkins* (see TOMMY, 4).

Chevy Chase. A face: rhyming s. (—1859); †by 1914, except as abbr., *chevy* or *chivvy*.

chew. A quid of tobacco: low coll; from ca 1820.

chew the cud. To be very thoughtful: coll from ca 1860. 2. To chew tobacco: from ca 1845.

chew the fat or **rag.** To grumble; resuscitate an old grievance: military: from ca 1880. Brunlees Patterson, *Life in the Ranks*, 1885.

chewing her oakum. (Of a wooden ship) beginning to leak, the caulking being bad: nautical: mid-C.19–20; ob.

***chewre.** To steal: c.: C.17–18.

chi-a(c)k, -hike, -ike, see CHIIKE.

chi-chi, n. and adj. Half-caste (girl, rarely boy): Indian Army and Anglo-Indian coll: C.19–20. Hindustani.

chib. A low Cockney corruption of the mainly dial. JIB, mouth, lower part of the face: 1899, Clarence Rook, *The Hooligan Nights*, 'He slings a rope . . . round her chib, and fastens it to a hook in the wall. Then [she] can stand, but can no longer argue.'

chic. Skill, dexterity, esp. in the arts; finish, style; elegance: coll: from ca 1855. Ex the Fr.; Lever; Yates, 1866, 'A certain piquancy and chic in her appearance'. 2. 'Style': artists' coll: late C.19–20.

chic, v. '*To chic up a picture*, or *to do a thing from chic* = to work without models and out of one's own head': artists' s. (—1891) verging on coll. F. & H. Ex preceding term.

chic, adj. Elegant, stylish: from late 1870s: coll after ca 1890. (Not so used in Fr.)

chice(-am-a-trice). Nothing; no good: low and vagrants': C.19. Egan's Grose has both forms and implies that the term was orig. Yiddish. Prob. ex Romany *chichi*, nothing, and the source of SHICER.

chick. A child: whether endearment or neutral term. From M.E. onwards. Coll almost S.E. 2. Anglo-Indian coll (—1866): abbr. *chickeen*, a Venetian coin (=4 rupees). Esp. in 'I'll buy you a chick.'

chickabiddy. A young girl: orig. (—1860) costers'. Ex the nursery name for a chicken often employed as an endearment (—1785) for a child. The *-biddy* may orig. have been *birdy*: W.

chickaleary cove. An artful fellow: costers'; from ca 1860, but anticipated by *chickaleary chap* in an underworld song quoted by W. A. Miles, *Poverty*, 1839. *The C. C.* was one of the famous Vance's songs ca 1869. Prob. CHEEKY + LEARY.

chicken. C.17–18 coll, 'a feeble, little creature, of mean spirit', B.E. Whence the †*hen-hearted* and *chicken-hearted*, adj., and *chicken-heart*, a coward, also coll. 2. A child (C.18–20, coll), *chick* being more usual. 3. In (—1851) c., a pint pot: cf. CAT-AND-KITTEN HUNTING. 4. A fowl of any age; *the chicken*, fowls collectively: coll: C.19–20.

chicken, no. Elderly. From ca 1700: coll.

Swift, '... Your hints that Stella is no chicken'; Fielding; Walpole; Sala, 'I am no chicken.'

chicken-butcher. A poulterer; also, anyone shooting very young game. Coll: late C.18–20; ob.

chicken-fixing, see GILGUY.

chicken-food. Blancmange: naval: late C.19–20.

chicken got the axe, where the. i.e. 'in the NECK'; severely, disastrously, fatally: a c.p. dating from ca 1896; slightly ob. cf. *where* MAGGIE WORE THE BEADS.

chicken-hammed. Bandy-legged: mid-C.18–19 coll.

chicken nabob. A man returned from India with but a moderate fortune: late C.18–early 19 coll.

chicken-perch. A church: rhyming s.: late C.19–20.

chickens before they are hatched, count one's. Unduly to anticipate a successful issue. C.16–20; coll till C.19, then S.E. Gosson, 1579; 'Hudibras' Butler, its popularizer.

chickery-pokery, see JIGGERY-POKERY.

chie, occ. **chai,** see CHAL.

chief (the chief). The Chief Engineer, or, loosely, the First Mate: nautical coll: mid-C.19–20. 2. A – gen. jocular – form of address: coll; from ca 1880. Partly ex sense 1.

chief buffer, the. The Chief Boatswain's Mate: naval: late C.19–20.

chief muck of the crib. 'A head director in small affairs', Bee: low: ca 1820–80. cf. *Lord* MUCK.

***chife.** An occ. variant of *chive*: see CHIVE-FENCER. As is *chiff* (*Lex. Bal.*).

chigger. A variant of GIGGER or JIGGER, esp. as a private still. 'Jon Bee', 1823.

chiïke, occ. **chy-ack (or chiack)** and **chi-hike;** rarely **chi-ak.** A street (orig. costers') salute; a hearty word of praise heartily spoken. From ca 1855; low coll. H., 1st ed.; *The Chickaleary Cove*, where it is spelt *chy-ike*. Echoic. Etymology? Prob. a perverse reduplication of *hi!* 2. Whence, in Australia, a jeering call, a piece of CHEEK: from ca 1880. cf.:

chiïke, chy-ack, v. To hail; praise noisily. Low coll; from ca 1855. 2. Among tailors: to chaff ruthlessly: from ca 1865. Also in New Zealand, since ca 1890. 3. Whence, in Australia, to CHEEK, of which it is a corruption: from mid-1870s. 4. v.i., to make a ROW, a din: low coll: from ca 1880.

chiïke with the chill off, give. To reprimand, scold, abuse. From ca 1866; ob.

child, eat a. 'To partake of a treat given to the parish officers, in part of commutation for a bastard child', Grose, 1st ed. Mid-C.18–mid-19 (coll).

child, this. Oneself; I, me: coll; orig. (—1850), U.S.; anglicized ca 1890.

children's shoes, make. To be fooled, mocked, depreciated: coll: C.17–19. Mrs Centlivre.

child's play. Something very easy to do: coll >, by 1880, S.E.; from ca 1839, but dating from late M.E. in form *child's*, or *childer, game*.

chill, v.t. and i. To warm (a liquid). Coll; from ca 1820. Dickens, in *Boz*, 'A pint pot, the contents ... chilling on the hob'. Abbr. *take the chill off*, also coll.

chill off, with the. A comment or exclamation indicative of dissent or depreciation or disbelief. Coll; from ca 1840. cf. *over the* LEFT.

chillum. (Anglo-Indian, from ca 1780) a hookah, the smoking thereof, a 'fill' of tobacco therein: coll rather than s. The orig. and proper meaning is that part of a hookah which contains the tobacco. Ex Hindi *chilam*.

chilo. Child: 'pidgin': mid-C.19–20.

Chiltern Hundreds, accept the. 'To vacate a favourable seat at the alehouse', Bee: public-house: ca 1820–60. Punning S.E. sense.

***chime.** In c., to praise, esp. highly or dishonestly; puff; CANOODLE mercenarily: C.19–20.

chime in, v.i. To join harmoniously in conversation, etc.: from ca 1830; coll soon S.E.

chime in with. To be in entire (subordinate) agreement with: from ca 1800; coll soon > S.E.

chimmel; chimmes. Resp., a stick; wood, or a stick: Shelta: C.18–20.

chimney. One who smokes (esp. a pipe) a great deal: from ca 1880; coll.

chimney-chops. A negro: coll; late C.18–mid-19 pejorative.

chimney-pot. The tall silk hat worn by men, also (long †) a riding-hat for women. Coll; from ca 1865. Abbr. *chimney-pot hat*. cf. BELL-TOPPER; STOVE-PIPE.

chimney-sweep(er). The aperient more gen. known as the black draught: ca 1850–1900. cf. CUSTOM-HOUSE OFFICER. 2. A clergyman: from ca 1870; ob. cf. CLERGYMAN = a chimney-sweep.

chimozzle. A variant (recorded in 1900) of SHEMOZZLE.

chimp. Chimpanzee: coll: Lear, *Laughable Lyrics*, 1877, 'The wail of the Chimp and Snipe'.

chin. A talk: s.: since late C.19. Prob. a shortening of CHIN-WAG, 2.

chin, v. To talk, esp. if loquaciously or argumentatively: orig. (—1880), U.S.; anglicized ca 1890.

chin, up to the. Deeply involved; extremely busy. Coll; from ca 1860.

chin-chin! A salutation; in C.20, a c.p. toast. This Anglo-Chinese term dates from late C.18; it was general in the Navy in late C.19 and, by 1909, common in 'club society' (Ware). Chinese *ts'ing-ts'ing*, please-please. 2. Hence also v., to greet: 1829, Yule & Burnell. Whence CHIN-CHIN JOSS. 3. See CHIN, v.

chin-chin joss. Religious worship: pidgin-English (in Chinese ports): mid-C.19–20. Ex preceding + JOSS, an idol.

chin-chopper. A blow under the chin: boxing, from ca 1870; ob.

chin-music. Conversation; oratory. Adopted ca 1875 ex U.S. where popularized by Mark Twain. Note, however, that Berkshire dial. had it as early as 1852.

chin-wag. Officious impertinence: ca 1860–1900. 2. Whence, talk, chatter: from ca 1875. *Punch*, in 1879: 'I'd just like to have a bit of chin-wag with you on the quiet.'

china; chiner. A PAL, a MATE: abbr. *china plate*, rhyming s. (from ca 1870).

China!, not for all the tea in. Certainly not!; on no account: Australian coll: from the 1890s.

China orange, see LOMBARD STREET.

China Street. Bow Street (London): c.: ca 1810–50. Ex proximity to Covent Garden and its oranges.

Chinee. A Chinese: coll; orig. and mainly U.S.; anglicized ca 1870. cf. CHINK, 3.

chiner, see CHINA.

Chinese compliment. A pretended deference to, and interest in, the opinion of another when actually one has fully made up one's mind: from ca 1880; coll soon S.E.

chink. Money, esp. in coins. In pl, either coin (collective) or ready cash: only the latter sense (C.16–20) has always been coll. After ca 1830, *chinker* is very rarely used, *chink* taking its place. Shrewdly honest Tusser, 'To buie it the cheaper, have chinks in thy purse'; Jonson. 2. The female pudend: low coll, C.18–20. 3. (**Chink.**) A Chinese: mainly Australian; from ca 1890. cf. CHINKIE and JOHN (abbr. JOHN CHINAMAN). 4. Prison: Devonshire s.: 1896, Eden Phillpotts in *Black and White*, 27 June. Ex lit. S.E. sense of *chink*, a hole, on s. CLINK, prison.

chinkers. Money, esp. in coin. Coll; from ca 1830. Sir Henry Taylor, 1834; Baumann in his Slang Ditty prefacing *Londonismen*, 1887. Derivatively developed from CHINK(s) and likewise echoic. 2. In C.19–20 c., handcuffs joined by a chain.

Chinkie. A Chinese: Australian; from ca 1880; ob. A. J. Boyd, *Old Colonials*, 1882. Morris. By perversion of *Chinaman*. cf. *Chink* (at CHINK, 3).

chinner. A grin: Winchester College: ca 1885–1900.

chinning, vbl n. A talk. See CHIN, v.

chinny. Sugar: Regular Army's: late C.19–20. Ex Hindustani *chini*.

chinqua soldi. (Properly *cinqua s.*) Fivepence: theatrical and Parlary from ca 1840. Ex It. via Lingua Franca.

chintz. A bed-bug: ca 1880–1900. G. A. Sala, in the *Daily Telegraph*, 14 Aug. 1885. Ex Sp. *chinche*.

chip. A child: late C.17–early 19. cf. *chip of the old* BLOCK. 2. A sovereign: from ca 1870. Miss Braddon in *Phantom Fortune*. 3. A slight fracture; a piece chipped off: coll; from ca 1870. 4. With *not to care, a chip* = at all; C.16–20, ob.; coll > S.E. by 1600. 5. See CHIPS. 6. A rupee: Regular Army's: late C.19–20.

chip, v. To CHEEK, interrupt with (gen. deliberate) impertinence: Australia and New Zealand; from ca 1890. e.g. in C. J. Dennis. Perhaps ex the 'flying-off' of wood-chips; cf. CHIP AT.

chip, brother. Orig. a 'brother' carpenter, then anyone of the same trade or profession. cf. CHIPS. Often = BROTHER SMUT. Coll; from ca 1810.

chip at. To quarrel with; to criticize adversely: coll: from ca 1800. cf. CHIP, v., and the U.S. phrase, *with a chip on one's shoulder*.

chip in, v.i. To join in an undertaking; contribute a share; interpose smartly in a conversation, discussion, or speech: orig. (ca 1870), U.S.; anglicized ca 1890. Perhaps ex CHIPS, 5.

chip in broth, pottage, porridge. Resp. C.17–early 19, late C.17–18, late C.18–20 (ob.); all coll for a thing or matter of no importance. *Church Times*, 25 June 1880,

'The Burials Bill ... is thought ... to resemble the proverbial chip in porridge, which does neither good nor harm.'

chip of the same or **old block**, see BLOCK.

chipper. A lively young fellow: 1821, Pierce Egan, *Life in London*; †by 1870. 2. A crisp blow or punch: pugilistic: ca 1840–90. Mayhew, *Paved With Gold*, 1857.

chipper. Well, fit; lively. Coll; orig. (1837), U.S.; anglicized ca 1880. cf. Northern dial. *kipper*.

chipperow, see CHUB-A-ROW!

chipping, vbl n. (Ex *to* CHIP.) Impudence; the giving of CHEEK: Australian: from ca 1890.

Chippy. The inevitable nickname of a man surnamed Carpenter: mostly military: late C.19–20. Ex CHIPS, 1.

chippy, adj. Unwell, esp. after liquor: cf. Fr. *gueule de bois*: from ca 1870. Ex CHEAP. 2. Apt to be impudent: coll (—1888). cf. CHIP IN.

chippy chap. A bluejacket of carpenter's rating: naval: late C.19–20. cf. CHIPPY. Ex:

chips. A carpenter: esp. in Army and Navy; from ca 1770; in C.20, coll. Grose, 1st ed.; Clark Russell. cf. the C.17–19 proverb, *a carpenter is known by his chips*. 2. Hence, in the Army of late C.19–20, a Pioneer sergeant. 3. Money: from ca 1850. cf. sense 5. 4. (At Wellington College) a kind of grill, from its hardness: C.19–20, ob. 5. Counters used in games of chance: orig. (—1880) s., soon coll (?ex U.S.).

chips, cash (or **throw in**) **one's.** To die: Canadian: adopted ca 1880 ex U.S. Ex the S.E. sense, to stop gambling at cards, esp. poker.

chiromancer, see CONJUROR.

chirp. To sing: coll; C.19–20. 2. In c., to talk; hence (—1864), to inform to the police.

chirper. A singer: C.19–20, coll. 2. A glass or a tankard: from ca 1845. Meredith in *Juggling Jerry*, 1862, 'Hand up the chirper! ripe ale winks in it.' 3. The mouth: C.19–20. 4. One who, gen. as member of a gang, haunts music-hall doors, tries to blackmail singers, and, if unsuccessful, enters the auditorium and hisses, hoots, or groans: music-halls', ca 1887–1914.

chirpiness. Liveliness; cheerfulness; pleasing pertness: coll, from ca 1865.

chirping-merry. 'Very pleasant over a Glass of good Liquor', B.E.; convivial: late C.17–early 19; coll. Either the orig. of CHERRY-MERRY, or its explanation. (The Lancashire dial. form is *cheeping-merry.*) Grose, 1st ed., adds: 'Chirping glass; a cheerful glass, that makes the company chirp like birds in spring.'

chirpy. Cheerful; lively: coll, from ca 1835. Justin M'Carthy; Besant.

chirrup. To cheer or hiss at a music-hall according as a singer has paid or not: coll: from ca 1888; ob. cf. CHIRPER, 4, and CHIRRUPER. 2. vbl n., *chirruping* (*Pall Mall Gazette*, 9 March 1888) suggests Fr. *chantage*.

chirruper. An additional glass of liquor: public-house coll: ca 1820–80. 2. A blackmailing hisser, occ. applauder, at a music-hall: coll 1888. James Payn in an article, 17 March, and *Pall Mall Gazette*, 6 March 1888. See CHIRRUP.

chirrupy. Cheery; lively; CHIRPY. Coll: from ca 1870. Burnand, 1874; but in U.S. at least as early as 1861.

***chise**; occ. **chis.** A variant of *chiv(e)*, knife: c. of ca 1820–40. cf. CHISER; CHIVE-FENCER.

chisel. To cheat: from ca 1800. Prob. orig. dial., it > gen. only ca 1840. Mayhew, who spells *chissel*; Sala, who prefers *chizzle*; also *chizzel*; even *chuzzle*. Hence the old conundrum, 'Why is a carpenter like a swindler? – Because he chisels a deal.' *Chiseller* and *chiselling* are natural but infrequent derivatives.

***chiser, chiver.** Variants (ca 1820–40) of CHIV(E), a knife: c. cf. CHIVE-FENCER.

chit. A letter or a note: used by Purchas in 1608, while its orig., *chitty* (still in use), is not recorded before 1673: Anglo-Indian coll. 2. Hence, an order or a signature for drinks in clubs, aboard ship, etc.: Society, ex India; from ca 1875; coll. (3. As a very young or an undersized girl, always S.E., but as a pejorative for any girl or young woman it has a coll flavour.) 4. A pill: showmen's: late C.19–20. Hence, *chitworker*, a fellow who sells pills on the markets.

chit-chat. Light and familiar conversation; current gossip of little importance. C.18–20; coll, by 1760 S.E. By alteration-reduplication.

chitterlings. Shirt frills: C.16–19: s.> coll, then – the frills going out of fashion – S.E. Lit., a pig's (smaller) entrails. cf. *frill*. 2. Hence, the human bowels: mid-C.18–19. Grose, 1st ed., 'There is a rumpus among my chitterlins, i.e. I have the cholick.'

chitty. An assistant cutter or trimmer: tailors': from ca 1870; ob.

chitty-face. One who, esp. a child, is pinched of face, C.17. In C.18–19, baby-face. A pejorative. Extant in dial., mainly an adj. in *-d.* S.O.D. ranks it as S.E., but the authors' and the recorders' names connote coll: Munday, 'Melancholy' Burton, B.E., *A New Canting Dict.* (ca 1725), Grose (1st ed.), H.

***chiv, chive,** see CHIVE.

chivalry. Sexual intercourse: late C.18–19: low: ex Lingua Franca. cf. CAVAULTING; CHAUVERING; HORSING (at HORSE, v.), and:

chivarl(e)y. Human coition: C.19 low. See preceding entry.

***chive** (or **chiv**) – of Romany origin – is C.17–20 c. for a knife, a file, a saw: Romany and c. for to stab, to cut or saw (through), to 'knife': mid-C.18–20.

***chive-fencer.** One who 'fences' or protects murderers from arrest: c. (—1909). Ex: 2. A street hawker of cutlery: costers': from ca 1850. See FENCE.

***chiver.** An occ. variant (—1887) of CHIVE, knife, esp. as v.

chivey. A knife: nautical ex Romany: from ca 1890. cf. preceding entry. 2. (Also *chivy*, *chivvy*.) A shout, greeting, cheer, esp. if rough or chaffing; a scolding. Coll; a corruption of *chevy* with sense deflected. From ca 1810, and pronounced *chivvy*. 3. In c., the face, with further variant *chevy*: from ca 1860; ob. cf. sense 4 of:

chiv(e)y, chivvy, v. To run, go quickly, as in Moncrieff's *Tom and Jerry*, 1823, 'Now, Jerry, chivey! ... Mizzle! ... Tip your rags a gallop! ... Bolt!' Perhaps ex S.E. *Chevy Chase*. 2. To chase round (—1830), as in H. Kingsley's *Austin Elliot*, 'The dog ... used to chivy the cats.' 3. Hence, to make fun of, GUY, worry: from ca 1850. All coll. 4. In c., to scold: C.19–20. 5. To keep (someone) up to the mark by word and gesture: Army: late C.19–20.

***chiving lay.** The robbing of coaches by cutting the rear braces or slashing through the back of the carriage: mid-C.18–early 19 c.

chivvy, n. A face; short for CHEVY CHASE. 2. Hence, as a term of address, 'old CHAP': lower classes, esp. Cockneys': late C.19–20. 3. The chin: military in Boer War. 4. See senses 2, 3 and 4 of CHIV(E)Y, V.

***chivy.** Adj., relating to the use of the knife as a weapon: C.19–20 (ob.) c. e.g. *chivy duel*, a duel with knives.

chizz. To cheat or swindle. Public and Grammar Schools': since ca 1880. Ex CHISEL.

chizzel or **chizzle,** see CHISEL.

chizzy wag. A charity boy: Christ's Hospital: late C.18–19. The reference in Leigh Hunt's *Autobiography* is valid for 1795.

Chloe, blind as; drunk as Chloe. Utterly drunk. The former, ca 1780–1860, occurs in *The New Vocal Enchantress*, 1791; the latter dates from ca 1815. The origin is lost in the mists of topicality, but the latter phrase became popular in Australia in connection with the painting mentioned at DO A CHLOE. See also the quotation at GRUBBING.

chlorhin. To hear: Shelta: C.18–20.

choak; choakee; choaker, see CHOKE; CHOKER; CHOKEY.

chobey shop. A second-hand shop: circus hands': late C.19–20. Perhaps cf. CHOVEY.

chock. To hit a person under the chin: Cockney coll; from ca 1860. A semi-dial. variant of *chuck* (*under the chin*).

chockablock with. Full of: coll: since ca 1880.

chocker, gen. **old chocker.** A man. Not, like CODGER, a pejorative. Cockney coll; from ca 1860. Ex CHOCK.

chocolate without sugar, give (a person). To reprove: military (—1785); †by 1890.

choice riot. A horrid noise: streets': ca 1890–1915.

choice spirit. The S.E. sense began with Shakespeare, but in C.18 s., the term meant 'a thoughtless, laughing, singing, drunken fellow', Grose, 1st ed.

choke. Prison bread: low: from ca 1880; ob.

choke, enough to make a black man. (Of medicine, food) extremely unpalatable: Cockney coll (—1887); ob.

choke away, the churchyard's near! (cf. CHURCHYARD COUGH.) A late C.17–early 19 c.p. jocular admonition to anyone coughing.

choke, chicken: more are hatching. A similar C.18–early 19 c.p., then dial., Job's comforting. Swift; Grose, 3rd ed.

choke-dog. Cheese: low coll; orig. and mainly dial. From ca 1820; ob.

choke-jade. 'A dip in the course at Newmarket a few hundred yards on the Cambridge side of the running gap in the Ditch,' B. & L.; turf: from ca 1860. It CHOKES OFF inferior horses.

choke off. To get rid of a person; put a stop to a course of action: coll (—1818) >, by 1890, S.E. 2. Silence by a reprimand or retort: military coll: late C.19–20.

choke one's luff. To assuage (someone's) hunger; to keep (him) quiet: nautical: 1818, Alfred Burton, *Johnny Newcome.*

choke-pear. A difficulty; a severe reproof; a SETTLER (2)†; a GAG†: from C.16. Ex the instrument of torture (named from an unpalatable kind of pear) so called. Coll > S.E. by 1700; first two senses, archaic.

choke you?, didn't that; it's a wonder that didn't choke you! c.p. comments on a bare-faced or notable lie: C.19–20. cf. the C.17–18 semi-proverbial 'If a lie could have choked him, that would have done it' (Ray).

choke your luff! Be quiet: nautical: from ca 1810; slightly ob.

chokee, see CHOKEY.

choker. A cravat; orig. a large neckerchief worn round the neck. Often WHITE CHOKER. First record, 1848, Thackeray (*Book of Snobs*): 'The usual attire of a gentleman, viz., pumps, a gold waistcoat, a crush hat, a sham frill, and a white choker'. 2. A high all-round collar: from ca 1868. 3. A garotter: from ca 1800; coll. cf. WIND-STOPPER. 4. In c., a cell; a prison: from ca 1860; rare. See CHOKEY. Also, 5, a halter, the hangman's rope: C.18–19. 6. A notable lie; a very embarrassing question: low: late C.19–20; slightly ob. Ex its supposed effect on the perpetrator.

chokered. Wearing a CHOKER. *London Review*, 7 April 1866; O.E.D. records it at 1865.

chokey, choky; rarely **cho(a)kee** or **chauki.** A lock-up; a prison. In Anglo-Indian form C.17, in Australia ca 1840, and adopted in England ca 1850. Michael Scott has it in his *Cruise of the Midge*, 1836. Ex Hindustani *chauki*, lit. a four-sided place or building. 2. Hence, imprisonment: from ca 1880; rare. 3. Prison diet of bread and water: 1884. cf. CHOKE. 4. A detention cell, occ. a guard room: from ca 1870.

choking (or **cold**) **pie** (or **pye**). 'A punishment inflicted on any person sleeping in company: it consists in wrapping up cotton in a case or tube of paper, setting it on fire, and directing the smoak up the nostrils of the sleeper,' Grose, 3rd ed.: coll (—1650); ob. by 1860; †by 1890. Howell's edition (1650) of Cotgrave's Dict.

choky. Having a gen. tendency or a momentary feeling of choking: from ca 1855; T. Hughes, 'To feel rather chokey', 1857.

chonkey(s). A mincemeat, baked in a crust and sold in the streets: low coll: mid-C.19–20; ob. Etymology obscure: perhaps ex some noted pieman.

choops! Be quiet, silent! Anglo-Indian and military: C.19–20. See CHUB-A-ROW for etymology.

choose. To wish to have; want: low coll: from ca 1760.

chootah. Small; unimportant: Anglo-Indian: C.19–20. Ex Urdu *chota*, small.

chop. In mid-C.18–early 19 boxing s., a blow with the fist.

chop, adj. In 'pidgin', C.19–20: quick. cf. CHOP-CHOP!

chop as in *first-*, *second-chop*, first- or second-rate or -class, rank or quality. Anglo-Indian and -Chinese coll, ex Hindi *chhap*, a print, a seal or a brand. The attributive use is the more gen. and dates from late C.18: thus Thackeray, 'A sort of second-chop dandies'. Yule & Burnell, whence *no chop* (see CHOP, NO).

chop, v. (The barter-exchange senses are S.E.) 2. To eat a chop: ca 1840–1900. Mrs Gore, 1841, 'I would rather have chopped at the "Blue Posts".' 3. To eat (a human being), gen. in passive: West Africa, from ca 1860; ob. But, simply as 'to eat', it is current, with corresponding n., 'food'. Either ex †*chop*, to devour, or suggested by *chopsticks.* 4. In c., to speak, as in *chop the* WHINERS, to say prayers: C.18–19. cf. CHOP UP. 5. Esp., however, to do, or speak quickly: c.: C.17–18. 6. To beat in a race: turf: from ca 1860. Ex hunting j. (to seize prey before it clears cover). 7. To hit (a horse) on the thigh with the whip: coach-drivers': C.19. (W. O. Tristram, *Coaching Days* . . ., 1888. This author notes *fan*, to whip (a horse), *towel*, to flog it, and the nn. *chopping*, *fanning*, *towelling.*)

chop, no (or **not much**). Inferior, insignificant, objectionable: coll: from mid-1880s; ob.

Chop-Back. (Gen. pl.) A Hastings fisherman: nautical: C.18–20; ob. Bowen, 'From an old-time incident in a fight with Dutch traders'. Also *Hatchet-Back*, for the same grim hand-lopped reason: E.D.D. (Sussex nicknames.)

chop by chance. 'A rare Contingence, an

extraordinary or uncommon Event', B.E.; coll: late C.17–18; never very gen.

chop-chop! Quickly; immediately: pidgin; from ca 1830. Ex Cantonese dial. 2. Also as v., to make haste.

chop-church. In C.16–early 17, S.E.; in late C.17–18, coll; in C.19, archaic S.E.: an unscrupulous dealer or trafficker in benefices.

***chop up.** To hurry through, esp. in c. *chop up the* WHINERS, to gallop through prayers: late C.17–19.

chopper. 'A blow, struck on the face with the back of the hand', Moore in *Tom Crib's Memorial*, 1819. Pugilistic; ob. Occ. in coll form, *chopping blow*. 2. A sausage-maker: tradesmen's: from ca 1860. 3. A sailor's broad-brimmed hat: naval: ca 1805–40. W. N. Glascock, *The Naval Sketch-Book* (II), 1826, 'I powders my pate, and claps on a broad-brimm'd chopper over all'. 4. A tail: mostly Cockney: late C.19–20.

chopper or **button on, have a.** To feel depressed: printers', from ca 1850; ob. See also *have a* BUTTON ON.

chopping. (Of girls) vain and ardent; sexually on-coming: late C.19–20; ob. Coll. Ex the S.E. sense. cf. the idea in Fr. *avoir la cuisse gaie*.

chopping-block. In boxing, an unskilled man who yet can take tremendous punishment. From ca 1830: coll.

chops. The mouth: C.18 coll. cf. S.E. senses.

chops, down in the. Depressed; melancholy; sad. Coll: from ca 1820; rare in C.20, when the form (as occ. from ca 1850) is *down in the mouth*, with sense of dejected.

chops, lick one's. To gloat: coll in C.17–18; S.E. thereafter, but hardly literary.

chops of the Channel, the. The Western entrance to the English Channel: nautical coll: C.19–20.

chores, do. To CHAR, do the cleaning work of a house: from ca 1745: coll when not dial. More gen. in U.S.

chortle. To chuckle gurglingly or explosively. Coined by 'Lewis Carroll' ex *chuckle* + *snort* (*Through the Looking Glass*, 1872) and soon popular, e.g. in Besant & Rice, 1876. For a while considered coll, but by 1895 definitely S.E. See my *Slang* at Portmanteau Words. 2. Hence, to sing: 1889, *Referee*, 29 Dec., 'Chortle a chansonette or two'. 3. Hence, *chortle about* or *over*, to praise excessively: 1897, *Daily Telegraph*, 31 March.

***chosen pals** or **pells.** Highwaymen robbing in pairs, esp. in London: c.: mid-C.18–early 19. Grose, 2nd ed. See PAL, n.

Chosen Twelve, the, see APOSTLES.

choter (or **chota**) **wallah,** see BARROW WALLAH (cf. CHOOTAH).

chounter. 'To talk pertly, and (sometimes) angrily', B.E.; late C.17–18. ?ex *chant* influenced by *counter*; or is it not rather cognate with Devon dial. ppl adj., *chounting* (the v. is unrecorded) = 'taunting, jeering, grumbling', E.D.D., which quotes it at 1746?

chouse. A SWINDLE; HOAX; HUMBUG, imposition: from ca 1700; ex *chouse* (= *chiaus*), a S.E. term of perhaps Turkish orig., the etymology remaining a partial mystery. From ca 1850 at Eton and, as we see in R. G. K. Wrench, at Winchester, a shame, as in 'a beastly chouse', or an imposition, whence (—1864) *chouser*, a SHARP lad.

chouse, v. To cheat; deceive; impose on: coll, from the 1650s; ob. Pepys, 15 May 1663, 'The Portugalls have choused us, it seems, in the Island of Bombay'; the anon. *Hints for Oxford*, 1823; Scottish Public-School s. at least as late as 1884. cf. DIDDLE. vbl n., *chousing*.

chouser, see CHOUSE, n.

chout. An entertainment: East-End Cockney, ca 1855–1910. Etymology slightly problematic: ?a perversion of *shout*; or rather an adaptation of E. Anglian and Norfolk *chout*, a frolic or a merry-making.

chovey. A shop: costers': from ca 1835; ob. Whence *man-chovey*, a shopman, and *Ann-chovey*, a shop-woman. ?etymology, unless a corruption of CASA (perhaps on CHOKEY).

chow. Food: from ca 1870, mainly nautical ex 'pidgin'. Abbr. CHOW-CHOW. 2. Talk; CHEEK: theatrical, from ca 1870; ob. 3. **(Chow.)** In Australia, a Chinese (—1882). Prob. ex sense 1.

chow, v. To talk much; grumble: theatrical; from ca 1870. cf. n., 2, and:

chow! An Anglo-Italian coll (esp. in London) salutation: mid-C.19–20. Ex It. *ciao* (coll for *schiavo*), at your service.

chow, have plenty of. To be very talkative: theatrical; from ca 1875.

chow-chow. Food of any kind (now CHOW); from ca 1860; cf. S.E. senses. 2. Also, CHIT-CHAT: from ca 1870. Ex 'pidgin', where, lit., a mixture. See esp. Lady Falkland's *Chow-Chow*, 1857.

chow-chow. To gossip, to chat: late C.19–20. Ex the n., sense 2.

chow-chow, adj. In Anglo-Indian coll, from ca 1870: assorted, general, as in *chow-chow cargo* or *shop*; very good, very bad (as context shows), esp. when preceded by *No. 1.*

chow-chow chop. In Anglo-Chinese from ca 1890: coll rather than s. 'The last lighter containing the sundry small packages to fill up a ship', S.O.D.

chow-chow water. Eddies in the sea: Eastern nautical: late C.19–20. Bowen, 'From the term used by Chinese pilots': cf. CHOW-CHOW, adj.

chowdar. A fool: from ca 1860. Anglo-Chinese, says H., 5th ed.; but is it not an abbr. of the dial. *chowder-headed*, i.e. *jolter-headed*?

Christ-killer. A Jew: proletarian and military ca 1850–1915. Mayhew; Ware.

christen. To call by the name of, give a name to: coll, from ca 1640. 2. To change the markings on a watch: from ca 1780 (G. Parker, 1781); orig. c.; not low s. until ca 1850, as in H., 1st ed. (1859), and in Doran's *Saint and Sinner*, 1868. (Equivalent C.19–20 c. is CHURCH.) vbl n., *christening*, late C.18–20. 3. To add water to wines or spirits; any light liquor with a heavier: from ca 1820. Scott, 1824, 'We'll christen him with the brewer (here he added a little small beer to his beverage).' cf. *drown the* MILLER. 4. To souse from a chamber-pot: from ca 1870. A school and college ceremony that is on the wane; but youth finds a chamber-pot symbolically ludicrous and emblematically important. 5. To celebrate (a meeting, a purchase, a removal, etc.): late C.19–20. 6. To soil, chip, damage (something new or hitherto unmarked): late C.19–20.

christened by a baker. ('He carries the bran in his face,' i.e. he is) freckled. Coll: mid-C.18–early 19.

christened with pump-water, he was. He has a red face. Coll; mid-C.17–early 18.

christening, be out in one's. To be in error: proletarian coll (—1887).

christening-wine. The 'champagne' used in launching ceremonies: nautical: mid-C.19–20; ob.

Christian. A decent fellow; a presentable person. Coll. In Shakespeare's *Two Gentlemen of Verona*, 1591, and until ca 1840, it meant merely a human being, not an animal, the mod. sense beginning, as so many mod. senses have begun, with Dickens (see *Slang*). 2. ca 1805–40, the term = a tradesman willing to give credit. 3. The adj. (of a person, 1577: humane; of a thing or action, 1682: civilized, respectable) follows the same course.

Christian poney or **pony.** A handcart man: Canadian, esp. in East: ?ca 1860–1905. 2. A sedan-chairman: late C.18–early 19. (W. N. Glascock, *Sailors and Saints* (II, 89), 1829.)

Christmas, Christmassing. Holly and mistletoe serving as Christmas decorations: from ca 1820, 1840. Dickens, the former; Mayhew, the latter. S.O.D. says it is nursery slang, F. & H. – coll. (The latter, I think.) 2. Something special to drink at Christmas time: Australian coll: late C.19–20.

Christmas, v. To 'provide with Christmas cheer': very rare: late C.16–17. Adorn with decorations for Christmas: from ca 1825. Celebrate Christmas: from ca 1806. All three senses, coll. See 'The Philology of Christmas', in *Words!*

Christmas! A mild, euphemistic expletive: late C.19–20.

Christmas beef, see BEEF, BE DRESSED LIKE CHRISTMAS.

Christmas box. A Christmas present: low coll (and dial.): from ca 1860.

Christmassing, see CHRISTMAS, n.

Christmas(s)y. Pertaining to, looking like, Christmas: coll: from ca 1880.

chronic. Unpleasant; objectionable; unfair; ROTTEN. Late C.19–20, ex the S.E. sense, acute (pain), inveterate (*c. complaint*). Ware, recording it for 1896, defines *chronic rot* as 'despairingly bad'.

chrony. A C.17 variant of CRONY, 1.

chub. An inexperienced person, esp. a callow youth: C.17–18. 2. A blockhead: ca 1600–1850; coll. Ex the short, thick river fish, whence also *chubby*, plump, S.E. (despite H.).

chub-a-row or **chubarrow!; chuprow!;** occ. **chipperow!** SHUT IT!: military, esp. the Regular Army's (resp. s., coll, s.): mid-C.19–20. Ex Hindustani *chuprao*.

***chubbingly.** A late C.17–early 18 c. variant of S.E. *chubby*. B.E., s.v. *bulchin*.

chuck. A coll endearment: C.16–20, but ob. by 1800. ?ex CHICK. 2. Food of any kind, but esp. bread or meat (—1850): orig. c. ?origin: cf. next 3 senses, esp. sense 5, and senses 7–9. Perhaps such food as one can chuck about without spoiling it. 3. Scraps of meat (cf. BLOCK-ORNAMENT): from ca 1860. 4. A particular sort of beefsteak: from ca 1855; ob. 5. A measure for sprats: Billingsgate, from ca 1840. Otherwise a *toss*; cf. next. 6. A toss, jerk, or throw: coll; from ca 1840. 7. Sea biscuit: nautical, from ca 1840. (As for the next two senses) cf. 2–4. 8. (Military) mealy bread: from ca 1855. 9. A schoolboy's treat: Westminster School: from ca 1855. 10. Abbr. *chuck-farthing*, a national sport: from ca 1710: coll. 11. See CHUCK, GET THE.

chuck, v. In c., to eat (—1876). Hindley's *Cheap Jack*. App. later than and ex the n., 2nd sense. 2. As to toss, to throw with little arm-action, it has always been S.E., but as throw in any other sense, it is low coll of C.19–20. 3. (Pigeon fanciers') to despatch a pigeon: coll, then j.; from ca 1870. 4. To spend extravagantly (—1876): coll, as is the gen. late C.19–20 form, *chuck-away*. 5. To abandon, dismiss, discharge (from gaol); (v.i.) give up: often varied as *chuck up*: from ca 1860. Whence *chuck it up!* = drop it! stop (talking, etc.)! 6. Also, in low coll, *chuck* often = do, perform (e.g. *chuck a jolly*, to begin bantering, chaffing, to support heartily, noisily): the sense and the connotation of all such phrases will be obvious from the definition of the complementary nouns. 7. v.i., to be sexually desirous: late C.18–mid-19. Perhaps suggested by the n., 1.

chuck, do a, see DO A CHUCK.

chuck, get or **give the.** To be dismissed, to dismiss: from ca 1880; low coll.

chuck, hard. A long or a difficult flight: pigeon fanciers': from ca 1875; in C.20 j. 2. Ship's biscuit: nautical: late C.19–20. See CHUCK, n., 7, and cf. HARD TACK.

***chuck a chest.** 'To throw forward the chest, as though prepared to meet the world': streets': late C.19–20. Ware.

chuck a curly. To malinger: military, from ca 1870; ob. *curly* = a writhing.

chuck a dummy. To faint on parade: military, from ca 1890. Ex CHUCK THE DUMMY.

chuck a fit. To pretend to have a fit: (low) coll: mid-C.19–20.

chuck a jolly. (Costermongers') from ca 1850: see CHUCK, v., 6.

chuck a shoulder. To give (a person) the cold shoulder: costers' (—1909).

***chuck a stall.** To attract someone's attention while a confederate robs him: c.: from ca 1850. See STALL.

chuck (oneself) **about** or **into.** To move or act quickly, vigorously (—1860): coll. The *into* phrase also (—1880) = fall into.

chuck-barge. 'Cask in which the biscuit of a mess is kept. Also equivalent to [fig.] BREAD-BASKET,' Ware: naval: late C.19–20. cf. CHUCK, n., 2.

***chuck-bread.** Waste bread: late C.19–20 vagrants' c.

chuck-farthing. A parish clerk: late C.17–early 18. Ex a character in the *Satyr against Hypocrites*.

chuck her up! In cricket, the fielding side's expression of delight: coll: from ca 1875.

chuck-hole. A coll variant for the game of chuck-farthing: from ca 1830; ob.

chuck in, v.i. To challenge: boxing; from ca 1820. Ex the old throwing a hat into the ring. Also, to compete.

chuck-in, have a. To try one's luck: ca 1860–1914; sporting.

chuck one's weight about. To SHOW OFF; orig. military (—1909).

chuck out. To eject forcibly (—1880).

chuck out hints. To hint (v.i.): low coll (—1887).

chuck out ink. To write articles: journalists' (—1909); ob.

chuck over. To abandon (e.g. a sweetheart): low coll (—1887). 2. Hence, n.: late C.19–20.

chuck seven. To die: low: late C.19–20. A dice-cube has no '7'.

***chuck the dummy.** To feign illness; esp. to simulate epilepsy: c. (—1890). Whence CHUCK A DUMMY.

chuck up, v. To vomit. Australian: late C.19–20.

chuck up the bunch of fives. To die: boxers' (—1909).

chuck up the sponge. See SPONGE. 2. Hence *chuck up* (often corrupted, says H., 5th ed. to *jack up*), to abandon: coll: from ca 1860.

chuckaboo. A street endearment: mid-C.19–20.

chuckaby. A C.17 endearment: coll. So is *chucking*. cf. CHUCK, n.

chuckaroo. A boy employed about a regiment: coll among soldiers in India (—1886). A corruption of Hindustani *chhokra*, a boy or youngster.

chuckaway, see BRYANT & MAY'S CHUCKAWAY.

chucked. Slightly drunk: from ca 1880. †. cf. SCREWED. 2. Disappointed; unlucky; SOLD. From ca 1870; ob., except among artists, who, from late C.19, apply it to a picture refused by the Academy. cf. that delightful ca 1879 ballad, *Chucked Again.* 3. Abbr. *chucked out*, forcibly ejected: see CHUCK OUT. 4. In c., amorous; FAST, 2: from ca 1800. Ex CHUCK, v., 7.

***chucked** or **chucked up, be.** To be acquitted or released: c.; from ca 1860.

chucked all of a heap. Fascinated; infatuated: London proletarian (—1909).

chucked-in. Into the bargain; for good measure. Coll; from ca 1875. *Punch*, 11 Oct. 1884, 'Arry at a Political Picnic, reproduced in Baumann's *Londonismen.*

***chucked up,** see CHUCKED, BE.

chucker. In cricket, either a bowler apt to throw the ball or a defaulting player. Both are coll and both date from ca 1880.

chucker-out. A man, often ex-pugilist, retained to eject persons from meetings, taverns, brothels, etc.: low coll (—1880). *Saturday Review*, 31 March 1883.

chucking-out. Forcible ejection (see preceding entry): from ca 1880. Occ. (1881+) an adj., esp. in *chucking-out time*, closing time at a PUB.

chuckler. Anglo-Indian coll: a native shoemaker. From ca 1750. Ex Tamil.

chucks. A naval boatswain: nautical: from ca 1820: cf. Mr Chucks in Marryat's *Midshipman Easy*, 1836.

chucks! Cave! Schoolboys'; from ca 1850. Perhaps cf. SHUCKS!

chucky. A coll endearment (cf. CHUCK, n.): from the 1720s; ob. except in dial. 2. A chicken or a fowl: late C.18–20; coll.

chuff. Stimulation of male member by lumbar thrust in coition: low: late C.19–20. In Durham dial., *chuff* = to cuff.

chuff it! Be off! Take it away! Coll: ca 1850; ob. Perhaps ex *chuff* as a term of reproach.

chul(l) or **chullo!** Hurry! Military and Anglo-Indian, from ca 1800. Hindi *chullo*, go along. Sala, in the *Illustrated London News* of 19 June 1886, says 'In Calcutta *chul* is a word that you may hear fifty times a day.'

chul(l), v. To succeed; be satisfactory: of things or plans, as in 'It won't chul,' i.e. answer, do. From ca 1860. Etymology obscure; but perhaps suggested by CHULL!

chum; in C.18, occ. **chumm.** First recorded in 1684 – Creech's dedication, 'to my chum, Mr Hody of Wadham College' – this term seems at first to have been university s., which it remained until ca 1800; a contemporaneous sense was 'a Chamber-fellow, or constant companion', B.E. Almost immediately the term came to mean, also, an intimate friend and, in C.18, a mate in crime: cf. COLLEGE CHUM. Either s. or coll in C.17–18, it has in C.19–20 been coll. Perhaps by abbreviation and collision of *chamber-fellow* or *-mate*: cf. the Fr. *chambrée* (a roomful of people, oneself included) and Grose's *camerade.* cf. MATE; PAL, and the U.S. *buddy.* See Terms of Address, in *Words!* 2. On the *Conway* Training Ship, from ca 1880 or a few years earlier, *chum* denoted anyone junior, *new chum* a newly joined cadet (Masefield, *The Conway*, 1933). 3. In Australia, a *chum* is an English immigrant: from ca 1890. It represents *new chum*, a newcomer – esp. from England: this term dates from (—) 1839, while *old chum*, an experienced settler, antedates 1846 (C. P. Hodgson, *Reminiscences of Australia*); the latter has never, after ca 1880 (see Morris), been much used. This use of *new* and *old* comes ex that, 4, in prisons for newcomers and old hands: c. (—1812); †by 1900.

chum, v. To live together: from ca 1730 (Wesley); coll, as is the rare C.19 v.t., put as a chum (Dickens in *The Pickwick Papers*).

chum, long-haired. A girl: military: from the 1890s.

chumm, see CHUM, n.

chummage. The practice of rooming together; more gen., money made, in several very different ways, from such practice: coll: 1837, Dickens. Hence, *chummage-ticket.* 2. Among prisoners in gaols, garnish, footing: low s. verging on c. Orig. a London term (—1777). Howard's *State of Prisons in England and Wales.* 3. See JURY, CHUMMAGE, AND COUTER.

chummery. Friendship; friendliness; rooms shared with a friend: coll, from ca 1870; never very gen.; ob., except in India, where it = 'a house where European employees of a firm . . . live together' (Lyell).

chumming or **chumming-up.** Same as *chummage*, esp. as to garnish, footing: C.19.

chummy. A chimney-sweep's boy: from ca 1835. Ob. by 1865, †by 1900. Dickens; Thackeray; Mayhew, in vol. II of *London Labour*, '. . . Once a common name for the climbing boy, being a corruption of chimney'. Also, since ca 1870, an adult sweep. 2. A coll diminutive of CHUM = friend, PAL. Charles Clewearing, *Simon Solus*, a one-act farce played and published in New York in 1843, contains this passage: '. . . Nicer fellows, stouter hearts, freer souls, than some of my chummies just paid off.' As Colonel Albert Moe, U.S.M.C., Ret., has remarked, 'As American naval speech of that period was taken almost entirely and directly from British naval speech, I suggest that [this passage] represents a British expression appearing in an American publication': with so great an authority on American naval speech, I gladly agree. 3. A low-crowned felt hat: ca 1858–1900. A friendly, comfortable piece of head-gear. 4. In Australia a post-1895 variant of NEW CHUM, an English newcomer: cf. CHUM, n., 3.

chummy, v. To 'go partners' (with someone); work along with: Australian: since ca 1870. 'Tom Collins', *Such is Life*, 1903, 'He chummied for a few weeks with a squatter.'

chummy, adj. Friendly, intimate; sociable: coll: from ca 1880.

chummy ships. Ships whose crews are 'friends': nautical coll: late C.19–20. See CHUMMY, adj.

chump. (S.E. or coll > S.E. in sense of a blockhead.) 2. The head; occ. the face: from ca 1860. Esp. in *off one's chump*, very eccentric; mad to almost any degree. 'Master . . . have gone off his chump, that's all,' Besant & Rice, 1877. 3. A variant of CHUM = friend; ca 1880–1920. *Punch*, 11 Oct. 1884.

***chump, get or provide one's own.** To earn one's own living: c.: ca 1860–1914. See esp. that prison classic, *Five Years' Penal Servitude*, anon., 1877, not to be confused with James Greenwood's *Seven Years' Penal Servitude*, 1884.

chump, or **chunk, of wood.** No good: rhyming s. (—1859). Also, a CHUMP or fool, ca 1870–1900.

Chumps Elizas. Champs Élysées: '*London*, Five Pounder Tourists', 1854 on', Ware.

chumpy. Eccentric; idiotic; insane. ca 1870–1914. Ex *off one's* CHUMP.

chunk. A thick solid piece or lump cut off anything (esp. wood or bread): coll and dial: mid-C.17–20. Ray's *Country Words*, 1691. App. ex CHUCK. 2. 'Among printers, a journeyman who refuses to work for legal wages', Grose, 2nd ed.: late C.18–early 19. cf. FLINT and DUNG among tailors. 3. A School Board officer: ca 1870–1910.

chunk of wood. No good: rhyming s., contemporaneous variant of CHUMP OF WOOD.

chunky. Thick set. From ca 1870; coll. Ex U.S. (1776).

chuprassy, in civilian use (—1865) a messenger, in military usage, an Indian orderly (from ca 1880), is Anglo-Indian coll, direct ex Hindi *chaprasi*, the wearer of a *chapras* or badge.

chuprow, see CHUB-A-ROW!.

***church.** Illicitly to disguise a watch by changing its 'innards': c.: from ca 1835; gen. as *church a* YACK. cf. CHRISTEN, 2.

church, n. An endearment; esp. *my church*, my dear: non-aristocratic: ca 1870–1910.

church, go to. To get married: coll; from late C.16. Shakespeare, 1599, 'Counte Claudio, when meane you to goe to Church?'

church, talk. To talk 'shop': coll; from ca 1850; ob.

church-folk. Members of the Church of England as opp. to CHAPEL-FOLK, Dissenters. From ca 1870; coll.

church parade. The walk-and-talk after church on Sunday mornings: coll: from ca 1870. cf. PRAYER-BOOK PARADE.

church-piece. A threepenny bit: Society (—1909); ob. Ware.

church-service. A church-service book, i.e. one containing the Common Prayer, the lessons, the psalms in metrical version, etc.: low coll (—1859). Sala.

church-work. Work that proceeds very slowly: coll; from ca 1600. Ex church-building.

churcher. A threepenny bit: Cockneys': late C.19–20.

churchify. To render CHURCHY: 1843, Miall: coll >, by 1900, S.E.

churchiness. The being CHURCHY: from ca 1880: coll >, by 1900, S.E.

churchwarden. A long-stemmed clay pipe: from ca 1855; coll. Hood, 1857, 'Hang a churchwarden by my side for a sabre.' Churchwardens affected this ob. instrument. cf. ALDERMAN; YARD OF CLAY.

churchy. Redolent of the Church; obtrusive in religious observance. Coll: from ca 1860.

churchyard clock, as many faces as a. (Of a man) unreliable: naval: ca 1860–1910.

churchyard cough. A severe cough: coll: late C.17–20. Mainly jocular.

churchyard luck. The death of a child in a large, poor family: proletarian coll (—1909).

churl upon a gentleman, put a. To drink

malt liquor immediately after wine: late C.16–early 19. Coll after ca 1700.

***chury.** A knife: c. of ca 1810–60. From Welsh Romany.

chuzzle, see CHISEL. **chy-ack** or **-ike; chyacke,** see CHIIKE.

cicisbeo. A ribbon-knot attached to hilt of sword, neck of walking-stick, etc.: ca 1770–1820: Society. (S.O.D. gives as an unassimilated Italianism, but this usage of the word is slangy.) Ex the C.18–20 sense, imported direct from Italy: a married woman's recognized gallant or 'servente'.

cider-and. Cider with something else (esp. if liquid): C.18–20; ob. Coll. Fielding in *Joseph Andrews*, 'They had a pot of cider-and at the fire.' cf. HOT WITH.

cig. A cigar: ca 1885–1900. 2. From ca 1890, a cigarette. Earliest record: 1895, W. Pett Ridge, *Minor Dialogues*.

cigaresque. Well furnished with cigars; smoking or 'sporting' a large or very expensive cigar. A jocular coll (1839) after *picturesque* or *picaresque*.

cinch, v.t. (In Canada, as in the Northern States of America, the *c* is hard; in England, as in the Southern States, it is soft; in other parts it varies.) CORNER, get a grip on, put pressure on: orig. (1875), U.S., anglicized ca 1900, though never gen.

cinder. Any strong liquor mixed with water, tea, lemonade, etc. (—1864); ob. H., 3rd ed., 'Take a soda with a cinder in it.' 2. A running track: abbr. *cinder-path* or *-track*: coll: from ca 1880. Occ. *cinders*.

cinder-garbler. A female servant: late C.18–early 19. Grose, 1st ed., adds: 'Custom House wit'. cf.:

cinder-grabber. A female drudge: C.19–20; ob. Ex preceding entry. cf. SLAVEY.

cinder-knotter. A stoker: naval (—1909); ob.

cinder-sifter. A woman's 'hat with open-work brim, the edge of which was turned up perpendicularly': Society: ca 1878–1912. Ware.

cinderella. Abbr. *Cinderella dance*, one ceasing at midnight: from ca 1880: coll >, by 1900, S.E.

cinders, see CINDER, 2.

cinquanter. An old 'hand' or 'stager': ca 1600–1800. Pedantic; ex Fr. *cinquante*, 50. 2. A 'gamester and scurrilous companion by profession': ca 1600–60. (O.E.D.)

cinque and sice, set at. 'To expose to great risks, to be reckless about' (O.E.D.): ca 1530–1720: s. > coll > S.E. cf. *at sixes and sevens*.

circle train. A London underground train: London coll: 1887.

circlers. Occupants of the dress-circle: theatrical (—1909).

***circling boy.** A ROOK, a swindler, a gambler's or a thief's decoy: C.17 c. Jonson. cf. *run* RINGS ROUND.

circs. Circumstances: trivial coll: from ca 1880. Prob. orig. commercial.

circumbendibus. A roundabout way (lit.): coll: from 1681 (Dryden); ob. Ex *bend* + L. *circum*, around, + L. dative and ablative pl, *-ibus*. Whence, 2, a long-winded story: coll: from ca 1780.

circumlocution office. A Government Office; any roundabout way of doing things. Coined by Dickens in *Little Dorrit*, 1857. Derisively coll; S.E. by 1900.

circus. A noisy and confused institution, place, scene, assemblage or group of persons: coll: American, anglicized ca 1895.

***circus cuss.** A circus rider: c.: from ca 1850. ?abbr. CUSTOMER.

ciss! see CESS! **cissie, -y,** see SISSIE.

cit. Abbr. *citizen*: pejorative coll; from ca 1640; ob. by 1830. Rarely applied, in a city, to other than tradesmen; in the country, to other than (gen. non-aristocratic) townsmen born and bred. 'The cits of London and the boors of Middlesex', Johnson. *Citess*, ca 1680–1750, is rare.

***citizen.** A wedge for opening safes: c.: from ca 1860. Whence, *citizen's friend*, a wedge smaller than a *citizen*, itself smaller than an ALDERMAN; larger still, though only occ. used, is a LORD MAYOR. The tools are used in the order of their size; the terms are ob.

citt. A C.17–early 18 variant of CIT.

City, something in the. In lit. vagueness, obviously S.E.; but, pointedly coll from ca 1890, it denotes a shady financier, a nondescript and none too honest agent, and esp. a criminal or even a burglar.

***City College.** Newgate: c. (—1791); †by 1890. cf. COLLEGE.

City of the Saints, the. Grahamstown: South African coll nickname of ca 1865–90.

City Road Africans. Harlots of that quarter: London streets': ca 1882–1910.

City sherry. Four-ale: East London: ca 1880–90. Ex colour (!).

city stage. The gallows: C.18–early 19. (Once in front of Newgate, London, E.C.4.)

civet. C.18–19, low coll: *pudendum muliebre*.

civet-cat. A person habitually using civet perfume: C.18; orig. – Pope, 1738 – S.E., it soon > coll and quickly ob.

civies, civvies. Civilian clothes: military: mid-C.19–20.

civil, do the. To do the civil – the polite – thing: coll: C.19–20. (A. Trollope, *Barchester Towers*, 1857.)

civil reception, a house of. A bawdy house: mid-C.18–early 19.

***civil rig.** In vagrants' c., C.19–20 (ob.), an attempt to obtain alms by extreme civility. RIG, a trick.

***civilian.** Any person, esp. a man, who is not a criminal: C.19–20 (ob.): c. 2. One who is unfailingly polite when drunk: ca 1650. 3. 'The surgeon, purser, and chaplain, are commonly designated . . . civilians,' W. N. Glascock, *The Naval Sketch-Book* (I, 12): naval: ca 1800–60.

civility money. A tip claimed by bailiffs for doing their duty with civility: C.18–early 19; orig. coll, it was S.E. by 1880. Motteux, 1708, 'four Ducats for Civility Money'.

civvies, see CIVIES.

civvy, civy. Civilian: coll: orig. military: from the 1890s.

clack. As chatter, gossip, S.E.; as tongue, coll: late C.16–20; ob. Greene, 'Haud your clacks, lads.' As 'a prattler or busybody' (Dyche), coll: C.17–early 18. cf. Wilkie Collins's character, Drusilla *Clack*. 2. A loud talk or chat, coll: from ca 1810; ob. James Payn, 1888, 'The old fellow would have had a clack with her.' Esp. in *cut your clack!*, SHUT UP! (2): late C.19–20. 3. The v. is S.E. The word is echoic.

clack-box. The mouth: C.19. 2. A persistent chatterer: C.19–20, ob. Both have a dial. tinge. Ex the S.E. sense, the container of a pump's clack-valve. cf.:

clack-loft. A pulpit: late C.18–20; ob. cf. HUM-BOX.

clagger. A duff made of flour and slush: nautical: late C.19–20. Ex dial. *clag*, to adhere.

***claim.** To steal: later C.19–20 c.; ob. cf. CONVEY; WIN. 2. To catch hold of, seize, grasp (a person): *Sessions*, 19 Nov. 1902, 'Tyler jumped out at the window – I *claimed* him and tustled [*sic*] with him.'

claim, jump a. To seize or gain possession of, fraudulently. Lit., S.E. ex U.S.; but fig. it is a coll anglicized ca 1880.

***clank.** In c., a pewter tankard: C.19; late C.17–18 (B.E.), a silver one. Hence, RUM CLANK, a double tankard, as in B.E., who also records *clank-napper*, a stealer of silver tankards.

clanker. A notable lie, cf. CLINKER, 5: ca 1690–1840. Ex the noise of heavy metal: cf. CLANK, and *clanker*, silver plate, C.17–18 c.

***clanker-napper.** A thief specializing in silver plate, esp. tankards: late C.17–early 19 c. cf. *clank-napper* (see CLANK).

clans, a or the gathering of the. Any considerable, or indeed inconsiderable, gathering-together of people, gen. of the same or similar character or pursuit or purpose. From ca 1890: coll. Ex Scottish warfare of C.16–18.

clap. Gonorrhoea: late C.16–20; S.E. until ca 1840, then low coll. Respectably 'They sing, they dance, clean shoes, or cure a clap' – almost the sole instance in Johnson's formal works (this occurs in *London*, an admirable satirical poem, 1738) of a monosyllabic sentence. Ex Old Fr. *clapoir*.

clap, v. To infect with gonorrhoea: from ca 1650. S.E. until ca 1840, then low coll. 2. Catachrestically for *clip* (to embrace) and *clepe* (to call): C.15, C.17 resp. 3. To take, seize: low (—1857); ob. Ex *clap one's hands on*.

clap, in a. Immediately; occ., instantaneously. Coll; from ca 1630; ob.

Clap-'em, see CLAPHAM.

clap eyes on. To see, esp. unexpectedly or finally: coll; Dickens, 1838.

clap in, v.i. To come or go decisively; enter vigorously; put oneself forward: coll: ca 1600–1780. Marvell, 1672, 'Hearing of a vacancy with a Noble-man, he clap'd in, and easily obtained to be his Chaplain.'

clap of thunder. A glass of gin: coll; ca 1810–40. cf. FLASH OF LIGHTNING.

clap on, v.i. To 'set to'; apply oneself energetically: coll; from ca 1850. Surtees.

clap on the shoulder, n. and v. (An) arrest for debt. C.18 (?also C.17) coll.

clap-shoulder. A bailiff or a watchman: rare coll; C.17–early 19. Adj. in Taylor the Water Poet. The gen. form is *shoulder-clapper*.

Clapham (or Clap-'em), he went out by Had'em and came home by. 'He went out a-wenching, and got a clap,' Grose, 1st ed.: mid-C.18–early 19 c.p. Punning CLAP, n.

clapper. The tongue (human); esp. that of a very talkative person: coll: 1638, H. Shirley.

clapper-claw. To thrash soundly and

crudely: late C.16–early 19. Coll. Lit., to scratch noisily. 2. Hence, to revile: late C.17–20; ob. coll, almost S.E.

***clapper-dogeon** or, more correctly, **-dudgeon.** A beggar born, a whining beggar; also as an insult. Mid-C.16–19: c. till ca 1800, then low s. with an archaic tinge. Harman; Jonson; Ned Ward; Sala. ?lit., one who assumes (CLAPS ON) grief, indignation, distress. Or, as O.E.D. suggests, *clapper* + *dudgeon*, the hilt of a dagger.

clapster. A frequent sufferer from CLAP; a very loose man. C.19–20; low coll.

Clare Market Cleavers. Butchers of that district: London coll: ca 1850–1900. 'The glory of Clare Market . . . was practically gone in '98,' Ware (whom see for an excellent account).

Clare Market duck. 'Baked bullock's heart stuffed with sage and onions – which gave a faint resemblance to the bird', Ware: London: ca 1850–1900. See the preceding.

claret. Blood: from ca 1600 (Dekker, e.g. in *The Honest Whore*, 1604). From ca 1770, mostly in boxing circles (e.g. in Moore's *Tom Crib's Memorial*, 1819). Ex the colour. cf. BADMINTON and BORDEAUX. Hence:

claret, v. (Usually in passive.) To draw blood from, to cause to be covered with blood. 'Purcell's *mug* was clareted,' *Boxiana*, II, 1818.

claret, tap one's. To draw blood: from ca 1770.

claret-jug. The nose: pugilistic; from ca 1840; ob. Ex CLARET.

clargyman. A rabbit: provincial, esp. Cheshire, s. (—1898), not dial.

clashy. Anglo-Indian coll for a native sailor or tent-pitcher, loosely for a labourer, a 'low fellow': late C.18–20. Ex Urdu.

class. Distinction; sheer merit: athletics and, slightly, the turf: from ca 1850: coll. 'He's not class enough,' 'There's a good deal of class about him': he is not good enough; pretty good. cf. CLASSY, and:

***class, do a bit of.** To commit a crime that is, by criminals, considered notable or, at the least, not below one's abilities: c.: from ca 1880. Clarence Rook, *The Hooligan Nights*, 1899.

class, no. Without distinction or merit: lower classes' coll: 1897, 'Soldiers! Why, soldiers ain't no class.' Ware. Ex CLASS.

class, take a. (Oxford) to take an honours degree: mid-C.19–20: coll >, by 1880, S.E.

classic. Excellent, splendid: from ca 1880: coll. Ex burlesque S.E. sense: 'approved, recognized "standard"', O.E.D.

classy. Stylish; fashionable; smart; well-turned-out: from ca 1890: coll, lower middle class downwards. cf. CLASS.

clattery, adj. Clattering: coll: from ca 1880.

***claw.** A stroke of the CAT-O'-NINE-TAILS: (—1876) c.; ob.

claw me and I'll claw thee. The C.17–early 19 form of the C.16 *claw me, claw ye* and the C.20 *scratch my back and I'll scratch yours*: coll. cf. SCRATCH MY BREECH . . .

claw off. Severely to defeat or thrash: late C.17–19, low coll, as is the sense, venereally to infect. 2. Also, to scold: same period and kind. Occ. *c. away*. cf. earlier S.E. senses.

claw-back, see CLAW-POLL.

claw-hammer (coat). The tail coat of full evening dress: coll; from 1869 in U.S.; anglicized in 1879. (The *coat* is gen. omitted.) Ex a *claw*-hammer.

claw-poll, more gen. **claw-back.** A toady: coll, resp. C.16–17, C.16–19. Both S.E. after 1600.

***claws for breakfast.** Punishment with the CAT-O'-NINE-TAILS: (—1873) c.; ob. James Greenwood, *In Strange Company*. cf. CLAW.

clay. Abbr. *clay-pipe*: coll: from ca 1860. Calverley in the *Ode to Tobacco*.

clay, moisten or **wet one's.** To drink: from ca 1700: coll verging on S.E. In C.19–20 also *soak*. Addison in the *Spectator*, 'To moisten their clay, and grow immortal by drinking'. cf. S.E. *mortal clay*.

clay-brained. Very dull-witted: coll >, by 1700, S.E.; late C.16–20, ob. Shakespeare.

clean, v.i. To change one's clothes: naval: late C.19–20. Bowen, 'Even "clean into dirty clothes" is permissible.' 2. To scold severely: to chastise: (low) Cockney: late C.19–20. 'I won' 'alf clean yer when I gits yer 'ome!' Ex the lit. sense of that threat.

clean, in several senses as adj. and adv. is almost coll, as in *clean off his head*. 2. But as 'expert, clever', it is wholly c. (—1811); †by 1890.

clean as a pig-sty (,as). An Anglo-Irish ironic c.p. applied to a dirty house: late C.19–20.

clean leg up, give (one) **a.** To help him (esp. to obtain a job): non-aristocratic coll (—1887); slightly ob. Ex giving a person assistance over a fence.

clean one's front, see FRONT, CLEAN ONE'S.

clean out. To deprive of money, gen. illicitly: orig. low, verging on c.: from ca 1810. Dickens, in *The Old Curiosity Shop*, 'He was plucked, pigeoned, and cleaned out completely.' 2. ca 1840–70, to thrash.

clean potato. The right, occ. the 'correct', thing, esp. morally: coll: from ca 1870; ob.

clean ship. A whaling ship returning whaleless to port: whalers' coll: late C.19–20.

Clean-Shirt Day. Sunday: lower-classes' coll: since ca 1820; †by 1900. *Sinks*, 1848.

clean-skins. (Rare in singular.) Unbranded cattle. Australia (—1881): coll.

clean straw. Clean sheets: Winchester College, ?C.16–20; ob. 'Before 1540 the beds were bundles of straw on a stone floor,' F. & H. The same meaning is extant at Bootham School.

clean the board. To clear the board, etc., of all it contains; make a clean sweep: coll (—1884).

clean the slate. To pay all debts: non-aristocratic coll: from ca 1860. (The *slate* on which, in public-houses, drinking debts are noted.)

clean wheat, it's the. i.e. the best of its kind: coll, ca 1865–1910.

clear. (Exceedingly) drunk: c. and low: from late 1680s; †by 1890. Vanbrugh, *The Relapse*, 'I suppose you are clear – you'd never play such a trick as this else.' cf. CLEAR AS MUD.

clear an examination paper. To answer all the questions: coll (—1893). On the analogy of *clear a dish*, eat all its contents.

clear as mud. Anything but clear; confused: coll: from ca 1890.

clear crystal. White spirits, esp. gin; loosely, brandy and rum. From ca 1860; ob.

clear decks. To clear the table after a meal: nautical coll: mid-C.19–20.

clear off or **out.** To depart: from ca 1830. The S.O.D. gives it as S.E., but in C.19, at least, the term had a coll taint, perhaps because it was used slightly earlier in U.S. – e.g. Neal, in *Brother Jonathan*, 1825, had 'Like many a hero before him, he cleared out.' Monetarily, *clear out* is gen. S.E., but as CLEAN OUT, or 'ruin', it is coll (—1850), as in Thackeray's *Pendennis*.

clearing-out at custom-house, n. and adj. Easing (or eased) of an encumbrance: nautical: ca 1820–60.

cleat. *Glans penis*: low: late C.19–20.

cleave, v.i. To be wanton (said of women only): C.18–early 19; low. The two opp. meanings of *cleave* – 'split', and 'cling closely', due to independent radicals – are present in this subtle term.

cleaved, see CLOVEN.

cleaver. A butcher: coll: C.18–19. Ex the butcher's cleaver or chopper. 2. In late C.18–early 19 low s., a forward woman; a wanton. See CLEAVE.

cleavin(g). Boastful: Clare Market, London: ca 1850–1900. Ex CLARE MARKET CLEAVERS.

cleft. The female pudend: coll, C.17–20. Ex the earlier S.E. (in C.19–20, dial.) sense: the body's fork. In late C.19–20 usage, as much euphemism as coll. 2. adj. See CLOVEN.

cleft stick, in a. In a very difficult position: from ca 1700; coll in C.18; in C.19–20, S.E.

clencher, see CLINCHER. **clenchpoop,** see CLINCHPOOP.

clergyman. A chimney-sweep: C.19. cf. CHIMNEY-SWEEP.

clergyman or **clerk, St Nicholas's,** see at NICHOLAS.

clericals. A clergyman's dress: coll; from ca 1860. cf. ACADEMICALS.

***clerk.** To impose upon; swindle: c. and low coll: C.18–early 19. Ex ignorance's suspicion of learning. 2. To act as a clerk: C.19–20; coll. The vbl n., *clerking*, occurs in C.17, the ppl adj. in mid-C.16. Lamb, in 1834, 'I am very tired of clerking it.'

clerk of the works. 'He who takes the lead in minor affairs', Bee: public-house: ca 1820–50. Punning S.E. sense.

clerks, St Nicholas's, see at NICHOLAS.

clerk's blood. Red ink: coll: C.19–20, ob. Charles Lamb.

clever. 'At first a colloquial and local word', S.O.D.; it still is coll if = 'cunning' or 'skilful' and applied to an animal or if = 'well', 'in good health or spirits' (mid-C.19–20). Esp. *not too clever*, indisposed in health; the health sense is common in Australia and New Zealand. 2. Convenient, suitable: coll: ca 1750–1820. 3. NICE; generally likable or pleasant: coll: from ca 1730; ob. 4. (Of persons) well-disposed, amiable: coll: ca 1770–1830, extant in U.S. Goldsmith, 'Then come, put the jorum about, | And let us be merry and clever.'

clever Dick. A clever or sly person: schools' (—1887); mostly London. cf.:

clever shins. A person sly to no, or little, purpose: schools', ca 1870–1910. cf. SLY-BOOTS.

clew up. To join another ship: naval: since ca 1895. Ex the 'clew' system of fixing hammocks.

***cleyme; occ. clyme** or **cleym.** An artificial sore: ca 1670–1830: c. Head; B.E. furnishes an excellent account of this beggar's device. ?etymology, unless ex CLY, to seize.

click. A blow, a punch: boxing; from ca 1770; ob. except in dial. Moore, in *Tom Crib's Memorial*, 'clicks in the gob'.

click, v. To 'stand at a shop-door and invite customers in', Dyche, 1748. C.18–early 19. Ex: 2. In c. and low, to seize: late C.17–early 19. 3. In printers' s., from slightly before 1860, 'A work is said to be "clicked" when each man works on his lines, and keeps an account thereof.' O.E.D. (Sup.).

clicker. A shop-keeper's tout: late C.17–19. Ned Ward in *The London Spy*: 'Women here were almost as Troublesome as the Long-Lane clickers.' 2. A foreman shoemaker apportioning leather to the workmen: orig. (C.17) s., soon j. 3. In printing, from ca 1770, a foreman distributing the copy: soon j. 4. In C.18–early 19 c., one who shares out the booty or REGULARS. 5. A knockdown blow: boxing, from ca 1815; ob.

clicket. Sexual intercourse: c. or low coll; late C.17–18. Gen. as *be at clicket*. Ex the S.E. term, applied to foxes.

clickman toad. A watch: late C.18–early 19. Perhaps orig. dial. Ex clicking sound. Whence, 2, a West-Countryman: s. (—1788) and dial.; †by 1890. Grose (2nd ed.), who tells an amusing anecdote of a countryman mistaking a watch for a toad.

clie, see CLY, n.

***clift.** To steal: mid-C.19–20; ob. ?ex *have in a cleft stick*.

***cligh,** see CLOY, v.

climb down. To abandon a position, an assertion or boast: from mid-1880s: coll >, by 1910, S.E.

climb the Mountain of Piety. To pawn goods: late C.19–20; ob. cf. Fr. *mont de piété*, a pawnshop.

climb the rigging. To lose one's temper: naval: late C.19–20. cf. REAR UP.

***climb the three trees with a ladder.** To ascend the gallows: c.: late C.18–early 19. Ex the three pieces of a gallows.

climb Zion. 'To rush up the fo'c'sle, chased by armed seniors', Masefield: *Conway* Training Ship, from ca 1890.

***clinch.** A prison cell: mid-C.19–20 c. (ob.). Hence *get*, or *kiss, the clinch* or CLINK, to be imprisoned.

clincher. A great lie: C.19–20; ob.; coll. cf. CORKER. 2. A conclusive statement or argument: coll; 1804 (O.E.D.).

clinchpoop, occ. **clenchpoop.** A lout: coll; ca 1570–1640.

***cling-rig,** see CLINK-RIG.

clinger. A female dancing very close to her partner: from ca 1890.

clink. A prison in Southwark, London: C.16–17. In C.18–20, any prison, esp. if small; a lock-up; a detention cell, this last nuance dating only from ca 1880 and being mainly military (cf. CLINCH). Barclay, 1515; Marryat, 1835, 'We've a nice little clink at Wandsworth.' Echoic from the fetters (see CLINKERS). 2. Money (cf. CHINK): Scottish coll rather than dial.: from the 1720s. Ramsay, Burns, Hogg. Also, a coin: mostly military: from ca 1870. 3. Very inferior beer: from ca 1860; ob. cf. BUM CLINK.

clink, v. To put in prison: from ca 1850. Also see CLINCH.

clink, kiss the. To be imprisoned. Low: late C.16–early 19. A C.19 c. variant, *get the* CLINCH.

***clink-rig;** occ. corrupted to **cling-rig.** The stealing of (esp. silver) tankards from public-houses: c.; ca 1770–1880. Ex CLANK.

***clinker.** In c. of ca 1690–1830, a crafty, designing fellow. 2. In c. C.18–19, any kind of chain. 3. A hard, or smartly delivered blow: from ca 1860; boxing. Thackeray. Ex S.E. *clink*, a quick, sharp blow. 4. A person or thing of excellent quality: sporting s. (ca 1860) >, ca 1900, coll. 5. A notable lie: mid-C.19–20; ob.

clinker-knocker. A naval stoker: nautical, esp. naval: late C.19–20.

***clinkers.** Fetters: c. and low; late C.17–early 19. Echoic; cf. CLINK. 2. 'Deposits of faecal or seminal matter in the hair about the *anus* or the female *pudendum*', F. & H.; low coll, from ca 1830. cf. CLINKERS IN ONE'S ... and the S.E. sense, a hot cinder.

clinkers in one's bum, have. To be restless; uneasy. Low coll, from ca 1840.

clinkerum. A prison; a lock-up: C.19. CLINK influenced by CLINKERS, 1.

clinking. First-rate; remarkably good: from ca 1855: coll; esp. in racing and games. *Sporting Times*, 12 March 1887, 'Prince Henry must be a clinking good horse.'

clip, a smart blow, has a coll look, but it is genuine S.E. The corresponding v., however, is coll, late C.19–20, and is always in forms *clip a person one* or *clip a person on the* (gen.) *ear*.

clip, v. To move quickly; run: coll, from ca 1830. Michael Scott in *Tom Cringle's Log*, 1833. Until ca 1844, rarely of anything but ships. 2. See preceding entry.

***clip-nit.** A dirty ruffian: c.: Ned Ward, 1703.

clip-up, v.i. A Cockney coll that, dating from ca 1890 (or earlier), has no synonym in S.E. and should therefore, by this time, have been considered S.E. It is a schoolboys' method of casting lots by approaching each other from opposite kerbs, with a heel-to-toe step. He who finds that the last gap is too small for the length of his foot is the loser.

clipe. To tell tales: schools', ca 1860–1900. cf. Chaucer's *clepe*, to speak of, and O.E. *clipian*, to call, to name.

clipper. A splendid or very smart specimen of humanity or horseflesh: orig. (—1835), U.S., anglicized ca 1845. Thackeray, 1848. Ex *clipper*, any fast-moving ship or (from ca 1830) the special kind of vessel; as horse, influenced by Dutch *klepper*. 2. A cutpurse: c.: Ned Ward, 1709.

clipping. (Of pace) very fast, 'rattling': coll: 1845, *Punch*. cf. CLIPPER. 2. Hence, excellent; very smart; dashingly showy: from ca 1855. Thackeray, *Philip*, 'What clipping girls there were in that barouche.' Ex (*to*) CLIP. adv. in *-ly*.

clique, v.i. and t. To act as, or form, a clique: coll: from ca 1880.

cliqu(e)y. Pertaining to or characterized by cliques: from ca 1875, though recorded in 1863 for U.S.: coll for a decade, then S.E.

clishpen. To break (a thing) by letting it fall: Shelta: C.18–20. cf. Shelta *clisp*, to fall or to let fall.

clo. Clothes: low (mostly Cockney) coll pronunciation, chiefly in the street cry, *clo! old clo!*: C.19–20.

***cloak.** A watch-case: C.19 c. Ainsworth.

cloak, Plymouth, see PLYMOUTH CLOAK.

cloak-father. 'A pretended author whose name is put forth to conceal the real author', O.E.D.: coll: ca 1639–1700. Fuller. The O.E.D. cites as S.E., but surely not?

***cloak-twitcher.** A thief specializing in cloaks: C.18–early 19: c.

clobber; occ. **clober.** Clothes: from ca 1850; at first, old clothes but from ca 1870 also new. Prob. ex Yiddish (*klbr*). (W. H. Davies, 'the super-tramp', considers it to be c.) 2. To redecorate (plain) china to enhance its value: antique dealers': late C.19–20.

clobber, v. See CLOBBER UP, 2.

***clobber at a fence, do.** To sell stolen clothes: c.; from ca 1855.

clobber up. To patch, 'transform' (clothes). Orig. a cobbling device. From ca 1850. 2. To dress smartly, v.t. and reflexive: from ca 1860. W. E. Henley. Also, occ. (gen. in passive), *clobber*: not before ca 1880.

clobberer. A transformer of old clothes: from ca 1855. ca 1880 it > j. *The Times*, 2 Nov. 1864. cf. CLOBBER UP, 1.

clober, see CLOBBER, n.

***clock.** A watch: C.19–20 c. and low. (In C.16–18, S.E.) If of gold, *a red c.*; if of silver, *a white c.*: gen. abbr. to *a red, a white, 'un*. 2. A face: from ca 1870, ex U.S. cf. DIAL. 3. A dynamite bomb: London: 1880s. Ex a topicality of the dynamite scare at that time.

clock, v.t. To time by a stop-watch: from ca 1880: sporting s.

clock, know what's o', see O'CLOCK . . .

clock-calm. (Of the sea) dead-calm: nautical coll: late C.19–20. Ex a clock's shiny face.

clock-setter. A busybody, a sea lawyer: nautical (—1890). Ex: 2. One who tampers with the clock to shorten his hours: nautical coll: from ca 1880.

clock stopped. No TICK, i.e. no credit. Tradesmen's c.p.: from ca 1840; now rare, but not ob.

clocking. Very fast time, esp. in athletics and racing: 1888; coll; ob.

clocky. A watchman: ca 1820–70. *Sinks*, 1848. He makes his rounds at regular intervals.

clod-crusher. A clumsy boot (gen. pl): coll: from ca 1850. cf. BEETLE-CRUSHER. 2. Hence, a large foot (gen. in pl): coll; from ca 1860. 3. Also, a heavy walker: coll; from ca 1870.

clod-hopper. A clumsy boor: coll: C.18–20, ex the C.17–18 sense, ploughman. After ca 1800, S.E.

clod-pate, clod-poll or **-pole.** A dolt: C.17–20, ob.; coll; S.E. after ca 1750. Like the preceding, in B.E., though the O.E.D. and S.O.D. say nothing of their almost certainly coll origin and beginnings.

cloddy. Aristocratic in appearance:

proletarian: late C. 19–20. Ex well-formed or *cloddy* bull dogs ('low to the ground, short in the back, and thickset'. Ex dial. *cloddy*, thickset, full-fleshed like a bull.) *Daily Telegraph*, 13 Nov. 1895.

clods. Copper coins: Cockneys': since ca 1870. *Clods* = *clodhoppers*, rhyming s. on COPPER(S).

clods and stickings. Skilly: paupers', from ca 1840; ob.

cloister-roush. At Winchester College, 'a kind of general tournament', Mansfield. Dating from early C.19, †by 1890.

***cloke**, see CLOAK.

Clootie; Cloots. The devil: Scots coll (and Northern dial.): from the 1780s. Burns has both; Barham has *Clootie*. Ex *cloot*, a division of a hoof; the devil has a cloven foot.

close as God's curse to a whore's arse or **as shirt and shitted arse.** Very close indeed: mid-C.18–early 19 c.p. or proverb.

close as wax. Miserly; stingy; secretive: from ca 1770: coll till mid-C.19, then S.E. Cumberland, 1772; Charles Reade. cf. the S.E. *close-fitted* (C.17–20, regarded by B.E. as coll).

close call. A near thing; an incident almost fatal: coll: U.S. (1880s) anglicized in late 1890s.

***close file.** A secretive or uncommunicative person: c. or low, from ca 1820; ob. FILE (cf. BLADE) = a man.

close in. Shut up: C.14–17; coll. soon S.E.

close one's dead-lights. To 'bung up' one's eyes: nautical: ca 1820–1910. Egan's Grose.

close thing. A narrow escape; an even contest. Coll > S.E.: late C.19–20. cf. CLOSE CALL.

Closh. Collective for Dutch seamen: mid-C.18–early 19. Ex Dutch *Klaas*, abbr. *Nicolaas*, a favourite Christian name in Holland. 2. Hence, a seaman from the Eastern counties of England: nautical: mid-C.19–20. Bowen.

cloth. One's profession: C.17–19; coll > S.E. in C.18. Esp. *the cloth*: the Church; clergymen: C.18–20; coll. Swift, 1701; Dickens, 1836, of another profession, 'This 'ere song's personal to the cloth.' 2. Also, from ca 1860 and coll, the office of a clergyman.

cloth, cut one's coat according to the. To act in sane accordance with the circumstances; esp., to live within one's means. Mid-C.16–20. Coll till C.18, then S.E.

cloth in the wind, shake (occ. **have**) **a.** To be slightly drunk: nautical; from ca 1810; ob. cf. SHEETS IN THE WIND.

cloth is all of another hue, the. That's a very different story: proverbial coll: C.15–17. cf. HORSE OF ANOTHER COLOUR.

cloth market. (Or with capitals). Bed. Late C.17–19: coll. (gen. with *the*). Ray, 1678; Swift. cf. BEDFORDSHIRE.

clothes-line, able to sleep (up)on a. Capable of sleeping in difficult place or position; hence, able to rough it, to look after oneself. Coll; from ca 1840.

clothes-pegs. Legs: rhyming s.: late C.19–20.

clothes-pin I am, that's the sort of. That's me! That's my nature. (Of men only.) Coll; from ca 1865.

clothes sit on her like a saddle on a sow's back, her. A late C.17–mid-18 c.p. applied to an ill-dressed woman.

cloud. Tobacco smoke. Late C.17–early 19 (cf. BLOW A CLOUD). B.E. gives it as tobacco, but his example shows that he means either tobacco being smoked or, more prob., tobacco smoke.

cloud, under a. As = out of favour, or in difficulties other than monetary, S.E.; as = in disgrace, coll in C.16–17, then S.E.

cloud-cleaner. Nautical of mid-C.19–20 (ob.). 'An imaginary cloud jokingly assumed to be carried by Yankee ships', Clark Russell.

cloud-compeller. A smoker, esp. of tobacco: from ca 1860: jocular-pedantic >, ca 1880, coll. (Like *cloud-assembler*, this is a Homeric epithet for Zeus.)

clouds, in the. Fantastic; fanciful; metaphysical. Also as adv. In C.17, coll; then S.E.

cloudy. In disgrace or disrepute; SHADY, 2: coll: 1886, Stevenson; ob. cf. *murky*.

clout. A heavy blow: M.E. onwards. S.E. until ca 1850, when it > low coll and dial.; indeed it was far from literary after ca 1770 (see Grose). 2. A handkerchief (unless of silk): the S.O.D. implies that this is S.E., but Jonson's *Gipsies*, B.E., John Hall's *Memoirs*, Fielding's *Jonathan Wild*, Grose (edd. of 1785–1811), Brandon, and H. tend to show that, from ca 1600, it was low coll verging on c. 3. A woman's sanitary towel: low coll, C.19–20, ob.

clout, v. To strike (a person) heavily: M.E. onwards; S.E. until ca 1850, when it > low coll and dial. cf. sense 1 of the n.

clout, wash one's face in an ale. To get drunk: coll (jocular): C.16–17.

clout-shoe, clouted shoe. A yokel; a boor:

ca 1580–1750: coll. cf. Spenser's *Colin Clout.*

***clouter.** A pickpocket; one specializing in handkerchiefs: c. (—1839); ob. 2. vbl n., *clouting.*

clouting. A thrashing or a cuffing: see CLOUT, v. 2. See:

***clouting lay.** The stealing of handkerchiefs from people's pockets: late C.18–19 c. Occ. abbr. to *clouting.*

clouts. A woman's underclothes, from the waist down. Also, her complete wardrobe. Low coll: C.19–20; ob.

cloven, occ. **cleaved** or **cleft,** ppl adj., spuriously virgin: C.18–early 19. cf. CLEFT, n.

clover, in. (Gen. with *be* or *live.*) In great comfort; luxuriously; in pleasant and most welcome safety or security: C.18–20: coll >, in late C.19, S.E. Ex cattle in clover.

clow. (Pronounced *clo.*) A box on the ear. Winchester College: C.19. Perhaps on the auditory analogy of *bout – bow, lout – low,* as F. & H. suggests. Also, v.t.

***clows.** (Gen. as pl.) A rogue: late C.17–18 c. Perhaps cognate with:

***cloy, cloye.** A thief; a robber: C.18–early 19 c. cf.:

***cloy, cligh, cly,** to steal, is – like its derivatives – c., not s.: C.17–early 19. cf. C.16–17 S.E. *cloyne,* cheat or grab.

***cloyer.** A thief habitually claiming a share of profits from young sharpers: C.17 c. 2. Also in c., the less specialized sense: a thief, a pickpocket: mid-C.17–early 19.

club. The *membrum virile*: low: C.19. 2. A very thick pigtail: coll; 1760–1920; S.E. after ca 1800. 3. Short for *benefit club*: coll; from ca 1880. *To be on the club* is to receive financial help from a benefit club.

club, v. (Of an officer) to get one's men into an inextricable position by confusing the order: from ca 1805: coll > S.E. by 1890. Thackeray, Whyte-Melville.

club-fist. A man rough and brutal: late C.16–17; coll > S.E. by 1620.

club-land. The social district of which St James's (London) is the centre: coll; from ca 1870.

clubbability. The possession of qualities fitting a person to be a member of a club: coll: from ca 1875.

clubs are trump(s). Brute force rules, or is to rule, the day: coll in C.19–20; S.E. in late C.16–18. Punning the card-suit.

clump. A heavy blow, gen. with the hand: mid-C.19–20: coll (mostly Cockney) and dial. 2. Incorrect for a *clamp*: C.19–20.

clump, v. To hit heavily: mid-C.19–20: coll and dial. The ppl adj. *clumping* = heavily walking.

clumper. A thick walking boot: coll, from ca 1875. Ex *clump,* an additional half-sole. 2. A heavy hitter: C.19–20: coll. Ex CLUMP, V.

clumperton. A countryman; a yokel; C.16–early 19; coll.

clumping, see CLUMP, V.

clumsy cleat. A wedge of wood against which a harpooner, for steadiness, braced his left knee: whalers' coll verging on j.

clumsy Dick. An awkward and/or clumsy fellow: non-aristocratic coll (—1887); ob.

***clush.** Easy, simple; 'cushy': c.: from ca 1840; ob. by 1880, †by 1900. Etymology?

clutch-fist. A miser: C.17–20; coll till ca 1800, then S.E. adj., *clutch-fisted,* as in B.E.

clutter. A crowded confusion, a mess or litter: in C.17–early 19, S.E.; then coll and dial. A variant of *clotter* (ex *clot*). Whence:

clutter, v. To litter confusedly and abundantly: ca 1670–1840, S.E.; now coll and U.S.

***cly.** A pocket; a purse; money: c., ?and low: late C.17–19. Indubitably c. is the late C.17–early 19 sense, money. So is FILE *a cly,* late C.17–18, to pick a pocket. As mid-C.16–18 v., to seize, take, to pocket, to steal: c., ?and low. See CLOY, n. and v.

cly, fake a, see FAKE A CLY.

***cly-faker.** A pickpocket: c. (—1812); ob. 2. Hence the vbl n., *cly-faking* (—1851); ob.

***cly off.** To carry off, away: C.17 (?18) c. Brome in his *Jovial Crew.*

***cly the gerke** or **jerk.** To receive a whipping, a lashing: c. of ca 1550–1850. See *cly the* JERK.

***clye.** A C.16–17 variant of CLY. ***clyme,** see CLEYME.

clyster-pipe. A doctor: C.17. 2. An apothecary: C.18–early 19. Both senses are low coll, the latter in Grose. Ex S.E. for a syringe.

***co.** (Also **coe.**) A shortening of *cofe* or COVE. 2. **Co.** or **coy,** so pronounced, is a sol. for *company*: early C.19–20. Esp., . . . *and Co.,* and the rest of them: coll: from ca 1880. 3. **co-,** where used jocularly, is either pedantic or coll, according to circumstances. 4. **in co;** esp. *act in co,* to be leagued together: coll (—1817); ob.

co, join; co, part. To join (the) company; to part company: since ca 1810.

co-op; co-op store. A co-operative store: the longer form, early 1870s; the shorter, early 1880s. Also a co-operative society: from early 1890s.

coach. A private tutor: at first (1848, says S.O.D.) a university word, orig. Cambridge; s., says Frank Smedley in *Frank Fairleigh*, 1850; but very soon coll. If not connected with a college, he was, until ca 1880, known as a *rural coach*. 2. As a trainer of athletes (1885), a coll now almost S.E. Whichever of CAB, a CRIB, and *coach* is the earliest, that one presumably suggested the others: since *cab* comes ex CABBAGE, the earliest is prob. *cab*.

coach, v. To travel, go, in a coach: coll: C.17–20; ob. Occ. with *it*. 2. To prepare (a pupil), teach him privately: from ca 1848; s. soon coll: orig. university, as in Thackeray. 3. To train athletes: from ca 1880; coll. 4. v.i., to read or study with a private tutor: from ca 1849; s. > coll.

coach-fellow, occ. **-companion.** A companion, fellow worker, mate: jocularly coll: ca 1590–1800. Shakespeare, in *The Merry Wives*, 'You, and your Coach-fellow Nim'.

coach-wheel. A crown piece: late C.17–20; ob. In late C.17–19, *fore c.-w.*, half a crown; *hind c.-w.*, a crown.

coach-whip. A Navy pennant: nautical: from ca 1890. cf. DUSTER, 2.

coachee, coachie, coachy. A coachman; late C.18–20; ob. Coll. Thomas Moore, 1819, in *Tom Crib's Memorial*, in form *coaches*.

coaches won't run over him, the. He is in gaol: coll (—1813); †by 1900. Ray, 1813. cf. *where the* FLIES WON'T GET AT IT.

coaching. Private instruction (actively or passively): from ca 1845. Coll. 2. (Rugby School) a flogging: C.19; ob. by 1891. 3. The obtaining of high auction prices by means of fictitious bidders: commercial (—1866); ob.

coachman on the box. Syphilis: rhyming s. (on POX): from ca 1870.

coachy, n., see COACHEE.

coachy, adj. Resembling a coach horse: coll (—1870). 2. Concerned with coaches or coach-driving: from ca 1880; coll.

***coal,** money: see COLE.

coal-box. A chorus: W. N. Glascock, *Sailors and Saints* (II, 119), 1829, '"Now, my boys, reg'lar coal-box."' Earlier in his *Sketch-Book*, II, 1826. It derives ex the din made by a coal-box being vigorously shaken.

coal-hole, a. Work down in the coal-hole, often given as punishment to a working hand: *Conway* Training Ship: from ca 1890.

coal-sack. Cul-de-sac: sol. (—1909). 2. (Gen. pl.) A dark patch of cloud near the Milky Way: nautical: mid-C.19–20.

coal-scuttle (bonnet), n. and adj. A poke bonnet: from ca 1830; ob., the fashion being outmoded by 1880 – if not earlier. Dickens, in *Nicholas Nickleby*, '... Miss Snevellici ... glancing from the depths of her coal-scuttle bonnet at Nicholas'.

coal up. To eat (heartily): stokers' (—1909); slightly ob.

coal-whipper. A dock coal-heaver: nautical: C.19. Bowen, 'Unloading ... by jumping off a staging in the days of primitive equipment'.

coaler. A coal-heaver: coll (—1887) verging on S.E. cf. COALY.

coaley, coalie, see COALY.

coaling or **coally.** (Of a part) effective, pleasant to the actor: from ca 1850, ob. Also, fond of, partial to: ca 1870–1910, e.g. Miss Braddon in *Dead Sea Fruit*. Theatrical.

coals, blow or **stir the.** To cause trouble between two parties: coll; resp. C.17–20, C.16–18; ob. Both soon > S.E.

coals, call or **fetch** or **haul over the.** To call to task; reprimand; address severely: coll, resp. C.19–20, late C.16–18, late C.18–20. Ex the treatment once meted out to heretics. See also HAUL, v., 2.

coals, carry no. To be unlikely to be imposed on, swindled, or tamely insulted: coll: C.16–19. B.E., whose definition is somewhat more racy. A C.16–17 variant, as in Skelton, is *bear no coals*.

coals, let him that hath need blow the. 'Let him Labour that wants,' B.E.; also, stop no man from working. Coll and proverbial: C.17–18.

coals!, precious, see PRECIOUS COALS!

coals, take in one's (or one's winter). To catch a venereal disease: nautical, C.19.

coals to Newcastle, carry. To do something ludicrously superfluous: late C.16–20, being coll till ca 1830, then S.E. Heywood, Fuller, Scott.

coaly, coaley, coalie. A coal-heaver or -porter: from ca 1810.

coast; coaster. To LOAF, a LOAFER, about from station to station: Australian coll (—1890); ob.

coat, baste or **coil** or **pay a person's.** To beat him: C.16–18: coll. cf. DUST ONE'S CASSOCK.

coat ..., cut one's, see CLOTH ...

coat, get the sun into a horse's. To allow a horse to rest from formal racing; hence, (of a trainer) to save oneself trouble: racing, from ca 1880; †. *Standard*, 25 or 26 June 1889: a forensic speech by Sir Charles Russell.

coat, turn one's. To desert one's cause or party: mid-C.16–19: coll >, by 1800, S.E.

coat, wear the King's. To serve as a soldier: from ca 1750; coll till C.19, when S.E.

coax. One who coaxes, or is skilled in coaxing: coll: from ca 1860. Ouida.

coax, v. To hide a dirty or torn part of one's stocking in one's shoes: mid-C.18–early 19; coll. 2. Hence, to deface or alter (a service-certificate): nautical: mid-C.19–20.

cob. A chignon: coll: ca 1865–1914. 2. (Winchester College, ca 1870–1903) a hard hit at cricket. Ex COB, v., 1. 3. In c., a punishment cell: from ca 1860; ob. 4. A testicle: low: late C.19–20.

cob, cobb, v. To strike, esp. on the buttocks with something flat (gen. a hand-saw, says Hotten): nautical (—1769). Marryat in *The King's Own*: 'Gentlemen, gentlemen, if you must cobb Mrs Skrimmage, for God's sake *let it be over all*,' i.e. with no clothes raised. Prob. echoic. 2. Hence, to HUMBUG, deceive: coll, C.19–20, ob., perhaps influenced by COD, v. 3. To detect, catch: schoolboys', C.19. A variant of COP, v.

Cobb, by. By coach: Australian coll: from 1870s; slightly ob. The Cobb who started a system of coaches long before 1860 was an American.

cobber. A great lie: C.19–20, ob. cf. THUMPER. 2. A friend, comrade, companion: Australians': C.20. A trustworthy correspondent (a writing man) tells me that he heard it among racing-men of the lower sort in the year 1900. Ex Yiddish *chaber*, a comrade. See *Words!*, pp. 27–8.

cobbing, vbl n. cf. COB, v., 1.

cobble. To detect; catch: schoolboys': C.19. Ex COB, v., 3.

***cobble-colter.** A turkey, late C.17–18 c., was resuscitated by Disraeli in *Venetia*, his most picaresque novel. *Cobble* = *gobble*.

cobbler. A drink of wine mixed with lemon-juice, sugar, and ice, gen. taken through a straw: coll; from ca 1840; ex U.S. ?short for *sherry-cobbler*; cf. *cobbler's* PUNCH; perhaps, however, 'as patching up the constitution', W. 2. The last sheep to be shorn: Australian: from ca 1890. Ex *the cobbler's last*.

cobbler's awls. Testicles: low rhyming s. ON BALLS: late C.19–20.

cobbler's door, knock at the; give the cobbler's knock. In sliding or, less often, in skating, to rap the ice in series of three taps with one foot while one moves rapidly on the other. This rapping is occ. called *the postman's knock*. Dickens in *Pickwick Papers*. Coll; from ca 1820.

cobbler's marbles. Sol. for *cholera morbus*, itself catachrestic for malignant or Asiatic cholera: from ca 1860; ob.

cobbler's punch, see PUNCH, COBBLER'S.

Cob's body(, by). In oaths, a coll corruption of *God's body*: C.18.

cobweb, in late C.17–early 18, seems to have been coll for transparent or flimsy: B.E. cites *cobweb cheat*, a swindler easily detected, and *cobweb pretence*.

cobweb in the throat, have a. To feel thirsty: coll: from ca 1830. 2. Hence, *cobweb throat*, a dry throat after drinking liquor: late C.19–20.

cocam. An occ. form of COCUM.

cochineal dye. Blood: pugilistic; ca 1850–1910. 'Cuthbert Bede', 1853: 'He would kindly inquire of one gentleman, "What d'ye ask for a pint of your cochineal dye?"' For semantics, cf. BORDEAUX and CLARET.

cock. The penis. Nathaniel Fields, *Amends for Ladies*, 1618, 'O man, what art thou when thy cock is up?' cf. F. & H.'s example from Beaumont & Fletcher's scabrous play, *The Custom of the Country*. Always S.E. but since ca 1830 a vulg. Prob. ex *cock*, a tap. 2. A plucky fighter; hence, a coll term of appreciation or address. Massinger, in 1639, has 'He has drawn blood of him yet: well done, old cock.' 3. As chief or leader, despite the coll tang of *cock of the walk*, *the school*, etc., it has, since 1800 in any case, been S.E., the term arising in early C.15. 4. A horse not intended to run or, if running, to win: racing; from ca 1840; ob. 5. In boxing, *a cock* = out, senseless, as in 'He knocked him a regular cock' or simply '. . . a cock', where the term > an adv.: ca 1820–1920, but ob. by 1900. 6. A fictitious narrative sold as a broadsheet in the streets: low coll, recorded by Mayhew in 1851 but prob. in use as early as 1840; †by 1900. From ca 1860 it derivatively meant any incredible story, as in the *London Figaro*, 1 Feb. 1870, 'We are disposed to think that cocks must have penetrated to Eastern Missouri.' Prob. ex COCK-AND-BULL STORY: mid-C.19–20. 7. In c., abbr. COCKNEY. 8. Among printers, a cock ensues when, in gambling with quads, a player receives another chance by causing one or more of the nine pieces to fall, not as desired but crosswise on another: from ca 1860. 9. Among tailors, from ca 1840, a *good cock* is a good, a *bad cock* a bad workman. 10. In ancient oaths, *cock* = God. 11. See OLD COCK. 12. See COCKS.

cock, v. To smoke (v.t.): C.19. cf. BROSELEY. 2. To copulate with, but gen. in the passive: low coll, C.19–20, ob. Whence vbl n., *cocking*, and cf. (*with*) *a cock in her eye*: sexually desirous. 3. To see, examine; speak of: gen. as *cock it*: tailors', from ca 1850; ob.

cock, adj. Ex the n., 3: chief; foremost: coll; from ca 1660; ob. Etherege, in *The Man of Mode*, 'The very cock-fool of all those fools, Sir Fopling Flutter'.

***cock-a-brass.** App. this c. term belongs to C.18–19. B. & L., 'A confederate of card-sharpers who remains outside the public-house where they are operating. When they have left, *cock-a-brass* protects their retreat by misleading statements to the victim on the direction taken by them.'

cock-a-bully. The gray (fish): New Zealand coll (—1896). A corruption of the Maori name, *kokopu*.

cock-a-doodle. A DONKEY-DROP: schoolboys': ca 1880–1910. Ex its 'high note'.

cock-a-doodle broth. Beaten eggs in brandy and water: 1856; very ob. (Very strengthening.)

cock-a-doodle(-doo). Nursery and jocular for a cock: C.18–20. Echoic ex its crow (1573, O.E.D.).

cock-a-hoop (incorrectly *-whoop*). From ca 1660: coll, in C.20 S.E.: in C.17–early 19, 'upon the high Ropes, Rampant, Transported' (B.E.), but only predicative or complementary; ca 1830 it > an ordinary adj. Ex the earlier *set* (*the*) *cock on* (*the*) *hoop* or, as in Shakespeare, *set cock-a-hoop*, which Ray explains by the practice of removing the cock or spigot, laying it on the hoop, i.e. on the top, of a barrel, and then drinking the barrel dry.

cock-a-loft. 'Affectedly lofty', O.E.D.: coll: from ca 1860; ob. Ex COCK-LOFT.

cock a snook, see COCK SNOOKS.

cock-a-wax; occ. cock-o-wax. A cobbler: ca 1800–50. Lit., a fellow working with wax. 2. Hence, anyone familiarly addressed: ca 1820–1900: coll. It occurs in Wm Maginn, *Whitehall* (p. 87), 1827, thus, 'What will you drink, my cock-of-wax, my Trojan, true as ever whistled.' Ex COCK, n., 2. Variant LAD O'WAX.

cock-ale. A strong ale: 'pleasant drink, said to be provocative', remarks B.E.: coll; ca 1680–1830.

cock-alley. Also *c.-hall*, *-inn*, *-lane*, *-pit*, and *Cockshire*. All low coll: C.18–20, the second and the third being †, the fifth and sixth ob. *Pudendum muliebre*. Ex COCK, 1.

cock-and-breeches. A sturdy boy, a small but sturdy man: low coll: from ca 1830; ob.

cock-and-bull story. In this form from ca 1700; as *story* or *tale of a cock and bull* from ca 1608: coll, passing ca 1850 to S.E. At first, a long rambling tale, then (C.18–20) an idle, silly or incredible story. John Day in *Law Tricks*, Sterne in *Tristram Shandy*, Mrs Henry Wood in *Henry Ludlow*. cf. the Fr. *coq-à-l'âne*, an irrelevance, an incongruous change of subject.

***cock and hen.** A £10 note: thieves' and low rhyming s.: from ca 1870. *Slang*, p. 243.

cock-and-hen. (Gen. with *club*, occ. with *house.*) adj.: admitting both sexes, for the once or constitutionally: coll; from ca 1815. Moore in *Tom Crib's Memorial*.

cock and (by) pie!, by. A mild oath: coll: mid-C.16–mid-19. Thackeray. Perhaps *Cock*, God + *pie*, a Roman Catholic ordinal.

cock-and-pinch. The beaver hat affected by dandies of ca 1820–30; †by 1900. Coll. (*Cock*ed back and front *and pinch*ed up at the sides.)

cock-bawd. A man keeping a brothel: ca 1680–1830: low coll.

cock-billed. With yards crooked as a sign of mourning: nautical: late C.19–20. cf. A-COCKBILL.

cock-brain. A silly light-headed person: late C.16–18; coll. adj., *cock-brained*.

cock-catching, see CATCH COCKS.

cock-chafer or **-teaser.** A girl or a woman permitting – and assuming – most of the intimacies but not the greatest: low coll (the latter term is far the commoner): *c.-c.*, C.19; *c.-t.*, C.19–20. Ex COCK, n., 1. 2. Also low coll is *c.-c.* = the *pudendum muliebre*, C.19–20, while, 3, in c. of ca 1860–90, it = the treadmill; the latter (H., 2nd ed.) is unhyphenated.

cock-cheese. Smegma: low: late C.19–20.

cock-eye. A squinting-eye: recorded in 1825; *cock-eyed*, squinting: Byron, 1821. Both are coll. Hence, 2, *cock-eye* and *cock-eyed*, from ca 1895, = crooked; inaccurate; inferior. Lit., like a tilted eye.

cock-eyed, see COCK-EYE, 2.

cock-fighting, beat. To be very good or delightful; to excel: coll, C.19–20, though foreshadowed in Gauden's *Tears of the Church*, 1659.

cock-hall, see COCK-ALLEY.

cock-hoist. A cross-buttock: late C.18–early 19: coll till C.19, then j.

cock-horse. Elated, COCK-A-HOOP, in full swing: ca 1750–1870; coll. Ex (*ride*) *a cock-horse*, a child's improvised horse.

Cock Inn. The female pudend: low: C.19–20; ob. cf. *Cupid's Arms* (at HOTEL) and see COCK-ALLEY.

cock-lane, see COCK-ALLEY.

cock-linnet. A minute: rhyming s. (—1909). 2. A dapper lad: East London (—1909).

cock-loft. The head: mid C.17–18; coll. Fuller, 1646 (Apperson). Lit., a garret; cf. the proverbial *all his gear is in his cock-loft* and GARRET and UPPER STOREY.

cock-maggot in a sink-hole, like a. Very annoyed or peevish: proletarian coll (—1887); slightly ob.

cock-my-cap. Some kind of strong liquor fashionable in the 1720s. Anon., *The Quaker's Opera*, 1728. See quotation at BUNTER'S TEA.

cock-o-wax, see COCK-A-WAX.

cock one's chest. The naval equivalent (—1909) of CHUCK A CHEST.

cock one's toes (up). To die: from ca 1860; slightly ob. cf. the much more gen. *turn up one's* TOES.

cock-pimp. A supposed, rarely an actual, husband to a bawd; i.e. a harlot's bully: late C.17–18 coll.

cock-pit, cockpit, the. A Dissenters' meeting house: late C.18–early 19. 2. The Treasury; the Privy Council: a London coll; from ca 1870. Ex an old Whitehall *cockpit*. 3. See COCK-ALLEY.

cock-quean. A man concerning himself unduly in women's affairs: either a sol. or a jocular perversion of *cotquean*: ca 1830–80.

cock-robin. A soft, easy fellow: coll: from ca 1690; ob. Montagu Williams, *Leaves of a Life*, 1890.

cock-robin shop. A small printery: printers', from late 1850s; ob.

cock-shot. Anything set up as a target; a shot thereat: coll: resp. ca 1840, 1880.

cock-shut. Twilight (also an adj.): coll > S.E. > dial. Recorded in 1598, 1594: 'perhaps the time when poultry are shut up', S.O.D.

cock-shy. Coll; in C.20 verging on S.E. Cock throwing and similar games: mid-C.19–20. Mayhew. 2. A free SHY at a target: from mid-1830s. 3. The missile: rare and ob.: from late 1830s. 4. The target (lit. or fig.): 1836. 5. A showman's cock-shy booth, etc.: from late 1870s. 6. *cock-shying*: see 1 and 2: late 1870s.

cock-smitten. Enamoured of men: low coll, C.19–20.

cock snooks or a snook. To put one's fingers derisively to nose: coll; late C.19–20. See SIGHT, n., 5.

cock-sparrow. A barrow: rhyming s.: late C.19–20.

cock-stand. A priapism: a vulg.: C.18–20.

cock-sucker. A toady: low coll: C.19–20. Mostly (?orig.) U.S.

cock-sure. Feeling quite certain (from ca 1660): dogmatically sure of oneself (from ca 1750). Coll till ca 1890, then S.E. Semantics obscure; perhaps ex the action of a *cock* or water-tap; perhaps a euphemism for *God-sure* (W.) – cf. COCK (10) for *God* in oaths. cf. COCKALORUM, COCKING, and COCKY, adj., 2.

cock-tail. A harlot: low coll; C.19–20, ob. 2. A person of energy and promptness but not a 'thoroughbred': from ca 1855; coll. Ex racing j. Hence, 3, a coward: coll; from ca 1860. 4. A whisked drink of spirits, occ. wine, with bitters, crushed ice, etc.: orig. (1809), U.S.; anglicized ca 1870. In senses 3 and 4, the usual spelling is *cocktail*.

cock-tail, -tailed, adj. Unsoldierly; guilty of 'bad form': military, ca 1880–1914. Either ex the n., 2nd and 3rd senses, or ex *turn cock-tail*, i.e. to cock the tail, turn, and run.

cock-tax. Alimony: Australian: since ca 1850.

cock-teaser, see COCK-CHAFER.

cock the eye. To wink; leer; look incredulous or knowing: from ca 1750: coll until ca 1800, then S.E. Smollett, in *Peregrine Pickle*, 1751, 'He . . . made wry faces, and, to use the vulgar phrase, cocked his eye at him.' (*Cock an eye* is merely to glance.) cf. *cock the nose*, (S.E. for) to turn it up in contempt.

cock-up. (Printers') a superior, i.e. a

superior letter, as the *o* in N^o; from ca 1860.

cock (up) one's toes. To die: c. and low; from early C.19. 'Fancy' Reynolds.

cock won't fight!, that. That won't do! That's a feeble story! Tell that to the MARINES! From the 1820s †: coll Scott, *St Roman's Well*, 1824. Ex the cock-pit.

cockalorum, occ. **cockylorum.** A very confident little man: coll: 1715. Often as slightly contemptuous vocative. As adj., self-confident or -important: 1884+. Ex *cock*, a leader (see COCK, n., 2, 3), pseudo-L. *orum*; cf. COCK-A-DOODLE-DOO.

cockalorum (jig), hey or **high.** A coll exclamation: from ca 1800; ob. Prob. ex an old song-refrain. – As a schoolboys' game (leap-frog), S.E.

cockatoo. A small farmer: orig. in the wool districts and by the big squatters: from ca 1863. Australian: coll. Henry Kingsley in *Hillyars and Burtons*, 'The small farmers contemptuously called cockatoos'. Like cockatoos, they try to live off a small piece of land.

cockatoo, v. To be a (small) farmer: coll (—1890). Boldrewood. Ex n.

cockatoo fence. A fence made by a small farmer: Australian coll (—1884). Boldrewood in *Melbourne Memories*.

cockatooer. A COCKATOO: Tasmanian: ca 1850–80.

cockatrice. A harlot; a kept woman: late C.16–18. Coll. Ben Jonson in *Cynthia's Revels*; Marston in his most famous work, *The Malcontent*: 'No courtier but has his mistress, no captain but has his cockatrice'; Taylor, 1630; Killigrew. 2. A baby: coll: C.18–19. Resp. ex the fascination of the fabulous monster's eye, and the egg from which it was fabulously hatched.

***cockchafer,** see COCK-CHAFER, 3.

cocked hat, knock into a. To damage very considerably (things, persons, and fig.): coll; from ca 1850. Orig. (1833: Thornton), U.S. An officer's cocked hat could be doubled up and carried flat.

cocker. A foreman: tailors': from ca 1860. 2. A coll Cockney term of address, dating from ca 1870; ob. Clarence Rook, *The Hooligan Nights*, 1899. An extension (influenced by COCKY, 3) of S.E. *cocker*, a supporter of cock-fighting.

Cocker, according to, see at ACCORDING TO COCKER.

cockie, see COCKY, 1, 3.

cockies' joy. Treacle: Australian: late 19–20. See COCKY, 5.

cockily. In a cocky manner: coll; from ca 1860.

cockiness. Conceit; undue self-assertion: coll: from early 1860s.

cocking. Pert; impudent: ca 1670–1830; coll. The *Spectator*, 1711, 'The cocking young fellow'.

cocking a chest like a half-pay admiral. Putting on SIDE: naval: late C.19–20.

cockish. 'Wanton, uppish, forward', B.E.: C.16–20: coll > S.E. ca 1800. As = lecherous it is applied gen. to women and, except in dial., it > ob. ca 1860.

cockles. (Always in pl.) *Labia minora*: C.18–20; low coll. *Play at hot cockles* – see Northall's *English Folk-Rhymes* – is, in addition to its S.E. sense, *feminam digitis subagitare*: C.18–20, low coll, ob.

cockles, cry. To be hanged: late C.18–mid-19: low. Ex the gurgling of strangulation.

cockles of the heart, rejoice, warm, tickle the. To please mightily, cheer up: coll; from ca 1669. Eachard, in his *Observations*, 1671, 'This contrivance of his did inwardly rejoice the cockles of his heart.' The S.O.D. mentions the proposed derivation ex the similarity of a heart to a cockle-shell and that ex *cardium*, the zoological name for a cockle; F. & H. refers to Lower's once famous *Tractatus de Corde* (*A Treatise of the Heart*), 1669, where the term *cochlea* is used. The first is the likeliest.

cockloche. (App. =) a foolish coxcomb: C.17. ?ex Fr. *coqueluche*.

cockney or **Cockney,** n. and adj. (One) born in the city of London: 1600+. Coll till ca 1830 and nearly always pejorative. Orig. and until ca 1870, 'born within the sound of Bow-bell', B.E. Ex *cockney* = a milksop, earlier a cockered, i.e. pampered, child, a sense that developed from (?) *cock's eggs*, small eggs. The full history of this fascinating word has not yet been written, but see esp. O.E.D., Sir James Murray in *The Academy* of 10 May 1890; also W. and Grose, P. For an account of Cockney 'dialect', see *Slang*, pp. 149–59.

Cockney's luxury. Breakfast in bed and defecation in a chamber-pot; in the truly Cockney idiom, *breakfast in bed and a shit in the pot*, which is often added to – indeed, constitutes the original form of – the c.p.: late C.19–20. Dating from the days of backyard privies.

Cockney-shire. London: C.19–20, ob.; coll.

Cockoolu, see MOUNSEER.

cockpit mess. Eating one's meals in the cockpit with a marine sentry at hand – a punishment in the old training ship *Britannia*: naval: late C.19–early 20.

cockroaches, get, see BOX THE JESUIT...

cocks. (In trade, applied to) anything fictitious: ca 1860–1910. Ex COCK, n., 6. 2. Hence, esp., concoctions: pharmaceutists' (—1909). 3. At Charterhouse (school), a gen. lavatory: from ca 1860; ob. Ex the taps over the wash-bowls. See esp. A. H. Tod, *Charterhouse*, 1900.

cock's egg, give one a. To send on a fool's errand, esp. on April the First. Coll: rare before C.19, and ob. in C.20. cf. MILK THE PIGEON, *strap-oil* (at STRAP 'EM), and see *All Fools' Day* in *Words!*

cock's tooth and head-ache, I live at the sign of the. A late C.18–early 19 c.p. answer to an impertinent inquiry where one lives.

Cockshire, see COCK-ALLEY.

cocksy, coxy. Pert; impudent; bumptious: 1825: (mostly schoolboys') coll. Ex COCKY after *tricksy*. For second spelling, cf. COXCOMB ex *cock's-comb*.

cocksy fuss. 'Billing and cooing', *Sinks*: ca 1825–80.

cocktail, see COCK-TAIL, esp. sense 4.

cocky. An endearment: coll: from ca 1680; ob., except among Canadians and Cockneys. Ex (OLD) COCK. 2. adj., very pert; saucily impudent; over-confident: 1768: coll (cf. COCKING). Hughes in *Tom Brown's School-Days*, 'It seems so cocky in me to be advising you.' 3. A low coll form of address, ex COCK: from ca 1730. 4. Brisk, active, as applied to the money market: Stock Exchange, ca 1860–1910. 5. Abbr. COCKATOO, a small farmer in Australia: from ca 1870.

cockylorum, see COCKALORUM.

cockyolly bird. Dear little bird: nursery and pet term (coll): from ca 1830.

cocky's joy, see COCKIES' JOY.

coconut (here, as in S.E., erroneously *cocoa-nut*); sol., *coker-nut*. The head: mainly boxing: from ca 1830. Ainsworth. cf. BOCO, and U.S. *coco(a)*.

coco(a)nut, have no milk in the. To lack brains; to be silly, even mad. From ca 1850. See COCONUT.

coco(a)nut, that accounts for the milk in the. A c.p. rejoinder on first hearing a thing explained: ca 1860–1910. Ex 'a clever but not very moral story', H., 5th ed. See COCONUT.

cocum (-am), cokum, kocum. Ability, shrewdness, cleverness; that which is seemly, right, correct; luck, advantage: rather low (—1851). Mayhew in *London Labour*; *The Flippity Flop Young Man*, a ballad, ca 1886. 2. A sliding scale of profit: publishers', ca 1870–1914. Ex Yiddish c. *kochem*, wisdom. cf.:

cocum, fight or **play.** To be cunning, wary, artful, esp. if illicitly: from late 1830s. Likewise, *have cocum*, to have luck or an advantage; be sure to succeed. Perhaps cognate with Ger. *gucken*, to peep or pry into; but see preceding entry.

cod. The scrotum: from M.E.; S.E., but in C.19–20 a vulg. Ex O.E., M.E., S.E. and dial. sense, a pod. 2. In pl, a sol. for testicles: also from M.E. 3. In c., a purse; whence *cod of money* = a large sum: late C.17–early 19. 4. A fool: from ca 1690; ob. Perhaps ex COD'S HEAD, also a fool: B.E. has both. *Sinks*, 1848, defines it as a 'haughty meddling fool'. 5. A friend, a PAL: from —1690, B.E. giving '*an honest Cod*, a trusty Friend'. Abbr. CODLING, says F. & H. with reason. 6. (Often as CODD) a pensioner of the Charterhouse: Charterhouse, ca 1820–1905. Thackeray in *The Newcomes*. Perhaps ex CODGER. 7. A drunkard; a drinking bout: tailors' (—1909). cf. n., 4, and COD, v., 2. 8. A foreman: builders': late C.19–20.

cod, v. To chaff; hoax; humbug; play the fool: v.t. and i.: from ca 1870. Ex COD, n., 4. 2. To go on a drinking or a womanizing spree: tailors'; from ca 1870; ob. 3. In C.18 c., to cheat.

cod, on the. Drinking heavily: tailors': late C.19–20. cf. COD, n., 7.

cod-banger. A gorgeously arrayed sailor: Billingsgate (—1909). Cod are banged on the head when wanted for market.

cod-hauler. A ship, or a man, from Newfoundland: nautical: mid-C.19–20. Ex the fisheries there.

cod-piece or collar?, do they bite in the (with slight variations). 'A jocular attack on a patient angler by watermen, &c.', Grose, 1st ed.: a mid-C.18–early 19 c.p. *Cod(-)piece*: fore-flap of a man's breeches, C.16–18.

Cod Preserves, the. The Atlantic Ocean: nautical: from ca 1840; ob.

cod-whanger. A man engaged in fish-curing in Newfoundland: nautical: late C.19–20. cf. COD-HAULER.

coddam, coddem, coddom. A public-house and extremely elementary guessing-game played with a coin or a button: from ca 1880; coll. i.e. *cod 'em*.

codder. One very fond of hoaxing or chaffing: from ca 1860. Ex COD, v., 1.

codding, vbl n. Chaff, humbug; fooling; nonsense: from ca 1860.

coddle. One who is coddled or who coddles himself: coll; —1830, when used by Miss Mitford in *Our Village*.

coddom, see CODDAM.

coddy. 'A temporary foreman over a stevedore's employees': nautical: late C.19–20. Bowen. He CODS 'em along.

coddy-moddy. A young gull: nautical: mid-C.19–20.

codger; occ. **coger.** (Whimsically pejorative of) an old man: low coll: 1756. Gen. with OLD, as in Colman's *Polly Honeycomb*, 'A clear coast, I find. The old codger's gone, and has locked me up with his daughter'; Smollett; Barham. 2. During the approximate period 1830–1900, it occ. = a FELLOW, a CHAP. Dickens. ?ex. *cadger*.

codling. A raw youth: ca 1600–1750; coll. In late C.18–early 19 (cf. C.19–20 ob. PIPPIN), a familiar term of address; an endearment.

codocity. Gullibility: printers': 1874; ob. Ex COD, n., 4, and v., 1.

cods. See COD, n., 2. 2. (cf. BALLOCKS.) A curate: mid-C.18–early 19 low. Often as *cods the curate*. 3. The *Bookseller*, 4 Nov. 1871: 'The Cods and Hooks were the Whigs and Tories of Dutch William's land.' 4. With variant *cod's*; a mid-C.16–early 18 perversion or corruption of *God's*.

cod's-head. A fool: ca 1560–1850. (Dunton in his ironically titled *Ladies Dict.*, 1694.) In mid-C.19–20 (ob.), as *cod's-head and shoulders*. Both forms are coll. Perhaps the source of COD = a fool.

cod's head and mackerel tail(, with). A sailing ship with the greatest beam well forward: nautical: mid-C.19–20; ob.

***coe,** see CO, 1.

coffee-and-b. Coffee and brandy: night-taverns': 1880; ob.

coffee-colour. (Applied to persons) of mixed parentage: Anglo-Indian coll (—1886). cf. ANNAS OF DARK BLOOD.

coffee-house. The *pudendum muliebre*: low: late C.18–19. Ex the popularity of coffee-houses in late C.17–18. 2. A water-closet (variant *coffee-shop*): late C.18–20, ob.

coffee-house, -houser, -housing. To gossip during a fox-hunt, esp. while the huntsmen wait for hounds to draw a covert; one who does this; the act of doing this: sporting: from ca 1875. Hawley Smart, in *Play or Pay*, ch. iv, 1878, speaking of horses: '... A hack, just good enough to do a bit of coffee-housing occasionally'.

coffee-mill. The mouth: ca 1800–70. Moncrieff, 'Come, come, silence your coffee-mill.' 2. A marine engine: nautical: late C.19–20.

coffee-mill, grind the (or **work the**). See *take a* GRINDER.

coffee-milling, vbl n. GRINDING, working hard. Dickens, 1837. Aytoun & Martin's 'coffee-milling care and sorrow' illustrates *c.-m.* as a v., to thumb one's nose at. i.e. *take a* GRINDER. Both ca 1830–1900.

coffee-pot. One of the former small tank-engines of the Midland Railway: railwaymen's: late C.19–20; ob.

coffee royal. 'The first mug of coffee in the morning under sail': nautical: late C.19–20. Bowen.

coffee-shop. See COFFEE-HOUSE, 2. 2. A coffin: proletarian: from ca 1880.

coffin-brig. An overweighted 10-gun brig: naval: early C.19. 2. Hence, any unseaworthy vessel: mid-C.19–early 20.

coffin-nail. A cigarette: from ca 1885.

***cog.** Money; esp. a piece of money: C.16–mid-18 c., mostly gamesters'. cf. DROP-GAME.

cog, v. To cheat, wheedle; beg: C.16–mid-19. Orig. either dicing s. or gen. coll: cf. B.E.'s *cog a dinner*, 'to wheedle a Spark out of a dinner'. The S.O.D., like the O.E.D., considers wholly S.E. Perhaps ex *cog*, a wheel. 2. Hence, v.i., to cheat by copying from another: Scottish Public-Schools': mid-C.19–early 20. 3. v.i., to agree well with another, as cog with cog: C.19; coll. (Running like cogs.) 4. 'In school slang, to chastise by sundry bumpings or "coggings" on the posteriors for delinquencies at certain games,' E.D.D., 1898.

cog over. To crib from another's book: schoolboys', C.19. cf. COG, v., 2.

coger, see CODGER. **cogey,** see COGUEY.

coggage; coggidge. Paper; writing paper; a newspaper: Regular Army coll: mid-C.19–20. Ex Hindustani *kaghaz*.

cogging, the cogging of dice, may orig. (—1532) have been c. or low s. G. Harvey in *Four Letters*.

***cogman.** A beggar pretending to be a shipwrecked sailor: c.: C.19.

cogue (occ. **cog**) **the nose.** To take, hot, a

good strong drink: nautical; C.19–20; ob. Ex *cogue*, to drink brandy, drink drams.

coguey. Drunk: ca 1820–60. Ex *cogue*, a dram. It is recorded in Staffordshire dial., as *cogy*, in 1816: E.D.D.

coigne. Money: printers' (—1909). Ware, 'A play upon coin and coigne or coin, or quoin, a wedge'.

coil up one's cables or **ropes.** To die: nautical: mid-C.19–20. Ex SLIP ONE'S CABLE.

coin, post the. (cf. *tip the* COLE.) To deposit money for a match: for a bet: sporting, ca 1840–1900.

coin money. To make money both easily and quickly: from ca 1860: coll. cf.:

coiny. Rich: coll: from ca 1890. cf. preceding and TINNY, adj.

coke, go and eat. Oh, run away! Pejorative coll: ca 1870–1920. F. & H. cites as a variant, *go and shit cinders.*

Coke upon Littleton. A mixed drink of brandy and text (a red Spanish wine): ca 1740–1800. Ex the famous legal textbook.

***coker.** A lie: ca 1670–1830; c. > low s. Coles, 1676; B.E.; Grose (=CAULKER). cf. CORKER: undetermined cognates. 2. C.19–20 sol. for *coco*, esp. in *coker-nut*.

coker-nut, see COCONUT. 2. In pl, 'Well-developed feminine breasts': low London (—1909). Ware.

cokes. A fool, a simpleton: ca 1560–1700. B.E. indicates that the term was first used at Bartholomew Fair and in plays; it is almost certainly (despite O.E.D.) either s. or coll, orig. at least. Perhaps ex COCKNEY.

cokum. An occ. variant of COCUM.

col. A Parlary form of COLE, or *coal*, money.

colander, in and out like a fart in a. Moving restlessly and aimlessly: low: mid-C.19–20. cf. FART IN A BOTTLE, LIKE A.

colcher; occ. **colsher.** A heavy fall; esp. *come a colcher*: dial. (—1888) >, by 1893, coll. Ex dial. *colch*, *colsh*, a fall.

(Colchester,) weaver's beef (of). Sprats: coll, mainly Essex: mid-C.17–mid-19. Fuller, 1662; J. G. Nall, 1866.

Colchester clock. A large, coarse oyster: from ca 1850; ob. A Londonism.

cold, have a bad. To be in debt. A *very bad cold* indicates a rent-unpaid departure: ca 1850–1920. Mostly a Londonism. 2. Gen., however, is the sense, to have gonorrhoea: C.19–20.

cold, leave out in the. To neglect (a person); to ignore him: from ca 1860: coll >, by 1890, S.E.

cold, the matter will keep. The matter may rest without harm or loss: coll; ca 1660–1800.

cold at that, you will catch. A c.p. or proverbial form of advice or warning to desist: coll: mid-C.18–early 19.

cold blood. A house with an off-licence only: from ca 1858 (ob.): licensed victuallers' and public-houses'.

cold burning. A private punishment by the pouring of water down a man's upraised arm so that it comes out at his breeches-knees: mid-C.18–early 19; military (rank and file).

cold by lying in bed barefoot, he (or **she**) **caught.** A mid-C.18–early 19 c.p. applied to a person fussy about his health.

cold coffee. A hoax: Oxford University, ca 1860–1910. Because cold coffee is, except in very hot weather, a poor drink. 2. Bad luck; misfortune: from ca 1860; ob. Variant, *cold gruel.* 3. A snub or other unkindness in return for a proffered kindness: nautical, then gen.: from ca 1870; ob. 4. Beer: artisans': ca 1874–1920.

cold comfort. Articles that, sent out on sale or return, or on approval, are returned: tradesmen's: from ca 1870.

cold cook. An undertaker: from the 1720s.

cold cook's shop or **cookshop.** An undertaker's premises: from ca 1830.

cold cream. Gin: from ca 1860. *The Comic Almanack*, 1864. cf. CREAM OF THE VALLEY.

cold enough . . . see MONKEY . . .

cold feet, get or **have (got).** To become, to be, discouraged, afraid: coll: 1904.

cold four. Inferior beer (*four* ale): public-houses' (—1909).

cold iron. A sword: coll, ca 1690–1800. B.E., who adds: 'Derisory Periphrasis'.

cold meat. A corpse: from ca 1780. Moore, in 1819, 'Cold meat for the Crowner'.

cold-meat box. A coffin: from ca 1820. E. Sue, *The Mysteries of Paris*, anon. translation, 1845.

cold-meat cart. A hearse: ?earlier than 'Peter Corcoran' Reynolds in *The Fancy*, 1820. cf.:

cold meat of one, make. To kill: prob. from ca 1820 (cf. preceding entry). Dickens, in *Pickwick*, causes a game-keeper to say to a bad shot, 'I'm damned if you won't make cold meat of some of us!' cf. COOK ONE'S GOOSE.

cold-meat train. Any train plying to a cemetery: from ca 1860. 2. Also, however, the last train by which officers can return to Aldershot in time for their morning duties: from ca 1870. R. M. Jephson in *The Girl He Left Behind Him*, 1876. Properly a goods train, it pulled one *ad hoc* carriage, called *the larky subaltern* (*coach*).

cold north-wester. A bucket of sea-water poured over a new hand, by way of initiation: sailing ships'; mid-C.19–20; ob.

cold pickles. A corpse: medical students'; from ca 1840.

cold pie (pye), see CHOKING PIE.

cold pig. The 'empties', i.e. empty packing-cases, returned by rail to wholesale houses: commercial travellers', from ca 1870; ob. 2. In c., a corpse (cf. COLD MEAT); a person robbed of his clothes: from ca 1850.

cold pig, v. From ca 1830: coll. Same meaning as:

cold pig, give. To awaken by sluicing with cold water or by pulling off the bed-clothes: s. passing to coll. Grose, 2nd ed.: J. R. Planché; Thackeray. From ca 1750 in this form (now ob.); but from ca 1600–1750, the form is *give a cold pie*: see CHOKING PIE.

cold shivers, the. A fit of trembling: coll; from ca 1840.

cold shoulder of mutton. A mid-Victorian s. variant of the S.E. *cold shoulder* in its fig. sense.

cold tea. Brandy: a coll of ca 1690–1890. (Esp. among women.) Also see TEA.

cold tongue. A senior's lecture or long reprimand: naval: ca 1840–1900.

cold-water army. The generality of teetotallers: coll: from ca 1870; ob. cf. WATER-WAGGON.

cold without. Spirits mixed with cold water without sugar: coll; from ca 1820. Barham; Bulwer Lytton, 1853, 'I laugh at fame. Fame, sir! not worth a glass of cold without.'

***cole,** much more frequent than *coal*, though the latter (money = coal = the fuel of life) is prob. correct, is money collectively; there is no pl. From ca 1670; it was c. until ca 1730. (For alternative etymologies, see COLIANDER and cf. CABBAGE, n., 1, for *cole* = cabbage; possibly ex foreigners' pronunciation of *gold* as *gōl*.)

***cole, tip the.** Hand over money: c. then low: ca 1660–1830. A C.18–20 variant is *post the* COLE (*coal*) or *the coin*.

cole (gen. coal) up! They're paying out!; there's a pay-parade!: military: late C.19–20. Ex COLE.

colfabi(a)s. A water-closet at Trinity College, Dublin: from ca 1820. Latinized Irish.

***coliander** or **coriander (-seed or seeds).** Money: c.: from ca 1690. Possibly the orig. form of COLE.

***coll.** A C.18 variant of CULL: c. Harper, 1724, 'I Frisky Moll, with my rum coll.' 2. College ale: 1726, Amherst; †by 1800. 3. College: schoolboys' and undergraduates': coll, prob. mid-C.19–20. As undergraduate s., prob. from mid-C.18. Also as adj., e.g. in *coll-chap*.

collah carriage. A railway carriage filled with women: nigger minstrels': ca 1880–1900. Ware, 'Collah being Yiddish for young girls'.

collapse. To CAVE IN; suddenly lose courage: coll: from ca 1860.

collar, v. To appropriate; steal: 1700. Leman Rede in *Sixteen-String Jack*; Dickens in *Bleak House*. 2. To seize: from early C.17: coll till ca 1680, then S.E. though somewhat loose and undignified.

collar, against the. (Working) against difficulties – or the grain: from ca 1850: coll till ca 1890, then S.E.

collar, in; out of. In: out of: employment. Coll; from ca 1850. Ex the stable.

collar, put to the pin of the. Driven to extremities; at the end of one's resources. A coll phrase ex hard-pulling horses: ca 1850–1910.

collar and elbow, n. The Cornwall and Devon style of wrestling: coll: from ca 1820.

collar-day. Execution day: late C.18–early 19; low. Ex the hangman's noose.

collar (or get) the big bird. To be hissed: theatrical: from ca 1840; ob.

collar-work. Severe, laborious work: coll from ca 1870; in C.20, S.E. Ex an uphill pull – all collar work – for horses.

collared. Unable to play one's normal game; FUNKY: C.19–20, mostly gaming.

collared on, be. To be in love with: Australian: ca 1860–1914. 'Tom Collins', *Such Is Life*, 1903.

collared up. Kept hard at work, close to business: coll; from ca 1850; ob.

colleckers, collekers. Terminal examinations with interviews: Oxford, from ca 1895. Ex *collections*.

colle'ct. 'A gathering (in line) for an

official purpose': Bootham School: late C.19–20.

collect, v. To retrieve (objects) from a place: coll: 1875.

collector. A highwayman; occ., a footpad: late C.18–early 19.

Colleen Bawn. An erection: rhyming s. (on HORN): since ca 1862.

***college.** A prison: this gen. sense arose ca 1720, the orig. sense (C.17) being Newgate, as indeed it remained until ca 1800, when, too, from c. the term > low s. 'Velcome to the college, gen'l'men,' says Sam Weller in Dickens. 2. (Often preceded by *New*) the Royal Exchange: late C.17–18: c. 3. (Gen. **the college.**) The workhouse: poor people's: late C.19–20. 4. A tavern with a green garland or painted hoop hung up outside: s. (—1650).

college, ladies'. A brothel: C.18–early 19; low.

***college chum, collegian, collegiate.** The first, C.19 and not very gen.; the second, C.19–20, as in Dickens; the third, the commonest, from ca 1660: the first and the third were c. before they > low s.: a prisoner (orig. of Newgate, *the City College*). 2. (Only *collegiate.*) A shopkeeper to a prison: c.: late C.17–early 19.

***college-cove.** A turnkey: c. (—1823); †by 1890. See COLLEGE, 1.

college telegraph; often shortened to *telegraph.* A college servant given to telling tales: Oxford: 1815–60. *Spy,* 1825.

colleger. The square cap worn at universities: the mortar-board. University and Public School: from ca 1880. cf. the S.E. senses.

collegers, see COLLECKERS. **collegian, *collegiate,** see COLLEGE CHUM. **collek(k)ers,** see COLLECKERS.

colli-mollie, see COLLY-MOLLY.

Collins. A letter of thanks sent by departed guest to hostess: 1904: coll. Ex the *Collins* of Jane Austen's *Pride and Prejudice.* cf. BREAD AND BUTTER LETTER. 2. A 'strong' drink; esp. *Tom C.,* made with gin, and *John C.,* made with rye whisky: since ca 1860; by 1900, coll. See JOHN COLLINS.

collogue. To confabulate: from ca 1810 (Vaux, 1812; Scott, 1811): coll, perhaps whimsical. The earliest sense, to wheedle or flatter, v.i. and v.t., may possibly be coll – it is hard to be dogmatic with C.16–17 words – as Nashe's and Rochester's usage and B.E.'s recording seem to indicate. ?ex Gr. λόγος, a word, influenced by *colloque* (or *colloquy*) and *colleague.*

colloquials. Familiar conversation: Society: ca 1890–1910.

colly-molly; colli-mollie. Melancholy, of which it is a C.17 jocular perversion. Nares. cf. SOLEMNC(H)OLY.

colly-wobbles. A stomach-ache: coll; from ca 1820. Ex *colic.* cf. the Australian *wobbles,* a cattle-disease from eating palm-leaves.

Colney Hatch. A match: rhyming s.: late C.19–20.

Colney Hatch for you! You're crazy: a c.p. of ca 1890–1914. Ex the famous lunatic asylum.

colo. Cold: 'pidgin': mid-C.19–20.

colonel's cure, the. Cockney term of ca 1870–1905, thus: 'I sent my yard-boy round for six-penn'orth o' physic, an' I took it all standing – one gulp, you know: what we useder call "the colonel's cure",' A. Neil Lyons, *Arthur's,* 1908.

Colonial goose. 'A boned leg of mutton stuffed with sage and onions': Australian (—1898); ob. Morris. Ex predominance of mutton as bushman's diet.

Colonial oath!, my. An Australian variant (late C.19–20) of *my* OATH! cf. Henry Lawson's story, 'His Colonial Oath', in *While the Billy Boils,* 2nd series.

colonist. A louse: ca 1810–70. David Carey, *Life in Paris,* 1822. A neat pun.

colory, see COLOURY.

colour. A coloured handkerchief: sporting, chiefly boxing: from ca 1840; ob. Adumbrated in Pierce Egan; Mayhew.

colour, off. Exhausted; debilitated; indisposed: from ca 1860; coll.

colour-chest. A locker for signal-flags: naval coll: C.19.

colour of a person's money, see the. To see his money; esp., to be paid. Coll: from ca 1710. Dickens.

colour one's or the meerschaum. To > red-faced through drink: from ca 1850; ob.

colour with, take. Ostensibly to ally oneself with: from ca 1700; coll > S.E. > †.

coloured on the card. With a jockey's colours inserted on a specific-race card: racing; from ca 1870; †.

coloury; occ. **colory.** Coloured; two-coloured: coll; from ca 1850. C. Brontë. 2. Hence of such colour as shows good quality: commercial coll: from ca 1880.

***colquarron.** The neck: late C.17–early 19 c. Prob. Fr. *col,* neck + c. QUARROM, body.

colsher, see COLCHER.

colt. A barrister attending on a serjeant-at-law at his induction (1765): legal, †. 2. A life-preserver, a NEDDY (4): a weapon affected by thieves and law-keepers: c. and low; from ca 1850. 3. In c., a man (esp. an inn-keeper) who hires horses to highwaymen, thieves or burglars; also, 4, a lad newly initiated into roguery: late C.17–early 19. 5. One acting as a juryman for the first time: ca 1860–90. 6. A professional cricketer in his first season: coll; from ca 1870. Ex *colt* in bowls.

colt, v. To make a newcomer pay his FOOTING: late C.18–20; coll. Ex COLT, a very old term for an inexperienced or a newly-arrived person. Whence the †*coltage*: such a fine.

colt veal. Very red veal: coll: late C.17–early 19. Because 'young', fresh.

colting. A thrashing: C.19 coll. Ex *colt*, to beat with a colt, which is S.E.

colt's tooth, have a. To be fond of youthful pleasures; to be wanton: late C.14–19: coll till ca 1790, then S.E.; †. Chaucer; Greene, 1588; Fletcher (the dramatist); Walpole; Colman. Ex the lit. sense, one of a horse's first set of teeth.

Columbine. A harlot: theatrical; from ca 1845; ob. Ex Harlequin's mistress.

Columbus. A failure: theatrical; from ca 1870; †.

column, dodge the, see DODGE THE COLUMN.

column of blobs (or **lumps).** Column of route: jocular military: from ca 1899.

columns. 'Rows of words, written vertically from a dictionary, as a punishment': Bootham School coll: late C.19–20.

com. A commercial traveller: 1884, G. R. Sims in the *Referee*, 28 Dec. 2. A comedian: theatrical (—1887). The *Referee*, 27 July, that year. 3. Commission in the agential or ambassadorial, not the pecuniary, sense: sporting: from ca 1860; slightly ob.

comb and brush. LUSH, n. and v.: rhyming s. (—1909); ob.

comb-brush. A lady's maid: ca 1749–1820; coll (?> S.E.). Fielding.

comb cut, have one's. To be humiliated; hence, down on one's luck. Coll soon > S.E.; from ca 1570. Middleton. cf. Scott's 'All the Counts in Cumberland shall not cut my comb.' But *be comb-cut*, to be mortified or disgraced, has always been coll (—1860); ob. Ex cock-fighting.

comb down. To ill-treat; thrash: Australian coll: from ca 1860.

comb one's head. To scold: C.18–19. A C.19–20 variant, esp. as to rebuke, is *comb one's hair*. 2. With the addition of *with a joint* or *three-legged stool*, it means – as sometimes it does in the shorter form – to beat, thrash. Shakespeare, 1596, 'Her care should be, | To combe your noddle with a three-legg'd stoole.'

comb the cat. To run one's fingers through the CAT-O'-NINE-TAILS in order to separate the tails: nautical and military; ca 1800–95.

combie. (Pron. *com-bĕe.*) Abbr. *combination-room*, the fellows' common room: Cambridge University, from ca 1860, ob. 2. A woman's combination(s): from ca 1870: women's, nursery, and shop.

come (occ. come off). 'To experience the sexual spasm' (F. & H.): low coll: C.19–20. Considered coarse, but it was orig. a euphemism and, in C.20, how, if the fact is to be expressed non-euphemistically, could one express it otherwise with such terse simplicity? 2. To perform; practise: coll, recorded in 1812 (Vaux) but prob. from ca 1800. 3. To play a dodge, a trick (v.t. with *over*): 1785; coll. Greenwood, in *Tag, Rag, and Co*, 1883, 'We ain't two . . . as comes that dodge.' 4. To act the part of: O.E.D. records it at 1825: coll or s.: cf. COME THE OLD SOLDIER. 5. To attain to, achieve: from ca 1885: dial. and coll. 6. To experience, suffer, as in *come a cropper*: this once coll usage is now S.E. where the complement is S.E. 7. See COME IT.

***come, to.** c. of ca 1810–50, as in Vaux, 1812: 'A thief observing any article in a shop, or other situation, which he believes may be easily purloined, will say to his accomplice, I think there is so and so *to come*.'

come a colcher, see COLCHER. **come a cropper.** See COME, 6, and CROPPER.

come about (one). To circumvent: C.18; coll. Mentioned by Johnson. 2. To have sexual intercourse with: C.19–20 (ob.); coll: said of men by women.

come-all-over-queer, n. A *je ne sais quoi* of discomfort: low coll: late C.19–20.

come aloft. To have an erection: coll: ca 1550–1840. Spenser, *The Faerie Queene*, 1590–6; Dryden, *The Maiden Queen*, 1668, 'I cannot come aloft to an old woman'.

come and have a pickle! 'An invitation to a quick unceremonious meal', Ware: Society: 1878–ca 1910.

come and have one!; come and wash your neck! Come and have a drink!: resp., gen. coll (from ca 1880) and nautical s. (from ca 1860). cf.:

come and see your pa! Come and have a drink! c.p.: ca 1870–1910.

come-at-able. Approachable; accessible: 1687 (S.O.D.); coll till ca 1900, then S.E.

come back. To fall back, lose position: sporting; from ca 1880; ob.

come-by-chance. A person or thing arriving by chance; a bastard. Coll: from ca 1760.

come Cripplegate. To attempt to hoodwink officers: nautical: C.19–20; ob. Ex the tricks of crippled beggars.

come-day, go-day with (a person), **it's.** He's extravagant: military: ca 1890–1915.

come dish about. A C.18 drinking c.p. Ned Ward, 1709.

come-down. A social or a financial fall or humiliation or *pis-aller*: from ca 1840.

come down, v. To give, subscribe, or lend money (or an equivalent): from ca 1700, perhaps ex late C.17 c. COME IT (6), to lend money. v.t. with *with*, from a few years later: coll. The v.i. in Steele's play, *The Funeral*; Thackeray's *Pendennis*. The v.t. in Gay's *Beggar's Opera*: 'Did he tip handsomely? – How much did he come down with?' 2. See DOWN, BE.

come down (up)on (a person) **like a ton of bricks.** To scold, blame, reprimand severely: coll; from ca 1850.

come home. (Of lost gear) to be restored to its proper place; (of an anchor) to drag: nautical: late C.19–20.

come in if you're fat! A C.18 c.p. Swift, ca 1708, 'Who's there? . . . come in, if you be fat.' A thin person is prob. more expensive to entertain.

come it. To cut a dash; to move (lit. and fig.) fast: coll (—1840); ob., except in Glasgow, where it = to TALK BIG. cf. GO IT. Thackeray, 'I think the chaps down the road will stare . . . when they hear how I've been coming it.' 2. To inform the police, disclose a plan, divulge a secret: c. (—1812). 3. To tell lies: low: ca 1820–80. 4. To show fear: pugilistic, ca 1860–1910. 5. To succeed, manage: ex U.S., anglicized ca 1895; coll, ob. 6. To lend money: c.: late C.17–19. 7. A late C.19–20 variant (low; military) of COME THE OLD SOLDIER. 8. To be quiet, esp. in imperative: c.: from ca 1880; ob.

***come it as strong as a horse.** (Of a criminal) to turn King's evidence: c. of ca 1810–50. Vaux, who cites the synonymous *be coming all one knows*. Elaborations of COME IT, 2.

come it as strong as mustard. An intensive of COME IT, esp. in sense 3, or of COME IT STRONG: low: ca 1820–90.

***come it at the box** (or **the broads**). To dice; to play cards: c.: from ca 1860.

come it over or **with.** To get the better of: s., > coll by 1900: from ca 1820 or earlier.

come it strong. To go to extremes; exaggerate; to lie: coll; from ca 1820. 'Jon Bee', 1823; Dickens in *Pickwick*; Barham; Thackeray. cf. *make it hot* and see COME IT AS STRONG AS MUSTARD.

come it with, see COME IT OVER.

come off, v.i. To pay: coll: ca 1580–1750. Variant of COME DOWN. 2. (Gen. of the man.) To experience the sexual orgasm: see COME.

come off the grass! Not so much SIDE! Don't exaggerate, or tell lies! Ex U.S.; anglicized ca 1890.

come one's mutton or turkey. To masturbate: low: late C.19–20.

come-out, adj. Execrable (*Sinks*, 1848): low: ca 1830–80.

come out. (Of girls) to make one's début in Society, gen. by being presented at Court: from ca 1780; a coll that, ca 1840, > S.E. 2. Abbr. *come out on strike*: coll at first; from ca 1890.

come out of that hat – I can't see yer feet! A boys' c.p. cry to a man wearing a topper: ca 1875–1900. (Mostly London.)

come out strong. To express oneself vigorously or very frankly: coll; from ca 1850. cf. S.E. *come out with*, to utter, and coll COME IT STRONG. 2. To be generous: Public Schools': from ca 1890.

come over. (cf. COME IT OVER.) To cheat; trick; impose on: C.17–20: until ca 1750, S.E., then coll. From ca 1860, gen. GET OVER; in C.19–20, occ. COME IT OVER. 2. With *faint, ill, queer, sick*, etc., to become suddenly faint, etc.: coll; from ca 1850.

come over on a whelk-stall, have. To be dressed to the nines: costers' (—1909).

come right on the night, it will all. This – dating from ca 1880 – is perhaps the commonest c.p. of the theatre. Ex mishaps and mistakes that, happening at a – esp. at the dress – rehearsal, will probably not recur.

come round. To persuade; make a deep impression on; influence: coll; from ca 1830. Thackeray, in *Vanity Fair*, 'The governess had come round everybody . . . had the upper hand of the whole house.'

come souse. To fall heavily: boxing: from ca 1815. Tom Moore, 1819.

come the artful. To try to deceive: coll: from ca 1840.

come the bag. An occ. variant of COME THE OLD BAG.

come (the) blarney over (someone). To be very sweet to; to flatter: since ca 1810 or a decade earlier.

come the don, see COME THE NOB.

come the gypsy. To attempt to cheat or defraud: coll; from ca 1840. cf. the two COME THE OLD ... entries.

come the heavy. To affect a much superior social position: from ca 1860.

come the lardy-dardy. To dress oneself showily: from ca 1860. Mostly London.

come the nob (occ. **the don).** To put on airs: from ca 1855; ob. Mostly lower classes'.

come the old bag or **man** or **soldier.** (v.t. with *over*.) To bluff; to shirk; to domineer: late C.19–20: resp. low, gen., and military. Manchon (*bag*); F. & Gibbons (the other two). Ex:

come the old soldier. (v.t., *over*.) To wheedle; impose on: coll: from (?—)1818, Alfred Burton, *Johnny Newcome*. The idea is adumbrated in Shadwell's *Humours of the Army*: 'The Devil a farthing he owes me – but however, I'll put the old soldier upon him.' 2. See preceding entry.

come the Rothschild. To pretend to be rich: ca 1880–1914; coll.

come the sergeant. To give peremptory orders: from ca 1855; coll.

come the spoon. To make love, esp. if sentimental: from ca 1865.

***come the Traviata.** In (harlots') c., to feign phthisis: C.19; †by 1891. *La Traviata* is a Verdi opera, in which the heroine is a consumptive *prima donna*, based, of course, on *La Dame aux Camélias*.

come the ugly. To make threats; from ca 1870; coll.

come through a side door. To be born out of wedlock: coll: from ca 1860; ob. In ca 1880 broadside ballad, *The Blessed Orphan.*

come to cues! Come to the point!: theatrical: late C.19–20. Ex rehearsal practice of giving a hesitant actor the cue line only.

come to grass; usually **coming ...** To come up to the surface of a mine: Cornish miners': mid-C.19–20. (R. M. Ballantyne, *Deep Down*, 1869.)

come to grief, see GRIEF, COME TO.

come to stay. (adj. phrase.) With the quality of – possessing – permanency. Gen. as (*it*) *has come to stay*. Orig. (—1888), U.S.; anglicized ca 1895. Coll.

***come to the heath.** To give or pay money: c. of ca 1810–40. Vaux suggests that there is a pun on *tipping* + *Tiptree Heath* (a place in Essex).

***come to the mark.** 'To abide strictly by any contract ...; to perform your part manfully ...; or to offer me what I consider a fair price ...', Vaux: c. of ca 1805–80. Whence the S.E. *come up to the mark*.

come to, or **up to, time.** In boxing, to answer the call of 'time!'; hence, in sporting circles, to be ready, to be alert. Whyte-Melville, *M. or N.*, 1869.

come tricks, see COME, 3.

come up smiling. To smile though (esp. if heavily) PUNISHED: boxing; from ca 1860. 2. Hence, to face defeat without complaining or flinching: coll; from ca 1870. John Strange Winter, in *That Imp*, 1887, 'And yet come up smiling at the end of it'.

come up to (the) scratch or **the chalk,** see SCRATCH ...

come Yorkshire over, see YORKSHIRE, v.

comedy-merchant. An actor: ca 1870–1914. (MERCHANT = CHAP, fellow, man.)

comether on, put one's or **the.** To coax, wheedle; influence strongly: Anglo-Irish coll (?dial.): from ca 1830. Ex *come hither*.

comfort. (Gen. with *to do*, occ. with *that* ...) A cause of satisfaction: C.19–20 coll; earlier, S.E. 2. A sort of strong liquor in vogue ca 1725–30. Anon., *The Quaker's Opera*.

comfortable. Tolerable: coll (—1720). 2. Placidly self-satisfied: coll; 1865.

comfortable importance or **impudence.** A wife: also a mistress virtually a wife: late C.17–20; ob. cf. Fr. *mon gouvernement*.

comfy. Comfortable: coll (orig. Society): from ca 1830. Prob. influenced by *cosy*.

comic, n. A comic periodical: coll; S.O.D. records it for 1889.

comic-song faker. A writer of comic songs; music-halls': 1880–1910.

comical, n. A napkin: ca 1870–1910. (Mostly proletarian.)

comical, adj. Strange, queer, odd: 1793 (S.O.D.); coll.

comical, be struck. To be astonished: low coll from ca 1870; ob.

comical farce. A glass: rhyming s.: late C.19–20; ob.

coming. (Gen. of women) forward; wanton: C.17–20; coll till ca 1850, then S.E.

Fielding. 2. Sexually capable: C.18–19; low coll. 3. Pregnant: coll; C.17–18.

coming! Directly! In a minute! Coll: from ca 1700. cf. *coming?, so is Christmas*, said, C.18–20, to a slow person.

***coming all one knows, be,** see COME IT AS STRONG AS A HORSE.

coming on, be. To be learning the ways of the world, e.g. of women: coll: mid-C.19–20. Ex S.E. *coming on*, growing (up).

comings. Seminal fluid: low coll: mid-C.19–20. Ex the relevant sense of COME.

commandeer. To gain illicit possession of, gen. by pure bluff: coll: Boer War+. cf. S.E. sense.

commandments, the ten. The finger-nails or 'claws' of a person, esp. of a woman: from ca 1540; ob.

commend me to. Give me preferably, by choice: coll; from ca 1710. (Orig. of persons; post-1850, things.)

***commercial.** In c., a thief or a tramp who travels considerably: ca 1855–1914. 2. Abbr. *commercial traveller*: from ca 1850: coll.

commercial legs. Legs unfitted for drill: recruiting sergeants': late C.19–20; ob.

commish. Abbr. *commission*, a percentage on sales: from ca 1895.

***commission.** A shirt: mid-C.16–early 19 c. Harman. Ex It. *camicia*. See CAMESA and MISH.

commissioner. A bookmaker: from ca 1860. Little used since ca 1890.

commissioner of Newmarket Heath. A footpad: late C.16–17. Nashe.

***commister.** A rare variant (H., 1st ed.) of CAMISTER, a clergyman.

committal, adj. Compromising; involving, committing; rashly revelatory: coll: 1884, *Punch*. Ex *non-committal*.

commodity. The *pudendum muliebre*: coll; late C.16–19. Shakespeare, in *King John*, 'Tickling commodity; commodity – the bias of the world.' 2. Occ., but only in c., a whore: late C.16. Greene.

common bounce. 'One using a lad as a decoy to prefer a charge of unnatural intercourse': low, orig. perhaps c.: from ca 1850; ob. in s.

Common Garden. A C.17–19 facetious variant of *Covent Garden*. Many *common* whores to be found there.

common garden gout. Syphilis: late C.17–18. Ex COVENT GARDEN (AGUE) after *common-(or-)garden*.

common jack. A harlot: military; C.19–20, ob.

common John. A species of marble (in the game of marbles): children's: late C.19–20.

common-roomed, be. To be brought before the head of a college: university coll (—1886).

common sewer. A drink; a taking or GO (n., 2) of drink: from ca 1860; ob. Ex *sewer* = a drain. 2. A cheap prostitute: low: from ca 1870; ob.

commoner. An ordinary harlot: late C.16–early 19; coll > S.E. by 1660. 2. An inexpert or amateur boxer: pugilistic: ca 1810–50.

commoner-grub. A dinner given, after cricket matches, by 'commoners' to 'college': Winchester College: C.19, †by 1890. (A 'commoner' is not on the foundation.)

commoney. A clay marble: schoolboys', ca 1830–1900. Dickens.

commons, house of. A privy: C.18–early 19; coll. The S.E. form is *common house*.

commonsensical. Possessing, marked with, common sense: coll; from ca 1870. 'The commonsensical mind' occurs in *Fraser's Magazine*, Sept. 1880. After *nonsensical*; the S.E. term being *common-sensible*.

communicator. A bell: jocularly coll; from ca 1840. Esp. in *agitate the communicator*.

***communion bloke.** A religious hypocrite: prison c.: from ca 1870. B. & L.

comp. A compositor: printers': from ca 1865. *Tit-Bits*, 31 July 1886, 'Applications for work from travelling comps are frequent.' cf. ASS, DONKEY, GALLEY-SLAVE.

company, see. To live by harlotry; esp., and properly, in a good way of business: low: from the 1740s; ob. John Cleland, 1749; Grose, 1st ed.

company (with), keep, v.i. and v.t. To court; to pay court to, or be courted by: low coll (—1861).

competition wallah. A competitioner, i.e. one who enters the Indian Civil Service by examination: the competition and the name began in 1856: Anglo-Indian coll. The WALLAH is ex Urdu *wala* = Arabic *walad* = L. *-arius*, signifying a 'doer', 'maker', 'actor'.

compile. In cricket, to make abundantly, score freely to the extent of, as in 'England compiled 480 (runs).' S.O.D. records it for 1884.

complaining. 'The creaking of a ship at sea': nautical coll verging on S.E.: C.19–20. Bowen.

compo. A monthly advance of wages:

nautical coll: from ca 1850. Prob. ex *compo*, j. for a composition paid by a debtor (see O.E.D.).

comprador. In India, but †by 1900, a house-steward; in China, a butler: coll: from C.16. The Portuguese *comprador*, a purchaser.

compulsory. That irregular kind of football which is now called *run-about*: Charterhouse coll: ca 1850–90. A. H. Tod.

compy-shop. A truck-shop: workmen's coll: ca 1850–1900. Ex *company-shop*.

con. Abbr. *confidant*, 1825; *conundrum*, 1841; *conformist*, 1882; *Constitutional*, 1883 (Ware); *contract*, 1889; *construe*, n. (1905); *con*sultation or *con*ference, late C.19. 2. A previous *con*viction: late C.19–20 c. Charles E. Leach. 3. A *convict*: low (—1909).

con, v. To rap with the knuckles: Winchester College, C.19–20; ob. Ex the much older n., perhaps cognate with the Fr. *cogner*. Wykehamists, pre-1890, traditioned it ex Gr. κόνδυλος, a knuckle. 2. In C.20 c., to subject to a confidence trick. 3. In late C.19–20 c., abbr. of *convict*. 4. To construe: Charterhouse: late C.19–20.

Conan Doyle. Boil: rhyming s.: from ca 1895.

***concaves and convexes.** A pack of cards devised for sharping: from ca 1840; ob. Low and c.

concern. Any object or contrivance: somewhat pejorative; from ca 1830; coll. 2. The male or female genitals: from ca 1840; s., whereas *thing* is perhaps more euphemistic than unconventional.

***concerned.** Often used in c. periphrasis or c.p.: late C.18–19. See e.g. ALDERMAN LUSHINGTON, BOLT-IN-TUN, *Mr* PALMER. 2. (Occ. *with* or *in drink*.) Intoxicated: from ca 1680; S.E. till ca 1860, then coll. Ob.

concert grand. A grand piano suitable for concerts: coll (—1893).

concertize. 'To assist musically in concerts', Ware: musicians' coll: 1885.

conchers. Cattle, either tame or quiet – or both: Australians': from ca 1870. †by 1912 and ob. by 1896.

conchologize. To study conchology; collect shells: coll: 1855, C. Kingsley.

condiddle. To purloin, steal: coll; ca 1740–1860; extant in dial., where it arose. Scott in *St Ronan's Well*, 'Twig the old connoisseur . . . condiddling the drawing.' Ex DIDDLE, a, and to, cheat.

condition, see DELICATE CONDITION.

condog. To concur: coll: ca 1590–1700; almost S.E. by 1660. *-dog* puns *-cur*.

Condolence, see BAY OF CONDOLENCE.

condom is a variant of CUNDUM.

conduit. The two Winchester senses (a water-tap, a lavatory) – see Wrench – are, now, almost certainly j.; but orig. (?ca 1850) they may have been s.

condumble, see YOUR HUMBLE C.

coney and its compounds: see CONY, etc.

confab. A talk together, or a discussion, esp. if familiar: coll; 1701 (S.O.D.). 'In close confab', Wolcott, 1789. Ex *confabulation*. Also as v.: from ca 1740: not much used. Richardson.

***confect.** Counterfeited: late C.17–18 c. O.E.D. considers it S.E.; perhaps it is c. only as *confeck* (Coles, 1676).

confess. Confession, as in *go to confess*: Roman Catholic: from ca 1890.

confess and be hanged! A proverbial c.p. equivalent of 'You lie!': late C.16–17. Lit., be shrived and be hanged!

confiscate. To seize as if with authority: from ca 1820; coll until C.20, when, for all its looseness, the word is S.E. 2. Hence *confiscation*, 'legal robbery by or with the sanction of the ruling power', O.E.D.: from ca 1865. 3. And *confiscatory*, adj. to 2: coll: 1886 (O.E.D.).

conflabberate. To upset, worry, perturb (gen. as past ppl passive): from ca 1860.

conflabberation. A confused wrangle; an AWFUL din.: from ca 1860. One of the half-wit jocularities so fashionable ca 1840–1900, e.g. ABSQUATULATE, SPIFLICATE, more popular in the U.S. than in the British Empire, which did but adopt them.

confloption. An unshapely or twisted thing, a distorted representation or grotesque figure: jocular (—1887); ob. Perhaps a perversion of CONTRAPTION. Contrast the dial. senses: flurry, confusion.

conflummox is an intensive of FLUMMOCKS: from ca 1860; virtually †.

confound it! A coll expletive: C.19–20. cf. sense 1 of:

confounded. Inopportune; unpleasant, odious; excessive. This coll, like AWFUL, BEASTLY, is a mere verbal harlot serving all men's haste, a counter of speech, a thought-substitute. From ca 1760. Goldsmith, in *The Vicar of Wakefield*, 'What are tythes and tricks but an imposition, all confounded imposture.' From ca 1850 its emotional connotation has been brutalized by association with *confound it!* = damn it! 2. Hence *confoundedly*, very: coll: C.18–20.

congee-house, see CONJEE-HOUSE.

conger. An association of London bookseller-publishers that, ca 1680–1800, printed and sold books as a close corporation, a none-too-generous 'combine': late C.17–early 19: coll >, by 1750, S.E. >, by 1830, historical. See esp. B.E. Prob. (*pace* the O.E.D.) ex the *conger* or sea-eel, a lengthy, unpleasant creature. 2. Whence, to enter into such an association: coll (—1785); †by 1823.

congrats. Congratulations. Anthony Hope, *The Dolly Dialogues*, 1894, 'Dear old Dolly, – So you've brought it off. Hearty congrats.'

conish. Genteel; fashionable: low (?also, or orig., c.); ca 1800–40. Perhaps = TONY and a corruption from TON, 2.

***conish cove.** A gentleman: Scottish c. of ca 1820–50.

conjee- or congee-house. A lock-up: military coll (in India mostly): from ca 1830. Ex Tamil *kañji*; *congee* – the water in which rice has been boiled – being a staple food of prisoners in India.

conjobble. To arrange, settle; discuss; v.i., to chat together: 1694; ob.: coll.

conjurer (-or), no. One lacking brains and/or physical skill: coll > S.E.; from ca 1660. 2. A C.17–18 sol. for 'Astrologers, Physiognomists, Chiromancers, and the whole Tribe of Fortune-tellers', B.E. 3. In c. of the same period, all those terms also = judge, magistrate. cf. CUNNING MAN, FORTUNE-TELLER.

conk. The nose, esp. if large: low: 1812, Vaux; H. Cockton, in *Valentine Vox*, 1840, 'Oh! oh! there's a conk! there's a smeller!' Prob. ex *conch*, L. *concha*: cf. L. *testa* (a pot, a shell) = head. 2. 'A spy; informer, or tell-tale': c. of ca 1810–40. Vaux, who shrewdly relates it to sense 1: cf. NOSE, an informer. Hence 3, a policeman: low: ca 1820–1910. 4. A blow on the nose: low: from ca 1870; ob. 5. **(Conk.)** A lower-middle class nickname for a large-nosed person: late C.19–20.

conker. A blow on the nose: from ca 1820; ob. (But *conkers*, the game, is S.E.)

conk(e)y. Having a large nose: from ca 1800. 'Waterloo' Wellington was called *Conkey* at least a decade before 1815; thereafter, *Old Conkey* or *Atty Conkey*, lit. 'Arthur the Long-Nosed'. 2. Hence, NOSEY, inquisitive: from ca 1840. cf. BEAK, BOWSPRIT, NOZZLE; for synonymy, see F. & H.

conner. Food: Regular Army's: late C.19–20. Ex Hindustani.

conny wobble. Eggs and brandy beaten up together: Anglo-Irish, C.18–19.

conqueror. (As in *play the conqueror*.) A deciding game: games coll: from ca 1870. cf. *decider*.

conscience. An association, gen. in a small company, for the sharing of profits: theatrical: ca 1870–1900.

conscience, in (all). Equitably; in fairness or in reason: coll; from ca 1590. Swift. A mid-C.16–17 variant is *of (all) conscience*.

conscience-keeper. 'A superior, who by his influence makes his dependents act as he pleases', Grose, 2nd ed.: coll: late C.18–mid-19.

consequence, of. As a result; by inference: low coll, C.19–20; earlier, S.E.

conshun's price. Fair terms or price: Anglo-Chinese; from ca 1850; ob. Ex *conscience*.

considerable bend, go on the. To engage in a bout of dissipation: from ca 1880; cf. BENDER, 4.

considering, adv. If one considers everything, takes everything into account: coll; from ca 1740. Richardson, 'Pretty well, sir, considering.'

consign. To send, wish, as in *consign to the devil*: coll, from ca 1900.

consols. Abbr. *consolidated annuities*: (1770) in C.18, Stock Exchange s.; then gen. coll; finally (from ca 1850) S.E. The consolidation of all Government securities into one fund took place in 1751.

consonant-choker. One who omits his 'g's and slurs his 'r's: ca 1870–1910.

constable, outrun – occ. **overrun** – **the.** To go too fast or too far (lit. and fig.), as in an argument (Butler's *Hudibras*, I, 1663): coll; †by 1850. 2. Hence, mid-C.18–20, to change the subject. 3. To fall into debt (Smollett, in *Roderick Random*; Dickens): coll >, ca 1880, S.E.; very ob.

constant screamer. A concertina: non-aristocratic: ca 1860–1915.

constician. A member of the orchestra: theatrical; from ca 1875; †.

constituter. The 'Oxford *-er*' form of the next: Oxford undergraduates': from late 1890s.

constitutional. A walk taken as exercise (for the good of one's constitution or health): coll: recorded by S.O.D. in 1829. Smedley, 1850, 'Taking my usual constitutional after Hall'; 'Cuthbert Bede', 1853.

constitutionalize. To take a walk for health: coll; from ca 1850. Like its origin, CONSTITUTIONAL, it is a university term, app. arising at Cambridge.

consumer. A butler: Anglo-Indian; from ca 1700. Semi-jocular on *consumah.*

***content.** Dead: C.18–early 19; c. and low. i.e. content in death.

conter, see JURY, CHUMMAGE, AND CONTER.

context. To discover, or approximate, the sense of a badly written word from the context: printers' and typists' coll (—1909).

continent, adj. and adv. On the sick list: Winchester College, C.19–20.

continental, not worth a; not care (or **give**) **a.** To be worth nothing; care not at all. Orig. (—1869), U.S.; anglicized ca 1895. In allusion to *continental money,* a worthless American currency note of ca 1775–8. cf. DAM . . .

continuando, with a. For days on end; for a long time. Often preceded by *drunk.* Coll: ca 1680–1750.

continuations. Trousers, for they continue the waistcoat: from ca 1840. Whyte-Melville, 1853. (cf. DITTOES, INEXPRESSIBLES, UNMENTIONABLES.) Ex *continuations,* gaiters (as continuing knee-breeches).

contract. An undertaking; esp. *it's a bit of a contract,* a rather difficult job: coll: U.S. (ca 1880) >, ca 1890, anglicized.

contraption. A contrivance, device; small tool or article: dial. (1825: E.D.D.) >, ca 1830, U.S. coll (Thornton) and, ca 1850, English coll. Perhaps ex '*contriv*ance' + 'inven*tion*'.

contrā'ry. Adverse, inimical, cross-grained, unpleasantly capricious: from ca 1850: coll. Prob. influenced by the Scottish *contrair*(*y*).

***control fortune.** Not a euphemism but a c. term: to cheat at cards: C.19–20; ob.

conundrum is s. in that sense, a pun, play on words, which arose at Oxford in 1644 or 1645; in C.18 coll; ob. by 1800, †by 1830. Prob. ex a lost parody of a scholiast phrase. Tom Brown, Ned Ward. W. notes the similarity of *panjandrum.* 3. Female pudend: ca 1640–1830. App. earliest in R. W., *A Pill to Purge Melancholy,* 1652.

convenience. A water-closet; chamber-pot: C.19–20; orig. euphemistic. (In C.17–18 c., with variant *-cy,* a wife or a mistress.)

***conveniency.** A mistress; primarily, however, a wife: c. and low: late C.17–early 19. cf.:

***convenient.** A mistress; also, a harlot: c. and low: ca 1670–1830. Etherege, 1676, 'Dorimant's convenient, Madam Loveit'. cf. COMFORTABLE IMPORTANCE.

convenient, adj. Handy, i.e. conveniently situated or placed: coll: 1848. Thackeray.

conversation, a little. Cursing and/or swearing: C.20; ob. Ware, 1909. cf. LANGUAGE.

convey. To steal: mid-C.15–20. Shakespeare: 'Convey, the wise it call.' Orig. euphemistic; but in mid-C.19–20 decidedly coll in its facetiousness.

conveyance, a theft, C.16–20; **conveyancer,** a thief, C.18–19; **conveyancing,** thieving, swindling, from ca 1750; **conveyer,** a thief, esp. if nimble (see Shakespeare's *Richard II*), late C.16–20. In C.19–20, all these are coll and more or less jocular, though *conveyance* and *conveyer* were ob. by 1890.

Convocation Castle. 'Where the . . . heads of colleges . . . meet to transact and investigate university affairs', Egan's Grose: Oxford University: ca 1820–40. Punning *Convocation.*

cony, coney. 'A silly Fellow', a simpleton: from ca 1590, archaic after 1820; coll. Greene, B.E., Grose. (Variant, TOM CONY.) Whence:

***cony-catch.** To cheat, trick, deceive: c. and low: late C.16–18. Greene; Shakespeare, in *The Taming of the Shrew,* 'Take heed, signor Baptista, lest you be conny-catched in this business.' Ex:

***cony-catcher.** A deceiver; trickster; sharper: c. and low; ca 1590–1840. John Day, Robert Greene, Walter Scott.

***cony-catching.** Trickery; cheating; swindling: c. and low: late C.16–early 19. Shakespeare, Middleton, Ned Ward; the *locus classicus,* however, is Greene's series of pamphlets on cony-catching: and very good reading they are (see Dr G. B. Harrison's reprints in the Bodley Head Quartos and my *Slang,* pp. 46–7). cf. GULL, WARREN. 2. As adj., cheating, swindling: late C.16–17. Greene.

***cony-dog.** One who assists in cheating or swindling: c.: late C.17–18.

cony-fumble. A constable: s.: Ned Ward, 1703.

cony-wabble. A dupe: s.: Ned Ward, 1703.

coo! indicates astonishment or disbelief: mostly lower classes' coll: from ca 1890.

Prob. ex *good gracious* (or *Lord*)*!*: cf. the frequent *coo* LUMME! and COR!

cooee, cooey. (The *oo* sound long drawn out.) The Australian black's signal-cry, adopted by the colonists. Recorded in 1790 see esp. Morris – it has, since ca 1840, been the gen. hailing or signalling cry. Coll > S.E. As early as 1864, H. can say that it is 'now not unfrequently [*sic*] heard in the streets of London'. E. S. Rawson, *In Australian Wilds*, 1889, 'the startling effects of Jim's cooee'. 2. The v.i. dates from 1827 – or earlier.

cooee, within. Within hail; hence, within easy reach. From ca 1880; coll.

cook. To manipulate, tamper with; falsify: coll; recorded in 1636 (S.O.D.). Smollett, 1751, 'Some falsified printed accounts, artfully cooked up, ... to mislead and deceive'. H., 5th ed., 'Artists say that a picture will not *cook* when it is excellent and unconventional and beyond specious imitation.' 2. To kill, settle, ruin, badly worst: from ca 1850. Mayhew. cf. COOK ONE'S GOOSE and COOKER. 3. (Of persons) to swelter in the heat: coll; from ca 1860.

cook one's goose. To ruin; defeat; kill: from ca 1850. 'Cuthbert Bede', 'You're the boy to cook Fosbrooke's goose'; Trollope, 1861, 'Chaldicotes ... is a cooked goose.' cf. *do* BROWN and *settle one's* HASH. (At this phrase, F. & H. gives an excellent synonymy of DO FOR in its various senses.)

cook up. To falsify (e.g. accounts): late C.19–20. Variant of COOK, 1.

***cook-ruffi(a)n.** A bad or bad-tempered cook: ca 1690–1830; c., then low. Prob. ex the proverbial saying recorded by Ray in 1670, *cook-ruffian, able to scold the devil in* (or *out of*) *his feathers.*

cooked. Exhausted, ruined, killed: since ca 1820. *Sessions*, 1825.

cookem fry. Hell: naval: since ca 1870. Granville. Presumably ex 'to cook and fry (in hell)'.

cooker. A decisive or a fatal act, a SETTLER or FINISHER: low (—1869), ob. cf. COOK, v., 2, and COOK ONE'S GOOSE. 2. See CAPTAIN COOK.

cookie, cooky. A cook, but rarely of a man: coll: from ca 1770.

cookie-shine. A tea-party: jocular coll: ca 1863–80. Reade. Ex *cookie*, a small cake.

Cook's (or Cooks') Own, the. The Police Force: ca 1855–90. Mayhew, ca 1860 (see *Slang*, p. 93). On names of regiments and ex police predilection for cooks.

cook's warrant. A surgical operation, esp. if amputation: nautical (—1887); ob.

***cool.** A cut-purse: late C.16–early 17 c. Greene in 2nd *Cony-Catching.*

cool. (Esp. with *fish* or *hand.*) Impertinent, impudent, audacious, esp. if in a calm way: from ca 1820; coll till ca 1880, then S.E. The same with the adv. *coolly.* 2. Stressing the amount in a large sum of money: from 1728 (S.O.D.); coll. Fielding, in *Tom Jones*, 'Mr Watson ... declared he had lost a cool hundred, and would play no longer.' 3. At Eton College, clear, effective, as in *cool kick*: mid-C.19–20. cf.:

cool, v. To kick hard and clear: Eton College: mid-C.19–20. 2. In back s. (—1857), look. Thus *cool him!* is a costers' warning to 'look out' for the policeman.

cool as a cucumber, adj. and adv. Cool(ly) and calm(ly): from ca 1700; coll. Gay, Scott, De Morgan. The C.17 form was *cold as cucumbers*, as in Fletcher.

cool crape. A shroud: C.18–early 19: low. *A New Canting Dict.*, 1725. Ex *c.-c.*, 'a slight Chequer'd Stuff made in imitation of Scotch Plad [*sic*]', B.E. Hence, *be put into one's cool crape*, C.18, is to die.

cool lady. A female camp-follower who sells brandy: late C.17–early 18. Ex:

cool Nant(e)s or **Nantz.** Brandy: ca 1690–1830; coll. Ex the city of Nantes.

cool one's coppers. To quench the morning thirst after over-night drinking: from ca 1860: coll. T. Hughes in *Tom Brown at Oxford.*

cool one's heels. To be kept standing; esp. waiting: from ca 1630; coll > S.E. by 1700. A slightly earlier form was *hoofs*, applied lit. to soldiers.

cool tankard. (Like COOL CRAPE – LADY – NANTES, it may be, but rarely is, spelt with a hyphen.) 'Wine and Water, with a Lemon, Sugar and Nutmeg', B.E. Coll: late C.17–18; in C.19–20 (ob.), S.E.

coolaman. A drinking vessel: Australian coll: from ca 1870. Ex Aborigine.

cooler. A woman: late C.17–early 19: low (?orig. c.). Ex the cooling of passion and bodily temperature ensuing after sexual intercourse. 2. Ale, stout, or porter taken after spirits (even with water): from ca 1820. Pierce Egan's *Tom and Jerry.* cf. DAMPER, 4. 3. A heavy punch: boxers' (—1823); †by 1900. 'Jon Bee.' 4. A prison: orig. (—1884), U.S.; anglicized, in c., ca 1890.

coolie, cooly. 'A common fellow of the lowest class': from ca 1800, orig. nautical. 2. Hence, a private soldier (—1859); †by 1900. Ex the Tamil for 'day labourer'.

coolth. Coolness: S.E. >, ca 1890, jocular coll.

cooly, see COOLIE.

coon. A man, esp. if sly and shrewd. Ex U.S., anglicized by *Punch* in 1860. 2. A negro: ex U.S. (—1870), anglicized ca 1890. Ex *racoon.*

coon, a gone. A person in serious, or indeed in a hopeless, difficulty: orig. U.S. (—1840), anglicized ca 1860. Origin doubtful: perhaps ex *racoon* after Scottish *gone corbie.* Calverley.

coon's age, a. A very long time, the racoon being notably long-lived: ex U.S. (—1845), anglicized ca 1870 but now ob.

***coop.** A prison: c.: *Sessions*, Sept. 1785.

cooped-up. In prison: low; from ca 1690. cf. COOP.

cooper. Stout HALF-AND-HALF, i.e. stout with an equal portion of porter: coll; from ca 1858. Ex the coopers of breweries. 2. A buyer or seller of illicit spirits; a ship engaged in such contraband: nautical coll: from ca 1880. Ex S.E. senses.

coopered. Made presentable: coll: 1829 (Scott). Prob. ex HORSE-CAPPER or –COOPER). 2. Illicitly tampered with; forged; spoiled; betrayed, ruined: c. and low, esp. the turf: from ca 1850. Mayhew. The other parts of the verb are rare. Cognate with SCUPPERED. (In vagabondia, denoted by the sign ▽.)

coopering. The vbl n. corresponding to COOPER, 2: the practice of such sales: nautical: mid-C.19–20.

Cooper's ducks with, be. To be all over with: London butchers' (—1902); slightly ob. Apperson from *Notes and Queries.* Presumably of anecdotal origin.

***coor.** To whip: Scottish c. of ca 1810–80. Haggart's *Life*, 1821. Prob. ex S.E. *coir.*

coot. A simpleton: orig. (1794), U.S.; anglicized ca 1850. Gen. as *silly coot* or *old coot.* Ex the common coot's stupidity.

cooter, see COUTER.

cooter-goosht. Bad food: Regular Army's: late C.19–20. Ex the Hindustani for 'dog's meat'.

cop. A policeman (—1859); abbr. COPPER. 2. An arrest, as in *It's a* (*fair*) *cop* (spoken by the victim): from ca 1870: low (?orig. c.). (In Cumberland dial. it = a prison.) Ex COP, v., 4. 3. An easy matter, gen. as *be no cop*: see COP, BE NO. In the Boer War, an English soldier wrote, 'We are going to a place called Spion Kop; and I don't think it will be much of a "kop" for our chaps' – it wasn't. (J. Milne, *The Epistles of Atkins*, 1902.)

cop, v. Catch, capture: from ca 1700, S.O.D. recording at 1704. 2. Hence to steal: low: mid-C.19–20. E.D.D. 3. In mid-C.19–20, it also = take, receive, be forced to endure, as in *cop it* (*hot*), to be scolded, to get into trouble. 4. As = arrest, imprison, perhaps as = steal, it was orig. (C.19) c., in C.20, low. 5. In racing c., C.20, if a 'bookie' wins on a race, he has 'copped'; and his clerk accordingly marks the book with a C; from ca 1860. The word derives prob. ex L. *capere* via the Old Fr. *caper*, to seize, whence the C.17 S.E. *cap*, to arrest: *cap* to *cop* is a normal argotic change. Whence COPPER.

cop! Beware! Take care! Anglo-Indian: mid-C.19–20; ob. ?ex the v., 3.

cop, be no (or not much). Of a task: to be difficult; of an object: valueless. From ca 1895. See COP, n., 3, and cf. *it's no catch*, which is earlier.

cop a mouse. To get a black eye: artisans' (—1909). Ware.

***cop bung!** 'A warning cry when the police make their appearance': c.: from ca 1875. B. & L. See COP, n., 1.

cop it (hot), see COP, v., 3.

cop on is the Northern equivalent of Southern *get off* (with a member of the other sex): late C.19–20.

***cop on the cross.** Cunningly to discover guilt: late C.19–20 c.

cop out. See COP, v., 3. 2. Also, to die: military in Boer War and, occ., later. J. Milne, *Epistles of Atkins*, 1902.

cop the brewery, the curtain, see BREWERY, COP THE, and CURTAIN, COP THE.

***copbusy.** To hand the booty over to a confederate or a girl: c. (—1839); ob. Brandon.

cope. 'An exchange, bargain; a successful deal': low: from ca 1840; ob. Carew, *Autobiography of a Gipsy*, 1891. Prob. independent of the same word recorded, for C.16–17, by the O.E.D.

(?*)copesmate. An accomplice: late C.16–early 17 c. or low s.; T. Wilson, 1570; Greene. cf. the S.E.

copper. A policeman, i.e. one who 'cops' or captures, arrests: orig. theatrical: from 1840s. 2. A penny or a halfpenny: from ca 1840. In pl, coll for halfpennies and pennies mixed. 'Still used of the bronze which has superseded the copper coinage', O.E.D., 1893.

copper, catch. To come to harm: C.16–17; s. > coll.

copper, worth one's weight in burnt. Of little worth: coll (—1887); slightly ob. (In copper instead of in gold.)

copper-belly. A fat man: cockneys': late C.19–20. The *copper* being that used on washing day.

copper-captain. A pretended captain: from ca 1800 (?orig. U.S.); coll > S.E.

copper-clawing. A fight between women: London streets': from ca 1820; ob. Ware suggests *cap-a-clawing*.

copper Johns. A sixpence: s.: Ned Ward, 1700.

Copper Knob. Nickname for a red-headed person, esp. man: since ca 1860.

***copper-man.** A policeman: Australian c.; ca 1870–1910. Ex COPPER, n., 1.

copper-nose. The red, pimply, swollen nose of habitual drunkards: coll; from early C.17; B.E. records the adj. *copper-nosed*, which until ca 1660 was S.E.

copper-rattle. (Irish) stew: naval (—1909); ob. Ware. Ex the noise made by the bones in the pot.

copper-slosher. One apt to GO FOR (2) the police: 1882.

copper-stick. The *membrum virile*: low: C.19–20; ob. Analogous is C.19 *coral branch*. 2. From ca 1880, a policeman's truncheon.

copper-tail. A member of the lower classes: Australian: late 1880s.

copper-tailed, see SILVER-TAIL.

coppers, clear one's. To clear one's throat: 1831, Trelawney. cf.:

coppers, cool one's, see COOL ONE'S COPPERS.

coppers, hot. The hot, dry mouth and throat ensuing on excessive drinking: coll, from ca 1840.

***copper's nark.** A police spy or informer: c.; from ca 1860. NARK = spy.

copper's shanty. A police-station: low: ca 1890–1915.

coppy, a tufted fowl; adj., crested: dial. (—1880) >, by 1885, coll. Ex dial. *cop*, the top of anything.

copus. A drink of wine or beer imposed as a fine in hall: Cambridge University, C.18–19. Johnson derives ex *episcopus* (cf. BISHOP); H. ex *hippocras*.

copy of (one's) countenance. A pretence, hypocrisy; sham, humbug: from ca 1570; coll passing in C.17 to S.E. In *Westward Ho*, a play of 1607: 'I shall love a puritan's face the worse, whilst I live, for that copy of thy countenance.'

copy of uneasiness. 'A copy of writ in any court', Bee: ca 1820–40.

cor. God, as a low expletive: C.19–20. Via GOR.

cor lummie (or -y)! A Cockney expletive: mid-C.19–20. i.e. *God love me!*

coral. Money: 1841, W. Leman Rede, *Sixteen String Jack*; †by 1900. *coral branch*, COPPER-STICK.

Cordle, Lord and Lady. Two finely bedecked canaries sitting in a little carriage: London street-performers' coll nickname (—1887).

cords. A pair of corduroy trousers; clothes of corduroy: from ca 1880: lower classes' s.

corduroys. (A pair of) corduroy trousers: from ca 1780; coll.

***core,** v.i. To pick up small articles in shops: ca 1810–60. vbl n., *cor(e)ing*. Perhaps ex Romany *čor*, to steal (Sampson).

***coriander (seed),** see COLIANDER.

Corinth. A brothel: C.17–19; coll >, by 1800, S.E. The ancient Greek city was noted for its elegance and modernity, also for its licentiousness.

Corinthian. A rake: late C.16–18; coll soon S.E., as is the adj. 2. A dandy, hence a fashionable man about town: ca 1800–50; coll > S.E., precisely as SWELL, which was in vogue by 1854, > S.E. One of the characters in Pierce Egan's *Life in London* is Corinthian Tom.

cork. Incorrect for *calk*, v. (late C.18–20) and n., a sharp point on a horse-shoe: C.19–20. 2. A bankrupt: ca 1870–1900. Ex his lack of 'ballast'. 3. In Scottish coll, from ca 1830, a small employer; a foreman. 4. See CORKS. 5. A workman bringing a charge against his fellows: workshops' (—1909). Ware derives ex *caucus*.

cork, draw a or the. In boxing, to draw blood: from ca 1815; ob. cf. *tap one's claret* (at TAP, v., 2).

cork and water. Any bottle of medicine: Bootham School: late C.19–20.

cork-and-water club. Old scholars at Oxford University: id.: id.

cork-brained. Foolish, light-headed: C.17–20; coll; S.E. after ca 1820. In B.E. as *corky-b*.

corked. (Of wine) tasting of cork: coll (—1864).

corker. Something that ends an argument

or a course of action; anything astounding, esp. a great lie. Recorded for 1837; app. orig. U.S. (O.E.D.): s. cf. CAULKER, SETTLER; WHOPPER, and esp. *put the* LID ON.

corker, play the. (Of persons) to be unusual, exaggerated, eccentric; in university and Public School, to make oneself objectionable. From ca 1870. Anstey in *Vice Versa*.

corking. Unusually large, fine, good: from early 1890s: mostly U.S., s. App. ex CORKER, on the model of other percussive adjj. WHACKING, WHOPPING, etc.

corks. A butler: from ca 1860. cf. CHIPS, a carpenter. 2. Money: nautical and military; from ca 1858. Ex the floating property of corks.

corkscrew! An evasion of *God's truth*: low London (—1909). cf. CHEESE AND CRUST.

corkscrew. To move spirally (1837). Coll. Dickens: 'Mr Bantam corkscrewed his way through the crowd.' 2. **corkscrew out.** To draw out as with a corkscrew: coll: 1852, Dickens.

corkscrewing. The uneven walk due to intoxication: from ca 1840; coll.

corkscrews. Abbr. *corkscrew curls*: coll; from ca 1880. Displaces BOTTLE-SCREWS.

corky. Frivolous; lively; restive: from ca 1600: coll; ob. Contrast the S.E. senses.

corky-brained. A coll variant (C.17–19) of CORK-BRAINED.

corn, a great harvest of a little. Much ado about nothing: coll; C.17–early 19.

corn, carry, see CARRY CORN.

corn, earn or **be worth one's.** To be worth one's wages – one's keep: coll, orig. farmers': mid-C.19–20.

corn fake; corn fake worker. A corn cure; a market-place or fair-ground chiropodist: showmen's: since ca 1880. cf. NOB FAKE. Mostly a corn-plaster.

corn in Egypt. Plenty, esp. of food: coll; from ca 1830.

corn-snorter. The nose: low: ca 1825–70. *Sinks*, 1848.

corned. Drunk (—1785). cf. *pickled* and *salted* for semantics. Not, as often supposed, an Americanism, as, however, *have corns in the head* (to be drunk) may possibly be. In dial., *corny*. 2. Pleased; content; tailors': from ca 1870.

cornelian tub. A sweating-tub: late C.18–early 19 coll.

corner. A money-market monopoly with ulterior motives. From the 1850s. Coll >, by 1900, S.E. 2. **The corner.** Tattersall's subscription rooms: mid-C.19–20, †; sporting. It is more than ninety years since 'Tatts' was near Hyde Park Corner. 3. Also, Tattenham Corner on the Derby course at Epsom: sporting, from ca 1870. 4. In c. (—1891), a share; the chance of a share in the proceeds of a robbery.

corner, v. Drive into a fig. corner: ex U.S. (1824), anglicized ca 1840: coll. 2. Monopolize a stock or a commodity: from the mid-1830s in U.S. (whence, too, the corresponding n.) and anglicized before 1860.

corner, be round the. To get ahead of one's fellows by unfair or dishonest methods: from ca 1860.

corner, hot, see HOT CORNER.

corner-boy. A loafer: Anglo-Irish coll: from ca 1880; but recorded in U.S. in 1855. Prob. suggested by CORNER-COVE. cf. CORNER-MAN.

corner-cove. A hanger-on: pugilistic: ca 1815–60. 2. A street-corner lounger or loafer: coll; from ca 1850. Mayhew.

corner-creeper. An underhand and furtive person: coll; ca 1560–1720; S.E. after 1600.

corner-man. A loafer: coll, from ca 1880 (recorded in 1885). Replacing CORNER-COVE. 2. An end man, 'bones' or 'tambourine', in a Negro-minstrel or an analogous show: from ca 1860; ob.

corner-shop. A guard-room: Army s. (—1900). It often stands at a corner of the barrack square.

cornerer. A question difficult to answer: coll (—1887). Ex CORNER, v., 1.

cornering. The practice of CORNER, v., 2.

corney, see CORNY-FACED.

cornichon. A MUFF (e.g. at shooting): Society, 1880–ca 1886. Ex Fr.

Cornish duck. A pilchard: trade: from ca 1865; ob. cf. YARMOUTH CAPON.

corns and bunions. Onions: rhyming s.: late C.19–20.

corns in the head, have. To be drunk: drinkers' (—1745); †by 1860.

cornstalk (or **C.**). A New South Welshman of European descent: coll: from ca 1825. Later (ca 1880), and loosely, any Australian of the Eastern states. Peter Cunningham, 1827, 'From the way in which they shoot up'; rather, ex tendency to tall slimness.

cornuted. Cuckolded: late C.17–18; coll. Ex a cuckold's horns. cf.:

Cornwall without a boat, send (a man)

into. To cuckold him: ca 1565–1830. Painter, *Palace of Pleasure*, 1567; Halliwell. Punning †*corn*(*e*), a horn, (in fortification) hornwork. Apperson. cf. CORNUTED.

corny-faced. Red and pimply with drink: ca 1690–1830. cf. CORNED.

coroner. A heavy fall: from ca 1870; ob. i.e. one likely to lead to an inquest.

corp. A corpse: nautical: late C.19–20. E. Pugh, *A Street in Suburbia*, 1895. Recorded in dial. in 1775.

corporal and four, mount a. To masturbate: low; late C.18–20, ob.

Corporal Forbes or **the Corporal Forbes.** Cholera Morbus: Regular Army (esp. in India): from 1820s. Shipp's *Memoirs*, 1829.

corporation. A prominent belly: from ca 1750; coll. C. Brontë, in *Shirley*, 'The dignity of an ample corporation'. Influenced by S.E. *corpulent*.

corporation's work, freeman of a. 'Neither strong nor handsome': c.p. of ca 1780–1820. Grose, 1st ed. (Not very complimentary to corporate towns.)

corpse. A horse entered in a race for betting purposes only: the turf, from ca 1870.

corpse, v. To blunder (whether unintentionally or not), and thus confuse other actors or spoil a scene; the blunderer is said to be 'corpsed': theatrical: from ca 1855; ob. 2. To kill: low; recorded in 1884. Henley & Stevenson in *Deacon Brodie*. Ex dial.

corpse lights. Corposants (St Elmo's fire): nautical coll: mid-C.19–20.

corpse-provider. A physician or a surgeon: from ca 1840; ob.

corpse-worship. A marked profusion of flowers at funerals: clubmen's: ca 1880–1900. Ware says that 'this custom, set by the Queen at the mausoleum (Frogmore) immediately after the death of the Prince Consort [in 1861], grew rapidly . . . Finally, in the '90s, many death notices in the press were followed by the legend, "No flowers".'

correct card, the. The right thing to have or do; the TICKET: from ca 1860, ex lit. racing sense. Often written *k'rect card.*

corro'boree, corro'bbery. A large social gathering or meeting (—1892). Perhaps ex: 2. A drunken spree: nautical: late C.19–20. Ex: 3. A fuss, noise, disturbance (—1874). Ex the lit. senses (Australian); properly a Botany Bay aboriginal word.

corroboree, v. To boil (v.i.); to dance. Australia: from ca 1880; ob. For v. and n., see Edward Morris's neglected dictionary, *Austral English*, 1898.

corruption, occ. in pl. Natural sinfulness, 'the old Adam': 1799; coll.

corsey. Reckless (betting or gambling): sporting coll: 1883; ob. Ex Fr. *corsé.*

Corsican, the. Something unusual: sporting; ca 1880–1913. Coined by F. C. Burnand (1836–1917), playwright and editor of *Punch*.

corybungus. The posterior: boxing; ca 1850–1900. Etymology?

'cos. Because: coll: C.19–20. Better spelt '*cause*.

***cosey.** A late C.19–20 variant of CARSEY = *casa* (2), CASE. 2. Ware, however, notes that, in the London slums, it is (from before 1909) 'a small, hilarious public-house, where singing, dancing, drinking, etc., goes on at all hours'. Prob. influenced by S.E. *cosy*.

***cosh.** A life-preserver, NEDDY (4), i.e. a short, thin but loaded bludgeon; also (rare before C.20) a policeman's truncheon. From ca 1870: orig. c., then low. Prob. ex Romany.

***cosh,** v. To strike with a cosh; esp. thus to render unconscious: late C.19–20 c. Ex the n.

***cosh-carrier.** A harlot's bully: c. (—1893). E.D.D. Ex COSH, n., 1. Hence, *cosh-carrying*: c. (—1896).

cosher, n., see KOSHER. 2. In late C.19–20 c., one who uses a COSH. 3. A policeman: Berkshire s. (—1905). 4. v.i., to talk familiarly and free-and-easily: coll: from ca 1830. cf. Scottish *cosh*, on intimate terms, ex *cosh*, snug, comfortable.

cosier. An inferior seaman: naval: C.19. Ex the †S.E. *cosier, -zier*, a cobbler.

coss. A blow, a punch: hatters' (—1909). Perhaps ex COSH + GOSS.

cossack. A policeman: from late 1850s. H., 1st ed.; the *Graphic*, 30 Jan. 1886, 'A policeman is also called a "cossack", a "Philistine", and a "frog".' All three terms are †.

cossid. A 'runner', i.e. a running messenger: Anglo-Indian coll: late C.17–20. Ex Arabic.

costard. The head: jocularly coll (—1530). Palsgrave; Udall in *Ralph Roister Doister*; Shakespeare; B.E.; Grose; Scott. Ex *costard*, a large apple. cf.:

coster. Abbr. (—1851) *costermonger* (C.16), orig. *costard-monger*, at first a seller of apples, then of any fruit, finally of fruit, fish, vegetables, etc., from a barrow. cf. COSTARD, and BARROW-MAN.

costering. Costermongering: from ca 1850; ob. Mayhew, 1851.

costermonger Joe. 'Common title for a favourite coster': commercial London (—1909). Ware.

costermongering. 'Altering orchestral or choral music, especially that of great composers': musical: ca 1850–1910. Ware. Ex Sir Michael Costa's adaptations of Handel.

costive. Niggardly: late C.16–20; coll, in C.20 S.E. and rare.

cot. Abbr. *cotquean*, a man meddling with women's work and affairs: coll: late C.17–18. Extant in dial.

cot, on the. 'A man of a bad character, trying to amend his ways – i.e. in a moral hospital, so to speak': military: late C.19–early 20.

cots. The shoe-strings of monitors: Christ's Hospital, ca 1780–1890. Charles Lamb. Ex *cotton*. 2. God's, in coll oaths: C.16–mid-18.

cotso. A variant of CATSO.

Cots(w)old lion. A sheep: mid-C.15–mid-19. Ex the sheep-fame of the Cotswolds. Anon., ca 1540; 'Proverbs' Heywood; Harington in his *Epigrams*. cf. ESSEX LION; CAMBRIDGESHIRE NIGHTINGALE.

cottage. Abbr. *cottage piano*: (—1880) coll > j. 2. A urinal: ca 1900–12.

Cotterel's salad; Sir James (Cotter's or) Cotterel's salad. Hemp: Anglo-Irish, C.18–early 19. A baronet of that name was hanged for *rape*.

cotton, v.i. Prosper; hence, agree together: coll; the former (†), from ca 1560; the latter, from ca 1600. In an old play (1605), 'John a Nokes and John a Style and I cannot cotton.' The primary sense ('prosper') may arise ex 'a fig. sense of raising a nap on cloth', W. 2. Hence, with *to*, GET ON (5) well with (a person), take kindly to (an idea, a thing): from ca 1800; coll. Barham, 'It's amazing to think, | How one cottons to drink!'

***Cotton, leave the world with one's ears stuffed full of.** To be hanged: Newgate c. of ca 1820–40. Ex the name of the Newgate chaplain, by a pun.

cotton-box. An American ship, bluff-bowed, for carrying cotton: nautical: C.19. Bowen, 'The old clipper men used to speak of them as being built by the mile and sawn off in lengths when wanted.'

cotton in their ears, die with. A variant of COTTON, LEAVE THE WORLD WITH ONE'S EARS STUFFED FULL OF.

cotton-lord, occ. **-king.** A wealthy manufacturer of, dealer in, cotton: 1823. Coll >, by 1880, S.E. cf. COTTONOCRACY, COTTONOPOLIS.

cotton-top. A loose woman preserving most of the appearances: ca 1830–80. Ex stockings cotton-topped, silk to just above the ankles.

cotton up. To make friendly overtures; v.t. with *to*. Both coll; from ca 1850. See COTTON.

cotton-wool, wrap in. To cosset, coddle: coll; from ca 1870; now almost S.E.

cottonocracy. Cotton magnates as a class: coll: 1845. cf.:

Cottonopolis. Manchester: from ca 1870: coll. cf. COTTON-LORD and ALBERTOPOLIS.

Cotzooks! A coll corruption of *God's hooks* (nails on the Cross): early C.18. cf. GADZOOKS!

***couch a hog's head.** Lit., to lay down one's head, i.e. to lie down and sleep: C.16–17 c.; in C.18, low. Recorded in Harman, B.E., Scott (as an archaism). Occ. *cod's head.*

***couch a porker.** A variant of the preceding: c.: (?)C.18.

cough(-)and(-)sneeze. Cheese: rhyming s.: since ca 1880.

cough-drop. A CHARACTER; a quick courter or 'love'-maker: low coll: 1895, the *Referee*, '"Honest John Burns" ... objects to being called "a cough drop".' Ware postulates '1860 on'.

cough-lozenge. A mishap; something unpleasant; esp. in *that's a cough-lozenge for* (somebody): a virtual c.p. of 1850–60. cf. preceding.

cough up. To disclose: from C.14, now ob. (not, as the S.O.D. says, †); S.E. in C.14–17; coll in C.19–20. 2. To pay, v.i. and t.: from ca 1895.

Coulson. A court jester: a coll nickname (—1553) soon > allusive S.E. Ex a famous fool so named.

coulter-neb. The puffin: nautical: C.19–20; ob. Ex its sharp beak.

council of ten. The toes of a man with inturned feet: ca 1858–90.

councillor of the pipowder court. A pettifogging lawyer: coll; ca 1750–1850. Ex *Court of Piepowders*, dealing summary justice at fairs; Fr. *pieds poudreux.*

***counsellor.** A barrister: Irish c. (—1889) and dial. (—1862). Ex Scots (C.19–20).

count. A man of fashion: ca 1840–60; coll. cf. DANDY; SWELL; TOFF.

count, out for the. (Often preceded by *put.*) Ruined; dead: from ca 1880. Ex boxing.

count, take the. To die: from ca 1890. Also ex boxing.

Count No-Account. 'A facetious title for one who, lacking funds, claims an aristocratic background' (Leechman): Canadian: ca 1895–1914.

count noses. To count the Ayes and *Noes*: Parliamentary: from ca 1885; ob.

counter. An inferior officer of a counter or prison: C.17.

counter-hopper. A Londoners' coll variant (ca 1850–1910; Mayhew, 1851) of the next.

counter-jumper. A shopman: coll: 1831, an American example (O.E.D. Sup.); S. Warren, 1841; G. A. Sala, 1864, 'He is as dextrous as a Regent Street counter-jumper in the questionable art of "shaving the ladies".' Baumann, 1887, has *counter-skipper*.

***counterfeit crank.** A sham-sick man: mid-C.16–18: mostly c. Burton's *Anatomy*.

counting-house. Countenance (n.): non-aristocratic, non-cultured: ca 1870–1910.

country, the. The outfield: from early 1880s: cricket s. Lillywhite's *Cricket Companion*, 1884 (O.E.D.). But *country stroke* appears as early as 1872. Also *country catching* (1888), *c. field(sman)* in 1890s.

country-captain. A very dry curry, often with a spatch-cocked fowl; Anglo-Indian: coll: from ca 1790. 2. Also (—1792,†), the captain of a COUNTRY-SHIP.

country cousin. A dozen: rhyming s. (—1909).

***country Harry.** A waggoner: mid-C.18–early 19 c.

country-put. 'A silly Country-Fellow', B.E.: coll; late C.17–early 19. See PUT, n.

country-ship. A vessel owned in an Indian port: Anglo-Indian coll (—1775); *country-boat* occurs as early as 1619.

country with (one), **be all up the.** To be ruin, or death, for: coll (—1887); virtually †.

country work. Work slow to advance: coll (—1811); ob.

county, adj. Wrapped up in the affairs of county society; apt to consider such society to be the cream of the social milk; very much upper-middle class. Coll: from ca 1880.

county-court. To sue a person in a county court: coll: from ca 1850.

county-crop. Abbr. *county-prison crop.* Hair cut close and as though with the help of a basin: a 'fashion' once visited on all prisoners: ca 1858–1910. 2. Hence, *county-cropped*: 1867, J. Greenwood (O.E.D.).

couple, a. A couple of drinks: coll: late C.19–20.

couple-beggar. A hedge priest: coll: C.18–19. Swift, in *Proposal for Badges to the Beggars*; prob. the earliest record; Lever, in *Handy Andy*. cf. BUCKLE-BEGGAR.

couple of flats. Two bad actors: theatrical: ca 1830–80. A pun on the two scene-screens.

coupling-house. A brothel: C.18–19; low coll.

couranne. A crown piece: theatrical: from ca 1860. Via Fr. *couronne.*

***courber,** see CURBER.

course with (a person), **take a.** To hamper him, follow him closely: coll: mid-C.17–early 19. Ex coursing.

court. To sue in a court of law: from ca 1840: coll. cf. COUNTY-COURT.

court card. 'A gay fluttering Fellow', B.E.; a dandy: coll: ca 1690–1800, then dial.

court cream; court element; court holy bread; court holy water; court water. Fair but insincere speeches, promises: C.17–18 the first; the others being C.16–18. All are coll, as, orig., was the C.17–18 *court promises.*

court martial. (Gen. hyphenated.) To try by court martial: from ca 1855; coll.

court martial, n. A tossing in a blanket: schoolboys': from ca 1870.

court noll, courtnoll. A courtier: coll, pejorative; ca 1560–1680. In C.17, S.E.

court of assistants. Young men to whom young wives, married to old men, are apt to turn: a late C.18–early 19 facetious coll punning the S.E. sense.

court tricks. 'State-Policy', B.E.: coll; mid-C.17–18.

court water, see COURT CREAM.

***cousin.** A trull: c.; —1863. S.O.D. 2. In late C.16 c., a (rustic) PIGEON (4). Greene.

cousin Betty. A half-witted woman: mid-C.19–20; ob.; coll. Mrs Gaskell, in *Sylvia's Lovers*, '. . . gave short measure to a child or a cousin Betty'. cf. COUSIN TOM. 2. Also, a strumpet: C.18–mid-19: c. and, latterly, low s.

cousin Jan or **Jacky.** A Cornishman: coll and dial.: from ca 1850.

cousin the weaver or, as in Swift and Fielding, **dirty cousin.** Prefaced by *my*, these two terms – the latter much the more gen. – were, in late C.17–18, pejorative forms of address: coll.

cousin Tom. A half-witted man: in C.18 if a beggar, in C.19 of any such unfortunate, though not applied to a person of standing. cf. COUSIN BETTY.

cousin trumps. One of the same occupation or, occ., character: mainly, like BROTHER SMUT, as a familiar tu-quoque. Coll; C.19.

couta. A rare form of COUTER. 2. A barracouta (fish); Australian coll: late C.19–20.

couter, occ. **cooter.** A sovereign: perhaps orig. c., certainly always low and mainly vagrants' and Cockney: from ca 1835. Brandon, 1839; Snowden's *Magistrate's Assistant*, 1846 (O.E.D.); H., 1st ed.; James Payn in *A Confidential Agent*, 1880. Ex Romany *kotor*, a guinea.

***cove.** A man, a companion, chap, fellow; a rogue: from ca 1560. In C.16 often *cofe*. In C.16–18, c.; still low. Dickens, in *Oliver Twist*, 'Do you see that old cove at the book-stall?' Prob. cognate with Romany *cova*, *covo*, that man, and, as W. suggests, identical with Scottish *cofe*, a hawker (cf. CHAP ex *chapman*). 2. Hence, in Australia, the owner, the BOSS (2), of a sheep-station: ca 1870–1910. This sense owes something to: 3. **the cove** (or **Cove**), 'the master of a house or shop', Vaux: c. of ca 1800–70. cf. next entry but one.

***cove of (the) dossing-ken.** The landlord of a low lodging-house: C.19 c. cf.:

***cove of the ken, the.** 'The master of the house', Egan's Grose: c. of ca 1820–70. Ex COVE, 3.

covee. 'A variant spelling of *covey*, a man': *Boxiana*, IV, 1824. The term was ca 1815–30 much applied to landlords of public houses.

Covent Garden. A farthing: rhyming s. on FARDEN (—1857).

Covent Garden abbess. A procuress: C.18–early 19. The Covent Garden district, in C.18, teemed with brothels. See esp. Beresford Chancellor's *Annals of Covent Garden*; Fielding's *Covent Garden Tragedy*; and Grose, P. cf. BANKSIDE LADIES and DRURY LANE VESTAL.

Covent Garden ague. A venereal disease: late C.17–early 19. cf. DRURY LANE AGUE, and see COVENT GARDEN ABBESS and COVENT GARDEN RAILS.

Covent Garden lady. A variant (ca 1800–30), noted in 1823 by Bee, of:

Covent Garden nun. A harlot: mid-C.18–early 19. cf. NUN and DRURY LANE VESTAL.

Covent Garden rails, break one's shins against. To catch a venereal disease: low: late C.18–early 19. cf. COVENT GARDEN AGUE.

Coventry, gone to; or he (she, etc.) has gone to Coventry. He doesn't speak (to me, to us, etc.) nowadays: tailors': late C.19–20. Ex:

Coventry, send one to. To ignore socially: mid-C.18–20; orig. military. Coll, > S.E. ca 1830. Origin uncertain: perhaps ex Coventry Gaol, where many Royalists were imprisoned during the Civil War (see e.g. Clarendon's *History of the Rebellion*, VI, § 83). Lytton, *Alice*, 'If any one dares to buy it, we'll send him to Coventry.' cf. the County Antrim *go to Dingley couch*, the Ulster *send to Dinglety-cootch*, and see esp. the O.E.D. and Grose, P.

***cover.** A pickpocket's assistant: c.: from ca 1810. cf. STALL. Ex:

***cover,** v.t. and i. To act as a (thief's, esp. a pickpocket's) confederate: from ca 1810: c. and low. 2. To possess a woman: low coll: C.17–20. Urquhart's *Rabelais*, 1653. Ex stallion and mare. cf. *tup*.

***cover, at the,** adj. and adv. Applied to a pickpocket cloaking the movements of the actual thief: c.: from ca 1840. Charles E. Leach. See COVER, n.

cover-arse gown. A sleeveless gown: Cambridge University, ca 1760–1860.

***cover-down.** A false tossing-coin: c.: C.19; †by 1891. See CAP, n., 4.

cover-me-decently. A coat: ca 1800–50. Moncrieff in *Tom and Jerry*.

cover(-)me(-)properly. Fashionable clothes: low: ca 1830–70. *Sinks*. Contrast:

cover(-)me(-)queerly. Ragged clothes: low: ca 1830–70. *Sinks*.

cover-slut. Apron, pinafore: coll; C.17–20, now archaic.

covered waggon. A fruit tart: *Conway* Training Ship (—1891).

covess. A woman: late C.18–mid-19. George Parker, Lytton. Ex COVE, 1.

covey. A man: low: from ca 1820; ob. Pierce Egan, 1821; Dickens in *Oliver Twist*, 'Hullo, my covey! what's the row?' Diminutive of COVE.

covey (of whores). 'A well fill'd Bawdy-house', B.E.; late C.17–early 19: coll.

***coving.** 'Theft of jewellery by palming it as a conjuror does': c.: from ca 1860.

cow. A woman: in C.18–20, low coll. Earlier, hardly opprobrious; Howell, in 1659, speaks of that proverb which, originating *temp.* Henry IV, runs, 'He that bulls the cow must keep the calf.' 2. A harlot: C.19–20; ob. 3. (Sporting) £1000: from ca 1860. cf. PONY (3), MONKEY. 4. Milk: Canadian: late C.19–20.

cow, sleep like a. (Of a married man) 'i.e. with a **** at one's a–se', Grose, 1st ed., who quotes the quatrain, 'All you that in your beds do lie, | Turn to your wives and occupy; | And when that you have done your best, | Turn arse to arse, and take your rest'; for a variant here unquotable, see Grose, P. A mid-C.18–mid-19 low coll.

cow and calf. To laugh: rhyming s. (—1859); ob.

cow-baby. A faint-hearted person: coll; from ca 1590. In C.19–20, dial.

cow-bridges. 'The fore and aft gangways in the waists of old men-of-war, before the days of completely planked main decks', Bowen: naval: C.19.

cow-cocky. A dairy-farmer: Australian: from ca 1890. See COCKY, n., 5.

cow come home, till the, C.17–18 coll. See COWS COME HOME . . .

cow-cow, v.i. and t. To be in a rage; to scold, reprimand severely: Anglo-Chinese; mid-C.19–20.

cow-(occ. bushel-, sluice-)cunted. Low coll pejorative applied to a woman deformed by child-bearing or by harlotry: C.19–20.

cow died of, the tune the old, see TUNE THE (OLD) COW . . .

cow-grease or **-oil.** Butter: coll: mid-C.19–20. In C.19, gen. *cow's-grease.* cf. COW-JUICE.

cow-gun. A heavy naval gun: naval s. (from ca 1900).

cow-handed. Awkward: late C.18–19 coll.

cow-heart. Either jocular or pedantically sol. for coward: C.19–20 (?earlier). Prob. suggested by:

cow-hearted. 'Fearful or Hen-hearted', B.E.; coll, verging on S.E.: mid-C.17–20, ob. cf. preceding.

cow-hitch. A clumsily tied knot: nautical (—1867). As in COW-GUN and COW-HANDED, the idea is of unwieldiness.

cow-hocked. Thick-ankled; large- or clumsy-footed. Coll; mid-C.19–20.

cow-horn. A brass mortar on shipboard: naval: late C.19–20; ob. A perversion of *coe-horn.*

cow in a cage, as comely (or nimble) as a. Very ungainly or clumsy: coll: 1399, Langland; 1546, Heywood; 1678, Ray; 1732, Fuller. cf. BULL IN A CHINA SHOP . . .

cow-juice. Milk: coll; late C.18–20. Grose, 3rd ed.; heard on the *Conway* Training Ship (—1890), says Masefield. Esp. opp. *tinned cow.*

cow-lick. 'A peculiar lock of hair, greased, curled, brought forward from the ear, and plastered on the cheek. Once common amongst costermongers and tramps.' F. & H.; H., 2nd ed., has it. Coll >, by 1900, S.E. It looks as if a cow had licked it into shape. (First used in late C.16, prob. of a fashion different from that of the costers.)

cow-oil, see COW-GREASE.

cow-pad. A third-term cadet employed in keeping the petty officers' quarters clean: Training Ship *Worcester*: late C.19–20.

cow-quake. A bull's roar: coll, mostly Irish and dial.: C.19–20.

cow-shooter. A DEER-STALKER hat, worn by seniors: Winchester College, C.19.

cow-turd. A piece of cow-dung: late C.15–20: S.E. until C.19, then a vulgarism.

cow-with-the-iron-tail. (Gen. without hyphens.) A pump, yielding water to be mixed with milk: jocular coll: from ca 1790.

cowan. A sneak, eavesdropper, Paul Pry; an uninitiated person; from ca 1850. Ex freemasonry, certainly the last nuance and perhaps the others. Ex Scottish *cowan* or *kirwan*, a rough stone-mason; or, less prob., Gr. κύων, a dog.

coward's castle or **corner.** A pulpit, 'six feet above argument': coll; C.19–20, ob.

cowardy (occ. **cowardly**) **custard.** A child's taunt: coll: C.19–20. A custard quivers and is yellow.

cowle. Almost any document of a promissory or warranty nature, e.g. lease, safe-conduct: Anglo-Indian, from late C.17.

cows-and-kisses. (But occ. unhyphenated.) The MISSIS: wife or mistress (of house); any woman. Rhyming s. (—1857).

cow's baby, occ. babe. A calf: late C.17–20; coll. 2. Hence, ca 1820–60, 'any lubberly kind of fellow', Bee, 1823.

cows come home, till the. An indefinite time; for ever: mostly Canada, Australia, New Zealand: coll: mid-C.19–20. Ex U.S. (1824: Thornton); orig. (1610), English, as *till the cow come home.*

cow's courant. A 'gallop and sh–[t]e', Grose, 2nd ed.: low coll: late C.18–early 19. *Courant* = *coranto*, a quick dance.

cow's grease (H., 1st ed.), see COW-GREASE.

cow's-spouse. A bull: late C.18–mid-19. Prob. *spouse* rather than *husband* by rhyming association: cf. BUBBLY JOCK.

cow's thumb, to a. Mid-C.17–20, ob.; coll. 'When a thing is done exactly, nicely [i.e. fastidiously], or to a Hair', B.E.: is this ironical?

cox. Abbr. *coxswain*: from ca 1880; coll. 2. The same applies to the v. (t. or i.).

coxcomb. The head: jocular coll, punning *cock's comb*; late C.16–19. Shakespeare. cf. S.E. senses. See esp. Weekley's *More Words Ancient and Modern.*

coxy, see COCKSY.

coy or **Coy,** see CO., 2.

coyduck. To decoy, v.t., rarely v.i.: C.19–20, coll and dial. Prob. ex *coy-duck* = *decoy-duck*, and not, as Farmer ingeniously suggests, a blend of *conduct* and *decoy.*

coyote. The *pudendum muliebre*: C.19. (cf. CAT, PUSSY.) Lit., the barking-wolf of the U.S.

coz. Abbr. *cousin*: used either lit. or to a friend: coll.; late C.16–early 19. Shakespeare.

coze. An intimate talk; a comfortable friendly time together: 1814, Jane Austen, *Mansfield Park*, 'Proposed their going up into her room, where they might have a comfortable coze': ca 1790–1860. Perhaps originally from Fr. *caus*erie.

cozier, see COSIER.

cozza. Pork: cheapjacks' and costers'; from ca 1850. Charles Hindley, 1876. Ex Hebrew *chazar*, a pig.

crab. A decoy at auctions: low, C.19–20, ob. 2. Abbr. *crab-louse*, a human-body louse, esp. and properly one of those unpleasant vermin which affect the pubic and anal hair: low coll, from ca 1800. In B.E.'s day, *crab-louse* itself was coll. 3. See CRABS. 4. The action, or an instance, of finding fault: coll: from ca 1890. Ex CRAB, v. 5. A midshipman: naval: late C.19–20.

crab, v. To 'pull to pieces', criticize adversely: low s. >, ca 1840, gen. s. >, ca 1870, coll; from ca 1810. Occ. as v.i.: mid-C.19–20. cf. the S.E. senses, to oppose, irritate, and the C.19–20 c. sense, to expose, inform on, insult, spoil. vbl n., *crabbing*.

crab, catch a, see CATCH A CRAB.

***crab, throw a.** A v.i. form (c. of ca 1810–40) of CRAB, V.

crab lanthorn. A peevish fellow: late C.18–early 19 coll. cf. CRAB WALLAH.

crab-louse, see CRAB, n., 2.

***crab-shells.** Boots, shoes: from ca 1780, perhaps orig. c., for in c. CRABS = feet. Grose, 1st ed.; Mayhew, 'With a little mending, they'll make a tidy pair of crab-shells again.' cf. TROTTER-BOXES.

***Crab Street, in.** 'Affronted; out of humour', Vaux: c. (—1812); †by 1890. A pun on *crabbed*. cf. QUEER STREET, IN.

crab wallah. An evil man: Regular Army's: late C.19–20. cf. CRAB LANTHORN and see WALLAH.

***crabs.** In c., shoes: ca 1810–1900. Also feet: from ca 1840. Abbr. CRAB-SHELLS. 2. In gaming, esp. at hazard, a throw of two aces, 'deuce-ace' (cf. DEUCE): from ca 1765: Lord Carlisle, 1768; Barham. Whence:

crabs, come off or **turn out or up (a case of).** Of things: to be a failure, unfortunate. C.19–20.

***crabs, move one's.** To run away: c.: mid-C.19–20; virtually †.

crabtree comb. A cudgel: jocular coll: late C.16–19.

crack. Abbr. CRACK-BRAIN, a crazy or soft-headed person: coll; C.17–18. Dekker, Addison. 2. A harlot: ca 1670–1820: orig. c., then low. D'Urfey, 1676; Farquhar, 'You imagine I have got your whore, cousin, your crack'; Vanbrugh; Dyche; Grose. ?ex *crack*, the female genitals: low, C.16–20. 3. A lie (the mod. form is *cracker*): ca 1600–1820; coll. Goldsmith, 'That's a damned confounded crack.' Whence, prob., the coll sense, a liar: C.17. 4. In mid-C.18–19 c., a burglar or a burglary: whence – both in Vaux – *cracksman*; and *the crack*, a (—1812) variant of (*the*) *crack lay*. 5. Any person or thing – though very rarely the latter in C.20 – that approaches perfection: coll; from ca 1700 for persons, from ca 1630 for things (cf. the adj.). 6. Hence esp. a racehorse of great excellence: from ca 1850, e.g. in those very horsey publications, *Diogenes*, 1853, *Derby Day*, 1864, and *From Post to Finish* (1884), the third by Hawley Smart, the less popular Nat Gould of the 80s and '90s. 7. cf. **the crack,** the fashion or vogue: ca 1780–1840: fashionable world, as rendered by Pierce Egan, his cronies and his rivals. cf. the adj. 8. A crisp and resounding blow: coll; S.O.D. records for 1838. Ex the crack of a whip or a shotgun. 9. Dry firewood: c., Gypsy, and low: from ca 1840 (recorded in Mayhew in 1851). Ex the crackling sound it emits when burning.

10. A narrow passage [or alley] of houses: London proletarian (—1909). 11. A fop: Ned Ward, 1703. Ex sense 5.

crack, v. To boast, brag: C.15–20, ob. S.E. till ca 1700, then coll and dial. Burton in his *Anatomy*: 'Your very tradesmen . . . will crack and brag.' 2. To fall into disrepair; into ruin: C.17–19 coll. Dryden. 3. To collapse; break down (v.i.): sporting, from ca 1870. 4. To break open, burgle: c. and low: from ca 1720. Dickens in *Oliver Twist*, 'There's one part we can crack, safe and softly.' Esp. in *crack a crib*, to break into a house, likewise c. and low. 5. Wholly c.: to inform; v.t. with *on*: ca 1850–1910. 6. To drink (cf. CRUSH): late C.16–20: coll. Gen. with *a quart* or *a bottle*. Shakespeare in the 2nd *Henry IV*, 'By the mass, you'll crack a quart together'; Fielding and Thackeray (*a bottle*). 7. v.i., a variant of CRACK ALONG: coll. 8. v.i., to fire (a rifle, shotgun, etc.); v.t., with *at*. Coll; from ca 1870. 9. In cricket, from ca 1880, to hit (the ball) hard. 10. To smite (a person): Australian: late C.19–20. e.g. 'He'll crack you one'; C. J. Dennis. 11. To devirginate: low: C.18–20. cf. CRACK A JUDY and CRACKED, 3.

crack, adj. First-class; excellent: from ca 1790; coll. Esp. of regiments, riflemen, and athletes. Thackeray, 1839, 'Such a crack-shot myself, that fellows were shy of insulting me.' cf. CRACK, n., 5, 6.

crack, fetch a, see FETCH . . . A CRACK.

crack, in a. Instantaneously: coll: from ca 1720. Byron, 1819, 'They're on the stair just now, and in a crack will all be here.'

crack, must have been sleeping near a, see SLEEPING NEAR A CRACK . . .

crack a bottle, see CRACK, v., 6.

crack a crib, see CRACK, v., 4.

crack a crust. To make a living; rub along. Superlatively, *crack a tidy crust*: coll, from ca 1850. Mayhew, 'Crack an honest crust'; H., 1874, 'A very common expression among the lower orders'.

crack a Judy, a Judy's tea-cup. (cf. the U.S. use of *Jane*, any girl.) To deprive a maid of her virginity. C.19–20, low, ob.

***crack a ken** or **a swag.** To commit a burglary: c.; the former, C.18; the latter C.19–20, ob.

***crack a whid.** To talk: C.19–20 (ob.) c. Vaux; Hindley's *Cheap Jack*. See WHID.

crack along or **on.** v.i., to make great speed. v.t., *crack on* or *out*, to cause to move quickly, often with connotation of jerkily. Both coll, recorded in 1541. In C.19, the adv. is often omitted.

crack-brain(ed), -headed, -skull, nn. and adjj. Indicative of craziness: all coll. quickly > S.E.; C.16–19. Here *crack* = CRACKED, 2.

***crack-fencer.** A seller of nuts: low or c.; from ca 1850; †by 1900.

crack-halter, -hemp, -rope, nn. and adjj. A GAOLBIRD: a good-for-nothing 'born to be hanged'. All coll passing rapidly to S.E.: the first and second, C.16–17; the third, C.15–early 19. Gascoigne and Dekker, *c.-halter*; Shakespeare, *c.-hemp*; Massinger and Scott, *c.-rope*.

crack-haunter or **-hunter.** The *membrum virile*: low, C.19–20. cf. CRACK, n., 2.

crack-hemp, see CRACK-HALTER.

crack into (reputation, repute, fame, etc.). To render (famous, etc.) by eulogy: coll (—1892); ob.

crack-jaw. Difficult to pronounce: coll: from ca 1870. Miss Braddon.

***crack-lay, the.** House-breaking: from ca 1785; ob.; c.

crack on, v.i. See CRACK ALONG. 2. To pretend; esp. pretend to be ill or hurt: ?orig. military: from the 1880s, if not earlier. See the Kipling quotation at BLIND, V.

crack (or break) one's egg or **duck.** To begin to score: cricket; from ca 1868.

crack-pot. A pretentiously useless, worthless person: coll: from ca 1860.

crack-rope, see CRACK-HALTER.

crack the bell. To fail; muddle things, make a mistake; ruin it: Cockneys' (—1909); slightly ob.

crack the monica. To ring the bell (to summon a performer to reappear): music-halls': ca 1860–90.

crack-up. To praise highly: coll; from ca 1840. James Payn, 'We find them cracking up the country they belong to.' Orig. (1835: Thornton), U.S. 2. v.i., to be exhausted; break down, whether physically or mentally: from ca 1850; coll. cf.:

cracked. Ruined; bankrupt: from early C.16; S.E. in C.16–17, rare in C.18, coll in C.19, ob. then † in C.20. Mayhew, who has the more gen. *cracked up*. 2. Crazy: C.17–20; S.E. until ca 1830. 3. (With variant *cracked in the ring*) deflowered: C.18–20, low, perhaps coll rather than s. 4. Penniless, ruined: low (—1860); ob.

'cracked in the right place', as the girl said. A FAST (esp. 3) c.p. reply to 'You're cracked' (=crazy): low: late C.19–20.

cracked-up, see sense 1 of CRACKED.

cracker. A lie; a (very) tall story: C.17–20, ob.: coll. 2. In C.18, a pistol. Smollett. 3. A very fast pace, a large sum, a dandy, and analogically: from ca 1870. *Daily News*, 1 Nov. 1871, 'The shooting party, mounting their forest ponies, came up the straight a cracker.' 4. A heavy fall; a smash: from ca 1865; ob. 5. (The mod. sense, a thin, crisp biscuit, may derive ex the C.17–18 c. and low *cracker*, a crust, as recorded by B.E.; cf. the early C.19 c. sense, 'a small loaf, served to prisoners in jails', Vaux.) 6. Leather, gen. sheepskin, trousers: South African coll (—1833). 7. In mid-C.17–early 19 c., the backside. 8. A heavy punch: pugilistic: from ca 1820.

cracker-hash. Pounded biscuit with minced salt meat: nautical coll: mid-C.19–20.

cracker-jack. Synonym of the preceding.

crackers, get the. To go mad: lower classes': late C.19–20.

crackey, see CRIKEY.

crackiness. Extreme eccentricity; craziness: coll: from ca 1860; ob.

cracking. Boasting. Burglary. See CRACK, v., resp. 1, 4.

cracking, adj. Very fast; exceedingly vigorous (—1880): slightly ob.

cracking a (tidy) crust, see CRACK A CRUST.

***cracking tools.** 'Implements of house-breaking', Egan's Grose: c. (—1823) >, by 1860, low; ob.

crackish. (Of women only) wanton: late C.17–early 19; coll. Ex CRACK, n., 2.

crackle, crackling. The velvet bars on the hoods of 'the Hogs', or students of St John's, Cambridge: from ca 1840. cf. *Isthmus of Suez*, a covered bridge at the same college: ex L. *sus*, a pig.

crackling, see CRACKLE. 2. Usually *bit of c.*, a girl, since ca 1890.

***crackmans, cragmans.** A hedge: C.17–early 19 c. Rowlands; B.E.; Grose. See -MANS. Perhaps ex a hedge's *cracks* or gaps.

***cracksman.** A house-breaker (see CRACK, v., 4): from ca 1810; orig. c. Vaux, Lytton, Barham, Dickens. The most famous of fictional cracksmen is Hornung's *Raffles*. 2. Hence, the *membrum virile*: from ca 1850.

cracky, see CRIKEY.

craft. A bicycle: youths': ca 1870–80. (Bicycles were still a novelty.)

crag, see SCRAG, n.

crag, long. A long purse: Aberdeen, either c. or low: late C.18–mid-19. Shirrefs, 1790 (E.D.D.). Perhaps because a long purse (vaguely) resembles a long neck.

***cragmans,** see CRACKMANS.

crail capon. 'A haddock dried unsplit': nautical: mid-C.19–20. Bowen.

cram. A lie, cf. the more frequent CRAMMER. From ca 1840. *Punch*, 1842, 'It soundeth somewhat like a cram.' 2. Hard, 'mechanical' study (gen. for an examination), both the action and the acquisition: coll; from ca 1850. 3. A CRIB, an aid to study: university and school; from ca 1850. 'Cuthbert Bede' in *Verdant Green*. 4. A coach or private tutor: from ca 1855. Dutton Cook, in *Paul Foster's Daughter*, 1861, 'I shall go to a coach, a cram, a grindstone.' 5. (Of a crowd) a crush or jam: coll: 1858, Dickens.

cram, v.i. and t. To tell lies; to ply, hence to deceive, with lies. From ca 1790 (recorded 1794, in the *Gentleman's Magazine*). Ex the idea of stuffing, over-feeding with lies. 2. To prepare oneself or another hastily, gen. for an examination (cf. the n., 2–4): coll, from ca 1800: university and school. *Gradus ad Cantabrigiam*. 3. To urge on a horse with spur and/or knee and/or hand or reins: sporting, from ca 1830. 4. To coït with (a woman): low: mid-C.19–20. For semantics, see sense 1: cf. STUFF, v., in its sexual sense.

cram-book. A book used for CRAMMING: coll; from ca 1855.

cram-coach. A tutor who CRAMS (2) pupils for examinations: coll; from ca 1880.

cram-paper. A list of prospective answers to be CRAMMED for examination: coll: from ca 1875.

crammable. Capable of being mechanically learnt or soullessly prepared: coll: from ca 1865.

crammed, ppl adj. (Of a person or a lesson) hastily prepared for an examination: coll: from ca 1835.

crammer. A liar: from ca 1860. cf. CRAM, n. and v. 2. A lie (cf. id.): from ca 1840. H. C. Pennell, *Puck on Pegasus*, 'I sucked in the obvious crammer as kindly as my mother's milk'; Trollope, 1880. 3. One who prepares students, pupils, for examination (cf. COACH; GRINDER): from ca 1810; coll. Maria Edgeworth in *Patronage*. 4. A pupil or student 'cramming' for an examination (like the preceding, ex CRAM, v., 2): coll, rare; from ca 1812.

crammer's pup. (Gen. pl.) The pupil of a CRAMMER (sense 3): military: since ca 1870.

cramming, vbl n. The act of studying, less often of preparing another, for an examination: coll; from ca 1820. 'Aspirants to honours in law . . . know the value of private cramming,' *Punch*, 1841; Herbert Spencer, 1869. 2. As adj., from ca 1830. Southey.

cramp. Prayer; to pray: Bootham School: late C.19–20. Ex the cramped position.

cramp, the. S.E. *cramp*: C.19–20; coll.

cramp-dodge. Simulated writer's cramp: schoolboys' coll, mostly London (—1887).

cramp in the hand. Niggardliness; 'costiveness': C.19–20, ob.; coll.

cramp in the kick, have. To be (very) short of money: from ca 1880. Here, KICK is one's pocket.

***cramp-rings.** Fetters: from ca 1560; c. in C.16–17, c. and low in C.18. Harman, Dekker, Coles, Grose. Ex the S.E. sense, a gold or silver ring that, blessed on Good Friday by the sovereign, was considered a cure for falling sickness and esp. for cramp.

cramp-word. CRACK-JAW word; a word either very hard for the illiterate to pronounce or for most to understand: from ca 1690: coll Mrs Cowley, 'Cramp words enough to puzzle and delight the old gentleman the remainder of his life'. 2. A sentence of death: C.18–early 19 c.

***cramped.** Hanged; derivatively, killed: c. and low: C.18–19. A development from †S.E. *cramp*, to compress a person's limbs as a punishment.

***cramping-cull.** The hangman: c.: C.18–early 19. CULL = man.

cranch, see CRAUNCH.

crane. To hesitate at an obstacle, a danger: from ca 1860: coll >, by 1890, S.E. Ex hunting j.

craner. One who hesitates at a difficult jump: hunting coll; from ca 1860.

cranium. Jocular coll; from ca 1640: the head. In S.E. it is an anatomical term.

crank. Gin and water: late C.18–mid-19. Perhaps ex *crank*, pert, lively, exceedingly high-spirited, which may itself in C.17–18, after being S.E. in C.16, have been coll (see B.E.), just as in C.19 it > coll. 2. A person odd, eccentric, very FADDY, mildly monomaniacal: orig. (—1881), U.S., anglicized ca 1890. Prob. ex CRANKY. 3. (Also *cranke*.) In mid-C.16–18 c., a beggar feigning sickness or illness; also, the falling sickness. Ex Ger. *krank*, ill. cf. COUNTERFEIT CRANK.

***crank-cuffin.** A vagrant feigning sickness. C.18 c. Ex CRANK, 3.

***cranke,** see CRANK, n., 3.

cranky. Crotchety; eccentric; slightly mad (rare): from ca 1820; coll >, by 1900, S.E. cf. the S.E. and c. senses of *crank*.

cranny. The *pudendum muliebre*: low coll; C.19–20; ob. Whence *cranny-hunter*, its male opponent. 2. A half-caste: Anglo-Indian coll: mid-C.19–20. Ex *cranny* as applied, orig. and mainly in Bengal, to a clerk writing English, itself ex Hindustani *karani*.

***crap** or **crop.** Money: from ca 1690. Orig. either c. or dial.; in C.19 either s. or dial. cf. DUST, n., for origin. 2. In c., C.19 gallows: cf. *to crop*, to harvest. Ex CRAP, v., 2. 3. (Printers') type that has got mixed; 'pie': from ca 1850 (*crap* only). 4. A defecation: low coll: mid-C.19–20. Esp. *do a crap*. Ex:

crap, v, To defecate, evacuate: low coll: mid-C.18–20. ?cf. *crop*, v.i., to take in the harvest. 2. In c., however, it = to hang: from ca 1780. cf. CROP, 3.

crape it. 'To wear crape in mourning': coll: late C.19–20.

crapping-casa, -case, -castle, or **-ken.** A w.-c.: low: C.18–20 for all except *-castle*, which is C.19–20; as *croppin-ken*, however, it occurs in Coles, 1676. Ob. 2. The third, in hospital, = a nightstool: C.19.

crapple-mapple. Ale (?): Perthshire s.: from ca 1880. Charles Spence, *Poems*, 1898.

Crappo. The French, collectively, esp. seamen or warships: late C.18–mid-19. (W. N. Glascock, *Sketch-Book*, I, 1825.) Ex Fr. *crapaud*, a toad. cf. FROG, 2, and JOHNNY CRAPOSE.

crash. Entertainment: C.17 (?18): S.E. or coll. Nares. 2. In C.16, revelry: S.E. 3. (Theatrical) the machine that produces 'thunder'; this or any analogous noise: from ca 1870; ob. 4. A failure, a fiasco: policemen's and warders': late C.19–20.

crash one's fences. To make mistakes: sporting, esp. hunting, coll: late C.19–20.

crasher. A person or thing exceptional in size, merit or, esp., beauty: coll: from ca 1908. 2. A lie: Cheshire s. (—1898); ob.

***crashing-cheats.** The teeth: ca 1560–1830. Until ca 1750, c.; then low. Lit., crunching-things. 2. In mid-C.16–early 17 c., fruit.

crater, crat(h)ur, see CREATURE.

craunch; occ. **cranch.** What can be crunched: coll: from ca 1870. A variant of *crunch* (v.).

craw. The human stomach: C.16–20: pejorative coll > S.E. (ob.). Whence *craw-thumper*, a Roman Catholic: from ca 1780. cf. BRISKET-BEATER. 2. Also, jocularly, a cravat falling broadly over the chest: coll: ca 1780–1830.

crawl. A workman given to currying favour with foreman or employer: tailors'; mid-C.19–20.

crawl, do a, see DO A CRAWL.

crawler. A cab that leaves the rank to search for fares; this the driver does by coasting the pavement at a very slow pace: coll; from ca 1860. Rarely applied to taxis. 2. A contemptible sycophant: coll; from ca 1850. *Evening News*, 21 Sept. 1885, 'The complainant call her father a liar, a bester [q.v.], and a crawler.' 3. A louse, a maggot, a nit: coll: ca 1790–1830. cf. CREEPER, 4.

crawling. Rotten: coll: mid-C.19–20. Short for *crawling with maggots*.

crawly. Having, or like, the feeling of insects a-crawl on one's skin: coll: 1860. cf. S.E. *creepy*.

crawly-mawly. Weakly; ailing: mid-C.19–20 (ob.) coll. Rhyming reduplication ex *crawl.* Adopted from Norfolk dial. of mid-C.17–20.

crayt(h)ur or **craychur,** see CREATURE.

crazy. Very eager (*for* or *about*, or *to do*, something): coll: from the 1770s.

crazy-back; crazy Jack. Baumann (whom the O.E.D. has unfortunately overlooked) defines, resp., as *närrischer Fant*, a silly coxcomb, affected 'puppy', and *verrücktes Weibsbild*, a crazy or a droll hussy: I know neither of these terms (London s. of ca 1880–1910), but I suspect that, by a printer's error, the definitions have been transposed.

creak in his shoes, make one. To make him smart for it, give him a devilish bad time: London coll (—1887); ob. (Creaking shoes are often painful.)

cream. 'Father-stuff', as Whitman has it: low coll, C.19–20. Hence, *cream-stick*, the *membrum virile*: C.18–20, low coll.

cream (or **green**) **cheese, make one believe the moon is made of.** To humbug; impose upon: coll; C.19–20. cf. BAMBOOZLE.

cream fancy (billy). A handkerchief, white or cream of ground but with any pattern. From ca 1830: mostly sporting. cf. BELCHER.

cream-ice jack. (Gen. pl and *c.-i.-J.*) A street seller of ice-creams: London streets' (—1909). Ware, 'Probably from Giacomo and Giacopo', common It. names, most such vendors being Italians.

cream jugs. The paps: low (—1891).

cream of the valley. (cf. COLD CREAM.) Gin: coll (—1858); ob. Mayhew in *Paved with Gold.* Prob. suggested in opp. to MOUNTAIN-DEW, whisky. Occ. *cream of the wilderness* (1873; O.E.D.), ob.

cream-pot love. Love pretended to dairy-maids for the sake of cream: late C.17–early 19 coll. Ray, 1678. i.e. CUPBOARD LOVE.

cream-stick, see CREAM.

creamy. First-class, excellent: coll; from ca 1880; slightly ob.

creases. Watercress: sol. when not a London street-cry, which latter is coll: (?mid-) C.19–20.

creation!, that beats or licks. That's splendid, incomparable: ex U.S. (1834); anglicized ca 1880; the LICK form has never quite lost its American tang.

creature, often **crater, crat(h)ur,** all with **the.** In late C.16–18, any liquor; in C.19–20, whisky, esp. Irish whiskey, though Bee, I think wrongly, applies it specifically to gin. Coll. Shakespeare, 'I do now remember the poor creature, small beer.' cf. S.E. *creature-comfort*.

credentials. The male genitals: jocular coll ex commerce: from ca 1895.

creek. 'Division between blocks of changing-room lockers; division between beds': Bootham School: late C.19–20.

creek mat. A bedside mat: id.: id.

creel. The stomach: Scottish: C.19–20. cf. BREAD-BASKET.

creeme. To slip or palm something into another's hand(s): coll in late C.17–18, dial. in C.19–20 (ob.): ?orig. dial. ?ex the smoothness of cream.

creep into favour with oneself. To become self-conceited: ca 1810–50. *Boxiana*, II, 1818.

creeper. A cringer; a cringing lick-spittle: C.17–20; coll. cf. CRAWL; CRAWLER. 2. A hack journalist; PENNY-A-LINER: from ca 1820; †by 1890. 3. A paying pupil to a Ceylon tea-planter: Ceylon: from ca 1890; ob. Yule & Burnell (at *griffin*). 4. A louse: low coll: mid-C.17–20. cf. CRAWLER, 3. 5. See:

creepers. The feet: C.19–20 (ob.); coll. cf. KICKERS.

***creeping**, vbl n. Men and women robbing together: late C.16–early 17 c. Greene.

creeping Jesus. A person given to sneaking and whining: ca 1818 (O.E.D. Sup.).

***creeping law.** Robbery by petty thieves in suburbs: late C.16–early 17 c. Greene. See LAW.

creeps, the. The odd thrill resulting from an undefined dread: coll: 1850, Dickens. Occ. (now ob.) *cold creeps.* cf. COLD SHIVERS. Edmund Yates, in *Broken to Harness*, '. . . In the old country mansions . . . where the servants . . . commence . . . to have shivers and creeps.' (The singular is rare.)

creepy. Given to creeping into the favour of superiors or elders: schoolboys': late C.19–20.

crevice. The *pudendum muliebre*: coll; C.19–20. cf. CRANNY.

crew, when – in C.16–20 – used derogatively of a set or a gang, is almost, not – despite B.E. and Grose – quite coll after ca 1660; before 1600 it is almost c., as in Greene's Cony-Catching pamphlets.

***crib.** In C.17–early 18 c., food; provender. This sense is extant in dial. 2. Abbr. *cribbage*: coll; from ca 1680. 3. (For origin, cf. sense 4.) An abode, shop, lodgings, public-house: from ca 1810; orig. c., then low. Dickens, in *Oliver Twist*, 'The crib's barred up at night like a jail.' 4. A bed: from ca 1820; c., then low. Maginn's *Vidocq*: 'You may have a crib to stow in.' Ex dial. sense (—1790), a child's cot. 5. Hence, a 'berth', a situation, job: 1859, H., 1st ed. 6. A plagiarism: from ca 1830; coll. 7. A literal translation illicitly used by students or pupils: coll: from ca 1825. 8. Stomach: c.: ?C.17–19.

crib, v. To pilfer; take furtively: from ca 1740. Foote, 1772, 'There are a brace of birds and a hare, that I cribbed this morning out of a basket of game.' 2. (For *crack a crib*, see CRACK, v., 4.) 3. To plagiarize: coll: 1778 (S.O.D.). 4. To use a CRIB (n., 7): from ca 1790; coll. 5. To cheat in an examination: coll; from ca 1840. *Punch*, 1841 (vol. I), 'Cribbing his answers from a tiny manual . . . which he hides under his blotting paper'. 6. To beat (a person) at fisticuffs: London streets': ca 1810–40. Tom Cribb defeated Belcher in 1807. 7. Hence, to thrash: low: from ca 1840. 8. v.i., to grumble: military: late C.19–20. Prob. a back-formation ex CRIB-BITER. In all senses, the vbl n. *cribbing* is frequent.

crib, do a, see DO A CRIB.

crib, fight a. To pretend to fight: pugilistic (—1791). Ex the bear-garden.

crib-biter. A persistent grumbler: coll; fróm late 1850s; ob. Ex the S.E. sense of a horse that, suffering from a bad digestion, bites its crib, i.e. manger.

crib-cracker. A burglar: low (?orig. c.): from ca 1850. G. R. Sims, 1880. 2. vbl n., *crib-cracking*, in *Punch*, 1852. cf. CRACK, v., 4.

Crib-Crust Monday, see PAY-OFF WEDNESDAY.

cribbage. The action of cribbing (CRIB, v., 3, 4); what is cribbed: rare coll; from ca 1830. Punning *cribbage*, the game.

cribbage-face(d), n. and adj. (A person) with a face pock-marked and therefore like a cribbage-board: from ca 1780; ob. cf. ROLLED ON DEAL BEACH.

cribber. One who uses a CRIB (n., 7): from ca 1830: coll. 2. A grumbler: military; from ca 1860. Prob. ex CRIB-BITER.

Cribbeys or **Cribby Islands.** Blind alleys, hidden lanes, remote courts: late C.18–early 19. Ex the Carribbee Islands, of which little – and that little unprepossessing – was known in C.18, and gen. applied to the western quarter of the Covent Garden district.

***cribbing.** Food and drink: C.17 c. 2. Also see CRIB, v., at end.

cricket, it's (that's, etc.) not. It's unfair: 1902 (S.O.D.), but adumbrated in 1867 (see Lewis): coll, almost imm. > S.E.

Cricket Quarter. Summer Quarter (i.e. term): Charterhouse coll: mid-C.19–20. A. H. Tod, *Charterhouse*, 1900.

crik(e)y!; occ. **crick(e)y** or **crack(e)y!**, the latter mostly American; also **by crikey.** Orig. an oath (*Christ*), but by ca 1835 merely an exclamation of surprise, admiration, etc. Barham, 'If a Frenchman, *Superbe!* – if an Englishman, Crikey!' cf. the ob. CRIMES!, in the same usages (Farquhar, 1700) CRIPES! and GEMINI!. These terms are either s. or coll, according to the philologists' point of view.

crim con. Abbr. *criminal conversation*, adultery. From ca 1770, orig. legal; then, by 1785, coll; then – from ca 1850 – S.E.

crimea. A (long or fierce-looking) beard: proletarian: 1856; very ob. Ex the hairiness of Crimean 'veterans'. 2. =FUSILIER.

crimes!; **crimine** or **criminy!** Variants (mid-C.19–20; late C.17–20) of CRIKEY or GEMINI. Farquhar, 1694, 'Oh! crimine!'

crimp. To play foul: low s. or c.: ca 1690–1750. Ex:

crimp, play. To play foul: low coll: ca 1660–1800. D'Urfey, Grose.

crimping-fellow. 'A sneaking Cur', B.E.: low coll: late C.17–18.

crimum. Sheep: Shelta: C.18–20.

crinckam, crincum, see CRINKUM.

crinkle-pouch. A sixpence: late C.16–early 17: coll.

crinkum, crincum; occ. **crinkom,** C.17, and **crinckam,** C.18. A venereal disease: C.17–18.

crinkum-crankum. The *pudendum muliebre*: ca 1780–1870. Ex the S.E. sense (cf. *crinkle-crankle*), a winding way. cf. CRINKUMS. 2. In pl (*crinkum-crankums*), tortuous hand-writing: coll (—1887); ob.

crinkums. A venereal disease: C.17–early 19. cf. CRINKUM and CRINKUM-CRANKUM.

crinoline. A woman: ca 1855–95. cf. PETTICOAT; SKIRT.

Cripes! Christ!: low: late C.19–20. Also *by cripes!* cf. CRIKEY.

cripple. A sixpence (—1785); ob. in C.20. Ex its aptness to be bent. cf. BENDER. 2. A clumsy person; a dull one: coll; mid-C.19–20. 3. (Wellington College) a dolt: mid-C.19–20. 4. A lobster minus a claw: nautical coll: late C.19–20.

cripple!, go it, you. An ironic, often senseless, comment on strenuous effort, esp. in sports and games; *wooden legs are cheap* was often added. Coll; C.19–20. Thackeray, 1840.

cripple-stopper. A small gun for killing wounded birds: sporting coll (—1881).

Cripplegate, see COME CRIPPLEGATE.

crisp. A bank or a currency note: from ca 1850; cf. SOFT, n., 2.

Crispin. A shoemaker: from ca 1640; orig. coll, by 1700 S.E. Hence *St Crispin's lance*, an awl, and *Crispin's holiday*, every Monday: both late C.17–19 coll. Ex Crispin, the patron saint of shoemakers.

crit. A critic: C.18 coll (?coined by Fielding).

cro or **cros** (pron. *cro*). A professional gambler: buckish s. of ca 1810–40. In, e.g., J. J. Stockdale, *The Greeks*, 1817. Ex Fr. *escroc*, a SHARP.

cro'-Jack-eyed. Squinting: nautical: mid-C.19–20. Ex work aloft.

***croak,** in c., means both to die and to kill; also (ob.) a 'last dying' speech: C.19–20. Vaux (to die); Egan, 1823 (to hang); H., 1st ed., the n. sense: hardly before ca 1850. Ex the death-rattle. Both senses appear also in dial.

***croaker.** In mid-C.17–18, c. for a groat; in C.19, s. for a sixpence. Perhaps a pun – suggested by CRIPPLE, 1 – on *groat*. 2. A beggar: low: from ca 1835. Ex his complaints. 3. A dying person, a doctor, a corpse: the second being c. and low s., the first low coll, and the third (H., 2nd ed.) low s.: mid-C.19–20. 4. Hence, a beast killed to save it from dying: 1892. 5. A pronounced and persistent pessimist: from ca 1630; coll until ca 1700, when it > S.E. Whence, prob., senses 2, 3.

croaker's chovey. A chemist's shop: C.19–20 low. cf. CROCUS-CHOVEY.

Croakumshire. Northumberland: mid-C.18–19. Ex that county's defective *r*.

croakus, see CROCUS (METALLORUM).

croc. A file of school-boys or, much more gen., -girls walking in pairs: from ca 1900; mostly school s. Abbr. CROCODILE, orig. university s. (—1891), now coll. 2. Also, of course, the crocodile itself: coll: rare before C.20.

crock. A worthless animal; a disabled person or (in C.20 rarely) a 'duffer': from ca 1879; coll. Either ex broken earthenware (1850) or the Scottish *crock*, an old ewe or (1879) a broken-down horse. 2. Hence, a boy or a man who plays no outdoor games: Public Schools' coll: from ca 1890. P. G. Wodehouse, *St Austin's*, 1903. 3. A bicycle: youths': ca 1870–80. Because a BONE-SHAKER?

crock up. To get disabled; break down; fall ill: from ca 1890. Ex preceding.

crocketts. A kind of makeshift cricket: Winchester College, C.19–20. (R. G. K. Wrench.) Hence:

crocketts, get. (At cricket) fail to score: from ca 1840; Winchester.

crocodile. A (gen. and orig. girls') school walking, two by two, in file (—1870): coll. The very rare v. occurs in 1889. 2. A support of a plank serving as a seat: *Conway* Training Ship (—1891).

***crocus,** see CROCUS (METALLORUM).

***crocus-chovey.** A doctor's consulting-room; a surgery: mid-C.19–20 c. See CHOVEY. Ex: 2. A chemist's shop: c. (—1791). B. M. Carew, quoted by E.D.D.

crocus (metallorum); in C.19–20 occ. *croakus*. A surgeon or a doctor (esp. a quack): low (—1785); ob. Grose, 1st ed.; Mayhew. Prob. ex CROAK after HOCUS-POCUS, though the O.E.D. mentions a

Dr Helkiah *Crooke* and Coles has *crocus Martis*, a chemical preparation of iron, and *crocus veneris*, one of copper. cf. CROAKER, by which also the old scientific term *crocus* was prob. suggested in this sense. At first, naval and military.

***crocus-pitcher.** An itinerant quack: mid-C.19–20 c.

***crocus-worker.** A seller of patent medicines: c., and Petticoat Lane traders': late C.19–20.

***crocussing rig.** The practising of itinerant quackery: mid-C.19–20 c.; ob.

crokus, see CROCUS (METALLORUM).

***crome.** The hook used by an ANGLER: late C.16 c. Greene, in *The Black Book's Messenger*.

crone. A clown: from ca 1850; mostly Parlary. Prob. *clown* corrupted.

cronk. (Of a horse) made to appear ill in order to cheat its backers: from the 1880s: racing s. >, by 1890, gen. Ex Ger. *krank*, sick, ill. 2. Hence, unsound; dishonestly come by: from ca 1890. (*Melbourne*) *Herald*, 4 July 1893. Both senses are Australian.

crony. 'A Camerade or intimate friend', B.E.: from 1650; university s. till ca 1750, then gen. coll. Pepys, 'Jack Cole, my old schoolfellow ... a great crony of mine'. Perhaps *crony* was Cambridge University's counterpart to the orig. Oxford CHUM. Its C.17 variant *chrony* indicates the etymology: Gr. χρόνιος, contemporary, ex χρόνος, time. W. cites an instance for 1652. Whence, 2, in c. or low s., an accomplice in a robbery: C.18–early 19. 3. In C.17–18, a tough old hen. 4. A Dumfriesshire c. term (C.19–20) for a potato. The E.D.D. cites the derivative *crony-hill*, a potato-field.

crook. A sixpence (—1789): low; ob. by 1860. Ex CROOK-BACK. 2. A swindler, a thief; a professional criminal: orig. (1870), U.S., anglicized ca 1895 as a coll. Perhaps ex CROOK, ON THE; cf., as W. suggests, Fr. *escroc*.

crook (or click), in the. In the act of cutting: tailors' coll: from ca 1860.

crook, on the. Dishonestly, illegally, illicitly; leading a life of crime: in England before 1874 (?first used in U.S.) and, there, perhaps orig. c. Prob. suggested by (*on the*) STRAIGHT: cf., however, *on the* CROSS.

crook-back. A sixpence (—1785); †by 1900. cf. BENDER; CRIPPLE; CROOK.

crook (occ. cock) one's or **the elbow (occ. ttle finger).** To drink (not of water): ex U.S. (1830: Thornton), anglicized ca 1875: coll.

crook one's elbow and wish it may never come straight. With the required pronominal adjustment, this phrase lent efficacy to an oath: late C.18–early 19 low coll.

crooked. Dishonestly acting (of persons), handled or obtained (things): mostly Australian; from before 1864. H., 3rd ed., 'A term used among dog-stealers, and the "fancy" generally, to denote anything stolen'; Rolf Boldrewood speaks of 'a crooked horse'.

***crooked,** adv. Illicitly, in a criminal manner; furtively: c.: (?) mid-C.19–20.

crooked as a dog's hind leg, see DOG'S HIND LEG. **Crooked Lane,** see BUY ONE'S . . .

crooked straight-edge or **the round square, go and fetch the.** C. pp. April Fool 'catches': carpenters': C.19–20. Among warehousemen, *go and fetch the wall-stretcher*; in engineers' shops, the *rubber hammer*: both from ca 1860.

crookshanks. A coll nickname for a man with bandy legs: 1788, Grose, 2nd ed. cf. the surname *Cruickshanks*.

crooky. To walk arm in arm; v.t., to court (a girl): coll: mid-C.19–20; ob.

croop. Stomach: lower classes': mid-C.19–20. ?*crop*.

Crop. 'A nickname for a Presbyterian', Grose; 'one with very short Hair', B.E. Resp. mid-C.18–early 19 and late C.17–early 18 coll. 2. money, see CRAP, n., 1. 3. to hang, to defecate, is a variant of c. CRAP, v., 1 and 2. cf.:

***crop, be knocked down for a.** 'To be condemned to be hanged', *Lex. Bal.*: c. of ca 1810–50.

Crop the Conjuror. 'Jeering appellation of one with short hair', Grose, 1st ed.: late C.18–early 19 coll. cf. CROP, 1.

cropoh. A Frenchman: nautical (—1887). Ex Fr. *crapaud*, a toad: cf. FROG, 2.

***croppen, croppin,** see CRAPPING CASA. 2. The tail of beast or vehicle: C.18–early 19: c.

cropper; esp. **come, or go, a cropper.** A heavy fall, fig. and lit.: from the late 1850s; coll. Trollope, 1880, 'He could not ... ask what might happen if he were to come a cropper.' Ex hunting.

croppie. A variant of CROPPY, 2. **croppin,** see CROPPEN. **croppin-ken,** see CRAPPING CASA.

croppled, to be. Fail in an examination, be

sent down at a lesson: Winchester College: mid-C.19–20. Ex (*to*) *crop* + *cripple*.

croppy or **Croppy.** An Irish rebel of 1798, when sympathy with the French revolutionaries was shown by close-cut hair: orig. coll, soon historical – therefore S.E. 2. Also, an ex-gaolbird: low (—1857).

crops, go and look at the. To visit the w.-c.: mid-C.19–20; ob. Ex agriculture. cf. PLUCK A ROSE.

***cross,** gen. with **the.** Anything dishonest: from early C.19; c. >, by 1870, low s. Opp. to *the* SQUARE as CROOKED is opp. to STRAIGHT. Trollope in *The Claverings*. 2. Esp. a pre-arranged swindle: c. (—1829). 3. Also, a thief: c. from ca 1830. (The term occurs mostly in compounds and phrases; these follow the v.)

cross, v. To bestride a horse: jocular coll; from ca 1760; ob. 2. Hence, to have intercourse with a woman: from ca 1790. 3. To play false, v.t. and (rarely), i.; to cheat: low: C.19–20. 4. In the passive, *be crossed*, mid-C.19 university, s. meant to be punished, e.g. by loss of freedom: 'Cuthbert Bede' in *Verdant Green*, 1853. Ex the cross against one's name.

cross, adj. Out of humour, temporarily ill-tempered: coll; from ca 1630. 2. Dishonest; dishonestly obtained: c.: from ca 1810. Ex CROSS, n.

cross, adv. Unfavourably, adversely; awry, amiss: from ca 1600; S.E. till ca 1840, then coll.

cross, come home by weeping. Finally to repent: C.18–early 19 coll.

***cross, on the.** Dishonest(ly), illegal(ly), fraudulent(ly): from ca 1810; orig. c. Henry Kingsley; Ouida, 1868, in *Under Two Flags*, 'Rake was . . . "up to every dodge on the cross".' See CROSS, n., 1.

cross, play a. Act dishonestly; esp. in boxing, to lose dishonestly: from ca 1820.

cross as the devil. A late C.19–20 coll variant, or perhaps rather intensive, of:

cross as two sticks, as. Very peevish or annoyed: coll: from ca 1830. Scott, 1831; Pinero, 1909. Perhaps ex their rasping together, but prob. ex two sticks set athwart (W.).

***cross-bite, cross-biting.** A deception, trick(ery), cheat(ing): from ca 1570; c. > s. > coll > S.E. >†, the same applying to the slightly earlier v. Marlowe, G. Harvey, Prior, Scott, Ainsworth. 2. In late C.16–18 c., 'one who combines with a sharper to draw in a friend', Grose; also v.

***cross-biter.** A swindler, cheat, hoaxer: late C.16–early 18; c. > s. > coll > S.E.

***cross-biting law.** 'Cosenage by whores'. Greene: late C.16–17 c. Greene. See LAW.

***cross-boy.** A crook, a dishonest fellow: Australian c. (—1890). Ex CROSS-CHAP.

cross-built. (Of persons) awkwardly built or moving: coll: ca 1820–70.

cross-buttock. An unexpected repulse or rebuff: coll (—1860). Ex a throw in wrestling.

***cross-chap, -cove, -lad, -man, -squire.** A thief. C.19–20 c.; *-squire* is †. Varied by *lad*, etc., *of the* CROSS. (See also the separate entries at CROSS-COVE and CROSS-MAN.)

cross-chopping. Argument: 1831, *Sessions*, 'There was a good deal of *cross-chopping* at the office as to whether it was on a Sunday': coll: C.19.

***cross-cove.** A swindler; a confidence trickster: c. (—1812); ob.

***cross-cove and mollisher.** A man and woman intimately associated in robbery: (—1859); c.; ob. H., 1st ed. See CROSS, n.; MOLLISHER: ex MOLL. ?after *demolisher*.

***cross-crib.** A thieves' and/or swindlers' lodging-house or hotel: c.; from ca 1810. Ex CRIB, n., 3.

cross-cut. A Jewess: low: late C.19–20. Ex the Gentile lower-class myth that she has to undergo an operation similar to her brother's.

***cross-drum.** A thieves' tavern: c.: from ca 1840. See DRUM.

cross-eye(s). A person with a squint: coll; from ca 1870.

***cross-fam** or **-fan.** (Also n.) To rob from the person, with one hand masking the other: c.: from ca 1810. See FAM, v., and FAN, v., 2.

***cross-girl.** A harlot who, specializing in sailors, gets all the money she can from the amorous and then bilks them by running away: c. (—1861); ob. Mayhew.

cross I win, pile you lose. A C.17 form of HEADS I WIN, TAILS YOU LOSE.

cross-in-the-air (or without hyphens). A rifle carried at the reverse: amateur soldiers': ca 1880.

cross-jack-eyed. Squint-eyed: ca 1800–70. *The Night Watch* (II, 88), 1828. cf. LOOK CRO'-JACK-EYED.

***cross-jarvey (-jarvis,** Baumann**) with a cross-rattler.** 'A co-thief driving his hackney-coach', Bee: c.: ca 1820–90. See CROSS, adj., 2.

cross-kid, n. KIDDING; BLARNEY; deception, imposition; irony: low: 1893, P. H. Emerson.

***cross-kid,** occ. **-quid.** To cross-examine: c. (—1879). Ex KID, n., 3, to quiz.

***cross-kiddle.** To cross-examine: c. (—1879); ob. Horsley (cited by F. & H. at *reeler*).

***cross-lad,** see CROSS-CHAP.

cross-legs. A tailor: low: ca 1850–1910.

***cross-life man.** A professional criminal, esp. thief: c. (—1878); ob.

***cross-man.** A thief; a swindler; confidence man: c. (—1823). See CROSS, n.

***cross-mollisher.** A female CROSS-COVE: c. (—1812); ob.

cross my heart! A c.p. of declaration that one is telling the truth: mid-C.19–20.

cross-patch. A peevish person: late C.17–20; coll. cf. the old nursery rhyme: 'Cross-patch, | Draw the latch, | Sit by the fire and spin.' Here, *patch* is a fool, a child. In late C.19–20, occ. *cross-piece*: Manchon.

***cross-squire,** see CROSS-CHAP.

***cross-stiff.** A letter: c.; from ca 1860; ob.

cross the damp-pot. To cross the Atlantic: tailors'; from ca 1860; ob.

cross the Ruby. To cross the Rubicon: 'Fast World, early 19 cent.' (Ware). Punning *ruby*, port wine.

crosser. An arranger of or participator in a dishonest act: sporting: from ca 1870.

crossish. Rather bad-tempered or peevish: coll: from ca 1740; rare and ob.

crotcheteer. 'A patron of crotchets': Society: ca 1880–1900.

crow. Gen. as a REGULAR *crow*. A fluke; unexpected luck: from ca 1850. Ex billiards; prob. the Fr. *raccroc*. 2. In c., with corresponding v., a confederate on watch; if a female, often CANARY (7). From early 1820s. 3. A clergyman: late C.18–20; ob. Ex black clothes. 4. A professional gambler: ca 1805–40. Pun on S.E. *rook*.

crow, v. To act as a 'crow' (n., 2): c.: from ca 1840. '*No. 747*', *The Autobiography of a Gipsy*, 1891 (E.D.D.).

crow, no carrion will kill a. A coll, semi-proverbial saying applied to gross eaters, tough persons: C.17–18.

crow a pudding, give or **make the,** see PUDDING, GIVE THE CROW A.

crow-bait. A scraggy, esp. if old, horse: among Englishmen in Canada and South America: from ca 1895. C. W. Thurlow Craig. 2. An aborigine: Australian coll: since ca 1830.

crow-eater. A lazy person (ex the eating habits of crows): Australia, South Africa: from ca 1875. 2. (Gen. in pl.) A South Australian: from the 1890s. Crows are very numerous in that State.

crow-fair. An assemblage of clergymen: late C.18–19; coll. Ex their black clothes.

crow in a gutter, strut like a. To be over-proud: late C.16–19; coll. Fulke; Spurgeon.

crow to pluck (in C.15, **pull;** rarely **pick) with anyone, have a.** To have an unpleasant or embarrassing affair to settle: from C.16; coll till C.18, when it > S.E. Shakespeare, 'Hudibras' Butler, Scott. The phrase 'suggests animals struggling over prey', W.

Crowbar Brigade, the. The Irish Constabulary: Anglo-Irish: 1848; ob. Ex 'crowbar used in throwing down cottages to complete eviction of tenants', Ware. Whence:

crowbar landlord. One who resorts to such methods: Anglo-Irish: ca 1850–90.

crowd. A company of people; set, LOT: Colonial (ex U.S.), from ca 1870.

crowder. A full theatre or 'house': theatrical: from ca 1870; ob. 2. A string: Shelta: C.18–20.

crowdy-headed Jock, see JOCK, 1.

crown; always **the crown.** The school tuck-shop: Charterhouse: C.19–20. (A. H. Tod, *Charterhouse*, 1900.) Perhaps ex the old Crown Inn. 2. The school pavilion: Charterhouse: late C.19–20. (ibid.)

crown, v. In c., to inspect a window with a view to burglary: C.19–20; ob.

crown and feathers. The female genitals: low: C.19–20.

crown-office. The head: late C.18–early 19.

crown-office, in the. Tipsy: late C.17–18. cf. preceding.

crowner. Coroner: in M.E. and early mod. E. (e.g. in Shakespeare's *Hamlet*), it is S.E.; then dial. and either coll or sol., in C.20 gen. the latter: esp. *crowner's quest*, a coroner's inquest. 2. A fall on the crown of one's head: sporting: from ca 1860. Whyte-Melville.

***crow's-foot.** In c., the Government broad arrow: from ca 1870; ob.

crow's-nest. 'Small bedroom for bachelors high up in country houses, and on a level with the tree-tops', Ware: Society: mid-C.19–20; ob. Ex nautical S.E.

cruel, cruelly, adj., adv. Hard, exceeding(ly): resp. since M.E. and C.16: S.E. until C.19, then coll. Pepys, 31 July 1662, 'Met Captain Brown . . . at which he was cruel angry'. The early history of the coll *cruel(ly)* significantly parallels that of the adv. BLOODY.

cruelty-van (or booby-hutch). A four-wheeled chaise: from ca 1850; †by 1910.

crug. Food: from ca 1820. Prob. ex *crug* (Christ's Hospital) bread: late C.18–19; Lamb, 'a penny loaf – our crug'. 2. (ibid.) a Christ's Hospital boy, esp. old boy: from ca 1830.

cruganaler, cruggnailer. (Christ's Hospital) a biscuit given on St Matthew's Day: C.19–20. Either ex *crug and ale* (see CRUG) or punning HARD AS NAILS.

cruggy. Hungry: C.19–20; Christ's Hospital. Ex CRUG.

cruiser. A harlot: C.19–20, ob. One who cruises the streets. 2. In c., a beggar: late C.17–early 19. Ex habit of 'cruising about'. 3. A highwayman's spy: c.: C.18–early 19.

cruity. A recruit: military: ca 1850–1914.

crumb. A pretty woman: military; from ca 1830. 2. Plumpness: from ca 1840. Dickens. cf. CRUMMY.

crumb and crust man. A baker: coll; from ca 1840.

crumbles. A set of mishaps causing one person to be blamed: nautical: late C.19–20.

crumbs, pick (in C.16, **gather) up one's,** see PICK UP ONE'S CRUMBS.

crummy. Plump; esp. (cf. BIT OF CRUMB) of a pretty woman who is full-figured, large-bosomed: from early C.18, as is, 2, the c. sense, rich: both ex *crumby* (bread). 3. Lousy: from ca 1840; perhaps orig. c., then Cockney (see H.), then low and military. Hence, the c. *crummy doss*, a lice-infested bed. ?ex a louse's vague resemblance to a small crumb. 4. Hence, dirty, untidy: nautical: mid-C.19–20.

crummy, the. Fat: sporting: ca 1818–40. Tom Moore, *Tom Crib's Memorial*, 1819, 'To train down the crummy'. Ex sense 1 of the adj.

***crump.** In late C.17–early 19 c., one who helps litigants to false witnesses. cf. CRIMP and CRIMPING-FELLOW. 2. A hard hit or fall: Winchester College, from ca 1850. S.E. *crump*, to hit briskly, the S.O.D. quoting 'We could slog to square-leg, or crump to the off,' 1892.

crumper. A hard hit or blow: from ca 1850: coll. cf. CRUMP, 2. 2. Whence, a great lie (cf. THUMPER): from ca 1880: schoolboys'. Miss Braddon.

crumpet. The head: late C.19–20; ob. cf. ONION, 2, and F. & H., s.v., for synonymy. 2. Woman as sex; women viewed collectively as instruments of sexual pleasure: low: from ca 1880. cf. BUTTERED BUN, 1, 2, and CRACKLING, 2. 3. A term of endearment: lower classes': from late 1890s.

crumpet-face. A face covered with smallpox marks: mid-C.19–20, ob.; coll. cf. CRIBBAGE-FACE.

crumpet-scramble. A tea-party: from ca 1860: coll. Derby Day, 1864, 'There *are* men who do not disdain muffin-worries and crumpet-scrambles.' cf. BUN-FEAST.

crumpler. A cravat: from ca 1830; coll. 2. A heavy fall: circus and music-halls' and, in C.20, hunting: from ca 1850, as in 'Guy Livingstone' Lawrence's *Hagarene*, 1874. cf. CRUSHER, 3, for semantics.

crunchiness; crunchy. Fit(ness) for crunching or being crunched: coll: from ca 1890.

crupper. The human buttocks: jocularly coll, from late C.16. Ex a horse's rump.

crush. A large social gathering, esp. if crowded: from ca 1830; coll. Whyte-Melville, 1854; H. D. Traill, in *Tea Without Toast*, 1890, 'And we settled that to give a crush at nine | Would be greatly more effectual, and far more intellectual, | Than at six o'clock to, greatly daring, dine.' 2. Hence (in the Army) a military unit: late C.19–20.

crush, v.t., with *bottle, cup, pot, quart*. Drink: late C.16–19; coll. Greene, 1592 (*a potte of ale*); Shakespeare (*a cup of wine*); Scott (*a quart*). cf. BURST, CRACK. 2. To decamp, run away: c. (?> low s.): from ca 1860. cf. AMPUTATE . . . and esp. next entry. 3. See CRUSH THE STIR.

***crush down sides.** To run away, esp. to a place of safety; also, to keep a rendezvous: Northern c.; from ca 1850.

***crush the stir.** To break out of prison: late C.19–20 c. See CRUSH, v., 2, and STIR, 2.

crushed on. Infatuated with: Society: 1895; almost †. Suggested by MASHED.

crusher. A policeman: from ca 1840. Thackeray; *Punch*, 1842; Sala. ?ex the size of his feet. ('He needs 'em big; he has to stand about for hours,' a friend, 1933.) cf. FLATTIE. 2. Any thing or person overwhelming or very large or handsome: coll: from ca 1840. Thackeray of a woman, 1849. cf. WHOPPER and CRUSHING. 3. A heavy fall: sporting coll (—1887); ob. cf. CRUMPLER, 2. 4. A ship's corporal: naval (—1909). Ex sense 1.

crushing. First-rate; excellent; very attractive: coll; from ca 1855; ob. cf. CRUSHER, 2, and CRASHER.

crust; occ. **upper crust.** The head: from ca 1870. cf. CRUMPET, 1.

crustily. Peevishly, snappishly: coll: C.18–20.

crusty beau. Late C.17–early 19; coll: 'One that lies with a Cover over his Face all Night, and uses Washes, Paint, etc.', B.E.

crusty-gripes. A grumbler: low coll, mostly London (—1887); slightly ob. cf. BELLY-ACHE, V.

crutches are cheap! (cf. *wooden legs are cheap* and see CRIPPLE! . . .) An ironic comment on strenuous physical effort, esp. in athletics: mid-C.19–20; ob.

cry. A crowd of people: pejorative coll >, by 1660, S.E.: late C.16–18. Shakespeare, in *Coriolanus*, 'You common cry of curs'. Ex hunting j. for a pack of hounds. 2. A fit of weeping: coll: from ca 1850.

cry, v.i. To weep: C.16–20; coll >, by 1700, S.E.; except in dignified contexts, where it still is indubitably coll and where *weep* is requisite.

cry! A libidinous good wish at nightfall; an exclamation indicative of 'surprise of a satiric character': London lower classes' (—1909). Ware: 'Shape of Carai – probably introduced by English gypsies passing from Spain'. cf. *caramba*. 2. An abbr. of CRIKEY: low: mid-C.19–20.

cry, or **call, a go.** To desist; give in. (With connotation: wisely and humorously.) Coll (—1880); the post-war *call it a day* is displacing it. Ex cribbage, where *cry a go* = *pass* in bridge.

cry and little wool, great (occ. **much**). A proverbial c.p. abbr. '*Great cry and little wool*', *as the Devil said when he sheared the hogs*. Much ado about nothing. From ca 1570.

***cry carrots and turnips.** To be whipped at the cart's tail: C.18 c.

cry cupboard. To be hungry: coll; from ca 1660. Swift in *Polite Conversation*, '*Footman*. Madam, dinner's upon the table. *Col*[*onel*]. Faith, I'm glad of it; my belly began to cry cupboard.' See also CUPBOARD, ONE'S GUTS CRY.

cry off. To back out of an engagement or project: from ca 1700; coll > S.E. by 1800.

cry, the less you'll piss!, the more you, see PISS THE LESS . . .

cry whore. To impute a fault, ascribe blame: coll: ca 1660–1800.

cub. An awkward, uncouth, uncultured or unpoised youth: from ca 1600; prob. coll at first; soon S.E. 2. In late C.17–early 19 c., a tyro gamester. 3. At St Thomas's Hospital, ca 1690–1740, a surgeon's assistant; a coll soon > official j.

cubic type. A non-existent type-face that green apprentices are sent to find: printers': late C.19–20.

Cubit, the; punishment by the cubit. The treadmill: low (—1823); †by 1890. Bee, '*Cubit* being the inventor's name.'

cuckold the parson. To 'sleep' with one's wife before she is: coll (—1791); †by 1890.

cuckoldshire, cuckold's-row. Cuckoldom: facetious coll; C.16–17. Likewise, in C.16–18, *Cuckold's Haven* or *Point*, a point on the Thames below Greenwich, was humorously used, with various verbs, to indicate cuckolding or being cuckolded.

cuckoo. A fool: from late C.16: coll. Shakespeare in *2 Henry IV*, 'O' horseback, ye cuckoo.' In C.19–20 gen. as *the*, or *you*, *silly cuckoo*. 2. A cuckold: late C.16–18; coll > S.E. Shakespeare. Prob. ex the Fr. *cocu*, a cuckold. 3. The penis: schoolboys', C.19–20, ob. Perhaps a perversion of COCK.

cuckoos. Money: C.17. ?c. Perhaps because the cuckoo sings and money talks.

cuckoo's nest. The *pudendum muliebre*: C.19–20. e.g. in a traditional Irish patter-song.

cucumber. A tailor: late C.17–early 19.

cucumber-time. The dull season: mid-July to mid-Sept. Tailors': late C.17–20; ob. B.E.: 'Taylers Holiday, when they have leave to Play, and Cucumbers are in season.' cf. the Ger. *die saure Gurken Zeit*, pickled-gherkin time, and the saying *tailors are vegetarians*, which arises from their living now on cucumber and now on CABBAGE.

cud. A chew of tobacco: until ca 1870, S.E., now dial. and coll, *quid* being much more usual.

cud, adj. Attractive, cosy; comfortable: Winchester College: 1st half C.19. Wykehamistically derived ex *kudos*. 2. Hence, pretty: ibid. mid-C.19–20. 3. At Christ's Hospital, mid-C.19–20: severe. Prob. ex CUDDY, adj.

cuddie. A variant of CUDDY.

cuddling. Wrestling: esp. among devotees of wrestling and boxing: C.19–20, ob.

cuddy. A nickname for a donkey: coll:

from ca 1710. ?ex *Cuthbert*. 2. The Captain's cabin: naval: late C.19–20.

cuddy, adj. (Of a lesson) difficult: Christ's Hospital, mid-C.19–20, ob. Perhaps ex *cuddy*, a stupid chap: cf. preceding. 2. Hence *cuddy-biscuit*, a small hard biscuit.

cuddy-jig. The capers of a landsman endeavouring to keep his balance: nautical: mid-C.19–20. Ex CUDDY, n., 1.

cuddy-leg. A large herring: (mostly Scots) nautical: late C.19–20.

cuds, cuds(h)o. In expletives, a corruption of *God's*: ca 1590–1750: coll.

cue. A small quantity of bread; occ. of beer. As CEE from C, so *cue* from Q (q = *quadrans* = a farthing). A university s. term that > S.E.: late C.16–18. The S.O.D. quotes a 1605 text: 'Hast thou worn Gowns in the university . . . ate cues, drunk cees?' cf. CEE.

***cue,** v. To swindle on credit: c.: from ca 1860. ?ex *Q.* = *query*.

cuerpo, in. 'Without the cloak, so as to show the shape of the body', S.O.D. Ex the Spanish for body, this phrase was presumably gallants' j. of C.17: its unconventional use appears, C.18, in the sense: without any clothing, naked, as in Smollett (coll).

cuff; often **old cuff.** A (foolish) old man: coll; ca 1610–1820. ?ex *cuffin*, mid-C.16–18 c. for a fellow, chap, itself prob. cognate with *cofe* = COVE. 2. Perhaps hence, a religious or a religious-seeming man: tailors'; C.19–20 ob. 3. A mean, surly or despicable fellow: s.: Ned Ward, 1703.

cuff Anthony, see ANTHONY, CUFF.
cuff or **beat Jonas,** see BEAT GOOSE, and ANTHONY, CUFF.

cuff of, up the. In the good graces of: tailors': late C.19–20.

cuff(-)shooter. A beginner: theatrical; from ca 1870. Ex his display of linen.

***cuffen.** A C.16 variant of *cuffin*, q.v. at CUFF.

cuffer. A lie; an exaggerated story: military: from ca 1870: often, *to spin cuffers*. Ex S.E. *cuff*, to strike with the fist. cf. THUMPER. 2. Hence, any story, a yarn: from mid 1880s.

***cuffin,** see CUFF, n., 1. **cuffin-quire,** see QUEER CUFFIN.

cufuffle. An amorous embrace: Anglo-Irish: late C.19–20.

cuirass. Same as CURE-ARSE: late C.18. Grose, to the B.M. 1st ed. copy, has added the term with the note, 'Quasi *cure-a-se*', but contrary to his gen. practice with these MS. addenda, he did not include it in the 2nd ed.

culch. Inferior meat: odds and ends of meat: low, mostly London: ca 1815–80. *Sinks*, 1848. Ex S.E. and S.W. English dial. *culch* or *culsh*.

***cule.** Abbr. *reticule*: c. (—1859); ob. H., 1st ed., implies it in CULLING.

***culing,** see CULLING.

***cull, cully.** In C.17 c., a constable. A deviation from: 2. In C.17–18, c. for a fool, esp. a dupe; in C.19–20, though anticipated in C.17 as *cully*, low s. for a man, companion, mate, partner: in C.17–18, however, *cull* tended to mean any man, fool or otherwise, *cully* 'a fop, fool, or dupe to women' (Grose), as in Congreve's 'Man was by nature woman's cully made' (*The Old Bachelor*, 1693): *cull* dates from ca 1660, *cully* from ca 1664. For etymology, see CULLS (cf. BALLOCKS, a parson); but perhaps ex †S.E. *cullion*; less prob. ex the Continental Gypsy radical for a man. 3. See RUM CULL.

***cull, bob** and **curst.** Resp. 'a sweet-humour'd Man to a Whore, and who is very Complaisant . . . An ill-natur'd Fellow, a Churl to a Woman', B.E.: c.: late C.17–early 19. See CULL, 2.

***culling,** or **culing.** Stealing from carriage seats: c. or low; from the mid-1830s. Ex *reticule*.

culls. Testicles: low coll, C.16–17. Ben Jonson. Abbr. *cullions*, the same. Ex Fr. *couillons*.

***cully.** See CULL. In late C.19–20, often as a Cockney, also as a low, term of address to a man.

***cully,** v. To dupe; to cheat or swindle: c. of ca 1670–1800. Thomas Dangerfield, *Don Tomazo*, 1680; B.E., 1690. Ex the n.

cully-gorger. A theatre manager (cf. RUM CULL); a fellow actor: from ca 1860: theatrical. Ex CULLY (see also CULL) + GORGER (3), a SWELL.

cully-shangy. Sexual intercourse: low: C.19. *Cully* ex CULLS, *shangy*, ex ?

culminate. To climb a coach-box: ca 1780–1870; Cambridge University.

culp. 'A kick, or blow; also a bit of any thing', B.E.: late C.17–early 19 low coll (later dial.). Prob., as Grose (2nd ed.) suggests, influenced by *mea culpa*.

culty-gun. The *membrum virile*: low: C.19. Ex L. *cultellus*, a knife.

culver-headed. Feebly foolish: coll ex dial.: C.19. A culver is a dove, a pigeon, whence

PIGEON, n., 4, an easy gull for the ROOK, n., 2.

cum used facetiously for 'with' or 'plus' is coll: from ca 1860.

cum-annexis. One's belongings, esp. one's wife and children: West Indies, from ca 1850; ob. Ex an official land-transfer locution affected at Demerara.

cum grano. A coll abbr. of *cum grano salis* (with a grain of salt): from ca 1850.

cummer, kimmer. A *female* intimate, acquaintance, or 'fellow' or CHAP. Orig. and still good Scots, these words have, in late C.19–20, occ. been familiarly used by Sassenachs in these senses and thus > coll. Ex Fr. *commère*.

cummifo. '*Comme il faut*': lower class coll: 1889, *Referee*, 28 April.

cumsha(w). A present; a bribe: Anglo-Chinese 'pidgin': from ca 1800. Ex Chinese for 'grateful thanks'. 2. Unexpected or additional money: nautical: mid-C.19–20.

cund. To say or determine which way (a shoal of fish) is going: nautical coll verging on j.: mid-C.19–20. Ex *cund* (gen. *cond*), to direct (a ship).

cundum. A ca 1665–1820 form of a safety-sheath (cf. FRENCH LETTER), ex the name of its deviser, a colonel in the Guards. In 1667 those three aristocratic courtiers, wits and poets, Rochester, Roscommon and Dorset, issued *A Panegyric upon Cundum*. (Coll rather than s.) 2. 'A false scabbard over a sword', Grose, 2nd ed.: late C.18–early 19: military. 3. (Likewise ex sense 1.) 'The oil-skin case for holding the colours of a regiment', ibid.: id.: id.

cundy. A small stone: Australian: late C.19–20. Ex E. dial. *cundy*, a conduit, e.g. a small conduit made of stone-work.

cunnel. A potato: Shelta: C.18–20.

cunning. Quaintly interesting, pretty, attractive: orig. (—1854) U.S.; anglicized ca 1880, but never very gen. cf. CLEVER.

cunning as a dead pig. Stupid: coll: ca 1705–50. Swift.

***cunning man.** 'A cheat, who pretends by his skill in astrology, to assist persons in recovering stolen goods', Grose, 1788: c.; †by 1850. Ex †S.E. for a seer, healer, or fortune-teller. 2. A judge: Egan: cf. FORTUNE-TELLER.

cunning shaver. A sharp fellow, orig. illicitly: mid-C.17–20, ob.; coll. See SHAVER.

Cunningberry (or -bury). A variant (ca 1820–50), recorded by 'Jon Bee', of:

Cunningham; often **Mr Cunningham.** Ironical coll for a simple fellow: mid-C.18–early 19.

cunny. The *pudendum muliebre*: low coll; C.17–20. Influenced by L. *cunnus*, it is actually an †form of *cony*, a rabbit. cf. PUSS.

cunny-haunted. Lecherous: C.18–20, ob.; low coll. Ex preceding term.

cunny-hunter. A whoremonger: C.17–early 19; low. Punning CUNNY = *con(e)y*.

cunny-thumbed. Given to closing his fist, as a woman does, with the thumb turned inwards under the first three fingers: low coll; late C.18–20. Ex CUNNY. 2. C.19–20 schoolboys': given to shooting a marble as a girl does.

cunny-warren. A brothel: low (—1785).

cunt. (In back s., *tenuc*, the *e* being intruded for euphony.) The female pudend. In one form or another, it dates from O.E.; it is unlikely to be related to L. *cunnus*, but is certainly cognate with O.E. *cwithe*, 'the womb' (with a Gothic parallel); cf. mod. English *come*, ex O.E. *cweman*. The *-nt*, which is difficult to explain, was already present in O.E. *kunte*. The radical would seem to be *cu* (in O.E. *cwe*), which app. = quintessential physical femineity (cf. sense 2) and partly explains why, in India, the cow is a sacred animal. Owing to its powerful sexuality, the term has, since C.15, been avoided in written and in polite spoken English: though a language word, neither coll, dial., c., nor s., its associations make it perhaps the most notable of all vulgarisms (technical sense, *bien entendu*), and since ca 1700 it has, except in the reprinting of old classics, been held to be obscene, i.e. a legal offence, to print it in full; Rochester spelt it *en toutes lettres*, but Cotgrave, defining Fr. *con*, went no further than 'A woman's, &c.', and the dramatist Fletcher, who was no prude, went no further than 'They write *sunt* with a C, which is abominable', in *The Spanish Curate*. Had the late Sir James Murray courageously included the word, and spelt it in full, in the great O.E.D., the situation would be different; as it is, no dictionary before the Penguin English Dict. (1965) had the courage to include it. (Yet the O.E.D. gave PRICK: why this further injustice to women?) 2. (cf. Romany *mindj* or *minsh*, the pudend; a woman.) In C.19–20 it also means woman as sex, intercourse with a woman, hence sexual intercourse. (It is somewhat less international than FUCK.) 3. Anybody one dislikes: late C.19–20.

cunt, drunk as a. Extremely drunk: low: late C.19–20. Prob. the commonest of all the CUNT similes.

cunt!, silly. A low pejorative address or reference to a person: late C.19–20.

cunt face is a low term of address to an ugly person: late C.19–20. More insulting than the synonymous SHIT-FACE.

cunt-itch and **-stand.** Active physical desire in women: vulgarism: resp. C.18–20, C.19–20.

cunt-pensioner. A male-keep; also, the man living on a woman's harlotry or concubinage: low coll or perhaps rather a vulg.: C.19–20; slightly ob.

cunt-stand, see CUNT-ITCH.

cunt-struck. Enamoured of women: C.18–20; either a vulg. (more correctly, I think) or a low coll. cf. COCK-SMITTEN.

cunting, adj., expressive of disgust, reprobation, violence: late C.19–20.

cup and can. Constant associates: ca 1540–1830; coll >, by 1600, S.E. Gen. *as merry as a cup and can*, or *be cup and can*. Ex the cup's being filled and replenished from a can.

cup-and-saucer player. A player in a comedy by T. W. Robertson (d. 1871), a pioneer of 'slick' yet natural and workmanlike society-drama: theatrical, ca 1866–90.

cup even between two parties, carry one's. To favour neither of them: coll C.17–early 19.

cup man, cup-man. A toper: coll > S.E.; ca 1830–1900.

cup of comfort or **of the creature.** Strong liquor: late C.17–20; slightly ob. See also CREATURE.

cup-shot. Tipsy: late C.16–early 19; coll >, by 1660, S.E. Fuller in *The Holy War*, 'Quickly they were stabbed with the sword that were cupshot before.' cf. SHOT, adj.

cup such cover, such; or **such a cup(,) such a cruse.** 'Implying similarity between two persons related in some way', O.E.D. Coll; both ca 1540–1700.

cup too low, a. Applied to one who, in company, is silent or pensive: late C.17–18; coll. The phrase is extant in dial.

cup too much, have got or **had a.** To be drunk: mid-C.17–19; coll. Ray, 1678. cf. the preceding phrase.

cup-tosser. A juggler: C.19; coll. Brewer suggests ex Fr. *joueur de gobelets*. 2. Whence, 'a person who professes to tell fortunes by examining the grounds in tea or coffee cups', H., 3rd ed.: from ca 1860; very ob.

Cupar justice. Hanging first and trying afterwards: C.18–mid-19: Scots coll >, by 1810 or so, S.E. In 1706, A. Shields refers to 'Couper Justice and Jedburgh Law'. cf. JEDBURGH JUSTICE, LYDFORD LAW, and *lynching*.

cupboard, the. The sea: nautical: late C.19–20. Ex DAVY JONES'S LOCKER.

cupboard, one's guts cry. One is hungry: low coll: C.18–mid-19.

cupboard love. Interested affection: C.18–20: coll; S.E. after ca 1820. 'A cupboard love is seldom true.' Hence *cupboard lover*, C.19–20, rare.

cupboardy. 'Close and stuffy': Cockneys' coll: late C.19–20. Ware.

Cupid. A harlot's bully-lover: C.19–20, ob.; low. 2. With variant **blind Cupid,** 'a jeering name for an ugly blind man', Grose, 1st ed.: mid C.18–early 19 coll.

Cupid's Arms or **Hotel,** see HOTEL . . .

Cupid's whiskers. Sweets with mottoes on them: coll: late C.19–20.

Cupid, blind, see CUPID, 2.

cuppa. A cup of tea; esp. *a nice cuppa*: Australian: since ca 1905.

cups, in one's. While drinking (rare in C.20); intoxicated. From ca 1580: coll (as in Nashe and Shadwell) until ca 1720, then S.E.

***cur, turn.** To turn informer or King's evidence: c.: mid-C.19–20; ob.

cur-fish. Small *dog*-fish: nautical: late C.19–20.

curate. Late C.19–20 coll: 'A small poker, or *tickler* [q.v.], used to save a better one; also a handkerchief in actual use as against one worn for show. The better article is called a *rector* [q.v.]. Similarly when a teacake is split and buttered, the bottom half, which gets the more butter, is called the *rector*, and the other, the *curate*,' F. & H.

curate's delight. A tiered cake-stand: from ca 1890.

curate's egg, see GOOD IN PARTS . . .

***curb.** A thief's hook: c.: late C.16–18.

***curb.** To steal, esp. with a hook; gen v.i.: late C.16–early 18 c. Greene. 2. In C.19 c., to strike.

***curber.** A thief that uses a hook: late C.16–18 c. Rowlands. See DIVER.

***curbing.** An abbr. of the following term. Greene.

***curbing law.** The practice of illegally hooking goods out of windows: late C.16–18 c. See LAW.

curbstone-broker. A guttersnipe: from ca 1865; ob. In U.S., an illicit street-broker.

curbstone-sailor. A harlot: from ca 1830. cf. CRUISER.

curby hocks. Clumsy feet: rather low: ca 1850–1910. (See HOCKS.)

curdler. A blood-curdling story or play; a writer thereof: coll (—1887); ob. cf. THRILLER.

cure. An eccentric, an odd person (1856); hence, a very amusing one (—1874). First printed in *Punch*, though 'he' has 'no mission to repeat | The Slang he hears along the street'. Perhaps abbr. CURIOSITY or, more prob., *curious fellow*; popularized by an 1862 music-hall song.

cure-arse. A late C.18–19 low coll: 'a dyachilon plaster, applied to the parts galled by riding', Grose, 3rd ed. cf. CUIRASS.

curio. Abbr. *curiosity*: from ca 1850 (at first among travellers); coll till ca 1880, then S.E.

curiosity. An odd person: ca 1840–70: coll. Displaced by CURE.

curious, do. To act strangely: low coll: mid-C.19–20; ob.

curiouser and curiouser. Ever more strange: coll: late C.19–20. Adopted ex Lewis Carroll.

***curl.** See CURLE. 2. (Gen. pl.) A human tooth 'obtained by the body-snatchers': c. (—1823); †by 1860.

curl, out of. Indisposed; vaguely ill at ease: coll: mid-C.19–20. Ex the hair.

curl one's hair. To chastise; scold, vituperate: C.19–20 coll; ob.

curl paper. Toilet paper: either coll or euphemistic: C.19–20; ob.

curl up. To fall silent, SHUT UP: from ca 1860; ob. 2. (Sporting.) To collapse: coll: from ca 1890.

***curle.** Clippings of money: late C. 17–18 c.

curled darlings. Military officers: Society: 1856–ca 60. Ware, who, noting that 'the Crimean War . . . once more brought soldiers into fashion', refers to 'the waving of the long beard and sweeping moustache'.

curls, see CURL, 2.

curly. A cane: *Conway* Training Ship: from ca 1885. Masefield. 2. **(Curly.)** The inevitable nickname of men with curly hair: coll (—1851). Mayhew.

curly-murly. A fantastic twist, esp. curl: ca 1720–1830. Also adj.: mid-C.19–20: coll.

currant bun. The sun: Cockneys' rhyming s.: late C.19–20.

currants and plums. A threepenny piece: rhyming s. (—1859) on *thrums* (see THRUMBUSKINS).

currency, n. and, occ., adj. of a person born in Australia, one of English birth being STERLING: Australians': from ca 1825. P. Cunningham, 1827; Charles Reade in *It is Never Too Late to Mend.*

curry-and-rice navy. The Royal Indian Marine: naval: late C.19–20; ob.

curry one's hide. To beat a person: coll: C.18–early 19. Ex S.E. *curry* in this sense.

curse, not to care or **be worth a.** i.e. extremely little: from M.E. onwards; coll. S.O.D. supports *curse = cress* (A.-S. *cerse*) but notes that *damn* in this sense is very early. Prob. *cress > curse* under the influence of DAMN; nevertheless, see DAM. Langland has 'Wisdom and witt now is worth not a kerse.' Whereas *not worth a rush* or *a straw* have > S.E., *not worth a curse* has remained coll because of its apparent meaning. Also *tinker's curse.*

curse (of Eve), the. The menses: feminine euphemistic or jocular coll: late C.19–20. Often expanded to: 'The curse is come upon me,' in jocular allusion to Tennyson's *The Lady of Shallott.*

curse of God. A cockade: coll: early C.19.

curse of Scotland. The nine of diamonds: from 1710. Coll > S.E. in C.19. Orig. problematic. Grose, 1st ed. The various theories are as interesting as they are unconvincing: see H., 5th ed. and W.

cursetor, cursitor. A vagabond: from ca 1560; coll. 2. In mid-C.18–early 19 c., 'broken petty-fogging attornies, or Newgate solicitors', Grose, 1st ed. Ex L. *currere*, to run. cf. the S.E.

***curtail, curtal.** A thief who cuts off pieces from unguarded cloth, etc., or from women's dresses; C.18 c. Also, a thief wearing a short jacket; C.16–17 c.

curtain, cop the. 'To gain so much applause that the curtain is raised for the performer to appear and bow': music-halls' (ca 1880) >, by 1890, theatres'. Ware. cf. CURTAIN-TAKER.

curtain-lecture. A reproof, or lengthy advice, given in bed by a wife to her husband: from ca 1630; orig. coll; by 1730, S.E. The occ. *curtain-sermon* was †by 1900.

curtain-raiser. A one-act play to 'play in the house': orig. (—1886) theatrical s.; by 1900, coll. Ex Fr. *lever de rideau.*

curtain-taker. 'An actor even more eager than his brethren to appear before the curtain after its fall': theatrical: 1882. Ware. cf. CURTAIN, COP THE.

curtains. 'A [soldiers', esp. officers'] name given to one of the first modes of wearing the hair low on the military forehead (1870). The locks were divided in the centre, and the front hair was brought down in two loops, each rounding away towards the temple. The hair was glossed and flattened', Ware. ca 1870–85.

***curtal.** A species of vagabond and thief: mid-C.16–18 c. Ex his short coat. See CURTAIL.

cuse. Weekly order; (a book containing) the record of marks in each division. Winchester College: C.19–20, ob. Ex *classicus paper*, the master's term.

***cushion.** To hide, conceal: c.: mid-C.19–20, ob. Ex S.E. sense, to suppress.

cushion, beside the. Beside the mark: coll: late C.16–early 19, verging on S.E. Ex billiards, a game played in England since C.16. cf. CUSHION, MISS THE.

cushion, deserve a or **the.** To have done his duty and therefore deserving of rest (of a man to whom a child has been born): coll: mid-C.17–early 19. Ray, 1678.

cushion, miss the. To miss the mark; to fail; coll (—1529); app. †by 1700. Skelton; Clarke, 1639.

cushion-cuffer, -duster, -smiter, and **-thumper.** A clergyman, esp. a violent preacher: coll: the first, ca 1680–1750; the second, ca 1720–1820; the third, from ca 1840 but ob.; the fourth, ca 1640–1900. Thackeray, 1843, 'For what a number of such loud nothings . . . will many a cushion-thumper have to answer.'

cushmawaunee! Never mind: among soldiers and sailors with Indian experience: mid-C.19–20; ob.

cuss. As a coll exclamation orig. (—1872) U.S. and partly anglicized ca 1900, it euphemizes *curse!* 2. A person; gen., a man: coll; both senses ex U.S. (—1848), anglicized ca 1880. Ex CUSTOMER, perhaps influenced by *curse*.

cussèd. A low coll form of *cursèd*, anglicized ca 1882.

cussedness. CANTANKEROUSness (persons); contrariness (things). Coll: ex U.S. (from ca 1850), anglicized ca 1885. The fourth general 'law' is, 'The cussedness of the universe tends to a maximum.'

***cussin.** A man: c. (—1887); virtually †. Ex CUSS, 2.

custom of the country. 'A bribe given to port officials to avoid delays': nautical coll: mid-C.19–20. Bowen.

customer. A man; chap, fellow: coll; from late C.16 but not common before 1800; gen. with QUEER or *ugly*. cf. CHAP; MERCHANT; ARTIST, and Scottish *callant*.

custom(-)house goods. 'The stock in trade of a prostitute, because fairly entered', Grose, 2nd ed.: mid-C.18–early 19 low coll.

custom(-)house officer. A cathartic pill: mid-C.19–20; ob. Also *customs*.

Cut; always **the C.** The New Cut, a well-known plebeian street near Westminster: London coll (—1887).

cut. A stage, a degree: coll from ca 1815; S.O.D. records in 1818; Dickens uses in 1835, (of a house) 'I really thought it was a cut above me.' 2. A refusal to recognize, or to associate with, a person: from ca 1790. The *cut(-)direct* (later *dead cut*) occurs ca 1820. 3. A snub or an unpleasant surprise: coll; ca 1850–1910. 4. (Theatrical) an excision, a mutilation of the 'book' of a play: C.18–20. Sheridan in *The Critic*, 'Hey . . . ! – what a cut is here!'; *Saturday Review*, 21 April 1883, 'Some judicious cuts.' 5. A spree: see CUT, adj. C.19. 6. See CUTS. 7. A share: Australian and New Zealand coll: late C.19–20.

cut, v. To talk; speak; make (of words): in mid-C.16–early 19, c. – *cut bene*, e.g., is to speak gently; from ca 1840 (?low) s. as in Thackeray's *Pendennis*, '(He) went on cutting jokes at the Admiral's expense.' 2. Ignore or avoid (a person); abandon (a thing, a habit): from ca 1630; coll. Samuel Rowley, in *The Noble Soldier*, 'Why shud a Souldier, being the world's right arme | Be cut thus by the left, a Courtier?' vbl n., *cutting*. With this usage, cf. 3, the university (orig. s., then coll, now almost S.E.) *cut lecture* or *hall* or *chapel*, to absent oneself from these duties (—1794). 4. Move quickly; run: coll; from ca 1780. Earlier forms – all S.E. – are *cut away* (Cotton, 1678), *cut off*, and *cut over* (Lambarde's *Perambulation of Kent*; Nashe). Dickens, in *Little Dorrit*, 'The best thing I can do is to cut.' A C.19 variant is CUT IT. After ca 1810, the gen. form is the orig. nautical *cut and run* (lit., cut the cable and sail away); *cut one's lucky* (—1840) being lower down the social scale, as also is (—1823) *cut one's stick*: with the last, cf. AMPUTATE ONE'S MAHOGANY, the idea being that of cutting a staff for one's journey; in gen., however, cf. U.S. *cut dirt* (1833): 'the horse hoofs make the dirt fly', Thornton. 5. (Theatrical) to excise: C.18–20. See n., 4. 6. Excel (cf. CUT OUT): coll; from ca 1840. Whyte-Melville, in 1853, has *cut down*.

cut, adj. Tipsy: from ca 1650. Head; B.E. cf. *Punch*, 1859, 'He goes on the Loose, or the Cut, or the Spree.' Whence a *deep cut* or *cut in the back* (or *leg*), very drunk, late C.17–early 19 (B.E.), and *a little cut over the head*, slightly drunk, late C.18–mid-19 (Grose, 1st ed.): cf. CUT ONE'S LEG. 2. Hence, stupid, silly: late C.19–20: esp. HALF-CUT.

cut! See CUT IT, 2.

***cut a bosh or a flash.** To cut a figure: mid-C.18–early 19: c. See BOSH.

cut a caper. To play a trick or prank; behave extravagantly or noisily: from late C.16; coll till ca 1700, when it > S.E.

cut a dash or **shine** or **splash.** To make a display, a notable figure; be very successful, prominent: resp. early C.18–20, C.19–20 (orig. U.S.), C.19–20: coll, the first being now S.E. Here, *cut* = make, do, perform. cf. CUT A BOSH.

cut a dido. To CUT A DASH: naval: ca 1835–60. Ex *cut up* DIDOES, with a pun on H.M. corvette *Dido*, very smart, of the 1830s. Bowen adds: 'The term was also applied to a sailing vessel tumbling about in a confused sea.'

cut a (e.g. fine, poor) figure. To make a . . . appearance: from ca 1760; coll until ca 1890, then S.E. Lever in *Harry Lorrequer*, 'He certainly cut a droll figure.' The earlier, more dignified, phrase is *make a figure*.

cut a finger. To break wind: low (—1909). cf. the Somersetshire *cut the leg*, to give off a foul smell.

cut a flash, see CUT A BOSH.

cut a shine or **splash,** see CUT A DASH.

cut a stick. To desert: naval: from ca 1830. cf. CUT, v., 4.

cut a tooth or **one's (eye-)teeth.** To become 'knowing', wide-awake: from ca 1820: coll. After ca 1870, occ. *cut one's wisdom teeth*. See also CUT ONE'S EYE-TEETH, HAVE.

cut above, a, see CUT, n., 1.

cut and come again. Abundance, orig. of 'Meat that cries come Eat me', B.E.: late C.17–20; coll. Swift, Wm Combe. 2. Whence, the female pudend: C.19–20; low.

cut and run. Depart promptly; decamp hurriedly: coll (—1810). Ex nautical j.

cut(-)away. A morning coat: from ca 1845: coll. (As adj., recorded in 1841, says the S.O.D., but anticipated in Jon Bee's description, 1823, of a dandy.)

***cut bene whids.** To speak fair: c., as in B.E.: mid-C.16–18. See WHIDS. Variant of BENAR.

cut caper sauce, see CAPER UPON NOTHING . . .

cut capers on a trencher. To dance within a very small compass: ca 1850–1910; coll, mostly Cockney; cf. CELLAR-FLAP.

cut dead (—1826) is a variant of CUT, v., 2.

cut fine. To reduce to a minimum, esp. in *cut it fine*, to leave a very small margin of money, space, or time: mid-C.19–20: coll >, by 1900, S.E.

cut for the simples, see SIMPLES, BE CUT FOR THE.

cut in, v.i. To intrude; interpose briskly into a game or a conversation: from ca 1820; coll till ca 1870, then S.E. Thackeray, '"Most injudicious", cut in the Major.' 2. Whence the n.: same period and promotion. Often written *cut-in*.

cut in the back or **leg,** see CUT, adj.

cut into. (Winchester College) orig. to hit with a 'ground ash'; hence, to correct in a manner less formal than TUND: C.19–20, ob.

cut it. To run, move quickly: C.19–20; coll. See v., 4. 2. Interjection: cease! or be quiet! Also as *cut!*, *cut that!*, in C.20 *cut it out!* From ca 1850; coll.

cut it fat. To make a display; cut a dash; show off; from ca 1830. Dickens, 1836, 'Gentlemen . . . "cutting it uncommon fat"'; Baumann, 1887. In the Dickens quotation, the sense of the whole phrase is perhaps rather, COME IT (*too*) STRONG. *Cut it too*, or *uncommon*, *fat*, is indeed a separate phrase = overdo a thing; now ob.

cut it out! see CUT IT, 2.

cut it short! Make your story, or account, shorter! Coll: C.19–20. Dickens.

cut mutton with. To partake of someone's hospitality: coll; from ca 1830.

cut of one's jib. General appearance: orig. and still mainly nautical: from ca 1820. Robert Buchanan, 1881, 'By the voice of you . . . and by the cut of your precious jib'.

cut of the simples, see SIMPLES, BE CUT FOR THE.

cut off without a shilling. A late C.19–20 jocular coll variant of the S.E. phrase.

***cut someone's cart.** To expose his tricks: (—1851) c.; ob. Mayhew.

cut one's coat according . . . see CLOTH . . . **cut one's comb,** see COMB CUT.

***cut one's eye.** To become suspicious: c.: from ca 1840. cf. CUTTY-EYE.

cut one's eye-teeth, have. To be alert or

'knowing': low (—1864). See also CUT A TOOTH.

cut one's leg, have. To be drunk: late C.17–mid-18. Ray, 1678 (Apperson). cf. CUT, adj.

cut one's lucky or (perhaps orig. c., as Egan states) **stick,** see CUT, v., 4, the latter ex the cutting of a staff before one begins a journey.

***cut one's own grass.** To earn one's own living: c.; from ca 1860; ob. cf. *get one's own* CHUMP.

cut one's painter, see CUT THE PAINTER.

cut one's stick, see CUT, v., 4.

cut out. To find, put in the way of: late C.17–19; coll. '*I'll cut you out business*, I'll find you Work enough,' B.E. 2. To supersede, outdo, deprive of an advantage: C.18–20; coll till ca 1860, then S.E.; orig. nautical, but very early of sexual (or analogous) rivalry, as in R. Cumberland, *Wheel of Fortune*, 1779. 3. In Australia (—1874), to detach (an animal) from the herd: orig. coll; soon S.E. 4. To steal (esp. service stores): naval: late C.19–20. Ex senses 1, 2. 5. To come to an end: Australian coll: late C.19–20.

cut out of. To deprive of; destroy one's participation in, chances of getting: C.17–20, ob.; coll, as in B.E.'s '*Cut another out of any business*, to out-doe him far away, or excell, or circumvent'. 2. To cheat out of: C.18–20; coll.

cut over the head, see CUT, adj.

***cut queer whids.** To speak offensively; use foul language: mid-C.16–early 19: c.

cut quick sticks. To depart hastily: C.19–20; ob. cf. CUT, v., 4.

cut that! see CUT IT. **cut the cackle,** see CACKLE, CUT THE.

***cut the line** or **rope** or **string.** To cut a long story short; to cease from keeping a person in suspense: c.: from ca 1810, 1860, 1810, resp.

cut the, occ. **one's painter.** To depart; decamp; depart in secret haste; to desert: orig., still mainly, nautical. From ca 1840. Hence, 2. To die: nautical: from ca 1850. cf. ALOFT. 3. **Cut a person's painter,** to send away, get rid of, render harmless: ca 1660–1840.

***cut the rope** or **the string,** see CUT THE LINE.

cut throat. (More gen. with hyphen.) A butcher (lit.): C.19–20, ob. 2. A dark lantern: coll: ca 1770–1840. 3. A game of bridge with three players only: coll (—1900). 4. An open-bladed razor: C.19–20.

cut under, v.t. To undersell, the gen. C.20 form being *undercut*. From ca 1870; coll at first, S.E. since ca 1895. L. Oliphant in *Altiora Peto*: 'Ned was all the time cutting under us by bringing out some new contrivance.'

cut up. To depreciate, slander; criticize very adversely: from ca 1750; coll till ca 1800, then S.E. Goldsmith, 1759,' The pack of critics . . . cutting up everything new'. cf. the sense, to mortify, which is gen. in the passive, to be vexed, hurt, dejected: from ca 1790; coll, in C.20 almost S.E. 2. In the passive, to be in embarrassed circumstances: coll; ca 1800–70. 3. To turn up, become, show (up): coll; ?late C.18, certainly C.19–20; ob. 4. To plunder, rob; to divide plunder: from ca 1770; c. till ca 1880, then (as in G. R. Sims's *How the Poor Live*) low. 5. To leave a fortune by will, v.i. (v.t. with *for*): from ca 1780. Gen. with *big*, *large*, *fat*, *rich* or *well*. Grose, 1st ed.; Disraeli, in *The Young Duke*, '"You think him very rich?" "Oh, he will cut up very large," said the Baron.' This 'likens the defunct to a joint' (of meat), W. 6. To behave: coll; from ca 1850. Hughes, in *Tom Brown's School Days*, 'A great deal depends on how a fellow cuts up, at first.' cf. CUT UP NASTY.

cut up didoes, see DIDOES, CUT UP.

cut up nasty, rough, rusty, savage, stiff, ugly, etc. To be quarrelsome, dangerous: coll; the gen. phrase dates from ca 1825. Dickens has *rough* in 1837, Thackeray *savage* in 1849, and *stiff* in 1856; *nasty* is the latest of those mentioned: hardly before 1900. Semantically similar to CUT, v., 5. 2. In a race, cut up *rough*, *badly*, etc., signifies to behave badly, unfairly: from ca 1880; orig. and gen. of horses.

cut up well. To look well when naked; be an attractive bed-fellow: in the language of (?) love: from ca 1860; ob. 2. See also CUT UP, 5.

cutcha, kutcha. Makeshift; inferior; spurious; bad: Anglo-Indian and hence military; coll; recorded in 1834, but in use in C.18 (see French quotation in Yule & Burnell). Ex Hindi *kachcha*, raw, uncooked, hence rural, hence inferior, etc. Opp. PUKKA.

cutcher(r)y. A court-house; business office: coll; Anglo-Indian, from early C.17. Ex Hindi *kacheri*, a hall of audience.

cute, 'cute, adj. 'Sharp, witty, ingenious, ready', Dyche, 1748: coll: from ca 1730. Foote has the adv. *cutely* in 1762, Goldsmith *'cuteness* (rare) in 1768. 2. cf. the U.S. *cute*, used of things (—1812), anglicized ca 1850, esp. by schoolboys. cf. the U.S. *cunning*.

cuts. Scissors. **small cuts:** button-hole scissors. Tailors': from ca 1850. 2. Persons no longer friends: orig. schoolboys' (—1871). Ex CUT, v., 2, or n., 2. 3. In expletives, a corruption of *God's*: C.17–18. 4. A humorous seaman: late C.19–20. Ex S.E. *comic cuts*. 5. Shorts, esp. football shorts: Charterhouse: late C.19–20. Prob. ex S.E. *cut short*.

cuts, have. To be excited: nautical: late C.19–20.

cuts and scratches. Matches (ignition): rhyming s.: late C.19–20.

cuttee, see CUTTY, 2. Baumann, 1887. (A rare form.)

cutter, swear like a. i.e. violently: C.19–20. Ex mid-C.16–early 19 c. *cutter* = a robber, a bully.

cutter's mainsail. 'Corvus', says Bowen without explanation: nautical: mid-C.19–20. Perhaps the black guillemot: see E.D.D. at *cutty*, 2.

cuttie, see CUTTY, 2.

cutting. Underselling; keen competition: (—1851); coll > S.E. cf. sense 2 of the adj. 2. Disowning or avoiding a person: see CUT, v., 2.

cutting, adj. Blood-curdling (story, play, etc.): low coll, mostly London (—1887). Perhaps ex *cut to the heart* or *the quick*. 2. Cutting prices; underselling: coll: 1851, Mayhew.

cutting-down. 'Cutting the clews of an unpopular shipmate's hammock and letting him down on deck': nautical coll: mid-C.19–20. Bowen.

***cutting-gloak.** A rough apt to use the knife in a quarrel: c.: ca 1810–50.

cutting-out party. A predatory gang of cadets, esp. in the officers' pantry: (—1891).

cutting-shop. A manufactory of cheap, rough goods: ca 1850–1900; coll.

cutting the wind. Sword drill: military: ca 1850–1914.

cuttle. A knife; in C.16–18 low or coll; cf. the c. *cuttle-b(o)ung*, C.16–18, a knife for cutting purses.

cutty. Abbr. *cutty pipe*: (—1727) coll: in C.19–20, S.E. cf. NOSE-WARMER. *Cutty* is a mainly dial. adj. = curtailed. 2. A coll, often humorous, semi-nickname for a testy, or esp. a naughty, girl: from ca 1820. Mostly in Scotland: see esp. the E.D.D. Often *cuttie*. 3. A black guillemot: (dial. and) nautical coll: C.19–20.

***cutty-eye,** v.i. To look, gaze, suspiciously: late C.18–early 19 c. v.t. with *at*.

***cutty-eyed.** Looking suspiciously; suspicious-looking: C.19–20 (ob.) c.

cutty-gun. A Scottish variant of CUTTY, 1: mid-C.19–20; ob.

cutzooks! An early C.18 variant of GADZOOKS! cf. CUTS, 3.

cuz. A workman free of the 'chapel': printers' coll > j.: from ca 1720; ob. Bailey. Ex COZ. 2. A defecation: *the cuzzes*, the latrines: Cotton College: mid-C.18–20. Said to be ex Hebrew *cuz*, a large metal refuse container outside the Temple at Jerusalem.

cycle. Abbr. *bicycle* or *tricycle*: from ca 1880: coll till C.20, then S.E.; the same applies to the corresponding v.i.

cycling fringes. 'Especially prepared fore-head-hair to be worn by such women bikers as had not abjured all feminine vanities': cyclists' coll: 1897–ca 1907. Ware.

cyclophobist. A hater of circulars: literary: 1882, *Daily News*, 6 Jan. 2. Whence a hater of cyclists: 1897, *Daily Telegraph*, 9 Dec. (Both are ob.)

***cymbal.** A watch: mid-C.19–20 c.; ob. cf. TICKER, 2.

Cyprian. A prostitute: adumbrated long before, this term as used *temp.* Regency and George IV was fashionable s.; now rare, archaic S.E. Ex *the Cyprian* (*goddess*), Venus.

D

d or dee. A penny: coll; from ca 1870; ob. except at Charterhouse: cf. FA'D and HA'D. Ex the abbr. for penny, pence; *d* = L. *denarius*, a rough equivalent of a penny. Hence, *be on the two d's*, to get the minimum pay: military: late C.19–early 20. 2. A detective: from ca 1840. (In c., any police officer whatsoever.) 3. A damn, hence an oath; esp. as *big d.* Coll: popularized in Gilbert & Sullivan's *H.M.S. Pinafore*, 1877, 'What, never use a big, big D?', though Dickens, in 1861, has 'with a D'.

d.a. or **d.as.** The menstrual flux: from ca 1870. Abbr. DOMESTIC AFFLICTION.

d. and d. Drunk and disorderly: police and, in C.20, gen.; from ca 1870. cf. OBSTREPERLOUS.

d.b. Damned bad: theatrical coll (—1909); ob.

D.I.O., see DAMME! I'M OFF.

d.m.t. A jam roll: *Conway* Training Ship cadets': ca 1890–1914. Masefield. Ex '**d**amn **t**art'.

d.t., from ca 1858; **d.ts**, from ca 1880: low coll abbr. of *delirium tremens* ('sometimes written and pronounced *del. trem.*', H., 5th ed.). G. R. Sims, 1880, and J. Payn, 1887, both use *d.t.*

d.t. centre. A minor club: literary: ca 1880–1900.

d.v. Doubtful – very: theatrical (—1909); ob. 2. **D**ivorce: Society: ca 1895–1915. Another pun on the abbr. of *Deo volente* (if God so wishes).

da. A family and a child's abbr. of *dada* (see DAD): coll (—1850).

da-erb. Bread: back s. (—1859).

da da! Good-bye!: mainly nursery coll: late C.17–mid-18. cf. TA TA. Origin ?perhaps from DAY, DAY!

***dab.** An adept or expert; DABSTER: late C.17–20: orig. c.; by 1740, low; by 1830, coll. Chesterfield, in letter of 17 Aug. 1733, 'Known dabs at finding out mysteries'. In C.18, it has, in c., the sense, expert gamester (Dyche), while in C.17–early 18 c. it means an 'expert exquisite in Roguery', esp. in form RUM DAB. In C.19–20, esp. among schoolboys. ?ex *dab*, to strike crisply, as the S.O.D. suggests, or ex L. *adeptus*, as H. proposes and I believe. 2. A bed: from ca 1810; c. or low. Vaux; Moncrieff in *Tom and Jerry*. ?origin and etymology. If any other example of back slang were recorded before 1850, I would postulate *bed > deb > dab*: prob., however, the term is a semantic development ex C.18–20 S.E. *dab*, a flattish mass (e.g. of butter dabbed on something else). Certainly, however, *dab* is a variant for DEB as back s. for a bed, in H., 1859. 3. cf. the rare C.18–early 19 coll sense: a trifle. 4. In C.19–20 c., the corpse of a drowned outcast woman: from 1850. Ex *dab*, a small flat fish. 5. A pimp; esp. a bawd: c.: late C.19–20. Prob. ex sense 1. 6. A flat fish of *any* kind. London street coll: C.19–20. 7. See SKEW, n., 2.

dab, adj. Clever; skilful or skilled; expert; very conversant. (Gen. with *at* or *in.*) C.18–20, but never very common: in C.19–20, coll. Ex DAB, n., 1. 2. Bad: in back slang: from ca 1845. Diprose, *London Life*, 1877. Esp. DAB TROS, a bad sort: occ. used as an adv.

dab down. To hand over; pay; SHELL OUT: coll, C.19–20. cf. Yorkshire *dabs doon*, immediate payment.

dab in, have a, v.i. To have a GO (n., 8): late C.19–20. (J. Milne, *The Epistles of Atkins*, 1902.)

***dab it up (with).** To pair off (with a woman); arrange or agree to lie with her: c. >, by 1820, low; from ca 1810. 2. 'To run a score at a public-house', Egan's Grose: public-house coll: ca 1820–60.

dab out, v.t. To wash: lower classes': from ca 1860. Perhaps ex dabbing clothes out on a scrubbing board.

dab!, quoth Dawkins when he hit his wife on the arse with a pound of butter. A mid-C.18–mid-19 c.p. applied to impacts.

dab, says Daniel. A nautical c.p., applied to 'lying bread and butter fashion' in bed or bunk: ca 1810–60. 'A Real Paddy', *Real Life in Ireland*, 1822.

dab tros. A bad sort: back s. (—1859). See DAB, adj., 2.

dabheno. A bad one, esp. a bad market: back s. (—1851). cf. DAB, adj., 2.

dabs. A rare abbr. of DABSTER: coll, mostly London (—1887); slightly ob.

dabster. A DAB; an expert: from ca 1700; s. >, by 1850, coll >, in late C.19, mainly dial. Ex DAB, n., 1.

***dace.** Twopence. Late C.17–19; c. and low. A corruption of DEUCE, 3.

dacey. Of native Indian origin: Anglo-Indian coll (—1876). Ex Hindi *desi*, country.

dacha-saltee. Tenpence; a franc: from ca 1850; Parlary and c. Reade, *The Cloister and the Hearth.* Ex It. *dieci soldi* via Lingua Franca. Also *dacha-one*, eleven(pence).

dad, dada, dadda. The first from before 1500, the others from before 1680: coll for father. Prob. ex child's pronunciation of *father*: cf., however, Sampson at *dad.* James I styled himself Charles I's 'Dear Old Dad'. 2. In oaths and asseverations, God: coll: 1678, Otway. In mid-C.19–20, dial. and U.S.

dad-dad, mum-mum; or **daddy-mammy.** A tyro's practice on a drum: military; from ca 1760.

daddle. The hand; fist. From ca 1780: low. The S.O.D. says dial.: this it may orig. have been, but its use by and *temp.* Grose (1st ed.), George Parker, and Tom Moore indicates that it was common in London. ?etymology: cf. PADDLE. F. & H. gives synonymy. cf. also FLIPPER.

daddler. (Gen. pl.) A hand: low: from ca 1870; ob.

daddy. Diminutive of DAD: father: coll from ca 1500. 2. A stage-manager: theatrical; from ca 1850. 3. The superintendent of a casual ward: from ca 1860: coll. 4. The man who, at a wedding, gives away the bride: ca 1860–85. 5. The person 'winning' the prize at a mock raffle, faked lottery: from ca 1860; c. then low. 6. The comic old man of a theatrical company: ca 1860–1910.

***dads.** An old man: c.: C.18. Anon., *Street-Robberies Consider'd*, 1728. A perversion of DAD. The *-s* indicates either familiarity or affection, or both: cf. *ducks* for DUCK (the endearment).

dad's will. Parental authority: Oxford University: ca 1820–40.

daff; daffy. Coll abbr. of *daffodil*: mid-C.19–20.

daffier. A gin-drinker: ca 1820–60. *Boxiana*, III, 1821. Ex DAFFY.

daffy (loosely **daffey); Daffy's Elixir.** Gin: from ca 1820; ob. 'Corcoran' Reynolds, 1821; Leman Rede, 1841. Ex a very popular medicine advertised as early as 1709, ca 1860 called *soothing syrup* (applied also to gin) and in 1891 known as *tincture of senna.* Hence, *daffy it*: to drink gin: ca 1820–60.

daffy, adj. Slightly mad; soft in the head: dial. (—1884) >, by ca 1895, s. Ex Northern dial. *daff*, a simpleton.

daffy-down-dilly. A dandy: ca 1830–80. Leman Rede in *Sixteen-String Jack.*

daftie. A daft person: coll: from ca 1870. Ex *daft.* (Slightly earlier in dial.)

dag. A HARD CASE; a wag; a CHARACTER: Australia, thence New Zealand: from ca 1890. Prob. ex DAGEN.

dag, adj. Excellent: Australian: from ca 1905.

dag at, be a. To be extremely good at: from the mid-1890s: Australians'. Ex preceding.

***dagen.** c. for an artful criminal or near-criminal, itself ex c. *dagen* or DEGEN, a sword.

dagged. Tipsy: (—1745) this term, perhaps orig., > solely, dial. ca 1800. Ex dial. *dag*, to sprinkle.

dagger-ale. Inferior ale: late C.16–17. Ex The Dagger, a low tavern fl. 1600 in Holborn. cf.:

dagger-cheap. Very cheap: C.17–18; coll and archaic after ca 1660. Bishop Andrewes, 1631, '[The devil] may buy us even dagger-cheap, as we say.' Lancelot Andrewes, d. in 1626. See preceding.

daggle-tail. A slattern; 'a nasty dirty Slut': from ca 1560; coll till 1700, when it > S.E.; ca 1830 it > dial. and low coll. cf. DRAGGLE-TAIL.

Dago. One of Latin race, but rarely of a Frenchman: ex U.S. (—1858) – though anticipated in 1832; anglicized ca 1900: coll. In C.17, *Diego* (James) was a nickname for a Spaniard. See *Words!* and O.E.D. (Sup.).

dags. A feat, piece of work. 'I'll do you(r) dags', i.e. 'something *you* can't'; (among schoolboys) 'do dags', play foolhardy tricks. Coll; from ca 1850. F. & H. proposes the A.-S. *daeg*, the O.E.D. *darg*, one's task, as the origin; ?a perversion of *dare* or *darings* (W.).

dags, on the. On furlough (as opp. a few days' leave): naval: late C.19–20. Prob. ex the preceding.

daily-bread. A wage-earner; the working head of the house: from ca 1890.

dairs. Small unmarketable fish: nautical coll: C.19–20; ob. Ex †dial. *dairns*, the same.

dairy or **dairies.** The paps; hence *sport*, later *air, the dairy*, expose the breast: low, from ca 1780. cf. CHARLEYS, CHARMS, MILKY WAY, and, in rhyming s., CABMAN'S REST.

daisies. A pre-1879 abbr. of DAISY ROOTS: boots.

daisies, turn up one's toes to the. To die: coll (—1842). Barham. cf. GRIN AT THE DAISY-ROOTS. Hence:

daisies, under the. Dead: from ca 1860; ob.

daisy, n. (and, in England, a rare adj., 1757), an excellent or first-rate person or thing: the n. came ex U.S. (—1876) and was anglicized ca 1890; Kipling used it in his poem, *Fuzzy Wuzzy*. 2. A chamber-pot: Midlands, esp. nursery: late C.19–20. Probably ex floral design on the inner base.

daisy, pick a. To defecate in the open air; also, to retire to urinate. Mostly women's; from ca 1860; orig. a euphemism; in C.20, coll. cf. PLUCK A ROSE.

daisy beat. To cheat; a cheat or swindle or minor crime: rhyming s.: late C.19–20.

daisy-beaters. Feet; the singular is very rare. C.19. cf. CREEPERS, with which it 'rhymes'.

daisy-cutter. A horse that hardly raises its feet from the ground: coll: late C.18–19. 2. Hence, any horse: C.19–20; ob. Scott, Charles Reade. 3. In cricket, a ball that keeps very low after pitching, esp. on being bowled: coll (1863); cf. *sneak(er)*.

***daisy-kicker.** A horse: c. and then low: from ca 1770; ob. cf. preceding. 2. The ostler of an inn, esp. a large inn: from ca 1770; ob. Both are in G. Parker's *View of Society*, 1781.

daisy recruits. (A pair of) boots: rhyming s.: ca 1855–70. cf.:

daisy roots. Boots: rhyming s. (—1874). I have never heard the singular used. Often abbr. to DAISIES. cf. the preceding term, which is less viable.

***daisyville, deuseaville.** The country: c. and (?) low: resp. C.19 and mid-C.17–early 19.

***dakma.** To silence: c.; rare in England and perhaps ex U.S.: C.19.

dam. DAMAGE: university: ca 1900–15.

dam, not be worth or **care a.** (See CARE A PIN.) Mid-C.18–20; coll. Prob. ex a small Indian coin; cf. CURSE. See esp. Yule & Burnell, W., and Grose, P. The *twopenny dam* is said to have been rendered fashionable by Wellington.

dam of that was whisker, the. A c.p. – coll and dial. – applied ca 1675–1810 to a great lie. Ray, 1678. Is it possible that *whisker* may orig. have been *whisper*? See also WHISKER, THE MOTHER . . .

damage. Expense; cost: from ca 1750; S.O.D. records it at 1755. Byron, 'Many thanks, but I must pay the damage.' Prob. ex *damage(s)* at law. In late C.19–20, gen. as *what's the damage?*, jocularly varying the much earlier *what's the shot?*

damaged. Tipsy: from ca 1865. cf. SCREWED.

damager. A manager: theatrical: ca 1880–1912. By sarcastic perversion and/or rhyming. 2. A damaging punch: pugilistic coll: from ca 1815, ob. *Boxiana* IV, 1824.

damask. To warm (wine): late C.17–early 19. B.E. has '*Damask the Claret*, Put a roasted Orange flasht smoking hot in it' ?the 'warmth' of damask, 'a rich silk fabric woven with elaborate designs and figures'.

***damber.** A man belonging to a criminal gang: c.: mid-C.17–18. cf. DIMBER; perhaps suggested by: DAMME-BOY.

dame. A house-master not teaching the Classics: Eton College: mid-C.19–20.

damfool; occ., jocularly, **damphoole** or **-phule.** A DAMNED fool: coll, n. and adj.: from, resp., ca 1880 and ca 1895. Whence:

damfoolishness. DAMNED foolishness: coll: late C.19–20.

damme, or **dammy,** or **damme (or -y)-boy.** A profane swearer gen. the single word): coll; ca 1610–1820. From mid-C.17–early 18 (the hyphenated term), 'a roaring mad, blustering Fellow, a Scourer of the Streets', B.E.; this latter is possibly c. (Perhaps *damme!* is itself coll.)

damme! I'm off. (Often *D.I.O.*) A men's c.p. of late C.18–early 19, satiric of initials on cards of invitation, etc.

damn'. DAMNED: coll: late C.18–20. cf. DAMN THE . . ., and see DAMNED.

damn, not be worth or **care a.** The form and etymology preferred by the O.E.D.: see DAM.

damn a horse if I do! A strong refusal or rejection: coll: ca 1820–60. 'Jon Bee', 1823, shrewdly postulates origin in *damn me for a horse if I do*.

damn the (e.g. **thing) can** (or **could) one** (e.g. **find).** Not a (thing) can one (find): a coll form of *not a* DAMNED *thing can one (find)*: somewhat rare (—1887).

damn well. Certainly; assuredly: coll: late C.19–20.

damnable. CONFOUNDED; objectionable: late C.16–20; S.E. till ca 1800, then coll or a vulgarism.

damnably. In degraded usage, very, exceedingly: C.19–20 coll or vulgarism. cf. preceding.

damnation, adj. and adv. From ca 1750: damned; excessive(ly), very. Coll.

damnation take it! A coll curse: C.19 (?18)–20.

damned. An adj. expressive of reprobation or of mere emotional crudity or as an ever-weakening intensive (cf. BLOODY): late C.16–20; S.E. till ca 1800, then coll. 2. adv., damnably; hence, very: mid-C.18–20; S.E. till ca 1850, then coll. In both senses, one tends to use *damned* before a vowel, DAMN' before a consonant.

damned!, I'll be; you be damned! A coll exclamation and a coll imprecation: C.17–20.

damned soul. A Customs House clearing clerk: from late 1780s. Ex a belief that he has sworn never to make true declarations on oath.

damp. A drink: Dickens in *Pickwick*; not very gen. elsewhere. Gen. *give oneself a damp*, or *something damp*. 2. Also, rather rare v. reflexive (—1862), whence prob.:

damp one's mug. To drink: low: from ca 1835; slightly ob.

damp(-)pot. The sea; esp. the Atlantic: tailors': from ca 1855. 2. A water-pot: tailors' coll: late C.19–20.

damp the sawdust. To drink with friends at the opening of a new tavern: licensed victuallers': from ca 1860.

***damper.** In c., *damper*, after ca 1860 gen. displaced by LOB, is a till: C.19. 2. A spoil-sport, 'wet blanket': coll: from ca 1815. 3. A sweating employer, a 'last-ouncer': tailors': from ca 1860. 4. Ale or stout taken after spirits (and water): from ca 1820. 5. A snack between meals: coll and dial.: from ca 1780; slightly ob. Maria Edgeworth. See 'The Art of Lightening Work' in *Words!*, p. 47, and cf. *snack*, *snap*, TIFFIN, and esp. BEVER. 6. A suet pudding preceding meat: schoolboys': C.19–20, ob. 7. (Australia and New Zealand) a kind of bread, unleavened and baked in ashes: orig. (ca 1825) coll but by 1910 accepted as S.E. Peter Cunningham, 1827. 8. A lunch- or, more gen., dinner-bill: Society: 1886–ca 1915. Ware notes the Fr. s. *douloureuse* and quotes Theodore Hook, 'Men laugh and talk until the feast is o'er; | Then comes the reckoning, and they laugh no more!'

damphool, -phule, see DAMFOOL.

damsel. A hot iron used to warm a bed: contrast a SCOTCH WARMING-PAN. The S.O.D. records it at 1727. Orig. it was undoubtedly either coll or s., but by 1800 it had > S.E.

damson-pie. Abuse; a slanging match. Either coll or dial.: Birmingham and 'the black country'; from ca 1865; ob. William Black, in *Strange Adventures of a House Boat*, 1888. The variant *damson-tart* occurs a year earlier (O.E.D.), but rather in the sense: profane language. Punning DAMN!

Dan. The inevitable nickname of anyone surnamed Coles: coll: late C.19–20.

Dan Tucker. Butter: rhyming s. (—1859), the rhyme being, as often, merely approximate.

***dance.** A staircase; a flight of steps: c. (—1857); †. Abbr. DANCERS.

dance, dance upon nothing (in a hempen cravat), dance the Paddington frisk or **the Tyburn jig.** To be hanged: low. The first, C.19–20, the second C.18–20, but both ob.; the third, late C.17–19. *Paddington* refers to Tyburn. Hence, *the dance (up)on nothing*, like *the dance of death*, = hanging, C.19–20. Hood, in *Miss Kilmansegg*, 'The felon . . . elopes | To a caper on sunny greens and slopes | Instead of the dance upon nothing.' 2. Among printers, from ca 1650, type is said to dance when, the forme being lifted, letters fall out. 3. **dance Barnaby,** see BARNABY DANCE.

dance, fake a, see FAKE A DANCE.

dance, lead (rarely **give**) **a person a.** To cause needless or excessive worry or exertion: from ca 1520; coll >, by 1900, S.E.

dance at your funeral, I'll or occ. **he'll, she'll.** 'An old slanging-match catchphrase' (Petch): late C.19–20.

dance barefoot. Applied to a girl whose younger sister marries before her: coll; ca 1590–1800. cf. the Yorkshire *dance in the half-pick*, 'to be left behind as a bachelor, on a brother's marriage', E.D.D.

dance to a person's whistle, pipe, etc. To follow his lead; unquestioningly obey. Coll > by 1700, S.E.; from ca 1560.

danceable. Fit to dance with: coll: 1860, Wilkie Collins. 2. (Of a tune) suitable for a dance: coll: from ca 1890.

***dancer.** A burglar who enters by climbing the roof: C.19 c. cf. GARRETER and DANCING-MASTER, 3.

***dancers.** Stairs; a flight of steps: from ca 1670; until ca 1840, c.; then low s. or archaic c. Because one 'dances' down them. 2. (Also *Merry Dancers*) the Aurora

Borealis: coll > S.E., though in C.20 mainly dial.: 1717.

dancing-dog. (Gen. pl.) A dancing man: from ca 1880; ob. Ware, 'A satirical title applied . . . when dancing began to go out'.

dancing-master. A species of MOHOCK *temp.* Queen Anne: coll. See esp. the *Spectator*, No. 324 (1712). This dandy-rough made his victims caper by thrusting his sword between their legs. 2. The hangman: late C.17–early 18; perhaps orig. c. 3. A burglar who enters by climbing the roof: ca 1860–1900. cf. DANCER and GARRETER.

dand. Abbr. DANDY, a fop: ca 1870–1900: perhaps more dial. than s. Hardy.

dander. Anger; a ruffled temper: coll; orig. (—1832) U.S., though perhaps ex English dial. as H. implies; (?re-)anglicized ca 1860. Thackeray, in *Pendennis*, 'Don't talk to me . . . when my dander is up.' The S.O.D. proposes derivation either ex *dander* = dandruff or ex *dunder* = ferment; the latter is preferable. But I suggest that the Romany *dander*, to bite – *dando*, bitten – may solve the problem. Whence *dandered*, angry, ruffled, anglicized ca 1880 but never gen.

dandification. The act or state of making look or looking like a DANDY: coll, 1825 +. Ex:

dandify. To make resemble, give the style of, a DANDY: coll; from ca 1820. Whence the ppl adj. *dandified.*

dandi, see DANDY, 5.

dandiprat; occ. **dandyprat(t).** A person physically, socially, or morally very insignificant: from ca 1550; coll till C.19. The anon. play *Lingua*, 1580; Scott, 1821. Ex the C.16–18 sense, a small coin worth 1½d.

dando. A heavy eater; esp. one who cheats restaurants, cafés, hotels, etc.: from ca 1840. Coll. Ex a 'seedy swell' so named and given to bilking. Thackeray; Macaulay, 1850, in *Journal*: 'I was dando at a pastry cook's.'

dandy; gen. **the d.** The TICKET; precisely the thing needed, esp. if fashionable. S.O.D. records it at 1784; *dandy*, fop, occurring only four years earlier (?ex DANDIPRAT), was perhaps s., or at the least coll, until ca 1830. 2. Anglo-Irish, a small drink or GO of whiskey (—1838); ob. 3. Anything first-rate; also adj.: orig. (1794: Thornton), U.S., anglicized ca 1905. 4. In the West Indies, with variant *dandy fever*, the coll name for *dengue* fever: 1828. 5. **dandy, dandi.** Anglo-Indian (coll rather than s.) for a boatman on the Ganges; from ca 1680. And for: a small hammock-like conveyance carried by two men; from ca 1870. 6. In c., a bad gold coin (—1883). Ex the modicum of pure gold. 7. A male homosexual: mid-C.19–20; also as adj.

dandy grey russet. A dirty brown: mid-C.18–early 19 coll. cf. dial. *dandy-go-russet*.

dandy horse. A velocipede: Society: ca 1820–40.

***dandy-master.** The head of a counterfeiting gang (—1883): c.

dandyfunk. Pounded biscuit mixed with water, fat, and marmalade, then baked: nautical: late C.19–20. Prob. ironic.

dandypratt, see DANDIPRAT.

dandysette. A female dandy: fast life: ca 1820–35. *Spy*, II, 1826. Also *dandizette* or *dandisette*.

dang. A curse, a damn: late C.19–20. Ex:

dang, v. To damn (e.g. *dang me!*): euphemistic dial. (from ca 1790) >, ca 1840, coll. Perhaps a blend of 'damn' and 'hang'.

dangle in the Sheriff's picture-frame. To be hanged: (c. or) low: late C.18–early 19.

***danglers.** A bunch of seals: c. (—1859): ?ex U.S. 2. Testicles: low: mid-C.19–20.

Daniel, take one's. To depart or decamp: low: ca 1860–1900.

***danna.** Human ordure: C.18–19 c. Hence *danna-drag*, the night-man's cart, C.19 c., and (*danna ken*), the C.18 c. form of the C.19–20 *dunnekin*, which, orig. c., > s. and then, ca 1900, low coll and which, early in C.19, pervaded dial.

Dansker. (Gen. pl.) A Dane: nautical coll: C.19–20. i.e. Danish *Dansker*, the same. cf. Shakespeare's use.

dant. A profligate woman; a harlot: C.16–17. Ex the Dutch, it is almost certainly c. or, at the least, low s.

dantiprat. A variant (C.17) of DANDIPRAT.

daps. Slippers: Regular Army's: late C.19–20. Perhaps cognate with dial. *dap*, to move quickly and lightly.

darbies. As handcuffs (from ca 1660), prob. orig. s., certainly soon coll; but as fetters (from ca 1670) always, though rare, s., ob. by 1860. Marryat, in *Japhet*, "We may as well put on the darbies, continued he, producing a pair of handcuffs." Ex a rigid form of usurer's bond called *Father Derby's*, or *Darby's, bands.* 2. Sausages: C.19–20, ob. Ex?

darbies and joans. Fetters coupling two persons: from ca 1735, ex *Darby and Joan.*

darble. The devil: a coll corruption, i.e. orig. a sol., of Fr. *diable.* From ca 1850.

darbs. (Playing) cards: rhyming s.: late C.19–20.

***darby,** see DARBIES. 2. Ready money: from ca 1675; orig. c., it > low ca 1780; †by ca 1850. Estcourt, in *Prunella*, a play (?1712), 'Come, nimbly lay down darby; come, pray sir: don't be tardy.' For etymology, cf. DARBIES. 3. A wholly c. sense is the mid-C.19–20 one, a thief's 'haul'.

darby roll. A gait that results from the long wearing of shackles: from ca 1820. Orig. a c. or a police term, it > low gen. s., never very common and now ob. cf.:

darby's dyke. The grave; death: C.19 low, prob. orig. c.: cf.:

darby's fair. The day on which a prisoner is removed from one prison to another for trial: C.19 low. cf. DARBIES and DARBY ROLL.

dard. The *membrum virile*: C.17–18; low, perhaps c. Ex Fr. *dard*, a dart.

dare. A challenge; act of defiance: from late C.16; S.E. till late C.19, when it > coll.

dark. Any person, place, thing not impregnated with Recordite principles: ecclesiastical: ca 1855–80. Perhaps ex *darkest Africa.*

***dark, get the.** To be confined in a punishment cell: c.: from ca 1880.

dark, keep it. Say nothing about it; gen. imperative. From ca 1856; coll. Prob. ex the long †, *keep a person dark*, i.e. confined in a dark room, as madmen formerly were; cf. the treatment of Malvolio in *Twelfth Night.*

dark as a pocket. Extremely dark: merchant-servicemen's: late C.19–20; ob.

dark (occ. **black**) **as Newgate knocker,** see NEWGATE KNOCKER, 2.

dark as the inside of a cow. (Of a night) pitch-black: nautical: from ca 1880. cf. DARK AS A POCKET.

***dark cull(y).** A married man with a mistress whom he visits only at night: C.18–early 19 c.

***dark engineer.** A rogue: c.: Ward, 1703.

dark horse. A horse whose form is unknown to the backers but which is supposed to have a good chance: the turf; from ca 1830. Disraeli, 'A dark horse . . . rushed past the grand stand in sweeping triumph,' 1831. Variant, from ca 1840, *dark un.* 2. Hence, a candidate or competitor of whom little is known: from ca 1860; in C.20, coll.

dark house. The coll form of *dark-room,* one in which madmen were kept: ca 1600–1850.

dark it. (Esp. in imperative.) To say nothing: s.: from ca 1880.

dark-lantern. 'The Servant or Agent that Receives the Bribe (at Court)', B.E.: ca 1690–1770.

darkened. Closed (eye): pugilistic. cf. 'I threatened him, that, if he was severe upon them, we would darken him' (give him a black eye), D. Haggart, *Life*, 1821.

darkey, see SWATCHEL.

***darkman.** A watchman: c.: C.18. Anon., *Street-Robberies Consider'd*, 1728. Independent of *darkmans*, for lit. it is a man working in the dark, i.e. at night.

***darkmans.** Night; twilight: mid-C.16–19 c. Harman, B.E., Scott. Occ. *darkman.* i.e. *dark* + -MANS.

***darkman's budge.** A nocturnal house-breaker's day-plus-night assistant: c.: late C.17–18. B.E.

***darkness, child of.** A bell-man: c.: late C.17–early 18.

darks, the; darky. The night; occ. twilight: low; mid-C.18–20, ob. G. Parker, 1789 (*darkey*).

***darky, darkey,** see DARKS. 2. A dark lantern: ca 1810–1910; either low or c. 3. A Negro: coll: orig. (1775: Thornton), U.S.; anglicized not later than 1840. 4. A white man with a dark skin: a generic nickname, from ca 1880. 5. The inevitable nickname of men surnamed Smith: military: late C.19–20. Prob. at first a Gypsy nickname. Also, ironically, of men surnamed White. 6. A beggar who pretends to be blind: c. (—1861). Mayhew.

Darling shower. A dust-storm: Darling-River vicinity (Australia): coll (—1898).

darn, darnation, darned. A coll form of *damn, damnation, damned.* ?orig. dial.; in C.19–20, mostly U.S. and euphemistic.

darning the water. 'Ships manoeuvring backwards and forwards before a blockaded port': nautical: C.19. Bowen. Ex darning socks.

dart. In boxing, a dart-like, i.e. straight-armed blow: from ca 1770; ob. 2. In Australia, idea, plan, scheme; ambition (—1887). Also, particular fancy, personal taste: from ca 1894. Ex the idea of a 'darting' or sudden thought. Hence: 3.

An illicit activity, a racket: Australian: since ca 1870.

dash. A tavern waiter: ca 1660–1830. Either ex his dashing about or ex his adding to drinks a dash of this or that. 2. See CUT A DASH. 3. A gift; a tip: West Africa: from ca 1780. Also v.: C.19. Ex *dashee*, a native word: in fact, *dashee*, n. and v., is the earlier, C.18 only, form of this 'Negrish' term.

dash, v.i. To CUT A DASH; coll; from ca 1780. 2. (Brewers' and publicans') to adulterate: from ca 1860. *The Times*, 4 April 1871, in leader on the Licensing Bill, '[The publicans] too often . . . are driven to adulterate or dash the liquor.'

dash! An expletive: coll always, but euphemistic only when consciously used as an evasion for DAMN!, which orig. it represented: from ca 1810. Ex the dash in *d–n.* The most frequent variants are *dash my wig(s)!*, ca 1810–80, and *dash it all!*, from ca 1870.

dash my buttons!, see BUTTONS! . . .

dash my wig(s)!, see DASH!

dash off; dash out. To depart with a dash; come out with a dash: coll: late C.18–20. Ex DASH, v., 1.

dash on, have a. To bet heavily and/or wildly: the turf; from ca 1865, ob.

dashed, dashedly, adj., adv. Euphemistic coll for *damned, damnably*: from ca 1880. See DASH!

dasher. One who cuts a dash; esp. a showy harlot: from ca 1790; coll. Dibdin, 'My Poll, once a dasher, now turned to a nurse.' 2. A brilliant or dashing attempt or motion: coll (—1884); ob.

dashing. A daring or brilliant action; a showy liveliness in manner, dress, gen. behaviour: coll: ca 1800–95.

dashing, adj. Fond of 'cutting a dash' (see at CUT . . .), making a show: from ca 1800; coll.

dashy. DASHING, adj.; coll; from ca 1820 (perhaps after FLASHY); never very common.

date. An appointment, esp. with a member of the opposite sex: coll: from ca 1905. Ex U.S. 2. The anus: Australian: low: late C.19–20.

date, v.i. To show its period, decade, year, etc., as in 'Fashion in dress dates so terribly.' Also, to be or become superseded, go out of fashion, quickly, as in 'Topicalities date so quickly.' Both senses are coll, somewhat cultured or, occ., snobbish, and arose ca 1900: ex the v.t. sense, likewise coll (1896: O.E.D. Sup.), to set definitely in a period.

date, up to. Coll as = (*brought*) up to the relevant standard of the time (—1890); almost S.E.

datoo. 'A westerly wind in the Straits of Gibraltar and Western Mediterranean': nautical coll: mid-C.19–20. Bowen. ?ex Arabic.

daub. An artist: low coll: mid-C.19–20. Ex *daub*, a bad painting. 2. A bribe: either c. or low s.: C.18.

daub, dawb, v. (vbl n., **daubing.**) To bribe, gen. v.i.; low, perhaps orig. c.; ca 1690–1850. cf. GREASE *a person's palms.*

David, david; davy. An affidavit: the former, C.19–20; the latter from ca 1760. In O'Hara's play, *Midas*, 1764, 'I with my davy will back it, I'll swear.' A facetious variant is *Alfred David* or *Davy*. Also as oath in '*so help me Davy*, gen. rendered "swelp my *Davy*"', H., 5th ed., the purer form occurring in H., 2nd ed. (1860). 2. **David Jones,** see DAVY.

David Jones; David Jones's locker, see DAVY JONES'(S) LOCKER.

David's (later Davy's) sow, (as) drunk as. Beastly, or very, drunk: coll; from ca 1670. Shadwell, 1671. In Bailey's *Erasmus*, 1733, 'When he comes home . . . as drunk as David's sow, he does nothing but lie snoring all night long by my side.' Origin obscure, but presumably anecdotal. (Apperson.) Also *drunk as a* SOW.

Davy, Davy Jones, Old Davy; David Jones. The spirit of the sea: nautical; from ca 1750, Smollett being, in *Peregrine Pickle*, the first to mention it in print. *Davy Jones* is the orig. form, *David Jones* is recorded by Grose in 1785, *Old Davy* occurs in Dibdin in 1790, *Davy* arises ca 1800. ?*Jonah* > *Jonas* > *Jones*, the *Davy* being added by Welsh sailors: such is W.'s ingenious and prob. etymology, perhaps suggested by DAVY JONES'(S) LOCKER. 2. See DAVID.

Davy Debet or **Debt.** A bailiff: coll verging on S.E.: ca 1570–90. Gascoigne. Apperson, 'Debt personified'.

Davy Jones'(s), later **Davy's, locker.** The sea, esp. as an ocean grave: nautical. *Journal of Richard Crosswell*, 1774–7, '"Damn my eyes," says he, "they are gone to Davy Jones's locker."' i.e. overboard. In Grose, 1785, *David Jones's locker*.

Davy Jones's natural children. Pirates; smugglers: nautical, C.19. (Mostly officers'.)

davy-man. That member of the crew of a

ship captured by a privateer who was left aboard in order to swear an *affidavit* as to her nationality: naval coll: C.19.

Davy putting on the coppers for the parson(s). A nautical comment on an approaching storm: from ca 1830; ob. This implies the sailors' belief in an arch-devil of the sea; cf.:

Davy's dust. Gunpowder: from ca 1830; ?orig. nautical. Ex *Davy* = the devil.

Davy's locker, see DAVY JONES'(S) LOCKER. **Davy's sow,** see DAVID'S SOW.

dawb, see DAUB.

dawg. A s. > coll variation of DOG: late C.19–20.

daxie, daxy. A dachshund: coll: 1899 (O.E.D. Sup.).

day! Good day!: coll: mid-C.19–20. cf. AFTERNOON!, MORNING!, and NIGHT! used in precisely the same voice- and manners-sparing way.

day, day! Good day!; good-bye!: C.17–18 coll; somewhat childish.

Day and Martin. A Negro: ca 1840–1910. Ware, 'Because D. & M.'s blacking was *so* black'. cf. BROWN POLISH.

day-bug. A day-boy: schoolboys': late C.19–20. cf. NIGHT-FLEA.

day-mates. The mates of the various decks: naval coll: C.19. Bowen.

day-opener. An eye; usually in pl: pugilistic: ca 1840–90. Augustus Mayhew, *Paved with Gold*, 1857. cf. the much more gen. DAYLIGHTS.

daylight. A glass not full: university, ca 1825–80. Ex the S.E. sense for the space between rim and liquor; the toast-tag, *No daylights* or *heel-taps* is still occ. heard. 2. For *burn daylight*, see BURN. 3. A space between a rider and his saddle: from ca 1870. 4. See DAYLIGHTS.

daylight into one (coll) or, both s., **the victualling department** or **the luncheon reservoir, let** or **knock.** To make a hole in, esp. to stab or shoot, hence to kill: in gen., from ca 1840; but *let daylight into one* is low coll recorded by the O.E.D. for 1793. In U.S., *make daylight shine through* (a person) occurs as early as 1774. cf. COOK ONE'S GOOSE, *settle one's* HASH.

daylights. The eyes: from ca 1750. Esp. in the pugilistic phrase, *darken one's daylights*. Fielding, 'D–n me, I will darken her daylights'.

dazzler. A showy person, esp. a woman; a brilliant act: from ca 1835. 2. A dazzling blow (—1883). 3. See BOBBY-DAZZLER.

deacon. 'Boy who collects bread plates for replenishment': Bootham School: late C.19–20.

dead. Abbr. *dead* CERTAINTY: racing, from ca 1870; ob.

dead, adj. (rarely) and adv. (often), has a coll tinge that is hard to define: this unconventionality may spring from one's sense of surprise at finding so grave a word used to mean nothing more serious than incomplete, inferior, or than very, directly, straight, etc. See the ensuing phrases. It is, however, doubtful if *dead drunk* and analogous terms were ever, despite one's subjective impression, coll: their antiquity is a hindrance to accurate assessment. The *dead* phrases may be spelt with or without a hyphen.

dead, on the. Off liquor, teetotal: military: late C.19–early 20. Prob. *on the dead t.t.* 2. Yet, ca 1890–1910, it seems to have been applied to one who has actively ceased to be a teetotaller.

dead!, you'll be a long time. Enjoy yourself while you can and may!: a late C.19–20 c.p. cf. the C.18 proverbial *there will be sleeping enough in the grave.*

dead against. Strongly opposed to: from ca 1850. Coll >, ca 1890, S.E. but not literary.

dead alive, dead and alive. (Of persons) dull, mopish, cf. DEADLY-LIVELY: C.16–20: S.E. till mid-C.19, then increasingly coll. 2. Hence of things, esp. places: dull, with few amusements, little excitement ('a dead-and-alive hole'): coll; from ca 1850; now S.E.

dead amiss. Incapacitated, as applied to a horse: the turf: ca 1860–1910.

dead and done-for look, have a. To look most woe-begone, wretched: coll (—1887).

dead! and (s)he never called me 'mother'! A c.p. satirizing, and quoting, melodrama. From ca 1880.

dead as a door-nail, a herring, Julius Caesar, mutton, a tent-peg. Quite dead. All coll orig.; all except the first still coll. The *door-nail* phrase occurs as early as 1350 and is found in *Piers Plowman* – it was S.E. by 1600; the *herring*, C.17–20, e.g. in Rhodes's *Bombastes Furioso*, 1790; the *mutton*, from (—)1770; the other two are C.19–20, though *tent-peg* has since ca 1910 been rare. Origins: *door-nail* is perhaps the striking plate of a door-knocker; a *herring* dies very soon after capture; *Julius Caesar* is deader than Queen Anne; *mutton* is by definition the flesh of a dead sheep; a *tent-peg*, like a *door-nail*, is constantly being hit on the head. Dial. has the synonyms: *dead as a hammer, maggot, nit, rag, smelt.*

dead beat. A worthless idler, esp. if a sponger as well: orig. (—1875) U.S., anglicized ca 1900 and now verging on coll. 2. In Australian s. (from ca 1870), a man down on his luck or stony-broke. Morris. 3. adj., completely exhausted: from ca 1820; coll. Pierce Egan in *Tom and Jerry*, 'Logic was . . . so dead-beat, as to be compelled to cry for quarter.'

dead bird. A certainty: Australian: from ca 1895; slightly ob. Morris, 'The metaphor is from pigeon-shooting, where the bird being let loose in front of a good shot is as good as dead.'

dead broke. Penniless; occ., bankrupt or ruined: coll: from ca 1850.

dead broker. A DEAD BEAT: Australian: from ca 1890.

***dead cargo.** Booty less valuable than had been expected: C.18–20, ob.; c.

dead cert, certainty, see CERT and CERTAINTY, A DEAD.

dead cinch. An intensive of CINCH in sense of 'dead CERT'.

dead cop. A sure way to win or make money: sporting: from ca 1870. cf. COP, v., 5.

dead earnest, in. In S.E., most earnest(ly); as coll, undoubtedly, in very truth: from ca 1870.

dead eyes for square? Shall I pass at divisions (examinations)?: *Conway* Training Ship: from ca 1890; ob.

dead-eyes under. (Of a ship) listing heavily: nautical: mid-C.19–20. Graphically proleptic.

dead finish, the. The extreme point or instance of courage, cruelty, excellence, endurance, etc.: Australian coll (—1881). Prob. ex FINISH, n.

dead frost. A fiasco, complete failure: theatrical; from ca 1875.

dead give-away. A notable indication, or revelation, of guilt or defect: from ca 1860.

dead gone. Utterly exhausted or collapsed: coll; from ca 1870.

dead head. One who travels free, hence eats free, or, esp., goes free to a place of entertainment (cf. PAPER, 2): coll: orig. U.S. (1849: Thornton), anglicized ca 1864. *Daily Telegraph*, 21 May 1883, '"Lucia di Lammermoor" is stale enough to warrant the most confirmed deadhead in declining to help make a house.' Whence v., and *dead headism.* Orig. of 'passengers not paying fare, likened to dead head (of cattle), as opposed to live stock', W.

dead heat. A race in which two (or more) competitors – animals or men – reach the goal simultaneously: from ca 1820 (Tom Hood); coll > S.E. by 1880.

dead horse. Work to be done but already paid for, work in redemption of a debt; hence, distasteful work. Often as *work for a* or *the dead horse*, C.17–20, or *draw* or *pull a* . . ., the former C.19–20, the latter C.17–18. Cartwright, 1651; B.E., who implies the use of *a dead horse* as also = a trifle. Coll. In Australia, *work off the dead horse.* 2. (West Indies) a shooting star: from ca 1850. Ex a native Jamaican belief.

dead horse, flog a or **the.** To work to no, or very little, purpose; make much ado about nothing; cry after spilt milk. Coll; from ca 1840.

dead lights. The eyes: nautical; from ca 1860.

dead-lock. A lock hospital: Cockneys': 1887; slightly ob.

dead low. (Of an atmosphere) absolutely still: nautical coll: C.19–20.

***dead lurk.** Robbing a house during divine service: c. and low (—1851); ob. Mayhew. See LURK.

dead man. (Very rare in singular.) An empty bottle or pot at a drinking-bout or the like: late C.17–20; orig. military. cf. the later DEAD MARINE. 2. A loaf charged for but not delivered, or smuggled away by a baker's man to his master's prejudice: bakers', from ca 1760. 3. Hence the † sense, a baker (—1860). 4. A scarecrow; non-aristocratic coll: from ca 1870; ob. 5. 'Why don't they tuck-in those dead-men out of sight' – glossed as 'the platted reef-points of the sails when carelessly hanging beneath the yard, when the sail is furled' (Glascock, *Sketch-Book*, I, 11, 1825): Naval: ca 1790–1850.

dead man, get a fart of a. Applied to anything extremely improbable: low coll: ca 1540–1720. Heywood, 1546; Robertson, 1681.

***dead man's lurk.** The extorting of money from a dead man's relatives: c.: from ca 1850. See LURK.

dead marine. An empty bottle at or after a carouse: orig. nautical; from ca 1820.

dead meat. A corpse: from ca 1860. cf. COLD MEAT; CROAKER; PICKLES; STIFF 'UN. 2. (Also *froze*
prostitute, as opposed to *fresh meat*, a non-prostitute: low: late C.19–20.

dead men. Empty bottles: see DEAD MAN, 1. 2. Among tailors, misfits, hence a scarecrow, lit. and fig.: from ca 1840. 3. See DEAD MAN, 5.

dead men's shoes, waiting for. Expecting inheritances: C.16–20: coll; S.E. after ca 1700. Phineas Fletcher, ''Tis tedious waiting dead men's shoes.'

dead nap. A thorough rogue: provincial low s., C.19–20, ob. cf.:

dead nip. An insignificant project turning out a failure: provincial s., C.19–20, ob.

dead number. 'The last number in a row or street; perhaps the *end* of the street': Cockneys': late C.19–20; ob. Ware.

dead oh!; deado, adv. In the last stage of drunkenness: naval; from ca 1850.

dead on, dead nuts on. Clever at; extremely fond of; hence, at first ironically, very inimical towards. Coll; from, resp., ca 1865 and 1870. cf. the earlier NUTS ON.

dead one, see DEAD UN.

dead pay. Money drawn by 'widows' men': naval coll: mid-C.19–20.

***dead set.** A persistent and pointed effort, attempt; esp. such an attack. From ca 1720. c. >, in the 1770s, s. or coll (low). *A New Canting Dict.*, 1725, '*Dead Set*, a term used by Thief-catchers when they have a Certainty of seizing some of their Clients, in order to bring them to Justice.' The *Globe*, 2 Nov. 1889, 'Certain persons . . . are making a dead set against the field sports of Britain.'

dead sow's eye. A button-hole badly made: tailors': from ca 1840; ob.

dead struck. (Of actors) breaking down very badly in a performance: theatrical; from ca 1860; ob.

***dead swag.** In c., booty that cannot be sold: C.19–20. cf. DEAD CARGO.

dead thick. Wide-awake and cunning (or clever): low Glasgow: late C.19–20.

dead to rights, adv. Certainly, undoubtedly; absolutely. ?orig. U.S.; in England from ca 1895, but never gen. and now ob. cf. RIGHTS. 2. In the (criminal) act: c. and low: late C.19–20.

***dead un** (or **'un**). In C.19–20 c., an uninhabited house. 2. A half-quartern loaf: from ca 1870. 3. A horse that will be either scratched, DOPED, or 'pulled' (cf. SAFE UN): the turf, from ca 1870. Hawley Smart in *Social Sinners*, 1880. 4. A bankrupt company: commercial: late C.19–20. cf. CADAVER. 5. A supernumerary who plays for nothing: theatrical: from ca 1860; ob.

dead uns, make. To charge not only for loaves delivered but for loaves not delivered: bakers': mid-C.19–20.

dead with, see SEEN DEAD WITH.

dead yet, not. Very old: a theatrical c.p. (1883; ob.) applied to 'an antique fairy' (Ware).

deader. A funeral: military: ca 1865–1910. 2. A corpse: from ca 1880. Conan Doyle. 3. *Be a deader* also = to be (very recently) dead: late C.19–20.

deadly. Excessive; unpleasant; very dull (gen. of places): from mid-C.17; coll. cf. AWFUL, GRIM. 2. adv., excessively; very: coll; from late C.16. The S.O.D. records *deadly slow* at 1688, *deadly dull* at 1865.

deadly-lively, adj. and adv. Alternately – or combining the – dull (or depressing) and the lively; with forced joviality, esp. to no purpose: coll: 1823, 'Jon Bee'. cf. DEAD ALIVE.

deadly nevergreen(s). The gallows: late C.18–early 19.

deady. Gin (—1812): Tom Moore, 1819. The S.O.D. says: 'Distiller's name'; F. & H.: 'From Deady, a well-known gin-spinner.' Ob., except in U.S. *dead-eye.*

deaf as the mainmast. Exceedingly deaf: nautical coll: C.19–20.

***deaf un, turn a.** (i.e., ear.) Not to listen: late C.19–20 c. Charles E. Leach.

deal, a. A lot (of . . .): coll: from C.16. 'Pregnantly for *a good* or *great deal*, etc.', O.E.D. 2. Hence, adv., much: coll: mid-C.18–20.

deal, do a. To conclude a bargain: coll; late C.19–20.

deal, wet the. To drink to the conclusion of a bargain(ing): coll; from ca 1860. Hindley, in *A Cheap Jack*, 'We will wet the deal'.

deal of glass about, there's a. A person or a thing is showy; first-rate, the TICKET. ?ex large show-windows. From ca 1880; ob.

deal of weather about, there's a. We're in for a storm: nautical coll: mid-C.19–20.

deal suit. A coffin, esp. if parish-provided: coll: from ca 1850. cf. ETERNITY BOX and the Fr. *paletot sans manches.*

dean. A small piece of wood tied round a small faggot: Winchester College; from ca 1850. cf. BISHOP, n., 3.

***deaner, occ. denar, deener,** or **dener.** A shilling: from ca 1835; orig. tramps' c.; in C.20, racing and low. Common in Australia. Prob. ex Fr. *denier* or Lingua

Franca *dinarly*. 2. (**Deaner.**) Dean of a college: Oxford undergraduates': *Daily Telegraph*, 14 Aug. 1899.

dear!; o(h) dear! Mild coll exclamations (cf. DEAR ME!): resp. C.19–20, late C.17–20. Perhaps *oh dear!* = *oh, dear God* or *Lord*; *dear* is an abbr. of *oh dear!*

Dear Joy. An Irishman: coll: late C.17–20; ob. Ex a favourite Irish exclamation. cf. *dear knows!*: C.19–20: coll: Northern Ireland and English provinces: abbr. *the dear Lord knows!* cf. quotations in Thornton.

dear me! A mild exclamation: coll: from ca 1770. Perhaps ex It. *Dio mi* (*salvi*)*!*, God save me!

dearee. A C.18 variant of DEARIE.

dearest member. The *membrum virile*. From ca 1740: orig. literary and euphemistic; from ca 1870, jocular and coll.

dearie, deary. A low coll form of address used by women: late C.18–20.

deary me! Slightly more sorrowful or lugubrious than DEAR ME!: coll (?orig. dial.): from ca 1780.

death, done to. Too fashionable; trite: coll (—1887) >, by 1910, S.E.

death, dress to. To dress oneself in the extreme of fashion: coll; from ca 1850. cf. DRESS TO (KILL) and KILLING.

death, like. (Or, much later, *like grim death.*) Very firmly or resolutely: coll; from ca 1780.

death, sure as. Absolutely certain: from ca 1760: S.E. >, ca 1800, coll.

death hunter, later **death-hunter.** One who, to newspapers, supplies reports of deaths: from ca 1730. Foote. 2. A seller of last dying speeches: from ca 1850; coll; ob. by 1895, †by 1910. Mayhew. 3. Robber of an army's dead (—1816): ob. by 1860, †by 1890. 4. An undertaker: late C.18–20. 5. Anyone else engaged in, living by, funerals: from ca 1870; ob.

death-hunting, n. The selling of 'last dying speeches': street vendors': ca 1840–1900. Mayhew, I, 1851.

death on. (With *to be.*) Very fond of; clever or capable at dealing with: orig. (—1847), U.S.; anglicized ca 1875. (cf. DEAD (*nuts*) ON, NUTS ON.) In U.S. (1842), it also = fatal to – a sense anglicized ca 1890.

death-warrant is out!, my (or **his** or **your**). A police c.p., dating from the late C.19. Clarence Rook, *London Side-Lights*, 1908, 'When a constable is transferred against his will from one division to another, the process is alluded to in the force in the phrase, "His death-warrant is out." For this is a form of punishment for offences which do not demand dismissal.'

death's head upon a mop-stick. 'A poor, miserable, emaciated fellow,' Grose, 1st ed.: late C.18–early 19.

deb. A bed: back s.: since ca 1845.

de-bag. An Oxford and (less) Cambridge term, from ca 1890: to remove the 'bags' or trousers of (an objectionable fellow student).

debblish. A penny: South Africa: from ca 1870.

deboo. A début: sol. spelling: from ca 1885.

debs. Debenture stock: Stock Exchange (—1896).

decencies. 'Pads used by actors, as distinct from actresses, to ameliorate outline', Ware: theatrical coll: late C.19–20.

decent, decentish. Passable; fairly good or agreeable; tolerable; likable. Senses 1–3 arose ca 1700 (the form in *-ish* ca 1814) and, in C.19–20, are S.E. The fourth sense is orig. and still Public-Schoolboyish (esp. in *decent fellows*).

deck. A pack of cards: late C.16–20; until ca 1720, S.E. (Shakespeare has it in the third *King Henry VI*); then dial. and, until ca 1800, coll; very gen. in U.S. In C.20 England, it is confined, more or less, to the underworld. 2. In Anglo-Indian coll, a look, a peep: C.19–20. Variant *dekh*. cf. DEKHO. 3. See DECKER, 3.

decker. A deck-hand: from ca 1800: coll >, by 1850, S.E. 2. A deck-passenger, from ca 1865: coll. 3. (**Decker.**) One who lives in 'the Deck' or Seven Dials district of London (W.C.): costers': late C.19–20; ob.

declare off, v.t. To cancel (an arrangement, a match, etc.); v.i., to withdraw, arbitrarily or unsportingly. Both coll; from the late 1740s. Fielding; George Eliot, 'When it came to the point, Mr Haynes declared off.'

decoct. Bankrupt: C.16; either pedantic or affectedly facetious coll. Lit., thoroughly cooked, i.e. done to a turn. cf. the C.17 *decoctor*.

decoy-bird or **-duck.** A swindling-decoy: C.17–20; low coll; S.E. after ca 1790.

***decus.** A crown piece: late C.17–19. Ex the L. motto, *decus et tutamen* on the rim. Shadwell; Scott, 'Master Grahame . . . has got the *decuses* and the *smelts*.' B.E. cites as c., as it prob. was for some years.

dee. See D. 2. In c., a pocket-book: from ca 1835; ob. Orig. Romany.

dee'd. Damned: C.19–20. Barham.

Dee-Donk. A Frenchman: Crimean War, when, by the way, the French soldiers called the English *I says*, precisely as the Chinese mob once did (see Yule & Burnell). cf. WI WI.

'deed. Ex Fr *Dis donc*! Abbr. *indeed*: coll: mid-C.16–20. Since ca 1870, mostly Scottish.

***deeker.** 'A thief kept in pay by a constable', Haggart in his *Life*, 1821: Scottish c.: †.

deener, see DEANER.

deep. Sly; artful: from ca 1780. *Punch*, 1841, 'I can scarcely believe my eyes. Oh! he's a deep one'; *a deep one* is defined by Grose (2nd ed.) as 'a thorough-paced rogue'. Ex the C.16–20 S.E. sense, profoundly crafty.

deep grief. Two black eyes: ca 1875–1900. Jocular on *full mourning*.

deep-sinker. The largest-sized tumbler; the drink served therein: Australian coll: 1897, *Argus*, 15 Jan. Ex deep-sinking in a mining shaft.

deer-stalker. A low-crowned hat, close fitting and gen. of felt (—1870); coll, soon > S.E.

deevie, -vy; dev(e)y. Delightful, charming: 1900–ca 1907, H. A. Vachell speaking of it in 1909 as †. A perversion of DIVVY, 3. O.E.D. (Sup.) records also the adv. in *-ily*.

deferred stock. Inferior soup: ca 1860–1900; in the City. The body or solid part of soup is stock.

definite. Dogmatic: late C.19–20; coll. (Of persons only.)

***degen,** occ. **degan; dagen.** In late C.17–early 19, c. for a sword. 2. A sense that engendered that of an artful fellow: C.19 low. cf. DAG. Ex C.17 Dutch *degen*, 'sword'; prob. introduced by returned soldiers. Sense 2 follows from sense 1: cf. Middle High German *ein sneller Degen*, 'a brave knight', and the C.17–18 Dutch *degen*, 'a brave soldier; an "old soldier"'.

degree, to a. To a serious, though undefined, extent: coll: from ca 1730.

***degrees, have taken one's.** To have been imprisoned in a COLLEGE or gaol: c.: ca 1820–50.

degrugger. A degree: Oxford undergraduates': from ca 1895. For the form, cf. TESTUGGER.

dekh, see DECK, 2, and cf.:

dekho; gen. dekko, n. (esp. **take a dekko**) and v. To see; to, or a, glance. Vagrants' (—1865), ex Romany *dik*, to look, to see (Sampson). In Army, common since ca 1890, via Hindustani.

del. trem., see D.T., 2.

***delicate.** A false subscription-book used by a pseudo-collector of alms, etc.: mid-C.19–20; c. and low. 2. In c. alone (—1845), a begging-letter.

delicate condition (late C.19–20) or **state of health** (1850, Dickens), **in a.** Pregnant: euphemistic coll.

delighted! Certainly!; with pleasure!: C.19–20; S.E. worn, in C.20, to coll.

deliver the goods, see GOODS, THE.

***delivered dodge.** A trick whereby one secures possession, without payment, of goods delivered to one's rooms: c.: mid-C.19–20.

***dell.** In mid-C.16–early 19 c., a young girl: but in C.17–early 19 low s., a young wanton, a mistress (cf. DOXY). Harman, Jonson, B.E., Grose, Ainsworth. Etymology?

delo diam, see DELO NAMMOW.

***delo nam o' the barrack.** In late C.19–20 c., the master of the house. *Barrack* = house, while *delo nam*, in back s., = old man.

delo nammow. An old woman: back s. (—1874). Earlier, DILLO-NAMO. There is also *delo diam*, an old maid (Ware).

delog. Gold: in back s. (—1873). Hotten. Earlier DLOG.

delve it. To work head down (as in digging) and sewing fast: tailors': from ca 1865.

dem, see DEMN.

demand the box. To call for a bottle: nautical: from ca 1820; ob.

***demander (or demaunder) for glimmer (or glymmar).** A pretended victim of fire: C.16–18 c.

demi-beau, see SUB-BEAU.

demi-doss. A penny bed: vagrants' and low; ca 1870–1914.

demi-rep. A woman whose general reputation or, esp., chastity is in doubt. First recorded in Fielding's *Tom Jones*, 1749, '... Vulgarly called a demi-rep; that is ..., a woman who intrigues with every man she likes, under the name and appearance of virtue ... in short, whom everybody knows to be what nobody calls her.' By 1800, coll; by 1840 (except in the occ. variant *demi-rip*) S.E.; by 1900, ob. Ex *reputation*,

demme!, a coll variant of DAMN ME!, is recorded by O.E.D. for 1753.

demn; dem. From late C.17 in profane usage; the latter the gen. form in C.19–20. Orig. euphemisms for *damn*; but rather are they jocular coll when facetious, esp. in derivatives *demd* (earlier *demn'd*) and *demnition* (as in *demnition bow-wows*, coined by Dickens in *Nicholas Nickleby*).

demon, n. and adj. Applied to 'a super-excellent adept'. Coll; from ca 1882.

demon chandler. A chandler supplying ship's stores that are very inferior: nautical coll: from ca 1871.

***dempstered,** ppl adj. Hanged: Scottish c.: mid-C.17–18. Ex *dempster*, that official whose duty it was, until 1773, to 'repeat the sentence to the prisoner in open court'.

demure as a(n old) whore at a christening, as. Extremely demure: late C.18–20: coll.

***demy.** An illicit die (i.e. dicing): C.16–17 c. > s. Greene.

demy-rep, see DEMI-REP.

den. A small lodging or, esp., room in which one – gen. a male – can be alone: from ca 1770: coll >, by 1900, S.E. cf. *snuggery*.

dena; denar, dener, see DEANER. **denarli,** see DINARLEE.

dennis. A small walking-stick: C.19. App. unrecorded before 1823. 2. **(Dennis.)** A pig: nautical: mid-C.19–20. Gen. in address (*Dennis*). Hence, *hullo, Dennis!*, an insulting or derisive nautical c.p. of late C.19–20; ob.

deolali tap, see DOOLALLY TAP. Also *deolalic tap*.

dep. A deputy, esp. a night porter at a cheap lodging-house: low (—1870). Dickens, in *Edward Drood*, 'All man-servants at Travellers' Lodgings is named Deputy.'

depends, it (all). Perhaps! Coll; late C.19–20. 2. Also, when *depend* is used elliptically with the following clause and it = 'to depend on it', it is coll (1700).

derack; deracks. A pack of cards; in pl, the cards themselves; military back s.: late C.19–20. Thus, *card* > *drac* > *derack*, and *s* is added.

derby, see DARBY. 2. **Derby dog.** The homeless dog that, at Epsom, is sure to appear on the course as soon as it has been cleared for the Derby: mid-C.19–20: coll >, by 1890, S.E. (The race was founded in 1780 by the 12th Earl of Derby.) 3. **derbies,** see DARBY. 4. Short for DERBY KELLY.

derby, v. To pawn: sporting: late C.19–early 20. Ware derives from: the pawning of watches being excused on the grounds of their being lost or stolen at Epsom on Derby Day.

Derby crack, a. An outstanding race for the Derby: Cockney (—1887).

Derby Kelly. Belly: rhyming s. (—1900). Gen. abbr. to *Derby Kell*.

dern, derned, see DARN, also DURN.

***derrey.** An eye-glass: c.: from ca 1860; ob.

derrey, take the. To quiz, ridicule: tailors', ca 1850–1900.

derrick. The gallows; hangman. As v., to hang. Orig. (1600) coll; by 1800, S.E. Ex *Derrick*, the name of the public hangman ca 1598–1610. cf. JACK KETCH. 2. A casual ward: tramps' c.: late C.19–20. 3. The *membrum virile*: low: C.19–20.

derrick, v.i. 'To embark on a disreputable cruise or enterprise': nautical: mid-C.19–20. Bowen. Ex the n., sense 1.

derry on, have a. To have a DOWN (3) on: Australian: from ca 1895. Morris derives ex the comic-song refrain *hey derry down derry*; but also operative is the dial. *deray*, uproar, disorder, itself ex Old Fr. *desroi*, *derroi*, confusion, destruction.

derwenter. A released convict: ca 1880–1900: Tasmanian. Boldrewood. Ex the penal settlement on the banks of the River Derwent, Tasmania.

derzy. A tailor: Regular Army coll: late C.19–20. Ex Hindustani *darzi*. Also, occ., *dhirzi*.

desert. A ladies' club: Society: 1892–ca 1915. Ware, 'From the absence [?lack] of members.'

deserve a (or the) cushion, see CUSHION, DESERVE A.

despatchers, dispatchers. False dice with two sets of numbers and no low pips: low; perhaps orig. c.: from mid-1790s. *The Times*, 27 Nov. 1856. They soon 'despatch' the unwary. cf. DISPATCHES.

desperate, desperately, adj. and adv. Both from early C.17 in loose sense of AWFUL. Coll; the adv. – esp. as an intensive (= extremely, very) – remaining so, the adj. having, ca 1750, > S.E.

desperately mashed. Very much in love: ca 1882–1910. cf. MASH.

detail! but that's a, In the 1890s, a current phrase humorously making light of something difficult or important.

detec. A detective: ca 1875–95. Superseded by TEC.

deten. Detention: school coll: late C.19–20.

detrimental. An ineligible suitor, also (and orig.) a younger brother to an heir to an estate: from ca 1830. 2. Hence, a male flirt: from ca 1850. All three nuances are Society slang.

deuce; occ. **deuse**, C.17–18; **dewce**, C.17; **dewse**, C.18; **duce**, C.17–19. Bad luck, esp. in exclamations (e.g. *the deuce!*): from ca 1650. Hence, perdition, the devil, esp. in exclamations (e.g. *the deuce take it!*): from ca 1690. cf. its use as an emphatic negative (e.g. *the deuce a bit*): from ca 1710. These three senses are very intimately linked; they derive either from old Fr. *deus*, L. *deus*, or from *the deuce* (Ger. *das daus*) at cards: cf. *deuce-ace*, a throw of two and one, hence a wretched throw, hence bad luck. 2. Whence also the two at dice or at cards (mostly among gamesters); and 3, twopence (mostly among vagrants and Dublin newsboys): both low and dating from ca 1680. No. 3 is in B.E. as DUCE.

deuce, go to the. To degenerate; to fall into ruin: coll; from ca 1840.

***deuce-a-vil(l)e,** see DAISYVILLE.

deuce and ace. (A) face: rhyming s.: late C.19–20.

deuce and all, the. Much, in a violent or humorous sense: coll (—1762). Sterne.

deuce to pay, the. Unpleasant consequences or an awkward situation to be faced: from ca 1830. Thackeray, 1854, 'There has been such a row . . . and the deuce to pay, that I'm inclined to go back to Cumtartary.'

deuce (or **devil**) **with, to play the.** To harm greatly; send to rack and ruin: from ca 1760.

deuced. (Of things) plaguy, confounded; (persons) devilish; (both) excessive. Also as adv. From ca 1774. Mme D'Arblay; Michael Scott, in *The Midge*, 1836, 'Quacco . . . evidently in a deuced quandary.' Ex DEUCE.

deuced infernal. Unpleasant: Society: ca 1858–70. H., 1st ed., Introduction (*jeuced* . . .).

deucedly. Plaguily; extremely: coll; from ca 1815. Thackeray.

***deuces.** In racing c., from ca 1860: odds of 2 to 1.

deuse, see DEUCE.

***deuseaville,** see DAISYVILLE. Hence *deuseaville-stampers*, country carriers: late C.17–18 c.

***deus(e)wins.** Twopence: 1676, Coles: c.

devey, see DEEVIE.

devil. The errand boy in a printery – perhaps orig. the boy who took the printed sheets as they issued from the press: (—1683) orig. printers' s. By 1800 printers' j. and gen. coll; by 1900, S.E. *Punch* in 1859 spoke of 'the author's paradise' as 'a place where there are no printers' devils'. 2. In law, a junior counsel who, gen. without fee, does professional work, esp. the 'getting-up' of cases, for another: from ca 1850. 3. Hence, a person doing hack work (often highly intelligent and specialized work) for another: from ca 1880; coll; after ca 1905, S.E. 'I'm a devil . . . I give plots and incidents to popular authors, sir, write poetry for them, drop in situations, jokes, work up their rough material,' G. R. Sims, 1889. 4. A (firework) cracker: from ca 1740; coll till ca 1800, when it > S.E. Hence, perhaps, the C.19–20 coll sense, a piece of firewood, esp. kindling, soaked in resin. 5. A grilled chop or steak seasoned with mustard and occ. with cayenne: late C.18–20; coll, soon S.E. Grose, 2nd ed., defines it as a broiled turkey-gizzard duly seasoned and adds, 'From being hot in the mouth'. cf. ATTORNEY. 6. Gin seasoned with chillies: licensed victuallers and then public-houses in gen.; from ca 1820. G. Smeaton, *Doings in London*, 1828. 7. (Fighting) spirit, great energy, a temper notable if aroused: coll: from ca 1820. 8. A sandstorm, esp. a sand spout: military (India and Egypt; by 1890, South Africa); from ca 1830. 9. Among sailors, any seam difficult to caulk: (?C.18,) C.19–20. 10. See DEVIL HIMSELF.

devil, v. To act as 'devil' to a lawyer: from ca 1860. 2. To do hack work: from ca 1880. See n., 2 and 3.

devil, a or **the,** followed by **of a(n).** An intensive of no very precise meaning: coll; from ca 1750. Esp. in *a, the devil of a mess, row, man, woman.* Michael Scott, 1836, 'A devil of a good fight he made of it.' 2. Also, *the devil* (without *of*) is used intensively as a negative, as in 'The devil a thing was there in sight, not even a small white speck of a sail,' Michael Scott in *The Midge*.

devil, American. A piercing steam whistle employed as a summons: workmen's, ca 1865–1910. *Manchester Guardian*, 24 Sept. 1872.

devil, go to the. To fall into ruin: late C.18–20; but the imprecation *go to the devil!* dates from C.14.

devil, hold a light or **candle to the,** see CANDLE TO . . .

devil!, how or what or when or where or who the. An exclamation indicative of annoyance, wonder, etc.: the second, from M.E. and ex Fr. *que diable!*; the others C.17–20: coll. The first occurs in Pope, the second in Garrick, the fifth in Mrs Cowley.

devil, little or **young.** A coll term of address, playful or exasperated: C.17–20.

devil, play the. To do great harm; v.t., *with.* Coll from ca 1810; earlier, S.E. Egan, 1821, 'The passions . . . are far from evil, | But if not well confined they play the devil.'

devil, the, see DEVIL, A.

devil a bit says Punch, the. A firm though jocular negative: ca 1850–1910; coll. (Without *says Punch*: from ca 1700.)

devil among the tailors, the. (Gen. preceded by *there's.*) A row, disturbance, afoot: late C.18–20, ob.; coll. Perhaps ex tailors' riot at the performance of *The Tailors: a Tragedy for Warm Weather.* cf. CUCUMBER-TIME.

devil (and all) to pay, the. Very unpleasant consequences to face: C.15–20; coll. Swift in his *Journal to Stella.* 'Supposed,' says the S.O.D., 'to refer to bargains made by wizards, etc., with Satan, and the inevitable payment in the end.'

devil and ninepence go with (her, etc.)**!, the.** A semi-proverbial coll: C.18. T. Brown (—1704), 'That's money and company.' In C.19–20 (ob.), with *sixpence* for *ninepence.*

devil and you'll see his horns or **tail, talk of the.** Applied to a person that, being spoken of, unexpectedly appears: coll proverbial, C.17–20.

devil beats or **is beating his wife with a shoulder of mutton, the.** 'It rains whilst the sun shines,' Grose, 3rd ed.: semi-proverbial coll: late C.18–mid-19.

devil by the tail, pull the. To go rapidly to ruin; to take an undue risk; to be at one's last shift. Coll; from ca 1750.

devil-catcher or **-driver.** A parson: late C.18–early 19. See also:

devil-dodger. A clergyman, esp. if a ranter: late C.18–20. Lackington, 1791. 2. (cf. HOLY JOE.) A very religious person: mid-C.19–20. 3. Also, a person that goes sometimes to church, sometimes to chapel (—1860); ob. Variants of sense 1: *devil-catcher* (rare), *-driver* or *-pitcher,* and *-scolder,* all slightly ob. cf. SNUB-DEVIL.

devil doubt you, the. (Often with addition of *I don't*: which explains it.) A proletarian c.p. of late C.19–early 20.

devil-drawer. A sorry painter: ca 1690–1830: coll.

devil-driver, see DEVIL-DODGER.

devil go with you and ninepence or **sixpence,** see DEVIL AND NINEPENCE . . .

devil himself, the. A streak of blue thread in the sails of naval ships: mid-C.18–early 19 nautical.

devil is blind, when the. Never; most improbably. Coll: mid-C.17–20; ob. cf. BLUE MOON.

devil-may-care. Reckless; spiritedly free and easy, with connotation of real or assumed happiness. ?before Dickens in 1837: coll.

devil may dance in his pocket, the. He is penniless: C.15–early 19 coll. Because there is no coin with a cross on it: no coin whatsoever.

devil-on-the-coals. A small, very quickly baked DAMPER (7): from ca 1860: Australian rural coll: >, ca 1900, S.E. The Rev. A. Polehampton, *Kangaroo Land,* 1862.

devil-pitcher, -scolder, see DEVIL-DODGER.

devil take . . .! Followed by *me, him,* etc. Variants of *take* are *fetch, fly away with, send, snatch.* Exclamations of impatience, anger. Coll: C.16–20; earlier in other forms.

devil to pay, see DEVIL (AND ALL) TO PAY, THE.

devil to pay and no pitch hot, the, see PAY AND . . .

devil's (occ. **the old gentleman's**) **bed-post(s)** or **four-poster.** At cards, the four of clubs, held to be unlucky: coll; from ca 1835. Captain Chamier, *The Arethusa,* 1837. cf.:

devil's bedstead, the. The thirteenth card of the suit led: whist players' coll (—1887).

devil's bones, or **teeth.** C.17–20, C.19: coll: dice. Etherege, 1664, 'I do not understand dice . . . hang the devil's bones!' cf.:

devil's books, the. Playing cards: C.18–20, ob.; coll till ca 1810, when it > S.E. Swift, 1729, 'Cards are the devil's own invention, for which reason, time out of mind, they are and have been called the devil's books.' Also, ca 1640–1720, *the devil's prayer-book,* likewise coll.

***devil's claw(s).** The broad arrow on convicts' uniforms: c.: from ca 1850; ob. 2. 'A split hook to catch a link of chain cable': nautical coll verging on j.: mid-C.19–20. Bowen. 3. A cable-stopper on a sailing ship: id.: id.

devil's colours or livery. Black and yellow: coll: mid-C.19–20, ob.

devil's daughter. A shrew: coll: mid-C.18–20; from ca 1820, mainly dial. Grose, 3rd ed., 'It is said of one who has a termagant for his wife, that he has married the Devil's daughter, and lives with the old folks.'

devil's daughter's portion. A mid-C.18–early 19 c.p. applied – on account of their impositions on sailors and travellers – to Deal, Dover, and Harwich; Helvoet and the Brill. Grose, 1st ed. (q.v.).

devil's delight, kick up the. To make a din, a disturbance: from ca 1850. Whyte-Melville in *General Bounce*.

devil's dinner-hour, the. Midnight: artisans': late C.19–20; ob. Ware, 'In reference to working late'.

devil's dozen. Thirteen: coll; ca 1600–1850. From the number of witches supposed to attend a witches' sabbath. cf. BAKER'S, *printers'* and *long dozen*.

devil's dust. Shoddy, which is made from old cloth shredded by the devil, a disintegrating machine: (—1840, when Carlyle uses it); coll recognized as S.E. by 1860. Popularized by a Mr Ferrand in the House of Commons on 4 March 1842, when, to prove the worthlessness of shoddy, he tore a piece of devil's dust into shreds. 2. Gunpowder: military; from ca 1870; ob. Hawley Smart in *Hard Lines*, 1883.

devil's guts, the. A surveyor's chain: mid-C.17–early 19; rural. Ray, 1678; Grose, 1st ed., 'So called by farmers, who do not like that their land should be measured by their landlords.'

devil's horns off, enough wind to blow the. A very strong wind: nautical: mid-C.19–20.

devil's in Ireland!, as sure as the. A coll asseveration (—1823); ob.

devil's livery, see DEVIL'S COLOURS.

devil's luck and my own (too), the. No luck at all: lower and middle classes' coll: late C.19–20. cf. DEVIL'S OWN LUCK.

devil's own, adj. Devilish; very difficult or troublesome or unregenerate, as e.g. in *devil's own dance* or *business*. Coll: C.19–20. W. N. Glascock, *Sketch-Book*, II (29), 1826, 'He led the boatswain the devil's own life.'

devil's own boy. A young blackguard; a notable 'imp of the devil': coll; C.19–20, ob.

devil's own luck. Extremely bad, more gen. extremely good, fortune: C.19–20; coll.

devil's own ship. A pirate: coll; C.19.

devil's paternoster, say the. To grumble: C.17–18; coll. Terence in English, 1614.

devil's picture-gallery, the. A pack of cards: coll: late C.19–20; ob.

devil's playthings, the. Playing cards: C.19–20, ob.; coll. cf. DEVIL'S BOOKS.

devil's prayer-book, the, see DEVIL'S BOOKS.

devil's smiles. April weather; alternations of sunshine and shower: C.19–20, ob.; coll.

devil's tattoo. An impatient or vacant drumming on, e.g. the table, with one's fingers, with one's feet on the floor. Coll; after ca 1895, S.E. Scott, Lytton, Thackeray.

devil's teeth. Dice: coll (—1860); ob. cf. DEVIL'S BONES.

devilish, adv. Much, very: from early C.17: coll; in C.19–20 almost S.E. Grose cleverly satirizes its use. Orig. it had the force of the C.20 *hellish* (adv.).

devils, blue, see BLUE DEVILS.

deviltry. A coll form of *devilry*: not gen. among the educated. From ca 1850 in England, influenced by U.S.; orig. and, except in facetious use, still mainly dial.

devor. A plum cake: Charterhouse, from ca 1875. Ex the L.

devotional habits. Applied to a horse eager, or apt, to go on his knees: the stables (—1860); ob.

devy, see DEEVIE.

dew. Whiskey; occ., punch: Anglo-Irish: 1840, Lever. Abbr. of MOUNTAIN-DEW, whiskey.

dew-beaters. Pedestrians out before the dew has gone: coll: mid-C.17–19. Hackett's *Life of Williams*. Whence, 2, the feet: c.: late C.18–20, ob. Scott. 3. In C.19 c. and (?) low: boots, shoes. Variants: *dew-dusters*, *-treaders*: mid-C.19–20 (ob.).

dew-bit. A snack before breakfast: mid-C.19–20; ob.; coll. cf.:

dew-drink. A drink before breakfast, as to farm labourers before they begin a non-union day's harvesting. Coll: mid-C.19–20. Like DEW-BIT, more gen. and early in dial.

dewce, see DEUCE.

dewitted, be. To be murdered by the mob, as were the brothers De Witt, Dutch statesmen, in 1672: from ca 1685; coll till ca 1720, then S.E.

***dews,** see DEUCE, 2. Esp. in *dews wins*, twopence. **dewse,** see DEUCE, 1.

***dewse-a-vyle.** cf. DEUSEAVILLE and see DAISYVILLE.

***dewskitch.** A thrashing, esp. a sound one: (—1851, ob.) vagrants' c., and low s.

dexter. (On the, belonging to the) right: facetiously coll ex heraldry. From ca 1870; in C.20, rare in England, very gen. in U.S., esp. in sport (e.g. baseball). Atkin in *House Scraps* (a humorous ballad of the Stock Exchange), 1887: 'His "dexter ogle" has a mouse; | His conk's devoid of bark.'

dhirzi, see DERZY.

dhobi, dhoby; sometimes anglicized as **dobie, dobey, dobee.** A native washerman: Anglo-Indian coll: C.19–20. Ex Hindi *dhōb*, washing. Among C.20 Regular Army soldiers as among post-1840 Europeans resident in India, occ. loosely of any washerman or -woman. (Not to be confused with *dhoti*, the Hindu loin-cloth.) 2. Hence as v.i. and v.t., gen. in form **dobeying** (vbl n.), clothes-washing: nautical: mid-C.19–20.

dhobi wallah. A variant, late C.19–20, of sense 1 of the preceding.

dial. The face: low: from ca 1830. Orig. *dial-plate*: *Lex. Bal.*, 1811. (cf. FRONTISPIECE, esp. CLOCK.) Variant, *dial-piece*. 2. In c., a thief or a convict hailing from Seven Dials (now part of W.C.1), London: ca 1840–90.

dial, turn the hands on the. To disfigure a person's face: ca 1830–1910; low.

dial-piece, -plate, see DIAL, 1. **alter one's dial-plate.** To disfigure his face: 1811.

diamond-cracking. Work in a coal mine: C.19–20; cf. BLACK DIAMONDS. 2. In Australian c., from ca 1870: stone-breaking.

dib. A portion or share: non-aristocratic: from ca 1860; ob. Prob. ex S.E. *dib*, a counter used in playing card-games for money. 2. See DIBS.

dibble. In C.17, a moustache (?). 2. The *membrum virile*: low coll; C.19–20. Ex the gardening instrument. 3. An affectionate form of *devil*: C.19–20; affected by lovers.

dibble-dabble. An irregular splashing; noisy violence; rubbish: mid-C.16–20: coll till C.19, then dial. By reduplication of *dabble*.

dib(b)s. Money: from ca 1800. Prob. ex *dibstones*, a children's game played with sheep's knucklebones or with rounded pebbles. 2. A pool of water: nautical coll: mid-C.19–20. Ex Scottish *dib*. 3. The game of knucklebones: schoolchildren's: (see sense 1): late C.19–20. 4. Prayers: Rugby s.: late C.19–20. See DICS.

***dice.** The names of false dice are orig. c. and few > s. The terms are: BRISTLES, *cinques*, *demies*, *deuces*, *direct contraries*, DOCTORS, FULHAMS, *gord(e)s*, *graniers*, LANGRETS, *sices*, and *trays* or *treys*. See also such terms as BARRED, FLATS, LONGS.

dice, box the. To carry a point by trickery: legal; from ca 1850.

dicer. A hat: ca 1800–40.

Dick. A man; lad, fellow. As in TOM, DICK AND HARRY (see *Words!*, pp. 70–71): late C.16–20. Ex *Richard*. (Coll rather than s.)

dick. A dictionary; hence, fine words: from 1860 in U.S., and in Britain from ca 1870. H., 5th ed. cf. RICHARD. 2. An affidavit: recorded in 1861 (Dutton Cook, in *Paul Foster's Daughter*). See DICK, UP TO. 3. A riding whip: from ca 1860; ?etymology. 4. The *membrum virile*: military, from ca 1860.

***dick,** v.t. and i. To look, peer; watch: North Country c.: from ca 1850. Ex Romany: cf. DEKHO.

Dick, in the days or **reign of Queen.** Never: coll: from ca 1660; ob. (cf. DEVIL IS BLIND, WHEN THE; BLUE MOON. Grose, 3rd ed., however, mentions that *that happened in the reign of Queen Dick* was applied to 'any absurd old story'; cf. DICKS' HAT-BAND. Perhaps alluding to the ineffectual Richard Cromwell.

dick, swallow the. To use long words; esp. to use them without knowledge of their meaning. Coll; from ca 1870. See DICK, n., 1.

dick, take one's. To take an oath: from ca 1861. See DICK, n., 2.

dick, up to. Artful, knowingly wide-awake; also, up to the mark, excellent: from ca 1870. J. Greenwood, *Under the Blue Blanket*: 'Aint that up to dick, my biffin?' As in the preceding term, *dick* abbr. *declaration*: cf. DAVY for *affidavit*.

***dick in the green.** Inferior; weak: c.: ca 1805–1900. cf. DICKEY, adj.

dicked in the nob. Silly, crazy: low: ca 1820–60. Perhaps ex DICK'S HATBAND, AS . . . AS.

dickens (also **dickins,** C.17–18; **dickings,** C.19; **dickons,** C.18–19, O.E.D.), **the,** rarely **a.** The DEVIL, the DEUCE, esp. in exclamations: late C.16–20; perhaps coll. Shakespeare, Urquhart, Gay, Foote, Sims; C. Haddon Chambers, 'What the dickens could I do?' In origin a euphemistic evasion for *devil*; either an attrition from *devilkin* (S.O.D.) or ex *Dicken* or *Dickon* (W.).

Dick(e)y. The second mate: nautical: mid-C.19–20. See sense 6 of:

***dickey, dicky.** A worn-out shirt: ca 1780–1800; c. or low. G. Parker. H.'s extremely ingenious TOMMY (ex Gr. *τόμη*) perversely changed to *dicky* won't quite do. 2. Hence (—1811) a sham, i.e. a detachable, shirt-front: low > respectable s. > coll, by 1900 > S.E. 3. A woman's under-petticoat (—1811): coll; †. 4. A donkey, if male: late C.18–20; coll, ?orig. dial. John Mills, 1841. *Lex. Bal.*, 'Roll your dickey; drive your ass.' 5. A small bird: mostly children's coll; from ca 1850. Abbr. DICKEY-BIRD. 6. A ship's officer in commission, gen. as *second dickey*, second mate: nautical (—1829). 7. A SWELL = London, ca 1875–95. ?ex *up to* DICK. 8. The *membrum virile*: schoolboys': from ca 1870. Ex DICK, n., 4. 9. An affidavit: lower classes': from ca 1865. Ex DICK, n., 2. 10. A detachable name-plate (the name being false) on a van: low London: from ca 1860. Ex sense 2. 11. See DICKEY-BIRD, 5.

dickey, dicky, adj. In bad health, feeling very ill; inferior, sorry; insecure; queer: from ca 1790; low at first. See DICKEY WITH. 2. Smart: London: ca 1875–1910. ?ex *up to* DICK. cf. DICKEY, n., 7.

dickey-, gen. **dicky-bird.** A small bird: coll: ca 1845. Barham. 2. A harlot: from ca 1820. In the broadside ballad, *George Barnwell*, ca 1830. Often as *naughty dick(e)y-bird*. 3. A louse: low: from ca 1855; ob. 4. Gen. in pl, a professional singer: from ca 1870; ob. Prob. influenced by dial. *dicky-bird*, a canary. 5. Word: rhyming s.: late C.19–20. Often shortened to *dickey*.

dick(e)y-diaper. A linen-draper: ca 1820–70. Lit., a fellow who sells diapers.

dick(e)y dido. A complete fool; an idiot: mid-C.19–20 (ob.): lower classes'.

Dick(e)y Dirt. A shirt: rhyming s.: late C.19–20.

dick(e)y domus. A small 'house' or audience: theatrical: from ca 1860;. ob. Ex DICKEY, adj., l, and L. *domus*, a house or home.

dick(e)y flurry. 'A run on shore, with all its accompaniments': nautical: late C.19–20. Bowen. See DICKEY, adj., 2.

dick(e)y lagger. A bird-catcher: from ca 1870; low. Ex *lag*, to seize.

dick(e)y run. A naval variant of DICK(E)Y FLURRY, same period.

Dick(e)y Sam. A native, occ. an inhabitant, of Liverpool: from ca 1860; coll ex Lancashire dial. *Athenaeum*, 10 Sept. 1870, 'We cannot even guess why a Liverpool man is called a Dickey Sam.'

dick(e)y with, all. (Rare, except in dial., in the absolute use exemplified in Thackeray, 1837, 'Sam ... said it was all dicky.') QUEER; gone wrong, upset, ruined; ALL UP WITH. From ca 1790. Poole, in *Hamlet Travestied*, 1811: 'O, Hamlet! 'tis all dickey with us both.' Moore; Barham. Origin?

dickings, dickins, dickons, see DICKENS.

Dick's hatband. A makeshift: proletarian and provincial: C.19–20; ob. Ex:

Dick's hatband, as . . . as. Any such adj. as *queer* relates the second *as*. An intensive tag of chameleonic sense and problematic origin, mid-C.18–early 19; surviving in dial., as in the Cheshire 'All my eye and Dick's hatband.' In C.19, occ. as *queer as Dick's hatband, that went nine times round and wouldn't meet.*

dickory dock. A clock: rhyming s.: from ca 1870. Ex the nursery rhyme.

dicks, see DICS.

dicksee, see DIXIE. **dicky,** see DICKEY, n. and adj., all senses.

dics, dibs (Rugby) or **dicks, digs** (Shrewsbury), **dix** (Tonbridge); to **dick.** Prayers; to pray: Public Schools': late C.19–20. Ex L. *dictare*, to say repeatedly, or *dictata*, lessons rather than precepts.

dictionary, up to. Learned: coll: C.19.

diddeys. A C.18 variant of:

diddies. The paps: low; from ca 1780. 1728, Anon., *The Quaker's Opera*. A corruption of TITTIES.

diddle. Gin: from ca 1720; in C.19, low, but orig. c. Prob. ex TIPPLE. 2. The sound of a fiddle: C.19–20 (ob.), low coll. 3. A swindle: low; from ca 1840, ex the v. *Punch*, 5 Sept. 1885, 'It's all a diddle.' Ex v., 1. 4. Among schoolboys, the penis: from ca 1870. ?an arbitrary variation on PIDDLE.

diddle, v. To swindle; DO; DO FOR, i.e. ruin or kill: from ca 1803 (S.O.D. recording at 1806). Moore; Scott, 'And Jack is diddled, said the baronet.' Ex JEREMY DIDDLER in Kenney's *Raising the Wind*, 1803. 2. To trifle time away (v.i.): from ca 1827, ob.; coll. 3. To shake (v.t.): coll, perhaps orig. dial: late C.18–20, ob. as coll. 4. Hence, to copulate with: low coll or s.; C.19–20.

***diddle-cove.** A publican: c. (—1858). Ex DIDDLE, gin.

diddle-daddle. Nonsense; stuff and nonsense: coll; from ca 1770.

diddle-diddle. Violin music: Ned Ward, 1703.

diddler. A sly cheat, a mean swindler; a very artful dodger; occ., a constant borrower. Coll; from ca 1800. cf. JEREMY DIDDLER: prob. ex dial. *duddle*, to trick.

diddling. Sly, petty cheating or meanly sharp practice; chronic borrowing. Coll; from ca 1810. Ex DIDDLE, v., 1.

diddlum buck. The game of crown and anchor; military: from ca 1880.

diddly-pout. The *pudendum muliebre*: low; from ca 1860. Probably ex POUTER, by elaboration.

diddums! Did you (or did he, etc.) then!: nursery coll, in consoling a child: late C. 19–20. Manchon. And see esp. Norah March's excellent article entitled 'Away with all the "Diddums" Jargon' in the *Evening Standard*, 28 May 1934. By perversion of *did you* (or *he*).

diddy, see DIDDIES. 2. A familiar diminutive of *didekei*, a half-bred gypsy: among the folk of the road: late C.19–20.

didoes, cut up (occ. **one's**). To play pranks: orig. (from ca 1830) U.S.; anglicized in the 1850s; slightly ob. Etymology?

die. (Gen. pl.) A last dying speech; a criminal trial on a capital charge: low: ca 1850–70. 2. See DIE OF IT.

die by the hedge. (Or hyphenated.) Inferior meat: provincial coll (?orig. dial.); C.19–20, ob.

die dunghill, see DUNGHILL, DIE.

die in a devil's or **a horse's nightcap; one's shoes** (later **boots**)**; like a dog; on a fish-day.** To be hanged: coll. All four were current in late C.17–18; the first and second survived in early C.19. The second, with *boots* and owing to U.S. influence, has since ca 1895 meant to die in harness, at work.

die like a rat. To be poisoned to death: C.17–18; coll. In C.19–20, S.E. and of a blunted signification. Like the preceding set of phrases, it is in B.E.

die (of it), make a. To die: coll: C.17–20; ob. Cotgrave, 1611.

Diet of Worms, be or **have gone to the.** To be dead and buried: ca 1710–1830. (cf. ROT-HIS-BONE.) When Luther attended the Diet at Worms in 1521, many thought that he would meet the fate of Huss. See also *Hamlet* IV iii on why 'the worm's your only emperor for diet'.

diff. A difference, esp. in 'That's the diff': coll, orig. Stock Exchange: from ca 1870. Ware, 'There is a great diff between a dona [a woman] and a mush. You *can* shut up a mush (umbrella) sometimes.'

different ships, different long-splices. A coll nautical variation, mid-C.19–20, of the landsman's *different countries, different customs*.

diffs. Monetary difficulties: theatrical: from ca 1870; ob. Contrast DIFF.

dig. In boxing, a straight left-hander delivered under the opponent's guard: from ca 1815; used by Tom Moore in *Tom Crib's Memorial*, 1819. (As = any sharp poke, S.E.) cf. such terms as AUCTIONEER; BIFF; CORKER; FLOORER; NOBBLER; TOPPER, 3. 2. A(n intensive) period of study; school coll (—1887); slightly ob. Baumann, 'He had a dig at his Caesar, *er hat seinen Cäsar geochst*.' cf. DIG AWAY. 3. Dignity: 'elegant' lower middle-class: from ca 1890. Prob. ex INFRA DIG. 4. An archaeological expedition: from ca 1890.

dig, v. To lodge: from ca 1900. Ex DIGGINGS.

dig, on. On one's dignity: schoolboys' (—1909).

dig a day under the skin. To shave every second day: from ca 1870; ob.

dig away, v.i. To study hard: school coll (—1887); slightly ob.

dig in. Eat lustily: from ca 1870.

dig in the grave. To shave: rhyming s.: from ca 1880.

dig (a person) **out.** Esp. *dig me out*, call for me,' tear me from lazy loafing in the house': Society: ca 1860–1910. cf. DIGGINGS.

dig up. To depart, make off: low: late C. 19–20. 2. To work hard: nautical: late C.19–20.

Digby chicken. A herring: mid-C.19–20. (Perhaps an error for DIGBY DUCK.) 2. A smoked herring: Canadian: from ca 1880. Ex Digby in Nova Scotia.

Digby duck. (Gen. pl.) A dried herring: Nova Scotian and nautical: late C.19–20. Prob. on BOMBAY DUCK.

digger. The guard-room: military (—1900); slightly ob. Ware, 'Short for "Damned guardroom"'. 2. A common form of address – orig. on the gold-fields – in Australia and New Zealand since ca 1855.

diggers. Spurs: late C.18–20, ob. cf.

PERSUADERS. 2. In cards, the spades suit: from ca 1840. cf. DIGGUMS and BIG DIGGER. 3. The finger-nails: low: from ca 1850: more gen. in U.S. than in the British Empire.

diggers' delight. A wide-brimmed hat made of felt: from ca 1880; ob.

digging, n. Kneeling down to pray in dormitory at night: Shrewsbury School: from ca 1880.

diggings. Quarters, lodgings, apartment: coll; orig. U.S. (1838), anglicized in late 1850s. (In S.E., *diggings*, gold-fields, and *digger*, a miner, date from the 1530s.) Clark Russell, 1884, 'You may see his diggings from your daughter's bedroom window, sir.'

diggums. A gardener: provincial coll or s.: C.19–20. 2. In cards (cf. DIGGERS, 2), the suit of spades: from ca 1840.

digital. A finger: facetiously and pedantically coll; from early Victorian days.

dignity men. (Extremely rare in singular.) 'The higher ranks and ratings of coloured seamen': nautical: late C.19–20. Bowen. Ex the dignity of brief office.

digs. Abbr. DIGGINGS, from ca 1890. Ex Australian; common in theatrical s. before becoming gen. 2. Prayers: Shrewsbury School: from ca 1880. cf. DICS.

dike, dyke. A w.-c.: (low) coll: mid-C.19–20. Ex S.E. sense, a pit. Hence, *do a dike*, to use the w.-c.

dikk; dikk-dari. Worry; worried: Anglo-Indian coll: from ca 1870. Ex Hindustani *dik(k)*, vexed, worried.

dilberries. Impure deposits about the anus or the pudend: low: C.19–20. cf. CLINKERS.

dilberry-bush. The hair about the pudend: low: mid-C.19–20. cf.:

dilberry-maker. The fundament: low (—1811); ob.

dildo. An imagic substitute for the *membrum virile*; a *penis succedaneus*. C.17–20; orig. coll; in C.19–20, S.E. 'Hudibras' Butler's *Dildoïdes*; Grose. Perhaps ex It. *diletto*, delight, hence this sexual substitute (cf. *dildo-glass*, a cylindrical glass), perhaps ex *dildo*, 'a tree or shrub of the genus *Cereus*'. See Grose, P.

dildo, v. To exchange sexual caresses with a woman: coll; ca 1630–1820. Ex preceding.

diligent like the devil's apothecary, double. Affectedly diligent: coll: mid-C.18–early 19.

dillo-namo. An old woman: back s. (—1851). Later, DELO NAMMOW.

dilly. A coach: coll; ca 1780–1850. 'The dillies', Grose, 1st ed., remarks, 'first began to run in England about the year 1779,' but (see O.E.D.) in France by 1742. Ex Fr. *diligence*. 'The Derby dilly, carrying | Three Insides,' Frere, 1789. 2. From ca 1850: a night cart. 3. A duck: coll; from ca 1840, ex the call to a duck. 4. A coll abbr. of *daffodilly*: 1878 (S.O.D.).

dilly-bag. A wallet; a civilian haversack: Australian coll: from ca 1885.

dilly-dally. A doubling of *dally*: orig. (?Richardson in *Pamela*) coll; S.E. by 1800. 'Prob. in coll use as early as 1600', O.E.D. 2. Also as coll adj. (—1909).

***dimber.** Pretty, neat; lively: low, prob. orig. (—1671), c.; †by 1840, except in dial. Whence the late C.17–19 (perhaps always c.) *dimber-damber*, leader or captain of criminals or of tramps, as in Head, B.E., and Ainsworth's *Rookwood*; *dimber* COVE, a handsome man, a gentleman (as in B.E.); and *dimber* MORT, a pretty girl. 2. Moreover, *dimber-damber* has become a Cockney adj.: C.19–20; ob.: 'smart, active, adroit' (Ware).

dime museum. 'A common show – poor piece': theatrical: 1884–ca 1900. Ware, 'From New York which has a passion for monstrosity displays, called Dime Museums – the dime being the tenth of a dollar.'

dimensions, take. To obtain information: police s.: from ca 1880; ob.

***dimmock.** Money: c. (—1812) >, by 1860, low. Hence, *flap the dimmock*, to display one's cash. Either ex *dime* = a tithe or ex *dime* = an American coin of 10 cents (minted ca 1785).

dimmocking bag. A bag for the collection of subscriptions in cash; an individual's 'savings bank' for the hoarding of money for, e.g., Christmas cheer: lower classes': mid-C.19–20; ob.

din-din. Dinner; hence, any meal; food: nursery coll: late C.19–20. In a certain house I know, one woman invites her baby to 'din-din', another calls 'din-din!' to her cats.

Dinah. A favourite girl or woman; a sweetheart: Cockney (—1890). DONA(H) corrupted.

dinarlee (or -ly); dinali (or -y), etc. Money: from ca 1845; low Cockney and (orig.) Parlary. Esp. in *nantee dinarlee*, [I have] no money. Mayhew in his *magnum opus*. Ex It. or Sp. (ultimately L. *denarii*) via Lingua Franca: the gen. view. Possibly, however, through the Gypsies ex the

Arabic and Persian *dinar* (itself ultimately ex L. *denarius*), the name of various Eastern coins.

dincum. A rare variant of DINKUM.

***dine.** Spite; malice: c. (—1688); †by 1820. Randle Holme. Origin?

dine out. To go without a meal, esp. dinner: mid-C.19–20; coll, 'among the very lower classes', says H., 5th ed. cf. *go out and count the* RAILINGS, DINING OUT, and:

dine with Duke Humphrey. To go dinnerless (cf. DINE OUT): late C.16–20; ob. Coll till ca 1820, then S.E. In *Pierce Penniless*, Nashe writes: 'I . . . retired me to Paules [St Paul'*s*], to seeke my dinner with Duke Humfrey'; Smollett; *All the Year Round*, 9 June 1888. Prob. ex the Old St Paul's Church part known as Duke Humphrey's Walk; Humphrey, Duke of Gloucester, Henry IV's youngest son. See esp. the O.E.D. and F. & H. cf.:

dine with St Giles and the Earl of Murray. A Scottish coll variant (C.18–20; ob.) of the preceding. The Earl was buried in St Giles' Church.

dines!, by God's. A coll oath of late C.16–early 17. Perhaps ex *dignesse*.

ding, v.t., to strike, seems to have a coll savour: actually, however, it is either S.E. (archaic in C.19–20) or dial. 2. To *ding a person* is to abandon his acquaintance, or to quit him: ca 1810–60, low. Ex: 3. As to snatch, to steal, to hide, it is C.18–19 c. (Capt. Alexander Smith, *A Thieves' Grammar*, 1719), whence *dinger*, a thief who, to avoid detection, throws away his booty. 4. As = DANG, a euphemism, mostly U.S. 5. Occ. confused with *din*, n.: mid-C.18–20.

***ding, knap the; take ding.** To receive property just stolen: c. (—1812); †by 1870.

***ding, upon the.** On the prowl: c.: C.19.

***ding-boy.** 'A Rogue, a Hector, a Bully, Sharper,' B.E.: late C.17–18 c. cf. DING, 3.

ding-dong. In (—1859) rhyming s., a song: ob. by 1910, except as theatrical.

ding-fury. Anger: either dial. or provincial s. – a discrimination sometimes impossible to make. C.19–20; ob.

ding the tot! Run away with the lot! Rhyming s.: from ca 1870; low.

***ding** (something) **to** (a PAL). To convey to a friend something just stolen: c. (—1812); †by 1870.

dingable. Worthless; easily spared: c. (—1812) >, by 1840, low; †by 1900. Ex DING, 2.

dingbats, the. Madness: Australian and New Zealanders': from ca 1905; ob.

dinge. A picture, esp. a painting: Royal Military Academy: from ca 1870; ob. Ex *dingy*.

dinge. To render dingy: from ca 1820: coll (ob.) and dial. Ex *dingy*.

***dinger.** See DING, 3. (Grose, 1788.) 2. A dingo: Australian coll: from ca 1830.

dingers. Cups and balls: jugglers', from ca 1840. Ex the sound.

dinges or dingus. WHAT-D'YE-CALL-'EM; WHAT'S-HIS-NAME: South African s. verging on coll: late C.19–20. Fossicker's 'Kloof Yarns' in the *Empire*, 27 Aug. 1898. Ex Dutch *ding*, a thing: cf., therefore, THINGUMMY.

dingey, see DINGY CHRISTIAN.

dinghy. A small rowing-boat, esp. for pleasure: from ca 1810; orig. Anglo-Indian coll; from ca 1870, S.E. Ex Hindi *dengi*, a river-boat. 2. **(D).** The inevitable nickname of men surnamed Reed (Read, Reid): naval and military: late C.19–20.

dingle. Hackneyed; used up: Society, ca 1780–1800. The *Microcosm* (No. 3), 1786. ?ex *dinged*, battered.

dingle-dangle. The *membrum virile*: low; from ca 1895. The term occurs in a somewhat Rabelaisian song. Ex *d.-d.*, a dangling appendage.

dingus, see DINGES.

dingy Christian. A mulatto; anyone with some Negro blood: mid-C.18–mid-19.

dining out. (Of a seaman) undergoing punishment, esp. cells: naval: late C.19–20. See also DINE OUT.

dining-room. The mouth: low from ca 1820; ob.

dining-room chairs. The teeth: low: from ca 1820. Ex DINING-ROOM.

***dining-room jump,** see JUMP, n.

dining-room post. Sham postmen's pilfering from houses: late C. 18–19; low or c.

dinkum, occ. **dincum.** Work, toil: Australian: 1888, Boldrewood, 'An hour's hard dinkum'; ob. Ex Derbyshire and Lincolnshire dial; cognate with Gloucestershire *ding*, to work hard: i.e. *dincum, -kum*, is prob. a perversion of *dinging*, with which cf. *dink*, to throw, toss, a variant of S.E. *ding*, to strike.

dinkum, adj. (Often *fair dinkum*, occ. *square dinkum*.) Honest; true, genuine; thorough, complete: Australian: from ca 1890. Perhaps ex DINKY, adj.; but actually *dinkum* prob. derives ex *fair dinkum*, for in Lincolnshire dial. we find *fair dinkum*, fair play, before 1898; the E.D.D. derives it ex Lincolnshire *dinkum*, an equitable share of work.

dinky. Neat, spruce; small and dainty: coll (from ca 1870) ex dial. *dinky*, itself ex Scottish *dink*, feat, trim, neat, as in Burns.

dinner for tea, be. To be easy, 'money for jam'; extremely pleasant or profitable: Cockney coll: from ca 1890.

dinner-set. The teeth: low: from ca 1870. cf. DINING-ROOM CHAIRS.

***dip.** In c., with corresponding v. (1817), a pickpocket, 'pick-pocketing' (from ca 1850). cf. DIVE, V., DIVER. 2. Abbr. *dip-candle*: orig. coll, soon S.E.: from ca 1815. Barham, 'None of your rascally dips.' 3. A pocket inkstand: Westminster School, C. 19–20, ob. 4. A tallow chandler: C.18–early 19. cf. sense 2. 5. Dripping, or melted bacon fat: (low) coll: mid-C.19–20.

dip, v. To pawn: mid-C.17–20; coll. Ex the C.17–20 S.E. sense, to mortgage, esp. lands, as in Dryden ('Never dip thy lands'). *Spectator*; Thackeray; B.E. has *dip one's terra firma*. 2. In the passive, to get into trouble; be involved in debt: c.: from ca 1670. 3. See n., 1. 4. To fail in an examination; more gen. *be dipped*: naval: late C.19–20. Ex the salute of dipping the ensign. cf.: 5. To lose (e.g. a good-conduct badge), forgo (one's rank): naval: late C. 19–20. Same origin.

Dip, the. A cook's shop that, in C.18–early 19, was situated 'under Furnival's Inn' (Grose, 2nd ed.) and frequented by the lesser legal fry.

dip into. (Gen. with *pockets*.) To pick pockets: from ca 1810.

dip one's beak. To drink: C.19–20; low. (cf. *wet one's* WHISTLE.) B.E.: '*He has dipt his Bill*, he is almost drunk'; low: late C. 17–early 19; extant in Cornish dial.

dip one's wick; bury it. (Of the male) to have sexual intercourse: low: from ca 1880, 1860 resp.

dip(t) stick. A gauger: C.18–19.

dipped, be, see DIP, v., 2, 4.

dipped in the wing. Worsted: C.19–20, ob.; coll.

dipped into one's (gen. **my**) **pockets, it** or **that has.** That has involved me in considerable expense: coll (—1887); slightly ob. Perhaps ex DIP INTO.

***dipper.** A pickpocket: mid-C.19–20; orig. c., then low. cf. DIVER. 2. An Anabaptist or a Baptist: the S.O.D., recording at 1617, considers it S.E., but – witness B.E. and Grose – it was prob. coll until ca 1820.

dipper (is) hoisted(, the). (There is) a strict rationing of water: nautical: C.19–20. Bowen, 'From the old sailing ship custom of hoisting the dipper to the truck after the water has been served out to prevent men stealing more than their regulation pint.'

***dipping.** Pick-pocketry: c. from ca 1855. See DIP, n., 1.

dipping-bloke. A pickpocket: mid-C.19–20; orig. c., then low. See DIP, n., 1.

dips. A grocer: s. > coll: C.19–20; ob. cf. 3. 2. The purser's boy: nautical: from ca 1870. Ex: 3. The purser himself: from ca 1830; nautical. Marryat. Ex *dip-candles*. 4. Dough-boys: Australian coll: mid-C.19–20.

directly minute. Immediately; forthwith; this very minute: lower-class, esp. Cockney, coll: from ca 1870. W. Pett Ridge, *Minor Dialogues*, 1895, ''Oist me up on this seat, Robert, dreckly minute, there's a good soul.'

dirk. The *membrum virile*: C.18–20; orig. Scottish, then low jocular coll.

dirt. Brick-earth: late C.17–20; coll. 2. Money: orig. (—1890), U.S.; anglicized ca 1900.

dirt (occ. **mud**), **cast, fling,** or **throw.** (v.t. with *at*.) To be vituperative, malicious: from ca 1640: coll till ca 1800, then S.E. Seldom with (*throw*); Ned Ward ('Fling dirt enough, and some will stick'); 'John Strange Winter' (*throw mud*).

dirt, eat. To submit to spoken insult, degrading treatment: coll; from late 1850s.

dirt and grease. Marine indications of a gathering storm: nautical: ?ca 1800–50. (W. N. Glascock, *Sailors and Saints* (I, 184), 1829.) cf. GREASY.

dirt-baillie. An inspector of nuisances: Scottish (s., not dial.): C.19–20.

dirty. A boy with a dirty mind: schoolboys': late C.19–20.

dirty a plate, see FOUL A PLATE.

dirty acres. An estate in land: mid-C.17–20; coll till ca 1820, then S.E. – still facetious.

dirty beau. Coll: ca 1680–1810: 'a slovenly Fellow, yet pretending to Beauishness', B.E.

dirty dishes. Poor relations: coll; C.19–20; ob. Somewhat low.

dirty dog. A lecher: coll, often jocular: from ca 1880.

dirty look. A look of contempt or strong

dislike, as in 'He gave me a dirty look': coll: late C.19–20.

dirty puzzle. 'A sorry slattern or Slut,' B.E.: low coll: ca 1680–1830.

dirty-shirt march. The sauntering of male slumdom before, on the Sunday morning, it dresses for the midday meal: coll; from ca 1870; ob.

dirty thing. Adolescent girls' term to, or for, a boy that becomes amorous: coll: late (?mid-) C.19–20.

dirzi, dirzy, see DERZY.

dis; sometimes **diss.** (Gen. v.t.) To distribute (type): printers' (—1889). 2. Hence, occ., as n.

disab(b)illy, see DISHABBILLY.

discourse. To yaw-off on both sides: nautical: late C.19–20. i.e. *discourse*, with a pun on divagation in spoken discourse.

discuss. To eat, drink: jocular coll: 1815, Scott. *Discussion*, the consumption of food or drink, does not follow until ca 1860.

disgorge, v.i. and t. To pay up: coll; C.19–20. Ex the S.E. sense, to surrender something wrongfully appropriated.

disgruntled. Offended; chagrined; ill-humoured (temporarily): late C.17–20. The S.O.D. records as S.E., but (witness B.E. and Grose) perhaps coll in C.17–18.

disguised. Drunk: s. or, perhaps rather, coll: late C.16–20; ob. In C.18–20, the gen. form (almost S.E., by the way) is *disguised in liquor*. Massinger, in *The Virgin Martyr*, 'Disguised! How? Drunk!' Goldsmith, of a handwriting in *She Stoops to Conquer*, 'A damned up and down hand, as if it was disguised in liquor.' Clark Russell, 1884, '. . . A third mate I knew, slightly disguised in liquor.' Ex the C.16–20 *disguise*, to intoxicate with liquor. (Then, *disguise*, intoxication, is rare and rather S.E. than coll.)

disguised public-house. A workmen's political club: political: ca 1886–1900.

dish. An act of 'dishing': 1891, Sir W. Harcourt. Ex:

dish, v. To cheat; baffle completely; disappoint, 'let down'; ruin. From ca 1798: and see DISHED UP. The *Monthly Magazine*, 1798; Moore; Moncrieff, 1821, 'I have been dished and doddled out of forty pounds today'; Disraeli, 1867, coined the famous *dishing the Whigs*. Ex meat being well cooked (*done*) and then served (*dished*): exactly analogous is *done* BROWN; cf. also COOK ONE'S GOOSE and *settle one's* HASH.

dish, have a foot in the. To get a footing; have a share or interest in: coll (—1682). †by 1800. Bunyan. Ex a pig in his trough.

dish, have got a. To be drunk: coll: ca 1675–1750. Ray.

dish-clout. A dirty and slatternly woman: late C.18–20; coll.

dish-clout, make a napkin of one's. To marry one's cook; hence, to make a misalliance: from ca 1750; ob.; a coll of the proverbial kind. Earlier (—1678) as *make one's dish-clout one's table-cloth* (Ray).

dish-jerker. A steward: nautical: late C. 19–20.

dish-water, dull as. A late C.19–20 coll variant of DITCH-WATER, AS DULL AS.

dis(h)ab(b)illy, n. Undress: which is pardonable. adj., undressed: which is ludicrous. From ca 1700; ob. Ex Fr. (*en*) *déshabillé*.

dished. (Of electrotypes) with letters having their centre or middle lower than their edge: printers'; from ca 1880.

dished up, be (whence DISH, v.), is recorded by Grose, 2nd ed., for 'to be totally ruined'. 2. 'To be attended to in the sick bay' (Bowen): nautical: mid-C.19–20.

dismal ditty. A psalm sung by a criminal just before his death at the gallows: ca 1690–1820: (perhaps orig. c., then) low, passing to low coll.

dismal Jimmy. Mid-C.19–20 coll, as in H. A. Vachell, *The Vicar's Walk*, 1933, 'Shown in his true colours, as a dog-in-the-manger, a spoil-sport, a wet blanket, a dismal Jimmy.'

dismals (, esp. in the). Low spirits: from ca 1760; coll till ca 1840, then S.E. Ex M.E. *in the dismal*. 2. Mourning garments: ca 1745–1830: coll. L. *dies mali*, unpropitious days.

dispar, disper. A portion (cut in advance) of a leg or a shoulder of mutton (cf. CAT'S HEAD): Winchester College: from ca 1830; ob. See esp. Mansfield's *School Life at Winchester College*, 1870, at p. 84. Prob. ex *to disperse* or perhaps *disparate* in the sense of unequal, or it may be a direct adoption of L. *dispar*.

dispatch. (*Despatch* is the inferior spelling.) v.t., to dispose quickly of food and/or drink: from ca 1710: coll. Addison.

dispatches; des-. False dice: from ca 1810; low, perhaps orig. c. cf. DESPATCHERS, and DOCTOR. 2. In C.18–early 19 legal: a mittimus.

disper, see DISPAR.

disremember. To fail to remember: Anglo-Irish coll, C.19–20; dial. and sol., mid-

C.19–20; fairly common in U.S., mid-C.19–20.

diss, see DIS, v.

dissecting job. Clothes requiring much alteration: tailors': from ca 1870.

distaff, have tow on one's. To have trouble in store, ex the sense of having work awaiting one, in hand: ca 1400–1800. Coll >, by 1600, S.E.

***distiller.** One easily vexed and unable to conceal his annoyance: Australian c.: ca 1840–90. Ex English c. *walking distiller*, the same: 1812, Vaux. See CARRY THE KEG.

distracted division. 'Husband and wife fighting', Egan's Grose, 1823; †by 1860.

distress, flag of, see FLAG OF DISTRESS.

district of sappers, the. 'Those who sap at [study hard] their quarto and folio volumes', *Spy*, 1825: Oxford: ca 1815–50.

ditch. To throw away: nautical: from ca 1870. Ex DITCH, THE, 2. cf. DITCHED.

ditch, the. The sea; **the D.** the Atlantic: coll: from ca 1860.

ditch-water, as dull as. Extremely dull: from ca 1800; coll till ca 1880, then S.E.

ditch-water, clear as. Fig., far from clear: coll: late C.19–20.

ditched. At a loss; nonplussed: coll: from ca 1890.

dither, v.i. To be very nervous on a given occasion; to hesitate tremulously or bewilderedly: coll when not dial.: from ca 1880. Ex DITHERS.

dithers. Trepidation; (an access of) nervous shiverings: from ca 1860: coll (orig. dial.). (Hence adj., *dithering*.) Perhaps ultimately ex *shiver*, via *didder*.

ditto. The same: coll when not used strictly in the way of business: late C.17–20. cf. DITTO(E)S.

ditto(-)blues. A suit of clothes made of blue cloth: Winchester College: C.19–20, ob.

ditto, brother smut, see BROTHER SMUT.

dittoes, better **dittos.** A suit all of one colour and material: C.19–20. Until ca 1860, the gen. form is *suit of dittos*, which the S.O.D. records, as *suit of ditto*, as early as 1755. James Payn, 1882: 'He was never seen in dittos even in September.' In C.19, occ. applied to trousers only. Both senses, imm. they > gen., are coll; orig. tailors' s.

ditty. (Gen. in pl.) A fib; a long circumstantial story or excuse. Coll (mostly Australian and New Zealand): late C.19–20. Ex dial.

ditty-bag. A small bag used by sailors for their smaller necessaries and sentimentalities: from ca 1860. Orig., according to H., 3rd ed., and F. & H., coll; in C.20, S.E. ?ex *dilli*: see DILLY-BAG.

ditty box. 'A small wooden box ... issued to seamen; displaced by the more convenient attaché case ... Believed to be a shortened form of "commodity box",' Granville: naval: from ca 1890.

div. A stock-and-share dividend: Stock Exchange: from ca 1880.

dive. A place of low resort, esp. a drinking-den: coll: orig. (ca 1880), U.S.; anglicized ca 1905, though it was fairly well known considerably earlier (e.g. in the *Referee*, 10 May 1885). Many 'dives' were, still are, in cellars or, at least, in basements. 2. A variant of DIVER, 2.

***dive**, v.t. and i. To pick pockets: from ca 1600; ob. In C.17, c.; then low s. Ben Jonson: 'In using your nimbles [i.e. fingers], in diving the pockets.'

dive for a meal (esp. *dinner*). To go down into a cellar for it: coll: late C.18–mid-19. cf. DIVE, n., 1, and DIVER, 3.

dive in the dark. An act of coïtion: C.19–20; low.

dive into one's sky. To put one's hand(s) in one's pocket(s); esp. to take out money. C.19–20, ob.; low.

dive the twine. Gen. *dived* ..., applied to a school of fish that, 'surrounded by a purse-seine net drops down through the net and escapes before it can be ... closed' (Bowen): Grand Banks fishermen's coll: late C.19–20.

***diver**, rarely **dive.** (*Diver* only.) He who, assisting a CURBER, sends in a boy to do the stealing: late C.16–early 17 c. Greene, Dekker. 2. A pickpocket: from ca 1600; c. till ca 1800, then low. Gay's *The Beggar's Opera* has a character named Jenny Diver. Baumann, 1887, 'Smashers and divers and noble contrivers.' cf. DIP. 3. One who lives in a cellar: low: late C.18–mid-19. cf. DIVE, n., 1. 4. See DIVERS. 5. 'A liner's boatswain in charge of the wash deck party': nautical: late C.19–20. Bowen (*the diver*).

divers. The fingers: C.19–20; low. cf. PICKERS AND STEALERS. cf. the U.S. c. term, *diving-hooks*, appliances for picking pockets (late C.18–19).

divi, see DIVVY, 1.

divide the house with one's wife. To turn her out of doors, give her the KEY OF THE STREET: mid-C.18–19.

divine punishment. Divine service: naval: 1869 (or a few years earlier); ob.

diviners; **divvers.** Divinity Moderations: Oxford undergraduates': from ca 1898. (Oxford *-er.*)

diving-bell. A basement-, esp. a cellar-, tavern. cf. DIVE. From ca 1885. This term may, however, be rather older and hence constitute the germ whence sprang the U.S. *dive.* 2. 'A sailing-ship that was very wet and plunged badly': nautical: C.19. Ex S.E. nautical sense.

divvers, see DIVINERS.

divvies, see sense 1 of:

div(v)y. (Also **divi:** 1897, O.E.D.) A share; a dividend (—1890): coll. 2. Also as v.i. and t., with variant *divvy up*: from ca 1880. 3. As an adj., divine: from late 1890s. cf. DEEVIE.

dix, see DICS.

dixie, dixy. An iron pot, esp. as used in the Army, for boiling tea, rice, stew, vegetables, etc. Popularized by soldiers, who adopted it (—1879) ex Urdu. 2. Also, the small, lidded can that, forming part of a soldier's equipment, is used for tea, stew, etc. Both senses were orig. s. or coll, but they soon > j.

dizzy, n. A clever man, esp. in *quite a dizzy*: middle classes': ca 1870–1914. Ex Disraeli's nickname.

dizzy, adj. Rather tipsy: 1791, *The New Vocal Enchanters*, p. 33; †by 1890. 2. Astounding: from ca 1895.

dizzy age, (of) a. Elderly: near-Society: ca 1860–1900. Ware, 'Makes the spectator dizzy to think of the victim's years.'

dlog. Gold: back s. (—1859). More gen. DELOG.

do. A swindle, a fraud; a trick: from ca 1810; perhaps coll. Dickens, in *Boz*, 'I thought it was a do, to get me out of the house.' Ex DO, v., 1. 2. Action, deed, performance, business, event; (a) success. In C.17–18, S.E., but from ca 1820, coll, esp. in *make a do* – a success – *of it*, which dates back to Mayhew, 1851, or a little earlier. 3. A joke: middle classes': ca 1900–15.

do, v. To swindle, cheat: from ca 1640. Kenney, in that amusing play, *Raising the Wind*, 'I wasn't born two hundred miles north of Lunnun, to be done by Mr Diddler, I know.' Hence, to deceive, trick, without illegal connotations: C.19–20. 2. In c., v.t. to utter base coin or QUEER: from ca 1810. 3. To give a bad time, punish: boxing; ca 1815–1900. Earlier, to defeat. Grose, 3rd ed., mentions that Humphreys, writing from the boxing ring, said: 'Sir, I have done the Jew' (Mendoza). Cognate is to kill: low: 1823, Bee, †by 1890. cf. DO FOR, 3. 4. Visit, go over, as a tourist or as a pleasure-seeker: coll; from ca 1850. Shirley Brooks, 1858, in the *Gordian Knot*, 'I did Egypt, as they say, about two years back.' 5. With *the amiable*, *polite*, *heavy*, *grand*, *genteel*, etc., *do* is coll, the exemplar being Dickens's *do the amiable* in *Boz.* 6. See the senses implicit in DONE-FOR; DONE-OVER; DONE-UP. 7. To suffice (*that'll do me*), to answer its purpose: ?orig. (1846: Thornton), U.S., anglicized ca 1860. 8. Hence, to please, meet the requirements of (a person): late C.19–20. e.g. '*You*'ll do me!'

do a beer, a bitter, a drink, a drop, a wet. To take a drink of something stronger than milk or water, the domestic trio (coffee, cocoa, tea), or soft drinks. *Do* here = drink; it dates from ca 1850. All, orig. s., are, except *do a wet*, coll in C.20. cf. *do a meal*, to eat a meal: same period and status.

do a bill. To utter a bill of exchange: commerce; from ca 1830. Barham, Thackeray.

do a bishop. To parade at short notice: military: C.19. Perhaps ex a full-dress parade turned out, at short notice, for a chaplain-general.

do a bit. To eat something: coll; from ca 1850. 2. (Of men) to possess, have, a woman: low coll; from ca 1860. 3. The cricket sense is ineligible.

do a bit of stiff. To draw a bill: low commercial: from ca 1850; ob.

do a bunk, a guy, a shift. To depart hastily or secretly: from ca 1860. The second, orig. c.; the commonest, the first.

do a bunk, a shift. To ease nature: low; from ca 1865.

do a cadge. To go begging: low coll: from ca 1820. See CADGE, n. and v.

do a cat. To vomit: low: from ca 1840. cf. CAT, SHOOT THE.

do a Chloe. To appear in the nude: Australian, esp. Melbourne: late C.19–20. A pre-1900 Melbourne Art Gallery reject of a nude painting of Chloe hangs in a well-known Australian hotel.

do a chuck. To effect an ejectment; to depart. Low: from ca 1850; ob.

do a crawl. To cringe: coll: late C.19–20.

***do a crib.** To burgle: c. then, in C.20, low: from ca 1840.

do a doss. To go to sleep: low from ca 1850. cf. DOSS.

do a drink (or drop), see DO A BEER.

do a duck, see DUCK, DO A.

do a fluff. To forget one's part: theatrical: from ca 1850.

do a grind, a mount, a ride, a tread. To have sexual intercourse (of men): low: from ca 1860.

do a grouse. To go a-seeking women: low: C.19.

do a guy, see DO A BUNK, A GUY . . . 2. Among workmen, to absent oneself, without permission, from work: from 1865. 3. In c., to make an escape: from ca 1860. Ex sense 1. 4. See GUY, DO A, 1.

do a job. To commit a burglary: *Sessions*, 12 March 1878.

do a knee-trembler, see DO A PERPENDICULAR.

do a meal, see DO A BEER.

do a mike or a mouch. To go on the prowl: from ca 1860; low.

do a mount, see DO A GRIND.

do a Nelson. To withstand danger, or extreme difficulty, in a confident spirit: mostly Cockney: late C.19–20. 'Knowing that whatever may befall, as upon Nelson on his column in Trafalgar Square, one will, like him, "be there" to-morrow'.

do a nob, see NOB, DO A.

do a perpendicular or a knee-trembler. To have sexual intercourse while standing: low: from ca 1860; the former, ob.

do a pitch – a rush, see PITCH – RUSH.

***do a push.** To depart; esp. to run away: c. (—1865); ob. 2. See PUSH, DO A.

do a ride, see DO A GRIND.

do a rural. To ease oneself by the wayside: low: from ca 1860; ob.

do a scrap. To have a fight: from ca 1840.

do a shift, see DO A BUNK (both senses).

do (one) a shot. To outwit; to swindle: South African coll (—1890). Occ. *do* (one) *a shot in the eye*.

do a sip. To make water: back slang on PISS: from ca 1860; ob.

do a smile, see SMILE, n. (a drink).

do a spread or a tumble. To lie down to a man: low coll: from ca 1840.

do a star pitch. To sleep in the open (*à la belle étoile*): low theatrical: from ca 1850. cf. HEDGE-SQUARE.

do a tread, see DO A GRIND.

do a treat, see TREAT, 3.

do a tumble, see DO A SPREAD. **do a wet,** see DO A BEER.

do as I do. An invitation to drink: ca 1860–1910: coll.

do brown, see BROWN, DO, 2.

do-do (pron. *doo-doo*). To excrete: excreta: children's: late C.19–20. Hence *do-do noise*, a fart.

do down. To cheat or swindle: from the 1890s. cf. DO, v., 1. 2. Hence, get the better of: coll: from ca 1908.

do for. To ruin, destroy; wear out (person or thing) entirely: coll; from ca 1750. Fielding. 2. To attend to or on, as a landlady or a char for a lodger, a bachelor: orig. S.E.; since ca 1840, coll. 3. In c., to kill: from ca 1740; in C.20, low. cf. DO, v., 3. 4. To convict: c.: from ca 1850.

do gospel. To go to church: low coll: from ca 1860.

do in. To kill: late C.19–20. cf. DO FOR, 3. 2. Hence, to denounce to the police: low: A. Niel Lyons, *Sixpenny Pieces*, 1909. 3. To steal: low: late C.19–20: *Sessions*, 1 July 1905.

do in the eye. To cheat: late C.19–20. Ex idea of a nasty punch in the eye. cf. DO, v., 1.

do it. To be in the habit of doing – or gen. ready to do – it, i.e. to have physical intercourse. As an evasion, euphemistic; otherwise, coll C.18–20.

***do it away.** To dispose of stolen goods: c.: from ca 1810. cf. FENCE, V.

do it brown, see BROWN, DO, 2.

do it on (someone). To swindle (v.t.), impose on: low: since ca 1890. *Sessions*, 19 Dec. 1901. 2. Hence (?), to forestall, anticipate; get the better of, outdo, be too good for; since ca 1905.

do it up, see DO UP, 2.

do it up in good twig. (See DO UP, 2.) To live comfortably by one's wits: low: C.19–20; ob.

do-little sword. A midshipman's dirk, indicative rather of authority than of violence: naval: mid-C.19–20.

do(-)me(-)dag; usually pl, do-me-dags. A cigarette: low rhyming s.: late C.19–20. Rhyming on FAG, 5.

do-more. A small raft, made of two logs: Canadian lumbermen's: late C.19–20. Because a riverman can do more on two logs than on one log.

do on one's head, with the left hand, while asleep, etc. To do easily: coll; from ca 1880. A variant is, *do on the b.h.*, i.e. on the, or one's, bloody head.

do one's balls on. (Of a man) to fall utterly in love with: low coll: late C.19–20.

***do one's bit.** In late C.19–early 20 c., to serve a sentence. Ware. 2. In late C.19–20 coll, do one's share, to help a general cause. In the Boer War, a soldier wrote of his fellows, 'They all do "their bit" well' (J. Milne, *The Epistles of Atkins*, 1902).

do one's business. To kill: C.18–20, low coll (Fielding, Thackeray, Reade), as is the sense, 2 (from ca 1850), to evacuate, defecate. 3. To have sexual intercourse with a woman (*one's* = her): low; from ca 1860.

do one's dags. Cigarettes: rhyming s. on FAGS: from ca 1890.

do one's stuff. To act as one intends; perform one's social task: coll: George Fox, the Quaker, in his Journal for the year 1663, wrote: 'A while after, when the priest had done his stuff, they came to the friends again.'

do oneself well, see DO WELL.

do over. Knock; persuade; cheat, ruin: low coll; from ca 1770. Parker, Dickens. 2. In C.19 c., to search the pockets of; c. FRISK. 3. To seduce; also, to copulate with: low; mid-C.19–20, ob.

do Paddy Doyle, see PADDY DOYLE, DO.

do proud. To flatter, act hospitably or generously towards: coll; from ca 1830.

do reason or **right.** To honour a toast: coll; C.19–20, ob.

do the aqua. To put water in one's drink: public-houses': mid-C.19–20. L. *aqua*, water.

do the downy. To lie in bed: from ca 1840. 'Cuthbert Bede', 1853, 'This'll never do, Gig-lamps! Cutting chapel to do the downy.' cf. BALMY.

do the graceful. To behave gracefully or fittingly: non-aristocratic coll: from ca 1880.

do the handsome, occ. **the handsome thing.** To behave extremely well (in kindness, money, etc.) to a person: coll; from ca 1840.

do the High. To walk up and down High Street after church on Sunday evening: Oxford University, ca 1850–90.

do the polite. To exert oneself to be polite; to be unusually polite: coll: 1856 (O.E.D.).

***do the swag.** To dispose of stolen property: c.: from ca 1840. cf. FENCE and DO IT AWAY.

***do the trick.** To gain one's object: from ca 1810: c. >, by 1830, s. >, by 1860, coll. 2. Hence, (of a man) to perform effectually the act of kind; (of a woman) to be devirginated: both low coll, from ca 1840.

do things by penny numbers, i.e. by instalments or spasms: mid-C.19–20. Ex novels so published ca 1840–80.

***do time.** To serve a sentence in prison: from ca 1870; c. till C.20, when s. > coll. *Cornhill Magazine*, June 1884, 'He has repeatedly done time for drunks and disorderlies, and for assaults upon the police.'

do to death. To do frequently and *ad nauseam*: coll; C.18–20.

do to rights. To effect or achieve satisfactorily; to treat (a person) well: proletarian: mid-C.19–20.

do up. To use up, finish; disable, wear out, exhaust; ruin financially: coll: from ca 1780; ob. 2. To accomplish one's object: coll: C.18–19. 3. In C.19–20 (ob.) c., to quieten, gen. in DONE-UP, silenced.

do-ut-des. Selfish persons: Society: 1883–ca 1905. A pun on L. *do ut des*, I give in order that you may give.

do well. To treat, entertain, well: from ca 1895. Esp. *do oneself well* (in food and comfort).

do while asleep; do with the left hand, see DO ON ONE'S HEAD.

do with . . ., (I) could. I would very much like to have: coll (—1887). By meiosis.

do without, able to. To dislike (esp. a person): late C.19–20. Ex Yorkshire dial. 'Well, I could do without him, you know.'

do yer feel like that? A satirical, proletarian c.p. addressed to any person engaged in unusual work or to a lazy one doing any work: late C.19–20; ob.

do you hear the news? see NEWS?, DO YOU HEAR THE.

do you know? An almost expressionless coll tag: 1883–ca 1890. It > gen. in 1884 owing to its adoption by Beerbohm Tree in *The Private Secretary*.

do you sav(v)ey? Do you know: middle classes': ca 1840–90. cf. DO YOU KNOW and DON'T YOU KNOW.

do you see any green in my eye? D'you think I'm a fool? What do you take me for? A c.p.: from ca 1850. cf. the Fr. *je la connais*, sc. *cette histoire-là*.

do you to wain-rights. An intensification of DO TO RIGHTS: East London c.p. of ca 1874–1915. Ex murderer Wainwright.

***doash.** In late C.17–early 19 c., a cloak. Etymology?

doasta. Adulterated spirit, esp. if fiery, served in sailors' lodging-houses: nautical: late C.19–20. ?ex Hindustani.

dobbin. A sorry horse: coll; C.19–20. Ex the S.E. sense, an ordinary draught horse. (Variant *dobin.*) 2. Ribbon: c. and low:

mid-C.18–19. Hence *dobbin*-RIG, the stealing of ribbon: late C.18–20 (ob.) c.

dobbs. Pork: military: late C.19–20. Origin?

dobee, dobey, or **dobie,** see DHOBI.

doc. A coll abbr. of *doctor*, in address and narrative: from ca 1850; app., orig. U.S. 2. See DOCTOR, 7.

***doccy,** see DOXY.

dock. Orig. (1586–1610), as in Warner and Jonson, prob. c. in its C.19–20 S.E. sense, an enclosure for prisoners on trial in a law-court. 2. Hospital; chiefly *in dock*. Late C.18–20: orig. nautical. 3. Among printers, the weekly work-bill or POLE: from ca 1860; ob.

***dock,** v. To deflower (a woman); hence, to 'have' a woman: from ca 1560; ob. by 1800, †by 1840. Prob. orig. c.; certainly always low. Harman, Middleton, B.E., Grose. (Gen. with *the* DELL.) F. & H. proposes Romany *dukker*, to ravish; but the S.E. *dock*, to curtail, with an implied reference to TAIL, is obviously operative. 2. At Winchester College, C.19–20, ob., to scratch or tear out or, as in R. G. K. Wrench, to rub out; to knock down. 3. To take from (a person) part of his wages as a fine: dial. (ca 1820) >, by 1890, coll.

dock, go into. To be treated for a venereal disease: late C.18–20, ob.; nautical.

dock-pheasant. A bloater: nautical: late C.19–20. cf. BILLINGSGATE PHEASANT.

dock-shankers. 'Dock-mates': nautical (—1823); †by 1870. Egan's Grose, where, I surmise, the real meaning is, companions in a venereal hospital.

dock-walloping. Perambulating the docks to look at ships: nautical: late C.19–20.

dock to a daisy, (as like as) a. Very dissimilar: coll (—1639); †by 1800.

docked smack smooth, be. To have had one's penis amputated: nautical: mid-C.18–19.

docker. A dock labourer: from ca 1880; coll till ca 1895, then S.E. 2. A brief from the prisoner in the dock to counsel: legal; from ca 1890.

dockers' ABC, the. Ale, baccy, cunt: British docksides, mostly dockers' (esp. Liverpool): late C.19–20.

docket, strike a. To cause a man to become bankrupt: legal and commercial j. > coll > S.E.: ca. 1805–60.

dockie (or **-y**). A dock labourer: coll: since ca 1880.

docking. 'A punishment inflicted by sailors on the prostitutes who have infected them with the venereal disease; it consists in cutting off all their clothes, petticoat, shift and all, close to their stays, and then turning them out into the street', Grose: low coll; ca 1700–1850.

docking herself. (Of a ship) taking the mud and forcing a position for herself: nautical coll: late C.19–20.

dockyard-crawl. The rate of work in the Royal dockyards: naval: late C.19–20. cf. GOVERNMENT STROKE.

dockyard-horse. An officer better at office-work than on active service: naval; from ca 1870. 2. (Gen. pl.) A man drawing stores for a (naval) ship: naval: late C.19–20.

dockyard matey. A dockyard worker: naval coll: prob. since ca 1810. Occurs in Kipling, *A Fleet in Being*, 1898; *Captain Sherard Osborn*, *Arctic Journal*, 1852, as Rear-Admiral P. W. Brock, D.S.O., tells me; and, very much earlier, in W. N. Glascock, *Sailors and Saints* (II, 115), 1829.

dockyarder. A skulker, esp. about the docks: nautical; from ca 1840. The U.S. equivalent is *dock-walloper*. cf. STRAW-YARDER.

***doctor.** A false die: Shadwell, 1688, constitutes the earliest record. Until ca 1740, c.; then low; in C.20 ob., very ob. Fielding, in *Tom Jones*, 'Here, said he, taking some dice out of his pockets, here are the little doctors which cure the distempers of the purse.' Ex a doctor's powers. Hence, late C.17–early 19 (as, e.g., in B.E.), *put the doctor(s) upon*, to cheat a person with loaded dice. 2. An adulterant, esp. of spirits (see Grose, 1st ed., 1785), but also of food, e.g. bread: among bakers (says Maton in *Tricks of Bakers Unmasked*), alum is called the doctor. O.E.D. records it at 1770. 3. Brown sherry: licensed victuallers', C.19–20, ob.; because a doctored wine. 4. Earlier (—1770), milk and water, with a dash of rum and a sprinkling of nutmeg: †by 1880. 5. The last throw of dice or ninepins: perhaps orig. c.: C.18–19, mostly among gamesters. 6. The headmaster: Winchester College, from ca 1830. 7. (Occ. **doc.**) A ship's cook: nautical, also up-country Australian: recorded by S.O.D. at 1860, but the evidence of H. shows that it must, among Englishmen, have been current some years earlier; it existed in the U.S. as early as 1821. Ex food as health-ensurer. 8. A variant of CAPE DOCTOR; always *the* *doctor* (or *Doctor*): 1856 (Pettman). But it is recorded for the West Indies as early as 1740. 9. A broker dealing specifically with overdue vessels: nautical and commercial s. (late 1890s). 10. A red-nosed drinker: University s. (—1650). 11. A synonym of PUNISHER, 3, as is also GENTLEMAN.

doctor, v. Confer a doctorate upon, make a doctor ('philosophy', not medicine): from ca 1590; now very rare, yet not quite a ghost-word. 2. To treat, give medicine to, of a doctor or as if of a doctor: from ca 1730. 3. Hence, to practise as a physician (—1865). 4. To adulterate; tamper with; falsify: from ca 1770. Now coll. 5. Hence, to repair, patch up; revise extensively, distort a literary work, a newspaper article: C.19–20. 6. To DOPE (a horse): sporting: from ca 1860; little used after ca 1910, *dope* being the fashionable word. 7. 'To undergo medical treatment': coll: from ca 1880. All these senses are coll, though the fourth and the sixth had orig. a tinge of s. 8. 'To prepare the warriors, by certain "medicines" and incantations, for war', Pettman: South African coll: from ca 1890. Ex *witch doctor*.

Doctor Brighton. Brighton: Society coll (from ca 1820) >, ca 1895, gen. coll. i.e., Dr Bright 'Un.

Doctor Doddypoll, see DODDYPOLL.

doctor draw-fart. An itinerant quack: C.19–20, ob.: low coll.

doctor (in one's cellars), keep the. Habitually to adulterate the liquor one sells: licensed victuallers', then public-houses': coll; from ca 1860.

Doctor Jim. A soft felt hat, wide-brimmed: lower classes': 1896–ca 1914. Ex Dr Jameson's 'Africander felt'. Whence JIMKWIM, JIMMANT.

Doctor Johnson. The *membrum virile*: literary: ca 1790–1880. Perhaps because there was no one that Dr Johnson was not prepared to stand up to.

doctor on one, put the. To cheat, orig. with false dice and, orig. perhaps, c.: late C.17–20; ob.

doctored, ppl adj. Adulterated; patched-up (fig.); falsified: C.18–20, coll. See DOCTOR, v., 4.

doctor's curse, gen. preceded by **the.** A dose of calomel (—1821): coll; ob.

doctor's stuff, occ. (C.19–20) **doctor-stuff.** Medicine: coll: from ca 1770. 'He could not take Doctor's stuff, if he died for it.'

doctors upon, put the, see DOCTOR, n., 1.

dod. A low coll(†) and dial. interjection: from ca 1670. Orig. a deformation of *God.*

dodder. 'Burnt tobacco taken from the bottom of a pipe and placed on the top of a fresh plug to give a stronger flavour,' F. & H.: mid-C.19–20, Irish. cf. S.E. *dottle.*

dodderer. A meddler; a fool. (In S.E., a tottering, pottering old man.) C.19–20, ob.; mostly Cockney. Variant, *doddering old sheep's head.*

doddies. A selfish person: proletarian: ca 1890–1915. A corruption of DO-UT-DES.

doddipool, see DODDYPOLL.

doddy, or **hoddy-doddy** ('all head and no body'). A simpleton, an idiot: mostly Norfolk and orig. and mainly dial.: C.19–20.

doddypoll. A M.E. and C.15–18 nickname for a doll, a fool; extant in dial. In late C. 16–mid-17, occ. *Doctor Doddypoll.* Apperson. Ex *dod*, to lop, poll, clip, and *poll*, the head. cf. preceding.

dodge. A shrewd and artful expedient, an ingenious contrivance: from ca 1830; coll in C.20. Dickens in *Pickwick*: ' " It was all false, of course?" "All, sir," replied Mr Weller, "reg'lar do, sir; artful dodge." ' (Ex the corresponding v., which, like its derivative, *dodger*, is S.E., though the latter has a slightly coll. tinge.)

***dodge,** v. To track (a person) stealthily: c.: from ca 1830: ob. Dickens, *Oliver Twist*.

dodge the column. To shirk one's duty: military: 1899 (Boer War).

dodger. See DODGE. 2. A dram of liquor: from ca 1820. 3. A shirker, malingerer: military: late C.19–20. 4. A mess-deck sweeper: naval: late C.19–20. He thus avoids other duties. 5. A clergyman, a priest: c. and low: mid-C.19–20. Mayhew, *London Labour*, vol. IV, 1861. Abbr. DEVIL-DODGER.

dodgy. Artful: (low) coll (—1887); slightly ob. 2. Hence, ingenious or neat: schoolboys': late C.19–20.

dodipol, see DODDYPOLL.

dodo. A stupid old man: Society: late C.19–20 (ob.); coll. Ex the extinct bird. cf.: 2. Scotland Yard: journalists': 1885–ca 1890.

***dodsey.** A woman: c.: late C.18–early 19. Prob. a corruption of *doxy*.

doe. A harlot: Ned Ward, 1700; R. Head, *Proteus Redivivus*, 1675. 2. A girl, a woman: mostly University of Oxford: late C.19–early 20.

doee, see DOOEE.

doer. One who cheats another: from ca 1840; ob. 2. A CHARACTER; an eccentric or very humorous fellow: Australian; from ca 1905.

does it? A sarcastically intonated coll retort: from ca 1870; ob.

does your mother know you're out? A c.p. of sarcastic or jocular implication: from 1838, says Benham in his *Book of Quotations. Punch*, 1841; The *Sun*, 28 Dec. 1864. F. & H., s.v., gives a very interesting list of such sapient phrases: all of which will be found in these pages.

does your mother want a rabbit? A c.p. of the 1890s and pre Great War C.20: non-aristocratic Ex the question of itinerant rabbit-vendors.

doesn't (or don't) give much away. Yield(s) few – or no – advantages; very keen: coll: from ca 1880.

doey, see DOOEE.

dog. Abbr. *dog-watch*: nautical: from ca 1890. 2. In the West Indies, a copper or a small silver coin, with variant *black dog*: (—1797) nautical. 3. God: in coll oaths: C.16. 4. See DOGS.

dog. To post (a student) for examination on the last day: Oxford University (—1726); †by 1800. 2. v.i. To have sexual connection on all fours, i.e. like a dog: C.19–20 low.

dog, an easy thing to find a stick to beat a. 'It costs little to trouble those that cannot help themselves,' B.E.: mid-C.17–18 coll.

dog, blush like a black, see BLACK DOG...

dog, – fight bear, fight. To fight till one party is overcome: C.16–20 coll; ob. Aphra Behn, Scott.

dog, he (she) worries the. A c.p. directed at a visitor whose approach repels even the house-dog: lower-middle classes' (—1909): ob.

dog, try it on the, see TRY IT ON THE DOG.

dog and cat, agree like, see CAT AND DOG...

dog at it, (an) old. Expert; habituated: coll; C.16–19. Nashe. The mod. form is *an old dog for a hard road.*

dog away one's time. To idle it away: Cockney (—1887); slightly ob.

dog-basket. 'The receptacle in which the remains of the cabin meals were taken – or smuggled – forward' in sailing ships: nautical: C.19.

dog before its master, the. A heavy swell preceding a gale: nautical c.p.: late C.19–20.

dog-biscuit. An Army mattress: military: late C.19–20; ob. Ex colour and shape. Also BISCUIT.

dog biting dog. Applied to one actor's adversely criticizing another's performance: late C.19–20 theatrical.

dog-bolt. A coll term of contempt: mean wretch. C.15–17, later use being archaic.

dog booby. An awkward lout; a CLODHOPPER: late C.18–early 19 military.

***dog-buffer.** A dog-stealer who kills all dogs not advertised for, sells the skins, and feeds the other dogs with the carcases: c.: late C.18–19.

dog-cheap. Exceedingly cheap: coll (C.16–20), F. & H.; S.E., S.O.D.: prob. the latter.

dog-collar. A 'stand-up' stiff collar, esp. a clergyman's reversed collar: from late 1860s; slightly ob. Grenville Murray, 'The dog-collar was of spotless purity.'

dog-drawn. Said (low coll) of a woman from whom a man has, in the act, been forcibly removed: C.19–20; ob.

***dog-fancier.** A receiver of stolen dogs and restorer of the same to their owners – for a fee: c. (—1861).

dog-gone, dog gone. Coll euphemism for and 'fantastic perversion of *God-damned*' (W.): U.S.; anglicized ca 1860. 2. Devoted: lower classes' (—1909).

dog-hole. A mean or a disgusting dwelling-place: coll: from ca 1570; ob.

dog in a blanket. A roly-poly pudding: coll: mostly nautical: from ca 1840.

dog in a doublet. 'A daring, resolute fellow', Grose, 3rd ed. C.16–early 19 coll. Ex German hunting-dogs, protected, in a boar-chase, with a leather doublet.

dog in a doublet, a (mere). 'A mean pitiful creature', Northall: coll (1577); now dial. cf.:

dog in a doublet, proud as a. Exceedingly proud: coll: late C.16–17.

dog in shoes, like a. Making a pattering sound: Anglo-Irish coll, C.19–20.

dog is dead?, whose. Variant, *what dog is a-hanging?* What is the matter? C.17–20 coll; ob. Massinger, 'Whose dog's dead now | That you observe these vigils?'

dog-Latin. Bad Latin; sham Latin. cf. APOTHECARIES' or BOG- or GARDEN-LATIN: from ca 1600; coll >, by 1820, S.E.

dog laugh, enough to make a. Extremely funny: coll: C.17–early 19. Pepys; Wolcot. cf. CAT LAUGH, ENOUGH TO MAKE A.

dog-leech. A quack: C.16–18 coll.

dog-nap. A short sleep enjoyed sitting: coll; from ca 1850. cf. CAT-NAP. The variant *dog-sleep* is S.E.

dog-nose, see DOG'S NOSE.

***dog on anyone, walk the black.** A punishment inflicted on a prisoner by his fellows if he refuses to pay his FOOTING: c.: late C.18–mid-19.

dog on it! An expletive affected, ca 1860–90, by boys. Perhaps euphemistic for *God damn it!* cf. DOG-GONE.

dog out in, not fit to turn a. (Of weather) abominable: coll (—1887).

dog-shooter. A volunteer: C.19 military then gen. 2. At the Royal Military Academy (—1889), a cadet who, unable or unwilling to become an engineer, joins a class in another branch. Ob.

dog-stealer. A dog-dealer: jocular coll (—1854). Whyte-Melville.

dog that bit you, a hair of the. A drink taken to counteract drunkenness; a drink the same as another the night before: coll (—1546).

dog-throw. The lowest throw at dice (cf. DEUCE): coll (—1880), verging on S.E.

dog to hold, give one the. To serve a person a mean trick: coll (—1678); †by 1800. Ray, 1678. cf. *holding the baby*. cf.:

dog-trick. A mean or 'dirty' action, trick: C.16–19 coll. cf. S.E. *dog's trick*.

dog-vane. A cockade: nautical: from ca 1785; ob. Songster Dibdin. Ex the S.E. sense.

dog-walloping. Picking up the ends of cigars and cigarettes: theatrical: ca 1810–50.

dogged, adv. Very, excessively: mainly sporting (—1819), prob. ex-dial., where only is it extant. Perhaps the orig. of the U.S. *dog-gone*.

dogged as does it!, it's. Perseverance and pluck win in the end: a coll c.p. dating from the mid-1860s.

dogger, v. To cheat; sell rubbish: Charterhouse; from ca 1860.

doggery. Manifest cheating: coll: from ca 1840; ob. cf. S.E. *dog's trick*. 2. Nonsense: proletarian: mid-C.19–20; ob.

doggess, see DOG'S LADY.

doggie, doggy. A pet name (coll) for a dog: from ca 1800. 2. In coal-mining, a middleman's underground manager (—1845). Disraeli in *Sybil*. 3. (Esp. a cavalry) officer's servant: military: mid-C.19–20; ob. 4. 'All-round upright collar': London youths' (—1909); ob. Ware.

doggo, lie. To make no move(ment) and say nothing; to bide one's time: C.19–20. Prob., 'like a cunning dog' (W.). The-*o* suffix is common in s.

doggy, adj. Stylish; smart, whether of appearance or of action: from ca 1885. Ex a SAD *dog*, *a bit of a dog*. 2. n.: see DOGGIE. 3. (Of Latin) debased: coll: 1898 (O.E.D. Sup.). Ex DOG-LATIN.

dogs. (Always pl.) Sausages: low: from ca 1860. Ex reputed origin. cf. BAGS OF MYSTERY.

dogs, go to the. To go to ruin; to lead an extremely dissipated and foolish life. C.16–20; coll till ca 1680, then S.E.

dogs, rain cats and, see CATS AND . . .

dog's body. Pease pudding: nautical (—1818). Clark Russell. 2. Any junior officer, R.N.; esp. a midshipman; hence, pejoratively, of any male: naval: late C.19–20.

dog's chance, not to have a. To have no chance at all: coll: late C.19–20.

dog's dram. A spit into his mouth and a smack on his back: mid-C.18–early 19 low.

dog's face. A coll term of abuse: coll > S.E.; from ca 1670; ob.

dogs have not dined, the. A c.p. to one whose shirt hangs out at the back: mid-C.18–early 19. (See *Slang*, p. 274.)

dog's hind leg, crooked as a. Very crooked (lit. only): coll: late C.19–20.

dog's home. Guard-room: Army s. (—1898). For 'lost' gay dogs.

dog's lady or **wife; doggess; puppy's mamma.** 'Jocular ways of calling a woman a bitch', Grose, 3rd ed.: coll: late C.18–mid-19.

dog's leg(s). The chevron(s), 'designating non-commissioned rank, worn on the arm, and not unlike in outline to the canine hindleg,' Ware: military: late C.19–20.

dog's lug. A small bight in a sail's leechrope: nautical: from ca 1880. A characteristic variant on *dog's ear*, nautical j.

dog's match of it, make a. To do the act of kind by the wayside: low coll: C.19–20; cf. DOG, v., 2.

dog's meat. 'Anything worthless; as a bad book, a common tale, a villainous picture, etc.', F. & H. Coll: from ca 1820. Ex lit. sense.

dog's nose. Gin and beer mixed: low (—1812); ob. Occ. *dognose*. 2. A man addicted to whisky: from ca 1850.

dog's paste. Sausage – or mince-meat: low coll: from ca 1850. cf. DOGS.

dog's portion. A LICK AND A SMELL, i.e. almost nothing: late C.18–20 (ob.) coll. In late C.18–19 occ. applied to a distant admirer of women. cf. DOG'S SOUP.

dog's rig. Sexual intercourse, to exhaustion, followed by back-to-back indifference: mid-C.18–19: low. cf. DOG'S MATCH.

dog's soup. Water: mid-C.18–20 (ob.) coll. cf. FISH-BROTH.

Dog's Tail. The constellation of the Little Bear: nautical: from ca 1860.

dog's vomit. Meat and biscuits cooked together as a moist hash: nautical: late C.19–20.

dog's wife, see DOG'S LADY.

dogun or **D-.** A Roman Catholic: Canadian: late C.19–20. Possibly ex that very Irish surname, *Duggan*.

dogways, adv. and adj. (Of coïtion) like a dog, *a retro*: workmen's coll: late C.19–20.

doing. A thrashing; a severe monetary loss: lower classes' coll (—1909). Ex dial. *doing*, a scolding: which in C.20 is coll.

doing!, nothing. 'Certainly not!' in retort to a dubious or unattractive offer or an amorous invitation: from late 1890s.

doing dab. Doing badly (in business): London low: since ca 1845. Mayhew, I, 1851. Here *dab* is back s. for *bad*.

doing of, be. To be doing: illiterate coll: C.19–20. In, e.g., An Old Etonian, *Cavendo Tutus*; *or*, *Hints upon Slip-Slop*, forming the second part of his *The Alphabet Annotated*, 1853.

dol. A dollar: lower classes' (—1909).

doldrum. A dullard: a drowsy or a sluggish fellow (—1812). Ex:

doldrums. Low spirits; dullness: from ca 1805; coll till ca 1890, then S.E. James Payn, 1883, 'Serious thoughts ... which she stigmatized ... as the doldrums.' Ex *dull* on *tantrum*, or ex nautical *doldrums*.

dole. A trick, a stratagem: Winchester College: from ca 1830. A development (though prob. straight from L. *dolus*) of the †S.E. sense, guile, fraud.

dolefuls. Low spirits: coll; from ca 1820. Miss Braddon. cf. DISMALS.

dolifier. One who contrives a trick: Winchester College; ex DOLE.

doll, n. Augustus Mayhew, *Paved with Gold*, 1858, records that among London crossing-sweepers (of the 1850s–1860s) 'the insulting epithet of "doll" was applied to every aged female' – precisely as 'the rather degrading appellation of "toff" was given to all persons of the male gender.' But in Anon., *The New Swell's Guide to Night Life*, 1846, at p. 29, *doll* occurs, twice in sense 'a girl': 'soldiers and their Dolls' followed by 'another resort for soldiers and their girls' – a clear anticipation of U.S. 'guys and *dolls*'. 2. A lady: Cockneys' (—1864); †by 1900. Mayhew, 'If it's a lady and gentleman then we cries, "A toff and a doll!"' Because well dressed.

doll, Bartholomew, see BARTHOLOMEW BABY.

***doll, mill.** To beat hemp in prison: c.: mid-C.18–early 19.

dollar. A five-shilling piece; five shillings: C.19–20 coll ex U.S. ex C.16–17 S.E. Hence *half-dollar* or HALF A DOLLAR, half a crown.

dollar, holy, see HOLY DOLLAR.

dollars to buttons, it's. It is a sure bet: coll: American >, before 1909, English.

dolled up like a barber's cat; usually all ... Extravagantly fashionable in dress: Canadian: late C.19–20.

dollop. A lot; *the whole dollop*, the whole lot, esp. sum (—1812): coll, †. 2. A lump, esp. if formless or clumsy: low coll, or perhaps a vulgarism, ex dial. (—1812). W. compares Norwegian *dolp*, a lump.

dolloping. The selling of goods at a ridiculously low price: cheapjacks' (—1876). C. Hindley.

dolly. A mistress: C.17–early 19. 2. Also (—1843), 'any one who has made a *faux pas*', *Punch*, 1843. cf. the C.17 S.E. *doll-common*, a harlot; in C.17–early 18 coll, surviving as dial., *dolly* also bore this sense, plus that of a slattern. 3. A pet, i.e. a coll name for a child's doll: from late C.18. 4. A piece of cloth serving as a sponge: tailors', from ca 1850. 5. A binding of rag on finger or toe: coll and dial. (—1888). 6. The *membrum virile*: low: C.19–20, ob. 7. A DONKEY-DROP: cricketers' (1906). 8. A servant girl: chimney sweeps': C.19. (George Elson, 1900.)

***dolly.** Perhaps only in *dolly pals*, dear friends or companions: c.: C.19. Possibly a perversion of *dear* suggested by DOLLY, n., 1. 2. adj., silly; foolish: from ca 1850; ob. Dickens, 'You wouldn't make such a dolly speech,' where, however, the term may = babyish.

dolly-catch. A slow, easy catch: cricketers' (1895).

Dolly Cotton; John Cotton. Rotten: rhyming s.: from ca 1890.

dolly-man, pitchy-man. A Jew: Anglo-Irish, esp. in the West: late C.19–20. Prob., *dolly-man* derives ex DOLLY-SHOP, *pitchy-man* ex a huckster's PITCH.

dolly-mop. A harlot: coll (—1833). Marryat. But in Cockney (—1855, †), an 'amateur' prostitute. Mayhew. 2. Also, a badly dressed maidservant: ca 1858–1905.

dolly-mopper. A womanizer, esp. if a soldier: military (—1887); ob. Ex preceding term, 1.

***dolly-shop.** An illegal rag-and-bone shop or pawn-shop: from ca 1840: c. > low coll. Mayhew; '*No. 747*' (reference to 1845). 2. A FENCE's, i.e. a receiver's parlour: c.; late C.19–20.

dolly-worship. The Roman Catholic religion: Nonconformists' (—1909). 'From the use of statues, etc.', Ware.

Dollymop, see DOLLY-MOP, 1.

dome. The head: coll; 'common', says F. & H. in 1891.

dome-stick. A servant: sol., or, when deliberate, jocular coll, †. (—1891.) Obviously suggested by the C.17–18 spelling of *domestic.* cf. DRAM-A-TICK.

doment. A variant of DO, n., 3: dial. and (†) low coll: from 1820s.

***domerar,** see DOMMERAR.

domestic afflictions. The menstrual period: coll: from ca 1850.

domin(i)e-do-little. An impotent old man: mid-C.18–early 19 coll.

domino. A knock-out blow: also as v.; from ca 1870. Ex: 2. As an exclamation, it expresses completion – of a punishment in the Victorian Army and Navy (1864, H., 3rd ed.); among bus-conductors to signify FULL UP (—1882); ob. All these senses are coll ex the game of dominoes. 3. See DOMINOES.

domino-box. The mouth: from ca 1820; orig. low, in C.20 inelegant and ob. Bee, 1823. Contrast *box of* DOMINOES.

domino-thumper. A pianist: from ca 1880; ob.

dominoes. (Never singular.) The teeth, esp. if discoloured (contrast IVORIES): from ca 1820. cf. DOMINO. 2. The keys of a piano: from ca 1880; ob. Hence:

dominoes, box of. A piano: from ca 1880. See preceding.

dominoes, sluice one's. To drink: low (—1823). Moncrieff in *Tom and Jerry,* Act II, scene 6. cf. DOMINOES, 1, and DOMINO-BOX.

***dom(m)erar or -er; dummerer.** A beggar pretending to be deaf and *dumb*: mid-C.16–18. Harman. 2. Also, ca 1670–1750, a madman. Coles, 1676. Both are c.

don. An adept, a SWELL OF TOFF; a pretentious person: coll; from ca 1820. In C.17–18 S.E. a distinguished person. Ex the Spanish dons, as is 2, the English university coll use, a fellow of a college: from ca 1660; orig. pejorative. 3. (Gen. pl, and always **D.**) A Spaniard; a Portuguese: nautical: C.19–20. Bowen, 'A more polite term than *Dagoes* [q.v.] but not applied to other Latins.'

don, adj. Expert, clever; excellent: from ca 1860; ob. Ex the preceding.

Don Caesar spouting. 'Haughty public elocution': Society: ca 1850–1900. Ware.

Don Peninsula. The world, the 'geographical' range, of the dons: Oxford University, ca 1820–40.

dona, donah (mostly in sense 2), **donna, doner,** rarely **donnay.** A woman; esp. the lady of the house: from the 1850s: Cockney and Parlary. Ex It. or Sp. via Lingua Franca. 2. Hence, in Australia, from ca 1880: a girl; a sweetheart. 'Never introduce your dona(h) to a pal' has long been an Australian c.p., from a Cockney song.

dona Highland-flinger. A music-hall singer: rhyming s. (—1909).

dona Jack. A harlot's bully: lower classes' (—1909).

***donaker.** A cattle-stealer: C.17–early 18; c.

Donald. A glass of spirituous liquor, esp. whisky: Scottish: 1869, Johnston, *Poems.*

Doncaster-cut. A horse: coll (—1529); †by 1600. Skelton. Doncaster famous for horses.

donderkop. In address, blockhead: South African coll (—1897). Lit., dunderhead.

done, it isn't. It is bad form: coll: from late 1870s. An upper-class counter, this.

done brown, see BROWN, DO.

done-for. Exhausted; cheated; ruined; in c., robbed, convicted to prison, or hanged: (—)1859: see DO FOR. The c. *done for a* RAMP = convicted for stealing (H., 1st ed.).

done-over. Intoxicated: C.19–20. 2. Possessed carnally (only of women): C.18–20; ob. 3. In c., same as *done*: see DO OVER.

done to death, see DEATH, DONE TO.

done to the wide; done to the world. Utterly exhausted, defeated, or baffled; ruined: from ca 1908: s. now verging on coll.

done-up. Used up, finished, or quieted: coll from ca 1820. 2. 'Ruined by gaming, and extravagances', Grose, 1st ed. ('*modern term*', he adds): ca 1780–1860.

doner, see DONA. And:

doner. One who is done for, ruined, fated to die: lower classes': *Sessions,* Jan. 1838.

donkey. A compositor (cf. PIG, n., 3): printers' (—1857). Variants MOKE, ASS. 2. A sailor's clothes-chest: nautical: from ca 1860. 3. A blockhead, a fool: coll, from ca 1840. 4. Even for an ass, *donkey* was orig. – ca 1780 – coll and remained so for some fifty years. cf. DONKEY DICK. Perhaps ex *Duncan* or *Dominic.* 5. *A regular donkey*, anything very long and big (as, e.g., a carrot). 6. And *a donkey's* = a large penis: low: late C.19–20.

donkey!, a penny (or twopence or threepence) more and up goes the. A (low) London c.p. expressing derision (—1841): coll: ex a street acrobat's stock finish to a turn; ob.

***donkey, ride the.** To cheat with weights and measures: c.: C.19. vbl n., *donkey-riding.*

donkey, ride the black, see RIDE ...

donkey, talk the hind leg off a, see TALK ...

donkey?, who stole the. Sometimes another person added, *the man in* or *with the white hat*: this latter represented also the occasion: ca 1835–1910. Ex an actual incident.

donkey dick. An ass: ca 1780–1820. A variant of DONKEY, which is prob. ex *Duncan.* From early C.19, DICKY (n., 4) came to be used by itself.

donkey-drops. In cricket, from ca 1887, slow round-arm bowling. A. G. Steel, 1888; the Hon. E. Lyttelton, in his *Cricket*, 1890. Also DOLLY (n., 7).

donkey-frigate. A 28-gun ship (between a frigate and a sloop): naval: C.19.

donkey has of Sunday, have as much idea (of it) as a. To be wholly ignorant: Cockney (—1887); ob.

donkey in one's throat, have a. To have phlegm there: Cockney (—1887); slightly ob.

donkey-rigged. Endowed with a large penis: low: late C.19–20. cf. DONKEY, 6.

donkey's breakfast. (Orig. a man's) straw hat: Cockneys': 1893; slightly ob. 2. A bundle of straw for a bed: nautical (—1901).

donkey's ears. A shirt-collar with long points, already old-fashioned in 1891: s. or coll: ca 1870–1900. 2. A false collar: *Sinks*, 1848.

donkey's years. A long time: suggested by the sound of *donkey's ears*, when illiterately pronounced *donkey's yeers*, and the length of a donkey's ears: from ca 1900. Also, as Sam Weller pointed out, 'Some wery sensible people' assert 'that post-boys and donkeys is both immortal.'

donna and **donnay,** see DONA. **donneken,** see DUNNAKEN. (Bee's spelling.)

donovan. (Gen. in pl) A potato: Anglo-Irish: from ca 1830. cf. MURPH. Ex the commonness of the surname.

don's or **dons' week.** The week before a general holiday; esp. a week out of work before it: tailors': from ca 1860; ob.

don't care a Pall Mall, (I). (I) don't care a damn: clubmen's: 1885–ca 1890. Ex the *Pall Mall Gazette*'s articles entitled 'The Maiden Tribute' in July 1885. *Pall Mall,* a GAL or girl.

don't dynamite! Don't be angry!: non-aristocratic c.p. of 1883–ca 1900. Ware, 'Result of the Irish pranks in Great Britain with this explosive.'

don't fear! see DON'T (YOU) FEAR!

don't know who's which from when's what, (I). (I, etc.) don't know anything about it: lower classes' c.p.: 1897–ca 1905.

don't look down, you'd soon find the hole if there was hair round it! A drill-sergeant's c.p., on the fixing of bayonets: late C.19–20.

don't lose your hair! KEEP YOUR HAIR ON!: non-aristocratic: from ca 1860; ob.

don't mention that. A c.p.: ca 1882–4, as the result of a libel case. Ex *don't* MENTION *it!*

don't-name-'ems. Trousers: jocular coll; from ca 1850. cf. INNOMINABLES.

don't seem to. Be incapable of; as in 'I don't seem to see it': coll (—1909).

don't sell me a dog! Don't deceive me!: Society: ca 1860–80.

don't think!, I. I do think so!: middle and lower classes': from ca 1880. cf. NOT HALF!

don't turn that side to London! A c.p. of condemnation: non-aristocratic (—1909). Ware, 'From the supposition that everything of the best is required in the metropolis.'

don't (you) fear! Take my word for it!; certainly not!: coll: mid-C.19–20. cf. *never* FEAR!

don't you forget it! see AND DON'T YOU FORGET IT!

don't you know. As you well know; please understand!: coll (—1887). Baumann,'Sehr gebräuchlicher Zusatz' (a very frequent tag).

don't you wish you may get it? A c.p. of ca 1830–50 = I don't like your chance! or I don't think! Barham; *Punch*, 1841, 1844.

doocid. An affected, also a Cockney variation of DEUCED. As:

dood is of DUDE.

doodle. A noodle: coll; from ca 1620. Ford; Grose; Cobden, 1845, 'The Noodles and Doodles of the aristocracy.' 2. (Gen. of a child) the penis: mid-C.18–20. ?Ex *cock-a-doodle-doo*, or COCK.

doodle, v. To make a fool of; cheat: from ca 1820. Moncrieff, 'I have been. . . doodled out of forty pounds today.' cf. DIDDLE.

doodle-dasher. A man indulging in self-abuse: C.19–20 low; ob.

doodle-doo, gen. preceded by *cock-a*. A child's or a childish name for a cock: C.17–20 coll.

doddle-doo man. A cock-breeder or -fighter: C.18–19; cockpit s.

doodle-sack. The *pudendum muliebre*: mid-C.18–20; ob. In S.E., a bagpipe: this origin, like so many in C.18, is crudely anatomical.

dooee, occ. **dooe; doee.** Two, as in *dooee salter*, two pence: Parlary: mid-C.19–20. It. *due soldi*.

doog. Good: back s. (—1859). Whence:

doogheno. A good one. *Doogheno hit*, one good hit, i.e. a bargain, a profit. Back s. (—1851).

doojie's joy. A poor specimen: *Conway* cadets': from ca 1885.

dook. See DUKES. 2. A sol. pronunciation of *duke*: C.19 (?earlier)–20. 3. A huge nose: lower classes': from ca 1840; ob. Ex the Duke of Wellington's nose: cf. CONKEY. 4. An upper-form boy: Public Schools'; late C.19–20. See NONDESCRIPT.

dook-reading. Palmistry: grafters': late C.19–20. cf. DOOKIN.

dookie; dukey. An unlicensed theatre; PENNY GAFF; theatrical: from ca 1860; ob. Perhaps ex a gaff-proprietor with a large nose: cf. DUKER and DOOK; 3.

dookin, dookering. Fortune-telling: gypsies', thence criminals': from ca 1835. Ex Romany *dukker*, to tell fortunes.

dookin-cove. A fortune-teller: low: from ca 1850. See COVE and DOOKIN.

dooks. (Extremely rare in singular.) The hands. More gen. DUKES.

doolally (or doolali) tap. Off one's head; mad: Regular Army. Late C.19–20. Ex *Deolali*, a camp in Bombay where time-expired men waited for homeward ships and often got in trouble through boredom; also ex Hindustani *tap*, fever.

doolie. An ambulance: Anglo-Indian coll: C.18–20. Ex the S.E. sense, a litter or a rudimentary palanquin (C.16+).

door, up to the, see DICK, UP TO.

door and hinge. 'Neck and breast of mutton, a joint which bends readily amongst the cervical vertebrae,' Ware: Cockney's: mid-C.19–20.

door-knob. A BOB (shilling): rhyming s.: late C.19–20.

door-knocker. A ring-shaped beard: proletarian: 1854–ca 1915. (Also adj.) 2. A Nordenfelt machine-gun (used by the Boers): military in Boer War. J. Milne, *The Epistles of Atkins*, 1902. Ex the noise.

door-mat. A heavy beard: 1856–ca 1882. cf. CRIMEA. 2. Hence, says Ware, 'by 1882 . . . applied to the moustache only, probably because about this time the tendency to shave the beard and wear only a very heavy moustache became prevalent'.

door-nail, see DEAD AS A DOOR-NAIL.

doorer. A doorsman or barker at an auction sale: London coll: from the 1880s. *Answers*, 12 Dec. 1891 (E.D.D.).

doorstep. A (gen. thick) slice of bread and butter: low (—1885).

dooshman. An enemy: Regular Army: late C.19–20. Ex Hindustani.

dope. A drug: 1889. 2. Drugging: from ca 1900. 3. Fraudulent information: 1901. All coll ex U.S., where orig. of any thick lubricant or absorbent (S.O.D.); itself ex Dutch *doopen*, to dip.

dope, v. To take drugs: from ca 1890. Ex n., 1. 2. To DOCTOR or drug a person or a race-horse: from ca 1900. Both senses were orig. U.S. The vbl n. is frequent.

dopey. A beggar's trull: low: mid-C.18–early 19. 2. The podex: C.18.

dopper. 'A heavy blanket overall once much favoured by North Sea fishermen' (Bowen): nautical coll verging on j. Ex Norfolk dial. *dopper*, a thick woollen jersey.

doption. An adopted child: low, verging on c.: from ca 1870. i.e. *adoption*.

dor. Permission to sleep awhile: Westminster School: C.17–early 19. Ex L. *dormire*, to sleep.

dorbie. An initiate: Scots Masonic: from ca 1850. Hence *the dorbies' knock*, a masons' signal-rap. Ex *dorbie*, a stone-mason, a builder.

dorcas. A sempstress, esp. in a charitable cause: coll; from ca 1880. Ex the S.E. *Dorcas society*, *D. basket*, ex Dorcas in Acts, ix, 36.

dork. A DOORSTEP: lower classes': since ca 1895. By 'telescoping' or conflation.

dorm. A dormitory: schools': late C.19–20.

dormie, see:

dormy; occ. **dormie.** A dormitory: at certain Public Schools, e.g. Rossall: late C.19–20. Desmond Coke, *The House Prefect*, 1908.

Dorothy, n. and, gen., adj. Rustic love-making: Society: late 1887–ca 1890. Ex a musical comedy (1887–8) so named.

dorse, see DOSS.

dorse, v. To knock down on to the back: boxing: ca 1810–80. Wilson, 1826.

dorse, send to. Knock out: boxing, ca 1820–70. See DOSS.

***dose.** A burglary: C.18–19 c. 2. A term of imprisonment, esp. one of three months' HARD: mid-C.19–20 c. cf. MOON, STRETCH, n., 2. ? ex: 3. A defeat: boxing, C.19–20, ob. Tom Moore, 1819. 4. As much liquor as one can hold – or somewhat more than is good for one: coll; from ca 1850. cf. *take a grown man's dose*, a great deal of liquor. 5. (?hence,) a venereal infection: low coll; from ca 1860.

dose, v.; gen. **be dosed.** To infect venereally: low: from ca 1870. Ex n., 5. cf.:

dose, cop a. A phrase corresponding to DOSE, n., 2 and esp. 5: low: from ca 1870.

dose of the balmy, have a. To sleep: coll; C.19–20, ob. See BALMY.

doser. A severe blow or punch: pugilistic: ca 1840–90. Augustus Mayhew, *Paved with Gold*, 1857.

doshed!, I'm. A variant, ca 1870–1910, of *I'm* DASHED.

***doss** (not before C.19); (after ca 1850, rarely) **dorse.** A, and to, sleep; lodging, to lodge; a bed. All implying extreme cheapness and/or roughness: late C.18–20; vagrants' c. > ca 1890, gen. s. G. Parker, 1789; Mayhew. Presumably imm. ex †*dorse*, *doss*, back; ultimately ex L. *dorsum*, the back. (cf. DORSE, V.)

doss, do a, see DO A DOSS.

doss-down, n.; **doss down,** v. A late C.19–20 variant of the following.

doss-house. A very cheap lodging-house: low: from ca 1880. On:

doss in the pure. To sleep in the open air: (mostly London) vagrants' c.: from ca 1890.

***doss-ken.** The same: c.; from ca 1800. cf. DOSSING-KEN.

doss-man. The keeper of a cheap lodging-house: low: from ca 1825.

doss-money. The price of a night's lodging: low: from ca 1870.

doss-ticket. A ticket for a night's lodging: tramps' (—1887).

dosser. A frequenter of doss-houses: low: from ca 1865. Whence *(h)appy dosser*, a homeless vagrant creeping in to sleep on chairs, or in passages or cellars: low (—1880). Sims in *How the Poor Live.* Presumably ex *happy* but just possibly ex *haphazard.* 2. **The dosser:** the father of a family: from ca 1885; ob. He who provides the *doss*.

***dossing-ken** or **-crib.** (cf.: DOSS-HOUSE; DOSS-KEN.) A cheap lodging-house: c.: the former —1838; the latter —1851. See DOSS.

dossy. Elegant; smart: from ca 1885. ?ex *dosser*, the ornamental cloth used to cover the back of a(n imposing) seat; or ex *D'Orsay*, for in Society, ca 1830–45, one spoke of a man as 'a D'Orsay' (a perfect gentleman) – ex the Comte D'Orsay (Ware).

do't. Do it: Society coll of early C.18. Scourged by Swift (see *Slang*, p. 66).

***dot.** A ribbon. Hence, *dot-drag*, a watch-ribbon: C.19 c. Haggart, 1821.

dot. v. To strike, gen. in form *dot* (a person) *one*, and esp. in sense 'give a black eye' (Ware): from the middle 1890s. W. Pett Ridge, 1895, *Minor Dialogues*; C. J. Dennis has *dot* (one) *in the eye*, to punch (a person) in the eye.

dot, the year. A date long ago: coll: late C.19–20. Lit., 'the year 0'. cf. 'I reckon *he* was born in the year dot, that 'orse was,' W. Pett Ridge, *Minor Dialogues*, 1895.

dot and carried. Married: rhyming s.: since ca 1880. cf. CUT AND CARRIED.

dot and carry, or **go, one.** A person with a wooden or a shorter or a limping leg. The mid-C.18–mid-19 form is *go*; the C.19–20, *carry*. Coll. Also as v. 2. An inferior writing or arithmetic master: late C.18–early 19. Ex an arithmetical process.

dots. Money: from ca 1880. Collective-pl synonyms are numerous.

dotter. A penny-a-liner; a reporter: from ca 1870; ob.

dotties man. A greedy or selfish man: proletarian ca 1885–1915. See DODDIES.

dotty. Weak; dizzy: sporting and gen. (—1870); ob. Esp. *dotty in the pins*, unsteady on one's legs. Perhaps ex *dodder*, v. 2. Hence, idiotic; (a little) mad: from ca 1888. 3. As n., a low harlot's fancy man: c. (—1891).

double. A trick: esp. in C.18–19 *tip*, C.19–20 *give the double*, to run away from one's creditors, then, from ca 1850, to escape;

and in *put the double on*, to circumvent (—1870). 2. An actor playing two parts; also v. (from ca 1800 and soon S.E.): theatrical (—1825). 3. Repetition of a word or sentence: printers': from ca 1870. 4. In c. a street-turning: from ca 1870. 5. (Gen. *a double*.) Two score: fisheries' coll: late C.19–20. Ex *double*, a basket containing from three to four dozen fish.

double, v. For the theatrical sense, see n., 2. 2. See DOUBLE UP. 3. To double one's effort or speed (v.i.): coll: from ca 1885.

double, make a. To repeat a line or a sentence: compositors' coll: C.19–20.

double-arsed. Large-bottomed: low coll or a vulgarism: C.19–20.

double back. To go back on an action, statement, opinion: coll: mid-C.19–20. Ex doubling back on one's tracks.

double-banked. 'Sleeping two in a cabin': nautical coll: late C.19–20. Bowen. Ex a rowing-boat double-banked.

double barrel. A field or opera glass: from ca 1880; ob. Traill.

double-barrelled. Applied to a harlot natural and unnatural (see FORE-AND-AFTER): low: from ca 1860. 2. Also to any person both normal and abnormal in sex: from ca 1900.

double-bottomed. Insincere: coll: C.19–20; ob.

double-breasted feet, occ. double-breasters. Club feet: coll: from ca 1850; ob.

double-breasted water-butt smasher. A well-developed man; an athlete: Cockney's: ca 1890–1914.

double Cape Horn. To be made a cuckold: nautical: late C.18–mid-19. John Davis, *The Post Captain*, 1805. Ex horns attributed to cuckolds.

double-cross or -double. Winning, or trying to win, after promising to lose a race: sporting: from ca 1870. The v. is *double*, *double-cross*, or *put the double on*, the last v.t. only: from ca 1870. 2. Later, *double-cross*, etc., is much used by criminals for betrayal (n. and v.) in a criminal transaction: from ca 1885.

double-cunted. Sexually large: low coll or vulg.: from ca 1800.

double dash! Emphatic DASH!: Cockney (—1887); ob.

double-decker. A ship having two above-water decks: from ca 1870. 2. A tramcar or bus with seats on top as well as below: from ca 1895. Both coll, the latter ex U.S.

double-diddied or -dugged. Large-breasted, n., *double dugs*. C.19–20; the n. is low coll; *double-diddied*, low s.; *double-dugged*, low coll.

double-distilled. (Esp. of a lie) superlative: coll: from ca 1840; ob.

double Dutch, see DUTCH, TALK. cf.:

double Dutch coiled against the sun. Unintelligible; nonsense: nautical: from ca 1840.

***double-ender.** A skeleton key with a ward at each end: c.: mid-C.19–20; ob. '*No. 747*'.

double event. Simultaneous syphilis and gonorrhoea (men), or defloration and conception: low: from ca 1870.

double finn. A £10 note: low (?orig. c.): from ca 1870. See:

***double finnip** (etc.). The same: c. (—1839). See FINNIF.

double guts, n.; **double-gutted,** adj. (Of a) person large-paunched: low coll; from ca 1820.

double-headed. (Of a train) with two engines, one at the front and the other at the back: late C.19–20: railwaymen's coll, now verging on S.E.

double-header. A coin with two heads: low coll: from ca 1875.

double-hocked. Having extremely thick ankles: low: from ca 1860.

double intenders. 'Knock-down blows – labial or fistful', Ware: non-aristocratic (—1909); virtually †.

double jug(g). The backside: late C.17–19. 2. In pl., the posteriors: C.17–20, ob. 'Melancholy' Burton.

double lines. Ship-casualty or casualties: nautical: from ca 1870. Ex the manner of their entry at Lloyd's.

double-mouth(ed). (A person) large-mouthed, n. and adj.: coll: C.19–20.

double on, put the, see DOUBLE-CROSS.

double-ribbed. Pregnant: low coll: C.19–20.

double scoop. 'Hair parted in centre, and worn low – gave way to the quiff', Ware: military: ca 1890–95.

double-shotted. (Of a brandy, or whisky, and soda) containing twice the usual proportion of alcohol: coll: from ca 1860.

double shuffle. A hornpipe step in which each foot is shuffled, rapidly and neatly, twice in succession: coll; from ca 1830, esp. among costermongers. Dickens. 2. Hence a trick, a piece of faking: from ca 1870.

double-shung. (Of men) excessively equipped sexually: C.19–20 (ob.): low. ?*double-slung*.

***double slangs.** Double irons or fetters: c. (—1812); ob.

double-sucker. Abnormally developed *labia maiora*: low: from ca 1870.

double thumper. An OUTSIZE in lies: from ca 1850: coll.

double-tide work. Extra duty: C.19–20: coll, orig. coastguardsmen's >, by 1880, gen. nautical.

double-tongued squib. A double-barrelled gun: coll. G. W. Reynolds, 1864. Ob.

double up. To cause to collapse (v.i. sense is rare): boxing (ca 1814). Moore, 'Doubled him up, like a bag of old *duds*.' 2. To pair off, e.g., in a cabin (rare as v.i.): coll: 1837. Occ. simple *double*.

doubler. A punch on side or belly: boxing: from ca 1810. 'Peter Corcoran', 1821, 'A doubler in the bread-basket'.

***doublet.** A precious stone endorsed with glass: in C.15–17, it was S.E.; then it > c. 2. See IRON D. and STONE D., a prison.

Douglas with one eye and a stinking breath, Roby. The breech: nautical: mid-C. 18–19.

dough. Pudding: Public Schools', C.19–20. 2. Money: U.S. (—1851), then (from ca 1870) Canada, then (from ca 1880) Australia, then – ca 1895 – Britain.

dough, one's cake is, see CAKE IS DOUGH, ONE'S.

dough-baked. Deficient in brains: coll: from late C.16; in late C.19–20, dial. Wycherley, 1675, 'These dow-baked, senseless, indocile animals, women'. cf. HALF-BAKED.

dough-cock. A half-wit aboard as seaman: nautical: late C.19–20.

doughy. A baker: coll (—1823). cf. CHIPS; DIPS. 2. Hence, the nickname of any man surnamed Baker: naval and military: late C.19–20.

doughy, adj. (Of complexion) pale or pasty: coll: from ca 1860; ob. cf. UNDER-DONE.

doughy-nosed. (Of a seaman) in love: nautical: late C.19–20.

doul. A FAG (boy): Shrewsbury: C.19–20. Ex Gr. δουλος, a slave.

douse, dowse. To put, esp. down or (of a candle, lamp, etc.) out: low coll: C.18–20, chiefly in *douse the glim*, put out the light. Scott, Reade. 2. n., rare, except in *dowse on the chops*, a blow on the jaw: low: C.17–19.

douser, a heavy blow; **dousing (dowsing),** a thrashing: resp. late C.18–19, C.19. Both, low coll.

Dove. A member of St Catherine's College, Cambridge: C.19–20: ob. Suggested by PURITAN. See Whibley in *Cambridge Wit*.

dove, soiled. A high-flying harlot: from ca 1870; coll. Dove = purity.

dove-cote. 'The quarters allotted to officers' wives on ... the old Indian troopships': military: late C.19–early 20. F. & Gibbons.

dove-tart. A pigeon pie: coll: from ca 1850; ob. 'Cuthbert Bede'.

dover. A re-heated dish: hotels': from ca 1870. i.e. 'do over again'.

Dover, Jack of. A sole: late C.14–17: coll; then, in C.18–early 19, dial. Chaucer. Dover is famed for its soles.

Dover Castle boarder. A debtor compelled to sleep within the rules of the Queen's Bench Prison: debtors': ca 1850–81 – the prison was demolished in 1881. Ex the Dover Castle, the most prominent tavern in that district.

Dover waggoner!, put this reckoning up to the. (Gen. addressed to a landlord.) Score this up against me: a c.p. of ca 1820–40. Bee, 'The waggoner's name being Owen, pronounced *owing*.'

Dovercourt beetle. A heavy mallet: nautical: mid-C.19–20. By a pun.

dovey or dovy, adj. Pretty; attractive; SWEET: domestic, esp. feminine, coll: from ca 1890.

dowdying. A drastic practical joke practised in C.18 by one Pearce, nicknamed *Dowdy* ex the burden, *dow de dow*, of one of his songs.

dowlas. A draper. Coll; from late C.18. Ex the towelling so named; popularized by Daniel Dowlas, a character in Colman's *The Heir at Law*.

dowling. A compulsory game of football: Public Schools (—1871); ob. Ex the Gr. word for (a slave, or that for) to enslave. Desmond Coke, *The Bending of a Twig*, 1906, of the game as it is played at Shrewsbury School: 'Any number from three hundred down (or up) can play a dowling; but it often happens that in reality some half-a-dozen punt the ball from end to end, while all the rest troop after it, like soldier-slaves round the great warriers of Ilium. And dowling is compulsory.' cf. the quotation at SKYTE.

***down.** Alarm; suspicion; discovery: c.; ca 1810–1900. 2. Hence *there is no down*, there is no risk; all's safe. 3. A tendency to be severe towards: coll (—1893). Ex DOWN ON, BE, 2. But cf.: 4. A prejudice against, hostility towards: Australian coll: from ca 1850. W. J. Dobie, *Recollections of Port Phillip*, 1856. Ex sense 1.

down, v. To trick; circumvent: C.19–20 coll. 2. The sense, to bring, put, throw, or knock down, is – despite F. & H. – S.E., but *down a woman*, physically to prepare her for the act, is definitely low coll if not s., from ca 1850: cf. UP, v.

down, adv. (often with adj. force). Esp. with *to be*: depressed; in low spirits: coll: C.17–20. Ben Jonson, 'Thou art so downe upon the least disaster.' 2. Wide-awake; suspicious; aware: low (?orig. c.): Vaux, 1912. Often with *to*, as in 'Down to every move,' Smedley, 1850. cf. *up to*, aware of.

down, be or **come.** To be PLOUGHED in a university examination: Australian coll: 1886; ob.

down, up or, see UP OR DOWN.

down a pit, be. To be greatly attracted by a role: theatrical: from ca 1860; †.

down along. (Sailing) coastways down the English Channel: nautical coll: mid-C.19–20.

down among the dead men. Dead drunk: ca 1850–1900. 'Cuthbert Bede', 1853.

***down as a hammer** (see also HAMMER, DOWN AS A) or **as a tripper.** To be alert, wide-awake: c.; ca 1810–40. Elaborations on DOWN, adv., 2.

down as a nail. A synonym of DOWN AS A HAMMER: 1817, J. J. Stockdale, *The Greeks.*

***down buttock and sham file,** see BUTTOCK AND TONGUE.

***down(-)hills.** Dice cogged to run low: late C.17–early 19: c. > low s. cf. UP-HILLS.

down in. Lacking in; short of: proletarian coll: mid-C.19–20. e.g. 'down in cash'.

down on or **upon, be.** To be aware of, alertly equal to: from ca 1790. 2. Hence, to pounce upon, treat harshly: s. (—1860) >, by 1900, coll. 3. See DOWN UPON.

down on (more gen. **upon) one, put a.** To inform on a person: from ca 1800.

down on the knuckle, see KNUCKLE, DOWN ON THE.

down pin, be. To be indisposed; depressed: C.19. Extant in dial. Ex skittles.

down south, esp. with **go** or **put.** (Of money) to go or be put in one's pocket, hence to be banked: from ca 1890.

down the drains. Brains: rhyming s.: late C.19–20.

down the hatch! 'Bung ho! (*Pause*). Down the hatch!': a drinking, esp. a toasting, c.p; mid-C.19–20; orig., nautical.

down the Lane and/or into the Mo. (To take a stroll) in the Drury Lane district: Central London Cockneys': ca 1850–1910. *Mo* derives ex the long-disappeared Mogul Music Hall.

down the road. Vulgarly showy: coll: (—1859); ob. Sala, 'A racing and down-the-road look.' Ex Mile End Road, says Ware.

down the wind, see WEATHER, GO UP THE.

***down to, drop.** To learn a person's designs or character: c. (—1812); ob. cf. DROP TO and:

***down to, put** (a person). To apprise one (of something); explain it to him: c. (—1812); very ob. See DOWN, adv., 2.

down to dandy. Artful; excellent: low: from ca 1860; ob. cf. *up to* DICK.

down to something, put one. To explain; prime; let into the 'know': from ca 1830.

down to the ground. Thoroughly; extremely well: coll: from ca 1865. Miss Broughton, 'Suited me down to the ground,' 1867. In C.16–17 S.E., *up and down.*

down upon (occ. on) a person, be. To scold, reprimand severely: coll: from ca 1810. Scott, 'We should be down upon the fellow . . . and let him get it well.' 2. See DOWN ON, BE.

down upon oneself, be or **drop.** To be melancholy: ca 1810–60.

downer. A sixpence: from ca 1835. Brandon, 1839; Whyte-Melville. Ex Romany *tawno*, little one. cf. TANNER. 2. A knock-down blow: boxing; from ca 1815; ob. Moore, 1819.

downish. Somewhat dejected: coll: ca 1670–1800.

downstairs. Hell: C.19 coll. Barham, 'Downstairs . . . old Nick.'

downy. An artful fellow: ca 1820–80. Pierce Egan. See the adj. Perhaps associated with DOWNY BIRD, but imm. ex DOWN ON, BE, 1. 2. A bed: from ca 1850; ob. Trollope, 'I've a deal to do before I get to my downy.' Ex the down mattress.

downy, adj. Artful; very knowing: from ca 1820. Moncrieff, 1823, 'You're a downy von'; Dickens; H. J. Byron, the dramatist. Ex DOWN, n., 1. cf. DOWNY, n., 2. Fashionable: ca 1855–90.

downy, do the, see DO THE DOWNY.

downy as a hammer. A variant of DOWN AS A HAMMER; *Boxiana*, III, 1821.

downy (or **D.**) **Bible.** Douay Bible: tailors': from ca 1860. Used as reference, like ACCORDING TO COCKER.

downy bird or **cove.** A clever rogue (—1875, —1821 resp.). In pl. gen. *the downies*. Egan; Leman Rede, 'the downiest cove'; Greenwood. The *bird* form was suggested by a bird's down (cf. DOWNY-BIT), but the *downy* is ex DOWN, n., 1.

downy bit. A half-fledged wench: low: from ca 1830; ob. 2. An attractive young girl: low: from ca 1880.

downy flea-pasture. A bed: from ca 1800. cf. BUG-WALK.

dowry. A lot; much: low; from ca 1850; ob. Prob. ex the S.E. word.

dowse, see DOUSE.

***doxe, doxey, doxie,** see DOXY.

doxology-works. A church, a chapel: from ca 1870; ob. cf. GOSPEL-SHOP and PREACHING-SHOP.

***doxy;** also **doxey,** C.17–19, and **doxie** or **doxey,** C.17; occ. **doccy,** C.16, and **doxe,** C.16–17. In mid-C.16–18 c., a beggar's trull, a female beggar. Prob. ex Dutch *docke*, a doll: cf., therefore, DOLLY. 2. Hence, in late C.16–20 (ob.), a mistress, a prostitute. Chapman, Dunton, Grose. 3. Hence, in C.19 low s., esp. in London and among patterers, a wife. Augustus Mayhew, *Paved with Gold*, 1857, notes that among London crossing-sweepers – prob. it holds good for ca 1840–80 – *doxy* is a girl, a young woman, however respectable. (Dial. takes up two analogous ideas: a sweetheart (—1818); app. later a slattern or (pejoratively) an old woman.) This *doxy* lends point to the quotation in 4. **doxy,** opinion: coll; 1730. ' "Orthodoxy, my Lord," said Bishop Warburton . . ., "is my doxy – heterodoxy is another man's doxy."'

Doyle, do Paddy, see PADDY DOYLE, DO.

dozen, talk (occ. **run**) **nineteen to the.** To talk very fast: from ca 1850; coll till C.20, then S.E. Reade (*talk*), 1852, Sala (*run*), 1860.

dozenth. Twelfth: coll; from ca 1710. (Hence, the rare *half-dozenth*.) Cobden, 'Let me repeat it – if for the dozenth time.'

dozing-crib. A bed: low (?c.): mid-C.19–early 20. cf. KIP, n., 2.

Dr Brighton; Dr Jim; Dr Johnson, see DOCTOR BRIGHTON . . .

drab. Poison; medicine: low (—1851). Ex Romany, where *drabengro* (the suffix *-engro* = a man) is a doctor: see esp. Smart & Crofton and Sampson.

drabbit! Abbr. (*G*)*od rabbit!* An old, mainly dial., expletive. cf. DRAT.

drabby. An Indian transport-driver: Regular Army coll: late C.19–20. Ex Hindustani.

drach (pron. *drăk*). A drachma: among the English colony in Greece: late C.19–20.

draft on Aldgate pump. A spurious bank-note; fraudulent bill: ca 1730–1850. Fielding, who notes it as 'a mercantile phrase'. Also at ALDGATE.

drag. A late C.18–19 four-horse coach, with seats inside and on top. Orig. s. or coll, as Moore's *Tom Crib*, Reynolds's *The Fancy*, and Lever's *Harry Lorrequer* (1819, 1820, 1839) clearly show; it > S.E. ca 1860. (In C.17–18 S.E., also a cart or waggon, whence the robbery senses.) 2. In late C.19–20 c., a van. Leach. 3. A chain: C.19 c. 4. A street or a road (—1851): low, mostly Cockney. Mayhew. 5. The robbing of vehicles: c., ca 1780–1830. G. Parker, 1781. Now *van-drag*. Hence *done for a drag*, convicted for such robbery, and *go on the drag*, to embark on, or to practise, such robbery: same period. But, from ca 1850 (ob.), *go on* (or, more gen., *flash*) *the drag*, is for a man to wear women's clothes for immoral purposes (*in drag*, thus dressed): low if not c. 6. A trick or stratagem: C.19–20, ob.; low. 7. Three months' imprisonment: c. (—1851). Henry Mayhew; Charles E. Leach. Now rather *three* MOON. 8. Its hunting senses are j. 9. An obstacle: coll (—1887). Baumann, 'That's where the drag is.' 10. 'Petticoat or skirt used by actors when playing female parts. Derived from the drag of the dress, as distinct from the non-dragginess of the trouser', Ware: theatrical (—1887). Perhaps rather ex *go on the drag* (see sense 5). Also as adj. 11. A harrow: Canadian coll: late C.19–20.

***drag,** v. To rob vehicles: c. of ca 1810–50. See the n., sense 5.

***drag, on the.** See DRAG, n., 5. 2. 'On the off-chance of attracting the attention of a customer': low or c.: from ca 1840. '*No. 747*', *Autobiography of a Gipsy*.

drag, put on the. To go slowly, ease off. *Put the drag on a person*, to apply pressure, esp. to make him ease off or cease. Coll: mid-C.19–20.

***drag-cove.** A carter: C.19, mainly Cockney and orig. c.

***drag-lay.** The practice of robbing vehicles: late C. 18–early 19 c. See also DRAG, n. 5.

drag on, put the, see DRAG, PUT ON THE.

***drag-sneak.** A practised robber of vehicles: c.; late C.18–19. Parker, Mayhew.

drag the pudding. To get the SACK just before Christmas: tailors': from ca 1870; ob.

dragged. Late for duty: military: late C.19–20; ob.

dragged or **dragged out.** Physically exhausted: coll; from ca 1860; ob.

dragged up. (Rare in other tenses.) Ppl adj., educated, nurtured, brought up: from ca 1690. Orig. Society s., B.E. remarking: 'As the Rakes call it'; in C.19–20 coll.

***dragger.** A vehicle thief. c.: late C.18–20. George Parker; Charles E. Leach. Ex DRAG, n., 5.

***dragging.** The practice of robbing vehicles: c.: C.19. See DRAG, V.

dragging-time. 'The evening of a country fair day, when the young fellows begin pulling the wenches about', H., 3rd ed.: provincial coll (—1864).

draggle-tail. 'A nasty dirty Slut,' B.E.: coll: late C.17–mid-19. See (anatomical) TAIL and cf. DAGGLE-TAIL. 2. Hence, a low prostitute: mid-C.19–20; ob.

dragon. A sovereign: ca 1825–90; low. Ex the device. Maginn. 2. A wanton: C.17–19 coll. Fletcher. cf. RIDING ST GEORGE.

dragon, water the. To urinate: low: C.18–20; ob. Perhaps suggested by *dragon-water*, a popular C.17 medicine. cf. NAG ...

dragon (up)on St George, see RIDING ST GEORGE.

dragoon it. To occupy two branches of one profession: coll: mid-C.18–19. Ex Army: orig. a dragoon was a mounted infantryman armed with a carbine.

dragsman. A coachman: coll: from ca 1810; ob. Egan. 2. A vehicle-thief: c., ca 1810–1900. Mayhew. Less gen. than DRAG-SNEAK.

drain. A drink: coll; from ca 1835. Dickens in *Boz*. Hence *do a drain* (cf. WET), to take a drink. Both, ob. 2. Gin: ca 1800–80. Ex its urinative property. 3. The *pudendum muliebre*; low: C.19–20.

drain, down the. Lost; wasted: coll: from ca 1870.

drain-pipe(s). Macaroni: (mostly London) school-children's (—1887).

drainings. A ship's cook: nautical: ca 1830–1910. cf. SLUSHY. cf.:

drains. A ship's cook: nautical: late C.19–20; ob.

***drake;** gen. in passive. To *duck* (a thief) in a pond: c.: ca 1810–50.

dram, dog's, see DOG'S DRAM.

dram-a-tick. A small glass of liquor served on credit: a late C.18–early 19 punning coll suggested by the C.17–18 spelling of *dramatic*. cf. DOME-STICK.

drammer, see DRUMMER.

drap. 'A nasty sluttish whore', Egan's Grose: low: ca 1820–50. A perversion of *drab*.

drapery miss. 'A girl of doubtful character, who dresses in a striking manner': non-aristocratic coll: ca 1870–1915. Ex the S.E. sense explained by Byron in a note to XI, 49, of *Don Juan*. cf. DRESS-LODGER.

drat! A mild expletive; occ. *drat you, him*, etc.; *drat it!*, curse it! Coll: from ca 1815; *dratted*, from ca 1840. Dickens, 'Drat you, be quiet! says the good old man'; Mrs Henry Wood, 'That dratted girl.' Ex *(G)od rot!*: cf. GAD for *God*.

draught on the pump at Aldgate, a, see DRAFT and ALDGATE.

draw. A drawn game: from ca 1870; orig. coll. 2. In cricket, a stroke made with the bat's surface inclined downwards: from ca 1860. 3. An attraction, whether newspaper article or a game, a play or a preacher: from ca 1880; coll. 4. A person, from ca 1810, or a thing, a decade later, employed to DRAW OUT a person. 5. One so 'drawn': from ca 1885.

draw, v.i. To attract public attention: coll; from ca 1870. Hawley Smart, 'He usually kept "his show" running as long as it would draw'; by 1900, virtually S.E. 2. v.t. To elicit information from: coll, 1857, Reade. More gen. DRAW OUT. 3. Flatter, tease, inveigle into vexation; hence, make game of: coll. From ca 1859. Thackeray, 'The wags ... can always, as the phrase is, "draw" her father, by speaking of Prussia.' 4. In low coll, the sense in DOG-DRAWN. 5. In c., to rob, pick the pockets of; steal: C.19–20. Also *draw* (one) *of*, rob him of: ibid.

draw blanks. To fail; be disappointed: coll, C.19–20, ob. In S.E., *draw a blank*. Ex lotteries.

draw-boy. A superior article offered at a very low price: trade: mid-C.19–20, ob.

draw (a person's) **cork.** To cause his nose to bleed: pugilistic (—1823); †by 1900.

draw-fart, occ. preceded by **doctor.** An itinerant quack: low coll: C.19.

draw for. To borrow money from, as in

'She drew him for a dollar': coll; C.19–20, ob.

draw it mild! (Rare in other moods.) Expressive of derision; incredulity; supplication: coll: 1837, Thackeray; *Punch*, 1841; Barham; Martin & Aytoun. ?ex public-houses; cf. Barham's 'A pint of double X, and please to draw it mild.'

***draw-latch.** A thief, esp. from houses: in C.14–15, S.E.; ca 1560–1740, a member of an order of rogues (B.E.); in mid-C.18–early 19, any house-robber. The sense 'loiterer' is S.E.

***draw of,** see DRAW, v., 5.

draw off, v.i. To throw back the body in order to hit the harder: orig. (ca 1860) pugilistic s., cf. the nautical *haul off*. 2. v.t. with variant *draw one's fireworks*, to cool a man's ardour by lying with him: a low, woman's term: C.19–20; ob. cf. COOLER.

draw out. To cause to talk, give an opinion; elicit information: coll; from ca 1775. cf. DRAW, v., 2. Ex *drawing a badger*.

draw plaster. To angle for a man's intentions: tailors'; from ca 1850; ob.

draw straws; or one's eyes draw straws. To feel sleepy: coll in late C.17–early 19, then dial. Swift, in *Polite Conversation*, No. 3. (Esp.) Apperson; but see also STRAWS, DRAW.

draw teeth. To wrench the handles and knockers from street doors: ca 1840–70. Orig. and chiefly medical students'. (Gen. as vbl n. *drawing teeth*.)

draw the bow up to the ear; draw (or **pull**) **the long bow,** see at BOW. **draw the cork,** see CORK. . . .

***draw the King's** or **Queen's picture.** To manufacture counterfeit coins: from ca 1780; c. After ca 1860, perhaps s.

draw the line at tick. (Of a woman) to be virtuous: serio-comics', esp. lady singers' (—1909); ob. Ware, 'A covered allusion to the textile fabric used for the covering of beds and mattresses.'

draw water. To weep: coll: ca 1820–90. Emily Brontë, *Wuthering Heights*, 1847. 2. In the late C.19–20 Navy, it is used, as coll, thus: 'He draws too much water for me' – outranks me.

draw wool or **worsted,** v.t. and i. To irritate; to foment a quarrel: tailors': C.19–20; ob.

drawer-on. An appetizer (not of drink, which has *puller-on*): coll, other senses being S.E.: C.17–20, ob.

***drawers.** (Only in pl.) Stockings, esp. if embroidered: c.: mid-C.16–18. Harman, Head, Grose. The origin? Perhaps it is because one *draws* them on and off.

dread! DRAT! as in 'Dread the fellow!'; Cockney (—1887); ob.

dreadful. A sensational story, article, print: coll; from ca 1884; ob. Earlier and more gen., PENNY DREADFUL. cf. AWFUL and SHOCKER.

dreadful, adj. Very bad, objectionable, etc., etc., etc.: coll: from ca 1860.

dreadfully. Very: coll; from ca 1600. cf.: AWFULLY; BLOODY; TERRIBLY.

dreadnought. A male pessary: low: from 1908. 2. A very high, stiff corset: low: from ca 1909; ob.

dreadnoughts. (Like the preceding, ex the battleship.) Close-fitting (gen. thick) woollen or flannel female drawers: from 1908; low.

dream, wet, see WET DREAM.

dredgerman. A sham dredger-man, actually a thief: (—1857); ob. See esp. Dickens's 'Down with the Tide,' in *Reprinted Pieces*. (Dickens's knowledge of unconventional English is very extensive, almost irreproachable.)

dredgy. A drowned sailor's ghost: nautical: late C.19–20. Because his corpse runs, or had run, the risk of being brought up by a dredge.

dress. At Winchester College, the players who come next in order after *six* or *fifteen*: because they attend matches ready to act as substitutes: from ca 1850.

dress, v., more often **dress down.** To beat, thrash; hence, scold severely: coll; from ca 1660. Mrs Centlivre, 'I'll dress her down, I warrant her.' i.e. to SET TO RIGHTS.

dress a hat. To practise a concerted robbery, from employers and by employees: low (—1864).

dress down, see DRESS, v.

dress for the part. To be hypocritical: theatrical (ca 1870) >, ca 1880, Society coll.

dress-house. A brothel: from ca 1820; ob.

dress in, v.i. To dress ready to play in a game: Winchester: from ca 1850. See DRESS, n.

dress-lodger. A woman lodged, boarded, and (gen. well) dressed by another, whom she pays by prostitution: from ca 1830; ob. Social-reform Kidd, 1836. 'The West End name for prostitutes,' T. Archer, *The Pauper, the Thief, and the Convict*, 1865. cf. DRAPERY MISS.

dress to death (later **to kill**) or **within an**

inch of one's life. To dress ultra-smartly: coll (—1859).

dressed like Christmas beef, see at BEEF...

dressing, gen. **dressing-down.** A thrashing; a severe scolding or reprimand: coll; from late 1760s. Jane Austen, 'I will give him such a dressing.'

dressy. Fond of dress: 1768. 2. Very smartly dressed (—1834). 3. Of clothes, extremely fashionable: 1818. All three – the first appears in Goldsmith – were orig. coll, but a generation later they were S.E.

drift. To go, walk: mostly Public Schoolboys' and Society coll (from ca 1905) now verging on S.E.

***drill.** To entice by degrees: c.: late C.17–mid-18. Ex the patience exercised in drill, or that in using a drill. 2. *Subagitare feminam*: C.18–20.

drill a hole in. To shoot (a person) with a rifle: from ca 1830. The p.ppl passive *drilled*, without complement, occurs in Marryat's *Peter Simple*. Both are coll.

drilling. 'Punishment by way of waiting, applied to needlewomen who make errors in their work,' Ware: workpeople's (—1885); ob.

drink, n. See BIG DRINK and cf. Thornton at *drink*.

drink, v. To supply with drink (water or stronger): coll: from ca 1880.

drink hearty! A coll nautical toast of mid-C.19–20.

drink like a fish, see FISH, DRINK LIKE A.

drink like a funnel. A C.19 variant of the preceding.

drink till one gives up one's halfpenny; only in past tense. (He) drank till he vomited: low: ca 1675–1770.

drinkite. Thirst: 1864, Surtees, *Mr Romford's Hounds*; †by 1900. cf:

drinkitite. Thirst, but *on the drinkitite* is 'on the drink': East London (—1909).

drip. Nonsense: Public Schools': from ca 1890. For semantics, cf. BILGE and S.E. *drivel*. 2. Hence, v.i., to be stupid, to be a terrible bore, to talk nonsense: id.: id.

dripper. A venereal gleet: late C.17–early 19: low coll.

dripping. A cook, esp. a bad one: from ca 1860; ob. cf. SLUSHY.

***driss.** An occ. form of DRIZ.

drive. A blow; a kick: coll; *Sessions*, May 1839. 2. Energy: coll: from ca 1905.

drive French horses. To vomit: mid-C.19–20; ob. Ex the *hue donc!* of French carters.

drive into. (Of the male) coït with: low coll: C.19–20.

drive oneself to the wash. To drive in a basket-chaise: C.19.

drive pigs to market, see PIGS TO MARKET, DRIVE ONE'S.

drive to the last minute. To protract or defer as late as possible: coll; from ca 1880.

driver. One who compels his employees to do more work for the same wages: s. (1851, Mayhew) >, by 1900, coll. 2. A captain notorious for crowding-on all possible sail: nautical coll: mid-C.19–20; ob.

driver's pint. A gallon: late C.19–20 (ob.): military.

***driz.** Lace. Hence *driz* FENCER, a seller of lace; a receiver of stolen lace, hence of other material. c.: from ca 1810. Vaux, Mayhew. Occ. *driss*.

***driz(-)kemesa.** A lace shirt: c. of ca 1830–70. Ainsworth, *Rookwood*, 1834, 'And sported my flashest toggery ... My thimble of ridge, and my driz kemesa.' cf. CAMESA.

droddum. Buttocks; breech: low: from ca 1860.

dromack(k)y. A harlot: North of England s.; ca 1830–1900. Ex (a strolling actress that used to play the part of) Andromache.

***dromedary.** A (bungling) thief; hence, 2, a burglar: resp., late C.17–18 c., C.18 c. or low s. Also in sense 1, *purple dromedary*, late C.17–18 c. In C.19–20 dial. (ob.), as in C.16–17 S.E., a dull or stupid person. Ex the dromedary's ungainliness.

***drommerars, -ers,** see DOMMERAR.

drooper. A drooping moustache: Cockney coll: from ca 1880.

***drop,** or rather **the drop.** Same as DROP-GAME. Vaux, 1812.

drop, v. To part with; give: from ca 1670; low. 2. Hence (1849), to lose, esp. money. 3. v.i., to understand: low (—1909). Abbr. DROP TO.

drop, give one the. To give him the slip: coll; C.18. Mrs Centlivre.

drop, the new or, in C.19, **last.** 'A contrivance for executing felons at Newgate, by means of a platform, which drops from under them,' Grose, 2nd ed.: ca 1780–1900; coll.

drop a brick, see BRICK, DROP A.

***drop a cog.** To practise the DROP-GAME: late C.17–early 19 c. See esp. Borrow's *Romano Lavo-Lil* (at *ring-dropping*).

drop a turd or **one's wax.** To defecate: low coll: C.18–20; C.19–20 (ob.).

drop anchor. To pull up a horse: the turf: from ca 1860; ob. 2. Also, but gen. with *one's*, to sit down; settle down: orig. nautical; C.19–20 coll.

drop (one's) **anchor in the Levant.** To abscond: ca 1815–60. David Carey, *Life in Paris*, 1822. A pun on synonymous S.E. *Levant*.

***drop-cove.** A specialist, C.19–20 c., in the DROP-GAME.

drop-dry. Water-tight: nautical coll (—1887).

***drop down to,** see DOWN TO, DROP.

***drop-game.** The letting fall a coin, pocket-book, etc., in order to cheat the innocent person picking it up; the piece so dropped is a *cog*. C.19–20 (ob.) c. The gen. mid-C.19–20 term is RING-DROPPING or FAWNEY RIG.

drop in one's or **the eye, have a.** To be slightly tipsy: from ca 1690; coll. Swift, 'You must own you had a drop in the eye, for ... you were half-seas over.' cf. dial. *drop in the head*.

drop – or **hang, slip,** or **walk** – **into.** To attack; later, to criticize adversely. From ca 1850; coll. The first, the most gen., prob. began in pugilism, where it means to thrash; the second is rare and †; the third is almost confined to physical aggression (including that of coïtion) and was orig. nautical; the fourth is common.

drop it! Stop! Esp., stop talking or fooling. Coll: *Sessions*, May 1847.

drop of good. A glass – or even a bottle – of liquor: mostly workmen's: late C.19–20.

drop of wet and warm, a. (A cup of) weak tea: lower-middle class domestic coll: ?since ca 1880.

drop off is coll for *drop off to sleep*: late C.19–20.

drop off the hooks. To die: coll (—1857); ?orig. nautical.

drop on. To call on, or 2, to scold or accuse, a person without warning; 3, to thrash (cf. *drop into*): the first, coll; the second, low; the third, pugilistic. All from ca 1850. ?cf. the U.S. *get the drop on*; certainly cf.:

drop on, have the. 'To forestall, gain advantage over', orig. and esp. 'by covering with a revolver': (U.S. and) Australian (—1894). Morris: cf. *get the drop on* in Thornton.

drop on to or, loosely, **onto.** A variant – prob. the imm. origin of – *drop on*. 'Ducange Anglicus', 1857.

drop one's flag. To salute; hence, fig. to lower one's colours, to submit: coll (orig. nautical); from ca 1840.

drop one's leaf. To die: coll; from ca 1820. Ex the autumnal fall of leaves. cf. HOP THE TWIG.

drop one's peak. Same as DROP ONE'S FLAG. Glascock, *Sailors and Saints*, 1829.

drop one's wax. To defecate: low: mid-C. 19–20.

drop short. To die: coll: from ca 1820. ?ex *drop short in one's tracks*, or is this latter, as I suspect, much more recent?

drop the cue. To die: billiard-players' (—1909). cf. DROP OFF THE HOOKS.

***drop the main toby.** To leave the high-road; turn off the main road: mostly vagrants': mid-C.19–20. See TOBY, n., 3.

drop the scabs in. To work button-holes: tailors': from ca 1850; ob.

drop to. To come to understand a plot or plan, a man or his (bad) character: late C.19–20: s. Ex *drop* DOWN TO. cf. TUMBLE TO, 2.

drop your tailboard. A CAMP c.p. of late C.19–20.

dropped. Born: Australian rural coll: mid-C.19–20. Ex calving and lambing.

dropped on. Disappointed: tailors': C.19–20; ob.

***dropper.** A specialist in the DROP-GAME: late C.17–19 c. 2. In late C.17–18 c., also a distiller: B.E. at RUM DROPPER.

dropping. A beating, thrashing, pugilistic or other: Royal Military Academy, ca 1850–80.

dropping member. The *membrum virile*, esp. if gonorrhoea'd: C.19 low.

dropping the anchor. Holding back a horse or merely not flogging it: turf: mid-C.19–20.

droppings. Porter; beer: low: ca 1820–70. *Sinks*, 1848. Ex colour.

drops, fond of one's. Addicted to liquor: Cockney coll (—1887). Ex *fond of a drop*, which is familiar S.E.

drouthy. Hesitant, wavering: Scottish (—1884).

drown the miller, see MILLER, DROWN THE.

drozel. A girl: s.: Ned Ward, 1714.

drudge. A cabin boy: nautical coll: late C.19–20.

drugs. Pharmacology: medical coll: late C.19–20. *Slang*, p. 192.

druid. A priest: Anglo-Irish: late C.19–20.

***drum.** In c., a road, highway, street: from ca 1840. Ex Romany *drom* (itself ex Gr.

δρόμος), a road. 2. A building, house, lodging, or (in C.20) a flat: c. and low (—1859). Charles E. Leach. 3. Hence, a cell: c.: late C.19–20. 4. (Ex FLASH *drum*) a brothel: low: from ca 1900. 5. Among tailors, a small workshop: from ca 1870. 6. In Australia, from ca 1860, a bundle of clothes carried on tramp: ob. by 1897, †by 1910. Hence, HUMP *one's drum*, to go on tramp: likewise †. Wm Stamer, *Recollections of a Life of Adventure*, 1866. cf. BLUEY and SWAG. 7. The ear: pugilistic: ca 1860–1900. Abbr. *drum of the ear*. 8. A tin for making tea, etc.: tramps' c.: from ca 1890. 9. A crowded social gathering: coll: late C.18. See quotation at SQUEEZE, n., 6.

drum, v. To obtain, esp. custom(ers), by solicitation: from ca 1840; coll. cf. U.S. *drummer*, a COMMERCIAL (2).

drum, empty as an old. Extremely hungry: (mainly Cockney) coll (—1885); slightly ob.

drum and fife. Wife: military rhyming s.: late C.19–20.

***drum up.** To make tea, esp. by the roadside: tramps' c. (—1864). Ex Romany *drom*, the highway.

drumbelo. A late C.17–early 19 coll variant of S.E. *drumble*, a dull, heavy fellow.

drummer. A horse with irregular fore-leg action: the turf: late C.18–19. Ex the flourishes of a kettle-drummer. 2. A rabbit: late C.19–20, ob. 3. In c., a thief that, before robbing, drugs his victim: from ca 1855; ob. 4. A trousers-maker: tailors': from ca 1860.

Drummond. An infallible scheme, certain event: low: ca 1810–50. Ex the banking-house of Drummond & Co.

drummy. A sergeant-drummer: military: ca 1870–1905.

Drum's entertainment, see JACK DRUM'S . . .

drums, pair of. Trousers: tailors': from ca 1860.

drumstick. The *membrum virile*: C.19–20 low; ob. 2. In Madras Presidency, a pod of the horse-radish tree: coll (—1885). 3. See DRUMSTICKS.

drumstick-cases. Trousers: low: C.19. Ex:

drumsticks. The legs: s. >, by 1840, coll: Foote, 1770, 'What, d'ye think I would change with Bill Spindle for one of his drumsticks?' Orig. of a fowl's leg.

drunk. A debauch: coll: from ca 1860. 2. A tipsy person: coll: from ca 1880. 3. A charge of being drunk (and disorderly): from 1883. (The various *drunk*(*en*) similes – Grose (3rd ed.), e.g., has *drunk as a wheelbarrow* – are recorded *passim*: see the key-nn. For a short synonymy, see F. & H. at *drunk*, and Apperson.)

drunk, on the, adj. Drinking continually for days: low coll: from ca 1870.

drunk as a besom. Exceedingly drunk: coll: ca 1830–90. 'Cuthbert Bede' in *Verdant Green*, 1853. cf. MOPS AND BROOMS.

drunk as a rolling fart. Very drunk: low coll: from ca 1860. Richards, 'In my old days it was a common sight by stop-tap to see every man in the Canteeen as drunk as rolling f**ts.'

drunk as Chloe (loosely **Cloe**). Exceedingly drunk: from ca 1815. Moore, 1819, has *like Cloe*, vigorously: a s. phrase †by 1890. It owes much of its Australian popularity to the painting mentioned at DO A CHLOE.

drunk to see a hole in a ladder, too, see HOLE IN A LADDER. **drunk with a continuando,** see CONTINUANDO.

drunkard, be quite the gay. To be somewhat tipsy: coll: ca 1870–1900.

drunkard, come the. To pretend tipsiness; rarely, to be tipsy (†): coll; from ca 1860.

drunken-chalks. Good conduct badges: military: ca 1870–1910. cf. CANTEEN MEDAL.

drunken sailor. A leaning type of chimney cowl, used to cure a smoking chimney: late C.19–20.

Drury Lane ague. A venereal disease: mid-C.18–early 19. cf. COVENT GARDEN AGUE, and cf.:

Drury Lane vestal. A harlot: mid-C.18–early 19. Grose, 1st ed. In the C.18, though little after ca 1760, this district was residentially infamous. cf. COVENT GARDEN NUN and *C.G. vestal*.

Drury-Laner, feel like a. To be indisposed: late C.19–20. Perhaps, orig., ill from dissipation.

dry as . . . See the key-nn.; Apperson has all – or most – of the phrases.

dry-bang, -baste, -beat, -rub. To beat severely: (*pace* O.E.D.) coll; C.17–18.

dry-bob. A cricketer, at Eton College: see BOB. 2. A smart repartee: C.17–18 coll. 3. Coïtion without (male) emission: mid-C.18–19 low.

dry boots. A dry humorist; late C.17–early 19 coll. cf. SLY BOOTS.

dry ducking. A man's suspension by a

rope to just above the water: nautical coll: mid-C.19–20.

dry fist. A niggard: C.17–18 coll. adj., *dry-fisted.*

dry flogging. Corporal punishment with the clothes on: nautical (esp. naval) coll: mid-C.19–20. cf. DRY DUCKING.

dry guillotine, the. Severe imprisonment esp. imprisonment at Cayenne, most malarious: journalistic coll: ca 1860–80.

dry hash. A BAD EGG, esp. one who will not SHOUT drinks; ne'er-do-well; LOAFER: Australia, ca 1870–95. 2. A baked pudding made of corned beef, tinned salmon, or anything else that comes in handy: mid-C.19–20: nautical coll.

dry holy-stoning. A flogging: nautical: ca 1800–70. *Boxiana*, II, 1818. Ex S.E. *holy-stones* (with which one cleans the deck).

dry land! You understand! Rhyming s. (—1859); ob. 2. For *dryland sailor*, see TURNPIKE-SAILOR.

dry lodging. Accommodation without board: lodging-house keepers', from ca 1870. cf. S.E. *dry*, without strong liquor; but imm. ex Scots *dry lodgings* (Galt, 1823).

dry nurse. A junior who, esp. in the Army and Navy, instructs an ignorant superior in his duties: coll: mid-C.19–20; ob. Ex the S.E. sense.

***dry room.** A prison: c.: C.19–20, ob.

dry-rot, see ROT, n. **dry-rub,** see DRY-BANG.

dry-shave. To annoy (a person) by vigorously rubbing his chin with one's fingers: lower classes' coll: from ca 1860.

dry smoke. A South African coll as in Parker Gilmore, *Days and Nights in the Desert*, 1888, 'In his mouth was stuck a short pipe, out of which he was taking, in colonial parlance, *a dry smoke* – that is, it was alike destitute of fire or tobacco.'

dry straight. To turn out all right (in the end): coll: from mid-1890s; ob.

dry-up. A failure (cf. esp. FROST): theatrical: mid-C.19–20.

dry up, v. Cease talking, notably in the imperative: from ca 1864. Ex U.S. (—1855). Rider Haggard, 1888, 'He ... suddenly dried up as he noticed the ominous expression on the great man's brow.' Ex 'the figure of the "babbling" fountain', W. 2. In c. of ca 1850–1910, to decamp, take to one's heels. 3. To slacken pace through exhaustion: turf: from ca 1870. Ex sense 1. 4. To cease work at lunch-time or at night; hence, leave a situation: printers': from ca 1870. Ex sense 1.

dry-walk, gen. **-walking.** A moneyless soldier's outing: military: ca 1860–1914. (*Dry*, liquorless, is a U.S. import.)

ds, on the two. On twopence a day: military: ca 1870–1910. Ex D, pence.

***dub.** A key, esp. a master or skeleton key: c.: late C.17–mid-19. Ex the v.

***dub,** v. To open: mid-C.16–18; (by confusion with DUP), to close, gen. in form *dub up*: early C.19 c. Prob. ex Walloon *adouber*, to strike, tap.

***dub, strike upon the.** To rob (a house): c.: late C.17–early 19. See DUB, n., 1.

***dub at a knapping jigger.** A turnpike keeper: (?late C.18-) early C.19 c. JIGGER, door or gate.

***dub-cove.** A turnkey, gaoler, as is DUBSMAN, occ. abbr. DUBS: c. of (?late C.18–) C.19. Vaux; the last in Henley.

***dub lay.** The robbing of houses by picking the locks: late C.18–early 19 c. B.E. has '*We'll strike it upon the dub, ...* we will rob that place.'

dub o' the lick. 'A lick on the head', Grose, 2nd ed.: late C.18–mid-19: low coll.

dub up. To FORK OUT; pay: s. (—1823), now verging on coll. Developed from DUB, v. 2. See DUB, V.

dubash. An interpreter; a commissionaire: Anglo-Indian; from late C.17. The former sense was †by 1902; the prevailing C.20 one being a European's native servant. Ex Hindi *dobashi*, a 'two-language man'.

dubber. The mouth; tongue: C.18–19 c., as, in late C.17–19, is the sense, 2, a picklock thief. 3. In Anglo-Indian coll, more properly *dubba*, a leather bottle or skin bag: from late C.17.

***dubbs,** see DUBS, 2.

dubby. Blunt; dumpy: dial. (—1825) >, by 1870, coll.

duberous (1818); **dubersome** (1837). In doubt; dubious: (low) coll and dial.

Dublin dissector. A cudgel: medical students', ca 1840–1900. *Punch*, 1841.

Dublin packet, take the. To run round the corner: (—1859) coll; ob. Punning *doubling.*

***Dublin packet, tip** (a person) **the.** To elude openly; give the slip quietly: c. (—1812) >, ca 1840, low, †by 1900.

Dublin tricks. (Rare in singular.) Bricks: rhyming s.: since ca 1860.

***dubs.** A jailer: c. (—1789); ob. Abbr. DUBSMAN. 2. (Also **dubbs.**) Money, esp. if of copper: c. (—1823); †by 1870. Ex *dub*, a fraction of a rupee.

dubs, adj. Double: Winchester College; from ca 1830; ob.

***dubsman.** A turnkey, see DUB-COVE.

***ducat,** see DUCKET.

ducats. Money, cash: theatrical (—1853), ob. Earlier, gen. coll: 1775. Prob. ex Shakespeare's Shylock. cf. the use of *shekels*.

***duce** (i.e. DEUCE) is twopence: c.: late C.17–18. Moncrieff.

duchess. A woman of an imposing presence: from ca 1690. Contrast DUTCH. 2. 'A woman enjoyed with her pattens on, or by a man in boots, is said to be made a duchess,' Grose, 1st ed.; †by 1890.

duchess, the. The mother or the wife (*the old duchess*) of the person addressed: proletarian: late C.19–20: cf. DUCHESS OF FIFE; DUTCH. 2. A living lay-figure: silk trade: from ca 1870. 3. See DUCHESS OF TECK.

Duchess of Fife. Wife: rhyming s.: mid-C.19–20; but by 1880, 'invariably reduced to *Dutch* ("my old Dutch"). It served as inspiration for Albert Chevalier's song of that title' – *My Old Dutch* – 'and is by that immortalized': Franklyn. See also DUTCH.

Duchess of Teck. A cheque: rhyming s.: late C.19–20. Often shortened to *duchess*.

duchessy, adj. Like a duchess (—1887); abounding in duchesses (—1870): coll.

duck. A decoy; C.19 coll. Abbr. *decoy-duck*. 2. A bundle of meat-scraps: low coll (—1864). cf. FAGGOT. 3. A coll endearment: from ca 1590. Shakespeare. Hence, in admiration, as is the adj. DUCKY. Leman Rede, 1841, 'Oh, isn't he a duck of a fellow?' 4. A soldier (gen. in pl) of the Bombay Presidency: Anglo-Indian: from ca 1800. Later, any official in the Bombay service. Ex BOMBAY DUCK. 5. A metal-cased watch: cheapjacks': ca 1850–1914. Hindley. 6. The face, as in *make a duck*, make a grimace: Winchester College: ca 1860–1920. In cricket, however, *make a duck*, or *duck's egg*, is to score nothing, while *save* (—1877) or *break* (—1900) *one's duck*, is to score at least one run: *duck* occurs in 1868, *duck's egg* in 1863, and *duck-egg* in 1868. 7. cf. the Anglo-Irish *duck* (*for dinner*), nothing to eat: late C.19–20. 8. Abbr. LAME DUCK: from ca 1780.

***duck, do a.** In c., to hide under the seat of a public conveyance so as to avoid paying (—1889); but in gen. coll, to depart hurriedly (—1900).

duck, make a, see DUCK, 6.

duck, fake the, see FAKE THE DUCK.

duck-egg, see DUCK, 6.

duck-footed, adj. Walking with toes turned inwards: coll: C.19–20; ob. But *duck-legged*, with very short legs, is S.E.

duck-fucker. The man looking after the poultry on a warship: mid-C.18–early 19; nautical.

duck in a thunderstorm, see DYING DUCK . . .

duck it. To 'waddle out as a lame duck', George Godfrey, *History of George Godfrey*, 1828: Stock Exchange: ca 1815–70.

duck of diamonds. A superlative of the admiring DUCK, 3: coll; from ca 1850; ob.

duck-pond. A canvas bathing-place for cadets: naval (—1909); ob.

duck-pot is a late C.19–20 variant of DUCK, n., 3.

duck-shover, -shoving. A cabman who is guilty of breaking the rank and thus unfairly touting for custom; this extremely reprehensible practice; Melbourne: ca 1869–95. 2. (*d.-shoving.*) Hence (?), an evasion of duty: military: late C.19–20.

ducket. Any ticket; esp. a raffle-card or a pawnbroker's duplicate: c. and low (—1874); ob. A corruption of *docket*. Also DUCAT.

duckey, duckie, see DUCKY.

ducking, go. To go courting: low coll: from ca 1850; ob. Ex DUCK, 3.

ducking-money. Money exacted from a sailor the first time he went through the Strait of Gibraltar: naval coll: C.19.

ducks, fine weather for, see FINE WEATHER . . .

ducks and drakes with, later of. To squander money or potential money: from late C.16; coll till C.19, then S.E. Chapman, 'Be like a gentleman . . . make ducks and drakes with shillings.'

duck's bill. 'A tongue cut in a piece of stout paper and pasted on at the bottom of the tympan sheet', F. & H.: printers'; from ca 1860; ob. Ex shape.

duck's egg. See DUCK, 6; *break one's duck's egg* occurs in 1867 (Lewis).

ducky; duckie, adj. Expressive of admiration (see DUCK, 3): coll; from ca 1830. 2. n., an endearment, thus a variant of DUCK, 3: from ca 1815; coll. The former solely, the latter mainly, a woman's term.

dud. A delicate weakling (†); person without ability and/or spirit: orig. Scottish (—1825), Jamieson speaking of 'a soft dud'; (?) used in U.S. in 1870; rare by 1896. The adj. dates from mid-1890s in the nuance 'worthless': *Sessions*, Feb. 1898, 'I have it, it is a *dud* lot' (watch and chain). These terms have prob. been influenced by the C.17–20 dial. *dudman*, a scarecrow, but the word may derive ultimately ex Dutch *dood*, dead. 2. See DUDS.

***dud(d)-cheats.** Clothes and household effects: c. (—1725); †by 1830. cf. DUDS, 1, 2.

***dudder** or **whispering dudder, dudsman** (q.v.), and **duffer** (q.v.). A pedlar of supposedly smuggled wares: late C.18–early 19; the first two being c., the third also c. but only at first. Ex DUDS.

duddering rake. 'A thundering Rake ... one devilishly lewd', *A New Canting Dict.*, 1725: C.18–early 19. See DUNDERING RAKE.

duddery. A clothier's booth: C.17–early 19 low coll. cf. the dial. senses, and:

dude. A SWELL, fop: orig. (1883), U.S. and almost imm. anglicized; coll till ca 1918, when it > S.E. Where the etymology is a mystery, but the occasion known to be the Aesthetic craze of ca 1882–7, it is perhaps permissible to guess at DUD influenced by *attitude*, the semantic transition being aided, maybe, by the dial. v.i. *dud*, to dress.

duds. Clothes: mid-C.16–17 c. (Harman, Head); in C.18–20, low (Grose, Trollope). Ex C.15 *dudde*, cloth, a cloak; cf. DUDDERY. 2. In C.16–20 coll, occ. rags or old clothes. 3. The sense 'portable property' is, orig. in mid-C.17–18, English c., but in C.19–20 it is mainly U.S. standard. 4. Female knickers: late C.19–20.

***duds, sweat.** To pawn clothes: C.19–20 c.

***dudsman.** A seller of so-called contraband clothes: c.; (?late C.18–)early C.19. cf. DUDDER.

***dues, the.** Money: orig. (—1812) c.; by 1860, coll; by 1890 ob.

duey. Twopence: circus s. via Parlary: mid-C.19–20. cf. DUCE.

duff. No good; inferior: Glasgow: late C.19–20. cf.:

***duff**, gen. preceded by **the.** The selling of actually or supposedly smuggled goods: late C.18–early 19 c. 2. Food: nautical coll: late C.19–20. Ex the specific S.E. sense.

***duff,** v. To sell inferior goods, esp. clothes, pretending they are stolen or smuggled: orig. (—1781) c.; by 1860, low. 2. Hence, to make old clothes appear new by manipulating the nap: coll; from ca 1835. 3. To alter the brands of stolen horses or, esp., cattle (—1869); hence, to steal cattle by changing the brands: Australian s. > coll; ob. Carton Booth in *Another England*, 1869; Boldrewood, *The Squatter's Dream*, 1890. 4. v.i. and t. To be a duffer (no good); to be a duffer at: ca 1880–1915. Ex DUFFER, 4.

***duff, man at the.** A seller of certain goods (see DUFF, n., 1): C.19 c. cf. DUFFER, 1.

duff days. Thursday and Sunday, when that pudding appeared at the gun-room's dinner: naval coll: C.19. cf.:

duff night. Guest night on a warship: naval officers': late C.19–20. cf. preceding.

duff out of. To cheat or rob (a person) of: from ca 1860; ob. cf. DUFF, v., 1, 3.

***duffer.** A seller of pretended stolen or smuggled goods: mid-C.18–19; orig. c.; by 1860 low and slightly ob. Also a maker of sham jewellery, ca 1820–90; Colquhoun, 1796, in *Police of the Metropolis*, 'A class of sharpers ... duffers'; Dickens; Thackeray. 2. A pedlar; a hawker, esp. of women's clothes: low coll: from late C.18; ob. 3. A 'renovator' of inferior goods, esp. clothes: low coll; from ca 1850. 4. A worthless object, esp. counterfeit jewellery and coin: low s. (—1840); ob. Also, a person of no ability (—1842), a dolt (from ca 1870): both coll. 5. A female smuggler: C.19 nautical. 6. ca 1820–50, a professional cheater of pawnbrokers: low if not c. 7. In Australia, a cattle-stealer (or illicit brander): s. > coll; from ca 1870, though unrecorded before 1889. 8. An unproductive mine-claim: Australian coll (—1861). H. Finch-Hatton, *Advance Australia*, 1885. cf. SHICER.

duffer- or **duffing-fare.** A person driving in a cab to oblige the driver: London cabmen's: ca 1900–10.

duffer out. (Of a mine) to become unproductive: Australia (—1885); coll > j. by 1910.

duffing. The practice of selling worthless goods as valuable: low > coll; from ca 1850. See DUFF, n. and v., and DUFFER, 1, 2. 2. In Australia, thieving of cattle (gen. preceded by *cattle-*): s. (—1881) > coll by 1900.

duffing, ppl adj. Inferior or counterfeit but offered as superior or genuine (—1851); of a person selling such goods (—1862). 2. Dull, stupid; foolish: from ca 1880; rare in C.20.

duffing-fare, see DUFFER-FARE.

duffman. Sick: rhyming s.: late C.19–20. In full: *Duffman Dick*.

Duffo. A Devonport bluejacket or ship: naval: late C.19–20. By 'telescoping'.

duffy. A ghost or spirit: West Indies, chiefly among the Negroes (—1864). ?ex DAVY JONES. 2. A quartern of gin: London: ca 1800–50. cf. *duffy bottle*, a bottle of gin. *The Port Folio*, 16 May 1807.

dufter. An orderly room: military (Regular Army): late C.19–20. Ex Hindustani *daftar*, an office.

dugs, of a woman's breasts or nipples, has, since ca 1880, been a vulg., though it is permissible in S.E. if used as a strong pejorative.

***duke.** A handsome man, esp. if of showy appearance: gen. as *rum duke* (B.E.): late C.17–early 18 c. 2. Hence (see RUM), 'A queer unaccountable fellow', Grose, 1st ed.: c.: late C.18–early 19; often as *rum duke*. 3. Gin: ca 1850–80; a below-stairs term. 4. A horse: cabmen's; ca 1860–1910. 5. In c. also, a burglary, a robbery: from ca 1840; ob. The first and second are derivable from the idea of aristocracy; the third is etymologically problematic; the fifth comes prob. ex Romany (cf. DOOKIN). 6. See DOOK, 2 and 3, and DUKES. 7. A navvies' nickname for a man with a large nose (ca 1850–1910). In compliment to the Duke of Wellington. cf. DUKER.

Duke Humphrey, see DINE WITH DUKE HUMPHREY.

Duke of Fife. A knife: rhyming s.: late C.19–20.

duke of limbs. An ungainly fellow, esp. if tall: coll: mid-C.18–mid-19.

duke o(f) Seven Dials. 'Satirical peerage bestowed upon any male party dressed or behaving above or beyond his immediate surroundings': proletarian London: ca 1875–1900. Seven Dials was a very poor quarter.

Duke of Teck. A cheque: rhyming s., mostly theatrical: late C.19–20. cf. DUCHESS OF TECK.

Duke of York. To talk: to walk, or a walk: rhyming s. (—1859 the latter, —1873 the former). 2. A storm trysail: nautical: from ca 1880. 3. A cork: rhyming s.: from ca 1890.

Duke of Yorks. Forks: rhyming s. (—1874); ob. 2. Hence, fingers; hence hands; hence DUKES.

duker. The proprietor of a large nose: streets': ca 1840–70. Ware. See DOOK, 3. 2. A lighter of a special type operating in the Mersey and Manchester Ship Canal: nautical: late C.19–20. Bowen. Why?

dukes, often, esp. in C.20, pronounced *dooks*. Hands; fists: low (—1874). Ex DUKE OF YORKS, 2. For such abridgements and similar ingenuity, see *Slang* at 'Oddities' and *Words!* at 'Rhyming Slang'.

dukes, grease the, v.i. To practise bribery; but the v.t. with *of* is much more gen.: low (—1877). Horsley, *Jottings from Jail*.

dukes, put up the. To prepare for fisticuffs: orig. low s.; in C.20, low coll. From ca 1880.

dukey, see DOOKIE.

dukkering, see DOOKIN

dulcamara. A quack doctor: cultured coll: ca 1845–1910. Ex a character in *L'Elisir d'amore*, by Donizetti, who adopts the medieval L. name for the herb gen. called bittersweet.

dull in the eye. Tipsy: coll: from ca 1840; ob.

dull-pickle. A heavy, dull, stupid fellow: late C.17–18 coll.

Dull Street, live in. i.e. in a dull quarter: coll (—1887) verging on S.E. cf. QUEER STREET.

dull-swift. A stupid fellow; a sluggish messenger: coll: mid-C.18–early 19.

dully. A dull person: coll: 1883 (O.E.D.). cf. STUPID, n.

***dum tam.** A bunch of clothes carried on his back, but under his coat, by a beggar: North Scottish c.: C.19. E.D.D., 'This seems to be a cant phrase denoting that although this is carried as beggars carry their children, it is mute.'

dumb arm. A maimed one: coll: late C.18–early 19.

dumb-cow. To brow-beat or cow: Anglo-Indian coll (—1886). Prob. ex Hindustani *dhamkana*, to chide or threaten, via the process of Hobson-Jobson.

dumb-fogged, -foozled, ppl adj. Confused, puzzled, confounded: coll; from ca 1860; ob.

dumb glutton. The *pudendum muliebre*: mid-C.18–19 low as is the synonymous *dumb squint*, C.19. Hence *feed the dumb glutton*, mid-C.18–19, or *the dummy*, C.19–20 (ob.), to have sexual intercourse.

dumb peal. A muffled peal of bells: coll (—1901).

dumb scraping. Scraping wet decks with blunt scrapers: nautical coll: late C.19–20. Bowen.

***dumb sparkler.** A silent match: c.: mid-C.19–20.

dumb watch. 'A venereal bubo in the

groin', Grose, 1st ed.: mid-C.18–early 19: low.

dumbfound. To perplex; put to confusion; silence: from ca 1650; coll until ca 1800, then S.E. 2. Also, to beat soundly, thrash: ca 1660–1820, as in B.E.'s 'I dumbfounded the sawcy Rascal.' After *confound.*

dumby. A variant, prob. the original, of DUMMY, 1. *Boxiana*, II, 1818.

dummacker. A knowing person; an astute one: ca 1850–1910. ?ironically ex dial. *dummock*, a blockhead.

***dummee.** A variant of DUMMY, 3.

***dummerer,** see DOMMERAR.

dummie. Bee's spelling of DUMMY, n., 3.

dummock. The posteriors: low: C.19–20; ob. Perhaps ex Romany *dumo*, the back (Sampson), + *ock* as in *buttock.*

dummy. A deaf-mute: coll; from late C.16. Ex *dumb.* 2. A person notably deficient in ability or brightness: coll; from ca 1795. 3. In c., a pocket-book: from ca 1810. 4. A dumb-waiter: from ca 1850. 5. An actor or actress who does not speak, a SUPER: theatrical; ca 1870–1920. 6. A makeshift, substitute, or rudimentary bill: Parliamentary s.; from ca 1860. 7. In Australia, the grip-car of a Melbourne tram: coll: ca 1893–1905. Ex *Dummy*, the Northumberland dial. nickname for a colliery carriage: 1843 (E.D.D.). 8. A loaf of bread: c. (—1909). Ware, 'Probably from the softness of the crumb'; cf. sense 2. 9. See DUMB GLUTTON.

dummy, v. To take up (land), nominally for oneself, really for another: Australian: since ca 1860. 'Tom Collins', *Such Is Life*, 1903, 'Bob and Bat dummied for ole McGregor.'

dummy, chuck a; chuck the dummy. See the two relevant entries at CHUCK.

***dummy(-daddle) dodge.** Pocket-picking under cover of a sham or 'dummy' hand or DADDLE: c. of ca 1850–1900.

***dummy-hunter.** A pick-pocket specializing in DUMMIES (3), pocket books: c.: ca 1810–1910.

dump. A small coin or sum of money: Australian coll and s. resp.; 1827, ca 1840. Both ob. by 1895, †by 1910. Ex a small coin, worth 6p, called in as early as 1823. 2. A button: c. (—1859). App. only in DUMB-FENCER. Ex sense 1.

dump, v. To throw or set down heavily; let fall heavily: ex U.S. (—1830), anglicized ca 1870 as a coll that, ca 1900, > S.E. cf. the M.E. *domp*, to fall heavily – whence *dump* perhaps on THUMP.

dump, not to care a. To care little or not at all: coll; from ca 1800. Ex a metal counter.

dump-fencer. A button-seller: ca 1855–1910: low, perhaps c. For FENCER = seller, cf. DRIZ-*fencer*. See DUMP, n., 2.

dumplin(g). A short, thick-set man or woman: from ca 1610: until ca 1800, coll then S.E.; now ob. cf. NORFOLK DUMPLING, an inhabitant of Norfolk, ex the prevalence of apple and, esp. plain, suet dumplings.

dumpling-depot. The stomach: C.19–20; ob.

dumplin(g) on, have a. To be pregnant: proletarian (—1909); ob.

dumplings. Breasts: low s.: ca 1700–25.

dumpling-shop. The human paps: lower classes': C.19–20; ob.

dumps, the. A fit of melancholy; depression: C.16–20; S.E. until ca 1660, then coll, esp. when preceded by *in. Spectator*, No. 176 (1711), 'when I come home she is in the dumps.' 2. Money: from ca 1835; ob. Barham speaks of suicide 'for want of the dumps'. Ex DUMP, n., 1.

dun. A creditor importunately asking for what is his: from ca 1628; orig. coll; in C.19–20, S.E. Wycherley, 'insatiable ... duns'. Possibly ex a stock name of the *John Doe*, TOMMY (4) *Atkins* type, as W.'s analogy from the Paston Letters seems to show.

dun, v. To persist in trying to get what is due to one: from ca 1626; in C.19–20, S.E.; before, coll. Killigrew, 'We shall be revenged upon the rogue for dunning a gentleman in a tavern.' Prob., despite recorded dates, ex the n.

dun, adj., see SCRUFF, n.

dun is the mouse, gen. dun's the mouse. A c.p. quibble made when *done* is mentioned, a mouse being *dun*-coloured; when spoken urgently it connoted 'keep still!' ca 1580–1640. A later C.17 form is *dun as a mouse*, which, implying no warning, prob. arises from the confusion of *'s* = *is* or *as* (or, though not here, *has*).

dun territory. 'Circle of creditory to be had', Egan's Grose: Oxford University: ca 1820–40.

***dunagan.** An early C.19 variant of DUNNAKEN.

***dunaker.** A stealer of cattle, esp. of cows: late C.17–early 19 c. Variants, *dunnocker*, *donnaker*. Ex DUNNOCK.

Dunbar wether. A red herring: Scottish: C.19–20; ob. cf. YARMOUTH CAPON.

duncarring. Homosexuality: late C.17–early 18. Prob. ex a person's name.

dundering rake. This (B.E., ca 1690) is almost certainly the correct spelling of Grose's DUDDERING RAKE. *Dunder* is a variant of the mainly Scottish *dunner*, to thunder.

dundrearies. A pair of whiskers that, cut sideways from the chin, are grown as long as possible: from Sothern's make-up in *Our American Cousin* (see the next entry); the fashion was antiquated by 1882, dead by 1892. This coll term (1858) survives. cf. PICCADILLY WEEPERS.

dundreary. A stammering, silly, long-whiskered dandy: coll; from 1858, the year of Tom Taylor's once famous comedy, *Our American Cousin*, in which Lord Dundreary appears; hence, from ca 1860, a foppish fool. The former †, the latter ob.

***dunegan.** An early C.19 variant of DUNNAKEN.

dung. A workman at less than union wages: C.19; in C.20, merely historical. 2. Mid-C.19–20, also a SCAB (2). 3. ca 1760–1840, a journeyman tailor satisfied with regulation wages. *Sessions*, 17–20 April (trial of Wm Milbourn *et al.*), 1765. Blood, a journeyman tailor, says, 'They that were agreeable to our rules we called *Flints* and those that were not were called *Dungs*.'

dung it. To be a traitor to the trade: tailors': mid-C.19–20.

dung-cart or **-fork.** A yokel; a country bumpkin: coll: C.19–20; ob.

dung-drogher. A guano ship: nautical coll: late C.19–20.

dungaree, adj. Low, coarse, vulgar: Anglo-Indian: from ca 1830; ob. Ex the coarse blue cloth and the name of a disreputable Bombay suburb.

dungaree-settler. A poor settler in or of Australia: Australian coll: ca 1840–70. Anon., *Settlers and Convicts*, 1852. Ex clothing himself, wife and family in clothes made of dungaree.

dunghill, die. To die contrite or cowardly; esp. to repent at the gallows: coll; ca 1755–1830.

dunk. To dip: Cockney-ex-Yiddish ex German *tunken*: mid-C.19–20.

dunnage. Clothes; baggage: nautical: from ca 1850. Mayhew. cf. DUDS. Ex the S.E. sense, matting or brushwood used in packing cargo.

dunnage-bag. A kit-bag: naval: late C.19–20.

***dunnaken** or **-kin; dunneken** or **-kin; dunnyken** or **-kin; dunagan, -egan.** A privy: late C.19–20; c. >, by 1860, low coll. In C.17–18, *dannaken*: orig. c., then low s.: see DANNA. Whence *do a d.*, to visit one: low: late C.19–20.

dunnaken-drag. A night-cart: ca 1820–60. cf. *danna-drag* at DANNA.

dunneken or **-kin,** see DUNNAKEN.

dunner. An importunate creditor: from ca 1690; coll till C.19, then S.E. See DUN, n. and v.

***dunnick-drag.** A variant pronunciation of *danna-drag* (q.v. at DANNA).

***dunnock.** A cow: (?C.17,) C.18–early 19 c. ?ex *dun*, adj.: *the dun cow* is famous and serves as a title to a satire by Robert Landor.

dunnyken or **-kin,** see DUNNAKEN.

dunop. A pound (gen. sterling): back s., from ca 1865. *Dnuop* > *dunop*, for the sake of euphony. See *Words!*, article 'Rhyming Slang'.

duns. Tradesmen dealing with a ship or its crew: nautical: late C.19–20. Bowen. They have the impudence to ask for their money.

***dup.** To open: mid-C.16–18 c.; now dial. Harman, Head. Elisha Coles, 1676, defines it as 'to enter [the house]'. Not *do up* but *do ope*(*n*).

durance. A prison: coll; ca 1690–1750. (This sense gives added point to *in durance vile*.)

Durham man. A knock-knee: late C.18–early 19 coll. Grose, 3rd ed.: 'He grinds mustard with his knees: Durham is famous for its mustard.'

***duria.** Fire: C.19 c. 'Ducange Anglicus', 1857. ?cf. Romany *dugilla*, lightning.

durn, durned. Variants of DARN, DARNED low coll: C.19–20.

durra, dhurra. Indian millet: Anglo-Indian coll: from late C.18.

***durrynacker.** A female lace-hawker, gen. practising palmistry 'on the side'. vbl n., *durrynacking*. Mayhew: mid-C.19–20 c.; ob. Ex Romany *dukker*, to tell fortunes: cf. DOOKIN.

durzee. A variant of DERZY.

dust. Money: coll: from ca 1600. Esp. in *down with one's* or *the dust*, to pay, as in Fuller, 1665: 'The abbot down with his dust, and glad he escaped so, returned to Reading.' Prob. abbr. *gold-dust*. 2. A disturbance, ROW, esp. in KICK UP *a dust*, cause a SHINDY: from ca 1750; s. until ca 1890, then coll. 3. Gunpowder: Australian coll: mid-C.19–20. 4. Flour: Australian: since ca 1860. 'Tom Collins', *Such Is Life*, 1903.

dust, v. To blind (fig.); befool, as in *dust the public*: Stock Exchange; from ca 1814; ob. Abbr. the S.E. *dust the eyes of.* 2. **dust** or **dust off (or out),** v. To depart hurriedly: in C.17 S.E.; in C.19 U.S. s., whence C.20 English s.

dust-bin. A grave: from ca 1850; ob.

dust (a ship) down. To sweep her decks: nautical: late C.19–20.

dust-hole. Guard-room: Army s. (—1898). Not because of dust, for usually it is spotlessly clean, but perhaps because it's a God-forsaken place for a soldier to be.

dust in the eyes, have. To be sleepy: cf. DRAW STRAWS and *the* DUSTMAN (2) *is coming*. Coll: (?C.18,) C.19–20; ob.

dust it away, gen. in imperative. To drink a bout, esp. quickly: late C.17–18: coll (*pace* the O.E.D.).

dust off, see DUST, v., 2.

dust one's cassock, coat, doublet, or **jacket,** with **for him (her)** occ. added. To thrash; †criticize severely. Coll: the first and third, C.18, Smollett; the second, late C.17–early 19, but anticipated in Tusser's 'What fault deserves a brushed cote'; the fourth and sole extant, from late C.17, as in Farquhar, Barham.

dust one's pants. To spank: coll: late C.19–20.

dust out, see DUST, v., 2.

dust-up. A variant of DUST, n., 2: C.19–20.

dust whapper (or whopper). A carpet beater: ca 1815–70. George Smeeton, *Doings in London*, 1828.

duster. A sweetheart (female): tailors': from ca 1850; ob. 2. (Also **the red duster.**) A red ensign: nautical: from ca 1895. cf. COACH-WHIP.

dustie, see DUSTY.

dusting. A thrashing; (nautical) rough weather: both from late C.18.

dustman. (Esp. *be a dustman.*) A dead man: late C.18–early 19. 2. Sleep personified, esp. in *the dustman's coming*, used chiefly to children: coll; from ca 1820; ob. 3. A gesticulatory preacher, apt to raise the dust: 1877, Blackmore. 4. A naval stoker: naval: late C.19–20.

dustman's bell, the. Time for bed: nursery coll: from ca 1840. See preceding entry, sense 2.

dustoor(y). Commission as 'rake-off'; *douceur*; bribe: Anglo-Indian, the shorter form, ca 1680–1830; then, mainly, the longer. Largely displaced by BAKSHEE.

dusty; dustie. A dustman: Cockney (—1887). cf. POSTIE. 2. 'A ship's steward's assistant – probably because this hard-worked official looks it': naval (—1909). 3. A nickname for any man named *Miller* or *Rhodes*: late C.19–20. Because millers and roads are gen. dusty.

dusty or **gritty.** Penniless: lower classes': from ca 1870; ob.

dusty, none or **not so.** Good (cf. *not* or *too* BAD): from ca 1854. Smedley, in *Harry Coverdale*, 'None so dusty that – eh? for a commoner like me.' Ex much earlier S.E. *dusty*, mean, worthless. cf. MOULDY, adj., 2.

dusty-bob. A scavenger: coll: ca 1850–1910.

dusty boy. A steward's assistant: naval: late C.19–20. cf. DUSTY, 2 and 3.

dusty-nob or **-poll.** A miller: coll: C.16–17 the latter; C.17–18 the former (rare). cf. DUSTY, 3.

Dutch. Beer: s. (—1650).

Dutch. Both n. and adj. were, in C.17–early 18 (owing to trade rivalry and naval jealousy) very opprobrious or derisive; the coll sense endured throughout C.18, some of the following phrases becoming S.E. in C.19; but the few terms or phrases coined in C.19 have remained s. or coll. See esp. 'Offensive Nationality' in *Words!* and Grose, P., s.v. *Dutch.*

dutch; esp. my old dutch. A wife: from ca 1885; mostly Cockney and esp. costermongers'. Prob. coined by Albert Chevalier, who explained it by the resemblance of 'the wife's' face to that of an *old Dutch clock*: cf. DIAL. (I used, with W., to consider it an abbr. of *duchess*, but Chevalier, I now feel tolerably certain, is right.) See also DUCHESS OF FIFE. 2. Beer: s. (—1650).

Dutch, beat the. To do something remarkable: coll (—1775). Esp. in C.19–20 *that beats the Dutch*, that beats everything, that's 'the limit', it's hardly credible.

dutch, do a. To desert; run away; abscond: military and Cockney: from ca 1870; ob.

dutch, old, see DUTCH.

Dutch (or double Dutch or Dutch fustian or High Dutch), talk. To talk a foreign tongue, or gibberish. The third, used by Marlowe, may never have > coll or gen.; *High*, ca 1780–1860; *Dutch* is C.19–20 (ob.); *double Dutch* (H., 1st ed.), easily the commonest since ca 1860. All are coll. A humorous variant for linguistic dexterity is the ca 1870–1900 *to talk double Dutch backwards on a Sunday.*

Dutch auction or **sale.** A mock auction or sale; either at 'nominal' prices, esp. after the goods have been offered at a high price: coll; mentioned in 1872 as 'the old Dutch auction', hence presumably much earlier. Ruskin has it in 1859.

Dutch bargain. i.e. one-sided: coll; from ca 1650. With variant *wet bargain*, it also means a business transaction concluded with a drinking together.

Dutch brig, the. Cells on board ship or in the naval prisons: naval: mid-C.19–20. Bowen.

Dutch build. (Of a person having) a thick-set figure: coll: mid-C.19–20; ob.

Dutch caper. A light privateering-ship, esp. if Dutch: naval: ca 1650–1720.

Dutch cheese. A bald-head(ed person): low Cockney: 1882–ca 1915. Ware, 'Dutch cheeses are generally made globular.'

Dutch clock; old D.c. A wife: almost imm. abbr. to DUTCH; †by 1900. 2. A bed-pan: from ca 1880; ob.

Dutch comfort. 'Thank God it is no worse,' Grose, 2nd ed.: coll; from ca 1787. A C.19 variant is *Dutch consolation* (H., 1st ed.).

Dutch concert or **medley.** Where everyone plays or sings a different tune: the former (Grose, 1st ed.) from ca 1780, the latter C.19–20 (ob.) and gen. of voices only. Coll.

Dutch consolation, see DUTCH COMFORT.

Dutch feast. 'Where the entertainer gets drunk before his guests', Grose, 1st ed.: coll; ca 1780–1880. cf. DUTCH TREAT.

Dutch gleek. Drinks: ca 1650–1870. Gayton, 1654.

Dutch have taken Holland, the. A C.17–early 18 form of QUEEN ANNE IS DEAD.

Dutch medley, see DUTCH CONCERT.

Dutch nightingale. A frog: 1769, Pennant: jocular coll >, by 1840, dial.; ob. cf. FEN-NIGHTINGALE.

Dutch palate. A coarse palate, lit. and fig.: coll: ca 1675–1800.

Dutch party, see DUTCH TREAT.

Dutch pennants. Untidy ropes: nautical (naval) coll: mid-C.19–20. Merely another of these little national amenities.

Dutch pink. Blood: 1853, 'Cuthbert Bede'. Ex the pigment so named.

Dutch pump. A punishment entailing vigorous pumping to save drenching or, occ., drowning: nautical coll: late C.17–early 19.

Dutch reckoning. A lump account, without particulars: ca 1690–1800: coll > S.E. cf. ALTAMAL, likewise in B.E. 2. Among sailors (—1867), 'a bad day's work, all in the wrong', Smyth.

Dutch red. A highly smoked Dutch herring: nautical coll: late C.19–20. Bowen.

Dutch row. 'A got-up unreal wrangle': Cockney coll (—1909); ob. Ware remarks that, even in his day, it was rarely heard.

Dutch sale, see DUTCH AUCTION.

Dutch street, eat (or lunch or dine) in. To eat with someone, each paying his own bill: late C.19–20. cf.:

Dutch treat. An entertainment at which each pays his share: coll; from ca 1875. Thornton records it for Iowa in 1903; in U.S.A. one finds also *Dutch lunch* and *D. supper*, while *D. party* is common to both England and U.S. in C.20. cf. DUTCH FEAST.

Dutch uncle, talk to a person like a. To give a firm but kindly rebuke. Coll; from ca 1830. Ex the Dutch reputation for extremely rigorous discipline and the gen. idea resident in *partruae verbera linguae* and Horace's *ne sis patruus mihi*, the particular idea in Dutch *baas* = BOSS = master; (ship's) captain.

Dutch widow. A harlot: coll; ca 1600–1750. Middleton, 1608. 'That's an English drab, sir.'

Dutch wife. A bolster: from ca 1880; ob. Ex the S.E. sense, an open frame used for resting the limbs in bed.

dutchess, see DUCHESS.

Dutchie. A Dutchman; occ. a German: allusive and nick-nominal: mid-C.19–20 coll. cf.:

Dutchman. A German; 'any North European seaman except a Finn': nautical coll: mid-C.19–20. 2. An irregular hard lump in brown sugar: late C.19–20.

Dutchman if I do!, I'm a. Certainly not! Coll; from ca 1850. Earlier (1837) is *I'm a Dutchman*, i.e. I'm somebody else: a coll equivalent for disbelief; Reade, 'If there is . . . gold on the ground . . ., I'm a Dutchman.'

Dutchman's anchor. Anything that, esp. if needed, has been left at home: nautical: from ca 1860. Bowen, 'From the Dutch skipper who explained after the wreck that he had a very good anchor but had left it at home.'

Dutchman's breeches (occ. breeks). Two streaks of blue in a cloudy sky: nautical coll (—1867). Smyth. Sailors gen. use it in form, *enough to make a pair of breeches for a Dutchman.*

Dutchman's Cape. Imaginary land on the horizon: nautical coll: mid-C.19–20. Bowen.

Dutchman's drink. One that empties the pot: coll; from ca 1860. cf.:

Dutchman's headache, the. Drunkenness: coll (—1869).

Dutchy, see DUTCHIE.

duty. Interest on pawnbrokers' pledges: respectable lower classes' (—1909). Ware, 'Evasive synonym'.

dwell. A pause: sporting coll (—1887); ob.

dye, see DIE.

dying duck in a thunderstorm, look like a. To have a ludicrously forlorn, hopeless, and helpless appearance: coll, orig. rural: from ca 1850.

dying man's dinner. Something edible or potable snatched, opportunity favourable, when a ship is in peril and all hands at work: nautical: late C.19–20; slightly ob.

dyke, see DIKE.

dynamite. Tea: middle classes': 1888–9. Ex Irish-American dynamiters' evasive term (*Daily News*, 4 Feb. 1888). cf.:

dynamiter. Any violent person: ca 1882–90.

dynasty of Venus, the. 'Indiscriminate love and misguided affection', Egan's Grose: Oxford University: ca 1820–40.

d'you feel like a spot? see HOW WILL YOU HAVE IT?

dyspepsia. Delirium tremens: military hospitals' (—1909).

dyspepsy. Dyspepsia: uncultured Canadian coll: late C.19–20.

E

E.C. women. Wives of City men: snobbish Society: ca 1881–1900. From the London postal district designated East Central.

'e dunno where 'e are! A c.p. of the 1890s, from a music-hall song.

e' knows. A c.p. punning *Eno*'s advertisements: from ca 1905.

E.P. or **e.p.** An experienced playgoer: theatrical: late C.19–early 20.

***eagle.** The winning gamester: late C.17–18 c.

eagle-hawking. The plucking of wool from dead sheep: Australian 'bush' (—1898). Ex this habit of the Australian eagle-hawk.

eagled. Punished by being spread-eagled: nautical: C.19–20; ob.

ear, pull down one's. To get money from (a person), esp. as a tip: Cockneys': from ca 1870. Clarence Rook, *The Hooligan Nights*, 1899, 'Well, we couldn't pull down their ear for more'n 'alf a dollar.' cf. BITE ONE'S EAR.

ear, put on one's. To set on: low coll: from ca 1890. Pugh (2): '"An' I s'pose", said Deuce, looking puzzled, "that it wouldn't be quite the thing, would it, to put a tiggy" – detective – "on his ear?"'

ear, send away with a flea in one's (or **the**) **ear,** see FLEA IN ONE'S EAR...

ear-biter; ear-biting. A persistent borrower; borrowing: see BITE ONE'S EAR, than which the two terms are slightly later.

Earl of Cork. The ace of diamonds: Anglo-Irish (—1830) coll. Carleton,'Called the Earl of Cork, because he's the poorest nobleman in Ireland'.

Earl of Murray, see DINE WITH ST GILES.

early. Keeping early hours; rising early: coll (—1893).

early, rise or **wake** or **get up very.** To be wide-awake, ready, astute: *rise*, C.18; the other two C.19–20, with *get up* the commoner in C.20. Orig. coll; in C.20, S.E. Swift.

early, small and, see SMALL AND EARLY.

early bird. A word: rhyming s.: late C.19–20. cf. DICK(E)Y BIRD, 5, above.

early door. A whore: rhyming s.: late C. 19–20.

early doors. A pair of (female) drawers: rhyming: since ca 1870.

early hour. A flower: rhyming: since ca 1880.

early on; late on. Early in the morning; late at night: coll: mainly North Country: late (?mid-)C.19–20.

early riser. An aperient: mid-C.19–20 coll. cf. *custom-house officer*. 2. A sharp, business-like person: coll: U.S. >, ca 1895, anglicized. Ware. Ex EARLY, RISE.

early worm. One who searches the streets at dawn for cigar and cigarette stumps: coll: from ca 1870; ob. Ex S.E. sense.

***earnest.** A share of the booty: mid-C.17–18 c. Head; B.E. cf. S.E. senses.

ears are (or **were**) **worth, it's** (or **it'd be**) **as much as one's.** It is, would be, very risky for him: coll: from ca 1860.

ears from one's elbows, know one's. To be sensible or shrewd: coll: mid-C.19–20. Perhaps a refined version of ARSE FROM ONE'S ELBOW...

'eart!, 'ave an, see HEART!, HAVE A.

earth. An early variant of ERTH, three.

earth-bath, take an. To be buried. By itself, *earth-bath* = a grave. C.19 low.

earth-stoppers. A horse's feet: ca 1810–80. Moncrieff, 1821. Alluding to those who stop up foxes' earths.

earthly, no; not an earthly. No chance whatsoever: coll: resp. 1899, 1907.

earwig. A private and malicious prompter or flatterer: coll > S.E. in C.18: ca 1610–1880. Scott. 2. In C.19 c. or low s., a clergyman. 3. 'A crony, or close friend' (*Sinks*, 1848): ca 1830–70. Ex the mutual whispering. 4. An inquisitive person: from ca 1880.

earwig, v. To prompt by covert assertions; whisper insinuations to; rebuke privately: C.19–20; S.E. in the latter. Marryat, 'He earwigs the captain in fine style.' Ex n., 1. The vbl n. *earwigging* is more frequently used than the v.

ease. To rob of, steal from: coll: C.17–20; in C.17, jocular coll; in C.18, c.; in late C.19–20, S.E. Jonson, 'Ease his pockets of a superfluous watch.'

ease one's arm; gen. imperative. To go steady: Cockneys': from ca 1885; ob.

ease oneself. To ejaculate seminally: coll: C.18–20. Prob. ex the S.E. sense, 'to defecate'.

east and south. The mouth: rhyming s.

(—1857). After ca 1895, *north and south.* Occ., ca 1880–1900, *sunny south.*

East Country ship. A ship trading in the Baltic: nautical coll: mid-C.19–20.

East of the Griffin. (In) East London: London coll: 1885, the *Referee,* 11 Oct.; very ob. Ware, 'Outcome of the city Griffin on his wonderful pedestal replacing Temple Bar'.

East (or e.) roll. A slow, gradual roll without jerks: nautical coll: late C.19–20.

eastery. Private business: cheapjacks' (—1876); ob. Hindley in his classic 'editing' of cheapjack life.

easy. A short rest, esp. as *take an easy*: coll; from ca 1880.

easy, v.i. To dispose oneself suitably to the sexual embrace: low coll; from ca 1900.

easy, adj. (Of a girl) easily picked up: coll: from ca 1890.

easy, adv. Without difficulty: in C.19–20, coll where not sol.; earlier, S.E. 2. Comfortably; at an easy pace, e.g. in *take it easy*; without severity, as in *let one off easy*. Coll (—1779). cf. the Irishism *be easy!*, don't hurry!

easy, honours. Honours divided: coll. (1884: O.E.D.) Ex cards.

easy, make. To gag; to kill: mid-C.18–early 19, low if not c. For the latter sense, *quiet* was occ. preferred.

easy as damn it or **kiss my arse** or **my eye** or **pissing the bed, as.** Extremely easy: coll: first, second, and third, C.19–20; fourth, C.18–20 (ob.). The polite variant and original of the second is (*as*) *easy as kiss my hand*, 1670, Cotton (Apperson). cf. Shakespeare's 'easy as lying' and Ray's (1678) *easy as to lick a dish. Easy as an old shoe* and *as falling off* (*a chair*, *a log*, etc.) were orig. dial., not earlier than 1800.

easy as taking money (or toffee) from a child; gen. preceded by **as.** Very easy (to do): coll: late C.19–20.

easy does it! Take your time: coll; from ca 1840; ob.

***easy mort.** Mid-C.17–18 c.: 'a forward or coming wench', B.E.

easy over the pimples or **stones!** Go slow! Be careful! Coll: from ca 1870. The former ex the barber's shop, the latter ex driving on bad roads.

easy virtue. 'An impure, or prostitute', Grose, 1st ed.: from ca 1780: s. >, by 1820, coll >, by 1900, S.E. cf. the S.E. *easy*, compliant.

eat a child, see CHILD, EAT A.

***eat a fig.** To break into a house: s. rhyming imperfectly on (CRACK a) CRIB (3): from ca 1855; ob. c.

eat a sword, eat iron. To be stabbed: C.16: coll.

eat bull-beef, see BULL-BEEF, EAT.

eat like a beggar man and wag one's under-jaw. 'A jocular reproach to a proud man', Grose, 1st ed.: late C.18–mid-19: coll c.p.

eat one's boots, hat, head. Gen. as *I'll* or *I'd eat my . . ., hat* being the commonest and earliest (Dickens, 1836). A coll declaration.

eat one's head off. To be idle; cost more than its, or one's keep. Orig. (—1736) of horses; then of servants (—1874).

eat one's terms, occ. **dinners.** To go through the prescribed course of study for admission to the bar: a legal coll (—1834). Ex the eating of a few meals each term at an inn of court.

eat the wind out of a ship. To get nearer the wind than another ship is: nautical coll (—1834). cf. WIPE (a person's) EYE.

eat up. To massacre (a man and his family) and confiscate his property (1838); hence, to vanquish in tribal battle (1859): coll. Prob. ex a Zulu metaphor. In late C. 19–20, gen. = to ruin, hence to be much too strong or too skilful for another.

eat vinegar with a fork, see FORK, EAT.

eaten a stake, see SWALLOWED A STAKE...

eatings. Board, meals, food: proletarian: C.19.

eautybeau. Beauty: music-hall transposition (—1909); ob.

ebb-water. Lack of money: late C.17–18. B.E. says it is c.; perhaps it is, rather, low s. or low coll.

ebenezer. In fives, a stroke that so hits 'line' as to rise perpendicularly: Winchester College. Title of Nonconformist hymn, 'Here I'll raise My Ebenezer.' Hence the stone that makes a fives ball rise. Moreover, Ebenezer = *stone of help* (Heb.).

ebony. A Negro: coll: ca 1860–1910. Abbr. *son of ebony* (1850).

ebony optic. A black eye; *e.o.* ALBONIZED, the same – painted white: C.19.

eccer. (Pronounced *ekker.*) Exercise: Oxford undergraduates': late C.19–20. 'Oxford *-er*'.

eccespie. Pieces: transposed or central s.; from ca 1860. 2. Hence, money: from ca 1880.

ecclesiastical brick. A holy stone: nautical, mostly officers'; late C.19–20. By elaboration.

***eclipse.** In gaming, a fraudulent manipulation of a die with the little finger: late C.17–18, c.

ecod! A mild oath (cf. ADOD and EDOD): coll: C.18–19. ?ex EGAD, itself C.17–20 (ob.).

edgabac. Cabbage: back s. (—1859).

Edgarism. Atheism; loosely, agnosticism: clubmen's: 1882. Ex *Edgar*, 'the villain-hero' of Tennyson's prose play, *The Promise of May*.

***edge!** Run away!, be off!: c. (—1886); ob. A deviation from S.E. *edge* (*away*).

edge, short top. A turned-up nose: tailors': from ca 1860.

edge, side. Whiskers: tailors' s.: from ca 1860, as is:

edge, stitched off the. Likewise tailors': (of a glass) not full.

edge off, or, v.t., **out of.** To slink away; to desist gradually: coll: from ca 1860. cf. the S.E. usages, whence it naturally develops.

edge on, have (got) an. To be impudent; put on SIDE: Public Schools': C.20. P. G. Wodehouse, 1903, 'Doesn't it strike you that for a kid like you you've got a good deal of edge on?'

edgenaro. An orange: back s. (—1859).

edgeways, not able to get a word in. To find oneself unable to take part in a conversation or discussion: coll; from ca 1870; earlier and S.E., *edgewise*.

edition, first, second, etc. One's first, second, or other child: journalists', authors', and publishers' s. fast becoming a gen. bookish coll: from ca 1890. (There is prob. a further pun on *addition*.)

edod! Rare coll variant of ADOD!: late C.17–early 18.

educated trimmer. An engineer officer: nautical, esp. executive officers': late C.19–20. Opp. BRIDGE-ORNAMENT.

ee; 'ee. Ye: coll abbr. (—1775); ob. Sheridan, 'Hark ee, lads.'

eekcher. Cheek: central s.: from ca 1880.

eel-skin(s). Very tight trousers: ca 1820–60. Bulwer Lytton, 1827, 'a . . . gilt chain . . . stuck . . . in his eel-skin to make a show'. 2. A very tight dress: Society coll: ca 1881–90.

e'en. Even (= just, nothing else but) 'prefixed' to vv.: mid-C.16–19 coll; in C.20, dial. Richardson, 1741. 'E'en send to him to come down.'

eenque; eetswe. Queen; sweet: transposed or central s.: from ca 1870.

effort. Something accomplished involving concentration or special activity: from ca 1870.

efink. A knife: back s. (—1859). *E-* is a common initial letter in back-s. words, for it ensures euphony.

***efter.** A theatre thief: c.; from ca 1860; ob. Perhaps *after* (*the* GOODS) perverted.

egad! A mild oath ('prob. for *ah God*', W.): C.18–20 (ob.); coll. Slightly earlier *igad*; occ. *egod* (C.18).

egg. A person: coll, esp. in *good egg* and, as exclamation, *good egg!*, late C.19–20, and *a bad egg*, a person (rarely a thing) that disappoints expectation: from early 1850s. 2. Abbr. *duck's egg*: cricketers': 1876. See DUCK, n., 6.

egg-box. A box for table napkins: Bootham School: late C.19–20.

egg-trot. A coll abbr. of *egg-wife's trot*, a gentle amble: ca 1680–1900. Ex her pace when riding to market.

eggs, teach one's grandmother to roast, more gen. **suck.** To inform or lecture one's elders, superiors, or intellectual betters: coll: from ca 1700. Earlier forms are *teach one's dame* or *grandame* (*grannam*) *to spin* or *to grope ducks* (or *a goose*) or *to sup sour milk*.

eggs (a penny, and four of them addled or **rotten), come in with five.** To interrupt fussily with worthless news or an idle story: coll: ca 1540–1880.

eggs are, be, or **is eggs, as sure as.** Undoubtedly; certainly: coll: the first two, late C.17–18 (e.g. Otway); the third from (—)1772. The last perhaps, as A. de Morgan suggested, influenced by *X is X*, the logician's statement of identity.

eggs for one's money, be glad to take. Gladly 'to compound the matter with Loss', B.E.: semi-proverbial coll: C.17–18. Shakespeare, 1610.

egham, staines and windsor. A private coachman's three-cornered gala hat: coll: ca 1870–1900. Ex a once-famous business firm.

ego, often with capital. Myself; yourself; herself, himself: jocular coll (—1824); ob. 2. **(ego!)** see QUIS?

egod! see EGAD!

Egyptian charger. A donkey: mostly London: ca 1820–50. Perhaps ex its frequent use by Gypsies, or because the infant Jesus escaped into Egypt on an ass; cf. JERUSALEM PONY.

Egyptian Hall. A ball: rhyming s. (—1859).

Egyptian medal, show an; esp. as c.p., *you're showing an E.m.* To have one's trouser-fly undone, to show a fly-button (or more than one): from ca 1884; orig. military; slightly ob. cf. ABYSSINIAN MEDAL.

eh? What's that (you say)?: coll: C.19–20.

eight eyes, I will knock out two of your. A mid-C.18–early 19 Billingsgate fishwives' c.p. The other six, as Grose, 2nd ed., enumerates them, are the two 'bubb*ies*' (q. v.), the bell*y* (prob. implying the navel), 'two pope's eyes' (?the anal and urinal orifices), and 'a *** eye' (?what): by the 'pope's eyes' he perhaps means rump and anus, while by the asterisks he almost certainly understands the sexual aperture.

eighteenmo. Octodecimo: book-world coll; 1858. Ex *18mo*, the abbr. form.

***eighter.** An 8-ounce loaf: c., mostly prisoners': from ca 1870.

Eiley Mavourneen. (More correctly *Kathleen Mavourneen*). A non-paying debtor: commercial (—1909); ob. Ex that song by Louisa Macartney Crawford, in which occur the words, 'It may be for years, and it may be for ever.'

Eine (dissyllabic). London: showmen's: since ca 1870. P. H. Emerson, *Signor Lippo*, 1893. A Parlary word: corruption of It. *Londra*.

ekame. A MAKE, i.e. a swindle: back s. (—1859).

ekker. An exercise (scholastic task): Public Schools' and universities' (orig. Oxford): from ca 1890. 'The Oxford *-er*'. cf. ECCER.

ekom. A MOKE, i.e. donkey: likewise back s. (—1859).

elbat, see HELBAT.

elbow, crook one's, see CROOK ...

elbow, knight of the. A gamester: coll: ca 1750–1840.

elbow, shake the. To play dice: coll: from ca 1690; ob. Vanbrugh, 'He's always shaking his heels with the ladies' – i.e. dancing – 'and his elbows with the lords'; Scott in *Nigel*.

elbow?, who is at your. A late C.17–18 c.p. caution or warning to a liar. cf. *watch your step!*

elbow-crooker. A hard drinker: coll; mid-C.19–20; ob. cf. POT-WALLOPER.

elbow-grease. Hard manual labour: coll (—1639). Clarke's *Paroemiologia Anglo-Latina*; Marvell; B.E., 'A derisory Term for Sweat'; Grose; George Eliot, 'Genuine elbow-polish as Mrs Poyser called it.' cf. the Fr. *huile de bras* or *de poignet* (recently *de coude*), the primary sense being that of vigorous rubbing. 2. Hence, energy: coll: Ned Ward, 1709.

elbow in the hawse, (there's) an. A nautical coll applied to a ship that, 'with two anchors down swings twice the wrong way, causing the cables to take half a turn round one another', Bowen: from ca 1800 or 1810.

elbow-jigger or **-scraper.** A fiddler: coll: from ca 1820; ob.

elbow-shaker, -shaking. A gamester; gaming, adj. and n.: coll: the first from early C.18, the second (—)1718; the third, C.19–20, ob.

elbows, out at. (Of an estate) mortgaged: coll; C.18–early 19.

elch(er)wer, see HELCHERWER.

elderly jam. An ageing woman: lower classes': ca 1880–1915.

eldest, the. The first lieutenant: naval s. verging on coll: C.19. Contrast *the old man*, the captain.

electrify. Violently to startle: from ca 1750; coll till ca 1850, when it > S.E. Burke; Barham.

elegant. NICE: coll verging on s.: C.18–early 19. cf. FAIR, adj., 1. 2. Hence, first-rate, excellent: coll; from ca 1840; ob. Prob. owing to influence of the U.S., where it was so used as early as 1765 (Thornton). As a jocular Irishism, it is spelt *iligant*: mid-C.19–20. cf. NICE.

Elegant Extracts. At Cambridge University, those students who, though 'plucked', were given their degrees: from ca 1850; ob.

elephant, bang through the; elephant, bang up to the, see BANG, etc.

elephant, see the. To see the world; gain worldly experience: coll; orig. (ca 1840), U.S., anglicized ca 1860. Laurence Oliphant; ob. 2. (Gen. *to have seen the elephant*.) To be seduced: from ca 1875; ob. cf. Fr. *avoir vu le loup*.

Elephant and Castle. The anus: rhyming s. (on illiterate *ars'le*): late C.19–20.

elephant dance. The double shuffle or cellar-flap: ca 1870–1920.

elephant's trunk. Drunk: rhyming s.; from ca 1855. By 1873, often abbr. to *elephant's* or *elephants*. cf. process in CHINA (*plate*).

elevate. To render slightly drunk; gen. in p. ppl passive used as an adj.: from ca 1700; in C.18, S.E.; then coll. Dickens, 'Except when he's elevated, Bob's the quietest creature breathing.'

elevation. Slight tipsiness: coll; from ca

1820. Scott. 2. Opium (—1850); ob. 3. Whence, a PICK-ME-UP: coll: mid-C.19–20; now mostly dial.

elevator. A crinolette: Society: 1882–ca 1900.

elevens, by the! A jocular expletive: coll: (?coined by) Goldsmith, 1773; †. Prob. punning *heavens!*

***elf.** Little: c.: late C.17–mid-18. *Street Robberies Consider'd.* Ex *elf*, a dwarf.

Ellenborough Lodge or **Park** or **Spike.** The King's Bench: ca 1810–50. Ex Lord Chief Justice Ellenborough (d.1818), fl. 1802–18 in that office.

***Ellenborough's teeth.** The *chevaux de frise* around the King's Bench Prison wall: c.; ca 1810–50. See preceding entry.

Elliot-eye. 'An eye splice worked over an iron thimble': naval coll: late C.19–20. Ex Admiral Elliot, its introducer into the Navy.

elpa, see HELPA.

elrig. A girl: back s. (—1859).

emag. Game; trick; dodge: back s. (—1873). Ware dates it 1870.

embroidery. Exaggerations; fancy-work manipulations of or additions to the truth: coll; from ca 1885. The corresponding v. is C.17–20 S.E.

emergency crew. A crew that, of men immune from the press gang, worked a ship for the real crew while danger threatened: nautical coll: mid-C.18–mid-19.

emit. Time: back s.: late C.19–20.

Emma, whoa! see WHOA, EMMA!

emperor, drunk as an. 'Ten times as drunk as a lord', Grose, 3rd ed.: late C.18–early 19. cf. the allusive *bloody drunk*: see BLOODY.

Empress pidgin. Discussion with Queen Victoria: naval: 1876–1901.

***empty.** Unpossessed of the riches reported: c.: C.18.

empty, get the. To be dismissed: Cockneys' (—1887). i.e. get the empty SACK.

empty bottle. A fellow-commoner: Cambridge (—1794); †by 1870. cf. FELLOW- and GENTLEMAN-COMMONER.

encore, get an; gen. as vbl n., **getting an encore.** To have to rectify a mistake in one's job: tailors': from ca 1870.

encumbrances. Children: coll: from ca 1830.

end, see BUSINESS END, THE.

end, at a loose. With nothing particular to do: coll; from ca 1900. Orig., without occupation or employment.

end, no, adv. Immensely; *no end of*, a great number or quantity of. The former is s., the latter coll: the former dates from ca 1850, the latter from ca 1620.

end is (or **end's**) **a-wagging, the.** The end of a job is in sight: naval: mid-C.19–20. Granville, 'From sailing days when, after much "pulley-haulley", the end of a rope was in sight.'

end of The Sentimental Journey. The female pudend: low coll: C.19–20; ob. Sterne's witty novel ends with a significant '——'.

end-on. Straight; standing on or showing its end: coll, C.19; S.E., C.20. *Be end-on*: to have a priapism: low coll: C.19–20.

end up, keep one's. To rub along; maintain one's status, reputation, etc. From the late 1870s: coll >, by 1910, S.E. Ex cricket.

Endacott, v.i. 'To act like a constable of that name who arrested a woman whom he thought to be a prostitute': journalistic coll: ca 1880–1900. B. & L.

endorse, see INDORSE.

ends, at loose. Neglected (of persons), (of things) precarious: coll; from ca 1860; ob. (cf. END, AT A LOOSE.) Orig. nautical, of an unattached rope.

enemy, the. Time; the clock, watch, etc.: coll; esp. as *how goes . . . ?* or – ob. in C.20 – *what says . . . ?* Dickens in *Nicholas Nickleby*, 1839. Hence *kill the enemy*, to pass time; ob.

engaged ring. Engagement ring: coll, mostly London (—1887).

English. A key-translation, a CRIB: Winchester College s. verging on coll: C.19–20. Ex *English*, to translate into English. 2. Ale: —1650.

English burgundy. Porter: mid-C.18–19. cf. BRITISH CHAMPAGNE.

English cane. An oaken plant; ?a cudgel: late C.17–mid-18.

English manufacture. 'Ale, Beer, or Syder', B.E.: late C.17–18: coll.

English pluck. Money: proletarian (—1909); virtually †.

enif, adj. Fine: back s. (—1851).

enin. Nine: back s. (—1859). *Enin* GEN, nine shillings; *enin yanneps*, ninepence.

eno. One: back s. (—1859).

enob. Bone: back s.: late C.19–20.

enough for anything after an adj. = either that adj. preceded by *very* or, gen., to satisfy anyone, in all conscience. Coll: mid-C.19–20.

enough to . . . see the key-nn. or -vv.

ensign-bearer. A drunken man; a drunkard. Esp. one with a very red face: mid-C.17–early 19. (It serves as a flag.)

enthuse. To be enthusiastic; speak enthusiastically: (mostly jocular or semi-jocular) coll: orig. (—1880), U.S.; anglicized ca 1900. cf. the U.S. sense (1859: Thornton), 'to kindle into enthusiasm'.

enthuzimuzzy. Enthusiasm: Society: ca 1870–1900.

envelope. A condom: coll: late C.19–20.

epip. A pipe: back s.: from ca 1865.

Epsom races. A pair of braces: rhyming s. (—1857). 2. Also, ca 1850–1900, faces, now 'rhymed' *airs and graces.*

Epsom salts. Coll from ca 1870, for *Epsom salt.*

equality (or E.) Jack. An officer treating those under him as equals: naval coll: from ca 1810.

equator. Waist: jocular: late C.19–20.

***equipped, equipt.** Rich; well-dressed: c.: late C.17–18.

Eric, or Little by Little. A c.p. directed at shy or sexually-slow youths: since ca 1860. Ex the phenomenal popularity of Dean F. W. Farrar's novel of school-life, *Eric; or Little by Little,* 1858, the story of Eric, a boy who, little by little, went to the dogs and a pathetic end.

erif. Fire: back s. (—1859).

***eriff.** A rogue 'just initiated, and beginning to practice', Grose, 1st ed.: C.18–early 19 c. Recorded first in *A New Canting Dict.,* 1725. Ex the sense, a canary (bird) two years old, for CANARY (BIRD) itself = a rogue.

erk. A lower-deck rating: nautical: late C.19–20. Perhaps ex dial. *irk,* to grow weary, or from officers' impatient 'They irk, me, these ——.' See also IRK.

errand, send a baby on an. To undertake a probable failure: coll: mid-C.19–20; ob.

error, and no, see MISTAKE, AND NO.

erth. Three: back s.: from ca 1845. Hence, *erth-pu,* 'three up', a street-game; *erth* SITH-NOMS, three months' imprisonment; *erth* GEN, three shillings; *erth yan(n)eps,* three pence. Also EARTH.

esclop. A policeman: back s. (—1851). The *c* is never pronounced, the *e* gen. omitted: hence the well-known SLOP.

Eskimo Nell is an imaginary Naval heroine – the central figure in a ballad almost as long as it is bawdy. Late C.19–20. cf. BALLOCKY BILL.

esroch. A horse: back s. (—1859). The *c* is added for naturalness. Occ. *esroph.*

Essex calf. A native of Essex: coll: from ca 1570; ob. G. Harvey, 1573; A. Behn. cf.:

Essex lion. A calf: from late 1620s (ob.): coll. 'Water Poet' Taylor, 1630. Essex being noted for its calves. cf. COTSWOLD LION; RUMFORD LION, and:

Essex stile. A ditch: coll: C.17–19. Camden, 1605. Ex the predominance of ditches over stiles in Essex.

establish a funk. 'To create a panic – invented by a great bowler, at cricket, who enlivened this distinction with some cannon-ball bowling': Oxford University (—1909); Ware. cf. BOWL FOR TIMBER.

esuch. A house: back s. (—1873); *c* for *o.* cf. ESROCH.

et cetera; etc. A bookseller: c.: early C.18. *Street Robberies Consider'd.* (Prob. ex booksellers' habit of short-titling books in their catalogues.)

eternal. Infernal; damned: in C.19–20, (dial. and) low coll; C.17–18, S.E. cf. U.S. *tarnal.* 2. In C.18, it occasionally means 'thorough-going', as in *Sessions,* 6th session of 1733, 'Kempton swore at me, *God damn your Blood and Liver, you eternal Bitch.*'

eternity-box. A coffin: late C.18–20; ob.

Europe morning, have a. To rise late from bed: Anglo-Indian coll: from ca 1870; ob. In India one has to rise early in order to get a good day's work done, work being unhealthy in the middle of the day.

Europe on the chest. Home-sickness: military: ca 1880–1915.

Evans, Mrs. 'A name frequently given to a she cat, owing, it is said, to a witch of the name of Evans, who frequently assumed the appearance of a cat', Grose, 1st ed.: coll: late C.17–mid-19.

evaporate. To run away: coll: from ca 1850. Dickens, 'The young man, looking round, instantly evaporated.' Ex S.E. sense, to disappear.

evatch. To have: back s. (—1874). Instead of 'un-English' *evah.*

***eve.** A hen-roost: C.18–early 19 c. Extant, though ob., in dial. Prob. ex S.E. *eaves.*

evening wheezes. False news: lower classes' (—1909); ob. Ex the lying rumours once more freely spread than nowadays.

evens, in. In even time (esp. of the 100 yards run in 10 seconds): late C.19–20: athletics' coll.

ever?, did you. (Self-contained.) Have you ever seen, or heard, such a thing?: coll: mid-C.19–20. See An Old Etonian, *The Alphabet Annotated,* 1853:

'Some exclaim, and think themselves so clever!
Did you *ever*? (answer) no, I never!'

ever a(n), e'er a(n). Any: in C.19–20 (ob.), low coll; earlier, S.E.

ever is (or **was**), **as.** A coll tag, orig. intensive, as in 'Bad riding as ever was', 1708. Now approximately = 'mark you' (parenthetic) and, mostly, rather illiterate.

ever so. Ever so much, as in *thanks ever so!*: mostly proletarian: from ca 1895. Edwin Pugh, *Tony Drum*, 1898, '"But I like you ever so," she faltered.'

ever the, adv. At all; any; e.g. 'Ever the richer', preceded by negative, = no richer. Coll; from ca 1620.

everlasting knock, take the. To die: sporting: 1889, *Referee*, 10 March.

everlasting shoes. The feet: coll: from ca 1870.

***everlasting staircase.** The treadmill: from ca 1835; ob. ca 1850–90, occ. *Colonel Chesterton's everlasting staircase*, ex its improver.

every man Jack; every mother's son. Absolutely everyone: coll; the former, from ca 1810, or even late C.18; the latter, C.14–20, e.g. in Shakespeare, Scott.

every time. On every occasion; without exception: coll, U.S. (1864) anglicized by 1880.

everything, in the predicate, = (something) very important, is coll; from ca 1870. e.g. 'Bring the money; that's *everything!*'

everything is lovely, see GOOSE HANGS HIGH...

everything is nice in your garden! 'A gentle protest against self-laudation': 1896–ca 1910. Ware supports with an anecdotal origin.

Eve's custom-house. The female pudend: late C.18–19. Grose, 2nd ed., '... Where Adam made his first entry.' Contrast CUSTOM-HOUSE OFFICER.

***evesdropper.** A thief lurking about doors and watching his opportunity: c. (—1725); †by 1800. 2. A robber of hen-roosts: mid-C.18–early 19 c. Ex *eaves*, see EVE.

evethee, see HEVETHEE.

evif. Five: back s. (—1851). Also EWIF.

***evil.** In late C.18–early 19 c., a halter. 2. In C.19 s., matrimony; a wife.

evlenet. Twelve: back s. (—1859). Naturally *evlewt*, looking un-English, was changed.

***ewe,** or **white ewe,** gen. preceded by **the.** An important, because very beautiful, woman in a band of rogues, a criminal gang: c.: late C.17–18.

ewe dressed lamb fashion, an old. An old woman dressed like a young girl: late C.18–19: coll. In C.19–20 the usual form is *mutton dressed up to look like lamb*; orig. and mainly Cockney.

ewe-mutton. An elderly harlot or amateur prostitute: C.19–20; ob.

ewif. A variant of EVIF, five; *ewif* being more euphonious.

ex. Exhibition; gen. **the Ex,** some specific exhibition, such as the Earls Court Exhibition in 1899: late C.19–20.

exactly! Certainly! excellent! Coll: from ca 1865. W. S. Gilbert, in *Bab Ballads*, 1869, '"I'm boiled if I die, my friends", quoth I, And "exactly so", quoth he.'

exalted. (Other forms, very rare.) Ppl passive, hanged: coll: C.19. Michael Scott, 1836.

exam. Examination: school s. >, in C.20, gen. coll; from ca the middle 1870s. James Payn, 'I read all about it for my exam.,' 1883.

exasperate or **hexasperate.** To over-aspirate one's *h*'s: from ca 1850; ob. 'Cuthbert Bede', 1853.

exceedings. 'Expenditure beyond income': Oxford University coll (—1909); ob.

Excellent's ulster. An oilskin: the (naval) Gunnery Schools', hence gen. naval: ca 1840–90.

exchange spits. To kiss: low: late C.19–20.

excite!, don't. Keep cool!: coll (—1899). i.e. *don't excite yourself.*

exciting, adj. Excellent; amusing, pleasant; unexpected: coll; from ca 1880.

excruciators. Very tight boots, esp. with pointed toes: coll: from ca 1865; ob.

excursioner, -ist. An excursion-agent: coll; from ca 1890.

excuse! Pardon me!, do not be offended: South African coll (—1906). Watkins, *From Farm to Forum*, at that date. Ex Dutch influence.

execute. To cane: Public Schools' jocular coll: late C.19–20. Ian Hay, *Pip*, 1907.

execution day. Washing day; Monday: late C.17–20 (ob.): low coll. Ex hanging clothes on the line.

exes. Expenses: coll (—1864). 2. Those who were once something else: coll; from ca 1820. Tom Moore, 'We x's have proved ourselves not to be wise.' 3. See TOMMY AND EXES.

exhibition of oneself, make an. To show oneself in an unfavourable light: coll; from ca 1880.

exis. Six; esp. in *exis*-EVIF GEN, 6 × 5

shillings, 30s., and *exis*-EWIF *yanneps*, 6 + 5 pence, 11d. Back s. (—1851).

Exmas. Christmas: (low) coll: late C.19–20.

expecting, adj. With child: lower classes' coll; from ca 1870.

expended. Killed: nautical: mid-C.18–early 19. Ex book-keeping accounts.

experience does it. A mid-C.19–20 coll rendering of *experientia docet*, (lit.) experiment teaches. Originated by Mrs Micawber in *David Copperfield*.

explosion. The birth of a child: low: from ca 1865; ob.

***export trade, the.** The procuring of women and shipping them to the Argentine: white-slavers' c.: from ca 1890.

extensive. Showy; given to, or actually displaying, wealth, fine clothes, conversational ability or effectiveness: (—) 1859; ob.

extinguish. To reduce (an opponent) to silence: from ca 1890, coll; earlier (1878), S.E.

extinguisher. A dog's muzzle (—1890). The *Standard*, 12 May 1890.

extracted. Included in the list of ELEGANT EXTRACTS. Ob.

Extradition Court. The Second Justice-room at Bow Street: London legal and political: 1883, *Daily News*, 10 April. Ex the numerous extradition cases there tried.

extrumps or **ex(-)trumps.** Extempore; without preparation (of a lesson): Winchester College, from ca 1860.

eye. A place where tradesmen (orig. and esp. tailors) hide stolen material: 'Called *hell*, or their *eye*: from the first, when taxed with their knavery, they equivocally swear, that if they have taken any, they wish they may find it in *hell*; or alluding to the second protest, that what they have over and above is not more than they could put in their *eye*,' Grose, 1st ed. (at *cabbage*): trade: mid-C.18–mid-19. 2. Incorrect for *nye*: C.15–mid-18.

eye, all in the. All nonsense, humbug: ca 1820–80. cf. BETTY MARTIN. . .

eye, be a sheet in the wind's. To be slightly drunk: nautical: 1883, Stevenson. Gen. abbr. to *be a sheet in the wind*.

eye, have a drop in the, see DROP IN ONE'S EYE.

eye, have in one's. To have in mind: coll: ca 1790–1860. 'To some true girl I'll be steering,/I've got one in my eye' – from an unidentified British poem anteceding 1806 and quoted in an American magazine, the *Port Folio*, 17 May 1806, p. 304.

eye, in the twinkling of an, see BEDPOST, IN THE . . .

eye!, mind your. Be careful! From ca 1850, low coll; earlier, S.E.

eye!, my or **all my,** see BETTY MARTIN and cf. EYES!, MY. 2. But also as a simple exclamation, as in Wm Maginn, *Whitehall*, 1827 (p.46), ' "Bless us, there's the Dover coach again. My eye, she's setting down all her passengers at Holmes's." '

eye, pipe the; or **put (the) finger in (the).** To weep: derisive coll; the former, C.19–20; the latter, C.16–early 19.

eye, to have fallen down and trod(den) upon one's. To have a black eye: mid-C.18–early 19.

eye, wet an or the. To drink: from ca 1830; ob.

eye-brows, see EYE-LASHES.

eye-glass weather, see HEYE-GLASS WEATHER.

eye-glassy. Characteristic of the wearers of monocles: coll: 1871, Meredith. 2. Hence, haughty, supercilious, haughtily contemptuous: coll: 1907. O.E.D. (Sup.).

eye-hole. See GARTER-HOLE. 2. *Introitus urethrae*: low: late C.19–20.

eye in a sling, have an; with one's. (To be) crushed or defeated: proletarian coll (—1909).

eye-lashes or **-brows, hang (on) by the.** To be extremely persevering, tenacious, esp. in a difficulty: coll; from ca 1850. The gen. ca 1770–1850 form is *hang by the eye-lids*, applied to a dangerous position.

eye-limpet. An artificial eye: ca 1875–1900.

eye of another shooter, wipe the. 'To kill game that he has missed' (S.O.D.): sporting: from ca 1885.

eye opened, have one's. To be robbed: ca 1820–80. (Alexander Somerville, *Autobiography of a Working Man*, 1848.) Hence the n. *eye-opening*.

eye-opener. The *membrum virile*: C.19–20 low; ob.

eye out of register. An inaccurate eye: printers' (—1887). Baumann. Ex printers' j. *out of register*.

eye peeled or **skinned, keep one's (best).** To be wary: coll: U.S. (1852: Thornton), anglicized in late C.19. cf. FLY; WIDO; *up to* SNUFF.

eye(-)sight, nearly lose one's. To obtain an unexpected and very intimate view of a member of the opposite sex: coll; from ca 1860.

eye-teeth, have (cut) one's. To be experienced, prudent: coll: C.18–20. Apperson.

eye-wash. Something done, not for utility but for effect: coll (—1884); prob. orig. military. C. T. Buckland, in *Sketches of Social Life in India*, 1884. 'Most officers of any tact understand the meaning of eye-wash.' (O.E.D.)

***eye-water.** Gin (—1823); ob. c. >, by 1850, low. Whyte-Melville; *Judy* (an 1880s rival of *Punch*), 4 Aug. 1886, 'He imbibed stupendous quantities of jiggered gin, dog's nose, and Paddy's eye-water.'

eyes, goo-goo, see GOO-GOO EYES.

eyes!, my. An exclamation indicative of surprise: ca 1780–1910. Dickens, in *Oliver Twist*, 'My eyes, how green! . . . Why a beak's a madg'strate.'

eyes are set, one's. One is drunk: coll: C.17. Shakespeare. O.E.D. (See also EYES SET.)

eyes chalked!, get your. To one not looking where he is going, or to a clumsy person: North Country: late C.19–20.

eyes draw straws, one's, see both DRAW STRAWS and STRAWS, DRAW.

eyes out, cry one's. To weep long and bitterly: coll; from ca 1705. Swift, 'I can't help it, if I would cry my Eyes out.'

eyes out, go. To make every effort: work exceedingly hard: Australian: since ca 1820.

eyes peeled or skinned, keep one's, see EYE PEELED.

eyes set (in one's or the head), have or be with one's or the. To be drunk: C.17–18 coll. Shakespeare, 'O he's drunke . . . his eyes were set at eight i'th 'morning.'

F

F.C.s. False calves: theatrical coll (—1909). Ware, 'Paddings used by actors in heroic parts to improve the shape of the legs.'

f.h.o.!; f.h.b. Family hands off! (sometimes explained as family hold off!); or, family hold back!: middle-class domestic coll c.p. indicating that a certain dish is not to be eaten by members of the family at a meal where guests are present: mid-C.19–20.

f sharp. A flea: from ca 1860; ob. Lyell, ' "F" being the initial letter, and "sharp" because of the bite'. cf. *b flat*, at B, 1.

face. A grimace: coll: from ca 1600 (S.O.D.). Shakespeare. 2. Great confidence, insolent boldness; impudence: from ca 1530; coll till C.18, then S.E. Face is a principal character in Jonson's *The Alchemist*. 3. Credit, esp. in *push one's face*, to obtain credit by bluff or bluster: coll: from ca 1760. Goldsmith. cf. U.S. *run* – or *travel on* – *one's face*, to go upon credit. 4. A contemptuous term of address: orig. and mainly Cockney: from ca 1875. cf. FEATURES.

face, v. To punch in the face: pugilistic: ca 1815–50. *Boxiana*, III, 1821. cf. BELLIER.

face, put on a. To change one's expression, usually to severity: coll: C.19–20. cf. *what a face*: how severe or disapproving you look!: coll: mid-C.19–20.

face, square, see SQUARE-FACE.

face-entry. Freedom of access to a theatre: theatrical (—1874); ob. cf. FACE, 3.

face but one's own, have no. To be penniless: prob. ex the gamesters' sense, to hold no court cards: late C.18–early 19.

face-fins. Moustaches: orig. nautical: late C.19–20. Frank Richardson.

face-fungus. Moustaches, beard, or both: late C.19–20. Frank Richardson.

face like a sea-boot. An expressionless face: nautical coll: late C.19–20.

face-making. Sexual intercourse: mid-C.18–early 19. cf. FEET FOR CHILDREN'S STOCKINGS, MAKE.

face the knocker. To go begging: tailors': from ca 1875.

face the music. To cope bravely with an unpleasant emergency: orig. (1850) U.S., anglicized ca 1880. Perhaps ex stage acting.

face ticket, have a. To be so well known to the janitors that one is not asked to present one's ticket; British Museum Reading Room coll (—1909).

facer. A glass full to the brim: late C.17–early 19: c. >, by 1800, low coll. B.E., 'A Bumper without Lip-room'. 2. A blow in the face: pugilistic coll: from ca 1810; ob. 3. Hence, a sudden check or obstacle: coll; from ca 1820. Thackeray, 'In . . . life every man must meet with a blow or two, and every brave one would take his facer with good humour.' 4. Hence, a problem: coll: early-C.19–20. 5. A dram: Anglo-Irish: mid-C. 19–20. 6. A glass of whiskey punch: from ca 1870; ob.

faces, make. To beget children: C.18–early 19. 2. **(make faces at.)** To deceive, disappoint, or verbally attack a friend: c.; ca 1870–1920.

facey. A workman facing another as he works: tailors'. Hence, *facey on the bias*, one not directly in front, and *facey on the two thick*, a workman just behind one's *vis-à-vis*. From ca 1870.

facias, see FIERI FACIAS . . .

facings, go or **be put through one's.** To be reprimanded or to show off: military s. > gen. coll: from ca 1865.

facings, silk. Beer-stains on the garments being made or altered: tailors': from ca 1870. Ex *watered silk*. cf. CANTEEN-MEDAL.

***Factory, the.** Old Scotland Yard: c. of ca 1860–90. '*No. 747*'. 2. Any police station: late C.19–20.

facty. Full of facts: coll but never very gen.: from ca 1880. 'A "facty" [newspaper] article', *Pall Mall Gazette*, 2 Nov. 1883.

facy. Impudent, insolvent: C.17–20; coll till C.19, then dial. Ex FACE, n., 2.

fa'd., fa-d., fa-dee, far-dee. A farthing: Charterhouse: from ca 1870. cf. HA'D.

fad-cattle. Easily accessible women: C.19. cf. CATTLE; FADDLE, to toy.

faddist, fadmonger. One devoted to a public or private fad: coll; from ca 1880. vbl n., *fadmongering*.

faddle. To toy or trifle: coll in C.19; †by 1890, except in dial. Hence, n., a busybody; also an affected and very effeminate male.

The v. arose ca 1680 (orig., to caress a child); the n. ca 1800, though the sense, triflery, foolery, BOSH, hardly before 1850.

faddy. Full of fads: coll: from ca 1820. Mrs Sherwood, 1824. Ex dial.

***fadge.** A farthing: late C.18–19 c. Duncombe, *Sinks of London*, 1848.

fadge, v. To suit; fit: late C.16–19. Succeed: from ca 1600. Both coll. The former in Nashe, Shakespeare, B.E., Horace Walpole; the latter in Cotgrave, Borrow, Nares: 'Probably never better than a low word; it is now confined to the streets.' Esp. in *it won't fadge*, it won't do or serve. 2. **fadge with,** to tolerate (a thing), agree or rub along with a person, is C.17–early 18 and rather S.E. than coll.

fadger. A glazier's frame: glaziers'; from ca 1860. Ex FADGE, v., 1. 2. A farthing: Cockneys': late C.19–20. By corruption. cf. FADGE, n.

fadmonger, FADDIST.

fag. cf. FAG, STAND A GOOD: possibly this phrase + *fag*, hard work, drudgery, weariness (1780), perhaps being a schoolboys' perversion of *fatigue*, led to: 2. A boy doing menial work for one in a higher form: schoolboys' s. (—1785) >, by 1850, gen. coll. Thackeray (of a young drudge in a painters' studio). Prob. ex the v., 1, but, despite the dates, perhaps ex the v., 2. 3. Eatables: Christ's Hospital, from ca 1800. Leigh Hunt, in his *Autobiography*, 'The learned derived the word from the Greek *phago*.' 4. See FAG, STAND A GOOD. 5. A cigarette; orig., an inferior cigarette: from ca 1887. Abbr. FAG-END and ?orig. military. 'Cuthbert Bede', in 1853, speaks of 'the fag-ends of cigars'.

fag, v. In c., to beat, thrash: late C.17–19; after ca 1830, low coll. 2. (?hence) v.t., to have (a boy) as one's fag: schoolboys': from ca 1785; ob. 3. v.i. To do menial jobs for a schoolfellow higher up in the school: from ca 1805: schoolboys' s. >, by 1860, gen. coll. Prob. ex the more gen. sense, 'to work hard, whether mentally or physically' – a sense app. current since ca 1770 and almost certainly deriving ex Southern Scottish and Northern English dialect. *Port Folio*, 30 May 1801, p. 175; *Dublin Magazine*, March 1834, p. 246.

fag, stand a good. Not to become easily tired: late C.18–19: coll. Hence, *fag*, anything that causes weariness; toil: coll (—1780). Hence, from ca 1880, a wearisome thing; a bore.

fag-end. The part nearest the end: Ned Ward, 1703.

fag out. To serve as a FAG; esp. in cricket, to field: from ca 1840: coll, schoolboys', orig. and esp. at Winchester College.

fagged out. Exhausted: coll (—1785). Perhaps ex dial. *fag*, to exhaust oneself in toil, and *fagged out*, frayed.

***fagger, figger or figure.** A boy thief who, entering by a window, opens the door to his confederates or even hands the booty out to them: c. (—1785); ob. Grose, 1st ed.; whereas *figger* (Grose, 1st ed.) arose in late C.18, *figure*, its derivative, is of C.19–20.

faggery, fagging. Serving as a FAG, in a school: schoolboys'; from ca 1850, 1820, resp. De Quincey in his autobiographical sketches, 1853, 'Faggery was an abuse too venerable and sacred to be touched by profane hands.'

fagging. A beating, thrashing, thumping: low: not recorded before 1775, but prob. used as early as 1700. Ex c. FAG, to beat. 2. See FAGGERY. 3. An exhausting experience or bout of work; late C.18–20.

fag(g)ot. A BAGGAGE; a pejorative applied to a woman (—1600), also – gen. preceded by *little* – to a child (—1859): low coll, the former in C.20 being dial. 2. A rissole: low coll; from ca 1850. Mayhew. Also, butcher's oddments or 'stickings' (?hence the name): low coll (—1859). 3. A man mustered as a soldier but not yet formally enlisted: late C.17–19. Hence, a man hired to appear at a muster or on a muster-roll: C.18–19. Both nuances are military; the latter, also naval.

fag(g)ot, v. In C.17–19, to bind, truss, i.e. as sticks in a faggot. Prob. coll; never, despite B.E., was it c. 2. c., however, is the sense, to garotte: late C.19–20. 3. In low s., v.t. and i., to copulate (with); to frequent harlots: C.19. Ex FAGGOT, n., 1.

fag(g)ot-briefs. A bundle or bundles of dummy briefs carried by the briefless: legal (—1859). Sala, 'Pretend to pore over faggot briefs'. Ob.

fag(g)ot-master. A whoremonger: low; from ca 1825; ob. cf. FAGGOT, v., 3.

fag(g)ot-vote. 'A vote secured by the purchase of property under mortgage, or otherwise, so as to constitute a nominal qualification', F. & H.: political coll (1817); S.E. by 1840. Gladstone, 25 Nov. 1879. Perhaps ex FAGGOT, n., 3. Hence *fag(g)ot-voter*.

fag(g)oteer. Same sense, period, and status as FAGGOT-MASTER.

fain I!; fains!; fain it!; fainits! A call for a truce; a statement of opposition: schoolboys': from ca 1810. See also FAYNIGHTS! Prob. a corruption of *fen!*, ex *fend*; or possibly ex *claim(s) I!* or *feign*. cf. BAGS (I)! its opposite. The earliest forms are FEN! and FIN (3) or FINGY.

faints, the. A tendency to faint: coll: from ca 1890.

***fair;** always **the fair.** 'A set of subterraneous rooms in the Fleet Prison', *Lex. Bal.*: c.: ca 1810–50.

fair, adj. NICE: coll verging on s.: C.17. In C.18, the word was ELEGANT. See *Slang*, p. 28. 2. Undoubted, complete, thorough: dial. (—1872) >, by ca 1885, s. See FAIR COP.

fair, adv. Fairly: coll: C.19–20. 2. Completely: dial. (1859: E.D.D.) >, in the 1880s, coll.

fair, see. To ensure fair play by watching: coll: Dickens, 1837. Ob.

***fair cop, it's a.** It's a clear arrest: c.: late C.19–20.

fair dinkum, see DINKUM.

fair-gang, the. Gypsies: coll; from ca 1830; ob. by 1900. From their frequenting fairs in gangs or communities. Prob. a corruption of *faw-gang*, itself ex *Faa*, a Scottish-Gypsy surname.

fair herd. A good attendance of strangers: Oxford University: 1883, *Daily News*, 13 June; ob.

fair itch. Utter imitation: low (—1909); ob.

fair rations. Fair dealings; honesty: sporting: from ca 1875.

***fair roebuck.** 'A Woman in the Bloom of her Beauty', *A New Canting Dict.*, 1725: c.: C.18. Ex *fair roebuck*, a roebuck in its fifth year.

fair speech!, you have made a. A late C.17–18 c.p. 'in derision of one that spends many words to little purpose', B.E.

fair trade, -trader. Smuggling; a smuggler: nautical (—1887).

fair wind, give (something) **a.** To pass (e.g. the salt): nautical: late C.19–20.

fairing. Cakes (or sweets) bought at a fair; esp. gingerbread nuts: coll when not dial.: from mid-C.18.

fairish. Fairly large: coll (—1865). 2. As adv., in a pleasant manner; to a fair degree: coll, 1836. Both perhaps orig. dial.

fairy. 'A debauched, hideous old woman, especially when drunk': proletarian (—1909); ob. Ware.

faithful, one of the. A drunkard: C.17 coll. *The Man in the Moon*, 1609. 2. A tailor giving long credit: late C.18–19, either c. or low or c. > low. Hence, *his faith has made him unwhole*, too much credit has bankrupted him.

faithfully. With obligating assurances: from late C.16; coll. 'He promised faithfully to send the book the next day,' O.E.D.

***faitor,** see FATER.

fake. An action, esp. if illegal; a dodge; a sham (person or thing): from ca 1825: low. James Greenwood, 1883, 'Naming the house in [this] ridiculous way was merely a fake to draw attention to it.' For etymology, see the v., though it may abridge FAKEMENT. 2. Anything used in illicit deception or manufacture: 1866 (O.E.D.). Hence: 3. A mixture for making a horse safe (cf. DOPE): ca 1870–90. 4. (Ex senses 1, 2.) A gadget; a THINGUMMY: Cockneys': from ca 1890. Clarence Rook, *The Hooligan Nights*, 1899. 5. (Ex sense 2.) Stuff used in patent medicines, a patent medicine; a (so-called) cure: showmen's: since ca 1870. Wm Newton, *Secrets of Tramp Life*, 1886. Ex CORN FAKE, corn cure, and NOB FAKE, hair-restorer. 6. Make-up: theatrical: since ca 1875.

***fake,** v. To do anything, esp. if illegally or with merely apparent skill or ability; to cheat, deceive, devise falsely; tamper with; forge; DOPE (a horse); to steal. In c. and then, by ca 1880, in low s., a verb of multiple usage: gen. only from ca 1830 (cf. however, FAKE AWAY!), though doubtless used in c. as early as 1810, Vaux recording it in 1812. vbl n., *faking*. Perhaps ex L. *facere*, to do, influenced by *faire* as understood in Fr. c., but more prob. ex Ger. *fegen*, (lit.) to sweep, itself in extensive s. use: cf. FEAGUE, which is either cognate or the orig. form. 2. To hurt: c. (—1812). Ex sense 1, possibly influenced by *ache*. cf. FAKE ONESELF. 3. See FAKE UP.

***fake a cly.** To pick a pocket (see CLY): c.; from ca 1810; ob.

fake a curtain. 'To agitate the act-drop after it has fallen, and so perhaps thereby induce a torpid audience to applaud a little, and justify the waiting actor to "take a curtain"', Ware: theatrical: 1884.

fake a dance, step, trip. To improvise a step when, in dancing, one has forgotten the correct one: theatrical: from ca 1860. cf.:

fake a line. To improvise a speech: theatrical; from ca 1860.

fake a picture. 'To obtain an effect by some adroit, unorthodox means': artistic coll: from ca 1860. Ware.

***fake a poke.** To pick a pocket: c.: late C.19–20. *People*, 6 Sept. 1896.

***fake a screeve.** To write a (begging) letter: c.; from ca 1810.

***fake a screw.** To make a false or a skeleton key: C.19–20.

fake a step or **trip,** see FAKE A DANCE.

***fake away!** Go it! Splendid – don't stop! c., perhaps only 'literary': ca 1810–1900. See FAKE, v.

fake one's pin, see FAKE ONESELF.

***fake one's slangs.** To file through fetters: c.; from ca 1810; ob. See SLANGS.

***fake oneself.** To disfigure or wound oneself: C.19 c. cf. *fake one's pin*, to 'create' a sore or wounded leg: likewise c.

***fake out and out.** To kill (a person): c.: C.19.

fake-pie. A pie containing 'left-overs': straitened Society: 1880; ob.

***fake the broads.** To STACK the cards; to work a three-card trick: c.; from ca 1840.

***fake the duck.** To adulterate drink; to swindle, cheat: c.; from ca 1830; †.

***fake the rubber.** To stand treat: c.; from ca 1850; ob.

fake the sweeteners, see SWEETENERS.

fake up; occ. simply FAKE, v.t. and reflexive. To paint one's face: theatrical; from ca 1870; ob. 2. To adapt for the theatre: theatrical (—1887). 3. To falsify: mid-C.19–20.

faked; occ. **faked-up.** Spurious; counterfeit: low coll; from the 1850s. See FAKE, v.

***fakeman-charley.** See sense 4 of:

***fakement.** A counterfeit signature (—1811), hence a forgery; a begging letter, a petition (—1839). 2. A dishonest practice (—1838); hence, any trade, action, thing, contrivance (—1857). 3. Small properties, accessories: theatrical; from ca 1875. The first senses, c.; the second group, low; the last, s. The term derives prob. ex FAKE, n., 1. 4. (cf. sense 1.) Also *fakeman-charley*. A private mark of ownership: c.; from ca 1810; ob. 5. Paint for the face: theatrical: from ca 1870. 6. Any letter; a note: 1826, *Spy*, II; †by 1910. Ex sense 1.

***fakement-chorley.** Ware's variant of *fakeman-charley*: see FAKEMENT, 4.

***fakement-dodge; -dodger.** The practice of writing begging letters; the beggar or impostor employing this DODGE: c.: mid-C.19–20; ob.

faker. A maker, or a faker, of anything: low (—1688). Randle Holme. cf. the U.S. *faker*, 'a street-vendor of gimcracks, &c.', Thornton. 2. In c., a thief (—1851); in C.20, a pickpocket. Borrow, in *Lavengro*, 'We never calls them thieves here, but prigs and fakers.' 3. A jeweller: c. (—1857). 4. A circus performer, esp. rider: circus, from ca 1875. Baumann (*fakir*). 5. A harlot's FANCY-MAN: low (—1891); ob.

fakes and slumboes. Properties; accessories: theatrical: from ca 1880; †.

faking, vbl n., corresponding with all senses of FAKE, v.: low s. > coll; (—)1845.

fakir, see FAKER, 4.

fal. A girl: rhyming s. (1868) on GAL; ob.

falderals (or -ols). Silly ideas: C.19–20. It occurs in a Charles Dibdin song quoted by the *Port Folio*, an American magazine, on 30 Nov. 1805 (p. 376, col. 2): 'He runs, while listening to their fal de rals,/Bump ashore on the Scilly Isles.' Ex *falderal*, a trinket, a trifle; imm. ex dial. sense: an idle fancy.

fall, v. To conceive a child: coll: C.19–20; ob. 2. In c., to be arrested (—1883).

fall, have a bad or **good** or **lucky.** To have a piece of bad, or good luck; make a (bad) strike: coll (—1887); ob.

fall across. To meet (a person) unexpectedly: from ca 1885; coll.

fall down the sink. A, to, drink: rhyming s.: late C.19–20.

fall-downs. Fragments of cookshop puddings; collected, they are sold cheaply. Cockney: C.19.

fall in. To be quite wrong: coll; from ca 1900.

fall in the thick. 'To become dead drunk . . . Black beer is called thick, so is mud': low (—1909). Ware.

fall of the leaf, (at) the. (By) hanging: low or c.: ca 1780–1840. George Parker.

fallen angel. A defaulter, a bankrupt: Stock Exchange: ca 1810–70. *Spy*, II, 1826.

fallen away from a horse-load to a cart-load. Grown fat: a late C.18–mid-19 c.p.

false alarms. Arms (of body): military rhyming s.: late C.19–20.

false hereafter. A dress-improver or bustle: Society: ca 1890–1900.

***fam**; occ. **famm** (B.E.) or **fem.** The hand: low, orig. c.: from ca 1690; †by 1870. ?abbr. FAMBLE. Hence, 2, a ring: c. of ca 1770–1850.

***fam**, v. To handle: C.19–20 (ob.) c. Hence *fam a* DONA, to caress a woman intimately; *fam for the* PLANT (2), to feel for the valuables.

***fam-grasp.** A hand-shaking: c.: late C.18–19. Ex the v.t., late C.17–19. The v. also = to agree, or to come to an agreement, with a person, a sense recorded by Coles in 1676. Lit., to grasp by the FAM or hand.

***fam-lay.** Shop-lifting, esp. of jewellery by one with viscous hands: c.: mid-C.18–19.

fam-snatcher. A glove: low: ca 1820–60. Pierce Egan may have coined it.

***fam-squeeze.** Strangulation: C.19 c. Contrast FAM-GRASP.

***fam-struck.** Baffled in a search; handcuffed: C.19 c.

***famble.** The hand: mid-C.16–20 c. Harman, B.E., Grose, Hindley. Prob. ex *famble*, to fumble. 2. Hence, a ring: C.17–early 19 c. Shadwell.

***famble-cheat.** A ring: mid-C.17–18 c. 2. A glove: mid-C.17–early 19 c.

***fambler.** A glove: C.17 c. Rowlands. 2. A seller of BRUM (3) rings (rarely *famble*): late C.17–18 c.

***fambling-cheat.** (Lit., a hand-thing;) a ring: mid-C.16–17 c. Harman; Rowlands.

familiar way, in the. Pregnant: jocular coll (—1891), punning *in the family way*. Ob.

familiars. Lice: C.19–early 20. Facetiously ex S.E. sense, a familiar spirit.

famillionaire, see VERY FAMILLIONAIRE.

***family, the.** The underworld of thieves: mid-C.18–19; c.: Bamfylde-Moore Carew, 1749. cf. FAMILY-MAN.

family, hands off! see F.H.O.!

family head. An elaborate figure head of several figures: nautical: mid-C.19–20. Bowen.

family hotel. A prison: coll; ca 1840–1900. *Punch*, 31 Jan. 1857, 'In a ward with one's pals, | Not locked up in a cell, | To an old hand like me it's a family hotel.'

***family-man.** A thief: c. (—1788); ob. In pl, occ. *family people*. Ex FAMILY. 2. Also, a FENCE: mid-C.19–20 c.

family of love. 'Lewd Women, Whores', B.E.; esp. a company thereof, Grose, 1st ed.: late C.17–20 (ob.).

***family people.** A c. (—1812) variant of FAMILY, THE.

family(-)plate. Silver money: jocular coll; from ca 1850.

family(-)pound. A family grave: from ca 1870.

***family-woman.** A female thief: c. (—1812). On FAMILY-MAN.

famine. Lack of bread at meals: Bootham School: late C.19–20.

***famm,** see FAM, n.

famous. Excellent; CAPITAL: coll: from the 1790s. Southey, '"But every body said", quoth he, "that 'twas a famous victory."'

famously. Excellently: CAPITALLY: coll; from ca 1600. Shakespeare, Lytton.

***fan.** A waistcoat: c.; ca 1835–1900. Brandon; Snowden, *Magazine Assistant*, 3rd ed. ?ex its spread. 2. ca 1680–1720, a fanatic: jocular coll gen. spelt *fann* or *phan*.

fan, v. To beat, whip; be-rate: low coll: late C.18–20. Now esp. *fan with a slipper*. 2. In c., to search a person, or his clothes: from ca 1850. Mayhew. cf. FRISK.

fan-qui, see FANQUI.

fan-tail, see FAN-TAIL.

fancy. (Always **the f.**) The boxing world (from ca 1810); boxers collectively (—1820): coll; by 1900, S.E.; somewhat ob. Pierce Egan, 'The various gradations of the Fancy hither resort, to discuss matters incidental to pugilism.' 2. 'His father took a great deal to the fancy . . . it meant dealing in birds, and dogs, and rabbits,' J. Greenwood, *The Little Ragamuffins*, 1884: poor Londoners' coll: from ca 1860.

fancy, v. To have a (too) high opinion of oneself, of another, or of a thing: coll: from ca 1860. 2. In the imperative, either as one word (*fancy!*) or two words (*fancy that!*) or preceding a phrase (e.g. 'Fancy you being in plus-fours!'), it expresses surprise: coll: ?earlier than 1834, when Medwin has 'Fancy me boxed up in the narrow vehicle.'

fancy-(bloak or) bloke. A sporting man: coll; from ca 1850. Ex FANCY, n. 2. A FANCY-MAN: from ca 1835. 3. Hence, any woman's favourite male: from ca 1880.

fancy frigate. A warship notable for smartness – but gen. 'very uncomfortable to live in': naval coll: late C.19–20; ob. Bowen.

***fancy house.** A brothel: prostitutes' c.: from ca 1860.

fancy Joseph. A harlot's 'boy' or bully (see FANCY-MAN): C.19 low. Either with an allusion to Joseph and Potiphar's wife or an amplification of JOE (5), a male sweetheart.

fancy-lay. Pugilism: low (—1819): ob. by 1890, †by 1918. Tom Moore. See LAY, 2.

fancy-man. (cf. FANCY-BLOKE and F. JOSEPH.) A harlot's protector and/or lover; her husband: low (—1818). Egan, 'Although "one of the fancy", he was not a fancy man.' Ex: 2. A sweetheart: from ca 1810: low s. >, by 1860, coll. 3. A male keep: low (—1811); ob. cf. sense 2. 4. Rarely a pugilist; often a follower of pugilism: but seldom used in the singular: from ca 1845; ob. by 1900. In all senses, *fancy* is either a corruption of Fr. *fiancé* or, much more prob., ex *the* FANCY. Notable synonyms of sense 1: MAC, PONCE, and PROSSER, 3.

fancy piece. A harlot: low (—1823). cf. Egan, *Life in London*, 1821, 'Fancy piece ... a sporting phrase for a "bit of *nice* game" kept in a preserve in the suburbs. A sort of *bird of Paradise*.'

fancy religion. Any religion other than C. of E., R.C., and Presbyterian: naval and military: from the 1890s or earlier.

fancy sash. A punch: Australian rhyming s. (on BASH or SMASH): from ca 1880.

fancy woman. A temporary mistress; a kept woman: low coll (—1850). cf. FANCY-MAN, 3. 2. In C.19–20, a man's favourite female – often jocularly: low s. >, by 1860, coll. cf. FANCY-MAN, 2.

fancy-work, take in. To make extra money by prostitution, 'do the naughty for one's clothes': low (—1891). The pun is best left unexplained; cf. FANCY-MAN, 1, 2.

fandangle. A fantastic or ludicrous ornament; foolery; nonsense: coll: from ca 1880. W. considers it an arbitrary deformation of *fandango*, ?after (*new-*)*fangle*(*d*).

fang-chovey. A dentist's 'parlour': low; from ca 1850. *Fang*, a tooth; CHOVEY, a shop. Also, *fang-faker*, a dentist: same comments. cf. CROCUS-CHOVEY.

***fann,** see FAN, n., 2.

fanning. A thrashing: late C.18–19. See FAN, v., 1. 2. In c., stealing: mid-C.19–20. See FAN, v., 2, and cf. CROSS-FAM.

fanny. The female *pudenda*; the pudend: low: from ca 1860 (perhaps much earlier). Variants, seldom used, are *fanny artful* and *fanny fair*. Perhaps ex *Fanny*, the heroine of John Cleland's *Memoirs of Fanny Hill*, 1749, the English classic of the brothel, as *La Fille Elisa*, 1877, or perhaps rather *La Maison Tellier*, 1881, is the French and *Bessie Cotter*, 1935, the American; the English novel, it may be added, is by far the most 'actionable'. 2. A can for liquor: naval: C.20. Ex:

Fanny Adams. Tinned mutton: naval (—1889) >, ca 1900, also military. Ex Fanny Adams, a girl who, ca 1812, was murdered and whose body, cut into pieces, 'was thrown into the river at Alton in Hampshire' (O.E.D. Sup.). cf. HARRIET LANE.

fanny a pitch. To SPIEL – talk glibly – until enough people have gathered: showmen's: late C.19–20.

***Fanny Blair.** The hair: rhyming s. (—1859); †. A c. and U.S. variant of BARNET FAIR.

Fanny Nanny (or n). Nonsense: nautical: late C.19–20. Prob. a reduplication on the hypocoristic shape of the first syllable of *fantastic*: cf. FANTOD.

fanqui, fan-qui. A European: Anglo-Chinese: from ca 1860; ob. Lit., a foreign devil.

fant, see PHANT.

fantadlins. Pastry: ca 1860–70: ?Cockney.

fantail, fan-tail. A 'sou'-wester' of the kind affected, in C.19, by coal-heavers and dustmen: from ca 1850; ob. J. Greenwood in *Dick Temple*, 1877. Abbr. *fan-tail hat*, which must date from early C.19.

fantail-boy. A dustman: low: ca 1820–50. 'Jon Bee', 1823. cf. preceding.

fantailer. A person with a tail-coat much too long for him: ca 1820–50.

fantastically dressed. 'With more rags than ribbons', Grose, 3rd ed.: ironic coll: late C.18–early 19.

fanteague, on the. On the spree or 'loose': low: ca 1875–1900. 2. cf. *fanteague* or *fantique*, dial. and coll for a fuss, commotion, excitement, passion; a vagary; a joke, a LARK: from ca 1830. Dickens, 1837. Ex *fatigue* (see E.D.D. at *fantigued*), or perhaps ex *frantic* after *fatigue* (the rare variant *fantique* occurs – see O.E.D. – in 1825).

fanteeg, fantigue, see FANTEAGUE, 2.

fantod. A fad; a faddy naval officer: these senses are prob. S.E. 2. **the fantods.** Restlessness, restless inquietude; esp. *give* (a person) *the fantods*, make him restless, uneasy, hence (in C.20) nervy: U.S. (1885), anglicized ca 1905. Imm. ex *fantad*, a fad, on Kentish *fantod*, restless; ultimately ex FANTEAGUE or fantasy.

far and near. Beer: rhyming s.: late C.19–20.

far-away. In pawn: lower classes': 1884; ob. From the hymn, 'There is a happy land, far, far away'. 2. Hence (—1909), to pawn: likewise ob. Ware, 'I far-awayed my tools this blessed day – I did!'

far(-)back. An inferior workman; hence, an ignorant fellow: tailors', from ca 1870. Ex an apprentice's position at the back of the work-room.

far-dee. see FA'D.

far-keeper. An eye: Northumberland s. (—1899), not dial. Ex *keek* = *peek* = peep, look.

far (enough) if . . ., I'll be. I'll certainly not (do so and so): Sheffield (low) coll – not dial.: from ca 1880.

farcidrama. Any light piece that fails: theatrical: 1885 – ca 90. Ex Ashley Sterry's name for H. J. Byron's posthumous half-finished comedy . . . *The Shuttlecock*, which was a FROST.

***farcing, farsing.** The picking of locks: c.: late C.16 – early 17. Greene's 2nd *Cony-Catching*, 1592. ?*forcing*.

farden. A farthing: Cockney: from ca 1840. (Also in dial.) cf. COVENT GARDEN.

fardy. A farthing: (mostly London) street-vendors': C.19–20; ob. Mayhew, I, 1851. cf. FARDEN.

fare-croft. A cross-Channel Government packet-boat: nautical: ca 1840–90.

***farger.** A false die: c.: late C.16–early 17. Perhaps a perversion of FORGER.

farm. A cheap establishment for pauper children (—1869); for illegitimate children (—1874). Also v. (—1838). Coll soon > S.E. See esp. Dickens, *Oliver Twist*, ch. ii. 2. In c., a prison hospital. Hence, *fetch the farm*, to be ordered hospital diet and treatment. From ca 1875.

farmer. A countryman; a CLOD-HOPPER: London coll (—1864). 2. An alderman: low or c. (—1848); prob. †. 3. See FARM, 1, with its v.: coll (—1869) > S.E. ca 1900, though gen. as *baby-farmer*. 4. Gen. *be a farmer*, to be off duty: nautical: from early 1880s. Ex the purely imaginary joys of a farmer's life. 5. Hence, an inferior seaman: nautical: from ca 1890. 6. A hare: Kentish s. (—1878). Ex its affection for the land.

***farsing,** see FARCING.

fart. An anal escape of wind, esp. if audible: C.13–20: S.E., but in C.18–20, a vulgarism, as is the v. Chaucer, Jonson, Swift, Burns. In 1722, there appeared the 10th edition of the anon. author's pamphlet *The Benefit of Farting Explain'd*, 'wrote' in Spanish [!] by Don Fart in Hando, Translated into English by Obadiah Fizle. 2. Hence a symbol of contempt: C.17–20. Crowne, 1685, 'A fart for your family.' 3. Hence, a contemptible person (cf. *silly* CUNT): low coll; from ca 1860. 4. Also in *not care* or *give a fart for, not worth a fart*: the former, C.17–20 (earlier *set not . . .*); the latter, C.19–20.

fart, let a brewer's. (Occ. followed by *grains and all*.) To befoul oneself: low: late C.18–mid-19. cf. the late C.18–19 low coll, *not to trust one's arse with a fart*, to have diarrhoea (ibid.).

fart about. To dawdle; to waste time; play about: low coll, late C.19–20. Ex dial.

fart-catcher. A footman or a valet (he walks behind): mid-C.18–19; low.

fart-daniel. The *pudendum muliebre*: low: C.19. Obscure: I surmise that *fart* = *farth*, alleged to = a litter of pigs, and that *daniel* – cf. ANTHONY – is the youngest pig (see E.D.D. at *daniel* and *farth*), hence that this strange term is orig. dial. (not in E.D. D.); it may, however, be merely a misprint for *fare-daniel*, dial. for a sucking pig that is the youngest of a litter.

fart in a bottle, like a. Flustered, agitated: low: late C.19–20. cf. *in and out like a fart in a* COLANDER (mid-C.19–20), used to describe restless and aimless movement.

fart-sucker. A parasite: low: C.19–20; ob.

farthing, not to care a brass. Not to care at all: coll >, by 1890, S.E.: from ca 1800. Earlier, without *brass*. (James II, debasing the coinage, issued brass farthings, half-pence, and pence.)

farthing dip. A piece of bread dipped in hot fat and sold by pork butchers: coll: ca 1820–80. Ex the candle so named.

farthing-faced chit. A small, mean-faced, insignificant person: Cockney (—1909); ob.

farthing-taster. 'Lowest quantity of commonest ice-cream sold by London . . . itinerant . . . vendors': Cockneys': ca 1870–1914. Ware.

fartick, fartkin. Diminutives of FART: C.19; low coll.

farting(-)clapper. The podex: mostly workmen's: late C.19–20.

***farting-crackers.** Breeches: late C.17–18: c. cf. CRACKER, 7.

farting-trap. A jaunting car: Anglo-Irish: C.19–20; ob.

fartleberries. Excrement on the anal hair: late C.18–19: low. cf. FARTING-CRACKERS.

fash one's beard. To get annoyed or exasperated: Scottish coll (?dial.): 1789, Davidson.

fast, v. To be short of money: ca 1850–1900.

fast, adj. Short of money: coll but orig. and mainly dial.: C.19. Perhaps semantically = *bound fast*. 2. Dissipated; 'going the pace': coll in C.18, S.E. in C.19–20. 3. Impudent: low coll: ca 1870–1900. *Don't you be so fast!* = mind your own business! 4. As in *I'm fast*, my watch is fast: coll (—1887).

fast and loose, play (orig. at). To be inconstant; variable; inconsistent: C.16–20. Coll till ca 1700, then S.E. G. Harvey, Ned Ward, Dickens. Ex the game now – though even this is ob. – known as prick-the-garter, and played with a string or a strap.

***fast-fuck.** A rapid or a standing coïtion: harlots': C.19–20.

***fast(e)ner.** A warrant for arrest: late C.17–early 19 c.

fastidious cove. A fashionable swindler: London: 1882–1915.

***fat.** In c., money: C.19. More gen. in U.S. than in Britain. 2. 'The last landed, inned or stow'd of any sort of Merchandize whatever, so called by the several Gangs of Water-side Porters, &c.': late C.17–early 19. 3. Hence, among printers, composition in which, e.g. in dictionaries and esp. in verse, there are many white spaces, these representing profit (—1788). 4. Hence (theatrical), a good part; telling lines and situations: from ca 1880. The *Referee*, 15 April 1888, 'I don't want to rob Miss Claremont of her fat, but her part must be cut down.' cf. GREASE, 3. 5. In journalism, a notable piece of exclusive news: from ca 1890 (S.O.D.). 6. A lower-class nickname for a fat person (gen. a man): late C.19–20. cf. FATTY. 7. Good luck: Army: late C.19–20: cf. senses 4, 5.

fat, adj. Rich: esp. with CULL: late C.17–early 19 c. ex C.16 S.E. 2. Hence, in C.19–20, abundant, profitable, very large, e.g. profits, income, takings. Also ironical, *a fat lot*, not much: from ca 1860. 3. Good: Australian (—1890): coll. The revival of a C.17 S.E. usage.

fat, bit of. Something profitable: see FAT, n., 3, 4: C.19–20. 2. Coïtion with a stout female: low: from ca 1850; ob.

fat, cut it, see CUT IT FAT.

fat, cut up, see CUT UP.

fat-arsed. Broad-bottomed: C.19–20 coll. cf. BARGE-, BROAD-, and HEAVY-ARSE, the third in Richard Baxter's *Shove to Heavy Arsed Christians*, i.e. slow, dull ones.

fat as a hen in the forehead or **as a hen's forehead.** Very thin: meagre: coll; the former, from ca 1600, is in Cotgrave and Swift, but rare after 1820, when the latter, now ob., > gen.

fat burnt itself out of the fire, the. (And in other tenses.) The trouble blew over: lower classes' coll (—1909). Ware, 'Antithesis of "All the fat's in the fire."'

fat-cake. 'A ridiculous name sometimes applied to *Eucalyptus leucoxylon*': Australian s. or coll (—1898); ob. Morris cites Maiden's *Useful Native Plants*.

fat cock. A stout elderly man: jocular: from ca 1850; ob. 2. A DOUBLE-SUCKER.

***fat cull.** See FAT, adj., 1. In B.E. and Grose.

fat-face. A term of derision or abuse: coll; 1741, Richardson.

fat-fancier or **-monger.** A man who specializes in fat women: low: the former, C.19–20; the latter, C.19.

fat flab. A slice from the fat part of mutton-breast: Winchester College: from ca 1860; ob.

fat or **full-guts.** A fat man or woman: low coll: late C.16–20, C.19 resp. Shakespeare, 'Peace, ye fat guts, lie down.'

fat-head. A fool: from ca 1840: coll. (As a surname, C.13.)

fat-headed, -pated, -skulled, -brained, -thoughted, -witted. Dull; slow; stupid. All coll: resp. C.18–20; C.18–19; C.18–19; C.19; C.19; C.16–19, but soon S.E. Shakespeare has *fat*, slow-witted.

fat is in the fire, (all) the. It has failed; (C.19–20 only) that's done it, it's all U.P.: coll: the first sense from ca 1600 (... *lies in the fire*, C.16; *cast all the gruel in the fire*, Chaucer), as in Dekker; the second and third in Henry James, G. B. Shaw.

fat Jack of the bone-house. A very fat man: coll; ca 1850–1910.

fat lot, a. Always in actual or virtual negative, which = nothing; very little: coll: from ca 1860. 1899, Cutcliffe Hyne, 'Shows what a fat lot of influence ... Congo has got.'

fat-monger, see FAT-FANCIER.

fat one or **un.** A particularly rank breaking of wind; a 'roarer' (Swift): low: C.19–20, ob.

fate. One's *fiancé* or *fiancée*: late C.19–20; jocular coll.

***fater, fator, faytor.** In C.17, a member of the Second Rank of the Canting Crew: in C.18–early 19, a fortune-teller: both c. In

C.16–early 17 S.E., a cheat or imposter. Prob. ex Anglo-Fr. *faitour*.

***father.** A FENCE or receiver of stolen property: c.: mid-C.19–20; ob. Prob. suggested by UNCLE, a pawnbroker. cf. FATHER'S BROTHER. 2. A master shipwright: nautical: C.19. 3. Head of a common lodging-house: low: since ca 1840.

father!, go to. Go to hell!: c.p.: late C.19–20; virtually †. Ex a music-hall song (father being dead). Prob. suggested by *go farther* and *ask father*.

Father Derby's or **Darby's bands,** see DARBIES.

father of a . . ., the. A severe; esp. *father of a hiding* (or *licking*), a very severe thrashing: coll: from ca 1890. cf. 'For three fardins I would take it from ye an' give ye the father an' mother of a good soun' blaichin'' in Seumas MacManus, *The Leading Road to Donegal*, 1895.

father's brother. A pawnbroker: jocular: from ca 1850. cf. FATHER.

fatness. Wealth: s. > coll: C.19.

***fator,** see FATER.

fatten-up. To write a telling part: theatrical: from ca 1875. See FAT, n., 4.

fatty. A jocular epithet, endearment, or nickname for a fat person: coll; C.19–20.

fat(t)ymus, fat(t)yma. A fat man, woman resp.: facetious or endearing: ca 1860–1900. Too artificial to last.

***faulk(e)ner.** (cf. the spelling of FAST(E)NER.) One that decoys others into dicing or card-playing; also a juggler: late C.17–18 c. Perhaps ex *falconer*, via †*fawkener*.

fault, at. At a loss: orig. (1833), hunting s.; coll by 1850, S.E. by 1870. 2. In fault: sol.: from ca 1870.

***fauney,** see FAWNEY.

favour 'To deal gently with; to ease, save, spare: C.16–20, S.E. till ca 1790, then coll and dial. 2. To resemble in face or features: orig. (early C.17), S.E.; since ca 1820, coll and dial.

favourite vice. One's usual strong drink: club or man-to-man's: ca 1880–1915. *Daily News*, 6 Oct. 1885, 'When the bottles and the cigar-case are to the fore, even a bishop may enquire of you, with a jovial smile of born companionship, What is your favourite vice?' Replaced by POISON.

***fawn(e)y,** occ. **forn(e)y,** rarely **faun(e)y.** A ring (hence *fawnied*, adj., ringed); ring-dropping (see FAWNEY-DROPPING): the former low, the latter c.: late C.18–19. Parker, 1781. 2. Also, though rare, a RING-DROPPER: late C.18–early 19 c. Prob. *fawney* derives ex Irish *fáinne*, a ring.

***fawney, go on the.** To practise FAWNEY-DROPPING: late C.18–19 c.

***fawney-bouncing.** Selling rings for a supposed wager: c.: mid-C.19–20; ob. See esp. H., 1st ed. A *fawney-bouncer* is one who does this.

***fawney-dropper.** A ring-dropper: see next entry. C.19 c. cf. MONEY-DROPPER.

***fawney-dropping** or **-rig** (or **-rigging:** '*No. 747*'). c.: C.19, late C.18–19 resp. Grose, 2nd ed., 'A fellow drops a ring, double gilt, which he picks up before the party meant to be cheated, and to whom he disposes of it for less than its supposed, and ten times more than its real, value.' See FAWNEY.

***fawn(e)y-fam'd** or **-fammed; fawnied.** 'Having one or more rings on the finger', Vaux: c.: ca 1810–60.

***fawney-rig,** see FAWNEY-DROPPING.

fawny, see FAWNEY.

fay appears in C.14–19 coll verging on S.E. expletives. † form of *faith*.

faynights. A late C.19–20 variant of *fainits!*, q.v. at FAIN I!

***faytor,** see FATER.

fe. Meat: chimney-sweepers': C.19–20. Adopted from Shelta *fe*, itself ex Irish *feóil*.

***feager** (properly **feaguer) of loges.** A beggar with forged papers: C.17 c. Rowlands. cf.:

feague. To GINGER UP, esp. a horse (gen. by enlivening but ugly 'fundamental' means): late C.18–early 19: low. Ex S.E. senses: beat; overcome, esp. by trickery: themselves ex Ger. *fegen*. Whence FAKE: a form anticipated by C.17 variant *feak*, to thrash.

***feaguer,** see FEAGER.

feak. The fundament: low: early C.19. Perhaps ex FEAGUE.

feaker, see FAKER.

fear. To frighten: since ca 1870, coll; earlier, S.E. Also common in dial.: C.19–20.

fear, for. Short for *for fear that* or *lest*: coll: from ca 1840.

fear!, never. No danger, or risk, of that!: coll: ?earliest in Bulwer Lytton, 1838. cf. DON'T YOU FEAR! 2. See NEVER FEAR.

fear!, no. Certainly not! Coll: from ca 1880. cf. FEAR, NEVER.

'feard, see AFEARD.

fearful, fearfully, adj., adv. A coll intensive (cf.: AWFUL; TERRIBLE): from ca 1880. Earlier in dial.

fearful frights. 'Kicks, in the most humiliating quarters': lower classes': ca 1890–1914. Ware.

fearnought. A drink to keep up the spirits. 1880, S.O.D.; ob.

feather. The female pubic hair: either coll or euphemistic: C.18–19. Prior, Moore. Perhaps ex S.E. *feather*, (of a cock) to tread. 2. See FEATHER AND FLIP.

feather, high or **low in the.** With one's oar well or badly held while out of the water: sporting: from ca 1870. Andrew Lang, *Ballad of the Boat Race*, 1878. Ex the S.E. *feather an oar*.

feather, in (full). Rich: coll: from ca 1860. Mrs Henry Wood, 1871, 'Clanwaring, in feather as to cash . . . was the gayest of the gay.' 2. In full dress: coll: from ca 1865. 3. Elated: from ca 1870. Earlier *in high feather*: ca 1815–70. Moore, 1819, 'The swells in high feather'.

feather, Jack with the. (Variant, *a plume of feathers*.) A trifling person: coll: late C.16–17.

feather, ride a. To be a jockey weighing less than 84 lb.: ca 1810–1900; sporting coll.

feather, show the white. To show oneself a coward: orig. coll; S.E. by ca 1895. It probably arose in the late C.18, for in Grose, 1785, we find, at *white feather*, 'He has a *white feather*, he is a coward. . . . An allusion to a game-cock, where having a white feather, is a proof that he is not of the true game breed.'

feather and flip. A bed; sleep: late C.19–20. Rhyming KIP. Often shortened to *feather*.

feather-bed and pillows. A fat woman: low: ca 1850–1910. Ex FEATHER, and *pillow*, a large breast.

feather-bed lane. A rough road or lane: coll: late C.17–20; ob.

feather-bed soldier. A persistent, expert whoremonger: C.19: coll. cf. CARPET KNIGHT.

feather-driver. A quill-driver, a clerk: coll; late C.16–17. Literary s.

feather in one's mouth, having (or with) a. Capable of showing temper, but holding it in: nautical: late C.19–20; ob. Ex that foam at a ship's cut-water 'which shows there either has been, or will be, dirty weather' (Ware).

feather one's nest. To enrich oneself with perquisites, licit and/or illicit; to amass money: C.16–20; coll till ca 1830, then S.E. Greene, Vanbrugh, G. Eliot.

feather to fly with, not a. 'Plucked': universities': late C.19–20; ob.

***feathers.** Money: wealth: c. or low: ca 1855–1905. 2. **(the feathers.)** Bed: from ca 1880; very ob.

features. A satirical term of address: ca 1900–14. cf. FACE.

***feck.** To discover a safe method of robbery or cheating: C.19 c. Duncombe, 1848. Ironically ex *feckless* or, more prob., a corruption of *feak* = FAKE.

fed-up. Bored: disgusted; (*with*) tired of: orig. military, possibly ex the Boers (witness Pettman): from ca 1899. G. W. Steevens (d. 1900), 'We're all getting pretty well fed-up with this place by now.' cf. Fr. *en avoir soupé*.

feed. A meal; an excellent meal: coll: both from ca 1805. Ex the stables. Bulwer Lytton, in *Paul Clifford*, 'He gave them plenty of feeds.'

feed, v. To take food: M.E.–C.20. Of animals, S.E.; of persons, coll since ca 1850. 2. In football, to back, v.i. and t.: from ca 1880: coll >, in C.20, j. > S.E. Ex rounders. 3. In the theatre, to supply (the principal comedian) with cues: from ca 1890. 4. In the universities, to CRAM: C.18–19.

feed, at. At meal; eating: coll: from ca 1880, *The National Observer*, 1890, vol. V, 'Statesmen at feed'.

feed, be off one's. To have no appetite: from ca 1830; s. > coll ca 1870. Michael Scott; Reade, 'No, doctor; I'm off my feed for once,' 1873. Variant with *oats*.

feed a part. (Theatrical.) To fill it out with small speeches or incidents (—1892); ob.

feed the fishes. To be sea-sick: coll (—1884). 2. Hence, though rarely, to be drowned: from ca 1890.

feed the press. To send copy to the compositors slip by slip: journalistic (—1891); ob.

***feeder.** In c., a silver spoon; any spoon: late C.18–20; ob. Hence *feeder-prigger*, a spoon-thief. 2. In university s., a COACH: mid-C.18–early 19. Goldsmith: 'Mr Thornhill came with . . . his chaplain and feeder,' 1766. 3. Actor or actress whose part simply feeds that of a more important comedian: theatrical coll: 1800; ob. Ware.

***feeding-birk.** A cookshop: c.: late C.19–20. Ware, '"Birk" being possibly a corruption of "barrack"'.

feeding-bottle. A woman's paps: low coll: C.19–20; ob.

feel. To take liberties with (one of the

opposite sex): low coll: C.18–20. 2. v.i., with infinitive, to feel, imagine, that one does: low coll (—1836); ob. cf. FEEL LIKE.

feel, have a. Same as FEEL, 1: low coll: mid-C.19–20.

feel cheap, see CHEAP, FEEL.

feel for (someone's) **knowledge box.** To aim a blow at an opponent's head: pugilistic: ca 1810–60. Anon., *Every Night Book*, 1827.

feel (something) **in one's water;** often preceded by *be able to* or *can.* To have a premonition: coll: late C.19–20.

feel like. To have an inclination for a thing or – esp. in form *feel like doing* – to do something: from ca 1870, orig. (—1855), U.S.: coll.

feel the collar. To perspire while walking: stable coll (—1909).

feel the shrimps, see CAN'T YOU FEEL THE SHRIMPS?

feele. A girl; a daughter; loosely, a child. In pl, occ. = mother and daughter. Low Cockney: from ca 1840. Ex It. *figlia*, via Lingua Franca. In Parlary, often *feelier*.

feeler. A tentative question, comment, or device: from ca 1830; coll till ca 1890, then S.E. *Tait's Magazine*, Sept. 1841, '*The Times* is putting out feelers on the corn-law question.' 2. The hand: c. (—1877); by 1890, low s.; ob. cf. FAMBLE.

feelier, see FEELE.

feet?, how's your poor. A c.p. rampant in 1862, nearly † in 1890.

feet, officer of. An infantry officer: military: ca 1750–1830. cf. FOOT-SLOGGER.

feet-casements. Boots; shoes: low: from ca 1840. cf. TROTTER-BOXES.

feet for children's stockings, make. To beget children: low coll: mid-C.18–early 19.

feet uppermost, lie. To receive a man sexually: low coll: C.19–20; ob.

fegary, figary; flagary. A whim; a prank: coll; ca 1600–1850. *Vagary* corrupted.

***fegs.** A late C.16–18, now dial., expletive: *faith* distorted; cf. FAY.

***feint.** A pawnbroker: c.: ca 1830–70. ?punning S.E. *feint* and c. FENCE.

feke. A conjurer's trick: magicians': since ca 1890.

felican. A little boy: showmen's: since ca 1870. cf. MOSIQUI for sense and FEELE for form; a diminutive.

Felix. A man who stands another a drink: military: late C.19–20; ob.

fell a bit on. To act craftily or underhandedly: tailors': from ca 1850; ob. *Fell*, in tailors' j., = to stitch down (a wide edge) so that it lies smooth.

fell-and-didn't. A person lame-walking: tailors': from ca 1840.

fella(h); feller. A coll pronunciation, the former somewhat affected and aristocratic, and form of *fellow*: resp. C.20 and from ca 1870.

fellow. As a male person it is S.E. of M.E.–C.20; as CHAP it is coll (—1711). Note *my dear* or *good fellow* and *what a fellow!* 2. A sweetheart: coll: late C.19–20. 3. Jocularly, C.19–20, of animals; coll.

fellow, a. One; anybody; even myself: coll: from ca 1860. Hughes, 1861.

fellow, old. A familiar, gen. affectionate, term of address: coll: C.19–20. 2. In some English schools it = a former member of the school (—1844); ob. 3. See OLD BENDY.

fellow-commoner. An empty bottle: Cambridge (—1785); ob. by 1900. The Oxford term was GENTLEMAN-COMMONER. Contrast EMPTY BOTTLE.

fellow-feeling. A ceiling: rhyming s.: late C.19–20.

***felon.** Felony: c.: C.18. The term had existed in this sense in C.14.

felon swell. A gentleman convict: Australian police and other officials': ca 1810–60. J. W., *Perils, Pastimes and Pleasures*, 1849.

felonious. Thievish: (somewhat low) coll: mid-C.18–20.

felt. A hat made of felted wool: coll until ca 1600, then S.E. Dekker; Moncrieff, 1823, 'Don't nibble the felt, Jerry.' (Caution: perhaps always S.E., even when, as occ. in C.17, used of any hat whatsoever.)

***fem,** see FAM, n. 2. A woman: Soho, London: late C.19–20. Ex Fr. *femme*: cf. FEME.

feme. In C.16–early 17 a coll, jocular in this survival of Anglo-Fr. legal usage, for a woman.

***fen.** A harlot; esp. a very low one: late C.17–early 19. Hence, 2, a procuress: C.18–early 19. Both are c. Prob. ex †*fen*, mud, filth. 3. A FENCE (n., 1): c.: late C.17–18.

fen! An early (—1815) variant of or alternative to FAIN I; esp. at marbles. cf. also FIN, and FINGY *that* or *you*, Winchester College and Christ's Hospital resp. As a gen. term of protest or warning it has the † variant *fen live lumber!* (—1877).

Note F. & H. at *fains!*, *fen*, *fin*, and *finjy!* Perhaps ex *fend*.

fen-nightingale. A frog; occ. a toad: coll: from ca 1860; ob. cf. CAMBRIDGESHIRE (or DUTCH) NIGHTINGALE.

***fence.** A purchaser or receiver, and/or a storer of stolen goods: late C.17–early 19 c.; then low; then, in C.20, increasingly gen. B.E., Dyche, Grose, Dickens. cf. BILLY-FENCER and FATHER. For etymology, see the v., 1. 2. A place where stolen goods are received or purchased, and/or stored: from ca 1700. Always c. cf. DOLLY-SHOP, FENCING-CRIB.

***fence,** v.i. To purchase or receive, and/or store, stolen goods: c. (—1610). Rowlands, *Martin Mark-All*. 2. v.t. To spend (money): late C.17–18: c. Both n. and v., 1, derive ex S.E. *fence* = *defence*, while *fence*, v., 2, is prob. a deliberate derivation from v., 1. 3. To sell: c. (—1839).

fence, over the. (Of a person) unashamed, scandalous; greedy; very unreasonable: New Zealanders' coll variation (late C.19–20) of S.E. *beyond the pale*. Perhaps ex local rules for cricket.

fence, sit (up)on the. (Rarely *ride*, occ. *be*.) To be neutral, waiting to see who wins: orig. political s., ex U.S. (—1830), anglicized ca 1870.

fence-shop. A shop where stolen property is sold: low coll: from ca 1780; ob.

***fencer.** A tramp; gen. with a defining term (as in DRIZ-FENCER), a(n itinerant) hawker: vagrants' c.: C.19–20. 2. A receiver of stolen goods: c. > low: from ca 1690; ob.

fences, crash one's, see CRASH ONE'S FENCES. cf. *rush one's fences*.

***fencing.** The 'profession' of purchasing or storing stolen goods: orig. (ca 1850) c.

***fencing-crib,** C.19–20, **-ken,** late C.17–early 19. A place where stolen property is purchased or hidden: c. The former, Ainsworth; the latter, B.E.

***fencing-cully.** A broker or receiver of stolen goods: mid-C.17–early 19.

Fenian, a. Threepence-worth of Irish whiskey and cold water: taverns': either from 1867, when the Fenians Allen, Larkin and O'Brien ('the Manchester Martyrs') were hanged for the murder of Police Sergeant Brett; or from 1882, when three Fenians were hanged – and therefore grew cold – for the murder of Cavendish and Burke in the Phoenix Park, Dublin. Also *three cold Irish*: which likewise was ob. by 1910.

Ferguson, you can't lodge here(, Mr). A London c.p., ca 1845–50. (Ex the difficulties experienced, in 1845, by a drunk, not a drunken, Scotsman named Ferguson, in getting lodgings.) In denial or in derision.

Feringhee. A foreigner: Anglo-Indian: from ca 1630. From ca 1880, contemptuous. Ex the C.10–20 Oriental, esp. the Persian and Arabic, hence also the Hindi adaptation of *Frank*, the *-ee* representing the ethnic suffix *-i*.

***ferm(e).** A hole: C.17–18: c. Dekker. 2. Occ. a cave, a prison. Ex Fr. *fermer*.

***fermedy** or **fermerly beggars.** All beggars that lack sham sores: c.: late C.17–18. Prob. ex Fr. *fermé*, closed, shut.

fernan bag. A small DITTY-BAG for tobacco and such trifles: nautical: C.19. Origin obscure; quite irrationally, I suspect a connection with Pernambuco: cf. the † S.E. *Fernanbuck*, (of) Brazil.

***ferret.** A dunning tradesman, esp. on 'young Unthrifts': late C.17–early 19 c. 2. Whence, a pawnbroker: c.: C.18–early 19. 3. A barge-thief: late C.19–20 c.

***ferret,** v.t. To cheat: c.: late C.17–mid-19. Ex the idea of sharpness. cf. n., 1.

ferreting. (From the male angle) the act of kind: ex the method of hunting rats and rabbits with a ferret. C.19–20; ob.

ferricadouzer. A knock-down blow: orig. pugilistic (—1851); ob. Mayhew. Ex It. *fare cadere*, to fell, + *dosso*, back, prob. via Lingua Franca.

ferrup(s) appears in C.17–19 exclamations; from ca 1830, dial. ?echoic.

fess. To confess; own up: coll: C.19–20. More gen. in U.S. than in England.

fess, adj. Proud: schoolboys': C.19–20; ob.

festive. 'Loud; fast; a kind of general utility word', F. & H.: ca 1870–1910. cf.: 2. (Of a new boy) 'who has not learnt his duty to his superiors and seniors', A. H. Tod: Charterhouse (—1900). Hence *festivity*, cheekiness. cf. FESS, adj.

fetch. A success: coll: C.19. 2. A likeness – ex the S.E. sense, an apparition – as in 'the very fetch of him': coll: from ca 1830. 3. Seminal fluid: coll: late C.19–20.

fetch, v. (As = to attract greatly, S.E. though not dignified.) 2. To deal (a blow), make (a stroke or other movement): M.E.–C.20: S.E. till C.19, then coll. 3. To obtain a summons against (a person): coll; from ca 1840. cf. FETCH LAW OF. 4. To go to (a certain prison), e.g. *fetch Pentonville*: c.: C.20. Also, more gen., to attain to, get access to: coll: from ca 1875. See FARM, 2. Ex nautical j.: to arrive at. 5. (Of a pump) to empty the bilge: *Conway* cadets' coll: from ca 1860. John Masefield, *The Conway*, 1860. Prob. an abbr. of *fetch the water up*. 6. Experience a seminal emission: coll: late C.19–20.

fetch a circumbendibus. Make a detour: C.19–20; ob.

fetch . . . a crack. To strike (a person): (?low) coll: 1853, Dickens.

fetch a howl. To weep noisily; cry out: low coll: C.19–20.

***fetch a lagging.** To be imprisoned; serve one's term: C.19–20 c.; ob.

fetch . . . a stinger. To strike (gen. a person) heavily: coll: from ca 1860.

fetch away. To part; separate: coll: from ca 1850; ob. 'A fool and his money are soon fetched away,' F. & H.

fetch down. To bring down by blow or shot: coll: from ca 1700. 2. To force down (prices, value): coll; from ca 1840.

fetch law of. To bring an action against: coll (—1832). cf. FETCH, v., 3.

fetch the brewer, see BREWER.

fetch the farm, see FARM, 2.

fetching. Attractive: from ca 1880: coll.

fetid waistcoat, see WAISTCOAT, 2.

fettle, in good or **proper.** Drunk: coll: from ca 1875.

fettle. (Of a man) to coït with: North Country workmen's: late C.19–20. Ex dial. *fettle*, to chastise, itself from a term in weaving.

few, a good. A fair number: coll (and dial.): from ca 1860. cf.:

few, (just) a, adv. Much, greatly; decidedly, certainly: s. > coll: from ca 1760; ob. Dickens, in *Bleak House*, 'Mr Smallwood bears the concise testimony, a few.' cf. RATHER!, the U.S. *some*, and the Fr. *un peu*, which last may be the source.

fi-fa. Abbr. FIERI FACIAS, a legal writ: legal: C.18–20.

fi-fi, see FIE-FIE.

fi-heath. A thief: back s. (—1859). By euphonic manipulation.

fib. A trifling falsehood: early C.17–20; a lie: C.17–20. Coll. Perhaps ex †*fible-fable* (on *fable*). 2. A liar: coll (—1861); an isolated pre-C.19 instance occurs in C.16. H. Kingsley, in *Ravenshoe*, '"Oh! you dreadful fib," said Flora.' 3. A blow: low coll or s.: from ca 1814 when boxing was at its palmiest. Ex FIB, v., 3, 4.

fib, v. To tell a trivial lie: late C.17–20. Dryden. Prob. ex FIB, n., 1. Hence, 2, to tell a lie: in C.18, chiefly among children (Johnson). Congreve, 1694, 'You fib, you baggage, you do understand, and you shall understand.' 3. To beat, thrash, strike: mid-C.17–18 c. Hence, 4, in C.19 pugilism, v.t. and i., to punch in rapid repetition. Southey, 1811; Thackeray ('My boy, fib with your right'). Origin obscure: but cf. possibly FAKE, v., and certainly FOB, V.

fibber. A liar, orig. small, soon great or small: coll; from ca 1720.

fibbery. The telling of lies: from ca 1850; ob.: coll.

fibbing. The telling of lies: coll; from ca 1740. Fielding. 2. In pugilism, C.19, a rapid pummelling; a sound beating. Tom Moore. See FIB, v., 4.

***fibbing-gloak.** A boxer: c.: early C.19. See FIB, v., 4. *Gloak*, a man (see GLOACH).

***fibbing-match.** A prize-fight: c.: C.19. Ex FIB, v., 4.

fice or foyse. 'A small windy escape backwards, more obvious to the nose than ears', Grose, 2nd ed.: late C.18–19; low coll. Earlier, S.E., esp. as *fist*.

fickle Johnny Crow. A man who does not know his own mind: West Indies coll: mid-C.19–20.

fid. A quid of tobacco: late C.18–20 (ob.): nautical. Ex *fid*, an oakum-plug for the vent of a gun.

fiddle. A sharper, occ. as *old fiddle*: C.18–early 19. Ex FIDDLE, v., 2. 2. A watchman's or policeman's rattle: low: ca 1820–50. Moncrieff. 3. A sixpence (cf. FIDDLER, 3): from ca 1850. 4. The female pudend: low: from ca 1800. cf. STRUM, v. 5. One-sixteenth of £1: Stock Exchange: from ca 1820; ob. 6. A writ to arrest: late C.17–early 19 c. 7. A whip: low: mid-C.19–20 (ob.). 8. A piece of rope and a long crooked nail for the picking of oakum: prison c. (—1877).

fiddle, v. To play the fiddle: M.E.–C.20: S.E. till ca 1820, then coll. 2. To cheat: C.17–20; S.E. until ca 1800, revived by the underworld ca 1840. Mayhew. 3. Hence, to make a living from small jobs done on the street (cf. S.E. sense, to trifle): mid-C.19–20; ob. 4. To punch: pugilistic: ca 1830–1900. 5. (In C.19–20, gen. with adv. *about*) to play about intimately with, to caress familiarly, a woman, v.t. (*with* in C.19–20): C.17–20: coll. In this sense 'to play as on a fiddle' is prob. cognate with '*fiddle*, fidget with the hands', which 'may belong . . . to Old Norse *fitla*, to touch with the fingers', W. 6. To drug (liquor): c. (—1899). Clarence Rook, *The Hooligan Nights*. Perhaps ex sense 2. 7. To be a petty thief: c.: late C.19–20.

fiddle, fine as a. Excellent: coll since ca 1590: 1598, Wm Haughton. Very fine: U.S.: recorded for 1811–27. cf.:

fiddle, fit as a. Excellent, most fitting or opportune: coll: since ca 1590: 1598, Wm Haughton; 1620, John Fletcher. 2. In good health, condition, form: coll since ca 1870: 1882, M. E. Braddon; 1883, R. L. S.; 1887, James Payn.

fiddle, get at the. To cheat: low and/or commercial: late C.19–20.

fiddle, hang up the. To desist, esp. from an enterprise: coll; from ca 1870.

fiddle, have a face as long as a. To look dismal, extremely depressed: coll; C.18–20.

fiddle, have one's face made of a. To be irresistibly attractive or charming: coll; from ca 1660. Smollett, Scott.

fiddle, play first (ob.) or **second fiddle.** To occupy an important, esp. the most important, part or to have but a secondary place: coll: from ca 1770. Dickens, 'Tom had no idea of playing first fiddle in any social orchestra,' 1843.

fiddle, Scotch and **Welsh,** see those adjj.

fiddle, second. An unpleasant job: tailors': ca 1870–1915.

fiddle and flute. A suit one wears: rhyming s.: late C.19–20.

fiddle-back. A chasuble having a fiddle-shaped back: coll: late C.19–20.

fiddle-bow. The penis: cf. FIDDLE, n., 4. Low: from ca 1830; ob.

fiddle-de-dee!, fiddle-faddle!, fiddlestick(s)! Coll interjections of resp. C.18–20 (ob.), C.17–early 19, C.17–20 (ob.).

fiddle-face. A wizened-faced person: dial. and coll: ca 1850–1900. H., 1st ed. Prob. ex: 2. One with a long, unhappy face: coll: late C.18–20; ob. Hence adj. *fiddle-faced.*

fiddle-headed. Plain; ugly: nautical: from ca 1840. cf. FIDDLE-FACE. 2. Empty-headed: coll, first recorded in 'You fiddle-headed brute!' (to a horse), Whyte-Melville, 1854.

fiddle when one comes home, hang up one's. To be merry or witty abroad, but not at home: coll: C.19–20. Ex the C.18–20 synonymous Derbicism *hang the fiddle at the door*.

fiddled stick. A flag-staff: nautical, esp. naval: ca 1805–60.

fiddler. A SHARP or a cheat: low: C.19–20; ob. Ex FIDDLE, v., 2. 2. A prize-fighter, esp. one who jumps about a great deal: pugilistic: ca 1830–1910. Ex FIDDLE, v., 4. 3. A sixpence: low (—1853). Prob. ex FIDDLER'S MONEY. (Whence FIDDLE, sixpence.) 4. Also a farthing: ca 1855–1900. 5. A capstan-house: nautical (—1874); very ob. Because, on some ocean-going ships, it was the only place where passengers were allowed to smoke and because, while the sailors worked the capstan-bars, a man sometimes played on the fiddle to cheer them at their toil. 6. A trumpeter: a bugler: military: late C.19–20; ob.

fiddler's bitch, drunk as a. Extremely tipsy: lower-class coll: mid-C.19–20.

fiddler's fare. Meat, drink, and money: coll: ca 1780–1850. cf. FIDDLER'S PAY.

Fiddler's Green. The traditional heaven of sailors, esp. of those who die ashore: from ca 1790: nautical coll. Marryat, in *Snarley-Yow*:

'At Fiddler's Green, where seamen true,
When here they've done their duty,
The bowl of grog shall still renew,
And pledge to love and beauty.'

Bowen defines it as 'a place of unlimited rum and tobacco'.

fiddler's money. All small change, esp. sixpences: coll: mid-C.18–early 19; since, dial. In C.18, each couple paid 6d. 'for musick at country wakes and hops', Grose, 1st ed. cf.:

fiddler's pay. 'Thanks and wine', B.E.: ca 1660–1750: coll. cf. preceding entry. In C.16–early 17, *fiddler's wages*, which gen. = thanks (without even the wine): likewise coll.

***fiddlestick.** A spring saw: Scottish c.: ca 1820–1910. 2. The male member: C.19–20, ob.; low. cf. FIDDLE-BOW. 3. A sword: late C.16–17 jocular. Shakespeare. 4. Substituted for another word in jocular derision (hence coll), as in '"He won a patriot's crown," said Henry. "A patriot's fiddlestick," replied Bill.' C.19–20. In this last sense, often replaced by FIDDLESTICK'S END.

fiddlestick, not to care a. To care not a whit: coll; from ca 1800.

fiddlestick's end(s). Nothing: late C.18–early 19: coll. cf. FIDDLESTICK, 4.

fiddling. A livelihood from odd street-jobs; esp. the selling of matches in the streets: low coll (—1851). cf. FIDDLE, v., 3. 2. In low s. (—1850), buying very cheaply and selling at a good price. 3. In c. esp.

among gamesters, gambling: mid-C.19–20; ob.

fidfad, fid-fad. A FUSS POT, a habitual fusser; a fiddling trifle: coll: from ca 1750; ob. Goldsmith, 1754, 'The youngest ... is ... an absolute fid-fad.'

fidge. Fidgeting (habit, action); fidgetiness: C.18–20. 2. A fuss: C.19. Likewise coll (when not dial.). 3. A fidgety person: coll or dial. (—1884). Also in phrase, *be in a fidge*, to be restless, fidgety. The term derives ex *fidge*, to fidget.

fidibus. A paper spill: cultured coll (—1829); ob. Ex C.17 Ger. students' s.

***fidlam-** (or **fidlum-)ben,** late C.18–19; **-cove,** C.19. A general thief: c. cf. FIDDLE, n., 1, and ST PETER'S SON.

fie-fie, occ. **fi-fi.** Of improper character (persons): coll; from ca 1810. 2. Hence, a woman of damaged repute: ca 1820–1900. 3. Smutty, indecent: cultured coll; from ca 1860. ?begun by Thackeray, referring to Paul de Kock's novels.

fie-for-shame. The female genitals: schoolgirls': from ca 1820. cf. MONEY, 2.

field, v.i. To back the field: turf coll: from ca 1870.

field. To support, take care of in swimming: Winchester College: mid-C.19–20. Wrench. Perhaps ex fielding at cricket.

field, crop the. To win easily: horse-racing: from ca 1870; ob. (Double pun.)

Field-Lane duck. A baked sheep's-head: late C.18–19. Ex a low London thoroughfare leading from the bottom of Holborn to Clerkenwell and, for the greater part, demolished ca 1870.

field of wheat. A street: rhyming s.: late C.19–20; rare.

field-running. The building of rickety houses rapidly over suburban fields: builders': ca 1860–1910.

fielder. One who backs the field, i.e. the rest, against the favourite: from ca 1850. Also, a bookmaker: ca 1865–90. The turf. cf.:

fielding. The laying of odds against the favourite; horse-racing (—1874); ob.

fields of temptation. 'The attractions held out to young men at the university', Egan's Grose: Oxford University: ca 1820–40.

fieri facias, to have been served with a writ of. Have a countenance habitually red: late C.16–20; in C.16–17, legal; in 18–19, gen.; in 20, † except in legal s. – and even there it is decidedly ob. (cf. FI-FA.) Nashe, Dryden, Grose, H. Ex the English pronunciation of the L. phrase (lit., cause to be done!), with a pun on *fiery face*.

fiery lot. A FAST (2) man: coll: ca 1880–1900.

fiery snorter. A red nose, SNORTER (4), being a nose: from ca 1840; ob. *Sinks*, 1848.

fif. Fifteen, in calling lawn-tennis scores: (trivial) coll: from ca 1890.

fifer. A waistcoat workman: tailors': from ca 1860.

fifteen-puzzle, a. Confusion; incomprehensibility: middle-class coll: ca 1880–90. Ex a type of puzzle (movable cubes) very fashionable in 1879.

fifteen years of undetected crime. (Applied to) the long service and good-conduct medal: naval (ca 1895) >, by 1910, also military.

fifteener. A book printed in C.16: bibliographical coll: 1830.

fifth rib, dig or **hit** or **poke one under the.** To hit hard; dumbfound: coll (—1890). Ex C.17–19 S.E. *smite under the fifth rib*, i.e. to the heart.

fig, occ. **fig of Spain.** A contemptuous gesture made by thrusting the thumb forth from between the first two fingers: whence *not to care* or *give a fig for a person* (see CURSE, DAM(N), etc.). In C.16–17 often as *fico*. Coll. Shakespeare, 'Fico for thy friendship'. 2. The *pudendum muliebre*: C.19–20 (ob.) low. Semantically connected with the gesture. 3. See FIG, IN FULL. 4. A coin (value unknown) issued by a counterfeiter: c. (—1798). Also *fig-thing*.

fig, v. To GINGER-UP (a horse): C.19–20; stables'. Ex FEAGUE. 2. In c., mid-C. 16–18, v.i., to steal. cf. FEAGUE and FAKE. 3. The same (late C.19–20) as its original:

fig, give (a person) **the.** To defy with contemptuous gesture (see FIG, n.): from late C.16; ob.

fig, in full. In full dress: s. >, ca 1880, coll: from ca 1830. *Dublin University Magazine*, April 1835 (p.388), 'It was alleged by his shipmates that he was rather fond of arraying himself in "full fig".' Perhaps ex FEAGUE (v.); perhaps *fig-leaf*; prob. abbr. *figure*.

***fig-boy.** A pickpocket: c. of ca 1550–1620. Ex FIG, v., 2.

fig-leaf. A small apron worn by women: from ca 1870; ob. Ex the fencing protective pad.

fig out, v.t. and reflexive. To dress in one's best: coll: from ca 1820; ob.

***fig-thing,** occ. **figthing,** see FIG, n., 4.

fig up. To restore, reanimate, enliven:

coll (—1819). T. Moore, 'In vain did they try to fig up the old lad.' Ex FIG, v., 1.

figaries. Roguery; pranks: low coll, mostly London (—1887). Ex the very gen. dial. form of *vagaries*.

figaro. A barber: cultured: from ca 1860; ob. Ex the popularity of the opera, *Le Nozze di Figaro*.

***figdean.** To kill: c. of ca 1810–80. ?ex Fr. *figer*.

***figger, figure,** see FAGGER and cf. DIVER. 2. A Levantine trading-ship or trader, orig. from Smyrna only: nautical: mid-C.19–20. Ex the staple *fig*.

***figging-law** or occ. **fagging-lay.** Pocket-picking: c. of C.16–early 19, 18–early 19. Ex FIG, v., 2.

figgins, see FIGS.

figgy-dowdy and **-duff.** A boiled fruit-pudding: nautical coll: mid-C.19–20, the former being used orig. and mainly by West Country seamen. Smyth (*-dowdy*); Bowden (both). cf. the Shropshire dial. *figgetty-dumpling*, a boiled pudding made with figs.

fight. A party, as in TEA-FIGHT: coll; from ca 1870. cf. CRUMPET-SCRAMBLE.

fight a bag of shit, not be able to. To be no good at fisticuffs: low Australian coll: from ca 1905.

fight at the leg. 'To turn every event to good account', Pierce Egan, *The Life of Hayward*, 1822: low: ca 1810–50. Ex fencing or cross-stick?

fight or **play cocum,** see COCUM.

fight cunning To box intelligently: coll: mid-C.18–early 20. James Woodforde, *Diary*, 6 Oct. 1781.

fight for love. To fight without being paid. *Sessions*, 5th session, 1734, 'Agreed to *fight for Love*, as they call it': pugilistic s. >, by 1800, coll >, by 1830, S.E.

fight in silver. To fight in silver spurs: cock-fighting coll (—1823).

fight space with a hairpin. To attempt the impossible: Oxford University coll: 1882–ca 1914.

fight the old soldier, see OLD SOLDIER, FIGHT THE.

fight (or **buck**) **the tiger.** To play against the bank, orig. and esp. at faro: U.S. (*fight*, 1851; *buck*, late C.19), anglicized ca 1900, but never wholly acclimatized.

fighting cove A pugilist, esp. one travelling with fairs: low; mostly tramps' (—1880).

fighting drunk. Quarrelsomely tipsy: coll; from ca 1890.

fightist. A fighter: jocular coll: 1877, *Daily News*, 8 Oct.; ob.

figlia. A child: *figlia homey*, a male child; *figlia polone* (or *poloney*), a female child: Parlary: late C.19–20. In the older Parlary, *figlia* is strictly a girl: cf. FEELE. In Italian, the m. form is *figlio*.

figs; occ. **figgins.** A grocer: coll: from ca 1870. Ex his commodities.

fig's end. A c.p. replacing another word: cf. FIDDLESTICKS' END and *nothing*. Coll; C.17–18. Shakespeare. 2. Also, same period, as exclamation.

figure. A price value; amount to be paid: coll; from ca 1840. Sala, 1883, 'The "figure" to be paid to Madame Adelina Patti for her forthcoming season'. 2. (Esp. in *no figure*.) The female breasts and buttocks: coll; from ca 1870. 3. A person untidy or, in appearance, grotesque (*quite a figure, such a figure*, etc.): coll, 1774. 4. See FAGGER.

figure, v. In billiards (—1891), to single out or 'spot'. 2. App. only as *figure on*, as in *The Gentleman's Magazine*, 1773, 'His antagonist ... figured on him ... at ... whist, about £200,' i.e. totalled against him: non-proletarian; †by 1900.

figure, cut a, see CUT A FIGURE.

***figure-dancer.** One who alters the face value of banknotes, cheques, bills, etc.: late C.18–19: c. Ex S.E. sense, a performer in a figure-dance.

figure-fancier. One who prefers his women to be large: low: ca 1870–1910. Ex FIGURE, n., 2.

figure-head. The face: nautical: from 1840 (in Marryat).

figure-maker. A wencher: low; from ca 1875. Ex FIGURE, n., 2.

figure of fun. An oddity: coll: from ca 1810; slightly ob. cf. FIGURE, n., 3.

figure on, see FIGURE, v., 2.

***figure,** occ. **number, six.** 'A lock of hair brought down from the forehead, greased, twisted spirally, and plastered on the face', F. & H. c. of ca 1840–95. Mayhew, 'Hair ... done in figure-six curls'. cf. AGGERAWATOR.

filbert. A very fashionable man about town: Society: ca 1900–20. Popularized by the song about 'Gilbert | The filbert, | Colonel of the Nuts'. See NUT and KNUT. 2. The head, as in:

filbert, cracked in the. Slightly – or very – eccentric; crazy: Cockney: from ca 1880; ob.

***filch.** A hooked stick or staff wherewith

to steal: c.: C.17–18. Fletcher, 1622. Abbr. FILCHMAN. Grose gives variant *filel*: almost certainly a misprint for FILER. 2. Something stolen: C.17–20, increasingly rare. 3. A thief: more gen. FILCHER: from ca 1770. Ex the v. 4. See FILCH, ON THE.

***filch,** v. To steal; pilfer; rarely, rob: c. in mid-C.16–early 18, then low s.: in late C.19–20, low coll. Awdelay. Possibly ex FILCHMAN; perhaps, however, cognate with FILE. 2. To beat, strike: c.: mid-C. 16–17. cf. FIB, v., 3.

***filch, on the.** On the watch for something to steal: c. (—1877). Anon., *Five Years' Penal Servitude*, 1777.

***filcher.** A thief, esp. an ANGLER. In mid-C.16–18, c.; then low; in C.20, low coll. See FILCH, n., 2, and v., 1.

***filching,** vbl n. Theft, thieving, robbery: mid-C.16–20; c. until C.18, low until ca 1850.

***filching cove, mort.** A male, female thief: late C.17–18: c.

***filchman.** A thief's hooked staff or stick: c.: mid-C.16–17; cf. FILCH, n., 1. Awdelay, Head. The *man* is prob. *-man*, -MANS, the c. suffix.

***file; occ. foyl- or file-cloy.** A pickpocket: mid-C.17–19 c. cf. BUNG-NIPPER and BULK. 2. Hence, a man, a CHAP; orig. a very cunning one: low (—1812). Vaux; Dickens. Often in combination, e.g. *old file*, an elder, or miser. Ob. The word may derive ex the tool; perhaps, however, it is connected with Fr. *filou*, a pickpocket: cf. also Fr. *lime sourde*.

***file,** v. To pick pockets; to pick the pockets of; occ., to cheat: c.: late C.17–19. cf. n., 1, and Fr. *filouter*.

***file-cloy:** C.17–19; in C.18 **file-cly:** whence FILE, n., 1. cf.:

***file-lifter.** Also a pickpocket: c. of ca 1670–1800. cf. FILE, n., 1.

***filel.** The same as FILCH, n., 1: q.v. as to form.

***filer.** A pickpocket: c. of ca 1670–1800. Rare. Ex FILE, v.

***filing-lay.** Pickpocketry: C.18–19 c. Fielding. Ex FILE, v.

filio, see SWATCHEL.

***fill, give** (a person) **a.** To put on the wrong scent; to deceive: c. (—1909).

fill a gentleman's eye. (Of a dog) to have thoroughly good points: sporting, esp. dog fanciers': from ca 1870.

fill one's pipe. To be able to retire from work: coll: ca 1810–1910. Egan, 'According to the vulgar phrase, to fill their pipe'.

fill one's pipe and leave others to enjoy it. To make a large fortune, which one's heirs or other relatives dissipate: 'a vulgar phrase', says Pierce Egan in *Life in London*, 1821: coll: ca 1805–60.

fill the bill. To STAR (2): theatrical: ca 1880–1910. Ex *bill*, a programme; *fill* refers to the large letters 'featuring' the star performer. 2. Hence (?ex U.S.) to be effective, very competent, and, now †, to be a whopping lie: coll; from ca 1885.

***filler.** A large coal, used in filling-out a sack with illicit intent: c. of late C.16–early 17. Greene, *A Notable Discovery*, 1591.

***fillet of veal.** A house of correction: c. (—1857); †by 1900. Rhyming s. on STEEL, THE.

fillibrush. To flatter; praise insincerely, ironically: coll: ca 1860–90. ?ex FILLY.

filling at the price. Satisfying: coll; from ca 1840; ob. *London Figaro*, 28 May 1870, concerning baked potatoes. Perhaps ex Dickens's remark about crumpets in *Pickwick*, ch. xliv.

fillip, give nature a, see GIVE NATURE A FILLIP.

fillup(pe)y. Satisfying: ca 1840–80. cf. FILLING AT THE PRICE.

filly. A girl; a wanton: from early C.17. Etherege, 'Skittish fillies, but I never knew 'em boggle at a man before.' 'Filly' has, since ca 1820, been, among the upper classes, a coll and an entirely inoffensive word for a girl, a young unmarried woman. Pierce Egan the Elder, a very close observer of the speech of his day, glosses, in *Finish to Tom, Jerry, and Logic*, 1828, the phrase 'fillies of all ages', thus: 'This phrase is now so commonly used in a sporting point of view, without meaning any offence to the fair sex, that it would be almost *fastidious* to make any objections to it in this instance' (a race-meeting). 2. In C.19–20 c., a daughter. Ex Fr. *fille*; cf. FEELE. 3. 'A lady who goes racing pace in round dances': ballrooms' (—1909); virtually †.

filly and foal. 'A young couple of lovers sauntering apart from the world': proletarian (—1909); ob. Ware.

filly-hunting. A search for amorous, obliging, or mercenary women: C.19–20 low.

filth. A harlot: late C.16–17 coll > S.E. and dial. Shakespeare.

filthy, the. Money: from ca 1875. Abbr. FILTHY LUCRE.

filthy fellow. A mild endearment: coll: C.18.

filthy lucre. Money: jocular coll: from ca 1850. Mrs Gaskell, *Cranford.*

fimble-famble. A poor excuse or an unsatisfactory answer: coll: C.19. Ex the ideas implicit in S.E. *famble*, *fimble*, and *fumble.*

fin. An arm; a hand: nautical > gen.: late C.18–20. Grose, 1st ed. (*one-finned*, having only one arm); Dickens; Thackeray. *Tip the fin*, to shake hands: from ca 1850; slightly ob. 2. Abbr. (occ. *finn*) of FINNIF. 3. Variant of FEN! cf. FAIN I and FINGY.

find. A mess of three or four upper-form boys, breakfasting or teaing in one another's rooms in turn. Hence, *find*-FAG, a younger boy attending to a 'find's' wants. Harrow: late C.19–20; ob. 2. See FIND, A SURE.

find, v. To suffer from, feel to an unpleasant extent (esp. the temperature): coll (ob.) and dial. in C.19–20; formerly, S.E.

find, a sure. A person, occ. a thing, sure to be found: coll: 1838, Thackeray.

find cold weather. To be ejected: public houses' (—1909). cf. give a person the KEY OF THE STREET.

***finder.** A thief, esp. in a meat-market: c., from ca 1850. 2. A waiter: university, esp. Gonville & Caius College, Cambridge: C.19.

***fine.** A punishment, esp. imprisonment. Hence, v., to sentence: c.: C.19–20 (ob.). A revival of C.16–18 S.E.

fine, adj. Very large: coll, from ca 1830. (cf. *wee little.*) Often followed by *big*, *large*, etc.

fine, cut. See CUT FINE. Also RUN (*it*) FINE.

fine and large, all very. A coll c.p. comment expressing admiration or, more gen., incredulity or derision. Popularized by a music-hall song much in vogue 1886–8.

fine as a cow turd stuck with primroses. Very fine; always satirical. Coll (low): late C.18–early 19. Perhaps suggested by:

fine (occ. **proud) as a lord's bastard.** Richly dressed or lodged: mid-C.17–18 coll; semi-proverbial.

fine as fivepence or **fip(p)ence.** Very fine; 'all dressed up': coll: from ca 1560. Wycherley, 'His mistress is as fine as fippence, in embroidered sattens.' Ex that coin's brightness. cf. *grand as* NINEPENCE. Dial. (see Apperson) has some picturesque variants; coll English, *grand* for *fine.*

fine day for the (young) ducks. An exceedingly wet day: C.19–20, ob.

fine days, one of these. Some day; in the vague future: coll: from ca 1850. ?a development ex the C.19 proverb, *one of these days is none of these days*, influenced by the Fr. *un de ces beaux jours.* In C.19, occ. *mornings.*

fine(-)drawing. The sly accomplishment of one's (gen. illicit) purpose: tailors': from ca 1860; ob. Very delicate stitching being almost invisible.

fine madam. A woman above her station: pejorative coll: from ca 1800.

fine twig, in. Finely, splendidly: low (—1812). (See GAMMON THE TWELVE.)

fine weather for ducks. (Very) wet weather: coll: 1840, Dickens.

fine words butter no parsnips! A sarcastic comment on fine-sounding statements or promises: coll; from ca 1750. C.17 variants are *fair words*, or *those words*, and *mere praise*, etc.

finger. Abbr. FINGER AND THUMB: 1868, says Ware.

finger. To caress a woman sexually: low coll; from ca 1800. cf. FEEL.

finger, a bit for the. An extremely intimate caress, the recipient being a woman: C.19 low.

***finger and thumb.** A road: c. rhyming on Gypsy DRUM: late C.19–20. 2. Also (—1851), rum: gen. rhyming s. 'Ducange Anglicus', 1857, records it as *finger-thumb*, a form soon > rare.

finger-fuck, v.i. (Of women only) to masturbate. vbl n. in *-ing.* C.19–20 low coll.

finger in (the) eye, put, see EYE, PIPE THE.

finger-post. A clergyman: late C.18–20. He points out the way to heaven, but does not necessarily follow it himself. 'Do as I say, not as I do.'

finger-smith. A midwife: C.19–20; low. 2. In c., a thief, a pickpocket (—1823); ob.

finger-thumb, see FINGER AND THUMB, 2.

fingers are made of lime-twigs, (e.g.) **his.** He is a thief: coll: late C.16–mid-18. Harington, 1596; Bailey, 1736. Apperson.

fingy or **finjy!** An exclamation of protest: Winchester College: from ca 1840. cf. and see FIN, 3, FEN, and esp. FAIN I.

finish. The 'end' of a person by death; social, professional, physical ruin: low coll; from ca 1820.

finish. To kill; exhaust utterly, render helpless: from ca 1600; S.E. until ca 1830, then coll. cf. SETTLE.

finisher. Something constituting, a person administering, the final or decisive blow or touch: coll (orig. pugilistic): from ca 1815.

finjy, see FINGY.

fink, see THINK!, I DON'T.

finkydiddle. Same as, and prob. a variant of, FIRKYTOODLE. Late C.19–20.

***finn,** see FINNIF. **finned,** see FIN, n, 1.

***fin(n)if, -ip, -uf(f), -up;** occ. derivatively **finny, finn, fin;** in C.20, occ. **finnio** (Chas. E. Leach). A £5 note, hence *double finnif* (etc.) = a £10 note, and *ready finnif* (etc.) = ready money. c.: from ca 1835. Brandon (1839); Snowden, *Magazine Assistant*, 1846. Ex Ger. *fünf*, five, via Yiddish.

fins, put out one's. To bestir oneself: C.15 (?—C.16); coll. Paston Letters.

***finuf** or **finup,** see FINNIF.

fi'pence, fippence. Five pence: coll: C.17–20. cf. U.S. *fip*.

***fi(p)penny.** A clasp knife: Australian c.: ca 1860–1910. Ex England, where recorded by Vaux in 1812.

***fire.** Danger; *on fire*, dangerous: C.19 c.

fire, v. To dismiss; expel: orig. (—1885), U.S.; anglicized ca 1905, though (says Ware) reaching England in 1896. Punning *discharge* (W.).

fire, catch on. To catch fire: either sol. or coll (—1886).

fire, like a house on, see HOUSE ON FIRE, LIKE A.

fire, pass through the. To be venereally infected: C.19–20 (ob.); low.

fire, set the Thames on. (Gen. ironically or in sarcastic negative.) To be very able or clever. Coll: late C.18–20. In late C.19–20, S.E. Foote, Jane Austen. See esp. Apperson and W.

fire, there's been a. A c.p. addressed to one wearing a new suit: Londoners': late C.19–20. Implying salvage.

fire a gun. To introduce a subject unskilfully, late C.18–19; lead up to a subject: C.19. Coll ?ex military s. 2. To take a (strong) drink: late C.18–mid-19. George R. Gleig, *The Subaltern's Log-Book* (I, 208), 1828. cf. FIRE A SLUG.

fire a shot. (Of the man *in coitu*) to have an emission: C.19–20 low.

fire a slug. To drink a dram: late C.18–20 (ob.); orig. military.

fire-and-light(s). A master-at-arms: naval coll (and nickname): late C.18–19.

fire away. (Gen. an imperative.) To go ahead: coll: from ca 1770. FitzGerald.

fire-box. 'A man of unceasing passion': ca 1900–15. Ware classifies it as 'passionate pilgrims''.

fire-eater. A rapid worker: esp. among printers and tailors: ca 1840–1920. 2. A bully; duellist: ca 1820–1900: coll > S.E. 3. In the 1860s, a SWELL, esp. if inclined to boast.

fire-escape. A clergyman: from ca 1850; ob. cf. DEVIL-DODGER.

fire-fiend. An incendiary: coll (—1897).

fire-flaw. A sting-ray: nautical coll: C.19–20. Bosen. Corruption of *fire-flair*.

fire in the air: 'To shoot in the bush', i.e. to ejaculate externally: low: C.19–20.

fire-out. Same as (*to*) FIRE. (In U.S., 1885; in England by 1896, says Ware.)

fire-plug. A (young) man venereally infected: low (1823); †by 1890. Suggested by FIRE-SHIP.

***fire-prigger.** One who, pretending to help, robs at fires: c. or low: C.18–early 19. See PRIGGER and esp. Defoe's *Moll Flanders*.

fire(-)ship. A venereally diseased whore: low: ca 1670–1850. Wycherley.

fire-shovel when young, to have been fed with a. Have a large mouth: late C.18–19 coll.

fire-spaniel. A soldier apt to sit long by the barrack-room fire: military: from ca 1870; ob. by 1910.

fire up, v.i. To light one's pipe: coll: from ca 1890. Ex a furnace.

fire(-)water. Very fiery spirits: ex. U.S. (—1826), anglicized ca 1850: coll that, by ca 1890, is S.E. 'Awful firewater we used to get,' T. Hughes in *Tom Brown at Oxford*. Perhaps so called because if one applied a match, the drink caught fire.

fireworks. A brilliant display of skill or virtuosity: C.19–20 coll > S.E.; often pejorative. 2. Among tailors, ca 1870–1915, a great disturbance or intense excitement.

fireworks on the brain, have. To be flustered: coll: ca 1870–1905.

Firinghee. A variant of FERINGHEE.

firk. To beat: late C.16–19, coll > S.E. ?cognate with FEAGUE and FIG, v.v.

firkin of foul stuff. 'A very Homely' – i.e. plain – 'coarse corpulent woman', B.E.: low: late C.17–mid-18.

firkytoodle (with frequent vbl n., **firkytoodling).** To indulge in physically intimate endearments, esp. in those provocative caresses which constitute the normal preliminaries to sexual congress. Coll: C.17–19. cf. FIRK.

firm. An association of two, three or four boys for the purchase and consumption of provisions: Shrewsbury School: late C.19–20.

firm, a long, see LONG FIRM.

first at the top-sail and last at the beef kid. (Of an A.B.) perfect: naval c.p. (—1909); ob. Ware; Bowen implies that it dates well back into C.19.

first-chop, see CHOP.

first(-)class. Exceedingly good: coll: 1870. 'From the universities [*first-class degree*] via the railways', while '*first-rate* is from the navy', W. 2. As adv.: extremely well: 1895. cf. FIRST-RATE.

first flight, in the. Active, or first in, at the finish of a race or a chase: from ca 1850: coll. ?ex fox-hunting. Contrast the S.E. sense.

first-floor. The tenant or lodger occupying the first floor: coll: from ca 1860.

first-night wreckers. A theatrical coll (1882–5) for a band of men intent on spoiling first-nights.

first-nighter. A habitué of first (orig. theatrical) performances: from ca 1885: journalistic s. >, ca 1900, gen. coll.

first of May. One's 'say' (firm speech, declaration); hence, the tongue: low (—1857): rhyming s.

first pop. At the first attempt; on the first occasion: late C.19–20. For *at the first pop*.

first(-)rate, adv. Excellently; in good health: coll: from early 1840s. (The adj., C.17–20, S.E.) See FIRST-CLASS.

first-rater. A person or thing that is first-rate: from ca 1805; coll till C.20, then S.E.

first-termer, see NEW FELLOW.

first thing. Early in the morning or the day: coll: mid-C.19–20. 'The boss wasn't here first thing.'

fisgig. Fun (gig) made at the expense of another's face (PHIZ): London jocular: ca 1820–30. See also PHIZ-GIG.

fish. A seaman; hence *scaly fish*, a rough, blunt sailor: late C.18–early 19. 2. A man. Gen. derogatively. Always in such combinations as COOL *fish*, LOOSE F., *odd f.* (prob. influenced by *odd fellow*), *queer f.* (after QUEER BIRD, and see QUEER CARD), SCALY F., *shy f.* Coll: from ca 1750, *queer* being the earliest, though *odd* and *scaly* are also of C.18; *loose* (—1831); *cool* (—1861); *shy* (—1891). Orig., presumably, an angler's term. 3. A piece, often collectively = pieces, cut out of a garment to ensure a better fit: tailors'; from ca 1870; ob. 4. The female pudend: low: from ca 1850. 5. An instance or an act of fishing, esp. in *have a fish*: coll; (?—)1880. 6. A whale: whalers' coll: C.19–20. 7. In oaths, as *God's fish!* (more gen. *Odds fish!*): C.18. Here 'fish' is euphemistic for 'flesh'.

fish, bit of. A coïtion (see FISH, n., 4): low: from ca 1850; ob.

fish, drink like a. To be constantly drinking (not innocuously): coll: from ca 1640. cf. C.17–19, *drunk as a fish*. See esp. Apperson.

fish, pretty (in late C.19–20, gen. **nice**) **kettle of.** A quandary; muddle: coll: C.18–20. Richardson. Perhaps ex Scottish *kettle of fish*, a picnic.

fish?, who cries stinking. Who would depreciate his own goods?: C.17–20; his own abilities?: C.18–20. Coll.

fish-bagger. A suburban tradesmen's derisive term of ca 1880–1915 for 'those who live in good suburbs without spending a penny there beyond rent', *Graphic*, 27 Sept. 1884.

fish-broth. Water, esp. if salt: jocular coll: late C.16–20; ob. Nashe, 'Belly-full of fish-broath'.

fish-eyes. Tapioca pudding: nautical: late C.19–20. Ex the appearance of that dish.

fish-face. A coll term of abuse: ca 1620–1750. Fletcher.

fish fag. A vixenish or foul-mouthed woman: coll: from ca 1810. Ex S.E. sense, a Billingsgate fishwife.

fish-fosh. Kedgeree. Cockney (—1887); slightly ob. Reduplication of *fish*.

fish-hooks. (Singular very rare.) Fingers; hence, hands; low, and nautical: from ca 1840.

fish-market. The lowest hole at bagatelle: gamblers': C.19–20. cf. SIMON. 2. A brothel: ca 1850–1910. Ex FISH, n., 4.

fish nor flesh, be neither. (In C.16, *flesh* occ. precedes *fish*.) To be hesitant, undecided, indeterminate: coll; C.16–20. Shakespeare, 'She's neither fish nor flesh.' Variants: *neither fish, flesh, nor fowl*; *neither fish, flesh, fowl, nor good red herring*, though, as in Dryden, the *fowl* is omitted at times.

fish of one and flesh or **fowl of another, make.** To exhibit partiality or make an invidious distinction: from ca 1630; coll till ca 1850, then S.E.

fish on one's fingers, find. To devise and/or allege an excuse: late C.16–early 17: coll. Greene.

fish to fry, have other. To have something

else to do: coll: mid-C.17–20. Evelyn, 1660; Swift; C. Brontë.

fisher. A toady: C.19.

fisherman's daughter. Water: rhyming s.: late C.19–20.

fisherman's walk, a. To which is gen. added *three steps and overboard*, which explains: nautical: C.19–20; ob.

fishing, go. To seek for an obliging or a mercenary woman: low: from ca 1850; ob. cf. FILLY-HUNTING, FISH (n., 4), GROUSING.

fishing-fleet. 'The wives and families of naval officers spending the season at Malta': naval: from ca 1890. Bowen.

fishmonger. A bawd: mid-C.16–early 17. Barnaby Rich; Shakespeare, *Hamlet*, II, ii, 174. Prob. a corruption of *fleshmonger*. Hence:

fishmonger's daughter. A whore: late C.16–early 17. Ben Jonson; Middleton.

fishy. Morally or financially dubious; equivocal, unsound: from ca 1844: s. >, by 1880, coll. *Punch*, 1859: 'The affair is decidedly fishy.' cf. FISH, n., 2. Whence *fishiness*, the corresponding abstract n. 2. SEEDY, indisposed: esp. in and ex *have a fishy*, i.e. a glazed, *eye.* Coll; from ca 1860.

fishy about the gills. Having the appearance of recent drunkenness: Cockneys' (—1909). cf. FISHY, 2. Ware, 'Drink produces a pull-down of the corners of the mouth, and a consequent squareness of the lower cheeks or gills, suggesting the gill-shields in fishes.'

***fisno.** A warning, esp. in *give someone the fisno*: c.: from ca 1840. '*No. 747*'. Origin?

fist. Handwriting: coll > s. > coll again; from ca 1470. In C.15–17, prob. S.E. 'A good running fist', anon., *Mankind*, 1475. 2. A workman (tailor): tailors': from ca 1860. Esp. *good* or *bad fist*. 3. Among printers, an index hand: from ca 1880. Jacobi.

fist, v. To apprehend; seize: coll: late C.16–20; ob. Shakespeare, 'An I but fist him once!' 2. Whence the C.19–20 low coll sense, take hold of: 'Just you fist that scrubbing-brush, and set to work', F. & H., 1891.

fist, give a person one's. To shake hands: coll: late C.19–20. Esp. in *give us your fist!*

fist, make a good, poor, etc., **at.** To do, or attempt to do, a thing, with a good, bad, etc., result: orig. (1834), U.S.; anglicized ca 1860. Coll.

fist, put up one's. To admit a charge: tailors': from ca 1860; ob.

fist-fucking. Masturbation: of males only (contrast FINGER-FUCKING): low: C.19–20.

fist it. (Of a woman) to grasp the *membrum virile* with sexual intent: low: C.19–20. 2. To use one's hands, e.g. in eating with one's fingers: Australia and New Zealand (—1846): ob. by 1870; †by 1890.

fist-meat, eat. To receive a punch or slap in the mouth: coll of ca 1550–1700.

fistiana. Boxing and all that pertains thereto: jocular coll; from ca 1840.

fistic. Related to boxing: (an increasingly low) coll adj.: from ca 1885.

fists, (esp. in one's). Grasp; clutches: M.E.+; S.E. till C.19, then coll.

fit. Fought: (dial. and) low coll: C.18–20.

fit, adj. In excellent health: coll: from ca 1870. Ex sporting j.

fit as a fiddle, see FIDDLE, FIT AS A.

fit as a flea. Extremely fit or healthy: sporting coll: mid-C.19–20; ob.

fit as a pudding. Very fit or suitable: coll: 1600, Dekker, ''Tis a very brave shoe, and as fit as a pudding'; app. †by 1700. Apperson, who implies that it is prob. an abbr. of *fit as a pudding for a friar's mouth* (ca 1575–1750) or, occ., *a dog's mouth* (1592, Lyly), itself a semi-proverbial coll.

fit end to end or **fit ends.** To have sexual intercourse: low: C.19–20; ob.

fit (in the arm). A blow or a punch: London slums': 1897–8. One Tom Jelly, arrested for striking a woman, declared that 'a fit had seized him in the arm': this was too good for the populace to miss.

fit like a ball of wax. (Of clothes), i.e. close to the skin: coll: from ca 1840.

fit like a glove. To fit perfectly: from ca 1770; coll till ca 1850, then S.E.

fit like a purser's shirt on a handspike. The nautical version of the next: from ca 1800: coll.

fit like a sentry-box, i.e. very badly: military coll: mid-C.19–20; ob.

fit (a garment, hat, etc.) **on a person** is coll: from ca 1860.

fit the head, not. A C.19 tailors' phrase, meaning that a garment, although faultless, is said by a customer to have some fault or other, the tailor then keeping it a while and sending it, untouched, back to the customer, who is thereupon delighted with it. *Saturday Evening Post*, 28 Sept. 1822 (p. 4, col. 1) – reporting a trial held in London.

fit to. (Of things) likely or enough to (do something): coll; from ca 1770; ob. 2. Ready to, angry enough to (do something): late C.16–20. S.E. till ca 1850, then coll and dial.

fit to a T. Gen. v.t., to fit to a nicety: coll: late C.18–20. Ex the T-square used by architects.

fit to kill. Immoderately, excessively: coll: U.S. (1856: Thornton), anglicized ca 1890.

fit(-)up. A stage easily fitted up; hence, a small theatrical company: from ca 1880: theatrical s. >, by 1910, coll. cf. FIT-UP TOWNS.

fit up a show. To arrange an exhibition: artists': from ca 1870; ob.

fit-up towns 'do not possess a theatre, and ... are therefore only visited by small companies carrying portable scenery, which can be fitted up in a hall or an assembly room', *Referee*, 22 July 1883: theatrical: from ca 1880; ob.

fits, beat into. To beat HOLLOW: coll; from ca 1835. Hood, 'It beats all the others into fits.'

fits, forty, see FORTY FITS, HAVE.

fits, give a person. To defeat humiliatingly: coll; from ca 1870. Orig. U.S.

fits, lick into. To beat HOLLOW: coll (—1887). Ex *give a person* FITS.

fits, scream oneself into. To scream excessively: coll: from ca 1840.

fits, throw (a person) **into.** To alarm or startle greatly: coll: from ca 1855.

***fitter.** A burglars' locksmith: c.; from ca 1860.

Fitz. A royal natural child: lower classes': late C.19–20. The prudent Ware thus wisely: 'Derivation obvious'. 2. A person of position or fortune going on the stage: theatrical: 1883.

five-barred gate. A policeman: Cockneys': 1886–ca 1915. Ware, 'The force being chiefly recruited from the agricultural class'.

five-boater, -master, -rater. These are nautical coll of obvious meaning, all three referring to ships: from ca 1887.

five(-)fingers. The 5 of trumps in the card game of don or five cards: C.17–19: s. > j. Cotton in *The Compleat Gamester*, 1674. cf. FIVES.

five-master, see FIVE-BOATER.

five o'clock, a. Afternoon tea at five o'clock: coll: from ca 1890. cf. Fr. *des five o'clock à toute heure.*

five or seven. Intoxicated; a drunkard: policemen's and Cockneys': 1885–ca 1914. Ex *five shillings or seven days*, 'the ordinary magisterial decision upon "drunks" unknown to the police' (Ware).

five over five, adj. and adv. Applied to those who turn in their toes: from ca 1820; ob.

five-pot piece, see POT, n., 5.

five-pounder. A cheap-excursionist: Jersey: 1883, *Graphic*, 31 March; ob.

five-rater, see FIVE-BOATER.

five-shares man. (Gen. pl) A fisherman, whaler, etc., working for a share of the profits: nautical coll: late C.19–20.

five shillings, the sign of. The tavern-sign of the crown. Hence *ten shillings*, *fifteen shillings*, the sign of the two, the three crowns. Mid-C.18–early 19.

fivepence, fine or **grand as,** see FINE AS FIVEPENCE.

fiver. Anything that counts five, but gen. a £5 note or occ. its equivalent: from ca 1850. Whyte-Melville, 'Or, as he calls it, a fiver'. 2. In c., a fifth term of imprisonment (—1872).

fives. A foot: C.17. 2. From ca 1820: fingers, i.e. hands, fists. 3. Hence, a street fight: low, esp. Cockney: from ca 1850.

fives, bunch of. A fist: from ca 1822. Ex preceding entry, sense 2.

***fives going, keep one's.** Constantly to thieve, esp. to pickpocket: c. or low s.: ca 1820–80.

fix. A dilemma: orig. (1833), U.S.; anglicized ca 1840; coll till ca 1890, then S.E.

***fix,** v. In c., to arrest: late C.18–early 19. 2. As a coll verb-of-all-work, it is an importation – rare before 1840 – ex the U.S. (1708: Thornton).

fix it. To arrange matters: ex U.S. (—1836); anglicized ca 1850: coll. cf.:

fix up. To arrange, e.g. a rendezvous, esp. for another: ex U.S., anglicized ca 1855. In C.20, occ. *be fixed up*, to have an appointment. 2. **fix** (a person) **up.** To provide him with lodgings or other quarters: coll: from ca 1888.

fixed bayonets. A brand of Bermuda rum: military: late C.19–early 20. Ex its sting and effects.

fixfax, see PAXWAX.

fixing. Strong drink: Australian (—1889); ob. by 1912.

fixings. See FIX, v., 2. 2. As furniture: 1887, Baumann.

fiz, fizz. Champagne; also, any sparkling wine: from ca 1860. 2. Occ., though very rarely in C.20, lemonade mixed with ginger-beer: from ca 1880. 3. A hissing sound: coll; 1842. 4. A fuss: from ca 1730. 5. Animal spirits: from ca 1850. These last two senses are coll – and ob. 6. Ned Ward, in 1700, has *fiz* for PHIZ.

fizzer. Any first-rate thing (e.g. a theatrical role) or, rarely, person: coll (—1866). 2. A very fast ball: cricketers' coll (1904). 3. A vendor of soft drinks: mostly Cockneys': 1895, H. W. Nevinson. Ex:

fizzer-man. A camp-follower selling soft drinks: military: 1894 (O.E.D.). Collectively the 'fizzermen' form the *fizzer-brigade*.

fizzing, adj. Excellent (—1859). 2. Also as adv.: from ca 1880; ob. cf. STUNNING.

fizzle. A ludicrous failure: orig. U.S., anglicized ca 1880: coll; by 1900, S.E.

fizzle out. To tail off; end lamely; become a failure; fail: orig. (ca 1848), U.S.; anglicized ca 1870; coll till ca 1905, then S.E. Ex fireworks, esp. if damp.

flab. Dripping (ca 1840–1900); (also *flib*) butter (C.20): Christ's Hospital. Marples. Ex its flabbiness.

flabagast, gen. **flabbergast.** To astound, physically or mentally; utterly to confuse (a person): coll: from ca 1772, when *The Annual Register* included it in 'On New Words'. Disraeli. Ex *flap* (or *flab*by) + *aghast*. 2. Hence the not very common and now ob. *flabbergastation*: 1845.

flabberdegaz. A GAG (4) or stop-gap words; a piece of bad acting or instance of imperfect utterance: theatrical: ca 1870–1915. Prob. ex:

flabbergast, see FLABAGAST.

***flag.** A groat or fourpenny piece: ca 1560–1890: c. Mayhew, 'A tremendous black doll bought for a flag (fourpence) of a retired rag-merchant.' 2. An apron: low, or low coll: from ca 1845. 3. A sanitary pad or towel. Hence, *the flag* (or *danger-signal*) *is up*: she is 'indisposed': from ca 1850. 4. Abbr. FLAG UNFURLED: late C.19–20; ob. 5. Words missed in composing: printers' (—1909). Ex the appearance of the 'out' words written at the side of the 'copy' or of the proof.

flag, fly the. To post a notice that workmen are needed: tailors': from ca 1860. cf. FLAG-FLYING.

flag-about. A strumpet: low, or low coll: ca 1820–70. cf. FLAGGER.

flag-flapper. A signaller: Navy: late C.19–20.

flag-flasher. One who, when off duty, sports the insignia of office – cap, apron, uniform, badge, etc.: from ca 1860. Ex FLAG, 2.

flag-flying. adj. and vbl n. corresponding to FLAG, n., 2 (cf. FLAG-FLASHER) and 3 (cf. CAPTAIN IS AT HOME, THE). 2. A bill's being posted up when hands are required: tailors' (—1889).

flag is up, the, see FLAG, 3.

flag of defiance. A drunken roisterer: nautical: mid-C.18–early 19. Ex:

flag of defiance or **bloody flag, hang out the.** To have a red face owing to drink; to be drunk: late C.17–early 19 nautical.

flag of distress. 'The cockade of a half-pay officer': naval: late C.18–mid-19. A MS. note by Grose to the B.M. 1st ed. copy: not, however, incorporated – as all such notes were orig. intended to be – in the 2nd ed. (1788). 2. An announcement-card for board, or board and lodgings: from ca 1850; coll. 3. Hence, any outward sign of poverty: orig. nautical: mid-C.19–20. 4. A flying shirt-tail: from ca 1855: low, esp. Cockney.

flag unfurled. A man of the world: rhyming s. (—1859); ob.

flag-wagging. Flag-signalling, esp. at drill: naval and military; from ca 1885.

flagger. A harlot, esp. one walking the streets: low (—1865); ob. Mostly London. Either ex pavement-*flags* or ex FLAG-ABOUT.

flags. Clothes drying in the wind: low coll: from ca 1860. cf. SNOW. 2. A flag lieutenant: naval nickname: late C.19–20.

flam, humbug, a trick, a sham story, after being S.E. in C.17–18, is in C.19 coll, in C.20 † except in dial. and Australian, the same applying dialectally to the rare adj. and the common v. Perhaps abbr. *flim-flam*, which, however, is recorded later: W. suggests that it derives ex Scottish *flamfew*, a trifle, gew-gaw. 2. The single beat of a drum: (—1791; ob.) orig. military s.; in C.19 gen. s. > coll. 3. In c., a ring: ca 1850–70.

flamdoodle, flam-sauce, see FLAPDOODLE.

flame. A sweetheart; a kept mistress: after being S.E., this term, esp. as *an old flame*, a former sweetheart or lover, is in C.19–20 increasingly coll and jocular. The modern semi-jocular use is perhaps directly ex C.17 Fr. '*flamme* and *âme* riming in the Fr. classics almost as regularly as *herz* and *schmerz* in Ger. lyrics', W. 2. In C.19 low coll or s., a venereal disease.

flamer. A person, incident, or thing very conspicuous, unusual, or vigorous; e.g. as in Cockton's *Valentine Vox*, 1840, a stiff criticism: ca 1808–1900. 2. In pl, a kind of safety-match giving a bright flame: from ca 1885; ob.

flames. A red-haired person; occ. as term of address or personal reference: coll: ca 1820–90. cf. CARROTS; GINGER, n., 4.

flaming. Very or too noticeable or vigorous; STUNNING: border-line coll: from ca 1780; ob. 'The first time I saw the flaming mot/Was at the sign of the Porter Pot' – from a popular ballad titled *Fal de Ral Tit*, ca 1800 or earlier. Ex the S.E. senses (C.17+), flagrant, startling. 2. (Of tobacco) very strong: low (—1887). 3. adj. and adv., BLOODY: euphemistic coll; from early 1890s. cf. RUDDY.

flamp. To sell Army property illegally: Regular Army: late C.19–20. cf. FLOG, 3.

Flanderkin. Late C.17–18 coll for 'a very large Fat Man or Horse; also Natives of that Country' (Flanders), B.E. cf. the next three entries.

Flanders fortune. A small one: late C.17–18; coll.

Flanders piece. A picture that looks 'fair at a distance, but coarser near at Hand', B.E.: late C.17–18: coll.

Flanders reckoning. A spending of money in a place unconnected with that where one receives it: coll: C.17–18. Thos. Heywood. cf. FLEMISH ACCOUNT.

flanges, see WINKERS, 2.

flank. To hit a mark with a whip-lash (—1830). 2. To crack a whip (v.t.): from ca 1830. Both are coll verging on S.E., the standard sense being, to flick; ob. 3. To push or hustle; to deliver (esp. a blow): coll; from ca 1860; ob. cf. Fr. *flanquer un coup à quelqu'un*, whence, presumably, it derives.

flank, a plate of thin. A cut off a joint of meat: low coll: from ca 1860; ob.

flanker. A blow, kick; retort: coll: ca 1860–1910. Whence *do a flanker*. 2. A shirker: military: late C.19–20; ob. Ex the 'advantages' of being on a flank.

flankey. The posterior: low (perhaps orig. c.): from ca 1840. Duncombe.

flannel, see HOT FLANNEL.

flannel- (often pron. **flannin)-jacket.** A navvy: contractors': from ca 1860; ob. From his flannel shirt or singlet. The *flannin* (or *-en*) form comes from dial.

flannel hammer or **left-handed spanner.** Imaginary tools, which an apprentice is sent to fetch: workmen's coll: late C.19–20.

flannels, get one's. To obtain a place in a team (orig. cricket): schools'; esp. and initially Harrow: from ca 1885. Coll. Ex *flannels*, flannel garments.

flannen or **-in,** see FLANNEL-JACKET.

flap. A blow: coll or dial.: C.16–18. Ex the S.E. v. 2. A female of little repute, a jade: C.17–20; coll, > dial. by 1800. 3. In c., sheet-lead used for roofing: mid-C.19–20 (ob.). Ex the noise it makes when loose in the wind. 4. A garment or hat that has a pendent portion: ca 1790–1920. 5. 'Any evolution on board or movement of warships': naval: late C.19–20. Bowen. Applied esp. to the bustle ensuing on an emergency order.

flap, v. To pay; FORK OUT. Esp. in *flap the* DIMMOCK (money). Low. From ca 1840; ob. 2. In c., rob, swindle: C.19–20; ob. 3. v.i., fall or flop down: coll, from ca 1660.

***flap a jay.** To cheat or swindle a greenhorn: c. (—1885). See FLAP, v., 2.

flap (in C.16–17, occ. *slap*) **with a fox tail.** A rude or contemptuous dismissal; a mild rebuke: coll: C.16–early 19. Palsgrave, 1530; Smollett; Scott.

flapdoodle. Empty talk; transparent nonsense: coll; from ca 1830. (?orig. U.S.) Marryat, 1833, 'Flapdoodle . . . the stuff they feed fools on'. Also a v., as is very rare with the variants: *flap-sauce*, *flam-sauce*, *flamdoodle*. 2. The *membrum virile*: late C.17–18 low coll. cf. DOODLE, 2. Like FLABBERGAST, *flapdoodle* is arbitrarily formed.

flapdoodler. An empty, inept, talkative political charlatan: journalists': ca 1885–1910; then gen. but ob.

flapdragon, flap-dragon, flap dragon. Syphilis or gonorrhoea: late C.17–early 19: low. Ex the S.E. sense, a raisin snatched from burning brandy and eaten hot. 2. A Dutchman; a German: pejorative coll: C.17.

***flapman.** A convict promoted for good behaviour: prison c. (—1893); ob.

flapper. The hand: low coll (—1833). Marryat; *London Miscellany*, 19 May 1866, 'There's my flapper on the strength of it.' cf. FLIPPER. 2. A slow or unskilful hunting man: sporting: from ca 1850; ob. Whyte-Melville. 3. A dustman's or a coal-heaver's hat: coll: ca 1850–1900. cf. FANTAIL. 4. In the low coll of sexual venery, the male member (cf. FLAPDOODLE, 2): C.19. 5. There too, a very young harlot, a sense linking up with that in gen. s., a young girl (?ex that, mainly dial., sense of a fledgling partridge or wild duck): both in F. & H., 1893, the latter being discussed in the *Evening News*, 20 Aug. 1892.

flapper-shaker. The hand: low coll; from ca 1850; ob. Ex FLAPPER, 1.

flapper-shaking. Hand-shaking; hence, a preliminary ceremony: from ca 1850. 'Cuthbert Bede', 1853.

flappers. Extremely long pointed shoes, esp. those worn by 'NIGGER minstrels': from ca 1880.

flapsauce, flap(-)sauce, see FLAPDOODLE. (No connection with the †S.E. term.)

flare. Anything unusual, uncommon: nautical; from ca 1850. 2. A quarrel, a row, a spree: coll: from ca 1840. cf. FLARE-UP.

flare. In its C.19–20 S.E. sense, to shine unsteadily, *flare* seems to have, ca 1660–1730, been c., then low s. and then, ca 1760–1830, coll: witness B.E. and Grose, all edd. Prob. ex Dutch or Low Ger.: cf. Ger. *flattern, fladdern,* and Dutch *vlederen.* 2. To swagger: low coll (—1841); ob. Leman Rede. 3. To whisk out (—1850); hence (—1851), to steal lightly, deftly. Mayhew. Both: c.

***flare, all of a.** Clumsily; bunglingly: c. of ca 1830–90. H. Brandon in *Poverty, Mendicity, and Crime*, 1839.

flare-up, rarely **-out.** A quarrel, commotion, or fight: coll; from ca 1835. Hence, a spree or orgy; a jovial party: coll (—1842). Justin M'Carthy, 1879, 'What she would have called a flare-out'. cf. the v.

flare up, v. To become extremely angry: coll (—1849). 'Father Prout' Mahony, '. . . Swore, flared up, and curs'd'; Thackeray.

flaring, adv. Exceedingly; vulgarly: coll: C.19–20; ob. e.g. in *flaring drunk*.

***flash,** n. and adj. (Underworld) cant; relating to the underworld or to its slang. Hence they often connote trickery, crime, low immorality. Orig. – 1756, 1700 resp. – themselves c., they rapidly > low s. > gen. s. > coll > S.E. Ultimately ex *flash* = sudden flame; intermediately ex *flash* = ostentation; imm. – of problematic birth. ca 1810–30, the s. of the man about town, chiefly the FAST (2) set and its hangers on (see esp. Jon Bee's *Dict. of the Turf*, 1823): s. > coll > S.E. cf. the ca 1760–1825 coll, verging on S.E., sense: fop, coxcomb. 2. In c., late C.17–mid-19, a peruke. 3. A showy swindler; a hectoring vulgarian or *nouveau riche*: C.17 coll. Shirley, 'The town is full of these vain-glorious flashes.' 4. A boast or great pretence uttered by spendthrift, QUACK, or sciolist: C.18. 5. A portion or, as in FLASH OF LIGHTNING, a drink: late C.18–19: low s. or low coll.

flash, v. To show; esp. excessively, vulgarly, or with unnecessary pomp or pretence: coll (—1785). In C.17, S.E. 2. v.t. with, e.g. *the gentleman*, to show off as, pretend to be, e.g. a gentleman: ca 1795–1850. 3. v.i., with variant *flash it*, to make a display, show off: ca 1770–1830. cf. FLASH IT ABOUT and FLASH IT AWAY. The term derives ex *flash* in the sense, 'show as in a flash, hence, brilliantly' (see esp. W.), prob. influenced by FLASH, n. and adj.

***flash,** adj. See FLASH, n., 1. 2. In c. of ca 1810–1900, knowing, expert; cognisant of another's meaning. 3. Orig. (—1785) c., by 1870 low: showy, vulgar; (in Australia, —1893) vainglorious, swaggering. Perhaps ex C.17–18 S.E. *flash*, show, ostentation. 4. Connected with boxing and racing: ca 1808–90. 5. In a set style: ca 1810–60: c. > low. Also n. Rare except in next entry. 6. Occ. adv., as in *to dress flash*, i.e. fashionably but showily and in bad taste. 7. Imitation; counterfeit: c.: from ca 1880; ob. (In the ensuing list of *flash* combinations, only such are given as are not imm. and accurately deducible from the mere collocation of n. and n., v. and n., and n. and adj.)

***flash, out of.** For showy effect or affectation: c. (—1812) >, by 1820, low s.; †by 1900.

***flash, put.** To put (a person) on his guard: c. (—1812); †by 1900.

flash a bit. (Of women) to permit examination; behave indecently: low: from ca 1840. cf. FLASH IT.

***flash a fawn(e)y.** To wear a ring: c.: from ca 1815; ob.

***flash-case, -crib, -drum, -house, -ken, -panny.** A lodging-house or tavern frequented by thieves and illegally favourable to them; in sense 2 of that n., FENCE: c. of resp. C.19–20 ob.; C.19; C.19–20 ob.; C.19–20; mid-C.17–19; and C.19, though extremely rare in these senses. 2. The meaning, a brothel, is derivative, and, though orig. c., it gradually > low: *flash-crib* is not used in this sense.

***flash-cha(u)nt.** 'A song interlarded with flash', i.e. with cant: c.: ca 1820–70. Also *flash song* (Vaux), 1812.

***flash-cove,** from ca 1810; **-companion,** from ca 1860. A thief; sharper; FENCE;

(only *flash-cove*) landlord of a FLASH-CASE.

***flash-covess.** A landlady of a FLASH-CASE: c.: C.19.

***flash-crib** and **flash-drum,** see FLASH-CASE.

***flash-dona.** A variant of FLASH GIRL: c.: late C.19–20.

***flash-gentry.** The high-class thieves: from ca 1820; ob.; c. Conflation of n. and adj.

flash girl, moll, mollisher, piece, woman. A showy harlot: low: from ca 1820.

***flash-house,** see FLASH-CASE.

flash in the pan. Coition *sans* emission: C.18–20 low coll. D'Urfey.

flash it, see FLASH, v., 3.

flash it or **flash one's meat.** (Gen. of men) to expose the person: low: from ca 1840.

flash it! Let me see it! Show it! A low, esp. a coster's reply to the offer of a bargain: from ca 1820; ob.

flash it about or **cut a flash.** To make a display – once, often, continuously; to lead a riotous or even a crapulous life: low: from ca 1860. cf. CUT A DASH. Developed ex:

flash it away. To show off; cut a figure: coll: ca 1795–1860. O'Keeffe.

flash-jig. A favourite dance: costers': ca 1820–90. Perhaps ex FLASH, adj., 3.

***flash-ken,** see FLASH-CASE.

flash kiddy. A dandy: low: ca 1820–60. cf. KIDDY, 3 and 4.

flash-lingo. Underworld slang: low: late C.18–19. See FLASH, n., 1.

***flash-man.** One who talks the s. of the underworld: c.: late C.18–19. 2. A chucker-out to a brothel: c.: C.19. Imm. ex: 3. A harlot's bully or PONCE: late C.18–20, ob.: low; prob. orig. c. 4. A patron of boxing: s. > coll: ca 1820–50. Moncrieff.

***flash mollisher.** A woman thief or swindler: c. (—1812); †by 1890. 2. See FLASH GIRL.

flash-note. A counterfeit banknote: C.19 low (?orig. c.).

flash o(f) light. A gaudily or vividly dressed woman: South London (—1909); virtually †. Rhyming s. on *sight* in nuance 'sorry sight'.

flash o(f) lightning. A dram of strong spirit, a glass of gin: from ca 1780. cf. (—1862) U.S. usage and CLAP OF THUNDER. 2. Gold braid on an officer's cap: nautical: mid-C.19–20; ob.

flash one's gab. To talk, esp. much; boast: low (—1819). Tom Moore, 'His lordship, as usual, . . . is flashing his gab.'

flash one's meat, see FLASH IT.

flash one's sticks. To expose or draw (*not* to fire) one's pistols: ca 1810–50: c.

flash one's ticker. To take out one's watch rather often: low: from ca 1850.

flash-panny, see FLASH-CASE.

***flash patter.** Cant (underworld slang): c.: C.19. e.g. in '*No. 747*'s autobiography, p. 410.

flash side, the. The 'knowing ones' or self-constituted judges: pugilistic: ca 1810–50. *Boxiana*, I, 1818. See FLASH, adj., 2.

***flash song,** see FLASH-CHA(U)NT. Perhaps low s. rather than c.

flash(-)tail. A harlot picking up TOFFS at night: low (—1868); ob.

flash the dibs. To spend one's money: low: from ca 1840; ob.

***flash the dicky.** To show one's shirt-front: c.: from ca 1820.

***flash the drag,** see DRAG, n., 5.

flash the flag, see FLAG-FLASHER.

***flash the hash.** To vomit: late C.18–19: c.

***flash the ivory** or **one's ivories.** To grin or laugh: c. of late C.18–19 and low s. of C.19–20 resp. Contrast *tickle the* IVORIES.

flash the muzzle. To bring forth a pistol: low (—1823); ob. by 1870, †by 1900.

***flash the screens.** To pay: c. of ca 1820–40. See PEW, STUMP THE.

flash the upright grin. (Of women) to expose one's sex: low: from ca 1860; ob.

***flash the wedge.** To FENCE one's 'haul', SWAG, or booty: c.: C.19.

***flash to, be.** To be aware of, to understand fully: c.: ca 1810–60.

flash toggery. Smart clothes: low (—1834). Ainsworth in *Rookwood.*

flash vessel. A very smart-looking ship that is undisciplined: nautical: ca 1860–1915.

***flash woman.** A harlot mistress of a FLASH-MAN (3): c. (—1823); †by 1890.

flash yad. A day's enjoyment: ca 1865–1910. YAD = *day* reversed.

flasher. A would-be wit; hence, an empty fop: ca 1750–90: coll that perhaps > S.E. Mme D'Arblay, 1779, 'They are reckoned the flashers of the place, yet everybody laughs at them.'

flashery. Tawdry elegance; showy or vulgar display or action: coll: ca 1820–80. Never much used.

flashily; flashly, see FLASHY.

flashing it, go. To have sexual connection: low: from ca 1840; ob. cf. FLASH IT and FLASH A BIT.

flashy. Showy, gaudy; ostentatious: in late C.18–20, coll; earlier, S.E. Hence advv. *flashly*, s., C.19–20, but very rare in C.20, and *flashily*, coll, C.18–20. Miss Braddon, 1864, 'He chose no . . . flashily cut vestments.'

flashy blade or **spark.** A dandy: ca 1815–30. 2. Hence, a cheap and noisy dandy or would-be dandy: ca 1830–75. Both, coll verging on S.E.

flat. A greenhorn; a fool; an easy GULL or dupe: from ca 1760. Barham, 'He gammons all the flats.' cf. the C.20 story of the girl who refused to live either with or in one. By contrast with SHARP.

flat, do or **have a bit of.** To have sexual connection: low: mid-C.19–20.

***flat, pick up a.** To find a client: harlots' c.: C.19–20.

flat as a flounder or **a pancake.** Extremely flat, lit. and fig.: coll. The former: C.17–19; the latter, C.18–20, but with *cake* as early as 1542. Ware notes the C.18–20 variant (likewise coll), *flat as a frying-pan.*

flat back. A bed bug: low: from ca 1840; ob. by 1900.

flat broke. Penniless; ruined: coll: from ca 1830.

flat-cap. A citizen of London: coll: late C.16–early 18. Marston, 'Wealthy flat caps that pay for their pleasure the best of any men in Europe'. *Temp.* Henry VIII, round flat caps were fashionable; citizens continued to wear them when they had become unfashionable. 2. A Billingsgate fishwife: s.: Ned Ward, 1703.

***flat-catcher.** An imposter, a professional swindler; a decoy: orig. (—1823), c.; then low. Moncrieff, Mayhew, Whyte-Melville. 2. Hence, 'an article to dupe the public', *Sinks*, 1848; ob. 3. Also applied to a horse that looks well and performs badly: ca 1840–1930. cf. FLAT.

***flat-catching.** Swindling: orig. (—1821), c., then low. J. Greenwood, 1869, 'Flat-catching, as the turf slang has it'.

flat chicken. Stewed tripe: proletarian (—1909); slightly ob.

flat-cock. A woman: low (—1785); †by 1890. Ex one of two possible anatomical reasons.

flat fish, gen. **a regular.** A dullard; occ., an easy prey: from ca 1850. Ex FLAT, stupid + *fish*, something hookable.

flat foot. A sailor not yet aged 21: naval (—1909). Ex: 2. Any sailor: naval, esp. marines': from ca 1895; ob.

flat-fuck. 'Fricatio mutua coniunctorum genitalium muliebrium': Lesbian coll: C.19–20. Also as v.

flat-iron. A public-house at a corner: low: from ca 1860; ob. Ex its triangularity.

flat-iron jeff. A master man in a small way: tailors': late C.19–20.

***flat move.** A plan that fails; folly or mismanagement: ca 1810–80: c. >, by 1823, low s. i.e. a FLAT's action.

flatch. A half: the rigid *flah* modified: back s. (—1859). 2. A spurious *half*-crown: coiners' c.: from ca 1870. 3. A *half*penny (—1859).

flatch yenork. A half-crown: back s. (—1859).

flatiron gunboat. A gunboat of the 1870s–80s, 'with a short turtle back': naval coll: that period. Bowen.

***flats.** Playing cards: c. (—1812); ob. by 1880, †by 1900. Vaux. cf. BROADS. 2. False dice: ? c.: ca 1700–1850. cf. FULHAM. 3. Counterfeit money: c. or low: ca 1780–1870. 4. **sharps and flats:** jocular coll for sharpers and their victims: C.19–20. And, 5, for recourse to weapons: 1818, Scott; †by 1900.

flats, mahogany. Bed bugs: low: from ca 1850; ob. cf. FLAT BACK.

flats and sharps. Weapons: coll: ca 1780–1850. Scott, in *Midlothian*, 'He was something hasty with his flats and sharps.' 2. See FLATS, 4.

flattened out, ppl. adj. Penniless: tailors': late C.19–20.

***flatter-trap.** The mouth: c. or low: from ca 1840; ob.

flattie, flatty. Among cheapjacks, one in a new PITCH: ca 1840–80. 2. A rustic; an uninitiated person: low coll: ca 1855–80. 3. Hence (see, however, FLATTY-GORY), a FLAT; an easy dupe: ca 1855–1915: c. or low. 4. A uniformed policeman: c. and low: late C.19–20. Because his feet go flat from so much 'promenading'. 5. A small flat-bottomed sailing-boat: coll, esp. among boys: from ca 1860. 6. One who goes out in a van in the summer but lives in a house in the winter: Gypsies' (—1897). Abbr. *flattybouch*, same meaning.

***flatty-gory.** A FLAT, a dupe or intended dupe: c.: ca 1810–40. Perhaps the origin of all senses of FLATTIE.

***flatty-ken.** A thieves' lodging-house where the landlord is not FLY to the tricks of the underworld: c. (—1851): ob. Mayhew. Ex FLATTIE, 2, + KEN, a place.

flavour, catch or **get the.** To be drunk: low coll: from ca 1860; ob. 2. To feel somewhat inclined for sexual intercourse: low: from ca 1870: ?ob.

flawed. Drunk: mid-C.17–19: orig. c., then low. In C.19, gen. = half drunk. 2. (Of women) no longer virgin though unmarried: coll: C.19–20.

flay or skin a flint. To be mean; miserly: coll > S.E.: mid-C.17–19, Marryat, 'She would skin a flint if she could.' cf. FLEA-FLINT.

flay (orig. and gen. **flea**) **the fox.** To vomit: coll: late C.16–19. Cotgrave; Urquhart. The mod. term is *whip the cat.*

flaybottomist, late C.18–19; **flaybottom,** C.19–20 (ob.). A schoolmaster: jocular coll. (cf. BUM-BRUSHER and KID-WALLOPER.) Punning *phlebotomist.*

flea, fit as a, see FIT AS A FLEA.

flea and louse. A (bad) house: rhyming s. (—1859).

flea-bag. A bed: low: ca 1835–1915. Lever in *Harry Lorrequer*. 2. From ca 1909, a(n officer's) sleeping-bag.

flea-bite, in C.16–17 occ. **-biting.** A trifling injury or inconvenience: coll: late C.16–18; in C.19–20, S.E. The former in Taylor, 1630, and Grose; the latter in Burton.

flea- or flay-flint. A miser: coll, > S.E. in C.19: C.17–20; ob. D'Urfey, 1719, 'The flea-flints . . . strip me bare.' Ex FLAY A FLINT.

flea in one's or the ear, have a. To be scolded or annoyed; to fail in an enterprise: coll: C.16–20. Heywood's *Proverbs*, 1546. (Anticipated in C.15.) cf.:

flea in one's (or the) ear, send away with a. To dismiss annoyingly or humiliatingly: coll (—1602). Middleton: George Eliot. cf. dial. *flea in the ear(-hole)* and *flea in the lug*, resp. a box on the ears and a scolding or sharp reproof.

flea the fox, see FLAY THE FOX.

fleas, sit on a bag of. To sit uncomfortably; be uncomfortable: coll: from ca 1830. If *of hen fleas,* then in extreme discomfort.

fleas for, catch (one's). To be very intimate with: of a man with a woman: low coll: C.19–20; ob.

flea's leap, in a. Very quickly or promptly: coll: from ca 1840.

fleece. An act of thieving or swindling: C.17 coll. The v. itself has a coll flavour in C.16–18. 2. The female pubic hair: (?C. 18); C.19–20: low coll. cf. FURBELOW.

fleece-hunter or **-monger.** A whoremonger: C.19–20 (ob.): low coll. Ex FLEECE, 2. Contrast TUFT-*hunter*.

fleecer. A thief or swindler: C.17–19 coll. Prynne. cf. Yorkshire *fleecery.*

fleet, go round or **through the.** 'To be flogged on board each vessel in the fleet', S.O.D.: from ca 1840: nautical s., > j.: ca 1880; ob.

Fleet, he may whet his knife on the threshold of the. He is not in debt: coll: ca 1650–1800. Fuller in his *Worthies*; Grose in his *Provincial Glossary*. The reference is to the Fleet Prison (London), where debtors used to be imprisoned.

***fleet note.** A counterfeit banknote: c.: ca 1810–60. Is this the dial. adj. *fleet*, shallow? Or *fleet*, the mainly dial. adj., skimmed?

Fleet Street. Journalism: in C.19 coll and pejorative.

Fleet-Streeter. A journalist: C.19–20 (ob.): coll. In C.19, 'a journalist of the baser sort; a spunging PROPHET; a sharking dramatic critic; a SPICY paragraphist; and so on', F. & H. 1893.

Fleet-Streetese. The English of the FLEET-STREETER; coll: in C.19, to quote the same authority, 'a mixture of sesquipedalians and slang, of phrases worn threadbare and phrases sprung from the kennel; of bad grammar and worse manners; the like of which is impossible outside of *Fleet Street* [q.v.], but which in *Fleet Street* commands a price, and enables not a few to live.'

Flemish account. A bad account; unsatisfactory remittance: coll (by 1800 S.E.): ca 1660–1830; but extant as s., among sailors as late as 1874. cf. FLANDERS RECKONING. 2. Hence, 'ship's books that will not balance': nautical: C.19–20; ob. Bowen.

flesh!; flesh and fire! As coll exclamations: late C.17–mid-18. Ex *God's flesh!* (Langland), where *flesh* has a spiritual or religious sense.

flesh and blood. Brandy and port equally mixed: from ca 1825: ob.

flesh-bag. A shirt; a chemise: low: from ca 1810; ob. Vaux, 1812; *The London Magazine* (the like of which we need today), 1820 (vol. I), 'They are often without a flesh bag to their backs.'

flesh-broker. A match-maker: a bawd: late C.17–early 19: low. B.E., who has also, *spiritual flesh-broker*, a parson.

flesh-creeper. A SHOCKER or BLOOD (n., 5) or DREADFUL: 1887, Baumann.

flesh, fish, nor good red herring, neither, see FISH NOR FLESH.

flesh it. (Other forms are S.E.) To 'know' a woman: C.16–20 (ob.); low coll. cf. FLESHING, and the S.E. *flesh one's sword.* (*Flesh*, generative organs, C.16–20 literary: see Grose, P., at *flesh-broker*.)

flesh-tailor. A surgeon: C.17: jocular, but ?coll or S.E. Ford, in *'Tis Pity She's a Whore.*

flesher. A shirt: military coll: late C.19–20; ob. In the Army, it is worn next to the skin.

fleshing, go a-. To go wenching: coll: late C.16–17. Florio, 1598.

fleshy part of the thigh. The buttock: jocular coll: 1899–ca 1912. Ex military news evasion. Ware, 'Came into use upon the news from S. Africa of Lord Methuen having been wounded in this region'.

flet. A halibut: nautical: C.19–20. Perhaps by perversion on perversion: which will, admittedly, explain anything, yet is undoubtedly operative now and then.

***fletch.** A counterfeit coin: c.: ca 1870–1910. Perversion of FLATCH.

flick, gen. old flick. Comical fellow: a low coll salutation, jocular in tendency (—1860); ob. *Punch*, 28 July 1883. 2. In C.17 c., a thief. Rowlands, where wrongly printed *afflicke*. Abbr. late C.16–early 17 *flicker*, a pilferer.

***flick,** v. To cut: c.: from ca 1670; ob. Disraeli in *Venetia.* ?ex the flicking of a whip.

***flicker.** A drinking-glass. A *rum f.*, a large glass; *queer f.*, an ordinary one. c.: mid-C.17–early 18. Perhaps ex its flickering lights.

flicker. To drink: c. (?C.18) C.19. Ex the n. 2. To grin; laugh in a person's face: late C.17–20; dial. after ca 1830.

flier, flyer. At association football, a shot in the air: sporting: from ca 1890. 2. See FLYER, all senses.

flier, take a. To copulate without undressing or going to bed: low from ca 1780; ob.

flies about (a thing, a person), **there are no.** It, he, etc. is particularly good: Australian (—1848); †by 1890. Whence:

flies on a person, there are no. (Occ. with *about* for *on.*) He is honest, genuine, not playing the fool: coll (—1864). But, 2, since ca 1895, and owing to U.S. influence, it has meant: he is wide-awake; esp. very able or capable.

flies won't get at it, where the. (Of drink) down one's throat: coll: late C.19–20, cf. (at COACHES) *the coaches won't run over him.*

flight, in the first, see FIRST FLIGHT.

flight o(f) steps. Thick slices of bread and butter: coffee-houses' (—1883). cf. DOORSTEP.

flim. Abbr. FLIMSY, n.

***flimp;** rarely **flymp.** To hustle; esp. thus to rob: c. (—1839). Hence *flimper*: a stealer from the person. 'cf. west Flemish *flimpe*, knock, slap in the face', O.E.D. 2. To have sexual intercourse with: from ca 1850. cf. KNOCK, 1.

***flimp, put on the,** gen. v.i. To rob on the highway; to rob and garotte: c.: from ca 1835; ob.

***flimper,** see FLIMP, 1.

***flimping.** Stealing from the person: c. (—1839).

flimsy. A banknote: from ca 1810: low. *Lex. Bal.* (*flymsey*). Occ. abbr. *flim* (—1870). Also, in pl, paper-money (—1891). Ex the thin paper. 2. Reporters' 'copy'; news: journalistic coll: from ca 1859. Ex the thin copying-paper. 3. Hence, a sheet of music, a street-song: tramps' c. (—1887). 4. 'An officer's report at the end of a commission or when leaving a man-of-war': naval: from ca 1890. Bowen. Likewise ex sense 2.

flimsy, v. To write on *flimsy* (sense 2): journalists': from ca 1885: coll.

flinch-gut. Whale's blubber: whalers': mid-C.19–20. 2. Hence the hold in which it is stored: whalers': late C.19–20.

fling. A sowing of one's wild oats; a spree: from ca 1825: coll soon S.E. Thackeray. (With *have.*)

fling, v. To cheat or trick; v.t. with *out*: coll: mid-C.18–20; almost †. Esp. *fling out of*, e.g. money.

fling, in a. In a fit of temper: coll: C.19–20.

fling-dust, occ. **-stink.** A harlot that walks the streets. C.17–18 (?later): coll. Fletcher, 'An English whore, a kind of fling-dust, one of your London light-o'-loves', 1621.

fling (or flap) it in one's face. Of a harlot: to expose the person: low coll: C.19–20.

fling out, v.i. To go out or away in noisy haste; esp., in a temper: coll > S.E.: C.18–20.

flint. A worker at union, mod. trades-union, rates: from ca 1760. Opp. DUNG.

Both terms are in Foote's burlesque, *The Tailors*. Ob. by 1890, †by 1910.

flint, old. A miser: coll (—1840). Dickens in *The Old Curiosity Shop*. Ob.

flip. 'Hot small Beer (chiefly) and Brandy, sweetened and spiced upon occasion', B.E., ca 1690: orig. nautical; but S.E. by 1800. (cf. SIR CLOUDESLEY.) Perhaps abbr. *Philip*. 2. A bribe or tip: low: C.19–20.

flip, v. To shoot, gen. v.t.: c. (—1812).

flip-flap. A flighty woman: coll > S.E.: C.18. Vanbrugh, 1702, 'The light airy flip-flap, she kills him with her motions.' 2. A step-dance (see CELLAR-FLAP); a somersault in which the performer lands on feet and hands alternately: the former, from ca 1860; the latter (showmen's), late C.17–early 19. 3. The arm: nautical (—1887). cf. FLIPPER. 4. The *membrum virile*: from ca 1650: cf. DINGLE-DANGLE. 5. A (fireworks) cracker (—1885); ob. 6. 'Broad fringe of hair covering the young male forehead': Cockneys': 1898–ca 1914. Ware.

flipper. The hand: from ca 1820: nautical, soon gen. One flips it about. 2. Esp. in *tip a person one's flipper*, shake hands with. *Punch*, 11 Oct. 1884. cf. FLAPPER, DADDLE, MAULEY. 3. That part of a 'scene' which, painted and hinged on both sides, is used in trick changes: theatrical coll: from ca 1870; ob.

flirt. A jest: coll: Ned Ward, 1709.

flirt-gill, C.16–17; **gill-flirt,** C.18–early 19. A wanton; a harlot. Orig. coll, soon S.E. Occ. *jill*; abbr. *Gillian = Juliana*.

flirtina cop-all (sc. men). A wanton: low coll: from ca 1860. ?after *concertina*.

flit, do a moonlight. To quit one's tenement, flat, or house, or one's lodgings, by night and without paying the rent or (board and) lodging: (low) coll: mid-C.19–20.

float. The row of footlights; (also in pl) the footlights: theatrical: ca 1860–1930. Before gas, oil-pans with floating wicks were used.

floater. A suet dumpling: Cockney, mostly costers' (—1864). Often it floats in gravy. cf. the U.S. *floating island*. 2. (Gen. pl) An Exchequer bill; any sound stock: Stock Exchange (—1871). Because a recognized security. 3. The penis: C.19. 4. A penny that does not spin: two-up players' coll: late C.19–20.

***floating academy.** The convict hulks: mid-C.18–mid-19 c. or low s. cf. CAMPBELL'S ACADEMY and FLOATING HELL.

floating batteries. Broken bread dipped in tea: military: ca 1890–1914.

floating coffin. A ship materially rotten: nautical coll: late C.19–20. Ex: 2. A 10-gun brig (also a COFFIN-BRIG): ca 1800–80.

floating hell; occ., in sense 2 only, **hell afloat.** The hulks: ca 1810–50. Ex the repulsive conditions. 2. Hence, a ship commanded by a brutal bully, hence by any rigid disciplinarian: nautical coll: from ca 1850.

flock of sheep. White waves (cf. 'horses') of the sea: coll: C.19–20; ob. 2. A dominoes-hand set out on the table: from ca 1870.

floey (or Floey), drunk as. Exceedingly drunk: proletarian (—1909). Perhaps ex some very bibulous Flora. cf. CHLOE.

***flog.** To whip: from ca 1670. Until ca 1750, c.; in C.19–20, S.E. Prob. an echoic perversion of L. *flagellare*. 2. To beat, excel: ca 1840–1910. 3. In late C.19–20 military, to sell illicitly, esp. Army stores.

flog a willing horse. To urge on a person already eager or very active: coll: mid-C. 19–20.

flog one's donkey. (Of a male) to masturbate: low (?orig. Cockney): late C.19–20. Also *flog one's mutton* – a variant of *jerk* . . . (see JERK OFF). Also *flog the* BISHOP.

flog the cat. To cry over spilt milk: nautical: mid-C.19–20.

flog the clock. To move its hands forward (—1894): coll. Prob. suggested by the nautical *flog the glass*, turn the watch-glass (—1769); †.

flog the dead horse, see DEAD HORSE . . .

***flogged at the tumbler.** Whipped at the cart's tail: c.: late C.17–18.

flogger. A whip: late C.18–19. George Parker, 1789. 2. 'A mop used in the painting room to whisk (charcoal) dust from a sketch': theatrical: ca 1870–1920.

flogging. 'A Naked Woman's whipping (with Rods) an Old (usually) and (sometimes) a Young Lecher', B.E.: C.17–18 c. 2. The frequent vbl n. of FLOG, v., 3.

flogging, adj. Mean; grasping: late C.19–20: coll. Ob. cf. FLOG, 2.

flogging, be. To be saving up one's money very carefully: proletarian: mid-C.19–20; ob.

***flogging-cove.** An official dealing out the corporal punishment: c.: late C.17–early 19. 2. A C.18 variant of:

***flogging-cully.** A man addicted to flagellation for sexual purposes: C.18–early 19: c. cf. FLOGGING, n.

***flogging-stake.** A whipping-post: late C.17–19, c. until late C.18, then low.

flogster. A person addicted to flogging as a punishment: coll: C.19–20; ob.

floor. That which nonplusses or discomfits one: ca 1840–1920; coll. 2. A miscalculation: coll: ca 1845–1910. The former ex FLOOR, v., 1; the latter, which has a corresponding but very rare v.i., is influenced by *flaw*. 3. As in FIRST-FLOOR.

floor, v. (Coll.) To vanquish, silence, or nonplus, esp. in an argument (—1835). L. Oliphant, 1870, 'I floor all opposition.' 2. To drink; 'get outside of' (—1851); ob. 3. (Of an examiner) to PLOUGH: ca 1840–1910. 4. (Also university) answer every question of; reply brilliantly to (an examiner): from ca 1850; ob. Prob. ex sense 5.: To do thoroughly; complete, finish: 1836. 6. See FLOORED, 2. 7. See ibid, 3.

floor, have or **hold the.** To be speaking; esp. too much or to another's displeasure: coll: from ca 1850. Ex S.E., orig. political sense.

floor one's licks. To 'shine'; do unusually well: low: ca 1840–1900.

floor the odds. (Gen. of a horse) to win despite heavy odds: the turf (—1882). *Daily Telegraph*, 16 Nov. 1882, 'The odds were ... floored from an unexpected quarter.'

floored, ppl adj. Senses as in FLOOR. 2. Dead drunk: from ca 1810. 3. Among painters: hung low at an exhibition, whether exhibit or exhibitor: from ca 1860. Opp SKIED.

floorer. A knockdown blow (cf. AUCTIONEER): pugilistic (—1819), > gen. ca 1860. 2. Hence, unpleasant news, decisive argument or retort; a notable check: from the 1830s. 3. In universities and schools: a question or a paper too difficult to answer: from ca 1850. 4. In skittles, a ball that knocks down all the pins: from ca 1840. 5. In c.: a thief that in assisting a man that he has tripped robs him: 1795 (O.E.D.).

floorer, first-, second-, third-. One who rooms on the first, second, third floor: lodging-houses' (—1887).

flooring. vbl n., in senses of FLOOR, v., but esp. among pugilists (—1819). Tom Moore.

flop. The act or sound of a heavy or a clumsy fall; a blow: late C.17–20 coll when not dial. 2. Hair worn low down over the forehead by women: low London: 1881–ca 1900. 3. A failure, e.g. of a book, a play, a project: from ca 1890: coll.

flop, v.t. In boxing: to knock down (—1888); ob. 2. In gen.: v.i., to swing loosely and heavily: coll; C.17–20. 3. v.i., move heavily, clumsily or with a bump: late C.17–20: coll. 4. v.t., throw with flopping suddenness: coll; from ca 1820. 5. To move, esp. wings, heavily up and down: coll (—1860). 6. See FLOP, DO A, 2.

flop, adv. With a heavy or clumsy fall. Often expletively. Coll: from ca 1725. J. Payn, 'She'll roll down, papa, and come flop.'

flop, do a. To sit or fall down: from ca 1870. 2. To lie down to a man: low: from ca 1875. Contrast *flop a judy*, to cause a woman to lie ready for the sexual act: low: from ca 1875.

flop about. To lie about, lazily and either lethargically or languorously: coll: from ca 1870.

flop in. To effect intromission: low: latter C.19 (?C.20).

flop on, e.g. the gills. A blow on the (e.g.) mouth: low coll: from mid-C.19.

flop out, v. Of a bather leaving the water with noisy awkwardness: coll: from ca 1870.

flop over, v.i. To turn heavily: coll: from ca 1860.

flop round. To loaf about: from ca 1865: coll.

flop-whop. Onomatopoeic for a 'flopping' impact: coll (—1887).

floppy. Apt to flop (see FLOP, v., intransitive senses): coll: 1858 (S.O.D.).

florence. A girl that has been tousled and ruffled: late C.17–early 19: coll. cf. the ob. Northants *florence* (to go about untidily dressed), by which the Christian name, as a type, was prob. influenced.

florid. Half-drunk; fuddled: ca 1770–1830. i.e. flushed with drink.

floster. A drink of sherry, soda-water, lemon, ice, and several other ingredients: from ca 1860; ob. by 1900.

flouch or **floush, fall** or **go.** To collapse; sag; coll. (—1819); ob. Tom Moore. 'Georgy went floush, and his backers looked shy.' Ex dial.; ultimately echoic.

flounce. 'The thick line of black paint put on the edge of the lower eyelid to enhance the effect of the eye itself': theatrical (1854) soon > Society. Ware.

***flounder.** The corpse of a drowned man: c.: from ca 1870. cf. DAB, n., 4.

flounder, v. To sell and re-purchase a stock, esp. when at a loss on each occasion: Stock Exchange (—1889). More gen. as *floundering*, vbl n.

flounder and dab. A cab: rhyming s. (—1857); ob.

flourish. To have money, esp. much, in one's pocket: coll. Ex the semi-coll sense, to be well off, itself ex the M.E.–C.20 S.E. sense, to thrive.

flourish, take a. (Of the man) to have a hasty coition: mid C.18–19 low or low coll.

flourish it. (Of either sex) to expose the person: low coll: mid-C.19–20.

flourishing. Flourishingly. Often in reply to 'How are you (getting along)?' Coll: C.19–20.

floush, fall or **go**, see FLOUCH.

flower, flower of chivalry, flower-pot. The female pudend: low: C.19–20. The second term puns the etymological meaning of its third vocable, alluding to RIDE.

flower-fancier. A whoremaster: whoremonger: low: C.19–20; ob.

flowers. Abbr. *monthly flowers*, the menstrual flux: C.15–20: until ca 1840, S.E.: then coll. Ex Fr. *fleurs* = *flueurs* = L. *fluor* ex *fluere*, to flow.

flowers and frolics; fun and frolics. Testicles: Anglo-Irish rhyming s. on BALLOCKS: late C.19–20.

***flowery.** Lodging; entertainment: c. and Parlary: from ca 1850; ob. Prob. ex It. via Lingua Franca.

flowery language. A jocularly euphemistic coll for obscenity and for blasphemy: from before 1893.

flowing hope. A forlorn hope: naval and military: ca 1850–1914. Orig. a sol.

'flu, flu; occ. **flue.** Influenza: coll, gen. with *the*: from late 1830s. Southey, 1839, 'I've had a pretty fair share of the flue.'

flue. The Recorder, esp. of London: ca 1750–1900. ?orig. c. corruption of FLUTE, 1. 2. See FLU. 3. See FLUE, IN, and the following entry.

flue, v. To put in pawn: low: from ca 1860. Ex FLUE, IN or UP THE.

flue, be up one's. To be awkward for a person, as in 'That's up your flue': from ca 1870; ob.

flue, in or **up the.** Pawned: from ca 1820. cf. *up the* SPOUT. *Flue* is itself s. for the spout in a pawnbroker's shop. cf.:

flue or **spout, up the.** As in preceding entry. 2. Collapsed, physically or mentally; dead: low: ca 1850–1910.

***flue-faker.** A chimney-sweep: c. or low s.: ca 1810–1900. 2. A low sporting man: ca 1855–1914. Because he bets on the great SWEEPS.

flue-scraper. A chimney-sweep: ca 1830–1910. Suggested by FLUE-FAKER.

fluence, put on the. To 'attract, subdue, overcome by mental force': Cockneys': ca 1850–85. Ware. Hence, 2. To hypnotize: Australian coll: from ca 1900.

fluff, occ. **fluffings.** Short change given by clerks: railway: from ca 1870. cf. MENAVELINGS. 2. Lines imperfectly learned and delivered: theatrical: from ca 1880. W. Archer, 'But even as seen through a cloud of fluff the burlesque is irresistibly amusing.' cf. MAJOR MCFLUFFER. 3. The female pubic hair: low: C.19–20. 4. See FLUFF, LITTLE BIT OF. 5. A tip (gratuity): railway workers': ca 1890–1920. Prob. ex sense 1. 4. Diffusely worded contribution to a newspaper: journalists' coll: late C.19–20. cf. S.E. *woolly*.

fluff, v. To give short change: railways': from ca 1870. 2. Disconcert, nonplus, FLOOR: from ca 1860. cf. FLUFF IN. 3. To forget one's part: theatrical: from ca 1880. George Moore, in *The Mummer's Wife*, 1885. 4. See FLUFF IT!, 5. (Which should, chronologically, be sense 1.) To disguise the defects of (a horse): 1822, David Carey, *Life in Paris*, 'He knew ... when a *roarer* had been *fluffed* for the purpose of sale.'

fluff, do a. To forget one's part: theatrical: from ca 1870.

fluff, little bit of. A girl: mostly Australian. C.20. O.E.D. records it at 1903.

fluff in. To deceive (a person) 'by smooth modes': lower classes' (—1909). Ware. Prob. ex FLUFF, v., 2.

fluff in the pan. A failure: from ca 1860: coll: ex Scottish.

fluff it! Go away! Take it away! (—1859). Ob.

fluffer. A drunkard: from ca 1880. cf. FLUFFINESS. 2. A player apt to forget his part: theatrical: from ca 1880. See FLUFF, V., 3.

fluffiness. Drunkenness: from ca 1885. *Fun*, 4 Aug. 1886. 2. A tendency to forget words: theatrical: from ca 1885.

fluffing; fluffings. The practice of, and the proceeds from, giving short change: railways': from ca 1870. See FLUFF, n., 1, and v., 1.

fluffy. Of uncertain memory: theatrical: from ca 1880. Ex FLUFF, n., 2. See also

MAJOR MCFLUFFER. 2. Unsteady; stupidly drunk: from ca 1885.

fluke. A stroke of luck: coll: from ca 1860. Ex billiards. Black, 1873, 'It is a happy fluke.' 2. An easy dupe, a FLAT: ca 1800–30. Ex *fluke*, a flat fish.

fluke, v. To do a thing (well) by accident: coll: from ca 1880. Hence, vbl n. and adj., *fluking*. Ex billiards. 2. To shirk: Eton (—1864).

flukes, peak or **turn the.** To go to bed: nautical: mid-C.19–20. Ex a whale's showing its tail-flukes in going under.

fluk(e)y, adj. Chancy, uncertain; achieved less by good management than by good luck: coll: from ca 1880.

flummergast, gen. as ppl adj. To astound or confound: coll (—1849); ob. Variation of FLABBERGAST.

flummery. Flattery; polite nonsense: from ca 1750: coll; after ca 1830, S.E. Ex the lit. sense, 'oatmeal and water boiled to a jelly', not 'over-nourishing', Grose, 1st ed. cf. BALDERDASH.

flummocks (rare), **flummox, flummux.** To perplex, abash, silence; victimize, 'best'; disappoint, dodge, elude: 1837: Dickens. Variant, †*conflummox*. Ex dial. cf. FLABBERGAST. 2. Hence, to confuse another player: theatrical: from ca 1880.

flummocky. In bad taste: coll (—1891). *Blackwood's*, March 1891. Ex preceding.

flummox. A failure: 1857, 'Ducange Anglicus'; ob. Ex:

flummox, v., see FLUMMOCKS.

flummox by the lip. To talk down; vanquish in a slanging match: low: from ca 1860; ob.

flummoxed. Silenced; disappointed, outwitted; spoilt; ruined; drunk; sent to or sure of a month in prison (c. only): from the 1850s. *Punch*, 30 Aug. 1890. 'I'm fair flummoxed.' ppl adj. ex *flummox*, see FLUMMOCKS. Whence:

***flummut.** A month in prison: vagrants' c. (—1851). Mayhew equates it to the beggars' sign. See FLUMMOXED.

flummux, flummuxed, see FLUMMOCKS, FLUMMOXED.

flump. An abrupt or heavy fall, making a dull noise; the noise: late C.18–20 (ob.) coll. cf.:

flump, v. To fall, or be set down, violently, thumpingly, or hurriedly: coll: v.i., 1816; v.t., 1830; as adv., 1790. Thackeray, 'Chairs were flumped down on the floor.' ?a blend of FLOP and *thump*.

flump, adv. With a 'flump': coll: late C.18–20.

flunk, v.t. and v.i. To fail in an examination: Canadian universities: late C.19–20. Adopted from U.S.; of hotly disputed – in short, of unknown – orig.

flunkey. A parasite, a toady: coll: from ca 1855; in C.20, S.E. Ex sense, a manservant esp. if in livery. 2. A ship's steward: nautical (—1883); ob. W. Clark Russell. 3. A wardroom attendant: naval: from ca 1880.

flunkey out of collar. A footman out of work: 1857, 'Ducange Anglicus'; ob.

flurry one's milk. To be angry, perturbed, worried: low coll: from ca 1820; ob. cf. Fr. *se faire du mauvais sang*.

flurryment. Confusion, bustle; excitement, agitation: low coll (—1848). Pleonastic on *flurry*, ?after *flusterment*.

flush, v.t. To whip: coll: mid-C.19–20; ob. Hence *flushed on the horse*, privately whipped in gaol: mid-C.19–20, ob.: prob. c. Perhaps ex *flush*, to cleanse, or to make red.

***flush,** adj., with *of*. Having plenty of money, esp. temporarily: C.17–20. In C.17, esp. as *flush in the pocket* or FOB (n., 2), c.; in C.18, low > gen.; in C.19–20, S.E. Dekker; Trollope, 'Long before that time I shall be flush enough.' cf. S.E. *flush of success* and *flush*, level, hence full. 2. Tipsy: C.19–20; ob. Ex *flush*, level with, i.e. full to, the top.

flush, adv. Full; directly: pugilistic, of a blow (—1888). Ex C.18 S.E.

flush a wild duck. To single out a woman for amorous attentions: low: C.19–20; ob. Ex shooting: *flush* = to cause to take wing.

flush hit. A clean hit; a punch fair on the mark: pugilism: ca 1810–1920; s. > j. by 1900.

flush on one, come. To meet a person suddenly, unexpectedly: coll > S.E.: C.17–20.

***flushed on the horse,** see FLUSH, v.

flute. (cf. FLUE, n.) A city recorder, esp. of London: ca 1690–1820: prob. c. 2. The male member: C.18–19: low. Variants *living flute*, *one-holed f.*, *silent f.* cf. the Romany *haboia* (English *hautboy*) in same sense. 3. A pistol: ca 1840–1910. Lover in *Handy Andy*. Ex shape and 'tune'.

flutter. A short visit or trip, esp. a joyous, informal one: coll: 1857 (O.E.D.). 2. A venture, an attempt ; a spree; a gamble: from ca 1870. *Saturday Review*, 1 Feb. 1890, 'Fond of a little flutter'. 3. The spinning of a coin: from ca 1872. 4. See FLUTTER, HAVE HAD A. All senses refer to the flutter of excitement; 3 also to the fluttering movement.

flutter, v.i. To gamble; from ca 1870. cf. sense 3. 2. Also, to indulge in pleasure: from ca 1880. 3. v.t., to spin (a coin), as in *flutter a brown*: from ca 1870; ob.

flutter, be on the. To be on the spree; sexually adept: low: ca 1875. cf.:

flutter, do or **have a.** To have a small gamble; go on the spree; (of either sex) to have sexual intercourse, for pleasure rather than passion: from ca 1870: s.

flutter, have had a. To have had sexual experience; to have lost one's virginity: low: from ca 1875.

flutter a judy. To pursue a girl; to possess one: low: from ca 1850.

flutter a skirt. To be a (street-walking) harlot: low: from ca 1850.

flutter for, have a. To try hard to do, get, etc.: coll (—1873).

flutter (or **fret) one's kidneys.** To agitate; greatly annoy: low: from ca 1860. cf. FLURRY ONE'S MILK.

flutter the ribbons. To drive (horses): coll: ca 1860–1910.

flux. To cozen, cheat, outwit: late C.18–early 19. Ex S.E. sense, to subject to a flux.

fly. A printer's devil: late C.17–mid-19: printers'. Ex *fly* = a familiar spirit, a devil. 2. A waggon: c.: late C.18–early 19. All other vehicle senses are S.E. 3. The act of spinning a coin: from ca 1870; cf. FLUTTER, n., 2. 4. A policeman: c. > low (—1857). Ob., except as a detective. 5. A customer: trade: ca 1840–1910. 6. A trick, DODGE: ca 1860–1910. 7. A blow, punch: boxing (—1887): ob.

fly, v. To give way; become damaged: pugilism (—1865); ob. 2. To toss; raise (e.g. a window): c. (—1857). 3. Send quickly, hastily: coll: ca 1845–1900. Darwin. 4. See FLY A KITE, a TILE; FLY THE MAGS. 5. v.t., (of a horse) to outdistance easily: sporting (—1887).

fly, adj. Artful, knowing; shrewdly aware: low (?orig. c.): from ca 1810. In Scots (*flee*), however, as early as 1724. Variants *a-fly*, *flymy*, *fly to the game*, *fly to what's what*. Perhaps ex the difficulty of catching a fly, more prob. cognate with *fledge*, *fledged*, as Sewel, 1766, indicates (W.); though Bee's assertion that it is a corruption of *fla*, abbr. FLASH, is, considering the devices of c., not to be sneered at. 2. Dextrous: from ca 1834: low. Ainsworth. 3. (Of women) wanton: low: from ca 1880. Ex senses 1 and 2. cf. U.S. *fly dame*, a harlot (—1888).

*__fly, beg on the.__ To beg from persons as they pass: c. (—1861). Mayhew. cf. FLY, ON THE, 2.

fly, let, v.t. To hit out: coll (—1859). *Punch*, 25 July 1859, 'Lord Lyndhurst let fly and caught him . . . an extremely neat one on the conk.'

fly, make the fur or **feathers.** To attack successfully (*one's* for *the*); to quarrel noisily: coll: orig. (1825), U.S.; anglicized ca 1860.

fly, not to rise to that. Not to 'bite', i.e. not to believe: coll: from ca 1870; ob.

fly, off the. Laid up; doing nothing: retired, esp. from the giving or the pursuit of pleasure: low: from ca 1850.

fly, on the. Off work; walking the streets for fun; on the spree: low: from ca 1850. 2. In c., in motion: from ca 1860.

*__fly, take on the,__ v.t. To beg from in the streets: c.: from ca 1845; ob. cf. *beg on the* FLY, above.

fly a, the, kite. To raise money by means of accommodation bills: from ca 1808. Whence *fly a bill*, to gain time by giving a bill (1860, O.E.D.). 2. Merely to raise money (—1880). Also *cash a dog*, *pay the bearer*. 3. In c., to depart by the window (—1860): esp. from low lodging-houses. 4. With *at*, to set one's cap at (—1863). Henry Kingsley. 5. (Gen. *fly the kite.*) To seek publicity: Society: from the 1890s; ob.

fly a tile. To knock off a man's hat: Stock Exchange: ca 1820–1900.

fly-away. A tricycle: coll (—1887); ob. by 1905.

fly-blow. A bastard: coll (—1875); ob. ?corruption of BY-BLOW.

fly-blown. Tipsy: from ca 1875; ob. 2. Penniless: Australian (—1889). 3. Exhausted: low: from ca 1880. 4. Devirginated; also, suspected of venereal disease: low: from ca 1885.

fly blue paper. To issue a summons: legal: from ca 1890; slightly ob.

fly-boy. A variant of FLY, n., 1.

fly-by-night. A sedan chair on wheels: coll; *temp.* the Regency. 2. A defaulting debtor; his defaulting: coll: 1823, 'Jon Bee'. 3. A harlot: from ca 1860. 4. The female pudend: C.19–20 low. 5. One who frequently moves about at night, e.g. a spreester: from ca 1865. 6. A term of contempt for a woman: coll: C.18–early 19.

Ex witches broom-flying by night. 7. A transient boarder who bilks his landlady: coll: late C.19–20.

fly-cage. The female pudend: C.19–20 low. Also:

fly-catcher. The same: id. 2. An open-mouthed ignorant person: coll: from ca 1820.

***fly cop.** A detective: U.S. >, by 1889, English c. Lit., 'a clever policeman'. Ex FLY, adj., 1.

fly-disperser soup. Oxtail soup: from ca 1860–1910.

fly-dusters. Fists: ca 1880–1920. Arthur Binstead, *Mop Fair*, 1905.

fly-flapped. Whipped in the stocks or at the cart's tail: ca 1785–1830. Ex the C.17–18 S.E. *fly-flap*, to beat.

fly-flapper. A heavy bludgeon: from ca 1840; ob.

fly flat. A would-be expert: the turf: ca 1885–1915.

fly high or **rather high.** To get or to be drunk: low: from ca 1860. 2. To keep good company and fine state; venture for big stakes: coll > S.E.; C.19–20.

fly in a tar-box (in C.19–20, **glue-pot), like a.** Nervously excited: coll (—1659); the former, ob. by 1800, †by 1900. Howell, 1659.

fly jerks. Small pieces of cork suspended from the brim of a tramp's hat to ward off flies: Australian: late C.19–20.

fly laugh, 'twould make a. Very amusing: (?C.17–) C.18 coll.

fly loo, see KENTUCKY LOO.

fly low. To be modest and retiring: from ca 1835: coll, > S.E. by 1895. 2. In c., to hide from justice: ca 1870.

fly my kite. A light: rhyming s. (—1857).

fly off the handle. To lose one's temper: orig. (1825), U.S.; anglicized ca 1860.

fly on a wheel, break or **crush a.** To make much fuss about very little (—1859): coll > S.E. by 1900.

fly on the wheel, the. One who considers himself very important: coll > S.E.: late C.16–20; ob. From Aesop's fable.

fly out. To grow angry; to scold: C.17–20; coll, > S.E. by 1700. Chapman, *Spectator*, Thackeray.

fly-rink. A bald head: lower classes': 1875; ob.

fly-slicer. A cavalryman: C.19–20 (ob.): orig. (late C.18), a Life Guardsman. Ex the brushing-away of flies with a sword.

fly-stuck (possibly S.E.); **stuck** (coll). Bitten by the tsetse: South African: from ca 1880 and esp. among hunters, as F. C. Selous, who uses both forms, makes clear in *A Hunter's Wanderings in Africa*, 1881.

fly the blue pigeon. To steal lead from roofs: see BLUE PIGEON: C.18–19 c. 2. To use the sounding lead: nautical: from ca 1870.

fly the flag. (Of harlots) to walk the streets: low: from ca 1840. 2. To have the monthly flux: low: from ca 1850.

fly the kite, see FLY A KITE.

***fly the mags.** To gamble; properly, by throwing up halfpence: c. (—1812) >, by 1850, low.

fly to, see FLY, adj., 1. cf. DOWN TO; UP TO . . .; FLASH TO.

fly-trap. The mouth: from ca 1790. cf. FLY-CATCHER. 2. The female pudend: C.19 low. cf. FLY-CAGE.

fly with, not a feather to. Penniless; ruined: coll: C.19–20; slightly ob.

flyer, see FLIER. 2. (Gen. in pl) A shoe: c.: late C.17–18. In C.19 low s., e.g. in Mayhew, *flyer* is an unwelted shoe. 3. In Winchester football, a half-volley: from ca 1850. 4. A swift kangaroo: Australian coll (—1848) >, by 1890, S.E. 5. A breeder of homing pigeons: sporting coll: mid-C.19–20.

flying, look as if the devil had shit him or **her.** To be filthy or deformed: low coll: C.19–20; ob.

flying bedstead. The open stall (on wheels) of a dealer in old clocks and bric-à-brac: Cockneys' (—1887).

***flying camp.** A couple, or a gang, of beggars: c.: late C.17–early 19. B.E.; Grose, 1st ed., 'Beggars plying in a body at funerals'. cf. S.E. sense.

***flying caper.** An escape from prison: c. (—1864); ob.

***flying-cat.** An owl: c.: late C.17–mid-18. cf. Fr. *chat-huant*.

flying county or **country.** A district where one can ride fast and safely: hunting: from ca 1850; s. > j. by 1900. Whyte-Melville, 'Leicestershire, Northamptonshire, and other so-called "flying counties" '.

***flying cove.** One who gets money by pretending to be able to supply robbed persons with such information as will lead to the recovery of the lost goods: c.: ca 1860–1940.

flying dustman. 'The defendant was what is termed a *Flying Dustman*, who . . . paying nothing to anyone, goes round the parish collecting all the ashes he can, to the great injury of the contractor,' says a witness in a trial of 1812 in *The New Newgate Calendar*, V, 519; J. Wight, *More Mornings at Bow Street*, 1827, for a most informative account: coll: ca 1805–70.

***flying gigger** or **jigger.** A turnpike gate: c.: early C.18–19.

flying kite. A fancy sail, esp. if temporary: nautical coll: early C.19–20; ob.

flying knacker. A horse-flesh butcher in a small way: Londoners': ca 1860–1900. James Greenwood, *Odd People in Odd Places*, 1883.

flying light. (Of a seaman who, when he joined his ship, was) possessed of nothing but the clothes on him: nautical coll: mid-C.19–20; ob.

flying man. In Eton football: a skilful skirmisher (—1864); ob.

flying mess, in a. Hungry and having to mess wherever one can: military (—1860). Ex the difficulty of obtaining a good meal on a forced march.

flying pasty. Excrement that, wrapped in paper, is thrown over a neighbour's wall: from ca 1790; †by 1893.

***flying porter.** An imposter who gets money by giving, to robbed persons, information that will (prob. not) lead to the arrest of the thieves: c.: late C.18–19.

flying stationer. A hawker of street-ballads, penny histories, etc.: late C.18–19: low. Ex the fact that such a hawker keeps moving. cf. the C.19 RUNNING PATTERER.

flying trapeze. Cheese: rhyming s.: late C.19–20.

flymp, see FLIMP.

flyms(e)y, see FLIMSY, 1.

flymy. Knowing, artful, roguish; sprightly; low (—1859). Henley. Ex FLY, adj., 1, on *slimy*.

flyness. The abstract n. of FLY, adj., 1: late C.19–20.

foal and filly dance. A 'dance to which only very young people . . . are invited': Society (—1909); ob. Ware. cf. FILLY AND FOAL.

foaled. Thrown from one's horse: hunting: C.19–20; ob. 2. Manchon asserts that it = FOGGED; I doubt the validity of this.

***fob.** A trick, cheat, swindle: orig. (1622), prob. S.E.; but in late C.17, c.; in C.18 low: in C.19, gen. s., almost coll; in C.20, †. Ex M.E. *fob*, an imposter, ex Fr. *fo(u)rbe*. 2. A breeches or a watch pocket: in C.17, c. or low; C.18, coll; C.19, recognized. The O.E.D. takes a rather different view of its status. 'Hudibras' Butler. Ex Ger. Variant, FUB.

fob, v. To pocket: C.19–20, ob.; coll. cf. *pocket*, v. 2. To cheat, rob; procure dishonestly: C.17–20; ob. Congreve; Wolcot, 'To use a cant [i.e. fashionable s.] phrase, we've been finely fobb'd.' cf. FOB, n., 1. 3. To deceive; trifle with: coll > S.E.: late C.16–20; ob. Shakespeare. In all senses, an early variant is FUB.

***fob, gut a.** To pick a pocket: low, ?c.: ca 1815–90. Moore, 1819, 'Diddling your subjects, and gutting their fobs'.

***fob-diver.** A pickpocket: c.: from ca 1880; slightly ob.

fob of, fob out of. To cheat or deprive illicitly (a person) of (a thing): coll: from ca 1840, 1850 resp. An extension of FOB, v., 2.

fob off. To put off, or ignore, contemptuously, callously, unfairly, dishonestly; deceive in any of these ways. (Variant *fub off*.) Coll > S.E.: late C.16–20; ob. Shakespeare, 'You must not think to fob off our disgrace with a tale.'

fob out of, see FOB OF.

***fob-worker.** A pickpocket specializing in the contents (esp. watches) of fobs: c.: from ca 1890. See FOB, n., 2.

fobus. A pejorative, gen. as term of address: C.17–18. Wycherley, 'Ay, you old fobus'. cf. FOGEY. 2. The *pudendum muliebre*: low (—1893); ob.

fodder. Abbr. BUM-FODDER: C.19–20 low, verging on coll.

foei(-tock). An interjection of surprise, sorrow, sympathy: South African coll: late C.19–20. Ex Dutch *foei*, for shame!, and *tock*, why, to be sure!

foetus, tap the. To procure abortion: medical (—1893).

***fog.** Smoke; occ. a smoke: c.: late C.17–early 19. ?abbr. FOGUS.

fog, v. To smoke a pipe: either low s. or c.: C.18–early 19. 2. Mystify, perplex; occ. to obscure: coll (orig. S.E.): from ca 1815. *Daily Telegraph*, 29 Sept. 1883, 'We turns what we say into tangle talk so as to fog them.' 3. v.i., to set fog-signals along the line: railwaymen's: from ca 1885.

fog-dog. The lower part of a rainbow: Newfoundland (esp. nautical): mid-C.19–20. cf. STUB, n., 2.

fog in. To see (a place) by chance, to achieve (a purpose) by accident: Society (—1909); virtually †.

fog(e)y; occ. **fogay, foggi(e); fogram** (q.v.). An invalid or, later, a garrison soldier or, derivatively, sailor: ?Scottish military: 1780. Grose, 1785, shows that, even then, *old* gen. preceded it. ca 1850, the sense > wholly that of an elderly person; an old-fashioned, occ. an eccentric, person: a meaning it possessed as early as 1780. Thackeray, 1855, 'A grizzled, grim old fogy'. Grose derives ex Fr. *fougueux*, W. ex FOGGY, 2. 2. Hence, an old maid: low coll (—1887). Baumann (*eine alte Schachtel*). 3. Whence *fogyish*, old-fashioned, eccentric (1873) – *fogeydom*, the being a fogey, fogeys as a class (1859) – *fogeyism*, an example of fogeydom, a fogeyish trait (1859): these three terms, somewhat coll at first, had > S.E. by 1880.

fogged. Tipsy: from ca 1840; ob. cf. FOGGY, 1, its imm. origin. 2. Bewildered, puzzled, at a loss: coll; from ca 1850.

fogger. A pettifogging lawyer: coll (—1600) > S.E.; †by 1700. Ex *Fugger*, the merchant-financier family.

foggie, see FOGEY. This form is recorded for 1812.

fogging, vbl n. Fumbling through one's part: theatrical: ca 1885–1915.

foggy. Tipsy; gen. slightly tipsy: from ca 1820; ob. cf. HAZY. 2. Dull, thick-headed: from ca 1770. cf. FOGEY. Ex *foggy*, moss-grown, boggy, thick, murky, ex *fog*, rank grass.

***fogle.** A (silk) handkerchief: c.: from ca 1810; ob. *Lex. Bal.*; Egan; Dickens in *Oliver Twist*. 'Ger. *vogel*, bird, has been suggested, via "bird's eye wipe",' W.; perhaps rather ex It. *foglia*, a pocket; cf. Fr. *fouille*. 2. Whence *fogle-hunter*, a thief specializing in silk handkerchiefs: from ca 1820; ob. And *fogle-hunting*, occ. *f.-drawing*: from ca 1820; ob.

fogles. A prize-fighter's colours: boxing: mid-C.19–20. Ex FOGLE, 1.

fogo, see HOGO.

fogram, fogrum. (cf. FOGEY.) 'A fusty old man', Grose 1st ed.; ca 1775–1850. 2. Liquor; esp. wine, beer, spirits of inferior quality: nautical (—1867); ob. 3. adj., stupid, old-fashioned: app. earlier than FOGEY: witness e.g. Mme D'Arblay in 1772 and O'Keeffe, in *A Trip to Calais*, 1778, 'Father and mother are but a couple of fogrum old fools,' the *fogrum old* being significant.

fogramite. An old-fashioned or eccentric person; coll: ca 1820–1900.

fogramity. An old-fashioned way or custom: Mme D'Arblay, 1796. 2. Hence, eccentricity. 3. A FOGEY. All coll. See preceding entry.

fogrum, see FOGRAM.

***fogus.** Tobacco: c.: mid-C.17–19. Head, Ainsworth. Perhaps *fog*, a mist, + *us* as in HOCUS-POCUS.

fogy, see FOGEY.

foie-gras. Pâté de foie gras: coll: 1818, T. Moore.

***foil-(or foyl-)cloy.** A pickpocket; thief; rogue: c.: late C.17–early 18. cf. FILE.

***foiler.** A thief: C.17 (?–18): c. Anon., *Nicker Nicked*.

***foin.** A pickpocket: c.: late C.16–early 17. Greene, 1591.

foin, v.t. and i. To have connection with a woman: low: late C.16–17. Ex S.E. sense.

***foist, foyst, fyst.** A cheat, rogue, sharper, pickpocket: late C.16–18 c. Greene; Jonson: 'Prate again, as you like this, you whoreson foist you.' 2. A trick, imposture, swindle: C.17 low or c. 3. A silent breaking of wind: low coll: C.16–early 19. Variants, FICE, *fiste*, *fyse*.

***foist, foyst, fyst,** v.t. and i. (very frequent as vbl n.). To pick pockets; trick, swindle: c.: late C.16–18. Greene, Dekker, Middleton, Grose. 2. To break wind silently: low coll: C.16–early 18. 3. The dicing senses may have begun as c., the same applying to:

***foister, foyster.** A pickpocket; swindler: low, ?c.: mid-C.16–17.

***foisting,** see FOIST, v., 1.

follow. To accompany (a corpse) to the grave; (also v.i.) to attend the funeral of (a person): coll: 1819 (O.E.D. Sup.).

follow-me-lads. Curls or ribbons hanging over the shoulder: coll (—1872). Contrast Fr. *suivez-moi jeune homme*.

follow your nose!, often with **and you are sure to go straight.** A c.p. (non-cultured) addressed to a person asking the way (—1854). Other forms, e.g. *and you will be there directly* (C.17), are earlier and the phrase is clearly adumbrated in C.14.

follower. A female servant's sweetheart or suitor, esp. if he frequents the house: coll: 1838. Dickens, 'Five servants kept. No man. No followers.' 2. A seaman serving always, if possible, under the one captain: naval coll: C.18. 3. A young officer doing the same with a view to promotion: id.: id.

fool, adj. Silly, foolish; often a pejorative intensive: C.13–20: S.E. till C.19, then (low) coll and dial. Esp. in *a*, *the*; or *that fool thing*.

fool around (with). To dally riskily, with one of the opposite sex: v.t. and i. Coll: from ca 1880. In U.S., v.t., without *with*.

fool at the end of a stick, a; a fool at one end and a maggot at the other: mid-C.18–19 c.p. 'gibes on an angler', Grose, 2nd ed.

fool-finder. A gen. petty bailiff: ca 1785–1880.

fool-monger. An adventurer, -uress; swindler; betting man: coll: late C.16–early 18.

fool-sticker. The male member. Occ. *fool-maker.* Low: C.19–20.

fool-taker, -taking. A sharper, sharping: low coll: late C.16–mid-17. Greene, 1592.

fool-trap. A FOOL-MONGER. 2. A stylish harlot. 3. The female pudend: low. All from ca 1840.

fooleries, the. April-fooling: coll: prob. from ca 1880.

***foolish,** adj. Of one who pays: harlots' c.: from ca 1788: ?ob. Grose, 2nd ed., 'Is he foolish or flash?'

foolocracy. Government by, or consisting of, fools: jocular coll: 1832. Sydney Smith.

foolometer. A means whereby to determine the public taste: jocular coll: 1837, Sydney Smith. cf. S.E. *foolocracy.*

foolosopher, foolosophy. A silly pretender to, pretence of, philosophy: jocular coll: from ca 1550. Greene, 'That quaint and mysticall forme of Foolosophie'.

fool's father. The pantaloon or OLD ONE (4): theatrical: ca 1870–1910.

fool's wedding. A party of women: coll: from ca 1875. cf. HEN-PARTY.

***foont.** A sovereign: c. (—1839). Ex either Fr. *vingt* or, prob., Ger. *Pfund.*

foot. Feet, as in 'Six foot two': coll: C. 15–20.

foot!; or **foot!, foot!** Get out of it!, go away!: coll: C.19–20; ob. Ware implies equivalence to Fr. *fous-moi le camp* and remarks that it is 'cast after the respectably dressed person who wanders into strange and doubtful bye-ways'.

foot, know the length of one's. To know a person well; discover his weakness: coll > S.E.: late C.16–early 18. Later, *have* or *get* . . .; slightly ob. Prob. orig. a shoemaker's metaphor.

foot!, me or **my.** Rubbish!; not at all!: low: late C.19–20. Occ. *pig's foot!*

foot a or **the bill.** To pay; settle an account: coll: from ca 1844. Until ca 1890, an Americanism.

foot-bath. A too full glass: late C.19–20; slightly ob.

foot in the grave, have one. To be seriously ill, near death; to be very old: from ca 1630: coll > S.E. ca 1850.

foot in(to) it, put one's. To get into trouble; cause trouble: coll: from ca 1790.

foot it. To walk: coll: from ca 1840. cf. Fr. *faire du footing.* 2. To kick, HOOF, use one's feet: from ca 1850: sporting, esp. football. 3. To dance: coll: late C.18–19.

foot land-raker. A footpad: C.16–17 coll (?jocular). Shakespeare.

foot-licker. A servant; toady: coll: C.17–19. Shakespeare in *The Tempest.*

foot(-)lights, smell the. To come to like theatricals: theatrical coll: from ca 1870.

foot-pad. A pedestrian highwayman: orig. (C.17), c. or low; C.18, coll; C.19–20, S.E. cf. LOW PAD and see PAD. For the vocabulary of foot-paddery, see the relevant essay in *Words!*

foot-riding, vbl n. Wheeling one's machine instead of riding it: cyclists' (—1887); ob. T. Stevens, *Round the World on a Bicycle.*

foot-rot. Fourpenny ale: public-houses': ca 1895–1915. Ware. cf. ROT-GUT.

***foot-scamp.** A FOOT-PAD: C.18–early 19, low or c. Parker. See SCAMP.

foot-slogger. An infantryman: military coll: from early 1890s. cf. FOOT-WABBLER and the Fr. equivalents, *pousse-cailloux, piou-piou.*

foot the bill, see FOOT A BILL.

foot up. To 'total' at the foot of a bill: coll: ex U.S. (1840), anglicized ca 1860. But as *foot* in S.E. for centuries before.

foot-wabbler, -wobbler. An infantryman: 1785, Grose; ob. by 1860: military. cf. MUD-CRUSHER, and FOOT-SLOGGER. (Grose is notable on early military s.)

footer. Football: orig. university s.: from ca 1880. 2. ca 1885–1905, a player of Rugby football: universities'. 3. One who potters, messes about: s. when not dial.: from ca 1750. It has a corresponding v. and vbl n.: variant spelling *fouter(ing).* See Grose, P., at *forty.* Ex Fr. *foutre.*

footing. Money paid, on beginning a new job, to one's fellow-workers: in C.18, coll: but thereafter S.E. cf. CHUMMAGE.

footle. Nonsense; twaddle: from ca 1893. Ex:

footle, v. To dawdle, potter, trifle about; act or talk foolishly; coll: from ca 1890; slightly ob. By *futile* out of dial. *footer, fouter* (ex Fr. *foutre*), to trifle. F. Anstey in *Voces Populi.*

footless stocking without a leg, a. Nothing: Anglo-Irish coll (—1909).

footling. Insignificant; trivial; pettily fussy: coll: from ca 1893. Ex FOOTLE, v.

footman's inn. A wretched lodging; a gaol: coll: ca 1600–1630.

***footman's maund.** An artificial sore, made to resemble a horse's kick or bite: late C.17–late 19 c. B.E. cf. FOX'S BITE and see MAUND.

Foot's horse, take or travel by (Mr). To walk: coll verging on S.E.: from ca 1820; ob. Bee. cf. SHANKS'S MARE.

footy. Despicable; worthless: coll from ca 1750: in C.20, ob. Ex Fr. *foutu.*

foozilow. To flatter, cajole: Anglo-Indian coll (—1886). Ex Hindustani.

foozle. A miss: sporting s. > gen. coll: 1890. Ex the v. 2. (Of a person) a bore; an old FOGEY: coll: 1860. Rhoda Broughton, 'Frumps and foozles in Eaton Square' (London, S.W.1). Prob. ex *fool* + FIZZLE: cf. next.

foozle, v. To miss; make a bad attempt at; bungle: sporting j. > gen. s. or coll. *Field,* 25 Feb. 1888, 'Park foozled his second stroke.' Ex FOOTLE + FIZZLE; or, more prob., dial. *footer* (to bungle) + *fizzle.*

foozled, foozly. Blurred; indistinct; spoilt: coll: from ca 1890.

foozler. A bungler: from ca 1895: sporting j. > gen. s.

foozlified. Tipsy: nautical (—1887); ob.

fop-doodle. A fop; a fool; an insignificant man: coll: ca 1640–1700.

fop's alley, Fops' Alley. The gangway between stalls and pit, orig. and esp. in the Opera House: theatrical: ca 1770–1830. Mme D'Arblay in *Cecilia,* 1782. Earlier *fop's corner* (nearest-the-stage corner of the pit): Wycherley, *The Country Wife,* 1675, in form *fop corner.*

for certain sure, see CERTAIN SURE, FOR.

forakers. A privy: Winchester College: C.19–20. Either L. *forica > foricas > foricus >,* ca 1860, *forakers* (W.): or *four acres,* a field (H.). W.c.s have had to endure much pedantic wit: cf. AJAX. R. G. K. Wrench gives it as *foricus*; he adds 'cf. Vulgars = Vulgus'.

foraminate. To have sexual connection with (a woman): C.19: low pedantic. Ex L. *foramen,* an orifice.

Force, the. The Police: coll: from ca 1850. cf. *the Profession* (see PRO, 2). Miss Braddon in *The Trail of the Serpent,* 1868. Abbr. *the Police Force.*

force-meat ball. Something inherently unpleasant endured under compulsion: C.19. ?ex the spiced, highly seasoned nature of *force-meat* and influenced by *force-ment.*

force the voucher, see VOUCHER, FORCE THE.

forced to be, be. To be necessarily: late C.17–20: S.E. until mid-C.19, then coll (increasingly low).

force(d) put. Compulsion: HOBSON'S (i.e. no) CHOICE: coll > S.E.: ca 1650–1820, then dial.

forceps. The hands: mainly and orig. medical: from ca 1820; ob.

fore. A mostly proletarian and military coll form of *before*: mid C.19–20.

fore-and-aft. To have sexual connection: nautical: mid-C.19–20; ob.

fore-and-aft rig. The single-breasted chief petty officer's uniform: naval: late C.19–20. Bowen.

fore-and-after. A harlot that is DOUBLE-BARRELLED: from ca 1850. ?ex, 2, the † nautical s. sense (—1867), a cocked hat worn with the peak in front, Smyth: recorded in Southern Scots in 1839.

fore-bitter. 'A narrative song sung round the fore bitts in the dog watches, as opposed to a shanty, or working song': nautical coll: mid-C.19–20. Bowen.

fore-chains, (there's) a rat in your. A nautical c.p., 'the final insult to a sloppy ship': late C.19–20. Bowen, 'Its origin is obscure.'

***fore-stall.** In garotting, a look-out in front; the one behind is the *back-stall.* c. of C.19–20, ob. See STALL.

forecastle, forecourt, forehatch, forewoman. The *pudendum muliebre*: all C.19–20 and decidedly ob. terms in Venus-venery.

forecastle rat. A seaman whom one suspects of being either the owners' or the officers' spy: nautical coll: late C.19–20.

forefoot. The hand: jocular coll: late C.16–20; ob. Shakespeare, Grose.

foregather. To come together in sexual intimacy: coll: C.18–early 19.

foreign line. Any line other than that on which the speaker is employed: railwaymen's coll (—1909).

foreign parts, gone to. Transported as a convict: ca 1820–70.

foreigneering, vbl n. and ppl adj. Foreign (matters); like a foreigner: low coll: from mid-1820s; slightly ob. i.e. *foreign* + pejorative suffix *-eer.*

foreman. The *membrum virile*: C.17, ?later: coll, perhaps literary. 2. In Beaumont & Fletcher's *Philaster,* ed. of 1622, at V, iii, presumably s. and prob. = a goose.

foreman of the jury. One who monopolizes the conversation: late C.17–early 19. It is the foreman who delivers the jury's verdict.

foreskin-hunter. A prostitute: low coll: C.19–20 (?ob.).

forest of debt. The payment of debts: Oxford University: ca 1820–40.

forever gentleman. 'A man in whom good breeding is ingrained': Society: ca 1870–1915. Ware. Contrast *temporary gentleman.*

***forger.** (Gen. pl.) A false die: gamblers' c.: late C.16–early 17. Greene, *A Notable Discovery*, 1591.

forget. A lapse of memory; an instance of such lapse: coll: from ca 1820; ob.

forget about. To fail to remember the facts of or about; fail to take action about: coll: from ca 1895. Actually, this is a slipshod, unnecessary elaboration of *forget.*

forget it!, don't you, see:

forget it!, (and) don't (you). An admonitory coll c.p.: U.S. (—1888) >, by 1900, anglicized.

forget oneself. (Of a child) to urinate or defecate unconventionally: euphemistic coll: late C.19–20. cf. Fr. *s'oublier.*

foricus, see FORAKERS.

***fork.** A pickpocket: c.: late C.17–early 19. Prob. ex *forks* in: 2. Also c.: app. from ca 1810: a finger; *the forks* (late C.17–20) being the fore and middle fingers. cf. DADDLES; FIVES; GRAPPLING-IRONS; PICKERS AND STEALERS. 3. A spendthrift: C.18: ?c. 4. As crutch of the body, S.E. though hardly literary. But *the old fork* is coll (late C.19–20), esp. in *get on the old fork*, (of either sex) to coït.

fork, v. To pick pockets; esp. by inserting the fore and middle fingers: late C.17–early 19: c. In C.19, variant: *put one's forks down.* cf. C.18–19 Edinburgh *fork for*, search for. 2. v.t. and i., to dispose (a woman) for the sexual act: low: mid-C.19–20 (?ob.). 3. Occ. abbr. FORK OUT. 4. To protrude awkwardly: coll: 1882 (?earlier).

fork, a bit on a. The female pudend; also, a sexual congress: low: C.19–20. Hence, *get on the old fork*, to copulate: low coll: late C.19–20. Ex FORK, n., last sense. cf. FORK, v., 2.

fork, eat (or have eaten) – or, properly, **have been drinking** (Baumann) – **vinegar with a.** To be sharp-tongued or snappish: proverbial coll: mid-C.19–20; ob.

fork, pitch the. To tell a sad or doleful story: low coll: from ca 1860; ob.

fork and knife. Life: rhyming s: late C.19–20.

fork in the beam! A late C.19–20 naval c.p., 'an order from the sub for all midshipmen to retire from the gunroom'. Ex a fork 'actually stuck into the beam in the old wooden ships'.

fork out; rarely – except in U.S. – **over** or **up.** Hand over (valuables or money); pay, SHELL OUT: from ca 1815: s. > coll by 1900: Dickens, 'Fork out your balance in hand.' Ex FORK = finger. cf. STUMP UP.

forker. A dockyard thief or FENCE: nautical: C.19–20; extremely ob. Ex FORK, v., 1. cf. FORKING. 2. See:

forker, wear a. To be cuckolded: via *cornuted*: C.17. Marston, 1606.

***forking.** Thieving; the practice of thieving: c.: C.19. Ex FORK, v., 1. 2. The undue hurrying of work: tailors': from ca 1850; ob.

forking the beam. The vbl n. corresponding to FORK IN THE BEAM!

***forkless.** Clumsy; unworkmanlike: c. (—1821); ob. As if without FORKS, hands or fingers – prob. the latter.

forks, see FORK, n., 2. 2. Only in pl, the hands: from ca 1820. An extension of FORK, n., 2.

forlo(o)per. A teamster guide: South Africa: from ca 1860: coll. The guide is gen. a boy who walks abreast the foremost pair of oxen. Dutch *voorlooper*, a 'fore-runner'.

forlorn hope. A gambler's last stake: coll: late C.17–19. Ex S.E. sense (orig. military).

form. Condition, fitness: orig. of horses (ca 1760) and s.; by 1870, coll; by 1900, S.E. Esp. *in* or *out of form.* Hawley Smart, in *Post to Finish*, 'When fillies, in racing parlance, lose their form at three years old, they are apt to never recover it.' 2. Behaviour, esp. in *bad* or *good form*: coll (1868) ex the turf, though anticipated by Chaucer and Shakespeare. In C.20, by the class that uses this magic alternative and formula, it is considered S.E. 3. Habit; occupation; character: low coll (—1884); ob. 4. The height of one's attainment: Public Schools': C.20. P. G. Wodehouse, 1902, 'He sneers at footer, and jeers at cricket. Croquet is his form, I should say.' 5. (Gen. with *in*) high spirits; 'concert' pitch: coll: from ca 1875.

form, a matter of. A merely formal affair; a point of ordinary routine: coll: 1824, H. J. Stephen. Ex the legal *a matter of form,* (cf.) 'a point of formal procedure' (ibid.).

***forney.** A (finger-)ring. A variant of FAWNEY: C.19–20 c.

fornicating-engine, -member, -tool. The male member: C.19–20 ob.: low coll. cf.:

fornicator. The male member. Whence *fornicator's hall*, the female pudend: C.19 low. 2. In pl, the old-fashioned trousers with a flap in front: †by 1880, the trousers being antiquated even earlier.

forra(r)der, get no or (not) any. To make (no) headway: coll (orig. illiterate, now mostly jocular): 1898, *Daily Telegraph*, 15 Dec.

Forties, the. A well-known gang of thieves of the 1870s–early 80s: low (1887 —); †by 1910. Ex *the Forty Thieves*.

Fortnum and Mason. A notable hamper: Society: mid-C.19–20. Ware, 'From the perfection of the eatables sent out by this firm of grocers in Piccadilly' – whence came also the cleverest advertising-matter known to this century. (The firm was established in C.18.)

fortune, a small. An extravagantly large sum paid for something, esp. for something small: coll: from ca 1890.

fortune-biter. A sharper, swindler: coll: C.18. D'Urfey.

***fortune-teller.** A judge or, occ., a magistrate: c.: late C.17–early 19. B.E., whose definition is so ambiguous that the term may, even there, bear the usual meaning: in which case that sense may orig. have been c. or, more prob., s. or low coll. Grose, 1st ed., seems, however, to be clear as to the 'judge' interpretation, though he may merely be glossing B.E. cf. LAMBSKIN MAN; CUNNING MAN, which Egan considers as = a judge.

forty is in C.17–20 S.E. as well as coll, used frequently to designate a large though indefinite number, or quantity, or degree: Shakespeare, who has 'I could beat forty of them,' twice employs 'forty thousand' in a highly hyperbolical manner common to the Elizabethan dramatists. *Forty pence*, a customary amount for a wager, C.16–17, and the later *forty thieves* may be operative reasons for the continuance of this coll or coll-tending *forty*.

forty-faced. Arrant; esp. shamelessly given to shameless deception: e.g. *forty-faced flirt* or *liar*.

forty fits, have. To be much perturbed or alarmed: coll: late C.19–20.

forty-foot, forty-guts. A fat, dumpy person (pejoratively): the former stressing the shortness, the latter the fatness: low coll: resp. from (—)1864, (—)1857. cf. GUTS, 2; TUBBY or *tubs*.

forty-jawed. Excessively talkative: coll: mid-C.19–20. cf. JAW and FORTY-LUNGED.

forty-legs. A centipede: late C.17–20: coll (ob.) when not dial.

forty-lunged. Stentorian – or very apt to be. Coll: from ca 1850.

forty-rod. Strong, crude illicit whisky: Canadian s.: since ca 1885.

forty to the dozen. Very quickly: with *talk*, more often *nineteen to the* DOZEN; with *walk off*, the sense is to decamp very speedily. Coll: from ca 1860.

forty-twa. A public urinal (Edinburgh): Scots coll: ca 1820–90. Ex the number of persons seatable.

forty winks. A nap, short sleep: coll: from middle 1820s. Egan, 1828; G. Eliot, 'Having "forty winks" on the sofa in the library', 1866.

forward station. 'A desirable coastguard station': nautical coll: ca 1850–1900. Bowen.

***foss; phos(s),** see PHOS.

fossick. (v.i., occ. with *about*; but v.t. only when used with *after*, *for*, *out*, *up*.) To search for anything: 1870; Australian s. > coll ca 1890. Ex the ideas, search for gold (1861), pick out gold (1852). 2. Whence vbl n. *fossicking*, which is commoner than the other parts of the v.; also adj. (1859). Ex dial. *fossick*, a troublesome person: cf. *fuss*.

fossicker. A persistent searcher: from ca 1890. Ex gold-mining senses. Australian.

fossicking, see FOSSICK, 2.

fossilize. To look for fossils: coll: 1845. Lyell.

fou, occ. fow. Drunk: late C.17–20, coll. Vanbrugh. Ex Scottish.

foul a plate (with). To sup or dine with a person: coll: late C.18–20; ob. except in Western Scotland in the form *dirty a plate*.

foul as an Indiaman. (Of a ship) dirty: naval: C.19. Ex jealousy.

foul-weather breeder, the. The Gulf Stream: nautical coll: mid-C.19–20.

foul-weather Jack. Any person supposed to bring bad luck to a ship while he is on it: nautical coll: late C.18–20.

***foulcher.** A purse: c. (—1877). Anon., *Five Years' Penal Servitude*, 1877. Is this cognate with or derived from Romany *folaso*, a glove?

foundling temper. A very bad temper: London: from ca 1880; ob. Ware, 'Proverbially said of the domestic servants poured upon London by the metropolitan Foundling Hospital'.

foundry. A pork-butcher's shop; loosely, any shop: proletarian (—1909); ob. Prob. ex 'the noisy vibrations of the sausage machine' (Ware).

fountain palace or **temple.** (Gen. pl.) 'Places of convenience, sunk below the roadways': London: the 1890s. Ware. Ex bright and cleanly appearance, the running water, etc.

four-and-nine(penny). A hat: ca 1844–80. Thackeray; Viator, *Oxford Guide*, 1849. Occ. a *four-and-ninepenny* GOSS. Ex the price set by a well-known London hatter.

four arf. A Cockney form of FOUR-HALF.

four bag. A flogging: naval: mid-C.19–early 20. The bluejacket received *four* dozen lashes; if also his discharge, then *four bag and a blanker*, the latter being his discharge ticket with one corner cut off.

***four-bones.** The knees: c.: from ca 1850; ob. *Punch*, 31 Jan. 1857.

four-eyes. A bespectacled person: uncultured coll: from ca 1870.

four-foot-one-and-a-half. A rifle: bluejackets': late C.19–20. Ex length.

four-half. Half-ale, half-porter, at fourpence a quart: 1884 (O.E.D.). cf. FOUR THICK.

four-holed middlings. Ordinary walking shoes: Winchester College: C.19; †by 1890.

four kings, the book (or **history**) **of the,** see HISTORY OF THE FOUR KINGS.

four-legged burglar-alarm. A watch-dog: jocular coll: from ca 1880.

four-legged fortune. A winning horse: Society: ca 1880–1914.

four-legged frolic. Sexual connection: low coll: from ca 1850. Perhaps ex the ob. C.16–20 proverb, 'There goes more, *or* more belongs, to (a) marriage than four bare legs in a bed.'

four-liner, n. and adj. (Something) very important: Society coll: ca 1890–1915. The origin appears in the *Daily News*'s words, 1890, cited by Ware, 'Four-lined whips [or messages] have been sent out on both sides of the House of Commons urging members to be in their places this evening.'

four-poster. A four-poster bedstead: coll: 1836, Dickens. 2. Hence, a four-masted sailing-ship: nautical: mid-C.19–20.

four seams and a bit of soap. A pair of trousers: tailors': from ca 1870.

four, but more gen. **three, sheets in the wind.** Drunk: nautical, from ca 1840. See SHEETS . . .

four thick. 'Fourpence per quart beer – the commonest there is (in London), and generally the muddiest': public-houses': late C.19–early 20. Ware. cf. FOUR-HALF.

four-wheeler. A four-wheeled cab: coll: from ca 1846; coll > S.E.; ob. cf. *four-poster*. 2. A steak: low coll; from ca 1880.

fourpenny. An old ill-favoured whore: low London: ca 1870–1920. Ex her tariff.

fourpenny cannon. Beef-steak pudding: London slums' (—1909); ob. Ex shape or, more prob., hardness.

fourpenny pit. A fourpenny bit: rhyming s.: late C.19–early 20.

fourteen hundred; or **f.h. new fives.** A warning cry = There's a stranger here! Stock Exchange: from ca 1885. Atkin, *House Scraps*, 1887. For a long time the Stock Exchange had never more than 1,399 members: the term has remained, though even as early as 1890 there were nearly 3,000 members.

***fourteen penn'orth of it.** Fourteen years' transportation: c.: 1820–60.

fourth. A w.c.; a latrine – the vbl phrases being *keep a fourth, go to the fourth*: *gone*[4] is the esoteric sign on an undergraduate's door. Cambridge s. (—1860). Not ex the Fourth Court at Trinity College, as explained by H., but perhaps (W.) ex a staircase-number. Or from the routine: 1, Chapel; 2, breakfast; 3, pipe; 4, defecation. (This Cambridge interpretation dates back to at least as early as 1886.) 2. See FIRST.

fourth, on one's. Very drunk: non-aristocratic: ca 1870–1910.

fourth estate, the. Journalists; journalism as a profession: S.E., applied by Burke, > literary s. (—1855) >, by 1910, outworn journalese: already in 1873 it was much in use among penny-a-liners.

fousty. Stinking: coll when not dial.: from ca 1810. ?ex FOIST, n., 2, influenced by FROUST, *frowst*.

fouter, v., and **foutering,** vbl n. See FOOTER, 3, for all remarks.

fouter or **footer, care not a.** To care not at all: coll: late C.16–20, ob.

foutie or **fouty,** see FOOTY.

fow, see FOU.

fowl. A troublesome seaman: nautical: late C.19–20. Also a BIRD (4) or an ERK. Perhaps there is a pun on *foul* and QUEER BIRD.

***fox.** An artificial sore: c. (—1862). Mayhew. cf. FOX'S BITE.

fox, v. To intoxicate: C.17–20; until ca 1760, S.E.; then coll. *Sporting Times*, 11 April 1891, 'And so to bed well nigh seven in the morning, and myself as near foxed as of old.' 2. To cheat, rob: Eton (—1859). 3. v.t. and v.i., to watch closely though slyly: London c. (—1859) > low s. v.i., *fox about*. cf. FOX'S SLEEP. 4. v.i., to sham: early C.17–20; S.E. until C.19, then coll and dial. Ex a fox's habit of pretending to be asleep. This is prob. the sense posed by 'Ducange Anglicus', 1857: to be half asleep. 5. To criticize adversely a fellow-actor's acting: theatrical (—1864). 6. To mend a boot by 'capping' it: from ca 1790 (?j. >) s. > coll > S.E.

fox, catch a; gen. **to have caught a fox** (B.E.). To be or become very drunk: C.17–19 coll. A late C.16–17 variant is *hunt the fox*. cf.:

fox-drunk. Crafty-drunk: late C.16–17: coll. Nashe.

fox (or fox's) paw, make a. To commit a blunder, esp. in society or (of women) by carelessly allowing oneself to be seduced: late C.18–19 low coll. A (prob. deliberate) perversion of Fr. *faux pas*.

fox to keep one's geese, set a. To entrust one's confidences and/or money to a sharper or an adventurer: coll: from ca 1630; Ob.

foxed. Tipsy. See FOX, v., 1.

foxing, vbl n. Ex FOX, v., but not for sense 1, rarely for senses 2 and 6; mostly for sense 3.

fox's bite. An artificial sore: schoolboys': from ca 1850; ob. cf. FOX, n.

fox's paw, see FOX PAW, MAKE A.

fox's sleep. A feigned sleep veiling extreme alertness: coll: C.17–20: ob. In S.E., *fox-sleep*.

foxy. Strong-smelling: coll, verging on S.E.: C.19–20.

***foy.** A cheat, swindler: late C.16–17. Perhaps c., certainly low. 2. A coll expletive: late C.16–early 18. i.e. FAY, faith.

***foyl-cloy,** see FOIL-CLOY. **foyse,** see FICE. **foyst,** n. and v., see FOIST. **foyster,** see FOISTER.

fragment. A dinner ordered by a master for a favoured boy, who could invite five school-fellows to share it: Winchester College: †by 1891. *Winchester Word-Book*. A *fragment* = three dishes or courses. 2. In Shakespeare, a pejorative term of address.

'fraid. Afraid: a coll, mainly childish, shortening: C.19–20.

'fraidy cat. A frightened or a timorous person: coll, mostly children's: from ca 1870.

frail. A courtesan: fast life: ca 1830–70.

frame. A picture: artists': ca 1890–1912. 2. See SWATCHEL.

***frammagem,** see FRUMMAGEM.

franc-fileur. 'A man who gets away quickly and won't dance'; Society: ca 1890–1915. Punning Fr. sense. Ware.

France and Spain. Rain: rhyming s.: late C.19–20.

frater. A beggar working with false papers, esp. a petition: mid-C.16–20. Awdelay, Fletcher.

fraud. A thing either deceptive or spurious: coll: late C.18–20. 2. An impostor, HUMBUG, hypocrite: coll: 1850, Dickens. Often jocularly.

freak. An actor who loses caste by performing in some eccentric show: theatrical: late C.19–early 20. cf. DIME MUSEUM.

***free,** v. To steal (gen. a horse): c. of ca 1835–90. cf. CONVEY. 2. To make (a person) free; to initiate: Public Schools' coll: late C.19–20.

free. Self-assured; impudent: Oxford University (—1864).

free and easy (often hyphenated). A social gathering (gen. at a public-house) where smoking, drinking and singing are allowed: (orig. low) coll; from ca 1796. The *Lex. Bal.*; Macaulay, 1843; Cassell's *Saturday Journal*, Sept. 1891. A ribald club or society, fl. 1810–11, was known as the Free-and-Easy Johns.

free-and-flowing. A seaman's uniform with square collar: naval: mid-C.19–20; ob.

free(-)booker. A piratical publisher or an under-selling bookseller: journalists': ca 1880–1914. Punning *freebooter*.

free fight. A general struggle or mellay: orig. U.S. (—1855) coll, anglicized by 1873. Occ. *a free-for-all fight*, the *fight* sometimes being omitted.

free-fishery. The female pudend: low: C.19–20 (?ob.).

free-fucking. A general sexual looseness; unpaid coition; fidelity to the other sex. Also adj. Low: rather a vulg. than a coll: C.19–20.

free gangway. 'General leave from a man-of-war': naval coll: late C.19–20. Bowen.

free, gracious (and) for nothing. A c.p. variant (only ca 1885–1900) of:

free gratis – for nothing; f., g., and for nothing. Costing nothing: coll, orig. low: from mid-C.18.

free(-)holder. A harlot's lover or FANCY-MAN: C.19–20 (ob.) low. 2. 'He whose Wife goes with him to the Ale-house', B.E.: from ca 1650.

free-lance. A persistent adulteress: ca 1888–1910. Ex the medieval mercenary earlier known as a *free companion* and renamed by Scott in *Ivanhoe*.

free object. A non-convict settler: Australian: ca 1810–70. A. Harris, *Settlers and Convicts*, 1847. Punning 'free subject'.

free of fumbler's hall or **Fumbler's Hall.** Impotent: (?late) C.18–early 19 low.

free of the bush. Extremely intimate (with a woman): low: from ca 1860.

free of the house. Intimate: privileged: coll in C.19, S.E. in C.20.

Free State coal. A South African coll euphemism (dating from ca 1880, and now slightly ob.) for dried cow-dung. R. Jameson, *A Trip to the Transvaal Gold-Fields*, 1886.

free trade or protection? (Women's) knickers loose and open or closed and tight-fitting: low coll: from ca 1905.

free with both ends for the busk, make. To caress a woman with extreme familiarity: C.18–20 (ob.).

freeman. The lover of a married woman: C.19–20 (ob.) low.

freeman, v.; **make a freeman of.** To spit on a (new boy's) penis: schools' (mostly Public): ca 1850–1920. Occ. *freemason*.

freeman of a corporation's work, see CORPORATION'S WORK . . .

freeman of Bucks. A cuckold: C.19 low. Punning *Buckinghamshire* and a *buck's* horns. Contrast BEDFORDSHIRE.

Freeman's!, it's Harry. There's nothing to pay: naval: from ca 1870.

Freeman's Quay, drink or **lush at.** To drink at another's expense: ca 1810–80. Ex *free* beer distributed to porters and carmen at this wharf near London Bridge.

freemason, v., see FREEMAN, V.

***freeze,** v. To appropriate or steal: c.: C.19. cf. FREEZE TO.

freeze, do a. To feel extremely cold: coll: late C.19–20.

freeze on to, see FREEZE TO.

freeze out. To compel to retire from business or society, by competition or social opposition: orig. (ca 1867), U.S.; anglicized ca 1895 as a coll.

freeze the balls . . . see MONKEY, COLD ENOUGH . . .

freeze to, in C.20 gen. **freeze on to.** To take a powerful fancy to: late C.19–20; ob. 2. Cling to, hold fast. Coll: Australian (ex U.S., where common): England slightly: in both countries from ca 1880.

freezer. A very cold day (from ca 1895, S.E.); a chilling look, comment, etc.: coll: from ca 1848. 2. An Eton jacket (without tail): coll or s.: from ca 1880. ?abbr. BUM-FREEZER or -PERISHER. 3. A sheep bred for frozen export: New Zealand (—1893); Australian, from ca 1900. Coll.

French, loose, see LOOSE FRENCH.

French article, cream, elixir, lace. Brandy: coll: resp. —1821, —1788, —1860, —1821. The second, gen. of brandy in tea or coffee – a French custom. See 'Offensive Nationality', in *Words!* for coll, dial. and S.E. variations on the *French* theme, which was at its height ca 1730–1820.

French crown, goods or **gout.** Syphilis: C.17–19: coll verging on S.E. *F. ache(s)*, *fever*, *disease*, *measles*, *marbles*, *mole*, *pox*, are S.E. cf. FRENCH FAGGOT-STICK.

French elixir, see FRENCH ARTICLE.

French faggot-stick, a blow with a. A nose lost through syphilis: late C.17–18: low.

French fare. Elaborate politeness: C.14–17: coll > S.E. In C.14–early 16 often *frankish fare*.

French goods, or **gout,** see FRENCH CROWN.

French King, to have seen the. To be drunk (—1650).

French lace, see FRENCH ARTICLE.

French leave, take. To depart without intimation or as if in flight; do anything without permission: from ca 1770: coll in C.18–mid-19, then S.E. Smollett, 1771. (cf. Fr. *filer à l'anglaise*.) Ex the C.18 Fr. custom of departing from a reception, dinner, ball, etc., etc., without bidding good-bye to host or hostess.

French (rarely **American, Italian** or **Spanish) letter.** A male sheath-pessary: low coll: from ca 1870. cf. Fr. *capote anglaise*.

French pie. Irish stew: City of London restaurants' (—1909).

French pig. A venereal bubo: C.19–20 (ob.) low.

French pigeon. A pheasant mistakenly shot in the partridge season: sportsmen's (—1893); ob.

French prints. Obscene pictures: coll: from 1850. Thackeray. Ob.

French tricks. Cunnilingism, penilingism: coll: mid-C.19–20.

Frencher. A Frenchman: pejorative coll: ca 1840–1900. C. Kingsley.

Frenchified. Venereally infected; esp. with syphilis: mid-C.17–19 coll. cf. FRENCH CROWN.

Frenchman. A (good, bad, indifferent) French scholar: coll: from *temp.* Restoration.

Frenchman, the. Any foreigner: naval coll (cf. later dial.): ca 1620–1720. 2. Syphilis: C.19 low. cf. old technical *morbus gallicus.* 3. (A bottle of) brandy: Society: mid-C.19–early 20. Ware, 'From this spirit being French'.

Frenchy. A Frenchman: coll: recorded 1883, ?considerably earlier. Ex ob. S.E. adj. Miss Yonge, 'The squires had begun by calling him Frenchy.' In dial., any foreigner whatsoever.

fresh, adj. In one's first university term: university (?orig. Cambridge); from ca 1800; ob. *Gradus ad Cantabrigiam*, 1803. Ex FRESHMAN. 2. Forward, impudent: orig. (—1848), U.S. (ex Ger. *frech*), anglicized ca 1895. 3. Slightly drunk: coll; from ca 1810. But in dial. at least twenty years earlier: E.D.D. Marryat, 'I could get fresh as we call it', 1829. 4. Fasting; opposed to eating and esp. drinking; sober: M.E.–C.20: until C.19, S.E.; in C.19 coll. 5. Uninitiated: mid-C.19–20.

fresh and blood. 'Brandy and port wine, half and half', *Spy*, 1825: Oxford University: ca 1815–60.

fresh as a daisy, a new-born turd, an eel, flowers in May, paint, a rose. Very healthy, strong, active: coll, the second being low: resp. from ca 1815, 1830, 1410, (1400–1600), 1440, 1850; the third and fifth soon > S.E. and indeed poetical, while the first is in C.20 almost S.E. For the first, third, fifth and sixth (perhaps orig. ironic for the first or the third) see esp. Apperson.

fresh bit. (Of women, in amorous venery) a beginner; a new mistress: low: from ca 1840. cf. *bit of fresh*, the sexual favour.

fresh hand at the bellows, (there's) a. A sailing-ship coll c.p. of mid-C.19–20 (now ob.), 'said . . . when the wind freshened, especially after a lull' (Bowen).

fresh milk. A newcomer, newcomers, to the university: Cambridge University: ca 1820–50. Egan's Grose. (cf. FRESHWATER BAY.) Punning *freshman.*

fresh on the graft. New to the work or job: from ca 1890. See GRAFT.

fresh water, a. By way of punishment for working hands, a turn at pumping various tanks: *Conway* cadets': from ca 1880.

fresh-whites. Pallor: lower classes': mid-C.19–early 20.

freshen hawse. To have an incidental drink: *The Night Watch* (II, 117), 1828, 'After we had been mustered at quarters, and the hammocks down, I went and freshened hawse with a nip of Tom's grog.' cf. FRESHEN THE HAWSE.

freshen one's way. To hurry: nautical (—1893) s. > j. Ex *freshening wind.*

freshen the hawse. To serve out a tot after extra fatiguing duty: nautical: late C.19–20. Bowen. cf. FRESHEN HAWSE.

freshen up. To clean, smarten; revive: coll: from ca 1850. An example of a S.E. term (*freshen*) being made coll by the addition of pleonastic adv.

fresher. An undergraduate in his first term: university, orig. (—1882) Oxford. Perhaps the earliest example of the Oxford *-er*. See *Slang*, pp. 208–9, and note that R. Ellis Roberts thinks that possibly it arose from a new man being described as *fresher than fresh.*

freshish. Verging on drunkenness, nearly tipsy: County s.: ca 1819–60. P. Egan, *London*, 1821.

freshman. A university undergraduate in his first year; at Oxford, in his first term: late C.16–20: orig., university s., but in C. 19–20 to be considered S.E. Nashe; Colman, 1767, 'As . . . melancholy as a freshman at college after a jobation'. Whence FRESHER. 2. Also an adj.: C.19–20, ob. 3. The C.17–20 *freshmanship* is, I think, ineligible.

freshman's Bible. The University Calendar: mostly Oxford and Cambridge: from ca 1870; ob.

freshwater bay, or F.B. The world of freshmen: Oxford University: ca 1820–40. cf. FRESH MILK.

freshwater mariner, seaman. A begging pseudo-sailor: ca 1550–1840, 1690–1840, resp. as are Harman and B.E. Perhaps c., orig.

freshwater soldier. A recruit: late C.16–18: orig. coll; but in C.17, S.E. Florio, 1598, defines as 'A goodly, great milkesoppe'. cf. S.E. *fresh-water seaman*, which may, just possibly, have at first been coll.

fret!, don't (you). You needn't worry: sarcastic coll c.p.: late C.19–20. cf. *I should worry!*

fret one's fat, giblets, gizzard or guts; one's cream, kidneys. To worry oneself with trifles: low coll: in gen., from ca 1850, the *gizzard* form ante-dating 1755, and the *fat* form being from ca 1880; ob., except for *gizzard*. cf. FLURRY ONE'S MILK.

friar. A white or pale spot on a printed sheet: printers': from ca 1680. Contrast MONK. In C.19–20, both are j.

Friar Tuck. Fuck, as n., v., and expletive: low rhyming s.: late C.19–20.

Friars. Blackfriars Station: London coll (—1909).

***frib.** A stick: C.18 c. *Discoveries of John Poulter*, 1754. ?etymology.

Friday, black, see BLACK FRIDAY.

Friday face. A glum, depressed-looking face or person: coll: from ca 1590; ob. by 1889. (adj., *Friday-faced*, from late C.16; ob.) Variant, C.18–20, *Friday look*. Ex Friday as a day of fasting.

Friday while. Week-end leave: naval coll: late C.19–20. *While* here = *until*, as in North Country dial.; the leave is from Friday noon until Monday.

fried carpet. 'The exceedingly short ballet skirt... especially seen at the old "Gaiety"': London theatrical: 1878–82. Ware. 2. 'An improved Cockneyism for "fish and 'taters"': from ca 1890; ob. *Tit-Bits*, 8 Aug. 1891. By jocular perversion.

friend. The man who keeps a harlot as his mistress: (better-class) whores' euphemistic coll: from ca 1870. 'Oh yes, I have a friend.'

friend, go and see a sick. To go womanizing: low: from ca 1860.

friend has come, my (little); I have friends to stay. The victim's announcement of the menstrual flux: C.19–20 low: ob. cf. CAPTAIN IS AT HOME.

friend in need. (Gen. pl.) A louse: low: C.19–20; ob. ?ex C.18 GENTLEMAN'S COMPANION; see also BOSOM FRIEND.

friendly lead. An entertainment organized to assist an unlucky, esp. an imprisoned man – or his wife and children: from ca 1870; orig. c.

friendly pannikin. A drink shared with another from that utensil: Australian coll: ca 1860–1910.

friends to stay, see FRIEND HAS COME...

frig. An act of self-abuse: low coll: C.18–20.

frig, v.t., i., refl. To masturbate: from ca 1590: low coll. Cotgrave; Robertson of Struan. The imperative with *it* is late C.19–20, occ. an exclamation: cf. FUCK IT! Ex L. *fricare*, to rub. 2. Hence, loosely, to copulate with: mid-C.19–20.

frig about, v.i. To potter or mess about: low coll: mid-C.19–20.

frig-pig. A fussy trifler: late C.18–early 19.

frigate. A woman: orig. (—1690), nautical. Esp. *a well-rigged frigate*, 'a Woman well Drest and Gentile' (i.e. Fr. *gentille*), as B.E. has it.

frigate on fire. A variant (ca 1810–50) of *fire-ship*.

frigation. A frigatoon: naval: C.19. By perversion of the S.E. term, with a pun on FRIG, V.

frigging. The practice, or an act, of self-abuse (cf. FRIG, n.): low coll: C.17–20. 2. Trifling; irritating waste of time: C.18–20, ob. except with *about*.

frigging, adj. and adv. A low coll intensive: *a frigging idiot* being an absolute fool; *frigging bad*, exceedingly bad. From ca 1820. cf. FUCKING, adj., adv.

fright. Any thing or person of a ridiculous or grotesque appearance: coll: from ca 1750.

fright hair. 'A wig or portion of a wig which by a string can be made to stand on end and express fright': theatrical coll (—1909). Ware.

frightful. An intensive adj.: coll: from ca 1740. (cf. AWFUL, TERRIBLE.) Dr Johnson notes its constant use 'among women for anything unpleasing'. 2. A low coll variant (C.19–20) of:

frightfully. An intensive adv.: coll: from late C.18, to judge by a passage (from *La Belle Assemblée*) in *The Port Folio* of June 1809.

frillery. Women's underclothing: low coll: ca 1888–1910. cf. FRILLIES.

frillery, explore one's. To caress a woman very intimately: low coll: ca 1888–1914.

frillies. Women's underclothing: coll: ca 1870–1910.

frills. Swagger, conceit, SIDE. Hence *put on one's frills*, to swagger; also, low coll or s., to grow very amorous. Also culture and accomplishments (music, dancing, foreign languages). Orig. (—1870), U.S.; anglicized ca 1890. Kipling, 1890, 'It's the commissariat camel putting on his blooming frills' (recurring, in book form, in 1892).

frills, have been among a woman's. To have 'known' her: ca 1860–1914.

fringe. Irrelevant matter: coll: from ca 1885; ob.

frint. A pawnbroker: low or c.: ca 1810–50. *Real Life in London*, 1821. ?*friend* perverted.

frisco, frisko(e). A term of endearment: coll: C.17. Variant *friskin.*

frisk. As frolic and a lively dance-movement, it is S.E. as also is *frisker*, a dancer; but as sexual connection it is low coll: C.19–20. 2. Only in *stand frisk*, to be searched: c. (—1812); †by 1900. Ex:

***frisk; occ. friz** (for senses 1, 2), v. To search (the person); examine carefully for police evidence: c. (—1781). 2. Hence to pick the pockets of, pick (a pocket, rob a till): c.: C.19. 3. To HAVE (4) a woman: low: C.19–20. 4. To hoax: ca 1820–60.

***frisk, dance the Paddington.** To be hanged: mid-C.18–early 19: low or c.

frisk and frolic. Carbolic: rhyming s.: from ca 1880.

frisk at the tables. 'A moderate touch at gaming': London coll: from ca 1880. Ware.

***frisker.** A pilferer: c.: from ca 1890. Ex FRISK, v., 2.

frisko(e), see FRISCO.

frisky. Whiskey: from ca 1890. Ex the popular saying (—1887), *whiskey makes you frisky.*

frisky, adj. Playfully amorous; fond of amorous encounters: coll: from ca 1890. 2. Bad-tempered: low London: from ca 1880; ob.

frivol, frivel, frivole. To behave frivolously: coll, almost S.E.: from ca 1865. W. Black, in *Yolande*, 1883, 'If you want to frivole . . . I shut my door on you.' Ex *frivolous*, ?on *fribble.*

frivoller; frivolling. A trifler; trifling: coll; resp. 1887 (Baumann), 1882 (O.E.D.).

***friz, frizz,** see FRISK, v., 1 and 2.

frizzle. Champagne: ca 1860–70. ?a perversion of FIZZ.

***frizzler.** A hawker: c.: from ca 1840. '*No. 747*'. Origin?

frock and frill. A minor ill, esp. a *chill*: rhyming s.: late C.19–20.

frock-hitcher. A milliner, esp. one in a small way: urban: ca 1880–1915. Arthur Binstead, *Mop Fair*, 1905.

***froe, occ. vroe.** A woman, wife, mistress, whore: c.: late C.17–19. Ex Dutch.

frog. A policeman: low s. verging on c.: from ca 1855. More gen. in U.S. than in Britain. Ex his sudden leaping on delinquents. 2. **(Frog.)** A Frenchman (also *Froggy*): from ca 1790. It has > the 'inevitable' nickname (also *Froggy*) of men with French surnames: lower classes'. (In Fr. s., orig. a Parisian.) Ex the toads on the Parisian shield and 'the quaggy state of the streets', F. & H., or ex the eating of frogs. 3. In C.17, however, it meant a Dutchman: cf. FROGLANDER. 4. A foot (cf. CREEPERS): low: C.19–20, ob. Ex the frog in a horse's hoof. 5. The bluejacket's 'frock, before the days of the jumper': naval coll: C.19. Bowen. Ex the tailors' frog.

frog and toad. A (main) road: rhyming s. (—1859). Perhaps cf.:

***Frog and Toe.** London: c. (—1857); †by 1900. Perhaps cognate with preceding entry.

Frog-Eater. A Frenchman: low coll: from late C.18; ob. cf. FROG, 2, and FROGGIE.

frog-skin. A sovereign (£1): Australian rhyming s.: late C.19–20.

frog-spawn. Tapioca pudding: Public School-boys': since ca 1890.

Froggie or Froggy. A Frenchman: from ca 1870. The *Referee*, 15 July 1883. Also adj. All the *frog* terms for a Frenchman refer to the eating of frogs. Contrast:

Froglander. A Dutchman: late C.17–19 (though after ca 1820 only among sailors), and, in U.S., C.19–20, though ob.

frog's march (gen. with **give the**); occ. **frog-march** or **-trot.** The carrying of a drunken man face downwards, e.g. to the police-station. Coll: from ca 1870. *Evening Standard*, 18 April 1871; *Daily News*, 4 Oct. 1884. 2. Also, from ca 1884, a v.t.

frog's wine. Gin: ca 1810–70. ?a reference to Holland: cf. FROGLANDER.

Froncey. French: low London: C.19. i.e., Fr. *français.*

***front,** v. To cover the operations of an associate pickpocket: c. (—1879): ob.

front, clean one's. To clean one's front door-step and proportionate share of the adjoining pavement: lower- and lower-middle-class coll: late C.19–20.

front attic, door, garden, parlour, room, window. The female pudend: low. None, I think, before 1800; Bee, 1823, has *parlour*; F. & H., 1893, all six.

front-door mat. The female pubic hair: low: C.19–20.

front(-)gut. The female pudend: low: C.19–20; ob.

front name. A Christian name, esp. the first: when not culturedly facetious, it is low coll (—1895). Ex U.S. (—1877).

front parlour, see FRONT ATTIC.

front piece. A CURTAIN-RAISER: theatrical coll: ca 1885–1912.

front room, see FRONT ATTIC.

***front-stall.** He who, in garotting or

robbery with strangulation, keeps a look-out in front: c.: from ca 1850; ob. See also BACK-STALL and NASTY MAN or UGLY MAN.

front window, see FRONT ATTIC.

front windows. The eyes; occ. the face: from ca 1860.

frontispiece. The face: pugilistic (—1818); ob. Egan, Buckstone. Anticipated, however, with jocular (?) pedantry by the C.17 and C.18, e.g. by Hume.

froom or **frume.** Religious in the orthodox sense: Jewish coll: late C.19–20. Ex Ger. *fromm*, pious.

frost. An utter failure or complete disappointment, whether thing, event, or person: theatrical s. > gen. coll: from ca 1885. *Star*, 17 Jan. 1889, 'The pantomime was a dead frost.' W. ingeniously suggests that *frost* derives ex Wolsey's *killing frost* in Shakespeare's *Henry VIII*. 2. Lack of work: as in *have the frost*, to be unemployed: from ca 1880. 3. A coolness between persons: late C.19–20, ob.

frosty-face. 'One pitted with the small pox', Grose, 1st ed.: low or c.: ca 1750–1910.

froudacious, froudacity, adj. and n. Inaccurate, -acy: Australia and, though much less, New Zealand: ca 1888–93. Ex Froude the historian's statements concerning those two countries: on *audacious*.

frought, see FROUT.

froust, frowst. A stink; stuffiness (in a room): coll: from ca 1870. cf. FUG. Ex FROUSTY. 2. Hence, at Harrow School, additional sleep allowed on Sundays and whole holidays: from ca 1875.

froust, frowst, v. Rest lazily: coll when not dial. (—1884); ob. in coll.

frouster, frowster. One who wears warm clothes in summer: Naval cadets': from ca 1880.

frousty, frowsty. Unpleasant-smelling; FUGGY: coll when not dial.: 1865 (S.O.D.). Origin obscure.

frout. Angry; annoyed; vexed: Winchester College: C.19–20. Ex the Hampshire dial. *frou(g)ht*, frightened, as R. G. K. Wrench suggests.

frow, see FROE. **frowst,** see FROUST. **frowsty,** see FROUSTY.

fruit of a gibbet. A hanged felon: coll: C.18. Gay.

fruitful vine. The female genitals: either low coll or dubious euphemism, the double pun being indelicate: C.19–20, ob.

fruity. Very rich or strong (e.g. language); very attractive or interesting or suggestive (e.g. story): coll: 1900. Prob. suggested by JUICY.

frume, see FROOM.

frumety-kettle, see FURMITY KETTLE. . .

***frummagem;** app. only as **frummagemmed,** choked, strangled, spoilt: c. of ca 1670–1830. Head, Coles, Grose, Scott (in *Guy Mannering*). ?etymology.

***frumper.** A sturdy fellow: c. of ca 1820–60. Kent, *Modern Flash Dict.*, 1825. Perhaps a survival of *frumper* = mocker, jester.

fry. To turn into plain English; gen. in passive: from ca 1880; ob. James Payn, in *Grape from a Thorn*, 1881.

fry in one's own grease. To suffer the (natural) consequences of one's own folly; 'dree one's weird': coll: C.14–20. See esp. Apperson.

***fry the pewter.** To melt pewter measures: c. of ca 1850–1910. ?suggested by *fry the potato*.

fry your face, go and. A c.p. retort indicative of contempt, incredulity, or derision: ca 1870–1905. cf. the Suffolk *fry your feet!*, nonsense!

frying-pan. A collier brig from Whitby: nautical: C.19. Ex the 'traditional wind vane, a large disc and a pointer' (Bowen). 2. See TURNIP. Mayhew, 1861; H., 5th ed., 1874; ob. On WARMING-PAN, 2.

frying-pan brand. 'A large brand used by cattle-stealers to cover the owner's brand', Morris: Australia (—1857); ob.

frying-pan into the fire, jump from or out of the. To be thus worse off: from ca 1520, with antecedents in Plato, Lucian, Tertullian: coll until ca 1890, then S.E. More, Harington, Garrick, Barham. See esp. Apperson.

fu-fu. Barley and treacle, 'a favourite dish in the early 19th century sailing ships': nautical: C.19. ?origin: perhaps Bowen is wrong about the 'early', and the term derives from S.E. *fufu*, yam or plantain pounded into balls. 2. Hence, 'an amateur band raised in the ship's company': nautical: late C.19–20. Bowen.

fuant. Excrement, esp. in pl and of vermin: C.17–18 low coll. ?Fr. *puant* corrupted.

fub, see FOB, n., 2, and FUBBS.

fub, v. See FOB, v., of which it is a late C.16–17 variant. 2. v.i., to potter about: cricketers' coll (—1906). (Ultimately ex sense 1.)

fubbery, trickery, cheating, stealing, occurs in Marston. See FOB, n. and v.

fub(b)s, n. 'A loving, fond Word used to pretty little Children and Women' (B.E.), esp. if (small and) chubby: C.17–18: coll. cf. the next two complete entries.

fubby, see:

fubs(e)y. Plump; (of things) well filled: C.17–20 (ob.) coll. 'Applied by Charles II to Duchess of Portsmouth', W.; Marryat, in *Snarley-Yow*, 1837, 'Seated on the widow's little fubsy sofa'. Variant, *fubby*. Ex FUB(B)S.

fubsiness. Fatness; 'well-filledness': coll: from ca 1780. Ex preceding term.

fubsy, see FUBSEY.

fuck. An act of sexual connection: from ca 1800. (Ex the v., for which see etymology, etc.) 2. A person (rarely of the male) viewed in terms of coïtion, as in 'She's a good f.': C.19–20. These two senses are excellent examples of vulgarism, being actually S.E. 3. The seminal fluid, esp. if viewed as providing the requisite strength (*full of fuck*, potently amorous): low coll: C.19–20.

fuck, v.t. and i. To have sexual connection (with): v.i. of either sex, v.t. only of the male: a vulg., C.16–20. Almost certainly cognate with the Latin v. *pungere* and n. *pugil*, both ex a radical meaning 'to strike'; semantically, therefore, *fuck* links with PRICK, 3. Transitive synonyms, many of them S.E., occur in Shakespeare (9), Fletcher (7), Urquhart (4), etc., etc.; intransitive in Urquhart (12), D'Urfey and Burns (6), Shakespeare (5), etc., etc. See esp. B. & P. (the Introduction); Grose, P.; and Allen Walker Read, 'An Obscenity Symbol' (sec. II) in *American Speech*, Dec. 1934 – all at this term. 2. See FUCK OFF.

fuck!, like. Expressive of extreme scepticism or aversion; 'certainly not!': low: late C.19–20. Synonyms: *like* BUGGERY! and *like* HELL! Also in form *did* (or *will*) I (etc.) *buggery* or *fuck* or *hell!*, I certainly didn't or won't.

fuck, to. A low intensive, as in 'Get to fuck out of it!': late C.19–20. Here, *fuck* is apparently n.

fuck about. To play the fool: low: mid-C. 19–20.

fuck all. A low variant of *damn all*: nothing: late C.19–20.

fuck-beggar. An impotent or almost impotent man whom none but a beggar-woman will allow to 'kiss' her: mid-C.18–early 19 low coll. Grose, 1st ed. See BUSS-BEGGAR.

fuck-finger, -fist. A female, a male, masturbator: low C.19–20, ob.

fuck-hole. The *pudendum muliebre*: C.19–20 low. ?on *bung-hole*.

fuck (it)! A low expletive: C.19–20. Very gen. among those for whom delicacy and aesthetics mean little – or rather nothing. cf. *frig it!* at FRIG, V.

fuck off. To depart, make off: low: late C.19–20. cf. BUGGER OFF, PISS OFF. 2. Esp. in the imperative: id.: id.

fuck-pig. A thoroughly unpleasant man: low Cockney: from ca 1870.

fuck you, Jack, I'm all right! A c.p. directed at callousness or indifference: (late C.19–20).

fuckable. (Of women) sexually desirable; nubile: low coll or a vulg.: C.19–20. cf. and contrast FUCKSOME.

fucked, adj. Extremely weary; (utterly) exhausted: late C.19–20. Ex FUCK, V.

fucked!, go and get; go and fuck yourself! Run away and stop bothering me!: low: mid-C.19–20.

fucked more times than she's had hot dinners, she's been. A low c.p. of late C.19–20.

fucker. A lover; a harlot's 'fancy man': C.19–20 low coll. 2. A pejorative or an admirative term of reference from ca 1850. 3. Hence, a man, chap, fellow: from ca 1895.

fucking, vbl n. The sexual act regarded generically: C.16–20: vulg.

fucking, adj. (C.19–20 low) 'a qualification of extreme contumely', F. & H., 1893.

fucking, adv. Very, exceedingly. Somewhat stronger and much more offensive than BLOODY. From ca 1840; perhaps much earlier – records being extremely sparse. cf. FUCKER, 3.

fuckish. Wanton (of women); inclined, even physically ready, for amorous congress (men and women); C.19–20 coll.

fucksome. (Of women) sexually desirable: a C.19–20 vulg.

fuckster, fuckstress. A (notable) performer of, an addict to, the sexual act: a C.19–20 vulg. 2. Hence, as a pejorative ('*vieux cochon*', says Manchon): late C.19–20.

fud. The pubic hair: coll when not Scottish or dial.: late C.18–20, ob. as coll. Ex dial. sense, a hare's or rabbit's scut.

fuddle. Drink; a drink: c. or low: ca 1680–1830. L'Estrange. Ex the v. 2. Intoxication, drunken condition: coll: from ca 1760. 3. A drunken bout: low coll, or perhaps s.: from ca 1810. 4. Derivatively: muddlement; mental 'muzziness': from ca 1825.

fuddle, on the. Engaged in drinking; on a drinking bout: coll: C.19. *Sessions*, May 1845 (Surrey cases).

fuddle, out on the. Out on a day's drinking: (low) coll: mid-C.19–20.

fudge. A lie, nonsense; exaggeration; humbug or a humbug: 1790. Also (e.g. in Goldsmith, 1766), an exclamation, roughly equivalent to, though slightly politer than, BOSH! Coll: C.18–20. Anecdotal orig. improbable; perhaps ex Ger. *futsch*, no good, corrupted by Fr. *foutu*, with the anecdote helping and FUDGE, v., reinforcing. 2. A forged stamp: schoolboys': from ca 1870. 3. A farthing: Dubliners', esp. newsboys': late C.19–20. Ex FADGE, n.: cf. the Manx *not worth a fudge*, worthless or useless.

fudge, v. To interpolate (as in Foote, 1776); do impressively very little (Marryat); fabricate (Shirley Brooks); contrive with imperfect materials, as e.g. writing a book of travel without travelling (Sala, 1859); forge (mostly schoolboys': from ca 1870). Coll: all nuances slightly ob. 2. Botch, bungle, v.t.: coll: from ca 1700. 3. v.i., to talk nonsense, tell fibs: from ca 1834. 4. Advance the hand unfairly in playing marbles: schoolboys': from ca 1875. 5. Copy, CRIB: also schoolboys' and -girls': from ca 1870. 6. At Christ's Hospital (—1877), v.i. and t., to prompt oneself in class; to prompt another; thence, to tell. Ex FADGE, prob. influenced by *forge*.

fug. A stuffy atmosphere: from ca 1888. ?ex *fog*, influenced by *fusty*, of which it is prob. a schoolboys' or a dial. perversion.

fug, v. To remain in a stuffy room: Shrewsbury School: from ca 1888. Ex the preceding. cf. FROUST, n., 2, and v.

fug-footer. An informal game played with a small ball: Harrovians': from ca 1880.

fug out. To clean or tidy (a room): Rugby School: since ca 1880. To take the FUG *out* of it.

fug shop, the. The carpenter's shop at: Charterhouse (—1900). A. H. Tod.

fug trap. A ventilator above a study door: Marlborough College: since ca 1870.

fugel, fugle, v.i. To cheat, trick: s. or dial.: C.18–19. D'Urfey.

fugger. A waste-paper basket: Tonbridge: late C.19–20. Marples. Smell, musty.

fuggy. A hot roll: schoolboys': from ca 1860. ?etymology.

fuggy, adj. Stuffy: orig. (—1888) schoolboys'; from ca 1910, coll. Perhaps a direct adoption of Scottish *fuggy, foggy*.

fugle, see FUGEL.

fugo. The rectum: C.17–18: low coll. Cotgrave, D'Urfey.

fulham, fullam. A loaded die: practically never in singular. Mid-C.16–early 19: low; in C.17, perhaps c. Nashe, Shakespeare, Jonson, Butler, B.E., Grose, Scott. Fulham in South-West London was either a main manufactory or a notorious resort of sharpers. (A *high fulham* was marked 4, 5, or 6; a *low*, below 4.)

Fulham virgin. A loose woman: coll: C.19–20; ob. by 1905. cf. – for same reason – BANKSIDE LADY and COVENT GARDEN NUN.

fulk. 'To use an unfair motion of the hand in playing at taw' (marbles), Grose, 3rd ed.: schoolboys', mid-C.18–early 19. Prob. ex dial., like so much other schoolboy s.; certainly it is extant in dial.

fulke. To have sexual intercourse (mainly v.i.): ca 1820–1900: low pedantic. Ex the last word of Byron's *Don Juan*.

fulker. A pawnbroker: coll: mid-C.16–17. Gascoigne, 1566, 'The Fulker will not lend you a farthing upon it.' Ex Ger. (cf. FOGGER).

full. Having eaten, occ. drunk, to repletion: low coll since ca 1830; earlier, S.E. 2. Tipsy: coll: from ca 1850. 3. Having already sufficient money laid against a particular horse: bookmakers': from ca 1880. 4. See FULL UP.

full against. Very inimical to: gen. coll from ca 1870, ex earlier racing j. (see preceding entry, sense 3).

full as a goat. Extremely drunk: taverns': C.18–19. Ware considers *goat* to be a corruption of *goitre*.

full as a tick. Replete (with food and/or drink): coll: mid-C.17–20; after ca 1850, mainly dial. 2. Completely drunk: from ca 1890: mainly Australian.

full as a tun(ne). Replete: coll: ca 1500–1660. Heywood the proverbist.

full belly. One who ensures that his belly be full: C.17 coll.

full blast, in. Very active; highly successful: coll (—1859). Orig. North Country and ex the engine-room, esp. furnaces.

full bob. Suddenly; in unexpected collision: C.17–18 coll. Marvell, 'The page and you meet full bob.'

full-bottomed, -breeched, -pooped. Having a broad behind: coll: C.19–20, the first and third being orig. nautical.

full dig, in. On full pay: ca 1860–1910.

full due, for a. For ever: nautical: late C. 19–20.

full feather, in, see FEATHER.

full fig, in. See FIG. 2. Adj. and adv., priapistic: low (—1893); ob.

full-fledged. Ripe for the sexual act (of a girl): low coll: C.19–20.

full frame, have a. To have obtained regular employment after being a temporary hand: printers': from ca 1860.

full guts. A large-bellied person: C.19–20, low coll. adj., *full-gutted.*

full in the belly. Pregnant. Occ. abbr. to *full of it.* C.19–20, low coll.

full in the hocks or **pasterns.** Thick-ankled: coll, orig. stable s.: C.19–20.

full in the waistcoat. Large-bellied: coll: C.19–20. cf. FULL GUTS.

full march by [e.g.] **the crown-office, the Scotch Greys are in.** The lice are crawling down his (e.g.) head: a low c.p. of ca 1810–30.

full mouth. A chatterer: late C.16–17 coll. Greene.

full of. Sick and tired of: Australian (—1898).

full of beans, see BEANS.

full of 'em. Lousy; full of fleas, nits: low coll: C.19–20.

full of emptiness. Empty: jocular coll: late C.18–20.

full of fuck and half starved. (Often preceded, occ. followed, by *like a straw-yard bull.*) A friendly reply to 'How goes it?' Low c.p., from ca 1870; ob.

full of guts. Vigorous; courageous; (pictures, books, plays, etc.) excellently inspired: coll: from ca 1885. See GUTS.

full of it. See FULL IN THE BELLY. 2. Much impressed by any event or subject already mentioned: coll (—1887).

full of oneself. Conceited; somewhat ludicrously arrogant: C.19–20 coll. Ex the C.18–19 proverb, *He's so full of himself that he is quite empty.*

full on. More than ready; eager: coll: from ca 1860. 2. Australian, from ca 1890: sated with, weary of, disgusted with. cf. FULL UP. 3. A bookmaker who is 'full on' a horse is one who has so many bets placed on that horse that he risks losing much money to the betters: 1868, *All the Year Round,* 13 June.

full on for it or **for one.** Ready and extremely willing: gen. of an indelicate connotation: coll; from ca 1860.

full-pooped, see FULL-BOTTOMED.

full suit of mourning, have or **wear a.** To have two black eyes: *half-mourning,* one black eye. Pugilistic: from ca 1870; ob.

full swing, in. Very or fully active or engaged; highly successful: coll (—1861). *In the swing* is C.18–20; *full swing* is C.16–18.

full to the bung. Exceedingly drunk: low coll: from ca 1850. cf. BUNG-EYED.

full up. Quite full; full: coll: C.19–20. Whence perhaps: 2. (Constructed with *of*) sated; weary; disgusted: Australian and, later, New Zealand, from ca 1890. Rolf Boldrewood in *The Miner's Right.* Variants *full* (if followed by *of*), *full on* (with object). cf. FED UP (*with*), the English counterpart.

fullam, see FULHAM.

fuller's earth. Gin: ca 1815–50. *Real Life in London,* 1821.

***fullied, be.** To be commited for trial: c.: from ca 1855. Ex *fully committed.*

fulness enough in the sleeve-top, there's not. A derisive reply to a threat; it implies lack of muscle. Tailors': ca 1870–1920.

fumble, v.t., i., and absolute. To caress a woman sexually: coll: C.16–20; ob. Dunbar, Shebbeare, Goldsmith.

fumble-fisted. Clumsy: nautical coll: from ca 1860.

fumbler. An impotent man, gen. old; an unperforming or inadequate husband: mid-C.17–19 coll. One of D'Urfey's titles is *The Old Fumbler.* Ex FUMBLE. 2. The adj. *fumbling,* sexually impotent, C.16–19, seems to have always been S.E. 3. But Ned Ward (1703) uses *fumbler* for 'a young debauchee'.

fumbler's hall. 'The place where such [i.e. fumblers] are to be put for their non-performance', B.E.: late C.17–18: coll. 2. The female pudend: late C.18–19. See FREE OF FUMBLER'S HALL. cf. the dial. *fumbler's feast* mentioned by Southey in 1818.

fun. The breech or the behind: late C.17–early 19. Prob. abbr. *fundament.* 2. A cheat, a trick: late C.17–early 19. Both senses were orig. c. ?ex *funny*: certainly *funny business* is cognate, while U.S. *phoney business* is from another radical. 3. Difficult work; exciting and/or dangerous events: military: from mid-1890s.

***fun,** v.t. Cheat, trick, outwit; with (*out*) *of,* deprive illicitly, dishonestly of: late C.17

–early 19: orig. if not always c. Now dial., ob.

fun, do or gen., **have a bit of.** To obtain or to grant, or enjoy together, the sexual favour: low coll: from ca 1850.

fun, have been making. To be tipsy: coll: from ca 1860; ob.

fun, like. Very quickly; vigorously: coll: from ca 1815: see LIKE. 2. Also ironically as a decided negative: from ca 1870.

fun at, poke. To joke (ob.), ridicule, make a butt (of). Also absolute without *at*. Coll: from ca 1835. Barham, 'Poking fun at us plain-dealing folks'.

fun (up)on, put the. To cheat, trick, outwit: late C.17–early 19: low. Ex FUN, n., 2.

functior, functure. A bracket candlestick made of iron and used for a night-light in college chambers: Winchester College (—1870). ?ex *fulctura*.

fundamental features. The posterior: cultured coll: 1818, Moore: ob. *Blackwood's Magazine*, 1828, has it in the singular. Punning *fundament*: cf. FUN, n., 1, and the jocular use of *fundamentally*.

funds. Finances; supply of (esp. ready) money: coll: 1728 (S.O.D.): in C.18 and C.20, S.E.; in C.19, coll. Esp. *be in funds*, to have (temporarily) plenty of money. Thackeray.

funeral, it's his, my, your, etc.; or negatively. It's his (not his, etc.) business, affair, concern, duty: orig., negative only and U.S. (1854), anglicized, mainly in the affirmative form, ca 1880.

fungus. An old man (cf. S.E. *fossil* and †S.E. *funge*): ?coll: ca 1820–90.

funk. Tobacco smoke; tobacco; a strong stink: resp. late and early C.17–early 18 c. B.E.; Ned Ward, 1703 (2nd nuance). 2. (A state of) fear, great nervousness, cowardice: orig. at Oxford, 1743, in *to be in a funk*. Often preceded by CURSED (Grose); MORTAL; AWFUL; BLUE, or, in C.19–20, BLOODY. 3. Among schoolboys, a coward: from ca 1860. Anstey in *Vice Versa*, 1882. The second and third senses derive ex the first (itself prob. ex Flemish *fonck*), as appears from:

funk, v. 'To smoke; figuratively, to smoke or stink through fear', Grose, 1st ed. The *stink* sense occurs in 1708; that of smoking a pipe, five years earlier, and that of blowing smoke upon a person, four years earlier still. As to fear, the v.i. is recorded for 1737, the v.t., fear, be afraid of, not until a century later, and that of shirk, fight shy of, not until 1857, while the †sense, terrify, occurs in 1819 (e.g. in Mayhew, 1858). 3. With sense 1, connect 'to smoke out', at least as early as 1720: D'Urfey, Moncrieff; with sense 2 (v.i.), of schoolboys' v.i. *funk*, unfairly to move the hand forward in playing marbles: from ca 1810; ob.: cf. FUDGE, v., 4. Perhaps n. and v. are ultimately derivable ex L. *fumus*, smoke, *fumigare*, to fumigate or smoke.

funk the cobbler. To smoke out a schoolmate (gen. with asafoetida): from late C. 17; ob. by 1830, †by 1895. Ned Ward. See FUNK, V.

funker. A pipe, cigar, fire: ca 1800–70. Ex FUNK, and v. 2. A coward: from ca 1860. 3. Among harlots, 'a girl that shirks her trade in bad weather', F. & H.: from ca 1865. 4. In the underworld, a low thief (—1848); ob. Duncombe.

funkster. A coward: Winchester College: from ca 1860. cf. FUNKER, 2.

funksticks. One who fears the fences (*sticks*): hunting: 1889. 2. Hence, in South Africa, any coward: 1897, Baden Powell.

funky. Afraid; timid: very nervous: coll: from ca 1837. Reade, 'The remaining Barkingtonians were less funky, and made some fair scores.' cf. *windy*, (*have the*) *wind up*.

funnel. The throat: coll: C.18–20, ob. cf. GUTTER-ALLEY.

funnily, funniness, ex FUNNY, adj., in the corresponding senses: C.19–20.

funniment. A joke, verbal or physical: from ca 1845 (ob.): coll. Suggested by *merriment* and prob. coined by Albert Smith. 2. The female pudend: low: mid-C.19–20, ob.

funny. A narrow, clinker-built boat for sculls; a racing-skiff: Cambridge and nautical s. > j.: from ca 1799. Barham; *Field*, 28 Jan. 1882. Probably ex Japanese *fune*, a boat.

funny, adj. Strange, odd, queer: coll: from early C.19. 2. Hence, in late C.19–20 coll: dishonest. 3. Intoxicated: mid-C.18–20; in late C.19–20, only as a euphemism. Toldervy, 1756; *Slang*, p. 23.

funny, feel. To feel ill: from ca 1895. 2. To be overtaken with drink or with emotion (e.g. of amorousness): the former(†), from ca 1800; the latter from ca 1850.

funny bit. The *pudendum muliebre*: iow: C.19–20.

funny bone. The extremity – at the elbow – of the *humerus*, the 'funniness' being caused by the ulnar nerve: coll: from ca

1840. Barham. Presumably by a pun on *humerus*, but greatly influenced by *funny feeling*, i.e. sensitiveness.

funny for words, too. Extremely funny: coll: late C.19–20. Prob. suggested by *too funny for anything*, which was orig. (the late 1860s) U.S.

funny man. A circus clown: from ca 1850. Mayhew, *London Labour*, III, 129. 2. A private joker: from ca 1860. Both coll.

funny party. 'A warship's minstrel troupe or entertainers of any kind': naval coll: late C.19–20. Bowen.

funster. A maker of fun: coll: 1887: ob. Modelled on and suggested by *punster*.

funt. A pound sterling (£1): a Yiddish word incorporated into Parlary: mid-C.19–20. Ex German *Pfund*.

fur. The (gen. female) pubic hair: low: C.18–20.

fur, adj. and adv. Far: sol.: C.19–20. Also *for*.

fur and feather(s). Game: sportsmen: from ca 1830; orig. s., then coll, then, in C.20, j. or S.E.

fur fly, make the, see FLY, MAKE THE FUR.

fur out, have one's. To be very angry: Winchester College: from ca 1870.

fur trade. Barristers: ca 1830–80. 'Multiple' journalist Reynolds, 1839.

furbelow. The female pubic hair: a C.17–early 19 pun: cf. FUR.

furious joy. The *feu-de-joie* of military j.: military: late C.19–20. By 'Hobson-Jobson'.

furk; also ferk, firk. To expel, drive away; send on a message: Winchester College: from ca 1850. Variants *furk down*, *f. up*.

***furman.** An alderman: c.: late C.17–early 19. Ex the fur-lined robes. cf. LAMBSKIN MAN.

furmity-faced. White-faced: coll and dial.: C.18–19. *Furmity*, also *fromenty* or *frum(m)ety*, is a dish of hulled wheat (L. *frumentum*) boiled in milk and variously flavoured.

furmity kettle, simper like a. To smile; look merry: coll: C.18–early 19. In form *frumety-kettle*, however, it occurs in L'Estrange in 1668; and *simper like a pot that's ready to run over* is recorded by Apperson for 1631.

furnish. An embellishing or setting off: coll: 1896; ob.

furnish, v.i. and t. To fill out; regain strength and (good) appearance: coll: from ca 1860. Rarely of persons, gen. of horses. Henry Kingsley in *Ravenshoe*. Orig. stable s.

furniture picture. A picture sold to fill a gap on somebody's wall; a picture painted solely as merchandise: artists' (—1889). cf. POT-BOILER.

furrow, or **Cupid's** or **the one-ended furrow.** The *pudendum muliebre*: low coll: C.19–20 (ob.). Whence *die* or *fail in the furrow*, do a DRY-BOB, and *fall in the furrow*, to 'emit'.

furry tail. A non-unionist; a 'rat' – whence the synonym. Esp. a workman accepting less than 'Society', i.e. trade-union, wages: from ca 1860; ob. Among printers, who, like tailors, have a large s. vocabulary. See *Slang* at 'Printers and Publishers' and 'Trades'.

furry thing. (Gen. pl.) A rabbit: North Sea fishermen's euphemistic coll: C.19–20. For these fishermen, the mere mention of a rabbit brings ill luck.

further first, I'll see you. I certainly won't! Coll (—1851). Mayhew, *London Labour and the London Poor*, I, 29.

fury, like. 'Like mad', furiously, very hard or vigorously: coll: from ca 1840.

furze-bush. The female pubic hair, viewed as an entity. Occ. *furze*, which, however, stresses the hair as hair rather than as a mass. C.19–20 low.

fusby. A woman: contemptuously pejorative: coll: ca 1719–1880. D'Urfey; *Punch*, 29 Nov. 1845. ?ex FUSBY influenced by FUSSOCK.

fusilier. Beer: military rhyming s.: from ca 1860: ob.

fuss, see SQUEEZE, n., 6.

fuss-arse. A fussy person: rural coll: from ca 1880. cf.:

fuss pot, fuss-pot. A very fussy person: coll (not the upper classes'): from ca 1890.

fussock, fussocks; a mere fussocks. 'A Lazy Fat-Ars'd Wench', B.E., who proceeds: '*A Fat Fussocks*, a Flusom [? fulsome], Fat, Strapping Woman'. Grose (1st ed.) has 'an old fussock; a frowzy old woman'. Coll and dial.: late C.17–19; † except as dial. Connected with FOSSICK.

fussockin, fussikin. A fuss: Cockney (—1887).

fustian, n. and adj., bombast(ic), has never, I think, despite F. & H., been other than S.E. 2. Wine; but gen. with *white* = champagne, *red* = port, the latter occurring in Ainsworth, 1834. Low: late C.18–19.

fustilarian. A low fellow, scoundrel: coll: late C.16–17. Shakespeare. ?*fusty* (see also next entry) + suffix *-arian* as a variation on the later-recorded:

fustilug(s), (Grose) **fusty luggs.** 'A Fulsom, Beastly, Nasty Woman', B.E. Coll: late C.17–19. Junius. Common in C.18–19 dial. as a big coarse person, a dirty slattern, a very untidy child. cf. preceding entry. Lit., dirty ears or dirty thing.

fut, go, see PHUT, GO.

futures, gen. with **deal in.** To speculate for a rise or a fall, esp. in cotton: Stock Exchange coll: from ca 1880.

fuzz. Abbr. FUZZ-BALL: coll: C.17–early 18. In Holland's *Pliny*.

fuzz. To make drunk, esp. in p.ppl passive, which = tipsy. Wood, 1685, 'The university troop dined with the Earl of Abingdon and came back well fuzzed.' Coll: C.17–18. Whence perhaps FUDDLE. Its own etymology is uncertain: perhaps abbr. S.E. *fuzzle*, to intoxicate. 2. To shuffle cards meticulously: change the pack: mid-C.18–early 19. E. Moore in *The World*, 1753. Prob. ex sense 1.

fuzz-ball. A puff-ball (the fungus *lycoperdon bovista*): coll: late C.16–20. Of such long usage as to be, C.19–20, virtually S.E.

***fuzz-chats.** People camping on commons in the *furze*; esp. Gypsies, showmen, cheapjacks: c. (—1909).

fuzziness. A drunken condition: hence incoherence, bewilderment; a temporary dense stupidity: coll: from ca 1800; ob. 2. An intentional blurring: artists' and, later, photographers' s. (—1866).

fuzzy, n. Abbr. FUZZY-WUZZY: military: late C.19–20. Kipling.

fuzzy, adj. Tipsy: coll: from ca 1770. 2. Hence, incoherent, temporarily 'dense', bewildered: coll: late C.18–20; ob. 3. Rough, e.g. 'a fuzzy cloth'; big, vigorous, e.g. 'a fuzzy wench'; and esp. fluffy (1825): of these three nuances, the first is coll, the second s., the third orig. coll but soon S.E. 4. Prob. ex sense 1 is the nautical sense: rotten, unsound (of a ship): from ca 1860.

Fuzzy-Wuzzy. A Soudanese tribesman, esp. as a dervish soldier: commemorated by Kipling in 1890 (reprinted in *Barrack-Room Ballads*, 1892) as 'a pore benighted 'eathen but a first-class fighting man'. Military: late C.19–20, ob. Ex his ''ayrick 'ead of 'air'.

fy oût. To spy out: (low) Cockney (—1887).

***fye-buck** (see also BUCK, n., 6). A sixpence: in late C.18, c.; in C.19, low; †by 1885; already ob. in 1859.

fylche, see FILCH.

fyst(e), see FOIST.

G

G.H.! see GEORGE HORNE!

g.y., abbr. GALLEY-YARN.

gab. The mouth: low coll: from ca 1720, orig. Scottish. (GOB is earlier.) Hence, 2, talk; idle chatter: coll: from ca 1790. Poole, 1811, 'Then hold your gab, and hear what I've to tell'; *Punch*, 10 Sept. 1887, 'Gladstone's gab about "masses and classes" is all tommy rot.' Ex GOB, or rather ex:

gab, v. To talk fluently, very well; too much: from ca 1670: (in C.19–20, low) coll. Coles, 1676; Burns, 'gab like Boswell'; *Punch*, 10 Sept. 1887, 'Gals do like a chap as can gab.' Perhaps abbr. GABBLE and prob. distinct from S.E. *gab*, to tell lies, speak mockingly, though Coles's definition ('to prate or lie') hardly supports such distinction.

gab, blow the. To inform, PEACH (v., 3): low coll: late C.18–mid-19; ca 1810, *blow the* GAFF > more gen. Ainsworth in *Rookwood*.

gab, flash the, occ. **one's.** To show off in conversation: low (—1819); ob. Moore.

gab, gift of the. 'A facility of speech, nimble-tongued eloquence', Grose, 1st ed.: low coll: from ca 1780. Shelley in *Oedipus Tyrannus*. Earlier (?ca 1640), *gift of the gob*, as in B.E.: the form prevalent until ca 1780.

gab, stop your. Be quiet! A C.19–20 low coll variant of Scottish *steek* (shut up) *your gob*.

gab-string. (Variant GOB-STRING.) A bridle: C.18–early 19 low.

gabber. A prater, ceaseless talker: coll: from ca 1790.

gabbey, see GABY.

gabble. A gossiper: coll: C.19. 2. A voluble talker: coll: C.19–20. 3. Rapid, continuous talk: from ca 1600: C.17–18 S.E. > pejorative coll.

gabble, v. Talk rapidly, volubly, inconsequently: late C.16–20; S.E. till ca 1820, then a decidedly pejorative coll. The same applies to *gabbling*, vbl n.

gabble-gabble. A contemptuous variation on GABBLE, n. and v.

gabble-grinder. A gossiping or voluble talker: coll: C.19–20; ob.

gabbling, see GABBLE, V.

gabby. Water: Australian: mid C.19–20. Ex aboriginal.

gabey, see GABY.

gable, gable-end. The head: orig. builders' s.: from ca 1870. Ob.

gabster. An empty or an eloquent talker: coll: C.19–20; ob. cf. GAB, n. and v.

gaby, or **gabey;** occ. **gabb(e)y.** A fool, dolt; boor: coll (—1791). H. Kingsley, 'Don't stand laughing there like a great gaby.' ?ex *gape* (cf. GAPE-SEED) influenced by *baby*; it occurs in Lancashire dial. in 1740. *Gaby* is not to be connected with the Scottish adj. *gabby*, garrulous.

gad. An idle or trapesing slattern: low coll (—1859). Abbr. *gadabout*.

gad! Coll abbr. of coll *by gad* (C.17–20): C.19–20; ob. cf. EGAD; BEDAD; *gads me*; *gads my life*. Ex *God*.

gad, (up)on the. Impulsively: suddenly: coll: C.17–18. Shakespeare. Here, *gad* = a spike: cf. *on the spur of the moment*. 2. Hence, on the move; constantly making visits, gossip: coll: from ca 1815. Jane Austen. 3. On the spree: low: from ca 1830. 4. Hence, from ca 1850, (of women) on the town.

gad the hoof. To go without shoes; hence to walk, roam about: low: from ca 1845. cf. PAD THE HOOF; HOOF IT.

gad up and down. To go a-gossiping: late C.17–18 coll.

gad yang. A Chinese coasting junk: nautical: late C.19–20. Bowen. Prob. *gad* because they gad about, and *yang* ex the Yangtse-kiang or as a typical Chinese name.

gadabout. A gossip moving from neighbour to neighbour; a housewife too frequently talking to or visiting others; a woman constantly out shopping, visiting, and otherwise enjoying herself: cf. the C.18 proverb, 'gadding gossips shall dine on the pot-lid'. Coll: from ca 1800. Also adj.: coll, 1817.

gadget; occ. **gadjet.** A small mechanical contrivance, a tool, a part of a mechanism: nautical coll: from ca 1855, though not in print before 1886. Prob. ex Fr. *gâchette*, a piece of mechanism; cf. however, S.E. *gasket*.

gadsbud! i.e. *God's bud!* (the infant Saviour): coll: late C.17–18. Congreve.

gadso. The penis: late C.17–mid-19: low coll. Variant CATSO. Ex It. *cazzo*. 2. As an interjection: late C.17–mid-19. Dickens, '"Gadso!" said the undertaker.' An interesting example of the (politely ob.) phallicism of many oaths and other expletives: cf. and see BALLS; BUGGER; CUNTING; FUCK; PRICK; TWAT.

gadzooks. A mild expletive: either ex GADSO or a corruption of *God's hooks* (*?hocks, houghs,* W.): coll: late C.17–20; but since ca 1870, only as deliberate jocularity or in 'period pieces'. There are many other *gad(s)* variations, but these need not be listed.

Gaelically utter. The Scottish accent 'when trying to produce English': Society coll: ca 1882–1901. Ware. Suggested by TOO-TOO.

***gaff.** A fair: c. of ca 1750–1845. *The Discoveries of John Poulter*, 1753. Also c., at least orig., are the senses: 2. A ring worn by the card-sharping dealer of the pack: early C.19: ex *gaff*, a hook. And 3, a hoax, imposture; stuff and nonsense (—1877): cf. Fr. *gaffe*, a social blunder. 4. An outcry; cry, 'bellow': low: ca 1820–50, C. M. Westmacott. 5. Any public place of entertainment: ca 1810–50: low (or c.). Hence, 6, a low and cheap music-hall or theatre: low coll: from ca 1850. Mayhew. Also and often *penny-gaff*, 1856. Prob. ultimately ex sense 1.

***gaff,** v.i. To toss for liquor: c. >, ca 1820, low s.: ca 1810–80. cf. GAFFING. Also, 2, to gamble: same period. 3. To play in a GAFF (n., 6): from ca 1860; ob.

gaff, blow the. To inform; divulge a secret: low (perhaps orig. c.): from ca 1810. (Earlier *blow the gab*, see GAB. See also BLOW.) Marryat.

gaff-topsail hat. A silk TOPPER (2): nautical: late C.19–20.

gaffer. A husband: C.18 coll or dial. 2. An old man, esp. if a rustic (cf. GAMMER), esp. as a term of address: coll and dial.: late C.16–20. Gay, Tennyson. Both these senses and the next six are ex *granfer* = grandfather. 3. Simply as term of address = 'my good fellow': coll: late C.16–20; slightly ob. 4. A master or employer: from ca 1650. Dyche, 1748, 'A familiar word mostly used in the country for master.' 5. Hence, a foreman: navvies': from ca 1840. 6. 'Mine host' at an inn: low or c. (—1887). 7. Among athletes, a trainer (—1888); ob. 8. The steward of a racecourse: the turf: late C.19–20. 9. A player at toss-penny: ca 1828–80. Ex GAFF, v., 1 or 2. 10. A market-master or fair-ground superintendent: grafters: from ca 1880. cf. GAFF, n., 1.

gaffer, v. To have sexual intercourse: C.19. ?ex the v. implied in CHAUVERING (sexual intercourse): app. a corruption thereof.

gaffing. A way of tossing three coins in a hat to say who is to pay for drinks; only he who calls correctly for all three is exempt from payment: low (?orig. c.): ca 1828–80. 2. Hence, toss-penny; tossing of counters: low coll (—1859).

gag. Something placed in the mouth to silence or prevent the subject's cries: mid-C. 16–20. Perhaps always S.E., but ca 1660–1800 it may have been c., then low; witness B.E. (at *to gag*) and Grose. 2. Boiled fat beef; more precisely, the fatty part of boiled beef: Christ's Hospital (—1813). Lamb. ?Etymology. cf. GAG-EATER. 3. A joke; invention; HOAX; imposition; HUMBUG; false rumour: from ca 1805: low s. >, ca 1880, coll: ob., *Daily News*, 16 May 1885. Ex sense 1. 4. Whence, interpolated words, esp. jokes or c.p. comments: theatrical (—1847). *Pall Mall Gazette*, 5 March 1890, 'Mr Augustus Harris pointed out that . . . actors and singers were continually introducing gag into their business.' In this quotation and often elsewhere, *gag* is collective, i.e. GAGGING, 3. cf. WHEEZE. Ex preceding sense, itself perhaps ex sense 1. 5. A criticism in Latin; an analysis of some historical work: Winchester College: from ca 1850. Mansfield. Ex *gathering*, an alternative name for this exercise. 6. A lie: c.: ca 1860–1920. ?ex theatrical *gag* (4). 7. (cf. 3.) A handbill: sporting: ca 1810–60. *Boxiana*, III, 1821.

gag, v. 'To put Iron-pinns into the Mouths of the Robbed, to hinder them Crying out', B.E.; in late C.17–early 18, app. c.; in C.19–20, S.E. Ex the victim's gurgle. 2. Hence, to hoax, v.t. and i.: low s. or coll (?orig. c.): from ca 1777; †by 1880. Parker, Bee. 3. To scold, nag at: *Sessions*, Sept. 1837. 4. To puff: low (—1876). Hindley in his *Cheap Jack*. 5. Make up words; speak 'gags' (see n., 4), v.i.: theatrical, perhaps orig. low Cockney (see *London Labour*, III, 149): ?first in 1852 in Dickens's *Bleak House*, 'The same vocalist gags in the regular business like a man inspired.' 6. As v.t., to fill up or enliven with a gag: 1861. 7. To lay information (v.t. with *on*): c. (—1891).

***gag, on the high,** adj. and adv. Telling

secrets; 'on the whisper': c.: ca 1820–80. Kent, Duncombe. cf. GAG, v., 7.

***gag, on the low.** In extreme destitution; in lowest beggary; with appalling bad luck; in utter despair: c.: ca 1820–80. cf. preceding entry.

gag, strike the. To desist from joking or chaffing: low (? c.): ca 1830–70. Ainsworth in *Jack Sheppard.* See GAG, n., 3.

gag-eater. A Christ's Hospital term of reproach: from ca 1800; ex GAG, n., 2, perhaps by way of GAG, v., 1.

gag-master, see GAGGER, 3.

gag-piece. (Theatrical) a play in which 'gags' (GAG, n., 4) are, or can effectively be, freely used (—1864).

gaga; incorrectly *ga-ga.* Showing senile decay; stupid, fatuous: theatrical s.: from ca 1875. Ex Fr. s. *gâteux*, an old man feeble-minded and no longer able to control his body, itself ex Standard Fr. *gâter*, to impair, damage, spoil.

gagarino, n. A melodrama performed by professional actors, usually of the lower ranks, in which the general outline of the plot is so familiar that it is not necessary to write a concrete play at all, everything being 'gagged' impromptu. Before C.20. Ex GAG, n., 4 + comic suffix *-arino.*

***gage.** A quart pot: c.: mid-C.15–19. Promptorium Parvulorum, Harman, B.E., Haggart. In C.18, occ. a pint (pot). In C.19 c., occ. a drink. Ex the measure. 2. A pipe (for smoking): mid-C.17–early 19 c. 3. A chamber-pot: C.18 coll. Variant spelling, *gauge.* 4. A small quantity of anything: low coll (—1864).

***gager.** An early form of GORGER. C. Hitchin, *The Regulator*, 1718.

***gagger.** In late C.18–mid-19 c., one of those 'cheats who by sham pretences, and wonderful stories of their sufferings, impose on the credulity of well-meaning people', Grose, 2nd ed. Ex GAG, v., 2. cf. RUM GAGGER. Called *high* and *low gaggers*: also cf. GAG, ON THE HIGH or LOW. 2. Hence, a tramp, esp. one who begs: tramps' c.: mid-C.19–20. 3. An actor or music-hall 'artist'; from late 1840s, esp. one that often employs 'gags' (GAG, n., 4): theatrical (—1823). *Fortnightly Review*, April 1887, 'Robson . . . was an inveterate gagger.' Variants: *gaggist* (rarely), *gag-master* (occ.), and *gagster* (fairly often). 4. The under-lip: Perthshire c.: C.19–20; ob. Also *gegger.* Prob. ex †S.E. *gag*, v.i., to project.

gaggery. A hoaxing kind of wit: ca 1819–50: coll. cf. GAG, v., 1. 2. The practice of employing 'gags' (n., 4): theatrical: from ca 1860. cf.:

***gagging.** The persuading a stranger that he is an old acquaintance and then 'borrowing' money from him: ca 1825–80: c. 2. Loitering about for fares: cabmen's: ca 1850–1910. Mayhew. 3. The frequent employment of 'gags' (n., 4): theatrical (—1883). Also as ppl adj.

gaggist, see GAGGER, 3.

***gaggler's coach.** A hurdle: c. of ca 1820–60. Duncombe. Ex *gaggler*, a goose. Or is this Kent's mistake, copied by Duncombe, for GAOLER'S COACH, also = a hurdle?

gagster, see GAGGER, 3.

Gaiety girl. (Gen. pl.) One of the 'dashing singing and dancing comedians in variety pieces – from their first gaining attention at the Gaiety Theatre': theatrical coll: from ca 1890; ob. Ware. cf.:

Gaiety step. 'A quick, high dancing pas, made popular at the Gaiety Theatre': theatrical coll: ca 1888–92. Ware.

gail. A horse: either low or c.: early C.19. ?connected with Romany *grei.*

gainst, 'gainst. Except in poetry, a late C.16–20 coll.

gal. A girl: originally (ca 1820) Cockney s.; later an upper-class coll. Perhaps ex New England pronunciation (—1796). 2. A servant-girl: lower-class coll: from ca 1850. 3. A sweetheart: low coll: from ca 1860. cf. CHAP; FELLOW. 4. A harlot: low coll (—1851); ob. Mayhew, 'Upon the most trivial offence . . . the gals are sure to be beaten . . . by their "chaps".'

gal-sneaker. 'A man devoted to seduction'; London lower classes': ca 1870–1915. Ware.

galaney, see GALENY.

galanty (occ. gallanty or gal(l)antee) show. A shadow pantomime: occ. a magic-lantern show, but of silhouettes only: from ca 1820. Ob. by 1900. This term, S.E. at origin and in C.20, seems to have been coll ca 1850–90. ?ex It. *galanti.*

galany, see GALENY.

galavant, see GALLIVANT.

***galbe.** 'Profile of a violent character, and even applied to any eccentricity of shape above the knees': c. (—1909). Ware derives from Fr. *Galbe*, the Emperor Galba of 'pronounced profile and terrific nose': but is it not a sense-perversion of Standard Fr. *galbe* (from It. *garbo*), bodily contour?

gale of wind dose. Very little whisky in

much water: nautical: late C.19–20. Opp. *second mate's nip*.

galee. Bad language: Anglo-Indian: from ca 1860. Ex Hindustani *gali*.

galen, Galen. An apothecary: coll: ca 1870–1910. By way of *Galen*, jocularly a physician. Ex the great physician of the 2nd century A.D.

galeny, galeeny, galan(e)y. A guinea-fowl: coll or dial.: late C.18–20. Ex L. *gallina*. *Temple Bar*, March 1887. 2. In late C.18–early 19, a fowl of any kind: c.

galimaufr(e)y, gallimaufr(e)y. As a medley, a jumble, and as 'a hodgepodge made up of the remnants and scraps of the larder' (Grose), it is S.E. But as a mistress, it is a late C.16–17 coll. Shakespeare in *Merry Wives*. 2. In 'love'-making s., the female pudend: C.19. Ex Fr.

galivant, see GALLIVANT.

gall. Effrontery; impudence: early C.19–20 low; more gen. in U.S., where app. it arose, than in England; cf. however, GALL IS NOT YET BROKEN, HIS.

gall, on the. On the raw, i.e. on a tender spot (lit. or fig.): coll, ? > S.E.: C.14–17. Chaucer, Skelton, Sanderson.

***gall is not yet broken, his.** A mid-C.18–early 19 c., esp. prison, saying of a man who appears dejected. Ironical on †*gall(s)*, courage.

gallantee (or gallanty) show, see GALANTY SHOW.

gallavant, see GALLIVANT.

***gallersgood.** Worthy of the gallows: c.: C.18–early 19. i.e. *gallows-good.*

gallery. A commoner bedroom: Winchester College: C.19. Ex a tradition of galleries in Commoners. cf. GALLERY-NYMPH. 2. A showing of oneself in a ridiculous light: Shrewsbury School: late C.19–20. Desmond Coke, *The Bending of a Twig*, 1906. cf. *play to the* GALLERY.

gallery, play the. To be, make an audience; to applaud: coll (—1870); ob. Ex the theatre. The *Echo*, 23 July 1870, 'We were constantly called in to play the gallery to his witty remarks.' cf.:

gallery, play to the. Orig. theatrical, then sporting, then gen.: to act so as to capture popular applause: from ca 1870: coll. Hence *gallery-hit*, *-play*, *-shot*, *-stroke*, etc., one designed to please the uncritical and those who like showy display.

gallery-nymph. A housemaid: Winchester College: C.19. Ex GALLERY, 1.

galley down-haul. An imaginary fitting, for the further confusion of a youngster for the first time at sea: nautical coll: mid-C.19–20.

galley down your back!, put a. Such-and-such a superior wishes to see you!: printers': from ca 1870; ob. The galley – an oblong tray – would serve as a screen.

galley-growler or **-stoker.** An idler; malingerer: naval: from ca 1850. The galley is, of course, the cook-house: cf. GALLEY-YARN.

galley-news; g.-packet, see GALLEY-YARN.

galley-slang. 'A landsman's attempt at nautical jargon': nautical coll: late C.19–20. Bowen.

galley-slave. A compositor: printers': late C.17–19. Moxon. Ex the oblong tray whereon the type is made up for page or column.

galley-stoker, see GALLEY-GROWLER.

galley-yarn. A lying or hoaxing story; a swindle: nautical (—1874). Henley & Stevenson in *Admiral Guinea*. Occ. abbr. to *g.y.* In this sense, ob. by 1910. 2. A rumour, esp. if baseless: early C.19–20 nautical. As a lie, an empty rumour, *galley-packet* is a frequent synonym, dating from ca 1790: prob. the earliest form. *Galley-news* is of ca 1880–1900. cf. *cookhouse yarn*; SHAVE, n., 3.

galleynipper, see GALLINIPPER.

gallied. 'Hurried, vexed, over-fatigued, perhaps like a galley-slave', Grose: C.18–early 19 coll. More prob. ex dial. *gally*, to frighten.

galligaskins, S.E. in C.16–17, is in C.18–20 (ob.) a gen. jocular coll for any loose breeches.

gallimaufr(e)y, see GALIMAUFREY.

gal(l)inipper, occ. **gall(e)ynipper.** A large mosquito: West Indians' (—1847). Ex U.S. usage (1801). Perhaps one that has a GALLOWS nip or bite.

gallipot. An apothecary: late C.18–20 (ob.) coll. Lit., a pot conveyed in a galley (vessel). Michael Scott; Thackeray in his *Book of Snobs*. cf. BOLUS.

gallipot baronet. An ennobled physician: Society coll: ca 1850–1910. See GALLIPOT.

gallivant, etc. 'A nest of whores', Bee: London low: ca 1820–40. ?a perversion of GALENY, 2.

gal(l)ivant, occ. **gal(l)avant.** To gad about with or after, 'do the agreeable' to, one of the other sex: coll: 1823. Bee; Dickens. Perhaps ex the n.; perhaps a perversion of *gallant*. 2. Hence, to gad about, TRAPES; occ. fuss or bustle about: coll: from ca

1825. Miss Braddon, 'His only daughter gallivanting at a theaytre'. A humorous variation of (*to*) *gallant*, as in Galt's 'The witches . . . gallanting over field and flood'. The vbl n. is common.

gallon distemper. Delirium tremens; the less serious after-effects of drinking: C.19–20 (ob.) coll or s. cf. BARREL-FEVER; HOT COPPERS.

galloot, see GALOOT.

gallop one's maggot. (Of males) masturbate: low: Cockneys': mid-C.19–20.

galloper. A blood horse; a hunter: ca 1810–60: low or c. 2. An aide-de-camp; an orderly officer: military: from ca 1870.

gallore, see GALORE.

gallow-grass. Hemp: mid-C.16–17: s. > coll. i.e. 'halters in the rough', F. & H. cf. NECK-WEED.

gallows. (As = one who deserves hanging: S.E.). 2. Gen. in pl. A pair of braces: low coll: 1730; then U.S. (1806); re-anglicized ca 1830; in C.19–20, mostly dial. Mayhew.

gallows, adj. Enormous; FINE; an intensive, cf. BLOODY: late C.18–20, ob. except in dial. Parker, 1789, 'They pattered flash with gallows fun.' Whence:

gallows, adv. Very; extremely: from late C.18. On 24 Aug. 1805, *The Port Folio* quotes an anon. English song, *Dustman Bill*:

'Why, jealous girls, 'tis all my eye,
Besides 'tis gallows silly.'

gallows, a child's best guide to the, see HISTORY OF THE FOUR KINGS.

gallows-apples of, make. To hang: low (?c.): ca 1825–80. Lytton.

gallows-bird. A corpse on, or from, the gallows: low coll (—1861); ob. Ex the S.E. sense, one who deserves to be hanged.

gallus. A frequent pronunciation and occ. spelling of GALLOWS, adv. cf. *allus* for 'always'.

gally-pot, see GALLIPOT.

gally-swab. A cook's steward: *Conway* cadets': from ca 1880.

***gallyslopes.** Breeches: early C.19 c. ?punning GALLIGASKINS.

galoot, occ. **galloot,** rarely **ge(e)loot.** A man, chap, fellow; gen. a pejorative, implying stupidity or boorishness or moral toughness: orig. (1866), U.S., anglicized ca 1880. Developed from the, 2, nautical s. sense (—1818; †by 1900), a young or inexperienced marine. Marryat in *Jacob Faithful*, 'Four greater galloots were never picked up.' Ex: 3. A soldier: low or c. (—1812); †by 1890. ?ex Dutch *gelubt*, a eunuch.

galoot, on the gay. On the spree: low, mostly Cockney (—1892). 'Ballads' Milliken.

galoptious, galuptious; goloptious; or any with **-shus.** Delicious; delightful; splendid; a gen. superlative: low: from ca 1855; ob. *Judy*, 21 Sept. 1887, 'The galopshus sum of 20,000,000 dollars'. A fanciful adj. of the CATAWAMPOUS, SCRUMPTIOUS type, perhaps via Norwich dial.

galore; occ. **†gallore, gol(l)ore.** In abundance: from ca 1670: coll till ca 1890, then S.E. – though far from literary. In C.19, also *in galore*. Prob. ex Irish *go leor*, in sufficiency. Ned Ward, Grose, Reade.

***gam.** PLUCK; *game*ness: c. (—1888). 2. With variant *gamb*, a leg, esp. if bow or otherwise ill-shapen; nearly always in pl: from ca 1780: c. In low U.S. s., only of a girl's legs. It is also, as *gamb*, the heraldic term for a leg. Ex Northern Fr. *gambe* or else ex It. *gamba*, via Lingua Franca. 3. A hammock: training-ship *Britannia*: late C.19.

gam, v. To have a yarn, esp. with one's opposite number on another ship: nautical: late C.19–20. Ex GAMMON, v., 1.

***gam, flutter a.** To dance: C.19 c. – But *lift a gam* = to break wind: c.: mid-C.19–20. Henley.

Gam-better. To humbug, deceive: political: ca 1879–82. Ex Gambetta (1832–82), that Fr. statesman of Italo-Hebraic origin whose popularity began to wane in 1879.

***gam-case.** A stocking: c.: late C.18–mid-19. G. Parker, 1781. Ex GAM, 2.

***gam it.** To walk; esp. to 'leg it', run away: C.19 c.

gamaliel. A pedant: a cultured coll: C.19–20. Ex the name of several Rabbis famous in the first two or three centuries A.D., by confusion with Gallio (Acts xviii, 12–17).

gamaroosh, -ruche, n. and, hence, v. (Of women.) (To practise) penilingism: late C.19–20 low. Ex Fr. (?ex Arabic).

***gamb(e),** see GAM, 2.

gamble. Anything, esp. course or procedure, involving risk: coll: from ca 1820. 2. An act of gambling: coll: from late 1870s. 3. Whence *on the gamble*, engaged on a course or spell of gambling: coll: from ca 1880.

gamble on that!, you can or may. Certainly! Assuredly! Coll: from ca 1870 in England; ex U.S. (1866, Artemus Ward).

gambler. A mid-C.18–early 19 class of sharper: low or c. Whence mod. S.E.

gamblous. Of, like to, gambling: Society coll: coined by Joseph Chamberlain on 29 April 1885, in a speech made at a dinner given by the Eighty Club; ob. Ex *gambling* + *hazardous*.

gambol. A railway ticket: railwaymen's: ca 1880–1914.

***game.** (Collective for) harlots, esp. at a brothel: c.: late C.17–early 19. 2. A simpleton, a dupe, a PIGEON (5); gen., however, a collective n.: c.: late C.17–early 19. 3. The proceeds of a robbery: c. of ca 1660–90. 4. A LARK or source of amusement: coll: Dickens, 1838. 5. Preceded by *the*, *game* refers to some occupation and, except among thieves (where it is c.), is to be demarcated as coll: among thieves it means thieving (1812, Vaux); among sailors, slave-trading (—1860); among C.17–early 18 lovers of sport, cock-fighting; in amorous venery, coïtion (C.17–20); among harlots, prostitution (C.17–20). 6. As plan, trick or DODGE (esp. in pl), the term – despite F. & H. – is gen. considered to be S.E.: nevertheless, I consider that *what is your* (*his*, etc.) *game* or *little game*, mid-C.19–20, is definitely coll. 7. Courage: pugilistic: ca 1810–50.

***game,** v. To jeer at; pretend to expose; make a game of: c.: late C.17–18.

***game,** adj. (Of men) knowing, wide-awake; (of women) prone to venery, engaged in harlotry: c.: C.18–20. cf. GAME PULLET.

***game, on the.** Thieving: c. (—1839); slightly ob. cf. GAME COVE. 2. Engaged in prostitution: harlots' c.: mid-C.19–20. See GAME, n., 5.

game, stashed up the, see STASH UP.

game, the national indoor. Sexual intercourse: late C.19–20; coll.

***game cove.** An associate of thieves: C.19 c. Ex GAME, n., 5.

game ever played, the first. Sexual congress: C.19–20, coll rather than euphemistic.

***game publican.** A publican dealing in stolen goods or winking at his customers' offences: C.19: c. >, ca 1830, low.

game pullet. 'A young whore, or forward girl in the way of becoming one', Grose, 1st ed.: late C.18–19 low (?orig. c.). cf. GAME WOMAN.

game ship. A ship whose captain and officers are susceptible to bribes for overlooking thefts from the cargo: nautical: ca 1830–90.

***game woman.** A harlot: C.18–19: c. >, ca 1830, low. cf. Etherege's 'the game mistress of the town'. See GAME, n., 5.

gamester. A harlot: C.17 coll. 2. In the sense of wencher, C.17, the term lies on the borderline of coll and S.E.

gammer, as rustic title, C.16–20 (ob.), is coll > S.E.; as term of address, = 'my good woman', it is coll. Ex *grandmother*. cf. GAFFER.

gammocks. Pranks; wild play: s. (—1823) and (in late C.19–20, nothing but) dial. Ex *game*.

gammon. Nonsense, humbug; a ridiculous story; deceitful talk; deceit: low, prob. orig. c. (—1805). Ex the late C.18–19 c. sense, talk, chatter, gen. GAMMON AND PATTER. (In C.18–early 19, often spelt *gamon*.) Hood, 'Behold yon servitor of God and Mammon ... Blends Gospel texts with trading gammon.' Perhaps ex C.17 sense, a beggar or seller of gammons of bacon. (cf. Fr. *boniment*(*s*).) 3. Wholly c.: one who engages the attention of a man to be robbed by a confederate: C.19. cf. COVER.

gammon, v.i. To talk, esp. plausibly (—1789). 2. (v.i. and t.) To pretend: from ca 1810. 3. Humbug or hoax; tell deceitful or extravagant stories to; deceive merrily or with lies or fibs; flatter shamelessly: from ca 1810. All senses orig. low; from ca 1850, low coll. Hume Nisbet, 1890, 'Oh, don't try to gammon me, you cunning young school-miss.' cf. BAM; COD, V.; FLAM; KID (n., 5, v., 2); *pull one's* LEG; SELL; SOFT-SOAP; TAKE IN. 4. v.i., act as COVER to a thief: C.19 (?C.18) c. Ex n., 3. 5. To cheat (v.i.) at gaming: late C.17–mid-18: c. Prob. the origin of senses 1–3 and of n., 1. Its own etymology is obscure: but cf. GAME, V.

gammon! Interjection = nonsense! bosh!: from ca 1825; low s. >, by 1860, low coll. Michael Scott, 1836, 'Gammon, tell that to the marines.' Ex n., 1, or ex *that's all gammon* (Vaux, 1812).

***gammon, give** or **keep in.** To engage a person's attention – the former connotes by mere propinquity, the latter by conversation – while another robs him: C.18–19 c. Capt. Alex. Smith, 1720; Haggart, 1821. cf. GAMMON, n., 3.

***gam(m)on and patter.** The language of the underworld, esp. of thieves: late C.18–early 19 c. G. Parker, 1781. 2. The commonplace or familiar (hence almost jargonistic) talk of any trade or profession: late C.18–20; ob. c. 3. A meeting; a PALAVER (not sense 1): from ca 1850: c. See GAMMON, n., and PATTER, n.

gammon and spinach. Nonsense; humbug; deceit: low coll: from ca 1845; ob. Dickens, 1849, 'What a world of gammon and spinnage it is.' An elaboration of GAMMON, n., 1, after previous entry.

***gammon lushy; gammon queer.** To feign tipsiness, illness: c.: C.19. See LUSHY, adj., 1.

gammon the draper. 'When a man is without a shirt, and is buttoned up close to his neck, to make an appearance of cleanliness, it is termed "gammoning the draper",' Pierce Egan, *Life in London*, 1821: ca 1810–50.

***gammon the twelve.** To deceive the jury: c. (—1812); ob. Vaux, who shows that *in fine twig*, cleverly or thoroughly, was often added. See GAMMON, v., 3.

gammoner. One who talks nonsense or humbug; a specious or ulterior deceiver: from ca 1830; slightly ob. Ex GAMMON, v., 1. 2. (cf. GAMMON, n., 1.) One who covers the action of his thieving confederate: C.19 c. cf. COVER.

gammoning. vbl n. and ppl adj. corresponding to GAMMON, v., in all senses, though rarely in the last – *gammoning* which was †by 1900, while the other *gammonings* are extant though slightly ob.

***gammoning academy.** A reformatory: c.: late C.19–20.

***gammy.** The language of the underworld: C.19: c. ?ex GAMMON AND PATTER. 2. A lame person (see the adj., 4): late C.19–20. 3. A fool: Australian: ca 1890–1910. Hume Nisbet in *The Bushranger's Sweetheart*, 1892.

***gammy,** adj. False, spurious; forged: c. (—1839). As in *gammy* STUFF, spurious, i.e. worthless, medicine; *gammy* MONAKER (4), a forged signature; *gammy* LOUR (*low(r)*), counterfeit money. Perhaps ex the n., 1. 2. Also c., but tramps': mean; hard (of householders): mid-C.18–20. Bampfylde Moore-Carew. Opp. BONE, adj. Hence *gammy* VILE or *vial*, a town in which unlicensed hawking is enthusiastically discouraged by the police. 3. Old; ugly: theatrical: from ca 1885; ob. ?ex next sense. 4. Halt and maimed: low coll: from ca 1870. *Gammy leg*, a lame leg; *gammy arm*, an arm injured permanently or temporarily; *gammy-eyed*, blind, or sore-eyed. Either a corruption of *game* = lame or ex GAM, n., 2. 5. Hence, disabled through injury or pain: (low) coll: from ca 1890. 6. Lazy; idle; navvies': ca 1860–1900. (D. W. Barrett, 1880.)

gamon, see GAMMON, n. and v.

gamp or Gamp. A monthly or sick nurse, esp. if disreputable; a midwife: coll (—1864); ob. Hence, 2, a fussy, gossiping busybody: coll (—1868). Brewer, quoting the *Daily Telegraph*, 'Mr Gathorne Hardy is to look after the Gamps and Harrises of the Strand.' Ex Mrs Sarah Gamp in Dickens's *Martin Chuzzlewit*, 1843: as also in next two entries. 3. An umbrella, esp. a large one loosely tied: coll: 1864. G. R. Sims.

gamp, adj.; **gampish.** Bulging, gen. of umbrellas: coll (1881, 1864); ob.

Gamp, Mrs. A variant of GAMP, n., 3: coll. (—1887).

gampy. A low coll variant (—1887) of GAMP, n., 3; ob.

gamut, in the. A picture, a detail, etc., in tone with its accompaniments or environment: artists': from ca 1870.

***gan.** The mouth; occ. the throat: c.: mid-C.16–early 19. ?ex Scottish *gane*. cf. GANS.

gander. A married man: C.17–20 coll; ob. cf. GANDER-MONTH.

Gander. A fop: London (mostly in Society): ca 1815–40. Ware, 'It is a perversion of Gandin, the Parisian description of fop.'

gander, v. Ramble; waddle (like a goose): coll (—1859). H. Kingsley.

gander, what's sauce for the goose is sauce for the. Let us be consistent! Coll (in C.20, ?S.E.): from ca 1660. Head, Swift, Byron. Apperson quotes Varro's *idem Accio quod Titio jus esto*. cf. the proverbs 'As is the goose so is the gander,' C.18, and 'Goose, gander, and gosling are three sounds, but one thing,' C.17.

gander-faced. Silly-faced: proletarian (mostly Cockney) coll (—1887); slightly ob.

gander-month or **-moon.** The month after childbirth, when in C.17–early 19 it was held excusable for the husband to err. Coll; †except in dial. Dekker, 1636. cf. STAG-MONTH.

gander-mooner. A husband during the GANDER-MONTH: C.17–19. Middleton, 1617.

gander-party. A party of men: opp. HEN-PARTY and cf. STAG-PARTY. Occ.

gander-gang. Coll: C.19–20, ob. Orig. (—1866), U.S.; anglicized ca 1880.

gander's wool. Feathers: coll of the COW-JUICE type: C.17–20; ob. Breton.

gang. A troop; a company; an underworld band of men: C.17–20. Only from ca 1850 has it ceased to be low coll. B.E., e.g., defines: 'An ill Knot or Crew of Thieves, Pickpockets or Miscreants'.

ganger. An overseer or foreman of a working gang: coll: from ca 1849. It > S.E. ca 1880. Mayhew; *Cornhill Magazine*, June 1884. 2. A member of the press gang: nautical coll: C.19.

gangway! Make way!: *Conway* cadets': from ca 1860: c.p. >, by 1900, j.

gannet. A greedy seaman: nautical: mid-C.19–20. Ex the bird.

***gans.** The lips: c.: late C.17–18. cf. GAN, and the differentiation of MUN; MUNS. The E.D.D. notes the Scandinavian dial. *gan*, a fish-gill.

ganymede. (As a sodomist, late C.16–19 literary.) A pot-boy; *Hebe's* 'opposite number': C.17–20 (ob.) jocular and cultured coll. Ex *Ganymede*, cup-bearer to Zeus.

gaol-bird. One who has been often or long in gaol: from ca 1680. Until ca 1860, coll. Smollett, 1762, 'He is become a blackguard gaol-bird.'

gaoler's coach. A hurdle: 'traitors being usually conveyed from the gaol, to the place of execution, on a hurdle or sledge', Grose, 3rd ed.: c. > low: late C.17–early 19. Possibly the orig. of GAGGLER'S COACH.

gap. The female pudend: S.E. only if strictly medical and contextual: C.18–20, low. Robertson of Struan, a bawdy poet who d. in 1746. 2. Mouth, esp. in *stop yer* (*your*) *gap!*, be quiet: low: late C.19–20. *Slang*, p. 243.

gap, blow the. To inform, PEACH (3): a ca 1820–90 variant of *blow the* GAFF.

gap-stopper. A whoremonger: mid-C.18–19 low. 2. The virile member: C.19–20 low. cf.:

gape. The female pudend; gen. as *g. over the garter*: C.19–20 low; ob. cf. GAPER.

gape-seed, gapeseed. A cause of astonishment; a marvellous event, extraordinary or unusual sight, etc.: coll: late C.16–20, ob. Esp. with *seek* or *buy*, a vbl phrase is frequent. (Florio, 1598, has the rare *gaping seed.*) Nashe; B.E.; Grose, 1st ed., 'I am come abroad for a little gapeseed'; C.19–20 dial., *be fond of* or *gather* or *sow g.*, or *have a little g.* A folk-pun on *gape*. 2. One who stares with open mouth: from ca 1880: coll; ob.

gape-seed, be looking for. To be lazy and inattentive to one's work: C.19 coll, C.20 dial. (ob.).

gaper, or g. over the garter. The *pudendum muliebre*: C.19–20 low; ob.

gapes, the. A fit of yawning; utter boredom: coll: from ca 1815. Jane Austen.

gapped, ppl adj. Worsted; defeated: coll: ca 1750–1820. Ex S.E. sense, with the edges notched or cut about.

gaps with one bush, stop two. To accomplish two purposes at one time: C.16–17; coll till C.17, then S.E. cf. *kill two birds with one stone*.

gar in oaths (*beggar!*, *by gar!*, *gar!*) is a corruption of *God* (cf. GAD!): late C.16–20. Rather Anglo-French than purely English: cf., however, the U.S. pronunciation of *God* as *Gard*.

Garamity, see GORAMITY.

garbage. 'The goodes gotten' in the 'lifting law' (criminal DODGE): c.: late C.16–early 17. Greene, *Second Cony-Catching*, 1592.

garden. The female pudend: C.16–20. When a euphemism, S.E.; when used in jocular or amatory reference, *without* euphemistic intentions, it is cultured coll. (Occ., *garden of Eden*, indubitably a euphemism.) cf. ROSE.

***garden, put** (one) **in the.** To defraud (a confederate), esp. of (part of) his monetary share: c.: from ca 1810; ob. Vaux (variants, . . . *bucket*, HOLE; WELL). cf. REGULARS.

garden-gate. A magistrate: rhyming s. (—1859). 2. The *pudendi labia minora muliebris*: low coll – very rare as a euphemism: C.19–20. cf. GARDEN-HEDGE.

Garden goddess. A harlot, not necessarily superior: C.19. cf. C.18 COVENT GARDEN ABBESS. The Covent Garden district was harlot-ridden in C.17–early 19. cf.:

Garden-gout. Syphilis; gonorrhoea: C.19 low. cf. C.18 COVENT GARDEN AGUE.

garden-hedge. The female pubic hair: C.19–20 low (ob.); rarely a euphemism.

Garden- or **garden-house.** A brothel: the *garden-* form is C.17 coll > literary; the *Garden-*, C.18–early 19 low coll. See GARDEN; GARDEN GODDESS, and the various COVENT GARDEN entries.

garden-Latin. Sham or extremely bad Latin: coll: C.19–20. cf. *kitchen* and APOTHECARIES' LATIN; BOG- and DOG-LATIN.

garden-rake. A tooth-comb: a low and jocular coll: from ca 1870.

garden steerage. Additional rest 'allowed to the blue jacket the morning after he has been busy on a night job': naval: late C.19–20. Bowen.

garden-violet, see VIOLET.

Garden whore. A harlot; a low harlot (cf. GARDEN GODDESS): C.19 low.

gardener. The male member: cf. and ex GARDEN: C.19–20; ob. 2. An awkward coachman: coll (—1859). Ex the gardener's occ. relieving the coachman. Cabbies, wishing to annoy real coachmen, used to shout, 'Get on, gardener' (H., 1864). cf. TEA-KETTLE GROOM.

gardening. Patting the pitch, picking up loose bits of turf: cricketers' jocular coll (—1897).

gards. 'Post guardship': nautical: C.19.

gardy-loo. Take care! Look out! A mid-C.18–early 19 Scottish coll. Ex Fr. *gardez* [*-vous de*] *l'eau* or (via the supposed Fr. *gare de l'eau*) ex Fr. *gare l'eau*, i.e. the slops thrown into the street. 2. Hence, the act of so emptying the slops: same period and status.

gargle. A drink; drink: orig. – ca 1859 – medical for physic; gen. by 1889, and usually of strong drink. cf. LOTION.

gargle, v.i. To drink; drink a lot, 'celebrate': orig. – ?ca 1880 – medical; gen. by 1889. *Morning Advertiser*, 2 March 1891, 'It's my birthday; let's gargle.'

gargle-factory. A public-house: from ca 1870. Ex GARGLE, n.

gargler. Throat: Cockneys': from ca 1890. Clarence Rook, *The Hooligan Nights*, 1899, 'There was the little bleeder gettin' black in the face froo its night-dress bein' tied too tight round its gargler.'

garlic, smell. To smell something FISHY, to have suspicions: Cockney (—1887); slightly ob.

garn! 'Get away with you!' Low coll: from ca 1875. Ex GO ON! Runciman, *The Chequers*, 1888; *Ally Sloper*, 19 March 1892.

Garnet, Sir, see SIR GARNET.

garnish, in late C.17–19 occ. *garnish money*. A fee exacted by gaolers and old HANDS from a newcomer to prison: late C.16–19: s. until ca 1790; then coll >, by 1830, S.E. Greene, B.E. (Abolished by George IV.) 2. Among workmen, mid-C.18–19, an 'entrance fee' – wholly informal: s. > coll > S.E. Goldsmith. Occ. *maiden-garnish*. Not quite † in Northern – mainly Yorkshire – dial. 3. In C.18–19 c., fetters, handcuffs. But, as the O.E.D. points out, this may well be a ghost-word due to a misapprehension by Johnson, copied by F. & H. 4. A bribe or tip: s.: Ned Ward, 1700, cf. sense 1.

***garnish,** v. To fit with fetters; handcuff: c. (—1755); †by 1900. Ex the n., 1. But see the n., sense 3.

garotte, see GARROTTE.

garret. The head: from ca 1785. Grose (2nd ed.), who also gives UPPER STOREY. cf. also COCK-LOFT. 2. Hence the mouth: low: C.19. 3. The FOB-pocket: c.: ca 1810–70. 4. 'A consultation of the members of a shop in relation to some trade or social difficulty': hatters': C.19–20; ob. Ware. cf. a printers' *chapel*.

garret, queer or **wrong in one's.** Crazy: s. when not dial. (—1869). Ex GARRET, 1.

garret-election. A ludicrous, low popular ceremony practised at Wandsworth, London, when a new parliament opens, the 'voting'-qualification being open-air coïtion in or near Garret, a mean hamlet: C.18–early 19. Coll: or perhaps rather a legitimate folk-lore term. See Grose, 1785.

garret empty or **unfurnished, have one's** (occ. **the**). To have no brains; be a fool, somewhat crazy: from ca 1790. cf. Kentish (*be*) *not rightly garreted*.

garret-master. A cabinet-maker who, working on his own account, sells direct to the dealers: cabinet trade: from ca 1850. Mayhew.

***garrete(e)r.** A thief specializing in entering houses by garret-windows or skylights: c.: mid-C.19–20 (ob.). cf. DANCER; DANCING-MASTER. 2. A literary hack: from ca 1730: journalists' s., > gen. coll ca 1780, > S.E. ca 1895: ob. Bentley, Macaulay. Ex S.E. sense, one who lives in a garret.

garrison-hack. A harlot: a soldier's drab: coll: from ca 1850; ob. 2. A woman who habitually flirts, somewhat indiscriminately, with garrison officers: from ca 1875. *Athenaeum*, 8 Feb. 1890, 'The heroine is a garrison-hack, but the hero is an Australian.'

garrison sports. Washing out quarters: Regular Army jocular coll: late C.19–20; ob.

***gar(r)otte.** To cheat with the aid of cards concealed at the back of the neck: card-sharping c.: from ca 1850.

***gar(r)otte, tip** (one) **the.** To rob during or after throttling the victim: c.: from ca

1850; †by 1900. The n. and the v., rob with or by throttling, with their natural derivatives, are S.E. ex the S.E. sense, execution by strangulation; see, however, BACK-STALL; FRONT-STALL, and UGLY or NASTY MAN. Ex Sp. *garrote*, a stick: cf. *garrot*, a surgical tourniquet.

***gar(r)otting,** vbl n. corresponding with GAR(R)OTTE, v., above.

garry, gharry. A (gen. light) carriage: Anglo-Indian coll: from ca 1800. Ex Hindi *gari*, a cart, a carriage.

garter, get over her or **the.** To take manual liberties with a woman: C.19–20 (ob.) low coll.

garter, in the catching up of a. In a moment; quickly: coll: from ca 1690; ob.

garter-hole or **eye-hole.** Fillet-hole: bell-ringers' (—1901), resp. s. and coll. (Rev. H. Earle Bulwer.)

garters. The irons; fetters: nautical (—1769); ob. Falconer. Pleasantly semantic.

gas. Empty talk; bombast; baseless boasting or threats: 1847, U.S.; anglicized ca 1860. *Chambers's Journal*, 29 June 1867, 'I've piped off Sabbath gas in my time.' 2. A jet of gas: coll: 1872.

gas, v. To supply with gas; to light with gas: coll: from ca 1885. 2. Talk idly or for talking's sake; boast unduly or arrogantly (—1874). 3. The sense, to deceive by such talk, is orig. and mainly U.S.

gas, give a person. To scold him; give a thrashing: ca 1860–90. See (*give one*) JESSIE, by which it was perhaps suggested.

gas, turn off the. To cease, cause to cease, from overmuch talk or from boasting: from ca 1880. Ex GAS, n., 1. cf.:

gas, turn on the. To begin talking hard or boasting: from ca 1880.

gas-bag. A person of too many words; a boaster: coll: from ca 1889. Ex GAS, n., 1. cf. *wind-bag* and *poison gas*. 2. A balloon, airship: pejorative coll: 1877; slightly ob.

gas-pipes. Very tight trousers: Cockneys': ca 1890–1915.

gas out of one, take the. To take down a peg, the conceit out of one: from ca 1885. See GAS, n., 1.

gas round, to. Seek information slyly: from ca 1890.

gaseous. Apt to take offence on insufficient grounds: coll (—1864). Ex the inflammability of gas.

gash. The mouth: orig. U.S. (1852) and rare in Britain except in jocular form, *an awful gash*: late C.19–20. 2. The female pudend: C.18–20: low coll.

gashion. Additional, free; often in pl as n., 'extra of anything' (cf. BAKSHEE): naval: late C.19–20. Prob. ex dial. *gaishen* (*gation*), an obstacle in one's way, perhaps via *additional*.

gaskins. Wide hose or breeches: (in C.18–19, jocular) coll: C.17–early 19. Johnson, 'An old ludicrous word'. ?abbr. GALLIGASKINS.

gasometer. A voluble talker; a boaster: from ca 1890; ob. cf. GAS-BAG.

gasp. A dram of spirits: from ca 1880. Ob. Ex its frequent effect.

gasp, v.i. To drink a dram of spirits: from ca 1880: †.

gasp my last if...!, may I. A non-aristocratic asseveration: coll (—1887); slightly ob.

gaspipe, occ. **gas-pipe.** A steamer whose length, instead of five, is nine or ten times that of her beam: nautical: ca 1880–1910. 2. An inferior or damaged roller: printers': from ca 1860; ob. 3. A rifle; esp. the Snider. *Daily Telegraph*, 9 July 1883, 'The old Snider – the ... gas-pipe of our Volunteers – continues to be used in many of the competitions.' Gen. ca 1880–1910; specific, ca 1875–95.

gaspipe-crawler. A tall thin man: gas-works': ca 1885–1914. cf. LAMP-POST.

gasser. A tremendous talker; a boaster: from ca 1888. Gen. with a modifying adj. cf. GAS-BAG and GASOMETER.

gassy. Full of empty talk or boasts; given to these: 1863. 2. Very apt to take offence: ?coll (—1860). cf. GASEOUS.

gat, gats. A quantity; number, group: schoolboys'; C. 19.

gate. The 'paying' attendance at any outdoor sport or game: from ca 1888. In C.19, coll. Ex: 2. (Occ. in pl) money paid for admission thereto: coll: 1887, Baumann. Ex *gate-money*. 3. Preceded by *the*: Billingsgate, C.18–20 fishmongers'; Newgate (Prison): C.19 c.

gate, v. To confine wholly or partially to college-bounds: university (1831): in C.20, j. or S.E. Anon., *The Snobiad*, 1835; Bradley ('Cuthbert Bede'), 1853; Hughes, *Tom Brown at Oxford*, 1861.

***gate, on the.** On remand: c.: late C.19–20; ob. cf. FENCE, (SIT UP) ON THE. Perhaps imm. ex: 2. Forbidden to leave barracks: military: from ca 1870.

gate of horn, or **of life.** The female pudend: the former, low; the latter, gen. euphemistic and ineligible. C.19–20. cf. HORN, n., 5.

gate-race (—1864) or **-meeting** (—1881). A contest arranged less for the sport than for the money: sporting s. > coll.

gater. A plunge, headlong, into a POT (8): Winchester College: C.19–20.

gates. The hour at which one must be in college; the being forbidden to leave college, either at all or, as gen., after a certain hour: university: from ca 1855. Bradley, *Tales of College Life*, 1856; Lang, *XXXII Ballades*, 1881.

Gates, be at. To assemble in Seventh Chamber passage: Winchester College, ca 1850–1910. Mansfield.

gates, break. To return to college after the latest permissible time: university: from ca 1860.

Gath, be mighty in. 'To be a Philistine of the first magnitude', F. & H. Gath, a city in Philistia, is here, as in the next two entries, employed for Philistia (the land of the Philistines) itself. Coll: mid-C.19–20; ob. All three entries verge on S.E.

Gath, prevail against. To deal the Philistines a rousing blow; coll: mid-C.19–20; ob.

Gath!, tell it not in. Fancy *your* doing that! Fancy your doing *that!* Coll: mid-C.19–20.

gather the taxes. To seek employment at one shop after another: tailors': ca 1870–1920. Hence, *tax-gatherer*, a tailor seeking work.

gathering, see GAG, n., 5.

gathers, out of. In distress (cf. *out at* ELBOWS): ?tailors' s. > gen. s. or coll. ca 1875–1915.

gations. An occ. spelling of *gashions* (see GASHION).

'gator. An alligator: Australian coll: late C.19–20. (Earlier in U.S.A.)

***gatter.** Beer. Frequently SHANT *of gatter*, a pot of beer: 1818. ?orig. c.: low s. >, ca 1860, low coll; ob. Maginn in *Vidocq Versified*; *Punch*, 1841. ?etymology: perhaps ex Lingua Franca (?*agua* + *water*).

gaudeamus. A students' feast, a drinking-bout; any merry-making: 1823, Scott. Ex first word (=let us rejoice) of a students' song in festive Latin.

gaudy, adj., app. always in negative sentences. Good, esp. with *chance* or *lot*; healthy: from ca 1880: slightly ob. Ex notion of brilliance.

gaudy, as the devil said when he painted his bottom pink and tied up his tail with pea-green ribbon, Neat but not. A c.p. that, in C.19, was addressed (by whom?) to old ladies dressed in flaming colours. For other variants see NEAT BUT.

gauge, see GAGE.

gauge of, get the. To SIZE up; discern a motive, penetrate a character: coll: from ca 1870; ob. Ex the S.E. *take the gauge of.*

gauge of it, that's about the. That is a tolerably accurate or equitable description: coll: from ca 1875.

gaum, see MAUM.

gaw(-)gaw. A useless seaman: nautical: late C.19–20. Perhaps ex GAWPUS.

gawblim(e)y, see GORBLIMY!

Gawd forgive (him) the prayers (he) said! (He) did curse and swear!: Cockney evasive c.p.: late C.19–20; ob.

gawdelpus. A helpless, sad, or woebegone person: Cockney: late C.19–20.

gawf. An inferior, red-skinned apple that can easily be made to look very attractive: costers' (—1851). Mayhew. (They are now more highly considered.)

gawk, a simpleton, a fool, or an awkward person, is S.E. according to the O.E.D. and S.O.D.: I cannot help thinking that at first, 1837, it was coll, though admittedly it was dial. as early as C.17 (E.D.D.), and is S.E. in C.20. Presumably ex *gawky*, n. (1724), and adj. (1724), always – it seems – S.E. The v. *gawk*, to gape or stare, to loiter about in a gaping manner, is orig. U.S. (1785); so far as it is used in Britain, it is coll, as also is *gawking*, vbl n. and ppl adj.; *gawkiness*, however, is late (1873) and S.E.

gawm (or **G.**), see GORM.

gawney, goney. A fool: coll when not dial.: from ca 1770. ?by SAWNEY out of GAWK.

gawpus. An idle seaman: nautical coll: from ca 1870. Ex dial. *gaupus* (*gawpus*), a simpleton.

gay. (Of women) leading an immoral, or a harlot's, life: 1825, Westmacott. 2. Slightly intoxicated: C.19–20; ob. Perhaps orig. a euphemism.

gay, all (so). 'All serene'; all correct, safe, excellent: C.19.

gay, feel. To feel amorous: C.19–20. Orig. euphemistic.

gay, turn. To become a prostitute: since ca 1870.

gay and frisky. Whisky: rhyming s.: late C.19–20.

gay as a goose in a gutter (, as). Very gay indeed: coll: late C.18–mid-19. (W. N. Glascock, *Sketch-Book*, 1826, at II, 30.)

gay bit. A harlot: from ca 1830; ob. Coll. See BIT (n., 7).

gay girl. A prostitute: non-aristocratic: mid-C.19–20; ob.

gay house. A brothel: C.19–20; ob. Perhaps orig. euphemistic.

gay in the arse or **groin** or **legs.** (Of women) loose: coll: C.19–20 low. cf. Fr. *avoir la cuisse gaie.*

gay it. (Of both sexes) to have sexual connection: C.19–20; ob.: coll.

gay life, lead a. To live immorally; live by prostitution: coll or s.: from ca 1860.

gay old. An occ. variant of HIGH OLD: ca 1885–1910.

gay tyke boy. A dog-fancier: ca 1840–80; low. Duncombe.

gaying instrument, the. The male member: C.19; low coll. cf.:

gaying it, vbl n. Sexual intercourse: C.19–20 (ob.); low coll.

gazebo, gazook. A foolish fellow: Australian: mid-C.19–20. cf. U.S. s. *gazabo,* a gawky or awkward fellow. Either ex Sp. *gazapo,* a shrewd fellow, or ex *gaze* + the comic suffix *-ebo.* cf.:

gazob. A silly fool; a (foolish) blunderer; a SOFTIE: low (?orig. Australian): late C.19–20. Perhaps a corruption of *galoot,* or a blend of GALOOT + *blob*: cf. the U.S. *gazabo,* which, dating from ca 1890, prob. derives ex S.E. *gazebo,* and may well represent the origin of *gazob.*

***geach.** A thief: c. (—1821); ob. by 1900. ?*thief* disguised. cf.:

***geach,** v.t. To steal: c. Haggart, 1821. ?*thieve* perverted.

gear. The genitals, male and, more gen., female: late C.16–19: S.E. until C.19, then coll >, very soon, s.

gear, the. (Always predicatively, e.g. 'That's the gear'.) Very good: low, but also Liverpool ordinary: late C.19–20.

gear or **gears, warm in one's.** Settled down to work: C.17–18 coll. cf.:

gears, in his. Ready dressed: late C.17–18: coll. B.E., who notes also *out of his gears,* out of sorts, indisposed: perhaps, orig., s. Ex earlier *in his gears,* ready for work.

ged! A coll variant of GAD! = *God!* Late C.17–19. cf. vowel in DEMME!

gee. A horse: s. (1887) >, ca 1900 coll. Orig. a child's word. Abbr. GEE-GEE.

gee. To fit, suit, be convenient or practical: only in negative phrases: late C.17–20; ob. 2. (Of persons) to behave as is expected or desired; agree, get on well together: C.18–20; ob. v.t. with *with.* Either ex next entry or a corruption of *go.*

gee! A command to a horse: gen. to turn to the right: coll; 1628 (S.O.D.). 2. See JEE!

gee-gee. A horse: s. (1869) >, ca 1900, coll. Reduplication of GEE! Mostly among sportsmen and 'turfites'. *Pall Mall Gazette,* 14 April 1889.

gee-gee dodge. The selling of horseflesh for beef: butchers': app. since ca 1860: James Greenwood, *Odd People in Odd Places,* 1883.

gee ho! or **ho, gee ho!** Equivalent to GEE!: from ca 1650: coll. Contrast GEE WHOA! Also, same period, v.i. and t., say *gee-ho* (to).

gee up, occ. **hup!** (To a horse) move forward! Move faster: C.18–20 coll. 2. To say 'gee up!': C.19–20 coll. *Blackwood's Magazine,* Oct. 1824, 'Mr Babb gehupped in vain.' The *(h)up* is not adv. but interjection.

gee whizz! see JEE!

gee whoa! (To a horse) stop! Rarer than *whoa!* Coll: C.18–20.

geebung. An old settler: Australian: since ca 1870. B., 1942. Aboriginal word.

***geekie.** A police-station: Scottish c. (—1893). ?ex *geek,* to peer about.

ge(e)loot, see GALOOT.

geese, the old woman's picking her. Applied to a snowstorm: C.19–20 proverbial coll, very gen. among school-children, who often add: *and selling the feathers a penny apiece.*

geese are swans, all his. He exaggerates in his praise, esp. of his own family or property: coll (—1529); in C.20, rather S.E. Skelton; Burton; Newman in his *Apologia,* 'To use the common phrase . . .'

geese go bare-legged!, fie upon pride when. A proverbial c.p. retort to undue pride in the lowly: late C.17–18.

geese on a common, like. Wandering, somewhat aggressively, at large: C.19–20, coll.

geese when the gander is gone, he'll be a man among the. A C.17–20 ob. coll variation (ironical and = He'll be a man before his mother) of the C.17–20 proverb *You're a man among the geese when the gander's away.*

geeser (rare) or **geezer;** occ. **geyser** (incorrectly); esp. **old geezer.** A person: in the 1890s, gen. of women; in C.20, gen. of men (cf. OLD BUFFER). Low coll: 1885 (O.E.D.). Albert Chevalier in his still-remembered *Knocked 'Em in the Old Kent Road*, 1890, 'Nice old geezer with a nasty cough'. Ex †*guiser*, a mummer, via dial. Note, however, that Wellington's soldiers may, ca 1811, have picked up Basque *giza*, man, fellow, and changed it to *geezer*.

***gegger**, see GAGGER, 4.

gel (hard g). A Cockney as well as an affected form of *girl*: C.19–20. Prob. ex dial. cf. GAL.

geld; occ. gelt. Money: South African s. verging on coll: from ca 1880. Ex Dutch *geld*, money, cash. cf.: GELT.

geloot, see GALOOT.

***gelt.** GILT, i.e. money: late C.17–early 19 c.: in C.16–early 17, S.E.; in C.19–20, grafters' s.; and see GELD. B.E., '*There is no Gelt to be got*, c., Trading is very Dead.' Ex Dutch *geld*, money.

***gelter.** Money: a C.19 c. elaboration of GELT. Duncombe.

***gem.** A ring: late C.17–early 18. 2. A gold ring: C.18. RUM *gem*, a diamond ring: C.18. All are c. 3. A 'jewel' or TREASURE: (gen. playful) coll: C.19–20; ob. Because prized.

gemini!, gem(m)iny!, jim(m)iny! (In the earliest example, *gemony*.) An orig. not so low coll oath or interjection, from ca 1660, expressing surprise, often preceded by *oh!* and occ. followed by *gig* (late C.18–early 19) or *figs* (C.19, chiefly Cockney). Dryden, 1672, 'O Gemini! is it you, sir?' Ex *Gemini*, the Twins (Castor and Pollux, who figure in an old Roman oath), says the O.E.D.; 'Folk Etymology' Palmer traces to a German and Dutch exclamation ex *O Jesu Domine!*: the former is preferable.

gemony! see GEMINI!

gen. A shilling: costers' (—1851). Either abbr. GENERALIZE, or abbr. Fr. *argent* – see GENT, 2. Mayhew. For back slang, see *Slang* at 'Oddities'.

gen-net, see GENNET.

gender, feminine. The pudend: (—1835) schoolboys' ob. s., as in the rhyme, quoted – in part – by Marryat in *Jacob Faithful*: '*Amo, amas,* | I loved a lass, | And she was tall and slender, | *Amas, amat,* | I laid her flat, | And tickled her feminine gender.'

general. A maid-of-all-work: coll: 1884 (O.E.D.); Ware dates it at 1880. Abbr. *general servant*. 2. Chandler's shop – where everything may be obtained: urban low classes' (—1909); slightly ob. Ware. 3. See GENERALIZE.

general, adj. Affable to all: late C.16–17: either S.E. or, more prob., coll. Shakespeare, 'Bid her be free and general as the sun.'

generalize or **ise.** A shilling: back – i.e. mainly costers' – s.: from ca 1850. *Saturday Review*, 14 May 1887, 'The difficulty of inverting the word shilling accounts for "generalize".' (cf. GEN.) Ware records the form *general*. 2. Hence (—1909) *Can you generalize?*, can you lend me a shilling?

generating place. The female pudendum: C.19–20 (ob.) low coll.

generating, or **generation, tool.** The male member: C.19–20 (ob.) low coll. Solus TOOL is prob. the older term.

Geneva print. Gin; mostly in *read Geneva print*, to drink it: C.17 coll. Massinger. (*Geneva* > *gin.*) Punning the kind of type used in Geneva bibles.

genitrave or **genitraf,** see GENNITRAF.

gennet, gen-net. Ten shillings, separately or as a sum: back s.: fl. 1859. See GENERALIZE, GEN, and NET-GEN.

gen(n)itraf or **-trave.** A farthing: back s.: from ca 1860. *Gnihtraf* euphonized.

genol. Long: back s.: from ca 1860. *Gnol* euphonized.

gent. A loudly dressed vulgarian: from ca 1560, though anticipated in C.15: in C.16–18, S.E.: ca 1800–40, coll; from ca 1840, low coll, except when applied derisively to those who use the term. Glapthorne, Burns; Thackeray, Disraeli. In 1846, magistrate Rawlinson: 'I hold a man who is called a gent to be the greatest blackguard there is.' 2. In c. (—1859), money, esp. silver money: ex Fr. *argent*: cf. GEN. 3. A sweetheart; mistress; *my gent*, my best girl. Low coll: from ca 1880: ob. Prob. ex Fr. (*une femme*) *gentille*.

genteel, well-dressed, *apparently* a gentleman or a lady, has, from ca 1880, been low coll – except when depreciatory.

gentish. Like, characteristic of, a GENT: ?S.E. or coll: 1847 (O.E.D.); ob.

***gentleman.** A crowbar: c.: from ca 1850; ob. See ALDERMAN. 2. See PUNISHER, 3.

gentleman, put a churl (or **beggar**) **upon a,** see CHURL.

gentleman-commoner. An empty bottle: Oxford University (—1785); †by 1900. cf. FELLOW-COMMONER; DEAD MAN; DEAD MARINE. Such a student was, in general repute, deficient in intelligence.

gentleman in black, the (old). The devil: from ca 1660: s. >, in C.19, coll. Dryden.

gentleman in black velvet, the (little). A

mole. This was a Jacobite phrase after the death of William III, whose horse was said to have stumbled over a mole-hill. C.18–19. Scott.

gentleman in blue. A policeman: satirical coll: mid-C.19–20; ob.

gentleman in brown. A bed bug: coll (—1885); ob. G. A. Sala.

gentleman in red. A soldier: 1774: either s. or jocular coll; ob.

gentleman of fortune. A pirate: C.19–20 (ob.): coll, punning the S.E. sense: adventurer.

gentleman of four outs, see GENTLEMAN OF THE THREE OUTS.

gentleman of observation. A (spying) tout: the turf: C.19.

gentleman of the back(door). A sodomist: *back door*, C.18–20, ob.; *back*, C.19: low coll. See also at BACK DOOR . . .

gentleman of the fist. A boxer: boxers' (—1819); ob. by 1900, †by 1910.

gentleman of the first head or **house; gentleman of the five outs,** see GENTLEMAN OF THE THREE OUTS.

gentleman of the green-baize road. A card-sharper: gamblers': C.19–20, ob. Punning *gentleman of the road*, S.E. for a highwayman.

gentleman of the nig. A cut-purse: s.: Ned Ward, 1709.

gentleman of the pad. A highwayman: 1718: sometimes s., sometimes jocular coll: †by 1870. See PAD and SCAMP.

gentleman of the round. An invalided or a disabled soldier begging for his living: late C.16–17 coll. Ben Jonson.

gentleman of the short staff. A constable: ca 1830–80. Ainsworth.

gentleman of (the) three ins. (But *the* is rare and does not appear before ca 1830.) 'In debt, in gaol, and in danger of remaining there for life; or, in gaol, indicted, and in danger of being hanged in chains', Grose, 1788; H., 1864, 'In debt, in danger, and in poverty'. A c.p. that > ob. ca 1890. Prob. suggested by the contrasted:

gentleman of (rarely, and not before ca 1830, **the) three outs.** 'Without money, without wit, and without mourners', Grose, 1785 – it is the earlier phrase. In 1788, he added, 'Some add another out, i.e. without credit.' Variants *four, five*; H., 1864, has *four* and refers to Ireland, where, he says, the retort to a vulgar fellow blustering of gentlemanliness was 'Yes, a gentleman of four outs – that is, without wit, without money, without credit, and without manners.' F. & H., 1893, cites 'Out of money, and out of clothes; | Out at heels, and out at the toes; | Out of credit, and in debt'. Ob. by 1893, but not yet †. cf. the C.16–17 *dunghill gentleman* and *gentleman of the first head* or *house*, which may themselves be coll or even s.

gentleman of three ins and **outs,** see previous two entries.

Gentleman Outer. A highwayman: s.: Ned Ward, 1709.

gentleman ranker. A broken gentleman serving in the ranks: military s. (—1892). See Kipling's famous poem, *Gentleman Rankers*.

gentleman who pays the rent, the. A pig! Anglo-Irish: mid-C.19–20; ob.

gentleman's companion. A louse: coll (—1785). Grose, 1st ed. cf. BOSOM FRIEND. 2. Possibly, in late C.17–18, it also = a flea. Ned Ward, 1709.

gentleman's master. A highwayman: ca 1780–1840. Ex gentlemen's obedience to his 'stand and deliver!'

gentleman's, occ. lady's, piece. A tit-bit: (mostly children's) coll: ca 1880–1910.

gentleman's pleasure-garden. The *genitalia muliebria*: low or jocular coll: C.19–20; ob. – Followed by *padlock*, it = a sanitary towel.

gentlemen's sons. The three regiments of Guards: coll: ca 1870–1914.

***gentry cofe,** mid-C.16–17; **gentry cove,** mid-C.16–early 19. A gentleman: c. (cf. C. 19 Devon *gentry man.*) 2. Whence *gentry cofe('s)* or *cove('s) ken*, a gentleman's house: likewise c.: †by 1850.

***gentry ken.** A (?C.18) C.19 c. abbr. of *gentry cove's ken* (preceding entry).

***gentry mort.** A lady: c.: mid-C.16–early 19. This and the preceding two terms are in Harman.

genuine, n. and v. Praise: from ca 1840, 1860 resp.: Winchester College. Wrench, 'Possibly from calling a thing "genuine".'

geo-graphy. 'Burned biscuit boiled in water': nautical: early C.19–20. Bowen.

geom. (Pronounced *jŏm.*) Geometry: schools': late C.19–20.

Geordie, geordie. A pitman; any Northumbrian: North Country coll: from ca 1760. Prob. ex the Christian name there so pronounced. 2. A North Country collier (boat): nautical: from ca 1880. 3. The *George* Stephenson safety-lamp: miners' (—1881). 4. A Scottish variant of the various senses of:

George, george. A noble (6s. 8d., *temp.*

Henry VIII): abbr. *George-noble*: late C.16–17. 2. A half-crown (piece): ca 1659–1820: c. Shadwell. 3. A guinea: rare unless in form *yellow George*: c. (—1785); †by 1870. 4. A penny: low: ca 1820–70. 5. See BROWN GEORGE.

George!, by. (Occ. in late C.19–20, simply *George!*) A mild oath: coll abbr. *by St George!*: 1731, Fielding; earlier *by St George*, *for George*, both in Ben Jonson, 1598; *before George*, 1678.

George, riding (or the dragon upon) St, see RIDING ST GEORGE.

George Horne! QUEEN ANNE IS DEAD! Occ. *G.H.* Printers': ca 1880–1910. Ex a romancing compositor so named.

Georges man. A vessel fishing on the Georges Bank: Canadian fisheries' coll: late C.19–20.

***Georgie (or-y); georgie.** A quartern loaf: c. (—1812); †by 1890. cf. BROWN GEORGE.

Georgie-Porgie or **Georgy-Porgy.** A coll pet form of *George*; any plump male child. (In 1883, R. L. Stevenson employed it as a v. = to fondle, but this use has not caught on.) From ca 1870. Ex, as well as suggestive of, the nursery rhyme, 'Georgy-Porgy, pudding and (*or*, *loosely*, puddingy) pie, | Kissed the girls and made 'em cry.'

Georgium Sidus. The Surrey side of the Thames: London Society (—1909).

geranium. A red nose: Cockneys': from ca 1882; ob. 2. A brigadier-general: Army officers': late C.19–20.

German bands. Hands: late C.19–20 rhyming s.

German duck. 'Half a sheep's head boiled with onions', Grose, 2nd ed.: late C.18–19 (†by 1893) coll. Because 'a favourite dish among the German sugar-bakers in the East End of London', H., 1864. 2. A bed bug: orig. and mainly Yorkshire: from ca 1860; ob.

German flutes. (No singular.) Boots: rhyming s. (—1857).

German gospel. Vain boasting, megalomania: Nov. 1897–ca 99. Ware, 'From a phrase addressed in this month by Prince Henry of Prussia to his brother of Germany at a dinner: "The gospel that emanates from your Majesty's sacred person", etc.'

***gerry.** Excrement: C.16 c.; cf. GERRY GAN. ?ex L. *gero*, I carry; perhaps rather cf. Devonshire *gerred*, bedaubed, dirty, itself connected with Fr. *bigarré*, streaked.

***gerry gan.** (See GAN and GERRY.) Lit., shit (in your) mouth: a brutal C.16–early 17 c. way of saying SHUT UP! (v., 2.).

gerswinty or **geswinty.** Hurried; engaged on an urgent job: Jewish Cockney tailors': C.19–20. Ex Yiddish.

gertcher. Get out of it, you!: low coll: late C.19–20. 2. Don't *pull my* LEG! id.: id.

gerund-grinder. A schoolmaster; esp. a pedantic one: coll: from ca 1710; ob. Sterne, 'Tutors, governors, gerund-grinders, and bear-leaders'. Also, C.19–20, *gerund-grinding*.

get. A trick, swindle; a cheating contrivance: posited by F. & H.; †by 1890. 2. A child, esp. in *one of his get*, one of his offspring, of his begetting: C.14–20: S.E. till ca 1750, then coll; after ca 1870, only of animals – unless pejorative.

get, v. To become; feel, e.g. 'He gets ill every winter,' 'He gets moody after drinking': late C.16–20; nominally S.E., but in C.19–20 more properly considered coll. 2. v.i., with intransitive past ppl; to complete an action: C.18–20; S.E. till ca 1860, then coll. e.g. 'I'd be glad to get gone from this town.' A rare construction. 3. v.i., *get* as an auxiliary (from ca 1650) is held by the O.E.D. to be S.E., but there is a coll taint in such locutions as 'I got caught in the storm,' 1887 (S.O.D.). 4. v.t., have, take, eat (a meal): coll (—1888), perhaps ex dial. 5. v.t., understand (rarely a thing), gen. as 'Do you get me?': ex U.S.; anglicized ca 1910. 6. To corner (a person); get hold of, find and bring him, there being an implication of subject's difficulty and/or object's reluctance: coll: 1879. 7. To depart: mostly in the imperative. See GET! 8. In c., to steal: ca 1820–60. cf. MAKE, v. 9. To get the mastery of: pugilistic: ca 1810–60. *Boxiana*, III, 1821.

get! Abbr. *get out!*, go away! clear out! Orig. (1884) U.S., where usually *git!* Anglicized ca 1900, but found in Australia ca 1890. Hume Nisbet in *The Bushranger's Sweetheart*, 1892, 'None of your damned impertinence. Get!'

get a bag! A cricket spectators' c.p., addressed to a fielder missing an easy catch: esp. in Australia and New Zealand: late C.19–20. The implication is that he would do better as twelfth man, who carries the bag, but also that, if he held a bag open, he might succeed.

get a bit. To obtain money – or a woman: low: late C.19–20.

get about, v.t., with **her**, to effect intromission: low coll (amorous venery): from ca 1880. Also, absolutely, *get about it*. 2.

v.i., (of news, gossip) to spread, either (e.g.) 'The story got about,' often with a *that* clause, or (e.g.) 'It got about that the firm was bankrupt': coll: from ca 1848; since ca 1880, S.E. 3. v.i., to move about or around, to travel, gen. with implication of frequency, though this may be defined, as in 'He gets about a lot, *or* a great deal': coll: from late 1890s.

get all over. To handle and examine (a person) – 'not necessarily for theft, but in all probability feloniously': low: mid-C. 19–20; slightly ob. Ware.

get along with you! Go away! Be quiet! Have done! Coll: 1837, Dickens.

get anything. To be infected, e.g.venereally; *get* replacing *catch*. Coll: from ca 1850. Merely a coll absolute form of S.E. *get* = catch, C.17–20.

get at. To assail; strike, as in 'Let me get at the foul-mouthed b——r': from ca 1890. 2. To banter, chaff, annoy, take (or try to take) a rise out of: from ca 1890. *Ally Sloper's Half Holiday*, 3 Jan. 1891, '"Your family don't seem to get on, missie . . ." "*On!* who're ye gettin' at?"' See also GET BACK AT. 3. To influence, bribe, corrupt a person or a group of persons; to NOBBLE (2) a horse: orig. s. (1865), then ca 1880, coll. J. S. Mill; *Graphic*, 17 March 1883, 'Without any suspicion of being got at'. 4. To mean; intend to be understood: gen. as 'What are you getting at?' Coll: from late C.19: ?ex sense 2.

get away, get-away, getaway. An escape: 1890. 2. A means of escape; hence an exit: from ca 1895; ex U.S., where in late C.19–20 c. it means a train or a locomotive.

get away! As = go away, S.E., but as = don't talk nonsense, don't flatter, it is coll: from ca 1830. The form *get away with you!* is prob. to be considered S.E. cf. GET ALONG WITH YOU!

get away closer! An 'invitation to yet more pronounced devotion': costers', hence gen. Cockneys' c.p.: late C.19–20; slightly ob. Ware.

get back at. To chaff, banter; satirize; criticize; call to account: coll: from ca 1885. cf. GET AT.

get back into your box! Be quiet! That's enough from *you!* Orig. (—1893), U.S.; anglicized ca 1900; slightly ob. Ex the stables.

get before oneself. To boast, threaten, be angry, unduly: low coll: late C.19–20; ob. Contrast GET BEHIND ONESELF.

get behind, v.t. An occ. variant of GET UP BEHIND. 2. See:

get behind oneself. To forget an appointment, the date of an event, etc.: lower classes' coll: mid-C.19–20.

get curly. To become troublesome: tailors': late C.19–20. ?ex rucking.

get down. To depress mentally; to exasperate or irritate: coll: late C.19–20.

get 'em. Have the D.T.S.: from ca 1900.

get encored. To have a garment returned for alterations: tailors: from ca 1875.

get even (with), v.i., t. To give tit for tat, have one's revenge (on): coll (from ca 1880). Ex S.E. *be even with*, on a par (or even terms) with.

get (one's) **fingers nipped.** To get into trouble for some misdeed: coll: late C.19–20. Perhaps suggested by S.E. *get one's fingers burnt.*

get fits. To be impatient under defeat: lower classes' (—1909); ob.

get forrader, see FORRADER.

get going. The v.t., set going, start, prepare, is S.E., but the v.i., to begin doing something (work or play) vigorously or very well, 'get into one's stride', is coll: from ca 1895. Esp. in 'Wait till I (he, etc.) get(s) going.'

get in, v.i.; **get into,** v.t. To effect intromission: low coll: C.18–20. cf. GET UP. 2. **(get in.)** To strike victoriously; e.g. 'Get in with both fists': coll (—1897). Ex *get a blow in.*

get inside and pull the blinds down! A c.p. addressed to a poor horseman: Cockneys': mid-C.19–20; ob.

get into. Put on clothes, boots, etc.: coll: late C.17–20. Lady Burghersh, 1813. **2.** See GET IN, 1. 3. To become accustomed to; to learn: coll: from ca 1870.

get into a hank. To get angry: nautical: late C.19–20.

get into hot water, see HOT WATER.

get it. To be punished, physically or morally; to be reprimanded: coll: from ca 1870. cf. CATCH IT. 2. To be venereally infected: low coll: from ca 1875.

get it hot. An elaboration, from ca 1872, of GET IT, 1.

get it in the neck. To be defeated, thrashed (lit. or fig.), to receive a shock, to be grievously disappointed, severely reprimanded: —1900. Elaboration of GET IT, 1. cf. *get it where the* CHICKEN *got the axe.*

get left, see LEFT, BE.

get off, v.t. Deliver oneself of, utter, esp. a witticism: orig. (1849), U.S.; anglicized ca

1875: coll; slightly ob. 2. To let off; excuse, esp. from punishment: mid-C.19–20. 3. To succeed in marrying one's daughters: coll: from ca 1820. 4. v.i., to be let off a punishment, an irksome duty: escape: from ca 1640: in C.17–early 19, S.E., then either coll or near-coll.

get (money, a BIT) **on.** To back a horse: racing s. (from ca 1869) >, ca 1880, gen. coll. 2. To have connection with (a woman): low coll: from ca 1870. Ex the lit. sense, to mount. 3. v.i., to succeed, prosper: coll: from ca 1780. *Pall Mall Gazette*, 29 Dec. 1871, 'That great Anglo-Saxon passion of rising in the world, or getting on'. 4. (?hence) to fare; feel (in health): coll: from ca 1880. 5. Hence, also v.i., agree – or disagree – with a person, with modifying adv.; also, occ., absolutely, to agree well (with a person). Coll: from ca 1815. Never of things. 'We got on like a house on fire'; 'Oh, we get on, you know!' 6. To become elderly, or, esp., old: coll: from ca 1885. Abbr. *getting on in years.*

get on one's nerves. To affect morbidly, e.g. 'The clock gets on his nerves': coll (from ca 1870) >, by 1900, S.E. cf.:

get (a person, a thing) **on the brain,** or (more gen. **have**) **on one's mind.** To be obsessed by, crazy about: coll: from ca 1870. cf. GET ON ONE'S NERVES.

get on the home stretch. To be in sight of one's goal: coll: late C.19–20. Ex cribbage.

get on to. To suspect; find out about: coll: late C.19–20.

get one on, v.t. and absolute. To land a punch (on): pugilists': from ca 1880; ob.

get one's or **another's back up,** see BACK UP, adj.

get one's leg across. To achieve mastery of (a woman): low coll: late C.19–20.

get one's own back. To have one's revenge (on), get even with: coll: from ca 1908. Ex the recovery of property.

get one's tail up. Gen. in pl and 'said of a crew which is getting out of hand and impudent to the officers': nautical: late C.19–20. Bowen.

get-out. A means of escape: coll. E. H. Hornung, *Raffles*, 1899.

get out, v. To depart; go away; gen. in imperative: coll: from ca 1710; cf. GET. 2. 'To back a horse against which one has previously laid', F. & H.: racing (—1884). Also *get round* (—1893). 3. On the Stock Exchange (—1887), to sell one's shares, esp. in a risky venture. 4. See ROUND THE CORNER, GET. 5. v.i. (of things), to lengthen: coll, mostly Cockneys': from ca 1880.

get out! *Tell that to the* MARINES! Don't flatter! Coll: from ca 1840. Dickens, 'Kit only replied by bashfully bidding his mother "get out".'

get out (of bed) on the wrong side. To be irritable, testy: coll: from ca 1885. Ex the S.E. *to rise on the right side is accounted lucky*, C.17–19. The *Globe*, 15 May 1890, 'If we may employ such a vulgar expression – got out of bed on the wrong side.'

get out of, e.g. **it, the scrape.** To escape the consequences of one's folly or mistake: be excused punishment or duty: coll: from ca 1880.

get outside, or **outside of.** To eat or drink, gen. a considerable and specified amount: low coll: from ca 1890. S. Watson, in *Wops the Waif*, 1892. 2. (Of women only) to receive a man sexually: low coll: from ca 1870.

get over. To overcome (an obstacle, a prejudice): coll: from ca 1700; since ca 1895, S.E. 2. To recover from (illness, disappointment): coll: mid-C.18–20; since ca 1900, S.E. 3. To dupe, circumvent, seduce: low coll: from ca 1860. cf. COME OVER and GET ROUND. 4. To astonish, impress: coll: ca 1890–1915. (J. Milne, *The Epistles of Atkins*, 1902.)

get religion. To be converted; become (very) religious: orig. (1826) U.S., anglicized ca 1880: in C.19, s.

get round. To circumvent, trick: coll; from ca 1855, ex U.S. (1849). 2. To persuade, cajole; hence, seduce (lit. or fig.), dupe: coll: from ca 1860. cf. GET OVER, 3. 3. To evade; arrange, to one's own satisfaction, concerning: coll: from ca 1895. 4. In racing, same as GET OUT, 2.

***get round the corner,** see ROUND THE CORNER, GET.

get set. To warm to one's work; become thoroughly used to or skilful at it: coll: from ca 1895. Ex the cricket sense: (of a batsman) to get one's eye in, itself s. in the 1880s, coll in the 90s.

get shut of, see SHUT OF.

get straight, v.i. To free oneself of debt; have a complication straightened out, one's home tidy, etc., etc.: coll: from ca 1875.

get stuffed! Oh, run away and 'play trains'!: low: late C.19–20.

get the ambulance! (Gen. *git* . . .) A c.p. addressed to a drunk person: urban: 1897; ob.

get the: BAG; EMPTY; GO-BY; LEAD; MITTEN; POKE; RASPBERRY; STICK, see the relevant nouns (for *sack* see BAG).

get the sads. Grow melancholy: lower classes' coll (—1909).

get the shilling ready! Prepare to subscribe!: a c.p. of 1897–8. With esp. reference to the *Daily Telegraph*'s shilling fund for the London hospitals – part of the charity characterizing the 60th year of Queen Victoria's reign.

get the shoot. To be dismissed: lower classes' (—1909).

get the spike. To lose one's temper: low London: from ca 1890; ob. cf. NEEDLE.

get there. To succeed in one's object or ambition; *with both feet*, notably, completely. Coll: orig. (—1883), U.S.; anglicized ca 1893. 2. To become intoxicated: ca 1890–1914. 3. (Of the man) to have sexual connection: low coll: from ca 1860.

get through, v.i. To pass an examination; succeed: coll: from ca 1850; in C.20, S.E. 'Cuthbert Bede', 1853, 'So you see, Giglamps, I'm safe to get through.' 2. v.t., to spend: late C.19–20; coll. 3. v.t., to complete; do: coll: late C.17–20: coll; then, in C.19–20, S.E. 'He gets through an astounding amount of work – largely because he loves work.' 4. To copulate with a woman (originally and strictly, with a virgin): low: late C.19–20.

get to. To begin to (do something): coll: from ca 1870. Nevinson, 1895.

get-up. Dress; general appearance, so far as it is prepared or artificial; coll: from ca 1847. Whyte-Melville, George Eliot. 2. Hence, a masquerade dress; a disguise: coll: from ca 1860. 3. 'Style of production or finish, esp. of a book, 1865', S.O.D.: publishers' coll.

get up, v. To make, esp. as regards appearance or embellishment: always with adv. or adv. phrase: coll: from ca 1780. Leigh Hunt, 'The pocket books that now contain any literature are got up, as the phrase is, in the most unambitious style.' 2. v. reflexive, to dress: coll: from ca 1855. Albert Chevalier, 1892, in *The Little Nipper*, ''E'd get 'imself up dossy.' Hence to disguise oneself: coll: from ca 1860. Also (though less gen.), from ca 1860, v.i., as in the anon. *Eton School Days*, 1864, 'He felt confident in his power of getting up so that no one would recognise him.' 3. v.i., to rise in the morning: from ca 1580: S.E. till ca 1880, then increasingly coll. 4. v.t., prepare (a case, role, subject, paper); arrange (e.g.) a concert: from ca 1770, though anticipated in late C.16–17; in C.19, coll; but from ca 1905, again S.E. 5. v.t., to have carnal knowledge of a woman: C.17–20: in John Aubrey's *Brief Lives*, written in 1679–96, we hear of Sir Walter Raleigh 'getting up one of the mayds of honour'.

get up! (To a horse) go! get a move on! Coll: from ca 1887 (O.E.D.).

get up and look at you. (Of the ball) 'to rise very slowly after pitching': cricketers' jocular coll (—1888).

get up behind. (v.t., with personal object) to endorse or back a man's bill or I.O.U. vbl n., *getting up behind.* Coll, mainly commercial: from ca 1870.

get up early, see EARLY, RISE . . .

***get up the mail.** To provide money for a prisoner's defence: c. (—1889). cf. *mail* in S.E. *blackmail.*

get your eye in a sling! This proletarian c.p. of late C.19–20 (ob.) constitutes a 'warning that you may receive a sudden and early black eye, calling for a bandage – the sling in question', Ware.

get your hair cut! A non-aristocratic c.p. of ca 1885–1912. 'Quotations' Benham. Ex a popular song.

getter, a sure. 'A procreant male with a great capacity for fertilization', F. & H.: Scottish coll: C.19–20.

getting a big boy now. Of age: a c.p. 'applied satirically to strong lusty young fellows': late C.19–20; slightly ob. Ex the 'leading phrase of the refrain of a song made popular by Herbert Campbell'. Ware.

getting ox-tail soup. The maiming of cattle by cutting off their tails: Anglo-Irish: ca 1867–83.

gharry, see GARRY.

ghastly. A vaguely pejorative or a merely intensive adj.: coll: from ca 1860. Thackeray, 'A ghastly farce'.

ghastly. A pejorative or merely intensive adv. e.g. 'ghastly early in the morning'. Coll: from ca 1870. cf. SHOCKING(LY).

ghaut serang. 'A crimp in the Indian ports': nautical coll: late C.19–20. Bowen.

ghost. One who, unknown to the public, does literary or artistic work for which another gets all the credit and most of the cash: from ca 1884: orig. journalistic or artistic s., then – ca 1890 – gen. coll, then – ca 1910 – S.E. 2. Meat: Regular Army's:

late C.19–20. Ex Hindustani. 3. Salary; but rare outside of *the* GHOST WALKS.

ghost, v.i. To do unrecognized, and prob. ill-paid, work for another in art or literature: from ca 1885: ex, and of the same social ascent as the n., 1. 2. To shadow, spy upon: coll: from ca 1880: ob. Rarely v.i. Ex S.E. sense, haunt as an apparition.

ghost of a chance, not the. No chance whatsoever: coll: 1857 (O.E.D.).

ghost walks, the; . . . does not walk. There is, is not, any money for salaries and wages: theatrical: 1853, in *Household Words*, No. 183. Ex *Hamlet*, I, i.

ghosty. A ghost, esp. if small or friendly: coll: from ca 1900. Ex the jocular but S.E. adj.

ghoul. A newspaperman chronicling even the pettiest public and private gossip or slander (cf. Oscar Wilde's witty differentiation): journalists': ca 1880–1915. Ex Arabic *ghul*, a body-snatching demon.

giant. (Gen. pl.) A very large 'stick' of asparagus: restaurants' coll: from ca 1880.

Gib. Gibraltar: military and civil service s. > gen. coll: from ca 1850. Once a convict settlement: whence the next entry. *Pall Mall Gazette*, 23 March 1892, 'Stormy Weather at Gib'.

***gib.** A gaol: c. (—1877); ob. by 1914. Ex the preceding. 2. See CUT OF ONE'S JIB. 3. A forelock: nautical: late C.19–20. Prob. ex a whale's gib.

gib or jib, hang one's. To pout: nautical s. (ca 1860) >, ca 1890, gen. coll.

gib cat, melancholy as a. Exceedingly depressed, dispirited: coll: C.16–19. *Gib* = male (ex *Gilbert*); not, in itself, eligible.

gib-face. A heavy jaw, an ugly face: coll: mid-C.19–20; ob. Ex *gib*, the lower lip of a horse.

gibberish, gib(b)rish, giberish, gibridge, gibrige, gibberidge. In C.16–early 19, in the sense of underworld s. and Gypsy j., the word seems to have had a coll, even a s., taint. Prob. not ex *gibber*, than which it is earlier recorded, but from *Egyptian*, which, until recently, was gen. associated with *Gypsy*. (For modern gibberish, in technical sense, see *Slang*, p. 278.)

gibby. A spoon: naval (—1909). Origin? Perhaps ex dial. *gibby* (*stick*), a hooked stick.

***gibel.** To bring: c. (—1837): †. Disraeli in *Venetia*, his underworld novel.

giblets. The intestines: coll (—1864). Browning. 2. A fat man: low coll: C.19.

giblets, join. To marry: coll verging on S.E.: 1681 as *j. g. together*, 1769 as *j. giblets*. 2. Whence, to copulate: late C.18–20 low. In C.19–20, also *do* or *have a bit of giblet-pie*. 3. To cohabit unmarried: late C.18–early 19.

Gibson or Sir John Gibson. 'A two-legged stool, used to support the body of a coach whilst finishing', Grose, 2nd ed.: coachbuilders': late C.18–early 19.

giddy, in coll speech, emphasizes the word it precedes: late C.19–20.

giddy goat, play the. To play the fool; be extremely happy-go-lucky; live a FAST (2) life: coll: from ca 1890. *Ally Sloper*, 19 March 1892, has *giddy ox*. There is also the vbl n., *giddy-goating*, 1891.

giddy kipper – whelk – whelp. A youth about town: London: ca 1895–1914. Ware derives the first from *giddy skipper*, the second from the first, the third from the second. 2. (*g.k.* only.) 'A term of reproach at the Cheltenham Grammar School,' E.D.D., 1900.

giddy limit, the. The 'last straw', the most outrageous person or thing: Cockneys': from ca 1890.

gift. Anything very easily obtained or won; an easy task: coll: from ca 1830. cf. BUNCE. 2. A stolen article sold very cheap: c. of ca 1850–90. Mayhew, 1851. 3. See GIFT-HOUSE.

gift, not to have as a; or in form **would not have as a.** Not to want at any price, even for nothing: coll: 1857, Thomas Hughes in *Tom Brown's School Days*.

gift-house, occ. abbr. *gift*. A benefit club: printers': from ca 1870; ob.

gift of the gab, see GAB, GIFT OF THE.

gifts as a brazen horse of farts, as full of. Miserly; mean with money: low coll: ca 1787–1870. cf. COSTIVE and PART, V.

gig, in C.17–18 often *gigg*. The nose: later C.17–early 19 c., as is the sense, *pudenda muliebria*. 2. A door: prob. c.: late C.18–early 19. Abbr. GIGGER = JIGGER. 3. (Esp. of a person.) An oddity: Eton, 1777: †by 1870. Colman. 4. A farthing: mid-C.19–20; ob. ?ex GRIG. 5. The mouth: low (—1871): †by 1900. Perhaps cf. GIB-FACE; H. considers it to derive ex GRIG.

gig, v. To hamstring. 'To gigg a Smithfield hank; to hamstring an overdrove ox', Grose, 1785: late C.18–early 19: either low or, less prob., c. Origin obscure, unless ex *gig*, to throw out, give rise to (see the O.E.D.'s v., 1).

gig-lamps. Spectacles: Oxford University, 1848: by 1860, gen. s. Ex the lamps on a gig. 2. One who wears spectacles: from ca 1854. Popularized by 'Cuthbert Bede'.

gigg, see GIG, n. and v.

gigger. A sewing-machine: tailors': from ca 1880. 2. Other senses: at JIGGER.

giggle-mug. 'A habitually smiling face': Cockneys' (—1909): Ware.

giggles-nest?, have you found a. Asked of one tittering, or laughing senselessly or excessively: low coll c.p.: C.19.

gigler, giggler, giglet, giglot, goglet. A wanton woman; a giddy, romping girl (not in *gig(g)ler* form). The *-er* term may be c., C.17–18; the other is S.E., the same applying to the adj. and to the adv. *gigletwise*.

gigs!, by. A mild, rather foolish oath: ca 1550–1700.

Gilderoy's kite, to be hanged (or hung) higher than. To be punished with excessive severity; hence and gen., out of sight, gone: mid-C.19–20; ob. Prob. of Scottish origin: see *Notes and Queries*, 7th Series, V, 357, and Thornton.

gilguy. Anything whose name has slipped the memory: nautical: from ca 1880; ob. R. Brown, *Spunyarn and Spindrift*, 'Sailors . . . if the exact name of anything they want happens to slip from their memory . . . call it a chicken-fixing, or a gadget, or a gill-guy.' Ex *gilguy*, 'often applied to inefficient guys' (for bearing boom or derrick), Smyth. cf. JIGGER; GADGET; THINGUMMY; WHAT'S-HIS-NAME.

***gilk or gilke.** A skeleton key: early C.17 c. Rowlands. ?GILT (2) corrupted.

gill. A fellow, a chap: low s. or c.: Vaux, 1812; extremely ob. Gen. with another term, says Vaux, who aligns GLOACH and GORY.

gill-ale. 'Physic-ale', says B.E., who, since a gill is only one-quarter of a pint, would seem to mean medicinal ale (?stout): coll: ca 1670–1750.

gill-guy, see GILGUY.

gilliflower. One wearing 'a canary or belcher fogle round his twist [neck]', Bee: low London: ca 1820–50. If he wears many more colours he is a TULIP (2).

gills. The flesh under the ears and jaws: since Francis Bacon's 'Redness about the cheeks and gills'; in C.19–20, *pace* the O.E.D., the term has a very coll hue, esp. in *rosy about the gills*, cheerful – *blue*, *green*, *yellow*, or *queer about* . . . dejected, indisposed – and *white* . . . frightened. 2. The corners of a stand-up collar: 1826; hence, 1859 (H., 1st ed.), a stand-up collar.

gills, a cant or dig in the. A punch in the face: pugilists': C.19–20; ob.

gills, grease the. To eat a very good meal: coll: C.19–20.

gilpy. A youth: naval: C.19. Perhaps suggested by HOBBLEDEHOY, likewise 'less than a man and more than a boy', but ex Scots *gilpy*, a lively young person.

gilt. Money: late C.16–20; S.E. until ca 1820, then s. cf. GELT. 2. A skeleton key: c.: ca 1670–1840. 3. Whence, since ca 1840, likewise in c., a crowbar. ('Pronounced *gilt*', says 'Ducange Anglicus'.) 4. Also c., a thief, esp. a pick-lock: ca 1620–1830. 5. 'A Slut or light Housewife', B.E.: late C.17–18.

***gilt-dubber.** A C.18–19 form of GILT. Also *rum dubber*.

gilt-edged. (Of 'paper', i.e. shares, bills, etc.) exceptionally easy to negotiate: ex U.S. (ca 1860); anglicized ca 1895. Ex *gilt-edged* note-paper. 2. Hence, first-class: coll: from ca 1898 in England.

gilt-horn. A complacent cuckold: C.18. Because well-fee'd.

gilt off the gingerbread, take the. To destroy an illusion; lessen a value: coll (—1830).

gilt-tick. Gold coins: costermongers': from ca 1840; ob. ?ex *gilded*.

***gilter.** A (pick-lock) thief: c.: late C.17–18 c. *Warning for Housekeepers*, 1676.

gimbal (occ. gimber)-jawed. Very talkative, in gen. and in particular: coll: C.19. Ex the lit. U.S. sense, loose-jawed (—1859).

gimcrack. 'A spruce Wench', B.E., it is perhaps s. (late C.17–early 19 low); as the female pudend, low or low coll: C.19–20.

gimmer. A woman, esp. an old one: pejorative, standard >, ca 1850, coll; Scottish: from ca 1770. cf. GAMMER.

gin. A native woman (—1830; anticipated in 1798): Australian. Hence, 1830, the wife of an Aborigine. Orig. coll, but by 1860 standard Australian. Ex Aborigine. 2. Hence, from ca 1880, occ. facetious of any woman or wife; also, an old woman (—1893); ob.

gin and fog. Hoarseness caused by alcohol: theatrical: from ca 1880.

gin-and-tatters. A dilapidated dram-drinker: coll (—1887).

gin-bottle. A 'dirty, abandoned, . . . debased woman . . . the victim of alcoholic abuse, within an ace of inevitable death': low urban (—1909); slightly ob. Ware.

gin-bud. A gin-induced tumour or pimple

on the face: low: ca 1820–95. cf. *brandy* BLOSSOM.

gin-crawl. A drinking-bout on gin: low coll. Ware quotes *The Bird o' Freedom* of 7 March 1883. cf. *pub-crawl.*

gin-ken. A gin shop: low: late C.18–19.

gin-lane. The throat: low: from ca 1830. cf. GIN-TRAP. 2. The habit of drunkenness, esp. on gin: from ca 1835. Ainsworth, 'Gin Lane's the nearest road to the churchyard.' cf. Hogarth's print, 1751.

gin-penny. Additional profit; BUNCE: costermongers': from ca 1850. Gen. spent on drink.

gin-spinner. A distiller: ca 1780–1900. On *cotton-spinner*. 2. Hence, a wine-vault: 1821, Pierce Egan, *Life in London*; † by 1890.

gin-trap. The mouth; the throat: low: ca 1825–1910. Pierce Egan, 1827.

gin-twist. A drink made of gin and water, lemon and sugar: orig. (—1823) coll; ob. cf. U.S. *gin-sling*.

gingambob, gingumbob; jiggumbob. A toy; bauble: late C.17–20 (ob.): coll. B.E. has the second, Grose the first spelling, the third being C.19–20. 2. (Gen. in pl.) The testicles: mid-C.18–20; ob. Grose (1st ed.), who adds: 'See *thingambobs*' (see THINGUMBOB).

ginger. Spirit, pluck, energy: from ca 1840: ?orig. U.S. R. L. Stevenson & Lloyd Osbourne in *The Wrecker*. 2. A cock with reddish plumage: from C.18. 3. A reddish or a sandy colour: from ca 1865, when used by Dickens. 4. A red- or sandy-haired person; CARROTS: 1823, Bee. Whence the profligate c.p., *Black for beauty, ginger for pluck*. 5. A fast, showy horse; one that is, or appears to have been, 'figged' (see FIG, v.): from ca 1815. 6. **(Ginger.)** The very frequent nickname of men surnamed Jones: naval and military: late C.19–20.

ginger, adj. Ginger-coloured; red- or sandy-haired (applied to persons and cocks): from ca 1825: also dial.

ginger-hackled. Red-haired (—1785): ob. Ex the cockpit. Also *ginger-pated*: coll (—1785).

ginger-pop. Ginger-beer: 1827 (S.O.D.): coll. 2. A policeman: 1887, 'Dagonet' Sims. Rhyming on SLOP.

ginger-up. To enliven: put mettle or spirit into: coll: from ca 1848: from ca 1890, S.E. Disraeli, 1849. Ex 'figging' (see FIG, v.) a horse (1823) or putting ginger in drinks (1825). Whence vbl n. *gingering-up*.

ginger-whiskers. A man, esp. a soldier, dyeing his whiskers yellow: ca 1820–60.

gingerbread. Money: from ca 1690; ob. Esp. in *have the gingerbread*, to be rich. 2. Showy but inferior goods: coll: mid-C.18–20; ob. Rare. Ex:

gingerbread, adj. Showily worthless: coll: 1748. Nautically, *gingerbread hatches* or *quarters*, luxurious accommodation or living (mid-C.19–20: coll); *g. work*, carved and gilded decorations (coll >, by 1800, S.E.: Smollett, 1757); *g. rigging*, wire-rigging (C.19: coll). 2. See GILT OFF THE GINGERBREAD.

gingerbread-office. A privy: C.17 coll. Ex GINGERBREAD, adj.

gingerbread-trap. The mouth: jocular coll: 1865, Dickens: ob.

gingerly, adj. and adv., is considered by F. & H. orig. to have been coll.

gingery. Red- or sandy-haired; CARROTY: from ca 1850: coll until C.20, when S.E. Miss Braddon, in *The Cloven Foot*, 'A false front of gingery curls'. 2. (Of horses) fiery: turf (—1823).

gingham. An umbrella (rightly, one made of gingham): coll: 1861.

gingle- (or jingle-)boy. A coin: C.17–18. Massinger & Dekker. 2. A gold coin: C.19. cf. YELLOW BOY and CHINKERS.

gingler or **jingler.** A coin: C.19–20; ob. Ex the preceding.

gingumbob, see GINGAMBOB.

ginnified. Stupefied with liquor, esp. and orig. with gin: coll: late C.19–20; ob.

ginnums. An old woman, esp. if fond of liquor, e.g. gin: low coll (—1893); ob.

***ginny.** 'An Instrument to lift up a Grate, the better to Steal what is in the window', B.E.: c.: ca 1670–1830. Head. ?ex dial. *ginny*, a (primitive) crane.

ginny. Affected by gin, applied esp. to the liver or the kidneys: coll: 1888. cf. *beery*.

gip. See GYP, all senses. 2. Abbr. GIPSY: from ca 1840: coll.

gip! Indicative of surprise or contempt; also = go away! C.16–17 coll. i.e. GEE UP.

gip (gyp, jip), give (a person). To thrash, punish, manhandle, give a bad time: dial. (—1898) >, by 1900 at latest, coll. Perhaps ex GEE UP.

'gip', quoth Gilbert when his mare farted (Howell, 1659); **'Gip with an ill rubbing', quoth Badger when his mare kicked** (Ray, 1678). A c.p. addressed to one who is 'pertish and forward'; †by 1800.

Gippoland. Egypt: military coll: from ca 1890.

Gippy, Gyppy. An Egyptian (soldier): military: late C.19–20.

Gippy tummy. Stomach-trouble in *Egypt* (hence also in Libya): Army: late C.19–20. Perhaps commoner in form *Gippo tummy*.

gipsy. A playful term of address to a woman, esp. if she is dark: 1858, George Eliot, but prob. in use some years earlier: coll. Ex. sense, a hussy (C.18–19); ex C.17–18 term of contempt.

girdle?, ne'er an M by your. Have you no manners? Esp., haven't you the politeness to say '*M*aster'? Coll: ca 1550–1850. Udall in *Roister Doister*; Swift; Scott.

girdle, under one's. In subjection; under one's control: ca 1540–1880: coll until C.18, then S.E.

girdle behind you, if you are angry you may turn the buckle of your. 'To one Angry for a small Matter, and whose Anger is as little valued', B.E.: late C.16–early 18 coll.

girl. One's sweetheart or *one's best* GIRL: coll: from ca 1790. e.g. 'Me and my girl'. 2. A mistress: coll: C.19–20: abbr. (*a*) *kind girl* (C.18). 3. A harlot: coll: from ca 1770. Abbr. *girl about*, or *of the town* (1711) and *girl of ease* (1756). cf. TART and see GIRLS.

girl, v.i. To consort with women; make love to a woman: Oxford University coll: from late C.18. See GIRLING.

girl, old. A woman of any age whatsoever: pet or pejorative term, in reference or in address: from ca 1845. 2. A term of address to a mare: a pet name: 1837, Dickens.

girl, one's best. The girl to whom one is engaged, or wishful to be; the fancy of the moment: coll: anglicized ca 1890; orig. U.S. cf. GIRL, 1.

girl and boy. A saveloy: rhyming s. (—1859). One of the comparatively few rhyming s. terms that – unless here an indelicate innuendo is meant – lack adequate reason or picturesqueness.

girl-catcher, see GIRLOMETER.

girl-getter. An affected, mincing, effeminate male: low coll: ca 1870–1910. Does *getter* here = *begetter*? For such a man usually disdains girls.

girl-shop. A brothel: low coll: from ca 1870: ob. cf. GIRLERY.

girl-show. A ballet or a revue, esp. one that in the 1890s was called a *leg-piece* and in C. 20 is known as a *leg-show* (see LEG-DRAMA): low coll: from ca 1880.

Girl Street, see HAIR COURT.

girl-trap. An habitual seducer: low coll: from ca 1870; ob.

girlery. A brothel (cf. GIRL-SHOP); a musical-comedy and revue theatre: the former from ca 1870, the latter from ca 1880: coll. Ex Lamb's *girlery*, girls collectively.

girlie. (Little) girl, mostly as an endearment: coll: late C.19–20.

girling, go. To go looking for loose women, professional or amateur: low coll: from late C.18. 'The maid said two men were missing, and the others said, God d..n them, they are gone a-girling,' *Sessions*, Jan. 1787.

girlometer, occ. **girl-catcher.** The male member: low jocular coll: from ca 1870; ob. Perhaps on FOOLOMETER.

girls, the. Harlots in the mass; lechery: coll: from ca 1850. cf.:

girls, to have been after the. To have syphilis or gonorrhoea: low coll: from ca 1860.

girls are (hauling) on the tow-rope, the. A coll naval c.p. = 'homeward bound'. Late C.19–20; ob.

girnigo-gaby the cat's cousin. A reproach to a weeping, a yelling child: C.19 coll. I surmise *girnigo-gaby* to be *crying-baby* corrupted; *cat's cousin* obviously refers to the shrill noise. But cf. GRINAGOG, which prob. suggested it by antiphrasis, and the dial. *girniga*(*w*), 'the cavity of the mouth'.

git! see GET! (Only occ. British.)

give, v. For phrases (e.g. *give the* GO-BY, *the* OFFICE (2), *the* TIP) not listed here, see the resp. nn.

give (someone) **a fair crack of the whip.** To 'play fair' with: North Country miners': late C.19–20.

give (a person) **a piece of one's mind.** Frankly to impart one's ill opinion of him in gen. or in particular: coll: 1865, Dickens.

give (someone) **a rap.** To reprove or reprimand: coll: mid-C.19–20; by 1890, S.E.

give (a woman) **a shot.** To coït with: low: C.19–20.

give and take. A race in which a horse is weighted according to its height: turf (—1769); ob. 2. A cake: rhyming s.: from ca 1860.

give away, give-away. The betrayal, whether deliberate or inadvertent, of a secret: from ca 1880.

give away, v. To betray; expose to punishment or ridicule: from ca 1878. In C.20 mainly – but not (?) orig. – U.S. Occ. *give dead away*. 2. v. reflexive, to let slip a secret: (—1883).

give-away cue. An underhand betrayal of a secret: low: from ca 1885.

give (a ship) **beans;** gen. **give her beans.** 'To crack on sail in a strong wind': nautical: late C.19–20; slightly ob. Bowen.

give (one) **best.** To acknowledge a person's superiority; admit defeat: orig. (—1883), in Australia, where also, as soon after in England, it = to give up trying at anything. Keighley, 1883, 'I went to work and gave the schooling best'; 'Rolf Boldrewood'. Prob. ex: 2. In c., to leave (a person), avoid or abandon him (—1877). Horsley, *Jottings from Gaol.*

give gip or **gyp,** see GIP, GIVE.

give her the rush. 'To run out of one's ground to hit the ball': cricketers' coll (—1888); slightly ob. – as is the practice.

give him a rolling for his all-over! Give him a *Roland* for his *Oliver*!: low Cockney (—1909).

***give in best.** To affect repentance: c.: from ca 1860.

give in . . . that. To admit, when close-pressed in argument, that . . .: coll (—1877).

give it a bone! Oh, stop talking!: from ca 1880. As if quieting a dog.

give it a drink! A c.p. hurled at a bad play or performance: theatrical and music-halls' (1897).

give it hot (with dative). To beat (soundly), scold (severely): coll: from ca 1870.

give it mouth! Speak up! Low coll: ca 1865–1910. Orig. and mainly to actors. H., 5th ed., cites 'He's the cove to give it mouth' as a 'low-folk' encomium. Perhaps on *to give tongue.*

***give it to** (a person) **for** (something). To rob or defraud one of: c.: ca 1810–50. 2. As to thrash or to scold, it was coll in C.18, but it soon > S.E. 3. To pull a person's leg: low (—1812); †by 1890.

give it (up) on?, what suit did you. How did you effect your purpose?: low (—1812); †by 1890.

give jessie, see JESSIE.

give lip to. To speak insolently to: from ca 1820: nautical >, ca 1860, gen. Haggart, 1821.

give (a ship) **muslin.** To make sail: nautical: late C.19–20; ob.

give nature a fillip. To indulge in wine and/or women: late C.17–19: coll.

give (a person) **one.** To give him a blow, a kiss, etc.: coll: C.19–20.

give (e.g. him) **one in the eye.** To thrash: occ. to scold: from ca 1880. cf. GIVE IT HOT; GIVE SOMETHING FOR HIMSELF; GIVE WHAT FOR.

give one's head for naught (late C.14–15) or **for the washing** (late C.16–mid-19). 'To submit to be imposed on', Halliwell.

give sky-high. To scold (a person) immoderately: proletarian: from ca 1870; ob.

give (a ship) **something else to do.** Constantly to work the helm in order to check rolling or pitching: nautical: late C.19–20.

give (a person) **something for himself.** To thrash; reprimand: coll: late C.19–20.

give the bag, bullet, kick-out, pike, road, sack. To dismiss from one's employ: coll: see the separate nn. *Bag* is the early form of *sack*, but see esp. BAG. *Pike* and *road* are rare; the former †, the latter ob. *Get* is commoner than *give the kick-out.*

give the crock. To yield victory: lower classes': from ca 1880; very ob.

give the go. To reject (a suitor): New Zealand: late C.19–20. (G. B. Lancaster, *Sons o' Men*, 1904.) For . . . GO-BY. Also *give the* MITTEN. 2. Also to abandon (a country, a job): New Zealand and Australian: late C.19–20. G. B. Lancaster, 1904.

give (a person) **the ros(e)y.** To blush at chaff: tailors'. From ca 1890.

give the slip; either with **us,** etc., or absolutely. To die: coll: since ca 1830. Emily Brontë, *Wuthering Heights*, 1847. Ex fox hunting.

give way. (Of women) to permit the sexual embrace (—1870). Perhaps orig. euphemistic and S.E., as often it still is; but it also is a humorous coll.

give what for; occ. **what's what.** (With dative.) To beat, thrash: scold, reprimand: coll, the former C.19–20, the latter C.20 and gen. jocular.

given the deep six, be. To be heaved overboard; to be buried at sea: nautical: late C.19–20. A body must be laid in not less than six fathoms of water.

giver. A good boxer, esp. one with a hard punch: pugilistic: ca 1820–1900. 'Peter Corcoran' Reynolds in *The Fancy.*

gixie. An affected, mincing woman; late C.16–early 17. 2. A wanton wench: C.17. Both senses coll on verge of respectability, the former being in Florio, the latter in Cotgrave, who remarks: 'A fained word'. Perhaps ex GIG after *tricksy* (*trixy* in an old spelling).

gizz. A face: Scottish: C.19. From *guise*, a mask. Perhaps influenced by PHIZ.

gizzard, fret one's. To worry oneself: low coll (—1755); ob. Johnson. cf. FRET.

gizzard, grumble in the. To be secretly annoyed: coll (—1765): anticipated in C.17 (?ex Yorkshire dial.). Whence *grumble-gizzard*, with which cf. GRUMBLE-GUTS.

gizzard, stick in one's. To continue to displease or render indignant: coll: from ca 1660. Pepys; Swift, 'Don't let that stick in your gizzard'; in late C.19–20, almost S.E. Ex the lit, sense, to prove indigestible.

***gladd(h)er.** (Often as vbl n.) To employ a certain unascertained trick to relieve good citizens of their money. c. of ca 1865; app. †by 1900. Either from Welsh Gypsy *glathera*, 'solder, pewter', ex Shelta; or direct from Shelta.

gladstonize. To say a lot and mean little: coll: ca 1885–1900.

***glanthorne.** Money: c.: late C.18–early 19. George Parker. ?*lanthorn* corrupted.

glarney (or **-ny**). A corruption of GLASSER: Cockney: late C.19–20.

Glasgow boat. A coat: Anglo-Irish rhyming s.: late C.19–20.

Glasgow magistrate. A superior herring: inferentially from H., from ca 1830. Ob. cf. ATLANTIC RANGER; BILLINGSGATE PHEASANT; DIGBY CHICKEN; DUNBAR WETHER; GOUROCK HAM; TAUNTON TURKEY; YARMOUTH CAPON.

***glasiers,** see GLAZIER, 2.

***glass.** An hour: c.: from ca 1860; ob.

glass, (to have) been looking through a. (To be) drunk: coll: from ca 1860; ob.

glass?, who's to pay for the broken. Who is to pay for the damages? Coll: C.19–20: ob.

glass about, there's a deal of. It is a fine (though vulgar) display: low coll. 2. A c.p. retort to the boast of an achievement: low coll. Both ca 1880–1914.

glass of beer. Ear: rhyming s.: since ca 1880.

glass of something. An alcoholic drink: coll, orig. euphemistic: late C.19–20. Elliptical for *glass of something strong*.

glass case: A face: Cockney rhyming s.: —1857.

glass-eyes. A person wearing spectacles: coll: ca 1785–1900.

glass-house. A guard-room, esp. detention barracks or cells for long-term prisoners: Army: from ca 1905.

glass-house, live in a. To lay oneself open to criticism: coll: from ca 1845; now virtually S.E. Prob. suggested by the C.17–20 proverb, *those who live in glass houses shouldn't throw stones.*

***glass-work.** A method of cheating at cards by means of a tiny convex mirror attached to the palm of the dealer's hand: ca 1820–1905: c.

glasser; glassy. A glass marble with coloured centre: from ca 1880: resp. Irish and London schoolboys'.

***glasyers,** see GLAZIER, 2.

***glaze.** A window: c. of ca 1690–1890. 2. Eye; eyesight: c. (—1788); †by 1900. See GLAZE, MILL A.

***glaze,** v. (Of the dealer) to cheat, with a mirror, at cards: low or c.: ca 1820–80. (See GLASS-WORK.) Pierce Egan.

***glaze, mill** or **star a** or **the.** To break a window: c.: ca 1785–1890. 2. Grose, 2nd ed. (1788), at *mill*, has 'I'll mill your glaze; I'll beat out your eye,' †by 1900.

***glaze, on the,** adj. and adv. (By) robbing jewellers' windows after smashing them: c.: from ca 1719. Johnson's *Pirates and Highwaymen.*

***glaze, spank a** or **the.** To break a window with the fist: c. (—1839).

***glazier.** 'One that creeps in at Casements, or unrips Glass-windows to Filch and Steal', B.E.: c.: mid-C.17–early 19. Head, 1673. 2. pl only (in C.16–17 often spelt *glasiers* or *glasyers*), the eyes: c. of ca 1560–1830. Harman. cf.:

glazier?, is, rarely **was, your father a.** A c.p. addressed to one who stands in the light – esp. in front of a window, a fire, a candle, or a lamp. Grose (2nd ed.), who adds: 'If it is answered in the negative, the rejoinder is – I wish he was, that he might make a window through your body, to enable us to see the fire or light.' From ca 1786.

***glaziers,** see GLAZIER, 2.

glean, v.t. and i.; **gleaning,** vbl n. To steal; stealing: c. or low: ca 1860–1910. Greenwood, *The Little Ragamuffin*, ca 1880, 'Pinchin', findin', gleanin', some coves call it.'

gleaner. A thief of 'unconsidered trifles': low or c.: ca 1860–1900. Ex the preceding.

***glib;** in C.18, occ. **glibb.** A ribbon: c.: mid-C.18–early 19. ?ex its smoothness. 2. The tongue: mid-C.19–20; ob. Esp. in SLACKEN YOUR GLIB! don't talk so much! ?ex *glib-t(ongued)*, which F. & H. wrongly include.

glib-gabbed or **-gabbet.** Smooth and ready of speech: nautical: mid-C.19–20; ob.

***glim, glym.** A thief's dark lantern: late

C.17–early 19 c. Perhaps abbr. *glimmer* (of light). 2. Hence, a candle: c. (—1714); †by 1840, except in *douse the* GLIM. 3. A light of any kind: c. (—1728). 4. A fire: c. (—1785). Abbr. *glimmer, glymmar* or *-er*. 5. Whence, ca 1840–90, the sham account of a fire sold by a FLYING STATIONER. 6. Low or c. is the sense, a venereal infection, ex that of fire: ca 1850–1900. 7. See GLIMS. 8. Eye-sight: c. of ca 1820–60. Ex GLIMS, 1. 9. A fiery drink (?gin): ca 1750–70. Toldervy, 1756. cf. RUSH-LIGHT.

***glim,** v. To burn, i.e. brand, in the hand: c.: late C.17–early 19. Ex preceding.

***glim, douse the.** To put out the light, gen. in imperative: orig., C.18, c.; ca 1840, it > s., mainly nautical. Ex GLIM, n., 1–4. See DOUSE.

***glim-fender.** An andiron: c. of ca 1670–1820. A RUM *g.-f.* was of silver. Ex GLIM, n. 2. A handcuff (but rare in singular): c.: ca 1820–70. Punning sense 1.

***glim-flash(e)y;** in C.17, occ. **glimflashy.** Angry: c.: late C.17–mid-19. Lytton, 'No, Captain, don't be glimflashy!'

***glim-glibber.** A jargon; applied esp. to underworld cant: low or perhaps c. (—1844): †by 1910. If *glibber* perverts GIBBER(ISH), then, lit., the term = a 'dark-lantern' gibberish or lingo.

***glim-jack.** A link-boy; occ. a thief operating at night: c.: mid-C.17–early 19.

***glim-lurk.** A beggar's petition alleging loss by fire: c. of ca 1845–80. Ex GLIM, n., 5. Mayhew. cf. LURKER and see LURK.

***glim-stick, glimstick.** A candlestick: c. of ca 1670–1830. A RUM *g.-s.* is of silver, a QUEER *g.-s.* is of brass, pewter, or iron. cf. GLIM, n., 2. See GLIM-FENDER.

***glimmer, glymmar** or **-er.** Fire: c. of ca 1560–1830. cf. GLIM, n., 4. 2. See GLIMMERS.

***glimmerer.** A beggar alleging loss by fire: ca 1600–1830: c. Dekker & Wilkins; B.E. cf. GLIMMER and:

***glimmering mort.** A female GLIMMERER: ca 1560–1660 c. See MORT.

glimmers. The eyes (pl only): from ca 1814: low: ob. Ex GLIMMER.

glimmery. (Of an actor) having no clear conception of his part: theatrical: 1892: ob. *Athenaeum*, 9 April 1892.

***glims,** pl only: eyes. From ca 1790: c. > low s.: ob. 2. Whence, in pl only, a pair of spectacles: orig. c., then low: from ca 1860: ob.

glims, puff the. 'To fill the hollow over the eyes of old horses by pricking the skin and blowing air into the loose tissues underneath, thus giving the full effect of youth', F. & H.: shady horse-dealing and veterinary surgery: from ca 1870.

glip. 'The track of oil left by a fast-swimming whale': whalers' and sailors': mid-C.19–20. Bowen. Perhaps cognate with Scottish and Northern *glid*, smooth (E.D.D.), possibly influenced by *slippery*: cf. Northern *gliddy*, oily.

***glist(e)ner.** A sovereign: c. >, ca 1830, low: from ca 1815. T. Moore. cf. SHINERS and YELLOW BOY.

***glister.** A glass or tumbler: c. (—1889). ?ex the S.E. n. and v., *glister*.

***gloach;** gen., **gloak.** A man: c. (—1795), Scottish according to Pierce Egan (1823); †by 1875. ?cognate with BLOKE. cf. GILL and GORY.

***globe.** Pewter; a pewter pot: c.: late C. 18–mid-19. Ex the shape.

globe-trotter. A merely quantitative or spatial traveller: coll (—1883): ob. Hence a long-distance or a frequent traveller: coll: from ca 1892. *Graphic*, 7 August 1886, 'Your mere idle gaping globe-trotter.'

globe-trotting is the vbl n. to GLOBE-TROTTER.

globes. The female breasts: coll: from ca 1860; ob.

glope. To spit: ca 1830–80: Winchester College. cf. dial. *gloup*, to gulp.

glorification. A festive occasion, a SPREE: coll: 1843. 2. A GLORIFIED variety or example of something usually inferior or unimpressive: coll: from ca 1885.

glorified. Changed into something glorious (often sarcastically): coll: from ca 1820. Lamb; Thackeray, 'A glorified flunkey.'

glorious. Divinely or ecstatically drunk: coll: 1790, Burns (O.E.D.); Thackeray, 'I was taken up glorious as the phrase is, . . . and put to bed.'

glorious sinner. A dinner: rhyming s. (—1859). ?satirizing gluttony.

gloriously. Ecstatically: always with *drunk* explicit or implicit. Coll: 1784. Cowper.

glory! is a low coll exclamation of delight (—1893). Quiller-Couch. Also *great glory!* and *how the glory!* Abbr. *glory be to God!*

glory, go to. To die: coll: 1814. *Punch*, 1841. Ex *glory*, 'the splendour and bliss of heaven', S.O.D.

glory, in one's. Extremely gratified: coll: 1895. 2. Esp. *leave one in his glory*, to depart, so that now he is (or sits) alone: 1887, Baumann.

***glory-hole.** A small cell in which, at the court, prisoners are kept on the day of trial: c.: 1845. 2. A Salvation Army meeting-place: low: 1887; ob. 3. The fore peak: nautical: late C.19–20; ob. 4. Hence, the stewards' quarters: nautical: late C.19–20.

gloss off, take the; gen. as c.p., it takes . . . It lessens the profit or the value: tailors': mid-C.19–20.

glove. A kind of drinking vessel: early C.17. Dekker in *The Gull's Horn-Book.*

glove, fit like a, see FIT LIKE A GLOVE.

gloves, go for the. To bet recklessly: the turf: from ca 1870; ob. Ex women's tendency to bet in pairs of gloves on the 'heads I win, tails you lose' principle.

gloves, win a pair of. To kiss a sleeping man: a kindly act meriting this reward: coll: from ca 1710: ob. Gay, Grose.

glow, adj. Ashamed: tailors': ca 1870–1914. Ex *a glow of shame.*

glow, (all) of a. Coll for *in a glow*: 1865, Dickens.

glow, got the, see GOT THE GLOW.

glue. Thick soup: C.19–20. It sticks to the ribs! cf. DEFERRED STOCK. 2. Gonorrhoea: low: from ca 1870.

glue did not hold, the. 'You were baulked . . . you missed your aim,' Ray, 1813: coll: C.19.

glue-pot. A parson: mid-C.18–20, ob. He joins couples together. 2. 'Part of the road so bad that the coach or buggy' – or motorcar – 'sticks in it', Morris: Australian coll: recorded in 1892, but prob. dating from the 1870s or even 60s; ob. 3. A convivial public-house: pub-frequenters': from ca 1880; ob. Ex its 'flypaper' attractiveness.

glue-pot has come unstuck, a or the. He gives off the odour of a genital exudation or of a seminal emission: a low c.p.: from ca 1890.

glum-pot. A gloomy or glum person: coll: late C.19–20.

glutman. A rush-time extra hand in the Customs: coll verging on S.E.: ca 1790–1850. See that interesting book, Colquhoun's *The Police of the Metropolis*, 1796.

glutton. A boxer that takes a lot of punishment before he is 'satisfied': pugilism: 1809. cf. the S.E. *glutton for work.* 2. A horse that stays well: racing s. > gen. from ca 1850.

gluttony. Willingness to take, fortitude in taking, punishment: pugilistic: ca 1810–60. *Boxiana*, 1818. cf. preceding.

***glybe.** A writing: c. (—1785); †by 1890. A perversion of GYBE.

***glym** and its derivatives are defined at the preferable GLIM, etc.

gnaff or **n'aff.** A low, irritating, no-account fellow, inaverse from petty theft or from informing to the police: low Glasgow: mid-C.19–20. cf. Parisian s. *gniaffe*, a term of abuse for a man; prob. of same origin as GONNOF.

***gnarl upon; gnarling,** adj. To spy or SPLIT (2) on (a person); doing this, apt to do this: c. of ca 1810–60. cf.:

***gnarler.** A watch-dog: c.: C.19. Lit., a snarler. cf. BLEATING *cheat.*

***gnarling,** see GNARL UPON.

gnasp. To vex: coll: C.18–early 19. Bailey has it.

***gnawler.** A late C.19–20 c. variant of GNARLER.

***gnoff,** see GONNOF.

gnomon. The nose: jocular coll: ca 1580–1820. Stanyhurst, Cowper.

gnostic. A knowing person, a DOWNY BIRD: 1815–1900, but already ob. in 1859. Moore, in *Tom Crib*, 'Many of the words used by the Canting Beggars in Beaumont and Fletcher's masque are still to be heard among the gnostics of Dyot Street and Tothill Fields.' 2. Also as adj. (†).

gnostically. Artfully; knowingly; flashily: ca 1820–95. Scott.

go. For the phrases not listed here, see the significant n. or adj.

go. A three-halfpenny bowl of gin and water, esp. – and orig. – if sold at the GO-SHOP: ca 1787–1820. 2. Whence (?) a draught, a drink: from ca 1800. *Punch*, 1841, 'Waiter, a go of Brett's best alcohol.' Specifically, a quartern of brandy: same period. Thackeray in *The Hoggarty Diamond*, 'Two more chairs . . . and two more goes of gin?' Synonyms of the former are: BENDER, 4; *coffin-nail*; DRAIN; FACER; GARGLE; LOTION; NOBBLER, 7; PEG; REVIVER; SLUG; *something*; SWIG; TOT, 4; *warmer*; WET; etc., etc. 2*a*. Hence, of food, as in 'We had a good go of cherries (of ices)', Baumann, 1887. 3. The fashion, esp. in ALL THE GO and, late C.19–20, *quite the go – the go* having > † ca 1840; the correct thing: from ca 1787 (Grose's annotations to 1st ed. copy in the British Museum): s. > coll. G. R. Sims, 1880, 'And all day long there's a big crowd stops | To look at the lady who's all the go.'

4. Hence, in the 1820s, a dandy, a notable swell. Egan, 1821, 'In the parks, Tom was the go among the goes.' 5. An affair, incident, occurrence: coll or low coll: 1796 (O.E.D.). Kenney, 1803, 'Capital go, isn't it?' (this stock phrase = a pleasant business); Dickens, 'A pretty go!' (stock, = a startling or awkward business or situation etc.); G. Eliot, 'A rum go' q.v. (stock, with variant *rummy* = a queer start, a strange affair). 6. Hence (—1877), an occasion, a time; e.g. 'I've twelve this go' = I have [received] twelve [years] this time. 7. High spirits; mettle, spirit; energy, enterprise: coll: 1825, Westmacott, in *The English Spy*. 8. A turn, an attempt: coll: U.S. (1825), anglicized ca 1835. Dickens, 'Wot do you think o' that for a go?' Gen. in *have a go at*, the object being anything from an abstruse subject to a woman. 9. A success, esp. in *make a go of it*, (C.20) *make it a go*: orig. (—1877), U.S.; anglicized ca 1895. 10. An occasion of coïtion: low: mid-C.19–20.

go, v. Abbr. GO DOWN, v., 1: from ca 1740; coll. Fielding. 2. Gen. with *for*, as *to go for to* (do something), to be so foolish, brave, strict, etc., as to . . . sol. or low coll: from ca 1750. 3. v.t., to wager, risk: 1768, Goldsmith: coll. Hence, to afford: from ca 1870. Also to stand treat: from ca 1875. 4. (Of things) to succeed: coll: from ca 1690; *London Opinion*, 13 Jan. 1866, 'His London-street railway scheme didn't go'; H. D. Traill, 1870. 5. Hence, to be accepted or acceptable; to be valid or applicable: coll; *The Night Watch*, 1828. 6. (Of a politician or a constituency, with adj., as in 'Chelsea went red', 'Mr Maxton went conservative') to become: coll: from ca 1889; ex U.S. 7. To ride to hounds: from ca 1840: sporting s. >, ca 1895, j. 8. v.t., to eat: nautical: late C.19–20. Prob. ex sense 4, nuance 1. 9. Hence, to digest: mostly Canadian: late C.19–20. 10. 'How do they go?' = How do they get along together?: upper class: late C.19–20. Ex a pair of carriage horses.

go, a little bit on the. Slightly drunk: ca 1820–80.

'go', from the word. From the start: coll: orig. (—1838) U.S.; anglicized ca 1890.

go, great and **little,** see GREAT GO; LITTLE GO.

go, high, see HIGH GO.

go, near. A narrow escape: coll: from ca 1825.

go, no. Either with *to be* or as an exclamation: from ca 1810: Dickens, 'I know something about this here family, and my opinion is, it's no go.' Occ. abbr. *n.g.* (ob.).

go, on the. On the verge of ruin or destruction: late C.17–18: coll. It survived till ca 1850 in the nuance (of tradesmen) 'about to abscond'. 2. In a (state of) decline: coll: ca 1725–1880. FitzGerald, 1842 (in a letter), 'As to poor old England, I never see a paper, but I think with you that she is on the go.' 3. Slightly drunk: 1821, Egan; very ob. 4. On the move; busy; restlessly active: coll: from ca 1840.

***go abroad.** To be transported: ca 1825–1900: c. >, by 1860, low. cf. ABROADED.

go-ahead, adj. Progressive: anxious to succeed – and usually succeeding: ex U.S. (like *going-ahead*, it occurs in 1840); anglicized ca 1865.

go ahead! All right! Proceed! Ex U.S. (1835), anglicized ca 1868.

go along with you! A variant (mid-C.19–20) of GET ALONG WITH YOU!

***go-along(er).** A fool; an easy dupe: c. of resp. ca 1845–1914 (Mayhew) and ca 1810–90 (Vaux). Because he goes along when bid. 2. A thief: c. (—1857). (This sense: only in the form *go-along*.)

go along, Bob!; come along, Bob! These two c.pp., of ca 1800–30, are of problematic and dubious meaning.

go-alonger, see GO-ALONG(ER).

go and (do something). Where the *go and* represents a mere pleonasm, the usage is coll: from C.15 or C.16. 2. If = to be so silly, foolish, or unlucky as to do something, it is also coll: from ca 1875. cf. BEEN AND GONE AND . . .

go and bust yourself! You *be* BLOWED!: low: from ca 1860; ob.

go and eat coke! A c.p. indicative of impatient contempt: London slums' (—1909).

go and fuck yourself! A low equivalent of 'You be blowed!': from ca 1880.

go as you please, adj. Unconfined by rules: athletics, ca 1880. Hence, characterized by a general freedom of action: 1884: coll.

go-ashore. 'An iron pot or cauldron, with three iron feet, and two ears, from which it was suspended by a wire handle over the fire,' Morris: New Zealand coll (—1834) >, by 1880, S.E. Ex Maori *kohua* by 'Hobson-Jobson'.

go-ashores. 'The seaman's best dress', Smyth, 1867: nautical coll: from ca 1850: ob.

go at. To deal vigorously with (something): ?late C.18–mid-19. 'They can "go" at the bottle, and "stick" at the table till "all's blue" ': John L. Gardner, *The Military Sketch-Book* (II, 28), 1831.

go at, have a, see GO, n., 8.

go-away. Abbr. *go-away dress* (a bride's): Society coll: 1886.

go back of, see GO BACK ON. 2. See GO BEHIND.

go back on, v.t. To desert, turn against, or to fail, a person; break a promise: ex U.S. (1868); anglicized ca 1895. Variant *go back of* (not with persons): 1888.

go bail!, I will or **I'll.** I'll be bound! I'm sure! Assuredly! Coll: from ca 1880. Rider Haggard, in *Dawn*, 'He won't marry her now, I'll go bail'. Ob.

go behind, v.t. 'To disregard the writing for the sake of ascertaining the fact', Thornton: orig. (1839; popularized in 1876), U.S.; anglicized as a coll ca 1890. The variant *go back of* (late C.19–20) is rare in Britain, frequent in U.S.

go beyond. Be transported as a convict: Anglo-Irish: ca 1810–70, i.e. beyond the sea.

go-by. The act of passing without recognizing (a person), dealing with or taking (a thing); an evasion or a deception. Esp. in *give* (e.g. him or it) *the go-by*, to ignore; to abandon; to refuse to recognize: from ca 1640: in C.17–18, and indeed until ca 1860, S.E.; then coll. Stevenson, 'A French ship . . . gave us the go-by in the fog.' Also common in *get the go-by*, the corresponding passive.

go-by-the-ground. 'A little short person', Grose, 2nd ed.: C.18–19 coll; ob. except in dial. In late C.16–17, *go-by-ground* (also, C.17, adj.). cf. Lincolnshire *go-by-the-wall*, a creeping, helpless person.

go close. Abbr. *go close to the winning-post*: sporting coll (—1909).

go dog on. To fail (a person); to betray: Australian: late C.19–20.

***go down.** To rob (someone): since ca 1880: c. until C.20, then low s. *Sessions*, 27 June 1901, 'I was along with two men, and they *went down* a man': i.e. down into his pockets.

go-down. A drink: mid-C.17–18: s. >, by 1700, coll. D'Urfey, Ned Ward. Later GO, n., 2. The term survives in dial.

go down, v.i.; **go down with,** v.t. To be accepted (by); be approved or allowed: C.17–20: in C.17–18, S.E.; then coll. Dekker; Pepys; Smollett, 'That won't go down with me.' cf. GO, v., 3. 2. v.i., be rusticated: university: ca 1860–1900. 3. To become bankrupt: coll (—1892): ob. Also GO UNDER.

go down one. To be vanquished: Cockneys' coll (—1909). Ex *going down one place* in school.

go due north. To go bankrupt: ca 1810–80. i.e. to White-Cross Street Prison, once (†before 1893) situated in the north of London.

go fanti. To return to primitive life: scientific: from ca 1880; ob.

go for. To attempt (to do); undertake: coll: from ca 1860; ob.; orig. (—1871), U.S. – cf. that U.S. sense, to be in favour of, support, vote for, which is occ. found in coll English ca 1880–1910. 2. To attack, physically, lingually, or in writing (hence, esp. in the theatre, to criticize adversely): ex U.S. (1838); anglicized ca 1870. Baumann, 1887; *Polytechnic Magazine*, 24 Oct. 1889, 'He went for the jam tarts unmercifully.'

go for the gloves, see GLOVES, GO FOR THE.

go-in, gen. followed by **at.** A lit. or fig. attack: 1858. 2. A turn of work (—1890). Both coll.

go in, v.i. To enter oneself; set about it; try: from ca 1835: from ca 1890, S.E. Dickens, 'Go in and win', advice offered to the weaker in a contest, esp. fisticuffs. 2. To die: military in the Boer War. J. Milne, *The Epistles of Atkins*, 1902. Ex dial. sense, 'to come to an end'.

go in at. To assail vigorously: coll: from ca 1810. In 1849, Dickens, 'Sometimes I go in at the butcher madly, and cut my knuckles open against his face.' Ob.

go in for. To seek; attempt to obtain; make one's object: coll: from ca 1860. Dickens, 'Go in for money – money's the article,' 1864. 2. Hence, apply oneself to, take up (e.g. as a hobby); to begin to do, to adopt as a profession, study as a subject: coll: from ca 1870. 3. To enter oneself as a candidate for: coll: from ca 1879. 4. To venture on obtaining or on wearing: coll: from ca 1890. 5. To court (a woman). Society s. of ca 1865–1900. Whyte-Melville in *M. or N.* cf. GO IN and GO FOR, 1.

go into. Attack vigorously; punch fast and hard: boxing: 1811: ob. by 1910.

go it; often **go it strong,** in C.20 occ. **go it thick.** To act vigorously and/or daringly; speak very strongly or frankly: coll: C.19–20. J. H. Lewis, *The Art of Writing*, 7th ed., 1816 (in reference to boxers fighting vigorously). Dickens, 'I say, young Copperfield, you're going it.' 2. Hence, to live expensively and/or dissipatedly: coll (—1821). Egan, in *Tom and Jerry*, 'To go it, where's a place like London?'

go it! Keep at it! Play, fight, etc., hard! Coll: from ca 1820. ?ex *go it, you* CRIPPLE, (*crutches are cheap*).

go it blind. To act without considering the consequences; esp. to 'speed', physically or morally: from ca 1840. 2. To drink heavily: Cockney: late C.19–20.

go it strong (or thick), see GO IT.

go-off. (Time of) commencement: coll: 1851 (O.E.D.). Esp. in the ob. *at one go-off* (1856) and in *at (the) first go-off*, at the very beginning: from ca 1879. 2. In banking s., from ca 1890, 'the amount of loans falling due (. . . going off the amount in the books) in a certain period', O.E.D.

go off, v. To die: C.17–20 (ob.): coll. Shakespeare; Dickens, 'She . . . was seized with a fit and went off.' 2. To be disposed of: goods by sale, women in marriage. Dickens, of the latter, in *Boz*. 3. To take place, occur; occ. it almost = to succeed. Coll: from ca 1804. Maria Edgeworth; Mrs Gaskell, 'The wedding went off much as such affairs do.' 4. To deteriorate in freshness or (e.g. a horse) in form: coll (—1883). 5. (Contrast sense 3.) Not to take place: Society: ca 1885–1915.

go off the hooks. To die: from ca 1830; ob.

go on. To talk volubly: coll: from ca 1860. With *at*, to rail at: coll: 1873.

go on! An exclamation of surprise, incredulity, or derision: coll: from ca 1875.

go on about; be always on about. To complain of or about; (*be* . . .) to do this habitually: coll: since ca 1880. cf. ON AT.

***go on, orig. upon, the dub.** To go housebreaking: late C.17–early 19 c. See DUB.

***go out,** v.i. To rob in the streets: c. (—1823); ob. Bee, ' "I don't *go out*, now," said by a reformed rogue'. cf. next entry. 2. To fall into disuse or into social disrepute: coll: 1840 (O.E.D.). *Punch*, 1841, 'Pockets . . . to use the flippant idiom of the day, are going out.' 3. To fight a duel: (?mostly Army) coll: late C.18–mid-C.19.

***go out foreign.** To emigrate under shady circumstances: c. (—1909). Ware.

***go out together.** To go, habitually, thieving in company: c. of ca 1810–90. cf. GO OUT, 1.

go out with the ebb. To die: nautical coll: late C.19–20. cf. GO WEST.

go over, to desert, is C.17–20 S.E.; but it is clerical s. when it = to join the Church of Rome (—1861). cf. VERT. 2. To die: coll: from ca 1845. Abbr. *go over to join the majority*. cf. GO OFF. 3. In c., to search and rob a person (—1889). cf. GO THROUGH.

go phut, see PHUT, GO.

go round, v.i. To pay an informal visit: coll: 1873, W. Black.

go round the buoy. To have a second helping of any food: nautical: late C.19–20. Bowen.

Go-Shop, the. The Queen's Head tavern in Duke's Court, Bow Street (London, W.C.2): late C.18–early 19. 'Frequented by the under players', Grose, 2nd ed. Ex GO, n., 1.

***go sideways.** To engage in a criminal enterprise: c.: from ca 1890; ob. Clarence Rook, *The Hooligan Nights*, 1899. 'Young Alf recounted this incident in his career, in order to illustrate his thesis that if you want to go sideways you have got to have your tale ready to pitch.'

***go the jump.** To enter a house by the window: c.: C.19.

go the whole hog. To act thorough-goingly: ex U.S. (1828); anglicized ca 1850. See esp. Thornton and W.

go through. To rob: ex U.S. (1867); anglicized ca 1895. 2. To possess a woman: low coll: from ca 1870.

go through the Chapter House. (Of the ball) to pass through the stumps, in the days when there were only two: cricketers': mid-C.18–early 19.

go through with. To complete (a difficult or distasteful task or duty): mid-C.16–20: S.E. until ca 1890, then of a coll tendency.

go to Bath, etc., see BATH; HALIFAX; HANOVER; JERICHO; PUTNEY.

go to do. To go and do; to do: proletarian coll: late C.19–20.

go to grass. To abscond; disappear suddenly. Gen. in present perfect tense or as ppl phrase, *gone to grass*. ca 1850–90. 2. See GRASS, GO TO. 3. To fall sprawling: pugilists': from ca 1840; ob.

go to grass! 'A common answer to a troublesome or inquisitive person', H., 1859: ob. by 1880, †by 1900 in England: orig. (—1848), U.S.

go to grass with one's teeth upwards. To be buried: from ca 1810. 2. Hence, to die: coll: from ca 1820: †by 1910. cf. and see LANDOWNER and cf. the Devonshire *go* *round land.* ?an elaboration of the C.17 *go to grass*, to succumb, be knocked down.

go to heaven in a string. To be hanged: coll: ca 1590–1800. Greene, 1592.

go to hell and pump thunder! A late C.19 c.p. indicative of utter incredulity or derision. See GOOSE, GO SHOE THE.

go to Hell or Connaught! Go where you like, but don't bother me with where you're going!: coll: from 1654. Ex a Parliamentary Act of that date.

go-to-meeting, adj. Best (of clothes): coll: ex U.S. (1825); anglicized ca 1850, 'Cuthbert Bede' having 'His black go-to-meeting bags'. Often preceded by *Sunday*.

go to pot, see POT, GO TO.

go to the dogs, see DOGS.

go under. To become bankrupt; disappear from Society: coll (—1879). 2. To succumb: coll (—1891). 'He had "gone under" in the struggle, as the terribly expressive phrase runs,' H. C. Halliday, 1891. 3. To die: orig. (—1849), U.S.; anglicized ca 1870, but never very gen.

go up. To be ruined, financially, socially, or politically: coll (—1864): ob. More gen. in U.S. than in Britain.

go up for. To sit for (an examination): coll: from ca 1885.

go up one! Good for you!: a c.p. of late C.19–20. Ex school-teacher's promotion of a successful pupil.

go west. To die: popularized in the First World War, but adumbrated in late C.16–18, as in Greene, *Cony-Catching*, Part II, 1592. 'So long the foists [thieves] put their villanie in practice, that West-ward they goe, and there solemnly make a rehearsall sermon at Tiborne.' The basic idea is that of the setting sun; pioneering in North America may have contributed. See esp. *Words!*

go with. (Of things) to harmonize or suit: 1710: S.E. until ca 1880, then of a coll hue. 2. To 'walk out with'; to affect in friendship or, gen., passion or love: low coll: from ca 1880. 3. To share the sexual congress with: low coll: from ca 1870.

***goad.** A decoy at auctions or horse-sales: c.: C.17–mid-18. Contrast:

***goads.** False dice: c.: C.18-early 19. cf. CHAPMAN.

goanna; gohanna; guana; guano. An 'iguana', i.e. a monitor lizard: Australian coll: resp. —1891; 1896 (Henry Lawson), but ob.; 1830 (†by 1910); and 1802 (Barrington) – but †by 1900.

goat, a lecher, is not unconventional, but *goat*, to thrash, is low coll of ca 1860–1910. *Derby Day*, 1864. 2. A Maltese: nautical (esp. naval): late C.19–20. 3. *Sinks*, 1848, s.v. 'stern', defines *the goat* as 'posteriors' – very much earlier than one had thought! 4. A fool: coll: late C.19–20.

goat, play the. To play the fool: 1879: coll. In late C.19–20, *giddy* is often added before *goat*. See also GIDDY GOAT. 2. To lead a dissipated life, esp. sexually: low: from ca 1885. 3. (Of the male) to fornicate hard: s. or low coll: C.19–20; ob.

goat, ride the. To be initiated into a secret society, esp. the Masons: low coll: from ca 1870. Ex the superstition that a goat, for candidates to ride, is kept by every Masonic lodge.

goat-house. A brothel: C.19 coll. Ex *goat*, a lascivious man.

goat-milker. A harlot: from ca 1820. cf. GOAT-HOUSE, brothel. 2. The female pudend; low: from ca 1840.

goatee. A tufted beard on the point of a shaven chin: from ca 1855: in C.19, coll; in C.20, S.E. Ex the tuft on a he-goat's chin.

goats and monkeys (at), look. To gaze lecherously (at): coll: 1749, Cleland; †by 1890 at the latest.

goat's gig(g) or jig. Gen. or specific copulation: mid-C.18–early 19: low coll. Grose, 1st ed., 'making the beast with two backs'.

goat's wool. Something non-existent: proverbial coll: late C.16–20; ob. Ex L. *lana caprina*.

gob. A slimy lump or clot, esp. of spittle: mid-C.16–20; S.E. till ca 1830, then dial. and low coll. 2. The mouth: s. when not, as in the North, dial.: mid-C.16–20. cf. GAB, n. 3. A portion: London schoolboys' (—1887). Also gen. s. (—1859).

gob, v. To swallow in large mouthfuls; gulp: low: C.18–20. Abbr. *gobble*. 2. To spit, esp. copiously: C.19–20 low coll.

gob, have the gift of the. To be wide-mouthed: late C.17–18. 2. To speak fluently, sing well: late C.17–early 19. cf. GAB, GIFT OF THE.

gob-box. The mouth: low: ca 1770–1910. Scott, in *Lammermoor*, 'Your characters . . . made too much use of the gob-box: they *patter* too much.' An elaboration of GOB, n., 2.

gob-full of claret. A bleeding at the mouth: boxing: ca 1820–90.

gob-spud. A potato held in the mouth to

round out sunken cheeks while shaving: lower classes': from ca 1870.

***gob-stick.** A silver table-spoon: c. (—1789): †except in dial. Parker. 2. A wooden spoon: nautical: mid-C.19–20.

***gob-string.** A bridle: mid-C.18–mid-19: either c. or low. cf. GAB-STRING.

gobbie, see GOBBY.

gobble. A quick straight putt at or into the hole: golf coll (—1878). 2. Mouth, esp. in *shut up your gobble!*, be quiet!: low (—1887). cf. GOBBLER, 3. 3. A C.19 schoolboys' variant of GOBBLER, 2.

gobble Greek. To study and/or speak Greek: Cambridge undergraduates': from ca 1855; ob. Pun on *gabble Greek*.

gobble-gut. A glutton: from ca 1630: S.E. until ca 1790, then low coll.

gobble-prick. 'A rampant, lustful woman', Grose, 1st ed.: low coll: mid-C.18–19.

gobble up. To seize; appropriate: use rapidly: coll: ex U.S. (1861), where earlier *gobble*; anglicized ca 1890.

***gobbler.** In mid-C.16–early 17 c., a duck. Harman. 2. A turkey cock: from ca 1720; orig. low coll, but now S.E. 3. The mouth: low coll: C.19–20; ob. 4. A greedy eater: from ca 1740: S.E. in Johnson's day: but since ca 1850, coll.

gobbling. Gorging: from ca 1630: S.E. until ca 1840, then coll. Thackeray, in *Vanity Fair*, 'The delightful exercise of gobbling'.

gobby, or **gobbie.** A coastguardsman: nautical: from late 1880s; ob. Ex GOB, n. 1; see GOBBY LOO. 2. A quarter-deck man: naval: ca 1830–90. Bowen, who adds: 'In the American [navy], any blue-jacket'.

gobby fleet. Coastguard and post-guard ships: nautical: from ca 1890; ob.

gobby loo, according to Bowen, is the orig. form of GOBBY, 1.

goblin. A sovereign: low: from ca 1880. Henley in Villon's *Straight Tip*, 'Your merry goblins soon stravag: | Boose and the blowens cop the lot.' Suggested by *sovrin*, the low coll pronunciation of *sovereign*, as the fuller *Jimmy o' Goblin* (or *g.*) shows.

God. 'Often oddly disguised in oaths, e.g. *swop me bob*, for *so help me God!*', W. As an oath, it occurs in many forms, but these are hardly eligible here. 2. **(god.)** A block pattern: tailors': from ca 1870: s. > j. 3. A boy in the sixth form: Eton (—1881): ob. Pascoe's *Life in our Public Schools*.

God-amighty. The coll and dial. form of *God-almighty*, lit. and fig.: C.17–20.

God bless the Duke of Argyle! A Scottish c.p. addressed to a person shrugging his shoulders, the insinuation being – lice. C.19–20; ob. Ex certain posts erected on his lands, for sheep to rub against. Shepherds, who were not uncommonly verminous, would scratch their backs on these posts, and when doing so blessed the Duke.

God bless you! A c.p. addressed to one who sneezes: C.18–20. cf. the C.18 proverbial 'He's a friend at a sneeze; the most you can get out of him is a *God bless you*,' 'Proverbs' Fuller, 1732.

God-box. A church; a chapel: atheists': since ca 1880.

God-forbid. A child. 2. A Jew. 3. A hat. Rhyming s. on KID; YID, and LID: all late C.19–20.

God have mercy (or, more gen. **Godamercy), horse!** 'An almost meaningless proverbial exclamation' that is also a coll c.p.: coll: ca 1530–1730. Heywood's *Proverbs*; 1611, in Tarlton's *Jests*, 'a by word thorow London'.

God knows: I don't. An emphatic reply: coll: C.19–20. The C.16–18 form is *God himself tell you, I cannot*: Florio, 1598. cf. BRAMAH KNOWS.

God-mamma. Godmother: coll, verging on S.E.: 1828, Miss Mitford.

God pays! A c.p. of soldiers and sailors, who assumed a right to public charity: C.17–18. The C.19–20 form is, *If I don't pay you, God Almighty will.* Ben Jonson, in *Epigrams*, 'To every cause he meets, this voice he brays, | His only answer is to all, God pays.'

God permit. A stage coach: late C.18–early 19. Stage coaches were advertised to start 'If God permit' or 'Deo volente'.

Godamercy, horse! see GOD HAVE MERCY, HORSE.

Godamercy me! God have mercy on me!: low (—1887).

Godblimey, see GORBLIMEY, the much more gen. pronunciation.

goddess. A young woman: coll of Englishmen in Malay: mid-C.18–early 19. Ex Malay *gadis*, a virgin, by the process of Hobson-Jobson. 2. The female 'galleryite': see GODS, 2: coll: 1812: very rare after 1890.

goddess Diana. A sixpence: rhyming s. on TANNER: ca 1855–1900. (Less gen. than LORD OF THE MANOR.) *Press*, 12 Nov. 1864.

godfather; in C.17, occ. **godfather-in-law.** A juryman: late C.16–early 19: coll. Shakespeare; Jonson, 'I will leave you to your god-fathers in law'; Grose. 2. He who pays the bill or who guarantees the rest of the company; esp. in 'Will you stand godfather? and we will take care of the brat,' i.e. repay you at some other time: late C.18–19 c.p.

godfer. A troublesome child: lower classes' (—1909); very ob. Ex GOD-FORBID.

godma. Godmother: familiar coll: since ca 1825. (A. Neil Lyons, *Hookey*, 1902.)

Godmanchester black pigs, see HUNTINGDON STURGEON.

godown. A warehouse; a store-room: Anglo-Chinese and Indian ex Malay *gadong*: from ca 1550. Coll >, in C.19, S.E. – though there's not the slightest need of the word. 2. A kitchen: Anglo-Indian: late C.18–19.

godpapa. Godfather: a childish or familiar coll: from ca 1825.

gods. In such oaths as *Gods me*, a corruption of *God save.* 2. Those occupying the gallery at a theatre: from ca 1750: s. that, ca 1840, > coll. Occ., but not since ca 1850, in the singular. *Globe*, 7 April 1890, 'The gods, or a portion of them, hooted and hissed while the National Anthem was being performed.' F. & H.: 'Said to have been first used by Garrick because they were seated on high, and close to the sky-painted ceiling'. cf. Fr. *poulailler* and *paradis.* 3. Among printers, the quadrats employed in JEFFing: from ca 1860. Perhaps rhyming on abbr. QUAD (5).

gods, sight for the. A cause of wonderment; coll only when ironic: from ca 1890. Hume Nisbet. cf. the literary *enough to make the gods weep.*

God's mercy. Ham (or bacon) and eggs: country inns': ca 1800–80. (cf. THREE SIXTY-FIVE.) Ex a pious expression of thanks.

Godspeed, in the. In the nick of time: coll: ca 1660–1820. L'Estrange.

goer. (Orig. of a horse.) An adept or expert; one well grounded in a subject. Gen. with an adj., e.g. *a fast* (or *a hell of a*) *goer*. Coll: from ca 1850. G. A. Lawrence in *Guy Livingstone.*

goes for my money, he. He's the man for me: coll: ca 1540–1660. Latimer, R. Harvey.

goffer, n. A blow, a punch: low: ca 1870–1910. *Sessions*, 11 Feb. 1886, 'Graham called out "Hop him, give him a *goffer*" . . . I then received a blow on my left shoulder.' cf.:

goffer, v. To BONNET a man: low London: from ca 1890; ob.

gog. In oaths, a corrupt form of *God*: mostly C.16–early 17: coll.

gog, v. Gen. as vbl n., *gogging*, 'the old sea punishment of scraping a man's tongue with hoop-iron for profanity' (Bowen): nautical: C.19. Either ex or cognate with Lancashire *gog*, a gag for the mouth.

goggle, v. To stare; roll the eyes: mid-C.16–20: S.E. till late C.18, then somewhat coll.

goggler. A goggle-eyed person: coll: from ca 1800; ob. 2. An eye: from ca 1820: low. Ob.

goggles. A goggle-eyed person: coll >, by 1830, S.E. C.17–19. Beaumont & Fletcher, 'Do you stare, goggles?' 2. The eyes, esp. if rolling or of a constrained stare: coll: from ca 1710. Byrom. Abbr. *goggle-eyes.* 3. Spectacles, esp. with round glasses: C.18–20: coll.

gohanna, see GOANNA.

going. The condition of the ground for traffic, walking, hunting, etc.: orig. U.S. (1859); anglicized ca 1870: coll till ca 1895, then S.E. *Daily Telegraph*, 23 Nov. 1883, 'Going . . . wonderfully clean for the time of year'.

going (h)ome. A-dying: proletarian (—1909); slightly ob.

going to buy anything? An evasive request for a drink: urban: 1896; ob.

going to Calabar. A-dying: naval (—1909); ob. Calabar is 'a white man's grave'.

going to keep a pianner-shop. Prosperous; smartly dressed: Cockneys' (—1909); ob.

going to see a dawg. i.e. a harlot or a kept woman: sporting: late C.19–20. cf.:

going to see a man. Going to get a drink: 1885, *Referee*, 6 Sept.

going tots. Trespassing on railway sidings: London schoolchildren: 1890s. See TOT, n., 5.

goings-on. Behaviour or proceedings, with a pejorative implication and gen. with a pejorative adj.: from ca 1770: coll until C.20, then undignified S.E. Douglas Jerrold, 'Pretty place it must be where they don't admit women. Nice goings-on, I daresay, Mr Caudle.'

gol-mol. (A) noise or commotion: Anglo-Indian (—1864).

gold-backed one or **un.** A louse: mid-

C.19–20; ob.: low coll. cf. GREY-BACKED.

gold-drop. A gold coin: late C.18–19. Mary Robinson, in *Walsingham.*

***gold-dropper.** A sharper who works the confidence trick by dropping money: see FAWNEY RIG. ca 1680–1830: c.

gold-dust. Tobacco, when supplies are short: nautical: late C.19–20.

gold-end man. A buyer of old gold and silver; an itinerant jeweller: C.17 coll. Jonson. ?a variation on *goldsmith's apprentice.*

gold-finder. An emptier of privies: coll: C.17–early 19. cf. the C.19 Warwickshire *gold-digger.* 2. A thief; a GOLD-DROPPER; early C.19.

gold hatband. An undergraduate aristocrat: university: ca 1620–1780. Earle's *Microcosmography.* Superseded by TUFT; see also HAT, 1.

gold-mine. A profitable investment: from ca 1850: coll till ca 1885, then S.E. *Saturday Review,* 28 April 1883, 'A gold mine to the . . . bookmakers'.

gold-washer. A 'sweater' of gold: C.16 low or low coll.

***golden cream.** Rum: c. (—1889); ob. Clarkson & Richardson, *The Police.*

golden grease. A fee; a bribe: coll: late C.18–19. cf. *palm oil.*

***goldfinch.** A rich man: C.17–early 19 c. Ex the colour of gold. 2. A guinea: C.17–early 19; a sovereign: ca 1820–1910. Both are either low or c. Same semantics. cf. CANARY, 4, and YELLOW BOY.

goldfinch's nest. The female pudend: low (—1827); ob. cf. CUCKOO'S NEST.

goldsmith's window. A rich working that shows gold freely: from ca 1890: Australian coll.

goldy- or goldie-locks; goldilocks. A flaxen-haired girl or woman: mid-C.16–20: orig. S.E.; in late C.19–20, archaic except when coll and applied to a child, often as a pet name.

goles!, by. A variant of *by* GOLLY!: 1734, Fielding; in C.19, lower classes': in late C.19–20, mostly dial.

Goliath. 'A man of mark among the Philistines': literary: ca 1880–1910.

goll. The hand: in late C.16–early 19 coll, verging on S.E.; in late C.18–19 mainly dial. Dryden, 'Mighty golls, rough-grained, and red with starching'. Origin obscure.

gollop. To gulp; swallow noisily and greedily: (low) coll: C.19–20. Ex *gulp.*

gollore, see GALORE.

gollumpus. A large, clumsy, loutish fellow: late C.18–mid-19 coll. Prob. an arbitrary formation on *lump* (cf. modern *you great lump, you!*).

golly! Abbr. *by golly,* an orig. Negroes' euphemistic corruption (1743) of *God*: anglicized in mid-C.19. cf. *by* GOLES!

golopshus, goloptious. See GALOPTIOUS. The best form is *goluptious,* for the term is a 'facetious perversion . . . of *voluptuous*; cf. rustic *boldacious*', W., *delicious* being the 'suggester'. The S.O.D. records it at 1856.

golore, see GALORE.

goloshes. India-rubber over-shoes: a coll spelling of *galoshes*: late C.18–20. *Galoshes* itself had a coll air at first. Ex Fr. *galoche*; Grose's derivation ex *Goliath's shoes* is one of his portly jests.

***gom.** A man: c.: C.17. Beaumont & Fletcher.

gom! Damn it: low: C.19–20; ob. *God* corrupted.

gombeen-man. A usurer; an extortionate middleman: Anglo-Irish: ca 1862–1900 as coll, then Standard. Ex Irish *gaimbīn* = Medieval L. *cambium.* (W.'s *umpteen,* suggested by this word?)

gomer. A large pewter dish: ?ex the †S.E. sense, a Hebrew measure. 2. Whence, a new hat. Both, Winchester College s. of ca 1850–1915.

gommed! Damned!: low: C.19–20. cf. GORMED, BE.

gommy. A dandy: C.19. Ex Fr. *gommeux.* 2. A fool: coll: ca 1870–1910. 3. 'One who calls Mr Gladstone a G.O.M., and thinks he has made a good joke', *Weekly Dispatch,* 11 March 1883: †by 1900.

gomus. A fool: Anglo-Irish: from ca 1830. cf. Yorkshire *gomo* and the gen. dial. *gaum.*

gone. Pregnant, as in 'She's six months gone': coll: mid-C.19–20.

gone coon, see COON, A GONE.

gone goose. A person left in the lurch, ship abandoned: nautical (—1867).

gone off his dip. Crazy, mad: low: from ca 1885. Arthur Binstead, *Mop Fair,* 1905.

gone on. Infatuated with: low coll: from ca 1885. *Illustrated Bits,* 29 March 1890, 'He must have been terribly gone on this woman.' S.E. has the absolute phrase *far gone.*

gone over a goodish piece of grass. (Of meat, esp. mutton) tough: lower classes (—1909).

gone phut, see PHUT, GO.

gone through the sieve. Bankrupt: commercial (—1909).

gone to Rome. (Of bells) silenced on Good Friday and Easter Saturday: Roman Catholics' coll: from the 1880s. When they resume ringing, they are said to **have** 'returned from Rome'.

gone west. Dead. See GO WEST.

goner. One who is undone, ruined, or dead; that which is (almost or quite) finished, extinguished, or destroyed: orig. (1847), U.S.; anglicized ca 1880. Nat Gould, 1891, 'Make a noise, or follow me, and you're a goner.'

goney, see GAWNEY.

gong. A medal; loosely, a decoration: Regular Army: late C.19–20.

goniv. An illicit diamond-buyer: South African diamond fields': from ca 1890; ob. Also *gonoph* and therefore a variant of GONNOF. 2. Whence (via Hebrew *genavah*, a theft, a thing stolen) *goniva(h)*, 'a diamond known to have been stolen or come by illicitly', Pettman: South African c.: 1887, Matthews, *Incwadi Yami*.

gonna. (e.g., I'm) going to (do something): dial. and, esp. in U.S., low coll: C.19–20.

***gon(n)of, gonoph, gonov, gnof(f).** (See also GUN, 4.) A thief; esp. a skilful pickpocket: c. from ca 1835. Ex Hebrew *gannabh* via Jewish Dutch *gannef* (W.). Brandon, Mayhew, Dickens, Hindley, Clarkson and Richardson ('gunneffs or gonophs'). cf. the C.14–20 *gnof*, a bumpkin, a simpleton, as in Chaucer: this, however, is a different word.

***gon(n)of,** etc., v. To steal; cheat; wheedle: c.: from ca 1850; ob. Whence *gonophing*, etc., vbl n.: Dickens in *The Detective Police*, reprinted 1857.

goo-goo eyes. Loving glances: Australian mostly: from ca 1905. Neil Munro, 1906; C. J. Dennis. Prob. first in the baby-talk of lovers. Hence, occ., *goo-goo*, such a glance.

gooby. A simpleton, a dolt: from ca 1890: coll (1892, *Ally Sloper*, 19 March). Prob. a corruption ex dial. *goff* or *goof*.

***good.** Easily robbed (e.g. *upon the* CRACK, 4, or *the* STAR): c. of ca 1810–1910. 2. Solvent; esp. *good for*, able to pay: coll: from ca 1890. Ex the (—1860) S.E. sense, 'safe to live or last so long, well able to accomplish so much'. But Vaux, 1812, says that 'A man who declares himself *good for* any favour or thing, means, that he has sufficient influence, or possesses the certain means to obtain it,' – which puts back the S.E. sense some fifty years and perhaps indicates that this S.E. sense was orig. s. or coll. 3. The omission of *good* before *afternoon, day, morning*, etc., in greetings is a mostly Colonial coll of late C.19–20.

good, adv., when modifying a v. and = well: in C.19–20, low coll; earlier, S.E.

good! Good night!: printers': from ca 1870.

good, be any or **some,** or, gen., **no.** To be to some extent useful; wholly useless: coll: from ca 1870. 2. When predicative with gerund following, coll from ca 1840. J. H. Newman, 1842, 'There is no good telling you all this.' 3. In *what good is it? are they?* etc., it is coll from ca 1865, Dasent using it in 1868. 4. (Of persons) *be no good*, to be worthless: coll: from early 1890s.

good, feel. To be jolly or in FORM: ex U.S. (1854: Thornton); anglicized ca 1895: coll.

good, for. Completely; permanently: coll: from ca 1880. Abbr. GOOD AND ALL, FOR.

good a maid as her mother, a (occ. **as).** A C.17 c.p. applied to a devirginated spinster. Howell's *Proverbs*, 1659.

good and all, for. Entirely; permanently; finally: from ca 1515. In C.16–early 19, S.E.; then coll. Horman in his *Vulgaria*, 1519; Wycherley, in *The Gentleman Dancing Master*, 'If I went, I would go for good and all'; Dickens.

good as . . ., as. It is extremely difficult to determine the status of the (*as*) *good as . . .* comparative phrases, many of which are either proverbs or proverbial sayings. G. L. Apperson lists the following: *as good as a Christmas play* (late C.19–20 Cornwall) – *a play* (C.17–20) – *ever drew sword* (late C.16–17) – ever *flew in the air* (C.17) – *ever struck* (C.17) – *ever the ground went upon* with such variants as *ever stepped* (late C.16–20) – *ever twanged* (mid-C.16–17) – *ever water wet* (C.17–18) – *ever went endways* (C.17?–18) – *George of Green* (C.17–18) – *gold* (mid-C.19–20) – *good for nothing* (C.17) – *goose skins that never man had enough of* (Cheshire: C.17–20) – *one shall see in* or *upon a summer's day* (late C.16–19). 2. But Vaux's *good as bread* and *good as cheese* = thoroughly competent or able (in some specific relation): low: ca 1810–50. Influenced by *the* CHEESE.

good as a play, gen. preceded by **as.** Very entertaining: proverbial coll: from ca 1630. Taylor the Water Poet.

good as ever pissed. Extremely good: low coll: from ca 1710; ob. D'Urfey. cf. the C.17–18 proverbial saying, *good as ever went endways* (in previous entry).

good as ever twanged (often preceded by **as**). Of women only: very good: coll: ca 1570–1700. (Apperson.) Lit., as good as ever responded to a man's sexual aggress.

good as gold. Very good: coll: 1843, Dickens. Gen. applied to children.

good as good(, as). Extremely good: coll: from ca 1880. Gen. applied to children: cf. GOOD AS GOLD. cf. Romance-languages emphasis by repetition of adjj. and advv.

good as they make 'em(, as). The best obtainable (things only): coll: from ca 1870.

good at it or **at the game.** An adept between the sheets: amatory coll: C.19–20.

good blood and so does black pudding, you come of. A proverbial c.p. reply to one boasting of good birth: C.19.

good books; bad books: be in one's, see BOOKS, IN A . . . 2. As *the Good Books* – a pun on *The Good Book*, the Bible – it means '(a pack of) playing cards': *The Night Watch* (I, 71), 1828. cf. BOOKS.

good cess! Good luck! Anglo-Irish (—1845). F. & H.: 'Probably an abbreviation of "success" ': but see BAD CESS, its opposite.

good chap. A late C.19–20 coll variant of GOOD FELLOW.

good enough, not. (Very) bad; esp., decidedly unfair: coll: from ca 1890.

good fellow, goodfellow. A roisterer, a boon companion: C.16–20: S.E. until ca 1660, then coll. cf. Grose, 1st ed., '*Good Man*, a word of various imports, according to the place where it is spoken; in the city it means a rich man; at Hockley in the Hole, or St Giles's, an expert boxer; at a bagnio in Covent Garden, a vigorous fornicator; at an alehouse or tavern, one who loves his pot or bottle; and sometimes, tho' but rarely, a virtuous man.' 2. In C.17 c., a thief. Middleton in his most famous comedy.

good-for, n. An I O U: South African coll: 1879. Rider Haggard in *Cetywayo*, 1882.

good form, see FORM.

good girl or **good one.** A harlot; a wanton wench: coll: the former, C.18–20, ob.; the latter, C.17–18. cf. GOOD AT IT.

good goods. Something worth having; a success: sporting (—1874): ob. *Sporting Times*, 17 July 1886, 'He was . . . rather good goods at a Sunday-school treat.' The superlative is *best goods* (—1874).

good gracious, see GRACIOUS!

good hunting! Good luck!: coll: from ca 1895. Orig. among sportsmen. Popularized, and perhaps generated, by Kipling's *Jungle Book*, 1894.

good in parts(, like the curate's egg). Now a potential proverbial saying, recently a 'battered ornament' (H. W. Fowler), it was in the first decade of the century a cultured coll. Ex an illustrated joke in *Punch*, 1895.

good man, goodman. See Grose's definition at GOOD FELLOW, above. 2. Gen. as one word: a gaoler: C.18–early 19: low or coll. 3. The devil, always with *the*: C.18–20 coll; ob. cf. OLD GENTLEMAN. 4. (cf. sense 1.) *good man turd.* A contemptible fellow: C.16–17 low coll. Florio.

good mark, see MARK, BAD.

good morning! have you used Pear's soap? A c.p. of the 1880s. Ex the famous old soap-firm's advertisement. cf. SINCE WHEN . . .

good night! A c.p. retort expressive of incredulity, comical despair, delight: from ca 1860; ob. An extremely suggestive adumbration occurs in Gabriel Harvey's *Four Letters*, 1592 (Bodley Head Quartos ed., p. 81): 'Every pert, and crancke wit, in one odd veine, or other, [is] the onely man of the University, of the Citty, of the Realme, for a flourish or two: who but he, in the flush of his overweening conceit? Give him his peremptory white rod in his hand, and God-night all distinction of persons, and all difference of estates.' cf. also Shakespeare, *I Henry IV*, I, iii, 194: 'If he fall in, good night!'

good old . . . A (—1891) familiar, i.e. coll, term of reference or address, gen. affectionate, occ. derisive. Albert Chevalier in *The Little Nipper*, 1892.

good one, see GOOD UN.

good people, the. Fairies: Anglo-Irish coll >, ca 1880, S.E.: from ca 1800; ob. Scott; C. Griffin; R. L. Stevenson. Orig. and mainly euphemistic: cf. *Eumenides*: see *Words!* at 'Euphemism'. In C.16–17 Scottish, *the good neighbours*.

good shit would do you more good, a. A low c.p., addressed to one who says that he 'could do with a woman': late C.19–20.

good sort, occ. **g. old s.** A generous, a sympathetic, or a readily helpful person: coll (—1892); orig. only of men. Hume Nisbet, 'He seems a good sort.'

good strange! A mild coll oath: late C.17–18. Perhaps *God's strings*.

good thing. As a *bon mot*, as something worth having, and as a successful speculation, it is hardly eligible, but as a presumed certainty it is racing s. (—1884).

good time. A carouse; amusement and entertainment; a sexually enjoyable occasion. Gen. as *have a good time*. In C.17, S.E. – Pepys has it; ob. till ca 1840, when it appeared in the U.S.; re-anglicized ca 1870 as a coll. Trollope, 1863, 'Having . . . what our American friends call a good time of it'.

good tune played on an old fiddle, there's many a. An oldish woman may make an excellent bedfellow: late C.19–20: a c.p.

good un. A person or thing of great merit: coll: from ca 1830.

good un (or one)!, that's a. What a fib (occ. good story)! Coll: C.19–20.

good woman. 'A non descript, represented on a famous sign in St Giles's, in the form of a common woman, but without a head', Grose, 1785; hence, 'a not uncommon public-house sign', H., 1864: the same authority adding that *the honest lawyer*, similarly represented, is another. The phrase is relevant because it was often employed allusively.

good-wool(l)ed. Plucky and energetic: s. when not, as prob. orig., dial.: from ca 1845. Halliwell. Ex sheep with a good fleece.

good young man. A hypocrite: proletarian c.p. of 1881–ca 1914. Sponsored by Arthur Roberts in a song, says Ware, who notes that its opposite is *bad young man*.

gooder; goodest. Deliberately used, it is coll: late C.19–20.

goodlish. Goodish: low coll (—1887). Prob. a confusion of *goodly* + *goodish*.

goodman; goodman turd, see GOOD MAN.

goodness in mild expletives is coll; mostly mid-C.19–20.

goods, bit (occ. piece) of. A woman, gen. as viewed in the light of her sexual attractiveness or potentialities: low coll: from ca 1860. cf. BIT; PIECE. 2. **(piece** only.) A person: coll: from ca 1870. 3. **(goods.)** A goods train: railwaymen's coll (—1887).

goods, the. (Precisely) what is needed, esp. if of considerable worth or high merit. Gen. in *have the goods*, to be a very able person, and *deliver the goods*, to fulfil one's promise(s): coll: anglicized, ca 1908, from U.S. (1870s). ?ex the U.S. sense (1852), the thing bargained for, the prize.

Goodwin sands, set up shop on. To be shipwrecked: ca 1540–1750. In C.16–17, often *Goodwins*.

goody. A matron – but used only of, or to, a social inferior or, among the lower classes, equal: mainly rural: C.16–20; ob.: in C.16–18, wholly S.E.; in C.19, increasingly coll. Ex *goodwife*, cf. AUNTIE; GAMMER; *mother*. See esp. Florio, Johnson, and O.E.D. Whence the occ. coll *goodyship* = the *ladyship* of jocular usage. 2. A religious hypocrite: coll (—1836); ob. 3. Gen. in pl, sweetmeats; buns, cakes and pastry: from ca 1760; occurring as *goody-goody* in 1745 (S.O.D.): until ca 1850, S.E.; then coll.

goody, adj. Officiously or hypocritically or ignorant-tiresomely pious: 1830: coll. D. W. Thompson in *Daydreams of a Schoolmaster*, 1864.

goody!, my. My goodness!: lower classes' (esp. women's) coll (—1887).

goody, talk. To talk in a weakly or sentimentally good way: from ca 1865. Coll.

goody-goody. Occ. a n. (ca 1872) but gen. an adj. (1871). Both coll in sense of a weakly or sentimentally good person. 2. See GOODY, n., last sense.

goodyear!, what a or **the.** A (now) meaningless expletive: ca 1550–1720. cf.:

goodyear(s). Syphilis: C.17 coll. Perhaps (!) ex *gougeer* ex *gouge*, a soldier's drab. But this may be deducing too much from the imprecative uses of *goodyear*, as in *a goodyear take ye!* and as in the preceding entry, in which the word = the deuce, the devil, a sense that may be operative in:

goodyer's pig, like. Explained by the occ. accompanying tag, *never well but when in* – or *he is doing* – *mischief*: mid-C.17–20. Mainly Cheshire. Who was Goodyer? cf.:

Goodyer's pigs did, they'll come again as. Never: proverbial coll: ca 1670–1750. Goodyer was prob. a notable farmer; cf. preceding entry (likewise in Apperson). But *Goodyer* may be only a personification of †Scottish *goodyer*, a grandfather.

goolies. Testicles: low: late C.19–20. Prob. ex dial. *gully*, a game of marbles.

goori. A dog: New Zealanders': late C.19–20. A corruption of Maori *kuri*.

goose. A tailors' smoothing iron, the handle being shaped like a goose's neck: 1605, Shakespeare: in C.17–18 coll; in C.19–20, S.E. Whence the C.17–19 proverbial saying, 'A tailor, be he ever so poor, is always sure to have a goose at his fire.' 2. Abbr. *Winchester goose*, a venereal disease; a harlot: low coll (—1778) †by 1870. 3. (Theatrical) a hissing: 1805 (S.O.D.), but not gen. before ca 1850: cf. GOOSE, GET THE. 4. A scolding or a reprimand: coll (—1865); ob. by 1910. Prob. ex the theatrical sense. 5. A woman; hence, the sexual favour: low: from ca 1870. 6. See GONE GOOSE; also GREENWICH GOOSE and GUINEA TO A GOOSEBERRY.

goose, v. To condemn by hissing; hiss: theatrical and gen.: 1848; in 1854, Dickens, 'He was goosed last night.' cf. BIG BIRD, GET THE. Hence, 2, to ruin; spoil utterly: coll (—1859). cf. COOK ONE'S GOOSE. 3. To befool, make a 'goose' of (—1899). 4. To possess (a woman): low: from ca 1875. 5. v.i., to go wenching: low: from ca 1870. 6. v.i., gen. as vbl n., *goosing*, 'Thames waterman afloat looking for jobs': nautical: late C.19–20.

goose, be sound on the. To hold orthodox political opinions: orig. U.S. (1857); anglicized ca 1890: ob. Milliken in his *'Arry Ballads*, 1892.

goose, find fault with a fat. To grumble without cause: late C.17–19: coll.

goose, get the. To be hissed: theatrical: ca 1860–1900. See GOOSE, v., 1.

goose!, (go) shoe the. A derisive or incredulous retort: late C.16–18. cf. the late C.19 equivalent, GO TO HELL AND PUMP THUNDER!

goose, guinea to a, see GUINEA TO A GOOSEBERRY.

goose, hot and heavy like a tailor's. A late C.17–mid-18 c.p. 'applied to a Passionate Coxcomb', B.E. See GOOSE, n., 1, and cf. GOOSE ROASTED ...

goose, not able or unable to say 'boh' to a. Very bashful or timid: coll: late C.16–20.

goose and duck. A copulation: rhyming s., from ca 1870, on FUCK.

goose-cap, goosecap. A dolt; a silly person: late C.16–early 19; S.E. until C.18, then coll, then, ca 1800, dial.

goose for, or that laid, the golden eggs, kill the. The proverbial forms: C.15–20. The coll form is *kill the goose with the golden eggs*: C.19–20.

goose-gob (rare); **goose-gog.** A gooseberry: homely coll: mid-C.19–20.

goose-grease. A woman's vaginal emission: low: from ca 1875.

goose hangs high, everything is lovely and the. All goes well: coll: C.19–20; ob. Ex a plucked goose hanging out of a fox's reach.

goose is in the house, the. A tense-variable expression for the hissing of a play, etc.: ca 1800–50. cf. GOOSE, n., 3, the v., 1, and GOOSE, GET THE.

goose-month. The period of a woman's confinement: coll: late C.18–mid-19. Ex GANDER-MONTH.

goose-persuader. A tailor: C.19–20; ob. Ex GOOSE, n., 1.

goose roasted, a tailor's. 'A Red-hot smoothing Iron, to Close the Seams', B.E.: late C.17–18. See GOOSE, n., 1.

goose-shearer. A beggar: C.19–20 coll: ob. Lit., cheater of fools.

goose-turd green. A light-yellow green: coll: C.17–18. Cotgrave.

goose without gravy. A severe blow that does not draw blood: nautical: ca 1850–1914. cf. GOOSER.

gooseberries. The human testicles: low: from ca 1850; ob.

gooseberry. A fool: coll (ob.): ca 1820–95. Ex *gooseberry fool*. 2. Hence (?), chaperon, or a save-appearances third person: 1837 (S.O.D.): dial. until ca 1860, then coll. 3. A (too) marvellous tale: journalistic s. (—1870) >, ca 1880, gen. coll; ob. by 1900. Occ. *giant* or gigantic *gooseberry*. See also GOOSEBERRY SEASON. 4. See GOOSEBERRY, PLAY OLD; and GOOSEBERRY, LIKE OLD, and, more fully, OLD GOOSEBERRY itself. 5. Short for GOOSEBERRY-PUDDEN. 6. Short for GOOSEBERRY TART.

gooseberry, do or play. To act as propriety-third or chaperon: the former, 1877, in Hawley Smart's *Play or Pay*, and †by 1900; the latter, ca 1837, and e.g. in G. R. Sims, 1880, and slightly ob. App. Devonshire dial. until ca 1860. cf. GOOSEBERRY, 2.

gooseberry, like old. Like the devil: coll (—1865). Ex next entry, *old gooseberry* being an † term for the devil. See 'The Devil and his Nicknames' in *Words!*

gooseberry, play old. (v.t. with *with*.) To play the deuce: coll (—1791); ob. The v.t. form (with variant *play up*) also = to silence, or defeat, summarily; quell promptly: coll: ca 1810–80. cf. preceding entry. 2. See GOOSEBERRY, DO.

gooseberry-eyed. Having 'dull grey eyes, like boiled gooseberries', Grose, 3rd ed.: coll: ca 1789–1880.

gooseberry-grinder, gen. preceded by **Bogey the.** The behind: late C.18–mid-19 low. Esp. in ASK BOGY *the g.-g.* (Grose, 1st ed.).

***gooseberry lay.** The stealing of linen

hanging on the line: C.19 c. ?from the notion 'as easy as picking gooseberries'.

gooseberry-picker. A GHOST; from ca 1885; ob. by 1910. 2. A chaperon: ca 1870–1900. *Cornhill Magazine*, Dec. 1884. Ex children accompanying young people on gooseberry-picking parties.

gooseberry-pudden (rarely **-pudding**). A woman: low rhyming s. (—1857); ob. 2. Hence, a wife: an OLD WOMAN: low: from ca 1860.

gooseberry season. The SILLY SEASON: journalists': ca 1870–1900. Occ. (see the *Illustrated London News*, 18 July 1885), *giant gooseberry season*, or *big g.s.* cf. GOOSEBERRY, 3.

gooseberry tart. Heart: rhyming s.: from ca 1860. Often abbr. to GOOSEBERRY.

gooseberry wig. 'A large frizzled wig', Grose, 3rd ed.: coll: ca 1788–1850. Perhaps, as Grose suggests, ex a vague resemblance to a gooseberry bush.

goosegog, see GOOSGOG.

gooser. A knock-out blow; a decisive coup: coll: from ca 1850; ob. ?ex COOK ONE'S GOOSE via GOOSE, v., 2. 2. No score; a 'goose-egg', U.S. for *duck's egg*, (see DUCK, n., 6): sporting: ca 1885–1910. 3. The male member: low: from ca 1871; ob. 4. A student at the Queen's College: Oxford undergraduates': late C.19–20.

goose's gazette. A lying story; a SILLY-SEASON tale: coll: ca 1810–60. cf. GOOSEBERRY, 3.

goose's neck. The male member: low: from ca 1872. Ex GOOSE, n., 1, 2, and 6. cf. GOOSER, 3.

goosey, goosy, adj. With a goose-flesh feeling: coll: mid-C.19–20. Jefferies in *Amaryllis at the Fair*.

goos(e)y-gander. A gander: coll: from ca 1815. Baby language has both *goos(e)y-goos(e)y*, a goose, and *goosey-goosey gander*, a gander; the latter occurs, e.g., in the well-known nursery rhyme recorded as early as 1842 by Halliwell in his *Nursery Rhymes*. 2. A fool: from ca 1880.

goosgog. A gooseberry: nursery and proletarian (—1887) ex dial. A variant of *goose-gog* (at GOOSE-GOB).

goosing, see GOOSE, v., 6.

Gor. God: low coll, esp. Cockneys': C.19–20. Also *Gaw*. Esp. in GORBLIM(E)Y.

Gor' damn. Jam: rhyming s.: late C.19–20.

Goramity; occ. **Garamity.** God almighty: West Indian Negroes' coll (—1834).

Gorblimeries, the. Seven Dials, London: policemen's (—1909); ob. Ex:

gorblim(e)y; gawlim(e)y! A corruption of *God blind me!*: orig. and mainly Cockneys': 1870, says Ware for the latter form; 1890, for the former.

gorblim(e)y, here come(s) the ——. A Cockney soldiers' derisive c.p. addressed to, or within the hearing of, another battalion or a section thereof: from late 1890s.

gordelpus. A person frequenting casual wards: low (—1909); ob. Ex *Gord (h)elp us!*

***goree.** Money; esp. gold money or gold: c.: late C.17–mid-19. Ex Fort Goree on the Gold Coast. cf. S.E. *guinea* and OLD MR GOREE.

gorge. A heavy meal: from ca 1820: coll until C.20, when S.E. Ex the S.E. v. 2. A manager: theatrical: ca 1873–1905. Ex GORGER, 1.

gorgeous as a loose adj. expressing approbation is coll: 1883 (S.O.D.).

gorger. A theatrical manager: theatrical (—1864). Occ. CULLY-GORGER. 2. An employer, a principal (—1864). Prob. ex: 3. A gentleman, a well-dressed man: low: from ca 1810: †by 1910. Ex Romany *gaujer, gaujo, gorgio*, anyone not a Gypsy, or, just possibly, ex *gorgeous* (H., 1859). 4. The sense, 'a man', is very rare: c.: 1857, 'Ducange Anglicus'. 5. A voracious eater: from ca 1790. App. coll, actually S.E., ex the S.E. v. Whence:

gorger, rotten. A lad who hangs about Covent Garden to eat discarded fruit: London: ca 1870–1900.

gorgery. A GORGE; a (school-)feast: coll: 1906, Desmond Coke, *The Bending of a Twig*. cf. S.E. *gorger*, a glutton.

gorgie. One who is not a Gypsy: grafters': late C.19–20. See GORGER, 3.

gorgio, see GORGER, 3.

gorm (or **G.**); **gawm.** God damn: low: mid-C.19–20. Esp. in GORMED, BE.

gorm, v. To gormandize: from ca 1890; virtually †. Ex U.S.A.

gormagon. ('Meaningless: pseudo-Chinese', O.E.D.: but it may be a confused blend of *Gorgon*+*dragon*.) A hypothetical monster of ca 1750–1830: coll. Grose, 1785, 'a monster with six eyes, three mouths, four arms, eight legs, five on one side and three on the other, three arses, two tarses [*penises*], and a **** [*pudendum muliebre*] upon its back; a man on horseback, with a woman [*riding 'side-saddle'*] behind him.' Relevant is the *Gormagons*, properly *Gormogons*, an English secret society – a lay offshoot from the Masons – of ca 1725–50: evidently there was some ridiculous rite (cf. GOAT, RIDE THE), for, in 1791, 'G. Gambado' in his *Horsemanship*, speaks of 'the art of riding before a lady on a double horse, vulgarly termed *à la gormagon*'. cf. SEVEN-SIDED ANIMAL.

gorman. A *cormorant*: nautical coll: C.19–20. cf. Scots and Northern *gormaw*.

gormed, be. Be 'God-damned' if . . .: low coll oath: 1849, Dickens. *God* corrupted after dial. *gaumed*. cf. GOMMED!

gormy-ruddles. The intestines: low: C.19. Ex dial. *gormy-ruttles*, 'strangles', i.e. horses' quinsies.

gorra. Got a: Cockney: C.19–20. *Slang*, p. 153. cf. NORRA.

gorsoon, see GOSSOON.

***gory.** See OLD MR GOREE and cf. GOREE. 2. A chap, a fellow: c.: ca 1810–40. Origin? cf. COVE; GILL; GLOACH.

gos, gosse. Gossip, as term of address: coll: ca 1540–1660. Abbr. *gossip*.

gosh is a corruption of *God* (cf. GOLLY): 1757; though in 1553 it occurs thus in the anon. *Respublica*: 'Each man snatch for himself, by gosse'.

gosh. To spit: Winchester College: late C.19–20. cf. GLOPE.

gosher. A heavy blow or punch: Cockney: ca 1890–1914. A. Neil Lyons, *Hookey*, 1902, 'On his snitch I gave him such a gosher.' Echoic.

gosoon, gosoun, see GOSSOON.

gospel, do. To go to church: low coll: from ca 1860: ob.

gospel-gab. Insincere talk about religion: low coll (—1892). Hume Nisbet, 'With a little gospel-gab and howling penitence, [I] got the church people interested.'

gospel-grinder, -postillion, -shark or -sharp, are more gen. in U.S. than in England: coll: from ca 1855. Besant & Rice speak of 'a Connecticut gospel-grinder', Mark Twain of a 'gospel-sharp' in *Innocents at Home*. But in U.S. they merely = a parson; in England they = a city missionary or a tract-distributor (H., 1st ed.) or a Sunday-School teacher ('Ducange Anglicus', 1857).

gospel of gloom, the. Gloomy house-decoration and dresses: Society: ca 1880–1900. Satirizing the Aesthetes.

Gospel of St Jeames, the. Snobbery: Society: 1847; ob. Ex Thackeray's *Jeames de la Pluche* in *The Yellowplush Papers*.

gospel of the tub, the. The mania for cold baths: Society coll: ca 1845–1910.

gospel-postillion or -shark, see GOSPEL-GRINDER.

gospel-shop. A church or chapel: gen. Methodist: coll: from ca 1780: after 1860, chiefly nautical. (*Gospel-mill* is a U.S. variation.) J. Lackington, 'Mr Wesley's gospel-shops', 1791.

gospeller. An Evangelist preacher: pejorative coll: from ca 1880. Ex the †sense, one of the four evangelists, and the rare one, a missionary. cf. HOT GOSPELLER.

goss. A hat; at first a FOUR-AND-NINE: coll: 1848. Ex *gossamer hat*, a light felt fashionable in the late 1830s. cf.:

gossamer. A hat (—1859); esp. and orig. a very light one: ca 1837–1900. Both Dickens and James Grant, in the late 1830s, mention 'ventilation' gossamers; Andrew Lang, in 1884, 'the gay gossamer of July'. cf. GOSS.

gosse, see GOS and GOSH. **gossip, up to one's**, see UP TO THE CACKLE.

gossip pint-pot. A hard drinker: C.16–early 17 coll. Hollyband. cf. 'Peace, good pint-pot' in Shakespeare, *I Henry IV*, II, iv, 438.

gossoon; earliest as **gosoun**; occ., C.19–20, **gosoon, gorsoon** (O.E.D.). A boy: Anglo-Irish: 1684: S.E. until ca 1850, then increasingly coll. Ex Fr. *garçon* via M.E. *garsoun*. 2. Hence, a silly awkward lout; nautical (—1867); ob.

got?, what has. What has happened to, become of? Coll: from ca 1820; ob. a century later. Scoresby, in *Whale Fishery*, 1823, 'They all at once . . . enquired what had got Carr.'

got a clock(, he's). (He is) carrying a bag: a London c.p. of 1883–4. Ex dynamitards' activities.

got a collar on. Conceited; vain; arrogant: lower classes' (—1909).

got a face on (her, him). Ugly: id.: id.

got 'em bad, has or have. To be in earnest; seriously affected (by illness, delirium tremens, love): low coll: from ca 1870. cf. *get them*.

got 'em on (occ. all on), have. To be very fashionably dressed, often with the implication of over-dressing: low coll: 1880 (*Punch*, 28 Aug.); broadside ballads of the 80s. Ob. See also GOT-UP (adj.) and RIG-OUT.

got line. (Of women). Graceful and vigorous in dancing: theatrical: 1870; ob.

got the glow. Blushing: London lower classes' (—1909); ob.

got the morbs, adj. *Morbid*, melancholy: Society: ca 1880–1910.

got the pants. Panting: low (—1909).

got the perpetual. Vigorous; enterprising: id.: id. Ex *perpetual motion.*

got the shutters up. Surely: id.: id.

got the woefuls. Sad; wretched: id.: id.

got to?, where has it, he, etc. What has become of it, him, etc.? From ca 1885: s. in C.19, then coll. Jerome K. Jerome in *Three Men in a Boat.*

got-up, n. An upstart: coll: ca 1880–1915. For form, cf. HAD-UP.

got-up, dressed (ppl adj.): see GET UP, v., 1. 2. Esp. well-dressed, in the low coll variations: *got-up regardless* (abbr. *regardless of expense*) – *to kill* – *to the knocker* – *to the nines*: all from ca 1880: the first and the third are ob.

gotch-gutted. Pot-bellied: coll when not, as gen., dial: late C.18–19. Ex *gotch*, a pitcher or a (large) round jug. A late C.17–mid-18 variant: *gotch-gutted.*

Goth. 'A fool, an idiot' (*Sinks*, 1848): ca 1825–70.

Gotham. Newcastle: North Country s. (—1900) rather than dial. Ex dial. *gotham*, foolish, ignorant.

Gothicky. Gothic-like: coll: 1893, Kate Wiggin in *Cathedral Courtship.*

Gotter-dam-merung. A grotesque form of swearing: Society: 1862–3. Ex the performance of Wagner's *The Ring* in London in 1862.

goujeers, prob. a 'made' word: see GOODYEAR . . .

gourd. (Rare in singular.) A hollowed-out false die: low, or c., > j.: ca 1540–1660. Ascham in *Toxophilus*, Shakespeare in *Merry Wives.* ?ex the fruit, influenced by Old Fr. *gourd*, a swindle.

Gourock ham. A salted herring: mostly Scottish: ca 1830–1900. Gourock was, before 1870, a well-known Clyde fishing village. cf. GLASGOW MAGISTRATE.

gout = venereal disease: e.g. in COVENT GARDEN, or SPANISH GOUT: late C.17–18.

gov, see GUV.

government house. The house of the owner or manager of an estate: a Dominions' jocular coll: from ca 1880; ob. Ex *Government House.*

Government man. A convict: Australian coll: ca 1825–85. Applied esp. to assigned servants: see J. West, *History of Tasmania*, 1852, at ii, 127.

Government securities. Handcuffs; fetters: from ca 1850; ob.

Government signpost. The gallows: mid-C.19.

Government stroke. A slow lazy stroke, hence a lazy manner of working: Australia: 1856. Trollope, 1873. Ex the anti-sweat motions of convicts: seen later in those of Government labourers, e.g. on the railway lines.

governor. A father: 1837: s. >, ca 1895, coll. Dickens in *Pickwick*; *Answers*, 20 April 1889, 'To call your father "The Governor" is, of course, slang, and is as bad as referring to him as "The Boss" [!], "The Old Man", or "The Relieving Officer".' (The last is never used as a term of address, OLD MAN practically never.) Occ. abbr. GOV or GUV. Ex the third sense, whereas the second follows from the first. 2. A term of address to a strange man: s. > low coll: from ca 1855. 3. A superior; an employer: coll (occ. in address): 1802 (S.O.D.), thus the earliest sense.

***gowk.** One ignorant of the various dodges: prison c. of C.19. Ex Scottish for a fool or a cuckoo.

gowk, hunt the. To go on (esp. an April) fool's errand: Scottish coll: C.18–20. See 'All Fools' Day' in *Words!*

***gowler.** A dog, esp. one given to howling and growling: North-Country c. (—1864). Prob. *growler* perverted or ex dial. *gowl*, to howl.

gown. Coarse brown paper: Winchester College: C.19, but †by 1890. ?suggested by the rhyme and the coarseness of gown-material.

gowsers. Gownboys' shoes: Charterhouse: ca 1830–75. A. H. Tod, *Charterhouse*, 1900. By telescoping.

goy; goya. Resp., a Gentile man, woman: Jewish coll: mid-C.19–20. Ex Yiddish. cf. GORGER, esp. sense 3.

grab. A professional resurrectionist: medical s. (1823) > coll: almost †. S. Warren's *Diary of a Late Physician*, 1830. 2. A policeman: 1849: coll: †by 1900. Albert Smith.

grab, v. To steal; to arrest: 1812, Vaux, therefore from a few years earlier: resp. low coll and c. >, ca 1870, s. >, ca 1880, low coll: so I believe, despite the O.E.D. Dickens in *Oliver Twist*, 'Do you want to be grabbed, stupid?'

grab-all. A greedy or an avaricious

person: coll: from ca 1870. 2. A bag wherein to carry odds and ends: coll: from ca 1890.

grab-bag. A lucky-bag: late C.19–early 20. Ex U.S.

***grab-coup.** The snatching, by a losing gambler, of all the available money and then fighting a way out: c. of ca 1820–80. The variant *-game* arose, prob. in U.S., ca 1850; *-racket* is certainly U.S. (—1892), as in Stevenson & Osbourne's *The Wrecker*.

***grab-gains.** The snatching of a purse and then running away: c. of ca 1840–1900.

***grab on,** v.i. To 'hold on', manage to live: low: from ca 1850; ob. Mayhew.

***grabber.** The hand, but gen. in pl: from ca 1810 (ob.): c. >, by 1860, low. cf. PICKERS AND STEALERS. 2. A garotter: c. (—1909).

grabble, to seize, also to handle roughly or with rude intimacy, seems, in late C.18–mid-19, to have been felt to be coll: the O.E.D., however, considers it S.E. cf.:

grabbling irons. A mid-C.19 variant of GRAPPLING IRONS: fingers.

grabby. An infantryman: military (mostly in contempt by cavalrymen) and hence naval: ca 1848–1912. Bowen, 'Borrowed from the Hindustani'. Perhaps rather ex dial. *grabby*, greedy, inclined to cheat.

grace before meat. A kiss: domestic: late C.19–20. A preliminary.

grace card. The six of hearts: Anglo-Irish: C.18–20; ob. The proposed etymology – see F. & H., or H. – is too anecdotal for inclusion here.

grace o' God. 'The copy of a writ issued upon a bill of exchange': commercial (—1909). Ware.

gracious, as H. shows in his Introduction, was, in mid-Victorian ecclesiastical s., made to = pleasant or NICE or excellent.

gracious! (C.18–20), **gracious alive!** (mid-C.19–20), **gracious me!** (C.19–20), **good gracious!** (C.18–20) are euphemisms > coll.

gracious!, 'pon my. GRACIOUS!: mostly Cockneys': from ca 1890.

graduate. An artful fellow: coll: from ca 1875; ob. 2. A spinster skilled in sexual practice: low coll: from ca 1885. 3. A horse that has proved itself good: the turf: from ca 1870. All ex the ob. S.E. sense, a proficient in an art or a craft.

graduate, to, v.i. Obtain a sound practical knowledge of life, love, society, a livelihood etc.: coll: from ca 1875; ob.

***gradus.** In card-sharping, the making of a card to project beyond the rest: c. of ca 1820–1910. Also known as *the step*. cf.:

gradus ad Parnassum. (Lit., step to Parnassus; properly, a dictionary of prosody.) A treadmill: literary s.: ca 1790–1870. Ex the ascent of Parnassus and of the mill.

graft. Work, labour: coll: from ca 1870. Esp. in *hard graft*, (hard) work. *Hard grafting* occurs in the *Graphic* of 6 July 1878. 2. Hence, any kind of work, esp. if illicit: low coll (—1874). Esp. in *what graft are you at?*, what is your line – your LAY (2)? cf. the U.S. (orig. s.) sense, illicit profit or commission (mainly in politics), which, adopted into S.E. ca 1900, prob. derives ex the Eng. term, as, ultimately, does its corresponding v.

graft, v. To cuckold, 'plant horns' on: low coll: late C.17–18. 2. To work; esp. to work hard: coll, mostly Australia and New Zealand: from ca 1870. Earlier (ca 1855–80), to go to work: English only. Esp. in *where are you grafting?* Prob. ex †*grave*, to dig, perhaps influenced by the gardening *graft* and even by *craft* (as in *arts and crafts*).

grafter. 'One who toils hard or willingly', C. J. Dennis: from late 1890s: mostly Australian. Ex GRAFT, v., 2. 2. A swindler: coll, orig. (—1900) U.S., partly anglicized ca 1910. cf. GRAFT, n., 2. 3. One who works a line in a fair or market: as fortune-teller, quack doctor, mock-auctioneer, etc.: late C.19–20.

gram-fed. 'Getting, or being given, the best of everything': Anglo-Indian: 1880 (O.E.D.): s. >, by 1910, coll. Ex *gram*, chick-pea.

gramophone record. A canteen bloater: naval: late C.19–20. Because out of a tin.

grampus. A fat man; esp. one who puffs freely: from ca 1836: coll until ca 1895, then S.E. Dickens. 2. A greedy, stupid person: Roxburghshire s.: C.19–20; ob.

grampus, blow the. To drench a person: nautical: from ca 1790. 2. To play about in the water: nautical s. > gen. coll: from ca 1790.

gran. A grandmother; esp. in address: dial. and nursery coll: late C.19–20. cf. GRANNY.

***granam.** A late C.16 form of GRANNAM, 2.

grand. Abbr. *grand piano*: 1840: coll till C.20, then S.E. *Morning Advertiser*, 28 March 1891.

grand, adj. A gen. superlative of admiration: coll: from ca 1815. In late C.19–early 20, mainly U.S., opp. *fierce*. 2. adv., grandly: (low) coll verging, in C.20, on sol.: mid-C.18–20.

grand, do the. To put on airs: coll: from ca 1885; ob. cf. LARDY-DAH.

grandad, grand-dad. A coll childish and/or affectionate variation of *grandfather*: 1819, Byron. cf. GRANNY; GRANTY; GRANDMA, and:

grandada, grand-dada; gran(d-)daddy. Grandfather: familiar coll: resp. late C.17–20 (ob.) and mid-C.18–20.

grandma. An affectionate abbr. (C.19–20) of *grandmamma* (1763), itself an affectionate form of *grandmother*: coll.

grandmother, all my eye and my, see ALL MY EYE AND MY GRANDMOTHER.

grandmother, see one's. To have a nightmare: coll: from ca 1850; ob.

grandmother, shoot one's. To be mistaken or disappointed. Often as *you've shot your granny*. Coll: from ca 1860.

grandmother!, so's your, see ALL MY EYE AND MY GRANDMOTHER.

grandmother!, this beats my. That *is* astonishing! Coll: from ca 1880: ob.

grandmother (or granny) how to (or to) suck eggs, teach one's. To give advice to one's senior; esp. to instruct an expert in his own expertise: from ca 1600. Cotgrave, Swift, Fielding. Occ., from ca 1790, abbr. to *teach one's grandmother* or *granny*. Earlier forms are *teach one's (gran)dame to spin*, C.16–17, *to grope ducks*, Cotgrave, 1611, or *a goose*, Howell, 1659, and *to sup sour milk*, Ray, 1670; ca 1620–1750, *grannam* (or *-um*) was often substituted (see GRANNAM); from ca 1750, *granny*. A coll phrase so gen. as almost to > S.E.

grandmother (or little friend or auntie) with one, have one's. To be in one's menstrual period: low coll: from ca 1830. This process has attracted much cheap wit.

grandmother's review, my. The *British Review*: ca 1820–60. Byron's nickname.

grandpa. Abbr. (C.19–20) of *grandpapa*, itself coll and affectionate – from 1753 – for *grandfather*. cf. GRANDMA.

granite boulder. (One's) shoulder: shoulder: rhyming s.: since ca 1870.

***granna.** A loose variant of sense 2 of the next. Recorded (at date 1690) among the Sackville papers: see the Hon. V. Sackville-West, *Knole and the Sackvilles*, 1922. However, this may be an error for:

grannam, occ. **grannum.** A coll form of *grandam* = grandmother: late C.16–early 19. Shakespeare; Cibber in his *Rival Fools*, 1709, 'Go, fools! teach your grannums: you are always full of your advice when there's no occasion for't.' 2. Corn: c.: ca 1560–1820. Ex L. (cf. PANNAM) influenced by *granary*.

grannam-gold. 'Old Hoarded Coin', B.E.; 'hoarded money', Grose (1st ed.) who prefers the preferable *grannam's* (or *-um's*) *gold*; the S.E. form is *grandam-gold*. Coll: late C.17–18. i.e., supposed to have been inherited from the grandmaternal hoard.

Granny. See GRANDMOTHER. 2. The inevitable nickname of men surnamed Hudson: military: late C.19–20.

granny; occ. **grannie, grannee** (C.17), **grany** (C.18), **grannie,** Scottish: O.E.D. Grandmother: by that softening and abbr. (via GRANNAM) which is typical of affection. Coll: 1663 (S.O.D.). 'An old Woman, also a Grandmother', B.E. 2. 'Conceit of superior knowledge': low (—1851): ob. Mayhew. ?ex *teach one's* GRANDMOTHER HOW TO SUCK EGGS. 3. A badly tied knot apt to jam: nautical: ca 1860. Abbr. *granny's knot*. 4. Nonsense: Australian: ca 1860–1914.

***granny,** v. To know, recognize; swindle: c. (—1851). Mayhew. cf. the n., 2. Ex: 2. To understand (v.t.): c.: ca 1845 in '*No. 747*' *Autobiography of a Gipsy*.

granny, shoot one's, see GRANDMOTHER, SHOOT ONE'S. **granny, teach one's,** see GRANDMOTHER HOW TO . . .

granty. Grandmother: a coll more familiar and less gen. than *granny*, of which it is an affectionate elaboration. From ca 1850. More usual in Australia and New Zealand than in Great Britain. cf. Scottish and Northern *grandy* (1747: E.D.D.).

granum. An occ. C.18 form of GRANNAM.

grape-monger. A tippler of wine: C.17 coll.

grape-shot, adj. Tipsy: ca 1875–1900.

grape-vine. Clothes line: rhyming s.: late C.19–20.

graph. Ex *chromograph*, *hectograph*, etc., for a copy-producing apparatus: coll: ca 1880–1912. Whence:

graph, v. To take a number of copies of, by means of a GRAPH: coll: from ca 1880.

grapple. To shake hands with: naval: ca 1790–1850. W. N. Glascock, *Sailors and Saints* (I, 138), 1829.

grapple. (Gen. in pl.) The hand: low (—1877). See GRAPPLER, more common.

grapple-the-rails. Whiskey: Anglo-Irish c. > coll (—1785); ob. Because, after drinking it, one had to do this to remain upright.

grappler. (Gen. in pl.) The hand: from ca 1850: ?orig. nautical. cf. GRAPPLE and:

grappling-irons. The fingers: nautical: from ca 1855. cf. GRAPPLE and GRAPPLER. 2. Handcuffs: ca 1810–70. Presumably ex nautical S.E.

grass. Ground: 1625 (O.E.D.). 2. Abbr. SPARROW-GRASS = asparagus: low coll: from ca 1830; earlier, S.E. 3. Green vegetables: Royal Military Academy and nautical: from ca 1860. 4. A temporary hand on a newspaper: Australia (—1889); ob. Whence the c.p. *a grass on news waits dead men's shoes.* ?ex the English printers' *grass* = casual employment (1888, O.E.D.) or ex GRASS-HAND. 5. Female pubic hair: low: late C.19–20.

grass, v. To bring to the ground: orig. (1814), pugilistic. Egan, Moore, Dickens. 2. Hence, to baffle completely, pugilistic (—1822); to defeat, ca 1880–1910, and to kill, ca 1875–1914. 3. To discharge temporarily from one's employment: trade (—1881): ob. Ex a horse's going out to grass. 4. To do jobbing or casual work: printers': from ca 1894.

grass, be sent to. To be rusticated: Cambridge: ca 1790–1880. Punning 'rustication'.

***grass, cut one's own,** see CUT ONE'S OWN GRASS.

grass, go to. (Of limbs) to waste away: coll: ca 1840–1910. 2. For other senses, see GO TO GRASS.

grass, hunt. To be knocked down: s. or coll: ca 1870–1914. 2. At cricket, to field: ca 1880–1910. A variation of *to* HUNT LEATHER.

grass, out to. (Of person) retired: Australian: late C.19–20. Baker. Ex retired horses.

grass, send one's calves out to, see CALVES.

grass, send to. To knock down: from ca 1875; ob. Hindley. It originated in the old prize-fights waged in a field and was, therefore, orig. boxing s. (*Galaxy*, Oct. 1868, on p. 557.)

grass, take Nebuchadnezzar out to. To 'take' a man: low: from ca 1870. *Take* = lead; NEBUCHADNEZZAR = the male member, since he ate grass, and GRASS = (female) pubic hair.

grass before breakfast. A duel: Anglo-Irish: mid-C.18–mid-19. Lover, in *Handy Andy*.

grass-comber. A countryman serving as a sailor: nautical: ca 1860–1910. Walter Besant, 1886, 'Luke was a grass comber and a land swab.' Earlier (ca 1830–60), a farm-labourer passenger on a ship. On BEACH-COMBER.

grass grow under one's feet, let no. To lose no time or chance: C.17–20: coll in C.17, then S.E. A † variant is *on one's heel* (or *under one's heels*): C.16–early 19.

grass-hand. A GREEN or new hand: printers': ca 1875–1915. cf. GRASS, n., 4.

grass-widow. An unmarried mother; a discarded mistress: C.16–early 19 coll. More; B.E. The former nuance is extant in dial. 2. A married woman temporarily away from her husband: coll: from ca 1858; orig. mainly Anglo-Indian. The second follows from the first sense, which prob. contains an allusion to a bed of straw or grass – cf. the etymology of *bastard.* 3. Occ. as a v.: coll: from ca 1890.

grass-widower. A man separated temporarily from his wife: orig. (1862), U.S.; anglicized ca 1880. On GRASS-WIDOW, 2.

grasser. A fall, esp. one caused by a punch: sporting (—1887).

grasses! 'A cry directed at any one particularly polite': printers' (—1909). Perhaps ex Fr. *gracieux*: cf. Scots *gracie*, well-behaved.

grasshopper. A policeman: rhyming s. (—1893) on COPPER. 2. A waiter at a tea-garden: ca 1870–1914. Ex his busyness on the sward. 3. A thief: c. (—1893). *Pall Mall Gazette*, 2 Jan. 1893.

grassing. 'Casual work away from the office', F. & H.: printers': from ca 1889.

grassville. The country: early C.19: low. Punning DAISYVILLE.

gratters. Congratulations: university and Public School s. (—1903).

graunie, see GRANNY.

grave-digger, like a. 'Up to the arse in business, and don't know which way to turn', Grose, 2nd ed.: ca 1790–1860.

grave-digger, the. Strong liquor: Anglo-Indian: late C.19–20. Contrast COFFIN-NAIL. 2. pl, the last two batsmen (in the batting-order): cricketers' jocular coll: 1887; ob.

gravel. A rapidly diminishing supply of money in the market: Stock Exchange: 1884. Semantics: as the tide recedes, it leaves the gravel bare.

gravel, v. To confound, or puzzle greatly; FLOOR: mid-C.16–20; coll for a century, then S.E. Shakespeare, 'When you were gravelled for lack of matter'. Orig. nautical: cf. *stranded.*

gravel-crusher. A soldier at defaulters' drill: military: ca 1880–1900. 2. Then, but soon ob. and now †, any infantryman: mostly cavalrymen's. cf. BEETLE-CRUSHER. Also *gravel-crushing*, n. and adj.

gravel-grinder. A drunkard: low: from ca 1860: ob. Ex:

gravel-rash. Abrasions resulting from a fall: coll: from ca 1855. Perhaps jocular on *barber's rash.* 2. **have the g.-r.,** to be extremely drunk: from ca 1860; ob. Ex the poor fellow's numerous falls.

gravelly. The adj. to GRAVEL, n.: 1887, Atkins, *House Scraps.*

Gravesend bus. A hearse: (low) coll: ca 1880–1920. cf. S.E. *journey's end.*

Gravesend sweetmeat. (Gen. in pl.) A shrimp: ca 1860–1920. Many being sold there.

Gravesend twins. Solid pieces of sewage: low (—1874); ob. Our sewage system!

graveyard. The mouth: from ca 1875; ob. Contrast TOMBSTONE, 2. 2. 'A berth made over the counter of a coasting steamer': nautical: from ca 1880. Bowen.

gravy. The sexual discharge, male or female: low coll: mid-C.18–20; ob. Whence *give one's g.*, to 'spend'; *gravy-giver*, penis or pudend: *g.-maker*, pudend only: all, C.19–20 (ob.) low, the first coll, the others s.

gravy!, by. A Scots exclamation: mid-C.19–20; ob. Stevenson & Osbourne, *The Wrecker*, 1892. Prob. a corruption.

gravy-eye. A pejorative term of address: C.19–20 low coll. Ex *gravy-eyed*, blear-eyed, a late C.18 coll > C.19 S.E. The adj. is in Grose, 1st ed. 2. A turn at the wheel, 4–6 a.m.: nautical: ca 1850–90. 3. The middle watch (12–4 a.m.): nautical: from ca 1890.

***grawler.** A beggar: Scottish c.: ca 1820–60. ?*crawler* perverted.

gray: see GREY all entries.

graze, send to. To dismiss, turn out: ca 1730–60. Swift, 1733, 'In your faction's phrase, send the clergy all . . .'

graze on the plain. To be dismissed: coll (—1869); ob. cf. preceding.

grease. A bribe: coll (—1823). Hence bribery. 2. Flattery, fawning (cf. BUTTER, n., 2): coll and dial.: from ca 1870. 3. Profitable work: printers': from ca 1850; ob. Ex FAT. 4. A 'struggle, contention, or scramble of any kind, short of actual fighting': Westminster School (—1909). Perhaps ex the resultant perspiration. 5. Butter: Australians' and New Zealanders' and *Conway* cadets': late C.19–20. If inferior, *axle-grease.* Perhaps ex Yorkshire *grease*, strong, rancid butter.

grease, v. To bribe: C.16–20: coll till C.19, then S.E. 2. To cheat, deceive: C.17 (?18): coll, mostly low. 3. To flatter: C.19–20: coll. Ex GREASE ONE'S BOOTS.

grease, melt one's. To exhaust oneself or itself by violent action: coll: from ca 1830: ob. Southey.

grease a fat sow in the arse. To (try to) bribe, to give money to, a rich man: coll: C.18–mid-19. Heywood. cf. the proverb, *every man basteth the fat hog* (sc. *and the lean one gets burnt*).

grease off. To make off; slip away furtively: low: 1899, Clarence Rook. Prob. suggested by GREASED LIGHTNING.

grease one's boots. To flatter; fawn upon: late C.16–mid-19 coll. Florio; Ray, 1813. cf. GREASE, v., 3.

grease one's gills. To make a very good meal: C.19–20 (ob.), low coll. cf. GREASY CHIN.

grease-spot. The figurative condition to which one is reduced by great heat: coll: mainly Colonial: from ca 1890. ?ex the U.S. (1836) sense, adopted in England ca 1860 (H., 2nd ed., 'a minute remnant') as 'an infinitesimally small quantity' (Thornton), without reference to heat and gen. in negative sentences.

grease the fat pig or **sow.** A C.17–20 variant (ob.) of GREASE A FAT SOW . . .

grease the ways. 'To make preparations in advance to secure influence to get an appointment or the like': naval coll: from ca 1880. Bowen. A variation of S.E. *grease the wheels.*

grease to. To make up to; to flatter: Public Schools': late C.19–20. Desmond Coke, *The School across the Road*, 1910, 'You don't *really* mean you've chucked Warner's just because old Anson greased to you by making you a prefect.' cf. GREASER, 4, and OIL UP TO.

greased lightning, gen. preceded by **like.** This coll emblem of high speed is orig. (1833) and mainly U.S.; anglicized ca 1850. It appears in cricket as early as 1871.

greaser. A Mexican: orig. (ca 1849) and mainly U.S.; anglicized ca 1875, though used by Marryat much earlier. Ex the greasy appearance. 2. A ship's engineer: naval: from ca 1860. 3. An apology:

Bootham School: from ca 1880. For semantics, cf. BUTTER (n., 2) and SOFT SOAP. cf.: 4. A flatterer, sycophant: Sherborne Schoolboys': late C.19–20. Occ. *greazer*. cf. GREASE TO and GREASING. 5. See GREASERS.

greaser, give (one). To rub the back of another's hand with one's knuckles: Winchester College: from ca 1860: ob.

greasers. Fried potatoes: Royal Military Academy: ca 1870–1910. cf. BOILERS.

greasing. Flattery; ingratiating manners; pretentiousness: Public Schools', esp. Shrewsbury School's: late C.19–20.

greasy. Stormy: nautical coll (—1887).

greasy chin. A dinner: ca 1835–80. Ex the mid-C.18–early 19 sense, 'a treat given to parish officers in part of commutation for a bastard', Grose, 1st ed. cf. *eating a* CHILD.

great, adj. Splendid; extremely pleasant; a gen. superlative: orig. (1809), U.S.; anglicized ca 1895: coll. cf. IMMENSE. 2. In *run a great dog, filly*, etc., the sense is: the dog, etc., runs splendidly, a great race: sporting: from ca 1897.

great big. A mere intensive of *big*: coll: late C.19–20. cf. FINE.

. **great Caesar!** An almost meaningless substitute for *great God!*: from ca 1890. *Tit Bits*, 19 March 1892, 'Great Caesar! There you go again!' Here may be noted *great Jehoshaphat!*, in Besant & Rice's *Golden Butterfly* (1876), which contains also the (by 1914) †*great sun!* See also GREAT SCOTT!

great dog or **filly,** see GREAT, adj., 2.

great go, or **Great Go.** The final examination for the B.A. degree: Cambridge (hence, Oxford): from ca 1820: s. >, by 1860, coll and, by 1870, ob.; by 1900, †. cf. LITTLE GO; GREATER; GREATS, and see also GO, n.

great gun. A person, occ. a thing, of importance: coll: from ca 1815. Whyte-Melville, 'The great guns of the party'. At Eton, ca 1815–50, it = 'a good fellow, a knowing one'. Variant BIG GUN: from ca 1865; ob. 2. A favourite or gen. successful WHEEZE (3) or practice: pedlars', mostly London: from ca 1850. Mayhew, 'The street-seller's great gun, as he called it, was to . . .' Ex the S.E. sense: 'a fire-arm of the larger kind which requires to be mounted for firing', S.O.D.

great guns. An intensive adv.: naval: since ca 1790. cf. BLOW GREAT GUNS and 'growling great guns' in W. N. Glascock, *Sailors and Saints* (II, 51), 1829. 2. An expletive: 1895; ob.

great guns, blow, see BLOW . . . **great house,** see BIG HOUSE.

great I am, the. Used jocularly of oneself, pejoratively of others, it connotes excessive self-importance: coll: from ca 1905. Ex *I Am*, the Self-Existent, God, as in Exodus iii. 14.

great intimate. This sense of *great* – such a phrase is app. independent of *great friend* – is †S.E., but we may quote Grose's (3rd ed.) low coll equivalent of 'very intimate': *as great as shirt and shitten arse*. For other synonyms, see THICK.

great joseph. 'A surtout. *Cant*,' says, in 1788, Grose, 2nd ed.; †by 1860. By *surtout* he prob. means overcoat, the gen. definition; and low s. is perhaps the more accurate classification. Ex Joseph's coat of many colours.

great on. Knowing much about; very skilled in: coll: from ca 1875. Jefferies, 1878, 'He is very "great" on dogs'.

great Scott! An exclamation of surprise: also a very mild oath: orig. U.S. but soon anglicized, F. Anstey using it in *The Tinted Venus* in 1885. ?ex General Winfield Scott, a notoriously fussy candidate for the presidency. cf. DICKENS.

great shakes, no, see SHAKES.

***Great Smoke, the.** London: orig. (—1874), c.

great sun! see GREAT CAESAR!

great unwashed, the. The proletariat: at first (late C.18), derisively jocular S.E.; but since Scott popularized it, (non-proletarian) coll – and rather snobbish.

great whipper-in. Death: coll (?orig. hunting s.): from ca 1860; slightly ob.

greater. The B.A. finals examination: Oxford (—1893). Ex GREATS. An early example of the Oxford *-er*.

greats or **Greats.** That Oxford variation of GREAT GO which was first recorded and presumably popularized by 'Cuthbert Bede' when, in *Verdant Green*, 1853, he wrote: 'The little gentleman was going in for his Degree, *alias* Great-go, *alias* Greats'; used again by T. Hughes in *Tom Brown at Oxford*. Until ca 1895, s.; since, coll and applied (as abbr. *Classical Greats*) esp. to the examination for honours in Literae Humaniores. cf. LITTLE GO.

greaze. A crowd, a gang: Westminster School: C.19–20. Strictly applied only to the annual pancake fight.

greazer, see GREASER, 4.

Grecian. As roisterer, esp. ca 1818–30, it is gen. considered S.E., though prob. it was orig. Society s. (cf. CORINTHIAN.) Ob. by 1840, †by 1860. 2. An Irishman, esp. a newly arrived Irish immigrant: (?low) coll: from ca 1850; ob.; a variation of GREEK, 3. cf. next entry. 3. A senior boy: Christ's Hospital: from ca 1820.

Grecian accent. An Irish brogue: coll: ca 1850–1930. See GRECIAN, 2.

Grecian bend. A stoop affected in walking by many women ca 1869–90. *Daily Telegraph*, 1 Sept. 1869, '. . . What is called the "Grecian bend"'. The phrase was anticipated by *The Etonian* in 1821 (of a scholarly stoop) and is rarely used after ca 1885. cf. ALEXANDRA LIMP and ROMAN FALL. 2. H., 1874, defines it as 'modern milliner slang for an exaggerated bustle' (dress-improver): a derivative sense soon †.

***greed.** Money: c. of ca 1850–1900.

greedy-gut or **-guts.** A glutton: (from ca 1840, low) coll: the former, mid-C.16–early 18; the latter, C.18–20. cf. the old schoolboys' rhyme (ob. by 1900), 'Guy-hi, greedy-gut, | Eat all the pudding up,' the † singular being retained for the rhyme.

greedy scene. One in which a STAR (3) has the stage to him- or herself: theatrical (—1909).

Greek. A comparatively rare abbr. of *St Giles Greek*, cant; cf. the C.17–20 *it is Greek to me*, halfway between S.E. and coll. Prob. orig. s., but soon merely allusive and therefore S.E.: C.17–early 19. 2. As a card-sharper, a cheat, it is C.16–19 S.E., as also is the C.17 *merry Greek*, a roisterer. 3. An Iri hman ('the low Irish', H., 1859): Anglo-Irish s. or coll, from ca 1820; ob. Also in Australian s. before 1872. 4. A gambler; a highwayman: c.: early C.19. 5. v., only as implied in GREEKING.

***Greek fire.** Bad whiskey: c. (—1889); ob. Ex the S.E. sense. cf. ROT-GUT.

Greeking, vbl n. and gerund. Cheating at cards: ca 1816–40. *Sporting Magazine*, 1817, 'A discovery of Greeking at Brighton, has made considerable noise . . . in the sporting world'. Displaced by S.E. *Greekery.*

green, n. An inexperienced or unworldly person: coll: ca 1830–90. (Francis Francis, *Newton Dogvane*, 1859.) 2. See RED, n.

green, v. To make to appear simple; to hoax: from ca 1884 (Eton has the (—1893) variant *green up*); slightly ob. T. C. Buckland in 1888, 'Green . . . as boys call it'. i.e. to treat as a green hand. 2. To swindle, take in: (low) coll or s.: 1884.

green, adj. Inexperienced: S.E. but cf. GREEN IN MY EYE, GREENER, etc.

Green, send to Doctor or **Dr.** To put (a horse) to grass: late C.18–19. A punning coll.

green apron. A lay preacher: C.18: coll. In mid-C.17–18, also an adj., as in Warren's *Unbelievers*, 1654, 'A green-apron preacher'. Ex the sign of office.

green as duckweed(, as). Extremely simple or foolish: low coll (—1887).

green as I'm (or **you are,** etc.) **cabbage-looking, (I'm,** etc.) **not so.** (I'm, etc.) not such a fool as I (etc.) appear to be: lower- and lower-middle-class c.p.: late C.19–20.

green-back. A frog: late C.19–20; slightly ob. 2. A Todhunter text-book in mathematics: universities': ca 1870–1905. Ex colour of binding; cf. *yellow-back*. Dr Todhunter (d. 1884) published his famous text-books in 1858–69.

green-bag. A lawyer: late C.17–early 19. Ex (the †) colour of brief-bag. Grose, 1st ed., is amusing on the subject. cf. BLACK BOX, and:

green bag?, what's in the. 'What is the charge to be preferred against me?', Barrère & Leland: from ca 1890; ob. cf. preceding entry.

green bonnet, have or **wear a.** To go bankrupt: coll: ca 1800–1910. Ex the green cap formerly worn by bankrupts.

green cheese, see CHEESE.

green cloth. Abbr. *board of green cloth*, a billiard table: from ca 1890: coll. 2. Coll, too, is the sense, the green baize covering the table: from ca 1870.

green goose. A harlot: late C.16–17 coll. Beaumont & Fletcher, 'His palace is full of green geese.' cf. idea in FRESH BIT.

green gown, give a, either absolute or with dative. To tumble a woman on the grass: late C.16–18: coll > S.E. 2. Hence, to have sexual sport, esp. (somewhat euphemistically) deflower a girl. C.17–early 19 coll. 'Highwaymen' Smith, 1719, 'Our gallant being disposed to give his lady a green gown'.

green-grocery. The female pudend: low: from ca 1850; ob. Ex GREENS, 4.

green grove. The pubic hair (gen. female): low: ca 1850–1910.

green-hand(l)ed rake, see PETER COLLINS.

green (in late C.19–20, occ. **green stuff) in my eye?, do you see any.** The most gen.

form of *to see (any) green in a person's eye*, to consider him a greenhorn or a fool: 1840: coll, mostly low. 'Quotations' Benham; Mayhew; *Ally Sloper*, 19 March 1892, 'Ally Sloper, the cove with no green in his eye'. Ex *green* as indicative of inexperience or, esp., gullibility.

***green kingsman.** A pocket-handkerchief – gen. of silk – with a green ground: c. and pugilistic: ca 1835–1910. cf. BELCHER.

green meadow. The female pudend: low: more coll than euphemistic: from ca 1850. cf. GREEN GROVE.

green rag. The curtain: theatrical: from ca 1840: †by 1900.

green-room, talk. To gossip about the theatre: 1839, Lever in *Harry Lorrequer*: coll until ca 1880, then S.E.

green stuff, see GREEN IN MY EYE.

green up. The gen. Etonian variation of GREEN, v., 1.

greenacre. 'The falling of a set of goods out of the sling': dockers': mid-C.19–20. Perhaps ex Greenacre, a murderer (who buried the victim in sections in various parts of London) hanged at Newgate in 1837: the rope broke.

greener. A new hand; esp. one replacing a striker; also a foreign workman newly arrived: ca 1888.

greenery-yallery. Characteristic of the Aesthetic movement in the art and literature of the 1880s. Coined in 1880 by W. S. Gilbert **in** *Patience*, which was first performed on 23 April 1881. Orig. s., it > coll by 1890 and had, by 1910, > S.E. (as, e.g., it is in Hugh Walpole's *Vanessa*). This colour-scheme was a favourite with the Aesthetes.

greenfinch. 'One of the Pope's Irish guard': 1865, *Daily Telegraph*, 1 Nov. – but prob. from a decade earlier.

greengage. In actors' rhyming s., from ca 1880: stage (n.).

greengages. Wages: rhyming s.: from ca 1870.

greenhead. A new hand, esp. if inexperienced: late C.16–early 19: coll until ca 1820.

greenhorn. A new hand; also, a simpleton: from ca 1680, but presumably several centuries older (see W.'s *Surnames* at *Greenhorn*). Coll until C.20, when S.E. In mid-C.18–early 19, esp. 'an undebauched young fellow, just initiated into the society of bucks and bloods', Grose, 1785. Ex a young horned animal, cf. GREENHEAD.

greenhouse. An omnibus: London bus-drivers': ca 1890–1914. Ex the large amount of glass in the windows.

greenie, greeny. The white-plumed honey-eater (*ptilotis penicillata*): Australian schoolboys' coll (—1896).

Greenland, come from. To be inexperienced: from 1838, Dickens; ob.: a punning coll.

Greenlander. A new hand; a simpleton: from ca 1840: ob. Ex preceding. 2. Occ. (—1874), an Irishman; ob.

greenman. A contractor speculating with money not his own: builders': ca 1875–1910.

***greenmans.** The country: green fields: c.: C.17–early 19. cf. DAISYVILLE; -MANS.

greens. Chlorosis: coll: C.18–early 19. D'Urfey, 'The maiden ... that's vexed with her greens'. Ex *green sickness*. 2. Inferior or worn-out rollers: printers': from ca 1870: ob. 3. Green vegetables, e.g. and esp. cabbage and salads: coll: 1725 (S.O.D.). 4. Sexual sport, esp. coïtion: low coll: from ca 1850. ?ex GARDEN. cf. the next six entries: all low s. that, except GREENS, FRESH, have > (low) coll and all dating from ca 1850.

greens, after one's, adj. (Of men) seeking coïtion: cf. GREENS, ON FOR ONE'S and see GREENS, 4.

greens, fresh. A new harlot. cf. BIT, and see GREENS, 4.

greens, get or **have** or **like one's; give one's.** To obtain or enjoy the sexual favour; to grant it. (Of either sex.) See GREENS, 4, and:

greens, on for one's. (Gen. of women) eagerly amorous. cf. GREENS, AFTER ONE'S; see GREENS, 4. Also, (of men) *go for one's greens*, to seek sexual intercourse.

greens, price of. The cost of a harlot's sexual embrace. See GREENS, 4.

greens (or taturs)!, s'elp me (my). A low oath, orig. obscene – though this was rarely realized: mid-C.19–20; ob. Mayhew, *London Labour*, iii, 144. See GREENS, 4.

Greenwich, get. To become a GREENWICH GOOSE: nautical coll: late C.18–20.

Greenwich barber. A retailer of sand from at and near Greenwich in Kent: mid-C.18–early 19. Ex 'their constant shaving the sand banks', Grose, 1st ed.

Greenwich goose. A pensioner of Greenwich Hospital: naval and military: mid-C.18–19.

Greeny, the greeny. The curtain: theatrical: ca 1820–95. Egan. 2. A freshman:

university coll: ca 1830–1900. Southey in *The Doctor*. 3. A simpleton: from ca 1850: mainly U.S. 4. See GREENIE.

greetin' fu'. Drunk: coll: C.19–20. The Scottish properly = crying-drunk, a sense here ineligible.

gregarine. A louse, esp. in the head: C.19. Ex It.

grego. A rough greatcoat: mostly nautical: ca 1800–80. Westmacott; Marryat; Bowen, 'Borrowed from the Levant'.

gregorian, Gregorian. A kind of wig: late C.16–20: a coll that by 1690 was S.E.; now historical. Ex one Gregory, the Strand barber who invented it, according to Blount, 1670.

Gregorian tree. The gallows: mid-C.17–early 19: s. >, by 1750, coll. Ex 'a sequence of three hangmen of that name', *Gregory*, says F. & H.; prob. ex Gregory Brandon, a hangman, fl. *temp.* James I; successor, his son, Richard, gen. called 'Young Gregory'. In mid-C.17, *Gregory* occ. = a hangman.

gregory. Abbr. *Gregory-powder*: 1897. Ex Dr James Gregory (d. 1822).

Greshamite. A fellow of the Royal Society: late C.17–18: coll soon > S.E.

***grey.** A halfpenny (or, in C.20, a penny) two-headed or two-tailed, esp. as used in 'two-up': c.: from ca 1810. Ex Romany *gry*, a horse; cf. the synonymous PONY, 5. 2. Abbr. GREY-BACK, 1: from ca 1855; ob. 3. Silver; hence, money: c. (—1909). Ex the colour, *silvery-grey*.

grey as a badger, be; as grannam's (or -um's) cat. To have grey or white hairs from age: coll: resp. C.18–20 (ob.), C.18–19.

grey-back, greyback. A louse: mid-C.19–20, ob.: when not dial. it is coll. cf. SCOTCH GREYS. 2. (Mainly and orig. U.S.) a Confederate soldier: coll: 1862, U.S.; 1864, England. 3. A big wave: nautical coll: late C.19–20.

grey-backed un. The same GREY-BACK, 1.

grey-cloak. An alderman above the chair: C.16–17 coll. Ex his grey-furred cloak.

grey goose. A big stone loose on the surface: Scots coll: C.19–20. Scott.

grey mare. A wife, esp. if dominant: C.19–20 coll. Ex the proverb.

grey matter. Intelligence: jocular coll: from ca 1895. Ex S.E. sense, 'the grey-coloured matter of which the active part of the brain is composed.'

grey parson; grey-coat(ed) parson. A lay impropriator of tithes: coll: the first, late C.18–early 19; the second, C.19; the third, ca 1830 (Cobbett) -1910.

greyhound. 'A hammock with so little bedding as to be unfit for stowing in the nettings', Smyth: nautical (—1867). Ex thinness. 2. Abbr. *Atlantic* or *ocean greyhound*, a fast ocean – esp. Atlantic – liner: from ca 1887, the first being the S.S. *Alaska*, as W. reminds us; ob.: journalists'. 3. A member of Clare College: Cambridge: ca 1830–80.

greys. A fit of yawning; listlessness: coll: from ca 1860: ob. cf. BLUES, 2.

***grick,** see GRIG, 1.

griddle, n. A violin: itinerant entertainers': late C.19–20. cf. BOSH, n., 3, and:

griddle, v. To sing in the streets (whence vbl n. *griddling*): low or c. (—1851). Mayhew, 'Got a month for griddling in the main drag.' ?ex GRIZZLE or perhaps ex Romany *ghiv*, to sing.

griddler. A street-singer, esp. without printed words or music: low or c.: from ca 1855. Ex GRIDDLE, v. 2. A tinker: tramps' c.: from ca 1860.

griddling homey or **polone.** A violinist, male or female: partly Parlary: late C.19–20. Ex GRIDDLE, n.

gridiron. A county court summons (—1859); ob. Sala, 'He . . . takes out the abhorred gridirons.' Ex, and orig., those of the Westminster Court, for its arms resemble a gridiron. 2. **(the g-)** 'The Honourable East India Company's striped ensign': nautical coll: C.19. 3. 'The Stars and Stripes of the United States. Also called the "Stars and Bars"': nautical: from ca 1860. 4. A public-house sweetheart: Anglo-Irish: ca 1810–60. 'A Real Paddy', *Real Life in Ireland*, 1822.

gridiron, on the. (Either absolute, C.19–20, or with defining circumstances, C.16–18.) Harassed; in a bad way: coll: late C.16–20; ob.

gridiron, the whole. The whole party: non-aristocratic: from ca 1860. Perhaps suggested by *the whole* BOILING.

gridiron and dough boys. The U.S. flag: nautical: ca 1860–1910.

gridiron grumbles at the frying-pan, the. 'The pot calls the kettle BLACK ARSE': coll: C.19.

***gridirons.** The bars on a prison-cell window: c.: from ca 1870.

grief. Trouble: coll (—1891); ob. *Sportsman*, 28 Feb. 1891, 'The flag had scarcely fallen than [*sic*] the grief commenced.' Ex GRIEF, COME TO.

grief, bring to. To involve in great trouble; cause to fail: from ca 1870: coll.

grief, come to. To get into serious trouble; fail: coll (—1857). 2. To fall from a horse or a carriage: coll (—1855), mainly sporting. Thackeray in *The Newcomes*, 'We drove on to the downs, and we were nearly coming to grief.'

griff. Abbr. GRIFFIN, 2: 1829. Also of GRIFFIN, 3, 8.

griff, v. To deceive, take in (a person): Anglo-Indian, from ca 1830; ob. Ex the n.

griffin. A greenhorn: from ca 1810. Ex: 2. A new arrival from Europe: Anglo-Indian: 1793. Perhaps ex the unfortunate Admiral Griffin commanding in the Indian seas in 1746–8. See Yule & Burnell, who quote, for 1794, from Hugh Boyd, 'Griffin [capital letter], . . . the fashionable phrase here' (Madras). 3. A naval cadet, or a subaltern: resp. ca 1820–90, and from ca 1865. 4. An unbroken horse: Anglo-Chinese: from ca 1875. Occ., esp. in senses 2 and 3, abbr. to *griff*, as, for the former in 1829, and for the latter in Besant & Rice's *By Celia's Arbour*, 1878. 5. A woman forbidding in appearance or manners: coll: 1824: very ob. cf. *gorgon* in S.E. 6. Hence, a chaperon; a caretaker: coll: ca 1830–1900. 7. An umbrella: FAST (2) male society, ca 1859–70. 8. In c. (—1888), a signal or warning. Occ. *griff*, as in Nat Gould's *Double Event*, 1891; rare in C.20. 9. 'A grinning booby, who hath lost a tooth or two at top, and the same at bottom': app. ca 1720–1850. 'Jon Bee'. 10. The derivatives *griffinage*, *griffinism*, are †: these refer mostly to senses 1–3.

griffins. The leavings from a contract feast: trade (—1893); ob.

griffish, adj. Of or like a newcomer to India, hence of any greenhorn: Anglo-Indian > gen.: 1836; ob. Ex GRIFF, n.

griffmetoll, griff-metoll. A sixpence: c.: ca 1750–1800. ?ex *metal* + a device on the coin.

***grig**; in early C.19, occ. **grick** (Bee). A farthing: c. of ca 1690–1860. B.E., Ainsworth. cf. GIG, n., 4. 2. In pl, cash: mid-C.17–early 19.

grig, merry as a. Very active and lively: C.18–20 (ob.) coll. Goldsmith, 'I grew as merry as a grig.' An extension of *a merry grig*, a jocose and lively person: C.16–18 coll > S.E. ca 1820, when also it > archaic. Cotgrave, Wycherley, Grose. Ex the cricket or possibly the young eel.

grigs, see GRIG, 2.

***grim.** To swindle: c.: late C.16–early 17, Greene, 1591, 'The Cheater, when he has no cosin to grime with his stop dice.' ?cognate with Fr. *grimer*.

Grim, Mr, see OLD MR GRIM.

grimness. Obscenity, eroticism in literature: literary coll: 1895, *Daily News*, 19 Jan.; ob.

grin, on the (e.g. **broad**), adj. Grinning, e.g. broadly: coll: from ca 1800. In C.18, *on the high grin*, as in Swift.

grin, stand the. To be ridiculed and laughed at: ca 1820–50.

grin, the. A quizzing: low: 1821, Pierce Egan, *Life in London*; †by ca 1860.

grin at the daisy-roots. To be dead and buried: Anglo-Indian (esp. Calcutta): from ca 1880; ob.

grin in a glass case. 'To be shown as an anatomical preparation', F. & H.: coll: mid-C.18–mid-19. Ex the bodies and skeletons of criminals, formerly glass-cased at Surgeons' Hall.

grin like a Cheshire cat, see CHESHIRE CAT . . .

grinagog, the cat's uncle. A 'Cheshiring' simpleton; one who grins without reason: mid-C.18–early 19. Punning *grin*. cf. GIRNIGO-GABY.

grincomes, grincums. Syphilis: a C.17 variant of CRINKUMS. Jones, in *Adrasta*, 1635, 'In [a nobleman] the serpigo, in a knight the grincomes, in a gentleman the Neapolitan scabb, and in a serving man or artificer the plaine pox'.

grind. Hard work; routine: coll: from ca 1850. 2. Study, esp. for an examination: schools' (—1856). T. Hughes. 3. A plodding student: schools': ca 1870–1900, now only U.S. cf. GRINDER, 2. 4. A walk, esp. a CONSTITUTIONAL: university (—1860). 5. A steeplechase: university (mainly Oxford): 1857, 'Cuthbert Bede'. 6. A training run; an athletic sports meeting: from ca 1870: Oxford University. *Chambers's Journal*, April 1872, 'The hero of a hundred grinds'. 7. The sexual act: late C.16–20: low coll. Florio. Esp. in *do a grind* (rarely of a woman), to coït: C.19–20.

grind, v. To study (hard); read a text; prepare for examination: all with *with a* COACH understood and all v.i. (v.t. with *at*): school and university: from ca 1835. 2. To work at a hard or a distasteful task, or at the daily routine: v.i., variants with *on* and *away*; v.t. with *at* or *through*: coll: from ca 1855. 3. v.t., to teach (a subject) in a plodding way, cf. GERUND-GRINDER; to COACH (a student): university: 1815: ob. 4. To ride in a steeplechase: 1857, G.A. Lawrence, in *Guy Livingstone*; slightly ob. 5. v.i., to have sexual intercourse: low coll (—1811). Less gen. than *do a grind.* 6. To exhaust; be (like) hard work for: coll: 1887; ob. Talbot Baines Reed.

grind, do a, see GRIND, n., 7, and v., 5.

grind, on the. (Of either sex) being, at the time, incontinent; gaining a living as a prostitute: low: C.19–20.

grind mustard with one's knees. To be knock-kneed: C.18–early 19. See DURHAM MAN.

grind-off, see GRINDO. **grind the coffee-mill,** see GRINDER, *take a.*

grind water for the captain's ducks. On a sailing-ship, to take the wheel at 6–8 a.m.: nautical: mid-C.19–20; ob.

***grind wind.** To work the treadmill: c. of ca 1880–1910.

grinder. A private tutor; a COACH: university > gen.: 1813, Maria Edgeworth, 'Put him into the hands of a clever grinder or crammer [q.v.].' Ob. by 1900. 2. A plodding student: schools': ca 1870–1900.

grinder, take a. 'To apply the left thumb to the nose, and revolve the right hand round it, as if to work a . . . coffee-mill', F. & H. A Cockney retort to an attempt on his credulity or good faith. cf. *take a* SIGHT (n., 5) and *work the* COFFEE-MILL. The term was ob. in 1900; already in *Pickwick* we hear that this 'very graceful piece of pantomime' is 'unhappily, almost obsolete'. A variation, presumably, upon 'cocking a snook' (see COCK SNOOKS).

grinders. Teeth: coll: C.17–20. Ex S.E. sense (molars), as in Horace Walpole's 'A set of gnashing teeth, the grinders very entire'.

grindery. Shoemaking-material: shoemakers' (—1887).

grinding, vbl n. of GRIND, v., at all senses.

grinding-house. A house of correction: C.17–18 coll. 2. A brothel: C.19–20 (ob.) low. cf. GRIND, n., 7.

grinding-mill. A tutor's house where students are prepared for examination: university: ca 1860–1900. Ex a coffee-mill.

grinding-tool. The male member: low: C.19–20; ob. Ex GRIND, n., 7.

grindo or **grind-off.** A miller: ca 1862–1910. Ex a character in the play, *The Miller and his Men.*

grindstone. The female pudend: low: mid-C.19–20. Ex GRIND, n., 7. 2. A private tutor; a COACH: university: ca 1850–1900. Ex GRIND, v., 3.

grindstone, hold or **keep one's nose to the.** To treat harshly: coll: *hold* in C.17–18; *keep* in C.19–20. Variants in C.19, *bring* or *put*. Ex C.16–17 S.E. sense, to torture. 2. In C.19–20, to study hard or toil unremittingly; to cause another to do so.

grindstone on his back, have the. To (go to) fetch the monthly nurse for one's wife's confinement: C.18–19.

grinkcome, grincum, see GRINCOMES.

grinning stitches. Careless sewing: milliners': from ca 1870; ob. Because the stitches are wide apart.

grip. A place, e.g. a town: non-aristocratic: late C.19–20.

grip, v.i. To seize sheep (for a shearer): Australian s. (1886) >, by 1910, coll. 2. To catch, seize, take; Public Schools' coll: late C.19–20.

gripe or **gripes.** A miser; a usurer; occ. a banker: coll: C.17–18. Burton, 1621. 2. **(gripe)** In late C.16–17 c., a cheating gamester. Greene.

gripe-fist, -money, -penny. A miser or a usurer: coll, resp. C.19, C.17, C.19. cf. *gripe-all*, a grasping, mean person, C.19: ?S.E.

***griper.** A collier bringing coal in barges to London: c.: late C.16–early 17. Greene, 1591. cf. GRIPE, 2.

gripes. Colic. When, in late C.19–20, it is used of persons, it is coll – either low or jocular. (Earlier, S.E.; as still of animals.) 2. See GRIPE.

gripes in a tangle, see TIP A DADDLE.

gripper. He who catches sheep for the shearers: 1886: ob. Ex GRIP, v., 1. 2. A miser: coll (—1887); ob.

gristle, the. The male member: low: C.17–20; ob. 1665, R. Head, *The English Rogue*, ch. X.

grit. Spirit; stamina; courage, esp. if enduring: orig. (1825, as *clear grit*), U.S.; anglicized as a coll ca 1860. Thackeray. (*Clear grit* was, in U.S., not a mere synonym but an intensive.) Ex its hardness. cf. U.S. *sand.* 2. A member of the Liberal or Radical Party: Canada: 1887; ca 1884–7, a *Clear Grit.* The adj. *gritty* (U.S., 1847) has never caught on in England.

grizzle. One who frets: coll: 1703, E. Ward. 2. A fit of weeping: Cockney:

late C.19–20. Perhaps on *drizzle* = light rain.

grizzle, v. To fret; complain whiningly or lachrymosely: coll: 1842, ballad. The low coll form is *grizzle one's guts.*

grizzle-guts, occ. **-pot.** A tearfully or whiningly ill-tempered or melancholy person: low coll: from ca 1875.

grizzler. A grumbler; a person given to fretting: dial. (—1900) and coll (C.20). Ex GRIZZLE, V., 1.

***groaner.** A thief specializing in funerals and revivalist meetings: c.: ca 1840–1900. Duncombe, *The Sinks of London,* 1848. Ex:

***groaner and sigher.** A wretch 'hired by methodists and others to attend their meetings for the purposes of fraud', Potter, 1795. cf. GROANER.

groat, a cracked or **slit,** gen. in negative. Something worthless; nothing: coll: C.17. Dekker, 'Peace, you cracked groats'; Penn, 'The People . . . that would not trust an Archbishop about a Slit Groat'.

groats. The chaplain's monthly stipend: nautical: ca 1850–1914.

groats, save one's. To come off handsomely: university: mid-C.18–early 19. Ex the nine groats deposited by every degree-candidate, who, with honours, recovers them.

groceries, the, see GROCERY, 2.

groceries sundries. 'Wine and spirits sold furtively to women on credit': grocers' (—1909). Ware. Because so 'itemed'.

***grocery.** Small change in copper; copper coins collectively: C.18–early 19: s. or, more prob., c. Bailey. 2. (With *the,* occ. in the pl) sugar: ca 1838–1910. Lytton, 1841, 'A pint of brandy . . . Hot water and lots of the grocery'. According to the E.D.D., however, *the groceries* is Anglo-Irish for a decanter of whiskey and a bowl of sugar: Anglo-Irish: 1839, Lever.

grog. Rum diluted: 1770. 2. Spirits and water: from ca 1790. 3. Strong drink in gen.: from ca 1820. Orig. s., all these senses were coll by 1840, S.E. by 1870. ?ex *grogram,* whence *Old Grog,* the nickname of Admiral Vernon, who, in the summer of 1740, ordered the Navy's rum to be diluted and who wore a grogram cloak. 4. A party at which grog is drunk: coll: 1888: ob. (O.E.D.). 5. A GROGGY (2) horse: 1818, *The Sporting Magazine,* vol. ii (O.E.D.).

grog, v. To drink grog: 1833 (S.O.D.): s. >, ca 1850, coll.

grog, seven-water. Extremely weak grog: nautical: from ca 1830. Marryat.

grog-blossom. A pimple caused by strong drink: low (—1791): ob. Thomas Hardy, 'A few grog-blossoms marked the neighbourhood of his nose.'

grog-fight. A drinking party: military (—1864): ob.

grog on board, have. To be drunk: C.19–20 (ob.) nautical.

grog-shop. The mouth: pugilistic: from ca 1840; ob. Thackeray.

grog-tub. A brandy bottle: nautical: ca 1860–1914.

grogged, be. To be tipsy: ca 1840–1900: coll. cf. Grose, 1796, 'A grogged horse; a foundered horse'. Ex GROG, V.

groggified. A late C.18–19 variant (Grose, 2nd ed.), latterly nautical, of the first sense of:

groggy. Tipsy: 1770: ob. Ex GROG, n., 1, 2. Whence, (of horses) tender-footed: stables s. > j.: 1828. Youatt, 1831, in *The Horse*: ob. 3. Whence, unsteady on one's feet: pugilistic and gen.: from ca 1830. Thackeray.

***grogham.** A horse, esp. if old: c. in late C.18–19, then low; ob. Origin? cf. PRAD.

groise, n. A SWOT: Harrow School: late C.19–20. 2. A GORGE or SPREAD (5) of edibles, etc.: Scottish Public Schools': since ca 1870.

groise, v.i. To work hard: Harrow School: late C.19–20.

gromal. An apprentice: nautical coll: mid-C.18–19. A corruption of dial. *gom(m)eral(l), -el(l), -il(l),* a simpleton (E.D.D.).

groom. A croupier: gamblers' c. > s.: late C.19–20.

groovy. Of settled habits or rutty mind: coll: only from ca 1880, although *grooviness,* likewise coll, is recorded by the O.E.D. as early as 1867.

***groper.** A blind man: c.: mid-C.17–mid-19. 2. (Gen. in pl.) A pocket: c. or low: late C.18–early 19. 3. A midwife: low (?orig. c.): C.18–mid-19. 4. The blindfolded person in blind-man's-buff: ca 1810–1914.

groperess. A blind woman: low: ca 1820–60. Ex GROPER, 1.

groping for Jesus. Public prayer: lower classes': 1882. Ex Salvationists' cry, *grope for Jesus – grope for Jesus!*

gropus. 'The coat-pocket – from the manner of groping for its lesser contents', says 'Jon Bee', 1823: ca 1820–50.

grote. An informer (?): low s. or perhaps c.: ca 1880–1920.

grouce, see GROUSE, V.

ground, go down to the. To defecate: C.17 coll. Middleton in his *Family of Love,* 'Do you go well to ground?' cf. C.19 medical j., *get to the ground.*

ground, suit down to the. To be thoroughly acceptable or becoming: coll: from ca 1875. Miss Braddon, 'Some sea coast city . . . would suit me down to the ground.' But *down to the ground* is occ. used with other vv. cf. the M.E. *all to ground.*

ground floor, let in on the. (Of the promoters) to allow to share in a financial or commercial speculation on equal terms: orig. U.S.; anglicized ca 1900: mainly Stock Exchange and commerce. From the opp. angle, *get,* or *be let, in on the g.-f.*

ground-parrot. A small farmer: Australian (—1898); ob. Suggested by COCKATOO, n., and ex the *ground-parrot* or *psittacus pulchellus.*

ground-squirrel. A hog, a pig: nautical: ca 1790–1860.

ground-sweat. A grave: c. or low: late C.17–mid-19. Esp. in *have,* or *take,* a *ground-sweat,* to be buried. cf. dial. *take a g.-s. about anything,* to worry oneself greatly, and the C.19 dial. proverb, 'a ground-sweat cures all disorders.'

ground (or floor) with one, mop (or wipe) up the. To thrash soundly; fig., to prove oneself vastly superior to: coll: from ca 1880. Henley & Stevenson, 1887, 'I'll mop the floor up with him any day.'

grounder. A low-keeping ball: cricketers' coll: 1849; ob. cf. *sneak(er).* 2. In angling, catching the ground: 1847, Albert Smith: s. > j. or coll. 3. A knock-down blow: from late 1880s: s.; in C.20, coll.

grouse. A grumble: orig. (ca 1890) soldiers' s.

grouse; occ., but not after 1914, **grouce,** v. To grumble: dial, from ca 1850 (see W.), >, by ca 1880, soldiers' s. that, ca 1919, > gen. coll. Kipling, 1892, 'If you're cast for fatigue by a sergeant unkind, | – Don't grouse like a woman, nor crack on, nor blind.' ?cognate with Old Fr. *groucier*; and ?cf. U.S. *grout,* to grumble (1836: Thornton). 2. To coït with a woman: dial. and s.: mid-C.19–20. Ex dial. *grouse,* to pry, search.

grouse, do a. To look for, or successfully follow, a woman: low: from ca 1850; ob. Either ex the 'running down' of the bird or ex *grouse,* to shoot grouse.

grouser. A grumbler: 1885, J. Brunlees Patterson, *Life in the Ranks*: soldiers'. Ex GROUSE, V., 1. 2. One who runs, sexually, after women: low: from ca 1855; ob. by 1914. 3. A rowing man, a 'wet BOB': sporting: ca 1880–1910.

grousing. A sexual search for women: the habit thereof. cf. *go grousing = do a grouse.* Both, low: from ca 1850; ob. 2. vbl n. of GROUSE, V., 1.

grout(e). To work or study hard: Marlborough and Cheltenham Colleges: from ca 1870. Ex the S.E. sense, dig with the snout.

grout-bag. One who studies hard: English schoolboys': since ca 1880.

grouty. Peevish; sulky: coll: orig. (1836), U.S.; anglicized ca 1870; ob. Ultimately ex Eng. dial. *grouty,* thundery.

***grow,** v.i. To be allowed to let one's hair and beard grow: prison c.: ca 1870–1915. Ex:

***grow one's feathers.** Gen. as *growing one's feathers,* 'letting one's hair and beard grow, a privilege accorded to convicts for some months before their discharge, that they may not be noticeable when free': prison c.: from ca 1870.

***growl.** Female pudend: c.: from ca 1890. Short for *growl and grunt,* rhyming s. on CUNT.

growl you may – but go you must! A nautical c.p. uttered 'when the watch have to turn out of their bunks to shorten sail in bad weather': late C.19–20. Bowen. The moderation of the language indicates the gravity of the need.

***growl-biter.** A cunnilingist: c.: late C. 19–20. Ex GROWL.

growler. A four-wheeled cab: coll: 1865. ?ex its own tendency to creak – or its driver's to grumble. 2. Hence, *work the growler,* to go in a cab from PUB to pub: low coll: late C.19–20; ob. 3. A dog: Anglo-Irish: C.19.

growlery. One's private sitting-room: jocular coll: ex Dickens's coinage in *Bleak House,* 1852–3. cf. DEN; *snuggery.*

grown. The corpse of an adult: undertakers': from ca 1870; ob.

grown-man's dose. A very large drink; much liquor: coll: from ca 1860.

grown(-)up. An adult: coll: from ca 1810. Dickens, in *Our Mutual Friend,* 'I always did like grown ups.'

groyze. To spit: *Conway* cadets' (—1891); ob.

grub. Food; provisions of food: 1659.

Until ca 1830, low. ca 1750–1830, gen. in *grub and* BUB, or *bub and grub*, food and drink: of the latter, Parker in 1789 says: 'A mighty low expression'. Maginn; Thackeray, 1857, 'He used to ... have his grub too on board.' 2. Whence, a meal, a feed: from ca 1855; ob. Hughes. 3. (For etymology, cf. sense 5.) A short, thick-set person (rarely a woman): coll: C.15–17. cf. 4. A dirty and slovenly, gen. elderly, person: coll: from ca 1890. 5. A low-keeping ball; a GROUNDER – and, like it, only of a bowled ball: cricketers': ca 1820–1910. Ex the lowly insect so named.

grub, v.i. To eat: from ca 1720: low until ca 1840. Dickens in *Pickwick*. Ex the n., 1. 2. Whence, v.t., provide with food: from ca 1810. 3. Whence, to beg food: low: ca 1840–1900. 4. To cut off a cock's feathers under the wings: cock-fighters': from ca 1700. Kersey's 'Phillips'.

grub, like. Greatly: enthusiastically. 'I am on like grub,' Baumann, 1887. Low; ob.

grub, ride. To be sullen: ill-tempered: coll (—1785); ob. by 1860, †by 1890. ?ex dial., which has *the grubs bite* (a person) *hard* in the same sense.

grub along. To get along, fig., as best one can: low (—1888).

grub-crib, see GRUB-SHOP.

grub-hamper. A consignment of sweet edibles from home: Public Schools': late C.19–20.

***grub-hunting,** vbl n. Begging for food: tramps': from ca 1845.

grub it. A variant of GRUB, v., 1: C.19–20; very ob.

grub-shite. To befoul; hence, make very dirty: low: ca 1780–1860. Lit., to befoul as a grub befouls.

grub-shop, -crib, -trap. The first and second, an eating-house: low: from ca 1840. Also, a workhouse: from ca 1850. 2. The first and third, the mouth: low: from ca 1860.

grub-spoiler. A ship's cook: nautical: late C.19–20.

grub-stakes. GRUB (1): non-aristocratic: from ca 1890. Richards. 2. Food-supply: coll: from ca 1890. Ex the U.S. and Canadian practice whereby someone with capital provided a gold-prospector with food and, if necessary, equipment.

***grub-stealer.** A beggar stealing food from another: tramps' c. (—1887).

Grub Street, as the ill-fed corpus of literary hacks, is S.E., but *Grub Street news*, 'lying intelligence' (Grose, 1st ed.) or 'news, false, forg'd' (B.E.) is, in late C.17–18, coll. Ex that C.17 hack-, i.e. 'grub-', inhabited street near Moorfields which has, since 1830, been known as Fore Street. See Grose, P., and Beresford Chancellor's *Annals of Fleet Street*.

grub-trap, see GRUB-SHOP.

grubber. An eater: low: from ca 1860. Ex GRUB, v., 1. 2. A workhouse: tramps' c. (—1900). J. Stamper, *Less than the Dust*. 3. A tuck-shop: Tonbridge School: from ca 1880. 4. A BONE-GRUBBER, esp. sense 1.

grubbery. An eating-house: from ca 1820. 2. A dining-room: from ca 1830. 3. Food: ca 1830–1905. Trelawney. Ex GRUB, v., 1. 4. The mouth: from ca 1870. All low, except the jocular third.

grubbing, vbl n. (see GRUB, v.). Eating: from ca 1815. Moore, 'What with snoozing, high grubbing, and guzzling like Cloe'. 2. Food: from ca 1865: ob.

***grubbing-crib or -ken.** An eating-house: low if not indeed c.: from ca 1830; ob. 2. (*-crib* only) a workhouse: tramps' from ca 1850. Mayhew. cf. MUNGARLY-CASA.

***grubbing-crib faker.** The proprietor, occ. the manager, of a low eating-house: low: from ca 1850: ob. Ex preceding term.

***grubby.** A c. diminutive of GRUB, food: C.19–20.

***grubby-ken.** A low eating-house: ca 1820–50: c. Ex preceding.

gruel. Punishment; a beating: coll: from ca 1795. Scott in *Guy Mannering*, '... Great indignation against some individual. "He shall have his gruel," said one.' Gen. in phrases. *Give one his*, or *get one's*, *gruel*, to punish, be punished; in boxing, knock out or be knocked out; in c., to kill, be killed. Also, *gruelled*, FLOORED; *gruelling*, a beating; heavy punishment: also adj. (Occ. *take one's gruel*, to endure a beating like a man, as in *Sporting Life*, 15 Dec. 1888.) cf. *settle one's* HASH and COOK ONE'S GOOSE and consider *serve one out*, pugilistic ex nautical SERVE OUT *grog*.

gruel, v. To punish; exhaust: coll: 1850, Kingsley. Ex the n.

grueller. A SETTLER (3); a knock-down blow; a poser: coll: 1856, Kingsley. Ex GRUEL, V.

gruelling, vbl n. and ppl adj.: see GRUEL, n. (1882: O.E.D.)

gruffle. To speak gruffly in a muffled way: dial. (—1825) >, by 1900, coll. Echoic.

grumble-guts. An inveterate GROUSER: C.19–20 coll, now mainly dial., which also has *grumble-belly* or *-dirt*. Variant, *grumble-gizzard*, C.19–20; ob. cf.:

grumble in the gizzard, C.18–20 (ob.); **of the gizzard,** C.17. To murmur or repine: coll.

grumbler. Fourpence-worth of grog: Londoners': ca 1820–50.

grumbles, be all on the. To be cross or discontented: low coll: from ca 1865. The O.E.D. records *the grumbles*, jocular coll for ill humour, at 1861.

grumbletonian. A (constant) grumbler: coll: from ca 1710; ob. Orig. – ca 1690–1730 – the nickname of the Count(r)y Party, in the opposition (Macaulay's *History*, ch. XIX). 'Coined on *Muggletonian*', W.

grumbly. Like a grumble: 1858, Carlyle. 2. Inclined to grumble: ibid. Both coll.

grummet. The female pudend: low: nautical: from ca 1860; ob. 2. Coïtion: nautical and low: mid-C.19–20. Ex nautical j.: sense 1 *b* or *c* in the O.E.D.

grumpish, grumpy. Surly; peevish: coll; in C.20, S.E.: resp. 1797, 1778 (O.E.D.). Sala, 'Calling you a "cross, grumpy, old thing", when you mildly suggest . . .'

grundy. A short fat person, rarely of a woman: rare coll: C.16. Foxe in *Acts and Monuments*, 1570.

***grunt.** Anon., *Street Robberies Consider'd*, 1728, defines it as a hog: if this is correct, the term is c.; but prob. it is an error of sense 1 of:

***grunter.** (In M.E., any grunting animal. Hence:) A pig: c. in mid-C.16–18; coll (mainly jocular) in C.19–20. Brome; Tennyson. 2. In C.17 c., also a sucking pig. Ex GRUNTING CHEAT. 3. A shilling: late C.18–early 19: low, ?orig. c. On HOG. But from ca 1840, sixpence: ob. *Household Words*, 20 June 1885, 'The sixpence . . . is variously known as a "pig", a "sow's baby", a "grunter", and "half a hog".' 4. A policeman: low (—1820): ob. *London Magazine*, vol. i, 1820. 5. A constant grumbler: tailors': from ca 1870.

grunter's gig. A smoked pig's 'face' or chap: late C.18–mid-19.

grunters' mums. 'Pigs' faces and the like' (as food): s.: Ned Ward, 1703. cf. MUMS and MUN.

***grunting cheat.** A pig: c.: ca 1560–1730. Fletcher in *The Beggar's Bush*. cf.:

***grunting peck.** Pork; bacon: c.: ca 1670–1850. See PECK and cf. BLEATING *cheat*.

gruts. Tea: low coll: from ca 1810: ob. Perhaps cognate with dial. *grout*, small beer.

guana, guano, see GOANNA.

guard. To see that horses or hounds from one stable are separated in a race: sporting s. > coll > j.: 1893 (O.E.D.).

guardy, -ie. An affectionate abbr. of *guardian*: coll: from ca 1850.

gubb. A young sea-gull: nautical: C.19–20. Origin?

gubber. A beach-comber on the look-out for odds and ends: nautical: mid-C.19–20.

gubbins as fish-offal is S.E., but as the name given to the primitive inhabitants of a Dartmoor district near Brent Tor, it is coll: from ca 1660; ob. by 1850, †by 1900. 2. Hence (?), a fool: military and schools': late C.19–20. 3. Rubbish, trash: coll: late C.19–20. Ex S.E. sense.

gubbrow. To bully, dumbfound, perturb: Anglo-Indian coll (—1886). Ex Hindustani.

gud. An expletive perversion of *God*: ca 1675–1750. Otway.

guess!, I. I'm pretty sure: coll: orig. (1798) U.S., anglicized ca 1885 but still recognized as from abroad. Ex the M.E.–early Mod. Eng. *guess*, (rather) think, suppose, estimate.

guess and by God (or, euphemistically, **Godfrey), by.** (Of steering) at hazard: naval (—1909).

guff. HUMBUG; empty talk; foolish bluff; nonsense: from ca 1888 (?orig. U.S.). Prob. ex *guff*, a puff, a whiff. cf. GUP. 2. Whence, impudence: Dartmouth College, where *guff rules* = 'privileges of the Senior Cadets': from ca 1890. Hence, *guffy*, impudent.

guffin. A person both clumsy and stupid: from ca 1860: s. when not dial.

guffoon. The Anglo-Irish form of the preceding. Ex It., says Ware.

guffy. A soldier: nautical: from ca 1880; ob. Clark Russell. ?ex GUFFIN.

guffy, adj. see GUFF, n., 2.

guggle. The windpipe: late C.17–20; ob. except in dial. Ex the v. 2. A gurgling sound: coll: from ca 1820.

guggle, v. To gurgle (of which it is the coll form): C.17–20. Johnson.

gugusse. 'An effeminate youth who frequents the private company of priests': Roman Catholics': from the early 1880s; ob. Ware, noting its Fr. origin, adds: 'In Paris (1880) the word was taken from the name of one of the novels specially directed about this time at the French priesthood.' i.e. *Gugusse*, a s. form of *Auguste*, often connoting 'fool'. cf. GUSSIE.

guide-post. A clergyman: late C.18–early 20. Inferentially from Grose (all edd.) at PARSON (a signpost). For a parallel vice-versality, cf. CHIMNEY-SWEEP and CLERGYMAN.

guiders. Reins: coll: from ca 1830; ob. 2. Sinews: low coll when not dial.: from ca 1820. cf. *leaders*.

guillotine, v.t. To place (a delinquent) with his head jammed under the shutter in the hammock netting and then aim missiles at the exposed portion of his anatomy: *Conway* cadets' (—1891).

guilt. Sense of guilt: a catachresis: ?only in Tillotson, 1690.

guinea, yellow as a. Very yellow: C.19–20: coll >, by 1900, S.E.; ob.

guinea-dropper. A sharper, esp. one who drops counterfeit guineas: late C.17–18. Gay in *Trivia*. cf. GOLD-FINDER (2) and RING-DROPPER.

Guinea-gold. Sincere; utterly dependable: coll verging on S.E.: C.18–early 19. Semantics: *sterling*. Moreover, Guinea gold, from which the guinea was coined in C.18, was 'of a magnificent yellow' (Ware).

guinea-hen. A courtesan; a harlot: C.17–early 18: s. >, by 1700, coll. Shakespeare. With a punning allusion to her fee.

guinea-pig. A gen. term of reproach: coll: ca 1745–1830. Smollett, 'A good seaman he is . . . none of your guinea-pigs.' cf. sense 6. 2. One whose fee is a guinea, esp. a VET, a medical man, a special juryman: coll: ca 1820–70. 3. From ca 1870, a public-company director, one who merely attends board meetings. 4. ca 1870–90, an engineer officer doing civil duty at the War Office. 5. Also, ca 1875–1915, a clergyman acting as a deputy. *Saturday Review*, 25 Aug. 1883. 6. A midshipman in the East Indian service: nautical: ca 1745–1930.

guinea-pigging. Acting as a company-director for the sake of the fee: 1890. 2. As a clerical deputy: 1887. Both coll.

guinea to a gooseberry, (it's) a. (It is) long odds: sporting: ca 1880–1910. Hawley Smart, 1884, 'Why, it's a guinea to a gooseberry on Sam!' A ca 1865–90 variant: *a guinea to a goose* (Baumann). cf. the City LOMBARD STREET TO . . .

guinea-trade. Professional services of the deputy, stop-gap, or the nominal kind: 1808 (S.O.D.); ob. Perhaps rather jocular coll than s. Punning *Guinea trade*.

guiver. Flattery; artfulness: theatrical: from ca 1890. 2. 'The . . . sweep of hair worn down on the forehead, lower and lower as the 1890s proceeded': among Cockney boy-SWELLS: from ca 1890; virtually †. Ware. Ex the Hebrew for 'pride', hence 'pretence' or 'swank'.

guiver, v.i. To humbug; fool about: show off: sporting (—1891); ob. Ex preceding.

guiver, adj. Smart; fashionable: low (—1866). Vance in *The Chickaleary Cove*.

guiver lad. A low-class dandy; an artful fellow: ca 1870–1900. Mainly Cockney.

gulf. (The group or position of) those who barely get their degree, 'degrees allowed': Cambridge University: 1827; Bristed, *Five Years in an English University*. 2. One who, trying for honours, obtains only a pass: Oxford University: from ca 1830: cf.:

gulf, v. To place in the GULF (1, occ. sense 2): university: from ca 1831, Cambridge; 1853, Oxford (O.E.D.). According to H., 1860, *gulfed* denoted a man 'unable to enter for the classical examination from having failed in the mathematical . . . The term is now obsolete.'

gulf, shoot the. To achieve a very difficult task; ironically, to achieve the impossible: coll: ca 1640–1760. Howell; Defoe, 'That famous old wives' saying'. Perhaps, as Defoe asserts, ex Drake's 'shooting the gulf' of Magellan.

gulf it. To be content with, or obtain, a place in the gulf: Cambridge University, 1827. Anon., *Seven Years at Cambridge*, 1827. Ob. by 1890. Ex GULF, n., 1; rarely sense 2.

gulfed, see GULF, v.

gull, as a simpleton, fool, or dupe or as a trick, fraud, or false report, is S.E., but as a trickster or swindler, late C.17–19, it is s. S.E. also is the v. in its various senses, though it may possibly have been orig. coll in that of dupe. Almost certainly S.E. are *gullage* and *gullery* – *gullable*, *gullible*, and *gullish* – and *guller*; perhaps, too, *gull-catcher*.

gull-finch. A simpleton; a fool: C.17 coll. 'Water Poet' Taylor.

***gull-groper.** One who (gen. professionally) lends money to gamblers: c.: C.17–early 19. Dekker, 'The gul-groper is commonly an old moneymonger.' Ex the S.E. *grope a gull*, to *pluck a* PIGEON (5).

gull in night-clothes. A rook (the bird): naval: late C.19–20. Ex the darkness of night.

gull-sharper. 'One who preys upon Johnny Raws', Smyth: nautical: ca 1850–1915.

gullet. The throat: always loose Eng., it was coll in late C.17–mid-18: B.E., 'a Derisory Term for the Throat, from Gula'.

gullfinch, see GULL-FINCH.

gully, the throat, is low coll: C.19–20 (ob.). Ex C.16–17 S.E. sense (GULLET). 2. As a large knife, it is, despite F. & H., ineligible, for it is dial. 3. The female pudend: low (? s. or coll): from ca 1850; ob. 4. In c. of C.19–20 (now virtually †), a person given to telling lies.

gully, v. Dupe; swindle: low: ca 1830–1910. Ainsworth, 'I rode about and speechified, and everybody gullied.'

gully-fluff. BEGGAR'S VELVET; orig. the fluff that forms in pockets: low coll: from ca 1820; ob. cf. S.E. *flue*.

gully-groper. A long cattle-whip: Australian: ca 1870–1900. cf. GULLY-RAKER, 3.

gully-gut. A glutton: mid-C.16–19 coll. In C.16–17, often *gulli(e)-gut*.

gully-hole. The gullet, the throat; the female pudend. C.19–20 (ob.); low.

gully-raker. A wencher: low: C.19–20. 2. The male member: low: C.19–20, ob. 3. In Australia, a long whip, esp. for cattle: from ca 1880. A C. Grant, *Bush Life in Queensland*, 1881. Ex the ca 1845–80 sense, 4, a cattle thief.

gully-raking. Cattle thieving: Australian: from ca 1845; ob.

gully-shooting, vbl n. Pointing oars upwards when rowing: *Conway* cadets' (—1891).

gulpin. A simpleton; a person (ignorantly) credulous: coll (—1860). Besant, 1886, 'Go then, for a brace of gulpins!' Because he will gulp down anything; imm. ex the next sense. 2. A marine: nautical: from ca 1800; ob. cf. *tell that to the* MARINES.

gulpy. Easily duped: coll: C.19–20; ob. cf. GULPIN, 1. 2. (Of the voice) broken by gulps of emotion: coll: from ca 1860.

gulsh, hold one's. To keep quiet, refrain from talking: from ca 1840: more dial. than (provincial) coll. Ex Northamptonshire *gulsh*, silly talk; ribaldry.

gum. Chatter: coll: ca 1750–1860. Smollett. 2. Abusive talk: coll or s.: ca 1780–1840. Grose, 1st ed., 'Come, let us have no more of your gum.' Ex the *gums* of the mouth. 3. Abbr. *chewing-gum*: orig. U.S.; anglicized ca 1905.

gum!, by. A mild oath: low coll and dial.: from ca 1825. Pierce Egan in *The Life of an Actor*. *God* corrupted; or, as Ware suggests, a telescoping and slovening of *God almighty*.

Gum, old mother. Pejoratively, an old woman: low coll: from ca 1850; ob.

gum-smasher or -tickler. A dentist: from ca 1860; ob. cf. SNAG-CATCHER.

gum-sucker. A native of Tasmania, inaccurately says F. & H.; properly, a person Victorian-born – loosely, a native of other States, inclusive of – and esp. – Tasmania. Coll: from ca 1820; slightly ob. Ex the habit, among boys, of eating gum from eucalyptus or acacia trees, as in P. Cunningham's *Two Years in New South Wales*. Hence 2, a fool: also Australian, but not very gen.: ca 1880–1900.

gum-tickler. A drink; esp., a dram: ca 1814–1915. Dickens, 'I prefer to take it in the form of a gum-tickler,' 1864. Perhaps adopted from U.S., where it is attested in 1810. 2. See GUM-SMASHER.

gum-tree, be up a. To be in a predicament; be cornered: Australian: from ca 1895. cf. the much earlier U.S. sense, be on one's last legs, whence prob. the Australian. ?ex an opossum being shot at. cf.:

gum-tree, have seen one's last. To be done for: Australian (—1893): s. > coll; ob. But Baumann, 1887, classifies the phrase as nautical: prob. both lexicographers are correct.

gum-tree!, strike me up a. Variant, *up a blue gum(-tree)*. An Australian coll expletive: from ca 1905. The gum-tree has very hard wood and is difficult to climb.

gumbler, see QUERIER.

gummagy. Given to scolding or snarling: low coll: C.19–20 (ob.). Ex GUM, 2.

gummed. (Of a ball) close to the cushion: billiards: from ca 1870.

gummer. A fighting dog now old and toothless: low London: mid-C.19–20; ob.

gummie, gummy. A toothless person: low coll: from ca 1840. Gen. as *old gummy*. Ex the extent of gum displayed. 2. A dullard; a fool: C.19–20; ob. Ex GUMMY, adj. 3. (More U.S. than British.) Medicine; properly, a medicament. Also *gummy stuff*. (—1859); ob. 4. A SWELL: sporting: ca 1875–1910. Ex Fr. *gommeux*, a young man of fashion; 'imported by English racing bookmakers'.

gummy, adj. Thick, fat: applied mostly to a drunkard, human ankles, and equine legs: coll, though by O.E.D. considered as S.E.: ca 1735–1890.

gummy! A late C.19–20 low variant of *by* GUM!

gummy, feel. To perspire: university: ca 1880–1914.

gummy composer. An old and insipid composer: musical coll (—1909). Ex GUMMIE, n., 1.

gumption. Common sense; shrewdness; practical intelligence: coll: 1719 (S.O.D.). Grose, in his *Provincial Glossary*, '*Gawm*, to understand . . . Hence, possibly, gawmtion, or gumption, understanding.' Orig. Scottish. A C.18–mid-19 variant is *rum gumption*, latterly one word, where RUM = first-class.

gumptious. Shrewd; coll: from ca 1880; ob. 2. Vain of one's ability: low coll: ca 1850–95. Lytton in *My Novel*.

gums!, bless her, his, its, your, etc. A facetious form of *bless your* SOUL! From ca 1860; ob.

gun. A flagon of ale: s. and – in C.20 wholly – dial.: 1645 (S.O.D.). cf. the Anglo-Irish sense (a toddy glass) and GUN, IN THE. 2. A tobacco pipe: jocular coll: from ca 1705; ob. 3. A lie: c.: ca 1680–1770. Perhaps ex the loud voice characterizing a liar or a lie. 4. A thief; a pickpocket: c. (1845 in '*No. 747*'; 'Ducange Anglicus', 1857) >, ca 1880, low s. cf. GUNNER and GUN-SMITH. Abbr. GON(N)OF, or *gon(n)ov*. 5. Hence, a rascal, BEGGAR, as a vaguely pejorative term of reference: from ca 1890; ob.: more Australian than English. 'Rolf Boldrewood'. 6. A revolver: orig. (—1889) and mainly U.S.; anglicized ca 1900. 7. In c. of ca 1810–50, a look, inspection, observation. Vaux, 'There is a strong *gun* at us, . . . we are strictly observed.' cf. the v. 8. Gonorrhoea: low: late C.19–20.

***gun,** v. To look at, examine: c. of ca 1810–95. Perhaps ex sighting an object before shooting at it. (Extant in Sussex dial.)

gun, in the. Tipsy: late C.17–early 19. Ex GUN, n., 1. This phrase may have suggested *have been in the* SUN.

gun, over the; chest, over the. Settlement, esp. judicial and domestic: *Conway* training-ship cadets': from before 1900.

gun, son of a, see SON and cf. SON OF A BITCH.

gun, sure as a. adv., with complete accuracy or certainty; adj., wholly certain, inevitable: coll: from ca 1680; ob. Jonson, 'He has spoke as true as a gun, believe it' (*as a gun* becoming inseparable from *sure* only in late C.17); 'Father Prout'; Manville Fenn.

gun-case. A judge's tippet: coll: from ca 1895.

gun-fire. Early-morning tea (or a cup of tea): military: from ca 1890. Prob. ex the morning gun of a garrison town, but perhaps by analogy, ex *gunpowder*, a coarse or common (though orig. a fine green) tea.

gun-runner. One engaged in illegally conveying firearms (and ammunition) into a country: coll: 1899, *The Athenaeum*, 21 Oct.

gun-smith. A thief: low (—1869); ob. An elaboration of GUN, 4.

gundiguts. 'A fat, pursy fellow', Grose, 1st ed.: low coll: late C.17–mid-19; ob. Ex Scottish *gundie*, greedy. cf. GREEDY-GUT(S).

gun(n)eah, guniah, guniar, see GUNYAH.

***gunnef,** see GONNOF.

***gunner.** A thief: low or c. (—1889): ob. Extension of GUN, 4. 2. One who lies in order to do harm: 1709, Steele: †by 1760. cf. GUNSTER. 3. 'A Merchant Service warrant officer in the East': nautical: late C.19–20. Bowen.

gunner's daughter, hug (C.19) or **kiss** (—1785) or **marry** (1821) **the.** To be flogged: nautical: †by 1900. Byron; Marryat. A *gunner's daughter* is a cannon: a nautical jocularity and prob. eligible here as s. > coll.

gunner's tailor. The rating who made the cartridge-bags: naval (—1867); †by 1900.

gunnery Jack. A gunnery lieutenant: naval: late C.19–20.

***gunning,** vbl n. Thieving – 'profession' or an instance: c. (—1868) > low. Ex GUN, n., 4.

gunnya(h), see GUNYAH.

***gunpowder.** An old woman: c.: late C.17–early 19. Either ex dry, yellow skin compared with the powder, or because, in the underworld, likely to be peevish, apt to 'go up in the air'. 2. Some fiery drink: ca 1755–80. Toldervy. cf. WILD-FIRE and SLUG.

gunster. 'A Cracker, or bouncing Fellow', a harmless liar (contrast GUNNER, 2): ca 1700–60. Steele in the *Tatler*, No. 88.

gunyah; occ. **guniah, guniar, gun(n)eah, gunnya(h), gunyer, gunyio.** 'A blackfellow's hut, roughly constructed of boughs and bark': this sense, late C.18–20, is S.E. But when applied to a white man's hut or, derivatively, house, it is coll: late C.19–20. Ex Aborigine. cf. HUMP(E)Y.

gup. Gossip, scandal: coll: Anglo-Indian, with stress on its idleness: *gup-gup* is recorded for 1809; *gup* doubtless soon followed. Familiarized in Britain in 1868 by Florence Marryat's *Gup*, a rather catty account of society in South India. Ex Hindi *gap*, tattle.

gup! Go up!; (to a horse) get up! A C.16–17 coll corruption of *go up*. G. Harvey. Followed by *drab*, *quean*, or WHORE, it is a c.p. form of address.

gurge. A whirlpool: nautical coll: C.19–20. Ex dial. *gurgise*, †S.E. *gurges* (direct ex L.), the same.

gurrawaun. A coachman: Anglo-Indian (—1864); ob. A native corruption of *coachman*.

gurrell. A fob: Westminster slums (?c.): ca 1850–80.

gush. A smell, a whiff (e.g. of tobacco): coll: 1838, Dickens: ob. 2. Talk too effusive and objectionably sentimental: coll: from ca 1865. *Church Times*, 17 Sept. 1886, 'Not mere gush or oratorical flip-flap'. 3. ca 1870–80, 'the newspaper work necessary for a continuance of the "largest circulation"'. 4. Hence, in late C.19–20, a newspaper article designed to this end.

gush, v. To talk (gen. v.i.) too effusively and sentimentally; often, also insincerely: coll: from early 1860s; Webster records it in 1864. Miss Broughton, Miss Braddon. Ex the burbling spring and the garrulous brook.

gusher. An over-effusive and (gen. insincerely) sentimental talker: coll: 1864, Edmund Yates in *Broken to Harness*.

gushing, adj. (The n., also coll, is rare.) Excessively sentimental and effusive, either inanely or insincerely: coll: 1864, *Fraser's Magazine*, p. 627, 'What, in the slang of translated Cockneys, is called the Gushing School'. 2. Coll adv. in *-ly*: 1865.

gushy, adj. The same as preceding adj.: coll (—1889).

gusset. The female sex: coll: late C.17–19. cf. PLACKET.

gusset, brother or **knight** or **squire of the.** A pimp: low coll: resp. late C.17–19, C.19–20, C.19.

gusset of the arse. The inner side of the buttocks: late C.18–19: low coll. Burns.

gusseteer. A wencher: C.19 coll, somewhat derisory. Ex GUSSET. cf.:

gusseting. Wenching: C.19 coll, low or jocular. Punning S.E. sense.

gussie. An affected and/or effeminate man: Australian: from ca 1890. Ex *Gus*, the Christian name. cf. NANCY, which, however, connotes sexual perversion.

gust. A guest: jocular: from ca 1905; ob. (See *Slang*, p. 17.) cf. *finance* for *fiancé*.

gut. The belly: low coll and dial. in C.19–20; until ca 1800, S.E. 2. Gluttony: low coll in C.19–20: ob.

gut. v.i. To cram the guts: low coll: 1616. This accounts for F. & H.'s 'to eat hard, fast, and badly' (schools'), now ob. 2. As to remove or destroy the contents or inside of (v.t.), it is, despite F. & H., good Eng., but *gut a house*, to rob it, is C.17–19 c. – *gut an oyster*, to eat it, low s. of late C.17–20 (ob.) – *gut a quart pot*, empty it, is C.18–20 low s. – *gut a job* (Moore in *Tom Crib's Memorial*), to render it valueless, is C.19 low s.

gut-entrance. The female pudend: low: from ca 1840. cf. FRONT-GUT.

gut-foundered. Extremely hungry: coll: mid-C.17–mid-19. In dial. it = 'diseased from the effects of hunger' (E.D.D.).

gut-fucker, -monger, -sticker. A sodomite: low: C.19–20; ob.

gut-head. A person stupid from over-eating: coll: C.17.

gut-pudding. A sausage: late C.17–18: ?coll or S.E.

gut-puller. A poulterer: low: from ca 1850. Ob.

gut-scraper. A fiddler: jocular coll: C.18–20. D'Urfey. Also *catgut-scraper*. A C.17 variant is *gut-vexer*.

gut-stick. The male member: low: C.19–20; ob. cf. CREAM-STICK. Hence *have a bit*, or *a taste, of the g.-s.*, (of women) to coït.

gut-sticker, see GUT-FUCKER. **gut-vexer,** see GUT-SCRAPER.

guts. The stomach and intestines: mid-C.16–20. Until ca 1830, S.E.; then coll; then, in C.20, low coll. 2. A (very) fat person; rarely of a woman: low coll from ca 1660 (earlier, S.E.); ob., unless preceded by an adj.; extant in dial. cf. Shakespeare's 'Peace, ye fat-guts.' 3. Abbr. GREEDY-GUTS: low: late C.19–20. 4. Spirit, real quality, energy: artists' s. and gen. coll: from ca 1890. 5. Whence, courage: coll: from ca 1892. cf. the exactly similar ascent of PLUCK. 6. The essentials, the important part, the inner and real meaning: coll: from ca 1908. 'Let's get at the guts of it' or 'of the matter': a very gen. locution. Ex the S.E. (1663) sense, 'the inside, contents of anything', S.O.D. cf. GUTS IN ONE'S BRAIN.

guts, v.i. and v.t. To eat; to eat greedily: Australian: since ca 1890.

guts, fret one's. To worry oneself greatly: low (?s. or coll): from ca 1840.

guts, ward-room officers have stomachs, and flag-officers palates, – midshipmen have. A naval c.p.: mid-C.19–20; ob. (cf. *horses sweat, men perspire, and women feel the heat.*)

guts, with or **without,** adj. Strong or weak, gen. of things, esp. books, pictures, etc. Low coll > coll (ob.): from ca 1890.

guts and garbage. A (very) fat man: mid-C.18–mid-19: low.

guts are ready to eat my little ones, my great; my guts begin to think my throat's cut; my guts curse my teeth; my guts chime twelve. I'm very hungry: coll (the first, low): resp. late C.18–mid-19; late C.18–20; late C.18–19; mid-C.19–20; ob. The first three are (?first) recorded by Grose, 1785, 1785, 1788, resp., the fourth by F. & H. Not 'cast-iron', but adaptable to other than the first person singular.

guts but no bowels, have plenty of. To be unfeeling; even hard, merciless: coll: late C.18–20; ob. cf. dial. *have neither gut nor gall in one*, to be heartless and lazy.

guts in one, have (no). To be spirited, energetic, a 'good fellow' – or the opposite, which is much the more gen.: coll: from ca 1890. cf. GUTS, 4.

guts in one's brain(s), have. To have a solid understanding; be genuinely intelligent: coll: ca 1660–1890. Butler, 1663; Swift, 'The fellow's well enough if he had any guts in his brain.' cf. *more* GUTS THAN BRAINS.

guts into it, put one's. Do your best, esp. physically; perhaps orig. aquatic, row the best you can. Coll: from ca 1880.

guts than brains, more, adj. Silly; brainless: late C.18–20.

guts to a bear, not fit to carry. Worthless; very uncouth: coll: ca 1650–1880. Howell, Wolcot, Scott.

gutser; occ. **gutzer.** A heavy fall: from ca 1905.

gutsiness. Energy; spirit: from ca 1890: s. > coll. Ex:

gutsy. Energetic; spirited: coll: from ca 1890.

gutted. Penniless; temporarily without cash: low: ca 1820–1910.

gutter. The female pudend: low: C.19–20 (ob.). cf. Sanskrit *cushi.*

gutter, v. To fall stomach-flat in the water: Winchester College: from ca 1860. cf. Fr. *piquer un plat-ventre.*

gutter, lap the. To be extremely drunk: low: from ca 1850. Perhaps suggested by GATTER: but cf.:

gutter-alley, -lane. The throat: C.17–19 the latter, C.19 the former. Jocular coll. (See also at GUTTER LANE.) 2. A urinal: from ca 1850; ob.

gutter-blood. A ragged rascal: Scottish coll (—1818); ob. Scott, *Midlothian.* 2. A vulgarian, a *parvenu*: mainly Scots coll: from ca 1855; ob.

gutter-chaunter. A street singer: low, mainly Cockney: ca 1840–1900.

gutter-hotel. The open air: tramps' c.: from ca 1870; ob. cf. HEDGE-SQUARE and DAISYVILLE.

gutter-kid. A street ARAB: Cockney coll (—1887).

gutter-lane. See GUTTER-ALLEY. 'Throat' synonyms are: BEER STREET; GIN- and RED LANE; PECK ALLEY. Ex L. *guttur*, the throat, fig. gluttony: indeed Bailey, 1721, spells it *Guttur Lane.* cf.:

gutter lane (or capitalled), **all goeth** (C.17) – or **goes** (C.18–20) – **down.** He spends all his money on his stomach. A proverbial coll: C.17–20; ob. Prob. suggested by Gutter Lane, London, with pun on L. *guttur*. cf. preceding entry.

***gutter-prowler.** A street thief: c.: ca 1840–1910.

gutter-slush, -snipe. A street ARAB: resp. s., ca 1885–1910, and coll, from ca 1880 (in C.20, S.E.). With the latter, which follows from the S.E. sense, a gatherer of refuse from the gutter, cf. Fr. *saute-ruisseau*, an errand-boy.

guttie, -y. A glutton: coll: C.19. 2. A very fat person: low coll: C.19–20; ob. Ex the Scottish adj. 3. A gutta-percha ball: golfers' s.: 1890.

guttle-shop. A tuck-shop: Rugby School: from ca 1860.

gutty, see GUTTIE.

guv or **gov.** Abbr. GOVERNOR: low: from ca 1880.

guv, adj. Expert: Oxford undergraduates': ca 1820–60. 'Cuthbert Bede', *Verdant Green*, 1853.

guvner, -or, = GOVERNOR. Occ. *gov'nor.*

guy, an ill-dressed or ugly person, is gen. considered S.E.: but was it not orig. (1823, Bee) coll? 2. A dark lantern: low, or c. (—1811) >, ca 1860, low: ob. by 1900. Esp. in *stow the guy*, conceal the lantern. Ex Guy Fawkes's plot. 3. A Christian as opposed to a Jewish crimp: ca 1830–80: low or c. 4. A jaunt or expedition: Cockney (—1889). *Sporting Times*, 3 Aug. 1889,

'A cheerful guy to Waterloo was the game.' cf. DO A GUY. 5. Whence, a decamping (—1898): low. 6. A man, FELLOW, chap: orig. (—1860), U.S.; anglicized by 1903. Perhaps ex Yiddish *goy*, a Gentile.

guy, v. To hiss: theatrical: from ca 1870; ob. 'If orig. U.S., may be . . . from Dutch *de guig aansteken*, to make fun', W. 2. Whence, to quiz, make an object of ridicule: coll: from ca 1880. cf. U.S. sense (e.g. in Thornton). 3. To run away; escape: c. or low (—1874). cf.:

***guy, do a.** To give a false name: c. (—1887): †by 1910. *Fun*, 23 March 1887. 2. To run away; escape: c. (—1889, Clarkson & Richardson) >, ca 1892, low. cf. GUY, v., 3. Referable to Guy Fawkes.

guy on, clap a. Put a stop to; cease (v.t.): nautical: 1814. Ex *guy-rope*.

guy to, give the. To run away from; give (someone) the slip (—1899). Ex GUY, n., 4, 5.

guying, n. Hissing: theatrical (—1885). Jerome K. Jerome. 2. Ridicule: coll: from ca 1890.

guzzle-guts. A glutton or a heavy drinker: low (—1788); ob.

g.y., all a. All on one side or askew; crooked: North Country coll (?and dial.). From ca 1860. cf. ALL OF A HOUGH.

***gybe.** A written paper: c. of ca 1560–1660. 2. A pass, esp. if counterfeit: ca 1560–1830: c. (Often spelt *jybe*.) Perhaps ex Ger. *Schreiben*, a writing.

***gybe,** v. To whip; castigate, esp. in past ppl passive: late C.17–18 c. Ex the S.E. sense.

gybing (i.e. gibing), occ. **gybery or gibery,** n. Mockery; jeering. In late C.17–18 (witness B.E. and Grose) it seems to have been coll.

gybs. Prayers: Charterhouse: late C.19–20. Why?

***gyger,** see JIGGER.

Gyles, see HOPPING GILES.

gym. Abbr. *gymnasium*: orig. and mainly schools' (—1887).

gymnasium. The female pudend: low jocular s.: from ca 1860.

gyp. A college servant: Cambridge University: from ca 1750. In C.19–20, also Durham University. cf. the Oxford *scout* and the Dublin *skip*. Etymologies proposed: Gr. γύψ, a vulture (symbolic of rapacity), by Cantabs, popularly; *Gipsy Joe*, by the *Saturday Review*; *gypsy*, by the S.O.D.; and, I think the most convincing, the C.17 *gippo* (Fr. *jupeau*), a garment, hence a valet – cf. the transferred sense of BUTTONS – by W. 2. A thief: mid-C.19–20: c. >, by 1900, low. Abbr. *gypsy*.

gyp! see GIP.

gyp, give (a person), see GIP, GIVE.

gyp-room. 'A room where the gyps keep table furniture, etc.': from ca 1870: Cambridge coll.

gype, adj. Looking like a boxer or a boxer's clothes, etc.: tailors': late C.19–20. Origin ?

gypper. A Gypsy: late C.19–20.

Gyppy, see GIPPY.

gypsy's warning. Morning: rhyming s.: mid-C.19–20.

gyro. A gyroscope: coll: from mid-1890s.

gyte. A child: pejorative low: from ca 1820: Scots. Ex *goat*. 2. A first-year pupil at the Edinburgh High School: Scots: from ca 1880. Ex Scots *gyte*, a foolish fellow.

gyvel. The female pudend: Scots low coll: C.18–20 (ob.). Burns.

H

h.o.p., on the. A jocular elaboration of *on the* HOP, 1; ob. s.

ha' d, ha-d, ha-dee. A halfpenny: Charterhouse: from ca 1870. Obviously *ha'* = half; *d* is the sign for pence. Also, rarely, *hadee.*

ha-ha. A defecation: nursery: late C.19–20. Echoic of baby's instinctive grunting.

hab or nab, hab-nab, habs-nabs; hob-nob, adv. At random, by hook or by crook, hit or miss: coll: from ca 1540: the *a* forms ob. by 1760, †(except in dial.) by 1800; the *o,* ob. by 1840, †(except in dial.) by 1860. 'Hob-nob is his word; give't or take't,' Shakespeare, whereas Udall revealingly spells *habbe* or *nhabbe*. cf. *hab or nab* (=*ne habe*), have or have not. Variant: *at*, or *by*, *hab or nab*. See also HOB AND NOB.

haberdasher. A publican: jocular coll: C.19. Moncrieff. Because he sells TAPE.

haberdasher of (nouns and) pronouns. A schoolmaster: late C.17–19; now archaic. The longer and orig. form, not after C.18.

habit-shirt. A profligates' s. term of ca 1820–50. As the exact meaning is obscure, Bee is quoted in full: 'A sham plea put in (on) to save appearances. Worn by the *ladies*; but gentlemen should "look well to't", as Hamlet says, or it will be all *Dickey*.' See DICKEY, n., and cf. BELLY-PLEA.

habitual, n. A confirmed drunkard, criminal, drug-taker, etc.: coll: 1884. Contrast CHRONIC.

hack. A harlot or bawd: s.: from ca 1730; almost †. Ex *hackster* or *hackney* (*woman* or *wench* or *whore*), which are rather S.E. than coll. 2. See GARRISON HACK.

hack and manger, at. (Gen. with *live.*) In clover: coll: ca 1660–1890. Ex *hack*, the rack that holds fodder for cattle. (Extant in dial.)

hack of a dress, make a. To wear it daily: coll (—1887); ob.

hackery. A bullock-cart: late C.17–20 Anglo-Indian. (Before 1880, at least) rarely used among natives: W., however, suggests ex Hindi *chhakra*, a two-wheeled cart.

hackle. Pluck, spirit. Whence *to show hackle*, to be willing to fight: coll (—1860). Ex *hackle*, a long shining feather on a cock's neck. cf. HACKLES UP.

hackle, cock of a different. An opponent of a different, gen. better, character: coll (—1865). See HACKLE and cf.:

hackles. Whiskers: jocular coll: from ca 1880; ob. cf.:

hackles up, with the. Very angry; at fighting-point: coll when, from ca 1880, applied to men. Ex cock-fighting.

hackslaver. To splutter, hesitate in speech, stammer: low coll (—1864); ob. Ex †S.E. *hack*, same meaning.

hackum, occ. **-am** or **-em.** A BRAVO, a blustering bully: coll: from ca 1650; ob. by 1820, † (in England) by 1860. Variant: *Captain Hackum*, in B.E. and Grose, the former designating it – wrongly, I think – as c. Obviously a variation of S.E. *hacker* ex *hack*, to gash. (But *hackster*, its variant, is S.E.)

hacky. Of, or like, a hack (horse): coll: 1870. 2. (Of a cough) hacking: coll: from ca 1899.

had, deceived, tricked: see HAVE.

Had 'em, Haddums. Rare except in *to have been at Haddums*, late C.17–18, or in the mid-C.18–early 19 c.p. *to have been at Had'em and come home by Clapham*, punning *Hadham* and *clap*: properly, to have caught CLAP or gonorrhoea; loosely, syphilis. (These topographical and coll puns were much commoner before ca 1830 than after.)

had enough(, have). (To be) tipsy: coll: C.19–20. i.e. more than enough.

had on! 'Sucks!', a term of triumph or defiance at certain schools: from the 1880s.

had-up. An examination (of a person) by the police: ca 1820–70. Ex S.E. *had up*, brought before a magistrate. 2. A person 'had-up': legal coll: late C.19–20.

haddie. A haddock: Cockneys', esp. costermongers', coll: C.19. Mayhew, I, 1851. (Prob. independent of Scottish dial.)

***haddock.** A purse: (low or) c.: from ca 1810; ob. Ainsworth. 2. Money: fishmongers' (—1874).

haddock to paddock, bring. To lose everything: C.16 coll and proverbial.

Haddums, see HAD 'EM.

ha-dee, see HA'D. (Rare.)

Hades. Hell: orig. euphemistic S.E.; in C.20, esp. in *go to Hades!*, jocular coll.

hadland. One who has lost the land he once owned: coll: ca 1590–1660. cf. *lackland.*

haeremai!; occ. horomai! (†by 1898). A 'Maori term of welcome, lit. come hither . . . It has been' – from ca 1880 – 'colloquially adopted': New Zealand. Morris.

hag, an old or ugly woman, is S.E., as is the †*hagged*, haggard. 2. At Charterhouse (school), any female; at Winchester College, a matron, as also at Charterhouse: both ca 1850.

***haggard.** A proposed dupe that keeps aloof: c. of ca 1592. Greene. Ex the S.E. sense: a wild, unreclaimed bird that does not return to the wrist.

Haggisland. Scotland: jocular coll: C.19–20; ob. (Until C.18, haggis – as is very little known – was a popular English dish.)

hagrerwa(i)ters is a variant of AGGERAWATOR.

hagship, your. A contemptuous term of address, occ. of reference, applied only to women: C.19–20 (ob.) low coll. Ex S.E. sense, personality of a hag.

hail up. To 'put up, as at an inn': Australian coll: ca 1880–1910. Ware. Does this represent a perversion of *hale oneself up*?

hailed for the last time, be. To die: nautical, coll rather than s. (—1891); ob. Clark Russell in *An Ocean Tragedy.*

hair. The female sex; women viewed sexually: low: ex *hair*, the female pubic hair. This, like the following, is C.19–20: *after hair*, looking for a woman, ob.; *bit of hair*, the sexual favour; *plenty of hair*, an abundance of girls; *hair-monger*, a womanizer; *hair to sell*, a woman prepared – at a price – to grant the favour.

hair, not worth a. Worthless: coll: C.19–20 (ob.).

hair about the heels. Underbred: coll when, from ca 1880, applied to persons. Orig. of horses. cf. HAIRY ABOUT THE FETLOCKS.

Hair Court. Sexual connection, esp. in *take a turn in Hair Court*, occ. amplified *take . . . Court, Girl Street*: C.19–20 (ob.) low.

hair cut, get one's. To visit a woman: low: late C.19–20. cf. SEE A MAN *about a dog.* 2. For **hair cut!, get your,** see GET . . .

hair-divider or **-splitter.** The male member: low coll: from ca 1850, 1810 resp.; ob. cf. BEARD-SPLITTER.

hair grows through his hood, his. 'He is on the road to ruin': coll: mid-C.15–early 18. Skelton, Deloney, Motteux.

hair on, hold or, more gen., **keep one's.** To keep one's temper: from late 1860s ('Quotations' Benham). Gen. in imperative. Variant, *wool.* 'App. playful advice not to *tear one's hair*', W.

hair-splitter, see HAIR-DIVIDER.

hair stand on end, make one's. To astound; frighten: orig. (C.17) coll, soon S.E.

hair than wit, having more. Often preceded by *bush natural.* (Rather) stupid, silly: C.16–19 coll > proverbial.

hairs, get or **have by the short.** So to hold (lit. and fig.) that escape is painful or difficult: (low) coll, esp. among soldiers: from mid-1890s. Ex the hair on one's nape or that around the genitals. It occurs in the U.S., in the form *get where the hair is short*, in George P. Burnham, *Memoirs of the United States Secret Service*, 1872.

hairy. A draught-horse; any rough-coated horse: military: 1899, Conan Doyle. 2. A hatless slum girl: low Glasgow: late C.19–20. MacArthur & Long, 'In Glasgow, as in Rome, the hat is a badge of feminine quality.'

hairy, adj. Difficult: Oxford University: ca 1850–1900. Clough. 2. Splendid, famous: from ca 1890; ob. Kipling, 'The Widow of Windsor with a hairy gold crown on her head.' 3. (Of women only) desirable: low: from ca 1860. 4. Ill-bred; bad-mannered: 1906 (O.E.D. Sup.). Ex HAIRY ABOUT THE FETLOCKS. 5. Angry, (angry and) excited: from ca 1900.

hairy, feel. To feel amorous: low: from ca 1860. cf. HAIRY, adj., 3.

hairy about (or **at** or **in**) **the fetlocks** (or **heel**). Ill-bred, bad-mannered. From late 1890s. Ex the stables.

hairy-arsed. No longer young: low: late C.19–20.

hairy bit. An amorous and attractive wench: low: from ca 1860.

hairy Jock, see JOCK, HAIRY.

hairy oracle or **ring.** The female pudend. Whence *work the hairy oracle*, to go wenching, to copulate. Low: from ca 1870.

hairy wheel. The female pudend: low Australian: from ca 1860. cf. last entry. 2. But also low English s. for the male genitals: since ca 1870.

Hairyfordshire. The female pudend: low: from ca 1865. Whence *go to Hairyfordshire*, to coït. Obviously punning *Herefordshire.*

hake's teeth. 'A series of deep soundings in the Bristol Channel': nautical: late C.19–20. Bowen. A hake's teeth being well defined.

hakim. 'A medical man. – *Anglo-Indian*', H., 1864: C.17–20. 2. (Yule & Burnell) 'the authority'; a governor. Anglo-Indian coll: late C.17–20. Both ex Hindi; the former ex *hakim*, wise, the latter ex *hakim*, a master.

halbert. *Carry the halbert in one's face*, (of officers) to show that one rose from the ranks, is C.18 military s. > coll.

half, v. Go halves: coll: 1889 (O.E.D.).

***half a bean** or **couter.** Half a guinea (Vaux) or sovereign: C.19 c., C.19–20 c. > low. See BEAN and COUTER; cf. HALF A QUID.

half-a-brewer. Tipsy: low: mid-C.19–20; ob.

half a bull or **tusheroon.** Half a crown: C.19; C.19–20 low. See BULL (n., 2) and TUSHEROON.

half a crack or **jiffy** or **tick.** Half a MO: low coll, s., low s., resp.: C.19, C.19–20 (ob.), C.19–20.

half a dollar. Half a crown: from ca 1900, due to U.S. influence. 2. A collar: rhyming s.: late C.19–20.

half a farthing I'd (do, have done it), for. It wouldn't take (have taken) much to make me . . .: coll (—1887); ob.

half-a-foot o' port. A glass of that wine at Short's in the Strand: London: mid-C.19–20. Because served in a long champagne-beaker.

***half a hog.** Sixpence: late C.17–19: c. then low. cf. GRUNTER (3) and HOG.

half a jiffy, see HALF A CRACK.

half a one. £500 ('one' being one thousand): Stock Exchange coll (—1895).

***half a quid.** Half a guinea (Vaux, 1812); by 1830, half-a-sovereign: c. >, by 1850, low.

half a stretch. Six months in prison: c. (—1859). See STRETCH, n., 2.

half a surprise. A black eye: Londoners': ca 1885–1905. Ex a music-hall song. The chorus began, 'Two lovely black eyes,/Oh, what a surprise!'

half a tick, see HALF A CRACK.

half a ton of bones done up in horsehair. 'A thin ill-conditioned young horse': sporting (—1909); ob. Ware.

half a tusheroon, see HALF A BULL.

half-a-yennork. Half a crown: low: from ca 1855. See YENNORK.

half an eye, see with. To be alert of mind; often with the implication that the deduction is easy to make. Coll: from ca 1530: in C.19–20, S.E. The nautical *have half an eye*, ex the same sense, is perhaps to be considered as coll.

half an ounce. Half a crown: C.18–early 19. Silver, in C.18, being assessed at five shillings an ounce.

half an Oxford. Half a crown: from ca 1870. On OXFORD SCHOLAR = DOLLAR.

half and half, gen. hyphenated. A drink of ale and beer, or ale and porter, in equal quantities: from ca 1710 (ob.): s. >, ca 1800, coll. Ned Ward, *A Vade Mecum for Maltworms*, 1715; 'Peter Corcoran' Reynolds, 'Over my gentle half-and-half'.

half and half, adj. Half-drunk: from ca 1715 (slightly ob.): in C.18, s.; in C.19 coll.

half-and-half coves, occ. **boys, men,** etc. Cheap would-be dandies: low: ca 1820–60. Moncrieff.

half-and-halfer. A person, an object, that is neither the one thing nor the other: coll: late C.19–20.

half-arsed. (Of things) imperfect; (of persons) ineffective, indecisive: Canadian: late C.19–20.

half-baked. Irresolute: ca 1800–60: coll. Ex the C.17 S.E. sense, not thoroughgoing. 2. (?hence) half-witted; silly: perhaps orig. (1842) U.S. and anglicized ca 1860, though recorded in dial. in 1855: coll. Besant, 1886, 'Not quite right in her head – half-baked, to use the popular and feeling expression'; *Notes and Queries*, 1864, records the Cornish proverb, 'He is only half-baked; put in with the bread and taken out with the cakes' – so perhaps *not* American in origin.

***half board** or **borde.** Sixpence: mid-C.17–early 19 c. Coles. See BORDE.

half-bull white, see WHITE, n.

half-chat. An Indian Army term dating from ca 1880, thus in Richards: 'Half-caste, or "half-chat" as the troops in my time [ca 1901–9] contemptuously called them.'

half-cock, go off at. (Variant *half-cocked.*) 'To ejaculate before completing erection', F. & H.: low: from ca 1850. Ex a gun.

half-cocked. Slightly intoxicated: Australian: 1888, Fergus Hume; ob. Ex dial., where recorded over fifty years earlier.

half-cracked. Somewhat unintelligent or mad: low coll (—1887). W. P. Frith, 'What is vulgarly called half-cracked', 1887.

half-crown ball. Generic for: 'a respectable, commonplace hop': middle-classes' coll: ca 1880–1914. Ware.

half-crown word. A rare or, esp., a difficult

word: low coll: from ca 1860; ob. cf. JAW-BREAKER and SLEEVE-BOARD.

half-crowner. A publication priced at 2s. 6d.: booksellers' coll: from ca 1880; ob.

half-cut. Half-drunk: lower classes': from ca 1860: ob. See CUT. 2. Stupid: silly; foolish: Australian: late C.19–20. i.e. with half one's virility and vigour removed.

***half flash and half polish.** Having a smattering of cant and an imperfect knowledge of the world: c. of ca 1810–50. cf. FOOLISH.

***half-fly flat.** A criminal's rough-worker: c.: from ca 1830.

half-go. 'Three pennyworth of spirits, for mixing with . . . water': public-houses': ca 1890–1914. Ware.

half-gone. Half-drunk: coll: late C.19–20.

half-hour gentleman. A man whose breeding is superficial: society coll: ca 1870–1914.

***half jack.** Half a sovereign: c., or low: mid-C.19–20; ob.

half-joe. Eight dollars: see JOE, 4.

half-laugh and purser's grin. A sneer or an unpleasant innuendo: nautical, esp. naval: ca 1880–1915. It derives ex the much earlier *half-and-half laugh and purser's grin* recorded by W. N. Glascock, *Sketch-Book*, II, 1826: naval: ca 1790–1880.

half-man. A landsman or a youth rated as an A.B., but not with his pay: nautical coll: ca 1860–1910. cf.:

half-marrow. An incompetent sailor; a seaman who, having served his time, is not yet rated as A.B.: (mainly Northern and Scots) nautical: ca 1850–1930. cf. mining *h.-m.*, a partner.

half-moon. A wig: coll: C.18–19. 2. The female pudend: C.17 low.

half-mourning. A black eye: rather low (—1864); ob. cf. *full mourning*, two black eyes.

half-nab or **-nap.** At a venture; hit or miss: a C.18–early 19 low corruption or perversion of HAB OR NAB.

half-off or **-on.** (Often without hyphens.) Half-drunk: low: from ca 1870. See ON, adj., 5.

half-ounce. To cheat (v.t.): rhyming s. (on BOUNCE, v., 2): late C.19–20.

half-past kissing time and time to kiss again(, it's). A low c.p. reply to a female asking a man the time: mostly London: ca 1870–1910. Ex a popular ballad. cf. *an hour past hanging time* in Swift's *Polite Conversation.*

half-rats. Partially intoxicated: low: 1897; ob. Ware, who notes the equally low variant, *half up the pole*, dating from a decade or so earlier.

half-rocked. Half-witted; silly: dial. >, ca 1860, coll. Ex a West Country saying that fools have been cradle-rocked bottom upwards. A West Country synonym (wrongly, I think, included by F. & H.) is *half-saved*: see Mortimer Collins's *Frances*, ch. 42. cf. ROCKED IN A STONE KITCHEN.

half round the bend. Not mad, but often doing very silly things: naval: late C.19–20.

***half-scrag.** (Collective n.) Half-castes: c.: from ca 1860. The reference in '*No. 747*' at p. 16 is to ca 1865.

half-screwed. Half-drunk: from ca 1835. Lever, 'He was, in Kilrush phrase, half-screwed . . . more than half tipsy.' See SCREWED.

half sea. Mid-Channel: nautical coll: from ca 1860.

half-seas over. Half or almost drunk: late C.17–20: nautical > gen.; in C.19–20, coll. B.E., Smollett, Thackeray. Either *half sea's over* or a corruption, as Gifford maintained, of *op-zee zober*, 'over-sea beer', a heady drink imported from Holland; but, in C.16, the phrase = halfway across the sea, which rather rebuts Gifford. cf. the nautical SLEWED; SPRUNG; THREE SHEETS.

half-slewed. Half-drunk: nautical > gen. See SLEWED; *half-slewed* may, however, have been prompted by HALF-SCREWED.

half-snags. Half-shares: low coll: C.19–20 (ob.). Ex *half-snack(s)*. See esp. Walford's *Antiquarian*, 1887, p. 252.

half-timer. A scholar working half the day and going to school the other half: primary schools' coll (from 1870) >, by 1900, S.E.

***half tusheroon.** Half a crown: c. (—1857).

half-un. A half-glass of spirits and water: low coll: from ca 1865; ob.

half up the pole, see HALF-RATS.

halfpenny good silver, think one's. To think extremely well of one's abilities: coll: ca 1570–1700. Gascoigne.

halfpenny howling swell. A pretender to fashion: ca 1870–80.

halfpennyworth of tar, lose the ship for a. To lose or spoil by foolish economy: a C.19–20 coll perversion of C.17–18 *sheep*, often – in dial. – pronounced *ship.*

halfperth, halfporth, halfp'worth, see HA'P'ORTH.

Halifax!, go to. Go to blazes!: coll: 1669 (O.E.D.); in C.19–20, mostly U.S. and re-anglicized ca 1870, esp. in dial. Euphemizing *hell* but ultimately ex the C.16–20 HELL, HULL AND HALIFAX. cf. BATH; JERICHO; PUTNEY.

hall. (Gen. pl.) A music-hall: coll (—1887).

hall, v. Dine in hall: Oxford University coll rather than s.: from ca 1860.

hall of delight. A music-hall: Australian: ca 1890–1910. Hume Nisbet. (I myself did not hear it; never, I believe, very gen.)

hallabaloo. An early form of HULLABALOO.

hallan(d)-, or hallen-, shaker. A vagabond; esp. a sturdy beggar: Scots coll: C.16–20; ob. *Hallan*, a partition wall in a cottage.

hallelujah gal(l)op. A hymn in a quick, lively measure, 'invented by General Booth to attract the multitude': Salvationists' coll: from the 1890s.

hallelujah-lass. A female member – esp. if young – of the Salvation Army: coll: from ca 1899.

halligator; properly **alligator.** A herring: eating- and coffee-houses': mid-C.19–20.

hallion, hallyon; hellion; hullion. 'A rogue; a clod; a gentleman's servant out of livery; also a shrew', F. & H.: Scots coll and Northern dial.: late C.18–19. Scott, 1817, 'This is a decentish hallion'; Crockett, 1895, 'I can manage the hullions fine.' ?ex Fr. *haillon*, a rag, a tatter.

hallo, baby! how's nurse? A military c.p. addressed to a girl pushing a pram: from ca 1908.

halloo-baloo; halloo-bo-loo; hallybaloo. Early forms of HULLABALOO.

halo racket, work the. To grumble, be discontented: low: from ca 1860. Ex the Heaven-placed saint dissatisfied with his halo. See RACKET.

halperthe, halp(w)orth(e). Early forms of HA'P'ORTH.

halter-sack. A gallows-bird; also as a gen. pejorative: late C.16–mid-17: coll. Beaumont & Fletcher, in *A King and No King*, 'Away, you haltersack, you.'

halvers! An exclamatory claim to something found: coll and dial. (—1816): ob. except in dial. Scott.

halves. Half-Wellington boots: Winchester College, ca 1840–85. (Pron. *hāves.*)

halves, cry or **go.** To claim, or to take, a half share or chance: coll: from late C.18. Mayhew, 'He'll then again ask if anybody will go him halves.'

ham and eggs. Legs: rhyming s.: from ca 1870.

ham-bone. A greenhorn or an amateur among itinerant musicians: showmen's: since ca 1880. P. H. Emerson, *Signor Lippo*, 1893.

***ham-cases, hams.** Trousers: c.: ca 1770–1860, ca 1720–1830 resp., though *ham-cases* may be the earlier: those things which encase the hams. cf. Romany *hamyas*, knee-breeches.

ham-match. A stand-up lunch: low (—1890); ob.: mostly London.

Hamburg. A 'bazaar', i.e. false, rumour: Anglo-Indian: late C.19–20; very ob. Semantics: *made in Germany*=bad.

***hamlet.** A high constable: c.: ca 1690–1830; it survived in U.S. till ca 1900. B.E. cf. Yorkshire *play Hamlet*, or *hamlet, with*, to play the devil with, to scold. 2. **(Hamlet.)** An omelette: theatrical: 1885. Ware, 'Started on Ash Wednesday [of that year] by the actors of the Princess's Theatre, where Mr Wilson Barrett was then playing *Hamlet*. These gay souls dined and supped at the Swiss Hotel, Compton Street, and necessarily therefore found themselves before omelettes.'

hammer. A vigorous puncher, esp. with the stronger arm: pugilistic: from ca 1830; ob. Also *hammerer*, as in Moore's *Tom Crib*, 1819, and *hammerman*, as in Bee's Dict. 2. Hence, a boxer; a stalwart bodyguard: late C.19–20. 3. An impudent lie: from ca 1840; ob. cf. WHOPPER.

hammer, v. To punish; beat: pugilistic s. (—1887) and then gen. coll. 2. To declare (a member) a defaulter: Stock Exchange (—1885). Ex the hammer-taps preceding the head porter's formal proclamation. Frequently as a ppl adj., *hammered*: see esp. A. J. Wilson, *Stock Exchange Glossary*, 1895, for the procedure. In the printing and allied trades a youth is said to be *hammered out* when he completes his apprenticeship and leaves the shop, at which point all those who are working in the shop seize a hammer and bang on a bench: this is a coll verging on j., and belongs to late C.19–20. 3. To depress (a market, stocks, prices): Stock Exchange: 1865. vbl n., *hammering*.

hammer, at or **under the.** For sale: auctioneers': from ca 1800; the phrase with *under* occurs in the *Port Folio*, 1 Nov. 1806, p. 266, quoting a British source. The *at* form is †.

***hammer, down as a.** Wide-awake, FLY: c.: ca 1810–1905. Vaux; Moore. See also DOWN AS A HAMMER. 2. (Variant, *down like a hammer*) very prompt to act;

peremptory, merciless: coll: from ca 1860. The *as a* form is †.

hammer, that's the. That's all right; that's excellent: (low) coll: from ca 1860; ob. cf.:

hammer, up to the. First-rate; excellent: from early 1880s: s. >, ca 1900, coll; ob. Lit., up to the standard.

hammer and tongs. Occ., as in Marryat's *Snarley-Yow*, an expletive (†); gen. an adv. = violently, and preceded by *at it*, as in G. Parker's 'His master and mistress were at it hammer and tongs.' Coll: from ca 1780; *with h. and t.*, ca 1708–80. Ex a vigorous smith's blows on the iron taken with the tongs from the fire.

hammer-headed. Stupid; oafish: coll, perhaps: the O.E.D. considers it S.E. Mid-C.16–20; ob. Nashe. Ex the hardness of a hammer. 2. Hammer-shaped: mid-C.16–20; S.E. till C.19, then coll. Dickens.

hammer into. To succeed, finally, in teaching (a person something) or convincing (a person of something): mid-C.17–20: S.E. until ca 1830, then coll.

hammer-man, see HAMMER, n., 1.

hammer on, v.i. To reiterate again and again: coll (—1888): ob.

hammer out. To discuss (v.t.) until settled, gen. with connotation of difficulty, occ. with that of obtuseness: late C.16–20; coll till ca 1720, then S.E. D'Urfey.

hammered. Married: metal workers': since ca 1880. 2. See HAMMER, v., 2.

hammerer, see HAMMER, n., 1.

hammering. Heavy punishment; a defeat: pugilistic s. > gen. coll: from ca 1830. 2. Overcharging for time-work, e.g. corrections (which are, from author's and publisher's stand-point, always over-charged): printers': from ca 1860; ob. 3. See HAMMER, v., 3.

hammering-trade. Boxing: boxers' coll (—1819); ob. by 1900. Moore, 'The other ... made, express, by Nature for the hammering trade.'

***hammerish.** Same as, and ex, DOWN AS A HAMMER: ca 1810–50.

hammers to one, be. 'To know what one means', F. & H.: (low) coll: ca 1860–1910.

Hammersmith, have been at or **gone to.** To be soundly drubbed: boxing coll: from ca 1820; ob. Punning the London suburb, part of which is 'tough', and HAMMER, n., 1.

hammock, the moon's stepping out of her. The moon is rising: nautical coll (—1887); ob.

hammock-man. A seaman attending to the midshipmen: naval: *The Night Watch*, 1828. cf. MIDSHIPMEN'S DEVIL.

hampered. Entangled: ca 1630–90, S.E.; late C.17–18 coll; then S.E. again. Ex *hamper*, a fetter, as in Browne's *Britannia's Pastorals*, 'Shackles, shacklockes, hampers, gives and chaines'.

Hampshire hog. A native of Hampshire: C.17–20: coll. Drayton in *Polyolbion*. Ex the county's famous breed of hogs.

Hampstead donkey. A louse: low: ca 1865–1900.

Hampstead Heath. The teeth: rhyming s.: from ca 1880. *Referee*, 7 Nov. 1887. cf. HOUNSLOW HEATH.

Hampstead Heath sailor. A landlubber: ca 1875–1905. cf. FRESHWATER MARINER.

Hampsteads. Teeth: a late C.19–20 abbr. of HAMPSTEAD HEATH.

Hampton Wick, often abbr. to **Hampton.** The penis: rhyming s.: late C.19–20. On PRICK, n., 3.

***hams,** see HAM-CASES.

›**hanced.** Tipsy: C.17 coll. Taylor the Water Poet. cf. ELEVATE.

hand. Orig. (C.17), nautical for a sailor, a sense it has retained; but as early as 1792 it had > gen. coll for one skilful at anything. 2. Of a person in reference to character (e.g. *a loose hand*): coll: 1798; ob. 3. A skilful touch with horses: coachmen's and sporting: from ca 1855, j. > s. or coll; ob. Whyte-Melville. 4. See HANDS, ALL.

hand!, bear a. Make haste!: coll: since ca 1720.

hand, bring down, or **off, by.** To masturbate (v.t.): low coll: from ca 1800; *down* is †. (Of men.)

hand, bring up by. Manually to induce a priapism: low: from ca 1850.

hand, cool or **fine** or **good** or **neat** or **old** or **rare.** An expert: coll: resp. 1845, —1880, —1748, —1892, —1861, (?—)1797. In *cool*, and occ. for the others, the stress is on character, not skill: this gen. coll tendency dates from ca 1798 (S.O.D.). 2. See HAND, OLD, below.

hand, get or **give a.** To be applauded or to applaud: theatrical: from ca 1870. Ex the S.E. *give one's hand*, as in Shakespeare.

hand, get or **have the upper.** To gain or have an advantage (v.t. with *of*): coll (—1886); in C.20, S.E.: ?always S.E. Stevenson, in *Kidnapped*.

hand, green. An inexperienced person, esp. workmen: C.18–20: orig. coll; but since ca 1860, S.E.

hand, heavy on; hot at hand. Hard to manage: coll: ca 1860–1912. cf.:

hand, light in. Easy to manage: coll: ca 1860–1910.

***hand, old.** An ex-convict: Australian: ca 1860–1905. T. McCombie, *Australian Sketches*, 1861; 1865, J. O. Tucker, 'Reformed convicts, or, in the language of their proverbial cant, "old hands".' 2. See HAND, COOL.

hand, stand one's. To pay for a round of drinks: Australian: ca 1890–1915. Hume Nisbet in *The Bushranger's Sweetheart*, 1892.

hand, such a thing fell into his. He has improved another's notion, invention, etc.: coll: ca 1660–1800.

hand and pocket shop, the first three words being often hyphenated. An eating-house where cash is paid for what one orders: coll: ca 1785–1840.

hand-Bible. A holystone: Naval: late C.19–20.

hand gunner. A machine-gunner: Artillerymen's: from ca 1890.

hand in, get one's, v.i. To practise so as to become proficient: coll: from ca 1875. Ex much earlier cognate S.E. phrases.

hand in one's checks or **chips,** see CASH ONE'S CHECKS.

***hand like a fist.** A handful of trumps; an unbeatable hand: gamblers' (at cards): from ca 1870.

hand like a foot. A large, rough hand; vulgar, clumsy handwriting: coll: from ca 1705; ob. Swift.

hand-me-downs. Second-hand clothes: low coll (—1874).

hand of it, make a. To turn something to account; profit by it: coll: C.17–early 19. Ex C.16 S.E. *make a hand*, v.i.

hand on, get a. To suspect; be distrustful of: tailors': from ca 1870; ob.

hand (or heart) on, e.g. **his halfpenny, have his.** 'To have an eye on the main chance, or on any particular object', Apperson: C.16–20: coll till C.19, then dial.

hand on it, get one's. To caress a woman genitally: low coll: from ca 1850.

hand over fist. Hand over hand; very quickly: coll: from ca 1810.

hand over head. Hurriedly; without method or reason; thoughtlessly: coll: from ca 1440: ob. except in dial. Latimer.

hand-running. Straight on; in due succession: coll when not, as gen., dial.: from ca 1825; † except in dial.

hand-saw. Same as CHIVE-FENCER: Cockney (—1859). Prob. the correct term (which is ob.) should be *hand-saw fencer*.

hand to fist. Cheek by jowl; intimate(ly): mid-C.17–19 coll. Ex the †S.E. *hand to hand*.

hand up. To betray; sneak on: Winchester College: ca 1860–1910.

handbasket portion. A woman whose husband receives numerous presents from her parents and/or relatives: late C.18–mid-19: coll.

hander. A second or assistant in a prize fight: sporting (—1860). 2. A cane-stroke on the hand: schoolboys' (—1868); ob. J. Greenwood, 'You've been playing the wag, and you've got to take your handers.'

handful of sprats. A sexual groping: low: late C.19–20.

handie-dandie, handy-dandy. Sexual connection; (mainly Scots) coll: C.16–18. Ex the child's game.

handle. A nose: low: ca 1790–1910. *Modern Society*, 27 Aug. 1887, 'A[n] . . . intriguing . . . old lady, with an immense handle to her face'. Ex the C.18 jocular *handle of the face*, as in Motteux. 2. A title: nearly always in form *handle to one's name*: coll: 1833, Marryat; 1855, Thackeray.

handle, v. To palm (cards): cardsharpers' c.: from ca 1860.

handle, fly off the, see FLY OFF THE HANDLE.

handle the ribbing. To punch (someone) in the ribs: pugilistic: ca 1830–70. *Sinks*, 1848.

handle the ribbons. To drive a coach or a carriage: coll (—1827): ob. Moncrieff; Milliken, 'He 'andled the ribbings to rights,' 1892 in his lively *'Arry Ballads*.

handle to one's name, see HANDLE, n., 2.

hands, all. 'All the members of a party, esp. when collectively engaged in work', O.E.D.: coll: from ca 1700. Farquhar, Dickens. Ex *all hands*, the complete (ship's) crew.

hands off! Keep off or away! Coll: from ca 1560.

hand's turn. A stroke of work: coll (—1881) ex dial. (1828).

hands up! Oh, stop talking!: (low) coll (—1888). Ex police command to surrender.

handsaw. A street seller of knives and razors: low: ca 1835–1900. Ex the lit. S.E. sense. cf. CHIVE-FENCER.

handsome. As an adv., esp. in *handsome is that handsome does* ('a proverb frequently cited by ugly women'; Grose), it was, in C.15–mid-18, S.E.; then coll; then, after ca 1850, low coll. As n.: see HANDSOME (THING) . . .

handsome-bodied in the face. Ugly: derisively coll (—1678): †by 1893, ob. by 1860.

handsome reward, ca 1785–1830, meant, as a jocular coll, a horse-whipping. Ex the ambiguous language of 'lost' advertisements.

handsome (thing), do the. To behave extremely well; esp. to be very generous: coll (—1887). Manville Fenn, in *This Man's Wife.*

handsomely over the bricks! Go cautiously; be careful: an ob. (—1893), mainly nautical coll elaboration of the nautical *handsomely!*, carefully!, not so fast! (From ca 1800.)

handspike hash. The enforcing of discipline: sailing-ships': late C.19–20. cf. BELAYING-PIN SOUP.

handsprings, chuck. To turn somersaults: low coll: from ca 1860.

handstaff. The male member: from ca 1850: coll (mainly rural). Ex the handling of a flail.

handy billy (or **B.**). A small tackle used for a variety of purposes: naval coll: from ca 1800.

handy blows. Fisticuffs: late C.16–mid-19. The O.E.D. considers it S.E.; F. & H., coll, as do B.E. and the editor of *A New Canting Dict.* Prob. coll ca 1660–1740.

handy-dandy, see HANDIE-DANDIE.

handy Jack. A lower classes' coll and pejorative form of JACK OF ALL TRADES: but C.19–20.

hang. The general drift or tendency, gen. in *get the hang of*: coll (—1847): perhaps orig. U.S., where recorded – see Thornton – in 1845 as *acquire the hang of.* Darley; *Daily Chronicle*, 4 April 1890, 'He gets what some call the hang of the place.' 2. (Always in a negative sentence.) A (little) bit: pejorative coll (—1861); ob. H. Kingsley, 'She can't ride a hang.'

hang, v. In expletive locutions, as *hang him!* (*and*) *be hanged!*, (*go and*) *hang yourself!*, *hang it!*, and *hang!*, it indicates disgust, annoyance, or disappointment, and sometimes *hang* (*it*)*!* = DAMN (IT)! Coll: late C.16–20, though anticipated in C.14, as in Chaucer's 'Jelousie be hanged be [*by*] a cable!' Shakespeare, 'He a good wit? Hang him, baboon!'; Grant Allen, 'Hang it all . . .' – a common form of the exclamation. cf. the †proverbial *hang yourself for a pastime* (—1678).

hang aback. A coll nautical variant of *hang back* (to show reluctance), in the specific sense, to shirk duty: C.19–20.

hang about or **around.** To haunt, v.t., loaf, v.i.: coll: orig. U.S.; anglicized ca 1895.

hang an arse. To hold (oneself) back; hesitate: late C.16–20, ob.: S.E. in C.17, then coll, then in C.19–20 low coll. Marston, Smollett, Tomlinson in his valuable *Slang Pastoral.* cf. S.E. *hang a leg* or †*the groin.*

hang-bluff. Snuff: rhyming s. (—1857); †. Displaced, ca 1870, by HARRY BLUFF.

hang-by. A hanger-on, a parasite: coll: late C.16–17; then dial. Jonson.

hang-dog. A pitiful rascal: C.18 coll. Fielding. Lit., fit only to hang a dog.

hang-gallows look. A villainous appearance: coll on verge of S.E.: late C.18–19.

hang in. To set to work; do one's best: low coll: C.19–20, ob.

hang-in-chains. 'A vile desperate fellow', Grose, 1st ed.: coll: ca 1780–1830.

hang in the bellropes. To postpone marriage after being 'banned' in church: coll: from ca 1750; ob. by 1900.

hang it! see HANG, V.

hang it on, see HANG ON, and cf.:

hang it on with (a woman). To make her one's mistress: low (—1812); †by 1900.

hang it out. To delay a matter: (?low) coll: Australian (—1890): slightly ob. Prob. ex: 2. To 'skulk' on a job – not to do justice when on time-work: printers': from ca 1870.

hang it up, see HANG UP, V. **hang of, get the,** see HANG, n., 1.

hang off, v.t. To fight shy of: printers': from ca 1860. A slight deviation from C.17–20 S.E. senses, to hesitate, hang back, raise objections.

hang-on. 'A hanger-on, a mean dependant' (O.E.D.): coll, I think, though given as S.E. by the O.E.D.: late C.16–early 17.

hang on, v. To delay a matter (gen. as *hang it on*): low: from ca 1810. 2. *Hang on!* 'Don't be hasty!', 'Be reasonable!': coll: mid-C.19–20.

hang on by one's eyelashes. To persist obstinately or most courageously: from ca 1860: coll.

hang on by the splashboard. To catch a bus, tram, etc., as it moves; hence, barely to succeed: from ca 1880: coll.

hang one's bat out to dry. To place one's

bat in an impotent position: cricketers': 1895, C. B. Fry.

hang one's hat up. To become engaged to a girl; *hanging one's hat up*, thus engaged: non-aristocratic: late C.19–20. cf. HANG UP ONE'S HAT.

hang one's latchpan. To look and/or be dejected; to pout: low coll when not dial.: C.19–20, ob. Ex *latchpan*, a pan to catch the drippings from a roast.

hang-out. A residence or lodging: low s. > coll: from ca 1820; ob. by 1910. 2. A feasting, an entertainment: Cambridge undergraduates': ca 1845–70

hang-out, v. To reside, live, lodge; be temporarily at (e.g. a dug-out in the trenches): orig. low or prob. c. (—1811); by 1835 gen. s.; in C.20, coll. *Lex. Bal.*, 'The traps [*police*] scavey where we hang out'; Dickens. Ex the ancient custom of hanging out signs. cf. (—1871) U.S. *hang out a shingle*, to carry on a business.

hang out the washing. To set sail: nautical: mid-C.19–20.

hang saving! 'Blow the expense!': coll c.p.: C.18. Swift, *Polite Conversation*, II. Nowadays, *hang the expense!*: C.19–20.

hang-slang about, gen. v.i. To 'slang', vituperate: low: ca 1860–1910. An elaboration of SLANG, V.

hang-up. A gallows-bird: coll: ca 1560–1660.

hang up, v. (Gen. as *hang it up.*) To give credit, lit. chalk it up: prob. orig. (—1725) c.; by 1785, low; ob. by 1890. 2. v.t., to rob, with assault, on the street; to garotte: c.: ca 1870–1915. cf. S.E. *hold up*. 3. v.t., to postpone, leave unsettled: coll: G. Rose, 1803. *Cornhill Magazine*, June 1887. 4. v.i., to be in dire straits, physical or monetary; e.g. *a man hanging* is one 'to whom any change must be for the better', F. & H.: low coll: ca 1860–1910. 5. v.t., to tie up a horse: Australian (—1860); coll. W. Kelly, *Life in Victoria*, 1860. Ex securing horses to posts.

hang up one's hat. To die: (?low) s. > coll: ca 1850–1914. 2. To make oneself very much at home: coll: from ca 1855. Occ. with an implication of 'honest' courting and often of a married man living in the wife's house, as in Trollope's *The Warden*. cf. HANG ONE'S HAT UP.

hang up the hatchet, see BURY THE HATCHET.

hang up the ladle. To marry: society: mid-C.18–early 19.

hanged. CONFOUNDED, gen. as in 'Oh that be hanged!' Coll: from the middle 1880s. Ex dial. where recorded in 1864. cf. HANG, V.

hangers. Gloves; esp. gloves held in the hand: ca 1875–1910. 2. (Gen. in POT-HOOKS AND HANGERS and very rare in the singular.) Strokes with a double curve, as ʃ: a nursery coll: from ca 1705. Swift.

hanging. Fit to be hanged: coll: C.19–20, ob. See HANG UP, 4.

hanging Johnny. The male member; esp. if impotent or diseased: low: C.19–20 (? ob.).

hangman. A pejorative term; a jocular endearment: mid-C.16–20, but rare after 1650. By the O.E.D. considered S.E.; the latter use is, I believe, coll.

hangman's day. Monday (in U.S., *hanging day*, Friday): low coll: ca 1830–1900.

hangman's wages. Thirteen-pence-half-penny: 1678, Butler, ob. by 1820, †by 1880: coll. Dekker, 1602, has 'Why should I eat hempe-seed at the hangman's thirteen-pence-halfpenny ordinary?', and *thirteen-pence-half-penny wages* occurs in 1659. The C.17 execution fee was a Scottish mark, fixed by James I at 13½d.

hangs-out, see HANG-OUT, n.

hank. A spell of rest or comparative (physical) ease: coll: from ca 1810; ob. *Sporting Life*, 7 Dec. 1888, concerning a boxing-match, 'The company ... called out, "No hank!"'

hank, v. To tease, bait, worry; persecute: coll: from ca 1820; ob. 2. To hesitate, be diffident; also as ppl adj., *hanking*: proletarian coll: from ca 1870. Nevinson, 1895, 'Lina's style, full of 'ankin' artful little ways'; 'Don't stand 'ankin' there; you're not the only person in the world.'

hank, in (a). In trouble; in difficulty: coll: C.17–19.

***hank, on the.** On the look-out (for booty): c., and low Cockney: from ca 1890. Clarence Rook, 1899.

hank, Smithfield. An ox infuriated by ill-treatment: ca 1780–1830.

hank (up)on one, have a. To have a profitable, e.g. a blackmailing, hold on a person: coll: ca 1600–1840 (extant in dial. and in U.S.). In Vaux it takes the form, *have* (a person) *at a good hank*. Ex *hank*, a coil of rope.

hanker, v.i. To long. v.t. with *after*. From ca 1640; it seems to have, ca 1680–1825, been considered coll – witness B.E., and Grose (edd. of 1785–1823). The same applies to the vbl n. *hankering*.

hankie, hanky; rarely **handky.** A handkerchief: coll: late C.19–20.

hankin, n. Passing off bad work for good: commercial: from ca 1870; ob.

***hankins.** Breeches: c.: C.18. Anon., *Street-Robberies Consider'd*, 1728.

hanktelo. 'A silly Fellow, a mere Codshead', B.E.: late C.16–early 19: coll verging on S.E. In Nashe as *hangtelow.*

hanky, see HANKIE.

hanky-panky. Legerdemain; hence, almost imm., trickery, double or underhand work: 1841, *Punch.* Also adj., as in *hanky-panky business*, conjuring or 'dirty work', and *hanky-panky tricks* or *work*, double-dealing. A reduplication of *hanky*, handkerchief – the conjuror's handkerchief used to assist the quickness of the hand in deceiving the audience's eye.

hanky-panky bloke. A conjuror: theatrical: from ca 1860. Ex preceding.

hanky-spanky. Dashing (of persons); esp., well-cut, stylish (of clothes): ?low: from ca 1880. Prob. ex SPANKING, by HANKY-PANKY.

Hannah, that's the man as married (occ. **that's what's the matter with the man. . .**). Excellent! Good for you! Most certainly! Orig. to designate a good or happy beginning. A rather low c.p., mostly Shropshire, then London: ca 1860–1905.

Hanover!, go to. Go to hell: Jacobites': ca 1725–80. cf. HALIFAX; JERICHO; BATH, etc. E.D.D. notes also the dial. *what the Hanover!* and, concerning the Suffolk *go to Hanover and hoe turnips!*, remarks: 'Said to date from the time of the [first two] Georges, who were very unpopular in the east [of England].'

Hanover (or to Hanover) jack. An imitation sovereign: low (?orig. c.): ca 1880–1914. Ware, who cites a police report of 1888, offers an unconvincing derivation.

Hans. A Dutchman; a German: coll: from ca 1570. Abbr. *Johannes*, John. cf. *Fritz.*

Hans Carvel's ring. The female pudend: C.17–19 low coll. Prior. Ex a tale by Poggio.

Hans-en(or in)-Kelder. An unborn child: low: perhaps orig. c.: often as a toast to the expected infant: ca 1630–1830. Brome, Dryden, Grose. Ex Dutch, lit. Jack in (the) cellar. For an interesting anecdote, see Thornbury, *London*, iii, 315.

hanseller, han'-seller. A low coll form of S.E. *hand-seller*, a cheapjack: ca 1850–1910. Hindley, in *Adventures of a Cheap Jack.*

hansom. A chop: costermongers': from ca 1870. ?punning the notions 'goes quickly' and 'good to look at', or ex the normal shapes.

hap-harlot. A rug, a coarse coverlet: coll: ca 1550–1760, then dial. Lit., a cover-knave. cf. WRAP-RASCAL. 2. A woman's undergarments: C.19.

hap worth a cop(p)eras, see HA'PORTH O'COPPERS.

ha'penny. A coll form (C.16–20) of *halfpenny.*

ha'p'orth. A coll contraction of *halfpennyworth*: 1728, Swift. Earlier contractions, also to be rated as coll, are – see the O.E.D. at *halfpennyworth* – *halpworthe*, ca 1490 – *halporthe*, 1533 – *halfperth*, 1692 – *halfp'worth*, 1719. Swift also has *halfporth*, but this is rare. A late (?before 1873, Browning) contraction is *ha'p'worth.*

ha'porth o' coppers. Habeas corpus: legal: from ca 1840; ob. Ex the C.18 sol. pronunciation *hap worth a coperas* quoted by Grose (3rd ed.).

ha'porth of liveliness. Music: costers': from ca 1845; ob. Mayhew. 2. A dawdler, a slow-coach: low (—1893); ob.

happen, adv. (Orig. a subjunctive: cf. *maybe*), perhaps, perchance: at first (—1790) and still mainly Northern dial., but from ca 1845 it has been increasingly used as a coll, esp. in the non-committal *happen it does, happen it* (*he*, etc.) *will.*

happen in, v.i. To pay a casual visit: coll: ex U.S. (—1855); anglicized ca 1895.

Happy. The inevitable nickname of anyone surnamed Day: late C.19–20: mostly naval and military. Ex *O, happy day!*

happy, adj. Slightly (and, properly used, cheerfully) drunk: coll: 1770 (O.E.D.). Marryat.

happy as pigs in shit, as. Completely happy: low: since ca 1870.

happy dosser, see DOSSER.

happy Eliza. A female Salvationist: 1887–ca 1910. Ex a broadside ballad that points to 'Happy Eliza' and 'Converted Jane' as 'hot 'uns in our time'.

happy family. A number of different animals living quietly in one cage: coll: ca 1850–1915. Mayhew.

happy hours. Flowers: rhyming s., mainly theatrical: late C.19–20.

happy hunting-ground. 'A favourable place for work or play', F. & H.: coll (—1892)

>, ca 1900, S.E. 2. The *pudendum muliebre*: low: from ca 1870.

happy returns. Vomiting: Australia: low: from ca 1880.

ha'p'worth, see HA'P'ORTH.

haramzeda. A scoundrel; very gen. as term of abuse: Anglo-Indian (—1864). Ex Arabo-Persian for 'son of the unlawful'.

***hard.** Hard labour: c. (—1890): in C.20, low. 2. Third class, on e.g. a train. 'Do you go hard or soft?', i.e. third or first: late C.19–20. Abbr. *hard seat* or *hard arse.* 3. Preceded by *the*, whisky: from ca 1850; ob. 4. See HARD UP, HAVE A. 5. Plug tobacco: from mid-1890s: coll.

hard, adj. (Of beer or cider) stale or sour: late C.16–20: S.E. till ca 1680; then coll till mid-C.19, then s. when not dial. 'Hard drink, that is very Stale, or beginning to Sower', B.E. 2. Intoxicating, spirituous: coll: orig. (ca 1874) U.S., anglicized in mid-1880s.

hard, die. To die fighting bravely: coll: C.19–20; ob.

hard, in the. In hard cash; cash down: coll (—1830); ob.

hard-a-Gilbert. Hard-a-port: naval: ?from ca 1860. Bowen, 'Gilbert being an old-time wine merchant whose port was supplied to ward-rooms'.

hard-a-weather. Weather-proof; physically tough: nautical coll: 1848. Clark Russell, 'They were hard-a-weather fellows.'

hard-arsed. Very niggardly, monetarily costive: low: from ca 1850.

hard as a bone; as nails. Very hard: unyielding; physically or morally tough: coll: resp. ca 1860–1930 and from 1838 (Dickens in *Oliver Twist*).

hard at it. Very busy, esp. on some particular work: coll: from ca 1870.

hard-bake. A sweetmeat of boiled brown sugar (or treacle) and blanched almonds: schoolboys' (—1825): in C.20, gen. considered S.E. Hone, 'Hardbake, brandy-balls, and bull's-eyes'.

hard-baked. Constipated: low coll (—1823); ob. by 1893. 2. Stern, unflinching: coll: ?orig. U.S. (—1847).

hard bargain. A lazy fellow; an incorrigible: coll: from ca 1850. 2. A defaulting debtor: trade: from ca 1860; ob. 3. Occ. as synonymous with HARD CASE, 4.

hard bit or **mouthful.** An unpleasant experience: coll: ca 1860–1910. 2. (Variant, BIT OF HARD) the male member in priapism; hence (for women) the coïtus.

hard case. An incorrigible: orig. (1842), U.S.; anglicized ca 1860. 2. In Australia and New Zealand, a person morally tough but not necessarily incorrigible; also a witty or amusing dare-devil – one who loves fun and adventure; a girl ready for sexual escapades: all coll from ca 1880. 3. A defaulting debtor: trade: from ca 1865. cf. HARD BARGAIN. 4. A brutal officer: nautical: from ca 1865. cf. HARD HORSE.

hard cheek, see HARD LINES.

hard cheese. Bad luck; orig., esp. at billiards: Royal Military Academy (—1893).

hard-cut. Dropped cigar-ends: low (?c.): ca 1890–1920. cf. HARD-UP, n., 1.

hard-drinking, vbl n. Drinking to excess: C.17–20: coll till ca 1750, then S.E.

hard-faced. Impudent: Liverpool; half-way between coll and dial.: late C.19–20.

hard for soft, give. (Of men) to have sexual intercourse: low coll: from ca 1860.

hard hit, be. To have had a heavy loss, esp. of money: coll: 1854. 2. To be very much in love: coll (—1888). Miss Braddon, in *Gerard.* Occ. *hit hard.*

hard horse. A brutal or tyrannical officer: nautical (—1893); virtually †.

hard in a clinch – and no knife to cut the seizing. In a very difficult position – and no app. way out: a nautical c.p.: late C.19–20. Here, *seizing* is cordage.

hard lines. Hardship: orig. nautical (—1855); ob. 1824, Scott, 'The old seaman paused . . . "It is hard lines for me," he said, "to leave your honour in tribulation."' ?ex ropes unmanageable from wet or frost; *lines*, however, was in C.17 *lot.* 2. Difficulty; an unfortunate occurrence, severe action: coll: from ca 1850. In South Africa, also *hard cheek*: late C.19–20.

hard-mouthed. Coarse-spoken: coll of ca 1860–1910. Ex the stables.

hard neck. Extreme impudence: Anglo-Irish and tailors': from ca 1870; ob.

hard nut. Abbr. *hard nut to crack*: a dangerous foe; a HARD CASE (1 and 2): coll (?orig. s.): from ca 1875.

hard-on, adj. With the *membrum virile* in erection: low: from ca 1860. 2. Also as a n.: from ca 1890 (?ex U.S.). cf. HORN, 4.

hard on the setting sun. A journalistic coll phrase indicative of scorn for the Red Indian: in 1897, *People*, 13 June, refers to it as 'a characteristic bye-word'; virtually and happily †. Ware.

hard-puncher. 'The fur cap of the London

rough', F. & H.: low: ca 1870–1905. Ex a vigorous boxer's nickname. cf. BENDIGO.

hard-pushed. In difficulties, esp. monetary: coll (—1871). cf. HARD-UP, adj., and:

hard put to it. In a – gen. monetary – difficulty: coll: cf. HARD-RUN. Prob. from ca 1690, for B.E., 1699, has the entry, '*Oxhouse. . . . The Black Ox has not trod upon his Foot*, of one that has not been Pinch'd with Want, or been Hard put to it.'

hard row to hoe. A difficult task: coll: orig. (1839), U.S.; anglicized ca 1860. Gen. as *he*, e.g., *has a hard . . .*

hard-run. Very short of money; HARD-UP: coll: late C.19–20.

hard Simpson. Ice: milk-sellers': ca 1860–80. See SIMPSON.

hard stuff. Intoxicating liquor: Australia, whence New Zealand: from ca 1890. Prob. ex U.S., where *hard* = intoxicating (1879).

hard tack, whether ship's biscuits or coarse fare, is S.E. in C.20; perhaps orig. (1841) nautical s. Lever in *Charles O'Malley*. 2. As = insufficient food, it is coll, mostly Cockneys': ca 1810–1910.

hard-up. A gleaner and seller of cigar-ends: low (—1851); ob. Mayhew. See also TOPPER-HUNTER and HARD-CUT. 2. Hence, a very poor person: low coll (—1857); ob. 'Ducange Anglicus'. 3. Hence, one who is temporarily penniless: from ca 1860. 4. A cigarette-end: low: prob. from ca 1870. Ex sense 1.

hard-up, adj. In want, gen. of money: s. >, ca 1880, coll: Alfred Burton, *Johnny Newcombe*, 1818. Hence *hard up for*, sorely needing. Haggart, Hook; *London Figaro*, 25 Jan. 1871, 'For years, England has been a refuge for hard-up German princelings.' Ex nautical j. (steering). cf. HARD-PUSHED – PUT TO IT – RUN; DEAD-BROKE; STONY. 2. Intoxicated: low coll: ca 1870–1900. 3. Out of countenance; exhausted, esp. in swimming: Winchester College: from ca 1850; ob. 4. Impeded, detained: naval: ca 1790–1850.

hard up, have a. To have a priapism: low: late C.19–20.

hard-upness, -uppishness, -uppedness. Poverty, habitual or incidental: coll: resp. 1876, 1870, ca 1905.

hardware. 'Ammunition in general, and shells in particular. Jocular', Ware: military and naval: from ca 1880.

***hardware bloke.** A native of Birmingham; a BRUM: c. of ca 1870–1915.

***hardware-swag.** Hardware carried by them for sale: tramps' c. (—1887).

hardy annual. A constantly recurring bill: Parliamentary: from ca 1880. 2. A stock subject: journalistic: from ca 1885. *Pall Mall Gazette*, 16 Aug. 1892, 'The readers of the *Daily Telegraph* are once more filling [its] columns . . . with "Is Marriage a Failure?" The hardy annual is called "English Wives" this time.'

hare, v.i. To run very fast: Shrewsbury School coll: late C.19–20.

hare, swallow a. To get exceedingly drunk: coll: late C.17–mid-19. Grose, 1st ed., proposes *hair*, 'which requires washing down', but the phrase was perhaps suggested by the old proverbial *to have devoured a hare*, to look amiable.

hare and hunt with the hounds, hold or run with the. To play a double game: C.15–20: orig. coll; then, in C.16, proverbial; then, in C.18–20, S.E.

hare in a hen's nest, seek a. To try to do something (almost) impossible: late C.16–17 coll. *Hare* synonyms, all (I think) S.E. rather than coll and all certainly proverbial, are *catch*, or *hunt for*, *a hare with a tabor*, C.14–20 – *take hares with foxes*, C.16–17 – and *set the tortoise to catch the hare*, C.18–20, ob.

hare of, make a. To render ridiculous; expose the ignorance of: coll, mostly and orig. Anglo-Irish: from ca 1830. Carleton; Lever, 'It was Mister Curran made a hare of your Honor that day.'

hare-sleep. Feigned sleep: C.17–18: coll > S.E.

hare's foot, kiss the. To be (too) late: coll: C.17–18. cf.:

hare's foot to lick, get the. To obtain very little – or nothing. Coll: C.19–20; ob. Scott, 'The poor clergyman [got] nothing whatever, or, as we say, the hare's foot to lick.'

hark-ye-ing. 'Whispering on one side to borrow money', Grose, 1st ed.: mid-C.18–early 19. The late C.17–early 18 preferred *harking*, as in B.E.

harlequin. A sovereign: theatrical: ca 1860–1905. Ex its glitter. 2. The wooden core of a (gen. red) india-rubber ball: Winchester College: ca 1870–1900.

harlequin Jack. 'A man who shows off equally in manner and in dress': lower classes': late C.19–20; ob. Ware.

***harman.** A late C.17–19 abbr. (as in B.E.; Lytton, *The Disowned*) of:

***harman-beck.** A constable: c. of ca

1560–1880. Harman; B.E.; Scott; Borrow. Prob. ex next + *beck* (=BEAK); but perhaps ex *hard man*, a severe one; or even ex postulated *har-man*, he who cries *ha*(*r*), stop! – cf. †*harr*, to snarl.

***harmans.** The stocks: c.: ca 1560–1820, though ob. by 1785. If the -MANS is the c. suffix found in DARKMANS, LIGHTMANS, etc., then the *har-* is prob. *hard*, for the notion, hardness = the gallows, is characteristic of c.

harness, the routine of one's work, as in *in harness*, at work, and *die in harness*, i.e. at one's post or still working, is held by the O.E.D. to be S.E. But I think that at first (say 1840–80) it was coll. ?suggested by Shakespeare's 'At least we'll die with harness on our back,' *Macbeth*, V, v.

haro. To yell: coll: C.19. Ex *cry haro*.

harp. The tail of a coin, esp. as a call in toss-halfpenny: Anglo-Irish (—1785); ob. by 1860. The tail of a coin bore Hibernia with a harp. cf. MUSIC (2) and WOMAN.

harper. A brass coin, value one penny, current in Ireland in late C.16–early 17: coll. Ben Jonson. Ex the harp thereon represented.

harpers!, have among or **at you (my blind).** A c.p. 'used in throwing or shooting at random among a crowd', Grose: ca 1540–1830. Considered proverbial as early as 1542 (Heywood).

harridan. A woman half whore, half bawd: c.: late C.17–18. 2. 'A hagged old woman', a disagreeable old woman: orig. (—1725) coll; S.E. by 1895.

Harriet Lane. 'Australian canned meat – because it had the appearance of chopped-up meat; and Harriet Lane was chopped up by one Wainwright': lower classes': ca 1875–1900. Ware. cf. FANNY ADAMS.

Harrington. A brass farthing: ca 1615–40 coll. Jonson, 1616, 'I will not bate a *Harrington* o' the sum.' Ex Lord Harrington, who, in 1613, obtained the patent of coining them.

Harry. A rustic: late C.18–early 19 c., then dial. 2. The 'literary' shape of 'ARRY: 1874: coll > S.E.

Harry!, by the Lord. Perhaps jocular ex app. later OLD HARRY, the devil: late C.17–20; ob. Congreve, Byron, Besant.

Harry, old. For this and *play old Harry*, see OLD HARRY.

Harry, – Tom, Dick, and. As generic for the MOB, any and everybody, it was orig. coll, but in C.20 it is S.E. See 'Representative Names' in *Words!*

Harry Bluff. Snuff: rhyming s. (—1874); ob. (cf. HANG-BLUFF.)

Harry Common. A womanizer: jocular coll: late C.17–18. cf. Shakespeare's *Doll Common*.

Harry Freeman's, see FREEMAN'S . . .

Harry gave Doll, what. Sexual connection: low coll: C.18–19.

Harry Lauder. A prison warder: rhyming s.: since ca 1905.

Harry Lauders. Stage hangings: theatrical rhyming s. (on *borders*): from ca 1905.

Harry-Soph. One who, having kept the necessary terms, ranks, by courtesy, as a bachelor: Cambridge University (—1720, as in Stukeley's *Memoirs*); > † before 1893 but after 1873. Earlier (—1661), *Henry Sophister*. ?ex *Henry VIII* – see Fuller's *Worthies*, p. 151 – and *Sophista*, in the form *sophista Henricanus*. A University joke refers to Gr. ἐπίσοφος, very wise.

Harry Tagg. A bag: rhyming s., mostly theatrical: late C.19–20.

***hartmans.** The pillory: c.: ?C.18–early 19. A variant of HARMANS.

harum-scarum. Four horses driven TANDEM: sporting: ca 1862–1900. cf. SUICIDE.

harum-scarum, adv., 1674; adj., 1751; n., 1784. Coll. Wild(ly); reckless(ly); giddy, giddily. Anon., *Round about Our Coal Fire*, 1740, 'Tom run harum scarum to draw a jug of ale.' Perhaps, as W. suggests, *hare'em, scare'em* ex †*hare*, to harass: cf. Smollett's *hare'um scare'um* and Mme D'Arblay's *harem-scarem*. cf. Westcott's famous novel, *David Harum*, 1899.

harvest for, of, or **about a little corn, make a long.** To be tedious about a trifle: coll proverbial: C.16–20; since ca 1820, mainly dial. – indeed, in C.20, otherwise †. Greene; Richardson in *Clarissa*.

has(-)been. Any antiquated thing or, more gen., person: coll from ca 1825; orig. Scots (C.17–19) as in Burns. Rare as adj. cf. NEVER-WASER.

hash. As a medley, S.E.; as a fig. mess, coll, esp. in *make a hash of*, to fail badly with or at: C.19–20. 2. One who 'makes a hash' of his words: coll when not Scots: mid-C.17–20, ob. Burns. 3. Work in school: Charterhouse (—1900). A. H. Tod. cf. HASH, v., 2.

hash, v. To spoil: coll but not very gen.: C.19–20. 2. Study hard: Cheltenham School: ca 1860–1915. Also at Charterhouse: witness A. H. Tod, 1900. cf. HASHER.

***hash, flash the.** To vomit: mid-C.18–mid-19 c.

hash, settle one's. To subdue, silence, defeat; kill: Isaac Cruikshank, *Olympic Games*, 16 June 1803; s. >, in C.20, coll. cf. COOK ONE'S GOOSE.

hash-up. A MESS, a bungling; fiasco: coll: from ca 1905. Ex:

hash up, v. To re-serve; mangle and re-present: coll (in C.20, S.E.): from ca 1740.

hasher. A football sweater: Charterhouse: from ca 1880. A. H. Tod, *Charterhouse*, 1900. cf. HASH, n., 3.

hask. A fish-basket: nautical (esp. fishermen's) coll: mid-C.19–20. Prob. ex dial. *hask*, hard; but perhaps cognate with *husk* (n.).

Haslar hag. A nurse at the Haslar Hospital: nautical: from ca 1880; †.

hassle. A fuss, a disagreement, a ROW; a HULLABALOO: Canadian: adopted, ca 1860, ex U.S. Leechman, who proposes a blend of *ha*ggle + tu*ssle*; I, one of *ha*ggle + wres*tle*.

Hastings sort, be none of the. To be too slow; slothful: esp. of one who loses a good chance by being dilatory: mid-C.16–mid-19: proverbial coll. Grose, 3rd ed., explains by 'the Hastings pea, which is the first in season'; but is not the phrase merely a pun? The personal is recorded before the vegetable sense; the capital *H* is folk-etymology. cf. HOTSPURS.

hasty, precipitate, 'very Hot on a sudden' (B.E.) – which dates from early C.16 – seems to have, ca 1680–1810, been coll.

hasty g. A hasty generalization: Cambridge University: ca 1880–1900.

hasty pudding. A muddy road: coll: ca 1790–1870. Grose, 3rd ed., 'The way through Wandsworth is quite a hasty pudding.' 2. A bastard: low: from ca 1870.

hat. A gentleman commoner; a TUFT. Cambridge University (—1830); ob. by 1900, †by 1920. In the *Gradus ad Cantabrigiam*, 1803, he is a *hat commoner*; in Earle's *Microcosmography*, 1628, a GOLD HATBAND. 2. An occ. abbr. of OLD HAT, the female pudend: ca 1760–1830. 3. Hence, an old-hand harlot: Scots: ca 1820–1910. Ex preceding sense. 4. In such asseverations as *by this hat* (Shakespeare), *my hat to a halfpenny* (ibid.), and *I'll bet a hat* (?C.18–early 19). 5. See BAD HAT. 6. A condition or state, thus *be in a* DEUCE *of a hat* = to be in a 'nice mess'; *get into a hat*, to get into a difficulty: low: late C.19–20; ob. 7. Price: showmen's: late C.19–20. Ex hat as collecting box.

hat!, all round my. A derisive and mainly Cockney c.p. retort; also, all over, completely: from ca 1830. Milliken. Perhaps ex the broadside ballad, 'All round my hat I wears a green willow.'

hat, bad, see BAD HAT. **hat, black,** see BLACK HAT.

hat, eat one's. Gen. as **I'll eat my hat, if . . .** A strong asseveration: C.19–20: coll; seemingly originated or, at the least, recorded first by Dickens in *Pickwick*, who also sponsors the much rarer *eat one's head*; there is, however, another form, . . . *old Rowley's* (Charles II's) *hat*.

hat, get a. To do the HAT-TRICK: cricketers': ca 1890–1914.

hat, get (occ. be) in(to) a or **the,** see HAT, 6.

hat, hang up one's, see at HANG. **hat!, I'll have your,** see HAT!, SHOOT THAT.

hat, old, see OLD HAT.

hat, pass (or send) round the. To make a collection: from ca 1857: coll.

hat!, shoot that; occ. I'll have your hat! A derisive c.p. retort: ca 1860–72: mainly London. cf. HAT!, ALL ROUND MY.

hat, talk through one's. To talk nonsense: coll, orig. (—1888) U.S., where at first it meant to bluster; anglicized ca 1900.

hat!, what a shocking bad. A Cockney c.p. remark on an objectionable person: ca 1890–1910; but possibly sixty years earlier, see quotation at BAD HAT. Anstey, 1892, 'Regular bounder! Shocking bad hat!' As a BOUNDER (3 and 4), a BAD LOT, BAD HAT survives: cf. OLD HAT.

hat?, where did you get that. A c.p. of ca 1885–1914. cf. HATTER?, WHO'S YOUR. Ex a popular song. ('Quotations' Benham.)

hat covers (e.g. his) family, (his). He is alone in the world: coll: from ca 1850.

hat-peg. The head: low: ca 1875–1915. cf. BLOCK, n., 2.

hat(-)trick. Three wickets with successive balls: cricket: 1882. Orig. s. *Sportsman*, 28 Nov. 1888, 'Mr Absolom has performed the hat trick twice.' In the good old days, this feat entitled its professional performer to a collection or to a new hat from his club.

hat up, hang one's, see HANG ONE'S HAT UP.

hat-work. Hack-work; inferior writing: journalists' (—1888). Rider Haggard in *Mr Meeson's Will*. Perhaps work that could be done with one's hat almost as well as with one's head.

hatband, (as) queer (occ. odd, tight, etc.) as Dick's or occ. Nick's. Very queer, etc.: late C.18–20, ob. Prob. ex some local half-wit.

hatch, be hatching. To be confined in childbed: low: from ca 1860; ob.

hatch, match, and dispatch column; or hatches, matches, despatches; or the hatched, matched, dispatched column. Births, marriages, and deaths announcements: journalistic: ca 1885–1914. Occ., also †, *cradle, altar, and tomb column.*

Hatch-Thoke. A Founder's Commemoration day: Winchester College: C.19–20. Wrench, 'Said to be from the old custom of staying in bed [see THOKE] till breakfast, which was provided at Hatch'.

hatches, under (the). In (gen. serious) trouble of any kind: coll: mid-C.16–20; ob. by 1890. 2. Dead: nautical: late C.18–early 20. Dibdin in *Tom Bowling*. In C.17, often *(be)stow under hatches*, to silence (as in Marston), distress; *bestowed under hatches* = the shorter phrase, C.17–early 18; *be under (the) hatches* dates from early C.17 and occurs in Locke. Ex the lit. nautical sense, below deck.

hatchet. A very plain or an ugly woman: tailors': ca 1870–1920. Ex HATCHET-FACED.

hatchet, bury (and dig up) the, see at BURY.

hatchet, sling or throw the. To exaggerate greatly; tell yarns; lie: low: the former —1789 and ob., the latter —1821. 2. (Gen. with *sling*.) To sulk; skulk; sham: nautical: from ca 1850. Whence the vbl nn. *hatchet-slinging* and *-throwing*; the former in G. Parker, 1789. 'App. a variant on *draw the longbow*', W.

Hatchet-Back, see CHOP-BACK.

hatchet-face(d), applied in S.E. to a long, thin face, was, ca 1680–1750, coll and = very plain or even ugly: B.E., '*Hatchet-fac'd.* Hard-favor'd, Homely' – whence, by the way, the U.S. as distinct from the mod. Eng. sense of *homely*.

hatchway. The mouth: nautical > low gen.: from ca 1820; ob. 2. The female pudend: nautical > low gen.: from ca 1865. cf. *fore-hatch*.

hatfler. A FLAT (person): centre s.: from ca 1860; ob.

hatful. Much, esp. money and in horse-racing: coll (—1859). Miss Braddon, 'He had won what his companions called a hatful of money on the steeple-chase.'

hatter. A miner who works alone: Australia, 1864: s. >, by 1890, coll. R. L. A. Davies, 1884, 'Oh, a regular rum old stick; he mostly works [as] a "hatter".' 2. Hence, a criminal, esp. a thief, working on his own: Australian c. (—1893); ob. By 1890, the term has the connotation, 'A man who has lived by himself until his brain has been turned', Marriott Watson, in *Broken Billy*: this sense was prob. prompted by the next entry, sense 1. Prob. ex (*his*) HAT COVERS HIS FAMILY.

hatter, (as) mad as a. Very mad; extremely eccentric: coll: orig. (1836, Haliburton) U.S., where *mad* meant angry, as generically it still does; anglicized in 1849 by Thackeray in *Pendennis*; well established in England by 1863, when appeared F. A. Marshall's farce, *Mad as a Hatter*; it was 'Lewis Carroll' who, in 1866, definitely fixed the English sense. 'The *hatter* may orig. have been *adder*, or Ger. *otter* ... both adder and otter. *Attercop*, spider ... has some support in *mad as a bed-bug*, [another U.S. phrase],' W. But hatters often suffered from mercury poisoning, the symptoms of which include tremors and twitches that may have suggested the idea of insanity.

hatter?, who's your. A London (chiefly Cockney) c.p. of ca 1875–85. cf. HAT?, WHERE DID YOU GET THAT.

hatting, vbl n. and ppl adj. corresponding to HATTER, 1: Australian (—1890) coll: ob.

hatty, an elephant: Anglo-Indian coll. See HUTTY.

haul. To worry, pester: coll: ca 1670–1750. Gay. 2. (Gen. with *up*) to bring up for reprimand: coll (—1865). Ex the more gen. *haul over the coals*, coll, 1795. cf. COALS, CALL OVER THE, and HAULABLE.

haul ashore. To retire from the sea: nautical: late C.19–20. cf. *swallow the* ANCHOR.

haul-devil. A clergyman: low: ca 1865–1910. cf. DEVIL-DODGER.

haul off and take a binge, see BINGE, HAVE A.

haul one's wind. To get clear: nautical coll (—1823). Ex lit. sense.

haul over the coals, see HAUL, 2.

haulable, adj. Applied to a girl whose company renders an undergraduate liable to a fine: university (Oxford and Cambridge): ca 1870–1914. Ex HAUL, v., 2.

hauling sharp. On half rations: nautical: late C.19–20.

häuser. A meat pie: Bootham School: late C.19–20. Origin?

havage, havidge. 'An assemblage or family of dishonest or doubtful characters', Bee: low: ca 1820–50. Ex dial. *havage*, lineage, family stock, + (*William*) *Habberfield*, a criminal whose family was such.

Havannah, under a canopy of. 'Sitting where there are many persons smoking tobacco,' *Sinks*, 1848: ca 1840–60.

have. (Gen. in pl.) One who has, esp. money and/or property; gen. contrasted with *have-not*, a needy person: coll: 1836 (S.O.D.). 2. A trick or imposture; a swindle: from ca 1880. Ex:

have, v. To cheat (—1805): perhaps orig. c. G. Harrington, in *The New London Spy*, 'Had, a cant word ... instead of ... cheated'. 2. Hence, to trick, deceive (1821): low. 3. Hence, to humbug, fool (—1893; prob. as early as 1825), low > gen. 4. To possess carnally: a vulgarism of C.16–20. In C.20, gen. of women by men, but previously said 'indifferently of, and by, both sexes', F. & H. 5. (Gen. *have it.*) To receive, or to have received, punishment, a thrashing, a reprimand: coll: late C.16–20. Shakespeare. 6. To have caught (someone) in discussion, argument, or put into a fix: coll: 1820.

have?, is that a catch or a. A low c.p. acknowledgement that the speaker has been 'had' or fooled. Should the other essay a definition, the victim turns the tables with *then you catch* – or, as the case may be, *have – your nose up my arse*. ca 1885–1900.

have a banana, see BANANA.

have a binge, see BINGE, HAVE A.

have a cab. To be drunk: London: late C.19–early 20.

have a down, see DOWN, n.

have a go. To hit the bowling, esp. if rashly: cricketers' coll: 1894, Norman Gale.

have a heart! see HEART!, HAVE A. **have a heat!** see HEAT!, HAVE A. **have any, not,** see ANY. **have by the short hairs,** see HAIRS, GET ...

have had it. To have been seduced: C.19–20 low coll.

have it, see HAVE, v., 5.

have it, let one. To strike hard; punish (lit. or fig.) severely: coll: ?orig. U.S., where it is recorded as early as 1848; anglicized in the 1880s.

have it in. To effect intromission: low coll: late C.19–20. Partly euphemistic.

have it in for (someone). To bear a grudge against: coll: since ca 1820. Alex. Harris, *The Emigrant Family*, 1849.

have (or take) it out of one. To punish; exact a compensation from: coll: from ca 1870.

have it out with one, (v.i., have it out). To reprove freely; come to a necessary understanding, or settle a dispute, with a person: coll: from ca 1860 (Ware). *Daily News*, 2 April 1883; John Strange Winter, 'Instead of ... having it out, he ... fumed the six days away.' ?ex the S.E. *have out*, to cause a person to fight a duel with one.

have-not. (Gen. in pl.) See HAVE, n., 1. 1836.

have on. To engage the interest or the sympathy of, esp. with a view to deceit (seldom criminally): dial. (—1867) > (low) coll ca 1870; slightly ob. cf. STRING ON, and the S.E. *lead on* and (see HAVE ON TOAST) the †S.E. *have in a string*.

have on the raws. To touch to the quick; tease: low coll: from ca 1860; ob. Lit., raw flesh, raw places.

have on the stick. To make fun of, pull someone's leg: ca 1870–1914. (William Westall, *Sons of Belial*, 1895.)

have on toast. To deceive utterly, hence to defeat heavily in argument: from ca 1870: (orig. low) s. > coll.

have one's cut. (Of a male) to coït: low: late C.19–20.

have the edge on, see EDGE ON.

have (a person) to rights. (Gen. in passive.) To defeat: lower classes' coll: from ca 1880.

have towards, occ. with or at. To pledge in drinking: the first and third, C.17–18 and S.E.; the second, C.19 and coll. Michael Scott, '"Have with you, boy – have with you," shouted half-a-dozen other voices.'

have you a licence? A c.p. addressed to one clearing his throat noisily: mid-C.18–early 19. Punning *hawking* and 'the Act of hawkers and pedlars'.

Havelock's saints. Teetotallers: military: mid-C.19–20; virtually †. Dating from a fact – and the time – of the Indian Mutiny.

haven-screamer. A sea-gull: nautical: late C.19–20.

haves. Half-boots: Winchester College. See HALVES, the better spelling.

hav(e)y-cav(e)y. (Of persons only) uncertain, doubtful, shilly-shally: also an adv. Late C.18–early 19: coll ex dial. A Northern and Midland anglicization of L. *habe, cave*, have (and) beware!

havidge, see HAVAGE.

***havil.** A sheep: c. (—1788): †by 1860 in England. Origin?

havildar's guard. The cooking of the fry of fresh-water fish spitted in a row on a skewer: coll, in and around Bombay (—1886). Ex *havildar*, a Sepoy non-commissioned officer.

havoc(k). In late C.17–mid 18, esp. in *make sad havoc*, this term app. had a strong coll taint.

havy-cavy, see HAVEY-CAVEY.

haw-haw, adj. Affected in speech (rarely of women); rather obviously and consciously English upper-class: (mostly Colonial) coll: mid-C.19–20.

hawbuck. An ignorant and vulgar rustic: 1805: coll. Ex *haw*, either the fruit of the hawthorn or a hedge + BUCK, a dandy.

hawcubite. A noisy, violent street roisterer, one of a band infesting London ca 1700–1; hence a street bully or ruffian. Coll > S.E. Except historically, used very rarely after ca 1720. F. & H.: 'After the Restoration there was a succession of these disturbers of the peace: first came the Muns, then followed the Tityre Tus, the Hectors, the Scourers, the Nickers, the Hawcubites, and after them the Mohawks.' ?ex HAWK; cf.:

***hawk.** A sharper, esp. at cards; a ROOK (2): orig. (C.16), c.; from ca 1750, low; ob. 2. A bailiff; a constable: C.16–early 19: s. > coll. Jonson, Ainsworth.

***hawk**, v. To act as a decoy (cf. BUTTON, n., 2) at a fair: c. (—1851); ob.

hawk!, ware. A warning, esp. when bailiff or constable is near: low coll: C.16–mid-19. Skelton has the phrase as a title.

hawk and buzzard, between. Perplexed and undecided: proverbial coll (—1639): ob. by 1780, †by 1820, except in dial. L'Estrange, 'A fantastical levity that holds us off and on, betwixt hawk and buzzard, as we say, to keep us from bringing the matter in question to a final issue.'

hawk and pigeon. Villain and victim: Society coll: late C.19–early 20.

hawk from a handsaw (when the wind is southerly), know a. (Gen. in negative.) To be discerning; occ. lit., have good eyesight, hence to be a person of sense: proverbial coll: C.17–20. Shakespeare and Barbellion, the longer form; Mrs Centlivre, the shorter in the negative.

hawk it. To be a prostitute on the streets: low: late C.19–20. Ex HAWK ONE'S MUTTON.

hawk one's meat. (Of a woman) to peddle, i.e. display, one's charms, esp. of breast: low: late C.19–20. cf. *sport one's* DAIRY.

hawk one's mutton. To be a prostitute: mostly Cockney: mid-C.19–20. Contrast HAWK ONE'S MEAT.

hawker, vbl n. **hawking.** Peddler, peddling: C.16–20; app. coll, ca 1680–1820, when it was applied specifically to newsvendors. 2. A severe cough: lower-class coll: from ca 1870. Ex hawking, or clearing one's throat.

hawks. An advantage: London: ca 1835–60. *Sinks*, 1848. Ex Fr. *haussé*.

hawse or **hawses, cross** or **come across** or **fall athwart one's.** To obstruct or check; fall out with: nautical: ca 1800–1910. A *hawse* being 'the space between the head of a vessel at anchor and the anchors, or a little beyond the anchors', O.E.D. cf.:

hawse, I'll cut your cable if you foul my. A nautical threat: from ca 1850. cf. preceding entry.

hawse-holes, creep (or **come**) **in** (or **through**) **the.** To rise from the forecastle: nautical, esp. the Navy (—1830); ob. Marryat, 'A lad who creeps in at the hawse-holes . . . was not likely to be favourably received in the midshipmen's mess.' Hence, *hawse-pipe officer*, one so risen: naval: mid-C.19–20. cf. HALBERT.

hawser, esp. in C.17–18, is occ. used in error for *hawse* (see HAWSE, CROSS . . .).

hay! or **hey!**, as interpellation or in address, evokes – not among the cultured – the c.p. reply, *no, thanks!* or *not today!* or, rarely, *straw!* Late C.19–20.

hay, make. (Transitively with *of*.) To cause confusion; defeat heavily whether manually or verbally; upset; kick up a ROW: university (—1817). H. Kingsley, the v.i.; v.t. in Maria Edgeworth and the *Pall Mall Gazette*, 9 June 1886, 'Sussex made hay of the Gloucestershire bowling.'

***hay-bag.** A woman: c. (—1851). Mayhew. 'Something to lie upon', F. & H.; also perhaps from the appearance of old drabs.

hay-band. An inferior cigar: low (—1864).

hay is for horses; occ. – with conversion of *hey* to *eh* – **'ay is for 'orses.** A c.p. used when someone says *hey!* or *eh?* for *I beg your pardon*: C.18–20. This, the oldest of all c.pp., is recorded in Swift's *Polite Conversation*, 1738: see esp. my *Comic Alphabets*, 1961, and commentary edition, 1963, of Swift's *Conversation*.

hay, lass, let's be hammered for life on

Sunday! A lower classes' c.p. of late C.19–early 20. Prob., at first, metal-workers'.

hay-seed. A countryman; esp. if very rustic: orig. (—1889), U.S.; anglicized as a coll, ca 1905 in Britain, but in Australia and New Zealand ca 1895. Ex hay-seeds clinging to outer garments. Also *hayseed.*

hay while the sun shines, make. Profitably to employ one's time: proverbial coll (—1546) >, ca 1800, a S.E. metaphor. Anticipated by Barclay in 1509.

haying. Haymaking: coll (—1887).

haymaking. Practical joking: University and Army: from ca 1880; extremely ob. Perhaps ex *making* HAY WHILE THE SUN SHINES.

haymaking drill. Bayonet exercise: military: late C.19–20; ob. Ex prodding sacks filled with straw.

Haymarket Hector. A whore's bully: C.17–19: coll. Marvell. cf.:

Haymarket ware. An ordinary prostitute: C.19–20. cf. preceding entry and cf. BARRACK-HACK.

hayseed, see HAY-SEED.

haystack, sails like a. Sails ugly or clumsy to look at: nautical coll: late C.19–20.

haystack, unable to hit a; I, he, etc., couldn't hit a haystack. A coll c.p. applied to a bad aimer, esp. a bad shot: mid-C.19–20.

***hazard drum; or h.-d.** A gambling den or house: c. (—1860); ob.

haze. To harass or punish with overwork or paltry orders; constantly find fault with: nautical coll > j. > gen. S.E.: Dana, 1840. Ex dial. *haze*, to ill-treat, frighten.

haze about. To LOAF; roam aimlessly about: coll: ob.: 1841, *Tait's Magazine*, VIII, '. . . Hazing about – a capital word that, and one worthy of instant adoption – among the usual sights of London.'

hazel-geld, -gild. To beat with a hazel stick: (?jocular) coll: late C.17–early 19; the former, perhaps an error, is in B.E.; the latter in Grose, 1st ed. (For *oil of hazel*, see OIL.)

hazy. Stupid or confused with drink: 1824, T. Hook: coll. Barham, 'Staggering about just as if he were hazy'.

he; hee. A cake. A *young he*, a small cake. Charterhouse (school): from ca 1860; ob. cf. SHE, 2. 2. It, where personification does not hold good: coll: C.19–20. Baumann cites 'Shut him up well,' close the door well.

he could fall into (the) shit (Canadian: **a shit-hole) and come up smelling of violets.** A low c.p., directed at an exceptionally lucky fellow: late C.19–20.

he-cups. Hiccoughs: mostly Cockneys': mid-C.19–20.

he-male. A very manly fellow indeed, all confidence and coïtion: middle classes': ca 1881–1910. On SHE-MALE.

he-man. A virile fellow; a CAVE-MAN; one who 'treats 'em rough': from ca 1906: s. cf. B.E.'s *great he-rogue*, 'a sturdy swinging Rogue'.

he-man stuff. CAVE-MAN methods: from ca 1908. ?orig. U.S.

he never does anything wrong! An ironic c.p. applied to one who never does anything right: music-halls' (1883), then gen.

he worships his creator. A Society c.p. (—1909) directed at a *self-made* man with a high opinion of himself. Ob. Punning *Creator*, God.

head. A man-of-war's privy: nautical, but perhaps rather j. than s. or coll: from early C.18. cf. REAR. 2. See HEADS. 3. A postage stamp: mid-C.19–20: dial. >, by 1860, coll. Ex the sovereign's head thereon. 4. A racing SHARP: c.: from ca 1885. Hence, a professional gambler, e.g. at TWO-UP: Australian c. and low: from ca 1890.

head, v.t. To toss (a coin); *head* BROWNS, to toss pennies: Australian: late C.19–20. Lit., to make a coin turn up heads.

***head, (can) do on one's.** To do easily and joyfully: c.: from ca 1880.

head, eat one's, see HAT, EAT ONE'S.

head, fat or soft in the. Stupid: coll: C.19–20.

head, get or have a big; or a swelling in the. To become or be conceited: ?orig. (—1888) U.S.; established in Britain, however, by 1893.

head, have a. To have a headache from drinking: coll: from ca 1870.

head, have maggots in the. To be eccentric; crotchety: low coll: from ca 1860. cf. BEE IN ONE'S BONNET.

head, have no. To be crack-brained, irresponsible: (?low) coll: from ca 1870.

head, hurt in the. To cuckold: C.18 coll.

head, knock on the. To destroy, kill; put an end to: low coll: from ca 1870. *Weekly Dispatch*, 21 May 1871, of a disorderly house.

head, off one's. Out of one's mind; crazy: coll: from ca 1845. Hood; Mark Pattison.

head, out of one's own. Imagined, invented, thought of by oneself: rather coll than S.E.: 1719, Defoe. 'Were not all these answers given out of his own head?', Jowett.

head (or neck) and heels, bundle out. To eject forcibly: low coll: from ca 1860. In S.E., *neck and crop*.

head-beetler. A foreman or ganger: (? orig. Anglo-Irish) workmen's (—1864); ob. 2. Hence, almost imm., a bully: workmen's. *Chambers's Journal*, 18 Sept. 1886, 'The "beetle" was a machine for producing figured fabrics by the pressure of a roller, and head-beetler probably means the chief director of this class of work.'

***head bloke,** see HEAD SCREW.

***head bully, or cully, of the pass (or the passage) bank.** 'The Top Tilter of that Gang, throughout the whole Army [*of criminals and vagabonds*], who Demands and receives Contribution from all the Pass Banks in the Camp', B.E., who has *bully*, Grose (1st ed.) preferring *cully*. c. of ca 1670–1820.

head bummaroo, the. A chief organizer; most important person present; manager: mid-C.19–20; virtually †. A perversion of BUMPER.

head cook and bottle-washer. One in authority (cf. HEAD-BEETLER); a foreman; a boss: low coll (—1876). Hindley. 2. A general servant: pejorative (—1887).

***head cully of the pass, or the passage, bank,** see HEAD BULLY . . .

head (or beard) for washing, give one's. To yield tamely: C.17 (?—18) coll. Butler, in *Hudibras*, 'For my part it shall ne'er be said, | I for the washing gave my head.' A late C.16–early 17 variant: . . . *polling*. cf. Fr. *laver la tête à quelqu'un*.

head full of bees, see BEES, HIS HEAD IS FULL OF.

***head-guard.** A hat; esp. a billy-cock: c. (—1889); †.

head in a bag, get or put the, see BAG, GET . . .

head is full of proclamations, one's; or have a head full . . . To be 'much taken up to little purpose', B.E.: coll: ca 1560–1770. Fenton's *Bandello*; Cotgrave; Berthelson's *English-Danish Dict.*, 1754.

head(-)lamp. An eye; usually in pl: pugilistic: ca 1840–90. Augustus Mayhew, 1857.

head like a sieve, have a. To be very forgetful: coll: mid-C.19–20.

head-mark, know by. To recognize (a cuckold) by his horns: low: mid-C.18–20, ob. Punning the S.E. sense.

head-marked, adj. Cuckolded, cuckold: low: mid-C.18–20; ob.

head off, argue or talk one's. To be excessively argumentative or talkative: coll: from ca 1885. Milliken. (In fact, *one's head off* is an adv. = excessively. We can speak of a person's *yawning his head off*.) cf.:

head off, beat one's. To defeat utterly: coll: from ca 1850. Thackeray, 'He pretends to teach me billiards, and I'll give him fifteen in twenty and beat his head off.' cf.:

head off, eat one's or its. To cost, in keep, more than one's or its worth: C.18–20: coll. Orig., of horses; gen. from ca 1860. Anon., *The Country Farmer's Catechism*, 1703, 'My mare has eaten her head off at the Ax in Aldermanbury.'

head on, have a. To be alert or knowing: low coll (—1893); ob. cf. the S.E. *have a head on one* or *on one's shoulders*.

head on, put a (new). To damage a man's face: ?orig. U.S. (—1870), anglicized by 1890. 2. Hence, to defeat, gen. heavily; get much the better of: ?orig. (—1880) U.S.; anglicized by 1890. Also *put a new face on*. 3. To make malt liquors froth: public-house s. > gen. coll: from ca 1860.

head on one, have a, see HEAD, HAVE A.

head or tail, see HEADS OR TAILS.

head over heels, for earlier and logical **heels over head,** was orig. coll – a popular corruption: from ca 1770. Thackeray.

head over tip. Head over heels: 1824, *Boxiana*, IV; ob. cf. *arse over tip*.

head-rails. The teeth: nautical (—1785) >, ca 1840, gen.; extremely ob. Grose, 1st ed.; 'Cuthbert Bede', in *Verdant Green*; Baumann, who compares the Homeric ἕρκος ὀδόντων, the hedge or fence of the teeth; Bowen.

head-robber. A plagiarist: journalistic: ca 1880–1914. 2. A butler: low (—1893); ob.

***head screw,** occ. **h. bloke.** A chief warder; prison c. (—1893).

head-serag. An overseer, master; one in authority or a BIG WIG: Bengali English coll and nautical s. (—1864) >, ca 1900, gen. s. Ex Persian *sarhang*, an overseer, a commander.

***head-topper.** A hat; a wig: c.: mid-C.19–20; ob.

headacher. A severe punch on the head: pugilistic: ca 1840–90. Augustus Mayhew, *Paved with Gold*, 1857.

header. A blow on the head: boxing: 1818; ob. 2. A notability: tailors': from ca 1860. cf. BIG WIG. Perhaps ex †S.E. sense, a leader. 3. See:

header, take a. To plunge, or fall, headlong into the water: coll: implied in 1849. 2. To leap, app. dangerously: theatrical: from ca 1860. 3. To go direct for one's object: coll (—1863).

heading-'em, vbl n. The tossing of coins for bets: low: from ca 1880.

headless, hop. To be beheaded: grimly jocular S.E. > coll: C.14–17.

headquarters (often capitalled). Newmarket: turf s. (—1888) >, in C.20, j. Because the most important racing and training centre.

heads, the. Those in authority, the singular being *one of the heads*: coll: from ca 1895: Colonial. 2. Seamen's latrines: naval coll: late C.19–20. Granville, 'Right forward'. Hence *the Captain of the Heads*, the rating responsible for their cleanliness. It prob. goes back much further: W. N. Glascock, *Sketch-Book*, II, 1826, has the variant *captain o' the head.* Naval s. of ca 1790–1850.

heads and tails, lie. To sleep heads to head-rail and foot-rail alternately: low coll: from ca 1860; ob.

heads I win, tails you lose. A mock bet; also = I cannot fail! Occ. used as an adj. Coll, orig. low (—1846). Anticipated by Shadwell, 1672, in *Epsom Wells*: 'Worse than *Cross I win, Pile you lose.*'

heads or tails; head or tail. A phrase used in tossing coins to gain a decision: coll: late C.17–20. Otway.

heady, intoxicating, was by B.E. considered coll, as it may well have been in his day.

heady whop. A person with an extraordinarily large head: Cockney: ca 1880–1900. Merely WHOPPING *head* corrupted.

heap. A large number, a great deal: coll: mid-C.17–20. Keats. Often, mid-C.16–20, in pl, as in Hughes, 'She will be meeting heaps of men.'

heap, adv. Much: orig. (1834), U.S.; anglicized ca 1850. Also, from ca 1880, *heaps.*

heap, go over the. To relieve oneself: colliery surface workers': late C.19–20. Ex using the slag heap for this purpose.

heap, strike (from ca 1895, often **knock**) **all of a.** To cause to collapse: coll (—1818). Scott, 'Strike, to use the vulgar phrase, all of a heap.' In C.18, the form was *strike all on a heap*, recorded for 1711, but Richardson adumbrated the mod. form with 'He seem'd quite struck of a heap,' 1741.

***heap o(f) coke.** A fellow, man, comrade: thieves' rhyming s. on BLOKE: 1851, Mayhew. In theatrical s., it refers to the GUV'NOR (father; managing director): from ca 1890.

heap o(f) saucepan lids. Money: rhyming s. on DIBS: from ca 1880.

heaped, ppl adj. Joined in the sexual act: C.16–20: low coll. Tourneur, 'O, 'twill be glorious to kill 'em . . . when they're heaped.' 2. HARD PUT TO IT, stumped (see STUMP, v., 2): racing: ca 1880–1915. Hawley Smart in *From Post to Finish.*

heaps, see HEAP, n. and adv.

***heapy.** Short for HEAP OF COKE. Ware, 1909.

hear. To attend church; v.t., sit under the preaching of: coll: ca 1780–1910. Cowper, 1783, in a letter, 'There are, however, many who have left the Church, and hear among the Dissenters.'

hear a bird sing. To learn privately: coll: late C.16–17. Shakespeare. In C.19–20, *a* LITTLE BIRD TOLD ME (*so*).

hear of it. To be blamed, reprimanded for it: coll: late C.16–20. Shakespeare. Occ. in C.19–20, *about.*

hearing. A scolding, a reprimand: coll when not, as gen., dial.: from ca 1810; ob. Scott in *Old Mortality.* Ex HEAR OF IT.

***hearing cheat.** (Gen. in pl.) An ear: c.: mid-C.16–early 19.

heart appears in various ejaculations, e.g. (*Lord* or *God* or *Lord God*) *bless my heart*: coll: C.19–20; *heart alive!*, C.19–20 coll. The earliest, *for God's heart*, appears in Chaucer.

heart!, have a. Show mercy!; steady!: coll: late C.19–20; slightly ob. Often jocular, esp. as *'ave an 'eart!* Ex *have the heart* (*to do* something).

heart, next the, adj. or adv. Fasting(ly): mid-C.16–17, coll; in C.18–19, dial. Nashe. Here, *heart* = the stomach: cf. S.E. *heartburn* and Fr. *mal au cœur.*

heart alive! see HEART.

heart and dart. A FART: rhyming s.: from ca 1860; ob.

heart in one's boots, one's. (In sentences with *is* or *sinks*; in phrases, preceded by *with.*) Afraid, extremely dejected: coll: C.19–20; anticipated by Garrick's 'soul and spirit . . . in her shoes', a form still heard. The C.15–early (?all) 18 form is *in one's hose*, as in Skelton, Breton, Motteux.

heart out, slave one's. To worry oneself to death: coll (—1887); ob.

heart to grass, take. A C.16–17 coll form

of *heart of grass*, a corruption of *heart of grace*, esp. when preceded by *take*.

heart up, enough to have one's. Enough to make one spew: low coll: from ca 1810.

heartbreaker. A lovelock; a pendent curl: coll: 1663, Butler, who applies it to Samson: ob. by 1860, †by 1900.

heartburn. A bad cigar: ca 1870–1925: mainly Cockney.

hearthstone. Butter: eating-houses'; late C.19–20. Prompted by DOORSTEP.

heartie, see HEARTY, MY.

***heart's ease.** (Occ. as one word without apostrophe.) A twenty-shilling piece: c.: late C.17–early 19. 2. Gin: c.: ca 1690–1830.

hearts of oak. Penniless: late C.19–20: (ironic) rhyming s. on BROKE.

hearty, n. and adj. Strong drink; drunk: low: from ca 1850.

hearty (incorrectly **heartie**), **my.** A Northern dial. (1803: E.D.D.) and hence a nautical form of address: from ca 1835; ob. Marryat. Whence, the only just S.E. sense, a sailor.

***hearty-choke (and, or with, caper-sauce) for breakfast, have a.** To be hanged: orig. (—1785), c.; in late C.19, low; in C.20, †, except in the doubly-punning *a (h)artichoke and a (h)oyster*, a hanging-breakfast. Danvers, in *The Grantham Mystery*, 'Compelled to have a hearty-choke for breakfast some fine morning'. Punning *artichoke*. cf. VEGETABLE BREAKFAST.

heat!, have a. Warm yourself (by the fire)!: Anglo-Irish c.p. invitation: late C.19–20.

heat, on, sexually excited, is low coll when applied, C.19–20, to women.

heathen philosopher. One whose breech is visible through his trousers: late C.17–18. Ex dress-despising philosophers.

heathenish. Abominable, offensive, BEASTLY: coll: from ca 1855. Ex S.E. sense of 'barbarous', as in Shakespeare.

***heave.** An attempt to cajole, deceive, or swindle, esp. in *a dead heave*, a flagrant attempt to do so: C.19, and prob. earlier: c.

***heave.** To rob, v.t.: c.: ca 1560–1830: extant, according to F. & H., in 1893 in Shropshire dial., but unrecorded by E.D.D. Esp. in *heave a bough*, rob a booth, mid-C.16–18, and *heave a* CASE, rob a house, C.18–early 19: occ., by confusion of these two senses, *heave a* BOOTH = to rob a house. Ex the S.E. sense, to lift: cf. LIFT, v. 2. To throw, toss, hurl: late C.16–20: S.E. until ca 1830, then nautical j. and gen. coll and dial.

heave ahead or on, v.i. To hurry, press forward: nautical coll: C.19. Marryat. Ex the advancing of a ship by heaving on a cable attached to some fixed object in front of her (Smyth). 2. Hence, gen. in imperative, get on with one's job or story: nautical coll: mid-C.19–20.

heave around. To proceed vigorously: *Conway* cadets' (—1891).

heave in sight. When not nautical j., this is gen. coll (from ca 1830).

heaven, feel one's way to. To caress a woman with progressive intimacy: low coll: C.19–20, ob. By itself, *heaven*, thus used, is a euphemism.

Heaven, Hell, and Purgatory. Three taverns situated near Westminster Hall: C.17. Jonson in *The Alchemist*.

heaven-tormentor. (Gen. pl.) A sail above the sky-sail: late C.19–20; ob.

heavenly collar; heavenly lapel. A collar, or a lapel, that turns the wrong way: tailors': from ca 1860.

heavenly plan. A man: Australian rhyming s. of ca 1885–1914.

heavens, adv. Very: a coll (ob.) and dial. intensive: from ca 1875. Esp. of rain and with *hard*, as in D. C. Murray's *The Weaker Vessel*, 'It was raining heavens hard.'

***heaver.** A thief; esp. one who steals tradesmen's shop-books: c.: late C.18–early 19. Ex HEAVE, v., 1. 2. A breast; the bosom: c.: mid-C.17–early 19. 3. (Gen. pl.) A person in love: low: C.18–19.

heavies, the. Bugs, esp. bed-bugs: low: ca 1850–1910. 2. In late C.19–20, the heavy artillery: military.

heavy, come or do the; occ. do it heavy. To put on airs; affect superiority: s. or low coll: from ca 1880.

heavy, the. Porter and stout: abbr. HEAVY WET: 1821; ob.

heavy-arse. A sluggard: low coll: late C.19–20. cf.:

heavy-arsed. Inert, lethargic, apathetic: C.17–18 coll. One of Richard Baxter's titles was, *Shove to Heavy-Arsed Christians*.

heavy brown. Porter: low: ca 1820–50. Bee, who is, however, ambiguous, thus: '*Heavy* – heavy wet, or brown – porter.' cf. HEAVY WET.

heavy cavalry or dragoons or horsemen or (the) heavy troop. Bugs; esp. bed-bugs: ca 1850–1910. The commonest are the first two; *h.d.* is recorded by H., in 1864, as of Oxford University. cf. HEAVIES, 1, and contrast LIGHT INFANTRY.

heavy grog. Hard work: workmen's: ca 1860–1914. Ex the drink.

heavy grubber. A hearty eater; a glutton: low coll: from ca 1858; ob. Dickens in *Great Expectations.*

heavy hand. Deep trouble: lower classes' coll (—1909).

heavy horseman. (Gen. pl.) A ship-looter working in the daytime, esp. on the Thames: nautical: C.19. 2. (pl) see HEAVY CAVALRY.

heavy line, the. Tragic or, at least, serious roles: theatrical: ca 1820–90. *Sessions,* Dec. 1840 (p. 286), 'He played various characters . . . perhaps the King, in Hamlet; he played what we call the "heavy line" of business.'

heavy merchant. He who represents the villain: theatrical (—1909).

***heavy plodder.** A stockbroker: c.: ca 1845–90. Duncombe.

heavy, or **howling, swell.** A man, occ. a woman, in the height of fashion: ca 1819–1910: perhaps rather coll than s. Anstey, 1892, 'We look such heavy swells, you see, we're all aristo-crats.' Punning *heavy,* having great momentum, and undoubtedly prompted by *heavy swell,* a sea running high.

heavy wet; occ. abbr. to **heavy.** Malt liquor; esp. porter and stout: 1821, Egan: ob. Lytton, 'I had been lushing heavy wet.' 1830. cf. WET, n., 2 and *twopenny* WET. 2. An extremely severe drinking-bout: ca 1850–1925.

hebdomadal. A weekly magazine or review: 1835 (S.O.D.): orig. jocular S.E.; in late C.19–20, journalistic; ob.

Hebrew. Unintelligible speech, jargon: coll: 1705, Vanbrugh, 'Mighty obscure . . . All Hebrew.' cf. *Greek,* a century older and S.E. 2. Hippocras: drinkers' s. (—1650).

heck!, by; what the heck! Orig. (—1892), Lancashire exclamations of surprise or indignation: by 1905, at latest, they had > gen. coll. Prob. ex dial. (*h*)*eck!,* indicating surprise or conveying a warning; *heck* is perhaps a euphemism for HELL: cf. the Lancashire *ecky,* a mild oath, and *go to ecky,* 'go to hell!', of mid-C.19–20, and possibly the Scottish and Irish *hech* (or *hegh*), as in *hech, sirs!,* though this expletive *hech* is more prob. an elemental like *ha* or *ho.*

Hector, hector, as a bully, a swashbuckler, is rather S.E. than coll, though (†1670) John Hacket's 'One Hector, a phrase at that time' – ca 1640 – 'for a daring ruffian' tends to show that at this period it was, by some at least, held to be coll. The *Hectors* were a swashbuckling band: see HAWCUBITE.

Hector's cloak, wear. To be rightly rewarded for treachery: coll: C.17–early 18. Ex Hector Armstrong who, the betrayer of Thomas Percy, Earl of Northumberland in 1569, died a beggar. But *take Hector's cloak,* C.17–early 18 (then dial., now †), is 'to deceive a friend who confides in one's fidelity', Apperson.

hedge, as adj., is a (mainly †) pejorative prefixed to nn. to connote 'connected with, born under, plying a trade under a hedge, esp. one by the roadside; hence low, paltry, rascally, ignorant'. That many of these terms had a coll taint appears from B.E. and Grose; yet it is more correct to regard as S.E. all *hedge* compounds except the few that follow.

hedge, (as) common as the. Applied to whore or strumpet: coll: late C.17–18. cf. the S.E. *hedge-whore,* 'a low beggarly prostitute' (Grose). Also with *highway.*

hedge, hang in the. (Esp. of a law-suit) to be undecided: coll: late C.17–18.

hedge, take a sheet off a. To steal openly: coll: C.17 (?18 also).

hedge and ditch. Often shortened to *hedge.* A PITCH (stall; stand): rhyming s.: late C.19–20.

hedge-bird. 'A Scoundrel or sorry Fellow', B.E.: C.17–mid-18 coll (?S.E. till ca 1680).

hedge-bit. A hedge-whore; a (gen. dirty) harlot favouring the open air: C.19–20 low; ob.

hedge-bottom attorney or **solicitor.** An unqualified or a disqualified attorney or solicitor doing business in the shelter of a proper solicitor's name: legal: mid-C.19–20; ob.

***hedge-creeper.** A robber of hedges: mid-C.16–early 19: coll till ca 1690, then low s. or c.

hedge-docked. Seduced in the open air: low: C.19.

hedge or by stile, by. By hook or by crook: late C.17–18: coll.

hedge-popper. 'A trumpery shooter', F. & H.; *hedge-popping,* the shooting of small birds in and about hedges. Both sporting s. > coll: from ca 1860; ob.

***hedge-square** (occ. **street**), **doss** or **snooze in.** To sleep in the open air, esp. in the country: vagrants' c. (—1876); ob. J.

Greenwood, in *Under the Blue Blanket*. cf. DO A STAR-PITCH.

hedgehog. A many-oared boat: nautical: C.19. Ex that animal's appearance. 2. Veal: London streets': ca 1840–1900. Augustus Mayhew, *Paved with Gold*, 1857. The two kinds of flesh, cooked, are not unlike.

hee, see HE, 1.

hee-haw. A donkey: nursery coll: mid-C.19–20.

heel, hairy at the, see HAIRY ABOUT . . .

heel-tap!, take off your. A toast-master's injunction to drain one's glass: coll: mid-C.18–mid-19.

heeler. A plunge, feet first, into water: Winchester College: from ca 1860. 2. A lurch to the side: coll: from ca 1890. 3. A fast sailing-ship: nautical coll: late C.19–20. Prob. ex dial. *heeler*, a quick runner.

heels, bless the world with one's. To be hanged: coll: ca 1560–1650. Painter in his *Palace of Pleasure*.

heels, cool or **kick one's**, see COOL ONE'S HEELS.

heels, his. The knave of trumps: cribbage s. > j.: late C.18–20. cf. NOB.

heels, kick up one's, see HEELS, TURN UP ONE'S.

heels, lift one's. (Of a woman) to lie down for coïtion: low coll: C.18–20.

heels, turn – occ. **tip, topple; kick, lay** – **up one's.** To die: coll. The first, much the most gen., C.16–20, e.g. Nashe, in *Pierce Penniless*; *topple*, late C.16–19, in Nashe's *Lenten Stuff*; none of the other three antedated C.17 or postdated C.19.

hefty. Big and strong: coll: orig. (—1867), U.S.: anglicized ca 1905 (Thornton defines it as 'heavy, bulky', which prob. derives ex Eng. dial., but in Eng. coll usage the connotation of strength is essential, unless the reference is to a thing – and then the tendency is to join it to another adj. as in 'a hefty great book'). 2. Hence, adv.: exceedingly: coll: late C.19–20.

heifer. A woman, gen. a girl: low coll: C.19–20; ob. 2. A charwoman: Charterhouse: †by 1900, as A. H. Tod notes in his *Charterhouse*.

heifer-paddock. A school for older girls: Australian: ca 1880–1900. Mrs Campbell Praed, *Australian Life*, 1885, 'I shall look over a heifer-paddock in Sydney, and take my pick.'

***heigh-ho.** Stolen yarn: Norwich c.: ca 1855–1910. Ex the form of apprising the FENCE of stolen yarn.

heights of connubial bliss, scale the. If jocular, it is coll: otherwise, obviously, it is a weak S.E. euphemism. C.19–20, ob.

heightth. Height: in late C.18–early 19, it was coll; since ca 1860, it has been low coll. This represents a comparatively rare spelling, a frequent pronunciation – until Johnson's day, in fact, a variant S.E. pronunciation. cf. COOLTH.

(h)elbat. A table: back s. (—1859). 'The aspirate is a matter of taste,' H.

helch(er)wer; helsh-. A welsher (see WELSH): centre s.: from ca 1860; ob.

helio, n. and v. Heliograph: by coll abbr.: from ca 1890. Kipling, in *Many Inventions*; *Daily News*, 4 Sept. 1897, 'Messages had to be helio'd under a hot fire at short range.'

hell is frequent in imprecations, esp. in *hell!*, *go to hell!*, *hell's bells!* (Colonial), and the quaint †*go to hell and pump thunder!* 2. As a gambling house, it may, orig., have well been coll or even c. – witness Anon.'s *Defence of Cony-Catching*, 1592 (pp. 57–8). 3. As the female pudend, C.18–20, it is low coll: see HELL, PUT THE DEVIL INTO.

hell, all to; occ. **gone to hell.** Utterly ruined: coll: C.19–20.

hell, give. To trounce, punish severely; vituperate: coll: from ca 1830.

hell, gone to, see HELL, ALL TO.

hell, kick up or **play.** To cause a (tremendous) disturbance or great trouble: coll: from ca 1840. See HELL AND TOMMY.

hell, lead apes in, see APES . . .

hell, like. With extreme vigour; desperately: coll: from late C.18. 'Cutting them up like hell' (severely criticizing them): W. N. Glascock, 1826. Or, as an expletive, 'certainly not!'

Hell, Little. 'A small dark covered passage, leading from London-wall to Bell-alley', Grose, 2nd ed.: mid-C.18–early 19.

hell, put the devil into. To have sexual connection: C.18–20 'literary' coll: ex Boccaccio.

hell, raise. To make a tremendous noise or disturbance: C.19 coll. Variant, HELL'S DELIGHT.

hell, silver. A gambling house where only silver stakes are allowed. This, like *dancing hell*, was orig. (ca 1840) coll but soon > S.E.

hell, to. Intensely. Always with *hope* or *wish*: low coll (—1891). Nat Gould, in *Double Event*, 'I hope to h— the horse will break his neck and his rider's too.'

hell and tommy, esp. in *play h. and t.* A

picturesque intensive (s. > coll): slightly ob. John L. Gardner, *Sketch-Book*, 1831; 1832–4, in *The Caesars*, by De Quincey, 'Lord Bacon played Hell and Tommy when casually raised to the supreme seat in the council.' Genesis obscure; *and tommy* is a tag added to (*play*) *hell*, precisely as *and Betty Martin* is tagged to ALL MY EYE. Ware, who does support *Hal and Tommy* (Henry VIII and Thomas Cromwell playing havoc with Church property), proposes *hell and torment* (by corruption or perversion) – than which I have not heard, nor can I think, of a likelier origin. In Northumberland dial. (1894: E.D.D., Sup.), *play hell and tommy with* = 'to set utterly at variance'.

hell-born babe, hell-cat, -hag, -hound, -kite. A man or a woman of a devilish character: C.16–20, ob. Perhaps orig. coll, but certainly soon S.E.

hell-box or **-hole.** A coll variation of *hell*, a receptacle for (esp. stolen) remnants. cf. CABBAGE. 2. (Only *hell-box.*) A galley-stove: nautical: late C.19–20. Bowen, 'Most frequently in the Canadian and American ships'.

hell breaks loose, gen. **hell is broke loose,** describes extreme disorder; *hell broke loose* as a n. = anarchy, noisy topsy-turvydom: coll soon > S.E.: late C.16–20. Byron, in *Vision of Judgement*, 'And realised the phrase of "Hell broke loose"'.

hell-broth. Bad liquor: (low) coll: from ca 1850; ob. Ex S.E. sense.

hell-cart. A hackney carriage: coll: ca 1630–1700. Perhaps orig. *hell-cart coach.*

hell-driver. A coachman: late C.17–mid-18 coll.

hell-fire, adv. Extremely, DAMNED, damnably, DEVILISH: coll (—1760); ob. C. Johnston, in *Chrysal*, 'The weather in summer is *hell-fire* hot, in winter *hell-fire* cold.' cf. and (?) ex HELL-FIRED.

Hell-Fire Jack. A violent or reckless officer, not necessarily unpopular: sailing-ships' nickname: mid-C.19–20.

hell-fired, adv. Extremely, DAMNED: coll: 1756; ob. Toldervy, in *The Two Orphans*, 'He is a h–ll-fir'd good creature.' Ex S.E. sense.

hell for leather, often hyphenated. Desperately and vigorously (or swiftly): coll: from ca 1875. Kipling, 1892, 'When we rode hell-for-leather, | Both squadrons together, | Not caring much whether we lived or we died'. Perhaps out of *all of a lather* by *leather*, skin as affected by riding.

hell, Hull and Halifax, – Good Lord deliver us, – from. A proverbial coll = save us from evil: C.16–20. (The most usual form is *from Hull, hell, and Halifax, Good Lord deliver us!*) Ex the celebrated Gibbet-Law of Halifax: this consisted in execution of prisoners and *subsequent* inquiry into their demerits; as early as 1586, *to have had Halifax law* had been extended to the procedure of inquiry made after condemnation. See HALIFAX!, GO TO.

hell-matter. Old, battered type: printers': from ca 1865; ?orig. U.S.: ob.

hell mend (him)! Curse (him)!: coll: late C.19–20.

hell of a (e.g. mess). Very much of a ——. A coll intensive: 1778 (S.O.D.). cf. DEVIL *of a* ——.

hell-scrapers. Shrapnel: a Boer name: 1899–1901. J. Milne, *The Epistles of Atkins*, 1902.

hell-ship. A ship with brutal officers: nautical coll: late C.19–20. Bowen, 'Borrowed from the Americans'.

hellish, adv. 'Sometimes a mere coarse intensive', O.E.D.: coll: from ca 1750.

hellite. A professional gambler: coll (—1838) >, ca 1870, S.E.; ob. by 1900.

hell's bells! HELL!: coll: late C.19–20.

hell's delight. A violent disturbance: coll: C.19–20. 'She would kick up hell's delight,' *Sessions* April 1835. See HELL, RAISE.

helpa. An apple: back s. (—1859). The *h* is optional: cf. HELBAT.

helpless. (Very) drunk: coll: from ca 1860. cf. PARALYSED.

helsh(er)wer, see HELCH(ER)WER.

helter-skelter. A privateer: naval: C.19.

hemispheres. The female breasts: literary coll when not a mere euphemism: C.19–20.

***hemp, stretch the.** To be hanged: c.: mid-C.19–20; ob.

hemp, young. 'An appellation for a graceless boy', Grose, 1785: coll: late C.18–early 19. Sure to be hanged one day.

hemp in the wind, wag. To be hanged: coll: ca 1530–1620. Sir Thomas More. (Never, I think, very gen.)

hemp is growing for the villain, the. A c.p. applied to a rogue: C.19. Earlier, *hemp is grown for you.*

hempen bridle. A ship's rope or rigging: coll: C.18.

hempen fever, die of a. To be hanged: mid-C.18–mid-19: (?s. >) low coll. Ainsworth, 'Three of her [*four*] husbands died of hempen fevers.' cf. Nashe's *hempen circle*, Skelton's *hempen snare*, Hoccleve's *hempen lane*, and Dekker's *hempen tragedies*.

hempen widow. A woman widowed by the gallows: late C.17–mid-19: (?s. >) low coll; perhaps orig. c.

hen. A woman: from ca 1620: jocular s. > coll. 2. A mistress: same period; ob.: low. 3. Drink-money: Cockney (—1892); ob.

hen-frigate. A ship BOSSED by the captain's wife: nautical (—1785); ob. cf. HEN-HOUSE; but prob. an abbr. of B.E.'s HEN-PECKED *frigate*.

hen-house. A house in which the woman rules: coll (—1785): ob. by 1870, †by 1900.

hen-party. An assemblage of women: coll (orig. low): from ca 1885. Occ. *-convention* or *-tea*. cf. BITCH-, CAT-, TABBY-PARTY.

hen-peck. (Of a wife) to rule, domineer over the husband: coll: 1688 (S.O.D.). Byron. Ex:

hen-pecked. Ruled, domineered over by a wife: coll: 1680, 'Hudibras' Butler; B.E. gives *hen-pecked frigate* (see HEN-FRIGATE) and *hen-pecked husband*; *Spectator*, No. 479, 'Socrates . . . the undoubted head of the sect of the hen-pecked'. Perhaps suggested by the C.16–18 proverb, *It is a sad house where the hen crows louder than the cock*.

hen-toed. With one's feet turned in as one walks: coll: C.19–20; ob.

hence the pyramids! A c.p. applied to a *non sequitur*, or used as an ironic jocular *non sequitur*: late C.19–20. Ex the very rude, very droll recitation *The Showman*, q.v. in Brophy and Partridge, *Songs and Slang of the British Soldier*, 3rd ed., 1931.

Henri Clark. To flatter: theatrical; esp. at Drury Lane: 1883–ca 90. Ware, 'From the flattering stage-mode of a singer of this name'.

Henry Hase. A bank or currency note: 1820, W. J. Moncrieff, *The Collegians*: 'A twenty pound Henry Hase'.

Henry Melville. Devil: rhyming s.: since 1887.

Henry Sophister, see HARRY-SOPH.

***hens and chickens.** Pewter measures; esp. quarts and pints: c. (—1851); ob. Mayhew.

hens' teeth, as scarce as. Very scarce indeed: mostly Australian: late C.19–20.

Her Majesty's carriage. A prison van: ca 1880–1901; then *His M. c.*, ob.

Her or **His Majesty's naval police,** see NAVAL POLICE.

Her Majesty's tobacco pipe. The furnace in which forfeited tobacco from the Customs is burnt: ca 1850–80. *Echo*, 27 Jan. 1871. This wasteful custom was changed ca 1880 and the forfeited tobacco went to workhouses (?always).

here, I'm not. I feel disinclined for work or conversation: tailors': ca 1860–1915.

here-and-thereian. A 'rolling stone': coll: ca 1700–1860. Cibber.

here endeth the first lesson. A (non-Catholic) c.p., used by the bored after a long speech or lecture or gratuitous exposition: since ca 1870.

here goes! Now for it!; there's not much chance, but I'll *try*: coll: *Edinburgh Weekly Magazine*, 16 Oct. 1783, p. 77. 2. Hence a toast, equivalent to *here's how!*: *Port Folio*, 6 Sept. 1806 (p. 144) reprints an unidentified British song, with the lines, 'So here goes what the world appals,/Old England and her wooden walls' (fighting ships).

here (or **yere**) **they come smoking their pipes!** A c.p. by Billingsgate fish-buyers when, at auctions, the bids were rapid and high: 1870s. Ware, 'It probably meant independence and determination.'

here we (or **you**) **are!** This is what's needed: coll: both from ca 1845.

here we are again! A C.20 c.p.; orig. (from ca 1880) a form of greeting. Possibly originated by Harry Paine (?Payne), that clown who, at Drury Lane in the 1870s and 80s, began the Boxing Night harlequinade with a somersault and a cheerful 'here we are again!'

Herefordshire weed. An oak: (when not Herefordshire dial.) coll (—1860).

here's a couple of match-sticks. A mostly workmen's c.p., addressed to someone sleepy early in the day: late C.19–20. To prop open his eyelids.

here's how! A late C.19–20 coll toast. ?used before Kipling, 1896, in *Seven Seas*.

here's looking to you, see HERE'S TO YOU!

here's luck! I don't believe you!: tailors': from ca 1860.

here's my (or **me**) **head, my** (or **me**) **arse is comin(g).** A workman's c.p., dating from ca 1895, in reference to a girl or woman who, wearing high heels, walks with the head and shoulders well forward and with posteriors (esp. if shapely or buxom) well behind. Originally, of any forward-sloping person.

here's to it! A most indelicately anatomical toast: C.19–20: coll. See IT.

here's to you! A toast: in some form or

other, from late C.16. At first coll (with ellipsis of *a toast*); by 1700, S.E. Late C.19–20 coll variants are *here's looking to you* and *here's looking towards you.*

heresy-shop. A Nonconformist church: Roman Catholic priests': C.19–20. cf. SCHISM-SHOP.

hermit, or **bald-headed h.** The male member: low: C.19–20, ob. 2. In Gypsy s., a highwayman: C.19. Longfellow.

hern, see OURN.

herohotic. (Of novels) sexually outspoken: literary: 1897–ca 1900. Punning *erotic* and *hot* (amorous) *hero.*

herring, dead as a (shotten). Quite dead: coll: late C.16–20, ob. Herrings very quickly die on being removed from the water.

herring, – neither fish, flesh, fowl, nor good red, see FISH NOR FLESH . . .

herring, neither (or **no,** or **never a,** or, gen., **the devil a) barrel the better.** All (gen. bad) alike: proverbial coll: mid-C.16–20. Bale, in his play, *King John,* ca 1540; Jonson, Fielding, FitzGerald.

herring (or, 1869, **a whale), throw a sprat to catch a.** To forgo a small in the hope of a great advantage: proverbial coll (—1826). Grant Allen, in *Tents of Shem,* 'He's casting a sprat to catch a whale.'

herring-gutted. Tall and very thin: coll: C.18–mid-19. Arbuthnot. 2. 'Gutless' (lacking courage): coll: mid-C.19–20. Perhaps ex sense 1.

herring-hog. A porpoise: nautical coll: mid-C.19–20. Ex dial.

Herring-Pond, be sent across the, or **cross the H.-P. at the King's expense.** To be transported (—1785): coll; perhaps orig. c.: †by 1870. By itself, *herring pond,* the sea, or *H.-P.,* the North Atlantic Ocean (1616), is jocular S.E. rather than coll. (In Cornish, *herring-pool.*)

herrings in a barrel, like. Very crowded; packed very close: coll (—1891).

Hertfordshire kindness. An acknowledgement – or a return in kind – of favours received; also and esp. a drinking twice to the same man: coll: ca 1660–1830. Ex a Hertfordshire custom, says Fuller in his *Worthies.*

he's saving them all for Lisa (or **Liza)!** A now ob. c.p. applied, from before 1909, by the lower classes to 'a good young man who will not use oaths or strike blows', Ware. Ex the youth who wouldn't give a beggar a penny because he was saving them all for his girl.

hevethee. A thief: centre s.: from ca 1860; ob.

hexasperate, see EXASPERATE. **hey!** see HAY!

hey(-)diddle(-)diddle. A violin: late C.19–20. Rhyming on *fiddle.*

hey-gammer-cock, play at. To coït: C.18–early 19. C. Johnson.

hey-nonny-no. Female pudend: ca 1590–1750. e.g. in a ballad in John Aubrey's *Lives.*

heye-glass weather, it's. It's foggy: a proletarian c.p. aimed at the wearer of a monocle or eye-glass: 1860; very ob.

***hiccius-doccius, hictius-doctius, hixius-doxius,** etc., the variants being unrecorded after ca 1790. A juggler; a trickster, a shifty fellow: c.: ca 1678–1810. Butler, Wycherley. Either an artificial word of spurious L. (cf. HOCUS-POCUS), or a corruption of *hicce est doctus.* The term was orig. (1676, Shadwell) and frequently used in jugglers' patter.

hiccius-doccius or **-doxius,** etc., adj. Slovenly: ca 1730–1800. North, in the *Examen,* 'The author with his hiccius-doxius delivery'. 2. Drunk: ca 1780–1820. Perhaps ex *hick,* to hiccup.

***hick.** An (easy) prey to sharpers: c.: ca 1685–1750. 2. Whence, a – gen. simple – countryman: s. > coll: ca 1680–1830. Common in Australia since 1890. Ex the familiar by-form of *Richard,* as *Bob* is of *Robert.*

Hickenbothom, Mr. 'A ludicrous name for an unknown person, similar to that of Mr Thingambob', Grose: coll (—1791); †by 1890. Grose's etymology, *Ickenbaum* (an oak-tree), is nonsense; the word is perhaps a pun on HICK, and BOTTOM, the posteriors; surnames with *-bottom* attract much cheap wit.

hickey. (Not quite) drunk: late C.18–19: low (?orig. c.); more U.S. than Eng. Ex HICCIUS-DOCCIUS, adj., or else ex dial. *hick,* to hiccup.

hickitserpu. A sticker-up (esp. of skittles): centre s.: from ca 1860; ob.

hide. The human skin: O.E.–Mod. Eng.: S.E. >, ca 1710, low coll. C. Coffey, in *The Devil to Pay,* 1731, 'Come, and spin, you drab, or I'll tan your hide for you.'

hide, v. To flog, thrash: low coll, prob. ex dial. (1825); ob. Ex TAN ONE'S HIDE.

***hide and find.** That strap trick in which the GULL is invited to put a pencil into the loop of a strap: c.: from ca 1885. Anstey, *The Man from Blankley's,* 1901.

hide and seek, he plays at. 'A saying of one who is in fear of being arrested . . . and therefore does not choose to appear in public', Grose, 1785; ob. by 1860, †by 1890.

hidey hole. A hiding-place: children's coll: mid-C.19–20. A hole to hide in.

hiding. A thrashing; occ., from ca 1890, a heavy defeat. Low coll: 1809 (S.O.D.). 'Cuthbert Bede', 1853, 'May the Gown give the Town a jolly good hiding.'

higgledy-piggledy, adv. and adj. In a confused jumble: coll: late C.16–20: from ca 1895, S.E. Florio; Miss Broughton, in *Nancy*, 'We are all higgledy-piggledy – at sixes and sevens.' Johnson, 'corrupted from *higgle* . . . any confused mass', and therefore connected with *higgler*, a hawker – *higgler* being S.E., not coll; but more prob. a 'reduplicated jingle on *pig*, with reference to huddling together', W.

high. Intoxicated: 1627, May in his *Lucan*: from ca 1880, mostly U.S. 2. As (of game) tainted, it is S.E., but as (of a prostitute) venereally infected, it is low coll. 3. Obscene: low coll; like preceding sense, from ca 1860.

high and dry. An epithet c.p. applied to the High Church party: from ca 1850. *Graphic*, 10 April 1886, 'In the Church have we not the three schools of High and Dry, Low and Slow, and Broad and Shallow?' See the other two terms.

high and mighty. Arrogant; imperious: coll (—1825). J. W. Croker; Nat Gould, 'None of your high and mighty games with me.'

high-bellied; high in the belly. Advanced in pregnancy: low coll: from ca 1850. Also *high-waisted*.

high collar and short shirts. A music-halls' (1882), hence urban c.p. directed at cheap SWELLS; †by 1900.

high eating. Eating skylarks in a garret: jocular coll: late C.18–early 19. cf. HIGH-LIVER.

high enough, you can't get. A jeering comment on failure: low coll: from ca 1850; ob. 'Probably obscene in origin', F. & H.

high feather, in, see FEATHER, IN FULL.

high-flier, see HIGH-FLYER.

high-fly, n. HIGHFALUTIN; SIDE: Cockney coll: late C.19–20. Pugh, 'She went in for so much style – sounding her "aitches", and all that kind of high-fly.' 2. **the h-f.,** see HIGH-FLYER.

***high-fly, be on the.** To practise the begging-letter game or LAY (C.16 *law*): c. (—1839); ob. Brandon in *Poverty, Mendicity and Crime*, 1839. Collectively, *the high-fly* is those who carry on this trade. 2. To tramp as a beggar: from ca 1850; ob.

high-flyer, -flier. A bold adventurer, a fashionable prostitute, an impudent and dissolute woman: from ca 1690, only the second nuance being extant. Perhaps s. is sense 3, a fast mail-coach: Scott, 1818, in *Midlothian*; †by 1870. Also old s. are: 4. One who frequents the gallery of a theatre: C.18. D'Urfey, 1719. 5. And, a gross exaggeration: ca 1770–1910. G. J. Pratt, in *The Pupil of Pleasure*. 6. In c., a genteel beggar (—1851), as in Mayhew's *magnum opus*; a begging-letter writer, from ca 1839. 7. Ex the c. senses comes that of a broken-down gentleman, as in the *Standard*, 20 June 1887; ob. 8. 'A swing fixed in rows in a frame much in vogue at fairs', F. & H.: circus (—1859). 9. A slave-ship: nautical: late C.19–20; ob.

***high-flying.** Begging, esp. by letter: from ca 1839; ob.

***high game, high-game.** A mansion: c. (—1889); ob.

high(-)gig, in. Lively: ca 1815–70: coll. Moore, 'Rather sprightly – the Bear in high-gig'. See GIG.

high(-)go. A frolic; a drinking-bout: low coll: from ca 1820; ob. cf. GO, n., 2 and 6.

high, home, and easy. Very slow, underhand lob bowling: cricketers': ca 1825–1900.

high hook. That angler of a party who *hooks* the heaviest fish: anglers' coll: from early 1890s. Prob. ex: 2. Same as HIGH LINE, 2.

high horse, be on or **get on** or **ride the,** see HORSE, RIDE THE HIGH. **high in the belly,** see HIGH-BELLIED.

high in the instep, be. To be (over-) proud: coll: from ca 1540; in C.19–20, mostly dial. Fuller, in his *Church History*.

***high jinks.** A gambler who, at dice, drinks to intoxicate his, gen. PIGEON (5), adversary: c.: ca 1770–1820. (In S.E., a dicing game for drinks.) 2. A frolic; a very lively, and often noisy, party or gathering or behaviour: coll (—1815). Hughes, in *Tom Brown at Oxford*, 'All sorts of high jinks go on on the grass plot.' Ex the S.E. sense.

high jinks, be at one's. To be stiffly arrogant in manner; 'ride the high horse': low coll: from ca 1865; ob.

high-kicker. A dancer specializing in the high kick; whence, almost imm., a wild 'spreester': coll: from ca 1870.

high-kilted. Indecorous; obscene: Scots coll: C.19–20. The same holds of *Highland bail*, the right of might, as in Scott's *Antiquary*.

***high law.** Highway robbery: c.: ca 1590–1660. Greene, *Cony-Catching* pamphlets, No.1.

***high-lawyer.** A highwayman: c.: late C.16–mid-17. Greene, 1591; John Day in *The Blind Beggar*, 'He wo'd be your prigger, ... your high-lawyer.' Lit., one who practises the high (i.e. the highway) LAW or LAY.

high line. A good catch: Grand Banks fishermen's coll: from ca 1890. 2. Hence, the most successful fishing boat or clipper of the season: from ca 1895: id. Also, occ., *high hook*.

***high-liver.** A thief lodging in an attic: C.19 c. Ex the gen. s. or jocular coll sense, one who lodges in garret or loft, with its vbl n., *high living* (—1788), as in Grose, 2nd ed. cf. HIGH EATING.

high-lows. Laced boots reaching up over the ankles: orig. (1801), trade s. >, ca 1860, gen. coll, and, by 1895, S.E. 'In contrast with "top" boots and "low" shoes', S.O.D.

***high(-)men** or **runners.** Dice so loaded that they fall 'high': orig. (1592), c.; by C.18, low s.; in C.19–20, gen. considered S.E. The *runners* form, 1670. (Extremely rare in singular.)

high-nosed. Arrogant; supercilious, 'superior': (low) coll: from ca 1860; ob.

high old. Excellent; very merry, jolly, or joyous: coll: from ca 1880: *high old time* occurs in the *Illustrated London News*, 10 Feb., and the *Referee*, 11 March 1883; *high old liar*, in J. Newman's *Scamping Tricks*, 1891; *high old drunk*, a mighty drinking-bout, before 1893. Orig. (—1869) U.S. All the *high old* phrases except *h.o. time* are ob. An extension of †*high time* in this sense.

***high(-)pad** or **-toby** or, occ., **-toby-splicer** or **-splice toby.** The highway, esp. as a place for robbery: c.: resp. mid-C.16–early 19, C.18–mid-19, first half C.19, latter half C.19. See PAD and TOBY (3) and cf. DRUM, and:

***high pad** or **high tobyman** or **high-toby gloak.** A highwayman, esp. if well armed and well mounted: c.: resp. C.17–early 19, C.19, C.19.

high part, the. The gallery: Dublin theatrical (—1909). cf. the GODS.

high-pooped. Heavily buttocked: nautical s. > low coll: from ca 1830; ob.

high-priori. A burlesque coll perversion of *a priori*: from ca 1740. ?'coined' by Pope ('We nobly take the high Priori Road').

high-rented. Hot: low coll: from ca 1850; ob. 2. Very well known to the police: c.: from ca 1860; ob. cf. HOT, adj., 3.

high ropes, be on the. To be excited: late C.17–early 19; (very) angry: C.18–mid-19; standing on one's dignity: C.19–20, ob. All coll. Resp. B.E., Grose (2nd ed.), Mrs Henry Wood (in *Trevlyn Hold*). ?ex circus tight-rope walking and trapeze-work.

high(-)runners, see HIGH MEN.

high-seasoned or **highly spiced.** Indelicate; obscene: coll verging on S.E.: C.19–20.

high shelf, the. The ground: lower classes' (—1909).

high- (or clouted-) shoe(s). A rustic: mid-C.17–early 19: coll > S.E. The occ. form, *high-shoon*, is often used as an adj.

high-sniffing. Supercilious; pretentious, 'superior': (low) coll: from ca 1860; ob. cf. HIGH-NOSED.

high-stepper. A very fashionably dressed or mannered person: from ca 1860: coll. adj., *high-stepping*: same period, same comment. Ex a high-stepping horse.

high-stomached. Very courageous: prob. S.E. rather than coll. 2. Disdainful, haughty: coll rather than S.E. Both from C.16; ob. and, since ca 1850, archaic.

high(-)strikes. Hysterics: if unintentional, a sol. (—1838); if deliberate, jocular coll: from ca 1850; ob.

high tea. An ample tea with meat: coll (1856); from ca 1895, S.E. *Sporting Life*, 15 Dec. 1888. Perhaps *high* is here merely intensive (W.).

***high(-)tide** or **water.** Temporary richness or plentifulness of cash: resp. late C.17–20, C.19–20: ob. (Contrast LOW TIDE.) Orig., prob. c.; by 1830, coll.

***high-toby.** Highway robbery, but only by mounted men: ca 1810–70. Vaux, Ainsworth.

***high-toby gloak,** see HIGH PAD.

***high-top(p)er.** A SWELL thief: c.: ca 1850–1900. Burton, *Vikram and the Vampire*, 1870.

high-up. High; fig., of high rank or position: dial. >, in late 1890s, coll.

high-waisted, see HIGH-BELLIED.

high-water, see HIGH TIDE.

high-water mark, up to (the). In excellent condition; also, a gen. approbatory locution: coll: from ca 1860; ob.

high wood, live in. To hide, esp. to lie low and keep quiet: low: from ca 1840; ob. by 1900. Ex High Wood, i.e. that H.W. which was the nearest to London. cf. HIDE AND SEEK.

highball. A drink of whisky served in a tall glass: 1899. Orig. and mostly American.

higher Malthusianism. Sodomy: cultured s.: ca 1860–1900. Ex Thomas Malthus, the political economist's (d. 1834) *Essay on Population*, 1798.

highfalute. To rant; use fine words: mainly and orig. U.S.: anglicized ca 1875 as s., but never very gen. cf.:

highfalutin(g). Rant or bombast: orig. (—1850), U.S.; anglicized ca 1865: coll. *Pall Mall Gazette*, 3 May 1886, 'A glib master of frothy fustian, of flatulent highfalutin', and of oratorical bombast'.

highfalutin(g); gen. without g. Bombastic, absurdly pompous, whether in conversation or in behaviour: orig. (1848), U.S. s.; anglicized, as coll, ca 1862; 'now common in Liverpool and the East End of London', H., 1864 – a very useful word. Friswell, in *Modern Men of Letters*, 1870, 'Highfalutin' nonsense'. Ex Dutch *verlooten*, says H.; more prob. an elaboration of *high-flown*, perhaps influenced by *floating*.

Highgate, sworn (in) at. Sharp, clever: coll (from ca 1840, mainly dial.): mid-C. 18–19. Colman, 1769, 'I have been sworn at Highgate, Mrs Lettice, and never take the maid instead of the mistress'; Hone's *Every Day Book* (ii, 79–87); Apperson. Ex a C.18 custom prevalent at Highgate public-houses – see Grose, P.

Highland fling. A speech, or series of speeches, delivered in Scotland: political: 1880–ca 1915. Applied orig. to Gladstone's famous Midlothian speeches.

Highland frisky. Whisky: rhyming s.: since ca 1870. Perhaps a blend of *Highland whisky* and GAY AND FRISKY.

highly spiced, see HIGH-SEASONED.

highty-tighty ; hoity-toity. A wanton, or, as B.E. phrases it, 'a Ramp, or Rude Girl'; resp. late C.17–18, C.18–early 19: orig. low, then gen., coll. But *hoity-toity* is rare as a n.; usually it goes with *wench*, as in Grose.

highty-tighty; hoity-toity, adj. Peremptory, quarrelsome: C.19–20. 2. Uppish: late C.19–20; this, the prevailing C.20 sense, comes ex dial. The *-i-* form is coll, the *-oi-* orig. coll, in C.20 S.E. 'The earliest record, *upon the hoyty-toyty* (1668), suggests the *high ropes* [q.v.] and *tight rope*, or simply a jingle upon *high*,' W. See esp. W.: *More Words Ancient and Modern*.

highway, (as) common as the, see HEDGE, (AS) COMMON AS THE.

higly-pigly. A ca 1660–1800 variant of HIGGLEDY-PIGGLEDY.

hike. To pull or drag about: coll, ex dial.: 1867. 2. To tramp about: Canadian: late C.19–20. Ex American usage, itself ex dial. (1809). 3. To arrest: low London: ca 1860–1914. Ex sense 1.

hike about. Wander about: coll ex dial.: C.19–20. Perhaps influenced by U.S. college use.

hike off. To run away: c. (—1788). 2. Also, to carry off; to arrest: both (low) coll: mid-C.19–20; the latter, ob.

hiked up, be. 'To be shanghaied, or shipped unwillingly': nautical: late C.19–20. Bowen. cf. HIKE, v., 1 and 3.

hill, over the, see OVER THE HILL.

hill-topper. A 'sex-novel': journalists': ca 1894–1900.

hillman. The foreman of the dustmen: Cockney (—1887); very ob.

hillo! Hello!, hullo!: non-aristocratic variant (coll and dial.): C.19–20.

hilltop literature. Solid advice: journalistic coll of ca 1898–1914. Ware, 'Derived from danger-board warnings to cyclists on the summits of steep hills'.

hilly. Difficult, as in *hilly reading* and *hilly going* (hard to do): coll: from ca 1870; ob. cf. STEEP.

hilt(s), loose in the. Unsteady; conjugally unfaithful: coll: mid-C.17–early 18.

him!, I've got. Now I know or have guessed (it): coll (—1887).

hinchinarfer. A woman of gruff voice and shrieking-sisterhood tendencies: proletarian: from ca 1880. 'Implying that her husband has but an inch and a half, hence her bad temper' (Julian Franklyn).

hind. Person, fellow, chap: coll: C.16. e.g. in Douglas's *Aeneid*.

hind boot. The breech: low: C.19–20, ob. cf. HINDER END.

hind coach-wheel. A five-shilling piece: late C.17–early 20; †. See COACH-WHEEL.

hing leg, kick out a. To make a rustic bow: coll: mid-C.18–20, ob.

hind leg off a horse (dog, donkey, etc.), talk the, see TALK THE ...

hind-shifters. The feet or heels: coll: ca 1820–70. Lamb, in *Elia*, 'They would show as fair a pair of hind-shifters as [anyone] in the colony.'

hinder end, parts, world. The breech: (low) coll: C.19–20; ob. cf.:

hinder entrance. The fundament: low coll: C.19–20; ob. cf.:

hinders. Hind-quarters: coll: from ca 1890; slightly ob. Ex dial.: 1857.

Hindoo punishment. The 'muscle-grind' (s.v. LEG-GRINDER) in gymnastics: circus (—1875): Frost, in *Circus Life*.

hinge and pluck. The heart, liver and lungs of a killed pig: butchers' (—1887).

hinges, off the, adv., adj. Confused(ly); slightly indisposed: coll: C.17–20; †by 1820, except in dial. Cotgrave, Motteux.

hinterland. The breech: (low) coll: cf. HINDER END, etc. 'Old', says F. & H. in 1893, but not, I feel sure, older than 1880, the S.E. sense being recorded only at 1890. F. & H. may well be thinking of *hinderlands*, rare for *hinderlings*, the posteriors. Perhaps cf. Romany *hinder*, to defecate.

hip (1762), **hip(p)s** (1710). Morbid depression: 1710: coll; ob. by 1870; †by 1910. (See HYP.) Usually 'spelt with *y* in the n. but with *i* in the v., etc.', S.O.D. Ex *hypochondria*.

hip, v. To depress the spirits of: coll: from ca 1840. Prob. ex HIPPED.

hip-hop, adv. Hoppingly: coll: from ca 1670. Villiers, in *The Rehearsal*; Congreve. Reduplication of *hop*. (The O.E.D., perhaps rightly, considers it S.E. – at least after ca 1700.)

***hip-inside.** An inner coat-pocket, *hip-outside* being an outer: c. (—1839); ob.

hip, Michael, your head's on fire! see MICHAEL . . .

hipe. A rifle; gen. in *slope hipe*: military: late C.19–20. *Rifle* being less easy to pronounce, *ripe* none too easy, and *slope* perhaps effecting the form.

hipped. Melancholy, bored, depressed; slightly indisposed: coll: 1710; ob. Ex *hypochondria*; cf. HYPO; HYPS; HIPPISH.

hippen. The green curtain: theatrical, but perhaps only in Northumberland; certainly never very gen.: ca 1870–1905. ?ex Scots coll *hippen* (i.e. hipping cloth), a baby's napkin.

hippish. Low-spirited: coll: 1706 (S.O.D.). Gay, 'By cares depress'd in pensive hippish mood'. cf. HIPPED; HIP; HYP.

hippo. An occ. variant, recorded for 1725, of HYPO. (Never *hipo*.) 2. Hippopotamus: coll: 1872 (O.E.D.). Selous. 3. Ipecacuanha: Anglo-Irish (1900).

hippy. Morbidly depressed: coll: from ca 1890. cf. HIPPED; HIPPISH.

hips, down in the. Dispirited; indisposed: coll: 1729, Swift; ob. by 1890, †by 1910. Ex a phrase applied to horses injured in the haunch-bone.

hips, – free of her lips, free of her. Proverbial coll: C.19–20; somewhat ob. *Hips* here = buttocks, hence sex.

hips, long in the. Broad-buttocked: coll: C.19–20; ob. cf. HIPS TO SELL.

hips, walk with the. 'To make play with the posteriors in walking', F. & H.: C.19–20 coll; ob. A lower rather than a middle- or upper-class allurement to lewdery.

hips to sell(, with). Broad-buttocked: low coll: C.19–20; ob.

hircarra(h), see HURKARU.

his (or his royal) highness. My husband: feminine, either jocular or derisive: mainly lower-middle class: late C.19–20. cf. HIS LORDSHIP.

his legs . . . see LEGS GREW.

his lordship. He: derisive coll: mid-C. 19–20. Feminine: *her ladyship*: same period.

his nabs, nibs, see NABS; NIBS.

hishee-hashee, see SOAP AND BULLION.

hisn, see OURN.

hiss, the. The warning of a master's approach: Winchester College: C.19–20.

hist, n. and v. (Pronounced *hīghst*.) Hoist: sol.: C.19–20.

historical. (Of a costume or hat) seen more than three times: Society: 1882, the *Daily News*, 26 Dec.

history of the four kings, study the. To play at cards: coll: mid-C.18–mid-19. cf. the mid-C.18–early 19 coll *a child's best guide to the gallows*, a pack of cards, as also in the n. part of the defined locution. cf. DEVIL'S BOOKS.

hit. A success: orig., I think, coll, *pace* the O.E.D.: from ca 1815. 2. An attempted crime, esp. theft or robbery: c.: late C.18–mid-19.

***hit,** ppl adj. Convicted: c.: orig. and mostly at the Old Bailey: from ca 1860.

hit, hard, ppl adj., see HARD HIT. **hit a haystack,** see HAYSTACK.

hit it off. To agree well with a person: coll on verge of S.E.: from ca 1780. Trollope, in *Barchester Towers*. 2. To describe accurately: the (from ca 1735) coll form of S.E. *hit*: Trollope, in *The Duke's Children*.

hit on the tail, v.t. To coït with: C.16–17 coll. Skelton.

hit or miss. A kiss: rhyming s.: late C.19–20.

hit with. (More gen. STRUCK with.) Prepossessed by: coll: ca 1885–1915.

hitch. Temporary assistance; unimportant help through a difficulty: coll: from ca 1890; ob.

hitch, v. To marry; gen. in *hitched*, ppl adj., married: orig. (1857) U.S., app. first as *hitch horses*: anglicized ca 1890.

Hittite, hittite. A prize-fighter: a pugilistic pun: ca 1820–1910. More gen., however, as Bee (1823) phrases it: '*Hittites* – boxers and ring-goers assembled'.

hive. The female pudend: low: from ca 1850; ob. Ex HONEY.

hive it. To effect coïtion: low: from ca 1860; ob. Ex preceding.

hixi(o)us-dixi(o)us, see HICCIUS-DOCCIUS.

ho gya, ho-gya, hogya. In trouble: nonplussed or stumped; failed: Anglo-Indians': mid-C.19–20.

ho, out of all. Beyond all bounds: coll: late C.14–20. Chaucer, Swift. (After ca 1870, † except in dial. Ex *ho!*) A late C.16–19 variant is *out of all (w)hooping*, which appears in Shakespeare's *As You Like It*, and, as *past all w.*, in Kingsley's *Westward Ho!*

hoaky or hokey, by (the). An expletive: mainly nautical, but perhaps orig. Scots: from ca 1820: ob. Barham, Lover, Manchon. ?ex HOLY POKER.

hoax, v. and n., and its derivatives *hoaxer* and *hoaxing*, were orig. (1788) coll, which they remained until ca 1830. Orig. university wit, says Grose. Prob. ex HOCUS (-POCUS); cf., possibly, Romany (*hoax* or) *hokano*, to cheat, and *hookapen*; a hoax, a falsehood.

hob. A dolt; a rustic clown: C.14–early 19: until ca 1680, S.E.; then coll when not dial. Ex *Robert*.

hob, be on the. To be a teetotaller: military: late C.19–20. F. & Gibbons, 'The tea-kettle on the hob'.

hob and nob, hob or nob, hob nob. Orig. mere variants, but the only C.19–20 forms, of HAB OR NAB (etc.). – The only specific individual senses are, 1, as v.: to drink together, 1763, coll: be on very friendly terms (v.t., *with*), 1828; coll. 2. As n.: a toast (very rarely as *h.n.*, occ. – in C.18–19 – as *hob a nob*), 1756, always coll; adv. or adj., on terms of close friendship or good-fellowship, 1851, coll. See also HOB-NOB. The *hab, nab* form was influenced by *Hob*, a familiar by-form of *Robert*.

Hob Collingwood. The supposedly unlucky four of hearts: C.18–19 Northern coll.

hob-job. An unskilled or clumsy job; an odd job: s. and dial.: from ca 1855.

hob-jobber. A man or boy alert for small jobs on the street: (low) coll: mostly London: from ca 1850; ob. – Also vbl n., *hob-jobbing*.

hob-nob. A c.p. gracing a 'mutual' drinking: ca 1760–1830: coll > S.E. 2. A drinking together or to each other's health: 1825: coll. (See HOB AND NOB.) 3. A familiar intimate conversation: coll (—1876).

hobbadehoy, hobbe(r)dehoy, see HOBBLEDEHOY.

hobber-nob(ber). A corrupted form of *hob or nob* (see HOB AND NOB): from ca 1800; ob.

Hobbes's voyage. Coll: late C.17–18. Vanbrugh, in *The Provoked Wife*, 'So, now, I am in for Hobbes's voyage; a great leap in the dark.' Some topical origin.

hobble, as amorous v. (see F. & H.), is ob. S.E.; but as an awkward or puzzling situation it is (from ca 1775) coll and dial.; and as to arrest, to commit for trial, it is c. (—1789) and ob. 2. To *hobble a plant* is to *spring* it (see PLANT, a cache, and PLANT, SPRING A): c.: ca 1810–50.

hobble, in a. In trouble; hampered; perplexed: coll: late C.18–20; ob. 2. In c., committed for trial: late C.18–20; ob.

***hobbled (upon the legs).** On the hulks; in prison; transported as a convict: c.: late C.18–mid-19. Parker, Vaux. 2. Whence (?) *hobbled*, committed for trial: c.: late C.18–20; ob.

hobbledegee or -jee. A jog-trot: coll (—1788): ob. by 1880, †by 1900. i.e. *hobble* + a fanciful ending.

hobbledehoy; also **hobba(r)d(e or y)hoy, hobbe(r)dehoy.** A boy not yet quite a man: coll: 1540, as *hobbledehoye* in Palsgrave. In C.18, gen. in rhyme, 'hobbledehoy, neither man nor boy'. Prob. HOB + some now indeterminable ending – perhaps Fr. *de haie, de haye*, of the hedge (see HEDGE) – with *-le-* (rare before 1700) or *-a(r)-*, *-e(r)-*, acting as a euphonic.

hobbledehoyish; hobbledehoyhood. Awkwardly youthful; the age when a boy is such: the former (—1812), coll: the latter (1836) hardly gen. enough to be coll.

hobbler. An unlicensed pilot; a landsman acting as tow-Jack: orig. (1800), nautical s.; by 1900, j. As a boatman, Isle of Man dial.

hobby. A translation: university. Whence *to ride hobbies*, to use CRIBS: ca 1870–1910.

Hobby, Sir Posthumous('s). A man fastidious or whimsical in his clothes: coll: ca 1690–1830. Punning *hobby*, an avocation.

hobby-horse. A wanton, a prostitute: late C.16–17: coll. Ex the S.E. sense, a horse in common use: cf. *hobby*.

hobby-horse, v. To romp; play the fool, esp. in horse-play: coll: ca 1630–1890.

hobby-horsical. Connected with, devoted to a hobby; whimsical: jocular coll: 1761, Sterne. 2. In late C.18–early 19, and perhaps orig., 'a man who is a great keeper or rider of hobby horses', i.e. hacks.

hobnail. A countryman; a boor: coll: from ca 1645; in C.19–20, S.E.; ob. Beaumont & Fletcher, in *Women Pleased*, 'The hob-nail thy husband's as fitly out o' th' way now.'

hobnailed. Boorish: coll till C.19, then S.E.: C.17–20; ob. Ex preceding. Occ. *hobnail* (earlier, by the way, as adj. than as n.).

hobson-jobson. 'A native festal excitement; a *tamāsha* . . .; but especially the Moharram ceremonies', Yule & Burnell: Anglo-Indian, prob. orig. (ca 1820) military; the form *hossy-gossy* occurs as early as 1673. Ex the Shia wailing-cry, *Yā Hasan! Yā Hosain.* (In S.E., a certain linguistic process.)

Hobson's, see sense 2 of:

Hobson's choice. That or none: coll: 1649, Somers Tracts, 'I had Hobson's choice, either be a Hobson or nothing'; Steele, in the *Spectator*, No. 509; Cibber, in *The Non-Juror*, 'Can any woman think herself happy that's obliged to marry only with a Hobson's choice?' The etymology ex Thomas Jobson, that Cambridge livery-stable keeper (d. 1630) who let out his horses only in strict rotation, is seriously damaged by Richard Cock's 'We are put to Hodgson's choice to take such privilegese as they will geve us, or else goe without,' 1617 – one of W.'s happiest discoveries. 2. A voice: theatrical rhyming s.: late C.19–20; now gen. abbr. to *Hobson's*.

hock, in. Laid by the heels; swindled: low: late C.19–20, ob. 2. In prison: c.: late C.19–20. Prob. ex Dutch s. *hok*, debt, and perhaps influenced by *hock*, a rod, a chain, with a hook at the end.

hock, old. Stale beer: late C.18–19: (low) coll. Ex *hock*, the white German wine – orig. *Hochheimer*, that made at Hochheim, on the Main.

***hock-dockies**; in C.19, occ. **hock(e)y-dockies.** Shoes: c. (—1789); †by 1893, perhaps by 1880. Rhyming reduplication on HOCKS.

hockelty; hocly. The *hock* or penultimate card, esp. in faro: from mid-1860s.

hockey. Drunk, orig. with stale beer: ca 1788–1880. Ex HOCK, OLD. cf. HICKEY.

***hock(e)y-dockies,** see HOCK-DOCKIES.

hocks. The feet: low coll (—1785); in C.19–20, gen. the feet and ankles; ob. Ex a quadruped's hocks.

hocky, see HOCKEY. **hocly,** see HOCKELTY.

hocus. A juggler, a conjuror; an imposter: ca 1650–1720. Abbr. HOCUS-POCUS. In Witts' *Recreations*, ca 1654, as *hocas*. 2. Jugglery; deception: from ca 1650; in C.19–20, S.E.; † except in sense of criminal deception, shady trickery. 3. Drugged liquor: orig. (—1823), s.: by 1890, S.E. Also *hocus-pocus*.

hocus, v. To HOAX: 1675: coll till C.19, then S.E. Whence *hocusser* and *hocussing*, C.19–20 nn. 2. To drug, esp. with liquor (—1821, *Boxiana*, III): cf. slightly later, now ob., sense, to stupefy with liquor (and then rob): 1831 (S.O.D.): coll until ca 1880, then S.E.: cf. SNUFF. To *hocus* horses as early as 1823. All senses ex the n.

hocus, adj. Intoxicated (—1725): ob. by 1830, †by 1860. Ex the v.

hocus-pocus; in C.17, often **hocas-pocas.** The name of, or for, a juggler: Jonson, in *The Staple of News*, 1624; in 1634, a title runs, 'Hocus Pocus Junior, *The Anatomie of Leger de main*'; in 1656, defined by Blount. 2. Hence, a trickster: from ca 1720. 3. A juggler's trick; hence, imm., deception, trickery: 1647. 4. As a juggler's formula: 1632. 5. A juggler's or impostor's stock in trade: from ca 1650. Also *hocus-trade*, C.17. 6. An astrologer: s.: Ned Ward, 1703. 7. Drugged liquor (—1823); †by 1893, *hocus* being then gen. – All these senses were orig. s., prob. low s., but soon > coll; by 1850, only the third, fourth, and fifth were much used; in C.20, only the third and fifth, both of which have, since ca 1810, been S.E. Either ex an actual juggler's name (slightly latinized, no doubt), or ex *hoc est corpus* (*filii*), mentioned (by

Tillotson) as a juggler's phrase, the latter theory being bolstered by the Scandinavian *hokus-pokusfiliokus*. N.B., the C.17 sense, a bag used by jugglers, was too rare to be coll.

hocus-pocus, v. To cheat, trick: from ca 1770. 2. v.i., to juggle, practise trickery: 1687, L'Estrange. Both orig. coll, but in late C.19–20, S.E. Ex the n.

hocus-pocus, adj. Juggling, cheating, fraudulent: 1668 (S.O.D.): coll until C.19, then S.E. Wycherley; Macklin, in *Love à la Mode*, 'The law is a sort of hocus-pocus science that smiles in yer face while it picks yer pocket.' The adv. is rare: *hocus-pocusly*.

hocus-pocus, play. To play the juggler (fig.): coll: ca 1659–1740. Bentley.

hocus-trade, see HOCUS-POCUS, n., 5.

hocus-trick. A juggling trick, hence a swindle: coll: ca 1675–1700. Ex HOCUS, n.

hod or **Hod**; occ. **Brother Hod.** A bricklayer's labourer: coll (—1791); ob. Ex the hod used for carrying bricks and mortar; abbr. *hodman*.

hod of mortar. A pot of porter: rhyming s. (—1859); ob.

hoddie-doddie; better **-y.** A squat person: coll: ca 1530–1900. In C.17–18, gen. in form of jeering rhyme or c.p., *Hoddy-doddy, All arse and no body*; the rhyme was, in a contemporary song, applied to the Rump Parliament. 2. A fool; a cuckold: ca 1595–1800; cf. HODDY-PEAK (the reference being to a snail's horns). Cognate with HODMANDOD, in being prob. a rhyming perversion of *dodman*, a snail. 3. A lighthouse's revolving light: nautical: late C.19–20; ob. Ex West Country dial.

hoddy-doddy, adj. Dumpy: coll: from ca 1820; † except in dial. Ex n.

hoddy-peak; in C.16, often **peke.** A fool, a dolt: C.16–early 17. 2. A cuckold: ca 1585–1640. Both senses orig. coll, but by 1590, at latest, S.E. The *hoddy*, as in HODDY-DODDY, may at first have been = a snail; cf. HODMANDOD. (*Hoddy-poll*, C.16, same meanings, may orig. have been coll.)

hodmandod. A shell-snail: coll: 1626 (S.O.D.); ob. except in dial. Ex *dodman*, a snail: cf. HODDIE-DODDIE. 2. A deformed person: coll: ca 1660–1900. 3. A Hottentot: low coll, almost sol.: 1686; †by 1850. Captain Cowley in *Harris's Voyages*.

hodmandod, adj. Short and clumsy: from ca 1820; ob.: coll when not dial. Ex preceding; prob. suggested by HODDY-DODDY.

***hog (pl hog).** A shilling: orig. (ca 1670), c.; in C.19–20, low s. 2. In C.18–early 19, occ. a sixpence: also c., whence the U.S. sense. Prob. ex the figure of a hog on a small silver coin. 3. A half-crown: ca 1860–1910. 4. A hogget (yearling sheep): Australian: late C.19–20.

hog, v. To coït: low: C.19–20, ob.

hog, go the whole, see GO THE WHOLE HOG.

hog-grubber. 'A narrow-soul'd sneaking Fellow', B.E.: coll: late C.17–early 19. Hence adj., *hog-grubbing*: C.18–early 19. 2. 'A Thames waterman, licensed by the Trinity House': London watermen's: ca 1840–80. Mayhew.

hog in a squall or **storm, like a.** Beside oneself; out of one's senses: nautical coll (—1887); slightly ob.

hog in armour. A lout in fine clothes: coll: from ca 1650. Hence Thackeray's 'Count Hogginarmo'. 2. Larwood & Hotten, in *Signboards*, 1867, 'a favourite epithet applied to rifle volunteers [from ca 1850] by costermongers, fishmongers, and suchlike.' 3. An iron-clad: naval: ca 1860–90.

hog-rubber. A(n ignorant) rustic: pejorative coll: C.17. Jonson, Burton.

hog-shearing; shearing of hogs, vbl n. Much ado about nothing: coll: C.17–18. Ex the full text of the *much cry and little wool* proverb, q.v. at CRY AND ...

hog-wash. Bad liquor, esp. ROT-GUT; 1699, B.E., 'Toplash, Wretched, sorry Drink, or Hog-Wash': coll >, by 1800. S.E. Hence, 2, worthless, cheap journalism journalistic: from ca 1880. cf. *slush*.

hog-yoke. Nautical, C.19, thus in Bowen: 'The old-fashioned wooden quadrant in American ships and Grand Bankers, so-called from its likeness to the wooden yoke put over hogs to prevent them breaking through fences'.

hoga, that won't. That won't do! Anglo-Indian (—1864); ob.

Hogan(-Mogan); Hogen(-Mogen). A Dutchman: a coll affected by satirists, ca 1670–1700. Ex *hoogmogendheien*, the Dutch for high and mighty lords, as applied to the Dutch States-General. See that fine scholar, G. Aitken's *Satires of Andrew Marvell* (1892), p. 128. 2. Hence, any 'high and mighty' person: coll: ca 1640–1750. 3. Also as corresponding adj., with additional sense, potent (of drink): ca 1650–1730. cf.:

hogan-mogan rug. A strong drink, esp. ale: coll: ca 1650–1720. Dryden, in *The Wild Gallant*, 'I was drunk; damnably drunk with ale; great hogan-mogan bloody ale.' cf. the preceding entry.

hogmagundy. Sexual intercourse: orig. Scots: ca 1820–90, (not very gen.) Southern coll. ?ex HOGMANAY.

hogmanay. A wanton: Scots C.19–20 (ob.) coll. Ex the Scots national festival of Hogmanay, New Year's Eve.

hogo, a flavour, a taint, may orig. – ca 1650 – have been coll, but it very soon > S.E. Ex Fr. *haut goût*. Also *fogo*, which is a C.19 corruption.

Hogs Norton, have been born at. To be ill-mannered, uncouth: proverbial coll: mid-C.16–mid-19. Often in orig. form, which adds: *where the pigs play on the organs*. The reference is to 'the village of Hock-Norton, Leicestershire, where the organist once upon a time was named Piggs!', so it is said (Apperson, q.v.).

hogs (or pigs) to a fair or fine market, bring one's. To profit; do well: coll: C.17–20, ob. 2. Also, ironically: C.18–20.

hogs (or pigs) to market, drive one's. To snore: C.18–20: coll. Swift, 'He snored so loud that we thought he was driving his hogs to market'; Grose, 1st ed., has the abbr. form *drive one's hogs*. Ex the notable grunting of driven pigs.

***hogshead, couch a.** To lie down and sleep: c. of ca 1560–1840. Ex *hog's head*, a person, 1515.

hoi polloi. Candidates for pass degrees: university: ca 1860–1915. Ex the Gr. for 'the many'.

hoick. A jerk as one's stroke begins or ends: rowing coll (—1898).

hoick, v. To raise, hoist, esp. with a jerk: coll: late C.19–20. Prob. ex HIKE, v., 1.

***hoise.** A C.19 variant of:

***hoist.** A confederate helping a thief to reach an open window: late C.18–mid-19 c. 2. Hence, a shop-lifter: C.19, c. > low. cf. 3, **hoist, the.** Shop-lifting: c. (—1812).

***hoist,** v. To rob by means of *the hoist* (n.); to shop-lift: c.: ca 1810–60. 2. Implied in HOISTING, 2. 3. v.i., to drink: (low) coll: from ca 1860; ob.

hoist, give a, v.t. To do a bad turn: tailors': from ca 1870; ob.

***hoist, go upon the.** To enter a building by an open window: c.: ca 1787–1860. cf. HEAVE, v., 1.

hoist, on the. On *the* DRUNK: (low) coll: from ca 1860.

hoist him in! A mid-C.19–20 nautical c.p. verging on j., for it constitutes an order 'to welcome the captain or senior officer over the side, a relic of the old way of embarking in bad weather with a whip on the yard arm'.

hoist in. A drink of liquor: ca 1865–1920. Ex HOIST, v., 3.

hoist in, do or have a. To have sexual intercourse: low: from ca 1850. (Rarely of women.)

***hoist-lay.** Shop-lifting: c.: ca 1810–60. 2. 'Shaking a man head downwards, so that the money rolls out of his pockets', F. & H.: ca 1830–1900: c. Also HOISTING, 2.

hoist one's pennants. To grumble; be severely critical: nautical: late C.19–20. A display of all pennants means 'I don't understand your signal.'

***hoister.** A shop-lifter; a pickpocket: c.: resp. C.19–20 and C.19. The latter is in J. H. Jesse's *London*, vol. i, 1847. Ex HOIST, v., 1. 2. A sot: (low) coll: from ca 1860; ob. Ex HOIST, v., 3.

***hoisting; hoist-lay.** Shop-lifting: late C. 18–19 c. 2. See HOIST-LAY, 2: c.: late C.18–early 19. 3. **(hoisting.)** Drinking: low coll: from ca 1860; ob. Ex HOIST, v., 3.

hoity-toity, see HIGHTY-TIGHTY.

hokey. Prison: low: late C.19–20. Perhaps ex CHOKEY on HOKEY-POKEY.

hokey!, by (the). See HOAKY. Occ. varied to *by the hokeys* and, in late C.19, to *by the hokey-pokey*.

hok(e)y-pok(e)y. A cheat, a swindle: low coll: from ca 1845. 2. Nonsense: low coll: from ca 1875. 3. A, indeed any, cheap ice-cream sold in the streets: low coll: from ca 1884. A C.19 street-cry ran 'hokey-pokey, pokey ho'; a C.19–20 children's derisive c.p., 'hokey-pokey, a penny a lump, the more you eat, the more you pump.' All these senses are ex HOCUS-POCUS; the third is not – as some wit proposed – ex It. *o che poco!*, oh, how little!

hokey-pokey, adj. Swindling; illegal, illicit: low coll (—1887). Ex n., 1.

Holborn Hill, ride backwards up (Grose, 1st ed.). To go to be hanged: mid-C.18–early 19 s.: perhaps orig. c., but certainly soon low coll. Congreve has *go up Holborn Hill*; *ride up Holborn* occurs at least as early as 1659 (see Nares), while Jonson, in *Bartholomew Fair*, alludes to *the heavy hill . . . of Holborn*. Such was the route to Tyburn, where criminals were hanged, the criminals riding backwards. The last execution at Tyburn, so therefore the last procession thither, was in 1784, the executions thereafter taking place near Newgate.

hold, v.i. To conceive a child: coll: C.18–20. Ex the C.17–20 S.E. sense of animal conception. Variant *hold it*. 2. In billiards, to hole, v.t.: s. > j.: 1869. 'A corruption of *hole*, by association of *holed* and *hold*', S.O.D. 3. (v.t.) To hold one's own against, be (clearly) a match for: sporting s. (—1883). 4. To be in funds: low coll (?orig. s.): at first, Cockney: from ca 1870.

hold a candle to, and **hold a candle to the devil,** see CANDLE.

hold a good wind. (Of a ship) to have 'good weatherly qualities': nautical coll: mid-C.19–20; slightly ob.

hold down (a claim). To reside long enough on a claim to establish ownership under the homestead law; mining s.: U.S. (1888) and Australia (ca 1890).

hold hard!; hold on! Wait a moment!; stop! Coll: the former (orig. in S.E., of pulling at a horse's reins) from ca 1760; the latter from ca 1860 and orig., and long mostly, nautical. Colman, 1761, 'Hold hard! hold hard! you are all on a wrong scent'; Edmund Yates, 1864, in *Broken to Harness*, 'I told Meaburn to hold on'.

hold in hand. To amuse; vividly to interest; have a marked ascendancy over: coll: from ca 1860; ob. Ex the †S.E. sense, keep in expectation.

hold it! Stay in precisely that position!: painters' s. (from ca 1895).

hold on! see HOLD HARD!

hold on by the eyebrows, or **eyelashes,** or **eyelids,** see EYELASHES ...

hold on like grim death; hold on to. To be courageously or obstinately persistent about; apply oneself diligently to: the former, coll; the latter, coll in C.19. Both from ca 1850; the former was perhaps orig. U.S.

hold on the slack. To do nothing: nautical coll: mid-C.19–20. i.e. the slack of the rope.

***hold-out.** A mechanical device, esp. in poker, for 'holding out', i.e. concealing, desirable cards until they are useful: gamblers' c.: ca 1860–1900, though app. not recorded before 1893. Maskelyne, in *Sharps and Flats*, 1894.

hold the stage. To have the eye of an audience: theatrical: from ca 1875. 2. To attract most of the attention; do all the talking: coll: from ca 1895.

hold-up, v. Rob on the highway, hence waylay and rob, hence to cheat: orig. (1887), U.S.; anglicized as a coll ca 1895. cf. Australian STICK UP. 2. In c., to arrest: ca 1880–1915.

hold up your dagger hand. A C.17 drinking c.p.

(hold up your head:) there's money bid for you. (Don't be so modest! for) people think well of you: C.17–mid-19: a semi-proverbial c.p. Swift, the longer form; Marryat, the shorter, preceded by 'as the saying is'.

hold with. To approve of; agree with: coll: from ca 1895. Ex S.E. sense, to side with: cf., in S.E., the †*hold on*, the ob. *hold of* or *for* (S.O.D.).

hold your jaw! Be quiet: (low) coll: from ca 1750. Foote. Occ. in other moods than the imperative. cf. HOLD HARD!

hole. The *pudendum muliebre*: low coll: C.16 (?earlier)–20. 2. Hence, like CUNT, it has come to signify coïtion or women viewed as sexual potentialities or actualities, as in 'He likes a, *or* his, bit of hole' or 'Hole means everything to that blighter.' 3. The anus: low coll in C.19–20, but in C.14–18 a vulgarism (as in Chaucer's ribald *Miller's Tale*). Abbr. ARSE-HOLE. – The following two senses were S.E. previous to ca 1870, then, *pace* the O.E.D., they > coll: 4, a small dingy abode or lodging (1616); 5, a monetary or social difficulty, a mess, a scrape: 1760, Smollett. 6. A tunnel: railwaymen's coll: mid-C.19–20.

hole. (Gen. v.t.) 'To effect intromission', F. & H.: low: C.19–20. Ex n., 1. The v.i. is gen. expressed by *to hole it*.

hole, bit of, see HOLE, n., 1 and 2.

***hole, put in the.** Contemporary with the synonymous GARDEN, PUT IN THE.

hole!, suck his. A low 'dovetail', or c.p. retort, on receiving 'Yes' to the question, 'Do you know So-and-so?': from ca 1870; ob.

hole-and-corner work. Sexual connection: mid-C.19–20 low coll.

hole in a ladder, unable (or too drunk) to see a. Excessively drunk: coll: from ca 1860.

hole in (anything), make a. To use up largely, esp. money or drink: coll: from ca 1660. 2. To interrupt, break; upset, spoil: coll: from ca 1850. Only in such locutions as: *make a hole in one's manners*, to be impolite (ob.); ... *in one's reputation*, (of a man) to seduce a girl, (of a girl) to allow herself to be seduced; ... *in the silence*, to make a noise, esp. an excessive (and occ. continuous or continual) noise: orig., these were prob. to be considered jocular S.E., but they promptly > coll.

hole in one's coat(, pick a). (To find) a cause for censure, a moral flaw: coll: late C.16–19. Shakespeare, 'If I find a hole in his coat, I will tell him my mind'; Burns on Grose, 'If there's a hole in a' your coats, I rede you tent it.'

hole in one's pocket, burn a, see BURN ...

hole in the water, make a. To commit suicide by drowning: (jocular > low) coll: from ca 1850. Dickens, 1853. cf. HOLE IN ANYTHING, MAKE A, 2.

hole it, see HOLE, V.

hole of content or **of holes.** The female pudend: C.16–19: orig. euphemistic, but in C.18–19 low coll. Also *queen of holes.*

hole to hide it in, give or **lend a.** To grant the sexual favour: low coll: C.19–20.

holed, ppl adj. (Of the woman, with *well-*, *large-*, etc.) having a pudend of a specified kind: C.19–20: low coll. 2. (Of a man) in, or at, sexual congress: C.19–20 low coll.

holer. A man promiscuously and actively amorous: low coll: C.16–20, ob. Also *hole-monger.* 2. A whore; a light woman: C. 18–mid-19: coll. This word, not nearly so gen. as F. & H. implies, is a reminiscence of the C.13–15 use, gen. as *holour*, applied only to men.

holey dollar, see HOLY DOLLAR.

holiday. (Gen. pl.) A spot carelessly left untarred or unpainted: nautical coll (—1785). Also builders' and house-painters': C.19–20. Hence, a gap left between slung hammocks or clothing hung up to dry: nautical: late C.19–20.

holiday, blind man's, see BLIND MAN'S HOLIDAY.

holiday, gone for a, adj. Imperfect, incomplete, flawed: coll: from ca 1860; ob. cf. HOLIDAY, n., 1, (—1785) and Cornish dial., resp. a spot left untarred or unpainted and a part left undusted, unswept, uncleaned.

holiday, speak. To use choice English: coll: late C.16–17. Shakespeare.

holiday, take a. To be dismissed, esp. from a job: (low) coll: C.19–20; ob. cf. *get the* BAG or SACK.

holiday at Peckham, have a. To go without dinner: coll: C.19. Ex:

holiday at Peckham or **with him, it is all.** It is all over with it or him: coll: ca 1790–1910. Punning on PECK, food, and PECKISH, hungry.

holiday cutter, a. A minor punishment, the delinquent pulling in the cutter instead of going ashore: *Conway* cadets': from ca 1890. Analogous is the *Conway*'s *holiday messenger*, the delinquent attending on lower deck instead of going ashore.

holing, n. Whoring; womanizing: low coll: C.19–20; ob. See HOLE, V.

holla-balloo. A variant, recorded by Baumann, of HULLABALOO.

Holland tape, see TAPE.

Hollanders. Pointed wax moustaches: South London: 1875–85. Ex W. Holland, a popular theatre-lessee owning 'the finest pair of black-waxed sheeny moustaches ever beheld'.

holler, v. To shout; cry for mercy: a low coll form of *hollo*, *holloa*, *hollow*: app. orig. (—1699), U.S., anglicized ca 1870.

holler, boys, holler. A collar: rhyming s.: late C.19–20. Often shortened to *holler, boys.*

hollow. Cooked poultry: gourmets' (—1823). Because disembowelled.

hollow, adj. Complete, thorough; very easy: coll: 1750 (S.O.D.). Esp. with *thing* and *victory* (or *defeat*), the former (synonymous with the latter) being a set phrase in C.18–early 19. Ex:

hollow, adv. Completely, thoroughly, very easily: 1668 (S.O.D.). Esp. with *beat*, as in Townley, 1759, 'Crab was beat hollow.' Skinner, in his fascinating *Etymologicon*, pertinently suggested that *hollow* = *wholly* corrupted. The mainly U.S. form, *all hollow*, occurs in Foote's *The Orators*, 1762.

hollow meat. 'Rabbit or hare ... unpopular when served out to a ship's company': nautical coll: late C.19–20. Bowen. Prob. suggested by dial. *h.m.*, poultry as opp. to butcher's meat.

Holloway. The female pudend: low, punning: from ca 1860; ob.

Holloway, Middlesex. The lower bowel: low, doubly punning: ca 1865–1910.

Holly. A philippic: Society: ca 1880–90. Ex John *Holl*ingshead, who, as lessee of the Gaiety Theatre, 'for many years issued scathing proclamations signed with his name, printed in the house bills' (Ware).

holt. A hold, a grip: low coll: from ca 1880, ex U.S. (1825), ex Eng. dial. of C.14–20.

holus-bolus. The head; occ. the neck: nautical: ca 1870–1905.

holus-bolus, adv. All together: completely; at a gulp; in confusion; helter-skelter: orig. (—1847), dial.; coll from ca 1860, perhaps thanks to T. Hughes (as dial.) in *Tom Brown's Schooldays*; Wilkie Collins, in *The Moonstone*, 'He put [the silver] back, holus-bolus, in her pocket.' The O.E.D. suggests by facetious latinization of (*the*) *whole bolus* or as through Gr. ὅλος βῶλος.

Holy Aunt. A High Anglican c.p. term for the Roman Catholic Church: late C.19–20. On the Roman Catholics' 'Holy *Mother* Church'.

Holy Cod. Good Friday: atheists': 1890; ob. Adopted from Fr. free-thinkers' *la Sainte Morue*.

holy day. 'In well disciplined ships of war, many officers devote a certain day in the week, purposely, that the crew "may overhaul their bags", and repair their clothes – gloss, on *holyday*': W. N. Glascock, *Sailors and Saints*, 1829, at I, 97.

holy dollar. A dollar out of which a DUMP has been punched: Australia: ca 1820–80. Elsewhere, ca 1850–1910, also as *holey d.* Referred to in the *Hobart Town Gazette*, 10 Aug. 1822, though not so named. Punning *holey*.

holy father. 'A butcher's boy of St Patrick's Market, Dublin, or other Irish blackguards [pl, *sic*], among whom the exclamation, or oath, *by the holy father*, (meaning the Pope) is common', Grose, 1785: Anglo-Irish: (prob.) ca 1750–1850. cf. HOLY LAMB.

holy fowl. A pious (esp. outwardly pious) woman: ecclesiastical: late C.19–20.

holy friar. A liar: rhyming s.: late C.19–20.

Holy Ghost shop. A church: low (—1909).

holy ground, see HOLY LAND. **holy iron,** see HOLY POKER.

holy Joe. One who is good at Scripture: *Conway* cadets': from ca 1865. 2. Hence (?), a pious person: coll: late C.19–20. Imm. ex: 3. A parson, a chaplain: nautical (—1874).

holy (jumping mother of) Moses! see MOSES and cf. the former of:

holy kicker!; holy smoke! Exclamations expressive of amazement: late C.19–20.

holy lamb. A thorough-paced villain: Anglo-Irish: ca 1760–1870. Orig., prob. blasphemous. cf. HOLY FATHER.

holy land or **ground** (occ. with capitals). St Giles's, London, or rather (Seven Dials) the underworld part thereof: perhaps orig. c.: the former —1821, the latter —1819; both prob. from ca 1810. Ob. by 1890. A pre-1819 chant runs: 'For we are the boys of the holy ground, And we'll dance upon nothing' – i.e. be hanged – 'and turn us round.' An early explanation has it that the name is 'in compliment to the superior purity of its Irish population, (*Fancy*, vol. i: 1821), while the *Licensed Victuallers' Gazette* of 3 April 1891 refers to 'the Irishmen of the Holy Land'. cf. PALESTINE. 2. Any neighbourhood affected by Jews: (low) coll: from ca 1875. cf.:

holy of holies. The Grand Hotel at Brighton: from ca 1890. Because a favourite with Jews. cf. preceding entry. 2. A private room; a DEN or 'sanctum': coll (—1875); in C.20, S.E., as indeed it was in C.19 except when jocular or derisive. Nat Gould, in *The Double Event*, 'Fletcher did not venture into that holy of holies.' 3. The female pudend: low: C.19–20. Punning *holey*.

holy poker or **iron.** A university bedel (rarely as *h. iron*): ca 1850–1910. 2. As an oath (in C.20, mild): the former (—1840) has variant *h. pokers*, without *the*; the latter (—1886). Ex the mace carried by an esquire bedel. 3. The penis: low: from ca 1860; ob. Punning HOLE, n., 1; cf. POKE, V.

holy show!; h. lance! A mild oath: ca 1850–1910: the latter, not gen. cf. HOLY POKER, 2.

holy smoke! see HOLY KICKER.

holy terror. A very formidable person; a person of tiresome manner or exasperating habits: coll: from ca 1890.

holy than righteous, more. (Of a garment) torn or holey; (of a person) wearing ragged or torn clothes: (orig. low) coll: from ca 1885.

holy water, as the devil loves. Not at all: coll: mid-C.16–20. (Holy water having, in theology, the virtue of routing the devil.)

holy-water sprinkler. A spiked club: coll: C.19 (and prob. centuries earlier). The S.E. is *h.-w.* †*springle* or *sprinkle*, though, in this sense, even those forms must orig. have been coll, as the sense, a fox's brush (C.18 and prob. C.17), was orig. sporting s.

Holy Week. Menstrual period: (Catholic) girls': late C.19–20. Abstention from intercourse.

holy workman, he is a. An ecclesiastical c.p. of C.16 applied to 'him that will not be saved by Christ's merits, but by the works of his own imagination' (Tyndale, 1528).

home, bring oneself, see HOME, GET, 3.

home, carry or **send.** To bury, to kill: coll: C.18–20, ob. Ex late C.16–20 coll > S.E. *send to one's last home*. cf. HOME, GO.

home, get. To LAND (3) a blow effectively: boxing s. > gen. coll: C.19–20. Ex S.E. *pay* or *touch home*. 2. To reach the winning-post: turf and athletics: late C.19–20, s. > coll. 3. Specifically games and the turf, orig., is the sense, to recover a loss, come out quits: from ca 1809. Also *bring oneself home*, from ca 1760, as in Miss Burney. 4. To induce the sexual spasm in a woman; also to get her with child: low coll: C.19–20.

home, go. To die: C.19–20 coll. Esp. in *gone home*, dead. Note, however, that *go to one's last home* is a S.E. euphemism. cf. HOME, CARRY.

home, make oneself at. To make oneself very comfortable in another's abode or lodging: coll (—1892).

home about, nothing to write, see NOTHING TO WRITE . . .

home and fried. 'Safe and correct': military: late C.19–20. Possibly rhyming s. on *home and dried*.

home-bird. A hen-pecked husband; a milksop: coll: from ca 1870.

home-folk(s). One's relatives and/or friends, neighbours: coll, orig. (ca 1880) U.S., anglicized ca 1900.

home, James! A c.p., dating from ca 1870 – if not earlier; *James* being the coachman, later the chauffeur. At first usually, and still occasionally, *home, James, and don't spare the horses*.

Home Rule or **h. r.** Irish whiskey: ca 1880–1914. cf.:

home-rulers. 'Roast potatoes, as baked in the streets': London: 1882–ca 1914. Ware. Because so many potatoes came from Ireland.

home-stretch, see GET ON THE HOME-STRETCH.

home sweet home. The female pudend; orig., no doubt, the conjugal one: low: from ca 1870; ob.

home with the milk, come or **get.** To reach home in the early morning: coll: since ca 1890.

homee. Rare for OMEE.

homesters. A team playing on their own ground: sporting s. (1891) >, ca 1900, coll.

homeward-bound stitches are designed to last only till one is paid off: nautical: from ca 1870. cf.:

homeward-bounder. A vessel bound for home: coll (—1867).

homey, adj., and **hominess**, see HOMY.

homo. A man: the orig., and a C.19 alternative (never gen.), of OMEE. Lingua Franca. Pierce Egan, *Life in London*, 1821.

homo genius. A genius: 1887, Baumann; virtually †. Punning *homogeneous* and *genus homo*.

***homon(e)y.** A woman; a wife; C.18 c. *The Discoveries of John Poulter*, 1754, 'My homoney is in quod.' cf. HOMO, with which it is cognate.

homy, occ. **homey**. Home-like; resembling or suggesting home; unobtrusively comfortable: coll: from ca 1855. Kingsley, 'I like to . . . feel "homey" wherever I be.' Whence *hominess*, homelikeness, quiet comfort: coll: 1885.

hondey. An omnibus: Manchester: ca 1860–1900. Abbr. *hondeybush* (i.e. *omnibus* corrupted).

hone. The female pudend: either euphemistic or low coll: C.18–19. D'Urfey, 'So I may no more pogue the hone of a woman.'

honest, chaste, was always S.E., despite F. & H., whose second sense, a coll one, immoral but within the law, arose ca 1850 and disappeared with the C.19. As an adv. (= *honestly*) it is coll only when, exclamatory, it means 'It's true – on my word it is,' or when, interrogatively, it means 'Do you mean it?' Both from ca 1880.

honest, the. The truth: non-aristocratic, non-cultured coll: late C.19–20.

honest a man as any (in the cards) when all the kings are out, as. A knave: C.17–mid-19 coll, the longer form being gen. till C.19.

honest as the skin between the brows or **horns(, as).** As honest as may be: coll: resp. mid-C.16–17, C.17. Still, Jonson, Shakespeare; Jonson. cf. the coll > S.E. similes *as honest a man as ever broke bread*, late C.16–20 (ob.); *as ever trod on shoe-leather*, late C.16–19; *as the sun ever shone on*, late C.18–20; and *as honest a woman as ever burnt malt*: late C.16–17.

honest broker. A matrimonial agent: lower middle classes': from ca 1880; ob.

honest fellow, see JEMMY, n., 2.

honest Indian, or, gen., **Injun!** HONOUR BRIGHT! Coll: orig. (—1884), U.S.; anglicized ca 1895, mostly owing to Mark Twain's books; ob.

honest man and a good bowler, an. A person who combines two qualities rarely found together – for, says Quarles in 1635, 'He hardly can Be a good bowler and an honest man,' the special combination soon being made generic and then proverbial. Coll: late C.16–early 18. Shakespeare, in *Love's Labour's Lost*, V, ii; Ray.

honest woman (variant **of**), **make an,** v.t. To marry a mistress: low coll (and dial.): from ca 1560. Wycherley, in *Love in a Wood*, '*Dap*. Why she was my wench. *Gripe*. I'll make her honest then.' 2. From ca 1890, often jocular and meaning simply to marry (as thus give a higher official status to), and, as such, ordinary coll.

honey. As the *semen virile* it is C.19–20 low s., and, in form *poor honey*, a harmless, foolish, good-natured fellow, it is C.18–early 19 coll when not dial.

honey-blob. (Gen. in pl.) A large and ripe yellow gooseberry: Scots coll. Horace Walpole, in a letter of 1744.

honey-fall. A piece of good fortune: ca 1820–50. Perhaps by fusion – or a confusion – of HONEY MOON and *windfall*.

honey for a halfpenny, sell. To think very poorly of: coll: late C.16–17.

honey moon. (In C.19–20, one word.) The first month after marriage: coll (at first low): mid-C.16–18. 2. In C.19–20, the holiday spent together by a newly married couple before they settle down in their home: at first, perhaps coll, but very soon S.E. Ex *sweetness* = tenderness. cf. the proverbial *it is but honeymoon with them*: C.16–17.

honey or all turd with them, it is all. They are either sworn friends or bitter enemies: coll c.p. or perhaps proverb: mid-C.18–mid-19. Grose, 3rd ed.

honey-pot. The female pudend: C.18–19 low s. > coll or euphemism > coll. D'Urfey. cf. HONEY.

Hong-Kong!, go to. Go away!: coll: late C.19–20. Hong-Kong is prob. a euphemism for Hell: cf. *go to* BATH; HALIFAX; JERICHO; JERUSALEM.

honky-donks. A marine's feet: naval: late C.19–20. Ex East Anglian *honka-donka*, thick, heavy boots. cf. HOCK-DOCKIES.

honour!; honour bright! Upon my honour!, or as an emphatic or anxious query. Coll, orig. Anglo-Irish and somewhat low: resp. ca 1840–80 (as in Selby's *Antony and Cleopatra Married*, 1843) and from ca 1819 (e.g. Moore's *Tom Crib* and W. Black's *Beautiful Wretch*).

hoo-ha. An argument, a ROW; an artillery demonstration: military: from ca 1905.

hood, by my. An asseveration: mid-C.14–early 17; coll. Shakespeare. Origin unknown.

hood, put a bone in one's. To cuckold: mid-C.16–17 coll. The anon. play, *The Nice Wanton*, 1560, 'I could tell you who putteth a bone in your hood.'

hood, two faces under one. Double-dealing, n.: coll: C.15–18. In early C.19, often *hat* for *hood*.

hood for this fool, a. A proverbial c.p. of ca 1550–1620.

hoodlum. (A boy rough: U.S. only: from ca 1872. Hence:) Any, esp. if dangerous, rough: orig. (ca 1876) and still mainly U.S.; anglicized ca 1895. Prob. by printer's error for *noodlum*, ex *Muldoon*, the name of the leader of a San Franciscan gang of *street* ARABS; another suggestion is that it comes from the gang-cry, *huddle 'em!*: unlikely. cf. HOOLIGAN; LARRIKIN; *tough*. 2. Also *hoodlumism*, coll, never very gen.

hoodman. A blind man (cf. GROPER): C.18–early 19: ?orig. c.

hoodman, adj. Blind: C.18–early 19. **2.** Intoxicated: C.19 low. Prob. ex:

hoodman blind. Blind drunk: C.19 low. ?ex HOODMAN, adj., 1.

hoof. A human foot: low coll: late C.16–20. 1836, in M. Scott's *Cruise of the 'Midge'*; Sydney Watson, 1892, 'Teddy, look out, yer've got yer hoof on my trotters.' cf. TROTTERS.

hoof, v.t. To kick: low coll: from ca 1860. cf. TOE, v., and HOOF OUT.

hoof, bang or **beat** or **pad the.** To walk, tramp, run away: low coll: resp. C.17, mid-C.17–mid-19 (in C.17, *beat it on the hoof*), and —1838 and ob.; the first in Cotton, the second in Grose and, the older form, in B.E., the third in Dickens. Also, occ., *be upon the hoof*, ca 1710–78. cf. HOOF IT, and Shakespeare's 'Rogues, hence, avaunt . . . Trudge, plot, away ith' hoof' (*Merry Wives*).

hoof, under the. Down-trodden: coll: from ca 1840.

hoof in, recognize or **see one's.** To discern personal interference or influence in a matter: coll: 1860, Thackeray. Ex *the devil's hoof*.

hoof it. To go on foot; tramp: low coll: late C.17–20. Cumberland, in *The Fashionable Lover*, has *hoof* without *it* – prob. for the metre, though the usage occurs from ca 1640. cf. HOOFING. **2.** To decamp: c.: from ca 1870.

hoof out. To eject; dismiss, discharge: low coll: from ca 1850. Ex HOOF, v.

hoof the pad. To go on tramp; be a tramp: Australian: mid-C.19–20.

hoof-padder. A pedestrian: low: C.19. cf. HOOF, n., and PAD, v.

hoofing, vbl n. Walking; tramping: (low) coll: mid-C.17–20. From ca 1850, gen. *hoofing-it*.

hoofy. Splay- or large-footed: low coll: C.19–20, ob.

Hooghly mud. Butter: nautical: late C.19–20. Bowen, 'Originating in the ships on the Indian trade'.

***hook.** (Gen. pl.) A finger: c.: from ca 1820; ob. Maginn, in *Vidocq Versified*. 2. A thief, esp. a pickpocket: c.: from ca 1560. *Jack Juggler*, an anon. C.16 play, 'So yonder cometh that unhappy hook.' 3. An advantage, 'catch', imposture: low coll (?s.): from ca 1860; ob. cf. HOOK, ON THE, 2.

***hook,** v. To rob, steal, esp. to steal small articles from a (gen. shop-)window by cutting a small hole in it and 'fishing' with a piece of string that has a hook attached: mid-C.16–18 c. in specific sense; C.17–20, low coll in gen. sense. 2. Overreach, trick, gen. in past ppl passive: low (?orig. c.): late C.17–18. 3. To obtain, esp. in marriage: coll: from ca 1800: gen. of a woman, as in John Strange Winter's *Army Society*, 'I wonder if Mrs Traff has contrived to hook him for her sweet Laura.' Ex *hook a fish*. 4. See HOOK IT. 5. To move with a sudden twist or jerk: M.E.–Mod. Eng.; till C.19, S.E.; then coll rapidly > s. and dial.

hook! An exclamation implying doubt: Oxford University: ca 1860–1910. ?ex '?' or ex the v., 3, or ex HOOKY WALKER.

hook, on one's own. On one's own account, at one's own risk and/or responsibility: coll: orig. (1812), U.S., anglicized ca 1845. Thackeray in *Pendennis*. Origin not yet properly determined.

hook, on the. At an advantage: coll: late C.17–18. Congreve, 'Consider I have you on the hook.' 2. On the 'thieve': c.: C.19–20; ob. Ex HOOK, v., 1, or n., 2.

hook, sling or **take one's.** To run away; depart, secretly or hastily, or both: low: from ca 1860. H. (*sling*); Baumann, 1887 (both forms); Kipling, 1892, 'Before you sling your 'ook, at the 'ousetops take a look.' cf. HOOK IT. 2. Nautical and only in the *take* form, is the sense, to weigh anchor: from ca 1890; ob. 3. To die: since ca 1860.

hook and eye, adv. Arm in arm: tailors': from ca 1860. Ex the S.E. term, a metallic fastening, as for a dress.

***hook and snivey; hook-em** (or **'em** or **hookem)-snivey,** a corruption dating from ca 1800; (after ca 1820, the corrupted) **hookum snivey.** (In C.20, *snivey* often > *snivv(e)y*.) Abbr. *hook and snivey, with nix the buffer*, an underworld trick for feeding a dog (BUFFER) and an additional man for nothing (NIX); see HOOK, n., 2. c.: ca 1775–1850. G. Parker's illuminating *View of Society*. 2. Hence (of course omitting *with nix the buffer*), an impostor specializing in this trick: ca 1790–1860. (cf. HOOK-UM-SNIVEY, v.) 3. Cognately, and gen., like the next sense, in form *hook-um* (or *hookum*) *snivey*, 'a crook of thick iron wire in a wooden handle, used to undo the wooden bolts of doors from without', F. & H.: likewise c.: ca 1800–1905. 4. A sarcastic or derisory affirmation accompanied with hand to nose, or as an irrelevant answer (= no one) to, e.g. 'Who did that?': low, orig. and mostly Cockney: ca 1850–1915. 5. Hence, adj. in senses 1 and 2: late C.19–20; mostly dial.

hook (at the end), with a. (Often tagged with *of it*.) A phrase implying 'Don't you believe it!'; low, ob.: the shorter form, (—)1823; the longer, (—)1864, and resp. Bee and Traill. Accompanied by a crooking of the forefinger. cf. *over the* LEFT for the practice, HOOKY WALKER for the phrase.

***hook 'em snivey.** A variant of HOOK AND SNIVEY.

hook it. To decamp; depart hastily: (low) coll: from ca 1830. *Sessions*, Aug. 1835, 'Hobbs said, "Hook it, you b——s."' As *hook*, v.i., however, it dates from much earlier and comes ex HOOK, v., last sense. Whence HOOK, SLING ONE'S.

hook, line and sinker. Completely, utterly: coll: late C.19–20. Ex fishing.

hook-me-dinghy. Anything whose right name has temporarily slipped one's memory: naval: from ca 1890. cf. WIFF-LOW GADGET and JIMMY FIXING.

hook off. To remove (illicitly): low (—1887). cf. HOOK, v., 1 and 5. 2. To go away: Cockneys': late C.19–20.

hook on to. To attach oneself to; follow up; (orig. low) coll: from ca 1890. Milliken, 1892, 'It's nuts to 'ook on to a swell.'

hook-pointed (Scots **-pintled).** Imperfectly erected: low amorous coll: C.19.

***hook-pole lay.** To plunder a man after pulling him from his horse by means of a long, hooked pole: c.: C.18. Smith's *Highwaymen*, 1720.

hook-um-snivey. To cheat, esp. by feigned sickness: low: ca 1855–80. The *and* of HOOK AND SNIVEY corrupted to *um*.

hooked, ppl adj. Duped, tricked: see HOOK, v., esp. in sense 2.

Hookee Walker (*Lex. Bal.* spelling), see HOOKY WALKER.

***hookem snivey,** see HOOK AND SNIVEY.

***hooker.** A thief, esp. an ANGLER: c.: ca 1560–1870. (One of the third rank of canters.) 2. A sharper: C.17–18 c. 3. A pickpocket, esp. a watch-stealer: c. (—1888); ob. *Tit Bits*, 17 Nov. 1888. cf. the C.19–20 U.S. c. sense, a harlot. 4. A ship: depreciative or affectionate nautical s. (1823) >, ca 1880, coll. Perhaps ex Dutch *hoeker*, huckster. Often *old hooker* (—1865).

hookerman. A ship: nautical coll (—1894). Ex preceding, last sense.

hookey, play. To play truant: from ca 1890. (Orig. American.)

Hookey (Walker), see HOOKY WALKER.

***hooks.** The hands: c.: from ca 1825. Ex *hook*, a finger. Also *hooks and feelers*, as in the anon. *Five Years' Penal Servitude*, 1877; a thief, referring to hard work in prison, says that, when a man is released, 'in a week or two [he] can bring his hooks and feelers into full trim again.' 2. Spurs: military: late C.19–20.

hooks, drop or **go** or **pop off the.** To die: low: resp. from ca 1800, —1872, and 1837. Perhaps ex a felon's corpse dropping, from sheer decay, off the hooks from which it has been suspended. 2. (Gen. with *go*) to get married, usually of women: coll (—1876); ob.

hooks, off the, adj. Ill-tempered, peevish: mid-C.17–mid-19. Pepys, 1662. 2. Out of sorts or order: C.17 (? also early C.18). 3. Slightly mad: late C.18–mid-19. Scott, 1825, 'Everybody that has meddled in this . . . business is a little off the hooks . . . in plain words, a little crazy.' cf. S.E. *unhinged*. 4. Dead: low: Thackeray, 1848. This sense from *drop* (etc.) *off the* HOOKS; all senses except the last, which is s., are coll.

hooks, off the, adv. To excess: coll: C.17. D'Urfey. 2. Immediately; summarily: coll: from ca 1860. Trollope, in *Castle Richmond*, 'Baronets with twelve thousand a year cannot be married off the hooks.'

***hooks and feelers,** see HOOKS.

hookum. A regulation; *the h.*, 'the correct thing': military coll: late C.19–20; ob. Ex Hindustani *hukam*.

***hookum-snivey,** see HOOK AND SNIVEY and HOOK-UM-SNIVEY.

Hooky. The inevitable nickname of any man surnamed Walker: late C.19–20: mostly naval and military. Ex HOOKY WALKER.

hooky, adj. Rural Canadian coll for a cow given to using her horns: mid-C.19–20.

hooky, by! see HOOKY WALKER!

hooky, do. To apply fingers and thumb contemptuously to one's nose: streets': from ca 1860.

hooky, play, see HOOKEY, PLAY.

Hooky Walker! A phrase signifying that something either is not true or will not occur: (low) coll, from ca 1810. Also *Hook(e)y!* and *by hooky!* 2. Be off!: (low) coll: from ca 1830. Since ca 1840, gen. abbr. to *Walker!*, as in Dickens's *Christmas Carol*, 1843, ' "Buy it," said Scrooge. "Walker!" said the boy.' According to Bee, ex John Walker, a prevaricating hook-nosed spy.

hoolerfer. A fool: centre s.: from ca 1860; ob. cf. HUGMER.

hooligan. A lively rough, not necessarily nor usually criminal: from ca 1895: s. till ca 1910, then coll. Ex a 'joie-de-vivre' Irish family (the Houlihans) resident, in the middle 90s, in the Borough (London): W. For a description of the career of Patrick Hooligan (Houlihan), see Clarence Rook, *The Hooligan Nights*, 1899, ch. 2.

hoop. The female pudend: low: C.19–20; ob.

hoop, v. To beat, thrash: late C.18–mid-19.

hoop, go through the. To pass the Insolvent Debtors' court: C.19. Ex circus tricks.

hoop it, see last entry. 2. To run away: c. (—1839); †by 1900. Perhaps a perversion of *hop it*.

hoop one's barrel. To beat, thrash: low (—1785). cf. HOOP, v.

hoop-stick. The arm: low: ca 1860–1910.

hooper's, or **hoopers, hide.** Coïtion: C.18–mid-19 low, but never very gen. D'Urfey, 1719, in the notorious *Pills*. Ex the S.E. sense, hide-and-seek.

hoops-a-daisy! A variant, or possibly the origin, of UPS-A-DAISY!, up!: coll: C.19–20.

hoosh. A thick soup with plenty of body: 1905, R. F. Scott, *The Voyage of the*

'*Discovery*'. Just possibly ex dial. *hoosh!*, used in driving or scaring away pigs or poultry: such soup is a staple dish of explorers; its frequent appearance may well have induced a vigorous *hoosh!*, go away, but cf. Irish dial. *hoosh*, to heave, to raise.

hoot. Money; payment, wage: compensation: New Zealand and soon Australia from the 1850s. Ex Maori *utu* (money), often pronounced with clipped terminal.

hoot, care a. Care infinitesimally; always in negative or interrogative – i.e. potentially or implicatively negative – phrases or sentences: coll: from ca 1905. Possibly ex S.E. *hoot*, a cry of disapprobation, a shout expressive of obloquy; prob. an adoption of U.S. *hoot*, an abbr. of, and used in the same sense as, U.S. *hooter*, an atom, the least bit.

hooting pudding. A plum-pudding containing so few plums that they can be heard hooting to one another across the void: provincial: from ca 1860; ob.

hop. A ball, if informal; a dance: coll: from ca 1730. Jane Austen, 'At a little hop at the park, he danced from eight o'clock till four.'

hop, on the. (Esp. *catch on the hop*.) Unawares: (orig. low) coll (—1868). In that famous ballad, *The Chickaleary Cove*. 2. In the nick of time: coll: ca 1872–1905. 3. At a disadvantage: coll: from ca 1880; ob. Perhaps ex *on the hip*. 4. (adj.) On the go; unresting: coll: from ca 1890.

hop-and-go-kick. A lame person: tailors': from ca 1860; ob.

hop and hang all summer on the white spruce. A Canadian lumbermen's c.p.: from ca 1890.

hop-harlot. See HAP-HARLOT, of which it is an occ. variant.

hop in. To arrive: coll: from ca 1820; virtually †. cf. *pop in*.

hop-merchant. A dancing-master: low coll: late C.17–19. Occ. HOPPY. cf. CAPER-MERCHANT. 2. A fiddler: C.19–20.

hop-o'-my-thumb. A dwarf: coll: C.16–20; slightly ob. (Palsgrave has *upon*, the usual C.16 form.) Smollett, 'You pitiful hop-o'-my-thumb coxcomb'. Cf. JACK SPRAT.

hop off. To die: 1797, Mary Robinson, 'Must look in upon the rich old jade, before she hops off'; ob. cf. Craven dial. *hop* and HOP THE TWIG, 2. 2. To depart: coll (?orig. Cockney): late C.19–20.

hop (or jump) over the broom(stick), see BROOMSTICK, JUMP . . .

hop-picker. A harlot: low (?orig. c.): from ca 1880. Also HOPPING WIFE.

***hop-pickers.** The queens of all four suits: gambling, c.: from ca 1885.

hop-pole. A tall, slight person: (low) coll: 1850, Smedley.

hop, skip and jump, – do with a. To do with ease: coll, mostly Cockneys': from ca 1890.

hop the Charley (or **-ie**). To decamp: low: from ca 1870; ob. Ex CHARLEY WAG.

***hop the twig.** To depart, esp. if suddenly: orig. (—1785), c.: from ca 1860, low; slightly ob. *All the Year Round*, 9 June 1888, '*To hop the twig* . . . and the like are more flippant than humorous.' Ex bird-life. Whence 2, to die: low: 1797, Mary Robinson, in *Walsingham* (cf. HOP OFF, above). *Punch*, in its 1st volume, 'Clare pines in secret – hops the twig and goes to glory in white muslin.' cf. CROAK; GO WEST; KICK THE BUCKET; *lose the number of one's* MESS; SLIP ONE'S BREATH; SNUFF IT.

hop the wag. To play truant or CHARLEY WAG: low: from ca 1850; ob. Mayhew, 'They often persuaded me to hop the wag.' cf. HOP THE CHARLEY.

hop-thumb. A C.16–17 variant of HOP-O'-MY-THUMB.

hop whore, pipe thief(, hangman lead the dance)! A proverbial c.p. of ca 1530–1660. 'Proverbs' Heywood; Davies of Hereford.

hopeful; much more frequently **young hopeful.** A boy, youth, young man: ironic coll: from ca 1855, ca 1720, resp. 'Cuthbert Bede', in *Tales of College Life*, has the former. Occ. of a girl.

Hopkins; Mr Hopkins. A lame person: jocular coll (—1785); ob. cf. HOPPY and:

Hopkins!, don't hurry. In mid-C.19–20 U.S., ironic to slow persons; but in C.17–18 England it implied, Don't be too hasty, and took the form *as well come* (or *hasty*) *as Hopkin(s), that came to jail over night, and was hanged the next morning*. cf. preceding term.

hopper. The mouth: low: mid-C.19–20; ob. 2. A grasshopper: Australian coll: late C.19–20.

hopper, go a. To go quickly: sporting: ca 1870–1915.

hopper-arsed. Large-bottomed: coll: late C.17–early 19. D'Urfey, 'Hopper-arsed Nancy'; Grose, 'from . . . resemblance to a small basket, called a hopper'. 2.

Sometimes, however, it appears to = shrunken-arsed: B.E.'s definition is susceptible of this meaning; not so Grose's.

***hopper-docker.** A shoe: c.: ca 1810–50. Perhaps a corruption of HOCK-DOCKIES.

hopping Giles. A cripple: s. (—1785) >, ca 1850, coll; ob. Ex *St Giles*, the patron of cripples. *Household Words*, 27 June 1885. cf.:

hopping Jesus. A lame person: low: from ca 1860; ob. cf. CREEPING JESUS.

hopping pot, the. The lot; esp. 'That's the hopping pot', the end of the day's work: rhyming s.: late C.19–20.

hopping wife, see HOP-PICKER. In Anon., *Indoor Paupers*, 1888.

hoppo. A customs-house officer: Anglo-Chinese coll: from ca 1710. Ex Chinese *hoo-poo*, the Board of Revenue; abbr. *hoppo-man*.

hoppy. A lame person: coll: C.19–20; ob. 2. A dancing-master: mid-C.19–20. 3. A fiddler: low coll (—1892); ob. S. Watson, in *Wops the Waif*.

horizontal. A courtesan: fast life: 1886; ob. Ex Fr. *horizontale*. cf. the next entry, sense 2.

horizontal refreshment. Food taken standing, esp. a snack at a bar: jocular coll: from ca 1890; ob. 2. Coïtion: low pedantic coll: from ca 1870. cf.:

horizontalize. To have sexual intercourse: low pedantic: from ca 1845; ob.

horn. The nose, esp. if noisy: C.19–20; ob. low coll. Also *horn(e)y*. 2. As a drink, almost wholly U.S. since C.18. 3. Gen. in pl, indicative of one's having been cuckolded: despite F. & H., this sense and the v. *horn*, to cuckold, are definitely S.E.: likewise S.E. are most of the *horn(s)* = cuckoldom terms listed by F. & H.; all that are relevant follow hereinafter. 4. The physical sign of sexual excitement in the male; in C.19 often used loosely of women. Low coll: mid-C.18–20. Always preceded by *the*; cf. HORN, GET THE. Hence, *get* (or *give*) *cheap horn*, to be sexually excited by smutty talk or reading-matter: late C.19–20. 5. The male member: coll: C.18; being the origin of the preceding sense.

horn, at the sign of the. In cuckoldom: late C.17–early 19 coll.

horn, come out of the little end of the. To get the worst of a bargain, be reduced in circumstances; after great efforts, to fail: coll: the first two senses, C.17–early 18; the third, from ca 1840 and mostly U.S. Moreover, in the C.17–18 usages, the form is almost always *be squeezed through a horn*.

horn, cure the. To have sexual intercourse: C.19–20, low coll.

horn, get or have the. To have a priapism: late C.18–20: low coll.

horn, in a. A phrase that advises disbelief or refusal: (ex Eng. dial.) mostly U.S., where recorded as early as 1840; it never > very gen. in Britain and was †by 1910.

horn, wind one's or the. To publish one's having been cuckolded: C.17–18. cf. the C.17–18 proverb, *he had better put his horns in his pocket than wind them.* 2. To break wind: C.18–mid-19 low. 3. To blow one's nose hard: from ca 1850.

horn and hide, all. (Of cattle.) Nothing but skin and bone: Australia (—1890).

horn and the hoof!, by the. C.17: 'A Butcher . . . sweares by the horne and the hoofe (a poor othe . . .)', Day, 1640.

horn-colic. A temporary priapism: mid-C.18–mid-19 low. cf. IRISH TOOTHACHE.

horn-fisted. With hard, callous hands: nautical coll: mid-C.19–20.

horn-grower or **-merchant.** A married man: coll: C.18.

horn in on. To intrude upon; to interfere in: Australian: late C.19–20. Ex cattle.

horn-mad. As stark-mad, even at being cuckolded, it is – like *horn-work* – S.E., but as extremely lecherous it is a C.19–20 (ob.) low coll.

horn-pipe or **hornpipe.** A cry of condemnation by the audience: theatrical: 1885, *Daily News*, 6 May; very ob.

horn-pipe, dance the. To be a cuckold: C.17–18 jocular coll.

horn-pipes in fetters. A jigging dance: Cockney (—1851); †by 1900. Mayhew.

***horn-thumb.** A pickpocket: ca 1565–1620. Jonson, 'A child of the horn-thumb, a babe of booty . . . a cut-purse'.

Horncastle, the member for. A cuckold: C.18–early 19 jocular coll.

horned range(s). A fife-rail; a shot-rack: nautical coll, the latter naval (and †by 1890): C.19–20.

Horner, Miss. The female pudend: C.19–20 (ob.): low.

hornet. A cantankerous person: (low) coll: from ca 1840; ob. Ex the S.E. sense, a virulent and persistent enemy. cf. the ironical Gloucestershire saying, *he is as mild as a hornet*.

horney and **hornie,** see HORNY.

hornification; hornify. A priapism; to procure one: late C.18–20; ob.: low coll.

horning, vbl n. and ppl adj. of HORN, 4.

Hornington, old. The male member: C.19 low. cf. HORN, n., 5.

hornpipe, see HORN-PIPE. **horns,** see HORN, n., 3.

horns. Cattle: Australian coll: late C.19–20.

horns, draw or **pluck** or **pull** or **shrink in one's.** To retract, withdraw, cool down: coll: from C.14, mid-C.17 (ob.), late C.16, and C.15 (†by C.17), resp. All were orig. coll, but they quickly > S.E.; then, excepting the last, they seem to have been coll ca 1760–1890, from which date they have certainly been S.E. cf. *retire into one's shell*, also ex a snail.

horns-to-sell. A loose wife: coll: C.18–mid-19. 2. A cuckold: coll: same period.

Hornsey, knight of. A cuckold: mid-C.17–early 19 punning coll. The anon. play, *Lady Alimony*. cf. HORNCASTLE.

hornswoggle. Nonsense, humbug: ca 1860–1905. Ex U.S. *hornswoggle*, to cheat, deceive (1852).

horny, horney, hornie. Scots coll for the devil: late C.18–20. Gen. *auld Hornie*. 2. A constable: c. of ca 1810–70. Extant in Anglo-Irish s.: witness E.D.D. 3. The nose: low: ca 1820–1910. Ex HORN, 1. 4. A street horn-player: proletarian: from ca 1880.

horny, adj. With rising *membrum*; disposed for carnal woman: C.19–20 low coll. Esp. in *feel horny*.

horny, old. (Or with capitals.) The male member: C.19–20 low coll. 2. See HORNY, n., 1.

horomai! see HAEREMAI!

horrible. Excessive; immoderate: mid-C. 15–20: S.E. till ca 1830, then coll. Lady Mary Wortley Montague, 1718, 'This letter is of a horrible length'. The same applies to the adv. cf.:

horrid. Offensive; detested; very bad or objectionable: coll: from ca 1665. Esp. as a feminine term of strong aversion.

horrid, adv. Horridly; very objectionably: 1615: coll till ca 1830, then low coll.

horrid horn. A fool, a half-wit: Anglo-Irish of the streets: ca 1850–1900. Ex Erse *omadhaun*, a brainless fellow.

horridly. An intensive before adjj. denoting qualities objected to: coll: late C.18–20.

horrors. (Gen. with *the*.) The first stage of *delirium tremens*: low coll: from ca 1859. 2. Low spirits, a fit of horror: coll: from ca 1765; ob. Goldsmith; Miss Ferrier; F. W. Robinson, in *Mr Stewart's Intentions*, 1864, 'Sermons always gave me the horrors.' 3. (Without *the*.) Sausages: see CHAMBER OF HORRORS. 4. In c., handcuffs: from ca 1860; ob.

Horrors, Chamber of, see CHAMBER OF HORRORS.

horrors, have the blue. To have *delirium tremens*: coll (—1887); slightly ob.

horse. A lottery ticket hired out by the day: ca 1725–80. Fielding. 2. A day's leave of absence from the Fleet Prison: debtors': ca 1815–50. Pierce Egan, *Life in London*, 1821. 3. Work charged for before completion: workmen's: 1760. Abbr. the orig. form, *horse-flesh*. 4. A £5 note: low: from ca 1860. 5. (With capitals.) Horsemonger Lane Gaol: c. of ca 1850–90. Mayhew. Also *the Old Horse*. 6. An arrogant or supercilious officer: nautical (—1867); ob. 7. Hence, a strict disciplinarian: naval: mid-C.19–20; ob. 8. See SALT HORSE. 9. A mud-bank, esp. in estuary waters: bargees': from ca 1880. If you *get astride* it on a falling tide you must keep your seat until rescued by the next flood.

horse, v. To possess a woman: coll: C.17–20, ob. Ex a stallion covering a mare. 2. To flog: C.19 coll. cf. HORSED, BE. 3. To outdo another, esp. at piece-work: workmen's: ca 1860–1910. *All the Year Round*, 13 July 1867. 4. See HORSE IT and cf. DEAD HORSE and HORSE, n., 3.

horse, all. (Of a jockey) very small: coll: 1860, O. W. Holmes. (Not typically U.S.)

horse, as good as a shoulder of mutton for or **to a sick.** Utterly useless or worthless: coll: mid-C.16–mid-18. Jonson.

horse, as holy as a. Extremely holy: C.16 coll, somewhat proverbial. Palsgrave.

horse, as strong as a. (Of a person only) very strong: coll: from ca 1700. Ned Ward; Douglas Jerrold, in *Mrs Caudle*, 'You're not as strong as a horse.'

horse, eat like a. To have a very large appetite: coll: C.18–20.

horse, flog (occ. mount on) a dead. To engage in fruitless effort: coll: from ca 1840. Ex:

horse, flog (also **work,** or **work for**) **the dead,** see DEAD HORSE and HORSE, n., 3.

horse, old and **one-,** see resp. OLD HORSE and ONE-HORSE.

horse, put the cart before the, see CART . . .

horse, put the saddle on the right. To apportion (esp. blame) accurately: coll:

C.17–18. cf. the C.17–mid-18 proverbial *the fault of the horse is put on the saddle.*

horse, ride (occ. mount) the high. To put on airs, stand on one's dignity; (haughtily) take offence: coll: from ca 1715. Addison has *great,* while in C.19–20 one occ. finds *be on* or *get on.* Prob. ex a *high hobby-horse* in the nursery.

horse, salt, see SALT HORSE.

horse, sick as a. Very sick *without* vomiting: late C.17–19: coll.

horse, talk. To talk big or boastingly: coll: 1891, Kipling. Ex *talk horse,* i.e. of the turf.

horse and cart. Heart: rhyming s. (—1909).

horse and foot. With all one's strength: coll: ca 1600–1760. (Extant in dial.) Horace Walpole.

horse and harness, come for. That is, for one's own ends: coll: C.15–16. Caxton.

horse and man. (Often preceded by *undone.*) Completely: C.17 coll. ?ex jousting.

horse!, and thou shalt have grass, – live. Well, let's wait and see! Later on, we'll see! In C.18–early 19, coll, as in Swift's *Polite Conversation*; then dial., mainly Lancashire.

horse and trap. Gonorrhoea: since ca 1870. Rhyming CLAP.

horse away. To spend in a lottery (cf. HORSE, n., 1).

horse-box. The mess-room of the sergeant-major(s) of Marines: naval: late C.19–20.

horse-boxes. (Rare in singular.) 'The senior military officers' cabins in the old naval troopers': naval: ca 1850–1910. Bowen.

horse-breaker. A woman hired to ride in the park: ca 1860–70: Society. 2. Hence, a courtesan given to riding, esp. in the park: Society (—1864); ob. by 1900. *Public Opinion,* 30 Sept. 1865, 'These *demi-monde* people, anonymas, horse-breakers, hetairae . . . are by degrees pushing their way into society.'

horse-buss. A resounding kiss; a bite: coll (—1785); †by 1890. A development from HORSE-KISS.

horse-capper (or -coper), -courser (or -coser), or -chaunter. A dealer in worthless or tampered horses. The last, C.19–20 (ob.), has always been low coll; *h-capper* is a corruption of *h.-coper,* which, despite its taint of unsavouriness, was always S.E.; both *-courser,* low coll after ca 1750, and *-coser* were orig. S.E., the latter being somewhat dial.

horse-collar. A halter: an occ. variation, mainly C.18, of HORSE('S)-NIGHTCAP. 2. The female pudend: low: C.19–20; ob. 3. A very long wide collar: tailors': from ca 1860.

horse-coser or -courser, see HORSE-CAPPER.

horse-duffing, see DUFF, v., and DUFFING (esp. *cattle-duffing*).

horse-faker. A horse-dealer: low (—1887). cf. HORSE-CAPPER.

horse-flesh: see HORSE, n., 3; HORSE IT; and DEAD HORSE. (*Horse-flesh* is orig. – C.17 – printers' s.)

horse foaled on an acorn, a or the. The gallows: ca 1670–1850: low proverbial > literary s. Smollett, Grose; Lytton, Ainsworth. 2. 'The triangles or crossed halberds under which soldiers were flogged', F. & H.: ca 1790–1870: military.

horse-godmother. 'A large masculine woman', Grose, 1st ed.: (rather low) coll: ca 1570–1890; now – and perhaps orig. – dial. Wolcot, 'In woman angel sweetness let me see, | No galloping horse-godmother for me'; Thackeray.

horse is soon carried, a short. 'A little Business is soon Dispatched,' B.E.: coll: ca 1670–1770.

horse is troubled with corns, that. That horse is foundered: jocular coll: mid-C.17–mid-18.

horse it. To charge, in one's week's tally, for work not yet completed, the unprofitable remainder being DEAD HORSE: workmen's (—1857). 2. See also HORSE, n., 3, and v., 2.

horse-kiss. A rough kiss: coll: ca 1670–1760. cf. HORSE-BUSS. Extant in dial. as 'a pretended kiss which is really a bite,' E.D.D.

horse ladder, send for a. To send on a fool's errand: rural (esp. Wiltshire) coll: mid-C.18–early 19. The victim was told that it was needed *to get up the horses* (*to finish a hay-mow*: Grose, 3rd ed.).

horse-latitudes. That space in the Atlantic which, lying north of the trade winds, is noted for baffling winds: nautical: from ca 1775; ob. 'Perhaps adapted from Sp. *golfo de las yeguas,* "the gulph of mares, so the Spaniards call the great ocean, betwixt Spain and the Canary Islands" (Stevens), supposed to be from contrast with the *golfo de las damas* (of ladies), from Canaries to West Indies, usually smooth and with favourable winds,' W.

horse-laugh. A guffaw: coll >, ca 1890,

S.E.: from ca 1710. Pope. ?punning *hoarse*.

horse-leech. An insatiable person; a whore: coll: mid-C.16–mid-17. Jonson. Prob. ex: 2. A quack: late C.16–17. Hall, in *Satires*, 1597, 'No horse-leech but will look for larger fee.' Ex lit. S.E. sense. 3. Whence too: an extortioner; a miser: coll: from ca 1545; ob.

horse-load to a cart-load, fall away from a. To put on weight suddenly: ironic coll: mid-C.17–early 19. Swift.

horse lop. A pudding – or puddings – of plumless suet: military: from ca 1870; ob.

horse-marine. An awkward person: ca 1820–60. Perhaps ex the heraldic and †*horse-marine*, a sea-horse. cf.:

horse-marines, the. 'A mythical corps, very commonly cited in jokes and quizzes on the innocent', F. & H.: coll: from ca 1820: ob., except in form *the marines*. Scott, 'Come, none of your quizzing ... Do you think we belong to the horse-marines?' Ex an incident in 1796, when the 17th Lancers, on a passage to the West Indies, did duty as marines. 2. Men that contract for the horse-traction of casual vessels: canal-men's (esp. in N.E. England): late C.19–20. cf.:

horse-marines!, tell that to the. Don't be silly!, or Do you think I'm a fool?! Coll: ca 1830–1910. (See MARINES!) Occ. amplified with *the sailors won't believe it* or *when they're riding at anchor*.

horse-milliner. As a dandified trooper, hardly eligible. 2. A saddle- and harness-maker: coll: ca 1815–80. Ex the S.E. sense.

horse-nails. Money, esp. cash: low (—1859). cf. BRADS; HADDOCK.

horse-nails, feed on. 'So to play as not so much to advance your own score as to keep down your opponent's,' F. & H.: cribbage: ca 1860–1914.

horse-nails, knock into. To defeat heavily: low coll: from ca 1870; ob. cf. *knock into a* COCKED HAT.

horse- or **horse's-nightcap.** A halter; esp. in *die in a horse('s)-nightcap*, to be hanged: low coll, ex low s. (?ex c.): late C.16–19. cf. ANODYNE NECKLACE; CHOKER, 5; *hempen cravat*; TYBURN *tippet*.

horse of another colour, (that's) a. (That is) quite another matter: coll: orig. (1790s) U.S., anglicized ca 1840 by Barham. Undoubtedly suggested by Shakespeare's 'My purpose is indeed a horse of that colour' (*Twelfth Night*, II, iii, 181).

horse-pox. An intensive of POX, esp. in adjuration of asseveration: mid-C.17–18 low coll. e.g. 'Ay, with a horse-pox'.

horse-Protestant. A churchman: tailors': from ca 1860; ob.

horse-sense. Common sense, esp. if unrefined and somewhat earthy: orig. (1833), U.S.; anglicized ca 1895 as a coll.

horse-shoe. The female pudend: C.18–20 (ob.) low. cf. HORSE-COLLAR.

horse sick, enough ... see SICK AS A CAT.

horse-sovereign. 'A twenty-shilling piece with Pistrucci's effigies of St George and the Dragon', F. & H.: coll (mostly low): ca 1870–1900. *London Figaro*, 26 Jan. 1871.

horse to a hen, a. Long odds: sporting coll: ca 1810–60. *Boxiana*, III, 1821.

horse to market, run before one's. To count unhatched chickens: coll: late C.16–17. Shakespeare.

horse with (or Bayard of) ten toes, ride (up)on a. To walk: coll: C.17–early 19. cf. MARROWBONE (punning *Marylebone*) STAGE and SHANKS'S MARE.

horsed, be. To be flogged; to take on one's back a person to be flogged: coll: ca 1675–1895. 'Hudibras' Butler; Smollett; *Notes and Queries*, 1 Jan. 1881. Ex the wooden horse used as a flogging stool.

horses and mares, play at. To coït: schoolboys': from ca 1850; ob.

horse's head is swollen so big that he cannot come out of the stable, his. He owes much money to the ostler: a C.17 c.p.

horse's leg. A bassoon: military bandsmen's (—1909). Ware, 'From its shape'.

horse's meal. Food without drink (esp. without strong liquor): ca 1780–1850: s. >, by 1820, coll. cf. *dog's supper* and dial. *horse-feast*.

horse's necklace. A contemporaneous variant of HORSE-NIGHTCAP.

horse's nightcap. See HORSE-NIGHTCAP, than which it is more gen.

horses together, they cannot set (occ. hitch or stable) their. They cannot agree: mid-C.17–18 coll as in Swift and Garrick; C.19–20 dial.

horsy-face. An unpopular officer, esp. if he had a long face: naval: mid-C.19–20; slightly ob.

hortus. A perfect example of C.18 pedantic s.: the female privy parts. L. for GARDEN.

hose, in my other. Expressive of refusal or disbelief: late C.16–17 coll. Florio. cf. *I don't* THINK!; *in a* HORN; *over the* LEFT.

hosed and shod. (Gen. preceded by *come in* and in past tense.) Born to a good estate:

ca 1670–1750. cf. *born with a* SILVER SPOON IN ONE'S MOUTH.

hospital game. Football, esp. Rugby: non-aristocratic coll: 1897; ob. Ware, 'From the harvest of broken bones it produces'.

hospitality, partake of Her or **His Majesty's.** To be in gaol: jocular coll: 1894.

hostel. An inn providing food for horses: s.: mid-C.17.

hot. A mellay at football; a crowd: Winchester College (—1878). The second sense is ob. 2. 'I . . . had a pot of *hot*, which is beer with gin in it,' *Sessions*, March 1847: public-houses': ca 1830–90. 3. A penny; *hots*, money: Felsted School: late C.19–20.

hot, v.i. To crowd, or form a mob: Winchester College (—1878); ob. Also *hot down* and *hot up*: R. G. K. Wrench. 2. To heat: coll from mid-C.19; earlier – from late M.E. – it was S.E.

hot, adj. Alive; vehement: coll: from ca 1860. 2. Very reckless, boisterous; careless of decorum; (of a literary work) licentious: coll: from ca 1885. J. Runciman, in *The Chequers*, 1888. 3. In c., well known to the police: from ca 1830; ob. 4. Venereally diseased: low: C.19–20 (?ob.). 5. Much betted-on. Esp. in *hot favourite*. Orig. (1894) racing.

hot, catch or **get it; give it hot.** To be severely thrashed, defeated, or reprimanded; to thrash, defeat, reprimand severely: coll: from ca 1860 for *give*, ca 1859 *catch*, and 1872 *get*.

hot, cop it, see COP, v., 3.

hot a stomach as to burn the clothes off his back, have so. To pawn one's clothes for drink: mid-C.18–early 19: coll.

hot and hot, adj.-adv. and n. (Dishes) served in succession, so soon as cooked: 1771, Smollett, the adj.-adv.; 1842, Tennyson, the n.: coll till ca 1880, then S.E. Occ. in fig. usage.

hot and strong, give it (to) a person. To punish severely, either physically or verbally: coll: late C.19–20.

hot-arsed. Extremely lascivious (only of women): low coll: C.17–20. cf. S.E. †*hot-backed*.

hot as similes to be considered for this dictionary are these: (Perhaps, but most probably not) *hot as (a) toast*, C.15–18, and *warm as (a) toast*, C.19–20, *hot as coals*, ca 1550–1620, and *hot as fire*; *hot as blazes*, C.19–20, however, is downright s., while *hot as hell* is merely coll; *hot as buggery* is low s. > low coll; (of a person only) *hot as if* (e.g.) *he had a bellyful of wasps and salamanders*, ca 1700–50.

hot at, see HOT ON. **hot beef,** see HOT MEAT.

***hot beef, give.** To cry 'stop thief': underworld rhyming s. (—1877); ob. Horsley, cf. BEEF, n.

hot blanketeer. 'A woman who pawns her blankets while they are warm from being slept in – she redeeming them before night-time': proletarian: late C.19–20; ob. Ware.

hot bricks, like a cat on, adj. and adv. Restive(ly); uncomfortable (or -ly): coll: from ca 1880. J. S. Winter, 'Lady Mainwaring looked . . . like a cat on hot bricks.'

hot cakes, like, see CAKES, LIKE HOT.

hot coppers. (Occ. singular.) The parched throat to be expected after a drinking-bout: low: 1806, John Davis; ob. Thackeray, ' "Nothing like that beer", he remarked, "when the coppers are hot." ' cf. COOL ONE'S COPPERS, also MOUTH, 4.

hot corner. 'A position in which one is threatened or bullied': non-aristocratic coll: '1854 on', says Ware.

hot cross bun. Son: theatrical rhyming s.: late C.19–20.

hot cup of tea, a. HOT STUFF: ca 1880–1914. William Westall, *Sons of Belial*, 1895.

hot down, see HOT, v., 1.

hot flannel; warm flannel; flannel. A drink of gin and beer, heated after the addition of sugar, nutmeg, etc.: coll: resp. 1789 (Parker), 1823 (Bee), and 1858 (Mayhew). cf. HOT-STOPPING.

hot gospeller. A fanatical preacher, or a preaching fanatic: coll (—1893).

hot lot. A late C.19–20 variant of HOT MEMBER.

hot meat; occ. **hot mutton** or **beef.** A fast woman, a prostitute; the female pudend: low: C.19. cf. BIT.

hot member; hot un. A debauchee, an either sex rake: C.19–20 (ob. the former). 2. A person contemptuous of the conventions: C.19–20. (Both senses are low coll.) 3. A dangerous and/or quarrelsome person: low s. > coll: from ca 1880, *h. m.* being very ob. (The earlier term – *h. m.* – may have been suggested by HOT SHOT.)

hot milk. The *semen virile*: low: C.19–20.

hot on. Unusually good or skilful at: from ca 1895: coll. Variant, *hot at*. cf. HOT STUFF.

hot place, the. Hell: orig. (ca 1840)

euphemistic; but from ca 1890, coll. *Blackwood's Magazine*, March 1891.

hot potato. A waiter: (approximately) rhyming s.: 1880: orig. and mainly music-halls'.

hot potato, drop like a. To abandon with – often callous or unseemly – alacrity: (orig. low) coll: from before 1893.

hot press. 'A particularly vigorous comb by the Press Gang': nautical: late C.18–mid-19. (The Press Gang was disenrolled in 1835.)

hot pudding for supper, have a. (Of women only) to coït: low: C.19–20. Ex PUDDING (2), the male member.

hot roll with cream, a. Coïtion: low: late C.19–20.

hot shot (indeed), a; hot shot in a mustard pot (when both one's heels stand right up), a. Always preceded by the v. *to be*, which is gen. in the present tense, and indicative of contemptuous irony: ca 1650–1750. Ex *hot-shot*, one who shoots eagerly with a firearm.

hot stomach, see HOT A STOMACH . . .

hot-stopping. Hot spirits and water: 1861, Whyte-Melville, 'No man can drink hot-stopping the last thing at night, and get up in the morning without remembering that he has done so.' ob. cf. HOT FLANNEL and HOT TIGER.

hot stuff. A person very excellent, skilful or energetic (*at*, e.g., a game): coll: from the early 1890s.

hot tiger. Hot-spiced ale and sherry: Oxford University (—1860); ob. cf. HOT FLANNEL; HOT-STOPPING.

hot time (of it), give (a person) **a.** To make him thoroughly uncomfortable; to reprimand severely: coll: late C.19–20. See also HOT, CATCH IT.

hot 'un. A severe punch or blow: pugilistic: mid-C.19–20. Augustus Mayhew, *Paved with Gold*, 1857. 2. See HOT MEMBER.

hot up, see HOT, v., 1.

hot water. (Constructed, sense 1 with *cost* (*one*), sense 2 with *be in.*) Trouble; great discomfort: coll: ca 1535–1750. 2. Hence, a scrape: coll: from ca 1760. Gayton, 1659, 'This same search hath not cost me hot water (as they say)'; Lord Malmesbury, 1765, 'We are kept, to use the modern phrase, in hot water'; *Punch's Almanack*, 29 Nov. 1846, 'The *Times* newspaper first printed by steam, 1814, and has kept the country in hot water ever since.' (Until ca 1890, *The Times*, until ca 1900 *Punch*, had much less of a reputation for respectability than they now enjoy (?).)

hot-water play. A farce: theatrical coll, adopted in 1885 from U.S.; ob. Ware, 'The actors [?characters] in the play always being in difficulties until the fall of the curtain'.

hot with. Spirits with hot water and sugar: coll: 1837; Thackeray, 1862, fig. cf. CIDER-AND and COLD WITHOUT, and contrast Fr. *café avec*.

hotel; occ. Cupid's hotel or Cupid's Arms. The female pudendum: low: C.19–20, ob. cf. COCK INN. (This kind of coll humour is moribund, thank heaven!)

hotel-barbering, n. Bilking; lodging at hotels and departing without paying the bill: low (—1892). *Daily Chronicle*, 28 March 1892.

hotel-beat. 'A frequenter of hotels with no means of payment': adopted, before 1909, from U.S. (Ware.)

Hotel Lockhart. A lower classes' c.p. 'satirical attack upon doubtful grandeur': ca 1890–1914.

hotel warming-pan. A chambermaid: C.19–20 ob. In C.18, SCOTCH WARMING-PAN. A C.19–20 variant: WARMING PAN.

Hotspurs, you are none of the. A c.p. retort to, or comment on, a noisy braggart, with the implication that he is a coward: ca 1720–1870. cf. HASTINGS SORT.

Hottentot. 'A stranger come from the West [sc. of London]', G. R. Sims: East End of London (—1880). Esp. in the playful street-cry, *Hottentots!* 2. A fool: low coll: C.19. Ex the Hottentots' reputation for stupidity.

hottie. An Edinburgh High School term for 'one who has something pinned to his back of which he knows nothing', E.D.D.: mid-C.19–20.

hound. An undergraduate not on the foundation: King's College, Cambridge: late C.18–early 19. *The Anecdotes of Bowyer*.

Hounslow Heath. The teeth: rhyming s. (—1857). Also HAMPSTEAD HEATH, which displaced it ca 1890.

hour-grunter. A watchman: s.: Ned Ward, 1703.

houri of Fleet Street. A harlot: orig. (ca 1880) journalistic, > gen. ca 1890, †ca 1910.

house. A brothel: c. and low: from ca 1860. 2. (Preceded by *the*.) The workhouse: proletarian coll (—1861). Mayhew. 3. The public-house: coll, mostly Cockney

(—1887). 4. A gambling form of lotto: military s. (from late 1890s). Its other name, *box and numbers*, partly explains the semantics.

house, be atop of (occ. **on) the.** A C.17 variant of HOUSETOP, BE AT THE.

House, father of the. The oldest-elected member of the House of Commons: from ca 1850: Parliamentary s. >, ca 1890, coll.

house-bit; occ. **-keeper** or **-piece.** A paramour servant: low: from ca 1850; ob.

house broke up. A military c.p. indicative of complete despair: from ca 1870; ob.

house-dog. House tutor: several Public Schools': from ca 1880.

house-dove. A stay-at-home: 1579: coll till ca 1660, then S.E.; †by 1800.

house-farmer or **-knacker.** Resp. London coll and s. for 'landlord', gen. pl, as in Baumann, who, in 1887, scathingly describes them as 'Londoner Blutsauger, die den Armen schlechte, wohlfeile Wohnungen vermieten.'

house of call. 'The usual lodging Place of Journey-men Tailors', B.E.: late C.17–18 tailors' s. > coll in early C.18 and S.E. by 1790. (Also of other occupations.)

house of civil reception. A brothel: C.18–early 19 coll.

House of Commons; house of office. A water-closet: the former, always s.; the latter, orig. coll but S.E. by 1690. Resp. mid-C.19–20, ob.; C.17–19. Chapman, in *May-Day*, 1611, 'No room save you turn out my wife's coal-house, and her other house of office attached to it'; Smollett.

house on fire, like a. Very quickly or energetically: coll: from ca 1805. W. Irving, 1809, 'like five hundred houses on fire'; 1837, Dickens.

house on one's head, pull (in **C**.19 occ. **bring) an old.** To involve oneself in trouble: coll: C.17–mid-19. Topsell.

house out of the windows, throw (in C.16–17 occ. **cast,** in C.17 often **fling) the.** To make a great noise or disturbance in a house: mid-C.16–mid-19 coll, then dial. Dickens, in *Boz*, quotes it in form 'regularly turned out o' windows', i.e. in an uproar.

house-roof, up in the, see HOUSETOP, BE AT THE.

house-tailor. An upholsterer: coll: late C.17–18.

house that Jack built, the. A prison: low: from ca 1860; ob. Baumann. 2. 'The first permanent building in the Whale Island Gunnery School': naval: late C.19–20; slightly ob. Bowen.

house (or **tenement** or **apartments) to let.** A widow: resp. mid-C.18–20 (ob.), C.18–19, C.19–20 (ob.).

house under the hill. The female pudend: low: C.19–20; ob.

house-wallah. One who, esp. a Gypsy who, lives in a house in contradistinction to a tent: Gypsies' coll (—1900), esp. in Hampshire.

housebreaker. A breaker-up of houses: industrial: from ca 1895.

household brigade, join the. (Of men) to marry: coll (—1881); ob. *Home Tidings*, April 1881. Punning the name of the English regiment.

houses, (as) safe as. Perfectly safe: coll: 1859. E. Yates, 1864, 'I have the means of doing that, as safe as houses.' Perhaps, as H. suggests, the phrase arose 'when the railway bubbles began to burst and speculation again favoured houses'.

housetop (or **top of the house** or, C.16–early 17, **house-roof), be at (**or **up in) the.** To be, become, very angry (cf. *hit the roof*): coll: *up in*, ca 1540–1660; *at*, ca 1630–1800, then dial. Anon., *Scoggin's Jests*, 1626. cf. *up in the* BOUGHS.

housewife. The *pudendum muliebre*: C.19–20 (ob.) low.

housey, adj. Belonging to the Hospital: Christ's Hospital: C.19–20.

housle. To hustle, of which, presumably, it is a corruption: Winchester College: from ca 1850.

hove-down. Bed-ridden, confined to bed: nautical (—1887).

hoveller. A beach-thief, a lawless boatman: nautical: from before 1769, when recorded by Falconer. Ex his living in a hovel. cf. BEACH-COMBER.

how!, here's, see HERE'S HOW!

how and about. Concerning; all about: coll: ca 1750–1830. Richardson, in *Grandison*, 'Emily wrote you all how-and-about it.'

how are you off for soap? A city c.p. of ca 1830–45. Marryat, in *Peter Simple*, 'Well, Reefer, how are you off for soap?'

how came, or **come, you so?** (Often hyphenated and occ. preceded by *Lord!*) Intoxicated: 1816: low s. >, by 1840, coll; ob. by 1880, †by 1900.

how do or **how-do.** A shortening of *how do you do?*: Society (—1887).

how-do-you-do, how-d'ye-do. A fuss, a

noisy difficulty, a 'mess': low coll: from ca 1835.

how do you like your eggs cooked or done? An Australian c.p. (from ca 1908), gen. as an unkind comment on misfortune: very soon, however, there was evolved the c.p. reply, *scrambled, like your brains, yer* (or *you*) *bastard!*

how-d'ye-do. A shoe: rhyming s.: from ca 1890.

How-howish, see HOWISH.

how much? What do you say, mean? A coll request for an explanation: from ca 1850. F. Smedley, 1852, ' "Then my answer must . . . depend on the . . ." "On the how much?" inquired Frere, considerably mystified.'

how the blazes! see BLAZES.

how we apples swim! A c.p. applied to a parvenu, a pretender, a person 'out of the water': mid-C.17–19. Hogarth, in *Works*, vol. iii, 'He assumes a consequential air . . . and strutting among the historical artists cries, how we apples swim.' In Ray's *English Proverbs*, 1610, and often in C.19, tagged with *quoth the horseturd.* cf. HUMBLE-BEE . . ., and APPLES . . ., q.v. for origins.

how will (gen. how'll) you have it? Either a specific or, hence, a vague general invitation to take a drink. Lyell gives, as the commonest coll invitations to drink, the following, all of which are of late C.19–20: *what'll you have?, what's yours?, how'll you have it?, what is it?, name yours!, let's have one!*

howdy, -ie. A midwife: low Scots coll (and Northern dial.): C.18–20, ob. ?ex *holdie* ex *hold*, friendly. Ramsay, Scott, Galt. 2. (only **howdy**) how do you do?: C.19–20 dial. and slightly ob. low coll.

howdydo? How do you do?: C.19–20: coll.

howish. Vaguely feeling somewhat indisposed: mid-C.18–early 19. 2. ALL-OVERISH: late C.18–mid-19. Both coll. In late C.17–early 19, also *I know not howish* and *I don't know howish*, while *how-howish* occ. occurs ca 1720–80. Dryden, 1694, 'I am – I know not howish.'

howl, fetch a, see FETCH A HOWL.

howler. A glaring (and amusing) blunder: from before 1890; recorded first in 1872 (S.O.D.) of a bitterly cold day; then, 2, at least as early as 1875 (though this sense is ob.), of a – lit. or fig. – heavy fall, a serious accident, esp. in *come*, or *go, a howler*, as in Stephens & Yardley's *Little Jack Sheppard*, 1886, 'Our hansom came a howler.' Lit., something that howls or cries for notice, or perhaps, as W. proposes, by way of contracting *howling blunder*. 3. A fashionably dressed man: London: 1896–ca 1914. Ex HOWLING *swell*:

howling, adj. A general intensive: 1860, H., 2nd ed.; 1865, Sala, 'howling swells', a *howling* SWELL, orig. low, being, ca 1865–1910, a very fashionably but over-dressed man. Applied also to e.g. a lie, a cad, trousers (e.g. *howling* BAGS) extravagantly cut or patterned: †by 1905. S.E. itself has *howling* as an intensive, as e.g. in the Biblical *h. wilderness*.

howling comique. A 'very bad comic singer indeed': music-halls' (—1909); ob. Ware. cf. HOWLER, 1, and HOWLING.

howlingly. A gen. intensive adv.: late C.19–20.

howling-stick. A flute: low, mostly London: ca 1840–90. Augustus Mayhew, *Paved with Gold*, 1857.

how's your (often yer) belly (off) for spots? A lower classes' c.p. (= how are you?) from ca 1900.

how's your poor (often pore) feet? A mainly London c.p. dating from the Great Exhibition of 1851: ob. by 1895.

howsomever. Nevertheless; however. M.E.–C.20: until ca 1750, S.E.; then (dial. and) coll; from ca 1830, low coll.

***hoxter.** An inside pocket: c.: ca 1810–80. ?ex *huck*, a hip, a haunch. 2. Additional drill: Royal Military Academy: ca 1885–1914. Ex *extra* via *hextra*. 3. Money: see HUXTER.

hoy. A coll exclamation of address at a distance (see also WHOY-OI), hence a summons to attention (esp. in *give a person a hoy*); also = *steady!*: late C.19–20. Used very much earlier in dial. A mean between archaic *ho!* and *hullo!*

***hoys, hoise,** see HOIST.

hub. A low coll abbr. of HUBBY: from ca 1810; ob. Combe, 1812; Hood, ca 1845.

hubbie. An incorrect form of HUBBY.

hubble-de-shuff. Quickly and irregularly: military s. > coll. 2. Hence, confusedly: coll. Both senses, C.18. 'Old military term', says Grose. ?ex Northern dial. *hobbleshow*, (a) tumult, rabble, confusion.

hubbub may possibly, in C.17–18, have been coll; in C.19–20, definitely S.E. Perhaps ex an Irish cry or interjection.

hubby. A husband: coll: E. Ravenscroft, in *London Cuckolds*, 1688; 1798, Morton, in the epilogue to his comedy, *Secrets Worth*

Knowing, 'The wife poor thing, at first so blithe and chubby, | Scarce knows again her lover in her hubby.' cf. HUB, and:

hubbykins. A still more hypocoristic form of *husband* as a vocative: coll: late C.19–20.

hubris. 'Accomplished, distinguished insolence' (Ware): academic s. >, by 1890, coll: from early 1880s; ob. Direct ex Gr. On 28 Oct. 1884, the *Daily News* wrote thus: 'Boys of good family, who have always been toadied, and never been checked, who are full of health and high spirits, develop what Academic slang knows as *hubris*, a kind of high-flown insolence.'

hubshee. Applied in India to anyone, or to a pony, with woolly hair: coll: from ca 1850. A corruption of Arabic *Habashi*, Persian *Habshi*, an Abyssinian, an Ethiopian, a Negro.

huck. To bargain: C.15–17: coll prob. in C.16 only, otherwise S.E.; in C.18–20 (ob.), dial. Holinshead, 1577, 'If anie man hucked hard with him about the price of a gelding, [he said]: "So God helpe me . . . he did cost me so much," or else, "By Jesus, I stole him."'

huckle. To chatter: s.: Ned Ward, 1703.

huckle-my-buff or **butt.** 'Beer, egg, and brandy, made hot', Grose, 1785, at which date Grose spells it *butt*; in the 2nd and 3rd edd., however, it is *buff*, as again in the *Lex. Bal.* and in Egan's ed.; Ainsworth, in *Rookwood*, returns to *butt*. Since the term is extant, though ob., in Sussex dial. as *h.-my-buff*, *butt* is prob. a misprint: see too HUGGLE-MY-BUFF.

huddle. To have sexual connection: low coll: C.18–20, very ob. Ex C.17 S.E., C. 18–20 dial., where it = to hug or embrace.

***hue.** To lash; punish (esp. severely) with the lash: late C.17–18 c. ?ex the resulting *hue* of the victim's flesh, or, more prob., ex S.E. *hue*, to assail or drive with shouts. 2. To beat with a cudgel: c.: C.19–20.

***huey.** A town or a village: tramps' c. of ca 1840–80. Mayhew. Origin?

huff, as a Winchester College abbr. of HUFF-CAP, is s. from before 1870 and now †. Mansfield, 1870; Adams, 1878. 2. In c. (—1832), now †, to rob by throwing one's arms over the victim's shoulders and then taking (esp. money) from the pockets. 3. As a low coll for a (mean) trick, an (artful) dodge, ca 1860–1910, it is prob. ex the removal of a piece at draughts, wherein *huff*, v. and n., is j.

huff, stand the. 'To be answerable for the reckoning in a public-house', Grose, 2nd ed.: coll (—1788); ob. by 1860, †by 1893. Prob. jocularly on *huff*, a slight blast.

huff and ding. 'To Bounce and swagger', B.E.: low coll: C.17–early 18. See DING.

huff-cap. Strong ale: orig. coll (1577), soon S.E., †by 1700. 'From inducing people to set their caps in a bold and huffing style', Nares.

huff-snuff, a bully, a person apt to take offence, was prob. coll orig., but if so it very quickly > S.E. (†by 1800). Lit., blow snuff, i.e. show resentment.

huffa! An exclamation: C.16–early 17. Ex C.15 interjectional *huff*.

huffle. To BAGPIPE, which, says Grose, 1785 (neither term appears in later edd.), is 'a piece of bestiality [?*penilingism*] too filthy for explanation'. Low: C.18–early 19.

hufty-tufty; huftie-tuftie, adj. Swaggering: coll: late C.16–early 17. Nashe.

***hug.** The act or (as in *put on the hug*) the practice of garrotting: c. (—1864); ob. by 1890, †by 1910. *Home Magazine*, 16 March 1864.

hug, close. (Gen. *the c. h.*) Coïtion: coll: C.18–early 19. D'Urfey, 'They've a new drug | Which is called the close hug.'

hug, give the. To close (with) and grapple the body (of): pugilistic: C.19–20, ob.

hug-booby. A married man: s.: Ned Ward, 1703.

hug brown Bess, see BROWN BESS.

hug-centre. 'Head-quarters of public love-making': coll: U.S. (—1882), anglicized ca 1885; ob.

hug it as the devil hugs a witch. To hold a thing as if one fears to lose it: coll: mid-C. 18–early 19.

hug the ground. To fall; be hit off one's legs: pugilistic: C.19.

hug the gunner's daughter, see GUNNER'S DAUGHTER.

hugger-mugger, in. Secretly: C.16–20; S.E. till ca 1830, then coll. The C.16 form is *in hucker-mucker*. 'Perhaps partly suggested by M.E. *huke*, . . . cloak', W.

***hugging,** n. Garrotting: c. of ca 1850–90. Ex HUG.

huggle-my-buff. A ca 1750–80 form of HUCKLE-MY-BUFF. Toldervy, 1756.

Hugh Prowler, see PROWLER, HUGH.

hugmatee. Some kind of ale: either c. or fashionable s. of ca 1698–1710. In *Letters to Phalaris*, Bentley names it along with HUMPTY-DUMPTY and *three-threads*; 'facetious' Tom Brown, ca 1704. Perhaps, as Murray (always ingenious on drinks – cf. his *bingo*) brilliantly suggested, ex *hug me t'ye*.

hugmer; ugmer. A fool: centre s. on MUG (n., 4): from ca 1860; ob.

hugsome. Sexually attractive (rarely of men); esp. sexually cuddlesome: coll: late C.19–20.

hulk, n. A hulk-ship report on a convict: ca 1810–70. Price Waring, *Tales*, 1897.

hulkey, see HULKY.

hulking, adj. Bulky, unwieldy; ungainly, clumsy: coll: late C.17–20. Ex S.E. *hulk*, an unwieldy mass (as in J. Beresford, 1806), a heavy ungainly person (as in Ned Ward, 1698). cf.:

hulky, adj. (Occ. as n.) Unwieldy; ungainly, clumsy: coll (—1785).

hull between wind and water, to. Possess a woman: C.19–20(†): nautical s. > low coll. cf. SHOOT BETWEEN WIND AND WATER.

***hull-cheese** 'is composed of . . . mault and water . . . and is cousin germane to the mightiest ale', Taylor the Water Poet, 1622: C.17 c. > s. By 1670 it was proverbial in the form *you have eaten some hull-cheese*, you are drunk, and as such, latterly only in dial., it remained in C.19.

Hull, hell, and Halifax, see HALIFAX, also HELL.

hullabaloo. A tumultuous noise or confusion; an uproar: from ca 1760: coll till ca 1840, then S.E. Prob. ex Northern or Scottish dial. Smollett, 1762, spells *hollo-ballo*; another frequent early form is *hallooba(l)oo*. Evidently a rhyming reduplication on *halloo*.

hullo yourself (or your own self) and see how you like it! A lower-classes' c.p. of ca 1890–1910. W. Pett Ridge, *Minor Dialogues*, 1895.

hulver-head. 'A silly foolish Fellow', B.E. Whence *hulver-headed*, adj. Coll in late C. 17–18, then dial. Lit., *hulver* = holly.

hum. Very strong ale: ca 1615–1720: coll. 1616, Jonson; Fletcher. Perhaps orig. c. cf. STINGO. 2. A hoax, a trick, a cheat: 1751; ob. by 1900. From ca 1850, the word was somewhat low. The *World*, No. 164 (1756); Lamb, 1806, 'I daresay all this is hum', where its derivation ex HUMBUG appears very clearly. 3. A lie: ca 1820–1900. Bee, '*Hum* – a whispered lie'. 4. A person at church: c.: C.18–early 19. ?ex *amen* mumbled into a resemblance to *hum!* 5. A stink: low: from ca 1890. Perhaps ex Northern dial. *humming*, anything gnawed and then left by rats.

hum, v. To be all astir, very lively: coll: 1726. Esp. in form *is* (*are*), *was* (*were*), etc., *humming*. 2. Cheat, BAMBOOZLE, humbug: 1751: ob. by 1860, †by 1880: orig., prob. s., but by 1760 it was coll. Goldsmith, in his *Life of Nash*, 'Here Nash, if I may be permitted the use of a polite and fashionable phrase, was humm'd.' Ex HUMBUG. 3. Hence, to cadge: military: late C.19–20. 4. To stink: low: from ca 1895. Prob. ex the corresponding n. (sense 5); Ware, however, implies that the v. is the earlier and that it dates from considerably before 1895, and states that 'this is an application from the humming of fermentation in an active manure heap.'

hum, make things. (cf. HUM, v., 1.) To accelerate, lit. and fig.; keep busy and moving: coll: orig. (—1887), U.S., but anglicized by 1895. Ex the *hum* of activity.

***hum-box.** A pulpit: c.: ca 1720–1895. Mayhew, in *Paved With Gold*. The idea: the box noted for humming and hawing. cf. CACKLE TUB, CLACK-LOFT.

***hum-box patterer.** A parson, esp. when preaching: c.: C.19. G. W. M. Reynolds.

***hum-cap.** 'Old, mellow, and very strong Beer', B.E.: late C.17–18 c. Ex HUM, n., 1.

hum-drum. A parson: s.: Ned Ward, 1709.

Humber keel, see BILLY-BOY.

humble-bee in a cow-turd thinks himself a king, a. A proverbial c.p. of ca 1650–1800. See also HOW WE APPLES SWIM!

humble-cum-dumble, your. Your humble servant: jocular (—1823); †by 1900.

humble-pie, eat. To apologize; be very submissive, even to humiliation: from ca 1830: dial. till ca 1850; coll till ca 1895, then S.E. Thackeray, 1855; Manville Fenn, 'Our savings are gone and we must eat humble pie for the future.' By a pun ex *umble pie*, i.e. one made from a deer's *umbles*; cf. dial. *to eat rue-pie*.

humbug. A †hoax, †befooling trick; an imposture, fraud, sham: coll: ca 1740; perhaps not till ca 1754, when F. Killigrew issued *The Universal Jester*, a collection of 'conceits . . . drolleries . . . bon-mots, and humbugs', tracked down (see ed. 1860) by H., who also discovered that 'Orator Henley [d.1756] was known to the mob as Orator Humbug'. The term however, occurs for certain in 1751 – in the *Student*, ii, 41, a notable locus. 2. An impostor, a cheat, a FRAUD (2): coll: 1804. Dickens in

Pickwick, 'You're a humbug, sir . . . I will speak plainer . . . An impostor, sir.' Prob. this sense dates back to ca 1762, for in 1763 we find a mention of the quasi-Masonic society, the *Humbugs*. 3. Deception, pretence, affectation: coll: 1825. cf. HUMBUG! Etymology obscure; perhaps ex *hum* (*and haw*) + *bug*(*bear*). cf., however, Nashe's 'without humdrum be it spoken', in *Saffron Walden*.

humbug, v. Impose upon, hoax, delude: coll: 1751, Smollett, 'The most afflicted of the two taking his departure with an exclamation of "Humbugged, egad!"' 2. v.i., to practise or be a humbug: coll: 1753. Whence HUMBUG ABOUT. 3. Change or transfer by fraud or trickery (v.t.): 1821: low coll; ob. 4. v.t. and, more often, i., to cajole: esp. in *h. of*, cajole or cheat out of something (ca 1760–1870), and *h. into*, cajole or hoax into doing something (from ca 1810). These four nuances are all coll. As used in the following quotation, *humbug* is ob.: H. Kingsley, in *Ravenshoe*, 'She was always ready to help him, provided, as she told him, "he didn't humbug".' cf. preceding entry for etymology.

humbug, adj., corresponding to senses 1 and 2 of the n.: coll: 1812.

humbug! Stuff and nonsense! Coll: from ca 1825. Ex the n., 3.

humbug about. To play the fool: C.19–20: coll. Ex the v., 2.

humbug-and-derricks. (Gen. pl.) A cargo steamer: sailing-ships': mid-C.19–20; ob.

humbug into and **†humbug of,** see HUMBUG, v., last sense.

humbug(g)able. Gullible: coll: 1825, Southey. But the seldom-used *humbug*(*g*)-*ability* is recorded as early as 1798.

humbugger. A cheat: low coll: ca 1751–1890. 2. A hoaxer: coll: from ca 1752; ob. 3. One who constantly fools about, an habitual deceiver: coll: from ca 1760. Henry Brooke, in *Poems*, at that 'On Humbugging': 'To you . . . the humbuggers of hearts', 1778.

humbuggery. Imposture; deception; pretence: from ca 1830; ob. More gen. in U.S. than in Britain, where the word is apt to recall *buggery*.

humbugging, n. Deception, hoaxing (C.18–20, ob.); pretence, foolery (C.19–20). Coll. A. Murphy, 1752, 'The never enough to be admired Art of Humbugging came into Vogue'; Henry Brooke, 1778, see HUMBUGGER, 3.

humbugging, adj. Swindling (ob.), hoaxing: from ca 1800: coll. 2. Deceitful, pretentious: coll: from ca 1830. Thackeray, 1840, 'Do you not laugh . . . at the humbugging anniversary of a humbug?' 3. Apt to cajole or to play the fool: (rather low) coll: from ca 1860.

humbuggism. An occ. coll variant, now ob., of HUMBUGGING, n.: from ca 1840. Tom Moore, 1842, 'By dint of sheer humbuggism'.

humdrum. A wife, occ. a husband: C.17–early 19 coll. By 'reduplication on *hum*, with reminiscence of *drum*', W.

humdudgeon; humdurgeon. An imaginary illness: coll (—1785). Grose, 1st ed., spells it *humdurgeon*, the O.E.D. *humdudgeon*, thus linking the word with *dudgeon*, ill humour. Grose, 'He has got the hum durgeon, the thickest part of his thigh is nearest his a*se; i.e. nothing ails him except low spirits.' The saying was †by 1890.

humdurgeoned, adj. Annoyed: late C.18–mid-19 coll. Lytton. Ex preceding.

humging. A whip-top: Restoration period. Lit., 'goes with a hum'.

humgruffin. A hobgoblin; a repulsive person. Also, a derisive term of address: 1842, Barham: coll; ob. Prob. *hobgoblin* corrupted by association with *griffin*.

humgumptious. Knowingly deceitful or artful: low: ca 1820–70. Ex †dial. *humgumption*, self-importance, nonsense, itself presumably ex HUMBUG + GUMPTION.

humm. A C.17–18 variant of HUM (esp. n., 1).

hummer. (cf. RAPPER; WHOPPER, 2.) A notable lie: late C.17–early 19 – being a special application of the sense, 'a person or thing marked by extreme energy, activity, etc. . . . 1681' (S.O.D.); of persons, it has since ca 1880 been mainly U.S. Ex HUM, v., 1. 2. An impostor, a pretender: s. > coll: ca 1760–1820. Henry Brooke, 'Our hummers in state, physic, learning, and law', 1778. A variant of HUMBUG, n., 3, which it may have preceded.

hummie. A callous growth, induced by continual friction, on the back of the neck: dockers' s. (—1887) > coll; ob. ?ex *hump* or *hummock*. 2. Bursitis (inflammation of a sac), caused by carrying weights: London dial. (see E.D.D.) >, ca 1890, coll. Apparently an easing of *humpy*.

humming. Extremely intense, active, busy, (of blows) hard, or (ob.) large: from ca 1650: s. >, ca 1790, coll. Fielding, 'Landlord . . . You seem to drive a humming trade here.' Ex HUM, v., 1. 2. (Of liquor) very strong: coll: 1675 (S.O.D.); ob. B.E., '*Humming Liquor*, Double Ale, Stout, Pharaoh [q.v.]'; *humming tipple*, Ned Ward, 1714. cf. HUM, n., 1; STINGO; HUMMING OCTOBER. Perhaps ex the hissing of frothy liquor, perhaps ex subsequent humming in the head.

humming, adv. Exceedingly: coll: C.18. Farquhar. Ex adj., prob. sense 1.

humming October. Very strong ale from the new season's hops: coll: from ca 1710; ob. by 1890, †by 1910. Often just *October*, lit. ale brewed in October.

hummum(s). A brothel: the form *hummum* is prob. coll, while *hummums* is either s. or, more prob., coll: late C.17–18. (See O.E.D. and esp. Beresford Chancellor's informative *Covent Garden.*) Ex Arabic *hammam*, a hot bath, some Turkish bath establishments (*hummums* in S.E.) being or becoming little better than brothels.

hump; sense 1 always preceded by **the.** Temporary ill humour; a sulky fit: from ca 1725, but not gen. before ca 1860. Esp. in *get*, or *have*, *the hump*: Jerome K. Jerome, in *Idle Thoughts*, 1886, 'He has got the blooming hump.' Also *have the hump on* or *up* (recorded by H., 1860): ca 1862–1900. Perhaps ex HIP on DUMP(S). 2. 'A long walk with a swag on one's back': Australia: ca 1890–1914. Boldrewood. See the v., 3. 3. **(the Hump.)** Portland: nautical: late C.19–20. Ex the Bill's shape and the feeling induced.

hump, v.i. To have sexual intercourse: ca 1760–1800, Grose in 1785 remarking: 'Once a fashionable word'. It was transported to the U.S., where it survives in c. 2. To spoil, botch: low (mostly Cockney): ca 1850–1900. Mayhew. 3. To shoulder and carry: Australia: from ca 1850, perhaps orig. gold-diggers' s., as W. Howitt's *Two Years in Victoria*, vol. i, 1853, tends to show. As early as 1857, one spoke of *humping it*, but gen. the phrase is *hump one's* SWAG (Howitt), *one's* DRUM (6) (—1886) as in Lawson's *When the World was Wide*, 1896, and in C.20 (*one's*) BLUEY, this last being recorded in 1890. cf. HUMP, n., 2. Ex the *hump* of a bent back. cf. the familiar-S.E. *hump oneself* (to depart). 4. See HUMP ONESELF.

hump, get or **have the,** see HUMP, n., 1.

hump on or **up, have the,** see HUMP, n., 1.

hump oneself. To hurry: Shrewsbury School: from ca 1880.

hump(e)y. As an Australian native hut, it is coll (1846 as *umpee*, 1873 as *humpy*) >, ca 1880, j.; but as a settler's small and primitive house, it is s. (1881) >, ca 1910, coll. A. C. Grant, R. M. Praed, 'Rolf Boldrewood', Gilbert Parker. Ex Aboriginal *oompi*; 'the initial *h* is a Cockney addition', Morris. cf. GUNYAH. 2. A hump-backed person: since ca 1870. *Sessions*, 30 June 1885. 3. A camel: Australian: late C.19–20.

Humphrey, dine with Duke, see DINE . . .

humpty-dumpty. Ale boiled with brandy: coll: late C.17–20, ob. Disraeli, in *Venetia.* 2. A short, dumpy, round-shouldered, gen. clumsy person: coll (—1785). Prob. by reduplication on *hump* by reminiscence of *dump*, with intrusive *t*; or perhaps a reduplication on a corrupt or diminutive form of *Humphrey*. 3. Also adj. Both n. and adj. are occ. abbr. to *humpty*.

humpy, n. See HUMPEY. 2. adj.: depressed; dispirited: 1907, P. G. Wodehouse, *Not George Washington.* See HUMP, n., 1.

hung, be. To have one's picture accepted and hung at an exhibition esp. that of the Royal Academy: artists' coll: mid-C.19–20.

hung beef. 'A dried bull's pizzle', esp. as an instrument of castigation: low (—1811); very ob.

hung up, be. To be held up, hence at a standstill, (ob.) in a fix: coll: 1879, says Ware, who implies that it came from America and that it is a Society phrase – which, it may be added, had > gen. by 1910 if not a decade earlier.

hungarian. A hungry person: C.17: ?orig. c. or merely and prob. jocular coll; certainly punning *Hungarian.* 2. Hence, a beggar, a thief, a freebooter: C.17, perhaps orig. c.

hunger drops out of one's nose. One is extremely hungry: proverbial coll: C.16–17. Skelton; Cotgrave; Howell in his *Letters.*

hungry as a hunter, as. Very and healthily hungry: coll: from ca 1800 or slightly earlier. Lamb, in a letter of 1800, 'I came home . . . as hungry as a hunter'; Marryat; Mrs Henry Wood. Other *hungry as* phrases, all coll, are *hungry as a church mouse* (C.17–20, dial. from ca 1800), *as a hawk* (from ca 1640, e.g. in R. L. Stevenson), *as a June crow* (C.19–20, ob., proverbial), *as a kite* (C.16–20, in C.19–20 dial.: cf. *as a hawk*), *as a wolf* (from ca 1540, e.g. in Lytton, cf. the C.19 Leeds *hungry as a dog*), and *as the grave* (C.19–20, ob., mainly dial.).

hungry quartz. Unpromising quartz: Australian mining s. >, ca 1900, coll: from ca 1880. Ex the S.E. application to poor land and fishless rivers.

hungry rock. 'Rock carrying little or no mineral' (Leechman): Canadian miners' coll: late C.19–20. cf. last entry.

hungry staggers, the. Faintness or staggering caused by hunger: proletarian coll: from ca 1860.

hunk, v. To clean: (naval and) military: late C.19–20. Origin? Also, among telegraph-messenger boys, *hunk up*, to polish (one's buttons).

hunkers, on one's. In a squatting position: Scottish coll: late C.18–20. R. L. Stevenson.

***hunt.** To decoy a PIGEON (4) to the gaming tables: c.: late C.17–19. Mostly as vbl n. 2. See HUNTED, BE.

hunt, in or out of the. Having a (good) chance or none; *in* (or not in) *the* SWIM: coll: late C.19–20.

hunt-about, n. A prying gossip: coll: from ca 1850; ob. 2. A harlot ever walking about: low coll: from ca 1860; ob.

hunt-counter. A beggar: late C.16–17 coll. Shakespeare.

hunt grass. To be knocked down: pugilists': C.19. cf. GRASS. 2. Occ., though mostly U.S., to be very puzzled (—1869); by ob 1900, †by 1910.

hunt leather or **the leather.** To field: cricket s. (—1892) >, ca 1900, coll. Now mostly journalistic j. – and something outmoded.

***hunt the dummy.** To steal pocket-books: c. (—1811); ob. A Catnach chorus: 'Speak to the tattler, bag the swag, | And finely hunt the dummy.' See DUMMY, n., 3.

hunted, be. 'A man whose turn comes for him to drink, before he has emptied his former glass, is said to be hunted,' Grose, 1st ed.: drinkers': ca 1770–1840.

hunters, pitch the, v., with vbl n. **pitching the hunters.** Low coll (mostly costermongers' and cheap jacks'): ca 1845–1914. Mayhew, 1851, 'Pitching the hunters is the three sticks a penny, with the snuff-boxes stuck upon sticks; if you throw [?*knock down*] your stick, and they fall out of the hole, you are entitled to what you knock off.'

hunter's moon, the. An October moon, the moon next after the harvest moon: rural coll >, in C.20, S.E.: C.18–20, ob. Kingsley, 1855.

***hunting.** The vbl n. corresponding to HUNT, v. The predominant C.19–20 sense is 'card-sharping'. 2. **hunting, good,** see GOOD HUNTING!

Huntingdon sturgeon. A native or an inhabitant of Huntingdon: 1667–ca 1900, though ob. by 1830. Ex a young, flood-drowned donkey thought, in May 1667, to be a sturgeon by the people of Huntingdon, a black pig by those of Godmanchester, the latter being called *Godmanchester black pigs*, the former *Huntingdon sturgeons*. Braybrooke's Pepys (the *Diary*), cited by Apperson.

Huntley and Palmer, take the. A variant (ca 1894–1928) of TAKE THE BISCUIT, *take the* CAKE. W. Pett Ridge, in his clever *Minor Dialogues*, 1895. Huntley & Palmer being the notable makers of biscuits.

Hunt's dog, (which) will neither go to church nor stay at home, – like. A mid-C.17–20 ob., mainly rural and latterly dial., proverbial c.p. applied to any very unreasonably discontented person. Grose, who explains it by a certain labourer's mastiff. (Ascribed to, or claimed by, various counties: see Apperson.)

hup, v.i. and t. To cry *hup* (to a horse) in order to urge on or to turn to the right: coll: from ca 1820. Scott in *St Ronan's Well*.

hupper sukkles. Upper circles: Society: ca 1845–70. Ware, 'Introduced by Thackeray in the *De la Pluche* [Yellowplush] *Papers*.' These Papers appeared in *Fraser's Magazine* in 1838–40; in book-form, in 1841.

hurdy-gurdy. As = barrel-organ, this was orig. (ca 1800) coll, for properly it meant a lute-like instrument.

hurkaru. A messenger: Anglo-Indian coll: from ca 1800; earlier as *hircar(r)a(h)*, *hurca*(or *u*)-*ca*(or *u*)*rra*(*h*). Ex Hindustani *harkara*, messenger, emissary, spy.

hurly-burly. Strife, a commotion, an uproar: mid-C.16–20. Until ca 1850, S.E.; since, increasingly though still but slightly coll. Also adj. and †adv. Ex S.E. *hurling and burling*.

hurrah-boat. An excursion steamer: naval (—1909).

hurrah clothes. One's best clothes: mostly naval: from ca 1905.

hurra(h)'s nest. The utmost confusion: nautical from ca 1845, but orig. (1829 or earlier) U.S.; prob. anglicized mainly by the popularity of R. H. Dana's *Two Years Before the Mast*, 1840. Rare in C.20; †by 1910 (i.e. in Britain).

hurricane. A very crowded – properly a fashionable – assembly at a private house: ca 1745–1815: fashionable s. > coll. Mrs Delany, Mrs Barbauld. (Occ. as v., spend at a 'hurricane'.) cf. BUN-STRUGGLE.

hurricane-jumper. A rating who joined the Navy as a youth without going to a training-ship: naval: late C.19. (See also NORTHO-RIGGER.)

hurroosh. A coll form of C.19–20 S.E. *hurroo*, a cry of triumph or joyous excitement. Kipling, 1891, in *Plain Tales*, 'There was a wild hurroosh at the Club.' 2. Also v.i. and v.t.: from ca 1890.

hurry. 'A quick passage on the violin, or a roll on the drum, leading to a climax in the representation', F. & H.: from ca 1835: musical s. > j. Dickens, in *Boz*, 'The wrongful heir comes in to two bars of quick music (technically called a hurry).'

hurry, be in no. To have, or take, plenty of time: coll (—1858). Buckle.

hurry, not . . . in a. Not very soon: coll: from ca 1835.

hurry-durry, hurrydurry. Rough, boisterous, impatiently wilful: mainly nautical coll: ca 1670–1720. Wycherley, in *The Plain Dealer*, ''Tis a hurrydurry blade.' Reduplication on *hurry*. 2. As a comparatively rare n., C.18, it is coll variant of Scottish *hurry-burry*. 3. A late C.17 exclamation of impatience or indignation: coll. Otway, Mrs Behn.

hurry-scurry. A (hurried, disorderly) rush or a crowded rushing-on or -about: coll: 1754. Ex the adj.

hurry-scurry, v. 'To run or rush in confused and undignified haste' (S.O.D.): coll: from ca 1770. Prob. ex the n.

hurry-scurry, adj. Characterized by hurried disorder: coll: 1732. A reduplication on *hurry* suggested by *scurry*.

hurry-scurry, adv. Pell-mell; in hasty and marked disorder: coll: 1750. Ex the adj.

hurry up. (Gen. in imperative.) To hurry: coll: late C.19–20; Ware, however, dates it from 1850, makes it Anglo-Indian, and goes so far as to say that it 'originated in the river steamer navigation of U.S.A.' at, presumably, a date earlier than 1850. N.B., both v.i. and v.t.

hurry-whore. A harlot ever walking: C.17 (—1630) coll. Taylor the Water Poet, 'Hyreling hackney carryknaves and hurry-whores'. Prob. with reference also to what is coarsely known as a SHORT TIME.

hurt, v.i. To suffer injury, esp. to feel pain: C.14–20: S.E. till ca 1880, then coll. e.g. 'Does your foot still hurt?'

husband's boat. The Saturday London-to-Margate boat in the summer season: (lowish) coll: ca 1865–1914. A Vance ballad, ca 1867, was entitled *The Husband's Boat*.

husband's supper, warm the. To sit, with lifted skirts, before a fire: low: from ca 1860; ob.

husband's tea. Weak tea: low coll: from ca 1850; ob. cf. WATER BEWITCHED.

***hush.** To kill, esp. to murder: c. of C.18–19. cf. SILENCE.

hush-crib, see HUSH-SHOP.

hush-money. Money paid to ensure silence; blackmail: C.18 coll (the O.E.D. records at 1709); C.19–20 S.E.

hush-shop, occ. **-crib.** An unlicensed tavern: low coll (*h.-crib* may well be c.): from ca 1843; ob. *Globe*, 18 Sept. 1872, 'At Barrow-in-Furness the new Licensing Act has had the effect of calling numerous hush-shops into existence'; first recorded in Bamford's *Life of a Radical*, 1844.

hush up, v.i. To be, more gen. become, quiet, silent, or still: coll: C.18–20, ob. cf. the v.t. sense, which is S.E.

husky. Gooseberry fool with the *husks* retained: Winchester College: ca 1840–80. Mansfield. Opp. *non-husky*. 2. An Eskimo or his language; esp. an Eskimo dog: 1864 (S.O.D.): coll till C.20, then S.E.: mostly Canadian. *Eskimo* corrupted.

***husky-lour, huskylour.** A guinea: c.: late C.17–18. Ex LOUR money, + *husky*, dry. (Dry money = hard cash = a specific coin.)

hussy, huzzy. When, in C.19–20, used jocularly as = woman, lass, esp. as a term of address, verges on coll; otherwise wholly S.E. 2. See HUZZY. Ex *housewife*.

hustings (occ. hoistings), you are all for the. A mid-C.17–18 proverbial c.p., app. = you're all due for trouble. ?ex *Hustings*, long the supreme law court of London. (The political sense of *hustings* did not arise before C.18.)

hustle, n. 'Push'; energetic activity: ex U.S. (ca 1890); anglicized, as a coll, ca 1905.

hustle, v.i. and t. To have sexual connection (with): low: ca 1830–1910.

***hustler.** A pickpocket who relies on jostling and hustling his victims: ca 1825–1910: c. 2. One who works energetically and impatiently: ex U.S. (1886), where, however, there is frequently a connotation of (often slight) unscrupulousness: anglicized ca 1905, coll.

hustling. 'Forcible robbery, by two or more thieves seizing their victim round the body, or at the collar', Bee: c.: from ca 1820; ob.

hutch. A place of residence, sojourn, or occ. employment: low coll: ca 1860–1915. Ex S.E. sense, a hut, cabin, small house. cf. DIGGINGS. 2. A study: Public Schools': late C.19–20.

hutty. An elephant: Anglo-Indian coll: post-1886 but pre-1892; *hatty*, however, was used prob. as early as C.18. Kipling, in *The Road to Mandalay*. Ex Hindustani *hattee*, properly *hathi*, an elephant.

huxter; occ. **hoxter.** Money: low, being 'much in use among costermongers and low sharpers', H., 1874, therefore prob. c. at first and mainly: ca 1860–1910. Also in pl. ?ex HOXTER.

huzzy, -ie; also **hussy.** A housewife's companion, i.e. a pocket-case for needles, thread, etc. A reduction of *housewife*: C.18–early 19. Richardson, Scott. 2. See also HUSSY.

hy-yaw! An exclamation of astonishment: Anglo-Chinese coll (—1864).

Hyde Park railings. A breast of mutton: West London street s.: late C.19–20; ob. Ex appearance of the bone-system.

hydromancy. 'He that weeps in his cups, and is Maudlen drunk, is said to study *Hydromancie*': drinkers' s.: *The English Liberal Science*, 1650.

hyena. A Society term of ca 1770–80. Scott, *Diary*, 9 May 1828, in reference to Foote's play, *The Cozeners*, 1774: 'She had the disposal of what was then called a hyaena, that is, an heiress.'

hymns and prayers. (Esp. unmarried) men and women: late C.19–20 ob. jocular coll. Suggested by *hims and hers*.

hyp (1736), gen. **the hyp**; also in pl, (*the*) *hyps* (1705). Low spirits: coll: ca 1705–1895. (See HIP, n. and v., and HYPO.) Ex *hypochondria*. Lamb, in *The Pawnbroker's Daughter*, 'The drops so like to tears did drip, | They gave my infant nerves the hyp.'

hyp, Michael, see MICHAEL . . .

hyper. Abbr. *hypercritic* and *hyper-Calvinist*: coll: resp. late C.17–early 18 (as in Prior) and mid-C.19–20, ob., as in Spurgeon.

hypernese. 'Ziph'; schoolboyish gibberish (e.g. *pegennapy*, penny): Winchester College: ca 1830–60. *Press*, 12 Nov. 1864.

hypo. Abbr. *hyposulphite* (now technically known as *thiosulphate*) *of soda*: from ca 1860: coll, though not perhaps till *thiosulphate* arose in 1873. Also adj. 2. See:

hypo; occ. **hyppo.** (Very) low spirits: coll: 1711; †by 1880. Abbr. *hypochondria*. (cf. HIP; HYPOCON; HYP.) In 1711 Mandeville brought out his *Treatise of the Hypochondriack and Hysterick Passion, vulgarly called the Hypo in Men and Vapours in Women*. In the same year, Joseph Collett, merchant, wrote from Rio de Janeiro, 'I have a better Stomach than usual and have perfectly forgot what the Hyppo means,' 15 Oct. in his *Private Letter Books*.

hypocon, occ. **hyppocon.** Abbr. *hypochondria*: coll: 1704 to ca 1710. 'Facetious' Brown. This is earlier than HIP(PS); HYP; HYPS.

hypped (1710) and **hyppish** (1732), see HIPPED, HIPPISH.

hyps, gen. *the hyps* (1705). See HYP and cf. HYPO. (For a tabulation of the earliest records of the various forms of the various HIP, HYP, words, see Grose, P., s.v. *hyp*.)

I

I believe yer or you, my boy! Of this c.p., not wholly disused even yet, the *Referee*, on 18 Oct. 1885, wrote: ''Tis forty years since Buckstone's drama, *The Green Bushes*, was first played at the Adelphi, and since Paul Bedford's [that most popular actor's] "I believe yer, my boy!" found its way on to tongues of the multitude.' cf. BEDFORD GO, and:

I believe you – but thousands wouldn't! A c.p. indicative of friendship victorious over incredulity: late C.19–20. Perhaps ex preceding.

I.D.B. An illicit diamond-buyer: South African coll: 1884. Ex *I.D.B.*, illicit diamond-buying.

I desire. A fire: rhyming s. (1859); ob. cf. I SUPPOSE.

I don't think! see THINK!, I DON'T.

I hope we shall meet in Heaven. A pious ecclesiastical convention (late C.17–20) that soon acquired a wider currency, as in Swift, *Polite Conversation*, 1738, first dialogue, in the opening exchange.

I refer you to Smith! An allusive imputation of a lie or a boast: 1897–ca 99. Ware, 'From a character named Smith with an affliction of lying in *The Prodigal Father* (Strand Theatre, 1897).'

I say! A coll exclamation, indicative of surprise, or used to attract attention: C.19–20. Ware implies that orig. it was proletarian.

I subscribe! Yes (on being offered a drink): coll: ca 1870–1910.

I suppose. The nose: rhyming s. (—1859). cf. I DESIRE.

I.T.A. IRISH TOOTHACHE, sense 2: proletarian (—1909).

I work like a horse – (so) I may as well hang my prick out to dry! A c.p. palliation of accidental or ribald exposure: late C.19–20.

ickitserpu, see HICKITSERPU.

ickle. Little: nursery coll: since when?

ictus. A lawyer: C.19 legal. A telescoped corruption of L. *iuris consultus*.

idder, see KIDDER?

iddy (or itty) umpty. A signaller: military: late C.19–20. Ex a phrase used in Indian for teaching Morse to native troops.

I'd hate to cough. A c.p. spoken by one who is suffering from diarrhoea: late C.19–20.

idea-box or **-pot.** The head: resp. C.19, late C.18–20 (ob.). cf. KNOWLEDGE-BOX.

ideas about, have; get ideas into one's head. To have or get amorous ideas (about a girl): coll: mid-C.19–20.

idee. (An) idea: C.15–20: S.E. till C.18, then low coll.

identical, the. The very same person, thing, or statement: coll (—1891). N. Gould, in *The Double Event*, '"I'm the identical," said Jack.'

identity. A person, esp. of some – gen. rather quaint – importance. Chiefly in phrase, *an old identity*: coll: orig. (1862) New Zealand; then (—1879) Australia. Ex a topical song by R. Thatcher. 2. In mid-C.19–20 Australia, mostly 'a person long associated with a locality', Jice Doone. 3. Hence, as adj., effete: New Zealand: ca 1870–90.

idiot-fringe. Factory-girls' hair combed down, fringe-wise, over the forehead: London jocular: ca 1885–1900.

idle fellowship. (Gen. pl.) A sinecure fellowship: Oxford and Cambridge Universities' coll (—1884); ob.

idlers, the. 'Officers or men who don't keep watch at sea, the Accountant Branch, for instance' (Granville): naval: since ca 1790 or even 1780. The O.E.D. cites it for 1794, and it occurs in, e.g., W. N. Glascock, *Sailors and Saints* (I, 166), 1829, where it is glossed as 'Surgeon, Purser, &c. &c.', and in his *Sketch-Book* (I, 15, 16), 1825.

idles, the. Idleness, whether healthily deliberate or morbidly lazy: C.17–20: coll. Gen. preceded by *sick of*, i.e. with.

if my aunt had been a man she'd have been my uncle. A C.18–mid-19 proverbial c.p. in derision of one who has laboriously explained the obvious.

if-shot or **-stroke.** An unsound stroke: cricketers' coll: 1897, Ranjitsinhji.

if your head was loose, you'd lose that too. A c.p., addressed mainly to children: late C.19–20.

ifs and ands. Conditions and stipulations: circumlocution: hesitation: coll: C.16–20, but since ca 1820, mainly dial. and rurally proverbial. More, 1513; Davenport, 1624; Richardson, 1748.

iggri, -ry. Hurry up!: coll of soldiers with service in Egypt: late C.19–20. Ex Arabic.

ignoramus. An ignorant person: C.17–20. In C.17, coll: then S.E. Ex *Ignoramus*, a nickname for the title-role lawyer in Ruggle's lawyer-satirizing play, 1615 – this latter being ex a Grand Jury's endorsement to a bill of indictment.

***Ikey.** A Jew, esp. a Jewish receiver of stolen goods: c. (—1864) in C.19, low in C.20. H., 3rd ed. also IKEY MO. Ex *Isaac.* 2. The 'inevitable' nickname of men with Jewish surnames or features: late C.19–20.

ikey, adj. Smart or smartly dressed: alert, wide-awake, artful: low: from ca 1870; ob. Ex the preceding, sense 1. 2. Hence, conceited: low (—1889); slightly ob.

ikey, play the. To play a sharp trick: Cockneys': from ca 1880. v.t. with *on.* Also in C. Rook, *The Hooligan Nights*, 1899: 'I don't think any Lambeth boy'll play on the ikey like that wiv them girls again.' Ex IKEY.

***Ikey Mo.** Same senses, period, and genesis as IKEY, n. Ex *Isaac Moses.*

ile. Dance (n. and v.): rhyming s. (—1909). Abbr. ISLE OF FRANCE.

iligant, see ILLIGANT.

ill, be. To vomit: C.19–20; euphemism.

ill-convenient and its n. in **-ence.** (The being) inconvenient, ill-suiting: C.18–20; S.E. till ca 1820; coll ca 1820–70; then low coll.

***ill fortune.** Ninepence (as a single coin): c.: late C.17–early 19. Because not a shilling. cf. *picture of ill luck*, its synonym.

I'll give you Jim Smith! i.e. a thrashing: (mostly London) streets' c.p.: 1887–ca 90. Ex a pugilist prominent in 1887.

I'll have your gal! 'A cry raised by street boys or roughs when they see a fond couple together': from ca 1880; ob.

I'll push your face in; I'll spit in your eye and choke you. Working-class threats, often playful: c.pp.; late C.19–20.

I'll tell your mother! A c.p. addressed to a young girl (or occ., one not so young) out with a boy: late C.19–20.

ill to, do. (Gen in negative.) To coït with (a woman): Scots coll: C.19–20; ob.

***illegitimate.** A counterfeit sovereign, *young illegitimate* being a SNIDE half-sovereign: c. of ca 1820–70. By a pun. 2. A low-grade costermonger: from ca 1840.

illegitimate, adj. 'Applied to steeple-chasing or hurdle-racing, as distinguished from work on the flat', F. & H.: racing (—1888): in C.19, s.

illigant; more correctly **iligant.** Elegant: Anglo-Irish: C.18–20; † except as an archaic jocularity or as a typical example of the Irish pronunciation of English. See also ELEGANT.

I'm afloat. A boat, or a coat: rhyming s. (—1859 the former; —1874 the latter).

I'm sure! Certainly; certainly it is (or was or will be, etc.): lower-class coll: from ca 1870.

image, esp. in *you little image.* A term of affectionate reproach: coll: from ca 1870: ob.

immense. A general superlative; splendid: from ca 1760. G. A. Stevens, 1771, 'Dear Bragg, Hazard, Loo, and Quadrille, | Delightful, extatic! immense!' cf. GREAT.

immense, adv. Immensely; very: 1754, Murphy, 'An immense fine Woman'.

immensely. As a mere intensive: coll: C.19–20. cf. IMMENSE, adj.

immensikoff. A fur-lined overcoat: ca 1868–1905. Ex a song, *The Shoreditch Toff*, sung ca 1868 by Arthur Lloyd, who described himself as Immensikoff and wore a coat heavily lined with fur.

immortal. Excessive; inhuman: coll: ca 1540–1650.

immortally. Infinitely; superhumanly: coll: from ca 1540.

imp. One who prepares cases for a (law) DEVIL (2): legal: from ca 1855; ob.

impale. To possess a woman: low: C.19–20: ob.

impayable, adj. Beyond anything; 'the limit', PRICELESS: coll: 1818 (S.O.D.); ob. Direct ex Fr.; cf. Fr. *c'est impayable!*

imperial, adj. (Of a fall) on one's head, sporting s.: 1861. Suggested by *imperial crown.* cf. CROWNER, 2.

imperial pop. Ginger beer: Cockneys': in 1854. The *imperial* was in honour of Napoleon III, who in that year passed in state through London.

implement. 'Tool, a Property or Fool, easily engag'd in any (tho' difficult or Dangerous) Enterprize', B.E.: coll: late C.17–18.

impo, see IMPOT.

importance. A wife: from ca 1640; in C.19–20, low coll; ob. Rochester. Less gen. than COMFORTABLE IMPORTANCE.

importunity of friends. Book-world c.p. or coll, ca 1660–1780: 'the stale Excuse for coming out in Print, when Friends know nothing of the matter', B.E. (Still a frequent make-believe.)

impose. To punish (a person) by an imposition: †university and ob. school s.: from ca 1885.

impost. That weight which, in a handicap

race, a horse has to carry: racing: 1883 (S.O.D.).

***impost-taker.** A usurer who, attending the gaming tables, lends money at exorbitant interest: ca 1690–1830: c. cf. SIXTY PER CENT.

impot; in Australia and New Zealand, occ. **impo.** A schoolboys' contraction of *imposition* (a punishment-exercise): from ca 1880.

improve the occasion, to turn to spiritual profit, seems, ca 1855–90 – nor is it yet † – to have been 'much in use among Chadbands and Stigginses', H., 5th ed. H. calls it s., but it is perhaps rather a Nonconformist c.p. Lawrence, in *Guy Livingstone*, 1857.

impudence. Penis: lower-middle and lower-class women's: ca 1760–1900. *Sessions*, July 1783 (No. VI, Part V, p. 723), Margaret Shehan, raped spinster, in evidence, '"He put his impudence ..." – "What, do you mean his private parts?" – "Yes."'

impudent stealing. 'Cutting out the backs of coaches, and robbing the seats', Grose, 2nd ed.: ca 1788–1830. (Not a mere description (hence S.E.), but a definition.)

impure. A harlot: fashionable s. until ca 1830, then coll: 1784. Ob. by 1890.

in, preposition: all phrases not found here – and only a few are listed here – must be sought at the dominant n. or pronoun. 2. If suppressed, as before *these days* (at this time or age), it produces a coll: C.19–20. 3. 'Within the sphere of (a particular class or order of things)': coll: 1866, Ruskin, 'The newest and sweetest thing in pinnacles.'

in, adv. In office: C.17–20: political coll >, in C.19, S.E. Shakespeare. 2. In season: from ca 1850, though anticipated in C.17: coll till C.20, then S.E. Mayhew, 1851, 'During July cherries are in as well as raspberries.' 3. Fashionable: coll: from ca 1860. 4. See IN IT and IN WITH. 5. At the wickets: from ca 1770: cricket coll >, ca 1860, S.E. 6. In c., in prison (—1862). 'It is the etiquette among prisoners never to ask a man what he is in for,' Anon., *Five Years' Penal Servitude*. cf. INSIDE, adv. 7. To the good; with a profit (of e.g. £1000): from ca 1890: s. >, ca 1905, coll.

in, well, see WELL IN.

in-and-in, play at. To have sexual connection: low coll: C.17–early 19. Glapthorne, Cotton, D'Urfey. cf. IN-AND-OUT, PLAY AT.

in-and-out. Variable, uneven (as applied to a horse's FORM): sporting s. (—1885) >, in C.20, coll. 2. An *in-and-out* is a pauper frequently returning, for short periods, to the work-house or casual ward: low: from ca 1880. 3. The nose: rhyming s. (on *snout*): late C.19–20. 4. Stout (the drink): rhyming s.: late C.19–20.

in-and-out, play at. To coït: C.17–20 low coll. cf. IN-AND-IN.

in everybody's mess and nobody's watch. A cadger chary of work: a naval c.p. of ca 1880–1910.

in for, gen. with **it.** Due to receive punishment, incur trouble: C.17–20. Coll till late C.18, then S.E. – though not dignified. cf. the modern *for it*.

in for (a person), **get it.** To remember to one's disadvantage: (rather low) coll: from ca 1860. *Derby Day*, 1864 (p. 121).

***in for patter,** adj. and adv. Waiting for trial: c. (—1859); ob. Also *in for pound* (1887, Baumann.)

in for the plate. Venereally infected: low: ca 1810–70.

in her Sunday best. With all canvas set: sailing-ships' coll: mid-C.19–20; ob.

in it, be. See IN WITH. 2. Sharing in the benefits of robbery or swindle: c. (—1812). 3. To be in trouble: coll: from ca 1880.

in it, for all there's. Esp. with *play one's hand*. To one's or its utmost capacity: (somewhat low) coll: from ca 1880.

in-laws. One's parents-in-law: 1894 s. >, ca 1905, coll. Attributed to Queen Victoria by *Blackwood's Magazine*, 24 Jan. 1894.

in Paris. Eloped: Society: mid-C.19–early 20. Because elopers so often went there.

in the tub. 'In the bad books of seniors'; (of a ship) having incurred the Admiral's displeasure: naval: late C.19–20. Bowen.

in the wind. Drunk: nautical (—1818); ob. See THREE SHEETS.

***in town.** 'Flush of money', Vaux: c. of ca 1810–60.

in with (or **in it with**), **be.** To be on guard against or 'even with' (a person): low coll: ca 1860–1905. 2. To be on intimate or profitable terms with: late C.17–20: coll till C.19, then S.E. Surtees, in *Hillingdon Hall*, 'He was in with the players too, and had the *entrée* of most of the minor theatres.' 3. Hence, to be in partnership with: (orig. low) coll; in C.20, S.E.: from ca 1810. 4. Hence, in the swim: coll:

from ca 1860. 5. To be compared with, count beside: coll (—1889).

inch before (or beyond) one's nose, not to (be able to) see an. To find oneself in the dark: C.17–20 coll. Apperson cites two examples of the now rare affirmative.

inch in, v.i. to encroach, seems to have been coll in C.17–18. So too the vbl n., *inching-in.*

incog. A coll abbr. of *incognito*, n., adj. and adv.: resp. from ca 1690, 1705, 1709. Gray, Disraeli. 2. Intoxicated: ca 1820–1900: low. Ex *cog(ue)*, a dram, by way of DISGUISED.

incognita. A disguised harlot: fashionable s. > coll: C.18. cf. ANONYMA.

incon(e)y. '? Rare, fine, delicate, pretty, nice': fashionable s. of the c.p. kind: ca 1585–1640. Shakespeare, 1588. ?etymology. Also adv.

incumbrances. Children: (?low) coll: C.19–20. Gen. ENCUMBRANCES.

indeed and indeed! Really and truly: coll: from ca 1670. Wycherley, 'Indeed and indeed, father, I shall not have him.'

indentures, make. To stagger with drink: C.17–18 coll. Rowlands; Franklin, *Drinker's Dict.*, 1745. (The legal documents had their tops or edges indented, mainly for identification.)

indescribables. Trousers: coll (jocular): 1794. Dickens. Of this orig. euphemistic, but by 1850 jocular and semi-satirical group, the two commonest synonyms are INEXPRESSIBLES and UNMENTIONABLES; others are: INDISPENSABLES; INEFFABLES; INEXPLICABLES; INNOMINABLES; *unutterables* and *unwhisperables*. The earliest is *inexpressibles* (1790). the latest *unutterables*. By 1900, all except *indescribables*, *indispensables*, *inexpressibles*, and *unmentionables* were †. Not belonging to this class, yet cognate, is SIT-UPONS (—1860).

index. The nose: sporting: 1817; ob. cf. GNOMON. 2. The face: (low) coll, or s. > coll: from ca 1818; ob. cf. DIAL.

India husband. That actual owner of an East Indiaman who chartered her to the Company: nautical coll: mid-C.18–mid-19. By deviation from S.E. *ship's husband.*

India wipe. A silk handkerchief: ca 1790–1840: low. See WIPE, n., 2.

indispensables. Trousers: coll: 1841 (O.E.D.); ob. by 1900. cf. INDESCRIBABLES.

individual, when merely = person, dates from ca 1740: until ca 1870, S.E.; then coll when contemptuous, low coll > sol. when unintentional. See esp. Fowler.

indorse; more gen. *endorse.* To cudgel. Esp. *indorse with a cudgel.* Coll (—1785); †by 1880. With a pun on †*dorse*, the back. 2. v.t. and i., to practise sodomy (on): low: from ca 1780. Whence:

indorser. A sodomite: low (—1785); ob. by 1870, †by 1900.

indulge, as in 'He doesn't indulge.' To take strong drink, whether habitually or incidentally: late C.19–20.

Indy. India: C.16–20: until C.18, S.E.; then coll till late C.19, when it > sol.

ineffable, the female pudend, is a literary synonym, but as one not to be named, an anonymous journalist (1859), or a tremendous SWELL (1861, †), it is coll, while *ineffables*, trousers, is a coll: 1823 (O.E.D.); ob. by 1880, †by 1900. Leigh Hunt, 'The eatables were given up for the ineffables.'

inexplicables. Trousers: coll: Dickens, 1836, in *Boz*: †by 1890. cf. last entry and:

inexpressibles. Trousers: coll: from ca 1790. Wolcot; Dickens, 'Symmetrical inexpressibles, and scented pocket-handkerchief'. cf. INDESCRIBABLES.

infant. Walter Hancock's steam-carriage, 1832: coll: 1832–ca 1840.

infantry. Children: from 1613: in C.17–18, S.E.; in C.19–20 (ob.), jocular coll. Jonson describes a teacher as 'terror to the infantry'.

infantry, light, see LIGHT INFANTRY.

Infants, the. The infantry: cavalrymen's: late C.19–20; ob. cf. the *Gee-Gees*, the Cavalry.

inferior. Any non-prefect member of the school: Winchester College: from ca 1840; ob. Mansfield.

infernal. Execrable, detestable, excessive: coll: 1764 (S.O.D.). 2. In C.17–early 19, sometimes an adv.: 1646, Lady Mary Verney, 'Besides coaches which are most infe[r]nell dear.'

infernally. An intensive adv.: C.19–20. Ex the idea of HELLISH.

influence, see FLUENCE . . .

infra dig. Unbecoming (act); undignified: coll: 1824 (S.O.D.). Scott. Abbr. *infra dignitatem.* Hence, 2. Scornful, proud: Winchester College: from ca 1860. Also *sport infra-dig duck*, to look scornful: ibid.

ingan, see INGUN.

***ingler.** A dishonest horse-dealer: ca 1820–1910. *The Modern Flash Dict.*, 1825.

ingot(t)ed. Rich: coll: ca 1860–1905. E. Yates. cf. INLAID.

ingun, occ. **ingan.** An onion: Cockney (—1823); ob.

Iniskillen men. The militia: late C.17–18 pejorative. Ex a famous regiment 'fam'd . . . in the late Irish Wars', B.E.

ink, sling. To be an author: coll: ex U.S., anglicized ca 1890. 2. To be a clerk: coll: C.20.

ink-bottle. A clerk: artisans' (—1909); slightly ob.

ink in one's pen, have no. To be penniless, occ. witless: C.16–17 coll.

ink-slinger. An author, a journalist: coll: orig. (1887), U.S.; anglicized ca 1890. Milliken. 2. Occ., in late C.19–20, a clerk; esp. in the Navy, who use it for a purser's clerk.

ink-slinging. Authorship, journalism: coll: from ca 1890.

ink-spiller. A clerk: Cockney (—1887). cf. INK-SLINGER, 2.

inky, adj., often as a one-word reply evasive of a direct answer; 'can't talk about it now!' Tailors': from ca 1860; ob. cf. S.E. *dirty*.

***inky smudge.** A judge: underworld rhyming s.: late C.19–20.

inlaid; well-inlaid. Rich; temporarily in funds: late C.17–early 19. cf. INGOTTED, and Yorkshire *inlaid for*, provided with.

inn of court. A tavern offering lodging: s.: mid-C.17.

innards. The stomach; guts: C.19–20; orig. euphemistic, then, ca 1870, coll; in C.20 regarded as low coll. Corruption of S.E. *inwards*.

innards, fill one's. To eat: low coll: from ca 1860.

inner man, the. The stomach; one's appetite: jocular coll: from ca 1855. Esp. in *satisfy the inner man*. Ex *the i. m.*, the mind, the soul. cf. INSIDE LINING and *M. le Ministre de l'Intérieur*.

innings, have (a) good. To be lucky, esp. in money matters: coll: from ca 1860. 2. To live a long time: coll (—1870). cf.:

innings, have a long. To live a long time; *have had a long innings*, to die at a ripe old age: coll: from ca 1860; in C.20, S.E. cf. *not out (96)*, 96 and still alive. 2. Also as for preceding entry, sense 1.

***innocent.** An undeserved term of imprisonment: c. (—1896).

innocent as a devil of two years old, (as). A mocking assent to a declaration of innocence: coll: ca 1660–1770. Ray, Swift.

innocent of. Free from, devoid of: coll: 1706. Addison.

innocents, massacre or slaughter of the. 'Devoting to extinction a number of useful measures which there was not time to pass', *The Times*, 20 July 1859: Parliamentary: the former from —1859, the latter from —1870.

innominables. Trousers: coll: ca 1835–90. Southey. cf. INDESCRIBABLES.

inns a court is a coll form of S.E. *inns of court*: C.17–early 19.

inquiration. An inquiry: London jocular: ca 1885–1900. Prob. ex Essex dial.

insane, when applied to things, is coll: from ca 1845.

insecty. Abounding in, or of the nature of, insects: coll: 1859, Alex. Smith.

inside, n. A passenger riding inside a vehicle: coll: 1798 (S.O.D.); ob. Scott. cf. OUTSIDE. 2. The entrails: coll and dial.: from ca 1740. Also in pl: from ca 1760.

inside, adj. Secret, intimate, trustworthy (information): from ca 1880: coll.

***inside,** adv. Inside a prison: c. (—1888).

inside and outside! A toast of ca 1805–50: low coll. Abbr. *the inside of a* CUNT *and the outside of a gaol.*

inside lining. Food and drink, a meal. Esp. in *get an inside lining*. Low coll (—1851); slightly ob. Mayhew. cf. INNER MAN.

inside of. Within (of time): mid-C.19–20: coll, mostly Colonial ex U.S. 'Rolf Boldrewood', 1888, 'He knocked the seven senses out of him inside of three rounds.'

inside of a(n). 'The middle or main portion of a period of time, exclusive of the beginning and end,' O.E.D.: coll: from ca 1890; ob. Hardy, in *Tess*, 'Home for the inside of a fortnight.' Ex preceding term.

inside of everything, know the. To be especially well informed: from ca 1880: coll till C.20, then S.E.

inside out of, take the. To empty (a glass); gut (a book): coll (—1843); ob. Moncrieff, 'Haven't you taken the inside out of that quart of gatter yet?' (See GATTER.)

inside running. An advantage: late C.19–20: orig. a sporting coll. 'The inside track of a curved race-course being shorter than the outside,' W. cf. INSIDE TRACK.

inside squatter. A settler in a civilized district: Australian coll: ca 1870–1900.

inside the mark. Moderate: coll: adopted from U.S. before 1909; slightly ob.

inside the mouth. Secretly in one's mind, to oneself, reserved: pidgin: C.19–20 Australian.

inside the probable. Probable; within

probability: coll (—1909); perhaps orig. American, certainly ob.

inside track, be on (or have) the. To be safe or at a point of vantage; (with *of*) to understand thoroughly: sporting s. >, by 1890, coll: from ca 1865; ob. See INSIDE RUNNING.

inside walkee. A screw-steamer: nautical: late C.19–20. Bowen, 'Borrowed from "Pidgin" English.'

inside worry, do an. To copulate: low coll: from ca 1840.

insides, see INSIDE, n., 2.

insinuator. A slow, twisting ball: cricketers' jocular coll: 1845; ob.

inspector of pavements. A person in the pillory: ca 1820–40. Egan. 2. A man out of work: from ca 1840; ob. by 1914.

inspector of public buildings. A man out of work: from ca 1870.

inspire. To impart – unavowedly – a tendential, esp. an official, tone to an article: journalists' (—1884): orig. coll. *Daily Telegraph*, 14 Feb. 1889, 'All the inspired papers keep laying stress upon this fact.'

inspired. Tipsy: coll: C.19–20; ob. 2. See last entry.

institution. A widely recognized and established practice or object; an idea, an invention: coll (1839): ex U.S. (1788). In C.20, almost S.E.

insurance-anchor. A spare bower: merchant-servicemen's jocular coll: late C.19–20.

***int.** A sharper: C.17 c. Brathwayte, 'His nipps, ints, bungs and prinados.' ?ex *interest* or ex L. *intus*.

intellects. Intellectual power(s); 'wits': late C.17–20: S.E. until ca 1860, then – when not an archaic survival – coll; from ca 1890, low coll.

intelligeneer. One who swears and lies when drunk: s. (—1650).

intended. A prospective and affianced husband or wife: coll: 1767 (S.O.D.). Gen. as *my*, *your*, etc. *intended*.

intense. Serious: soulful: coll: from ca 1878.

intentions. One's hitherto unavowed intention in regard to a proposal of marriage: coll: 1796, Jane Austen (S.O.D.). Only of the man, esp. if bashful or 'dishonourable'.

interesting condition, be in an. To be with child: coll: from ca 1745. Smollett, 'I cannot leave her in such an interesting condition'; Dickens, in *Nicholas Nickleby*.

interloper. An unlicensed trader, interfering smuggler; hanger-on; busybody: C.16–20; ob. Coll till ca 1750, then S.E. Minsheu; B.E.

internatter. An international player: Oxford undergraduates': from the middle 1890s.

into (a person) **for** (a sum of money), **be.** To owe a person so-much, to have let him down for a stated amount: Canadian coll: late C.19–20.

into (a man), be. To fight: coll (—1864). cf. PITCH INTO; SLIP INTO.

into (a woman), be or **get.** 'To possess a woman carnally,' F. & H.: low coll: C.19–20. cf. *be* or *get* UP, prep.

into next week. Violently; fatally; into insensibility: coll: mid-C.19–20. Gen. with *knock*; occ. with *hit*, *skid*, etc. See the entry at *knock into a* COCKED HAT.

intro. An introduction (to a person): coll: 1899, Clarence Rook; Michael Harrison.

introduce (the) shoemaker to (the) tailor. To kick on the posterior: lower classes' (—1909); ob.

invalidish, invalidy. Valetudinarian; rather ill: coll: resp. 1855, 1894. S.O.D.

inveigle. To wheedle (one) out of something: coll: from ca 1845; ob. E. E. Napier, 1849, 'He managed to "inveigle" me out of sixpence.'

invest, v.i. (v.t. with *in*). To spend money (on), lay out money (for): coll: from ca 1860.

inveterate. Obstinately prejudiced; malignant, virulent; embittered: C.16–20. S.E. till ca 1860, then coll. Dickens, 1861, 'I felt inveterate against him.'

invite. An invitation: late C.16–20. S.E. until ca 1815, then coll; in C.20 low coll if not indeed sol. Dickens, 'The invites had been excellently arranged.'

ipecac. A coll abbr. of *ipecacuanha*: late C.18–20: S.E. until ca 1890, then coll.

ipsal dixal. An unsupported statement: Cockney (—1860); ob. by 1895, †by 1910. Ex *ipse dixit*.

Irish, n. Irish whiskey: from ca 1650; ob.: coll verging on S.E. Crackanthorpe. 2. Anger: orig. dial. >, ca 1870, s. See also IRISH UP and cf. PADDY, a synonym. Presumably ex Irish impetuosity.

Irish, adj. A derogative: from ca 1690. In addition to the ensuing phrase, there are many in dial. (see esp. Grose, P.). Probably ex Irish uncouthness and lack of general education before C.19.

Irish, weep. To shed insincere tears: C.19–20. Coll verging on S.E.

Irish, you're. You're talking gibberish: low coll: C.19–20.

Irish apricot. A potato: late C.18–19. C.19 variants, *Irish apple* or *lemon.* 'It is a common joke against the Irish vessels, to say that they are loaded with fruit and timber; that is, potatoes and broomsticks,' Grose.

Irish Arms, the; occ. **Irish arms.** Thick legs: mid-C.18–mid-19. 'It is said of the Irish women', remarks Grose, 1st ed., 'that they have a dispensation from the Pope to wear the thick end of their legs downwards'. Also *Irish legs.*

Irish assurance. 'A bold forward behaviour', Grose, 1st ed.: mid-C.18–mid-19. cf. *dipped in the* SHANNON.

Irish battleship or **man-of-war.** A barge: naval: mid-C.19–20; ob.

Irish beauty. A woman with two black eyes: mid-C.18–early 19. With allusion to pretty, black-eyed colleens.

Irish draperies. Cobwebs: English lower classes' (—1909).

Irish evidence. False evidence; a perjured witness: late C.17–mid-19: B.E., 1699, has '*Knight of the Post*, c. a Mercenary common swearer, a Prostitute to every Cause, an Irish Evidence'.

Irish fortune. *Pudendum muliebre* and pattens: C.19. cf. WHITECHAPEL FORTUNE.

Irish horse. Salt meat; corned beef: nautical (—1887); ob.

Irish hurricane. 'A flat calm with drizzling rain': nautical: mid-C.19–20. Bowen.

Irish legs, see IRISH ARMS. **Irish lemon,** see IRISH APRICOT.

Irish man-of-war. A barge: Thames-side: late C.19–20. Jocular.

Irish mile. A mile plus: coll: late C.19–20.

Irish pennants. Fag-ends of rope, etc.: nautical: C.19–20; ob. Bowen.

Irish promotion, see IRISH RISE.

Irish rifle. A small comb: from ca 1840.

Irish rise. A reduction in pay or position: coll: ca 1850–1910. Also *Irish promotion.*

Irish root. The penis: low: ca 1830–1914. cf. IRISH TOOTHACHE.

Irish theatre. A guard-room: military (—1864): ob. by 1900, †by 1914. cf. MILL, 7.

Irish toothache. A priapism: low: C.19–20; ob. In late C.19–20, gen. simply *toothache.* cf. IRISH ROOT. 2. Pregnancy: lower classes' (—1909).

***Irish toyle.** A thief in the semblance of a pedlar: mid-C.16–18 c. 2. A member of the twelfth order of rogues: C. 17 c.

Irish up, get one's. To become angry: low: from ca 1880. See IRISH, n.

Irish wedding. The emptying of a cesspool: low: ca 1820–50. cf.:

Irish wedding, to have danced at an. To have two black eyes: coll: from ca 1840; ob.

Irish welcome. An invitation to come at any time: coll verging on allusive S.E.: late C.19–20.

Irish whisper, see MITCHAM WHISPER.

Irish whist(, where the jack takes the ace). Coïtion: low: from ca 1850; ob.

Irishman's dinner. A fast: C.19–20 jocular coll; ob.

Irishman's harvest. The orange season: London costermongers': ca 1840–1910. cf. IRISH APRICOT.

Irishman's hurricane. A dead calm: nautical: C.19–20, ob. cf. IRISH HURRICANE.

Irishman's promotion or **rise.** A reduction in wages: coll (—1889). Also IRISH RISE.

Irishman's reef. 'The head of a sail tied up': nautical s. (—1880) > j.

Irishman's rest. 'Going up a friend's ladder with a hod of bricks': lower classes' (—1909).

Irishman's rise, see IRISHMAN'S PROMOTION.

irk. A troublesome seaman: nautical: late C.19–20. Abbr. *irksome.* Also BIRD (4) and FOWL. cf. ERK, which is prob. a derivative.

iron. Money: ca 1780–1840. 2. A portable firearm, esp. a pistol or a revolver: from ca 1835.

iron, v. To kill: low: late C.19–20.

iron, bad. A failure; a mishap; bad luck: workmen's: from ca 1860; ob. cf. *in bad* BREAD.

iron, thieving, see THIEVING IRONS.

iron-bound. A hard-baked pie: low: ca 1870–1915.

iron-bound, adj. Laced with metal. e.g. *iron-bound hat*, a silver-laced hat. Coll: ca 1780.

iron cow. The village pump: C.19 coll. cf. COW-WITH-THE-IRON-TAIL.

iron doublet. A prison: C.18–early 19. A variation of STONE DOUBLET.

Iron Duke. A lucky chance: late C.19–20. Rhyming on FLUKE.

iron face. Stern, obdurate, severe, cruel: pidgin: mid-C.19–20.

iron hoop. Soup: (military and Cockney) rhyming s.: late C.19–20.

iron horse. A locomotive: from ca 1860, ex U.S. (1846). In C.19 coll; in C.20, outworn S.E. 2. A bicycle; occ. a tricycle: cyclists': ca 1875–1900. 3. (Of coins) a toss: late C.19–20. cf.:

iron horse, v. Toss: Cockneys': from ca 1880. Most Cockneys pronounce *toss* to rhyme with *horse.*

iron making. 'Occupying a berth or billet where money is to be put by': non-aristocratic: from ca 1870: ob.

iron rations. Tinned meat: nautical and military coll: from ca 1860.

iron toothpick. A sword: military: ca 1870–1910. Contrast TOOTHPICK.

iron with one's eyebrow(s), polish the King's. To look out of grated, esp. prison, windows: ca 1780–1840.

ironbark, adj. Unyielding; hard: Australian (—1888); ob. 'Rolf Boldrewood', in *Robbery under Arms,* 'I always thought he was ironbark outside and in.' cf.:

ironclad, adj. Severe, hard; unyielding: ca 1884–1910. Mostly U.S., ex the vessel.

ironmonger's shop by the side of a common, keep an. (To which is often added: *where the sheriff sets one up.*) To be hanged in chains: ca 1780–1830.

irons, fresh or **new off the.** Fresh from school or college; inexperienced; brand-new: coll: from ca 1680; ob.

irons in the fire (or **on the anvil), have many** or **other.** To have many interests; to employ various means to one end: C.16–20; coll; in C.20, S.E. The *on the anvil* form, recorded in 1612, was ob. by 1850, †by 1900. For *many, other* or *more* is occ. found. Ex a smithy.

irrigate (one's canal), v.i. and t. To take a drink; pour drink down: jocular coll: C.18–20; ob. Ex the L. sense, to moisten.

is it cold up there? A jocular c.p., to a tall person: late C.19–20.

Isabella. An umbrella: rhyming s.: from ca 1855.

ishkimmisk. Drunk, tipsy: Shelta: C.18–20.

island, drink out of the. To drink until – and after – one sees the rising bottom of a wine bottle: drinking s.: late C.18–early 19.

Island of Bermuda, see BERMUDAS.

Isle of Bishop. 'Orthodox', i.e. good, mead: Oxford University: ca 1820–40.

Isle of Bull-Dogs. The area within the proctors' authority: Oxford University: ca 1820–40.

isle of fling. A coat: East End of London: ca 1875–1910. ?origin. Perhaps rhyming on *lining.*

Isle of Flip. Eggs and sherry: Oxford University: ca 1820–40.

Isle of France. A dance: rhyming s. (—1859); ob.

Isle of Matriculation. Entrance into the University: Oxford University: ca 1820–40.

ism. A doctrine or a theory: 1680 (O.E.D.): coll. Ex such words as *Jesuitism, Puritanism.*

issues, pool one's. To work in profitable unison: coll: from ca 1860; ob.

ist. A holder of an ISM: from ca 1810: coll till ca 1880, then S.E.

it. As an indefinite object of a v., as in *walk it, cab it*: orig. S.E.; but from ca 1880, coll. (So too in curses.) 2. A chamber-pot: C.19–20; ob. 3. The female, occ. the male, sexual organ: C.19–20; orig. and still mainly euphemistic.

it, of. As in 'We had a nice time of it': coll, gen. ironic (—1887).

it ain't all honey! It isn't wholly pleasant: c.p. of ca 1904–14. cf. 'It ain't all honey and it ain't all jam, | Wheelin' round the 'ouses at a three-wheeled pram' in a music-hall song of Vesta Victoria's, ca 1905.

it isn't a hanging matter. Well, after all, it's not so very serious, is it?: c.p.: late C.19–20.

it isn't done, see DONE, IT ISN'T.

it snowed! A c.p. indicating misery or disaster: lower classes': adopted, before 1909, from U.S.A.

Italian quarrel. 'Death, poison, treachery, remorselessness' (Ware): Society (—1909).

itch. To feel a sexual urge: C.17–20 low coll. cf. ITCH IN THE BELLY.

itch and scratch. A match (ignition): rhyming s.: late C.19–20.

itch-buttocks, play at. To have sexual intercourse: late C.16–19; coll. Florio.

itch in the belly, have an. To be sexually excited: ca 1660–1900: coll. Cotton, D'Urfey.

itcher. The female pudend: C.19–20 low; ob. Ex ITCH, v. Also *itching Jenny.*

itching Jenny, see ITCHER.

Itchland. Wales: late C.17–early 18. **2.** Scotland: C.18–mid-19. cf. SCRATCHLAND.

Itchlander. A Scotsman: C.18–mid-19. Ex preceding term.

itchy. Affected with or like an itch: C.16–20: S.E. until ca 1840, then coll.

***item.** A hint or a warning: c.: C.19. Bee, 'It was I that gave the item that the traps were a coming.'

it's a way they have in the Army! A

military (mostly officers') c.p. from ca 1880 or earlier. From a popular song.

it's all in a lifetime. It's no use grumbling: c.p.: (?)mid-C.19–20.

it's Friday, so keep your nose tidy. A c.p., employed only on a Friday (a folklorishly unlucky day) and meaning either 'keep out of mischief' or 'mind your own business': non-aristocratic, non-cultured: late C.19–20.

it's naughty but it's nice. A c.p., since ca 1900, in reference to copulation. Ex a popular song. In the U.S., Minnie Schult sang and popularized it in the 1890s.

itty umpty, see IDDY UMPTY.

ivories. The teeth: from ca 1780, ob. Egan; Thackeray, 'Chatter your old ivories at me;' *Punch*, 1882, 'Sluicing his ivories' (cf. IVORIES, RINSE ...). 2. Dice; billiard-balls: from ca 1830. (Very rare in singular.) 3. See IVORIES, TICKLE THE. 4. Checks and counters: card-players': from ca 1860.

ivories, box of. A set of (good) teeth in one's mouth: low (—1860). Also *cage of ivories*.

ivories, flash the. To show one's teeth: low: C.18–20; ob. See FLASH THE IVORY. 2. Occ., to smile.

ivories, rinse or **sluice** or **wash one's** or **the.** To drink: C.19–20; ob. Moncrieff. See IVORIES, 1.

ivories, tickle the. To play the piano: mid-C.19–20 coll. cf. IVORY-HAMMERER.

ivory. See IVORIES, various senses. Rare in singular, except when collective. 2. A pass-ticket on a railway, to a theatre, etc.: ca 1855–1910.

ivory, black. (African) Negroes as merchandise: 1873 (S.O.D.); slightly ob.

***ivory, flash the,** see FLASH THE IVORY.

ivory, touch. To play at dice: (—)1864; ob. Sala.

ivory box. The mouth: pugilists': ca 1880–1910.

ivory carpenter. A dentist: low jocular coll: ca 1885–1915.

ivory-hammerer or **-thumper,** occ. **-spanker.** A pianist: from ca 1860; ob. cf. IVORIES, TICKLE THE.

ivory-snatcher. A dentist: from ca 1880; ob. (G. B. Shaw, *You Never Can Tell*, 1897.) cf. IVORY CARPENTER.

ivory-turner. A skilful dicer: fast life: ca 1820–40. *Spy*, 1825. cf. IVORIES, 2.

ivy bush, like an owl in an. Having a large wig or very bushy hair: anticipated in 1606 (Day) but properly of ca 1705–1840. Swift, Grose.

ivy cottage. An outside privy: a late C.19–20 euphemistic coll. Formerly, often ivy-covered.

ivy-leaf, see PIPE IN ...

J

J. or **j.** See JAY. Also *J.A.Y.* 2. A Jesuit: Catholic coll: mid-C.19–20. 3. Jesus: Anglo-Irish: late C.19–20.

jab. A poke, prod, or stab: coll and dial. (Scottish form of *job*): from ca 1820. 2. In boxing s. (in C.20, gen. coll), an abrupt blow with the fist: from ca 1850.

jab, v.i. and t. To poke, prod, stab, thrust: coll and dial.: from ca 1830. Both n. and v. may have owed their widespread coll usage in part to U.S. influence. 2. Hence, to strike smartly (e.g. *jab him one!*): late C.19–20.

jabber. Chatter; incoherent, inarticulate, or unintelligible speech: in C.18, coll; then S.E. Ned Ward, in *Hudibras Redivivus*, 'And stopp'd their bold presumptuous labour, By unintelligible jabber.'

jabber, v. To chatter; speak fast and indistinctly, talk gibberish: from ca 1500: coll till C.19, then S.E. Pope, in *The Dunciad*, 'Twas chatt'ring, grinning, mouthing, jabb'ring all.' Imitative: cf. GAB(BLE) and *gibber*.

jabberer. One who jabbers (see the v.): from ca 1675: coll till C.19, then S.E. with a coll tinge. 'Hudibras' Butler.

jabbering. vbl n. of JABBER, V.: C.16–20: coll till C.19, then S.E. 2. The same applies to the adv. in *-ly*.

jabber(k)nowl, see JOBBERNOWL.

Jab(b)er(s) or **Jabez** or, rarely, **Japers, by** (Anglo-Irish **be**). A low oath: first recorded in 1821 and as *by jappers*. Presumably a corruption of *Jesus* via the Anglo-Irish *Jasus*. cf. BEGORRA.

jabberwock. A weird monster: coined by Lewis Carroll in *Through the Looking Glass*, 1871. In C.19, s.

jabez, see JABBERS.

jack. (The capital is fairly gen. where a person is designated; otherwise the initial letter is in lower case.) The c. senses are a farthing (late C.17–early 18); a seal (C.17–18, a corruption of JARK); an abbr. (not later than 1845) of JACK IN A BOX, 6; and a policeman (ca 1865) – this last > gen. Australian s. ca 1910. 2. Almost c. is the (—1851) gaming sense, a counter resembling a sovereign. 3. The least bit: coll: ca 1500–1650. (In negative and interrogative sentences.) 4. A variety of polyanthus: coll (—1879). 5. A single carnation (sold as a choice carnation): horticultural s. (—1878). 6. A variety of tea-rose: coll: abbr. *Jacqueminot*: 1883. 7. A jack-boot: coll: C.19–20; ob. 8. A Jacobin pigeon: coll: ca 1740–1830. 9. A coll abbr. of *jackal*: from ca 1890. 10. Orig. s. or coll but long recognized as S.E. are the senses: the small bowl aimed at in the game of bowls (C.17–20), as in Shakespeare's *Cymbeline*; a pitcher, gen. one of leather and often as *black jack* (late C.16–20); a boot-jack (late C.17–20); an ape (from ca 1500; long ob.); a peasant (C.16–20; ob. by 1800); a male, as in *jack-hare, -rabbit*, etc. (C.16–20); a male sweetheart (C.15–20; now archaic) – cf. *Jill*; a term of contempt (from C.14, but rare after C.18). 11. Orig. (ca 1660) S.E., but in C.19–20 coll, is the sense a knave in a suit of cards. 12. Mid-C.18–19 coll: a jakes. 13. Nautical: the Union Jack: from ca 1650. Kipling. 14. A sailor: coll: from ca 1700. Dibdin. Earlier as *sailor Jack, Jack the sailor*. 15. A Jacobite: coll: ca 1685–1750. Swift. 16. A post-chaise: low: ca 1810–50. 17. In amorous venery and low s., both the penis and an erection thereof: C.19–20, ob. 18. See JACK IN THE WATER. 19. **(Jack.)** A low coll term of address to any man one doesn't know: C.19–20. Prob. orig. nautical. 20. A native soldier: Anglo-Indian coll: 1853; †by 1886. Abbr. JACK-SEPOY. 21. Horse-flesh salted and so washed as to lose its horsy flavour: 1904. 22. The inevitable nickname of any man surnamed Sheppard (etc.): naval and military: late C.19–20. Ex the C.18 prison-breaker. 23. See JACK IN A BOX, 11.

***jack,** v. In c., to run away quickly: from ca 1840; ob. 2. In low s., to copulate: C.19–20, ob. 3. App., to lock, as in *gig(g)ers jacked* in Anon., *The Catterpillars of the Nation Anatomized*, 1659: c.: C.17. 4. See JACK UP.

Jack, Cousin, cf. *Cousin Jack*. **Jack, every man,** see EVERY MAN JACK. Occ. *every Jack man*, †.

jack, lay (occ. be) on the, v.i. and t. To thrash or to scold soundly: coll of ca 1550–1640. In *Jacob and Esau*, a play, 'If I wrought one stroke to-day, lay me on the jack'; North, 1579, 'Lay it on the jacks of them.'

jack, play the. To play the rogue: C.17. 2. To play the fool: C.19. Both coll. 3. v.t. with *with*, as in Shakespeare's *The Tempest*, 'Your fairy . . . has done little better than play the jack with us.'

Jack, poor. (A) dried hake: 1667: coll till ca 1705, then S.E. Also *dry* or *dried Jack*.

Jack-a (occ. -o')-dandy; occ. **Jack Dandy.** A little fop, a petty dandy, an insignificant little fellow: coll: ca 1630–1820. Brome, Cumberland, Ainsworth. See also BOX-LOBBY PUPPY. 2. Brandy: rhyming s. (—1857): gen. as *Jack Dandy*.

Jack-a-green, see JACK IN THE GREEN.

Jack-a-Lent, occ. **Jack o' Lent.** A dwarf, a puppet: late C.16–18: coll till ca 1660, then S.E. Shakespeare. 2. A simpleton, a nobody: C.17–19: coll till C.18, then S.E. Both ex the puppet thrown-at during Lent.

Jack Adams. A fool: late C.17–19: coll till ca 1850, then nautical s. for a foolish and stubborn person.

Jack Adams'(s) parish. Clerkenwell: C.18–early 19. Prob. ex an actual idiot.

Jack and Jill. A till; a bill: from ca 1890.

Jack ashore. A lower classes' coll (—1909) for a LARKY, rather tipsy sailor.

Jack at a pinch. A person employed in an emergency; esp. a stop-gap clergyman: coll: from ca 1620; very ob., except in dial.

Jack at warts. A conceited little fellow: C.19 coll. Ex dial. *Jack at the wat*, the small bag of a pig's intestines.

Jack Barrel. A minnow: nautical: late C.19–20.

Jack Blunt. A blunt fellow: 1898: coll till ca 1910, then S.E.

Jack boot(s). The BOOTS (2) at an inn: ca 1800–50: coll till ca 1820, then S.E.

jack-boy. A postillion: low: ca 1810–50. See JACK, n., 16.

Jack Brag(ger). A boaster: C.16–20 coll; almost †.

Jack Dandy, see JACK-A-DANDY.

Jack Drum's entertainment. Ill-treatment, esp. an ignominious dismissal: coll: ca 1570–1660. Gosson; Nashe, 'I would give him Jacke Drummes entertainment, and send him packing'; John Taylor, 1649. Occ. *Tom Drum's entertainment*, as in Holinshed.

Jack Dusty; Jack in the dust. A ship's-steward's assistant: resp. nautical, mid-C. 19–20, and naval, from ca 1800. cf. DUSTY BOY.

Jack Frost. A coll personification of frost: from ca 1825; ob.

Jack-hold-my-staff. A too humble servant: coll: C.17. Mrs Behn.

Jack in a (or the) box, gen. hyphenated. A child's toy: recorded in 1702, but prob. much earlier: coll, soon > S.E. 2. A sharper, a cheat: c.: ca 1570–1830. Dekker. Prob. ex the fifth sense. 3. A street pedlar: late C.17–18: coll. Ned Ward. 4. See JACK IN THE CELLAR. 5. The consecrated host: pejorative coll: ca 1545–1700. 6. A small but powerful screw, used by burglars: c. of ca 1840–1910. '*No. 747*', in a 'locus' valid for 1845, likewise valid for the abbr. *Jack* (pp. 423, 439 resp.); Albert Smith, 1848. Prob. ex the nautical s. > coll sense (—1801), 7, a large wooden male screw. 8. The male member: C.19–20 ob. Ex sense 1. 9. A game in which one throws at an object placed on the top of a stick set in a hole, beyond which the object, if hit, must fall clear to become the thrower's property: C.19–20 ob. (low) coll. 10. A coll, mainly Australian, name of the plant, *stylidium graminifolium*: from ca 1850. Ex the sensitive stigma-column. 11. Syphilis: since ca 1870. Often abbr. to *Jack*. Rhyming on POX.

Jack in (C.17–18 an) office. An imperious petty official: from ca 1660: coll till C.19, then S.E. cf. JACK IN THE PULPIT.

Jack in the basket. A mark (orig. a basket) on top of a pole to serve as a beacon: nautical coll: mid-C.19–20; ob. Bowen.

Jack in the cellar or **low cellar** (occ. **the box**). A child in the womb: ca 1750–1900. Smollett. cf. HANS-EN-KELDER. The latter occurs in Wycherley, *Love in a Wood*, 1672.

Jack in the dust, see JACK DUSTY.

Jack in the green. A chimney-sweep enclosed in a framework of boughs in a First of May procession: from ca 1800; ob. by 1890: coll >, ca 1850, S.E.

Jack in the orchard, get. To achieve sexual intromission: C.19–20 low.

Jack in the pulpit. A pretender; an upstart: coll: C.19.

Jack in the water; occ. **Jack.** A handy man at boat-house or landing-stage: (low) coll; from ca 1835. Dickens in *Boz*.

Jack Ketch; occ. **J. Kitch.** A hangman, an executioner; c. >, ca 1750, s. > coll in C.19: ca 1705–1880. Earlier allusions are to the actual person; e.g. Anon., 1676, 'There stands Jack Kitch, that son of a Bitch.' Ex the famous executioner of ca 1670–86. cf. DERRICK.

Jack Ketch's kitchen. That room in Newgate in which the hangman boiled the quarters of those dismembered for high treason: C.18: perhaps orig. c. Ex preceding.

Jack Ketch's pippin. A candidate for the gallows: C.18 low. Also called a GALLOWS APPLE.

Jack Muck. A merchant seaman: naval: ca 1870–1914.

Jack Nasty. A sneak; a sloven: (low) coll: from ca 1855; ob. T. Hughes. cf.:

Jack Nasty-Face. A common sailor: nautical: late C.18–early 19. 2. A cook's assistant: C.19–20 nautical. 3. A dirty fellow: mid-C.19–20 coll. (now ob.), prob. orig. nautical. 4. Female pudend: low: ca 1820–70.

Jack northwester. The north-west wind: nautical coll: from ca 1740; ob.

Jack-o'-Dandy, see JACK-A-DANDY.

Jack of all trades. One who (thinks he) can do everything: C.17–20: coll till C.18, then S.E. and gen. contemptuous. Minshull, Dryden.

Jack of legs. An unusually tall man: coll: ca 1770–1890. 2. A large clasp-knife; late C.18–19. (A corruption of *jocteleg*.) Also as JACKYLEG.

Jack of or **on both sides.** A neutral; a runner with both hare and hounds: coll: ca 1550–1880: extant in dial. Nashe, Defoe, Spurgeon.

Jack out of doors. A vagrant: C.17: coll, quickly > S.E.

Jack out of office. A discharged official: derisive coll: ca 1540–1790. Shakespeare, 'But long I will not be Jack-out-of-office.' Contrast JACK IN OFFICE.

Jack pudding (or **Pudding**). A merry Andrew; a clowning assistant to a mountebank: coll: 1648; ob. by 1830, †by 1900. cf. Fr. *Jean Potage*.

Jack rag, every. A C.19 (mainly dial.) variant of EVERY MAN JACK.

Jack Randall. A candle: rhyming s. (—1859). Ex the famous boxer.

Jack Robinson. The penis: low: C.19–20, ob. cf. JOHN THOMAS, 2.

Jack Robinson, before one can say. Instantly: late C.18–20 coll. Fanny Burney, Dickens, Hardy. According to Grose, 1st ed., 'from a very volatile gentleman . . . who would call on his neighbours, and be gone before his name could be announced': which seems improbable.

Jack (S)(s)auce. An impudent fellow: coll: ca 1560–1750. (cf. SAUCEBOX.) G. Harvey, 'A Jack-Sauce, or unmannerly puppy'. See SAUCE, n., 1.

Jack-Sepoy. A native soldier: Anglo-Indian coll: ca 1840–70.

Jack Shalloo. A braggart: naval: ca 1850–1900. Perhaps ex dial. *shallock*, a dirty, lazy fellow. But see JACK SHILLOO for more prob. orig.

Jack Shay; jackshea. A tin quart-pot: Australia (—1881); ob. ?prompted by CHAR, n., 2; more prob. punning, or rhyming on, *tay*, †S.E. and present Irish pronunciation of tea; possibly at first *Jack Shea* (rhyming with *tay*).

Jack Shilloo. A boaster: naval: late C.19–20; ob. A *Jack*-personification of Anglo-Irish *shilloo*, a loud shouting, as in Lover, 1840. Also JACK SHALLOO.

Jack Snip. An inferior tailor: C.19–20; ob. cf. SNIP, n.

Jack Sprat. An undersized man or boy: mid-C.16–20; ob., except in dial. Pejorative *Jack* with pejorative *sprat*; perhaps, in its post-1850 career, rhyming s. on *brat*. Whence presumably *Jack Sprat could* (or *would*) *eat no fat, his wife could* (or *would*) *eat no lean*. 2. Fat (of meat): rhyming s.: late C.19–20.

Jack stickler. A busybody: coll: ca 1570–1690.

Jack Straw. A nonentity: coll: ca 1590–1910. Nashe, 'These worthless whippets and Jacke-Strawes'. Ex the C.14 rebel (cf. *Guy Fawkes*).

Jack Straw's castle. The female pudend: C.19 low.

Jack Surpass. A glass (of liquor): beggars' rhyming s.: 1851. Mayhew, 1: app. †by 1910.

Jack tar (Tar). A sailor: 1781, George Parker: coll: often abbr. *jack*, occ. TAR. 2. A hornpipe: ca 1820–90.

***jack the interim.** To be remanded: c. of ca 1860–1914.

***Jack the Jew.** A Jewish thief or FENCE of the lowest order: c. of ca 1820–60.

Jack the Painter. Very strong tea, drunk in the bush: Australia: from ca 1850; ob. G. C. Mundy, *Our Antipodes*, 1855. Ex mark it leaves around one's mouth.

Jack the Ripper. A kipper: late C.19–20. Rhyming s.

***Jack the slipper.** A treadmill: c.: from ca 1860; ob.

jack up. To give way, collapse, become bankrupt, become utterly exhausted. 2. v.t., to ruin; exhaust utterly; destroy. Both from ca 1870 and both coll (perhaps orig.

dial.: see E.D.D.). Perhaps ex JACKED. 3. To abandon, give up: late C.19–20; slightly ob. Edwin Pugh, *Tony Drum*, 1898. Originally navvies', and apparently rhyming s. on *pack up*.

Jack Weight. A fat man: coll: late C.18–mid-19.

jack whore. 'A large masculine overgrown wench,' Grose, 1st ed.: ca 1760–1860. (Extant in Hampshire dial. for 'a strong Amazonian sailors' trull', E.D.D.) 2. A wencher: low: mid-C.19–20; ob.

jackanapes – 'old colloquial', says F. & H. – was prob. such only in the C.16–17 sense, a tame ape or monkey; otherwise S.E.

jackanapes, (as) full of tricks as a. Exceedingly mischievous: C.17–18. cf. the C.17–18 proverb, *there is more ado with one Jack-an-apes than* (*with*) *all the bears.*

jackaroo, jackeroo. A young Englishman learning sheep- and/or cattle-farming: Australia (—1878): s. >, by 1900, coll. Either ex JOHNNY RAW after *kangaroo* or ex the Brisbane Aborigines' name (orig. for a garrulous bird) for a white man. cf.:

jackaroo, v. To lead the life of a JACKAROO: Australia (ca 1887); ob.: s. > coll.

jackass. A stupid, ignorant fellow: coll > S.E.: from ca 1830; ob. Barham. 2. A rowing boat that plies between ships and shore: naval: ca 1805 (?earlier)–1880. W. N. Glascock, *Naval Sketch-Book*, 1825.

jackass frigate. A small frigate that sails slowly: nautical s. > coll: ca 1830–70. Marryat, in *Peter Simple*.

jackdaw. The jaw: rhyming s. (London streets'): 1857, Augustus Mayhew, *Paved With Gold*.

jacked. (Of a horse) spavined, lamed: late C.18–19 coll. In late C.19–20, *jacked up*. (See JACK UP.) Perhaps ex *to jerk*.

jackeen, Jackeen. (Often *Dublin jackeen.*) A self-assertive but worthless fellow; esp. a Dublin rough: Anglo-Irish: from ca 1840; ob.: coll. Ex *Jack* + pejorative *-een*, as in *squireen*.

***jacken-closer.** A seal: ca 1820–60: c. Corruption of JARK.

jacker (or J.). A boy in a training-ship: naval: late C.19–20; ob.

jackeroo, see JACKAROO.

Jackery. (Gen. in pl.) A favoured station-hand: Australia: ca 1885–1910.

jacket. 'A soldier who wears a jacket (chiefly cavalry or horse artillery)': military (—1909); extremely ob. Ware.

***jacket,** v. To swindle; betray; deprive of one's birthright or situation: c. of ca 1810–50. 2. To thrash: coll: from ca 1875. Ex the vbl n., itself ex *fall upon*, or *dust* or *lace, the jacket of* (s.v. DUST ONE'S . . .). 3. To put in a strait jacket; threaten to lock (a person) up as a madman: lower classes' (—1909).

jacket, dust (a person's), see DUST ONE'S . . .

jacket, give a red-laced. To flog: military: ca 1800–50.

jacket, line one's. To fill one's stomach: C.17–early 19: coll.

jacket, send in one's. To resign: jockeys': ca 1870–1905. Hawley Smart.

jacket-reverser. A turn-coat: jocular coll: C.19.

jacketing. A thrashing; severe reprimand: coll (—1848). Mayhew, 'I don't work on Sundays. If I did, I'd get a jacketing.' cf. JACKET, V., 2.

***jacketing concern.** The vbl n. of JACKET, v., 1,: c.: ca 1810–50.

jackety. Of or like a jacket: coll: from ca 1850. Surtees.

jack(e)y. Gin: orig. (1799) either c. or low. W. S. Gilbert, in *H.M.S. 'Pinafore'*, 'I've snuff, and tobacky, | And excellent jacky.' cf. OLD TOM for the semantics.

***jackrum.** A marriage-licence: c. of ca 1800–50. cf. JUKRUM.

jacks, be upon their. To have an advantage: coll: C.17–18. Ex bowls.

Jack's alive. A sharp run round: coll (—1894); ob. Ex the mainly Scottish game.

Jack's delight. A sea-port harlot: sea-port s. > coll: from ca 1840; ob.

jackshea, see JACK SHAY.

jacksie (or -y). The posteriors: Army and Navy: late C.19–20. cf. JACKSY-PARDY.

Jackson, jammed like, see JAMMED LIKE JACKSON.

Jackson's hens, fly up with. To become bankrupt: from ca 1570: coll till C.19 then dial. 2. Hence, *make one fly with Jackson's hens*, to ruin a person: C.17–18.

Jackson's pig, it's gone over Borough Hill after. It is lost: rural coll verging on dial. (esp. Northants): mid-C.19–20; ob.

jacksy-pardy (occ. -pardo). The posteriors: low: from ca 1850; ob.

jacky, see JACKEY.

Jacky (or Johnny) hangman. A Jack hanger, i.e. *lanius collaris*: Natal coll (mostly juvenile): from ca 1890. Ex 'the bird's habit of hanging his captures on thorns until they are to his taste', Pettman.

Jacky Winter. The brown flycatcher, a

small bird common about Sydney: coll, New South Wales: from ca 1890. 'It sings all through the winter, when nearly every other species is silent,' Morris.

jackyleg(s). A large pocket-knife: Scots coll: late C.19–20, ob. Ex *jocteleg*.

***jacob.** A ladder: C.18–20 c. >, by 1900, low. *Memoirs of John Hall*, 1708. Perhaps, as Grose suggests, ex Jacob's dream. 2. A thief using a ladder: c. of ca 1710–80. 3. A familiar name for a jay: C.18–mid-19. cf. POLL, 5. 4. Hence, a soft fellow; a fool: ca 1810–60. 5. The male member: C.19 low. cf. DICK, n., 4.

Jacobite, jacobite. A sham shirt; a shirt collar: late C.17–mid-19.

Jacob's ladder. A rent in which only the woof threads remain, e.g. 'a longitudinal flaw in the leg of a ballet-girl's tights,' H.: theatrical > gen. s. (—1859); ob. Sala. 2. The female pudend: C.19 low. cf. JACOB, last sense, and LADDER, first sense.

jag, (a bout of) intoxication, **on a jag,** on a drunken spree, and **have a jag on,** gen. supposed to be U.S., were orig. - C.17–20, ob. - Eng. dial., whence U.S. and Eng. s. usage in late C.19–20. Lit. sense, a load. 2. An injection: medical: adopted, ca 1905, from U.S. Cognate with JAB.

jag, v.t. To hunt, pursue: South African coll: 1850, Gordon Cummings, *A Hunter's Life in South Africa*. Ex Dutch *jagen*, to hunt, chase.

***jagger.** A gentleman: c. of ca 1835–1910: more U.S. than Eng. ?ex Ger. *Jäger*, a sportsman.

Jaggers. Undergraduates at Jesus College: Oxford undergraduates' (—1899). 2. A messenger-boy: late 1890s and early C.20. Ex the name of one who went from London to Chicago at a moment's notice in the nineties.

***jague.** A ditch: c. of mid-C.17–mid-19. ?cognate with JAKES.

jail-bird. A prisoner; a thorough scoundrel: C.17–20: coll till C.19, then S.E. Davies of Hereford. cf. QUEER BIRD.

jail-khan(n)a. A gaol (jail): Bengal Presidency coll (—1886). A hybrid ex KHANNA, a house, a room.

jakes. A privy: from ca 1530; slightly ob.: S.E. till ca 1750, then coll. Shakespeare, in *Lear*, 'I will tread this unbolted villain into mortar, and daub the walls of a jakes with him'; Sir John Harington's *Metamorphosis of Ajax*. Prob. an abbr. of *Jack's place*.

jalouse. To infer; to guess: Scottish coll: from ca 1860.

jam. Clear profit, an advantage, or a certainty of winning: late C.19–20 s. (orig. racing) > coll. 2. A sweetheart; a mistress: low: from ca 1870. (Also *bit of jam*, esp. as an attractive girl.) Hence, *lawful jam*, a wife: late C.19–20, ob. 3. The female pudend: C.19–20, ob. Whence *have a bit of jam*, to coït. 4. The pool at the game of nap: gaming s.: from ca 1850.

***jam,** v. To hang: c.: mid-C.18–early 19. ? = *jamb*. 2. To spread with jam: coll: from ca 1850.

jam, adj. Smart; neat: low: ca 1880–1905.

jam, bit of. A very pretty girl: lower classes': from ca 1890; ob. See, e.g., BIT OF CRUMB, and cf. JAM-TART, 2.

jam, not all. Despite its apparently coll tinge the phrase is S.E. But *real jam* is coll, †*jam and fritters* is s.: ex JAM, n., 1.

jam on it. Something pleasant: naval (—1900) > military. See JAM, n., 3, and cf. JAMMY.

jam-pot. A high collar: Australian: ca 1880–1900. 2. The female pudend: low: C.19–20.

jam-tart. A mart: rhyming s.: mid-C.19–20. 2. Whence, a sweetheart; a wife; a mistress; a harlot: low: from ca 1860. 3. The market, esp. if favourable; buyers and sellers thereat: Stock Exchange: ca 1880–1914.

jam-up, adj. and adv. (In) the pink of perfection: low coll: ca 1850–90. Also *real jam*: from ca 1880. cf. JAMMY.

Jamaica discipline. 'The regulated distribution of booty among the crew of a pirate': nautical coll: C.19–20; ob. Bowen.

jamboree. A frolic, a spree: s. >, in C.20, coll: orig. (—1872) U.S.; anglicized, esp. in Australia, ca 1890. Origin unknown.

***james.** A crowbar: c.: C.19–20 ob. cf. JEMMY. 2. A sovereign (money): c.: from ca 1855; ob. Mayhew, in *Paved with Gold*. 3. A sheep's head: low: from ca 1825; ob. cf. BLOODY JEMMY.

Jamie Duff. A professional mourner: mid-C.19–20. Prob. ex the name of a firm that supplied them.

Jamie Moore, have been talking to. To be tipsy: Scots coll: C.19–20 ob.

jammed, be. To be hanged (see JAM, v.), hence to meet any violent death: ca 1800–50.

jammed like Jackson. A C.19–20 naval c.p. verging on the proverbial, 'and when something goes seriously wrong, or leads to a disaster', F. & Gibbons. Ex John Jackson who, in 1787, refused to listen to his pilot and 'nearly wrecked his ship in consequence'.

Jammy. (Gen. pl.) A native of Sunderland: nautical: late C.19–20. Possibly a corruption of SAMMY.

jammy. Exceedingly lucky or profitable: from ca 1870: (low) coll. Hence, in C.20, excellent, 'topping'. Ex JAM, good luck. cf. JAM ON IT and JAM-UP.

jammy bit of jam. An intensive of JAM, n., 3: 1883, says Ware.

jams. Abbr. JIM-JAM, 2. Always *the ams.*

***jan.** A purse: C.17 c. Rowlands, in *Martin Mark-All*; Jonson.

***jane.** A sovereign: c. of ca 1860–1910. *The Times*, 14 April 1864. Prob. suggested by the †S.E. sense, a small silver coin of *Genoa.*

Jane Shore. A whore: rhyming s.: mid-C.19–20. More gen. RORY O' MORE. Ex the famous mistress of Edward IV.

jannock, jonnick, jonnock, jonnuk. Honest, loyal, equitable; proper, customary; conclusive: dial. > current s. ca 1820 (*Sessions*, 1825, as *jonnock*). Whence the C.19 *die jannock*, to die game or with bravado. In Australia, where it dates from ca 1880, it is rather s. than coll and is gen. pronounced *jonnuk.* 2. Also adv.

janty. A ship dressed with flags: nautical, esp. naval: C.19. Ex *jaunty*, elegant.

January chickens, have. To have children in old age: proverbial coll: C.19.

Jap. A Japanese: late C.19–20 coll. 2. Also adj.: dated by Ware as early as 1860 and classified, as to *Jap crock*, as a Society term. (cf. CHINK, 3.)

japan. To ordain (a priest): from ca 1755; ob.: mainly university. Ex the clerical black coat.

Japanese knife-trick. Eating with one's knife: low: ca 1885–1910.

jap(p)ers, be or **by**, see JAB(B)ERS.

jar. (A source of) annoyance: Public Schools' coll: 1902, P. G. Wodehouse, *The Pothunters.*

jar, on or **upon a** or **the.** Ajar: from ca 1670: S.E. till ca 1850, then coll.

jarbee. An able seaman: naval (—1909); ob. A perversion of *A.B.*

jargoozle. To mislead, lit. and fig.: C.19–20 ob.: coll. Prob. by BAMBOOZLE ex †S.E. *jargogle*, to confuse.

***jark;** often **jarke.** A seal: c.: mid-C.16–19. Often corrupted to *jack.* ?cf. Romany *jarika*, an apron. 2. Whence, a safe-conduct pass: C.19–20, ob. 3. A watch: low (?orig. c.): C.19–20, ob. More gen. YACK.

jark it. To run away: low: ca 1820–60. ?ex *jerk*: cf. C.20 *put a jerk into it.* 2. In C.17–18 c., it occurs in *blot the scrip and jark it*, where *jark* = to seal.

***jarkman.** A writer of begging letters; a habitual carrier, or a fabricator, of false papers: c.: mid-C.16–mid-19.

jarrehoe. A man servant: Wellington College: C.19–early 20. ?origin.

Jarvey, the Fighting. Bill Wood: pugilistic: ca 1810–30. Ex:

jarvis or **jervis; jarv(e)y, jarvie.** A hackney coachman: s. >, ca 1870, coll: the *-is* forms in late C.18–early 19: the *-(e)y, -ie* forms from 1819, ob. by 1898, †by 1910 except as = the driver of an Irish car. Serjeant Ballantine in his *Experiences.* 2. Hence, a hackney coach: ca 1819–70. Moncrieff. 3. Occ. as v.i., to drive a carriage: 1826. Ex the proper name, 'perhaps in allusion to *St Gervase*, whose attribute is a whip or scourge'; W.

jas(e)y or **jaz(e)y.** A (worsted) wig: ?orig. c.: by 1840 coll: by 1870, S.E.: 1789, George Parker. Ex *Jersey (flax).*

jasey (or jazey), cove with a. A judge: ?orig. c.: C.19.

***Jason's fleece.** A citizen swindled out of his money: late C.17–early 19: either c. or low s.

jasy, see JASEY.

***jaum.** To discern; discover: c. of ca 1815–1900. Haggart; Egan's Grose, where it is spelt *jaun.* Origin? Possibly cognate with dial. *jaum* (=*jam*), to corner in an argument (E.D.D.).

jaundy. A master at arms: naval (—1909). Ware, 'Supposed to be from "gendarme"' The more gen. form is *jaunty*, recorded by the O.E.D. (Sup.) for 1904. Also *jonty.* Whence:

jaunty's boat's crew. The men remaining in one of the old naval hulks after the ships had drawn their companies: ?ca 1800–40 – a dating that affects JAUNDY.

javel. A dock-loafer, gen. also a thief: nautical: C.18. An extension of †S.E. *javel*, a low fellow, a rogue.

jaw. (Continual) talk; impudence: coll: mid-C.18–20. Smollett, '"None of your jaw, you swab," . . . replied my uncle.' 2. A talk, speech, lecture: low coll: from ca 1800.

jaw, v. To chatter; speak, esp. if impudently or violently; (v.t.) abuse grossly: (low) coll: mid-C.18–20. Smollett, 'They jawed together . . . a good spell'; Thackeray. 2. To address abusively, scold or address severely: low coll: from ca 1810. Marryat. 3. To go: tramps' c.: from ca 1860. B. & L. derive ex Romany *java*, I go, and cf. Anglo-Indian *jao* (or *jaw*)*!*, go, of mid-C.19–20.

jaw, hold or **stow one's.** To fall or be silent: coll > ca 1890, undignified S.E.: from ca 1780. Foote (*hold*). In C.19–20, often *stop*, as in H. Kingsley's *Geoffrey Hamlyn*.

jaw-bone. Credit (TICK, n., 2): Canadian (ca 1860) >, ca 1880, military. 2. Hence, *call one's jaw-bone*, to live on credit: from ca 1890.

jaw-breaker. A word difficult of pronunciation: coll: W. N. Glascock, *Sketch-Book*, 1826. Baumann, 1887, has the rare variant, *break-jaw*. cf. the U.S. form, *jaw-cracker*. 2. A hard punch on the jaw: pugilistic coll of ca 1860–1900. 3. A cheap, large, hard or sticky sweet: late C.19–20.

jaw-breaking, adj. Difficult to pronounce: coll: from ca 1840. Thackeray. 2. The adv. in *-ly* is recorded for 1824.

jaw like a sheep's head, all. Nothing but talk: coll: from ca 1870. Hindley.

jaw-mag. Talk: mostly Cockneys': from ca 1880; ob. Pugh (2): 'He made her head ache, she declared, with his noisy jaw-mag.'

jaw-me-dead. A very talkative fellow: late C.18–mid-19. Baumann (1887) has *jaw-me-down*, which he classifies as nautical: so, too, Bowen.

jaw-smith. A (demagogic) orator: coll: ca 1860–1900: more U.S. than English.

jaw- (or **jawing-**)**tackle.** The organs of speech: nautical: from ca 1830, 1858 resp.; ob. Trelawney, 1831; C. Reade, 'Ah! Eve, my girl, your jawing tackle is too well hung.' Baumann, 1887, records the variant *jawing-gear*.

jaw-twister. A (—1874) ob. coll elaboration of JAW-BREAKER.

jaw-work! 'A cry used in fairs by the sellers of nuts', Grose, 1st ed.: coll or c.p.: mid-C.18–mid-19.

jawaub, see JUWAUB.

jawbation. (Also JOBATION.) A general confabulation: coll and dial.: C.19–20. Ex: 2. A scolding: coll: C.18–20. cf.:

jawing. A talk: (low) coll: late C.18–20. 2. A scolding: low coll: C.19–20.

jawing-gear, see JAW-TACKLE.

jawing-match. Wordy warfare: (low) coll: from ca 1815; ob. Moore.

jawing-tackle on board, have one's. 'To be saucy or impudent', Egan's Grose: from ca 1820. cf. JAW-TACKLE.

jawkins. A club bore: clubmen's coll: ca 1846–50. Ex Thackeray's *Book of Snobs*.

jay. A wanton: late C.16–early 17 coll > S.E. Shakespeare. 2. An amateur; an inferior actor: theatrical: ca 1870–1905. 3. A simpleton (occ. as *j*): coll (—1889); ob. (Ware dates it at 1880.) *Punch*, 22 Feb. 1890, 'She must be a fair j as a mater.' The *j* prob. abbr. JUGGINS.

jay, flap a; play or **scalp one for a.** To befool or swindle (a simpleton): low coll (—1887); ob.

jaz(e)y, see JASEY.

jeames. A flunkey; a footman: 1846: coll in C.19. Thackeray instituted the term in the *Diary of C. Jeames de la Pluche, Esq.*

Jedburgh, Jeddart, or **Jedwood justice.** Hanging first and trying afterwards: C.18–20: Scots coll > historical S.E. A. Shields, 1706, 'Couper Justice and Jedburgh Law'. Ex a piece of summary justice done at this Scots border town. cf. CUPAR JUSTICE; LYDFORD LAW.

Jee! or **Gee!** An orig. euphemistic, now mostly U.S. coll corruption of *Jesus!*: mid-C.19–20. Whence, **jee whizz!**, indicative of surprise: late C.19–20, as in C. J. Dennis.

jeer, see JERE.

jeff. A rope: circus s. >, by 1900, j.: from ca 1850. Dickens in *Hard Times*. 2. A man, chap, fellow: tailors': late C.19–20. Gen. in combination: e.g. FLAT-IRON JEFF.

jeff, v. 'To throw or gamble with quadrats as with dice', Jacobi: printers' (—1888). Ex U.S. (1837).

jeffy, see JIFF.

***jegger,** see JIGGER, n., 1. **Jehoshaphat,** see JUMPING JEHOSHAPHAT. (A sonorous name for the mild purpose.)

jeldi (or **-y**), see JILDI.

jellico, occ. **jeelyco.** Angelica sylvestris: coll (—1853) >, ca 1880, S.E.

jelly. A buxom and pretty girl: low: ca 1840–1910. Perhaps ex Scots *jelly* = excellent. 2. The *semen virile*: low coll: C.17–20; ob. Fletcher, in *The Beggar's Bush*. cf.:

jelly-bag. The scrotum. 2. The female pudend. Both low coll: C.17–20, ob.

jelly-belly. A fat person: low coll: C.19–20. cf. *forty-guts* (at FORTY-FOOT).

jelly-dog. A harrier (dog): sporting (—1897). With harriers, one hunts hares, which are gen. eaten with jelly.

jelly-dogging, vbl n. Hunting with harriers: sporting s.: 1889, R. S. S. Baden-Powell.

***jem.** A gold ring. (A RUM *jem* = a diamond ring.) Mid-C.18–mid-19 c.

Jem (occ. Jim) Mace. A face: rhyming s.: late C.19–20. Ex the noted pugilist.

jemima. A chamber-pot: low: C.19–20; ob. 2. A servant girl: Londoner's jocular coll (—1887); ob. cf. BIDDY, 2 and 3. 3. A dressmaker's dummy: domestic: since ca 1880.

jeminy!, often preceded, occ. followed, by *o(h)*. A variant of ob. GEMINI.

jemmily. Neatly: coll: ca 1830–90. Ex JEMMY, adj., 1.

jemminess. Neatness, spruceness: low coll: ca 1755–1890. See JEMMY, adj., 1.

jemmy (in C.19, occ. *jimmy*). A short crowbar used by housebreakers: ?orig. (—1811) c.: by 1870, coll. Dickens, in *Oliver Twist*. Earlier JENNY; ca 1810–30, occ. called a *jemmy rook*; in U.S., *jimmy*. cf. JAMES. 2. A dandy: coll: ca 1752–1800, thereafter gen. *jemmy jessamy* (†by 1900), though the two terms were orig. distinct. *Adventurer*, No. 100, 1753, 'The scale . . . consists of eight degrees; Greenhorn, Jemmy, Jessamy, Smart, Honest Fellow, Joyous Spirit, Buck, and Blood.' See also JEMMY JESSAMY, adj. 3. Hence, a light cane, orig. and esp. one carried by a 'jemmy' or dandy: ca 1753–1800. 4. Hence, also, a finicky fellow: naval: ca 1760–1800. Bowen, 'Adopted by the mutineers of 1797 for all officers'. 5. A sheep's head cooked: coll: from ca 1820; ob. It occurs in *Sinks*, 1848, as 'the head', human or animal. cf. BLOODY JEMMY. 6. A shooting-coat; a greatcoat: coll: ca 1830–1910. Dickens, 'Your friend in the green jemmy.' 7. A term of contempt, esp. as *all jemmy* (more gen. *all* JIMMY), all rot!: ca 1860–1910. 8. A sovereign (coin): 1857, Augustus Mayhew, *Paved with Gold*. Short for JEMMY O' GOBLIN.

***jemmy,** v. To open (a door, a window, etc.) with a JEMMY (n., 1): late C.19–20: c.

jemmy, adj. Dandified, smart, neat: coll: ca 1750–1860; extant in dial. G. A. Stevens, 'Dressed as jemmy . . . as e'er a commoner in all England.' Ex †*gim*, smart, spruce. 2. Hence, sharp, clever: ca 1760–80. 3. A pejorative: low: ca 1860–1910. Ex the n., last sense.

Jemmy Donnelly. A jocular coll name given to three kinds of large timber tree: Queensland: from ca 1880; ob.

Jemmy Ducks. (Occ. *Billy D.*) The ship's poulterer: nautical: ca 1860–1905.

Jemmy Grant, see JIMMY, n., 2, and JIMMY GRANT, 2.

jemmy jessamy (gen. with capitals), adj. Dandified, effeminate: ca 1755–1860. Variant, *Jemmy Jessamine*, not before 1823. See JEMMY, n., 2. Ex Eliza Haywood's *The History of Jemmy and Jenny Jessamy*, 1753.

jemmy-john. A low coll corruption (—1864) of *demijohn*. T. B. Aldrich.

Jemmy o' Goblin. A sovereign: (orig. theatrical) rhyming s.: from ca 1850. More frequently *Jimmy o' Goblin*.

jemmy rook, see JEMMY, n., 1.

Jemmy Squaretoes. The devil: nautical: C.19–20. cf. OLD SQUARE-TOES.

Jenkins' hen, die like. i.e., unmarried: Scots coll: C.18–19.

jenny. A small housebreaking crowbar: late C.17–early 19 c. cf. JEMMY, n., 1.; BESS; BETTY, and the Ger. *Peterchen, Klaus, Dietrich*. 2. A she-ass: C.19–20: coll >, by 1890, S.E. Abbr. *jenny ass*. 3. 'A losing hazard into the middle pocket off a ball an inch or two from the side cushion,' F. & H.: 1856 (S.O.D.): billiards s. > j. 4. A hot-water bottle: coll: from ca 1880; ob.

***jenny,** v. To understand: c. (—1909). Perhaps a perversion of GRANNY, v., or JERRY, v.

Jenny Darbies. Policemen: ca 1830–70. Charles Martell, *The Detectives' Note Book*, 1860, 'Well, I joined the [police] force. . . . There was a good deal of animosity against us for a long while and all sorts of opprobrious epithets were bestowed upon us. We were "Bobbies", "Bluebottles", "Peelers", and "Jenny Darbies" (gens d'armes).'

Jenny Hills. (Very rare in singular.) Pills: rhyming s.: late C.19–20. Ex a music-hall star famous in the 1870s.

Jenny Lea or Lee. Tea: rhyming s.: late C.19–20. Also ROSY LEE and YOU AND ME.

jenny linda or -er, Jenny Linda or -er. A window: rhyming s. (—1857). On *winder*, the low coll pronunciation, ex Jenny Lind, the famous mid-C.19 singer.

Jenny Wren. A wren: coll: mid-C.17–20. An excellent example of the people's poetry ('twopence coloured').

jere or jeer. (The latter is rare and erroneous.) A turd: c.: C.17–18 (?–19). 2. Hence (?), one's posterior: low; esp. showmen's: C.19–20.

Jeremiah, v. To complain: lower classes' coll (—1909). cf.:

Jeremiah-mongering. 'Deplorable and needless lamentation': Society: 1885–6. 'Invented to describe the behaviour of those who after the fall of Khartoum' – the country is going to the dogs, sir! – 'went around maintaining that England had indeed come to a finality' (Ware).

jeremy diddler (or with capitals). A shark or sharper; a shabby and dishonest borrower: coll: 1803, Kenney names thus a man in *Raising the Wind*; ob. Personification of DIDDLER.

Jericho. A place of banishment, retirement, concealment, or desirable distance, esp. in *go to Jericho*, which in the imperative = go to the devil!: s. > coll: from ca 1635. Ex II Samuel x, 4–5. cf. HALIFAX. 2. A privy: from ca 1750: low: †.

Jericho, have been to. To be tipsy: C.18–early 19: drinkers'. cf. JERUSALEM, BE GOING TO.

Jericho to June, from. A long way: coll: ca 1835–1915.

jerk, v. To write, as in *jerk a poem*: (low) coll: ca 1770–1905. 2. To accost eagerly: coll or s.: ca 1740–1810. 3. To rob (a person of): c.: from ca 1880.

***jerk, cly the.** To be whipped at the post: C.17–18 c.

Jerk, Dr. A flogging schoolmaster: coll: ca 1740–1830. Foote.

jerk, in a. Instantly: coll: ca 1760–1820. G. A. Stevens, 'Put wine into wounds, | You'll be cured in a jerk.' Extant in dial.

***jerk a gybe.** To forge a licence: mid-C.17–18 c.

jerk a part, see SLING A PART.

jerk a wheeze. To tell a WHEEZE with brilliant effect: theatrical: 1860, says Ware, but he, I believe, antedated it by a decade – perhaps even by two decades.

jerk chin-music. To talk: ca 1870–1910: coll, mostly U.S.

jerk-nod, see YERKNOD.

jerk off, v.i. and v. reflexive. To masturbate: low coll: C.18–20. An ob. low s. variant is *jerk one's jelly* or *juice* or *mutton* or *turkey*.

jerk the cat, see CAT, SHOOT THE.

jerk the tinkler. To ring the bell: jocular: from ca 1830. Dickens, in *Oliver Twist*.

jerker. A tippler: low: ca 1830–1900. ?ex *jerk one's elbow*. 2. A steward: nautical: from ca 1850; ob. 3. A harlot: urban (mostly London): from ca 1860; ob. Ex JERK, v., 2. 4. A chamber-pot: low: from ca 1870; ob.

jerks. Delirium tremens: coll: from ca 1820.

jeroboam. A chamber-pot: ca 1820–80. Whence JERRY, 3.

jerran. Anxious; (greatly) concerned: Australia: ca 1820–1900. Peter Cunningham, 'Rolf Boldrewood'. Ex *jirrand*, Botany Bay Aborigine for afraid.

jerrawicke. Australian-made beer: Australian coll: ca 1850–60. ?ex Aborigine.

***jerry.** A fog, a mist: c. of ca 1810–80. 2. Also c. (—1887), a watch: ob. 3. A chamber-pot: low: from ca 1825. A water-closet (—1850). Ex JEROBOAM. Hence, 3 *a*, a cup, as in *the cricket* or *sports jerry*: Charterhouse: late C.19–20. 4. A (hard, round) hat: ca 1840–1900. Abbr. TOM-AND-JERRY *hat*. 5. A celebration of completed indentures: printers': from ca 1870; ob. 6. A low beer-house: from ca 1850: coll >, ca 1880, S.E. Abbr. JERRY-SHOP. 7. A jerry-builder: 1890 (S.O.D.): s. 8. A recognition, discovery, TUMBLE: low: from ca 1880. Ex the v. 9. A variant of GERRY.

jerry, v.i. and t. To recognize; discern, discover, detect; understand: low: from ca 1870. Prob. ex JERRYCUMMUMBLE. cf. RUMBLE, itself prob. suggested by TUMBLE, the latter prob. ex *jerrycummumble*. 2. To jibe (at); chaff maliciously: low: ca 1850–90. Ex *jeer*.

jerry, adj. Unsubstantial; constructed unsubstantially: from ca 1880: coll. cf. next two entries. ?etymology: perhaps ex *Jerry*, familiar and/or contemptuous for *Jeremiah*. More prob. a corruption of *jury* (as in *jury-mast*, *-leg*, etc.), as W. suggests.

jerry-builder. 'A rascally speculating builder,' F. & H.: recorded in 1881 but arising in Liverpool ca 1830. The vbl n. *jerry-building* occurs in a Liverpool paper of 1861.

jerry-built. Unsubstantial(ly built): 1883: coll. *Daily Telegraph*, 23 March 1883; J. Newman in *Scamping Tricks*, 1891. ?ex *Jeremiah*, or = *jury-built* (W.): see JERRY, adj.

jerry-come-tumble. A water-closet: lower classes' (—1860). Ex JERRY, n., 3, influenced by JERRY-GO-NIMBLE or by JERRYCUMMUMBLE or by both.

***jerry-getting, -nicking, -stealing.** The stealing of watches: c. (—1888); ob.

jerry-go-nimble. Diarrhoea: coll: C.19. Earlier, THOROUGH-GO-NIMBLE. 2. An antic or JACK PUDDING: C.19 coll > S.E. Henley & Stevenson.

Jerry Lynch. A pickled pig's-head: low: mid-C.19–20; ob.

***jerry-nicking,** see JERRY-GETTING.

Jerry Riddle (or **Riddell),** n. and v. Urination; to urinate: mid-C.19–20. Rhyming on PIDDLE. cf. JERRY, n., 2.

jerry-shop. A (low) beer-house: from ca 1830: s. > coll >, ca 1860, S.E. Often abbr. JERRY (n., 6) as in Mayhew, 'A beer-shop or, as he called it, a jerry.'

jerry sneak. A henpecked husband: 1763, Foote instituted the character in *The Mayor of Garratt*: coll: †by 1860. 2. In c., a watch thief: C.19–20; ob.

***jerry-stealing,** see JERRY-GETTING.

jerry wag. A spreester, esp. if half drunk: ca 1820–70.

jerry-wag shop. A coffee shop or stall: ca 1820–70.

jerry(cum)mumble. To shake, tousle, tumble: C.18–early 19. Cibber the shorter, Grose (1st ed.) the longer form. Perhaps on *stumble*. Whence, perhaps, TUMBLE, to understand (v.t. with *to*), JERRY, the same, and RUMBLE, the same.

jersey. A red-headed person: Australian: from ca 1870.

Jersey hop. 'An unceremonious assembly of persons with a common taste for valsing; from Jersey, U.S.A.': ca 1883–1900. Ware.

Jerusalem! Indicative of surprise. Mid-C.19–20. Perhaps the origin of JEE! cf. JERUSALEM, GO TO.

Jerusalem, be going to. To be drunk: drinkers': C.18–early 19. cf. JERICHO, HAVE BEEN TO. Both terms occur in Franklin's *Drinker's Dict.*, 1745.

Jerusalem!, go to. Go to blazes! C.19–20. cf. JERICHO!, GO TO.

Jerusalem artichoke. A donkey: rhyming s., on MOKE, 1: from ca 1870.

Jerusalem pony. An ass: from ca 1820; ob.: s. >, ca 1850, coll. Ex Christ's entry into Jerusalem on an ass. cf. EGYPTIAN CHARGER. 2. Hence, a needy clergyman doing *locum tenens* work: clerical: from ca 1850; ob. cf. GUINEA-PIG.

Jerusalem the Golden. Brighton: from ca 1870. Ex the numerous rich Jews there.

jervis, see JARVIS.

jessamine. A C.19 variant of:

jessamy. As n., a fashionable man next above a JEMMY (see n., 2): ca 1750–1830. 2. As adj., dandified, effeminate: ca 1680–1850. Head, G. A. Stevens. (For both, see also JEMMY JESSAMY. Like *jessamine*, of which it is a corruption, it is ex the flower (*jasmine*).)

jessie or jessy, give (a person). To thrash: non-aristocratic (—1860); slightly ob. Ex Isaiah xi, 1, 'There shall come forth a rod out of the stem of Jesse.'

Jesso. The inevitable nickname of anyone surnamed Read: naval and, hence, military: late C.19–20. Why?

jester. A JOKER, CHAP, fellow: coll: ca 1860–1905. See also ARTIST; MERCHANT. A very interesting s. and coll synonymy exists for a fellow.

jesuit. A sodomite: coll: ca 1630–1820. Whence *jesuits' fraternity*, the world of sodomy, as in Rochester, 'The Jesuits' fraternity | Shall leave the use of buggery.' cf. BOX THE JESUIT and the opprobrious sense attaching to *Jesuit* even in S.E. The Society of Jesus is here made the scapegoat for all monastic orders – against whom, as against sailors, the charge of masturbation is often laid. 2. A graduate or an undergraduate of Jesus College, Oxford: Oxford University: ca 1760–1890. Smollett, in *Humphrey Clinker*.

Jesuit, box the, see BOX THE JESUIT . . .

Jesus'-eyes. Forget-me-nots: Roman Catholic coll (—1909).

***jet.** A lawyer: c.: C.18–early 19. cf. AUTEM *jet*, a parson.

jet one's juice. (Of men) to experience the sexual spasm: low: C.19–20; ob. cf. COME.

jeuced infernal, see DEUCED INFERNAL.

Jew, n. A ship's tailor: nautical: late C.19–20. cf. JEWING.

jew, v. To drive a very hard bargain, to overreach or cheat: coll: 1845.

Jew(-)bail. Insufficient or worthless bail: mid-C.18–mid-19: coll.

Jew-balance. A hammer-headed shark: nautical: late C.19–20.

Jew boy. A (young) Jewish male: mid-C.19–20: coll. Mayhew, 1861.

Jew fencer. A Jewish street buyer or salesman, esp. of stolen goods: low: from ca 1850. See FENCER (not FENCE).

***Jew-Jack,** see JACK THE JEW.

Jew parade. Sunday cookhouse fatigue for those who dodge the church parade, whether they are Jews or not: Army: late C.19–20.

jewing, vbl n. Tailoring; sewing: nautical: late C.19–20. cf. JEW, n. Hence, *jewing-bag*, the bag in which a sailor keeps his sewing-gear: id.: id.

Jewish nightcap. Foreskin: low: late C.19–20. With reference to circumcision.

Jew's compliment, see JUDISCHE COMPLIMENT.

Jew's eye, worth a. Extremely valuable: late C.16–20; ob. Perhaps ex eyes put out by medieval torturers to enforce payment. G. Harvey, 'Let it everlastingly be recorded for a soverain Rule, as deare as a Jewes eye'.

Jew's(-)harp. A hair-comb with tissue paper applied to one side: on humming against the other, one can produce queer music: C.19–20: s. >, ca 1890, coll. Punning the S.E. musical instrument so named.

Jews on a pay-day, (as) thick as two. (To be) intimate: Cockney (—1887).

Jew's poker. One who lights Jews' fires on Saturdays (the Jewish Sabbath): from ca 1870. *Lloyd's Weekly*, 17 May 1891.

Jezebel. The male member: C.19–20 low. Perhaps ex II Kings ix, 33: 'And he said, throw her down. So they threw her down.'

jib. The underlip (as in *hang one's jib*, to look dejected); also, the face (as in nautical CUT OF ONE'S JIB, one's personal looks or look): coll and dial.: from late C.18. 2. A first-year undergraduate: Dublin University: from ca 1840; ob. Lever. 3. A horse given to jibbing: 1843 (S.O.D.): coll >, ca 1895, S.E. Mayhew. 4. See JIBB. 5. A flat-folding, 'chimney-pot' hat, closed by springs set in centre of vertical ribs: Society: 1848–80. Ex Fr. *gibus* (from the inventor's name).

jib, v. To depart (esp. hastily or slyly): low coll: from ca 1850.

jib-and-staysail Jack. The seaman's name for an officer given, whether inexperienced or a martinet, to tormenting the men by constantly 'making and shortening sail' to keep the ship in station when it forms one of a fleet: naval: late C.18–mid-19.

jib draw!, long may your big. 'Good luck!', esp. to a man leaving the service: naval (—1909). Of erotic origin.

jib of jibs. An impossible sail: nautical coll: ca 1850–1910. Ex nautical j. for the outermost jib (a triangular stay-sail). cf. *sky-scraper*, a 'sky sail'.

***jibb.** The tongue; hence language, speech: C.19–early 20 tramps' c. Ex Romany *chib, jib*.

jibber the kibber. To deceive seamen and thus wreck ships 'by fixing a candle and lantern round the neck of a horse, one of whose fore feet is tied up; this at night has the appearance of a ship's light,' Grose, 2nd ed.: late C.18–early 19. The phrase is mysterious: *jibber* – by itself, however, unrecorded before 1824 – gen. = to talk confusedly, here prob. = to confuse. But what is *kibber*? unless it be a rhyme-tag?

jickajog. A pushing; a commotion: low: C.17–mid-19. Jonson. Euphonic reduplication on *jog*. cf. JIG-JOG.

jiff (1790, ob.); gen. **jiffy** (1785); occ. **jeffy** (—1791). A moment: coll. Rare except when preceded by *in a*. Grose, 3rd ed.; H. & J. Smith; Thackeray; Milliken (*jiff*). ?etymology, perhaps suggested by *jiffle*, to fidget.

jiffess. An employer's wife: tailors': from ca 1860; ob.

jiffy, see JIFF.

jig. Abbr. JIGGER, c. senses. 2. Applied to a person, a domestic animal, etc.: jocular coll: C.18–19. Bentham, 'This Lord and Lady Traction are the queerest jigs you ever saw.' 3. A swindler: Winchester College: ca 1840–70. 3*a*. Hence, a clever fellow: ibid.: from ca 1860. 4. A swindle, a low joke, an object of sport: ibid.: from ca 1870.

jig, on the. Fidgety: coll: from ca 1880. Jefferies, in *Wood Magic*.

jig, the feather-bed or **the buttock-** or **Moll Peatley's.** Copulation: low coll: C.17–20; ob.

jig-a-jig; in C.19 often **jig-jig.** n. and v. for sexual intercourse: low: v. from ca 1840, n. from ca 1900. In the 1840s there was a street-ballad entitled *Jig Jig to the Hirings*, wherein *jig-jig* occurs as a v. Echoic. cf. JIG-JOG, JIGGLE and ZIGZIG,

jig by jowl. Cheek by jowl: late C.17–18 coll. D'Urfey.

jig is up, the. The game is up: late C.18–20: S.E. till ca 1850, then coll.

jig-jog, jigga-jog(gy). A jolting movement: coll verging on S.E. C.17–20. Marston.

jig(g)amaree. A trick; a fanciful contrivance: recorded in England from ca 1845; ob.: coll, esp. in U.S. (where recorded in 1824). Ex various dial. Halliwell. Fanciful on *jig*.

jiggalorum. A fanciful, gen. worthless, trifle: coll: C.17–18. cf. COCKALORUM.

jig(g)ambob, occ. **jiggembob,** see JIGGUMBOB.

Jigger. An 'inevitable' nickname of men surnamed Lees: mostly naval and military: late C.19–20.

***jigger.** Its c. senses are: A door: mid-C.16–19. Also as *jig, gigger, gyger, jegger*. 2. A door-keeper: C.18–20, ob. Parker. Also *jigger-dubber*. 3. A key, a lock: ca 1815–70. 4. A whipping-post: C.18–early 19. John Hall. 5. A private or secret still: ca 1820–1910. Its s. senses: 6. A fiddlestick: C.18–19. 7. A bridge or rest: billiards: 1847. 8. The curtain: theatrical: from ca 1850; ob. 9. A prison cell: 1896, Max Pemberton. Ex next. 10. A guardroom: military (—1882). 11. The penis: low s.: C.19–20. 12. The female pudend: id.: id.

jigger, v.t. and i. To shake and jerk often and rapidly: coll: 1867. Ex *jig*, v. of motion. 2. To circumvent, damage, ruin: from ca 1860. Ex JIGGERED! cf. JIGGERED UP. 3. To imprison, shut up: 1887, Hall Caine; ob. Gen. with *up*.

jigger, not worth a. Worthless: (low) coll: 1861, *Punch*, 'The churches here ain't worth a jigger – no, not half-a-jigger.'

***jigger-dubber.** A door-keeper, turnkey: c.: ca 1770–1880. See JIGGER, esp. 1, 2, 3.

jigger-stuff. Illicitly distilled spirits: ca 1840–1900: low (?orig. c.).

jigger-worker. A vendor of illicitly distilled spirits: ca 1840–1905. 2. A drinker of whisky, esp. if illicitly distilled: low (—1896); ob.

jiggered, ppl adj. Made from a secret still: from ca 1880. *Judy*, 4 Aug. 1886, 'Jiggered gin'. Suggested by JIGGER-STUFF.

jiggered!, be. As in *I'm*, or *I'll be, jiggered!*, *you be jiggered!* Marryat, 1837. Possibly a deliberate fusing and perversion of *Jesus* and *buggered*; cf., however, SNIGGERED.

jiggered up. Exhausted: nautical (—1867). cf. JIGGER, v., 2, but prob. ex last entry.

jiggery-pokery; occ. jackery-pokery. Humbug; underhand work: ?orig. (ca 1880) tailors' s.; coll by 1900. Ex Scottish *joukery-paukery* ex *jouk*, a trick. cf. HANKY-PANKY; HOCUS-POCUS, W.

jigget, occ. **jiggit,** v.i. To jig, fidget, hop about, shake up and down: coll: 1687. Mrs Behn, Miss Mitford, Kipling. Diminutive of *jig*.

jiggety, jiggity. Having a hopping or jerky movement: coll: from ca 1880.

jiggle, v.i. and t. To have sexual intercourse with: low: from ca 1845. Ex the S.E. sense. Hence *jiggling-bone*, the male member. cf. JIG-A-JIG.

***jiggot o' mutton.** A leg of mutton: c. (—1909). Fr. *gigot*.

jig(g)umbob. Also *jig(g)ambob, -embob, -ombob*; *gig(g)umbob*, etc.; *gingam*(or *um*)*bob*. Something odd or very fanciful; something unspecified: coll: C.17–20; ob. Beaumont & Fletcher, 'What Giggombob have we here?' Rare of a person. Ex JIG, n.: cf. THINGUMBOB.

jil-crow-a-berry. The anglicized pronunciation and spelling of the aboriginal name for the indigenous *Rat-tail Grass*: Australian coll (—1898).

jildi, jildy; jildo; occ. **jeldi (-y);** very often **jillo,** adj. and adv. Lively; look sharp!: Regular Army's: late C.19–20. Ex Hindustani. (Also, as adv., *on the jildi.*) cf. Romany *jido, jidilo*, lively.

***jilt.** A crowbar: c. (—1859); ob. In pl, housebreaking tools in general. 2. A harlot: s.: Ned Ward, 1703.

***jilt, v.** Enter a building slyly or on false pretences, and then steal: c.: from ca 1860; ob.

***jilter.** A thief acting as in JILT, v.: c.: from ca 1860. Also called a *note-blanker*. (Such thieves work in pairs.)

Jim Brown. Town: rhyming s. (—1893).

Jim Crow, see BILLY BARLOW.

jim-jam. A knick-knack: coll (—1592); †by 1700. A reduplication on the first syllable of *gimcrack*. 2. Delirium tremens: in pl only (*the j.-j.*): 1885. Often called *the jams* (ob.). Perhaps influenced by WHIM-WHAM. 3. Also pl only: peculiarities: coll (—1899).

Jim Mace, see JEM MACE.

jimbugg. A sheep: Australia: from ca 1850; ob. More gen. is *jumbuck* (—1845): orig. the natives' pidgin English: the word meaning, in Aborigine, a white mist, the only thing with which a flock of sheep could be compared.

jiminy, see GEMINI.

jimkwim; jimmant. Corruptions of DOCTOR JIM.

jimmy. A mainly U.S. variant of JEMMY, n., 1. 2. **(Jimmy.)** A new chum or immigrant: Australian (—1859); †by 1897. Also (—1867) *Jimmy* (or *Jemmy*) *Grant*, presumably after *immigrant*, though see JIMMY GRANT, 2. (Only *Jimmy*:) In South Africa (esp. Natal) by 1878, notes Pettman. 3. A contrivance; anything faked; a concealed helper: showmen's: from ca 1850. 4. Abbr. *Jimmy o' Goblin*, JEMMY O' GOBLIN. 5. 'The nickname used as an alternative to Shiner for all naval Greens' (Bowen): late C.19–20.

jimmy, adj., see JEMMY, adj.

jimmy, all. All nonsense: Cambridge University: ca 1860–1910. See also JEMMY, n., 7.

Jimmy Bung(s). A cooper: naval (—1909). Prob. ex *bung-hole*. Also BUNGS.

Jimmy Ducks. The rating in charge of the ship's poultry: naval: ca 1800–50. cf.

DUCK-FUCKER. 2. Hence, a galley boy, a butcher's assistant: nautical: mid-C.19–20.

jimmy (or **J.**) **fixing.** 'A mechanical contraption of any description': merchant service: late C.19–20. Bowen. cf. HOOK-ME-DINGHY.

Jimmy Grant. See JIMMY, n., 2. 2. An emigrant: rhyming s.: New Zealand, from 1840s. Also *Jemmy Grant.*

Jimmy Low. A eucalyptus timber-tree: Australia (—1889). After some New South Wales CHARACTER. cf. JEMMY DONNELLY.

Jimmy o' Goblin, see JEMMY O' GOBLIN.

Jimmy Riddle. To urinate: rhyming s. (on PIDDLE): late C.19–20.

Jimmy Round. (Gen. pl.) A Frenchman: naval: late C.18–early 19. Ware derives it from the Fr. *je me rends,* I surrender.

Jimmy Skinner. A dinner: rhyming s. (—1896).

Jimmy the Bunting. A signalman: naval: late C.19–20. With a pun on *Baby Bunting* and *bunting*, flags in the mass.

jingbang, occ. **jimbang.** (Sometimes hyphenated. Always preceded by *the whole.*) A lot, or group, complete: mainly Scots coll (—1891). Stevenson, 'The only seaman of the whole jing-bang.'

***jingle-box.** A leathern drinking vessel tipped with silver and hung with bells, in C.17 use among topers: C.17–18.

jingle-boy, see GINGLE-BOY.

jingle-brains. A wild HARUM-SCARUM fellow: C.17–18; coll. Extant in dial.

***jingler.** A horse-dealer frequenting country fairs: early C.17–18 c.

jingo!, by the living. A C.19–20 (ob.) elaboration of:

jings!, more gen. *by jingo*; in late C.18–20 Scotland, always (*by*) *jing*(*s*). A mild oath: coll: from ca 1694 as an exclamation, but in 1670, and prob. much earlier, it was a piece of conjurer's gibberish. The word comes prob. ex Basque *J*(*a*)*inko*, God, via the Basque harpooners on British whalers.

jiniper-, in C.18–19 **juniper-lecture.** A scolding: late C.17–mid-19: coll. B.E.'s *jiniper-l.* is obviously a misprint, but it may have reproduced a Cockney pronunciation.

jink. Coin, money: late C.19–20. Perhaps on CHINK. 2. In pl, see HIGH JINKS.

jink one's tin. To pay, SHELL OUT; rattle one's money: low: from ca 1850; ob.

jinker. A light sulky, with room for only one person; esp. one used in speed-trotting trials: Australian coll (from ca 1875). Ex *jinker*, a vehicular contrivance for the transport of tree trunks.

jinket. To be very merry; dance about: coll, the former 1742, ob., the latter 1823, ob. Ex *jink.*

jinks. See HIGH JINKS. 2. **Jinks the Barber.** A secret informant: middle classes': mid-C.19–20; ob. Ware, 'The general barber being such a gossiper. Jinks is a familiar name' – coll, from ca 1820 – 'for an easy-going man'.

***jinny.** A Geneva watch: c.: late C.19–20; ob. Ex *Geneva.*

Jinny Spinner (or **j.-s.**). A cockroach: nautical: late C.19–20.

***jintoe.** A girl of poor reputation; a whore: South African (low s. and c.): late C.19–20.

***jip;** esp. **stick of jip.** Indian ink: c.: mid-C.19–20. '*No. 747*'. cf. JIPPING.

jip, give one, see GIP, GIVE.

jipper, jippo. Gravy: nautical: from ca 1850. Occ. it = juice, syrup, or even dripping. Perhaps ultimately ex †*jippo*, a tunic, hence a scullion. Just possibly, a *Gippo* being a man of brown colour, ex sense 2; but I shouldn't be surprised if it were proved to be a corruption of *sipper*. 2. *Jippo*, an incorrect form of *Gyppo*, an Egyptian.

***jipping,** vbl n. Staining (part of a horse) with Indian ink to conceal a blemish: c.: mid-C.19–20. '*No. 747*': cf. JIP.

jippo, see JIPPER.

jirrand, see JERRAN.

jo. See JOE, n. 2. An exclamation, a warning: Australia: from ca 1853; ob. Also *joe, joey.* Ex Charles Joseph La Trobe, the Victorian Governor at that time. W. Howitt, *Two Years in Victoria*, 1855. Also a v. (—1861), with variant *joey.* T. McCombie, *Australian Sketches*, 1861.

jo-jo. A man with much hair on his face: Melbourne (Australia): low: ca 1880–1905. Ex a Russian 'dog-man', ostensibly so named, exhibited in Melbourne ca 1880.

joan, Joan. A fetter, esp. in *Darby and Joan*, fetters coupling two prisoners. C.18–19. Suggested by DARBIES, handcuffs or fetters.

Joan, homely. A coarse, ordinary woman: C.17–18 coll. In dial., *Joan Blunt.*

Job. A henpecked husband: lower and lower-middle classes' coll: coined by Douglas Jerrold, in *Mrs Caudle's Curtain Lectures*, 1846; ob. Ex the Biblical character.

job. A guinea: c. of ca 1670–1830.

Whence *half a job*, half a guinea. Occ. *jobe*. 2. A robbery: C.18–20, c. >, ca 1850, low. Defoe, in *Moll Flanders*, 'It was always reckoned a safe job when we heard of a new shop.'

job, v. To coït with: coll: C.16–20. Anon. play of *Thersites*, 1537; Burns. Ex *job*, to prod; cf. JAB, v., 2. 2. See JOBE.

job, be on the. 'To mean honestly; to be genuine; to "run straight"; to work quickly and steadily; to achieve complete success; to be bent on', F. & H. Coll: from ca 1880.

job, do a. To conduct a funeral: undertakers' coll (—1864). 2. See DO A JOB. 3. To defecate: both children's and adults': late C.19–20. Euphemistic.

job, have got the. To have a commission to bet on a horse: racing: from ca 1875.

job for her, do a woman's. To accomplish the sexual act with her – and to her pleasure. Low coll: from ca 1850.

job for him, do a man's. To ruin; knock out; kill; low coll: from ca 1860.

job for oneself, do a. To defecate: late C.19–20: (?orig. low) coll.

job of it, make a clean. To do thoroughly: coll: from ca 1885. Anstey, *Voces Populi*, II, 1892.

Jobanjeremiah. A maunderer: lower classes' (—1909); ob. Ware, 'Combination of the two doleful patriarchs'.

jobation. A (tedious) reproof or rebuke: coll: from ca 1765; ob. Ex JOBE, v. The alternative form JAWBATION has been influenced by JAW, n. and v. Colman, 1767, in *The Oxon in Town*, 'As dull and melancholy as a fresh-man ... after a jobation'.

jobbed, that job's. It's finished: coll: 1840, Marryat, 'That job's jobbed, as the saying is.'

***jobberknot, -nut.** (Or hyphenated.) A tall, clumsy fellow: C.19 c.

jobbernowl, -nol(l), -nole. A fool's head; a fool: coll: late C.16–20; ob. ?ex *job(b)ard*, a simpleton. The *-nol(l)* forms not before ca 1670, and rare after 1750. 2. adj., stupid: coll: from ca 1825; ob.

jobbing. Sexual intercourse: mainly Scots coll: C.17–20.

***jobe**, see JOB, n., 1.

jobe, occ. **job.** To rebuke lengthily and tediously: coll: ca 1670–1830. 'Cambridge term', Grose, 2nd ed. (following Ray). Ex the lengthy reproofs of Job's friends.

Job's dock, be laid up in. To be treated in hospital for a venereal disease: coll: C.18–early 19. A malicious interpretation of Job's 'sore boils'. cf. JOB'S WARD.

Job's tears. The seeds of *Coix lachryma*, 'which are used for necklace-making by the native tribes on Cape York peninsula, are there called *Job's tears*', Morris. Australia (—1897). But also of the natives of Papua, where they are worn only by widows as a sign of mourning: cf. Job when 'separated' from his family.

Job's turkey, as poor as. Exceedingly poor: coll of ca 1820–1910: mainly and perhaps orig. U.S.

Job's ward. The ward for venereal patients in St Bartholomew's Hospital: mid-C.18–mid-19: prob. orig. medical.

Job's wife. A wanton and scolding woman: coll: C.19. cf. JOB.

joby. A vendor of sweets and refreshments: Eton College: late C.19–20.

Jock. A North Country seaman, esp. a collier: coll: mid-C.18–19. Also *crowdy-headed Jock*, 'Jock being a common name, and crowdy the chief food, of the lower order of the people of Northumberland,' Grose, 2nd ed. 2. A Scot. Coll: from ca 1870. In C.16–19 dial., *Jocky*. 3. Hence, the 'inevitable' nickname of men with a Scottish surname or accent: late C.19–20.

jock. 'Private parts of a man or woman,' Potter, *Dict. of Cant and Flash*, 1790: low. (Of a woman, very rare after ca 1880.) See the v. 2. Abbr. *jockey*: coll: from ca 1825; ob.

***jock**, v. To coït with a woman: late C.17–19: c. till C.19, when low. cf. JOCKUM-CLOY; also JOCKUM, which it prob. abbr.; hence the n., 1.

Jock, hairy. (Gen. pl.) A variant of JOCK, 2, second nuance – but not in his hearing!

Jock Blunt, look like. To be out of countenance through disappointment: C.18–early 19. Ramsay. Contrast JACK BLUNT, and its dial. counterpart *Joan Blunt*.

***jockam**, see JOCKUM.

jockey, v. To appropriate, engage, supplant: Winchester College: from ca 1820; ob.

jockey not!; jockey up! Winchester College ob. cries of (*a*) exemption, (*b*) participation. (cf. BAGS!) Mid.C.19–20.

jockey (or bag) the over. So to run as to get all the bowling to oneself: cricketers': from ca 1860.

jockeying. 'Vehicular racing': London streets': C.19. Ware.

jockeys. Top-boots: trade: from ca 1850; ob. Mayhew.

***jockum;** occ. **jockam.** The penis: c.: mid-C.16–early 19.

***jockum-cloy.** To coït with (a woman): C.17–early 19 c. Ex JOCKUM + CLOY. cf. JOCK, v. 2. Also n.

***jockum-gage.** A chamber-pot: c.: C.17–19. Ex JOCKUM.

***jockum-gagger.** A man living on his wife's harlotry: ?C.18–early 19: c.

***jocky.** 'A Man's Yard', Holme, 1688; whence JOCK, n.

joe. Abbr. JOE MILLER: 1834. 2. (Also JOEY.) A fourpenny piece: ca 1840–1910. Ex *Joseph* Hume, politician and financial expert (1777–1855). E. Hawkins, *Silver Coins of England.* 3. A marine: nautical: ca 1850–1900. Abbr. JOSEPH. 4. A Portuguese and Brazilian gold coin: 1772: coll >, ca 1880, S.E. Ex *Johannes*, recorded in 1762 in U.S., where *jo* occurs in 1765. Derivatively a nautical name for the sum of sixteen dollars: ca 1790–1850: John Davis, *The Post Captain*, 1805. 5. **Joe** or **Joey.** A police-trooper: Australian miners' derogatory in the 1850s. Prob. of same origin as JO, 2. 6. As *Joe*, it = an imaginary person, as in '"Who did that?" – "Joe"': ca 1830–70. *Sinks*, 1848.

joe, v.i. To poke fun; to take liberties with text or audience: theatrical: ca 1865–1900. Kingsley. Ex Australia, where (—1861) it means – gen. as v.t. – to ridicule; insult grossly; now ob. See JO, 2, also JOEY.

Joe, not for, see JOSEPH, NOT FOR.

Joe Blake. A cake: rhyming s.: late C.19–20.

***Joe Blake the Bart(h)lemy,** v. To visit a prostitute: c. and low (—1859); ob.

Joe Brown. (A) town: rhyming s., ?orig. showmen's: 1893, P. H. Emerson, *Signor Lippo.*

Joe Manton. A fowling-piece made by Joseph Manton (d. 1837), a well-known London gunsmith: coll: 1816 (S.O.D.); ob. by 1890, †by 1910. Also *Manton.* See next entry, sense (2):

Joe Miller. A jest-book: coll: 1789, George Parker; ob. Ex comedian Joseph Miller (1684–1738), whose name was identified with a book pub. in 1739 but not compiled by him. 2. Hence, a jest, esp. if a stale one: coll: 1816. Scott, 'A fool and his money are soon parted, nephew; there is a Joe Miller for your Joe Manton.' cf. CHESTNUT, 2.

Joe Miller of it, I don't see the. I don't see the joke; or the fun of doing it: coll: ca 1830–95.

Joe O'Gorman. A foreman: rhyming s.: late C.19–20.

Joe Poke. A justice of the peace: lower classes'; from ca 1875. By elaboration of *J.P.*

Joe Savage. A cabbage: rhyming s. (—1859). As is also:

Joe Skinner. Dinner: late C.19–20.

joey. A fourpenny piece: from ca 1855; †. H., 1859, 'The term originated with the London cabmen.' See JOE, n., 2. 2. (Gen. with capital.) A marine: nautical: from ca 1830; ob. 'Taffrail', 'A Royal marine is a "bullock", "turkey", or "Joey", while a soldier is a "grabby" or "leather neck",' cf. JOE, n., 3; but prob. ex JOLLY, n., 2. 3. A clown: theatrical: from ca 1830. Ex Joe Grimaldi, who to the early C.19 was what Grock is to C.20. 4. A very young kangaroo: Australian coll: 1839. Hence, a hewer of wood and drawer of water (1845), punning *kangaroo* as typical of an Australian; from ca 1870, any other young animal; hence, from ca 1880, a little child, a baby. Ex Aborigine *joé.* 5. See JO, 2. 6. A newly entered prisoner in a convict prison: c.: ca 1865 is the date of the reference in '*No. 747*'. 7. See JOE, 5. 8. A humbug: prison c.: mid-C.19–20. Mayhew. Perhaps cf. HOLY JOE.

joey, v. See JO, 2, and JOE, v. 2. To MUG or attract the public's attention, while the MUGGER (2) is up-stage: theatrical: mid-C.19–early 20. Ex the n., 3.

joey! see JO, 2.

jog the loo. To pump briskly: nautical coll: C.19–20. Obviously *loo* is water (Fr. *l'eau*).

jogger. To play and sing: theatrical or, rather, Parlary (—1893); ob. Ex It. *giocare*, to play.

joggering omee (or omey). A musician, esp. if itinerant: Parlary (—1893); ob. See last entry.

***jogue.** A shilling: c. of ca 1810–60. ?the origin of BOB (2). It seems to have survived among chimneysweepers till ca 1900 in the form *jug.*

***jogul.** To PLAY UP, or simply to play, at any game, esp. cards: gaming c. (—1859). Ex Sp. *jugar.*

John. A first-year cadet: Sandhurst: from ca 1860. Ex JOHNNY RAW. 2. A chap, a fellow (C.19–20). Ex JOHNNIE, 1. 3. A Chinaman: U.S. (ca 1870), anglicized ca

1890. 4. Dried fish: nautical: late C.19–20. 5. A coll term of address, C.19–20.

John-and-Joan. A homosexual: C.18–mid-19 coll.

John Audley; occ. Orderly! Abridge the performance!: theatrical: from ca 1810. Ex the actor-manager John Richardson (d. 1837), who used to ask 'Is John Audley here?' whenever another 'house' was waiting, though tradition (H., 1864) has it that John Audley or Orderly taught him the WHEEZE.

John Barleycorn, or Sir J. B., is nobody with him. He's no drinker: proverbial c.p.: C.17–18.

John Barleycorn's, or Sir John Barleycorn's, the strongest knight. Malt liquor is strong stuff: proverbial c.p.: C.17–18. Ray.

John Blunt, see JACK BLUNT.

John Chinaman. A Chinese: C.19–20, ob.

John Collins. A drink made of soda water, gin, sugar, lemon and ice: Australia: from ca 1860. The *Australasian*, 24 Feb. 1865, 'That most angelic of drinks for a hot climate . . .'

John Company; occ. Johnny Company. The Honourable East India Company: coll: from ca 1785; now only historical. Ex Dutch *Jan Kompanie*, by which the Eastern natives speak of the Dutch East India Company and government.

John Cotton, see DOLLY COTTON.

John Crap(p)o, see JOHNNY CRAPOSE.

John Drawlatch. A sneaking person: coll > S.E.: C.16–17. Heywood's *Proverbs*, 1546.

John Fortnight. The tallyman: London workmen's: late C.19–20; ob. Ware, 'From his calling every other week'.

John Gray's bird, like. Fond of company, even if it be rather above one: coll: C.16. Gascoigne.

John Long (in C.18–19, occ. **Tom Long) the carrier, stay for** or **send by.** To wait, or postpone for, a long time: coll: C.16–19. Cotgrave.

John o' Groat. A coat: rhyming s.: since ca 1800.

John Orderly, see JOHN AUDLEY.

John Roberts. A, or enough, drink to keep a man drunk from Saturday to Sunday night: Anglo-Welsh (—1886). Ex the author of the Sunday Closing Act.

John Roper's window, see ROPER'S WINDOW.

John Thomas. A flunkey: low coll: ca 1860–1910. 2. The male member: upper-class: from ca 1840. cf. DICK.

John (occ. Joan) Thomson's man. An uxorious husband: Scots coll: C.16–19. Dunbar.

John Trot. A bumpkin: upper classes': ?ca 1710–70. (A letter, dated 17 Dec. 1733 and cited in *Lord Hervey and His Friends*, edited by the Earl of Ilchester, 1950.)

John Tuck. A Chinese mandarin: nautical: late C.19–20. cf. JOHN, 3.

John Willie (or Willy), come on! A North Country c.p. of exhortation to a slow-witted or mentally deficient youth or man: late C.19–20. Also, Julian Franklyn tells me, a London streets c.p. of ca 1910: 'I believe from a song.'

Johnnie, Johnny. A fellow, a CHAP; a sweetheart: coll: from ca 1670; ob. Ramsay, Kipling. 2. A (fashionable) young man about town: from ca 1880. 3. A tiger: sportsmen's: 1815. 4. A penguin: nautical (—1898). 5. A policeman: low: from ca 1850. Occ. (ca 1860–80) *Johnny Darby*, perhaps influenced by DARBIES and Fr. *gendarmes*. Mayhew, Besant & Rice. 6. A half-glass of whiskey: Anglo-Irish: from ca 1860; ob. (Earlier (—1827), Dumbartonshire dial.) 7. A Greek: nautical: late C.19–20. Perhaps ex prevalence of the name *Johannides*. 8. The nickname of men surnamed Walker: naval and military: late C.19–20. Ex the celebrated whisky. 9. Penis: late C.19–20.

Johnnie Rutter. Butter: rhyming s.: from ca 1880. Contrast JOHNNY HORNER.

Johnny Bates'(s) Farm, see BATE'S FARM.

Johnny Bono. An Englishman: East End of London: from ca 1850; ob.

Johnny Bum. A male donkey: jocular: late C.18–mid-19. Ex a euphemism for *jack ass*, *ass* being pronounced ARSE.

Johnny cake. A cake cooked in a frying pan or baked in the ashes: Australia (—1861): coll. Adoption of a U.S. term, which (orig. – 1775 – *journey-cake*) denotes a thin cake made of Indian meal and toasted before a fire.

John(ny) Crapose. Frenchman: low: C.19–early 20. The singular is *Crapo* or *Crappo* – but not very frequent. Ex Fr. *crapaud*, a toad (not a frog). 2. (Gen. *John Crappo.*) Hence, a British seaman wearing a moustache: nautical: ca 1815–50.

Johnny Darby. See JOHNNY, 5. 2. In pl, handcuffs: ca 1860–1915.

Johnny hangman. See JACKY HANGMAN. (Woodward, *The Birds of Natal*, 1899.)

Johnny Haultaut. A man-of-warsman:

merchant service: ca 1870–1910. Clark Russell. Perhaps ex *haul taut*.

Johnny Horner. Round the corner; i.e. to, at, a PUB: rhyming s. (—1909).

Johnny Newcome. A new-born child: coll: from ca 1830; ob. 2. An inexperienced youth; a landsman: nautical: from late C.18; ob.

Johnny Randall. A candle: navvies' rhyming s.: ca 1860–1900. (D. W. Barrett, 1880.)

Johnny Raw. A novice; a recruit: coll: 1813; ob. *Sydney Bulletin*, 26 Feb. 1887, 'He was a new-chum – a regular Johnny-Raw.' 2. A morning drink: provincial: from ca 1870; ob.

Johnny Scaparey, do a. To abscond: circus-employees': mid-C.19–20. It. *scappare*, to escape.

Johnny Warder. An idler who hangs about public-houses in the hope of a free drink: Australian: ca 1880–1920. Ex *John Ward*, the landlord of a low PUB in Sydney.

Johnson. The penis: low: mid-C.19–20.

joined, be. To be married. Coll: C.19–20. cf. *join* GIBLETS.

***joint.** In c. (—1885) partnership; a concerted robbery (—1887, Baumann): ob. 2. 'An outside bookmaker's paraphernalia of list-frame, umbrella, etc., some of which are joined together in movable pieces,' O.E.D.: the turf: from ca 1896. 3. Any place or building: low: app. Anglo-Irish in origin – 'A Real Paddy', *Real Life in Ireland*, 1822, 'I slips the joint' (ran away from the place – a boarding school).

***joint, work the.** To swindle with a jockeyed lottery table: c. (—1895).

jokee. The 'victim' of a joke: coll: from ca 1870.

joker. A man, CHAP, fellow: from ca 1810. (Pepys's 'At noon . . . to the Trinity-house, where a very good dinner among the old jokers' is misleading.) cf. ARTIST; MERCHANT; SHAVER.

***joker, little,** see LITTLE JOKER.

jolah. A haversack: Regular Army's: late C.19–20. Ex Hindustani.

Jollies, the. See JOLLY, n., 2, quotation from Bowen: ?C.17–early 19.

jollification. Jollity; a merry-making: coll: 1798 (S.O.D.). Scott. Whence:

jollify. To behave merrily; become, occ. make, slightly drunk: coll: from ca 1820.

jollily. Excellently, splendidly; delightfully: from ca 1560: S.E. till ca 1850, then coll; slightly ob. (cf. JOLLY, adj., 1 and 2.) M. C. Jackson, 1878.

jollocks; jollux. A parson: low: late C.18–19. Possibly a euphemizing (suggested by JOLLY, adj.) of BALLOCKS (cf. CODS, a curate); prob. ex dial. *jollock*, jolly, hearty. 2. (*jollux.*) A fat person: ca 1795–1815.

jolly. The head: late C.18–mid-19. Also *jolly* NOB. 2. A Royal Marine: nautical: from ca 1820. Also (—1867) a *Royal* (or *royal*) *jolly*. (cf. *tame jolly*, a militiaman.) Marryat; Kipling; Bowen, 'Taken from the old nickname of the City Trained Bands'. 3. The confederate of a thief or a swindler; esp. a sham purchaser: c. (—1856); ob. Mayhew, Greenwood. 4. A pretence; an excuse: c.: from ca 1850; ob. J. W. Horsley. 5. Praise, a recommendation; chaff, abuse: low (orig. Cockney) coll: from ca 1855. Vance, in *The Chickaleary Cove*. 6. Hence, a cheer: from ca 1870; slightly ob. Esp. in *give* (e.g. *him*) *a jolly*, chiefly in imperative.

jolly, v.t. and i. To joke; rally, chaff; vituperate: from ca 1860. 2. To cheer: from ca 1890. 3. v.i., to make a sham bid (at an auction): 1869: c. > low; ob. 4. To impose upon, to act as an accomplice or abettor: c.: from ca 1860.

jolly, adj. Excellent; fine; indicative of general approbation (in mid-C.19–20, often ironical): C.14–20; S.E. till C.19, then coll. *Daily Telegraph*, 1869, 'He is annoyed when young ladies use slang phrases, such as awfully jolly.' 2. Extremely pleasant, agreeable, suitable, charming: mid-C.16–20: S.E. till ca 1860, then coll. 3. Slightly drunk: from ca 1650; euphemistic S.E. till C.19, then coll. 4. Healthy and well developed; well conditioned; plump: coll and dial.: from ca 1660. Whence: 5. Fat; too fat: the turf: from ca 1885.

jolly, adv. with adv. or adj. (In mid-C.19–20, often ironical.) Very; exceedingly: mid-C.16–20: S.E. till C.19, then coll. Dickens in *Oliver Twist*, '"He is so jolly green," said Charley.'

jolly, chuck a, see CHUCK A JOLLY.

jolly boys. 'A group of small drinking vessels connected by a tube, or by openings one from another,' F. & H.: coll: from ca 1890; slightly ob.

jolly dog. A boon companion, merry fellow: coll (—1785) >, ca 1870, S.E.: slightly ob. cf. S.E. *jolly fellow*.

jolly for. To support a friend with kindly chaff or praise: ca 1850–1925: mostly Cockney. cf. JOLLY, n., sense 6.

jolly jumper. A light sail set above a

'skyscraper': nautical (—1883); ob. Clark Russell.

jolly nob, see JOLLY, n., 1.

jolly Roger. A pirate's flag: nautical coll > S.E.: from ca 1880. Stevenson, in *Treasure Island*, 'There was the jolly Roger – the black flag of piracy – flying from her peak.'

jolly-up. A BEANO; a drinking-bout: lower-middle class: from ca 1905; ob.

jolly utter. Unspeakable: London cultured: 1881–ca 1890. *Punch*, 1881; W. S. Gilbert's *Patience*, 1881; *Referee*, 18 Feb. 1883.

jolly well. An intensive adverb: middle-class coll: apparently since the 1880s.

jolt. To coït with (a woman): C.19–20.

jomer. A fancy girl; a sweetheart: c. (—1839) >, ca 1850, theatrical and Parlary; † as theatrical. Perhaps a corruption of It. *donna* (cf. DONA(H)) it is always – in contradistinction to BLOWER (2), BLOWEN – a complimentary term, says Brandon.

Jonah's whale. Tail: rhyming s.: from 1887. It first occurs in G. R. Sims's 'Tottie', a Dagonet Ballad published in the *Referee*, 7 Nov. 1887.

Jones, Mrs, see MRS JONES.

jonnick, jonnock, jonnuk, see JANNOCK.

jordan; in C.17–18, often **jordain;** in C.16–17, occ. **jurdain(e), jurdan** or **jurden.** A chamber-pot: C.14–20; ob.: S.E. till ca 1840, then dial. and low coll. (In C.19, occ. a slop-pail.) 'Prob. an application of the baptismal name *Jordan*, very common in M.E.', W.; perhaps reinforced by the Biblical 'waters of Jordan'. 2. A blow with a staff: c.: late C.17–mid-19. 3. The Atlantic: journalists': ca 1870–1910.

Jordan, over; this side of Jordan. Resp., dead; alive: coll (—1889). Ex its use in 'pietistic language to symbolise death' (O.E.D. Sup.).

jorrie. A girl: low Glasgow: late C.19–20.

Joseph. A marine: nautical: C.19–20; ob.

Joseph!, not for. A scornful refusal: 1844, C. Selby, *London by Night*: ob. by 1900. Also (—1867) *not for joe!*

Josephine. See NOT TONIGHT, JOSEPHINE!

Joseph's coat. A many-coloured coat; a dress of honour: coll: from ca 1890. Kipling, 'A Joseph's jury-coat to keep his honour warm'.

Josephus rex, you are. You're joking: a late C.18–early 19 c.p. *Jo-king*, *rex* being L. for king.

josh. A fool; a sleepy fellow: coll: mid-C.19–20; ob. ?ex:

joskin. A country bumpkin: low: from ca 1810; ob. Prob. ex dial. *joss*, to bump, after *bumpkin* itself. 2. Hence, 'a green hand under sail': nautical: from ca 1830; ob. 3. Hence, a recruit: military: C.20.

joss. An idol: Anglo-Chinese 'pidgin': C.18–20. Ex Portuguese *Deos*, God. Whence *joss-house*, an idol temple: mid-C.18–20. cf. CHIN-CHIN JOSS. 2. Luck: nautical: late C.19–20. Ex sense 1.

joss-house man; joss-pidgin man. A priest; a missionary: pidgin: from ca 1860.

josser. A simpleton (—1886); ob. except among tailors. Prob. ex JOSKIN. 2. An old roué (—1892); †. 3. (Gen. with *old*.) A fellow: from ca 1890. Perhaps ex JOSKIN. 4. A parson: Australia: ca 1885–1910. 5. A SWELL: Hong-Kong (—1909). Prob. ex JOSS, as sense 4 is – even more prob. 6. An outsider: Parlary: (?late C.19–)C.20. Prob. ex sense 1 influenced by JOSKIN, 2; also *josher*.

jossop. Syrup, juice, sauce, gravy: schoolboys': from ca 1860; ob. Perhaps a corrupt blend of *juice* + *syrup*.

***jostle.** To cheat: c.: late C.18–20. (cf. *hustle*, v., and HUSTLER.) Whence:

***jostler.** A swindler: Glasgow c.: C.20 – and prob. from well back in C.19.

jottle (v.i.); **do a jottle; go jottling.** To copulate: low: C.19–20; ob.

journey, not one's. Not a successful day: turf: from ca 1860; ob. Ex Fr. *journée*.

journey, this. On this time or occasion: coll: 1884; slightly ob.

journeyman parson. A curate: London: ca 1820–1900. Because apt to be moved about far more than is a full-blown clergyman.

journeyman soul-saver. A scripture-reader: ca 1860–1900.

***jovah.** Gaol: c.: from ca 1870. Pugh (2): 'All I can say is, you never kept your brains clear while you was in jovah.' Perhaps a perversion of *jail* suggested by *chokey*.

Jove!; by Jove. A coll exclamation, asseveration: from ca 1570. Shakespeare, 'By Jove, I always took three threes for nine'; Miss Ferrier.

jow. (Gen. in imperative.) To go away; be off: Anglo-Indian: from ca 1860; slightly ob. Ex Hindustani; cf. Romany *jaw* (and Sampson's *ja*).

jowl-sucking. Kissing, kisses: lower classes': from ca 1865; ob.

jowler. A lane between back-to-back houses: Liverpool: late C.19–20. You pass cheek-by-jowl.

joy of my life. A wife: rhyming s., mostly military: from ca 1880. cf. the much more general TROUBLE AND STRIFE.

joyful, O be, see O BE JOYFUL. 2. cf. *sing* 'O BE JOYFUL' ON THE OTHER SIDE OF ONE'S MOUTH.

joyous spirit, see JEMMY, n., 2. (Transient s.)

jube. A coll abbr. of *jujube* (the lozenge): from ca 1840.

jubilee. A very pleasant time: Winchester College: C.19–20; ob. 2. Posterior: sporting and inferior society: 1887–ca 1897.

Judaic superbac(e)y. A 'Jew in all the glory of his best clothes': Covent Garden Theatre and vicinity: 1887–ca 1899. Ware.

jude. A harlot: low (—1886). Henley. Also JUDY.

***judge.** An expert, sagacious thief or swindler: c.: ca 1810–50.

judge and jury. A mock trial, the fines being paid in beer: tailors': from ca 1870.

judgmatic. Judicious; judicial. So *judgmatical*, adv. *judgmatically*. All coll and slightly ob.; resp. 1835, 1826, 1814. But *judgmatical* was orig. U.S., Thornton recording it at 1774. On *dogmatic*.

Judische (or Jew's) compliment. A large penis but no money: low: from ca 1850; ob. cf. YORKSHIRE COMPLIMENT.

judy. A girl, esp. one of loose morals: from ca 1810: prob. orig. c.; always more or less low; common among C.19 sailors. Also, later, *jude*. Vaux. 1812; Runciman, *The Chequers*. Ex *Punch and Judy*, or, like *jane*, direct ex the Christian name. 2. A simpleton, a fool: orig. (1824), U.S.; anglicized ca 1850. Esp. in *make a judy of oneself*, play the fool, act the giddy goat.

judy-slayer. A LADY-KILLER: London Jews' (—1909). cf. JUDY, 1.

***jug.** A prison: C.19 c., C.20 low. Also *stone jug* (s.v. STONE DOUBLET). Ainsworth, 1834, the first English user, the term occurring in U.S. in 1815; Dickens, Thackeray. Ex Fr. *joug*, a yoke, via ob. Scots *joug(s)*, a pillory. 2. As a mistress and as a term of contempt, it is despite F. & H., indubitably S.E. 3. Abbr. JUGGINS. 4. A bank: c.: from ca 1860. *Cornhill Magazine*, 1862.

***jug,** v. To imprison; lock up: orig. (ca 1840) c.; by ca 1860, low. See the n., and cf. Scots *joug*, to confine in the jougs. 2. To deceive humorously or, more gen., illicitly: low: from ca 1870; ob.

jug-bitten. Tipsy: coll: ca 1620–1750. Taylor the Water Poet.

jug-loops. Hair worn with tiny curls on the temples: low Cockney: ca 1885–1905.

***jugelo(w).** A dog: c. of ca 1810–50. Ex Romany *juggal*, pl *juggalor*.

jugful, not by a. Not by a long way: coll: ex U.S. (1834), anglicized ca 1850; ob. by 1910.

jugged. Arrested, imprisoned: see JUG, v., 1.

juggins; occ. jug. A fool: s. >, in C.20, (low) coll: 1882 (S.O.D.). *Punch*, 17 July 1886, 'Yah! Wot a old juggins he is!' Prob. suggested by MUGGINS.

juggins-hunting. 'Looking for a man who will pay for liquor' (Ware): taverns' (—1909). Ex preceding. Contrast:

juggins's boy. 'The sharp and impudent son of a stupid and easily ridiculed father': low London: 1882. Ware.

***juggler's box.** The branding-iron: c.: late C.18–early 19.

***juggling law.** In late C.16–early 17 c., it is a branch of criminal activity practised among the devotees of certain games. Greene, *A Disputation*, 1592, '*The Juggling Law*, wherein I will set out the disorders at Nyneholes and Ryfling [i.e. dicing], how they are only for the benefite of the Cutpurses.'

juice. Emoluments, profits of office or profession: coll: ca 1520–1640. Latimer, Sir E. Hoby. 2. Money: ca 1695–1730. Ned Ward in *The London Spy*, 1698 (see *Slang*, p. 69). 3. Juiciness of colour: C.19–20 artists. cf. JUICY, 5. 4. Petrol: 1909. 5. Electricity; electric current: 1903; electricians' s.

juice, bright-work, see BRIGHT-WORK JUICE. **juice, bug.** Hair-oil. **juice, cow,** see COW-JUICE. **juice, fresh.** Fresh water. All four terms are *Conway* cadets' s.: from ca 1890.

juice for jelly, give. (Of a woman) to experience the sexual spasm: low: C.19–20. (Otherwise, *juice* in this sense is rare.) cf. JELLY.

juicy. As (of women) amorous, it is S.E. 2. Piquant, bawdy: low coll (—1880). Greenwood. 3. (Of weather) wet, very rainy, drenching: coll: 1837. 4. Rich in money, etc.: coll: from ca 1620. Contrast *dry*. 5. In artists' s.: characterized by rich liquid colouring, 1820.

***jukrum.** A licence: late C.17–early 19 c. cf. JACKRUM.

Julius Caesar. The male member: low: from ca 1840; ob.

Julius Caesar, dead as. Certainly, or long, dead: coll: C.19–20; ob.

Julius Caesar was a pup, not since. In, or for, a devilish long time: from ca 1890.

jumbaree. Jewellery: theatrical: ca 1870–1905. ? ex JAMBOREE.

jumble, v.i. and t. To have sexual intercourse (with): late C.16–18: S.E. >, ca 1650, coll. Stanyhurst, Barnfield, Randolph, D'Urfey. 2. To take for a drive: coll: C.19–20; ob. For origin, cf.:

jumble-gut lane. A rough road: low coll: late C.17–early 19.

jumbler. A performer of the sexual act: coll: C.17–18. Ex JUMBLE, v., 1.

jumbo. A clumsy, heavy fellow: from ca 1820: coll >, ca 1900, S.E. 2. An elephant: coll: from ca 1882. 'Chiefly in allusion to a famous elephant at [the London] Zoo (d. 1885),' W.; it was sold to Barnum in Feb. 1882. 3. Whence *Jumbo*, the Elephant and Castle Tavern in South London: public-house frequenters': from 1882. 4. 'The big fore-staysail': Grand Banks fishermen's: from ca 1883.

Jumbo's trunk. Tipsy: rhyming s. on *drunk*: esp. ca 1880–85. On ELEPHANT'S TRUNK.

jumback, see JIMBUGG.

***jump;** occ. **dining-room jump.** 'Robbery effected by ascending a ladder placed by a sham lamp-lighter, against the house intended to be robbed. . . . Because, should the lamp-lighter be put to flight, the thief . . . has no means of escape but that of jumping down,' Grose, 2nd ed.: c. from ca 1787; †by 1890. 2. A window (on the ground floor): c.: C.19–20. Vaux. 3. pl. see JUMPS. 4. The n. corresponding to the v., 5: same period. Esp. *have a jump*. 5. A fright: coll: late C.19–20. 6. A journey from one 'stand' to another: circus and fair-ground: late C.19–20.

***jump,** v. To seize and rob (a person): c.: ca 1780–1890. Also to rob (a building) by way of the n., 1: c.: C.19. 2. To seize and arrest: Australian: ca 1870–1900. 'Rolf Boldrewood'. 3. To possess oneself of a mining right, in the owner's absence. Gen. with *a* or *the claim*. From ca 1854, when in *The Melbourne Argus*; *jumping of claims*, however, occurs in U.S. in 1851 (Thornton): coll >, ca 1870, S.E. Marryat, in *Mountains and Molehills*, 'If a man jumped my claim, . . . I appealed to the crowd.' 4. Hence, in South Africa, to appropriate (goods) wrongfully: 1871, *The Queenstown Free Press*, 18 Aug., 'Five thousand bricks were jumped the other night from . . .'s brickyard at Klipdrift.' Pettman. 5. To copulate, v.i. and t.: C.17–20 coll; ob. 6. To try a medicine: medical: from ca 1860; ob.

jump, at the first. At the very beginning (of proceedings): coll: ca 1570–1700.

jump, from the. From the beginning: coll (in C.20, tending to S.E.): app. orig. U.S. (1848) and anglicized ca 1870.

***jump, go the.** To rob as in JUMP, n., 1: c.: C.19.

jump, not by a long. Not by a long way: non-aristocratic coll (—1887); ob.

jump, on the. On the move; active; restless: coll: 1900, *Daily News* (of 4 May), 'Keeping the foe on the jump'.

jump, see how the cat will. To watch the course of events before committing oneself: coll: from ca 1820. Scott, Bulwer-Lytton.

jump a bill, to dishonour an acceptance, like *jump one's bail*, to abscond, is orig. and mainly U.S., partly anglicized ca 1890.

jump at. To accept eagerly: coll >, ca 1905, S.E.: 1769 (S.O.D.). J. Payn, 1882, 'He might well have jumped at such an offer.' 2. To guess: coll: from ca 1890.

jump-down. 'The last place . . . in course of erection on the outskirts of . . . civilised life', Staveley Hill, in *From Home to Home*, 1885: Colonial: ca 1880–1910.

jump down a person's throat. A variant (—1806) of JUMP UPON.

jump on, see JUMP UPON.

jump one's horse over a or the bar. To sell horse, bridle and all, to the landlord of a public-house: Canadian: ca 1880–1905. *Daily Telegraph*, 20 March 1886.

jump out of one's skin. To be greatly startled: coll: C.19–20.

jump up. To get the best of (a person); or the reverse: tailors': from ca 1850.

jump up behind. To endorse the bill of a friend: commercial: from ca 1870. cf. INDORSE.

jump (up)on. To criticize severely: coll: 1868. M. E. Braddon, 'In vulgar phraseology, to be "jumped upon"'.

jumpable. 'Open for another to take': Australian coll: 1884, Boldrewood. Ex JUMP, v., 3.

jumped-up. Conceited, arrogant: (orig. low) coll: from ca 1870. Ex dial. 2. Upset nervous: low coll: ca 1880–1910. cf. S.E. *jumpy*.

***jumper.** A thief entering houses by the windows: c.: from ca 1787; ob. See JUMP, n., 1. 2. A tenpenny piece: Scottish c. of ca 1820–50. Haggart. 3. The illegal appropriator of another's mining-claim: from ca 1855: coll>, ca 1880, S.E. 4. 'Now the technical term for the seaman's upper garment, but originally [ca 1850–75] a slang term for a duck jacket slipped on to protect clothing during a dirty job on deck', Bowen. 5. The 'inevitable' nickname of a man surnamed Collins or Cross: naval and military: late C.19–20. The latter ex *jump across*, the former of anecdotal origin. 6. A (gen., travelling) ticket-inspector: orig. (1900), railwaymen's. 7. A light buggy; also a crude sled: Canadian: from ca 1830 or -40. 8. A flea: ca 1810–60.

jumping cat, the cult of the. The practice of waiting before committing oneself: coll (—1896).

jumping-jack. A sea-gull: nautical (—1896): coll rather than s.

jumping Jehoshaphat or **Jupiter** or **Moses(, by the).** Mild oaths: mid-C.19–20 coll; ob. *Jehoshaphat* is occ. employed alone, often in the sol. form *Jehosophat*.

jumping-off place. A point of departure: coll: orig. (1826), U.S.; anglicized ca 1870.

jumping over the fat-pot. A stipulation that all players should assist in the old-fashioned pantomime, *The Man in the Moon*: theatrical of ca 1830–80. Ex flame from burning fat in the days before gas was in gen. use for lighting.

jumping-powder. A stimulant: c. >, ca 1890, coll: ca 1825–1914. Blaine, 1840, in *Encyclopaedia of Rural Sports*, 'Fortified . . . by a certain quantum of jumping powder'.

jumps. Delirium tremens (—1879). 2. The fidgets: coll (—1881). (Both with *the*.) 3. Excitement, craze: ca 1880–1900.

junior. Smaller; lower; the less good. (So *tight junior*, the smallest, lowest.) Winchester College: C.19–20; ob. The opp. is *senior*.

juniper. Gin: from ca 1820; Bee, 1823; J. E. Ritchie, in *The Night Side of London*. Gin = *de genièvre* = juniper, though *gin* is actually abbr. of *geneva*.

juniper-lecture, see JINIPER-LECTURE.

junk, as old or inferior cable, fig. salt beef, is S.E. Whence, however, sense of (*a*) miscellaneous, second-hand stuff, hence (*b*) rubbish: orig. (1842), U.S.; anglicized as coll, resp. ca 1880 and ca 1900.

junket, v. To exult (*over*): Winchester College: from ca 1850; ob. Ex the S.E. v.

junket! Indicative of self-congratulation: Winchester College: C.19–20; ob.

Jupiter. Used in mild oaths of C.17–20: literary until C.19, then coll if used with a smile.

Jupiter Scapin. 'A tricky minister': political and Society's coll: late C.19–early 20. Ex the Parisians' nickname, ca 1810, for Napoleon I, Scapin being a rogue in a play by Molière.

***jurk.** A rare C.19 variant of JARK.

jury. An assertion; a profession of faith, etc.: costermongers': from ca 1850; ob.

jury, chummage, and couter. Knife, fork, and spoon: Regular Army's: late C.19–20. Ex Hindustani.

jury – hang half and save half. The jury may be *a Kentish*, *a London*, or *a Middlesex jury*: a proverbial c.p.: resp. C.18–19; late C.18–mid-19; C.17–19. The implication, as Middleton in 1608 suggested of the third, 'Thou . . . wilt make haste to give up thy verdict, because thou wilt not lose thy dinner.'

just. Certainly; indeed; RATHER!: 1855: coll. Milliken, 1892, 'Wouldn't I just!'

justass. A mid-C.18–early 19 coll pun on *justice* (a person).

justice, do. To pledge (a person); drink to: late C.17–18.

Justice Child, do. To inform to the police or to a magistrate: c. of ca 1690–1750. The reference is prob. to Sir Francis Childe, the elder (1642–1713); *A New Canting Dict.*, 1725, makes *child* a vocative – which seems less likely and certainly less pointed.

justices' justice. Justice (esp. if severe) of the kind administered by petty magistrates: from ca 1830: coll till ca 1890, then S.E.

jutland, Jutland. The posteriors: low punning coll: C.18–mid-19.

juvenile. (Gen. pl.) A book for children: booksellers' and publishers': from ca 1898.

juwaub, a refusal, a dismissal; as v., to refuse, reject. Anglo-Indian: from ca 1830. Ex Hindustani *jawaub* (better spelling).

jybe, see GYBE.

K

k. See KA' ME, KA' THEE. 2. For such obscure words gen. spelt with a *c* as are looked-for in vain under *k*, see **c.**

K.A.B.G.N.A.L.S. These letters, which, in back s., form *back slang* (the needless *c* being omitted), are 'uttered rapidly to indicate that this mode of conversation will be agreeable to speaker' (Ware): mostly Cockneys' (—1909). Also *kabac genals.*

k.d. or **K.D.!** Say nothing about it!: printers' c.p.: from ca 1860. i.e. **keep** it **dark.**

k-legged. Knock-kneed; shaky on one's legs: printers': from ca 1860. In dial., *k* or *kay* denotes 'left', as in *k-pawed*, Cheshire and Lancashire for left-handed.

k-nut, see KNUT.

ka' me, ka' thee. One good turn deserves another: proverbial coll (—1546) >, ca 1700, S.E. Other forms *k, kay, kawe, kob*; Ray, C.17, has *claw*, which, being also the earliest form, may provide the origin. cf. the late C.19–20, *scratch my back and I'll scratch yours*, and SCRATCH MY BREECH.

kabac genals, see **K.A.B.G.N.A.L.S.**

kadi, see CADY.

kadoova, off one's. Insane: New South Welsh: ca 1870–1910. Ex Aborigine.

kaffir. A prostitute's bully; hence, a low fellow: low: ca 1860–1910.

Kaffir piano. The marimba, a musical instrument: South African coll: 1891.

Kaffir's (occ. Çaffre's) lightener. A full meal: South African: from ca 1860; ob.

kai-kai. Food; feasting: New Zealand: mid-C.19–20. Reduplication of Maori *kai* (food).

kail through the reek, give one his. To reprimand, or punish, severely: Scots coll: C.19–20. Scott. Ex the unpalatableness of smoke-tasting soup.

kaio. A popular corruption in the South Island of New Zealand of *Ngaio*, the Maori name for *myoporum laetum*, a tree whose wood is used for gun-stocks: from ca 1870.

kakker-boosah. Prematurely voided excrement: low (—1823); †by 1890. See CACK.

kan du! A military variant of CAN DO, 2. As if ex Hindustani.

kanga. Abbr. *kangaroo*: Australian coll: from ca 1890.

kangaroo. A native – not an Aborigine – of Australia: 1827 (S.O.D.): coll >, ca 1860, S.E. 2. 'A tall thin man, especially ill-shaped and round-shouldered': nautical coll: late C.19–20; ob.

kangaroo-droop or, more gen., **-hop.** A feminine affectation, hands being brought, palm downward, to the breast: cf. GRECIAN BEND, ROMAN FALL. Coll, Australian: ca 1875–1900.

kanits. A stink: back s. (—1874). Whence *kanitseno*, a stinking one. Ob.

kant, see CANT. **kanurd.** A loose form of KENNURD.

kapai. Good; agreeable; (mostly North Island) New Zealand: mid-C.19–20. *New Zealand Herald*, 14 Feb. 1896. Borrowed direct from Maori, where *kapai* = this is good.

karibat. Food: Anglo-Indian (—1864). Ex Hindustani for curry and rice, the staple dish of both Europeans and natives in India.

***kate.** A master or skeleton key: c. of late C.17–mid-19. cf. JENNY; JIMMY: esp. BETTY. 2. Hence, a picklock: C.18–mid-19. 3. (Also *katy, Katy.*) A wanton: (mainly Scots) coll: C.16–early 19.

Kate and Sydney. A steak-and-kidney pudding: rhyming s.: from ca 1880.

Kate Karney or **Carney.** The Army: military rhyming s.: late C.19–20. Ex the name of a very popular comedienne of the 1890s.

katterzem. A parasite: Scottish (—1909). Ex Fr. *quatorzième*, fourteenth: he being willing to go, at a moment's notice, to prevent the number of guests being thirteen.

keck-handed. Left-handed: schools' and dial.: C.19–early 20. cf. K-LEGGED.

kedge. To CADGE: Cockney (—1887).

kedger. A fisherman; a mean fellow: nautical (—1867). Prob. CADGER influenced by *kedger*, a kedge-anchor. Imm. ex: 2. A beggar specializing in fees for trivial services: c. (—1823); †by 1890. Bee adds *kedgers' coffeehouse* and *hotel*, a resort resp. daily and nightly of 'every kind of beggars'.

kedgeree-pot. A round pipkin: Anglo-Indian coll: C.19–20.

kee-gee. 'Go, vigour': East London: ca

1860–1915. Prob. ex *qui-vive*, for cf. KEY-VEE.

keek-cloy, see KICKS.

***keekers.** The eyes: Scots c.: C.19–20. Ex *keek*, to look. cf. PEEPERS.

keel. The posteriors: Scots coll: C.19–20; ob.

***keel-bully.** A lighterman carrying coals to and from the ships: late C.17–18: c. >, ca 1770, s. >, ca 1800, coll >, ca 1860, S.E. Mostly derisive.

keelie. A (gen., street) rough: from ca 1850: Scots s. >, ca 1870, coll. Ex *the Keelie Gang*, an Edinburgh band of young blackguards, ca 1820. cf. HOODLUM and HOOLIGAN; see also LARRIKIN.

keen (on). Fond (of); eager (for); greatly interested (in): coll (—1897).

keep, v. To live; reside; lodge: C.14–20: S.E. till ca 1770, then coll and mainly Cambridge and U.S. Shakespeare.

keep a cow, – as long as I can buy milk I shall not. Why have the expense of a wife when one can visit a whore? Proverbial c.p.: C.17–20; ob.

keep a pig. To have a lodger: Oxford University: mid-C.19–early 20. Esp. of a freshman quartered on a senior undergraduate.

keep a stiff upper lip is coll orig. – ca 1815 – (U.S.) >, in C.20, S.E. Not to show fear or sorrow.

keep [a person] back and belly. To clothe and feed: coll: C.18–20; ob.

keep 'cave!' To watch, and give warning: Eton College: C.19–20.

keep chapel, see CHAPEL.

keep company. To be or act as a sweetheart; coll: from ca 1830. Dickens in *Sketches by Boz*, 'Mr Wilkins kept company with Jemima Evans.'

keep down the census. To abort; to masturbate: low: mid-C.19–20; ob.

keep hold of the land. To hug the shore: nautical coll: late C.19–20; slightly ob.

keep in with. To maintain, esp. friendly, relations with: late C.16–20: S.E. till ca 1875, then coll. W. Black, in *Yolande*, 1883.

keep it dark, see DARK, KEEP IT.

keep it up. To prolong a debauch: from ca 1780: coll. Ex the S.E. sense, to continue doing something.

keep off the grass! Be cautious!: a coll c.p. orig. proletarian: late C.19–20. Ex notices in parks.

keep one's appointment, to be unable to – or cannot. To fail to come-to in time: pugilistic: ca 1810–60. Anon., *Every Night Book*, 1827.

keep one's (or the) boiler clear. (Esp. in the imperative.) To 'watch your stomach – in reference to health' (Ware): engineers': mid-C.19–20. As a C.20 wit has said, in approximately these words: 'What a lot of trouble people would spare themselves if only they would keep their bowels open and their mouths closed.'

keep one's eyes skinned. To maintain a sharp look-out: coll: U.S. (1846), anglicized ca 1860. Occ. *peeled* for *skinned.*

keep oneself to oneself. Coll form of *keep to oneself*, i.e. avoid the society of others: from ca 1890.

***keep open house.** To sleep in the open air: tramps' c.: from ca 1850; ob. See also HEDGE-SQUARE; STAR-PITCH.

keep out of the rain. To avoid, evade trouble: Australian coll: late C.19–20.

***keep sheep by moonlight.** (v.i.) To hang in chains: C.18–early 19 c.

keep sloom. To remain quiet; say nothing: tailors': from ca 1860. Here, *sloom* = slumber, as in Scottish and Northern dial.

keep the doctor. To sell adulterated drinks: low coll: C.19–20; ob.

keep the door. To be a brothel-keeper: low coll: C.18–mid-19.

keep the line. To behave becomingly, decently: ca 1815–50. Pierce Egan, *London*, 1821.

keep up to the collar, v.t. Keep hard at work: coll (—1861); ob. T. Hughes, 'Hardy kept him pretty well up to collar.'

keep your hair on! A c.p. from ca 1867, offered on any mishap. 'Quotations' Benham. See HAIR ON, KEEP ONE'S.

keep your nose clean! Avoid drink!: military c.p. (—1909).

keep your pecker up! Keep your spirits up: since ca 1840. See PECKER, 2.

keep your thanks to feed your chickens! I don't need, desire, any thanks: semi-proverbial c.p. (—1681); very ob. W. Robertson, *Phraseologia Generalis.*

keep yourself good all through! Be entirely good!: a Society c.p.: 1882–ca 1890.

***keeping-cully.** 'One who keeps a mistress, as he supposes, for his own use, but really for that of the public', Grose, 1st ed.: c.: ca 1660–1840.

keeping the pot boiling; winding the chain. In R. W. Vanderkiste, *A Six Years' Mission among the Dens of London*, 1852, these two proletarian phrases are explained thus, 'They ran up stairs, jumped out of the window, up stairs again, and so on – called by them "Winding the chain", and "Keeping the pot boiling"': men and boys': ca 1830–80. Also of several persons on an ice-slide: Dickens, *Pickwick*, ch. 30.

keeps, for. For good; permanently; in cricket, defensively: coll: from 1880 in Australia (app. earliest in cricket sense), ca 1890 in England. i.e. to keep for good.

***keffel.** A horse: c. late C.17–mid-19. (It survives in dial., where first recorded in 1825. Ex Welsh *ceffyl*, E.D.D.)

keg. The stomach: from ca 1885 (orig. dial.).

keg, little bit o(f). Human copulation: low (—1909). Lit., a small piece of common meat.

keg-meg. Tripe; derivatively *keg-meg shop*: low (—1857). A variant of dial. CAG-MAG, inferior meat, refuse. 2. Hence (?), an intimate talk: (low) coll: 1883, J. Payn in *Thicker than Water*.

kegged, be. To be jeered at: nautical: mid-C.19–20; ob. Ex CAG.

keifer. 'Generic for MUTTON,' F. & H.: see MONOSYLLABLE.

kelder. Belly; womb: low coll: mid-C.17–early 19. cf. HANS-IN-KELDER.

kelp. Hard-earned money; wages: workmen's: late C.19–20. Opp. BUNCE, money for overtime work. Ex *kelp*, large seaweed. 2. See also CALP.

***kelp,** v.t. To lift one's hat to (a person): c. of ca 1800–50.

kelter; occ. **kilter.** Money: c. of ca 1780–1820. George Parker, 1789. Also dial.: ?before it was c. – the earliest dial. record being 1808.

kemesa, see CAMESA.

Kemp's shoes to throw after you!, would (that) I had. I wish I could bring you good luck: a C.17–early 19 c.p. Ex a lost topical reference.

***ken.** A house (in compounds, house or place): c.: ca 1560–1860; thereafter somewhat literary – except in compounds. Harman, B.E., Lytton, Henley & Stevenson. The O.E.D. essays no etymology, W. proposes abbr. *kennel*, I suggest a corruption of Romany *tan*, a place, or a corruption of the original whence *tan* itself springs. (H., 3rd and later edd., refers us to '*khan*, Gipsy and Oriental'. The word does not exist in Romany in this form; but there is the Hindustani KHAN(N)A, a house, a room, which appears, in various forms, in the various Gypsy dialects.) See also BOB KEN and BOOZING KEN.

***ken, bite or crack a.** To rob a house: c.: resp. late C.17–18, late C.19–20 ob.

***ken, burn the,** see BURN THE KEN.

***ken-crack lay.** Housebreaking: c.: C.19–20, ob. See KEN and LAY, 2.

***ken-cracker, -miller.** A housebreaker: c.: resp. late C.18–20 (ob.), late C.17–early 19.

kenird. Drink: back s. (—1887). cf. KENNURD for the euphonic *e*.

kennedy. A poker: low London: ca 1820–1900. Ex one Kennedy killed in 'tough' St Giles's by a poker. Hence, *give one kennedy*, hit one with a poker, as in Henley's *Villon's Good Night*. 'Frequently shortened to *neddy*', H., 1859.

***kenner.** A C.19 (?–20) variant of KEN. Influenced by KHANNA.

kennetseeno. Stinking: manipulated back s. or central s. (—1859).

***kennick.** 'A mixture of flash-patter [i.e. cant] and padding-ken [or low lodging-house] talk', says '*No. 747*' at p. 17 in a reference valid for the year 1865. Fanciful ex KEN.

kenning by kenning, vbl n. 'Increasing a seaman's wages by the work he does, a term principally used by the old whalers'; nautical coll: from ca 1860; ob. Bowen. A natural development ex Scottish and Northern dial. *kenning*, a little.

ken(n)urd. Tipsy: back s. (—1859) on *drunk*. (Since *knurd* is ugly.) Mayhew has it in 1851 in form *kanurd*.

kent. A coloured cotton handkerchief: low: from ca 1810; ob. Also:

Kent clout or rag. See preceding entry. H., 1859.

Kent-Street ejectment or distress. The removal, by the landlord, of the street door when rent is in arrears: (low) coll: ca 1780–1830. Ex a Southwark practice.

Kentish knocker. A Kentish smuggler: C.19: local coll > S.E. Ex *Kentish Knock*, the sandbank facing the Thames-mouth.

Kentish long-tail. A native of Kent: coll nickname: C.13–20; since ca 1750, dial. The legend behind the name is in Layamon's *Brut*, vv. 19555–86.

Kentucky loo; fly loo. Betting on certain antics of flies: students': mid-C.19–20; virtually †.

kenurd, see KENNURD.

kep. An occ. variant of KIP, n., 3.

Keppel's snob, put up at the. To be a snob: naval: ca 1870–1910. i.e. at *The Keppel's Head*, an inn named after Admiral Keppel (d. 1786): pun on NOB, head.

kerbstone broker. A stockbroker operating outside the Stock Exchange: orig. (1860), U.S.; anglicized ca 1890 as coll.

kerel. A chap, a fellow: South African coll: late C.19–20. Also (simply *kerel*), a term of address = old CHAP. Ex Dutch; cf. †S.E. *carl* (cognate with *churl*).

kerr'b. To hit, strike, punch: Shelta: C.19–20.

Kerry security. 'Bond, pledge, oath – and keep the money,' Grose, 1785. Coll: late C.18–mid-19.

Kerry witness. One who will swear to anything: coll: from ca 1825; ob.

kerte(r)ver-cartzo. A venereal disease, esp. syphilis: low London: ca 1850–90. (cf. CATEVER and CATSO.) Ex Lingua Franca, ex It. *cattivo*, 'bad'.

kervorten. A quartern: a Cockneyism: mid-C.19–20; ob. '*No. 747*' (=reference of 1845). By perversion.

ketch. To catch; also as n.: Cockney (—1887). cf. KEDGE. Whence *ketched*, caught.

Ketch; Jack Ketch, see JACK KETCH.

kettle. The female pudend: low coll: C.18–20; ob. D'Urfey. 2. An ironclad or other iron-built vessel: nautical: ca 1870–1914. 3. In c., a watch. A *red kettle* is a gold watch; a *white*, a silver one. Mid-C.19–20.

kettle, cook the. To make the water in the kettle to boil: South African coll: from the late 1890s.

kettle and coffee-mill. Boiler and engine: from ca 1870; ob. Bowen remarks that it was applied by sailing-ship men to windjammers ruined by the intrusion of 'these monstrosities'.

kettle black, pot calling the, see BLACK ARSE and cf. the proverbial *the kiln calls the oven burnt house* (C.17–19).

kettle brandy. SCANDAL BROTH, i.e. tea: ca 1870–1910.

kettle on the hob; often shortened to *kettle.* A shilling: rhyming s. (on BOB, n., 2): late C.19–20.

kettle of fish, a pretty, see FISH, PRETTY.

kettledrum. An afternoon tea-party on a big scale: coll: from ca 1860; ob. Mrs Henry Wood, 'Bidding the great world to a kettle-drum.' cf. DRUM, 8, †S.E. for 'tea-party'. 2. **kettledrums,** or **Cupid's kettledrums,** a woman's breasts: low: ca 1770–1850.

kew. A week: back s. (—1859). Pl either *kews* or *skew.*

key. The penis: C.18–20, ob.: sometimes euphemistic, but gen. low coll. 'Lets a man in and the maid out', F. & H. (cf. LOCK, 6.) Whence *keyhole*, the female pudend, for which F. & H.'s *keystone of love* is a mere literary euphemism.

key, his wife keeps the. He is addicted to drinking on the sly: proletarian (—1887).

key of the street, have the. To be shut out for the night; to have no home: from ca 1835: coll. Dickens in *Pickwick.*

key under the door (occ. **threshold**), **leave the.** To go bankrupt: C.17–19: coll. Swift; Ray, 1670, *lay the key* . . ., a variant.

key-vee(, on the). Alert: lower classes': 1862. Ex *qui-vive.* cf. KEE-GEE.

keyhole, see KEY, n.

keyhole (occ. **keyholed**), **be all.** To be tipsy: low: from ca 1860; ob. Perhaps because a drunk man has difficulty in finding the keyhole.

***keyhole-whisperer** or **-whistler.** A night's lodger in barn (see SKIPPER, whence SKIPPER-BIRD) or outhouse: tramps' c., resp. 1845 ('*No. 747*') and 1851 (Mayhew); ob.

keystone under the hearth(, keystone under the horse's belly). A C.19 smugglers' c.p. > proverbial, the reference being to the hiding of contraband spirits below the fireplace or in the stable. Wise, *The New Forest*, 1863.

khabbar, khubber, see KUBBER.

khalishee. (Gen. pl.) A native Indian sailor: nautical coll: mid-C.19–20; ob. ?a corruption of *Khalsa(h)*, the Sikhs collectively.

khanna. A house, compartment: often used very incongruously in Anglo-Indian coll: late C.18–20. (See also KEN.)

Khyber Pass. Glass: rhyming s.: since ca 1885. Often merely *Khyber.* 2. Backside: late C.19–20. Almost invariably in shorter form. Rhyming, of course, on ARSE.

kia ora! Good health to you!; good luck!: New Zealand (and occ. Australian): from ca 1870. Ex Maori *keora ta-u* and *k. tatu.*

kibber, see JIBBER THE KIBBER.

kibosh. (The *i* gen. long.) Nonsense; anything valueless: low: 1860 (H., 2nd ed.): ob. *Punch*, 3 Jan. 1885, ''Appy New Year, if you care for the kibosh, old chappie.' Occ. *kiboshery.* By BOSH, nonsense, out of KIBOSH ON, PUT THE. 2. Fashion; the correct thing: low: from ca 1888; ob. e.g. 'That's the proper kibosh.' 3. See KIBOSH ON, PUT THE.

kibosh, v. To spoil, ruin; check; bewilder;

knock out (lit. and fig.): from ca 1880 (E.D.D.). Milliken in his *'Arry Ballads*.

kibosh, put (a person) **on the.** To calumniate: low: late C.19–20. Ex the n., 1. Contrast:

kibosh on, put the. Same senses as in KIBOSH, the v.: 1836, Dickens, in *Boz*, '"Hooroar," ejaculates a pot-boy . . ., "put the kye-bosh on her, Mary!"' Probably ex Yiddish *Kabas*, *Kabbasten*, to suppress; but Julian Franklyn proposes the heraldic *caboshed* and Scots hunting *caboche* or *cab(b)age*, to cut off a deer's head close behind the horns – a theory which would also explain CABBAGE, n., 1 and v., 1.

kiboshery, see KIBOSH, n., 1.

kick. The fashion; vogue: from late C.17; very ob. Preceded by *the*. (If preceded by *a*, a singularity is indicated.) Hence, *high kick*, 'the top of the Fashion', B.E.; *all the kick*, 'the present mode', Grose. 2. A sixpence: from ca 1700; slightly ob., except in *two and a kick*, half-a-crown. Only in compound sums, e.g. 'fourteen bob and a kick', Moncrieff. 3. The hollow in the butt of a bottle: trade: from ca 1860. (Occ. *kick-up*.) Mayhew. ?cognate with *kink*, W. pertinently asks. 4. A pocket: c.: from ca 1850. Mayhew. Prob. ex KICKS. 5. A moment (cf. JIFFY): low coll: from ca 1855; ob. Esp. *in a kick*. 6. (cf. *the boot*) dismissal from a job: 1844 (S.O.D.). Preceded by *the* and esp. in *get the kick*. cf. KICK OUT, GET THE. 7. A complaint, a GROUSE; a refusal: coll: mid-C.19–20; orig. (1839), U.S. e.g. 'He has a kick coming.' Ex the C.14–20 S.E. v., to resist, be recalcitrant. 8. A chance; an attempt, GO (n., 8), as in 'Let's have one more kick' (Baumann): coll (—1887); ob.

kick, v. To die: ?c. (—1725) > s. 2. To escape: C.18 c. Also *kick away*. In C.19–20, but ob., is *kick it*: low. 3. v.t., ask for (money); borrow from (a person): low: from ca 1790; ob. Mayhew, 'Kick him for some coppers.' cf. BREAK SHINS and KICK FOR THE BOOT. 4. v.t., demand money, work, a rest, etc., from (a person): esp. tailors': 1829 (O.E.D.).

kick, get the, see KICK OUT, GET THE.

kick, have the. To be lucky: athletic ex football: ca 1880–1915.

kick a (person's) **lung out.** To castigate severely: low (—1909). Prob. ex U.S.

kick at waist. To fit badly at the waist: tailors': from ca 1870.

***kick away,** see KICK, v., 2.

kick coming, a. A (gen. a serious) objection; obstacle. 2. An effort. Both late C.19–20 coll. cf. KICK, n., 7, 8.

kick for the boot. To ask for money: tailors': from ca 1850. cf. KICK, v., 3, and:

kick for trade. To ask for work: tailors': from ca 1855; ob. cf. preceding.

kick, or **odd kick, in one's gallop.** A whim; strange fancy: mid-C.18–19 coll.

kick in the guts. A dram of spirits: low: ca 1770–1860.

kick it, see KICK, v., 1 and 2.

kick-off. A start: City s. (—1875) >, ca 1900, gen. coll. Esp. *for a kick-off*. Also v. Ex football.

kick on one's side, have the. To have the luck: sporting coll (—1887); slightly ob.

kick one's heels. See COOL ONE'S HEELS. 2. See KICK UP ONE'S HEELS.

kick out, v.i. To die: 1898 (O.E.D.). Prob. ex U.S. cf. *kick the* BUCKET.

kick out, get or **give the (dirty).** To be dismissed; to dismiss (from employment): C.19–20: with *dirty*, s.: without, coll till ca 1920, then S.E. Also *get* or *give the kick*: coll: late C.19–20 (Lyell).

kick over the traces. To 'go the pace'; to be recalcitrant: from ca 1860: the former sense verging on S.E., the latter S.E. since ca 1905. Ex a fractious horse.

kick-shoe. A dancer; a buffoon: coll: 'old', says F. & H. – but how old?

kick the bucket, see BUCKET, KICK THE.

kick the cat. (Gen. **he kicked the cat.**) To show signs of domestic dissatisfaction: lower classes' coll (—1909).

***kick the clouds** or **the wind.** To be hanged: resp. c. (—1811), ob., often amplified with *before the hotel door* (*Lex. Bal.*), and s. or coll: late C.16–early 19 (Florio).

kick the eye out of a mosquito, can or **be able to.** This coll Australian expression (—1888; ob.) indicates superlative capacity. 'Rolf Boldrewood'.

kick the stuffing out of. To maltreat; to get the better of: orig. U.S.; anglicized, as low, ca 1900.

***kick the wind,** see KICK THE CLOUDS.

kick-up. A disturbance; quarrel: late C.18–20: coll. Wolcot, 'There'd be a pretty kick-up – what a squall'; Dickens. 2. A dance: late C.18–early 19. 3. As a v., it is, in itself, S.E., even when = to die and even in *kick up a* BREEZE; DUST, n., 2; SHINDY, etc.

kick up a lark. To cause a commotion or disturbance: ca 1810–60. Pierce Egan, 1821. See KICK-UP.

kick up at. To reprimand: at certain Public Schools, esp. Marlborough: late C.19–20.

kick up Bob's-a-dying. To make an unnecessary fuss or noise or commotion: New Zealand: since ca 1890.

kick up Meg's devotion. To make a ROW, cause a disturbance: naval: late C.19–20. Some piece of naval folklore; perhaps also a prompting by *commotion* or a pun on *diversion.*

kick up one's dust in the park. To stroll there: Society (—1909); ob. Ex Fr. *faire sa poussière . . .*

kick up one's heels. To die: C.16–19: orig. coll but soon S.E. cf. KICK, v., 1, KICK OUT, and *kick the* BUCKET.

kicker. A dancing-master: coll: ca 1830–70. (cf. HOP-MERCHANT.) Selby, 1838. 2. A horse: nautical (—1887). 3. An auxiliary motor fitted into a sailing ship: Canadian (and U.S.) nautical coll: from ca 1890; ob. Ex its action on the ship.

kickeraboo or **-poo.** Dead: West Indies 'pidgin': late C.18–19. Prob. ex *kick over the bucket* rather than ex *kick the* BUCKET.

kickers. The feet: low: C.19–20; ob.

kicking-in. A fag's duty at football: Winchester College: ca 1820–70.

kicking-strap. An elastic strap inside a garment: tailors': from ca 1860. Ex the strap adjusted on a horse to prevent his kicking.

***kicks.** Breeches: late C.17–early 19; trousers: C.19–20, ob. The former, c.; the latter, low. Moore, 'That bedizen'd old Georgy's bang-up togs and kicks.' cf. KICKSEES.

kicks than halfpence or **ha'pence, more.** Esp. with *get*, more trouble than profit or money; hence, more unkindness than kindness: coll. 1824, Scott, 'Monkey's allowance . . . more kicks than halfpence.' cf. MONKEY'S ALLOWANCE.

kicksees, kickseys, kicksies. Breeches: C.18–mid-19. 2. Trousers: mid-C.19–20, ob. (As breeches, perhaps orig. c.) cf. KICKS. 3. Shoes: low (—1823): †by 1895.

kicksie, see KICKSY. **kicksies,** see KICKSEES.

kicksies-builder. A tailor: c. or low (—1887); ob. Ex: 2. A trousers-maker: c. or low (—1857).

***kicksters.** A pair of breeches: c. (—1839); †by 1900.

kicksy; occ. **kicksie.** Disagreeable; apt to give trouble: ca 1850–90. i.e., apt to kick.

kicky, adj. Kicking (ball): cricketers' coll: 1888, A. G. Steel.

***kid.** (The 1599 Middleton-Massinger quotation given by both F. & H. and the O.E.D. may belong to sense 1; perhaps to sense 3.) A child, esp. if young: late C.17–20: orig. c. or low; ordinary s. in C.19–20. J. Payn, 'He thinks how his Missis and the kids would enjoy the spectacle.' Ex the young of a goat. 2. A thief, esp. a young and expert one: c. (—1812); ob. by 1880, †by 1896. 3. A man, esp. if young: low (—1823); ob., except in U.S. and, in England, except when applied to a (clever) boxer, e.g. Kid Berg; this boxing nuance is allied to the preceding sense. Bulwer Lytton. 4. A policeman: c. of ca 1875–1905. Thor Fredur. 5. Chaff, leg-pulling, 'gammon [q.v.] and devilry', Hindley; low (—1874) >, ca 1900, ordinary s. Esp. in *no kid* (! or ?). Ex the v., 2. 6. See KIDS. 7. (Gen. *kiddy.*) A flat dish wherein sailors measure their ration: nautical (—1825). 8. Cheese: Winchester College: late C.19–20. cf. origin of sense 1. 9. One's younger brother or sister (gen. *the kid*): mostly Cockneys': from ca 1880.

kid, v. To lie in; v.t., get with child: low coll, low s., resp.: C.19–20; ob. 2. To cheat; hoax; wheedle, flatter: from ca 1810, orig. c. 3. Hence (mostly v.t.), to chaff, quiz: low (—1859) >, ca 1900, ordinary s. cf. KID ON. Senses 2 and 3 ex the idea: to treat as a child. 4. Hence, v.i. (often with *that . . .*), to pretend, to give the impression . . . : from late 1870s. Esp. *stop kidding!*, let's talk seriously: late C.19–20.

***kid, nap the.** To become pregnant: c. (—1811); ob.

kid, no, see KID, n., 5. **kid, with,** see KIDDED.

kid-catcher. An official who seeks non-attendants-at-school: London School Board's: late C.19–early 20.

***kid-ken,** see KIDDEN.

***kid-lay** and **-rig.** The robbing of apprentices or errand-boys of the parcels entrusted to them: c.: resp. late C.17–early 19 and C.19 (ob. by 1859). cf. KINCHEN-LAY. 2. (Only **kid-lay.**) One of the gang practising this LAY (2): c.: C.18.

kid-leather. Generic for young harlots: low: C.19–20. cf. LEATHER, n., 2.

kid on. To lead on, persuade, by GAMMON or by deceit: c. (1839, Brandon) > low (1851, Mayhew) >, ca 1900, ordinary s. cf. KID, v., 2. Contrast:

kid oneself; occ. **kid oneself on.** To be conceited; to delude oneself: low > ordinary s.: from ca 1860. See KID, v., 2, and KID ON.

***kid-rig,** see KID-LAY.

kid-stretcher. A man fond of young harlots (see KID-LEATHER): low: C.19–20; ob.

kid-walloper. A schoolmaster: coll: late C.19–20. Recorded in Yorkshire dial. in 1889.

kidded; occ. **with kid.** Pregnant: low: C.19–20; ob. See KID, v., 1.

***kidden,** slurring of less usual *kid-ken*; occ. *kiddy-ken*. A lodging house frequented by thieves, esp. by young thieves: c. (—1839); ob. by 1890. Brandon in *Poverty, Mendicity and Crime*. See KEN.

kidder. A glib, persuasive speaker; an expert in chaff: low (—1859) >, ca 1900, ordinary s. 2. Hence, one given to pretending: low (—1880) >, by 1900, gen.

kidder? Where?: Regular Army's: late C.19–20. Ex Hindustani. Opp. IDDER!, here! id.: id.

kiddey, kiddie, see KIDDY.

kiddier. A pork-butcher: low: from ca 1860; ob. ?pejorative on *kid*, a young goat.

kiddily. Fashionably, smartly, showily: low: from ca 1820; †by 1914.

kidding. vbl n. of KID, v., 2 and 3. cf. KID, n., 5.

kiddish. Childish: 1897, *Daily News*, 13 Dec.: s.

kid(d)l(e)ywink. A raffle: low (—1884); ob. 2. A small village shop: from ca 1855; ob. 3. A beerhouse (cf. TIDDLY-WINK): mid-C.19–20. See the teetotallers' song quoted by G. B. H., *Teetotalism Unmasked*, 1845, p. 58. Whence, 4, the late C.19–20 nautical sense, 'a seaman's beershop in the Western English ports': from ca 1870. 5. A woman of unsteady habits: from ca 1860; ob. 6. A loosely used, humorous word for a place, esp. a building, as in 'a sartain kidlie wink that is called the "House of Commons"': J. H. Lewis, *The Art of Writing*, 7th ed., 1816.

kiddo. A term of address to a girl or, mostly by the father, to a daughter of any age whatsoever: from the late 1880s. cf. BOYO.

kiddy. A man, youth, boy: low (—1810); ob. by 1910. 2. A little child: 1888, 'Rolf Boldrewood', 'They'd heard all kinds of rough talk ever since they was little kiddies': s.. Occ. *kidlet*. Ex KID, n., 1. 3. A FLASH, but minor, thief: 1780, Tomlinson in his *Slang Pastoral*: ob. by 1875. Whence *rolling kiddy*, a dandy thief (1840, Lytton). 4. (Only with difficulty separated from preceding sense.) A dandy, esp. one who dresses like a flash thief (see preceding sense): low: ca 1820–1910. Byron, 'A kiddy . . . a real swell'. 5. A harlot's bully: c. (or perhaps low): ca 1830–1910. 6. 'A hat of a form fashionable among "kiddies"': ca 1860–1900: c. or low. 7. A stage-coach driver, says F. & H., citing Dickens in *Boz*: actually Dickens uses it as the adj. 8. See KID, n., 7.

kiddy, v.t. To hoax, HUMBUG: low (1851) >, ca 1880, ordinary s.; ob. Mayhew.

kiddy, adj. Fashionable, smart, showy, FLASH: low: ca 1805–1900. Also, arrogant: nautical (—1887); ob. Baumann. Moncrieff, 'That kiddy artist . . . the dandy habit-maker'; Dickens, 'In the celebrated "kiddy" or stage-coach way.'

***kiddy-ken,** see KIDDEN.

***kiddy-nipper.** 'Taylors out of work, who cut off the waistcoat pockets of their brethren . . . thereby grabbling their bit', or money, says Grose, 1st ed.: c.: late C.18–mid-19.

kiddyish. Stylish; somewhat showy: low: ca 1815–60. 'Think of the kiddyish spree we had,' *Jack Randall's Diary*, 1820. Ex KIDDY, adj. 2. Gay; frolicsome: low (—1860); ob.

kidknapper. A C.17–18 form of KIDNAPPER.

kidlet, see KIDDY, n., 2, and KID, n., 1. cf.:

***kidling.** A young thief, esp. if his father is in the same profession: c. of ca 1820–60. 2. A baby; a little child: 1899: s. verging on coll.

kidment. HUMBUG; GAMMON; BLARNEY: c. (—1839) >, by 1860, low; ob. Brandon. 2. Hence, a false story, a begging letter, etc.: c.: from ca 1845. 3. Professional patter: cheapjacks' s.: from ca 1850. 4. A pocket handkerchief, esp. 'one fastened to the pocket, and partially hung out to entrap thieves': c. of ca 1835–1910. 5. Hence, from ca 1860, any inducement to crime: c.; ob.

kidna, kitna. How much: Anglo-Indian (—1864); ob.: coll.

***kidnap.** To steal children: orig. (late C. 17), c. >, ca 1750, s. >, ca 1800, coll >, ca 1840, S.E. Ex KID, n., 1 + NAP, v., 3 = *nab*, to steal. Recorded four years later than:

***kidnapper**; occ. †**kidknapper.** A child-stealer, orig. one who sold the children he stole to the plantations in North America: 1678 (S.O.D.). In late C.18 used also 'for all recruiting crimps', Grose. For rise in status, see back-formational KIDNAP.

kidney-hit. A punch in the short ribs: boxing: from ca 1860.

kids. Kid gloves: coll: from ca 1885. In *Illustrated Bits*, 13 July 1889, a shop-dialogue runs: 'Certainly, miss ... Some undressed kids.' – 'Young man! I only require gloves.'

***kid's-eye.** A fivepenny piece: Scottish c. of ca 1815–50. Haggart.

***kidsman.** One who teaches boys how to steal, esp. one who also boards and lodges them: c. of ca 1835–1900.

kiff. Tea, coffee, cocoa: Christ's Hospital: since ca 1870.

kift. A BOOZE(?): Ayrshire s.: 1892, Hew Ainslie, *A Pilgrimage to the Land of Burns*, 'To ... invite them all to that ancient hostelry for a "kift owre a chappin".'

***kilkenny.** A frieze coat: late C.17–early 19: c. > low ca 1760. 2. A penny: from ca 1870.

kill. A ruined garment: tailors': from ca 1860.

kill, v. 'To hurt badly, put *hors de combat*,' Wrench: Winchester College: C.19–20. Prob. ex the Anglo-Irish use: cf. KILT. 2. To ruin a garment: tailors': mid-C.19–20.

kill, dressed (or **got-up**) **to,** see DRESS TO ...

kill-calf or **-cow.** A butcher; a murderous ruffian; a terrible person: coll: ca 1580–1750: coll quickly > S.E.; extant in dial. 2. Also as adj., murderous. 3. An arrant boaster: lowest classes': C.19–20.

kill cobbler. Gin: ca 1715–60. Anon., *The Quaker's Opera*, 1728. Contrast KILL GRIEF.

kill-devil. Rum, esp. if new: mid-C.17–20, ob.: coll (orig. West Indian). Thus also in C.18 America. 2. A gun: C.18. Ned Ward, 1703.

kill grief. Some kind of strong liquor, prob. rum (cf. KILL-DEVIL) fashionable in the 1720s. Anon., *The Quaker's Opera*, 1728.

kill-priest. Port wine: provincial: late C.18–20, ob. cf. preceding.

kill-the-beggar. Inferior whiskey: Anglo-Irish: from ca 1850. cf. KILL-DEVIL and -PRIEST.

kill the canary. To evade, or malinger at, work: bricklayers' (—1909).

kill-time. A pastime; a stop-gap: mid-C.18–20: coll >, ca 1890, S.E. 2. Also adj.

kill who? ca 1870–1915, a proletarian c.p., 'satirical protest against a threat' (Ware).

killed off. Removed from (or lying under) the table because intoxicated: ca 1805–1900. Bee, 1823, 'Borrowed from a phrase used of our brave defenders by Mr Windham, minister-at-war' (William Windham, 1750–1810).

killers. Eyes (never in singular): Society s. of ca 1775–1800. C. Whibley, in *Cap and Gown*, quotes one Mansell (1780): 'Their eyes (in fine language ... killers)'.

killick. A petty officers' arm-badge: bluejackets': late C.19–20. It is shaped like an anchor or killick.

killing. Extremely funny: coll: from ca 1890.

kilt, ppl adj. Killed (gen. as a gross exaggeration and merely = severely hurt, beaten, defeated): Anglo-Irish and jocular: C.19–20. Marryat.

kilter, esp. in U.S., see KELTER.

kiltie (-y), or K. A Highland soldier: coll: from late 1840s, orig. Scottish. J. Milne, *Epistles of Atkins*, 1902. Ex their kilts. cf. JOCK.

kim kam (occ. hyphenated), adv. and adj. (In) the wrong way; out of order: coll: late C.16–early 19, then dial. In Cotgrave and Shakespeare, *clean kam*; North, 1740, *chim-cham*. Prob. *clean* (wholly) *cam* (awry, crooked).

***kimbaw.** To cheat, trick; esp. beat severely and then rob: c. of ca 1690–1830. Ex *a kimbo* (*akimbo*): cf. CROSS, v., 3.

***kin.** A thief; *the kin*, thieves collectively: c.: C.18.

***kinchen, kinchin.** A child; a young boy (or girl), a young man: c.: from ca 1600, though forty years earlier in combination. In C.19–20, convicts' c. Ex Ger. *Kindchen*, a little child. cf. next three entries.

***kinchen-** (or **kinchin**) **co** (C.16–18) or **cove** (C.17–19). A boy brought up to stealing: c.: from ca 1560. (Before C.19, rare in *cove* form.) See CO and COVE. 2. (Only as *k. cove.*) A small man (cf. KINCHEN): c. of ca 1660–1830. 3. A man who robs or kidnaps children: c.: C.19. 4. See KINCHEN-MORT, 1.

***kinchen** (or **-in**) **-lay.** The practice of robbing children: c. of ca 1835–80. Dickens in *Oliver Twist*. cf. KID-LAY.

***kinchen-mort** or **-cove.** One of 'Beggars' children carried at their mother's backs,' Grose (2nd ed.), who, to distinguish from the second sense, adds *in slates*, i.e. in sheets: c.: ca 1560–1830. cf. KINCHEN-CO. 2. Also a young girl trained to thieve: mid-C.18–early 19 c.

kincob. 'Uniform, fine clothes, rich embroidered dresses,' H., 3rd ed.: Anglo-Indian coll: from ca 1840; ob. Loosely ex proper sense, gold brocade (1712). Persian-Hindustani origin.

kind, adv. Kindly: C.17–20: S.E. till ca 1820, then coll; since ca 1880, sol. Dickens, 1849.

kind-heart. A dentist: jocular coll: ca 1610–40. Jonson.

kind of, adv. In a way, somewhat; as it were: coll: orig. (—1800), U.S.; anglicized ca 1850, Dickens using it in *David Copperfield.* (cf. SORT OF.)

kind of a sort of a. A coll (gen. jocular) variation of *kind of a* and *sort of a*, themselves both coll forms of KIND OF, SORT OF (e.g. *thing*).

kindly, adv. Easily, readily, spontaneously, congenially: C.15–20; S.E. till ca 1880, then coll.

King Death. Breath: rhyming s.: mid-C. 19–20. In C.20 only in abbr. form, *king*. Clarence Rook, *London Side-Lights*, 1908.

King Dick. A brick: rhyming s.: late C.19–20.

King John's men, one of. Occ. amplified with *eight score to the hundred.* A little under-sized man: late C.18–19: from ca 1850, mainly nautical.

King Lear. An ear: from ca 1870.

King of Spain's trumpeter, see SPANISH TRUMPETER.

kingdom come. The after-life: late C.18–20: s. Wolcot, 'The Parson frank'd their souls to kingdom-come.' Hence, *go, send, to k.c.*, to die, kill. Ex *thy kingdom come* in the Lord's Prayer.

King's (or Queen's) bad bargain, see BAD BARGAIN.

King's-Bencher. A notable galley orator: nautical: late C.18–early 20. cf. BUSH LAWYER.

King's birthday, the. Pay day: military: from ca 1908.

king's books; books or **history of the four kings.** A pack of cards: ca 1650–1850: coll >, ca 1800, S.E. Urquhart, Foote. cf. DEVIL'S BOOKS.

King's English, clip the. To be drunk: drinking s. (—1722) >, ca 1800, coll; †by 1890.

King's hard bargain. An early C.19–20 variant of *King's* BAD BARGAIN.

***King's (or Queen's) Head Inn.** Newgate Prison: c. of ca 1690–1830. Also called *the Chequer Inn in Newgate Street.* 2. Any prison: c.: ca 1790–1850.

king's horse, (you, he, etc.) shall have the. A c.p. directed at a liar: ca 1670–1840.

King's keys, the. Crowbars and hammers used to force locks and doors: legal: ca 1810–60. Scott in *The Black Dwarf.*

King's man or **K.-m,** see KINGSMAN.

King's parade, the. The quarterdeck: naval: C.19. Ex the display made by the officers.

king's peg. Champagne laced with brandy: late C.19–20.

***King's (or Queen's) Pictures.** Money; esp. coins: C.17–20, ob.: c. >, ca 1780, s. >, ca 1850, coll. Also, in C. 19–20, *King's* (or *Queen's*) *portrait.*

King's plate. Fetters: low (—1811); ob. by 1880, †by 1910.

King's whiskey. Customed whiskey (the illicit stuff being plain *whiskey*): Anglo-Irish coll: mid-C.19–20.

kingsman. A handkerchief green-based, yellow-patterned: costermongers' (—1851); ob. Mayhew; 'The favourite coloured neckerchief of the costermongers,' F. & H. A very emphatic one is a *kingsman of the rortiest* (see RORTY).

Kingswood lion. An ass: ca 1820–90: coll or s. cf. JERUSALEM PONY.

***kinichin.** A rare C.19 variant of KINCHEN.

kinkling. (Gen. pl.) A periwinkle: nautical: mid-C.19–20. By corruption. Also in Dorset dial. (—1851).

kinyans. Spirituous liquor(s): naval: ca 1860–1910. Origin?

***kip.** A brothel: 1766, Goldsmith, 'Tattering a kip' – wrecking a brothel – 'as the phrase was, when he had a mind for a frolic': low (? orig. c.): †by 1880, except in Dublin, where it has > s. Ex Danish *kippe*, a hut, a mean alehouse; ?cf. Romany *kipsi*, a basket, and *kitchema*, an inn. 2. A bed; a hammock: low (—1879, perhaps orig. c.) and nautical. cf. DOSS; LETTY; LIB; LIG. 3. A lodging or a lodging-house, a doss-house: low (—1883). *Answers*, 31 Jan. 1891. 4. 'A small chip used for tossing pennies in the occult game of two-up', C. J. Dennis: late C.19–20: s. Perhaps a corruption or a perversion of *chip.*

***kip,** v. To play truant: low (?c.): ca 1815–60. Haggart. 2. To lodge; sleep: c.: from ca 1880.

kip in. To 'shut up'; low: late C.19–20. Ex KIP, to go to bed (and sleep).

***kip-house.** A tramps' lodging-house: tramps' c.: from ca 1885.

kipper. A stoker (from being roasted): naval (—1909); ob.

kirb. A brick: back s. (—1859).

kirk and a mill of, make a. To make the best of: C.18. 2. To use as one wishes: C.19–20. Galt. Both senses are Scots coll.

***kirkling; cracking a kirk,** vbl nn. Breaking into a dwelling while its occupants are at *kirk* or church: c.; from ca 1850. cf. U.S. **kirk-buzzer*.

kisky. Drunk; stupid with drink: from ca 1860; ob. Perhaps ex fuddled speech or ex Romany *kushto*, good (cf. *feel pretty good*) or else, as Baumann suggests, on FRISKY and *whisky*.

kismisses. 'The raisins issued as rations in Indian waters': nautical: late C.19–20. Bowen. ?ex Hindustani.

kiss. A drop of wax by the side of the seal of a letter: coll (mostly rural): from ca 1825; ob. Thackeray, Dickens.

kiss-curl. A small curl lying on cheek or temple: coll: from 1854, says Ware. *Punch*, 1856, 'those pastry-cook's girl's ornaments called kiss-curls'.

kiss me, Hardy! An occasional, jocular c.p.: late C.19–20. Ex Nelson's famous, and prob. mythical, last words. Some historians (?) have supposed that he said *Kismet, Hardy* – which I doubt.

kiss-me-quick. A small bonnet, once fashionably worn on the back of the head: 1852 (O.E.D.): coll >, ca 1890, S.E. 2. A KISS-CURL: from ca 1890; ob.: coll.

kiss my ——. See ARSE. (Also as adj.) cf. the old proverbs, *He that doth kiss and do no more, may kiss behind and not before* and *Kiss one where one sat on Saturday* (or *Sunday*).

kiss my foot! Rubbish!: Australian: late C.19–20.

kiss my hand, as easy as, see EASY AS DAMN IT.

kiss the book on that!, you can. A coll c.p. dating from ca 1890 and = 'it's a dead cert!' (s.v. CERT.)

kiss the Clink, the Counter. To be confined in the Clink (see CLINK, n.) or in the Counter prison: mid-C.16–18 coll. J. Wall, Rowlands.

kiss the hare's foot, see HARE'S FOOT.

kiss the maid. To lose one's head in an early form of the guillotine: late C.17–mid-18.

kiss the master. To hit the jack: bowls: ca 1570–1660. Gosson.

kisser. The mouth: pugilists' (—1860) >, ca 1900, gen. low s. cf. KISSING-TRAP. 2. In pl, the lips: likewise pugilistic (—1896); ob.

kissing cousins. Cousins sufficiently close or familiar to allow mutual kissing; hence, loosely, friends unrelated by either blood or marriage: Canadian coll: late C.19–20.

kissing-crust. 'The soft-baked surface between two loaves; also the under-crust in a pudding or pie,' F. & H.: coll: 1708, W. King's *Art of Cookery*; Barham, 'A mouldy piece of kissing-crust as from a warden pie.'

kissing-trap. The mouth: low and boxers': from ca 1850; ob. On POTATO-JAW or -TRAP.

kistmutgar, see KITMEGUR.

kit. A dancing-master, a fiddler: ca 1720–1830. Ex *kit*, a small fiddle formerly much used by dancing-masters. 2. A set, collection of things or (rarely in C.20) persons, esp. in *the whole kit*: coll: 1785, Grose; Shelley, in *Oedipus Tyrannus*, 'I'll sell you in a lump the whole kit of them.' cf. the U.S. *whole kit and boodle*. Prob. ex the military sense. 3. (*the whole kit.*) In low C.19–20: *membrum virile* and *testes*.

Kit has come. The monthly period is here: feminine: late C.19–20. cf. (*the*) CAPTAIN IS AT HOME.

kitchen. The stomach (cf. VICTUALLING DEPARTMENT): low coll: from ca 1850. 2. The female pudend: low: from ca 1860.

***kitchen co, kitchen mort.** Awdelay's variants (1561) of KINCHEN-CO and KINCHEN-MORT.

kitchen, go into the. To drink one's tea out of the saucer: non-aristocratic: from ca 1860. Ex servants' tendency so to drink their tea.

***kitchener.** A thief haunting a 'thieves' kitchen': c : from ca 1840.

kitchy-koo. The noise made by adults when tickling an infant: C.19–20. Ex Irish dial.

kite. An accommodation bill; a bill of exchange, esp. if worthless: commercial: 1805. Hence *fly a kite*, to raise money or get credit by such bills.

kite, v. To move like a kite through the air; also fig.: coll: 1863, Le Fanu, 'He has been "kiting all over the town".' 2. v.i., same as *fly a kite*: see the **n.**: from ca 1860: commercial. 3. As v.t., to convert into an accommodation bill, it is not very gen.: from ca 1900: commercial.

kite, blow out the. To have a full stomach: Cockneys' (—1909); ob.

kite, fly a. See KITE, n.: 1805; app. orig. Anglo-Irish. 2. See KITE-FLYING, 2.

***kite, pull a.** To make a face, a grimace: c. (—1887).

kite-flyer. One who raises money or maintains credit by the issuing of bills of exchange and/or accommodation: commercial: from ca 1830. See KITE, n.

kite-flying. The vbl n. corresponding to the preceding: from ca 1820. 2. Whoremongering: low: ca 1820–60.

kitmegur. An under-butler, a footman: Anglo-Indian (Bengal) coll: from ca 1750. More correctly *kitmutgar* or *khedmutgar*, *khid-*; *kistmutgar* is an † sol.

kitna, see KIDNA.

***kitten.** A pint or half-pint pewter pot: c.: from ca 1850; ob. See CAT, n., 7.

kitten, to. To be brought to bed of a child: low coll: C.19–20.

kitties, kittys. Effects, furniture, stock: s. or coll: late C.18–mid-19.

kittle-pitchering. 'A jocular method of hobbling or bothering a troublesome teller of long stories' (Grose, 1st ed.) by constant inquiries about minor points: ca 1780–1850.

kitty. The prison at Durham; hence, esp. in the North of England, any prison: 1825: s. and dial. Hone. ?ex *kid-cote*. 2. In card games, the pool: 1892, *Daily Chronicle*, 5 March: coll >, in C.20, S.E. 3. A pet-name form of *kitten*: C.18–20: coll till C.19, then S.E. 4. for *kittys*, pl only, see KITTIES. 5. **(Kitty.)** The inevitable naval, hence military, nickname of any man surnamed Wells: late C.19–20. Ex some naval celebrity or 'character'. 6. The female pudend: mostly card-players': late C.19–20. Suggested by the synonymous *pussy*, q.v. at PUSS, 1.

kivey. A man, fellow, chap: from ca 1850; ob.: low. Bradley, in *Verdant Green*. This diminutive of COVE (see also COVEY) was possibly influenced by L. *civis*, a citizen.

klep. A thief: from ca 1880. A somewhat low abbr. of *kleptomaniac*.

klep, v. To steal: from ca 1885; ob. Ex the preceding.

klip. A diamond: South African diamond fields' s.: from the middle 1880s. Matthews, *Incwadi Yami*, 1887. Ex Cape Dutch *klip*, a rock, a pebble. cf.:

klip, v. To put a stone behind (a wheel) to prevent a vehicle from running backwards: South African coll: 1878, Roche, *On Trek in the Transvaal*. For origin, cf. the n.

klobber, see CLOBBER.

klondyke, adj. Mad: lower classes': 1897–ca 1914. Ex Klondyke gold-fever.

kloop. A coll imitation of a cork being drawn: from ca 1870.

knab, knap, and compounds, see NAB, NAP, etc. But see also KNAP.

knacker. An old and worn-out horse: coll ex dial.: from ca 1858. W. Bradwood.

***knacker,** v., gen in passive. To kill; ruin: c. or perhaps merely low s. (—1887). Ex S.E., a horse-slaughterer. 2. (Rare except as *knackered*, ppl adj.) To rob (a person) of something: *Conway* cadets' (—1891). 3. To geld, emasculate: Australian: since ca 1860. Ex:

knackers. The testicles, occ. of animals: low: C.19–20. Prob. ex dial. *knacker*, a castanet or other 'striker'.

knap. A cheating trick at dice: ca 1650–1720: ?orig. c. > j. > S.E. 'Hudibras' Butler. 2. 'A manual retort rehearsed and arranged', F. & H.: theatre: ca 1850–1900.

***knap.** Its various senses, receive, endure, steal, all derive from that of 'to take': c. or low: from ca 1810. Vaux; H., 1864, 'Oh, my! won't he just knap it if he can!', i.e. take anything if there's a chance. (cf. the Whitby *knap*, a person not strictly honest.) In combination: *knap a* CLOUT, to steal a handkerchief; *knap the* SWAG, to grab the booty; *knap* SEVEN PENN'ORTH, to be sentenced to seven years: all being c.

knap, give or take the. To give or to get a sham blow: ca 1850–1900: s.

knap a hot un. To receive a hard punch: boxing: from ca 1820; ob.

***knap a jacob from a danna- (or dannaken-, dunnigen-)drag.** To steal a ladder from a nightcart: c.: ca 1810–90.

Knap is concerned, Mr; Mr Knap's been there. She is pregnant: low: ca 1810–1910.

***knap the glim.** To catch a CLAP: c.: from ca 1810; ob.

***knap the rust.** To become (very) angry: c.: from ca 1810; †by 1910.

knap the stoop. To be made INSPECTOR OF PAVEMENTS: c.: ca 1820–70.

knapped, be. To be pregnant: low: ca 1820–90.

knapper. The head: low: from ca 1840. Because the RECEIVER GENERAL (2). 2. (Rare in singular.) The knee: from ca 1760: since ca 1820, dial.; ob. T. Brydges.

***knapper's poll.** A sheep's head: late C.18–early 19 c.

***knapping-jigger.** A turnpike or toll gate: c. of ca 1830–95. Ainsworth.

***knapping-jigger, dub at the.** To pay at the turnpike: c. (—1859); †by 1900.

Knap's been there, Mr, see KNAP IS CONCERNED.

knapsack descent. A soldier or soldiers in every generation of a family: non-aristocratic coll: late C.19–20.

knark. A ca 1850–1900 variant of NARK.

knat. A hard task; a tyrant; a person not easily fooled: tailors': from ca 1860; ob. ?the perversion – or the survival of an †form – of *gnat*.

knave. A dunce: Christ's Hospital: from ca 1820; ob.

knave in grain. A late C.17–mid-19 jocular coll for a corn-factor, a miller.

knave's grease. A flogging: C.17 jocular coll.

knee, break one's. To be deflowered; made pregnant: coll: C.19–20; ob.

knee-drill. Kneeling, to order, for prayers: Salvation Army j. (1882) >, ca 1895, jocular coll, gen. used loosely as = praying.

knee-high to a(n) ... Very small or young, esp. in *knee-high to a grasshopper*, *a mosquito* or *a duck*: orig. (1824), U.S.; anglicized ca 1890.

knee-trembler. A standing sexual embrace: low coll: from ca 1850.

knees, sit on one's. To kneel down: coll: C.19–20.

kneller, see KNULLER.

knick-knack, see NICK-NACK.

knickers. Men's knickers; women's drawers: a coll abbr. of *knickerbockers*: 1881 (S.O.D.).

knife. A sword: M.E.–mod. Eng.: literary till C.19, when it > military coll. 2. A shrew: lowest London: C.19. Ware, 'Suggestive of being "into you" in a moment'. 3. To 'bluepencil' (a manuscript): theatrical: ca 1880–1915. Punning CUT, v., 5.

'knife', before one can or could say. Very quickly, swiftly, or suddenly: coll: 1880, Mrs Parr, *Adam and Eve*; 'Rolf Boldrewood'; Kipling. cf. JACK ROBINSON ...

knife and fork, lay down one's. To die: low coll: from ca 1860.

knife and fork tea. High tea: lower-middle class's coll: 1874; slightly ob.

knife-board. A seat running lengthways on the roof of an omnibus: 1852 (S.O.D.): coll >, ca 1890, S.E. Leech's cartoon in *Punch*, 15 May 1852.

knife it. To decamp; esp. as imperative; stop!, go away!, run!: low (—1812); ob. cf. CUT IT, 2.

knifer. A sponging SHARK: low: from ca 1890; ob. 2. A rough apt to stab with a knife: low (—1905).

kniff-knaff. Some kind of jest: ca 1680–1700. E. Hooker.

knifish. Spiteful: tailors': from ca 1860; ob.

knight and barrow pig. 'More hog than gentleman. A saying of any low pretender to precedency,' Grose, 1st ed.: c.p. of ca 1780–1840.

knight of the ... 'Forming various jocular (formerly often slang) phrases denoting one who is a member of a certain trade or profession, has a certain occupation or character, etc.', O.E.D. Most are ironical (cf. CARPET-KNIGHT) and orig. were, prob., derisive of the many sets or classes of knights and/or of the various orders of knighthood. Some are c., some s., some coll, some S.E., even literary, and long demoded. A few arose in C.16, many in C.17–18; the numerous C.19 additions are s. or coll; the practice is, fortunately, †. The principal phrases – drawn from F. & H. and O.E.D. – are these: **awl,** a cobbler (—1848). **blade,** a bully: late C.17–18: c. > s. **brush,** an artist (—1885): coll; also, a housepainter: jocular coll: from ca 1890; ob. **brush and moon,** a drunken fellow (—1848). **cleaver,** a butcher: jocular coll: from ca 1830; ob. **cloth,** a tailor: ca 1790–1860. **collar,** one who has been hanged: ca 1550–1660. **cue,** a billiard-marker: jocular coll: 1887 (O.E.D.); ob. **elbow,** a sharping gambler: late C.17–mid-18. **field,** a tramp: C.16–early 17. **forked order** or (without **the**) **Hornsey**: jocular: a cuckold resp. ca 1660–1750, ca 1630–1700. (Contrast *order of the fork*, below.) **grammar,** a schoolmaster: perhaps merely literary: ca 1690–1740. **green cloth,** a gambler: orig. (—1881), U.S.; anglicized ca 1885; ob. **hod,** a bricklayer. **Hornsey,** see above. **industry** (**the** being occ. omitted): from ca 1650: prob. literary. Fr. *chevalier d'industrie*. **jemmy,** a burglar: Society: late C.19–early 20. **knife,** a cutpurse: C.17. Jonson. **lapstone,** a cobbler: jocular coll: C.19–20; ob. **napkin,** a waiter: from ca 1850: jocular; ob. **needle, shears, thimble,** a tailor: resp. 1778, Foote; from ca 1780; late C.18–20. All orig. jocular s. or coll but by 1860, almost S.E. **order of the**

fork, one who digs with a fork: jocular coll: from ca 1620. J. Taylor the Water Poet. Contrast *forked order*, above. **pen,** a clerk or (cf. *quill*) an author: from ca 1860; ob.: resp. jocular coll and near-literary **pencil,** a bookmaker: jocular: from ca 1880; ob. or †. **pestle,** an apothecary: C.17–20; ob.: jocular coll. **petticoat,** a brothel's bully: low coll: ca 1880–1910. **piss-pot,** a physician or an apothecary: from ca 1860; ob. **pit,** a fancier of cock-fighting: from ca 1870; ob.: jocular coll or perhaps journalistic. **post,** a notorious and/or a professional perjurer: from ca 1580; ob.: c. till ca 1750, then s.; since ca 1840, S.E. Also, *the K. of the P.*, Titus Oates of the Popish Plot: C.17. (The most widely used of all.) Nashe, Ford, Mrs Centlivre, W. T. Moncrieff. ?ex (*fit for*) *the whipping-post*. F. & H.'s other sense is suspect: see KNIGHTED IN BRIDEWELL. **quill,** an author: late C.17–20; ob.: coll soon > S.E. **rainbow,** a footman: ca 1780–1880. **road,** a highwayman, esp. a notable one: from ca 1660: c. till ca 1750, then s.; from ca 1840, S.E. and literary. In C.19, occ. a footpad and in C.20 a tramp. In late C.19–20, occ. a COMMERCIAL. **rumpad,** the same: c.: ca 1815–40. Moore. **shears,** see above at *needle*. **spigot,** tapster or publican: from ca 1820; ob.: jocular coll. Scott. **sun,** an adventurer: literary: from ca 1720; †by 1910. Punning *the Knights of the Golden Sun*, an order of chivalry. **thimble,** see above at *needle*. **trencher.** A good trencher-man: from ca 1780: jocular. **vapour,** a smoker: C.17; perhaps a nonce-word (Taylor the Water Poet). **wheel,** a cyclist: prob. S.E.: from ca 1880; ob. **whip,** a coachman: from ca 1810; ob.: jocular s. > coll. **whipping-post,** a disreputable person, esp. a sharper: ca 1815–60. Scott. **yard,** a shop-assistant: ca 1885–1910.

knighted in Bridewell or **bridewell, be.** To be whipped in prison: late C.16–17. cf. KNIGHT OF *the post* and *the whipping-post*.

knights, be the guest of the cross-legged. To go dinnerless: C.18–early 19. Ex the effigies in the Round Church (in the Temple, London), a rendezvous of hungry men looking for jobs from the lawyers and their clients. cf. DINE WITH DUKE HUMPHREY.

knitting-needle. A sword: military: ca 1850–1910. cf. TOOTH-PICK.

knob. The head: from ca 1720. Hence, *one on the knob*, a blow on the head. Gen. NOB. 2. Abbr. KNOBSTICK: 1838. 3. A NOB (4) or BIG WIG. cf.: 4. An officer: naval: ?mid-C.17–mid-19. Bowen, 'Apparently introduced into the British service with the amalgamation with the Scottish Navy'. 5. (Also *nob*.) A double-headed penny in the game of two-up: Australian, hence also New Zealand: late C.19–20. 6. (Also *nob*.) Penis; *playing with one's nob*, male masturbation: low: late C.19–20. With ref. to *glans penis*. Indeed, *knob* also = *glans penis*.

knob, v. To hit: 1818: from ca 1815. Prob. ex *hit on the* KNOB.

knob of suck. A piece of sweetmeat: provincial: C.19–20; ob.

knob on to. To pay court to; fall in love with: Cockney (—1887); slightly ob.

knobs, make no. Not to hesitate or be scrupulous: coll: ca 1670–1770.

knobstick; occ. **nobstick.** A non-unionist; a workman who takes less than the agreed price or one who works while his fellows are on strike: workmen's: from ca 1825; ob.: s. >, ca 1870, coll >, ca 1900, S.E. 2. A master paying less than union wages: workmen's: from ca 1850: s. >, ca 1880, coll >, ca 1905, S.E. Mayhew.

knock. A copulation: low coll: C.16–17. See the v. 2. The penis: C.18–20. More gen. KNOCKER (2). 3. A lame horse: horse-dealers': from ca 1860. *London Review*, 18 June 1864, 'The knock ... is a great favourite for horse-coping purposes, as he is often a fine-looking animal.'

knock, v.t. and i. (Of a man) to have sexual intercourse (with): low coll: late C. 16–20. Florio, '*Cunnata*, a woman nocked'. See NOCK, n., for possible etymology, and cf. the mainly U.S. *knocked-up*, pregnant. 2. To rouse or summon one by knocking at his door, v.t.: coll: C.18–19. Abbr. C.19–20 S.E. *knock up*. 3. To astound, alarm, confuse; to FLOOR: coll: from ca 1715; ob. except in *that knocks me!*, that confounds or is too much for me. 4. To impress greatly, to 'fetch', to surprise: 1883, *Referee*, 6 May, ' "It's never too Late to Mend" ... is knocking 'em at the Pavilion.' cf. Albert Chevalier's song title, 1892, *Knocked 'em in the Old Kent Road*.

knock, get the. To drink too much, become drunk: from ca 1860; ob. 2. To be dismissed from employment: from ca 1860; ob. cf. *get the* SACK or BAG.

knock, take the. To lose to the bookmakers more than one can pay: the turf (—1890). Hence, from ca 1895, to suffer a financial loss.

knock about, v.i. To wander much, roam,

gen. aimlessly: coll: from ca 1800. Mayhew, 'I've been knocking about on the streets.' Also v.t., as in Glascock, 1829, 'Had you been served as I was – kept knocking about the North Seas . . .' 2. To pass round, esp. in *knock about the bub* (drink): low (—1781); ob.

knock-about, adj. Noisy and violent (e.g. comedians): theatre: 1891. 2. The n., a 'knock-about' performer or performance, is recorded four years earlier. 3. Abbr. of next.

knock-about man or **hand.** A handy man: Australian coll: from ca 1875. W. Harcus, 1876, 'Knockabout hands, 17*s*. to 20*s*. per week'. Also (—1889) *knock(-)about*. cf. *rouseabout*.

knock acock. To FLOOR; astound: coll: C.19. See COCKED HAT.

knock all of a heap, see HEAP . . .

knock along. An Australian variation (commented-on in the Tichborne case, 1874) of KNOCK ABOUT, v.i.; very ob. Ware.

knock at the cobbler's door, see COBBLER'S DOOR.

knock bandy. To astound, FLABAGAST: tailors': from ca 1860.

knock (someone's) **block off.** To punch him on the head; esp. as a jocular threat, *I'll k. your b. off*: since ca 1870.

knock (or **let**) **daylight into,** see DAYLIGHT INTO . . .

knock-down. Strong liquor: late C.17–19. In mid-C.18–20, but ob., *knock-me-down*.

knock down, v. To call upon, nominate, urgently invite: coll; slightly ob.: 1759, Goldsmith, '. . . Had knocked down Mr Spriggins for a song.' 2. To reduce considerably in amount or degree: coll: from ca 1865. e.g. *to knock down prices, colours*. 3. To spend in drink or other riotous living: Australia: 1869, Marcus Clarke, 'Knocked down thirteen notes, and went to bed as light as a fly.'

knock 'em down. To gain applause: proletarian (—1887).

knock-'em-down business. Auctioneering: low coll: from ca 1860.

knock-'em-downs; k.-me-d. A coconut shy: coll: from ca 1825. 2. Loosely, skittles: from ca 1860.

knock for six. To overcome drastically, foil utterly, inconvenience gravely: from ca 1899.

knock-in. The game of loo; a hand at cards: from ca 1860: low s. > coll. 2. The same as KNOCK-OUT, n., 1.

knock in, v.i. To return to college after the gate is closed: university: 1825, C. M. Westmacott. 2. To join in (cf. CHIP IN) a game of cards: clubmen's and gamblers': from ca 1860. 3. To make money: costermongers': from ca 1870. i.e., into the pocket.

knock in the cradle. A fool; but gen. as *to have got a knock . . .*, be a fool. Coll: ca 1670–1850.

knock into. To encounter: coll: late C.19–20.

knock into a cocked hat, see COCKED HAT. **knock into fits,** see FITS. **knock into** (gen. **the middle of**) **next week,** see WEEK. **knock spots off** or **out of.** These four = to defeat utterly, be much better than: C.19–20. The first and second are coll, the others s.

knock it down. To applaud by hammering or stamping: low: from ca 1860; ob.

knock it out of one. To exhaust; punish severely: coll >, ca 1910, S.E. *Punch*, 1841, 'The uphill struggles . . . soon knock it all out of him.'

knock-me-down, see KNOCK-DOWN, n., 1. 2. As adj., violent, overpowering, overbearing: coll: 1760, Foote, 'No knock-me-down doings in my house.'

knock-me-downs, see KNOCK-'EM-DOWNS.

knock off. To die: C.18–20; very ob. Tom Brown in a letter of 1704. 2. To complete or despatch easily or hastily: coll: from late C.18. Peacock; *Pall Mall Gazette*, 29 Nov. 1891, 'A specimen of the "consumptive manner" as knocked off by Mr Lang'.

knock off corners. To be successful: music-halls': ca 1880–1914. Ware cites *Entr'Acte*, 16 April 1885: 'Just as Arthur Williams had commenced to "knock corners off" at the music hall, he is once more summoned to the Gaiety. More study!'

knock-out; occ. (—1860) **knock-in.** One who, at auctions, combines with others (hence, also, the combination) to buy at nominal prices: from ca 1850: coll. Ex: 2. *knock-out* an illegal auction: from ca 1820: coll >, ca 1890, S.E. (These auction senses are also used as adjj.) 3. Applied in admiration, or by way of outraged propriety, to a person, esp. one who does outrageous things; also to an astounding or outrageous thing. Chiefly as *a regular knock-out*. From ca 1885. Perhaps ex boxing, a *knock-out* being a champion, but more prob. ex KNOCKER, 3.

knock out, v. Corresponding to the n., senses 1 and 2: from ca 1870: coll >, ca 1905, S.E. 2. To make (very) quickly or roughly: coll: from ca 1855. Dickens, Hardy. 3. Hence, to earn: Colonial: from ca 1895. Ex KNOCK UP, 3. 4. To render bankrupt: from ca 1890. 5. To leave a college by knocking at the gate after it has been shut: university: from ca 1860. cf. KNOCK IN, v., 1. 6. 'To bet so persistently against a horse that from a short price he retires to an outside place', F. & H.; to force out of the racing quotations: from ca 1870: mostly the turf. 7. To fail (a candidate) in an examination: late C.19–20. Ex boxing.

knock out an apple. To beget a child: 1818, Keats in a letter of 5 Jan.; †by 1890.

knock out of time, v.t. To punch so hard that one's opponent cannot rise at 'Time': boxers': from ca 1880: s. >, ca 1890, coll.

knock-outs. Dice: gamblers' s.: from ca 1850.

knock over, v.i. To give way; to die: from ca 1890: s. >, ca 1905, coll; ob.

knock round, see KNOCK ABOUT, v., 1.

knock saucepans or **smoke out of.** To attack violently; gen., however, to defeat utterly: Australia: ca 1885–1905. 'Rolf Boldrewood', both uses in *Robbery under Arms*.

knock-softly. A fool; a simpleton; a too easy-going person: coll: 1864; ob.

knock spots off. See the group at KNOCK INTO A COCKED HAT.

knock the bottom (or **filling** or **inside** or **lining** or **stuffing** or **wadding) out of.** To confound, defeat utterly; render useless, valueless, or invalid: coll: resp. 1875, ca 1880, ca 1890, ca 1890, 1889, ca 1895. The O.E.D. compares *it won't hold water*.

knock the shit out of. To thrash; (of a job) to exhaust or strain: low coll: late C.19–20.

knock-toe. A 'Deal lugger-rigged galley-punt, in which there was little room for the feet': nautical: C.19. Bowen.

knock up. To gain, in class, a place (v.i. and v.t., e.g. 'He knocked Jones up'): Christ's Hospital: from ca 1830. cf. OX UP. 2. Make (so many runs) by hitting: cricket coll: 1860. Ex: 3. To earn: coll: from ca 1885. cf. KNOCK OUT, V. 4. See KNOCKED UP, its only part. 5. To arrange (e.g. a dance): (low) coll (—1887).

knock-upable. Easily fatigued: coll: from ca 1870. George Eliot.

knockabout, n. and adj., see KNOCK-ABOUT.

knocked-knees and silly and can't hold his water. A pejorative c.p.: Public Schools': late C.19–20.

knocked off one's pins. FLABAGASTED: coll (—1880). Trollope.

knocked one's link out, to have. To be tipsy: ca 1730–70. See quotation at LINK, TO HAVE . . . Here, *link* = torch.

knocked out. Unable to meet engagements: commercial coll: from ca 1860.

knocked up. Exhausted: see KNOCK UP, 1. 2. Pregnant: low: C.19–20; mainly U.S. Ex KNOCK, v., 1.

Knocker. An 'inevitable' nickname of men surnamed Walker or White: naval and military: late C.19–20.

knocker. A (notable or frequent) performer of the sexual act: C.17–20; ob.: low coll. Barry, in *Ram Alley*. 2. The penis: from ca 1650; ob.: low (?coll). 3. One of striking appearance: C.17–19. Whence KNOCK-OUT, n., 3. 4. A (kind of) pendant to a wig: ca 1818–38.

knocker, up to the. (Very) healthy, fit, or fashionable; adv., exceedingly well: 1844, Selby, in *London by Night*.

knocker-face or **-head.** An ugly-face (or its owner): low: from ca 1870; ob.

knockers. Small curls worn flat on the temples: coll: ca 1890–1915.

knocking. Sexual intercourse: low coll: late C.16–20, ob. except in combination.

knocking-house or, more gen. **-shop.** A brothel: low: mid-C.19–20.

knocking-jacket. A nightgown, nightdress: low coll: ca 1700–1850. D'Urfey.

***knocking-joint.** A brothel: C.20: c. >, by 1915, low s. Ex KNOCK, v., 1.

knocking-shop, see KNOCKING-HOUSE.

knot. The swelling (or shoulder) of the *glans penis*: coll: mid-C.19–20.

knot, tie with St Mary's. To hamstring: coll: C.19.

knot it. To abscond: low: from ca 1860; ob.

knot with the tongue that cannot be undone or **untied with the teeth, knit** or **tie a.** To get married: coll: late C.16–mid-19; then dial. Lyly, Swift, Scott.

know, be all. To be a bookworm: proletarian coll (—1887).

know, don't you, see DON'T YOU KNOW.

know, in the. Possessing special and/or intimate knowledge: coll: 1883, *Referee*, 29 April, 'As everybody immediately interested knows all about them, perhaps Refreaders would like to be in the know likewise.'

know, we or **you** or **do you (?).** A mildly

exclamatory or semi-interrogatory (virtual) parenthesis: coll: from ca 1710. Addison, 1712; Jane Austen, 'Do you know, I saw the prettiest hat you can imagine.'

know a great A from a bull's foot, (2) a thing or two, (3) a trick or two, (4) a trick worth two of that, (5) how many blue beans make five, (6) how many days go to the week, (7) how many go to a dozen, (7a) one's book, (8) one's life, (9) one's way about, (10) something, (10a) the price of old iron (or old rags), (11) the ropes, (12) the time of day, (13) what's o'clock, (14) what's what, (15) which way the wind blows. To be well-informed, experienced, wide-awake, equal to an emergency. Nos. 5 and 14 are s., the others coll; nos. 7, 9 and 15 are almost S.E. – No. 1, C.18–20, ob.; no. 2, late C.18–20 (Holcroft); no. 3, C.18–20, ob.; no. 4, late C.16–19 (Shakespeare); no. 5, C.19–20; no. 6, C.17–18; no. 7, from ca 1850; no. 7a, from ca 1880; no. 8, from ca 1890, ob.; no. 9, from ca 1860; no. 10, from ca 1870, ob.; no. 10a, late C.19–20; no. 11, from ca 1850, orig. nautical; no. 12, from ca 1890; cf. no. 13, from ca 1520 (Dickens); no. 14, *what is what* from ca 1400, *what's what* from ca 1600 (e.g. in Jonson and Wycherley): see esp. Apperson; no. 15, from ca 1540; ob. by 1890; †. cf. KNOW ONE POINT MORE THAN THE DEVIL.

know B from a battledore, not to, see B FROM A . . . and cf. above.

know it!, not if I. Not if I can help it: coll: 1874, Hardy.

***know life,** in the C.19 underworld, meant, to know the shady tricks and the criminal acts, but not necessarily to be a criminal oneself.

know of, not that I. So far as I know: coll: from ca 1880.

know of, not that you. A defiant expression addressed to someone in reference to something he proposes or is about to do: coll: ca 1740–1820. Richardson, 'As Mr B. offer'd to take his Hand, he put 'em both behind him. – Not that you know of, Sir!'

know one point, occ. an ace, more than the devil. To be (very) cunning: coll: C.17–18. Prob. ex Spanish. cf. the Cornish *know tin* – tin occurring in many forms. Both are much stronger than *know a thing or two*, etc.

know one's book. Be correctly informed: coll: from ca 1875.

know one's way about, the ropes, the time of day, what's o'clock (etc.), see KNOW A GREAT A, etc.

knowing. Stylish; knowing 'what's what' in fashion, dress, manners: coll: ca 1795–1860. Jane Austen; T. Hughes, 'Tom thought his cap a very knowing affair.'

knowing bloke. A sponger on recruits: military (—1887); ob. Brunlees Patterson in *Life in the Ranks*. For *knowing codger* (—1859) see *knowing* + CODGER.

knowledge-box. The head: (—1765) coll >, ca 1890, S.E.

knowledgeable. Having or showing knowledge or mental ability: from ca 1830: dial. >, ca 1860, coll. Hence *knowledgeably* (—1865) and *knowledgeableness* (—1886).

known, n. A well-known person: coll: 1835. Never very gen.

knows, all one. (To) the best of one's ability; (to) the utmost: coll: from ca 1870. Other forms are possible: *all one knew, all they know* or *knew*.

***knuck.** A thief, esp. a pickpocket: c. of ca 1810–60. Ainsworth, in *Rookwood*. Ex:

***knuckle.** A pickpocket, esp. an expert: c. of ca 1780–1840. 2. Abbr. KNUCKLE-DUSTER; never very common: coll: from ca 1870.

***knuckle,** v. To pick pockets, esp. if expertly: c. of ca 1785–1870. 2. To pummel, punch, fight with one's fists: c.: from ca 1860; ob.

***knuckle, down on the.** (Almost) penniless: either c. or low: from ca 1840; ob. '*No. 747*' (reference to year 1845).

***knuckle, go on the.** To practise pickpocketry: c. of ca 1810–70.

knuckle, lie on the, see LIE ON THE KNUCKLE.

knuckle, near the. Slightly indecent: coll (1895, W. Pett Ridge). cf. the c.p., *the nearer the bone the sweeter the* MEAT.

knuckle-bleeders. Those spiky balls of the plane tree with which children hit one another over the knuckles: Cockneys': from ca 1880.

***knuckle-bone, down on the.** Penniless: c.: from ca 1880.

***knuckle-confounders** or **-dabs.** Handcuffs: c. of ca 1780–1850.

knuckle-duster. A knuckle-guard that, made of metal, both protects the hand and gives brutal force to the blow: orig. (—1858), U.S. and c.; anglicized, ca 1865, as coll; by 1900, S.E. *The Times*, 15 Feb. 1858. 2. Hence, a large and either heavy or over-gaudy ring: low: from ca 1870.

knuckled. Hand-sewn: tailors': from ca 1860; slightly ob.

***knuckler.** A pickpocket: c.: ca 1810–90. Ex KNUCKLE, v., 1. cf.:

***knuckling-cove.** The same: id.: id. Ex KNUCKLE, v., 1.

knuller; occ. **kneller.** A chimney-sweep given to soliciting custom by knocking or ringing at doors: low: ca 1850–1900. ?ex *knell.* 2. A clergyman: low: ca 1860–1910. Ex sense 1 via CLERGYMAN.

knut, k-nut. (The *k*- pronounced.) A very stylish (young) man about town; a dandy: from ca 1905. Prob. NUT orig. = head and *knut* has perhaps been influenced by KNOB. See also FILBERT.

ko-tow, kotow! (Properly **k'o-tou, k'o-tou!**) Thank you!: Anglo-Chinese coll: C.17–20.

kocks nownes! A coll perversion of *God's wounds*: C.16–mid-17.

kokum. Sham kindness: Australian c. (—1896); ob. Also COCUM. Perhaps this strange word is cognate with Sampson's *χοχano*, lying, counterfeit: cf. *χοχani*, a sham horoscope (Welsh Gypsy).

konk, see CONK.

***konoblin rig.** The stealing of large pieces of coal from coal-sheds: c. (—1811); †by 1900. This may be the original of NOBBLE: but what is its own etymology?

kooferred, be. To be killed: naval (African Squadron): ca 1860–1910. Bowen, 'Borrowed from the Swahili'.

kool. To look: back s. (—1859).

kop-jee. The head: lower classes': 1899–1901. (Boer War influence.) cf.:

kopje walloper. A diamond-buyer visiting the Kimberley fields: from ca 1886; ob. Ex *kopje*, a small hill.

kosal kasa. One shilling and six pence: Yiddish trading coll: C.19–20. Ex Hebrew words for '1' and '6'.

***kosh, occ. kosher.** A short iron bar used as a weapon: c. (—1874). Prob. ex Romany *kosh(t)*, a stick. Occ. spelt COSH(*er*). 2. In late C.19–20, to hit (a person) with a kosh, as 'He'll cosh him one.'

kosher; occ. **cosher.** See KOSH. 2. adj. Fair; square: East End of London: from ca 1860. Ex Hebrew *kasher*, lawful, esp. as applied to meat.

***kradying-ken.** A low lodging-house: c.: 1845. '*No. 747*', p. 419. A corruption of (the only app. later) PRATTING-KEN.

krop. Pork: back s. (—1874).

Kruger-spoof. Lying: 1896–7. Ex promises made by President Kruger in 1896 – but not kept.

Kruger's tickler or **tiddler.** A little feather brush used, in the celebrations after Ladysmith and Mafeking, to tickle fellow-celebrants' faces: coll: Boer War.

kubber, properly **khubber,** occ. **khabbar** (or **-er**). News: Anglo-Indian (—1864). Hindustani *khabar*, news – esp. of game.

kudize. To esteem, honour; praise, extol: students' (—1887); virtually †. Ex:

kudos. Glory, fame: university s. (from ca 1830) >, ca 1890, gen. coll. Gr. κῦδος. As rare †v., *kudos* occurs in 1799, *kudize* in 1873: both, pedantically ineligible.

kutcha, see CUTCHA.

kwy. Death: fast life: ca 1800–40. Ex *quietus.*

kybosh, see KIBOSH and cf. KYEBOSK.

kye. Eighteen pence: costermongers': from ca 1860. Abbr. Yiddish *kye*, 18, + *bosh*, pence. cf. KIBOSH. 2. Hence (?), a bluejacket mean with his money: naval: late C.19–20. ?cf. U.S. s. *kike*, a Jew.

kye-bosh, see KIBOSH ON. **kyebosh,** see KIBOSH.

kyebosk. A low Cockney variant of KIBOSH.

kynchen, see KINCHEN.

'kyou! (Pronounced as the letter **q.**) Thank you!: slovenly coll (verging on sol.) abbr.: late (?mid) C.19–20.

kyrie eleison, give or **sing a.** To scold (v.t. with *to*): ecclesiastical (1528, Tyndale) >, ca 1600, gen. coll (as in Taylor the Water Poet): † by 1780. Ex the Gr. for 'Lord, have mercy'.

kysh. A cushion; a small, flat, square squab used for sitting on and for carrying books: Marlborough College: late C.19–20. By corruption of *cushion.*

L

L.L. (Slightly) fraudulent: financial: 1870. i.e. *limited liability*. 2. The best whiskey: Dublin taverns': late C.19–early 20. Ex *Lord Lieutenant*.

Ls, the three. Lead, latitude, look-out: nautical coll: from ca 1860. Smyth; Clark Russell. Dr Halley added a fourth, *longitude*.

L.S.D. Money: coll: from ca 1835: in C.20, S.E. Hood, 'But, p'raps, of all the felonies de se, . . . Two-thirds have been through want of £ *s. d.*'

la! An exclamation: C.16–20: polite till ca 1850, then low coll and dial. cf. LA, LA! 2. (Often pronounced *law*): in C.17–20, a low coll euphemism for *Lord!*, this sense merging with the preceding. cf. LOR'; LAWK.

la-di-da, or occ., as in Baumann, **la-de-da;** also LARDY-DARDY. Very stylish; affectedly smart of costume, voice, manners: from ca 1860: coll. 'Its great vogue was due to a music-hall song of 1880 – *He wears a penny flower in his coat, La-di-da!*', W., who suggests imitation of affected HAW-HAW speech. 2. Also, from 1883 (O.E.D.), a n.: derisive coll for a SWELL. cf. †U.S. *la-la*, also a 'swell'. And: 3. 'Elegant leisure, and liberal expenditure': (mostly London) streets' (—1909); ob. 4. Occ. as v.: 1867, S. Coyne, 'I like to la-di-da with the ladies.'

la, la!, or **la-la!** A coll imitation of a French exclamation: C.18–20. 2. Also, C.16–20 (ob.), an expression of derision: polite >, ca 1850, somewhat trivial and coll. cf. LA!

la-li-loong. A thief; thieves: pidgin: mid-C.19–20.

labbering. 'The struggling of a hooked fish': nautical coll: late C.19–20. Bowen. Ex dial. *labber*, 'to dabble or splash in water.'

lac, lack, lakh, esp. in pl. A large number or quantity: Anglo-Indian: from ca 1885. Kipling. Ex Hindustani *lak(h)*, a hundred thousand. 2. Earlier, in (—1864) Anglo-Indian coll that, ca 1910, > standard, it meant 100,000 rupees.

lace. Strong liquor, esp. spirits, added to tea or coffee: coll >, ca 1750, S.E.: C.18–20, ob. *Spectator*, No. 488 (i.e. in 1712). 2. By inference, sugar: C.18. Ex:

lace. To intermix with sugar: ca 1690–1720: prob. s. or coll. Ex lace as an adornment, an accessory. 2. To wear tight stays (v.i.) from ca 1870; coll >, ca 1895, S.E.; ob.

lace-ups. Laced-up boots: coll (—1887).

laced, ppl adj. Sugared: ca 1690–1750: s. or coll.

laced mutton. A woman, esp. a wanton: ca 1575–1860. Whetstone, 1578; Shakespeare, in *Two Gentlemen*, 'She, a lac'd mutton, gave me, a lost mutton, nothing for my labour.' cf. MUTTON and MUTTON DRESSED AS LAMB.

lacing. A flogging: coll: C.17–20.

Lack(e)ry. The Regular Army nickname for any man surnamed Wood: late C.19–20. Ex: 2. *lack(e)ry*. A stick, piece of wood: Regular Army: mid-C.19–20. Ex Hindustani *lakri*.

lad. A dashing fellow: coll: late C.19–20; anticipated in Udall's *Roister Doister*, ca 1553, 'I trowe they shall finde and feele that I am a lad.' cf. LAD OF THE VILLAGE. Also sometimes applied to a humorous or saucy girl.

lad o' wax. A cobbler: coll: from ca 1790; ob. by 1890. Baumann notes the variant, COCK-A-WAX. 2. A boy; a poor sort of man (contrast *man of wax*, a 'proper' man): C.19 coll.

***lad of,** occ. **on, the cross,** see CROSS, n.

lad of the village, gen. in pl. A dashing fellow or cheerful companion, esp. if a member of a set: late C.19–20 coll. Perhaps an extension of LAD (or vice versa), or, more prob., ex: 2. (Gen. in pl.) One of a set of thieves and pickpockets congregating at a given spot: c. of ca 1820–80.

ladder. The female pudend: C.19–20 low. Semantics fairly obvious. 2. A vertical flaw in a stocking: orig. (ca 1830) coll: by 1890, S.E. cf. JACOB'S LADDER.

ladder, climb or **go up** or **mount the.** To be hanged: semi-proverbial coll: ca 1560–1870. In C.17–19, *to bed* or *to rest* is gen. added. Harman, *climb three trees with a ladder*. cf. (and see) the following few of many synonyms: *catch* or *nab the* STIFLER; *cut a* CAPER UPON NOTHING; *dance the* PADDINGTON FRISK; *preach at* TYBURN *cross*; TRINE (2); *die of a* HEMPEN FEVER.

ladder, groom of the. A hangman: either S.E. or jocular coll: ca 1640–1700.

ladder, unable to see a hole through a, see HOLE IN A LADDER.

laddie, laddy. A coll endearing form, mainly Scots, of *lad*: mid-C.16–20; also actors': from mid-C.19.

laddle. A lady: chimney-sweeps' (esp. on 1 May): mid-C.19–early 20. On that date, the sweepers' wives, collecting money for the men, carried brass ladles. 'Ducange Anglicus', 1857, classifies it as c.

ladidah, see LA-DI-DA.

ladies. Cards: gambling (hence almost c.): 1890, *Standard*, 15 March.

ladies' finger or **wish.** A tapering glass of spirits, esp. if gin: (low) coll: ca 1850–1910. 2. In Australia, but gen. as *lady's finger*, a very short, thin banana: from ca 1890: coll on the verge of S.E.

ladies' grog. Grog that is hot, sweet, strong, plentiful: from ca 1840; ob.

ladies' tailoring. Sexual intercourse: low: from ca 1815; ob. cf. STITCH.

ladle. To enunciate solemnly and pretentiously: theatrical coll: from ca 1870; ob.

lady. A hunchbacked woman: ca 1690–1870. cf. LORD, by which suggested. 2. A wife (esp. *my* OLD LADY: cf. OLD WOMAN): low coll: from ca 1860; earlier, S.E. cf. LADY, YOUR GOOD. 3. Madam, as term of address: M.E.–C.20: polite till ca 1860, then increasingly coll and low. (See W.'s comment.) 4. The reverse of a coin: low: C.19–20, ob. Ex *tail*, via sex. 5. A quart or a pint pitcher upside down: low: C.19–20, ob. 6. He who attends to the gunner's small stores: nautical (—1711). Whence, in the same period, the †*lady's hole*, the place where such stores are kept. Both terms were coll by 1750, S.E. by 1800 at latest. 7. With sense 2, cf.: mother, gen. *the* OLD LADY: (jocular) coll (—1887).

lady, old. The female pudend: low: C.19–20, ob. 2. A coll term of address to animals, esp. mares and bitches: from ca 1840. See also OLD LADY.

lady, perfect. A prostitute: low when not jocular: from ca 1880. Ex the claims of such women – or ex male irony.

lady, your good. Your wife: C.18–20: S.E. till ca 1860, then low coll. cf. *your* or *the* MISSIS and Fr. *votre dame.* (Rare in other 'persons'.)

lady-bird, ladybird. A whore: C.16–20; ob. cf. BIRD, 5.

Lady Dacre's wine. Gin: ca 1810–50.

lady-finder. A woman who sits by the fire, being too proud to do housework: servants': C.19–20, ob.

***lady green,** or with capitals. A clergyman, esp. a prison chaplain: c.: from ca 1880; ob. ?ex inexperienced mannerism.

Lady in mourning. A Hottentot girl: ca 1830–60. *Sinks*, 1848.

lady, or **Lady, Jane.** The female pudend: low: from ca 1850; ob. 2. 'A stout, handsome, cheery woman': Society: 1882–ca 1915. Ware.

lady-killer. A male flirt: from ca 1810: coll >, ca 1890, S.E. Whence **lady-killing,** n. and adj., which arose, the adj. in 1825, the n. in 1837 (O.E.D.): same change of status. cf. MASHER.

lady of easy virtue, see EASY VIRTUE.

lady of the gunroom. A C.19 variant (coll verging on S.E.) of LADY, 6.

lady of the manor. An occ., late C.19–20 variant of LORD OF THE MANOR, sixpence.

lady-sitter. A lady who allows herself to be appraised – and painted: painters' (—1887); ob.

ladyfied. Having the appearance (*l'air mais pas la chanson*) of a fine lady: coll: from ca 1880.

lady's finger, see LADIES' FINGER.

lady's hole, see LADY, 6.

lady's ladder. Rattlins set (too) close: nautical: from ca 1850.

lady's low toupee, see TOUPEE.

lady's pocket-handkerchief. 'Any light fancy sail or flying kite': nautical pejorative: C.19–20; very ob. Bowen.

ladyship, her. Our ship: nautical coll rather than s. (—1887); slightly ob.

***lag.** (Also LAGE.) Water: c.: ca 1560–1870. 2. Also, wine: c.: late C.16–19. 3. Hence (also *lage*), a 'wash' of clothes: c.: ca 1560–1860. Esp. in *lag of* DUDS, in C.17–18 often corrupted to *lag-a-duds.* 4. A transported convict: c. (—1811); †by 1895. Prob. ex the v., 4. (It may well date back to 1740 or so.) Hence, any convict: from ca 1830: also c. Prob. via *returned lag.* 5. A sentence of transportation: c. (—1821); †by 1895. Hence (also *lagging*) a term of penal servitude: c.: from ca 1850. 6. A ticket-of-leave man: c.: from ca 1855. Usually *old lag* (—1856), which also = a one-time convict. 7. A fag: Westminster School (—1881).

***lag,** v. To urinate: c.: ca 1560–1850. 2. To wash (gen. with *off*): c.: ca 1560–1700. 3. Also v.t., to water (spirits): c. of ca 1810–60. 4. To transport as a convict: c.: from ca 1810; †by 1900. Dickens. Ex

†*lag*, to carry away. 5. To send to penal servitude: c.: from ca 1850. 6. Midway between these two senses: to arrest: from ca 1823: c. >, by 1900, low and military. De Quincey; Nat Gould. 7. To inform on (a person) to the police, to SHOP (3): c.: from ca 1870.

***lag, old**, see LAG, n., 6. **lag-a-duds**, see LAG, n., 3.

***lag-fever.** Illness feigned to avoid transportation: c. ca 1810–90.

***lag-ship.** A convict transport: c. of ca 1810–80.

***lage.** See LAG, n., 1, 3. Esp. *lage of* DUDS. Ex Old Fr. *l'aige* or *l'aigue*, the water: ?cf. *newt* for (a)*n ewt*. 2. v., see LAG, v., 1–3. 3. Weak liquor: C.17–18. Ex sense 1. Brome, *A Jovial Crew*, 1652.

***lagger.** A sailor: low (?orig. c.) > nautical: from ca 1810; ob. Perhaps ex *lag*, to loiter. 2. A convict during or after imprisonment: c.: 1819; ob. 3. An informer to the police: from ca 1870: c. Ex LAG, v., 7. 4. A bargeman who, lying on his back, pushes the barge along with his feet on the roof of a subterranean canal: nautical: from ca 1880. An extension of sense 1, possibly influenced by sense 2.

***lagging and a lifer.** Transportation for life: c. of ca 1835–90. Dickens. Ex LAG, v., 4.

***lagging-dues will be concerned.** He will be transported: c.: ca 1810–60.

lagging-gage. A chamber-pot: low if not indeed c.: C.18–19. Ex LAG, v., 1.

***lagging-matter.** A crime potential of transportation: c. of ca 1810–60. 2. Hence, a crime likely to result in penal servitude: c.: from ca 1860.

laid. A pollack: nautical: mid-C.19–20. Possibly ex dial. *laidly*, ugly: it is not a handsome fish, for its lower jaw protrudes.

laid on the shelf; laid (up) in lavender. Pawned: resp. C.19–20, late C.16–20 (slightly ob.). 2. (The latter phrase only:) ill; out of the way: turf: from ca 1870.

laid on with a trowel. (Of flattery or lies.) Grossly exaggerated or obvious: mid-C.19–20: coll, > S.E. by 1910.

lairy. 'Slow, slack; also cunning': *Conway* cadets' (—1891). A corruption of LEARY.

laker-lady. An actor's whore: theatrical: C.18–early 19. ?ex *lady of the lake* or ex *lake* (now dial.), to play amorously.

lakin!, by (our). A (low) coll form of *by our Lady!*: C.15–mid-17.

lakh(s), see LAC.

lall-shraub. Claret: Anglo-Indian coll: from ca 1780. Ex Hindustani *lal-sharab*, red wine. Yule & Burnell, 'the universal name . . . in India'.

***lally.** Linen; shirt: c. (—1789); †by 1890. Gen. LULLY.

lam. A hard hit: cricketers' coll (—1902).

lam, v.; lamb; old spelling **lamm(e).** To beat, thrash: 1596, though implied in 1595 in *belam*: S.E. >, in C.18, coll; in late C.19–20, low coll. Dekker, 'Oh, if they had staid I would have so lamb'd them with flouts.' Cognate with Old Norse *lemja*, lit., to lame; fig., to flog, thrash. cf. *lamback*, LAMBASTE, *lambeak*, LAMB-PIE. 2. To hit hard: cricketers' coll: 1855.

lam (it) into one; lam out, v.i. To hit out; give a thrashing: mainly schoolboys': from ca 1875.

lamb. An elderly woman dressed like a young one: C.19–20, coll mostly Cockney, and gen. as MUTTON DRESSED AS LAMB, EWE DRESSED LAMB-FASHION . . .

lamb, v., see LAM. **lamb, skin the**, see SKIN THE LAMB.

lamb and salad, give, v.t. To thrash: mid-C.19–20; ob. Elaboration on LAM. cf. LAMB-PIE.

lamb-down. To make a man get rid of his money to one: 1873, Marcus Clarke: low Australian; ob. 2. To spend in drink: Australian: 1873, J. Brunton Stephens; ob. Ex LAM.

lamb-fashion, see LAMB, n. Earliest (?) in *The London Guide*, 1818, 'Old harridans . . . dress out lamb-fashion, wear false curls, and paint a little.' cf. EWE DRESSED LAMB-FASHION.

lamb-pie. A thrashing: low coll: C.17–mid-19. cf. LAMB AND SALAD.

lambaste. To beat, thrash: 1637: S.E. >, in C.18, coll; in C.19–20, (dial. and) increasingly low coll. Davenant, 'Stand off awhile, and see how Ile lambaste him.' Ex LAM, on BUM-BASTE.

lambasting. A thrashing: 1694, Motteux, 'A tight lambasting': S.E. >, ca 1750, coll; from ca 1860, low coll and dial.

Lambeth, n. and v. Wash: South London (—1909); very ob. Ware, 'From the popular cleansing place in S. London being the Lambeth baths'.

lambie, see LAMBY.

lambing, see LAMMING.

lambing-down, vbl n. of LAMB-DOWN.

***lambskin (occ. lamb-skin) man.** A judge: c. of ca 1690–1830. Ex judge's gown, lined and bordered with ermine. cf. FURMAN.

lamby. (Gen. pl.) A mizzen-top man: naval (—1891).

lame as a tree, see TREE, LAME AS A.

lame as St Giles, Cripplegate(, as). Very lame indeed – 'applied to badly-told untruth': coll: C.17–19. Ware. Ex the frequenting of that church by cripples, St Giles being their patron.

lame duck. A defaulter, esp. on the Stock Exchange: ca 1760–1870. 2. A scapegrace: Australian coll (—1895); ob.

lame-hand. An inferior driver: coaching: ca 1800–70.

lame post, come by the. To be late (esp. of news): from ca 1650: coll >, ca 1700, proverbial S.E. Fuller, 1732, records, 'The lame post brings the truest news.'

lamentable. Despicable, wretchedly bad: late C.17–20: jocular S.E. verging on, indeed occ. descending to, the coll.

lamm(e), see LAM.

Lammermoor lion. A sheep: C.18–mid-19 mainly Scots jocular coll. cf. COTSWOLD LION; contrast ESSEX or RUMFORD LION.

Lammie Todd! I would – if I got the chance! From ca 1860; ob.: tailors'. Prob. ex a well-known tailor's name.

lamming. A beating, thrashing: 1611, Beaumont & Fletcher, 'One whose dull body will require a lamming': S.E. till C.18, then coll; from ca 1850, low coll.

lammy. A term of address: dustmen's (—1823); †by 1900. Bee suggests derivation ex Fr. *l'ami*, as in 'Ohé! l'ami.'

lamp. An eye: late C.16–20: S.E. till C.19, then s., gen. in pl. In C.19 c., a *queer lamp* is a blind, squinting, sore or weak eye. cf. Fr. c. *lamper*, to gaze at. 2. (Extremely rare in singular.) Spectacles: late C.19–20: low, mostly Cockney. Abbr. GIG-LAMPS.

lamp country. 'Walking out at night without money in one's pockets': military: from ca 1880; virtually †. i.e. when the lights are lit.

lamp-lighter, (off) like a. (Off) *like a* STREAK: coll: from ca 1840; ob. E.D.D., which notes the variant *like lamp-lighters*.

lamp-post. A tall, very thin person: (low) coll: from ca 1870. cf. HOP-POLE.

lamp-post, between you and me and the. In confidence: urban coll (—1887); slightly ob. cf. BED-POST . . .

lamps, see LAMP, both senses.

Lancashire lass. (Gen. pl.) A tumbler: rhyming s. (on *glass*): from ca 1880.

lance-jack. A lance-corporal: military coll: late C.19–20.

***lance-knight, lanceman, lanceman-prigger.** A highwayman: c. of ca 1590–1640. The first in Nashe, the other two in Greene. See PRIGGER. Prob. ex S. German *Landsknechte*, the mercenary soldiers who looted and murdered all over Germany in C.16–17, at a period when touring companies of English actors were popular over there.

***lancepresado, lanspresado, lansprisado.** One who comes into company with but two pence in his pocket: c. of ca 1650–1800. Ex *lancepesade*, *lanceprisado*, a lance-corporal in an army of mercenaries.

land. To cause a horse to win (v.t.); (v.i.) to win: sporting coll: 1853, Whyte-Melville. 2. To establish, set one 'on his feet', make safe: 1868, Yates; Hindley, 'I bought a big covered cart and a good strong horse. And I was landed.' 3. (v.t.) to deliver, get home with: boxers' (—1887). 1888, J. Runciman, 'Their object is to land one cunning blow.' Earlier *lend*, playful for *give*.

land!, my. A mild Canadian (and U.S.) oath: mid-C.19–20. Ex English dial.; *land* = *Lord*.

land-face, see SHIP ONE'S LAND-FACE.

land or lands in Appleby?, who has any. A c.p. directed at one who is slow to empty his glass: late C.17–early 19. Perhaps orig. of cider.

land lies, see how the. To ask how stands one's account or bill, esp. at a tavern: coll: late C.17–early 19.

land-loper or **-lubber.** A vagabond, a pilfering tramp: C.17–early 19 coll; after ca 1860, low. The earlier form, *land-leaper*, was S.E.

***land navy, the.** Pretended sailors: vagabonds' c. (—1909).

land of incumbents. Good clerical livings: Oxford University: ca 1820–70. See also next two entries.

land of promises. A freshman's ambitions: Oxford University s. > coll: ca 1820–60. cf. last entry and:

land of sheepishness. The being a schoolboy: Oxford University: ca 1820–50. cf. preceding two entries.

***land-pirate, -rat.** A highwayman, footpad, or vagabond thief: C.17–early 19: the former, c.; the latter, S.E.: resp. Dekker, Grose; Shakespeare.

land-raker. A vagabond, esp. if a thief: late C.16–mid-18: coll. Shakespeare. cf. preceding entry.

land-security. A C.19 variant of LEG-BAIL.

land-shark. A usurer: C.19–20 (ob.) coll, mostly low when not U.S. 2. A custom-house officer: coll: 1815; Scott, in *Guy Mannering*; ob. 3. A lawyer: nautical (—1860): coll.

land-swab. A landsman; an incompetent seaman: nautical: from ca 1840. See also SWAB.

landed estate. The grave: coll: C.19–20, ob. cf. DARBY'S DYKE and LANDOWNER. 2. Dirt under one's nails: low coll: from ca 1870; ob.

landies. Gaiters: Winchester College: ca 1840–80. Ex *Landy & Currell*, the firm that supplied them.

landlady, bury the. To decamp without paying: low: C.19–20, ob. cf. BURN THE KEN and MOONSHINE; contrast BURY A MOLL.

landowner, become a. To die: late C.19–20. Prob. a development ex LANDED ESTATE.

Land's End or land's end, at (the). At last; sooner or later: proverbial coll: ca 1540–1600. 'Proverbs' Heywood. Ex the geographical feature, perhaps; prob., however, in reference to *land-end*, 'a piece of ground at the end of a "land" in a ploughed field'.

Land's End to John o' Groats, from. All the way; thoroughly: proverbial coll: from ca 1820; ob. Scott, Peacock.

land's sake!; for the land's sake! A non-aristocratic exclamation: late C.19–20. i.e. *Lord's sake*. cf. LAND!, MY.

lane. The throat: from ca 1550. Udall. Gen. preceded by *the*. Esp. *the narrow lane* (Udall, 1542: †by 1800) or *the* RED LANE (1785, Grose) and *Red Lion Lane* (1865; now †). cf. GUTTER LANE.

Lane, another murder down the. Another (melo)drama at Drury Lane Theatre: theatrical: from ca 1880; ob.

Lane, Harriet. Preserved, gen. tinned, meat: nautical and military: ca 1870–1910. Ex a girl, so named, found chopped into small pieces.

langolee. The male member: low: mid-C.19–20; ob. ?a perversion of Welsh Gypsy *trangluni*, tools (Sampson).

***langret.** A die so loaded that it shows 3 or 4 more often than any other number: mid-C.16–18: c. > s. > coll > j. >, by 1700, S.E. and archaic. Greene. Ex *lang* = long.

Langtries. Fine eyes: Society: ca 1880–1900. 2. Female breasts: id.: id. Lily Langtry, 'the Jersey Lily', shone as one of the most beautiful women of her time (1852–1929); went on the stage in 1881 and had a tremendous success; married Sir Hugo de Bathe in 1899.

language. Bad language; swearing, obscenity: 1886 (S.O.D.): low coll. Besant. Often in the imperative = 'Mind your bad language!'

language of flowers, the. 'Ten shillings – or seven days; the favourite sentence of Mr Flowers, a very popular and amiable magistrate' at Bow Street Police Court: 1860–83. Ware. Contrast FLOWERY LANGUAGE.

lank comes a bank, after a. A proverbial c.p. in reference to pregnant women: ca 1650–1820.

lanspresado, -prisado, see LANCEPRESADO.

lantern (late C.18–19) or **lanthorn** (late C.17–19), **dark.** A servant or an agent receiving a bribe at court: ca 1690–1820.

lantern, Ballarat. A candle set in the neck of a bottle whose bottom has been knocked off: coll, Victoria (Australia): ca 1870–1910. Wood & Lapham, *Waiting for the Mail*, 1875. Ballarat is a noted mining town.

lap. Any potable: from ca 1565; ob. In C.16–19 c., butter-milk, whey (Harman); in late C.17–19 c., also pottage (Head). In C.18–20, also tea (G. Parker) and, from 1618, less gen. strong drink: low except, as often in mid-C.19–20, when jocular. Among C.19–20 (ob.) ballet-girls, it gen. denotes gin. Ex the v.

lap, go on the. To drink (strong liquor): low s. > low coll: from ca 1885; ob. *Punch*, 25 Sept. 1886, 'Grinds 'ard, never goes on the lap, | Reads Shakespeare instead o' the *Pink 'Un*.'

lap-clap. A copulation; a conceiving: low coll: C.17–mid-18. Hence, *get a lap-clap*, to become pregnant.

lap-feeder. A silver table-spoon: low: C.19–20; ob.

lap the gutter, see GUTTER, LAP THE.

lapel, ship the white. To be promoted from the ranks; esp. to become an officer of marines: naval coll: mid-C.18–early 19. (In 1812, marine officers began to wear, not white lapels but epaulettes.)

lapful. A husband, a lover; an unborn child: resp. low s., low coll: C.19–20, ob.

lapland; Lapland. The female pudenda: low: from ca 1840. 2. The society of women: low coll: from ca 1850. Punning *lap* and *Lapland*.

***lapper.** Drink, esp. if liquor: c.; C.19–20,

ob. 2. But *rare lapper* = a hard drinker. 3. A lap-dog: late C.19–20.

***lappy cull.** A drunk man: c.: C.18. C. Hitchin, *The Regulator*, 1718. cf. LUSHINGMAN.

laprogh. A goose: a duck; loosely, a bird of any kind: Shelta: C.18–20.

larboard peeper, one's. One's left eye: nautical (—1887); ob.

larbolians, -ins (both in Smyth); **larbowlines** (Bowen). Men in the *larboard*, or port, watch: nautical (—1867); ob.

lardy; lardy-dardy; lardy-dah, adj. Affected, SWELL, though *lardy* (abbr. LARDY-DARDY) very rarely = affected. Somewhat low: resp. 1890 and ob., 1861 (Miss Braddon), ca 1870 and a mere variant of LA-DI-DA.

lardy-dah; also LA-DI-DA. A fop, a SWELL: from ca 1880; somewhat low.

lardy-dah (or la-di-da), come or **do the.** To dress for the public; to show off in dress and manner: low: from ca 1883. See LA-DI-DA, of which *lardy-dah* is a corruption.

lardy-dardy, v.i. To act the SWELL; be affected; show off: 1887, G. R. Sims, 'Other men were lardy-dardying about . . . enjoying themselves.' cf. LA-DI-DA, 4.

lareover (or **lare-over**); **lay-over, layer-over.** A word used instead of one that must, in decency, be avoided: late C.17–early 20: the first, coll and dial.; the others, S.E. cf.:

lareovers for meddlers. 'An answer frequently given to children, or young people, as a rebuke for their impertinent curiosity', Grose: c.p.: C.18–early 19; then dial., gen. as *layers for meddlers*.

large, adj. gen. used as adv. Excessively: (low) coll: from ca 1850. Thus, *dress large*, i.e. showily; *go large*, i.e. noisily; *play large*, i.e. for high stakes; *talk large*, i.e. boastfully. cf. FINE AND LARGE.

large house. A workhouse: low coll: from ca 1850. cf. BIG HOUSE.

large order. Something big or exaggerated or very difficult: coll: 1890, *Pall Mall Gazette*, 17 Feb. Ex commerce.

larikin. An occ. variant of LARRIKIN.

lark. A game; piece of merriment or mischief; trick: *Sessions*, April 1802: s. >, ca 1870, coll. Dickens, in *Pickwick*, '"Here's a lark!" shouted half a dozen hackney coachmen.' For etymology, see the v. 2. A boat: from ca 1785: c. > s. >, ca 1850, nautical s. >, ca 1870, nautical j.; ob. Prob. *ark* perverted. 3. Abbr. MUDLARK. 4. A line of business: grafters': late C.19–20. cf. LAY, 2, and LAW.

lark, v. See the amorous and the sporting sense of LARKING. 2. To play (esp. the fool); be mischievously merry; go on the SPREE: 1813, Colonel Hawker; Barham, 'Don't lark with the watch, or annoy the police.' 3. To ride in a frolicsome way or across country: 1835, 'Nimrod': sporting s. >, ca 1870, coll. 4. v.t., tease playfully: 1848, Thackeray: s. >, ca 1880, coll. 5. v.t., to ride (a horse) across country: from ca 1860: sporting s. >, ca 1880, coll; ob. 6. To jump (a fence) needlessly: 1834, Ainsworth; ob. Ex the n., which is ex the Northern dial. *lake*, sport. Whence SKYLARK.

lark, go on or **have** or **take a.** To be mischievously merry: go on the spree: from ca 1815: s. >, ca 1870, coll. cf.:

lark, knock up a. Same as preceding: 1812, Vaux; †by 1890: prob. c. > low s.

larker. A person given to (mischievous) fun: from ca 1825: s. >, ca 1870, coll.

larkin. A girl: Shelta: C.18–20. 2. A very strong spiced punch: Anglo-Indian: from ca 1860. Prob. ex concocter's name.

larking, n. Cunnilingism: low: C.18–19 (?20). Grose, 1st ed.; absent in latter edd. 2. Fun; a mischievous frolic: from ca 1812: s. >, ca 1870, coll. Beddoes, 'Professors of genteel larking'. 3. Sporting senses of LARK, V.

larking, adj. Given to 'larks' (see LARK, n., 1); sportive: W. N. Glascock, 1826: s. >, ca 1870, coll.

larkish. Fond of, or of the nature of, a LARK: from ca 1880. Whence *larkishness*.

larksome. Fond of a LARK, apt to indulge in 'larks': coll: from ca 1870.

larky. Ready or inclined to play 'larks' (see LARK, n.): 1841: s. >, ca 1870, coll. H. Mayo, 'When the Devil is larky, he solicits the witches to dance round him.'

larky subaltern's train, see COLD-MEAT TRAIN. **Larrence,** see LAZY LARRENCE.

***larries.** A C.18 variant of *lurries* (s.v. LURRY). *The Scoundrel's Dict.*, 1754.

larrikin; occ. **larikin.** A (gen. young) street rowdy: orig. and mainly Australian: 1870 or a few years earlier: s. >, ca 1890, coll >, ca 1910, S.E. *Melbourne Herald*, 4 April 1870, 'Three larikins . . . had behaved in a very disorderly manner in Little Latrobe-street.' cf. HOODLUM; HOOLIGAN. Also as adj.: 1870, Marcus Clarke. See esp. Morris. Etymologies proposed: LEARY KINCHEN (see separate words), fantastic; a pronunciation of *larking*, ineptly fantastic; *Larry*, a common Irish pet-form of *Lawrence*, + *kin*, O.E.D.; perhaps orig. Cornish, where *larrikin* = a LARKER, suggested by W., not to the exclusion of the preceding, which seems the most likely.

lar(r)ikiness. A female larrikin: 1871: same remarks as for preceding.

larrikinism. The habits and tricks of larrikins: 1870: remarks as for LARRIKIN. *Australian*, 10 Sept. 1870, 'A slight attempt at "larrikinism" was manifested.'

larrup; occ. **larrop** and **†lirrop.** To beat, thrash: coll and dial.: from ca 1820. Fonblanque, 1829, 'Is this a land of liberty, where a man can't larrop his own nigger?' ?ex *lee-rope*, as an early glossarist proposed, or, as W. proposes, suggested by LATHER, LEATHER, v., and WALLOP.

larruping. vbl n. of preceding: a thrashing. Coll and dial.: from ca 1825.

larry. A familiar form of LARRIKIN.

Larry, (as) happy as. Very happy: Australian coll: late C.19–20.

Larry Dugan's eye-water. Blacking: mostly Anglo-Irish: ca 1770–1820. Ex a very well-known Dublin shoe-black.

lascar. A tent-pitcher; (in full, *gun-lascar*) an inferior artilleryman: Anglo-Indian coll: from late C.18; both ob.

lash, v. To envy. Gen. as *lash!*, used as a taunt: the Blue Coat school (—1877); ob.

lash-out. 'A sudden burst of work on the approach of an officer' (Granville): naval: since ca 1905. Ex a (horse's or a) boxer's lashing out.

lash-up. Anything makeshift: naval coll: late C.19–20. i.e. lashed together.

lash up, v. To stand (someone) treat: naval: since ca 1905. Granville, '"I'll lash you up to a couple of pints when we have a run ashore", originated from lashing up a messmate's hammock.'

lashin(g)s. (Gen. of drink, occ. of food, rarely of anything else.) Plenty: coll, orig. Anglo-Irish: 1829, Scott, 'Whiskey in lashings'; 1841, Lever, 'Lashings of drink', these quotations illustrating the gen. forms; the former is ob. Perhaps ex, or for, *lavishings* (W.); prob. ex †S.E. *lash* (*out*) to squander. cf.

lashin(g)s and lavin(g)s. Plenty and to spare: Anglo-Irish coll: from ca 1840.

la'ship. A coll form of ladyship: C.18–early 19.

lashool. Pleasant: Shelta: C.18–20.

lass in a red petticoat. A wife well-endowed: proverbial coll, esp. in *the lass in the red petticoat shall pay for*, or *piece up, all*: ca 1660–1800. J. Wilson, *The Cheats*, 1664.

lassitudinarian. A person of infirm health: Society: 1894–1914. Punning *Latitudinarian* and *valetudinarian*.

last. A person's most recent joke, witticism, etc.: coll: 1843. e.g. 'X's last is a scream.'

last, the. The end of one's dealings with something: coll: 1854. Dickens, 'If it ever was to reach your father's ears I should never hear the last of it.'

last bit o(f) family-plate, the. The final silver coin: artisans' (—1909).

last card of one's pack. The back: rhyming s.: Mayhew, 1857.

last compliment. Burial: coll: from ca 1780; ob.

last drink, take one's. To die by drowning: Canadian lumbermen's coll: late C.19–20.

last shake o(f) the bag. Youngest child: proletarian: C.19–20; ob.

last ship, a. A nautical coll (C.19–20), thus in Bowen, 'Anything that is the epitome of excellence, for the sailor always has good things to say, and odious comparisons to make, of his last ship, no matter what she was like.'

laster. The flow of the tide: nautical: C.19. ?the ebb-flow, 'the last of it'.

lasting, adj. (Of a horse) having staying power: sporting: from ca 1810.

***latch.** To let in: c. of ca 1720–1850.

latch-key. A crowbar: Irish Constabulary's: 1881–2. Because so often used by them in evictions.

latch-pan. The under lip. Hence, *hang one's latch-pan*, to pout, be sulky: coll and dial.: C.19–20. Ex lit. sense.

late. Keeping late hours: coll: from ca 1630. Having to do with persons or things that arrive late: coll: 1862, 'the "late" mark'.

late play. A holiday beginning at noon: Westminster School: C.19–20 coll.

latest, the. The latest news: coll: C.19–20. Baumann, 'What's the latest?'

lath-and-plaster. A master: rhyming s. (—1857).

lather. The sexual secretion: low: C.19–20; ob. Hence *lather-maker*, the female pudend.

lather, v. To beat, thrash: from ca 1795: coll >, ca 1890, S.E. cf. LACE; LEATHER; LARRUP.

Latin. Alicante wine: s. (—1650).

Latin for 'goose'. A dram: ca 1820–50. Ex BRANDY IS . . .

Latiner. A Latin scholar; one who speaks Latin: coll: 1691.

latitat. An attorney: coll, though perhaps orig. legal s.: 1565, Cooper's *Thesaurus.* Foote, in *The Maid of Bath*, 'I will send for Luke Latitat and Codicil, and make a handsome bequest to the hospital.' †by 1860 in England, the term derives ex an old form of writ.

latter end. The posteriors: early C.19–20: jocular coll >, ca 1910, S.E. According to Baumann, a careful observer, it was at first a boxing term.

latty, see LETTY.

laugh and joke. A smoke: rhyming s. (—1880).

lauk! see LAWK!

launch. A lying-in: coll: from ca 1786; ob. by 1880. Prob. ex nautical v., but perhaps cognate with †dial. *launch*, to groan.

launch, v. (Gen. in passive.) To reverse a boy's bed while he is asleep: Public Schools: ca 1810–90. G. J. Berkeley, *My Life*, 1865.

Laurence on one's back, have; have a touch of old Laurence. To be lazy: coll: C.19–20; ob. except in dial. See LAZY LARRENCE.

lavender, not all. Not all fun or pleasant: coll: from ca 1880.

lavender, lay (up) or **put in.** (The *put* form not before C.19.) To pawn: from ca 1590; slightly ob. Greene, in his *Upstart Courtier.* Like the next sense, ex the preservative virtues of lavender. 2. 'To put out of the way of doing harm, as a person by imprisoning him or the like': from ca 1820; ob. Scott, in *Nigel.* 3. See LAID ON THE SHELF, 2.

lavender-cove. A pawnbroker: low: from ca 1850; slightly ob. Ex preceding.

law. A phase of crime, esp. of theft; a trick or LAY (2): c.: ca 1550–1650. Esp. in Greene's 'coney-catchers'. See also LURK, PACKET, RIG, SLUM.

law! or **Law!** LORD!: late C.16–20; in C.19–20 low coll, perhaps orig. euphemistic. Prob. arising from cumulative force of LA!, *lo!*, and LOR'. See also LAWK!; LAWS! and LORS!

law-lord. A judge having, by courtesy, the style of 'Lord': Scots coll: from ca 1770.

lawed, it is, was, etc. It is settled by law: coll and dial.: C.19–20; ob.

lawful blanket or **jam.** A wife: low: the former from ca 1810; the latter from ca 1850; ob. Henley, 1887, 'Gay grass-widows and lawful jam'. cf. DUTCH, contrast JAM-TART.

lawful picture. A coin; in pl, gen. money: coll: C.17–18.

lawful time. Playtime: Winchester College: C.19–20; ob.

lawk!, lawks! Lord!: coll (rather low): from ca 1765; earliest as *lauk*, latest as *lawks.* Dickens in *Pickwick*, 'Lawk, Mr Weller . . . how you do frighten me.' Occ. (C.18–20, ob.) *lawk-a-daisy* (*me*) i.e. *lackadaisy* = lackaday!, and (C.19–20) *lawk-a-mussy*, the latter a corruption of *Lord have mercy!* Either ex *lack* as in *good lack!* or ex *Lord* influenced by *lack* and LA! or LAW! See also LOR'!

lawless as a town-bull. Quite lawless; very unruly: proverbial coll: ca 1670–1800.

lawn. A handkerchief, esp. if of white cambric: low coll: from ca 1810; ob.

Lawrence, see LAURENCE and LAZY LARRENCE.

laws!; laws-a-me!; lawsy! A low coll form (cf. LAW!; LAWK!; LORS) of LORD!: from ca 1875.

lawt. Tall: back s. (—1859).

lawyer. An argumentative or discontented man, esp. one given to airing his grievances: military coll: late C.19–20.

***lawyer, high** (occ. **highway**). A highwayman: c.: ca 1590–1640. Greene. Ex LAW. cf. MARTIN; OAK; SCRIPPER; STOOP.

lawyer must be a great liar, a good. A frequent c.p. in conversations turning on the law: ca 1670–1780. Ned Ward, 1703.

lawyering, n. and adj. (Concerning, of) a lawyer's profession: coll: from ca 1860.

lawyers go to heaven, as. (Gen. preceded by *fairly and softly* or *by degrees*, etc.). Very slowly: from Restoration days: proverbial coll; in C.19–20, mainly dial.

lay, a wager, is S.E. 2. An occupation, esp. if criminal; a 'line'; a trick: from ca 1705: c. >, ca 1840, low. Hence AVOIRDUPOIS LAY; FANCY-LAY, pugilism, C.19 low; KINCHEN-LAY; etc., etc. Prob. ex LAW. 3. Hence, a hazard, chance: 1707, Farquhar: c. >, ca 1800, low: †by 1850. See LAY, STAND A QUEER. 4. A quantity: c.: ca 1815–50. Haggart. Perhaps ex fusion of senses 1 and 2. 5. Hence, some; a piece: Northern c.: from ca 1850; ob. 6. ?hence, a share in the capture: whale-fishers' (—1887). 7. (Also from sense 5.) Goods: c.: ca 1820–50. Haggart. 8. (Butter)milk: c.: C.17. Middleton & Dekker in *The Roaring Girl.* Ex Fr. *lait.*

lay, a good. Anything advantageous; esp.,

an economical way of cutting: tailors': C.19–20 >, ca 1890, coll.

***lay, on the.** At (illicit) work: C.18–20 c. 2. On the alert, e.g. for something to steal: C.19–20 c. See LAY, n., 2.

***lay, stand a queer.** To run a great risk: c.: from ca 1720; †by 1850. See LAY, n., 3.

lay a duck's egg. In cricket, to score nothing: sporting: from ca 1870; ob. See DUCK (6) and BLOB.

lay a straw. To stop (v.i.); mark a stopping-place: coll: C.16–mid-17. Barclay, Bullein, Barnaby Rich.

lay a or in water. To defer judgement; esp. too long: coll: C.15–early 17; *in* not before C.16. (The *a* is, of course, the preposition as in *a-board.*) Lyly, 'I see all his expeditions for warres are laid in water; for now when he should execute, he begins to consult.'

lay at. To (attempt to) strike: C.15–20: S.E. till C.19, then dial. and coll.

lay by the heels. To put in stocks (†) or in prison: C.18–20: coll >, ca 1860, S.E.

***lay down,** gen. **lay them down.** To play cards: c.: mid-C.19–20; ob.

lay down one's ears. To drink heartily: s. (—1650).

lay down one's, or the, knife and fork. To die: low coll (—1859); ob.

lay down the law. To dogmatize: coll: 1885. Ex lit. sense, declare what the law is.

lay, or lay himself, down to his work. (Of a horse, etc.) to do his best: sporting: from ca 1885; slightly ob. *Illustrated Sporting and Dramatic News*, 20 May 1893.

lay in, v.i. To attack with vigour: coll: from ca 1888. 2. v.i., to eat vigorously: from ca 1800: S.E. >, ca 1880, low coll.

lay, occ. **cast, in one's dish.** To object to something in a person; accuse of: coll: mid-C.16–mid-19. T. Wilson in *Rhetorique*, Harington in *Epigrams*, Butler in *Hudibras*, Scott in *Old Mortality*.

lay into. To thrash: 1838, Douglas Jerrold: s. >, ca 1870, coll. cf. PITCH INTO.

lay into its collar. (Of a horse) to pull hard: Canadian coll: late C.19–20.

lay or lie on the face. To be exceedingly dissipated: lower classes' (—1909); slightly ob.

lay one's shirt. To stake one's all: sporting s. > coll: mid-C.19–20. If the stake is lost, one *does* (or *has done*) *one's shirt*: late C.19–20 sporting.

lay out. To overcome or disable, esp. with a punch, also to kill: s.: orig. (1829), U.S.; anglicized ca 1860. Ex the *laying-out* of a corpse.

lay-over, see LAREOVER.

***lay the razor.** A term, ca 1865, in racing c. (or perhaps s.), as in '*No. 747*'; of obscure meaning. Possibly, to judge precisely when to spur one's horse to win the race.

lay-up. A drink, a GO: low (—1891); ob. Newman, in *Scamping Tricks*, 'A strong lay-up of something neat.'

lay up in lavender, see LAVENDER.

laycock, see MISS LAYCOCK.

layer. A bookmaker; a betting-man: mid-C.19–20: sporting s. >, ca 1880, coll.

layer-over, see LAREOVER.

laze. A lazy rest: coll: from ca 1860.

lazy as Joe the marine who laid down his musket to sneeze. Exceedingly lazy: C.19 semi-proverbial coll. Prob. ex LAZY AS THE TINKER ...

lazy as Ludlam's, or (David) Laurence's, dog. (Sussex dial. has *Lumley's.*) Extremely lazy: proverbial coll from ca 1660: ob. by 1870, †except in dial. by 1900. According to the proverb, this admirable creature leant against a wall to bark. cf. preceding entry.

lazy as the tinker who laid down his budget to fart. The acme of laziness: late C.18–early 19 low, semi-proverbial coll. cf. two preceding entries.

lazy-bones. A loafer or a very lazy person: coll: from ca 1590. Harvey, 'Was ... vivacitie a lasie-bones?' cf. LAZY-BOOTS. 2. Lazy-tongs or, as it is occ. called, lazy-back: coll (—1785); ob.

lazy-boots. A LAZY-BONES: coll: from ca 1830; ob. Mrs Gaskell. cf. SLY BOOTS.

lazy Larrence, Laurence, Lawrence. The incarnation of laziness: from ca 1780 or perhaps even from ca 1650: coll (ob.) and dial. Perhaps in reference to the gen. heat of St Lawrence's Day, 10 Aug., or to the legend of the martyred St Lawrence being too lazy to move in the flames. (Apperson; E.D.D.; Prideaux's *Readings in History*, 1655.) See also LAURENCE ...

lazy-legs. A LAZY-BONES: coll: 1838, Dickens; ob.

lazy man's load. An excessive load carried to save a second journey: coll (—1791).

lazy-roany. Lazzaroni, or Neapolitan beggars: nautical (—1887).

Lea toff. 'One who displays his distinction, in a hired boat, rowing up and down the River Lea': Cockneys' (—1909); ob. Ware.

lead. Abbr. *friendly lead*, an entertainment designed to assist some unfortunate: from ca 1850: c. >, ca 1880, s.

lead, get the. To be shot: late C.19–20.

lead apes in hell, see APES IN HELL.

lead-off. The first or most important article in a newspaper: journalists' coll (—1887).

lead towel. A pistol: low: mid-C.18–early 19.

leaden fever, esp. in *die of l.f.*, to die from a bullet wound: late C.18–mid-19.

leader. A remark or question intended to lead conversation (cf. FEELER). (1882): coll; slightly ob.

leading article. The nose: coll (—1886); ob. 2. The female pudend: low: mid-C.19–20; ob. 3. 'The best bargain in the shop – one that should lead to other purchases': tradesmen's: from ca 1870; ob. Ware.

leading heavy. (Gen. pl.) The role of a serious middle-aged woman: theatrical: from the late 1880s; prob. from U.S.A.

leading-strings. The yoke-lines on a ship's rudder: nautical: late C.19–20.

leaf, drop one's. To die: low (?orig. c.): C.19–20; ob. Ex:

***leaf, go off with the.** To be hanged: Anglo-Irish c. > low: from ca 1870; ob. Either ex the autumnal fall of leaves or ex a hanging-device shaped like the leaf of a table. cf.:

***leafless tree.** The gallows: c. of ca 1825–70. Lytton in *Paul Clifford.*

leak. The female pudend: low: C.18–20; ob. Gay. 2. A urination: a vulgarism or a low coll: mid-C.19–20. Esp. in *do* or *have a leak*. cf.:

leak, v. To make water: a vulgarism: from ca 1590; ob. Shakespeare.

leak, spring a. To urinate: low: ca 1860–1910. Ex nautical j.

leaky. Talkative when drunk: proletarian coll: from ca 1880.

lean, adj. and n. Unprofitable (work): printers' (—1871). From C.17 in a different sense, but this (e.g. in Moxon) is j. Contrast FAT. 2. Unremunerative: (dial. and) coll (—1875).

lean and fat. A hat: rhyming s. (—1857).

lean and lurch. A church: rhyming s. (—1857).

lean as a (1) rake, (2) shotten herring. Extremely thin: resp. late C.16–20, S.E. >, ca 1700, coll, but in C.19–20 mainly dial.; and proverbial coll from ca 1650 (after ca 1830, mainly dial.).

lean-away. A drunkard: Australia: ca 1890–1910.

lean off it or that! Cease leaning on it!: coll: 1829, Marryat, 'Lean off that gun'; ob.

***leap!** All safe!: c.: C.18.

leap, do a. To copulate: low coll: C.19–20.

leap (occ. go) a whiting, let. To let an opportunity slip: proverbial coll: ca 1540–1780. Heywood, Breton.

leap at a crust. ?To be very hungry; or, snatch at any chance whatsoever: semi-proverbial coll: ca 1630–1750. Draxe; Swift.

leap at a daisy. To be hanged: coll: ca 1550–1620. Anon., *Respublica*; Greene; *Pasquil's Jests*, 1604, 'He sayd: Have at yon dasie that growes yonder; and so leaped off the gallows.'

leap at Tyburn or in the dark, take a. To be hanged: low (?orig. c.): C.17–early 19. D'Urfey, 'All you that must take a leap in the dark . . .'

***leap-frog.** A crab: c. (—1857).

leap in the dark or up a ladder. A copulation: C.18–20 low; ob. 2. Being hanged: cf. LEAP, DO A, and LEAP AT TYBURN.

leap over nine hedges, ready to. Exceedingly ready: coll: ca 1660–1800. Ray.

leap over the hedge before one comes to the stile. To be in a violent hurry: proverbial coll: ca 1540–1800. Heywood, Gascoigne, Ray, Motteux.

leap (or jump) the besom, broom(-stick), sword. (U.S., book.) To marry informally: C.18–19 coll. See BESOM and BROOMSTICK separately. The *sword* form, military.

leap the stile first, let the best dog. Let the best or most suitable person take precedence or the lead: coll: C.18–early 19.

leapt, to have. (Of frost) to thaw suddenly: coll, mainly rural: 1869, H. Stephens, 'When frost suddenly gives way . . . about sunrise, it is said to have "leapt".'

learn. To teach: from M.E.; S.E. till ca 1760, then coll; from ca 1810, low coll; since ca 1890, sol. Chiefly in *I'll learn you!* (often jocularly allusive). cf. Fr. *apprendre*, to learn, also to teach.

learned men. C.19 nautical coll, thus: 'In the old coasters, certified officers shipped for foreign voyages to satisfy the regulations.' Bowen.

learning-shover. A school-teacher: Cockneys': 1869; ob.

***leary, leery.** Artful; wide-awake; (suspiciously) alert; c. >, ca 1830, low: from ca 1790. Prob. ex dial. *lear*, learning, cleverness (cf. S.E. *lore*). cf. PEERY. 2.

FLASH; showy of dress and manners: low: ca 1850–75. cf. CHICKALEARY COVE. 3. (Of personal appearance) somewhat wild: from ca 1850.

leary bloke. A showy dresser, gen. of lower classes: low (—1859); †by 1880. cf. LEARY, 2, and CHICKALEARY COVE.

leary-cum-Fitz. A vulgarian actor: theatrical: ca 1890–1914.

least in sight, play. To hide; make oneself scarce; keep out of the way: low: ca 1780–1870.

leastaways. A C.19–20 variant of:

leastways; leastwise. At least: C.16–20: S.E. till C.19, then coll. In C.19–20, also dial.

leather. Skin: C.14–20: S.E. till ca 1700, then coll till ca 1780, when it > s. Hence, *lose leather*, C.18–20 (ob.), to be *saddle-galled.* 2. Hence, the female pudend: C.16–20 low coll. Whence, *labour* or *stretch leather*, to coït, C.16–19 and C.18–20, and *nothing like leather*, nothing like a good CUNT, C.19–20.

leather. To beat, thrash: from ca 1620: coll >, ca 1820, S.E. Prob. at first with a strap. cf. LATHER; TAN; DUSTING.

leather-bumper. (Gen. pl.) A cavalryman: infantrymen's: late C.19–20.

leather-flapper. A keen horseman: sporting: from ca 1865; virtually †. '*No. 747*'.

leather-head(ed), n. and adj. (A) blockhead: late C.17–20; ob. Davenant. 2. A swindler: Canadian: from ca 1870; ob.

leather-jacket. Applied to various Australian trees: Australian coll (—1898) verging on S.E. Ex their tough skin. 2. A rough-and-ready pancake: Australian coll: 1846, G. H. Haydon, *Five Years in Australia Felix*, '... Dough fried in a pan'. Tough eating!

leather-lane. The female pudend: C.18–20 low; ob. 2. As an adj., paltry, it is c. of ca 1810–60. Always as *Leather Lane concern.*

leather-neck. A soldier; more gen., a Royal Marine: nautical and esp. naval: late C.19–20; ob. According to 'Taffrail', however, it is a bluejackets' name for a soldier: see quotation at JOEY, 2.

leather-stretcher. The male member: C.18–20, ob.: low. Ex LEATHER, n., 2. Hence, *go leather-stretching*, to have sexual intercourse.

leathering. A thrashing: from ca 1790: coll. Ex LEATHER, v.

leathern convenience, -cy. A stage-coach; a carriage: Quakers' j. >, ca 1790, jocular coll; †by 1860. B.E.; C. K. Sharpe, 1801, 'I left Oxford with Stapleton in his mama's leathern conveniency.'

leathers. A person wearing leggings or leather breeches, e.g. a postboy: coll: ca 1835–1910. Dickens; Thackeray, in *Pendennis.* cf. BOOTS; BUTTONS. 2. The ears: low: from ca 1860.

leave. A (favourable) position for a stroke: billiards: from ca 1850.

leave, take French, see FRENCH LEAVE.

leave ... be. To let be; cease, or abstain, from interfering with: coll: from ca 1825.

leave an R in pawn. To desert: naval: C.19. Bowen, 'The man's name in the ship's books being marked "R" for "run".'

leave cold, see COLD, LEAVE OUT IN THE.

leave go (of), hold (of), (loose of), v.i. To let go: coll: from ca 1810.

leave in the air, see AIR, IN THE.

leave in the briers or seeds. To bring to, or leave in, (grave) trouble: semi-proverbial coll. 1533, Udall (*briers*); ca 1590, Harvey (*seeds*). Rare since ca 1820.

leave it all to the cook!, I'll. I won't take that bet: sporting c.p. of ca 1820–40. (A cook is a good judge of meat, a betting-man of horseflesh.)

leave the minority. To die: Society: 1879; ob. On *join the majority.*

leave the sea and go into steam. To transfer to a steam-driven ship: sailing-men's c.p.: ca 1860–1900.

leave-yer-(h)omer. 'A handsome, dashing man ... Derived, very satirically, from "That's the man I'm goin' to leave me 'ome for"' (Ware): lower-class women's: late C.19–20.

leaver. A paroled convict: Australian: ca 1840–70. One who is on ticket-of-leave.

leaving-shop. An unlicensed pawnbroker's shop: low coll (—1857); ob. *Morning Chronicle*, 21 Dec. 1857; J. Greenwood. 2. Hence, allusively, the female pudend: low: from ca 1860; ob.

leccers. (Pron. *lekkers.*) Lectures: Oxford undergraduates': from late 1890s. (Oxford *-er.*)

lechery-layer. A harlot: s.: Ned Ward, 1703.

led-captain. A toady, sponge, pimp: from ca 1670: coll >, ca 1800, S.E.; †by 1880. Wycherley, in *Love in a Wood*, 'Every wit has his culley, as every squire his led captain.' Prob. ex *a led horse.*

leddy, the. A ship's figurehead, no matter what it represents: nautical: mid-C.19–20. Ex the old Scots and dial. *leddy*, a lady.

ledger. (Gen. in pl.) A ledger-clerk: bank-clerks' coll: late C.19–20. cf. VOUCHER.

leek. A chimney-sweep not brought up to the trade: ca 1850–1910: low. Mayhew. Ex his *greenness.* 2. A Welshman: very late C.17–early 19 c. *Street Robberies Considered*, ca 1728.

Leekshire. Wales: low: C.18–19. Ex the racial emblem.

***leer.** A newspaper: c. of ca 1785–1870. G. Parker, in *Life's Painter*, 1789. ?ex Ger. *lehren*, to teach; much more prob. ex *the* LURE.

***leer, roll the,** see ROLL THE LEER.

leerily. The adv. of LEARY: 1859. Farrar, in *Julian Home*, 1859.

***leery,** see LEARY.

leetle. Little: late C.17–20: on borderland between S.E. and (gen. jocular) coll. cf. LICKELL.

leeward, go to. To put oneself at a disadvantage: nautical coll: mid-C.19–20. cf.:

leeward of (occ. **on**), **get to.** 'To fall foul of a man': nautical coll: late C.19–20. Bowen. Ex nautical j.

lef, see LEP.

left, be or **get.** To fail; be outdistanced metaphorically; be placed in a difficult position: coll: orig. (ca 1890), U.S.; anglicized ca 1895. Abbr. *be* or *get left in the lurch.*

left, over the; over the left shoulder. In the wrong way. But gen. a c.p. used to negate one's own or another's statement, the thumb being sometimes pointed over that shoulder: from ca 1610; slightly ob. In C.19–20, when the phrase is somewhat low, *shoulder* is gen. omitted. Cotgrave; H. D. Traill, 1870, 'Don't go? . . . It's go and go over the left . . . it's go with a hook at the end.'

left-forepart. A wife: mid-C.19–20; ob. ?ex *left rib.* cf. DUTCH.

left hanging Judas. (Of a rope) left hanging over the side: naval: late C.19–20.

left her purse on her piano. A c.p. constituting a 'satirical hit at self-sufficiency': non-aristocratic: late C.19–early 20. Ware.

left-off, gen. in pl. Left-off clothes: coll: from ca 1890.

left in the basket, see BASKET!

left shoulder, over the, see LEFT, OVER THE.

Lefty. A proletarian 'inevitable nickname' (late C.19–20) for a left-handed man.

leg. A swindling gambler at race-courses: 1815; ob. Abbr. BLACK-LEG (n., 1). Dickens in *Pickwick*, 'He *was* a horse-chaunter: he's a leg now.' 2. A point: card-players': from ca 1860. 3. See LEGS. 4. A footman: fast society: ca 1860–1910. Ware, 'From the display of the lower limbs'.

leg, v. To trip up: from ca 1880: also dial. *Saturday Review*, 22 April 1882, 'They legged the copper, and he fell to the ground.'

leg, as right as my. As right as may be; decidedly: from ca 1660; ob.: low coll. 2. Occ. as adj., perfectly right, 'a bit of all right': C.18–20; ob.

leg, break a. To give birth to a bastard: low coll: from ca 1670; ob. R. Head, in *Proteus Redivivus*. The proverbial form gen. added *above the knee*; gen., too, as *to have broken her leg*. See also BROKEN-LEGGED.

leg, cut one's. To get drunk: C.18–early 19: coll.

leg, get one's. To obtain a person's confidence: tailors': from ca 1865.

leg (or **arm** or **throat**), **have a bone in one's.** To be incapacitated: coll, as a playful refusal: from ca 1540. Udall, 1542, 'Allegeing that he had a bone in his throte and could not speake'; Torriano, 1666, 'The English say, He hath a bone in his arm and cannot work'; Swift, ca 1706 (pub. 1738), 'I can't go, for I have a bone in my leg.' In C.19–20 dial., to *have a bone in the arm* or *leg* is to have a shooting pain there.

leg, lift one's. To coït: low: C.18–20; ob. Anon., in *Duncan Davidson*, a song.

leg, pull one's. To befool; impose on: coll (—1888); now on verge of S.E. Ex tripping-up.

leg, show a. To rise from bed: orig. naval coll: from ca 1830.

leg, swing the. To loaf; malinger: nautical: from ca 1860. Ex a dog running on three legs, sometimes to rest the fourth, sometimes to elicit sympathy (Mr H. G. Dixey, in a letter to the author). cf. LEG-SWINGER, -SWINGING.

leg-and-leg, adv. and adj. (Of a game) when each player has won a LEG or point; level: cards coll: from ca 1860. In Anglo-Irish, *horse-and-horse.*

leg-bags. Trousers: from ca 1855; ob. 2. Stockings: ca 1870–1910.

leg-bail (and land-security), give or **take.** To escape from custody; to decamp: from ca 1760: semi-proverbial coll >, ca 1700, S.E.; slightly ob.

leg-business. Sexual intercourse: low coll:

C.19–20; ob. 2. Ballet-dancing: from ca 1870. cf. LEG-SHOP and LEGGY.

leg-drama, -piece, -show. A play or a ballet distinguished for the amount of leg shown by the female participants: resp. from ca 1870, 1880, 1890.

leg-grinder. A revolution round the horizontal bar as one hangs by one's legs: gymnastic coll (—1887). cf. *muscle-grinder*, the same exercise as one hangs by one's arms.

leg in, get a. To win another's confidence, esp. to gain proof of confidence and/or esteem: coll: from ca 1890. Nat Gould.

leg in, own a. To have an interest, a share in (horses): sporting: from ca 1865; ob. '*No. 747*'.

leg-lifter. A male fornicator: C.18–20 (ob.) low. So *leg-lifting*, fornication.

leg-maniac. An 'eccentric, rapid dancer': theatrical coll: ca 1880–1915. Ware.

leg of mutton. A sheep's trotter: low: from ca 1850.

leg of the law. A lawyer: C.19–20; ob.: low. Varying *limb of the law*.

leg on or over, lay or lift a. To coït with a woman: low coll: C.18–20. D'Urfey, Burns. cf. LEG, LIFT ONE'S; LEG-LIFTER.

leg-piece, see LEG-DRAMA.

leg-shaker. A dancer: (low) coll: C.19–20; ob.

leg-shop. A theatre specializing in the display of the female form: from ca 1872; ob. cf. LEG-BUSINESS (2), -DRAMA.

leg-swinger. A loafer; malingerer: nautical: from ca 1860. (Corrupted by the Army to *lead-swinger*.) Ex LEG, SWING THE. cf.:

leg-swinging or swinging the leg. Loafing; pretended illness or injury: nautical: from ca 1860. See LEG, SWING THE.

***leger.** A giver of short weight in coals. **legering** (LAW), this practice. ca 1590–1650: c. Greene. Ex Fr. *léger*, light.

***legged.** In irons: c. > low: ca 1830–70.

***legger.** One pretending to sell smuggled, but actually selling shop-worn, goods: ca 1785–1830: c.

leggings. Stockings: (somewhat low) jocular coll: from ca 1870; ob.

leggism. The art or the character of a LEG (1), from ca 1820; ob.

leggo! 'Leg it!'; run!: low: late C.19–20.

leggy. Notable for the display of leg: from ca 1865. cf. LEG-BUSINESS; -SHOP. *Daily Telegraph*, 10 Jan. 1866, 'Leggy burlesques'.

leggy-peggy. A (little) leg: nursery (—1887).

legitimacy. The reason for much early emigration to Australia, i.e. transportation: Australia: ca 1820–60. Ex the legal necessity of the voyage. Peter Cunningham. cf. LEGITIMATES.

legitimate. A sovereign (coin): Londoners': ca 1820–50. Prob. ex *legitimate sovereign* (king).

legitimate, adj. Applied to flat racing as opp. to steeplechasing: racing (—1888).

legitimate, the. Legitimate drama, i.e. good (mainly Shakespearean) drama, as opp. to burlesque: theatrical (—1887).

legitimates. Convict emigrants: Australian: ca 1820–60. See LEGITIMACY.

legs. A tall, thin person, esp. if a man: coll: C.19–20. cf. LAMP-POST.

legs, be or get on one's hind. To be speaking, rise to speak, esp. if formally: jocular coll (—1897).

legs, give – or show – (a clean pair of). To run away; decamp: coll (—1883).

legs, have. To be (considered) fast (e.g. of ship, train, runner): coll: from ca 1870.

legs, make indentures with one's. To be tipsy: C.18–early 19. Ray.

legs, merry, see MERRY-LEGS.

legs and arms. Weak beer: tailors': from ca 1860. Because without body.

legs grew in the night, therefore could not see to grow straight, – his. A jeering c.p. addressed to a crooked-legged man. cf. BUY ONE'S BOOTS . . .

legs in a bed, more belongs or goes to marriage than four bare. A c.p., > proverbial when applied to a portionless couple: from ca 1540; ob. Heywood, 1546; Swift; Scott; Apperson. cf. the C.17–18 proverb, *there belongs more than whistling to going to plough*.

legs on one's neck or to ground, lay one's. To decamp; run away: coll: C.17–early 19, C.17–20, the latter extant only in dial.

legs up to her bum, she's got. A mid-C.19–20 c.p. addressed by men to boys in order to imply a common humanity: 'She has legs too, you know; just like you, son.'

Legshire. The Isle of Man: C.19–20; ob. Ex the heraldic bearings.

***legsman.** A race-course swindler who invites one to 'find the lady': c.: late C.19–20.

Leigh whisper, see MITCHAM WHISPER.

leisure hours. Flowers: rhyming s. (—1909).

lel or lell. To take, seize, arrest: low London s. verging on c.: from ca 1860. Ex Romany.

lemon, squeeze the. To make water: C.19–20: low. Ob.

lemon-rob. Lemon- or lime-juice as an anti-scorbutic: nautical (—1867); slightly ob. Subjectively pejorative.

lemoncholy. Melancholy: London (—1909); ob. By jocular transposition and slight distortion of *melan.* cf.:

lemonjolly. A jocular distortion of *melancholy*: ca 1860–1910. Occ. *lemon colly, lemon* punning *melan.* cf. COLLY-MOLLY.

lemons, adv. With a will; vigorously: Australian: ca 1860–1910. 'Tom Collins', *Such Is Life*, 1903, ' "Grass up over yer boots, an' the carrion goin' into it lemons," he remarked.'

lend. A loan: coll from ca 1825 ex C.16–20 dial. 'For the lend of the ass you might give me the mill,' old ballad.

lend, v. Give, as in 'Lend me a lick of the ice-cream!': proletarian coll (—1887).

lend us your breath to kill Jumbo! A proletarian c.p. of 1882–ca 1910. Ware, 'Protest against the odour of bad breath'. (See JUMBO, 2.)

lend us your pound! Pull your weight (on the rope): a jocular nautical c.p.: late C.19–20.

length. 42 lines: 1736 (O.E.D.): theatrical s. >, ca 1880, theatrical coll. Fielding; G. Parker; Dickens, 'I've a part of twelve lengths.' 2. Six months' imprisonment: c.: from ca 1850. cf. DOSE; MOON; STRETCH.

length of a . . ., go the. To lend as much as a (guinea, etc.): coll (—1887).

length of one's foot, get the, see FOOT, KNOW THE LENGTH OF ONE'S.

lep; occ. **lef.** Left, esp. in words of command: military: C.19–20. In the same way, *right* > *ri*, as in *ri turn!, ri wheel!*

leracam. Mackerel: back s. (—1859). Occ. *luracham.*

lerry-come-twang. A fool: Restoration period. Ex a popular refrain-tag of the time.

Lesbian. A woman sexually devoted to women: coll (—1896). Ex the Sapphic legend.

'less or less. Unless: Canadian (and U.S.) coll: mid-C.19–20. Ex English dial. usage. cf. 'CEPT.

let alone. (Prepositional phrase.) Much less; not to mention: coll: 1816, Jane Austen; Barham, 'I have not had . . . [a] brown to buy a bit of bread with – let alone a tart.' Occ. *letting alone* (1843; ob.). 2. **let me, him, etc., alone (†for doing,) to do something**: coll: C.17–20. Shakespeare, 'Let me alone for swearing'; Dryden, 'Let me alone to accuse him afterwards.'

let daylight into. To stab, shoot; kill: coll: C.19–20. See also at DAYLIGHT . . .

let-down. A disappointment; deception: coll (—1894).

let down easily or gently. To be lenient to: coll: 1834, M. Scott, 'By way of letting him down gently, I said nothing.' 2. Occ. = *let down,* to disappoint: late C.19–20: coll.

let fly, see FLY, LET.

let 'em all come! A c.p. expressive of cheeky defiance: 1896: lower classes'. Ware relates its origin to the manner in which the British received the German Emperor's message of congratulation to Kruger, on the repulse of the Jameson Raid, the U.S.A.'s communication concerning the English boundary dispute with Venezuela, and the shortly ensuing tricoloured agitation in the French press. cf. LET HER RIP!

let 'em trundle! CLEAR OFF!, go away: app. ca 1695–1730. Congreve, *The Way of the World*, 1700 (cited by G. H. McKnight).

let go. To achieve sexual emission: low coll: C.19–20.

let go the painter, see PAINTER, LET GO THE.

let her fizzle. To keep on all possible sail in a strong wind: Canadian (and U.S.) nautical: from ca 1870; ob. cf.:

let her rip! Let it (etc.) go freely!; damn the consequences!: coll: mid-C.19–20. Perhaps orig. U.S. (as Ware and Thornton think).

let in, v. To victimize; deceive, cheat: coll: from ca 1830. Thackeray, 'He had been let in terribly . . . by Lord Levant's insolvency.' Ex ice giving way. 2. v.i., to deal, gen. followed by *with*: university (mostly Oxford): from ca 1860; ob. T. Hughes, *Tom Brown at Oxford*, cf.:

let (another or oneself) **in for.** To involve in: coll: late C.19–20. Always with – occ. jocular – implication of unpleasantness.

let into. To attack; abuse; beat: from ca 1850; ob. Mayhew, 'Those that let into the police, [got] eighteen months.' cf. S.E. *let out at.*

let it run. To write as fully as the facts allow: journalistic coll: late C.19–20.

let loose, see LET ONESELF LOOSE.

let-loose match. A bull-baiting: sporting: ca 1820–40.

let me die! A synonym of CARRY ME OUT ...: ca 1860–1914.

let on. To admit; betray: dial. (—1725) >, ca 1830, coll. Haliburton, 1835; Boucicault, 'Don't let on to mortal that we're married.' 2. Hence, mostly in Australia and New Zealand and from ca 1880, occ. to pretend, make believe, give to understand: coll: orig. dial. >, by 1828, Southern U.S. (Thornton).

let oneself loose. To speak or act without restraint: coll: C.19–20.

let out. To disclose a secret, information, v.i.: from ca 1870: coll, mostly U.S. 2. A gen. v.i. of action, but esp., v.t., to give a horse his head; v.i., to ride at greater speed: coll: from ca 1885. 'Rolf Boldrewood'. 3. See LETS OUT HER FORE-ROOMS ...

let out a reef. To unbutton after a meal: from ca 1850: nautical >, ca 1880, gen. coll.

let rip. See RIP, but cf. LET HER RIP.

let-up. A pause, a cessation: orig. (1837) and still mainly U.S.: partially adopted ca 1880: coll.

let up on. To cease to have – esp. anything pejorative – to do with: coll: orig. (1857) and still mainly U.S.

letch-water. The sexual secretion: low coll: late C.18–20; ob. See S.E. *letch.*

let's! Let us (sc. do something expressed or implied)! Coll: late C.19–20. Often *yes, let's!*

lets, no. Without hindrance or modification: schoolboys': from ca 1850. cf. FAIN I and FEN!

let's have one! see HOW WILL YOU HAVE IT?

lets out her fore-rooms, – she lies backwards and. She is a harlot, esp. one not professed: proverbial coll: ca 1630–1850. Motteux.

lettary. A lodging; lodgings: grafters': late C.19–20. A variant of LETTY.

letter. Abbr. (—1896) of FRENCH LETTER.

letter, go and post a. To coït: low: mid-C. 19–20; ob. cf. SEE A MAN *about a dog.*

letter cloth, see SWATCHEL.

letter-fencer. A postman: low London (—1909).

letter in the post office, there is a. See FLAG, n., 3; it is synonymous with the phrase there: late C.19–20; ob.

letter-man. (Gen. pl.) A steward doing his first trip with a company: nautical: late C. 19–20. Because presumed to have had a letter of introduction to the seniors.

***letter Q.** An underworld dodge known also as the BILLIARD SLUM or MACE. Hence, *go on the* (*letter*) *Q*, to practise this dodge: c.: ca 1810–60. Vaux, 'Alluding to an instrument used in playing billiards'.

***letter-racket.** Begging by letter: vagrants' c.: from ca 1810.

***lettered.** Branded; burnt in the hand: C.18–early 19 c. cf. CHARACTERED.

letting alone, see LET ALONE, 1.

letty. A bed; a lodging. Also v.i., to lodge. Parlary (—1859); in C.20, mainly theatrical. Ex It. *letto*, a bed, via Lingua Franca. J. Frost, *Circus Life*, 1875. Also occ. *latty.*

level, on the, adj. and adv. Honest(ly), fair(ly): coll, orig. (—1900) U.S., anglicized by 1905. Perhaps ex U.S. (*act* or *work*) *on a broad level*, be trustworthy. cf. SQUARE; STRAIGHT, and contrast CROOK (2), CROSS, ON THE.

level, one's. Esp. **do one's level,** do one's utmost: coll esp. Cockneys': from ca 1890. Clarence Rook, *The Hooligan Nights*, 1899. Ex:

level best. One's best or utmost: coll: orig. (1851), U.S.; anglicized ca 1870. E. Hale, 1873, 'I said, "I'll do my level best, Doctor."'

level-coil, play. To coït: C.17–early 18: low. Ex S.E. †*level-coil*, a rough, noisy game.

level pegging. (Of competitors) keeping level; also n.: s.: (—1900).

leven. 'In back s., is sometimes allowed to stand for *eleven*, for ... it is a number which seldom occurs. An article is either 10*d*. or 1*s*.', H., 1859.

leviathan. A heavy backer of horses: sporting journalists' (—1887); virtually †. Ex S.E. sense.

levy. A shilling: low: from ca 1860. H., in 3rd ed., says Liverpool. Ex U.S. *levy* (1832), an abbr. of *eleven* or perhaps even *elevenpenny bit*: see esp. Bartlett, 1848, and Thornton.

Lewis Cornaro, gen. **a.** A water-drinker: London: ca 1820–40. (Topical.)

liar myself, I'm a bit or something of a. A c.p. reply to a liar: orig. (—1896), U.S.; adopted in British Empire ca 1900 as a coll.

***lib.** Sleep: c. of ca 1670–1800. R. Head. 2. A bank-note: c.: C.19. 3. (**Lib;** gen. pl.) A Liberal: 1885, *Punch* (Baumann). 4. (Always **the Lib.**) The Library: Charterhouse (—1900). A. H. Tod, 'A collection of Library books is "Lib. Coll."' 5. A liberty: trivial Cockney: from ca 1895.

***lib**, v. To sleep, lie down; also to coït: c. of ca 1560–1870. Also *lyp* (C.16–17).

***lib-beg, libbege; lyb beg(e), lybbeg(e); lib-(b)edge.** A bed: c. of ca 1560–1860. Harman, Rowlands, Head, B.E., Grose.

***lib-ken, libken; lipken, lypken; lib-** or **lybkin.** A house; lodging: c. of ca 1560–1880. Harman, Jonson, B.E., Grose, Scott, Mayhew. Ex LIB + KEN. cf.:

***libben.** A private house: c. of ca 1670–1860. Ex preceding.

library. A drinking school; a convivial club, meeting at a tavern: drinkers' or taverns': ca 1640–90. Anon., *The Eighth Liberal Science*, 1650.

licence?, have you a, see HAVE YOU A LICENCE?

licet. Allowed, permissible: Winchester: C.19–20. Ex L. *licet*, it is permissible.

lick, a blow, is S.E. and dial. But see LICKS. 2. A hasty wash; a dab of paint: coll: from ca 1650. cf. LICK AND A PROMISE and LICKED. 3. A drinking bout: low (—1886); ob. *Daily Telegraph*, 3 March 1886. 4. A turn of speed or works, esp. if great or vigorous: (dial. and) U.S. and Australian coll: 1837 (S.O.D.). See LICKS, BIG.

lick, v. To beat, thrash: perhaps orig. c. or low (it's in Harman) >, ca 1700, gen. s.: from ca 1535. (See also LICK INTO FITS.) 2. To defeat, surpass: s.: from ca 1800. De Quincey. 3. To astound, puzzle: from ca 1855. See LICKS ME, IT. 4. v.i., to ride at full speed: Australian (—1889); ob., except of a motor-car. See LICK, (AT) A GREAT. 'Rolf Boldrewood'. 5. See LICKED.

lick, (at) a great or, more gen., **full.** At a great or at full speed: coll: U.S. (?orig.) and Australian: from ca 1888. 'Rolf Boldrewood'.

lick and a promise, a. A piece of slovenly work, esp. a hasty, inadequate wash of hands and/or face: coll: from ca 1870.

lick and a smell, a. Almost nothing, esp. as to food; a DOG'S PORTION: coll: mid-C.18–20.

lick-fingers. A cook: coll: Ned Ward, 1703.

lick into fits. To defeat thoroughly: from ca 1875. Ex LICK, v., 1.

lick of the tar-brush, a, the. A, the, seaman: nautical: late C.19–20. Ex the utility of tar on shipboard. 2. (Also **a touch . . .**). Applied to one who has a touch of coloured blood in his make-up: coll: mid-C.19–20.

lick one's (more gen., **the**) **eye.** To be well pleased: low coll: mid-C.19–20; ob.

lick out of. To drive (something) out of (a person) by thrashing: from ca 1880; ob.

lick-spigot; l.-twat. Resp. *fellatrix, fellator*. Low: resp. C.18–20, ob.; C.17–20.

lick-up. Trade s. of mid-C.19–20 as in quotation at SMOTHER.

lick you, I'll. This threat in C.18–early 19 evoked the following 'dovetail', i.e. c.p. reply: *If you lick me all over, you won't miss my* ARSE.

licked, lickt, ppl adj. Applied to 'Pictures new Varnished, Houses new Whitened, or Women's faces with a Wash', B.E.: coll: late C.17–20.

lickell. Little: C.18–mid-19 coll. Ex *little* on *mickle*. cf. LEETLE.

licker. Anything excessive, in size, degree, quality: C.18–20; ob. cf. LICKING, adj.; SPANKER (2); THUMPER; WHOPPER, and LICK, v., 3, its imm. origin. cf. the mid-C.19–20 Cockney, *it's a licker to me*, I don't understand it. i.e. *it licks* (beats) me.

licking. A thrashing: from ca 1755: s. >, cà 1800, coll. Toldervy. 2. A defeat: from ca 1800: s.

licking, adj. First-rate, splendid, excellent: from ca 1680; ob. by 1900. Cotton, Eden Phillpotts. cf. LICKER.

licks, with **my, your, his,** etc. A thrashing: late C.18–20: coll(†) and dial. Burns. Ex LICK, n., 1.

licks, big. Hard work; also adv., by hard work, 'great guns': Australian, from ca 1888 (e.g. in 'Rolf Boldrewood'), but ob.; orig. (—1861), U.S. cf. LICK, (AT) A GREAT.

licks me, it. It's beyond my comprehension: coll: from ca 1855. Anon., *Derby Day*, 1864. Ex LICK, v., 2; cf. *it beats me.* (The past tense occurs: e.g. in 'It licked me how the bottom itself did not tumble clean away from the ship,' *Durham County Advertiser*, 10 Nov. 1871.)

lid. A hat, a cap or (in Glasgow, at least) even a bonnet: from ca 1905.

lid, – like pot, like (pot-); or with **such** for **like.** (Also **a lid worthy of such,** or **the, kettle.**) A proverbial coll expressive of suitability, similarity, adequacy: C.16–18. Palsgrave, Urquhart, Fuller.

lid on (it), that's put the. (cf. LIE WITH A LID ON.) That's done it; nothing more's to be said; that's finished it; GOOD NIGHT!: late C.19–20 c.p.

lie, n., see LOUD ONE and LIE WITH A LATCHET.

lie, v. To be in pawn: C.17: coll. Anon., *The Man in the Moon*, 1609.

lie as fast as a dog can lick a dish; as fast as a dog (or horse) will trot. To tell lies LIKE ANYTHING; semi-proverbial coll: resp. C.16–17; C.16–20, but in C.19–20 mainly dial.

lie back and let, etc., see LETS OUT HER FORE-ROOMS.

lie by one, not to let anybody. To be a liar: C.17–18 coll. Ray.

lie by the wall. To be dead: C.15–20: coll till C.18, then dial.

lie doggo, see DOGGO.

lie down. To take a reprimand, a lie, a beating, etc. abjectly. Only in *take lying down*. 1888, *Saturday Review*, 4 Aug.

lie flat. See LIE LOW; †by 1910.

lie in. To remain in one's room when one is supposedly out on leave: Royal Military Academy: ca 1870–1914. Ex the S.E. sense.

lie in state. To lie between two women: low: C.18–20 (?ob.). Recorded in *A Compleat Collection of Remarkable Tryals*, 1721: in vol. IV, p. 248.

lie like a flat-fish. To tell lies adroitly: nautical: late C.19–20. By pun on *lie*.

lie like truth. To tell a lie with seemly verisimilitude: coll (—1876). C. Hindley, '[Cheapjacks] are always supposed, and by common consent allowed, to lie like truth.'

lie low. (Also **†lie flat.**) To hide one's person or one's intentions; occ., but †by 1910, to keep to one's bed: coll: from ca 1845. F. Anstey, 'So you've very prudently been lying low.'

lie off. 'To make a waiting-race', F. & H.: the turf (—1896).

lie on the knuckle. (Of a ship) to be 'drawn alongside the entrance to a dock, generally waiting for a tug': nautical coll: late C.19–20. Bowen.

lie out of one's ground. To LIE OFF too long and so, unintentionally, lose the race: the turf (—1896).

lie with a latchet. A thorough-going lie: coll: C.17–20, but since 1820, only dial. Ray, Fuller. Also known as a *†lie made of whole cloth*, or (in dial.) *out of the whole stuff*, and one *laid on with a trowel*.

lie with a lid on, gen. preceded by **that's a.** Coll, but mostly dial.: 1880, Spurgeon.

life, bet your, see BET YOUR BOOTS. **life, know,** see KNOW LIFE. **life, lag for,** see LIFER, 1; also LAG.

life, not on your. Certainly not!: coll: from middle 1890s.

life and everlasting, for. (Esp. of sales) final; without appeal: lower and lower-middle classes' coll: mid-C.19–early 20.

life of him, me, etc., for the; for my, etc., **life** (ob.). Gen. preceded by *cannot*. To save one's (exaggerated) life: coll: 1809, Malkin, 'Not knowing how for the life of him to part with those flattering hopes.'

life-preserver. The penis: low: from ca 1840; ob.

***lifer.** One sentenced, for life, to transportation (1830; †by 1890) or (from ca 1860) to penal servitude: c. R. Dawson, *The Present State of Australia*, 1831; Dickens. Also LAG *for life* (ob.). 2. Penal servitude (orig. transportation) for life: 1832: c. Besant 'Twenty-five years . . . as good as a lifer'. cf. LAGGING AND A LIFER.

***lift.** A thief, esp. from shops: c.: late C. 16–early 19. Greene, 'A receiver for lifts, and a dishonourable supporter of cut-purses'. cf. LIFTER; SHOP-LIFT, -LIFTER. 2. A theft; plunder: c.: late C.16–mid-19. Also LIFTING. 3. A kick: coll: orig. footballers': late C.19–20. 4. Conceit, SIDE; presumption: Shrewsbury School: from ca 1885. (Desmond Coke, *The Bending of a Twig*, 1906.) Whence the adj., *lifty*, recorded by the same author. cf. ROLL, 2.

***lift,** v. To steal, v.i. and t.: c. (1526) >, ca 1750, gen. s. Skelton, Greene. From ca 1850, gen. applied to stealing cattle and horses. 2. Hence, to transfer matter from one periodical to another: journalists' and printers' (—1891). 3. To bring (a constellation) above the horizon in sailing, etc.: coll: 1891. Kipling.

lift, a good hand at a dead. A person reliable in emergency: coll >, by C.19, S.E. C.17–mid-19.

lift-leg. Strong ale; STINGO: C.18–mid-19: low. cf.:

lift-leg, play at. To have sexual intercourse: C.18–mid-19 low. Also *lift one's leg*.

lift or **raise one's elbow, hand, little finger.** To drink, esp. to excess: late C.18–20: s. >, ca 1860, coll. The *hand* phrase admits the addition of *†to one's head* (Grose, 2nd ed.). cf.:

lift (up) the hand(s); occ. the arm. To do a little physical work: from ca 1890. 'Rolf Boldrewood'. See also the preceding entry.

lifted, be. To be promoted unexpectedly or undeservedly: naval coll: C.19. Bowen.

***lifter.** A thief, esp. from shops: c.: ca 1590–1830; from ca 1750, gen. s. Shakespeare, 'Is he so young a man and so old a lifter?' Ex LIFT, v., 1. 2. (Gen. in pl.) A crutch: S.E. or coll in C.16–mid-17, then low or c. until ca 1870, when it fell into disuse. Coles and B.E. classify it as c. 3. A heavy blow: from the late 1880s. 4. A horse given to kicking: stables' coll (—1909).

***lifting.** Thieving; theft; late C.16–20; ob. except for the stealing of live stock: c. >, ca 1750, gen. s. Greene. Also in late C.16–mid-17, *lifting* LAW (Greene, *passim*).

***lig.** A bed: c. of ca 1720–1840. Perhaps LIB influenced by dial. *lig*, to lie (down). cf. U.S. c. *lig-robber* in Irwin. 2. A weighted fish-hook: nautical coll: late C. 19–20. Ex East Anglian *lig*, a load.

light. Credit: low or rather workmen's: from ca 1820. Bee, 1823, says that it is orig. printers' s. and gives '*strike a light*, to open an account, of the minor sort, gen. applied to ale-house scores'. 2. Hence *get a light*, obtain credit: *have one's light put out*, exhaust one's credit.

light!, he (she, etc.) wouldn't give you a. He (she, etc.) is exceedingly mean: Cockney c.p.: late C.19–20. i.e. a light (or match) for one's cigarette; possibly with a pun on LIGHT, n., 1.

light, make a, see MAKE A LIGHT.

light, not worth a. Worthless; useless: low coll: late C.19–20.

light, put out one's. To kill: C.17–20: S.E. till ca 1820, then (increasingly low) coll; in C.20, indeed, it is s. *Graphic*, 27 Sept. 1884, 'So now, the malefactor does not murder, he "pops a man off", or "puts his light out".'

light!, strike a. A late C.19–20 coll exclamation. Prob. ex the imperative of the lit. S.E. phrase. 2. See LIGHT, n., 1.

light and dark. A park: late C.19–20.

light-blue. Gin: ca 1820–40. 'Peter Corcoran' Reynolds; Randall's *Scrapbook*; Egan's Grose. cf. LIGHT-WET.

light bob. A light-infantry soldier: 1785, Grose: military s. >, ca 1880, S.E. Whyte-Melville, 'A light-bob on each side, with his arms sloped'.

light-comedy merchant. A comedian pure and simple: theatrical: 1887, *Referee*, 13 March.

light fantastic, the. The foot as the means of dancing; dancing: coll: from ca 1840. Stirling Coyne, 'Then you're fond of sporting on the light fantastic.' Ex Milton's 'Come and trip it as you go | On the light fantastic toe' (*L'Allegro*).

***light-feeder.** A silver spoon: c. from ca 1850; ob.

light food. Tobacco for chewing instead of a meal to eat: lower classes' (—1909).

light frigate. A woman of loose morals: ca 1690–1760. cf.:

light horse. A courtesan; a harlot: ca 1620–1700: Society s. > coll. 2. Highwaymen, collectively: s.: Ned Ward, 1700.

***light horseman.** A thief operating as one of a gang on the Thames: C.19–20; ob. Colquhoun; *Daily News*, 9 Jan. 1899.

light-house, lighthouse. A red-nosed person, gen. male: ca 1810–90. 2. A pepper-castor: naval (—1909). 3. A watch-house: Londoners': ca 1805–40. Pierce Egan, *Life in London*, 1821.

light infantry. Fleas: C.19–20; ob. cf. LIGHT TROOPS, contrast HEAVY CAVALRY.

light master. A go-between to the landlord of a house of call and the workmen using it: printers': from ca 1840. Ex LIGHT, n., 1.

light-o! A request for more light, shouted to anyone standing in the light: *Conway* cadets' coll (—1891).

light out. To leave hastily and, gen., secretly: from ca 1800.

light the lamp. (Of a woman) to have sexual intercourse: rather literary: late C. 19–20.

***light the lumper.** To be transported: c. of ca 1795–1830. Perversion of LUMP THE LIGHTER.

light-timbered. (Of persons) limber; slender-limbed; weak: coll: late C.17–mid-19. cf. the S.E. *light(ly) built*.

light (or candle) to the devil, bear or hold a, see CANDLE TO . . .

light troops. Lice: ca 1810–90. cf. LIGHT INFANTRY and HEAVY CAVALRY.

light up, v.i. To light one's pipe, cigar, cigarette: coll: from ca 1860. T. Hughes. 2. v.i., to light the lamps; put on the lights: coll: late C.19–20.

light-wet. Gin: ca 1820-60. Randall's *Scrapbook*, 1822. cf. LIGHT-BLUE; BLUE RUIN; SATIN; LIGHTNING.

***lighter,** see LUMP THE LIGHTER and LIGHT THE LUMPER.

***lightmans.** Daylight, dawn, day: c. of ca 1565–1860. Opp. to DARKMANS. Ex *light*; see -MANS.

lightning. Gin: low (perhaps orig. c.): from ca 1780; ob. G. Parker. (cf. BLUE

RUIN.) Hence, *flash o' lightning*, a glass of gin (—1811).

lightning, like greased. Very swiftly: orig. (1833, *as g. l.*), U.S.; anglicized ca 1845 as a coll. Hood, 1842, 'I will come, as the Americans say, like greased lightning.'

lightning curtain-taker. A performer rushing in front of the curtain on the least approbation: theatrical coll: 1884.

lights. The eyes: from ca 970: S.E. till ca 1810, then boxing s. *Sporting Magazine*, 1815, 'He mill'd the stout Caleb and darken'd his lights'; 1820, 'Peter Corcoran,' Reynolds. Also DAYLIGHTS and TOP LIGHTS. 2. A fool: low: ca 1858–1910. Ex an animal's *lights*, influenced by *light-headed.*

lights up! A play-goers' c.p. indicative of condemnation: ca 1900–15.

lignum. *Polygonum*, a wiry plant: Australian coll (—1880). By contraction.

like, n. Always preceded by *the* and (esp. from ca 1860) gen. in the pl and followed by *of* (rarely †*to*): such a person or thing, in C.19–20 often pejorative: coll: from ca 1630, the first record being a letter by Rutherford in 1637, 'In a broken reed the like of me'; *likes* occurring in 1787 ('the likes of me'); Cobbett, 'the like of this'; Du Maurier, in *Trilby*.

like, adv., at the end of a phrase or a sentence. Somewhat, not altogether; as it were, in a way; in short, expressive of vagueness or after-thoughted modification: (dial. and) low coll: 1801, 'Of a sudden like'; Scott, Lytton, De Quincey, E. Peacock.

like, anything – nothing – something, in comparison (e.g. Payn, 'Not that Pye is an archangel, nor anything like it'), are S.E.; but the elliptical *something like*, something like what is obligatory, intended, or desired, is late C.18–20 coll. The O.E.D. quotes '"This looks something like, Sir," said she,' 1798. Often by itself.

like, feel, see FEEL LIKE. **like, most** or **very,** see LIKE AS NOT.

like?, what. (Absolutely or as in 'what like is he?') Of what character, nature, quality?: dial. (—1820) > coll 1860, (low) coll.

like a . . ., like anything, etc., where speed, energy, or intensity is indicated, have a coll tendency that often > coll or, if the second member is coll or s., even s. Many of the following phrases, which are s. unless otherwise designated, are found at the resp. n., pronoun, adj., or adv.: *like a* BASKET OF CHIPS (Moore, 1819), †; *l. a bird* (from the 1860s: 'Quotations' Benham), coll; *l. a dog in a fair* (Barham), †; *l. a* HOUSE ON FIRE (1857), s. > coll; *l. a* SHOT (1850, Smedley), coll; *l. a* STREAK (—1890), coll; *l. a thousand*, or *a ton*, or *a cart-load, of bricks* (from ca 1840), cf. BRICK; *l. a tom-tit on a horse-turd*; LIKE ANYTHING (from ca 1680; *as anything*, 1542), coll; *l. be(-)damned* (late C.19) – cf. *smart as be damned*, i.e. 'damned smart'; *l.* BEANS (ca 1820–1900); *l.* BILLY-O (late C.19–20); *l.* BLAZES (—1845; Disraeli, De Quincey), cf. *l. a* HOUSE ON FIRE; *l.* †*boots* or *old* BOOTS (1868, Miss Braddon; prob. earlier), cf. *l. the very devil*; *l. bricks* s.v. BRICK (1835, Dickens); *l.* BUGGERY; *l.* FUN (1819, Moore), s. > coll; *l.* HELL; *l. hot* †*cake* or CAKES (—1888), orig. U.S.; *l. mad* (from ca 1660), coll, as in Pepys's 'A mad coachman that drove like mad'; *l. one o'clock* (from before 1847: orig. 'of a horse's movement' (very rapid), says Halliwell), contrast LIKE ONE O'CLOCK HALF-STRUCK, separate entry; *l.* SHIT TO A SHOVEL (late C.19–20, low, ob.); *l.* SMOKE (C.19–20); *l. thunder* (from ca 1830, ob.; M. Scott); *l. the very devil* (from ca 1830; M. Scott); *l.* WINKY (—1896) and *l.* WINKING (Barham).

like a birch-broom in a fit, see BIRCH-BROOM.

like a book, see BOOK, SPEAK LIKE A.

like a halfpenny, or a penny, book, you talk. A c.p. remark to a fluent or an affected or pedantic speaker: low coll: ca 1880–1910.

like a whale, see WHALE.

like as not(, as); like enough; most (ob.) or **very like.** Probably: coll and dial.: resp. —1897 (but *as like as*, without *not*, occurs in 1681); 1563, Foxe; 1611, Shakespeare, 'Most like I did'; 1610, Shakespeare, 'Will money buy 'em? . . . Very like.'

like Christmas beef, see BEEF. **like greased lightning,** see LIGHTNING.

like it but it doesn't like me, I. Applied to food, drink, work, etc., implying that it makes one ill: a semi-jocular coll c.p.; late C.19–20.

like it or lump it. To like or, disliking, put up with it: from ca 1860: coll. See LUMP, v., 3.

like it you may do the other thing!, if you don't. Equivalent, and allusive to, the preceding: coll (—1864).

like mother makes it, see MOTHER MAKES IT, LIKE.

like one o'clock half-struck. Hesitatingly: 1876, Hindley: low; ob. Contrast *like one o'clock*, s.v. LIKE A . . .

like that!, I. A derisive or indignant 'Certainly not', 'I certainly don't think so': coll: late C.19–20. cf. NOT HALF.

like to meet her in the dark(, he'd, I'd, etc.). Plain: lower classes': from ca 1884; slightly ob.

likely!, not. Certainly not!: coll: prob. from late C.19.

***likeness, take a.** To take a criminal's measurements and record physical characteristics, almost solely of the face: c. of ca 1810–1910. Ex *likeness*, a portrait.

likes, the; likes of, the, see LIKE, n.

l'il. Little: a drunken or an endearing contraction: C.19–20 coll.

***lil(l).** A pocket-book: c.: from ca 1810. Prob. ex Romany *lil*, paper, a book. See esp. Sampson. cf. Borrow's *Romano Lavo-Lil*, i.e. *Romany Word-Book* or *Glossary*. 2. Hence, any book: from ca 1840: tramps' c. 3. A five-pound note: c. (—1896); ob.

lill for loll (or **law**). Tit for tat: C.15–17: coll. Perhaps jinglingly ex A.-S. *lael*, a bruise.

lily benjamin. A white greatcoat: C.19 low. See BENJAMIN; cf.:

lily shallow. A white driving-hat: Society, esp. the 'whips' ': ca 1810–30.

***lily-white.** A chimney-sweep: c. of ca 1690–1830. 2. A Negro: C.18–early 19: low.

lily-white groat. A shilling: low: ca 1890–1914. See WHITE.

limb. A very mischievous child: 1625, Jonson, 'A limb o' the school, . . . a little limb of nine year old': coll; slightly ob. 2. Hence, depreciatively, of older persons: coll: C.18–20; ob. except in combination, e.g. *limb of Satan* (Estcourt, 1706).

***limb,** v. To tear to pieces; to thrash: c. or low (—1857); ob. 2. To cheat: c. (—1878); ob. Hatton, *Cruel London*. 3. To bring to the stocks: low: C.19.

limb!, blow of my last. A coll asseveration: nautical (—1887); ob.

limb of the bar. A barrister: 1815: coll >, ca 1860, S.E. Ex:

limb of the law. A lawyer; a lawyer's clerk: 1730: coll >, ca 1800, S.E.

limbo. A prison; any place of confinement: from ca 1590; †by 1910: coll till C.18, then s.; in C.19–20, c. Anon., *Five Years' Penal Servitude*, 1877, 'It was a heartless, cruel robbery . . . Before that occurred he had never been in limbo.' Ex the theological sense, esp. the phrase *in limbo patrum*. 2. Pawn; a pawnshop: ca 1690–1820. Congreve. 3. The female pudend: C.19 low. 4. Bread: military: late C.19–20. Perhaps because often it is, on active service, 'as hard as *hell*'.

limbs, duke or **duchess of.** A GAWK: from ca 1780; ob.: low.

Limburger, that's the. That's *the* CHEESE, i.e. excellent, correct, splendid: late C.19–early 20.

lime-basket or **-kiln, as dry as a.** Exceedingly dry: coll: from ca 1835. Dickens, Hume Nisbet.

lime-juice. Lime-light: theatrical: from ca 1875. (Thus does sound generate sense!) 2. A new CHUM (n., 3): Australia (—1886); ob. by 1896, †by 1910. Ex the lime-juice served on outgoing ships. cf.:

lime-juicer. The same as LIME-JUICE, 2: ibid.: ca 1858–1900. Cornwallis, *The New World*, 1859. 2. An Englishman; an English sailor. Wm Kelly, *Life in Victoria*, 1859. 3. An English sailing ship: Canadian, ex U.S.: since ca 1860: ob. Lime-juice was served on British ships as an anti-scorbutic.

lime twig, -twig, limetwig. A thief: late C. 16–early 17: c.: Greene, *Third Cony-Catching*, 1592.

***limiting law.** In c. of late C.16–early 17, as explained by Greene in *A Disputation*, 1592, '*The lymitting Lawe*, discoursing the orders of such [professional criminals] as followe Iudges, in their circuites, and goe about from Fayre to Fayre.'

limmick. Salt: Regular Army: late C.19–20. A perversion of Hindustani *namak*.

limping Jesus. A lame person: low: C.19–20; ob. cf. DOT AND CARRY ONE.

Lincoln and Bennett. A superior men's-hat: Society coll: ca 1840–1910. Ex the maker's name. cf. *Dunn's three-and-ninepenny* for any cheap bowler hat, this make being the best of the lower-priced hats: coll: late C.19–early C.20.

Lincoln's Inn. A £5 note: racing rhyming s. on synonymous (orig. underworld) *finn*, s.v. FINNIF: late C.19–20. 2. A hand: rhyming s. on FIN, 1: late (?mid) C.19–20. 3. Gin (the drink): rhyming s.: late C.19–20.

Lincolnshire Yellow-Belly (or **y—b—**). A native of Lincolnshire: C.18–20. Ex the yellow-bellied frogs of the Lincolnshire fens.

line. A hoax: low coll: ca 1850–1910. Esp.

in *get* (e.g. *him*) *in a line*, get some sport out of him. cf.:

***line (or string), cut the.** To end suspense: c.: ca 1810–60. cf. 2nd nuance of LINE, GET INTO A.

line, draw the. 'To lay down a definite limit of action beyond which one refuses to go,' S.O.D.: from ca 1885: coll.

line, fake a, see FAKE A LINE.

***line, get into, or on, a; keep in a (tow-) line.** To end suspense; to engage in conversation a person to be robbed by one's confederate(s), also *get in a string* – cf. LINE, 2; to keep in suspense, also *keep in tow* or *in a string*. c. of ca 1810–60.

line, the devil's regiment of the. Felons; convicts: coll: ca 1870–1914.

line-age; also **linage.** Payment by the line: journalists': from ca 1888: s. till C.20, then j. Punning *lineage*.

line-o'-battler. A battle-ship: naval coll (—1887); slightly ob.

line of the old author, a. A dram of brandy: late C.17–early 19.

lined, be. (Gen. of women) to be married: lower classes' (—1909). Ex LINES, 1.

linen, the. The stage curtain: theatrical: ca 1880–1910. cf. RAG, n., 5.

linen, wrap up in clean. To couch smutty or sordid matter in decent language: coll: C.18–19. We still say *nicely wrapped up*.

***linen-armourer.** A tailor: late C.17–mid-19: c. >, ca 1800, jocular S.E.

linen-draper. Paper: rhyming s. (—1857). 2. Esp. a newspaper.

liner. A picture hung on the line: artistic s. (—1887) >, in C.20, coll. W. P. Frith in his *Autobiography*. 2. A battle-ship: naval (—1810); very ob. cf. LINE-O'-BATTLER.

lines. A marriage certificate: from ca 1825: dial. and coll >, ca 1900, S.E. Anon., *Fast Life: An Autobiography*, 'Those good-natured ladies who never had their lines'. 2. Reins: from ca 1850: dial. and (mostly U.S.) coll.

lines like a butter-box. A nautical c.p. (late C.19–20) applied to 'a clumsy, full-bodied ship' (Bowen). cf. SARDINE-TIN.

liney, liny. Wrinkled: coll (—1887). e.g. 'a liney face'.

ling-grappling, vbl n. Caressing a woman sexually: low: C.19–20; app. ob.

***link.** To steal from a person's pocket: c.: ca 1820–60. Haggart.

link and **froom.** These related terms in Yiddish and hence in low London s. date, as to the latter at any rate, from the 1880s. See FROOM, of which *link* is the opp.

link, to have knocked out one's. *Sessions*, 1754 (No. IV, Part iii), 'He said he supposed she had knocked out her link (meaning she was drunk)': Londoners': ca 1730–80. Here, *link* = torch.

linkister. A linguist; esp. an interpreter: nautical (—1867). (Also dial.)

linkman. A general man-servant about kitchen or yard: West London coll (—1909). An extension of S.E. sense.

linnen, see LINEN, THE.

lino. A coll abbr., from ca 1880, of *linoleum* (1863).

lint-scraper. A surgeon, esp. if young: coll: 1763, Foote; Thackeray. Ex the lit. S.E. sense.

lintie. (Gen. pl.) A sprite: theatrical: from ca 1870; ob. Prob. ex Scottish *lintie*, a linnet; perhaps influenced by Fr. *lutin*.

liny, see LINEY.

lion. A great man's spy: C.18: coll, perhaps > S.E. 2. An inhabitant of, or a visitor to, Oxford: Oxford University: from ca 1780; in C.20, ob. 3. A citizen: London smart s.: ca 1780–1800. 4. A hare: ca 1825–35: coll verging on S.E. Westmacott, Lytton. Ex certain restrictions on game.

lion, as valiant as an Essex. Timid: C.18–early 19. cf.:

lion, Cotswold or **Lammermoor; lion, Essex** or **Romford.** Resp., a sheep; a calf. COTSWOLD LION or *lion of Cotswold*, mid-C.15–mid-19. Anon., *Thersites*; Ray; Grose. See also ESSEX L., LAMMERMOOR L., RUMFORD L.

lion, tip the. To squeeze a person's nose and flatten it to his face: late C.18–mid-19.

lion comique. A leading comic singer: music-halls' coll: ca 1880–1905.

lion's den. The headmaster's study: various schools': late C.19–20.

lion's lair. A chair: since ca 1860: rhyming.

lions in the Army, they tame. A Regular Army c.p.: late C.19–20. In reference to military discipline.

lip. Impudence; abuse: low: from ca 1810 (perhaps orig. c.). Haggart, 'giving him plenty of lip'. 2. A house: c.: ca 1820–50. Ex LIB-KEN.

lip, v. To sing: c. (1789, G. Parker) >, ca 1860, low s.; ob. Esp. in *lip a chant*, sing a song. 2. To speak, utter: coll: from ca 1880. *Punch*, 10 Jan. 1885, 'I had great power, millions lipped my name.'

lip, button one's. Gen. in imperative. C.19–20: s. verging on coll; once (—1868) common among schoolboys.

lip, carry or **keep a stiff upper,** see KEEP . . .

lip-lap. A child born in the East Indies: esp. if Eurasian: East Indian coll: mid-C. 18–20. Perhaps ex Javanese *lap-lap*, a dish-clout. cf. CHEE-CHEE.

lip-thatch or **-wing.** A moustache: jocular coll verging on S.E.: resp. 1892 (Kipling), 1825 (Westmacott): ob.

lipey; occ. **lippy.** A low London term of address: ca 1870–1915. Ex German *liebe*, 'beloved'?

lipish or **lippish.** Impudent: ca 1835–70. *Sinks*, 1848. Ex LIP, n., 1.

***lipken,** see LIB-KEN.

lippy. Impertinent: from ca 1890. Ex LIP, n., 1. 2. See LIPEY.

lips hang in your light, your. (Occ. **his, her,** etc.) A proverbial c.p. = you're a (born) fool. C.16–17. Skelton (*eye* for *light*); Davies of Hereford; 'Phraseologia' Robertson.

liq, see WHAT WILL YOU LIQ?

liqueur of four ale. A glass of bitter: City (—1909); ob. Also CITY SHERRY.

liquid fire. Bad whisky: (low) coll: C.19–20; ob.

liquor. A drink: from ca 1860; mostly U.S. Also *liquor-up*. 2. The water used in adulterating beer: publicans' (—1909). (Obviously, a euphemism.)

liquor, v.t. To supply, or to ply, with liquor: mid-C.16–20: S.E. till C.18, then coll till ca 1850, then s. Also, late C.19–20, *liquor up*. Surtees. 2. v.i., to drink alcoholic liquor: orig. (1836), U.S.; anglicized ca 1840. Marryat. Also, from 1845, *liquor up*. 3. To thrash, esp. in *liquor someone's hide*: ca 1680–1800. D'Urfey. Punning LICK.

liquor?, what's your. What will you drink?: coll (—1887); slightly ob. cf. *what's your* POISON?

liquor one's boots. To cuckold: C.18: T. Brown. 2. To drink before a journey (cf. S.E. *stirrup-cup*); among Roman Catholics, to administer extreme unction: ca 1780–1890.

liquor up, see LIQUOR, v., 1 and 2; and the n.

liquored, drunk, 1667, now gen. **liquored up** (not before C.19); **liquorer,** a hard drinker (—1885; ob.); **liquoring,** vbl n., hard drinking, C.19–20, now gen. **liquoring-up.** All ex the v., 1 and 2. cf.:

Liquorpond Street, to have come from. To be drunk: ca 1825–1910. Buckstone, in *23, John Street, Adelphi*, 'I don't know where you are, sir; but you seem to have just come from Liquorpond Street.'

***lispers.** The teeth: c. of ca 1785–1860. G. Parker. cf. LISTENER. 2. The lips: C.18–mid-19.

list. Short for *list of geldings in training*: the turf: 1890. Hence, *put on the list*, to castrate. See ADDED . . .

list, on the. In disfavour: coll: from 1885; ob. Introduced in *The Mikado*, 1885. Abbr. S.E. *on the black list*.

listen, n. An act or period of listening: coll: since ca 1890. Usually *have a good listen* (coll) or *do a listen* (s.).

listen to oneself. To think: Anglo-Irish coll: C.19–20.

listener. An ear: low and boxers': from ca 1805; ob. (Gen. in pl.)

listman. A ready-money bookmaker: from ca 1885; ob.: the turf. Ex the list of prices exhibited by his side.

***lit, smack the.** To divide the booty: c.: ca 1850–90. Burton, *Vikram and the Vampire*, 1870. (The term is suspect.)

literature. Any printed matter whatsoever, as in 'the literature of patent-medicines': coll: 1895.

***little alderman.** A sectional JEMMY: c. (—1889). cf. ALDERMAN.

Little Barbary. Wapping: s. > coll: late C.17–early 19.

little beg. Little beggar, as a 'friendly term applied by upper form to lower form boys': Public Schools': late C.19–20. Ware.

***little ben.** A waistcoat: c.: C.19–20; ob. Ex BENJAMIN.

little bird told me, a. A semi-proverbial c.p. (C.19–20) in reply to the (not necessarily expressed) question, 'Who told you?'

little boy, see LITTLE MAN IN THE BOAT, 2.

little breeches. A familiar term of address to a boy: ca 1770–1850.

little brother. *Membrum virile*: low: mid-C.19–20. On analogy of LITTLE SISTER.

little cheque, a. A c.p. *à propos* of the repayment of a loan: ca 1893–5. Ex *Two Roses*, a popular comedy, in which this phrase is often spoken by Digby Grant played by a famous actor.

little clergyman. A young chimney-sweep: ca 1787–1860. See CLERGYMAN; contrast CHIMNEY-SWEEP.

little Davy. The penis: low: C.19–20; ob.

little devil, see DEVIL, LITTLE.

little end of the horn, the. A difficulty; distress: hence, *come out at the little end of the horn* = to come to grief, be worsted. Coll: C.17–20; after 1800, mostly dial. and U.S.

Little England. Barbados: West Indies': C.19–20, ob. cf. BIM.

Little England beyond Wales. Pembrokeshire: late C.16–20; coll till C.19, then S.E. See esp. E. Laws's *History of Little England beyond Wales*, 1888. But *Little London*, Penrith, is prob. dial., as is *Little London beyond Wales*, Beaumaris.

little fields have big gates. A c.p. – ?rather an unrecorded rural proverb – referring to the fact that many little women bear large families: (?)C.19–20. The true reason is that they possess an invincible vitality.

little finger, cock one's. To drink often – and much. Coll: C.19–20.

little finger laugh, letting one's. Board-school girls' term, from ca 1890, thus in W. Pett Ridge, *Mord Em'ly*, 1898: 'One of the most painful jibes that a girl could offer to another in school was to point her finger, and inflect it slightly – an act called "letting one's little finger laugh".'

little go. The first examination to be passed for one's B.A. degree: university coll: 1820: Oxford (†by 1864) and Cambridge. Thackeray. 2. Hence, one's first imprisonment: c. (—1909). Ware, 'First invented by a fallen university man.'

little-house. A privy: from ca 1720: S.E. till ca 1850, then dial. and, in New Zealand, coll. Ex PETTY-HOUSE.

***little joker.** The hidden pea in the thimble-rigging game: c.: from ca 1870. ?ex the card-game sense of *joker*.

little man. A footman: Eton College: ca 1850–1915.

little man in the boat. The navel: trivial: late C.19–20. (Also in a very indelicate metaphorical c.p.) 2. Clitoris: trivial: late C.19–20. Also *little boy*.

little Mary. The stomach: coll: 1903. Ex Barrie's *Little Mary*.

little more Charley behind. 'More lumbar width – speaking of feminine dress or costume': theatrical (—1909); ob.

little shillings. 'Love money' (*Sinks*): ca 1830–70.

little side. A game between houses only: Rugby school: from ca 1870: coll > j.

little sister. The female pudend: low: C.19–20; ob. cf. LITTLE BROTHER.

***little snakesman.** A young thief who, entering by a window, opens the door to the gang: c. of ca 1780–1890. G. Parker.

little spot, see SPOT, n., 1.

Little Witham, be born at; go to school at; belong to, etc. To be stupid: coll (more or less proverbial): late C.16–mid-19; extant only in dial. Punning *wit*; Nashe, e.g., has *small Witam . . . little Brainford*.

little wooden hill, the. The stairs: nursery coll: mid-C.19–20. Esp. in 'Now we'll go up the little wooden hill to Bedfordshire'; cf. BEDFORDSHIRE.

littleish. Rather small: coll: since ca 1825. *Sessions*, 1832.

live. Jocular s. verging on coll, esp. as *a real live* ——; e.g. 'A real live glass milk jug', 1887 (S.O.D.), 'A real live philosopher', 1890 (ibid.).

live bach(e). To live as a bachelor: Society coll (—1909).

live eels. Fields: rhyming s. (—1857).

live even in a gravel pit, he would. A semi-proverbial, mainly rural, c.p. applied, ca 1660–1750, to a cautious, niggardly person. Ray, Fuller.

live horse. Work additional to that included in the (gen., week's) bill: workmen's: C.19–20; ob. Opp. to, and suggested by, DEAD HORSE.

live in one's chest(s). (Of midshipmen) to sleep in a hammock in the gun-room; where one's chest is kept: naval coll: late C.19–20.

live lumber. Soldiers or passengers on board ship: nautical: ca 1780–1910.

live message. (Gen. pl.) A message in course of transmission: telegraphers' coll (1870) >, by 1910, j.

live-on. A fine girl or woman: low: late C.19–20; ob. cf. LEAVE-YER-HOMER.

live sausage, see SAUSAGE.

live stock. Fleas; lice; in short, body vermin: from ca 1780. 2. In C.19, also cattle.

live up to one's blue china. To live up to or beyond one's means: from ca 1860; ob. cf.:

live up to the door (or the knocker). To live up to one's means: proletarian: mid-C.19–20; ob.

lively. A lively person: coll: 1889, Clark Russell, in *Marooned*.

lively kid. 'A funny fellow, a brave man,' *Sinks*, 1848: coll.

liven. To make, or to become, lively: coll: 1884.

livener. A PICK-ME-UP; a morning dram: s. (—1887) >, by 1910, coll.

liver, have a. To be irritable, bad-tempered: coll: from ca 1890.

liver-faced. Pale- or white-faced; cowardly: low (—1857).

liver-jerker. A tricycle: ca 1890–1914. G. & W. Grossmith, *The Diary of a Nobody*, 1894.

liver-pad. A chest-protector, usually of flannel: ca 1850–1905.

liver-shaker. A riding hack: late C.19–20.

liverish. LIVERY; having the symptoms attributed to a liver out of order: coll: 1896. *Daily News*, 9 July 1896, an advertisement.

Liverpool button. 'A kind of toggle used by sailors when they lose a button', F. & H.: nautical s. > j.: from ca 1850; ob.

Liverpool house. The midship deckhouse: sailing-ship coll: C.19.

Liverpool tailor. A tramping tailor (status of workman): tailors': ca 1870-1910.

Liverpool weather. 'In the Merchant Service, a special brand of dirty weather': coll: late C.19–20. Bowen.

livery. LIVERISH: coll: from ca 1895.

livery, be one of the. To be a cuckold: ca 1680–90. Betterton.

Liveyer(e), Livyere. A permanent inhabitant of the Labrador coast: Canadian coll (—1901). Ex *live here*.

living with mother now. A females' c.p. addressed to proposals of marriage or mistress-ship: 1881–ca 1914. Ware notes that orig. it was 'the refrain of a doubtful song'.

Liza, he's saving them all for, see HE'S SAVING ...

Liza!, outside. Be off! A low c.p. of ca 1880–1905.

'lo! Short for *hollo(a)*, *hullo*: late C.19–20: coll, mostly Colonial.

load, v.i. To buy heavily; *unload*, v.i. and t., sell heavily: Stock Exchange: 1885: coll. 2. v.t., to conceal a horse's broken wind by putting well-greased shot into its throat: c.: from ca 1860. '*No. 747*'.

load, a; loads. A great quantity or number: coll: both being of C.17–20. Shakespeare; Clough, 'Loads of talk with Emerson all morning'. 2. A venereal infection: Australia: late C.19–20: low. Hence *get a load*.

load of hay. A day: rhyming s. (—1859).

loaded-up, be. Have in hand large quantities of a thing – e.g. stocks – as security. Stock Exchange: from ca 1886: coll.

loads of, see LOAD, A.

loaf. A dawdle; a lounge: s. > coll: orig. (ca 1855), U.S.; anglicized ca 1870. Ex the v., which, however, probably comes ex LOAFER. 2. See LOAF OF BREAD, 2.

loaf, v. To lounge, idle, take things very easily: coll. Orig. (ca 1838), U.S.; anglicized ca 1850, though Dickens uses it in 1844. H. Kingsley, 'This one loafed rather energetically.' cf. LOAF AWAY.

loaf, be in a bad. To be in trouble, in a difficulty: ca 1780–1850.

loaf away. Pass (time) in idling: from ca 1850 (orig. U.S.). coll. cf. LOAF, V.

loaf o(f) bread. Dead. 2. The head (gen. *loaf*): rhyming s.: late C.19–20.

loafer. An idler: coll: orig. (1835), U.S.; anglicized ca 1850, though Dickens uses it earlier in his *American Notes*. Prob. ex Low German (*land*)*läufer*, a landloper.

loafing, vbl n. Aimless lounging; deliberate idling: orig. (1838), U.S.; anglicized ca 1850 as a coll. cf.:

loafing, adj. Lounging; deliberately idle: orig. (ca 1838), U.S.; anglicized ca 1850 as a coll >, by 1905, S.E. T. Hughes, 'A ... poaching, loafing fellow'.

loamick, see LOMICK.

loap. A C.18 variant of LOPE.

***loaver.** Money: c. (—1851) >, ca 1880, low s. Mayhew. Prob. a corruption of *lowre* (= LOUR) by Romany *luva* (pronounced *loover*) – cf. Sampson at *lovo*. Lingua Franca, says H. in 1864.

***lob;** in C.18, often **lobb.** A snuff-box; any box; a till: c.: resp. 1718 (†by 1800); ca 1750–1810; from ca 1810 (slightly ob.), as in valuable Vaux. 2. **lob, the:** see LOB, GO ON THE. 3. The head: boxing: ca 1850–1910. 4. A partial priapism: low coll: C.18–19. 5. A yorker: Winchester College cricketers': ca 1850–90.

lob, v. To droop; sprawl: late C.16–20; ob.: S.E. >, ca 1800, s.

***lob, dip** or **frisk** or **pinch** or **sneak a.** To rob a till: from ca 1810: c.: all slightly ob. See also LOB-SNEAK.

***lob, go on the.** To go into a shop to get change for gold and then secrete some of the change: c.: ca 1750–1820. C. Johnson; Grose, 2nd ed. cf.:

***lob, make a good.** To steal much money from a till: c. of ca 1810–60. cf.:

***lob-sneak, -crawler; lob-sneaking.** A till-robber; till-robbing: c.: from ca 1865; slightly ob. See LOB, n.

***lobb,** see LOB, n., 1.

lobcock, a blockhead, is S.E. 2. A large relaxed *membrum virile*: mid-C.18–19 low coll. Ex LOB, v. 3. An alderman: s.: Ned Ward, 1703.

***lobkin.** A house; a lodging: c.: late C. 18–early 19. A survival and perversion of LIB-KEN.

loblolly-boy. A doctor's assistant: naval s. (1748, Smollett) >, ca 1860, S.E., and merchant-service s., in C.19, for a steward, also for a spiritless boy at sea (from ca 1850; ob.), while *loblolly-doctor*, a ship's doctor or surgeon, is nautical s. of C.18. Both ex *loblolly*, gruel.

lobs. An under-gamekeeper: from ca 1860. 2. Abbr. LOBSTER. 3. Talk: tramps' c. of ca 1840–1910. A perversion of Romany *lavaw*, pl of *lav*, a word.

lobs! Look out!: schoolboys': ca 1850–1910.

lobscouse, a meat-and-vegetable hash, is nautical j. and dial., but **lobscouser,** a sailor, is nautical s. (—1884) >, in C.20, S.E. and ob. cf. SCOUSE.

lobster. A British soldier: 1687, T. Brown, is app. the earliest indisputable record; ob. by 1901. Also LOBSTER, BOILED. Ex the red coat. 2. Hence, a marine, as in W. N. Glascock, *Sketch-Book*, I and II, 1825–6. 3. See LOBSTER, RAW.

lobster, v. To cry; cry out: Winchester College: ca 1850–1910. Prob. ex the Hampshire dial. *louster*, to make an unpleasant noise.

lobster, boil one's. (Of a clergyman) to turn soldier: military: ca 1785–1840. Because clerical black is exchanged for red and because an unboiled lobster is bluish-black, a boiled one is red. cf.:

lobster, boiled. Same as LOBSTER, n., 1: ca 1875–1905. In contradistinction to, and suggested by:

lobster, raw or **unboiled.** A policeman: 1829–ca 1910: s. >, ca 1870, coll. Ex the blue uniform equated with the colour of a raw lobster: see LOBSTER, BOIL ONE'S.

lobster-box. A military transport: nautical: 1833, M. Scott, 'Lobster-box, as Jack loves to designate a transport'. 2. A barrack: mainly military (—1860). Ex LOBSTER, n., 1.

lobster-cart, upset one's. To knock a person down: coll: orig. (1824) and mainly U.S.; †in England. cf. APPLE-CART.

lobster-kettle of my cunt, I will not make a. 'A reply frequently made by the nymphs of the Point at Portsmouth, when requested by a soldier to grant him a favour', Grose, 2nd ed.: ca 1785–1860. Ex LOBSTER, n., 1.

lobster-pot. The female pudend: C.19–20 low; ob.

lobster-smack. A military transport (cf. LOBSTER-BOX): 1829, Marryat (O.E.D.): jocular coll >, ca 1880, S.E. Ex LOBSTER, n., 1.

lobster soldier. A marine: naval: late C. 19–20.

lobtail. To sport or play: nautical: ca 1850–1910. Ex a whale smacking the water with his flukes.

loc man. (Gen. pl.) A pilot: nautical: ca 1850–1910. Perhaps abbr. *local man.*

***lock.** A place for storing stolen goods: c.: late C.17–early 19. 2. Hence, a receiver of such goods: c. of ca 1690–1870. (This sense is also expressed by LOCK-ALL-FAST.) 3. A line of business or behaviour: ca 1780–1830: low; perhaps orig. c. 4. A chance, gen. in *stand a queer lock*, have a poor one: c. of ca 1720–1860. Hence, prob., the next sense. 5. As in Grose (1st ed.), *to stand a queer lock*, bear an indifferent character; †. 6. The female pudend: mid-C.18–20: low. Also *lock of all locks* (G. A. Stevens, 1772). The male counterpart is KEY.

***lock-all-fast.** A late C.17–18 variant of LOCK, 2.

***lock-up chovey.** A covered cart: c. >, ca 1860, low: ca 1810–1910.

lock-ups. Detention in study: Harrow School: from ca 1830; ob.

lockees. Lockhouse: Westminster School: C.19–20.

***locker.** A thieves' middleman: C.18 c. C. Hitchin, 1718. Ex LOCK, 2. 2. A bar-room: nautical coll: from ca 1850; ob. 3. The female pudend: C.19–20 low, mainly nautical.

locker, Davy Jones's, see DAVY JONES'(S) LOCKER. **locker, shot in the,** see SHOT...

lockers, be laid in the. To die: nautical (1813, Scott) >, ca 1890, S.E. cf. *lose the number of one's* MESS.

locksmith's daughter. A key: ca 1780–1890. Grose, 1st ed. cf. BLACKSMITH'S DAUGHTER.

loco. A coll abbr. of *locomotive*, an engine: 1896.

locomotive. A hot drink of burgundy, curaçao, egg-yolks, honey, and cloves: coll: ca 1885–1910.

locomotive tailor. A tramping workman tailor: tailors': from ca 1870.

locomotives. The legs: from 1841; ob. by

1900. W. T. Moncrieff, in *The Scamps of London.*

locum. Abbr. *locum tenens*: medical, clerical: from ca 1900. *Scotsman*, 11 March 1901, 'Acting . . . as "locum" . . . during the severe illness of the minister.'

***locus,** see LOCUST, v.

locus away. To remove under the influence of drink: low (?orig. c.): 1831. Ex LOCUS(T), v., and see:

***locust.** Laudanum: c.: from ca 1850; ob. Mayhew. Also *locus(s)*, esp. when used in the wider sense, a drug ('generally . . . snuff and beer', H., 1st ed.). The term occurs in combination (*locus-ale*) as early as 1693. Perhaps ex Sp. *locos*, pl of *loco*, lunatic. 2. In Australia, 'popularly but . . . erroneously applied to insects belonging to two distinct orders', cicadas and grasshoppers: 1846. 3. A very extravagant person: Society (—1909); ob. A resuscitation of the C.16–17 S.E. sense.

***locust,** v. To drug a person and then rob him: c. (—1859). H., 1st ed., where spelt *locuss*. 2. Earlier (*locus*, 1831), to stupefy with drink. cf. LOCUS AWAY and the n., 1.

loddy. A perverted abbr. of *laudanum*: ca 1810–70. L. M. Hawkins. cf. dial. *lodlum* and *lodomy* (E.D.D.).

lodger. A person of no account: low: from ca 1840; ob. Ex 'It's only a lodger!' cf. LOG. 2. A convict awaiting his discharge: prison-authorities' (—1889). 3. (Gen. pl.) Applied chiefly to head lice but also to all vermin – even rats and mice: mostly Cockneys': from ca 1870.

***lodging-slum.** The stealing of valuables from high-class lodgings hired for the purpose: c. of ca 1810–70. See SLUM, n., 4.

lodgings. Prison: Australian: late C.19–20.

log. The lowest boy in form or house: Public Schools': ca 1860–1910. 2. Abbr. *logarithm*, coll: C.19–20: universities'. 3. See LOGS, 2.

log-juice. Cheap port-wine: 1853, 'Cuthbert Bede'; slightly ob.

log-roller. A political or a literary ally, gen. not too scrupulous: orig. (ca 1820), U.S.; anglicized ca 1865: coll. See:

log-rolling. 'Co-operation in the pursuit of money, business, or praise', F. & H.: orig. (1823), U.S.; anglicized ca 1865: coll till ca 1895, then S.E. Ex mutual assistance in the actual rolling of logs. 2. Also adj.

log up, v.i. To make a log-support for a windlass: Australia (—1890): coll. Morris, who quotes 'Rolf Boldrewood', 1890, *The Miner's Right.*

***loge.** A watch: c.: late C.17–early 19. Ex Fr. *horloge*.

***loges.** A pass or warrant: c.: early C.17. Hence, FEAGER OF LOGES, a professional beggar with false passes. Rowlands.

logged. (Of a ship) on her beam-ends: nautical coll: late C.19–20. Perhaps ex dial. *log*, v.t., to rock.

loggo. Logs, esp. in 'Any loggo?': a London street-cry: mid-C.19–20.

logie. Sham jewellery: theatrical: from ca 1860; in C.20, S.E. and ob. Ex David *Logie* the inventor. Sala, 'The plastering of girdles with zinc "logies" '. 2. Sewage: Winchester College: from ca 1870; ob.

***logier.** A pocket-book: c. of ca 1820–50. Ex Dutch or Yiddish.

logs. A lock-up; a minor prison: Australian coll (—1888). 'Rolf Boldrewood', 1888, 'Let's put him in the Logs.' Morris, 'In the early days' – see G. Barrington, in his *History of New South Wales* – 'a log-hut, and often keeping its name when made a more secure place'. Ob. however, by 1910. cf. the †U.S. *log-box*. 2. (Rare in singular.) Fines inflicted at sea, officially logged by the captain: nautical coll: late C.19–20.

loke. A locum tenens: medical: from ca 1905. Ex LOCUM.

lol; occ. **loll.** A students' social evening or spree: Stellenbosch students': ca 1885–1900. Pettman, who derives it ex Dutch '*lollen*, to sit by the fire, to chat'.

loll-shraub, -shrob. Claret: Anglo-Indian coll: from ca 1815. Ex Hindustani for 'red wine'.

loll-tongue, play a game at. To be salivated for syphilis: ca 1785–1850. ?ex panting from the effects of the treatment.

lollipop, lollypop. A sweetmeat: coll: *London Chronicle*, 17–20 Jan. 1784, p. 72: '. . . sweetmeats, called lollypops'. ?ex Northern dial. *lolly*, the tongue. 2. The *membrum virile*: C.19–20 (ob.); low. Also *ladies' lollipop*. 3. Fig., over-sweet writing from ca 1850; ob.: coll. 4. As an adj., from ca 1835; coll. cf.:

lollipop dress. A 'stripy dress, generally red and white, suggestive of sticks of confectionery': theatrical coll: 1884. Ware.

lollop. A lounger, loafer: coll: from ca 1840. Ex the v. 2. The action or an act of lolloping: coll: 1834 (S.O.D.). Ex the v.

lollop. To lounge about: coll: 1745, C. H. Williams, 'Next in lollop'd Sandwich, with negligent grace.' Ex *loll*, v. 2. To bob up and down: coll: from ca 1850. Mayhew, 'Its head lolloping over the end of the cart.' 3. To proceed clumsily by bounds: coll: 1878, Lady Brassey, 'We lolloped about in the trough of a heavy sea.' But for date cf. LOLLOPING, 2.

lolloping. vbl n. of *lollop*, v., in all senses: coll. 2. adj., lounging, slovenly, idle: coll: 1745. 3. Moving by clumsy bounds: coll: 1844, Stephens in *Advice of a Gentleman*, '[Long-pasterned horses] have usually a lumbering lolloping action, neither fast nor pleasant.'

lollopy. Lazy: coll: from ca 1855. cf. LOLLOPING, adj.

lollpoop. 'A lazy, idle Drone': a C.17–18 coll verging on S.E.

lolly. A sweetmeat: 1862 (O.E.D.): dial. and, in Australia and New Zealand, coll. Ex LOLLIPOP. 2. The head: boxers': ca 1855–1910; ob.

lolly-banger. A ship's cook: nautical: ca 1872–1914. Perhaps ex LOLLY influenced by LOBLOLLY-BOY.

lollypop, see LOLLIPOP. **lolpoop,** see LOLLPOOP.

Lombard fever. The 'idles': coll: 1678, Ray; †by 1870. A perversion of the S.E. †*fever-lurden* (cf. S.E. †*lurden*).

***Lombard Street, in.** In prison: c. of ca 1810–60. See LUMBER, n. and v. (esp.); LUMBERED; LIMBO.

Lombard Street to a Brummagem sixpence, a China orange (the commonest form), **an egg-shell, ninepence.** (Gen. preceded by *all.*) In C.20, the second occ. > *all China to an orange.* A c.p. indicative of very heavy, indeed the longest possible odds; a virtual certainty: coll: resp. 1826, G. Daniels, ob.: 1849, Lytton; 1752, Murphy, †; 1819, Moore, ob. Ex the wealth of this London street. (See esp. Apperson.) Also *Chelsea College to a sentry-box* (1819) and *Pompey's pillar to a stick of sealing-wax* (1819, likewise in Tom Moore).

lomick; loamick. The hand: Shetland and Orkney islanders' s., not dial.: from ca 1880. Ex Orkney dial. *lomos*, the hands.

London, agree like the clocks of. To disagree at, and on, all points: proverbial coll: late C.16–early 18. Nashe, Ray. The elder Disraeli ascribes it, tentatively, to some Italian clock-maker.

London, put or **show** or **turn the best side to.** To make the best display one can: coll: 1873, *Cassell's Magazine*, Jan. Ware, 'Making the best of everything'.

London flitting, see MOONLIGHT FLIT.

London fog. A dog: rhyming s.: late C.19–20.

London ivy; L. particular. A thick London fog (cf. PEA-SOUPER): coll: both 1852, in Dickens's *Bleak House*. 2. (Only **London ivy.**) Dust: Cockneys' (—1909).

London jury, see JURY – HANG HALF . . .

London ordinary. Brighton beach: ca 1864–1915. Trippers feed there.

London smoke. A yellowish grey: Society coll: ca 1860–90. Ware, 'Became once a favourite colour because it hid dirt.'

London waggon. 'In the days of the Press Gang [abolished in 1835], the tender which carried the victims from the Tower of London to the receiving ship at the Nore': nautical: ca 1770–1840.

Londrix. London: ca 1860–80. Prob. ex Fr. *Londres.*

lone duck or **dove.** A woman no longer 'kept'; a harlot 'working' in houses of accommodation: low: from ca 1860; ob.

lonesome, all on one's. Alone: coll: since ca 1890.

long. A BULL (n., 5): Stock Exchange (—1888); ob. 2. A rifle: Fenian: from ca 1885. cf. SHORT, a revolver. 3. See JOHN LONG. 4. See LONG, THE.

long, adj. Tall: M.E.–C.20: S.E. till ca 1870, then coll, mostly jocular. 2. (Of numbers, or of numbered things) large. Chiefly in *l. trump*, *l. suit* (both in cards), *l. family, odds, price*: 1746 coll.

long!, so. Good-bye: coll: 1834. In the Colonies, often pronounced *soo'-long.* ?ex *for so long as you're away good luck!*

long, that. Thus or so long: low coll: late C.19–20.

long, the. The summer vacation: university coll: 1852, Bristed; Reade, 1863.

Long Acre. A baker: rhyming s. (—1857).

long and slender like a cat's elbow. A C.18–mid-19 ironic proverbial c.p. T. Fuller, *Gnomologia*, 1732.

long attachment. One tall, one short (other-sex) person walking together: coll: from ca 1860; ob. In jocular S.E., *the long and* (*the*) *short of it.*

long balls; gen. **l. bowls.** Long-range firing: naval: C.19. Bowen. Ex *long bowls*, whether in sense of ninepins or in the Scottish one of a game played by throwing heavy bullets is not certain.

long beer, drink. A large measure of liquor: coll: 1859, Trollope.

***long bill.** A long imprisonment: c.: from

ca 1860. cf. LIFER. A short term is *a short bill*.

long-bow, draw or **pull the.** To tell unlikely stories: coll: resp., from ca 1668, C.19–20. L'Estrange; Thackeray, 'What is it makes him pull the long-bow in that wonderful manner?'

long-bow man. A liar: coll: ca 1678–1830. Ray, Motteux.

long bowls, see LONG BALLS.

long chalk, see CHALK, BY A LONG.

long clay. A long clay pipe: coll: from ca 1860. cf. CHURCHWARDEN.

long-cork. Claret: 1829, Marryat: †by 1900. Ex the long corks.

long-crown. A clever fellow, esp. in the proverb, 'That caps long-crown, and he capped the devil': coll and dial. (—1847); † except in dial.

long dispar(s). The loin: Winchester College. See DISPAR.

long drink, see LONG BEER.

long Eliza. A blue and white vase ornamented with tall china-women: sailors' and traders': from ca 1880. See esp. the *Pall Mall Gazette*, 4 Dec. 1884. Ex Ger. *lange Lischen*, tall Lizzies.

long enough, I, you, etc., **may** (do something). It's pretty hopeless: coll: C.16–20. In C.19–20 gen. followed by *before* + v. Palsgrave, Browning.

long eye. The female pudend: pidgin: from ca 1850.

long face. A solemn or a downhearted expression: coll: from ca 1785.

long-faced one. A horse: military (—1896).

long feathers. Straw; bedding stuffed with straw: military (—1879).

long fifteens. Some class of lawyers: C.17. L. Barry, in *Ram Alley*.

long firm. A swindling group of phantom capitalists: 1868: commercial coll. *Orchestra*, 2 Jan. 1869. Presumably ex *long* (!) credit expected, or ex 'choosing its victims at a distance'.

long fork. A stick used as a toasting fork: Winchester College: ca 1830–70.

long gallery. The act or the practice of trundling the dice the whole length of the board: ca 1790–1850.

long ghost. A tall, awkward person: ca 1860–1910. cf. LAMP-POST.

long glass. A very long, horn-shaped glass filled with beer on special occasions: Eton College s. > j.: ca 1820–70. Brinsley-Richards, *Seven Years at Eton*, 1883.

long-haired chum. A female friend or sweetheart: from ca 1870: tailors' >, in C.20, soldiers' and sailors'.

long hogs. A sheep's first growth of wool: coll: ca 1840–1900.

long home, one's. The grave: C.14–20: S.E. >, ca 1820, coll. Dickens.

long hope. Long expectations in studying for a degree: Oxford University: ca 1820–40.

long hundred. Six-score fresh herrings: Billingsgate coll: from ca 1870. Ex *long hundred*, 120.

long in the arm. Addicted to theft: from ca 1870. *Sessions*, Sept. 1893 (Surrey cases). Of one who *will* reach for things.

long in the mouth. Tough: low coll: from ca 1850; ob.

long-jawed. (Of rope) so strained and so far untwisted that it coils both ways; (of an eye-splice) badly tucked: naval: late C.19–20.

long lady. A farthing candle: late C.18–early 19 coll.

long lane. The throat: C.19–20; ob. See LANE.

long lane, for the. Of something borrowed without intention of repayment or restoration: coll: C.18–mid-19. ?ex the proverb *it's a long lane that has no turning*.

long leg. 'A big difference in the draught forward and aft in a sailing ship': nautical coll: mid-C.19–20; ob. Bowen. Ex nautical j. *long-legged*, (of a ship) drawing much water.

long legs; long un. A tall person: C.18–20 coll. cf. LAMP-POST.

long Meg. A very tall woman: late C.17–early 19. Ex an actual woman, known as Long Meg of Westminster.

long nose, make a. To put a derisive thumb to the nose: 1868.

long oats. 'A broom or fork-handle used to belabour a horse', F. & H.: military: ca 1870–1914 See ASH BEANS.

***long one** or **'un.** A hare: poachers': from ca 1810. 2. A pheasant: poachers' (—1909). Prob. suggested by LONG TAIL, 4. 3. See LONG LEGS.

long paper. Paper for impositions: Winchester College: from ca 1860.

long pig. Human flesh as food: 1852, Mundy, in *Our Antipodes*: nautical >, ca 1895, S.E. Prob. ex Fijian phrase.

long-shanks. A tall man: coll: late C.17–20.

long shilling. A drive 'from the Royal Exchange to the east corner of Catherine-street, in the Strand', Grose: London hackney-coachmen's: ca 1740–80.

long ship. A ship 'in which it is a long time between drinks': nautical: C.20. Bowen.

long-shore butcher. A coastguardsman: nautical: ca 1820–1905.

long-shot. A bet laid at large odds: turf s. (—1869) >, in C.20, gen. coll. *Leisure Hour*, May 1869.

long sight, not by a. Not by a long way: coll: late C.19–20.

***long-sleeved top.** A silk hat: c. (—1889); ob.

long-sleeved 'un. A long glass (of liquor): Australian: from ca 1890; ob. Ex:

long-sleever. The same; also the glass itself: Australian (—1888).

long stomach. A greedy eater: ca 1780–1870: coll.

long streak of misery. A (very) tall, thin person, even if not miserable-looking: late C.19–20.

long tail, as applied to one of the riff-raff, is S.E. 2. A native of Kent: from ca 1620: coll till ca 1750, then dial. Also KENTISH LONG-TAIL. 3. A Chinaman: nautical: from ca 1865; ob. 4. A pheasant: sporting coll: 1854, Smedley. 5. A greyhound: coursers' and dog-fanciers' (—1864); ob. 6. One or another: c.: ca 1730–70.

long-tailed bear, (that's) a. You lie!: non-aristocratic evasive c.p.: late C.19–early 20. Ware, 'Bears have *no* tails.'

long-tailed beggar. A cat: low (mostly nautical) coll: from ca 1830; ob. Marryat.

***long-tailed finnip** or **'un.** A bank-note of high denomination: c.: from ca 1835. Brandon; Snowden's *Magazine Assistant*. cf. FLIMSY; FINNIF.

long tea. Tea poured from a high-held pot; urine: schoolboys': ca 1850–1910.

long time dead, you'll be. A c.p. to anyone failing to make the most of life: late C.19–20.

long togs. A landsman's clothes; esp. full-dress clothes: nautical: from ca 1810. Also adj. as in Marryat's 'them long-tog, swallow-tailed coats'.

long Tom. A large, long-range gun: nautical (also †*long Tom Tuck*: Bowen) and military coll: from ca 1865. cf. LONG-WINDED WHISTLER. Also, a nickname for specific cannon. 2. Hence, a penis: low: from ca 1898. (Whence an obscene riddle current during the Boer War.)

long-tongued as Granny. Very apt to blab: coll: ca 1720–1830. Ex Granny, an idiot (d. 1719) that could lick her own eye.

long tot. A lengthy set of figures for addition, esp. in examinations: from ca 1885: coll. Ex TOT, itself abbr. *total*.

Long Town. London: Anglo-Irish (—1823). †by 1900.

long trail, the. 'In the China clippers, the homeward route round Australia': mid-C.19–20; virtually †. Bowen.

long trot, to do the. To go home: low London: from ca 1860; ob. B. & L.

long 'un. A tall person: coll: mid-C.19–20. Also as vocative. 2. See LONG LEGS and LONG ONE.

long vac. The summer holiday: at schools, some universities (cf. LONG, THE), the law-courts: coll: late C.19–20.

long-winded paymaster. A person who takes long credit: late C.17–early 19.

long-winded whistler. A chase-gun: nautical: ca 1865–90. Smyth. cf. LONG TOM.

long word, a. A word indicative of a long time: coll: from ca 1860. 'Since I've been in London, and that's saying a long word,' *Cornhill Magazine*, Dec. 1861; '"Never" is a long word,' *Standard*, 28 July 1883.

longa in 'pidgin' represents 'at', 'for', 'of', 'to'. Ex *belonging to*.

***longs and shorts;** also **longs and broads.** 'Cards so manufactured that all above the eight are a trifle longer than those below it,' F. & H.: card-sharpers' c.: from ca 1860. 2. Orig. (—1823), *longs and broads* = cards.

longshore lawyer. An unscrupulous lawyer: coll (—1823); ob.

longshore owner. (Gen. pl.) A shipowner that sent ill-found ships to sea: nautical coll: ca 1850–1910.

loo! Milk!: milkmen's cry (—1823); ob. Ex Fr. *lait*.

loo. A lieutenant: naval: ca 1880–1914.

loo, the. The water closet: late C.19–20. Ex Fr. *l'eau*. Or perhaps rather ex GARDY-LOO.

looard. A nautical spelling of *leeward*: coll (—1887).

looby. A fool; an idle, dull fellow: C.14–20: S.E. till ca 1820, then coll and dial. Disraeli, 'Her looby of a son and his eighty thousand a year'. cf. LOOPY.

loocha, -cher. 'A blackguard libertine, a lewd loafer': Anglo-Indian coll: from ca 1820. Ex Hindustani *luchcha*. Whence *Loocha Point*, Louisa Point, Matheran, India.

loof-faker. A chimney-sweep: 1859, H.,

1st ed.; ob. Doubtless *loof* is an approximate back-s. perversion of *flue*: *flue* > *floo* > *oolf* > *loof*.

look. To look surprised; stare: C.17–20: S.E. till ca 1850, then coll.

look a gift-horse in the mouth. To criticize a gift or a favour: C.16–20: coll till C.18, then S.E. 'Hudibras' Butler.

look alive. To be alert; bestir oneself: coll: C.19–20. Also, in late C.19–20 lower classes' coll, *look slimy* (ob.). cf. LOOK SHARP and LOOK SLIPPERY.

look as if butter would not melt in one's mouth, see BUTTER WOULD NOT . . .

look as if one had eaten live birds. To be unwontedly lively: from ca 1867: ob. *Quarterly Review*, cxxv, p. 231.

look at, cannot. To have no chance against: coll: 1895 (O.E.D.). Ex cricket, where it appears as early as 1862.

look at, have a. To look at for the purpose of examining: coll: 1885.

look at every woman through the hole in one's prick. To regard every woman as a mere potential instrument of pleasure: low coll: late C.19–20.

look at him (it, me, you, etc.), to. Judging from his (my, etc.) appearance: coll: 1846, Bentley's *Miscellany* (vol. xx), 'No one would think me more than five- or six-and-thirty, to look at me.'

look at the maker's name. To drain a glass: coll: from ca 1860; ob. Also *bite one's name in the pot*.

***look at the place.** (Of thieves) to examine a house, etc., beforehand, to see if there is anything unusual about it: C.19–20: c.

look behind one, not or never to. Advance or prosper without interruption: coll: 1852, Serjeant Bellasis. The gen. C.20 form is *never to look back* (1893, O.E.D.). Perhaps ex racer leading easily.

look big, see BIG. **l. blue,** see BLUE.

look Cro'-Jack-eyed. To squint: nautical: mid-C.19–20.

look down one's nose. To look glum: coll: C.19–20; ob.

look down one's nose at. To despise: coll: from ca 1840.

look'ee. A low coll form of *look you!* (C. 18–20) = mind this! cf. LOOK HERE!

look for a needle in a bottle of hay or **in a haystack.** To look for something virtually impossible to find: proverbial coll: resp. late C.16–19, C.19–20.

look goats and monkeys at, see GOATS AND MONKEYS.

look here! Mind this!; mind what I say!: coll: C.17–20. Shakespeare. Also *look you!*: late C.16–20. Shakespeare, 'Look you how he writes.'

look in. A chance of success: sporting: 1870, *Bell's Life*, 12 Feb.

look into the whites. To be about to fight: lower classes': from ca 1885; ob. Sc. *of each other's eyes*.

look like a billy-goat in stays. To look very silly: nautical: late C.19–20.

look like a tooth-drawer. To be thin and meagre: coll: C.17. Beaumont & Fletcher, in *Philaster*; Ray (as a semi-proverbial phrase).

look lively. To be drunk: low coll: from ca 1850.

look marlinspikes. To 'look daggers': nautical, esp. naval: ca 1790–1860. *Night Watch* (II, 119), 1829, 'Then comes the captain with the articles of war in his hand, looking marlinspikes, and calls for Paddy.'

look nine ways for Sunday(s). To squint: nautical: from ca 1850; ob. Ex the C.16–18 coll *look nine ways* confused with the dial. *look both* (later *all*) *ways for Sunday*.

look old. To be severe or cautious: streets' coll (—1909).

look on, v.i. Applied to a horse meant not to do its best: the turf: from ca 1870. 2. To read (a book, etc.) at the same time (*with* another person): coll: late C.19–20.

look on the wall and it will not bite you. A derisive c.p. addressed to a person 'bitten with mustard', Ray: ca 1670–1760.

look one way and row another. To do the opposite of what one seems to intend to do: coll: ca 1580–1880. Melbancke, 1583; D'Urfey; Spurgeon, 1869.

look out, that is X's. That is X's concern or sole business: coll: 1844.

look-out house. The watch kept 'by ordained masters on defunct incumbents', Egan's Grose: Oxford University: ca 1820–40.

look-see; occ. **looksee.** A look-round, an inspection: from early 1880s. Almost certainly ex pidgin, hence nautical, *look-see*, to look and see.

look-see, v. See preceding.

look sharp. To be quick; to hasten: coll: from ca 1815. Cobbett, 'They shall look sharp if they act before I am ready for them'; Dickens; Manville Fenn. cf. the next two entries.

look slimy, see LOOK ALIVE.

look slippery. To be quick: see SLIPPERY. (Ware, 1909, considers it essentially naval.)

look slippy, see SLIPPY.

look-stick. A telescope: naval: late C.19–20. cf. LOOK-SEE.

look through a glass. To become tipsy: low coll: from ca 1840; ob.

look through a hempen window. To be hanged: coll: ca 1625–1700.

look to, or watch, one's water (for him). To follow a person's movements, watch him very closely: coll (semi-proverbial): from ca 1540: in C.19–20, dial. only. Heywood, 1546; Manley, *The New Atlantis.*

look towards one. To drink his health: low coll: 1848, Thackeray; ob. See also LOOKS TOWARDS.

look up, v.i. To improve: s. >, in C.20, coll (in C.19, mainly commercial): 1822, *The Examiner*, 'Foreign Securities are generally looking up.' 2. v.t., to visit, gen. informally: coll: late C.18. *Sessions*, Jan. 1788.

look up nor-west-and-by-well. Look cheerful: naval (?gen. nautical): late C.18–mid-19.

look you! see LOOK HERE!

looking all ways for Sunday, see LOOK NINE . . .

looking as if he hadn't got his right change. Mad- or wild-looking: Cockneys' (—1909).

looking as if one could not help it. Looking like a simpleton or a faint-heart: coll: late C.18–20; ob.

looking for a big penny for a little ha'-penny. A North of England coll, almost a c.p., applied to those who always want the best of a bargain: late C.19–20.

looking for maidenheads. A lower-class c.p. directed at people looking for something unprocurable or, at the least, very scarce: since ca 1890.

looking-glass. A chamber-pot: ca 1620–1830, then dial. (N.B. the E.D.D. entry.) Beaumont & Fletcher. Prob. ex the attention paid to it by physicians.

looking lively. Slightly intoxicated: coll: late C.19–20.

looking seven ways for Sunday. Squinting: London lower and lower-middle classes': late C.19–20. cf. LOOK NINE WAYS . . .

lookit ——! Look at ——!: Canadian (and U.S.): from ca 1880.

looks towards you!, I. Your good health!: lower classes' coll: mid-C.19–20.

looksee, see LOOK-SEE. **looney,** see LOONY.

***loonslate, loonslatt.** Thirteen pence halfpenny: c.: late C.17–18. cf. HANGMAN'S WAGES.

loony; often **looney;** occ. **luny.** Crazy: (lower classes') coll: 1872. 2. Hence, a fool; a lunatic: id.: 1869. Ex *lunatic* influenced by *loon.* DOTTY; LOOPY, and:

loony, be taken. To go crazy, mad: (proletarian) coll: late C.19–20.

loony-bin. A lunatic asylum: Cockneys': from ca 1890. Ex LOONY, 2.

loop, up the. Mad: military: from ca 1870. Prob. by fusion of LOOPY and *up the* POLE.

loopy. Slightly mad: s. (or coll): late C.19–20. ?ex LOOBY, influenced by ironic allusion to Scots *loopy*, crafty. Occ. *looby.*

loos-wallah. A rascal; a thief: Regular Army: late C.19–20. In Hindustani, 'thief-fellow'.

loose, adj. (Of time) not strictly observed: coll: 1892, Sir H. Maxwell, 'Breakfast is not on the table till a loose ten.'

loose, have a screw, see SCREW. **loose, play fast and,** see FAST AND LOOSE.

loose, on the. Earning money by prostitution: low coll: from ca 1860. 2. Out of prison: proletarian: mid-C.19–20; ob.

loose, run. (Of a horse) to race unbacked: the turf: 1884, Hawley Smart.

loose, turned. (Of a horse) handicapped at a very low rate: the turf: from ca 1880; ob. cf. preceding entry.

loose a fiver. (To have) to pay extravagantly for any pleasure or purchase: proletarian (—1909).

loose-box. A carriage kept for a kept woman's use: C.19. cf. MOT-CART.

loose end. A late C.19–20 variant of LOOSE FISH, 2.

loose end, at a (†after or on a). Not regularly employed; not knowing what to do: from ca 1850 (*at a* . . . recorded first in 1860): coll ex dial. Ex freedom from tether. cf.:

loose end, leave (a matter) at a. To leave unsettled: coll: from ca 1864.

loose ends, at. Neglected: coll: from ca 1870; ob. cf. preceding entry.

loose fish. A harlot: coll: 1803, *The Port Folio*; †by 1895. 2. A person of irregular, esp. of dissipated habits: coll: 1827, Egan, 'Known among the loose-fish who frequent races by the name of thimble-rig'. 3. An independent member: Parliament: 1864; ob.

loose French. (Gen. *loosing F.*) To use violent language in English: urban (mostly Cockney): ca 1890–1915.

loose hold. To let go: coll: from ca 1695. Dryden. cf. LEAVE GO.

loose-hung. (Of persons) unsteady: low coll: from ca 1820; ob.

loose (or loosen) out. To unspan a team (of, e.g., draught cattle): Australian coll: mid-C.19–20. In, e.g., 'Tom Collins', *Such Is Life*, 1903 (both forms). cf. South African *outspan.*

loose screw, a. Variant of a SCREW LOOSE, 1: 1821, Pierce Egan, *Life in London.*

loose-wallah. An occ. variant of LOOS-WALLAH.

loosen (a person's) **hide.** To thrash: 1902, *Daily Chronicle*, 11 April.

loot. Pillage; plunder: 1788: military coll >, ca 1870, S.E. Ex Hindustani *lut*, but prob. influenced by *lootie*, a native irregular of India, hence a bandit. 2. A lieutenant: late C.19–20 naval and military. Ex mispronunciation as *lootenant.* cf. LUFF.

loot, v. To plunder; carry off as booty: from ca 1840: military coll >, ca 1870, S.E. The same ascent characterizes *looter* and *looting.*

lop. A slight choppiness of the sea: naval: late C.19–20. Granville. cf. North Country *lope*, v.i., 'to curdle'. 2. A wave that, in a choppy sea, is 'big enough to break inboard in a rowboat or dory' (Leechman): Newfoundland coll: late C.19–20.

lope. To run; run away: from ca 1570: S.E. till ca 1690, then s. and dial. Grose, 'He loped down the dancers.' 2. To steal: c. (—1874).

loper. Abbr. LANDLOPER.

lor', Lor'! A slovenly form of *Lord*: low coll: 1835 (S.O.D.). cf. LAW!

lor (or Lor')-a-mussy! Lord have mercy! (= surprise): low coll: 1865 (prob. much earlier). Dickens. cf. LORD-A-MERCY!

lord. A hunchback: late C.17–20; ob. Lamb, 'A deformed person is a lord.' A hunchback used often to be addressed as *my lord.* Perhaps ex Gr. λορδός, bent backward, a technical and medical term. cf. LADY. 2. An occ. abbr. of LORD OF THE MANOR.

Lord! In C.14–16, dignified; in C.17–20, trivial when not profane. Shakespeare, 'O Lord, I must laugh.'

lord, drink like a. To drink hard: proverbial coll: C.17–18. Whence:

lord, drunk as a. Very drunk: from ca 1670: coll till C.19, then S.E. cf. EMPEROR.

lord!, my, see LORD, 1.

lord, swear like a. To swear copiously and/or vigorously: coll > S.E.: C.16–17.

Lord-a-mercy (on us)! 'The Lord have mercy (on us)!' as an exclamation of surprise: low coll when not sol.: C.19–20. Eleanor Smith, 1808, 'Lord-a-mercy upon those that had a hand in such a business.'

Lord Baldwin, see QUEEN ANNE.

Lord Harry, see OLD HARRY.

Lord have mercy (up)on me. The 'iliac passion', a 'colic' of the small guts: late C.16–17 medical coll used, according to *Junius' Nomenclator*, by 'the homelier sort of Phisicians'.

Lord John Russell. A bustle or dress-improver: rhyming s. (—1859); †by 1900.

Lord knows how or what or who, the. Some person or thing of unspecified but considerable potentialities; phrases indicative of irritation, wonderment, admiration, or, as gen., the completeness of one's own ignorance. Coll: late C.17–20. *The Gentleman's Journal*, March 1691–2, 'Here's novels, and new-born adventures . . . and the Lord knows what not.'

Lord love us! A jocular, also a low coll, form of *Lord love me!* (itself trivial): late C.19–20.

Lord Lovel. A shovel: rhyming s. (—1857).

Lord lumme or lummy! see LUMME!

Lord Mansfield's teeth. The spikes along the top of the wall of the King's Bench Prison: ca 1790–1830. Ex Sir Charles Mansfield (1733–1821), Lord Chief Justice.

***lord mayor.** A large crowbar: c. (—1889). D. C. Murray. Opp. ALDERMAN. See CITIZEN.

lord mayor, v. To swear: rhyming s.: late C.19–20.

lord mayor's coal. A (piece of) slate: coll: ca 1840–80. Barham.

Lord Mayor's fool, like my or the. Fond of everything good: proverbial coll: from ca 1670. Ray; H. Kingsley in *Geoffrey Hamlyn*: †by 1910. Often as *the Lord Mayor's fool, who likes everything that is good.* Swift has *like my Lord Mayor's fool, full of business and nothing to do.*

Lord Muck, see MUCK, LORD.

lord of the foresheet. A sailing-ship's cook: jocular nautical: late C.19–20.

lord of the manor. A TANNER, i.e. sixpence: rhyming s. (—1839). Brandon. This is the earliest record of a rhyming s. term; its inclusion in Brandon, moreover, significantly implies that 'Ducange Anglicus', 1857, was right in classifying all such terms as c.

lords, the. The first cricket eleven: Winchester College: from ca 1860; ob.

lordsake. For the Lord's sake: Scots coll: from ca 1860.

lordy! or **Lordy!** Lord!: (dial. and) low coll: mid-C.19–20. cf. LAWK!; LAWKS!; LOR'. Abbr.:

Lordy me! A (dial. and) low coll corruption of *Lord* (*have* or) *help me*: C.19–20.

lors! Lord!: low coll: 1860, George Eliot. cf. LAW!

***lorst, in the.** Engaged in shoplifting: c.: ca 1850–1900. Burton, *Vikram and the Vampire*, 1870. (The term is suspect.)

lose. The act, or an instance, of losing (a horse-race): racing: 1884.

lose one's legs. To become tipsy: from ca 1770; ob.

lose out, v.i. To lose; be swindled or merely fooled: coll: Australia: late C.19–20. Perhaps ex the †S.E. *lose out*, recorded by O.E.D. at 1869.

lose the number of one's mess, see MESS.

lot. A group of associated persons, or of things of the same kind: from ca 1570: S.E. until ca 1875, then (except for merchandise and live stock) coll. W. Benham, 1879, 'Their crew seems to have been a lazy lot.' 2. A person, gen. pejoratively as in *a bad lot*, or ironically as in *a nice lot*: from ca 1846: coll. Thackeray, in *Vanity Fair*, (apropos of Miss Sharp) 'A bad lot, I tell you, a bad lot'. Ex the auction-room.

lot, a; lots. A considerable quantity or number; adv., a good deal. Coll: *lots* from ca 1810, *a lot* from ca 1835. Also with adj. as in *a good lot* (Keble, 1835), *a great lot*. Either followed by *of* or absolutely.

lot, hot, see HOT MEMBER.

lot, the; the whole lot. The whole of a stated quantity or number: coll: 1867, Mrs Henry Wood, 'He's crunching the lot' (a quart of gooseberries).

Lothbury, go by way of. To be loth: coll: ca 1560–1660. Tusser. For punning topicalities, cf. CLAPHAM; NEEDHAM; PECKHAM.

lotherwite. Corrupt for *lairwite* (a fine for fornication or adultery): C.16–17.

lotion. A drink – rarely of aught but liquor, and esp. of gin: 1876, Hindley. cf. †*lotium*, a low coll form of *lotion*.

lotman. A pirate: nautical coll: ?late C.18–mid-19. Smyth; Bowen. 'Alleged', says O.E.D.: but why should Admiral Smyth fabricate the word? Ex *lot*, a share (in the booty).

lots, see LOT, A.

Lot's wife. Salt: nautical: late C.19–20. cf.:

Lot's wife's backbone, (as) salt as. Extremely salt: lower classes' (—1909). Ex the Biblical story.

Lotties and Totties. Harlots: orig. (—1885) and mainly theatrical. Ex the frequency of those diminutives in that class.

lotus, n. and esp. v. (To) hocus: low rhyming s.: 1885. Influenced by LOCUST.

loud. (Of dress or manners) showy: 1847, Albert Smith, 'Very loud patterns': coll.

loud one, a. A big lie: coll: ca 1670–1850. Ray; Scott, in *Ivanhoe*, ' "That's a lie, and a loud one," said the Friar.' 2. A noisy breaking of wind: low: mid-C.19–20.

loudly. Showily, of dress or manners; 1849, Thackeray: coll.

lounce. A drink: nautical: from ca 1850; ob. Ex *allowance*. 2. See LOWNCE.

lounge. A chief meal; a treat: Eton and Cambridge: 1844, Disraeli; *Press*, 12 Nov. 1864, 'I don't care for dinner . . . .Breakfast is my lounge.'

***lour, loure, lowr(e).** (See also LOAVER.) Money; in C.19, gen. of coin: c.: from ca 1565. Harman, Head, Grose, Brandon, Richardson (author of *The Police*, 1889). Ex C.14–16 S.E. *lower*, a reward, recompense, itself ex Old Fr. *louier*, a reward; cf. Romany *loor*, to plunder, and *looripen*, plunder, booty.

***lour, gammy.** Counterfeit coin: c. (—1839).

louse, mean as a. Stingy; miserly: non-aristocratic coll (—1887).

louse, prick a. To be a tailor: coll: C.17–mid-19. Hence *louse-pricking*, vbl n., tailoring, also as adj.: C.18–mid-19, e.g. in Toldervy. cf. PRICK-LOUSE.

louse a grey head of his own, he will never. A c.p. of C.18–early 19: He will never live to be old.

louse-bag. 'A black bag worn to the hair or wig', Grose, 1st ed.: coll: ca 1780–1830.

louse for the sake of its skin or hide, skin a. To be extremely thrifty: coll: late C.16–18. In C.19–20, *flea* is substituted for *louse*.

louse-house. A lock-up; a prison: late C. 18–early 19.

louse-ladder. 'A stitch fallen in a stocking', Grose, 1st ed.: ca 1780–1840. Extant in dial. cf. LADDER, 2.

Louse-Land; Louseland. Scotland: late C.17–early 19. cf. ITCHLAND.

louse miss its footing on one's coat it will break its neck, if a. To have a very threadbare coat, clothes: proverbial coll: mid-C. 14–mid-18. Langland, Palsgrave, 'Gnomologia' Fuller.

louse-trap. A fine comb: low: late C.17–20. In B.E., a *Scotch l.-t.*

louse-walk. A back-hair parting: low: ca 1820–80.

lousy. Contemptible; mean; filthy: late C.14–20: S.E. till C.20, when coll and used as a mere pejorative. 2. (Of paint) full of skin from too long keeping: painters': from ca 1860; ob.

lout. Anyone of the poorer classes: Rugby school: from ca 1855; ob. T. Hughes in *Tom Brown's Schooldays*.

lovanenty!; occ. **lov(e)anendie!** A C.19–20 Scots coll exclamation of surprise.

love. An endearing term for a person or a thing; a DUCK (3): coll: 1814, Jane Austen, 'The garden is quite a love.'

love-curls. Hair that, cut short, is worn low over the forehead: Society coll: ca 1880–1914.

love 'em and leave 'em, adj. and n. Given to philandering; a philanderer: coll: late C.19–20.

love-lane. The female pudend: C.19–20; ob.: low coll verging on S.E. euphemism. Hence, *a turn* or *an ejectment in l.-lane*, an act of copulation.

love of Mike!, for the. For goodness' sake!: low coll: mid-C.19–20: Anglo-Irish > gen.

love-penny. A miser: s.: Ned Ward, 1703.

love-pot. A drunkard: C.19 coll. cf. LUSHINGTON.

love us!, Lord, see LORD LOVE US!

love your heart!, or **you** or **it, Lord.** A low coll exclamation (cf. LORD LOVE US!): resp. 1833 (T. Hook), †by 1910; 1841, Lytton; 1843, Dickens.

loveage. Tap-lashes; ALLS; ULLAGE: coll (—1860); ob.

lovely, adj. Attractive, delightful; excellent: coll: C.17–20. Marham, 1614; Walton, 'This trout looks lovely.'

lover's knot, tie the true. To coït: C.19–20; ob. ?low coll or euphemistic S.E.

lovey; in C.18, occ. **lovy.** A term of endearment; from ca 1730: S.E. till ca 1820, then increasingly low coll. Fielding, 1731; Foote, 'I go, lovy.' cf.:

lovey-dovey. An endearment, whether in address or in reference: (low) coll: 1819 (O.E.D.). A reduplication of LOVEY. It may have been current throughout C.18 as well, for *Sessions*, 1735, has '"Why; Dovee," says she . . .'

low or **Low,** adj. Low Church: coll: 1854, S. Wilberforce: 1881, Trollope, 'Among [these Low Church prelates] there was none more low, more pious, more sincere.'

low, lie. To bide one's time; keep quiet: from ca 1881: s. >, ca 1910, coll. Orig., presumably U.S., for the popularity of Joe Chandler Harris's *Uncle Remus* (1880) put the phrase into gen. circulation. Low coll, or rather sol., is *lay low* in this sense.

low and slow. An epithet-c.p. applied to the Low Church: from ca 1855; ob. cf. HIGH AND DRY.

low comedy. A low comedian: theatrical: 1884, Jerome K. Jerome. Prob. an abbr. of *low-comedy merchant*, a low comedian: recorded by Ware for 1883.

low countries; Low Countries. (Preceded by *the*.) The female pudend: low: C.18–mid-19. cf. LOWLANDS.

low-country soldier. A heavy drinker: s. (—1650).

***low Fulhams.** See LOW MEN. (From ca 1670; †by 1850.)

***low in the lay.** Almost, or quite, penniless: c.: 1830, Lytton; ob.

***low men.** False dice so loaded as to show low numbers: late C.16–19: prob. orig. c., but by 1700 prob. S.E. Nashe, Florio. Also LOW FULHAMS, and *low-runners* (C.17–18), the latter being almost certainly c.

***low pad.** A footpad: c. of mid-C.17–mid-19. Contrast HIGH PAD, and see also PAD, n. and v.

low runners, see LOW MEN.

low tide or **water, be at, in.** To be in difficulties, rarely other than monetary: coll: resp. late C.17–early 19, late C.18–20. Dickens, 'I'm at low-water mark, only one bob and a magpie.' Nautical in origin: stranded by ebbing tide.

***low toby** and **low-toby man,** see TOBY.

lowance. A coll form of *allowance*: esp. nautical: mid-C.19–20. cf. LOWNCE.

lowdah. 'A native pilot in Eastern waters': nautical coll verging on j.: late C.19–20. Bowen. ?ex Hindustani.

lower. To drink (a glassful, etc.); low coll: C.19–20.

lower regions. Hell: from ca 1870: coll.

***lowing(-)cheat** or **(-)chete.** A cow: c.: ca 1560–1750. See CHEAT.

***lowing-lay** or **-rig.** The stealing of cattle, esp. cows: c. of ca 1810–60. See LAY (2) and RIG.

lowlands, the. The female pudend: low: late C.18–mid-19.

lownce or **lounce.** A ration of food: naval coll: late C.19–20. i.e. *(al)lowance*. 2. See LOUNCE.

***lowr, lowre,** see LOUR.

lowze (occ. written *lowse*). A whistle

indicating the end of a shift; knocking-off time: North Country miners': late C.19–20. Ex *loose?*

lozenge. A rifle bullet: military: John L. Gardner, *The Military Sketch-Book* (II, 17), 1831.

£.s.d., see at L.

lubber. A sailor: s.: Ned Ward, 1703.

lubber's(-)hole; until ca 1830, occ. **lubber-hole.** An opening in the maintop, preferred by tyros and timids to the shrouds: from ca 1770; ob. by 1910: nautical s. >, ca 1840, coll >, ca 1880, S.E. Captain Cook; Wolcot; D. Jerrold, 'Go up through the futtock-shrouds like a man – don't creep through lubber's-hole.' **2.** Hence, any cowardly evasion of duty: nautical (1860); ob.

lubra. A woman: low pejorative coll: late C.19–20 rural Australian. Ex the S.E. sense, on Aborigine woman, recorded first in 1834. Much less gen. then GIN.

lubricate. (Of the male) to copulate with: raffish London; C.18–early 19. It occurs in, e.g., Boswell's *London Journey.* 2. To ply (someone) with drink; v.i. to drink: since ca 1880.

luck; good luck. A treading in (esp. human) dung; a beraying: C.18–early 19. See LUCK, SHITTEN.

luck, down on (occ. **in**) **one's.** Unlucky; impoverished: from ca 1848: s. Thackeray, 'When Mrs C. was particularly down on her luck, she gave concerts and lessons in music.'

luck, fisherman's. The being wet, hungry, and 'fishless': coll: from ca 1855.

luck, greasy. A full cargo of oil: whalers': from ca 1830.

luck, shitten. Good luck: ca 1670–1830. Ex the proverb, 'shitten luck is good luck.' Ray, Grose. cf. the belief that a bird's droppings falling on a person confer good luck on him. cf. MUCK FOR LUCK!

luck!, worse. More's the pity!: coll: 1861, Miss Yonge.

luck to (e.g. him, it)!, bad or **good.** A c.p., pejorative or approbatory (occ. ironically or jocularly congratulatory): coll: C.19–20.

***lucky.** Plunder: c.: from ca 1850; mostly U.S.; ob.

lucky, adj. (Of persons) handy: C.18 coll.

lucky, cut (occ. **make**) **one's.** To decamp: low London: from ca 1820; slightly ob. M. C. Dowling, 1834, 'You'd better cut your lucky.'

lucky!, strike me. A mild asseveration ('agreed!'; SURE!): coll (—1887).

lucky, touch. To experience good luck: coll: late C.19–20.

lucky bag. The female pudend: mid-C. 19–20; ob.: low. Punning the S.E. term.

***lucky bone.** The small bone of a sheep's head, this being considered a charm: c. (—1883). Sala, *Illustrated London News,* 10 Nov. 1883.

lucky man, the. The bridegroom: coll: late C.19–20. Used by women, not by men.

lucky piece. An illegitimate son (occ. daughter) by a well-to-do father, generous enough to set up the mother in comfort: lower classes' (esp. rural): late C.19–20. Lit., a lucky coin.

lud! A trivial ejaculation: coll: ca 1720–1850. Ex LORD! 2. In address to a judge (*my Lud* or even *m'Lud*): a form so minced as to be coll or, at the least, near-coll. ?recorded in law before 1898, Besant, ' "My Lud," said Mr Caterham, "my case is completed." ' In the House of Lords, the clerks used *my Lud* as early as 1830.

Ludgate, take. To go bankrupt: coll, mostly commercial: 1585, Higgins; †by 1700. Ludgate Prison was mainly for bankrupts and debtors.

Ludgate bird. A person imprisoned for debt; a bankrupt: C.17. John Clarke, 1639.

Ludlam's dog, see LAZY AS LUDLAM'S ... DOG.

***Lud's bulwark.** Ludgate Prison: c.: ca 1690–1830. cf. LUDGATE, TAKE.

luff. Speech, talk: low: ca 1820–60. Egan, 1821, 'Hold your luff.' 2. A lieutenant: naval: from ca 1800; ob. Ex the gen. pronunciation (*le'f-tenant*). cf. the now more gen. LOOT, 2. (Rare except as *first l., second l.*)

luff, spring one's. To display agility in climbing: jocular nautical coll (ex the S.E. sense). The term (slightly ob.) app. arose in the 1860s.

luffed in for, be. 'To be put in the way of something either pleasant or unpleasant. "We got luffed in for paint ship," ' Granville: naval: late C.19–20. Ex the S.E. senses – as, e.g., in *luff the helm.*

lufftackle. A lieutenant (?of marines): naval lowerdeck: late C.18–mid-19. John Davis, *The Post-Captain,* 1806; W. N. Glascock, *Sailors and Saints* (I, 16), 1829. Moe. A lowerdeck pun.

lug. An ear: standard in Scots; in late C.16–20 English, s. – mainly jocular. Lyly, 'Your clumsy lugs'; Moncrieff, 'He napp'd it under the lugs, too.' **2.** See LUGS. 3. A pawn-shop: see LUG, IN.

lug, v. To pull violently, carry with effort, there being the implication of ponderousness in the object: without that implication, S.E.; with it, coll of mid-C.17–20.

lug, in. In pawn: low (?orig. c.): from ca 1840. Ex:

***lug-chovey.** A pawnbrokers' shop: c.: from ca 1830.

lugow. To fasten, place, put: Anglo-Indian coll: from 1830s. Ex Hindustani *lagana.*

lugs. Affected manners, AIRS, SWANK. Hence, *put on (the) lugs*, put on style, be conceited. Both low coll from ca 1890. 2. See LUG, n., 1.

lugs!, if worth his. (Sc. *he would . . .*) If worth his while! Scots coll: C.14–20. Ex LUG, n., 1.

***luke.** Nothing: c. of ca 1820–70. D. Haggart, 1821. Problematically ex dial. *luke*, a leaf (hence a trifle) or, more prob., Northern dial. *luke*, a look (?not worth a look); H., 1864, describes it as North Country cant; also, note the earliest record.

lullaby. The male member: low: mid-C.19–20. (?ob.)

***lullaby-cheat.** A baby: c. of ca 1670–1840. Head, Ainsworth. See CHEAT.

***lully** (occ. LALLY). Wet or drying linen: c. of ca 1780–1870. 2. Hence, a shirt: low: from ca 1860.

***lully-prigger, -prigging.** A stealer, stealing, of linen, esp. hanging on the fence or line: c. of ca 1780–1880.

***lumb.** Too much: c. of ca 1720–1800. ?a perversion of *lump.*

***lumber.** A room: c. of ca 1780–1830. Ex the Lombard Room (for the storing of valuables). 2. A prison, only in LUMBER, BE IN.

***lumber,** v. To pawn: somewhat low (?orig. c.): from ca 1810; ob. Ex S.E. *put to lumber*, hence ultimately ex *Lombard.* (Pepys in 1668 uses *Lumber Street* for *Lombard Street.*) 2. To arrest, imprison: c. of ca 1810–90; rare except, and extant only in, the passive (see LUMBERED).

***lumber, be in.** To be in detention; in prison: C.19–20 c.; ob. cf. LUMBERED; LOMBARD STREET; LIMBO.

lumber, live, see LIVE LUMBER.

***lumber-house.** A house for the storage of stolen property: c. (—1811). *Ally Sloper's Half-Holiday*, 4 May 1889. Ex S.E. *l.-house*, a pawnbroker's.

lumbered, ppl adj. Pawned: from ca 1810; ob.: low (?orig. c.). 2. Arrested; in prison: c. (—1812). cf. LIMBERED.

lumberer. A tramp, a vagrant: ca 1760–1820: perhaps orig. c.; certainly low. 2. A swindling tipster: low: from ca 1887. 3. Hence (?), a lying adventurer: Society: ca 1890–1914. 4. A pawnbroker: C.19–20, ob.: S.E. till ca 1880, then (mostly U.S.) c.

lumme!, lummy! Esp. as *Lord l.!* A low coll exclamation: C.19–20. Ex *love me.*

lummy. See LUMME! 2. First-rate: low: 1838, Dickens in *Oliver Twist*; Milliken, 1892, ''Ardly know which is lummiest.' Prob. ex dial.: cf. the N. Yorkshire *lummy lick*, a delicious mouthful.

lump. (Also in pl.) A great quantity; adv. (*a lump*), a lot, greatly : s. (in C.20, perhaps rather coll) and dial.: *a lump* from ca 1710, *lumps* from ca 1520. Skelton; Leigh Hunt; Farmer, 'I like that a lump.' 2. (Gen. *the lump.*) The workhouse: vagrants' c.: from ca 1870. Also *Lump Hotel.* cf. PAN, n., 3, and SPINNIKEN. 3. Short for LUMP OF LEAD: late C.19–20.

lump, v. To thrash; ca 1780–1840; then dial. 2. To punch, strike: low: ca 1780–1830. Like preceding sense, ex the S.E. meaning, to thresh. 3. To dislike, be displeased at: coll: orig. (1833), U.S.; anglicized ca 1860. Dickens, 1864, 'If you don't like it, it's open to you to lump it.' i.e. swallow it whole, however distasteful.

Lump Hotel, see LUMP, n., 2.

lump and bump. A fool; a simpleton: rhyming s. (on CHUMP): late C.19–20.

lump into. To do (a job) with vigour: Cockneys': late C.19–20. Esp. as adjuration, *lump into it!*

lump of, a. A large quantity; much: Australian coll: late C.19–20.

lump of coke. A man, chap, fellow: s. rhyming on BLOKE (—1859).

lump of ice. Advice: rhyming s. (—1909).

lump o(f) jaw on(, have a). (To be) talkative: low (—1909).

lump of lead. The head: rhyming s. (—1857). cf. POUND OF LEAD.

lump of school. A, rarely to, fool: rhyming s. (—1909).

***lump o(f) stone.** A county jail: c. (—1909). cf. STONE-DOUBLET.

***lump the lighter.** To be transported: c. of ca 1780–1875. Perhaps *lump* here = strike, hit (as in *hit the track*), i.e. unpleasantly or forcibly meet with.

lumper. A riverside thief: ca 1780–1840: c. G. Parker. 2. A contractor for loading and unloading ships: from ca 1780, ob.: s.

>, ca 1870, coll. Grose, 1785; Mayhew. 3. Such a fraudulent seller of clothes-material as makes the worse seem the better cause, e.g. the old new, the flimsy solid: c.: ca 1850–1910. Mayhew. cf. the somewhat different DUFFER. 4. A potato: from ca 1840: Anglo-Irish coll.

lumping. Great; heavy: bulky; awkward, ungainly: coll and dial.: 1678, 'lumping bargains'; 1887, 'a lumping yokel'. Stigmatized by Johnson as 'low'.

lumping pennyworth. A (great) bargain: coll: ca 1700–1860; then dial. Arbuthnot. Hence:

lumping pennyworth, get or **have got a.** To marry a fat woman: coll verging on c.p.: C.18–early 19.

lumps, see LUMP, n.

lumps out of, knock. To command much applause: theatrical: ca 1884–1910. Coun, *Nutts about the Stage*, 1885.

lumpshi(o)us. Delicious: low coll (orig., prob. s.): 1844, Buckstone; ob. ?by SCRUMPTIOUS out of LOVELY. cf. LUPTIOUS.

lumpy, pregnant, is low coll verging on S.E. 2. Tipsy: from ca 1810; ob. by 1910. *Punch*, 1845. 3. Costly: booksellers': ca 1890–1915.

lumpy roar. A grandee, or a 'swell of the first water': low London: 1855–ca 1860. Ware says that it may represent *l'Empereur* Napoleon III, 'who became popular in 1855 by his visit to England . . . and [by] his encouragement of English trade'.

lun. A harlequin: late C.18–early 19: theatrical. By 'collision'. 2. A clown: C.19, mainly U.S. and theatrical. ?a contraction of *harlequin* or, more prob., ex Shakespearean *lunes*, mad freaks, as in *Winter's Tale*, II, ii, 30.

***lunan.** A girl: vagrants' c.: from ca 1835. Ex Romany *loobni* (cf. Sampson at *lubni*), a harlot.

lunar, take a. To glance, look, keenly; properly, upwards: late C.19–20. Ex *take a lunar observation.*

lunch. Luncheon: 1829 (S.O.D.): coll. Abbr. *luncheon.* For *lunch(eon)* and its synonymy, see 'The Art of Lightening Work' in *Words!*

lunch. To provide lunch for: coll: 1892.

luncheon reservoir. The stomach: low jocular: from ca 1860; ob. cf. BREAD-BASKET and VICTUALLING DEPARTMENT. cf.:

lung-box. The mouth: low: from ca 1850. cf. POTATO-JAW.

lunger. A person diseased or wounded in the lungs: coll: 1893. Kipling.

lungs. 'A large and strong-voiced man', Johnson: coll: ca 1680–1740. 2. An underworkman in the 'chymical art', Johnson: ca 1610–1750: coll >, ca 1700, S.E. Jonson, 'That is his firedrake, his lungs, his zephyrus, he that puffs his coals.'

Lunnon. London: (dial. and) low coll: C.18–20.

luny, see LOONY.

luptious. Lovely; delicious: late C.19–20; ob. Ex *voluptuous* + *delicious.* cf. LUMPSHIOUS and SCRUMPTIOUS. (This type of 'made' words was common in the Victorian period; the vogue has waned.)

luracham, see LERACAM.

lurcher, a rogue, is S.E., but *lurcher* or *lurcher of the law*, 'a bum bailiff, or his setter' (Grose, 1st ed.), is s. of ca 1780–1840. Ex dial.: *lurch*, to slink about.

***lure.** 'An idle pamphlet', B.E.: c. of ca 1690–1780, when it > LEER.

***lurk** 'is mostly applied to the several modes of plundering by representations of sham distress', Mayhew: c.: from ca 1850; ob. Prob. ex the v. cf. LAW; LAY, 2; RACKET; RIG, 2; SLUM; BEREAVEMENT LURK; DEAD LURK; LURKER. 2. In Australian low s. verging on c., it = 'a plan of action; a regular occupation', C. J. Dennis: late C.19–20. 3. In app. temporary c. of ca 1840–60, it = an eye or eyesight. '*No. 747*', with valid reference to the year 1845. Ex Shelta. 4. An occasional customer: grafters': late C.19–20.

***lurk,** v. To beg with faked letters: c.: from ca 1850; ob. Mayhew. Perhaps a corruption of dial. *lurch*, to slink about: cf. LURCHER. 2. *be lurked.* 'To be ordered to do some unpleasant job without a chance of avoiding it': nautical: mid-C.19–20. Bowen. cf. (?ex) the †S.E. *lurk*, to shirk work.

***lurk, go on** or **upon a.** To get money by a LURK: c.: from ca 1850; ob.

***lurker.** A none too honest Jack of all trades: c.: from ca 1860; ob. 2. A begging impostor equipped with sham documents, false letters, faked seals and crests and signatures, etc.: c.: from ca 1850; ob., except as a professional teller of the piteous tale. See esp. Mayhew's *London Labour*, I, 233, and 'Stuart Wood', *Shades of the Prison House*, pp. 78–9. Also *lurksman.*

***lurking,** n. and adj. Fraudulent begging; being a LURKER (sense 2): c.: both from ca 1850 and both in Mayhew's *London Labour*, vol. I.

lurkman. A petty criminal: Australian: since ca 1870.

***lurksman,** see LURKER, 2.

***lurries.** The more gen. form of:

***lurry.** (Gen. in pl.) Money: c. of ca 1670–1830. R. Head in *The Canting Academy*. In the pl, the sense is rather 'all manner of cloaths', Coles, 1676, or 'Money, Watches, Rings, or other Moveables', B.E. Prob. a corruption of LOUR, *lowre*, influenced perhaps by dial. *lurry*, to pull, drag.

lush. Drink, i.e. strong drink: from ca 1790; ob. ?orig. c.; certainly low. Lytton, '"Bring the lush and the pipes, old bloke!" cried Ned ...; "we are never at a loss for company."' 2. A drink: low (—1892); ob. Hume Nisbet. 3. A drinking-bout: from ca 1840; ob.: low. Colonel Hawker's *Diary*; *Licensed Victuallers' Gazette*, 16 Jan. 1891. 4. A drunkard: low: from ca 1890; ob. Abbr. LUSHINGTON. These four senses are either ex S.E. *lush*, adj. (cf. the adj., below), as the O.E.D. proposes, or ex *Lushington*, a well-known London brewer, as F. & H. claims, or ex *the City of Lushington*, or, as W. suggests, ex Shelta *lush*, to eat and drink. 5. A dainty: Eton College: C.19. Either ex *lush*, as above, or ex *lush*, S.E. adj.

lush, v. To drink, v.i.: from ca 1810; ob.: low. *Lex. Bal.* Also *lush it*: from ca 1830; ob. cf. BOOZE; BUB; LIQUOR; SOAK; WET. 2. To drink, v.t.: low: perhaps from ca 1810 (see *Lex. Bal.*); certainly from 1830, when used by Lytton in *Paul Clifford*, 'I had been lushing heavy wet'; Dickens, 1838, 'Some of the richest sort you ever lushed.' 3. To treat, ply with drink: low: from ca 1820; ob. Haggart, 'We had lushed the coachman so neatly, that Barney was obliged to drive.' Ex the n., first three senses. For an excellent synonymy of all three senses, see F. & H. at *lush*, v.

lush, adj. Tipsy: low: from ca 1811; ob. Vaux. Also *lush(e)y*, from ca 1810. *Lex. Bal.*, 'The rolling kiddeys ... got bloody lushy.' Either ex S.E. adj. *lush* or ex the n., above. 2. Dainty: Eton: from ca 1860; ob.

lush at Freeman's Quay. To drink at another's expense. See FREEMAN'S QUAY and HARRY FREEMAN'S.

***lush cove.** A drunkard: c. (—1839).

***lush-crib.** A low public-house; a gin-shop: c.: from ca 1810; ob. cf. LUSH-KEN. Ex LUSH, n., 1. cf. BOOZER, 2; DRUM; PANN(E)Y; PUB; TOM AND JERRY *shop*, and see CRIB, n., 3.

***lush-house.** The same: c. or low (—1896); ob.

lush it, see LUSH, v., 1.

***lush-ken.** A low public-house or ale-house; a gin-shop: c.: from ca 1790; ob. Ex LUSH, n., 1. cf. LUSH-CRIB and LUSHING-KEN.

lush-out. A drinking-bout: low (—1823).

***lush-panny.** Same (—1896) as LUSH-KEN: c. or low; ob. See PANN(E)Y; cf.:

lushery. A low public-house: low (—1896).

lushey, see LUSH, adj., 1.

lushing. The vbl n. of LUSH, v., all senses. cf.:

lushing, adj. Given to drink: low: mid-C. 19–20; ob. Mayhew, 1861, speaks of a harlot nicknamed Lushing Loo.

***lushing-ken.** A low public-house, a drinking bar: c.: from ca 1880. L. Wingfield, 1883, 'Unable ... to steer clear of lushing-kens'.

***lushing-man.** A drunkard: c. of ca 1850–1910, mostly U.S. Ex LUSH, v.

lushing-muzzle. A punch on the mouth: boxing and nautical: ca 1820–1900. See LUSHING and MUZZLE, v.

lushington or **Lushington.** A drunkard: rather low: from ca 1840; ob. *The Comic Almanack*, 1840; Mayhew; 'Rolf Boldrewood', 1890, 'The best eddicated chaps are the worst lushingtons when they give way at all.' cf. BOOZER; GIN-CRAWL; POT-WALLOPER; SOAK. Either ex LUSH, n., 1, and punning the surname *Lushington*, or ex *Lushington the brewer*, or else ex *the City of Lushington*, a convivial society that, flourishing ca 1750–1895, had a 'Lord Mayor' and four 'aldermen': cf. the next three phrases.

Lushington, deal with. To take too much drink: ca 1820–90. cf.:

Lushington is concerned, Alderman. Applied to one who is drunk: low: ca 1810–1900. Vaux, where also *he has been voting for the Alderman.* cf.:

Lushington is his master. He is apt to drink too much: ca 1825–90.

lushy, see LUSH, adj., 1.

lushy cove. A drunkard: c. (ob.): from ca 1810. Vaux; Mayhew. Also *lush cove.*

lux. An excellent or splendid thing: Christ's Hospital: from ca 1840; ob. Prob. ex *luxuriant*, says Blanch, the Hospital's annalist. cf.:

luxer. A handsome fellow: Winchester College: ca 1850–1915. Either ex *luxury*, as Adams suggests, or ex L. *lux*, a light.

lyb-beg, lybbege, see LIB-BEG.

Lyceum, the, see ACADEMY, THE.

Lydford law. To hang first and try afterwards; hence, any arbitrary procedure in judgement: late C.14–20 (ob. by 1870, except in dial.): coll >, by 1700, S.E. Langland, T. Fuller, 'Molière' Ozell, Kingsley. Ex Lydford, 'now a small village on the confines of Dartmoor . . . formerly the chief town of the stannaries', O.E.D. cf. JEDBURGH JUSTICE.

lyesken chirps. Fortune-telling; telling a fortune: Shelta: C.18–20.

lying down, take it, see LIE DOWN.

lylo! Come here!: Anglo-Chinese (—1864).

***lymitting law,** see LIMITING LAW.

***lyp.** To lie down: c. of ca 1560–1700. (cf. LIB, the gen. form.) Whence:

***lyp-ken, lypken,** see LIB-KEN and cf. LIBBEN and LOBKIN.

M

'm. Abbr. MA'AM: low coll: C.18–20. Pronounced as brief and indistinct *um* or *em*.

m.b. coat and/or **waistcoat.** A long coat and/or a cassock waistcoat worn by some clergymen: clerical: from ca 1840, but not recorded till 1853, in Dean Conybeare; ob. Ex '**m**ark of the **b**east' in reference to Popery.

m.d. or **M.D.** A physician; a person holding the degree of Doctor of Medicine: coll when spoken, i.e. pronounced *em dee*: mid-C.18–20. 2. Money down: political coll (in reference to electioneering bribery): 1857.

m.p. A policeman: from ca 1860. ?ex '**m**ounted **p**oliceman'.

m.t. An empty truck, van, or gen., carriage: railway: from ca 1860. By pun on *empty*. cf. MOLL THOMPSON'S MARK. 2. An empty bottle: from ca 1858; ob. More usual in U.S. than in the British Empire. cf. DEAD MARINE.

M (occ. **by** but gen.) **under the girdle, carry** or **have an.** To be courteous of address: coll: ca 1550–1850; extant in dial. as *keep 'Master' out of sight*, to be lacking in respect. Udall, 'Ne'er an M by your girdle?'; Haughton in a late C.16 play, 'Hark ye . . . methinks you might do well to have an M under your girdle'; Swift. Ex 'master' and 'mistress'.

ma. Abbr. *mamma*: from ca 1820 (?orig. dial.): coll >, ca 1890, low coll. cf. PA. 2. At certain Public Schools, *ma* and *mi* indicate (Smith) *major* and (Smith) *minor*: mid-C.19–20. These terms are rather coll than s. 3. One's wife: lower middle-class form of address: mid-C.19–20.

ma'am. A coll contraction of *madam*: 1668, Dryden. Very gen. in C.18–mid-19 in Society, and still etiquette in addressing a queen or a royal princess; since ca 1850, chiefly parenthetical or terminal. 'Also written as vulgar *marm, mem, mim, mum, -m*', S.O.D.

ma'amselle. A coll abbr. of *mademoiselle*: late C.18–20. Fr. *ma'm'selle*.

mab. A cabriolet: ca 1820–95. Moncrieff; Baumann. A personifying perversion of *cab-*.

mab, gen. **mab up.** To dress carelessly: late C.17–early 19: coll verging on S.E. Ray (*mab*), B.E. (*mab up*). Gen. in ppl S.E. form *mabbed up*. Ex *mab*, a slattern.

mac, occ. **mack.** Abbr. MACKEREL, a pimp: 1887, Henley: low s. 2. (Only as **mac.**) A coll abbr. of *macadam*: 1851, Mayhew; slightly ob. 3. A rare spelling of MACK, 2.

macaroni, occ. **maccaroni,** a dandy (1760–75), is S.E., as is the adj. 2. A merry fool, esp. if an Italian: coll: C.18. Addison, 1711, *Spectator*, No. 47. 3. An Italian: somewhat low: C.19–20. Ex the national dish, as is the preceding sense. 4. A pony: rhyming s. (—1857).

macaroni-stake. A race ridden by a gentleman rider: ca 1820–30. Prob. ex MACARONI, 1.

maccacco, see MURKARKER. **maccaroni,** see MACARONI.

***mace.** 'A rogue assuming the character of a gentleman or opulent tradesman, who under that appearance defrauds workmen, by borrowing a watch, or other piece of goods, till one [that] he bespeaks is done' (i.e. swindled), 1785, Grose: c. of ca 1780–1850. Parker, 1781. 2. Any dressy swindler of tradesmen: from ca 1850; ob. 3. Swindling; fraudulent robbery: c.: from ca 1800. 4. A sham loan-office: c. (—1879); ob. Presumably ex *mace*, a club, a metal-headed staff.

***mace,** v.t., occ. v.i. To swindle, defraud, whether gen. or in sense of the n., 1.: from ca 1790, when recorded by Potter; 1821, Egan, in *Life in London*: c. Ex the n., 1. 2. To WELSH: c. (—1874).

***mace, get stuff on the;** often as vbl n., **getting . . .** To obtain goods by false pretences: c.: late C.19–20.

***mace, give it him** (a tradesman) **on** or **upon the.** To obtain goods on credit and never pay for them: c. (—1812); ob. cf. MACE, STRIKE THE.

***mace, man at the.** An operator of a sham loan-office: c. (—1879); ob.

***mace, on (the).** On credit: c. (—1893). P. H. Emerson, in *Signor Lippo*. 2. (Only *on the mace*.) On the MACE racket: c.: C.19–20. Vaux, 1812; W. T. Moncrieff, 1830, 'He's been working on the mace.' cf. MACER; MACING.

***mace, strike the.** The v.i. form of MACE,

v.; esp. as a variant of MACE, GIVE IT ON THE: c.: from ca 1810.

***mace-cove, -gloak, -man** (and MACER). A swindler: c.: resp. from ca 1810 (e.g. in *Lex. Bal.*); 1812, Vaux, †; from ca 1780, and often spelt *maceman.* 2. The third is also, from ca 1870, a WELSHER, and, ca 1880–1900, a SWELL-MOBSMAN. Ex MACE, n.

***mace the rattler.** To travel in a train without paying: c.: from ca 1880.

***macer.** A swindler, whether gen. (from ca 1819) or, ca 1820–50, as an exponent of MACE, n., 1: c. Ex the v. 2. A WELSHER: c. (—1874).

***MacGorrey's Hotel.** Chelmsford Gaol: c.: C.19. Ex a governor so named.

machine. The male member, the female pudend: low coll: C.19–20; ob. Prob. ex Fr. *machine*, the male member. (cf. THING and Fr. *machin.*) 2. A FRENCH LETTER: low coll: ca 1790–1860.

***macing.** See MACE, v. 2. 'Severe, but regulated, thrashing by fists': non-aristocratic: mid C.19–early 20. Ex *Jem Mace*, a notable English pugilist.

***macing-cove.** A variant of MACE-COVE. Mayhew, 1861.

mack. See MAC, 1. 2. A coll abbr. of *mac(k)intosh*: late C.19–20. 3. A Celtic Irishman: derisive coll: ca 1615–1700.

mack!, by (the); occ. simply **mack!** A trivial, coll asseveration: ca 1560–1670. Anon., *Misogonus*; Cotton. Ex *by the Mass* prob. influenced by *by Mary*.

Mackay, the real. The real thing, *the* GOODS: coll: from well before 1900: orig. Scottish.

macked steamer. Nautical, thus: 'In the middle 19th century, . . . a shoddily built . . . steamer' (Bowen): nautical. i.e., a 'made' steamer in Northern dial.

mackerel, a pimp, is S.E., despite F. & H.'s inclusion and despite B.E.'s classification as c. 2. adj., smeared; blurred: printers': from ca 1730; ob. A corruption of *mackled*, ex S.E. *mackle.*

mackerel-back. 'A very tall, lank Person', B.E.: late C.17–18. Hence *mackerel-back(ed)*, long-backed: late C.18–early 19.

Macready pauses! A theatrical c.p. applied to an actor who pauses too long: since ca 1885. Wm Macready (1793–1873) had a habit of pausing inordinately in any emphatic or dramatic speech.

mad, adj. (Construction: *mad at*, with a person; *mad about*, about a thing or person.) Angry, vexed: C.14–20: S.E. till C.19, then coll and mostly U.S. Nat Gould, 1891, 'My eye! won't he be just mad.' 2. (Of a compass-needle) with its polarity disturbed: nautical coll: late C.19–20. Suggested by *erratic.*

mad, like, see the entry at LIKE A . . .

mad!, – you are of so many minds, you'll never be. A semi-proverbial c.p. of ca 1670–1750.

mad as a buck. Very angry; crazy: late C.16–17: proverbial coll. Shakespeare, 'It would make a man mad as a buck to be so bought and sold.' cf. dial. *mad as a tup* (ram).

mad as a cut snake. Very mad; exceedingly angry: Australian: from ca 1890. Here, *cut* = castrated.

mad as a hatter, see HATTER, and cf. MAD AS A WEAVER.

mad as a March hare. (In late C.14–15, e.g. in Chaucer, *March* is omitted.) Eccentric; mad: proverbial coll: from ca 1500. Skelton, 'Thou mad March hare'. Ex sexual excitement. cf.:

mad as a weaver. Very angry; crazy: proverbial coll: C.17.

mad as May-butter. Exceedingly eccentric; mad; excited: C.17: proverbial coll. Fletcher, 1626. Ex difficulty of making butter in May.

***mad dog.** Strong ale: c.: ca 1580–1620. Harrison's *England.*

Mad Greek. A heavy drinker: s. (—1650).

mad nurse. 'A nurse attending on insane patients' (O.E.D.): coll: mid-C.18–20; ob. (*The World*, 1753.)

mad on, have a. To be in an ugly mood: Canadian coll: from ca 1870. i.e. a mad fit. Ex *mad*, a fit of anger: same period and status.

***mad Tom.** A rogue who counterfeits madness: C.17–18 c. See also TOM O' BEDLAM.

mad up, get one's. To become very angry: from ca 1880; mostly U.S. ex (—1847) Eng. dial.

mad woman. An empty coach: coaching: ca 1800–70.

madam. A pocket handkerchief: c. (—1879); ob. Perhaps because a mark of at least outward respectability. 2. As *proper madam*, it = a girl with a bad temper; a *proper little madam*, a girl child with one: lower-middle and lower classes': C.19–20.

madam-sahib, see MEM-SAHIB.

***Madam Van.** A whore: late C.17–early 19 c.

madame, the. The owner or the manageress of a brothel: mid-C.19–20. So often she is French . . .

Madame Bishop. A drink (port, sugar, nutmeg): Australian: from ca 1880. Ex a formerly well-known hotel-keeper.

maddy. A large mussel: nautical coll: C.19–20. Ex ob. (?†) Scots *moddy*, the same.

made, see MAKE, v.

made beer. College SWIPES bottled with rice, nutmeg, etc., to recondition it: Winchester College coll: ca 1840–90. Mansfield.

made in Germany. Bad, valueless: late C.19–20: coll.

made to walk up Ladder Lane and down Hemp Street. Hanged at the yard-arm: nautical: C.19. By 'allusive topography': cf. GUTTER-LANE.

madge, occ. **madge howlet.** The female pudenda: low: from ca 1780; ob. 2. A woman: Scots coll: C.19. Jamieson. 3. See MAG, n., 8.

***madge-cove** or **-cull.** A sodomite: resp. ca 1820–60 (Bee) and c. of ca 1780–1850 (Grose, 1st ed.).

madza. Half. Hence *madza caroon*, half a crown; *madza saltee*, a halfpenny; *madza poona*, half a sovereign; also *madza-beargered*, half drunk, and *madza round the bull*, half a pound of steak. Parlary: from ca 1850. Ex It. *mezzo*, a half, via Lingua Franca, and gen. pronounced *medzer*.

maffick, to rejoice wildly as a crowd, orig. s., rapidly > coll and, by 1902, S.E. Ex the rejoicing at the relief of *Mafeking* (South Africa) on 17 May 1900.

mag. Talk; chatter: coll: 1778, Mme D'Arblay, 'If you have any mag in you, we'll draw it out'; slightly ob. Ex *magpie*. 2. A chatterer: coll: from ca 1890. 3. A magazine: coll: C.19–20. Wolcot, 'Hawkesbury . . . who wrote in mags for hire.' 4. A halfpenny: c.: 1781, G. Parker. Ex MAKE, a halfpenny influenced by MEG, a guinea. cf. MAGPIE, 3. 'Ducange Anglicus' defines it as a penny (1857). 5. A magpie: C.19–20 coll verging on S.E. 6. A MAGPIE (5): shooting: 1895. 7. A face: low: 1899, Clarence Rook. Perhaps ex the v., 1. 8. (Pron. *madge*). A magistrate; policemen's: from ca 1870.

mag, v.i. To talk (noisily), chatter; to scold: coll: 1810. Ex the n., 1. 2. To steal: Scots c.: from ca 1815; ob. Scott.

***mag, on the.** On the look-out for victims: c. of ca 1845–60. '*No. 747*'. Perhaps, via MAG, n., 5, a perversion of *on the* MAKE.

***mag-flyer; mag-flying.** A player of, a game of, pitch and toss: c.: resp. 1882, 1883. Ex MAG, n., 4.

***mag-stake.** Money obtained by the confidence trick: c.: from ca 1838; ob. See MAGSMAN.

Magdalen marm. An unsatisfactory servant: Southwark coll: ca 1840–90. Ware, 'A servant from the Magdalen, a refuge for fallen women in the Blackfriars Road, which existed there until about the middle of the [19th] century. The women who went out as servants had been too often pampered there.'

magg. A variant of MAG, n., 4.

magged. Irritable, irritated; (of a rope) frayed: nautical: late C.19–20. cf. Bedfordshire *magged*, exhausted, itself prob. ex the very old dial. *maggle*, to tease, to exhaust, itself perhaps cognate with L. *mactare* (to afflict or punish), as Joseph Wright seems to imply.

Maggie Miller. That method of washing clothes which consists in towing them over the stern while the ship is under way: naval: late C.19–20. Granville, 'The origin, like that of most naval slang terms, is lost in obscurity': true; yet perhaps it is *Maggie* because that is a name common among washerwomen, and as for *Miller* – well, see ANDREW MILLAR. The Navy's washerwoman?

Maggie Rab or **Rob(b).** A bad halfpenny or wife: Scots coll: C.19–20.

Maggie wore the beads, where. *In the* NECK, i.e. disagreeably, disastrously: a c.p. from ca 1905. cf. *where the* CHICKEN GOT THE AXE.

magging. Talk(ing); chatter: 1814, Pegge. Ex MAG, v., 1.

maggot at the other, a fool at one end and a. A c.p. directed at an angler: late C.19–20.

maggot-boiler. A tallow-chandler: from ca 1786; ob.

magistrate. A herring: Scots: C.19–20, ob. cf. GLASGOW MAGISTRATE.

magnet. The female pudend: low coll: C.18–20; ob.

Magnificat, correct. To find fault unreasonably and presumptuously: mid-C.16–mid-18: coll till C,17, then S.E. Palsgrave, Nashe, L'Estrange. Ex the idea of changing the Church service.

Magnificat at matins, like or **sing.** (To do things) out of order: late C.16–17: coll soon > S.E. Bishop Andrewes, 1588; Urquhart, 1653.

magnificent. In pl 'a state of dignified resentment': 1836, Marryat, 'Jack walked his first watch in the magnificents.'

magnify. To signify: from ca 1710; after ca 1870, dial. Steele, 'This magnified but little with my Father.'

magnolious. Large, splendid, magnificent: from ca 1870; almost †. Ex the splendour of the magnolia.

magpie. An Anglican bishop: C.18–20 coll. Ex the black and white vestments. 2. His vestments: coll: from ca 1880. 3. A halfpenny: c.: 1838, Dickens. An elaboration of MAG, n., 4. 4. A pie: low: C.19–20, ob. 5. 'A shot striking a target, divided into four sections, in the outermost but one', F. & H.: 1884, *The Times*, 23 July: military coll >, by 1900, j. Ex the black and white disk (cf. a magpie's colour) with which such a shot is signalled from the butts.

magpie's nest. The female pudend: low coll: C.18–20; ob.

mags. A gratuity expected by servants: Scots coll: from ca 1830; ob.

***magsman; occ. megsman.** A street swindler; a confidence trickster: 1838, *Town*, 27 Jan.; Mayhew; G. R. Sims. Ob. Ex MAG, n., talk. 2. In '*No. 747*', the reference being to 1845 – the sense was †by 1900 – he is a fashionably dressed swindler travelling in or awaiting trains.

mahcheen. A merchant: Anglo-Chinese (—1864). Ex Chinese pronunciation.

mahogany. A dining-table: coll: 1840, Dickens, 'You three gentlemen with your legs under the mahogany in my humble parlour.' Also MAHOGANY TREE. 2. A drink of two parts gin to one part treacle: from ca 1790: s. ex Cornish dial.; long † except in dial. Boswell. Ex the colour. 3. A strong mixture of brandy and water: from ca 1815; ob. 4. Salt beef: nautical; from ca 1840; ob. Ex its hardness.

mahogany, amputate one's. To run away: from ca 1850; very ob. cf. *cut one's stick* (s.v. CUT, v., 4).

mahogany, have one's feet under another man's. To live on another: coll: from ca 1845; ob. cf. MAHOGANY TREE. Ex: 2. To dine with another person: 1840, Dickens (see MAHOGANY, 1).

mahogany-flat. A bug: ca 1860–1905. cf. HEAVY CAVALRY and NORFOLK HOWARD.

mahogany slosh. Cook-shop, or coffee-stall, tea: Cockneys': ca 1870–1914. Ex the colour and the taste.

Mahogany Top. Nickname for a red-headed man: ca 1860–1900.

mahogany tree. A dining-table: 1847, Thackeray: coll. cf. MAHOGANY, 1.

Mahometan gruel. Coffee: ca 1787–1900; coll. Because orig. coffee was drunk mostly by the Turks.

maid, kiss the. To be executed by the MAIDEN: C.17–18 coll.

maid, – neither wife, widow, nor, see MAIDEN-WIFE-WIDOW.

Maid Marian. A big woman: Leicester Square, London: ca 1882–90. Ex a giantess so named.

maidan (pronounced *mydahn*). A plain, an open space; parade-ground: Regular Army's, resp. coll and s.: late C.19–20. Ex Hindustani.

maiden. A decapitating machine: late C. 16–19: coll (mostly Scots) >, ca 1800, S.E. 2. A maiden speech: Parliamentary coll: late C.19–20. 3. Cloves; peppermint: Australian: from ca 1870.

maiden-wife-widow. The widow of a man 'that could never enjoy her maidenhead', Randle Holmes, 1688: coll: ca 1680–1800. 2. A whore: coll: ca 1670–1850. Ray, Fuller. Gen. *neither maid, wife, nor widow*.

maidenheads. Parentheses: Canadian printers': late C.19–20. cf. PARENTHESES.

maiden's water. Any weak drink, esp. of beer: since ca 1880. Whence, probably, MAID'S WATER.

maids adorning. The morning: rhyming s. (—1859).

maid's ring. The hymen: Cockney coll: C. 19–20.

maid's water. Any weak drink; esp. of tea: Australian: late C.19–20.

Maidstone jailor. A tailor: rhyming s. (—1857); ob.

maik. A frequent variant, in Scotland and Dublin (esp. among the Dublin newsboys), of MAKE, n., 1.

mail. To post (a letter): orig. (1828), U.S.: anglicized ca 1860 as coll.

***mail, get up the.** To find the money for a prisoner's defence: c.: from ca 1840; ob. Ex *mail*, payment: cf. *blackmail*.

maillhas or mailyas. Fingers: Shelta: C.18 –20. Whence MAULEY.

main. The main line: railwaymen's coll (—1887).

main, turn on the. To weep: 1837, Dickens; 'Cuthbert Bede', in *Verdant Green*, 'You've no idea how she turned on the main and did the briny.' cf. *turn on the* WATERWORKS, 2.

main avenue. The vagina: low: C.19–20; ob.

main-brace, splice the. To give out a double ration of grog, to celebrate some special event; hence, to drink: nautical: 1805 (O.E.D.). Perhaps ex the strengthening influence of good liquor (W.). Hence, (*with*) *main-brace well spliced*, thoroughly drunk.

main-sheet. Strong drink; esp. brandy: Jamaica: from ca 1880.

***main toby.** A main road: c. of ca 1800–90. See TOBY, n., 3.

Major McFluffer; Fluffy. A 'sudden lapse of memory, and use of words to call the attention of the inattentive prompter': theatrical (—1887). 2. **fluffy** is also an adj. See FLUFF, v., 3. Ware gives an anecdotal origin.

mak gauw! Be quick: South African coll: late C.19–20. Ex Dutch *maken*, to make, to do; *gauw*, quick. Pettman, who confines it to Dutch-speaking districts.

***make.** A halfpenny: c., from ca 1545; since ca 1860, only dial. and Scottish and Dubliners'. 2. A successful theft or swindle: c. (—1748); †by 1910.

make, v. To steal: late C.17–20: c. >, in C.20, low. cf. the exact synonym in Fr. c.: *faire*. 2. Hence, to appropriate: Winchester College: late C.18–20 (Wrench). Ex dial. 3. With ellipsis of infinitive: coll: not recorded before, but prob. at least ten years earlier than, 1888, *The Times*, 11 Aug., 'The enemy will not play the game according to the rules, and there are none to make him.' 4. To catch (a train, boat, etc.): from ca 1885. Ex the C.17–20 S.E. sense, orig. nautical, 'arrive at'.

***make, on the.** Intent on booty or profit: orig. (—1887), c. >, by 1900, s. Adopted from U.S.

make a kick. To raise an objection: proletarian: from ca 1860. cf. KICK, n., 7.

make a light. To see, look; to find: Australian 'pidgin' (—1859). Henry Kingsley.

make a mess of, see MESS.

make a row over the stones. (Of a ship) to pound heavily in the sea: nautical: late C.19–20; ob. Bowen.

make a straight arm. To offer a bribe: nautical: late C.19–20.

make a wry mouth. To be hanged: semi-proverbial coll: C.17. Cotgrave.

make all right. To promise to pay for vote: electioneering coll: mid-C.19–early 20.

make and mend. The naval half-holiday on Thursday, nominally for attending to one's clothes: naval: recorded in 1899.

make buttons, see BUTTONS, ONE'S ARSE MAKES.

make dead men chew tobacco, see TOBACCO, MAKE . . .

make down. To remake so as to fit a smaller wearer: coll: from ca 1890.

make 'em, as —— as they. A coll variant of *as —— as they* MAKE THEM, exceedingly, as —— as possible. Prob. mid-C.19–20.

make ends meet. To coït: low jocular: C.19–20; ob.

make hay. To cause confusion, disorder, trouble: coll (—1863); ob. H. Kingsley.

make horns. A †coll variant of *make* FACES.

make indentures, see INDENTURES, MAKE.

make it fly. To spend money very freely; go *on the* SPREE: coll: late C.19–20.

make it warm for. To punish, thrash: coll: from ca 1880. cf. *dust one's* JACKET.

make leg. To become prosperous: London lower classes' (—1909).

make mouths. To grin: jeer: coll: late C.16–20: S.E. >, ca 1880, coll (Shakespeare, *Hamlet*, IV, iv).

make one's coffin. To charge (a person) too highly for an article: tailors' (—1909).

make one's money. To make money 'on the side', e.g. by giving short change, purloining cigarette-cases: waiters': late C.19–20. Cf. MAKESURES.

make one's pile. To amass a fortune: orig. (1861), U.S.; anglicized ca 1875: coll.

make out. In *how do you make it out that . . .*, or *how do you make that out*, in what way do you come to believe that? Coll: 1887, Lewis Carroll.

make settlement in tail, see TAIL, MAKE SETTLEMENT IN.

make the chimney smoke. To cause the female to experience the orgasm: low: mid-C.19–20.

make them, as good, bad, etc., **as they.** As good, bad, etc., as may be: from ca 1870: coll. George Moore, in *Esther Waters*, 'You are as strong as they make 'em'; Grant Allen, 'As clever as they make them'.

make tracks. To depart hurriedly: orig. (1833), U.S.; anglicized ca 1860.

make up, v.i. **make up to,** v.t. To make love (to a person): coll: from ca 1820.

make up one's leg. To make money: costermongers' (—1909). cf. MAKE LEG.

make up one's mouth. To obtain one's living: low coll: from ca 1880; ob. cf. †S.E. sense, to finish a meal with something very delicious.

makes one (esp. you) shit through the eye of a needle, to which is often added **without splashing the sides.** A low, mostly Cockneys', c.p. applied to any substance that causes diarrhoea: late C.19–20.

makesures. Petty pilferings: potmen's: C.19–20; ob. cf. MAKE ONE'S MONEY.

makings. (Small) profits, earnings: coll: 1837, H. Martineau.

maknoon. Mad; silly: coll among troops in Egypt: late C.19–20. An Arabic word.

male-mules; callibisters. (Human) testicles: C.16–17. In Rabelais, *callistris* = the penis.

malkin. The female pudend: low Scots: from ca 1540; ob. cf. PUSS.

malkin-trash. A person dismally dressed: coll: late C.17–early 19.

mall. Credit (TICK, n., 2): metal trades' (—1909). Possibly ex *mall* (or *maul*), a heavy hammer.

mallet, on the. 'Having goods on trust', *Sinks*: low: ca 1825–80.

malleting bout. A bout with fisticuffs: low: ca 1820–50. On HAMMERING.

malley. A gardener: Anglo-Indian (—1864).

malt. To drink malt liquor: low coll: 1813, Colonel Hawker; 1835, Marryat, 'Well, for my part I malt.'

malt, shovel of. A pot of porter: London public-houses': ca 1820–60.

malt above the meal, water, wheat, – have the. To be tipsy: Scots coll: resp. C.19–20; from ca 1670; from ca 1540, ob. Heywood, 1546 (*wheat*); Ray (. . . *water*); Scott (. . . *meal*). (Apperson.)

malt-horse (or M. H.). A native of Bedford: C.17–20. 'Because of the high quality of malt produced from [Bedfordshire] barley', Hackwood; cf. Drayton's *Polyolbion*, XXIII (1622).

malt-pie. Liquor: jocular coll: C.17. Heywood the dramatist.

***maltooling.** The picking of pockets in omnibuses: c. (—1861); ob. Mayhew. Properly by a woman (*mal* = MOLL); and cf. TOOL, to drive.

maltoot, maltout. A sailor, esp. in address or as a nickname: 1785, Grose; †by 1880. (After that, MATLO(W).) Ex Fr. *matelot*, a sailor.

malty. Tipsy: from ca 1820; ob. cf. MALT.

malty cove. A beer-drinker: low London: ca 1825–80.

malum. To understand (gen. v.t.): Regular Army's: late C.19–20. Direct ex Hindustani.

mam. Mother: childish coll: C.16–20; ob. cf. MAMMY; DAD. 2. Also a variant abbr. of *madam*: coll: C.17–20. cf. MA'AM.

mammy. Mother: except perhaps when used by children, coll: from ca 1520. Skelton, 'Your mammy and your dady | Brought forth a godely babi!'

mamsell. Mademoiselle: coll: from ca 1840. Thackeray. 2. A French girl: coll: late C.19–20.

man. A husband, a lover: C.14–20: S.E. till ca 1850, then coll and dial. Esp. in *my* or *her man*. 2. The 'head' of a coin in tossing: coll: 1828, Bee. Contrast WOMAN. 3. In *the late* or *the present man*: the former, the present holder of a post, an office: coll: 1871, Beaconsfield. 4. As used in c., see -MANS.

man, v. To coït with a woman: low coll: C.19–20; ob.

man, dead. A supernumerary: coll: ca 1650–1800. Pepys.

man, get behind a. To endorse a bill: C.19–20, ob.: mostly commercial.

man, go out and see a. To have a drink: C.19–20. Ex the excuse.

man, – if my aunt had been an uncle, she'd have been a. A derisive c.p. (in C.19–20 occ. varied by the scabrous . . . *she'd have had a pair of balls under her arse*) applied to a ridiculous surmise: mid-C.17–20. Ray. cf. *if pigs had wings, what lovely birds they'd make.*

man, nine tailors make a, see NINTH . . .

man, old. A chief, a captain, an employer: coll: 1847, Howitt. 2. A father: coll: from ca 1850. 3. A husband: coll: from ca 1855. cf. OLD WOMAN. 4. A term of address: (?) mid-C.19–20: coll. 5. The penis: late C.19–20. 6. See also OLD BENDY.

man-a-hanging. A person in difficulties: coll: C.18–19.

man alive! A term of address, esp. in surprise or reproof: coll: ca 1829, J. B. Buckstone.

man among the geese when the gander is gone, he'll be a. He'll be important if nobody of importance is there; also a gen. c.p. derisive of a man's ability: C.18.

man before his mother, he'll be a, see MOTHER, HE'LL BE . . .

man-box. A coffin: ca 1820–70. 'Peter Corcoran' Reynolds in *The Fancy.*

man-chovey, see CHOVEY.

man-eater. A horse prone to biting (people): coll: 1879, Mrs A. E. James. 2. 'A particularly tough officer': (mostly Atlantic) sailing-ships': late C.19–20; virtually †. Bowen.

man for my money, the. The right person: coll: 1842, Lever.

man Friday. A factotum: C.19–20; ob.: coll verging on S.E.

man-hunters. Women, esp. spinsters and widows: jocular coll: late C.19–20.

man in blue. See BLUE, MEN IN. (Contrast S.E. *man in black*, a parson.)

man in the boat, the little, see LITTLE MAN . . .

man in the moon, as a dolt, is S.E. 2. 'A mythical personage who finds money, for electioneering, and for such electors as vote straight,' F. & H.: jocular coll, ob.: 1866, *John Bull*, 1 Sept.

man in the street. The average person: 1831, Greville: Newmarket s. >, ca 1840, coll >, ca 1890, S.E. cf. U.S. *man in the car* and see 'Representative Names' in *Words!*

man-killer. 'Porter, stout, cooper – the black beers' (Ware): teetotallers' (—1909). 2. 'A hard-working sailing ship in which accidents were frequent': nautical coll: ca 1850–1910. Bowen.

man(-)man. Gradually: little by little: pidgin: from ca 1860. Ex It. *mano mano* in same sense.

man of cash. A gambler in luck: London sporting: ca 1820–60.

man of many morns. A procrastinator: Scots coll: C.18–20; ob.

***man of the world.** A professional thief: c.: from ca 1870: ob.

man of wax, see LAD O' WAX.

man-root, see ROOT, n., 2.

man shall have his mare again, the. All will end well: a proverbial c.p.: late C.16–mid-19. Shakespeare, Addison, Creevey.

man Thomas. The penis: low: C.19–20. cf. JOHN THOMAS, 2.

man-trap. A widow: coll (mostly low): 1773, Goldsmith. cf. the macaronic pun *vir-gin* (late C.19–20). 2. The female pudend: low: from ca 1775. Ex preceding sense. 3. A lump of excrement: low: C.19–20; ob.

manablins, manav(i)lins, see MENAVELINGS.

manage. To succeed against odds; contrive to make the inadequate serve: coll: 1899, *Speaker*, 29 July, 'He managed almost without a hitch.'

mana(r)vel. To pilfer small stores: nautical: from ca 1865. Perhaps ex, or at the least prompted by:

manav(i)lins, see MENAVELINGS.

***Manchester, manchester.** The tongue: c.: 1812, Vaux; ob. by 1900. ?via YARN; perhaps rather a pun on MANG.

Manchester-bred. Explained by the gen. affixed tag, *long in the arms and short in the head*: a c.p. (—1869) > proverbial. W. Carew Hazlitt.

Manchester school of nutrition. 'High-feeding, emphatically introduced by certain medical men of that city': Society: ca 1860–70. Ware.

Manchester silk. Cotton: commercial: from ca 1850.

Manchester sovereign. A shilling: low: from ca 1860; ob.

mand, see MAUND.

***mander.** A remand: c. (—1877); ob. Greenwood. Ex *remand.* 2. A remanded prisoner: c. (—1887).

mandozy. A telling hit: low: ca 1800–70. Ex Daniel *Mendoza*, the Jewish boxer, who (1764–1836) did not, however, possess a powerful punch and who published a book on boxing in 1789 and took an inn in Whitechapel ca 1800; perhaps with a pun on *man dozy.* 2. Hence, an endearment among London's East-End Jews: from ca 1820.

mandrake. A bugger (in the legal sense): among folk of the road: prob. since C.17. In Nov. 1948, an octogenarian didekei was heard, in S.W. England, to remark of a certain man: ''E's a bloody mandrake. 'E's a bugger, that's what 'e be, a bugger. Small boys and such.' (My distinguished informant wishes to be nameless.) See *mandrake* in the glossary of *Shakespeare's Bawdy*, in reference to *2 Henry IV*, I, ii, 15, and esp. III, ii, 324–5 (Shakespeare Head edition). Yet, when that book appeared in 1947, several ivory-tower'd scholars accused me of seeing evil where none existed. I wonder what they'd do 'on the road' – yell for a policeman?

***mang.** To talk; boast: (mainly Scottish) c. of ca 1810–90. ?a corruption of MAG, to talk, influenced by Romany *mong*, beg, request.

***mangaree, mangarlee** or **-ly,** see MUNGAREE.

***mange.** A variant (—1909) of MUNGAREE. Ex It., through the organ-grinders' lodging-houses (Ware).

mangle. The female pudend: low: from ca 1860; ob.

manhandle. To handle roughly; maltreat: from ca 1864: s. >, ca 1910, coll. ?*handle as a man would* or, as W. suggests, ex Devon dial. *manangle*, to mangle.

manhole. The female pudend: low: from ca 1870. Ex S.E. sense.

manners, after you is. A c.p. indicative of the speaker's – gen. jocularly assumed – inferiority: ca 1650–1850.

manny. A derivative of MANDOZY, 2: Jewish East London: from ca 1880. Ware defines it as 'a term of endearment or admiration prefixed to Jewish name, as "Manny Lyons".' Contrast dial. senses.

manoeuvre, see APOSTLES, MANOEUVRE THE.

man's, a. A man-sized, esp. a large, *membrum virile*: low coll: C.19–20.

***-mans.** (Always preceded by *the*.) A c. suffix of ca 1560–1890, though † in most words by 1840. It means either 'state of being' or 'thing' according as an abstraction or an object is indicated; though it may simply be a disguise-appendage, a deliberately misleading amplification, as a glance at the *-mans* words shows. Perhaps ex L. *mens* via the Fr. advl ending *-ment*, or simply a perverted and extended use of *man*, a human being. cf., however, the Welsh Gypsy suffix *-imen* (?a variant of the much commoner Romany and Welsh Gypsy *-ben*), found in words adopted direct ex English, as *aidlimen*, idle, *gladimen*, glad, *madimen*, mad, and its radical form *-men*, which Sampson derives ex the Gr. 'middle passive participle – μενος' and notes as orig. attached to loan-v.v., as in *zilvimen*, jealous (§201); certainly relevant is the Welsh Gypsy *-moni*, app. derived ex Bengali *-man*, with which cf. Sanskrit *manaḥ*, mind, mood (Sampson, §205). See such words as CRACKMANS; DARKMANS; HARMANS; LIGHTMANS; RUFFMANS; TOGEMANS.

Mantalini. A male milliner: middle-class coll: ca 1840–60. Ex the milliner's husband in Dickens's *Nicholas Nickleby*.

Manton, see JOE MANTON.

manual compliment or **subscription.** A blow: C.19–20, ob.: coll.? prompted by Fielding's 'manual remonstrances'.

manufacture. Liquor prepared from English products: ca 1720–1850: coll.

map. A dirty proof: printers': from ca 1860. Ex the markings. 2. A young whiting: nautical: ?mid-C.19–20. Origin?

mapsticks!, cry. I cry you mercy!: low coll: ca 1705–50. Swift. Prob. *mapsticks* is a low perversion of both *mopsticks* and *mercy*; see MOP-STICK.

Marble Arch. The female pudend: low: from ca 1850. Punning some such phrase as (*at*) *the entrance to Hyde Park*. 2. A guard-room: Army s. (—1898). Within Marble Arch itself there was a small lock-up for use by the police.

marbles. Furniture, movables: somewhat low: 1864, H., 3rd ed.; 1867, Trollope; ob. Ex Fr. *meubles*, furniture. Hence, *money and marbles*, cash and effects. 2. Testicles: low: C.19–20. cf. PILLS, 2.

march, see DIRTY-SHIRT MARCH. **March hare,** see MAD AS A ... **march in the rear of a whereas,** see WHEREAS.

mare, Shanks's. See SHANKS ... (cf. the Fr. s. *par le train II*.)

mare (to) go, money makes the. Money can do most things: proverbial coll: late C.16–20; ob. Florio, Breton, N. Bailey, Kingsley. Perhaps punning *mayor*.

mare or lose the halter, win the. To play double or quits: coll: C.17–18. In Northants dial., *saddle* for *halter*.

mare to market, go before one's or the. To do ridiculous things: ca 1670–1830: coll.

mare with three (occ. two) legs; (two- or) three-legged mare. The gallows: coll: ca 1565–1850. Ainsworth, in *Rookwood*.

mare's dead?, whose. What's the matter?: rural coll: late C.16–mid-18. Deloney, Shakespeare, Swift.

margarine mess. (Gen. pl.) A motor-car: Nov. 1897–8, mostly in London. Ex BUTTER-COLOURED BEAUTIES.

marge. Margarine: from ca 1905. (*Margarine* itself, 1873: O.E.D.)

Margery. An effeminate: low London: ca 1850–1900. cf. NANCY.

Margery Jane. Margarine: lower-classes: ca 1900–20. Mary Higgs, *Glimpses into the Abyss*, 1906. cf. MARGE.

***margery-prater.** A hen: c. of ca 1570–1820. cf. CACKLING CHEAT.

Maria, see BLACK MARIA.

Maria Monk. SPUNK, in all senses: rhyming s.: late C.19–20. See also VICTORIA MONK.

marigold; occ. marygold. A gold coin, esp. a sovereign: ca 1660–1700. Cowley. Ex the colour. 2. One million pounds sterling: City men's: from ca 1855. H., 1st ed.

***marinated.** Transported as a convict: c.: ca 1670–1830. Head, Grose. Ex the salt-pickling fish undergo in Cornwall.

marine. An ignorant and/or clumsy seaman: nautical: from ca 1810; ob. 2. An empty bottle: from ca 1800; ob. John Davis, *The Post Captain*, 1805 (ed. R. H. Case, 1928); Trelawney. Also DEAD MARINE. cf. *marine officer*, Grose, 1785, the term being †by 1840, and *marine recruit* (—1860; †), in H., 2nd ed. See esp. Mark Lemon's *Jest Book* (1864), p. 161, for anecdotal etymology.

***mariner, freshwater,** see FRESHWATER.

marines!, tell that (tale) to the. *I* don't believe it, whoever else does!: c.p.: John Davis, 1806. Also (—1823) *that will do for the marines* (*but the sailors won't believe it*), as in Byron. Orig. nautical: cf. the opinion held by sailors of marines implicit in MARINE, both senses.

mark. A fancy or preference: 1760, Foote, 'Did I not tell you that old Moll was your mark?': coll; in late C.19–20, low coll. 2. A person: c.: from ca 1850. cf. MARK, BAD. 3. A victim, esp. a prospective victim: c. (—1885). 4. Abbr. MARK OF THE BEAST. 5. *the mark,* the pit of the stomach: boxing: 1747, J. Godfrey, *The Science of Defence*. Also (—1823; †) *Broughton's mark*, ex the famous C.18 boxer. 6. See MARK, BAD. 7. A humorist: mid-C.19–20. Prob. ex Mark Lemon (1809–70), co-founder and first editor of *Punch*.

***mark,** v. To watch; pick out a victim: c.: from ca 1860; perhaps, however, implied in Brandon, 1839, '*Marking* – watching, observing'.

mark, bad or **good.** A man who does not, or does, pay his employees regularly and in full: Australian: from ca 1840; ob. R. Howitt, 1845. A *good mark* was the earlier. cf. MARK, n., 2.

Mark Lane, walk penniless in. To have been cheated and to be very conscious of the fact: proverbial coll: late C.16–early 17. Greene.

mark of the beast. The female pudend: low: from ca 1715. D'Urfey. Also *mark*. 2. 'The white patches on the collar of a midshipman's uniform': naval: late C.19–20. Bowen. 3. See M. B. COAT.

mark on . . ., a. A person with a very pronounced fondness for (something): dial. and s.: from ca 1880; ob. Miss Braddon, 'Vernon was . . . a mark on strawberries and cream.'

mark up. To know or learn all about (a person): tailors': from ca 1870. 2. To give credit for: coll: 1899, *Tit-Bits*, 22 July, 'I shaved a gentleman who asked me to mark it up.'

marker. A receiver of stolen goods: late C.16–early 17 c. Greene. 2. Something worthy to be compared: 1895, H. P. Robinson, 'It ain't a marker to what's ahead'; ob.

market. The betting-ring: racing: from ca 1880.

market, go to. To attempt something: coll: 1890, 'Rolf Boldrewood'; ob.

market, on the. (Of a girl) available for marriage: coll: late C.19–20. (Maud Diver, *The Great Amulet*, 1908.)

market-dame, a harlot, is C.18 coll verging on S.E.

market-fever, see PENCIL-FEVER.

market-horse. A horse kept on the lists simply for the betting: turf: from ca 1873. cf. MARKET and MARKETEER.

market-place. The front teeth: provincial s. verging on dial.: from ca 1850; ob.

marketeer. A betting-man specializing in the study of horses that are favourites: racing s. verging on c.: from ca 1870; ob.

***marking.** A watcher; a watching: c.: from ca 1830; mostly U.S., though see MARK, V.

marley-stopper. A splay-footed person: streets' (—1887); ob. Ex *marble* and the stopping of a marble with one's feet.

marm. See MA'AM. 2. Marmalade: low coll: late C.19–20. cf. MARGE.

marm-puss. A wife: tailors': from ca 1870; ob. 2. (Also *marm-poosey.*) A showily dressed landlady: public-house frequenters': 1863; slightly ob.

marmaid. A mermaid: nautical: mid-C. 19–20.

Marquis of Granby. A bald-headed person: C.19–20, ob. Ex one.

marquis of marrowbones, see MARROWBONES, MARQUIS OF.

marriage, there belongs more to, see LEGS IN A BED . . .

marriage face. A sad face: middle classes' (—1909); ob. Ware, 'Because generally a bride cries a good deal, and so temporarily spoils her looks.'

marriage music. The crying of children: late C.17–mid-19.

***married.** Chained or handcuffed together: c.: mid-C.18–20, ob.

married but not churched. A living-together unmarried: almost a c.p.: late C.19–20.

married crocks. Men and wives married on the strength of a regiment: military:

from ca 1885. Only men over 26 with five years' service were allowed to marry on the strength.

married on the carpet and the banns up the chimney. Living together as though man and wife: coll (somewhat low): C.19–20; ob.

married the widow, have. To have made a mess of things: C.19. Ex Fr., with pun on the guillotine – 'the widow'.

married to brown Bess. (Having) enlisted: military: late C.18–19. Ex *hug* BROWN BESS.

marrowbone(-and-cleaver), like **marrow-pudding,** is low for the penis, as obviously is *a bellyful of marrow-pudding*, pregnancy: C.19–20, ob.

marrowbone (occ. **Marylebone**) **stage** or **coach, go in** or **ride by the.** To walk: ca 1810–1910. Prob. suggested by *Marybone* = *Marylebone*. cf. BAYARD OF TEN TOES and SHANKS'S MARE.

marrowbones, the knees, is jocular S.E., but as pugilists, C.17, e.g. in Fletcher, 1625, and as fists (regarded as weapons), ca 1810–1910, it is s.

marrowbones, marquis or **marquess of.** A lackey: late C.16–17. Nashe.

marry! An exclamation: C.14–mid-19. Orig. an oath, it soon > harmless. Ex (*the Virgin*) *Mary*. Often, in C.16–19, with asseverative tags or with GIP, *up*, etc. cf.:

marry! come up, my dirty cousin. A c.p. addressed to one affecting excessive delicacy: from ca 1670; in C.19–20, dial.

marry the mixen for the sake of the muck. To marry an undesirable person for the sake of the money: proverbial coll: from ca 1730; since ca 1850, dial. A *mixen* is a dung-heap; *muck* is a pun.

marry up. To bind or busy in marriage: coll: from ca 1820. J. Flint, 1822, 'I believe that the girls there are all married up.'

Marshall or **marshall.** A £5 Bank of England note: ca 1860–80. Ex a Bank of England official. cf. ABRAHAM NEWLAND.

Marshland, arrested by the bailiff of. Stricken with ague: coll: from ca 1660; in C.19–20, dial. 'Proverbial' Fuller, Grose (*Provincial Glossary*), Smiles.

martialist. An officer in the army: Society: 1885, *Daily News*, 31 Dec.

***martin.** An honest victim of rogues: c.: late C.16–mid-17. Greene. ?ex the bird. 2. A boot: tramps' c. (—1893); ob. P. H. Emerson. ?origin. 3. See ST MARTIN'S. 4. See ALL MY EYE . . .

Martin 'Enries. REACH-ME-DOWN clothes: Liverpool: late C.19–20. Apparently ex a manufacturer's name, *Martin Henry*.

martingale. The doubling of stakes at every loss: 1815: s. >, by 1850, j. Whence:

martingale, v.i. To double the bet at every loss: s. (—1823) >, by 1850, j.

Martin's hammer knocking at the wicket. Twins: C.18–mid-19 coll. In C.19–20, dial. and gen. in form, *she has had Martin's hammer knocking at her wicket*, she has twins. Halliwell. Ex the Fr. *Martin* (or, as in Lafontaine, *Martin-Bâton*), a man armed with a staff.

martins. The hands: low (and Parlary?): ca 1860–1914. P. H. Emerson, *Signor Lippo*, 1893. Ex It. *mani* (cf. Fr. *mains*?).

marwooded, ppl adj. Hanged: lower classes': ca 1875-83, executioner Marwood dying at the latter date.

Mary or **mary.** An aboriginal woman; occ. of a Kanaka: Queensland: from ca 1880; ob. cf. BENJAMIN, 3.

Mary! or **mary!** (In 'jeffing' with quads, s.v. JEFF, v.) no score!: printers': from ca 1870; ob. Ex MARRY! For the very interesting printers' s., see *Slang*.

Mary Ann. A female destroyer of recalcitrant labour-sweaters: ca 1865–90: mostly Sheffield. 2. A dress-stand: dress-makers': from ca 1870. 3. A sodomite: from ca 1890; ob. (cf. MARGERY; NANCY; SISSIE.) *Reynolds's Newspaper*, 2 June 1895. Hence, 4, an effeminate actor: theatrical: late C.19–20.

Mary Blane. A train: underworld rhyming s.: ca 1880–1914. 2. Rain: rhyming s.: ca 1860–1910.

Mary Jane or **mary jane.** The female pudend: low: from ca 1840; ob.

marygold, see MARIGOLD. **Marylebone stage,** see MARROWBONE STAGE.

Marylebone kick. A kick in the belly: ca 1820–80. *Sinks*, 1848.

mas; Mas John or **mas john;** also **mess-John.** By itself, *mas* is a low coll abbr. of *master*: ca 1570–1730, as in Whetstone and Mrs Centlivre. *Mas John*, however, is jocular or contemptuous coll, ca 1660–1840, for a Presbyterian minister as opp. to a Roman or an Anglican clergyman (in C. 19, S.E.), as in Jeremy Taylor, Burke, and Scott.

mascot. A person or thing that brings, or is believed to bring, good luck: 1881: s. >, ca 1905, coll. Ex E. Audran's opera, *La Mascotte*, played in London on 29 Dec.

1880, the word deriving ex Provençal *masco*, a sorcerer.

mash. A sweetheart: 1882. Also MASHER. 2. A dandy: from ca 1883; †. cf. MASHER. Ex the v. 3. Only in *make* (Society) or *do* (rather vulgar) *a mash*, to make a 'conquest': 1883–ca 1912. Ex the v.

mash, v.t., occ. v.i. To court or ogle or (attempt to) fascinate a girl or a woman; not often used of a woman 'bewitching' a man: 1882, Leland, 'These black-eyed beauties' – Gypsies – 'by mashing men for many generations ....'; ob. Prob. ex the S.E. sense, to crush, pound, smash utterly, but perhaps, as Leland suggests, ex Romany *mash* (*masher-ava*), to allure, entice. Orig. (ca 1860), U.S. Also *mash it* and:

mash, make a, see MASH, n., 3.

mash, on the. Constantly courting or ogling women: 1888.

mash that! Hold your tongue!: low London (—1909). Prob. ex S.E. sense of MASH, v.

mash-tub. A brewer: coll: from ca 1850; ob. Hence, ca 1870–1900, the *Morning Mash-Tub*: the *Morning Advertiser*, because of its brewery interests: Fleet Street.

mashed, adj. Flirtatious; 'smitten'; amorous: 1883. Ex MASH, v., but perhaps suggested by SPOONEY (3), 'mash being regarded as spoon-diet', W. Also *mashy* (Baumann, 1887).

mashed on. In love with: from ca 1883. See esp. the *Pall Mall Gazette*, 11 Oct. 1883. Ex MASH, v.

masheen. A cat: Shelta: C.18–20.

masher. A LADY-KILLER: 1882, but not very gen. till 1883; ob. Ex MASH, v. 2. A dandy, a fop: 1883; ob. The two senses merge, for the term was almost always applied to a flirtatious dandy, as T.A. Gartham in the *Pall Mall Gazette*, 11 Oct. 1883, makes clear.

masher, adj. Smart; dandified: 1884, *Globe*, 7 Feb., 'What are . . . masher canes to students immersed in Mill or Emerson . . .?'

masher blue. A weak blue, with tiny white dots: ca 1884–90. Affected by 'mashers' for their waistcoats. *Girl's Own Paper*, Nov. 1884.

masherdom. The world of the MASHER: coll: 1883. Also MASHERY.

mashers' corners. 'The O.P. and P.S. entrances to the stalls of the old Gaiety Theatre': Society: late 1882–ca 85. Ware. Ex MASHER, n., 1.

mashery. MASHERDOM: 1887, Baumann.

mashing. Dandified flirtation by men; as adj., given to or characterized by such flirtation: 1883; ob. Ex MASH, v. 2. 'A little screw of paper containing tea and sugar mixed': lower classes': late C.19–20.

mashy, see MASHED, adj.

maskee! Never mind!; it doesn't matter: Anglo-Chinese (—1864). Origin problematical: cf., however, *ma'alish*, ex the Arabic, and Skeat's ingenious derivation ex Portuguese *mas que*.

***maskin.** Coal: c.: C.18–mid-19. ?origin.

maskins!, by the. A corruption of *by the mass!*: C.17–20; in C.19–20, dial.

***mason.** A person, esp. a horse-dealer, giving worthless notes in payment for horses: c. of ca 1750–1800. *The Discoveries of John Poulter*, 1753. Ex superstitions regarding masonry. 2. Also, v.i.

***masoner.** The same as MASON, n. Poulter.

masonics. Secrets: Society coll: mid-C.19–early 20. Ware, 'From the secret rites of Freemasonry. Not that there are either secrets or rites in Freemasonry – at all events in England – where combined secrets are neither wanted nor expected.'

***masoning.** The giving of worthless notes for horses purchased: c. of ca 1750–1800. See MASON.

masonry. Secret signs and passwords: coll: 1841, Lytton; ob. Ex S.E. sense.

***mason's maund.** A sham sore that, above the elbow, counterfeits a broken arm: c.: late C.17–early 19. cf. MAUND.

massa; occ. mas'r. Master: in Negroes' English: recorded 1774, Foote; doubtless in use very much earlier. Mostly in U.S., but not to be considered U.S.

massacre of the innocents, see INNOCENTS.

massacree. 'Unlettered pronunciation for massacre', Bee, 1823. (Also in dial.)

***masse-stapler.** A rogue disguised as a woman: c.: C.18–early 19. ?origin.

master of (a person), **get the.** To become, or act the, master over: proletarian coll (—1887).

master of impediment. 'Troublesome preparation for the schools', Egan's Grose: Oxford University: ca 1820–40.

***master of the black art.** A beggar: c.: late C.16–17.

master of the mint. A gardener: jocular coll: mid-C.18–19. cf.:

master of the rolls. A baker: mid-C.17–20, ob.; jocular coll. Peacham, Grose. cf. BURN-CRUST; DOUGHY.

master of the wardrobe. One who pawns his clothes to buy liquor: ca 1780–1830. cf. two preceding entries.

master-vein, be hit on the. To take a man; to conceive: late C.16–17. Greene, 'My faire daughter was hit on the master vaine and gotten with child.' cf.:

masterpiece. The female pudend: low: C.18–20; ob. cf. MASTER-VEIN.

masterpiece o(f) night work. A very pretty harlot: low (—1909).

mat. (A) matter, esp. in *what's the mat?*: schoolboys': late C.19–20.

mat, on the. Up for trial (from late 1890s): military. Ex the small square mat on which the accused soldier stood in a barracks orderly-room.

match!, a. Agreed!; done!: coll >, by 1650, S.E.: late C.16–early 18. Shakespeare, 'A match, 'tis done'; Farquhar.

match and pocket the stake(s), lose the. (Of women only) to coït: C.19–20: low.

match! quoth Hatch (or Jack or John) when he got his wife by the breech or when he kissed his dame, – a. A c.p. of ca 1670–1750. Ray, 'Proverbial' Fuller.

mate. A companion, partner; comrade; friend: late C.14–20: S.E. except in Greene's *Third Cony-Catching* (1592), where it verges on c., and except when – from ca 1450 – it is used as a vocative, this being (in C.19–20, somewhat low) coll: orig. nautical. Stanyhurst, Miss Braddon. cf. MATEY.

mater. Mother; one's mother: from ca 1860: chiefly schoolboys' and undergraduates'. Hemyng in *Eton School Days*, 1864. Simply the L. word adopted in English. cf. PATER.

materials. Whiskey-punch: Anglo-Irish evasive coll: late C.19–20.

maternal. A mother: 1867, Routledge's *Every Boy's Annual*, Dec.; ob. Either short for *maternal parent* or the adj. used as a n.

mat(e)y. A mate, companion, comrade: from ca 1830: eligible only as a term of address (for it is then coll), as in H. Kingsley's *Geoffry Hamlyn*, '"Matey," says I, (you see I was familiar, he seemed such a jolly sort of bird,) "matey, what station are you on?"' Slightly ob. 2. (Gen. in pl and as *maties.*) A dockyard labourer: nautical: C.20. 'Taffrail'. 3. A (hospital) matron, esp. in a workhouse: 1857, A. Mayhew, *Paved with Gold*; ob.

Matilda, see WALZING MATILDA.

***matin-bell.** A thieves' meeting-place: c.: C.19–20; ob.

matinée dog. Mostly in *try it on the matinée dog*: theatrical: ca 1885–1915. Ware. Satiric both of vivisection and of frequenters of matinées, at which the dramatic performance is gen. inferior to the acting done in the evening. Whence TRY IT ON THE DOG.

matineer. A frequenter of matinées: theatrical coll: from either 1884 or 1885, the two years during which there was a rabies for matinées. Punning *mutineers.*

matlo(w). A sailor: from ca 1880: mainly nautical and, in C.20, military, and often as a nickname. Ex Fr. *matelot*, a sailor: cf. MALTOOT.

matric. A coll abbr. of *matriculation*: 1885, *Punch*, 16 March.

matrimonial. Coïtion in the usual position: occ. *m. polka.* Low: from ca 1850; ob. Known among English-speaking South-Sea Islanders (noted for their ingenuity in these matters) as *the missionaries' position*: late C.19–20.

matrimonial peacemaker. The penis: mid-C.18–20. It is doubtful whether this is not sometimes a mere S.E. euphemism.

matrimony. A mixture of two drinks or edibles: s. and dial.: 1813.

matspeak. 'Sixpence from everyone for the seats in the cathedral': church s.: ca 1870–1900.

matter, as near as no. Very near(ly) indeed: coll: from ca 1890.

matter with?, what is the. What troubles or ails or is amiss with ...?: coll: 1715, Defoe, 'I beseech, what is the matter with you.' 2. In late C.19–20, it also = What objection is there to ...?: jocular coll.

mattress-jig. Sexual intercourse: low coll when not S.E. euphemism: C.18–19.

maty, see MATEY.

maukes, maux, see MAWKES. **maukin,** see MALKIN.

maul. A, or to, wrestle for the ball when, in Rugby football, it is 'held' over the goal-line. London schools' coll: ca 1875–1914.

mauled. Exceedingly drunk: late C.17–mid-19.

mauler. (Gen. pl.) A fist: early C.19–20. Prob. suggested by:

mauley; occ. mawley or morley. A fist, the hand: low: 1781, G. Parker; Moncrieff; Miss Braddon. Hence SLANG THE MAULEY, to give a person one's hand, shake hands with; *tip a mauley*, give a hand; FAM *the mauley*, shake hands. 2. Hence, a finger; virtually always in pl: c.: 1845 in

'*No. 747*'; ob. 3. Handwriting, 'a fist'; a signature: low: from ca 1850; ob. Mayhew. The term derives ex *maul*, v.; or is perhaps 'a transposition of Gaelic *lamh*, hand, used in tinkers' s. or Shelta', W., 'in form *malya*'; the Romany s. is *mylier*.

maum, in phrase *maum and gaum* and gen. as *mauming and gauming*. To 'paw' (a person): low coll: ca 1735–1860. Perhaps cognate with dial. *malm*, to besmear.

***maund.** Begging; (with prefixed word) some specified begging imposture: C.17–early 19 c. Rowlands, B.E., Grose (MASON'S MAUND). cf. MAUNDER.

***maund,** v.t. and v.i. To beg: c.: ca 1565–1800. Harman, Beaumont & Fletcher, B.E. Prob. ex Fr. *mendier* or *quémander* influenced by Romany *mang*. 2. To ask: c.: ca 1565–1700.

***maund, mason's,** see MASON'S MAUND.

***maund abram.** To beg as a madman: C.17–18 c. Rowlands. See ABRAM.

***maund it.** To go a-begging: c.: C.17–18. Ex the v.

***maunder.** A beggar: c.: C.17–mid-19. Rowlands, Lytton. Ex MAUND, v.

***maunder,** v. To beg: c.: ca 1610–1770. Middleton & Dekker; Dyche. Ex MAUND, v., of which it is a mere extension, perhaps suggested by Fr.

***maunder on the fly.** To beg of people in the streets: c.: ca 1850–90.

***maunderer.** A professional beggar: c.: ca 1610–1840. Middleton & Dekker; Ainsworth, in *Rookwood*. Ex MAUNDER, v. cf.:

***maundering,** ppl adj. Begging; given to begging: c.: ca 1610–1700.

maund(e)ring-broth. A scolding: late C.17–early 19. Ex *maunder*, to grumble.

***maunding.** The, or an, act of begging: c.: 1610, Rowlands; †by 1850. 2. adj., begging; given to or characteristic of begging: c.: ca 1600–1720. W. Cartwright, 'Some counterfeiting trick of such maunding people'.

***maunding cove.** A beggar: c.: C.17–18. Anon., *Sack for my Money*, ca 1603.

maw!, hold your. Stop talking: coll: C.18–19. Ex S.E. *maw*, jaws or mouth of an animal.

maw-wallop. A filthy dish of food: low coll: late C.18–mid-19. Ex S.E. *maw*, belly.

maw-wormy. Captious; pessimistic: coll – theatrical, and non-aristocratic: 1885, *Entr'Acte*, 6 June. (Stomach-worms cause peevishness.)

mawkes. A whore: coll: C.17–18. Lodge, *Street Robberies Considered*. 2. A slattern, esp. if dirty or vulgar: coll verging on S.E.: late C.17–20; dial. after ca 1820.

mawkish. Slatternly: ca 1720–70.

mawley, see MAULEY. **mawpus,** see MOPUS.

max. Gin; properly, very good gin: low: ca 1810–1900. Byron, 'Oh! for a glass of max'; Mayhew, Baumann. Abbr. *maxima, -e, -us*, or *-um*. cf.:

maxie. A great error, big mistake: Scottish: 1868, G. MacDonald, *Robert Falconer*, 'Horror of horrors! a maxie'; ob.

May. The college Easter Term examination, says Bristed, 1852; more safely defined as the college May examination: Cambridge coll > j. > S.E. Occ. *Mays*.

May-bees don't fly all the year long. A c.p. reply to one beginning a statement with *it may be*: mid-C.18–20; ob. In Swift, *May-bees don't fly now*. Also *this month*. The Scots form is *maybes* (or *May-bees*) *are no aye honey-bees*.

May-game of one, make a. To befool a person: coll > S.E.: late C.16–early 19. B.E., who defines *May games* as 'Frolicks, Plaies, Tricks, Pastimes, &c.'.

***May-gathering.** Sheep-stealing: c.: C.19.

may God blind me. 'The original invocation' – †by 1909 – 'of the gutterling': whence GORBLIMEY, etc. Ware.

May hill, to have climbed or got over (or up). To have survived the late spring, gen. considered a tricky month: proverbial coll: from ca 1660: ob. Perhaps in allusion to an actual May Hill.

mazard, see MAZZARD.

mazarine. A common-councilman of London: coll: from ca 1760; ob. *The Annual Register*, 1761. Ex the gown of mazarine blue. 2. A platform under the stage: theatrical: from ca 1860; ob. ?ex It. *mezzanino*.

mazer, see MAZZARD:

mazzard; also **mazard** and **mazer.** The head: jocular coll verging on S.E.: *mazer*, ca 1580–1660; *maz(z)ard*, C.17–20, ob. 2. The face (not *mazer*): ca 1760–1890: jocular coll verging on S.E. Horace Walpole, 'His . . . Christian's mazard was a constant joke'. Sense 2 ex sense 1, which, as to *mazzard*, derives ex *mazer*, a drinking-bowl. 3. (Again, not *mazer*) the head of a coin: Anglo-Irish: C.19–20; ob. Maria Edgeworth.

mazzard. To knock on the head: C.17–18 coll verging on S.E. (Not very gen.)

McKie, see MACKAY, THE REAL

meal-mouth. 'A sly sheepish Dun', B.E.: coll or s.: late C.17–18.

meal-sack, gen. **-tub.** A stock of sermons: clerical: from ca 1860; ob.

mealer. One pledged to drink intoxicants only at meals (—1890). 2. One who, lodging at one place, eats elsewhere: coll: orig. (1883), U.S.; anglicized ca 1887.

mean, disobliging, petty, (of a horse) vicious, is U.S. 2. The phrase *to feel mean*, to feel ashamed or guilty, is recorded by Marryat in 1839 as U.S., but it > anglicized ca 1860 as s.

mean, v. To intend with determined purpose: coll: from ca 1840. e.g. 'Well, anyway, I *mean* to do it!' Esp. in *mean business*.

mean as a Christian, as. Very mean: Jewish coll: C.19–20. Tit for tat.

mean to do without 'em!(, I). i.e. without women: a c.p. popularized on the music-halls by Arthur Roberts in 1882; †by 1910.

mean to say, I. A coll tautological form, dating from the early 1890s, of *I mean*, itself verging on coll when, as frequently, it connotes apologetic modification or mental woolliness. (The phrase occurs in Yorkshire and Cheshire dial. before 1900.)

meaning-like. In earnest: low coll (—1887).

meant. (Of a horse) meant to win: turf: from ca 1840; ob. By cryptic abridgement.

measle, v.i. To become pitted with measle-spots: coll: from ca 1880.

measly. Contemptible; of little value: 1864, Miss Braddon, 'To think that the government ... should have the audacity to offer a measly hundred pounds or so for the discovery of a great crime!' 2. Miserable-looking, 'seedy': ca 1860–1900.

measure, be (a person's). To be just the person needed: low s. (—1857) >, by 1880, non-aristocratic coll. Baumann, 'He's our measure, *das ist unser Mann*.'

measure, get (late C.18–mid-19) or **take** (late C.17–early 19) **one's.** To coït with; to marry: coll, the former sense being low. Lacy, in *Sir Hercules Buffoon*, 'Gin I'd let him alane, he had taken measure o' th' inside of me as well as o' th' out.'

measure (someone's) **daylights for mourning.** To give (him) a black-eye: boxing: ca 1810–50. George Godfrey, *History*, 1828.

measure out. To knock down; to kill: low coll (—1891) verging on s.

measured, be. To be exactly suited, e.g. with a part written to one's fancy or ability: theatrical: 1859, Blanchard Jerrold.

measured for a suit of mourning, be. To receive a black eye: boxing: 1819, Moore in *Tom Crib's Memorial*; ob. by 1900.

meat. Something profitable or pleasant: coll: from ca 1885. *Westminster Gazette*, 28 Dec. 1897, 'There is a good deal of meat for the actors.' 2. Generic for the human body (rarely the male) as an instrument of sexual pleasure; hence, for the female pudend and/or the male: low coll: late C.16–20; slightly ob. Gosson; Killigrew, 'Your bed is big enough for two, and my meat will not cost you much.' cf. MUTTON and the ensuing entries and MEATY.

meat, a bit of. Coïtion: low (s. rather than coll): C.18–20. 2. A harlot: low: late C.19–20. See MEAT, 2.

meat, cold, see COLD MEAT.

meat, flash. To expose the person: late C.18–20: low.

meat, fond of. Frequently amorous: low: C.19–20.

meat, fresh. A harlot new at her trade: low: C.19–20.

meat, hot, see HOT MEAT.

meat, price of. The cost of a sexual embrace: low: C.19–20.

meat, raw. A harlot (less gen., any woman) naked in the sexual act: low: C.19–20. Contrast MEAT, FRESH.

meat, the nearer the bone the sweeter the. A mid-C.19–20 low c.p. applied by men to a thin woman viewed as a bed-mate. Ex the old proverb, *the nearer the bone the sweeter the flesh* (mid-C.16–20).

meat and drink. An amorous carouse: low: C.19–20; ob. 2. A cocktail in which an egg is beaten up: West Indian: from ca 1870.

meat-drink-washing-and-lodging. A spirituous liquor, prob. gin: ca 1720–50. Anon., *The Quaker's Opera*, 1728 (see quot'n at BUNTER'S TEA).

meat-flasher, -flashing. An exposer, the exposure, of the person in public: low: C.19–20. Ex MEAT, FLASH.

meat-fosh. A (warm) meat-hash: Cockneys' (—1887). ?Fr. *farci*.

meat-hook. A curl on the temple (as worn by the London coster): Cockneys' (—1887); slightly ob.

meat-house. A brothel: low: C.19–20; ob. cf.:

meat-market. A rendezvous of harlots; the female breasts; the female pudend; low: C.19–20.

meat-merchant. A bawd: low: C.19–20; ob.

meat-mincer. The mouth: pugilistic: ca 1840–90. Augustus Mayhew, *Paved with Gold*, 1857. The prototype of mechanical mincers.

meat-monger. A man given to wenching: low: C.18–19.

meat of, make (cold). To kill: orig. (1848), U.S.; anglicized ca 1870.

meater. A cowardly dog (lit., one that will bite only meat), hence a cowardly man: low (mostly Cockneys'): late C.19–20.

meaty. Sexually enjoyable: low coll: from ca 1820.

mebbe. Perhaps: (dial. and) proletarian coll: C.19–20. Lit., *maybe.*

med, medic, medical, medico. A doctor, whether physician or surgeon or both combined; a student of medicine. Thus, *med*, orig. (1851) U.S., was anglicized ca 1860 and in C.20 is ob.; *medic*, as doctor, is C.17–18 S.E., C.19 rare coll, and as medical student is s., orig. (1823) U.S. and very rare in Great Britain, where it is ob. in C.20; *medical* is coll in both senses, and, though recorded first (1823) in Hawthorne, it may be orig., as it is mainly, English (Halley, 1834; Masson, 1864); *medico*, student, is C.19–20, but the more gen. sense of doctor arises in late C.17, is S.E. till ca 1850, and is thereafter coll.

medal (or medals) today, you're wearing your; or **medal showing!** Your fly is undone; you have a fly-button showing: mid-C.19–20: jocular c.p. verging on euphemistic S.E.

meddlers, lare-overs for, see LAREOVERS.

meddling duchess. An 'ageing, pompous woman who fusses about and achieves nothing': lower classes': ca 1880–1915. Ware. See the corresponding sense of DUCHESS.

Medes and Persians. Jumping on a boy when he is in bed: Winchester College: ca 1840–1910.

medic and **medical,** see MED.

medical Greek. 'Marrowskying' (see p. 11): coll verging on S.E.: from ca 1800; ob. Also known as *Gower Street dialect*.

medicine. Liquor: from ca 1850; ob. Mayhew. cf. POISON. 2. Sexual intercourse: from ca 1855; ob. Hence *take one's medicine* = to drink; to copulate.

medicine, take (†a). To take a purgative: coll: 1830, Southey.

medico, see MED.

medium. 'A person engaged by a squatter, part of whose "run" is offered by Government at a land lottery' or ballot. 'The medium takes lot-tickets . . ., attends the drawing, and, if his ticket is drawn before his principal's land is gone, selects it, and hands it over on payment of the attendance fee,' F. & H.: Australian coll: from ca 1880: coll >, ca 1900, S.E.; ob.

medlar. The female pudend: low: C.17–mid-19.

medza, medzer, see MADZA. cf.:

medzies; metzes. Money: Parlary and theatrical: (?late C.19–) C.20. Ex It. *mezzo*: cf. MADZA. Hence, NANTEE *metzes*, BROKE, penniless.

meech, meecher, meeching, see MIKER, etc., and MOOCH, etc.

meer-swine. A porpoise: nautical coll: mid-C.19–20; ob. By Ger. influence ex *sea-hog*; but imm. ex Scots.

meerschaum. The nose: boxing (—1891); ob. *Sporting Life*, 25 March 1891.

***meg;** occ. **megg.** A guinea: c.: ca 1685–1820. Shadwell. cf. MAG (n., 4). 2. In Ned Ward (1703), a *meg* is any copper coin; in late C.19–20 dial. and till ca 1860 in c., a *meg* is a halfpenny; in the U.S. C.19–20 underworld, *me(i)g* is a five-cents piece. ?etymology. 3. See MEG OF WESTMINSTER.

***meg,** v. To swindle: c. (—1887).

Meg of Westminster, as long as. Very tall (esp. if of a woman): coll: late C.16–18. *The Life and Pranks of Long Meg of Westminster*, 1582; Grose. In C.18, LONG MEG was a nickname for any very tall woman. Ex a legendary character.

***megg,** see MEG, n.

***megging,** n. and adj. Swindling: c. (—1887).

***megsman,** see MAGSMAN.

meisensang. A missionary: Anglo-Chinese (—1864). Ex Chinese pronunciation of the English word.

***mejoge.** A shilling: c. of ca 1750–80 and perhaps much later. John Poulter. ?ex MEG.

melancholy as . . ., as. Apperson (to whom praise be!) cites the following four coll similes: *as melancholy as a* (gen. *gib*) *cat*, ca 1590–1840, e.g. Lyly, Shakespeare, D'Urfey, Lamb; *as m. as a collier's horse*, ca 1650–1750; *as m. as a sick monkey*, from ca 1830 (ob.), as in Marryat's *Midshipman Easy*; and *as m. as a sick parrot*, ca 1680–1840, as in Mrs Behn.

***mell.** The nose: c. of ca 1720–1850. ?ex the †S.E. sense, a mace or club. 2. A smell: nursery: mid-C.19–20. Ex baby-talk.

mell, dead as a. Quite dead: Scots coll: late C.18–20; ob. cf. preceding.

mellish. A sovereign: mostly Londoners' low s.: ca 1820–50. Also, money in general: mainly pugilistic or, rather, sporting: ca 1815–60. *Boxiana*, IV, 1824, 'The victor ... handing him over a little Mellish, "Welcome sweetener of human ills"'; the inner quotation suggesting that the etymology is Latin *mel*, 'honey'.

mellow. Almost drunk: C.17–20: coll till C.19, then S.E. Cotgrave, Garrick.

melon. A new cadet: Royal Military Academy: from ca 1870; ob. Ex his greenness, as is 2, the Australian and New Zealand sense (late C.19–20), a simpleton, a fool. 3. Abbr. *paddy-melon*, a small kangaroo: Australian coll: from ca 1845.

***melt.** To spend (money): c. from ca 1690; ob. Also *melt away* (C.18). 2. Hence, to cash (a cheque or a bank-note): 1868, Reade and Boucicault in *Foul Play*: low s. verging on c. 3. v.i., to be spent on drink: ca 1760–1800. Foote. 4. To defeat: boxers' (—1823); †by 1900. 5. To experience the sexual spasm: (slightly euphemistic) coll: mid-C.19–20.

melt in the mouth, look as if butter would not, see BUTTER WOULD NOT... **melted, 'twill (not) cut butter when it's,** see BUTTER WHEN IT'S ...

melted butter. The *semen virile*: low: C.18–20.

melter. He who administers a sound beating: boxing: ca 1820–1900.

melthog. A shirt: Shelta: C.18–20. Whence MILL-TAG.

melting. A sound beating: pugilistic: ca 1820–1900. Ex *malleting*, says 'Jon Bee'; much more prob. ex Scots *melt*, to knock down, orig. by a stroke in the side, where lies the *melt* or spleen (Jamieson).

melting moments. The coïtion of a fat man and woman: low: ca 1810–90. 2. Hence, ardent passion: non-aristocratic coll (—1887).

melting-pot. The female pudend: low: C.19. cf. MELTED BUTTER.

melton. Dry bread: tailors': from ca 1860; ob. Prob. ex *Melton* (*cloth*), a strong smooth cloth with close-cut nap.

mem. A low coll form of MA'AM: 1700, Congreve. 2. A memorandum: of which word, as of *memento* (Baumann, 1887), it was orig. a mere written abbr.: coll, 1818, Moore. cf. MEMO.

mem, the. The mistress of the house: coll (India and the F.M.S.): late C.19–20. Abbr.:

mem-sahib, the. One's wife: Anglo-Indian (orig. Bengal Presidency) coll: late C.19–20. Adoption of the Indian alteration (itself dating from ca 1857) of MA'AM, *madam*. cf. (the now ob.) *madam-sahib*, the form used at Bombay, and BURRA BEEBEE.

member. A person: C.16–20: S.E. till mid-C.19, then s. and dial. Gen. as *hot m.*, *warm m.*, etc. Ex *member of the community*.

'member. To remember: childish coll: C.18–20.

member for Cockshire, the. The penis: from ca 1840; ob. Punning *male* (or *privy*) *member* and COCK.

member-mug. A chamber-pot: low coll: late C.17–19. Ex *member*, the male member. 2. An out-of-doors boy: Westminster School: ca 1850–1910.

memo. Orig. (1889) a mere written abbr. of *memorandum*, it was by 1895 a gen. accepted coll.

memory-powder, you want a little. Your memory is bad: c.p. of ca 1885–1910.

men, see MAN for all senses and phrases.

menagerie. The orchestra: theatrical (—1859); ob. Ex the noise.

menavelings; maniv(i)lins, the usual form. Odd money in the daily accounts: railway clerks': from ca 1863. 2. Hence, in low s. of late C.19–20, odds and ends, extras, broken victuals.

mend. To bandage: lower classes' coll: mid-C.19–20; ob. 2. To produce (e.g. a story) better than (somebody else): coll: from ca 1870; earlier, S.E.

mend as sour ale mends in summer. To become worse: from ca 1540: coll till C.19, then dial. 'Proverbs' Heywood, Wither, Swift.

mend the Magnificat, see MAGNIFICAT, CORRECT.

mending, vbl n. Something to be repaired; nautical for repairing (as in *mending wool*): coll: from ca 1860.

mention it!, don't. A phrase in deprecation of apology or thanks: coll: 1854, Wilkie Collins. Prob. an abbr. of *don't mention it, for it's a trifle.*

mentisental. Sentimental: East London (—1909); ob. By transposition: cf. LEMONCHOLY.

mephisto. A foreman: tailors': from ca 1870; ob. Abbr. *Mephistopheles.*

mercer's book, the. Proverbial coll, ca

1590–1602, for debt, esp. the debts of a gallant. Nashe, 'Divers young Gentlemen shall creepe further into the Mercers Booke in a Moneth, then they can get out in a yere'; Jonson.

merchant. A fellow, CHAP: S.E. in mid-C.16–early 17, lapsed till ca 1880, then revived as a coll (esp. among actors) verging on s. cf. CUSTOMER and *client*.

merchant of capers. A variant of CAPER-MERCHANT.

merchant of eel-skins. No merchant at all: semi-proverbial coll: ca 1540–1670. Ascham, in *Toxophilus*; A. Brewer, 1655.

merchantable, see SCRUFF, n.

mercy, cry (one). To cry mercy; beg a person's pardon: coll when *I* is omitted: late C.16–18. Shakespeare, 'Oh, cry you mercy, sir, I have mistook.'

mere country put, a. A virtually c.p. elaboration of PUT, n., 1: ca 1690–1750.

meridian. A drink taken at noon: app. ca 1815–1910: Scots coll verging on S.E.

Merino(e)s, pure. (Members of) the 'very first families': Australian, esp. New South Wales: from ca 1825; ob. Peter Cunningham, 1827. 'The pure merino is the most valuable sheep,' Morris.

merits. ca 1820–50 as in 'Jon Bee', 1823: 'High flash' – i.e. fashionable s. – 'for the extreme of a thing, used negatively in general; as, "Sir, you do not enter into the merits of – the wine, the joke", &c.'

merkin. An artificial vagina for lonely men: coll (?, rather, S.E.): mid-C.19–20. Ex the two S.E. senses, 'female pudend' and 'artificial hair for a woman's pudend'.

merp. A species of marble (as used in the game of marbles): children's: late C.19–20. Ex dial. *mirk*, 'dusky, dingy, drab'?

Merry Andrew. The Royal Navy: naval: late C.19–20. cf. ANDREW (not sense 1). A pun on the archaic S.E. *merry-andrew*.

merry-arse(d) Christian. A whore: low coll: ca 1810–70.

merry as . . . Of the following similes listed by Apperson, all or nearly all must orig. have been coll: *merry as a cricket* (mid-C.16–20); *m. as a Greek* (mid-C.16–18); *m. as a grig* (from ca 1560; in C.20, dial.); *m.* or *happy as a king* (mid-C.16–mid-19); *m. as a (mag)pie* (late C.14–early 17); *m. as a beggar* (ca 1650–1750); (*who so*) *m. as he that hath nought to lose*(?) (ca 1660–1780); *m. as mice in malt* (ca 1630–1880); *m. as the maids* (ca 1630–90); *m. as three chips* (ca 1540–90); *m. as tinkers* (ca 1650–1700).

merry bit. A willing wench: C.19–20 low; ob. cf. MERRY-LEGS.

merry bout. A copulation: ca 1780–1830. *The Newgate Calendar*, 1780.

merry Cain, see CAIN, RAISE.

merry dancers. The Northern Lights: from ca 1715: coll and dial. Also (*the*) *dancers*.

Merry Dun of Dover. A legendary ship – drawn from Scandinavian mythology – 'so large that, passing through the Straits of Dover, her flying jib-boom knocked down Calais steeple; while the fly of her ensign swept a flock of sheep off Dover Cliff. She was so lofty that a boy who went to her mast-head found himself a grey old man when he reached the deck again,' F. & H.: nautical: ca 1840–1900.

merry-go-down. Strong ale: ca 1470–1620 (Golding, Nashe); then dial. Not c., though described as such by F. & H.: see esp. Apperson.

merry-go-round. A pound (£1): rhyming s.: late C.19–20.

merry-go-sorry. Hysteria: coll verging on S.E.: late C.16–early 17. Breton.

merry-go-up. Snuff: ca 1820–50. Egan, 1821, 'Short but pungent like a pinch of snuff.'

merry grig; merry snob. A pleasant or a boon companion: s.: ca 1700–1725. Ned Ward, 1715.

merry-legs. A harlot: low coll: C.19–20; ob.

merry-maker. The male member: low: mid-C.19–20; ob.

merry men of May. Currents caused by the ebb-tides: nautical: C.19–20; ob.

merry snob, see MERRY GRIG.

meshuga. (Tolerantly humorous.) Crazy: Jewish coll: mid-C.19–20. Ex Yiddish; cf. Hebrew *meshuga*, error.

Mesopotamia ring, the true. Pleasing, high-sounding, and incomprehensible: coll: ca 1880–1910. Ex *the* or *that blessed word Mesopotamia*, itself almost eligible on the same count, with the same meaning, and arising ex a plausible ascription of spiritual comfort.

mess. A difficulty, notable failure, muddle: 1833, *Sessions*, 28 Nov.: coll till ca 1890, then S.E. Hence, *make a mess of*, to bungle; *clear up the mess*, to put things straight; *get into a mess*, to involve oneself in difficulties.

mess. To interfere unduly: gen. as vbl n. *messing*, applied to police interference:

low coll: from ca 1870; ob. Also *mess about*, extant.

mess, be scratched out of one's. A variant (Baumann, 1887; now ob.) of:

mess, lose the number of one's. To be killed: naval. From early C.19: 1818, Alfred Burton, *Johnny Newcome.* In the Boer War, a military variant was *lose one's number*, as in J. Milne, *The Epistles of Atkins*, 1902.

mess about. See MESS, v. 2. To take (sexual) liberties: low coll: from ca 1873. v.t. form *mess about* or *m. a. with*. 3. v.i. and t., to play fast and loose; swindle, put off: low coll: from ca 1890.

mess clout. The duster supplied weekly to each mess: *Conway* cadets' coll (—1891).

mess-John, see MAS.

mess of, make a, see MESS, n.

mess-traps. Cooking utensils: nautical, esp. naval, coll (—1887); ob. Here *traps* = odds-and-ends, 'things'.

mess treat. A 'tip given by an old boy to his former mess to provide a special feed (usually at tea)': *Conway* cadets' coll (—1891).

messer. A bungler, muddler: coll (slightly ow): from ca 1905.

mesty, mestee, mestez. A half-caste: Anglo-Indian coll: mid-C.19–20; ob. Ex Spanish *mestizo*, a half-caste, itself ex L. *mixtus*, mixed.

metal. Money: coll: C.19–20, ob. Ex *precious metal*. 2. See METTLE. 3. Sweetmeats: Anglo-Indian (—1864); nearly †.

metal rule. An oath; an obscenity. Also as v., in *you be metal-ruled!*, you be damned! Printers': from ca 1860; ob. Ex the dash (—) in print.

metal (or, as gen., **mettle) to the back.** Constantly courageous and/or energetic: coll: ca 1590–1760. Shakespeare; Coffey, 1733, 'The girl is mettle to the back.'

metallician. A bookmaker: racing: ca 1870–90. Ex bookmakers' use of metallic pencils and even books.

metals. Rails: railwaymen's coll (—1887).

meter. A term of abuse in the Army: late C.19–20. Ex Hindustani: lit., a scavenger.

Methusalem. Esp. in *old as Methusalem*. Methuselah: mid-C.17–20: always corrupt; in mid-C.19–20, low coll. Cowley. Influenced by *Jerusalem*.

mettle. The *semen virile*: low coll: C.17–20; ob. Field, 1612 (*mettle of generation*). The gen. late C.19–20 term, esp. in the Colonies, is SPUNK (2). Ex S.E. *mettle*, (of animals) natural ardour and vigour. 2. Hence, *fetch mettle*, to masturbate: C.18–19. 3. See METAL TO . . .

metzes, see MEDZIES.

mew-mew! *Tell that to the* MARINES!: tailors': from ca 1860; ob.

mi, see MA, 2.

mia-mia (pron *mi-mi*); occ. **miam, mimi** or **mi-mi.** An aboriginal hut: Australian coll (—1845) >, ca 1870, 'standard'; in 1871 and later, applied to any hut: coll >, by 1880, 'standard'. Ex Aboriginal. cf. GUNYAH and HUMP(E)Y.

mibbies. Marbles: Cockney schoolchildren's: late C.19–20.

mice-feet o', make. To destroy utterly: Scots coll: C.18–19.

Michael, your head's on fire. (Often preceded by *hip!*) A (low) c.p. addressed to a red-headed man: mid-C.18–mid-19.

Michaelmas rent in Midsummer noon, spend (one's). To spend money that should be laid by for a definite purpose: proverbial coll: ca 1600–1860. Camden.

miching Malicho, or **mallecho** in Shakespeare's *Hamlet* is prob. s.: meaning and etymology are alike uncertain, though *miching* prob. = skulking, perhaps = a dirty trick (O.E.D.). Note, too, Romany *malleco*, false (Smart & Crofton), and Welsh Gypsy *maleko!*, look out for yourself! (Sampson). Moreover, Ware states that in April 1895, he 'heard a man in the gallery of the Palace of Varieties (London), after several scornful phrases, say derisively, "Oh – ah – minchin maleego".' I believe that the phrase may = our modern 'dirty dog!', for the Romany *malleco* is prob. cognate with Turkish Gypsy *maklo*, spotted. (L. *maculatus*.)

mick; mickey or **micky**; occ. **mike.** (Or with capital initial.) An Irishman: orig. (—1869), U.S.: anglicized ca 1890: more gen. in Canada, Australia, and New Zealand than in Britan. Ex *Michael*. 2. Hence, an Irish seaman (nautical: late C. 19–20) or soldier (military: same period). cf. JOCK. Both *Jock* and *Mick* are now vocatives of a wide range. 3. See MICKY, 3.

micky. See MICK. 2. A young bull running wild: Australia: from ca 1880. Grant, 1888, 'There were two or three mickies and wild heifers.' Prob. ex 'the association of bulls with Irishmen', Barrère & Leland. 3. A New Zealand corruption (—1898) of Maori *mingi*, orig. *mingi-mingi*, a shrub or small tree (*cya-*

thodes acerosa). 4. (Also *Mikey.*) Sick, esp. after liquor: low: late C.19–20. Ex BOB, HARRY and DICK, the same: rhyming s.: 1868. 3. The penis: Anglo-Irish: late C.19–20. 4. A casual ward: tramps' c.: late C.19–20.

mid. A midshipman: coll: 1798, Mrs Ann Bennett. Also MIDDY.

mid vire. A midday WIRE or telegram, 'giving last prices in the coming-on races': sporting men's, orig. (—1909) and mainly in Paris; ob.

midden. A filthy slattern: Scots coll: C.19–20. 2. *eating midden*, a glutton: Scots coll: C.19–20.

middle. A social, literary or scientific article for the press: 1862: coll. Abbr. *middle article*. Hence *middle(-)man*, a writer of such articles; ob. 2. A finger: c.: early C.17–mid-19. 3. A middle-weight: boxing coll: 1902, P. G. Wodehouse, *The Pothunters*.

middle, v. To cheat, befool: ca 1869–1905. E. Farmer, *Scrap-Book*.

middle-age spread. Paunchiness coming in middle-age: coll: late C.19–20.

middle finger or leg. The male member: low: C.19–20.

middle pie. The stomach: non-aristocratic: ca 1870–1910. cf.:

middle piece. The chest: boxing: ca 1800–1870. 2. *Sinks*, 1848, defines it as the stomach or belly. Perhaps the midriff is implied both in sense 1 and in sense 2.

***middleman.** One who, professionally, recovers property from the thief or thieves concerned: c.: ca 1830–90.

middle storey. The stomach: ca 1670–1800: jocular coll. Crowne.

middle-watcher. The slight meal snatched by officers of the middle watch (about 2.30 a.m.): nautical coll (—1867).

Middlesex clown. (Gen. in pl.) A native or an inhabitant of Middlesex: jocular coll: mid-C.17–early 19. Fuller; Grose, in the *Provincial Glossary*.

Middlesex jury, see JURY – HANG HALF...

Middlesex mongrel. A C.18 variant of MIDDLESEX CLOWN. (Lord Hailes, 1770.)

middling. Moderately large: late C.16–20: S.E. till ca 1850, then coll (somewhat low) except in *middling size, stature, degree*. Blackmore, 'A middling keg of hollands, and an anker of old rum'.

middling, adv. Moderately, tolerably: C.18–20; S.E. till ca 1830. 2. Fairly well (success, health): coll: from late C.18, as in 'I did it pretty middling' (in a Charles Dibdin song).

middlingish, adv. Somewhat; moderately (low) coll and dial.: 1820.

middy. A midshipman: coll: 1818, Alfred Burton, *Adventures of Johnny Newcome*. Ex MID.

midge-net. A lady's veil: (low) coll: ca 1858–1910.

Midlands, the. The female pudend: low jocular: from ca 1830; ob.

midnight's arse-hole, as white as. Black as pitch: low coll: ca 1550–1640. Anon., *Jacob and Esau*, ca 1557 (in Dodsley's *Old Plays*).

midshipman's half-pay. Nothing: nautical: from ca 1850.

midshipman's nuts. Broken biscuit, esp. and properly if hard (as dessert): nautical coll: *The Night Watch* (II, 50), 1828; ob.

midshipman's roll. A hammock badly rolled: naval coll: from ca 1800 or a little earlier.

midshipman's watch and chain. A sheep's heart and pluck: ca 1780–1850: orig. nautical. Grose, 1st ed.

midshipmen's devil. 'The steward who looked after the midshipman's mess in the Blackwallers': naval: latter half of C.19. Bowen.

midshipmen's parade. The lee side of the quarter-deck, the weather side being reserved for seniors: naval: ca 1820–60.

midshipmite. A midshipman: when not nautical, it gen. connotes smallness (*mite*): 1833, Marryat: coll. A perversion.

midsummer, be but a mile to. To be somewhat mad: coll: ca 1460–1570. *The English Chronicle*. cf.:

Midsummer noon. Madness. Gen. as *'tis Midsummer noon with you*, you are mad: late C.16–mid-19. cf. Shakespeare's *midsummer madness, midsummer noon*, popularly associated with lunacy, and the old proverb, *when the moon's in the full, then wit's in the wane*.

midzer. A half, as in *midzer caroon*, a half-crown: showmen's: since ca 1860. Variant of MADZA.

midzers. Money; esp., cash, coins: showmen's: late C.19–20. cf. MEDZIES.

miff. A petty quarrel; a tantrum, a fit of anger: coll and dial. (since ca 1850, mainly dial.): 1623, C. Butler, '... Lest some of the bees take a miff.' cf. MIFFY and MIFTY.

miffiness. A tendency to take offence: coll

and dial.: 1845, Ford's *Handbook of Spain*.

miffy. The devil: (low) coll: C.19. ?ex MIFF. Also in dial.; the E.D.D. derives it ex Old Fr. *maufé*, devil.

miffy, adj. Easily offended: coll and dial.: C.18–20. Cibber, Blackmore. Whence MIFFINESS. Also:

mifty. Apt to take offence: late C.17–18. Like preceding, ex MIFF.

mighty. Very considerable in amount, size, degree: late C.16–20: S.E. till ca 1840, then familiar S.E., rapidly > coll. Borrow, 'mighty damage'.

mighty, adv. Very greatly: C.13–20: S.E. till ca 1750, then coll. Johnson, 'Not to be used but in very low language'. (In C.19–20, often ironical.)

mighty!; mighty me! Coll interjections: Scots: from ca 1865. (Also in dial.)

mighty, high and, see HIGH AND MIGHTY.

mike or **Mike.** An Irishman, esp. if a labourer: coll: from ca 1873. cf. MICK, and, like that term, ex *Michael*. 2. A wasting of time; idling, esp. in *do*, or occ. *have, a mike*, to idle away one's time: low: 1825, Egan. Prob. ex S.E. *mich(e)*, to skulk. cf.:

mike, v. To hang about, either expectantly or idly: low: 1859, H., 1st ed. Where tramps are concerned, the gen. word is *mooch, mouch*. Ex S.E. *mich(e)*. cf. MIKER.

mike, do a, see MIKE, n., 2.

miker. A LOAFER; a scrounger: low: from ca 1880. Ex MIKE, v. cf. MIKING.

Mikey, see MICKY, 4.

miking, n. and adj. Idling; skulking; scrounging: low: from ca 1880. Ex MIKE, v.

***milch-kine.** (The singular, *milch-cow*, is very rare.) Applied by gaolers to their prisoners, who, when they BLEED freely, will 'have some Favour, or be at large', B.E.: c.: late C.17–early 19.

mild, draw it, see DRAW IT MILD.

mile. (With a plural numeral) miles: late C.13–20: S.E. till C.19: ca 1800–50, coll: since ca 1850, dial. and low coll. Dickens, 1850, 'I'd go ten thousand mile.'

mile of an oak, within a. Near enough; somewhere (derisively): late C.16–18: coll; sometimes a c.p. Porter, 1599, 'Where be your tools? . . . Within a mile of an oak, sir'; Aphra Behn; D'Urfey, 'Your worship can tell within a mile of an oak where he is'; Swift.

***miler.** Also *myla*. A donkey: vagabond c.: from ca 1850. Ex Romany *meila*, occ. *moila*, prob. ex dial. *moil, moyle*, a mule, and perhaps ultimately ex L. *mulus*. cf. Romany *Meilesto-gav*, lit. donkey's town, i.e. Doncaster. (Smart & Crofton.) 2. A man or a horse specially trained or qualified for a mile race: sporting: from ca 1886. 3. *-miler*. A journey, esp. a walk, of a stated number of miles: coll: 1856, Dickens, 'I went out this morning for a 12-miler.'

Miles's boy. A very knowing boy in receipt of much information: tailors': from ca 1860.

milestone. A yokel, a country boy: low (?orig. c.): from ca 1810; ob. by 1890, †by 1910. cf. MILESTONE-MONGER.

milestone, let run a. To cause a die to run some distance: gaming: 1680, Cotton; †by 1800.

milestone-monger. A tramp: coll: from ca 1860; ob. cf. MILESTONE.

milikers. Militia: low London: 1870; ob. By slovenly slurring.

military. Porter (the drink): taverns': ca 1885–1900. Ex its strength.

milk. Sexual 'spendings': low coll: from ca 1660; ob. John Aubrey. cf. MILK, v., 1. 2. A milksop; proletarian (—1887).

milk, v. To cause sexual ejaculation: low coll bordering on S.E.: C.17–20; ob. Jonson, in *The Alchemist*; D'Urfey. 2. To bet against one's own horse knowing that it cannot win; to keep (a horse) a favourite at short odds when he has no chance or may even be scratched: sporting: ca 1860–95. 3. To obtain possession, or sight, of by trickery or artifice: from ca 1860: coll till ca 1910, then S.E. e.g. *milk a telegram*, to see it before the addressee does. Prescott, *Electrical Inventions*, 1860, '. . . a wire could be milked without being cut or put out of circuit.'

milk, Bristol, see BRISTOL MILK.

milk, cry over spilt, see SPILT MILK . . .

milk, give down one's. To pay: coll, almost S.E.: ca 1590–1800. Marlowe, L'Estrange.

milk, hot, see HOT MILK.

milk and water! BOTH ENDS OF THE BUSK!: a late C.18–early 19 toast.

milk boiled over, (e.g.) **his.** He was careless: proverbial coll: ca 1730–1800. 'Proverbial' Fuller. (Occ. in other persons but rarely in other tenses.)

milk-bottle. A baby: lower classes' (—1909).

milk-fever, see PENCIL-FEVER.

milk horse. 'A horse entered at a race to make money on, and always scratched before the affair comes off': turf: ca 1865–1910.

milk in the coco-nut, no. Silly; mentally deranged: low: from ca 1850; ob. cf. the U.S. *account for the milk in the coconut*, to solve a puzzle (1853, says Thornton).

milk-jug or **-pan**; also **milking-pail.** The female pudend: low: C.18–20; ob. Ex MILK, n., 1.

milk off one's liver, wash the. To rid oneself of cowardice: coll: C.17–mid-18. Cotgrave.

milk over the fence. To steal milk from neighbours' cows: from ca 1870. Gen. as vbl n. phrase, *milking over* ... *Milk Journal*, Sept. 1871.

milk-shop or **-walk.** The female breasts: low: C.19–20; ob. cf. MILKY WAY.

milk the pigeon. To attempt an impossibility: coll: mid-C.18–20; ob. The corresponding S.E. phrases are *milk the bull* or *the ram.*

milk-woman. A wet-nurse: Scots coll: C.19–20. Hence, *green m.-w.*, one recently delivered. 2. A female masturbator: low: C.19–20; ob.

milken, see MILL-KEN.

milker. An interceptor of telegrams: from ca 1865: coll. Ex MILK, v., 3. 2. The female pudend (cf. MILK-JUG): low: C. 19–20. 3. A masturbator: low: C.19–20; ob.

milker's calf. A mother's child, esp. if a boy: Australian rural (—1888); ob. 'Rolf Boldrewood'. Ex standard sense, a calf still with the cow.

milking. vbl n. of MILK, v., 2. *The Times*, 2 Jan. 1862.

milking-pail, see MILK-JUG.

milking-pail, carry or **work the.** Racing s.: ca 1860–95. For meaning, see MILK, v., 2.

milkman. (cf. MILKER, 2; MILK-WOMAN, 2.) A masturbator: low: C. 19–20: ob.

milkman's horse. Bad-tempered: angry: rhyming s. (on *cross*): late C.19–20.

milky. A milkman: non-aristocratic coll (—1887). cf. POSTIE.

***milky,** adj. White: C.19–20 (ob.) c. Only in *milky duds*, white clothes (see DUDS), and *m. ones*, white linen rags.

milky way. The female bosom: from ca 1620: poetical S.E. till ca 1800, after which it rapidly > low s.: ob. cf. MILK-SHOP.

mill. A chisel: c.: ca 1605–1830. Dekker, Grose. 2. Hence (?), a housebreaking thief: C.17: c. Dekker. ?abbr. MILL-KEN, recorded much later. 3. The female pudend: C.18–20; ob.: ?low coll (or perhaps s.) or euphemistic S.E. D'Urfey. 4. A fight, esp. with the fists: from ca 1819: s. >, ca 1860, coll >, ca 1890, S.E. T. Moore, in *Tom Crib's Memorial*; 1825, Westmacott; T. Hughes, 'A good hearty mill'. ?ex *windmill* or ex the v. 5. See MILL, GO THROUGH THE, 2. 6. The treadmill: c.: 1842, Barham; †by 1910. 7. A prison: c.: 1838, Dickens; Mayhew, 'A month at the mill'.

***mill,** v. To rob (a building): c. of ca 1565–1840. Until C.17, only in *mill a* KEN. Harman. 2. To steal (v.t. and i.): c.: C.17–early 19. Middleton & Dekker; Jonson, 1621, 'Can they cant or mill?' 3. To beat, thrash, punch, pummel: C.18–20 (ob.): orig. c.; by C.19, low s. (cf. MILL ... GLAZE.) Hence v.i., to box, fight (occ. *mill away*): C.19–20, ob.; as in Thackeray. Also v.t., to fight with (a person): at Public Schools, esp. Harrow: from ca 1860 (?). 4. To kill: c.: from late C.17. (N.B., senses 3 and 4 derive ex sense 1, which connotes 'break in(to)' or 'through', 'knock out'). 5. To send to the treadmill, hence to prison: c.: ca 1838–1910. Dickens, in *Oliver Twist*. cf. LAG, v., 4, 5, 6. 6. See MILL ... GLAZE. 7. (Ex sense 3.) Esp. *mill the bowling*, to wear it down: cricketers': 1833, Nyren; ob.

mill, go or **pass through the.** To have (severe) experience: S.E. 2. Hence, to go through the bankruptcy court: coll or s.: from ca 1840; ob. 3. To go to prison: c. (—1889). *Daily News*, 4 July 1889.

mill, ground and bolted. – I've been through the. I'm too experienced for that!: nautical: mid-C.19–20; ob. cf. MILL, GO THROUGH THE.

mill, in the. (Imprisoned) in the guardroom: military: ca 1880–1915.

mill, safe as a thief in a. Not safe or honest at all: coll: ca 1660–1780. With allusion to 'a Miller, who is a Thief by his Trade', B.E.

***mill a quod.** To break out of gaol: c. (—1753); †by 1890. Poulter.

mill-clapper. The tongue, esp. of women: late C.17–20, ob.: coll.

***mill doll** or **M.D.** A prison: ca 1780–1830: c. Messink, Bee. 2. According to Vaux, 1812, it is 'an obsolete name for Bridewell house of correction, in Bridge-street, Blackfriars, London'.

***mill doll,** v. To beat hemp in prison: c.: ca 1750–1840. Fielding. Also *mill dolly*, recorded in 1714 in Smith's *Lives of the Highwaymen.*

***mill . . . glaze.** While *m. a* or *the glaze* is to break open a, the window (late C.17–mid-18, B.E.), *m. one's g.* is to knock out his eye (C.18–early 19, Grose): both are c.

***mill-ken.** A housebreaker: c.: ca 1669–1870. *The Nicker Nicked*; Fielding. See MILL, v., 1, n., 2. cf.:

***mill-lay.** Burglary: c.: ca 1780–1870. Ex MILL, n., 2.

***mill-tag, -tog, -tug, -twig.** A shirt: c.: resp. from ca 1850 (Mayhew), 1835 (Brandon), 1745 (B. C. Carew), and 1820 (Haggart, Egan: Scots c.): all these are ob. Perhaps ex MILL, n., 6. cf. CAMESA and MISH.

mill-wash. Canvas for lining of waistcoats and coats: tailors': from ca 1860; ob.

miller. A murderer: late C.17–early 19: c. Ex MILL, v., 4. 2. A boxer: 1812, *Sporting Magazine*; 1823, Bee; ob. by 1890. Ex MILL, v., 3. 3. A vicious horse: 1825, Westmacott: sporting: †by 1890. Ex senses 1 and 2. 4. A JOE MILLER. 5. A white hat: coaching: ca 1830–80. Ex the whiteness of flour. 6. A housebreaker: c.: C.17–mid-19. Ex MILL, v., 1.

miller (also †miller's thumb), drown the. To add too much water, esp. to flour or to spirits: coll: from ca 1815. Also *put out the miller's thumb*, 1767, and *put out the miller's eye*, 1678, Ray, and 1834, Esther Copley. 2. (Only *drown the miller.*) To go bankrupt: Scots coll: ca 1800–80. A. Scott, 1805.

miller, give (one) the. To pelt with flour, etc., in thin paper bags, which naturally burst immediately on contact: coll (—1864); ob.

miller's daughter. Water (n.): rhyming s.: late C.19–20.

miller's eye. (See MILLER, DROWN THE, 1.) A lump of flour in a loaf: coll: from ca 1830; ob.

miller's mare, like a. Clumsily: C.17: coll, semi-proverbial. Beaumont & Fletcher; Killigrew. A miller being no trainer of good horses.

miller's waistcoat (that takes a thief by the neck every day), as stout as a. A C.18–early 19 c.p., which glosses the proverb *many a miller many a thief* and that of miller, tailor and weaver in a bag.

milliner's shop. The female pudend: low: from ca 1840; ob.

milling. A beating, a thrashing: 1810, Combe, 'One blood gives t'other a milling'; ob. 2. A fight; fighting: 1815, *Sporting Magazine*; ob. 3. Robbery; theft: c.: ca 1565–1840. (For the origin of these three senses, see MILL, v., resp. 3, 3, 2 or 1.) 4. (Of horses) kicking: sporting (—1897). cf. MILLER, 3.

milling, adj. Fighting, pugilistic: from ca 1810; ob. As in:

milling-cove. A pugilist: low: ca 1810–1905. Vaux, Ainsworth. And in:

milling-match. A prize-fight; boxing-match: sporting: 1819, Moore.

million to a bit of dirt, (it's) a. (It's) a sure bet: sporting: from ca 1860; ob. cf. LOMBARD ST . . .

millstone, look or **see through a.** To be very perceptive or well-informed or shrewd of judgement: from ca 1530: coll till C.18, then S.E. Occ. *see into* (C.16–17); occ. . . . *a brick wall* (C.19–20). Often *see as far into a millstone as another* (Palsgrave, 1540).

millstone (occ. milestone or **brick wall), run one's head against a.** To resist stupidly: attempt the impossible: from ca 1835: coll verging on S.E.

millstones, one's eyes drop; weep m. Applied to one unlikely to weep: late C.16–17: coll. 1594, Shakespeare, 'Your eyes drop millstones when fools' eyes drop tears.'

milt. The semen. Hence *milt-market* or *-shop*, the female pudend; *double one's milt*, to ejaculate twice without withdrawal. Low: C.19.

milton. An oyster; coll: 1841, Thackeray; Aytoun & Martin, 'These mute inglorious miltons are divine', which offers a clue to the semantics: cf. the S.E. phrase, *close as an oyster*.

***milvad.** A blow: Scots c.: 1821, Haggart; †by 1900. Hence *milvader*, to strike. Origin?

***milvadering,** n. Boxing: Scots c.: 1821, Haggart; †by 1910. Ex preceding. Perhaps cf. the dial. *mulvather*, to confuse or bamboozle.

mim. A low coll variant, C.19–20, of MA'AM. cf. MEM; *mum*.

mimming mugger. A buffoon mimic: theatrical: mid-C.19–20; ob. i.e. *miming* (corrupted) + MUGGER, 2.

mimpins. Some kind of pretty sweetmeat: schoolboys': 1820; long †. Leigh Hunt.

mince. An abbr. of MINCE-PIES: late C.19–20, esp. in boxing; ob.

mince, v.t. and i. To dissect: medical students': from ca 1840.

mince-pies. Eyes: rhyming s. (—1857). Later, *minces* or occ. †MUTTON-PIES.

minchin malacho (or **maleego),** see MICHING MALICHO.

mind! Note what I say!: coll: 1806, J. Beresford, 'So I bar Latin, mind!'

mind, if you don't. If you're not careful (to avoid . . .): coll: from ca 1835. M. P. R. James, 1839, 'They'll see you, if you don't mind.'

mind!, never. Don't let that trouble you!; mind your own business!: coll: ca 1814, anon. in *Gonzanga*, 'Never mind, father, don't be obstreperous about it.'

mind one's book. (Of a schoolboy) to be diligent in one's studies: coll: from ca 1710; ob. Addison, 'Bidding him be a good child and mind his book'.

mind the grease! Let me pass, please!: lower classes', presumably rhyming s. (—1909).

mind the step! see STEP!, MIND THE.

mind to, have a. To be disposed (to do something). With the infinitive suppressed, it is coll: from ca 1850. Mrs Stowe, 'I don't need to hire . . . my hands out, unless I've a mind to.' Prob. ex such sentences as 'enquire what thou hast a mind to', 1671.

mind your eye! Be careful!: coll: 1737, Bracken. cf.:

mind your helm! Take care: nautical: C. 19–20. cf. preceding.

mind your ps and qs, see PS AND QS.

minder. A child left to be taken care of: 1865, Dickens: coll till ca 1890, then S.E.

mine arse, see BANDBOX . . .

mine in a Portuguee pig-knot. 'Confused, not knowing where to begin a yarn': nautical: late C.19–20. Bowen. The key is in YARN.

mine-jobber. A swindler: City coll: from ca 1880. Ex the frequent flotation of worthless companies.

mine uncle('s), see UNCLE.

mingy. Greedy: Cockney s.: ca 1890–1915. 2. Miserly, mean: coll: from ca 1900. A thinning of *mangy*, and prob. influenced by *stingy*.

minikin, tickle (the). To play the lute or viol: coll: ca 1600–40, mostly by the dramatists with a sexual innuendo (*minikin*, an endearment for a female). Marston(?), 'When I was a young man and could tickle the minikin . . . I had the best stroke, the sweetest touch, but now . . . I am fallen from the fiddle, and betook me to [the pipe].'

Minnie P. play. A play in which a little-maid variety-actress has the chief part: theatrical coll: 1885–ca 1900. Ware, 'From Miss Minnie Palmer's creations, chiefly in *My Sweetheart*'.

minor. A younger brother: schools' (orig. and esp. Eton): 1863, Hemyng, *Eton School Days*, ' "Let my minor pass, you fellows!" exclaimed Horsham.'

minor clergy. Young chimney-sweeps: ca 1787–1900.

mint. While *mint of money* is prob. to be considered S.E., *mint* (money), which dates from C.8, is S.E. till ca 1550, coll till ca 1850, then low s. In C.19–20, gen. MINT-SAUCE. 2. Gold: mid-C.17–18 c.

mint-hog. An Irish shilling: Anglo-Irish: low: C.19–20; ob.

mint-sauce. Money: from ca 1825; ob.: low. Egan; J. Greenwood, 1867, 'The requisite mint sauce (as that horribly slangy and vulgar B.P. terms money).' The corresponding U.S. term (now ob.): *mint-drops* (1837, J. Quincy Adams; prob. earlier). Thornton. See MINT, n., 1.

minus. (Predicatively) without; short of: coll: 1813. (Baumann, however, dates it from mid-C.18.) As in '*minus* one horse', 1840, or 'He was considerably minus at the last Newmarket meeting' (1813). Rarely †*minus of*. 2. As an adj., lacking, non-existent: from ca 1850: coll. Bristed, 1852, 'His mathematics are decidedly *minus*.'

mis. A variant of MISS.

mischief, ruin or a mischievous person, is S.E., but *the mischief*, the devil, is coll: 1583, Hollyband, 'What the mischief is this . . .?'; Beaumont & Fletcher, ca 1616, 'In the name of mischief . . .'

mischief, go to the. To go to the bad: coll: 1818, Susan Ferrier, 'Boys may go to the mischief, and be good for something – if girls go, they're good for nothing I know of.'

mischief, load of. A wife: C.18–early 19: coll bordering on S.E. Grose, 'A man loaded with mischief. . . with his wife on his back'.

mischief, play the. (v.t., **with.**) To play havoc: coll: 1867, Trollope, 'That butcher . . . was playing the mischief with him.'

mischievious. Mischievous: a frequent sol.: (?)C.17–20. Ex C.15–17 stressing of 2nd syllable.

misegun. Mazagan (a kind of bean): low coll or a sol.: C.19–20. Scott.

miserable. Close-fisted, stingy: Australian coll: since ca 1860. 'Tom Collins', *Such Is Life*, 1903.

miserable as a rat in a tar-barrel. Thoroughly depressed: nautical coll: late C.19–20.

miserables, the. A splitting headache after 'the night before': proletarian coll (—1887); ob.

miserere seat. A seat so constructed that if the occupant falls asleep he falls off: ecclesiastical coll: C.19–20; ob.

misery. Gin: low: ca 1820–1910. 2. (In cards) misère: coll: from ca 1830.

misery, be a. To be peevish; be a peevish person: lower classes', esp. Cockneys', coll: from ca 1880.

misery, streak of, see STREAK OF MISERY.

misery-bowl. 'Relief-basin – at sea': tourists' (—1909); slightly ob.

Misery Junction. 'The angle forming the south-west corner of the York and Waterloo Roads . . . From the daily meeting here of music hall "pros" who are out of engagements, and who are in this neighbourhood for the purpose of calling on their agents, half a dozen of whom live within hail' (Ware): theatrical: ca 1880–1914.

misfit. A clumsy man: tailors': from ca 1850.

misfortune, have or **meet with a.** To give birth to an illegitimate child: coll and dial.: C.19–20. Mrs Carlyle, Marryat. Hence, *misfortune*, a bastard: from ca 1860. Carlyle.

***mish.** A shirt; a chemise: c.: from ca 1670; †by 1870. Abbr. COMMISSION, the anglicized form of CAMESA. 2. A missionary: late C.19–20.

***mish-topper.** A coat; a petticoat: ca 1670–1850: c. Lit., that which 'tops' or goes over a MISH.

mislain, miesli, misli. To rain: Shelta: C.18–20. 2. To go: see MIZZLE.

misle, misli, see MIZZLE.

miss; more correctly **mis.** A miscarriage: women's: W. Somerset Maugham, 1897.

miss a tip. To have a fall: circus-men's: mid-C.19–20. Seago. See also TIP, n.

Miss Adams is an occ. variant of *sweet* FANNY ADAMS.

Miss Brown. The female pudend: low: late C.18–19. cf. BROWN MADAM; MISS LAYCOCK.

miss is as good as a mile, a. A narrow escape serves as well as an easy one; 'a failure by however little is still a failure'; proverbial coll: from ca 1820. Scott. Earlier, *an inch in a miss is as good as an ell.*

Miss Laycock. The female pudend: low: late C.18–19. Punning on COCK.

Miss Molly, see MOLLY, MISS.

Miss Nancy. An effeminate man: coll: from ca 1880. Ex dial. (—1824). Also NANCY. Hence, *Miss-Nancyism*, effeminacy: from ca 1885. cf. SISSY.

miss of, feel the. To feel the lack or the loss of: from ca 1855: S.E. till ca 1880, then (low) coll. George Eliot, 1860; Baumann, 1887; 'Rita', 1901, ''Tis now you'll feel the miss o' your mother.'

miss of, find or **have (a).** (The *miss* often preceded by *great, heavy, little, no.*) To feel regret at, or the disadvantage of, the loss or absence of some person or thing: C.13–20: S.E. till C.19, then coll (from ca 1880, low) and dial. Anna Seward.

miss of, there is no (great). There is no (great) regret or disadvantage in the loss, privation, or absence of some person or thing: C.14–20: S.E. till ca 1820; then dial. and coll (increasingly low), the latter being ob.

miss one's figure. To miss a chance; to make a mistake: non-aristocratic: from ca 1860; ob.

Miss Right, see RIGHT, MR. **miss the cushion,** see CUSHION, MISS THE.

miss the globe. To miss the ball altogether: golfers': from ca 1898. With a pun on *globe*, a sphere, and on *globe*, the world.

missing. Courting, courtship: ca 1830–70. *Sinks*, 1848.

missionaries' position, see MATRIMONIAL.

'missioner (or without apostrophe). An agent bullying or seducing men into the Navy or, come to that, the Army: naval coll rather than s.: ca 1770–1830. Short for *commissioner*? W. N. Glascock, *Sailors and Saints* (I, 82), 1829.

missioning. Mission-work: coll (—1887), now almost S.E.

missis; gen. **missus.** (Occ. written as *Mrs*, and always occurring as either *the missus* or, less gen., *my, your, his*, etc., *missus.*) A wife: orig. (—1839), dial. >, ca 1847, low coll. Thackeray, 1848, 'Bowing to the superior knowledge of his little Missis'. 2. (Among servants) a mistress of the house: low coll: 1837, Dickens. In this sense, often without *the, my*, etc.

missle, see MIZZLE.

missuses. The pl of MISSIS, *missus.*

missy. (In address.) Miss: coll: C.19–20. More gen. in U.S. than in England.

mist, Scotch, see SCOTCH MIST.

mistake, and no. Undoubtedly; for certain: coll: 1818, Lady Morgan, 'He is the real thing, and no mistake'; Thackeray. Also *and no error* (—1887), as in Baumann.

mister. In address with the name omitted: mid-C.18–20: S.E. (=*sir*) until ca 1820; then coll; by 1860, low coll. *Punch*, 22 Jan. 1901, 'Please, mister, when are we going to get through?'

mistress roper, or with capitals. A marine: ca 1840–95. Because he is clumsy with ropes: ?punning *miss the ropes* (a *miss-the-roper*).

mistura God help 'em. A mixture of dregs and drugs administered as a last resort: medical: from ca 1860; ob.

Mitcham whisper. A shout; almost a shout: 1880, Spurgeon, *Ploughman's Pictures*: coll. cf. *Irish whisper*, a very audible whisper. At Leigh (in Lancashire), a *Leigh whisper* is an unearthly yell.

mitching, vbl n. Playing truant: Canadian coll: mid-C.19–20. Ex Eng. dial.: see E.D.D.

mite; occ. in C.19–20, **mitey.** A cheesemonger: 1765, Foote, 'Miss Cicely Mite, the only daughter of old Mite the cheesemonger'; ob. 2. A particle, a tiny bit: C.17–20: S.E. till ca 1840, then coll (increasingly low). 3. A whit or a jot: late C.14–20: S.E. till mid-C.19, then coll. C. D. Warner, 1886, 'Not a mite of good'.

mitey, see MITE, 1.

mitre. A hat: universities' (—1896); ob.

mitt. A glove: from ca 1811; ob. Ex first sense of:

mitten. A hand; a fist: low (mostly pugilistic): from ca 1810; ob. 2. A boxing glove: ?orig. (—1859), U.S.; anglicized ca 1880. J. Greenwood.

mitten, get or **give the.** (In U.S., occ. simply *mitten* for *give the mitten to*.) To be jilted or to jilt: *get the m.*, orig. (1838), U.S., but anglicized ca 1870, also meaning to be dismissed; *give the m.*, orig. (1848), U.S., and anglicized ca 1870, with further sense, to dismiss. Both slightly ob. Prob. ex MITTIMUS with allusion to *mitten*.

mittens, easy as, adj. Free in speech and/or manner; free and easy: low (s. bordering on coll): from ca 1890; ob. Mostly London. Milliken.

mittens, handle without. To handle roughly: coll soon > S.E.: from ca 1675; ob. Ray, Johnson. In late C.19–20, gen. *handle without gloves* or *with the gloves off*.

mittimus. A dismissal from one's post, as in *get one's m.*, which also means to receive one's quietus. Coll: from late C.16. Nashe, 'Out of two noblemen's houses he had his mittimus of ye may be gone.'

mivey or **mivy.** A landlady: mostly Cockneys': from ca 1870.

mivvy. An adept; a very smart person: c.: from ca 1870. Pugh (2): '"He's a mivvy at makin' things easy." "For himself. No doubt o' that."' Perhaps ex *master* + *skilful*, but probably from S.E. *marvel*. By 1900, low Cockney.

mix. A MESS, a muddle; a state of confusion: coll: from ca 1880. cf. MIX-UP.

mix 'em, see MIXUM.

mix (C.19) or **join** (late C.18–19) **giblets.** To marry: low. See GIBLETS.

mix it up, see MIX UP, V.

mix-metal. A silversmith: late C.18–mid-19: coll.

mix them. To mix one's bowling: cricketers' coll: from mid-1890s.

mix-up. Confusion; a MESS, a muddle: coll: from ca 1895. cf. MIX.

mix up, v. Mainly as *mix it up*, 'to agree secretly how the parties shall make up a tale, or colour a transaction in order to cheat or deceive another party', Bee: ca 1820–95.

mixed. Confused, bewildered: coll: from ca 1870. *Punch*, 4 Sept. 1880, 'Rather mixed after twenty-one hours' continuous sitting'. 2. Slightly drunk: low coll: from ca 1871; ob. *Leeds Mercury*, 29 Aug. 1872.

mixum; occ. **mix 'em.** An apothecary: coll: ca 1630–1720. Glapthorne, 'Mr Mixum, your apothecary'.

***mizzard.** The mouth: c.: from ca 1890; ob. P. H. Emerson. Corruption of MAZZARD.

***mizzle** or **mis(s)le**; occ. **†misli.** To decamp; depart slyly: orig. (ca 1780), c. >, ca 1820, low s. G. Parker, 'He preferred mizzling off to France.' Ex Shelta *misli*. 2. Hence, to die: boxers': ca 1810–60. 3. To rain: Shelta: C.19–20.

mizzle, do a. (As n., *mizzle* does not otherwise occur.) To decamp: low: from ca 1850. Ex preceding; cf. the next entry.

mizzle one's dick. To miss one's passage: nautical: since ca 1880.

***mizzler.** A fugitive; one who departs slyly: orig. (—1834), c. >, ca 1840, low s. Ainsworth. Hence, *rum mizzler*, one clever at getting away.

mo. A *mo*ment, esp. in *half a mo*: low coll: late C.19–20.

moab. A hat; esp. the turban-shaped hat in feminine vogue, 1858–9: university (mainly Cambridge): ca 1858–80. Ex

'Moab is my washpot,' Psalm lx, 8: the approximate shape. 2. A lavatory at Winchester College: from ca 1860; †. 3. A receptacle for dirty plates: Haileybury: since ca 1870. Derivation as for sense 1.

Moabite. A bailiff: late C.17–19. cf. PHILISTINE.

moach, see MOOCH. **moak,** see MOKE.

mob. The rabble, the disorderly part of the population (1688). The populace, the crowd (1691). s. till ca 1750; coll ca 1750–1820; then S.E. Burke, 1790, 'A mob (excuse the term, it is still in use here) which pulled down all our prisons'; T. Hale, 1691, 'the beliefs of the mob', in the second sense. cf. the C.18–mid-19 proverb, 'The mob has many heads but no brains.' Abbr. MOBILE, itself a shortening of *mobile vulgus*, the fickle or excitable crowd. 2. A gang of criminals, esp. of thieves: orig. (1845 in '*No. 747*') c. > low by 1851 (Mayhew); as early as 1843 as *swell mob*. Prob. ex: 3. (Gen. in pl.) A companion in crime: c. (—1839); †by 1890. 4. In Australia, a gang of roughs: late C.19–20: s. > coll. Ex: 5. A group or crowd of persons, esp. if possessing common interests: coll: Australia, from ca 1880. 'Rolf Boldrewood' speaks, in 1884, of 'the "Dunmore *mob*"'. (N.B., mob as (part of) a herd, a flock, is 'standard' Australian now recognized as S.E.) cf. *mob* as 'party of men' in whalers' s. of ca 1820–1900. 6. In late C.19–20, a military unit, esp. a battalion or a battery. (Not disrespectful.) s. rapidly > coll. 7. A harlot (cf. *mab*): c.: 1665, Head; 1697, N. Lee; Grose. †by 1830. 8. A RAG (concerted mischief): Charterhouse: late C.19–20.

mob, v. To crowd; hustle; attack in a disorderly mob: from early C.18: coll till ca 1800, then S.E. Ex MOB, n., 1 and 2. Whence MOBBING. 2. To RAG: Charterhouse: late C.19–20. cf. MOB, n., 8, and next two entries.

mob-up. To hustle (a person): Charterhouse: ca 1870–1910. A. H. Tod, *Charterhouse*, 1900. cf. MOB, v.

mobbing, vbl n. corresponding to MOB, v., 1: 1734, North: coll >, ca 1800, S.E. H. Walpole, 'The night will be full of mobbing, bonfires, and lights.' (Perhaps the same holds of the adj. *mobbish*, late C.17–20, ob.)

mobile. The rabble, the rough part of the population: 1676, Shadwell, 'Do you hear that noise? the remaining rogues have raised the mobile.' 2. Whence, the populace: from ca 1680. Shadwell, 'The mobile shall worship thee.' Both senses, orig. coll, were S.E. by 1700; ob. by 1830, †by 1850 except historically. cf. MOB, n., 1 and 2.

mobility. The low classes: 1690, B.E. and Dryden: s. till ca 1750, coll ca 1750–1810, then S.E.; ob. by 1840, † (except historically) by 1915. In the *Maccaroni and Theatrical Magazine*, Jan. 1773, appeared this notice: 'Pantheon's: the *Nobility's*, Oxford Road; the *Mobility's*, Spawfields' (see Chancellor, *Pleasure Haunts of London*). Ex MOB, n., 1, on *nobility*.

mobocracy. The rabble as a ruling body: 1754, Murphy: coll till ca 1810, then S.E. Ex MOB, 1, and, though much less, 2.

***mobsman.** A pickpocket: from ca 1850; ob. Mayhew. 2. But orig. (ca 1845), a member of the 'swell mob' (properly SWELL MOBSMAN); hence, any well-dressed swindler (—1859).

moche, see MOOCH.

mocho. Mocha coffee: low (—1887); ob.

mock-duck or **-goose.** A piece of pork that, stripped of crackling, is baked with a stuffing of sage and onions: coll: from ca 1875. O.E.D.

***mock-litany man.** A sing-song beggar: Anglo-Irish c. (—1909).

mockered. Full of holes; (of a face) pitted: low: from ca 1850. Ex Romany *mockodo*, *mookeedo*, dirty, filthy (*moker*, to foul).

mocteroof, v.t. and i. To doctor damaged fruit or vegetables: Covent Garden: from ca 1860; ob. e.g. chestnuts are shaken in a bag with beeswax. ?etymology. Perhaps a corruption of *new-proof*.

model of, the (very). Some person or thing that very closely resembles another: orig. (—1849) and still dial., > coll ca 1890.

modest quencher. A small drink: from ca 1860; ob.: coll.

modicum. An edible thirst-relish: 1609, Dekker; soon †. 2. The female pudend: low: ca 1660–1840. Cotton. (cf. †S.E. jocular sense, a woman: cf. BIT, 7; PIECE.)

mods or **Mods.** The first public examination for B.A. degrees: Oxford University: coll: 1858, J. C. Thomson, 'Between the "little-go" and "mods" he learns nothing new.' Ex *Moderations*.

modsman. A candidate for MODS: Oxford coll (—1887).

moey; occ. **mooē(y).** The mouth: low: from ca 1850; ob. Ex Romany *mooi*, mouth, face. 2. The female pudend: low: from ca 1855; ob.

moffling chete, see MUFFLING CHEAT.

mofussil. Rather provincial; countrified: from ca 1840: coll >, ca 1890, S.E. Ex the n., which (*the Mofussil*) is standard Anglo-Indian for the country districts or anywhere out of a capital city. Ex Hindustani. Hence:

mofussilite. An inhabitant of a rural district: Anglo-Indian coll: from ca 1845. Ex preceding term.

mog. A lie: 1848, *Sinks*. Prob. ex Fr. (*se*) *moquer* (*de*); cf. MOGUE.

moggy. An untidily dressed woman: low: from ca 1880; ob. (Also dial.) Ex dial. *moggy*, a calf, a cow. 2. A cat: Cockneys' (and dial.): late C.19–20.

mogue, v.t. and i; n. To mislead; joke, gammon: low and tailors': 1870, Bell's *Life*, 19 June. Whence *no mogue*, honestly, and *moguing*, n., GAMMON. Prob. ex Fr. (*se*) *moquer* (*de*).

moguey. A coll corruption of Maori *moki* (or *mokihi*), a raft: mid-C.19–20.

mohack, see MOHOCK.

mohair. A civilian; a tradesman: military: 1785, Grose; ob. by 1870, †by 1890. Ex the mohair buttons worn by civilians; soldiers have metal buttons.

mohawk, see MOHOCK.

mohican. A very heavy man who rides a long way in an omnibus for sixpence: ca 1845–60. *Tait's Magazine*, 1848, 2nd Series, vol. XV.

mohock; occ. mohack or mohawk. (Or with capitals.) An aristocratic ruffian night-infesting London, ca 1710–15. From 1711: coll > S.E.; ob. by 1760, except historically. Ex *Mohawk*, a member of a Red Indian tribe. Swift, 'A race of rakes, called the Mohocks, that play the devil about this town every night'.

moiety. A wife: coll > S.E.: from ca 1735; ob. Punning BETTER HALF.

moist one's clay. To drink: from ca 1830.

moisten, v.i. To drink: from ca 1840; ob. Also *moisten one's* CLAY or CHAFFER, 2 (—1864).

moke. An ass: s. and dial.: 1848, J. L. Tupper; Thackeray. ?ex MOGGY, or perhaps Romany *moila*, an ass (cf. MILER), or rather ex Welsh Gypsy *moxio* or *-a*, a donkey: Sampson supports the third origin and notes that *moxio* existed at least 50 years before the first recorded instance of *moke*; moreover, Brandon, in 1839, records *moak* as a c. word of Gypsy origin and, at that time, mainly Gypsy use. Yet Gypsy *moxio* may well be an adaptation of the dial. *Mock*(*e*), a nickname for either a horse or an ass, precisely as MOGGY, in several dial., is a nickname for cow, calf, or ass, and *Mog* is a cat. *Mog* (cf. *Meg*) and *Moggy* (cf. *Meggy*) and even *Moke* are diminutives of *Margaret*, perhaps via *Molly*. We have, then, the interesting fact that both of the modern names for an ass represent diminutives: DONKEY of *Duncan*; *moke* of *Margaret*. cf. MOKUS. 2. A fool: orig. (1871), U.S.; anglicized ca 1890; ob. 3. A very inferior horse: Australia: 1888, 'Rolf Boldrewood', 'I am regular shook on this old moke.' cf. sense 1. 4. A variety artist who plays on several instruments: theatrical (—1890). 5. A compositor: printers' (—1857). A variant of DONKEY, ASS.

moko. A pheasant mistakenly shot before the shooting season: sportsmen's: from ca 1860.

mokus. An occ. s. (ob.) and dial. variant of MOKE, 1, 3: mid-C.19–20. Prob. ex *moke* + *-us*, a 'characteristic Romany termination of masculine loan-words', Sampson.

molasses in winter, slow as. Exceedingly slow: coll: late C.19–20. In winter, molasses is very stiff.

mole. The penis. Whence *mole-catcher*, the female pudend. Low: C.19–20, ob.

***moll.** A harlot: C.17–20: c. >, ca 1890, low. Middleton, 'None of these common molls neither, but discontented and unfortunate gentlewomen.' Ex the familiar form of *Mary*. 2. An unmarried female companion of a criminal or a tramp: c.: from ca 1820. cf. the U.S. *gun moll*, a woman who carries a revolver for her 'man'. 3. A girl: from ca 1835: c. >, ca 1860, low. 4. Hence, a sweetheart: low: from ca 1890.

moll, v.; **molling,** vbl n. To go – going – about with women; act – acting – effeminately: low: from ca 1860; ob. Ex the n.

Moll(-)Blood. The gallows: Scots coll: ca 1810–50. Scott.

***moll-buzzer.** A pickpocket specializing in women: c.: from ca 1855. Perhaps orig. U.S. Whence *moll-buzzing*, this practice.

***moll hook.** A female pickpocket: c.: from ca 1860.

moll-hunter. A man 'always lurking after women': low: late C.19–20. Ware. See MOLL, 1 and 3.

moll Peatley's, or – prob. erroneously – **Pratley's, gig.** Copulation: C.18–early 19:

low. Budgell, in the *Spectator*, 'An impudent young dog bid the fiddlers play a dance called Moll Patley.' Ex MOLL, 1, perhaps allusively to some whore surnamed *Patley* or *Peatley*.

***moll-sack.** A lady's hand-bag; occ. a small market basket: c.: from ca 1838.

***moll-slavey.** A maid-servant: c. of ca 1810–70.

Moll Thompson's mark. 'M.T.' = empty. 'Empty packages are said to be so marked,' F. & H.: ca 1780–1890.

***moll-tooler.** A female pickpocket: c.: from ca 1858; ob.

***moll-wire.** A pickpocket specializing in robbing women: c.: from ca 1865; ob.

***molled;** gen. **molled up.** Sleeping with a woman not one's wife: c.: 1851, Mayhew. 2. Accompanied by, esp. arm in arm with, a woman: low: from ca 1860. Both senses ex MOLL, but resp. ex sense 1 (or 2) and sense 3.

***mollesher;** more gen. **mollisher.** A – gen. a low – woman; a thief's mistress: c.: from ca 1810; ob. Ex MOLL, 1.

moll's three misfortunes, a. In the B.M. copy of the 1st ed., Grose has written: 'Broke the [chamber-]pot, bes–t the bed and cut her a–se.' But this low c.p. of ca 1785–1820 was included in no ed. whatsoever.

molly. An effeminate man; a milksop: coll: 1879, L. B. Walford, though possibly existing a century earlier: the entry in Grose (1st ed.) is ambiguous. Ex MISS MOLLY. 2. A sodomite: coll: 1709, E. Ward; ob. cf. *pansy*. But ca 1895–1914, a merely effeminate fellow was often called a GUSSIE; in C.20, a sodomite is a NANCY, a *Nancy-boy*, or a SISSY, this last also applying to a milksop. 3. A wench; a harlot: coll: 1719, D'Urfey, 'Town follies and Cullies, And Molleys and Dollys, for ever adieu'; ob. (As a country lass, it is dial.) All ultimately ex *Mary*: cf. MOLL.

molly, v.t. 'to bugger (someone)'; hence, adj. *mollying*, 'addicted to buggery'. *The Ordinary of Newgate's Account*, 1744, contains both – e.g. 'You mollying dog'. Ex sense 2 of the n.

Molly, Miss. A milksop, an effeminate fellow: from ca 1750; ob.: coll >, ca 1890, S.E. cf. MOLLY, all senses, and MISS NANCY. (But *Miss Mollyism*, C.19–20 (ob.), is S.E.)

molly-head. A simpleton: from ca 1900; ob. ?orig. U.S. Ex MOLLY, 1.

Molly Maguires. An Irish secret society that, ca 1843, aimed to intimidate bailiffs and their like: app. not recorded before 1867 (W.S. Trench): coll, quickly > S.E. Ex their usually dressing in women's clothes and ex Connor Maguire, a noted C.17 conspirator, says Dawson.

molly-mop. An effeminate man: coll: 1829, Marryat; ob. Ex MOLLY, 1.

Molly O'Morgan. An organ: late C.19–20.

mollygrubs, see MULLIGRUBS.

molly's (or Molly's) hole. The female pudend: low: C.19–20; ob. Ex MOLLY, 3.

molo(c)ker. A renovated hat: trade (—1892); ob. Ex *molo(c)ker*, v., to renovate an old hat by ironing and greasing: trade (—1863). Sala. ?ex the inventor's name.

molrower. A wencher, esp. a whoremonger: low: from ca 1860; very ob. Ex:

molrowing, vbl n. Whoring: low: from ca 1860; ob. Ex: 2. Caterwauling: low: from ca 1858; ob. Milliken, 'Beats 'Andel's molrowings a buster'. Perhaps a fusion of *miauling* and *caterwauling*.

mompyns, see MUNPINS.

monaker, monarch, etc. A sovereign (coin): from ca 1855; ob.: low. Orig. (—1851), a guinea. Mayhew. 2. The ten-oared boat: Eton College: ca 1890–1915. 3. A name or title: orig. tramps' c., it >, in all extant forms, gen. though somewhat low s. ca 1900. The forms are these: *monaker*, from ca 1860 (though Baumann implies from mid-C.18), not very gen.; *monarch* (—1879), ob., *Macmillan's Magazine*, 1879, vol. XL; *monarcher* (cf. MONARCHER, 2), app. first in P. H. Emerson, 1893; *monekeer*, 1851 (Mayhew), †; *moneker*, from ca 1852, while *monneker* arises ca 1855; *monica*, from ca 1890; *monnaker* (cf. *monaker*), from ca 1865; *mon(n)ick* (—1895), as in *The Times*, 11 Nov. 1895; *mon(n)icker*, a frequent form, from ca 1880; and *mon(n)iker*, the most gen. form of all (—1874), H., 5th ed. The etymology is mysterious: H. proposes *Ste Monica*, *Monica* deriving from L. *monitor*, an adviser, ex *monere*, to advise, to warn; Ware asserts that it derives 'from Italian lingo for name, Monaco being the Italian for monk'. W., however, thinks that it may be a Shelta word, and gives the meaning as 'sign'; but recent opinion favours *monogram*, which, I freely admit, is supported by: 4. A signature (—1859). This sense, however, causes me to wonder if the term be not a blend of *monogram* + *signature*; and this sense may possibly be earlier than sense 3. In a letter of 4 April 1959, Mr Jacob Jaffe suggests that it might be back-s. for *ekename*. This theory presupposes that a back form *emaneke* becomes *maneke* (trisyllabic), varied to *moneke* (trisyllabic) whence *monaker* etc. The chronologies of *ekename* and *monaker* do not exclude the possibility, but I prefer the derivation ex *monogram*.

monaker (etc.), **tip** (a person) **one's.** To tell one's name: low: from ca 1860.

monarch(er). See MONAKER (esp. 3). 2. **monarcher, big.** An important person: tramps' c. (—1893); ob.

Monday, adj. An intensive: from ca 1890; very ob.: low. Kipling, 1892, in *Snarleyow*, 'You may lay your Monday head | 'Twas juicier for the niggers when the case began to spread.' ?by misunderstanding or by corruption ex MULTY.

Monday, black, see BLACK M. **M., bloody,** see BLOODY M. **Monday, St,** see ST M.

Monday mice. The numerous black eyes seen that morning after the week-end drinking: London streets': late C.19–20; slightly ob.

Monday pop. One of the celebrated popular concerts at St James's Hall, London: coll: 1862, Geo. Eliot in letter of 26 Nov.

moneke(e)r; monekeur (very rare), see MONAKER, 3.

money. Money's worth; a way of investing money: coll: 1851, Mayhew, 'In February and March . . . green fruit's not my money'; ob. 2. A (gen. very young) girl's private parts: low: from ca 1780; ob. 3. Bubbles in a cup of tea: since ca 1870.

money, a pot – or pots – of. A large amount of money; a fortune: coll: from ca 1870. Mrs H. Wood, 1871, *pots*; Trollope, *a pot*.

money, eggs for. An excuse, a trick. Esp. in *take eggs*, to suffer a trick, accept an excuse. Coll: C.17. Shakespeare, *The Winter's Tale*.

money, hard. Coin, as *soft money* is notes: coll: from ca 1848.

money, it's like eating. This is a costly business: semi-proverbial coll c.p. (—1887).

money, not (a person's). Not to one's taste or choice: coll: late C.19–20. Esp. as in Manchon, 'You ain't everybody's money.' Prob. suggested by *(the)* MAN FOR MY MONEY.

money, (so and so) for my. (So and so) is what I like, desire, would choose: coll: C.17–20. W. Haughton, 1616, *English-Men for my Money* – a title.

money, Spanish. Fair words and compliments: late C.17–18.

money, the man for (e.g.) **my,** see MAN FOR MY MONEY.

money-bag lord. An ennobled banker: Society coll: 1885–ca 1914. cf. GALLIPOT BARONET.

money-box, -maker, and (†) **-spinner.** The female pudend: low: C.19–20; ob.

money-bug. A millionaire: anglicized in 1898 from U.S.A.; ob.

money burns in (e.g.) **his pocket(, e.g. his).** He cannot keep money; is impatient to spend it: from ca 1530: coll till ca 1860, then S.E. More, Cornwallis (1601), Farquhar, T. Hughes.

***money-dropper.** A swindler who, dropping counterfeit money, gets good change from some FLAT: c.: 1748, Smollett. †by 1905. cf. RING-DROPPER.

money makes the mare to go, see MARE (TO) GO.

money talks. Money is very powerful: semi-proverbial c.p. bordering on S.E.: 1586, Pettie, 'The tongue hath no force when gold speaketh'; 1666, Torriano, 'Man prates, but gold speaks.'

mongar(l)ey, see MUNGAREE.

***mongrel.** A sponger; a hanger-on among cheats: c.: ca 1720–1890.

***monic** or **monick.** A mainly c. variant of MONAKER: late C.19–20.

monica, monick, monicker, moniker, see MONAKER, 3.

monish. Money: mostly Yiddish (—1887). Ex *money* or rather *moneys*. But also, ca 1840–80, jocular, with a humorous imitation of Jewish pronunciation: *Sinks*, 1848.

monk. A term of contempt: low: from ca 1860. 2. A dark or an over-inked spot in a printed sheet: printers': 1683, Moxon: s. >, ca 1830, j. Perhaps ex the Westminster Abbey associations of Caxton's press. cf. FRIAR. 3. Abbr. *monkey*, the animal: mid-C.19–20: (low) coll. 4. A sickly parrot: from the 1890s. Ex head indrawn and dejected.

***monkery;** occ. **monkry.** The country: tramps' c.: 1790, Potter; Egan; Mayhew; P. H. Emerson. 2. (Preceded by *the*) tramps or other vagrants collectively: tramps' c.: 1851, Mayhew. 3. The practice of going on tramp: tramps' c.: from ca 1850. Mayhew, 'He had followed the "monkry" from a child.' 4. Hence, *on the monkery*, on tramp (Mayhew, 1851).

All senses are directly ex Shelta of C.18–20; all, too, are ob. cf. DEUSEAVILLE. 5. (Ex senses 1 and 4.) A district: grafters' s.: from ca 1880.

***monkery, on the,** see MONKERY, 4.

monkey. £500 (in U.S. $500): 1856, *The Druid*; Whyte Melville. (The O.E.D. cites an 1832 text in which, prob. erroneously, it = £50.) Among stockbrokers, however, *monkey* (in C.20) = £50,000 of stock, i.e. 500 shares of £100. cf. PONY, 3. 2. 'A vessel', i.e. a container, 'in which a mess receives its full amount of grog', F. & H.: nautical (—1867): s. >, ca 1890, j. Prob. ex MONKEY, SUCK THE. 3. A hunting flask (for drinking): hunting s. or coll: ca 1850–80. Surtees. 4. See MONKEY UP. 5. A sheep: rural Australian: from ca 1880. A. C. Grant, *Bush Life*, 1881. 6. The instrument that propels a rocket: military (—1860): s. >, ca 1895, j. 7. A hod: bricklayers' (—1885): s. >, ca 1905, j. 8. A small bustle or dress-improver (—1889); †by 1896: coll. *Notes & Queries*, 22 June 1889. 9. A padlock: c. (—1812). 10. A mortgage (see MONKEY ON A HOUSE); a writ on a ship: nautical: late C.19–20. 11. A clerk, esp. if unimportant: mechanics' (—1909). 12. A greatcoat: naval: ca 1810–60, Glascock, 1838. cf. senses 2, 8. 13. 'In English vulgar speech the monkey is often made to figure as a witty, pragmatically wise, ribald simulacrum of unrestrained mankind. Of the numerous instances, "You must draw the line somewhere, as the monkey said, peeing across the carpet" is typical. The phrase "... as the monkey said", is invariable in this context' (Atkinson): esp. since ca 1870.

monkey, cold enough to freeze the balls off a brass. Exceedingly cold: low coll (mainly Australian): late C.19–20.

monkey, suck the. To drink liquor, esp. rum, from a cask with a straw through a gimlet hole (cf. ADMIRAL, TAP THE): nautical: 1785; ob. cf. MONKEY, 2; perhaps it is a telescoping of the idea expressed in sense 3. 2. To drink liquor from a bottle; hence, to tipple: gen. s.: 1797; ob. 3. To drink rum out of coconuts, from which the milk has been drawn off: nautical: 1833, Marryat; ob.

monkey-board. The conductor's or the footman's place on an old-style omnibus or on a carriage: coll: 1842, Mrs Trollope; J. Greenwood. †by 1895.

monkey-boat. A small boat used in docks: 1858. 2. A long, narrow canal boat: 1864. Both senses are nautical s. >, ca 1905, j.

monkey-cage. A grated room from which a convict sees his relatives and friends: low: from ca 1870. cf. Fr. *parloir des singes*.

monkey-coat, -jacket. A close-fitting, short jacket, 'with no more tail than a monkey': nautical: from ca 1810: s. >, ca 1890, coll; app. orig. U.S.

monkey-hangers. Port Glasgow men: Greenock seamen's: late C.19–20. Topical: Bowen gives the anecdote.

monkey is up, see MONKEY UP. **monkey-jacket,** see MONKEY-COAT.

monkey island. 'The uppermost tier of a big ship's bridge': nautical: late C.19–20. Bowen.

monkey-motions. Physical drill: military: ca 1890–1914. Also naval: late C.19–20; ob.

monkey off one's back, take the. (Gen. in imperative.) To calm oneself: low (—1887). See MONKEY UP.

monkey on a gridiron. A cyclist: Cockneys'; late C.19–20. J. W. Horsley, *I Remember*, 1912.

monkey on a, gen. **one's** or **the, house; monkey on** or **up the chimney.** A mortgage on a house: mainly legal: 1875; ca 1885. Ob. cf. MONKEY WITH A LONG TAIL. 'Prob. suggested', says the O.E.D., 'by the initial *m* of *mortgage*'.

monkey on or up a stick. A thin man with jerky movements: coll: ca 1880–1920. Ex the now seldom seen toy so named (1863).

monkey on a wheel. A bicyclist: from ca 1880; ob.

monkey on horseback without tying his tail?, who put that. A low c.p. applied to a bad horseman: late C.18–early 19.

monkey on one's back, have a. A ca 1880–1910 variant of MONKEY UP.

monkey-parade, see MONKEY'S PARADE.

monkey-poop. 'The half deck of a flush decked ship': nautical coll verging on j.: late C.19–20. Bowen.

monkey-pump. The straw in MONKEY, SUCK THE, 1: nautical (—1867); ob. Smyth.

monkey-shines, monkey-like antics or tricks, is U.S. (1847) and has never been properly anglicized, though it was occ. heard, ca 1875–1905, in Britain.

monkey-tail, hold on by somebody's. To take someone's word for a story: nautical (—1887). Baumann. Punning *tale*; cf. *monkey about*, (S.E. for:) to play the fool.

monkey up, get one's. To make, but gen. to become, angry: s. (—1859) and dial.

Also, in predominant sense, *one's monkey is up* (1863, O.E.D.) or †*have a* or *the monkey on one's back* (—1864). Anon., 1877, *Five Years' Penal Servitude*, 'My monkey was up, and I felt savage'; 'Rolf Boldrewood', 1888, 'The mare, like some women when they get their monkey up, was clean out of her senses.' 'Perhaps alludes to animal side brought uppermost by anger', W. cf. BACK UP, adj.

monkey up, put one's. To anger a person: from ca 1830. cf. preceding entry.

monkey up a (or the) stick, like a. Performing queer antics: coll: late C.19–20. Ex the once popular toy.

monkey up the chimney, see MONKEY ON A HOUSE and:

monkey with a long tail. A mortgage: legal (—1886); ob. cf. MONKEY ON A HOUSE.

monkey with a tin tool(, like a). A low coll phrase denoting self-satisfaction or impudence: from ca 1863; ob.

monkey's allowance. More rough treatment than money: 1785, Grose; Marryat, 1833, 'When you get on board you'll find monkey's allowance': s. >, ca 1840, coll; ob. 2. Short rations: naval: late C.18–very early 20. W. N. Glascock, *Sailors and Saints* (I, 166), 1829.

monkey's fist. 'A knot at the end of a heaving-line to ensure its safe passage from a ship to jetty', Granville: naval coll: late C.19–20.

monkey's grease, (as) useless as. Useless: C.18: coll. 'Proverbial' Fuller. (Monkeys are thin.)

monkey's island. An occ. variant of MONKEY ISLAND. (F. & Gibbons.)

monkey's money. Payment in kind, esp. labour, goods, or, most of all, fair words: ca 1650–1800: coll. Urquhart, 1653, 'Paid for in court fashion with monkey's money'. cf. MONEY, SPANISH.

monkey's orphan. '19th century naval name for the disappearing ship's fiddler', Bowen.

monkey's parade. A (length of) road frequented by lads and lasses, esp. with a view to striking an acquaintance ('clicking'): (low) urban, esp. London: from ca 1895. Also **monkey-parade.**

monkey('s)-tail. A short hand-spike: nautical s. >, ca 1860, j.: 1823, *The Night Watch.* 2. A nail: rhyming s.: late C.19–20.

Monmouth Street finery. Tawdry clothes, furniture, etc.; pretence, pretentiousness: ca 1850–80: low coll. Mayhew. Monmouth (ca 1890 > Dudley) Street was long a well-known market for second-hand clothes.

monnaker, monneker, monnicker, monniker, see MONAKER, esp. 3.

monocular eyeglass. The breech: low: ca 1860–1910.

monosyllable. The female pudend: either polite s. or a vulgarism; ob. by 1880, † (except among the cultured) by 1915. Anticipated in Lucas's *The Gamesters*, 1714, thus, 'Perhaps a bawdy monosyllable' – i.e. *cunt* – 'such as boys write upon walls' but app. first 'dictionaried' in 1788, Grose, 2nd ed. (which, by the way, has been shamefully neglected by lexicographers), as 'a woman's commodity' (see COMMODITY). Omitted by O.E.D., as is CUNT, the word both connoted and denoted by *the monosyllable*, of which 'Jon Bee' remarks, in 1823, 'of all the thousand monosyllables in our language, this *one* only is designated by the definite article; therefore do some men call it "the article", "my article", and "her article" as the case may be.' For a fuller treatment, see my edition of Grose.

mons. A crowd; to crowd (v.i.): Winchester College: ca 1860–1920. ?L. *mons*, a mountain, or an abbr. of *monster* or *monstrous.* 2. (Gen. *Mons.*) A catachrestic abbr. of *monsieur*: C.18–20; ob. ('Regarded in Fr. as intentional impertinence', W.)

Mons Meg. The female pudend: low: C.19. ?ex the C.15 gun in Edinburgh Castle.

monstrous, adj. An intensive (very great, iniquitous, etc.): coll: ca 1710–1840. Swift, 'We have a monstrous deal of snow'; F. Burney, 'this monstrous fatigue'; Cobbett, 'Here is a monstrous deal of vanity and egotism.'

monstrous, adv. A general intensive (cf. AWFUL; BLOODY): coll: ca 1590–1850. Shakespeare, 'monstrous desperate'; Congreve; Mrs Trollope, 'monstrous good friends'.

Mont. A tramp or a beggar: Cockneys': late C.19–20; ob. Origin prob. anecdotal – perhaps in a picturesque tramp named Monty.

month, a bad attack of the end of the. Shortness of money: jocular coll: from ca 1870. i.e. waiting for the month's salary to be paid.

month of Sundays. A long time: coll: from ca 1830. Marryat, 1832.

monthlies, the. Menstruation: 1872: a

vulgarism >, ca 1895, low coll. cf. FLOWERS.

month's end, an attack of the, see MONTH.

***montra.** A watch: c.: ca 1810–50. Ex Fr. *montre*.

moo-cow. A cow: childish coll: 1812, Combe, 'The moo-cow low'd, and Grizzle neighed'; Thackeray. cf. BOW-WOW; COCK-A-DOODLE-DOO.

mooch. An idling, scrounging, skulking, hanging about, looking for odd jobs. Hence, *on the mooch*, adj. and adv., engaged in one of these 'activities'; in Wiltshire dial., shuffling(ly). H., 1st ed., 1859; *London Herald*, 23 March 1867. Also *mouch*. (cf. MIKE, 2.) Ex the v. 2. See sense 5 of:

mooch, v. (Also *mouch*; cf. MIKE, 2.) To idle, sneak, hang about (often with *about*); slouch (with *along*): low: 1851, Mayhew. Also dial. Prob. ex MIKE, v., influenced by Fr. *mucher*, to hide, skulk. 2. 'To sponge, slink away and allow others to pay for your entertainment', Barrère & Leland: ca 1855–1910. 3. v.t., to steal, pilfer: 1861, Mayhew (to steal things one finds lying about); ob.: prob. c. > low s. and dial. 4. To be a tramp: tramps' c.: late C.19–20. Gen. as vbl n.: *mooching*. cf.: 5. 'To walk round and round the decks in company': *Conway* cadets' (—1891). Also *come* (or *go*) *for a mooch*.

mooch, do a, see DO A MIKE.

moocher; moucher. A lazy loiterer or hanger-about; a loitering thief (gen. a pilferer); a tramp: a (professional) beggar: low: from ca 1855. Also *mutcher*. cf. dial. senses: see E.D.D. Ex the preceding.

moochi. An Indian shoemaker: Regular Army coll: late C.19–20. Ex Hindustani.

mooching, mouching, vbl n., see MOOCH, v. 2. adj., from ca 1860. Also dial.

mooë, mooey, see MOEY.

mooer. A cow: coll: ca 1820–1910. Ex *moo*, v. cf. MOO-COW; MOWER.

mooi. Fine; handsome: South African Midlands coll: from ca 1880. Ex the Dutch *mooi* (handsome, pretty, fine), which, among the Cape Dutch, 'has to do duty for almost every shade of appreciation', Pettman.

***moon.** A month's imprisonment: c.: 1830, Moncrieff, 'They've lumbered him for a few moons, that's all.' Hence, *long moon*, a calendar month. cf. DRAG, n., 7.

moon, v. (Gen. with *about*, *along*, or *around*.) To idle, lounge, or wander as in a dream: coll: 1848, Albert Smith; Charlotte Yonge, '. . . When you were mooning over your verses'. 2. Occ. v.t. with *away*, as in Besant & Rice, 1877, 'I might have mooned away the afternoon in the Park.'

moon, a blue, see BLUE MOON.

moon, find an elephant in the. To find a mare's nest: ca 1670–1830. Butler, *The Elephant in the Moon*. Ex the C.17 Sir Paul Neal, who thought that a mouse in his telescope, as he looked through it, was an elephant in the moon.

moon, shoot (occ. bolt or shove) the. To depart with one's valuables and, if possible, furniture, by night without paying the rent: coll: 1823, Egan's Grose, *shove* (†by 1870), c.; *bolt*, †by 1905, occurring in 1825, and *shoot* in 1837. cf. MOONLIGHT FLIT.

moon and the milkman, go between the. To *shoot the* MOON: proletarian: ca 1860–1910.

***moon-curser.** A link-boy, esp. one that lights his clients into a pack of rogues: c.: 1673, Head; †by 1840. (In dial., a shipwrecker.)

moon-eyed hen. A squinting wench: ca 1780–1890.

moon-faced. Japanese-faced: non-aristocratic (—1887); ob.

moon, God bless her!, – it is a fine. A proverbial c.p. greeting the new moon: from ca 1670; ob. Aubrey.

moon is made of green cheese, make believe the, see CHEESE, BELIEVE . . .

moon knows about Sunday, know no more about it than the. To know nothing about it: coll (—1887); slightly ob.

***moon-man; moon's man.** A Gypsy: C.17–early 19: c. (after 1800, perhaps low s.): Dekker, B.E., Grose. 2. A robber by night: late C.16–17: coll. Shakespeare (*moon's man*); 1632, Sherwood, who defines as a brigand.

moon-raker. A Wiltshire man: from ca 1765: coll, slightly ob. Grose, 2nd ed., says that some Wiltshire rustics, seeing the moon in a pond, tried to rake it out: Wiltshire people prefer a more complimentary legend. 2. Hence, ca 1830–1900, a smuggler: dial. (mostly) and coll. 3. A blockhead: from ca 1840, ob.: coll >, ca 1900, S.E. Ex sense 1. 4. A real or imaginary sail above the skysail: nautical, resp. (—1867) j. and (—1896) s.

moon-raking, vbl n. and ppl adj.: from ca 1865; ob. Coll >, ca 1895, S.E. See MOONRAKER.

moon-shooter. See MOON, SHOOT THE. From ca 1890.

mooner. A dreamy idler, lounger, wanderer: coll: 1848, Albert Smith.

mooney. A variant spelling of MOONY.

moonlight. Smuggled spirits: from ca 1809; > ob. ca 1890. Scott. Ex the night-work of smugglers: cf. MOONSHINE.

moonlight flit, flitting. A removal of household goods by night without paying the rent: resp. dial. (—1824) >, ca 1865, s.; s. (—1721) >, ca 1880, coll. O.E.D.; F. & H., where the occ. late C.19–early 20 variant, *London flitting*, is recorded. cf. MOON, SHOOT THE.

moonlight wanderer. One who does a MOONLIGHT FLIT or 'London flitting': ca 1820–70.

moonlighter. A harlot: from ca 1850; ob.

moonraker, see MOON-RAKER. **moon's man,** see MOON-MAN.

moonshee. An Indian teacher of, an amanuensis in, languages. This sense (1776) is prob. to be rated as 'standard'; but as = a learned person (—1864), *moonshee* is coll, as in 'Indian interpreter': military: late C.19–20. Also *moonshi, munshi, munshee.*

moonshine. Smuggled spirits: 1785, Grose: coll >, ca 1890, S.E. Often with a specific sense: white brandy, in Kent, Sussex; gin, Yorkshire.

moonshine, gilded. Bogus bills of exchange: ca 1820–1910, but ob. as early as 1880. Ex the metaphorical S.E. sense of *moonshine*: unreality.

moonshine in the mustard pot (for it). Nothing: coll: ca 1630–1700. Gen. preceded by *one shall have*. cf. S.E. *moon(shine) in (the) water*. (Apperson.)

moony. A noodle: coll: from ca 1850. Ex: 2. adj., silly, which is S.E. 3. But *moony*, drunk, (gen.) slightly drunk, is s.: 1854 (O.E.D.).

moored in Sot's Bay (or s. b.). 'Drunk and incapable': nautical: late C.19–20. Bowen. cf. GUTTER-LANE.

Moorgate rattler. A SWELL of that London district: Cockneys': 1899–1910.

Moorish. Mohammedan: C.16–20: S.E. till ca 1830, then coll, increasingly low; ob.

mootch, see MOOCH.

mop. A drinking-bout. Hence *on the mop*, on the DRUNK or the drink. Low: from ca 1860, ob., as is: 2. A drunkard, same period. cf. LUSHINGTON: see also LUSH.

mop, v. To empty a glass or pot: ca 1670–1810. Cotton. cf. MOP UP, 1. 2. To collect, obtain, appropriate: coll: from ca 1850; †by 1905. cf. MOP UP, 2.

mop-eyed, see MOPE-EYED.

mop out. (cf. *wipe out*.) To FLOOR, kill; ruin (—1892); †by 1910: low. Gen. in passive. Milliken, 1892, in his *'Arry Ballads*. cf. MOP UP, 5.

mop-squeezer. A housemaid: low: 1771. Ob. cf. SLAVEY.

mop-stick. A ninny, a simpleton: low (—1887); slightly ob. Also *mopstick.*

mop (or wipe) the †earth, floor, †ground with one. (Occ. with *up* after *mop*.) To knock a person down (—1887).

mop-up. A severe trouncing, in single fight or, gen., in battle: C.20; ob. Conan Doyle, 1900, 'Better six battalions safely down the hill than a mop-up in the morning.'

mop up, v. To empty (e.g. a glass): from ca 1810. cf. MOP, v., 1. 2. Also, to eat: rare before ca 1890. 3. To collect, obtain, appropriate: from ca 1855. Mayhew. 4. v.i., to stop talking, gen. in imperative (—1887); ob.: low. Walford, the *Antiquarian*, April 1887. 5. To kill, slaughter: mainly military and naval (—1887). Baumann: Rider Haggard. cf. the n., and *wipe out.*

mope-eyed (occ. mop-eyed) by living so (or too) long a maid, you are. A proverbial coll or c.p. of ca 1645–1720. Herrick, Ray, B.E. (Lit. *mope-eyed* = purblind.)

Mope-Eyed Ladyship, her. Fortune: Ned Ward, 1703. Notoriously blind.

moper. A deserter: military (—1887); virtually †.

mopes, the. Low spirits, esp. if shown: from ca 1825: coll. Hone, 'I have got the mopes'; Thackeray.

moph. A variant (Bee, 1823) of MUFF (n., 2), a fool.

mophy. (Of a youth) delicate and well-groomed: seamen's: late C.19–20.

moppery. The head: 1821, Pierce Egan, *Life in London*, †by 1870. The site of one's *mop.*

***moppy.** Drunk: c.: from ca 1820; †by 1915.

mops, in the. A perversion, ca 1830–1910, of *in the* MOPES.

mops and brooms. Half-tipsy: coll: 1814, *Sporting Magazine*; Hardy; ob. With *be*. Ex the drinking customary at *mops* (statute hiring-fairs), the girls carrying a mop or a broom to indicate the kind of work they desired. Hence:

mops and brooms, feel all. To be full of bitterness and sorrow: low (—1887).

mops(e)y. A (gen. short) homely or, esp.,

dowdy woman: late C.17–20: coll till ca 1830, then S.E.; †by 1910. Ex *mopsy*, an endearment.

mopstick, see MOP-STICK.

mopus. A moping, or a dull, stupid, person: coll: ca 1690–1820; then extant only in dial. Ex S.E. *mope*, n. and v. 2. A small coin: ca 1690–1860: c. >, ca 1750, s. Tait's *Edinburgh Review*, 1841. 3. In pl (often *mopusses*), money: ca 1765–1905: low. Anon., *The Stratford Jubilee*, 1769, 'If she had the mopus's, I'll have her, as snug as a bug in a rug'; 1892, M. Williams. ?ex Sir Giles *Mompesson*, an early C.17 monopolist.

moral. Likeness; counterpart. Rare except in *the very moral of*: low coll: 1757, Smollett; G. Parker, Smedley, 'Rolf Boldrewood'. Slightly ob. Perhaps ex the †S.E. sense, a symbolical figure, but prob. by a sol. for *model*. 2. A 'moral certainty', which it shortens: orig. and still mainly racing: 1861, Whyte-Melville; 1869, J. Greenwood, 'Everything that is highly promising becomes, in the slang of the advertising tipster, a moral.'

moral-shocker. A novel dealing with sex: ca 1890–1914: Fleet Street. Loose for *morals-shocker*. cf. HILL-TOPPER.

Moray coach. A cart: from ca 1805; ob.: Scots jocular coll.

more power to your elbow! A c.p. of encouragement: late C.19–20. Of Anglo-Irish origin.

more R than F. A c.p. applied, ca 1860–1910, to one who is more rogue than fool; esp. to a servant that *seemed* foolish.

more sauce than pig, ca 1670–1750, like **more squeak than wool,** C.18, indicates greater show than substance. Proverbial coll: resp. B.E., Swift; North. cf. the C.19–20 dial. *more poke* (bag) *than pudding*.

more than the cat and his skin, you can't have. A semi-proverbial, non-aristocratic c.p. (—1887); ob. A variant of *having one's cake and eating it*.

more war! A Cockney c.p. directed at a street quarrel, esp. among women: 1898. In reference to the Spanish-American War.

more wind in your jib! The c.p. of sailors in a ship with foul wind on meeting another with a fair wind: mid-C.19–20. (Thus will the wishers' ship gain a fair wind.)

moreish (occ. **more-ish**); **morish.** That makes one desire more: coll: from ca 1706, though not in print till 1738. Swift, '*Lady S.* How do you like this tea, Colonel? *Col.* Well enough, Madam; but methinks 'tis a little more-ish.'

morepork (kind of a fellow). A 'dull dog'; a fool: Australian coll: from ca 1840; very ob. R. Howitt, 1845; 'Rolf Boldrewood', 1890. Ex the bird named more properly *mopoke*.

morgan rattler. 'A cane or stick with a knob of lead at one or both ends, and short enough to be carried up the sleeve': low s. (—1902) ex dial. (—1866); †by 1910. Prob. ex a man's name. cf. COSH, and NEDDY, 4.

***mork.** A policeman: c. (—1889); ob. Clarkson & Richardson. Prob. a corruption of Romany *mo(o)s(h)kero*, a constable.

morley, see MAULEY.

morning. An early drink: 1718, Ramsay; 1854, R. W. Van der Kiste: mostly Scots: coll till ca 1860, then S.E. Also, from ca 1890, *morning-rouser*. 2. See:

morning! or **morning to you!**, or **the top of the morning to you!** (Cheerily) good morning!: from ca 1870: orig. and still mainly Anglo-Irish: coll.

morning-drop. The gallows: ca 1810–90: ?orig. c.

morning pride. See PRIDE OF THE MORNING.

morning-rouser, see MORNING, 1.

***morning sneak.** One who robs houses or shops while – before the household is up or the staff arrived – the servant or the shopman is cleaning steps, windows, etc.: c. (—1812); ob. by 1890. 2. In C.18 c., *the morning sneak* is 'to walk about the Streets in a Morning betimes, and 'sping [*sic*] any Body to go out of Doors, then immediately the Thief goes in,' as *The Regulator*, 1718, has it.

morning's morning. A variant (ca 1895–1914) of MORNING, 1.

morocco, in. Naked: Gypsy s.: C.19–20; ob. Longfellow. cf. LEATHER, n.

morocco man. An agent of a fraudulent lottery assurance: ca 1795–1830: s. > coll. Colquhoun, *Police of the Metropolis*, 3rd ed., 1796.

Morpheus, in the arms of. Asleep: coll: C.19–20. Morpheus is properly the god of dreams.

morrice, morris. To be hanged: c. of ca 1720–70. 2. (Often with *off*.) To decamp; depart: from ca 1760; ob. Cowper, 1765; Grose; Dickens; Grenville Murray, 'The fellows . . . flirt with them, and morris off to town in spring for better amusement.' 3. To move rapidly: sporting: ca 1825–60. 4. To die: boxing s.: ca 1810–60.

morrice (or morris), do a. A variant (?from ca 1770; ob.) of MORRICE, 2.

Morse (or Moss) caught his mare, as. Asleep. See NAPPING, CATCH.

***mort;** occ. **morte** (early). A woman; c.: ca 1560–1890. Awdelay: B.E., 'a Wife, Woman, or Wench'; Disraeli. 2. A harlot; a near-harlot: from ca 1565: c., †by 1910. 3. A yeoman's daughter: c.: late C.17–18. Also *mot*, late C.18–19 only: 'Arabian' Burton. All senses prob. cognate with or ex Dutch *mot* as in *mot-huys*, a brothel (Hexham); note, however, that Dr John Sampson, in *The Times Literary Supplement* of 21 June 1928, derived *mort* ex *amourette*.

***mort, autem-, dimber-, kinchen-,** see AUTEM, adj.; DIMBER; KINCHEN.

***mort, strolling** or **walking.** A female tramp: c.: late C.16–19. Chetle (*walking*).

mortal. Very great; AWFUL: coll: from ca 1715; ob. Countess Cowper, 1716, '[They] take mortal pains to make the Princess think well of the Tories'; Dickens. 2. As an emphatic expletive (with *any*, *every*, or a negative): coll: 1609, Jonson, 'By no mortal means(!)'; 'every mortal thing', 1843. cf. *no* EARTHLY chance. 3. Tediously long: 1820, Scott, 'Three mortal hours'; Stevenson, 'They performed a piece . . . in five mortal acts.' 4. Short for *mortal drunk* (cf. at MORTALLY): from ca 1808: Scots and Northern coll and dial.; ob.

mortal, adv. Excessively; DEADLY: C.15–20; ob.: S.E. till ca 1750; then, as in Warburton, coll till ca 1820, after which it is low coll (as in Thackeray's 'mortal angry') and dial.

mortallious. Very drunk: mostly lower classes': C.19–20. Ex '*mortal* drunk'. cf.:

mortally. Extremely; AWFULLY: coll: mid-C.18–20. e.g. *mortally drunk*. cf. preceding.

mortar. Abbr. of MORTAR-BOARD: low coll: from ca 1870. 2. The female pudend: low: C.19–20; ob. cf. PESTLE.

mortar, bricks and. Houses; house property: coll: from ca 1905.

mortar, have one's finger in (the). To dabble in building: coll: ca 1630–1750. Berkeley MSS., 1639; Gerbier, *Discourse of Building*, 1662; Swift.

mortar and trowel. A towel: rhyming: since ca 1870.

mortar-board. A trencher-cap, worn at universities and some Public Schools: coll: 1853, 'Cuthbert Bede', ' "I don't mind this 'ere mortar-board." '

mortar-pounder. A ship's doctor: nautical: late C.19–20.

mortgage-deed. A pawn-ticket: from ca 1860; ob. cf. TOMBSTONE.

moschkener, see MOSKENEER.

Moses!; by the holy (jumping mother of) Moses!; by the piper that played before Moses!; holy Moses! A (low) coll asseveration: resp. from ca 1858, ob.; 1876, Hindley (in full), ob.; 1890, Hume Nisbet, †; 1855, Strang.

Moses, prickly. The mimosa: Australian bushmen's (—1887).

Moses, stand. 'A man is said to stand Moses when he has another man's bastard child fathered upon him, and he is obliged by the parish to maintain it,' Grose, 3rd ed.: ca 1790–1920. Contrast dial. *say Moses*, to make an offer of marriage. 2. Hence, absolutely (of a man only). To adopt a child: lower classes'; mid-C.19–20.

mosey; occ. **mosey off.** To decamp; depart quickly: orig. (1836), U.S.; anglicized ca 1890.

mosey along. To jog along: orig. (—1877), U.S.; anglicized ca 1890; slightly ob. Kipling, 1891, 'I'll mosey along somehow.'

***mosh.** To leave a restaurant without paying: c.: from ca 1860; ob. A deliberate corruption of MOOCH, v., 2.

***mosh, the.** The practice of 'moshing' (see preceding entry): c. (—1857); ob.

mosiqui. A little girl: showmen's: from ca 1870.

mosk. To MOSKENEER, which it shortens: from ca 1900: perhaps orig. c.

moskeneer; occ. **moskeener, moshkeneer, moschkener, moskuiner.** To pawn (v.t. or i.) for more than the article is worth: ?orig. (—1874), c. > low. Henley, 1887, 'Fiddle, or fence, or mace, or mack; Or moskeneer, or flash the drag'. Ex modern Hebrew *mishken*, to pawn, by Yiddish corruption. 2. Hence, he who does this (—1893), as in P. H. Emerson. cf. MOSKER.

moskeneering. The profession of pawning at unfair prices: see preceding.

mosker. A professional pawner at prices unfair to the pawnbrokers: low (?orig. c.): 1883: *Daily Telegraph*, 9 July, in a long article.

mosky. A dolphin: nautical: late C.19–20. Whence?

mosque. A church: a chapel: either c. or low: ca 1780–1830. G. Parker.

***moss.** Lead: c.: from ca 1787; ob. Grose, 2nd ed., 'Because both are found on the tops of buildings'. cf. BLUE PIGEON. 2. Money: ?orig. (—1859), U.S., though adumbrated in early C.17; ob. Prob. ex *a rolling stone gathers no moss.*

Moss caught his mare, as, see MORSE ...

mossker. An occ. variant of MOSKER.

mossoo. Monsieur; a Frenchman: low coll (almost sol.): 1870; slightly ob. cf. MOUNSEER.

mossy. Dull; stupid: s. or jocular coll: ca 1595–1605. 'Mossy idiots', 1597. For etymology, cf. U.S. *mossaback* and:

mossy-back. An old-fashioned person: orig. U.S.; anglicized as coll ca 1890; ob.

mossyface; old mossyface. The ace of spades: low: from ca 1860; ob. 2. In late C.18–mid-19, however: the female pudend.

most of you!, all there but the. A low c.p. applied to copulation: from ca 1850; ?ob.

***mot, mott.** A girl: c.: 1785, Grose; ob. by 1880, †by 1915, except in Ireland, where it has, since late C.19 (if not earlier), been used in low s., not necessarily pejoratively. But *mot of the* KEN (Mayhew) = matron of the establishment. A thinned form of MORT. 2. A harlot: c.: from ca 1790; ob. A variant of MORT.

mot, v.i. To go wenching: c.: C.19–20; ob. Ex MOT, n., 2.

mot-cart. A brougham: ca 1820–70: low (prob. orig. c.). 2. A mattress: low: (—1890). Ex MOT, n., 2.

***mot-case.** A brothel: c.: mid-C.19–20; ob. Ex MOT, n., 2.

mote, v.i., with vbl n. *moting.* To drive or ride in a motor-car: coll: 1890–ca 1907. A prospectus of June 1890 (*moting*); *Westminster Gazette,* 18 Jan. 1898, 'Leaving London about midday we shall mote to Ascot.'

moth. A harlot: from ca 1870; very ob.: low. Either ex the attraction of night-lights or ex †S.E. sense, 'vermin'.

mother. A female bawd: low coll: late C. 17–20, but in C.18 gen., and in C.19–20 only, applied to the keeper of a brothel. Also, in reference, *the mother.* Also *mother* ABBESS (C.18–mid-19); MOTHER DAMNABLE; MOTHER MIDNIGHT; MOTHER OF THE MAIDS. 2. One's wife, if she is also a mother: Cockney coll: from ca 1880.

mother?, did you tell your, see MOTHER KNOW ...

mother, he'll be a man before his. A derisive c.p. either in retort or, more gen., in comment: from C.17; ob. Not in polite circles.

mother and daughter. Water: rhyming s. (—1864).

Mother Bunch. Water: Cockneys': ca 1590–1640. Dekker, *The Shoemaker's Holiday* (performed in 1599), IV, iv, Firk, 'Am I sure that Paul's steeple is a handful higher than London Stone, or that the Pissing-Conduit leaks nothing but pure Mother Bunch? Am I sure that I am lusty Firk? God's nails, do you think I am so base to gull you?' Mother Bunch was a well-known London ale-house 'hostess', as mentioned in *Pasquil's Jests,* 1604.

Mother Carey's chickens. Snow: nautical (—1864). 2. Applied to faring alike and paying the same: ca 1820–50.

mother damnable. A female brothel-manager: C.19–20; ob. See MOTHER.

Mother Hubbard. A cupboard: rhyming s.: late C.19–20. Ex the nursery rhyme.

mother-in-law. A mixture of 'old and bitter' (sc. ales), hence the etymology: 1884, *Daily Telegraph,* 3 July; ob. Mostly public-house.

mother-in-law's bit. A small piece: coll: from ca 1780. Grose, who thereby designates a step-mother – the meanness of such being notorious.

Mother Knab-Cony. A bawd: s.: Ned Ward, 1709.

mother know you're out?, does your. A derisive c.p. addressed to a person showing extreme simplicity or youthful presumption: 1838, in Bentley's *Miscellany,* '"How's your mother? Does she know that you are out?"' Baumann, 1887, has *what will your mother say?* and *did you tell your mother?* 2. Also in more gen. circumstances (—1895).

mother makes it, like. Very well cooked; extremely tasty: lower classes' coll: late C.19–20. Collinson. Prob. with allusion to many married men's stock complaint, 'Umph! not like (my) mother makes it.'

mother midnight. A female bawd: low: late C.17–18. 2. A midwife: low: late C.17–20; ob. The latter sense always predominated.

mother of all saints or souls, – of masons, – of St Patrick. The female pudend: low: resp. G. A. Stevens, 1785; Grose, 3rd ed. (say 1791), likewise ob.; ca 1810–70, 'Jon Bee'; *Lex. Bal.,* 1811. Anglo-Irish and ob. All are low.

mother of pearl. A girl: rhyming: since ca 1870. But this very Cockney term occurs only in *my old mother of pearl*, my old girl, my wife; often shortened to *mother* – to the confusion of non-Cockneys.

mother of the maids. A female brothel-keeper: low coll: ca 1787–1830. Ex – and in derision of – the ca 1570–1800 title of the head of the maids of honour in a Royal household.

mother sold her mangle?, has your. An urban (mostly London) c.p. of no special application: somewhat low: ca 1870–1900.

mother or **grandmother to suck eggs, teach one's,** see EGGS, TEACH . . .

mother's blessing, or **M.B.** Proletarian (—1861; ob.), as in Mayhew, 'My husband's bedridden, and can't do nothink but give the babies a dose of "Mother's Blessing" (that's laudanum, sir, or some sich stuff) to sleep 'em when they's squally.'

mother's milk. Gin: from ca 1820; ob.: low. Moncrieff. 2. Hence, spirits of any kind: from ca 1840; very ob. *Sinks*, 1848.

mother's (or **mothers'**) **ruin.** Gin: late C. 19–20. Perhaps it is rhyming s.

mother's white-haired boy. A mother's darling: coll, gen. derisive: from ca 1895.

motor. A FAST (2) man about town: London Society: 1896–ca 99. 2. A tutor for examinations: Oxford University: 1897–ca 1900. Simply a pun on COACH.

***mott,** see MOT.

motter. 'Name given to the motor carriage on its very first official appearance in London on Lord Mayor's Day, 1896': Cockneys': 1896–8 (or 9). Ware.

motting, vbl n. Wenching; whoring: C.19–20 low; ob. Ex MOT, v.

mottob, n. Bottom: back s. (—1859).

mouch; moucher; mouching, see resp. MOOCH; MOOCHER; MOOCHING.

mouchey, Mouchey. A Jew: low: from ca 1860; ob. Ex or cognate with *Moses*: cf. Ger. *Mauschel*. cf. YID.

moulder. 'A lumbering boxer, one who fights as if he were moulding clay,' Bee, 1823: pugilists': ca 1820–1900.

mouldies. Old clothes; *moult the mouldies*, get rid of, change, one's old clothes: Cockney: 1895, James Greenwood, *Inside a 'Bus*. i.e. clothes going mouldy. cf. MOULDY, adj., 2.

mouldy. A purser's steward: nautical: from ca 1875; very ob. Ex *mouldy provisions*.

mouldy, adj. Grey-headed: from ca 1860; ob. cf. MOULDY-PATE. 2. Worthless: coll: from ca 1890, as in 'a mouldy offer'. Anticipated in 1876 by Stevenson, 'I have had to fight against pretty mouldy health.' Ex the S.E. senses, decaying, decayed, lit. and fig.

mouldy-grub. (Gen. in pl.) A travelling showman; an open-air mountebank: low: from ca 1860; ob. Hence, vbl n., *mouldy-grubbing*, the work of such persons. In S.E., the term is † for *mulligrubs*.

mouldy one or **'un.** A copper coin: low: from ca 1850; ob. Ex colour.

mouldy-pate. A lackey with powdered head: ca 1860–1900.

moulies. Copper coins: low Cockney: late C.19–20. i.e. *mouldies*, ex the colour. cf. MOULDY ONE.

mounch-present (as in Awdelay), see MUNCH-PRESENT.

mounseer or **Mounseer.** A Frenchman: mid-C.17–20: S.E. till C.19, then (low) coll when not jocular S.E.; ob. W. S. Gilbert, e.g. in *Ruddigore*. cf. MOSSOO. Baumann, 1887, has the nautical *Mounseer Cockoolu*.

mount. A bridge: c.: C.18–19. But only in **Mount, the.** 2. A saddle-horse: coll: 1856, Whyte-Melville, 'A dangerous and uncontrollable mount'. 3. A copulation: low coll: from ca 1856; ob. cf. RIDE. 4. Hence (?), a wife or a mistress: from ca 1856: low.

mount, v. To get upon in order to copulate with: late C.16–20: S.E. till C.19, then (of animals) coll or (of persons) low coll. 2. To supply, 'set up': ca 1770–1890. D. Graham, 1775, 'The old woman . . . mounted [Tom] like a gentleman.' 3. (Occ. v.i.) to prepare for representation on the stage: theatrical (—1874) coll. 4. In c., v.i., to swear falsely, commit perjury, for money: from ca 1780; ob. G. Parker; *Daily Chronicle*, 6 March 1902. vbl n., *mounting*. 5. (Likewise in c.) *mount for* = BONNET FOR. Vaux, 1812; †by 1900.

Mount Pleasant. The *mons veneris*: low: from ca 1880; ob. Ex the London district and the pubic eminence. cf. SHOOTER'S HILL.

mount the ass. To go bankrupt: coll: late C.18–mid-19. Ex the old Fr. custom of mounting a bankrupt on an ass, face to tail, and leading him through the streets.

mount the cart. To be hanged: lower classes' coll: C.18–early 19. The victims proceeded in a cart to the place of execution.

mountain-dew. Scotch whisky: 1816, Scott: coll >, ca 1860, S.E. Bee, 1823, defines it, however, as contraband whisky.

mountain of piety, climb the. To pawn

some of one's effects: jocular coll (—1891); ob. By itself, *mount(ain) of piety* is S.E., C. 17–20, ob.

mountain-pecker. A sheep's head: low (—1859); †by 1910. cf. JEMMY, n., 5.

mounted pitcher. 'A grafter who talks and demonstrates from the top of his stall high above the crowd': grafters' coll, verging on j.: late C.19–20. Hence, *work mounted*, to do this: id.: id.

mounteer. A hat: s.: Ned Ward, 1703.

***mounter.** A swearer of false evidence, a giver of false bail: c.: from ca 1780; ob. Implicit in G. Parker, 1781; Vaux. Ex MOUNT, v., 4.

mourning. As n., two black eyes. Hence, *half-mourning*, one black eye. Gen., however, *in mourning*, bruised, black, either (of eyes) *to be in mourning* or (of persons) *have one's eyes in mourning*: mostly pugilistic: 1814 (O.E.D.), *Sporting Magazine*; 1820, 'Peter Corcoran' Reynolds. See also *have been to* BLACKWALL. 2. Both vbl forms are likewise, from ca 1880, applied to dirty finger-nails. 3. 'When a ship, or square-rigged vessel appears in mourning, the yards on each mast are alternately topped on end': W. N. Glascock, *Sailors and Saints* (I, 215), 1829. A naval phrase, dating late C.18–19.

mourning, (full) suit of. Two black eyes (—1864).

mourning-band. A dirty, esp. a black, edge to a finger-nail: from ca 1880.

mourning-coach horse. 'A tall, solemn woman, dressed in black and many inky feathers': London middle classes': ca 1850–90. Ware.

mourning shirt. A flannel shirt, as it needs comparatively little laundering (—1908).

mouse. A raised bruise: pugilistic: 1854, 'Cuthbert Bede'; ob. Ex the bluish colour. 2. Hence, a black eye (cf. MOURNING): from ca 1860. 1895, *Westminster Gazette*, 'A black eye in true cockney slang is known as a mouse.' 3. F. & H. says that it also = the face, the mouth: prob. this is fleeting s. of the 1890s, but I find no other record of these two senses. 4. The penis: low: C.19–20; ob. 5. A woman, esp. a harlot, arrested for brawling or assault: London police's: ca 1780–1800. R. King, 1781. 6. A barrister; occ. a solicitor (cf. the c. sense of MOUTHPIECE): ca 1888–1910: low (?orig. c.). Nat Gould.

mouse! Be quiet, or talk low!; softly!: low: C.19. Mostly U.S.

mouse, (as) drunk as a. Very drunk: C. 14–20; ob.: proverbial coll. Orig. (*as*) *drunk as a drowned mouse*.

mouse-buttock, see MOUSE-PIECE.

mouse-digger. Winchester College, ca 1840–1910. Mansfield, 1866, 'Plying the mouse digger (a kind of diminutive pick-axe) in search of mice'.

mouse-foot!, by (the). A mild coll oath: ca 1560–1640. A. Dent, 1601, 'I know a man that will never sweare but by Cocke, or Pie, or Mouse Foot. I hope you will not say these be oaths.'

mouse-hunt. A wencher: coll: late C.16–mid-17. Shakespeare. ?also *mouse-hunter*.

mouse in a cheese, speak like a. i.e. faintly; indistinctly: proverbial coll: late C.16–20; ob.

mouse in a churn, warm as a. Very snug: proverbial coll: ca 1670–1720. Ray.

mouse-piece or **-buttock.** (In beef or mutton) that part immediately above the knee-joint: coll and dial.: C.19–20; ob. In S.E., *mouse*.

mouse tied with a thread, as sure as a. Very far from sure: proverbial coll: ca 1540–1600. 'Proverbs' Heywood.

mouse-trap. The mouth: low: C.19–20; ob. 2. The female pudend: low: from ca 1850; ob. 3. A sovereign: low: from ca 1855. Ex 'a fancied resemblance of the crown and shield to a set trap', F. & H.

mouse-trap, the parson's. Marriage: late C.17–19.

mouser. The female pudend, the CAT (5): low: C.19–20; ob. 2. A battalion man, because, like a cat, he remains in quarters, to watch the mice: militia: C.19. C. James, in his *Military Dict.*, 1802. 3. A detective (—1863; ob.): low (?orig. c.).

mouth. A noisy, prating, ignorant fellow: late C.17–mid-19; anticipated in Shakespeare. Dyche. cf. MOUTH ALMIGHTY. 2. A dupe (Cotton, 1680); hence, a fool (1753, Poulter): c. >, as in H., 3rd ed., low s.; ob. 3. Spoken impudence (cf. CHEEK and esp. LIP): C.19–20; ob. Not very gen. 4. The dry or furry mouth caused by a debauch: low coll: from ca 1870. 'He has a mouth this morning.' cf. HOT COPPERS.

mouth, occ. **face, laugh on the wrong** (occ. **other) side of one's,** is S.E., but **sing on the . . .** is coll: from ca 1760.

mouth!, shut your. Stop talking!: low coll (—1895). cf. Fr. *ferme!*

mouth almighty. A noisy, talkative person: low: ca 1860–1910.

mouth and will die a lip, you are a. A low,

abusive c.p. of ca 1860–80. Ex MOUTH, n., 1.

mouth-bet. A verbal bet: the turf: from ca 1860; ob.

mouth half cocked. A person gaping and staring ignorantly at everything he sees: coll: late C.17–early 19.

mouth-pie. A feminine scolding or wrangle: Cockneys' (—1909).

mouth thankless. The female pudend: low Scots: mid-C.16–early 17. Kennedy, A. Scott.

mouth that cannot bite or **says no words about it.** The female pudend: C.18–mid-19: low coll; occ. euphemistic S.E. D'Urfey (latter form).

mouth wide, open one's. To ask a high price: coll: from ca 1890. C. Roberts, 1891, 'To use a vulgarism, he did not open his mouth so wide as the other.'

mouther. A blow on the mouth: boxing: 1814; slightly ob.

mouthful. A long word, esp. a name, that 'fills' the mouth: coll: 1884. cf.:

mouthful, say a. To say something important or arresting: English of ca 1780–1880, then U.S. Clearly adumbrated in *Sessions*, Sept. 1790, 'I never said a *mouth full of ill against her* in my life.'

mouthful of moonshire, give one a. To feed on fair words: late C.18–mid-19: coll. Ray, ed. of 1813.

***mouthpiece.** A defending counsel; a solicitor: c. (—1857).

movables, see MOV(E)ABLES.

move, a (gen. clever or sly) action or movement, is S.E., but FLASH *to* (e.g. *every*) *move*, 1812, was perhaps orig. c. (†by 1900), FLY *to* . . . is low s.; *up to* (—1859), perhaps orig. coll, is S.E. in C.20.

move, v.i. To depart, make a start; move away or off: mid-C.15–20: S.E. till ca 1750, then coll. Toldervy, Haliburton.

move in the blind. To *shoot the* MOON: low: ca 1860–1910. Here, BLIND = darkness.

move off. To die: coll: from ca 1760; ob. Foote, 'Whether from the fall or the fright, the Major mov'd off in a month.'

move on, get a, v.i. To hurry; make progress: coll: orig. U.S.; anglicized ca 1907.

move the previous question. To speak evasively: Society (—1909); ob. Ex Parliamentary j.

move to. To bow to (a person): app. ca 1900–20.

***mov(e)ables.** Swords, jewellery, small objects of value: c.: ca 1690–1830.

mow. To copulate with: Scots and Northern dial. or coll: C.16–early 19. The word, occ. as a n., survived in low s. till late C.19. Scots, either dial. or coll, is *mowdiwark* or *-wort*, the penis.

***mow-heater.** A drover: c.: mid-C.17–mid-19. Ex the drovers' habit of sleeping on hay mows.

***mower.** A cow: c.: ca 1670–1830. Perversion of MOOER.

Mowree. A New Zealand seaman: nautical: late C.19–20. Ex *Maori*.

Mozzy. Judy; cf. SWATCHEL, *Punch*. Showmen's: from ca 1850. ?via Lingua Franca ex It. *moglie*, wife.

Mr, see MISTER. **Mr Ferguson, Knap, Nash, Palmer, Right.** See each name, but for **Mr Pullen** see PULL IN.

Mrs Evans, see EVANS, MRS.

Mrs Gamp, Mrs Harris. (Gen. together.) The *Standard*, the *Morning Herald*, esp. when they were owned by a Mr Baldwin: ca 1845–60: journalists'. Ex Mrs Gamp and her imaginary friend Mrs Harris in Dickens's *Martin Chuzzlewit* and the way those inter-appealing newspapers had of pretending to be independent.

Mrs Jones. A water-closet: low: from ca 1860; ob. Gen. as *visit* or *go to see Mrs Jones*. cf. MY AUNT (JONES) and SIR HARRY.

Mrs Kell(e)y!, you must know. A c.p. 'with no particular meaning', gen. addressed to 'a long-winded talker': London: 1895–1905. Ex a 'phrase used for two years at all times and places by Dan Leno'. Ware.

***Mrs Lukey Props.** A female brothel-keeper: tramps' c. (—1896); ob.

Mrs Partington. 'A personification of impotent and senile prejudice': 1831; ob.: coll >, ca 1890, S.E. Sydney Smith. 2. Also, 'a kind of Malaprop', F. & H.; coll, in C.20 verging on S.E. but very ob. Besant & Rice, 1872, 'As Mrs Partington would say, they might all three have been twins.'

Mrs Suds. A washerwoman, a laundress: 1757, Foote; ob.: coll.

Ms and Ws, make. To be drunk, esp. walk unsteadily: printers': from ca 1860.

mubblefubbles. Low spirits: ca 1585–1670. Lyly, Gayton. ?echoic; cf. MULLIGRUBS.

much?, how, see HOW MUCH?

much!, not. *Not* LIKELY! or certainly not!: coll: from ca 1885.

much matter of a wooden platter. Much fuss about a trifle: ca 1630–1750. A proverb verging on coll.

much of a . . ., with a negative. A great . . .; a . . . of a noteworthy quality or to any great degree. Coll: from ca 1840. Dickens, 'He don't lose much of a dinner.'

much of a muchness. Of much the same size, degree, value or importance; very much alike; coll: 1728, Vanbrugh; 1860, *Punch*; 1876, G. Eliot, 'Gentle or simple, they're much of a muchness.'

much wit as three folks – two fools and a madman. Always preceded by *as*; gen. also with *have*. (To be) tolerably clever or cunning; also (to be) a fool. A derisive c.p. bordering on the proverbial. Mostly Cheshire. Ray, Lytton.

muck. A very untidy, an uncleanly condition: (low) coll: 1766, Goldsmith, 'She observed, that "by the living jingo, she was all of a muck of sweat".' (cf. MUCK-SWEAT.) Gen. *be in a*, or *all of a*, *muck*. 2. Filth, dirt, esp. if an oozing mass: C.14–20: S.E. till ca 1840, then coll, increasingly low. Dickens, Calverley. 3. Anything (soil, gravel, clay) excavated: Public Works' coll: late C.19–20. 4. Anything vile or disgusting: coll: 1888, *Sportsman*, 28 Nov., 'Drinking sech like muck'. 5. A coarse brute: low coll: from ca 1885. Anticipated in 'Muck: that's my opinion of him,' 1884, Henley & Stevenson. 6. Hence, an infantryman, the infantry: cavalrymen's (—1909). 7. A heavy fall, lit. or fig.: from ca 1892, ob. Abbr. MUCKER. 8. A failure: Public Schools' coll: late C.19–20. D. Coke, *The Bending of a Twig*, 1906, 'Make a muck of it.' cf. sense 4 of:

muck, v. To make dirty: from ca 1830: S.E. till ca 1895, then coll (increasingly low). 2. To excel; beat: low: from ca 1850; ob. Mayhew, 'He'd muck a thousand!' 3. Hence, to ruin (a person): low: from ca 1840. Milliken, 'I'm mucked, that's a moral.' 4. To fail in or at: from ca 1840. Kipling, 'I shall muck it. I know I shall.' cf. MUCK UP, 2.

muck, chief. (Of a person) a TRUMP: low (—1887); ob. cf.:

Muck, Lord. A person unjustifiably, or in the speaker's opinion unjustifiably, important or esteemed: (low) coll: from the 1890s. Prob. suggested by the preceding term.

muck about. To fondle or caress very intimately: low, mostly costers': from ca 1880. Stronger than MESS ABOUT. 2. v.i., wander aimlessly; potter about: s.: 1896, Kipling, 'Our Colonel . . . mucks about in 'orspital.'

muck and halfpenny afters. A bad, pretentious dinner: lower-middle classes' (—1909); virtually †.

muck and truck. Miscellaneous articles: commerce (—1898); ob.

muck-cheap. 'Dirt-cheap': coll: from ca 1870; ob. Ex MUCK, n., 2. cf. the Fr. *salement bon marché* (Manchon).

muck-fork. A finger; occ. a hand: low: from ca 1850.

muck for luck! a c.p. to someone getting his boots soiled with dog's excrement, or similarly befouled: late C.19–20. cf. LUCK SHITTEN.

muck-heap. A filthy sloven: coll: ca 1860–1910. cf. MUCK-SUCKLE.

muck of, make a. A coll variant of MUCK UP, 2: from late C.19.

muck out. To clean out (of money); ruin: low: from ca 1855.

muck-rag. A handkerchief: low: C.19. 'A Real Paddy', *Real Life in Ireland*, 1822.

muck-shifter. A navvy: navvies' coll: ca 1800–1910. (D. W. Barrett, *Navvies*, 1880.)

muck-snipe. A ruined person, esp. gambler: low: ca 1850–1910. Mayhew.

muck-spout. A foul-mouthed talker: low: from ca 1870; ob.

muck-suckle. A filthy woman: low coll: ca 1860–1900. cf. MUCK-HEAP.

muck-sweat. Perspiration; orig. and properly if dust or dirt has accrued: proletarian coll: since ca 1830. *Sessions*, 22 June 1843. cf. MUCK, n., 1.

***muck toper feeker.** An umbrella-maker: Scots c.: ca 1820–80. Prob. the form should be *mush-topper feaker*: see MUSH and MUSH-FAKER.

muck-train. A commissariat train: military: ca 1850–90.

muck up. To litter: late C.19–20: (low) coll. Mrs Caffyn, 'Mucking up my rooms.' 2. To spoil, ruin, e.g. a person but esp. a plan: from ca 1885. cf. MUCK, v., 3. 3. Hence, as n., a complete failure; confusion or muddle.

muck-worm. A contemptible fellow: s.: Ned Ward, 1703.

muckcook. To laugh behind one's back (v.i.): low: ca 1880–1905. Origin?

mucked out, ppl adj. Penniless: low: from ca 1820; ob.

muckender. A swab: s.: Ned Ward, 1703.

mucker. A heavy fall: from ca 1850. Esp. in *come* or (ob.) *go a mucker*; often fig., come to grief. Kingsley, 1852, 'Receiving a mucker' (lit., of a horse); J. Payn, 1876, 'A regular mucker' (fig.). Because frequently caused by road-filth or muck. 2. A quartermaster: military: ca 1885–1910.

mucker, v. To have a heavy fall; hence fig., come to grief: from ca 1860; ob. Kingsley. 2. v.t., to ruin (one's chances): 1869, 'W. Bradwood'. ob.

muckhill at one's door, have a good. To be rich: proverbial coll: ca 1670–1720. Ray. Here, as in next, *muckhill* = dung-heap. (Mostly rural.)

'muckhill on my trencher', quoth the bride, – 'you make a'. A c.p. of ca 1670–1750 and =You carve me a great heap. Ray, Fuller.

muckibus. Tipsy: low: ca 1755–1850. Horace Walpole, 1756. Ex MUCK, n.

muckin; occ. **mucking** or **mukkin.** Butter: Regular Army's: late C.19–20. Ex Hindustani *makkhn.*

mucking. An act of 'messing about': coll: 1904, Kipling, 'His photographic muckings'. ?no singular. Ob.; see MUCKING-ABOUT. 2. Rubbish, a mess: coll: 1898, Kipling, 'She's only burning muckings.' 3. See MUCKIN.

mucking, adj. Dirty; disgusting: low coll (—1887).

mucking-about. A 'messing about': s. > coll: from ca 1905. 2. An intimate fondling: low (mostly costers'): from ca 1880. See MUCK ABOUT.

mucking-togs; muckintogs. A mackintosh: low perversion: 1842, Barham; ob.

mud. A fool, 'a dull, heavy-headed fellow', Dyche: low (?orig. c.): ca 1710–1850. Whence *one's name is* MUD (Bee, 1823): > coll: extant. 2. A non-society (i.e. non-trades-union) man: printers': from ca 1786: ob. by 1900.

mud, one's name is. One has been heavily defeated; one is in disgrace: from ca 1820. '"And his name is mud!" ejaculated upon the conclusion of a silly oration, or of a leader in the *Courier*', 1823, 'Jon Bee'. See also MUD: the sense has changed, for in C.20 mire, not a dull fool, is understood to be the origin.

mud, sure as. Absolutely certain: school s.: 1899, Eden Phillpotts.

mud-crusher. An infantryman (not often applied to an officer): military: from ca 1872. Sir G. Chesney, 1893, '"You are too good to be a mud-crusher, Tommy," said the Major . . . patronisingly.' cf. BEETLE-CRUSHER; SWADDY; TOE-BUSTER; WORM-CRUSHER, and the Fr. *pousse-cailloux*, pebble-pusher. See esp. *Words!*

mud-fog association. A scientific association in gen., or some particular one: coined by Dickens, 1838, in *Bentley's Magazine*; referred to by C. Dickens, Jr, in *Household Words*, 1 May 1886. ca 1860–75, it was rarely used for other than the British Association for the Promotion of Science, esp. at the universities. Coll: †by 1896.

mud-head or **mudhead.** A stupid person: coll: 1838, Haliburton; D. C. Murray, 1883, 'That old m.-h.'. The adj., *mud-headed*, 1793, is S.E. but likewise ob.

mud-hen. A female speculator: Stock Exchange: U.S., anglicized by 1896.

mud-hole. 'A salt-water lagoon in which whales are captured', F. & H.: whalers' (—1893): coll. Ex the churning-up of the water.

mud-honey. Mud; esp. street slush: low: ca 1870–1914.

mud-hook. An anchor: nautical (—1884).

mud in one's eye. A tie: rhyming s.: late C.19–20.

***mud-lark** or **mudlark.** A waterside thief that, hiding under a ship at low tide, receives small stolen packets from the crew: c. (—1796). 2. By 1820, a sea-shore scavenger, who often waded out up to his, or her, waist. The first in Colquhoun's *Police of the Metropolis*, the second (also *mud-larker*, or *mudlarker*) in Egan's Grose and in Mayhew; the first, ob. by 1890, the second > s. by 1850, coll by 1900. Suggested by *skylark*. 3. A man that scavenges in gutters, esp. for metal, e.g. horse-nails: c. or low: ca 1820–50. 4. Hence an official cleaner of common sewers: coll (—1859); ob. 5. A street ARAB: coll: 1865, *Saturday Review*, 4 July. 6. A member of the Royal Engineers: military coll (—1878). 7. Any person that, belonging to bank, counting-house, etc., has often, in the course of his work, to be out in the open air: City (London): from ca 1860; ob. 8. A hog: ca 1780–1830. 9. A duck: ca 1810–30.

mud-larker. See MUD-LARK, 2. 1840, Marryat. Ob.

mud-major. An infantry major: military (—1896). Because, on parade, he was on foot. cf. MUD-CRUSHER and:

mud-picker. A military policeman in garrison: military: ca 1815–1910.

mud-pilot. The pilot who takes a ship from Gravesend to the entrance of her dock: nautical: late C.19–20. Bowen.

mud-pipes. Gum-boots: lower classes': prob. since early C.19, for *Sinks*, 1848, defines the term as 'thick boots'.

mud-player. A batsman fond of a wet wicket: cricket: ca 1890–1914.

mud-plunger. An infantryman: (mainly) military: from ca 1860; ob. cf. MUD-CRUSHER, and see 'Soldiers' Slang of Three Nations' in *Words!*

***mud-plunging.** A tramping through mud in search of alms: tramps' c.: from ca 1880. *Daily Telegraph*, 8 Feb. 1883.

mud-pusher. A crossing-sweeper: urban lower classes': from ca 1870.

Mud-Salad Market. Covent Garden: low London: from the late 1870s; ob. *Punch*, 14 Aug. 1880, 'Mud-Salad Market belongs to his Grace the Duke of Mudford [!]. It was once a tranquil Convent Garden.'

mud show. An outdoor show, esp. an agricultural one: Society (—1909); ob.

mud-slinger; -slinging. A slanderer; slander: coll (orig. low): from ca 1890.

mud-student. A student of farming: from ca 1855.

mudding-face. A fool; a soft fellow: low: ca 1870–1915. Presumably ex MUD, a fool, and prob. by a pun on *pudding-face.*

muddled. Slightly tipsy: coll: since ca 1780. *The New Vocal Enchantress*, 1791.

muddle on. Though half-drunk, to continue drinking: coll: late C.17–18.

muddler. A clumsy horse: turf coll: from ca 1886; ob.

***mudge.** A hat: c. (—1888). *Sportsman*, 22 Dec. 1888. ?etymology: is it perchance a sense- and form-perversion of MUSH, an umbrella?

mudger. A milksop: low: 1830, Lytton, 'Girl-faced mudgers'; ob. by 1880, †by 1910. ?ex dial. *mudge*, to move, budge, hence one moving very quietly.

mudlark, mudlarker, see MUD-LARK.

muff. The female pudend, outwardly: late C.17–20; ob.: orig. c.; by 1920, low. B.E., who quotes the toast, *to the well-wearing of your muff*, MORT. 2. 'A foolish silly person', Vaux, 1812: orig. c. >, by 1880, gen. s.; ob. ca 1850–75 it occ. connoted weakness of mind: H., 2nd ed., '*muff* has been defined to be "a soft thing that holds a lady's hand without squeezing it".' Perhaps (cf. sense 1) ex (the *softness* of a) *muff*, the covering for female hands; Vaux less prob. suggests that it is a perversion of MOUTH, 2. 3. Whence, orig. in athletic sport, a clumsy and/or a stupid person: 1837, Dickens, '"Now butterfingers" – "Muff" . . . and so forth': s. >, ca 1880, coll. 4. A failure: 1871, *Punch*, 25 Feb., of a book; ob. Esp. (1896), anything badly bungled. Coll. Ex the v. 5. See MUFF, NOT TO SAY.

muff, v. To bungle, physically or otherwise, esp. at games: 1846, 'Muffed their batting' (Lewis); 1857, G. A. Lawrence, 'I don't see why you should have muffed that shot.' 2. v.i., to fail in an examination: 1884, Julian Sturgis: orig. Eton College s. >, ca 1890, gen. coll; ob.

muff, not to say; say neither muff nor mum. To say not a word: mid-C.15–20: coll till C.18, then dial. Stapylton. Ex *muff*, an echoic word 'representing an inarticulate sound', O.E.D.

muff it. To die: boxers' s.: ca 1810–60.

muffed, ppl adj. Bungled; clumsily spoilt, missed: from ca 1860: s. > coll.

muffin. A fool: low: 1830, W. T. Moncrieff; †by 1910. Ex MUFF, n., 2, prob. by a pun on the light flat cake. 2. Whence, at games a constant misser of a shot or a ball: coll (—1895); ob. 3. One's 'girl', by arrangement, for the social life of a season: Canadian: 1856, Miss Bird: ob. 4. A cap of the 'pill-box' type: late C.19–early 20.

muffin, cold. Mediocre; (almost) worthless: Cockney: ca 1890–1910. Milliken.

muffin-baker. A Quaker: rhyming s. (—1859). Perhaps restricted to the low Cockney s. QUAKER, excrement long retained.

muffin-countenance or **-face.** A hairless one, says F. & H.; an expressionless one, says the O.E.D. with reason: resp. 1823, ob., and 1777 (I. Jackman). Whence:

muffin-faced. Having an expressionless face: C.19–20, ob. Bee, however, in 1823, implies that it indicates a face with protruding muscles: †by 1890.

muffin-fight; muffin-worry. A tea-party: coll: resp. ca 1885–1910 and 1860, H., 2nd ed. (also in Ouida, 1877). cf. BUN-FEAST; TEA-FIGHT.

muffin-puncher. A muffin-baker: Cockneys' (—1909).

muffin-walloper. (Gen. pl.) A scandal-loving woman delighting to meet others at a tea-table: London middle classes': ca 1880–1914.

muffing, ppl adj., bungling, from ca 1840. John Mills. n., clumsiness, clumsy failure: from ca 1860. Both s. > coll ca 1890.

muffish. Foolish, silly; esp. clumsy: coll: 1858, Farrar. See MUFF, n., 2, 3.

muffishness. The quality of being a MUFF, 2, 3: coll: 1858, Farrar.

muffism. Foolishness; an action typical of

a MUFF, 2, 3: coll: 1854, Lady Lytton: ob. by 1900.

muffle, a boxing-glove, is prob. S.E. (ca 1810–40). So, perhaps, is:

muffler, in the same sense: mid-C.18–20; ob. 2. A stunning blow: boxing: ca 1820–1905. 3. A crape mask: 1838, Glascock: c.; ob. Ex:

***muffling-cheat.** A napkin; a towel: c. of ca 1560–1840.

mufti. Plain clothes worn by one who, at work, wears a uniform: 1816: s. >, ca 1880, coll >, ca 1910, S.E. 'Quiz'; Marryat, 1833, 'In a suit of mufti', the post-1850 form being *in mufti*. O.E.D. Perhaps jestingly ex *mufti*, a Mohammedan priest, via the theatre, which, in early C.19, represented officers off duty wearing 'flowered dressing-gown and tasselled smoking cap', W. 2. A chaplain on a man-of-war: naval: ca 1830–50. Marryat, in his *King's Own.*

mug. The face: 1708, *The British Apollo*, 'My Lawyer has . . . a Temple-Mug.' Prob. ex mugs 'made to represent a grotesque human face'. 2. Hence, the mouth: 1820, J. H. Reynolds, 'Open thy mug, my dear.' Ob. by 1900. 3. A cooling drink: coll (1633, S.O.D.) >, ca 1850, S.E.; ob. 4. A fool; an easy dupe; a DUFFER (4): 1857, 'Ducange Anglicus'; Mayhew. i.e. something into which one can pour anything. 5. An examination: from ca 1852; ob.: university and school. 6. Hence, one who studies hard: school: from ca 1880. 7. A mist, a fog: s. and dial.; the former (as in Ash's Dict., 1775), ca 1770–80; the latter, extant, with further senses, a drizzle, gloomy damp weather.

mug, v. To grimace: theatrical >, ca 1880, gen.: 1855, Dickens, 'The low comedian had "mugged" at him . . . fifty nights for a wager.' Slightly ob. cf. MUG UP. Prob. ex *mug*, to pout: see sense 11, below. 2. To strike, esp. punch, in the face: boxing: 1818; ob. Ex the n., 1. Hence, 3, (—1859), to fight (v.t.), chastise, thrash. 4. To bribe with liquor: s. (†) and dial.: 1830 (O.E.D.). Also, in s. and dial., v.i. and v. reflexive, to get drunk: from ca 1840. 5. Hence, to swindle, to rob (esp. by the garrotte): low: from ca 1860; ob. Mayhew. 6. v.i., to study hard: 1848: mostly school and university. (v.t. with *at.*) Perhaps ex the theatrical sense. Occ. *mug away* or *on.* 7. Also v.t., to study hard (at): from ca 1880. More gen. *mug up*. Hence, 8, to take pains with (e.g. a room): Winchester College: from ca 1870; ob. 'He has mugged his study and made it quite cud' (i.e. comfortable), F. & H. 9. (Gen. with *together*), v.i., to crowd in a confined space (—1878). 10. See MUG ONESELF, 2. 11. To pout; to sulk: s. (ob.) and dial.: from ca 1730. Collins the poet. Perhaps ex dial. *mug*, v.i., to drizzle, rain slightly. cf. sense 1.

mug away or **on.** See MUG, v., 6: resp. 1893, 1878. (Prob. years earlier.)

mug-faker, see MUGGER, 2.

***mug-hunter.** A robber of drunken men, esp. at night: c. (—1887) >, ca 1900, low.

mug oneself. See MUG, v., 4. 2. To make oneself cosy: low: from ca 1880; ob. cf. MUG, v., 8.

mug-trap. A duper or swindler of fools: 1892, Milliken: low. cf. MUG-HUNTER.

mug up. v.i., and, more gen., v.t., to study hard: mostly school, university and Army: from ca 1860; ob. 2. v.t. and v.i., to paint one's face: theatrical: 1859, H.; 1892, Milliken, 'You're mugged up to rights.' 3. To eat: mostly in the Grand Banks schooners: late C.19–20.

mugger. One who studies hard: mostly schools' (—1883). James Payn. 2. (Also *mug-faker:* 1887, Baumann.) A comedian specializing in grimaces: theatrical: 1892 (also prob. earlier), *National Observer*, 27 Feb., 'None had ever a more expressive viznomy than this prince of muggers.' 3. A punch or blow to or on the MUG or face: pugilistic: ca 1810–60. *Boxiana*, III, 1821. See quote at BOX OF DOMINOES.

***muggill.** A beadle: c. of ca 1600–20. Rowlands, in *Martin Mark-All.* ?etymology.

mugging. vbl n. to MUG, v., 1, 2, 3, 5, 6.

muggins. A simpleton, JUGGINS, fool: U.S. (ca 1870), anglicized ca 1880. Ex MUG, n., 4, suggested by the surname *Muggins.* 2. A borough-magnate or a local leader: ca 1890–1910. 3. See:

muggins, talk. To say silly things: 1881, *Punch*, 10 Sept.

***muggled.** An adj. applied to cheap goods offered for sale as contraband: c.: from ca 1850; ob. Mayhew. A perversion of *smuggled.*

muggles. Restlessness: ca 1740–1800. Robertson of Struan, in *Poems*, 1750.

muggy. Drunk: low: from ca 1858; ob. Ex dial. *muggy*, damp.

mugs, cut. To grimace: theatrical: from ca 1820; ob. cf. MUG, n., 1.

mug's corner. The fielding position at mid-on; that at short leg: cricketers': ca 1890–1910.

mug's game. A silly – esp., an unprofitable – thing to do: late C.19–20.

mugster. One who studies hard (see MUG, v., 6): schools' (—1888); ob.

mugwump. A great man; an important one: from ca 1830, and orig. and mainly U.S.: perhaps orig. coll, but certainly soon S.E. Ex the Red Indian for a chief.

mukkin, see MUCKIN.

mule. A sexually impotent man: low coll: from ca 1870. A mule being unable to generate. 2. A day hand in the composing room: printers': from ca 1860; ob.

mule, shoe one's. To embezzle: coll: ca 1650–1720. Nares.

mull. A muddle, a mismanagement, a failure: 1821, Egan, 'Somebody must make a mull': s. >, ca 1860, coll. Esp. in *make a mull of*. Prob. ex *muddle* on analogy of *mell, meddle*, or perhaps ex dial. *mull*, to pulverize, cause to crumble. 2. Hence, or perhaps ex the v., from ca 1865, a simpleton; a clumsy fellow. Chiefly *old mull, regular mull*. 3. A Civil Service officer of the Madras Presidency: Anglo-Indian: from ca 1835. Abbr. *mulligatawny*. cf. DUCK, n., 4; QUI-HI.

mull, v. To spoil, muddle: orig. and mainly athletics': coll: 1862, *Sporting Life*, 14 June, 'Pooley here "mulled" a catch'. Ex the n., 1.

muller, v.t. To cut down a tall hat into a low-crowned one (occ. called a *muller*): trade: 1864–ca 85. *Builder*, Nov. 1864. The hat was also called a *Muller-cut-down*. Ex *Müller*, a murderer who attempted to disguise himself in this way.

mulligatawny. See MULL, n., 3. ca 1810–20. 'Quiz', 1816. ?ex the high seasoning of this East Indian soup and the peppery temper of many officials.

mulligrubs; in C.19–20, occ. **mollygrubs.** Colic: from ca 1615: S.E. till C.19, then coll. Fletcher, in *Monsieur Thomas*; 'Cuthbert Bede', 1853. Ex: 2. (Esp. in *be in one's mulligrubs*.) Depressed spirits (cf. MUBBLE-FUBBLES): C.17–20 (anticipated in 1599 by Nashe's *mulligrums*, which persists in dial.): S.E. till C.19, then coll. Scott (of a drink), 'Right . . . as ever washed mulligrubs out of a moody brain'. Both senses, esp. the latter, are ob. A fantastic formation, perhaps on *mouldy grubs*.

Mullingar heifer. (A development from MUNSTER HEIFER.) A thick-ankled girl: Anglo-Irish: from ca 1860; ob.

mullock. Rubbish; a worthless thing: Australian coll: from ca 1850. Ex the mining-j. senses, rock without gold, refuse of gold-workings, ex Eng. dial. 2. Hence, an ignorant or worthless person: since ca 1880.

mullock over. To shear incompletely or very carelessly: Australian shearers': from ca 1890. The *Age*, 23 Sept. 1893. Ex MULLOCK.

multa, multie, multi, multy. Very: Parlary: mid-C.19–20. e.g. in:

multee kertever (or -iver) or multicattivo. Very bad: theatrical (—1887) ex (—1859) Parlary; very ob. in the former. Ex It. *molto cattivo*, very bad, via Lingua Franca.

multy. An expletive and/or intensive adj.: low and Parlary: mid-C.19–20. Henley, 1887, 'How do you melt the multy swag?' Ex It. *molto*, much, very. 2. adv. See MULTA.

mum. Silence, esp. if connoting a refusal to speak: coll: 1562, J. Heywood; Butler; *Pall Mall Gazette*, 7 Jan. 1890, 'If the policy of "mum" continues'. ob. Ex *mum*, a representation of an inarticulate sound: cf. MUFF, NOT TO SAY. 2. See MUMS. 3. Mother, gen. as term of address: orig. (—1823), dial.; > coll ca 1880. Abbr. MUMMY. 4. A low coll variant of MA'AM: C.19–20. cf. MEM.

mum, as a quasi-adv. (strictly silent), esp. in *to stand mum*, is coll: C.16–19. Archaic except in dial. R. Bridges, 1894, 'Don't stand there mum.'

mum-tip. (A payment of) hush-money: ca 1815–50. Pierce Egan, *Life in London*, 1821.

***mum your dubber!** Silence!: from ca 1780; ob.: c. See DUBBER.

mumble-crust. A coll nickname for a toothless person: ca 1550–1620.

mumble-matins. A coll nickname for a priest: ca 1560–1630.

mumble-mumper. An old, sulky, inarticulate, unintelligible actor: theatrical: from ca 1860.

mumble-news. A tale-bearer: 1588, Shakespeare, 'Some mumble-news, some trencher-knight, some Dick': coll >, in C.19, S.E.; ob. by 1860, †by 1900.

mumble-peg. The female pudend: low: C.19. ?ex the old type of mole-trap.

mumble-sparrow. 'A cruel sport practised at wakes and fairs', a handicapped man (gen. with arms tied behind his back) attempting to bite off the head of a handicapped cock sparrow. Coll > S.E.: ca 1780–1820. Grose.

mumbo-jumbo. Meaningless jargon: coll: from ca 1850. Ex the S.E. sense: an object of senseless veneration, itself ex a West African word.

mumchance that or who was hanged for saying nothing, look or **sit like.** A c.p. applied to a silent, glum-looking person: late C.17–mid-19. Cheshire substitutes *mumphazard* and *stand.*

mummer. An actor: contemptuous s.: 1840, Carlyle. Ex the S.E. sense, an actor in a dumb show or in a mumming. Whence *mummerdom*, rather S.E. than unconventional. 2. The mouth: low, esp. boxing: ca 1780–1870. Ex MUNS and MUMS.

mummery-cove. An actor: low: ca 1830–80. cf. CACKLING-COVE.

mumming-booth. 'A wandering marquee in which short plays are produced': theatrical coll: mid-C.18–20; ob. Ware.

mummy. Mother, esp. as term of address: orig. (—1790), dial.; > coll ca 1880 and 'in recent years fashionable in England', O.E.D., 1908. Ex *mother* or MAMMY.

mump. To deceive, overreach, cheat: ca 1650–1740: s. >, ca 1710, coll; very gen. until ca 1705. Fuller, Wycherley, North. Ex Dutch *mompen*, to cheat. 2. To disappoint: coll: ca 1700–40. Kersey. Both senses constructed with *(out) of.* 3. v.i., to beg, be a parasite: from ca 1670; ob.: orig. c. >, ca 1750, low s. Head, Macaulay. 4. v.t., to obtain by begging: from ca 1680; ob. F. Spence. 5. v.t., to call at (a house) on a begging round: from ca 1865: c. >, ca 1890, low s.; ob. 6. To talk seriously: low (—1857); ob. 7. Short for MUMPER: Ned Ward, 1709.

***mump, on the.** A-begging: vagabonds' c.: late C.19–20.

***mumper.** A beggar: from ca 1670; ob.: c. >, by 1720, low s. Until ca 1720, a genteel, then any beggar (witness Head, 1673, and Grose, 1785). Extant also as dial. 2. Hence, a sponger: ca 1720–1830. Macaulay, 1849, 'A Lincoln's Inn mumper was a proverb.' 3. A half-bred Gypsy: ca 1870–1900: c. Hindley.

***mumper's brass.** Money: c.: Ned Ward, 1709.

***mumper's (or -ers') hall.** A beggar's alehouse: late C.17–mid-19: c. until ca 1720, then low s.

***mumping,** vbl n. and ppl adj. Begging: resp. from ca 1690 (c. > low s.) and from ca 1825 (low s., ob.): n. in Motteux, adj. in Lytton. cf. the dial. *Mumping Day*, Boxing Day: C.19–20; ob.

mumple-mumper. An occ. C.19 variant of MUMMER, 1.

mumps, the. Very low spirits: non-aristocratic coll (—1887). cf. DUMPS.

***mumpus.** A perversion of MUMPING.

mums. The lips: late C.18–19. More gen. MUNS. cf. also MUN. 2. See MUM, n., 3.

mum's the word! Silence: coll: C.18–20. T. Brown. Earlier, *mum for that!* (S.E.).

mumsie or **-y.** Mother: domestic and nursery coll: late C.19–20. cf. MUMMY.

mun; often **munn,** (early) **munne.** The mouth: C.14–20; s. (†by ca 1880) and dial. Ex Norwegian dial. *munn*, the mouth. Also MUNS and MUND. 2. One of a band of London street ruffians ca 1670: coll. Shadwell, 1691. cf. SCOURER; MOHOCK. ?etymology if not ex *mun*, the mouth: perhaps they were very loud-mouthed fellows.

munch-present. A servant that tastes of his master's presents to a friend: app. c.: ca 1560–90. Awdelay. 2. A glutton: C.16 (?–17): coll. 3. A taker of bribes: late C. 16–17: coll.

mund, munds. A C.19 variant of MUN, 1, and MUNS.

mundane. A person of fashion: Society coll: ca 1890–1910. Ex Fr. *mondain(e).*

munduc. The seaman left to take charge of the boat on the pearl fishery, while the others are diving; pearl-fishers': late C.19–20. Bowen. Prob. ex the Malayan *munduk*, a mole: a sense that accords well with nautical humour.

***mung.** To beg, gen. v.i.: tramps' c.: from ca 1810; ob. *Lex. Bal.*, Mayhew, P. H. Emerson. Ex Romany *mong*, request, beg (*mongamengro*, a beggar). cf. MANG and MUMP.

***mungaree** or **munjari; mungarly.** Food; scraps of bread; a meal: Parlary and tramps' c.: from ca 1855. Mayhew, Hindley, Emerson. Ex It. *mangiare* (cf. Fr. *manger*), to eat, hence food, via Lingua Franca. For the form, cf. DINARLEE. Also *mange.*

***mungarly-casa** or **-cass(e)y.** A baker's shop: Parlary and tramps' c.: from ca 1858. *The Times*, 18 Oct. 1864. Ex preceding + It. *casa*, a house.

***munge,** n. Dark, darkness: c.: C.18. C. Hitchin, *The Regulator*, 1718. Origin?

munging, vbl n. Begging: Northern s. (ob.) and dial. (—1859). Ex dial. *munge*, to grumble in low, indistinct tones.

mungo. An important person, a SWELL: 1770, Colman, in the *Oxford Magazine*: soon †, presumably s. ?ex *Mungo*, a common name for a Negro (1768).

mungy. Food: naval and military: from

ca 1860. Either ex Fr. *manger*, to eat, or a re-shaping of MUNGAREE. Hence, *mungy-wallah*, a man working in the cook-house: military: late C.19–20.

munjari or **-y,** see MUNGAREE.

munns, see MUNS.

munpins or, better, **mompyns.** The teeth: C.15–mid-16: coll. Lydgate. Lit., mouth-pins (see MUN, 1). Also *mone pynnes* (as in Lydgate) and *munpynnys* (as in Skelton).

***muns**; in C. 17–early 18, occ. **munns;** in C.19, occ. **munds.** The face: from ca 1660: c. >, ca 1720, low s. See MUN, 1. 2. Occ. the lips (cf. MUMS), the mouth (—1823), the jaws: C.18–20, ob. Foote, 1760, 'Why, you jade, . . . I must have a smack at your muns.'

munshi, see MOONSHEE.

Munster heifer. A thick-legged and/or thick-ankled woman: Anglo-Irish: ca 1810–60. cf. MULLINGAR HEIFER.

Munster plums. (Singular app. unrecorded.) Potatoes: Anglo-Irish >, ca 1850, gen.: from ca 1780; ob. cf. IRISH APRICOTS and MURPH.

***muogh.** A pig: Shelta: C.18–20.

mur. Rum: back s. (—1859).

murder, cry blue. To make an excessive outcry: 1887, 'John Strange Winter'.

murder, look like God's revenge against. To look angrily: coll: C.18–mid-19.

murder is out, the. The mystery is solved: C.18–20: S.E. >, ca 1830, coll. Ex the proverbial *murder will out* (late C.13–20), Apperson.

murderin' Irish!; orig. **murder an' Irish!** A lower classes' exclamation indicative of a climax: mid-C.19–early 20.

***murerk.** The mistress of the house: tramps' c.: from ca 1855. ?*burerk* (BURICK) perverted.

murkarker or **murkauker.** A monkey: ca 1850–80: low coll seldom heard outside London. Ex *Jacko Macauco* or *Maccacco*, a famous fighting monkey of ca 1840–5 at the Westminster Pit. (In S.E., *macaco* is any monkey of the genus *macacus*.) Also *maccacco*.

murph, but gen. **murphy.** A potato: from resp. ca 1870, ca 1810. Thackeray. Ex the very common Irish surname: cf. DONOVAN.

Murphy's countenance or **face.** A pig's head: from resp. ca 1810 (†by 1890) and ca 1860.

Murrumbidgee whaler, see WHALER.

murtherer. (Gen. pl.) A cannon for use against rather the men than the material of a ship: naval coll: C.18–early 19.

muscle-grinder, see LEG-GRINDER.

Museum headache. Extreme ennui; impatient boredom: London writers', authors', journalists': 1857–ca 1914. Ware, whose quotation from the *Daily News* of 11 Dec. 1882 shows that the phrase referred to the waiting for books in the British Museum Reading Room.

museuming. The visiting of museums: coll: 1838, 'A day or two museuming'.

mush, *mush-top(p)er, mushroom. An umbrella: resp. low (—1851), Mayhew, but recorded in a compound in 1821; from ca 1820, †by 1880, c., as in Haggart; low, 1856, very ob., Mayhew. Ex the shape. 2. (Only *mush*: pronounced *moosh*.) The mouth: boxing, then low: mid-C.19–20; prob. U.S., orig. Ex the softness of mush and the mouth. 3. (Only *mush*, in senses 3–6.) A cab-proprietor in a small way; (also *little mush*) a cab-driver owning his own vehicle: from ca 1890; ob. by 1910. Abbr. MUSHER. 4. The guard-room; cells: military: late C.19–20. Origin? Perhaps ex dial. *mush*, to crush. 5. See MUSHROOM. 6. Porridge: nautical coll: C.19–20; slightly ob. A particularization of the S.E. sense. 7. A man: c.: late C.19–20. Only in combination: e.g., *coring mush* and *rye mush*. Ex Romany *moosh*, a man. 8. Sentimentality: since ca 1880: coll. cf. SLOPPY.

mush-faker, *mush-top(p)er-faker, mushroom-faker. A mender of umbrellas: resp. low (—1851), Mayhew; c. of ca 1820–50, Haggart; c. or low (—1839), ob. by 1860, Brandon, Mayhew. Ex MUSH, 1, and FAKER. cf.:

mush-faking, occ. **mushfaking.** Umbrella-mending: low: from ca 1857. P. H. Emerson.

mush, gush, and lush. 'Mean interested criticism – critiques paid for either in money or feastings': authors' and journalists': ca 1884–1905. Ware.

mush-top(p)er, see MUSH, 1. **mush-top(p)er-faker,** see MUSH-FAKER.

musha. An interjection connoting strong feeling: from ca 1830: Anglo-Irish coll >, by 1870, S.E. Lover. Ex Irish *maiseadh*, if it be so.

musher. Same sense as MUSH, 3: 1887, *Globe*, 22 April (O.E.D.); ob. by 1900. Seldom used outside of the cab-trade.

mushing, vbl n. 'Cab-owning on a small scale': cab-men: ca 1887–1915. cf. MUSH, 3, and MUSHER. *Globe*, 22 April 1887.

mushroom. See MUSH, 1. 2. A circular

hat with a low crown, esp. a lady's with brim down-curving: coll: from ca 1864; ob. 3. The female pudend: low: C.19. 4. The great clock to be seen in most taverns: tavern-frequenters' (—1909). Ware. Ex shape.

mushroom-faker, see MUSH-FAKER.

mushy. Insipid; gushingly sentimental: from early 1870s: coll >, by 1910, S.E. George Eliot, 1876, 'She's not mushy, but her heart is tender.'

music. A C.18 abbr. of *the* MUSIC'S PAID. 2. The reverse or tail of a coin, but only in calling the toss: Anglo-Irish: ca 1780–1930. Ex the harp on the reverse of an Irish farthing or halfpenny.

music, face the, see FACE THE MUSIC.

music, it makes ill. Applied to unwelcome news: coll: late C.17–mid-18.

music as a wheelbarrow, you make as good. A semi-proverbial c.p. to one who plays badly or is unpleasantly noisy: C.18. 'Proverbs' Fuller.

music-box. A piano: jocular coll: 1849, Thackeray: C. Reade, in *Hard Cash*.

music-hall howl. The singing heard in music-halls: musicians' coll (—1909). Ware, 'The result of endeavouring rather to make the words of a song heard than to create musical effect'.

***music's paid, the.** 'The Watch-word among High-way-men, to let the Company they were to Rob, alone, in return to some Courtesy', B.E.: c.: late C.17–early 19.

muskin, gen. preceded by *unaccountable*. A CHAP, FELLOW, man, esp. if odd: ca 1750–60. Johnson, 'Those who . . . call a man a cabbage, . . . an odd fish, an unaccountable muskin'. ?a perversion of the C.16 endearing *muskin*.

muslin. Sails, collectively; esp. the lighter sails: nautical: from ca 1820; ob. *Blackwood's Magazine*, 1822, 'She shewed as little muslin as required.' 2. The fair sex: from ca 1883; ob. by 1910. Hawley Smart, 1884. (cf. SKIRT.) Gen. as:

muslin, a bit of. A woman, a girl: 1823, Moncrieff, 'A bit of muslin on the sly'; C. Griffin; Thackeray. Ob. by 1910. cf.:

muslin, a piece of. The same: ca 1840–1900. W. T. Moncrieff, 1843. Much less gen. than preceding term; prob. influenced by PIECE, a girl.

mussy, see MUZZY, 1.

musta or **muster.** The make or pattern of anything; a sample: Anglo-Chinese and -Indian: C.16–20; in 1563 as *mostra*, which is the Portuguese origin. Coll. H., 3rd ed., 'Very gen. used in commercial transactions all over the world'.

mustard-plaster on his chest!, put a. A c.p. applied to 'a doleful and dismal pallid young man': lower-classes': ca 1880–1914. Ware. Ex a comic song written in connection with Colman's mustard by E. Laman Blanchard (1820–89).

mustard-pot. The female pudend: C.19–20: low. 2. A carriage with a light yellow body: lower classes': late C.19–20; ob.

muster, see MUSTA.

muster one's bag. To be ill: nautical, esp. naval: late C.19–20. Ex taking one's kit-bag to the sick-bay.

mustn't-mention-'ems. Trousers: ca 1850–1910. cf. UNMENTIONABLES.

***mutcher,** see MOOCHER.

mute. An undertaker's assistant acting as a mourner silent supposedly from grief: from ca 1760: coll till ca 1840, then S.E.

mute as a fish. Silent: C.15–20; ob.: coll >, by 1600, S.E. In late C.18–20, often *mute as fishes*, and dial. offers at least six variants.

mutiny. The rum-ration: naval: late C.19–20. Because, without it, the men would mutiny.

mutton. A loose woman; prostitutes collectively: 1518, Skelton; Shakespeare; D'Urfey. Ob. by 1820, †by 1900. Rare in C.19 except as LACED MUTTON. 2. Sexual pleasure; the female pudend; the sexual act: from ca 1670; ob. e.g. in *fond of his mutton*, fond of the act. Almost solely from the man's stand-point. 3. A sheep: late C.16–20: in C.19–20, jocular but still S.E.

mutton, bow-wow, see BOW-WOW.

mutton, cut one's. To dine: low s. bordering on coll: from ca 1850; ob. Ex the S.E. *eat* or *take a bit of*, or *one's, mutton with*, to dine with (C.18–20, ob.).

mutton, give (a person) **the cold shoulder of.** A non-aristocratic punning elaboration (—1887; ob.) of *give the cold shoulder*.

mutton, in her. Having carnal knowledge of a woman: low: C.19–20, ob. Ex MUTTON, 2.

mutton, jerk one's, see JERK OFF.

mutton?, who stole the. A c.p. of ca 1830–50 addressed jeeringly to a policeman. Ex the Force's failure to detect the culprit in a theft of mutton.

mutton-chopper. A mutton-chop (sc. whisker): ca 1890–1900: mostly Cockney. Milliken.

mutton-chops. A sheep's head: low (—1864); ob.

mutton-cove. A MUTTON-MONGER: low: from ca 1830; ob. 2. **(M.C.)** The Coventry-Street end of Windmill Street, once a resort of harlots: ca 1840–70: low London. Ex MUTTON, 1.

mutton dressed as lamb or (ob.) **lamb-fashion.** An old woman dressed like a young one: low: mostly Cockney: from ca 1860. cf. the older form, *an* OLD EWE DRESSED LAMB-FASHION. Possibly with a pun on the culinary sense of 'dressed'.

mutton-eyed. 'Sheep's-eyed': from ca 1850; ob. Mainly jocular.

mutton-fist or **-hand.** A large coarse hand, esp. if red: resp. 1664, Cotton, 'Lifting his Mutton-fists to th' skies'; from ca 1820 and not very gen. 2. A printer's index-hand: printers' (—1888). Jacobi.

mutton-head. A dull or stupid person: coll: 1804. Ex:

mutton-headed. Dull; stupid: s. (1788) and dial. Ex the well-known stupidity of sheep.

mutton in a silk stocking, leg of. A woman's leg or calf: low: late C.17–20.

mutton in long coats. Women: low: late C.17–19. cf. preceding entry.

mutton-monger. A wencher: from ca 1530; ob. by 1830, †by 1850. More, 1532; Florio; Chapman, 'As if you were the only noted mutton-monger in all the city'. Ex MUTTON, 1. cf. MUTTONER. F. & H. provides a long synonymy. 2. A sheep-stealer: ca 1660–1750. 3. A considerable eater of mutton: mid-C.17. W. M., 1649, 'A horrible Mutton-monger, a Gorbelly-Glutton'.

mutton of, make. To kill (a person): low coll: late C.19–20.

mutton-pies. The eyes: rhyming s.: ca 1880–1910. *Referee*, 7 Nov. 1887, 'Bright as angels from the skies | Were her dark-blue mutton-pies.' cf. the very much more gen. MINCE-PIES.

mutton-quad. An em quad: printers' (—1871). Ex *m* for *mutton.* cf. MUTTON-THUMPER.

mutton-shunter. A constable: policemen's: 1883–ca 1915. Policemen keep harlots moving.

mutton-thumper. A bungling workman; a young apprentice bookbinder: late C.18–20: bookbinders'. Ex the sheepskin used in binding.

mutton-tugger. (Prob.) a MUTTON-MONGER: presumably s.: ca 1600. 'The nurseries of wickedness, the nests of mutton tuggers, the dens of formall droanes,' (O.E.D.)

mutton-walk (or with capitals). The saloon at Drury Lane theatre: ca 1820–80: London fast life. Egan, 1821, *Real Life.* 2. (?hence) any resort of harlots, esp. Piccadilly: from ca 1870.

muttoner. A MUTTON-MONGER: C.17–early 19. Halliwell. Ex MUTTON, 1. 2. A blow on the knuckles from a cricket-ball: Winchester College: ca 1850–90. cf. MUTTON-FIST.

muttongosht. Mutton: domestic Anglo-Indian coll (—1886). Lit., mutton-flesh. For its hybridity, cf. JAIL-KHANNA.

muttonous. Slow; monotonous: low: ca 1880–1910. Ex *monotonous* on *gluttonous.*

muzz; occ. **muz(†).** One who studies hard, reads much and studiously. *Trifler*, No. 5, 1788, 'The almost indelible stigma of a Muz'; 1899, W. K. R. Bedford. Ob. Ex:

muzz, v.i. To study diligently; to MUG, 7 (v.t. with *over*). S. J. Pratt, 1775, 'For ever muzzing over a musty book'. Since ca 1890, mainly at Westminster School: cf. the Eton SAP. ?ex *muse, (be)mused.* 2. v.t., to fuddle; make MUZZY: 1787, 'Fred. Philon', 'Apt to get muzzed too soon'. cf. MUZZLE, v., 4. 3. v.i., to loiter or HANG ABOUT: ca 1778–1810. Mme D'Arblay, 1779, 'You would not dare keep me muzzling here.' ?cognate with *muse*, v.

muzzed. Fuddled; stupidly tipsy: 1787, see quotation at MUZZ, v., 2.

muzzing, vbl n. of MUZZ, v., all senses. 2. ppl adj., studying hard; given to intent study: 1793, J. Beresford: ob.

muzzle. A beard, esp. if long, straggly, and/or dirty: ca 1690–1830. Ex S.E. *muzzle*, the mouth.

muzzle, v. To strike on the mouth: low, esp. pugilistic: from ca 1850; ob. Mayhew, 1851, 'Just out of "stir" [q.v.] for muzzling a peeler.' 2. Hence, to fight; to thrash: low (—1859); ob. 3. Hence, to throttle, garotte: c.: from ca 1860; ob. 4. To drink to excess: s. from ca 1850 ex (—1828) dial.; ob. as s. Also, v.t., to fuddle: s. (from ca 1850; ob.) ex dial. (—1796). 5. To take, BAG, get: orig. (1890, 'Rolf Boldrewood'), Australian > gen. ca 1895; ob. Prob. ex S.E. *muzzle*, put a muzzle on.

(muzzled) bull-dog. A main-deck gun: naval: ca 1865–1905. Admiral Smyth, 1867. 2. 'The great gun which stands housed in the officers' wardroom cabin', ibid.: ca 1865–80.

muzzler. A blow on the mouth: from ca

1810: boxing. 2. A dram; a (quick) drink: low: from ca 1850; ob. Ex *muzzle*, the mouth. 3. A strong head wind: from the middle 1870s: nautical coll >, by 1910, S.E. cf. NOSE-ENDER, 2.

muzzling, vbl n. Hitting on the mouth: boxing: 1819; ob. cf. MUZZLER, 1.

***muzzling cheat.** A napkin: c. (—1688); †by 1900. Randle Holme (*musseling c.*).

muzzy. (Of places) dull, gloomy; (of weather) overcast: coll and dial.: 1727, Mrs Delany, who spells it *mussy*; 1821, Coleridge, 'This whole long-lagging. muzzy, mizly morning'. Prob. ex dial. *mosey*, hazy, muggy. 2. Stupid, hazy of mind, spiritless: coll: 1728, Mrs Delany; Keats, 1817, 'I don't feel inclined to write any more at present for I feel rather muzzy'; Thackeray. cf. MUZZ, v., 2. Perhaps ex dial. *mosey*, stupefied with liquor, or ex *bemused.* 3. Stupefied, more gen. stupid, with liquor: coll and dial.: 1775, Thomas Campbell; Thackeray; J. Payn. Ex preceding senses. 4. Blurred, indistinct: coll: from ca 1830. Washington Irving, 1832. Ex senses 1, 2, and esp. 3.

my!; oh my! A (low) coll exclamation: 1707, J. Stevens, 'Such . . . Sayings are a Discredit . . .: As for Instance . . . my, Whither d'ye go'; 1849, Mrs Carlyle, 'Oh, my! if she didn't show feeling enough.' Abbr. *my God!* 2. *o(h) my* is an abbr. of *o(h), my Gawd*, a sword: late C.19–20.

my arse . . ., see ARSE, MY!

my aunt! A coll interjection: late C.19–20.

my aunt (Jones). A water-closet: low euphemistic: from ca 1850; ob. The longer form, ca 1870–1905, gen. dispenses with *my*. cf. MRS JONES.

my boy!, I believe you, see I BELIEVE YOU, MY BOY. **my colonial oath!** see COLONIAL OATH!, MY.

my eye! Occ. **my eyes!** (†by 1860). A coll exclamation of surprise, wonderment, or admiration: slightly ob. Moore, 1819, 'My eyes! how prettily Tom writes'; M. E. Braddon, 1876, 'My eye, ain't I hungry!' Also, *my eyes and limbs!*: ca 1805–50. 2. *my eye, all,* see ALL MY EYE.

my Gawd. A sword: rhyming s.: late C.19–20.

my gracious! my land! my lord. my nabs. my oath! my pippin. my star (and garter)! my uncle. my watch. my wig(s). my word! In all cases, see the noun.

***myla,** see MILER, 1.

mylier. An occ. C.19–20 form of MAULEY, 3.

***myll,** see MILL, n. and v. **mynt,** see MINT.

myrtle, my. A low London term of address: late C.18–early 19. cf. JESSAMY and TULIP, 2.

mystery. A sausage: somewhat low: from ca 1885; ob. More gen. is *bag of mystery* (see BAGS . . .), as in Henley, 1887, and much more gen. is *mystery bag*, as in the *Sportsman*, 2 Feb. 1889.

N

n.a.d. Shamming: military hospitals'. (—1909): ob. Ex the initials of *no appreciable disease.* cf. N.Y.D.

n.c. 'Nuff ced, i.e. enough said: from ca 1870. (Ware states American origin.) cf. O.K.

n.c.d. (N.C.D.), see NO CAN DO.

n.d. (Of a woman) trying to look young: Society: late C.19–early 20. Ex librarians' *n.d.*, no date.

n.e. or N.E., see NORTH-EASTER.

n.f. A smart or cunning tradesman: printers': from ca 1865; ob. Abbr. NO FLIES. 2. Among artisans (—1909), it means *no fool.*

n.g. No go; no good: orig. (1840), U.S., anglicized ca 1890; ob.

N.H. A bug: from ca 1875; ob. Abbr. NORFOLK HOWARD.

n.n. A **n**ecessary **n**uisance, esp. a husband: Society (—1909).

n. (or **N.**) **wash,** see NOTERGAL WASH.

n.y.d. Drunk: military hospitals' (—1909); ob. i.e. *not yet diagnosed.* cf. N.A.D.

***nab;** occ. **nabb** or **nab(b)e.** The head: c. of ca 1560–1750. Harman (as *nabe*); Head. cf. NOB and NAPPER, 4. 2. The head of a stick: c.: early C.17. Dekker. 3. A hat; a cap: c. of ca 1670–1830. Shadwell, Fielding, Grose. cf. NAB, A PENTHOUSE. Abbr. NAB-CHEAT. 4. A fop: c.: ca 1690–1750. 5. One who 'nabs' (see the v.), esp. a police officer: 1813: c. >, ca 1860, low s.; ob. 6. See NABS.

***nab;** occ. **nab(b)e** or **nabb,** v. To catch; to arrest: from ca 1685: c. >, ca 1860, low s. F. Spence, Shadwell. cf. NAP and NOBBLE. 2. It soon > a gen. c. v. of action: see NAB THE RUST, THE STIFLES, etc. 3. Linking senses 1 and 4 with the n., sense 3, is B.E.'s '*I'll Nab ye*, i.e. I'll have your Hat or Cap.' 4. To seize; to steal: low s.: from ca 1814. *Sporting Magazine*, 1814, 'All was lost, save what was nabb'd to pay the cost.' 5. To cog (a die): C.18 c. or low s.; in its orig. form, NAP, v., 5 (B.E.), it was certainly c. 6. v.i., to snatch at something: C.19–20; ob.: low. 7. (cf. senses 1, 4.) To detect (an incident): Shrewsbury School: late C.19–20. 8. To take something to which one is entitled, but which is not in plentiful supply: mostly Australian: late C.19–20.

nab, a penthouse. A large hat: c. or low s. of ca 1750–1820.

nab, queer, see QUEER NAB.

nab-all; also **nabal(l).** A fool: early C.17 s. > coll. Rowlands. 2. As a churl or a miser, C.17–20 (ob.), it is S.E.

***nab-cheat** or **-chete.** A hat or cap: c. of ca 1530–1830. See CHEAT.

***nab-girder.** A bridle: c. of ca 1670–1870, though ob. as early as 1820. Also *nob-girder.* Ex NAB = NOB, the head, + *girdle* perverted.

nab it (on the dial). To receive a blow (on the face): low: from ca 1820. But *nab it*, like *nap it*, also = to receive (gen., unexpected) punishment: low and dial.: C.19–20. cf. COP IT.

nab the bib. To weep: from ca 1830: low. An earlier variant, *nab one's bib*, dating from late C.18, occurs in a ballad, the *Rolling Blossom*:

> At the new drop I nabb'd my bib,
> While Will, my man, was swinging,
> At the gin ken I took a swig,
> Reel'd home, blind drunk, a-singing.

Later (1860 +), with variant *nap one's bib*, it also meant, to carry one's point, by weeping, then by any similar means.

***nab the regulars.** To divide a booty: c.: from ca 1840.

nab (or, in C.19–20, **nap) the rust.** To take offence (cf. RUSTY, adj.): from ca 1850: low and dial.; ob. Ex: 2. The turf sense, (of a horse) to become restless (—1785). 3. To receive unexpected punishment: C.19–20 (ob.): c. > low s. Prob. influenced by NAB THE TEIZE.

***nab the snow.** To steal linen, esp. from hedges: c.: from ca 1780.

***nab the stifles.** To be hanged: c.: C.19–20; ob. See STIFLER.

***nab** or **nap the stoop.** To stand in the pillory: late C.18–early 19 c.

***nab** or **nap the teize.** To be whipped, privately, in prison: late C.18–mid-19 c. ?ex *tease*, for in C.19 it is often spelt *teaze.*

nabb; occ. **nabbe,** see NAB, n. and v.

nabber. A bailiff; a constable: low: from ca 1810; ob. 2. A thief, esp. a pilferer: low and (—1808) Scots dial. Ex NAB, v., 1. cf.:

***nabbing-cheat.** The gallows: c. (—1719); †by 1850. 'Captain' Alexander Smith.

***nabbing-cull.** A bailiff; a constable: c.: ca 1775–1840. Tomlinson. cf. NABMAN.

nabby. A Scottish form of NOBBY, adj.

***nabe,** see NAB, n. and v.

***nabman.** A constable: c. of ca 1815–40. Ex NAB, v., 1.

nabob. (Gen. pl.) 'Senior passengers in the East Indiamen': nautical: late C.18–early 19. 2. A capitalist: ca 1858–90. Ex the S.E. sense.

***nabs;** in C.19, occ. **knabs.** (Mainly North Country) c. >, ca 1830, low s.: from ca 1790; ob. Potter. *His nabs*, he; (rare) *your nabs*, you: but *my nabs*, either I, myself, or my friend (cf. C.16 *my* NOBS, my darling). cf. WATCH. Perhaps a corruption of NEB, a nose, a face: for semantics, see NIBS, which is a variant.

***nabs on.** A hall-mark: c. (—1889); ob. Ex NAB = head.

***nace,** see NASE.

nack. A horse: c. (—1889). Ex NAG.

nackers. Properly KNACKERS: low and dial. C.19–20. The testicles.

naf. The female pudend: ?back s. on *fan*, abbr. FANNY: from ca 1845. If not obscure dial. of independent origin – ex or cognate with *naf(f)*, the navel (—1866), or with *naf(f)*, the hub of a wheel (—1796), E.D.D. – then this is perhaps the earliest of back-s. terms.

nag. A riding horse (esp. if small) or pony: C.15–20: coll except in Scotland and North of England, where dial. Anon., *The Destruction of Troy*, ca 1400: 'He neyt [= neighed] as a nagge, at his nose thrilles [= nostrils]'; Coryat; Johnson, 'A horse in familiar language'; Henley. 2. The penis: low: ca 1670–1750. Cotton. Ex preceding sense (semantics: to RIDE). cf. NAGS.

nag. To scold or persistently to find fault (v.t. with *at*): orig. (—1828), dial. >, ca 1840, coll >, ca 1890, S.E. Orig. sense, to gnaw.

nag, tether one's. To coit: low Scots: C.19–20. Contrast:

nag, water one's or **the.** To make water: low: mid-C.19–20; ob. cf. DRAGON . . .

***nag-drag.** A three-months' imprisonment: c.: from ca 1850; ob. See DRAG, n., 7.

naggie. See NAGGY. The female pudend: low: C.19–20; ob. cf. NAG, n., 2.

naggle. To toss the head stiffly and affectedly: coll (†by 1910) and dial.: from ca 1840. Halliwell. cf. S.E. *naggle*, to haggle, quarrel.

naggy or **naggie.** A pony; a very small riding horse: coll and dial. from ca 1780. Blackmore, 'Then the naggie put his foot down.'

nags. The testes: low: C.19–20; ob. cf. NAG, n., 2: ?on NACKERS.

nail. 'A person of an over-reaching, imposing disposition' – i.e. a SHREWDY, a crook – 'is called a nail, a dead nail, a nailing rascal,' Vaux, 1812: low: ca 1810–1915. Ex the v., senses 2 and 4. 2. 'The central sconce at the east and west ends of the school were so called,' Adams's *Wykehamica*: from ca 1840: Winchester College. Whence *stand up under the nail*, to stand there throughout school time for having told a lie; later a liar received a BIBLER or was 'bibled', Mansfield.

nail, v. To catch or get hold of or secure: 1760, Foote, 'Some bidders are shy . . .; but I nail them.' 2. Hence, to rob or steal: low: from ca 1810. 3. To catch or surprise (a person) in a fix, a difficulty: 1766, Goldsmith, 'When they came to talk of places in town, . . . I nailed them.' 4. Hence, in late C.19–20 c. > low s.: to arrest (a person). 5. To strike smartly, to beat: Scots s.: from ca 1805; ob. 6. Hence, to succeed in hitting: Dowden, 1886, but prob. very much earlier. In Scots at least as early as 1785. 7. To overreach; to cheat: low: ca 1810–30. 8. To backbite: printers': from ca 1870. Also *brass-nail*; cf. NAIL-BOX. 9. 'To impress for any kind of fagging. Also, to detect': Winchester College (—1889). Ex sense 1.

nail, naked as my, see NAKED. **nail, dead as . . .** see DEAD AS . . .

nail, off the. Tipsy: Scots coll: from ca 1820. Galt, 1822, 'I was what you would call a thought off the nail.' cf. Scots *off at the nail*, mad.

nail, on the. At once: late C.16–20: coll >, ca 1870, S.E. Nashe (*upon*, as is gen. till C.18); Gay. Ex hand-nail and a drinking custom: see SUPERNACULUM and cf. Fr. *payer rubis sur l'ongle.* 2. Under discussion: coll: ca 1885–1910. W. T. Stead, 1886.

nail!, no. I beg your pardon; sorry, but it's true!: printers': from ca 1870.

nail-bearer. (Gen. in pl.) A finger: C.18–mid-19: ?S.E. or coll.

nail-box. A favourite spot for backbiting: printers': from ca 1870.

nail-groper. One who sweeps or scours

the streets in search of nails, old iron, etc.: Londoners': ca 1830–70. *Sinks*, 1848.

nail in one's coffin. A drink of liquor: coll: from ca 1820. Gen. as *here's another nail in your*, occ. *my*, rarely *his*, *coffin*. 2. See COFFIN-NAIL.

nail in one's coffin, drive, or, occ., **put a.** To do anything likely to shorten one's life: C.19–20: coll till C.20, then S.E. In 1789, Wolcot anticipated, thus: 'Care to our coffin adds a nail, no doubt.'

nail on the ready. To catch someone in the criminal act: police s.: ca 1830–80. *Sessions*, Feb. 1839. See NAIL, v., 3.

nail-rod or **nailrod.** Orig. (ca 1885), a stick of 'Two Seas' tobacco. Ex the shape. 2. Hence (—1896), any coarse, esp. if dark, stick of tobacco; ob. Both senses, New Zealand and then Australian. *New Zealand Herald*, 8 Nov. 1886; 1896, H. Lawson.

nailed-up drama. Drama dependent upon elaborate scenery: theatrical: ca 1881–1914. First used in reference to just such a drama, *The World*.

nailer. An exceptionally good or marvellous event, thing or person (esp. a hand *at* . . .); a gen. term of excellence: 1818, Macneill; ca 1890, Marshall in '*Pomes' from the Pink 'Un*, 'At guzzling the whole lot were nailers'. cf. the ob. U.S. *nail-driver*, a fast horse. 2. An extortioner, a usurer, from ca 1888. Ex NAIL, v., 2. 3. See NAILOR. 4. An obvious, gross lie: late C.19–20. Ex dial. 5. (*the nailer.*) See BOY WITH THE BOOTS.

nailing, vbl n. See NAIL, v., all senses. 2. adj.: excellent: 1883, *Pall Mall Gazette*, 29 March. 3. adv.: very, exceedingly: 1884, Mrs E. Kennard; 1894, George Moore, 'A nailing good horse once'. Ex NAIL, v., 1, influenced by NAILER, 1.

***nailor;** more correctly **nailer.** (Constructed with *on.*) A prejudice (against): c. (—1887) >, by 1900, low.

nailrod, see NAIL-ROD.

nails often occurs in late C.14–early 17 oaths and asseverations. e.g. (*by*) *God's nails*.

nails, eat one's. To do something foolish or unpleasant: coll: C.18–19. Swift.

nails, hard as. In good condition: from ca 1860: coll till ca 1905, then S.E. 2. Unyielding, harsh, pitiless: coll (—1889).

nails, right as. Perfectly fit: coll: from ca 1890. Ex preceding, sense 1.

nails on one's toes, before one had. Before one was born; long ago: coll: C.17. Shakespeare, in *Troilus and Cressida*, 'Whose wit was mouldy ere your grandsires had nails on their toes'.

nair. Rain: back s.: from ca 1870; ob., as, except among costers, is all back s.: see *Slang* at 'Oddities'. cf. NIRE.

naked, n. Raw spirit: somewhat low: from ca 1810; ob. Ex the adj.

naked similes were prob. all coll in origin, but their very force soon made them S.E. and proverbial. The chief non-dial. ones are: **naked as a cuckoo,** C.17–20, latterly dial. and in Dekker as **naked as the cuckoo in Christmas; naked as a needle,** mid-C.14–20 (ob.), in P. J. Bailey, 1858, **nude as a needle; naked as a shorn sheep,** C.17–18 (Gayton, 1654); **naked as a stone,** C.14–15; **naked as a worm,** C.15–16; **naked as one's** (gen. **my) nail,** ca 1530–1700 (Heywood, 1533, – Massinger – 'Phraseologia' Robertson); **naked as truth,** C.17 (suggested by the late C.16–20 S.E. *the naked truth*), 'Lest it strip him as naked as truth', in the Somers Tracts.

nale, an ale-house, is Scots (prob.) coll: C.18–early 19. Extant in Gloucestershire.

nale or **nael, neel.** Lean: back s. (—1859). (Often adj., rarely v.)

nam. A man: back s. (—1859).

namase, see NAMMOUS.

namby-pamby. Affected; effeminate: from ca 1745: coll till ca 1780, then S.E. Ex Carey's, Pope's, and Swift's nickname (1726 +) for *Ambrose* Philips, poetaster (d. 1749).

name!, give it a; name yours! Invitations to drink: coll: late C.19–20. See HOW WILL YOU HAVE IT?

name, to one's. Belonging to one: coll: 1876, Whyte-Melville.

name in vain, take one's. To mention by name: coll: C.18–20. Swift. Ex the Biblical *take the name of the Lord in vain*.

name into it, put one's. To advance a matter greatly: tailors': from ca 1860; ob. Ex putting the tailors' name on a garment.

name is mud, his, see MUD.

name of, by the. Having the name (of): from ca 1670: S.E. till ca 1830, then coll and U.S. Thackeray, 1841, 'A grocer . . . by the name of Greenacre'.

name of . . .(, in the). Some of these asseverations are C.19–20 coll; e.g. *name of goodness*, which is also dial.

name to go to bed with, a nice. An ugly name: dial. >, by 1887, coll. cf. the Fr. s. *un nom à coucher dehors*.

name yours! see NAME!, GIVE IT A.

nameless creek, the. 'A lucky place whose

whereabouts is for that reason untold', F. & H.: anglers' j. > coll: from ca 1860; ob.

namesclop. Policeman: back s.: 1851, Mayhew, I; virtually †by 1910.

***nammous** or **namous;** occ. **nammus** or **nommus;** rarely **namus** and **†namase.** To depart, esp. furtively and/or quickly: c., esp. among costermongers: from ca 1855. J. E. Ritchie, *The Night Side of London Life*, 1857; *London Miscellany*, 3 March 1866. Slightly ob. Prob. a corruption of VAMOS, *vamoose*, perhaps shaped by NIM and Ger. *nehmen*. H. postulates back s. on *someone* ('simplified' presumably, as *summon*): wrongly, I believe.

nam(m)ow. A woman; esp. DELO NAMMOW, an old woman: back s. (—1851).

***nammus, namous, namus,** see NAMMOUS.

nan. A serving-maid: C.18: coll (somewhat low). Ex *Nan*, a by-form of *Anne*. 2. grandmother: lower classes' coll: mid-C.19–20. cf. GRAN, GRANNY, NANNY.

nan! What did you say?: mid-C.18–20: coll (e.g. in Foote) till ca 1810, then dial., where ob. Ex *anan*, *anon*.

nan-boy. An effeminate man: late C.17–20; ob.: coll. cf. NAN, n. 2. A catamite: C.19–20: coll. ?influenced by NANCY.

nan-nan. A man's straw hat: Australian: ca 1880–1914. Ex Aborigine?

Nana; Nana-ish. Outrageous; indecent: clubmen's coll: late 1880–ca 85. Ex Zola's *Nana*, that novel which, dealing with a SWELL courtesan, owes its best scene to Otway.

nana. A banana: nursery coll: late C.19–20.

Nancy, Miss Nancy, Nancy boy. A catamite: (low) coll: C.19–20. Also as adj.: rare before C.20. 2. Also, an effeminate man: C.19–20; ob. except in dial. cf. MOLLY. 3. (Only as *nancy, Nancy*.) The breech, esp. in *ask my Nancy*: low (perhaps orig. c.): ca 1810–1910. See ARSE!, ASK MY.

Nancy Dawson. Grog: naval: C.19–20; very ob. Bowen, 'Men were summoned to draw it by that popular old air.' 2. An effeminate, lackadaisical youth: ca 1887–1910. cf. NANCY.

Nancy homey. An effeminate man, esp. a homosexual: late C.19–20. See NANCY, 1 and 2; *homey* is a Parlary word.

Nancy Lee. A flea: rhyming s.: from ca 1860.

nanna. An occ. variant of sense 3 and 4 of:

nanny. A whore: late C.17–19: coll. Ex *Nanny*, the female name. Mostly in combination: see, e.g., NANNY-HOUSE. 2. A she-goat: from ca 1890 as a coll, but in dial. before 1870. Abbr. NANNY-GOAT. 3. (A) nursemaid: 1864. 4. GRANNY: lower classes' coll: mid-C.19–20.

nanny-goat. A she-goat: coll: 1788, T. Day. cf. NANNY, 1, and BILLY-GOAT. 2. An anecdote: 1860, Haliburton; ob. Semi-rhyming s.

nanny(-)hen, as nice as a. Very affected; delicate; prim: C.16–17: coll. The *nanny-hen* is merely *nun's hen* (see NICE AS A NANNE) and may, in fact, have rarely been used: see Apperson at *nice*.

nanny-house or **shop.** A brothel: low coll: resp. late C.17–19; C.19–20, slightly ob. F. & H. give an imposing synonymy: e.g. *academy* (see ACADEMICIAN); FLASH-CASE, -DRUM; KNOCKING-SHOP, -HOUSE; MOLLY-SHOP; PUSHING-SCHOOL; TRUGGING-*ken*, -HOUSE; VROW-CASE.

***nantee; nanti** (rare), **nanty.** No; not, or nor, any. Also absolutely: I have none; 'shut up!' (abbr. NANTEE PALAVER); stop! (e.g. 'Nanty that whistling!'): from ca 1850: Parlary and c. > also, by 1900, gen. theatrical. Mayhew. Among grafters: beware! Ex It. *niente*, nothing, via Lingua Franca, as is most Parlary. 2. Hence adj.: of no account: Parlary (—1909).

nantee medzies or **nanty metzes,** see MEDZIES.

nantee narking. Great fun: low taverns': ca 1800–50. Egan's *Life in London*. Lit., 'no crabbing'.

nantee palaver! Hold your tongue!: from ca 1850. Lit., no talk. cf.:

nantee panarly! Be careful!: from ca 1850. See NANTEE.

nantee worster. No worse; a person no worse: low London: late C.19–20.

nanti, nanty, see NANTEE.

***nap.** An infection of syphilis or gonorrhoea: c.: late C.17–18. 2. An instance of: 'By Cheating with the Dice to secure one Chance', B.E.: c.: late C.17–18. Rare: the v. is much commoner. 3. An arrest: throughout C.18: c. or low s. *Street Robberies Considered*, ca 1728. 4. Presumably, a sheep, the term occurring only in *napper of naps*, a sheep-stealer: late C.17–18: c. These four senses derive ex the c. v. 5. A hat: c. of C.18. Ex NAB, n., 3. 6. Strong ale or beer: Scots coll: late C.18–19. Tarras, 1804; Jamieson. Ex NAPPY. 7. A

Napoleon, i.e. a twenty-franc piece: coll: 1820, Moore. By abbr. 8. A pretended blow: theatrical: from ca 1850. Mayhew. See NAP, TAKE THE. ?ex KNAP. 9. A very pointed moustache: London: 1855–ca 70. Re-introduced by Napoleon III, who visited London in 1855.

***nap**, v. See the n., 1 and 2: same period and status. The infection is gen. conveyed by *nap it* (B.E., Grose). The etymology, like the relation to NAB, is vague; cf. the cognate S.E. *knap*. 2. To seize, catch; arrest: c.: from ca 1670; ob. Head, 'If the Cully naps us, And the Lurries from us take'; D'Urfey. In John Poulter, 1753, the sense weakens: 'Nap my kelp (hold my hat).' 3. Hence, to steal: c.: from ca 1690; ob. e.g. *nap the* WIPER, steal the handkerchief. 4. To receive severe punishment (prob. ex sense 1): gen. as *nap it*: low: from ca 1815; ob., except in dial. 5. To cog (a die): late C.17–18 c. cognate with sense 2: both prob. ex KNAP. 6. Hence, v.i. and t., to cheat: c. of ca 1670–1760. 7. A low variant of S.E. *knap*: late C.17–20. 8. The horse-racing v. is j., not s.

nap, go. To risk everything: ca 1884, Glover, *Racing Life*: coll (?orig. racing s.).

nap, take the. To pretend to have been struck, 'by slapping the hands together unseen by the audience': theatrical: from ca 1860.

***nap a winder.** To be hanged: c.: C.19. Lit., catch something that winds one.

***nap it.** See NAP, v., 1 and 4. e.g. *nap it at the nask* (see NASK), to be lashed at Bridewell: late C.17–18 c.

nap-nix. An amateur playing minor parts for experience: theatrical: from ca 1860; ob. Ex NAP, to take or receive, + NIX, nothing.

***nap on.** To cheat, try a cheating trick on: ca 1670–1760: c. 2. Also, however, it means to strike or to strike at: C.17–early 18. (See, e.g., the O.E.D.'s quotation from Head & Kirkman, where the sense is ambiguous.) Here, *nap* (cf. Greene's 'worse than nabbing on the neckes to Connies') is prob. S.E. *knap* corrupted.

nap on, go. To bet everything one has on: from the 1880s: racing coll >, by 1900, S.E.

nap or nothing. All or nothing: clubmen's: 1868–ca 1900.

***nap the bib, the regulars, the rust, the teize**, see NAB THE BIB, etc.

nap the rent. See PEW, STUMP THE: with which it is contemporaneous as well as synonymous.

nap (or knap) the slap. To know how to receive a blow without being hurt in rough-and-tumble clownery: showmen's: from ca 1860. Hindley.

nap toco for yam. To get the worst of it, esp. in fisticuffs: low: ca 1820–70. ?ex Gr. τόκος, interest. See TOCO.

napkin, be buried in a. To be asleep; half-witted: C.19–20, ob.: coll.

napkin, knight of the. A waiter: C.19–20, ob.: coll bordering on S.E.

napkin, take sheet and. To sleep and eat (with someone): coll: C.17–18. Mewe.

napkin-snatching. The stealing of handkerchiefs: ca 1820–60: low or c.

napkin under one's chin, stick a. To eat a meal: from ca 1750; ob.: coll. Foote.

***napp,** see NAP, n. and v.

***napper.** A cheat; a thief: c. of ca 1670–1840. Esp. in *napper of naps* (see NAP, n., 4). 2. A false witness: low or c.: C.18. 3. See RAIN-NAPPER. 4. The head: s. and dial.: from ca 1720. Esp. in *go off one's napper*, go mad. ?etymology, unless ex NAB, the head (cf. NAP, 5.) 5. Hence, the mouth: low: late C.19–20. 6. A hat: c. of ca 1800–70. See NAP, n., 5. 7. See:

napper's null. A sheep's head (as food): s.: Ned Ward, 1703. *Null* = NOLL.

***napping.** Cheating: from ca 1670; ob.: c. until C.19, then low s. 2. See NAP, v.

napping, as Moss (in late C.18–mid-19, often **Morse,** as in Grose) **caught his mare.** Asleep; by surprise: a coll proverbial c.p. of ca 1569–1870; in C.19, dial. 'The allusions to this saying and song in C.16–17 are very numerous,' Apperson. App. one Moss caught his mare by feeding her through a hurdle (Apperson, quotation of 1597).

napping, catch or **take.** To take by surprise or in the act: 1562, Pilkington; Grose, in the elaborated form (see preceding entry): coll till C.19, then S.E. Lit., to catch asleep.

nappy. Beer: early C.18–19. Ned Ward. 2. A napkin: nursery coll: prob. from mid-C.19. Collinson.

nappy, adj. (Of a horse) that has 'these here little lumps along the neck and withers about as big as a nut' ('*No. 747*'): horse-copers': mid-C.19–20. 2. 'A horse that refuses to answer to the hand or leg, tries to go the way home instead of the way you want, or plays other tricks, is spoken of as "nappy". It is very common speech with all who own horses': sporting: since ca 1860. *Sessions*, Sept. 1880. It is often applied to persons if they are recalcitrant or unamenable. Ex NAB (or NAP) THE RUST.

narang. Small: Australian pidgin: C.19. John Lang, *The Forger's Wife*, 1855.

narangy. A SWELL: Australian: ca 1870–1910. 'Tom Collins', *Such Is Life*, 1903. Ex Aboriginal.

***nark.** A police spy; a common informer: c. (—1864). '*No. 747*'; Arthur Morrison, in *Mean Streets*. Often COPPER'S NARK, i.e. NOSE. Ex Romany *nak*, the nose. cf.:

***nark,** v. To watch; occ., look after: c. (—1859). Ex the n. cf. TOUT, v. 2. Hence, to see: low (—1886). 'Pomes' Marshall. 3. v.i., to act the informer: 1896, A. Morrison, in *Child Jago*, 'It was the sole commandment that ran there: "Thou shalt not nark".' cf. NOSE; STAG.

narp. A shirt: Scots, either c. or, less prob., low s. (—1839). Origin?

narrative. A dog's tail: middle-class jocular: ca 1900–14. Punning *tail – tale – narrative*.

narrish. Thrifty: coll (—1889); ob. London society, Oct. 1889. Ex S.E. *narrowish*.

narrow. Never (a); not (a), not (one): coll and dial.: 1750, Fielding, 'I warrants me there is narrow a one of all those warrant officers but looks upon himself to be as good as arrow a squire of £500 a year.' Ex *ne'er a*. 2. It is low coll or s. as = stupid, foolish, ignorant: from ca 1850; ob. 3. The bowling sense, 'When the Bias of the Bowl holds too much', B.E., is either j. or coll of late C.17–20.

narrow, 'tis all. 'Said by the Butchers one to another when their Meat proves not so good as expected', B.E.: late C.17–18 c.p.

narrow lane, the, see LANE.

narrow-striper. A Royal Marine Light Infantryman: naval: late C.19–20.

nasal. The nose: boxing: 1888, *Sporting Life*, 21 Nov., 'Planted a couple of well-delivered stingers on Harris's nasal'.

***nase.** Also *nace*, *naze*, *nazie*, *nazy*. Drunken; (of liquor) intoxicating: c.: from ca 1530; fl. till ca 1690 as *nace*, *naze*; then only as *nazie*, *nazy*, or *nazzy*: see NAZY. ?ex *nose*, Fr. *nez*. Or ex Ger. *nass*, wet.

***nase nab.** A red nose; a drunkard: c. (—1688); †by 1820. Randle Holme. See NASE.

***nash.** To go away from, to quit, person(s) or place: c. of ca 1810–50. Vaux, 'Speaking of a person who is gone, they say he is nash'd.' Ex Romany *nash*, *nasher*, to run.

***Nash is concerned, Mr.** He has gone away: c. of ca 1810–50: Vaux, see quotation, preceding entry.

nasie (Coles, 1676), see NAZY.

***nask** or **naskin.** A prison: c. of ca 1670–1830. Coles, 1676 (*naskin*); Higden, 1686, Juvenal (*10th Satire*), *naskin*; ca 1690, B.E., *nask* and *naskin*; Grose, id. ?ex †Scots dial. *nask*, a withe + c. KEN, a place, *nask* being an abbr. Whence, *the Old Nask*, the City (London) bridewell; *the New Nask*, the Clerkenwell bridewell; and *Tuttle* (in Grose, *Tothillfields*) *Nask*, that in Tothill Fields: all in B.E. and all c.

nasty, cheap and. Outwardly pleasing, actually worthless: coll (—1864) until ca 1905, then S.E. In London, ca 1860–80, the phrase often ran '. . . like Short's in the Strand', with reference to a cheap restaurant that now has a much better reputation.

nasty face, see JACK NASTY-FACE.

***nasty man.** He who, in a garrotting gang, does the critical work; or he who, for a CRACKSMAN on a desperate job, acts as a garrotter: c.: from ca 1840; ob. The Reference (p. 419) in '*No. 747*'s *Autobiography* is valid for 1845; Trevelyan in *The Competition Wallah*.

nasty one. A fig. blow, a set-back: coll: 'Ouida', 1880. Also *a nasty one in the eye* (—1902).

Natal rum. 'A vile spirit distilled from sugar refuse and nothing behind "Cape smoke" [q.v.] in its effects', Pettman: 1885, W. Greswell, *Our South African Empire*.

Nathaniel, (down) below. Even lower than hell: ca 1860–1915. Nathaniel being Satan, says Ware: but *Nathaniel* may be rhyming s. on *hell*.

nation as n. is S.E., as an adv. = very (—1771) it is coll (†by 1870) and dial.; as adj. (very great or large) it is C.19–20 dial. As all three, common in late C.18–20 U.S. The adj. derives ex the n. (Sterne, 1762, 'The French have such a nation of hedges') and occurs in U.S. as early as 1765 (*nation profit*), while the adv., in U.S., 1781 (*nation fawdy*), derives either ex the U.S. adj. or the n. The word itself is a euphemistic abbr. of DAMNATION (adv.).

native; gen. collectively **the natives,** 'silly people, generally; the untravelled population of any town, wrapped up in incipient [?*innate* or *insipid*] simplicity are *natives*', Bee: London coll: from ca 1820; ob. cf.:

native cavalry. 'The unbroke horses of countrymen, when they resort to races, fairs, fights, &c.', Bee: London: ca 1820–60. cf. preceding entry.

nat'ral. Natural: low coll (—1887).

natty. A 'natty' person: coll: 1820, Moore; ob. Ex:

natty, adj. Orig., and in c., app. clever, smart with the hands: see NATTY LAD. 2. Smartly neat, spruce: from ca 1785 (implied in the adv.): s. till ca 1860, then coll. Surr, 1806, 'A natty spark of eighteen'. 3. Of things, very neat, dainty: s. till ca 1860; coll ca 1860–1910; then S.E. 1801, Wolcot, 'Thy natty bob'. 4. Hence, of persons, daintily skilful: from ca 1820: s. >, ca 1860, coll. Prob. ex NATTY LAD. For etymology, cf. the †S.E. *netty*, *nettie* (e.g. in Tusser, 'Pretty ... fine and ... nettie'), but prob. a corruption of *neat* or perhaps ex Fr. *net*. N.B., the other parts, *nattily*, *nattiness*, mid-C.19–20, were, prob., orig. coll, but they soon > S.E.

natty, adv. Nattily, i.e. smartly, daintily neatly, hence skilfully: from ca 1785: s. >, ca 1860, (low) coll. G. Parker, 1789, 'A kind of fellow who dresses smart, or what they term natty'. Ex the adj.

***natty lad.** A young thief, esp. if a pickpocket: c. of ca 1780–1870. See NATTY, adj., 1, and the etymology.

natural. A mistress, a harlot: ca 1685–1830: perhaps orig. c.; never better than low s. Shadwell, 'My natural, my convenient, my pure'. 2. A child: coll: late C.18–early 19. By abbr. ex *natural child*, *daughter*, *son*. 3. Ace and 10 at vingt-et-un: from ca 1900. Perhaps because such a hand naturally makes 21.

naturally! Of course: coll: late C.19–20.

naughty. Flash; loudly smart: low: ca 1860–1910. Vance, 1864, speaks of trousers as 'werry naughty'. Prob. *naughty*, immoral, influenced by NATTY, adj., 3.

naughty, do the. To play the whore; to coït (of women only): from ca 1850: low coll. Also, ca 1860–1910, occ. *go naughty*: ordinary coll.

naughty, the. The female pudend: mid-C.19–20.

naughty house, if used by the prim, is S.E.; if by the lewd, a coll: a brothel: C.19–20.

nauseous. Objectionable: coll: C.18–early 19. e.g. *nauseous toad*, a mild endearment.

nautical triumvisetta. 'A singing and dancing nautical scene by three persons, of whom two are generally women': music-halls' (—1909); very ob. Ware. Perhaps a blend of *triumvirate* + *set*, with an Italianate suffix (*a*).

nav. Abbr. NAVIGATOR.

naval police, Her or His Majesty's. Sharks: nautical: mid-C.19–20; ob. They are sharp deterrents of desertion at sea.

navel, gall one's. To grow wanton: C.18 coll; cf. the C.17–18:

navel, proud below the. Amorous: coll bordering on S.E., as in Davenant's *Albovine*, 1629, 'Whenever I see her I grow proud below the navel.'

navel-tied. Inseparable: C.18–early 19 coll. Gen. *they have tied their navels together*, as in Ray's *Proverbs*, ed. of 1767.

navels, wriggle. To copulate: C.19: low coll. cf. GIBLETS, JOIN.

navigator. A TATER, i.e. potato: rhyming s. (—1859). Occ. *nav* (—1902).

navigator Scot. A hot TATER; gen. a hot baked potato: rhyming s. (—1859).

navvy. A labourer working on excavation, earthworks, or similar heavy tasks: 1832, De Quincey: coll >, by 1865, S.E. Ex *navigator*, S.E. (ca 1770–1870), same sense. 2. The navigating officer: nautical: late C.19–20.

navvy's Prayer Book, the. A shovel: navvies': ca 1870–1910. (D. W. Barrett, *Navvies*, 1880.) Ex the prayerful attitude involved in its use.

Nawpost, Mr. A foolish fellow: late C.17–18: c.p. coll. Presumably, one foolish enough, if hungry, to gnaw a post.

'Nay, stay!' quoth Stringer when his neck was in the halter. A c.p. applied to one speaking too late: ca 1670–1750. Ex a topical instance, perhaps of an innocent man.

Nazarene foretop. 'The foretop of a wig made in imitation of Christ's head of hair, as represented by the painters and sculptors', Grose, 2nd ed.: ca 1785–1820: on the border-line between S.E. and coll.

naze, see NASE.

nazie, see NAZY.

nazold. A silly person; a vain fool: 1607, Walkington: coll till ca 1840, then only as dial. cf. S.E. *nazzard*, which app. = dial. *azzard* and, significantly, *azzald*, which may be cognate with *ass*.

***nazy;** occ. **nazzy.** Drunken: from early 1670s: c. (ex NASE) until ca 1780, then low; from ca 1830, dial. Coles, 1676 (*nasie*); B.E. (as *nazie*); *A New Canting Dict.*, 1725, *nazy*-COVE and -MORT, a male and a female drunkard; Grose (*nazie*, 1785; *nazy*, 1788): Robinson's *Whitby Glossary*, 1855 (*nazzy*). cf.:

***nazy-nab.** A drunken coxcomb: c.: C.18.

***ne-dash,** see NEDASH.

neagues; neakes, see 'SNEAKS!

Neapolitan favour. Syphilis: euphemistic coll: late C.16–mid-17. Greene, *Notable Discovery*, 1591.

near and far. The bar: public-house rhyming s. (—1909).

near – in C.17 occ. **like – as fourpence to a groat, as.** For practical purposes the same: mid-C.16–20: coll till C.19, then dial.

near the knuckle, see KNUCKLE, NEAR THE.

neardy. A master, a foreman, a parent; a BOSS (2): Northern coll: from ca 1860; ob.

nearer the bone, see MEAT, THE NEARER THE BONE . . .

neat. (Ironically) rare; fine: ca 1825–1915; ob. by 1890. T. Creevey, 1827, 'So much for my new find! Is he not a neat one?'

neat as a band-box, a new pin, ninepence, wax. As neat as possible; very neat indeed: coll: resp. C.19–20, C.19–20, C.17–20 (see at NINEPENCE), ca 1840–1910.

neat but not gaudy. Sprucely neat: orig. serious (ca 1630–1800) and presumably S.E.; then – even in Lamb's 'A little . . . flowery border . . ., neat not gaudy', 1806 – it takes an ironical turn (cf. NEAT), which finds itself recognized as a c.p. when, in 1838, Ruskin, in the *Architectural Magazine* for Nov., writes, 'That admiration of the "neat but not gaudy", which is commonly reported to have influenced the devil when he painted his tail pea green.' In 1887, *Lippincott's Magazine* for July has, 'The whole thing "Neat, but not gaudy, as the monkey said" on the memorable occasion "when he painted his tail sky-blue",' which presents a diversion from the orig. sense and likewise constitutes a c.p. But by 1902, F. & H. can give as a 'common', i.e. gen., c.p.: *neat, but not gaudy, as the devil said when he painted his bottom red and tied up his tail with sky-blue ribbon.*

neb. A face, esp. a woman's: (low) coll: C.17–18. Extant in dial. Ex *neb*, a bird's bill.

Nebuchadnezzar. The penis, esp. in *take N. out to* GRASS, (of a man) to have sexual intercourse: low: ca 1860–1915. Ex its liking for GREENS, 4. 2. A vegetarian: ca 1870–1910. Ex the Biblical Nebuchadnezzar's eating of grass.

necessary. A bedfellow, esp. a woman: coll: C.18–early 19. 2. With *the*: *ad hoc* money, funds: coll: 1897, *Daily News*, 6 Sept. cf. NEEDFUL.

neck, v. To hang: coll: C.18–mid-19. cf. S.E. senses, strike on the neck, behead; imm., however, prob. ex the *neck* hanging phrases. 2. To swallow, drink: coll: from ca 1820. cf. the C.16 coll usage: Barclay, 1514, 'She couthe well . . . necke a mesure . . .: she made ten shylynge [i.e. little] of one barell of ale.' 3. To choke (a person): c.: mid-C.19–20.

neck, in the. With unpleasant results; severely: U.S. (ca 1890), anglicized by H. G. Wells in 1908: s. Esp. with *get it*. cf. *where* MAGGIE WORE THE BEADS and *where the* CHICKEN GOT THE AXE.

neck, lose or **win by a.** To lose or win by very little: from ca 1820: coll. For origin, cf. NECK AND NECK.

neck, put it down one's. See NECK, WASH ONE'S, cf. the U.S. *shot in the neck*, drunk.

neck, talk through (the back of) one's. To talk extravagantly, catachrestically: 1904.

neck, wash one's or **the.** To drink: low: ca 1820–1900.

neck and crop. Violently; all of a heap; entirely: 1816, Hone: coll >, ca 1890, S.E. Hardy, 1872; Hall Caine in *The Manxman*, 1894.

neck and heels. Impetuously; wholeheartedly: coll (—1887).

neck and neck. Almost equal; close: from ca 1835: coll. Ex horses running almost level in a race. W. S. Landor to Browning, 11 Feb. 1860, 'You and your incomparable wife are running neck and neck, as sportsmen say.'

neck as long as my arm, I'll first see thy. I'll see you hanged first; you be hanged! A mid-C.17–mid-18 c.p. Ray, 1678.

neck-basting. Liquor-drinking: low (—1887); slightly ob.

neck-cloth. A halter: low coll: ca 1815–70. cf. NECKTIE.

neck it, unable to. Lacking moral courage: low coll: from ca 1840; slightly ob. Ex NECK, v., 2. cf. the S.E. *swallow* = to tolerate.

neck-oil. Liquor; esp. beer: low coll: from ca 1830. cf. NECK, v., 2.

neck or nothing. Desperate(ly): from ca 1675: coll till ca 1850, then S.E. Ray; Cibber; Swift, 'Neck or nothing; come down or I'll fetch you down'; Byron. Either a hanging or a steeplechasing phrase.

neck-squeezer. A halter: low coll: ca 1810–70. cf. NECK-CLOTH; NECKLACE.

***neck-stamper.** A pot-boy at a tavern: c.: ca 1670–1820.

neck-weed. A halter (cf. GALLOWS-

GRASS): ca 1560–1830: coll >, ca 1600, S.E.

neckerchief on the way to Redriffe, the Devil's. The halter; the gallows: low coll: ca 1810–60. *Notes and Queries*, 1886.

necklace. A halter: C.17–mid-19: coll, soon > S.E. cf. NECK-CLOTH, and:

necktie, a halter; *wear a hempen necktie*, to be hanged: C.18–early 19 coll. cf. the U.S. *necktie sociable* (—1878), *n. party* (—1893), a lynching.

necky. Impudent, cheeky: *Conway* cadets' (—1900). Ex *neck*, n. (=CHEEK).

Ned. The inevitable nickname, from the 1890s, of Australian men surnamed Kelly. Ex the notorious bushranger, Ned Kelly.

***ned.** A guinea: c. of ca 1750–1890; then in U.S. as a 10-dollar piece. *Discoveries of John Poulter*. 2. Abbr. NEDDY, 1: from ca 1830.

Ned Fool. A noisy fool or idiot: coll: late C.16–early 17. Nashe.

Ned Skinner. Dinner: rhyming s. (—1909.)

***nedash.** Of no use; nothing: c. of ca 1810–50. Ex Romany *nastis*, *nastissa*, *nestis*, I, you, he, etc., cannot; ?ultimately L. *nequeo*.

neddy. An ass: C.17–20: coll. Wolcot, 1790. Ex *Edward*. Occ. abbr. *ned*; also called *Jack* or *Tom*. (The very few pre-1790 examples are not indisputable.) 2. Hence, a fool: coll and dial.: from ca 1820. Thackeray, 'Long-eared neddies, giving themselves leonine airs'. 3. A guinea: c.: ca 1760–1850. See NED, 1. 4. A life-preserver: c.: 1845 in '*No. 747*' (p. 423); 1857, 'Ducange Anglicus'; 1859, H.; 1864, *Cornhill Magazine*. Also BILLY, 2; COSH. According to Brewer, ex one Ken*nedy*, whose head was smashed in with a poker; prob., however, semantically ex sense 2 above. 5. A large quantity; plenty: Anglo-Irish: from ca 1860; ob.

neddyvaul (or N.). The chief, leader, conqueror: street boys' (mostly London): late C.19–early 20. A corruption of *Ned* (the head) *of all*.

neecee peeress. 'An E.C. [East London] or city [rather, City] bride of little or no family, and an immense fortune, both of which are wedded to some poor lord or baronet': Society (—1909); ob. Lit., a*n E.C.* peeress.

needful, the. *Ad hoc* money: coll: 1771, Foote, 'Then I will set about getting the needful'; *The Comic Almanack*, 1836, 'Needy men the needful need'; Dickens; *Free Lance*, 6 Oct. 1900. cf. NECESSARY.

Needham. Poverty: allusive S.E. of ca 1570–1890. Prob. coll in *on the high-road*, or *in the high-way, to Needham*. Fuller, Ray, Spurgeon. Needham (in C.16, occ. *Needham*; in C.17, occ. *Needom* or *Needome*): a small town near Ipswich.

Needingworth, it comes from. It is worthless or inferior: coll: C.17. John Clarke, 1639. cf. preceding: another topographical allusion on the borderline between S.E. and coll.

***needle.** A sharper; a thief: c. of ca 1780–1850. Potter, 1790. Abbr. NEEDLE-POINT: ex the notion of extreme sharpness. 2. The penis: both low coll and, in C.18, S.E. (e.g. in Nabbes, Dorset, Rochester). 3. With *the*: irritation; nervousness: 1887, *Punch*, 30 July, 'It give 'im the needle ... being left in the lurch this way'; 1900, G. Swift, the nervousness sense, which is mainly athletic, esp. rowing. Prob., as W. suggests, influenced by *nettle* (e.g. †*get the nettle*, become angry), but imm. ex NEEDLE, COP THE. 4. Hence (without *the*), ill feeling: 1899, Clarence Rook, *The Hooligan Nights*, 'It was a fight with the gloves. But there was a bit of needle in it. It was all over Alice.'

needle, v. To irritate, annoy: 1881, G. R. Sims. Also, and ex, *cop* or *give the* NEEDLE, below. 2. v.i., to haggle over a bargain and if possible gain an advantage: c. of ca 1810–50. Ex the n., 1: but cf. n., 3.

needle, cop, get, or take the; needle, give the. To become annoyed; to annoy: resp. (—1874), 1898, 1897; 1887. cf. NEEDLE, n., 3, and v., 1. Ware classifies it as, orig., tailors' s.: 'Irritated, as when the needle runs into a finger'. 2. (Only *get the needle*.) To lose much money at a game: card-players': from ca 1870.

needle and pin. Gin: rhyming s.: late C.19–20.

needle and thread. Bread: rhyming s. (—1859); ob.

needle-book or **-case.** The female pudend: low: C.19–20; ob. cf. NEEDLE-WOMAN.

needle-dodger. A dressmaker: from ca 1860; ob. ?on DEVIL-DODGER.

needle-jerker. A tailor: from ca 1805; ob. cf. last entry.

***needle-point.** A sharper: c. of ca 1690–1890. (Occ., C.19, *needle-pointer*.) Because so sharp. cf. NEEDLE, n., 1, and v., 2.

needle-woman. A harlot: coll: 1849, Carlyle; ob. cf. NEEDLE-BOOK, and NEEDLE, n., 2.

***needy.** A nightly lodger; a beggar; a

tramp: c. verging on low s.: from ca 1859. P. H. Emerson. Ex:

***needy mizzler.** A very shabby person; a tramp that departs without paying for his lodging: tramps' c.: from ca 1810; ob. See MIZZLER.

***needy-mizzling.** c.: from ca 1820. *Temple Bar*, 1868, 'He'll go without a shirt, perhaps, and beg one from house to house.' Ex preceding.

neel, see NALE, second entry.

ne'er a face but his own. Penniless: low: late C.17–18. Obviously alluding to the heads and faces on coins. Occ. *nare* . . .; often *never* . . .

ne'er-be-lickit. Nothing whatever: Scots coll: from ca 1870. *The Encyclopaedic Dict.*, 1885, 'Nothing which could be licked by a dog or cat'.

neergs. Greens (vegetables): back s. (—1859).

neetewif; neetexis; neetrouf, see NETEWIF; NETEXIS; NETROUF.

neggledigee; niggledigee or **gée.** Negligee, 'a woman's undressed gown' (Grose): low coll when not a sol.: mid-C.18–early 19. Shebbeare; Grose, 2nd ed. (N.B., *néglígé* comes later.)

Negro, wash a. To attempt the impossible: coll: C.17. Middleton & Dekker; Barrow, in *Sermons*, ca 1677, 'Therefore was he put . . . to wash Negros . . . to reform a most perverse and stubborn generation.'

negro's-head, gen. in pl **(negroes' heads).** A brown loaf: nautical: late C.18–early 19. Ex the colour; also ex the hardness of the Negro's Head nut. cf. BROWN GEORGE.

negro-nosed. Flat-nosed: late C.17–20; ob. Coll (e.g. in B.E.) till C.19, then S.E.

neither buff nor bum. Neither one thing nor the other: proletarian coll: from ca 1860; slightly ob.

neither sugar nor salt, be. Not to be delicate; esp. not to fear rain: proverbial coll: C.18–20: ob. Swift. Ex sugar dissolving in rain.

Nellie, -y. A giant petrel: nautical coll (—1875).

Nelson. One pound, one shilling and one penny: bank cashiers': late C.19–20. Folklore derives it ex 'Nelson's one eye, one arm and one anus'.

Nelson's blood. Dark rum: naval: (?mid-) C.19–20. Naval lore has it that Nelson's corpse was pickled in rum to preserve it on its passage to England.

nenanecking. A variant of *shenanecking*, i.e. SHENANIGAN: nautical: late C.19–20.

nenti. A late C.19–20 form of NANTEE. P. H. Emerson, 1893.

Neptune's sheep. A nautical variant of *white horses* (waves white-crested): late C.19–20.

nerve. A dashing dandy: Society coll: ca 1750–60. *Adventurer*, No. 98, 1753, 'Buck, Blood, and Nerve'. 2. Impudence; supreme CHEEK: coll: from ca 1880; orig. Etonian. Ex the S.E. sense, courage, assurance, esp. Disraeli's 'You have nerve enough, you know, for anything,' 1826. cf. NERVY.

nerver. A PICK-ME-UP drink of strong liquor; a tonic: Cockney (—1887); ob.

nerves, get on one's, see GET . . .

nerving is an illicit tampering with a horse to make it more spirited and saleable: horse-copers': mid-C.19–20. '*No. 747*'. cf. NERVE, 2.

nervy. Very impudent; impudently confident: 1897: middle 1890s; slightly ob. Ex S.E. *nervy*, boldly brave. 2. 'Jumpy', having bad nerves; excitable or hysterical: coll: 1906.

nescio, sport a. To pretend not to understand anything, esp. in an old university custom: university: ca 1810–50 (perhaps 150 years earlier: cf. next).

nescio, stay with. To circumvent with pretended ignorance: Cambridge University: C.17–18. J. Hacket's *Life of Archbishop Williams*.

nest; gen. **nest in the bush.** The female pudend: low coll when not euphemistic S.E.: C.18–20; ob. G. A. Stevens (longer form), Burns (the shorter).

nest, v. To defecate: C.17–early 18: ?coll or dial. (Scots) or S.E.

nest-egg. A sum of money laid by: late C.17–20: coll till C.19, then S.E. Orig. (as in B.E.), gen. as *leave a nest-egg*. Ruskin.

nestling, keep a. To be restless and/or uneasy: late C.17–18 coll. Ex the restlessness and anxiety of a mother bird for her chicks.

nestor. An undersized boy: Winchester College: from ca 1860; ob. Ex wizened, shrunken Nestor, who in allusive S.E. = an old man.

***nests.** (App. never in singular.) Varieties: c. (—1851); ob. Mayhew. ?perversion of *sets*.

net. Ten: back s. Mayhew, I, 1851. 2. A guard-room: Army s. (—1898). It catches all offenders.

net, all is fish that comes to. All serves the purpose: proverbial coll: mid-C.17–20. In late C.19–20, rarely without *my*, *his*, etc., before *net*.

netenin. Nineteen: back s. (—1859). cf.:

netewif. Fifteen: back s. (—1859). Also *neetewif.*

netexis. Sixteen: back s. (—1859). cf. preceding two entries.

netgen. A half-sovereign; the sum of ten shillings: back s. (—1851). Composed of NET, 10 + GEN, a shilling.

Netherlands, the. The male or the female privities: low: C.18–20; ob.

netnevis. Seventeen: back s. (—1859).

netrouf. Fourteen: back s. (—1859). Also *neetrouf.* cf. preceding and following entries.

nettheg, often written **net-theg.** Eighteen: back s. (—1859).

nettle, to have pissed on a. To be peevish, ill-tempered; very uneasy: mid-C.16–18 coll, then dial. Heywood; Greene, in *The Upstart Courtier*.

nettle in, dock out. A phrase implicative or indicative of fickleness of purpose; or of senseless changing of order: proverbial coll: mid-C.14–18.

nettle stuff. The special rope yarn used for making hammock clews: nautical coll: mid (?) C.19–20. Bowen.

neux, n. and v. A fag; to fag; Woolwich: mid-C.19–20; ?†. Ex *new* (boy, lad, chap).

nevele; loosely **nevel.** Eleven: back s. (—1859).

never a face but his own, see NE'ER A FACE . . .

never fear. Beer: rhyming s. (—1859). 2. See FEAR!, NEVER.

never greens. Eucalyptus: Australian: late C.19–20. Ironic.

Never-mass, at. Never: coll: mid-C.16–17. Anon., *Thersites*, ca 1550; 1631, R. H., 'As our Country Phrase is, when Hens make Holy-water, at new-Never-masse'.

never-mention-'ems. Trousers: coll: 1856; ob. cf. UNMENTIONABLES.

never mind! see MIND!, NEVER.

never never; or with capitals. Abbr. *never never country* or *land*, the very sparsely populated country of Western Queensland and Central Australia: Australian coll: 1900, H. Lawson, 'I rode back that way five years later, from the Never Never.' Because, having been there, one swears *never, never* to return; the derivation ex an Aboriginal word for unoccupied land is prob. invalid. 2. Also with *country* or *land*: the future life, esp. heaven: Australian coll: from ca 1888; ob. 'Rolf Boldrewood'.

never no more. Never more, never again: c.p.: late C.19–20.

never out, the. The female pudend: low: C.19–20; ob.

never-squedge. 'A poor pulseless, passionate youth – a duffer': low London (—1909). Ware. Perhaps *never-squeeze* (a girl).

never-too-late-to-mend shop. A repairing tailor's: tailors': from ca 1860; ob.

never trust me! A c.p. oath = never trust me if this doesn't happen: (mostly low) coll and mostly London: late C.16–20; ob.

never-waser. (Rarely of things.) One who never was a success: orig. (ca 1890) circus s. >, ca 1905, gen. *Sportsman*, 1 April 1891. cf. HAS BEEN.

neves(s); more gen. **nevis.** Seven: back s.: from ca 1845. Whence:

***nevis-stretch.** Seven years' hard labour: c.: from ca 1860. Ex preceding.

nev(v)y; nev(v)ey. Nephew: occ. low coll but gen. dial.: C.19–20.

new. A fresh arrival: *Britannia* training-ship (—1909). (cf. NEW FELLOW.) Whence *new, new!*, the cry of a senior cadet wanting something done by a youngster: Bowen.

new!, tell us something. A coll c.p. retort on stale news: late C.19–20. Lyell.

new bug. A new boy: orig. (ca 1860), Marlborough School; in C.20, fairly gen.

new chum; new-chum. A new arrival, esp. if from Great Britain or Ireland: Australian coll, often slightly contemptuous. T. L. Mitchell, 1839, 'He was what they termed a "new chum", or one newly arrived'; R. M. Praed, 1885; Mrs H. E. Russell, 1892. Whence the rare *new chumhood* (1883, W. Jardine Smith). See also CHUM.

new-chum gold. Iron pyrites: Australian: mid-C.19–20. Very deceptive.

new collar and cuff. To refurbish an old sermon: clerical: from ca 1870; ob.

new drop. 'The scaffold used at Newgate for hanging criminals; which, dropping down, leaves them suspended', Grose, 1788: ca 1785–1850: perhaps orig. c.: certainly never better than low s.

new fellow. A naval cadet in his second term, a 'first-termer' being a *cheeky new fellow*: *Britannia* training-ship: late C.19–early 20. cf. NEW.

new Gravel Lane bullock, fifty ribs a side. A red herring: nautical: late C.19–20. cf. BILLINGSGATE PHEASANT.

new guinea, a or the. The first possession of an income: Oxford University: ca 1820–40.

new hat. A guinea: cheapjacks': ca 1870–1915. C. Hindley, 1876.

new head, give a. To supply a new title and a few lines of introduction to old matter, to deceive the reader into thinking the whole article or item new: journalistic coll: late C.19–20.

new iniquity. Australian immigrants: New Zealand (mostly Otago): coll: ca 1862–80. Opp. *old* IDENTITY.

New Light; occ. **new light.** A Methodist: coll: from ca 1785; ob. 2. One who attends the gaols in order to engineer escapes: c.: ca 1820–50.

new lining to his hat. A bluejacket's pay, 'still received on the cap instead of in the hand': naval: late C.19–20. Bowen.

new Navy. Comforts and improvements introduced into the Navy: naval coll (old bluejackets'): from ca 1920; ob.

new pair of boots, that's a. That's quite another matter: middle-class coll: 1883, *Entr'Acte*, 17 March; ob.

new pin, bright or **clean** or **neat** or **nice** or **smart as a.** Extremely bright, etc.; very smart; first-class: coll: from ca 1880. R. L. Stevenson, 1882 (*clean* . . .); Elworthy, 1886 (*neat*); P. H. Emerson, 1893 (*smart* . . .). Obviously, however, *as a new pin* often merely = wholly; it dates back at least as far as Scott, 1829, 'Clear as a new pin of every penny of debt.'

New River Head (or h-), the. Tears: a London c.p. of ca 1820–30. Bee, 'A watery head hath the wife, whose nob, like Niobe's, is all tears; sometimes termed "the New River head", after an elevated backwater near Islington.'

new scum. A new boy; collectively, new boys: Shrewsbury School: from ca 1870. cf. NEW BUG.

new settlements. A final reckoning: Oxford University: ca 1820–40.

Newcastle, carry or **send coals to,** see COALS TO . . .

Newcastle hospitality. Roasting a friend to death; more gen., killing a person with kindness: North Country coll: mid-C.19–20. (Rather coll than dial.)

Newcastle programme. 'Extreme promises difficult of execution': political coll: 1894–ca 1900. Ware. Ex 'a speech of extreme Radical promise made by Mr John Morley at Newcastle'.

Newgate, specifically, from C.13, the prison (demolished in 1902) for the City of London, was by 1590, 'a common name for all prisons' (Nashe). (cf. NEWMAN'S.) Whence the following; of which it is exceedingly difficult, if not impossible, to determine the exact status:

Newgate, as black as. Frowning; soiled (dress): low coll: ca 1820–80. cf. NEWGATE KNOCKER, 2.

Newgate, may soon be afloat at Tyburn, – he that is at a low ebb at. A c.p. of ca 1660–1810: condemnation at Newgate might well end in a hanging (one's heels afloat) at Tyburn; also fig. Fuller in his *Worthies*, Grose in his *Provincial Glossary*.

Newgate bird or **nightingale.** A gaol-bird; a thief, a sharper: *bird*, C.17–19 coll, e.g. in Dekker; *nightingale*, C.16 coll, e.g. in Copland.

Newgate collar (rare: gen. **Tyburn collar), frill, fringe.** 'A collar-like beard worn under the chin', F. & H.: resp. ca 1820–90 (c. or low s.); ca 1860–1900 (c. or low s.); ca 1860–1920 (id.). cf. NEWGATE KNOCKER and NEWGATE RING.

Newgate frisk or **hornpipe.** A hanging: c. or low s.: resp. ca 1830–90; ca 1825–80. Esp. preceded by *dance a*. Maginn has 'toeing a Newgate hornpipe'.

Newgate knocker. 'A lock of hair like the figure 6, twisted from the temple back towards the ear', F. & H.: low coll: from ca 1840; ob. Mayhew. The fashion was at its height ca 1840–55. cf. AGGERAWATORS, and NEWGATE RING. 2. (cf. NEWGATE, AS BLACK AS.) *As black*, or *dark*, *as Newgate knocker*, extremely black or (esp. of a night) dark: coll: from ca 1880; ob.

Newgate ring. Moustache and beard worn as one, without whiskers: s. or low coll: ca 1820–90. cf. NEWGATE COLLAR and NEWGATE KNOCKER.

Newgate saint. A condemned criminal: ca 1810–80: c. or s. or low coll.

Newgate seize me (if I do, there now)! Among criminals, an asseveration of the most binding nature: c. of ca 1810–60.

Newgate solicitor. A pettifogging attorney: c. or s. or low coll: ca 1785–1840.

Newgate steps, born on. Of criminal, esp. thievish, extraction: late C.18–mid-19: c. or low s. or low coll. Bee, 1823, 'Before 1780, these steps . . . were much frequented by rogues and w—s connected with the inmates of that place.'

Newland, see ABRAHAM NEWLAND.

***Newman's.** In C.17, *Numans*; in C.18, no record; ca 1805–50, *Newmans*. Newgate: c. The *New* of *Newgate* + MANS, a place. But while *Numans* stands by itself, *New-*

man's is rare except in the following combinations:

***Newman's Hotel.** Newgate: c. of ca 1805–50. Ex preceeding.

***Newman's lift.** The gallows: c. of ca 1805–50. Contrast:

***Newman's Tea-Gardens.** Newgate: c. of ca 1805–50. cf. NEWMAN'S HOTEL.

Newmarket Heath, a fine morning to catch herrings on. A c.p. = the C.20 *a fine day for ducks*. C.17–mid-18. John Clarke, 1639.

Newmarket Heath commissioner. A highwayman: coll: ca 1800–50. Ex notorious locality.

news?, do you hear the. A nautical c.p. (amounting indeed to a formula) 'used in turning out the relief watch': mid-C.19–20. Bowen.

news!, tell me. Often preceded by *that's ancient history*. A c.p. retort to an old story or a stale jest: C.18–20; ob. Swift. cf. QUEEN ANNE IS DEAD.

newsy. Gossipy; full of news: late C.19–20: coll.

Newtown pippin. A cigar: low: ca 1880–1910. Ex its fragrance.

newy. 'The "cad" paid to look after the canvas tent in "Commoner" field', F. & H.: Winchester College: ca 1860–1915. See CAD.

next, as – as the. As (any adj.) as possible: coll: late C.19–20.

next time you make a pie, will you give me a piece? A man's c.p. suggestion to a girl that she should cooperate: Canadian: ca 1895–1914.

next way, round about, is at the far door. You're going a long way round: a C.17 proverbial c.p. John Clarke, 1639. (N.B., *next* = nearest = shortest.)

n.f.; n.g.; N.H., see at the beginning of N.

***nib.** A gentleman: from ca 1810; ob.: c. until ca 1880, then low. (Also from ca 1840, *nib-cove*). Whence *half-nib(s)*, one who apes gentlemen. ?ex the C.17 Cambridge, esp. King's College, *nib* (either s. or j.), a freshman. More prob., as W. points out, a thinned form of NOB: cf. NAB and (*his*) NABS; see NIBS. 2. A fool: printers': from ca 1860; ob.

***nib,** v. To catch; arrest: from ca 1770: c. until ca 1850, then low s.; ob. Ex NAB. 2. To nibble: C.17–20: S.E. until C.19, then low coll(†) and dial. Ex *nibble*.

***nib-cove,** see NIB, n., 1.

nibbets. A Canadian synonym, late C.19–20, of CLINKERS, 2.

***nibbing cull.** A (petty) thief; occ. a fraudulent dealer: c.: ca 1770–1820.

***nibble.** To catch: C.17–20; ob.: c. >, ca 1860, low s. Middleton, 'The rogue has spied me now: he nibbled me finely once.' 2. To steal, pilfer: c.: C.19–20; ob. 3. To copulate: low: C.19–20; ob. 4. To consider, eagerly but carefully, e.g. a bargain, an offer. v.t. with *at*. Coll: C.19–20.

nibble, get a. To obtain an easy job: tailors': from ca 1850; ob.

nibble, have a. 'To have the best of the bargain, or an easy, well-paid job' (B. & L.): tailors': mid-C.19–20.

***nibbler.** A (petty) thief; occ. a cheating dealer: c.: C.19–20; ob.

nibby. A late C.19–20 low variant of and derivative ex:

***niblike.** (See also **nibsome.**) Gentlemanly: from ca 1830; ob.: c. until ca 1860, then low s. Ainsworth, 'All my togs were so niblike and splash.'

***nibs.** (See also NABS.) Self: *my nibs*, myself; *your nibs*, you or, as term of address, 'friend'; *his nibs*, the person mentioned; also (—1860), the master or a shabby genteel (cf. NIB, n., 1). From ca 1820: c. >, ca 1840, low s. >, ca 1890, gen. s. Haggart, 1821; Mayhew; Chevalier, 1893, in his song, *Out Little Nipper*. Ex NABS. There is prob. some connection with NIB, n., 1: cf. HIS LORDSHIP, jocularly applied to anyone, with which cf. *his royal nibs*, him, in A. Adams's *Log of a Cowboy*, 1903. Note also the analogous NOSE-WATCH.

nibso. A ca 1880–1915 variant of the preceding, 1: low.

***nibsome.** Gentlemanly; (of houses) richly furnished, etc.: from ca 1835; ob.: c. >, ca 1860, low s. G. W. M. Reynolds, 1839, 'Betray his pals in a nibsome game'.

nice. Agreeable; delightful: coll: 1769, Miss Carter, 'I intended to dine with Mrs Borgrave, and in the evening to take a nice walk'; Jane Austen; Mary Kingsley. (Often with an *ad hoc* modification.) cf. NICE AND.

nice, not too. A Society coll: from ca 1870. Ware, 'First degree of condemnation – equals bad'.

nice and. Nicely, in sense of 'very': coll: 1846, D. Jerrold, 'You'll be nice and ill in the morning.'

nice as a ha'porth of silver spoons. Ridiculously dainty or fastidious: proverbial coll: C.16. 'Proverbs' Heywood, 1546; anon., *Jack Jugeler*. cf.:

nice as a nanne, nanny, or nun's hen. Very affected or fastidious: proverbial coll: C. 15–early 18. Wilson in his *Rhetoric*, 1560; Ray.

nice as nasty. Objectionable: lower classes' (—1909). A euphemism.

nice as nip. Precisely what's needed; exactly: Northern and Midlands coll: from ca 1850.

nice joint. A 'charming, if over-pronounced, young person': urban, mostly Cockneys' (—1909).

nice place to live out of, it's a. A c.p. (—1909) indicating unpleasantness; ob.

nice thin job. The mean evasion of a promise: lower classes' coll: 1895–ca 1914.

niche-cock. The female pudend: low coll: C.18–20; ob. (By itself, *niche* is S.E.)

(nichels or**) nichils in a bag** or **in nine holes, nooks,** or **pokes.** Nothing whatsoever: late C.16–20: coll till C.19, then dial. R. Scot, 1584 (*in a bag*, †by 1700); Fuller; Bailey, 'Nichils are ... debts ... worth nothing.' Ex L. *nihil.*

Nicholas, Saint. The devil: jocular coll verging on S.E.: late C.16–early 19. Whence (*Old*) *Nick*. Ex the patron saint of scholars and ?thieves.

Nicholas, clergyman or **clerk** or **knight of St.** Or as *St Nicholas's clergyman*, etc. A highwayman (?ever in the singular): ca 1570–1820 (*knight* not before late C.17): coll >, by 1660, S.E. Foxe, Shakespeare, John Wilson, Scott (*clerk*); R. Harvey, 1598 (*clergyman*). Ex preceding entry, perhaps by a pun on †S.E. *St Nicholas('s) clerks*, poor scholars.

Nicholas Kemp. A proverbial coll, only in the phrase quoted by Quiller-Couch in *Troy Town*: 'Like Nicholas Kemp, he'd occasion for all.' From ca 1880; ob.

nick. The female pudend: low coll: C. 18–20; ob. Robertson of Straun, who, like G. A. Stevens, tended to obscenity. 2. Abbr. OLD NICK, the devil: coll: 1785. 3. Only in NICK AND FROTH. 4. (*the nick.*) The proper, the fashionable, thing or behaviour: ca 1788–1800. Lord R. Seymour in *Murray's Magazine*, vol. 1. 5. (*the nick.*) Good physical condition or health: almost always *in the nick*: late C. 19–20, or perhaps far older; it occurs in a song 'attributed to Ben Jonson' published in the *Port Folio*, 14 April 1804: 'Or else, unseen, with them I go, | All in the nick | To play some trick ...' 6. A winning throw at dice: gamblers': ca 1660–1750. Shadwell, *The Sullen Lovers*, 1668; Dryden, *An Evening's Love*, 1668; Otway, *The Atheist*, 1684. cf. sense 1 of the v. 7. Natal cleft at the fold of the buttock: low: late C.19–20.

nick, v. To cheat, defraud (*of*): coll: late C.16–20; very ob. Taylor the Water Poet. 2. To catch, esp. unawares: from ca 1620. Fletcher & Massinger. 3. Hence, in C.19–20, to arrest: low s. or perhaps c. *The Spirit of the Public Journals*, 1806, 'He ... stands a chance of getting nicked, because he was found in bad company.' 4. To steal; purloin: 1826; 1869, *Temple Bar*, 'I bolted in and nicked a nice silver tea-pot': c. >, by 1880, low s. 5. To in-dent a beer-can: C.17–18: either coll or, more prob., S.E. So too the vbl n. 6. To copulate with: low coll: C.18–20; ob. 7. v.i., to drink heartily: Scots s.: late C.18–19. Jamieson.

Nick, old, see OLD NICK.

***nick, on the.** Stealing; going to steal: c. (—1887). Ex NICK, v., 4.

nick, out of all, adv. Past counting: excessively; coll: late C.16–17. Shakespeare, in *Two Gentlemen*, 'He lov'd her out of all nick.'

***nick, out on the,** adj. and adv. Out thieving: c.: from ca 1870.

nick and froth. A false measure (of beer); cheating customers with false measures: coll: C.17–mid-18. Anticipated, however, in Skelton's *Elynour Rummynge*, 'Our pots were full quarted, | We were not thus thwarted | With froth-canne and nick-pot.' The *nick* was a dent in the bottom of the beer-can, the *froth* implied an excessive amount. 2. Hence, a publican: ca 1660–1800: coll. Ned Ward has *nick and froth victualler* (1703).

nick me! An imprecation of ca 1760–80: coll. Foote. Ex v., sense 2.

nick-nack; also **knick-knack.** The female pudend: low: C.18–20; ob. 2. In pl only, the human testicles: low: C.18–20. cf. KNACKERS.

nick-ninny. 'An empty Fellow, a mere Cod's head', B.E.: late C.17–early 19.

nick-pot. A tapster; an inn-keeper: C.17–18: s. or coll. Rowlands. 2. A fraudulent measure or beer-pot: C.17–18: s. or coll. See NICK AND FROTH, 1.

nick the pin. To drink not too much, i.e. fairly: coll: ca 1690–1730. Kersey, 'To the Pin plac'd about the middle of a Wooden Bowl or Cup'.

***nicker.** One who, at cards, is a cheat: ca

1660–1730: s. or low coll, though perhaps orig. c. 2. One of a band of disorderly young men delighting in the breaking of windows by throwing copper coins at them: ca 1715–20: coll. Gay, in *Trivia*, 'His scatter'd Pence the flying Nicker flings.' Ex *nick*, to hit the mark.

nickerers. New shoes: Scots c. or, more prob., s.; certainly it soon > s. C.19. Jamieson. Ex the creaking sound: see NICK, n. and v. (and in E.D.D.).

nickery. A nickname: low coll: ca 1820–30. By corruption.

nickey; nickin, see NIKIN and OLD NICK.

nicks. See NIX. 2. Stolen goods: Londoners' (—1890). Ex NICK, v., 4.

***nickum.** A sharper; a cheating tradesman or inn-keeper: c.: late C.17–mid-18. Ex *nick 'em*, cheat them. (In Scots dial., a wag; a tricky person.)

nicky, see NIKIN and OLD NICK.

Nicodemus. A fanatic: Restoration period. Ex Biblical history and Church dissension.

niff, v.i. To smell unpleasantly: Dulwich College: from late 1890s. ?back-formation ex NIFFY, or ex dial.

niffle. To smoke: *Conway* cadets': late C.19–20. Rather by a blend of NIFF and *sniffle* than ex the latter only.

niffy, adj. Smelly: Sussex dial. >, ca 1890, low s. Ex dial. n. and v., *niff*, smell; stink.

nifty. Smart, fashionable; fine, splendid; (somewhat blatantly) skilful: orig. (1868), U.S.; anglicized ca 1890. Bret Harte's 'Nifty! Short for magnificat' is a joke, but the term may be a perverted telescoping of *magnificent*.

***nifty,** n.; gen. **bit of nifty.** Sexual intercourse: c., and low: late C.19–20.

***nig.** A clipping of money; such clippings collectively. Gen., however, in pl: clippings. Late C.17–early 19 c. Prob. NICK perverted. 2. A Negro: (low) coll: orig. (1864), U.S.; anglicized ca 1870. Abbr. NIGGER. 3. Gin: back s. (—1859). 4. A trick or DODGE: Blue Coat Schoolboys': from ca 1840.

***nig,** v. To clip money: late C.17–early 19 c. Implied in B.E.'s *nigging*. 2. To catch; arrest: mid-C.18 c. ?NICK, v., 3, influenced by NAB, v., 1. 3. To have sexual intercourse: low: C.18. Abbr. NIGGLE.

nigger, sometimes (†) **niggar.** A Negro: coll, often pejorative: 1786, Burns; 1811, Byron, 'The rest of the world – niggers and what not'. Ex †S.E. *neger* (L. *niger*). Hence, 2, a member of some other dark-skinned race: somewhat catachrestically coll: from ca 1855.

nigger-driver; -driving. One who works others excessively hard; this practice: coll: from ca 1860. Ex the cruelty of some overseers of slaves.

nigger-spit. The lumps in cane sugar: low: from ca 1870; ob.

niggers! An oath: low coll: C.17. Whence *niggers-noggers!* cf. JIGGERED! ex *Jesus*. Often, ca 1640–80, abbr. to *nigs!*, preceded by (*God'*)*s* or CUDS.

niggers in a snow-storm. Curry and rice; stewed prunes and rice: naval: late C.19–20.

***niggle;** in C.16–early 17, often **nygle;** in C.17–18, often **nigle.** Occ. the n. of: *niggle*, etc., v.i. and v.t., to have sexual connection with a woman: ca 1565–1820: c. >, ca 1720, low s. Harman; Rowlands, who says that, ca 1610, WAP was more gen.; in 1612, however, Dekker has 'And wapping Dell that niggles well, and takes loure for her hire'. Whence NIGGLER, 1.

niggledigee or **niggledigée.** see NEGGLEDIGEE.

***niggler** or **nigler.** A lascivious or very amorous person: c.: C.17–18. Marston. 2. A clipper of money: c.: late C.17–18. Ex NIG, v., 1.

***niggling.** Keeping company with a woman, sexual intercourse: c.: C.17–early 19. Dekker. Ex NIGGLE, v. cf. NIGGLER, 1.

nigh, adj. Near; close (e.g. 'a nigh fit'): low coll: C.19–20.

night! Good night!: coll: late (?mid-)C. 19–20. cf. DAY!; EVENING!; MORNING!

night!, good. That's done it! Coll: late C.19–20; ob. cf. *that's* TORN IT!

night and day. A play: rhyming s. (—1859).

night-cap. A nocturnal bully: coll: ca 1620–30. Webster in *The Duchess of Malfi*. 2. See HORSE NIGHT-CAP.

night-flea. A boarder: Essex schools' (—1909). Contrast DAY-BUG.

night-fossick, n. To steal gold quartz or dust, by night: Australian: mid-C.19–20. See FOSSICK.

night hawk. (Gen. pl.) A night-watchman steward: nautical: late C.19–20.

night of it, make a. To spend the night in gambling and/or drinking and/or whoring: coll: from ca 1870.

night-physic or **-work.** Copulation: late C.16–early 18: jocular coll when not euphemistic S.E. Massinger, 'Which ... ministers night-physic to you?'

night-snap. A nocturnal thief: C.17: low s. Fletcher.

night to run away with another man's wife, a fine. A fine night: a proverbial c.p. of late C.16–18. Florio, Rowley, Swift (*a delicate night*).

night-walker. A bellman; a watchman: either c. or low s.: late C.17–mid-18. All other senses (e.g. a harlot), despite B.E., are S.E.

night with you and a file of the morn's morning!, all. 'A slang form of saying "good-night!" ': Aberdeenshire: 1882; ob.

nightie, nighty. A night-dress: coll: from early 1890s. 2. Hence, occ., a surplice: from ca 1897: jocular coll. Abbr. *night-dress* or *n.-gown* + familiar *ie, y*.

nightingale. See CAPE; CAMBRIDGESHIRE; DUTCH; FEN-; NEWGATE (BIRD or); SPITHEAD NIGHTINGALE. 2. A soldier who, being punished, 'sings out': military: ca 1770–1830. 3. A harlot: low: from ca 1840. Because most active at night.

nightshade or **deadly n.** 'A shameless prostitute of the very lowest class' (B. & L.): from ca 1860.

nighty, see NIGHTIE. **nigle; nigler; nigling,** see NIGGLE; NIGGLER; NIGGLING.

nigmenog, see NIMENOG.

nignog. A fool: Army: late C.19–20. Perhaps ex NIMENOG.

nigs, see NIG, n., 1. Also abbr. NIGGERS!

nihil-ad-rem. Vague (of things); unconscious: Winchester College: ca 1860-1910. e.g. 'He sported nihil-ad-rem duck.' L., lit. 'nothing to the purpose'.

nikin; occ. nickin; also nikey, i.e. **nick(e)y;** also **nis(e)y, nizey** or **nizzie.** A soft simpleton: coll: late C.17–18. The *-k-* forms are prob. ex *Nick*, the *-s-* and *-z-*, ex Fr. *niais*, foolish. 2. (Only *nickin, nikin, ni(c)k(e)y*.) Abbr. *Isaac*: C.17–19.

nil, n. and adj. Half profits, etc.; half: low: from ca 1859; ob.

***nim; occ. nym.** A thief: c. of ca 1620–40. Taylor the Water Poet. Ex:

***nim; occ. nym.** (Whence Shakespeare's Nym.) To steal, pilfer (v.i. and v.t.): C.17–20: low c. till mid-C.17, then c.: from ca 1850, still c. but archaic. John Day, 1606, in his *Isle of Gulls*; 'Hudibras' Butler; Gay, in *The Beggars' Opera*; G. P. R. James, *The Gipsy*. Ex A.-S. *niman*, to take.

nimak; occ. nimma(c)k. Salt: Regular Army's: late C.19–20. Ex Hindustani. cf. MUCKIN.

nimble as similes are coll: **(as) nimble as a cat (up)on a hot backstone,** late C.17–early 19 (**backstone,** occ. **bakestone** in C.19), the gen. C.19–20 form being **(up)on hot bricks; (as) nimble as a bee in a tar-barrel,** C.19–20, ob., a cognate phrase being **to bumble like a bee in a tar-tub; . . . as a cow in a cage,** C. 19–20 (ob.) jocular; **. . . as a new-gelt dog,** C.19–20 (ob.), mainly rural; **. . . as an eel (wriggling in the mud; in a sandbag),** C.17–20, being in C.19–20 mainly dial.; **. . . as ninepence,** from ca 1880, also dial., prob. ex the proverb, **a nimble ninepence is better than a slow shilling** (C.19–20; latterly dial.), with which cf. the late C.19–20 Gloucestershire **a nimble penny is worth a slow sixpence.**

nimble-hipped. (Gen. of women.) Active in the amorous congress: C.19–20; ob. Coll verging on S.E.

***nimbles.** The fingers: c.: early C.17. Jonson, 1621, 'Using your nimbles | In diving the pockets'.

nimenog; occ. nigmenog. 'A very silly Fellow', B.E.; a fool: late C.17–18: coll. Presumably cognate with *nidget* and the dial. *nidyard*, S.E. *niddicock*.

***nimgimmer; nim-gimmer.** A surgeon, doctor, apothecary, 'or any one that cures a Clap or the Pox', B.E.: c.: late 17–early 19. Ex NIM + ?

nimma(c)k, see NIMAK.

***nimmer.** A thief: see NIM, v., for period and changing status.

***nimming.** Theft; thieving: see NIM, v., for period and status.

nimrod. The penis: low: C.19–20; ob. Because 'a mighty hunter'. cf.:

nimshod. A cat: low: from ca 1870; ob. ?a corruption of *Nimrod*, or is it a mere coincidence that the vocable may = NIM, to take, + *shosho* or *shoshi*, Romany for a rabbit. Not ex dial.

nin. Drink: children's coll: C.16–17. Cotgrave ('Before they can speak'). By corruption.

nincum-noodle. A NOODLE with *no income*: jocular London: ca 1820–40. Baumann has *nincum*, a NOODLE.

nine-bob-square. Out of shape: C.19–20: coll (†by 1902) and dial. In dial., cf. *nine-bauble-square* and *nine-bobble-square*. ?lit. 'nine-cornered-square'.

nine corns. A small pipeful, a half-fill, of tobacco: mid-C.19–20: coll (†by 1902) and dial. (ob.; mostly Lincolnshire).

nine lives and (or but) women ten cats' lives, cats have. A mid-C.18–mid-19 c.p.

nine shillings. Nonchalance; cool audacity: late C.18–20; ob. A perversion.

***nine-tail bruiser** or **mouser.** The CAT-O'-NINE TAILS: prison c.: ca 1860–1910.

nine ways or **nine ways at thrice** or **nine ways for Sunday(s), look.** To squint: coll: resp. C.16–20 (ob.), as in Udall; C.17, as in G. Daniel; and C.19–20.

nine winks. A short nap: ca 1820–50. cf. FORTY WINKS.

nine words at once, talk. To speak fast or thickly: C.17: coll. Cotgrave.

ninepence, bring one's noble to, see NOBLE TO NINEPENCE . . .

ninepence, grand or **neat** or **nice** or **right as.** Extremely neat, nice, right: coll: C.17–20 for *neat* (e.g. Howell, 1659), C.19–20 for the three others: *grand*, Dickens; *right*, Smedley, 1850; *nice*, T. Ashe, 1884, but implied in H., 2nd ed. See also NEAT AS A BANDBOX.

ninepence, nimble as, see NIMBLE AS . . .

ninepence, right as. A coll variant (from ca 1885) of NIMBLE AS *ninepence*. Baumann suggests an influence by *ninepins*.

ninepence, the devil and, see DEVIL AND NINEPENCE . . .

ninepence to nothing, as like as. Almost certainly: coll: C.17. Ray.

ninepence to nothing, bring (one's). To waste or lose property: C.18–20: coll till ca 1850, then dial. In C.16–17, *bring a shilling to ninepence*.

ninepins. The body as life's container; life in gen.: low: 1879, G. R. Sims, in the *Dagonet Ballads*, 'It's a cold . . . as has tumbled my ninepins over.' Ob.

niner. A convict serving nine years: coll: 1897, Waring. 2. (Gen. pl.) A senior naval cadet: in the training-ship *Britannia*: late C.19–early 20. ?ex *ninth term*.

nines (rarely **nine**, †), **to** or **up to the.** To perfection; admirably: coll: late C.18–20. (ca 1870–80, *up to the nines* also = up to all the dodges.) Burns, 1887, *to the nine*, as also Reade in *Hard Cash*; T. Hardy, 1876, *up to the nines*, a form that appears to be recorded first in 1859, H., 1st ed., in the phrase *dressed up to the nines*. ?ex *nine* as a mystic number connoting perfection. Also *got-up to the nines*.

nineteen bits of a bilberry, he'll make. A pejorative c.p. of ca 1660–1700. Ray.

nineteen to the dozen, see DOZEN, TALK . . .

ninety dog; always in form: **90 dog.** A pug-dog: streets' (—1909). Ware, 'Referring to aspect of tail'.

ninety-eight out of, have. To get one's own back on (a person): tailors': late C.19–20.

ninety-nines, dressed up to the. An elaboration of *dressed* (*up*) *to the* NINES: coll (—1887); ob.

ninety-seven (gen. **97**) **champion frost.** A lower-classes' c.p. applied in 1897–9 to motor-cars, which, in 1896–7, were something of a FROST or failure.

ning-nang. A worthless thoroughbred: veterinary: from ca 1890. Ex horse-dealers' s. (—1864). In Northern dial., *ning-nang* is applied also to a worthless person.

***ninny.** 'A canting whining Beggar', B.E.: c. of late C.17–mid-18. Ex S.E. sense, or perhaps imm., as prob. the S.E. is, from *an innocent*, as the O.E.D. suggests.

ninny-broth. Coffee: late C.17–18. Ned Ward in *The London Spy*.

ninth, occ. in C.18 **tenth, part of a man.** A tailor: C.18–20; ob.: coll. Foote, 1763, 'A journeyman-taylor . . . this whey-faced ninny, who is but the ninth part of a man.' Ex the proverbial *nine tailors make a man* (late C.16–20): in C.17 also *two* (Dekker & Webster) or *three* (Apperson).

niog ot takram. Going to market: back s. (—1859).

***nip.** A thief, esp. a cut-purse or a pickpocket: c. of late C.16–18. Greene. ?ex the v. 2. A cheat: c.: late C.17–early 19, when it was the prevailing c. sense, a cut-purse gen. being a BUNG-NIPPER. 3. s. of ca 1820–50: 'Passengers who are taken up on stage-coaches by the collusion of the guard and coachman, without the knowledge of the proprietors, are called nips,' De Quincey, 1823. 4. See NIPS.

***nip,** v.; also **nipp(e), nyp.** To steal, esp. to pick pockets or to cut purses: c.: ca 1570–1830. (v.i. and v.t.) Harman (the stock phrase, *nip a* BUNG (n., 2), to cut a purse), Greene, Cleveland; B.E., 'to Pinch or Sharp anything'. Ex the S.E. sense, to pinch (cf. s. PINCH), and ex: 2. To catch, snatch, seize neatly, take up smartly (also with *away*, *out*, *up*): from ca 1560: chiefly dial. (earliest record) and s. H. Scott (dial.), F. Godwin, C. B. Berry. 3. To PINCH (4), i.e. arrest: c.: from ca 1560. R. Edwards, ca 1566, 'I go into the city some knaves to nip'; Mayhew. 4. (Prob. ex preceding sense.) To move, to go, almost always quickly or promptly: orig. (—1825), dial. > s. ca 1880. Often with *out* (*Daily Telegraph*, 2 Jan. 1883, 'I nipped out of bed') or *up*; *nip in* = to slip in, *nip along* = to depart hurriedly or rapidly, or to move with speed. 5. To detect: Shrewsbury School coll: from ca 1880.

nip, as white as. As white as snow: proletarian (—1887); slightly ob. Ex dial. (—1861) and the herb cat-mint, covered with a fine white down.

nip along, in, out, up, etc. See fourth sense of NIP, v.

nip and tuck, adv. and adj., occ. a virtual n. (a NECK-AND-NECK race). Neck and neck; almost level or equal(ly): coll: orig. U.S.; anglicized ca 1890. In U.S., *rip and tuck*, 1833; *nip and tack*, 1836; *nip and chuck*, 1846; *nip and tuck*, 1857: an illuminating example of semantic phonetics or, rather, phonetic semantics.

nip-cheese. A ship's purser : nautical s.: 1785, Grose; Marryat; 1867, Smyth; Bowen. Ob. by 1907. Ex some pursers' 'pinching' part of the cheese and other food.

nip-louse. A tailor: low: from ca 1850; ob. cf. NIP-SHRED.

nip-lug. A teacher: Scots s. or coll: C.19–20; ob. They pull bad pupils' ears.

nip-lug, at. At logger-heads: Scots coll: C.19–20: ob.

nip-shred. A tailor: mid-C.17–mid-18: s. > coll. K. W., 1661, 'Though her nimble nipshred never medles with the garments'. cf. NIP-LOUSE.

nipp, nippe, see NIP, v., 1–3.

nippence, no pence, | half a groat wanting twopence. Nothing, a groat being fourpence: a C.17 rhyming c.p. Ray, Fuller.

***nipper.** A thief, esp. a cut-purse or a pickpocket: c.: ca 1580–1830. Fleetwood, 1585, 'A judiciall Nypper', i.e. a very skilful one, this being a stock phrase. Ex NIP, v., 1. 2. 'A boy who assists a costermonger, carter, or workman', O.E.D.: low coll (and dial.): from ca 1850; ob. Mayhew, 1851. Prob. because he 'nips' about, therefore presumably dial. orig. (see NIP, v., fourth sense). 3. Whence, a boy, a lad (in C.20, esp. if under say 12): from ca 1859. *Daily News*, 8 April 1872; *Referee*, 11 Nov. 1888, 'Other nippers – the little shrimps of boys . . .'; Chevalier in *The Idler*, June 1892, 'I've got a little nipper, when 'e talks | I'll lay yer forty shiners to a quid | You'll take 'im for the father, me the kid,' which rather bears out the O.E.D.'s quotation from Williams's *Round London*, 1893, 'The mind of the East End "nipper" is equal to most emergencies.' 4. Whence(!), a boy or CAD; Marlborough School: from ca 1875; ob. 5. See NIPPERS. 6. A frosty day: coll (—1887); ob. 7. A cabin-boy: sailing-ships': from ca 1865; slightly ob. 8. A prawn: Australian: late C.19–20.

***nipper,** v. To catch; to arrest: c. (>, ca 1830, low s.): ca 1820–50. Egan (1824, in vol. IV of *Boxiana*). Ex NIP, v., 3.

***nippers.** Handcuffs or, occ., shackles: c. of ca 1820–1920. Haggart; Egan's Grose; Matsell. Ex NIP, v., 3. 2. 'A burglar's instrument used from outside on a key', F. & H.: c.: from ca 1840. Also *American tweezers*. 3. Eye-glasses, esp. pincenez (whence the name): from ca 1875 and prob. ex U.S. (Lowell, 1876). 4. A policeman: c. (—1887).

nippiness, see NIPPY, adj., 2.

***nipping,** n. and adj. See NIP, v., 1: same period and status. Esp. in Greene.

nipping Christian. A cut-purse: low s. of ca 1800–60.

nipping-jig. (A) hanging: early C.19: ?c. > low s.

nippitate; -ato, atum, -aty (occ. **-ati).** Strong, prime liquor, esp. ale: ca 1575–1700. The O.E.D. considers both the n. and the derivative adj. as S.E., prob. rightly; F. & H. thinks it may have been c. Laneham, Stubbes, Nashe, Oliffe, Urquhart. Etymology obscure: but cf. NIP, v., 2.

***nipps,** see NIPS.

nippy. The penis: children's: from ca 1850; ob. ?ex PEE.

nippy, adj. Lively, nimble, active, sharp or prompt: 1853, Surtees; Burleigh, 1898, 'He. . . liked to see them keen and "nippy" at every soldierly task.' 2. Fairly cold: coll: late C.19–20. cf. 'It's a bit nippy', as understatement of the fact that it's damned cold. Ex English dialect.

***nips; nipps, nyps.** Shears for clipping money: c.: late C.17–mid-19.

nipsitate. A C.17 variant of NIPPITATE. Davenport, 1639.

nire. Rain: Cockney back s. (on *rine*): before 1859. cf. NAIR.

nisey or nisy, see NIKIN and NIZEY.

nit. 'Wine that is brisk, and pour'd quick into a Glass', B.E.: coll: late C.17–mid-18. ?ex †*nitty*, full of air bubbles.

nit, dead as a. Quite dead: coll and dial.: late C.18–20; ob. except in dial. Wolcot, 1789; Hardy, 1874, '[The Sheep] will all die as dead as nits.'

nit-squeeger, i.e. **nit-squeezer.** A hair-dresser: low: 1788, Grose, 2nd ed.; ob.

nitraph. A farthing (pronounced *farthin'*): back s. (—1859).

nits will be, gen. become, lice. A proverbial c.p., > in C.18 a proverb, applied to 'small matters that become important', B.E.: mid-

C.17–18. Isaac D'Israeli ascribes it to Oliver Cromwell.

nitty. A disturbance, racket, squabble: naval: from ca 1810, or even ca 1790. 1830, Marryat, 'I never seed . . . such a nitty kicked up 'tween decks, in my life.' Ob. Prob. ex dial. *nitter* or *nitty-natter*, to be constantly grumbling.

***nix; nicks.** Nothing; occ., in mid-C.19–20 but ob., nobody. Orig. c. >, ca 1815, low s. >, ca 1860, gen. s. G. Parker, 1789, 'How they have brought a German word into cant I know not, but nicks means *nothing* in the cant language'; prob. ex coll Ger. *nix* (= *nichts*) via coll Dutch, as the O.E.D. implies. Also NIX MY DOLL.

nix! A warning, esp. among schoolboys and workmen, of somebody's approach. Esp. in *keep nix*, to keep watch. Ob. H., 2nd ed., 1860; Routledge's *Every Boy's Annual*, 1869. Also (recorded in 1883) *nix* (,e.g. *lads*,) *buttons!* Prob. ex Romany *nisser*, to avoid, influenced by NIX MY DOLLY.

nix, deberr! No, my friend: London: ca 1810–30. 'Jon Bee', 1823, 'Borrowed of the Russians who lay in the Medway, 1810.'

***nix my doll.** Nothing: c. of ca 1810–30. A mystifying elaboration of NIX, when the latter began to > well known.

***nix my dolly.** Never mind!; prob. a mere variant of NIX MY DOLL, nothing (to worry about): 1834, Ainsworth, 'Nix my dolly, pals, fake away,' in a popular song that popularized the phrase, which soon >, as it may orig. have been, merely 'literary' c.; certainly †by 1890 and ob. by 1860.

nix(e)y! No!: circus-workers' (—1887). Ex NIX and NIX!

niz-priz. A writ of *nisi prius*: legal: mid-C.19–20.

nizey, nizi, nizy, nizzie, nizzy. (Also nisey, nisy.) A dunce, simpleton, fool: coll: mid-C.17–early 19. (The rare *nizi*, only C.17; *nisy* only C.18.) Either ex Fr. *niais*, foolish, or ex †S.E. *nice*, foolish. Coles, 1676; Ned Ward; Johnson, 'a low word'. 2. A coxcomb: late C.17–early 18: coll, I think, though B.E. says c. See also NIKIN.

no. 1., see NUMBER ONE.

no battle. Not worth-while, no good: printers': from ca 1870; ob. Because not worth fighting for or because there's no fight to see.

no-beyond jammer. A perfectly beautiful woman: low (—1909); virtually †. Ware. Lit.: as JAM (n., 2 and 3), incomparable.

no can do. Cannot do; impossible: pidgin and 'passe-partout' English: mid-C.19–20. Whence *N.C.D.*, the naval refusal of an invitation: late C.19–20.

no catch(, it's, etc.). (It's) very hard work, very disappointing, unpleasant, dangerous: coll: late C.19–20. See CATCH, n., and cf. the equivalent *no cop* at COP, 3.

no cop, see COP, BE NO. **no earthly,** see EARTHLY, NO. **no end,** see END, NO. **no error, and,** see MISTAKE, AND NO. **no fear,** see FEAR!, NO.

no flies; also **no(-)fly.** Artful, designing: printers': from ca 1870. Also N. F. 2. 'An emphatic addition made to an assertion . . . It really means "no error" or "no mistake" . . . as "A jolly fine girl, and no flies!"' H., 5th ed. (1874).

no go(, it is, etc.). No use!; it's impracticable or impossible: prob. from ca 1800; 1824, *Boxiana*, IV; 1852, *Notes and Queries*, 17 Jan., 'My publisher coolly answered that it was no go'; 1896, Farjeon, 'But it was no go'.

no good to me! Won't satisfy me by far!: coll c.p.: from ca 1880. (Anstey, *Voces Populi*, I, 1890.)

no grease! An engineers' c.p. (—1909) inputing lack of *polish* or manners.

no hank! or **?** A Cockney speech-tag meaning 'there is no deception (is there?)': from ca 1870. Ex HANKY-PANKY.

no-how, no-howish, see NOHOW, NOHOWISH.

no kid. No mistake; lit., without deception: from ca 1890. P. H. Emerson.

no matter for that,you shall carry the rake. 'If you tax a Girl with playing the loose [i.e. being unfaithful], she shall immediately reply, *No matter* . . .,' Anon., *Tyburn's Worthies*, 1722: Essex c.p.: ca 1715–40. A rural piece of sexual imagery: 'You shall have the raking, the harrowing' (compare the Lucretian *plough the fields of woman*).

no mistake, and, see MISTAKE, AND NO.

no more wit than a coot(, have). (To be) stupid: C.16 coll.

no moss! No animosity!: tailors': from ca 1870; ob.

no name, no pull. If I don't mention names, there can – or should – be no offence, no libel action: tailors': from ca 1870; ob.

no odds! It doesn't matter; never mind: coll: 1855, Dickens.

no. one or **1; no. two** or **2,** see NUMBER ONE; NUMBER TWO.

no peace (or rest) for the wicked!, occ. preceded by **there's.** A c.p. uttered either by or about someone who isn't wicked at all but is being kept extremely busy: late (?mid) C.19–20. Partly an ironic jocularity, partly ex several Biblical references.

no possible probable shadow of doubt, no possible doubt whatever is a c.p., either independent, or in retort on, or confirmation of, *of that there is no possible doubt*. Late C.19–20, among the cultured. Ex Gilbert & Sullivan.

no rats! A proletarian c.p. (—1909; ob.): 'He (or she) is Scotch.' Ware, 'A Scot is always associated with bagpipes, and . . . no rat can bear . . . that musical instrument.'

no repairs, see REPAIRS, NO.

no return ticket! A London lower-classes' c.p. (—1909): He, or she, is mad! Abbr. *he's going to Hanwell* [lunatic asylum] *and has no return ticket*.

no show without Punch, there's. A c.p. applied to, or directed at, a ubiquitous person: mostly lower-middle class: late C.19–20.

no wanchee. Pidgin English for 'I don't want it, thank you': much used in the Navy, esp. on 'China-side': late C.19–20.

Noah's ark. An overcoat, long and closely buttoned: coll: from ca 1858; ob. by 1905. 2. A LARK (whether bird or, more gen., fun): rhyming s.: 1887, *Referee*, 7 Nov.

Noakes, see NOKES.

nob. (In C.18, also *nobb*.) The head: from ca 1690: c. >, ca 1750, low s. >, ca 1810, gen. s. K. O'Hara, 1733, 'Do pop up your nob again, | And egad I'll crack your crown.' cf. (?ex) NAB, the head. 2. A blow on the head: from ca 1810; very ob.: orig. sporting. 3. In cribbage, 'the knave of the same suit as the turn-up card, counting one to the holder', O.E.D.: 1821, Lamb. See also NOB, ONE FOR HIS. 4. A person of rank, position, or wealth: 1809 (O.E.D.); *Lex. Bal.*, 1811; Westmacott, 1825, 'Nob or big wig'; Dickens, Thackeray; Anstey. (In the C.19 Navy, a lieutenant.) Earlier in Scots dial. as *nab* or *knab(b)*: 1742, R. Forbes. These Scottish forms militate against abbr. *nobility*; this sense prob. derives ex sense 1: cf. *the* HEADS, important persons. 5. Hence, a fellow of a college: Oxford University: ca 1820–60. 6. Abbr. KNOBSTICK: workmen's coll: from ca 1865; ob. J. K. Hunter, *Life Studies*, 1870. 7. A sovereign (coin): ca 1840–90. Ex the head. 8. The game of PRICK- (or cheat-) THE-GARTER: c. of ca 1750–1800. John Poulter, 1753, 'We got about three pounds from a butterman at the Belt or Nobb.' 9. The nose: Scottish and North Country s.: 1796. cf. sense 1. 10. See KNOB, n., 5. 11. Linking with sense 4 is that of: an expert or a champion in sport, esp. in boxing: since ca 1810. Thus, 'Several new *nobs* have made their appearance in the pugilistic hemisphere since April 1818,' *Boxiana*, III, 1821. 12. See KNOB, n., 6.

nob, v. To punch on the head, v.t. and v.i.: boxing: 1812, both in the *Sporting Magazine*; ob. 1823, Moncrieff, 'I've nobb'd him on the canister.' 2. To collect (money); make a collection from (persons): showmen's: both 1851, Mayhew, e.g. 'We also "nobb", or gather the money', and 'We went to "nob" them.' Perhaps ex cribbage or ex NOB (n., 7) = a sovereign. 3. See NOB IT.

nob, come the. To give oneself airs: from ca 1820; ob. Ex NOB, n., 4.

nob, do a. A variant (—1875) of NOB, v., 2. T. Frost, *Circus Life*.

nob, one for his. A point in cribbage for holding the knave of trumps: 1870, Ware & Hardy in *The Modern Hoyle*. 2. Hence, a punch on the head: boxing: from ca 1870.

***nob, pitch the.** See PRICK(-IN)-THE-GARTER. From ca 1820; †by 1890; prob. c.

nob-a-nob, adj. Friendly, intimate: 1834, Ainsworth; †by 1890. Corrupted HOB-NOB.

nob-cheat or **-chete,** see NAB-CHEAT.

nob-girder, see NAB-GIRDER.

nob fake. Hair-restorer: showmen's: since ca 1885. See FAKE, n., 6.

***nob in the fur trade.** A judge: c.: ca 1838, G. W. M. Reynolds, 'Let nobs in the fur trade hold their jaw'; †by 1880. Ex the fur on the robe.

***nob it.** To prosper without much work; to succeed by shrewdness: c. of ca 1810–40. Also *to fight nob-work*, gen. as vbl n.

***nob-pitcher.** c. of ca 1810–90. Vaux, 1812, 'A general term for those sharpers who attend at fairs, races, etc., to take in the flats at prick-in-the-garter, cups and balls, and other similar artifices.'

nob-stick, see KNOBSTICK.

nob-thatch. Hair (of the head): 1866, Yates, 'You've got a paucity of nob-thatch, and what 'air you 'ave is gray.' Ob. Ex NOB, n., 1. cf.:

nob-thatcher. A wig-maker: from ca 1790; ob. 2. A (gen. female) straw-bonnet maker: 1823, Moncrieff: ca 1820–1900. cf. NODDLE-THATCHER.

nob the glazes. To collect money from persons at first-floor windows, performers standing upon each other's or even one another's shoulders: showmen's and circus s. (—1875). T. Frost, *Circus Life*. See NOB, v., 2, and GLAZE.

nob-work. Mental occupation: low: from ca 1820. Ex:

***nob-work, fight,** see NOB IT. **nobb,** see NOB, n., 1 and v., 2.

nobba; occ. **nobber.** Nine, gen. as adj.: Parlary via Lingua Franca: from ca 1850. e.g. *nobba saltee*, ninepence. Ex Sp. *nova* or It. *nove*. cf. the interchangeable *b* and *v* of *sabe*, *savv(e)y*. 'Slang introduced by the "organ-grinders" from Italy', H., 1864: from ca 1850.

nobber. See preceding entry. 2. A blow on the head: boxing: 1818; ob. Moore, 1819, 'That flashy spark . . . received a nobber.' Ex NOB, v., 1. 3. A boxer skilful at head-punches: boxing: from ca 1820; ob. *Sporting Magazine*, 1821, 'Randall . . . a nobbler of first-rate excellence'. 4. A collector of money, esp. for showmen or minstrels, or, in C.20, for a beggar: 1890, *Echo*, 30 Oct., 'Only a nobber can know the extraordinary meanness of the British public'; P. H. Emerson. Ex NOB, v., 2. cf.:

nobbet; esp. *n. round*. To collect the money; esp. in turn: itinerant minstrels' and tavern-singers': from ca 1860. Ex Romany but suggested by NOB, v., 2.

nobbily. Smartly, esp. if rather showily: from ca 1858. Ex NOBBY, adj.

nobbing. The giving or the getting of blows on the head: boxing (—1825). Ob. The corresponding adj. is recorded at 1816. 2. Going round with the hat (—1859): showmen's. In the pl, money collected: 1851, Mayhew, 'Fifteen shillings of nobbings'. Ex NOB, v., 2. cf. NOBBING-SLUM.

***nobbing-cheat,** see NUBBING-CHEAT.

nobbing-slum. The bag (or the hat) for collecting money: showmen's: from ca 1890. cf. NOBBING, 2, and NOB, v., 2.

nobbish. A variant of NOBBY, adj. From ca 1860; ob.

nobble. To strike on the head; to stun: low: from ca 1880; ob. Ex NOB, n., 1. 2. To tamper with a horse, e.g. by laming it, to prevent it from winning: the turf: 1847. Lever, 1859, 'A shadowy vision of creditors "done", horses "nobbled"'. 'App. a modern frequentative of NAB', v., q.v. (W.) 3. Hence, to obtain a person's help or interest by underhand methods: 1865. 4. To appropriate dishonestly, even to steal: 1854, Thackeray, 'After nobbling her money for the beauty of the family'. 5. To swindle out of: 1854, Thackeray, 'I don't know out of how much the reverend party has nobbled his poor old sister at Brighton.' 6. To seize, catch, get hold of: low (?orig. c.): 1877, Greenwood, 'There's a fiver . . ., and nine good quid. Have it. Nobble him, lads, and share it betwixt you.'

nobble-tree. The head: provincial: ca 1870–1910. Ex NOB, the head.

nobbled, ppl adj. See NOBBLE, v.

nobbler. A blow on the head: boxing: from ca 1840. 2. Hence, any finishing blow or stroke: from ca 1840. 3. An assistant of thimble-riggers (see THIMBLE-RIG, 2) and card-sharpers, i.e. a decoy; also, a pickpocket working in the vicinity of these riggers and sharpers: c.: from ca 1835. 4. One who disables horses a little before a race: the turf: 1854, Whyte-Melville. See NOBBLE, v., 2. 5. A pettifogging lawyer: North Country: from ca 1860; ob. 6. A drink, esp. of spirits: Australian coll: 1852, G.E.P., 'To drain a farewell "nobbler" to his Sally'; 1859, Fowler, *Southern Lights and Shadows*, 'The measure is called a nobbler, or a break-down': coll.

nobblerize. To drink frequent 'nobblers' (see NOBBLER, 6): Australian coll: 1864, J. Rogers.

nobbling, vbl n. See NOBBLE, all senses. 2. adj., in good health: coll: ca 1820–40. *The Spirit of the Public Journals*, 1825. Cognate with NOBBY, adj.

nobby, n. Always *the nobby*. The smart thing: 1869, E. Farmer; ob. Ex NOBBY, adj. 2. Inevitable nickname (*Nobby*) for any man surnamed *Clark(e)*: late C.19–20. Because city clerks used to wear top hats, i.e. *nobby* hats.

nobby, adj. Very smart, elegant, or fashionable. Of persons: from ca 1808. A broadside ballad of ca 1810, 'A werry nobby dog's meat man'. (cf. NIFTY.) Of places or things: 1844, C. Selby, 'My togs being in keeping with this nobby place'; 1852, 'The nobbiest way of keeping it quiet'. Ex Scots *knabbie* or *knabby* (1788, Picken, 'Mony a knabbie laird'); see also NOB, n., 4.

noble blood to market and see what it will bring, send your. A C.18 c.p. addressed to one boasting about or trading on his high birth.

noble to ninepence, bring a or **one's.** To dissipate money idly or wantonly: semi-proverbial coll: from ca 1565; ob. by 1820, except in dial. Fulwell, 1568, 'For why

Tom Tosspot, since he went hence, | Hath increased a noble just unto nine pence'.

nobs. An endearment applied to a woman: coll: ca 1520–80. Skelton. ?origin.

Nobs' House, the upper. The House of Lords: low: ca 1820–50. cf.:

Nobs' Houses, the. The Houses of Parliament: low: ca 1820–50.

nobsey. A mistress: coll: mid-C.16. Harpsfield. Ex NOBS.

nock. The female pudend: low: late C.16–18. Florio, Cotton. Lit., *a notch*. cf.:

nock, v. To 'occupy' a woman, gen. v.t.: low coll: late C.16–18. Florio; Ash in his Dict. In C.19–20, KNOCK, which was prob. suggested by this.

nockandro. The posteriors, esp. the breech: coll: C.17. Cotgrave, Urquhart, Gayton. Prob. *nock*, a notch, + Gr. ἀνδρός, of a man. cf. NOCK, n.

nocky. 'A silly, dull Fellow', B.E.: late C.17–early 19; *nocky* extant in dial. Also, as in Grose (1st ed.), *nocky boy*. The etymology is obscure: but perhaps via KNOCK IN THE CRADLE.

nocturne. A harlot: Society s. bordering on euphemistic S.E.: ca 1875–1915. Prob. ex ob. S.E. *nocturnal* (late C.17–20): a night-walker, a harlot.

nod, land of. (Occ. with capitals; always preceded by *the*.) Sleep: C.18–20: coll till C.19, then S.E. Swift, 'I'm going to the land of Nod'; Grose; Scott, 1818, in *The Heart of Midlothian*. Punning the Biblical place-name.

nod, on the. On credit: coll: from ca 1880. *Rag*, 30 Sept. 1882, 'A pay-on-the-nod, | An always-in-quod young man'. Contrast the C.18 proverb, *a nod of an honest man is enough*.

nod is as good as a wink to a blind horse, a. A semi-proverbial c.p. applied to a covert yet comprehensible hint, though often stupidity in the receiver is implied. C.19–20. Dorothy Wordsworth, *Journal*, 1802.

noddle. The head: coll (orig., perhaps jocular S.E.): 1664, Butler, 'My Head's not made of brass | As Friar Bacon's noddle was'; L'Estrange; Thackeray. Ex the S.E. sense of C.15–mid-17 *noddle* (cognate with NOLL): the back of the head. 2. The head as the seat of intelligence – or the lack of it. Coll; often playful, often derisive: 1579, Tomson; 1611, W. Baker, 'The wit enskonsed in thy noddell'; Dickens.

noddle-case. A wig: coll: ca 1700–80. Facetious Tom Brown. cf.:

noddle-thatcher. A wig-maker: coll: ca 1715–1800. cf. NOB-THATCHER.

noddleken, see NUDDIKIN.

noddy-headed. Drunk: coll: ca 1850–1910.

noffgur. A fashionable harlot: low: ca 1885–1910. Barrère & Leland quote from an anon. song: 'Wrong 'uns at the Wateries, | Noffgurs at the Troc, | Coryphées by Kettner, | Tartlets anywhere.' Etymology obscure: ?*naughty girl* telescoped.

noggin. The head: s. or coll: ca 1800–60. Ex S.E. sense.

nohow; occ. **no-how.** The adj. (=indistinct) is S.E., as is the adv. (by no means, in no manner). Preceded by *all*, it = out of sorts, and is coll: from ca 1850. Dickens.

nohowish. Unwell: nautical (—1887). Ex NOHOW.

***noisy-dog racket.** The stealing of brass knockers from doors: c. of ca 1810–60. ?ex the accompanying barks of a provoked dog or simply ex the noise the operation was apt to make.

nok. Nose: showmen's: mid-C.19–20. Direct ex Romany.

nokes; Nokes. 'A Ninny or Fool', B.E.: coll: ca 1690–1890.

Nokkum. (Gen. pl.) A Scottish Gypsy tinker: their own word: mid-C.19–20. The reference in '*No. 747*' (p. 49) is valid for 1865.

nol. Long: back s. (—1859).

noll; occ. **nol, nole, nolle,** these three being †by 1750. The head: C.9–20: S.E. till C.18, then coll till ca 1820, then (except as jocular archaism) dial. 2. A person, esp. as a simpleton, gen. with *dull* or *drunken*: late C.14–mid-17: S.E. verging on, indeed sometimes actually, coll.

nominate, see POISON. **nomm(o)us,** see NAMMOUS.

non-com. A non-commissioned officer: coll (orig. military): from ca 1862. J. S. Winter, 1885, 'Well-tipped quartermasters and their favourite tools among the non-coms.' cf. the Fr. s., *sous-off* = *sous-officier*.

non compos. Not in one's right mind: coll: mid-C.19–20. Elliptical for the legal *non compos mentis*.

non-con., Non-Con., Non-con. A Nonconformist: coll: from ca 1680; ob.

non est. Absent: coll: 1870, Brewer. Lit., he is not (sc. found, L. *inventus*). Abbr.:

non est inventus, adj. Absent: coll: 1827, De Quincey, *Murder as One of the Fine Arts*; ob. by 1890, †by 1915. Ex legal S.E.

non-husky, see HUSKY.

non-licet, adj. Illegal; esp. unbefitting a Wykehamist: Winchester College: from ca 1890. 'Don't sport non-licet notions,' Wrench, *The Winchester Word-Book*, 1891. Ex the legal S.E.

non me. A lie: lower classes', mostly Cockney: 1820–ca 30. Ex Queen Caroline's trial, whereat the Italian witnesses said *non mi ricordo* (I don't remember) to every important question.

non-plus, catch (a person) **on the.** To catch at unawares: coll (—1887); ob.

nondescript. A boy in the middle school: certain Public Schools': late C.19–20. In the same schools, SQUEAKER (3) and DOOK (4).

nonesuch, nonsuch. The female pudend: low: C.18–20; ob. 2. In allusive S.E. bordering on semi-proverbial coll (gen. ironic): late C.16–17. Wither, 'A spotless Church, or perfect Disciplines | Go seek at None-such.' Ex Nonsuch, near Epsom in Surrey. cf.:

Nonesuch, he's a Mr. He's very conceited: c.p. of ca 1885–1910.

nonny-nonny. A meaningless refrain useful esp. for palliating obscenity: C.16–18; extant only as an archaism. Perhaps coll rather than S.E. F. & H. give it as = a simpleton: but is this so? I find no support.

nonplush. Nonplus; occ. nonplussed: sol. when not dial., nor, as ca 1820–40, jocular.

nonsensational. Sensationally nonsensical: critics': 1897, *People*, 28 Feb.; †by 1909. On *non-sensational* and telescoping *nonsensically sensational*.

nonsense. 'Melting butter in a wig', Grose, 3rd ed.: late C.18–early 19. 2. Money: c. or, more prob., low s.: from ca 1820. Egan, 1821, 'Shell out the nonsense: half a quid Will speak more truth than all your palavers.' By antiphrasis.

nonsuch, see NONESUCH.

noodle, a simpleton (from ca 1750): perhaps orig. coll; otherwise, always S.E.

noodles. Nickname for a NOODLE: Society: from ca 1840; ob.

Noodles, the House of. The House of Lords: ca 1820–60. cf. NOBS' . . .

nooky. Sexual intercourse: middle-class and almost polite; certainly a kind of baby-talk: late C.19–20. Perhaps ex S.E. *nooky*, resembling a nook, characterized by nooks, but probably related to NUG, v.

Noolucks or Newlicks. An imaginary person: 1848, *Sinks*; †by 1890. cf. CHEEKS, 3, and JOE, 6.

noom. Moon: back s. (—1859).

noose, nooze. To hang: from ca 1670; ob.: ?orig. c.; certainly low s. till C.19, then coll.

nope. A blow, esp. on the head, from ca 1720: s. (†by 1870) and Northern dial. Cognate with C.15 *nolp*, of equally obscure origin: cf. CULP.

nor. Than: dial. (from C.15) and, in C.19–20, low coll. Thackeray, 1840, 'You're no better nor a common tramper.'

Nor' Loch trout. A joint or leg of mutton: Scots s.: ca 1770–1810. Jamieson, 'This was the only species of *fish* which the North Loch, on which the shambles were situated, could supply.'

nor'-wester. A glass of potent liquor: nautical coll: 1840, Marryat; ob.

Noravee yawl. A Norway yawl: nautical coll: C.19–20.

Norfolk capon. A red herring (cf. GLASGOW MAGISTRATE): coll: from ca 1780; ob. Grose, 1st ed. Smith, *The Individual*, 1836, 'A Norfolk capon is jolly grub.' cf. also YARMOUTH CAPON.

Norfolk dumpling. An inhabitant, esp. a native, of Norfolk: coll: C.17–20. Day, in *The Blind Beggar*, 1600; Ray, 'This referres not to the stature of their bodies; but to the fare they commonly feed on and much delight in.' True, Mr Ray; nevertheless, this dish does tend to make children and even adults round and fat. cf. NORFOLK TURKEY.

***Norfolk dumpling, the.** The (practice of) sending convicts to Norfolk Island: Australian c.: ca 1820–70. Conditions on Norfolk Island (800 miles east of Sydney) were appalling; Norfolk dumplings lie heavy on the stomach – fair 'settlers', as was a term on the Island.

Norfolk Howard. A bed-bug: coll: from ca 1863; ob. Ex one Joshua Bug, who in June 1862 changed his name to Norfolk Howard.

Norfolk turkey. An inhabitant, esp. a native, of Norfolk: coll: C.19–20; ob. Anon., *Ora and Juliet*, 1811, 'The boorish manners of those Norfolk turkeys'. cf. NORFOLK DUMPLING, see NORWICHER, and note the C.16–20 (ob.) proverb *Essex stiles* (ditches), *Kentish miles*, *Norfolk wiles*, *many men beguiles*, with variants; glance also at YORKSHIRE and at NORTH, 1.

***nork.** A variant (virtually †) of NARK, n.

norp, gen. v.i. To insert phrases apt to 'fetch' the gallery, i.e. to 'gag to or for the gods': theatrical: from ca 1870; ob. Perhaps ex Yorkshire dial. (at least as early as 1869: E.D.D.) *norp* or *naup*, to hit the mark, to succeed, ex the much earlier *norp, naup*, to strike, e.g. with a stick, gen. on the head.

norra. Not a: Cockney: C.19–20.

Norsker. A Norwegian: nautical coll: mid-C.19–20. Ex Scandinavian *Norsk* (Norse).

north, adj. Intelligent; mentally and socially alert; cunning: from late C.17; ob. Rare except in *too far north*, too clever or knowing, as in Smollett, 1748, and Mrs A. M. Bennett, 1797; Ashton, in his *Social Life in the Reign of Queen Anne*, quotes however this illuminating passage: 'I ask'd what Countrey-man my Landlord was? answer was made, Full North; and Faith 'twas very Evident, for he had put the *Yorkshire* most damnably upon us.' cf. the C.19–20 dial. *to have been as far North as anyone*, to be no more of a fool than the next man. 2. Strong, gen. of drink: nautical: from ca 1860. Hence, *due north*, neat, without water, and *too far north*, drunk; contrast this phrase in sense 1. *Glasgow Herald*, 9 Nov. 1864. cf. ANOTHER POINT (, STEWARD)!

north about, he's gone. A nautical c.p. referring (from ca 1860) to a sailor who has met his death by other than drowning.

north and south. The mouth: rhyming s.: from ca 1850.

North Country compliment. An unwanted gift of no value to either the donor or the recipient: coll: from ca 1870; ob.

north-easter. A bluejacket who, on pay day, finds he is not entitled to receive any: naval: late C.19–20. Ex the bitterness of a north-east wind.

north eye. A squint: showmen's s. and Southern dial.: from ca 1850. P. H. Emerson, 1893. cf. the other dial. phrases in E.D.D.

North Pole. Anus: since ca 1870. Rhyming s. on HOLE.

North Sea pheasant. A kipper: nautical: late C.19–20.

Northallerton. (Rare in singular.) A spur: coll: ca 1790–1880. Grose, 3rd ed., 'That place, like Rippon, being famous for making them'.

Northern Glance, the. The Aurora Borealis: nautical coll: mid-C.19–20. Presumably suggested by S.E. *Northern Lights*.

northo-rigger. (Gen. pl.) 'In the late Victorian and Edwardian Navy, ratings who had entered as youths instead of through the harbour training ships. Now seldom heard', Bowen, 1927. Also *hurricane-jumper*.

Northumberland's arms, Lord. A black eye: mid-C.17–20: s. >, ca 1680, dial. († except in Northumberland). Either from the dark-colour fusils (i.e. light muskets) carried by the Percys' retainers or from the black and red predominant in the spectacles-resembling badge of this powerful family. Note the heraldic sense of *fusil*.

Norway neck-cloth. 'The pillory, usually made of Norway fir', Grose, 1st ed.: ca 1784–1830.

Norwegian house-flag. One of the windmill pumps that used to be compulsory in Norwegian sailing ships: nautical: ca 1850–1910. Bowen. i.e. as inevitable as a house-flag.

Norwicher. One who drinks too much from a shared jug, glass, etc., i.e. an unfair drinker: ca 1860–1900. *Athenaeum*, 15 Aug. 1896 (?relevant). Origin obscure; but see *Norfolk wiles* in the 'cf.' part of NORFOLK TURKEY. These territorial amenities are common enough (cf. YORKSHIRE).

***nose.** An informer (1789, Parker: '*Nose*. Snitch'), esp. – from ca 1810 – a paid spy: c. Often, from ca 1870, *a policeman's nose*. Also NOSER, 4. 2. Hence, a detective policeman, as in Greenwood's *Dick Temple*, 1877: c. of ca 1875–1910.

***nose.** v.i. To inform the police; to turn king's evidence: c.: from ca 1810; ob. *Lex. Bal.*, 'His pal nosed, and he was twisted for a crack,' i.e. hanged for burglary. cf. NOSE UPON.

nose, at one's (very). Very close: from ca 1520: coll and dial.

nose, †candles or **dewdrops in the.** Mucus depending from the nose: low: late C.18–20.

nose!, follow your. A C.17–20 c.p. 'said in a jeer to those that know not the way, and are bid to Smell it out', B.E. In C.19–20, often *follow your nose, and you* (or *for it*) *can't go wrong*.

nose, good. A smell-feast: low coll: late C.17–20; ob.

nose, make a bridge of someone's. To pass him by in drinking: late C.17–20; ob. Swift. 2. Hence, to supersede: same period; ob. Ray.

***nose, on the.** Watching: c. (—1839) >, ca 1900, low s.; ob.

nose, parson's, see PARSON'S NOSE. cf.:

nose, recorder's. The rump of a fowl: coll: ca 1820–90. Westmacott, 1825.

nose, wipe (a person's), see at NOSE OF.

nose and chin. A WIN, i.e. a penny: low (orig. c.) rhyming s. of ca 1855–1905. 2. Gin: rhyming (—1909). cf. NEEDLE AND PIN.

nose-bag. Such a visitor as carries his own food: waiters'; 1860, H., 2nd ed. 2. A hospitable hotel or boarding-house: middle classes': late C.19–20; ob. cf. sense 1. 3. A veil: low: ca 1865–1915. 4. A hand-bag: from ca 1885; ob. *Cornhill Magazine*, April 1887, 'So I yesterday packed up my nosebag, and away I posted down to Aldgate.' All these senses ex the S.E. one.

nose-bag, put on the. To eat either hurriedly or at work – or both. (Low) coll: from ca 1870. Ex the stables. cf. NOSE IN THE MANGER.

nose-bag in one's face, have the. To have been 'a private man, or rode private', Grose, 2nd ed.: military: ca 1780–1830. Ex S.E., *nose-bag*. cf. HALBERT.

nose-bagger. A variant, from ca 1865, of NOSE-BAG, 1. Ware.

nose cheese first, see the. To refuse contemptuously: low: C.19–20; ob.

nose-cough. A heavy breathing through the mouth on account of a stoppage in the nose: non-aristocratic (—1887).

nose em, see NOSE MY.

nose-ender. A straight blow on the nose: boxing: 1854, 'Cuthbert Bede'. cf. NOSER. 2. A strong head-wind: nautical coll: mid-C.19–20. cf. MUZZLER, 3.

***nose-gent; nosegent.** A nun: c.: ca 1565–1830. ?etymology.

nose in, shove one's. To interfere, interpose rudely: low coll (—1887).

nose in the manger, have or put one's. To eat, esp. to eat heartily: coll: from ca 1860; ob. T. Hughes, 1861, *Tom Brown at Oxford*. Ex the stables.

nose is a lady's liking, a long. A low c.p. of C.19–20. Length of the male nose being held to denote a corresponding length elsewhere, as the size of a woman's mouth is supposed to answer to that of another part. cf. BIG CONK ...

nose is dirty, his. He is a heavy drinker: s. (—1650).

nose itches!, my. A C.18–20 c.p. invitation to kiss, the dovetail being either, as in Swift, 'I knew I should drink wine, or kiss a fool,' or, in C.18–20, 'I knew I would shake hands with a fool,' or, in C.19–20, 'I knew I was going to sneeze *or* to be cursed, *or* kissed, by a fool.'

nose my ('Ducange Anglicus', 1857) is itself ex NOSER-MY-KNACKER: mid-C.19–20; ob. Also *nose em*, *nose 'm*.

nose of. To cheat, swindle (a person) of (something): ca 1650–90. O.E.D. gives as S.E., but the O.E.D.'s quotations (Brome; Brian, *Piss-Prophet*) indicate coll. cf.:

nose of, wipe one's. To deprive or defraud (one) of (something): late C.16–mid-18. Again the O.E.D. gives as S.E; again I suggest coll. Bernard, 1598, '... Who wipes our noses of all that we should have'; Cibber, 1721, 'Thou wipest this foolish Knight's Nose of his Mistress at last', which, by the way, recalls 'He'll wipe your son Peter's nose of Mistress Lelia' in Anon.'s *Wily Beguiled*, ca 1606. cf. NOSE-WIPE, and WIPE.

nose of wax; or waxen-nose (†by C.18). Anything, esp. any person, very pliable, exceedingly obliging or complaisant or easy-going: coll verging on S.E.: ca 1530–1830. Scott, 1815, 'I let ... the constable ... manage the business his ain gate, as if I had been a nose o' wax.'

nose-paint. Alcoholic drink: South Lancashire jocular s. (—1905), not dial.

nose-rag. A pocket-handkerchief: from ca 1835: low. Haliburton. cf. NOSE-WIPER.

nose swell, make one's. To make a person jealous or envious: coll: from ca 1740; ob. *State Trials*, 1743, 'He heard Lord Altham say, ... my wife has got a son, which will make my brother's nose swell.' cf. the S.E. *put one's nose out of joint*, of which it is prob. a jocular elaboration, and the C.18 (?S.E.) variant, *make one's nose warp*.

nose to light candles at, a. A (drunkard's) red nose: coll: late C.16–20; ob. Nashe, 'Their noses shall bee able to light a candle.'

nose up my arse!, your. An expression of the utmost contempt: mid-C.19–20. cf. the milder ASK MINE OF MY ARSE!

nose upon, v.t. To tell something of a person so that he be injured and, if possible, one's self profited: low coll: from ca 1810; ob.

nose-warmer. A short pipe: from ca 1880.

***nose-watch.** I; me: c. of ca 1570–1630. cf. NIBS (esp. *my nibs*), which affords a very significant analogy. Harman, 'Cut to my nose watch ... say to me what thou wilt.' See WATCH.

nose-wipe. A pocket-handkerchief: low: from ca 1820. cf. NOSE-WIPER.

nose-wipe, v.t. To cheat, deceive: coll: ca

1620–1750. Burton. Again, reluctantly, I differ from the O.E.D. as to status: cf. NOSE OF, WIPE ONE'S.

nose-wiper. A pocket-handkerchief: from ca 1894. Lord C. E. Paget, 1895, 'Charged with my relay of nose-wipers, I was close to his Majesty on the steps of the throne.' Ex NOSE-WIPE, n.

nosebag, see NOSE-BAG. **nosegent,** see NOSE-GENT. **nosender,** see NOSE-ENDER.

nosegay. A blow on the nose: boxing: ca 1820–50.

nosegay to him as long as he lives, it will be a. A mid-C.17–early 18 semi-proverbial c.p. applied to one who has a very big and/or long nose. Ray, 1678.

noser. 'A bloody or contused nose', H., 1859; pugilistic; very ob. Ex: 2. A blow on the nose: mostly boxing: from ca 1850. Mayhew. 3. A strong head-wind: nautical coll: from ca 1850. 4. A paid spy: c. of ca 1860–1910. *Cornhill Magazine*, vol. II, 1862, 'There are a few men and women among thieves called nosers . . . They are in the secret pay of the police.' Ex NOSE, v. 5. One who inspects – esp. by smelling – fruit or flowers but does not buy: Covent Garden (—1909).

noser-my-knacker. Tobacco (pronounced *tobakker*): rhyming s. (—1859).

nos(e)y. Inquisitive: from ca 1906. Esp. *Nosey Parker*, a prying person (from not later than 1910): hence *nosey-parkering*, inquisitive(ness).

nosh, v. To acquire furtively: children's: C.19–20. Origin? Perhaps ex Ger. *naschen*, to eat on the sly, to nibble secretly; cf. Ger. *Nascherei*, a nibbling of dainties on the sly. Also spelt *nash*. Hence, *nosher*, one who samples food before buying; a greedy person: mid-C.19–20. If ex German, it comes via Yiddish.

nosper. A person: back s., low London (—1909). 2. Hence (—1909), a stranger.

nosrap. A parson: back s. (—1859).

nossall or **-oll.** A horse given to kicking and/or other vicious behaviour: London farriers': late C.19–20. Perhaps cf. dial. *nozzle*, to strike violently, to do things vigorously.

nosy, see NOS(E)Y.

not all there, see THERE, ALL.

not-class. Not first-rate: coll (—1887).

not likely!, see LIKELY!, NOT. **not much!,** see MUCH!, NOT.

not half, adv. Much, very; as in 'not half screwed, the gent was!': (mostly Cockney) ironic coll: C.20. 2. As exclamation, esp. of emphatic assent; as in '"Did you like it?" – "Not half!"': id.: from ca 1905.

not Jack out of doors nor yet gentleman. One not quite a gentleman; one of ambiguous status: C.17 semi-proverbial coll. John Clarke, 1639.

not meant. (Of a horse) not intended to win: the turf: ca 1860–1910.

not much frocks. Socks: rhyming s. of ca 1880–1910. Pugh (2): 'Never doin' no honest work out o' quod from the time when they was in not much frocks an' nickin' the baby's milk to when their poor ole shakin' legs got them lagged on the kinchin lay.'

not so old nor yet so cold. A late C.17–mid-18 semi-proverbial c.p. of doubtful and perhaps dubious meaning. Swift, *Polite Conversation*.

not tonight, Josephine! A c.p. used – or said to be used – by husbands, lovers, boy friends, refusing a request for sexual intercourse: late C.19–20. Apocryphally attributed to Napoleon refusing Josephine.

not worth a . . . These similes all have a coll – several, indeed, a s. – ring. Some will be found at the key n., but for convenience I summarize Apperson's masterly forty, and add one: **not worth a bands' end,** mid-C.19–20 dial.; **bean,** late C.13–20, but in C.19–20 only = penniless; **button,** C.14–20, ob; **cherry,** late C.14–15; **chip,** C.17; **cobbler's curse,** late C.19–20 dial. (cf. *tinker's curse*); **cress,** C.14–15; ?hence, **curse,** C.19–20; **dodkin, do(i)tkin,** or **doit,** from ca 1660, ob.; **fart,** C.19–20, low; **farthing,** C.17–20; **fig,** C.16–20; **flea,** C.15–17; **fly,** late C.13–20, ob.; **gnat,** late C.14–16; **gooseberry** (Shakespeare); **groat,** C.16–early 19; **haddock,** C.16; **hair,** early C.17; **haw,** late C.13–16; **hen,** late C.14–mid-16; **herring** (cf. *haddock*), C.13; **leek** or **two leeks,** C.14–mid-17; **louse,** late C.14–20, latterly dial.; **needle,** C.13–15; **nut,** late C.13–mid-14; **pea** or **pease,** late C.14–early 17; **pear,** C.14–16; **pin,** from ca 1530, ob.; **point** or **blue point,** ca 1540–1690; **potato** (Byron, ? nonce-use); **rush,** occ. **bulrush** or **two rushes** (cf. *leek*), mid-C.14–20, ob.; **sloe** (cf. *haw*), C.13–14; **straw,** late C.13–20; **tinker's curse,** mid-C.19–20, orig. dial.; **rotten apple,** mid-C.15–early 16; **egg,** C.15–19; **ivy leaf,** late C.14–mid-15; **onion,** C.16; **shoe-buckles,** C.17; **three halfpence,** mid-C.17–early 18.

notch. The female pudend: low coll: late C.18–20; ob. cf. NOCK.

note. Intellectual signature, political war-cry: Society coll: from ca 1860; ob. Ware quotes the *Daily News*, 18 Nov. 1884, 'Culture is the "note" of Boston.' 2. A £1 note; hence, the sum of £1: coll: since ca 1870.

note, change one's. To tell a (very) different story: late C.17–20: coll till ca 1850, then S.E. Ex modulated singing.

***note-blanker,** see JILTER.

note-shaver. A usurious bill-discounter: commercial coll (—1902). Orig. U.S.

noter. A note-book: Harrow School: late C.19–20. Oxford *-er*.

notergal wash; occ. abbr. to **n.** (or **N.**) **wash.** Grubbiness: lower classes': 1857–ca 80. Either ex *no wash at all* or ex *Nightingale wash*, Florence Nightingale having stated that a person could, if necessary, keep himself clean with a pint of water per day.

nothing. See DANCE; NECK; SAY NOTHING. 2. Ironically spoken it = something very considerable: coll, mostly Australian: late C.19–20.

nothing, no. Nothing whatever: coll: from the 1830s. *Harper's Magazine*, March 1884, 'There is no store, no post-office, no sidewalked street – no nothing.' cf. the (—1854) Northants dial. *a new nothing to hang on one's sleeve*, nothing at all.

nothing but up and ride? A semi-proverbial c.p. = Why, is it all over?; is that the end? ca 1650–1750. Howell, 1659; Ray; Fuller, 1732.

nothing doing! see DOING!, NOTHING.

nothing like leather. A c.p. applied to anything that smacks – esp. if one-sided or tendentially – of the doer's or the speaker's trade (orig. that of a currier): late C.17–20. L'Estrange, 1692; Mrs Gaskell, 1855. The anecdotal 'etymology' is that a cobbler once extolled leather for its value in fortifications. For an implied obscenity, see LEATHER, 2.

nothing to do with the case! That's a lie!: a polite c.p. dating from W. S. Gilbert's *The Mikado*, 14 March 1885; ob.

nothing to make a song about, see SONG ABOUT.

nothing to write home about. Unremarkable; usual; mediocre: coll: late C.19–20.

***notice to quit.** Danger of dying, esp. from ill-health: from ca 1820: c. until ca 1850, then coll; ob. Esp. *have notice to quit*, to have a fatal illness and to know that it is fatal.

notionable. Sensible: shrewd: coll, mostly Cockney': from ca 1890. Pugh, 'Not a notionable idea to his conversation from beginning to end.' Contrast the Wiltshire *notionable*, having an inclination for something.

nottamizer. A dissecting surgeon: ca 1825–60. Smeaton, 1828. Ex *anatomy*.

nottub. A button: back s.: late C.19–20.

nouns! A C.16–18 oath = (*God's*) *wounds*; coll. Earliest as *Cock's* or *Od's nouns*, *nouns* by itself being unrecorded in print before 1608.

nourishment, sit up and take. To become alert or healthy after apathy or illness: from ca 1890: coll. Ex the sick-room + S.E. *take notice*, (esp. of babies) 'to show signs of intelligent observation', Dickens, 1846.

nous. Intelligence; esp. common sense: academic s. >, by 1890, S.E. 1706, Baynard, 'A Demo-brain'd Doctor of more Note than Nous'; 1729, Pope, who, as still sometimes happens, writes it in Gr. characters (νοῦς); Barham; Reade. 'Curiously common in dial.', W. Ex the Gr. philosophic sense of mind or intellect, as in Cudworth, 1678. 2. App., ca 1820–40, it = uppishness. Bee; therefore London fashionable s. 3. Ex sense 1, the rare *nous*, to understand: from ca 1858; ob.

nous-box. The head: 1811, *Lex. Bal.*: s. >, ca 1880, coll; ob. Ex preceding.

nouvelle. New; stylish: smart society: ca 1815–25. Passim in *Boxiana*, 1818–24; castigated by Jon Bee in 1823. An aping of the French *nouveau, nouvel, nouvelle*, new.

nova. Nine, gen. in sums of money: from ca 1890, but much less gen. than NOBBA: Parlary. P. H. Emerson, 1893. Ex It. *nova*.

Nova Scotian pump. A bucket with a line attached to draw water from overside, referring to the hard work in Nova Scotian ships: nautical: late C.19–20. Bowen. cf. the next three entries.

Nova Scotian soda. Sand and canvas supplied, instead of soda, for cleaning paintwork: nautical: late C.19–20. cf.:

Nova Scotian sun(-light). The moon(-light): nautical: late C.19–20. A moonlight night being, in a hard-worked Nova Scotian ship, considered as opportune for some job, by the men deemed unnecessary.

Nova Scotian towing. Towing a boat with the dories out forward, to save expense of a tug: Grand Banks fishermen's: late C.19–20. Bowen. cf. the preceding three entries.

novelty, the, the female pudend, C.18–20 (ob.), may be euphemistic S.E.

novi. (pl. **novis**). A new boy: several

English Public Schools': late C.19–20. Ex L. *novi* (*homines*), the newcomers, the new-rich.

now. Really, truly, indeed: coll: mid-C.19–20. As in: 'Did you now?'

now or never. Clever: rhyming s. (—1909).

now we shall be shan't. A jocular perversion of *now we* SHAN'T BE LONG: a non-aristocratic c.p.: Dec. 1896–ca 1900.

now we shan't be long, see SHAN'T BE LONG.

now we're busy! A c.p. implying action: 1868: ob. Ware, 'Also an evasive intimation that the person spoken of is no better for his liquor, and is about to be destructive': a c.p. dating from the 1880s.

nowhere, be. To be badly beaten, hopelessly out-distanced: 1755. From ca 1820, often figurative. In gen. use from ca 1850. J. Greenwood, 1869, 'The brave Panther when he has once crossed the threshold of that splendid damsel . . . is, vulgarly speaking, nowhere.' Contrast the U.S. sense, utterly at a loss, completely ignorant.

nowheres, see SOMEWHERES.

nozzle. The nose: mainly pugilistic: 1755, Johnson; Meredith, in *Harry Richmond*, 'Uncork his claret . . .; straight at the nozzle.' Ex S.E. sense, a small spout, etc., the word itself being a diminutive of *nose*.

nozzle, v.t. To shrink (gen. clothes): tailors': from ca 1870; ob. Prob. ex steaming-process. 2. Hence, to pawn: also tailors': from ca 1875.

nozzler. A blow, esp. a punch, on the nose: mostly pugilistic: 1828.

***n^{th}*, esp. to the *n^{th}* (or *n^{th}* plus one or 1).** To the utmost; loosely, exceedingly: 1852, Smedley, 'Minerva was . . . starched to the *n^{th}*': coll: largely, university and scholastic. Less gen. (except in S.E., i.e. lit. usage), *n^{th} power*, *n^{th} degree*.

***nub.** The neck: c.: ca 1670–1830. Extant, though very ob., in East Anglian dial. as the nape of the neck. Perhaps cognate with dial. sense, knob; but cf. the app. earlier v., to hang. 2. (?hence,) the gallows: c.: late C.17–early 19. 3. Copulation: c.: C.18–early 19. ?ex dial. sense, a protuberance: cf., however, the C.18–20 dial. v., to jog or shake. 4. A husband: c. > low s.: late C.18–19. Either ex preceding sense or ex *an hub*.

***nub,** v.t. To hang (a person) by the neck: c. of ca 1670–1840. Head; Fielding. ?origin, the earliest dates of n. and v. being somewhat hazy.

nubbies. Female breasts: Australian low: late C.19–20.

***nubbing,** vbl n. Hanging: c.: ca 1670–1840. 2. Sexual intercourse: mid-C.18–early 19: c. Ex NUB, n., 3.

***nubbing-cheat**; occ., in C.19, **-chit.** The gallows: c.: ca 1670–1840, then only as an archaism. Head, B.E., Grose, Maher, ca 1812 (*nubbing-chit*), Ainsworth. cf. NUBBLING-CHIT. See CHEAT. F. & H. gives a brave synonymy: e.g. BEILBY'S BALL-ROOM; CRAP (n., 2); *hanging*-CHEAT, (*the*) QUEER-'EM, (*the*) *stifler*, TYBURN *cross*, WOODEN-LEGGED MARE.

***nubbing-cove.** The hangman: c.: mid-C.17–early 19. See NUBBING, 1.

***nubbing-ken.** The sessions-house: c. of mid-C.17–early 19.

***nubbling-chit.** A corrupt, rare variant of *nubbing-chit* (see NUBBING-CHEAT): C.19 only. Martin & Aytoun in their picaresque *Bon Gaultier Ballads*, 1841.

nubbly. Smutty: late C.19–20; ob.

nucloid. A reserve ship with only a *nucleus* crew: naval officers': ca 1890–1910. cf.:

nuddikin. The head: low: C.19–20; ob. Also *noddleken*. cf. dial. *noddle-box*.

nuff. Enough, esp. in *to have had one's nuff*, to have had enough, i.e. more than enough, drink; to be drunk: military: ca 1880–1910.

nuff ced or said, see N.C.

***nug.** An endearment, gen. with *my* (*dear*): c.: late C.17–early 19. Ex:

***nug,** v. To fondle; to coït with, though occ. v.i. The word is very rare in print, but it is implied in NUGGING-DRESS and -HOUSE. c. of late C.17–mid-19. ?a corruption of *nudge*: cf. dial. *nug*, to nudge, jog with the elbow, knock or strike.

nugget. A thick-set young beast (esp. heifer or calf): Australian, mostly rural: from ca 1850: coll >, ca 1890, S.E. Mundy's *Antipodes*, 1852. Often *a good nugget*. 2. Hence, a short, thick-set person: Australian coll: from ca 1890. Often as a nickname. This usage is paralleled in late C.19–20 Eng. dial. Ex shape. cf. NUGGETY.

nugget, v. (Gen. v.t.) To appropriate (usually one's neighbour's) unbranded calves: Queensland s. >, ca 1900, gen. Australian s. Mrs C. Praed, 1885; R. M. Praed, 1887. Ex the n., 1. (Whence vbl n., *nuggeting*: 1887.)

nuggets. Money, esp. cash: coll: from ca 1890; ob. Milliken, 1892.

nuggety. Thick-set, esp. if short: Australian: from ca 1885: coll >, ca 1905, S.E. *Daily News*, 9 April 1887. Ex NUGGET, n., 1.

***nugging,** vbl n. Sexual intercourse: late C.17–mid-19 c. Mainly in next four.

***nugging-cove.** A fornicator: C.18–mid-19 c. Ex NUG, v.

***nugging-dress.** An odd or exotic dress; esp. a loose dress affected by, and characteristic of, harlots: late C.17–mid-19: c.

***nugging-house.** A brothel: c.: mid-C.18–mid-19. Ex NUG, v.

***nugging-ken.** The same: c.: mid-C.18–early 19. Ex NUG, v.

***null.** To strike, beat, thrash: c. of ca 1780–1870. Ex S.E. *annul.*

***null-groper.** One who sweeps the streets in search of nails, old iron, etc.: c. of ca 1820–60. Prob. *nail-groper* perverted.

***nulling-cove.** A boxer: ca 1810–1910: c. >, ca 1850, pugilistic s. Ex NULL.

***Numans.** Newgate: C.17 c. Rowlands. i.e. *New* + MANS. Later *Newmans*, NEWMAN'S.

***Number Nine** or **9.** The Fleet Prison: c. of ca 1820–50. It was situated at No. 9, Fleet Market.

number nip. The female pudend: low: C. 19–20; ob.

number of one's mess, lose the, see MESS.

number one. One's self or one's own interests, esp. in *look after*, or *take care of, number one.* C.18–20: S.E. until C.19, then coll. T. Pitt, in *Diary*, 1704–5; Dickens; *Judy*, 29 July 1871, 'If a man doesn't take care of No. 1, he will soon have *0* to take care of.' cf. ONE, 1. 2. Urination; occ., a chamber-pot: children's: late C.19–20. Manchon, 'I want to do number one.' cf. NUMBER TWO, 1. 3. The CAT-O'-NINE-TAILS; punishment therewith: prison j. and prison c. (—1889); ob. cf. NUMBER TWO, 2. 4. The first lieutenant: naval (—1909). 5. See NUMBER ONES.

number one (or 1) chow-chow. (Of a meal) exceptionally good; (of an object), utterly worthless: Anglo-Indian coll (—1882). See CHOW-CHOW.

number one (or 1), London, – be at. To have the menstrual discharge: low: mid-C. 19–20; ob. cf. NUMBER ONE, 2.

number ones. A seaman's best uniform: naval: late C.19–20.

number six, see NEWGATE KNOCKER.

number sixes, see SIXES.

number two. Defecation: nursery: late C. 19–20. cf. NUMBER ONE, 2. 2. The birch: prison j. and prison c.: from ca 1885; ob. cf. NUMBER ONE, 3.

numbers, by. In an orderly, indeed somewhat too 'regimental', manner: military coll: late C.19–20. Ex drilling by numbers, esp. instructions to recruits.

numbers, consult the book of. To call for a division, put the matter to the vote: Parliamentary: ca 1780–1850. cf. (*the*) BOOK OF WORDS. Ex the Biblical Book of Numbers, which contains a census of the Israelites.

numbers the waves, he. (Other persons, rare.) He wastes his time or engages in an impossible task: late C.18–mid-19 semi-proverbial c.p. Ray, 1813.

***numms, nums.** A dickey; a clean collar on a dirty shirt: late C.17–early 19 c. ?etymology.

nun. A courtesan; a harlot: from ca 1770, ob.: S.E. >, ca 1810, coll or s. (Perhaps much earlier: see NUNNERY.) cf. ABBESS.

nunky (occ. nunkey); nunks. Coll forms of †S.E. *nuncle*, an uncle: resp. late C.18–20; from ca 1840 (ob.). Charlotte Smith, 1798, 'Old nunky looks upon you as still belonging to him.' *Comic Almanack*, 1841, 'Come, nunks, one game at Blindman's-buff.'

nunnery. A brothel: late C.16–20; ob.: S.E. till ca 1780, then s. Nashe; Fletcher, in *The Mad Lover*, 1615. cf. NUN.

***nunquam.** A very dilatory messenger: c.: ca 1560–1620. Awdelay. Ex L. *numquam*, never. cf. S.E. *numquid*, an inquisitive person.

nuntee (or -y). An occ. variant of NANTEE.

nunyare. Edibles; a meal: Parlary: from ca 1855. A corruption of MUNGAREE. Ex It. *mangiare*, to eat. Mayhew, *London Labour*, III, 201.

nuppence. No money: from ca 1885; ob. Ex *no pence* after *tuppence.*

Nuremberg egg. A watch, egg-shaped: C.16–early 18: coll. Invented there.

nurse. An old man's maid-*cum*-mistress: low coll: C.19–20; ob. 2. A capable first lieutenant 'nursing' a figure-head captain: naval coll: ca 1800–40.

nurse, v. To cheat (gen. *out of*): either c. or s.: from ca 1780; ob. 2. (Of trustees) to eat up property: from ca 1858. cf. NURSE, BE AT. 3. To cheat a rival company's omnibus of passengers by keeping close to it; gen. by having one bus before, one behind: 1858: omnibus drivers' and ticket-collectors'. 4. To hinder a horse in a race by hemming it in with slower ones: the turf: from ca 1892. P. H. Emerson, 1893.

nurse, be at. To be in the hands of (esp. dishonest) trustees: ca 1780–1840. (cf. NURSE, v., 2.) Gen. of the estate.

nursed in cotton, be. To be brought up very, or too, tenderly: late C.18–mid-19 coll. Ray, 1813.

nursery. A race for two-year-olds: the turf: from ca 1882. Coll 2. (*the n.*) The female pudend: low: C.19–20; ob.

nursery business. The playing of successive cannons: billiards: from ca 1890.

nursery noodle. A very fastidious critic: literary: ca 1900–14.

nurse's vail. A nurse's petticoats wet with urine: low: C.19–20; ob. by 1890. Punning *vail*, a gratuity.

nursey, nursie. A coll, mainly children's, form of *nurse*, n.: from ca 1810.

nut. The head: 1858, Mayhew, 'Jack got a cracker' – a heavy punch – 'on his nut.' 2. Hence, brains, intelligence: 1888, J. Runciman; ob. 3. A person: coll: 1887, Manville Fenn, 'He is a close old nut'; slightly ob. Esp. *an old nut*; cf. *a silly* CHUMP. 4. A tough youth: Australian s. or coll: 1882, A. J. Boyd, 'He is a bully, a low, coarse, blasphemous blackguard – what is termed a regular Colonial nut'; ob. cf. the Staffordshire dial. sense, a hard-headed fellow, and the Yorkshire one: a troublesome, disobedient boy. 5. Whence, a dare-devil: Australian: from ca 1895. Esp. *the nut*. 6. A dandy, esp. if in a cheap way: from late 1903; ob. except as KNUT. Cf. FILBERT. Prob. ex NUTTY, 3. 7. A drink, esp. of liquor: low: from ca 1898; ob. 8. A present; an action designed to please: c. or low s.: ca 1810–50. cf. the v., 1. 9. See NUTS.

nut, v. To curry favour with; to court, to ogle: ca 1810–90: ?orig. c. cf. NUT, n., 8, and NUTS, 1. 2. To punch on the head, gen. v.t.: boxing: from ca 1870; ob. Ex the n., 1.

nut, crack a. To drink a (gen. silver-mounted) coconut shell full of claret: Scots coll: ca 1820–80. Scott; *Notes and Queries*, 1889 (7 S., viii, 437).

nut, off one's. Crazy: 1873, Miss Braddon. Ex NUT, n., 1. 2. In liquor, drunk: low: 1860, H., 2nd ed.; ob. by 1910.

nut, sweet as a, see SWEET AS A NUT.

nut, work one's. To think hard; to scheme: orig. (—1902), dial. >, ca 1905, s., esp. in Australia. cf. NUT OUT.

nut at, be a. To be extremely good at (e.g. a game): from ca 1900. Whence NUT (n., 6), dandy.

nut-crack. Nut-crackers (the instrument): from ca 1570: S.E. till C.19, then low coll.

Nut-Crack Night. Hallowe'en: coll (C.18–19) and dial. (C.18–20; ob.). Brand, 1777. Because nuts were, in C.18, flung into the fire.

nut-cracker. The head; hence a sharp blow thereon: boxing: from ca 1870; ob. Ex NUT, n., 1. In the pl: 2. A pillory: c.: late C.17–early 19. ?ex the shape. 3. The fists: boxing: from ca 1870; ob. 4. A curved nose and protuberant chin: C.19–20 (ob.): coll. Ex S.E. *nut-cracker* as adj. describing 'the appearance of nose and chin . . . produced by the want of teeth'. 5. The teeth: coll: C.19–20.

nut-cut. Roguish, mischievous: ca 1860–1914. H., 3rd ed. ('Anglo-Indian'). cf. NUT, n., 6.

nut out. To consider; work out: military from ca 1908. F. & Gibbons, 'I've got to nut it out.' Prob. ex NUT, n., 2, and NUT, WORK ONE'S.

nut-worker. A schemer; a shirker; a malingerer; military: from ca 1906. Ex NUT, WORK ONE'S.

nutmeg-grater. A beard: 1848, *Sinks*; †by 1900.

nutmegs. The human testicles: low coll: C.17–20; ob. cf. NUTS, n., 2, and APPLES.

nuts. A delightful thing, practice, experience: from ca 1589 (Apperson): S.E. until ca 1780, then coll until ca 1850, then s.; ob. Fletcher, Cotton, Lamb, Milliken. Almost an adj., as in Grose, 1st ed., 'It was nuts for them; i.e. it was very agreeable to them.' (A particularly good example occurs in Head & Kirkman, 1674, 'It was honey and nuts to him to tell the guests.') Prob. ex C.16 *nuts to*, an enticement to, 'recorded in a letter from Sir Edward Stafford to Burghley (1587)', W. cf. NUT, v., 1. 2. The (gen. human) testicles: low coll: late C.18–20. Perhaps suggested by the †S.E. sense, the *glans penis*.

nuts, for. (Always with a negative, actual or implied.) At all: coll: 1895, W. Pett Ridge in *Minor Dialogues*; 1899, *The Times*, 25 Oct., 'They can't shoot for nuts; go ahead.'

nuts on or **upon, be.** To set high value upon; be devoted to; fond of or delighted with (person or thing): 1785, Grose: *on* not before ca 1840; *upon* rare after ca 1870. *Punch*, 1882 (LXXXII, 177), 'I am nuts upon

Criminal Cases, Perlice News, you know, and all that.' 2. Hence, to be very clever or skilful at: from ca 1880. 3. Hence, to detest: 1890, *Punch*, 22 Feb. Ex cleverness or skill directed *against* some person or thing. cf.:

nuts on or upon, be dead. The same as the preceding in all three senses: from ca 1890, though 1894 is the earliest O.E.D. record. Orig. an intensive, it >, by 1910, merely the more gen. form of *be nuts on.* Anticipated in 1873 by William Black's 'My aunt is awful nuts on Marcus Aurelius.'

nutted, ppl adj. Deceived or tricked by a friend: low: from ca 1860; ob. Ex NUT, v., 2, possibly influenced by sense 1, and NUTS, 1.

nutting, vbl n. Ogling; paying of court; currying of favour: ca 1810–90. See NUT, v., 1.

nutty. Amorous; with *(up)on*, fond of, in love with, enthusiastic about: 1821, Egan, 'He was so nutty upon the charms of his fair one.' Slightly ob. Ex NUTS ON, BE. 2. Not quite right in the head: *Pall Mall Gazette*, 27 May 1901. Semantically ex sense 1: cf. S.E. *be mad about a girl.* 3. Spruce; smartly dressed or turned out: 1823, Byron (of a girl), 'So prim, so gay, so nutty, and so knowing'; ob. Perhaps ex NUTS, 1; cf. NUT, n., 6. 4. Whence, agreeable: ca 1890. Milliken, 1893, 'Life goes on nutty and nice.' 5. Spicy; piquant: 1894, Sala in *London up to Date*, 'The case, he incidentally adds, promises to be a nutty one'; slightly ob. Ex the nuts in a cake via the idea of fullness of detail. 6. (*Nutty.*) The inevitable nickname of men surnamed Cox: naval and military: late C.19–20. Prob. ex sense 3 or sense 4, but perhaps ex NUTS, n., 2, by indelicate association.

***nux.** The object in view; the LAY (2) or 'game': c., orig. and mainly North Country: from ca 1860; ob. ?ex L. *nux*, a nut, hence a nut to crack.

***nygle,** see NIGGLE. **nym,** see NIM.

nymph of the pave. A harlot: s. (—1851); ob.

nyp, see NIP. **nypper,** see NIPPER.

O

o (or oh) be easy, sing. 'To appear contented when one has cause to complain, and dare not', Grose, 3rd ed. Coll: ca 1785–1830.

o (or, more gen. **oh) be joyful.** A bottle of rum: nautical: ca 1850–1910. 2. Earlier (—1823), of brandy or any other good liquor; †by 1860.

'o (or oh) be joyful' on the other side of his mouth, make one sing. (Gen. I'll make you . . . your mouth.) A c.p. threat: mid-C.18–early 19.

o-be-joyful works. A public-house: late C.19–early 20.

o beggar me, ex the alternative **o Bergami!** You're a liar!: London lower classes': ca 1820–30. Ex Bergami, a lying Italian witness at Queen Caroline's trial. cf. NON ME.

o.d.v. or **O.D.V.** Brandy: jocular (—1887): virtually †. i.e. *eau-de-vie*.

o.k.; gen. **O.K.** All right; correct; safe; suitable; what is required; comfortable, comfortably placed: orig. U.S. s.; >, ca 1880, Eng. s. and, ca 1895, Eng. coll. Alfred Glanville Vance, 'the great Vance' of the music-halls (from the middle sixties to the late eighties, C.19), used to sing:

> The Stilton, sir, the cheese, the O.K. thing to do,
> On Sunday afternoon, is to toddle to the Zoo.

The expression was taken to England by Artemus Ward and was well acclimatized by 1880 at the latest. Thornton records it for the U.S. at 1828 and gives an anticipation (likewise by Andrew Jackson) at 1790: but on these two instances the O.E.D. throws icy water and gives 1840 as the date. Dr Allen Walker Read, 'The Evidence on "O.K."' – in the *Saturday Review of Literature*, 19 July 1941 – has argued for dating it back to 1840 and to a semi-secret political society known as 'The Democratic O.K.', wherein the letters O.K. are used as a cabalistic symbol, perhaps for 'Old Kinderhook', the nickname of Martin Van Buren. However, it has recently been shown by Dr David Dalby ('The Etymology of O.K.', *The Times*, 14 Jan. 1971) that similar expressions were used very early in C.19 by Negroes of Jamaica, Surinam and South Carolina; a Jamaican planter's diary of 1816 records a Negro as saying 'Oh ki, massa, doctor no need be fright, we no want to hurt him.' The ultimate origin is to be sought in West African languages, either in the Mandingo *o ke* 'that's it' or 'all right', or the Wolof *waw kay* 'yes indeed'. The use of *kay* alone is recorded in the speech of black Americans as far back as 1776; significantly, the emergence of *O.K.* among white Americans dates from a period when refugees from southern slavery were arriving in the north. At the time (ca 1839) its etymology was a puzzle to white Americans, who usually 'explained' it as = *oll* (or *orl*) *korrekt* (or *k'rekt*). In the 1930s it was fashionably thought to derive from the Amerindian Choctaw (*h*)*oke*, 'it is so'. (Such fanciful etymologies as *aux Cayes* and *och aye!* can be summarily dismissed; *o.k.* is an evergreen of the correspondence column.)

o.k.; O.K., v.i. and, more gen., v.t. To pass as correct: orig. (—1885), U.S.; anglicized as a coll ca 1900. e.g. *to o.k. an account, a document.*

O my, see MY!, 2.

o.p.; O.P. Opposite the prompter. (cf. *p.s.*, prompt side.) Theatrical s. (—1823) >, ca 1870, coll >, ca 1900, j. 2. Earlier (ca 1809–20, though recorded later), old price(s), in reference to the demonstrations at Covent Garden Theatre, London, in 1809, against the proposed new tariff of prices. Byron alludes to it in a letter of 12 June 1815 to Moore. 3. (Of spirits) overproof: j. when lit.; when fig., it is coll, as – to borrow from the O.E.D. – in Walch, *Head over heels*, 1874, '"Pshaw", cried Sandy (Clan MacTavish) in his beautiful O.P. Scotch.'

o.p.h.; O.P.H. Off, as in 'Dammit! I'm off.' Jocular: late C.19–20. (Obviously, *off* is perverted to *oph*; but the pronunciation, gen. slow, is *O–P–H*.)

***o per se o;** or with capital Os. A crier: early C.17 c. Dekker.

o.t. (or O.T.), it's. It's (very) hot: non-aristocratic: from ca 1880.

o.v. or **O.V.** The oven, or that open space below the stage in which the Pepper's-ghost illusion is worked: showmen's and low actors': late C.19–early 20.

O.V.O. A low phrase listed by Ware with

the remark, 'Quite inexplicable. No solution ever obtained from the initiates.' Perhaps it's just as well.

o yes! A jocular perversion of *oyez!*: from before 1887; slightly ob.

oaf. A wiseacre: coll: late C.17–mid-18. Ex S.E. sense.

***oak.** He who, in highway robbery, keeps watch on behalf of the highwayman: c.: late C.16–early 17. Greene, 1591. He affords security. 2. A man of good substance and credit: late C.17–mid-19: c. >, ca 1750, s. Ex the solidity of oak. cf. †U.S. *oak*, strong. 3. An oaken, hence an outer door, esp. in *sport oak*, in C.19–20 gen. *sport one's oak*, to shut one's outer door as a sign that one is engaged. 1785, Grose: university s. >, ca 1820, coll. 4. A joke: rhyming s.: late C.19–20.

oak, close as. Very retentive of secrets; secretive: semi-proverbial coll: C.17–18. Shakespeare: Colman, 1763, 'I am close as oak, an absolute free-mason for secrecy.'

oaken towel. A cudgel, orig. and mainly of oak; hence *rub one down with an oaken towel*, to cudgel, to beat him: low (?orig. c.): C.18–mid-19. In U.S. c., *an oak towel* is a policeman's club.

oaks, felling of. Sea-sickness: C.17 coll. Jocular, as Withals (1608) shows in his *Dict.* ?ex vomiting upon the oak of a ship.

oakum, pick. To be in a poor-house: lower classes' coll (—1887). Ex the same phrase in S.E. (to be in prison).

oar in, put or **shove an** or **one's.** To interfere: resp. coll from ca 1730, as in Moncrieff, 1843; s. from ca 1870, as in Mrs Henry Wood (1874). Coffey, 1731, 'I say, meddle with your own affairs; I will govern my own house, without your putting in an oar.' Ex following entry; there is, however, the transitional *put an* (or *one's*) *oar in every man's boat*, as in Brathwait, 1630.

oar in every man's boat, occ. **†barge, have an.** To be concerned in everyone's affairs: mid-C.16–20, ob.: coll >, ca 1650, S.E. Udall, Florio, Howell, cf. preceding entry.

oars. A waterman: C.17–19: either coll or S.E.

oars, first. A favourite, esp. in *be first oars with*: coll: 1774, C. Dibdin's song, *The Jolly Young Waterman*, 'He was always first oars when the fine city ladies | In a party to Ranelagh went, or Vauxhall': whence the origin.

oars, lie or **rest (up)on one's.** To take things easily: resp. 1726, Shelvocke; 1836, Lady Granville: both coll till ca 1850, then S.E. Ex leaning on the handles of one's oars.

oat. An atom or particle, but esp. in *have not an oat*, to be penniless: from ca 1870 (ob.): low. Perhaps suggested by *groat*, but more prob., as H. suggests, *iota* corrupted.

oat-stealer. An ostler: C.19–20; ob. Jocular coll. Ex OSTLER.

oath, Highgate, see HIGHGATE, SWORN AT.

oath!, my. A mild expletive: mostly Australian and New Zealand: late C.19–20. Ex the more trivial senses of S.E. *oath*. See also COLONIAL OATH.

oath, take an. To drink (liquor): low: C. 19; mostly U.S.

oatmeal. (Gen. in pl.) A profligate roisterer (one of a set): coll: ca 1620–40. Ford, in *The Sun's Darling*, 1624; see also Nares. Semantics obscure.

oatmeal, all the world is (gen. not). Everything is delightful (or not): proverbial coll: ca 1540–1700. Udall, Swetnam. (cf. BEER AND SKITTLES.) ?ex oatmeal as food.

oatmeal, give (a person) **his.** To punish: rebuke severely: mid-C.18–early 19. Boswell.

oatmeal party. Scotsmen: naval coll: late C.19–20. Ex the staple Scottish food.

oats, earn a gallon of. (Of horses) to fall on the back and roll from side to side: provincial coll: C.19. Halliwell.

oats, feed of. A whip; a whipping: mostly rural: C.19–20; ob.

oats, wild. A dissolute young man: coll: ca 1560–1620. Gen. a nickname. Becon (d. 1570), 'Certain light brains and wild oats'. Prob. ex, though recorded some twelve years earlier than, *sow one's wild oats*, to commit youthful follies, while *to have sown* . . . indicates reform: coll; in late C.19–20, S.E.: 1576, Newton, 'That wilfull . . . age, which . . . (as wee saye) hath not sowed all theyr wyeld Oats'. Ex the folly of sowing wild oats instead of good grain; cf. Fr. *folle avoine*.

Oats and Barley. Charley: rhyming s. (—1859).

oats and chaff. A footpath: rhyming s. (—1857); ob.

ob. Abbr. OBIT: Winchester College: C. 19–20.

ob and sol. Scholastic, hence any subtle disputation: late C.16–17: coll. 1588, 'Very skilful in the learning of ob and sol'. Also *obs and sols*, as in Burton, 1621; occ. *sols* *and obs.* Abbr. *objection and solution* in C. 16 books of theology. The derivative *ob-and-soller*, a subtle disputant, is either a nonce or a very rare usage.

Obadiah. A Quaker: C.18–mid-19: coll. Ex the common Quaker name.

obfuscated; obfusticated. Drunk: coll: from ca 1855; ob. The former is in 'Ducange Anglicus', 1857; the latter (30 Dec. 1872) is a sol. Also *obfuscation*: H. Kingsley, 1861,'In a general state of obfuscation'. Ex S.E. sense, to stupefy.

obit. An obituary notice: journalistic: 1874, W. Black in the *Athenaeum*, 12 Sept., 'It was the custom of his journal to keep obits in readiness.' Prob. ex *obituary*, not a revival of mid-C.15–17 S.E. *obit*, the same.

object. A laughing-stock; GAPE-SEED: coll: from ca 1820. cf. '*little object* (of children) = a half-playful half-angry endearment', F. & H. Ex S.E. *object of pity, mirth, derision*, etc.

obligate. To make indebted, to bind, a person by a kindness or a favour: late C. 17–20: S.E. till ca 1860; then – except in U.S. (where coll) – slightly sol., or at least catachrestic; ob.

oblige. To favour a company (*with*, e.g., a song): coll: 1735, Pope. 2. (Of a charwoman) to work for: charwomen's coll: late C.19–20. 'The lady I "oblige"'.

***observationist.** One (gen. a pedlar, hawker, etc.) who spies out likely booty for thieves: c. (—1889); ob.

obsquatulate. An occ. form of ABSQUATULATE.

obstreperlous, -olous, -ulous; obstropalous, -olous, -ulous; also **abstrepolous, -ulous.** Obstreperous: from ca 1725: sol. when not deliberately jocular; Halliwell, however, in 1847, characterizes it as 'genuine London dialect'. Resp. first recorded: ca 1780, ca 1760, 1727; 1736 (*Sessions*), ca 1770, 1748 (Smollett); *ab*-forms only in C.18. Commonest: *obstropolous, -ulous*.

obvious. (Of women) stout: Society: 1897 –ca 1914. Ex the signs of pregnancy.

obviously severe. 'Hopelessly rude of speech': Society: ca 1890–1914. Ware.

occabot. Tobacco: back s. (—1851). (TIB *fo occabot*, bit of tobacco.)

occasion. A notable celebration, a special ceremony, an event of note: coll: from ca 1860.

occasion, improve the. To offer a prayer; give a homily or moral address: coll (mostly clerical): from ca 1860. G. Macdonald, 1865, in *Alec Forbes*.

occifer. An officer: late C.19–20. Also *ossifer*.

occupant. A harlot: late C.16–early 17: a vulg. Marston, 1599. Ex OCCUPY. 2. A brothel: C.17: a vulg. cf. NANNY-HOUSE. Ex preceding sense.

occupy. (v.t. and v.i.) to cohabit (with); lie with: C.16–early 19: S.E. in C.16, then a vulg., as in Florio, Rowley, Hexham, Rochester, D'Urfey, Grose. In consequence of its vulgar use in this sense, this verb was little used in literature in the 17th and 18th century: cf. [Shakespeare, *2 Henry* IV, at II, iv, 159] 'as odious as the word *occupy*'. cf. L. *occupare amplexu* and see FUCK.

occupying-house. A brothel: late C.16–17: a vulg. Florio.

ocean pearl. A girl: rhyming s.: late C.19–20. Also *ivory pearl*.

oceans. A (very) large quantity or number: from ca 1840: coll almost S.E.

***ochive;** also **oschive.** A knife: c.: C.18–20; ob. *A New Canting Dict.*, 1725, defines *oschive* as a bone-handled knive, as if ex L. *os*, a bone + *chive*, a knife, but *oschive* may be an etymologizing theory and perversion of *ochive*. Ex Romany *o chif*, the knife. More gen., *chive*; occ. *chif(f)*. See CHIVE-FENCER.

ochorboc. Beer: Italian organ-grinders' (—1909). It. *bocca* (mouth), thus: *occa* + *b* + intrusive *oc*.

***ochre.** Money: c. >, ca 1870, low s.: 1854, Dickens, 'Pay your ochre at the doors'; ob. Also, gold, money. Ex the colour of gold. cf. with caution, GILT.

o'clock, know what's. To be alert; shrewd: low coll: from ca 1835. Dickens, Thackeray. Ex the S.E. sense, to know the real state of things. cf. WHAT'S WHAT; TIME OF DAY, 3, 4.

o'clock, like one; see LIKE A . . .

October; october. Blood: boxing: from ca 1850; ob. 'Cuthbert Bede', 'Now we'll tap your best October.' Ex *October* (*ale* or *cider*). cf. CLARET.

od, 'od; occ. **odd.** Also with capitals. God, in oaths and asseverations: coll, though orig. euphemistic S.E.: C.17–early 19. Whence *od rabbit it!*, 1749, Fielding; *od rat it!* (also in *Tom Jones*), whence DRAT (*it*)*!*; *od rot it!*, from ca 1810; *od save's!* (lit., God save us), C.19–20, mainly and in C.20 only dial.

odd, adj. Homosexual: partly euphemistic, partly coll: from ca 1890. cf. C.20 *queer*, homosexual.

odd-come-short. In pl, odds and ends: rural coll: 1836, T. Hook; slightly ob. 2. Some day, coming shortly: coll: from ca 1875; ob. Usually *one of these odd-come-shorts* (as in Harris's *Uncle Remus*); but except in U.S., much less gen. than:

odd-come-shortlies. Some day soon: coll: C.18–20; ob. Swift, 'Miss, when will you be married? . . . One of these odd-come shortly's, Colonel.'

odd fish, see FISH.

odd job man. One 'who professes to do anything and only does his employer': trades' (—1909). Ware.

odd-trick man. A hanger-on, for profit, at auctions: auctioneers': mid-C.19–20. James Greenwood, *In Strange Company*, 1873. Ex card-playing.

oddish. Tipsy: low coll: from ca 1850; ob. cf. QUEER, adj., 2.

odds! see ODS.

odds, it is or **makes no.** It makes no difference (for good or ill): C.17–20: S.E. till C.19, then coll. T. A. Guthrie, 'But there, it's no odds.'

odds?, what's the. What difference does it make?: coll: mid-C.19–20. App. earliest as *what odds?*: 1826, *Sessions*, 'I asked Jackson whose they were – he said, "What odds; they are mine." '

odds?, where's the. A low coll form (—1887) of the preceding.

odds, within the. Possible or possibly; esp. just or barely possible: sporting coll (—1887) >, by 1890, gen. coll.

odds of, be no. As in 'It's no odds o' mine' (Greenwood), no concern of mine: (low) coll: mid-C.19–20.

odno. Lit., nod. Rare except in *ride on the odno*, to travel by rail without paying: back s.: 1889, *Sporting Times*; ob.

ods, od's; odds. (Also ADS; UDS.) God's, gen. in combination, in late C.16–early 19 coll oaths and asseverations; extant as a jocular archaism. The second member is frequently perverted, as in *bud* ex *blood*, NOUNS or OONS ex *wounds*, ZOOKS ex *hooks*. cf.:

ods bobs. A C.18 reduction of and corruption of:

ods bodkins, a jocular exclamation, is a late C.19–20 perversion of *ods bodikins*, lit. God's little body, a C.17–19 oath. See ODS.

of?, what are you doing. What are you doing? (dial. and) low coll: C.19–20. Abbr. or slovenly corruption of †*what are you in the doing of.*

of it, see IT, OF.

off, v. To depart, go away: low coll: 1895, *Westminster Gazette*, 21 Sept., 'He took down his hat, and off'd.' In C.20, gen. *off it*. Ex dial.: 1889 (E.D.D.). 2. *off with,* to remove or take off instantly: from ca 1890: sol. when not jocular (coll). *Daily News*, 23 Feb. 1892, 'They offed with his head.' 3. To refuse, reject: 1908, A. S. M. Hutchinson, *Once Aboard the Lugger*, 'I haven't offed that yet – haven't refused it, I mean'; ob.

off, adj. Out of date; no longer fashionable: coll: 1892, *Illustrated Bits*, 22 Oct., 'Theosophy is off – decidedly off.' Perhaps ex restaurant j. ('Chops are off'). 2. Hence, stale; in bad condition, e.g. of a cricket pitch: low coll: from ca 1895. 'Smells a little bit off, don't it?', F. & H. Abbr. *off colour*. 3. Hence, out of form: coll: from ca 1896. 4. Hence, in ill health: coll: from late 1890s.

off, n. Start of a horse-race: sporting coll: late C.19–20. 'You can bet, on the course, right up to the off.' Ex the cry 'They're *off*.'

off, be. To depart; run away: coll (—1887). Baumann; 1892, *Ally Sloper*, 27 Feb.

off, cannot (or could not) be. As in Greenwood, ca 1880, 'I couldn't be off likin' it,' I could not help – or refrain from – liking it: (low) coll: mid-C.19–20.

***off, have the bags.** To have independent means – and live on them: c. (—1887).

off bat. Point, in cricket: Winchester College: coll or j.: mid-C.19–20.

off chump. Having no appetite: stables' (—1909). Perhaps *off champing*.

***off duty.** Not engaged in stealing: c. (—1887).

off-go. A start, a beginning: Scots coll: 1886, R. L. Stevenson.

off it. See OFF, v. 2. A variant of *off one's* CHUMP or NUT or ROCKER, etc. See those nn.

off one's chump, coconut, nut, onion (2), rocker, see the nn. **off one's feed** or **oats,** see FEED.

off the hinge. Out of work: low: from ca 1850; ob. Ex:

off the hinges. Out of order; upset; disheartened: coll till C.18, then dial., where it gen. = in bad health, spirits, or temper. Cotgrave. Ex a door unhinged.

off the hooks. Crazed, mad (gen. temporarily); coll: C.17–mid-19. Beaumont & Fletcher; Scott. 2. Crestfallen (this sense was ob. by 1750, †by 1800); ill-humoured: coll (ob.): from ca 1630; in C.19–20, mainly dial. Davenport, 1639. (3. In dial., also shabby, worn out, ailing.) 4. Out of work: coll: C.18. North, *Lives of the Norths*, 1740. (This interpretation is not perfectly certain.)

off the horn. (Of steak) very hard: low: from ca 1870; ob.

off the rails, see RAILS, OFF THE. **off with,** see OFF, v., 2.

offer up. To lift; to help to raise: London labourers', esp. in the building trade: late C.19–20.

offhandish. A coll form (—1887) of *off hand*, brusque, inconsiderate, casual.

office. One's *office* is one's 'ordinary Haunt, or Plying-[?playing-]place, be it Tavern, Ale-house, Gaming-house or Bowling-green', B.E.: late C.17–18. 2. A signal, a (private) hint; a word of advice; (in sporting s.) valuable information: C.19–20: ?orig. c. Esp. in *give the office* (1803) and *take the office* (1812, likewise in Vaux), the latter slightly ob.

office, v. To give information (about something); warn, intimate to: low (?orig. c.): 1812, Vaux; Moore, 1819, 'To office . . . To the Bulls of the Alley the fate of the Bear'.

office, cast of (e.g. your). 'A Touch of your Employment': coll: late C.17–18. B.E. prob. means a helping hand from one in a (good) position.

office, cook's. The galley: nautical: from ca 1850; ob.

office, give one the, see OFFICE, n., 2.

office-sneak. A stealer of umbrellas, overcoats, etc., from offices: coll: from ca 1860.

officer's mount. A harlot: military (the ranks'): late C.19–20. Punning Army j. for a horse.

officers of the 52nds. Young men rigidly going to church on the 52 Sundays in a year: city of Cork (—1909). As if of the 52nd regiment.

offish. Distant; reserved: coll: from ca 1830. L. Oliphant, 1883. cf. *stand-offish.*

offishness. Aloofness; reserve: coll: from ca 1880. Ex *offish* and, like it, of persons only.

ofter. A frequenter or habitué: sporting: ca 1884–1910. Ex *oft*, often.

ogg or og. (Usually pl.) Stones of fruit, e.g. CHERRY-OGGS: non-aristocratic: mid-C.19–20. Origin?

ogging ot tekram. Going to market: back s. (—1859).

ogle. See OGLES. 2. 'An ocular invitation or consent, side glance, or amorous look', F. & H.: coll: C.18–20. Cibber, 1704, 'Nay, nay, none of your parting ogles.' Ex:

***ogle,** v.i. and t. To look invitingly or amorously (at): from ca 1680: c. until ca 1710, coll till ca 1790, then S.E. Implied in B.E.'s *ogling*, 'casting a sheep's Eye at Handsom Women'; and in the Shadwell quotation at OGLING; D'Urfey. Ex Low Ger. *oegeln*, same meaning. 2. To look; to look at: c. and S.E.: from ca 1820; ob. Haggart, 1821, 'Seeing a cove ogling the yelpers'. Ex S.E. sense, to examine.

***ogled,** with determining word, e.g. QUEER-OGLED, squinting: late C.18–20; ob.; c. >, ca 1840, low s.

***oglen, rum.** 'Bright, piercing eyes', Bee: c.: ca 1820–50. cf. etymology of OGLE, v., 1.

ogler. A punch in the eye: boxing s. (—1887); ob.

***oglers.** Eyes: c.: from ca 1820; ob. Haggart. A variation on:

***ogles.** (Extremely rare in singular.) Eyes: mid-C.17–20: c. until ca 1805, then boxing s. until ca 1860, finally low gen. s.; ob. 'Cuthbert Bede'; Thackeray. Ex the v. Hence, QUEER *ogles* (see also OGLED), cross eyes; RUM *ogles*, bright or arresting eyes.

ogling, vbl n. The throwing of amorous or insinuating glances: from ca 1680: c. until ca 1710, then coll, then, by 1790, S.E. Shadwell, 1682, 'They say their Wives learn ogling in the Pit,' a marginal gloss reading: 'A foolish Word among the Canters for glancing.'

oh, see O BE. . . .

oh, after you! That'll do!; stop talking!: tailors' c.p.: from ca 1870. Ironic.

oh, dummy! Nonsense!; HUMBUG!: tailors' c.p.: from ca 1860.

oh, my leg! A low c.p. addressed, ca 1810–50, to one recently liberated from gaol. A gibe at the gait caused by fetters.

oh, swallow yourself! Hold your tongue!: don't bother!: proletarian: from ca 1875; ob.

oh well! it's a way they have in the Army, see IT'S A WAY . . .

oick or oik. A townee; a CAD: at certain Public Schools in the North and the Midlands: late C.19–20.

oil. An oil-painting: coll: from ca 1890. (Gen. in pl.) 2. See OILS, 2. 3. In addition to its popularity in proverbs and proverbial sayings (there are 89 in Apperson), *oil* is of frequent occurrence in various humorous and/or ironic phrases that began as coll and may have > S.E.; indeed, since it is arguable that all except **oil of giblets** were always S.E., it is better to list them all together: **oil of angels,** a gift, a bribe, late C.16–17, as in Greene (and see below); **oil of barley** or **malt,** beer, mid-C.17–early 19, as in B.E.; **oil of Baston** (a topographical pun; *basting*), a beating, C.17, Withals – with which cf. **oil of gladness** (Grose, 2nd ed.), **hickory** (gen. as **h. oil**), **holly** (C.17), **rope** (C.18, Mrs Centlivre), **stirrup** (late C.18–mid-19, Grose, 2nd ed.: also as **stirrup-oil**), **strappem** (C.19), and **whip** (mid-C.17–mid-18, Fuller), and also the C.18–20 dial. (ob.) **birch, hazel** (also in form **h. oil,** coll and dial.), **oak, strap,** the form **strap-oil** occurring as C.19–20 jocular coll; **oil of giblets** or **horn,** the female spendings (this, certainly, is low s.!), C.19–20; **oil of palms** (Egan's Grose), or **palm-oil,** a bribe, C.19–20, ob. – cf. *oil of angels*; **oil of tongue,** flattery, with which cf. the late C.14–mid-15 S.E. **hold up oil,** to consent flatteringly (Apperson), and the rare **oil of fool,** flattery, as in Wolcot.

oil, v. To cheat: Charterhouse: late C.19–20. Hence OILER, 2. 2. v.i., to toady: Harrow School: late C.19–20. cf. OIL UP TO, and the corresponding sense of GREASE. 3. To act in an underhand way; to obtain unfairly: Rugby School: from ca 1880. Hence, *oiler*, one who does this. 4. To evade; an evasion: Winchester: late C.19–20.

oil, strike. To have good luck, be successful: orig. U.S.; anglicized ca 1875. Ex the S.E. sense, to discover oil-springs.

oil-butt. A black whale: whalers': late C.19–20. Ex the abundance of oil which its carcase yields.

oil of . . ., see OIL, n., 3.

oil-painting, be no. To be plain-looking; ugly: coll: late C.19–20. cf. PICTURE, 3.

oil the knocker. To fee the porter: from ca 1850; ob.

oil the wig. To become tipsy, while *oil one's wig* is to make a person tipsy: provincial s. or coll: late C.18–19.

oil up to. To toady to: Harrow School: late C.19–20. cf. OIL, v., 2.

oiler. An oilskin coat: coll, orig. (middle 1880s), U.S., anglicized, esp. in the Navy, by 1900. cf. OILIES. 2. A cheat: Charterhouse: late C.19–20. Ex OIL, v. cf. BUMFER.

oilies. The same as OILER, than which, in English use, it is slightly earlier: coll: late C.19–20. Also in dial.

oils. See OIL, 1. 2. (Very rare in the singular.) An oilskin coat: coll: 1891, J. Dale, *Round the World*. cf. OILER and OILIES.

oiner. A cad: university: ca 1870–1915. Etymology obscure: ?Gr. οἰνίζω, smell of wine.

ointment. Money: coll: C.15–17. Ex the C.13 fabliau, De la Vieille qui Oint la Palme au Chevalier. 2. The *semen virile*: low: C.18–20, ob. 3. Butter: medical students': from ca 1859.

old. Money: low: 1900, G. R. Sims, *In London's Heart*, 'Perhaps it's somebody you owe a bit of the old to, Jack.' ?abbr. *old stuff*. 2. Much: coll: early C.19, but rare. See the Scott quotation in the adj., 2. 3. *the old*, the master: ca 1860–1910. Abbr. *the old man*.

old, adj. Crafty, clever, knowing: from ca 1720; ob. Defoe, 'The Germans were too old for us there.' Esp. in such phrases as OLD BIRD, DOG, FILE, HAND, SOLDIER, STAGER. 2. A gen. intensive = great, abundant, excessive, splendid: coll: mid-C.15–20. Anon., ca 1440, 'Gode olde fyghting was there'; Tarlton, 1590, 'There was old ringing of bells'; Cotton, 1664, 'Old drinking and old singing'; Grose; Scott, 1814, 'So there was old to do about ransoming the bridegroom.' From ca 1860, only with *gay*, *good*, *grand*, *high*, and similar adjj., as in the *Referee*, 11 March 1883, 'All the children . . . had a high old time,' and with *any* as in 'any old time' or 'any old how'. 3. Ugly: c.: late C.18–early 19. Perhaps ex OLD HARRY, NICK, ONE, ROGER, etc., the devil. 4. (Mostly in terms of address.) Indicative of affection, cordiality, or good humour: coll: 1588, Shakespeare, 'Old Lad, I am thine owne'; B.E.; Grose; Hume Nisbet, 1892, 'Now for business, old boy.' Also *old bean*, CHAP, FELLOW, *man*, THING, *top*, etc. 5. Hence, of places familiar to one: coll: late C.19–20. Often *good old*. 6. A gen. pejorative: C.16–20: S.E. or coll or s. as the second member is S.E. or coll or s.; the practice itself is wholly (orig., almost wholly) unconventional. e.g. OLD *block*, *fizgig*, FOGEY, STICK IN THE MUD. 7. In combination with (e.g.) HARRY, NICK, ONE, SCRATCH, the devil: coll: from Restoration days, the earliest record in the O.E.D. being *Old Nick* in L'Estrange,

1668; *old*, however, was, in S.E., applied to Satan as early as C.11. Ex the S.E. sense in this connection: primeval. See also OLD BENDY.

old, any, see OLD, adj., 2.

old, good. An approving phrase that gives a coll and familiar variation to *good.* C.19–20. Perhaps ex OLD, adj., 2 and 4.

old Adam. The penis: low coll: C.19–20. Ex S.E. sense, natural sin.

old as Charing Cross or **as Paul's** (i.e. St Paul's) or **as Paul's steeple.** Ancient; very old indeed: coll: ca 1650–1820. Howell, 1659 (*Paul's steeple*); Ray, 1678 (*Charing Cross*). Other topographical similes are †*old as Aldgate* and, in dial., †*Cale Hill*, †*Eggerton*, †*Glastonbury Tor*, †*Pandon Gate*; cf. S.E. *old as the hills*.

old as my tongue and a little older than my teeth, as. A c.p. reply to an inquiry as to one's age: coll (slightly ob.) and dial.: C.18–20. Swift, *Polite Conversation*, Dial. I.

old as the itch, as. Extremely old: (low) coll: C.18. Fuller.

old bach. A confirmed bachelor: coll: from early 1870s.

old bag. An elderly, slatternly prostitute, hence pejoratively of an unpopular younger one: low: late C.19–20. Franklyn 2nd proposes a rhyme on *old* HAG, but I doubt this: cf. BAG, n., 4.

Old Bailey underwriter. A forger on a small scale: ca 1825–50. Moncrieff, *Van Diemen's Land*, 1830. ?orig. c.; certainly low.

old beeswing. A s. vocative (ob. by 1910). See BEES-WING, and OLD COCK.

old (or, as with all names for the devil, **Old) bendy** or **Bendy.** The devil: C.19–20 dial. rather than coll. Dial. also are (all with *old*): *a'ill thing*; BOGY; *botheration*; BOY; *carle*; *chap*; *child*; *cloots* or CLOOTIE; *dad*; FELLOW; GENTLEMAN; *hangie*; HARRY (!); *hooky*; HORNY; *lad*; *Mahoun*; *man*; NICK or *Nicker* or *Nickie* or *Nickie Ben*; ONE; *Sam*; *Sanners* or *Sanny* or *Saunders*; *Scrat(t)*, SCRATCH, *Scratchem*; *Smith*; *smoke*; *sooty*; *soss* or *Soss*, and *thief*. See under the coll and s. terms; cf. also OLD, adj., last sense. My essay 'The Devil and his Nicknames' in *Words!*

old Billy. The devil, but rarely except in *like old Billy*, like the devil, i.e. hard, furiously, etc. Astley, 1894. cf. the *like* similes.

***old bird.** An experienced thief: c.: 1877. 2. An experienced, knowing person: coll: from ca 1887. cf. OLD DOG; OLD HAND; OLD SOLDIER; OLD STAGER.

old blazes. The devil: low: 1849; ob. See OLD, adj., 7.

old block, see BLOCK. **old bloke,** see BLOKE.

old boots. The devil. Only in ... *as old boots* and esp. *like old boots*, a gen. intensive adv. Smedley, 1850, 'was out of sight like old boots'; Milliken, 'I jest blew away like old boots.' See OLD, adj., 7. 2. See OLD SHOES, RIDE IN ...

old boy. A coll vocative: C.17–20. Shakespeare. cf. OLD CHAP. See OLD, adj., 4. 2. See entry at OLD BENDY: coll and dial.: C.19 (?earlier)–20. 3. Any old or oldish man, or one in authority, esp. one's father, a headmaster, the managing director, etc.: coll: C.19–20. cf. OLD MAN. This (like the preceding sense) always, except in the vocative, goes with *the*. 4. A strong ale: brewers' coll: ca 1740–80.

old buck. A coll term of address: late or even mid-C.19–20: but it occurs as early as 1829 in Glascock, *Sailors and Saints*, and so, as a naval usage, may go back to ca 1810, 1800 or even 1790.

old buffer. An old fellow: C.19. It occurs in, e.g., W. N. Glascock, *Sailors and Saints* (I, 30), 1829, '... all for that old buffer on the hill'.

old buster. Old chap, gen. as vocative: 1905, H. A. Vachell in *The Hill*, 'You funny old buster!'

old chap. A coll vocative (—1823). Egan's Grose: Anstey. See CHAP and OLD, adj., 4.

old China. A variant, mostly as a vocative, of CHINA, a mate or companion.

old chum. See CHUM, 3. (ca 1840–1900; increasingly rare. C. P. Hodgson, *Reminiscences*, 1846.)

old clo! A c.p. applied to anything worn out, exhausted, behind the times: proletarian: from ca 1860; ob. Ex the street cry.

old cock. COCK (=man, fellow) + OLD, adj., 4. Used both in address, from before 1800, (Mark Lemon, 1867, 'Mr Clendon did not call Mr Barnard old cock, old fellow, or old beeswing') and in reference = an (old) man (Marriott-Watson, 1895, 'He was a comfortable old cock ... and pretty well to do').

old cockalorum (or **-elorum).** A very familiar variation (—1887) of the preceding, slightly ob.

old codger. See CODGER (Colman, 1760), and OLD, adj., 6.

old crawler, esp. preceded by **regular.** A

pejorative, whether in reference or in the vocative: late C.19–20: (mainly Australian) coll or s. 'Rolf Boldrewood', 1888. Prob. ex *pub-crawler* or CRAWLER (2), a contemptible person, a toady.

old cuff. See CUFF, 1, in relation to OLD, adj., 4.

old Davy. The devil: coll, mainly lower classes': from late C.18. 2. DAVY JONES, the 'spirit of the sea', hence the sea itself: ca 1780–1830.

old ding. The female pudend: low: C.19–20; ob. ?ex DING, to strike.

old dog. See OLD DOG AT IT. 2. Abbr. *gay old dog*: coll: C.19–20. 3. (Of a person) 'a lingering antique', F. & H.: coll: 1846, Dickens; ob. Ex sense 1. 4. A half-burnt plug of tobacco remaining in a pipe: low: from ca 1850; orig. prison c.

old dog at common prayer. (Of a clergyman) 'A Poor Hackney that cou'd Read, but not Preach well', B.E.: late C.17–mid-18. cf.:

old dog at it, be. To be expert at something: coll: ca 1590–1880. Nashe, 'Olde dogge at that drunken, staggering kind of verse'. cf. the S.E. proverbial *old dog for a hard road.*

***old donah.** A mother: tramps' c. (—1893) >, by 1914, also Cockney s. P. H. Emerson. See DONA; cf. OLD GIRL or WOMAN.

old driver. The devil: low: C.19–20; ob. cf. SKIPPER, 3.

old dutch or Dutch, gen. preceded by **my,** occ. by **your** or **his.** One's wife: from the middle 1880s. When Albert Chevalier introduced the term into one of his songs (cf. the later, more famous, poem, *My Old Dutch*), he explained that it referred to an old Dutch clock, the wife's face being likened to the clock-face. Prob. influenced by DUCHESS.

old enough to know better. A mostly feminine c.p. reply to 'How old are you?': late (?mid) C.19–20. cf. OLD AS MY TONGUE...

old ewe dressed lamb-fashion, an. An old woman dressing like a young one: coll: 1777, *The Gentleman's Magazine*, 'Here antique maids of sixty three | Drest out lamb-fashion you might see'; Grose, 1785, as above. †by 1900. See MUTTON DRESSED AS LAMB, the mod. form, and LAMB-FASHION.

***old fake.** A criminal undergoing his second probation: Australian c.: ca 1830–70.

old fellow. A coll vocative: 1825, C. M. Westmancott. See FELLOW.

old file. A miser: see FILE. 2. An old, or rather an experienced, man: low: from ca 1850; ob. Ex sense 1; cf. OLD, adj., 6.

old floorer. Death: low: from ca 1840; ob. cf. S.E. *the leveller*.

old fogy, see FOGEY. **old gal,** see OLD GIRL. **old geezer,** see GEESER.

old gentleman. The devil: s. > coll; also dial. C.18–20. T. Brown, 1700; Barham. 2. A card slightly larger and thicker than the others: cardsharpers' c.: 1828, G. Smeeton, *Doings in London*. Ex sense 1 (the very devil for the sharped). 3. Time personified: C.18. Ned Ward (1703): cited by W. Matthews.

old gentleman's bed-posts. A variant (—1874) of DEVIL'S BED-POSTS.

old geyser. i.e. *old geezer*: see GEESER.

old girl or gal. A wife; a mother: resp. low (—1887) > respectable coll, and, from ca 1895, low s. that has remained such. Baumann (*my old girl*, my wife); *The Idler*, June 1892 (*the old gal*, wife). cf. OLD WOMAN.

old gooseberry. The devil: low: from ca 1790. Grose, 3rd ed.; 1861, H. Kingsley in *Ravenshoe*; ob. App. orig. only in the next entry. 2. Hence (?), wife: low London (—1909).

old gooseberry, play (up). To play the devil: coll: from ca 1790; ob. H. Kingsley, 1865, 'Lay on like old gooseberry.'

old gown. Smuggled tea: low: from ca 1860; ob.

old grabem pudden. Old woman – whether wife or mother: rhyming s.: since ca 1870.

old hag, the. The matron: Preparatory Schools': late C.19–20. cf. HAG.

old hand. An experienced person; an expert: coll: 1785, Grose. See OLD, adj., 1. cf. OLD BIRD, DOG, FILE, SOLDIER, STAGER. 2. An ex-convict: c. (mostly Australian): 1861, T. McCombie, *Australian Sketches*. 3. *The Old Hand*: a coll nickname for Gladstone from 1886 until his death.

Old Harridan, the. Fortune personified: C.18. Ned Ward, 1700.

old Harry. The devil: coll: from ca 1740; ob. cf. *by the Lord* HARRY!, 1687, Congreve. 2. In B.E.: 'A Composition used by Vintners, when they bedevil their Wines', which explains the semantics.

old Harry, play. To play the devil: coll: 1837, Marryat, 'They've played old Harry with the rigging.' cf. OLD GOOSEBERRY,

PLAY. Ex preceding entry. H.'s etymology (*old hairy*) is very ingenious: but, I fear, nothing more.

old Harvey. The large boat (launch) of a man-of-war: nautical: from ca 1850; ob.

old hat. The female pudend: low: from late C.17: Fielding; Grose, 'Because frequently felt'. Ob.

old horney (horny) or **Hornington.** The penis: low: C.18–20; ob. cf. the indelicate sense of HORN and *Miss* HORNER, the female pudend. 2. The devil (only with *horney* or *horny*): see HORNY.

old horse; also **salt horse.** Salt junk: nautical: from ca 1858. 2. (Also and esp. *old hoss.*) A coll vocative: orig. U.S., 'but now in common use here among friends', H., 5th ed.

Old Horse, the, see HORSE, n., 5.

old house on or over one's head, bring an. To get into trouble: from ca 1575 (ob.): coll till C.19, then proverbial S.E. Gascoigne; Sedley.

old huddle and twang. App. a coll intensive of *old huddle*, a miserly old person: ca 1575–1640. Both are in Lyly, 1579. cf. OLD FILE.

old identity, see IDENTITY.

old image. A very staid person: coll: 1888, 'Rolf Boldrewood', 'You're a regular old image, Jim, says she'; slightly ob. ?ex *graven image*.

old iron. Shore clothes; *work up* (i.e. refurbish) *old iron,* to go ashore: nautical: C.19–20, ob. Ex the re-painting of rusted iron. cf. CLOBBER.

old jacker. A senior boy retained to show the youngsters the ropes: training-ships': late C.19–20; ob.

old Jamaica. The sun: nautical rhyming s.: late C.19–20. Abbr. *old Jamaica rum.*

old lad. A coll vocative: late C.16–20. See OLD, adj., 4.

old lady. A term of address to a woman come down in the world: low (—1823); †by 1900. 2. A card broader than the rest: cardsharpers' c.: 1828, G. Smeeton. See OLD GENTLEMAN. 3. The female pudend: low: C.19–20. cf. OLD MAN, n., 1. 4. One's wife or mother: coll: from late C.18. Mostly U.S.

Old Lady of Threadneedle Street, the. The Bank of England: coll: 1797, Gilray; *Punch*, 1859, 'The girl for my money. The old lady of Threadneedle Street'. Ex its position in London, its age, and its preciseness.

old lag, see LAG, n., 6.

old ling. The same as OLD HAT: low: mid-C.18–mid-19.

old man. The penis: low: C.19–20. cf. OLD LADY, 3, and OLD WOMAN, 4. 2. The captain of a merchant or a passenger ship: from ca 1820; orig. U.S.; anglicized ca 1860. W. Clark Russell, *Sailors' Language*, 1883. 3. Whence, the officer in charge of a battalion: military: C.20. 4. A husband: low (also jocular) coll: 1768, Sterne; 1848, Thackeray; 1856, Whyte-Melville. 5. A father: low coll: 1792, U.S.; 1834, British. cf. OLD WOMAN, 2. 6. A coll vocative: 1885, *Punch*, 24 Aug. cf. OLD BOY, CHAP, FELLOW. 7. A full-grown male kangaroo: Australian coll: 1827, Peter Cunningham, *Two Years in New South Wales*; J. Brunton Stephens, 'The aboriginal corruption is *wool-man.*' 8. A master, a BOSS (2): late C.19–20: s. ?orig. U.S. 9. 'The ridge between two sleepers in a feather bed', F. & H.: low (—1890). 10. A blanket for wrapping up a baby or young child: nurses': late C.19–20.

old-man, adj. Large; larger than usual: Australian coll: 1845, R. Howitt; slightly ob. Ex the kangaroo: see preceding entry sense 7. cf. PICCANINNY, adj.

old man's milk. Whisky: low coll: from ca 1860; ob. (Different in dial.)

old mother Hubbard, that's. That's incredible: non-aristocratic c.p. of ca 1880–1910. Ex the nursery-rhyme.

old moustache. An elderly vigorous man with grey moustache: lower classes': ca 1880–1914.

***old Mr Goree** or **Gory.** A gold coin: mid-C.17–early 19: c. >, ca 1750, s. Perhaps ex the bright colour; ?cognate with Romany *gorishi*, a shilling, ex Turkish *ghrush*; most prob., however, ex the place (*Goree*).

old Mr Grim. Death: coll: C.18–mid-19. cf. OLD FLOORER.

old Nick. The devil: coll: 1668, L'Estrange. (The date of F. & H.'s earlier record is suspect.) Suspect also is 'Hudibras' Butler's etymology: 'Nick Machiavel had no such trick, | Though he gave's name to our Old Nick.' Often abbr. to *Nick.* Certainly ex *Nicholas*, perhaps influenced by Ger. *Nickel*, a goblin. cf. OLD HARRY; see OLD, adj., last sense. 2. See BOY WITH THE BOOTS.

old one, often spelt **old 'un.** The devil: C.11–20: S.E. until C.18, then coll; ob. See OLD, adj., 7. 2. A quizzical familiar term of address: coll (—1811); slightly ob.

3. Hence, one's father: coll: 1836, Dickens. (Like preceding senses, with *the.*) 4. Hence, the pantaloon (who was gen. the fool's father): theatrical: from ca 1850; ob. 5. A horse more than three years old: from ca 1860: racing coll > S.E. 6. The headmaster: Public Schools': late C.19–20.

old oyster. A low vocative: from ca 1890; ob. Milliken, 1892, 'Life don't want lifting, old oyster,' which puns the Shakespearean tag.

old palaver, see PALAVER, n., 1.

old paste-horn. (Gen. a nickname for) a large-nosed man: mostly shoemakers': from ca 1856; ob. See PASTE-HORN and cf. CONKEY.

old peg(g). 'Poor Yorkshire cheese, made of skimmed milk', Grose, 1st ed.: late C.18–mid-19 coll, C.18–19 dial. ?because hard and dry.

old pelt. 'Applied to old and worn-out pressmen – referring to the old ink pelts used in olden times by these individuals for distributing the ink' (B. & L.): printers': mid-C.19–20; ob.

old pharaoh. A variation of PHARAOH: late C.17–early 19. G. Meriton.

old plug, see PLUG, n., 3.

old poker; Old Poker. The devil: coll: 1784, Walpole, 'As if old Poker was coming to take them away'. Perhaps 'he who pokes', but more prob. *poker* = hobgoblin, demon (cf. *Puck*, and Irish *pooka*): if the latter, then S.E. until C.19, then coll, after ca 1830, mainly U.S.; except in U.S., †by 1880. cf. *by the holy* POKER, which it may have suggested.

old pot. An old man: late C.19–20: see OLD, adj., 4 and 6, and POT, 6 and 13. 2. **the old pot,** one's father: low: late C.19–20; ob. P. H. Emerson.

old pot and pan. OLD MAN = husband, father; occ. OLD WOMAN = wife, woman: mid-C.19–20 rhyming s.

old put, see PUT, 2.

old rip, see RIP. 2. An old prostitute showing signs of age: low: late C.19–20.

old Robin. An experienced person: coll: ca 1780–1830. J. Potter, 1784. cf. OLD BIRD, HAND, SOLDIER, STAGER. See OLD, adj., 1.

old Roger. The devil: coll: ca 1720–1840. cf. OLD HARRY; OLD NICK. 2. The pirates' flag: 1723; by 1785, replaced by *jolly* ROGER.

***Old Ruffin.** An early C.19 form of RUFFIN, the devil: c. Ainsworth.

old salt. An experienced sailor: nautical coll: C.19–20. See OLD, adj., 1.

old scratch or **O— S—.** The devil: low coll: 1740; Smollett; Trollope. In late C.19–20, mostly dial. See also SCRATCH.

old shaver. See SHAVER. cf. the more gen. *young shaver*.

old shell. An old (sailing-ship) sailor: nautical: mid-C.19–20; ob. Ex S.E. *shell-back*.

***old shoe.** Good luck: c.: C.19. 'Prob. alluding to shoes and slippers thrown at a newly married couple' (B. & L.).

old shoes. Rum: low: late C.19–20; ob. Why?

old shoes (occ. boots), ride in (or more gen., **wear) another man's.** To marry, or to keep, another man's mistress: coll: C.19–20; ob.

old shoes! up again! 'No rest for the wicked!': semi-proverbial coll (—1887); ob.

old shopkeeper, see SHOPKEEPER.

old shovel penny. 'The paymaster, who is generally an ancient' (Ware): military (—1909).

old six. Old ale at sixpence a quart: proletarian: ca 1860–1914.

old soldier. An experienced, esp. if crafty, man: coll: 1722, Defoe, 'The Captain [was] an old soldier at such work.' See OLD, adj., 1. cf. COME THE OLD SOLDIER. Contrast: 2. A simple fellow, gen. in the proverbial *an old soldier, an old innocent*: mid-C.19–20; very ob. R. L. Stevenson in *St Ives*, 1894. 3. An old quid of tobacco; a cigar-end: low: late C.19–20. 4. One who can drink for three days on end (—1650). 5. See *old* SOLDIER, 2.

old-soldier, v. To COME THE OLD SOLDIER over (a person): coll: 1892. cf.:

old soldier, fight the. To shirk duty; sham sick: nautical: early C.19. John Davis, *The Post Captain*, 1805. i.e. like an OLD SOLDIER.

old son. My fine fellow: my dear chap: Australian coll: from ca 1870; ob.

old split-foot. The devil: low jocular: ?orig. U.S. (Lowell, 1848); very ob.

old sport. A coll term of address: 1905. Ex *sport*, a good fellow.

old square-toes. A coll nickname for a pedantic, old-fashioned man: from ca 1860; ob. *Sun*, 28 Dec. 1864. 2. But *square-toes* appears as early as 1785 for 'one's father' or 'father'; †by 1860.

old stager. A very experienced person: coll: 1711, Shaftesbury, whence we see that the term was orig. applied to travellers by stage-coach; the gen. sense was well established by 1788. 2. See OLD STICKER.

old stander. A naval seaman transferring from ship to ship as his captain is transferred: naval coll: C.18–mid-19, Bowen virtually implies. cf. last entry.

old stick. A pejorative applied to a person (cf. STICK, n., 3): coll: C.19–20; ob. See OLD, adj., 6. cf. next entry. 2. A complimentary vocative: ca 1800–70. Halliwell. cf. OLD, adj., 4.

old stick in the mud. (In vocative and reference) a very staid person: coll: from ca 1820. Moncrieff, 1823, *Tom and Jerry*.

old sticker. Army officers' s. of ca 1810–50, as in John L. Gardner, *The Military Sketch-Book*, 1827, '"Good-tempered Old Stagers" and "Old Stickers", meaning thereby that they can "go" at the bottle, and "stick" at the table till "all's blue".'

old strike-a-light. One's father: ca 1850–60. Ex his exclamation on being asked for loans.

old stripes, see STRIPES.

old sweat. An old soldier, esp. of the Regular Army: military: from ca 1890. Ex his strenuous efforts. cf. OLD SOLDIER.

Old Tay Bridge. A middle-aged lady bank-clerk: bank-clerks' nickname: late C.19–20. The old bridge across the Firth of Tay at Dundee was blown down in 1879.

old thing (Old or **Ould Thing, the).** The language of the Irish tinkers: those tinkers' (—1891). O.E.D. at *Shelta*. 2. Female pudend: lower classes': mid-C.19–20 (perhaps very much earlier). Orig., euphemistic. 3. Beef and DAMPER (7): Australian coll: ca 1845–80. Prob. ex '—, the same old thing!'

old-timer. One given to praising old times: coll: 1860, *Music and Drama*; ob. Mostly U.S. 2. One long established in place or position: from ca 1810: coll.

old toast. The devil: low: C.19–20; ob. Occ. *old toaster*, likewise ob. (cf. the U.S. *old smoker*.) Prob. ex: 2. 'A brisk old fellow', Grose, 1st ed.: c. or low s.: ca 1690–1830.

old Tom. Gin; esp. very good strong gin; low: from ca 1820; ob. Brewer's etymology ex one Thomas Chamberlain, a brewer of gin, may be correct.

old trout. A C.19–20 survival, now slightly ob., of *trout*, a dowdy woman.

old truepenny, see TRUEPENNY. **old 'un,** see OLD ONE.

old whale. An old sailing-ship seaman: nautical: from ca 1860; ob.

old whip, see WHIP, OLD.

old whiskers. A cheeky boys' salute to a working-man whose whiskers are a little wild and iron-grey: mid-C.19–20. Ware.

old wigsby. A crotchety, narrow-minded, elderly man: middle classes' coll: C.19–20; ob. Ware. cf. Fr. *perruque*.

old wives' Paternoster, the. 'The devil's paternoster', i.e. a grumbling and complaining: coll: ca 1575–1620. H. G. Wright, 1580, 'He plucking his hatte about his eares, mumbling the olde wives' Paternoster, departed.'

old woman. A wife: low (except when jocular) coll: 1823, 'Jon Bee'. cf. OLD MAN, 3. 2. A mother: low coll: orig. (1834), U.S.; anglicized ca 1850. cf. OLD GIRL. 3. A prisoner who, unfit for hard work, is put to knitting stockings: prison c.: from ca 1860. 4. The female pudend: low: C.19–20. cf. OLD MAN, 1.

old woman's poke. A shuffling of cards by the juxtaposed insertion of the two halves of the pack: card-players' coll (—1887).

olds. Old persons; old members of a set, class, etc.: coll: 1883, Besant, 'Young clever people . . . are more difficult to catch than the olds.'

oldster. The nautical sense (a midshipman of four years' service) is j. 2. An elderly or an experienced person: coll: 1848, Dickens in *Dombey and Son*. On YOUNGSTER.

olive-branch. A contemporaneous synonym of RAINBOW.

olive oil! *Au revoir!*: 1884, orig. music-halls'; ob.

***Oliver; occ. oliver.** The moon: c.: ca 1780–1900; nearly †by 1860. Esp. in *Oliver is up* or *O. whiddles*, the moon shines, and *O. is in town*, the nights are moonlight. Ainsworth, in *Rookwood* (1834), has 'Oliver puts his black night-cap on,' hides behind clouds. Perhaps *Oliver* was coined in derision of Oliver Cromwell: cf. OLIVER'S SKULL. 2. Among tramps conversant with Romany, *Olivers* (rare in singular) are stockings: from before 1887. 3. A fist: abbr. (—1909) of rhyming s. *Oliver Twist*.

Oliver Twist. See OLIVER, 3. (Mid-C.19–20; ob.)

Oliver's skull. A chamber-pot: low: ca 1690–1870; ob. by 1820.

oll. All: (dial. and) low coll: C.19–20.

ollapod. A (gen. country) apothecary: coll: ca 1802–95. Ex George Colman's *The*

Poor Gentleman, 1802. (Sp. *olla podrida*; lit., putrid pot.)

'oller, boys, 'oller! A collar: rhyming s.: late C.19–20.

***olli compolli.** 'The by-name of one of the principal Rogues of the Canting Crew', B.E.: c.: late C.17–mid-19. What was his role, unless he were, perchance, the JACK-OF-ALL-TRADES? And what the etymology of this rhymed fabrication unless on *olio*?

olly, olly! An invitation to a schoolfellow to play with one or to accompany one on an errand; occ., a term of farewell: Cockney children's: from ca 1870. Perhaps ex *ho there!* or ex Fr. *aller* – or ex both.

***omee; omer; omey; homee, homey.** A man; esp. a master, e.g. a landlord: c. and Parlary (>, in late C.19, also gen. theatrical): from ca 1840. Ex It. *homo* via Lingua Franca. See quotation at PARKER. 2. Hence, an inferior actor: theatrical: since ca 1890.

omnes. A mixture of odds and ends of various wines: wine-merchants' (—1909). Ex ALLS, L. *omnes* meaning all.

omni gatherum; or as one word. A variant of OMNIUM GATHERUM.

omnibus. The female pudend: low: from ca 1840. 2. A harlot: low: ca 1850–1910. Available 'to all'.

omnium(-)gatherum; also **o. getherum,** C.17; **o. githerum,** C.16. A mixed assemblage of things or persons: coll: 1530. Mock L. ending added to *gather*. 2. Hence a medley dance popular in mid-C.17: coll. 3. Omnium (in S.E. sense): coll: ca 1770–95.

omnium gatherum, adv. Confusedly, promiscuously: mid-C.17: coll. Ex preceding.

on, adj. Concupiscent: low coll: C.18–20; ob. Halliwell. 2. Whence, ready and willing: coll: from ca 1870. e.g. *are you on?*, are you agreed, prepared, willing? 3. Whence, fond of: 1890, L. C. O'Doyle, 'Woddell was not much on beer': coll. 4. No: back s. (—1859). e.g. ON DOOG, no good. 5. Tipsy: low, esp. public-house: C.19–20. Gen. *a bit on*. Perhaps ex *on the* BOOZE. 6. Present; nearby; likely to appear: Winchester Coll.: from ca 1830; ob. ?ex *on view*.

on, adv. or adv.-adj. Having money at stake, a wager on (something): from ca 1810: racing coll until ca 1885, then S.E. *Sporting Magazine*, 1812; *Standard*, 23 Oct. 1873, 'Everyone ... had something on.' Since ca 1870, gen. *have a bit on*, as in George Moore's *Esther Waters*: this phrase is coll. 2. Hence, standing or bound to win: racing (—1874) > gen. coll. 'You're on a quid if Kaiser wins,' H., 5th ed.

on phrases: see the key words.

on, hot, see HOT ON.

on and off, n. Lemonade on tap: Tonbridge: late C.19–20.

on at, be. To nag (someone); reprove constantly: Australian coll: late C.19–20. cf. GO ON ABOUT.

on doog. No good: 1851, Mayhew, I. Back sl.

once. Energy, vigour; impudence: low: 1886, *Referee*, 24 Oct., 'I like Shine – I cannot help admiring the large amount he possesses of what is vulgarly called "once"'; virtually †. Ware, 'The substantivising of "on" – most emphatic.'

once, in. First time; at the first attempt: low coll: late C.19–20. G. R. Sims, 1900, 'You've guessed it in once, father.' cf. S.E. *in one*.

once a week. A magistrate: rhyming s. (on BEAK): mid-C.19–20.

once-a-week man; or **Sunday promenader.** A man in debt: London: ca 1825–40. Egan, *Real Life in London*. Sunday was the one day on which he could not be arrested for debt.

once aboard the lugger and the girl is mine! A jocular c.p. late C.19–20. Ben Landeck, *My Jack and Dorothy*, a melodrama produced at the Elephant and Castle theatre. ca 1889–90.

once before we fill and once before we light. A drinking c.p. recorded by Ned Ward in 1709.

oncer. A person in the habit of attending church only once on a Sunday: coll: from ca 1890. cf. TWICER, 2.

onces. Wages: artisans' (—1909); ob. Ex *once a week*.

oncoming. (Of women.) Sexually responsive: coll: late C.19–20.

one. Oneself; one's own interest: coll: 1567, R. Edwards, 'I can help one: is not that a good point of philosophy'; †by 1830. In C.19–20, NUMBER ONE. 2. A grudge; a score; a blow, kiss, etc.: 1830, Galt, 'I owed him one': s. >, ca 1890, coll. 3. A lie: late C.19–20: s. Esp. 'That's a big one!'

one, a. A very odd or amusing person: from ca 1905. 'He's a one!'

one a-piece, see. To see double: coll: 1842, *Punch* (ii, 21); ob.

one and a peppermint drop. A one-eyed person: low London (—1909).

one and elevenpence three farden. Garden; pardon: rhyming s.: since ca 1870.

one-and-thirty. Drunk: semi-proverbial coll: mid-C.17–18. Ray. Ex the scoring of full points at the old English game of one-and-thirty.

one and t'other. Brother: rhyming s.: late C.19–20.

one-armed landlord. A pump: Somersetshire s. (—1903) rather than dial. Ex the cheapness of water compared with beer.

one better, go. To do better, to SCORE: from ca 1890: s. *Spectator*, 7 May 1892. Ex play at cards.

one-bite. (Gen. pl.) A small, sour apple – thrown away after being tested with one bite: costers': from ca 1870.

one consecutive night. A c.p. denoting 'enough': Society and theatrical: 1890, *Daily News*, 15 Aug.

one-drink house. A public-house where only one drink is served within (say) an hour: coll of London lower classes: ca 1860–1905.

one-er, †onener, oner, wunner. A person, a thing, of great parts, remarkable (e.g. a notable lie), most attractive, dashing; an expert: 1840, Dickens, 'Miss Sally's such a one-er for that, she is'; 1857, Hughes, *wunner*; 1861, Dutton Cook, *onener* (pron. *wun-ner*); 1862, Thackeray, *oner*. Perhaps *oner* is ex *one*, something unique, influenced – as W. suggests – by dial. *wunner*, a wonder. (cf. ONE, A.) 2. Esp. a knock-out blow: 1861, Dutton Cook, as above. 3. Something consisting of, indicated by, characteristic of or by, '1': coll: 1889 (of cricket). Esp. of one church-going a day. 4. Esp. a shilling: low: late C.19–20; ob. 5. A clay marble all of one colour: London schoolchildren's: from ca 1880. Opp. TWOER, 4.

one five. Hand: low: ca 1860–1910.

one for his nob, see NOB, ONE FOR HIS.

one hand for yourself and one for the ship! Be careful: a nautical c.p. (C.19–20) addressed to a youngster going aloft.

one-horse. Insignificant; very small: coll: orig. (1854), U.S.; anglicized – mostly in the Colonies – ca 1885. Goldwin Smith, 1886, 'Canada has been saddled with one-horse universities.'

one in, adj. 'Hearing another's good fortune and wishing the same to oneself', F. & H.: tailors': from ca 1870. Contrast ONE OUT.

one in ten. A parson: coll: late C.17–19. Ex *tithe*.

one in the box, have. To be pregnant: lower classes': late C.19–20.

one in the eye. A misfortune, a set-back, a snub, an insult: late C.19–20. G. R. Sims, 1900, 'It was . . . "one in the eye" for her aunt.'

one-legged donkey. The single-legged stool which the old coastguard was allowed for purposes of rest, designed to capsize the moment he drowsed off: nautical: C.19.

one lordship is worth all his manners. A C.17 c.p. punning *manors*.

one nick or **nitch.** A male child, TWO NICK (*nitch*) being a baby girl: printers': from ca 1860. Ex an anatomical characteristic.

one o'clock, like, see LIKE A . . .

one of my cousins. A harlot: coll: late C.17–early 19. Ex a lie frequently told by the amorous-vagrant male.

one of them or **us.** A harlot: coll: resp. C.19–20 (extant only with stressed *them*); mid-C.18–mid-19. cf. ONE OF MY COUSINS. 2. (Only *one of them*.) A shilling: urban lower classes' (—1909).

one of those, I (really) must have. A non-aristocratic c.p. of ca 1880–3. Ex a comic song.

one on (him, you, etc.)!, that's. That is a point against you!: coll: late C.19–20.

one out, adj. I'm lucky!: tailors': from ca 1870. Contrast ONE IN. cf.:

one out of it! I'm keeping out of this!: tailors': from ca 1870.

one side to his mouth, on. (Of a horse) that feels the bit on only one side of his mouth: turf coll: from ca 1850.

one two, preceded by **a, his, the,** etc. Two blows in rapid succession: boxing coll: from ca 1820. Egan, 'Belcher . . . distinguished for his one two'.

one-two; or the old one-two. Male masturbation: low, mostly Cockney: late C.19–20.

one under the arm. An additional job: tailors': from ca 1870; ob. Ex things carried comfortably under the arm.

one up, have. To be a second lieutenant or a lance-corporal: Army coll: late C.19–20.

one or a marble (up)on another's taw, I'll be! I'll get even with him some time!: low: ca 1810–50.

one with t'other, the. Sexual intercourse: low: C.17–18. Anon. song, *Maiden's Delight*, 1661, in Farmer's *Merry Songs and Ballads*, 1897.

onee. One: low theatrical: from ca 1850; ob. Influenced by Parlary.

onener, oner, see ONE-ER.

one's eye. A hiding-place for CABBAGE: tailors': from ca 1850; ob.

***onicker.** A harlot: c.: from ca 1880; ob. Walford's *Antiquarian*, 1887. cf. ONE NICK.

***onion.** A seal, gen. in pl. *bunch of onions*: c.: 1811, *Lex. Bal.*; ob. Esp. if worn on a ribbon or a watch-chain; occ. applied to other objects there worn. Ex the shape. 2. The head, esp. in *off his onion*, crazy: from ca 1890: low. Ex the shape.

onion, it may serve with an. An ironical C.17 c.p. Howell.

onion, off one's, see ONION, **2.**

***onion-hunter.** A thief of seals worn on ribbons, etc.: c.: 1811. See ONION, 1.

onions, give (someone). To strike; assault, PITCH INTO: *Sessions*, Nov. 1874; †by 1910. Ex their strong smell or ex their tendency to make one's eyes water.

onker. A sailing-ship on the Baltic timber trade: Thames-side: late C.19–20. Ex the interminable *onk-urr onk-urr* of the windmill pumps carried by these old ships, many of them since to be broken up.

oodles. A large quantity, esp. of money: orig. U.S.; anglicized ca 1890. *Overland Monthly*, 1869 (iii, 131), 'A Texan never has a great quantity of anything, but he has "scads" of it or oodles or dead oodles or scadoodles or "swads".' Prob. ex (*the whole*) *boodle* (O. W. Holmes), with which cf. CABOODLE.

oof, ooftish. Money: low: resp. from ca 1880; from ca 1870 (and ob.). *Sporting Times*, 26 Dec. 1891, 'Ooftish was, some twenty years ago, the East End [Yiddish] synonym for money, and was derived from [Ger.] *auf tische* [properly *auf dem tische*], "on the table", because one refused to play cards for money unless the cash were on the table'. cf. PLANK, 3.

oof-bird. A source, gen. a supplier, of money: 1888. Ex preceding on *the golden goose*. Whence *the feathered oof-bird*, (a supplier, a source of) money in plenty.

oof-bird walk, make the. To circulate money: low: from ca 1888; ob.

oofless. Poor; temporarily without cash: from ca 1889. See OOF. Contrast OOFY.

ooftish, see OOF.

oofy. Rich; (always) with plenty of cash: low: from ca 1889. See OOF.

oolfoo. A fool: low: late C.19–20. By transposition and addition. Also *oolerfer*: centre s.: from ca 1860.

oons; occ. **oun(e)s.** A coll variation, late C.16–20 (very ob.), of 'ZOUNDS.

ooperzootics. An unspecified complaint: s. Chorus of a popular song about 1890:

Father's got 'em, Father's got 'em,
He's got the ooperzootics on the brain,
He's running round the houses
Without his shirt and trousis,
Father's got 'em coming on again.

oops-a-daisy! A c.p. of consolation as one picks up a child that has fallen: late (?mid) C.19–20.

opaque. Dull; stupid: London: ca 1818–40. (Adumbrates *dim.*)

open-air. An open-air meeting: Salvation Army's coll: 1884.

open arse. A medlar: C.11–20: S.E. till ca 1660, then low coll till ca 1820, then dial. Grose, 1st ed. (at *medlar*), cites a C.18–early 19 c.p.: (*it is*) *never ripe till it is rotten as a t—d, and then* (*it is*) *not worth a f—t.* 2. Hence, a harlot: C.17–mid-18. Davies, *The Scourge of Folly*, ca 1618, puns thus on *meddler*, *medlar*: 'Kate still exclaimes against great medlers . . . I muse her stomacke now so much shoulde faile | To loath a medler, being an open-tail.' See also OPEN UP.

open c or **C.** The female pudend: low: C.19–20; ob. (?orig. printers'.)

open house, keep, see KEEP OPEN HOUSE.

open lower-deckers. To use bad language: naval: late C.18–mid-19. Bowen, 'The heaviest guns were mounted on the lower decks.'

open one's mouth too wide. To bid for more than one can pay for: from ca 1880. Stock Exchange.

open the ball, see BALL, OPEN THE.

open to. To tell, or admit, to (a person): London lower classes': 1895, *People*, 6 Jan., 'I knew then that Selby had got a bit more [money] than he opened to me'; slightly ob.

open up, v.i. (Of a woman, sexually) to spread: low coll bordering on S.E.: mid-C.19–20. Ex S.E. sense, to become open to view. cf. the rare C.17 *open-tail*, a harlot, a light woman, and OPEN ARSE.

opera buffer. An actor in opera bouffe: theatrical: 1888; ob. Punning *opera-bouffe*.

opera house. A workhouse: C.19. Ex L. *opera*, work. 2. A guard-room; detention-quarters or -cells: military: from the 1890s.

operation. A patch, esp. in trousers-seat: tailors' (—1909).

operator. A pickpocket: coll bordering on

S.E.: C.18–mid-C.19. Ex the †S.E. sense, one who lives by fraudulent operations.

opposite, n. The saloon bar: public-house coll: late C.19–20. *Opposite* the less 'superior' bar.

opt. The best scholar: schools' (—1887). Abbr. L. *optimus*.

optic. (Gen. in pl.) An eye: C.17–20: S.E. till ca 1880, then jocular coll. *Licensed Victuallers' Gazette*, 10 April 1891, 'A deep cut under the dexter optic'.

or out goes the gas! A c.p. threat to put an end to whatever is going on: ca 1880–1905.

or something. A vague, final tag, either to avoid full details or explanation or because the speaker doesn't know: coll: late C.19–20.

***oracle.** A watch: C.18 c. or low s. Swift, 'Pray, my lord, what's o'clock by your oracle?' Prob. S.E. *oracle* influenced by L. *hora* (cf. Romany *ora*, hour, watch). 2. The female pudend: low: C.18–20. Gen. HAIRY ORACLE.

oracle, work the. To raise money: from ca 1820. J. Newman, *Scamping Tricks*, 1891. Hence, 2, to contrive, a robbery: c. (—1887) ex S.E. sense, to obtain one's end by (gen. underhand) means. 3. **work the double, dumb,** or **hairy oracle,** (gen. of the man) to copulate: low: C.19 (?earlier)–20; ob.

orange. The female pudend: Restoration period.

orange dry, squeeze or **suck the.** To exhaust, drain, deplete: late C.17–20 (*squeeze* > † ca 1860): S.E. until ca 1880, then coll.

orate. To hold forth, 'speechify': C.17–20: S.E. till ca 1830, then lapsed until ca 1865, when, under the influence of U.S. (where still serious), it was revived as a jocular term.

oration, v.i. To make a speech: coll: from ca 1630; slightly ob. J. Done, 1633, 'They . . . had marvailous promptitude . . . for orationing.'

oration, n. A noisy disturbance; a clamour, a din: low: ca 1820–60. 'She kicked up such an oration,' *Sessions*, 1833. By a confusion of *uproar* and *oratorio* and *oration*.

oration box. The head: ca 1815–60. *Spy*, II, 1826.

orchard. The female pudend: low: C.19–20; ob. See JACK IN . . .

orchestra; in full **orchestra stalls.** Testicles: rhyming s.: late C.19–20. On BALLS.

orchid. A titled member of the Stock Exchange: from ca 1880. Because decorative.

order, a large. An excessive demand or requirement: *Pall Mall Gazette*, 24 July 1884, '. . . An agreeable piece of slang, a very large order.'

order of the . . ., the. e.g. . . . *of the* BATH, a bath; . . . *of the* BOOT, a kick, a violent dismissal; . . . *of the* PUSH (5), a dismissal. All are coll and essentially middle-class; from ca 1880. Perhaps suggested by such *knight* mock-titles as KNIGHT OF THE *pigskin*, a jockey.

order of the day, the. The most usual thing to do, think, etc., at a given period: coll: from ca 1790. Arthur Young, 1792.

***order-racket.** The obtaining of goods from a shopkeeper by false money or false pretence: ca 1810–70. See RACKET.

ordinar'. Ordinary: lower-class coll: mid-C.19–20. (Nevinson, 1895.) Also in Scottish: in England, until C.19, it was S.E.

ordinary. A wife: low coll: C.19–20; ob. cf. OLD DUTCH.

ordinary, adj. Ordinary-looking, plain: from ca 1740: S.E. till ca 1880, then coll and (esp. in Cambridgeshire) dial. *Knowledge*, 10 Aug. 1883.

ordinary, out of the. Unusual: coll: late C.19–20. (cf. the etymologically equivalent *extraordinary*.)

organ. A pipe: ca 1780–1850. Hence, *cock one's organ*, smoke a pipe. Presumably ex the resemblance to an organ-pipe. 2. A clothes' trunk: Scottish servants': C.19–20; ob. 3. A workman lending money to his fellows at very high interest: printers': from ca 1860. Hence, *play the organ*, to apply for such a loan, and, among soldiers, *want the organ*, to be trying to borrow money.

organ, carry the. To shoulder the pack at defaulters' or at marching-order drill: military: ca 1870–1910.

organ, want the, see ORGAN, 3.

organ-pipe. The wind-pipe, the throat; hence the voice: low s. > coll: from ca 1850; slightly ob. Ex the shape and purpose of both. 2. In pl it was, ca 1840–90, used among boxers for the nostrils, as in Augustus Mayhew, *Paved With Gold*, 1857.

or noko, pron. *orinoker*. A poker: rhyming s. (—1857); ob. 2. A variant of ORONOKO.

orlop, demons of the. Midshipmen and junior officers: naval jocular coll (—1887); virtually †.

ornary, ornery. Ordinary: illiterate coll (and dial.): C.19–20. Contrast the American sense: unpleasant, intractable, bad-tempered, etc.

ornicle. A policeman, magistrate, or anyone in authority: showmen's: from ca 1870. Oracle? as having the last word.

ornithorhynchus. A creditor: Australian: ca 1895–1915. i.e. a duck-billed platypus: F. & H. explain as 'a beast with a bill'.

Oronoko. Tobacco: 1703, Ned Ward. Rare. Perhaps influenced by Mrs Aphra Behn's *Oroonoko, or The Royal Slave*, 1688.

orphan collar. A collar unsuitable to the shirt with which it is worn: jocular (—1902). Orig. U.S.

orts of, see OUTS OF. **oschive,** see OCHIVE.

Oscar. A male homosexual: coll: late C.19–20. Ex Oscar Wilde.

ossifer, see OCCIFER.

ossy. Horsey (adj.): 1881, Earl Grenville.

ostiarius. A prefect doing, in rotation, special duty, e.g. keeping order: Winchester College coll or j.: C.19–20. Revived by Dr Moberly ca 1866. L. *ostiarius*, a door-keeper. 'The official title for the Second Master', Mansfield, 1866; ob.

ostler. An oat-stealer: late C.18–mid-19. I suspect that this is rather a Grose (1st ed.) pun than, except jocularly, an actual usage. cf. OAT-STEALER.

other thing!, if he doesn't like it he may do the. i.e. LUMP (3) it, or go to hell: coll (—1887).

otherguess. Different: from ca 1630: S.E. until ca 1820, then coll and dial. cf. †S.E. *othergates*.

otomy; occ. **ottomy.** A C.18–19 form of the dial. and (low) coll ATOMY. Swift, Grose, Ainsworth. Whence OTTOMIZE.

otter. A sailor: C.18–20; very ob. *Street Robberies Consider'd*. 2. n. and adj.; also *otto*. Eight: occ. eightpence: Parlary and costers' s.: from ca 1850. Ex It. *otto*, via Lingua Franca. P. H. Emerson, 1893, 'I'll take otto soldi.'

otto, see OTTER, 2.

ottomize. To anatomize: mid-C.18–mid-19: low coll. Ex OTOMY.

ottomy, see OTOMY.

ought. Nought (a cipher): sol. and dial.: from ca 1840. Dickens, 1844, '"Three score and ten", said Chuffey, "ought and carry seven".' Prob. ex *a nought* > *an ought*. Hence, *oughts and crosses*, a children's game: 1861, Sala.

ould. Old: low coll (and dial.): C.19–20.

***ounce.** A crown (coin): c. of ca 1720–1830. Silver being formerly estimated at five shillings an ounce.

'ounds. A coll form of *wounds* (e.g. God's wounds): C.18. cf. 'ZOUNDS.

our – –. A familiar way of referring to a member of one's family: Cockney, Northern and Scottish coll: C.19–20.

ourick. A Gentile (gen. pl): pejorative Jewish coll: late C.19–20. Ex Yiddish.

ourn. Ours: mid-C.17–20: dial. and low coll. Partly ex †S.E. *our(e)n*, our; partly ex *our* on *mine*. cf. HERN; HISN; YOURN.

Our Venerable Aunt. The R.C. Church: Protestants': since ca 1870. Punning *Mother* Church. Also HOLY AUNT.

out, n. (Mostly in pl.) One out of employment or (esp. political) office: 1764: coll till ca 1790, then S.E. Goldsmith, Chatterton. Ex the adj.-adv. 2. A dram-glass: public-house and low: ca 1835–1910. Dickens, in *Sketches by Boz*. These glasses are made *two-out* (half-quartern), *three-out* a (third), *four-out* (a quarter). 3. An outing or excursion; a holiday: from ca 1760: dial. and, from ca 1840, coll; very ob. as the latter. 4. An outside passenger on a coach, etc.: 1844; ob.: s. >, ca 1850, j. J. Hewlett, 1844, 'Room for two outs and an in'. 5. (Also in pl.) A loss: lower classes' coll (—1909).

out, v. To disable; knock out: *Sessions*, Aug. 1857: boxing s. Ex *to knock out*. 2. Hence, in c. to kill: 1899, *Daily News*, 11 Sept., but prob. dating from 1897 or 1898: see OUT, adj., 9. 3. See OUT IT and OUT WITH. 4. To dismiss from employment: late C.19–20.

out, adj. Unfashionable: coll or, as the O.E.D. classes it, S.E.: 1660, Pepys in *Diary*, 7 Oct., 'Long cloakes being now quite out'; ob. ?ex *go out of fashion*. 2. (Of a girl, a young woman) at work, in domestic service: coll >, ca 1890, S.E.: 1814, Jane Austen. 3. Tipsy: C.18–mid-19. ?ex *out*, astray. 4. Having been (esp. recently) presented at Court: Society coll >, ca 1890, S.E.: *The Night Watch* (I, 258), 1829, 'She has been out these two seasons.' Ex *to come out at Court*. 5. Wrong, inaccurate: coll or, as the O.E.D. holds, S.E.: mid-C.17–20. Ex *out in one's count, guess, estimate*. 6. Having a tendency to lose: s. verging on coll: from ca 1850; ob. Ex *out of luck*. 7. Not on sale: from ca 1830: market-men's coll > j. Ex *out of stock*. 8. In c.: (recently) released from gaol: from ca 1880. Ex *out of gaol*. 9. Dead: c.: 1898, Binstead, *The Pink 'Un and the*

Pelican. Ex *to knock out*. cf. OUT, v., 2. 10. See next entry, 3. 11. See OUT WITH.

out, adv. The orig. form of all the adj. senses: see preceding entry. 2. See ALL OUT. 3. In existence; one could find: coll >, ca 1905, S.E.: from ca 1856. G. A. Lawrence, 1859, 'Fanny was the worst casuist out.' ?ex *out before the world* or *out on view*.

out?, does your mother know you're. See MOTHER . . . The c.p. reply is, *Yes, she gave me a farthing to buy a monkey with! are you for sale?*

out, play at in and, see IN-AND-IN and IN-AND-OUT.

***out-and-outer.** A very determined, unscrupulous fellow: c. of ca 1810–70. Ex *out and out*, adv. 2. Hence, a person or thing perfect or thorough of its kind: from ca 1814; ob. 3. Hence, a WHACKING great lie: from ca 1830; ob. 4. A thorough-going supporter: coll: 1833; slightly ob. 5. An out-and-out possessor of some quality: coll: 1852, Thackeray. 6. A thorough scoundrel: from ca 1870. Ex sense 1. 7. A thorough bounder, an 'impossible' person: from ca 1905.

out at elbows, see ELBOWS.

out at leg. (Of cattle) feeding in hired pastures: rural coll: C.19–20; ob.

out for an airing. (Of a horse) not meant to win: the turf: *Sporting Times*, 29 June 1888. Opp. *be on the* JOB.

out it. To go out, esp. on an outing: coll: 1878, Stevenson, 'Pleasure-boats outing it for the afternoon'. Ex ob. S.E. *out*, v.i.

out of (occ. **Christ's,** but gen.) **God's blessing** (occ. **heaven's benediction,** Shakespeare in *Lear*) **into the warm sun.** From better to worse: proverbial coll: mid-C. 16–mid-19. Palsgrave, 1540, 'To leappe out of the halle into the kytchyn, or out of Christ's blessynge in to a warme sonne'; Howell; 1712, Motteux, who misunderstands it to mean 'out of the frying-pan into the fire'. Skeat derives it ex the congregation hastening, immediately after the benediction, from the church into the sun. Occ. *out of a* or *the warm sun into God's blessing*, from worse to better (Lyly).

out of collar. (Of servants) out of place: 1859, H.; †by 1910.

out of commission. Requiring work: clerks' coll (—1909).

out of flash, see FLASH, OUT OF.

out of it, the hunt, the running. Debarred; having no share, no chance; wholly ignorant: from ca 1880: coll. Ex sport.

out of print. Dead: booksellers': from ca 1820; very ob.

out of register. (Of a drunken person) walking crookedly: printers': from ca 1860. A page *out of register* is a type-area not square on page or sheet.

out of sorts, see SORTS, OUT OF.

out of the cupboard, come. To go out to work on one's first job: lower classes' (—1909).

***out of the way (for so and so).** In hiding because wanted by the police (for such and such a crime): c.: from ca 1810; ob.

***out of town.** 'Out of cash; locked up for debt', Bee: c.: ca 1810–50. Opp. IN TOWN.

***out of twig.** Reduced by poverty to the wearing of very shabby clothes: c. of ca 1810–60. Vaux, who notes *put out of twig*, to alter a stolen article beyond recognition, and *put oneself out of twig*, to disguise oneself effectually.

out or down there. Turn out or be cut (or knocked) down: boatswains' c.p. to lazy seamen: C.19.

out with. To bring out, show: coll: *Sessions*, Dec. 1783 (p. 15): 'He *out* with the knife and shewed it me.' 2. Hence, to utter, esp. unexpectedly, courageously, etc.: coll: 1870, Spurgeon, 'He outs with his lie.' 3. Gen. *be out with*, to be no longer friendly towards: (mostly nursery) coll: from before 1885.

outcry. An auction: C.17–19: †S.E. in England by ca 1800, but surviving in India as a coll until late C.19.

outface it with a card of ten, see CARD OF TEN.

outing. A pleasure-trip, an excursion: orig. (—1821), dial. >, ca 1860, coll >, ca 1905, S.E. *Sun*, 28 Dec. 1864, blames H. for omitting this term. 2. The vbl n. of OUT, v., 2.

***outing dues.** Execution (for murder): c.: late C.19–20; ob. G. R. Sims. Ex OUT, v., 2.

outrun the constable, see CONSTABLE.

outs, be (at). To quarrel; to be no longer friends: coll: C.19–20; ob.

outs, drink the three. To drink copiously: a coll c.p.: C.17. Two specific meanings: S. Ward, 1622, 'Wit out of the head, Money out of the purse, Ale out of the pot'; T. Scott, 1624, 'To drink by the dozen, by the yard, and by the bushell'.

outs, gentleman of (the) three. See GENTLEMAN OF . . . (Baumann, 1887, has *four outs*: without wit, money, credit, or good manners.)

outs of, make no. To fail to understand; misunderstand: (somewhat low) coll: C.19–20; ob. Possibly influenced by, or a corruption of, *make orts of*, to undervalue; cf. S.E. *make* (a person) *out*, to understand him.

outside. An outside passenger: 1804: coll till ca 1890, then S.E. 2. The utmost: coll: from ca 1690. Esp. in OUTSIDE, AT THE.

outside, preposition. More than, beyond: (low) coll: from before 1887. Baumann cites novelist Greenwood, 'Tuppence outside their value'.

outside, at the. At the (ut)most: from ca 1850. Esp. of number or price: e.g. 'In a few weeks, at the outside, we may expect to see ...' *Literary Gazette*, Jan. 1852. Ex OUTSIDE, n., 2.

outside!, come. Fight it out!: coll: late C.19–20. Ex lit. sense.

outside, get, see OUTSIDE (OF), GET.

outside, Eliza or **Liza!** Get out of this!: a low c.p.: from ca 1850; ob. Ware defines it as 'drunk again, Eliza' and says that it is 'applied to intoxicated, reeling women'.

outside (of), get. To eat or drink (something): from ca 1890. Also *be outside of*: same period: ob. cf. the U.S. sense, to understand. 2. (Of a woman) to coït with: low: from ca 1870.

outside of a horse. On horseback: coll, mostly Australian: 1889, 'Rolf Boldrewood'.

outside the ropes. Ignorant (of a particular matter); being merely a spectator: 1861, Lever, 'Until I came to understand ... I was always "outside the ropes".'

outside walkee. A paddle-steamer: nautical: late C.19–20. Ex pidgin: cf. INSIDE WALKEE, the reference being to the position of the motive power.

outsider. One who fails to gain admission to the ring: the turf: coll: from ca 1860. Ex *outsider*, a non-favourite horse, a sense that, despite the O.E.D., may have been coll at its inception (1857). 2. A person unfit to mix with good society: coll: from ca 1870.

***outsiders.** Nippers with semi-tubular jaws used in housebreaking: c. and j.: 1875 (O.E.D.).

outsize. A person (gen. female) rather larger than the majority: from ca 1890. Ex drapery j. The O.E.D. records it for 1894 as *rather an out size* and as S.E.; yet I believe that spelt as one word (C.20) it is to be considered coll.

outward-bounder. A ship outward-bound: nautical coll: 1884, Clark Russell.

ovate. To greet with popular applause, with an ovation: journalistic coll: 1864, Sala; *Saturday Review*, 3 May 1890, 'Mr Stanley ... was "ovated" at Dover.'

ovator. One who participates in a popular welcome (to another): journalistic coll: 1870, *Evening Standard*, 22 Oct. Like preceding, ex S.E. *ovation*.

oven. The female pudend: low: C.18–20, ob. D'Urfey. Perhaps with reference to the C.16–19 (extant in dial.) proverb, *he* (or *she*) *that has been in the oven* [as a hiding-place] *knows where to look for son, daughter*, etc. 2. A large mouth: ca 1780–1910. Ex S.E. *oven-mouth*, a wide mouth. 3. See O.V.

oven, in the same. In the same plight: low coll: C.19–20; ob.

over! A variant (—1860) of *over the* LEFT *shoulder!*, I don't believe you!

over, do. To possess a woman: low coll: C.18–20; ob.

over, get. To get the better of: coll: 1870, Hazlewood & Williams.

over-and-over. An acrobatic revolution of oneself in the air, a complete turn (or more): acrobats' coll (—1887).

over at the knees. Weak in the knees: C.19–20: stable coll.

over backs; hence **overs.** Leap-frog: resp. Cockney coll (mid-C.19–20) and Cockney s. (from ca 1890).

over-boyed. (Of a ship) officered by youths: naval coll: ?mid-C.18–mid-19.

over-day tarts. The darkened and damaged appearance about the gills and fins of a herring more than 24 hours caught: fish trade (1889). Ex the blood there extravasated and its resemblance to an overflowing jam tart.

over-eye. To watch (carefully): non-aristocratic coll: C.19–20; ob. Ex *oversee*.

over goes the show! A proletarian c.p. of ca 1870–1900 referring to a disaster or to a sudden change.

over one's time. (Of women) having passed the date on which the period should have begun: mostly feminine coll: mid-C.19–20.

over-rate it. To overdo one's part: theatrical: from ca 1860; ob.

over shoes, over boots. Completely: coll: late C.16–early 19. Shakespeare, Breton, Welsted (1726). Scott. cf. the S.E. *over head and ears*.

over the bender, see BENDER. **over the broomstick,** see BROOMSTICK, JUMP.

over the chest, see GUN. **over the coals, call over the,** see COALS.

over the door, put. To turn (someone) out into the street: coll: C.18–mid-19. cf. *give the* KEY OF THE STREET.

over the gun, see GUN, OVER THE.

over the hill. Past mid-Atlantic; occ. (of a ship) over the horizon: nautical: late C.19–20.

over the left (shoulder), see LEFT, OVER THE.

***over the letter.** (Of a partridge or a pheasant) shot before the season begins: poachers' c. (—1909).

over the mark. Tipsy: coll: ca 1820–80. In a letter written in 1846 – from what is now Winnipeg – Robert Clouston, a Scot, remarks, 'Those not accustomed to dine at these parties will get over the mark (tipsy) before they have any idea of it.'

over the stile. (Sent) for trial: rhyming s. (—1859).

***over the water.** In King's Bench Prison: London c.. ca 1820–50. The reference is to the 'other' side of the Thames.

overdraw the badger, see BADGER, OVERDRAW.

overflow and plunder. A method of fleecing the audience by sending them from dearer to yet dearer seats: theatrical: ca 1880–1900.

overheat one's flues. To get drunk: low, mostly Cockney (—1887).

overrun the constable, see CONSTABLE, OUTRUN.

overseen. Somewhat drunk: late C.15–20: S.E. till C.17, then coll till ca 1820, then dial. L'Estrange. cf. OVERSHOT; OVERTAKEN.

overseer. A man in a pillory: mid-C.18–early 19. Ex the C.16–17 S.E. sense, one who looks down at anything, hence a spectator.

overshot. (Very) drunk: C.17–20; ob. Marston, 1605; Lyell. cf.:

oversparred. Top-heavy; unsteady; drunk: nautical: 1890, Clark Russell; ob.

overtaken. Drunk: late C.16–20: S.E. till C.18, then coll till ca 1850, then dial. Hacket, 1693, 'I never spake with the man that saw him overtaken'; Congreve; Halliwell; Mrs S. C. Hall. Ex *overtaken in* or *with drink*.

overtoys box. A cupboard-like box for books: Winchester College: from ca 1880.

owl. A harlot: C.19–20 (ob.): coll verging on S.E. 2. A member of Sidney Sussex College, Cambridge: Cambridge University: ca 1810–90.

owl, v.i. To smuggle: coll: ca 1735–1820. Ex OWLER. 2. To sit up at night: from the 1890s; ob.

owl (or by owls), live too close to the, or **near a, wood to be frightened by an.** To be not easily frightened: C.18–early 19 as proverbial coll, then dial. Swift, however, has 'Do you think I was born in a wood to be afraid of an owl?'

owl, take the. To become angry: coll: late C.18–mid-19.

owl in an ivy-bush, like an, see IVY-BUSH.

owl-light, walk by. To fear arrest: coll: ca 1650–1700.

owler. A person, a vessel, engaged in smuggling sheep or wool from England to France: late C.17–early 19: orig. c. or s. Ex ob. S.E. v., *owl*. cf.:

owling. Such export: late C.17–early 19. See preceding entry for status.

owls to Athens, bring. To bring 'coals to Newcastle': proverbial coll: late C.16–18. Melbancke's *Philotinus*, 1583; Hacket's *Williams*, 1693. The owl is Athene's bird.

own, on its or **one's.** On its or one's own account, responsibility, resources, merits: from ca 1895: coll.

own up. To confess; admit (v.t. with *to*): coll: 1880, Trollope, 'If you own up in a genial sort of way, the House will forgive anything.'

owned, be. To make many converts: clerical: ca 1853–75. cf. SEAL, n.

owners' man. A captain or officer protecting the owner's interest by cheese-paring; an officer related to the owners: nautical coll: late C.19–20.

ownest. (e.g. *my*) *ownest own*, (my) dearest one: Society (—1887) >, by 1910 at latest, rather cheap.

owt. Two: back s. (—1859).

ox has (hath) trod on his foot, the black. He knows what poverty, misfortune, ill-health, old age, etc. is: proverbial: from ca 1530: coll till ca 1750, then S.E.; ob. Tusser, Ray, Leigh Hunt.

ox-house to bed, go through the. To be cuckolded: late C.17–early 19: semi-proverbial coll. Obviously because he has horns.

ox-pop. A butcher: low: ca 1810–80.

ox up; knock up; mob. To promote (a pupil): Christ's Hospital: resp. ca 1840–80, from 1850, 1890.

oxer. An ox-fence: fox-hunting: 1859, G. A. Lawrence, 'A rattling fall over an "oxer"'; Whyte-Melville; Kennard, *The Girl in the Brown Habit*, 1886.

oxford; Oxford. A crown piece: low: ca 1885–1914. Hence *half-oxford*, a half-crown piece: ob. Binstead, *The Pink 'Un and the Pelican*, 1898. It is an abbr. of OXFORD SCHOLAR. 2. As in 'Are you Oxford or Cambridge?', i.e. 'Are you at (or, were you at) Oxford or Cambridge University?': coll: C.19–20.

Oxford, – send verdingales (farthingales) **to Broadgates at or in.** A c.p. of ca 1560–1670 (later in dial.) in reference to farthingales so big that their wearers could not enter an ordinary door except sideways. Heywood (1562), Fuller, Grose's *Provincial Glossary*.

Oxford clink. The C.18–mid-19 sense, a play on words, a mere jingle, is prob. S.E. 2. A free pass: theatrical: ca 1890–1915.

Oxford scholar. Five shillings (piece or sum): from ca 1870, in the S.W. of England; now ob. Rhyming s. on DOLLAR.

oyl, see OIL, 3.

oyster. A gob of phlegm: low coll: late C.18–20. 2. The female pudend: low: C.19–20; ob. (cf. *the oyster*, the semen.) 3. Profit, advantage: jocular: ca 1895–1915. Ex a prophet's (*profit!*) and an oyster's beard. 4. (Gen. in pl.) One of the holes in a cooked duck's back: domestic: late C.19–20.

oyster, a choking or stopping. A reply that silences: coll: ca 1525–1600. Skelton (*stopping*); Udall (the same); J. Heywood, 1546 (*choking*).

oyster, as like as an apple to an. Very different: coll: ca 1530–1680. More, 1532, 'Hys similitude . . . is no more lyke then an apple to an oyster'; L'Estrange, 1667. In 1732, Thomas Fuller has the form, *as like as an apple to a lobster*.

oyster, old, see OLD OYSTER.

oyster-faced. Needing a shave: low (mostly London): ca 1895–1915. See OYSTER, 3.

oysters, drink to one's. To fare accordingly (esp., badly): coll: mid-C.15–early 16. J. Paston, 1472, 'If I had not dealt ryght corteysly . . . I had drownk to myn oystyrs.'

P

p and q; P. and Q. Of prime quality: C.17–20: coll in C.17, dial. thereafter. Rowlands (*Pee and kew*, as it is sometimes written). Origin obscure.

p.b. or **P.B., the.** The public: theatrical. (—1909). Also *the pub.*

p.c. (or **P.C.**). Poor classes: Society: from ca 1880; ob.

p.d. or **P.D.** An adulterating element in pepper: trade: from ca 1870. i.e. 'pepper-dust'.

p.d.q.; P.D.Q. Pretty damn(ed) quick: late C.19–20. *Free Lance*, 6 Oct. 1900, 'I'd be on my uppers if I didn't get something to do P.D.Q.'

p- (or **P-**)**maker.** The male, the female pudend: low: mid-C.19–20. See PEE.

***p.p.!** or **P.P.!** A pickpocket: c. (—1887). 2. Play or pay, i.e. go on with the arrangement or forfeit the money; esp., the money must be paid whether the horse runs or not: mostly the turf: from ca 1830; slightly ob.

p.p.c. A 'snappish good-bye': middle classes': late C.19–early 20. Ex *p.p.c.* (i.e. *pour prendre congé*, to take leave) written on a visiting card. 2. Hence, *to p.p.c.*, to quarrel with and CUT (2) (a person): Society: from ca 1880; virtually †.

p.s. or **P.S.** See O.P., 1. 2. An advance on wages: hatters' (—1909). Ex *postscript* written *p.s.*

ps and qs (or **Ps and Qs**), **learn one's.** To learn one's letters: coll; 1820, Combe. Ob. Prob. ex children's difficulty in distinguishing *p* and *q*, both having tails. cf.:

ps and qs (or **Ps and Qs**), **mind one's.** To be careful, exact, prudent in behaviour: coll: 1779, Mrs H. Cowley, 'You must mind your *P's* and *Q's* with him, I can tell you.' Also *peas and cues*; occ. (and ob.) *be on* (or *in*) *one's ps and qs.* Perhaps influenced by P AND Q; perhaps cognate with preceding entry; perhaps, as F. & H. suggests, ex 'the old custom of alehouse tally, marking "p" for pint and "q" for quart, care being necessary to avoid over- or under-charge'. 2. Grose, 2nd ed., shows that ca 1786–1830, there was the more dignified sense, 'to be attentive to the main chance'.

p.t. A pupil teacher: teachers' coll: late C.19–20.

P. W. Abney. A high, feminine hat appearing in 1896: lower classes': late 1896–7. Ex *Prince of Wales Abney Cemetery*, the hat being worn with 'three black, upright ostrich feathers, set up at the side . . . in the fashion of the Prince of Wales's crest feathers' (Ware).

pa. A mainly childish abbr. of PAPA: (in C.20, low) coll: 1811, L. M. Hawkins, 'The elder sat down . . . and answered "Yes, Pa'!" to everything that Pa said.' 2. Hence, the relieving officer of a parish: lower classes' (—1909). cf. DADDY, 3.

pa-in-law. Father-in-law: Society (—1887). See PA, 1.

pac. A cap: back s. (—1859).

pace, alderman's. A slow, dignified gait: coll: from ca 1580; ob. Melbancke, 1583; Cotgrave; 1685, S. Wesley the Elder, 'And struts . . . as goodly as any alderman'.

pacer. Anything (esp. a horse) that goes at a great pace: coll (—1890).

paces, show one's. To display one's ability: coll: from ca 1870. Ex horses.

pack-thread, talk. To speak bawdily in seemly terms: coll: late C.18–20; very ob. (In North Country dial., merely to talk nonsense.) Ex *packing-thread*, used for securing parcels. cf. WRAPPED-UP.

packet. A false report: coll: mid-C.18–19: mostly Northern. cf. PACKETS!

packet-rat. A seaman in the old trans-atlantic sailing packets: nautical coll: C.19. Bowen.

packet to, sell a. To hoax; lie to; deceive: coll: 1847 (E.D.D.); ob. Hardy, 1886, *The Mayor of Casterbridge*, ch. xliii. cf. PUP, SELL A.

packets! An expression of incredulity: mid-C.19–20; very ob. Ex PACKET.

packing. Food: low (—1909). cf. S.E. *stuff oneself with food* and INSIDE LINING.

***packing-ken.** An eating-house: c. (—1909). Ex the preceding.

packing-penny to, give a. To dismiss: coll: late C.16–early 19. Jonson. By pun.

packs. Storm-clouds: nautical coll (—1887).

packstaff, see PIKESTAFF.

Pad. A not very gen. abbr. (—1887) of PADDY.

***pad.** A path; a road. Esp. *the high pad*, the highway; in C.16–17, occ. *padde.*

From ca 1565: c. until C.19, then dial. Harman; Middleton & Dekker; Prior; Scott. Ex Old High Ger. *pfad*. 2. An easy-paced horse: 1617, Moryson: coll until C.19, then S.E. Also PAD-NAG. 3. A highway robber: c.: ca 1670–1840. Head, B.E., Messink, Byron. Ex next sense. See also PAD, HIGH and LOW, and PADDER. 4. Robbery on the highway: 1664, Etherege, 'I have laid the dangerous pad now quite aside'; Bee; Henley & Stevenson: c. until C.19, then low s.; very ob. 5. (Ex sense 3, 4.) A street-robber: low: ca 1820–50. cf. *pads and wods* in Ned Ward (1709), for 'highwaymen'. 6. A bed: ca 1570–1890: low s. verging on c. Drayton, Broome, Defoe, Grose, Brandon. In C.16–17 also *padde*. Ex the S.E. sense, a bundle of straw, skins, etc., on which to lie. 7. Occ. (—1874) an itinerant musician. Ex sense 3. 8. A walk: c. (—1839). Ex sense 1 of:

***pad**, v. To travel on foot as a vagrant: C.17–20: c. until C.19, then mainly dial. Rowlands, 1610, 'O Ben mort wilt thou pad with me?' Ex S.E. *pad*, to walk (1553, O.E.D.). Prob. cf. the n., sense 1. See also PAD THE HOOF. 2. To rob on foot or on the highway: ca 1635–1840: orig., prob. c.; never better than low s. Ford, 1638, 'One can . . . cant and pick a pocket, Pad for a cloak or hat.'

pad, gentleman of the. Also *knight* (ca 1670–1840), *squire* (ca 1700–1830) *of the pad*. A highwayman: C.18–mid-19: low s. > low coll. Farquhar. See PAD, n., 4.

***pad, go (out up)on the.** To (go out to) rob on the highway: c.: late C.17–mid-19. B.E., who notes the variant *go a-padding*. See PAD, n., 1.

***pad, high.** The highway: ca 1565–1800; c. 2. Hence, C.17–early 19, a robber on the highway, esp. a highwayman. Contrast:

***pad, low.** A footpad: c.: late C.17–early 19. Ex PAD, n., 1. cf. preceding.

***pad, on or upon the.** (Engaged in robbery) on the highway: c.: late C.17–early 19; prob. low s. after ca 1790. L'Estrange. 2. Hence, on tramp: C.19–20, though not with certainty recorded before 1851, Mayhew. Both senses ex PAD, n., 1; the former, gen. *upon*; the latter, *on*.

***pad, rum.** 'A daring or stout Highwayman', B.E.: c.: late C.17–early 19. See RUM, adj., 1; PAD, n., 3; and cf. PAD, HIGH, 2.

***pad, sit**, see: **pad, stand.** To beg by the wayside: c.: 1859, H.; 1862, Mayhew; ob. Properly, while remaining stationary – and standing. Obviously *sit pad* is to beg from a sitting position: recorded in 1851, likewise in Mayhew. In both, the beggar gen. has a piece of paper inscribed 'I'm starving – blind – etc.' Also *stand Paddy*.

pad, upon the, see PAD, ON THE.

***pad, water.** 'One that Robbs Ships in [esp.] the Thames,' B.E.: c.: late C.17–early 19. See PAD, n., 3.

pad-borrower. A horse-thief: s. > low coll: ca 1780–1840.

pad-clinking. 'Hobnobbing with footpads,' says F. & H., defining it as c.: Kingsley's note to the sole record, 1865, says 'Alluding to the clinking of their spurs'.

pad-horse. An easy-paced horse: from ca 1630; ob. Coll quickly > S.E. Jonson.

pad in the straw. A hidden danger: coll: 1530, Palsgrave; not quite † in dial. Still, *Gammer Gurton's Needle*; Ray. Ex †S.E. *pad*, a toad.

pad it. To tramp along, esp. as a vagrant: late C.18–20, or perhaps from as early as 1690: s. >, ca 1840, low coll >, ca 1890, S.E.

pad-nag. An easy-going horse: from ca 1650; ob. Coll >, ca 1810, S.E. 1654, Whitelocke, 'A sober . . . well-paced english padde nagge'.

pad round. To pay excessive attention to a customer: tailors' coll: from ca 1870. Ex the S.E. *pad*, (of animals) to walk, etc., 'with steady dull-sounding steps.'

pad the hoof. To go on foot: from ca 1790. On *plod o' the hoof* (Shakespeare), *beat the hoof* (mid-C.17–early 19). cf. PAD IT.

pad-thief. A horse-thief: late C.17–early 19: coll >, ca 1750, S.E. Shadwell.

padde, see PAD, n. **padden-crib** or **-ken**, see PADDING-CRIB. (*Answers*, 11 May 1889.)

***padder.** A robber on the highway; esp. a footpad: C.17–20; ob.: orig. c. >, in C.18, low s.; in late C.19–20, archaic S.E. Rowlands, Scott. cf. PADDIST. Ex PAD, v., 1, influenced by PAD, n., 3. 2. See:

padders. Feet; shoes or boots: low: from ca 1825; ob. Egan, *Finish to Tom and Jerry*, 1828, 'My padders, my stampers, my buckets, otherwise my boots'.

***paddin-ken.** See PADDING-CRIB. P. H. Emerson in *Signor Lippo Lippi*, 1893.

***padding.** Robbery on the highway: c.: ca 1670–1840. (see PAD, GO . . .). 2. Short, light articles in the magazines: journalistic coll (—1887); ob. Baumann notes that the term is used 'in opposition to the serial stories'. 3. Talk: s.: Ned Ward, 1703.

***padding,** adj. Practising highway robbery: c. of ca 1670–1840. Eachard, fig.

***padding-crib, -ken;** loosely **padden-c.** and **-k.** A lodging-house for the underworld, esp. for vagrants: c.: from ca 1835; ob. Ex PAD, v., 1., and n., 5. Brandon distinguishes thus: *p.-c.*, a boys' lodging-house; *p.-k.*, a tramps' lodging-house: a distinction that seems to have been lost as early as the 1850s.

***Paddington fair (day); or P. Fair(-day).** A hanging (day): c.: late C.17–early 19. Tyburn was in the parish of Paddington. Ex 'a rural Fair at the Village of that Name, near that Place' (Tyburn), B.E. cf.:

***Paddington frisk, dance the.** To be hanged: c.: ca 1780–1830. cf.:

***Paddington spectacles.** The cap drawn over a criminal's eyes at his hanging: either c. or low s.: early C.19. cf. the preceding pair of entries.

paddist. A professional highwayman: ca 1670–1800: Scots s. >, in C.18, coll.

paddle. A hand: late C.19–20: low and ob. ?suggested by DADDLE.

paddle, v. To drink strong liquor: low: from ca 1860; ob. ?ex noisy drinking. Hence, *to have paddled*, to be intoxicated. 2. To run away; to abscond: c. (—1860) >, by 1890, low. Ex S.E. *paddle*, to toddle.

paddle one's own canoe, see CANOE, PADDLE . . .

paddler. A paddle-steamer: coll: from ca 1890.

Paddy. A nickname (cf. PAT) for an Irishman: coll: *Sessions*, 1748; 1780, A. Young, 'Paddies were swimming their horses in the sea to cure the mange.' Ex the very common Irish name, *Patrick*, of which *Paddy* is the Irish diminutive. Also *Paddylander* (see PADDY LAND), PADDY-WHACK. cf.:

paddy. A rage, a temper: coll: 1894, Henty. Also PADDY-WHACK. cf. IRISH, and see esp. *Words!* at 'Offensive Nationality'. 2. Erroneous for *baddy*: Motley and recent dictionaries. 3. A paddy-whack (i.e. unlicensed) almanac: coll and dial. (—1876). 4. A hobby, a fad: non-aristocratic (—1887). Ex PAD, n., 2.

Paddy, stand, see PAD, SIT.

Paddy Doyle, do. To be a defaulter: naval and military: late C.19–20.

Paddy Land or Paddyland. Ireland. Hence, *Paddylander*, an Irishman. Coll: from ca 1820.

paddy-melon, see MELON, 3.

paddy over, come (gen. the). To BAMBOOZLE, KID (2), HUMBUG: from ca 1820; slightly ob. Ex PADDY, and the Irishman's reputation for BLARNEY.

Paddy Quick. A stick. 2. Thick. Both rhyming s. (—1859); the latter, ob. 3. A kick: rhyming s.: mid-C.19–20.

Paddy rammer. A hammer: rhyming s., esp. among urban labourers: late C.19–20.

paddy-row. 'More jackets off than blows struck, where sticks supply the place of fists', Bee: coll: from ca 1820; ob.

Paddy Wester; occ. paddywester. A bogus seaman carrying a dead man's discharge-papers; a very incompetent or dissolute seaman: nautical: from ca 1890. Bowen, 'After a notorious boarding-house keeper in Liverpool who shipped thousands of green men as A.B.'s for a consideration.'

paddy-w(h)ack, paddyw(h)ack, paddy w(h)ack; or with capitals. An Irishman (in C.18–early 19, only if big and strong): coll: 1785, Grose (at *whack*); cf. O.E.D. date. Humorous on PADDY. 2. Whence, on the analogy of PADDY, 1, a rage, a temper: coll: 1899, Kipling, 'He'll be in a ravin' paddy-wack.' 3. A paddywhack (unlicensed) almanac: coll (—1886); †by 1910. cf. PADDY, 3. 4. A smack; a smacking: Australian children's: late C.19–20. Elaboration: *paddy(-)whack the drumstick.* Partly echoic, partly rhyming.

Paddy's hurricane. A dead calm: nautical: from ca 1840: ob. Also *Irishman's h.*

Paddy's Land. Ireland: coll (—1864). Also PADDY LAND.

Paddy's lantern. The moon: nautical: late C.19–20. Prob. after PARISH-LANTERN.

Paddy's market. A market for the sale of second-hand goods, esp. clothes: coll: mid-C.19–20.

paddywester. An occ. form of PADDY WESTER.

paddyw(h)ack, see PADDY-W(H)ACK.

padre. A chaplain: naval (1888, *Chambers's Journal*, 14 Jan.) and military (—1900). Ex Portuguese (lit. a father) as used, from ca 1580, in India for any priest or parson.

paff! A coll interjection (contemptuous): mid-C.19–20; ob. Hence *piff and paff*, jargon.

page of your own age, make a. Do it yourself: semi-proverbial coll: Draxe,

Bibliotheca Scholastica Instructissima, 1633; Ray; Swift.

pagoda-tree, gen. preceded by **shake the.** (To obtain) rapid fortune in India: s.; by 1870, coll: 1836, T. Hook, 'The amusing pursuit of "shaking the pagoda-tree" once so popular in our Oriental possessions.' Slightly ob. by 1886. App. ex a coin that, owing to the design of a pagoda thereon, was called a pagoda.

pahny. An occ. variant of PARNEE.

paid. Tipsy: ca 1635–70. Shirley, *The Royal Master*, 1638.

'paid' to, put. 'To regard a matter as finished, as over and done with': S.E. of an account, coll in such fig. connections as 'Oh, don't worry; you can *put paid* to any friendship that ever existed between him and me; I've found out the sort of fellow he really is!' (Lyell): late C.19–20.

paint. Money: esp. among house-painters (—1866); ob. cf. BRADS; SUGAR. 2. Jam: military: from the 1890s. Ex its inferior quality.

paint, v.i. To drink (something strong): 1853, Whyte-Melville, 'Each hotel ... called forth the same observation, "I guess I shall go in and paint".' Ob. 2. v.t., to make numerous corrections on (a proof): printers' (—1909). Ex resulting appearance.

paint-brush baronet. An ennobled artist: Society coll: 1885, *Referee*, 28 June; extremely ob. cf. GALLIPOT BARONET.

paint one's eye for him (her, etc.). To give him a black eye: low (—1887).

paint the town red, see RED, PAINT THE TOWN.

painted mischief. Playing cards: 1879, *Daily News*, 8 March. Ob.

painter, cut one's. To prevent a person's doing harm: late C.17–mid-18 nautical s. 2. Hence, to send a person away: nautical s. (—1785). 3. (Of oneself) *cut one's* or *the painter*, to depart unceremoniously: nautical (—1867). 4. Hence, to sever one's connection: gen. coll (—1888) >, ca 1905, S.E. ('The painter being the rope that holds the boat fast to the ship', Grose.) Occ. *slip the painter*, in senses 3, 4: from ca 1865.

painter, let go the. To deliver a (heavy) punch: boxers' (—1887); ob. Ex nautical j. cf. PAINT ONE'S EYE.

painter, what pleases the. A late C.17–mid-18 c.p. in the world of art and literature: 'When any Representation in the Productions of his or any Art is unaccountable, and so is to be resolv'd purely into the good Pleasure of the Artist,' B.E.

pair of. *Pair* is coll (and often humorous) when used of 'the two bodily members themselves, as "a pair of eyes, ears, lips, jaws, arms, hands, heels, legs, wings", etc', O.E.D.: late C.14–20.

pair o(f) compasses. Human legs: London: ca 1880–1910. The term arose when the male leg began to be narrowly encased.

pair o(f) drums, see DRUMS, PAIR OF.

pair of hands. A man: coll: from ca 1630.

pair of lawn sleeves. A bishop: coll: 1844, Macaulay.

pair of oars. A boat rowed by two men: coll verging on S.E.: C.17–20.

pair of shears, see SHEARS.

pair of shoes, a different or **another.** A different matter: coll: 1859, Thackeray; 1865, Dickens. Both have *another*.

pair of spectacles, see SPECTACLES.

pair of wheels. A two-wheeled vehicle: coll: from ca 1620. Cockeram.

***pair of wings.** (A pair of) oars: ca 1790–1890: c. Ex speed. 2. Sleeves: tailors': late C.19–20.

pair off with. To marry: coll: 1865, Miss Braddon in *Sir Jasper*. Ex S.E. sense, to go apart, or off, in pairs.

pakeha. A white man: a Maori word colloquially adopted in New Zealand ca 1850. Perhaps ex a Maori word meaning a fairy; perhaps a Maori attempt at BUGGER, 'said to have been described by Dr Johnson (though not in his dictionary), as "a term of endearment amongst sailors" ', a theory app. supported by Morris. (Pronounced as a molossus, the *a*s being, as always in Maori, given the Continental value.)

pakka, see PUKKA.

***pal.** An accomplice: c. (—1788). Grose, 2nd ed. (*chosen pells*, *pell* being an occ. C.18–19 form); Vaux, 1812, *pall*. In late C.19, this sense > low s. 2. Earlier and from ca 1850 the prevailing sense, a CHUM, a friend: 1681–2, the Hereford Diocesan Register, 'Where have you been all this day, pall?': s. >, ca 1880, low coll. Ex Romany *pal*, brother, mate (cf. c. and Romany *blo(w)en*), ex Turkish Gypsy, *pral*, *plal*, brother; ultimately related to Sanskrit *bhratr*, a brother (cf. L. *frater*). (cf. PALLY.) Hence:

pal, v.i. To associate (*with*); become another's 'pal' (q.v.): perhaps orig. c.; certainly, at best, low s. (—1879) >, ca 1905, (decreasingly low) coll. Often, esp.

in C.20, *pal in with*, *pal up* (*to* or *with*); in C.19, occ. *pal on*. 'The Autobiography of a Thief', in *Macmillan's Magazine*, 1879, 'I palled in with some old hands at the game.' 2. (Gen. *pall*) to detect: c.: 1851, Mayhew; ob. Perhaps ex the n., 1, or, more prob., ex the Romany preposition *palal*, *palla*, after, as in *av palla*, lit. to come after, i.e. to follow, and *dik palla*, to look after, i.e. to watch: cf. *be after a person*, to pursue him, desire strongly to find or catch.

palace. A police-station: policemen's: from ca 1870; somewhat ob.

palampo. A bed-spread, a quilt: Anglo-Indian coll (—1864). A corruption of *palempore*, itself of doubtful etymology.

***palarie,** v.i. and t. To talk, speak: vagrants' c. (—1893); ob. P. H. Emerson, 'She used to palarie thick [cant] to the slaveys.' A variant of PARLARY (see p. 11) influenced by PALAVER, V.

palatic. Drunk: 1885, *The Stage*, 'Sandy told me he last saw him dreadfully palatic': theatrical; very ob. i.e. *paralytic* corrupted.

palaver. A fussy, ostentatious person: Scots coll: C.19–20; ob. Gen. *old palaver*. Presumably ex: 2. Conversation or discussion, gen. idle, occ. (in C.19–20) flattering or wheedling; JAW: nautical s. >, ca 1790, gen. coll: 1748, Smollett, 'None of your palaver.' Ex S.E. (orig. trade and nautical) sense, a parley, a conference, esp. one with much talk, itself ex Portuguese *palavra* (cf. Sp. *palabra*), used by the Portuguese in parleying with the natives on the African coast. cf. the v. 3. Hence, business, concern: from middle 1890s. C. Hyne, 1899, 'It's not your palaver . . . or mine.'

palaver, v. To talk much, unnecessarily, or (in C.19–20) plausibly or cajolingly: from ca 1730: s. or coll > in C.19–20 definitely coll, latterly almost S.E. Ex the preceding, but until ca 1775 unrecorded except as *palavering*. 2. Hence, to flatter; wheedle: from ca 1780; ob.

***palaver to** (a person) **for** (a thing). To ask one for something; beg it: tramps' c. (—1859). Ex PALAVER, V., 2.

palaverer, occ. **palaverist.** One who palavers; one given to palavering: from ca 1785 (ob.); coll. Ex PALAVER, V., 1. cf.:

palavering, vbl n. and ppl adj. Copious or idle talk; very talkative: resp. 1733, 1764 (O.E.D.): s. or coll until C.19, then definitely coll. Foote, 'He is a damned palavering fellow.' Ex PALAVER, V.

pale. Pale brandy: London coll: mid-C. 19–20; ob. Mayhew, 1861, 'A "drain of pale", as she called it, invigorated her.'

Palestine in London. Low: ca 1820–50. Egan, 1821, 'That portion of the parish of St Giles, Bloomsbury, inhabited by the lower Irish.' cf. HOLY LAND.

palette. A hand: late C.18–19. cf. DADDLE and PADDLE.

pall. See PAL, n., 1, and v., 2. 2. To detect: c. or low s.: 1859, H.; †by 1900. 3. To stop, e.g. *pall that!*, stop (doing) that!, and *pall there!*, silence!: nautical (—1864); ob. Ex *pall*, properly *pawl*, an instrument used to stop the windlass. See PAWL, the earlier, more gen. form. 4. To appal; daunt (as in C.14–17 S.E.): nautical (—1864). (cf. PALLED.) Abbr. *appal*, or ex the nautical order *ease and pall*.

pallaver, see PALAVER, esp. v., 2.

palled, be. Not to dare to say more: low coll (—1864). Ex *appal*, or PALL, V., 3 or 4.

***palliard.** A vagrant that lies on straw; but esp. 'he that goeth in a patched cloke', Awdelay: c. of ca 1560–1830; ob. by ca 1750. 2. In C.17–early 18, the seventh 'rank' of the underworld: born beggars affecting hideous sores. Ex Fr. *paillard*, itself ex *paille*, straw.

palliasse. A harlot: low: C.19–20; ob. Ex *palliasse*, a straw, i.e. cheap, mattress.

palliness. Comradeship; the being pals (see PAL, n., 2): from ca 1890. cf. PALSHIP.

pallish. Friendly, CHUMMY (adj.): mostly schools': 1892 (O.E.D.); ob. Ex PAL, n., 2. cf.:

pally. Friendly; THICK: from 1895 or slightly earlier. Ex PAL, n., 2. cf. preceding.

palm-acid or **-oil.** A caning on the hand: schoolboys': from ca 1860; ob.

palm-oil ruffian. An old-time trader on the West Coast of Africa: since ca 1860. Buying oil and drinking gin.

palm-soap. Money; a bribe: low (—1860); ob. On S.E. *palm-oil*, a bribe.

***palmer.** A beggar that, under the pretence of collecting 'harp' halfpence, by palming steals copper coins from shopkeepers: c. (—1864). Contrast PALMING. 2. A shy fellow: Durham School: from ca 1870; ob.

Palmer is concerned, Mr. A c.p. applied, ca 1810–50, to a briber or a bribee. Ex the S.E. *palm-oil*, a bribe. Contrast PALM-ACID and cf. PALM-SOAP.

Palmer's twister. (Gen. pl.) A strychnine pill: medical: ca 1870–1910. The medicine employed by Palmer of Rugeley in getting rid of Cooke.

***palming.** The robbing of shops by pairs, the one bargaining, the other palming desirable articles: c. (—1839); slightly ob. Contrast PALMER, 1.

***palming-racket.** 'Secreting money in the palm of the hand', Vaux: c. (—1812); ob.

palone, see POLONE.

palship. Friendship; being pals: 1896 (O.E.D.); ob. Ex PAL, n., 2. cf. PALLINESS.

Paltock's Inn or **inn.** A poverty-stricken place: ca 1578–1610: coll almost imm. > S.E. Gosson, 'Comming to Chenas, a blind village, in comparison of Athens a Paltockes Inne'. Presumably ex some wretched inn, the host one Paltock.

pam or **Pam.** The knave of clubs: 1685, Crowne; ob. Coll. Pope, 'Ev'n mighty Pam, that Kings and Queens o'erthrew.' Abbr. Fr. *pamphile*, a card-game and esp. this card, which, in trumping, ranks highest. 2. A card-game rather like nap: from ca 1690; ob. Coll >, ca 1780, S.E. Addison, in *The Guardian*, 1713, 'She quickly grows more fond of Pam than of her husband.'

Pamp, (as) snug as old. Very comfortable: lower classes' (—1887); ob. Who was Pamp? The name is prob. fanciful ex *a pampered person*. 2. (*pamp* or *P.*) A Pampero, i.e. a River Plate gale: nautical: late C.19–20.

***pan.** A bed: c.: C.18. Hall, 1708. 2. Money: c.: mid-C.18–mid-19. Halliwell. 3. (*the pan*). The workhouse: tramps' c. (—1893). P. H. Emerson. The etymologies are extremely obscure, as are the connexions – if any. Perhaps all three are cognate with Romany *pan(d)*, to 'shut, fasten, close, tie, bind, etc.', Smart & Crofton; sense 1 may, via dial., be ex *pan*, a beam of wood.

pan, v. To catch; capture: coll, mostly U.S. and Colonial: 1887.

pan, shut one's. To hold one's tongue: from ca 1830; ob. Marryat, in *Peter Simple*, 'Shut your pan.' Ex that part of an †gun or pistol which holds the priming. cf. S.E. *flash in the pan*.

pan on, have a. To be low-spirited: printers': from ca 1860. ?ex Fr. *panne*, a failure, a FIZZLE, a breakdown, e.g. *pannes de métro*.

pan out, v.i. To turn out; (of an event) be: coll: orig. (1871), U.S.; anglicized ca 1895, but common in South Africa (the paradise of American mining-engineers) as early as 1891: witness Pettmann. *Referee*, 7 April 1901, 'We do not want to know about . . . the M.C.C.'s big roller . . . or how the members' luncheon pans out as a commercial speculation.' Ex mining (the shaking of gold-bearing gravel in a pan). 2. v.t., to yield: Australian (and U.S.) coll: 1884, *Melbourne Punch*, 4 Sept.,'The department . . . only panned out a few copper coins.'

pan-pudding, stand to one's. To hold one's (lit. or fig.) ground: coll: late C.17–early 18. Motteux's *Rabelais*. (A heavy pudding, gen. of flour.)

panam, see PANNAM.

Pancridge parson. A term of contempt: C.17–18. Field, 1612; Halliwell.

pandemonium. A gambling-hell: educated gamblers' (—1823); †by 1900. 'Jon Bee', who implies a pun on *hell* being the place of *all the devils*. 2. The lower deck subalterns' quarters in the old naval troopships: naval and military: ca 1850–1910. Bowen.

pandie, pandy. A stroke from cane or strap on the hand as punishment: coll, mostly school and nursery and mainly Scots: A. Scott, 1805. Ex L. *pande palmam* or *manum*, hold out your hand! 2. (*pandy*): a 'revolted Sepoy in the Indian Mutiny of 1857–9': coll: 1857; ob. Ex *Pande*, the surname of the first man to revolt in the 34th Regiment. 3. Hence, an Indian soldier: Regular Army: late C.19–20; ob.

pandie, pandy, v. To cane, strap: coll (mostly school and nursery): 1863, Kingsley, 'She . . . pandied their hands with canes.' Ex the n., 1.

pane of glass. A monocle: Regular Army: since ca 1870.

***panel-crib, -den, -house.** A brothel where theft is (deliberately) rife: c. (—1860); ?orig. U.S. Bartlett, 1860 (*panel-house*, low s.). Whence the next two entries.

panel-dodge or **game.** Theft in a panel-house: low s. > low coll: resp. 1885, Burton, *Thousand Nights*; *Century Dict.*, 1890. Ex PANEL-CRIB, etc.

panel-thief, -thieving. A thief, theft, in a PANEL-CRIB: low s. (—1860) > low coll; perhaps orig. U.S. (see Bartlett, ed. of 1860).

***panem,** see PANNAM.

panicky. Like, given to, panic: very or excessively afraid or nervous: coll: 1869, *Echo*, 12 Oct. 'Hence the delays, mystification, and consequent panicky results'.

***pan(n)am; panem; pan(n)um.** Bread: c.: resp. mid-C.16–20, C.17–18, C.17–20.

Harman; Brome (*pannum*); B.E. (*panam*); Bee (*panum*); Vance. Ex L. *panis*, and prob. ex the accusative *panem*, via Lingua Franca. cf. Fr. s. *panam*, bread.

***pannam(, etc.)-bound.** Deprived of one's food-, esp. bread-, allowance: prison c.: mid-C.19–20. Ex preceding. cf. PANNAM-STRUCK and:

***pannam(, etc.; or cokey)-fence** or, more gen., **-fencer.** A street pastry-cook: c.: from ca 1840. Ex PANNAM, and see FENCE.

***pannam(, etc.)-struck.** Starving: c.: C.19–20; ob. Ex PANNAM.

***pann(e)y.** The highway: c. of ca 1750–1830. John Poulter, 1753, 'I'll scamp on the panney.' Etymology obscure: perhaps ex Romany. 2. A house; lodgings, rooms: c. of ca 1785–1880. 3. Whence FLASH *pann(e)y*, often simply *panny*, a brothel; a public-house frequented by thieves: c. of ca 1820–1920. 4. A burglary: c.: implied in Grose, 1788; ob. Ex preceding sense, via *do a* PANN(E)Y. cf. PANN(E)Y-LAY. 5. A fight between two, among more than two women: low (—1909). Cognate with Devonshire *panel*, to hurt, or pain, and Nottinghamshire *panneling*, a severe beating.

***pann(e)y, do a.** To rob a house: commit a burglary: c.: Grose, 1788; Lytton; ob. Ex preceding entry, sense 2. cf. CRACK (v., 4) *a crib*.

***pann(e)y-lay.** A burglary: c.: from ca 1820; ob. See PANN(E)Y, 2.

***pann(e)y-man.** A housebreaker: c.: C.19–20; very ob. Ex PANN(E)Y, 2.

pannier. A robed waiter at table in the Inner Temple: coll: 1823. Origin unknown, says S.O.D.; but is not the term an abbr. of *pannier man*, 'a servant belonging to the Temple or Gray's Inn, whose office is to announce the dinner', Grose, 3rd ed., 1796 (= 1790 or 1791)? W. compares with BOOTS and BUTTONS.

pannier, fill a woman's. To render her pregnant: C.17–18: low coll. Cotgrave.

pannikin-boss or **-overseer.** An overseer in a small, 'unofficial' way on a station: Australian coll (—1896); ob.

pannikin into another shed, roll one's. To seek work with another employer: Australian coll (—1902); ob. cf. the preceding entry.

***pannum,** see PANNAM. **panny,** see PANN(E)Y.

pannyar. 'The old name for the slave trade on the African coast', says Bowen: nautical: ?C.18–mid-19. Prob. ex *pannier*, a basket.

panorama (pron. *panorammer*). A hammer: rhyming s.: since ca 1870. D. W. Barrett, *Navvies*, 1880.

pantables, stand upon one's. To stand on dignity: coll: ca 1570–1760. G. Harvey, Cotton, Horace Walpole. Moreover, *pantable* is corrupt for *pantofle*, a slipper, a shoe. Other corruptions are *pantacle, pantocle, pantap(p)le, pantaphel, pantop(p)le, pantible*.

***panter.** A hart: c.: late C.17–early 19. Grose, 'That animal is, in the Psalms, said to pant after the fresh water-brooks' (1785 revised by 1796). 2. The human heart: from ca 1720 certainly; possibly from late C.17: low s., prob. orig. c.; slightly ob. A song of ca 1725, quoted in *Musa Pedestris*; Grose, 2nd ed., 'Frequently pants in time of danger'. 3. See:

panters. The female breasts: low: C.19–20; ob. Ex PANTER, 2. cf. HEAVERS.

panteys; in C.20, gen. **panties.** Pantaloons: ca 1848–60: coll: orig. and mainly U.S. (Burton, *Waggeries*, 1848). 2. Women's or children's drawers: 1905: coll.

pantible, see PANTABLES.

pantile. 'Erroneously applied to flat Dutch or Flemish paving tiles, and so' – in the pl – 'to the Parade at Tunbridge Wells which was paved with these', O.E.D.: ca 1770–1830. Properly 'a roofing tile transversely curved to an ogee shape' (id.). cf. PANTILE-HOUSE. 2. A hat: ca 1859–90. Ex shape. cf. TILE. 3. A flat cake, jam-covered: schoolboys': from ca 1863. Ex sense 1. 4. A hard biscuit, esp. one of those carried by Liverpool ships: nautical: from ca 1880; ob. Ex sense 1.

pantile(-)house, (-)shop. ca 1780–1830: s. rapidly > coll: resp. 1785, Grose; 1796, Grose (hence, 1790 or 1791). 'A Presbyterian, or other dissenting meeting house, frequently covered with pantiles, called also a cock pit', Grose, 1st ed.

Pantile Park. London's roofs and chimney-pots: jocular coll: mid-C.19–20; extremely ob.

pantiler. A Dissenter: coll: app. ca 1720–1890, but not recorded before 1863, according to F. & H., 1889 according to the O.E.D.; it occurs in H., 1860. Ex PANTILE, 1. 2. Hence, a religious prisoner: prison-staff s.: early C.19. Mayhew, 1856, 'The officers . . . used to designate the extraordinary religious convicts as "pantilers".'

pantocle, pantofle, pantople, see PANTABLES.

pantry shelves. Female breasts: domestic: since ca 1870; ob.

pants. Pantaloons: low coll: orig. (1842; 1846, O. W. Holmes) and mainly U.S.; ob. cf. sense 4 and PANTEYS, 1. 2. Pantalettes: coll: orig. (1851), U.S.; ob. 3. Hence, coll (in shops, only of men's) for drawers: 1874, H., 5th ed., 'American term for trousers. Here used to represent the long drawers worn underneath'; 1880, *Daily News*, 8 Nov., 'Pants and shirts sell rather freely.' cf. PANTEYS, 2. 4. Hence, trousers: orig. (—1874), U.S.; low coll, mostly Colonial: late C.19–20.

***panum,** see PANNAM.

panupetaston. A loose, wide-sleeved overcoat: Oxford University: ca 1850–80. H., 5th ed., 1874, 'Now out of fashion'. Prob. ex Gr.

***panzy.** A burglary: c. (—1857); †by 1900. A perversion of PANNEY, 3.

***pap.** Paper; esp. paper money: c.: 1877, Horsley, *Jottings from Jail*, 'A lucky touch for half-a-century' – £50 – 'in pap'. Ex *paper* influenced by S.E. *pap*: or the other way about.

pap, (e.g. his) mouth is full of. A c.p. applied to one still childish: late C.18–early 19. Ex *pap*, babies' food. cf. the C.18 proverb, *boil not the pap before the child be born.*

***pap-feeder.** A spoon: c. of ca 1850–90. Mayhew, 1858.

pap with a hatchet, give. To punish as if one were doing a kindness or conferring a benefit: ca 1589–1719; ob. by 1650. Coll. Lyly or Nashe, 1589; G. Harvey, 1589; D'Urfey, 1719. Halliwell's 'to do any kind action in an unkind manner' perhaps misses the irony.

papa; (C.18) pappa. Father: from ca 1680: S.E. until ca 1780: then a childish coll; since ca 1880, ob. except when jocular. Ex Gr. πάπ(π)ας via Fr.; ultimately cognate with *pap*, a breast (see esp. W., *Adjectives and Other Words*): cf. MAM. See also DAD; DADDY.

paper. Broadsides and similar publications: coll (—1851); ob. Mayhew. cf. PAPER-WORKER. 2. Free passes to an entertainment; collectively, the recipients of such passes: 1870, *Figaro*, 15 July, 'The best sort of paper for a theatre is Bank of England notes.' Also OXFORD CLINK and STATIONERY. cf.:

paper, v.t. To fill (a theatre, etc.) by means of free passes: before 1879. Webster, *Supplement*, 1879. Ex the n., 2. cf. PAPERY.

paper, adj. corresponding to the n., 2: theatrical (—1909). Esp. in *paper house.*

paper, reading the. The excuse given for taking a nap: c.p.: from ca 1880.

paper-boat. Any lightly built vessel, esp. a paddle excursion-steamer: nautical coll: late C.19–20.

paper-collared swell. A 'white-collar worker' (esp. a clerk): New Zealand: ca 1860–1900. A. Bathgate, *Colonial Experiences*, 1874.

paper-fake. A DODGE or LAY (2) with paper, e.g. selling ballads: Cockney: ca 1850–80. Mayhew.

***paper-maker.** A rag-gatherer, gutter-searcher: c. >, by 1860, low: from ca1835; ob. Brandon. 2. One who, pretending to be the agent of a paper-mill, collects rags free and then sells them: c. (—1839); ob.

paper-man. An officer 'who, being employed on the staff', is 'not available for regimental duty', *Standard*, 24 Oct. 1892; prob. it was used some few years earlier: military coll: ob.

paper-marriage. A Society wedding: from ca 1890. Ex fees paid in banknotes.

paper-mill, the. The record office of the Court of Queen's Bench: legal: ca 1840–1900.

paper-minister. A minister who reads his sermons: Scots coll: 1854, H. Miller. The E.D.D. records, at 1828, *paper-ministry*, 'a ministry of preachers who read their sermons'.

paper-padded. (Of foot-wear) shod with paper instead of with leather: shoemakers' s. (—1887) >, by 1910, coll.

paper-scull (or -skull). A silly or foolish fellow. Also adj. Coll: late C.17–early 19.

paper-sculled (-skulled). Silly, foolish: coll: C.18–early 19.

paper-stainer. A clerk: coll: mid-C.19–20; ob.

paper-worker. A vendor of broadsides: low coll: from ca 1850; ob. Ex PAPER, n. 1. cf. RUNNING PATTERER.

paperer. The issuer of PAPER, n., 2: theatrical: 1879, says Ware. Ex PAPER, v.

papery. Occupied by persons with free passes: 1885, *Referee*, 8 Nov., 'The stalls were partly papery, and partly empty.' Ex PAPER, n., 2.

paplar or papler, see POPLARS.

pappy. Father: childish coll: 1763, Bickerstaff; 1897, 'Ouida'. Diminutive of

PAPA. 2. A nursery form of *pap*, infants' food: coll: 1807, E. S. Barrett; ob.

par. Abbr. *paragraph*, esp. of news; journalistic coll: 1879, W. Black; Ware, however, dates *par-leader* (a short leading article in one paragraph) at 1875. 2. An occ. variant of PA.

par-banging. Tramping, seeking for work: urban lower classes' (—1909). Ware. i.e. banging the *pavé*.

***parachute.** A parasol; umbrella: c. (—1864) >, by 1873, gen. low s.; ob.

parade, burn the, see BURN THE PARADE.

paradise. The gallery of a theatre: 1864; always felt to be French; ob. by 1910. Fr. *paradis*. cf. the cognate *the* GODS (2) and contrast the Fr. *poulailler*.

paradise, get or have a penn'orth of. To get, have, take a drink, esp. of gin: low: ca 1860–1915.

parafinelly. Over-dressy clothes: (low) Glasgow s.: ca 1880–1905. Ex *paraphernalia*.

paralysed. Tipsy: s. verging on coll: ca 1890.

paralytic fit or **stroke.** A badly fitting garment: tailors': from ca 1870; slightly ob. By a pun on that affliction.

***param, parum.** Milk: c.: late C.16–17. Harman. Also YARRUM.

parcel. The day's winnings; a pocket-book: the turf: late C.19–20. *The Pink 'Un and the Pelican*, 1898 (former); *Sporting Times*, 6 April 1901 (latter). 2. An English girl sold into a brothel abroad: c. or low (—1887).

parcel-finder. One who, for lost packets, goes to the pawnbrokers: pawnbrokers' coll (—1887).

parchment. A bluejacket's certificate of service: naval coll: late C.19–20.

pard. A partner; a CHUM: orig. (—1872), U.S.; anglicized ca 1885, chiefly in the Colonies. A coll abbr. of *partner* via *pardner*: itself a coll (—1887), recorded by Baumann – but orig. U.S.

parding. Pardon: sol., esp. among Cockneys: C.19–20. Mayhew, 1861.

Paree. Paris: coll: from ca 1850. Often *gay Paree*. Ex Fr. pronunciation.

parentheses. Bandy legs: printers': from ca 1870. Ex the shape: ( ).

parenthesis, have one's nose in. To have it pulled: ca 1786–1850. Hence, *parenthesis*, the having one's nose pulled: ca 1820–40.

parenthesis, iron. A prison: ca 1810–50. cf. CAGE.

parenthesis, wooden. A pillory: ca 1810–40. cf. preceding.

pariah brig. A deep-sea native vessel of India: nautical: late C.19–20. Punning *pariah*.

***parings.** Illicit clippings of money: c.: late C.17–mid-19. A special application of the S.E. sense. (Grose's *chippings* is an error.)

parings of one's nails, not to give, lose, part with the. To be a miser: semi-proverbial coll: from ca 1540; in C.19–20, mostly dial. 'Proverbs' Heywood, Deloney, Mabbe, 'Phraseologia Generalis' Robertson, Northall.

***parish-bull, -prig, -stallion.** A parson: c.: resp. 1811, *Lex. Bal.*; 1864, H., 3rd ed.; F. & H., 1902. Prob. *prig* = PRICK influenced by PRIG, v., 3. cf. the ambiguous C.17 proverb, *the parson gets the children.*

parish-lantern. The moon: dial. and s. (—1847). cf. OLIVER.

parish pick-axe. A prominent nose: lower classes' (—1909); ob.

parish-rig. A poorly found ship or an ill-clothed man: Canadian (and Eastern U.S.) nautical: late C.19–20. Bowen. Ex S.E. *parish-rigged*, cheaply rigged.

parish-soldier. ca 1780–1850. 'A jeering name' – prob. coll rather than s. – 'for a militia man, from substitutes being frequently hired by the parish from which one of its inhabitants is drawn.'

parish-stallion, see PARISH-BULL.

parishes, his stockings are of (later, **belong to) two.** A c.p. applied to one whose stockings or socks are odd: ca 1790–1860.

park. A prison: low s. and Northern dial.: ca 1820–70. Perhaps ex the privileged circuit round the King's Bench and/or the Fleet Prison. 2. A back yard, a small strip of garden in a town: jocular coll: from ca 1890; ob. 3. See BUSHY PARK.

park, in the, see BUSHY PARK, AT.

park-paling(s), -railings. Teeth: low: 1811, *Lex. Bal.* (*paling*); *railings* from ca 1860. 2. A neck of mutton: low: from ca 1880. Ex the appearance.

parker. A very well-dressed man frequenting the parks: low London: mid-C.19–20; ob.

***parker,** v.i. and t. To speak (about); ask; beg: c.: from ca 1890; ob. P. H. Emerson, 1893, 'Have you parkered to the owner for your letties?' Ex It. *pargliare*, via Lingua Franca, or a corruption of *Parlary*. 2. To hand out (money): id.: id.

Pugh, '"If I'd a brighfull o'posh," she said, "I wouldn't parker no wedge to you."'

parker from (or **with**) **denarly.** To pay up: Parlary, esp. cheapjacks': from ca 1870. Pugh, cheapjack *loquitur*: '"I like the Birmingham people," I said. "They are nice people, sensible people, and they 'parker from denarly' without fuss."' Lit., part from money; *parker* represents It. *partire*; for *denarly*, see DINARLEE.

parkering ninty. Wages: Parlary: since ca 1860. (P. H. Emerson, *Signor Lippo*, 1893.)

parky; incorrectly **parkey.** Cold; chilly. (Only of weather; in Midland dial., however, it = witty, smart or sharp of tongue.) From 1898 or a little earlier. Prob. ex *perky*, *parky*, characteristic of a park; cf. dial. *parkin*, ginger-bread.

parleyvoo. Occ. **parlyvoo, parl(e)y-vous, parlezvous.** The French language: coll: 1754, Foote, 'A French fellow . . . with his muff and parlevous.' 2. The study of French: coll: late C.19–20. 3. A Frenchman: 1815 (O.E.D.): slightly ob. cf. Fr. *goddam*, an Englishman: even C.15 Villon alludes to the oath. Ex *parlez-vous*, do you speak (e.g. French)?

parleyvoo, adj. French: 1828, Moir. 2. Loosely, foreign: late C.19–20. Both coll.

parleyvoo, v.i. To speak French: s. when not jocular coll: 1765, Foote, 'You know I can't parler vous.' Ex the n., 1, q.v. also for variant spellings. 2. Hence, to speak a foreign language: from ca 1880; ob. cf. SLING THE BAT.

parliament!, kiss my. A rude c.p., based on 'the *Rump* Parliament': early Restoration period. Pepys, Feb. 1660, 'Boys do now cry, "Kiss my Parliament".' 2. Also *parliament house*. A privy: late C.19–20. Because one sits there.

parliament whiskey. Whiskey on which inland-revenue dues have been paid: Anglo-Irish coll: from the 1820s.

Parliamentary press. 'An old custom of claiming any iron, which happens to be in use, for the purpose of opening the collar seam', Barrère & Leland, 1889. Tailors': ob.

parlour; front parlour. The female pudend: low: C.19–20. Whence:

parlour and lie backward, let out one's. To be a whore: low: C.19–20; ob. cf. LETS OUT HER FORE-ROOMS, etc.

parlour into the kitchen, out of the. From good to bad: coll: late C.16–17. Florio. cf. OUT OF GOD'S BLESSING INTO THE WARM SUN.

***parlour-jump,** v. Ex PARLOUR-JUMPING: c.: 1894, Arthur Morrison.

***parlour-jumper.** One who specializes in PARLOUR-JUMPING: c.: from ca 1870, says Ware.

***parlour-jumping.** Theft from rooms, esp. by entering at the window: c.: from not later than 1879.

parlous. Extremely clever, shrewd, mischievous; extraordinary: C.15–20 (ob.): S.E. until ca 1840, then dial. and coll (= AWFUL, terrible).

parly. A Parliamentary train: railwaymen's (—1887).

parlyvoo, parlyvous, see PARLEYVOO, n. and v.

parnee, parn(e)y; in India, mostly **pawnee.** Water: orig. (—1862) among strolling actors (Mayhew); by 1890, fairly gen. low s., though – witness Yule & Burnell – popular in Anglo-Indian, e.g. in BRANDY-PAWNEE, by 1865. English usage derives ex Romany *pani*, *paani*, *pauni* (Smart & Crofton), itself ultimately the Hindustani *pani*. 2. Rain: Anglo-Indian (—1859); slightly ob. (The term is now common in Parlary and in the s. of Petticoat Lane.)

parnee(-), but gen. **pawnee(-)game.** Water-drinking, esp. as abstinence from liquor: low: 1893, P. H. Emerson, 'He sticks to the pawnee game.' See PARNEE.

parrot and monkey time. A period of quarrelling: ca 1885–1915. Adopted ex U.S., Ware noting that it 'started from a droll and salacious tale of a monkey and a parrot'. Whence *parroty time*.

parrot must have an almond, the. A c.p. applied to or hinting of incentive, reward, or bribery, very common ca 1520–1640. Skelton; Nashe, *Almond for a Parrot*, 1590; Shakespeare; Jonson; 'Water Poet' Taylor. Ex parrot's delight in almonds.

parroty time. The same as PARROT AND MONKEY TIME: 1886, *Daily News*, 12 Oct. †.

parsley. The pubic hair: low: C.18–20; almost †. cf.:

parsley-bed. The female pudend: low: from ca 1600 (see Mabbe quotation in O.E.D.); 1659, Anon., *The London Chanticleers*, a play; Ned Ward, 1719. Esp. *take a turn in the parsley-bed*, to coït with a woman; ob. (In folklore – cf. Mabbe, 1622, and R. Brome in *The Antipodes*, 1640 – little girls come from the parsley-bed, little boys from the nettle-bed or from under a gooseberry bush.)

parsnips!, (I) beg (your). I beg your pardon!: low jocular coll (—1887).

parson. Any minister of religion except a priest: coll and, except in country districts, gen. pejorative: mid-C.17–20. South, Hannah More, George Eliot. 2. A sign-post, 'because like him it sets people in the right way', Grose, 1785: prob. from ca 1750, mainly dial.; ob.

parson, v. To marry; to church after child-delivery: coll: from ca 1880.

Parson Mallum!, remember. 'Pray drink about, Sir!': late C.16–18: c.p. Like the next, it must have had its origin in some topicality.

Parson Palmer. 'One who stops the circulation of the glass by preaching over his liquor', Grose, 1785: coll: C.18–early 19. Swift, *Polite Conversation*, Dialogue II. An elaboration of *no preaching* – or *dangerous to preach – over your liquor*, as in Aphra Behn, 1682, and app. a semi-proverb, it is a c.p. cf. preceding.

parsoned, ppl adj. Married in church or chapel: coll (—1886). Esp. *married and parsoned*, duly and legally married: coll.

parsoness. A parson's wife: coll, mostly jocular: 1784 (O.E.D.). cf.:

parsonet. A parson's child: coll, gen. jocular: 1812, G. Colman; ob. 2. A newly fledged or a very unimportant parson: jocular coll: 1834, Gen. P. Thompson, 'fashionable parsonets'; P. Brooks, 1874, 'parsonettes'.

parson's barn, see BARN, PARSON'S.

parson's journeyman. A curate: from ca 1810; ob. An assistant curate does most of the itinerant work of his vicar or rector.

parson's nose. A chicken's or a goose's rump: coll (—1864). cf. POPE'S NOSE by which it was, to Protestants, prob. suggested.

parson's side, pinch on the. To withhold, cheat him of, his tithes: coll > almost proverbial. Lyly, 1579; T. Adams, 1630.

parson's week. A holiday from Monday to the Saturday of the following week: Cowper's letter of 28 June 1790 to Lady Hesketh; also, mid-C.19–20, Monday to Saturday of one week. Coll: late C.18–20.

parson's wife, kiss the. To be lucky in horse-flesh: semi-proverbial coll: late C.18–mid-19.

part, v.i. To pay, give, restore: from ca 1862: s. >, ca 1910, coll. G. R. Sims, 1880, 'The [people on the] top floor rarely parted before Monday morning.' Ex S.E. *part with*, C.14–20.

part brass-rags. To quarrel: naval (from ca 1890) >, by 1900, military. Bowen, 'From the bluejacket's habit of sharing brass cleaning rags with his particular friend'.

part co. To part company: ?orig. naval: ?since ca 1790; by 1850, ob.; by 1910, virtually †.

parter. A payer or giver of what is due or advisable; by itself, 'a free, liberal person' (H.); a bad payer is *a bad parter*. From ca 1862: s. Ex preceding.

partial. Crooked; over-inclined (lit.): coll: late C.18–early 19.

partial to. Liking; fond of: coll: 1696, Prior, 'Athens . . . where people . . . were partial to verse'; A. Lang, 1889, 'Cold sausage (to which Alphonso was partial)'.

particular, n. Something very characteristic or especially liked, e.g. *a glass of one's particular*, i.e. of one's favourite drink: s.: C.19–20. Earliest and mainly in PARTICULAR, LONDON. 2. A very close friend; a favourite mistress: dial. (—1828) >, ca 1830, coll; slightly ob. Gen. P. Thompson, 1830.

particular, adv. Especially: low coll: mid-C.19–20. 'I want to speak to you awfully particular,' *Boy's Own Paper*, cited by Baumann, 1887. (The O.E.D., giving an example of 1600, describes the usage as rare and †.)

particular, London. A Madeira wine imported especially for the London market: coll: 1807, Washington Irving: ob. by 1900. Perhaps the origin of *glass of one's particular* (see PARTICULAR, n., 1). 2. Hence, ex the colour, a London fog: 1852, Dickens: s. >, ca 1890, coll. Also called *London ivy* (London fog in gen.; not a particular one): 1889; somewhat ob. cf. PEA-SOUPER.

particular, one's. The favoured gallant of a courtesan: brothel coll: 1749, John Cleland; ?ob.

partinger. A partner: jocular (—1887); ob.

partners. Two men working together: tailors' coll (late C.19–20) verging on j.

partridge. A harlot: low: late C.17–mid-18. Anon. song of ca 1700. cf. PLOVER, by which – plus *partridge(-shot)*, case-shot – it was prob. suggested.

parts, play (a person) any, or one, of one's. To play a nasty trick on a person: low coll (—1887). Baumann, 'Don't play me any of your parts.'

party. A person: mid-C.17–20: S.E. until ca 1760, then coll (Foote, 1770); from ca 1850, low coll (Bagehot, 1855, 'A go-ahead party'). Esp. *old party*, an old person. Ex such legal phrases as *guilty party*, *be a party to*. See notably Alford's *The Queen's English*, 1863.

pasear; paseo. A walk: U.S. (—1840), anglicized ca 1890. Ex Sp. *paseo*, a walk; *pasear*, to walk. 2. (Only *pasear*.) To walk: id., id.

***pash.** A 'small' coin; a COPPER (2): c. (—1839); †by 1900.

pass in one's checks. To die: orig. (—1872) and chiefly U.S.; anglicized, esp. in Canada and Australia, ca 1890. Nisbet, 1892, 'Mortimer . . . passed in his checks . . . unexpectedly.' Also *hand in*; also, with either v., *chips*, which, however, is rare outside U.S. Ex settling one's accounts at poker.

pass in one's dinner pail. To die: mostly Cockneys': ca 1890–1914. Binstead, *Mop Fair*, 1905.

pass out. To die: coll: 1899. Prob. abbr. *pass out of sight*.

pass the compliment. To give a gratuity: low coll: late C.19–20; ob. Perhaps ex (the ?orig. U.S.) *pass the compliments of the day* (cf. next).

pass the time of day. (In passing) to exchange greetings and/or fleeting gossip: coll and dial.: 1834, A. Parker, 'Two Indians . . . halted . . ., stared . . ., and then civilly passed the time of day.'

passenger. An ineffective member of a racing-boat crew: 1885 (O.E.D.). 2. Hence, such a member of any team or (C.20) on a business or other staff: 1892 (O.E.D.): s. Ex travel by ship. 3. A passenger-train: railwaymen's coll (—1887).

passing-out number. A second-year naval cadet in the training-ship *Britannia*: late C.19–early 20.

passy. (Of a master) severe; bad-tempered: Christ's Hospital: ca 1790–1870. Superseded by VISH. Ex *passionate*, says Blanch in his reminiscences.

past. Beyond (the power or ability of a person): coll: C.17–20. Beaumont & Fletcher, 1611, 'You are welcome . . .; but if you be not, 'tis past me | To make you so; for I am here a stranger.'

past dying of her first child, be. To have had a bastard: coll: mid-C.17–18. Ray, 1678.

past praying for. (Esp. of persons.) Hopeless: coll: mid-C.19–20.

paste. Brains: printers': late C.19–20; ob. Ironically ex PASTE AND SCISSORS.

paste, v. To thrash; implied in 1851, Mayhew, 'He . . . gave me a regular pasting'; H., 5th ed. F. & H. suggests ex bill-sticking; perhaps on BASTE.

paste and scissors. Extracts; unoriginal padding: journalistic coll: late C.19–20. Usually *scissors and paste*, gen. considered as S.E. Ex cutting out and pasting up.

paste away, v.i. To keep on punching: coll: since ca 1870. *Sessions*, Jan. 1882. See PASTE, V.

paste-horn. The nose: shoemakers': 1856, Mayhew; ob. Ex an article of the trade. See also OLD PASTE-HORN. cf. CONK; SMELLER, 2.

pasteboard. A visiting-card: 1837, T. Hook. cf. PASTEBOARD, DROP ONE'S. 2. A playing-card; playing-cards collectively: 1859, Thackeray.

pasteboard, v.t. To leave one's visiting-card at the residence of: 1864; ob. by 1900. Ex preceding and following entry.

pasteboard, drop, leave, lodge, shoot one's. To leave one's visiting-card at a person's residence: mid-C.19–20.

pasteboard-customer. A taker of long credit: trade: from ca 1860; ob. Either ex cards and compliments or ex S.E. *pasteboard*, something flimsy.

pasting, vbl n. A drubbing: see the quotation at PASTE, V.

pastry. Collective for: young and pretty women: from ca 1885; slightly ob.

pasty. A book-binder: mostly among publishers, booksellers, and their carmen: from ca 1860; ob. Ex the paste used in binding books.

pasty, adj. Of the complexion: S.E. 2. Hence, indisposed: (orig. low) coll: 1891, Newman, *Scamping Tricks*, 'I feel pasty.' 3. Hence, angry: low coll: 1892; ob. Milliken, in the *'Arry Ballads*, 'Miss Bonsor went pasty, and reared.'

Pat. An Irishman; often in address: coll: 1806, *Port Folio*, 11 Oct. Ex *Patrick*, the commonest Irish Christian name. cf. PATESS; PATLANDER; PADDY.

Pat and Mick. The penis: Anglo-Irish: late C.19–20. Rhyming on PRICK, 3.

Pat and Mike. A BIKE: rhyming s.: late C.19–20.

patch. The nickname of Sexton, Cardinal Wolsey's domestic jester. T. Wilson, 1553; J. Heywood, 1562. 2. Hence, any 'fool' or jester: ca 1560–1700: coll, soon > allusive S.E. Shakespeare. 3. Hence, an ill-natured or bad-tempered person: C.19–20: coll and dial. Esp. as *cross-patch*. Scott, 1830. 4. The female pudend: low: C.19–20. ?ob.

patch (up)on, not a. Not to be compared with: coll: 1860, Reade, 'Not a patch on you for looks' – a very frequent comparison. Anticipated by Daniel Webster, 1850, in *but as a patch on.*

patched like a whaleman's shirt. (Of a sail or garment) patched as much as it can be: nautical coll: late C.19–20.

patch(e)y. A, gen. the, harlequin: theatrical: from ca 1860; ob. Ex costume.

patchy, adj. Bad-tempered; fractious: coll (ob.) and dial.: 1862, Trollope, 'He'll be a bit patchy . . . for a while.' Ex PATCH, n., 3.

pate. The head, esp. the part normally covered with hair: C.13–20: S.E. until C.19, then coll and gen. jocular. Barham, 'His little bald pate'.

***patent-coat.** An 'inside skirt coat pocket', Brandon: c. of ca 1835–90.

patent-digester. Brandy: coll: from ca 1835; ob. Dickens. Ex its digestive properties.

patent(-)Frenchman. An Irishman: tailors': from ca 1870; ob.

patent-inside, -outside. 'A newspaper printed [first] on the inside (or outside) only, the unprinted space being intended for local news, advertisements, etc.', F. & H.: journalists' (mostly provincial): from ca 1880; very ob.

pater. A father; also in address: mostly among schoolboys: 1728, Ramsay; Miss Braddon, who italicizes it. Direct ex the L. cf. MATER.

***pater-cove,** see PATRICO.

paternoster. A fishing-line with hooks and weights at regular intervals: anglers' coll (in C.20, j.): 1849, Kingsley. Abbr. S.E. *paternoster-line.* Ex rosary-beads.

paternoster, devil's. A muttering, grumbling; a blasphemous exclamation: coll: late C.14–20, but ob. by C.18. (Chaucer;) Terence in English; Congreve.

paternoster-while, in a. In a moment (the time needed for a paternoster); quickly: from ca 1360 (ob. by 1890): coll bordering on S.E. Paston Letters.

Patess. An Irishwoman: coll: 1825, Scott.

patience!, my. An exclamation of surprise: coll: recorded 1873 (E.D.D.); prob. much earlier.

patience on a monument. An extremely patient and long-suffering person: coll: from ca 1890. Henley & Stevenson, 1892, use it as an adj. Prob. ex the seeming patience of all statues, as seen in the immediate origin, Shakespeare's 'She sat, like Patience on a monument, | Smiling at grief.'

patience with, have no. To find too hard to tolerate; be irritated by: coll: 1855, Thackeray, 'I have no patience with the Colonel.'

Patland. Ireland: C.19–20. Earlier than, for it is the origin of:

Patlander. An Irishman: 1820, *Sporting Magazine*; ob. cf. PADDY; PAT.

***patrico.** One of the fifteenth 'rank' of the underworld, a strolling (pseudo-)priest: c.: C.16–20, but ob. by 1820. 2. Hence, C.17–20 (ob. by 1840), any parson or priest: c. The forms include *patriarch-(patriarke-) co*, C.16 rare, as in Awdelay; *pattering-* or *patring-cove*, C.16, Copland; *pater-cove*, late C.17–19 (e.g. in B.E., Grose, and Lytton), *patri-cove* (*A New Canting Dict.*, 1725), and *patter-cove*, C.19–20, as in Henley & Stevenson. (A C.18 song spells it *patrico-coe.*) Prob. ex PATER + CO(VE).

***patrin;** incorrectly **patteran.** 'A gipsy trail, made by throwing down a handful of grass occasionally', H., 5th ed.: vagrants' c. Whyte-Melville, 1876, in *Katerfelto*; 1898, Watts-Dunton in *Aylwin.* Ex Romany *pat(r)in*, a leaf, or (and in C.20 only) a trail-sign. (The Romany for trails is *patreni* or *patrinaw.*)

***patring-cove,** see PATRICO.

pattens, run on. (Of the tongue) to clatter; go *nineteen to the* DOZEN: ca 1550–1620. Udall; (?) Shakespeare. Ex the noise made by clogs.

***patter.** Any secret or technical language: S.E. (says O.E.D.; but prob. orig. c.) of mid-C.18–20. cf. GAMMON AND PATTER. Ex S.E. *patter*, to talk rapidly or glibly. 2. A cheapjack's oratory; JAW; speechifying: from ca 1780; c. >, ca 1840, s. Parker, Vaux, Mayhew. 3. Hence, mere talk; gabble: coll: 1858, Gen. P. Thompson, 'A patter . . . about religion'. 4. A judge's summing-up; a trial: c. or low s.: 1857, 'Ducange Anglicus'. 5. The words of a song, a play, etc.: coll: from ca 1875. J. A. Fuller-Maitland, 1880, 'Mozart and many other composers often introduce bits of "patter" into buffo solos.' 6. A piece of street literature: low (—1889). *Answers*, 11 May 1889. Ex sense 2 or 5, or perhaps ex PATTERER, 3. 7. Food: 1855, John Lang, *The Forger's Wife.* cf. the v., 5.

patter, v. To talk, speak, esp. as a cheapjack or a conjuror: pedlars' s. (—1851). Mayhew. Ex: 2. To talk the secret language of the underworld: c.: from ca 1780.

Parker, *View of Society*. For derivation, see: 3. To speak (some language): c.: 1812, Vaux. Esp. in PATTER FLASH. Ex S.E. *patter*, C.15–20, to talk glibly, rapidly. 4. To try (a person) in a court of justice: c. of ca 1810–50. 5. v.t., to eat: Australian pidgin English: 1833, Sturt, 'He himself did not patter . . . any of it'; ob. App. ex an Aboriginal dialect.

***patter, flash the.** To talk; esp. to talk s. or c.: c. (from ca 1820) >, ca 1880, low s. Prob. ex PATTER FLASH. See PATTER, n., 1 and 2, and FLASH, v.

***patter, stand – occ. be in for – the.** To stand for trial: c.: from ca 1810; ob. Vaux, Haggart. See PATTER, n., 1. (The legal talk.)

***patter-cove,** see PATRICO.

***patter-crib.** A lodging-house, or an inn, frequented by the underworld: c.: from ca 1830. See PATTER, n., 1, and CRIB, n.

***patter flash.** To talk; also to talk s. or c.: c. (—1812) >, ca 1860, low s. cf. PATTER, v., 2; PATTER, FLASH THE.

***patteran.** Incorrect form of PATRIN.

patterer. One who speaks c., low s., or Romany: 1849, Ainsworth: c. rapidly > low s. > s. >, by 1900, coll. Ex PATTER, v., 2. 2. Whence, one who 'speechifies', esp. a cheapjack: s. (—1851) >, ca 1890, low coll. Mayhew. 3. A vendor of broadsides, etc.: from ca 1850; ob. by 1880: s. >, ca 1870, low coll. Esp. RUNNING PATTERER (cf. FLYING STATIONER), one always on the move, and STANDING PATTERER, one selling from a pitch. Mayhew. cf. PATTER, n., 6.

***patterer, humbox-.** A parson: c.: from ca 1838; ob. Serialist Reynolds.

pattering, vbl n. The pert or vague replies of servants: coll: from ca 1690; ob. by 1880. Ex *patter*, to talk glibly. 2. Talk intended to interest a prospective victim: c. or low s.: 1785, Grose.

***pattering-cove,** see PATRICO.

pattern. Delightful; brilliant: Anglo-Irish: late C.19–20. Ware derives it thus: *pattern fair* ex *patron fair*, i.e. *patron saint's fair*.

pauca! Speak little!; say nothing: (?) c.: late C.16–17. i.e., L. *pauca verba*, few words.

paul, see PAWL. **Paul, rob Peter to pay,** see PETER TO PAY.

pauler, see PAWLER. Also, something very puzzling; a poser: as in Captain Glascock, *Land Sharks and Sea Gulls*, 1838.

Paul's, old as, see OLD AS CHARING CROSS.

Paul's (or Westminster) for a wife, go to. To go whoring: coll: late C.16–18. Shakespeare (implied: *2 Henry IV*, I, ii, 58); Ray. Old St Paul's was a resort of loungers and worse (cf. S.E. *Paul's men, walkers*, loungers).

Paul's pigeon. (Gen. pl.) A pupil at St Paul's School, London: from ca 1550. Fuller.

Paul's (steeple), old as, see OLD AS CHARING CROSS.

Paul's work. A bungled job; a MESS: coll: C.17. Dekker, 'And when he had done, made Poules work of it'.

Pauly. (Gen. pl.) A follower of Paul Kruger; a Boer: mostly journalists': 1899–1900.

paunch. To eat: coll: C.17. cf. equivalent *pouch* and Scots *paunch*, swallow greedily.

paunches, join. To copulate: low: C.19–20; ob. cf. *join* GIBLETS.

paup along. Bravely to make ends meet: middle and upper classes': from ca 1880. (Edward Burke, *Bachelor's Buttons*, 1912.) By back-formation ex *pauper*.

paved, have one's mouth. To be hard-mouthed: coll: C.18. Swift, 'How can you drink your Tea so hot? Sure your mouth's pav'd.'

pavio(u)r's or **pavio(u)rs' workshop.** The street: ca 1786–1890. Ex *pavio(u)r, paver*, a paving stone, extant in dial.

paw. A hand: coll: from ca 1590. Chapman, 1605, 'I . . . layd these pawes | Close on his shoulders'; Dryden; Scott. Jocularly ex *paw*, a foot. Also *fore paw*, the hand; *hind paw*, the foot: both recorded in 1785 (Grose) and ob. 2. Handwriting, esp. a signature: coll: C.18–20; ob. Ex sense 1.

paw, v. To handle awkwardly, roughly, coarsely, indelicately: coll: 1604, T. M., 'His palm shall be pawed with pence'; Farquhar; Tennyson. Extension of S.E. senses.

paw, adj. Improper; scrabrous: ca 1660–1740: s. >, ca 1720, coll. Davenant, 'A paw-word' – a stock phrase (gen. unhyphened); Cibber. App. a variant of *pah*, 'nasty, improper, unbecoming', adj. use of *pah*, interjection. cf. PAW-PAW.

paw-case. A glove: low (—1864); very ob. Ex PAW, n.

paw-paw. Naughty; esp. improper; from ca 1720 (S.O.D.): s. >, ca 1820, coll; slightly ob. Grose, 2nd ed., 'An expression used by nurses, &c., to children'. Ex PAW, adj.

paw-paw tricks. Naughty tricks: nursery s. > coll: from ca 1785. Whence, 2, masturbation: low: C.19–20. Ex preceding.

paw-pawness. Nastiness, impropriety: coll: 1828 (O.E.D.); ob. Ex PAW-PAW.

pawked-up stuff. Bad horses or dogs; poor horsemen: sporting (—1909). Ex Scottish (and Northern dial.) *pawk*, a trick, an artifice.

pawl. To check, stop, baffle: nautical coll: from ca 1820. Ex S.E. *pawl*, to secure or stop by means of a pawl. 2. v.i., to cease, esp. talking: nautical coll (—1867). Ex sense 1. Also spelt PALL, and, as in Smyth, *paul.* (Esp. *pawl there!*, stop arguing!)

pawl my capstan!, you. You're too good for me!: naval: late C.19–20; ob. cf. PAWL, 1.

pawler. A final argument or unanswerable objection: nautical coll: from ca 1820. Ex PAWL, 1. (Also spelled *pauler.*)

pawn. Mast of trees: incorrect for *pannage*: ca 1660–1700. 2. A pawnbroker: s. or low coll: 1851, Mayhew; ob. By abbr.

pawn. To slip away from (a person) and leave him to pay the reckoning: low (prob. orig. c.): ca 1670–1750. 2. In error for *palm*: from ca 1785. Marryat, 1832, 'Pawned them off on me'.

pawnee, pawny, see PARNEE.

pax. See PAX ON . . .! 2. A friend: from ca 1780: mostly Public Schools'. At first in *good pax*. 'Winchester' Wrench explains, rightly I think, as a pl of *pack*, though L. *pax* is clearly operative. cf.:

pax! Silence!; truce!: schoolboys' (—1852). Kipling, in *Stalky & Co.*, 1899, '*Pax*, Turkey. I'm an ass.' Ex L. *pax*, peace.

pax, be good. To be good friends: mostly Public Schools': 1781, Bentham, 'We may perhaps be good pax.' See PAX, 2, and cf. PAX! and PAX, MAKE.

pax!, have. An elaboration of PAX!: schoolboys': from ca 1860.

pax, make. To form a friendship: Public Schools': from ca 1840. See PAX, 2.

pax on (it!, him!, etc.). CONFOUND IT!, etc.: low coll: ca 1640–1730. Brome, 'Pax o' your fine Thing'; Addison. Corrupted POX.

paxwax; occ. **pax-wax, packwax.** The nuchal ligament: from late M.E.: S.E. until ca 1850, then coll and dial. A C.19–20 variant is *paxy-waxy*; a late C.17–early 18 one is *fixfax*, which is a sol. 2. The *membrum virile*: C.19–20.

pay. A paymaster: naval coll: late C.19–20. Abbr. *pay-bob*: id.: id.

pay, v. To beat, punish: from ca 1580: S.E. until ca 1750, then coll; from ca 1820, s. and dial. cf. PAY OVER . . ., PAY YOU . . .; PAY OUT. 2. To deliver (e.g. a letter): Anglo-Chinese coll (—1864).

pay, be good (etc). To be sure to discharge one's obligations, esp. one's debts: coll: 1727, Gay, 'No man is better pay than I am'; slightly ob.

pay?, what's to. What's the matter, trouble?: coll: C.19–20. Ex lit. sense.

pay and no pitch hot or ready!, the devil to. A nice mess!: nautical: late C.18–19. Punningly ex the paying, i.e. smearing, of a ship's bottom with pitch to stop a leak.

pay away. To proceed; continue (v.i.), the v.t. form being *pay it away*. Coll: 1670, Eachard (of talking); in C.19–20, mainly nautical. cf. PAY IT OUT! 2. To fight manfully: mainly nautical s. (—1785) >, ca 1850, coll; ob. 3. To eat voraciously: nautical (—1785); almost †.

pay-bob, see PAY, n.

pay down. To send all heavy weights below: nautical coll: late C.19–20.

pay for one's whistle. To pay excessively for one's fancy or whim: non-aristocratic: from ca 1870; ob.

pay into. To PITCH INTO, to strike or punch vigorously: (low) coll (—1887). cf. PAY, v., 1.

pay it out! Keep on talking!: nautical (—1887). Besant, 'Pay it out. [I don't care] – not . . . a rope's yarn.' Ex paying out a rope.

pay off, v. To throw (a thing) away: naval: late C.19–20. Ex paying off a crew.

Pay-off Wednesday. A schoolboys' term (—1864; ob.) for the Wednesday before Advent. H., 3rd ed., cites also *Crib-Crust Monday* and *Tug-Mutton Tuesday*.

pay one's corner. Pay one's share, esp. for drinks; mostly Lancs. and Yorks.: late C.19–20.

pay out. See PAY IT OUT. 2. To give (a person) his deserts: coll: 1863, Cowden Clarke, 'They, in return, (as the vulgar phrase has it,) "pay him out".'

pay out the slack of one's gammon. To relate (too) many stories: low (—1887). Prob. nautical at first.

pay over face and eyes, as the cat did the monkey. To give a terrible beating about the head: a low c.p. (—1860); ob. Ex PAY YOU AS PAUL PAID THE EPHESIANS.

pay the bearer. (Gen. as vbl n.) To cash a

cheque against non-existent funds: bank-clerks': late C.19–20.

pay the shot. To pay the bill: C.16–20: S.E. till C.19, then coll; ob. Hackwood, *Old English Sports,* 1907, '[they] called for their ale . . . and . . . expected the losers "to pay the shot".'

pay up and look pretty, occ. **big.** Gracefully to accept the inevitable: 1894, Sala (*pretty*); *big* is very, *pretty* slightly ob.

***pay with a hook.** To steal: Australian c.: from ca 1870. Brunton Stephens, in *My Chinese Cook,* 1873, 'You bought them? Ah, I fear me, John, | You paid them with a hook.' ?ex HOOK, to steal.

pay with pen-powder. To write fair promises but fail to pay: semi-proverbial coll: ca 1630–80. John Clarke, 1639.

pay (or pay debts) with the fore-topsail. To slip away to sea in debt: nautical: mid-C.19–20. Bowen. The military variant is *with the drum.*

pay you as Paul paid the Ephesians, I will. Explained by the part gen. added: *over the face and eyes and all the damned jaws.* A low c.p.: ca 1780–1850. An elaboration of PAY!; cf. PAY OVER FACE AND EYES, the later form of the phrase.

pea. The favourite; one's choice: low: 1888, *Sporting Life,* 11 Dec., 'Sweeny forced the fighting, and was still the pea when "Time!" was called'; ob. Ex *this is the pea I choose* in thimble-rigging. 2. The head: c.: from ca 1840; ob. '*No. 747*'. Prob. ex *pea-nut*: cf. NUT, 1.

pea, pick (occ. **do**) **a sweet.** To urinate: low (mostly among – or of – women): from ca 1860. Punning PEE. cf. PLUCK A ROSE.

pea-man or **-rigger,** see THIMBLE-RIG.

pea-soup. A French-Canadian: Canadian: late C.19–20. Ex the frequency of that dish on French-Canadian tables: late C.19–20.

pea-souper. A dense yellowish fog: coll: 1890, J. Payn. Ex the next.

pea-soupy. (Esp. of a dense, yellowish fog) resembling pea-soup: coll: 1860 (O.E.D.).

pea-whacker. A nautical variant (late C.19–20) of PEA-SOUPER.

peace, see PIECE.

peach. A detective; esp. one employed by omnibus, and formerly by stage-coach, proprietors to check receipts: from ca 1835; ob. 2. An attractive girl or (gen., young) woman: orig. (1870s), U.S.; anglicized before 1889. Gen. *a regular peach* or *a peach of a girl.* cf. DAISY.

peach, v. As v.t., it is S.E. = †to impeach; extant when it = to divulge, esp. in *peach a word* (1883, O.E.D.); ob. 2. v.i., to blab: coll: 1852, Thackeray, 'The *soubrette* has peached to the *amoureux.*' Ex: 3. v.i., to inform (against a person); turn informer: late C.16–20: S.E. (as in Shakespeare) in C.16–17; coll in C.18–mid-19 (as in Fielding, Hughes); s. in mid-C.19–20. Either absolute or with *against* or (*up*)*on.* Aphetic form of *a-peche,* to appeach. cf. BLOW THE GAB; *give the* OFFICE, n., 2; PUT AWAY, 3; SNITCH; SQUEAK; SQUEAL; TIP THE WINK; WHIDDLE.

peaching, vbl n. Giving of information against a person: turning or being an informer: mid-C.15–20: S.E. until C.18, then coll.

peaching, ppl adj. See preceding entry. C.17–20: S.E. till C.18, then coll. Moore, 1818, 'The useful peaching rat'.

peacock. A horse with a showy action: racing coll: 1869. cf. PEACOCK-HORSE.

peacock, v. To pay (esp. on ladies and gen. brief) morning calls, at which beer was served: Anglo-Indian: from ca 1850; ob. *Graphic,* 17 March 1883. Prob. ex the spotless clothes worn by the visitors. 2. v.t. and i., to buy up the choicest land so as to render adjoining territory useless to others: Australia: from ca 1890; ob. Ex *picking out the* '*eyes*' of the land: punning the *ocelli* on a peacock's feathers. cf. PEACOCKING.

peacock-horse. A horse with showy mane and tail, and with a fine action: undertakers' coll (—1860). cf. PEACOCK, n.

peacocking. The practice mentioned in PEACOCK, v., 2 – than which it is much commoner. 1894, W. Epps, *Land Systems of Australasia.*

peacocking business. A formal, esp. a ceremonial, parade: military: 1870, *Daily News,* 19 April. Ex the gorgeous display of a peacock.

peacock's tail, the. Euclid, Bk III, proposition 8: C.16 coll. Ex the figure.

***peak.** Lace: c. (the O.E.D., however, considers it S.E.): mid-C.17–early 19. Ex S.E. *peak,* a lace ruff. 2. The nose: low: C.19–20.

Peak, send a wife to the (devil's arse-a-). To send a woman about her business when she proves vexing: ca 1663–5. Pepys, *Diary,* 19 Jan. 1663. Ex a courtier's wife being sent home to the Peak in Derbyshire. N.B., *the devil's arse-a-,* or *in the, Peak,* earlier *Peaks arse,* is the Peak Cavern.

peaked. Sickly-looking; pinched, thin, esp. from illness: from ca 1830: mostly coll. Ex sharpness of features.

peaking. Remnants of cloth: drapers', cloth-warehousemen's, from ca 1859. Presumably related to *peak*, to dwindle. cf. CABBAGE.

peakish. Rather thin, pinched, sickly: from ca 1835: coll and dial. Perhaps ex PEAKED.

peaky, peeky. Feeble, puny, sickly: coll and dial.: from ca 1850. Ruskin, 'A poor peeky little sprouting crocus'. Suggested by PEAKED.

peaky (occ. **peeky)-blinder.** A railwayman from Birmingham: railwaymen's: late C.19–early 20. Ex the peaked caps worn by Birmingham 'toughs': cf. the entry in the E.D.D.

peakyish. Rather PEAKY: coll: 1853, 'Cuthbert Bede'; ob. cf. PEAKISH.

peal. The peal of the Chapel bell: Winchester College: from ca 1840: coll > j. > S.E. Mansfield. 2. 'A custom in Commoners of singing out comments on Praefects at Cloister-time', F. & H.: Winchester: mid-C.19–20; ob. 3. ibid., same period, ob.: 'Cheers given on the last three Sundays of the Half for articles of dress, etc., connected with going home', F. & H.

peal, ring (a person) **a;** occ. **ring a peal in one's ears.** To scold him: late C.18–19. cf. the dial. *be* or *get into a peal*, i.e. a temper.

pealer. Incorrect form of PEELER.

peam(e)y. A seller of peas: ca 1820–70. *Sessions*, 1833. A blend of '*pea-merchant*'.

pear. To appear: C.14–20: S.E. till C.18, then coll and dial. Gen. *'pear*. 2. To obtain money from both sides, e.g. from police for information, from underworld for a warning: c.: from ca 1850. Ex:

***pear-making.** To take bounties from more regiments than one: c.: ca 1810–60. ?the making of *pairs*, double-crossing.

pearl in a hail-storm, like a. Impossible to find: non-aristocratic coll (—1887); slightly ob.

pearl on the nail, make a. To drink: coll: C.17–18. Ray. Ex the (late C.16 +) lit. sense, to drop the moisture remaining in a cup, glass, etc., on to one's nail – a drinking custom recorded by Nashe.

pearlies. (The singular hardly exists.) Pearl buttons, esp. on a coster's clothes: from ca 1885: low coll. Henley. 2. Teeth: non-aristocratic: late C.19–20.

peas. Abbr. PEAS IN THE POT: from 1895, says Ware.

peas, as like as two. Very similar indeed: late C.16–20: coll >, in C.19, S.E. In C.16–17, *as . . . pease*; Horace Walpole; Browning, in *James Lee's Wife*.

peas and cues, see PS AND QS, MIND ONE'S.

peas in the pot. Apt to be amorous: low London rhyming s. on *hot*: from ca 1890. 2. Also, hot in the gen. sense.

pease-field, go into the. To fall asleep: coll: ca 1670–1800. Ray. A semi-proverbial pun on *peace*. cf. BEDFORDSHIRE.

pease-kill, make a. (v.t. with *of.*) To squander lavishly: Scots coll: C.18–20. Likewise, *a pease-kill* = a very profitable matter.

pebble. A person or animal difficult to handle: Australia: from ca 1890; slightly ob. 'Boldrewood', 1890, 'A regular pebble'. From ca 1905, it has, esp. in the big towns, meant rather a FLASH fellow; a LARRIKIN. Ex his 'hard-boiled' ways (cf. HARD NUT). Also *peb*. 2. A familiar term of address: ca 1840–60. Moncrieff, *The Scamps of London*, 1843. Occ. *pebbles*.

pebble-beach, v. To clean out of money: ca 1885–1905. Marshall in '*Pomes*'.

pebbles. The human testicles: low: C.19–20; very ob. Suggested by STONES.

pebbles, my. See PEBBLE, 2. Moncrieff, 1843.

pebbly beach, land on or sight a. To be very short of money; faced with ruin: ca 1885–1905. Marshall in his '*Pomes*' (*sight a . . .*). cf.:

pebbly-beached. Penniless – or nearly so. ca 1885–1905. Ex STONY-BROKE.

pec. Money; Eton College: C.19. Ex L. *pecunia*.

***peck;** in C.16–mid-17, occ. **pek.** Food; GRUB: from ca 1565: c. until C.19, then low s. Harman, Jonson, Centlivre, Moncrieff. cf. PECKAGE. 2. A business or concern, as 'a racing peck' (P. H. Emerson, *Signor Lippo*, 1893): low: ca 1870–1910. Perhaps ex sense 1.

***peck,** v.i. and v.t. To eat: mid-C.16–20: c. until C.19, then s. till ca 1860, then coll. Copland; Egan; Dickens, 'I can peck as well as most men.' Ex a bird's pecking; ?cf., however, Welsh Gypsy *pek*, to bake or roast. 2. To pitch forward; (esp. of a horse) to stumble: coll (mid-C.19–20) and dial.: from ca 1770. Ex †S.E. v.i. *peck*, to incline.

***peck** combinations, *peck* being the second member: **gere-peck,** a turd, C.17–19; **grunting-peck,** pork, C.17–20, ob.;

ruff-peck, bacon, C.17–19; **rum-peck**, good eating, an excellent meal: late C.17–early 19.

***peck, off one's.** Off one's appetite: c.: C.18–19.

peck-alley. The throat: low: C.19–20. Ex PECK, n.

peck and booze or **tipple.** Meat and drink: low (BOOZE orig. c.): C.18–20, the former; C.19–20, the latter. Mrs Delany, 1732. cf. BUB and GRUB and:

peck and perch. Food and lodging: low (?orig. c.): 1828, O.E.D.; slightly ob.

***peck-kidg**, see:

***peckage**; occ. **peckidge.** Food; food-supply: c.: C.17–18. Rowlands, B.E. Ex PECK, n. and v., 1.

pecker. The appetite: mid-C.19–20. Ex PECK, v., 1. Possibly ex the next sense. 2. Resolution, courage: 1848 (S.O.D.); 'Cuthbert Bede', 1853, 'Keep up your pecker, old fellow.' Perhaps *pecker* implicitly = beak (hence, head), app. ex the alert sparrow. 3. (With an adj.) an eater, esp. *a good* or *rare pecker*: from ca 1860. Ex PECK, v., 1. 4. The penis: low: C.19–20; ob. A pun on COCK?

Peckham, all holiday at, see ALL HOLIDAY.

Peckham, go to. To go to, sit down to, a meal: jocular coll: C.19. Bee, 1823; Halliwell.

***peckidge**, see PECKAGE.

peckish. Hungry: 1785, Grose: in C.18, perhaps c.: C.19, (orig. low) s. George Moore, 1894, 'I feel a bit peckish, don't you?' Ex PECK, n.

pecky. Choppy (sea, as in Blackmore); (of a horse) inclined to stumble. Coll: from ca 1860, though unrecorded before 1864. 2. (Esp. of kisses) like a bird's peck: coll: 1886, F. C. Philips, 'Flabby, pecky kisses'.

pecnoster. The penis: low: C.19–20, ob. Ex PECKER, 4; punning *paternoster*.

peculiar. A mistress: coll: late C.17–19. Ex the S.E. sense of the adj.: private. 2. A member of the Evangelical party, ca 1837–8: coll nickname at Oxford. Newman. 3. (Of a bowled ball) odd; peculiar to the bowler: cricket coll: 1864; very ob.

peculiarly. More than usually: coll: from ca 1890. Helen Harris, 1891, 'The Arabs regard the spot as peculiarly sacred.' By confusion with S.E. *particularly*, very.

ped. A professional runner, walker: 1863, Anon., *Tyneside Songs*. Abbr. *pedestrian.*

peddler's French. See PEDLAR'S FRENCH. (**peddling French** is a rare C.16 variant.)

pedestrian digits. The legs: schoolboys': ca 1890–1910.

Pedlar. The 'inevitable' nickname of men surnamed Palmer: mostly military: late C.19–20. Ex the medieval palmers or pilgrims.

pedlar's or **peddler's French.** Underworld slang: 1530, Palsgrave: in C.16, c. or low s.; C.17, s.; C.18, coll; C.19–20, S.E. but long very ob. 2. Hence, any unintelligible jargon: late C.17–early 19: coll.

pedlar's news. Stale news: coll: C.19. cf. PIPER'S NEWS.

pedlar's pad, occ. **horse, pony.** A walking-stick: from ca 1780: coll (†) and dial. (ob.). cf. PENANG LAWYER, contrast SHANKS'S MARE.

pee. A urination: coll, mostly nursery: C.19–20. Ex:

pee, v. To make water: coll, esp. nursery: 1788, Picken, (of a cat) 'He never pee'd his master's floor.' A softened perversion of PISS.

pee and kew, see P AND Q.

pee-pee, do. A variant of PEE, v.: children's coll: late C.19–20. cf.:

pee-wee. Either sexual organ: nursery: C.19–20. Prob. ex the v. 2. A small marble: schoolboys': ca 1880–1910. ?ex its yellowish colour.

pee-wee, v. To make water: nursery: C.19–20. An elaboration of PEE, V.

peechy; rarely **peachy.** Soon; presently: Regular Army coll: late C.19–20. Hindustani *pichhe*.

peek-a-boo. A girl's blouse with perforations: ca 1880–1914.

peeky, see PEAKY.

peel. To undress: v.i., 1785, Grose. 2. Hence, v.t., to strip, 1820, 'Corcoran' Reynolds. Both pugilistic j. > gen. coll. Ex peeling fruit. cf. PEELED.

peel eggs. To stand on ceremony: s. or low coll: from ca 1860; ob.

Peel (occ. **peele**) **Garlic,** see PILGARLIC.

peel off. To obtain money by a Stock Exchange transaction: financial: from ca 1860. Ware.

peel one's best end. To effect intromission: low: C.19–20.

peeled. Naked: coll: 1820.

peeler, Peeler. (cf. BOBBY.) A member of the Irish constabulary: 1817, Parliamentary Debates; †by 1860 as a distinct term. 2. Hence, any policeman: 1829, *Blackwood's Magazine*: s. > coll. Ex Mr (later Sir) Robert Peel, Secretary for Ireland, 1812–18. 3. One ready to strip for a fight: boxing: 1852, Anon., *L'Allegro*. Ex PEEL.

peenicker pawnee (or **-ie**). A frequent variant of PINNICKY PAWNEE.

***peep.** To sleep: c.: late C.17–mid-18. On *sleep*.

peep-bo. Bo-peep: coll: 1818, Alfred Burton; 1837, Dickens, 'A perpetual game of peep-bo'.

peep o' day tree. 'Providential stage machinery', e.g. a tree whereby escapes and/or rescues are effected: theatrical coll: 1862; ob. Ware. Ex such a tree in *Peep o' Day*, an extremely successful piece produced at the Lyceum Theatre in 1862.

peep-by, see PEEPY-BY.

peep-o(h)! (To and by children.) Look at me!: here I am!, esp. as one emerges from hiding: coll: C.19–20; perhaps centuries earlier.

***peeper.** A looking-glass: c.: from ca 1670; ob. Coles, 1676. Also, as in B.E., *peepers*. Ex *peep*, v. 2. A spy-glass: c.: late C.18–early 19. 3. An eye: from ca 1690: c. >, ca 1750, low s. Gen. in pl. cf. GLAZIER, 2; GLIMS; OGLES. 4. In pl, spectacles: c.: C.19–20; ob. 5. (Almost always pl.) A policeman: late C.19–20.

peeper, single. A one-eyed person: late C.18–mid-19: low (?orig. c.).

peepers. See PEEPER, 1, 4. 2. *painted peepers, peepers in mourning*: black eyes: C.19–20; ob. Egan, 1818, 'Peepers . . . taken measure of for a suit of mourning'; H., 1860, 'Painted peepers . . .' Pugilistic in origin, mainly such in use.

***peeping.** Drowsy, sleepy: c.: mid-C.17–early 19. cf. PEEPY.

peeping Tom. An inquisitive person: 1785, Grose: coll >, ca 1850, S.E. Ex the Coventry legend of Lady Godiva.

peepsies. The pan-pipes: street-performers' s., almost j.: late C.19–20; ob.

***peepy.** Sleepy: late C.17–20: c. >, ca 1750, s. >, ca 1820, coll (ob.) and dial. Ex PEEP. cf. PEEPING. 2. Given to peeping: coll: 1898, M. P. Shiel, 'Peepy little bewitching eyes'.

peepy-by, go to. To fall asleep: from ca 1840. Also *go to peep-by*: from ca 1850; ob. Both, coll and dial. Ex PEEPY.

peer. To make (a man) a peer; ennoble: coll: 1753. 2. To be circumspect: c.: late C.18–mid-19. Ex PEERY, adj.

***peery,** n. (Gen. *there's a peery*.) A being observed, discovered: c.: late C.18–mid-19. Grose, 1785, 'There's a peery, 'tis snitch, We are observed, there's nothing to be done.' Ex:

***peery;** occ., in C.17–mid-18, spelt *peerie*; adj. Sly: c.: late C.17–20; extremely ob. Ex *to peer*. cf. LEARY. 2. Shy, timid, suspicious: from ca 1670; slightly ob. in last, †by 1850 in first and second nuance. Coles and B.E. give it as c., O.E.D. as S.E.; almost certainly, until mid-C.18, either c. or low s. 3. Hence, inquisitive: from ca 1810 (ob.): low.

***peeter.** See PETER. Coles's and B.E.'s spelling.

peety. Cheerful: C.18: c., says F. & H., but is it? Perhaps ex *peart*.

peg. A drink (esp. of brandy and soda-water): Anglo-Indian: 1860, H., 2nd ed., is app. the earliest record; 1864, Trevelyan, '. . . According to the favourite derivation, because each draught is a "peg" in your coffin'; actually ex *peg* as one of the pins in a drinking-vessel. 2. A blow, esp. a straight or a thrusting one: s. and dial.: 1748, Smollett. 3. A wooden leg: coll: 1833, M. Scott. 4. A tooth (esp. a child's): late C.16–20: S.E. till C.19, then dial. and nursery coll. 5. A shilling: Scottish c.: 1839, Brandon. 6. A cricket stump: coll: 1891, W. G. Grace. 7. See OLD PEG. 8. A, or the most, telling point in a play: theatrical coll: 1884. Ware, 'Something upon which the actors, or more probably an actor, can build up a scene'.

peg, v. (See PEG INTO; PEG IT; PEG IT INTO; PEG OUT; PEG UP.) 2. drive: 1819, Moore, 'I first was hir'd to peg a Hack' (i.e. a hackney-coach); ob. 3. (Also with *away, off, along*) to move, or go, vigorously or hastily: dial. >, ca 1855, coll. Le Fanu, 1884, 'Down the street I pegged like a madman.' 4. To work persistently, 'hammer' away; coll: C.19–20. Esp. PEG AWAY, in eating, and PEG ALONG. 5. To tipple: 1874, H., 5th ed. Ex PEG, n., 1. 6. (Gen. *peg up* or *down*.) To copulate, v.t., occ. v.i.: low coll: from ca 1850. 7. v.t., to fix the market price of: Stock Exchange: from ca 1880: s. Gen. as PEG UP. 8. To starve (v.i.): Australian: late C.19–20.

peg, old, see OLD PEG.

peg, on the. Under arrest. 2. Fined; having had one's pay stopped. Both military: late C.19–20.

peg, put in the. To stop giving credit: coll ex dial.: late C.19–20. 'A peg of wood above the latch inside . . . effectually locked it,' Dr Bridge.

peg, put (oneself) on the. To be careful, esp. as to liquor, behaviour, etc.: late C.19–20 military; ob. Perhaps suggested by the preceding entry as well as by PEG, ON THE. cf. PIN, KEEP IN THE. 2. *put* (another) ... To arrest: military: late C.19–20. See PEG, ON THE.

peg a hack. See PEG, v., 2. 2. 'To mount the box of a hackney coach, drive yourself, and give the *Jarvey* a holiday': c.: ca 1820–50. Egan's Grose.

peg along. To 'hammer' away: coll: mid-C.19–20. See PEG, v., 3, and cf. the equivalent:

peg away, v.i.; peg away at, occ. and ob. **on.** Coll: from ca 1825. Dickens, 1837, '... The breakfast. "Peg away, Bob," said Mr Allen encouragingly.' Ex 'industrious hammering in of pegs', W. See preceding entry.

peg down, see PEG, v., 6.

peg into. To hit; let drive at: coll: from ca 1880. Ex PEG IT INTO.

peg (or nail) (in)to one's coffin, add or **drive a.** To drink hard: from ca 1860; ob. Ex the old peg-tankards: cf. PEG LOWER; PEG TOO LOW.

peg it. A variant, from ca 1860, of PEG, v., 2. 2. Inseparable part of:

peg it into. To hit: 1834, Dowling, 'You peg it into him, and pray don't spare him': coll; ob. cf. PEG INTO and PEG IT.

peg-leg. A person with a wooden leg: (low) coll: C.19–20. Ex S.E. sense, a wooden leg.

peg lower, go a. To drink to excess: coll: C.19–20; very ob.

peg out. To be ruined: ca 1880–1910. Ex: 2. To die: ?orig. U.S. (1852); certainly anglicized by 1860. Prob. ex cribbage, where pegs are used to keep score; whoever pegs out first, wins. '"My uncle's pegged out," he said. "His game of cribbage is done."' Morley Roberts, *Maurice Quain*, 1897. 3. To go to – and use – the w.c.: a certain Oxfordshire girls' school: (?) late C.19–20. Ex the feminine posture involved and its resemblance to an old-fashioned clothes-peg.

peg-puff. An old woman dressing young: Scots coll: from ca 1810; ob. (Perhaps dial.)

peg too low, a. Tipsy: ca 1870–1915. **2.** Hence, (fig.) depressed: from ca 1880.

Peg Trantum's, gone to. Dead: from ca 1690. †by 1860. Occ. *Peg Crancum's* (Ned Ward). Note that in East Anglia *Peg Trantum* is extant for a hoyden.

peg up. See PEG, v., 6 and 7. (*Pall Mall Gazette*, 8 April 1882, 'Arbitrarily raising prices ... "pegging prices up", it is called.'

pegged out, be. To be notorious: low: 1886, *Tit-Bits*, 31 July; ob.

pegger. A hard drinker: ca 1873–1915: coll. Ex PEG, a dram, and the v. cf.:

pegging. Tippling: from ca 1870; ob.

peggy. A thin poker bent for the raking of fires: coll: from ca 1860; ob. cf. CURATE; RECTOR. 2. (Gen. *Peggy.*) 'A hand ... called upon to do all the odd jobs in a watch': nautical: C.19. Bowen. Ex his 'feminine' duties. 3. (Gen. pl.) A tooth: children's coll: late C.19–20. Ex PEG, n., 4. 4. A man with only one leg: navvies' nickname: ca 1860–1910. (D. W. Barrett, 1880.)

pego. 'The penis of man or beast', Grose: C.18–mid-19. Ned Ward, 1709. Ex Gr. πηγή, a spring, a fountain.

pegs than square holes, there are always more round. There are always more applicants than jobs: coll: late C.19–20; ob. Ex S.E. *round peg in a square hole* (or *square peg ...*).

pek, see PECK.

pelf. Ill-gotten money: workmen's (—1887). Implied by Baumann. Ex S.E. *pelf*, money.

***pelfry.** The booty obtained by picking locks: c.: late C.16–early 17. Greene, 1592. Ex S.E. *pelf*.

***pell,** see PAL.

pelt. The human skin: coll (jocular) and dial.: C.17–20. Rowley, ca 1605, 'Flay off her wicked skin, and stuff the pelt with straw.' 2. Hence, a man: Yorkshire and Pembrokeshire s., not dial.: 1882.

pelt, v. To sew thickly: tailors': from ca 1860. Prob. suggested by *pelts*, garments made of furry skins.

pelter. A heavy shower: coll: 1842, Barham, 'The rain ... kept pouring ... What I've heard term'd a regular pelter.' Ex the weather v.i. 2. Anything large: coll (—1892) ex dial. (—1851); ob. Milliken. 3. A whoremonger: tramps' c.: from ca 1850; ob.

pelter, out for a. In a very bad temper: proletarian: from ca 1860; ob.

peltis-hole. A Scots coll pejorative addressed to women: late C.16–17. i.e. *pelts-hole*, i.e. tan-pit.

pempë. An imaginary object for which a newcomer is sent: Winchester College: C.19–20; ob. Ex πέμπε τὸν μῶρον πρότερον, send the fool further; i.e. keep the idiot moving! cf. *oil of* STRAP-'EM.

pen. The male member: late C.16–20 low; ob. (cf. PENCIL.) Ex shape of a pen + abbr. *penis*. See next entry. 2. A **peniten**tiary; a prison: low, almost c.: from ca 1820. 3. A threepenny piece: Colonial, says F. & H.; but which Dominion?: app. ca 1870–1910. Origin? 4. The female pudend: low: mid-C.19–20. Properly of sows. 5. (As n. or v.) Stink: low: late C.19–20. Abbr. of PEN AND INK.

pen, have no more ink in the. To be temporarily impotent from exhaustion: low: late C.16–17. e.g. in Weever's *Lusty Juventus*. Ex PEN, 1.

pen and ink. A stink: rhyming s.: from ca 1858. 2. Hence, to stink: id.: from ca 1870. 3. To kick up a STINK (n., 2), i.e. to yell (with pain): Cockney: late C.19–20.

pen-driver. A clerk; occ. a writer: coll: from ca 1885; very ob. Suggested by QUILL-DRIVER.

pen-gun; crack like a p.g. To chatter. Scots coll: C.19–20. Scott. Occ. *penguin*. (A toy gun made from a quill.)

penal. A sentence or a term of penal servitude: coll: from ca 1890. 2. See PENALS, 2.

penals. Lines as punishment: mid-C.19–20: Shrewsbury School s. >, by 1890, coll >, by 1900, j. Desmond Coke, *The Bending of a Twig*, 1906. 2. Hence, *penal* is a set of 25 lines: from ca 1870: s. > coll >, by 1900, j. ibid.

***penance-board.** A pillory: c.: late C.17–early 19.

Penang lawyer. The stem of a species of palm much used for walking-sticks, hence a walking-stick so made: coll: from ca 1820; ob. Prob. *Penang liyar* (the wild areca), corrupted. 2. Whence a bludgeon: Singapore: from ca 1870.

***penbank.** A beggar's can: c.: C.18. Bailey. Origin?

pencil. The male member: low: late C.19–20. Ex shape. cf. PEN, 1.

pencil, knight of the. A bookmaker: the turf: 1885, *Punch*, 7 March; ob. cf. PENCILLER.

pencil-fever. The laying of odds against a horse certain to lose, esp. after it has at first been at short odds: the turf: from ca 1872; ob. Also *market-fever* and *milk-fever*. Ex the pencilling of the horse's name in betting-books. Whence PENCILLER.

pencil-in dates. To make engagements to perform: theatrical coll: 1896; slightly ob.

pencil, open, lost, and found. Ten pound (sol. for ten pounds sterling): rhyming s.: from ca 1870; ob.

pencil-shover. A journalist: printers' (—1887); ob. On QUILL-DRIVER.

penciller. A bookmaker's clerk: the turf; *Daily News*, 24 Oct. 1879. See PENCIL-FEVER. cf.:

pencilling fraternity. Bookmakers, collectively: the turf: from ca 1890; ob.

pendulum. The penis: low: C.19–20; ob. cf. DINGLE-DANGLE.

pene(r)th, see PENN'ORTH.

Peninsular. A veteran of the Peninsular War: coll: *Quarterly Review*, 1888, but prob. in use from ca 1840. Ob. by 1900, †by 1910. 2. (Also called a *moll tooler*, H., 1st ed.) A female pickpocket: c.: (—1859); very ob.

***penman.** A forger: c.: late C.19–20.

***pennam.** A rare variant of PANNAM.

pennel, see PINNEL.

pen(n)e(r)th. C.16–17 forms of PENN'ORTH.

pennif. A five-pound note: back sl: 1862. *Cornhill Magazine*.

penniless bench, sit on the. To be poverty-stricken: coll: late C.16–19. Massinger, 'Bid him bear up, he shall not | Sit long on penniless bench.' Ex a certain London seat so named. cf. S.E. *Pierce Penniless*.

penn'orth, pennorth, pen'orth; penn'worth. Abbr. *pennyworth*: coll: resp. C.17, C.18–20, C.18–19 (H.); C.17. cf. PEN(N)E(R)TH; PENWORTH.

pennorth, take a, esp. in the imperative. To go away: Cockney: late C.19. Of fresh air? Or ex PENNORTH OF CHALK?

penn'orth of bread. Head: navvies' rhyming s.: ca 1860–1910. (D. W. Barrett, *Navvies*, 1880.)

penn'orth (or ball) of chalk. A walk: late C.19–20.

pennorth o(f) treacle. A charming girl: low London: 1882–ca 1912. Ex JAM, 2.

penny, clean as a. Completely: coll (and dial.): 1820–1910. cf. the 'brightness = completeness' semantics of *clean as a whistle*.

penny, turn and wind the. To make the most of one's money: coll: late C.17–18. An elaboration of S.E. *get* or *turn a* or *the penny*, to endeavour to live, hence to make money.

penny-a-liar. A jocular variation (—1887; ob.), recorded by Baumann, of:

penny-a-liner. A writer of paragraphs at a cheap rate, orig. a penny a line; hence, a literary hack: 1834, Ainsworth: journalistic coll >, ca 1905, S.E.

penny-a-mile. A hat: rhyming s. (on TILE): from ca 1870. 2. Hence, head: late C.19–20.

penny a pound; often merely *penny.* Ground: rhyming s.: late C.19–20.

penny(-)awful. An occ. variant of PENNY DREADFUL: ca 1875–1910.

penny-boy. A boy haunting cattle-markets in the hope of some droving: coll: C.19. Because paid a penny a beast. Also ANKLE-BEATER.

penny(-)buster. A small new loaf, or a large bun or roll, costing one penny: ca 1870–1910. H., 1874. But a *penny starver* is a stale one or an unusually small one (†by ca 1910); orig., however, a *starver* meant a halfpenny loaf, or, occ., a bun: H., 1874.

penny death-trap. A penny paraffin-lamp: low London: 1897–ca 1915. Made in Germany, these lamps caused numerous deaths.

penny(-)dreadful. A sensational story or (†by 1910) print: coll: H., 1874; *Pall Mall Gazette,* 17 Nov. 1892, 'A Victim of the Penny Dreadful', title. Occ. *penny †awful* or (ob.) *horrible*; cf. BLOOD-AND-THUNDER TALES; SHILLING SHOCKER; (U.S.) *dime novel.*

penny-farthing. An old-fashioned, very high bicycle with a large and a small wheel: coll: from ca 1885; ob.

penny for your thought(s). A c.p. addressed to one preoccupied: from ca 1540. Heywood's *Proverbs,* 1546; Greene; Swift. The *-s* form, which is not found before C.17, > gen. in C.18; *a penny for 'em* is late C.19–20.

penny(-)gaff. A low-class theatre, music-hall: 1851, Mayhew; slightly ob. Also *penny-room.* Ex GAFF, 6.

penny gush. 'Exaggerated mode of writing English frequently seen in a certain London daily paper': journalistic coll: ca 1880–5. Ware.

penny hop. A cheap (country) dance: C.19.

penny-horrible. A PENNY DREADFUL: coll: 1899, *Daily News,* 13 June; ob. cf. PENNY AWFUL.

penny lattice-house. A low ale-house: coll: C.18–early 19.

***penny loaf.** A man afraid to steal: c. (—1909). Lit., one who would prefer to live on a penny loaf.

penny locket. A pocket: rhyming s. (—1909).

penny or paternoster. Pay or prayers; only in *no paternoster, no penny* (no work, no pay): proverbial coll: mid-C.16–early 18. Heywood.

penny pick. A cigar: London: ca 1838–45. Ware derives ex Dickens's Pickwick: *?pick-wick.*

penny plain and tuppence coloured, originally (as in R. L. Stevenson's title for an essay published 1880) *a penny plain and twopence coloured,* has, since ca 1890, been a c.p. Meaning 'plain or fancy', the phrase seems to have, at first, referred to cheap fiction, costing one penny with plain jacket and, with coloured-picture jacket, twopence.

penny pots. Pimples on a tippler's face: low: from ca 1850; ob.

penny puzzle. A sausage: low: ca 1883–1914. Costing a penny, 'it is never found out'.

penny silver, think one's. To think well of oneself: coll: late C.16–early 18. Gabriel Harvey; Breton; Fuller, 1732. In early quotations, gen. *good silver.*

penny(-)starver. See PENNY BUSTER. 2. A penny cigar: low (—1909); ob.

penny stinker. A bad cigar: mostly Cockney: from ca 1880. ?ex last entry, 2.

penny-swag. A man who sells articles at a penny a lot in the streets: Cockneys' (—1851); ob. Mayhew. i.e. a 'swag-barrowman' (see SWAG-BARROW) specializing in sales at one penny.

penny to bless oneself with, not a. No, or extremely little, money: from ca 1540: coll >, by 1700, S.E. (Semi-proverbial: see Heywood's *Proverbs.*)

penny toff. 'The lowest description of toff – the cad imitator of the follies of the *jeunesse dorée*' (Ware): London: ca 1870–1914.

penny-white. Ugly but rich: coll: late C.17–18. (Rarely of men.)

pennyworth, Robin Hood's. Anything sold at a robber's price, i.e. far too cheaply: coll: C.17, and prob. earlier. cf. the C.19 proverb, *pirates may make cheap pennyworths of their pillage.*

pennyworth out of, fetch one's. To make a person earn his wages, its cost, etc.: coll: late C.17–18. A variation on *a pennyworth for one's penny.*

pen'orth, see PENN'ORTH.

pension!, not for a. Not for all the money in the world: lower classes' coll (—1887); ob.

***pensioner.** A harlot's bully: from ca

1810: c. > low s.; ob. Prob. an abbr. of the †S.E. *petticoat-pensioner* or *petticoat-squire*, i.e. any male keep. 2. A blind musician who has a regular round: London itinerant musicians' (—1861).

***penthouse-nab.** A broad-brimmed hat: c.: late C.17–early 19. B.E. (*pentice*); Grose.

penwiper. A handkerchief: from ca 1860. 2. The female pudend: low: from ca 1850; ob. cf. PEN, 1.

penworth, pen'worth. Coll abbr. of *pennyworth*: C.16–17, C.17. cf. PENN'ORTH, etc.

people. In *people say*, etc., it is coll: C.19–20. J. H. Newman, in a letter of 1843, 'People cannot understand a man being in a state of doubt.' 2. Coll too in *my*, *your* (etc.) *people*, my or your relatives, esp. the members of the family to which one belongs: 1851, Carlyle, 'Mrs Sterling had lived ... with his Father's people.' cf. PEOPLE-IN-LAW. 3. Thieves: c. (—1887); ob.

people-in-law. One's husband's or wife's relatives, esp. parents, brothers, sisters: coll: from ca 1890.

pepin. A C.17 form of PIPPIN, 1.

pepper, v.t. To put in the accents of a Greek exercise: university: from ca 1880. Ex sprinkling with black pepper. 2. v.t., to HUMBUG, to KID: from ca 1870; ob. Ex *throw pepper in the eyes of*. The v.i. form is *use the pepper-box*. 3. To SALT (v., 5) a gold-mining claim: Australian: since ca 1860.

pepper, snuff. To take offence: coll: C.17. On *take* PEPPER IN THE NOSE.

Pepper Alley or **pepper alley.** Rough treatment, esp. hard punching, as in the *Sporting Magazine*, 1820, 'His mug ... had paid a visit to "pepper alley"': pugilistic; ob. Punningly on the name of a London alley. cf. GUTTER-LANE.

pepper-box. A revolver: ca 1840–1910. (Revolver invented in 1835.) 2. A ship's lighthouse at the break of the forecastle: C.19 nautical. Also, a shore lighthouse: late C.19–20 nautical (now ob.). Ex the shape.

pepper-box, use the, see PEPPER, v., 1.

pepper-castor (occ. **-er**). A revolver: 1889; ob. Suggested by PEPPER-BOX.

pepper in the nose, take. To take offence, grow angry: C.16–mid-18: coll till C.17, then S.E. cf. *snuff* PEPPER.

pepper on one's nut, have. To be punched on the head: boxers' (—1887); ob.

pepper-proof. (Not, of course, immune to, but) free from venereal disease: low coll: late C.17–18. cf. PEPPERED OFF.

peppered, be. To have laid a large stake: turf: from ca 1870. 'He was peppered in one dangerous quarter alone to the extent of three or four thousand pounds,' quoted by B. & L.

peppered off. 'Damnably Clapt or Poxt', B.E.: low coll: late C.17–18. (†S.E. *peppered.*) cf. PEPPER-PROOF.

peppermint in one's speech, have a. To stammer: coll, mostly Cockney: from ca 1890. i.e., an *impediment*.

pepperminter. A seller of peppermint water: London lower-class coll (—1851); very ob.

pepst. Tipsy: s. or coll: ca 1570–90. Kendall, 1577, quoted by Nares. Origin?

per usual (, as), see USUAL.

perambulator. A costermonger: ca 1860–1900: s. Perhaps ineligible: F. & H. not convincing.

perch. A small and gen. high seat on a vehicle: coll: from ca 1840. 2. Death: C.18. Ex such phrases as *knock off the* PERCH; *drop the* PERCH.

perch, v. To die: ca 1880–1915. *Sporting Times*, 3 Aug. 1886. cf. next entry. Ex *hop* or *drop the* PERCH.

perch, be off to. To go to bed: from ca 1860; ob.

perch, drop or **fall** or **hop the; perch, pitch** or **tip** or **turn over the.** To die: first three, late C.18–20, all slightly ob.; the fourth, late C.16–17, e.g. in Hakluyt; the fifth, C.18 (Ozell's *Rabelais*, Richardson); the sixth, late C.16–17 (Nashe). Scott, *The Pirate*, 'I always thought him a d—d fool ... but never such a consummate idiot as to hop the perch so sillily.' cf. HOP THE TWIG. 2. Also, though rarely, *hop the perch*, to be defeated: same periods.

perch, knock off the. To perturb; defeat; kill: from ca 1850. Also *throw over the perch*, C.16–17, as in Fulwell, 1568; *turn over the perch*, C.17–18, as in facetious Tom Brown; occ. *give a turn over the*. The second and third senses > coll.

perch, pitch or **tip** or **turn over the,** see PERCH, DROP ...

percher. A dying person: C.18–19. Bolingbroke, 1714. Ex PERCH, DROP ..., etc. 2. A Latin cross made horizontally against the name of an absentee: Winchester College (—1891).

peremptory. Utter, unmitigated; complete: coll: late C.16–17. Ben Jonson. Prob. ex:

peremptory, adv. Entirely, absolutely: coll: C.16–17. Jonson.

perfect. (Mostly pejorative.) Sheer; unmitigated; utter: mostly coll: 1611, Shakespeare, 'His complexion is perfect gallows.' The phrase *perfect nonsense* is late C.19–20 coll.

perfect lady. A harlot: from ca 1880; slightly ob. Origin prob. anecdotal, as Ware says.

perforate. To take the virginity of: low: C.19–20.

perform, v.i. To copulate: low: C.19–20. 2. To make a (considerable) fuss, to GO ON ABOUT: C.20: s. > coll.

perform on, v.t. To cheat, deceive: low: from ca 1870.

performer. A whoremonger: low: C.19–20.

perger, see PURGER.

period, girl of the. A modern girl: Society coll: ca 1880–1900. Coined by Mrs Lynn Linton, who fulminated in this strain in a series of articles published by the *Saturday Review*.

perish, do a. Nearly to die from lack of water: Western Australia (—1894).

perishable cargo. Fruit; slaves: nautical: ca 1730–1800. cf. LIVE LUMBER.

perisher. A short-tailed coat: from ca 1880; ob. 2. An extreme, e.g. in drunkenness or betting: 1888, 'Rolf Boldrewood', 'Then he . . . went in an awful perisher . . . and was never sober day or night the whole [month].' Ob. 3. Hence, pejoratively of a person: a good early example: 'You bleeding little perisher', *Sessions*, April 1898. This sense probably goes back at least as far as 1850: cf. 'He had no name. In the thaw they buried him in the pass, and his epitaph was *some poor bloody perisher.* 1864': Ruth Park, *One-a-Pecker, Two-a-Pecker*, 1958, concerning the Otago goldrush of the 1860s.

perishing. Very cold: Cockneys': late C.19–20.

periwinkle. The female pudend: low: mid-C.19–20; ob.

perk; perks. Perquisites: (the singular, rare, ca 1890–1910;) 1887, *Fun*, 30 March, 'The perks, etc., attached to this useful office are not what they were in the "good old times".' In Scots, *perks* is recorded as early as 1824 (E.D.D.).

perk up. To recover health or good spirits: coll and dial.: from ca 1650. Ex †S.E. *perk*, to carry oneself smartly, jauntily.

perking. 'Any pert, forward, silly Fellow', B.E.: coll: late C.17–mid-18. Ex adj.

Perkins, perkins. Beer: ca 1860–90: 'dandy or affected shortening', H., 1864. Ex the better-known s. phrase, BARCLAY (AND) PERKINS, perhaps influenced by S.E. *perkin*, weak cider or perry. cf. PURKO.

perks, see PERK.

Perks, Board of. Board of Works: jocular: 1889, *Pall Mall Gazette*, 27 Sept., as title: 'Provincial Boards of Perks'.

permanent. A permanent boarder: hotels, boarding-houses: late C.19–20: coll.

permanent pug. A fighting man around the door of the premises: journalists', printers', tavern-frequenters': late C.19–20; ob.

pernicated dude. A swaggering dandy: Canadian: ca 1885–1910. B. & L.

peroney (or -nee). For each man; hence, for each person: Parlary, esp. among buskers: mid-C.19–20. Probably an 'easement' or, less likely, a deliberate distortion of *per* OMEE, per man. cf. a song current among buskers: 'Nantee dinarly; the omee of the carsey | Says due bionc peroney, manjaree on the cross. | We'll all have to scarper the letty in the morning, | Before the bonee omee of the carsey shakes his doss.'

peroon. For each, apiece; hence, each: Parlary: mid-C.19–20. Lit. 'for one': Italian *per uno*. cf. the entry preceding this.

perpendicular. A buffet meal; a party at which the majority of the guests have to stand: 1871, 'M. Legrand', '. . . An invitation to a Perpendicular, as such entertainments are styled.' 2. Coïtion between two persons standing upright: low: mid-C.19–20. Also a KNEE-TREMBLER, an UPRIGHT, 2. Contrast with a HORIZONTAL.

perp(endicular)!, strike me. A Cockney asseveration: late C.19–20; ob.

perpetrate. To make (e.g. a pun); do (anything treated as shocking): coll: 1849, C. Brontë, 'Philip induced . . . his sisters to perpetrate a duet.'

perpetration. The doing of something very bad, or atrociously performed: coll: from ca 1850. (Gen. a humorous affectation by the narrator.)

***perpetual staircase.** The treadmill: c.: late C.19–20. Also *everlasting staircase*.

perspiry. Full of, covered with, perspiration: coll: 1860.

persuader. A spur, gen. in pl: from ca 1786; ob. Grose, 2nd ed., 'The kiddey clapped his persuaders to his prad, but the traps boned him.' 2. A pistol: 1841,

Leman Rede; slightly ob. 3. Hence, any other weapon: from ca 1845, but anticipated by Marryat in 1833 ('three rattans twisted into one', to enforce submission). 4. A whip: coachmen's (—1887). 5. A JEMMY or other burglar's tool: c.: from ca 1850; ob. cf.:

***persuading plate.** c., from ca 1880; ob. 'An iron disk used in forcing safes: it revolves on a pivot, and is fitted with a cutting point,' F. & H.

persuasion. Nationality, sex; sort, kind; description: 1864 (S.O.D.). 'A dark little man ... of French persuasion'. Ex *persuasion*, religious belief, opinion.

pert as a pearmonger, as. Very cheerful: from ca 1560: coll till C.19, then dial. Harding, 1564; Gay; Swift. Dial. has at least four synonyms, with *pert* spelt *peart*.

pertish. Fairly drunk: coll: ca 1760–1820. *Sessions*, 1772.

pestilent, adv. Extremely: coll: late C.17–early 18.

pestle. A leg: coll verging on S.E.: C.16–17. Skelton, '[Her] myghty pestels ... | As fayre and as whyte | As the fote of a kyte'. cf. PESTLE OF PORK. 2. A constable's staff: coll: early C.17. Chapman. 3. A penis: low: C.19–20 ob. Contrast MORTAR (2), the female pudend.

pestle, v.i. To coït (of a man): low: C.19–20; ob. Ex the n., 3.

pestle, knight of the, see the KNIGHT paragraph.

pestle of a lark. Anything very small; a trifle: late C.16–early 18: coll >, by 1690, S.E. Fuller calls Rutlandshire 'Indeed ... but the Pestel of a Lark'.

pestle of a portigue. A portague, a C.16–early 17 Portuguese gold coin worth about £4: jocular coll (C.17) verging on S.E. Fletcher, 1622.

pestle of pork. A leg: low coll: C.19–20; very ob. Ex dial., where the phrase = the shank end of a ham, etc., or pork cooked fresh.

petard. A trick or a cheating at dice, prob. by some kind of bluff or by the use of loaded dice: gamblers' s. (?orig. c.): Restoration period. J. Wilson, *The Cheats*, 1662. Prob. ex, or suggested by, *hoist with his own petard*.

Pete Jenkins. An auxiliary clown: circus: from ca 1860; very ob. Ex Pete Jenkins (fl. 1855), who planted 'rustics' in the audience.

Peter. A coll abbr. of *Peter-see-me* (itself ex Peter Ximenes, a famous cardinal), a Spanish wine: C.17. Beaumont & Fletcher, *Chances*.

***peter.** A trunk, portmanteau, bag; (in C.19–20) a box or a safe: c.: 1668, Head; Smollett; Grose; Lytton; Horsley, 1879. Ex *Peter*, a rock. 2. Hence, any bundle, parcel or package; a tramp's sack: c.: from ca 1810. 3. A kind of loaded dice, hence the using of them: c.: ca 1660–1750. Wilson, *The Cheats*. Prob. the correct form is *petard*, as above: it is F. & H. that lists under *peter*. Wilson's spelling is *Petarrs*. 4. A punishment cell: Australian c.: from ca 1880; ob. 5. A partridge: poachers': from ca 1860. 6. The penis: low: mid-C.19–20; ob. cf. JOHN THOMAS. 7. A prison cell: c.: late C.19–20. cf. sense 4.

***peter,** v.t. To cease doing, e.g. speaking: low s. (prob. orig. c.): 1812, Vaux; ob. by 1900. Ex the n., 1: for *peter that!* = *stow that!* 2. v.i., (in whist) to call for trumps by discarding an unnecessarily high card: cards (—1887). Ex *the blue Peter*, which indicates that a ship is about to start. *Notes and Queries*, 7th Series, iv, 356. 3. Hence, v.i. and t., to run up prices: auctioneers': from ca 1890. 4. See PETER OUT.

***peter-biter.** A stealer of portmanteaux: c.: late C.17–20; ob. Also *biter of peters*, as in B.E. See PETER, n., 1.

peter (or Peter) boatman. Gen. pl. A river pirate: ca 1798–1840. cf. PETER-MAN.

***peter-claimer.** A stealer of portmanteaux, esp. a carriage-thief: c.: late C.19–20. See PETER, n., 1.

***peter-claiming.** The stealing of parcels and/or bags, esp. at railway stations: 1894, A. Morrison, 'From this, he ventured on peterclaiming.' Ex PETER, n., 1.

Peter Collins. An imaginary person on whom the GREEN are asked to call for a *green-handed* (or *handled*) *rake*: theatrical and circuses' (—1889); ob.

***peter-cutter.** An instrument for cutting iron safes: 1862, Mayhew. See PETER, n., 1.

***peter-drag.** See PETER-HUNTING. c.: C.19–20; ob. See PETER, n., 1, and DRAG, n., 5, 6.

Peter Funk. A member of a gang operating 'shadily' (see SHADY, 2) at public auctions: late C.19–20.

Peter Grievous. A fretful child: coll: mid-C.19–20; ob. 2. 'A miserable, melancholy fellow; a croaker': from ca 1850: coll. ?a euphemizing of CREEPING JESUS.

peter-gunner. A poor shot with a gun: coll: C.17–20; ob. Anon., *The Cold Year*,

1615 (quoted by Nares). Perhaps ex *petre*, saltpetre. cf.:

Peter Gunner will kill all the birds that died last summer. A C.18–mid-19 (?also late C.17) c.p.: 'A piece of wit commonly thrown out at a person walking through a street or village near London, with a gun in his hand', Grose, 2nd ed. Ex preceding entry.

***peter-hunting.** The stealing of portmanteaux, boxes, etc., esp. from carriages: c.: Vaux, 1812; ob. Also PETER-DRAG and PETER-LAY. See PETER, n., 1. Whence:

***peter-hunting jemmy.** 'A small crowbar used in smashing the chains securing luggage to a vehicle', F. & H.: c.: from ca 1810; ob.

***peter-lay.** The same as PETER-HUNTING, and as PETER-DRAG. C.18–20 c. See PETER, n., 1.

Peter Lug. A drinking laggard. Chiefly in *Who is Peter Lug?*, a c.p. addressed to one who lets the glass stand before him: ca 1680–1830.

***peter-man, peterman.** One who uses 'unlawful engines in catching fish in the river Thames', Bailey: late C.17–early 18: c. Ex *peterman*, a fisherman. 2. One who specializes in stealing bags, etc., from carriages: from ca 1810; ob. 1812, *Sporting Magazine*; Anon., *The Story of a Lancashire Thief*, 1863. Ex PETER, n., 1.

peter out. To cease gradually; come to an end: U.S. (1854), anglicized as a coll almost imm. *Saturday Review*, 9 Jan. 1892, 'Human effort of all kinds tends to "peter out".' Orig. U.S., of stream or lode of ore. ?from Fr. *péter* . . .; ?cf. to FIZZLE OUT.

Peter Pipeclay. A Royal Marine: naval: ca 1820–90. Ex his enforced use of pipeclay. cf. PICK HIM UP . . .

peter that! see PETER, v., 1.

Peter to pay Paul, rob; in C.17–19, occ. *borrow from*, as in Urquhart. To take from one person to give to another: C.15–20; proverbial coll >, ca 1820, S.E. Barclay, 1548, has *clothe* (surviving till C.18). Lytton, *Paul Clifford*, 'If so be as your name's Paul, may you always rob Peter [a portmanteau] in order to pay Paul.' Prob. not ex the relations of the two Apostles but 'merely a collocation of familiar names, *Pierre et Paul* being used in Fr. like *Tom, Dick and Harry* in Eng.': W.

***peterer.** The same as PETER-MAN, 2: c. of ca 1840–70.

peterman, see PETER-MAN.

peters, biter of, see PETER-BITER.

Peter's needle, go or pass through St. (Of children) to be severely disciplined: C.19–20 semi-proverbial coll and dial. ?ex the Biblical eye of a needle.

petticoat. A woman: s.: Ned Ward, 1709.

petticoat, up one's. Unduly, or very, familiar with a woman: low: C.18–20; ob.

petticoat-hold. A life-interest in a wife's estate: coll: late C.18–19.

petticoat-merchant. A whoremonger: low coll: C.19–20; ob. On S.E. *petticoat-monger* or *petticoat-pensioner*.

pettifogger, see PETTY FOGGER.

pettiloon. A pantaloon: coll: 1858, Whyte-Melville; ob. Blend of *petticoat* + *pantaloon*.

pettitoes. Feet: law s.: ca 1700–1725.

petty fogger; perhaps more correctly **pettifogger.** A Customs man: nautical, esp. quay-hands': late C.19–20; ob.

petty-house. A water-closet: coll: C.19–20; slightly ob. 'Widely prevalent in familiar use', Murray, 1905. Whence LITTLE HOUSE.

***petty lashery; petulacery.** Petty theft: c.: late C.16–early 17. Both forms in Greene.

pew. A seat, esp. in *take a pew*, *park oneself in a pew*, etc.: C.20. P. G. Wodehouse, *A Prefect's Uncle*, 1903, 'The genial "take a pew" of one's equal inspires confidence.'

pew, stump the. To pay: low: ca 1820–30. Moncrieff, *Tom and Jerry*, 1823, 'It's every thing now o' days to be able to flash the screens – sport the rhino – show the needful – post the pony – nap the rent – stump the pew.' Prob. *pew* is an abbr. of PEWTER, 1.

pew-opener's muscle. A muscle in the palm of the hand: medical (—1902). Sir James Brodie, 'because it helps to contract and hollow the palm of the hand for the reception of a gratuity'.

***pewter.** Silver: c. (—1823); †by 1900. 2. Hence, money, esp. if of silver; prize-money: low: 1821, W. T. Moncrieff. 3. A tankard: mostly London coll (1839), verging on S.E.; ob. Abbr. *pewter tankard*. Hence, 4, a pot sought as a prize: rowing men's (—1874); ob.

pewter, unload. 'To drink porter out of a quart pot' (*Sinks*): public-house: ca 1830–70.

pewy. (Of country) so enclosed by fences as to form a succession of small fields: sporting (esp. hunting): 1828 (O.E.D.). Ex the shape of the old-fashioned, big, enclosed pews.

phan, see FAN, n., 2.

phant; or **fant;** in the North of England, often *peeble*, by evasion. A phantom-glass, i.e. that sheet of plate-glass, which, set obliquely on the stage, reflects from below, or from the side, the illusion known as Pepper's ghost: showmen's (—1909).

pharaoh; occ. **pharoh.** A strong ale or beer: late C.17–early 19. Gen. as OLD PHARAOH. Prob. ex strength derived from oldness – 'old as Pharaoh'.

Pharaoh's lean kine, one of. A very thin person: coll: 1598, Shakespeare, 'If to be fat be to be hated, then Pharaoh's lean kine are to be loved.' 2. In C.19–20, with the qualification of looking '(1) as though he'd run away from a bone-house; or (2) as if he were walking about to save funeral expenses' (F. & H.); ob.

pheasant. A wanton: low: C.17–19; ob. cf. PLOVER and QUAIL. 2. See BILLINGSGATE PHEASANT.

pheasantry. A brothel: low: C.19–20; ob. Ex PHEASANT, 1.

phenomenon. A prodigy; a remarkable person, occ. animal, or thing: coll: 1838, Dickens, 'This is the infant phenomenon – Miss Ninetta Crummles.'

phi, occ. in Gr. form Φ or φ. A book deemed by the Bodley's librarian to be indelicate, and so catalogued under the the Greek letter *phi*: Oxford coll. Prob. coined by E. W. B. Nicholson, the eccentric and sarcastic Bodley's librarian 1882–1912. Punning *fie*!

Philadelphia lawyer. A smart attorney; a very shrewd person. Esp. in *puzzle* or *beat a P.l.*, to be extremely puzzling, and *be as smart* or *know as much as a P.l.* A U.S. coll (1803), introduced into England ca 1820; ob. cf. BUSH LAWYER.

philander, 'to ramble on incoherently; to write discursively and weakly', H., 1874, like the sense, 'to wander about' (as in Arthur Sketchley, quoted by Baumann), is a half-sol., half-coll of ca 1865–1910. ?influenced by *meander* and *wander*.

***Philip.** A policeman, mostly in *Philip!*, the police are coming!: c.: from ca 1860; ob. Possibly by a punning reference to *fillip*. Whence PHILIPER.

Philip and Che(i)n(e)y. Two of the common people considered typically: coll: ca 1540–90. Tusser has *Philip, Hob and Cheyney*. cf. TOM, DICK AND HARRY.

***Philiper, philip(p)er.** A thief's accomplice: c.: 1860, *The Times*, 5 Sept.; ob. See PHILIP.

Philippi, meet at. To keep an appointment without fail: literary coll: ca 1780–1830. Mrs Cowley, 1782, ' "At seven, you say?" ... "Exactly." ... "I'll meet thee at Philippi!" ' Ex Shakespeare's *Julius Caesar*, IV, iii, where the ghost speaks thus.

Philistine. (Gen. pl.) A drunkard: late C. 17–18.

Philistines. Earwigs or other such insects: provincial coll, and dial.: late C.17–20. Ex 'The Philistines are upon thee,' Judges xvi.

***phinney.** A burial: c.: C.18 (?–19). C. Hitchin, *The Regulator*, 1718. Origin?

Phip. A sparrow: coll and dial.: C.14–16. Less a contraction of *Philip* (in same sense) than ex the onomatopoeia for a sparrow's chirp.

phis. B.E.'s spelling of PHIZ. cf. *phys*, 1693 (O.E.D.). Both occur also in C.18.

phiz (phizz), phyz; physog. (cf. PHIS.) Face; expression of face: *phiz*, etc., is a jocularly coll abbr. of *physiognomy*; *physog*, however, is the abbr. of PHYSOGNOMY. Shadwell, 1688; Swift, 'Abbreviations exquisitely refined; as ... *Phizz* for Phisiognomy.' But PHYSOG not till C.19. A RUM *phiz* is an odd one: low: late C. 18–20.

phiz-gig. An old woman dressed young: C.19. 2. 'A pyramid of moistened gunpowder, which, on ignition, fuses but does not flash', F. & H.: schools': from ca 1840.

phiz-maker. A maker of grimaces: C.18: coll.

phizog, see PHYSOG; also PHIZ.

phos, phoss, even **foss.** Phosphorus: s. >, ca 1890, coll abbr.: from ca 1810. 2. Esp., in c. of early C.19, a bottle of phosphorus, used by cracksmen to get a light. Whence:

phossy, occ. **fossy, jaw.** Phosphorus necrosis of the jaw: coll: 1889.

photo. A photograph: coll abbr.: 1870, Miss Bridgman, 'I should like her photo.' 2. As v.: coll: 1870, Carlyle. 3. As adj.: likewise coll (technical): 1889.

phunt. One pound sterling: grafters': late C.19–20. Perhaps derived ex PONTE and influenced by Ger. *Pfund*.

phut, go. To come to grief; fizzle out; be a failure: coll: 1892, Kipling; A. S. M. Hutchinson, 1908. Partly echoic, partly ex Hindustani *phatna*, to explode.

phys, see PHIS.

physic. Sexual attentions; coïtion: coll: C.17–mid-18. Massinger, 'She ... sends for her young doctor, | Who ministers physic to her on her back'; D'Urfey. 2.

Medicine: late C.16–20: S.E. till ca 1850, then coll. Mrs Henry Wood, 1862, 'You'll take the physic, like a precious lamb:' 3. Losses; wagers, points: gaming: from ca 1820; ob. 4. Hard hitting: pugilistic: from ca 1830; ob. cf. PUNISHMENT. 5. Strong drink: from ca 1840. cf. MEDICINE; POISON.

physic, v. To treat, dose, with medicine, esp. with a purgative: C.14–20: S.E. till ca 1850, then coll. cf. the n., 2. 2. 'To punish in purse or pocket': 1821, Egan; ob. cf. the n., 3.

physic-bottle. A doctor: non-aristocratic (—1909).

physicking, n. and adj. Corresponding to PHYSIC, n., 2., and PHYSIC, v., 1 and 2: mid-C.17–20: S.E. until ca 1810, then coll. Bee, 1823, both n. and adj.

physiog. A coll abbr. of PHYSIOGNOMY: ca 1865–1920. cf. PHIZ and PHYSOG.

physiognomy. The face or countenance: (low) coll: C.17–20; ob. Fletcher & Shirley, 'I have seen that physiognomy: were you never in prison?' cf. PHYSOGNOMY.

physog; occ. **phizog, physog.** See PHIZ. App. recorded first in the *Lex. Bal.*, 1811. cf. PHYSIOG.

physognomy. Physiognomy: sol.: C.19–20. See PHYSIOGNOMY.

phyz. See PHIZ; cf. PHYSIOG, PHYSOG; note PHYSIOGNOMY.

phyzog, see PHYSOG.

pi; gen. **pie.** A miscellaneous collection of books out of the *alphabet*: booksellers' coll: from ca 1880; ob. Ex *printers' pi(e)*. 2. (Only *pi.*) A pious exhortation: Public Schools' and universities': 1870. 3. cf. the adj., whence *pi*, a pious person: late C. 19–20; ob. Ex *pious*.

pi, adj. Pious; virtuous; sanctimonious: schools' and universities': 1870, O.E.D., whose first record of the adj., however, is for 1891. cf. the n., 2.

pi-gas, -jaw. A serious admonition or talk: schools' and universities': ? *-jaw* from ca 1875; *-gas*, ca 1880–1915. See JAW and GAS. Ex:

pi-jaw, v. To give moral advice to; admonish: schools' and universities': from middle 1880s. Ex PI, adj. F. & H., 1902, quoting a glossary of 1891, 'He pi-jawed me for thoking.' cf. PI-GAS, and:

pi-man. A pious fellow: from ca 1900; ob. *To-day*, 22 Aug. 1901. Ex PI, adj., but prob. also containing a pun on *pieman*.

piache. Mad; on *stone-mad*, often *stone-piache*: Regular Army: late C.19–20. Ex Hindustani.

pialler. To speak; speak to: New South Wales and Queensland 'pidgin': mid-C. 19–20. R. M. Praed, 1885. Ex an Aboriginal dialect: cf. YABBER.

pianny. Tipsy: Regular Army: late C.19–20. Ex PARNEE.

piano. To sing small, take a back seat: Society: ca 1870–80. Ex musical *piano*, softly.

piazzas, walk the. (Of prostitutes) to look for men: ca 1820–70. Ex the piazzas – wrongly so called – of Covent Garden. 2. Hence, ca 1870–1910, to walk the streets: likewise of prostitutes.

picaninny, see PICCANINNY.

picaro, on the. 'On the make', prowling for easy money: coll: C.18. Smollett, trans. of *Gil Blas*, 'I see you have been ... a little on the picaro.' Ex Sp. *picaro*, a rogue, via the English *picaroon* (Sp. *picarón*).

Piccadilly crawl. A style of walking prevalent in Society in the Eighties. Ob. cf. ALEXANDRA LIMP; GRECIAN BEND; ROMAN FALL.

Piccadilly fringe. Front hair of women cut short and brought down, and curled over the forehead: lower classes': ca 1884–1900. Presumably suggested by PICCADILLY WEEPERS. Ware states that the 'fashion originated in Paris about 1868'.

Piccadilly weepers. 'Long carefully combed-out whiskers of the Dundreary fashion', H. 1874. Ob. Because worn by dandies on Piccadilly, London. cf. DUNDREARIES. cf.:

Piccadilly window. A monocle: London (non-aristocratic): the 1890s; ob. Because frequently seen in Piccadilly.

piccaninny; occ. **picaninny** or **pickanin(n)y.** A child: coll bordering on S.E.: 1785, Grose; 1817, 'The little pickaninny has my kindest wishes.' Orig. applied, in the West Indies and America, to Negro and other coloured children. Ex C.17 'Negro diminutive of Sp. *pequeño* or Portuguese *pequeno*, small ...; cf. Port. *pequenino*, tiny. It is uncertain whether the word arose in Sp. or Port. colonies, or in the E. or W. Indies, but it has spread remarkably,' W.

piccaninny, adj. Little: Australian coll: from 1840s; slightly ob. Ex preceding.

piccolo and flute. A suit (of clothes): rhyming s.: since ca 1870. cf. WHISTLE AND FLUTE.

picey, adj. Mean: Regular Army: late C. 19–20. Perhaps ex *pice*, a quarter-anna.

pick. An abbr. (—1887) of S.E. *pickwick*, a very inferior cigar; ob. 2. A toothpick: coll (—1890). 3. An anchor: nautical: late C.19–20.

pick, v.i. To eat: 1786, Capt. T. Morris, 'If it wasn't for shame, I could pick till to-morrow at dinner': s. till C.20, then coll. Ex S.E. sense, to eat daintily.

pick, adj. Chosen; best: coll: 1819, Lady Morgan; ob. Ex *pick*, choice.

pick a hole in (a person's) **coat.** To be censorious: coll verging on S.E.: late C.16–19. Anon., *Mar-Prelate's Epitome*, 1588; Ray; Manning in a letter to Lamb. Whence S.E. *pick holes in.*

pick a soft plank! Sleep easy!: a nautical c.p. addressed to young seamen sleeping on deck for the first time: mid-C.19–20; ob. Bowen. 2. Hence, to find an easy job: nautical coll: late C.19–20.

pick and cut. To pick pockets: low coll (?orig. s.): C.17. Shakespeare, *Winter's Tale*, 'I picked and cut most of their festival purses.'

pick-and-dab. A meal of potatoes and salt: Scots coll: C.19–20.

pick-axe. 'A fiery mixture of Cape smoke, pontac' – a dark, dry wine medicinally valuable – 'and ginger-beer, in much request in the diamond fields', Pettman: South African: ca 1870–90. Boyle, *To the Cape for Diamonds*, 1873. Ex its 'brutality'.

pick flies off. To find fault with: tailors': from ca 1860; ob.

Pick- (or **Picked-) Hatch,** see PICKT-HATCH.

pick him up and pipeclay him and he'll do again! A bluejackets' c.p. remark on a Royal Marine fallen on the deck, esp. if he fell hard: ca 1860–1910.

pick-it-up. The diamond bird: Australian boys' coll: from mid-1890s. G. A. Keartland, 1896, gives the origin in this bird's 'treble note'.

pick-me-up. A stimulating liquid, orig. and mainly liquor: coll: 1867, Latham, 'To drink home-brewed ale . . . instead of pick-me-ups'. 2. Hence, any person or thing (e.g. seaside air) with a bracing effect: 1876, 'Ouida' (of a person).

pick off. To hit (a person) with a stone: Winchester College: mid-C.19–20.

pick out robins' eyes. To side-stitch black cloth or any delicate material: tailors': from ca 1860.

pick-penny. A miser: coll bordering on S.E.: C.18–19. Ex S.E. sense, a greedy amasser or stealer of money. 2. A sharper: coll: ?C.17–18.

pick-up. A chance (esp. if carnal) acquaintance (gen. female): low coll (—1895). Ex the S.E. *pick up with*, to make acquaintance with someone casually met. 2. A pick-up match: coll: late C.19–20. One in which the opposing sides are chosen by the two captains selecting one player alternately.

pick up, v. To cheat, grossly deceive (a person): low (—1860); †by 1900. Ex: 2. To 'establish contact' with an unwary person: c.: from ca 1780; ob. 3. To meet casually, esp. of a man on the look-out for a girl: late C.19–20. cf. preceding entry. Orig. of harlot 'picking up' a man: c. or low: from ca 1720. cf. the dial. nuances recorded by the E.D.D. 4. (cf. senses 2, 3.) To rob a man thus: he is allured into speaking with a harlot, whose bully then comes up to extort money or who herself decamps after taking his money 'in advance' and perhaps his watch as well: c. (—1861). Mayhew.

pick up one's crumbs. To be convalescent: coll: 1580, Lyly; 1754, Berthelson; in mid-C.19–20, dial. i.e. to put on weight as well as to eat healthily.

pickanin(n)y, see PICCANINNY.

***picker-up.** A thief or a swindler 'picking up' an unwary person: c. (—1812); ob. See PICK UP, V. 2. Hence, a harlot: c.: mid-C. 19–20. ob. 3. 'A dealer buying on quotations trickily obtained from a member trapped into giving a wrong price', F. & H.: Stock Exchange: from ca 1890.

pickers and stealers. Hands: coll: C.17–20; slightly ob. Shakespeare, 'So I do still, by these pickers and stealers.' Ex the Catechism 'To keep my hands from picking and stealing', which dates from 1548–9. Baumann considered Shakespeare's use to be s.; the O.E.D. considers the phrase, at no matter what period, to be S.E.

picking gooseberries! Goodness knows!; doing God knows what!: a c.p. of early C.19. John Davis, *The Post Captain*, 1805.

pickle. A predicament, sorry plight, unpleasant difficulty: mid:-C.16–20: S.E. till C.19, then coll. Byron, 'The Turkish batteries thrash'd them . . . into a sad pickle.' A fig. use of the lit. secondary S.E. sense, pickled vegetables. 2. Hence, perhaps via *rod in pickle*, a mischievous or – ob. – a troublesome child; any person constantly causing trouble: coll: the former late C.18–20; the latter, late C.18–19,

Anon., *History of a Schoolboy*, 1788,' He told Master Bloich he was a pickle, and dismissed him to his cricket.' 3. Hence, a wild youth or young man: s. or coll: ca 1810–40. 4. A wretchedly produced, cheap book: booksellers' (—1887); ob. Esp. one that won't sell.

pickle, v. To HUMBUG; to GAMMON; C.19. Perhaps ex nautical S.E. sense, to rub salt or vinegar on the back of a person just flogged.

pickle, in. Venereally infected: low coll: late C.17–early 19. Ex salivation. 2. Drunk: late C.17–mid-18. Farquhar (*in that pickle*); Vanbrugh. (*Slang*, p. 65.)

***pickle-herring.** A wag; a merry companion: c. (—1887).

pickle-jar. A coachman in yellow: ca 1850–1910.

pickle-manufacturer. A publisher of cheap, badly produced books: booksellers': ca 1885–1914. See PICKLE, n., 4.

pickle-me-tickle-me, play. To coït: low coll: mid-C.17–18. Urquhart.

pickled. Roguish; waggish: coll verging on S.E.: late C.17–early 19. cf. PICKLE, n., 2.

pickled pork. Conversations: since ca 1890. Rhyming s. on *talk*.

pickles. Dissection specimens (straight) from the operation theatre: medical: from ca 1860. 2. As an exclamation, nonsense! or BALLS!: from ca 1850; ob. Also *all pickles*.

pickles, case of. A quandary; a serious breakdown: C.19–20; ob.

pickling-tubs. 'Wellington, or top boots' (*Sinks*): low: ca 1830–70.

Pickt-Hatch (often Pict-, occ. **Pick-,** and properly **Picked-Hatch), go to the Manor of,** late C.16–mid-17; **go to Pickt-Hatch Grange,** ca 1620–40. To go whoring; to whore: c., says Grose; more prob. s. or low coll. In Shakespeare's time, specifically a brothelly tavern in Turnmill Street, Clerkenwell; hence, from ca 1620, any brothel or low locality. A pickt hatch, i.e. a hatch with pikes, was a common brothel-sign. Shakespeare, in *Merry Wives*; Jonson; Randolph, 'Why the whores of Pict-Hatch, Turnbull or the unmerciful bawds of Bloomsbury.'

picnic. A rough-and-tumble; noisy trouble: coll: from ca 1895. F. & H. records it at 1898. Prob. ex: 2. 'An awkward adventure, an unpleasant experience, a troublesome job', Morris: Australian coll: at least as early as 1896. Ex the U.S. coll sense, 'an easy or agreeable thing'.

Pict-Hatch, see PICKT-HATCH.

picture. A portrait, a likeness, of a person: C.16–20: S.E. until ca 1890, then coll when not affected. 2. A fine example; a beau-ideal: coll (—1870). e.g., 'a picture of health'; often ironical as in 'a pretty picture', a strange figure (F. & H., 1902). 3. Hence, a very picturesque or beautiful object: coll: from ca 1890. e.g. 'She's a picture.' In Berkshire dial. as early as 1859. See also OIL-PAINTING.

picture, fake a, see FAKE A PICTURE.

picture, lawful, see LAWFUL PICTURE.

picture, not in the. Inappropriate, incongruous; (in racing) unplaced: coll: late C.19–20.

picture or **portrait, King's** or **Queen's,** see QUEEN'S PICTURE.

picture-askew. A jocular perversion of *picturesque*: coll: from ca 1870. cf. GUST.

picture-frame, see SHERIFF'S PICTURE-FRAME.

pictures. A jocular name for the flitches of bacon, &c., when hanging to a ceiling or against a wall: South Lancashire s. (—1905) rather than dial.

piddle. Urine; occ., the act of making water: coll, mostly nursery: C.19–20. Ex:

piddle, v. To urinate: late C.18–20: coll. esp. childish; in C.20, low coll. Ex PISS influenced by *paddle*; perhaps an unconscious blend. 2. Hence, of rain: low (—1887). Baumann, 'It piddled buckets.' 3. Ex sense 1, metaphorically of ineffectual writing. Scott, letter of 10 Nov. 1814, concerning a play: 'He piddles through a cullender.'

pie, see PI; PYE.

pie!, by cock and, see COCK AND (BY) PIE!, BY.

pie, like. Zestfully, vigorously: s. verging on coll: from ca 1885; ob. Henley, 1887, 'I goes for 'Olman 'Unt like pie.' ?ex zestful eating of pie.

pie, make a. To combine with a view to profit: coll: ca 1820–1910. Ex concerted cooking.

pie, put in, see PUT IN PIE.

pie, put into the. At book sales, to put into a large lot, to be sold at the end: auctioneers': from ca 1860.

pie and one. Son: rhyming s.: late C.19–20.

pie-ard. A term of abuse in the Regular Army: late C.19–20. Ex Hindustani for a pariah dog.

pie-jaw or **piejaw.** Incorrect forms of PI-JAW. A. H. Tod, *Charterhouse*, 1900.

pie-pusher. A street pieman: low coll (—1900).

pie-shop. A dog: low London: 1842–ca 1915.

piebald. v.t., formed (—1909) ex, and corresponding to:

piebald eye. A black eye: low: late C.19–20.

piebald mucker sheeny. A low old Jew: East London (—1909).

piece. A woman or girl: C.14–20: S.E. until late C.18, then (low) coll and gen. pejorative. Esp. sexually, as in Grose, 3rd ed.: 'A damned good or bad piece; a girl who is more or less active and skilful in the amorous congress'. (Also C.19–20 dial.) cf. the Cambridge toast, ca 1810–30, 'May we never have a piece (peace) that will injure the Constitution.' In C.19–20, usually considered as short for *piece of tail*; see TAIL, 2 and 3. 2. A slice of bread: Scottish, esp. Glaswegian, coll: late C.19–20. 3. See PIECE, THE. 4. Patter: pitch-holders' in any open market, e.g. the old Caledonian, that in Portobello Road, the Sunday market in Petticoat Lane: late (?mid) C.19–20.

piece, the. The thing, matter, affair; it: lower classes': late C.19–20. e.g., 'He'll fight the piece out with you.'

piece of entire. A jolly fellow: ca 1820–80. cf. later *bit of all right*.

piece of muslin. A female, esp. a girl: (low) coll: ca 1875–1910. Prob. an elaboration of S.E. *piece of goods*. cf. the C.20 *bit of skirt*.

piece of mutton. A female viewed as a sexual partner: low coll: C.17–early 19.

piece of pudding. A piece of good luck; a welcome change: proletarian: from ca 1870; ob.

piece of stuff. A woman: naval: ca 1790–1860. *The Nightwatch* (I, 151), 1828.

piece of thick. A piece of pressed cake tobacco: non-aristocratic: from ca 1860.

piece of work. A commotion, fuss, disorderly bustle: coll: 1810, 'He kept jawing us, and making a piece of work all the time.'

piece-out. Employment, a job (esp. if temporary), a loan: tailors': from ca 1860. Ex the S.E. v. sense, 'to enlarge by the addition of a piece': cf. also S.E. *piece-work*.

piecee one. First rate: pidgin (mid-C.19–20) > naval (C.20). Granville.

***pieces.** Money: c.: mid-C.19–20; ob. Perhaps ex *pieces of eight*.

pieces, all to. Gen. with *be* or *go*. Exhausted; collapsed; ruined: from ca 1665: till C.19, then S.E. Pepys, 29 Aug. 1667, 'The Court is at this day all to pieces'; Ray, of a bankrupt.

pieces, fall or **go to.** To be brought to childbed: mid-C.19–20: s. > coll.

piejaw, see PI-JAW.

pieman. The player who cries at pitch-and-toss: from ca 1850; ob. Ex the real pieman's cry, 'Hot pies, toss or buy, toss or buy'. 2. See PI-MAN.

piercer. A piercing eye: 1752, Foote, 'She had but one eye . . ., but that was a piercer.' s. until C.19, then coll; slightly ob.

piffing. An †variant of SPIFFING.

piffle. Very ineffective talk; feeble, foolish nonsense: from ca 1890: s. ex dial. (C.19–20). Ex echoic *piff* (W.), though imm. ex the v. *Saturday Review*, 1 Feb. 1890, '. . . "piffle" (to use a University phrase . . .'.

piffle, v. To talk, to act, in an ineffective, esp. in a feeble, manner: dial. (—1847) >, ca 1880, s. For origin, see the n.

piffler. An ineffective trifler; a twaddler; 'an earnest futility, i.e. a person with a moral end in view, and nothing to back it but a habit of talking, or writing sentimental rubbish', F. & H.: 1892.

***pig.** A sixpence: c.: from ca 1620; ob. Fletcher, 1622. cf. HOG. 2. A policeman, a detective; esp. (also GRUNTER, 4) a police-runner: c. of ca 1810–90. H., who, in 1873, writes, 'Now almost exclusively applied by London thieves to a plain-clothes man, or a "nose".' 3. A pressman: printers': 1841, Savage's *Dict.* cf. DONKEY. 4. A garment completely spoiled: tailors': from ca 1860; ob. Also PORK. 5. Hence, goods returned by a retailer to a wholesaler, or by wholesaler to manufacturer: drapers': from ca 1870. 6. A small piece, esp. a bit, i.e. a section, of orange: children's, mostly Cockney (—1887).

pig, bleed like a. To bleed much: coll: C.17–20. Dekker & Webster, 1607, 'He bleeds like a pig, for his crown's crack'd.' In C.17–20, occ. *stuck pig*.

pig, China Street. A Bow Street officer: ca 1810–30: c., or low s, See PIG, 2.

pig, cold. The pulling of bedclothes off sluggards and leaving them to lie in the cold: coll: ca 1780–1870. 2. Goods returned from on sale: ca 1820–80. 3. A corpse: medical: from ca 1840; very ob.

pig, follow like an Anthony, see ANTHONY. **pig, Goodyer's,** see GOODYER'S.

pig, in. Pregnant: rural upper classes': since ca 1870.

pig, keep a. To occupy the same rooms as another student: Oxford undergraduates' (—1887); ob.

pig, long, see LONG PIG.

pig, stare like a stuck. To look fixedly or in terror: coll: 1749, Smollett, 'He stared like a stuck pig at my equipment.'

pig-a-back. A corruption, esp. children's, of *pick-a-back*. See PIGGY-BACK.

pig and goose, brandy is Latin for. A c.p. excuse for drinking a dram of brandy after eating pig or goose: ca 1780–1880.

pig at a tater, go at it like a. To act like a bull in a china shop: late C.19–20: orig., Black Country dial.

pig at home, have boiled. To be master in one's own house, 'an allusion to a well-known poem and story', Grose, 1785: coll: ca 1780–1830.

pig by the ear, pull the wrong. To make a mistake: ca 1540–1870; from ca 1750, also *get the wrong pig* or *sow by the ear*. Coll. Heywood, 1546.

pig-eater. An endearment: C.19.

pig-faced lady. The boar-fish: Tasmanian coll: ca 1840–90.

pig in a poke. A blind bargain: mid-C.16–20: coll till C.19, then S.E. A *poke* here = a bag; indeed, *bag* is occ. substituted.

pig in shit, (as) happy as a. Very happy (though perhaps rather dirty): low coll, the ordinary coll form being ... *in muck*. C.19–20. cf. U.S. *pig in clover*.

pig (or **sow**) **in the arse** or **tail, grease** or **stuff a fat.** To give unnecessarily, e.g. to a rich man: the *grease ... arse* form, ca 1670–1830; the *stuff ... tail*, late C.18–19: low coll.

pig in the sun, snore like a. To snore vigorously or stertorously: coll: mid-C.19–20.

Pig Islander. A New Zealander: Australian coll: late C.19–20. Ex the (formerly) numerous wild pigs in rural N.Z.

pig it. Late C.19–20 coll form of ob. S.E. *pig*, live filthily together.

pig-jump, -jumper, -jumping. 'To jump ... from all four legs, without bringing them together': a horse that does this; the doing thereof: Australian: resp. 1893, 1892, 1893.

pig-market. The proscholium of the Divinity School at Oxford: Oxford University: late C.17–early 18. 'Oxonienses' Wood, 1681.

pig-meater. A bullock that will not fatten: Australian: 1884, 'Rolf Boldrewood'. Because fit only for pigs' food.

pig-months. Those months in which there is an *r* (September-April): non-aristocratic: C.19–20; ob. Ware, 'The months in which you may more safely eat fresh pork than in the ... summer months.'

pig, no good alive, – like a. Selfish; greedy; covetous: coll and dial.: late C.16–20; in C.19–20, mainly dial. In C.16–18, gen. *hog*, and nearly always in form ... *he'll do no good alive*.

pig of his or **one's own sow,** (gen. **give one a).** To pay one back in his own coin: semi-proverbial coll: ca 1530–1890. 'Proverbs' Heywood; Fielding; Reade.

pig on pork; esp. *draw pig on pork*, to draw post-dated cheques: commercial: ca 1810–80. J. W., *Perils, Pastimes and Pleasures*, 1848.

pig-poker. A swineherd: coll and dial.: C.19.

pig-running. The chasing, in sport, of a short-tailed, well-greased and/or -soaped, preferably large pig: coll verging on S.E.: ca 1780–1890.

pig-sconce. A dullard; a lout: coll: ca 1650–1900. Massinger; Meredith.

pig-sticker. A pork-butcher: low: from ca 1850. 2. A long-bladed pocket-knife: from ca 1880. 3. A sword: from ca 1890. cf. PORKER.

pig-sty. The press-room: printers': from ca 1845. Ex PIG, 3. 2. An abode, a place of business: jocular coll: from ca 1880. Ex *pig-sty*, a miserable hovel. cf. DIGGINGS; DEN.

Pig-Tail. A Chinese: 1886, *Cornhill*, July: coll till ca 1905, then S.E. 2. (*pig-tail*, or as one word.) An old man: low urban coll: ca 1810–45. Ware, 'From the ancients clinging to the 18th century mode of wearing the hair'. 3. A roll of coarse tobacco: ?ca 1780–1860.

pig-tail, adj. Chinese, as in *pig-tail brigade, party, land*: coll: late C.19–20.

pig to play on the flute, teach a. To attempt the impossible; do something absurd: coll: C.19.

pig-tub. The receptacle for kitchen-refuse: lower classes' (—1887); slightly ob.

pig-widgeon, -widgin. A simpleton; a fool: coll: ca 1685–1890. An intensive of *widgeon*, fig. used of a fool (—1741), just possibly influenced by *gudgeon*. Prob. related to S.E. *pigwiggen, -in*.

pig will make a good brawn to breed on, a

brinded. 'A red-headed man will make a good stallion,' Ray: a c.p. of ca 1670–1750.

pig-yoke. A quadrant; a sextant: nautical: 1836, Marryat, 'This was the "ne plus ultra" of navigation; . . . old Smallsole could not do better with his pig-yoke and compasses.' Somewhat ob. Ex the roughly similar shape.

pigeon. See PIGEON, FLY A BLUE. 2. Gen. in pl., one of a gang of lottery-sharpers that specialize in insuring tickets: late C.18–early 19 c. Grose, 3rd ed., where see a full description. 3. Hence, any person hastening with news surreptitiously obtained: c. of ca 1820–50. 4. A simpleton; a dupe: from ca 1590. G. Harvey, 1893. Esp. in *pluck a pigeon*, to fleece someone. cf. the v. 2. 5. (occ. *pidgin.*) Business, concern, duty, task: from early 1800s. e.g. 'This is *his* pigeon.'

pigeon, v. See PIGEON THE NEWS. 2. To deceive grossly; dupe; swindle: 1675, Cotton; 1807, E. S. Barrett, 'Having one night been pigeoned of a vast property', O.E.D., which classifies as S.E.: but surely s. (cf. the n., 4.)

***pigeon, fly a blue.** To steal lead from a roof, esp. of a church: c.: from ca 1785; ob. Grose, 2nd ed.; 1823, Bee (*fly the pigeon*). 2. But *fly the b. p.* is nautical s.: to heave the deep-sea lead: 1897 Kipling.

pigeon, milk the, see MILK THE . . .
pigeon, Paul's, see PAUL'S PIGEON.
pigeon, pluck a, see PIGEON, n., 4.

pigeon and kill a crow, shoot at a. To blunder deliberately: coll: from the 1630s; ob.

***pigeon-cracking.** Same as PIGEON-FLYING, 1859, H.; ob.

***pigeon-fancier.** A professional gambler: gamblers' c. of ca 1800–50. J. J. Stockdale, *The Greeks*, 1817. Pun on PIGEON, n., 4.

***pigeon-flying.** Stealing lead from roofs on buildings: c.: C.19–20. Also *bluey-cracking*. See *fly a blue* PIGEON.

pigeon-hole. A too-wide gap between two words: printers': 1683, Moxon; ob. cf. RAT-HOLE. 2. A small study: Winchester College: from ca 1850. 3. The female pudend: low: C.19–20; ob. 4. (Extremely rare – ?, indeed, non-existent – in singular.) The stocks; the instrument confining the hands of a prisoner being flogged: c.: late C.16–17. Greene, Eachard.

pigeon-hole soldiers. Clerks and orderlies: military coll: from ca 1870; ob. *Echo*, 1 July 1871.

pigeon-holes, see PIGEON-HOLE, 4.

pigeon the news. To send news by carrier-pigeon: s. verging on coll: from ca 1820. cf. PIGEON, n., 3.

pigeoner. A swindler or a sharper: 1849: coll >, ca 1900, S.E. Ex PIGEON, v., 2.

pigeons with one bean, catch (or **take**) **two.** To 'kill two birds with one stone': semi-proverbial coll: ca 1550–1700. North's *Dial of Two Princes*, 1557.

piggies. Toes of baby or small child: domestic: late C.19–20. Ex the nursery rhyme 'This little piggy went to market, this little piggy stayed at home.'

piggot, Piggot; Pigott. To forge: political coll: 1889–ca 1895. 'A reminiscence of the Parnell Commission: the expression was born in the House of Commons, 28th Feb. 1889,' F. & H. 2. Ware shows that it was used also as 'to tell an unblushing lie to', gen. in the passive; that there was a n. corresponding to this sense of the v.; that the term derived from the forger *Pigott* – which is the correct spelling.

Piggy. The 'inevitable' nickname of any man surnamed May: naval and military: late C.19–20.

piggy-back. A nursery and dial. variant of *pick-a-back*: C.19–20. Also PIG-A-BACK.

piggy-wig; piggy-wiggy. A pet pig; hence, a humorous endearment: coll: resp. 1870, Lear; 1862, Miss Yonge.

pight. The p. tense and p. ppl of *pitch* used wrongly as a present tense: late C.16.

Pigot, pigot; properly **Pigott,** see PIGGOT.

pigs, abbr. of PIG'S-EAR, 2.

pigs, please the. If circumstances permit: coll: late C17–20; ob. Facetious Tom Brown, Lytton. Perhaps orig. Irish; perhaps a corruption of *pix* (*pyx*), or more prob. ex *pixies*, fairies.

pigs and whistles, go to. To be ruined: Scots coll: from ca 1780. Mrs Carlyle, 1862, uses *make p. and w. of* as = to upset, or perturb, very greatly. In Scots, *pigs and whistles* is fragments.

pig's back, on the. In luck's way. Anglo-Irish (—1903). Perhaps ex a golden amulet in the shape of a pig.

pig's-ear or **-lug.** A very large lapel or collar flap: tailors': from ca 1860; ob. 2. Beer; rhyming s.: late C.19–20.

pig's eye. In cards, the ace of diamonds: low (—1864). Ex appearance.

pig's foot! see FOOT!, MY.

pigs fly, when. Never: coll: C.17–20; ob. Withals, in his Dict., defines *terra volat* as 'pigs flie in the ayre with their tayles forward'. (cf. BLUE MOON, *Greek kalends*; *Queen* DICK; etc.) In C.19–20, much less common than the S.E. *pigs might fly!*, perhaps!

pig's fry. A tie: from ca 1880.

pig's-lug, see PIG'S-EAR.

pigs (occ. hogs) to a fair – more gen. **a fine – market, bring one's.** To do well; make a profit: C.17–20: coll >, by 1800, S.E. Rowlands, Urquhart, Murphy (*carry*), Planché.

pigs (or hogs) to market, drive one's. To snore: coll: C.18–20; ob. (In C.19–20, mainly dial.) Origin explained in Swift's 'I'gad he fell asleep, and snored so hard, that we thought he was driving his hogs to market.' New Zealanders (late C.19–20) say *drive the pigs home*, esp. *driving . . .*

pig's(-)whisper. A grunt: low coll: C.19–20. Whence:

pig's whisper, in a. Very quickly indeed; in a very short time: s. > low coll: implied in Bee, 1823; 1837, Dickens, 'You'll find yourself in bed in something less than a pig's whisper'.

pigskin. A saddle: sporting: from ca 1860. Dickens. Hence:

pigskin, knight of the. A jockey: sporting: 1898, *Sporting Times*, 26 Nov., 'Riding rings round their crack knights of the pigskin.'

pigsn(e)y; (occ. in pl. -yes.) An endearment: C.14–early 19: S.E. till C.18, when (Grose, 1785) low if used to a woman. Lit., pig's eye, with intrusive or prosthetic *n.*

pigsty, see PIG-STY.

pigtail, see PIGTAIL.

pijaw. An occ. form of PI-JAW (see also PI-GAS).

pike. A turnpike road: coll and dial.: from ca 1830. (Mostly U.S.) 2. A toll-bar or -gate: coll and dial.: 1837, Dickens. Abbr. *turnpike.* 3. The toll paid thereat: coll: 1837, Dickens, fig. of death. 4. A tramp: c.: from ca 1860; ob. Ex *turnpike road* or perhaps ex PIKER.

***pike,** v. To depart: from ca 1520: S.E. until 1650, then s.; in C.18–20, low s. verging on c. Ex *pike oneself*, same sense. 2. In C.18–20 c., to go; occ. to run: Shirley, *The Triumph of Wit*, 1724. 3. Hence, to die: late C.17–20: low s. All senses often in form PIKE OFF.

pike, bilk a. To cheat a toll-keeper: low: C.18–19.

pike, go. To walk; depart: coll and dial.: C.16–17. cf. PIKE, V., 1.

pike, prior, see PIKE I!

***pike, tip a.** To walk; to depart; esp. escape, give the slip to: c.: C.18–mid-19. Song, 1712, 'Tho' he tips them a pike, they oft nap him again.' cf. PIKE OFF and PIKE ON THE BEEN.

pike I! An interjection implying prior claim or privilege: schools': C.19–20; ob. ? = I go first. (cf. BAGS; PLEDGE.) Also in the form, *prior pike!*

***pike it.** To go, depart: c. > low s.: late C.18–20. G. Parker, ca 1789, 'Into a booze-ken they pike it.' Elaboration of PIKE, V., 1. cf.:

pike it!, if you don't like it take a short stick and. A London c.p., rhyming variety, of ca 1870–1900. Ex preceding.

pike-keeper. A toll-keeper: coll and dial.: 1837, Dickens. Abbr. *turnpike-keeper.*

***pike off.** To depart; run away: c.: late C.17–20; ob. In mid-C.19–20, it is also common in dial. 2. To die: c.: late C.17–20; ob. Elaborations of PIKE, go, die.

***pike on the been (or bene).** To run away as fast as possible: c.: mid-C.17–18. Origin, meaning of *been*? Prob. it = *bien, bene*, excellent: hence, run away on a good road, i.e. to good purpose.

***piked off,** ppl adj. Clear away, safe; dead: c.: late C.17–20; ob.

pikeman. A toll-keeper: coll and dial.: 1857, 'Tom Brown' Hughes. cf. PIKE-KEEPER.

***piker.** A tramp or a vagrant; occ. a Gypsy: c. (—1874) ex dial. (—1838). Borrow, *Lavo-Lil*, 1874. Ex PIKE, V., 1, or PIKE IT. 2. The nose: North Country (mostly Northumberland) low s.: late C.19–20. 3. Gen. in pl, wild cattle: Australia: late C.19–20; ob. Ex PIKE (OFF), go, depart.

pikestaff. The penis: low coll: C.18–20; ob. **pikestaff, plain as a,** see PLAIN . . .

***pikey.** A tramp, a Gypsy: c. (or low s.) and dial.: mid-C.19–20. cf. PIKE and PIKER.

pilcher. A coll term of abuse: ca 1600–40. Ben Jonson. Perhaps *pilcher*, a pilchard.

pile, go the whole. To GO THE WHOLE HOG: lower classes' (—1887).

pile, have a. To have a difficult task, a hard time: Canadian coll: late C.19–20.

pile, make one's. To make a fortune: coll: from ca 1850. Mostly Colonial and U.S.; *pile* itself (1731) is S.E. Ex idea of a pile of coins.

pile-driver. The male member: low: mid-C.19–20: ob. 2. A heavy blow or punch: sporting coll: mid-C.19–20.

pile-driving. Sexual intercourse: low: mid-C.19–20. cf. preceding term. 2. Steaming or sailing into a heavy head sea: nautical: late C.19–20. Bowen.

pile it on is a coll form of **pile on the agony,** see AGONY.

pile up. To run (a ship) ashore: nautical coll: late C.19–20.

Pilgarlic(k); in C.18, occ. **Peel(e) Garlic,** as in Grose (1st ed.). Used of oneself; almost always *poor Pilgarlic*: coll and dial.: C.17–20; rare after ca 1880. Anticipated in Skelton; Beaumont & Fletcher, 'There got he a knock, and down goes pil-garlick'; Echard, 1694; Swift, 'They all went to the opera; and so poor Pilgarlick came home alone'; Grose; *Punch*, 21 April 1894, 'No! 'tis Bull is pilgarlic and martyr'; Collinson, 1927, 'The once popular "Everybody's down on poor Pilgarlic" . . .' Ex S.E. sense, a bald head (which resembles a peeled head of garlic). 2. A fop: early C.18. Ned Ward.

pilgrim-salve or **pilgrim's salve.** Excrement: coll: mid-C.17–early 19. Anon., *A Modern Account of Scotland*, 'The whole pavement is pilgrim-salve.' The O.E.D. considers it euphemistic S.E., but I very much doubt this classification.

pilgrim's staff. The *membrum virile*: low: C.18–19.

pill. A physician: 1860, H., 2nd ed.: military from ca 1855; †by 1915. cf. BOLUS. Also *pills*, 1899, *Cassell's Saturday Journal*, 15 March. 2. A ball, esp. a black balloting-ball or a tennis ball: late C.19–20. cf. PILLS, 2, and the v., 1. 3. (Of a person) a bore: 1897, Maugham, *'Liza of Lambeth*, 'Well, you are a pill!'; slightly ob. 4. Punishment; suffering; a sentence of imprisonment: low coll: from the mid-1890s. Abbr. *bitter pill*; often 'That's a pill, *that* is!' 5. A drink: from ca 1899; ob. 6. As a cannon-ball or a bullet, *pill* (C.17–20) is rather jocular S.E. than coll in C.17–mid-19, then coll. 7. (In billiards) see PILLS, 3.

pill, v. To reject by ballot: 1855, Thackeray, 'He was coming on for election . . . and was as nearly pilled as any man I ever knew in my life.' 2. v.i., to twaddle, talk platitudinously: university: ca 1885–1910.

***pill and poll,** v.t. To cheat (a comrade) of (his REGULARS): c.: from ca 1835. Ex S.E. sense.

pill-box. A small brougham: coll: 1855, Dickens, referring, however, to a few years earlier; ob. by 1895. 2. A doctor's carriage: ca 1870–1910. 3. A pulpit: jocular coll: from ca 1870; ob. 4. A soldier's cap: ca 1890–1910.

pill-driver. An itinerant apothecary: coll: mid-C.19–20. Ex S.E. *pill-monger*, *-peddler*. cf. PILL-PUSHER.

pill-pate. A friar; a shaveling: C.16 coll. Bacon, 'These smeared pill-pates, I would say prelates, . . . accused him.' i.e. *pilled* or *shaven pate*.

pill-pusher. A doctor: lower classes' (—1909). cf. (?ex) PILL-DRIVER.

pill-yawl. A Bristol Channel pilot boat: nautical: late C.19–20. Bowen.

pillar and post. A ghost: 'the ghost' (monetary, see GHOST WALKS . . .): theatrical rhyming s.: late C.19–20.

pillars to the temple. A woman's legs: Public Schoolmen's: late C.19–20. Not so much euphemistic as playfully allusive.

pil(l)icock, pil(l)cock, pillock. The penis: a vulgarism: C.14–18. Lyndsay, Florio, Cotgrave, Urquhart, D'Urfey. 2. Hence an endearment, addressed to a boy: late C.16–17: a vulgarism. Florio. Whence:

pil(l)icock (etc.)-hill. The female pudend: low: C.16–17. Shakespeare, in *King Lear*, puns thus on Lear's *pelican* daughters: 'Pillicock sat on pillicock-hill.'

pilling. The vbl n. of PILL, v., 1. Recorded in 1882; but prob. 27 years earlier.

pillocks; pillocky. 'He's talking pillocks' (nonsense) and 'Don't talk so pillocky' (so foolishly and nonsensically): Cockney: late C.19–20. Blend of PILL(S), testicle(s), and its synonym BALLOCKS.

pillory. A baker: late C.17–mid-18. ?semantics.

pillow-mate. A wife; mistress; harlot: coll: C.19–20.

pillow-securities. Safe scrip: financial coll: ca 1860–1915. Ware quotes the *Daily Telegraph*, 8 July 1896, '"Pillow securities" – those which do not trouble an investor's dreams at night and which a man need not worry about.'

pillows under folk's, men's, or **people's elbows, sew.** To give them a false sense of safety or security: coll: late C.14–17. The Geneva Bible; Wycherley.

pills. A physician, esp. in Army and Navy: see PILL, n., 1. 2. Testicles: low: late C.19–20. Ex PILL, n., 2. 3. Billiards, esp. in *play pills*: 1896, *Westminster Gazette*, 28 Oct., 'We can play pills then till after lunch, you know.' cf. PILL, n., 2. 4. The inevitable nickname of any man surnamed Holloway: naval and military:

late C.19–20. Prob. ex the well-known Holloway's Pills and Ointment.

pilot, sky, see SKY PILOT.

pilot's grog. Additional liquor served in an Indiaman beating up the Hughli under a pilot: nautical coll: mid-C.19–early 20.

pimgenet, pimgim(n)it. 'A large, red, angry Pimple', B.E.; any pimple, O.E.D.: s. > coll: late C.17–18; extant in C.19 as dial. cf. the C.18 c.p. *nine pimgenets make a pock royal.*

Pimlico, walk in. (Of a man) to be handsomely dressed: ca 1670–1720. Aubrey. The walks called *Pimblico-Path*, near the Globe Theatre, London, were frequented only by well-dressed men. cf. the C.19 Devonshire *to keep it in Pimlico*, to keep a house clean and attractive.

pimp. A male procurer: C.17–20. 'The word is app. of low slang origin, without any recorded basis,' *The Century Dict.*; B.E. and Grose still consider as s. or coll, but prob. S.E. by 1660. Perhaps ex Old Fr. *pimpreneau*, a scoundrel. 2. 'A small faggot used about London [and the Southern counties] for lighting fires, named' – orig., Defoe tells us, by the woodmen – 'from introducing the fire to the coals,' Grose, 1st ed. Coll: from ca 1720; ob., except in Surrey.

pimp-whisk, from ca 1700; **pimp-whiskin(g),** 1638, Ford. A PIMP, esp. a notable pimp: s. or low coll, †by 1830. 2. 'Also a little mean-spirited, narrow-soul'd Fellow', B.E.: coll: late C.17–mid-18. Obviously *whiskin(g)* is an elaboration or a diminutive of WHISK, a whipper-snapper.

pimple. A boon companion: late C.17–early 18. Congreve, 1700, 'The sun's a good Pimple, an honest Soaker.' 2. The head: low: C.19–20; ob. (With these senses, considered together, cf. C.20 *old top.*) 3. A hill: lower classes': from late 1890s. 4. The nose: pugilistic: ca 1815–60. 'A Real Paddy', 1822. 5. A baby's penis: women's: late C.19–20.

pimple and wart. A quart: public-house rhyming s.: late C.19–20. 2. Port wine: public-house rhyming s.: late C.19–20.

pimple in a bent. Something minute: coll: ca 1580–1650. Stanyhurst, 'I should bee thoght over curious by prying owt a pimple in a bent.' A *bent* is either a grass-stem or a flower-stalk. cf. *thimble in a haystack.*

pin. See PINS. 2. The penis: low coll: C.17–20. Glapthorne. cf. PIN-CASE. 3. A trifle; almost nothing, as in *not worth a pin, care not a pin.* Perhaps orig. (C.14) coll, but very soon S.E. 4. 4½ gallons; the vessel holding it: 1570, O.E.D.: perhaps coll in C.16–17, but thereafter, if not from the first, S.E.

pin, v. To seize: 1768, the Earl of Carlisle, 'I am sure they intended to pin my money'; ob. 2. Hence, to steal, esp. if rapidly: c.: C.19–20; ob. cf. NAB; PINCH; SNAFFLE. 3. To catch, apprehend: c. (—1864). 4. To pawn clothes (v.i.): low: from ca 1880; ob. Prob. a corruption of *pawn.*

pin, be down. To be indisposed: coll: C.19–20; ob. cf. PEG TOO LOW.

pin, keep in the. To abstain from drinking: from ca 1835: dial., and s. >, ca 1880, coll. Prob. suggested by PIN, PUT IN THE. cf. PEG, PUT ON THE,.

pin, let loose a. To have an outburst, esp. go on a drinking-bout: from ca 1850: dial., and s. >, ca 1880, coll; ob.

pin, nick the. To drink fairly: coll: mid-C.17–18. cf. PEG phrases. In old-fashioned tankards, there were often pegs or pins set at equal perpendicular distances.

pin, put in the. To cease; esp. to give up drinking: from ca 1830: dial., and s. >, ca 1880, coll. Mayhew. For semantics, cf. preceding entry; perhaps, however (as the O.E.D. suggests), ex a pin or a peg used for making something fast or for checking motion, the pin being a linch-pin. As a c.p. it = 'put a sock in it!', i.e. close your mouth!, SHUT UP!: ca 1860–90.

pin-basket. The youngest child in a completed family: coll in C.18–mid-19, then dial.

pin-buttock. A thin or a bony buttock or behind: late C.16–20 (ob.): coll >, ca 1660, S.E. Shakespeare, *All's Well*, 'The pin-buttock, the quatch-buttock, the brawn-buttock, or any buttock'. Opp. BARGE-ARSE, and comparable with S.E. *pin-tail.*

pin-case or **-cushion.** The female pudend: low: C.17–20; ob. See PIN, n., 2.

pin-money. A woman's pocket-expenses: late C.17–20: coll till C.19, then S.E. Orig. a settled allowance: see, e.g., Grose. 2. Money gained by women from adultery or occasional prostitution: late C.19–20; slightly ob. Allusion to PIN, n., 2.

pin-pannierly fellow. A covetous miser: coll: ?C.17. Kennett MS. (Halliwell). One who pins up his panniers or baskets; one who hates to lose a pin.

pinch. A certainty: racing: from ca 1885. Marshall, *Pomes, from the Pink 'Un*, 1886–

96. ?by confusion with U.S. *cinch.* 2. *pinch, the.* Pilfering during purchase; exchanging bad for good money, or giving short change: c.: late C.18–20; slightly ob.

***pinch,** v. To steal: from ca 1670: c. until ca 1880, then also low s. Head, 1673, 'To pinch all the lurry he thinks it no sin.' Ex the pinching movement of predatory fingers. cf. MAKE; NAB; NICK; WIN. 2. Hence (gen. *pinch . . . for*), to rob (a person): C.19–20, ob.; c. until ca 1860, then also low s. 3. v.i., to pass bad money for good: c. of ca 1810–60. Ex sense 1. cf. the n., 2. 4. To arrest: c.: 1860, H., 2nd ed.; 1861, Mayhew, 'He got acquitted for that there note after he had me pinched.' Similar semantics. cf. GRAB; PULL IN. 5. To urge (a horse), esp. press it hard; exhaust by urging: racing coll: 1737, Bracken, 'It is the vulgar Opinion that a Horse has not been pinch'd . . . when he does not sweat out.'

pinch, on a. A somewhat illiterate variant of *at a pinch*: prob. from ca 1800.

***pinch, on the.** A-stealing, either as at PINCH, n., 2, or gen. From ca 1800.

pinch-back, -belly, -commons, -crust, -fart, -fist, -gut, -penny, -plum. A miser; a niggard: all coll > S.E.: *-back*, C.17–19; *-belly*, 1648, Hexham; *-commons*, Scott, 1822, 'niggardly pinchcommons', ob.; *-crust*, C.17–18, as in Rowlands, 1602; *-fart*, late C.16–17, as in Nashe; *-fist*, late C.16–20, ob.; *-gut*, a niggardly purser: nautical (—1867), ex *pinch-gut*, a miser, mid-C.17–20, slightly ob. – in C.19–20, a vulgarism. cf. PINCH-GUT MONEY; *-penny*, C.15–mid-18, as in Lyly, 'They accompt one . . . a pynch penny if he be not prodygall'; *-plum*, from ca 1890.

pinch-bottom, -buttock, -cunt. A whoremonger: low coll: C.19–20; ob. cf. PINCH-PRICK.

pinch-fart, pinch-fist, see PINCH-BACK.

***pinch-gloak.** A shoplifter: c.: from ca 1810; ob. See GLOACH and PINCH, v., 1, and n., 2.

pinch-gut. See PINCH-BACK and cf. PINCH-GUT MONEY. 2. Hence, a badly fed ship: nautical coll: mid-C.19–20.

Pinch-Gut Hall. 'A noted House' –?a tavern-brothel – 'at *Milend*', – i.e. Mile End Road, East London – 'so Nicknam'd by the *Tarrs*, who were half Starved in an *East-India* Voiage, by their then Commander, who Built (at his return) that famous Fabrick, and (as they say) with what he Pinch'd out of their Bellies', B.E. Late C.17–mid-18.

pinch-gut money. 'Allow'd by the King to the Seamen, that Serve on Board the Navy Royal, when their Provision falls Short; also in long Voyages when they are forced to Drink Water instead of Beer', B.E. Coll, from ca 1660; ob. Smyth, who gives it as *pinch-gut pay* (1867).

pinch-gut vengeance, see WHIP-BELLY.

pinch on the parson's side, see PARSON'S SIDE. **pinch-penny, -plum,** see PINCH-BACK.

pinch-prick. A harlot: a wife keen, and insistent, on her conjugal rights: low coll: C.19–20; ob. cf. PINCH-BOTTOM, etc.

***pinch the regulars.** To take an undue share, or keep back part of the booty: c.: C.19–20. See PINCH, v., and REGULARS.

pinch-wife. A churlish, vigilant husband: (rather low) coll: C.19–20; ob.

***pincher.** A thief, esp. a shoplifter: c.: C.19–20. 2. One who indulges in the act of PINCH, v., 3: same status, period, and authority. 3. *Pincher* is the 'inevitable' nickname, mostly naval and military, of any man surnamed Martin: late C.19–20. Bowen, 'After Admiral Sir William F. Martin, a strict disciplinarian, who was constantly having ratings "pinched" for minor offences'.

***pinching lay.** The giving of short change or bad money: c.: late C.18–20; ob. Also *the pinch.* See PINCH, v., 3, and n., 2.

pincushion, see PIN-CASE.

ping. To speak in a quick singing high voice: sportsmen's: first half of C.19. Ware, 'From the sharp ping of the old musket'.

pink. An outstanding SWELL or dandy: buckish: ca 1815–40. Pierce Egan, 1821.

pink, adj. Smart; exceedingly fashionable: 1818, Lady Morgan, 'It was Lady Cork's "Pink night"; the rendezvous of the fashionable exclusives': †by 1890, except in U.S. Ex †S.E. sense, exquisite.

pink, Dutch. Blood: boxing: 1853, Bradley's *Verdant Green*, 'That'll take the bark from your nozzle, and distill the Dutch pink for you, won't it?' Ob. by 1910. Ex the S.E. sense (1758).

pink spiders (occ. **elephants**). Delirium tremens: late C.19–20: mostly low. Ob.

pink wine. Champagne: military (—1909); ob. Prob. an evasion.

pinkany, -eny; variants in **-ck-;** also **pink nye, pinken eye,** etc. (As an endearment) darling, pet: nursery coll > S.E.: late

C.16–early 17. Nashe, Massinger. Lit. *pink* (a narrow, hence little, hence dear) *eye*. Influenced by PIGSNEY.

pinked, ppl adj. Carefully and beautifully made: tailors': mid-C.19–20.

pinker. A blow that draws blood: pugilistic: ca 1880–1914..

pinkie, pinky. Anything small; orig. and esp. the little finger: Scots coll, mostly among children: C.19–20. Lit., the little pink one. 2. Red wine: since ca 1890; ob.

pinking dindee. A sweater or mohawk: Irish coll: C.18. Lit., a 'turkey-cock' given to pinking with a rapier.

pinky, see PINKIE.

pinna, pinner, pinny. A pinafore: resp. C.19–20, coll; from ca 1845, coll (†by 1910) and dial.; from ca 1855 (G. Eliot, 1859), coll, mostly nursery. (cf. the forms NANNY, NANNA.)

***pinnel,** occ. **pennel.** Penal servitude: c.: from ca 1860; ob. By abbr. and corruption of the two defining words. H., 1874, 'As "four-year pinnel"'. cf. PENAL.

pinner, see PINNA.

***pinner-up.** A seller of broadside songs and ballads: c.: 1851, Mayhew; ob. by 1900. Even in 1873, H. could write, 'There are but one or two left now.' Songs were usually pinned-up on canvas against a wall.

pinnicky pawnee (or -ie) and numerous other spellings. Drinking-water: mid-C.19–20: Indian >, by 1900, gen. Army s.

pinnock to pannock, bring. To cause ruin: coll: C.16–early 17. Huloet, 1552, 'Brynge somethynge to nothynge, as the vulgare speache is, to brynge pynnock to pannock.' Origin obscure.

pinny, see PINNA.

pins. (Rare in singular.) Legs: coll and dial.: 1530, Anon., *Hickscorner*, 'Than wolde I renne thyder on my pynnes As fast as I might goe'; 1781, General Burgoyne in one of his sprightly comedies, 'I never saw a fellow better set upon his pins.' Ex the primary sense of *pin*: a peg. cf. PEG-LEG.

pins, on one's. Alive; faring well (cf. S.E. *on his legs*); in good form: coll and dial.: from ca 1810.

pins and needles. The tingling that accompanies the restoration of circulation in a benumbed limb: coll: 1844, J. T. Hewlett; 1876, G. Eliot, 'Pins and needles after numbness'. Ex the feeling of being pricked with those articles.

pin's head in a cartload of hay, look for a. To attempt the impossible: coll: mid-C.16–18. Calfhill, 1565. Hence *find a pin's head . . .*, to do wonders. cf. *thimble in a bottle of hay* or *in a haystack*.

pinsrap. A parsnip: back s.: from ca 1880.

pint. Praise; recommendation: tailors': from ca 1860; ob. A pint is sufficient recommendation?

pint, the price of a. A sum sufficient to buy a pint of ale or beer: coll: late C.19–20.

pint of mahogany. (A glass of) coffee: low (—1909). Ex its colour.

pint-pot. (A nickname for) a seller of beer: coll: ca 1560–1620. Shakespeare.

pintle. The penis: *pintel* in A.-S., it is S.E. until ca 1720, then (dial. and) a vulgarism (ob.): cf. the degradation of PIZZLE and PRICK.

pintle-bit or **-maid.** A mistress; a kept whore: low coll: C.19–20; ob.

pintle-blossom. A chancre: low: C.18–20; ob. Contrast GROG-BLOSSOM.

pintle-case. The female pudend: low: C.19–20; ob. See PINTLE.

pintle-de-pantledy. 'Sadly Scared, grievously put to it', B.E. at *pit-a-pat*: coll: mid-C.17–early 19. Skinner, 1671.

pintle-fancier or **-ranger.** A wanton: low: C.19–20; ob. cf. PINTLE-MERCHANT.

pintle-fever. Syphilis or gonorrhoea: low coll: C.19–20; ob.

pintle-keek. An inviting leer: low Scots coll: C.19–20.

pintle-maid, see PINTLE-BIT.

pintle-merchant, -monger. A harlot: C.18–20: low. Ob. cf. Yorkshire *pintle-twister*.

pintle-ranger. See PINTLE-FANCIER and cf. PINTLE-BIT and PINTLE-MERCHANT.

pintle-smith, -tagger. A surgeon: low coll: from ca 1780.

pints round! A c.p. request to one dropping his shears: tailors': from ca 1850; very ob. by 1902. cf. PINT.

pinurt pots. Turnip tops: back s. (—1859).

pioneer. An early convict in Australia: Australian ironic coll: mid-C.19–20.

pip, preceded by *the*. Syphilis: coll verging on S.E.: late C.16–17. Ex the poultry disease. 2. The mark on a playing-card: coll (—1874). H., 5th ed., 'The ace is often called "single pip".' 3. See PIP, GET THE and GIVE THE.

pip, v. To blackball: clubs': 1880, Huth's *Buckle*. Prob. suggested by PILL, v. 2. To take a trick from (an opponent): cards: from ca 1885. 3. To hit with a missile, esp. a bullet; to wound; to kill: military: 1900. Perhaps ex sense 1 or as with a fruit-pip, or ex: 4. To beat, defeat, e.g. in a race: 1891. Ex senses 1 and 2. 5. To fail (a candidate): 1908.

pip, get or **have the.** To be depressed; (ob.) to be indisposed: coll: from ca 1885. Marshall, in *Pomes*, 'It cost a bit to square up the attack; | For the landlord had the pip.' Ex the poultry disease via the Thackerayan 'The children ill with the pip, or some confounded thing', 1862. cf. Devonshire dial. *take the pip*, to take offence: occurring as early as 1746.

pip, give the. To depress; from ca 1890: coll.

pip-pip! A 'hue and cry after anyone, but generally a youth in striking bicycle costumery': low (—1909). Ex the cyclist's warning by horn. Ware. 2. Good-bye!: from ca 1904.

pipe. The human voice: C.17–20: S.E. until late C.19, then coll; slightly ob. Ex *pipe*, a bird's note or song. 2. A boot; esp. a top-boot: low (?orig. c.): from ca 1810. Ob. (Extremely rare – ?non-existent – in the singular.) 3. The female pudend: low: C.19–20. 4. The urethra: late C.19–20. Abbr. *water-pipe*. 5. A satirical song, ballad, or prose-piece written on paper, which was then rolled up in the form of a pipe and left at the victim's door: Tasmanian coll: early C.19. 6. A good look (*at* . . .): low: from ca 1880. Ex the v., 4.

pipe, v. To talk; speak: coll: late C.19–20. Esp. in *pipe-up*, speak up, as in Whiteing's remarkable novel, *No. 5 John Street* (1899), 'Nance is called to oblige with a song. She is shy . . . But the Amazon brings her forward . . . "Pipe up, yer blessed little fool".' Ex playing on a pipe. 2. To weep: low: 1797, Mrs M. Robinson; ob. Ex PIPE AN (or ONE'S) EYE, than which it has been much less gen. 3. To follow, to dog: detectives' s. (—1864). 4. (Also *pipe off*.) Hence, to watch; spy: c.: from ca 1870. H., 1874; 'Pomes' Marshall; 'Dagonet' Sims. 5. v.i., to pant, breathe hard from exertion or exhaustion: boxing: 1814. De Quincey, 1827, 'The baker came up piping'; Dickens, 1848. Ex *pipes*, the lungs.

pipe, Her Majesty's or **the Queen's (tobacco-).** 'The kiln in the great East Vault of the Wine-Cellars of the London Docks, where useless and damaged goods that have paid no duty are burnt: as regards tobacco, a thing of the past, stuff of this kind being distributed to workhouses, &c.', F. & H., 1901 (pub. 1902). Coll: from ca 1840.

pipe, take a. To weep: 1818, Hogg; ob.: Scots coll. cf. PIPES, TUNE ONE'S, and:

pipe an or **one's eye, occ. one's eyes.** To weep: 1789, C. Dibdin: nautical s. >, ca 1860, gen. coll. 'An obscure variation on to *pipe away* . . ., with allusion to the boatswain's whistle', W. Earliest, *pipe one's eye*; *pipe one's eyes*, from ca 1810, ob. in C.20; *pipe an eye* is loose and rare. cf. PIPE, v., 2.

pipe and smoke it!, put that in your. Digest that if you can!: coll: 1824, Peake; Dickens in *Pickwick*; Barham; Miss Braddon.

pipe down. To be quiet: nautical coll: mid-C.19–20. Ex S.E. sense, 'to dismiss by sounding the pipe', and cf. PIPE, v., 1.

pipe in (or occ. **with) an ivy-leaf.** To busy oneself, either to no purpose or, more gen., as a consolation for failure; to do any silly thing one likes, gen. as *you may go pipe in an ivy-leaf*: coll: C.14–20; very ob. – indeed, rare since C.17. Semi-proverbial. An ivy-leaf being emblematic of very small value, and it being a notable art of country boys to produce shrill sounds by blowing through folded leaves or grass-blades.

pipe-layer, -laying. Political intriguer, intrigue: orig. (ca 1835), U.S.; partly anglicized ca 1890: coll. Ex a water-supply camouflaging an electoral plot.

***pipe off,** see PIPE, v., 4.

***pipe on.** To inform against: c.: from ca 1875; ob. See PIPE, v., 4.

pipe one's eye. A variant of PIPE AN EYE.

pipe-opener. (An) exercise taken as a 'breather': coll: 1879. Ex *pipes*, the lungs. – Ware classifies it as a university term and defines it as the 'first spurt in rowing practice – to open the lungs'.

pipe out, put one's. To spoil one's chance, sport, or showing; to extinguish: 1720, Ramsay, 'Their pipe's put out': coll till C.19, then S.E. and dial.; ob. 2. Hence, to kill: low: from ca 1860; ob.

pipe up. See PIPE, v., 1. 2. Also, to call, shout: same period.

pipeclay. v.t., to put into meticulous order (esp. accounts): 1833, Marryat; 1853, Dickens: nautical coll >, ca 1860, gen. coll. Ex *pipe-clay*, a white cleaning-material. 2. v.i. and t., to hide defects in material or mistakes in workmanship: from ca 1850. Ex sense 1.

piper. A broken-winded horse: 1785, Grose; 1831, Youatt: s. >, ca 1825, j. cf. ROARER. Connected with S.E. *pipes*, lungs. 2. A detective or spy: c.: from ca 1850. Esp., ca 1860–1910, a person employed to spy on the conductor of an omnibus: low.

piper!, by the. A mild, proletarian asseveration (—1887); slightly ob. Ex dial.

piper, drunk as a. Very drunk: 1770, Graves, *Spiritual Quixote*, 'Jerry . . . proceeded so long . . . in tossing off horns of ale, that he became as drunk as a piper': coll >, early in C.19, S.E.; †by 1890. (Dial.: *piper-fou.*)

piper (occ. **fiddler**), **pay the.** To pay the bill, lit. and fig.: 1681, Flatman; Congreve; Smollett; Brougham; Carlyle: coll till C.19, then S.E.

piper's cheeks. Puffed, swollen, or very big cheeks: coll: late C.16–17. Withals, 1602.

piper's news. Stale news: Scots coll: from ca 1820; ob. Hogg.

piper's wife. A whore: coll: late C.18–19.

pipers. Lungs: pugilistic: mid-C.19–20; ob.

pipes. See PIPE, n., 2. A boatswain: nautical nickname: early-C.19–20. Ex the giving of orders by sounding a pipe.

pipes, pack, or **put,** or **shut up one's.** To cease from action, more gen. from speech: coll: mid-C.16–18; in C.18, virtually S.E. Olde, 1556, *put up*; Nashe, *pack up.* While *shut up* is C.18 and perhaps early C.19. Ramsay has *poke up.* Ex the 'musical tube'.

pipes, set up one's. To cry aloud; yell: ca 1670–1800: coll >, by 1710, S.E.

pipes, tune one's. (To begin) to weep or cry: Scots coll and dial.: late C.18–20. Ex PIPE, voice, and *pipes*, lungs.

piping, n. Weeping, crying: s. >, ca 1850, coll: 1779, Seward, 'No more piping, pray'; Marryat, 1837. Ex PIPE, v., 2, though *piping* is recorded the earlier.

pipkin. The female pudend, esp. in *crack her pipkin*, to deflower a girl or woman: low: late C.17–early 19. Ned Ward, 1709; Grose. Ex cook's breakages, *pipkin* being a small earthenware pot. 2. The head; pugilism: from ca 1820; ob. Jones, *The Truc om'd Boxer*, 1825. 3. H., 1860, gives *pipkin*, the stomach, as Norwich s. (or coll): perhaps rather dial. Extremely ob.

pippin. A pejorative term of address: ca 1660–1820. Cotton, 1664, 'Thou'rt a precious Pepin, | To think to steal so slily from me.' Whence: 2. (Gen. *my p.*) An endearment, mostly costermongers': C.19–20; ob. cf. RIBSTONE. N.B. Byron called his wife 'Pippin'.

pippin, sound as a. Rosy-cheeked; very healthy: lower classes' coll (—1887). Ex the apple's 'high colour'.

pippin-squire. An APPLE-SQUIRE: s. or coll: C.17. Rowlands.

pippy. Shaky (of stocks): Stock Exchange: from ca 1890. ?ex PIP, GET THE.

pipy. Apt to PIPE AN EYE: from ca 1860: s. >, by 1890, coll.

pirate. Gen. pl. Naval small craft on any irregular or detached duty: naval coll: late C.19–20. Bowen.

pirler. An occ. form of PURLER.

piscatorial. Dubious: jocular: since ca 1845, but never common. (Francis Francis, *Newton Dogvane*, 1859.) A word-play on FISHY, 1.

piso. A miserly or stingy fellow: military: late C.19–20. cf. the †Northern dial. *pesant*, 'a stern, hard-hearted miser'.

piss, n. Urine: late M.E. + : S.E., but in C.19–20 a vulgarism. Ex:

piss, v. To urinate: M.E. + : S.E., but considered a vulgarism from ca 1760. (Because of its 'shocking' association, wrongly regarded as low coll. cf. ARSE; CUNT; SHIT.) Ex Old Fr. *pisser*, prob. echoic.

piss!, a. A vulgar Restoration expletive. Etherege, *The Man of Mode.*

piss, do a. To make water: low coll: C.19–20. See PISS, n.

piss, rods in. A prospective punishment, scolding: low coll: from ca 1620. Mabbe, 1623; Cotton, *Virgil Travestie*, 1678. Ob. Like brine, urine hardens canes.

piss, so drunk that he opened his shirt collar to. Blind drunk: low coll: C.19–20; ob.

piss-a-bed. The dandelion: coll verging on S.E.; also dial.: mid-C.16–20; †by 1900, except in dial. Ex (not its colour but) its diuretic virtues. cf. Fr. *pisse-en-lit.*

piss blood. To toil: low coll: late C.19–20. Ex strain of effort. cf.:

piss bones or **children** or **hard.** To be brought to childbed: low coll: C.19–20; ob. cf. the preceding entry.

piss down one's back. To flatter him: low coll: late C.18–19.

piss-factory. A public-house: C.19–20 (ob.): low. Liquor makes rapid urine.

piss-fire. A blusterer: C.18–19: (low) coll and dial. ?ex the old proletarian habit of extinguishing a fire by pissing it out. cf. the †proverb, *money will make the pot boil though the devil piss in the fire.*

piss in a quill. To agree on a plan: coll: C.17–19.

piss-kitchen. A kitchen maid: low coll: C.18–19.

piss-maker. A great drinker: low coll: late C.18–19.

piss money against the wall. To squander, waste money, esp. in liquor: late C.15–19: S.E. until C.18, then (low) coll.

piss more than one drinks. Gen. *pisses . . . he . . .* A semi-proverbial c.p. preceded by *vain-glorious man* and applied to a boaster: late C.17–early 19.

piss off. To depart, esp. to depart quickly: low: late C.19–20.

piss on a nettle. See NETTLE, TO HAVE PISSED ON A, and cf. the proverbial *as surly as if he had pissed on a nettle.*

piss one's tallow. To sweat: C.17–20; very ob. Urquhart, 'He's nothing but Skin and Bones; he has piss'd his Tallow.' Ex S.E. sense of a deer thinning in the rutting-season.

piss out of a dozen holes. To have syphilis: low: late C.19–20.

piss pins and needles. To have gonorrhoea: low coll: from ca 1780.

piss-pot. A nickname for a medical man: coll: late C.16–17. Ex: 2. A chamber-pot: mid-C.15–20: S.E. until mid-C.18, then a vulg. 3. An objectionable fellow (a STINKER): late C.19–20.

piss-pot emptier. A cabin steward: Merchant Navy: late C.19–20.

piss-proud. Having a urinal erection: low coll: late C.18–20. Grose, 2nd ed., where occurs the c.p. *that old fellow thought he had an erection, but his – – was only piss-proud,* 'said of any old fellow who marries a young wife'. cf. PRIDE OF THE MORNING.

piss pure cream. To have gonorrhoea: low: C.19–20, ob. cf. PISS PINS AND NEEDLES.

piss the less, – let her cry, she'll. A semi-proverbial c.p.: late C.18–20; ob. Supposed to have orig. been addressed by consolatory sailors to their harlots. In Grose, 3rd ed., it occurs in the form *the more you cry, the less you'll p–ss.*

piss (up)on, as good . . . as you would desire to. Excellent; extremely, as in Tom Brown's 'There are some Quacks as Honest Fellows as you would desire to Piss upon', 1700: (low) coll: late C.17–early 19. cf. PISSED, AS GOOD . . . and POT, AS GOOD . . .

piss-warm, adj. Distastefully tepid: low coll: late C.19–20.

piss when one can't whistle. To be hanged: low: from ca 1780; ob.

pissed, as good – occ. as very – a knave as ever. As good a man, etc. – as big a knave – as may be: (low) coll: C.18–20; C.18–19. See POT, AS GOOD . . ., and cf. PISS UPON . . .

pissed in the sea, – 'every little helps', as the old woman (or lady) said when she. A c.p. applied to urinating in sea or stream, hence to any very small contribution: mid-C.19–20. Adumbrated in the proverbial saying, 'Everything helps, quoth the wren, when she pissed into the sea' – quoted by *The Oxford Dictionary of Proverbs* for the date 1623.

pisser. The penis; the female pudend: low s. or coll: C.19–20. 2. A urinal: low coll: late C.19–20.

pisser, vinegar-. A niggard; miser: coll: C.18. 2. ? (in C.17) a sour fellow: cf. Anon.'s *2nd Return from Parnassus,* 1602, 'They are pestilent fellowes, they speake nothing but bodkins, and pisse vinegar.'

pisses my goose, such a reason. A very poor reason: C.18–19: low coll. cf. PISSETH . . . GOOSE.

pisseth, by fits and starts as the hog. Jerkily; intermittently: coll: C.18–19.

pisseth, when the goose. Never. Often preceded by *you'll be good.* Coll: C.18–20; ob. cf. PISSES MY GOOSE, SUCH A REASON.

pissing, vbl n. As in *the tin-whiffin is when you can't shit for pissin(g),* a low rhyming c.p.: ca 1870–1910.

pissing, adj. Paltry; brief: coll verging on S.E. (cf. *piddling*): C.16–early 19.

pissing candle. A small make-weight, or any very inferior candle: coll almost S.E.: C.18–19.

Pissing Conduit. A conduit with a flow resembling a stream of urine, esp. 'one near the Royal Exchange set up by John Wels (Lord-mayor, 1430),' F. & H.: late C. 16–17. Shakespeare, *1 Henry the Sixth,* IV, vi: 'I charge and command that, of the city's cost, | The pissing conduit run nothing but claret wine, | The first year of our reign.'

pissing-while. A very short time; an instant: coll: C.16–mid-19. Palsgrave; Still, *Gammer Gurton's Needle,* 'He shall never be at rest one pissing-while a day'; Shakespeare; Ray's *Proverbs.*

pissy pal. A public house crony: mostly Cockney: late C.19–20. Ex their simultaneous use of the urinal for the discharge of their heavy cargo.

pistol. A swaggering bully: coll >, ca 1640, allusive S.E. Shakespeare, *Merry*

Wives, dramatis personae, 'Bardolph, Pistol, Nym, sharpers attending on Falstaff'. cf. Florio's definition of *pistolfo*. 2. The male member: late C.16–20; low coll verging on euphemistic S.E.; ob. See esp. Shakespeare, *King Henry the Fifth*, II, ii, the play on Pistol's name and *pistol*.

pistol-shot. A drink: ca 1850–1910. cf. (*drink a*) SLUG and S.E. *pocket-pistol*.

***pit.** A breast-pocket; a fob: c.: from ca 1810; ob. 2. The female pudend. It is an open question whether *pit* and its variants, *pit-hole* and *-mouth*, *pit of darkness*, and *bottomless pit*, are low coll or euphemistic S.E. C.17–19.

pit, fly or **shoot the.** To turn tail: coll verging on S.E. and indeed, in C.19, achieving it: ca 1670–1890. The form with *shoot* occurs in a letter written by Andrew Marvell in 1675. Richardson, *Pamela*, 'We were all to blame to make madam here fly the pit as she did.' As does a cowardly cock in cock-fighting.

pit, knight of the, see the KNIGHT paragraph.

pit, shoot the, see PIT, FLY THE.

pit and boxes (or, in C.19–20, **back and front shops) into one, lay.** To remove or destroy the division between anus and vagina: from ca 1780; ob. 'A simile borrowed from the playhouse, when, for the benefit of some favourite player, the pit and boxes are laid together,' Grose, 1785.

pit(-)circler. An occupant of the pit: theatrical: ca1880–1910.

pit-hole. A grave: lower classes' coll (—1887). 2. See PIT, 2.

***pit-man; pitman.** A pocket-book carried in the breast-pocket: c. (—1812); †by 1900. Ex PIT, n., 1 + -MAN(S), the c. suffix.

pit-pat's the way! Go on!; don't stop!: proletarian c.p.: ca 1870–1914.

pit-riser. A burst of powerful acting which evokes an enthusiastic acclamation from the pit: theatrical: from ca 1814; ob. Ex a saying by Edmund Kean.

pitch. A place of sale or entertainment; a stand: 1851, Mayhew: showmen's and tramps' s. >, ca 1870, low coll >, ca 1880, coll >, ca 1910, S.E. Prob. ex *pitch a tent*. 2. Hence, a sale, a performance: low (showmen's, tramps'): from ca 1860. Vance, *The Chickaleary Cove*, ca 1864; Hindley, 1876, 'When I had done my pitch and got down from the stage.' 3. A short sleep: low: from ca 1870; ob. 4. A talk, chat: 1892, *Pall Mall Gazette*, 7 Sept.: in Australia, prob. since ca 1870. Ex PITCH A TALE.

pitch, v.i. To sit down; take a seat (and a rest): late C.18–20; coll; ob., except in dial. (where *pitch oneself*). Ex S.E. sense, to place oneself. 2. To do business: showmen's and tramps': from ca 1880. Henley, 1887, 'You swatchel-coves that pitch and slam'. Esp. among circus folk, 'To go on tour': prob. since ca 1865. Like the n., 1, this may orig. have been c. Also PITCH, DO A. 3. See PITCH A OF THE FORK, A TALE. 4. To utter base coin: c. (—1874). 5. To go to bed for less than the ordinary time; have a short sleep: esp. among bakers, busmen, etc.: from ca 1870. Perhaps because they pitch themselves down on the bed.

pitch, do a. See PITCH, n., 2, and v., 2. From ca 1860. Henley, 1887, 'A conjuror Doing his pitch in the street.'

pitch, make a. (Of a cheapjack) to attempt to do business: low coll (—1874).

pitch, queer the. To spoil a sale, a performance: showmen's and cheapjacks': 1875, Frost, *Circus Life*. See PITCH, n., 1, 2.

pitch a or **the fork, a tale.** To tell a story, esp. if romantic or pitiful: resp. s., ca 1859–1920; from ca 1865; s. Anon., *A Lancashire Thief*, 'Brummagem Joe . . . could patter and pitch the fork with any one'; *London Herald*, 23 March 1867, 'If he had had the sense to . . . pitch them a tale, he might have got off.' cf. PITCH IT STRONG. 2. See PITCH THE FORK.

pitch-and-Fill. Bill = William. Rhyming s. (—1859).

pitch and pay, v.i. To pay on the nail: coll: C.15–mid-19. Tusser; Shakespeare, *Henry the Fifth*, 'Let senses rule; the word is "pitch and pay"; | Trust none'; Evans, *Yorkshire Song*, 1810. Ex a Blackwell Hall enactment that a penny be *paid* by the owner of every bale of cloth for *pitching*.

pitch-fingers. A pilferer. Whence *pitch-fingered* thievishly inclined. Coll: from ca 1840.

pitch in, v.i. To set vigorously to work: coll, chiefly U.S. and Colonial: 1847 (O.E.D.). 2. Hence, to take a hand; to begin eating: coll: from ca 1850. Perhaps ex:

pitch into. To attack energetically, with blows or words (hence, to reprimand): *Sessions*, 1827, 'Beddis . . . began to pitch into Joseph Durden with his fists'; Dickens,

1852 (with words); Grant Allen, 1885 (of eating heartily). Coll.

pitch it. To desist; leave one's job; to cease doing something: tailors': late C.19–20.

pitch it mild. Usually in imperative. Don't exaggerate: a Canadian coll variant of DRAW IT MILD: late C.19–20. cf.:

pitch it (too) strong. To exaggerate: from ca 1870: s.

pitch-kettled. Puzzled; 'stumped': ca 1750–1830. Cowper, 'I ... find myself pitch-kettled, | And cannot see ... | How I shall hammer out a letter.' Lit., stuck fast, as in a kettle of pitch.

pitch-pole, pitchpole. To sell at double the cost price: coll: ca 1850–90.

pitch the fork. See PITCH A FORK. 2. Hence, to put a penny on the counter for, say, bacon and to receive both the bacon and the penny: vagrants' c.: from ca 1870. Thus the tramp avoids a charge of mendicancy.

pitch the hunters, see HUNTERS.

pitch the nob, see PRICK-THE-GARTER.

pitch-up. One's family or chums; a group or crowd: Winchester: from ca 1850. Hence:

pitch up with. To associate with: Winchester: from ca 1860.

pitched. CUT: tailors': from ca 1860.

pitcher. The female pudend: low coll: C.17–20; ob. Wycherley. 2. A street vendor: since ca 1870: s. 3. See SNIDE-PITCHER.

pitcher, bang a. To drain a pot: coll: C.19–20; ob. cf. †S.E. *pitcher-man*, a toper.

pitcher, crack a. To take a virginity; whereas *crack one's pitcher* is to lose it: C.18–20; ob. Coll, almost S.E. See PITCHER, 1, and cf.:

pitcher, cracked. A harlot still faintly respectable: coll: mid-C.18–mid-19. Smollett.

pitcher that holds water mouth downwards, the miraculous. The female pudend: a conundrum c.p. of mid-C.18–mid-19.

pitcher-bawd. 'The poor Hack' – worn-out whore – 'that runs of Errands to fetch Wenches or liquor', B.E.: low coll: late C.17–mid-18.

pitching, go (a). To turn somersaults: circus (—1887).

pitchpole, see PITCH-POLE. **pitchy-man,** see DOLLY-MAN.

***pitman.** An occ. form of PIT-MAN.

pitman's crop. A very close hair-cut, usual among miners on account of the dirty nature of their work: mining-towns' coll: late C.19–20.

pitster. One in, a frequenter of, the pit: theatrical coll (—1887). Perhaps on TIPSTER.

pittite. One sitting in the pit at a theatre: coll: 1807 (S.O.D.). Thackeray. Occ. *pitite*.

Pitt's picture. A bricked-up window: ca 1787–1800: political. Done by the poor and the miserly, to save paying Pitt's window-tax.

pity the poor sailor on a night like this! A semi-jocular c.p. *à propos* of a stormy night: late C.19–20.

piz or **pizz.** A young man-about-town: Society: ca 1760–80. cf. PUZ(Z).

pize on, upon, of; pize take it; etc. Coll imprecations: C.17–20. Since ca 1840, only dial. Cognate, prob., with *pest*, POX, and possibly POISON. Middleton, Shadwell, Smollett, Scott.

pizzle. The penis of an animal, esp. of a bull: from ca 1520. Hence, C.17–20, of a man. S.E. until ca 1840, then dial. and a vulg. Ex Flemish *pezel* or Low Ger. *pesel*, orig. a little sinew.

pizzle, v. (Of the male) to coït with: C.18–20: low coll. Ex the n.

place. An abode; a place of business: coll: mid-C.19–20. 2. A privy, a w.c.: coll: C.19–20; ob. 3. *the place*, the privities: low coll or perhaps euphemistic S.E.: C.18–20. Sterne, 'You shall see the very place, said my uncle Toby. Mrs Wadham blushed.'

place, v. To identify (thoroughly); remember in detail: orig. (ca 1855) U.S.; anglicized as a coll ca 1880.

place, hot, see HOT PLACE.

place of sixpenny sinfulness. The suburbs; esp. a brothel there: coll: C.17. Dekker.

placebo, be at or **go to the school of – hunt (a) – make – play (with) – sing (a).** To play the sycophant, be a time-server or servile: coll: resp. approx. mid-C.16–early 17 (Knox); 1360–1600 (Langland); 1480–1600 (Caxton); 1580–1650; 1340–1700 (Chaucer, Bacon). Ex the Office for the Dead. Lit., L. *placebo* = I shall be acceptable.

***placer.** A woman in an official brothel, e.g. in France: c., esp. white-slavers': from ca 1895.

placket. A woman, as sex; the female pudend: low coll: resp. C.17; C.17–18. With second sense, cf. *placket-racket*, the penis (Urquhart). Ex *placket*, a petticoat-slit or (dress or petticoat) pocket-hole, occ. a chemise.

placket-stung. Venereally infected: coll: mid-C.17–18. Ray.

plague. Trouble: coll: 1818, Scott, 'Deil a ... body about my house but I can manage when I like ...; but I can seldom be at the plague', i.e. of doing it. (Slightly ob.) Like the next seven entries, ex the weakening of S.E. sense of the respective words. 2. The menses: women's: mid-C. 19–20. cf. the CURSE.

plague, v. To trouble, bother; tease, annoy: late C.16–20: S.E. until C.18, then coll. Gay, 1727, 'Husbands and wives ... plaguing one another'; 1833, Harriet Martineau.

plague! In 'a plague (up)on, of', or 'take': from ca 1560; ob. Coll verging on S.E. and, after ca 1720, better considered as S.E. Also *how the*, or *what a, plague!*: late C.16–18: coll > S.E.

plagued. PLAGUILY: coll (—1887). Baumann, 'I'm plagued hard up.'

plaguesome. Troublesome, teasing, annoying: C.19–20: S.E. > coll ca 1860; ob.

plaguily. Exceedingly: coll: C.18–20. Swift; Landor, 1828, 'Ronsard is so plaguily stiff and stately.' Ob. by 1850.

plaguy. 'Pestilent'; CONFOUNDED; excessive, very great: coll: late C.17–20; ob. Motteux, 1694, 'Women that have a plaguy deal of religion'; *Punch*, 17 May 1879, 'A plaguy rise in the price'.

plaguy, adv. Exceedingly, very: coll: from ca 1740, earlier examples connoting a degree of some quality that troubles one by its excess. Richardson, in *Pamela*, 'I'm a plaguy good-humoured old fellow.' Ob. Ex preceding entry.

plain. Unwatered, undiluted, neat: coll: from ca 1850. Only of drinks.

plain as a pack-saddle. Obvious; very open: coll: mid-C.16–mid-18. T. Wilson, 1553; Wither; Ray; Bailey.

plain as a packstaff. The more gen. C.16–17 form (Becon, J. Hall) of:

plain as a pikestaff. Very clear or simple; beyond argument: late C.16–20: coll >, ca 1750, S.E. Shacklock, 1565; Greene, 1591; Smollett; D'Urfey; Trollope. cf. preceding and:

plain as a pipe-stem. Exceedingly plain, clear: coll: late C.17–18. cf. last three, and next two, entries.

plain as Salisbury. The same: coll: 1837, Dickens; curiously adumbrated, as the O.E.D. indicates, in Udall, 1542. Punning *Salisbury Plain*. (By the way, *plain as the sun at noonday* is S.E.) cf. Shakespeare's *plain as way to parish-church*.

plain as the nose on one's or **your face.** The same: coll: late C.17–20. Congreve, '"As witness my hand" ... in great letters. Why, 'tis as plain as the nose on one's face.'

plain-headed. Plain(-looking): Society: ca 1880–1910.

plain over (someone), **put the.** To search: Scottish (esp. Glasgow) policemen's: since ca 1880. Ex-Inspector Eliot, *Tracking Glasgow Criminals*, 1904.

plain statement. An easy piece of work; a meal plain to indifference: tailors': from ca 1860; slightly ob. Ex a statement contrasted with an invoice.

Plains of Betteris. 'The diversion of billiards', Egan's Grose: Oxford University: ca 1820–40.

plaister, see PLASTER.

***planet.** A candle: c.: 1840, Longfellow; ob. by 1890. (As source of light.)

plank, v. To put or set down; deposit: s. and dial.: 1859 (O.E.D.). Perhaps ex U.S. sense (no. 3),though this may well come ex Eng. dial. Note, however, that, 2, Egan's Grose, 1823, has *plank*, to conceal, and classifies it as Scottish c. – which suggests that, in this sense, the term is a perversion of PLANT, v., 1. 3. To table (money); pay readily: earliest Eng. record, 1835, Crockett (*plank up*); the U.S. dates (see esp. Thornton) are: *plank*, 1824; *plank up*, 1847; *plank down*, 1850. Both nuances are prob. a fusion of *put on the plank(s)* and *plank* as an echoic v. expressing violent action (cf. *plonk*); note that Ware has *plank the knife in(to)*, to stab deeply.

***plant.** A hiding-place (orig. at a FENCE's): c.: from ca 1787. Ex the v., 1. 2. Hence, hidden plunder or valuables (*the plant*): c.: from ca 1810. 3. 'A position in the street to sell from', H., 1st ed.: low: from ca 1858; slightly ob. 4. A swindle or a cleverly planned robbery: c. >, ca 1890, low s.: 1825, Westmacott. 5. A spy; detective: c.: 1812, *Sporting Magazine*; ob. Hence, 6, a decoy: c.: from ca 1830; ob. 7. A cordon of detectives: c.: 1880. 8. Loosely, a trick, a deception: 1889, *Notes and Queries*, 'The dispassionate scholar finds the whole thing a "plant".' (Senses 1–3: ex the v., 1; the other senses, derived from these.) 9. (Extremely rare in singular.) A foot: (?) low: C.17–18. Ex †S.E. *plant*, the sole of the foot.

***plant.** To conceal, hide: c.: C.17–20. Rowlands, *Martin Mark-All*, 'To plant, to hide'. Now esp. Australian, says the O.E.D. in 1909. Ex the planting of a seed, perhaps influenced by sense 2. cf. the, n., 1, 2. 2. Hence, to hide (esp. horses) until a suitable reward is offered: Australian: 1840, *Sydney Herald*, 10 Feb. 3. To place or set in position; to post (a person): mid-C.16–20: S.E. till ca 1705, then coll >, by 1780, low coll. J. Drake, 1706; Zangwill, 1892. 4. Whence, to achieve, or to assist, sexual intromission: C.17–20: low coll. cf. PLANT A MAN. 5. To bury: Grose, 1785; Mark Twain, *Innocents at Home*. 6. To abandon: s. or coll: 1821, Byron; rare and ob. cf. Fr. *planter là*. 7. To select a person or a building for a swindle or a robbery: c.: C.19–20; ob. 8. To plan, or devise, or prepare by illegal methods: c. or low s.: 1892, *Daily News*, 27 May, 'The affair was "planted" between two brothers.' 9. To utter base coin: c.: C.19–20; ob. 10. To HUMBUG; deceive: c.: C.19–20; ob. 11. To dispose cards for cheating: c.: from ca 1840. 12. (In mining) to SALT: c. almost imm. > low s.: from ca 1850. Reade, 1850. 13. In conjuring, to prepare a trick by depositing an object in the charge of a confederate: coll: from ca 1880. 14. To deliver (a punch); to drive (the ball) into the goal or 'into' another player: boxing, football: from 1808 and ca 1880 resp.: s. >, as to football, coll in C.20. 15. Hence, to hit: at certain Public Schools, esp. Marlborough: late C.19–20. C. Turley, *Godfrey Marten, Schoolboy*, 1902, 'You would plant him every time if you were taught properly.'

***plant, in.** In hiding; hidden: c.: 1812, Vaux. Ex PLANT, n., 1.

***plant, rise the.** 'To take up and remove anything that has been hid, whether by yourself or another', Vaux, 1812: c. cf.:

***plant, spring a.** To unearth another's hidden plunder: c.: 1812, Vaux. cf. preceding.

plant a man. To copulate: coll: C.18–19. (Rarely of a woman.)

plant home. To deliver (a, or as a, blow); hence, in argument, to make a point, and, in gen., to succeed (*plant it*, or *one*, *home*). From ca 1885: s. A special use of PLANT, v., 14

***plant the books.** To stack the cards: c.: mid-C.19–20: ob. See PLANT, v., 11.

***plant (the) whids and stow them.** To be very wary of speech; purposely say nothing: c.: C.17–mid-19. Rowlands, Grose. cf. STOW *it!*; WHID = word.

***plant** (a person) **upon** (another). 'To set somebody to watch his motions': c. (—1812); ob. Vaux. Merely a special application of PLANT, v., 3.

planter. A blow; esp. a punch in the face: sporting: from ca 1820; ob. *Sporting Magazine*, 1821, 'Smith put in a dreadful planter on Powell's throat.' 2. A horse apt to refuse to budge: (orig. Anglo-Indian) coll: 1864, 'Competition Wallah' Trevelyan. 3. A stealer and then hider of cattle: Australia: 1890, 'Rolf Boldrewood'. Ex PLANT, v., 1; cf. PLANT, v., 2, and:

planting, adj. Cattle-stealing: Australia: 1890, 'Rolf Boldrewood'. cf. PLANT, v., 2; PLANTER, 3.

planting, n. A burial: Welsh: mid-C.19–20. cf. PLANT, v., 5.

plants, see PLANT, n., 9.

plants, water one's. To shed tears: C.19.

plaster. A huge shirt or applied collar: non-aristocratic: ca 1890–1914. Ware. This looks like a corruption of Fr. *plastron*, a (stiff) shirt-front.

plaster, v. To shatter (a bird) with shot, blow it into a pulp: sporting: 1883, Bromley-Davenport. cf. quotation at PLASTERER. 2. To flatter (a person): proletarian: from ca 1860; ob.

plaster of warm guts. 'One warm Belly clapt to another', B.E.: 'a receipt frequently prescribed for different disorders', Grose, 1785. A late C.17–mid-19 low coll, almost a (men's) c.p. cf. the frequent, and often well-meant c.p. advice, *what you need is a woman*: mid-C.19–20.

plasterer. A clumsy shot with a gun (cf. PETER GUNNER): sporting: 1883. Bromley-Davenport, *Sport*, 1885, 'The plasterer is one who thinks nothing of the lives and eyes of the men who surround him, and blows his pheasant to a pulp before the bird is seven feet in the air.' cf. PLASTER.

plasterer's trowel and Seringapatam. Fowl and ham: rhyming s. (—1909); ob.

plate, be in for the. To be venereally infected: ca 1780–1850. 'He has won the *heat* . . . a simile drawn from horse racing,' Grose, 1785.

plate, foul a, see FOUL A PLATE.

plate-fleet comes in, when the. When I make or get a fortune: coll: ca 1690–1830. The Plate fleet was that which carried to Spain the annual yield of the American silver mines. cf. the C.19–20 *when my ship comes in*.

plate it. To walk: from ca 1890: rather low, slightly ob. Ex PLATES.

plate of meat. A street: rhyming s. (—1857). Contrast PLATES OF MEAT.

plated butter. A piece of butter genuine superficially, internally lard: low London (—1823); †by 1900.

plates. Short for PLATES OF MEAT: from ca 1885. Marshall, '*Pomes*', 'A cove we call Feet, sir, on account of the size of his plates'.

plates of meat. Feet: rhyming s. (—1874).

play, v. See PLAY IT OFF and PLAY OFF. 2. To make fun of: coll: 1891, Kinglake, in *The Australian at Home*, 'They do love to play a new chum.'

play a big game. To try for a big success: low (—1909).

***play a cross,** see PLAY ACROSS.

play a dark game. To conceal one's motive: coll, verging on S.E.: from ca 1885. Milliken, 1888, 'Bin playing some dark little game?'

***play across; occ. play a-cross or a cross.** Same as *play* BOOTY: c. of ca 1810–70.

play artful. To feign simplicity; keep something in reserve: low coll: from ca 1840.

play at hell and turn up Jack was a nautical elaboration (?ca 1790–1860) of *play hell*, to cause a tremendous commotion or much damage. John Davis, *The Post-Captain*, 1806.

play at push-pin or **two-handed put,** see PUSH-PIN . . .

play board. The stage in Punch and Judy: showmen's coll: mid-C.19–20.

play camels. To drink too much: to get drunk: Anglo-Indian (—1909). Ex a camel's drinking habits.

play diddle-diddle, v.i. To play tricks; to wheedle: coll: C.16. Skelton.

play it off. To make an end; the imperative = it's time you finished: s. or coll: late C.16–mid-17. See esp. Shakespeare, 1 *Henry the Fourth*, II, iv, 'They call drinking deep, dyeing scarlet; and when you breathe in your watering, then they cry hem, and bid you play it off.' Lit., orig., and gen., however, this is merely a form of PLAY OFF, v., 2.

play it (too) low; occ. play low. To take (a mean) advantage: s. > coll: resp. 1892, Zangwill; *Referee*, 15 Aug. 1886. 2. v.t., *play* or *play it* (*low*) *down on*: U.S. (1882), anglicized ca 1890: s. > coll. Marie Corelli, 1904.

play least in sight, v.i. To hide; keep out of the way: coll: C.17–mid-19. R. West, 1607.

play low, play low down (on), see PLAY IT (TOO) LOW.

play off; play with oneself. To masturbate: low: C.18–19; C.19–20. 2. To toss off or finish (liquor): late C.16–mid- or early 17. See quotation at PLAY IT OFF; Dekker, 1607, 'He requested them to play off the sacke and begon.'

play off one's dust. To drink: ca 1870–1910. (Remove it from one's throat.)

play owings. To live on credit: sporting (—1909): s. verging on coll.

play possum, see POSSUM. **play square,** see SQUARE. **play straight,** see STRAIGHT.

play tapsalteerie. To leap backwards; fall head over heels: Scots coll: 1826, John Wilson. The Scots adv. *tapsalteerie* (?ex *top* + Fr. *sauter*) = topsy-turvy.

play the ace against the jack. (Of a woman) to grant the favour: low: C.19–20; ob. A figure that, taken from cards, is suggested by *jack* = JOHN THOMAS.

play the duck. To show oneself a coward: coll: C.17. Urquhart.

play the game. To act honourably: coll: 1889, *Daily Chronicle*, 2 May 1904. 'Men do not talk about their honour nowadays – they call it "playing the game".' (Lit., playing to the rules; cf. *it's not* CRICKET and PLAY UP, 1.)

play the (giddy) goat, see GOAT, PLAY THE, and GIDDY GOAT.

play the Jack. To play the knave: coll: ca 1560–1700. Golding; Ray.

play the whole game. To cheat: ca 1780–1840. Grose, 1785. Perhaps lit., play every trick one can: as well as one knows.

play to the gallery. To court applause, esp. if cheaply and coarsely: theatrical coll: from ca 1890.

play to the gas, says the *Daily Mail* of 16 March 1899, 'is used in the general sense in reference to small audiences, but strictly it means that an audience was only large enough to render receipts sufficient to pay the bill for the evening's lighting.' Theatrical s.: ca 1890–1905.

play up. To do one's best: coll: from ca 1895. Newbolt, 1898, 'Play up, play up, and play the game!' See also PLAY THE GAME: prob. both phrases are taken from the playing-fields, but *play up* may have been suggested by PLAY UP TO. 2. To be troublesome: coll: late C.19–20. Of animals, esp. horses, and persons.

play up to. To take one's cue from another:

to humour another, back him up, or to meet him on his own ground; to flatter: coll: from ca 1825. (Implied in) Disraeli, 1826. cf. PLAY UP, 1. Ex: 2. So to act in a play as to assist another actor: theatrical s.: 1809, Malkin, 'You want two good actors to play up to you.'

play with oneself, see PLAY OFF.

play with (the ease of) a tooth-pick v.t. To play (one's opponents' bowling) with ease: cricket coll: 1899, J. C. Snaith; slightly ob.

please God we live. God permitting: lower classes' coll (—1887).

please, I want the cook-girl! A London c.p. directed at, or said of, 'a youth haunting the head of area steps': ca 1895–1915. Ware.

please oneself. To do just as one likes: coll, esp. in *please yourself!*: late C.19–20. Ex the S.E. sense, to satisfy, esp. to gratify, oneself.

please the pigs, see PIGS, PLEASE THE.

pleased as a dog with two choppers. Delighted: mostly lower-class: late C.19–20. With two tails. cf.:

pleased as a dog with two tails. Delighted: coll: late C.19–20.

pleased as Punch, (as). Extremely pleased: 1828, *The Night Watch* (II, 126).

pleasure-baulker. A petticoat: buckish: ca 1810–40. David Carey, *Life in Paris*, 1822.

pleasure-boat. The female pudend: low: C.19–20; ob.

pleasure-garden padlock. A menstrual cloth: C.17–early 19. ?coll or euphemistic S.E.

pleb or plebs. At Westminster School, a tradesman's son: pejorative: mid-C.19–20; slightly ob. Ex L. *plebs*, the proletariat. 2. (Only as *pleb.*) Any plebeian: 1823, 'Jon Bee'. cf. U.S. *plebe*, a newcomer at West Point, and:

plebbish; plebbishness. Plebeian (character or condition); caddish(ness): 1860, O.E.D. See preceding.

plebs, see PLEB, 1.

pleceman, pliceman; or **p'l.-** A policeman: low coll (—1887).

pledge. To give away. Esp. in *pledge you!*, after you (with that)!, and *I'll pledge it you when I've done with it*. Winchester: C.19–20. See esp. R. G. K. Wrench, *Notions*, 2nd ed., 1901.

plenipo. A **plenipo**tentiary: coll: 1687, Dryden; rare in C.19–20. Vanbrugh, 1687, 'I'll . . . say the plenipos have signed the peace, and the Bank of England's grown honest.' 2. The male member: low: C.18–19. cf. Captain Morris's scabrosity, *The Plenipotentiary*, ca 1786.

plenipo, v.i. To be or act as a plenipotentiary: coll: 1890. Rare.

pliceman, see PLECEMAN.

plier. A hand: from ca 1830: somewhat low. In C.20, ob. 2. (Gen. *plyer.*) A crutch: c.: mid-C.17–early 19. 3. A trader: coll: C.18–early 19. The idea of plying one's trade is latent in all three senses.

ploll-cat. A whore: C.17. A corruption of †S.E. *pole-cat*, the same.

plotty. Full of intrigue, having an intricate plot, as in Edwin Pugh, *Tony Drum*, 1898, 'Novels of a common type, plotty and passionate, but gilt-edged with the properties.'

plough, n. Ploughed land: hunting s. >, ca 1900, hunting coll: 1861, Whyte-Melville, 'It makes no odds to him, pasture or plough.' Ex East Anglian dial., where it occurs in 1787. 2. Rejecting a candidate in an examination, whether action or accomplished fact: 1863, Charles Reade. (cf. PLOUGHING.) Ex:

plough, v. To reject in an examination: university (orig. Oxford): 1853, Bradley, *Verdant Green*; 1863, Reade, 'Gooseberry pie . . . adds to my chance of being ploughed for smalls.' cf. S.E. *pluck*, concerning which, in relation to *plough*, Smyth-Palmer in his *Folk-Etymology* makes some interesting, by no means negligible, suggestions.

plough the deep. To (go to) sleep: rhyming s. (—1859).

plough with dogs!, I might as well. This is useless, or very ineffective!: C.17–20: a c.p. >, by 1700, semi-proverbial; from ca 1860, only in dial.

ploughed, ppl adj. See PLOUGH, v. 2. Tipsy: low: ca 1852–1910. cf. SCREWED.

ploughing. A plucking in an examination: university: 1882, Emma Worboise. Ex PLOUGH, v., and cf. PLOUGH, n.

plouter, see PLOWTER.

plover. A wanton (cf. PHEASANT and QUAIL): c.: C.17. Ben Jonson. 2. A dupe or a victim: c.: ca 1620–40. Esp. *green plover*, as in Jonson and Chapman, 'Thou art a most greene Plover in policy, I Perceive.' Prob. suggested by equivalent PIGEON, and cf. GREEN.

plowed, see PLOUGHED.

plowter; occ. **plouter.** To copulate: low: C.19–20; ob. ?*plough* corrupted or ex *plouter, plowter,* to splash about in mire or water.

'ploy, ploy. To employ: dial. (late C.17–20) and, hence coll, late C.19–20. As a n., it is used in the Public Schools for a task.

pluck. Courage: 1785, Grose: boxing s. >, ca 1830, gen. coll. Scott, in 1827, called it a 'blackguardly' word, and ladies using it during the Crimean War were regarded with the same shocked admiration as one felt towards those who in the War of 1914–18 used the exactly analogous *guts*; it is now almost S.E. Ex *pluck*, the heart, lungs, liver (and occ. other viscera) of an animal, hence, ca 1710, of a person. 2. In photographs, boldness, distinctness of effect: photographic: 1889. cf. PLUCKY, 2.

pluck, against the. Reluctantly: ca 1785–1850: s. > coll.

pluck a pigeon, see PIGEON, n., 4.

pluck a rose. To visit the privy: coll: C.17–19. Chiefly among women and because the rural w.c. was often in the garden.

pluck Sir Onion or the riband. To ring the bell at a tavern: resp. late C.17–mid-18; late C.17–early 19. Prob. *riband* refers to a bell-push; perhaps *onion*, the round 'handle'.

pluck-up fair. 'A general scramble for booty or spoil', O.E.D.: ca 1570–1650: coll.

plucked. Courageous: gen. preceded by *cool-*, *good-*, *rare-*, or *well-*; or by *bad-*. Coll: 1848, Thackeray (*good plucked*); Hughes, 1857 (*bad plucked*); 1860, *plucked 'un.*

plucked, hard-. Hard-hearted: coll: 1857, Kingsley; ob. cf. *bad-*PLUCKED and PLUCKLESS.

pluckily. Bravely: coll: 1858, Trollope.

pluckless. Faint-hearted: coll > S.E.: from ca 1820; ob. Ex PLUCK, 1.

plucky. Courageous, esp. over a period or by will-power: coll: 1842, Barham, 'If you're "plucky", and not over-subject to fright'; Disraeli, 1826, had 'with as plucky a heart'. Ex PLUCK, n., 1; cf. PLUCKED. 2. (Of negative or print) bold, distinct: photographic coll: 1885. cf. PLUCK, n., 2.

pluff. A shot from a musket, etc.: coll: 1828, J. Wilson. Ex the echoic S.E. (mainly Scots) *pluff*, an explosive emission of air (1663). cf. PLUFFER. 2. As adv. or interjection: coll, mainly Scots: 1860. cf. S.E. *phit.*

pluffer. A shooter, a gunner: coll (orig. Scots): 1828, J. Wilson. See PLUFF, 1.

plug, n. A punch; a knock (occ. fig.): 1798, Pitt, 'The bill ... in spite of many Plugs from Sir W. Pulteney, will certainly pass.' 2. A draught of beer: 1816, 'Come, sir, another plug of malt,' O.E.D. Ob. 3. An inferior horse: s.: Colonial and – prob. ex – U.S.: 1872, in U.S. Also *old plug*, ob. Ex *plug*, a stop-hole, perhaps influenced by *plug-tobacco*, often inferior and rank. But in Australia, from ca 1880, a good, steady, though slow horse, and in New Zealand, late C.19–20, a horse that is 'a good sort'. 4. Hence, an inferior, deteriorated, or damaged object or person: from ca 1890. 5. Hence, a workman with irregular apprenticeship: mostly artisans': from ca 1875. 6. Any defect: low: from ca 1895. Ex senses 1, 3. 7. A translation: school and university: 1853, Bradley, *Verdant Green*, 'Those royal roads to knowledge ... cribs, crams, plugs, abstracts, analyses, or epitomes'. Ob. by 1900. 8. A 'plug-hat', i.e. a top hat: U.S. (—1864), partly anglicized ca 1890; Kipling, e.g., uses it in 1891. Prob. because 'the head fits in it like a plug'.

plug, v. (Of the male) to coït with: low: C.18–20. cf. PLUG-TAIL. Ex S.E. sense, drive a plug into. 2. To punch, esp. *plug in the eye*: 1875, P. Ponder, 'Cries of ... "Plug him!" ...'. cf. sense 1. 3. To shoot (v.t.): 1875, J. G. Holland; 1888, 'Rolf Boldrewood', 'If that old horse ... had bobbed forward ... you'd have got plugged instead.' 4. To continue, persist, doggedly: 1865, at Oxford (O.E.D.); soon gen. 5. 'To labour with piston-like strokes against resistance': 1898, G. W. Steevens (that brilliant unfortunate). 6. to kick (a person's) behind: from ca 1870; ob.

plug-tail. The penis: low: late C.17–18. Ned Ward, *A Walk to Islington*, 1699.

plugger; plugging. An impersonator, -ation, at elections: Canadian coll: 1897, *Westminster Gazette*, 1 Dec. ?ex *plug*, to insert something closely (as a stop-gap). 2. e.g. a rower, a runner, who 'plugs' along; the corresponding effort: coll: late C.19–20. Ex PLUG, v., 4.

pluggy. Short and stumpy: dial. (—1825) >, ca 1860, coll. Agnes Strickland, 1861, 'A short, pluggy (thick) man, with a pug nose'. Ex S.E. n. *plug*.

plum; in C.17–18, gen. **plumb.** A fortune of £100,000: 1689, the Earl of Ailesbury. Steele, 'An honest gentleman who ... was worth half a plumb, stared at him'; Thackeray. Slightly ob. 2. Hence, loosely, a fortune: coll: 1709, Prior, 'The Miser must make up his Plumb,' though here, as in most other instances, the specific sum may be intended. Slightly ob. 3. (?hence) a rich man; orig. and properly, the possessor of £100,000; C.18–early 19. Addison, 1709, 'Several who were Plumbs . . . became men of moderate fortunes.'

plum, give a taste of. To shoot (a person) with a bullet: low: 1834, Ainsworth; †by 1900. i.e. *plumb*, lead.

plum-cash. Prime cost: pidgin English (—1864).

plum-duff. Plum-pudding or dumpling: 1840: coll, orig. nautical, >, ca 1890, S.E.

plum pudding. A coach-dog (the dog with dark spots which runs after carriages): Mayhew, II, 1851. Ex the markings; it is a sort of Dalmatian.

plum-tree!, have at the. A c.p., either semi-proverbial or in allusion to a song: C.18–19. Punning S.E. *plum-tree*, the female pudend (Shakespeare). cf:

plum-tree shaker. 'A man's yard', Cotgrave, 1611, at *hoche-prunier*. C.17–18.

plumb, n. See PLUM. 2. v.t., to deceive: ca 1850–1910: low. ?ex *plumb*, to fathom. 3. v.i. (1889) and v.t. (C.20), to work (properly, in lead) as a plumber: coll. W. S. Gilbert, 'I have plumbed in the very best families.' Ex *plumber*.

plumb, adv. As an intensive: quite; completely: 1587, Anon., 'Plum ripe': coll >, by 1750, also dial. In mid-C.19–20, mainly U.S., but wherever used, in this period rather s. than coll.

plummy. Rich; desirable; very good: 1812, Vaux: s. >, ca 1880, coll. *London Herald*, 23 March 1867, 'Ain't this 'ere plummy?' Ex S.E. *plum*, something good.

plummy, adv. Well; 'nicely': Cockney: 1851, Mayhew, I; †by 1910. Ex adj.

***plummy and slam.** All right: c.: ca 1860–1910.

plump. A heavy fall or sudden plunge: coll verging on S.E.: from ca 1450. 2. Hence, a blow (cf. PLUMPER): 1763, C. Johnston; 1785, Grose, 'I'll give you a plump in the bread basket': s. >, by ca 1810, coll. Ob. by 1850.

plump, v. To utter suddenly, abruptly; blurt out: coll verging on S.E.: 1579, Fulke, 'A verie peremptoire sentence, plumped downe . . .' 2. To come (very suddenly, i.e.) plump; plunge *in*, burst *out*: coll, bordering on S.E.: 1829, Lamb. 3. To shoot; hit hard, punch: 1785, Grose, 'He pulled out his pops and plumped him'; †by 1860.

plump, adj. Big; great; well-supplied: coll, verging on S.E.: 1635, Quarles, 'Plump Fee'; B.E., '*Plump-in-the-pocket*, flush of Money'; Pollok, 1827. Slightly ob. 2. (Of speech) blunt, flat: coll verging on S.E.: 1789, Mme D'Arblay, 'She . . . made the most plump inquiries.' Slightly ob. cf. the adv., 2, PLUMPLY, 1, and PLUMPNESS.

plump, adv. With a sudden fall or encounter: late C.16–20: coll verging on and sometimes merging in S.E.: 1610, Jonson. 2. Bluntly, flatly: 1734, North, 'Refuse plump': coll. cf. the adj., 2.

plump currant. In good health; gen. in negative: ca 1787–1850.

plumper. A heavy blow: 1772, Brydges, 'Gave me a plumper on the jaw, | And cry'd: Pox take you!' †by ca 1860. 2. An arrant lie: low coll: 1812. Ob. 3. Something that, in its kind, is uncommonly large: coll: 1881, *Punch*, 1 Oct. 4. Hence, all one's money staked on one horse: turf coll: from ca 1881.

plumply. Unhesitatingly; plainly, flatly: coll bordering on S.E.: 1786, Mme D'Arblay, 'The offer was plumply accepted.' Slightly ob. cf. PLUMP, v., 1, and adj., 2; also PLUMPNESS. 2. With a direct impact: same status: 1846, O.E.D. cf. PLUMP, n., 1; PLUMP, v., 2.

plumpness. (Of speech) directness, bluntness: coll verging on S.E.: 1780, Mme D'Arblay.

plunder. Gain, profit: from ca 1850. Mayhew, 1851, '*Plunder* . . . a common word in the horse trade.' Ex the S.E. sense of property acquired illegally or shadily. 2. A grafter's stock or goods: grafters': from ca 1890. Perhaps ex sense 1.

plunge, n. A reckless bet: from ca 1877: racing s. >, ca 1890. gen. coll. Ex:

plunge, v. To bet recklessly; speculate deeply: 1876, Besant & Rice, 'They plunged . . ., paying whatever was asked.' (Orig. and mostly) racing s. >, ca 1890, gen. coll. Lit., 'go in deep'.

plunger. A cavalryman: military: 1854, Thackeray, 'Guardsmen, "plungers", and other military men'. Prob. *plunge* (of a horse), to throw by plunging. 2. A reckless better, gambler, speculator: 1876, 'The prince of plungers'. Ex *plunge*, to dive. 3. A Baptist: Church s.: C.19–20. Ex plunging (immersion) in water at baptism.

plunging. Reckless betting, deep speculation: 1876: racing s. >, ca 1890, gen. coll.

plunk. A fortune; any large sum: 1767, Josiah Wedgwood; †by 1850. cf. the U.S. *plunk*, a dollar. As it precedes *plunk*, the v., by some thirty years, the word may be ex PLUM, 1, on CHUNK or *hunk*.

plush. The pubic hair: low: C.19–20. cf. FLEECE, 2. 2. Over*plus* of grog: nautical: 1825, Glascock, *The Naval Sketch-Book* (I, 24). Slightly ob. 3. Hence, that over-*plus* of gravy which goes to the cook of each mess: nautical (—1867).

Plush, John. A footman: coll: from ca 1845; ob. Ex *plushes*, such plush breeches as are worn by footmen, + Thackeray's *The Yellowplush Papers*, 'by Charles Yellowplush, Esq.', the former recorded in 1844 (O.E.D.), the latter pub. in 1837.

***plyer,** see PLIER.

***Plymouth cloak.** A cudgel: 1608: c. >, ca 1660, low s. >, ca 1700, s.; †by 1830, except historically. Dekker, 'Shall I walk in a Plymouth cloak (that's to say) like a rogue, in my hose and doublet, and a crab-tree cudgel in my hand?' The staff, cut from the woods near Plymouth by sailors recently returned from a long voyage, was jocularly supposed to serve as a cloak to those walking *in cuerpo*, i.e. in hose and doublet: Ray's *Proverbs*. Bowen notes that in the old Navy it = 'an officer's or warrant officer's cane'.

po. A chamber-pot: C.19–20: coll >, ca 1880, low coll. (When, as rarely, written or pronounced *pot*, it is S.E.) Ex the pronunciation of *pot* in Fr. *pot de chambre*.

poach. To blacken (the eyes): boxing s. > gen. ca 1890: ca 1815–1920. Moore, *Tom Crib*, 'With grinders dislodg'd, and with peepers both poach'd'. Ex Fr. *yeux pochés*. 2. v.t., to gain unfairly or illicitly (an advantage, esp. a start in a race): the turf: from ca 1891. Ex S.E. sense, to trespass (on).

po'chaise; po-chay or **po'chay; pochay.** Abbr. *post-chaise*: coll: resp. 1871, Meredith; 1871 (id., *po'chay*); 1827, Scott, in *Chronicles of the Canongate*.

poacher. A broker dealing out of, or frequently changing, his market: Stock Exchange coll: from ca 1890.

poaching country. 'Resort of all who go shooting', Egan's Grose: Oxford University: ca 1820–50.

pock. Small-pox; syphilis: from M.E.: S.E. until C.19, then dial. and low coll. Gen. *the pock*. cf. POX and POCKY.

pock-nook, come in on one's own. 'As we say in Scotland when a man lives on his own means', Sir A. Wylie, *Works*, 1821. Late C.18–20; ob. Coll. A *pock-nook* is a sack-corner or -bottom.

pock- (Eng. poke-)pudding. An Englishman: Scots coll: C.18–20. Burt, *Letters*, 1730; Herd. Lit., a bag-pudding; hence, a glutton. In C.18, also *pock-pud*.

pocket, he plays as fair as if he'd picked your. A c.p. applied, in C.19, to a dishonest gambler.

pocket and please yourself!, if not pleased put hand in. A mid-C.17–18 c.p. retort addressed to grumblers. Ray, *Proverbs*.

***pocket-book dropper.** A sharper specializing in, or adept at, making money by dropping pocket-books (gen. containing counterfeit) and gulling the gullible: c.: C.19–20; ob. cf. DROP-GAME and FAWNEY RIG.

pocket-hank(y). A pocket-handkerchief: resp. low coll and gen. coll: late C.19–20.

pocket pistol. 'For a Pocket Pistol alias a dram bottle to carry in one's pocket, it being necessary on a journey or so, at Nicholl's pd 0.1.0' (paid one shilling): entry of 29 June 1763, in James Woodforde's *Diary*: ? ca 1740–1840. Ex shape.

pocket the red. To effect intromission: billiard-players' erotic s.: late C.19–20.

pocket-thunder. A breaking of wind: low coll: C.19–20; ob.

pockets to let(, with). Penniless: jocular coll: ca 1820–1900. Moncrieff, in *Tom and Jerry*, 1823, 'Clean'd out! both sides; look here – pockets to let!'

pocky. A coarse pejorative or intensive: a vulg.: ca 1598–1700. Jonson, 'These French villains have pocky wits.' Ex S.E. sense, syphilitic.

pocta. A member of the Society for Prevention of Cruelty to Animals: coachmen's: ca 1885–1910.

pod, in. Pregnant: low (—1889). cf. PODDY.

pod, old. A big-bellied man: proletarian: from ca 1860. cf. PODDY.

poddy, n. A 'poddy calf', i.e. a calf fed by hand: Australian coll: late C.19–20. Jice Doone. Prob. ex dial.

poddy, adj. Obese, esp. as to the waist-line: coll: 1844, Edward FitzGerald. Prob. ex dial. *pod*, a large, protuberant abdomen. 2. Tipsy: (low) coll: ca 1860–1910. ?ex sense 1. cf. POGY.

podge. A short, fat person; such an animal: dial. and coll from ca 1830. 2.

Occ. a nickname: from ca 1840. Cognate with PUDGE. 3. A special application is: an epaulette, as in Marryat, 1833: nautical; †by 1890.

podgy. Squat; short, stout, and (if of an animal) thick-set: dial. and coll >, ca 1905, S.E.: from ca 1835. Occ., as a n., a nickname. Ex PODGE, 1. 2. A C.19 variant of POGY.

pody cody! A low coll perversion of *body of God!*, an oath: late C.17–early 18. Perhaps, however, of Urquhart's invention (1693 in his *Rabelais*).

poge, pogh, pogue, see POKE, n. **pogey,** see POGY.

***poge-hunter.** A thief specializing in the removal of purses: from ca 1870. e.g. in Pugh (2). Ex *poge* = POKE, n., 7 = a purse: mid-C.19–20.

poggle; puggle or **puggly.** An idiot: Anglo-Indian coll (—1886). Ex Hindustani *pagal*, a madman or idiot. 2. Hence, in the Army (late C.19–20), mad.

poggle (or puggle) pawnee. Rum; any spirituous liquor: Regular Army: late C. 19–20. Ex POGGLE, 2.

poggled; puggled. Mad-drunk; mad: id.: id. Ex preceding.

pogram. A Dissenter; a (gen. Nonconformist) formalist; a religious humbug: 1860; †by 1902. H., 3rd ed.: 'from a well-known dissenting minister of the name'.

***pogy.** (Hard *g.*) Tipsy: c. >, in C.19, low: ca 1780–1890, but surviving in U.S. c. Etymology problematic: but perhaps cognate with Romany *pogado*, crooked, ex *pog(er)*, to break, or ex POGGLE. cf. POGY AQUA; cf., too, PUGGY-DRUNK.

***pogy (or pogey) aqua!** Make the grog strong! (lit., little water!): c. or low: ca 1820–1910. Ex It. *poca aqua*.

point. A point to which a straight run is made; hence, the cross-country run itself: sporting (esp. hunting) coll: 1875, Whyte-Melville, *Riding Recollections*. 2. See POINTS, GET, and POINTS TO, GIVE. 3. 'The region of the jaw; much sought after by pugilists', C. J. Dennis: coll: late C.19–20.

point, make his or **their.** (Gen. of a fox) 'to run straight to the point aimed at': hunting coll: 1875, Whyte-Melville, ib. cf. POINT, 1.

point-failure. Failure in examination: Oxford University: ca 1820–40.

Point Nonplus. 'Neither money nor credit' (*Sinks*): ca 1820–70.

point to, show a. To swindle; act dishonourably towards: New Zealand coll: late C.19–20. cf. POINTS TO, GIVE.

pointer. The penis: low: C.19–20. 2. A hint or suggestion; a useful piece of information: U.S. (1884) anglicized ca 1890: coll. But perhaps ex dial. (Pointing what to do.)

points, get. To gain an advantage: 1881 (O.E.D.): coll variant of S.E. *gain a point* in the same sense. Cognate with:

points to, give. To be superior to, have the advantage of: coll: from ca 1880. Ex S.E. sense, to give odds to (an opponent).

poison. Liquor; a drink of liquor: coll: adumbrated in Suckling's *Brennoralt*, approached in Lytton's *Pelham*, first indubitably used by the Americans, Artemus Ward and, in 1867, Pinkerton ('Name your poison'), and generalized in England ca 1885. Marshall, *Pomes*, ' "My favourite poison", murmurs she, "is good old gin" '; Milliken, 1888, 'Wot's yer pison, old pal?' Hence, ca 1885–90, *nominate your poison*, say what you'll drink.

poison, like. Extremely: gen. in *hate each other* (or *one another*) *like poison*: coll. Palsgrave, 1530, has 'Hate me like poison', but *hate like poison* > gen. only in C.19. Barham, 'And both hating brandy, like what some call pison'.

poison-pate(d). Red-haired: coll: late C. 17–early 19. B.E. (*poison pate*, prob. also n.); Grose's *poisoned-pated* should doubtless read *poison-pated*.

poisoned. Pregnant: (?orig. c. >) low s. or coll: late C.17–early 19. Ex the swelling that often follows poisoning.

pojam. A poem set as an exercise: Harrow School: late C.19–20; ob. A blend: *poem* + *jam* (or perhaps *pensum*, an imposition, with intensive *j.*).

***poke.** Stolen property: c.: from ca 1850; ob. *The Times*, 29 Nov. 1860. Ex *poke*, a bag, pocket, etc. 2. 'A blow with the fist', Grose, 2nd ed.: from ca 1787. Ex the corresponding v. 3. An act of sexual intercourse: low coll: C.19–20. Ex sense 2 and v. 4. Hence, a mistress, permanent or temporary. A *good*, a *bad poke*: a woman sexually expert or clumsy (or cold). Low: C.19–20. 5. A poke-bonnet: coll verging on S.E.: from ca 1840. Hood, ca 1845, 'That bonnet we call a poke.' 6. A fish's stomach: coll and dial.: 1773, Barrington. 7. A purse: c.: mid-C.19–20. Ex †a bag, etc.

poke, v. To coït with (a woman): low coll

C.19–20. Ex *poke*, to thrust at. cf. the n., 3, and POKER, 2. 2. (With *up*) to confine in a poky place: coll: 1860, Miss Yonge. Gen. as (*be*) *poked up*. 3. v.i., to project very noticeably: dial. and coll: from ca 1828.

poke, get the. A Scottish (esp. Glaswegian) variant of *get the* BAG, to be dismissed: late C.19–20. Also in Yorkshire dial., which has the corresponding *give the poke,* to dismiss.

poke a smipe. To smoke a pipe: Medical Greek or marrowskying: ca 1840–90. See *Slang* at 'Spoonerisms'.

poke bogey. (v.t. with **at.**) To HUMBUG: s. or low coll: ca 1880–1910. cf. S.E. *poke fun.*

poke-bonnet. A bonnet projecting-brimmed: coll: 1820, O.E.D., where the earliest quotation suggests an origin in poking people's eyes out; more prob. ex *poke*, to thrust forward. 2. Occ. applied to the wearer of one: coll: late C.19–20.

poke borak or **borax,** see BORAK.

poke fly. To show how: tailors': from ca 1860. See FLY, adj.

poke full of plums!, a. An impertinent c.p. reply to *which* (*is the*) *way to* (e.g.) *London?*: ca 1580–1680. Melbancke, 1583; Torriano, 1666.

poke-hole; poking-hole. The female pudend: low coll: C.19–20; ob. Ex POKE, v., 1.

poke in the eye, see THUMP ON THE BACK.

poke-pudding, see POCK-PUDDING. **poke up one's pipes,** see PIPES, PACK ...

poker. A sword: jocular s. or coll: late C.17–20; ob. cf. CHEESE-TOASTER. 2. The penis: low: from ca 1810. Ex POKE, v., 1. 3. (Also HOLY POKER.) An Oxford or Cambridge University bedell carrying a mace before the Vice-Chancellor: university: 1841. Because he carries a mace or 'poker' (jocular S.E.) 4. A single-barrelled gun: sporting: C.19. Ex the shape. 5. A clumsy fencer: fencing coll: C.19–20; ob. 6. A casual labourer in the dockyard timber-trade: Londoners': from ca 1850. Mayhew, 'From their poking about the docks for a job.' 7. See OLD POKER.

poker, burn one's. (Cf. men) to get a venereal infection: low: C.19–20; ob. See POKER, 2.

poker!, by the holy. (Occ., ca 1840–90, the wholly Irish *by the h.p. and tumbling Tom!*) Occ., ca 1870–1910, *by the holy iron!* A mainly jocular expletive, of uncertain meaning (cf., however, OLD POKER) and Irish origin: 1804, Maria Edgeworth.

poker, chant the. To exaggerate: to swagger: s. or low coll: C.19. ?ex preceding.

poker, Jew's, see JEW'S POKER. **poker, old,** see OLD POKER.

poker-breaker. A wife: low: C.19–20; ob. See POKER, 2. cf. Yorkshire *pintle-twister.*

poker-pusher. A naval stoker: naval: late C.19–20.

poker-talk. Fireside chit-chat: coll: 1885, Mrs Edwardes. Ex the fireside poker.

pokey. A Yorkshire s. (not dial.) term for goods paid for on the 'truck' system: from ca 1870. 2. (Usually *the pokey.*) Prison: low Australian: late C.19–20. Ex *poky* place?

poking-hole, see POKE-HOLE.

pol! By Pollux!: a coll asseveration: late C.16-early 17. Nashe, Dekker. 2. *the pol* or *Pol:* see POLL, n.

pole. The weekly wages account: printers': from ca 1850. ?because affixed to a pole or because it resembles a pole by its length; or, more prob., a corruption of *poll*, head, i.e. a 'per capita' account. 2. The male member, esp. when erect: low: C.19–20; slightly ob.

pole, get on the. To verge on drunkenness: low (—1909). Prob. ex POLE, UP THE, 3.

pole, up the. In good repute; hence, strait-laced: military: ca 1890–1910. Perhaps *up the pole = high up.* 2. (Gen. *up a pole*: Manchon.) In difficulties; e.g. overmatched, in the wrong: low: from ca 1890. 'Pomes' Marshall, 'But, one cruel day, behind slops he chanced to take a stroll, | And ... he heard himself alluded to as being up the pole.' Perhaps ex *pole*, the part of the mast above the rigging. 3. (Rather) drunk: 1896, says Ware. 4. Annoyed, irritated: nautical: late C.19–20. 5. In Australia, 'distraught through anger, fear, etc.; also, disappeared, vanished', C. J. Dennis: late C.19–20.

pole-axe. A low jocularity on *police*: ca 1860–70.

pole-axing. The reducing of wages to the point of starvation: printers' (—1887); ob.

pole, (with) lead at both ends, – he is like a rope-dancer's. A c.p. applied to a dull, sluggish fellow: ca 1787–1830.

pole-work. COLLAR-WORK, and which explains it; a long wearisome business: coll: from ca 1870. Ex North Country dial. of late C.18–20. 2. Sexual intercourse: low: mid-C.19–20; ob. Also *poling.*

poley; polley. (Of cattle) hornless; lit., polled: English dial. and, from ca 1840,

Australian coll. 2. In Australian coll, from ca 1880, also a hornless beast.

police-nippers. Handcuffs; occ., leg-irons: low: mid-C.19–20; ob.

policeman. A fly; esp. a BLUE-BOTTLE fly, which inversely = a policeman, esp. a constable. Mostly London (—1860). E. D. Forgues, *La Revue des Deux-Mondes*, 15 Sept. 1864. 2. A sneak, a mean fellow, an untrustworthy man: c. (—1874). 3. Under sail, the member of the watch who keeps on the alert to catch an order and rouse his mates: nautical: late C.19–20. Bowen.

policeman always a policeman, once a. A late C.19–20 c.p., imputing 'habit is second nature'. cf. the proverbial *once a captain always a captain* (Peacock, 1831); *once a knave and ever a knave* (C.17); and *once a whore and ever a whore* (C.17–18) – all three cited by Apperson.

poling, see POLE-WORK, 2.

polish, v. To thrash, to PUNISH: ca 1840–1910. Ex POLISH OFF.

polish (or **pick** or **eat) a bone.** (Gen. of eating with another.) To make a meal: ca 1787–1915. Contrast:

polish off. Summarily to defeat an adversary: boxing s., 1829 (O.E.D.) >, ca 1835, gen. coll = to finish out of hand, get rid of (esp. a meal) quickly. Dickens, 1837, 'Mayn't I polish that ere Job off?' Ex *polish*, to give the finishing touches to by polishing.

polish one's arse on the top sheet. (Of men) to coït: low: late C.19–20.

polish the King's iron with one's or **the eyebrows.** 'To be in gaol, and look through the iron grated windows', Grose, 1st ed.: ca 1780–1840: (prob. c. >) low s.

polite, do the, see DO THE POLITE.

politician's porridge, carmen's comfort, porter's puzzle, are found in Ned Ward's *The London Spy Compleat*, 1703, as = beer. At the best, they are very rare; at the worst, they merely represent Ward's alliterative ingenuity.

polka, matrimonial. (Gen. *the m.p.*) Sexual intercourse: low coll: 1842.

poll. (Occ. *pol.*) A pass in the examination for the ordinary, not the Honours, B.A. degree. Gen. as *the Poll*, the passmen, and as *go out in the Poll*, to be on the list of passmen. Hence, *poll*, a passman; occ. *poll-man*. Cambridge University s. first recorded ca 1830, *poll* is prob. ex Gr. οἱ πολλοί, the many, 'the general run'. Bristed, 1855, 'Several declared that they would go out in the Poll'; J. Payn, 1884, 'I took . . . a first-class poll; which my good folks at home believed to be an honourable distinction.' 2. A wig: C.18–early 19. Hall, 1708; Grose, 1788. Ex *poll*, the head. 3. A woman; esp. a harlot: nautical: from ca 1860. P. H. Emerson, 'A poll gave him a bob.' 4. A decoy bitch used in stealing dogs: c.: from ca 1870. 5. *Poll.* Mary, as a gen. name for a parrot: C.17–20: coll soon > familiar S.E. As *Peg* = *Meg*, Margaret, so *Poll* = *Moll*, Mary.

***poll,** v. See PILL AND POLL. From ca 1835: c., as in Brandon, 1839; P. H. Emerson, 1893, 'He accused us of polling.' 2. To defeat; outdistance: printers' and sporting: from ca 1870. 3. To snub: low: from ca 1875; ob.

Poll, Captain of the. The highest of the passmen: Cambridge University (see POLL, n., 1): ca 1830–90.

poll-man, see POLL, n., 1.

poll off. To become drunk: low: from ca 1860; ob. ?ex *poll*, head.

poll parrot, or with capitals. A talkative, gossipy woman: low, mostly London: from ca 1870.

***poll-thief.** A thief; an informer: c.: from ca 1890.

poll up. To court; live in concubinage with: low: from ca 1870. cf. *polled up*, living in unmarried cohabitation; in company with a woman: H., 1859. cf. MOLLED UP.

pollaky!; or **o(h) Pollaky** (or **p.**)! An exclamation of protest against too urgent enquiries: a non-aristocratic c.p.: ca 1870–80. Ex the advertisements in *The Times* agony column by an Australian detective resident at Paddington Green – one *Pollaky* (accented on second syllable).

***poller.** A pistol: c. of ca 1670–1750. *A Warning for Housekeepers*. Lit., a plunderer. 2. The same as POLL-THIEF. P. H. Emerson, 1893.

polley, see POLEY.

pollrumptious. Unruly or restless; foolishly confident: coll or s.: from ca 1860. ?ex *poll*, head + RUMPUS. (Much earlier in dial.)

***polly.** ?a boot, a shoe: from ca 1890. P. H. Emerson, 1893, 'All I get is my kip and a clean mill tog, a pair of pollies and a stoock, and what few medazas [?*mezadas*] I can make out of the lodgers and needies.' 2. **Apolli**naris water: 1893, G. Egerton. 3. As a name for a parrot: C.17–20: coll soon > familiar S.E.

***polly, do.** To pick oakum in jail: c.: from ca 1860. cf. MILL DOLL.

Polly Flinder. A window: Cockney rhyming s.: late C.19–20.

Polly, put the kettle on, and we'll all have tea. A c.p.: from ca 1870; ob. Ex the well known nursery song and country dance (—1797).

polone; palone. A girl or woman: low theatrical. The word goes back to ca 1850 and is often used in combination as adj. 'female', as in STRILL *polone*, a female pianist. Ex Romany: cognate with BLOWEN.

polony, drunk as a. Exceedingly drunk: London lower classes' (—1909). Ware derives ex Fr. *soûl comme un Polonais* (drunk as a Pole).

polore; palore, erroneous for POLONE.

polrumptious. A variant of POLLRUMPTIOUS.

polty; dolty. Easy: cricketers', ca 1890–1910. ?cognate with Kentish *polt*, saucy.

Polyphemus. The penis: C.19–20 (ob.) cultured. Via *Monops*, the one-eyed one.

pom. A Pomeranian dog: coll: C.19–20. cf. *peke*. Aldous Huxley has somewhere remarked that 'there is no inward, psychological contradiction between a maudlin regard for poms and pekes and a bloodthirsty hatred of human beings.'

pom-pom. A Maxim automatic quick-firing gun: 1899: echoic coll >, by 1905, S.E.

pommy, Pommy. A newcomer from Britain, esp. from England: Australian: C.20. The O.E.D. Sup. records it at 1916, but it was current before the Great War. Origin obscure; possibly a corruption of TOMMY imported by Australian soldiers returning from the Boer War (1899–1902). Or perhaps ex *Pomeranian*, a very 'superior' sort of dog. It may also have developed from JIMMY GRANT thus: *Jimmy Grant* > *immy-granate* > *pomegranate* > *pommy*.

pompaginis, see AQUA POMPAGINIS.

Pompey (or the black dog Pompey) is on your back! A c.p. (—1869) addressed to a fractious child: provincial coll, and dial. cf. the old South Devonshire *your tail's on your shoulder*. W. Carew Hazlitt.

Pompey's pillar to a stick of sealing-wax. Long odds: coll: ca 1815–60. Tom Moore, 1819. cf. ALL LOMBARD STREET TO A CHINA ORANGE.

pompkin, Pompkinshire, see PUMPKIN, 1.

'pon my life. A wife: rhyming s.: late C.19–early 20. More gen. TROUBLE AND STRIFE.

ponce; pounce-spicer; pouncey. A harlot's bully or keep: (prob. c. >) low s.: resp. 1872, ca 1890, 1861 (Mayhew). H., 5th ed., 1874, 'Low-class East-end thieves even will "draw the line" at ponces, and object to their presence in the boozing-kens'; Henley, 1887, 'You ponces good at talking tall.' Prob. ex *pounce on*, though possibly influenced by Fr. *Alphonse*, a harlot's bully, or by Fr. *pensionnaire*, 'boarder, lodger', conceivably with a pun on English pensioner. cf. BOUNCER; FANCY-COVE; MACK; PROSSER, 3; SUNDAY MAN, 2.

ponce on. To live on the earnings of (a prostitute): low: late C.19–20.

***poncess.** A woman who supports a man by prostitution: c. from ca 1870; ob.

poncho. A loose overcoat: 1859, H.; †by 1900. Ex Castilian *poncho*, a military cloak.

Pond, the. The North Atlantic Ocean: from ca 1830: (mainly nautical) s. >, ca 1880, gen. coll >, ca 1905, S.E. Ex the C.17–19 S.E. sense, the ocean. Occ. *the Big Pond*, as in Haliburton and Sala; also *the Herring Pond*, and even *the* PUDDLE.

poney, see PONY.

pong. A stink: low: from ca 1850. ?origin; cf. the v., 1, its prob. origin. 2. Beer: low: from ca 1860. H., 3rd ed., where spelt *ponge*.Variants *pongelo(w)* (H., 1864), *pongellorum* (F. & H., 1902), these being fanciful endings. Origin obscure: ?suggested by PARNEE (*pawnee*). Ware, who defines it as 'pale ale – but relatively any beer', classifies the term as 'Anglo-Indian Army'.

pong, v. To stink: low: from ca 1850. cf. the n., 1. Prob. ex Romany *pan* (or *kan*), to stink. 2. (Also *ponge*.) To drink (esp. beer): low: from ca 1870. Less gen. than the n. 3. v.i., to vamp, or amplify the text (of a part): theatrical: from ca 1890; slightly ob. Perhaps cognate with *pong*, a ringing blow, a bang. 4. To perform, esp. to turn somersaults: circus: from ca 1850. Perhaps via Lingua Franca ex L. *ponere*. 5. Hence, to talk, esp. to GAS: theatre, music-hall, circus: from ca 1890. cf. sense 3.

ponge, pongelo(w), pongellorum. See PONG, n., 2, and v. 2. But whereas *pongelow* is recorded (H., 1864) as a v., *pongellorum* is not so recorded.

ponging, n. Somersaulting: circus s.: mid-C.19–20. See PONG, v., 4.

pongo. A monkey: showmen's: mid-C.19–20. In S.E., properly 'a large anthropoid African ape'; loosely, indeed erroneously, the orang-outang, 1834. Native name.

pongy. Evil-smelling: late C.19–20. Ex PONG, n., 1.

ponte. A pound (sterling): showmen's, from ca 1850. Ex It. *pondo*. cf. POONA.

pontic. Credit: London s. (—1823) > Lincolnshire s. (—1903). Abbr. *upon tick* (see TICK, n., 2).

Pontius Pilate. A pawnbroker: late C.18–19. Grose, 1785. Why? 2. The drugget-covering tied to the thwart to prevent chafing: Oxford rowing men's (—1884); ob. Why?

Pontius Pilate's counsellor. A briefless barrister: legal: from ca 1780; ob. One who, like Pilate, can say, 'I have found no cause of death in him.' Grose, 1785. cf. Fr. *avocat de Pilate*.

ponto. A pellet kneaded from new bread: school: late C.19–20. *St James's Gazette*, 15 March 1900 (Matthew Arnold ponto-pelted at school). ?origin: possibly connected with the punto of ombre and quadrille (the card-game): cf. sense 2. 2. Punto, at cards: a corruption: 1861.

pontoon. Vingt-(et-)un, the card-game: 1900: military coll >, by 1910, gen. S.E. A corruption of, more prob. an approximation to, *vingt-un*.

Pony. An 'inevitable' nickname of men surnamed Moore: military: from ca 1885. Ex 'a well-known sporting character': actually 'Pony' Moore of the Moore & Burgess Minstrels.

pony. A bailiff; esp. an officer accompanying a debtor on a day's liberty: coll: C.18–mid-19. 2. Money: low: ca 1810–40. *Lex. Bal.*, Moncrieff (see quotation at PEW, STUMP THE), Ainsworth. Prob. ex: 3. £25: 1797, Mrs M. Robinson, 'There is no touching her even for a poney.' In *Sinks*, 1848, it = £50. Perhaps because only a small sum, as a pony is a small horse. (cf. PONY UP.) N.B., among brokers, a *pony* is £25,000 of stock, i.e. 25 £1000-shares. cf. MONKEY. 4. A *small* glass of liquor: 1884, in U.S.; anglicized ca 1890, chiefly as a small measure of beer. 5. In gambling, a double-headed or double-tailed coin: c. > low s.: late C.19–20. For origin, see GREY. 6. Short for PONY AND TRAP.

pony, post the. To pay: a C.19 variant of *post the* COLE: see POST, v., 3, and PONY, 2.

pony (occ. **lady**), **sell the.** To toss for drinks: low: late C.19–20. Ex PONY, 2, 5. Hence, he who has to pay, *buys the pony*.

pony and trap. To defecate: rhyming s. on CRAP: late C.19–20. cf. TOM-TIT.

pony up, v.i. and t. To pay; settle: a mostly U.S. variant and derivative of *post the* PONY: 1824, U.S.; partly anglicized ca 1840. Prob. ex PONY, 2.

pooch, see POUCH.

poodle. Any dog: (sarcastic) coll: from ca 1880; slightly ob.

pooja, puja. (Gen. pl.) Prayers: Anglo-Indian: 1863, Trevelyan in *The Competition Wallah*. Ex Sanskrit *puja*, worship.

poon. To prop (a piece of furniture) with a wedge: Winchester College (—1891). Wrench, *Notions*. Prob. ex L. *ponere*, to place. Imm. ex: 2. v.i., to be unsteady: ibid.: ca 1830–70. Wrench, 'Hence you wedged the leg that pooned.'

poona. £1; a sovereign: costermongers': from ca 1855. ?*pound* corrupted or ex Lingua Franca (cf. PONTE) or, less likely, *pound* influenced by *poonah*, a painting, etc., on the analogy of QUEEN'S PICTURE.

poonts. The paps: low: from ca 1870. Etymology obscure.

poop. The seat at the back of a coach: coll: ca 1614–80. Ex the poop of a ship. 2. The posteriors: low coll: from ca 1640. Ned Ward, 'While he manages his Whip-staff with one Hand, he scratches his Poop with the other.' Ob. cf. sense 1. 3. A breaking of wind: low coll: late C.18–20. Ex v., 2; cf. †S.E. *poop*, a short blast, a toot.

poop. To coït: C.17–18: low coll. cf. POOP-NODDY. 2. To break wind: dial. and low coll: C.18–20. Bailey, 1721, '*To Poop*, to break Wind backwards softly'. Ex S.E. *poop*, to make an abrupt sound; to toot. Occ. *poupe*. 3. Hence, to defecate (L. *cacare*): (?late) C.19–20: low coll, mostly of and by children.

poop-downhaul. An imaginary rope: nautical coll (—1883). cf. the operation, equally imaginary, of 'clapping the keel athwart-ships'. Clark Russell's glossary.

poop-noddy. Sexual intercourse: low coll: C.17. (cf. POOP, v., 1.) Anon., *Wily Beguiled*, 'I saw them close together at poop-noddy.' So F. & H.; the O.E.D. suggests that it = *cony-catching*, occ. *cony-catcher*, *noddy* being a simpleton.

poop-ornament. An apprentice: nautical: ca 1850–90. *Athenaeum*, 8 Feb. 1902, 'Miscalled "a blarsted poop ornament", the drudge even of ordinary seamen'.

pooped. Exhausted; very tired: since ca 1890. 'Must stop for a bit; I'm pooped.' Probably ex the nautical S.E. v. *poop*: a sailing ship was temporarily disabled when a following sea came inboard from over the stern.

pooper. A great wave coming over the stern (formerly called the *poop*): nautical coll: late C.19–20.

poor. Unfortunate; in pitiable condition or circumstances: C.13–20: S.E. until ca 1855, then coll. Mrs Carlyle, 1857, 'He looked dreadfully weak still, poor fellow!' 2. When said, as from ca 1785, of the dead person whom one has known, *poor* verges on coll.

poor as a Connaught man. Extremely poor: Anglo-Irish coll: ca 1802, Maria Edgeworth.

poor as a rat, as. Extremely poor: a C.18–20 (ob.) coll variation of *as poor as a church-mouse*. E. Ward, 1703, 'Whilst men of parts, as poor as rats . . .'

poor creature. (Gen. pl.) A potato: low London: ca 1820–50.

poor knight of Windsor. See next: coll and dial.: C.19. Scott, *The Bride of Lammermoor*, 1818, has this footnote, 'In contrast . . . to the baronial "Sir Loin"', concerning:

poor man (of mutton). The blade-bone of a shoulder of mutton: Scots coll: C.19–20. Scott: see preceding entry. 2. (*poor-man.*) As a heap of corn-sheaves, four upright and one a-top, it is prob. dial.: Scots, C.19–20.

poor man's blessing. The female pudend: low coll: C.19–20.

poor man's goose. Bullock's liver, baked with sage, onions, and a little fat bacon: (low) coll (—1909). cf. POOR MAN'S TREACLE. (In Warwickshire dial., it is 'a cow's spleen stuffed and roasted', E.D.D., 1903.)

poor man's oyster. A mussel: coll: 1891, *Tit-Bits*, 8 Aug.: ob.

poor man's side, or with capitals. The poor man's side of the Thames, i.e. South London: a coll (—1887; very ob.) verging on S.E. Baumann. Opp. *rich man's side*, the North side of the Thames: same period.

poor man's treacle. An onion: (low) coll: late C.19–20.

poor Robin. An almanach: coll: ca 1660–1760. Ex *Robert* Herrick, who issued a series of so-called almanachs.

poor soldier who can't stand his comrade's breath, it's a. A military c.p. proffered by the culprit when his companions complain of wind-breaking: from the 1890s.

poorly. (Always in the predicate, except in POORLY TIME.) In poor health; unwell: from ca 1750: S.E. until ca 1870, then near-coll.

poorly time. The monthly period: lower-class women's coll (—1887).

pooser. A huge, uncouth thing: low Northumberland s. (—1903). Ex dial. *poose* (or *pouse*), to strike. cf. WHOPPER.

poot. A shilling: East London (—1909). Ex Hindustani. Oriental beggars were, before that date, common there.

pooty is a favourite mid-Victorian adjective meaning 'pretty' – of which, via *purty*, it is a perversion. 'A pooty little bit of money', W. M. Thackeray, *Pendennis*, 1849–50.

pop; Pop. A club chiefly of Oppidans: Eton College: C.19–20. Founded in 1812; see e.g. *Etoniana*, 1869. Traditionally derived ex L. *popina*, a cook-shop, the rooms having long been over a confectioner's. 2. A **pop**ular concert: coll: 1862. W. S. Gilbert, 'Who thinks suburban hops more fun than Monday Pops'. cf. PROM. 3. (Gen. in pl.) a pistol: C.18–20; ob. Hall, 1714; Harper, 1724, 'Two Popps Had my Boman when he was ta'en'; Grose; Marryat. Like the next, ex the sound. 4. A drink that fizzes from the bottle when the cork – 'pop goes the cork' – is drawn; gen. ginger-beer: coll: 1812, Southey. Occ., but †by 1870, champagne, as in Hood, 'Home-made pop that will not foam.' cf. FIZ. 5. An, the, act of pawning: 1866, Routledge's *Every Boy's Annual*. Ex the v., 3. 6. See POP, IN. 7. As = father, orig. and almost wholly U.S. (1840). Also *poppa* (—1897), *popper* (—1901): likewise mainly U.S. Ex *papa*.

pop, v. To fire a gun: coll: 1725, *A New Canting Dict.*; ob. 2. v.t., to shoot: s. or coll >, in C.20, S.E. Gen. with *down* (1762) or *off* (1813). 3. To pawn: 1731, Fielding; Barrie, 1902, 'It was plain for what she had popped her watch.' cf. POP-SHOP; *pop up the* SPOUT. 4. See POP OFF and POP THE QUESTION. 5. To lose one's temper: tailors': late C.19–20.

pop, in. In pawn: from ca 1865: low. The n., only thus. cf. POP, v., 3, and n., 5.

pop, let fly the. To fire the pistol: midway between c. and low s.: late C.18–mid-19.

pop goes the weasel!, now gen. regarded as a nursery-rhyme tag, was in the 1870s and 80s a proletarian (mostly Cockney) c.p. Ware, 'Activity is suggested by "pop", and the little weasel is very active. Probably erotic origin. Chiefly associated with these lines – Up and down the City Road | In and out the Eagle, | That's the way the money goes, | Pop goes the weasel!'

pop it in, v.i. To effect intromission: low coll: C.19–20. Contrast:

pop it on, v.t. To ask for more, esp. a higher price: coll: 1876, Hindley. 2. To make a bet: from ca 1890.

pop-lolly. A sweetmeat: cheapjacks' s. or coll: 1876, Hindley, 'Lollipop and pop-lolly'.

pop off. See POP, v., 2. 2. To die: 1764, Foote, 'If Lady Pepperpot should happen to pop off'. Also *pop off the hooks*, from ca 1840, as in Barham.

pop-shop. A pawn-shop: 1772, *The Town and Country Magazine*; 1785, Grose. Ex POP, v., 3.

pop the question. To propose marriage: 1826, Miss Mitford, 'The formidable interrogatory ... emphatically called "popping the question"': s. Ex S.E. *pop the question*, to ask abruptly.

pop up the spout. Same as POP, v., 3: low: 1859, H., 1st ed. See SPOUT.

pop visit. A short visit: society coll: C.17–18. Jonson in *The Alchemist*.

pop-wallah. A teetotaller: military: late C.19–20. Lit., a ginger-beer fellow. See POP, n., 4, and WALLAH.

pope. As a pejorative (*a pope of a thing*), as an imprecation ('A pope on all women,' 1620), in *as drunk as a pope*, and in (e.g. *know*, *read*) *no more than the pope*, i.e. nothing, the term is on the borderland between S.E. and coll: all these phrases are † except in dial. 2. See POPE OF ROME.

Pope o' Rome, see TROT THE UDYJU, and:

pope of Rome. A home; home, adv.: rhyming s. (—1859). Often abbr. *pope* (Ware, 1909).

poperine pear. The penis: low coll: late C.16–mid-17. Shakespeare, *Romeo and Juliet*, in the quarto edition; passage afterwards suppressed. Ex shape.

pope's eye. The thread of fat, properly 'the lymphatic gland surrounded with fat', in (the middle of) a leg of mutton: from ca 1670: S.E. till C.19, then coll. Shirley Brooks, 1852, 'The pope's eye on a Protestant leg of mutton'. Presumably *eye* ex its rounded form.

pope's (occ. **Turk's**) **head.** A round broom, with a long handle: from ca 1820: coll >, ca 1890, S.E.; ob. Maria Edgeworth, in *Love and Law*, 'Run ... for the pope's head.'

pope's nose. A turkey's, a fowl's rump: coll: late C.18–20. cf. PARSON'S NOSE.

pope's size. Short and fat: trade s. > j.: from ca 1885; ob. Mostly tailors'.

***poplars, popler(s), poppelars;** rarely, **paplar.** Porridge; esp. milk-porridge: c.: C.17–early 19. Dekker (*poplars*); Middleton (*popler*); Grose, 1st ed. (*poplers*). Prob. a corruption of *pap* (for infants, invalids).

poppa, see POP, n., 7.

popped. Annoyed; esp. in *popped as a hatter*, very angry: tailors': from ca 1860. ? = *popped off*, *apt to pop off*. cf. *mad as a* HATTER.

***poppelars,** see POPLARS.

popper. A pistol: 1750, Coventry; ob.: s. > coll in late C.19–20, also a rifle or a shotgun (E. Seago, 1933). 2. See POP, n., 7.

poppite. A performer at (1895), a frequenter of (1901), the popular concerts: coll. Ex POP, n., 2.

poppy, adj. Popping, exploding: coll: 1894, Kipling, 'Little poppy shells'. 2. (Of the ground) causing the ball to 'pop' (itself, j.): cricket coll: from 1874.

poppy-show. A display, esp. if accidental, of underclothes; orig. and properly, of red or brown flannel underclothes: low coll: late C.19–20. Ex dial. *poppy-show*, a peepshow, a puppet-show.

***pops and a galloper, his means are two.** He is a highwayman: late C.18–early 19: c. or low s. i.e., two guns and a horse.

popsy. An endearment for a girl: nursery coll: 1862. Ex S.E. *pop*, similarly used: see the next entry.

popsy-wopsy. A foolish endearment: (mostly nursery) coll (—1887). 1892, *Ally Sloper's Half-Holiday*, 19 March, 'Bless me if the little popsy-wopsy hasn't been collecting all the old circus hoops and covering them with her old muslin skirts.' Reduplicating *popsy* ('archaic *pop*, darling, short for *poppet*', W.).

porangi. (Extremely) eccentric, crazy; (very) stupid: New Zealand coll: late C.19–20. Adoption of Maori word.

porgy, see GEORGIE-PORGIE.

pork. A spoiled garment; goods returned by a customer: tailors': from ca 1860. cf. PIG, n., 5. 2. Women as food for men's lust: low: C.18–20; ob. cf. MUTTON.

pork, cry. To act as an undertaker's tout: low: late C.18–mid-19. The raven, 'whose note sounds like ... *pork*', is 'said to smell carrion at a distance'.

pork-boat. (Gen. pl.) A Worthing fishing-boat: nautical: ca 1860–1910. cf. the Sussex *pork-bolter*, a Worthing fisherman. Presumably opprobrious, fishermen having a superstitious dread of pigs.

pork-pie. A coll abbr. of *pork-pie hat* (a style modish ca 1855–65): 1863; ob. 2. A 'toreador' hat, modish in the 1890s: coll: *Spectator*, 26 Dec. 1891, 'The bull-fighter's hat known in England as the "pork-pie"'.

***porker.** A sword: c. of ca 1685–1740. Shadwell, *The Squire of Alsatia*, 1688, 'The captain whipt his porker out.' cf. PIG-STICKER, 3; but *porker* is more prob. a perversion of POKER, a sword. 2. A Jew: low: ca 1780–1900. Because, traditionally, Jews never eat pork: on the principle of *lucus a non lucendo*.

porky, adj. Of, concerning, resembling pork; obese; coll: 1828.

porpoise. A very stout man: late C.19–20: coll.

porps! porps! 'The old time whalers' cry when porpoises were sighted', Bowen: C.19.

porridge-bowl. The stomach: low: mid-C.19–20; ob. cf. BREAD-BASKET and contrast PORRIDGE-HOLE.

porridge-disturber. A punch in the belly: pugilistic: from ca 1815; ob.

porridge-hole. The mouth: lower-class Scots' (—1909).

port for stuffs. 'Assumption of a commoner's gown', Egan's Grose: Oxford University: ca 1820–40. The double pun is obvious.

port-hole. The fundament; the female pudend: low coll: from ca 1660; ob.

Port Mahon sailor. An inferior seaman: naval: C.19. 'A perfectly safe port' in Minorca: Chisholm's Gazetteer.

port wine. Blood: pugilistic: ca 1840–90. Augustus Mayhew, *Paved With Gold*, 1857. Much less gen. than CLARET.

portable property. Easily stolen or pawned valuables – especially plate: coll: 1885, *Referee*, 7 June. Ware.

portcullis. A silver halfpenny: coll bordering on S.E.: late C.16–early 17. Jonson. Ex portcullis design.

porthole, see PORT-HOLE. **portigue,** see PESTLE OF A PORTIGUE.

portmanteau. A 'big high explosive shell, a name introduced during the Russo-Japanese War': naval; ob. Bowen.

portmantle, portmanty. A portmanteau: C.17–20: S.E. till C.19, then resp. dial. and low coll.

portrait, see QUEEN'S PICTURE.

portrait, sit for one's. To be inspected 'by the different turnkeys ... that they might know prisoners from visitors', Dickens in *Pickwick*: prison: ca 1835–80.

Portug(u)ee. A Portuguese: low coll, largely nautical: 1878, Besant & Rice. 2. Any foreigner except a Frenchman: naval: late C.19.

Portug(u)ee parliament. A forecastle discussion which degenerates into all talkers and no listeners: nautical: late C.19–20. Bowen.

Portuguese man-of-war. A nautilus: nautical coll verging on S.E.: C.19–20; ob.

Portuguese pumping. A nautical phrase (—1909), of which Ware was unable to discover the meaning. Nor have I; but I agree with Ware that 'it is probably nasty': it refers almost certainly to either defecation (suggested by PUMP SHIP) or masturbation.

pos, poss, poz, pozz. Positive: coll abbr.: resp. 1711, 1719, 1710 (Swift), 1710 (Swift), all †by 1860. The most frequent, *poz*, may date from as early as 1706 or 7, occurring as it does in *Polite Conversation*; *poss* (e.g. D'Urfey, 'Drunk I was last night, that's poss') is rather rare. 2. As adv., positively: coll: late C.18–early 19, but adumbrated in Swift. 3. Only *pos* and *poss* (gen. the latter): possible; usually in *if poss*. Low coll: from ca 1885; slightly ob.

posa. A treasurer: Pidgin English (—1864). A corruption of *purser*.

***posh.** Money; specifically, a halfpenny or other coin of low value: c. (—1839); ob. Ex Romany *posh*, a half, as in *posh-horri*, a halfpenny, and *posh-koorona*, a half-crown. 2. A dandy: Society s. (—1897). ?ex sense 1; i.e. a moneyed person (cf. PLUM, 1, 3). Or perhaps a corruption of (*big*) POT (6).

positive. Certainly no less than; downright; indubitable, 'out-and-out': coll: 1802, Sydney Smith, 'Nothing short of a positive miracle can make him ...'

poss, see POS.

posse mobilitatis. The mob: coll: ca 1690–1850. On *posse comitatus*.

possible. A coin, gen. in pl. money: ca 1820–50. 2. Hence, means or necessaries; supplies: 1824 (O.E.D.). 3. (Orig. *highest possible*.) The highest possible score, esp. in rifle-shooting: coll abbr.: 1866.

possle; more correctly **postle.** An earnest advocate: lower classes' satirical (—1909). i.e. *apostle.*

possum. Opossum: C.17–20: S.E. till mid-C.19, then coll.

possum, play. To pretend; feign illness or death: orig. U.S. (—1824); partly anglicized ca 1850. Ex the opossum's feigned death.

possum-guts. A pejorative, gen. in address: Australian: 1859, H. Kingsley; ob.

post. Such mail as is cleared from one receiving-box or as is delivered at one house: coll: from ca 1890.

post, v. Often *post up* and gen. in the passive, esp. in the past passive ppl: to supply with information or news: U.S. coll (1847), anglicized ca 1860; > S.E. ca 1880. Prob. ex posting up a ledger. 2. To summon (a candidate) for examination on the first day of a series: Oxford University: C.18. Amherst, 1721, 'To avoid being *posted* or *dogged.*' (See DOG, v.) Ex S.E. *post,* to hurry a person. 3. To pay: from ca 1780; ob. Esp. *post the* COLE, orig. c., 1781, C. Johnston; *post the neddies,* c., 1789, G. Parker; *post the pony,* 1823, Moncrieff – see PONY; *post the tin,* 1854, Martin & Aytoun. After ca 1870, the term is influenced by *post,* to send by post. 4. To promote (someone) to post-captain: naval: ca 1790–1850.

post, bet on the wrong side of the. i.e. on a losing horse: turf coll (—1823); †by 1900.

post, between you and me and the (bed-; in late C.19–20, often **gate-).** In confidence: coll >, ca 1910, S.E.: 1832, Lytton; Dickens.

post, knight of the, see KNIGHT.

post, make a hack in the. To use, consume, a considerable part of a thing: from ca 1840: coll >, by 1870, S.E.; ob.

post, on the. Dealing with postage; applied esp. to the clerk dealing with this: commercial and insurance coll: late C.19–20.

post a letter. To defecate: euphemistic: since ca 1890.

post-and-rail. A wooden match, as opposed to a wax Vesta: Australian: from ca 1880; ob.

post-and-rails tea. Ill-made tea: from ca 1850; ob. Only Australian. Ex floating stalks and leaves; the reference being to post-and-rail fences.

post-chaise. To travel by post-chaise: coll: 1854, Thackeray. Ob.

post-chay, post-shay. A post-chaise: ob. coll: 1757, F. Greville. cf. PO'CHAISE.

post-horn. The nose: ca 1820–90: (low) coll. Ex noise and shape.

post-mortem. The examination after failure: Cambridge: 1844, *Punch,* 'I've passed the post-mortem at last.' Punning the examination of a corpse.

post-nointer. A house-painter. 1785, Grose; †by 1850.

post-shay, see POST-CHAY.

post te, e.g. **chum** or **hat.** A Charterhouse c.p., from ca 1870, to indicate disapproval (of, e.g., hat or companion). A. H. Tod, *Charterhouse,* 1900, implies derivation ex a *post te of* (anything), the right to use a thing after the 'owner' has done with it (mid-C.19–20); itself ex *post te* (in L., 'after thee') as in *post te math. ex,* 'May I glance over your mathematical exercise?'

post the blue. To win the Derby: racing-men's (—1909). cf. POST, v., 3; *the blue* is *the blue riband of racing,* the Derby.

Postage Stamp, the. Any hotel, etc., known as the Queen's Head: taverns': 1837–ca 85. Ex the design on stamps.

postie; occ. **posty.** A postman: coll (—1887). It is recorded in dial. in 1871. For form, cf. *goalie,* goal-keeper.

postil(l)ion of the Gospel. A gabbling parson: 1785, Grose; †by 1870.

postman's sister, the. An unnamed or secret informant: middle-class coll: ca 1883–1914. cf. JINKS, 2.

postmaster general. The Prime Minister: a late C.17–early 19 nickname. Grose, 1785, '... Who has the patronage of all posts and places'.

posty, see POSTIE.

pot. (The money involved in) a large stake or bet: 1823, 'Jon Bee': sporting. e.g. Lever, 'The horse you have backed with a heavy pot.' 2. Hence, any large sum: coll: 1870, L. Oliphant, 'Harrie ... won a pot on the French horse.' 3. Any horse heavily backed, i.e. gen. the favourite: 1823, 'Jon Bee'; H., 'Because [he] carries a pot of money'. 4. A prize, orig. and esp. if a vessel (gen. of silver), given at sports and games: 1885, O.E.D. 5. (A) sixpence: medical students': ca 1858–1915. H., 2nd ed., 1860, 'A half-crown ... is a five-pot piece'; *Household Words,* 20 June 1885, 'Because it was the price of a pot or quart of "half-and-half".' 6. A person of importance, gen. as a *big pot*: coll: 1880, Hardy; 1891, *The Licensed Victualler's Gazette,* 9 Feb., 'Some of the big pots of the day'. Coll. >, by 1910, S.E. Cf. the naval nuance (—1909); an executive officer. 7. A steward: nautical: ca 1870–1920. 8. **the pot** or **Pot,** the Canal: Winchester College: from ca 1840. Hence, *pot-cad*, a sawyer on the Canal; *pot-gates*, lock-gates; *pot-houser*, a leap into the Canal from the roof of a house called *pot-house*. 9. Top: back s. (—1859). 10. See POTS. 11. A woman: c. (—1857); virtually †. 12. A stew: nautical coll: late C.19–20. Abbr. (the inevitable) *pot of stew*. 13. A person: in pejorative s. or coll combinations, as FUSS-POT, a fussy person and SWANK-*pot*, a conceited one: late C.19–20. cf. sense 6. 14. A POT-HAT: ca 1890–1914.

pot, v. To shoot or kill for the pot, i.e. for food; to kill by a pot-shot: coll: 1860 (O.E.D.). 2. v.i. to have a pot-shot, v.t. with *at*: 1854 (O.E.D.): coll till C.20, then S.E. cf. POT AWAY. 3. To win, BAG: 1900, H. Nisbet, 'He has potted the girl.' cf. the v., 1, and n., 4. 4. See POT, PUT ON THE. 5. To deceive; outwit: mid-C.16–20: S.E. until C.19, then s., as in Tom Taylor's *Still Waters*, 1855, 'A greater flat was never potted'; ob. 6. See POT ON. 7. To stake a large sum on (a horse): turf: from ca 1870. cf. the n., 1.

pot, as good a piece as ever strode a. As good a girl as you could find: low coll: mid-C.19–20. cf. PISSED, AS GOOD AS EVER, and PISS UPON . . .

pot, give moonshine in a mustard. To give nothing: coll: ca 1660–1800. Ray.

pot, go to. To be ruined or destroyed; to get into a very bad condition: mid-C.16–20: S.E. till C.19, then coll; in C.20, low coll. (Whence *go to pot!*, go to the devil: coll: late C.17–20.) Orig., *go to the pot*, lit. 'to be cut in pieces like meat for the pot'.

pot, gone to. Dead: C.19. See preceding entry.

pot, on the. At stool: low: ca 1810–60. 2. In trouble, vexed: low: ca 1840–80. *Sinks*, 1848.

pot, put in the. Involved in loss: turf (—1823); †by 1900.

pot, put on. To exaggerate, e.g. to overcharge: from ca 1850; ob. 2. (Also *to pot.*) To wager large sums: sporting: 1823, 'Jon Bee'; ob. See POT, n., 1.

pot, put on the big. To snub; to be patronizing: from ca 1891: coll. (Occ., *big* omitted.)

pot, upset the. To beat the favourite: sporting: from ca 1860. Ouida.

pot and spit. Meat boiled and meat roasted: coll verging on S.E.: late C.17–18. Ex the respective modes of cooking.

pot away, v.i. To keep shooting: coll: from ca 1855. Ex POT, v., 2.

pot-boiler. Any literary or artistic work done for money: coll: 1803 (S.O.D.). i.e. something that will keep the pot boiling. 2. Hence, a producer of 'pot-boilers': coll: 1892, G. S. Layard.

pot-cad, see POT, n., 8.

pot calls the kettle black arse, the, see BLACK ARSE.

pot-faker. A hawker, a cheapjack, esp. in crockery: low: from ca 1870; ob.

pot-gates, see POT, n., 8.

pot-hat. In *Notes & Queries*, 1891 (7th Series, xii, 48), we read: 'Until lately . . . always . . . short for "chimney-pot hat", less reverently known as a "tile"; but at the present time . . . often applied to a felt hat,' the latter – to be precise a BOWLER – being, by 1930, slightly ob., the former historical. Coll: 1798, Jane Austen.

pot-head. A stupid person: coll: 1855, Kingsley. App. ex:

pot-headed. Thick-headed, stupid: coll: More, 1533. Whence preceding entry.

pot-hooks and hangers. Shorthand: coll: C.19.

pot-house. An easy-going club: clubmen's coll (—1909). Jocular on S.E. sense.

pot-houser, see POT, n., 8.

pot-hunter. One who follows sport for profit, lit. for pots: coll: 1874, H., 5th ed. See POT, n., 4. Ex S.E. sense, one who hunts less for the sport than for the prey. cf. the next entry. 2. In very local c. of late C.16, the same as a BARNACLE. Greene, 1592.

pot-hunting. The practising of sport for the sake of the prizes: coll: 1862, *Saturday Review*, 7 July; *Good Words*, 1881, 'Some men are too fond of starring or pot-hunting at "sports".' cf. POT-HUNTER.

pot in the pate, have a. To be the worse for drink: coll verging on S.E.: ca 1650–1780. Bracken, in his interesting *Farriery Improved*, 1737, 'An Ox . . . would serve them to ride well enough, if they had only a Pot in the Pate.'

pot joint. In grafters' s. of late C.19–20, thus in P. Allingham, *Cheapjack*, 1934, 'An enormous number of crockery sellers are Lancashire men, and their great stalls, where they sell all kinds of china by mock auction, are usually called "pot joints".'

pot(-)mess. 'A stew made of bits and

pieces too numerous for specification,' Granville: naval coll: late C.19–20. cf. POT, n., 12.

pot of all. A leader-hero, a 'demi-god': Cockney: ca 1883–1914.

pot of beer. Ginger beer: teetotallers' (—1909).

pot o(f) bliss. A fine tall woman: taverns': from ca 1876; ob.

pot of O is the abbr. of *pot of O, my dear*: rhyming s. for beer: 1868, says Ware; ob.

pot on. To be enthusiastic for: non-aristocratic s. (—1887) >, by 1900, coll; ob. Baumann quotes *Punch*: 'When their fancy has potted on pink' (*Wenn sie sich in Rosa verliebt haben*).

pot on, put the. See PUT THE POT ON. 2. To exaggerate: from ca 1870; ob. 3. To overcharge: tradesmen's: mid-C.19–20.

pot scum. 'Bad or stinking dripping', *Sinks*: domestic coll: ca 1825–1910.

pot walks, the. A c.p. applied to a drinking bout: ca 1560–1750.

pot-walloper. A heavy drinker: coll: late C.19–20; ob. Ex: 2. A tap-room loafer; (theatrical) a PROSSER: low: from ca 1870. 3. A scullion; a cook on a whaler: s. (—1860) > coll. 4. A pejorative term of address: 1820: coll >, ca 1870, S.E. Ex the S.E. political sense = *potwaller*. 5. Incorrectly (prob. on preceding sense) applied to anything very big and/or clumsy: late C.19–20.

pot-walloping. Making vigorous but clumsy movements: catachrestic: 1899 (O.E.D.). Ex preceding, 5.

pot with two ears, make a or the. To set one's arms akimbo: coll: ca 1670–1760. Cotton, 1675, '. . . A goodly port she bears, | *Making the pot with the two Ears*.'

pot-wrestler. The cook on a whaler: nautical: from ca 1840. cf. POT-WALLOPER, 3.

potato. A pejorative coll, as in Smollett's 'I don't value [him] a rotten potato': ca 1750–1850. cf. POTATOES. 2. A large hole in fleshings or stockings: coll: late C.19–20.

potato, hot, see HOT POTATO.

potato!, take a red-hot. A c.p. (ca 1840–60) 'by way of silencing a person . . . a word of contempt', *Sinks*, 1848. A very hot potato in one's mouth is a sharp deterrent from loquacity.

potato, the or **the clean.** The best; the correct or most apposite thing: resp. 1822, 1880. Esp. in *quite* or *not quite the* (*clean*) *potato*. 2. A non-convict; a person of good character: Australian: ca 1825–70.

potato-box. The mouth (cf. POTATO-JAW): from ca 1870.

potato-finger. A long thick finger; a penis; a dildo: (low) coll: C.17–18. Esp. in Shakespeare's *Troilus and Cressida*. Ex supposed aphrodisiac virtues of the sweet potato.

potato-jaw or **-trap.** The mouth: resp. 1791, Mme D'Arblay; 1785, Grose. Orig. Irish.

potatoes, abbr. of:

potatoes in the mould. Cold: from ca 1870.

potatoes, small. Nothing much, nothing great: orig. U.S. (1836), anglicized ca 1860. cf. POTATO, 1.

potching. The taking of tips from a person whom one has not served: waiters' (—1883). *Graphic*, 17 March 1883. Prob. = *poaching*.

potle-bell, ring the. 'To confirm a bargain by linking the little fingers of the right hand', F. & H.: Scots dial. and coll, mostly among children: C.19–20.

pots. Potatoes: greengrocers' coll: since ca 1870.

pots and pans, make. 'To spend freely, then beg', Bee, 1823: ca 1820–1900.

pottage. The Book of Common Prayer: C.17. Frequent in the less reputable writings of the time. Esau sold his birthright for a mess of pottage.

potted; occ. potted out. Confined (e.g. in a lodging): coll: 1859, *The Times*, 21 July; ob. by 1890. 2. Dead and buried: from ca 1860; ob. Ex horticulture. 3. Snubbed, suppressed: non-aristocratic: from ca 1880; ob.

potted fug. Potted meat: either dial. or local s.: Rugby (town): from ca 1860.

potter-carrier. An apothecary: low coll and dial. form of *pothecary*: ca 1750–1820. Foote, 1764, 'Master Lint, the potter-carrier'.

potting. Shooting; esp. the taking of pot-shots: coll: 1884 (O.E.D.). Ex POT, v., 2.

pottle. A bottle (of hay): incorrect: ca 1730–1850. Fielding.

potty. A tinker: lower classes' (—1909). Ex his *pots* and pans.

potty, adj. Indifferent; shaky; very unpromising (business scheme): 1860, H.; rather ob. 2. (Of a stroke) feeble; clumsy: cricketers': from 1870. 3. Trivial, insignificant: 1899, Eden Phillpotts. Ex *potter* (*about*). 4. Easy, simple; safe: 1899: s.

pouch. A present of money: 1880, Disraeli: s.; ob. Ex sense 1 of the v.

pouch, v. To supply the pouch, i.e. the purse or pocket, of; to tip: s. >, in C.20, (low) coll: 1810, Shelley; 1844, Disraeli, 'Pouched in a manner worthy of a Marquess and of a grandfather'. Slightly ob. 2. To eat: low coll: 1892, Milliken, 'Fancy pouching your prog on a terrace.' Ex S.E. sense, to swallow.

pouch-mouth, n. and adj. A ranter; ranting: coll, somewhat rare: early C.17. Dekker, 'Players, I mean, theaterians, pouch-mouth stage-walkers'. i.e. *ore rotundo.*

pouchet. A pocket: either coll or a corruption of *pocket* by Fr. *pochette.* Radcliffe, 1682, 'Did out of his Pouchet three nutmegs produce.' †by 1800.

poudering-tub, see POWDERING-TUB.

pouf. A would-be actor: theatrical: ca 1870–1910. Ex *poof!, pouf!*

poulain. A chance: low coll: 1785, Grose; ob. Ex Fr. *poulain.*

poulderling. An undergraduate in his second year: university: C.17. Anon., *The Christmas Prince,* 1607. ?origin.

***poulterer.** A thief who steals and guts letters: c.: C.19. ?ex *quill* = a quill pen, perhaps via metaphor of feathers as letters.

poultice. A fat woman: Society: ca 1880–1900. 2. A very high collar, suggestive of a neck poultice, ring-like in shape: Society: ca 1882–1912. 3. See POULTICE OVER.

poultice-mixer. A sick bay attendant: naval (—1909). cf. POULTICE-WALLAH.

poultice over the peeper. A punch or blow on the eye: low (—1909).

poultice-wallah. A physician's, esp. a surgeon's, assistant: military: from ca 1870. See WALLAH and cf. POULTICE-MIXER and:

poultice-walloper. A sick-bay attendant: naval: late C.19–20.

poultry. Women in gen.: coll: C.17–20. Chapman. Hence, *celestial poultry,* angels, ex the wings. cf. HEN; HEN-PARTY, and contrast COCK.

***poultry-rig.** The DODGE noted at POULTERER: c.: C.19.

pounce. A variant of PONCE.

pounce, on the. Ready to leap verbally: Anglo-Irish: 1887, when brought into fashion by E. Harrington, M.P. *Daily News,* 10 Oct. 1890, '"On the pounce", as the irreverent phrase goes.'

pounce-shicer, and **pouncey,** see PONCE.

pound, v., see POUND IT and POUNDED.

pound. Pounds, whether weight or sterling: S.E. until mid-C.19, then coll and dial. 'He's worth a thousand pound if he's worth a penny'; 'That bullock weighs eight hundred pound.' (In combination, however, the uninflected pl is S.E.: e.g. 'a four pound trout'.)

pound, go one's. To eat something up: military: ca 1870–1914. Ex the fact that a soldier's ration of bread used to weigh 1 lb., his ration of meat nearly 1 lb. (actually ¾ lb.), as mentioned in the *Pall Mall Gazette,* 1 July 1885.

***pound, in for.** Committed for trial: c.: C.19–20; ob. Ex *pound* = prison.

pound, shut (up) in the parson's. Married: 1785, Grose: †by 1860.

pound and pint. The bare Board of Trade ration scale: nautical: late C.19–20. Bowen.

pound-and-pint idler. A naval purser: naval: late C.19–early 20. Ex preceding.

pound it. To bet, wager, as on a virtual certainty, esp. in *I'll pound it*: 1812, Vaux; ob. by 1900. Ex offering £10 to 2s. 6d. at a cock-fight. Dickens, 'I'll pound it that you han't.' cf. POUNDABLE.

pound (of lead). Head: rhyming s. (late C. 19–20).

pound the stones. To walk a beat: police: C.20. Via the coll *pound the beat* (late C.19–20).

pound-text. A parson: coll: late C.18–20; ob. cf. CUSHION CUFFER.

pound to an olive(, it's a). It's a certain bet: Jewish coll (—1909). Perhaps ex Jewish fondness for olives.

poundable. (Esp. of the result of a game, the issue of a bet) certain, inevitable; or considered to be such: low (?c.): 1812, Vaux; ob. by 1890.

pounded, ppl adj. Discovered guilty of impropriety: male Society: ca 1820–50. Egan, *Life in London,* 1821. Ex the pounding of strayed animals.

pounders. (Rare in singular.) Testicles: coll: late C.17–18. Dryden's *Juvenal,* VI, 117.

poundrel. The head: coll: 1664, Cotton, 'Glad they had scap'd, and sav'd their poundrels'; †by 1830. Origin obscure, though prob. connected with weight.

poupe, see POOP, n., 3, and v., 2.

pour. A continuous rain; esp. *a steady pour* (all the morning): coll: late C.19–20.

pouter. The female pudend: low: C.19–20; ob. cf. DIDDLY-POUT.

poverty. Some strong liquor that was in

vogue in the 1720s. Anon., *The Quaker's Opera*, 1728. See BUNTER'S TEA.

poverty-basket. A wicker cradle: s. or coll: ca 1820–70.

powder, v.i. To rush: coll and dial.: lit., in Quarles, 1632, 'Zacheus climb'd the Tree: But O how fast ... he powder'd down agen!'; fig., from ca 1730. Ex the rapid explosiveness of powder. 2. Hence, to spur (a horse) to greater speed: sporting (—1887). 3. v.t., to camouflage the fact that a horse is glandered: horse-copers': from ca 1860. '*No. 747*', p. 20.

powder-monkey. A boy employed to carry powder from magazine to gun: 1682, Radcliffe, 'Powder-monkey by name': naval coll till C.19, then S.E.

powder or shot, not worth. Not worth cost or, esp., trouble or effort: 1776, Foote: coll till ca 1850, then S.E.

powdered chalk, (take a). (Go for) a walk: rhyming s.: late C.19–20. Not very common, but perhaps the origin of U.S. *take a powder*.

powdering (one's) hair, be. To be getting drunk: taverns': C.18–20; extremely ob. Ware, 1909, remarks: 'Still heard in remote places. Euphemism invented by a polite landlord.'

powdering-tub. A salivating cradle or pit, used against syphilis: late C.16–early 19: humorous S.E. until C.18, then coll. Shakespeare. 2. With capitals, 'the Pocky Hospital at *Kingsland* near *London*', B.E.: low coll: late C.17–mid-18.

Powell it. To walk: sporting coll: ca 1810–50. *Boxiana*, II, 1818. Ex the name of a famous early C.19 walker.

power. A large number of persons, number or quantity of things; much: from ca 1660: S.E. until ca 1820, then dial. and (low) coll. Dickens, 'It has done a power of work.' 2. Penis: low and rather rare: mid-C.19–20. Prob. suggested by sexual *potency*.

poweration. A large number or quantity; much: coll: ca 1830–1910. Also dial.

powerful. Great in number; in quantity: dial. and low coll: 1852, in U.S.; anglicized in 1865, by Dickens, 'A powerful sight of notice'.

pox. Syphilis: C.16–20: S.E. until mid-C. 18; then a vulg. That the word was early avoided appears in Massinger's 'Or, if you will hear it in a plainer phrase, the pox', 1631. Often *French pox* (Florio, 'The Great or French poxe'); occ. *Italian*, *German*, *Spanish*, *Indian pox*, also (*the*) *great pox* – Swift has *the greater pox*; cf. FRENCH CROWN. Altered spelling of *pocks*, orig. applied to the pustules of any eruptive disease. See also POWDERING-TUB. cf. POX!, and:

pox, v. To infect with syphilis: late C.17–20: S.E. until mid-C.18, then a vulg. Amory, 1766, 'She ... lives ... to ... pox the body.' cf.:

pox! (cf. the n. and v.) In imprecations and irritated exclamations, esp. *a pox of* or *on ...!*, (*a*) *pox take ...!*, *a pox!*, *what a pox!*, *with a pox!*, *pox on it!* Late C.16–mid-19: S.E. until C.18, then a vulg. Shakespeare, 1588, 'A pox of that jest'; Fielding, 1749, 'Formalities! with a pox!'

poxed, poxt, ppl adj. Infected with syphilis: late C.17–20: S.E. until mid-C.18, then a vulg.

poyson; poysoned, see POISON; POISONED. **poz, pozz,** see POS.

pozzy. Jam: military: late C.19–20. Perhaps ex a South African language, for the Africans of S.A. 'used the word, before 1900 at least, to designate any sort of sweetmeat or preserve.'

practicable, n. A door, window, staircase, etc., actually usable in a play: theatrical coll: 1859, Wraxall. Ex the corresponding theatrical adj. (1838).

practicable, adj. Gullible; illicitly accessible; facile: 1809, Malkin. Ex S.E. *practicable*, feasible.

practical, n. (Rare in singular.) A *practical* joke; a trick: 1833, M. Scott. Ob.

practical politician. A public-house, self-appointed orator or spouter: coll: late C. 19–20.

practise in the milky way. To fondle a woman's breasts: low cultured coll: verging on, but not achieving, S.E.: C.17–20; ob. Carew, 1633.

***practitioner.** A thief: c.: from ca 1865; ob. J. Greenwood, 1869.

***prad.** A horse: c.: app. not recorded separately before 1799, but implied in Grose, 2nd ed., 1788, in PRAD-LAY. Egan, Dickens, Mayhew, Marriott-Watson. Ex Dutch *paard*, a horse. cf. CHARING CROSS; GEE; PRANCER; and esp. PROD, 2.

***prad-cove.** A horse dealer: c.: from ca 1820; ob.

***prad-holder.** A bridle: c.: 1798, Tufts, *A Glossary of Thieves' Jargon*.

***prad-lay.** Cutting bags from behind horses; the stealing of bridles, etc.: c.: 1788, Grose.

***prad-napper; -napping.** A horse-thief; horse-thieving: c.: C.19–20; ob. See PRAD.

***pradback.** Horseback: c. (—1812); ob.

***prag, pragge.** A thief: c. of ca 1590–1600. Greene, 1592. Prob. ex PRIG, n., and v.

praise. (The name of) God: a Scots euphemistic coll: C.17–early 19. Callander, 1782, '*Praise be blest*, God be praised. This is a common form still in Scotland with such as from reverence, decline to use the sacred name.' Ex †S.E. *praise*, 'an object or subject of praise'.

pram. A perambulator (for infants): coll abbr.: 1884, *Graphic*, 25 Oct., 'Nurses . . . chattering and laughing as they push their "prams"'. 2. Hence, a milkman's hand-cart: coll: 1897.

prams. Legs: low Glasgow s., verging on c.: late (?mid-)C.19–20. Prob. a corruption of the old c. term, GAM(s).

prance. To dance, caper, gambol: mid-C. 15–20: S.E. until ca 1850, then coll.

***prancer.** A horse: c.: ca 1565–1860. cf. the S.E. usage: a prancing or mettlesome horse. See also PRANKER. 2. A highwayman: C.17: c. >, ca 1680, low s. Day, Head. 3. Hence, a horse-thief: c.: C.18–mid-19. Anon., *The Twenty Craftsmen*, 1712, 'The fifteenth a prancer . . . If they catch him horse-coursing, he's nooz'd once for all.' 4. A cavalry officer: military: from ca 1870; ob.

***Prancer, the Sign of the.** The Nag's Head (inn): from ca 1565 (very ob.): c. >, in C.19, low s. Also *the Sign of the Prancer's Poll.*

***prancer's nab** or **nob.** A horse's head as a sham seal to a counterfeit pass: c.: late C.17–mid-19. cf.:

***prancer's poll.** The same: late C.17–mid-18. 2. See PRANCER, THE SIGN OF THE.

***pranker.** A horse: c.: late C.16–17. Greene. Prob. a corruption of PRANCER, 1.

prannie or **pranny.** Female pudend: low: late C.19–20. A term of contempt among men.

p'raps. Perhaps: coll abbr. (in C.19, rather low): 1835, Hood; prob. much earlier.

***prat, pratt.** A tinder-box: c.: late C.17–early 19. ?origin. 2. (Gen. in pl.) A buttock; a thigh: mid-C.16–20: c. >, ca 1820, low. 3. A behind: late C.16–20: c. >, in C.19, low. Rowlands, 1610, 'And tip lowr with thy prat'; Marriott-Watson, 1895, 'We ain't to do nothing . . . but to set down upon our prats.' cf. U.S. c. sense, a hip-pocket. 4. The female pudend: low: C.19–20.

***prat,** v. To go: c.: 1879, Horsley. Connected perhaps with the n., 3, but prob. with Romany *praster*, to run. 2. Hence, *prat oneself* – or, more gen., *one's frame – in*, to butt in, come uninvited, interfere: low: late C.19–20. 3. To beat, to swish: late C.16–20 (ob.): low. App. ex the n., 3. Shakespeare, *Merry Wives*, IV, ii.

prat about. To potter, mess about: low: late C.19–20. cf. PRAT, n., 2, 3, and v., 2.

prate-roast. A talkative boy: ca 1670–1840: low: Glanvill; B.E.; Grose (1st ed.), who, by the way, certainly errs when he describes it as c.

pratie, praty. A potato: dial. and Anglo-Irish: 1832, a Scots song; Marryat; Reade, 1857, has the very rare spelling *pratee*. A slurred abbr. Also see TATER (-UR); TATIE.

***prating cheat.** The tongue: c.: ca 1565–1860. See CHEAT, a thing.

***pratt,** see PRAT, n.

***pratting-ken.** A low lodging-house: c.: from ca 1860. '*No. 747*'. Ex PRAT, n., 2. cf. KRADYING-KEN.

prattle-box. A chatterer: coll: Ned Ward, 1703. cf. S.E. *chatterbox*.

prattle-broth. Tea: late C.18–mid-19. Grose, 1788. cf. CHATTER-, SCANDAL-BROTH.

***prattle-cheat,** see PRATTLING-CHEAT.

prattling-box. A pulpit: low: late C.18–mid-19. cf. HUM-BOX.

***prattling-cheat.** An occ. variant of PRATING CHEAT.

prattling-parlour. A private apartment: ca 1820–60. Moncrieff, 1821.

***pratts,** see PRAT, n.

praty. Talkative: coll (gen. low): C.19–20; ob. Ex S.E. *prate*, (idle) talk. 2. See PRATIE.

prawn, silly. A pejorative applied to persons; gen. *you silly prawn* or *the s.p.*: coll: from ca 1905; slightly ob. It may date from ca 1890, for in 1895 W. Pett Ridge, *Minor Dialogues*, has: 'Ah, I expect you're a saucy young prawn, Emma.'

pray with knees upwards. (Of women) to coït: low: 1785, Grose.

prayer-bones. The knees: low coll: from ca 1850; ob.

prayer-book. A small holy-stone (cf. BIBLE): nautical s. >, ca 1870, nautical coll (ob.): 1840, Dana, 'Smaller hand-stones . . . prayer-books . . . are used to scrub in among the crevices and narrow places, where the large holystone will not go.'

prayer-book parade. 'A promenade in fashionable places of resort, after morning service on Sundays', F. & H.: from ca 1880; very ob. cf. CHURCH-PARADE.

prayers, at her last. (adj. applied to) an old maid: late C.17–mid-19. cf. *lead* APES IN HELL.

prayers, say. (Of horses) to stumble: sporting: C.19–20; ob. cf. DEVOTIONAL HABITS.

prayers backwards, say. To blaspheme; to curse: coll: late C.17–early 19. Ray's *Proverbs*; Ned Ward, 1706, 'They pray . . . backwards'; Nathan Bailey's *Erasmus*, 1725.

pre. A prefect: Public-Schoolboys': late C.19–20. Also *prae*.

preach. An act of preaching; a sermon; a discourse; tediously moral talk (cf. PI-JAW): C.16–20. Mrs Whitney, 1870, 'I preached a little preach.' Slightly ob.

***preach at Tyburn Cross.** To be hanged: c. or low s.: ca 1810–60.

preachification. vbl n. of next: coll: 1843, Lockhart. cf. PREACH.

preachify. To deliver a (tedious) sermon; moralize wearisomely: coll: 1775, S. J. Pratt.

preachifying. Tedious moralizing: coll: 1828.

preachiness. The being PREACHY: coll: 1861, O.E.D. cf. preceding entry.

preaching-shop. A church; more gen., a chapel: coll: from ca 1840. Thackeray. Pejorative on *preaching-house* (1760), Wesley's name for a Methodist Chapel.

preachy. Given to preaching; as if, as in, a sermon: coll: 1819, Miss Mitford, 'He was a very good man . . . though preachy and prosy.'

preachy-preachy. Tediously moral or moralizing: coll: 1894, George Moore, 'I don't 'old with all them preachy-preachy brethren says about the theatre.'

precious. Egregious; arrant; (pejoratively) thorough; occ. an almost meaningless intensive: coll: late M.E.–C.20. Lydgate; Jonson, 1605, 'Your worship is a precious ass'; Darwin, 1836.

precious, adv. Exceedingly; very: coll: 1837, Dickens (who, as W. remarks, popularized this use), 'We've got a pair o' precious large wheels on'; Baumann, however, implies its use as early as the 1740s. Ex the adj. cf. PRECIOUS FEW.

precious coals! A coll expletive: ca 1570–1620. Gascoigne. Prob. ex *precious!* = *precious blood* or *body*, recorded by the O.E.D. in 1560.

precious few. Very few: coll: 1839 (O.E.D). Ex PRECIOUS, adv. Perhaps ex U.S.A., where it is recorded in 1802.

preciously. Exceedingly; very: coll: 1607, Middleton; Thackeray. cf. PRECIOUS, adv.

predeceased. Obvious: ca 1890–1915; orig. legal. Perhaps ex *Queen Anne's dead.*

pref. A prefect: Scottish Public Schools': since ca 1870. Contrast PRE.

prefer room to company, as in 'She prefers my room to my company' and a hint, 'I prefer your room to your company': virtually a c.p.: late C.19–20.

premises. The female pudend: low: C.19–20.

premune. A praemunire (= a predicament): coll abbr.: ca 1755–1800. Mrs Lennox, 1758.

prep. Preparation of lessons; the period of such preparation: school s.: 1862, O.E.D.; Eden Phillpotts, in *The Human Boy*, 1899. 2. Abbr. of next: school s.: from 1900 at the latest.

prep school. A preparatory school: school s.: 1899 (O.E.D. Sup.), but prob. earlier.

Prescott. A waistcoat: rhyming s. Gen. *Charley Prescott* (—1859).

present. A white spot on a finger-nail: coll: C.19–20; slightly ob. Suggested by S.E. *gift* in the same sense. The white spot on the finger-nail has a different meaning for each nail. Starting with a thumb the verse runs – 'A gift, a friend, a foe; a letter to come, and a journey to go.'

presenterer. A whore: low coll: ca 1820–70. (A presenter of herself.)

preserve (of long bills). A collection of outstanding debts: Oxford University: ca 1820–50.

press, hot, see HOT PRESS.

pressed off, ppl adj. Finished: tailors' coll: late C.19–20.

preterite, n. and adj. (A) very old (person); Society: ca 1870–1900. Ware, 'Especially applied to women'. cf. ANNO DOMINI and HAS BEEN.

prettification. Rendering finically or cheaply pretty: coll: from ca 1855.

prettified, adj. (Made) pretty in a too-dainty or in a cheap way: coll: from ca 1851. Ex:

prettify. To make pretty, esp. if cheaply or pettily: to represent prettily: coll: 1850, Mrs Trollope, 'Your money to prettify your house'.

pretty. This S.E. adj. has, since ca 1850, had a slightly coll tinge. 2. The adv. (C. 16–20) has been almost coll since ca 1890: i.e. in sense of 'rather', 'considerably'. Contrast:

pretty, adv. Prettily: 1667 (O.E.D.): S.E. until C.19, then coll; in C.20, low coll.

pretty, do the or **speak** or **talk.** To affect amiability or courtesy in action or speech: low coll: from ca 1890. J. Newman, *Scamping Tricks,* 1891, 'We can talk pretty to each other.'

pretty-behaved. Prettily behaved: coll: late C.18–20. cf. PRETTY-SPOKEN.

pretty-boy clip. Hair brought flat down over the forehead, and cut in a straight line from ear to ear: Society: ca 1880–1900. Ware.

pretty dancers, the. The Aurora Borealis: Scots coll: C.19–20. cf. MERRY DANCERS.

pretty-face. The whip-tail kangaroo: Australian coll: from ca 1885.

pretty Fanny's way, only. Characteristic: c.p. (in C.19, a proverb) on *only her* (*his*) *way*: ca 1720–1900. Ex Parnell, ca 1718, 'And all that's madly wild, or oddly gay, | We call it only pretty Fanny's way.'

pretty much. Almost; to a large extent: coll: since ca 1860.

pretty-pretties, pretty things, knick-knacks, 1875, and **pretty-pretty,** rather too, or prettily pretty, 1897, are given by O.E.D. as S.E.: but orig. they were almost certainly coll.

pretty-pretty. Ornamental work on shipboard: nautical coll: from ca 1880. Bowen. Ex preceding.

pretty-spoken. Speaking prettily: coll: 1809, Malkin. cf. PRETTY-BEHAVED (12 years earlier).

prettyish. Rather pretty: coll: 1741, Horace Walpole, 'There was Churchill's daughter, who is prettyish and dances well.'

preventive. A preventive officer: nautical: 1870, E.D.D.

previous; gen. **too previous.** Premature; hasty: s. >, ca 1895, coll: 1885, *Daily Telegraph,* 14 Dec., 'He is a little before his time, a trifle *previous,* as the Americans say, but so are all geniuses.' Whence:

previousness. The coming too soon or being premature, hasty: coll: 1884 in U.S.; anglicized ca 1890. Ex preceding term.

***prey.** Money: c.: late C.17–early 19. Ex S.E. sense.

price —?, what. (Occ. admiring, but gen. sarcastic; in reference to a declared or well-understood value.) What do you now think of —? Just consider, look at —!: orig. racing ('What odds —?'), then gen.: from ca 1890. P. H. Emerson, 1893, 'What price you, when you fell off the scaffold.'

priceless. (By itself, it =) ludicrous; extremely amusing. With n., egregious: e.g. 'priceless ass' (of a person): s. from ca 1906.

prick. A pimple: coll: C.17–18. Jonson, Marston, *et al.,* in *Eastward Ho!,* III, ii, 'I have seen a little prick no bigger than a pin's head . . . swell to an ancome,' i.e. a boil or ulcer; this is a quibble on sense 3. 2. An endearment: late C.16–17. (cf. PILLICOCK, 2.) Ex: 3. The penis: 1592: S.E. until ca 1700; in C.18–20, a vulg. verging, in C.20, on low coll. Shakespeare; Robertson of Struan, Hanbury Williams, Burns. Ex basic sense, anything that pricks or pierces. cf. COCK. See esp. Grose, P., and Allen Walker Read, *Lexical Evidence,* 1935 (Paris; privately printed). (The variant *prickle,* dating from ca 1550, has always been S.E.: in C.19–20, literary only.) 4. An offensive or contemptuous term (applied to men only), always with *silly*; gen. *you silly prick,* occ. *the s.p.*: low: late C.19–20. 5. '*Perique*: Issue tobacco wrapped in canvas and lashed with spun yarn into a cylindrical shape tapered to a point', Granville: naval: since ca 1890.

prick, v. To mark a course on (a chart): naval officers' coll: late C.19–20.

prick-ear or **-ears;** or with capitals. A Roundhead: a coll nickname: 1642; †by 1690. Though influenced by PRICK-EARED (or *-lugged*), *prick-ear* derives mainly ex the fact that 'the Puritan head-gear was a black skull-cap, drawn down tight, leaving ears exposed,' F. & H., or, as B.E. defines *prick-eared fellow,* 'a Crop, whose Ears are longer than his Hair'.

prick-eared, adj. Roundhead: ca 1640–1700: coll verging on S.E. cf. preceding.

prick for a (soft) plank. To find the most comfortable place for a sleep: nautical: C. 19–20.

prick has no conscience, see STANDING PRICK. . .

prick-(in-)the-garter; also **prick-(in-)the-loop.** A fraudulent game, in which pricking with a bodkin into the loop of a belt figures largely: C.19. In C.17–18 called *prick-(in-)the-belt*; in C.18 s., *the old nob.* Orig. coll, but almost imm S.E.

prick-louse; occ. as in Burns, **prick-the-louse.** (Also *nip-louse.*) A tailor: coll: C.16–

20; in C.19–20, mainly dial. Dunbar, L'Estrange.

prick-teaser. A late C.19–20 variant of COCK-TEASER. Often abbr. to *p.t.*

prick-the-garter, play at. To coït: C.18–19: low. Ex PRICK-IN-THE-GARTER.

prick-the-louse, see PRICK-LOUSE.

pricket. A sham bidder: auctioneers': C. 19–20; ob. cf. PUTTER-UP.

prickly Moses, see MOSES, PRICKLY.

pride-and-pockets. Officers on half-pay: coll: ca 1890–1915. P. H. Emerson, 1893.

pride of the morning. A morning erection due to retention of urine: late C.19–20 (low) coll. Also *morning-pride*. Perhaps suggested by the S.E. and dial. *p. of the m.*, an early morning shower of rain, and cf. †proud, 'swollen'.

***pridgeman,** see PRIGMAN.

priest, a great. An ineffectual but strong desire to stool: Scots coll: C.18–19.

priest-linked, see PRIEST SAY GRACE, LET THE.

priest of the blue bag. A barrister: coll: from ca 1845; ob. Kingsley, 1849, 'As practised in every law quibble . . . as if he had been a regularly ordained priest of the blue bag'. cf. GREEN-BAG.

priest say grace, let the, v.i., To marry: coll: C.17–18. Hence, *priest-linked*, joined in matrimony: late C.17–early 19.

priest spoke on Sunday, know more than the. To be worldly-wise: coll: C.15–20; in C.19–20, mostly dial. Bale, ca 1540.

priestess. A priest's wife: coll: 1709, Mrs Manley.

***prig;** in C.16–18, often **prigg.** A tinker: c.: 1567; †by 1690. Perhaps ex dial. *prig*, v.i., to haggle about the price; prob., however, connected closely (see, e.g., PRIG, PRINCE) with: 2. A thief: 1610, Rowlands: c. >, ca 1750, low s. In C.19–20, gen. a petty thief. Ex the v., 1. 3. Hence, a cheat: late C.17–early 19: c.>, ca 1750, s. 4. See PRIG-NAPPER, 2. 5. A fop, coxcomb: late C.17–early 19. B.E., 'A Nice beauish, silly Fellow, is called a *meer Prig*'; Grose, 'a conceited coxcomical [sic] fellow.' 6. Hence, a vague pejorative (dislike, contempt): late C.17–18 coll. Shadwell, 1679, 'A senseless, noisie Prig'. 7. A religious precisian, esp. a dissenting minister: coll: late C.17–mid-18. Facetious Tom Brown, Arthur Murphy. 'Perhaps partly a violent shortening of *precisian*,' W. Hence, 8, a precisian in manners, a purist in speech, esp. if conceited, didactic, or tedious: coll >, in C.19, S.E.: 1753, Smollett; George Eliot, in *Middlemarch*, 'A prig is a fellow who is always making you a present of his opinions.'

***prig; prigg** (as for n.), v. To steal: 1561, Awdelay; Harman: c. >, in C.19, low s. In C.19–20, gen. applied to petty theft. ?a corruption (cf. that in sense 4) of †*prick*, to pin, to skewer. 2. Hence, to cheat, to swindle: low s.: 1819, *Sporting Magazine*, '[He] shook hands with me, and trusted I should soon prig the London cocknies.' 3. v.i., to beg, importune: 1714, Woodrow; G. Douglas, 1901: coll and dial. Prob. ex *prig*, to haggle. 4. To ride: 1567, Harman: c. and dial.; †by 1850. Cognate with S.E. *prick*, as in Spenser's 'A gentle Knight was pricking on the plaine.' 5. Hence, v.i., to coït: c.: late C.17–early 19.

***prig, prince.** c. of late C.17–early 19: B.E., 'A King of the Gypsies; also a Top-thief, or Receiver General', i.e. a notable (or important) thief, or a very important FENCE. Ex PRIG, n., 2.

***prig (or prigging-lay), work on the.** To thieve: c.: C.19–20; ob. cf.:

***prig and buzz,** n. and v. Picking of pockets! resp. 1789, G. Parker (*p. and b., work upon the*), ob.; C.19–20, ob. Both, c. See BUZZ, n., 2 and PRIG, n., 2, and v., 1.

***prig-man,** see PRIGMAN.

***prig-napper.** A thief-taker: c.: late C.17–early 19. 2. A horse-stealer: c.: mid-C. 17–mid-18. This sense leads one to posit an unrecorded PRIG, n., a horse, ex PRIG, v., 4.

***prig-star.** A rival in love: c.: mid-C.17–18. Ex PRIG, n., 2, or v., 1. Obviously, *star* may = *-ster*. 2. cf. PRIGSTER.

***prigg,** see PRIG, n. and v.

***prigger.** A thief: c. >, in C.19, low s.: 1561, Awdelay. e.g. *p. of cacklers, prancers*, a poultry-, horse-thief. Ex PRIG, v., 1. (In C.16, often *priggar*.) 2. A highwayman: C.17 c. Ex *prig*, to ride; *prigger* also meaning any rider: c. (or low s.) and dial. 3. Hence, a fornicator: c. (?> low s.): C. (?18–)19. Ex PRIG, v., 5. cf. PARISH-*prig* or -BULL.

***priggery.** Thievery; petty theft: c.: C.18–early 19. Fielding, 1743. cf. PRIGGISM.

***prigging,** vbl n. to PRIG, v. e.g. B.E., 'Riding; also Lying with a Woman'; Greene, 1591, 'This base villany of Prigging, or horse-stealing'. From ca 1820, mostly of petty theft; and, as such, low s.

***prigging,** adj. Thieving; thievish: from ca 1567: c. >, in early C.18, low s. Ex PRIG, v., 1.

***prigging law, lay.** Theft; esp. pilfering: c.: resp. late C.16–17 and C.19–20; ob. Greene; Maginn, 1829, 'Doing a bit on the prigging lay'. (Prob., despite a lack of examples, the *law* form endured till ca 1750, when – again prob. – the other arose: see LAW and LAY.) Ex PRIG, v., 1.

***priggish.** Thievish; dishonest: c.: late C.17–early 19. Ex PRIG, n., 1.

priggism. Thieving: (c. or) low s.: C.18. Fielding, 1743, 'The great antiquity of priggism'.

***prigman;** occ. **prig-man.** A thief: c. of ca 1560–1600. Awdelay (*prygman*); Drant, 1567 (*pridgeman*). Ex PRIG, n., 2, or, more prob., v., 1.

***prigster.** A thief: c. >, by 1840, low s.: C.19. Ex PRIG, v., 1. 2. A vague pejorative: 1688, Shadwell; †by 1750. Ex PRIG, n., 6. 3. See PRIG-STAR, 2: B.E. and Grose both spell without hyphen: *prigstar*.

prim. 'A silly empty starcht Fellow', B.E.: late C.17–19: low s. >, by 1750, coll and dial. Ex both the adj. and the v.

prime as a universal approbative adj. ca 1810–40 is a coll almost s.

prime, adv. Excellently; in prime order: coll: 1648, Gage, 'Prime good'; C. Scott, *Sheep-Farming*, 'The hoggets will be prime fat by Christmas.'

prime kelter, in. (Of a ship, esp. her rigging) in excellent condition: nautical coll: C.19–20.

primitive. Unmixed; undiluted: society s. of ca 1890–1910.

primo. The chairman, or master, of a Buffalo lodge: friendly societies': from ca 1880: coll >, in C.20, j. Ex L. *primus*, the first.

***prinado.** A sharper, prob. female: c. of ca 1620–60. Dekker; Brathwait, *Clitus's Whimzies*, 1631, 'His Nipps, Ints, Bungs, and Prinado's ... ofttimes prevent the Lawyer by diving too deep into his Client's pocket.' Origin obscure: the O.E.D. hazards Sp. *preñada*, pregnant: unmarried pregnant women of the lower classes used to tend to become criminals.

Prince Alberts. Burlap wound round the feet when a man's socks are worn out: sailing-ships': from ca 1860: ob. 2. Hence rags used in the same way: from ca 1860. 'Tom Collins', *Such Is Life*, 1903, 'Unlapping from his feet the inexpensive substitute for socks known as "prince alberts" '. cf. S.E. *albert*, a watch-chain.

***prince prig,** see PRIG, PRINCE.

Prince's points. Shilling points at whist: Society and clubmen's coll: 1877–1901. H.R.H. (afterwards King Edward VII) argued that 'the best whist-players were not necessarily the richest of men,' Ware.

princock, -cox. The female pudend: low coll: C.16–mid-19. Ex S.E. sense.

princod. 'A round, plump person', Grose, 1st ed.: Scots coll: ca 1780–1860. Ex S.E. sense, a pincushion. (Possibly, however, it never emerged from dial.)

princum. Nicety of dress, fastidiousness of behaviour: coll: late C.17–18. D'Urfey. 1690. A mock-Latin perversion of PRINK. cf.:

princum-prancum, see PRINKUM-PRANKUM.

Princum Prancum, Mistress (B.E.) or **Mrs** (Grose, 1st ed.). A fastidious, precise, formal woman: coll: late C.17–early 19. See PRINKUM-PRANKUM, stressing *prink* rather than *prank*.

prink, n. An act of making (gen. oneself) spruce: coll: 1895 (O.E.D.). Ex:

prink, v.t. To make spruce; in reflexive, to dress oneself up: coll: 1576, Gascoigne, 'Now I stand prinking me in the glasse.' The v.i., in the reflexive sense, is also coll: C.18–20 (D'Urfey); in C.19–20, much the more gen. Cognate with equivalent *prank*.

prinked. The ppl adj. of PRINK, v.t., and = 'all dressed up'. Coll: 1579, North.

prinker. A very fastidious dresser of self: coll: from ca 1860. Webster, 1864. cf.:

prinking. A fastidious adorning, mostly of oneself: coll: 1699, Farquhar. See PRINK, v.

prinkum-prankum. A prank: coll: late C.16–17. Nashe. A reduplication on *prank* with *um* (see PRINCUM) added to each element. 2. (gen. pl.) Fine clothes; fastidious adornment: C.18–early 19: coll. Here the stress is laid on PRINK (see the v.). See also PRINCUM PRANCUM, MISTRESS.

print, out of, see OUT OF PRINT.

printed character. A pawn-ticket: low s. (? > coll): from ca 1860; ob.

Printing House Square, adj. Powerful, crushing, *ex cathedra*; from *The Times* being published in that locality: London clubmen's coll: ca 1810–80. Ware.

prithee. I pray thee; i.e. please!: coll: 1577, G. Harvey; †, except as an archaism, by 1880. Addison, 'Pr'ythee don't send us up any more Stories of a Cock and a Bull.' An abbr. corruption.

prittle-prattle. Chatter; coll: Ned Ward, 1703. Reduplication of S.E. *prattle*.

private business. Additional work done with a tutor: Eton College: late C.19–20.

Private Leak. One whose position cannot be discovered: nautical: late C.19–20. Bowen.

private property. The generative organ: low coll: C.19–20. Suggested by *privity* (*-ies*), *privates*.

privateer. A woman competing with prostitutes but not depending on prostitution for her whole livelihood: Society: ca 1890–1914.

prize faggots. Well-developed breasts in women; low London (—1909). Ware. A *faggot* is a kind of rissole.

prize-packet. A novice who pays to play: theatrical: late C.19–20. *Globe*, 27 July 1899, 'Another man spent a happy holiday as . . . a prize packet.' Punning S.E. *prize-packet* and, I suggest, *surprise-packet*.

prizer. A prize-winner: coll, somewhat rare: mid-C.19–20.

pro. A pro-proctor: university (esp. Oxford) coll: from ca 1750, if not earlier. It occurs in *The Gentleman's Magazine*, May 1784. 2. An actor: theatrical (—1859). i.e. one who belongs to the profession, i.e. acting. (N.B., *the profession* is rather j. than coll, though orig. it may possibly have been theatrical coll.) 3. Hence, any professional as opp. to an amateur: e.g. cricketer, 1867; journalist, 1886; golfer, 1887. Coll. 4. A probationer nurse: medical: late C.19–20.

pro-donna. An actress: music-halls'; from ca 1880; ob. Lit., professional lady.

proby. A probationer: Australian prison warders': ca 1820–90. Louis Becke, *Old Convict Days*, 1899.

procesh. A procession: late C.19–20. (Never as v.; contrast:)

process. To be part of, go along with a procession: coll: 1814. Ex *procession*, on *progress*.

process-pusher. A lawyer's clerk: legal (—1909). He serves writs.

procession, as applied to a race, esp. a boat-race (above all, one in which there are only two crews), implies 'an ignominious defeat' (*Graphic*, 24 March 1883): in C.19, coll; in C.20, S.E.

procession, go on with the. To continue (esp. in the imperative): coll: late C.19–20; very ob.

proctors' dog or **bulldog.** The orig. of *bulldog*, one of the university police: Oxford and Cambridge University: 1847, Tennyson in *The Princess*, 'He had climbed across the spikes . . . | And . . . breath'd the Proctor's dogs.'

***proctour,** i.e. **proctor.** Awdelay, 1561, 'Proctour is he, that will tary long, and bring a lye, when his Maister sendeth him on his errand,' i.e. of the 12th of the 25 orders of knaves: c.: mid-C.16–early 17. Ex S.E. sense, one licensed to beg for a hospital. 2. A drunkard who talks copious nonsense: s. (—1650).

prod, n. and v. (Of a man) the act of coïtion; to coït: C.19–20: low coll. cf. POKE, V. 2. A horse; esp. an old horse: from ca 1890. A perversion of PRAD.

prodigious. Prodigiously; very greatly; very: from ca 1670: S.E. until ca 1750, then coll; in late C.19–20, low coll; ob. E. de Acton, 1804, 'A prodigious high hill'. cf.:

prodigiously. Exceedingly; very: coll: C.18–20; ob. Swift, 1711, 'It snowed . . . prodigiously.'

prof; often, in C.19, **proff. A professor:** U.S., 1838; anglicized ca 1860.

profesh. Profession; esp. *the p.*, the stage: (lower-class) actors': from ca 1885.

profession, the. See note at PRO, 2.

prog. Food in gen.: 1655, Fuller, 'The Abbot also every Saturday was to visit their beds, to see if they had not shuffled in some softer matter or purloyned some progge for themselves'; Swift; Disraeli. Prob. ex corresponding v. 2. Hence, food for a journey, a picnic: coll: 1813 (O.E.D.).

prog, v. To poke about for food; to forage: C.17–20: in C.17, (low) s.; C.18, s. > low coll: C.19–20, mainly dial. Origin obscure. 2. To **prog**nosticate: printers': from ca 1870.

prog-basket. A provision-basket on journey or picnic: coll: mid-C.19–20. Ex PROG, n., 2.

progger. A beggar: late C.17–20: s. until ca 1750; then coll till ca 1850; then dial. Ex PROG, V., 1.

progging, n. Foraging: mid-C.17–20: s. >, by 1700, coll; ob. J. Chappelow, 1715, 'All their . . . progging is for themselves.' Ex PROG, V., 1.

progging, adj. Begging; foraging: from ca 1620: s. >, by 1700, coll; very ob. Ex PROG, V., 1.

proggins. A proctor: from ca 1898.

prognostic. An artistic eater: literary, ca 1900–10. i.e. PROG, n., 1 + *gnostic*, one who knows, obviously with pun on S.E. *prognostic*.

proing, vbl n. Being a professional (esp.

actor, showman, singer): coll (—1887); slightly ob.

prom. A **prom**enade concert: 1902, *Free Lance*, 4 Jan. 1902, 'There is never one of the programmes at the Proms ... unworthy of the ... most cultured music-lover.'

promenade. A promenade concert: coll now verging on S.E.: 1901, *Westminster Gazette*, 18 Sept.

promiscuous. Carelessly irregular; haphazard; casual: low coll: 1837, Dickens; L. Oliphant, 1883. 2. Casually; incidentally: 1885, Grant Allen. cf. sense 2 of:

promiscuously. Unceremoniously; promptly: coll: C.17. Rowlands, 1609. 2. Casually; incidentally: coll: 1812. Leslie Stephen, 1871, 'The stone was dropped promiscuously.'

promise. Declare; assert with assurance: coll: mid-C.15–20. Esp. in *I promise you*, I assure you; I tell you confidently or plainly.

promo. A promotion: Charterhouse: from ca 1880. A. H. Tod, *Charterhouse*, 1900. An unexpected, perhaps an undeserved promotion was, ca 1890–1905, a *Stedman*.

promoss. To talk rubbish; play the fool: Australia: ca 1885–1910. ?origin.

promoted. Dead: Oct.–Nov. 1890. Ex the public funeral of Mrs Booth, General Booth's wife, and Salvation Army j.

promoter. A fool-catcher: coll: from ca 1880. Ex *company-promoter*.

promotion, be on one's. To behave with marriage in view and mind: coll: 1836 (O.E.D.); 1848, Thackeray, '"Those filthy cigars," replied Mrs Rawdon. "I remember when you liked 'em, though," replied her husband . . . "That was when I was on my promotion, Goosey," she said.' Ex *on promotion*, on approval or trial.

prong. A table fork: waiters': from ca 1880. Anstey, *Voces Populi*, II, 1892.

Prooshan, -in. (A) Prussian: low coll: C.19–20. cf. quotation at PRUSSIAN BLUE.

Prooshan blue, my, see PRUSSIAN BLUE.

prop. See PROPS, 2–4. 2. Any stage requisite; a portable article used in acting a play: theatrical: 1864, H., 3rd ed. Ex *property*. Gen. in pl: *actor's props*, acting material provided by himself; *(manager's) props*, articles provided by the manager for stage use. cf. PROPS, n., 4. 3. A breast-pin; a tie-pin: c.: 1850, Dickens, 'In his shirt-front there's a beautiful diamond prop.' Perhaps ex *prop*, a support; more prob. ex Dutch *prop*. 4. The leg: s. and dial. (1793); the arm extended: s. only: 1869. See PROPS, 3. Hence partly: 5. A straight hit; a blow: pugilistic and low street: *Sessions*, Dec. 1856; 1887, *Licensed Victuallers' Gazette*, 2 Dec., 'Ned met each rush of his enemy with straight props.' Ex the v., 1. 6. The gallows: Punch and Judy s. verging on j.: from ca 1860. 7. A **propo**sition, as in geometry: schools': 1871, 'M. Legrand'.

prop, v. To hit; knock down: pugilistic and low: 1851, Mayhew, 'If we met an "old bloke" . . . we "propped him".' Perhaps by antiphrasis ex *prop*, to support, influenced by *drop*; but cf. the n., 5.

prop, kick away the. To be hanged: low coll: early C.19.

***prop-nailer.** A stealer of pins or brooches: c.: 1856, Mayhew. Ex PROP, n., 3.

prop on, put the. To seize an opponent's arm and thus prevent him from hitting: pugilistic: from ca 1860; ob. cf. PROPS, 3.

propensities, have musical. (Of a horse) to be a ROARER: sporting, esp. journalists' (—1887); ob.

proper. (Of things.) Excellent; admirable: from late M.E.: S.E. >, ca 1850, coll >, ca 1890, low coll. 2. (Of persons.) Respectable; decorous: 1818, Moore: somewhat, and increasingly, coll. 3. Thorough; complete; perfect: C.14–20: S.E. till C.19, then dial. and coll. Miss Yonge, 'Old Markham seems in a proper taking.' cf. sense 1.

proper, adv. Excellently; thoroughly; without subterfuge; handsomely: an intensive adv. = hard ('Hit him proper!'), very much: mid-C.15–20: S.E. until ca 1820, then coll; since ca 1880, low coll. Conan Doyle, 1898, '"Had 'em that time – had 'em proper!" said he.'

proper, make oneself. To adorn oneself: low coll: from ca 1870. cf. Fr. *propre*, clean.

proper bit of frock. A pretty and clever well-dressed girl: London lower classes': ca 1873–1910. Ware.

properly. Admirably; handsomely; well: C.14–20: S.E. until C.19, then coll; in C.20, low coll. 2. Thoroughly, perfectly; very: C.15–20: S.E. until ca 1850, then coll. *Daily News*, 18 March 1896, 'The accused said he got "properly drunk".'

propers, adj. Rejected, refused: lower classes' (—1909). Ware implies an erotic connotation.

property, alter the. To disguise oneself: late C.17–early 19: coll >, by 1750, S.E.

prophet. A sporting tipster: journalistic:

1884, *Pall Mall Gazette*, 3 May; slightly ob.

prop'ly, proply. Properly: slovenly coll: C.19–20.

propose, v.i. To offer marriage: coll: 1764, Gray in his poem *The Candidate.*

proppy. Like a prop or pole: coll, but rare: 1870, O.E.D.

propriet. To own: journalistic: 1887, *Referee*, 31 July; ob. Ex *proprietor*.

props. See PROP, n., 2. 2. Crutches: late C.18–20. i.e. things that support. 3. The arms; not, as Manchon defines it, fists: low: 1869, *Temple Bar*, vol. XXVI, 'Take off your coat and put up your props to him.' cf. PROP, v., 1. Prob. same semantics as for sense 2; cf. PROP, n., 4. 4. (Also *propster.*) The property-man: theatrical: from ca 1889. cf. PROP, n., 2.

propster, see PROPS, 4.

pros; occ. pross. A water-closet: Oxford and Cambridge University (—1860). Abbr. πρός τινα or τὸν τόπον. cf. the old undergraduate WHEEZE: 'When is *pote* used [or, put] for *pros*? | When the nights are dark and dreary, | When our legs are weak and weary, | When the quad we have to cross, | Then is *pote* put for *pros*': doubtless a double pun, for *pote* = (*chamber-*) *pot*, *pros* = a w.c., and *pote* = Gr. πότε, when?, *pros* = Gr. πρός, to. cf. TOPOS.

pros, adj. Prosper: low London (—1887); ob. ?ex *prosperous*. 2. Occ. as adv.

prose, n. and v. A lecture; to lecture: Winchester College: from ca 1860. Ex S.E., a prosy discourse or ex: 2. Familiar talk; a talk: coll: 1805, Mrs Creevey; ob. by 1890. Ex: 3. *prose*, v. To chat; gossip: coll: 1797, Tweddell; ob. by 1890. 4. A prosy, esp. if dull, person: coll: 1844, Dickens. Ex sense 2.

pross. One who, to an (itinerant) actor, throws money: low theatrical: 1851, Mayhew; very ob. Prob. ex *prosperous*: cf. PROS, adj. 2. Hence, a cadged drink: theatrical: from ca 1860. 3. A **prostitute**: low (mostly London): from ca 1870. 4. See PROSS, ON THE, and cf. PROSSER and the v. 5. A variant of PROS, n.

pross, v. To cadge (a meal, a drink); occ. v.i.: theatrical: from ca 1860. Either ex the n., 2, or the v., 2. Anon., ca 1876, 'I've prossed my meals from off my pals.' 2. 'To break in or instruct a stage-infatuated youth', H., 1st ed.: theatrical: from ca 1858; ob. This sense may have been influenced by Romany *pross*, to ridicule.

pross, on the, adj. and adv. Looking for free drinks, etc.; on the cadge: theatrical >, ca 1890, low gen. s.: from ca 1860. P. H. Emerson, 1893. 2. Breaking in (and sponging from) a stage-struck youth: theatrical: from ca 1865.

pross about. To MOOCH or hang about: low: from ca 1890. Pugh (2), 'Afternoon I prosses about in 'Ampstead.' Ex PROSS, v., 1.

prosser. A cadger of refreshment, stomachic or pecuniary: theatrical: from ca 1880. cf. *Prossers' Avenue* and 'For he don't haunt the Gaiety Bar, dear boys, | A-standing (or prossing for) drinks,' *Referee*, 18 Nov. 1883. 2. Hence, a LOAFER, a hanger-on: 1886, *Cornhill Magazine*, Nov. Senses 1 and 2, prob. ex: 3. A PONCE: low: from ca 1870. Ex PROSS, n., 3.

prossie. An Australian late C.19–20 variant of PROSS, n., 3.

prostituted. (Of a patent) so long on the market that it has become known to all: commercial coll (—1909).

protected man. 'A merchant seaman unfit for the Royal Service and therefore free of the press-gang', F. & H.: naval coll: ca 1800–50.

proud, do one. To flatter (ob.); to honour; to treat very generously: coll: 1819 (O.E.D.); 1836, Clark, *Ollapodiana Papers*, 'I really thought, for the moment, that "she did me proud".' cf. '*the Cull tipt us Rum Prog*, the Gentleman Treated us very High,' B.E. and:

proud, do oneself. To be delighted (ob.); to treat oneself well, live comfortably: coll: from ca 1840. Ex preceding entry.

proud as an apothecary. Very proud or conceited: a C.17 coll. cf.:

proud as old Cole's dog. Exceeding proud: C.19: coll. Southey explains that this animal 'took the wall of a dung-cart and got squeezed to death by the wheel'. Anecdotal origin.

prov, on the. Out of work and on the provident funds of a trade society or union: workmen's: from ca 1870; > ob. on the Dole's arrival.

***provender.** 'He from whom any Money is taken on the Highway', B.E.: c. of late C.17–early 19. Ex *provender*, food, a provider thereof. 2. Hence, money taken from a person on the highway: c.: C.18.

provender pricks one. One grows amorous: coll: ca 1540–1750. Heywood, E. Ward.

providence. One who appears, or acts, in the character of Providence: coll: 1856, Emerson.

province of Bacchus. Drunkenness: Oxford University: ca 1820–40.

provost. A garrison or other cell for short-sentence prisoners: military coll (—1890) >, ca 1905, S.E.; ob. Abbr. *provost-cell.*

prow. A bumpkin: naval: ca 1800–90. ?ex ob. *prow*, good, worthy.

prowl. To womanize: low coll: late C.17–20. B.E., as *proling* [sic]. (Like a wild beast for meat: cf. MUTTON.) 2. To wait for 'the GHOST (3) to walk': theatrical: from ca 1870; ob. 3. To go about, looking for something to steal: c. (—1887).

Prowler, Hugh. A generalized (?low) coll nickname for a thief, a highwayman: mid-C.16–17. Tusser, 'For fear of Hugh Prowler get home with the rest.'

proxime. *Proxime accessit*: coll abbr. (schools', universities'): 1896.

pruff. Sturdy: Winchester College: from ca 1870. Ex *proof against pain.* Pascoe, 1881, 'Deprive a Wykehamist of words . . . such as quill . . . pruff . . . cad . . . and his vocabulary becomes limited.'

prugg(e). A female partner; a doxy: C.17: either (low) s. or c. Nares (1822); Halliwell (1847). Prob. cognate with PRIG and perhaps with PROG.

Prunella, Mr; or prunella. A clergyman: late C.18–mid-19. Clergymen's, like barristers', gowns were formerly made from this strong (silk, later) worsted stuff.

Prussian blue, my. An endearment: ca 1815–70, though app. not recorded before 1837, Dickens, '"Vell, Sammy," said the father. "Vell, my Prooshan Blue," responded the son.' Punning the colour; ex the tremendous popularity of the Prussians after Waterloo: cf. the old toast, *Prussian blue.*

prygge, see PRIG, n. and v. **prygman,** see PRIGMAN. **pr'ythee,** see PRITHEE.

Ps and Qs. See imm. after P.S or P.S. 2. Shoes: rhyming s.: late C.19–20.

psalm-smiter. A ranting nonconformist; a street preacher: low: from ca 1860; ob. ?ex *psalm-singing*, noisily religious. cf. CUSHION-CUFFER.

pub. A **public**-house (see PUBLIC, n.): 1859, H., in his first ed.: s. >, ca 1890, coll. Anon., *The Siliad* ca 1871, 'All the great houses and the m or pubs.'

pub (always **pub it).** To frequent pubs: coll: 1889, Jerome K. Jerome. Ex preceding.

public. A **public**-house: coll: 1709, a churchwarden's account; ob. Scott '"This woman keeps an inn, then?" interrupted Morton. "A public," in a prim way, replied Blane,' cf. PUB.

public, adj. In, of, a public-house: coll: mid-C.18–20. Ex preceding.

public buildings, inspector of. An idler; a loafer: from ca 1850; ob. Hence, one in search of work: from ca 1860.

public ledger. A harlot: low: late C.18–20; very ob. 'Because like that paper, she is open to all parties', Grose, 2nd ed. Punning the *Public Ledger*, a London commercial newspaper, established 1760.

public line, something in the. A licensed victualler: coll. Dickens, who, in 1840, originated – or, at the least, gave currency to – the phrase; prob. on *the public business.*

public man. A bankrupt: ca 1810–80. Perhaps suggested by †S.E. *public woman* (Fr. *femme publique*), a harlot.

***public patterer.** A SWELL MOBSMAN (see both words) who, pretending to be a Dissenting preacher, harangues in the open air to attract a crowd for his confederates to rob: c.: ca 1860–1910. See PATTERER.

pucka, pucker, adj., see PUKKA.

pucker. Excitement; (a state of) agitation: coll: 1741, Richardson; Smollett, 1751, 'The whole parish was in a pucker: some thought the French had landed.' Rare except as *in a pucker*, which Grose, 2nd ed., defines as 'in a dishabille', a sense †by 1880; 'also in a fright', which is a little too strong. Common, moreover, in dial.; cf. the Lancashire *puckerashun*, vexation or agitation. Ex the puckering of facial skin. See PUCKER UP.

pucker, v. To talk privately: showmen's s. (perhaps orig. c.): 1851, Mayhew, 'The trio . . . began puckering . . . to each other in murdered French, dashed with a little Irish.' ?a corruption of Romany *rok(k)er*, or *vok(k)er*, to talk: cf. ROCKER.

pucker up. To become angry: coll: C.19–20. Ex the n., and S.E. v., primary sense.

pucker-water. An astringent employed – esp. by 'old experienced traders', i.e. prostitutes – to counterfeit virginity: low coll: Grose, 1785; †by 1890. Gen., water impregnated with alum. (cf. post-parturition astringents.) Ex *pucker*, to contract.

***puckering,** vbl n. Private talk: c. and showmen's s. (—1859). Ex PUCKER, v.

puckerow; occ. **pukkaroo.** To seize: Anglo-Indian and military (—1864). Ex Hindustani, where this, as in all the Anglo-Indian *-ow* vv., is the form of the imperative, not of the infinitive.

pud. A (child's) hand; an animal's forefoot: a nursery coll: 1654. Lamb, 1823, 'Those little short . . . puds'. Origin unknown: but cf. Dutch *poot*, a paw, and the later *pudsy*, plump, chubby. 2. Pudding: lower and lower-middle classes': late C.19–20.

pud, v. To greet affectionately or familiarly: proletarian coll: from ca 1860; ob. Ex the n., 1.

pudden. Pudding: dial. and low coll: C.16–20. 2. A MESS or failure: Cockney coll: late C.19–20.

pudden, v. C.17–20. To supply with pudding; treat with a pudding(-like substance): low coll. 2. Esp., in c., to silence a dog by throwing a narcotic ball to it: 1858, Youatt.

pudden club, put in the. To render pregnant: low: late C.19–20. See also PUDDING, WITH A BELLYFUL OF MARROW-.

***pudding.** Liver drugged for the silencing of house-dogs: c.: 1877, but prob. much earlier – see PUDDEN, v., 2. Horsley, *Jottings from Jail.* cf. the old saying 'Pudding is poison when it is too much boiled' (Swift). 2. Coïtion; the penis; the seminal fluid: low coll: from Restoration days. *Wit and Mirth*, 1682; D'Urfey. 3. See PUDDINGS.

pudding, give or **make** or **yield the crow(s) a.** To die; also and orig., to hang on a gibbet: late C.16–19. Shakespeare, 'He'll yield the crow a pudding one of these days.'

pudding!, not a word of the. Say nothing about it: coll c.p. of late C.17–early 18.

pudding, ride post for a. To exert oneself for a small cause: coll: C.18–19 coll.

pudding, with a bellyful of marrow-; in the pudding club. Pregnant: low: C.19–20; ob. cf. PUDDING, n., 2.

pudding about the heels. Thick-ankled: low coll: C.19–20; very ob.

pudding for supper, have a hot, see HOT PUDDING.

pudding-bag. A stocking pennant used as a vane: nautical: late C.19–20. Bowen. Ex shape.

pudding-bellied. With great paunch: coll: C.18–20.

pudding-filler. A glutton: Scots coll: C.16–19. Dunbar. See PUDDINGS.

pudding-house. The stomach, the belly: low: late C.16–20; ob. Nashe. cf. BREAD-BASKET. 2. A workhouse: low: ca 1830–70. *Sinks*, 1848.

***pudding-ken.** A cook-shop: c.: C.19–20; ob. P. H. Emerson. cf. PUDDING-SNAMMER.

pudding-sleeves. A clergyman: ca 1720–1860. cf. PRUNELLA.

***pudding-snammer.** A cook-shop thief: c. (—1839); slightly ob. Brandon.

puddings. The guts: mid-C.15–20: S.E. till C.18, then dial. and low coll. Shakespeare; Brydges, 1772; Grose, 1st ed., 'I'll let out your puddings,' i.e. disembowel you.

puddings and pies. Eyes: rhyming s. (—1859). Later, MINCE-PIES.

puddle. The female pudend: low: C.19–20. 2. *the Puddle* or *puddle*, the Atlantic Ocean: coll: from ca 1880. cf. *the* POND. 3. A muddle, a mess: late C.16–20: S.E. till ca 1850, then coll and dial.

puddle, v. To tipple: low coll: from ca 1870; ob. ?ex PIDDLE on FUDDLE.

Puddle-Dock, the Countess or **Duchess of.** An imaginary aristocrat: coll: C.18–mid-19. Swift, '*Neverout.* I promised to squire the Countess to her box. *Miss.* The Countess of Puddledock, I suppose.' Ex an almost permanent, large and dirty pool in Thames Street, which runs parallel to the river, London, E.C.4.

puddling, adj. A vague pejorative: coll: 1764, Foote; ob. Ex PUDDLE.

pudge. A short squat person; anything both short and thick: coll and dial.: 1808, Jamieson. Of obscure origin but prob. cognate with PODGE.

pudsy. A foot: late C.18–20: a nursery coll. A diminutive of PUD.

pudsy, v. To greet affectionately or with familiarity: coll: C.19–20; ob. Ex *pudsy*, a term of endearment, esp. to a baby, itself ex *pudsy*, plump.

puff. A decoy in a gambling-house; a mock-bidder at auctions: resp. 1731 and (—1785). 2. A sodomist: tramps' c.: from ca 1870. 3. Breath, 'wind': s. and dial.: 1827, *Sporting Magazine.* Hence, *out of puff*, out of breath: same status and period. 4. Life; existence: tailors' > (low) gen.: from ca 1880. As in *never in one's puff*, never, and as in 'Pomes' Marshall, 'He's the winner right enough! It's the one sole snip of a lifetime – simply the cop of one's puff.'

puff, v. To break wind: low: late C.19–20.

puff and dart. Beginning, commencement: rhyming s. (on *start*): late C.19–20. Barrett, *Navvies*, 1880.

puff-ball, v.t. In the 1890s, John Masefield tells us in his history (1933) of the *Conway* training ship, 'large cakes of soft bread were moulded in tea at tea-time to the size and similitude of dumplings and then thrust down the victim's neck between his shirt and the skin': a mess's punishment of an 'impossible' member.

puff-guts. A fat man: low coll: 1785, Grose; slightly ob.

puff-puff. A locomotive; a railway-train: nursing coll: from ca 1870. Echoic. cf. PUFFER and PUFFING BILLY.

puff the glim. Horse-coping s. from before 1890, thus: 'Old horses are rejuvenated by puffing the glim, . . . filling up the hollows . . . above [the] eyes by pricking the skin and blowing air into the loose tissues underneath,' *Tit-Bits*, 11 April 1891. (Verging on c.)

puffer. A steam-engine: coll: verging on S.E.: 1801 (O.E.D.). cf. PUFF-PUFF.

puffickly. Perfectly: proletarian coll: mid-C.19–20. Anstey, *Voces Populi*, II, 1892.

puffin, plump as a. Very plump: coll > S.E.: C.19–20. Ex corpulence of young bird.

puffing Billy or **billy.** A locomotive: coll: late C.19–20. cf. PUFF-PUFF and PUFFER.

pug. A boxer: sporting: 1858, Mayhew, 'Known by his brother pugs to be one of the gamest hands in the ring'. Abbr. *pugilist*. Hence *Pug's* or *Pugs' Acre*, that corner of Highgate Cemetery where Tom Sayers and other 'pugs' lie buried. 2. A dog of no matter what breed: coll: from ca 1860. See sense 7. 3. A bargeman: coll: late C.16–early 17. Lyly, 1591, 'With a good winde and lustie pugges one may goe ten miles in two daies.' 4. A ship's boy: coll: late C.16–17. 'Hudibras' Butler. 5. A harlot: coll: C.17–early 18. Ned Ward. 6. An upper servant in a large house (etc.): from ca 1840. Halliwell. 7. A nickname for a dog or a monkey: coll: resp. (—1731), Bailey; 1664. † except in dial. 8. Hence, like 'monkey', to a child: mid-C.18–20, but since ca 1850, † except in dial. 9. A fox; gen. as a nickname: C.19–20: coll. R. S. Surtees, 1858, 'Pug . . . turns tail, and is very soon in the rear of the hounds.'

pug-Nancy. A woman: C.17–19: Ned Ward, 1703.

pug-nasty. A dirty slut: coll: late C.17–early 19. Ex PUG, 5. cf. PUG-NANCY.

***puggard.** A thief: c.: C.17. Middleton, 1611. Ex *pug*, to tug, pull.

puggle, puggly, see POGGLE. **puggle pawnee,** see POGGLE P. **puggled,** see POGGLED.

puggy. A coll endearment to a woman or a child: C.17–early 18. 2. A monkey: Scots coll: from ca 1820. Ex PUG, 7. 3. A nickname for a fox: coll: 1827. Ex PUG, 9.

puggy-drunk. Extremely drunk: rather low: late C.19–20. Prob. ex POGY influenced by POGGLE, 2, and with an allusion to PUGGY, a fox (cf. FOXED, drunk).

pugified. Snub-nosed: coll: late C.18–mid-19. cf. S.E. *pug-nosed.*

Pug's or Pugs' Acre, see PUG, 1.

pug's or **pugs' hole, parlour.** The housekeeper's room in a large establishment: coll (—1847). Halliwell (*pugs'-hole*). The latter not till late C.19.

puja, see POOJA.

pukaroo. To break (something), ruin (a plan), confuse (an issue): New Zealand coll: late C.19–20. Ex Maori *pakaru*, to destroy.

puker. A good-for-nothing: a Shrewsbury School coll: C.19–20. Prob. ex the famous Shakespearian passage beginning: 'The infant Mewling and puking in the nurse's arms'. 2. An orange: preparatory schools': from ca 1870.

pukka, often *pucka*; also *pakka, puckah, pucker*. Certain, reliable; genuine; excellent: Anglo-Indian coll: from ca 1770. Grant Allen, 1893, 'That's a good word . . . Is it pucker English, I wonder.' In *pukka sahib* it connotes the acme of gentlemanliness. 2. Permanent, as of an appointment: mid-C.19–20: coll. Ex Hindu *pakka*, substantial.

pukkaroo, see PUCKEROW.

***pull.** A mechanical 'catch' or knack; an ulterior and hidden motive: c.: 1812, Vaux; †by 1890. Prob. ex pulling of strings and wires. 2. Hence, an illicit trick or manipulation: card-sharpers' c. (—1861). 3. See PULL IN. 4. An anxious moment: lower classes' (—1909); slightly ob. Ex the pull at one's heart.

***pull,** v. To arrest: c.: 1811, *Lex. Bal.* cf. PULL IN and PULL UP. 2. Hence, to raid: c. (—1871); ob. *Figaro*, 15 April 1871. 3. To steal; occ., to cheat: c.: 1821, Haggart; Mayhew. †by 1900.

***pull, in.** Under arrest: c. of ca 1810–70. Ex PULL, v., 1.

pull a cluck. To die: low from ca 1870. Echoic.

pull a horse's head off; esp. a vbl n., *pulling* . . . So to check a horse's progress that he does not win: turf: from ca 1860.

pull a kite. To look or be serious: low: C.19–20; ob.

pull a soldier off his mother!, ('pull'? He or you) wouldn't. A c.p. directed at laziness or slacking: nautical (from ca 1880) >, by 1900, military.

pull about. To treat roughly or without ceremony: coll and dial.: C.19–20. Ex S.E. sense, to pull this way and that. 2. Hence, to take liberties with a woman: low coll: from ca 1860. cf. PULLY-HAULY, PLAY AT; MUCK ABOUT. 3. *pull oneself about*, to masturbate: low coll: C.19–20.

pull-back. A retarding or repressing act or influence: late C.16–20: S.E. till C.19, then coll and dial.

pull-down. The moustache that succeeded the NAP, n., 9: Society: ca 1870–90. Ex its shape.

***pull down,** v. To steal from shop doors: c. (—1839).

pull down the blind! A c.p. addressed to couples love-making: London lower classes': from ca 1880; ob.

pull down the shutter. Butter: rhyming s.: late C.19–20.

pull foot. To decamp; run hard: coll: 1818. M. Scott, 'The whole crew pulled foot as if Old Nick had held them in chase,' 1833. cf. PULL IT and dial. *pull feet* or *hot-foot*, to walk fast.

pull-guts. A fishmonger: s.: Ned Ward, 1700.

***pull in.** To arrest: c. >, ca 1890, low s.: C.19–20. Implicit in Vaux, 1812, 'To pull a man, or have him pulled, is to cause his apprehension for some offence; and it is then said that Mr Pullen is concerned.' cf. PULL, V., 1; PULL OVER; PULL UP.

pull in the pieces. To make money; receive good wages: proletarian: from ca 1860; ob.

pull it. To decamp; run as fast as possible: coll: 1804 (O.E.D.). cf. PULL FOOT.

pull off. To obtain (some benefit): sporting: 1870 (O.E.D.). Ex sporting j., to win. 2. Hence, to succeed with, or in effecting, something: 1887, Black, 'We haven't pulled it off this time, mother.'

pull one's load. To do all one can: coll, mostly Canadian: late C.19–20. (Esp. in present perfect.) cf. the S.E. *pull one's weight*.

pull one's pudden or **wire.** (Of the male) to masturbate: low: late C.19–20.

pull oneself off. (Of the male) to masturbate: low: late C.19–20.

pull out. To hurry work in hand: tailors' s. verging on j.: from ca 1860. 2. To buy or sell for ready money: Stock Exchange coll: ca 1805–1910. 3. (v.i.) To exaggerate: low: ca 1830–80. *Sinks*, 1848. 'To stretch it a bit.'

pull over. To arrest: low: mid-C.19–20; very ob. cf. PULL, V., 1, and PULL UP. 2. *pull* (oneself) *over* (an edible). To eat: London lower classes': 1886, *Referee*, 6 June; very ob. cf. *get* OUTSIDE OF.

pull the ladder up, Jack, I'm all right! A late C.19–20 variation of FUCK YOU, JACK...

pull the string. To use all one's influence: tailors' coll: mid-C.19–20. 2. To do well: proletarian: from ca 1870; ob.

pull-through. A very thin man: military: from ca 1905. Ex the rifle pull-through.

***pull up.** To arrest: 1812, Vaux: c. >, by 1835, low s. >, by 1870, coll >, by 1910, S.E. Dickens in *Boz*. Ex the act of pulling up, of checking, a fugitive. cf. PULL, V., 1.

***pull up a Jack.** To stop a post-chaise on the highway with a view to robbery: c. of ca 1810–50.

pull up one's boot. To make money: costermongers' (—1909). Ware, 'When a man prepares for his day's work, he pulls on and strings up his boots.'

pull your ear! Try to remember!: lower classes' c.p. of ca 1860–1910.

pulled, see PULL, V., 1. **pulled up,** see PULL UP.

pulled trade. Secured work: tailors' coll: from ca 1860.

Pullen is concerned, Mr, see PULL IN.

pullet. A young girl: coll: C.19–20: ob. cf. PULLEY.

pullet, virgin. 'A young woman ... who though often trod has never laid', Bee, 1823: low: ca 1820–70. Ex PULLET; and cf.:

pullet-squeezer. A womanizer who 'likes 'em young'; a 'chicken-fancier': from ca 1830; somewhat ob. Ex PULLET; cf. PULLET, VIRGIN.

***pulley.** A confederate thief, gen. a woman: c. (—1859); very ob. Ex Fr. *poulet*.

pulling the right string?, are you. Are you correct?; are you going the right way about it?: cabinet-makers' c.p.: from 1863, says Ware. Ex small measurements being made with string.

pully-hauly (in Grose, **-hawly**). A rough-and-tumble; a romp: coll: late C.18–19.

pully-hauly, play at. To romp with women; esp. to copulate: coll: late C.18–20; slightly ob. The idea, however, is extant in dial. *pulling and hauling time* and *dragging time*: cf. the †dial. *pulling time.* See Grose, P.

pulpit-banger, -cackler, -cuffer, -drubber, -drummer, -smiter, -thumper; pulpit-cuffing, -drubbing, etc. A ranting parson; a violent sermon or moral exhortation: coll bordering on S.E.: late C.17–20; *-drubber* (*-drubbing*), †by 1850; *-cuffer* and *-drummer*, very ob.

pum-pum. A fiddler: coll: C.18–mid-19. Echoic.

pump. The female pudend: low coll: late C.17–20; ob. Also (as in Ned Ward) *pump-dale.* 2. The penis: low: C.18–20; ob. Also *pump-handle.* 3. A breaking of wind: Scots low coll: C.19–20. 4. A public-house: Scots coll: C.19–20; ob. 5. A solemn NOODLE: low: mid-C.19–20; ob. 6. See PUMPS.

pump, v. To coït with (a woman): low: C.18–20; ob. 2. To urinate: low coll: C.18–20; ob. except in form PUMP SHIP. 3. To break wind: Scots low coll: C.19–20. 4. To duck under the pump: coll: late C.17–mid-18. Esp. as treatment applied to bailiffs, constables, and pick-pockets. 5. To weep: low: 1837, Marryat, 'And she did pump | While I did jump | In the boat to say, Good bye.' Ob. Partly ex S.E. sense, partly ex PUMPS.

pump, ignorant as a. Extremely ignorant: coll verging on S.E.: late C.19–20.

pump, purser's, see PURSER'S.

pump at Aldgate, draught on the, see ALDGATE.

pump-dale. See PUMP, n., 1.

pump-handle, n. See PUMP, n., 2. 2. v. In greeting, to shake (a hand or person by the hand) as if working a pump: coll: 1858, R. S. Surtees. Also v.i.

pump-handler. A hand-shake as in preceding: coll: J. T. Hewlett, 1844, 'Exchanged the salute for a most hearty old English pump-handler'.

pump is good but your or the sucker's dry, your. A c.p. addressed to one trying to pump, i.e. extract information: from ca 1780; ob.

pump (oneself) off. To masturbate: low: C.19–20; ob. cf. FRIG.

pump ship. To make water: nautical s. (—1788) >, ca 1870, gen. gentlemanly coll. 2. To vomit: nautical: late C.18–mid-19.

pump-sucker. A teetotaller: low: from ca 1870; ob.

pump-thunder. A blusterer: coll: C.19–20. 2. Also, without hyphen, a v.; likewise ob.

pump-water, christened in or with. Red-faced: coll or, in form *he* (*she*) *was christened* . . ., c.p.: late C.17–mid-19.

pumper. Any effort that puts one out of breath: coll (—1886).

pumping. The vbl n. of PUMP, v., 4.

pumpkin; pompkin. A man or woman of Boston: late C.18–early 19. Grose, 1785, 'From the number of pompkins raised and eaten' there. (Whence, perhaps, the orig. and mainly U.S. *some* – occ. *big* – *pumpkins*, persons – occ. things – of importance. Coll: mid-C.19–20.) 2. The head: mid-C.19–20.

pumpkins of oneself, think. To think well of oneself: 1897, Ouida, *The Massarenes*; ob. cf. PUMPKIN, 1 (parenthesis); cf. POTATOES, SMALL.

pumps. Eyes: low: 1825, Buckstone, 'Your pumps have been at work – you've been crying, girl': ob. by 1910. cf. PUMP, v., 5.

pun. Punishment: Harrow School: mid-C.19–20. Abbr., s. > coll. cf. PUN-PAPER. 2. Pound or pounds (£): sol.: C.19–20. cf. Northern dial. *pund.*

pun (v.i.) **or pun of** (v.t.), at Hertford; **pun out** (v.i. and t.), London. To inform (against): Christ's Hospital, orig. at the country section: mid-C.19–20. Ex dial. *pun*, to pound.

pun-paper. Ruled paper for impositions: Harrow. See PUN, n., 1.

punce. An occ. variant of PONCE. 2. To kick (someone) with one's clogs: Lancashire: late C.19–20. Ex S.E. *punch* and s. PURR.

punch (or P.); Suffolk punch. An inhabitant of Suffolk: coll nickname (—1884). Ex the famous breed of horses. 2. (*Punch* only.) A short, thickset man: navvies' nickname: mid C.19–20. (D. W. Barrett, *Navvies*, 1880.)

punch, v. To deflower: coll: C.18–19. Ward and Grose imply it in PUNCHABLE. Ex S.E. *punch*, to pierce. 2. (Gen. *punch it.*) To walk: c.: 1780, Tomlinson, 'Now she to Bridewell has punch'd it along'; Grose; Haggart. 3. v.i., to drink punch: 1804, Coleridge.

punch, cobbler's. Urine with a cinder in it: low: ca 1810–60.

Punch and Judy. Lemonade: *English Illustrated Magazine*, June 1885.

punch-clod. A farm-labourer; clodhopper: rural coll: C.19–20; ob.

punch-house. A brothel: coll: late C.17–mid-19. Ex the S.E. sense, a tavern where punch may be had, and ex PUNCH, v., 1.

punch it, see PUNCH, v., 2.

punch one's ticket. To hit (a man) with a bullet: from 1899 (ob.), mostly military. J. Milne, *The Epistles of Atkins*, 1902.

***punch outsides.** To go out of doors: c.: C.19–20; ob. See PUNCH, v., 2.

punchable. 'Ripe for man': (low) coll: C.18–19. Ex PUNCH, v., 1. cf.:

punchable nun. A harlot: Ned Ward, 1709.

Puncheous Pilate. A lower classes' c.p. (—1909) 'jocosely addressed to a person in protest [against] some small asserted authority', Ware. Punning Punch and Pontius Pilate.

puncture. To deflower: cyclists' low s.; late C.19–20. Ex punctured tyres. 2. v.i. and in passive, (of cycle or rider) to get a puncture: coll: from ca 1893. Ex the tyre's being punctured.

pundit; occ., before C.20, **pundet.** An erudite expert: coll: 1816. *Saturday Review*, 15 March 1862, 'The doctors of etiquette and the pundits of refinement'. Ex Hindi *pandit*, a learned man.

punish. To handle severely, as in boxing (1812); food and drink (1825); the bowling, at cricket (1845); a horse (1856); a plant (1882): s. 2. To hurt, pain: coll and dial.: from mid-C.19.

punisher. A hard hitter: in boxing, 1814, *Sporting Magazine*; at cricket, 1846. 2. A heavy task: coll: 1827, ibid., 'Fifty miles' road-work this day . . . a punisher'. 3. A farrier who visits forges and cadges from his fellows without doing any work or rendering any service for the loan: London farriers': late C.19–20.

punishing, adj. Exhausting; handling severely; esp. hard-hitting: s. >, ca 1850, coll: 1819, Moore, 'An eye that plann'd punishing deeds'; in boxing, 1820, J. H. Reynolds; in cricket, 1846; *Field*, 28 Jan. 1882, 'Each course today was of the most punishing kind.'

punishment. Severe handling, orig. that dealt out by a cricketer or a boxer: s. >, ca 1890, coll: 1846, W. Denison (Lewis); 1856, H. H. Dixon. 2. Pain; misery: coll and dial.: from mid-C.19.

Punjab head, have a. To be forgetful; *Punjab head*, forgetfulness: Anglo-Indian, esp. Indian Army's: from the 1880s. An allusion to the (supposed) fact that service in the Punjab saps the memory.

punk. A punctured tyre: cyclists': late C.19–20; ob. cf.:

punk, v. To puncture (a tyre): cyclists': late C.19–20; ob. cf. the n.

punker. A frequenter of (S.E.) *punks* or harlots: ca 1735–1800. Addison.

punse. The female pudend: Yiddish and low London: late C.19–20.

punt. An occ. C.19 variant of POONA, £1.

punt, v. To act as a decoy: auctioneers' (—1891). See PUNTER, 1. Prob. ex: 2. To bet upon a race, etc.: 1873, implied in PUNTER; *Pall Mall Gazette*, 13 Sept. 1887. Ex punting at faro, baccarat, etc. 3. Hence, to be a purchaser, to buy something: grafters': late C.19–20. cf. sense 4 of PUNTER.

punt-about. An irregular form of football: Charterhouse coll (—1900). A. H. Tod. cf. SHOOTABOUT.

punter. An auctioneer's decoy or mock-bidder: auctioneers': from ca 1880. See esp. *Answers*, 2 April 1891. Prob. suggested by PUNTING. 2. An outsider betting on horses in a small way: s. (—1874) >, by 1900, coll. 3. Hence, a small-scale speculator 'watching the fluctuations in speculative securities' (A. J. Wilson); from the early 1890s: s. >, by 1910, coll. 4. (Prob. ex sense 2.) A grafter's customer, client, or victim: grafters': late C.19–20. Ex PUNT, v., 3.

punting. (Gen. of an outsider) a betting on horse-races: from ca 1873. See PUNT, v., 2.

punting-shop. A gambling den: 1874, H., 5th ed. cf. PUNT, v., 2.

pup. A pupil: school and college s.: 1871, 'M. Legrand'. Jocularly approximated to *pup* = a puppy. cf. PUPE.

pup, v. To be brought to childbed: low coll: from ca 1860. (As a BITCH.)

pup, in. Pregnant: low coll: from ca 1860. As a BITCH: cf. PUP, v.

pup, sell a. To swindle, v.i. Gen. *sell one a pup*. c. >, ca 1905, gen. coll: late C.19–20, though not recorded before 1901, *Daily Chronicle*, 4 May, 'There is a poetical phrase in our language, "to sell a man a pup".' cf. SEE A MAN *about a dog*.

pupe. A pupil-room: Eton College: mid-C.19–20. cf. PUP, n.

***puppy,** n. and adj. (A) blind (man): c. > low s.: from ca 1850; ob. Mostly U.S. (e.g. in Matsell). Ex the blindness of new-born puppies.

puppy-dog. A puppy: children's coll: late C.16–20. Shakespeare.

puppy-match. A snare: coll: ca 1690–1750. J. Smyth's *Scarronides*, 'He . . . might catch | Us Trojans in a puppy-match.' ?ex the stealing of puppies.

puppy's mamma, see DOG'S LADY.

pupsie, pupsy. A puppy: a children's coll: C.17–20. Cotgrave. cf. POPSY.

***purchase.** Stolen goods; booty: c.: late C.16–mid-17. Greene; Shakespeare. 2. Those from whom it is taken: c.: late C.16–early 17. Greene, 1592.

***pure.** A mistress, esp. a kept mistress; a wanton: ca 1685–1830: c. >, ca 1750, low s.: 1688, Shadwell, 'Where's . . . the blowing that is to be my natural, my convenient, my pure?' By antiphrasis. 2. A 'pure' physician, a 'pure' surgeon. (i.e. the one, not the other; not a general practitioner.) Medical coll: 1827, *Lancet*. 3. 'Dog's-dung is called pure, from its cleansing and purifying properties,' Mayhew: coll >, ca 1905, j.: 1851.

pure, adj. Excellent; splendid: very pleasant. (Indeed, a gen. intensive.) ca 1675–1900, though ob. by 1850; it is, however, extant in several diall. Wycherley, 1675; Cibber, 1704, 'She looks as if my master had quarrelled with her . . . This is pure'; Henley & Stevenson, 1884, 'O, such manners are pure, pure, pure!' cf. PURELY. 2. See PURE AND . . .

***pure, purest.** 'A Top-Mistress, or Fine Woman', B.E.; 'a courtezan of high fashion', Grose: ca 1690–1830: c. >, ca 1750, (low) s. Ex PURE, n., 1.

pure and . . . (another adj.). Nice, or fine, and . . .; also quasi-adverbially, excellently, very well, thoroughly. 1742, Fielding, '[The hogs] were all pure and fat': coll >, ca 1840, dial.

pure-finder. A street collector of dogs' dung: coll from ca 1850; in C.20, j.; slightly ob. Mayhew, 1851. See PURE, n., 3.

pure Merinoes, see MERINOES, PURE.

purely. Excellently; very well: 1695, Congreve: s. >, ca 1750, coll. Hood.

purge. Beer: military and low gen.: from ca 1870. cf. the barrack-room c.p. rhyme, recorded by F. & H. in 1902, *Comrades, listen while I urge; | Drink, yourselves, and pass to purge.* Copious liquid prevents costiveness.

purger or **perger.** A teetotaller; hence, a pejorative: ca 1860–1920: low. Vance, ca 1864, in *The Chickaleary Cove*, 'My tailor serves you well, from a purger to a swell.' ?one who, to keep himself fit, takes laxatives or purges instead of beer: cf. PURGE.

puritan, Puritan. A whore: coll: C.18. Prob. ex Puritans' reputed hypocrisy.

purko. Beer: military: ca 1870–1910. Ex the name of the makers, Barclay, **Perkins** and Co. Perhaps influenced by PURGE and suggested by PERKINS.

purl. A fall, or a dive, head foremost or head over heels: 1825, *Sporting Magazine*: s. >, ca 1870 coll. Ex S.E. *purl*, to whirl or spin round. cf. PURLER and:

purl, v.i. and v.t. To turn head over heels: coll and dial.: 1856, Reade. Ex the n. 2. To dive: Winchester College: late C.19–20. Ex the n.

purler. A headlong fall; a throw head foremost; a knock-down blow, esp. a blow that casts one head foremost: coll: 1867, Ouida, in her best-known story, *Under Two Flags*. Ex PURL, v., influenced by PURL, n. Variant *pirler*; *pirl* is frequent in dial. for the preceding pair of terms.

purple, adj. Glorious; ROYAL: coll, 1894, *Pall Mall Gazette*, 20 Dec., 'A purple time of it'. Ex the purple of royal robes (cf. *born in the purple*).

purple. Blood: Scottish: 1804, Couper, *Poetry*; ob. cf. CLARET.

purpose, a- or **o'.** On purpose: S.E. (gen. *a purpose*) >, ca 1790, dial. and low coll.

purpose as the geese slur upon the ice (or **as to give a goose hay), to as much.** Uselessly: semi-proverbial coll: late C.17–19, C.18–20. cf. *to no more purpose than to beat your heels against the ground* or *wind.*

purposes, for (e.g. **dancing**). For (e.g.) dancing: coll, tautological: late C.19–20.

purr, n. 'A rushing-in, Lancashire fashion, with the head against the opponent's guts', Bee, 1823: pugilistic: ca 1810–50. It causes the opponent to *purr* or grunt.

purr, v. To kick (a person), esp. with clogs: Lancashire: late C.19–20.

purse. The female pudend: low coll: C.17–20. (Beaumont & Fletcher.)

purse, v.i. To take purses; to steal: late C.16–17: low coll (?orig. s.). Lyly, 1592. Beaumont & Fletcher, in *The Scornful Lady*, 'Why I'll purse: if that raise me not, I'll bet at bowling alleys.'

purse, no money in his. Impotent: low: C.19–20. Ex PURSE, n.

purse a purgation, give a person's. To take money from one: coll: ca 1540–80. Heywood.

purse-catcher, -emptier, -lifter, -snatcher. A stealer of purses: s. or coll verging on S.E.: resp. C.17, C.17, late C.19–20, late C.19–20.

purse-finder. A harlot: low: C.19–20, ob.

purse-proud. Lecherous; amorous: low: C.18–20, ob. See PURSE, n.

***pursenets.** c. of ca 1608–1830: 'Goods

taken upon Trust by young Unthrifts at treble the Value', B.E.; but first in Dekker. cf. the dial. *purse-net*, the movable net in which ducks are snared, and RABBIT-SUCKER. 2. Also, though prob. in the singular form: a small purse: ca 1690–1750: app. likewise c.

purser's. Contemptuous or derisive in PURSER'S DIP, an undersized candle; *purser's quart* (Smollett), a short quart; etc.: nautical coll: C.18–20; slightly ob. Because a purser, i.e. ship's storekeeper and treasurer, was often dishonest. cf.:

purser's (gen. pusser's) crabs. Navy uniform boots, with toe-caps: naval: late C. 19–20: Bowen. See CRAB-SHELLS.

purser's (gen. pusser's) dagger. A service clasp-knife: naval: late C.19–20. cf.:

purser's (gen. pusser's) dip. A candle: nautical: mid-C.19–20; slightly ob.

purser's (gen. pusser's) dirk. Same as PURSER'S DAGGER: naval: late C.19–20.

purser's (gen. pusser's) grin. A hypocritical grin; a sarcastic sneer: nautical coll: C.19–20; ob. Esp. in the c.p., *there are no half laughs or purser's grins about me*; *I'm right up and down like a yard of pump water*.

purser's grind. A coïtion bringing the woman no money but some consolation in the size or potency of the member: low nautical: mid-C.19–20.

purser's name. A false name: nautical coll >, in C.20, S.E.: C.19–20; ob. Ex false name given to the purser by a passenger travelling incognito.

purser's (gen. pusser's) pack. The Slop Chest: naval coll: late C.19–20.

purser's pump. A siphon, because prominent in a purser's stores; a bassoon, 'from its likeness to a syphon', Grose, 1788: nautical of ca 1785–1890.

purser's shirt on a handspike(, like a). (Of clothes) ill-fitting: nautical: C.19–20; ob.

purser's (gen. pusser's) stocking. A metaphorical article in the Slop Chest: naval: mid-C.19–early 20.

purser's (gen. pusser's) tally. A name assumed by a seaman, esp. if naval: (naval) coll: C.19.

purser's (gen. pusser's) yellow. Naval soap: naval coll: late C.19–20.

purting glumpot. A sulky person: dial. and low coll: from ca 1850. Ex *glum*, gloomy, and dial. *purt*, to sulk.

push, n. A thronging, a crowd, of people: low s. (perhaps orig. c.) >, in C.20, gen. s.: 1718, C. Hitchin, 'A push, alias an accidental crowd of people'; Vaux, 1812, 'When any particular scene of crowding is alluded to, they (the underworld) say, the push . . . at the . . . doors; the push at the . . . match.' Ex the inevitable pushing and jostling. 2. Hence, a gang or a group of convicts, as in Davitt's *Prison Diary*, 1888; or a band of thieves, as in Anon., '*No. 747*', reference to the year 1845; or, in Australia, a gang of LARRIKINS, as in the *Melbourne Argus*, 26 July 1890, and esp. in Morris's dictionary: in C.19, c.; in C.20, low s., as indeed the 'larrikins' sense was from the first. 3. A robbery; a swindle; a dealing out of profits: c.: from ca 1860; slightly ob. Not unnaturally ex sense 2. 4. See PUSH, DO A. 5. Mostly in *give* or *get the push*. A dismissal, esp. from employment: from ca 1870: s. Anon., ca 1875, 'The girl that stole my heart has given me the push.'

push, adj. Stylish, smart; (of clothes) best, splendid: university s. by 1903, when P. G. Wodehouse, in *Tales of St Austin's*, says of a brightly coloured waistcoat that it is 'quite the most push thing at Cambridge'. This is the earliest form of *posh*, adj., and may itself be ex POSH n., 2, or possibly a corruption of Scottish *tosh*, clean, neat, trim.

push, v. See PUSH OFF and PUSHED. 2. v.i. (occ. **push on**), rarely v.t., to coït (with): low coll, gen. of the male: C.18–20. Robertson of Struan.

push, do a. To coït: low, gen. of the male: late C.19–20. 2. See DO A PUSH.

push, stand the. (Of a woman) to coït: coll: C.18–19. cf. PUSH, DO A.

push about the bottle. To drink heavily: naval officers': ca 1790–1870.

push-cycle. A foot-propelled bicycle, as opposed to a motor-cycle: coll: from ca 1904.

push-cyclist. A bicyclist, opp. to a motor-cyclist: coll: from ca 1905.

push off. To depart: mid-C.18–20. Semantics: pushing off a boat. *Sessions*, May 1740 (trial of Eliz. Pooley), 'He . . . heard somebody cursing and swearing and a woman . . . say, *d–n it*, *push off*, or *go off*.'

push one's barrow. To move on, away; to depart: mostly costers': from ca 1870.

push out the boat, see BOAT, PUSH OUT THE.

push-penny. A coll variant (—1903) of SHOVE-HALFPENNY.

push-pin, occ. **-pike, play at; play at put-pin.** To coït: low coll: resp. C.17–18, late C.17–18, and mid-C.16–mid-18. Rycharde's

Misogonus, 1560; Massinger, 1623, 'She would never tell | Who play'd at pushpin with her'; Ned Ward, 1707, 'When at push-a-pike we play | With beauty, who shall win the day?' cf. PUSH, V., 2; PUSH, DO A; and PUSHING-SCHOOL.

pushed. Short of money: coll: from ca 1825. Abbr. *pushed for money*. 2. Drunk: ca 1870–1910. Perhaps ex the tendency to fall; cf.:

pushed?, did she fall or was she. A c.p. dating from ca 1908, orig. applied to a girl losing her virginity. A woman named Violet Charlesworth was found dead near Beachy Head at the foot of the cliff. Suicide was at first presumed, but later a suggestion of foul play was made and the newspaper headline appeared 'Did she fall or was she pushed?' The innuendo caught the public fancy and for a long time the phrase was used on every possible and impossible occasion.

pusher. A fledgeling canary unable to feed itself: ca 1690–1750. Perhaps because it pushes with its bill. 2. A girl, a woman: low. Also SQUARE-PUSHER, a virtuous girl. See also SQUARE-PUSHING. Late C. 19–20. 3. A blucher boot: shoemakers': from ca 1860. 4. A finger of bread used as a feeding-implement: nursery coll: from ca 1880. 5. In pickpocketry, he who pushes the prospective victim against the actual thief: c.: late C.19–20.

pushing-school. A brothel: low: late C.17–19. Ex the S.E. sense, a fencing-school: cf. also PUSH, V., 2, and PUSH, DO A.

***pushing-tout.** A thieves' scout or watchman that brings intelligence of an accidental crowd or assemblage: c.: C.18. C. Hitchin, 1718.

puss. The female pudend: low: C.17–20. Cotton, 'Aeneas, here's a Health to thee, | To Pusse and to good company.' Also, in C.19–20, *pussy*, *pussy-cat*. 2. A cadet of the Royal Military Academy: ca 1820–80. Ex the short jacket with pointed tail. Also *pussy*. 3. A hare: coll: late C.19–20.

puss-in-boots. A swaggerer: military: from ca 1908. Ex the fairy tale.

pusser's crabs, dagger, dip, dirk, grin, pack, stocking, tally and yellow, see PURSER'S, etc.

pusserpock. Bad, hard salt-meat: naval (—1909); ob. A corruption of *purser's pork*, the purser being the purchaser.

pussy, see PUSS.

put. A rustic; a dolt: 1688, Shadwell; Grose (*country put*, a frequent variant): s. until ca 1750, then coll until ca 1830, then S.E. and archaic. The discrimination of *put*, a blockhead, and *country put*, a bumpkin, is logical: but the distinction cannot be pressed. 2. Hence, loosely, a chap, fellow: coll: ca 1800–30. Gen. applied, somewhat contemptuously, to elderly persons: cf. Thackeray in *Vanity Fair*, I, xi, 'The captain ... calls [his father] an old put.' 3. A harlot: ?C.17–18: F. & H., but who else?! (Ex Fr. *putain*, a whore.) 4. See:

put, do a; have a put-in. To coït: low coll: C.19; C.19–20 (ob.).

put, play at two-handed. To coït: low: C. 18–early 19. cf. PUSH-PIN.

put (or lay) a churl upon a gentleman, see CHURL ...

put a hat (up)on a hen. To attempt the impossible: proverbial coll: mid-C.17–mid-19. Ray.

put a nail in (a person's) **coffin.** To talk ill of: tailors': mid-C.19–20.

put a new face (or head) on. To disfigure by punching; hence, to get the better of: U.S. (—1870), anglicized by 1890.

put a poor mouth on (a position). To complain (moaningly) about: Anglo-Irish (—1884).

put a steam on the table. To earn enough money to obtain a hot Sunday dinner: lower classes': from ca 1860. Ware, 'Refers chiefly to boiled food'.

put-away. An appetite; a (considerable) capacity for food or drink: low: late C.19–20. Ex the v., 1. 2. Imprisonment: late C.19–20; ob. Ex the v., 2. 3. An information to the police: (c. or) low s.: late C.19–20. Ex the v., 3.

put away, v.t. To eat, drink, gen. in large quantities: 1878, Besant & Rice, 'I never saw a man put away such an enormous quantity of provisions at one time.' 2. To put in gaol: s. >, in C.20, coll: 1883 (O.E.D.). 3. To inform against: (c. or) low s.: from ca 1890; app. orig. Australian. 4. To pawn: s.: 1887, *Daily News*, 22 Oct. 5. To kill: coll: 1847, Anne Brontë.

put away proper. To give a good funeral: lower-classes' coll: late C.19–20.

put down. To eat: lower classes', esp. Cockney coll (—1909). 2. To cash (a cheque): c., and police s.: late C.19–20.

put down south, see SOUTH.

put 'em up! Raise your arms!: from ca 1860: coll. 2. Put up your fists!: coll: late C.19–20. A variant is *stick 'em up!*, in both senses. Contrast PUT IT UP!

put-in, n., see PUT, DO A.

put in, v. To pass (a period of time), gen. at or with the help of some occupation: coll: C. G. Gibson, 1863.

***put in a hole.** To defraud: c.: from ca 1860. A variant of *put in the* HOLE.

put in one's eye, as much as one can. (Virtually) nothing: coll: late C.17–early 19.

put in one's motto. To LAY DOWN THE LAW; butt rashly into a conversation: low coll: from ca 1880.

put in pie. To spoil or bungle (a thing), lead (a person) astray: printers' (—1887); ob. Ex the jumble of printers' pie.

***put in the garden, hole, peg, pin,** or **well.** See at the nn.

put in the pudden club, see PUDDEN CLUB, PUT IN THE.

put it in, v.i. To achieve intromission: perhaps rather a S.E. approximation to euphemism than a coll: when, however, there is no thought, intention or subconscious impulse towards euphemism, it may be considered a coll and not, from the psychological nature of the case, S.E.

put it on, v. i. To SHOW OFF: late C.19–20. Prob. ex *put on airs.* 2. v.t. To extract money from (a person) by threats, lying or whining: low London: late C.19–20. *People*, 6 Jan. 1895.

put it on her. To drive a ship hard in a strong breeze: nautical coll (sailing-ships'): mid-C.19–20. The *it* = her set of sails.

put it over, see PUT OVER.

put it there! Shake hands: coll: late C.19–20. Mostly Colonial.

put it up! Have done!; stop!; shut up!: low (—1859); †by 1910.

put it where the monkey put the nuts! Go to blazes!: a low c.p.: late C.19–20. An elaboration of the low familiar S.E. *stick it up your arse!*

put off. To disconcert, disturb: s. (—1909).

put-on. A deception, subterfuge, excuse: coll: from ca 1860. 2. An 'old woman mendicant who puts on a shivering and wretched look': c. or low (—1909). Ware.

put on, v. To begin to smoke: coll: prob. from ca 1870. It occurs in Conway Edwardes's play *Heroes*, 1876, 'Put on a smoke'. 2. To initiate (a person): coll: from ca 1860; ob.

put on a boss. To assume a malevolent look: low (—1909). Ware, 'Squinting suggests malevolence.' Ex BOSS-EYED.

put on a cigar. To assume gentility: lower classes': mid-C.19–20; ob.

put on the flooence (unnecessary spelling) or **fluence,** see FLUENCE. **put on the peg,** see PEG, PUT ON THE.

put on the pot. To give oneself airs: late C.19–20. See POT, n., 6.

put one's bones up; put up one's forks. To be prepared to fight: proletarian: from ca 1865.

***put one's forks down.** To pick a pocket: c.: mid-C.19–20; ob.

put one's hair in(to) a curl or **put a curl in one's hair.** To make one feel (very) fit: coll: from ca 1870; slightly ob.

put oneself outside. To eat; occ., to drink: from ca 1860. cf. *get* OUTSIDE OF.

***put out.** To kill: c. and low: late C.19–20. Ex:

***put out** (a person's) **light.** To kill: c. and low: 1884, *Graphic*, 24 Sept.

put over. To knock over with a shot, to kill: Australian: 1859. H. Kingsley; ob.

put 'paid' to, see 'PAID' TO.

put-pin, see PUSH-PIN.

put stuff on, see STUFF ON THE BALL.

put that in your pipe . . .! see PIPE AND SMOKE IT.

***put the gloves on.** To improve (a person): Scots c.: 1868; slightly ob.

put the lid on, see LID ON . . .

put the miller's eye out, see MILLER, DROWN THE.

put the pot on. To bet too much money on one horse: sporting: from ca 1820. See POT, n., 1.

put the strings on, see STRINGS ON.

put the traveller on, see TIP THE TRAVELLER.

put the value on. To sign (a canvas): artists' (—1909); ob.

put the windows in. To smash them: low urban (—1909).

put through. To succeed with (some plan, e.g.) by swindling: low: late C.19–20; ob. Ex the S.E. (orig. – 1847 – U.S.) sense, carry to a successful issue.

put to bed. To defeat: music-halls' (—1909); ob.

put to find. To put in prison: low (—1909).

put together with a hot needle and burnt thread. To fasten insecurely: ca 1660–1850: semi-proverbial coll.

***put-up.** A laying of information against a fellow-criminal: c. (—1823); ob. Bee, who implies that *put-up* serves also as n. to PUT UP, v., 2.

put up. To show, achieve, e.g. *a good fight*: coll: from ca 1890. *Field*, 30 Jan. 1892, 'Pettitt put up a good game.' 2. To plan in advance (a robbery, a swindle, a fraud): c.: from ca 1810. 3. Hence, to preconcert anything devious or underhand or disingenuous: from ca 1890. 'Barclay put up a job to ruin old Overton,' *Sporting and Dramatic News*, 13 Aug. 1892. 4. See PUT IT UP.

put up a stall. To act or speak misleadingly: low: late C.19–20. cf. STALL, n., 3.

***put-up job.** (The chief use of the adj. *put-up*.) A pre-arranged crime or deception: as the former, c. (from ca 1838); as the latter, s. A *put-up robbery* occurs in 1810, a *put-up affair* in 1812 (Vaux).

put up one's hat; put one's hat up. To pay serious court; often *put your hat up there!*, I see you mean to make one of the family: lower classes': late C.19–20.

put (a person) **up to.** To enlighten or forewarn about; inform of; instruct in: coll: 1812, Vaux. 2. To incite or excite to (some act, to do something); to induce, persuade (to do something): coll: 1824 (O.E.D.).

put your head in a bag! Be quiet: (low) coll: from ca 1890. A horse with its head in the nose-bag does not trouble about other things.

Putney!, go to. Go to the devil!: from ca 1840; ob. From ca 1850, occ. *go to Putney on a pig*, by a typical assonantal addition. Kingsley, 1863, 'Now, in the year 1845, telling a man to go to Putney was the same as telling a man to go to the deuce.' cf. BATH; HALIFAX; HONG-KONG; JERICHO.

putt. See PUT, n., 1, of which it is a C.17–18 variant.

***putter-up.** One who plans and prearranges robberies, frauds, swindles; esp. 'a man who travels about for the purpose of obtaining information useful to professional burglars', H., 5th ed.; also, in C.20, an instigator to crime: c. >, ca 1910, low s. and police coll: 1812, Vaux.

puttock. A whore; a greedy person: coll verging on S.E.: C.16–20.

putty. Money: mostly (?and orig.) U.S.: mid-C.19–20; ob. Prob. glaziers' at first. 2. A glazier, a house-painter; in the Navy, any painter rating: from ca 1820. Ex frequent use of putty. 3. Sticky mud at the bottom of a body of water: 1880, P. H. Emerson: dial. and s.

putty, could not fight. I am, he is, you are, etc., a very poor fighter (with one's hands); hence, also of, e.g., an army. Coll: late C. 19–20.

putty and plaster on the Solomon knob, the. Be silent!; the *Master*'s coming: a Freemasons' c.p. intimation: from ca 1870. Masonic punning on Masonic j.

putty and soap. Bread and cheese: low: ca 1830–80. *Sinks*, 1848.

***putty cove or covess.** An unreliable man or woman: c. of ca 1820–90. Ex softness of putty.

putty medal. (A satirical recommendation to) a reward for mischief, incompetence, or injury: non-aristocratic coll: 1856, says Ware, who adds: 'No medal at all'.

putty wallah. A messenger or orderly attached to an office: Bombay: mid-C.19–20.

puv. A field: chimney-sweeps': C.19. (George Elson, *The Last of the Climbing Boys*, 1900.) Ex the synonymous Romany *phuv*, itself related to Sanskrit *bhumi*.

puz(z). A young man about town: London Society: ca 1760–80. cf. PIZ.

puzzle the monkey. A coll variant, since ca 1880, of S.E. *monkey-puzzle* (the *Araucaria imbricata*).

puzzle-cause; *-cove. A lawyer: resp. coll of ca 1780–1830; c. or low of ca 1830–1900, mostly U.S. (Matsell). But while *p.-cove* = any lawyer, *p.-cause* is one 'who has a confused understanding'. cf. PUZZLE-TEXT.

puzzle-headed spoon. An Apostle spoon: C.19: coll.

puzzle-text. A clergyman; esp. 'an ignorant, blundering parson', Grose, 1st ed., 1785: ob. by 1830. †by 1870. cf. PUZZLE-CAUSE.

puzzling arithmetic. A statement of the odds: gamblers' coll (? > j.): C.17. Webster, 1613, 'Studying a puzzling arithmetic at the cockpit'.

***puzzling-sticks.** The triangle to which culprits were tied for flagellation: (prob. c. >) low s.: 1812, Vaux; †by 1870.

pyah. Weak; paltry, inferior; useless: mainly nautical (—1864). Ex *pariah*.

pye. A contraction of *pariah-dog*: Anglo-Indian military (—1886).

pygostole. An 'M.B.' coat or waistcoat: Church: 1844. Lit. rump-stole, ex Gr. πυγή.

pyke; occ. pike. A civilian that stands an impecunious soldier a drink: military: ca 1870–1910. ?ex Fr. s. *pékin*, a civilian.

pyke off, see PIKE, V.

pysoe. A close-fisted seaman: nautical: late C.19–20. Cognate with †Scottish *pyster*, to hoard up.

pyze. A variant of *pize*: see PIZE ON.

Q

***q,** see LETTER Q.

q, que, cue, kue, not worth a. Of negligible value: coll > S.E.: C.16. Skelton, 'That lyberte was not worth a cue.' Ex *q*, half a farthing. 2. See P AND Q; PS AND QS.

Q.b.b. A Queen's bad bargain: reign of Queen Victoria: coll. cf. K.b.b., and see BAD BARGAIN. Also (*K.h.b.* and) *Q.h.b.*, Queen's hard bargain, as in the *Cornhill Magazine*, Feb. 1865. cf. *Queen's* or *King's bad shilling*.

q (or Q) in a corner. Something not at once seen but brought to subsequent notice: legal: from ca 1870; ob. Perhaps = *query in a corner*, suggested by the old game of *Q in the corner* (prob., puss in the corner). cf.:

Q-in-the-corner cove. A keen (and cautious?) follower of boxing: pugilistic: ca 1815–60. *Boxiana*, IV, 1824, 'Great doubts have been expressed by the "Q-in-the-corner coves", whether Randall is *actually well*, or only "patched up".' Here, *Q* app. = 'query' or 'question'.

Q.S. QUEER STREET: non-aristocratic: late C.19–20; ob.

q.t. (or Q.T.), on the; or on the strict q.t. On the quiet: resp. ca 1870, 1880. Anon., *Broadside Ballad*, 1870, 'Whatever I tell you is on the Q.T.'

***qua; qua-keeper.** A prison; a gaoler: c. of late C.18–early 19. Tufts (dict. of flash), 1798. I suspect an error for *quad* = *quod*.

quack. A pretended doctor: 1659 (O.E.D.): coll till C.19, then S.E. Abbr. QUACKSALVER. See esp. the essay entitled 'Quacks and Quackery' in my *Literary Sessions*. 2. A duck: late C.19–20. More often, QUACK-QUACK. cf. QUACKING-CHEAT.

quack, v. Play the quack (see the n., 1): C.17–20: coll till C.19, then S.E. 2. To change (the title of a book), v.t.: C.18: booksellers'. Centlivre, 1715, 'He has an admirable knack at quacking titles ... When he gets an old good-for-nothing book, he claps a new title to it, and sells off the whole impression in a week.' Ex *quack*, to palm off as a quack would.

quack, in a. In a mere moment: Scots coll: from ca 1840.

quack-quack. A duck: an echoic nursery coll: recorded 1865 (O.E.D.), but prob. – as indeed with all such words – used much earlier. cf. BOW-WOW.

quacker. A duck: coll: C.19–20. cf. QUACK, n., 2, and:

***quacking-cheat.** A duck: c.: from ca 1565; †by 1860. See CHEAT.

quacksalver. A pretended doctor: 1579, Gosson: coll till ca 1660, then S.E.; ob. One who sells his salves by quacking (noisy patter). cf. QUACK, n., 1.

***quad.** A prison: c.: late C.18–20. Also and much more gen. QUOD. Prob. ex *quadrangle*. 2. A **quad**rangle: 1820 (O.E.D.): Oxford s. >, ca 1860, gen. coll. Trollope, 'The quad, as it was familiarly called ...' 3. A horse: low: 1845, '*No. 747*' (p. 416); 1885, *English Illustrated Magazine*, April, 'The second rider ... got his gallant quad over, and ... went round the course alone.' Abbr. *quadruped*. 4. A bicycle for four: 1888 (O.E.D.). Abbr. *quadruple*. 5. A **quad**rat: printers': from ca 1880: coll >, by 1890, j. 6. Hence, a (printer's) joke: printers': 1884.

quaedam. A harlot: cultured coll: late C.17–18. Hacket. Lit., a certain woman: cf. *one of those*, euphemistic for a harlot.

quaegemes or **quae-gemes.** A bastard: coll: C.18–early 19.

quail, a harlot, or a courtesan – C.17–early 18 – may orig. have been coll or even s., but it is gen. treated as S.E.: cf., however, PHEASANT and PLOVER. C.17–18. Motteux, 'With several coated quails, and lac'd mutton, waggishly singing'. Ex the bird's supposed amorousness. It is interesting to note that in U.S. university s. (now ob.), *quail* is a girl student.

quail-pipe. A woman's tongue: late C.17–19. 2. The throat: late C.17–18 (Dryden, Pope): on border-line between coll and S.E., the O.E.D. treating it as the latter. Ex the pipe with which quail are decoyed.

quail-pipe boot. (Gen. in pl.) A rather coll or illiterate form of *quill-p. b.*: C.17–18.

quaint. In C.14–15, *queinte* or *queynte*; in C.15–16, also *quaynt*(*e*). The female pudend: C.14–20: in C.14–16, a vulg.; in C.17–20, dial., now † except in parts of the North Country, where ob. Florio, '*Conno*, a woman's privie parts or quaint, as Chaucer calls it.' If not a mere variant of, certainly cognate with CUNT: 'Chaucer may have combined Old French *coing* with M.E. *cunte*, or he may have been influenced by the Old Fr. adjective *coint*, neat, dainty, pleasant,' Grose, P., q.v. for fuller discussion.

quake-breach or **-buttock.** A coward; dolt; sot: coll verging on S.E.: late C.16–17.

Quaker. A member of the Society of Friends: 1653, H. R., (title) *A Brief Relation of the Irreligion of the Northern Quakers* (O.E.D.): coll until ca 1810, then S.E., but never recognized, though in mid-C.19–20 often used, by the Society. Orig. a pejorative nickname, ex supposed 'agitations in preaching', Grose. 2. A rope or lump of excrement: low: C.(?18–)19. cf.:

Quaker, bury a. To defecate: low: C.(?18–)19. See QUAKER, 2.

Quaker's bargain. A '*yea* or *nay*' bargain; a 'take it or leave it' transaction: coll: late C.18–19. Ex the well-known directness, reliability and integrity of the Quakers.

Quaker's or Quakers' burying-ground. A privy; a w.c.: low: C.19. Ex QUAKER, 2.

***quaking cheat.** A calf; a sheep: c. of ca 1560–1850. See CHEAT.

qual. Abbr. *the* QUALITY: s.: Ned Ward, 1715.

qualified. Damned, bloody, etc.: euphemistic coll: 1890, Kipling, 'He was ... told not to make a qualified fool of himself.'

qualify, v.i. To coït: cultured s.: late C.19. ?ex *qualify as a man.*

quality, the. The gentry: late C.17–20: S.E. until ca 1830, then dial. and low coll. Mrs Centlivre notably omits *the*; A. Trollope, 1857, 'The quality, as the upper classes in rural districts are designated by the lower ...' Whence:

quality hours, the. Late hours for rising and for eating: lower classes' ironic coll: mid-C.19–20.

qually. (Of wine) 'Turbulent and Foul', B.E.: late C.17–mid-18: coll rapidly > j. ?*cloudy* corrupted.

quamino or **Q.** A Negro on shipboard: nautical: mid-C.19–20. ?ex a Negro name. cf. QUASHEE.

quandary. A state of perplexity; the difficulty causing it: coll till C.19, then S.E.: 1579, Lyly, 'Leaving this olde gentleman in a great quandarie'. Occ., C.17–early 18, as a v.: the Rev. T. Adams (d. 1655), 'He quandaries whether to go forward to God, or ... to turn back to the world.' The O.E.D. concerning the etymology, rejects M.E. *wandreth*, abbr. *hypochondry*, and Grose's and Baumann's *qu'en dirai-je?* Prob. L. *quam dare?* or *quando dare?*, less likely *quantum dare?*

quantum. A drink: from ca 1870; very ob. Ex S.E. sense, a sufficiency.

quantum suff. Enough: coll: C.19–20; slightly ob. J. Beresford, 1806; 1871, Anon., *The Siliad*, 'I, too, O comrade, *quantum suff.* would cry.' Ex the medical formula in prescriptions: *quant*(*um*) *suff*(*icit*), 'as much as suffices'.

quarrel-picker. A glazier: coll (?orig. s.): late C.17–18. A pun on *quarrel*, a small pane of glass, ex Old Fr. (cf. *carreau*).

***quarrom(e)** or **-s; quarron** or **-s.** A or the body: c. of ca 1565–1830. Harman and Grose, *quarromes*; Brome and B.E., *quarron*; Anon., *The Maunderer's Praise* ..., 1707, *quarrons*. Perhaps ex Fr. *charogne* or It. *carogna.*

quarry. The female pudend: C.18–19: coll, bordering on S.E. euphemism.

quart. A quart-pot, esp. as a drinking vessel: Australian coll: late C.19–20. Perhaps ex Devonshire usage (1865: E.D.D.).

quart-mania. Delirium tremens (cf. GALLON-DISTEMPER): ca 1860–1910.

quart-pot tea. Tea brewed over an open fire in a tin pot holding a quart: Australian coll: Mrs H. Jones, *Long Years in Australia*, 1878; 1885, Finch-Hatton, *Advance Australia*; ob.

quarter-decker. An officer with manners (much) better than his seamanship: naval coll: from ca 1865; slightly ob. Ex deck used by superior officers and/or cabin-passengers. Like the next, recorded first in Admiral Smyth's *Sailor's Word-Book*, 1867. cf. QUEEN'S PARADE.

quarter-deckish. Punctilious: naval coll: from ca 1865; slightly ob. Ex preceding.

quarter flash and three-parts foolish. A fool with a smattering of worldly knowledge: c.p.: ca 1815–50. Pierce Egan, *London*, 1821.

quarter of a sec!, (wait) a. A Society intensification of *half a* SEC!: ca 1900–14.

quarter pound bird's eye. A quarter-ounce of tobacco: lower classes' (—1909).

quarter sessions! A jocose form of swearing: legal coll (—1909).

quarter-sessions rose. A 'perpetual' rose: gardeners' coll: from ca 1880. Ex the Fr. *rose de quatre saisons*, i.e. all the year round.

***quarter stretch.** Three months' imprisonment: c.: (?)from ca 1815. See STRETCH, n., 2.

quartered, see RIDER, 2. A coll.

quartereen. A farthing: (low) theatrical and showmen's: from ca 1850. (cf. QUATRO.) Perhaps suggested by U.S. *quarteroon*, a quadroon, but more prob. by the It. *quattrino.*

quarterer. Four, esp. in *quarterer saltee*, four-pence: Parlary: mid-C.19–20. Ex It. *quattro.*

quartern of bliss. A small, attractive woman: low London: from ca 1882; ob. cf. POT OF BLISS.

quarto; Mr Quarto. A bookseller; a publisher: coll: mid-C.18–mid-19.

quashee, -e; occ. **quassy.** A Negro; above all, a Negro seaman from the British West Indies; esp. as a nickname: coll: from ca 1830. e.g. Michael Scott, 'I say, quashie.' Ex a Negro proper name.

quat. A contemptuous pejorative applied to a (gen. young, nearly always male) person: early C.17. Shakespeare, Webster. Ex *quat*, a pimple.

quat, go to. To defecate: low coll: C.19–20; very ob. Ex *quat*, to squat.

quatch, as in Shakespeare's *quatch-buttock*, may be coll and may = flat.

quatro. Four: from ca 1850: Parlary. Ex It. *quattro*. cf. QUARTERER.

quaver. A musician: low coll or s.: from ca 1860; ob.

quean; incorrectly **queen.** A homosexual, esp. one with girlish manners and carriage: low: late C.19–20; ob. except in Australia. Prob. ex *quean*, a harlot, influenced by *Queenie*, a girl's name, and dial. *queanish*, effeminate. cf. QUEANIE.

Quean Street, see QUEEN STREET.

queanie; incorrectly **queenie.** A NANCY: late C.19–20: Australian. See QUEAN.

queen, see QUEAN.

Queen Anne – Queen Elizabeth – my Lord Baldwin – is dead. A c.p. retort on old news: coll: resp. 1722; C.18, e.g. in Swift; ca 1670–1710, as in Ray. A ballad of 1722, cited by Apperson, 'He's as dead as Queen Anne the day after she dy'd'; Barham. Swift, 'What news, Mr Neverout? *Neverout*. Why, Madam, Queen Elizabeth's dead.' The first was occ., ca 1870–1910, elaborated to *Queen Anne is dead and her bottom's cold*. cf. the Yorkshire *Queen Anner*, 'an old-fashioned tale; a tale of former times'.

Queen Anne's fan. Fingers to nose: coll: mid-C.19–20; ob. See SIGHT, 5.

Queen Dick, see DICK ... 2. **Queen Dick, to the tune of the life and death of.** To no tune at all. Late C.18–early 19 coll.

Queen Elizabeth. See QUEEN ANNE. 2. The street-door key: c.: ca 1860–1910. On BETTY.

Queen Elizabeth's pocket-pistol. 'A Brass Cannon of a prodigious Length at *Dover Castle*', B.E.: a coll nickname, ca 1680–1780. Smollett.

queen (or Queen) goes on foot or **sends nobody, where the.** A water-closet: low coll: ca 1860–1915.

queen of the dripping-pan. A cook: coll: from ca 1850; ob.

Queen Street, live in; or **at the sign of the Queen's Head.** To be governed by one's wife: coll: ca 1780–1850.

queenie. See QUEANIE. 2. *queenie!* A 'mock endearing name called after a fat woman trying to walk young': Cockney: 1884–ca 1914. Ex *Queenie, come back, sweet*, addressed in a Drury Lane pantomime of 1884 to H. Campbell, who, exceedingly fat, was playing Eliza, a cook.

Queen's Arms, The; or **The Hen and Chickens.** Home: commercial travellers': from ca 1890. It comes into conversations concerning hotels; thus: ' "Where do you stay in York?" "Oh, at The Queen's Arms (or, The Hen and Chickens)." ' With punning reference to wife or to wife and children.

Queen's bad or **hard bargain** or **bad shilling,** see Q.B.B. and BAD BARGAIN.

***Queen's bus** or, as in Baumann, **carriage.** A prison van: ca 1860–1901: c. (But *the King's bus* did not 'take on'.)

Queen's gold medal. (Gen *the.*) A shilling: lower classes' (—1887); †by 1902.

Queen's head. A postage stamp: (low) coll: ca 1840–1901. *King's head*, †by 1910. Moncrieff, *The Scamps of London*, 1843.

queen's or **Queen's parade.** The quarter-deck: naval coll: ca 1865–1901.

Queen's or **King's picture** or **portrait.** Money; coins: coll verging on S.E.: C.17–20; slightly ob. Brome; Ned Ward, 'Queen's pictures, by their features, | Charm all degrees of human creatures'; *Judy*, 27 April 1887. 2. A sovereign: C.19–20; ob. Mayhew.

Queen's pipe, see PIPE, HER MAJESTY'S. Orig. *Queen's tobacco-pipe.*

Queen's or **queen's stick.** A stately person: (low) coll: ca 1870–1910.

Queen's woman. (Gen. in pl.) A soldier's trull: military coll, bordering on S.E.: ca

1860–1905. A Royal Commission report of 1871.

***queer,** adj. (Orig. opp. to RUM, excellent, which in C.19–20 has approximated to *queer*.) Base, criminal; counterfeit; very inferior: c.: C.16–20. First in Scots, 1508, as = odd, eccentric, of questionable character, prob. coll (*not* c.) and soon > S.E., this sense being perhaps independent of the c. (not attested before 1561); by 1560 very gen. in Eng. c. Awdelay, as *quire*; Harman, *quyer*, of liquor; Dekker, *quier*; Fletcher the dramatist, *quere*; B.E., *queere*; *Spectator*, *queer*, as in Grose. Origin obscure, but perhaps ex *quire* = *choir*: Awdelay, 'A Quire bird is one that came lately out of prison': cf. Grose's definition of QUEER-BIRD, and see CANARY; or, as H. suggests, ex Ger. *quer*, crooked. 2. Not until C.19 do the derivative senses occur: drunk, 1800, W. B. Rhodes, 'We feel ourselves a little queer.' 3. Hence, unwell; giddy: s. from ca 1810, e.g. in Vaux. cf. QUEERY. 4. Unfavourable, inauspicious: coll: late C. 19–20. 5. Not honest; SHADY: coll: late C.19–20. 6. Shrewd; alert: c.: late C.18–early 19. But this may merge with preceding sense. 7. Of strange behaviour; (slightly) mad, orig. (*a bit*) *queer in the head*: coll: 1840, Dickens. This links with sense 3, but prob. deriving imm. ex *queer in one's attic*. (In gen., cf. the n. and v.; also the *queer* combinations and phrases.) For the relation of this word to RUM, see E. Partridge, 'Neither Cricket nor Philology' in *A Covey of Partridge*, 1937.

***queer,** n. Counterfeit money: c.: from ca 1810. Vaux; Egan, 1821, 'The dealer in Queer'. cf. SHOVER OF THE QUEER, a counterfeiter. 2. An inferior substitute for soot: dealers in soot: (low) s.: ca 1815–70. Egan in *Boxiana*, vol. ii. 3. A hoax, a quizzing: low: late C.18–20, ob. Ex the v., 1. 4. A look: low s. verging on c.: Henley & Stevenson, 1892, 'Have a queer at her phiz'; ob. 5. See QUEER, TIP THE, and QUEER, IN.

queer, v. To ridicule; to puzzle: from ca 1790: s.; ob. 2. To hoax; cheat: trick: evade: c. or low s.: late C.18–20. Anon., 1819, 'There's no queering fate, sirs.' 3. To spoil, ruin: from ca 1790: c. >, ca 1840, low s. cf. PITCH, QUEER THE. e.g. *queer the* OGLES, blacken someone's eyes. 4. Hence, 'to put (one) out; to make (one) feel queer', S.O.D.: 1845, W. Cory, 'Hallam was rather queered'; Hindley, 1876, 'Consumption was queering him.'

***queer, in.** Wrong, e.g. with the police: c.: late C.19–20.

***queer, shover of the,** see QUEER, n., 1.

Queer, Sir Quibble. 'A trifling silly shatter-brain'd Fellow', B.E.: late C.17–mid-18.

***queer, tip** (one) **the.** To pass sentence of imprisonment on: c.: from ca 1820; ob.

queer as a three-dollar bill. Very odd (or strange) indeed: Canadian: late C.19–20. 'There are no $3 bills' (Leechman).

queer as Dick's hatband, see DICK'S HATBAND.

***queer bail.** Fraudulent bail: c.: 1785, Grose; ob.

queer belch. Sour beer: low: ca 1825–70. *Sinks*, 1848.

***queer bird;** in C.16–mid-17, **quire bird.** One only recently out of gaol but already returned to crime: c.: mid-C.16–early 19. Awdelay. 2. An odd fellow: from ca 1840: s. cf. QUEER COVE.

***queer bit, cole, money, paper, screens, soft.** Base money, *q. paper* and *soft* obviously applying only to notes: resp. c., late C.18–20; late C.17–20, ob., c.; C.19, s. or low coll; C.19–20, low; C.19–20, c. (ob. in C.20); mid-C.19–20, c.

***queer bit-maker.** A coiner of counterfeit: c.: 1785, Grose; Ware. cf. QUEER COLE-MAKER.

queer bitch. 'An odd out-of-the-way fellow', Grose, 1785; recorded 1772; †by 1870.

***queer bluffer.** 'A sneaking, sharping, Cut-throat Ale-house or Inn-keeper', B.E.; 'the master of a public house, the resort of rogues and sharpers', Grose, 1st ed.: c.: late C.17–early 19. See also BLUFFER.

***queer booze.** Poor lap, SWIPES; 'small and naughtye drynke', Harman: c. >, ca 1750, low s.: ca 1560–1830. See also BOOZE.

***queer bung** or **boung.** An empty purse: c.: mid-C.17–early 19.

queer card, fellow, fish; in pl, also **queer cattle.** A person odd in manner, strange in opinion: coll: resp. C.19–20; 1712, *Spectator*; 1772, 'Gods are queer fish as well as men'; (gen. of women), 1894, G. Moore – but prob. much earlier – coll.

queer checker. A swindling box-keeper: low theatrical: late C.18–mid-19.

***queer clout.** 'A sorry, coarse, ord'nary or old Handkerchief, not worth *Nimming*' (i.e. stealing), B.E.: c.: late C.17–18.

***queer cole.** Counterfeit money: c.: from ca 1670. See QUEER BIT.

***queer-cole fencer.** A receiver, or utterer, of false money: c.: late C.17–19.

***queer cole-maker.** A counterfeiter: c.: late C.17–20; ob.

***queer cove.** A rogue: c.: late C.16–mid-19. 2. A strange fellow: low >, by 1900, gen. s.: from ca 1830. cf. QUEER BIRD.

***queer cramp-rings.** Bolts; fetters: c. (—1567); †by ca 1750.

***queer cuffin,** occ. **q. cuffen** or **cuffing;** even **cuffin quire** (Elisha Coles, 1676). A magistrate: c.: C.17–19. Dekker, 'Because he punisheth them belike' and 'Quier cuffin, that is to say, a Churle, or a naughty man', which gives the secondary sense, 'a churl', recorded by B.E. and Grose.

***queer cull.** 'A Fop, or Fool, a Codshead; also a shabby poor Fellow', B.E.: c.: late C.17–mid-19: c. See CULL.

***queer degen.** 'An Iron, Steel, or Brass-hilted Sword', B.E.; 'an ordinary sword', Grose, 1st ed. c. of ca 1670–1830. Opp. RUM DEGEN.

***queer diver.** A bungling pickpocket: c.: mid-C.17–early 19.

***queer doxy.** A jilting jade; an ill-dressed harlot: c.: mid-C.17–mid-18.

***queer drawers.** 'Yarn, coarse Worsted, ord'nary or old Stockings', B.E.: c.: late C.17–18.

***queer duke.** A decayed gentleman: a starveling: c.: mid-C.17–18.

***queer 'em** or **'um** or **'un; queerum.** The gallows: c.: ca 1820–60. Bee, 1823 (*queer 'em*); *Sonnets for the Fancy*, 1824, 'The queerum queerly smear'd with dirty black'. ?*queer them* or *queer one*.

queer fella, the. The person who happens to be in command: Regular Army: late C. 19–20.

queer fellow; queer fish, see QUEER CARD.

***queer fun.** A bungled trick or swindle: c.: late C.17–18.

***queer-gammed.** Very lame; crippled: c., in C.20 slightly ob. George Parker, 1789, 'Though fancy queer-gamm'd smutty Muns | Was once my fav'rite man.' See GAM, n., 2.

***queer gill.** A shabby fellow: c.: ca 1800–40. Ainsworth, in *Rookwood*, 1834, 'Rum gills and queer gills'. See GILL and cf. CULL.

queer in one's (occ. the) attic. A variant – ca 1820–1910 – of QUEER, adj., 7. Ex QUEER, adj., 3. 2. Hence, perverse, wrong-headed: low (—1887); ob.

***queer it,** see QUEER, v., 3. cf. PITCH, QUEER THE.

***queer ken.** A prison: c.: 1608, Dekker; Grose, †by 1850. 2. A house not worth robbing: c.: late C.17–18. Here, *queer* = worthless. cf.:

***queer-ken hall.** A prison: c.: 1610, Rowlands, who spells *quirken hall.* C.17; on *queer ken.* Prob. genuine c., but Rowlands often 'improved on' Dekker, who, although he used Harman somewhat *à la Molière*, prob. knew the underworld intimately.

***queer kicks.** 'Coarse, ord'nary or old Breeches', B.E.: c.: late C.17–early 19.

***queer money,** see QUEER BIT.

***queer mort.** 'A dirty Drab, a jilting Wench, a Pockey Jade', B.E.: c.: C.17–early 19. Grose (2nd ed.) records only 'a diseased strumpet'. Contrast RUM MORT.

***queer nab.** A shabby hat, or a cheap one: c.: late C.17–early 19. B.E., who uncompromisingly defines it as 'A Felt, Carolina, Cloth, or ord'nary Hat, not worth whipping off a Man's Head'.

***queer-ogled.** Squint-eyed: c. (—1887).

***queer on** or **to.** To rob; treat harshly: resp. c. and low s.: C.19–20; ob. cf. QUEER, v., 3, 4.

***queer paper,** see QUEER BIT.

***queer peeper.** An interior mirror: late C.17–18.

***queer peepers.** Squinting or dim-sighted eyes: c. >, by 1830, low s.: C.18–20; ob.

***queer place, the.** Prison: c.: late C.19–20. By euphemism. cf. QUEER KEN, 1.

***queer plunger.** One who works a faked rescue of a drowning man: c.: 1785, Grose. It applies both to the 'victim' and to the 'rescuer'. In order that the 'rescuer' WANGLE a guinea from a humane society; moreover, the supposed 'suicide' often got a small sum.

***queer prancer.** An inferior or a foundered horse: late C.17–early 19 c. B.E.; Grose, 1st ed., who records also 'a cowardly . . . horse-stealer': c.: late C.18–early 19.

queer put. 'An ill-looking, foolish fellow' (*Sinks*): low: prob. ca 1800–60.

***queer roost, dorse (or doss) or sleep (up-) on the.** To live together as supposed man and wife: c.: late C.18–mid-19.

***queer rooster.** A police spy residing among thieves: c.: 1785, Grose; †by 1890.

***queer-rums.** Confusing talk: c. of ca 1820–50. Lit., bad-goods.

***queer screen.** A forged bank-note: c. (—1812). cf. QUEER BIT.

***queer-shover** or **shover of the queer.** See QUEER, n., 1. From ca 1870.

***queer soft,** see QUEER BIT.

queer stick. A very odd, or incomprehensible, fellow: coll: late C.19–20. cf. dial. *rum stick* and the c. and dial. RUM DUKE.

queer start. A strange business: ca 1820–80: low >, by 1860, gen. Anon., *Autobiography of Jack Ketch*, 1836. See START, n., 3.

***Queer Street, in.** In a serious difficulty; very short of money: (—1811); c. >, ca 1840, s. >, ca 1890, coll. 1837, Lytton, 'You are in the wrong box – planted in Queer Street, as we say in London'; Dickens.

queer the pitch, see PITCH, QUEER THE.

queer the stifler, see STIFLER.

queer thing, the. A basket or sack hoisted in a Grand Banks schooner to recall the dories: fishermen's: late C.19–20. Bowen.

***queer to,** see QUEER ON.

***queer topping.** A frowsy or inferior wig or other head-dress: c.: late C.17–18.

***queer wedge.** Base gold or, more gen., silver: c.: ca 1800–60. 2. A large buckle, says Grose, in his 3rd ed.: c.: late C.18–early 19.

***queer whidding.** A scolding: c.: C.18–mid-19. Ex:

***queer whids.** Esp. in *cut queer whids*, to give evil words: c.: 1567, Harman. Ob.

queered. Tipsy: 1822, Scott, 'You would be queered in the drinking of a penny pot of malmsey.' †by 1850. See QUEER, adj., 2.

queerer. A quizzer, a hoaxer: ca 1810–50. Colman, 1812, 'These wooden wits, these quizzers, queerers, smokers'. Ex QUEER, v., 1.

queerish. Somewhat QUEER, in various senses: coll: mid-C.18–20. Also in dial.

***queerly.** Like a criminal: c.: late C.17–early 19.

***queerum,** see QUEER 'EM.

queery. Shaky: low, esp. boxing: ca 1820–70. Jones, *The True-Bottomed Boxer*, 1825.

queint(e), see QUAINT. **queme,** see QUIM.

quencher; frequently *a modest quencher.* A drink: coll: 1840, Dickens.

querier. A chimney-sweep irregularly soliciting custom, e.g. by knocking at the doors of houses: low: from ca 1845. Mayhew (also GUMBLER). cf. KNULLER.

querry and **quetry** in Greene's *Second Cony-Catching*, 1592, are prob. misprints for *quarry*; nevertheless they are late C.16 c. and = a surety (to be victimized).

question, ask (a horse) **a.** To test before racing: the turf: *Licensed Victuallers' Gazette*, 7 Nov. 1890, 'A thorough judge of horses . . . and . . . not afraid of asking them a question, like some trainers we know of.'

question, pop the, see POP THE QUESTION.

***question lay.** 'To knock at the Door, and ask for the Gentleman of the House, if a Bed [a-bed] you desire the Servant not to disturb him, but you will wait untill he rises, and then an opportunity to steal something', C. Hitchin, *The Regulator*, 1718: c.: C.18.

queynte, see QUAINT. **Quhew,** see WHEW, THE.

qui, get the. To be dismissed: printers': from ca 1875. Ex *quietus*.

qui-hi or **-hai** or **-hy.** An Anglo-Indian, esp. of the Bengal Presidency: Anglo-Indian coll: 1816, Anon., *Quiz*; Thackeray, 'The old boys, the old generals, the old colonels, the old qui-his . . . paid her homage.' Ex Urdu *koi hai*, 'Is anyone there?' – in India a summons to a servant. Yule & Burnell, who cf. (*Bombay*) DUCK, n., 4 and MULL, n., 3. 2. In the Regular Army, *qui-hi* is used (mid-C.19–20) in its lit. sense.

qui tam; qui-tam, quitam. A solicitor who seeks such a conviction that the resultant penalty goes half to the informer (i.e. the lawyer himself), half to the Crown: also adj., as in Moncrieff, 1843, 'The quitam lawyer, the quack doctor'; *qui tam*, as n., app. recorded first in this sense in H., 3rd ed., 1864; in C.20, ob. except as legal s. 2. The adj., however, figures also in the earlier *qui-tam horse*, 'one that will both carry and draw', Grose, 3rd ed.: legal, †by 1860. Ex the legal action so named; L., 'who as well'. 3. But *qui tam*, an informer, occurs as early as 1816 in 'Quiz's' *Grand Master*: coll.

Quibble Queer, Sir, see QUEER, SIR QUIBBLE.

quick. Dapper and clever: Society: 1870s and 1880s.

quick and nimble; more like a bear than a squirrel. A c.p. addressed to one moving slowly when speed is required: C.18–mid-19.

quick stick(s). Rapidly: hurriedly. Esp. in the s. phrase, *cut quick sticks*, to start or depart thus (cf. CUT ONE'S STICK): coll: from ca 1860. Occ. *in quick sticks* (*Dublin University Magazine*, April 1835). The first phrase and the last occur also in various diall.

quicker than hell would scorch a feather. Promptly: sailing-ship officers' c.p. 'duly impressed on all youngsters': mid-C.19–20; ob. Bowen. cf. *an icicle's chance in hades.*

quicumque (loosely **quicunque**) **vult.** A very compliant girl (sexually): 1785, Grose; †by 1850. Also an *Athanasian wench.* Ex *quicumque vult salvus esse,* whosoever will be saved, the opening words of the Athanasian Creed.

***quid.** A guinea: c.: 1688, Shadwell; †by 1800. Perhaps L. *quid,* what?, for 'the wherewithal': cf. QUIDS. Hence, 2, a sovereign, or the sum of twenty shillings: low: C.19–20. 3. A shilling, says Grose, 3rd ed., but this I believe to be an error. 4. As a pl = *quids,* sovereigns or £, as in Dickens, 1857, ' "Take yer two quid to one", adds the speaker picking out a stout farmer.' 5. See QUIDS. 6. The female pudend: low: C.19–20; ob.

'quid est hoc?' 'hoc est quid.' A late C.18–early 19 punning c.p. As H. explains, the question is asked by one tapping the bulging cheek of another, who, exhibiting a 'chaw' of tobacco, answers *hoc est quid.* Lit., 'What is this? This is a quid [of tobacco].'

quid-box. A snuff box: ?1790–1850. (Wm Maginn, *Whitehall,* 1827, at p. 53.)

***quid-fishing.** Expert thieving: c. (—1909). Ex QUID, 2.

quid to a bloater, (it's) a. (It's) a certain bet: low urban (—1909); slightly ob.

quidding, vbl n. The chewing of tobacco: *Conway* training ship (—1900).

***quids.** Money, or rather cash, in gen.: late C.17–20 (ob.): c. >, ca 1750, low s. Moore, 1819, 'If quids should be wanting, to make the match good'. Ex QUID, 1.

***quids, tip the.** To spend money: c.: late C.17–19. 2. To lend money: c.: mid-C. 18–mid-19. See QUIDS.

quien. A dog: low (?orig. c.): mid-C.19–20; ob. Reade, 1861, ' "Curse these quiens," said he.' Origin obscure, but obviously cognate with L. *canis,* Fr. *chien,* a dog. Perhaps ex Northern Fr. dial.

quier, see QUEER, adj., 1.

quiess kateer? How are you: Regular Army (late C.19–20). Direct ex Arabic for 'well, very'.

quiet, on the. Quietly, unobtrusively, secretly: s. >, ca 1910, coll: 1860, H., 2nd ed. Whence Q.T., ON THE.

quiet as a wasp in one's nose(, as). Uneasy, restless: coll: 1670, Ray; ob.

quiff. 'A satisfactory result: esp. an end obtained by means not strictly conventional', F. & H.: low: from ca 1875; ob. Ex dial. *quiff,* a dodge or trick, a knack, a 'wrinkle'. 2. Whence, 'an idea, fancy, movement, suggestion': Anglo-Indian (—1909). 3. As an oiled lock of hair plastered on forehead, the S.O.D. considers it S.E., W. as s., orig. East End of London. Perhaps ex It. *cuffia*; cognate with *coif.* F. & H., 1902 (first record), says 'military'; Ware dates it at 1890.

quiff, v.i. To copulate: C.18–20 (very ob.): low. D'Urfey, 'By quiffing with Cullies, three Pound she had got'; Grose, 2nd ed., gives *quiffing,* copulation. Not in O.E.D.; origin problematic. 2. v.i., to do well; jog along nicely, merrily: from ca 1870. Prob. ex the dial. n. *quiff* (see QUIFF, n., 1); cf.:

quiff, adj. Smartly dressed (esp. for a particular occasion): military: from ca 1908. Ex the n., 1.

quiff in the press. To move a breast pocket to the other side: tailors': from ca 1870. cf. the Somersetshire dial. use (E.D.D.).

quiff the bladder. To conceal baldness: low: from ca 1870. Lit., to coif the bladder-resembling head; more prob. – cf. QUIFF, n., 1 – ex dial. *quiff,* a DODGE, a trick.

quiffing, see QUIFF, v., 1.

quifs. Manoeuvres: military: late C.19–20; virtually †. Ex QUIFF, n., 1 or 2.

quill. To curry favour: Winchester College: C.19–20. Perhaps ex *jump in quill,* to act in harmony, and *in a* or *the quill,* in concert. cf. QUILLED.

quill, brother – knight – of the, see BROTHER . . . and KNIGHT.

quill-driver. Anybody on shipboard doing clerical work: nautical coll: late C. 19–20. Bowen. Ex S.E. sense.

quilled, adj. Pleased: Winchester College: C.19–20. Prob. ex QUILL.

quiller, occ. **quilster.** A toady: Winchester: C.19–20. Ex QUILL.

quim. The female pudend: a vulg.: C.17–20. Variants, *queme, quim-box, quimsby, quin,* all † except the second, itself ob. Prob. ex Celtic *cwm,* a cleft, a valley. Hence such C.19–20 compounds as *quim-bush, -whiskers, -wig,* the female pubic hair; *q.-stake* or *-wedge,* the penis; *q.-sticker,* a whoremonger; *q.-sticking* or *-wedging,* and *quimming,* sexual intercourse.

quimsby, quin, see QUIM.

quinsy, choked by a hempen. Hanged: C.16–early 19.

***quire,** see QUEER, adj., 1.

***quirken,** see QUEER-KEN HALL.

quirklum. A puzzle: Scots: late C.18–19. ('A cant term' in Jamieson = s.)

quis? Who wants some?: Public-Schoolboys': mid-C.19–20. The answer is *ego!* Direct ex Latin.

quisby. An idler: 1837 (O.E.D.). Desmond, *Stage Struck*, 'That old quisby has certainly contrived to slip out of the house.' ?ex QUIZ, an eccentric. See QUISBY, DO.

quisby, adj. Bankrupt, 1853; out of sorts, 1854; queer, not quite right, 1887, *Punch*, 30 July, 'Arter this things appeared to go quisby.' ?ex QUIZ, an eccentric, or ex the n.

quisby, do. To idle: 1851, Mayhew. Ob. See QUISBY, n.

quisi. Low; obscene: Anglo-Chinese (—1864).

quitam, see QUI TAM.

quite!; quite so! Yes!; no doubt!; I agree: coll: from the mid-1890s. cf. Fr. *parfaitement* and our EXACTLY! and RATHER!

quite a bit. Fairly often; a fair amount (n.), rather (adv.): coll: late C.19–20. 'It hurts quite a bit.'

quite too nice. Nice: female aesthetic Society: 1880s and 1890s.

quitsest. A release, discharge: late C.16–early 17: prob. coll. Holinshed. ?ex *quietus est*.

quius kius! Hush!; cease!: theatrical c.p. of ca 1880–1910. The *kius* reduplicates *quius* ex *quietus*.

quiz. (Of arbitrary origin, perhaps on QUEER, adj.; cf. QUOZ.) An eccentric person: 1782, Mme D'Arblay: Oxford s. >, ca 1830, gen. coll and, ca 1860, S.E. 2. Hence, an odd-looking thing: coll: 1798, Jane Austen; ob. 3. A monocle: from ca 1810: coll. Abbr. *quizzing-glass*, as in Thackeray, 1843, 'The dandy not uncommonly finishes off with a horn quizzing-glass.' Ob. Prob. ex sense 1.

***quiz,** v.i. and t. To watch; play the spy: c.: from ca 1890. Ex dial.

quockerwodger. A politician acting under an outsider's orders: political (—1859); †by 1887. Ex dial. *quocker-wodger*, a puppet on strings.

***quod or quad.** A prison: late C.17–20: c. until ca 1780, then low s. B.E.; Fielding; Tarras, *Poems*, 1804 (*quad*). Gen. *in quod*. Prob. ex *quadrangle*. cf.:

***quod,** v. To imprison: from ca 1810: c. >, ca 1840, low s. Vaux, Tom Taylor. Ex n.

***quod-cove.** A turnkey: c.: 1812, Vaux; †by 1910. Ex QUOD, n. cf.:

***quod-cull.** A prison warder: c.: C.18. C. Hitchin, *The Regulator*, 1718.

quodded, adj. In prison: low: from ca 1820. Ex QUOD, imprison.

***quodding dues are concerned.** It is a case of imprisonment: c. (—1812); †by 1890.

quodger; quodjer. By what law?: legal: 1864. Ex L. *quo jure*.

quoniam. A drinking-cup of some kind: drinking s.: early C.17. Healy, 1609, 'A Quoniam is a glasse . . . well knowne in Drink-allia.' 2. The female pudend: low: C.17–18. ?a learned pun, suggested by QUIM, on L. *quoniam*, whereas (all males desire it).

***quota.** App. c. for a share (esp. of plunder): late C.17–early 18. cf. EARNEST.

quote. A quotation, 1885. 2. A quotation-mark, 1888. Literary, publishing, and printing coll >, ca 1910, S.E., but certainly not dignified S.E.

quoz. An odd or absurd person or thing: coll: ca 1790–1810. Also, as in Mme D'Arblay, as a plural. A jocular perversion of QUIZ, n., 1. 2. As an ejaculation or a retort, indeed a monosyllabic c.p.: same period. This word is the subject of an entire song in *The New Vocal Enchantress* (a song-book), 1791, at pp. 32–4. Also occ. as diminutive *quozzy*.

***quyer,** see QUEER, adj., 1. (A variant spelling of *quire*.)

R

r.i.p. (or **R.I.P.**), **let him, her, it,** etc. Let him, her, etc., rip; i.e. don't bother about him, her, etc.: late C.19–20. Ex the abbr. of *requiescat in pace*, on tombstones. cf. RIP!, LET HER.

R.M.D. (separately articulated). Immediate payment: (unexalted) financial coll: late C.19–20. Ex *ready money down.*

R.O., see RELIEVING OFFICER.

rabbit. A new-born babe, mostly in *rabbit-catcher*, a midwife: low: ca 1780–1850. Grose, 1785. 2. Political (ob.) as in report of the House of Commons Election Commission, 1866, 'Out of £50 . . . he had paid a number of rooks and rabbits. . . . In general . . . the rabbits were to work in the burrow and the rooks to make a noise at the public meetings.' 3. 'A rabbit, as a horse that runs "in and out" is sometimes called', 1882, The *Standard*, 3 Sept.: racing. 4. See BUNNY, 2.

rabbit, v. In imprecations, it = confound, as in Fielding's '"Rabbit the fellow!" cries he,' 1742, and Smollett's 'Rabbit it! I have forgot the degree,' in the same decade. cf. DRABBIT! (—1787), and *od(d) rabbit*. The O.E.D. considers *rabbit* an alteration of *rat* in *od rat*, DRAT; F. & H.'s *rot it* won't 'fit'.

rabbit or **rabbits, buy the.** To have the worst of a bargain; to be a dupe: orig. (1825), U.S.; anglicized ca 1850; very ob. cf. the C.16 proverb, *who will change a rabbit for a rat?*

rabbit, fat and lean like a. A mid-C.17–early 19 coll. Ray, 1678; explained in Swift's *Polite Conversation*, Dialogue I: 'I am like a Rabbit, fat and lean in Four-and-twenty Hours,' a rabbit responding very promptly to food.

rabbit, live. The male member: low: C.19–20; ob. Whence *skin the live rabbit* or *have a bit of rabbit-pie*, to coït: cf. RABBIT-PIE. cf. dial. *rabbit*, 'to coït' – as in John Masefield, *Reynard the Fox*, 1919, '"I'll larn 'ee rabbit in my shed!"'

rabbit-catcher, see RABBIT, n., 1.

rabbit-hunting – or (a) **coney-catching** – **with a dead ferret, go.** To undertake something with unsuitable or useless means: coll: ca 1670–1820. Ray; Fuller, 1732.

rabbit-pie. A harlot: low: mid-C.19–20; ob. Ex RABBIT, LIVE, q.v. also for phrase.

rabbit-pie shifter. A policeman: low London: ca 1870–1920. Barrère & Leland quote a music-hall song of ca 1870, 'Never to take notice of vulgar nicknames, such as "slop", "copper", "rabbit-pie shifter", "peeler".' He tells harlots to 'move along'.

rabbit-pulling. A variant of BABY-PULLING; cf. *rabbit-catcher* at RABBIT, 1.

rabbit-skin; occ. **cat-skin.** An academical hood: university: from ca 1850; ob. cf.:

rabbit-skin, get one's. To obtain the B.A. degree: university: from ca 1850; ob. Ex preceding; the trimming is of rabbit's fur.

***rabbit-sucker.** A young spendthrift 'taking up Goods upon Tick at excessive rates', B.E.: c. of C.17–early 19. Dekker. Prob. ex Shakespearian sense, 'baby' rabbits. cf. PURSENETS. 2. Also, a pawnbroker; a tally-man: c. or low s.: ca 1720–60.

rabbiter. A side-handed blow on the nape of the neck: Winchester College: from ca 1875. As in killing a rabbit. 2. In pl, a form of punishment: Charterhouse: C.19. A. H. Tod, *Charterhouse*, 1900.

rabbits! see WHITE RABBITS!

rabsha(c)kle. A profligate: coll: ?C.17–18. F. & H.: but who else? cf. S.E. *ramshackle.*

Rachel or **rachel,** v. To rejuvenate; renovate: ca 1890–5. Ex Madame Rachel, the 'beautiful for ever' swindler. (The C.20 is kinder to such impositions.)

rack. A bone, gen. in pl: slaughterers' coll >, ca 1890, j.: 1851, Mayhew. 2. A rib of mutton: Winchester School coll (—1870). Ex S.E., a neck of mutton.

rack off. To make water: low coll: late C. 19–20; ob. Ex wine-making.

rack-rider. The samlet: Northern fishermen's coll: late C.19–20. Because gen. it appears in bad weather.

rackaback. A GORMAGON: ca 1785–1850.

rackabimus. 'A sudden or unexpected stroke or fall', Jamieson, who adds that 'It resembles *racket*': Scots: late C.18–19.

***racket.** A DODGE, trick; plan; line, occupation, esp. if these are criminal or SHADY: c. (—1812) >, ca 1860, low s. Ex *racket*, noise, disturbance. 2. Esp. as in *be in a racket*, be privy to an illicit design, and as set forth in Egan's Grose, 1823,

'Some particular kinds of fraud and robbery are so termed, when called by their flash' – i.e. underworld – 'names; as the Letter-racket; the Order-racket . . . In fact, any game' – i.e. illicit occupation or trick – 'may be termed a racket . . . by prefixing thereto the particular branch of depredation or fraud in question.' Whence the various U.S. 'rackets': see esp. Irwin. cf. RACKET-MAN.

***racket, stand the.** To take the blame for one's gang: c. (—1823) >, by 1850, s. >, by 1900, coll. 2. Hence, to pay the bill, stand the expense: since ca 1830: s.

***racket-man.** A thief: c.: from ca 1850; ob. Mayhew. Ex RACKET, 2.

racket(t)y. (Of places) low, SHADY: Cockney: ca 1840–90. Mayhew, I, 1851. Ex RACKET, 1.

***raclan.** A married woman: tramps' c.: from ca 1830. cf. Romany *rakli*, a girl.

rad. A Radical: political s., in C.20 coll: 1831, *Lincoln Herald*, 7 Jan. Disraeli in *Coningsby*, 'They say the Rads are going to throw us over.' 2. A radiator: servants': from ca 1905.

raddled. Tipsy: late C.17–18. Motteux. cf. dial. *raddle*, to do anything to excess; but more prob. ex *raddle*, to colour coarsely with red.

radical; Hunt's breakfast powder. Roasted corn: ca 1820–60. *Sinks*, 1848. Prob. at first *radical Hunt's* . . ., then divided into a pair of synonyms. This was 'Orator' Hunt the Radical's favourite breakfast dish.

rafe or **Ralph.** A pawn-ticket: low; esp. at Norwich: from ca 1860; ob.

raffle-coffin. A ruffian, lit. a resurrectionist: C.19 low coll. Corruption of *rifle*(-*coffin*).

raffs. 'An appellation given by the gownsmen of the university of Oxford to the inhabitants of that place', Grose, 1785: coll: ca 1780–1920. cf. *riff-raff.*

rag. A farthing: c.: ca 1690–1850. Because of so little value. 2. A bank-note: 1811, *Lex. Bal.*, which proves that *rag* also = bank-notes collectively. 3. Hence, money in gen.: from ca 1810. 4. A flag: from ca 1700: coll till C.20, then S.E. Kipling, 1892. cf. RAG, ORDER OF THE. 5. The curtain: theatrical and showmen's: from ca 1875. 6. Hence, a dénouement, a 'curtain': id.: from ca 1880. 7. A street tumbler: circus: 1875, *The Athenaeum*, 24 April. 8. See RAG, ORDER OF THE. 9. The tongue: from ca 1825. Ex RAG, RED. 10. Talk; banter, abuse: from ca 1880. Gen. *ragging.* cf.: 11. A jollification, esp. and orig. an undergraduates' display of noisy, disorderly conduct and great high spirits, considered by the perpetrators as excellent fun and by many outsiders as 'a bloody nuisance': university >, ca 1910, very common in the Army and Navy; 1892, *Isis*, 'The College is preparing for a good old rag tonight'; *Daily Mail*, 10 March 1900, 'There was keen excitement at Cambridge yesterday when the magistrates proceeded to deal with the last two prosecutions of students arising out of the notorious rag in celebration of the relief of Ladysmith'; but in existence from ca 1860 (O.E.D. Sup.). Ex the S.E. v., to annoy, tease. 12. See RAG, THE. 13. See RAGS.

rag, v.t. and i. To question vigorously or jocularly; waylay, or assail, roughly and noisily; *Sessions*, June 1739 (trial of Samuel Bird and Suzannah Clark), 'On Monday night Bird and Clark came to their House to *ragg* (scold) her Grandfather for what he had talk'd of concerning them.' 2. To create a disturbance, hold a 'rag' (see n., 11): university: *Isis*, 1896, 'The difficulty of "ragging" with impunity has long been felt'; but implied by Baumann in 1887 and, in the first nuance, recorded by O.E.D. (Sup.) for 1891. Perhaps abbr. of *bully-rag.* Origin: see RAG, n., 11. 3. Hence, to wreck, make a mess of, by way of a rag: Public Schools': 1904, P. G. Wodehouse, *The Gold Bat*, 'Mills is awfully barred in Seymour's. Anybody might have ragged his study.' In c. (mainly of Norwich) to divide (esp. plunder): 1860, H., 2nd ed. Prob. ex, or at the least cognate with, the †S.E. sense, to tear in pieces. Also *go rags.*

rag, chew the. To scold, complain; sulk or brood: low and military, 1888. Ex RAG, n., 9, tongue.

rag, dish of red. Abuse: low: from ca 1820; ob. Egan, *Anecdotes of the Turf*, 'She tipped the party such a dish of red rag as almost to create a riot in the street.' See RAG, RED.

rag, have two shirts and a. To be comfortably off: coll: ca 1670–1800. Ray.

rag, order of the. (Preceded by **the.**) The military profession: coll: 1751, Fielding; slightly ob. See RAG, n., 4.

rag, red. (Also RED FLANNEL.) The tongue: low: late C.17–20; slightly ob. B.E., Grose, Combe, Bruton (1826, 'Say

. . . why that red rag . . . is now so mute'), W. S. Gilbert, 1876. See RAG, n., 9.

Rag, the. (Also **the rag**). The regimental brothel: Indian Army (non-officers'): from ca 1880.

rag, too much red. Loquacious: low: from ca 1840. See RAG, RED.

***rag, win the shiny,** see SHINE-RAG . . .

rag, without a; not a rag (left). Penniless: coll: late C.16–20; ob. Shakespeare, 'Not a rag of money', though here *rag* rather = *scrap*.

rag a holiday, give the red. To be silent: low: from ca 1850; ob. See RAG, n., 9.

rag-(and-bone-)shop. A very dirty and untidy room: coll: from ca 1880; ob.

rag-and-snatcher man. A rag-and-bones man: chimney-sweeps': C.19. (George Elson, 1900.) Here, *snatcher* apparently = a bone; if so, it probably comes ex dogs *snatching* bones.

rag-bag or **-doll.** A slattern: coll: from ca 1862.

rag-box or **-shop.** The mouth: low: from ca 1890. Kipling, 1892, 'You shut up your rag-box and 'ark to my lay.'

rag-carrier. An ensign: 1785, Grose; †by 1890. Ex RAG, n., 4.

rag-fair. An inspection of soldiers' kit-bags, etc.: 1785, Grose: military. Ex the S.E. sense, an old-clothes market at Houndsditch, London: which, contrary to F. & H., is certainly S.E.

rag-gorger or **gorgy,** see RAG-SPLAWGER.

rag-mannered. Violently coarse or vulgar; coll: C.19–20; ob.

rag money. Bank notes, bills of exchange, etc.: from ca 1860: coll till C.20, then S.E.

rag on every bush, – (oh,) he has a. He is, or is in the habit of, paying marked attention to more than one girl at a time: from ca 1860; ob.

rag out, v.i. To show the white flag or feather: ca 1880–1910.

rag out, get one's. To bluster (ob.); to grow angry: low: from ca 1880. Explained by the synonymous *get one's* SHIRT OUT, and by RAG, n., 9.

rag-sauce. Chatter; impudence: low: from ca 1840. Ex RAG, n., 9.

***rag-seeker,** see RAG-SOOKER.

rag-shop. See RAG-BOX. 2. See RAG(-AND-BONE) SHOP. 3. A bank: c. or low s.: 1860, H., 2nd ed.; ob. See RAG, n., 2.

rag-shop boss or **cove.** A banker: from ca 1865; ob. 2. See:

rag-shop cove. A cashier: low: from ca 1865. 2. See preceding entry.

***rag-sooker,** occ. **-seeker.** c. as in Anon.'s *The Tramp Exposed*, 1878, 'The ragsooker, an instrument attached to the end of a long pole for removing clothes-pins from the lines, and afterwards dragging the released clothes over the fence'. cf. ANGLER.

rag-splawger. A rich man: low (if not orig. c.): ca 1858–1900. Gen. 'used in conversation to avoid direct mention of names'. Also *rag-gorger* or (Vaux) *gorgy*: low (perhaps orig. c.): ca 1820–1900. See GORGER.

rag-stabber. A tailor: from ca 1870; ob. Also STAB-RAG. cf. SNIP.

rag-stick. An umbrella, esp. if loose and unreefed: lower classes' (—1909).

rag-tacker. A coach-trimmer: ca 1820–70. 2. A dressmaker: ca 1850–1920.

rag-tailed. Tattered; of, or like, a ragamuffin: coll (—1887).

rag-time, adj. Merry: coll: from 1901 or 1902.

rag-trade. The purchasing of false bank-notes, which are then palmed off on strangers: 1843, Marryat: mostly U.S.; ob. 2. Tailoring; dress-making; the dry-goods trade in gen.: from ca 1880: coll.

rag-water. Any inferior spirits: late C.17–early 19. 2. Esp. gin: ca 1780–1850. Grose, 2nd ed., 'These liquors seldom failing to reduce those that drink [*such spirits*] to rags': which is not an etymology but a pun.

rage, the. The fashion or vogue: 1785, *The New Rosciad*, ''Tis the rage in this great raging Nation, | Who wou'd live and not be in the fashion?' Coll till ca 1850, then S.E. cf. GO, n., 3.

rager. An old, fierce 'bullock or cow that always begins to rage in the stock-yard', Morris: Australian coll: 1884, 'Rolf Boldrewood'.

ragged. Collapsed: rowing s., says F. & H., 1902. 2. Inferior, wretched (game, form, display): coll (—1887). 3. (Of time, a period) wretched, unfortunate, ill-starred: coll (—1887). Baumann, 'A ragged week'. 4. Unwell; tired and unwell: Australian coll: late C.19–20.

ragged-arse, adj. Tattered; fig., disreputable, ruined: a vulg.: from ca 1880.

ragged robin. A keeper's follower: New Forest s. or dial.: from ca 1860. (Rare in singular.)

ragged soph, see SOPH.

raggery. Clothes, esp. women's: coll bordering on S.E.: very ob. Thackeray,

1855, 'Old hags ... draped in majestic raggery'. cf. Fr. *chiffons.*

raggie, raggy. A particular friend (ex the sharing of brass-cleaning rags: Bowen); but gen. in pl, as *be raggies,* to be steady chums: naval (—1909). Ware implies that it is mildly pejorative.

raggy, adj. Annoyed, SHIRTY: 1900, G. Swift. Ex RAG OUT, GET ONE'S.

raging favourite. A coll variant (—1887) of *a hot favourite.*

rags. See RAG, n., 3. 2. *rags, go.* See RAG, v., c. sense. 3. Old lace used for decorative purposes: art s. verging on coll and j.: from ca 1880; ob. Ware. 4. A steward in charge of the linen: nautical: late C.19–20.

rags, flash one's. To display, gen. ostentatiously, one's bank notes: low (?orig. c.): from ca 1860.

rags, in the. In trouble or disgrace; in a dispute: tailors': from ca 1860.

rags (on), have the. To be having one's period: women's low coll: from ca 1860.

rags a gallop, tip one's. To move; depart, esp. if hastily: low: 1870, Hazlewood & Williams, in *Leave It to Me,* 'I see; told you to tip your rags a gallop, and you won't go.' Here *tip* = give.

rags and jags. Tatters: coll: from ca 1860; very ob.

rags and sticks. A travelling outfit: showmen's and low theatrical: from ca 1870. Hindley, 1876, 'Rags and sticks, as a theatrical booth is always termed'.

rail-bird. A tout watcher of race-horses being exercised: sporting, esp. turf: from ca 1890; slightly ob. Ex his vantage-point on gate or hurdle.

railings, count the. To go hungry: low: from ca 1860; slightly ob. See also SPITALFIELD(S) BREAKFAST.

rails, see HEAD-RAILS.

rails, dish of. 'A lecture, jobation, or scolding from a married woman to her husband', Grose, 1st ed. (where misplaced): late C.18–mid-19.

rails, front. The teeth: low: C.19–20; slightly ob. Also HEAD-RAILS.

rails, off the. Not in normal or proper state or condition; morally or mentally astray: 1859, Gen. P. Thomson: coll.

railways. Red stockings worn by women: railwaymen's (—1909). Ex red signal.

rain, (know enough to) get out of the. To (be shrewd enough to) look after oneself, e.g. to refrain from meddling: to be common-sensical: coll: 1848, Durivage, 'Ham was one of 'em – he was. He knew sufficient to get out of the rain'; but anticipated by H. Buttes in 1599: 'Fooles ... have the wit to keep themselves out of the raine.' In Australia, *to keep out of the rain.*

rain, right as, see RIGHT AS ...

rain-napper. An umbrella: low: ca 1820–1910.

rainbow. A discoloured bruise: from ca 1810; ob. An excellent example of what G. K. Chesterton well names the poetry of slang. 2. A mistress: ca 1820–70. Egan, *Life in London,* 1821, 'The pink of the ton and his rainbow'. Because dressed in a variety of colours. 3. A footman: from ca 1820; very ob. Egan, ibid., 'It was the custom of Logic never to permit the Rainbow to announce him.' Abbr. RAINBOW, KNIGHT OF THE. 4. A pattern-book; ca 1820–60. Egan, ibid. Ex the variety of colours. 5. A sovereign: costers': from ca 1850; ob. Perhaps suggested by RHINO, for *rainbow* is in Costerese pronounced *rinebo*; perhaps, however, ex rainbow as a sign of better weather – as a sovereign is of better times. 6. A gay young spark: ca 1835–70. *Sinks,* 1848.

rainbow, knight of the. A footman in livery. Grose, 1785. See KNIGHT.

rains, the. The rainy season: Anglo-Indian coll (in C.20, S.E.): 1616, Sir T. Roe.

raise. A rise in salary: coll: late C.19–20. Ex U.S. sense, an(y) improvement (1728: O.E.D. Sup.).

raise a barney, see RISE A BARNEY. **raise Cain,** see CAIN.

raise-mountain. A boaster: coll: ?C.17–18.

raise the colour. To find gold: Australian coll: mid-C.19–20.

rake. A comb: jocular: from ca 1860. Also, *garden-rake* and, ca 1840–60, *raker:* low.

rake it in. To make money fast: coll: late C.19–20. 'He's simply raking it in!'

rake-jakes. A blackguard: C.18–20; ob. Rhyming on JAKES. cf. S.E. *rake-kennel.*

rake-out. A fill of tobacco: Cockney: from ca 1890; very ob.

rake out. To coït with (a woman): low: C. 19–20.

rake the pot. To take the stakes: racing: from ca 1825. See POT, n., 1.

raked fore and aft. Desperately in love: naval: late C.19–20. Ex damage done by well-directed shelling.

raker. A very fast pace: coll: 1876 (S.O.D.). Perhaps ex *rake,* (of hunting dogs) to run head down. 2. A heavy bet: sporting: 1869, Bradwood, *The O.V.H.*; 1884, Hawley Smart, in *From Post to Finish*; 1891, *Sportsman*, 25 March, 'Jennings ... stood to win a raker ... over Lord George.' Esp. in *go a raker* (cf. sense 1), to bet heavily or, more gen., recklessly (1869). 3. See RAKE, n. 4. A good stroke: golfers' coll: 1899.

rakes, carry heavy. To swagger; put on SIDE: C.17 coll. Terence in English, 1614.

ral, the. The admiral: naval (—1909).

ralizo, see RARZO.

rally-o(h)! Proceed vigorously: *Conway* cadets' c.p. of encouragement (—1891).

Ralph, ralph. See RAFE. 2. In printers' s., from ca 1810, 'The supposed author of the tricks played upon a recalcitrant member of a *chapel*', F. & H.

Ralph Spooner. A fool: coll: late C.17–early 19. In Suffolk dial., *Ralph* or *Rafe* means the same thing (E.D.D.).

ram. An act of coïtion: low: C.19–20. cf. S.E. *ram-rod*, the penis. Ex v., 1. 2. A crowd; a crush: Shrewsbury School: from ca 1880. Ex the force of a battering ram. cf. v.t., 2.

ram. To coït with (a woman): low: C.19–20. cf. POKE; RIDE. 2. v.t., to get (a boy) off a punishment: Shrewsbury School: from ca 1880.

ram and dam(n). A muzzle-loading gun: jocular coll: 1866; ob.

ram booze, see RUM BOOZE.

***ram-cat; ram-cat cove.** A man wearing furs: c.: from ca 1860. Ex *ram-cat*, a he cat.

ram-jam. A surfeit: s. and dial.: from ca 1885. Ex RAM-JAM FULL.

ram-jam, v. To stuff (esp. with food): from ca 1885. Ex:

ram-jam full. Packed absolutely full: dial. and (mostly U.S.) s.: 1879, Waugh.

ram-reel. A dance, men only: Scots coll (in C.20, S.E.): C.19–20. D. Anderson, 1813, 'The chairs they coup, they hurl an' loup, | A ram-reel now they're wantin''. cf. BULL-DANCE; STAG-PARTY.

ram-rod. A ball bowled along the ground: Winchester School: from ca 1840. (Also *raymonder*.) Mansfield. Ex the straightness of its 'flight'. 2. The penis: low: mid-C.19–20.

ram-skin (or one word). A bailiff: Anglo-Irish: C.19. 'A Real Paddy', *Real Life in Ireland*, 1822, 'He would take even a mat made of a ram's fell.'

ram-struck mutton. 'Tough meat from old ewes past breeding' (Baker): Australian: late C.–1920.

Ramasammy or **r.** A Hindu: Southern India. An Indian coolie in Ceylon: Ceylon. This coll (—1828) is a corruption of *Ramaswami*, a frequent Hindu surname in Southern India.

rambler. A whore: C.17. In, e.g., *The English Rogue*.

rambounge. 'A severe brush of labour', Jamieson: Scots: late C.18–mid-19. This *ram* is the dial. prefix = strong; very. cf.:

rambustious, ramgumption. See RUMBUSTIOUS, RUMGUMPTION. (cf. U.S. *rambunctious*, 1854.)

ramfeezled. Exhausted, worn out: mostly dial., whence, ca 1890–1910, coll.

ramjollock. To shuffle (cards): C.19. ?lit., jumble well. Also late C.19–20 Shropshire dial.

rammaged. Tipsy: Scots coll or, more prob., dial.: late C.18–20. Ex *ramished.*

***rammer.** An arm: c.: late C.18–20; ob. 2. The leg: pugilistic: ca 1840–80. Augustus Mayhew, *Paved With Gold*, 1857, 'Jack got a "cracker on his nut" which knocked his "rammers" from under him.' *Cracker*, as 'a heavy punch', occurs earlier – in, e.g., *Boxiana*, IV, 1824. 3. The penis: low: mid-C.19–20.

ramming. Forceful, pushing: 1825, *Sporting Magazine*, 'The most ramming ... cove you ever saw perform'; ob. by 1900. Ex *ram*, the animal.

rammo. The former naval evolution, 'Prepare aloft for action': bluejackets': late C.18–mid-19. Bowen. Ex *ramming a ship.*

***ramp.** A robbery with violence: c.: Vaux, 1812; ob. Moncrieff, 1830, 'And ramp so plummy'. Ex *ramp*, to storm, rage, violently, or v.t., to snatch, tear. 2. A swindle: c. >, by 1905, s.: from ca 1880. G. R. Sims. 3. A footpad and garrotter: c.: from ca 1870; ob. cf. RAMPER. 4. A race-course trickster: c.: from ca 1860. Also, *rampsman* (H., 1st ed., 1859) and *ramper*, as in H., 5th ed., 1874, and in Runciman's *Chequers*, 1876, 'A man who is a racecourse thief and ramper hailed me affably': cf. the quotation at RAMPER. 5. A hallmark: c.: 1879, Horsley. Ex the rampant lion forming part of the assay stamp for gold and silver.

***ramp,** v.t. To thieve or rob with violence: c. (—1811) >, ca 1860, low s. See the n., 1, for origin. cf. RANK; RANT. 2. Esp. to force (a person) to pay an alleged debt: c.:

1897, *Daily News*, 3 Sept., 'Charge of "ramping" a book-maker'; but it must be at least as early as the horse-racing sense of RAMPER (see the n., 4).

***ramp, on the.** Engaged in swindling: c: late C.19–20.

rampage, on the. Storming about: coll: 1860, Dickens, *Great Expectations*.

***ramper** and ***rampsman.** See RAMP, n., 4. cf. *Daily News*, 12 Oct. 1887, ' "Rampers", i.e. men who claimed to have made bets to bookmakers, and hustled and surrounded them if they refused to pay'. cf. RAMPING. 2. (*ramper* only.) A noisy, turbulent street-ranger, esp. if a youth: low London (—1909): ob.

***ramping.** The practice described in sense 1 of preceding entry: c. (—1891) >, by 1905, s. 2. 'Calling at houses where parcels [have] just been delivered from tradesmen to customers, and obtaining possession of them under various pretences': c.: from ca 1870.

ramping, adj. and adv. Rampant(ly): lower classes' coll (—1887). Baumann has *ramping mad*.

ramps, the. A brothel: Regular Army: late C.19–20. Perhaps ex *rampant* or *on the* RAMPAGE.

***rampsman,** see RAMPER. **ramrod,** see RAM-ROD.

***ran-cat cove,** see RAM-CAT. **ran-tan, on the,** see RANTAN.

Randal's-man or **randlesman.** A green handkerchief white-spotted: pugilistic (—1839); ob. Ex the colours of Jack Randal, the famous early C.19 boxer.

randan, see RANTAN.

randem-(or random-)tandem. Three horses driven tandem: from ca 1870: coll >, ca 1890, S.E.; ob. Ex: 2. adv. In that manner in which three horses are harnessed tandem: 1805: coll >, by 1870, S.E. Ex S.E. *randan* on *tandem*. Also, as in H., 1860, *random*.

randle. 'A set of nonsense verses, repeated in Ireland by school boys, and young people, who have been guilty of breaking wind backwards, before any of their companions; if they neglect this apology, they are liable to certain kicks, pinches, and fillips, which are accompanied with diverse admonitory couplets,' Grose, 1785; ob. by 1880. Whence:

randle, v. To punish (a schoolboy) for breaking wind: C.19. Halliwell. Ex preceding. 2. See RANDLING which is much commoner than the v. proper.

randlesman, see RANDAL'S-MAN.

randling. The punishment, by hair-pulling, of an apprentice refusing to join his fellows in taking a holiday: mostly at Birkenhead: 1879, *Notes and Queries*. Ob.

random, see RANDEM-TANDEM.

randy. Violent; esp. sexually warm, lecherous: from ca 1780: dial. and coll; in C.20, mainly dial. Burns, 1785; *Lex. Bal.*, 1811; Halliwell, 1847; E.D.D. ?ex *rand*, to rave, perhaps †Hindustani *randí-baz*, a lecher.

randy beggar. A Gypsy tinker: Northern coll (—1874) and dial. (—1806). Ex preceding.

randyvoo. A tavern that is the resort of recruiting sergeants: military (—1909). 2. Hence, noise and wrangling: mostly military (—1909). Ex *rendez-vous*.

ranger. The penis: low: C.18–20. Ex *range*, to be inconstant. 2. See ATLANTIC RANGER.

***rank.** To cheat: c. and low s. (—1864). Prob. *ramp* corrupted, with some influence exercised by U.S. *outrank*, 1842, and *rank*, 1860, to take precedence of. cf. RANT.

rank and riches; or hyphenated. Breeches: rhyming s.: 1887, 'Dagonet' Sims.

rank and smell. A common person: lower classes': ca 1870–1905. Punning *rank*, smelly and (*high*) *rank* + SWELL.

rank outsider. A vulgar fellow, a cad: from ca 1880; coll >, 1910, S.E. Ex the turf.

ranker. An officer risen from the ranks: 1874, H., 5th ed.; 1878, Besant & Rice, 'Every regiment has its rankers; every ranker his story': coll. 2. A corruption of *rank* DUFFER: low London: from ca 1870; ob. 3. See GENTLEMAN RANKER.

rant. To appropriate forcibly: low (—1887). Walford's *Antiquarian*. Corruption of RAMP, v. 2. To be unduly free with (females): low (—1887). Ibid. Perhaps ex RAMP, v., 1, influenced by S.E. *rantipole*, v.; more prob. a dial. form of *rend*.

rantallion. 'One whose scrotum is so relaxed as to be longer than his penis', Grose, 1st ed.: low: ca 1780–1850. Cognate with, perhaps even a blend of, '*rant*ipole' and 'rapsc*allion*', so closely related to each other in meaning.

rantan; ran-tan; also **randan.** A spree: from ca 1710: coll >, in C.19, S.E. except as in the next entry; by itself, *randan* (etc.) is extremely ob. ?ex *at random*. 2. Hence, a riotous person: coll soon > S.E.: 1809; ob. by 1890.

rantan, on the. On the spree; drunk: coll: from ca 1760; slightly ob.; since 1853, gen. in the form, *on the ran-tan*. See preceding.

rantipole, ride. Same as *ride St George* (see RIDING . . .). Low: late C.18–19.

rantum-scantum. Copulation, esp. in *play at r.-s.*: low: mid-C.18–early 19. ?a rhyming combination ex †S.E. *rant*, to be boisterous or noisily gay; cognate with *rantipole*. 2. A wordy and mutual recrimination: low: ca 1820–95.

Ranzo. 'A native of the Azores, from the number named Alonzo who shipped in the whalers, where "Rueben [*sic*] Ranzo" was a favourite shanty': nautical coll: mid-C.19–20. Bowen.

rap, v.t. To barter; SWAP: late C.17–20: s. (†by 1850) and dial. Perhaps ex ob. S.E. sense, to transport, remove. 2. v.i., to take a false oath: c.: from ca 1740; †by 1890. Fielding, in *Jonathan Wild*, 'He [is] a pitiful fellow who would stick at a little rapping for a friend'; id., *Amelia*, I, ch. X, the footnote establishing the c. origin. Perhaps ex *rap (out) an oath*. 3. Also, v.t., to swear (something, *against* a person): 1733, Budgell, 'He ask'd me what they had to rap against me, I told him only a Tankard.' 4. To knock out; to kill: c., esp. Australian > low s.: 1888, Rolf Boldrewood, 'If he tries to draw a weapon, or move ever so little, he's rapped at that second'; ob. Ex Scots *rap*, 'to knock heavily; to strike'.

rap, not care a. To care not at all: 1834: coll >, ca 1850, S.E. Ex *rap*, an Irish counterfeit halfpenny.

rap, on the. On a bout of dissipation; slightly drunk: low (—1893). Milliken, 'The way the passengers stared at me showed I was fair on the rap.'

rape. A pear: back s. (—1859).

rapless. Penniless: coll: from ca 1880: very ob. Binstead.

rapped, ppl adj. Ruined: from ca 1870; ob. 2. (Killed) dead: low (?orig. c.): from ca 1888. See RAP, v., last sense.

rapper. An arrant lie: S.E., declares O.E.D.; coll, F. & H. Arising early in C.17, this sense is prob. best considered as coll until ca 1850, then S.E.; in C.20, it is mostly dial. See esp. Grose, P. 2. A dealer who raps at doors to find out whether there is anything worth buying: secondhand (e.g. curio) dealers' coll: late C.19–20.

rapping. Perjury: mid-C.18–19. See RAP, v., 2 and 3.

rare. Excellent, fine, splendid, as applied to comparatively trivial objects; often ironically. Coll: 1596, Shakespeare, 'Master Bassanio, who indeed gives rare new liveries'; 1878, Mrs Henry Wood, 'Guy will about die of it . . . Rare fun if he does.' 2. As an intensive: coll: 1833, Harriet Martineau, 'They put me in a rare passion.'

rare and (another adj.). A coll intensive: 1848, Mrs Gaskell, 'We got a good supper, and grew rare and sleepy'; slightly ob. except in Northern dial.

rarzo (or **rahzo**). A red-nosed man: Cockney: late C.19–20. 'Whatcher, rarzo!' Ex *raspberry* colour, whence also RAZZO.

rascal. 'A man without genitals', Grose, 1785: low: ca 1750–1850. Ex deer.

rasher of bacon. Some fiery liquor: ca 1750–70. Toldervy, 1756. See quotation at SLUG, n., 1.

rasher of wind. A very thin person: from ca 1860; slightly ob. cf. YARD OF PUMP-WATER. 2. Any person or thing of negligible account: from ca 1890. *Daily Telegraph*, 7 April 1899, 'Lets 'em howl, an' sweat, an' die, an' goes on all the time, as if they was jest rashers o' wind.'

rasp. The female pudend: low: C.19–20; ob. 2. See RASP, DO A.

rasp, v.i. and t. To coït (with): low: C.19–20; ob. Rare compared with:

rasp, do a. To coït: low: C.19–20. Gen. of the male: for semantics, see PUCKER-WATER, which not only astringes but roughens and hardens.

raspberry. A disapproving, fart-like noise, described by F. & H. as stable s., but gen. considered to be theatrical of late C.19–20. Ex RASPBERRY-TART, 1. 2. Hence, a gesture or a sign made in disapproval: theatrical: from the middle 1890s. 3. Abbr. RASPBERRY-TART, 2: low, mainly military: late C.19–20.

raspberry, get or **give the.** To 'get the bird' (see BIRD, n., 2), to be hissed; to hiss: theatrical: late C.19–20. Mainly and properly when the disapprobation is shown by a RASPBERRY, 1.

raspberry-tart. A breaking of wind: low rhyming s. on FART: from ca 1875. 2. The heart: rhyming s.: from ca 1890. 'Pomes' Marshall, in the *Sporting Times*, 29 Oct. 1892, 'Then I sallied forth with a careless air, | And contented raspberry-tart.' (In U.S., though now ob., a dainty girl: cf. Eng. JAM-TART, 2.)

rasper. A difficult high fence: hunting s.

(1812) >, ca 1840, j. >, ca 1870, S.E. Ainsworth, 1834, 'A stiff fence, captain – a reg'lar rasper'. 2. A person or thing of sharp, harsh, or unpleasant character: 1839, Dickens, 'He's what you may a-call a rasper, is Nickleby.' 3. Anything that, in its own way, is extraordinary; e.g. a large profit on the Stock Exchange: from ca 1860.

***raspin, the.** A house of correction; a gaol: c.: early C.19. ?lit., the unpleasant thing, perhaps a pun on *grating*, adj., and *gratings*, n. cf. the †Scots *rasp-house*, as in Scott, 1818.

rasping. (High and) difficult to jump: 1829: hunting coll >, ca 1870, S.E. Dr J. Brown, 1858, 'You cannot ... make him keep his seat over a rasping fence.' See RASPER, 1.

***rasping gang.** 'The mob of roughs and thieves who attend prize-fights', H., 1864: c.; ob.

***rat.** A drunken person taken into custody: c.: late C.17–early 19. ?ex idea of a drowned rat or, more prob., ex *drunk as a* RAT. 2. A clergyman: C.17. 'Microcosmography' Earle, 'A profane man ... nicknames clergyman ... rat, black-coat, and the like.' Prob. current also in C.18, since Grose puns thus: '*Rats*. Of these there are the following kinds: a black rat and a grey rat, a py-rat and a cu-rat,' esp. as, in C.17–early 18, *rat* occ. designated a pirate. 3. A police spy: c.: from ca 1850. Ex the gen. term of contempt. 4. An infernal machine for the foundering of insured bottoms: nautical coll (from ca 1880) > j. 5. See RATS and RATS! 6. In Australia, a street urchin; a wharf labourer: C. J. Dennis: late C.19–20.

rat!, rat it! or rat me! A low coll imprecation: late C.17–20; ob. Vanbrugh, Hoadly, Thackeray, Conan Doyle. Ex *rot*. cf. DRAT!

rat, do a. To change one's tactics: coll: from ca 1860. Ex S.E. *rat*, to desert.

rat, drunk as a. Hopelessly tipsy: coll: mid-C.16–17. Boorde, 1542.

rat, smell a, see SMELL A RAT.

rat and mouse. A house: rhyming s.: late C.19–20.

rat back-clip. Short hair: lower classes': ca 1856–1900.

rat-castle. A prison: s.: Ned Ward, 1703. Rats both lit. and fig. abound there.

rat-firm, -house, -office, -shop. A workshop, etc., where less than full union rates are paid: trade unions' coll (—1888).

rat-hole. Too large a gap between printed words: printers': from ca 1870.

rat it!; rat me! See RAT! **rat-office,** see RAT-FIRM.

rat-shop. A shop or factory that employs non-union workers: lower classes': from ca 1875. See also RAT-FIRM.

rat-trap. A bustle or dress-improver: ca 1850–1900. cf. BIRD-CAGE.

rate of knots, at the. Very fast: naval coll: mid-C.19–20. Granville. Current also in Australia and New Zealand since ca 1860.

rather! (In replying to a question) I should think so; very decidedly: coll, orig. somewhat low: 1836, Dickens, '"Do you know the mayor's house?" inquired Mr Trott. "Rather," replied the boots, significantly, as if he had some good reason for remembering it.' Occ. *rayther*, from ca 1860: very affected; ob. by 1905. cf. the very genteel QUITE! Often emphasized by stressing the second syllable.

rather of the ratherest. Slightly in excess or deficit: dial. and coll: 1787, Grose's *Provincial Glossary*; 1860, H., 2nd ed.

ratherish, adv. Slightly; somewhat: coll, orig. U.S. (1862), anglicized ca 1890. Ob.

rations. A flogging: naval and military: ca 1880–1910.

rats. A star: back s.: from ca 1875. (Not very gen.) 2. See RATS, GET. 3. *the rats*, delirium tremens: from ca 1865. Ex RATS, GET, 3.

rats! A contemptuous retort = BOSH: (low) coll: orig. U.S., but anglicized ca 1891. 'Pomes' Marshall, 'One word, and that was Rats!' Prob. ex:

rats, get or **have** or **see.** To be out of sorts (rarely with *see*): 1865, E. Yates, '"Well ... old boy, how are you?" ... " .. Not very brilliant ..." "Ah, like me, got rats, haven't you?"' 2. To be drunk; very drunk: from ca 1865. Likewise ob., very ob. 3. (Rarely *get* or *have*.) To have delirium tremens: low: from ca 1865. 4. Hence (though not with *get*), to be eccentric: (low) coll: from ca 1880. 5. Hence, from ca 1885, to be crazy.

rats, give (one) green. To malign; slander: ca 1860–1910. Perhaps ex *rats*: *sick 'em!*, a call to a dog ... Perhaps not.

rats, in the. Suffering from delirium tremens: low and military: from ca 1880. Ex RATS, 3.

rats and mice. Dice: from ca 1860.

rats in the garret or **loft** or **upper storey.** Eccentric; mad: from ca 1890; ob. Prob.

ex BATS IN THE BELFRY and RATS, GET . . ., 3, 4, 5.

rat's-tail. A writ: legal: from ca 1870. ?ex scroll on cover. 2. A pigtail: s.: Ned Ward, 1714.

rattat, see RUTAT.

***rattle.** A coach: c.: late C.18–early 19. Grose, 1785. Rare except in *rattle and pad*, a coach and horses. More gen. is RATTLER: yet cf. RATTLE, TAKE. 2. The commander's report of defaulters: naval: late C.19–20. Bowen. cf. the †S.E. *rattle*, a sharp reproof. 3. A quarrel: s.: Ned Ward, 1703.

rattle, v. To move or work quickly and/or noisily: s. and, from ca 1850, dial.: late C.17–20. Esp. in *rattle away* or *off*.

rattle, spring the. (Of a policeman) to give the alarm: policemen's (—1887); ob.

***rattle, take.** To depart hurriedly: c.: late C.17–mid-18. B.E., '*We'll take Rattle*, . . . we must not tarry, but whip away': a quotation that may possibly premise RATTLE, a coach, as early as late C.17; otherwise we must suppose that *rattle*, v., has been substantivized.

rattle, with a. With unexpected rapidity: turf (—1909). Coll.

rattle and drive (or hyphenated). Scamped work: workmen's coll (—1887).

rattle-bag, devil's (Scots **deil's**). A bishop's summons: coll: from ca 1725; †by 1900. Scott.

rattle-ballocks. The female pudend: low: late C.18–20; ob.

rattled. Very drunk: coll: late C.19–20. Lyell. cf. FLOORED, 2.

***rattler.** A coach: early C.17–mid-19: c. >, ca 1750, s.: 1630, J. Taylor the Water Poet. Like RATTLE, because it rattles. 2. Hence, a cab; ca 1815–1910: Moore, 1819; Egan, 1821, 'At length a move was made, but not a rattler was to be had.' 3. A train: c. (1845: '*No. 747*') >, by 1874 (H., 5th ed.), low.

***rattler, mace the.** To travel, esp. on a train, without a ticket: c.: mid-C.19–20.

rattlers. Teeth: s. > low coll: C.19–20; ob. 2. A railway (—1859); ob. by 1900. cf. RATTLER, 3.

rattles, the. A or the death-rattle: (low) coll: from ca 1820. 2. (With *the* often omitted.) The croup: somewhat coll: C.18–20.

rattletrap. The mouth: from ca 1820. Scott. 2. A chatterbox: coll: 1880, Anon., *Life in a Debtors' Prison*, 'You're as great a rattletrap as ever.' Both senses tend to be low; the former is somewhat ob.

***rattling cove.** A coachman: c.: mid-C.17–early 19. cf. RATTLE, n. and v. cf.:

***rattling mumper.** A beggar plying coaches and carriages: c.: mid-C.17–early 19.

***rattling-peeper.** A coach-glass: c.: mid-C.18. *The Scoundrel's Dict.*, 1754.

ratty. Wretched, miserable; mean: orig. (—1885), U.S. and Canadian, anglicized ca 1900. *Blackwood's Magazine*, Nov. 1901, 'Both were pretty "ratty" from hardship and loneliness.' Ex lit. sense, infested with rats. 2. Angry, irritated: from ca 1906. ?ex U.S.; cf. RATS IN THE GARRET and RATS! But prob. ex the appearance of a cornered rat.

raughty, see RORTY.

rave. A strong liking; a craze; a passion: from ca 1899; ob. by 1910. F. & H., 1901 (pub. 1902), 'X has a rave on Miss Z.' Ex the ob. late C.16–20 S.E. sense, a raving, a frenzy, excitement.

raven. A small bit of bread and cheese: taverns' (—1909); ob. Ex the story of Elisha and the ravens.

'Ravilliac, any Assassin', B.E.: coll: ca 1610–1750. Properly *Ravaillac*. Ex François Ravaillac, who, the assassinator of Henry IV of France, died in 1610.

raw chaw. A dram of spirituous liquor: low s.: ca 1810–60. Captain Glascock, *Land Sharks and Sea Gulls*, 1838.

raw lobster. A policeman: C.19. In contrast with LOBSTER, a soldier. 2. A sailor dressed in blue: ca 1800–55. Contrast *boiled* LOBSTER.

raw meat. The penis: low coll: mid-C.18–20. Anon., *The Butcher* (a song), 1766. 2. A nude (female) performer of the sexual act: low: C.19–20; ob.

raw recruit. A nip of undiluted spirits: from ca 1860; very ob.

raw uns or **'uns, the.** The naked fists: pugilistic: 1887, *Daily News*, 15 Sept., 'This encounter was without gloves, or, in the elegant language of the ring, with the raw uns'; 1891, *Sporting Life*, 26 March, 'Even Jean Carney . . . has been obliged to abandon the raw-un's for gloves pure and simple.' Slightly ob. (Here, *raw* = unprotected or uncovered.)

rawg. A waggon: Shelta: C.18–20.

rawniel or **runniel.** Beer: Shelta: C.18–20.

raws, the. Bare fists (cf. RAW 'UNS): coll: from ca 1895. In 1899, Clarence Rook says of the hooligan that 'He has usually done a bit of fighting with the gloves . . . But he is better with the raws, and is very bad to tackle in a street row.'

***ray.** The sum of 1s. 6d.: c.: 1861, Mayhew. ?ex or cognate with the already long † S.E. *ray*, a small piece of gold or gold leaf.

ray-neck. A landsman in a clipper packet's crew: nautical: mid-C.19–20; ob. Bowen thinks that it may represent a corruption of *rawneck*.

raymonder, see RAM-ROD. **rayther,** see RATHER.

razor, real. A defiant, quarrelsome, or bad-tempered scholar: Westminster School: from 1883; ob. Ware.

razor-strop. A copy of a writ: legal: from some date after 1822, when the lit. sense appears (O.E.D.).

razors. Inferior liquor: Regular Army: late C.19–20; very ob. Ex the gripe it produces.

razzle. Abbr. of RAZZLE-DAZZLE, 2. Esp. in *on the razzle*, on the SPREE.

razzle-dazzle. 'A new type of roundabout ... which gives its occupants the ... sensations of an excursion at sea', *Daily News*, 27 July 1891. 2. A frolic, a SPREE; riotous jollity: U.S. (1890, Gunter), anglicized ca 1895, esp. in *on the razzle-dazzle*, gen. of a drunken spree. Binstead, *More Gal's Gossip*, 1901, 'Bank-holidayites on the razzle-dazzle'. An echoic word expressive of rapid movement, bustle, active confusion, but orig., I think, a reduplication on *dazzle* as in Gunter's 'I'm going to razzle-dazzle the boys ... with my great lightning change act,' 1890, in *Miss Nobody*.

razzle-dazzle, v. To dazzle: anglicized ca 1895 ex U.S.; ob. See preceding, 2. cf.:

razzle-dazzler, gen. in pl. A sock that dazzles: 1897, *Daily News*, 10 Aug., 'Two dozen pair of plain socks and half a dozen pair of the sort known as "razzle-dazzlers" '. Ex RAZZLE-DAZZLE, V.

***razzo.** The nose: c.: from ca 1895. Clarence Rook, *The Hooligan Nights*, 1899. For origin, see RARZO.

razzorridge. Shaving: s.: Ned Ward, 1703. On *razor*.

re-dayboo. Re-debut: music-halls' coll: 1899–ca 1903. Lit., a first appearance for the second time.

re-raw, occ. **ree-raw.** Esp. *on the re(e)-raw*. A drinking-bout: low: from ca 1850; ob. Dickens, 1854. Prob. ex Scots *ree*, excited with drink, + Anglo-Irish *ree-raw*, noisy, riotous.

reach-me-down, adj., 1862; **reach-me-downs,** n., 1862. Thackeray; Besant & Rice. Ready-made, or occ. second-hand, clothes; in late C.19–20, often of such, hence of any, trousers: perhaps always S.E. (ex U.S.). Coll.

***reacher.** A beggar who walks always with a female mate: c.: early C.17. Dekker. 2. A gross exaggeration: coll: 1613, Purchas; †by 1720. 3. A blow delivered at one's full reach: boxing: late C.19–20; ob.

***read,** v.i. Rarely v.t. To steal: c.: Anon., *A Song*, ca 1819, 'And I my reading learnt betime, | From studying pocket-books, Sirs.' Ex READER, 1.

read and write. To fight: rhyming s. (—1857). 2. A flight: id. Rare.

read between the lines. To discern the underlying fact or intention: from ca 1865: coll.

read me and take me. (In reference to riddles) a Restoration c.p. equivalent to *get me?* or *get me!* Dryden, *Marriage à la Mode*.

read of tripe. Transported for life: rhyming s. (—1859). H.'s approximation; †by 1900.

read the paper. To have a nap: coll: from ca 1860. A very common excuse.

***reader.** A pocket-book: c.: 1718, C. Hitchin, *The Regulator*. 2. Whence, a newspaper, a letter, etc.: c.: from ca 1840. 3. A marked card: c. or gamblers' s.: 1894, Maskelyne, 'The preparation of "faked" cards or "readers" '.

***reader-hunter.** A pickpocket specializing in pocket-books: c. (—1812). Ex READER, 1. See quotation at READ.

***reader-merchant.** (Gen. in pl.) 'Pickpockets, chiefly young Jews, who ply about the Bank to steal the pocket-books of persons who have just received their dividends there', Grose, 2nd ed.: late C.18–20; ob. Ex READER, 1, and see MERCHANT.

***readered.** Wanted by the police: c.: from ca 1845. '*No. 747*' (p. 412). Ex READER, 2, and the fact of being 'advertised' in the *Police Gazette*.

***ready, or the ready.** Money, esp. money in hand: c. until C.19, then low s. till ca 1870; by 1930, rather ob. Shadwell, 'Take up on the reversion ...; and Cheatly will help you to the ready'; Arbuthnot, 1712, 'He was not flush in ready'; Egan, 1821, 'The waste of ready'. Abbr. *ready money*. Often with RHINO: *ready rhino* (T. Brown, 1697) is adumbrated in Shadwell's *the ready, the rhino* (1688).

ready, v. To pull a horse so that he shall

not win: racing: Black, 1887. 2. To contrive, manipulate, engineer, WANGLE: from ca 1890. 'Pomes' Marshall, 'He made us all . . . believe he could ready his chance.' (Sense 1 is ex †S.E. sense, prepare, put in order.) cf. READY UP. 3. Hence, to bribe: low (—1909).

ready, (at) a good. Thoroughly alert; occ. dead certain: low (?orig. c.): from ca 1890; ob. cf. *on the* SPOT.

ready gilt. Money (in hand): a C.19 variant of READY, n. See also GILT.

***ready thick'un.** A sovereign (coin): c.: from ca 1860.

ready to drop. (Of a person) exhausted: late C.19–20: coll.

ready up. To prepare, or contrive, illicitly or not honourably: Australian: 1893, *Melbourne Age*, 25 Nov., 'A great deal has been "readied up" for the jury by the present commissioners.' Prob. ex READY, v., 3.

readying, readying-up. vbl nn. of READY, v., and READY UP.

real, adv. Extremely, very: coll: from ca 1880 in England, earlier in Scotland and U.S.; esp. in *real nice*. Ex *real* as adj. before another adj., esp. when no comma intervenes (J. Fox, 1718, 'An Opportunity of doing a real good Office'.)

real jam. A very delightful person or thing: s. verging on coll: 1879, Justin McCarthy, 'Real jam, I call her'; *Punch*, 3 Jan. 1885, 'Without real jam – cash and kisses – this world is a bitterish pill.' Earlier, a sporting phrase for anything exceptionally good: from ca 1870.

real Kate. A kind matron: Clare Market, London: ca 1882–1900. Ex *Kate*, the charitable queen of the market.

real live, see LIVE, adj.

real peacer (or P.). A 'dashing' murderer: low coll: late C.19–early 20. Ex Charles *Peace*, the celebrated murderer.

real raspberry jam. The superlative of JAM-TART, a girl: low: ca 1883–1915.

real thing, the. The genuine article (fig.): 1818, Lady Morgan, 'He is the real thing, and no mistake.'

***ream.** Genuine; honest, honourable, above-board: an occ. C.19 c. variant of RUM, adj. very rare outside London. Mayhew, 1851, 'A "ream" . . . concern'. cf.:

ream-penny. (Gen. in pl.) = Peter-pence. C.17: coll and dial. Ex *Rome-penny*.

ream-pennies, reckon (up) one's. To confess one's faults: coll: ca 1650–1700. Ray. Ex REAM-PENNY.

rear, rears, the. The latrine: university: from ca 1880. cf.:

rear, v. To visit the latrine; to defecate: from ca 1890: university >, ca 1905, gen. s. Perhaps of military origin: a man 'taken short' is told to 'fall out to the *rear*'.

rear up, v. To become extremely angry: coll: late C.19–20. Ex horses.

rearer. The upsetting of a vehicle – the wheel(s) on one side going into a ditch, drain, etc. – so that the vehicle turns underside up: 1827 (O.E.D.); very ob. 2. A battledore: Restoration period.

rec, the. The recreation ground: lower-class, esp. Cockney, coll: from ca 1890 or earlier.

receipt. Punches received: boxers': mid-C.19–20; extremely ob. *Bell's Life*, 'He showed strong symptoms of receipt.' cf. RECEIVER-GENERAL, 2.

receipt of custom (or hyphenated). The female pudend: C.19–20; ob. cf. Grose's CUSTOM-HOUSE GOODS. (Where Adam made the first entry.)

receiver-general. A harlot: C.19. *Lex. Bal.*, 1811. Ex S.E., a chief receiver of public revenues. 2. 'A boxer giving nothing for what he gets', F. & H.: boxing: *Boxiana*, III, 1821.

recep. Reception by an audience: theatrical and music halls': late C.19–20.

reckon up. To talk of, maliciously or even slanderously: non-aristocratic: from ca 1870.

reckoning, cast up one's. To vomit: low (—1788); very ob. More gen. *cast up one's* ACCOUNTS.

reckoning, Dutch. A bill that, if disputed, grows larger; a sharing of the cost or the money, plunder, etc.: coll: late C.17–20; ob. Swift. See the paragraph on DUTCH.

record, smash the. To go one better: coll, esp. in athletics: from ca 1890. *Break, cut* (†), *lower the record* are S.E.

recruit, n. See RECRUITS. 2. 'To get a fresh supply of money', Grose, 1785: coll. cf. the next two entries.

recruiting service. Robbery on the highway: ca 1810–40: s. verging on c. (*Lex. Bal.*) Ex:

***recruits.** Money, esp. expected money: late C.17–early 19: c. B.E., '*Have you rais'd the Recruits*, . . . is the Money come in?' Ex Army.

rector. 'A poker kept for show: *curate* [q.v.] = the work-a-day iron; (2) the bottom half of a tea-cake or muffin (as getting more butter), the top half being the *curate*, and so forth', F. & H.: coll: from ca 1860; ob.

rector of the females. The penis: C.17–20; ob. Either low coll or, more prob., euphemistic S.E. Rochester.

red, n. The port side of a ship; it shows a red light; cf. *green*, the starboard side, which shows a green one: nautical coll: late C.19–20.

***red,** adj. Made of gold; golden: C.14–20: S.E. till C.17, then c. See esp. RED CLOCK, ROGUE, STUFF, TACKLE, TOY, 'UN.

red, paint the town. To have a riotously good time: U.S. (—1880), anglicized ca 1890 as a coll. Anon., *Harry Fludyer at Cambridge*, 'Won't he paint the whole place red on Tuesday night!'

red ace; occ. **red C.** The female pudend: low: mid-C.19–20.

red and yellow, Tom Fool's colours. A c.p. (semi-proverb) in allusion to brightly coloured clothes: already old in 1874. Ex a jester's parti-coloured dress.

red beard. (App.) a watchman or constable: C.17: ?c. Dekker & Webster, 1607, 'White haires may fall into the company of drabs as red beardes into the society of knaves.' 2. A red marble: London schoolboys' (—1887).

red breast, redbreast. A Bow Street runner: C.18–early 19, though app. first recorded by Dickens in 1862. Ex red waistcoat.

***red clock.** A gold watch: c.: from ca 1860. Also RED 'UN. cf. RED LOT.

red cross. An English ship: nautical coll: C.17. Smith, 1626.

red-currant jelly. (Not as n., but as adj. in the predicate.) 'He's red-currant jelly' is County s., of ca 1840–1900, applied to a tradesman or merchant who, retiring to the country, out-Counties the County. Usually, however, simply *currant jelly*. (A staple produce on the shop-keeper's shelves.)

red(-)dog. Prickly heat: Anglo-Indian coll: ca 1740–1800.

red duster. The Red Ensign: naval: late C.19–20.

red eel. A term of contempt: coll: C.19.

red flag, see RED RAG, MOUNT THE.

red flag at the mast-head. In dead earnest: naval coll: mid-C.19–20; ob. Ex a single-flag signal enjoining either 'close action' or 'no quarter'.

red flannel. The tongue: low: C.19–20; ob. cf. RED RAG, 1.

***red fustian.** Red wine, esp. port or claret: c.: late C.17–early 19. 2. Porter: C.19.

red-headed. Zealous: *Conway* training-ship cadets': late C.19–20.

red heart. 'Redheart' rum; hence, any rum: London taverns': ca 1870–1910. (Coll rather than s.)

red herring. A soldier (1827; very ob.). cf. SOLDIER, a red herring.

red herring ne'er spake word but e'en, Broil my back, but not my weamb or womb (i.e. stomach). A c.p. of ca 1670–1700. (The *weamb* form is dial.)

red hot. 'Extreme; out-and-out', C. J. Dennis: coll: late C.19–20. Not as, e.g., *a red-hot socialtst*, but as *that's red hot, that is!*

red-hot treat. An extremely dangerous person: lower classes' (—1909); ob.

red-ink. Blood: pugilistic: ca 1840–90. Augustus Mayhew, *Paved With Gold*, 1857.

red inside (allee) same as Queen Victoria. A c.p., used of – and reputedly by – dark-skinned races: late C.19–20. i.e. a dark skin does not preclude moral merit.

red lamp. A brothel: coll: late C.19–20. Ex U.S. *red light district*.

red lane. The throat: coll: late C.18–20. Grose, 1st ed.; 1812, Colman; ob. Also in dial.

red-letter man. A Roman Catholic: coll: late C.17–early 19. Ex *red-letter day* and cf. RED NECK.

red(-)liner. ca 1840–80, as in Mayhew's *London Labour*, II, 564, 'The Red Liners, as we calls the Medicity officers, who goes about in disguise as gentlemen, to take up poor boys caught begging'. ?ex putting a red line under an offender's name.

Red Lion Lane, see LANE.

red lobsters. The original Metropolitan Police: Londoners': ca 1830–60.

***red lot.** Gold watch and chain: c., and low: late C.19–20. See RED, adj.

red neck. A Roman Catholic: Northern (esp. Lancashire) coll and dial.: C.19.

red-nosed rooter. A port-maintopman: *Conway* cadets': 1890s.

red one, see RED 'UN and cf. RUDDOCK.

red petticoat shall pay for it, the lass in the, see LASS IN . . .

red rag. The tongue: mid-C.17–20, ob. cf. RED FLANNEL. 2. A menstrual cloth: low coll: C.19–20. cf.:

red rag, flash the. To menstruate: low: C.19–20. Ex RED RAG, 2.

red rag, mount the. To blush: coll: C.19–20. Occ. *red flag*.

red ribbon. Brandy: ca 1820–1910. After 1890, c. (Contrast RED FUSTIAN.)

***red rogue.** A gold coin: c.: C.17. Fletcher, in *The Mad Lover*. See RED.

***red-sail (yard) docker.** A buyer of 'stores stolen out of the royal yards and docks', Grose, 1st ed.: c. of ca 1780–1840.

***red shank, red-shank, redshank.** A duck: c.: mid-C.16–19. 2. A turkey: C.18. Ex the pool-snipe so named. 3. A woman wearing no stockings: Connaught coll: from ca 1840. Ex the historical S.E. *redshank*.

***red shirt.** A back scarified with the cat-o'-nine-tails: Australian c.: ca 1820–70.

red steer, the. A bush fire: Australian rural: late C.19–20. cf. the South German *der rote Hahn* (the red cockerel), meaning 'fire', usually in a phrase translatable as 'putting the red cock on someone's roof'.

***red stuff.** Gold articles: c.: late C.19–20. David Hume.

***red tackle.** A gold chain: c.: 1879, *Macmillan's Magazine*, 'I touched for a red toy . . . and red tackle.'

***red tape.** Red wine: c. of C.19. Lytton in *Paul Clifford*. cf. RED FUSTIAN.

red tie. Vulgarity: Oxford University coll: ca 1876–1900.

***red toy.** A gold watch: c.: 1879 (see quotation at RED TACKLE).

***red 'un.** The O.E.D. instances *red ones* in C.16: prob. coll. But *red 'un* is c.: from ca 1860. Gen., a gold coin and usually a sovereign; occ. an object made of gold (Sims, in the *Referee*, 12 Feb. 1888); e.g. a gold watch: c. (—1864), as in H., 3rd ed. cf. REDDING.

red, white and blue. Cold salt beef: *Conway* cadets': late C.19–20.

redbreast, see RED BREAST.

redding. A gold watch: c. of ca 1860–1915. A corruption of RED 'UN, perhaps influenced by dial. *redding*, oxide of iron, red ochre.

redemptioner. A man who works his passage: nautical coll: C.19.

Redfern. A perfectly-fitting lady's coat or jacket: Society coll: ca 1879–1915. Ex a celebrated ladies' tailor.

***redge,** see RIDGE.

redraw. A warder: low back s. (—1875). Greenwood, in *Low-Life Deeps*, 'Shying a lump of red oakum at the redraw'.

reds. Blushes: coll and dial.: C.19–20. 2. The menses: mid-C.16–20; S.E. till C.18, then coll; almost †.

redshank, see RED SHANK.

redundant. Impertinent: City of London: 1899–1900. Ex a phrase by Horatio Bottomley.

redwop. Powder: back s.: from ca 1890.

ree-raw, see RE-RAW.

reeb. Beer: back s. (—1859).

***reef.** 'To draw up a dress-pocket until a purse is within reach of the fingers', F. & H.: c.: from ca 1860. Ex nautical S.E.

reef (or two), let out a. To undo a button or so, esp. after a meal: from ca 1870: nautical > gen.

reef taken in, need a. To be drunk: from ca 1880: nautical > gen.

reefer. A midshipman: nautical: 1818, Burton. Because, says Smyth, he has to 'attend to the tops during the operation of taking in reefs'.

***reek.** Money: c.: early C.19. ?ex *reek-penny*.

reel, dance the miller's; dance the reel o' stumpie or of bogie. To have sexual intercourse: low Scots coll: C.18–20; ob.

***reeler.** A policeman: c. (—1879); ob. Presumably on PEELER.

reeling, n. Feeling (gen. pl): rhyming s. (—1909).

***reener.** A coin (less, app., than a florin): tramps' c.: from ca 1890. P. H. Emerson, 1893, 'The old man never give her a reener.' ?DEANER corrupted.

reesbin. A gaol: tramps' c., and tinkers' s. verging on c.: 1845, reference in '*No. 747*' (p. 413). Prob. a corruption of *prison* on Romany *stariben* (whence STIR, n., 2).

ref. A reformer: political (—1909); ob.

refresh. A refreshment, esp. of liquor: coll, verging now on s.: from ca 1884. Ex:

refresher. A drink: coll: 1841, T. Hook. cf. the pun in 'As a rule barristers don't object to refreshers,' *Ally Sloper's Half-Holiday*, 3 Aug. 1889. cf. PICK-ME-UP.

reg. duck-egg. An egregious '0': cricketers': late C.19–20. See DUCK, n., 6.

regardless, see GOT UP, 2.

regent. 'Half a sovereign' (coin): ca 1820–60. *Sinks*, 1848. By a not despicable pun.

regimental sports. Coal-carrying fatigue: Regular Army: late C.19–20; ob.

regular. A drink taken at a fixed hour: coll: from ca 1850. 2. See REGULARS. 3. One who quits a pleasure-party at 11 or 12 at night. A laugh at his regular, wholesome habits.

regular, adj. Thorough, absolute; perfect: coll: 1821, Shelley, 'A regular conjuror'; 1850, Smedley, 'A regular sell'; 1888, *Cornhill Magazine*, March.

regular Callao. A free-and-easy ship lax of discipline: nautical coll: late C.19–20.

regular tradesman. Anyone who thoroughly understands his business or occupation: proletarian coll: mid-C.19–20; ob.

regularly. Thoroughly; wholly: coll: 1789, 'Regularly dissipated'. cf. REGULAR, adj.

***regulars.** A division of booty: c.: from ca 1810. *Lex. Bal.*, Vaux, Moncrieff, 'Gypsy' Carew. Abbr. *regular share(s)*.

regulated, be. To go through the Press Gang's perfunctory medical examination: naval coll: ca 1750–1840. Bowen.

regulator. The female pudend: low coll: late C.18–19. Prob. ex the S.E. sense, a regulating power or principle (1766, O.E.D.).

rehoboam. A shovel hat: coll of ca 1845–70. C. Brontë, 1849. 2. A quadruple magnum, a double jeroboam, gen. of champagne: from ca 1860; ob.

***reign.** A period of wrongdoing; a successfully criminal period out of gaol: c.: from ca 1810. cf.:

***reign,** v. To be at liberty, esp. at profitable liberty: Australian c. >, by 1910, gen. c.: late C.19–20.

reign of Queen Dick, see DICK, QUEEN.

relation. A pawnbroker: Londoners': ca 1845–1900. Mayhew, II, 1851. Suggested by synonymous UNCLE.

relations (or country cousins) have come, her. She is in her menstrual period: lower classes' c.p.: mid-C.19–20.

reliever. An old coat usable by all (the workmen): ca 1845–1900. Kingsley.

relieving officer (rarely **a**). One's father, because he pays one's debts: 1857, G. Lawrence. Grenville-Murray, 1883, 'The Relieving Officer, or ... the "R.O.", was a term of endearment which [he], in common with other young noblemen and gentlemen at Eton, applied to his father.' Slightly ob.

religion, get, see GET RELIGION.

religious. (Of a horse) apt to go down on his knees: late C.18–mid-19. cf. DEVOTIONAL HABITS and contrast the old West American *religious* applied to horses: free from vice.

religious painter. 'One who does not break the commandment which prohibits the making of the likeness of any thing in heaven or earth, or in the waters under the earth', Grose, 2nd ed.: ca 1780–1820. Either a little joke of Grose's or painters' s. – he was a painter and draughtsman.

relish. Coïtion with a woman: low: C.19. cf. GREENS, 4.

Relish, the. The (sign of the) Cheshire Cheese: late C.18–mid-19.

rem-in-re, esp. **be caught with.** Copulation, esp. be taken in the act of: low: from ca 1860; ob. Lit., a thing in a thing.

***remedy.** A sovereign (coin): c.: ?mid-C.18–early 19. Ex the technical S.E. *remedy*, the permissible variation of weight in coins (also called *tolerance*).

remedy-critch. A chamber-pot: late C.18–early 19. A *critch* = any earthenware vessel; *remedy*, because therewith discomfort is remedied.

remember Parson Mallum (or Meldrum, Malham, or Melham)! see PARSON MALLUM ...

remi. A holiday: Westminster School: from ca 1860. Ex *remedy* in that sense.

reminisce. To relate reminiscences, esp. if freely: coll: from ca 1880. Ex the jocular *reminisce*, v.i. and t., to recollect, + *reminiscences*.

removal. A murder: political: 1883–5. Ex a witness's euphemism in the Phoenix Park assassination case.

***rent.** Plunder: c.: late C.18–mid-19. Implied in Grose's COLLECTOR. 2. See RENTS. 3. Money; cash: lower classes': late C.19–20.

rent, collect. To rob on the highway: c.: late C.18–mid-19. See RENT, n., 1; also in Bee, 1823. See esp. RENT-COLLECTOR.

rent, pay (someone) **his.** To punish: coll: C.14–(?)16. S. Oliphant's *New English*. (?)

***rent-collector.** A highwayman, esp. one who fancies money only: c.: (?late C.18–) early 19. cf. COLLECTOR; RENT.

rents (in C.17, rent) coming in. Ragged; dilapidated: a punning coll c.p. of C.17–mid-18. Withals, 1616, '"That hath his rent come in"'; Swift, *Polite Conversation*, Dialogue I, 'I have torn my Petticoat with your odious Romping; my Rents are coming in; I'm afraid, I shall fall into the Ragman's Hands.'

rep. Reputation: coll: ca 1705–50 (extant in U.S.). Shippery, 'Upon rep'; D'Urfey, 'Dames of rep'; Fielding. (See REP, ON.) 2. Hence, a man (ob.) or woman (†by 1850) of loose morals: coll: 1747, Hoadly. Here, *rep* is ex *reprobate*, influenced by sense 1, and suggested by DEMI-REP. 3. Hence, a worthless or inferior object: coll: 1786, Wolcot, 'The fiddle... though what's vulgarly baptiz'd a *rep*'. Very ob. 4. A repetition (lesson): school s., esp. at Harrow: from ca 1860. Anstey. At Charterhouse, esp.: poetry as repetition: late C.19–20. cf. PREP.

rep, on or **'pon** or **upon.** On (my) word of honour, lit. on my **reputation**: coll: C.18, though rare after ca 1750. See REP, 1. Swift, 'Do you say it upon Rep?'

repairs, no. Reckless; neck or nothing: from ca 1880; ob. (Gen. of contests.)

reparty. A repartee: Society: 1874–ca 90. (Satirical.)

repentance curl. The English society form of the curl known in Fr. as *repentir*: 1863–ca 90.

reporter. A (hair-trigger) pistol: coll, mostly Irish, verging on S.E.; †by 1910. Jonah Barrington, 1827. Ex the suddenness of the report.

reposer. A final drink; a nightcap: coll: from ca 1870. (Repose-inducing.)

repository. A lock-up, a gaol: ca 1780–1830.

republic of letters, the. The Post-Office: ca 1820–50. Punning S.E. sense.

reservoir!, au. *Au revoir!*: jocular coll (—1897); ob. cf. OLIVE OIL!

residential club. A usual assemblage of idlers, esp. those frequenting the British Museum for warmth or shelter: jocular coll verging on S.E.; from ca 1890; ob., as (thanks be!) is the practice.

resin up. To smarten up (a man) at his work: nautical: late C.19–20. Ex resining a fiddle.

responsible. A sensible actor able to take the lead: theatrical coll: from ca 1890.

respun; occ. **rispin.** To steal: tinkers' s., bordering on c.: from ca 1850. ?origin. Just possibly ex or cognate with Scots *risp*, to rasp, to file.

rest, v. To arrest: mid-C.15–20: S.E. until C.19, then dial. and low coll.

rest?, and the. A c.p. retort on incompleteness or reticence: from ca 1860.

rest and be thankful, the. The female pudend: C.19–20; ob.

resting. Out of work: theatre, music-hall: late C.19–20.

resurrection-bolly. Beefsteak pudding: preparatory schools': late C.19–20.

resurrection-cove. A body-snatcher: low: ca 1810–95. Vaux; Baumann.

resurrection-jarvey. A nocturnal hackney-coachman: ca 1820–60. Westmacott.

resurrection(-pie). A dish made from remains: from ca 1864: coll till C.20, then S.E.: orig. and esp. a schoolboys' term.

reswort. Trousers: back s. (—1874).

ret. A reiteration in printing: printers' (—1874).

***retoure**, see TOUR.

***retriever.** A 'verser' (see VERSING LAW): local c. of ca 1592. Greene.

retsio. An oyster: back s. (—1874).

returned empty. A Colonial bishop returning to, and gen. taking up a post in, Britain: Church: from ca 1890.

revenge in lavender. A vengeance reserved: coll bordering on S.E.: late C.17–early 19. See LAVENDER . . .

reverence, see SIR REVERENCE.

review of the black cuirassiers. A visitation by the clergy: late C.18–early 19. Grose, 1785. Ex priestly black and shining crosses and/or crucifixes. cf. CROW-FAIR.

reviver. A drink (rarely of non-intoxicants): orig. Society: 1876, Besant & Rice, 'It was but twelve o'clock, and therefore early for revivers of any sort.' cf. REFRESHER.

revlis. Silver: back s. (—1859).

reward. Dogs' or hounds' supper: kennels' s.: C.19–20. Ex S.E. sense, entrails given to hounds imm. after the kill.

r'ghoglin or **gogh'leen.** To laugh: Shelta: C.18–20.

***rheumatic dodge.** The gaining of sympathy – and alms – by a pretence of (acute) rheumatism: c. (—1887).

rheumaticky. Afflicted with rheumatism: coll: from ca 1850.

rheumatics; often **the r.** Rheumatism: late C.18–20: coll: from ca 1890, considered increasingly low coll.Ex the adj. cf. RHEUMATIZ and RHEUMATICKY.

rheumatism in the shoulder. Arrest: low: from ca 1820; ob. Esp. *have r. in the s.*, to be arrested.

rheumatiz, r(h)umatiz; occ. (esp. until ca 1830) **rheumatise** or **-ize**, or **rheumatis.** Rheumatism: dial. and low coll: 1760, Foote, 'My old disorder, the rheumatise'.

***rhino**; occ. **rino, ryno,** but not after C.18. Money: 1688, Shadwell; B.E.; Grose; Barham. c. until ca 1820, then low s. >, ca 1870, gen. s. Often READY *rhino*. Origin problematic; there is prob. some allusion to the size of a rhinoceros, or to the price which almost any part of its corpse will fetch as an aphrodisiac: cf. next three entries. c. synonyms are: BIT; COLE; GELT; LOAVER; LURRY; PEWTER; QUIDS; REEK; RIBBIN; the s. and coll synonyms are too numerous to list – see F. & H. at *rhino* and H. at pp. 61–5. **2.** Rhinoceros: coll abbr.: 1884.

rhino-fat. Rich: C.19. Ex preceding; suggested by RHINOCERICAL; cf.:

rhinoceral. Rich: from ca 1860. See RHINO; abbr. cf.:

***rhinocerical.** Rich: c. until C.19, then s.; †by 1860. Shadwell, B.E., Grose. As Shadwell has both *rhino* and *rhinocerical* in 1688, the latter may well be the origin of the former. See RHINO.

rhubarb. A loan: dockers': late C.19–20. Ex its ruddy length, or from the illiterate pronunciation *rubbub*, rhyming on SUB (n., 7), a loan. 2. Genitals, male, or, occ., female. e.g. 'How's your rhubarb coming up, Bill?' 3. See next entry. 4. A rumpus, ROW; a loud confused noise; noises off, esp. those of a mob: theatrical: late C.19–20. Ex off-stage actors intoning the sonorous word 'rhubarb' to represent the noise of a mob. The custom goes back at least to the time of Charles Kean, ca 1852.

rhubarb (pill). A hill: rhyming: late C.19–20.

rhumatiz, see RHEUMATIZ.

rhyme-slinger. A poet: coll: from ca 1850.

ri, see LEP.

rib, crooked. A cross-grained wife: coll: late C.18–20, ob. (The S.E. *rib*, a wife, is Biblical in origin and affected esp. by Scottish poets.)

rib-baste or, much more gen., **-roast.** To thrash: coll: resp. late C.16–17, late C.16–20, ob. Occ. a n., with variant *rib-roasting*, *-basting*. Gascoigne, 'I hope to give them al a rybbe to roste for their paynes'; Smollett, 'He knew he should be rib-roasted every day, and murdered at last'; H., 1874, '*Ribroast* . . . Old; but still in use'. cf. next two entries.

rib-bender or **-roaster;** occ. **rib of roast; ribber.** A punch on the ribs: boxing: from ca 1810; the 2nd and 3rd, very ob. Tom Moore has *ribber*, 'Cuthbert Bede' *rib-roaster*, Hindley *rib-bender*. cf. the next entry. 2. A ball rising so high as to endanger the batsman's body: cricket: 1873; ob.

rib-bending or **-roasting; ribbing.** The vbl n. counterparts of RIB-BENDER, etc.

rib-roast, -roaster, see RIB-BASTE and RIB-BENDER.

rib-shirt. A front or dickey worn over a grubby shirt: lower classes': from ca 1880; ob.

rib-tickle; rib-tickler. To thrash, also *tickle one's ribs*. A punch in the ribs; thick soup. From ca 1850; slightly ob. cf. RIB-BASTE and -BENDER.

ribband, see RIBBIN. **ribber,** see RIB-BENDER.

***ribbin;** also **ribband, ribbon.** Money: c.: late C.17–mid-19. ?cf. FAT, being ex *ribbing* (cf. RIBS), or ex *ribbon*, gen. of rich stuff. cf.:

***ribbin runs thick** or **thin, the.** There is, he (etc.) has, much or little money: late C.17–mid-19. See RIBBIN.

***ribbon,** see RIBBIN. 2. See RIBBONS. 3. A bell-pull: c.: late C.17–mid-18. B.E., '*Pluck the Ribond*, . . . ring the Bell at the Tavern'. Ex likeness of ribbon to rope. 4. Esp. BLUE RIBBON: gin: c.: from ca 1810; ob. Prob. suggested by SATIN. 5. After ca 1860, *ribbon* (but not BLUE RIBBON) = spirits in gen.; ob. H., 3rd ed. ('Servants' term').

ribbons. Reins: 1813 (O.E.D.): sporting coll >, ca 1880, S.E. Dickens in *Pickwick*. Esp. in *handle* or *†flutter the ribbons*.

ribs. (A nickname for) a stout person: coll: C.19–20; ob. They do *not* show.

ribston(e). A Cockney's term of affectionate address: 1883, Milliken in *Punch*, 11 Oct. Abbr. *ribston(e)* PIPPIN.

rice-bags. Trousers: a trifle low: ca 1890–1910. On BAGS, trousers.

rice Christian. An Aboriginal 'accepting' Christianity for food: Society coll: 1895, *Referee*, 11 Aug.; ob.

rich. Very entertaining – preposterous, ridiculous – outrageous: mid-C.18–20 S.E. verging on coll. 2. Spicy; indelicate: coll: from ca 1860.

rich as a new-shorn sheep. An ironic, semi-proverbial c.p. of C.16–mid-18. Churchyard, Breton, Fuller.

rich as crazes. Rich as Croesus: Anglo-Irish (—1909).

rich man's side, see POOR MAN'S SIDE.

rich one. The wealthy wife of 'a man who finds home not to his liking': better-class harlots' coll (—1909).

Richard, Richard Snary, Richardanary. A dictionary: s., low coll, sol.: resp. late C.18–20, e.g. in Grose, 2nd ed., an abbr. of *R. S.*; from ca 1620, as in 'Water Poet' Taylor; C.19–20 (also dial.), a corruption of *R. S.* All ob. cf. DICK, which indicates the semantics.

Richard the Third. A bird: rhyming s.: late C.19–20. 2. A TURD: id.: id.

Richardanary, see RICHARD.

rick(-)ma(-)tick. Arithmetic: school s. and gen. sol.: C.19–20. On *'rithmetic*, as in the three Rs, *reading*, *'riting and 'rithmetic*.

rick-rack. A policeman's whistle: Manchester children's: ca 1860–80. Jerome Caminada, *Detective*, II, 1901. Echoic.

ride. (Gen. used by women.) An act of coïtion: low: C.19–20. Ex the v. (cf. the scabrous smoke-room story of the little boy that wanted 'a ride on the average'.) Esp. in *have* or *get a ride*.

ride, v. To mount a woman in copulation: v.i. and t.: M.E.–C.20: S.E. till ca 1780 then (low) coll. D'Urfey has *ride tantivy*. cf. RIDER, 1. 2. See RIDER, 2. (3. For relevant phrases not under *ride*, see the second member; e.g. *ride* BODKIN.) 4. To cart: South African coll: 1897, Ernest Glanville, *Tales from the Veld*, 'I want you to ride a load of wood to the house.'

ride as if fetching the midwife. To go in haste: coll: late C.17–mid-19. Ray.

ride behind, see RIDER, 2.

ride (a man) **down like a main-tack.** To overwork him: nautical coll: mid-C.19–20.

ride out. To be a highwayman: coll: C.17–18. Anon., *The London Prodigal*, 1605. cf. Chaucer's *riden out*, to go abroad, serve on a military expedition (the description of the knight, in the *Canterbury* Prologue).

ride rantipole, see RANTIPOLE, RIDE. **ride rusty,** see RUSTY, RIDE. **ride St George,** see RIDING ST GEORGE.

ride the black donkey. To be in a bad humour: coll: mid-C.19–early 20.

***ride the donkey.** To cheat in weight (weighing): c. (—1857).

ride the fore-horse. To be early; ahead of another: coll: ca 1660–1840. Etherege; Scott.

ride the fringes. To perambulate the boundaries of a chartered district: Irish coll of ca 1700–1820. Anon., *Ireland Sixty Years Ago*, 1847. A corruption of *ride the franchises*.

ride the mare. To be hanged: (c. or) low: late C.16–17. Shakespeare. See THREE-LEGGED MARE.

ride the wild mare. To play at see-saw; hence, I conjecture, to act wildly or live riotously: coll: late C.16–mid-17. Shakespeare; Cotgrave, 'Desferrer l'asne . . . we say, to ride the wilde mare.'

rider. An – esp. customarily – actively amorous man: low coll: C.18–20; ob. Ex RIDE, V. cf. RIDING ST GEORGE. 2. 'A person who receives part of the salary of a place or appointment from the ostensible occupier, by virtue of an agreement with the donor, or great man appointing. The rider is said to be quartered upon the possessor, who often has one or more persons thus riding behind him,' Grose, 3rd ed. Coll of late C.18–mid-19. 3. A passenger: cabmen's coll (—1887); ob.

***ridg.** An early variant of:

***ridge;** occ., in C.19, **redge.** Gold: c.: from ca 1660; ob. by 1840, †by 1900. Head (implied in RIDGE-CULLY). A CLY *full of ridge*, a pocketful of money. 2. Hence, a guinea: ca 1750–1830. ?ex *ridge*, a measure of land.

***ridge,** adj. Good; valuable: Australian c.: late C.19–20. Ex the n., 1.

***ridge, thimble of.** A gold watch: ca 1830–60: c. Ainsworth, 1834.

***ridge-cully.** A goldsmith, lit. a gold-man (see RIDGE and CULLY): c.: 1665, Head. Very ob. by 1880. Whence, prob.:

***ridge-montra.** A gold watch: C.19 (?–20): c. See RIDGE and MONTRA.

riding. Adroitness; ability: sporting (—1886); ob. Ex a jockey's skill.

riding-hag. A, the, nightmare: coll: C.19–20; ob.

riding St George or the dragon upon St George, n. and adj. (The position of) the woman being on top in the sexual act: late C.17–mid-19. (This posture was supposed to be efficacious if the parents wanted their child to be a bishop.) A pun on the legend of St George and the dragon, adumbrated in Fletcher's *Mad Lover*. Also known as *riding* RANTIPOLE.

riffle. A shuffle 'in which . . . the thumbs "riffle", or bend up the corners of the cards', Maskelyne: from ca 1890: sharpers' s. verging on c. cf.:

riffle, v. To do this (see the n.): same period, status and authority. 2. See:

rifle; in C.17, often **riffle.** To coït with, or to caress sexually, a woman: coll verging on S.E.: C.17–20; ob. Prob. ex the S.E. *rifle*, (of a hawk) to tread (the hen).

***rifler.** In PRIGGING LAW (horse-stealing), app. he who takes away the stolen horse: c. of late C.16–early 17. Greene's *Second Cony-Catching*, 1592.

rifting, vbl n. Cleaning gear, harness, etc.: Regular Army: late C.19–20. Perhaps ex dial. *rift*, 'to break up (grass-land) with the plough'.

rig. Ridicule, esp. in *run one's rig upon* a person: from ca 1720: s. till C.19, then coll; in C.20, dial. Thackeray. 2. A trick or DODGE; a swindling scheme or method: 1775, Anon., 'I'm up to all your knowing rigs.' cf. RIG SALE. 3. A prank; a mischievous or a wanton act: coll: from ca

1720; ob. 4. A (somewhat SHADY) manipulation of the money-market; a corner: 1877 (O.E.D.); s. >, ca 1890, coll. (Senses 2–4 follow naturally ex sense 1.) 5. Outfit; (style of) dress: coll: mid-C.19–20. Ex the rig of a ship; but cf. the v., 3. Also RIG-OUT and -UP.

rig, v. To play tricks on, to befool: from ca 1820: s. >, ca 1860, coll. Ex the n., 1 and 3. 2. Hence, to manipulate illegally or illicitly: from ca 1850: s. >, ca 1880, coll; slightly ob. cf. RIG THE MARKET and RIG UP, v. 3. To clothe; supply with clothes: from ca 1530: S.E. until C.19, then coll. *Sporting Magazine*, 1821, 'The gentlemen were neatly rigged, and looked the thing to a T.' cf. RIG OUT, V.

rig, run a or **the; run one's rigs.** To play pranks, even if wanton ones; run riot: s. >, ca 1820, coll: thus, Cowper, 1782, 'He little dreamt, when he set out, | Of running such a rig!'; *r. the r.*, 1797; *r. one's rigs*, 1802.

rig-me-role. See RIGMAROLE. Only in C.18.

rig-mutton. A wanton: coll: C.17–18. Elaboration of *rig*, a wanton.

rig-my-role or **-roll.** See RIGMAROLE. C.18 only.

rig-of-the-day, the. The Service dress to be worn on the day concerned: naval coll: since ca 1880.

rig-out, n. An outfit; (esp. a suit of) clothes, a costume: coll: from ca 1820. cf. RIG, n., 5, v., 3; RIG-UP; and:

rig out, v. To dress; provide with clothes: from ca 1610: S.E. until C.19, then coll.

rig sale. An auction-sale under false pretences: 1851, *Chambers's Journal.*

rig the market. To engineer the (money-) market in order to profit by the ensuing rise or fall in prices: 1855, Tom Taylor, 'We must rig the market. Go in and buy up every share that's offered.' Ex RIG, v., 2, and n., 4.

rig-up, n. An outfit; (style of) dress: coll: from ca 1895; ob. cf. RIG-OUT, n.

rig up, v.t. To send (prices) up by artifice or manipulation: commercial s.: 1884, *Pall Mall Gazette*, 14 Feb. Ex RIG, v., 2.

rigby, see RIGSBY.

rigged. Ppl adj. of RIG, v., 2: O.E.D. records at 1879, but prob. considerably older. 2. Of v., 3.

riggen (riggin; properly, **rigging), ride the.** To be extremely intimate: dial. and low coll: C.19–20; ob. Here *riggen* (*rigging*) is the back(bone), though the coll use may have been influenced by sartorial RIGGING.

rigger. A racing boat: Durham School: late C.19–20. ?ex: 2. Outrigger: coll abbr.: late C.19–20. 3. A thimble-rigger: from ca 1830: low coll >, by 1900, S.E. 4. One who 'rigs' an auction (1859) or the market (1883): s.

riggers. Clothes made to look like new: low: ca 1820–80. *Sessions*, Oct. 1840 (p. 1044). Ex RIG, v., 2, with pun on RIG, n., 5.

rigging. See RIGGEN, RIDE THE. 2. Clothes: C.17–20; ob. Not c., as B.E. asserts, but s. 3. The vbl n. of RIG, v., 2.

rigging, climb the, see CLIMB THE RIGGING. **rigging, ride the,** see RIGGEN, RIDE THE.

***rigging, rum.** Fine clothes: c.: late C.17–18.

riggmonrowle. An occ. C.18 form of RIGMAROLE.

right, adj. See RIGHT, ALL; RIGHT AS ... RIGHT ENOUGH; RIGHT YOU ARE! 2. Favourably disposed to, trustable by, the underworld: c.: ca 1865, '*No. 747*' has *right screw*, a 'good fellow' warder.

right, a bit of all. Excellent; most attractive, delightful: coll: from ca 1870. Often applied by a fellow to a girl, with the connotation that she is very pretty or very charming or, in the sexual act, ardent or expert (or both). Slightly ob. cf. the mock-French translation: *un petit morceau de tout droit.*

right!, all. Certainly!; gladly!: 1837, Dickens: coll. Like next entry, prob. ex c. sense (ca 1810–50), 'All's safe *or* in good order *or* as desired': *Lex. Bal.* cf. RIGHT YOU ARE!

right, all, adj. and adv. As expected; safe(ly); satisfactor(il)y: coll: 1844, Edward FitzGerald, 'I got your letter all right.' Ex preceding entry.

Right, Mr; Miss R. The right person – the person one is destined to marry (i.e. he or she who, before marriage, seems to be the right life-partner): coll: Sala, 1860, 'Mr Right'; Kipling, 1890, 'Miss Right'.

right as . . . There are various coll phrases denoting that one is quite well or comfortable or secure, that a thing, a job, a prospect, etc., is dependable or quite safe: **right as a fiddle** (—1903; F. & H.), an ob. corruption of the much earlier *fit as a fiddle*; **. . . a line** (C.15–early 17; e.g. Chapman); **. . . a trivet** (1837, Dickens); **. . . anything** (—1903; F. & H. Very gen.); **. . . my glove** (1816, Scott; ob.); **. . . my leg** (C.17–18;

e.g. Farquhar); ... **ninepence** (1850, Smedley), in C.19 often *nice as ninepence* (H., 5th ed.); ... **rain** (1894, W. Raymond); ... **the bank** (1890, 'Rolf Boldrewood', ?on *safe as the Bank of England*).

right as a ram's horn. (Very) crooked: ironic coll: C.14–17 (?early 18). Lydgate, Skelton, Ray. cf. the late C.19–20 coll *as* STRAIGHT (occ. *as crooked*) AS A DOG'S HIND LEG.

right away. Immediately, directly: U.S. (—1842), perhaps ex Eng. dial.; anglicized as coll by 1880.

right cool fish. 'One who is not particular what he says or does', *Spy*, 1825: Eton: ca 1810–90.

right-coloured stuff. Money: Norfolk s. (—1872), not dial.

right-down. Downright, outright; veritable: low coll (—1887). Baumann, 'A right-down swindle'. Ex dial., which has also *right-up-and-down*.

right down, adv. Wholly, quite: coll: Jan. 1835, *Sessions*, 'I was *right down* certain that the money was bad'; ob.

right enough, adj. Esp. in *that's right enough* = that's all right so far as it goes (but it doesn't go nearly far enough); or, that's all right from *your* point of view. Coll: late C.19–20. Contrast:

right enough, adv. All right, well enough; esp., all right (or well enough) although you may not at present think so. Coll: from ca 1880; 1885, Anstey's *The Tinted Venus*. cf. preceding entry.

right eye, or **hand, itches, – (and) my.** A coll c.p.; the former denotes prospective weeping, the latter (an unexpected) heritage or gift of money: C.18. Swift.

right forepart. (One's) wife: tailors': late C.19–20. Ex tailoring j.

right in one's, or the, head. (Gen. preceded by *not*.) (Un)sound of mind: coll: C.19–20. App. orig. dial.: cf. the Scottish *no richt*.

right off, put. To give a violent distaste for a thing, a plan, or dislike for a person: coll: late C.19–20.

right sort. Gin: low: ca 1820–50. 'Peter Corcoran' Reynolds.

right tenpenny on the cranium, hit. To hit the nail on the head: non-aristocratic jocular coll: ca 1890–1915.

right up and down, like a yard of pump-water. Straightforward and in earnest: nautical: mid-C.19–20. cf. RIGHT-DOWN.

right you are! ALL RIGHT!; certainly!; agreed!: s. (—1864). Churchward, 1888 'Right you are; I don't think I'll go up.'

righteous. Excellent, e.g. 'a righteous day', a fine one: coll: from ca 1860. Contrast WICKED.

righteous, more holy than. Very holey or tattered: late C.19–20. Applied to both persons (now ob.) and, always more gen., garments, esp. socks, stockings. (This kind of pun is rare among the upper and upper-middle classes.)

***rights, be to.** To have a clear (legal) case against one: c. of ca 1850–1910.

***rights, catch (bang) to.** To catch (a person) doing something he ought not to do: c.: from ca 1860. cf. last entry.

rigmarole; in C.18, occ. **rigmarol.** A string of incoherent statements; a disjointed or rambling speech, discourse, story; a trivial or almost senseless harangue: coll: from ca 1730. Mme D'Arblay, 1779. A corruption of *ragman roll*, C.13–early 16, a rambling-verse game; also a list, a catalogue. (Other C.18 variations are *rig-me-role*, *my-roll* or *-role*, and *riggmonrowle*.) 2. (Without *a* or *the*.) Such language: coll: C.19–20.

rigmarole, adj. (With variant spellings as for the n.) Incoherent; rambling: trivially long-winded: coll: from ca 1750. Richardson, 1753, 'You must all ... go on in one rig-my-roll way'; 1870, Miss Bridgman, 'A rigmarole letter'.

rigmarole, v.i. To talk rigmarole: coll: from ca 1830.

rigmarolish. Rather like a rigmarole: coll: 1827, J. W. Croker. The adv. (*-ly*) is too seldom used to be eligible.

rigs. See RIG, n., 1, and RIG, RUN A.

rigs, up to one's or **the.** Wide-awake, FLY; expert: s.: C.19–20; ob. In late C.18–early 19, *up ... rig*.

rigsby. A wanton; a romping (lad or) girl: coll: from ca 1540. In late C.17–20, only dial. In C.16, occ. *rigby*. Ex *rig*, a wanton.

rile. To vex, anger: coll: U.S. (1825), anglicized ca 1850, though the consciousness of its U.S. origin remained until ca 1890; the v.i. *rile up*, grow angry, has not been acclimatized in Britain. A later form of S.E. *roil*.

riled, ppl adj. Vexed, annoyed, angry: see RILE. *riling*, annoying, etc.: id.

rim-rack. To strain or damage (a vessel), esp. by driving her too hard in a sea: Grand Banks fishermen's coll: late C.19–20. Prob. cognate with the Aberdeen *rim-raxing*, a surfeit (-ing).

rimble-ramble, n. and adj. Nonsense, nonsensical: late C.17 coll. Reduplication on *ramble*.

rimp. To sprint; a sprint: Christ's Hospital: late C.19–20. Ex the Homeric adverb *ῥίμφα*, swiftly.

rinder. An outsider: Queen's University, Belfast: mid-C.19–20. Ex rind of fruit.

ring (gen. with the). The female pudend: low coll verging on euphemistic S.E. – or is it the other way about? C.16–20, but rare after C.18. Also *black – hairy – Hans Carvel's ring*. 2. 'Money extorted by Rogues on the High-way or by Gentlemen Beggers', B.E.: c. of late C.17–early 19. By 1785, it applied to any beggars; 'from its ringing when thrown to them', Grose. 3. Anus (also *ring-piece*): low: late C.19–20.

ring, v. To manipulate: change illicitly: from ca 1785: perhaps orig. c.; certainly low s. (See *ring the* CHANGES.) 2. Simply to change or exchange: from ca 1810: orig. low, then gen. s. 3. Hence, or ex sense 1, to cheat (v.i.; also *ring it*): low: late C.19–20. 4. v. reflexive: c. from ca 1860, as explained in the *Cornhill Magazine*, 1863 (vii, 91), 'When housebreakers are disturbed and have to abandon their plunder they say that they have rung themselves.' 5. See RING IN. 6. v.i. (of cattle), to circle about: Australian coll (—1884) >, ca 1910, S.E. 'Rolf Boldrewood'. 7. Even more essentially Australian is *ring*, v.i. and v.t., to shear the most sheep in a day or during a shearing (at a shearing-shed): from ca 1895: coll. A. B. Paterson (*Banjo* as Australians affectionately call him), 1896, 'The man that "rung" the Tubbo shed is not the ringer here.' See RINGER, 2. 8. See RING A PEAL.

ring, cracked in the. No longer virgin: late C.16–20; ob.: coll. In C.16–17, occ. *clipped* (*with*)*in the ring*. Lyly; Beaumont & Fletcher. See RING, n., 1. Punning on the †S.E. use, of coins so damaged as to be valueless.

ring, go through the. To go bankrupt: commercial: ca 1840–80. ?ex circus.

ring, lose one's. To lose one's virginity: coll: C.19–20. cf. RING, n., 1, and *cracked in the* RING.

ring (a person) **a peal.** To scold: coll: C.18–mid-19. Grose, 2nd ed., 'Chiefly applied to women. His wife rung him a fine peal!'

***ring-dropper, -faller.** One who practises RING-DROPPING: c.: resp. from ca 1795 and ca 1560–1600. cf. FAWNEY-DROPPER, and:

***ring-dropping.** The dropping of a 'gold' ring and subsequent prevailing on some MUG (n., 4) to buy it at a fair price for gold: c.: from ca 1820.

ring in. To insert, esp. to substitute, fraudulently: from ca 1810: orig., perhaps c., certainly at least low s. (Notably in gambling.) cf. RING, v., 1.

ring it. The v.i. form of the preceding: low: late C.19–20. 2. See RING, v., 2.

ring-man. The ring-finger: from ca 1480: coll till C.18, then dial. Ascham.

ring-neck. A jackaroo: Australian coll: 1898, Morris, 'In reference to the white collar not infrequently worn by a Jackaroo on his first appearance'.

ring-pigger. A drunkard: coll: ca 1560–1600. Levins.

ring-tail. A recruit: military: ca 1860–1914. cf. ROOK(E)Y; SNOOKER. 2. A novice: Canadian: late C.19–20, ex U.S.

ring the changes, see CHANGES, RING THE.

ringer. A bell: (low) coll: late C.19–20; ob. 2. An excellent person or thing, esp. with REGULAR: Australian: 1894, *Geelong Grammar School Quarterly*, April, 'Another favourite [school] phrase is a "regular ringer".' Ex *ringer*, that shearer who does the most sheep.

ringie, the. The man who, at two-up, keeps the ring, arranges the wagers, and pays out the winnings: Australian and New Zealand coll: late C.19–20.

***ringing castors.** The practice of substituting bad hats for good: c. (—1812); virtually †. Ex RING, v., 2.

ringing the horse-shoes. A welcome to a man who has been out boozing: tailors': mid-C.19–20.

rings. Abbreviated reference to an officer's rank, denoted by the number of rings on his sleeve: since ca 1890 in the Navy.

rings round, run. To beat hollow: Australian s. (—1891). *Argus*, 10 Oct. 1891. Ex sport, prob. ex Rugby, or ex Australian football. cf. CIRCLING-BOY.

rink, get out of one's. To sow wild oats: coll: from ca 1870. Perhaps ex skating; prob. ex Scots *rink*, 'the sets of players' forming sides at curling and quoit-playing.

rino, see RHINO.

rinse. A wash: coll: 1837, Dickens, '"I may as vel have a rinse," remarked Mr Weller.' 2. A drink: from ca 1870; ob.

rinse, v. i. To drink, esp. liquor: from ca 1870. Prob. ex *rinse down* (with liquor).

rinse-pitcher. A toper: coll: ca 1550–1640. Bullein.

Rio. Rio de Janeiro: coll, mostly nautical: mid-C.19–20.

Riot Act (to), read the. To reprove, administer a reproof: coll: from ca 1880.

rip. A mild term of reproof: coll and dial.: C.19–20. Ex *rip*, a rake, which may be ex *reprobate*. Rarely applied to a female. 2. A quick run, a rush: coll ex dial.: from ca 1870; ob. in coll. 3. A sword: ca 1690–1750. Ned Ward, 1700. Proleptic.

rip! An exclamation: coll: late C.16–mid-17. cf. RIP ME!

rip!, let her or **him.** A callous punning on *r.i.p.*, i.e. *requiescat in pace*, let him (her) rest in peace. Late C.19–20. cf. R.I.P.!, LET...

rip and tear. To be very angry: from ca 1870 (ob.): coll and dial. Prob. on *rip and swear*, an intensive of dial. *rip*, to use bad language, to swear.

rip into. To attack, to fight, (someone) with one's fists: Australian: late C.19–20.

rip me! A low coll asseveration: mid-C. 19–early 20. Marriott-Watson.

ripe. Drunk: C.19–20; ob. Either ex *reeling-ripe* (Shakespeare, Tennyson) or ex *ripe*, (of liquor) fully matured, with the occ. connotation of potent, or merely suggested by *mellow*.

ripper. A person or thing esp. good: 1838, of a ball bowled extremely well at cricket; 1851, Mayhew. Prob. ex RIPPING, adj. 2. In boxing, a knock-down blow: from ca 1860; very ob. 3. A notable lie: from ca 1860; ob. cf. WHOPPER. 4. One behaving recklessly; a RIP: 1877 (O.E.D.); ob. 5. A longshoreman taking his fish inland to sell: fishermen's: late C.19–20.

ripping, n. A ceremony (involving the ripping of his gown), 'incidental to the departure of a Senior Colleger for King's College, Cambridge', F. & H.: Eton College: C.19–20: s. > coll > j.

ripping, adj. Excellent; very fast; very entertaining: 1826, *Sporting Magazine*, 'At a ripping pace'; 1858, 'Ripping Burton' (ale). cf. RATTLE, V.; STUNNING; THUNDERING. 2. Occ. it verges on the adverbial, as in 'A ripping fine story' (Baumann, 1887) and 'A ripping good testimonial' (Conan Doyle, 1894). cf.:

rippingly. Excellently: capitally; splendidly: 1892, Hume Nisbet.

ripstone. An incorrect form of RIBSTONE: Dickens in *Pickwick*.

rise. A rise in salary: coll >, ca 1890, S.E.: 1837, Dickens, 'Eighteen bob a-week, and a rise if he behaved himself'. 2. In Australia, 'an accession of fortune', C. J. Dennis: coll: late C.19–20. 3. A fit of anger: Eton s. (—1880); Cockney coll (—1895). 4. A disturbance or commotion: low: ca 1840–70. *Sinks*, 1848.

rise, v. To raise, grow, rear: coll: 1844, Dickens, 'Where was you rose?' O.E.D. 2. To listen credulously, often with the connotation of to grow foolishly angry: coll: 1856, Whyte-Melville. Ex a fish rising to the bait: cf. BITE, V., 3 and the S.E. *get*, *have*, or *take a rise out of* a person.

rise, get a. To experience an erection: coll: late C.19–20. 2. To cause someone to BITE (3): coll: late C.19–20. Ex angling.

rise a barney. To collect a crowd: showmen's: from ca 1855.

rise and shine, see ROUSE AND SHINE.

rise (or raise) arse upwards. To be lucky: coll: ca 1670–1800. Ray. Rising thus from the ground was regarded as lucky.

rise the plant, see PLANT, RISE THE.

risk, take a. To risk venereal infection: euphemistic coll: mid-C.19–20.

risky. Secretly adulterous: Society coll: ca 1890–1905. 'John Strange Winter'.

rispin, see RESPUN.

Rit, rit. A ritualistic Anglican clergyman: university: ca 1870–1910.

ritualistic knee. A sore knee caused by kneeling at prayers: medical coll: ca 1840–60.

River Lea. Tea: rhyming s. (—1859); until ca 1900. 2. The sea: id.: (—1903).

River Ouse. A drink; a drinking-bout: rhyming s. (on BOOZE): late C.19–20.

river(-)rat. 'A riverside thief: specifically one who robs the corpses of men drowned', F. & H. In the former sense, S.E.; in the latter, c.: from ca 1880.

river tick; gen. **River Tick.** Standing debts discharged at the end of one's undergraduate days: Oxford University: ca 1820–50.

rivets. Money: from ca 1840. Prob. suggested by BRADS.

rivet(t)ed, ppl adj. Married: app. ca 1695–1730. Congreve, *The Way of the World*, 1700. cf. 'the modern *spliced* and *tied up*, the Scottish *buckled*, and the Australian *hitched* or ... *hitched up*', *Slang*, p. 64.

rizzle. To enjoy a short period of absolute idleness after a meal: provincial s.: 1890, *Cassell's Saturday Journal*, 2 Aug., 'the newest of new verbs'. Perhaps ex dial.

rizzle, to dry by the heat of sun or fire, via the notion of sunning oneself.

roach, sound as a, see SOUND AS . . .

roach and dace. The face: rhyming s. (—1874).

road. A harlot: coll: late C.16–17. Shakespeare. 2. The female pudend. C.(?)17–20, very ob.: either low coll or S.E. euphemism. cf. ROAD-MAKING. 3. Way, manner; esp. in *any road*, occ. *anyroad*: non-aristocratic, non-cultured coll: late C.19–20. In dial. before 1886; Australian by 1888 (Boldrewood). Ex: 4. Direction; esp. *all roads*, in every direction: (mostly lower-class) coll: mid-C.19–20.

road, gentleman or **knight of the.** A highwayman: C.18–19: coll > journalistic S.E. See the paragraph at KNIGHT.

road-hog. An inconsiderate (cyclist or) motorist: 1898 (O.E.D.), though, in U.S., as early as 1891, of a cyclist: coll.

road-making; road up for repairs. A low phrase indicating menstruation: mid-C.19–20. See ROAD, 2.

***road-starver.** A long coat without pockets: mendicants' c.: ca 1881–1914.

roader. 'A parcel to be put out at a roadside station', *The Times*, 14 Feb. 1902: railway coll. 2. A young SWELL in the Mile End Road: East London (—1909).

roadster. A tramp: late C.19–20.

roaf. (cf. ROUF.) Four: back s. (—1874). Ex the sol. pronunciation of *four* as *foär* or *foër*. 2. Whence (same period) *roaf* GEN, four shillings; *roaf yanneps*, fourpence.

roam on the rush. (Of a jockey) to swerve from the straight line at the finish [of a race] when the rush takes place: turf: from ca 1870.

roar. (Of horses) to breathe noisily: 1880: coll >, in C.20, S.E. cf. ROARER, 1. 2. (Of cattle) to low continuously, whence the n. *roaring*: Australian coll: late C.19–20.

roar up. To speak abusively to; shout at: lower classes': from ca 1905.

roaratorio, see RORATORIO. **roaration**, see RORATION. **roaratorious**, see RORITORIOUS.

roarer. A broken-winded horse: from ca 1810: coll >, ca 1900, S.E. *Lex. Bal.* cf. ROAR, v. 2. A riotously noisy reveller or bully: late C.16–early 18: coll. D. Rowland, 1586; 1709, Steele. Ex *roar*, *rore*, to riot. 3. A noisy or a rousing song: 1837, Marryat: coll.

roarin' horn. An urgent erection: low Australian: late C.19–20. cf. ROARING JACK below.

roaring. The disease in horses noted at ROAR and at ROARER, 1. From ca 1820: coll >, by 1900, S.E.

roaring, adj. Brisk, successful, esp. in *roaring trade*: from ca 1790: coll >, ca1860, S.E. 2. Boisterous; (of health) exuberant: 1848, Thackeray.

roaring blade, boy, girl, lad, ruffian. A street bully; a riotous, noisy, lawless female: C.17–mid-18 (later, only archaic): coll. A *roaring blade*, 1640, Humphry Mill; *r. boy*, 1611, J. Davies; *r. girl*, 1611, Middleton & Dekker (title); *r. lad*, 1658, Rowley, etc. (but current from ca 1610); *r. ruffian*, 1664, Cotton.

roaring forties, R.F. 'The degrees of latitude between 40° and 50° N – the most tempestuous part of the Atlantic', F. & H.; occ. the corresponding zone in the South Atlantic. Nautical coll. From ca 1880.

roaring Jack, have a. To have an urgent erection: low: late C.19–20. Clamant – and cf. JACK IN A BOX, 8.

roaring ruffian, see ROARING BLADE.

***roast.** To arrest: c.: late C.17–early 19. Perhaps on *(ar)rest*, via the idea of giving a person a hot time. 2. (Also *roast brown.*) To watch closely: c.: 1888, G. R. Sims, 'A reeler was roasting me brown.' cf. ROASTING, n., c. sense. 3. To ridicule, to quiz (a person), severely or cruelly: 1726, Shelvocke: s. >, ca 1760, coll; ob. cf. to WARM. 4. In telegraphy, to click off a message so fast that it cannot be followed by (a person; v.t.): 1888 (O.E.D.): telegraph-operators'.

roast, smell of the. To get into prison: coll: ca 1580–1640. Nares.

roast a stone. To waste time and energy: coll: ca 1520–1620. Skelton.

roast-beef dress. Full uniform: naval coll: C.19. cf. *roast-beef coat* in Alfred Burton, *Johnny Newcome*, 1818. Either ex ROAST-MEAT CLOTHES, or ex the uniform of the royal beef-eaters.

roast (h)and an(d) new (or noo). Roast shoulder (of mutton) and new potatoes: eating-house waiters' (—1909).

roast meat, cry. To talk about one's good fortune or good luck: coll: C.17–early 19. Camden, B.E., Grose, Fielding, Lamb. Northall, 1894, notes that in dial. it also = to boast of women's favours.

roast meat and beat with the spit, give (a person). 'To do one a Curtesy, and Twit or Upbraid him with it', B.E.: coll: ca 1670–1820.

roast-meat clothes. Sunday or holiday clothes: coll: late C.17–mid-19.

roast meat for worms, make (one). To kill: coll: late C.16–early 18. Shakespeare. cf. the jocular S.E. *food for the worms*.

roast snow in a furnace. To attempt the absurd or unnecessary: coll: C.19–20; ob.

roaster. An extremely hot day: a heat wave: coll: late C.19–20.

roasting, vbl n. of ROAST, v., in all senses except the first; sense 2 occurs mostly in *give* (one) *a roasting*, recorded for 1879, and *get a roasting*, to be very closely watched.

roasting-jack. The female pudend: low: mid-C.19–20; ob. Ex S.E. sense.

rob(-o')-Davy. Metheglin: a mid-C.16–mid-17 coll variation of *roberdavy*. Taylor the Water Poet.

rob Peter to pay Paul, see PETER TO PAY PAUL, ROB.

rob the barber. To wear long hair: lower classes' coll: late C.19–20.

rob(-)the(-)ruffian. The female pudend: low coll: C.19–20; ob.

roba, see BONA ROBA.

robbo. A cab or buggy plying for hire: Australian: ca 1880–1910. Ex *robber*.

robe. A wardrobe: furniture-dealers' coll: late C.19–20. cf. BOARD, n.; they may be written *'board* and *'robe*.

***Roberdsmen, Robert's men,** etc. 'The third (old) Rank of the Canting Crew, mighty Thieves, like *Robin-hood*', B.E.: c.: C.16–17. In other than this technical sense, it covers the period C.14–20 and is S.E., though long archaic. Prob. on *Robert* + *robber*.

Robert; Roberto. A policeman: coll: resp. 1870, ca 1890; both ob. Ex Robert Peel. cf. PEELER. 2. A shilling; esp. in *accept Her Majesty's Robert*, to enlist in the Regular Army: military: ca 1860–1901. On BOB.

robin. See ROBIN REDBREAST. 2. A penny: low: from ca 1890; ob. 3. A 'little boy or girl beggar standing about like a starving robin': c. and low: late C.19–20; ob. Ware.

Robin Hog. (Prob.) a constable: coll: early C.18.

Robin Hood. An audacious lie: coll: ?C. 18–19. Abbr. *tale of Robin Hood*.

Robin Hood, adj. Good: from ca 1870.

Robin Hood('s) bargain. A great bargain: coll: C.18. cf. PENNYWORTH, ROBIN HOOD('S).

Robin Hood's choice. This – or nothing. Coll: C.17.

Robin Hood's mile. A distance two or three times greater than a mile: coll: ca 1550–1700. Almost proverbial.

Robin Redbreast; r.r. A Bow-Street runner: ca 1820–70. Also *robin* and RED BREAST.

Robin Ruddock. Gold coin: ?late C.16–mid-18. See RUDDOCK, 1.

robin's-eye. A scab (sore): low: mid-C. 19–20; ob. Ex shape.

Robinson, see JACK ROBINSON.

Robinson Crusoe. Do so: from ca 1890.

robustious was, ca 1740–90, a coll. See esp. Johnson.

Roby Douglas. The anus: nautical: ca 1780–1850. Grose, 1785, 'One eye and a stinking breath': which indicates an allusion to one so named.

Rochester portion. 'Two torn Smocks, and what Nature gave', B.E.: late C.17–early 19. (N.B., *portion* is marriage-portion, *dot*; *what* = physical charms in gen., but esp. the genitals in particular.) cf. the C.18–19 equivalent, a WHITECHAPEL PORTION. Pegge, 1735, cites *R. p.* as a Kentish proverb.

rock. School (opp. to baker's) bread: Derby School: from ca 1850. Less s. than coll > j. 2. A medium-sized stone: Winchester School coll: from ca 1860. Perhaps owing to U.S. and Australian use of *rock* as a stone however small.

***rock,** v. To speak: tramps' c. (—1893); very ob. Abbr. ROCKER.

rock-a-low. An overcoat: dial. and (low) coll (—1860); ob. by 1890. = Fr. *roquelaure*.

rock-creeper. A coastal ship: nautical: since ca 1870.

rock-nosing. Inshore boat work in the old whalers: whalers' coll: ca 1850–1910. Bowen.

rock of eye and rule of thumb, do by. To guess instead of measuring precisely: tailors': from ca 1860. Presumably *rock* = a movement to and fro.

Rock(-)Scorpion. A mongrel Gibraltarine: naval, military: 1818, A. Burton. cf. S.E. *Rock English*, the Lingua Franca spoken at Gibraltar (Borrow, 1842).

rocked. Absent-minded, forgetful: low (—1812); †by 1900. Ex:

rocked in a stone kitchen. A little weak in the head; foolish: coll: late C.18–mid-19. Grose, 2nd ed., 'His brains having been disordered by the jumbling of his cradle' on the stone floor. cf. HALF-ROCKED.

***rocker** (or **rokker**); (occ. ROCK). To speak: tramps' c.: from ca 1850; since ca 1900, gen. low s. (—1818). C. Hindley, 1876, 'Can you rocker Romany . . .?'; A.

Morrison, 1894, 'Hewitt could rokker better than most Romany chals themselves.' Ex Romany *roker* (Sampson's *raker*), to talk, speak, with variant *voker* (cf. L. *vox, vocare*); cf. Romany *roker(o)mengro*, lit. a talk-man, i.e. a laywer.

rocker, off one's. (Temporarily) mad; extremely eccentric: low: 1897 (O.E.D.). Ex the piece of wood that enables a chair or a cradle to rock.

rockiness. Craziness: from ca 1898. Ex S.E. term influenced by *off one's* ROCKER.

rocks, on the. Without means: coll (—1889). Ex stranded ship.

rocks, pile up the. To make money: U.S. (*rocks*, money, 1847), partly anglicized ca 1895. Kipling uses it in 1897. Prob. ex *rock* = a nugget: cf. ROCK, n., 2.

rocks and boulders. (The) shoulders: rhyming s.: late C.19–20.

rocky, adj. A vague pejorative: e.g. unsatisfactory (weather), unpleasant or hard (for, on a person): 1883 (O.E.D.). Ex S.E. *rocky*, unsteady, unstable, tipsy. Hence *go rocky*, go wrong.

rod. The penis: coll: C.18–20. Also *fishing-rod*: C.19–20: s. cf. the Fr. *verge*, which is literary.

rod, v.i. and t. To coït (with): low: C.19–20. Ex the n.

rod at, or **under, one's girdle.** With various vv., it implies a whipping, present or past: coll verging on S.E.: ca 1579–1620. Lyly, Jonson.

rod-maker. 'The man who made the rods used in BIBLING', Mansfield, referring to ca 1840: Winchester School: coll > j.

roddy. A rhododendron: London lower-class coll: 1851, Mayhew.

rodger, see ROGER, v.

rodney or **R.** A (very) idle fellow: coll: ca 1865–1910. Ex dial., where still extant, in the North and Midlands. cf. the sad declension of SAWNEY.

roe. The semen: low: from ca 1850; ob. Hence, *shoot one's roe*, emit. Ex fish-roe. Possibly extant far earlier, in view of Mercutio's jibe at Romeo, 'Without his roe, like a dried herring' (*R & J*, II, iv).

rofefil; occ. **ro(u)f-efil.** A life sentence: back s. (—1859) of *for life*. On *for life*.

***roge, roging.** C.16–17 forms of ROGUE, ROGUING.

***roger.** A beggar pretending to be a university scholar: c. of mid-C.16. Copland. cf. ROGUE. 2. A goose: c.: mid-C.16–18. Also *Roger* (or *Tib*) *of the buttery*: C.16–18. 3. A portmanteau: c.: late C.17–early 19. Perhaps a corruption of *poge* (see POKE, n.). 4. A thief-taker: c. of ca 1720–60. ?via postulated *rogue-er*, a taker of rogues. 5. The penis: from ca 1650: perhaps orig. c. Ex the name *Roger*: cf. DICK, 4; JOHN THOMAS. 6. A ram: rural coll of ca 1760–1900. Ex the name. 7. A bull: coll (—1785); ob. 8. See ROGER, JOLLY. 9. See OLD ROGER.

roger; often **rodger,** v. To coït with (a woman): perhaps orig. c. In *The Secret Diary of William Byrd of Westover, 1709–1712*, this gentleman of Virginia was using *roger* for all his sexual relations with his wife, e.g. 'I rogered her lustily' (26 Dec. 1711) and 'I lay abed till 9 o'clock this morning . . . and rogered her by way of reconciliation' (1 Jan. 1712). Grose, 1st ed., 'From the name Roger, frequently given to a bull.'

Roger, jolly; in late C.19–20, occ. **Roger.** A pirate's flag: 1785, Grose: coll >, ca 1850, S.E. Earliest record, 1723, as OLD ROGER (W.). (A white skull in a black field; ironic.)

Roger Gough. Scrub (or brush) bloodwood: Australian coll: from early 1880s. 'An absurd name', Morris: either ex the general that won the battles of Sobraon and Ferozeshah, or, as the *Australasian*, 28 Aug. 1896, suggests, a corruption of an Aboriginal word now lost.

***Roger (or Tib) of the buttery; or r. (or t.)** . . ., see ROGER, n., 2.

Rogers. A ghastly countenance: Society: ca 1830–50. Ware. Ex *Rogers*, the poet, when old, or ex *the Jolly* ROGER of the pirates.

roglan. A four-wheeled vehicle: Shelta: C.18–20.

***rogue.** A professed beggar of the 4th Order of Canters: c.: mid-C.16–17; then historical. Awdelay implies it in *wild rogue*; Dekker; B.E.; Grose. Whence S.E. senses. Perhaps an abbr. of ROGER, n., 1, of problematic origin, unless a perversion of †*rorer*, a turbulent fellow, on L. *rogare*, to ask. 2. Short for ROGUE AND VILLAIN.

***rogue,** v. To be a beggar, a vagrant: c. of ca 1570–1630. Ex the n.

***rogue, wild.** A born rogue ever on tramp or a-begging: c.: ca 1560–1700. Awdelay.

***rogue and pullet.** A man and woman confederate in theft: c.: mid-C.19–20.

rogue and villain. A shilling: rhyming s. (—1857). On *shillin'*.

rogue in grain. A corn-chandler: ca 1780–1840. Lit., a great rogue. cf.:

rogue in spirit. 'A distiller or brandy merchant', Grose, 2nd ed.: ca 1780–1840. Prob. suggested by ROGUE IN GRAIN, with a pun on *spirit(s)*.

rogue with one ear. A chamber-pot: late C.17–early 18. Randle Holme.

rogue's salute. The single gun on the morning of a court-martial: naval jocular coll: late C.19–20. Bowen.

rogue's yarn. 'Coloured thread found in the heart of government rope to prevent its being stolen' (Granville): naval coll: C. 19–20.

***roguing,** n. Tramping as rogue or vagrant: ca 1575–1720: prob. orig. c. Harrison, 1577. The c. origin is postulated, for *roguing* is ex ROGUE, n., via the v. cf.:

***roguishness.** The being a ROGUE: late C.16–early 17: prob. orig. c.

rogum pogum, or **dragum pogram (-um).** The plant goat's beard eaten as asparagus: late C.18–mid-19: less s. than dial. and low coll. Grose, 3rd ed., 'So called by the ladies' – ironic, this – 'who gather cresses, &c.'

***roister, royster.** In C.17–early 18 c., one of a band of 'rude, Roaring Rogues', B.E.

roker. A ruler (esp. *flat roker*): stick; poker: schools': from ca 1850. Ex *roke*, to stir a fire, a liquid: Halliwell.

***roker** (rare), **rokker,** v., see ROCKER.

roll, n. See ROLLS. 2. Conceit; SIDE; presumption: Shrewsbury School: from ca 1870. By pun ex the words *roll from side to side*.

roll, v. To rob (a drunken person): nautical: since ca 1810. Alfred Burton, *Johnny Newcome*, 1818.

roll in every rig. To be up to every trick; be up-to-date: low. Old song, 1790, 'We roll in every knowing rig.'

***roll in one's ivories** or **ivory.** To kiss: 1780, Tomlinson in his *Slang Pastoral*, 'To roll in her ivory, to pleasure her eye'. After ca 1850, always *ivories*. c.; ob. cf. *ivory*, IVORIES; e.g. *flash the* IVORIES.

roll into. To pitch into; to thrash: coll: Australian (and U.S.): 1890, 'Rolf Boldrewood'.

roll me in the dirt (occ. hyphenated). A shirt: rhyming s. (—1874); †by 1915. In late C.19–20, DICKY (or *Dicky*) *dirt*.

roll me in the gutter. Butter: rhyming s.: late C.19–20.

roll-me-in-the-kennel. A spirituous liquor (?gin): ca 1720–50. See quotation at BUNTER'S TEA.

***roll of snow.** (A piece of) linen; (bundle of) underclothing: c. (—1839). See SNOW.

roll one's hoop. To go ahead; be successful (both with a connotation of playing safe): coll: from ca 1870; ob.

roll out. To rise (esp. in the morning): coll: from ca 1880. Abbr. *roll out of bed*.

***roll the leer.** To pick pockets: c.: from ca 1820; †by 1900. Egan, *Boxiana*, III, 'The boldest lad | That ever mill'd the cly, or roll'd the leer'.

roll up. A roly-poly pudding: coll; in C. 20, S.E. and ob.: 1856 (O.E.D.). 1860, George Eliot. cf. DOG IN A BLANKET. 2. A meeting: Australian: 1861: coll; anticipated in Grose (at *Hussar-Leg*). 'Rolf Boldrewood', 1890, 'As if you'd hired the bell-man for a roll-up'.

roll up, v.i. To assemble: Australian s. 1887, J. Farrell, 'The miners all rolled up to see the fun.' cf. ROLL UP, n., 2.

rolled on Deal Beach. Pitted with smallpox: nautical: late C.19–20. Bowen. Ex 'the shingly nature of that beach'.

roller. A roll-call: Oxford University: 1883 (O.E.D.). Occ. *rollers*. Oxford *-er*. 2. See:

***rollers.** The horse and foot (police) patrols: c.: ca 1810–40. Presumably because they rolled along at a great pace. 2. U.S. rolling stock: Stock Exchange: from ca 1885. 3. See ROLLER.

rolling. Smart, clever: low: ca 1770–1870. ?ex *rolling blade*; cf. ROLLING KIDDY. 2. Very rich: coll: 1905, H. A. Vachell, 'He's going to marry a girl who's simply rolling.' Abbr. *rolling in money* (or *wealth*).

rolling billow. A pillow: rhyming s.: late C.19–20.

***rolling Joe.** A smartly dressed fellow: app. ca 1830–90. cf. ROLLING, 1.

***rolling kiddy.** A smart thief: c.: ca 1820–90. Egan, 'With rolling kiddies, Dick would dive and buy'; Lytton.

rolling off a log, (as) easy as. Very easy, easily: U.S. (1847), anglicized as a coll ca 1870.

rolling-motion dickey. The three-*wavy*-lined blue jean collar worn by the Royal Naval Volunteer Reserve before the First World War: naval: late C.19–early 20.

rolling-pin. The male member: low: mid-C.19–20. cf. ROLY-POLY, 3.

rolls. A baker: C.19–20. coll; ob. Also, but rather S.E. than coll, *master of the rolls*: mid-C.18–20; slightly ob. Adumbrated by Taylor the Water Poet.

roly-poly. Un-deux-cinq (a game): Londoners': ca 1820–50. 2. A jam roll pudding: 1848, Thackeray: coll till ca 1880, then S.E. Abbr. *roly-poly pudding*, also in Thackeray (1841). Also ROLL UP and DOG IN A BLANKET. 3. The penis: low: mid-C.19–20; ob.

rom. See RUM (adj.). 2. Occ. among tramps, *rom* = a male Gypsy: from ca 1850. In Romany, *rom* is a bridegroom, a husband; any (adult) male Gypsy.

Roman. 'A soldier in the foot guards, who gives up his pay to his captain for leave to work; serving like an ancient Roman, for glory and the love of his country', Grose, 1st ed.: military: ca 1780–1830. 2. See SKY.

Roman Candle. A Roman Catholic: mostly Army: late C.19–20. Ex the use of candles.

Roman fall. That affected posture in walking which throws the head well forward and puts the small of the back well in; mostly among men, the women favouring the GRECIAN BEND: coll: ca 1868–71. *Orchestra*, 25 March 1870.

Romany, patter. To talk Romany: C.19–20: low. Vaux; Ainsworth.

Romany rye. A gentleman who talks and associates with Gypsies: mid-C.19–20: coll. Ex Romany *rai* or *rei*, a gentleman. Popularized by Borrow's *The Romany Rye*, 1857.

***romboyle, or -s.** The watch (early police): mid-C.17–18 c. Occ. *rumboile*, *-boyle*.

***romboyle.** To make hue and cry; search for with a warrant: c.: late C.17–early 19. Esp. *romboyled*, wanted by the constables. Whence RUMBLE.

rombullion, see RUMBULLION. **rombustical, rombustious,** see RUMBUSTICAL, RUMBUSTIOUS.

***rome.** See RUM, adj., 1. So for combinations, e.g. *rome mort*.

Rome, gone to. See GONE TO ROME. cf. *return from Rome*, (of bells) to resume ringing after the forty-eight hours' Easter silence: Roman Catholic coll (—1890).

Rome-runner. A person, esp. a cleric, constantly running off to Rome in search of spiritual and monetary profit: coll: mid-C.14–15.

***Rome Ville, Romeville;** in C.16–early 17, often **-vyle**; also **Rumville.** London: c.: mid-C.16–mid-19. Lit., excellent city. See RUM, c. adj., 1.

***romely,** see RUMLY.

***Romeville,** see ROME VILLE. **Romford,** see RUMFORD.

romp. To move rapidly (and with ease): racing: from ca 1890. J. S. Winter, 1891, 'To use the language of the turf, she romped clean away from them.' cf.:

romp away with. To win (a race) easily: racing s.: from ca 1890. Ex ROMP. cf.:

romp home or **in,** v.i. To win very easily: racing s. >, in C.20, gen. coll: 1888, 'Thormanby' (*romp in*); *Sporting Life*, 20 March 1891 (*romp home*, fig. of the winner of an athletic half-mile).

ronny, see ROUNY.

roo, 'roo. A rake: Society coll: mid-C.19–20; ob. i.e. *roué*. 2. A kangaroo: Australian: late C.19–20. Properly a termination: cf. *kangaroo*, *potoroo*, *wallaroo*.

roof. A hat: 1857, Hughes; ob. 2. The head: 1897, 'Pomes' Marshall; slightly ob.

roof!, come off the. A non-aristocratic c.p. addressed to a person being high and mighty: from ca 1890; ob. W. Pett Ridge, *Minor Dialogues*, 1895.

roof-scraper. A spectator at the back of the gallery: theatrical coll (—1909).

Rooinek. A British immigrant (1897); in Boer War, a British soldier: Boers' nickname: late C.19–early 20. In South African Dutch, lit. red-neck. The name replaced *rooibatje*, red coat.

***rook.** A housebreaker's JEMMY or crow (whence *rook*): ca 1786–1850. 2. As a swindler or a sharper, from ca 1575, and until C.19, s. (in C.18, coll); perhaps orig. c. cf. HAWK. 3. A clergyman: 1859, H., 1st ed.; ob. Ex black clothes. 4. A sloven: tailors': from ca 1870; ob. ?because his laziness 'rooks' (see the v.) others of their time. ?or because rooks' nests are untidy. 5. A swindle: Australian: late C.19–20. cf. sense 2.

rook, v. To cheat; defraud, and defraud of; charge extortionately: late C.16–20: s. (?orig. c.) >, in C.19, coll.

rookery. A gambling-hell: coll: 1751, Smollett; ob. Like the next, ex ROOK, to cheat. 2. A brothel: coll: 1821, Egan; ob. 3. A densely populated slum: coll: 1823, Bee: coll till C.20, then S.E. Ex *rookery*, a colony of rooks. 4. The subalterns' quarters in barracks: military (—1860). Ex the noise. 5. A scolding-match, a row, disturbance: s. > coll: 1824 (O.E.D.). Also dial. cf. preceding sense.

rook(e)y; rookie. A (raw) recruit: military: 1893, Kipling. A perversion of *recruit*, no doubt; but with a pun on *rooky*, rascally, scampish.

rooking, vbl n. of ROOK, v.: mid-C.17–20.

room(e), adj., see RUM, adj., 1.

roomer. A lodger, esp. if occupying only one room: coll: anglicized ca 1875 ex U.S.

***roon**; though rare in singular. A mushroom: tramps' c.: late C.19–20. By perversion of Kentish *'room.*

***roosher.** A constable: c.: from ca 1870; ob. Either a corruption of ROZZER, or ex Scots *rooser, ruser*, a braggart.

roost. A garret: low Scots coll: C.19–20. Jamieson, 1808. 2. A resting-place; a bed: coll. *The London Guide*, 1818. 3. A city-dweller affecting a hyphenated name was, in the 1890s, stigmatized by the country-dweller thus: Robb-Smith became Roost-Smith; Carter-Jones became Roost-Jones; and so forth.

roost, v.i. To perch; seat oneself: coll: 1816, Scott. Ex fowls. 2. v.t., to imprison: military: ca 1870–1910. ?ex *roster*. 3. v.i., to cheat; v.t., roost over: also, to take a rise out of a person: low: from ca 1880; ob.

***roost-lay.** The practice – and art – of stealing poultry: c.: from ca 1810.

rooster. The female pudend: low: mid-C. 19–20; ob. Where the COCK roosts. 2. See QUEER ROOSTER. 3. A member who makes himself heard: Parliamentary: from ca 1860; ob. 4. An angler keeping to one place: River Lea anglers' (—1909). 5. Penis: low: C.19–20. Orig. euphemistic for COCK. Contrast sense 1.

***roosting-ken.** A lodging-house; a 'doss-house': c. (—1887).

root. Money: coll (—1899); ob. Abbr. *root of all evil.* 2. (Also *man-root.*) The penis: low coll: C.19–20. 3. Whence, a priapism: low: late C.19–20. Esp. in *have the, get the r.* cf. ROOTLE. 4. A kick on the posterior: late C.19–20; orig. Public Schools'. Ex:

root, v.t. To kick (a ball, a person): late C.19–20. Semantics: *uproot, root up.* Perhaps orig. Public Schools'.

root, the old. The male member: perhaps rather coll than s.: C.19–20.

root-about. Promiscuous football practice: schools' (orig. Leys): late C.19–20.

root about, v.i. To indulge in such practice: id.: same period.

rooter. Anything very good, of prime quality. 1860, H., 2nd ed. e.g. a very smart dress, a brilliant gem. 2. Hence, anything (or any act) very flagrant (e.g. a lie) or brutal (attack, blow, ?orig. kick): from ca 1865. Both senses very ob.

rooti, see ROOTY.

rootle, v.i, To coït: low: from ca 1850; ob. Ex S.E. sense, to grub, poke about. 2. Also, as n., in *do a rootle*, from ca 1880. cf. ROOT, n., 2, 3.

rooty; rooti. Bread: military: in India, from ca 1800; fairly gen. from 1881, when the Army was reorganized. First recorded in 1883, G. A. Sala (a notable slangster) in the *Illustrated London News*, 7 July. Ex Hindustani *roti.*

rooty gong. A long-service medal: Regular Army: late C.19–20. Ex preceding + GONG. Occ. *rooty medal.*

rope, v.t. To hold a horse in check so that it shall not win: racing coll: 1857, G. Lawrence. Also, in late C.19–20, *rope in.* 2. v.i., to hold back in order to lose a race: racing and athletic coll: 1874, H., 5th ed.

rope, cry (a). To cry a warning: late C.16–17: coll. Shakespeare, 'Winchester Goose, I cry a rope! a rope!'; Butler, 1663, 'When they cry rope'. ?ex hanging rope.

rope, for the. Due, or condemned, to be hanged: police coll: late C.19–20. Charles E. Leach.

rope-hooky. (Of hands) with fingers curled in: nautical coll: late C.19–20. Esp. an old SHELL-BACK's, from years of handling ropes.

rope in. See ROPE, 1. 2. To decoy; enlist the services of: U.S. (—1848), anglicized, as a coll, ca 1890; after ca 1918, S.E. Prob. ex lassoing. 3. Hence, *rope in the pieces*, to make money: coll: late C.19–20.

rope to the eye of a needle, put a. To attempt the absurd, the impossible: semi-proverbial coll: C.19.

Rope-Walk (or r.w.), go into the. 'In the law . . . a barrister is said to have gone into the rope-walk, when he has taken up practice in the Old Bailey,' Temple Bar, 1871; ob. As Serjeant Ballantine shows in his *Reminiscences*, 1882, when he says, 'What was called the Rope-Walk [at the Old Bailey] was represented by a set of agents clean neither in character nor person', *the rope-walk* meant also a set of shysters battening on Criminal Law; moreover, he implies that the term dates back at least as early as 1850.

rope-yarn Sunday. A Sunday off: nautical coll (—1887); slightly ob. 2. More correctly, a synonym of MAKE AND MEND: nautical coll: late C.19–20.

ropeable. Angry; quick-tempered: from ca 1890: Australian. Ex *ropeable* (i.e. *wild*) *cattle.*

roper. A hangman: †, says Bee in 1823. See *Mr* ROPER. 2. One who 'ropes' a horse (1870) or, in athletics, himself (1887): coll. See ROPE, 1 and 2. Occ. (of a horse only), *roper-in*.

Roper, Mr; or the roper. The hangman: jocular coll: ca 1650–1750. (cf. *John* ROPER'S WINDOW.) cf. *Roper's news*, no news, in the Cornish *that's Roper's news – hang the crier!*

Roper, Mrs. A Marine; the Marines: naval (—1868); ob. 'Because they handle the ropes like girls, not being used to them' (Brewer). cf. the C.17 S.E. sense of *roper*: one deserving the rope.

Roper, marry Mrs. To enlist in the Marines: naval (—1864); ob. Ex preceding.

roper-in. See ROPER, 2. 2. A decoy to a gambling den: U.S. (—1859), anglicized ca 1880: coll. See ROPE IN.

Roper's window, John. A rope-noose: ca 1550–1640: coll. Huloet.

ropes. One who plays at half-back in football: schoolboys': from ca 1880; ob.

ropes, be up to or **know the.** To be well-informed, expert; artful: coll: 1840, Dana, 'The captain . . . knew the ropes'; *be up to*, not before ca 1870 and only in 'artful' sense.

ropes, on the high, see HIGH ROPES.

ropes, pull or **work the.** To direct; exercise one's influence: coll: from ca 1880.

ropes, put up to the. To inform fully; to 'put wise': from ca 1875: coll. Ex ROPES, BE UP TO THE. Besant & Rice, 1877, have 'You've put me up to ropes'; *up to the . . .* is much commoner, at least in C.20.

roping, vbl n., see ROPE, V.

***ropper.** A scarf; a comforter: tramps' c.: 1873, Greenwood. ?*wrapper* perverted, asks F. & H.: this seems viable, for cf. †Scots *roppin*, to wrap.

***roram.** The sun: c.: late C.18–mid-19. Tufts. ?ex *Roland*, suggested by OLIVER, c. for the moon, as F. & H. ingeniously suggests.

roration; rarely **roaration.** 'An oration pronounced with a loud unmusical voice', Grose, 1785; †by 1890: jocular coll or s. As in RORATORIO, *roar* is punned. cf.:

roratorio or **roaratorio.** '*Roratorios* and *Uproars*, oratorio's and opera's', Grose, 1785; †by 1890. Sometimes sol. (cf. the Northamptonshire *roratory*, an oratorio), sometimes jocular coll or s. cf.:

roritorious; roaratorious. (Jubilantly) noisy: ca 1820–60. Egan, 1821, 'The Randallites' – i.e. partisans of the great boxer – 'were roritorious and flushed with good fortune.' Punning *oratorio* and *uproarious*, and perhaps *notorious*. cf. the S.W. dial. *rory-tory*, 'loud, noisy, stirring'.

rork (or rorke), rorker. A town boy, a CAD: Tonbridge: since ca 1870. Perhaps ex *raw*.

rortiness; rarely **rortyness.** The abstract n. of:

rorty; occ. **raughty.** Of the best; excellent; dashing; lively; jolly; sprightly: costers': from ca 1860. 'Chickaleary' Vance, ca 1864, 'I have a rorty gal'; Milliken, 1893, 'We'd a rare rorty time of it'; Whiteing, 1899, 'A right-down raughty gal'. Ware ranks a *rorty toff* as inferior to a *rorty bloke*. W. suggests a rhyme on *naughty*; B. & L. suggest ex Yiddish *rorität*, anything choice. 2. Amorous: low: from not later than 1893.

rorty, do the. To have a good time: costers' (—1893). Milliken. Ex RORTY, adj., 1.

rorty dasher; 2, rorty toff. A fine fellow; 2, an out-and-out swell: costers': from ca 1880.

rory; R. Short for:

Rory o' More. A whore (—1874; ob.); a floor (—1857); a door (—1892). Resp. H., 5th ed.; 'Ducange Anglicus'; 'Pomes' Marshall, 'I fired him out of the Rory quick.'

rose. The female pudend; a maidenhead: C.18–20. A debasement of medieval and Renaissance literary symbolism. 2. A bitch: showmen's: from ca 1860. 3. An orange: 1860, H., 2nd ed. ?ex the sweet smell.

rose, pluck a. To take a virginity; (among women) to ease oneself in the open air: both coll verging on euphemistic S.E.: C.18–20. Swift (2nd sense).

rose, strike with a feather and stab with a. To punish playfully: coll: ca 1888–1914. Ex a music-hall refrain; cf., however, Webster's '*M.* If I take her near you, I'll cut her throat. *F.* With a fan of feathers,' 1612. cf. RUN THROUGH THE NOSE WITH A CUSHION.

rose, under the. In confidence; *on the* QUIET; secretly: mid-C.16–20: S.E. >, ca 1660, coll >, ca 1850, again S.E. Dymock, 1546. Here, *rose* = rose-bush; *sub rosa* is modern, not Classic, L. Grose, 2nd ed., mentions that the rose was 'sacred to Harpocrates, the God of Silence', as does Sir Thomas Browne.

rose in judgement. Turned up: tailors': from ca 1860.

rosebud. Mouth: Cockney: late C.19–20.

rosebuds. Potatoes: rhyming s. (on *spuds*): late C.19–20.

rosella. A European working bared to the waist: Northern Australia (—1898). 'The scorching of the skin . . . produces a colour which probably suggested a comparison with the bright scarlet of the parrakeet so named,' Morris.

Rosemary Lane to a rag shop. Heavy odds: coll: ca 1810–90. *Boxiana*, III, 1821.

roses and raptures. A literary c.p. (ca 1830–90) applied to the *Book of Beauty* kind of publication.

rosey, see ROSY.

rosh; roush. To horse-play: Royal Military Academy: from ca 1880. Hence, *stop roshing!*, be quiet! Perhaps a corruption of *rouse*.

rosin. A fiddler: coll: 1870, *Figaro*, 31 Oct., 'They playfully call me "Rosin" . . . yet I must . . . go on with my playing.' Ex the rosin used on violin bows. 2. Fiddler's drink: coll: early C.17–20; ob. Ex S.E. *rosin*, to supply with, or to indulge oneself in, liquor.

rosin-back. A horse that has had its back rubbed with rosin in order to ensure a firmer seat for the bareback rider: circus coll: late C.19–20.

rosin-the-bow. A fiddler: coll (—1864); very ob. Ex a song so titled. cf. ROSIN, 1.

rosser, see ROZZER. **rost** = ROAST.

rost, turn roast to. From arrogant to become humble: coll: C.16. Halliwell. Prob. ex the humbling of a boastful cook, *rost* being rust.

rosy, always preceded by **the.** Wine: 1840, Dickens, 'Richard Swiveller finished the rosy, and applied himself to the composition of another glassful.' Orig. and properly, red wine; cf. Fr. s. *le rosé*, which Kastner & Marks have omitted in their excellent Glossary. 2. Blood: sporting (—1891); ob. *Sporting Life*, 25 March 1891. Suggested by CLARET. 3. Good fortune: Cockney (—1893). Milliken. Ex *rosy*, favourable, of good omen.

rosy, do the. To have a ROSY (3), i.e. pleasant, time: Cockney (—1893); ob. Milliken, 'A-doin' the rorty and rosy as lively as 'Opkins's lot'.

Rosy Lee. Tea: rhyming s.: late C.19–20.

rot. Nonsense, trash, BOSH: s.: 1848, O.E.D.; 1861, H. C. Pennell, '"Sonnet by M. F. Tupper". A monstrous pile of quintessential rot.' Like ROTTER, 'app. first at Cambridge', W. Ex *rot*, dry rot, decay. Also TOMMY-ROT, and *dry rot*: coll (—1887).

rot, v. To chaff severely: 1890, Lehmann, 'Everybody here would have rotted me to death'; slightly ob. Ex the n. 2. To talk nonsense: 1899, Eden Phillpotts; ob. 3. In imprecations: late C.16–19: coll. Shakespeare, 1588, 'But vengeance rot you all.' Semantics: 'may you go rotten!' Also in *rot it!*, C.17–18, and *rot (up)on*, C.17. In *rot um!*, *um* = *'em*, them. 4. To spoil; mar nonsensically or senselessly: 1908, A. S. M. Hutchinson, 'He was rotting the whole show.' Also *rot up*; orig. Public Schools'.

rot! Nonsense!; BOSH!: from ca 1860. Henley & Stevenson, 1892, 'Oh, rot, I ain't a parson.' Ex the n.; quite independent of the v., 3. cf. ROTTEN!

rot about. To waste time from place to place; to play the fool: from late 1890s.

rot-funk. A panic: cricketers': ca 1890–1914.

rot-gut; occ. rotgut. Any unwholesome liquor; esp. inferior weak beer: late C.16–20: coll >, by C.19, S.E. G. Harvey, 1597. Occ. as adj.: C.18–20. T. Hughes, 'rot-gut stuff'. Grose, 1785, rhymes thus, '*Rot gut*, small beer, called beer a bumble, | Will burst one's guts before 'twill make one tumble.'

Rot-his-bone, be gone to. To be dead and buried: late C.18–early 19. Punning Ratisbon. cf. *be gone to the* DIET OF WORMS.

rot it!; rot on!; rot um!; rot upon! see ROT, v., 3. For **rot up,** see ROT, v., 4.

rotan. A wheeled vehicle: 1725, *A New Canting Dict.*; Grose; †by 1870. Prob. c. Ex L. *rota*. Whence, according to Bee, comes *Rotten Row*: which etymology may be correct.

Rothschild, see COME THE ROTHSCHILD.

rotten. In a deplorable state or ill-health; ill; worthless; BEASTLY: from ca 1880. R. L. Stevenson, 1881, 'You can imagine how rotten I have been feeling.' 2. *rotten!* An expletive corresponding to sense 1: from ca 1890.

Rotten Row. 'A line of old ships-in-ordinary in routine order', Smyth, 1867: nautical; ob. 2. A bow: rhyming s. (—1909).

Rotten Row, belong to. (Of ships) to be in ordinary: naval: C.19. 2. Whence (likewise of ships) to be discarded as unserviceable: nautical: from ca 1800; ob. A pun on *Rotten Row*, perhaps via *rotten borough*.

rotten sheep. A useless person (esp. male),

a mean traitor: Fenian: 1889, *Daily News*, 3 July; ob. Ex a sheep affected with the rot.

rotter. An objectionable person: 1894, George Moore. Ex ROT, n., and ROTTEN. Perhaps orig. U.S., where it is —1839, but see comment at ROT, n.

rouf. Four: back s.: Mayhew, I, 1851. cf. ROAF.

rouf-efil, see ROFEFIL.

rouge, n. A force-down in Rugby football: London schools': ca 1875–1900. Pun on *rough*?

rouge route, the. The 'red light' district of London: Londoners': ca 1660–1700. William Boghurst's contemporary account of the Great Plague of London. The term shows the French influence of the Restoration Court.

rough, n. A rough rider: coll: 1899, *Daily News*, 23 Feb.; ob.

rough, adj. See ROUGH ON. 2. Of food, esp. fish: coarse, inferior, stale: London coll: from ca 1850; slightly ob. Mayhew, 'The . . . "rough" fish is bought chiefly for the poor.'

rough, a bit of. A woman, esp. if viewed sexually: low: from ca 1870.

rough, cut up, see CUT UP NASTY.

rough and tough. A (?rhyming) coll variant of *rough*: ca 1880–1915. =*rough neck*, a rough, ignorant fellow.

rough and tumble (often hyphenated). A free fight; a go-as-you-please fight: from ca 1810: boxing coll >, ca 1910, S.E. (The adj. is S.E.) 2. The female pudend: low: from ca 1850. Also *the rough and ready*. cf. ROUGH, A BIT OF, and ROUGH MALKIN.

rough as a tinker's budget (bag). Very rough: ca 1650–1700. Howell.

rough as I run or it runs. Though I am rough, coarse, ignorant; it's certainly rough: coll: late C.17–mid-19. T. Brown, 1687, 'If you don't like me rough, as I run, fare you well, madam'; Ray, 1813, 'Rough as it runs, as the boy said when the ass kicked him'.

rough diamond. A person of good heart and/or ability but no manners: from ca 1750: coll till ca 1880, then S.E. *The Adventurer*, 1753; Lytton.

***rough fam or fammy**; occ. hyphenated. A waistcoat pocket: c.: ca 1810–50. In c., FAM is the hand: ?ex the habit of putting one's thumb in the pocket.

rough-knot. A Marine: naval: ca 1780–1850. John Davis, *The Post Captain*, 1806; W. N. Glascock, *Sailors and Saints* (I, 213), 1829.

rough Malkin (or m.). The female pudend: low Scots: C.16. 'Malkin' is a cat's name; cf. PUSS.

rough off (a horse). To break-in without troubling about 'the fancy stuff', esp. for station work: Australian rural coll: late C.19–20.

rough on. Hard for; bearing hardly on: coll: U.S. (1870, Bret Harte), anglicized ca 1885 (e.g. Besant, 1887). ?ex *rough luck* (cf. tough luck). 2. Severe on or towards (a person): coll: U.S. (1870), anglicized ca 1890. Recorded in Australia in 1878. cf.:

rough on rats; gen. it's . . . Rough luck: from ca 1890. Ex the name of a rat-poison.

rough ride. To ride an unbroken horse; hence, to domineer over a person: Australian coll: resp., late C.19–20 and since ca 1910.

rough-rider's (or -ers') wash-tub. The barrack water-cart: military: ca 1890–1915.

rough-up. A contest arranged at short notice; an informal contest: orig., boxing: 1889, *Referee*, 26 Jan. 2. A violent quarrel, a 'free for all': since ca 1890. *Sessions*, 22 June 1896, 'There was a little rough-up, and I found myself stabbed in the arm.'

roughing, vbl n. A students' interrupting of a university teacher of whom they disapprove by scuffling their boots on the floor: Scottish undergraduates' s. (late C.19–20).

round. A shirt collar: 1859, H.; †by 1910. Perhaps ex trade names *all rounds, all rounders*.

round, v.i. To PEACH (3), lay information: low: from ca 1859. v.t., *round on*. Prob. a development of *round on*, to turn upon and berate.

round. Languid: tailors': from ca 1870; ob. ?ex circular padding.

round, bet. To bet upon – or against – several horses: the turf: from ca 1820.

***round-about.** A treadmill (invented ca 1821): prison coll rather than s. or c.: from ca 1823; ob. 2. A female thief's all-round pocket: c.: from ca 1820. 3. A house-breaking tool that cuts out a round piece (about five inches in diameter) from shutter or door: c.: from ca 1820. Occ. *round Robin*, C.19.

round and square. Everywhere: rhyming s. (—1903). Not very gen.

round betting, see ROUND, BET.

round dozen. Thirteen lashes with the CAT-O'-NINE-TAILS: naval coll: C.19.

round me houses. The earliest form of ROUND THE HOUSES.

round mouth, gen. preceded by **the.** The fundament: low: ca 1810–70. Also *brother r.m.*, esp. in *Brother round mouth speaks*, he has broken wind.

round-mys. Trousers: rhyming s. (—1909). Abbr. ROUND ME (*my*) HOUSES.

round o (or O). A notable lie: coll: C.17. Ex the *oh!* of remonstratory surprise. 2. No runs; batsman's score of '0': cricket coll: ca 1855–65. Reade in 1863 refers to it as 'becoming obsolete'.

round one or **'un.** A notable lie: mid-C.19–20; ob.

round robin. The host: low coll: mid-C.16–17. Coverdale, Foxe, Heylin. cf. JACK IN A BOX. 2. A housebreaker's tool: see ROUND-ABOUT, 3. 3. 'A good hearty swindle', Clarkson & Richardson, 1889: c.

round shaving. A reprimand: (low) coll: from ca 1870; ob. Ex dial.

round the bend. Crazy; mad: naval: mid-C.19–20; ob.

***round the corner, get** (one). Deliberately to annoy an irritable person: c.: ca 1810–50. Vaux, who notes the variant *get* (one) *out*.

round the corner, wrong (all). Having had something strong to drink: lower classes': from the middle 1890s; slightly ob.

round the houses. Trousers: rhyming s. (1857) on sol. pronunciation, *trousies*. An improvement on orig. form, ROUND ME HOUSES.

round 'un, see ROUND ONE.

***roundem.** A button: c.: from ca 1860. A disguising of *round* (cf. ROUNDY).

rounder. One who peaches: low: 1884 (O.E.D.). Ex ROUND, v. 2. A short, close-fitting jacket: coll: mostly Cockney: from ca 1890. Milliken, 1893, 'That's me in plaid dittos and rounder.' Ex *roundabout* in same sense.

Roundhead. A Puritan: coll: 1641; S.E. by 1800. Ex cropped head. cf. SQUARE HEAD.

rounding. A betraying of one's associates: low: 1864. See ROUND, v.; cf. ROUNDER, 1.

***rounds.** Trousers: tramps' c.: from ca 1890. P. H. Emerson. Ex ROUND THE HOUSES.

rounds of the galley. Openly expressed abuse of a seaman by his mess-mates: naval: ca 1850–1910.

***roundy(-ken).** A watch-house or lock-up: c. of ca 1825–60. Egan. Lit., round place.

***rouny.** A potato: c. of ca 1820–70. Haggart. Also (?misprint), *ronny*. A corruption of *roundy*, a round object: cf. dial. *roundy*, a lump of coal.

***rouse,** v.i. To fight: c.: 1888, *Evening Standard*, 26 Dec.; ob.

rouse and shine (naval, C.19); **rise and shine** (naval and military, C.20). A c.p. order to get out of bed.

rouser. A formidable breaking of wind: coll: C.18. Swift. 2. A handy man: Australian coll: C.20. Lawson, 1902. Ex *rouse-about*.

roush, see ROSH.

roust. An act of coïtion: coll: late C.16–17. Hall, *Satires*, 'She seeks her third roust on her silent toes.' Ex *roust*, a roaring or bellowing.

roust, v.i. To coït: coll: late C.16–17. Ex the n.; the corresponding S.E. sense is 'to shout, bellow'. 2. To steal: c.: ca 1820–80. Haggart. Ex dial. *roust*, to rout out.

roustabout. A rouseabout or handy man, esp. at a shearing: Australian: 1883: coll >, by 1905, S.E. Ex U.S. *roustabout*, a deck hand or wharf labourer.

***router-putters.** Cows' feet: c.: ca 1820–60. Haggart. Ex *router*, (Scots dial. for) a cow.

rovers. Thoughts: Scots coll: C.19–20; ob. Jamieson. Ex *wandering thoughts*.

row. A disturbance; a noisy quarrel: perhaps orig. c. (John Poulter, *Discoveries*, 1753) > s. >, ca 1910, coll. Esp. in *make a row* (1787), *kick up a row* (1789, O.E.D.), and *get into a row*. Origin obscure; W. suggests that it is cognate with *rouse* = *carouse*. 2. A noise: 1845 (O.E.D.); s. >, ca 1910, coll. *Eton School Days*, 1864, 'Chorley cried, Hold your row, will you?'

row, v. To assail roughly: attack (a person or his rooms): 1790 (O.E.D.): s. until ca 1890, then coll; ob. Ex the n., 1. 2. v.i., to make a disturbance; to quarrel: 1797 (O.E.D.). 3. To RAG (2), v.i.: university: ca 1820–80. 4. To scold severely, to reprimand (v.t.): from ca 1810: s. Byron. 5. To criticize harshly or sharply: from ca 1825. 6. See ROW IN THE BOAT.

row?, what's the. What's the noise about? What's the matter or trouble?; 1837, Dickens, 'What's the row, Sam?'

row in. To conspire: low: from ca 1860. Ex next entry.

***row (in the boat).** To go shares (*with*): c. of ca 1810–60.

row up. To reprimand severely: 1845 (O.E.D.): coll; in C.20, S.E. but ob. ?ex: 2. To rouse noisily: C.19–20; ob. s. >, ca 1890, coll.

rowdy. Money: from ca 1840: low. Ob. Leman Rede (*rowdy*); Thackeray (*the r.*). ?ex RUDDY, n.

rowdy, adj. (Of horse or bullock) troublesome: Australian s. (—1872) >, by 1900, coll. C. H. Eden, 1872; A. B. Paterson, 'And I can ride a rowdy colt, or swing the axe all day.' Extension of S.E. sense.

rowdy-dow. Abbr. of next, or ex *row-de-dow*, a din. From ca 1860. H., 2nd ed., 'Low, vulgar; "not the cheese", or thing'.

rowdy-dowdy. Noisily rough; turbulently noisy: from ca 1850. Reduplication on ROWDY.

rowing, vbl n. To ROW, v., esp. in senses 1 and 4.

rowing man. A spreester, fast liver: university: ca 1875–1910. Ex ROW, v., 2, and 3.

rowl. Money: low: C.19. Prob. a corruption of ROYAL (IMAGES).

rowlock (phrase), see RULLOCK.

rows, the. The rows of hovels in the miners' section of a mining town: miners' (and their families') coll: since ca 1870.

royal. A member of the Royal Family: coll: 1788 Mme D'Arblay. 2. A privileged labourer working regularly enough but not on the staff: dockers' coll: 1883, G. R. Sims.

royal, adj. Noble; splendid; excellent: coll: from ca 1580; but not gen. before ca 1850. e.g. *a royal time*.

royal bob. Gin: ca 1729–70. cf. ROYAL POVERTY. ?origin.

royal image. A coin: mid-C.18–early 19: coll or perhaps S.E.; coll, however, is *royal images*, money: mid-C.18–mid-19. On *royal* (*ryal*), the coin; on the analogy of (*King's* and) QUEEN'S PICTURE.

royal poverty. Gin: ca 1725–80. N. Bailey. cf. ROYAL BOB. Perhaps because, though a ROYAL drink, gin is apt to lead to poverty.

royal-roast. Roast meat and vegetables for, and on, the lower deck: naval coll: late C.19–20. cf. *royal roast and straight bake*, roast meat and baked potatoes: id.: id.

***royal scamp.** A highwayman that, without brutality, robs only the rich: c.: late C.18–early 19. See SCAMP.

Royal Standbacks, the. 'A regiment imagined by others . . . not to have shewn particular keenness about going into action': military coll: C.19–20; slightly ob.

royally. Splendidly; excellently: coll: 1836, E. Howard, 'Royally drunk'.

***royster,** see ROISTER. **rozin,** see ROSIN.

***rozzer;** occ. **rosser.** A policeman: c.: from ca 1870. See ROOSHER for possible etymology; cf., however, Romany *roozlo* (or *-us*), strong.

rub. A rubber in card-games: 1830, 'An occasional rub or two of whist', O.E.D.: coll till C.20, then S.E. 2. A loan (e.g. of a newspaper): military: ca 1880–1910.

rub, v. See RUB DOWN, IN, OFF, OUT, RUB, TO, UP. 2. F. & H. postulates *rub* as a variant of RUB OFF and RUB UP; I doubt its independent existence. 3. As the base of RUB TO, it occurs in 1737. 4. B.E. and Grose describe *rub*, to go, run away, as c., but it is familiar S.E.

rub-a-dub, n. A pub; a club: late C.19–20 rhyming s.

rub and a good cast! A c.p. warning: ca 1635–90. Clarke; Ray. Ex bowls.

rub-belly. Coïtion: low coll: C.18–20.

***rub-down,** n. corresponding to the ensuing v.: c. of late C.19–20.

rub down. To search (a prisoner) by running the hands over his body: coll: 1887. More gen., *run the* RULE OVER. 2. To scold, reprimand: from ca 1895; ob.

rub in. To emphasize annoyingly; insist vexatiously or unkindly upon; remind naggingly of. Esp. as *rub it in*. *Daily News*, 26 May 1870. 'Rubbing it in is a well-known phrase amongst the doubtful portion of the constabulary,' esp. as = to give fatal evidence (Ware). cf. dial. *rubber*.

rub of the thumb, give (a person) **a.** To explain something to; esp. to show him how to do something: coll: mid-C.19–20; ob. Ex some trade. cf.: 2. To show appreciation for good work: tailors': late C.19–20.

rub-off. A copulation: coll: late C.17–early 19. Congreve. 2. A masturbation: low: C.19–20; ob. In this sense, RUB-UP is much more gen.

rub off, v. In same senses and periods as RUB-OFF. 2. See RUBBED OFF.

rub on. To make do, 'rub along': coll: ca 1870–1910. *Sessions*, 18 Sept. 1893.

rub out. To kill: orig. (1848), U.S.; anglicized ca 1870: S.E. until C.20, then coll. Ex erasing. 2. To cut (a pattern): tailors': mid-C.19–20.

rub, rub! 'Us'd on the Greens when the Bowl Flees too fast, to have it forbear, if Words wou'd do it', B.E.: a bowling c.p. soon > j.: late C.17–18.

***rub to.** (See RUB, v.) To send, carry off, to (prison): c.: ca 1670–1840. Anon.,

Warning for Housekeepers, 1676. Prob. a development of *rub*, to go, to run.

rub-up. See RUB-OFF, 2. From ca 1620: low coll. Esp. *do a rub-up*. Also *rubbing-up*. Ex:

rub up. The v. corresponding to RUB OFF, 2, and RUB-UP, n. Low coll: C.17–20. This sense is almost inseparable from: 2. So to caress a person that he or she becomes actively amorous: low coll: from ca 1620. Fletcher's *Martial*.

rubacrock; gen. **rubbacrock.** A filthy slattern: coll: C.19–20; ob. Ex S.W. dial.; the word occurs in the famous *Exmoor Scolding*, 1746.

rubba(d)ge; rubbi(d)ge; occ. **rubbich.** Rubbish: C.19–20. When not dial. (see esp. E.D.D.) it is low coll, verging indeed on sol.

rubbed about, be. (Of a person) to be made a convenience: tailors': from ca 1870.

rubbed down with the book (or **B.**), **be.** To be sworn on the Bible: London proletarian: from ca 1880. Nevinson, 1895.

rubbed off. Bankrupt and gone, indeed run, away: coll: late C.17–18.

rubbed(-)out. Dead: see RUB OUT. 'Of late frequently used in fashionable novels', H., 1864.

rubbedge, rubbege, see RUBBADGE.

rubber. A caoutchouc eraser: coll: late C.18–20. 2. Some illicit device or swindling trick: c.: early C.17. Dekker, 'Betting, Lurches, Rubbers, and such tricks'. Prob. connected with the *rubber* of games of skill and/or chance.

rubber, fake the, see FAKE THE RUBBER.

rubber(-)neck; (-)necking. A very inquisitive person; excessive curiosity or inquisitiveness: U.S. (—1900), partly anglicized, esp. in Australia, ca 1905; slightly ob. Ex 'considerable craning and stretching', as though one's neck were made of rubber: as in the *Pall Mall Gazette*, 8 March 1902.

rubber-up. The agent expressed in RUB UP, v.: low coll: C.19–20.

rubbich, see RUBBADGE.

rubbing-up. The act in RUB UP, v. Also RUB-UP.

rubbish. Money: low: ca 1820–60. Egan, 1821, 'She shall stump up [q.v.] the rubbish before I leave her.' cf. S.E. *dross* and *filthy lucre*. 2. Luggage, esp. household effects and furniture: Anglo-Indian military: early C.19.

rubigo. The penis: (low) Scots coll: late C.16–17. R. Sempill. ?ex L. *ruber*, red, on L. *rubigo* (or *robigo*), rust (on metals), perhaps influenced by L. *prurigo*, lasciviousness.

rubric, in or out of the. In, out of, holy orders: coll: late C.17–18. Farquhar.

ruby. Blood: boxing: 1860, *Chambers's Journal*; 'Pomes' Marshall, ca 1886, 'You'd be sure to nark the ruby round his gilt.' cf. CARMINE; CLARET. 2. See:

Ruby, cross the. To cross the Rubicon: fast life: early C.19, when *ruby* was s. for port wine.

***ruck,** v. To lay information (see also RUCK ON): c. >, by 1900, low s.: from ca 1884. 2. To grow angry or irritated: low: from ca 1890; ob. Ex sense 1, or independently ex *ruck* (*up*), as applied to clothes; origin of sense 1 is hazy.

ruck, come in with the. 'To arrive at the winning-post among the unplaced horses' (B. & L.): turf: from ca 1860.

ruck (or **rucket**) **along.** To walk quickly: ca 1890–1910: Oxford University. While *ruck*, prob. the earlier form, may derive ex dial. *ruck*, to go, *rucket* may be an elaboration suggested by *rocket along*.

***ruck on; occ. ruck upon.** To SPLIT ON A PAL; BLAB about (a person): c. >, ca 1900, low s.: 1884, *Daily News*, 'I told the prisoner that I was not going to ruck on an old pal.' 2. To go back on; to disown: Cockney: late C.19–20. Pugh (2), '"I don't care," said Deuce, defiantly ... "I ain't goin' to ruck on Dad."'

ruckerky. Recherché: Society: 1890s. Ware quotes the *Daily Telegraph* of 4 April 1898.

rucket along, see RUCK ALONG.

rucktion; gen. **ruction.** A disturbance, uproar, noisy quarrel, ROW: dial. (—1825) >, ca 1830, coll. In the pl, trouble, esp. noisy and avoidable trouble. The C.19 variant *'ruction*, combined with Lover's use of the word, points to origin in *insurrection*; P. W. Joyce, in *English in Ireland*, postulates 'the Insurrection of 1798, which was commonly called "the Ruction" '.

***ruddock.** A gold coin: 1567, Turberville: †by 1750; ob. indeed by 1650. Occ. *red* or *golden ruddock*. Prob. ex *ruddock*, a robin (redbreast); cf. RUDDY. 2. In pl, money, gold; esp. gold money: late C.16–17. Also *red* or *golden r*. Heywood, ca 1607 (printed 1631), 'They are so flush of their ruddocks.' cf. GLISTENER and RIDGE and RED ONE.

***ruddy.** A sovereign: c. and low sporting (—1887). Baumann has *thirty ruddy*, £30. Ex colour. cf.:

ruddy, adj. BLOODY; CONFOUNDED:

euphemistic s.: from ca 1905. (Synonymous colour; rhyme.)

***ruff, the wooden.** The pillory: c.: ca 1690–1830. Punning the neck-wear.

***ruff-peck.** Bacon: c. of ca 1565–1750. Harman, Dekker, Shirley (1707). ?lit., rough food.

***ruffelar** or **-er**, see RUFFLER.

***ruffemans.** A variant of RUFFMANS.

ruffer. One who is rough: lower classes' (—1909).

***ruffian.** See RUFFIN. 2. In boxing s., a boxer disregarding science in his desire for victory: ca 1820–50.

Ruffians' Hall, he is only fit for. A c.p. applied to an apprentice overdressed: London: coll: ca 1640–1820. Fuller; Grose's *Provincial Glossary*. Ex a part of Smithfield where, ca 1590–1860, 'Trials of Skill were plaid by ordinary Ruffianly people, with Sword and Buckler.' Blount, 1764.

***ruffin** or **Ruffin;** also spelt **Ruffian.** The devil: c.: 1567, Harman (*ruffian*); Dekker (*Ruffin*); B.E. (*Ruffin*); Grose (*Ruffian*); Ainsworth (*Old Ruffin*). *Ruffin*, the name of a fiend (C.13–early 16), influenced by *ruffian*, a cut-throat villain. 2. Whence, a justice of the peace: c.: ca 1620–1820. Fletcher, ca 1622 (*Ruffin*); B.E. (*Ruffin*); Grose (*ruffin*, 1st ed.; 2nd ed., *ruffian*).

***ruffin, to the,** see NINES, TO THE.

ruffin cook ruffin, who scalded the devil in his feathers. A c.p. applied to a bad cook: ca 1780–1860. Prob. influenced by PUFFIN.

***rufflar,** see RUFFLER.

***ruffle,** (gen. in pl.) A handcuff: c.: ca 1780–1850. Punning on the wrist-ornament.

***ruffler;** also **ruffelar** or **-er, rufflar, ruffleer, rufler.** A vagabond: c.: ca 1530–1620. Copland. 2. Esp. one of the 1st or the 2nd order or rank of 'canters': C.17–18. 3. A beggar pretending to be a maimed soldier or sailor: c. of ca 1560–1830. Awdelay; Grose, 1st ed. (The term derives ex *ruffle*, to deport oneself arrogantly.)

***ruffmans.** A hedge: c. of ca 1620–1840. Fletcher (1622). Lit., rough time. 2. Harman and B.E. define it as the wood, a bush; Grose as a wood, a bush, or a hedge: as wood or bush, it is a special application of sense 1: ca 1565–1840. See -MANS.

rufler, see RUFFLER.

rufus or **Rufus.** The female pudend: low: mid-C.19–20; ob. Ex *rufous*.

Rug. A Rugbeian: Rugby School (—1892).

rug, see RUG, AT.

***rug, all.** Safe; certain: c. > gaming s.: late C.17–18. B.E., '*It's all Rug*, ... the Game is secured.' 2. Hence, 'safe' in general: C.18–early 19: s. Rowe, 1705, 'Fear nothing, Sir; Rug's the Word, all's safe.' Perhaps ex the warmth and snugness afforded by rugs. cf.:

rug, at. In bed; asleep: low (?c.): ca 1810–60. Prob. *rug* (of bed) influenced by *all rug*: an interesting clue is offered by the Devonshire *rug*, warm. cf. RUGGINS.

Rugby, real. Cruel: Public Schools' (—1909); virtually †. Ex the roughness of Rugby football.

rugger. Rugby football: s. (1893). Ex *Rugby* on Oxford *-er*.

***ruggins;** more gen., as in Vaux and in Egan's Grose, **Ruggins's.** Bed: c. of ca 1810–70. Lytton, 1828, 'Toddle off to ruggins'. An elaboration of *rug* of bed, influenced by *all rug* and *at rug*; or perhaps merely *rugging* (coarse blanket cloth) pluralized or genitivized (*rugging's*), with *g* omitted.

***ruggy.** Safe; withdrawn, secluded: c. (—1887); ob. See RUG, ALL.

ruin. See BLUE RUIN. By itself, rare: 1820, J. H. Reynolds.

rule of three(, the). Penis and testes; low: C.18–20. D'Urfey. 2. Hence, copulation, C.19–20. Other mathematical indelicacies are *addition*, *multiplication*, *subtraction*, all implying the juxtaposition of opponent genitals.

***rule over, run the** (occ. **a**). To search: c. (—1874). H., 5th ed.; Horsley; 'Pomes' Marshall, 'Run the rule through all | His pockets.' cf. RUB DOWN, which has remained low s., and FRISK, ob. c. '*No. 747*' has it for 1845: (of a pickpocket) to feel over the person of (a prospective victim).

ruler, v. To rap, beat, with a ruler: coll: 1850, Dickens; ob.

rullock. A rowlock: nautical coll (—1825). Baumann has *shove one's ear into a seaman's rullock* (to seek a quarrel with a sailor), which is ob.

rum, n. A needy rural clergyman in Ireland: ca 1720–40. Swift. Perhaps ex the adj., 1, as a mark of appreciation. 2. A 'rum', i.e. questionable, person (gen. male): ca 1800–50. Ex the adj., 2. 3. An old, hence an unsaleable book: ca 1810–30. 'Anecdotes' Nichols. Ex the adj., 2.

rum, v. To cheat: ca 1810–20. 'He had rummed me,' 1812. Ex the adj., 2.

***rum,** adj.; variants: *rome*, C.16–18; *room(e)*, C.17. Excellent; fine, good;

valuable; handsome; great: c.: ca 1565–1910; but comparatively rare after ca 1810. The sense varies with the n.: see the ensuing list of terms, to many of which there is a precisely contrasted sense afforded by QUEER with the same n. Harman, 1567; Jonson; B.E.; Grose; Vaux; H.; Smyth (RUM-GAGGER). Quotations are here unnecessary: see the combinations, which illuminate and objectify this strange adj. It may well, as H. suggests, derive from *Rome* ("the glory that was Rome") as a city of splendid repute and fame; the dial. *ram*, very or strong, is ineligible, for its history does not go far enough back; Romany *rom*, a male (Gypsy), is a possibility, but not so probable as *Rome*. (cf. REAM.) Note that in Turkish, 'Roman' is *Rûm*; the Gypsies passed through Turkey – indeed there is a Turkish Gypsy dialect. Note, too, that L. *Roma* is cognate with, perhaps actually derived ex, that Teutonic radical *hruod* (fame) which occurs in *Roger* and *Roderick*, and in Ger. *Ruhm* (fame), whence *ruhmvoll*, famous: cf. the s. sense of FAMOUS itself. 2. Either hence, by ironic 'inversion', or ex *Rom*, a Gypsy, used attributively (for the adj. is *Romano* or *-ani*) – *A New Canting Dict.*'s (1725) and Grose's remarks (1785) at *Gypsies* make it clear that, even so early, the Gypsies had a 'rum' reputation – comes the sense 'queer, odd, eccentric, strange, questionable, disreputable': such terms as RUM BITE, RUM BOB, 2, RUM BUBBER, (esp.) RUM COVE, RUM CULL, RUM FUN, RUM NED, taken along with those C.18 strictures on the Gypsies, may have caused the change of sense from excellent, fine, etc., to queer, strange, etc. The earliest record is of 1774, but this sense does not > gen. until ca 1800, as the O.E.D. points out. The remarkable merging with the c. sense of QUEER, of which, from ca 1820, it is mostly a mere synonym, is due, in part, to the vitality of *queer* itself, for in c. *queer* was more potent after ca 1790 than *rum* was. H. Kelly, 1774, 'Rum tongue' (language); Grose; Dickens, 1837, 'There's rummer things than women in this world.' See also 'Neither Cricket nor Philology' in *A Covey of Partridge*. cf. RUMMY. 3. Strangely silly: late C.17–18. This is an extremely rare sense: I know it only in RUM NED, where the silliness may reside only in the second member. (N.B. Of the clear instances in Grose, 3rd ed., forty belong to sense 1; three to sense 2; only one to sense 3. And practically all of Grose's terms were already in B.E.; B.E.'s terms, with one exception (RUM NED), are all in sense 1.)

rum, come it. To talk oddly: low: ca 1820–70. 2. Hence, to act oddly: low: mid-C.19–20; ob.

***rum beak** or **beck.** A justice of the peace: c.: late C.17–early 19. See BEAK, BECK.

***rum bing,** see RUM BUNG.

***rum bit** or, mostly, **bite.** A clever trick or swindle; c.: late C.17–early 19. See BITE, n., 2. 2. (Only *bite*.) Hence, a clever rogue: c.: early C.19.

***rum bleating cheat.** A (very) fat wether: c.: late C.17–early 19. See CHEAT.

***rum blowen** (C.19) or **blower** (late C.17–18). 'A handsome wench', Grose, 1st ed.; esp. one 'kept by a particular Man', B.E. See BLOWEN; BLOWER, 2.

***rum bluffer.** A jolly inn-keeper or victualler: c.: late C.17–18. See BLUFFER.

***rum bob.** 'A young Prentice; also a sharp, sly Trick, and a pretty short wig', B.E.: late C.17–early 19, except the third (†by 1780).

rum-boile. A variant of ROMBOYLE, n.

***rum booze, bouse, bouze, buse, buze.** (See BOOZE, n.) Good wine (mid-C.16–19) or other liquor (C.17–19): c. 2. 'Flip made of white or port wine, the yolks of eggs, sugar and nutmeg', *Spy*, 1825: Oxford University: ca 1815–50.

***rum-boozing welts.** Bunches of grapes: c.: mid-C.17–early 19. Lit., excellent-liquor lumps or bunches.

rum-bottle. A sailor: naval: ca 1860–1900. Ex his fondness for rum.

***rum bub.** Very good liquor: c.: late C.17–18.

***rum bubber.** 'A dexterous fellow at stealing silver tankards from inns and taverns', Grose, 1st ed.: c.: late C.17–18. Ex BUB, liquor.

***rum buffer** (C.18–early 19) or **bughar,** gen. **bugher** (late C.17–early 19). A handsome and/or valuable dog: c. See BUFFER.

***rum bung** (occ. **bing).** A full purse: c.: late C.17–early 19.

***rum chant** or **chaunt.** 'A song', Grose, 3rd ed.; 'a good song', Vaux, 1812: the latter seems to be the correct definition. A late instance of RUM, adj., 1.

***rum chub.** 'Among butchers, a customer easily imposed on', Grose, 1st ed.: c.: late C.17–early 19.

***rum clank.** A gold or silver cup or tankard: c.: C.18–early 19. See CLANK.

***rum clout, wipe, wiper.** 'A Silk, fine Cambrick, or Holland Handkerchief', B.E.: c.: late C.17–19; *wipe* not before C.19.

***rum co** or **coe.** A smart lad: late C.16–early 17. cf. RUM COVE.

***rum cod.** A full purse (esp. of gold); a large sum of money: c.: late C.17–early 19. B.E.; cf. RUM BUNG.

***rum cole.** 'New Money'; 'Medals, curiously Coyn'd', B.E.: c.: late C.17–early 19. See COLE. Also, in first nuance, *rum* GELT.

***rum coll.** A rhyme-needed variant, early C.18, of RUM CULL, 1.

***rum cove.** 'A great Rogue', B.E.: c.: C.17–mid-18. Rowlands; Dekker's use stresses *rum*, rich. 2. Hence, 'a dexterous or clever rogue', Grose, 1st ed.: c.: mid-C.18–mid-19. (cf. COVE.) A very operative term: see RUM, adj., 2. 3. A 'queer fish' (see QUEER CARD): low: mid-C.19–20.

***rum cull.** 'A rich Fool, that can be easily . . . Cheated . . .; also one that is very generous and kind to a Mistress', B.E.: c.: ca 1670–1840. cf. the U.S. *sugar-daddy*. 2. A manager: low theatrical: from ca 1860. Esp. the master of a travelling troop (—1864). Perhaps ex: 3. An intimate friend (gen. in the vocative): low: ca 1840–90. Selby, 1844, 'What's in the wind, my rum cull?'

***rum cully.** Elisha Coles's variant (1676) of RUM CULL, 1.

rum customer. A person, an animal, that it is risky, even dangerous to meddle with or offend: late C.18–20. cf. *queer* CUSS (2). 2. Hence, in the pugilistic circles of ca 1800–50, a hard-punching, a skilful, attacking boxer, known also as a *swishing hitter*.

***rum cuttle.** A sword: c.: early C.17. Rowlands, 1609. A CUTTLE is a knife.

***rum dab.** 'A very Dextrous fellow at fileing, thieving, Cheating, Sharping, &c', B.E. (at *dab*, not at *rum*): late C.17–early 18: c.

***rum degen** or **tol** or **tilter.** A splendid sword; esp. a silver-hilted or silver-inlaid one: c.: late C.17–18.

***rum dell, doxy, mort.** A handsome whore: C.17–early 19. Jonson (*roome mort*); B.E. (in this sense, *dell* and *doxy*); Grose (id.). See separately RUM DOXY and RUM MORT.

***rum diver.** A skilful pickpocket: c.: C.18–mid-19. Also *rum file*.

***rum doxy.** A beautiful woman, a fine wench: c.: late C.17–early 19. 2. A 'light Lady', B.E.: late C.17–early 18.

***rum drawers.** Silk, or very fine worsted, stockings: c.: late C.17–18.

***rum dropper.** A vintner (wine-merchant); landlord of a tavern: c.: mid-C.17–18. Coles, 1676; Ned Ward (1709); Grose.

***rum dubber.** A dexterous picklock: c.: late C.17–18.

***rum duchess.** A jolly, handsome woman: c.: late C.17–mid-18. cf.:

***rum duke.** A jolly, handsome man: c.: late C.17–18. B.E.; Grose, who (1785) adds, 'an odd eccentric fellow', or, as he defines at *duke*, 'a queer unaccountable fellow': c.: late C.18–mid-19. Extant in East Anglian dial. in 1903. 3. Gen. in pl, 'The boldest and stoutest fellows lately among the Alsatians [see ALSATIA], Minters, Savoyards, and other inhabitants of privileged districts, sent to remove and guard the goods of such bankrupts as intended to take sanctuary in those places', Grose: c.: late C.17–mid-18.

***rum fam** or **fem.** A diamond ring: c.: ca 1850–90. See FAM.

***rum file.** See RUM DIVER: late C.17–early 19.

***rum fun.** A sharp trick; a clever swindle: c.: late C.17–18.

***rum gagger.** One of those impostors 'who tell wonderful stories of their sufferings at sea, or when taken by the Algerines', Grose, 1st ed.: c. of ca 1780–1850; then nautical s. (witness Smyth, 1867), with the Algerian gambit omitted; ob.

***rum gelt** or **gilt**, see RUM COLE.

***rum gill.** A clever thief; a handsome man: c. of ca 1820–50. Ainsworth.

***rum glimmer,** gen. spelt **glymmar** (or **-er).** The chief of the link-boys: c.: late C.17–18. See GLIM.

rum go. A puzzling and not too respectable contretemps; a mysterious (not merely because wholly unexpected) occurrence or, esp., development of a plot, situation, etc.: late C.18–19. Perhaps orig. c.: in Oct. 1783 (*Sessions*, p. 952), a thief says, 'By God, this is a rum go.' Thackeray, 1850, and George Eliot, 1876; *rummy go* is in *Punch*, 1841. See RUM, adj., 2, and GO, n.

***rum going.** Fast trotting: c. or low s.: ca 1820–60. Jones, 1825, *The True Bottom'd Boxer*.

***rum gut(t)lers.** Canary wine: c.: mid-C.17–18. cf. S.E. *guzzle*. 2. 'Fine Eating', *A New Canting Dict.*, 1725: c.: C.18.

***rum hopper.** A drawer at a tavern: c.: late C.17–18. One who hops or 'springs to it' with great alacrity.

rum johnny or **Johnny.** A native wharf-labourer: Anglo-Indian: C.19–20; ob. Prob. ex RUM, adj., 2; but see Yule & Burnell. 2. A whore: naval and military: mid-C.19–20. Ex Hindustani *ramjani*, a dancing-girl.

***rum Joseph or joseph.** A very good coat or cloak: c.: late C.17–18. B.E. at *Joseph*.

***rum ken.** A popular inn, tavern, brothel: c. of ca 1810–60. Egan, 1821.

***rum kicks.** 'Breeches of gold or silver brocade, or richly laced with gold or silver', Grose, 1st ed.: c.: late C.17–early 19.

***rum kiddy.** A clever young thief: c.: late C.18–early 19. G. Parker, 1781.

***rum maund (**or **mawnd).** 'One that Counterfeits himself a Fool' while begging: late C.17–18. B.E., Grose. See MAUND. cf.:

***rum maunder.** A late C.18–19 early form of the preceding. F. & H., where it is defined as 'a clever beggar'.

***rum mizzler.** A thief clever at escaping: c.: ca 1780–1900. cf. NEEDY MIZZLER and see MIZZLE.

***rum mort.** See RUM DELL. 2. A queen; the Queen: c.: Harman, 1567 (*Rome mort*); B.E.; Grose. †by 1840. 3. Hence, a great lady: c.: late C.17–early 19. See MORT.

***rum nab.** 'A Beaver, or very good Hat', B.E.: late C.17–early 18, the former (Shadwell, 1688); until ca 1830, the latter. See NAB, n., 3.

***rum nantz** or **Nantz.** Good French brandy: c.: late C.17–early 19.

***rum ned** or **Ned.** 'A very silly fellow', B.E.; 'a very rich silly fellow', Grose: c.: late C.17–18. cf. RUM CULL, 1; cf. RUM, adj., 2.

rum one or **un ('un).** (Gen. *r. one*) a settling blow, punch: boxing: early C.19. 2. (Gen. *r. un*). An odd or eccentric fellow; a strange-looking animal or object; a strange affair: from ca 1825. Dickens. Prob. ironic on: 3. (Only *rum un.*) A 'stout fellow'; a capital chap: c.: ca 1820–50. Jones, 1825; Moncrieff, 1830, in the vocative. cf. RUM CULL, last sense.

***rum omee** (or **omer**), occ. **rum homer, of the case,** see OMEE.

***rum pad;** Moore writes it *rumpad.* The highway: c.: late C.17–early 19. The v. *rum-pad*, to attack, rob, on the highway, is only 'literary' c. of late C.19. 2. A highwayman: an error or a catachresis: C.17–mid-18. J. Shirley; *The Scoundrel's Dict.*

***rum(-)padder.** One of 'the better sort of Highwaymen, well Mounted and Armed', B.E.: mid-C.17–early 19: c. Ex RUM PAD.

***rum peck.** Good food: c.: late C.17–early 19.

***rum peeper.** A silver looking-glass: c.: late C.17–18.

rum phiz or **phyz.** 'An odd face or countenance'; Grose, 1st ed.: low: from ca 1780; ob.

***rum prancer.** A very fine horse: c.: late C.17–early 19.

***rum quid(d)s.** A large booty; a great share of spoil: c.: late C.17–early 19.

***rum ruff peck.** Westphalia ham: c.: late C.17–18. Contrast RUFF-PECK.

***rum slim or slum.** Punch: c.: ca 1780–1890. Parker (*slim*); Egan (*slum*); H., 3rd ed. (*slim*). ?the 'originator' of *rum sling*, rum punch (cf. *gin sling*).

***rum snitch.** A hard blow on the nose: c.: late C.17–early 19.

***rum squeeze.** Copious drink for the fiddlers: c.: id.

rum start. An odd occurrence: s. and dial.: from ca 1840; slightly ob. as s. Recorded in '*No. 747*' as used in 1845.

***rum strum.** A long wig, esp. if a fine one: c.: late C.17–18. 2. A handsome wench or harlot: c.: late C.17–early 18. See STRUM, n., 1 and 2.

***rum tilter; rum tol** (see TOL). A RUM DEGEN: c.: late C.17–early 19.

***rum Tom Pat.** A clergyman (not a hedge-priest): c. of ca 1780–1840. See quotation at ADAM, v.

***rum topping.** A rich head-dress: c. of ca 1670–1810. Orig. of the style designated by *commode*.

rum touch, see TOUCH, RUM. **rum un ('un),** see RUM ONE.

***Rum ville or vyle; Rumville.** London: c.: C.17–19. See ROME VILLE.

***rum wipe or wiper,** see RUM CLOUT and quotation at RUMMY, adj.

rumble, n. An (improvised) seat for servants at the back of a carriage: 1808: coll till ca 1840 > then S.E.; ob. Abbr. RUMBLE-TUMBLE. 2. A stage-coach: coll: ca 1830–50. This differentiation (F. & H.) is open to dispute.

***rumble,** v. To rule *out* unceremoniously, handle roughly: ca 1810–50. Ex ROMBOYLE, v. 2. Hence, to test, try; handle; examine: c. of ca 1820–1900. Haggart. 3. Hence, v.i. & t., to detect; fathom, understand; low: from ca 1875. Binstead, 1898, 'I soon rumbled he was in it when I heard . . .' cf. TUMBLE TO, by which this sense may have been suggested and has certainly been influenced. 4. To experience stomachic gurgles, whether audible or inaudible: coll: late C.19–20.

rumble-tumble. See RUMBLE, n., 1. C.19: coll till ca 1830, then S.E. Ex the noise. 2. Any wheeled vehicle that rumbles: 1806, J. Beresford; †by 1910. Coll till ca 1840, then S.E. and dial.

rumbler. Same as RUMBLE, n., 1: coll: ca 1800–20. 2. A hackney coach: ca 1815–60: coll. Moncrieff, 1823, 'A rattler . . . is a rumbler, otherwise a jarvey.' 3. Hence, a four-wheeled cab: ca 1860–1910. 4. Prison: low: Australian: ca 1820–70. A perversion of RUMBO, n., 2.

***rumbler, running.** A carriage-thief's confederate: c.: ca 1820–80. ?ex:

rumbler's flunkey. A footman; one who, for tips or wages, runs for cabs, etc.: low: ca 1815–90. Anon., *The Young Prig* (song), ca 1819. See RUMBLER, 2, 3.

rumbo. Rum-punch: ca 1750–1840, then archaic: coll till C.19, then S.E. Smollett, 1751, 'He and my good master . . . come hither every evening, and drink a couple of cans of rumbo apiece.' Either fantastic on *rum* or ex RUMBULLION. 2. A prison: c. of ca 1720–1830. Also *rumboken* (Harper, 1724). Perhaps ironic on RUM, adj., 1. 3. Stolen rope: nautical and dockyard s. (—1867). cf. RUMBO-KEN, 2. 4. See:

rumbo, n. and adj. Plenty, plentiful; sufficiency, sufficient; good: low: 1870, Hazlewood & Williams; 1876, Hindley, '"Chuck rumbo (eat plenty), my lad"'; *Pall Mall Gazette*, 21 Dec. 1895 (horses and carts described as *rumbo*, good). Prob. ex coll Sp. *rumbo*, liberality, generosity (cf. *rumbosamente*, grandly, liberally), via Lingua Franca.

rumbo! Splendid!: lower and lower-middle classes': ca 1860–1915. Ex Sp. via the Gypsies.

***rumbo-ken.** See RUMBO, n., 2. 2. A pawnbroker's shop: c.: (?) ca 1700–1850.

rumbowling. Anything inferior or adulterated: nautical (—1864). (Occ. as adj.) Prob. a corruption of S.E. *rombowline*. 2. Grog: nautical (—1885). Ex sense 1, but perhaps influenced by RUMBO and:

rumbullion, -ian; occ. **rombullion.** Rum: ca 1650–1750: coll soon > S.E. ?etymology.

rumbumptious. Obstreperous: coll: ca 1786–1895. H., 5th ed., 'Haughty, pugilistic' (?quarrelsome). Ex dial. *ram* (see RUMBUSTIOUS) + *bump* on *fractious*. (N.B., BUMPTIOUS is later than *rumbumptious*, GUMPTION earlier than RUMGUMPTION.)

rumbustical; occ. (†) **rombustical.** Boisterous, very noisy; unruly: coll and dial.: 1795, O.E.D. Prob. on †S.E. *robustic* ex RUMBUSTIOUS. cf.:

rumbusticate. To coït with (a woman): late C.19–early 20. Ex RUMBUSTICAL on SPIFLICATE.

rumbusticator. A moneyed man: ca 1890–1910. cf. preceding two entries.

rumbustious; occ. (†in C.20) **rombustious.** Same as RUMBUSTICAL: coll: 1778, Foote, 'The sea has been rather rumbustious.' Lytton, 1853, *rambustious*. Prob. a perversion of *robustious* on dial. *ram*, very, strong, and RUM, adj., 1. (This type of word >, ca 1840, very gen. in U.S.: cf. CATAWAMPUS.)

Rumford (properly, **Romford), ride to.** To get a new pair of breeches, or an old pair new-bottomed: coll: ca 1780–1830. Grose, 1st ed.; in the 2nd he adds, 'Rumford was formerly a famous place for leather breeches.' But cf.: *you* (*one*, etc.) *may* or *might ride to Romford* (*up*)*on a* (*this*, etc.) *knife*, a c.p. imputing bluntness: ca 1705–1860. Swift, 'Well, one may ride to Rumford upon this knife, it is so blunt'; *Notes & Queries*, 1901, referring to ca 1850–70, 'You might ride to Romford on it.'

Rumford or **Romford lion.** A calf: coll: C.18–mid-19. More gen. is ESSEX LION: calves being very numerous in Essex.

rumgumption. Common sense: coll (mostly Scots and Northern): from ca 1770. A strengthened form of GUMPTION.

***rumly.** Finely; excellently; gallantly; strongly: c. of ca 1670–1770. In C.17, often *romely*, as in Rowlands, 1609. Ex RUM, adj., 1. 2. Oddly; eccentrically: s.: 1819, Moore, 'Thus rumly floored'. Ex RUM, adj., 2.

rummage. To caress a woman sexually; possess her: low coll: C.19–20; ob. Ex S.E. *rummage*, to disarrange, disorder; to knock about.

rummagy. Such as may be found, obtained, by *rummaging* in rubbish: coll: 1899, Baring-Gould, 'The "rummagy" faces'; slightly ob.

rummily. Oddly, queerly: 1827, Scott: s. >, ca 1890, coll. Ex RUMMY, adj.

rumminess. Oddness; singularity: 1899, Eden Phillpotts: s.

rummish. Rather odd or peculiar: 1826. Ex RUM, adj., 2.

rummy, adj. Odd; singular: 1828, *Sporting Magazine*, 'A neat, but rather rummy looking blue pony'. Moncrieff's 'rummy Spitalfields wipes' may mean odd handkerchiefs, but it might be a variant on RUM WIPE, a silk handkerchief.

***rummy,** adv. Capitally, excellently, well: c. of ca 1825–40. Moncrieff, 1830, has 'We chaunt so rummy' (cf. RUM CHANT) and 'We frisk so rummy.' Ex RUM, adj., 1, via some of the **rum* combinations.

rump. To flog: ca 1810–90: coll. Vaux, 1812. 2. (Of the male) to coït with, esp. dorsally: low: from ca 1850; slightly ob. As v.i., of either sex: cf. RUMPER. cf. *loose in the* RUMP; RUMP-SPLITTER.

rump, he hath eaten the. A semi-proverbial c.p. applied to one who is constantly talking: ca 1670–1800. Ray.

rump, loose in one's or **the.** (Of women) wanton: coll: C.18–mid-19. D'Urfey.

rump and a dozen. An Irish wager, 'A rump of beef and a dozen of claret', Grose, 2nd ed.: coll: late C.18–mid-19. Also called *buttock and trimmings* (Grose).

rump-and-kidney men. 'Fidlers that Play at Feasts, Fairs, Weddings, &c. And Live chiefly on the Remnants, of Victuals', B.E., who – wrongly, I think – classifies it as c.; Grose doesn't. (Prob.) coll: late C.17–early 19.

rump(-)and(-)stump, adv. Completely; utterly: dial. and coll: from ca 1820; ob. Lit., rump and tail; cf. *lock, stock, and barrel.* A rhyming phrase perhaps suggested by (*utterly*) *stumped.* The synonymous *rump and rig* is wholly dial.

rump-splitter. The penis: low coll: ca 1650–1800. Urquhart. cf. RUMP, 2. Whence, a whoremonger: low: C.19–20; ob. cf. *loose in the* RUMP, and:

rump-work. Copulation: low coll: C.19–20; ob. cf. RUMP, 2, and RUMPER.

rumpad, see RUM PAD.

rumper. A whore; a whoremonger: low: C.19–20; very ob. Ex RUMP, 2, though partly a pun on *Rumper*, a member of the Rump Parliament.

rumption. A rumpus: 1802: coll till ca 1820, then dial. Prob. ex RUMPUS on GUMPTION.

rumpty. One thirty-second of £1: Stock Exchange: 1887.

rumpus. An uproar or, †in C.20, a riot; a ROW, quarrel: coll: 1764, Foote, 'Oh, Major! such a riot and rumpus!' Always in collocation with *riot* before ca 1785; Grose has it in his 2nd ed. Also without article, gen. as riotousness, noise, quarrelling: 1768, O.E.D.; slightly ob. W. suggests a s. use of Gr. ῥόμβος, spinning top, also commotion, disturbance; tentatively, I suggest a fanciful perversion of *rumble*, used, esp. as v., of the noise made by the bowels (C.16 onwards), for Grose, 1785, says 'There is a rumpus among my chitterlins, i.e. I have the cholick.' 2. A masquerade: c.: ca 1810–40.

rumpus, v. To make a rumpus: coll: 1839, Hood; ob. (See the n.)

rumtitum. In fine condition, gen. of a bull or a whoremonger: from ca 1810. cf. *rumtitum, rumtiddy(-tum)*, in refrains, though these are unrecorded before 1820. *Sinks*, 1848, has *rum ti tum with the chill off* (excellent), with a pun on the spirit *rum.* The term *rum-ti-tum* is an elaboration of *rum-tum*, a rhyming reduplication of RUM, adj., 1.

***Rumville,** see ROME-VILLE.

***rumy.** A good girl or woman: tramps' and Gypsy c. (—1859). A perversion of Romany *romeni*, a bride, a wife.

run. To manage: U.S. (1827), anglicized as coll ca 1860. 2. To tease, irritate, nag at: Australian coll (1888); rather ob. 'Rolf Boldrewood'.

run, get the. To be discharged from employment: from ca 1870.

run, give the. To dismiss from employment: since ca 1875. Prompted by preceding entry.

run, have a. To take a walk, a CONSTITUTIONAL: coll: from ca 1880. 2. Esp. *have a* RUN FOR IT. 3. To desert ship: naval: late C.18–mid-C.19.

run, let it, see LET IT RUN.

***run, on the.** Wanted by the police: orig. (late C.19), c. In c., however, it implies leaving the usual haunts when one is wanted by the police.

***run a rule over,** see RULE OVER.

run-about. From ca 1890: coll. See COMPULSORY. 2. Usually in pl **run-abouts** (or one word), 'cattle allowed to graze freely': Australian coll: late C.19–20.

run about after (someone's) **arse.** To be obsequious or subservient to: low: late C.19–20.

run across. To meet by chance: late C.19–20: coll.

run as swift as a pudding would creep. To be very slow: coll: early C.17.

run away and play marbles! An insulting c.p. rejoinder or dismissal: late C.19–20. C. H. Bacon, a Sedbergh boy, aptly pointed out, in July 1934, that an exact equivalent occurs in Shakespeare's *Henry V*: where the Dauphin sends the King a present of tennis balls.

run big. (Of a horse.) To be forced to race when too fat: sporting: late C.19–20; ob.

run down. The gangway or bridge between stage and auditorium: conjurors' coll (from ca 1880).

run (something) **fine.** (Esp. *run it* or *that fine.*) To leave only a very small margin (gen. of time): coll: 1890.

run for it, have a. To make a fight: coll: from ca 1890; slightly ob.

run for one's money, a. An ample *quid pro quo*; extended liberty; a good time in exchange for one's money: C.19 racing s. >, ca 1890, coll.

run goods. 'A maidenhead, being a commodity never entered', Grose, 2nd ed.: ca 1786–1840. Punning the nautical sense, contraband, and see COMMODITY.

run in. To arrest: coll: 1872.

run of one's teeth or **knife and fork, the.** Victuals free: s., 1841 (in C.20, coll); coll (ca 1860). Ex *the run*, freedom, *of a place*.

run off one's legs. Bankrupt; gen. *he is run off his legs*. Coll: ca 1670–1760. Ray. (Apperson.) cf. RUN OVER SHOES.

run on. To run up an account: lower classes' coll (—1887).

***run on** (a person), **get the.** To play a dirty trick on (him): c. (—1887). 2. See RUN UPON.

run one way and look another. To play a double game: coll: from ca 1850; ob.

run one's face, or shape, for. To obtain an article on credit: coll: orig. (—1848) and mainly U.S.; anglicized ca 1880; ob.

run one's tail. To be a whore: from ca 1850. See TAIL.

run out on. To embroider, enlarge on: coll: late C.19–20; ob.

run over him, the coaches won't. He is in gaol. Also *where the coaches . . .*, gaol. A coll c.p. ca 1820–70. cf. *where the* FLIES WON'T GET AT IT.

run over shoes; be run over shoes. To get, be, heavily in debt: coll: late C.16–early 17.

run rings round, see RINGS ROUND.

run rusty, see RUSTY.

run straight. To remain faithful to one's husband: Society s. (from ca 1870) >, by 1910, gen. coll. Ex the language of the stable.

run the rule over, see RULE OVER.

run thin. To back out of a bargain: from ca 1880; ob. Ex dial.

run through the nose with a cushion. To strike playfully: coll: late C.17–early 18. cf. *stab with a* ROSE.

run to. To understand, comprehend: coll (—1859). 2. To afford, be able to pay: 1859, H.: coll till C.20, then S.E. Always in the negative or the interrogative. Ex horse-racing, thus:

run to it!, won't. A sporting c.p. (—1909; ob.) applied to a horse that has insufficient staying power to reach the winning-post.

run to seed; occ. hyphenated. Pregnant: low coll: from ca 1860; ob. 2. Shabby: coll: 1837, Dickens, 'Large boots running rapidly to seed'.

run upon (a person), **get the.** To have the upper hand of; be able to laugh at: coll (—1859) >, by 1890, S.E.; very ob. Also *get the run on.*

runner. A clothes-thief entering a house in the dark: c.: late C.17–early 18. cf. BUDGE. 2. A wave: coll: from ca 1870; ob. 3. A dog-stealer: c. (—1909).

runner-up. A docker employed by gangers to liven up the gangs and expedite the work: nautical: late C.19–20. Bowen.

***running glasier, glazier.** A thief posing as a glazier: c. of ca 1810–70.

running horse or **nag.** A gleet, a CLAP: low: ca 1780–1860.

running leather, have shoes of. To be given to wandering or rambling: semi-proverbial coll: from ca 1850; ob.

running (occ. flying) patterer or **stationer.** A hawker of books or, more gen., broadsheets, newspapers, about the streets: C.19, c. > low s. (Mayhew); late C.17–19, coll.

***running ramp.** In *The Post Boy robbed of his Mail*, Anon., 1706, it was – to reconstruct an apparent misprint – defined as 'formed of those Home-Beggers that scout for Weddings and Burials': c.: ?ca 1700–60.

***running rumble, the.** The practice of a *running* RUMBLER: ca 1770–1830.

***running rumbler,** see RUMBLER.

***running smobble.** 'Snatching goods off a counter, and throwing them to an accomplice, who rushes off with them', Grose, 2nd ed.: c. of ca 1787–1840. Cognate with SMABBLE (or SNABBLE); cf. the next entry; as *running smabble*, it occurs in 1718, in C. Hitchin, *The Regulator*.

***running snavel.** A thief specializing in the KINCHEN-LAY: c.: C.18. cf. preceding entry and see SNAFFLE, of which SNAVEL is a corruption on SNABBLE.

running stationer, see RUNNING PATTERER.

runs, the. Diarrhoea: coll: late C.19–20. Ex frequent hasty visits to the w.c.

ruof. Four: back s. (—1874). 2. Hence, four shillings: from ca 1880.

rural, do a. To ease oneself in the open air: coll: C.19–20; ob. Obviously suggested by Swift's *pluck a* ROSE.

rural coach. A tutor not attached to a college: undergraduates' (—1887); ob.

***rush,** n. (See also RUSHER.) A robbery (specifically with violence) of many objects at one rush: c.: from ca 1785. cf. U.S. *rush,* a street encounter, which Thornton records at 1860. 2. Hence, any swindle: c. or low s.: from ca 1840. cf. the v., 1.

rush, v.t. To cheat (gen. *rush out of*); esp. to charge extortionately: 1885, former; ca 1895, latter. F. & H., 'I rushed the old girl for a quid.' The semantics being: not to give time to think. 2. To arrest: c.: from ca 1890; ob. Clarence Rook, *The Hooligan Nights,* 1899.

rush, do a. To back a safe horse: racing: from ca 1860; ob. 2. To lay a dummy bet: bookmakers': from ca 1870. i.e., rushing the public into betting on this horse.

***rush, give it to** (one) **upon the.** To make a violent effort to get in or out of a place: c.: ca 1810–40.

rush, give one the. To sponge on a person all day and then borrow money from him at the finish, 'or pursue some such procedure', H.: low: from ca 1860.

rush, roam on the. In horse-racing, to swerve as the finishing spurt begins: sporting: from ca 1880; ob. cf. ROPE, v., 1.

rush-buckler. A violent bully: coll: ca 1530–90. Robinson's More, 'Bragging rush-bucklers'.

***rush-dodge,** see RUSH, n., 1, and RUSHER, 1.

rush for and **rush out of,** see RUSH, v.

rush-light. Some strong liquor: ca 1750–80. Toldervy, 1756. See quotation at SLUG, n., 1.

rush up the frills or **petticoats** or **straight.** To coït with a woman without any preliminary blandishments: low coll: from ca 1850; ob. The third comes from horse-racing (cf. RUSH, ROAM ON THE).

***rusher,** gen. in pl. 'Thieves who knock at the doors of great houses, in London, in summer time, when the families are out of town, and on the door being opened by a woman, rush in and rob the house; also house breakers, who enter lone' – unoccupied – 'houses by force', Grose, 1st ed.: c. of ca 1780–1850. cf. RUSH, n., 1. 2. A person (gen. male) of a GO-AHEAD nature or habits: coll: late C.19–20; ob.

***rushing-business.** Robbery by adroitness or with apparent fairness: c.: from ca 1880.

***russia; R.** A pocket-book: c. (—1877); ob. The reference in '*No. 747*' is valid for 1845. Because made of *Russia* (leather).

Russian. A 'difficult', unruly animal: Australian: 1888, 'Rolf Boldrewood'; ob.

Russian law. 'A 100 blowes on his bare shins', John Day, 1641: mid-C.17 coll.

rust, n. Old metal: London (—1884); ob. cf. RUSTING and RUST, V. 2. Money: low: ca 1855–1910. Mayhew, 1858, 'There's no chance of nabbing any rust (taking any money).' 3. See RUST, NAB THE. 4. See RUST, IN.

rust, v.i. To collect and sell old metal: London (—1884); ob.

rust, in. Out of work: theatrical: 1889; ob. Punning *rest* (see RESTING) and *rusty.*

***rust, nab the.** To be refractory (orig. of horses); hence, take offence: c. of ca 1780–1890. cf. RUSTY. 2. To be punished: c.: from ca 1890; †by 1850. cf. *nab the* BIB, *the* STOOP. 3. See RUST, n., 2.

rust, take (the); also **nab the rust.** (Of horses) to become restive: coll: 1775, Colman (*take rust*).

rustiness. Annoyance (state of); bad temper: 1860, Whyte-Melville; ob. Ex RUSTY, adj.

rusting. The frequent vbl n. of RUST, v.

rustle. To bestir oneself, esp. in business: U.S. (—1872), anglicized ca 1885 as a coll. But *rustler* (adopted by Morley Roberts in 1887) has not caught on.

***rusty.** An informer: c.: 1830, Lytton, 'He'll turn a rusty, and scrag one of his pals!'

rusty, adj. Ill-tempered; annoyed: coll: 1815, Scott, 'The people got rusty about it, and would not deal.' Esp. *cut up,* or *turn, rusty.* 2. Amorous, lecherous: Australian: late C.19–20.

rusty (or grub), ride. To be sullen: coll: ca 1780–1840. Ex *reasty,* restive, applied esp. to a horse.

rusty ballocks. A red-headed man: mostly naval: late C.19–20.

rusty guts, rusty-guts; rustyguts. 'An old blunt fellow', B.E.: late C.17–mid-18. 2. Then, though now slightly ob., any 'blunt surly fellow', Grose, 1785. Both B.E. and Grose consider it a 'jocular misnomer of *rusticus*'.

rut, keep a. To make mischief: coll: late C.17–18. ?ex dial. *rut*, friction (itself ex *rub*); the O.E.D. considers it ex †*rut*, noise, disturbance, which is the more likely, for dial. *rut* may not date back so far.

rutat; occ. **rattat.** A potato: back s. on TATE(OR U)R. Mid-C.19–20. H., 1st ed.; Ware, '*Ruttat-pusher* (1882). Keeper of a potato car' (i.e., barrow).

***rutter.** One of a party (gen. numbering four) of swindlers; he stood at the door: c.: late C.16; Greene.

rux, v. To reprimand, or blame, scold, severely: T. M. Ellis, 1899. Prob. ex dial. *rux*, shake; to tread upon. 2. In Public School s., *rux up the arse* = a, or to, kick: since ca 1880. The ultimate source of all these senses is perhaps *rough-house*, n., as it is of U.S. and Canadian *ruckus*.

ry. A sharp trick; a dishonest practice: Stock Exchange: from ca 1860; ob. It may possibly be a distorted abbr. of RIG, n. Brewer's anecdotal origin may just conceivably be correct.

rybeck. A share: low London (mostly Yiddish): 1851, Mayhew.

ryder. A cloak: low: ca 1870–1910. Prob. ex Romany *ruder*, to clothe.

rye, see ROMANY RYE.

ryno, see RHINO.

S

'S; rarely **'s.** A coll euphemistic abbr. of *God's* in oaths; gen. continuous with governing words as in 'SBLOOD and 'SLIFE: C.16–20; from mid-C.18, only 'literary'.

s. and b.; S. and B. An occasional variant (—1887; very ob.) of B. AND S.

S.S.; P.P. SHIMM(E)Y showing; petticoat peeping: hortatory c.pp. from one girl to another, in ref. to dress disarranged: ca 1895–1915.

S.W.A.K. 'Sealed with a kiss' on the back of an envelope: coll: late C.19–20. Also *S.W.A.L.K.*, where *L.* = loving.

sa. Six: showmen's, mostly Parlary: from ca 1850. P. H. Emerson, 1893, 'I was hired out . . . for sa soldi a day.' Ex Lingua Franca.

sa'. Save, esp. in *God sa' me*: C.17–mid-19: S.E. till ca 1660, then coll. Shadwell, 1668, 'As God shall sa' me, she is a very ingenious Woman.'

sa soldi. Sixpence: see SA.

sabe, save, see SAVVY.

sable Maria. A variant of BLACK MARIA.

sabby. A pidgin English variant (—1864) of SAVVY.

saccer. The sacrament: Harrow School: late C.19–20. By the Oxford *-er*.

***sack.** A pocket: c.: late C.17–mid-19. B.E.; Mayhew, 1858. 2. A hammock: naval: C.19.

sack, v. To 'pocket', take (illicit) possession of: coll: C.19–20; ob. E. S. Barrett, 1807, 'He sacked the receipts, without letting them touch one farthing.' 2. To dismiss one from employment or office: from ca 1840. Gen. in passive. Ex (*get* and/or) *give the sack*, see BAG. 3. To defeat (in a contest, esp. in a game): from ca 1820 (orig. Anglo-Irish); rare after ca 1860. ?ex *sack*, to plunder. 4. To expel: Public Schools': from ca 1880. Ex sense 2.

sack, bestow or **confer the order of the,** see SACK, THE ORDER OF THE.

sack, break a bottle in an empty. To make a cheating bet, a hocus wager, 'a sack with a bottle in it not being an empty sack', Grose, 2nd ed.: coll: late C.18–mid-19.

sack, buy the. To become tipsy: s. > coll: ca 1720–1840. Ex *sack*, generic for the white wines formerly imported from Spain.

***sack, dive into a.** To pick a pocket: c.: late C.17–early 19.

sack, get or **give the,** see BAG, and SACK, v., 2. cf.:

sack, the order of the. Gen. as *get* or *give* (occ. *bestow, confer*) *the order* . . . A dismissal from employment, a discharge from office, a being discarded by sweetheart or mistress (rarely lover): from ca 1860. Yates, 1864, 'I'd . . . confer on him the order of the sack.' cf. ORDER OF THE . . .

sack 'em up men. Resurrectionists: ca 1830–70.

sack of coals. A black cloud (gen. black clouds) in the Southern Hemisphere: nautical: late C.19–20.

***sacking.** Prostitution; *sacking law*, harlotry as practised by the underworld with a view to further gain: c. of late C.16–early 17. Greene, 1592, 1591 resp. Ex the S.E. v., *sack*, to lay waste.

sacks to the mill!, more. Pile it on!; there's plenty here!: coll: late C.16–18, then dial. Nashe; Middleton & Rowley in *The Spanish Gipsie*; Richardson.

sacred lamp. A ballet-girl burlesque: theatrical: 1883–ca 1900. Ex a cynicism by John Hollingshead ('The sacred lamp of burlesque'), parodying Ruskin.

sacrifice. A(n alleged) loss: coll >, ca 1880, S.E. Dickens, 1844, 'Its patterns were last Year's and going at a sacrifice.' Esp. *alarming* or *astounding s.*

sacrifice. To sell, or claim to sell, at less than cost price: from ca 1850: coll >, ca 1880, S.E. Ex the n.

sad. Mischievous, troublesome, merry, dissipated: late C.17–20 (ob. except in *sad dog*): coll. Chiefly of a place ('London is a sad place,' Mackenzie, 1771) and a person, esp. in *sad dog*, in C.18–mid-19 a debauched fellow, and thereafter rare except in playful reproach. Farquhar, 1706, '*S.* You are an ignorant, pretending, impudent Coxcomb. *B.* Ay, ay, a sad dog.'

sad vulgar. A vulgarian: Society: ca 1770–1820. Ware cites the *St James's Gazette* of 17 Aug. 1883.

saddle. The female pudend; woman as sexual pleasure: coll verging on euphemism: C.17–20, but rare since C.18. 2. 'An additional charge upon the benefits' from a benefit-performance: 1781, Parker: theatrical.

saddle-back, see SADDLEBACK. **saddle becomes . . .,** see SADDLE SUITS . . .

saddle-leather. The skin of the posteriors: coll: mid-C.19–20. Punning S.E. sense.

saddle on the right or **wrong horse, put the.** To blame – occ., to praise – the right or wrong person (loosely, act, thing): coll: from ca 1750. Ex the earlier *set* . . . (1607) and *lay* . . . (1652), both †by 1840. An occ. variant: *place*, mid-C.19–20, ob. Also *s. upon* . . .

saddle one's nose. To wear spectacles: coll: late C.18–mid-19.

saddle-sick. Made ill or very sore by riding: coll and dial.: late C.18–20; ob. cf. SADDLE-LEATHER.

saddle suits a sow, suit one as a. To suit, become, fit ill; be very incongruous: coll: C.18–19. Swift, who has *become* for *suit*.

saddle the spit. To give a meal, esp. a dinner: coll: late C.18–mid-19. Ex S.E. *saddle a spit*, to furnish one.

saddle upon . . ., see SADDLE ON . . .

saddleback. A louse: C.19–20; ob. (Not in the best circles.)

saddling-paddock. A place where lovers tend to congregate: Australian (—1909). Semantics: RIDE, *riding*.

***safe.** (Gen. **the safe.**) Inside waistcoat pocket: c.: late C.19–20. Esp. among pickpockets.

safe . . ., a. e.g. 'He is a safe second', i.e. he is sure to obtain second-class honours: coll: late C.19–20.

safe (and sound), be or **arrive.** To have duly arrived, be at one's destination: coll: 1710, Swift, 'I send this only to tell that I am safe in London.'

safe as . . ., as. Very safe: coll: none recorded before 1600, thus: **as safe as a church,** 1891, Hardy (not very gen.); **safe as a crow (occ. sow) in a gutter,** ca 1630–1730, Clarke, Ray; **as a mouse in a cheese,** ca 1670–1750, Ray; **as a mouse in a malt-heap,** ca 1630–1700, Clarke, Ray; **as a mouse in a mill,** ca 1600–50, Davenport; **as a thief in a mill,** ca 1620–1750 (then dial.), Beaumont & Fletcher, Swift; **as anything,** from ca 1895, F. & H. (1903); **as Chelsea** is dial.; **as coons,** 1864, †by 1920; **as houses,** 1864, Yates; **as safe,** 1860, Whyte-Melville; **as the bank,** 1818; **as the bellows,** 1851, Mayhew (mostly Cockney).

safe card. An alert fellow: from ca 1870; slightly ob. cf. CARD, 2.

safe un. A horse that will not run, certainly will not (because meant not to) win: the turf: 1871, 'Hawk's-Eye', *Turf Notes*, 'The safe uns, or "stiff uns" . . . horses that have no chance of winning'.

sag. To drift off a course: nautical coll: late C.19–20. Bowen. 2. To be illicitly absent from work: Liverpool: late C.19–20.

saha! Good-night!: naval: late C.19–20. Ex Maltese.

sahib. A thoroughly honourable gentleman: mainly in the Services: late C.19–20. Ex Arabic and Urdu term of respectful address.

said than done, no sooner; 2, (that's) easier. Both these phrases, obvious in meaning, are C.19–20 coll.

saïda; saïda bint or **girl,** see BINT.

sail about. To saunter about: coll: late C.17–mid-18.

sail in, v.i. To arrive, to enter: coll: from ca 1870. Ex S.E. *sail in*, to move in a dignified or a billowing manner. 2. Hence, to begin boldly (to act): from ca 1880. 3. Hence the special sense, to begin to fight: 1891, *Morning Advertiser*, 30 March. cf.:

sail into. To attack, e.g. with one's fists: from ca 1891. 2. To begin vigorously on (e.g. a meal). cf. SAIL IN, 3. 3. To enter (a building, a room, etc.): C.18–20. Tom Brown, 1700, 'From thence I sailed into a Presbyterian Meeting near Covent-Garden': cf. SAIL ABOUT.

sailor is a Regular Army term of ca 1855–1910. 'A "sailor" was the slang term for any person whose nature was so generous, and whose finances so sound, as to allow the quaffing of many cups at his personal charge,' Robert Blatchford, *My Life in the Army*, 1910.

sailor-teasers. 'Studding sails and flying kites which the sailor disliked intensely': nautical coll: C.19. Bowen.

sailor's blessing. A curse: nautical: from ca 1880. cf. FUCK YOU, JACK, I'M ALL RIGHT.

sailor's champagne. Beer: lower classes' jocular coll. (—1909); ob.

sailor's friend, the. The moon: nautical coll: mid-C.19–20.

sailor's pleasure. 'Yarning, smoking, dancing, growling, &c.', Clark Russell, 1883; ob. As applied to the first three, it is S.E.; to the last, coll.

sailor's waiter, the. A second mate on a sailing-ship: nautical (—1840); ob.

sailor's weather. 'A fair wind and just enough of it': sailing-ships' coll: C.19–20.

sails. A sail-maker: nautical (—1840). cf. CHIPS.

sails, take the wind out of one's. To nonplus; surprise, gen. unpleasantly: mid-C. 19–20: coll (orig. nautical) >, ca 1905, S.E.

sails like a haystack, see HAYSTACK.

saint. 'A piece of spoilt timber in a coach maker's shop, like a saint, devoted to the flames', Grose, 2nd ed.: ca 1785–1850.

saint and sinner. Dinner: rhyming s.: late C.19–20.

St Alban's clean shave. The clean-shaven face of a high churchman: ecclesiastical: late C.19–early 20.

St Anthony, dine with. A variant of DINE WITH DUKE HUMPHREY, to go without dinner or, loosely, any other meal: 1749, Smollett, translation of *Gil Blas*.

St Anthony pig, see ANTHONY. **St Benedict, St Francis,** see ST PETER.

St Geoffrey's day. Never: coll: ca 1786–1850. cf. *Queen* DICK.

St George, riding and **the dragon upon,** see RIDING ST GEORGE. And cf.:

St George a-horse-back. The act of kind: C.17–18. Massinger, ca 1632, omits *St*.

St Giles, dine with, see DINE WITH ST GILES.

St Giles's carpet. A sprinkling of sand: Seven Dials, London: C.19.

St Hugh's bones. Shoemaking tools: coll: C.17–mid-18; then dial., extant in Cheshire. Dekker, 1600; E. Ward, 1700.

St John's Wood donas. Harlots, courtesans: taverns'; ca 1880–1912. Many once lived there.

St Lubbock's day. August bank-holiday: 1871: coll; ob. Ex Sir John Lubbock, the institutor, who brought in an Act in that year. Ware records *St Lubbock*, an orgy or drunken riot: lower London: ca 1880–1914.

St Luke's bird. An ox, 'that evangelist being always represented with an ox', Grose, 1st ed.: c. or low: ca 1780–1850.

St Marget's ale. Water: coll: 1600, Munday & Drayton; †by 1800. cf. *Adam's ale*.

St Martin's (le Grand). A hand: Londoners' rhyming s.: late C.19–20.

St Martin's lace. Imitation gold-lace: coll: 1607, Dekker. (cf. etymology of *tawdry*.) S.E. cf.:

St Martin's ring. A copper-gilt ring: coll: C.17–early 18. Anon., early C.17, *Plain Percival*, 'I doubt whether all be gold that glistereth, sith Saint Martin's rings be but copper within, though they be gilt without.'

St Martin's the Grand. A hand: rhyming s. (—1857).

St Mary's knot, tie with. To hamstring: Scots coll: 1784, *The Poetical Museum*.

St Monday. Monday: South African coll (—1896). Because observed as a holiday by the Malays. Ex: 2. Esp. *keep Saint Monday*, to be idle on Monday as a result of Sunday's drunkenness: 1753, *Scots Magazine*, April, (*title*) 'St Monday; or, the tipling tradesmen'.

St Nicholas, see NICHOLAS.

saint of the saucepan. A good cook: coll verging on S.E.: 1749, Smollett; ob.

St Patrick. The best whisky: coll: ca 1650–1850. Ex *drink at St Patrick's well*: coll: 1648, anon., *A Brown Dozen of Drunkards*; †by 1850.

St Peter, silence and mortification; **St Radegonde,** a small cross studded with nails; **St Benedict,** a hair-shirt; **St Francis,** the discipline, i.e. the whip or scourge: Roman Catholic ecclesiastical s.: late C.19–20. Ex incidents recorded in hagiology.

***St Peter's son.** (Gen. in pl.) A general thief, 'having every finger a fish-hook', Grose, s.v. FIDLAM BEN: c. of ca 1710–1850.

St Radegonde, see ST PETER.

St Thomas a' Waterings, the 'Spital (or **'spital) stands too nigh.** A semi-proverbial c.p. derived ex London topography, *waterings* being a pun: C.17–mid-18; e.g. in the anon. play, *The Puritan*, 1607. 'Widows who shed most tears are sometimes guilty of such indiscretions as render them proper subjects for the public hospitals,' Hazlitt. (There is a cynical early C.17 play dealing with a woman successfully courted at her husband's funeral. cf. the classical Widow of Ephesus.)

sakes (alive)! A (low) coll exclamation: from ca 1840: mostly dial. and U.S.

sal. A salivation, or treatment for syphilis: 1785, Grose, who adds '*in a high sal*, in the pickling tub or under a salivation'. †by 1860. 2. A salary: theatrical: 1859, H., 1st ed.; 1885, *Household Words*, 29 Aug.

sal hatch, or **S.H.** An umbrella: lower classes' (—1909). Perhaps ex a proper name: cf. MRS GAMP and †S.E. *sal hatch*, a dirty wench.

sal slappers. A common woman: costers' (—1909).

salad. After having been wakened, to have another nap: nautical, applied only to officers (—1877). cf. the C.16–early 17 S.E. *pick a salad*, to be trivially engaged.

salad march. A 'march of ballet girls in green, white, and pale amber – from the usual colours of salads': late C.19–early 20 theatrical coll. Ware.

salamander. A fire-eating juggler: circus (—1859).

***salamon.** A C.17–19 form of SALMON.

sale, house of. A brothel: coll: late C.16–17. Shakespeare in *Hamlet*.

salesman's dog. A shop-tout: ca 1690–1840. On BARKER, 3.

Salisbury. A civil lie; a polite evasion: political: ca 1890–1900. *Pall Mall Gazette*, 5 March 1890, 'The famous Salisbury about the Secret-Treaty . . . must henceforth be read "*cum grano salis*-bury".' Ex the statesman.

Sallenger's (or Sallinger's) Round, dance. To wanton; copulate: coll: C.17–early 18. *Sallenger's Round* was an indelicate ballad of ca 1600; lit., *St Leger's*.

Sally, see AUNT SALLY.

***sally,** v.; **sallying,** vbl. n. These c. terms, valid for 1865 in '*No. 747*', are of obscure sense; it is, however, clear that they refer to some not very skilled DODGE for illicitly obtaining money.

Sally Nixon (occ. s.n.). Salenixon (sal enixum): workmen's: from ca 1880. By 'Hobson-Jobson'.

salmagundy. A cook: coll: C.18–early 19. Ex the dish so named.

***salmon;** occ. **salamon, salomon** or **-an,** and **solomon.** The Mass; Harman defines as also an altar, a sense not recorded after C.16. Rare except in *by salmon!*, by the Mass!, the beggar's expletive or oath, or in the C.18–early 19 *so help me salmon!*: c. of ca 1530–1830. Copland, Overbury, Moore-Carew, Scott. Prob. a corruption of the Fr. *serment*, an oath. 2. A corpse fished from a river, esp. the Thames: water-rats' c.: mid-C.19–20.

salmon and trout. The mouth: rhyming s. (—1859); ob. H., 1st ed., as *salmon trout*, which is rare after ca 1870; the 5th ed. has *s. and t.*

salmon-gundy. A (rather low) coll, indeed almost sol. form of *salmagundy*: late C.18–early 19. (See also SALMAGUNDY.)

***saloman, -mon.** The former a frequent, the latter a rare variant of SALMON: resp. C.17 and mid-C.16–early 19. Resp., Overbury; Harman, Middleton, Shirley.

salt. A sailor; esp. one of long experience, when often *old salt* (as in Hughes, 1861): coll: 1840, Dana, 'My complexion and hands were enough to distinguish me from the regular salt.' Occ., though by 1910, ob.: *salt-water*. 2. (An instance of) sexual intercourse: coll: mid-C.17–early 18. Ex *salt*, amorous, lecherous. cf.:

salt, v.i. To copulate: coll: (?)C.17–early 18. Ex the S.E. adj.: cf. the n., 2. 2. v.t., to admit (a freshman) by putting salt in his mouth, making him drink salty water, or practising on him some similar burlesquery: students': ca 1570–1650. 3. In an invoice or account, to price every article very high, gen. in order to allow a seemingly generous discount on settlement (*salt an account, an invoice*, etc.): commercial: 1882, Ogilvie. Perhaps directly ex next sense: 4. To insert in the account books fictitious entries with a view to enhancing the value of a business to a prospective buyer: commercial: from ca 1850. (Gen. *salt a book, the books*, etc.) Prob. suggested by: 5. In mining, to sprinkle or plant an exhausted or a bogus claim with precious dust, nuggets, or gems: orig. (—1864), of gold in Australia; of diamonds, ca 1890; of oil, ca 1900. H., 3rd ed.; *Pall Mall Gazette*, 22 Dec. 1894, 'Even experienced mining men and engineers have been made victims by salters.'

salt, adj. Dear, costly, excessive in amount (of money): C.18–20 dial. >, ca 1850, s.: as s., slightly ob. H., 2nd ed., '"It's rather too salt," said of an extravagant hotel bill'; F. & H., '*as salt as fire* = salt as may be'. Also *salty*. 2. Aristocratic; wealthy: 1868; slightly ob. Ex *the salt of the earth*, a phrase that began ca 1840 to be used of the great in power, rank, wealth – a trivial use that, during the First World War, > ob. 3. Drunk: late C.19–early 20. Abbr. SALT JUNK.

salt, we shan't take. Our box office returns will be very small: theatrical c.p. (—1909). Ware, 'We shall not take enough money to pay for salt, let alone bread.'

salt and batter. Assault and battery: partly s., partly illiterate: since ca 1830. An Old Etonian, *Cavendo Tutus*; *or, Hints upon Slip-Slop*, being the 2nd part of his *The Alphabet Annotated*, 1853.

salt and spoons, come after with. To be slow or dilatory: coll: late C.17–18. B.E., 'One that is none of the Hastings'; cf. HASTINGS SORT.

salt-beef flag. 'The Blue Peter, in anticipation of the diet': nautical: late C.19–20. Bowen.

salt-beef squire. More usual than SALT-HORSE SQUIRE.

***salt-box.** A prison cell; esp. the condemned cell at Newgate: c. of ca 1810–90. Ex (?smallness and) bitterness.

***salt-box cly.** A flapped outside pocket: c.: ca 1810–40.

salt-cellar. The female pudend: low: C. 19(?–20). cf. SALT, n., 2.

salt down. To put by (money, 1873, or stock, 1897); store it away. Ex *salt*, to preserve with salt.

salt eel. A rope's end, in *have (a) salt eel for supper*, to receive a thrashing: ca 1620–1830: naval coll. Mabbe, Congreve, B.E., Smollett, Colman, Grose.

salt horse or **junk.** Salted beef: nautical coll >, ca 1870, S.E.: resp. 1840 (O.E.D.); 1837, Marryat. Whence *salt-horse squire.*

salt-horse squire. A warrant as opp. a commissioned officer: naval: mid-C.19–early 20.

salt junk, adj. Drunk: rhyming s.: ca 1890–1910. n.: see SALT HORSE.

salt on one's, its, the tail, – cast or **fling** or **lay** or **put** or **throw.** To ensnare, capture: coll: mid-C.17–mid-19, C.18–19, late C.16–mid-19, mid-C.19–20, and C.19–20. Lyly; 'Hudibras' Butler, 'Such great atchievements cannot fail | To cast salt on a woman's tail' (see TAIL); Swift (*fling*); Lamb, 1806, 'My name is . . . Betty Finch . . . you can't catch me by throwing salt on my tail'; Dickens, 1861 (*put*).

salt-pits. A or the store of Attic wit: Oxford University: ca 1820–40. Ex *Attic salt.*

salt-water. See SALT, n., 1. (Ainsworth, 1839.) 2. Urine: coll: late C.17–18. Tom Brown.

Saltash luck. 'A wet seat and no fish caught': naval: late C.19–20. Bowen. Ex *Saltash*, a small town four miles N.W. of Devonport.

salted. Experienced: of horses, coll, 1879; of persons, s., 1889. 2. See SALT, v., 5.: recorded by O.E.D. in 1886, but doubtless twenty years older.

saltee. A penny: Parlary: mid-C.19–20. Reade, 'It had rained kicks all day in lieu of saltees.' Also *saulty.* Ex It. *soldi.*

salter. One who salts mines: from ca 1890. See SALT, v., 5.

salting, vbl n., see SALT, v., 2 and 5.

salts. Smelling salts: coll: 1767; slightly ob. 2. Epsom salts: coll: 1772.

salts and senna. A doctor: a nickname from ca 1860; ob. Ex *salts.*

salt's pricker. A thick roll of compressed Cavendish tobacco: naval (—1909). Ware.

salty. See SALT, adj., 1: mostly U.S. (1847, Robb).

salubrious. Drunk: from ca 1870; ob. 2. In reply, esp. to a query as to health, 'Pretty *or* very well, thanks!': from ca 1880; ob. Perhaps via SCRUMPTIOUS.

Salvation jugginses – rotters – soul-sneakers. Members of the Salvation Army: London lower classes': 1882–4. Ware.

salve, n. Praise; flattery: 1859, H., 1st ed.; rather ob. cf. S.E. *lip(-)salve*, flattery.

salve over. To persuade or convince by plausibility or flattery: coll: 1862 (O.E.D.).

Sam; occ. **sam.** A Liverpudlian: dial. and s.: from ca 1840. Perhaps ex SAMMY, 1. Also and gen. *Dicky Sam* (1864, H., 3rd ed.). 2. A fool: 1843, Moncrieff, 'I'm a ruined homo, a muff, a flat, a Sam, a regular ass.' Ex SAMMY, n., 1, and adj. 3. See SAM, UPON MY, and SAM, STAND.

sam, v. Abbr. (—1909; proletarian) of the next. 2. To slam (esp. a door): Lancashire rhyming s. (—1905) rather than dial.

sam, or **Sam, stand.** To pay the reckoning, esp. for drinks or other entertainment: 1823, Moncrieff; 1834, Ainsworth, 'I must insist upon standing Sam upon the present occasion'; Henley. Prob. the *sam* is cognate with that of *upon my* SAM, and derives either ex SALMON, as I prefer, or ex *Samuel*, as the O.E.D. suggests; H.'s theory of U.S. origin (*Uncle Sam*) is, I feel sure, untenable.

Sam, uncle, see UNCLE SAM.

sam!, upon my; more gen. **'pon my sam! A** jocular asseveration: 1879, F. J. Squires. See SAM, STAND for etymology; it is, however, not improbable that *'pon my sam* is a corruption of dial. *'pon my sang(s)*, recorded as early as 1860, *by my sang* occurring at least as early as 1790, and *my sang* ca 1840 (E.D.D.). cf. *on my* (*sammy*) SAY-SO.

Sambo, gen. in address. A Negro: coll: from C.18. John Atkins, *A Voyage to Guinea, Brasil and the West Indies*, 1735. 2. A Negro rating: nautical. Ex S.E. sense, a Negro with a strain of Indian or European blood.

same here; same there. What you say applies equally to me; to you: resp. from ca 1880 and from ca 1870, the latter being orig. a tailors' c.p.

same like. Same as; exactly like: coll, almost sol.: from ca 1870. W. Pett Ridge, *Mord Em'ly*, 1898, 'Beef Pudding same like Mother makes' – a cheap eating-house's advertisement.

same o.b. Same old BOB (shilling): lower classes' c.p.: ca 1880–1910. Ex usual entrance-fee.

same old 3 and 4. Three shillings and four pence a day wages: workmen's (—1909).

samkin. An occ., now ob., variant (—1886) of SIMKIN, 2.

Sammy or **sammy;** occ. **sammy soft** or **S.S.** A fool: from ca 1830; slightly ob. Peake, 1837, 'What a Sammy, give me a shilling more than I asked him!' cf. SAM, n., 2. 2. (*Sammy.*) A Hindu idol (e.g. of Siva): British soldiers' (in India): late C.18–20. Ex *Swamy*, ex Sanskrit *suamin*, Lord.

sammy, adj. Foolish: from ca 1810; ob. Whence the n., 1. cf. SAMMY SOFT.

sammy-house. An idol-temple: British soldiers' (in India): 1859. Ex SAMMY, n., 2.

Sammy Soft (or s.s.). A fool: from ca 1840; slightly ob. See SAMMY, n., 1.

sample. To caress intimately, or to 'occupy', a woman for the first time: coll: C.19–20. Ex *sample*, to 'obtain a representative experience of'. cf.: 2. To drink: from ca 1845. Porter, 1847, 'Old T. never samples too much when on business.' Via 'drink as a test or trial'.

sample-count. A commercial traveller: commercial coll: 1894, Egerton; very ob.

sampler. The female pudend: C.19–20; ob. Semantics: needlework.

sam(p)son or **S.** A drink of brandy and cider, with a little water and some sugar: dial. and s.: from ca 1840; ob. Halliwell. Also, mainly dial. and from ca 1880, *Samson with his hair on*, which denotes a very strong mixture of the same ingredients, as in 'Q', *Troy Town*, 1888. 2. A baked jam pudding: Durham School: from ca 1870. Both senses ex the sense of power, the second perhaps also ex toughness.

samshoo. Any spirituous liquor: Anglo-Chinese (—1864). Ex *samshoo*, a specific fiery spirit, rice-distilled.

san skillets, or **S.S.** The *sans-culottes* of Paris: proletarian: late C.18.

sanakatowmer. A heavy fall; a violent blow: nautical: late C.19–20. Bowen. Echoic.

sancipees, see SANK.

***sand.** Moist sugar: c. of ca 1810–50. 2. Money: C.19. cf. DUST. 3. Constancy of purpose; courage: stamina: orig. (ca 1870), U.S.; anglicized ca 1895, but never very gen. cf. GRIT. 4. Salt: nautical: mid-C.19–20. 5. Any sugar: Canadian, and at Bootham School: late C.19–20. cf. sense 1.

sand, eat. (Gen. of the helmsman) to shorten one's watch by turning the hour-glass before it has quite run out: nautical s. or coll: ca 1740–1820. *Memoirs of M. du Gué-Trouin* (properly Du Guay Trouin or Duguay-Trouin), 1743. Ex the sand in the glass.

sand-bag, -boy, -man, -paper. See these as single words.

sand-rat. A moulder in a foundry: engineers': from ca 1875. 2. An Indian Army term, dating from ca 1880. Richards, '... These native girls, who being in the last stages of the dreaded disease and rotten inside and out, only appeared after dark. These were the sand-rats and it was a horrible form of suicide to go with them.'

sand-storm medal. (Gen. pl.) An Egyptian Army decoration: military: late C.19–20.

***sandbag.** A long sausage-shaped bag of sand used as a weapon: orig. (—1871), c.; by 1900 gen. s. Pocock, *Rules of the Game*, 1895.

***sandbag,** v. To fell with a sandbag: orig. (—1890), c. >, ca 1910, gen. s. App. both weapon and word were first used in U.S.

***sandbagger.** A ruffian using a sandbag as a weapon: c., orig. U.S. (1884), anglicized ca 1890.

sandbeef. A sandwich: Anglo-Indian (—1887).

sandboy (properly **sand-boy), as happy** or **jolly** or **merry as a.** Very happy, etc.: resp. late C.19–20, never very gen.; 1823, 'Jon Bee', this being the usual form; 1841, Fitz-Gerald, 'We will smoke together and be as merry as sandboys.'

sandman (from ca 1870, occ. **sandy man) is coming, the.** Addressed to, or remarked of, children showing signs of sleepiness: a nursery coll: 1861. cf. DUSTMAN. Ex rubbing eyes as if sand were in them.

sandpaper. To rub out or off; to remove: 1889, *Answers*, 9 Feb., ' "Can't do it," said Lancaster, "and I hope to be sandpapered if I try".' Ob.

sandpapering the anchor. Doing unnecessary work aboard ship: nautical jocular coll: mid-C.19–20. Bowen.

sands, leave or **put a person to the long.** To abandon; place in a difficulty: Scots coll of ca 1670–1700. J. Brown, 1678, 'How quickly they were put again to the long sands (as we say).' Ex *sands*, a desert or perhaps a sand-bank.

sandwich. A sandwich-man: 1864 (H., 3rd ed.) though adumbrated by Dickens ca 1836: coll >, ca 1910, S.E. 2. A gentleman between two ladies: from ca 1870; ob. Perhaps ex Thackeray's 'A pale young man . . . walking . . . *en* sandwich' (*Vanity Fair*, 1848). Rather coll than s.

sandwich, v. To set or insert between dissimilars: from ca 1860: coll.

sandwich board. A police-ambulance stretcher: lower classes': ca 1870–1914.

Sandy. A Scotsman: a coll nickname (—1785), mostly Scots. Ex *Sandy*, abbr. *Alexander*, a very gen. Scottish name. 2. (*sandy*.) Gen. pl; Thames barge-men who dredge for sand in the river: nautical coll, esp. Thames-side: late C.19–20. Bowen.

sandy man, see SANDMAN.

sangaree. A bout of drinking (to excess): coll: ca 1820–70. Ex S.E. sense, a cold drink made of spiced wine diluted.

Sangster. An umbrella: London: ca 1850–70. Ex the inventor of a special kind.

sanguinary, jocular for BLOODY, is s. verging on coll (—1909).

sanguinary James. (cf. BLOODY JEMMY, its origin.) A (raw) sheep's-head: 1860, H., 2nd ed.; ob.

sank, sanky, occ. **sancipees (or centipees** – F. & H. erroneously **centipers).** A tailor employed by a clothier in the making of soldiers' clothing: ca 1780–1870. Perhaps ex Yorkshire dial. *sanky*, boggy, spongy, but prob. cognate with dial. *sank*, to perform menial offices as servant in a dining-room, itself a variant of *skink*, to wait on the company.

sank-work. The making of soldiers' clothes: coll: ca 1850–1920. Mayhew, 1851; Baumann. This word bears a curious resemblance to the C.14 S.E. *sank*, to bring together; see, however, remarks at SANK, whence it derives, and cf. Mayhew's suggestion that the origin resides in Fr. *sang* (Norman *sanc*), blood, in reference to a soldier's work or to the colour of his coat.

Santa. Santa Claus: coll, mostly of the nursery: from ca 1880. cf. SANTY.

***santar** or **-er.** He who, in a trio of thieves working together, carries away the booty: c.: late C.16–early 17. Greene, 1591. i.e. to sanctuary.

Santy. Santa Claus: coll, mostly Canadian: late C.19–20. cf. SANTA.

sap. A fool or a simpleton: 1815, Scott: coll >, ca 1900, S.E. Milliken, ca 1893, 'Sour old sap'. Abbr. *sapskull*, and cf. *sap-head*. 2. One who works, esp. studies, hard; a book-worm: schools': 1798, Charlotte Smith; 1827, Lytton, 'When I once attempted to read Pope's poems out of school hours, I was laughed at, and called a sap'; Goschen, 1888, '. . . Those who . . . commit the heinous offence of being absorbed in [work]. Schools and colleges . . . have invented . . . phrases . . . such as "sap", "smug", "swot", "bloke", "a mugster".' Whence:

sap, v. To be studious or a great reader: schools': 1830 (O.E.D.), but implied in SAPPING.

sap-head. A sot: s.: Ned Ward, 1703.

sap out. To work up (a subject); resolve (a problem or a 'construe'): Shrewsbury School: from ca 1880. cf. SAP, v.

sap the tlas. A Cockney c.p. used when the drink does not go round freely: ca 1880–1910. Back s. for *pass the salt*.

sapper. One who studies hard: Eton: 1825, Westmacott. cf. SAP, v. and n., 2. 2. A gay, irresistible fellow: music-halls': late C.19. Ex Fr. *sapeur*.

sappiness. Foolishness; folly: coll: late C.19–20. See SAP, n., 1.

sapping. Hard study: schools': 1825, Westmacott. cf. SAP, n., 2, and v.

sappy. (Of a caning) severe: Durham School: from ca 1870. Ex S.E. sense: vigorous, rich in vitality, perhaps influenced by dial. sense, putrescent. (As = foolish, *sappy* dates from C.17; certainly S.E. up till ca 1860; by 1870, it seems to have > coll: see e.g. H., 5th ed.)

sarcy. A low coll form of SAUCY: C.19–20. Moncrieff, 1843. Prob. influenced by *sarcastic*: see SARKY.

sard, to copulate, C.10–17, seems to have, in late C.16, > a vulg.

sardine-box. A prison-van: lower classes' (—1909); ob. (Packed as if with sardines.)

sardine-tin. A clumsy steamer: nautical: late C.19–20.

sardines, packed like. Crowded, huddled: mid-C.19–20: coll till C.20, then S.E. Ex the close packing of sardines in tins. Occ. *like sardines* (*in a tin*). cf. the U.S. *sardine*, a sailor on a whaling ship.

Sarey Gamp. An elaboration of GAMP (n., 3), an umbrella: mid-C.19 London.

sargentlemanly. So gentlemanly: satirical low coll: ca 1870–1900.

sark. To sulk: Sherborne School: from ca 1880. Prob. ex *sarcastic*; cf.:

sarky. Sarcastic: (low) coll: late C.19–20. cf. SARK.

sarvice. Service: low coll and dial.: C.18–20. Ex the older S.E. pronunciation.

sass, get too much. To become too bold, or powerful, or wicked: 'English Negro s.' of the West Coast of Africa: from ca 1870. i.e. SAUCE.

sassage. A sausage: either sol. or low, esp. Cockney, coll (—1887). cf.:

sassenger; sassinger. A sausage: col., mostly children's: late C.19–20; slightly ob.

sat. Satisfaction: universities': ca 1860–1900. (Ex L. *satis.*) 2. A fag: Public Schools' (—1909); ob. Abbr. *satellite*, a jocular name for a fag.

sat-upon. Repressed, humiliated; down-trodden: coll: from ca 1890.

satchel-arsed fellow; satchel-arsed son of a whore. A man fitted by Jon Bee's indictment in 1823: 'Some chaps put on certain habiliments in a very bag-like manner': †by 1900.

sate-poll. A stupid person: low s. > coll: late C.19–20. ? = *sated poll* (head).

satin. Gin: from ca 1860, ob. Ex *white satin*, see WHITE RIBBON. cf.:

satin, a yard of. A glass of gin: mostly among women (—1864). cf. RIBBON and TAPE, esp. among servants.

Saturday pie. A RESURRECTION PIE: lower classes' (—1909); ob.

Saturday soldier. A volunteer: 1890, *Globe*, 11 Aug.; ob. Also *cat-shooter*.

Saturday(-)to(-)Monday. A mistress for the week-end: coll (—1903); very ob.

***satyr.** A professional stealer of cattle, horses, sheep: C.18 c. 'Highwaymen' Smith, 1714. Prob. ex the Roman representation of satyrs as goat-like.

sauce. Impudence, impertinence: coll and dial.: 1835, Marryat; perhaps much earlier (see *more* SAUCE THAN PIG and SAUCEBOX). Ex SAUCY. 2. A venereal infection: coll: C.18–early 19. Vanbrugh.

sauce, v. To charge (a person) extortionately: coll (or jocular S.E.): late C.16–early 17. Shakespeare. 2. To strike; to thrash: coll: 1598, Jonson; †by 1750. 3. Hence, in C.17–18, to reprimand (severely); rebuke smartly: coll. Shakespeare. 4. Hence, to address impertinently: low coll: from ca 1860. Dickens, 1865, 'Don't sauce me in the wicious pride of your youth.'

sauce, carrier's or **poor man's.** Hunger: mid-C.19–20: coll; but the latter soon S.E.

sauce, eat; gen. **to have eaten sauce.** To be saucy: coll: C.16. Skelton, who has the variant *to have drunk of sauce's cup.*

sauce than pig, (have) more. (To be) very impudent, impertinent: coll: late C.17–18. cf. SAUCEPAN RUNS OVER.

saucebox. An impudent or impertinent person: coll: 1588, Marprelate's *Epistle*; ob. Tylney, 1594, 'You master saucebox, lobcock, cockscomb'; Fielding; Miss Mitford. cf. SAUCE, n., 1. 2. 'In low life it also signifies the mouth'; H., 3rd ed., 1864.

saucepan lid. A Jew: rhyming s. (on YID): late C.19–20. 2. A child: rhyming s. (on KID, n., 1): late C.19–20. 3. A mild deception, a leg-pulling; hence also v., as in 'Now you're saucepan-lidding me': rhyming s. (on KID, n., 5, v., 2–4): late C.19–20.

saucepan on the fire, have the. To be desirous of, ready for, a scolding bout: coll and dial.: mid-C.19–20; almost † as coll. cf.:

saucepan runs (occ. boils) over, your. You're very saucy: a late C.17–18 c.p. or coll. cf. SAUCE THAN PIG.

saucer, off one's. Not in the humour; indisposed: Australian: ca 1860–1910.

saucers. Eyes, esp. if wide-opened or very large: coll: 1864, Mark Lemon, 'I always know when he has been in his cups by the state of his saucers.' Ex S.E. *eyes like* (or *as big as*) *saucers, saucer-eyes* (or *-eyed*), etc.

saucy. Impudent or rude; impertinent: coll: late C.18–20. Ex C.16–18 S.E. senses (insolent, presumptuous). 2. Hence, smart, stylish: coll: from ca 1830. An East End tailors' broadside advertisement of ca 1838 runs, 'Kicksies made very saucy.'

saucy box. A SAUCEBOX (1): coll: 1711, Swift; †by 1780.

saucy jack. An impudent fellow: coll: ca 1550–1700. cf. JACK SAUCE.

saulty, see SALTEE.

sausage; live sausage. In sexual sense, it is on the marches of coll and S.E. 2. (*sausage* or *S.*) A German: lower classes': late C.19–20. Suggested by *German sausage.* 3. (*sausage.*) Short for *sausage and mash*, cash: rhyming: since ca 1870.

sausage toad. Sausage toad-in-the-hole: eating-houses' coll: late C.19–20.

sausages. Fetters: low: ca 1820–65. *Sinks*, 1848. Shape: string of sausages = a chain. 2. Side whiskers: mid-C.19–20.

sausanmash. A sausage and mashed potatoes: junior clerks' (—1909).

savage, adj. Furiously angry; unsparing in speech: from 1820s: mostly coll.

save, v.t. To protect oneself, or one's book of bets, by hedging; to keep (a horse) on one side, not betting against it, thus making it a clear winner for oneself: the turf: 1869.

save!; save? see SAVVY.

save-all. One of 'boys running about gentlemen's houses in Ireland, who are fed on broken meats that would otherwise be wasted', Grose, 1785: Anglo-Irish coll: mid-C.18–mid-19. Prob. ex the save-all candlestick.

save oneself. To hedge: racing coll: 1869, Broadwood, *The O.V.H.*, 'Most who received the news at least saved themselves upon the outsider.' See SAVE, v.

save-reverence, see SIRREVERENCE.

saved by the bell. Saved by a lucky intervention: coll; often as a c.p.: late C.19–20. Ex the bell signifying the end of a round in a boxing match.

saver. A prudent covering bet: the turf: from ca 1890. Nat Gould, 1891, 'I've put a saver on Caloola.' Ex *save (oneself)*, to bet thus.

savers! Halves!: boys': late C.19–20.

savey, savie, see SAVVY. **saving!, hang,** see HANG SAVING!

saving chin. A projecting chin: coll: ca 1776–1840. Bridges; Grose, 'That catches what may fall from the nose'. cf. the proverb *he would save the droppings of his nose*, applied to a miser.

savvy; also **sabby, sabe, savey, savie, savvey, scavey,** n. Common sense, good sense; GUMPTION: 1785, Grose; 'Rolf Boldrewood', 1888, 'If George had had the savey to crack himself up a little'. Hence, acuteness, cleverness: 1864, H., 3rd ed. Forms: *savvy*, mid-C.19–20; SABBY (—1864); *sabe*, since ca 1820, now rare; *savey*, 1785; *savie*, Scottish, C.19–20; *savvey*, from ca 1880; *scavey*, C.19. Ex Negro-izing of Fr. *savoir*, to know, or more prob. of Sp. *sabe usted*, do you know; imm. ex:

savvy; also **sabby, sabe(e); savey; savvey; scavey,** v. (Resp. C.19–20; mid-C.19–20; C.18–20; C.19–20; C.18.) v.t. (in C.20, occ. v.i.), to know: 1785, Grose, ' "Massa me no scavey".' For etymology, see end of n. 2. In pidgin English, also to have, to do, etc., etc.: C.19–20.

saw, held at the (occ. **a) long.** Held in suspense: coll: ca 1730–1830. North's *Lord Guildford*, 1733, 'Between the one and the other he was held at the long saw over a month.'

saw your timber! Go away!: low: from ca 1855; ob. On CUT (v., 4) *your stick*; a further elaboration is AMPUTATE ONE'S MAHOGANY.

sawbones. A surgeon: from ca 1835, Dickens in 1837 saying, 'I thought everybody know'd as a sawbones was a surgeon.'

sawder, rare except as **soft sawder.** Flattery; soft speech: 1836, Haliburton; Grant Allen, 'I didn't try bullying; I tried soft sawder.' Prob. ex the v.; perhaps ex *solder*, n. cf. BLARNEY.

sawder, v. To flatter; speak softly to: 1834, Lover. Prob. on to *solder*, perhaps influenced by:

sawdust. Same as SAWDER, n.: rather low (—1887). 1893, Milliken, 'True poetry ... not sawdust and snivel'; ob. Either SAWDER (n.) corrupted or ex *sawdust* as used, in various sports, to soften a fall.

sawdust bloke. A circus rider: circus coll: from ca 1860.

sawdusty. The adj. of SAWDUST: low: 1884, *Punch*, 11 Oct., 'Me doing the sawdusty reglar'; ob.

Sawney; occ. **Sawny.** A Scot: a (mainly pejorative) coll nickname: C.18–20. Tom Brown; Gay, 'He sung of Taffy Welch, and Sawney Scot.' Ex *Alexander*; cf. SANDY.

sawn(e)y. A fool; a stupid or very simple (gen., man): late C.17–20. In late C.19–20, through (non-Scottish) dial. influence, it often = a soft, good-natured fellow. Prob. ex *zany* (in 1567 spelt *zawne* in Edwards's *Damon and Pythias*), though conceivably influenced by SAWNEY. 2. Bacon: c. (—1812). Vaux; Mayhew, who restricts to stolen bacon. ?ex *sawn*, bacon being cut off in slices (rashers). cf. SAWNEY-HUNTER.

sawn(e)y, v. To wheedle or whine: coll: ca 1805–90. Southey, 1808, 'It looks like a sneaking sawneying Methodist parson.' Ex the adj., perhaps also in part ex, or influenced by, the East Anglian *sanny*, 'to utter a whining, wailing cry without apparent cause'. 2. To be soft; to fool about: coll: mid-C.19–20. Ex n., 1, and adj., 2.

sawn(e)y, adj. Whining, wheedling: ca 1800–50. cf. the v., 1. 2. Foolish; softly good-natured or sentimental: s. > coll: C.19–20. Rhoda Broughton, 1873, 'There is no sawny sentiment in his tone, none of the lover's whine.' Ex the n., 1.

***sawn(e)y (rarely sawny)-hunter.** One who purloins bacon and/or cheese from grocers' shops: 1856, Mayhew, *The Great World of London*. See SAWNEY, n., 2.

saxpence!, bang goes. A c.p. (—1890) addressed to a person excessively careful about small expenses. Originated by Charles Keene, *Punch*, 5 Dec. 1868; re-popularized by Sir Harry Lauder.

say. Yes: back s. (—1851). (Logically but not actually *sey*.) 2. Six: Parlary: mid-C.19–20. Ex It. *sei*.

say!; I say! An introductory interjection; a mere exclamation: coll: resp., orig. U.S., anglicized ca 1900; C.17–20. Beaumont & Fletcher, 1611, 'I say, open the door, and turn me out these mangy companions.'

say, see APE'S PATERNOSTER; BO; JACK ROBINSON; KNIFE; MOUTHFUL; PRAYERS; WHEN!

say away! Speak, then!; 'fire ahead!': coll: mid-C.19–20. cf. FIRE AWAY.

say for oneself, have nothing to. To be, by habit, silent: coll: mid-C.19–20.

say it again! I heartily agree with you: tailors' c.p.: from ca 1870.

say nothing when you are dead. Be silent!: c.p. of ca 1670–1750.

say-so, on my (sammy). On my word of honour: coll: mid-C.18–20 (. . . *sammy* . . . not before ca 1880); ob. cf. *upon my* SAM.

say so!, you don't. Expressive of astonishment (occ. of derision) at a statement: coll: from ca 1870.

saying one's prayers, be. To be scrubbing the floor: jocular domestic: late C.19–20.

says, it. The book mentioned, or its author, says: C.10–20: S.E. until mid-C.19, then coll.

says he. Said he: coll: late C.17–20. Congreve. cf.:

says I; says you. I say; you say: sol. or jocular coll: late C.17–20. Dryden, Bage.

'Sblood or **'sblood!** A coll form of *(by) God's blood!*: late C.16–mid-18, then archaic. See 'S and cf. the following more or less coll oaths: *'Sbobs* (i.e. *Od's bobs*), late C.17–mid-19; *'Sbodikins* (=*God's bodikins*), ca 1670–1800, then archaic; *'Sbody* (*God's body*), C.17; *'Sbores* (like *'Sbobs*, obscure in meaning), C.17; *'Sbud(s)*, which = *'Sbodikins*, ca 1670–1760, then archaic.

scab. A pejorative applied to persons, a 'scurvy' fellow, a rascal or scoundrel: from ca 1590; slightly ob. except in next sense; not after C.18 applied to women. Occ., as in Lyly, a constable or a sheriff's officer (not after C.18). Shakespeare, Defoe, Kipling. Ex the skin-disease or the crust forming over a sore: cf. SCURF, 1. Hence, 2, a workman refusing to strike, esp. one working while his companions are on strike: orig. (1811), U.S., anglicized ca 1880. Occ. attributively. 3. Among tailors, a buttonhole: from ca 1870; ob. Ex the shape of a sore-crust.

scab, v. To behave as a, be a, SCAB (n., 2): C.20, O.E.D. recording at 1905.

scab-raiser. A drummer: military: ca 1850–95. Because one of his duties was to wield the CAT-O'-NINE-TAILS, thus raising sores.

scabbado. Syphilis: mid-C.17–mid-18: coll verging on S.E. Bailey's *Erasmus*, 1725. Ex S.E. *scab* + *ado*, a mock-foreign suffix.

scabby. Vile, contemptible, beggarly: C.18–20: S.E. until mid-C.19, then coll. Smollett; Meredith, 1861, 'A scabby sixpence?' Ex lit. S.E. sense. 2. Among printers, unevenly or blotchily printed: from ca 1870. Ex sense 1. 3. At Christ's Hospital, stingy: mid-C.19–20. cf. quotation in sense 1. 4. Pertaining to one who does not employ union labour: from ca 1890: Australian s. Ex SCAB, n., 2.

scabby neck (or **S.N.**). A Dane; esp. a Danish sailor: nautical (—1864); ob.

scadger. A mean fellow, a contemptible begger of loans: low: from ca 1860; ob. Perhaps ex CADGER on Cornish *scadgan*, a tramp. At Winchester College, a rascal: †by 1901.

scaff. A selfish fellow: Christ's Hospital: mid-C.19–20. (cf. SCABBY, 3, and SCALY.) Perhaps influenced by dial. *scaff*, one who wanders idly about, or derived ex †dial. *scaff-and-raff*, the rabble.

scaffold-pole. A fried potato-chip: low London (—1909).

scalawag; more gen. **scallawag** and (esp. in C.20) **scallywag;** occ. **scal(l)iwag, scallowag, skallewag,** but very rarely in C.20. A ne'er-do-well or disreputable fellow; a scoundrel. (Esp. in C.20, frequently playful like *rascal*.) U.S. s. (—1848), anglicized ca 1860 and >, ca 1910, coll. Bartlett, 1st ed.; Haliburton, 1855, 'You good-for-nothing young scallowag'; *Melbourne Argus*, 1870, 'Vagrants are now [in Melbourne] denominated scalawags.' The earliest recorded dates (considerably earlier ones prob. occur in unpublished letters) of the various forms are: *scalawag*, 1848; *scallawag*, 1854; *scallywag*, 1864; *scalliwag*, 1891; *scallowag*, 1855; *skallewag*, ca 1870. Origin problematic: prob. cognate with, or a survival of, the †Scottish *scurryvaig*, a vagabond: itself perhaps ex L. *scurra vagas*, a wandering buffoon (O.E.D.); W. suggests origin in dial. *scall*, skin-disease. 2. Hence, in politics, an impostor or a rascally intriguer: 1864, Sala: s. >, ca 1890, coll. 3. Ex sense 1, in trade-union s., one (rarely of women) who will not work: 1891, in the Labour Commission glossary; ob.

scalawag, etc., as adj., dates in England from ca 1865.

scald. To infect venereally: coll: late C.16–20; ob. (Lit., to burn.) cf.:

scald, adj.; **scalded.** Venereally infected: coll: resp., C.17–18; C.18–20.

scald-rag. A dyer: a C.17 coll nickname. 'Water Poet' Taylor.

scalder. A venereal infection, esp. a CLAP: low: from ca 1810; ob. cf. SCALDING-HOUSE. 2. Tea, the beverage: low: from ca 1890. Sydney Watson, *Wops the Waif*, 1892, 'I'm good at a hoperation, I can tell yer, when it's on spot and scalder (which being interpreted, meant cake and tea).' Ex the heat.

scalding-house(, Cupid's). A brothel: late C.16–17: on border-line between coll and S.E. Middleton's quotation, cited by F. & H., makes it, however, appear as if the term had no such gen. meaning, though it may have been so used in allusively jocular S.E.

scaldings! A warning, esp. among sailors and at Winchester: 'get out of the way!'; 'be off!'; 'look out!': mid-C.19–20; slightly ob. Smyth's *Word-Book* and Adam's *Wykehamica*. Ex *cry scaldings*, to announce loudly that one is carrying *scaldings*, i.e. boiling liquid.

***scaldrum.** A beggar: tramps' c.: mid-C.19–20; ob. Prob. ex:

***scaldrum-dodge.** Tramps' c. of mid-C.19–20 (ob.), as in Mayhew, 1851, *London Labour*, I, 'By then Peter was initiated into the scaldrum-dodge, or the art of burning the body with a mixture of acids and gunpowder, so as to suit the hues and complexions of the accident to be deplored.' Practised chiefly by 'schools of shallow coves', groups of men pretending to have escaped from shipwreck, fire, or similar perils. Prob. a perversion of *scald* or *scalding* (nn.).

scale. To mount a woman: coll: C.17–20. Wentworth Smith, *The Puritan*, 1607. 2. To impress; to astound: low (—1887); ob. Perhaps ex S.E. *scale*, take by escalade.

scaley, see SCALY. **scaliwag, scallawag, scalliwag, scallowag, scallywag,** see SCALAWAG.

scalp. A charm worn on a bangle: Society: 1896–1914. Ware, 'Given by young men to young girls'.

scalp. To buy very cheap so as to sell at less than ruling price: Stock Exchange coll: 1888, *Pall Mall Gazette*, 15 Oct.,'. . . "Scalped" the market on a big scale for a small profit per bushel'. One who does this is a *scalper*, which occurs in the same article; *scalping* arose about the same time: both coll.

scaly; incorrectly **scaley.** Shabby, poor, in poor health: late C.18–20; ob. Southey, 1793. Ex S.E. skin-disease sense. 2. Hence, stingy: from ca 1810; like sense 1, slightly ob. Egan, 1821, 'If you are too scaly to tip for it, I'll shell out and shame you.' The sense is very common at Christ's Hospital (cf. SCAFF). 3. Ex senses 1 and 2, despicable: mid-C.19–20. Besant & Rice, 1875, 'If I were an author – they are a scaly lot, and thank Heaven I am not one.'

scaly-back. A sailor: nautical: mid-C.19–20. Perhaps suggested by:

scaly fish. An 'honest, rough, blunt sailor', Grose, 2nd ed.: late C.18–19.

scamander. To loaf: 1860, H., 2nd ed., 'To wander about without a settled purpose'. Coll. cf. (perhaps ex) Yorkshire dial. *skimaundering* (hanging about), which may – or may not! – derive ex the Classical river *Scamander*.

scammered. Tipsy: low: from ca 1840; ob. Carew's *Autobiography of a Gipsy*, 1891 – the reference being valid for the year 1845. Perhaps ex SCUPPERED on dial. *scammer*, to climb or scramble.

***scamp.** A highway robber: 1781, Messink, 'Ye scamps, ye pads, ye divers'. Ex v., 1. 2. Hence, highway robbery (cf. *scampery*): 1786; like sense 1, †by 1840 or, at latest, 1850. 3. A cheat or a swindler: ca 1805–40: rather s. than c. Ex sense 1.

***scamp,** v. To be, or go out as, a highway robber: c.: ca 1750–1840; implied, however, as early as C.16 in *scampant*, 'used in imitation of *rampant* in a rogue's burlesque coat of arms', W. *The Discovery of John Poulter*, 1753, 'I'll scamp on the panney,' i.e. go out and rob on the highway. Prob. ex SCAMPER. 2. v.t., to rob (a person) on the highway: c. (—1812); †by 1870.

***scamp, done for a.** Convicted (esp. for highway robbery): c. of ca 1810–50.

***scamp, go (up)on the.** To rob as occasion offers: c. of ca 1820–1910. (Applied to tramps and beggars, not to professional thieves.)

***scamp, royal.** 'A highwayman who robs civilly', Grose, 1st ed.: c. of ca 1780–1840.

***scamp, royal foot.** A footpad who does this: ibid. and id.

scamper. To run hastily; to BOLT: 1687, 'Facetious' Tom Brown: s. until mid-C.18, then coll till ca 1830, then S.E. Either ex *scamp*, v. of motion, or ex †Dutch *schampen*, to go away, to escape.

***scamperer.** A street ruffian: C.18–early 19: prob. orig. c. Steele.

***scamping,** adj. Dishonest: ca 1820–60: orig., prob. always, c. Bee, 1823, 'Fellows who pilfer in markets, from stalls or orchards, who snatch off hats, cheat publicans out of liquor, or toss up cheatingly – commit scamping tricks.'

***scampsman.** A highwayman: c.: late C.18–mid-19. Ex SCAMP, n., 2.

scandal-broth, -potion, -water. Tea: coll; resp. 1785 (Grose), 1786 (Burns), 1864 (H., 3rd ed.): all ob. by 1900.

***scandal-proof.** adj. applied to 'a thorough pac'd ALSATIAN or Minter', B.E.: prob. c.: late C.17–mid-18.

***scandalous.** A wig: c.: late C.17–18.

scanmag, from ca 1850; *scan-mag*, from ca 1820; *scan. mag.* (or *S.M.*), 1779, Sheridan. Scandal. Abbr. *scandalum magnatum*, an old law term for a scandal of magnates.

scapa. An occ. form of SCARPER. cf. SCAPER.

Scaparey, see JOHNNY SCAPAREY.

scape. A snipe: a coll nickname: from ca 1860. Ex flushed snipe's cry. 2. See 2 in:

scape. 'To neglect one's brush', Bee: artistic: ca 1820–50. 2. n. and v. (To) escape: S.E. in Shakespeare, but by 1850 it is coll.

scaper. An occ. variant of SCARPER. Mayhew.

Scarborough warning; in C.19, occ. **S. surprise.** A very or too short notice, or none at all: coll: mid-C.16–20; ob. 'Proverbs' Heywood, Fuller, Grose, P. H. Emerson. 'In 1557 Thomas Stafford entered and took possession of Scarborough Castle before the townsmen were aware of his approach,' E.D.D.

scarce, make oneself. To retire; to absent oneself, disappear: coll: 1785, Grose; 1821, Scott, 'Make yourself scarce – depart – vanish!'

scare the shit out of; scare shitless. To scare very badly indeed: low: late C.19–20.

scare up. To find, discover (e.g. *scare up money*): coll: from ca 1850. Ex shooting game.

***scarecrow.** c.: 1884, Greenwood, 'The boy who has served [a thief] until he is well known to the police, and is so closely watched that he may as well stay at home as go out'. Ob.

scarehead. A headline in large, thick type meant to arouse attention: journalistic coll: from ca 1900. Abbr. *scare headline.*

scarlet. A MOHOCK or aristocratic street ruffian: coll or s.: ca 1750–60. J. Shebbeare, 1755. Either ex colour of dress or on BLOOD.

scarlet, dye. To drink deep or hard: late C.16–early 17. Shakespeare.

scarlet beans, see SOW POTATOES.

scarlet countenance, wear a. To be impudent or shameless: coll: late C.19–20. Ex S.E. *scarlet*, (of an offender) deep-dyed.

scarlet-fever. (A) flirtation with or passion for a soldier: jocular: ca 1860–1910. With reference to the scarlet uniform. 2. A great admiration for soldiers: jocular (—1889).

scarlet horse. A hired horse: ca 1780–1840. Punning *high-red.*

scarlet runner. A Bow Street officer: mid-C.19. Ex the scarlet waistcoat. 2. A footman: from ca 1860. Partly ex sense 1, partly ex the vegetable. 3. A soldier: late C.19–very early 20. Also *scarlet runners*, the old-fashioned red-jacketed uniform: same period.

***scarper.** To run away; v.t. to decamp from: Parlary and c.; as latter, it > low Cockney ca 1905. Selby, 1844, 'Vamoose – scarper – fly!' Ex It. *scappare* via Lingua Franca. See *Slang*. 2. On the stage, it = to leave a play without notice: from ca 1900.

scarper the letty. To leave one's lodgings without paying: mid-C.19–20: Parlary >, by 1900, theatrical. Ex SCARPER, 1, and see LETTY.

scarve. A finger-ring: Parlary: late C.19–20. Not from any Italian word, but app. – this is a mere guess – a Parlary'd shape of an English term: *scarf*-ring.

scat! Go away: coll: 1869 (O.E.D.). Hence, occ. as jocular v. Mostly U.S. Prob. abbr. of S.E. *scatter.*

scatter. To make water: proletarian: from ca 1860.

scavenger's daughter. An instrument of torture: coll: C.17. (Afterwards, merely historical.) *Journals of the House of Commons*, 14 May 1604. On *Skevington's* (or *Skeffington's*) *torture*, the technical S.E. term being *Skevington's gyves* (1564) or *irons*. Invented ca 1545 by Leonard

Skevington (or Skeffington), Lieutenant of the Tower of London.

scavey, see SAVVY. **scawfer,** see SCOFFER.

***scellum,** see SKELLUM.

scene-rat. A supernumerary in ballet or pantomime: theatrical: from ca 1880; ob.

scent, on the. On the road; travelling about: show- and circus-men's: from ca 1865.

scent-bottle. A water-closet: euphemistic s. (—1887).

scent-box. The nose: pugilistic: from ca 1825; virtually †. cf. SMELLER, 2.

sceptre; in C.18, occ. **scepter.** A sceptred gold unite: coll: C.18–20; in mid-C.19–20, virtually S.E. In 1736, Folkes writes, 'Sovereigns or Unites [properly, unites], vulgarly called Scepters'.

***scew,** see SKEW. **schack-stoner,** see SHACK-STONER.

scheme. A collection of the questions likely to be asked in the various subjects of examination: universities': ca 1775–1810. *Gentleman's Magazine*, 1780. 2. A practical joke at Winchester, ca 1840–1910. Wrench, 'The candle on reaching a measured point ignites paper, which by burning a string releases a weight; this falls on the head of the boy to be waked.' cf. old S.E. *scheme*, 'a party of pleasure', and the more relevant dial. sense, an amusement.

schemozzle, see SHEMOZZLE. **schice(r),** see SHICE(R). **schickster,** see SHICKSTER.

schism-shop. A Nonconformist place of worship: Anglican pejorative coll: late C.18–20. cf. HERESY-SHOP.

schitt. A goal at football: Winchester: ca 1830–60. Prob. ex *shot*.

schlemihl. A booby: Jewish coll: late C.19–20. Ex Yiddish.

schlemozzle, see SHEMOZZLE.

***schlenter.** Dubious, untrustworthy; make-believe: South African (diamond fields): from ca 1890: c. >, by 1900, low s. The Comtesse de Brémont, *The Gentleman Digger*, 1891. Whence, 2, as a n.: imitation gold: 1898, *Cape Argus*, weekly ed., 16 March. 3. (Also n., only in pl.) Imitation diamonds: 1899, Griffith, *Knaves of Diamonds*. Senses 2, 3 were prob., at first, c. Ex Dutch *slenter*, a trick.

***schliver.** A clasp-knife: c. (or low): ca 1820–1910. Ex CHIVER.

schnorrer. A Jewish beggar: Yiddish coll: 1892, Zangwill. Ex *schnurren*, to beg.

schofel or **-ful,** see SHOFUL.

schol. A scholar: Harrow: mid-C.19–20. 2. A scholarship: late C.19–20, ibid.

scholar. In illiterate use, one whom the speaker regards as exceptionally learned: mid-C.17–20. Often merely, one who is able to read and write: C.19–20. Not s. but coll.

scholar as my horse Ball, as good a. No scholar at all: a coll, semi-proverbial c.p. of ca 1630–70. John Clarke, 1639.

scholard, schollard. A scholar: resp. C.19–20; C.16–20: low coll >, ca 1850, sol. Also in senses indicated at SCHOLAR.

school. A number or a group of persons met together in order to gamble: from ca 1810: perhaps orig. c. > low s. ca 1880. cf. SCHOOLING, 2. 2. Hence, a MOB (n., 2) or gang of thieves or beggars: mostly c. (in C.20, however, s.): mid-C.19–20. Mayhew. (The term may apply to four, three, or even two persons.) See quotation at SCALDRUM-DODGE.

School Board will be after you!, the. Take care!: London lower classes': ca 1881–1900.

School-Board worrier. A school-inspector: London teachers' (—1887).

school-butter. A flogging: C.17–19. Pasquil's *Jests*, 1604.

school of Venus. A brothel: coll: late C.17–19.

schoolie or **-y.** A school – as opp. to a house – prefect: Scottish Public Schools': from ca 1880.

***schooling.** A term of confinement in a reformatory: c. (—1879); slightly ob. 2. 'A low gambling party', H., 1859: c. >, ca 1890, low s. See SCHOOL, 1. 3. Hence, a, or the, playing of pitch and toss: c. (—1888); slightly ob.

schoolman. A fellow-member of a SCHOOL: c. or low s.: 1834, Ainsworth; ob.

schoolmaster. (Gen. in training other horses) a horse good at jumping: stables' coll: late C.19–20. Prob. ex S.E. sense, the leader of a school of fishes; esp. of a bull whale.

schoolmaster, bilk the, see BILK . . .

schooly, see SCHOOLIE.

schooner; frigate; full master. Among youths, new-comer; handy fellow; passed master in navigation: naval: late C.19–early 20.

schooner on the rocks. A cooked joint surrounded by potatoes: naval: late C.19–20.

schooner-rigged. Destitute: sailing-ships': late C.19–20; ob.

s(c)hroff. A banker; treasurer; confidential clerk: Anglo-Indian coll: mid-C.16–20. Ex Arabic.

schwassle-box, see SWATCHEL. **science, blinded with,** see BLINDED WITH SCIENCE.

science, the. Boxing or, as in Dickens (1837), fencing: from ca 1830: s. >, ca 1870, coll. cf. *the profession* (see note at PRO, 2).

scientific. A scientist: coll: 1830, Lyell; De Morgan. Slightly ob.

scientifics. Scientific matters: low coll: ca 1840–70. Lover.

scissorean operation. Gutting a book: literary: ca 1890–1915. On *Caesarean operation.*

scissors!; oh, scissors! Indicative of disgust or impatience: 1843, Selby; ob. cf.:

scissors, give (a person). To treat drastically, pay out: mid-C.19–20; ob. ?ex CUT UP.

sciver. A shoemaker's knife: shoemakers': from ca 1890. A corruption of CHIVER.

scoach. Rum: Regular Army: late C.19–20.

scobolotcher, scobberlotcher. An undergraduate walking round a quadrangle, hands in pockets, deep in thought and/or counting trees. C.16–20. Used by Dr Ralph Kettle (1563–1643), President of Trinity College, Oxford (Aubrey's 'Life' of him, 1697). The O.E.D. attempts no etymology, but does compare the North Country and East Anglian *scopperloit, scoppoloit,* a time of idleness or of play, and the rare *scoterlope,* to wander aimlessly.

scoff. Food: South African coll: 1856, the Rev. F. Fleming, *Southern Africa*; 1879, Atcherley. Ex Cape Dutch: see the v. 2. Hence, a meal: id.: late C.19–20. (The term, ca 1890, > gen. among tramps and sailors, often as *scorf.*) cf.:

scoff; often **scorf;** in South Africa, gen. **skoff.** v.t. To eat voraciously: s. (—1864) and dial. (1849). Prob. ex dial. *scaff.* 2. Hence, modified by South African usage (see the n.), v.t., simply to eat: from ca 1880: outside of South Africa, nautical (W. Clark Russell, 1883). 3. Occ. v.i.: late C.19–20 and rare outside South Africa. But this may be the primary sense, as we see from Lady Barnard's *South African Journal,* 1798, '[The Boer] concludes that the passengers want to scoff (to eat)': see W. 4. (Ex sense 1.) To seize; to plunder: 1893, Kipling, 'There's enough [gold-leaf] for two first-rates, and I've scoffed the best half of it.'

***scoffer;** occ. **scawfer.** Gold or silver plate: c.: mid-C.19–20; ob. 'Gypsy' Carew: a reference that is valid for 1845.

scold. A scolding: coll and dial.: from ca 1725; ob. except in Scots.

scold, v.i. To be constantly uttering reproofs: coll: mid-C.18–20.

***scoldrum (dodge).** A variant of SCALDRUM (DODGE).

scold's cure. A coffin: low: ca 1810–60. Esp. *nap the s.c.,* be coffined.

scollogue. To live or act dissipatedly, wildly: low (—1857); †by 1900. Perhaps ex SCALAWAG.

scolopendra. A harlot: ca 1630–1700. D'Avenant. Ex sting in centipede's tail.

sconce. The head; esp. the crown of the head: 1567, *Damon and Pythias*; Thackeray. Perhaps ex *sconce,* a fort, or its Dutch original, *schans.* 2. Hence, wit, sense, judgement, ability: coll: mid-C.17–20; ob. 3. Occ. the person himself: coll: ca 1570–1750. Kendall, 1577. 4. See SCONCE, BUILD A.

sconce, v. To fine, mulct: university (orig. – see Minsheu, 1617 – and mainly Oxford): C.17–20. Until C.19, of officials fining undergraduates; in C.19–20, of undergraduates fining one of themselves (gen. a tankard of ale) for a breach of manners or convention. Randolph, 'Honours of Oxford' Miller, Colman the Elder, 'C. Bede'. Perhaps ex the n., 1 (via 'so much a head'). 2. (Gen. *sconce off.*) To reduce (the amount of a bill, etc.): coll: 1768, Foote; †by 1910. Occ. *to sconce one's diet,* to eat less: coll (very ob.): C.19–20. 3. v.i. and v.t., to hinder; get in the way (of): Winchester, mainly in games (e.g. a catch at cricket): late C.19–20. *Public School Magazine,* Dec. 1899. Prob. ex preceding sense.

sconce, build a. 'To run a score at an alehouse', Bailey (1730); 'run deep upon tick', B.E. defining *build a large sconce.* There is often the connotation of lack of intention to pay the account, for Grose, 1785, defines it as 'a military term for bilking one's quarters'. ca 1640, Shirley; Tom Brown; Goldsmith. †by 1840. Ex *sconce,* a (small) fort.

sconce off; sconce one's diet, see SCONCE, v., 2.

sconcing is the vbl n. of SCONCE, v., all senses. Very gen.

scoodyn. The fouling of a ship's bottom: nautical coll: C.19–20; ob. Possibly by antiphrasis ex dial. *scud,* to clean, scrape clean; but prob. ex Shetlands dial. *scovin*, crust adhering to a vessel in which food has been cooked.

scoop. Male hair worn low and flat on the forehead: military: ca 1880–90. 2. See SCOOP, ON THE. 3. News obtained (and, of course, printed) in advance of a rival newspaper: journalistic: orig. U.S., anglicized ca 1890: s. 4. In the money-market, a sudden reduction of prices enabling operators to buy cheaply and to profit by the ensuing (carefully planned) rise: Stock Exchange: orig. (—1879) U.S., anglicized ca 1890. 5. An advantage, a (big) haul, a very successful or, more properly, a lucky stroke in business: 1893, Kipling; *Daily Chronicle*, 27 July 1909, 'Her engagement . . . at the Palace is a big "scoop".' This last sense follows ex nos. 3, 4, which, in their turn, derive ex the S.E. sense, an act of scooping.

scoop, v. (Gen. *scoop in*, occ. *scoop up*.) To obtain (a lot of money), make a big haul of; to appropriate in advance: orig. (ca 1880) U.S., anglicized ca 1890. Ex S.E. sense, to heap up by means of a scoop. 2. (Occ. *scoop out*.) To get the better of (a rival) by anticipating him or by obtaining what he has failed to obtain: journalistic; orig. U.S., anglicized ca 1890. Elizabeth Banks, *The Newspaper Girl*, 1902, 'Miss Jackson . . . [is] going to print it in to-morrow's paper, and I shall be scooped.'

scoop, on the. On the drink; engaged in dissipation: 1884 (O.E.D.); ob.

scoop out, see SCOOP, v., 2. **scoop up,** see SCOOP, v., 1.

scoot, occ. **skoot** or **skute.** A scooting (see the v.): s. and dial. from ca 1860. Esp. in *do a scoot*, run away, late C.19–20, and *on the scoot*, on the run (lit. and fig.), 1864.

scoot; occ. – though, as to the n., very rarely in C.20 – **skoot, skute; skewt** seems to have remained U.S. (Gen. with *about*, *along*, *away*, *off*, *round*, etc., as adv.) To go (away) hurriedly or with sudden speed: orig. (ca 1840) U.S.; anglicized ca 1860: s. *Quarterly Review*, 1869, 'The laugh of the gull as he scoots along the shore'. Ex the mainly nautical s. *scout*, to dart, move quickly: see SCOUT, v., 1.

scoot-train. An express train: late C.19–20; ob. Ex SCOOT, n., but see v.

scooter. One who goes with sudden swiftness or hurriedly: dial. (—1825) and (from ca 1860) s. >, ca 1910, coll. See SCOOT, v.

scorch. A very fast run on (motor-)cycle or motor-car: 1885 (O.E.D.): coll >, ca 1905, S.E.

scorch, v.i. To ride a bicycle, drive a motor-car, etc., at considerable or very great speed: coll (—1891) >, ca 1905, S.E. Implied in n. and in:

scorcher. A furious propeller of cycle or car (etc.): 1885: coll. *Daily Telegraph*, 7 Jan. 1901, 'The police have been keeping a sharp look-out for scorchers.' Ex the v. 2. An exceedingly hot day: coll: 1874. Often *a regular scorcher*. 3. Any thing or person severe, notably eccentric, deplorably hasty; a scathing remark, vigorous attack, etc.: orig. schoolboys': 1885, Hawley Smart. 4. Hence, a sensation-causer, habitual or incidental, deliberate or unintentional: 1899, Conan Doyle; ob. 5. A rotten potato: greengrocers' (—1887).

scorching, n. Furious riding (of cycle) or driving (of car, etc.): from ca 1890: coll till ca 1905, then S.E. Ex SCORCH, v.

scorching, adj. Very hot; esp., immoral or indelicate: coll: 1897, *Referee*, 24 Oct.

score, n. The gaining of a point or points in games: coll: from ca 1840. 2. Hence, a notable or successful hit in debate, argument, or keen business: likewise coll: from ca 1890. cf. the v. 3. Twenty pounds (£20): c.: late C.19–20.

score, v.i. and v.t. To gain (a success): from ca 1880: coll. cf.:

score off. To achieve a success over, make a point at the expense or to the detriment of (gen. a person): coll: 1882, 'Lucas Malet', 'For once she felt she had scored off her adversary.' Ex scoring at games: cf. the n., sense 1.

scorf. See SCOFF. (A low variant, more frequent of the v. than the n.)

scorny; occ. **scorney.** Scornful: low coll: 1836, Haliburton. Also Cornish dial.

scorp. A late C.19–20 naval and military abbr. of:

scorpion. A civilian native inhabitant of Gibraltar: military: 1845. Also, from ca 1870, as in H.M. Field, 1889, 'A choice variety of natives of Gibraltar, called "Rock scorpions" '. Ex the scorpions that infest the Rock of Gibraltar.

Scot. A very irritable or quickly angered person: from ca 1810; slightly ob. Bee, 1823, shows that, orig. at least, it may have been a butchers' term, 'the small Scots oxen coming to their doom with little resignation to fate'. 2. Hence, gen. *scot*, a temper, or passion of irritation: 1859, H.,

1st ed. cf. SCOTTY and SCOTTISH, adj., and PADDY, n.

Scotch or (though very rare in C.19) **scotch.** (A drink of) Scotch whisky: from ca 1885: coll. >, ca 1905, S.E. ('Pomes' Marshall, 'He had started well on Scotches.') 2. A leg: abbr. SCOTCH PEG.

Scotch, adj. Mean (of persons); ungenerous (of acts): coll: C.19–20. Esp. *be Scotch*, as in 'He's (*or* He must be) Scotch.' (The Scot's, like the Jew's, meanness is actually apocryphal.) Ex following combinations.

Scotch bait. A halt and a rest on one's staff as practised by pedlars: coll: ca 1780–1850.

Scotch bum. A kind of (dress-)bustle: coll: C.17.

Scotch casement. A pillory: late C.18–mid-19.

Scotch chocolate. Brimstone and milk: coll: ca 1780–1850. cf.:

Scotch coffee. Hot water flavoured with burnt biscuit: from ca 1860; ob. Orig. and mainly nautical; prob. suggested by SCOTCH CHOCOLATE.

Scotch fashion, answer. To reply to a question by asking another (*à la Jésus*): coll: 1834, Michael Scott, *The Cruise of the Midge*; slightly ob.

Scotch fiddle. The itch: coll: 1675, Rochester; ob. Also WELSH FIDDLE.

Scotch fiddle, play the. To work the index finger of one hand like a fiddle-stick between the index and middle finger of the other: coll: from ca 1820. H., 2nd ed. To do this 'provokes a Scotchman in the highest degree, it implying that he is afflicted with the itch', H.

Scotch (occ. Scots) Greys or greys. Lice: C.19–20. Punning the regiment. Hence, *headquarters of the Scotch Greys*, a lousy head: from ca 1820 (ob.).

Scotch hobby. A scrubby little Scotch horse: coll: C.17–early 19.

Scotch or (mid-C.19–20) **Scottish mist.** Rain: coll: 1589, Anon., *Pap with a Hatchet*; 'Phraseologia' Robertson, 1681; Grose, 1st ed., 'A sober soaking rain; a Scotch mist will wet an Englishman to the skin'; Scott.

Scotch ordinary. A privy: ca 1670–1750.

Scotch peg. A leg: rhyming s. from mid-1850s. H., 3rd ed., has it in full, whereas H., 1st ed., only implies it in '*scotches*, the legs'; it occurs, however, in 'Ducange Anglicus', 1857.

Scotch pint. A bottle holding two quarts: from ca 1820; ob.

Scotch prize. A capture by mistake: coll, mostly nautical (—1818); ob.

Scotch rabbit. A WELSH RABBIT (cf. SCOTCH FIDDLE): ca 1740–70. Mrs Glasse, the C.18 Mrs Beeton, gives a recipe in 1747.

Scotch seamanship. Seamanship by brute force: nautical coll from ca 1890; slightly ob. *St James's Gazette*, 9 April 1900. cf. SCOTCH PRIZE.

Scotch tea, see TEA.

Scotch or occ. **Scottish warming-pan.** A wench: coll: ca 1670–1880. Ray; S. Wesley the Elder; Grose. An elaboration of WARMING-PAN, 1. 2. A breaking of wind: low: ca 1810–1910.

scotchie (or **S.**). A marble with gay stripes: schoolboys' (—1887). In reference to tartan. 2. (Gen. in pl.) A leg: late C.19–20. Ex SCOTCH PEG. 3. See SCOTCHY.

Scotchman. A florin: South Africa, esp. among the Africans (—1879). (Atcherley, whom Rider Haggard repeats in *Jess*, 1886.) Ex that canny Scot who, among the Kaffirs, passed off a number of florins as half-crowns; which may account for a story related in J. Milne's *The Epistles of Atkins*, published in 1902 and dealing with the Boer War. 2. A Scotch fir: coll: 1901, 'Lucas Malet'.

Scotchman hugging a or the Creole, often without *a* or *the* before *Scotchman*. A clusia or kind of creeper: West Indian coll: 1835, M. Scott.

***Scotchmen.** Lice: c. (—1887). Ex SCOTCH GREYS.

Scotchy. A coll nickname for a Scotsman: C.19–20. cf. JOCK, 2.

Scots Greys, see SCOTCH GREYS.

Scott!, great, see GREAT SCOTT!

Scottish. Irritable; easily angered: low: ca 1810–80. Ex SCOT, 1.

Scottish mist, warming-pan, see SCOTCH M., W.-P.

Scotty. A Scotsman: coll: late C.19–20. Prob. ex SCOTCHY.

scotty. Angry; apt to grow easily annoyed: C.19–20. Ex SCOT, 2. It is defined in *Sinks*, 1848, as 'savage, wild, chagrined'.

***scour;** often spelt **scow(e)r, scowre.** To decamp, run away, depart hurriedly: ca 1590–1870: s. with more than a tinge of c., as have the next three senses. Greene, Shadwell, Grose. Ex S.E. *scour*, to move rapidly or hastily. 2. v.i. to roam noisily about at night, smashing windows, waylaying and often beating wayfarers, and attacking the watch: ca 1670–1830. Shadwell, Prior. 3. Hence, v.t., to ill-treat (esp. the watch or wayfarers) while street-roistering: ca 1680–1750. Dryden, 'Scowring the Watch grows out of fashion wit.' 4. v.t. to roister through (the streets): ca 1690–1830. 5. To wear, esp. in *scour the* CRAMP-RING(S) or DARBIES, i.e. to wear, or to lie in chains: ca 1450–1840 (*cramp-rings* not before mid-C.16, *darbies* not before late C.17): s. >, ca 1560, c. Awdelay, B.E., Egan's Grose. Ex *scour*, to cleanse by rubbing. (Ex this sense comes SCOURING, n.) 6. To coït with (a woman): coll: C.17–19.

scourer, often **scowrer.** One who behaves as in SCOUR, 2: s. verging on c.: ca 1670–1830. Wycherley. cf. HAWCUBITE; MOHOCK; MUN, 2; NICKER, 2; TITYRE-TU. 2. Hence, a night-thief: c.: late C.17–18. Anon., *The Gentleman Instructed*, ca 1700, '[In London] he struck up with sharpers, scourers, and Alsatians.'

***scouring.** (An) imprisonment: c.: 1721, Defoe; †by 1820. 2. adj. to SCOUR, v., 2–4.

scouse. Any kind of stew: naval coll, from ca 1820, or earlier. 2. (*Scouse*) A native of Liverpool: s.: late C.19–20. Abbr. LOBSCOUSE.

Scouseland. Liverpool: nautical and (Liverpool) dockers': late C.19–20. cf. SCOUSE.

scousy or **scowsy.** Mean, stingy: Christ's Hospital: since ca 1860; ob. Marples, 'Perhaps SCABBY + LOUSY'.

scout. A college servant at Oxford (cf. the Cambridge *gyp*): Oxford University: C.18–20: coll till ca 1850, then S.E. Hearne, 1708; Grose, 1st ed.; 'Cuthbert Bede'. Prob. ex the military, just possibly ex the †cricket, sense. 2. A member of the watch: c. of mid-C.17–early 19. Coles, 1676; Shadwell, 1688; Haggart, 1821. Ex †*scout*, a watchman.

scout, v.i. To dart; go, move, suddenly and swiftly: mid-C.18–early 19: orig. and mainly nautical. Captain Tyrrell, 1758; Anon., *Splendid Follies*, 1810, 'Sponge was actually obliged to scout out of the room to conceal his risible muscles'. Ex Swedish *skjuta*, v.i., to shoot. cf. SCOOT, v. 2. See SCOUT ON THE LAY. 3. 'To shoot pigeons outside a gun-club enclosure', F. & H.: coll: from ca 1880. Ex S.E. pigeon-shooting sense of the n.

***scout-cull.** A watchman: c.: C.18. C. Hitchin, *The Regulator*, 1718.

***scout-ken.** A watch-house: c. of ca 1810–40. Ex SCOUT, n., 2.

scout-master, scoutmaster. A schout (Dutch chief magistrate): catachrestic: ca 1650–1700.

***scout on the lay.** To go searching for booty: c.: late C.18–19. See LAY, n., 2.

scow, v. To be illicitly absent: mostly Liverpool: late C.19–20. Short for:

scowbank, n. (1861). See SCOWBANKER. 2. v., to loaf: dial. (—1868) >, ca 1880, s. ?etymology.

scowbanker; also **skow-,** occ. **skull-** and, ca 1890–1910, **showbanker.** A loafer, a tramp: mostly Australian (—1864). Ex U.S., where it dates from mid-C.18. Perhaps of Irish origin.

Scowegian. (Pron. *Scow-wegian.*) A Scandinavian: West Canadian and nautical: late C.19–20. Ex *Scandinavian* + *Norwegian.*

scow(e)r, see SCOUR. **scowre(r),** see SCOUR, v., and SCOURER.

***scrag.** A person's neck: c.: from ca 1750; slightly ob. ?ex *crag*, Scottish *craig*, the neck. 2. The gallows: C.19 c. Ex the v. 1, or abbr. SCRAG-SQUEEZER. 3. At Shrewsbury School (—1881), a rent across a paper signifying 'no marks'. Perhaps ex the v., 4, to handle roughly. 4. A very rough tackle at Rugby football (cf. the v., 4): Public Schools': (—1903).

***scrag,** v.t. To hang by the neck: from ca 1750 (slightly ob.): c. until ca 1840, then s. Toldervy; Tomlinson; Grose; Barham. 2. Hence, to wring the neck of: from ca 1820. 3. To garotte: c. or low s.: mid-C.19–20. 4. To manhandle, properly (as in Rugby football), to twist the neck of a man whose head is conveniently held under one's arm: early C.19–20. Kipling, *Stalky & Co.*, 'Don't drop oil over my "Fors", or I'll scrag you.' (*I'll scrag you* has > a vague threat and c.p., esp. among schoolboys.) Ex dial.

***scrag a lay.** 'To steal clothes put on a hedge to dry', Tufts: c.: late C.18–early 19. cf. SNOW.

***scrag-boy.** A hangman: c.: from ca 1780; ob. Ex SCRAG, n., 1 and v., 1.

***scrag-'em fair.** A public execution: c. of ca 1810–50. Ex SCRAG, v., 1.

scrag-hole. The gallery: theatrical (—1909); ob. Ex the craning of scrags or necks.

***scrag-squeezer.** A gallows: ca 1820–1900: c. Henley, 1887; Villon's *Straight Tip,*

'Until the squeezer nips your scrag.' Ex SCRAG, n., 1.

***scragged.** Dead by hanging: c.: mid-C. 18–20; ob.

***scragger.** A hangman: c. or low s.: 1897, P. Warung.

***scragging.** An execution: C.19–20: c. >, ca 1880, low s.; slightly ob. Ex SCRAG, v., 1.

***scragging-post.** A gallows: c.: from ca 1810; slightly ob.

***Scragg's Hotel.** The workhouse: tramps' c.: from ca 1880; ob. *Daily Telegraph*, 1 Jan. 1886.

***scran;** occ., though – except in dial. – very rare in C.20, **skran.** A reckoning at a tavern or inn: c. of ca 1710–40. In *Bacchus and Venus*, 1724, 'Frisky Moll's Song' by Harper. App. this sense, without leaving any record that I have found, survived until 1903, when listed as low s. by F. & H. ?etymology. 2. ?hence (or perhaps cognate with *scrannel*), food, esp. broken victuals: s. (—1785) and dial. (—1808); in mid-C.19, the word verged on c. 3. Hence, refuse (of food): mostly dial. (—1808) and, as s., †by 1910. 4. Ex sense 2, a meal: from ca 1870: mostly military. 5. See SCRAN TO, BAD. 6. See SCRAN, OUT ON THE.

scran, v.t. To provide with food: c. (in C.19–20, low s.): from ca 1740; slightly ob. (This entry seems to show that the n., 2, existed half a century before our earliest record.) 2. v.i. to collect broken victuals: c. (?orig. dial.) >, ca 1880, low s.: from the 1830s. Ex the n., 2.

***scran, out on the.** Begging for scraps of food: c. (—1864). Prob. ex SCRAN, v., 2. cf. SCRANNING.

***scran-bag.** A receptacle for scraps of food: c.: from ca 1850. Burn, *Autobiography of a Beggar-Boy*, 1855. Ex SCRAN, n., 2. 2. Hence, a haversack: military (—1864). 3. A receptacle for the impounding of articles carelessly left about: nautical: late C.19–20.

***scran-pocket.** A c. variant (—1887) of SCRAN-BAG, 1; ob.

scran to, bad. Bad luck to —!: Anglo-Irish coll: from ca 1840. Lever, P. H. Emerson. Perhaps ex SCRAN, n., 2. cf. BAD CESS TO.

***scrand.** An occ. variant of SCRAN, n.

***scranning,** vbl n. A begging of scraps of food: Scots dial. (—1839), whence c. (—1859), as in H., 1st ed. Ex SCRAN, v., 2; cf. SCRAN, OUT ON THE.

scrap. A blow, a punch: c. of early C.17. Rowlands in *Martin Mark-All*. cf. sense 3, of independent origin. 2. (In C.18–19, occ. *scrapp*) An intention, design, plot, always either vile or villainous: ca 1670–1830: either c. or low s. ?ex *scrape*. 3. ?hence, a struggle, scrimmage, fisticuffs: from ca 1873. cf. U.S. *scrape*, a rough encounter, 1812 (Thornton).

scrap, v.i. To fight, esp. with the fists (—1874). Ex the n., 3. 2. To scrimmage (—1891). 3. Ex sense 1, v.t. to box with: 1893, P. H. Emerson, 'I was backed to scrap a cove bigger nor me.'

scrap, do a, see DO A SCRAP.

scrap-up. An occ. variant of SCRAP, n., 3.

scrape. A shave: jocular coll (—1859). cf. v. and SCRAPER. 2. Cheap butter: 1859, H., 1st ed. 3. See SCRAPE, BREAD AND. 4. Short shrift: coll: 1899, *Pall Mall Gazette*, 5 April, 'From the French adventurers he was only likely to get what schoolboys call scrape.'

scrape, v.i., v.t., and v. reflexive. To shave: jocular coll: from ca 1770.

scrape, bread and. Bread with but a smear of butter: orig. schools': coll: 1861; 1873, Rhoda Broughton, 'Happiness thinly spread over their whole lives, like bread and scrape!' Ex S.E. *scrape*, a thin layer. 2. Hence, short commons: coll: from ca 1865.

scrape!, go. Go away!: contemptuous coll: early C.17. Cotgrave.

scrape the enamel. To scratch the skin by falling: cyclists': from ca 1890; ob.

scrape the kettle. To go to confession: lower-middle-class and proletarian Catholic: late C.19–20.

scraper. A barber: pejorative coll: from ca 1790. 2. A razor: jocular coll: from ca 1860. See SCRAPE, v. 3. As a cocked hat, esp. if gold-laced, naval coll of ca 1790–1840, verging on S.E. 4. A short one to two-inch whisker, slightly curved: Society: ca 1880–90. Ware. 5. See:

scrapers, take to one's. To make off: Anglo-Irish: from ca 1820. Here, *scraper* = a foot, esp. a heel; cf. *scrape* with one's feet.

scraping-castle. A water-closet: low: ca 1850–90.

scrapings of his nails!, he wouldn't give you the. A semi-proverbial, coll c.p. (—1887), applied to a very mean person; slightly ob.

scrapp, see SCRAP, n., 2.

scrapper. A pugilist; any fighter, whether with fists or weapons: from ca 1820.

scrapping. Fighting or boxing: from ca 1890. See SCRAP, v., and cf. SCRAPPER.

scrappy. A farrier: Regular Army: late C.19–20. Ex the scraps of iron or hoof he leaves about.

Scratch. Gen. and orig. *Old Scratch.* The devil: coll: 1740. In late C.19–20, mostly dial. Ex *scrat*, a goblin, on *scratch.*

scratch. A competitor starting from *scratch* in a handicap contest: coll: 1867. 2. In billiards, a fluke: coll: from ca 1890.

scratch, bring to the, come (up) to the or **toe the.** To bring oneself or another to the requisite point, lit. or fig.; to do, or cause to do, one's duty: coll >, ca 1890, S.E.: resp. 1827, Scott; 1834, Ainsworth; 1857, 'Cuthbert Bede'. Ex the line drawn on the ground or floor to divide the boxing-ring.

scratch, no great. Of little value or importance: orig. (1844), U.S., anglicized ca 1858; slightly ob. Lit., not very painful.

scratch a beggar before you die, you'll. You will die a beggar: a semi-proverbial c.p. of ca 1630–1800. Clarke, Ray, Fuller.

scratch-down. The public scolding of a man by a woman: low (—1909). Ware.

scratch-me. A lucifer match: London's lower classes' (—1909).

scratch my breech and I'll claw your elbow. Let us indulge in reciprocal flattery: C.17–19: a semi-proverbial c.p. cf. *ca me, ca thee*, and S.E. *scratch me and I'll scratch thee.*

scratch one's arse with, not a sixpence to. Penniless: low coll: mid-C.19–20; ob.

scratch one's wool. To puzzle; wonder greatly: tailors': from ca 1870. On S.E. *scratch one's head*; and see jocular S.E. *wool*, hair.

scratch-platter, see TAILOR'S RAGOUT.

scratch-rash. A scratched face: artisans' (—1909). cf. GRAVEL-RASH.

scratched. Tipsy: C.17 c. or s. 'Water-Poet' Taylor, 1622.

scratcher. A lucifer match: proletarian (—1909). cf. SCRATCH-ME. 2. A paymaster, or his clerk: naval: late C.19–20; ob. Ware, 'From the noisy times of quill pens'. 3. A toe: Anglo-Irish: C.19. 'A Real Paddy', *Life in Ireland*, 1822. 4. Usually pl, *scratchers.* The hand (*Boxiana*, IV, 1824): ca 1815–60. 5. A small ship: Merchant Navy: late C.19–20. It scratches the dock wall in entering at ebb tides.

scratching one's balls (or ballocks), be or sit. Instead of being either active or alert, to sit or loll in idleness and vacancy: low coll: late C.19–20.

scratching rake. A comb: proletarian: from ca 1870; ob.

Scratchland. Scotland: ca 1780–1890. cf. SCOTCH FIDDLE.

scratchy. (Of a batsman) lacking sureness and confidence in his strokes: cricket coll: 1904.

***scream,** v. (Of a thief, robbed by another) to apply to the police: c.: from ca 1885.

***scream the place down.** To go to Scotland Yard to report one's loss: c. from ca 1900.

screamer. An animate or inanimate of exceptional size, intensity, attractiveness: orig. U.S., anglicized in 1850 by Frank Smedley. Runciman, 1888, 'She's a screamer, she's a real swell.' 2. A startling, exaggerated, or extremely funny book, story, etc.: 1844, Dickens. 3. Hence, one who tells exaggerated or very funny stories: 1849, Albert Smith. 4. 'A thief who, robbed by another thief, applies to the police', F. & H.: c.: from ca 1890.

screaminess. The quality of being SCREAMY: coll: from ca 1880.

screaming. Splendid; excellent: orig. theatrical (—1859). Ex SCREAMER, 1.

screaming gin and ignorance. Bad newspaper writing: sporting reporters': 1868–ca 80.

screamy. Apt to scream; (of sound) screaming; fig., very violent, exaggerated, or unseemly in expression; (of colour) glaring: coll: in 1882, *Spectator* describes two of Swinburne's sonnets as 'thoroughly unworthy and screamy'. cf. SCREAMER, 2.

***screave,** see SCREEVE.

screech. Whisky: low: from ca 1880; ob. ?ex its strength or possibly ex its tendency to make some females screech. See also SCREIGH.

screed. ca 1870–90 a journalistic coll (later S.E.) for 'an illogical or badly written article or paper upon any subject', H., 5th ed. 2. Hence, a picture execrably painted: artists' (—1887); ob.

***screen.** A bank or currency note: esp. if counterfeit: from ca 1810: c. (cf. *queer* SCREEN) ca 1820–50, it often meant esp. a £1 note (cf. SCREEVE, n., 2), as in Egan, 1821. The word, which may be a witty perversion of SCREEVE, was ob. by 1900.

***screen, queer.** A forged note: c. (—1812). Vaux, Lytton, Ainsworth. See SCREEN.

***screen-faking.** The forging of notes: c.: 1830, Moncrief. See SCREEN.

***screeve** (1801); also **screave** (1821), **scrieve** (from ca 1850), **scrive** (1788). Any piece of writing: 1788; Scots s. or coll. 2. Whence, a banknote: (mainly Scottish) c.: ca 1800–90. *Sporting Magazine*, 1801, 'The one-pound screeves'; Haggart. 3. A begging letter, a petition, a testimonial: c.: from ca 1810. (From ca 1890, letter is the predominant sense.) 4. A drawing in chalk on the pavement: c.: from ca 1855. Ex the v., 2; and see SCREEVING. The etymology is not so simple as it looks: prob. ex dial. *scrieve*, to write, or ex the Dutch *schrijven*; ultimately ex L. *scribere*; cf.:

***screeve; occ. scrieve.** v.t. to write (esp. a begging letter, a petition): c. and East-End s.: mid-C.19–20. '*No. 747*', reference 1845; Mayhew, 1851. Ex It. *scrivere* via Lingua Franca; perhaps imm. ex the n., 1–3. 2. Whence, v.i., draw on the pavement with chalk; to do this as a livelihood: c.: 1851, Mayhew.

***screeve, fake a,** see FAKE A SCREEVE.

***screeve-faker.** The same as SCREEVER, 1: ca 1850–1910.

***screever; occ. scriever.** One who, for a living, writes begging letters: c.: 1851, Mayhew. Ex SCREEVE, v., 1. 2. A 'pavement artist': c. and East-End s.: implied by Mayhew in 1851 (see quotation at SCREEVING) and recorded by H. in 1859. *Punch*, 14 July 1883, 'Here is a brilliant opening for merry old Academicians, festive flagstone screevers and "distinguished amateurs" '.

***screeving.** vbl n. of SCREEVE, v., 1 and 2. Mayhew, 1851, 'By screeving, that is, by petitions and letters'; ibid., 'Screeving or writing on the pavement'.

screigh; occ. skreigh. Whisky: Scottish s.: C.19–20. Lexicographer Jamieson. i.e. a screech: proleptic usage.

***screw.** A skeleton key: c.: 1795, Potter; slightly ob. 2. ?hence, a turnkey or prison warder: 1821, Egan: c. until ca 1860, then low s. 3. A robbery effected with a skeleton key: c. of ca 1810–90. 4. *the screw*, the doing of this, esp. as an occupation: c.: ca 1810–80. 5. An old or otherwise worthless horse: 1821; 'Nimrod' Apperley, 1835, 'Mr Charles Boultbee, the best screw driver in England'. Coll >, ca 1890, S.E. Perhaps by the semantic process illustrated by RIP or orig. of a race-horse that can, by 'screwing', be made to gain a place. 6. Wages, salary (—1859). 7. Hence (?), a dram, a PICK-ME-UP: 1877. cf. 7*a*, a bottle of wine: Anglo-Irish (—1827); ob. Barrington. 8. See SCREW, FEMALE. 9. (Whence, or more prob. ex the v., 2,) an act of copulation: C.19–20: low. 10. Whence, a woman *qua* sexual pleasure: low: late C.19–20. 11. See SCREWS, THE. 12. A glance, a look; esp. *take a screw at*. 13. A tight-fisted person: coll: ca 1820–90. 'He would call her an old screw, or skinflint' (*Hogg's Instructor*, Nov. 1855, 'Memoranda by a Marine Officer').

***screw,** v. To break into (a building) by using a skeleton key: c.: from ca 1810. Arthur Morrison. See the n., 1, 2, and 3. 2. To copulate with (a female): low (—1785).

screw, all of a. Very crooked or twisted: coll (—1887). Perhaps influenced by *askew*.

***screw, fake a,** see FAKE A SCREW.

screw, female; occ. simply **screw.** A harlot: resp. ca 1780–1850 and ca 1720–1870.

screw, under the, see UNDER THE SCREW.

screw-driver. A hammer: carpenters' and joiners' jocularity: late C.19–20.

screw-jaws. A wry-mouthed person: coll (—1788) verging on S.E.; ob.

screw loose, a. A phrase indicative of something wrong: from ca 1820: s. until ca 1840, then coll till ca 1880, then S.E. Egan, 1821; Dickens; Trollope. Ob. in this gen. sense. 2. Hence, (slightly) crazy or mad, gen. as *have a screw loose*: coll: from ca 1870.

screw one's nut. To dodge a blow aimed at the head: London lower classes': from the early 1890s. *People*, 6 Jan. 1895. A double pun – on NUT and on *screw*.

screw-thread, drunken. A defective helical ridge of a screw: a technological coll: from ca 1850. Ronalds & Richardson, *Chemical Technology*, 1854.

screw up, v.i. To force one into making a bargain: coll: late C.17–mid-19. Ex S.E. sense, to tighten up with a screw. 2. To garotte: c.: 1845 (p. 419 of '*No. 747*'); ob.

screw up (someone's) **ogle.** To punch so hard in the eye that it closes: boxing: ca 1805–40. *Plymouth Telegraph*, early 1822.

screwed. Tipsy: 1838, Barham, 'Like a four-bottle man in a company screw'd, | Not firm on his legs, but by no means subdued.' s. >, ca 1870, coll. For semantics, cf. TIGHT. cf. SCREWY, 2; BLIND; BLOTTO; CORNED; FUZZY; PARALYSED; SCAMMERED; *three* SHEETS IN THE WIND; SQUIFFY; WET. F. & H. gives a magnificent synonymy; H., in the Introduction, a good one.

screwed on right or **the right way, have one's head.** To be shrewd and business-like; be able to look after oneself: coll: mid-C.19–20.

screwed up. Vanquished: Oxford and Cambridge undergraduates': late C.19–early 20. Ex 'the ancient habit of screwing up an offender's door', Ware. 2. (Also *screwed up in a corner.*) Penniless: artisans' (—1909). Ware, 'Without money – can't move'.

***screwing.** A house- or shop-breaking: c.: from ca 1810. See SCREW, v., 1.

screws, the. Rheumatism: coll and dial.: mid-C.19–20. Ex instrument of torture.

***screwsman.** A thief using a skeleton key: c. (—1812). Ex SCREW, n., 1–3.

screwy. Mean, stingy: 1851, Mayhew, 'Mechanics are capital customers ... They are not so screwy.' Coll >, ca 1890, S.E. Ex S.E. *screw*, a miser. 2. Drunk (cf. SCREWED): 1820, Creevey: coll >, ca 1890, S.E.; ob. 3. (Of horses) unsound: 1852, Smedley, 'It's like turning a screwy horse out to grass': coll >, ca 1890, S.E. Ex SCREW, n., 5.

scribbler's luck. 'An empty purse and a full hand', *Pelican*, 3 Dec. 1898: coll from ca 1890.

scribe. A bad writer: journalistic: ca 1870–90.

***scrieve,** see SCREEVE.

scrimmage. A free-fight, scuffle, or confused struggle: coll: 1780, Johnson (*skrimage*); 1826, Fenimore Cooper (*skrimmage*); 1844, *Catholic Weekly Instructor* (*scrimmidge*); 1859, H., 1st ed. (*scrimmage*). Ex S.E. sense, a skirmish, prob. via dial.

scrimshander, see SCRIMSHAW.

scrimshank, n., see SCRIMSHAW.

scrimshank; occ. **skrim-.** v.i., to shirk work: military (—1890). Kipling, 1893. Prob. a back-formation from:

scrimshanker; occ. **skrimshanker.** A shirker: military (—1890). *Tit-Bits*, 26 April 1890, 'Besides the dread of being considered a skrimshanker, a soldier dislikes the necessary restraints of a hospital.' Etymology obscure: perhaps a perversion of SCOWBANKER. The importance of the subject may be gauged from the fact that in 1843 there appeared a book entitled *On Feigned and Factitious Diseases, chiefly of Soldiers and Seamen.*

scrimshanking; skrim-. vbl n. and ppl adj. ex SCRIMSHANK, v.

scrimshaw (work); occ. **scrimshander, -y.** Mostly U.S. Small objects, esp. ornaments, made by seamen in their leisure: nautical: from ca 1850: s. >, ca 1880, coll >, ca 1910, S.E., as the v. has prob. always been. Etymology unknown, though the word is prob. either ex, or influenced by, the surname *Scrimshaw*. On whaling-ships, also *scrimshank*, which may be the source of SCRIMSHANKER.

scrip. A small (gen. written-upon) piece of paper: from ca 1615: S.E. until ca 1680, then c. till early C.19, then dial.; in c., esp. in BLOT THE SCRIP, it occ. = a bond. ?ex *scrap*: cf.:

scrip-scrap. Odds and ends: coll: C.19–20. Reduplication on *scrap*.

***scripper.** He who, in a swindle, keeps watch: c.: late C.16–early 17. Greene, describing 'high law'. ?etymology, unless ex †Scots *scrip*, to jeer.

***scrive,** see SCREEVE, n.

***scroby,** or **claws, (for breakfast), be tipped the.** 'To be whipt before the justices', Grose, 1st ed.: c. (orig. at least) of ca 1780–1850. The C.18 form is *be tipped the scroby*; *claws* came ca 1810, *for breakfast* (rare with *scroby*) was added about the same time; from ca 1850 (†by 1890), the term survived as *get scroby* (H., 1st ed., 1859, 'to be whipped in prison before the justices'). See TIP, v.; with *claws* cf. CAT-O'-NINE-TAILS; *scroby* is a mystery unless perchance it = *scruby*, scurvy, here used fig. (cf. *do the dirty on*).

scroo(d)ge, see SCROUGE, v.

scroof. A sponger: c. or low (—1823); †by 1890. A variant form of *scruff*, scurf, hence anything worthless.

***scroof,** v.i. To sponge or live on a person; v.t., *scroof with*: c.: ca 1840–1910. Perhaps ex the n. Whence *scroofer*, a parasite: same status and period.

***scrope.** A farthing: c. of ca 1710–1820. Hall; Grose, 2nd ed. ?origin.

scroudge, see SCROUGE, v.

scrouge; occ. **scrowge.** A crush; a crowd: low coll: 1839. C. Keene, 1887, 'I went to the Academy "Swarry" last night – the usual scrouge.' Ex:

scrouge, the earliest and gen. form; also **scroo(d)ge** (C.19–20), **scroudge** (C.19–20), **scrowge** (C.19–20), **skrouge** (C.19–20), and **skrowdge** (C.18). v.t. to crowd; to inconvenience by pressing against or by encroaching on the space of: low coll: mid-C.18–20. Ex *scruze*, to squeeze, 'still preserved, at least in its corruption, *to* *scrouge*, in the London jargon', Johnson, 1755. 2. v.i. in same senses: from ca 1820. (The vbl n. *scrouging* is fairly gen.)

scrouperize. To coït: a rather literary coll: mid-C.17–early 18. Translations of Rabelais. cf. later S.E. *scroop*, to scrape.

scrousher. An old, esp. if broken-down, gold-prospector or digger: New Zealand: since ca 1862; long merely historical. Perhaps an imitative word. 2. Hence(?), a prostitute: low Australian: late C.19–20.

scrovie, -y. A useless hand shipped as an able-bodied seaman: nautical: late C.19–20. Cognate with S.E. *scruffy*: cf. SCROOF.

scrowge, see SCROUGE, V.

scrub. 'One who pays not his whack at the tavern', Bee: public-house coll: ca 1820–60. Ex *scrub*, a shabby fellow. 2. A small (dirty or slovenly) boy: Christ's Hospital: since ca 1860. 3. Handwriting: Christ's Hospital: mid-C.19–20. Ex sense 2 of:

scrub, v. To drudge: coll: late C.19–20. Ex scrubbing floors, steps, etc. 2. v.t. to write fast: Christ's Hospital: mid-C.19–20. Ex L. *scribere.* 3. To reprimand: naval: late C.19–20.

scrub and wash clothes. A substitute expression in reading aloud for a word suddenly come upon which the reader cannot pronounce: naval coll: late C.19–20.

scrub-dangler. A wild bullock: ca 1885–1920. cf. SCRUBBER, 1.

scrub(b)ado. The itch: mid-C.17–early 19; coll on †S.E. *scrub*, the same.

scrubber. An animal living in the scrub: Australian coll >, ca 1900, S.E.: 1859, H. Kingsley in *Geoffrey Hamlyn.* 2. Hence, a person living there: 1890, 'Rolf Boldrewood'. 3. An outsider; in university circles, 'one who will not join in the life of the place' (cf. the Oxford SMUG): Australian: 1868; slightly ob. Ex sense 1, as is: 4. Any starved-looking or ill-bred animal: Australian coll (—1898). cf. the Australian j. *scrub-bull*, an inferior bull or bullock.

scrubbing. A flogging of four cuts: Winchester: ca 1840–1900. Mansfield, 'The ordinary punishment was called scrubbing.' Ex gen. coll of ca 1810–50, often in sense of defeat.

scrubbing-brush. The pubic hair: low: mid-C.19–20. 2. A loaf containing more bran and chaff than flour: Australian: from ca 1880.

scruey. See SCREWY, 2. Thackeray, 1855.

scruff. Newfoundland s. of ca 1860–1900. *Figaro*, 25 Nov. 1870, quoting from the *Montreal News*, on 'Codland Habits': 'The best society is called "merchantable", that being the term for fish of the best quality; while the lowest stratum is "scruff" or "dun".' Ex ob. S.E. *scruff* applied to anything valueless or contemptible.

scruff, v. To hang: C.19 coll. Ex *scruff*, the nape of the neck. 2. To manhandle; to attack: Australian coll: late C.19–20. i.e. take by the scruff of the neck.

scrum. A scrimmage in Rugby football: coll: 1888. 2. Hence, a crowd or RAG (11): Rugby School from the 1880s.

scrumdolious. SCRUMPTIOUS, of which it is an elaboration; late C.19–20.

scrump, see SKRIMP.

scrumptious. First rate, excellent, 'glorious': coll: 1859, H., 1st ed.; 1865, Meredith, 'Hang me, if ever I see such a scrumptious lot.' Ex U.S. coll sense, stylish (of things), handsome (of persons). 2. The sense 'fastidious, hard to please' is by the O.E.D. queried as U.S. only: perhaps orig. U.S. (whence the O.E.D.'s quotation, 1845), but app. current in England ca 1855–75, for the life-time edd. of H. define the word as 'nice, particular, beautiful'. Prob. ex dial. sense of mean, stingy; sense 1, therefore, as W. points out, may have been influenced by *sumptuous.*

scrumptiously. The adv. of the preceding: coll: from not later than 1880.

scruncher. A glutton: coll: from ca 1860. Ex *scrunch*, to bite *crushingly.*

scud. A fast runner: schools': 1857, Hughes in *Tom Brown*, 'I say . . . you ain't a bad scud'; ob. Ex *scud*, to move quickly. 2. Hence, a fast run: from ca 1870; slightly ob. cf.:

scud, v. (Of persons) to run: naval: late C.18–mid-19. Ex the S.E. nautical sense.

scuddick, the gen. form; also **scuddock, scurrick, scuttick** (mostly dial.), **skiddi(c)k** (id.), and **skuddick.** An extremely small sum or coin, amount or object: s. and dial.: from ca 1780; in C.20, only dial. 'Jon Bee', 1823, 'Used negatively; "not a scuddick" . . . "Every scuddick gone"; "she gets not a scuddick from me".' Perhaps ex †S.E. *scud*, refuse; more prob. ex dial. *scud*, a wisp of straw, despite the fact that this sense is not recorded until 1843 – many dial. terms were almost certainly existent 'ages' before their earliest appearance in print. 2. In c. of ca 1820–60, a halfpenny: only in form *scurrick.*

***scuff.** A(ny) crowd: c.: from late 1870s. *Macmillan's Magazine*, 1879 (XL, 501), 'This got a scuff round us': 'Dagonet' Sims in the *Referee*, 12 Feb. 1888. Ex more gen. S.E. sense, a noisy crowd.

***scuffle-hunter.** One who hangs about the docks on the pretence of looking for work but actually to steal anything that comes his way: c. and nautical s. from ca 1790; ob. Colquhoun's *Police of the Metropolis*, 1796.

scuffy. Inferior, contemptible: Christ's Hospital (—1887). Prob. ex *scurfy*.

***scufter.** A policeman: Northern c. (cf. BULKY): ca 1855–90. Ex either *scuffe*, to throw up dust in walking (cf. dial. *scuff*, to shuffle), or, more likely, *scuff*, to buffet.

scug; skug. (Latter very rare in C.20.) An untidy or ill-mannered or morally undeveloped boy: a shirker at games; one 'undistinguished in person, in games, or social qualities': Eton and Harrow: from ca 1820. Westmacott, 1825, refers it to *sluggish*; perhaps, however, ex Scots and Northern *scug* (*skug*), a pretence; ex Yorkshire and Lancashire dial. *scug*, scum; but possibly SCADGER.

scuggish; scuggy. adj. to the preceding.

scull. The head of a college: university (—1785); ob. by 1864 (see H., 3rd ed.), †by 1890. Punning *skull*. 2. 'A one horse chaise or buggy', Grose, 1st ed. (also *sculler*): ca 1780–1830. 3. See SCULLS.

scull-race. An examination: university: ca 1810–70. Ex SCULL, 1.

scull-thatcher. A wig-maker: coll (—1785); ob. 2. Whence, a hatter: C.19–20; ob.

sculler, see SCULL, 2.

scullery-science. Phrenology: jocular coll: ca 1830–60. Chorley, 1836. Punning *skull*.

sculls. A waterman plying sculls: coll: C.18–20. cf. OARS.

sculp. A piece of sculpture: coll: 1883, *Daily News*, 18 Jan. cf.:

sculp, v.t. To sculpture: from ca 1780: S.E. until ca 1880, then (gen. jocular) coll. R. L. Stevenson, 1887. 2. Hence, v.i.: coll: 1889, W. E. Norris; 1893, Kipling, 'Men who write, and paint, and sculp'.

***scum.** Enough: c. of ca 1720–50. *Street Robberies Consider'd*, 1728. ?etymology.

scupper. To take by surprise and then massacre: military: 1885 (the Suakin Expedition). 2. Hence, to kill: military: late C.19–20. ?ex COOPER, to ruin.

scuppered. Killed, dead in battle: naval, hence military: late C.19–20. Ex preceding.

scurf, adj. (Of labour) cheap: Cockney: ca 1845–90. Mayhew, II, 1851, cf. the n., 2.

scurf. A mean, a 'scurvy' fellow: ca 1850–1915. Mayhew, 1851, '"There's a scurf!" said one; "He's a regular scab," cried another.' cf. SCAB, n., 1. 2. A SCAB (n., 2): from ca 1850. 3. Also, an employer paying less than the standard wage: from ca 1850. Like sense 2, first in Mayhew.

***scurf,** v. To apprehend, arrest: c. of ca 1810–50. ?ex S.E. *scruff*.

***scurrick,** see SCUDDICK.

scuse or **'scuse.** (Esp. in *'scuse me!*) To excuse: late C.15–20: S.E. until C.19, then (when not, as occ., deliberately humorous) coll verging on illiteracy. T. E. Brown, 1887, ''Scuse me, your honour.'

scushy. Money: Scottish: late C.18–mid-19. Shirrefs, *Poems*, 1790. Origin?

scut. The female pudend or pubic hair: coll: late C.16–20; ob. Ex *scut*, a short upright tail, esp. of hare, rabbit, deer. (Implied in Shakespeare, Cotton, D'Urfey, and several broadsides, but not, I believe, defined as the pudend before Grose, 1st ed.) Also, the behind: C.18. Ned Ward, 1709. 2. A person; occ. a number of persons: coll and dial., either jocose or pejorative: from early 1890s. Ex S.E. sense.

scutter. To go hastily and fussily or excitedly or timorously: coll and dial.: from ca 1780. Mrs Delany, 1781, 'She staid about 24 hours, then scutter'd away to Badminton.' The vbl n. is frequent, the ppl adj. rare. Prob. ex *scuttle* on *scatter*. Imm. ex dial.

scuttick, see SCUDDICK.

scuttle. An undignified withdrawal: political: 1884; slightly ob. Ex:

scuttle, v.i. To withdraw with unseemly haste from the occupation, or the administration, of a country: political: 1883, Lord Randolph Churchill in a speech delivered on 18 Dec.; slightly ob. Ex S.E. sense, 'to run with quick, hurried steps'. 2. v.i. to shout in order to attract the attention of the masters to one's being roughly treated: Christ's Hospital: mid-C.19–20; ob. Whence *scuttle-cat*, one who does this: †by 1903. 3. To deflower: orig. nautical: mid-C.19–20. Whence *scuttle a ship*, to take a maidenhead. 4. To stab: c.: from ca 1860; ob. 5. To go, to depart: schoolboys' s. (from ca 1906) now verging on coll. cf. S.E. *scuttle away*. 6. See SCUTTLE A NOB. 7. See SCUTTLING, 2.

scuttle, do a back. To engage in an act of sodomy: low: late C.19–20.

scuttle, on the. On a bout of drinking or a round of whoring: from ca 1870; slightly ob. cf. preceding entry and see SCUTTLE, v., 3.

scuttle a nob. To break a head: pugilistic: from ca 1810; ob. Randall.

scuttle a ship, see SCUTTLE, v., 3. **scuttle-cat,** see SCUTTLE, v., 2.

scuttle-mouth. A small oyster in a very large shell: costermongers': 1848, though first recorded in vol. I (1851) of Mayhew's *London Labour*.

scuttler. An advocate of SCUTTLE (see the n.): political: 1884 (O.E.D.); ob.

scuttling. The policy implied in SCUTTLE, v., 1: political: 1884; ob. 2. As street-fighting between youthful groups, *scuttling*, like *scuttle* the v. (1890) and the n. (1864), is gen. considered S.E.: perhaps orig. coll or dial.

'sdeath!, 'sdeynes!, 'sdiggers! Abbr. *God's death!*, *deynes* or *dines!*, and *diggers!*: resp. C.17–18, then archaic; early C.17 (Jonson); late C.17. All coll except perhaps the first, which should perhaps be considered S.E.; all may be euphemistic, though this is to underestimate the power of colloquialism, which is at least as great as that of euphemism.

'sdheart, see 'SHEART.

sea?, who wouldn't sell a farm and go to. A nautical c.p. spoken when something unpleasant or extremely difficult has to be done: mid-C.19–20.

sea-blessing. A curse; curses: jocular nautical coll: late C.19–20.

sea-coal. Money: C.19, mainly nautical. On *sea-cole* = sea kale. See COLE. 2. Smuggled spirits: mid-C.18–mid-C.19.

sea-cook, son of a. A term of abuse: nautical coll: 1806, John Davis, *The Post-Captain*. M. Scott, 1836, 'You supercilious son of a sea-cook'.

sea-coot. A seaman, esp. if of fresh water or scant ability: nautical (—1887); ob. Prob. ex preceding, with a pun on (*silly*) COOT.

sea-crab. A sailor: nautical: ca 1780–1890. cf. SCALY FISH.

sea daddy. A staid rating: naval: since ca 1900. Granville, 'Usually a badgeman who acts as mentor to new entries'.

sea-grocer. A purser: a nautical nickname: from ca 1860; ob.

sea-lawyer. A shark; esp. a tiger-shark: coll nickname: from ca 1810. 2. A grey snapper: id. (—1876). 3. Ex sense 1, a captious and argumentative, or a scheming, fo'c's'le hand: nautical coll: from ca 1820. (cf. BUSH LAWYER.) Whence *sea-lawyering*, such behaviour: mid-C.19–20.

sea-pheasant. A bloater or a kipper: nautical: late C.19–20.

sea-pork. The flesh of young whales: id.: id.

sea-rover. A herring: mostly London (—1890). Gen. in *a doorstep and a sea-rover*, a slice of bread and a herring, and *doorsteps and* (*a*) *sea-rover*, a herring sandwich, as in Whiteing's *No. 5 John Street*, 1899.

sea-toss. 'A toss overboard into the sea' (*Century Dict.*): coll: late C.19–20.

sea-wag. An ocean-going vessel: nautical: late C.19–20; ob.

sea William. A civilian: naval: ca 1800–50.

seagly, see SEDGLEY CURSE.

seagull. An old sailorman retired from the sea; nautical: late C.19–20; ob.

seal. A preacher's convert: ecclesiastical: ca 1850–80. Conybeare, 1853. Either ex *set one's seal to* or ex *under* (*one's*) *seal*. cf. OWNED, BE.

seal, v. To impregnate (a woman): C.19–20; ob. cf. SEW UP.

***sealer.** 'One that gives Bonds and Judgements for Goods and Money', B.E.: c.: late C.17–early 19. Shadwell, Grose. Also known as SQUEEZE-WAX.

seals. Testicles: C.19–20; ob. Because they seal a sexual bargain.

seaman if he carries a millstone will have a quail out of it, a. A mid-C.17–mid-18 semi-proverbial c.p. alluding to the ingenuity displayed by sailors as regards meat and drink.

seaman's disgrace. A foul anchor: nautical coll: late C.19–20.

sear; sere. The female pudend: coll: late C.16–17. Partly ex *sear*, the touch-hole of a pistol, and partly ex *light* (or *tickle*) *of the sear* or *sere*, wanton.

seaside moths. Bed vermin: middle classes' (—1909); ob.

seat. A rider: sporting coll (—1887). Ex *have a good seat* (*in the saddle*).

seat of honour, shame, vengeance. The posteriors; jocular coll (in C.20 ob.): resp. 1792, Wolcot (adumbrated in Bailey's *Erasmus*, 1725); 1821, Combe, and rare; 1749, Smollett – likewise rare. Ex the fact that 'he was commonly accounted the most honourable that was first seated, and that this honour was commonly done to the posteriors' (Bailey).

seat of magistracy. 'Proctor's authority', Egan's Grose: Oxford University: ca 1820–50.

Sebastianist. A Mr Micawber, one who believes that something good will turn up some day: coll (late C.19–20) among the English Colony at Lisbon. Ex the Portuguese. In 1578, King Sebastian was defeated in Morocco and never again heard of: but half Portugal, refusing to credit his death, believed that he would return and lead them to victory.

sec. A second: coll: from ca 1880.

second; third. Second mate; third mate: nautical coll: mid-C.19–20. Often in address, as in 'Go easy, third!' 2. (Also adj.) Second-hand; *seconds*, second-hand goods: dealers' coll: C.19–20.

second dickey. The second mate: nautical: late C.19–20.

second fiddle, see FIDDLE, SECOND.

second greaser. Second mate under sail: nautical: late C.19–20. Bowen.

second-hand daylight. The light of another world: non-aristocratic: ca 1890–1910. Ex a music-hall song. cf.:

second-hand sun. Refracted sunlight: poor people's coll (—1909).

second-hand woman. A widow: Army in India: 1859–ca 1900.

second-liker. A second (e.g. drink) like – the same as – the first: taverns': 1884; slightly ob.

second mate's nip. A full measure of liquor: nautical coll: late C.19–20. Bowen.

second over the head. Rather worse than the first: *Conway* cadets': late C.19–20.

second picture. The 'tableau upon the rising of the curtain to applause, after it has fallen at the end of an act, or a play': theatrical coll: 1885. Ware.

second-timer. A prisoner convicted for the second time: coll: late C.19–20.

secret, in the grand. Dead: coll: from ca 1780; ob. cf. *join the great majority* and contrast:

***secret, let into the.** Swindled, e.g. at horse-racing, sports, games: late C.17–early 19: c. >, ca 1730, s. Contrast preceding entry.

sect. Sex: C.13–20: S.E. until C.19, then coll until ca 1850; then low coll till C.20, when sol. unless deliberately humorous. cf. PERSUASION.

Sedgley (occ. Seagly) curse. A semi-proverbial coll of ca 1620–1840. Fletcher, ca 1625, 'A seagly curse light on him, which is, Pedro: The feind ride through him booted, and spurd, with a Sythe at's back'; Ray; Defoe; Scott. Ex a town in Staffordshire; but I cannot improve on Apperson's 'I know not why'.

see, v.i. To coït: low s. verging on c., for it is a prostitutes' word: C.19–20 (? ob.). Also *see stars lying on one's back*.

see! or **you see.** A conversational tag among those who possess a meagre vocabulary: late (?mid-) C.19–20.

see, I. I agree or understand (as comment on an explanation or an argument): coll: C.19–20.

see a man or, occ., **a friend(, go and).** To have a drink: late C.19–20, as is *see a man about a dog*, loosely in same sense, properly to visit a woman sexually. Often, too, = to go to the lavatory (to urinate only): men's: late C.19–20.

see about it, I'll. A coll evasion: mid-C.19–20.

see and . . . (another v.). To take care to (do something): coll: from ca 1760; slightly ob. Mrs F. Sheridan, ca 1766, 'David . . . told me he'd see and get me another every jot as pretty.'

see anything, as in 'Have you seen anything?' – 'Have you had your monthly courses?': a lower and lower-middle class feminine euphemism: mid-C.19–20 >, 1910, coll.

see (someone's) **arse for dust, you couldn't.** He departed in a tremendous hurry: c.p.: late C.19–20.

see as far into a millstone (or **milestone**) **as . . .** see MILLSTONE, LOOK. **see candles,** see SEE STARS.

see (a person) **coming.** To impose on; esp., to charge too much: coll: late C.19–20. Gen. in some such phrase as 'He saw you coming,' i.e. saw you were gullible and so took advantage of you. Perhaps ex the Fr. *voir quelqu'un venir*, which means the same.

see him (her, etc.) damned or **further** or **hanged** or **to hell** or **to the devil first, I'll.** I certainly don't or won't agree to his proposal, etc.: coll: resp. 1631, Heywood; mid-C.19–20; 1596, Shakespeare; C.19–20.

see London, see SHOW LONDON.

see one's aunt. To defecate: euphemistic s. > coll: mid-C.19–20; ob.

see-otches, see SEEO.

see stars or **spots** or **candles.** To be dazed: coll: resp. late C.19–20, mid-C.19–20, and mid-C.18–mid-19. Smollett, 1749, 'He . . . made me see more candles than ever burnt in Solomon's temple.'

see stars lying on one's back, see SEE, 1.

see the breeze. To enjoy the fresh air (on a heath): Cockney: ca 1877–1900. cf. TASTE THE SUN.

see the devil. To become drunk: mid-C. 19–20; ob.

see the king. To be very experienced, knowing, alert: ca 1870–90. An English modification of the orig. U.S. *to see the* ELEPHANT.

see things. To experience hallucinations: coll: late (?mid-) C.19–20.

see through. To 'get through' (a meal): coll: 1863 (O.E.D.); slightly ob.

seed, run to, see RUN TO SEED.

seed-plot. The female pudend: C.19–20 (ob.): coll verging on S.E.

seedy. Of a SHADY character: low: ca 1780–1910. G. Parker, 'A queer procession of seedy brims and kids'. Ex *seedy*, shabby. (In other senses – shabby, almost penniless, in poor health – perhaps orig. coll; but the O.E.D. does not think so.)

seedy(-boy). A Negro: Anglo-Indian coll: mid-C.19–20. Also *sidi(-boy)*. Ironically ex Urdu *sidi*, my lord.

seek others and lose oneself. To play the fool: coll: late C.16–17. Florio.

Seeley's pigs. Pig iron, orig. and properly in Government dockyards: nautical: ca 1870–1910. Ex Mr Seeley, the M.P. for Lincoln, who revealed that some of the yards were half-paved with iron pigs.

seems to me. Apparently: coll: 1888, 'John Strange Winter', 'Seems to me women get like dogs – they get their lessons pretty well fixed in their minds after a time.'

seen dead with, (he, I, etc.) would not be. I detest (properly a person, loosely a thing); it, he, etc., is disgusting: coll: late C.19–20. Lyell.

seen the elephant, see ELEPHANT.

seen the French King, to have. To be drunk: s.: (—1650).

seeo (occ. see-o). Shoes: back s. (—1859). (Instead of *seohs*.) Baumann records the form *see-otches*.

***seer.** An eye (gen. *the seer*): c. (—1785) > low s.; very ob. cf.:

sees. The eyes: c. or low s.: from ca 1810. Moore, 1819, 'To close up their eyes – alias, to sew up their sees', in a boxing context. cf. SEER and DAYLIGHTS.

seldoms, the. Money, esp. cash: mostly naval: ?ca 1810–50. Because seldom come by, hard to get.

self, be. (e.g. *be himself.*) To be in one's normal health or state of mind: coll: 1849, Macaulay; *Daily News*, 23 May 1883, on a cricket match, 'Mr Grace was all himself.' Also, late C.19–20 (very rarely of things), *to feel like* (e.g. *one-)self*. cf. *be one's own man or woman.* 2. Hence, of things, be in its usual place: mid-C.19–20.

self and company (or **wife,** etc., etc.) is jocular coll, excusable only as a jocularity: late C.19–20.

sell. A successful deception, hoax or swindle: 1850, Smedley. Ex the v. 2. Hence, a planned hoax, deception, swindle: from ca 1860. 3. Ex sense 1, a (great) disappointment: 1860, H., 2nd ed.; 1874, Mrs H. Wood, 'It's an awful sell . . . no hunting, and no shooting, and no nothing.'

sell, v. To take in, deceive; impose on, trick, swindle: C.17–20. Jonson, 1607, Volpone, 'When bold, each tempts the other again, and all are sold'; Smedley; 'Rolf Boldrewood'. Prob. ex *sell*, to betray (a person, cause, party, or country). **2.** See SOLD OUT.

sell (a person) **a pup,** see PUP, SELL A.

***sell** (a person) **blind.** To deceive or swindle utterly: c. (—1887).

selopas. Apples: back s. (—1859). (A few back s. terms are only in the pl: cf. PINURT POTS; SEEO; SPINSRAP; STARPS; STOOB.)

s'elp (loosely, **selp**). So help, esp. in *s'elp me God*: C.14–20: S.E. until C.19, then coll. Kipling, 1888, 'S'elp me, I believe 'e's dead.' cf. SWELP and:

s'elp me, Bill Arline!; s'elp me tater! Synonyms of S'ELP ME BOB!: proletarian: resp. ca 1870–1910 and from ca 1855 (ob.).

s'elp me Bob (bob)! So help me God!: low coll: from ca 1823, 'Jon Bee'. J. Payn; 'Pomes' Marshall. cf. preceding entry and S'ELP MY GREENS.

s'elp me never! 'May God never help me if I lie now': low (—1909).

s'elp my greens! So help me God!: low coll: ca 1850–1910. Mayhew. Obviously *greens* (q.v., however) jocularly varies *Bob*, which itself euphemizes or perverts *God*. See preceding three entries and SWELP and SWOP MY BOB!

semi-bejan, see BEJAN.

semi-quotes. Single (instead of double) quotation-marks: coll: world of books, esp. and orig. printing: late C.19–20. See QUOTE.

seminary. The female pudend: mid-C.19–

20; ob. Punning *seminary*, a school, college, etc., and *semen* = *liquor seminale.*

senal pervitude. Penal servitude: cheap urban witticism: ca 1900–14. In addition to the switch-over of initial letters, there is a glancing pun on *senile.*

send, see COVENTRY; FLEA IN (ONE'S) EAR; and the next entries.

send along. To send to gaol; esp., to cause to be arrested: Australian coll: since ca 1870.

send for Gulliver! A Society c.p. (1887–ca 95) on 'some affair not worth discussion. From a cascadescent incident' in Part I of *Gulliver's Travels* (Ware).

send (a person) **for yard-wide pack-thread.** To despatch on a fool's errand: coll: ca 1800–60.

send her down, Hughie! An Australian c.p. expressing urgent desire for rain: late C.19–20.

send in. To drive in: ca 1810–60. *Lex. Bal.*, 'Hand down the jemmy and send it in; apply the crow to the door, and drive it in.'

send-off. A God-speed: coll: orig. (1872), U.S.; anglicized ca 1875. 2. Hence, a start in life, in business, etc.: 1894, A. Morrison, 'A good send-off in the matter of clothes'. 3. Occ. as adj.: 1876, Besant & Rice, 'A beautiful send-off notice'.

send round the hat, see HAT, PASS ROUND THE.

send up. To commit to prison: orig. U.S. (1852); anglicized by 1887, when Baumann recorded it without comment on its American origin. *Westminster Gazette*, 30 April 1897, 'Two prisoners . . . occupied the prison-van . . . Burns was being "sent up" for wife-beating, and Tannahill for theft': s.

sender. A severe blow: from ca 1800: boxing s. Perhaps ex *send spinning.*

senior, see JUNIOR.

sensation. Half a glass of sherry: Australian: ca 1859–90. Prob. ex sense 3, though this is recorded later. 2. In England, a quartern of gin: 1859, H., 1st ed. 3. A (very) small quantity, esp. of liquor, occ. of food, rather rarely of other things: mid-C.19–20: coll. Lit., just so much as can be perceived by the senses; cf. the French *soupçon.*

sense, it stands to. It stands to reason, it's only sensible: coll: 1859, George Eliot. Ex †*it is to* (*good*) *sense*, on *it stands to reason.*

sensitive plant. The nose: pugilistic c.: ca 1815–60. *Boxiana*, II, 1818; III, 1821; IV, 824.

sent. Sent to prison: lower classes' coll: late C.19–20. *People*, 20 March 1898.

sent ashore. Marooned: nautical coll: late C.19–20.

sent to the skies. Killed, murdered: lower middle classes' (—1909).

sentimental hairpin. An affected, insignificant girl: Society: ca 1880–1900. Ware.

sentimental journey, arrive at the end of the. To coït with a woman: from ca 1870; very ob. F. & H. says 'common' (i.e. used by the lower classes): should not this be read as 'cultured'? Ex the conclusion of Sterne's *Sentimental Journey*, 'I put out my hand and caught hold of the *fille-de-chambre's* —. FINIS.' The unworldly postulate 'hand'; the worldly, 'CUNT': to those who know their Sterne, *verb. sap.*

sentinel. A candle used at a wake. Anglo-Irish coll: mid-C.19–20. Punningly: because it keeps watch.

sentry, on. Drunk: rather low: ca 1885–1914. Ex *on sentry-go*: but why? Perhaps home-service sentries are tempted to take a tot too many in the laudable desire to keep out the cold on night-duty.

sentry-box, Chelsea Hospital to a, see LOMBARD STREET TO A . . .

***separate**; but extremely rare in the singular. A period of separate confinement in prison, esp. during the first year of a sentence: from ca 1860: prison c. >, ca 1890, low s. *Cornhill Magazine*, 1862, vol. vi, p. 640; Anon., *Five Years' Penal Servitude*, 1877. Abbr. *separate confinement.*

Sepoy. Any Indian foot-soldier, esp. an infantryman: Regular Army coll: late C.19–20.

sepulchre. A large, flat cravat: London middle classes: ca 1870–85. Ex the 'sins' it covered.

serag, see HEAD-SERAG.

seraglietto. 'A lowly, sorry Bawdy-house, a meer Dog-hole', B.E.: coll: late C.17–18. A diminutive of:

seraglio. A brothel: coll: late C.17–early 19. Ex *seraglio*, a harem, though *seraglio* itself was orig. incorrect when used for *serai*, a Turkish palace. (The term > gen. ca 1750 with Mrs Goadby, 'the great Goadby', who kept an excellent house in Berwick Street, Soho: Beresford Chancellor, *Pleasure Haunts of London.*)

sere, see SEAR. **serene, -eno,** see ALL SERENE.

Sergeant Kite or **Snap.** A recruiting sergeant: allusive coll: from ca 1850; ob. by 1900.

sergeant-major. A fat loin of mutton: butchers': late C.19–20. Ex the usual plumpness of sergeant-majors, with whom the cooks and the quarter-master's staff know that it pays to stand well. 2. A large piece of mutton in the rib part: butchers' (—1889). Barrère & Leland, 'From the white stripes like sergeant's stripes'. 3. In c., dating from ca 1840 but now ob.: 'a large cold-chisel . . . for cutting through metal plates', p. 422 of '*No. 747*', *The Autobiography of a Gipsy*, 1891 – the reference valid for 1845.

sergeant-major's brandy and soda. A gold-laced stable jacket: military: ca 1885–1914.

sergeant-major's wash-cat. A new kit: cavalry: ca 1885–1910. 2. A troop's store-man: ca 1885–1914. ?because he supplied a basin.

Sergeant Snap, see SERGEANT KITE.

Seringapatam. Ham: rhyming s.: late C.19–early 20. (J. Redding Ware, *Passing English*, 1909.)

serpent, stung by a. Got with child: coll: C.19–20; ob. Ex swelling.

serpent by the tail, hold a. To act foolishly: coll: C.19–20; ob. Ray, 1813.

serve, v. To treat in a specified – and, gen., unpleasant or inequitable – manner: C.13–20: S.E. until 1850, then – except in formal contexts – coll. 2. To rob, thus 'I served him for his thimble,' I robbed him of his watch: c.: from ca 1810; ob. 3. To convict and sentence: c.: from ca 1810; ob. 4. To injure, wound, treat roughly: c.: ca 1810–90. cf. next two entries. 5. To serve a term of imprisonment: criminals' coll (rather than c.): late C.19–20. 6. To impose a punishment: Bootham School coll: late C.19–20.

serve out, v. To take revenge on, to punish; retaliate on (a person) *for* . . .: from ca 1815: boxing s. >, ca 1830, gen. coll. *Sporting Magazine*, 1817, 'The butcher was so completely served out, that he resigned all pretentions to victory.' By 'an ironic application of nautical *serve out* (*grog*, etc.)', W. 2. To smash (a fence): hunting s.: 1862.

***serve out and out.** To kill: c. of ca 1810–90. cf. SERVE OUT.

serve out slops. To administer punishment at the gangway: naval: ca 1790–1890. cf. SERVE OUT, 1.

serve right. Coll only in (*and*) *serve* (e.g. *you*) *right!*, and *serves* (e.g. *you*) *right!*, which indicate satisfaction that someone has got his deserts: from ca 1830. Dickens, 1837, 'Workhouse funeral – serve him right.'

serve the poor with a thump on the back with a stone. To be a miser: semi-proverbial coll: ca 1670–1750; Ray.

serves you right! see SERVE RIGHT.

service. An imposition: Bootham School: late C.19–20.

service-book, to have eaten one's, see TEETHWARD.

***service lay.** The DODGE by which one hires oneself out as a servant and then robs the house: c.: C.18. C. Hitchin, *The Regulator*, 1718.

sessions. To commit (one) to the sessions for trial: 1857, Mayhew.

sessions! Well, I'm blowed!: late C.19–20; ob. Ex dial. *sessions*, a fuss, disturbance, argument, difficulty, task.

set. Abbr. *dead set* (see SET, DEAD): 1829, *The Examiner* (O.E.D.): s. >, ca 1860, coll >, ca 1900, S.E.

set, v. To fix on as prey or victim; to watch with a view to robbing; make a SET at: from ca 1670: perhaps orig. c., as also in late C.19–20 Australian. Gay, in *The Beggar's Opera*, 1727, 'There will be deep play to-night at Marybone, . . . I'll give you the hint who is worth setting.' cf. SET, DEAD, 3, and SET, HAVE.

set, adj.; gen. **all set.** In the late C.17–18, applied to 'desperate fellows, ready for any kind of mischief' (Duncombe). 2. See SET, HAVE.

***set, dead.** Esp. in *make a dead set at*. '*Dead Set*, a Term used by Thief-catchers when they have a Certainty of seizing some of their Clients', *A New Canting Dict.*, 1725: †by 1850. 2. Also, ca 1780–1860, 'a concerted scheme to defraud a person by gaming', Grose, 1st ed.: like sense 1, it is c. 3. The extant senses – a determined onslaught, an incessant attempt, and (in sport) an abrupt stop – date from ca 1820, derive from those two c. senses, and are gen. considered S.E.: prob., however, they were orig. coll.

set, have (a person). 'To have [him] marked down for punishment or revenge', C. J. Dennis: low (esp. in Australia): from ca 1890. cf. SET, DEAD.

set about. To attack, set upon: coll: 1879, Horsley, 'He set about me with a strap till he was tired.'

set (one's) child a-crying. (Of a watchman) to spring or sound one's rattle: fast life: ca 1810–40. *Spy*, 1825.

set (something) **in a crack.** To settle (a matter) quickly; e.g. *set a bet in a crack*, to wager smartly at two-up; *be set in a crack*, (of persons) to be comfortably placed (lit. or fig.), to be very pleased with circumstances: New Zealanders': from the 1890s. Perhaps ex the idea of doing a thing as sharply as the crack of a whip.

set jewels; gen. as vbl n., **setting jewels.** To purloin the best parts of a little-known (esp. if clever) book for incorporation in a new work by another author: literary coll: 1873, when originated by Charles Reade *à propos* of a flagrant instance published at Christmas, 1872; ob.

set-me-up, often preceded by **young.** One who sets himself up to be somebody: often pejoratively: late C.19–20.

set-out. A set or display of china, plate, etc.: coll: 1806, J. Beresford. 2. (Of food) a SPREAD (5): coll: 1809, Malkin. 3. A 'turn-out', i.e. a carriage 'and all': a mainly sporting coll: from ca 1810. 4. A person's costume or manner of dressing (cf. RIG-OUT); an outfit, equipment: coll: from ca 1830. 5. A public show or performance; an entertainment for a number of people; a party: coll: 1818, Lady Morgan. 6. Hence, a company or a set of people: from ca 1850: coll. 7. A to-do or fuss: (low) coll: late C.19–20.

set the hare's head to the goose giblets. To balance matters, to give as good as one gets: coll: C.17–early 18.

set to rights. To set right: coll: C.19–20. (Glascock, *Sketch-Book*, II, 1826.)

set-up. Bearing, carriage, port: coll (slightly ob.): 1890, T. C. Crawford.

set-up, adj. Conceited: coll and dial.: mid-C.19–20.

set up for, be. To be well supplied with: coll: 1863, Mrs Henry Wood, 'I'm set up for cotton gownds.' Ex S.E. *set up*, to establish or to equip in business, etc.

setta; occ. **setter.** Seven; sevenpence: Parlary (—1859). Ex It. *sette*.

***setter.** See SETTA. 2. An enticer to liquor or gambling; a confederate of swindlers or sharpers: c.: late C.16–17. Greene, 1592; ob. Ex the dog. 3. Hence, a person used by criminals to watch intended victims: c.: from ca 1640; ob. *Memoirs of John Hall.* 4. Hence, 'a Sergeant's Yeoman, or Bailiff's Follower, or Second, and an Excise-Officer to prevent the Brewers defrauding the King', B.E.: c. of late C.17–early 19. Also *setting-dog*. 5. A police spy; an informer to the police: from ca 1630: S.E. until ca 1850, then c. and low s. 6. A runner-up of prices: late C.17–20 (ob.): mostly among auctioneers.

setter, clock-. One who, to shorten a spell of duty, tampers with the clock: nautical coll: mid-C.19–20; slightly ob. cf. *eat* SAND. 2. Hence, a SEA-LAWYER (3): late C.19–20 (ob.): nautical.

***setting-dog,** see SETTER, 4. **setting jewels,** see SET JEWELS.

settle. To stun, finish, knock down: C.17–20: S.E. until ca 1750, then coll. Dickens; Kipling. 2. To give (a person) a life-sentence: c.: mid-C.19–20. ca 1850–70, it also = to transport as a convict. cf. WINDED-SETTLED.

settle (a person's) **hash,** see HASH, SETTLE ONE'S.

settlement-in-tail. An act of generation: legal: C.19–20; ob. (Pun.)

settler. A parting drink: mid-C.18–20; ob. M. Bishop, 1744. Because it is supposed to 'stabilize' the stomach. 2. A crushing remark: coll: from ca 1815. 3. A knockdown blow: coll: 1819, Moore, 'He tipp'd him a settler.' 4. Hence, any 'finisher' whatsoever: from ca 1820: coll.

settler's clock; settler's matches. A kookaburra; readily inflammable strips of bark: Australian coll: since ca 1870.

seven, be more than. To be wide-awake; knowing: coll: from ca 1875; slightly ob. A music-hall song of ca 1876 was entitled *You're More Than Seven*; Gissing, 1898. Occ. *more than twelve*.

seven, throw a. To die: Australian: late C.19–20; ob. A die has no '7'.

seven bells out of a man, knock. To knock him out; give him a thrashing: nautical: late C.19–20.

Seven Dials raker. A harlot 'who never smiles out of the Dials'; London costers' (—1909); very ob.

***seven(-)pennorth; sevenpence.** Seven years' penal transportation: c. of ca 1820–70.

seven-sided animal. (U.S. variant, C.19, *s.-s. son of a bitch.*) 'A one-eyed man or woman, each having a right side and a left side, a foreside and a backside, an outside, an inside, and a blind side,' Grose, 2nd ed.: low jocular, also Somersetshire dial.: ca 1785–1890. cf. GORMAGON.

seven-times-seven man. A 'hypocritical religionist': proletarian-satirical (—1909); ob. Perhaps *seven-times-seven* is meant to rhyme *heaven*; ?or because he outdoes Psalm cxix, 164.

seven ways for Sunday, looking, see LOOKING SEVEN WAYS . . .

sevendible. Very severe, strong, or sound: Northern Ireland: mid-C.19–20. 'Derived from sevendouble – that is, sevenfold – and . . . applied to linen cloth, a heavy beating, a harsh reprimand, &c.', H., 3rd ed. Coll rather than s., as in the adv. *sevendibly*: same period.

sevener. A criminal sentenced to seven years: coll: from the 1890s.

***sevenpence,** see SEVEN(-)PENNORTH.

severe. Excellent; very large or strong or hard to beat: orig. (1834) U.S. (esp. Kentucky), anglicized ca 1850. De Quincey in 1847 refers to it as 'Jonathan's phrase'.

severely. Greatly, excessively: coll: mid-C.19–20. Whyte-Melville. Ex SEVERE.

sew up. To impregnate (a woman): coll: C.19–20; ob. 2. See SEWED UP, 1–8.

sew up a person's stocking. To silence, confute: coll: 1859, C. Reade; ob.

sewed(-)up; occ. sewn up. Pregnant: coll (not upper nor middle class): C.19–20; slightly ob. 2. Exhausted: from ca 1825 (orig. of horses; not till 1837 of persons): as in Dickens's *Pickwick*; Smedley, 1850, 'I thought she'd have sewn me up at one time – the pace was terrific': slightly ob. 3. Cheated, swindled: 1838, Haliburton. 4. At a loss, nonplussed, brought to a standstill: 1855, Smedley; 1884, Clark Russell; slightly ob. 5. Severely punished; esp. with 'bunged-up' eyes: boxing: from ca 1860; ob. 6. (Ex senses 2, 7.) Sick: late C.19–20; slightly ob. 7. Drunk: —1818; 1829, Buckstone, 'This liquid . . . will sew him up'; ob. 8. Grounded: nautical coll: mid-C.19–20. Also *sued up*.

sewer, common. An indiscriminate tippler: coll bordering on S.E.: C.19–20. 2. The throat: mid-C.19–20; ob. cf. RED LANE.

sewn up. A variant of SEWED UP, esp. in senses 4, 6, 7.

'sflesh!, 'sfoot!, 'sgad! Coll euphemisms for *God's flesh!*, *foot!*, and *Egad!*: C.18, C.17, C.18.

shab. A low fellow: 1637, Bastwick; 1735, Dyche & Pardon, '*Shab*, a mean, sorry, pitiful Fellow, one that is guilty of low Tricks, &c'; 1851, Borrow. Ex *shab*, a sore. cf. SCAB, n., 1.

shab, v.i. To play low or mean tricks: mid-C.18–19; extant in dial. Johnson. Ex SHAB, n. 2. v.t., to rob; perhaps rather, to cheat or to deceive meanly: coll: ca 1780–1800. W. Hutton, 1787. 3. v.i., to run away: tramps' and Gypsies' c.: C.19–20. cf. much older S.E. *shab off*, to sneak away.

shab-rag. Shabby, damaged, very worn: from ca 1760: s. till mid-C.19, then dial. T. Bridges. Ex SHAB, n. The n., C.19–20, is solely dial. cf.:

shab(a)roon; also shabbaroon (C.18–19), **shabberoon** (C.17–18). A ragamuffin; a mean, shabby fellow; an otherwise disreputable or a mean-spirited person: late C.17–mid-19. B.E.; Ned Ward; Halliwell. Ex SHAB, n., on *picaroon* (cf. PICARO).

shabby, cut up, see CUT UP NASTY.

shabroon, see SHAB(A)ROON.

shack. A misdirected or a returned letter: Post Office: late C.19–early 20. Perhaps ex *shack*, 'grain fallen from the ear, and available for the feeding of pigs, poultry, etc.' (O.E.D.), or ex dial. *shack*, a vagabond, a worthless fellow.

shack, go. To share a parcel with one's school-fellows: Felsted: since ca 1875; ob. cf. Christ's Hospital *shag*, a share: ?*quelque-chose pour chaque personne* (or . . . *pour chacun*).

shack-per-swaw. Everyone for himself: London's East End and gen. London sporting (—1864). A corruption of Fr. *chacun pour soi*.

shack-stoner; occ. schack-s. A sixpence: low s., perhaps c.: ca 1890–1910. P. H. Emerson, *Signor Lippo*, 1893. ?ex *six-stoner*.

shade. A very small portion or quantity added or taken away: coll: mid-C.19–20. Ex *shade*, 'a tinge, a minute qualifying infusion' (O.E.D.).

***shade,** v. To keep secret: c.: late C.19–20; ob. Ex *shade*, to hide.

shadow. A new boy in the care of one who is not new (the 'substance') and learning the ropes from his temporary guardian: Westminster School: from ca 1860. Wm Lucas Collins, *Public Schools*, 1867. 2. A woman watching 'dress-women' prostitutes: c.: ca 1860–1910.

shadow never grow (occ. be) less!, may your. May you prosper: a Persian phrase introduced to England by Morier in 1824 and, ca 1880, generalized as a coll. *Referee*, 2 Jan. 1887.

shady. Uncertain, unreliable, inefficient; unlikely to succeed: 1848, Clough (of a tutor), 'shady in Latin': coll; though perhaps orig. university s. 2. Hence, disreputable; not quite honest, not at all honourable: coll: 1862, *Saturday Review*, 8 Feb., 'Whose balance-sheets are "shady"'.

shady side of, on the. Older than: 1807, W. Irving, 'The younger being somewhat on the shady side of thirty': coll.

shaft or a bolt of it, make a. To determine that a thing shall be used in one way or another: late C.16–20: coll till ca 1660, then proverbial S.E.; in C.19–20, merely archaic. Nashe, 1594; Isaac D'Israeli, 1823.

shaft(e)sbury; S. A gallon-potful of wine with cock: s. > coll: late C.17–early 19. Presumably ex the Dorsetshire town of Shaftesbury.

shag. A copulation; also, copulation generically: C.19–20. Ex: 2. A performer (rarely of a woman) of the sexual act, esp. in '*he is but bad shag*; he is no able woman's man', Grose, 2nd ed.: late C.18–mid-19. Ex the v., 1. 3. 'Any coat other than an "Eton" or "tails" is a "shag"', R. Airy, *Westminster*, 1902: Westminster School: late C.19–20. Ex *shaggy*.

shag, v.t. To coït (with a woman): late C.18–20. Prob. ex †*shag*, to shake, toss about. cf. n., 1, 2. 2. Whence perhaps, v.i., to masturbate: Public Schools: certainly ca 1900 and prob. many years earlier.

shag, miserable as a. Very miserable indeed: Australian coll: late C.19–20. cf.:

shag, wet as a. Very wet indeed: a mainly rural coll: from ca 1830. Marryat. Ex *shag*, a cormorant.

shag back. To hang back; refuse a fence: hunting coll: from ca 1870.

shag-bag. A poor, shabby fellow; a worthless fellow: coll: late C.17–20; slightly ob. Ex *shake-bag* on *shag-rag*, via cock-fighting.

shag-bag, adj. Shabby; worthless; inferior: coll: 1888 (O.E.D.). Ex preceding.

shag off. To go away: low: late C.19–20. Prompted by FUCK OFF.

shagged out. Exhausted, utterly weary: Clifton College: late C.19–20. Of same origin as SHAG.

shags, go. To go shares: Public Schools': late C.19–20. cf. *go* SHACK.

shah. A tremendous SWELL: mostly Cockney: ca 1880–1910.

shake. A harlot: low London (—1860); ob. Ex Northern dial. Whence (or ex the v., 1), 2, a copulation: from ca 1860; ob. 3. See SHAKES, NO GREAT. 4. Abbr. *milk shake, egg-shake*, etc: coll (—1903): ?orig. U.S. 5. Generic for instantaneous or very rapid action: from ca 1815: by C.20, coll. Esp. *in a shake* (late C.19–20), *in the shake of a hand* (1816), *in a brace* (1841) or *a couple* (1840) *of shakes, in two shakes* (from ca 1880), *in the shake of a lamb's tail* (—1903) or jocularly, from ca 1905 *of a dead lamb's tail*. 6. Hence, a moment: (?late C.19–) C.20. E. Nesbit, 1904, 'Wait a shake, and I'll undo the side gate.' 7. Hence also, *a great shake*, a very fast pace (—1903). 8. See SHAKES, THE.

shake, v.t. To coït (with a woman): coll: ?C.16–20; ob. In late C.19–20, rare except in *shake a tart*. Halliwell, 'This seems to be the ancient form of *shag*, given by Grose' (see SHAG, v., 1). 2. ?hence, v. reflexive, to masturbate: C.19–20. cf. SHAG, v., 2. 3. v.t., to rob (a person): low s., or perhaps c.: C.19–20. *Lex. Bal.*; in C.20, mainly Australian. cf. the C.15–16 S.E. *shake* (a person) *out of* (goods, etc.). 4. (?hence) to steal: from ca 1810: c. >, ca 1880, low s. Vaux; H. Kingsley, 1859, 'I shook a nag, and got bowled out and lagged.' See also SHOOK. 5. See SHOOK ON. 6. See SHAKE THE ELBOW. 7. See:

shake! Shake hands!: from ca 1890; mainly U.S. Often *shake on it!* (Other forms are very rare, except for, e.g., 'Well satisfied, they shook on it.')

shake a cloth in the wind. To be hanged: late C.18–mid-19. 2. Gen. as ppl adj., *shaking* ... To be slightly intoxicated: nautical: W. N. Glascock, *The Naval Sketch-Book* (II, 33), 1826.

shake a fall. To wrestle: C.19–20; ob.

shake a flannin. To fight: navvies': ca 1870–1914. A *flannin* is a flannel shirt or jacket.

shake a leg. (Gen. in imperative.) To hurry: coll (mainly military and nautical): late C.19–20. Anstey, 1892, 'Ain't you shot enough? Shake a leg, can't yer, Jim?' Ex S.E. *shake a foot, leg*, etc., to dance.

shake a loose leg. To go *on the* LOOSE: coll: mid-C.19–20.

shake a toe. To dance: ca 1820–80. *Sinks*, 1848.

shake and shiver. A river: theatrical rhyming s.: late C.19–20.

shake-bag. The female pudend: low: mid-C.19–20.

shake-buckler. A swashbuckler or bully: coll nickname: mid-C.16–mid-17. Becon.

shake (a person's) **fleas.** To thrash: low: C.19.

***shake-glim.** A begging letter, or petition, on account of fire: ca 1850–90.

shake hands with an old friend. To urinate: euphemistic: since ca 1880.

***shake-lurk.** The same as SHAKE-GLIM, only for shipwreck: c. of ca 1850–1900. Mayhew, 1851. See LURK, a DODGE or LAY (2); and cf. LURKER.

shake one's shambles, see SHAMBLES . . .

***shake one's toe-rag.** To decamp: vagabonds' and beggars' c. (—1909). cf. TOE-RAGGER.

shake-out. A 'sudden revulsion and following clearance – due to panic': Stock Exchange coll: from ca 1880.

shake the bullet. See BULLET. 2. To threaten to discharge a person: tailors': from ca 1870; slightly ob.

shake the (occ. one's) elbow. To dice: C.17–20 (ob.): coll >, ca 1800, S.E.

shake the ghost into. To frighten (a person) greatly: mid-C.19–20; ob.

shake the gum out of a sail. To test new canvas for the first time in bad weather: nautical coll: late C.19–20.

shake up, v.i. To masturbate: C.19–20; ob. cf. SHAG, v., 2. 2. v.t., to hurry: nautical coll: late C.19–20. Ex S.E. *shake up*, to rouse with, or as with, a shake.

shake-up. An unnerving experience: coll: late C.19–20.

shake your ears!(, go). c.p. advice to one who has lost his ears: ca 1570–1790. G. Harvey, 1573; Shakespeare; Mrs F. Sheridan, 1764.

shaker. A hand: low coll: mid-C.19–20; ob. 2. A shirt: from the 1830s: c. >, ca 1870, low s. 3. An omnibus: busmen's from ca 1870; rather ob. cf. BONE-SHAKER. 4. A beggar who pretends to have fits: c. (—1861). Mayhew.

shakes, in a brace or couple of, see SHAKE, n., 5.

shakes, no (occ. not any) great. Nothing remarkable or very important or unusually able or clever: from ca 1815: coll till C.20, then familiar S.E. Moore, 1819, 'Though no great shakes at learned chat'. Ex dicing.

shakes, the. Any illness or chronic disease marked by trembling limbs and muscles: coll: from the 1830s. 2. Hence, delirium tremens: coll: from ca 1880. *Cornhill Magazine*, June 1884, 'Until she is pulled up by an attack of delirium tremens, or, as she and her neighbours style it, a fit of the shakes'. 3. Hence, extreme nervousness: coll: from ca 1880.

***shakes?, what.** What's the chance of stealing anything?: c. (—1859).

Shakespeare-navels. A 'long-pointed, turned-down collar': London youths': ca 1870–80. Ware. Precisely why?

shakester, see SHICKSTER.

shakings. Litter, e.g. fragments of paper or thread: Naval: ca 1800–50. W. N. Glascock, *Sailors and Saints* (I, 143), 1829.

shaler, see SHEILA.

shall us? Let's. A c.p., esp. among juveniles: ca 1895–1914. Perhaps it originates in the Cockneys' *shall us?* for *shall we?*

shaller dodge, see SHALLOW DODGE.

***shallow.** A hat: c. of ca 1810–40. 2. See SHALLOW BRIGADE, COVE, DODGE, MORT, SCREEVER. Perhaps ex dial. *shalleygonahey*, *shallegonaked* (i.e. shall I go naked?), used chiefly of insufficient clothing.

***shallow, do the; go shallow.** To practise the SHALLOW DODGE: c. (—1887). The earliest shape of the phrase is *go on the shallows*. cf. SHALLOW, RUN.

shallow, lily-. A white whip-hat, i.e. a low-crowned one: fashionable s.: ca 1810–40.

***shallow, live.** To live in discreet retirement when wanted by the police: c.: from ca 1870; slightly ob. Contrast SHALLOW, DO THE.

***shallow, run.** To practise the SHALLOW DODGE: c. (—1893). *Ripon Chronicle*, 23 Aug. 1893, 'By running shallow I mean that he never wears either boots, coat, or hat, even in the depths of the most dismal winter.' A synonym of *do the* SHALLOW.

shallow brigade. Perhaps merely a more or less literary synonym for *school of* SHALLOW COVES. Mayhew, 1851. See:

***shallow cove; s. fellow.** C.19–20 tramps' c. (first recorded in 1839 and now ob.), as in Brandon and in Mayhew, 1851, 'He scraped acquaintance with a "school of shallow coves"; that is, men who go about half-naked, telling frightful tales about shipwrecks, hair-breadth escapes from houses on fire, and such like . . . calamities.' Also a SHIVERING JEMMY. cf.:

***shallow dodge.** The capitalizing of rags and semi-nudity: c.: 1869, Greenwood, 'A pouncing of the exposed parts with common powder blue is found to heighten the frost-bitten effect.'

shallow fellow, see SHALLOW COVE.

***shallow mort or mot(t).** A female practiser of the SHALLOW DODGE: 1842, *Edinburgh Review*, July. cf. SHALLOW COVE.

***shallow screever, scriver,** etc. A man who, very meagrely dressed, sketches and draws on the pavement: c. (—1859). See SHALLOW DODGE and SCREEVER, n.

***shallows, go on the,** see SHALLOW, DO THE. **shally-shally,** see SHILLY-SHALLY.

sham. A trick or hoax, an imposture, a fraud: 1677: orig. s., it had by 1700 > S.E. The same with the corresponding v., also in Wycherley in 1677. Prob. ex *shame*, n. and v.: cf. *cut a sham*, 'to play a Rogue's Trick', B.E., late C.17–18, and *upon the sham*, fraudulently (late C.17 only), and *put a sham upon*, to SELL, to swindle; ca 1680–1830 – all three, by the way, s. only for a year or two before being made S.E. 2. Hence, a false testimonial, certificate, or subscription list: c.: from ca 1840; ob. '*No. 747*'. 3. As false sleeve or shirt-front, prob. always S.E. 4. **Champagne**: 1849, Thackeray. cf. the early C.20 album c.p.: 'A bottle of champagne for my real friends; of real pain for my sham friends.' Occ. (—1874) *shammy*, as in H., 5th ed.: very ob.

sham, v. To ply with, or treat oneself to, champagne: rare: from ca 1820. Byron. cf. CHAM, n.

sham Abra(ha)m, see ABRA(HA)M-SHAM.

sham-legger. A man who offers to sell very cheaply goods that are very inferior: low s. (mostly London) of ca 1870–1910.

sham the doctor. To malinger: military: from the 1890s.

shambles, shake one's. (Gen. in imperative.) To be off: late C.17–mid-18: either low s. or perhaps, orig. at least, c.

shambly. Shambling, lurching: nautical coll: late C.19–20. W. E. Llewellyn has described sailors thus: 'Their hands were in a grab half-hook [i.e. as though grasping a grapnel], always, and their shoulders shambly.'

shame. Anything very ugly, painfully indecent, disgracefully inferior: coll: 1764, Gray, 'His nose is a shame'; 1815, Scott, 'Three [hens] that were a shame to be seen'.

shame to take the money, (it's) a. That's money very easily come by: c.p.: late C.19–20.

shammy, see SHAM, n., 4.

shamrock. A prick with a bayonet: military: ca 1850–1905.

shamrock, drown the. To drink or go drinking on St Patrick's Day, properly and nominally in honour of the shamrock: 1888, *Daily Telegraph*, 22 March, but prob. in spoken use many, many years earlier: coll.

***shan(d).** Base or counterfeit coin: c. (—1812); very ob. Ex dial. *shan*, paltry. cf. SHEEN.

shanghai. To stupefy and then put on a vessel requiring hands: nautical s. (orig. U.S.): 1871 (U.S.) and 1887 (England). Ex *Shanghai* as seaport, or perhaps as propelled from a *shanghai* or catapult.

Shanghai gentleman. One definitely not a gentleman: naval (—1909).

Shanks'(s) mare, nag, naggy, pony. One's legs as conveyance: coll (in C.20, S.E.): resp. 1795 (S. Bishop); *nag*, 1774 (Ferguson), and *naggy*, 1744 (an anon. Scottish song), the former being mostly, the latter wholly Scots; *pony*, 1891, *Globe*, 5 June. Jocular on *shanks*, the legs, and gen. as *ride S. m.* (or *n.*, or *p.*).

Shannon, to have been dipped in the. To be anything but bashful, the immersion being regarded as a cure completely effectual and enduring against that affliction: coll: ca 1780–1880. cf. BLARNEY.

shanny. Idiotic, silly; mad: Cockney (—1887). Ex Kentish dial.

***shant.** A quart or a pot; a pot of liquor (esp. *shant of* GATTER, a pot of beer): mid-C.19–20: c. and low s. Mayhew, 1851; P. H. Emerson, 1893. ?etymology: cf. SHANTY; SHANTY-LIQUOR.

shan't! A somewhat uncouth and gen. angry or sullen form of:

shan't!, I. I shall not (do so): a coll peremptory refusal: C.18–20.

shan't be long!, now we. It's all right!: a c.p. of ca 1895–1915. *Daily Telegraph*, 8 Sept. 1896; Maugham, *Liza of Lambeth*, 1897, '"Now we shan't be long!" she remarked.' Ware derives it from 'railway travellers' phrase when near the end of a journey'.

shan't play!, I. I'm annoyed!; I don't like it: Australian c.p.: from ca 1885; ob. Ex children's peevishness in games.

shanty. A public-house; a SLY-grog shop; showmen's s. (prob. from ca 1850) >, by 1860, Australian coll; in New Zealand —1862. H. Lawson, 1902, 'They got up a darnse at Peter Anderson's shanty acrost the ridges.' Prob. ex Fr. *chantier*; nevertheless, derivation direct ex SHANT is not impossible: cf. senses 3 and 4. 2. Hence, a brothel: nautical: from ca 1890. 3. A quart of liquor, esp. of beer or ale: 1893, P. H. Emerson. Prob. ex SHANT. 4. Beer-money: 1893, P. H. Emerson, 'Any shanty in your sky-rocket'. Prob. sense 3 is slightly earlier than, and the imm. source of, sense 4.

shanty, v. To drink often, habitually, at a SHANTY (sense 1): 1888: Australian coll. 'Rolf Boldrewood', 1888, 'The Dalys and us shantying and gaffing'.

shanty-bar. The bar in a SHANTY: late C.19–20: Australian coll. H. Lawson, 1902, 'Throwing away our money over shanty bars'.

shanty-keeper. One who keeps a SHANTY (1): from 1875: Australian coll. cf. preceding and ensuing entry.

shanty(-)liquor. SLY-grog-shop drink: Australian coll: 1886, H. C. Kendall, 'He'll . . . swig at shanty liquors.' Ex SHANTY, n., 1.

shap, see SHAPO.

shape, spoil a woman's. To get her with child: coll: late C.17–20; ob. Facetious Tom Brown, 'The . . . king who had spoil'd the shape . . . of several mistresses'. By an indelicate pun.

shape, travel on one's. To live by one's appearance, to swindle: coll: C.19.

shape for you!, there's a. A c.p. in respect of an extremely thin person or animal: mid-C.19–20; very ob. cf.:

shapes. An ill-made man, often in vocative: late C.17–mid-19. 2. Hence, a very tightly laced girl: ca 1730–1910. 3. 'An ill-made irregular Lump of Flesh, &c', Dyche & Pardon: ca 1730–1830.

shapes, cut up or **show.** To frolic; exhibit flightiness: mid-C.19–20; ob. cf.:

shapes, show one's. To 'turn about, march off', B.E.: late C.17–mid-19. 2. 'To be stript, or made peel at the whipping post', Grose, 1st ed.: mid-C.18–early 19. 3. To come into view: coll: 1828, Scott; ob.

shapes and shirts. Young actors' term, ca 1883–1900, for 'old actors, who swear by the legitimate Elizabethan drama, which involves either the "shape" or the "shirt" – the first being the cut-in tunic; the . . . shirt being independent of shape'. Ware.

***shapo,** rare; gen. **shappeau** or **shappo;** rarely **shop(p)o;** less rarely **shap.** A hat: late C.17–early 19: c. B.E., '*Shappeau*, c. or *Shappo*, c. for *Chappeau*' – properly Fr. *chapeau* – 'a Hat, the newest Cant, *Nab* being very old, and grown too common'.

***shark.** A pickpocket: c. of C.18. J. Stevens, 1707. 2. (?hence) a customs officer: ca 1780–1880. 3. See SHARKS. 4. (Also *black shark.*) A lawyer: nautical coll: (—1806). 5. A recruit: military: ca 1890–1910. ?on ROOKEY, a rook being a shark. 6. A sardine: jocular nautical: late C.19–20. cf. WHALE.

shark out. To make off; decamp slyly: dial. (—1828) >, by 1880, low coll.

sharks, the. The press-gang: 1828, D. Jerrold; †by 1900.

shark's mouth. An awning shaped to fit round a mast: nautical coll verging on j.: late C.19–20.

sharp. A swindler; a cheat: coll: 1797, Mrs M. Robinson; Maskelyne's title for a most informative book, *Sharps and Flats.* 2. Hence, an expert, connoisseur, actual or would-be wise man: coll: 1865, *Pall Mall Gazette*, 11 Sept., '"Sharps" who advertise their "tips" in the sporting journals'. Ex *sharp*, alert. 3. (Gen. in pl.) A needle: c.: late C.19–20. Ex S.E. *sharps*, one of three grades of needles, including the longest and most sharply pointed.

sharp and blunt. The female pudend: late C.19–20 rhyming s. on CUNT.

sharp as the corner of a round table. Stupid: coll (lower classes'): from ca 1870; ob. Prob. by opposition to S.E. *sharp as a needle* or *razor* or †*thorn.*

Sharp come in yet?, has Mr. A traders' c.p. addressed by one (e.g.) shopman to another to signify that a customer of suspected honesty is about: from ca 1860. cf. TWO-UPON-TEN.

sharper's tools. Fools: rhyming s.: late C.19–20.

***sharping omee.** A policeman: c. and Parlary: ca 1850–90. See OMEE.

Sharp's Alley bloodworms. Beef sausages; black puddings: ca 1850–1900. Ex a well-known abattoir near Smithfield.

sharp's the word and quick's the motion. A c.p. implying that a person is 'very attentive to his own interest', Grose, 2nd ed.: late C.18–20; slightly ob. Ex *sharp's the word*, an enjoining of promptitude.

sharpy. A derisive coll nickname for a person self-consciously alert: late C.19–20.

'shart, see 'SHEART.

shat. A tattler: ca 1709–20. Steele in the *Tatler*, No. 71, 1709.

shave. A narrow escape: 1834, R. H. Froude: coll >, ca 1860, S.E. Ex S.E. sense, 'a slight or grazing touch'. 2. Hence, passing an examination by a 'shave': university (orig. Oxford): 1840, Theodore Hook; slightly ob. 3. A definitely false, or at the least, an unauthenticated report: military: 1813, Capt. R. M. Cairnes, so that Sala was wrong when, in 1884, he implied that the term arose (instead of saying that it > gen. popular) during the Crimean War, though he may have been right when he said that as = a hoax, it arose then; the latter nuance, unless applied to a deliberately false rumour, was †by 1914. 'From a barber's shop, the home of gossip' (B. & P.). 4. 'The proportion of the receipts paid to a travelling company by a local manager', F. & H., 1903: theatrical. Ex *shaved-off*. 5. 'A money consideration paid for the right to vary a contract, by extension of time for delivery or payment, &c.', F. & H.: orig. U.S.; anglicized ca 1900. 6. A drink: proletarian: ca 1884–1914. Perhaps ex the excuse of going for a shave. 7. A customer for a shave: barbers' coll: 1895, W. Pett Ridge.

shave. To deprive a person of all his money or goods; to charge him extortionately: late C.14–20: S.E. until C.19, then coll verging on s. cf. SHAVING THE LADIES. 2. Hence, to steal (v.t.): late C.16–mid-18. D'Urfey, 'The Maidens had shav'd his Breeches.'

shave through, v.i. Abbr. *just shave through*: from ca 1860: university coll >, ca 1890, S.E. A variant is *make a shave*: see SHAVE, n., 2.

shaver. A fellow, chap; also a joker, a wag: late C.16–20: coll. From ca 1830 (though *young shaver* occurs as early as 1630) only of a youth, and gen. preceded by *young* or *little*, very often depreciatively – except that, at sea, *old shaver* = a man throughout C.19. Marlowe, 1592, 'Sirrah, are you not an old shaver? . . . Alas, sir! I am a very youth'; 1748, Smollett, 'He drew a pistol, and fired it at the unfortunate shaver'; Dickens; P. H. Emerson. Ex *shaver*, one who shaves (for barbers have always been 'cute, knowledgeable fellows); or perhaps ex *shaver*, an extortioner (esp. *cunning shaver*). 2. Very rarely applied to a woman: prob. only in C.17, e.g. Cotton, 1664, 'My Mother's a mad shaver, | No man alive knows where to have her.' (This instance may, however, be merely an extension of the C.17 coll *mad shaver*, a roysterer.) cf. the C.20 sporting women's use of CHAP in address or application to women. 3. A short jacket: late C.19–early 20: lower classes. Because it gen. fits close; cf. BUM-FREEZER, -PERISHER.

shaving. A defrauding, whether process or completed act: C.17–20. Dekker. Hence *shaving terms*, the making all the money one can: C.19–20.

shaving-brush. The female pubic hair: from after 1838; ob.

shaving-mill. An open boat, sixteen-oared, of a type used as privateers in the war of 1812: Canadian.

shaving the ladies. A drapers' phrase for overcharging women: 1863, Ouida, 'We have all heard of an operation called shaving the ladies'; ob. Ex SHAVE, n., 1.

shavings. Illicit clippings of money: late C.17–20: c. >, ca 1750, s. >, ca 1800, coll >, ca 1860, S.E.

shawk. An Indian kite: Anglo-Indian: from ca 1870. A blend of *shit-hawk*: in allusion to the scavenging characteristics of this bird.

shawly. An Irish fisherwoman, esp. of Dublin: Anglo-Irish: late C.19–20. Ex the great shawl they wore.

she. A woman: mid-C.16–20: S.E. until mid-C.19, then coll; in C.20, low coll when not jocular. 2. (Also *shee*.) A plum pudding: Charterhouse: late C.19–20. A. H. Tod, *Charterhouse*, 1900. cf. HE.

she couldn't cook hot water for a barber. A c.p. (from ca 1880) directed at a poor house-keeper, esp. a girl unlikely to be able to 'feed the brute'.

she didn't seem to mind it very much. A proletarian ironic c.p. intimating jealousy: ca 1885–1900.

she-dragon. A termagant or a forbidding woman, esp. if elderly: from the 1830s: coll bordering on, in C.20 >, S.E. 2. A kind of wig, says F. & H.: ?early C.19: prob. coll.

she-flunkey. A lady's maid: coll (lower classes'): from ca 1875.

she has (or she's) been a good wife to him. An ironic proletarian c.p. 'cast at a drunken woman rolling in the streets' (Ware): from ca 1905.

she-house. A house under petticoat rule: late C.18–mid-19.

'She' is a cat's mother. A c.p. addressed to (esp.) a child constantly referring thus to his mother: mid-C.19–20; slightly ob.

she-lion. A shilling: from ca 1780; very ob. By a pun.

she-male, n. and adj. Female: orig. – ca 1880 – London lower classes'. Pairing with HE-MALE.

***she-napper.** A female thief-catcher; a bawd, a pimp: late C.17–mid-19: c. > ca 1750 low s.

she-oak. Native ale: Australian (1888), hence New Zealand; ob. cf. SHEARER'S

JOY. Ex the Australian tree so named: quite! but why? Whence:

she-oak net. A net spread under the gangway to catch seamen drunk on SHE-OAK: nautical: late C.19–20; ob.

she-school. A girls' school: C.19–20 (ob.): coll. cf. SHE-HOUSE.

she will go off in an aromatic faint. A Society c.p. of 1883–ca 86, 'said of a fantastical woman, meaning that her delicate nerves will surely be the death of her' (Ware).

shearer's joy. Colonial beer: Australian coll: 1892, Gilbert Parker. cf. SHE-OAK.

shears, there's a pair of. They're very like: coll: C.17–18. Ex the more gen. *there goes* or *went but a pair of shears between* (e.g.) *them.*

'sheart; occ. **s'heart, shart, s'harte,** incorrectly (C.18) **'sdheart.** A coll euphemism for *God's heart!*: late C.16–18. Occ. *s'hart.*

sheath!, by my. A trivial oath: coll: ca 1530–50. Heywood, More.

sheave-o, sheaveo, sheavo or **sheevo.** A drunken bout; a free-fight: nautical. A late C.19–20 derivative of: 2. An entertainment: naval: C.19–20. Indeed, F. & Gibbons records it for 1798 thus: 'Sir John Orde gave a grand chevaux' (letter of Lieut. Charles Cathcart, 6 May).

shebang. As a hut, room, dwelling, shop, it has remained U.S.; but derivatively as a vehicle (Mark Twain, 1872) it was anglicized in the late 1890s. Prob. ex Fr. *cabane.*

sheckles, see SHEKELS.

sheckles! A s. Cockney expletive of late C.19–20; ob. Pugh (2). Perhaps cf. SHUCKS!

shed. To give; give away (something of little value); drop, let go: coll: 1855, Dickens, 'Would shed a little money [for] a mission or so to Africa'.

shed a tear. To make water: mid-C 19–20. 2. (?hence by antiphrasis) to take a dram, hence – from ca 1860 – any drink: 1876, Hindley, 'I always made time to call in and shed a tear with him.' Less gen. and very ob.

shee, see SHE, 2. **sheela(h),** see SHEILA.

***sheen.** Counterfeit coin: c. (—1839). Occ., from ca 1880, as adj. Ex SHAN(D), very prob. (cf. Brandon's and H.'s designation as Scottish); but perhaps influenced by:

sheeny (gen. **S.**); occ. **sheeney, -nie,** or **shen(e)y.** A Jew: from ca 1810: somewhat offensive. Thackeray, 1847, 'Sheeney and Moses are . . . smoking their pipes before their lazy shutters in Seven Dials.' From ca 1890, occ. as adj., as in the *Licensed Victuallers' Gazette*, 23 Jan. 1891, '"Don't like that Sheeney friend of yours," he said.' 2. Hence, a pawnbroker: mid-C.19–20. W. risks the guess that *sheeny* may derive ex Yiddish pronunciation of Ger. *schön*, beautiful, used in praising wares; very tentatively, I suggest that the term arose from the *sheeny*, i.e. glossy or brightly shiny, hair of some English Jews: cf. SNIDE AND SHINE.

sheeny or **S.**; etc. adj. See the n., 1. 2. Fraudulent (person); base (money): late C.19–20. A rare sense, due prob. to SHEEN.

sheep. A second-classman: Aberdeen University: 1865, G. Macdonald.

sheep-biter. A butcher: s.: Ned Ward, 1703.

sheep by moonlight, keep. To hang in chains: late C.18–mid-19. A. E. Housman's note to *The Shropshire Lad* (1898), ix.

sheep-guts, old. A term of contempt: coll: C.19–20; ob.

***sheep-shearer.** A cheat or swindler: c.: late C.17–mid-18.

***sheep-walk.** A prison: c. of ca 1780–1840. Messink, 1781.

sheep-wash. To duck: Winchester: from ca 1890. Ex sheep-dipping.

sheep's head, all jaw, – like a. A c.p. of a very talkative person: late C.18–20; ob. See JAW, n.

sheep's tail. Sheep's-tail fat: South African coll (—1888).

sheepskin-fiddle. A drum: ca 1810–60. Whence *sheepskin-fiddler*, a drummer (*Lex. Bal.*).

sheet, on the. Up for trial; 'crimed': military coll: from ca 1905.

sheet-alley or **-lane.** Bed: mid-C.19–20; ob. cf. BEDFORDSHIRE and BLANKET FAIR, and Baumann's (*go*) *down sheet lane into Bedfordshire*, to go to bed.

sheet in the wind or (less gen.) **wind's eye, a.** Half drunk: 1840, Dana, in adumbration; 1862, Trollope, 'A thought tipsy – a sheet or so in the wind, as folks say'; R. L. Stevenson, 1883 (*wind's eye*). s. >, ca 1890, coll. Ex *three* SHEETS IN THE WIND.

sheet of tripe. A plate of tripe: low urban (—1909).

sheets, between the. In bed: from ca 1860: coll.

sheets in the wind, three. Drunk: 1821,

Egan; 1840, Dana: mainly sporting s. > ca 1860, coll.

sheevo, see SHEAVE-O.

Sheffield handicap. A sprint race with no defined scratch, the virtual scratch man receiving a big start from an imaginary 'flyer': Northern coll and dial.: late C.19–20; ob.

sheila or **-er;** occ. **shiela(h)** or **sheela(h).** A girl: Australian, hence New Zealand: late C.19–20. A perversion of English dial. and low s. *shaler.*

shekels; occ. **sheckles.** Coin; money in gen.: coll: 1883, F. Marion Crawford, but prob. used at least a decade earlier – cf. Byron's anticipation of 1823. Ex *shekel,* the most important Hebrew silver coin.

shelf, on the. In pawn: C.19–20. 2. Under arrest: military: from ca 1870; ob. 3. Transported: ca 1850–70: c. 4. Dead: from ca 1870.

shell. An undress, tight-fitting jacket: military: from ca 1880. *St James's Gazette,* 22 Dec. 1886, 'Tunics and shells and messing-jackets and caps.' Abbr. S.E. *shell-jacket* (1840, O.E.D.). 2. The female pudend: C.19–20: coll verging on euphemistic S.E. 3. See SHELLS.

shell, in one's Sulky; not inclined to talk: coll: mid-C.19–20.

shell, old, see OLD SHELL.

shell-back. A sailor of full age, esp. if tough and knowledgeable: nautical coll (—1883). Perhaps for the reason given by W. Clark Russell in *Jack's Courtship* (1883), 'It takes a sailor a long time to straighten his spine and get quit of the bold sheer that earns him the name of shell-back.'

shell out. To disburse; pay (out): coll: C.19–20. Maria Edgeworth, Tom Moore, Headon Hill. Scott, in 1816, has *shell down,* but this form is very rare. Ex *shell,* remove a seed from its shell (etc.). 2. As v.i., to hand over what is due or expected, pay up: coll from ca 1820. 3. To club money together, gen. as vbl n.: ca 1820–50. 4. v.t., ex sense 1, to declare: a rare coll of ca 1860–1910. Mrs Henry Wood.

shelling peas, as easy as. Very easy: coll: C.19–20.

***shells;** occ. **shels.** Money: coll of ca 1590–1620. Greene. (cf. the use made of cowries.)

shels, see SHELLS.

s'help. See S'ELP. (1904, O.E.D.); cf. S'WELP.

shelve, gen. v.t. To hold over part of (the weekly bill): printers' coll: from ca 1870. Contrast HORSE, n., 3.

shemozzle; occ. **shimozzel, s(c)hlemozzle,** even **chimozzle.** A difficulty or misfortune; a ROW: from late 1880s: East End, orig. (esp. among bookmakers) and mainly. *Referee,* 1 Dec. 1889, *schlemozzle*; Binstead, 1899, *shlemozzle*; Anon., *From the Front,* 1900, *chimozzle*; J. Maclaren, 1901, 'If Will comes out of this shemozzle'. A corruption of Ger. *schlimm* and Hebrew *mazel*; lit. and orig., 'bad luck'.

shemozzle (etc.), v. To make off, decamp: orig. (ca 1901) and mostly East End.

shenan(n)igan or **-in;** occ. **shenan(n)iken, shi-** (with either ending), and, nautical, **shenanecking** (Bowen). Nonsense, chaff; (the predominant C.20 sense:) trickery, 'funny' games: orig. (ca 1870), U.S.; anglicized ca 1890. R. Barr, 1902, 'If I were to pay them they might think there was some shenanigan about it.' Perhaps fantastic on the Cornish *shenachrum,* a drink of boiled beer, rum, sugar, and lemon; but much more prob. the base is *nenan(n)igan* (etc.) and the origin the East Anglian and Gloucestershire *nanna(c)k, nan(n)ick,* to play the fool, with imm. origin in the vbl n. *nannicking* (etc.). It has, however, been suggested by Mr A. Jameson (of Sennan) that the term derives from the Erse *sionnach* (pronounced *shinnuch*): cf. Anglo-Irish *foxing,* hiding or malingering. 2. Hence, as v.i. and t.: late C.19–20.

shenan(n)i(c)ker. A shirker: from the middle 1890s. Ex preceding, 2.

shen(e)y, see SHEENY.

shepherd, n. 'Every sixth boy in the cricket-bill who answers for the five below him being present', F. & H.: Harrow: late C.19–20.

shepherd, v.t. To shadow; watch over (e.g. a rich relative, an heiress, a football or hockey opponent): 1874, H., 5th ed., 'To look after carefully, to place under police surveillance': s. Perhaps ex the tending of sheep. 2. To follow (a person) in order to cheat or swindle him, or else to get something from him: from ca 1890: Australian s. 3. To force (the enemy) into a difficult position: military s. (Boer War). *Daily Telegraph,* 2 April 1900, 'Cronje was shepherded with his army into the bed of the Modder by a turning movement.'

shepherd's friend. The dingo: Australian ironic coll: late C.19–20.

shepherd's plaid. Bad: from ca 1870. Contrast ROBIN HOOD, adj.

sherbet. (A glass of) any warm alcoholic liquor, e.g. a grog: s. (—1890) ex catachresis. (Not among the upper classes.) cf.:

sherbet(t)y. Drunk: 1890, *Licensed Victuallers' Gazette*, 8 Feb., 'By the time one got to bed Tom was a bit sherbetty'; ob. Ex SHERBET.

sheriff's ball. An execution: ca 1780–1850.

sheriff's ball and loll out one's tongue at the company, dance at the. To hang (v.i.): ca 1780–1850. cf. *go to rest in a horse's nightcap* ibid. (see HORSE-NIGHTCAP), and a variant of the entry-phrase: DANCE *on nothing at the sheriff's ball* (Grose in his *Olio*).

sheriff's basket or tub. A receptacle set outside a prison for the receipt of charity for the prisoners: resp. late C.16–mid-17 (Nashe) and ca 1630–60 (Massinger).

sheriff's bracelets. Handcuffs: ca 1780–1850.

sheriff's hotel. A prison: ca 1780–1850.

sheriff's journeyman. A hangman: early C.19.

sheriff's picture-frame. The hangman's noose: ca 1780–1850.

sheriff's posts. 'Two painted posts, set up at the sheriff's door, to which proclamations were affixed', O.E.D.: late C.16–mid-17. Jonson.

sheriff's tub, see SHERIFF'S BASKET.

sherk, see SHIRK.

Sherlock Holmes! A c.p. directed at detection of the obvious: from ca 1898; very ob. Obviously with reference to Conan Doyle's famous detective. Often abbr. to *Sherlock!*

sherry; shirry. A scurry; a rapid or furtive departure: from ca 1820; even in dial., very ob. Haggart, 1821, 'The shirry became general – I was run to my full speed.' Ex the v. 2. A sheriff: low (—1859); ob. 3. Cheap ale: taverns': late C.19–early 20.

sherry, v. (Also *sherry off.*) To run away (esp. hastily): 1788, Grose, 2nd ed. In C.19–20, often *shirry* (as in Haggart, 1821) and, from ca 1850, † except in dial. The O.E.D., prob. rightly, suggests ex (*to*) *sheer* (*off*); less likely a perversion of Fr. *charrier*, to carry off; less likely still, though not impossibly, ex an offensive-nationality idea, *sherry* the wine being from *Xeres* (now Jerez) in Spain.

sherry, go to. To die: circus-workers' (—1887). Ex SHERRY, n. and v.

sherry-cobbler. A cobbler made with sherry: coll: 1809; ob. Ouida.

sherry-fug. To tipple sherry: university: ca 1870–1915.

sherry off, see SHERRY, v.

shevoo. 'A "Chiveau", or merry dinner', 'Jon Bee', *A Living Picture of London*, 1828. The word occurs as *shiveau* in A. Harris, *The Emigrant Family*, 1847: an Australian usage. cf. SHEAVE-O, 2.

shevvle. ca 1860–90, as in the *Daily News*, 2 Dec. 1864, 'This is a term recently introduced as a genteel designation for cat's meat, and evidently derived from *cheval*, French for horse, as mutton from *mouton*, &c.'

***shew a leg.** To run away: c. (—1823); †by 1900. 2. (Gen. in imperative.) To rise from bed: mid-C.19–20: nautical >, ca 1910, military. Lit., show a leg from under the bed-clothes. John Masefield, *The Conway*, 1933, notes that the full call on that training ship has, from before 1891, been: 'Heave out, heave out, heave out, heave out! Away! | Come all you sleepers, Hey! | Show a leg and put a stocking on it.'

shew-leg day. A windy day: London coll (—1887); ob. 2. A very muddy day: London coll: from ca 1880. Often pron. *shulleg-day*.

***shice;** occ. **chice, schice, shise.** Any worthless person or thing: c. of ca 1860–1910. Rare. Prob. ex: 2. Nothing, as *work for shice*: c. or low s. (—1859). 3. Counterfeit money: c.: 1877, Anon., *Five Years' Penal Servitude*, 'I ascertained while at Dartmoor that a very large "business" is done in shise.' Either ex SHICER, 1, or direct ex Ger. *Scheisse*, excrement, or ex the v., sense 1. 4. 'An unprofitable undertaking. A wash-out. "To catch a shice" = to have an unremunerative deal': grafters': late C.19–20.

***shice,** v. To deceive, defraud, leave in the lurch, betray; v.i., to WELSH: c.: from ca 1860. Ex n., 2. 2. To befoul: low (—1887).

***shice (chice, schice, shise),** adj. No good: c. or low s. (—1859). H., 1st ed. at *chice*, 'The term was first used by the Jews in the last century.' ?ex Ger. *Scheisse*. (See also SHISH.) 2. Whence (or directly ex the n., 3), spurious, counterfeit: c.: 1877, 'Two shice notes' (source as in n., 3). N.B.: Senses 1 and 2 have variants *shicery*, *shickery*. 3. Drunk: low: late C.19–early 20. Presumably ex sense 1 influenced by SHICKER, adj.

shice, catch a, see SHICE, n., 4.

shicer; occ. **schicer, shiser,** and, in sense 2, rarely **skycer.** An unproductive claim or (gen. gold-) mine: Australia: 1855, (*Melbourne*) *Argus*, 19 Jan.: s. >, ca 1880, coll >, ca 1910, S.E. (The occ. spellings are, in this sense, merely illiterate and, in any case, very rare.) Either ex SHICE, adj., 1, or n., 2, or – as W. suggests – direct ex Ger. *Scheisser*, a voider of excrement; or, just possibly, ex SHICERY. 2. (?hence, or ex SHICE, adj., 1.) A worthless person (the predominant, and virtually the only, C.20 sense); a very idle one; a mean, sponging man; a HUMBUG: low (—1857). Also SHYSTER (H., 1874). 3. A welsher or defaulter: Australian racing: from mid-1890s. Ex sense 1 or 2 – or both.

shicery. Bad; spurious: c. or low s.: from ca 1860; very ob. F. & H., giving no illustration. Either ex SHICER, 2, or a perversion of SHICKERY.

shicker, v.i.; occ. **schicker, shikker, shikkur.** To drink liquor; get drunk: prob. from late 1890s: cf. next entry: mostly Australian and not gen. considered respectable. Ex Hebrew *shikkur*, drunk, as is:

shicker, etc., adj. Drunk: from late 1890s. (?ex the v.) Binstead, 1899, 'She comes over shikkur and vants to go to shleeb.' cf.:

shickered; shick. Tipsy: C.20 (?also very late C.19). Ex SHICKER, v. cf. 2 in:

shickery; rarely **shickerry.** (cf. SHICERY.) Shabby, shabbily; bad, badly: c. or low s.: 1851, Mayhew, 'The hedge crocus is shickery togged.' ?ex SHICE, adj., 1. 2. Occ., in late C.19–20, drunk. Perhaps ex SHICKER, adj. Cf. SHICKERED. 3. Spurious: see SHICE, adj.

shi(c)ksel. A nice Gentile girl: Jewish coll: mid-C.19–20. A diminutive of *shiksa*: see sense 2 of:

shickster; occ. **shickser, shiksa, shikster, shickster,** and (†by 1903) **shakester.** A lady: 1839, Brandon, *shickster*; 1857, Snowden (*Magazine Assistant*, 3rd ed.), *shikster*; 1859, H., 1st ed., *shakester* and *shickster*; 1899, Binstead, *shiksa*. 2. Hence, any (Gentile) woman or girl: mostly Jewish and pejorative: late C.19–early 20. Contrast SHICKSEL. 3. A Gentile female servant: among Jews: late C.19–20. 4. A none-too-respectable girl or woman: mid-C.19–20: low. Carew, *Autobiography of a Gipsy*, 1891, p. 414, 'As I was leavin' the court, a reg'lar 'igh-flying shickster comes up,' refers to mid-C.19; cf. H., 3rd ed., 'A "gay" lady'. Possibly the term derives ex SHICE, adj., 1: that *shickster* is, in any case, from Yiddish is a virtual certainty; that senses 1 and 4 may orig. have been c. is a possibility, as appears also in:

***shickster-crabs.** Ladies' shoes: tramps' c. (—1864); ob.

shie, see SHY, v. **shielah** (Jice Doone), see SHEILA, **shier,** see SHYER.

shif. Fish: back s. (—1859).

shift, v.t. To dislodge (a body of the enemy): coll: 1898. 2. To murder: 1898. 3. (The operative origin of senses 1, 2) to dislodge from its back, i.e. to throw (of a horse throwing its rider): coll: 1891. 4. To eat; more gen. to drink: s. (—1896) >, ca 1910, coll.

shift, do a. To stool: low: from ca 1870; slightly ob.

shift-monger. A young man-about-town: taverns': ca 1881–90. Ex stiff shirt-front of evening dress.

***shifter.** A sly thief; a sharper: ca 1560–1640: c. >, ca 1600, s. or coll. Awdelay, Florio, Withals. Prob. ex S.E. *shift*, to use shifts, evasions, expedients, though this is not recorded before 1579. 2. 'An alarm, an intimation, given by a thief to his *pall*', Vaux: c. of ca 1810–40. Because it causes him to shift. 3. A drunkard: from ca 1896; ob. Ex SHIFT, V.

***shifting.** A warning; esp. an alarm conveyed by the watching to the operating thief: c.: from ca 1820; ob. cf. SHIFTER, 2.

shifting ballast. Landsmen – esp. soldiers – aboard: nautical: late C.18–mid-19.

shifty cove. A trickster: from ca 1820 (ob.): low. See COVE; cf. SHIFTER, 1.

shig. A shilling: Winchester: from ca 1840; ob. Mansfield. cf. SHIGGERS. 2. Hence, *shigs*, money, esp. silver: East End: from ca 1860.

shiggers. White football shorts costing 10s.: Winchester: mid-C.19–20. Ex SHIG, 1.

shigs, see SHIG, 2.

shikerry, see SHICKERY. **shikker, -ur,** see SHICKER. **shiksa, shikster,** see SHICKSTER. **shiksel,** see SHICKSEL.

shilling, take the Queen's or **King's.** To enlist in the Army: C.18–20: coll >, by 1830, S.E. Also *take the shilling*.

shilling(-)dreadful (†in C.20), **shocker.** A (short) sensational novel sold at one shilling: coll >, ca 1905, S.E.: 1885, *Athenaeum*, 14 Nov., 'Mr R. L. Stevenson is writing another shilling-dreadful'; *s. shocker*, July 1886. The earlier term is on the analogy of PENNY DREADFUL; the latter, due to desire for variation. cf. THRILLER.

shilling to ninepence, bring a, see NINEPENCE TO . . .

shilly-shally. To be undecided; to hesitate; vacillate: 1782, Miss Burney: coll till ca 1850, then S.E. Ex the n. (1755, Shebbeare), itself ex the adj. (1734, Chesterfield), in its turn ex *stand shill I, shall I* (Congreve, 1700), earlier *stand shall I, shall I* (Taylor, 1630); *shilly-shally* as n. and (in C.20, ob.) adj., orig. coll, both > S.E. early in C.19.

shimmey (1837, Marryat); more gen. **shimmy** (1856, H. H. Dixon). A chemise: coll; not, as the O.E.D. asserts, merely dial. and U.S. 2. The game of *chemin de fer*, of the first two syllables of which it is a corruption: Society: late C.19–20.

shimozzel, -le, see SHEMOZZLE.

shin. A kick on the shin-bone: (esp. London) schoolboys' coll (—1887).

shin off. To depart: mostly Cockney: since ca 1870.

shin out. To pay up (v.i. and v.t.): proletarian: from ca 1860; ob.

shin-plaster. A bank-note: U.S., anglicized ca 1860; ob.

***shin-scraper.** A treadmill: c.: 1869, J. Greenwood, 'On account of the operator's liability, if he is not careful, to get his shins scraped by the ever-revolving wheel'.

shin-stage, (take) the. (To go) a journey on foot, not by stage-coach: non-aristocratic coll: mid-C.18–mid-19. cf. SHANKS'S MARE.

shin up. To climb (v.i.): C.19–20. (W. N. Glascock, *Sailors and Saints*, 1829, at I, 21.)

shinan(n)igan or **-in** or **-i(c)kin,** see SHENAN(N)IGAN.

shindig. An altercation, a violent quarrel, a tremendous fuss: late C.19–20. Ex SHINDY, 3.

shindy. A spree or noisy merrymaking: from ca 1820. Egan, 1821, 'The Jack Tar is . . . continually singing out, "What a prime shindy, my mess mates".' Either ex 'the rough but manly old game of "shinty"' (J. Grant, 1876) or, more prob., ex sense 3, which therefore presumably derives ex *shinty*. 2. A (rough) dance among sailors: nautical (—1811). 3. See SHINES. (The sense, a row or a commotion, from the 1840s, is gen. considered S.E., but it may orig. have been coll. ?ex sense 1 or 2.)

shine. A fuss, commotion, ROW: coll: from ca 1830. Dickens, 1852. Esp. *make* (or *kick up*) *a shine*. Perhaps ex *shine*, brilliance, influenced by SHINDY, 1. Hence, 2, boasting; chaff(ing); esp. *no shine*, honestly, sincerely, genuinely: tailors': mid-C.19–20. 3. Money: from ca 1840: (?c. >) low s. ?ex *shiners*. cf. SHINEY; SHINO. 4. See SHINE TO, TAKE A.

shine, v.i. To raise money, or display it: late C.19–20; ob. Ex *shine*, to excel. 2. To boast: tailors': from ca 1860; ob. cf. SHINER, 4.

shine, cut a. To make a fine show: coll: 1819 (O.E.D.). Occ. (†by C.20), *make a shine.*

shine from or **out of, take the.** To deprive of brilliance; to surpass, put in the shade: coll: 1818, Egan, *Boxiana*, I, *out of*; 1819, Moore, *from*, which is † in C.20.

shine-rag, win the. To lose; be ruined; London, ca 1850–1910. Occ. *shiney-rag*, as in H., 1st ed., 'Said in gambling when any one continues betting' after the luck sets in against him.

shine to, take a. To take a fancy to or for: coll: U.S. (—1850), adopted ca 1890 by Australians. cf. dial. *shiner*, a sweetheart, one's flirt.

shiner. See SHINERS. 2. A mirror; esp. a card-sharper's: from ca 1810: perhaps orig. c. 3. A clever fellow: coll and dial.: from ca 1820. 4. A boaster: tailors': from ca 1860. cf. SHINE, v., 2. 5. A silk hat: coll: 1867, F. Francis. 6. A stone so built into the wall of a house that its thick end is outward: South African: 1881, Douglass, *Ostrich Farming*. 7. A diamond: South African: 1884, *Queenstown Free Press*, 15 Jan. cf. SHINERS. 8. (*Shiner.*) The inevitable nickname of any man surnamed Green or Wright, Black or White, Bryant (Bryant & May's matches) or Bright: naval and military: late C.19–20.

shiners. Money; coins, esp. guineas and/or sovereigns: 1760, Foote, 'To let a lord of lands want shiners, 'tis a shame.' Occ. in singular as a gold or, less gen., a silver coin: C.19–20: Surr, 1806; 'Pomes' Marshall. cf. SHINE (n., 3); SHINEY; SHINO.

shines. Capers; tricks: U.S. (1830), anglicized ca 1860: coll. cf. SHINDY with its sense-history very similar to that of SHINE, *shines*, nn. 2. ?hence, copulation between human beings: from ca 1870.

shines like a shitten barn door, it. It shines most brilliantly: a low coll of C.18–mid-19. Swift, *Polite Conversation*, 'Why, Miss, you shine this morning like a sh— barn-door.'

shiney, properly **shiny.** Money; esp. gold

nuggets: 1856, Reade; very ob. cf. SHINERS; SHINO.

shiney-rag, see SHINE-RAG.

shingle short, have a. To *have a* TILE LOOSE, to be mentally deficient: from ca 1850: Australian s. >, ca 1910, gen. coll. Mundy, 1852; Mrs Campbell Praed, 1885.

shingle-splitting. The bilking of creditors by retiring to the country: Tasmanian: 1830, *The Hobart Town Almanack*; †by 1900. Here, *shingle* = a piece of board.

shingle-tramper. A coastguardsman: naval coll (—1867); ob. by 1900. Because he constantly walked the shingle of the (pebbly) shore.

shining saucepan and rusty pump. A nautical c.p. (late C.19–20) applied to a happy ship.

Shinkin-ap-Morgan. A Welshman: a coll nickname: mid-C.17–mid-18, when TAFFY > gen. A broadside ballad of ca 1660 (see Farmer's *Musa Pedestris*) has: 'With Shinkin-ap-Morgan, with Blue-cap, or TEAGUE, | We into no Covenant enter, nor league.'

shino. An ob. variant of SHINE, n., 3: from ca 1860. On RHINO. cf. SHINERS.

shins, break (one's). To borrow money (cf. U.S. *shinner*, *shinning*): late C.17–20; slightly ob. Ex the old Russian custom of beating on the shins those who have money and will not pay their debts.

shins, clever, see CLEVER SHINS.

shiny, the, see SHINEY. cf. SHINE (n., 3); SHINERS; SHINO.

shiny rag, win the, see SHINE-RAG.

ship. A body of compositors working together: printers' coll: 1875, Southward's *Dict. of Typography*. Abbr. *companionship*. cf. STAB, n. 2. See SHIP, OLD. 3. See SHIP, OUT OF A.

ship, v.t. To pull out of bed, mattress on top: Sherborne School: from ca 1860. 2. To turn back in a lesson: Shrewsbury School: from ca 1860. Both are prob. ex *ship (off)*, to send packing. 3. To drink (v.t.): nautical coll (—1887). Lit., take on board.

ship, old. A jocular coll address to a sailor: orig. and mostly nautical, to a former *ship*-mate: mid-C.19–20; ob. Cupples, *The Green Hand*, 1849.

ship, out of a. Out of work: theatrical: ca 1880–1910.

ship a bagnet. To wear a bayonet: naval: late C.18–mid-19.

ship a swab. To receive a sub-lieutenant's commission: naval: early C.19–early 20. The 'swab' was the single epaulette conferred by this rank. In W. N. Glascock, *Sketch-Book*, I, 1825, p. 113, it = to be a fully qualified captain. To *ship an epaulette* occurs in Glascock's *Sailors and Saints*, 1829, at II, 14; at I, 5, occurs *ship swabs*, thus 'Boys' shipping swabs before they shave' – glossed as 'Mounting epaulettes, which in his day denoted a captain'.

ship blown up at Point Nonplus. (Indicates that a man is) plucked penniless or politely expelled: Oxford University: ca 1820–50. *Point Nonplus* is a punningly imaginary geographical feature.

ship for a ha'porth of tar, lose (or spoil) a. Erroneous for *lose a sheep . . .*: mid-C.19–20. 'Tar is used to protect sores or wounds in sheep from flies, and the consequent generation of worms,' Apperson; *tar* being the cause of the error. (The proverb dates from late C.16.)

ship-husband. A sailor seldom on shore and even then anxious to return to his ship: nautical coll: from ca 1840; ob. Marryat, 1842. Punning the now ob. *ship's husband*, an agent that looks after a ship while it is in port.

ship in full sail. (A pot of) ale: rhyming s. (—1857).

ship-mate with, be. To have personal knowledge (of a thing): nautical: late C. 19–20. Bowen, 'e.g. "I've never been shipmate with single top-sails".'

ship one's land-face. To revert to one's sea-going attitude: nautical: late C.19–20; ob. With hard-case skippers a significant c.p. was *fetch me a bucket of water to wash off my land-face*: a hint to the crew of squalls ahead.

ship's cousin. A rating or apprentice berthed aft, but working with the men: nautical: late C.19–20. Prob. suggested by S.E. *ship's husband*.

ship's lungs. De Hall's patent bellows for ventilating men-of-war: naval coll: late C.19–early 20.

shipwrecked. Tipsy: East London (—1909). cf.:

shipwrecky. Weak; 'shaky': mid-C.19–20; coll (not very gen.). Hughes, 1857.

shiralee; shirralee. A swag or bundle of blankets, etc.: Australian: from ca 1880; ob. Ex an Aboriginal word. cf. BLUEY.

shirk. At Winchester, from ca 1860, *shirk in* is to walk, instead of plunging, into water, while *shirk out* is to go out without permission. cf. SHIRKSTER.

shirk, in its orig. sense, 'shark, sharper',

'needy parasite' and 'to live as a parasite' (C.17–18), may have been coll or s. or even c. Also *sherk*, *shurk*. A variant of SHARK.

shirkster. One who shirks: Winchester: from ca 1860. Ex SHIRK.

shirralee, see SHIRALEE. **shirry,** see SHERRY, n. and v.

shirt, fly round and tear one's. To bestir oneself: coll: C.19–20; ob.

shirt, lose one's. To become very angry: from ca 1865. Ex SHIRT OUT . . .

shirt!, that's up your. That's a puzzler for you! Mid-C.19–20; ob.

shirt collar. (The sum of) five shillings: rhyming s. (on *dollar*): from ca 1850; ob. OXFORD SCHOLAR is more usual.

shirt does!, do as my. Kiss my ARSE!: low c.p.: C.18–20; ob. D'Urfey.

shirt full of sore bones, give one a. To beat him severely: coll: C.18. Thomas Fuller, *Gnomologia*, 1732.

shirt in the wind. A piece of shirt seen through the fly or, much more gen., through a hole in the seat: late C.19–20; ob. Gen. *flag in the wind.*

shirt on, bet or **put one's.** To bet all one's money on, hence to risk all on (a horse): from ca 1890.

shirt out, get or **have** (a person's). To make or become angry: from middle 1850s. 'Ducange Anglicus' (*have*); H., 1st ed. (*get*). Ex the dishevelment caused by rage. cf. SHIRTY.

shirt-sleevie. A flannel dance: Stonyhurst: late C.19–20. 'The costume is an open flannel shirt and flannel trousers,' F. & H.

shirtey. Incorrect for SHIRTY.

shirtiness. The n. (late C.19–20) formed from:

shirty. Angry (temporarily); ill-tempered (by nature); apt to become quickly angered: from late 1850s. Maugham, 1897, *Liza of Lambeth*, 'You ain't shirty 'cause I kissed yer?' Ex SHIRT OUT.

shise, shiser, see SHICE; SHICER.

shish. A late C.19–20 variant of SHICE, adj., 1, and the v. Perhaps on SHIT.

shit, shite. Excrement; dung: late C.16–20 (earlier as diarrhoea, a sense †by C.15): S.E., but in C.19–20 a vulgarism. As n., *shite* is in C.19–20 comparatively rare except in dial. As excrement, prob. ex the v., common to the Teutonic languages: cf. SHICE; SHICER. i.e. it is ultimately cognate with *shoot.* 2. As a term of contempt applied to a person (rarely to a woman), it has perhaps always, C.16–20, been coll; in C.19–20, it is a vulgarism. In C.19–20, esp. *a regular shit*, in late C.19–20 *an awful s.* N.B., many compounds and all proverbs (even Swift's *shitten-cum-shites*) from n. and v. are S.E., but where they survive (e.g. *shit-breech*) they survive as vulgarisms: they (e.g. *shit-fire*, *s.-word*) do not here receive separate definition unless (e.g. SHIT-SACK) in a specifically unconventional sense: all those which are hereinunder defined have always been coll or s. See Grose, P., and A. W. Read, *Lexical Evidence*, 1935 (Paris; privately printed), for further details.

shit, shite, v. To stool: C.14–20: S.E., but in C.19–20 a vulgarism; at the latter stage, *shite* is less gen. than *shit*. See n., 1. **2.** To vomit: low coll (—1887).

shit!; rarely **shite!** An exclamation: rather low coll than a vulgarism: C.19 (?earlier)–20. cf. Fr. *merde!*

shit, fall in the. To get into trouble: low coll: since ca 1870. cf. SHIT, IN THE.

shit, happy as a pig in. 'Happy, even if lacking in grace' (Atkinson): non-aristocratic coll: late C.19–20.

shit, in the. In trouble: low coll: mid-C.19–20. Often *land* (another) *in the shit.*

shit, only a little clean. A derisive c.p. addressed to one bedaubed or self-fouled: C.19–20. In Scottish, gen. . . . *clean dirt.*

shit a brick. To defecate after a costive period: low: late C.19–20. cf. BAKE IT.

shit-bag. The belly; in pl, the guts: low: mid-C.19–20. 2. An unpleasant person: low: late C.19–20.

shit cinders!, go and eat coke and. A low, derisively defiant c.p. of late C.19–20; ob. (A good example of popular wit.)

shit-face is a low, late C.19–20 term of address to an ugly man.

shit-hole. The rectum: low: coll: C.19–20.

shit-hunter. A sodomist: cf. STIR-SHIT. low: C.19–20.

shit in your teeth! A retort on disagreement: C.18–mid-19: coll.

shit it in silver, swallow a sovereign and. A semi-proverbial c.p. indicative of the acme of convenience: C.19–20 (ob.) vulgarism.

shit not far behind that, there's. A workmen's c.p., evoked by a noisy breaking of wind: late C.19–20.

shit on. To impose on, use shamelessly: low: late C.19–20. 'He's shitting on you.'

shit on your own doorstep, you don't. You don't 'foul your own nest': c.p.: late C.19–20.

shit or bust with (e.g.) **him, it's.** He loves

bragging: low coll: late C.19–20. Key: 'He's all *wind*.'

shit-pot. A thorough or worthless humbug (person); a sneak: low s., and dial.: mid-C.19–20; ob.

shit-sack. A Nonconformist: 1769, Granger's *Biographical History of England*, concerning Wm Jenkin; this coll term may have arisen in late C.17; †by 1860. Grose, 2nd ed., repeats Granger's anecdotal 'etymology'.

shit-shark. A nightman: low: mid-C.19–20; ob.

shit-shoe (occ. **s.-shod**). 'Derisive to one who has bedaubed his boot', F. & H.: a low coll of mid-C.19–20; very ob. cf. *only a little clean* SHIT.

shit-stirrer. One who, by his actions, causes everybody unnecessary trouble: low: late C.19–20. The Canadian form is *shit-disturber*. Contrast STIR-SHIT.

shit through one's or **the teeth.** To vomit: low: late C.18–mid-19. Grose, 2nd ed., gives the following c.p., (*Hark ye, friend,*) *have you got a padlock on your arse, that you shite through your teeth?*

shit to a shovel, like. Very adhesive(ly) indeed: low coll: mid-C.19–20.

shit(-)wallah. A sanitary man: Army: late C.19–20.

shit weighs heavy! A low Canadian c.p., directed at a boaster: late C.19–20.

shite! see SHIT!

shite-poke. The bittern: Canadian: since ca 1880. 'From popular belief it has only one straight gut from gullet to exit, and has therefore to sit down promptly after swallowing anything' (D. E. Cameron in letter of 23 Aug. 1937). But Dr Leechman says that the *shit-* or *shite-poke* (euphemistically *shy-poke*) is a bird of the heron family and that it is so named because 'it habitually defecates on taking flight when alarmed'.

shits, the. Diarrhoea: coll: mid-C.19–20.

shitten door, see SHINES LIKE . . .

shitten look, have a. To look as if one needed to defecate: workmen's coll: late C.19–20.

Shitten Saturday. Easter Saturday: (dial. and) schools': from ca 1855; ob. Ex *Shut-in Saturday*, for on it Christ's body was entombed.

shitters. Diarrhoea: dial. and low coll: C.19–20.

shittle-cum-shaw, shittle (or shiddle)-cum-shite, shittletidee. Occ. as nn. in allusion, often as exclamations: both contemptuous: C.19–20 (ob.) dial and low coll reduplications on SHIT and *shite*, app. influenced by *shittle*, fickle, flighty.

shivareen is the Canadian shape of SHIVAROO: from ca 1870.

shivaroo. A spree; a party: Australia: 1888, (*Sydney*) *Bulletin*, 6 Oct., 'Government House shivaroos'; slightly ob. On Fr. *chez vous* (cf. SHEVOO) ex U.S. *shivaree*, a noisy serenade, itself a corruption of *charivari*, itself echoic.

shiver my timbers! see TIMBERS!, MY.

shivering Jemmy (occ., in late C.19–20, **James**). A beggar who, on a cold day, exposes himself very meagrely clad for alms: low, mostly London (—1860). Perhaps ex *s. J.*, dial. for *shivering grass*. cf. SHALLOW COVE and see SHALLOW DODGE.

shivers, the. The ague: coll: 1861, Dickens, in *Great Expectations*. 2. Hence (often *cold shivers*), horror, nervous fear: coll: from ca 1880.

shivery-shakes. The same; chills: coll: mid-C.19–20. Whence:

shivery-shaky. Trembling, esp. with ague or the cold: coll: mid-C.19–20. Anon., *Derby Day*, 1864, 'He's all shivery-shaky, as if he'd got the staggers, or the cold shivers.'

shlemozzle, see SHEMOZZLE. **shlenter,** occ. variant of SCHLENTER. **shoal,** see SHOOL.

shoal-water off, in. e.g. 'In shoal-water off the horrors', on the brink of delirium tremens; 'near' in any fig. sense: nautical coll: late C.19–20; ob.

shobbos of, make. To set in good order; to tidy up: Jewish: late C.19–20. To make clean and neat as if for the *Shobbos* or Sabbath.

shock-a-lolly, see WALLY.

shocker. See SHILLING SHOCKER, which, from 1890, it occ. displaces. Coll > S.E.

shocking. Extremely shocking or disgusting or objectionable: coll: 1842, Browning, 'Shocking | To think that we buy gowns lined with Ermine | For dolts . . .,' but doubtless in spoken use a decade earlier at least. cf. SHOCKINGLY, and:

shocking, adv. Shockingly: low coll: 1831, '"Vot a shocking bad hat!" – the slang Cockney phrase of 1831, as applied to a person: in 1833, Sydney Smith describes New York as "a shocking big place"'.

shockingly. Extremely or very, esp. in pejorative contexts: 1777, Miss Burney,

'Dr Johnson ... is shockingly near-sighted.' cf. SHOCKING, adj. 2. Shockingly ill: coll: 1768, Goldsmith, 'You look most shockingly to-day, my dear friend.' 3. Hence, from ca 1880, 'abominably', very badly. W. G. Marshall, 'Shockingly paved.'

shod, come in hosed and. To be born to a good estate: coll: C.19–20, ob. cf. *be born with a* SILVER SPOON IN ONE'S MOUTH.

shod (all) round, be. To know all about married life: coll: C.18–early 19. Swift, in *Conversation*, I, ' "Mr Buzzard has married again ..." "This is his fourth wife; then he has been shod round." ' 2. 'A parson who attends a funeral is said to be shod all round, when he receives a hat-band, gloves, and scarf: many shoeings being only partial,' Grose, 2nd ed.: late C.18–mid-19. *Four* items, in each case.

shoe-buckles, not worth. Worthless: coll: late C.17–18. Ray.

shoe is on the mast, the. 'If you like to be liberal, now's your time': a c.p. of C.19: sailors' > gen. lower classes'. In C.18, 'when near the end of a long voyage, the sailors nailed a shoe to the mast, the toes downward, that passengers might delicately bestow a parting gift.'

***shoe-leather!** Look out!; be careful!: c.: mid-C.19–20; ob. Perhaps cf. Warwickshire dial. *s.-l.*, a kicking.

shoe pinches him, his. He is drunk: coll: C.18. Franklin's *Drinker's Dict.*

shoe the cobbler. 'To tap the ice quickly with the fore-foot when sliding', F. & H.: coll: from ca 1840; ob. cf. COBBLER'S DOOR ...

shoe the goose. To undertake or do anything futile or absurd: coll: C.15–18. Hoccleve, Skelton, Breton. By late C.18, it has > a proverb, gen. in form *shoe the goslings*, usually, however, applied to a busybody smith. 2. To get drunk: coll: C.17. Cotgrave. Extant in Shropshire and Herefordshire dial.

shoe the (wild) colt. To demand an initiation-fee from one entering an office or employment: dial. (—1828) and coll; very ob. as the latter. Punning *colt*, a greenhorn. Also part of the ceremony of being *sworn in at* HIGHGATE, and of apprentices' initiations in various trades.

shoemaker. The large Antarctic gull: nautical (—1867). Perhaps jocular on its scientific name, *skua antarcticus*.

shoemaker's pride. Creaking boots or shoes: dial. and coll: mid-C.19–20. cf.:

shoemaker's stocks, be in the. To be pinched by strait shoes: ca 1660–1910. Pepys, 1666; Ray, 1678; B.E.; Grose. cf. last entry.

shoes, die in one's. To be hanged: ca 1690–1910: S.E. until C.19, then coll.

shoes, make children's. To be occupied absurdly or trivially; (to be made) to look ridiculous: coll: late C.17–19; in C.19, mainly dial. Behn, 1682, 'Pox! shall we stand making children's shoes all the year? No: let's begin to settle the nation, I say, and go through-stitch with our work.' cf.

shoes, make feet for children's. To coït: late C.18–mid-19. Ex preceding.

shoes are made of running leather, my, your, etc. I, you, etc., am – are – of a wandering disposition, or very restless: semi-proverbial coll: from ca 1570; ob. Churchyard, 1575; Hone, 1831.

shoesmith. A cobbler: jocular coll: C.19–20; ob. On S.E. sense, a shoeing-smith.

shoey. A shoeing-smith: military: late C.19–20. 2. (*Shoey.*) The 'inevitable' nickname of men surnamed Smith: military: late C.19–20.

***shoful** (1828, *Sessions*); occ. **schofel(l)** (1839), **schoful** (1859), **shofel** (1839), **shofle** (1862), **shouful** (—1914), (?only in sense 4) **shovel** (1864); often **showfull** (1851). (Only in sense 1 as an adj.) Counterfeit money: Brandon, 1839; 1851, Mayhew: Carew's *Autobiography of a Gipsy*. Yiddish almost imm. > Cockney s. verging on c., which indeed it may orig. have been – as Smythe-Palmer, 1882, says it was. Ex Yiddish *schofel*, worthless stuff, ex Ger. *schofel*, worthless, base, ex Yiddish pronunciation of Hebrew *shaphel* (or *-al*), low, as the O.E.D. so clearly sets forth. (Also SHOFUL MONEY: cf. SHOFUL-MAN.) 2. A low-class tavern: low: ca 1850–1910, and perhaps never very gen. Mayhew, 1851. Prob. directly ex the adj. *schofel* (see sense 1) with *place* or *tavern* suppressed. 3. A humbug, an impostor: ca 1860–90. See sense 1. 4. (Often spelt *shofle*, occ. *shovel.*) A hansom cab; among cabmen, a 'shoful' cab, according to Mayhew (*London Labour*, III, 351), is one infringing Hansom's patent: 1854, *Household Words*, vol. viii. There is little need to suppose with the O.E.D., that this sense may have a distinct origin, though H., 3rd ed., suggests the similarity of a hansom to a shovel or a scoop, and his successor in the 5th ed. cites (*à titre de curiosité*) a friend's 'shoful, full of show, *ergo*, beautiful – handsome – Hansom'. 5. See:

***shoful (jewellery).** Sham jewellery: 1864, H., 3rd ed., but prob. a decade older: c. Here, SHOFUL may be adj. or n.: cf. SHOFUL MONEY.

***shoful-man.** A counterfeiter of coins, notes, etc.; occ. = SHOFUL-PITCHER: c.: 1856, Mayhew.

***shoful(-)money.** Counterfeit money: c.: from the 1850s. See SHOFUL, 1.

***shoful** (etc.)**-pitcher.** A passer of counterfeit money: c. (—1839).

***shoful-pitching.** Passing of counterfeit money; c. (—1857). 'Ducange Anglicus'; H., 2nd ed.: but the reference in Carew's *Autobiography of a Gipsy* is to some twelve years earlier than in 'Ducange Anglicus'.

shoful pullet. 'A "gay" woman', H., 2nd ed.: low (?c.): ca 1860–90.

shoke. A hobby; a whim: Anglo-Indian: mid-C.19–20.

***sholl.** (Gen. v.t.) To crush the wearer's hat over his eyes: c.: from ca 1860; ob. ?ex *shola* (*hat*), a sola topee.

shonky, n.; shonk. A Jew: low: mid-C.19–20. Hence:

shonky, adj. Mean, money-grubbing: late C.19–20.

shont. A foreigner: Cockney: from ca 1880. cf. SHONK.

shoo to a goose, cannot say. To be timid, bashful: from ca 1630: coll till C.19, then S.E. – with BOO much more frequent.

***shook,** ppl (adj.), itself sol. Robbed; lost by robbery: c. of ca 1810–80. Vaux, 1812, 'I've been *shook* of my *skin*, I have been robbed of my purse.' See SHAKE v., 3 and 4, and cf. next entry. 2. A synonym, ca 1810–50, of ROCKED.

***shook?, have you.** Have you succeeded in stealing anything?: c. of ca 1810–80. See SHAKE, v., 4, and cf. SHOOK.

shook on. (Sense 1, gen. of a man; 2, of either sex.) In love with, or possessed of a passion for: Australian: 1888, 'Rolf Boldrewood', 'He was awful shook on Madge; but she wouldn't look at him.' 2. Having a great fancy for (a thing): 1888, 'Boldrewood', 'I'm regular shook on the polka.' cf. the very Australian *crook*, ill.

shook-up; esp. **reg'lar s.u.** Upset; nerve-racked: low coll: late (?mid-) C.19–20.

shool; Shool. A church or chapel: East London: from ca 1870. Ex the Jews' term for their synagogue.

shool; occ. **shoole** (Grose, 2nd ed.) or **shoal** (C.19); often **shule** (C.18–20), v. To go about begging, to sponge, to 'scrounge': dial. and s.: from 1730s. Smollett, 1748, 'They went all hands to shooling and begging'; Lover, 1842. Perhaps ex *shool*, a shovel, via dial. *shool*, to drag the feet, to saunter. 2. Hence, to skulk: dial. and s.: from ca 1780; ob. 3. To impose on (a person): 1745, Bampfylde-Moore Carew. Ex sense 1. 4. To carry as a 'blind': 1820, Clare: dial. and s.; ob.

shooler or **shuler;** occ. **shoolman.** A beggar, vagabond, 'scrounger', loafer: 1830, Carleton, 'What tribes of beggars and shulers'. cf. SHOOL, v., 1.

***shoon.** A fool; a lout: c. of late C.19–20; ob. ?on *loon*.

shoot. Amount, number: see SHOOT, THE WHOLE.

shoot, v.i. (Also *shoot a bishop*.) To have a wet dream: low: from ca 1870; ob. 2. v.t., to unload: railway: 1872, *Echo*, 29 July; slightly ob. Prob. on *shoot rubbish*. 3. To experience the sexual spasm: low: mid-C.19–20. Whence sense 1. cf. *flog the* BISHOP.

shoot, the whole. The entire amount or number or price, etc.: 1884 (O.E.D.) or perhaps from as early as 1880 (Ware): s. Occ. *the entire shoot* (?first in 1896).

shoot-about, see SHOOTABOUT.

shoot between or **(be)twixt wind and water.** To coït with a woman: coll: late C.17–20; ob. Implied in Congreve, 1695. A double anatomical allusion. 2. To infect venereally: late C.17–early 19. Gen. in the passive, punning the S.E. sense, 'to receive a shot causing a dangerous leak'.

shoot in the eye. To do (a person) a bad turn: coll: late C.19–20.

shoot in the tail. To coït with (a woman); to sodomize: low: mid-C.19–20.

shoot into the brown. To fail: Volunteers': ca 1860–1915. Ex rifle-practice, at which the poor shot misses the target, his bullet going into the brown earth of the butt.

shoot on the post. To catch and pass an opponent just before the tape: sporting: from ca 1870; ob.

shoot one's linen. To make one's shirt cuffs project beyond one's coat cuffs: coll: 1878, Yates, in *The World*, 16 Jan. cf. SHOOT YOUR CUFF!

shoot one's lines. To declaim vigorously: theatrical: from ca 1870.

shoot one's milt or **roe.** To ejaculate seminally: low: mid-C.19–20.

shoot one's star. To die : late C.19–20; ob. Ex evanescent shooting stars.

shoot over the pitcher. To brag of one's shooting: coll: C.19.

shoot that! Oh, be quiet!: late C.19–20. Possibly ex such Americanisms as *shoot that hat!* 2. Stop talking (about), as in *shoot the shop!*: late C.19–20.

shoot the cat, see CAT, SHOOT THE.

shoot the crow. To depart without paying: 1887, *Fun*, 8 June; ob. cf. BURN THE TOWN.

shoot the moon, see MOON, SHOOT THE; SHOVE THE MOON.

shoot up the straight, do a. To coït with a woman: low: mid-C.19–20. cf. *do a* RUSH, and SHOOT IN THE TAIL.

shoot white. To ejaculate: low: from ca 1870. Whence a Boer War conundrum.

shoot your cuff! 'Make the best personal appearance you can and come along' (Ware): lower classes': ca 1875–90. The semantics are those of SHOOT ONE'S LINEN.

shootabout. An irregular form of football: schools', esp. Charterhouse: late C.19–20. Also *shoot-about*, as in A. H. Tod, *Charterhouse*, 1900. cf. PUNT-ABOUT and COMPULSORY.

shooter. A gun or pistol; esp. a revolver: resp. 1840, 1877: s. >, ca 1910, coll. 2. A shooting-stick: printers': from ca 1860. Prob. on sense 1. 3. A black morning coat as distinguished from the tail coat worn by the Fifth and Sixth Forms: Harrow: from ca 1870.

shooter's hill. The *mons veneris*: low: late C.19–20; ob. Punning *Shooter's Hill*, London. 2. Whence *take a turn on Shooter's Hill*, to coït. Ex SHOOT, 3.

shooting stick. A gun: ca 1825–1900.

shop, always preceded by *the*. A place of business; where one works: coll: 1827, Thomas Surr, *Richmond*. An extension of the basic sense (a building, a room, where things are sold). 2. Often, Oxford or Cambridge University: from ca 1840: s. >, ca 1880, coll; slightly ob. Clough in his *Long Vacation Pastoral*, 'Three weeks hence we return to the shop'; Thackeray, 1848. Esp. *the other shop*, which is often used of a rival (chiefly, the most important rival) establishment of any kind. 3. Linked with the preceding sense is the jocular one, place – any place whatsoever. Thus, in political s., the House of Commons, as in Trollope's *Framley Parsonage*, 1861; among small tradesmen, one's house or home; among actors, the theatre, from ca 1880. Mid-C.19–20. cf. SHOP, ALL OVER THE. 4. Hence, in racing, a 'place' (1st, 2nd, or 3rd): from ca 1870. 5. An engagement, 'berth': theatrical: 1888, Jerome K. Jerome, 'Being just before Christmas . . ., there was no difficulty in getting another shop.' From twenty years earlier in dial. (Also gen. s.: 1898, W. Pett Ridge, *Mord Em'ly*.) 6. A prison: c.: late C.17–18. cf. the v., 1. 7. ?hence, the mouth: dial. and s.: from ca 1860. Whence *shut your shop!*, be silent! 8. (Certainly ex 'prison' sense.) A guard-room: military: mid-C.19–20. 9. A public-house: buckish: ca 1810–40.

***shop,** v. To imprison: late C.16–20: S.E. until mid-C.17, coll till late C.17, then c. 2. To put (an officer) under arrest in the guard-room: military (—1864). 3. To lay information on which a person is arrested: c.: early C.19–20. Ex sense 1. 4. Whence, or directly ex sense 1, to kill: c.: late C.19–20. Perhaps influenced by *ship*, to send packing. 5. To dismiss (a shop-assistant): from ca 1860; ob. Prob. ironically on S.E. *shop*, to give a person work (1855, O.E.D.). 6. *be shopped, get a shop*; to gain 1st, 2nd or 3rd place: the turf: from ca 1890 and 1870 resp. Ex the corresponding n. 7. (Gen. in passive.) To engage a person for a piece: theatrical (—1909). Ex the n., 5. 8. To punish severely: pugilistic: ca 1870–1910.

shop, all over the. Much scattered, spread out, dispersed; erratic in course: 1874 (= 1873), H., 5th ed., 'In pugilistic slang, to punish a man severely is "to knock him all over the shop", i.e. the ring, the place in which the work is done'; 1886, *Pall Mall Gazette*, 29 July, 'Formerly, the authorities associated with our fisheries were "all over the shop", if a vulgarism of the day be permissible': coll. Ex SHOP, n., 3.

shop, come or **go to the wrong.** To come (go) to the wrong person or place to get what one requires: coll: late C.19–20. Lyell. See SHOP, n., 3.

shop, get a, see SHOP, v., 6.

shop, shut up. To cease talking: mid-C.19–20. cf. SHOP, n., 7. 2. *shut up* (a person's) *shop*. To make him cease; to kill him: late C.19–20; ob.

shop, sink the. To refrain from talking shop: coll: late C.19–20. Prob. on *sink the ship*.

shop-bouncer. Mid-C.19–20; ob. low s., bordering on c. A variant of SHOP-LIFT. Ex:

***shop-bouncing.** Shop-lifting; c. (—1839).

shop-door. Trouser-fly: from ca 1890. Also *your shop-door is open!*

***shop-lift.** A shop-thief; esp. one who, while pretending to bargain, steals goods from the shop: ca 1670–1830: c. until ca 1700, then S.E. Head, 1673. See LIFT.

***shop-lifter.** The same: 1680, Kirkman: c. or s. until C.19, then coll till ca 1840, then S.E. cf. SHOP-LIFT. (Perhaps always S.E.: *shop-lifting*.)

shop lobber. A dandified shop-assistant: ca 1830–70. *Sinks*, 1848.

shop-masher. A very well, or much, dressed shop-assistant: lower classes': ca 1885–1910.

shop-mumper. A beggar operating in shops: c. (—1887).

shop-pad. A shop-thief: C.18: s. > coll. Dunton, 1705. See PAD, n., 5.

shop-'un. A preserved as opp. to a fresh egg: coll: 1878, dramatist Byron, 'I knows 'em! Shop-'uns! Sixteen a shilling!'

shopkeeper. An article still, after a long time, unsold: 1649, G. Daniel, who uses the frequent variant *old shopkeeper*.

shore loafer. Any civilian: bluejackets' pejorative coll: late C.19–20.

shore saints and sea devils. A nautical (mid-C.19–20; ob.) c.p. applied to such sailing-ship skippers as were lambs with the owners and lions with the crew. cf. SHIP ONE'S LAND-FACE.

Shoreditch, the Duke of. A mock-title: coll verging on S.E.: ca 1547–1683. See esp. Ellis's *History of Shoreditch*, p. 170.

short. A card (any below the 8) so tampered-with that none above the 8 can be cut, thus reducing the chances of an honour's turning up to two to one: gaming: mid-C.19–20. (Not to be confused with *shorts*, short whist.) 2. The same as SHORT, SOMETHING: coll: 1823, Egan's Grose, cf. the adj. 3. A revolver: Fenian: from ca 1885.

short, adj. Undiluted: coll: from ca 1820. See n., 2, and SHORT, SOMETHING. 2. A cashier's 'Long or short?' means 'Will you have your notes in small or large denominations?', *short* because thus there will be few notes, *long* because many, or because the latter method is short, the former long: bankers' > gen. commercial coll: from ca 1840. 3. 'A conductor of an omnibus, or any other servant, is said to be short, when he does not give all the money he receives to his master,' H., 3rd ed.: from ca 1860; ob. cf. SHORT(-)ONE.

short, bite off. To dismiss, or refuse, abruptly: tailors': from ca 1870. Prob. ex the habit of biting instead of cutting thread or cotton.

short, something. (A drink of) undiluted spirits: coll: from ca 1820. Either because, as Egan (1823) suggests, 'unlengthened by water' or, as O.E.D. proposes, ex short name – e.g. 'brandy', not 'brandy and water'.

short, taken, see TAKEN SHORT.

short and sweet, like a donkey's gallop. A coll elaboration of *short and sweet*: late C.19–20: coll and dial.

short and thick, like a Welshman's prick. A low c.p. applied to a short person very broad in the beam: mid-C.19–20.

short-arse. A short person: coll, mostly Cockney: from ca 1890. Ex:

short-arsed. (Of a person) that is short: coll: from ca 1870.

short cock. Cheese: Yorkshire s. (—1904), not dial.

short hairs, have by the, see HAIRS, GET BY THE SHORT.

short(-)head. A horse that fails by a short head: racing coll: 1883, J. Greenwood, 'That horribly anathematized short head'.

short home, come. To be put in prison: coll: C.17–18. Ex S.E. sense, to fail to return (orig. and esp. from an expedition).

short(-)length. A small glass of brandy: coll (Scots, esp. Glasgow): 1864, *Glasgow Citizen*, 19 Nov., 'The exhilarating short-length'.

short-limbered. Touchy: late C.19–early 20. cf. SHORT-WAISTED.

short of a sheet. Mentally deficient: late C.19–20; ob. cf. SHINGLE SHORT.

short(-)one. A passenger not on the way-bill: coaching: ca 1830–70. Because the way-bill is short of this passenger's name: cf. SHORT, adj., 3. 2. See SHORT 'UN.

short(-)stick. (Occ. collective.) A piece, or pieces, of material of insufficient length: drapers': from ca 1860. *Once a Week*, 1863, viii, 179.

short time. A visit to a prostitute for one copulation only: low coll: late C.19–20.

short 'un. A partridge: poachers' (—1909). Ware derives ex 'the almost complete absence of tail feathers'. Contrast LONG ONE, and see TALL 'UN.

short-waisted. Irritable; touchy: esp. among tailors: from ca 1870. cf. SHORT-LIMBERED.

***shortening,** vbl n. Clipping coins (as a profession): c.: ca 1865; ob.

shorter. A coin-clipper: low s. verging on c.: 1857, Borrow's *Romany Rye*.

shot. Amount due for payment; one's share thereof: late C.15–20: S.E. until late C.18, then coll. cf. *the whole* SHOOT. 2. A corpse disinterred: body-snatchers' s. > j.: 1828, *Annual Register*; ob. by 1900. App. ex *a good shot for the doctors*. 3. A meridional altitude ascertained by *shooting the sun*: nautical (—1867).

shot, v. To make a weak-winded horse seemingly sound: horse-dealers' (—1874). By dosing with small shot to 'open his pipes'.

shot, adj. Tipsy: from ca 1870. Ex being wounded by a shot. cf. the U.S. *shot in the neck*, perhaps the imm. origin, and SHOT-AWAY, and OVERSHOT.

shot! Look out, a master's coming!: Royal High School, Edinburgh: late C.19–20. 2. Abbr. *good shot!*; gen. 'shot, sir!': late C.19–20: coll.

shot, be. 'To make a disadvantageous bet which is instantly accepted', F. & H.: the turf: from ca 1880. 2. To be photographed: photographers' coll: from ca 1885.

shot, do a, see DO A SHOT.

shot, hot, see HOT SHOT.

shot, like a. Very quickly; immediately: coll: 1809, Malkin. 2. Hence, very willingly, unhesitantly: coll: late C.19–20.

shot, pay the, v.i. and t. To coït (with a woman): coll: C.17–19. F. & H. quotes two C.17 broadside ballads. Ex *pay the shot*, to pay the bill or one's share of it, now coll (see SHOT, n., 1).

shot-away. Tipsy: nautical: late C.19–20. cf. SHOT, adj.

shot-bag. A purse: 1848, Durivage, 'Depositing the "tin" in his shot-bag'; slightly ob. Ex SHOT, money, as in *not a* SHOT IN THE LOCKER.

shot between or **(be)twixt wind and water,** see SHOOT BETWEEN ...

shot-clog. A simpleton tolerated only because of his willingness to pay the SHOT: mid-C.19–20; ob. cf. SHOT-SHIP.

shot first, I'll see (him, her, gen.) **you.** Damned if I'll do it!: low coll: 1894, 'John Strange Winter'.

shot himself! A c.p. applied to someone breaking wind in or near a company of men, often with the c.p. comment, *if he's not careful, he'll shit himself*: late C.19–20.

shot if —; I'll (or may I) be. Mildly imprecatory or strongly dissenting: low coll: 1826, Buckstone, 'He, he he! I'll be shot if Lunnun temptation be onything to this.' H., 1st ed., has the ob. variant, *I wish I may be shot if* —. cf. SHOT FIRST ...

shot in the eye. An ill turn: coll: late C.19–20; slightly ob. *Pearson's Magazine*, Sept. 1897, 'Getting square with the millionaire who had done him such an unscrupulous shot in the eye'.

shot in the giblets or **tail.** Pregnant: low: mid-C.19–20.

shot in the (or one's) locker, have still (or **still have) a.** To be still potent: late C.19–20.

shot in the locker, not a. Destitute of money, ideas, or anything else: naval coll: mid-C.19–20. Much earlier, in a positive form, in an unidentified British song reprinted in the *Port Folio* of 17 May 1806:

Then with shot in my locker, a wife and a cot,
Tobacco, grog, flip, and no purser,
I'll sit down contented with what I have got,
And may each honest tar do no *worser*.

It occurs also in W. N. Glascock, *The Naval Sketch-Book* (I, 207), 1825; but earliest of all in George Brewer, *Bannian Day* (a farce), 1796, 'I've always got a shot in the locker.'

shot of. A mid-C.19–20 Cockney variant of SHUT OF. *Sessions*, Oct. 1836.

shot on the post, be. To have a competitor pass one as one easies for, or wearies at, the finish: athletics coll: 1897. Ex: 2. The same of horses in racing: adumbrated in 1868: coll.

shot-ship. 'A company sharing and sharing alike', F. & H.: printers': from ca 1875.

shot-soup. Inferior pea-soup: nautical: late C.19–20; ob. Ex peas like bullets.

shot 'twixt . . . see SHOOT BETWEEN ...

shouful, see SHOFUL.

should say (suppose, think), I. I'm very much inclined to say, etc.; I certainly do say, etc.: coll: 1775, C. Johnston, 'I should rather think he has a mind to finger its finances.'

shoulder, v.i. and t. To take passengers without entering them on the way-bill, thus defrauding the employer: coaching: ca 1810–70. 'Jon Bee', 1823; cf. his *Picture of London*, 1828 (p. 33). 2. Hence, v.t., of any servant embezzling his master's money: from ca 1860. Both senses very frequent as vbl n.

shoulder, over the (left), see LEFT, OVER THE.

shoulder, slip of the. (Of the woman 'victim') seduction: coll: C.19.

shoulder-feast. A dinner for the hearse-bearers after a funeral: ca 1810–60.

shoulder-knot. A bailiff: ca 1825–80. Ex hand clapped on victim's shoulder.

***shoulder-sham.** A partner to a FILE: c.: late C.17–early 19.

shoulder-stick. A passenger not on the way-bill, i.e. one whose fare goes into the pockets of driver and guard: coaching: ca 1825–70. cf. SHORT-ONE and SHOULDER.

shouldering, see SHOULDER.

shout. 'A call to a waiter to replenish the glasses of a company: hence, a turn in paying for a round of drinks. Also, a free drink given to all present by one of the company; a drinking party', this last being rare: Australian, hence New Zealand; mid-C.19 as, e.g., in Wm Kelly, *Life in Victoria*, 1859: 1863, H. Simcox, 'Many a "shout" they're treated to.' Ex the v.i. 2. Hence, one's turn to entertain another: same period. e.g. 'It's my shout this time.' 3. An alarm: fire-brigades': from ca 1880.

shout, v. To stand drinks to the company, hence to even one person: v.i., 1859, H. Kingsley; v.t., to pay for drinks for (a person, persons), hence for (say) 'smokes', 1867, Lindsay Gordon; hence, late C.19–20, to entertain (a person, persons). Australian, hence New Zealand; by 1864 well-known in England. Ex shouting to the waiter to fetch drinks.

shout, go on the. To embark on a bout of drinking; to drink to excess: from ca 1890: orig. Australian; by 1905, gen. Kipling. See SHOUT, n., and cf. next two entries.

shout, stand (a). To pay for drinks all round: 1887, 'Hopeful', 'There is a great deal of standing "shout" in the Colonies.' See SHOUT, n., 1.

shout oneself hoarse. To get drunk: gen. s. (—1903). Punning lit. sense of the whole phrase and the s. sense of SHOUT, v.

shouted, be. To have one's wedding banns proclaimed: since ca 1860. (Williams Westall, *Sons of Belial*, 1895.)

shouter. One who 'shouts': 1885, Douglas Sladen. See SHOUT, v. cf.:

shouting, vbl n. (Issuing) an 'all-in' invitation to drink: see SHOUT, v.

***shov.** A knife: c. (—1909). Ex *chiv(e)* (see CHIVE-FENCER) on *shove*.

shove, n. See SHOVE, THE; SHOVE, ON THE; also SHOVE IN THE EYE, THE MOUTH. 2. A coïtion: coll: C.18–20. Ned Ward, 1707. Esp. in *give* (a woman) *a shove*. cf. the v., 2, and PUSH, v., 2. 3. Empty talk; self-glorification: coll, at first (ca 1880) low urban, but by 1887 (at latest), gen. Prob. ex: 4. Energy; initiative: (low) coll: from the 1870s; ob. Presumably suggested by equivalent *push*.

shove, v.t. To thrust, put, carelessly or roughly or hurriedly into a place, a receptacle: familiar S.E. often merging into coll: 1827, Scott, 'Middlemas . . . shoved into his bosom a small packet.' Also *shove aside* (1864) or *away* (1861). 2. Gen. v.t. To coït (with): coll: C.17–20; ob. 3. See vbl phrases here ensuing. 4. (Of cabmen) 'to adopt unfair methods to obtain fares', Baker: Australian: from ca 1880.

shove, be on the. To keep moving, to move: coll: late C.19–20.

shove, get and **give the,** see SHOVE, THE.

shove, on the. On the move; moving: coll: late C.19–20. Milliken, 1893, 'There's always some fun afoot there, as will keep a chap fair on the shove.'

shove, the. A dismissal: 1899, Whiteing in *No. 5 John Street*, has both *get the shove* and *give the shove*, to be dismissed, to dismiss. cf. PUSH, n., 5.

shove along, v.t. To cause sailing ships to make as much speed as possible: naval coll: late C.18–19. (W. N. Glascock, *Sketch-Book*, I, 1825.)

shove-along, in. In echelon: soldiers' and sailors': late C.18–mid-19. (Glascock, I, 1825.) By the process of 'Hobson-Jobson'.

shove for. To go to; make a move towards: coll: 1884, Mark Twain, 'Me and Tom shoved for bed.' cf. SHOVE, BE ON THE, and modern coll *shove off*.

shove-halfpenny. A gambling game akin to shovel-board: 1841, *Punch*, 27 Nov., 'The favourite game of shove-halfpenny': s. >, ca 1910, coll. On the †*shove-groat, slide-groat*, and *shove-board* (later *shovel-board*).

shove in (a thing). To pawn it: low coll: late C.19–20.

shove in one's face. To put in one's mouth: low coll: late C.19–20.

shove in the eye, etc. A punch in the eye, etc.: coll: late C.19–20. Whiteing, 1899, 'Mind your own bloomin' business, or I'll give yer a shove in the eye.'

shove in the mouth. A drink: 1811, *Lex. Bal.*; ob.

shove on. To lay a bet of so much on (a horse): turf coll: late C.19–20.

shove the moon. To slip away with one's goods without paying the rent: low: 1809, G. Andrewes, slang-lexicographer; †by 1880. cf. *shoot the* MOON.

***shove the queer,** the article being occ. omitted. To pass counterfeit money: c.: mid-C.19–20: ?orig. U.S. Matsell. See QUEER, n.

***shove the tumbler.** To be whipped at the cart's tail: c.: late C.17–early 19. Hall's *Memoirs*, 1708, 'Those cast for Petit-larceny shove the tumbler'. A TUMBLER (2) is a cart.

shove underground. To bury: coll: from ca 1870.

***shove-up.** Nothing: c. or low s. of ca 1810–60. Ex †*shove-up socket*, a GADGET enabling a candle to burn right out.

shovel. A hansom cab. See SHOFUL, 4. 2. An engineer in the Navy: nautical: ca 1855–70. Because they were rough and ignorant.

shovel, or fire-shovel, he or she was fed with a. A c.p. applied to a person with a very large mouth: ca 1780–1850.

shovel, put to bed with a. To be buried: coll: from ca 1780; very ob. In C.19, occ. *with a spade*.

shovel, put up one's. To cease work: workmen's coll: from ca 1890; slightly ob.

shovel!, that's before you bought your. That is one against you; that *settles your* HASH: coll: ca 1850–1910.

shovelling is a form of bullying at Sandhurst, ca 1830–55: coll. 'Spread-eagling the victim on the table and beating him with racquet-bats and shovels', A. F. Mockler-Ferryman, *Annals of Sandhurst*, 1900.

***shover.** A passer of base coin: c.: orig. U.S.: anglicized ca 1890. Abbr. SHOVER OF THE QUEER. 2. (Also *shuvver, shuffer.*) A chauffeur: jocular coll: 1908.

***shover of the queer.** The same: c.: U.S., anglicized ca 1870. *Figaro*, 20 Feb. 1871, 'A saloon ... headquarters of all the counterfeiters and shovers of the queer in the country'. See QUEER, n.

show. Any public display (a picture-exhibition, a play, a fashionable assembly or ceremony, a speech-making, etc.): coll: 1863, Sala. Ex *show*, an elaborate spectacle. 2. Hence, a matter, affair, concern: 1888, Rider Haggard, in the Summer Number of the *Illustrated London News*, 'Their presence was necessary to the show.' 3. A group or association of persons. Mostly in *boss the* SHOW, and implicatively in *give the* SHOW AWAY.

show, v.i. In boxing, to enter the ring as a combatant: boxing coll of ca 1813–50. 2. Hence, to appear in society or company; at an assembly, etc.: coll: 1825, Westmacott, 'He *shows* in Park'; 1898, Jean Owen, 'If the king was in the cabin ... no subject might show on deck.' In C.20, this sense is ob., *show up* being much more gen.: *show up*, likewise coll, occurring first in W. Black's *Yolande*, 1883 ('Don't you think it prudent of me to show up as often as I can in the House ... so that my good friends in Slagpool mayn't begin to grumble about my being away so frequently?') and meaning also to turn up for an appointment. 3. To exhibit oneself for a consideration: coll: 1898, *Daily News*, 2 April, 'He got a living by "showing" in the various public-houses.'

show, boss or run the. To assume control; act as manager: 1889, BOSS (perhaps orig. U.S.); in C.20, often *run*. See SHOW, n., 2, 3.

show, do a. To go to a public entertainment: coll: from ca 1906. See SHOW, n., 1.

show, run the, see SHOW, BOSS THE. **show a leg!** see SHEW A LEG, 2. **show a point to,** see POINT TO.

show away, give the. To blab, confess; to expose the disadvantages or pretentiousness of an affair, esp. one in which a group is concerned: 1899, Delannoy, *£19,000*, 'I didn't want to give the show away': s.

show-box, the. The theatre: theatrical: from ca 1870; ob.

show-leg day, see SHEW-LEG DAY.

show (him) **London.** To hold one, upside down, by the heels: schools': from ca 1880. Opp. *see London*, to be thus held; also, to hang by the heels from a trapeze, a horizontal bar, etc.

show off, v.i. To act, talk, ostentatiously or in order to attract attention to oneself: coll: from ca 1790. Gilbert White; D. C. Murray.

show up, see SHOW, v., 2.

showbanker, see SCOWBANKER. **showful(l),** see SHOFUL.

showing, a front. A short-notice parade: military: late C.19–20; ob. Because while one might possibly pass muster in front, at the back ...

***shrap.** Wine used in swindling: very local c. of ca 1592. Greene, *The Black Book's Messenger*. Prob. ex †*shrap(e)*, a bait, a snare.

shred(s). A tailor: late C.16–early 19. cf.:

shreds and patches. A tailor: coll: C.18–20; ob.

shrewdy. A shrewd, esp. a cunning, person; a trickster: coll: late C.19–20. Mostly military and Australian.

Shrewsbury clock, by. A coll phrase lessening or even cancelling the period of time – or the fact – mentioned: late C.16–20; ob. Shakespeare; Gayton, 'The Knight that fought by th' clock at Shrewsbury'; Mrs Cowley, 1783; Stevenson, 1891.

shriek. An exclamation-mark: coll: 1864, Dean Alford; ob.

shrieking sisterhood. Women reformers, hence female busybodies: journalistic coll: ca 1890–1910. Milliken, 1893, 'This yere shrieking sisterhood lay ain't 'arf bad.'

shrift!, he hath been at. An ecclesiastical c.p. of C.16: applied to one who has been betrayed he knows not how. Tyndale, *The Obedience of a Christian Man*, 1528. The implication is that the priest to whom he confessed has betrayed him.

shrimp. A harlot: ca 1630–70. Whiting, 1638, in *Albino and Bellama*.

shroff, see SCHROFF.

shrubbery. (Gen. the female) pubic hair: coll: late C.19–20.

shtumer, see STUMER.

shucks! Nonsense!; *I* don't care!: coll: 1885: U.S. partly anglicized ca 1900. Ex *shuck*, typifying the worthless, itself orig. (and still) a husk or shell.

shuffer, see SHOVER, 2.

shuffle, v.t. To feign, as in *shuffle asleep*, pretend to be asleep. Whence *shuffler*. Winchester: mid-C.19–20. Ex S.E. sense, act evasively.

***shuffler.** (App.) a drinker; prob. one who WANGLES or scrounges drinks: Brathwait, 1652. Always with RUFFLER and SNUFFLER. 2. Usually in pl (*shufflers*), the feet: pugilistic: ca 1840–90. Augustus Mayhew, *Paved With Gold*, 1857. The old-time boxer used to shuffle about on his feet; it was Jim Corbett who introduced – or at least popularized – 'ballet dancing' in the ring.

shule; shuler, see SHOOL; SHOOLER.

shulleg-day, see SHEW-LEG DAY.

'shun! Attention!: military coll (from the middle 1880s). cf. HIPE.

shunt. To move aside (—1859); to kill (—1909): railwaymen's coll. Ex lit. sense.

***shurk.** A variant of SHARK. See SHIRK.

shut-eye. A deception, trick or swindle: s.: naval, 1899.

shut it! Be silent!; stop that noise!: from mid-1880s. 'Pomes' Marshall, ca 1890, 'Oh, shut it! Close your mouth until I tell you when.'

shut of, be or get. (See also SHOT OF.) To be free from, rid of: late C.16–20: S.E. until C.19, then coll; in late C.19–20, low coll. 'Rolf Boldrewood', 1888, 'Father)... gets shut of a deal of trouble . . . by always sticking to one thing'; R. L. Stevenson, 1891, 'What we want is to be shut of him.' In active mood from ca 1500, whence this passive usage. cf. dial. *be shut on*, as in Mrs Gaskell's *Mary Barton*, 1843, and *shut*, a riddance.

shut up. To end (a matter): coll: 1857, Dickens, 'Now, I'll tell you what it is, and this shuts it up.' 2. (Gen. in imperative: cf. SHUT IT! and SHUT YOUR FACE!) To cease talking; stop making a noise: 1853, 'C. Bede'; Mursell, *Lecture on Slang*, 1858, 'When a man . . . holds his peace, he shuts up'; Maugham, 1897. s. >, ca 1890, coll. Ex S.E. sense, to conclude one's remarks. The C.17 equivalent was SNECK (or SNICK) UP! 3. v.i. 'To give up, as one horse when challenged by another in a race', Krik, *Guide to the Turf* (*Krik* being the pseudonym of B. Reid Kirk, *Amicus Equus . . . And a Guide to Horse Buyers*, 1884): racing coll (?orig. s.). cf.:

shut up, adj. Completely exhausted: ca 1860–1900.

shut-up house. The land headquarters of the local Press Gang: naval coll: late C.18–mid-19. Bowen.

shut up shop, see SHOP, SHUT UP.

shut up shop-windows, have. To be bankrupt: coll: ca 1675–1850. Ray, 1678. cf. SHUTTERS, PUT UP THE, 2.

shut up your garret! Hold your tongue!: low (—1909). cf.:

shut your face, head, neck, rag-box! Be quiet!; stop talking: low: from mid-1870s: perhaps (except for last, which occurs in Kipling, 1892) orig. U.S., for *shut your head!* is recorded first in Mark Twain in 1876 and this appears to be the earliest of these phrases; *shut your neck* is in Runciman, *Chequers*, 1888; *shut your face*, from before 1903. All on the analogy of *shut your mouth!*, which, though admittedly familiar, is yet S.E. cf. SHUT IT! and SHUT UP, 2.

shuts. As n., a hoax, a SELL; as interjection, 'sold again!' Christ's Hospital: from ca 1860.

shutter, gen. pronounced *shetter*. To convey a drunk on a shop-shutter to the police-station, the police carrying him: low Cockney (—1909); very ob.

***shutter-racket.** The practice of stealing from a building by boring a hole in a window-shutter and taking out a pane of glass: c. of ca 1810–60.

shuttered (often pron. *shettered*). In a state of complete ignominy: low (—1909). Perhaps ex sense 2 of:

shutters, put up the. To 'bung up' the eyes of one's opponent: boxing: mid-C.19–20; slightly ob. 2. To stop payment, announce oneself bankrupt: coll: mid-C.19–20. Ex S.E. sense, to close a shop for the day. cf. SHUT UP SHOP-WINDOWS.

shutters up, got the, see GOT THE SHUTTERS UP.

shuttle-bag, swallow the. To get husky-throated: (?dial. and) coll: mid-C.19–20.

shuvly-kouse. A public-house: low urban (—1909); virtually †. Ware, 'This phrase spread through London from a police-court case, in which a half-witted girl used this phrase.'

shy. A quick and either jerky or careless (or jerkily careless) casting of a stone, ball, etc.: coll: 1791, Brand. Ex v., 1. 2. Hence, a GO (n., 8), attempt, experiment, chance: coll: 1823, Egan's Grose; 1824, Egan (vol. IV of *Boxiana*), 'I like to have a shy for my money.' 3. Fig., a 'fling', a jibe or sarcasm (*at* . . .): 1840, De Quincey, 'Rousseau . . . taking a "shy" at any random object'. 4. The Eton Football sense, orig. (1868) coll, soon > j. 5. A thrower, esp. in cricket: coll: 1884.

shy, v. (In late C.19–early 20, occ. *shie.*) v.i., to throw a missile jerkily or carelessly or with careless jerkiness: coll: 1787, Bentham, 'A sort of cock for him . . . to shie at'. Perhaps ex SHY(-)COCK. 2. Hence, v.t.: To throw, toss, jerk: coll: lit., 1824, Egan; fig., Scott, 1827, 'I cannot keep up with the world without shying a letter now and then.'

shy, adj. Short, low (of money): low: 1821, Haggart, 'Although I had not been idle during these three months, I found my blunt getting shy.' †by 1900. 2. Whence *shy of*, short of (money; hence provisions, etc.): Australia and Canada: late C.19–20. cf. U.S. *shy*, *shy of*, lacking, short of, a usage perhaps influencing, but not originating, the Australian. 3. Disreputable; not quite honest: 1849, Thackeray, 'Mr Wagg . . . said, "Rather a shy place for a sucking county member, ay, Pynsent?"'; 1864, H. J. Byron, 'Shy turf-transaction'. s. >, ca 1900, coll. Prob. ex S.E. sense, timid, bashful. 4. ?hence, doubtful in quantity and/or quality: 1850, Thackeray, 'That uncommonly shy supper of dry bread and milk-and-water'; Mark Lemon, 1865, 'Her geography is rather shy, and I can make her believe anything.'

shy, coconut. An amusement (and its means) consisting in throwing balls at coconuts: 1903: coll.

shy(-)cock. A wary person, esp. one who keeps indoors to avoid the bailiffs: 1768, Goldsmith. 2. Hence, a cowardly person: 1796, F. Reynolds. Both senses †by ca 1850, the latest record being of 1828. Prob. ex lit. sense, a cock not easily caught, one that will not fight.

***shy of the blues.** Anxious to avoid the police: c.: from ca 1870.

shyer; shier. One who throws as in SHY, v.: coll (—1895).

shyin', see SHINE, adj.

shyster. An unprofessional, dishonest, or rapacious lawyer (1856); hence, anyone not too particular as to how he conducts business (1877); hence (—1903), a generic pejorative: U.S., anglicized resp. ca 1890, 1900, 1905. Either ex SHY, adj., 3, or ex SHICER: cf. next sense. 2. 'A duffer, a vagabond,' H., 3rd ed.: from ca 1860. This sense, independent of U.S. *shyster*, is a variant of SHICER, 2.

si quis. A candidate for holy orders: from ca 1860; ob. Ex the public notice of ordination, so named because it began *Si quis*, if any . . .

***sice.** Sixpence: c.: ca 1660–1850. Tatham, 1660; *Covent Garden Drollery*, 1672; B.E.; Grose; Lytton. Ex *sice*, the six in dice.

sick. Disgusted; exceedingly annoyed or chagrined: from ca 1800. 1853, Surtees, 'How sick he was when the jury . . . gave five hundred pounds damages against him.' Ex *sick* (*of*), thoroughly weary (of), prob. via *sick and tired* (*of*).

sick, n. Mostly in *give* (someone) *the sick*, to disgust: low coll: ca 1840–1930. *Sessions*, Nov. 1849, 'If I have many such markets as this, it will give me the sick.'

sick, enough to make a horse, see SICK AS A CAT. **sick, the,** see SICKS, THE.

sick as a cat, cushion, dog, horse, rat, – as. Very sick or ill indeed: coll verging on S.E.: resp. 1869, Spurgeon; ca 1675–1800, Ray, Swift; late C.16–20, G. Harvey, Garrick, Mrs Henry Wood; ca 1680–1830 (Meriton,

1685; Sterne; Grose), then coll; late C.19–20, ob. As a horse does not vomit, to be *as sick as a horse* connotes extreme discomfort. Northamptonshire dial. is logical in that it applies the phrase to a person 'exceedingly sick without vomiting' (Miss Baker, 1854).

sick-bay moocher. A malingerer: *Conway* cadets': from before 1891. See MOOCHER.

sick friend, sit up with a. (Of a man) to excuse oneself for absence all night from the conjugal bed: from ca 1880; slightly ob. cf. SEE A MAN *about a dog*.

sick of the fever burden. To be BONE-LAZY: coll: C.16–17. e.g. in Fulwood's *Enemy of Idleness*, 1593, 'You have the palsey or eke the fever burden'; Ray. cf. SICK OF THE LOMBARD FEVER.

sick of the idle crick and the belly-work in the heel. As preceding: coll: ca 1670–1750. Ray, 1678, thus: *sick o'th'idle crick, and the belly-work i' th' heel*, therefore prob. orig. Northern dial. Derisive, presumably, of an illness alleged to excuse idleness. cf.:

sick of the idles. Exceedingly lazy; idle without the will to work: coll: 1639, John Clarke; Ray, 1670. Ob. by 1850, but not yet †. cf. preceding two entries and:

sick of the Lombard fever. The same: coll: ca 1650–1720. Howell, 1659; Ray, 1670. cf. SICK OF THE FEVER BURDEN.

sick of the simples, see SIMPLES, BE CUT FOR THE.

sick up, v.i. and t. To vomit: low coll: late (?mid-) C.19–20.

sickrel. 'A puny, sickly Creature', B.E.: late C.17–early 18. O.E.D. says that it is c.: but B.E. does not so classify it. Pejorative on *sick*: cf. *cockerel* on *cock*.

sicks (occ. sick), the. A feeling of nausea. Esp. in *give one the sicks*, to get on a person's nerves: late C.19–20.

side. Conceit, swagger; pretentiousness. Earliest and often *put on side*, to give oneself airs, to SWANK. Hatton, 1878; 'Pomes' Marshall. Ex *side*, proud, or more prob., as W. suggests, by a pun on *put on side* at billiards.

***side!** Yes: Northern c. (—1864); ob. ?on 'I side with you!'

side, on the. In addition; not downright illegally, yet dubiously, in unacknowledged commissions, tips, bribes: coll: late C.19–20.

side-boards. A shirt-collar: low (—1857); †by 1900. Prob. the same collar as that defined at SIDEBOARD. 2. Whiskers: from ca 1890.

side-lights. Eyes: nautical: late C.19–20.

side-pocket, want as much as a dog (or toad) wants a. A c.p. applied to one who desires something unnecessary: late C.18–20; ob. Grose, 1st ed., *toad* (at *toad*); *dog* in Grose, 2nd ed., where also the variant *as much need of a wife as a dog of a side-pocket*, applied to a debilitated old man. Quiller-Couch, 1888, 'A bull's got no more use for religion than a toad for side-pockets.' Occ. *monkey*, unrecorded before 1880; very rarely *cow*, as in Whyte-Melville, 1862.

side-scrapers. SIDE-WINGS: London middle classes': ca 1879–89.

side-sim. A fool: C.17 coll. Nares records for 1622. ?opp. *Sim subtle*, a crafty person or a subtle one. *Sim* = Simon. cf. *simple Simon*.

side up with. To compare, or compete, with: 1895, *Punch*, 23 Feb.; ob.

side wind. A bastard: naval: ?ca 1780–1850. ?punning BY-BLOW.

side-wings. Whiskers: late C.19–20; ob. Contrast SIDE-BOARDS.

sideboard. A 'stand-up' shirt-collar: 1857, 'Ducange Anglicus'; ob. Gen. in pl. (H., 1st ed., shows that the term was applied to the collars of ca 1845–55.)

sideboards. Whiskers: from ca 1890; very ob. cf. SIDE-WINGS.

'sides. Besides; moreover; late C.16–20: S.E. until C.19, then coll and dial.

sidey, see SIDY. **sidi-boy,** see SEEDY(-BOY).

sidledywry. Crooked: late C.18–early 19. Grose, 2nd ed. Ex *sidle* + *awry*.

sidy; occ. – but incorrectly – **sidey.** Conceited; apt to SWANK it: 1898 (O.E.D.): s. >, ca 1910, coll; ob. Ex SIDE.

sif, siff, see SYPH.

***sift,** v.t.; occ. v.i. To steal small coins, i.e. such as might be conceived of as passing through a sieve: thus F. & H. (1903); but in 1864, H. says that it = to purloin 'the larger pieces, that did not readily pass through the sieve'! It appears, however, that F. & H. is right, for in H., 1874, we find 'To embezzle small coins, those which might pass through a sieve – as threepennies and fourpennies – and which are therefore not likely to be missed'.

sight. A multitude or a (great) deal: late C.14–20: S.E. until mid-C.18, then coll (in C.20, virtually s.). Sheridan & Tickell, 1778, 'They wear . . . a large hat and feather, and a mortal sight of hair.' 2. As adv.: coll >, ca 1890, s.: 1836, T. Hook; 1889, Grant Allen, 'You're a sight too clever for me to talk to.' 3. An oddity, often pejoratively ('You've made yourself a perfect *or* regular sight'): late C.17–20: S.E. until C.19, then coll. cf. FRIGHT. 4. An opportunity or chance. Esp. *get within sight*, to near the end, and *get within sight of*, to get anywhere near. Coll: late C.19–20. 5. 'A gesture of derision: the thumb on the nose-tip and the fingers spread fan-wise: also *Queen Anne's fan*. A *double sight* is made by joining the tip of the little finger (already in position) to the thumb of the other hand, the fingers being similarly extended. Emphasis is given by moving the fingers of both hands as if playing a piano. Similar actions are *taking a* GRINDER ... or *working the* COFFEE-MILL ...; *pulling* BACON: ...; *making a nose* or LONG NOSE; COCKING SNOOKS, &c,' a passage showing F. & H. to advantage. (The custom seems to have arisen in late C.17: see the frontispiece to the English *Theophrastus*, 1702, and cf. *Spectator*, 1712, 'The prentice speaks his disrespect by an extended finger.') T. Hook, 1836, 'Taking a double sight'; Dickens, 1840, 'That peculiar form of recognition which is called taking a sight'. Ex nautical j., the outstretched fingers roughly resembling a quadrant.

sight, give a. Variant of *take a sight* (SIGHT, 5): *Sessions*, 6 April 1847.

sight, put out of. To consume; esp., to eat: coll: from ca 1870. cf. GET OUTSIDE.

sight, take a, see SIGHT, n., 5.

***sighter.** A minute dot on a card: card-sharping c. (—1894).

sign of a house or **a tenement to let.** A widow's weeds: 1785, Grose; ob. by 1900. In American low s., a *house for rent* (Irwin).

sign of the cat's foot, live at the. To be hen-pecked: C.19–20; very ob.

sign of the feathers, the. A woman's best good graces: mid-C.19–early 20.

sign of the five, ten, fifteen shillings, the. An inn or tavern named The Crown, Two Crowns, Three Crowns: late C.18–20; ob.

sign of the horn, at the. In cuckoldom: C.19–20; very ob.

sign of the prancer, the, see PRANCER ...

sign of the three balls, the. A pawnbroker's: C.19–20: coll.

signboard. The face: from ca 1870; very ob. cf. DIAL.

signed servant. An assigned servant: Australian coll: ca 1830–60. Ex that convict system under which convicts were let out as labourers to the settlers.

sigster. A short sleep: low: ca 1830–60. *Sinks*, 1848.

***sil,** see SILVER-BEGGAR.

Silas Hocking. A stocking: theatrical rhyming s.: late C.19–20. Silas Hocking's very popular novels appeared over a period of fifty years or more, beginning in ca 1879.

silence. To knock down, to stun: implied in 1725 in *A New Canting Dict.* (at *silent*). 2. Hence, to kill: C.19–20.

silence in the court, the cat is pissing. A c.p. addressed to anyone requiring silence unnecessarily: ca 1780–1850. cf.:

***silence-yelper.** An usher in a court of law: c. (—1909). i.e. 'silence!'-yelper.

silencer. A blow that knocks down or stuns: C.19–20. Ex SILENCE, 1.

***silent.** Murdered: c. (—1725). cf. SILENCE, 2.

silent beard. The female pubic hair: coll: late C.17–early 19. T. Brown (d. 1704): *Works*, ii, 202.

silent flute. The male member: late C.18–mid-19.

silk. A Q.C. or K.C.: 1884 (O.E.D.): coll till ca 1905, then S.E. Abbr. *silk-gown*, a Q.C.: 1853, Dickens, 'Mr Blowers, the eminent silk-gown'. A Counsel's robe is of silk; a Junior Counsel's, stuff. 2. A bishop: ecclesiastical: late C.19–early 20. The apron is of silk.

silk, carry or **sport.** To ride in a race: turf coll: 1884, Hawley Smart. Ex the silk jacket worn by jockeys.

silk, obtain, receive, take. To attain the rank of Counsel: legal coll >, ca 1905, S.E.: *obtain*, very rare before C.20, and perhaps always S.E.; *receive*, 1872, *Standard*, 16 Aug.; *take*, 1890, *Globe*, 6 May. Contrast:

silk, spoil. To cease being Counsel; esp. on promotion: legal coll >, ca 1900, S.E.: 1882, *Society*, 4 Nov., 'Ere long he "spoiled silk" (as the saying is), and was made a Serjeant.' ?ex *despoil oneself of.*

silk-gown, see SILK, 1.

silk-port. Assumption of a gentleman commoner's gown: Oxford University: ca 1820–60.

***silk-snatcher.** A thief addicted to snatching hoods or bonnets from persons walking in the street: c. of ca 1720–1840.

silks and satins, support one's. To parade, or prank oneself out in, silk and satin: modistes' coll (—1887); slightly ob.

silkworm. A woman given to frequenting drapers' shops and examining goods without buying: coll: C.18. Steele, 1712, in the *Spectator*, No. 454.

sillikin. A simpleton: 1860, G. A. Sala.

silly. A silly person: coll: 1858, K. H. Digby, 'Like great sillies'.

silly, adv. Sillily: C.18–20; S.E. until mid-C.19, then (low) coll and dial.

silly, v. To stun: coll: ca 1850–1900. *Sessions*, 10 May 1859, 'I felt great pain from the blows . . . it half *sillied* me at the time.' cf.:

silly, knock. To infatuate: coll: from ca 1890. (Lit., to stun, stupefy.)

silly (or S.) Billy. A clown's juvenile butt: coll: ca 1850–1900. Mayhew, 1851, 'Silly Billy . . . is very popular with the audience at the fairs.' 2. Hence, gen. affectionately, a SILLY: coll: late C.19–20. cf. SILLY WILLY.

silly season. In Great Britain, the months of August and September, when – owing to recess of Parliament and to other prominent persons' being on holiday – there is a shortage of important news, the lack being supplied by trivialities. 1871, *Punch*, 9 Sept., 'The present time of the year has been named "the silly season"': coll till ca 1910, then S.E. Whence:

silly-seasoner, -seasoning. A typical silly-season article or story (1893); the writing and publishing of such matter (1897). Still coll.

silly Willy. A simpleton: coll: C.17 (?–C.19). cf. SILLY BILLY, 2.

***silver-beggar** or **-lurker.** c.: *s.-b.*, 1859, Sala; *s.-l.* from ca 1860; both ob. 'A tramp with BRIEFS or FAKEMENTS concerning bogus losses by fire, shipwreck, accident, and the like; guaranteed by forged signatures or SHAMS of clergymen, magistrates, &c., the false subscription-books being known as DELICATES. Also' – from ca 1870 – '*sil* = (1) a forged document, and (2) a note on "The Bank of Elegance" or "The Bank of Engraving",' i.e. a counterfeit banknote; likewise ob.

silver-cooped. (Of a naval seaman) deserting for the merchant service: nautical coll: late C.18–early 19. Ex the bounties offered to the crimps. 2. Hence, (of any merchant seaman) 'shipped through the crimps': nautical coll: C.19.

silver fork. A wooden skewer, used as a chopstick when forks were scarce: Winchester: †by 1870.

silver hell. A low-class gaming saloon or den: coll: from ca 1840; ob. Moncrieff, 1843, 'He's the principal partner of all the silver hells at the West End.' Only or mainly silver was risked.

silver hook, catch fish with a. To buy a fish (or several fish) to 'conceal unskilful angling', as F. & H. delicately say: anglers': C.19–20; ob. Perhaps on the proverbial *angle with a silver* (or *golden*) *hook*, to get things by bribery, or only through paying for them.

silver-laced. Lousy: low s. (?orig. c.) of ca 1810–1910. Ex the colour of lice.

silver spoon in one's mouth, born with a. Born rich: C.18–20: coll till ca 1850, then S.E. Motteux, 1712; Buckstone, 1830, 'Born . . . as we say in the vulgar tongue, with . . .' Anticipated by John Clarke in 1639, ***born with a penny in one's mouth.***

silver-tail; silver-tailed, n. and adj. (A) SWELL: Australian bushmen's coll. (—1890); ob. Opp. *copper-tailed*, democratic. A. J. Vogan, *The Black Police*, 1890.

simkin or **simpkin;** or with capitals in sense 1. The fool in (comic) ballets: theatrical coll from ca 1860. Mayhew, 1861. Ex *simkin*, a fool. 2. (*simkin*; occ. *samkin*.) Champagne: Anglo-Indian coll (1853); slightly ob. Ex native pronunciation.

simon (or S.). A sixpence: c.: late C.17–19. Prob. by a fancy on the name: since TANNER, 6d., is unrecorded before 1811, *simon* cannot derive from 'the old joke . . . about St Peter's banking transaction, when he "lodged with one Simon a tanner"' (*Household Words*, 20 June 1885), but *tanner* may well have come from *Simon* in this connection. 2. A trained horse: circus: from ca 1850; ob. Is this a pun? On what? 3. A cane: King Edward's School, Birmingham: ca 1850–90. Ex Acts ix, 43.

Simon Pure (occ. Simon- or simon-pure), the or the real. The real or authentic person or, from ca 1859 (H., 1st ed.), thing: coll: *the real S.P.*, 1815, Scott; *the S.P.*, 1860, W. C. Prime. Ex *Simon Pure*, a Quaker who, in Mrs Centlivre's *A Bold Stroke for a Wife*, 1717, is, for part of the play, impersonated by another character; see esp. Act V, scene 1. 2. Its use as an adj. is mainly, as it certainly was orig. (Howells, 1879), American.

***Simon soon gone.** In Awdelay, *Simon soone agon*, 'He, that when his Mayster hath any thing to do, he will hide him out of the way': c. of ca 1560–90.

simper like a furmity kettle, see FURMITY KETTLE.

simpkin, see SIMKIN.

simple infanticide. Masturbation: pedantic coll or s.: late C.19–20.

***simpler.** A simple or foolish man much given to lust: c. of late C.16–early 17. Greene, 1592; Rowlands, 1602. i.e. *simple* + *er*.

simples, be cut for (in C.17–early 18 of) the. To be cured of one's folly: mid-C.17–20: s. (not c.) until ca 1820, then mainly, and in C.20 nothing but, dial. In C.18 often in semi-proverbial form, *he must go to Battersea, to be cut for the simples*, as in Grose, 1st ed., where also the corrupt variant, . . . *to have their simples cut*, for at Battersea *simples* (medicinal herbs) were formerly grown in large quantities. Cognate is the C.18 semi-proverbial *sick of the simples*, foolish: coll.

simpson; occ. incorrectly, **simson.** Also with capital. Water used in diluting milk: dairymen's: 1871, *Daily News*, 17 April, 'He had, he stated on inquiry, a liquid called Simpson on his establishment.' Ex the surname *Simpson*, that of a dairyman who, in the late 1860s, was prosecuted for such adulteration. 2. Hence, inferior milk: 1871, *Standard*, 11 May, Police Report, 'If they annoyed him again he would christen them with Simpson, which he did by throwing a can of milk over the police.' 3. Almost co-extensive is the sense, 'That combined product of the cow natural and the COW WITH THE IRON TAIL', *Standard*, 25 Dec. 1872. See also SIMPSON, MRS; cf. CHALKER and SKY-BLUE, 2, and next entry. 4. A milkman: mostly London (—1887); †by 1910.

simpson or **S.**; incorrectly **simson.** To dilute (milk) with water: 1872, *The Times*, 24 Dec. Ex n., 1. Also SIMPSONIZE, gen. v.t.

Simpson, Mrs. The (village) pump: mostly among dairymen (—1874). Also *Simpson's cow* and:

Simpson-pump. A pump as a means of diluting milk: dairymen's: from ca 1879. *Punch*, 31 Jan. 1880. cf. preceding entry.

Simpsonize, -ise. Gen. v.t., to dilute milk with water: dairymen's: 1871, *Echo*, 13 Dec. Ex SIMPSON, n., 1; and cf. the v.

Simpson's cow. See SIMPSON, MRS: dairymen's (—1903).

sin. (e.g. 'It's a sin that *or* to . . .') A shame; a pity: C.14–20: S.E. until C.19, then coll. cf.:

sin, like. Very vigorously; furiously: late C.19–20. Here, *sin* = the devil.

Sinbad. An old sailor: nautical: ca 1860–1910. Ex the legendary figure.

Sinbad the Sailor. A tailor: rhyming: late C.19–20.

since when I have used no other. A c.p. applied to any (gen. domestic) article: from ca 1890. Ex the witty Pears' Soap advertisement of a tramp ('Twenty years ago I used your soap, since when I have used no other'). cf. GOOD MORNING! . . .

sines. (Generic for) bread, whereas *a sines* is a small loaf: Winchester: from ca 1870; †by 1915. Perhaps a pun on *natural sine*(*s*) and *sign*(*s*).

sing a bone is the Australian Aboriginal practice of *pointing the bone* at someone under a curse: the former is s., the latter is S.E.: *sing a bone*, late C.19–20. For the practice, see Archer Russell, *A Tramp Royal in Wild Australia*, 1934.

sing it!, don't; or **don't chant the poker!** Don't exaggerate!: proletarian c.p. of ca 1870–1910.

sing like a bird called the swine. To sing execrably: coll: ca 1675–1750. Ray, 1678; Fuller, 1732.

***sing out.** c. of ca 1810–40. Scott, 1815, in a note to *Guy Mannering*, ch. xxviii, says, 'To sing out or whistle in the cage, is when a rogue, being apprehended, peaches against his comrades.' (N.B., the phrase is not *sing out in the cage*.) cf.:

***sing out beef.** To call 'Stop thief': c. of ca 1810–40. (More gen. *cry* BEEF or *give* (*hot*) *beef*.) Possibly a rhyming synonym.

sing placebo (or P.), see PLACEBO.

sing small. To make less extravagant or conceited claims or statements: coll: 1753, Richardson, 'I must myself sing small in her company'; Clement Scott, 1885. Perhaps suggested by S.E. *sing another*, or *a different*, *tune*, to speak, act, very differently, though it may follow naturally ex C.17–early 18 *sing small*, to sing in a small voice: cf. Shakespeare's 'Speaks small like a woman'.

single-peeper. A one-eyed person: ca 1780–1850. On *single-eyed*.

single-pennif. A five-pound note: back s. on *finnup* (see FIN(N)IF-): from 1850.

single-ten or **singleten.** See senses 1, 2 of:

singleton. 'A very foolish silly Fellow', B.E., where spelt *single-ten*: late C.17–early 19. Grose, 1st ed. Prob. ex †S.E. *single*, (of persons) simple, honest, on *simpleton*, but possibly ex *single*(-)*ten*, the 10 in a card-suit, thus: the '10' is below and next to the knave and – by the age-old juxtaposition of fools and knaves – is therefore a fool. 2. 'A nail of that size', says B.E. puzzlingly; Grose, who likewise has *singleten*, is no clearer with 'a particular kind of nails'. Late C.17–early 19. Possibly one that was one inch long. 3. 'A cork screw, made by a famous cutler of that name [*Singleton*], who lived in a place called Hell, in Dublin; his screws are remarkable for their excellent temper,' Grose, 1st ed.: coll: ca 1780–1830.

sink. A toper: coll: mid-C.19–20; ob. cf. *common* SEWER. 2. *the sink.* The throat: mid-C.19–20. 3. A heavy meal: Leys School: late C.19–20. cf. STODGE. 4. Hence, a glutton: ibid.: late C.19–20. 5. *the sink* (or *S.*). The Royal Marine office in a battleship: naval: late C.19–20.

sink, fall down the. To take to drink: late C.19–20: ?rhyming s. cf.:

sink-hole. The throat: low: ca 1830–90. *Sinks*, 1848. cf. last entry.

sink me! A coll imprecation: 1772, Bridges, 'But sink me if I . . . understand'; very ob. Prob. orig., and mainly, nautical.

***sinker.** A counterfeit coin: c. (—1839). Gen. in pl, bad money, 'affording a man but little assistance in keeping afloat', H., 3rd ed. 2. A small, stodgy cake (of the doughnut kind): late C.19–20. Gen. in pl.

sinks. The five: dicing coll (—1860). Ex Fr. *cinq*.

sinner. A publican: coll: from ca 1860; ob. Ex Luke xviii. 2. Affectionately for a person (usually male), as in 'You old sinner!'; coll: late C.19–20. cf. the affectionate use of SCAMP, SCALAWAG; BASTARD, etc.

sip. A kiss: London lower classes': ca 1860–1905. Ware. Ex the bee sipping: cf. that popular early C.20 song in which the male warbles, 'You are the honeysuckle, I am the bee.'

sip. To make water: back s. (—1903) on PISS.

sip, do a, see DO A SIP.

sipper. Gravy: low: late C.19–20. ?ex dial. *sipper-sauce* (ex C.16–17 S.E. *sibber-sauce*), sauce, influenced by *to sip*. cf. JIPPER. 2. A tea-spoon: low: ca 1810–90.

Sir Berkeley. Female genitals; hence, sexual intercourse (from the male angle), late C.19–20. Short for *Sir Berkeley Hunt*: mid-C.19–20 variant of BERKELEY *Hunt*.

Sir Cloudesley. A choice drink of small beer and brandy, often with a sweetening and a spicing, and nearly always with lemon-juice: nautical: late C.17–mid-18. Ex *Clowdisley* Shovell (1650–1707), knighted in 1689 for naval services, esp. against pirates.

Sir Garnet; often all Sir Garnet. All right: whether as predicate or as answer to a question: from ca 1885. 'Pomes' Marshall, 'And the start was all Sir Garnet, | Jenny went for Emma's Barnet.' In C.20 often corrupted to (*all*) *sirgarneo*. Ex *Sir Garnet* (later Viscount) Wolseley's military fame.

Sir Garny. A Cockney variant, dating from ca 1890, of SIR GARNET. E. Pugh, *Harry the Cockney*, 1912.

Sir Harry. A privy; a close-stool. Esp. in *go to*, or *visit*, *Sir Harry*: C.19–20: coll and (in C.20, nothing but) dial.; app. orig. dial. cf. MRS JONES; SIR JOHN.

Sir Jack Sauce, see JACK SAUCE.

Sir John. A close-stool: coll (C.19) and dial. (C.19–20); ob. cf. SIR HARRY.

Sir Oliver, see OLIVER. **sir reverence,** see SIRREVERENCE.

Sir Roger, (as) fat as. A real Falstaff in girth and weight: lower classes' coll: ca 1875–1900. Ex Sir Roger Tichborne of the famous law-suit.

Sir Sauce, see JACK SAUCE.

***Sir Sydney.** A clasp-knife: c. of ca 1810–50. Why?: unless Sydney, Australia, already had a notorious underworld.

Sir Thomas Gresham, sup with. To go hungry: C.17 coll. Hayman, 1628, 'For often with DUKE HUMPHREY thou dost dine, | And often with sir Thomas Gresham sup.' Sir Thomas Gresham, 1519–79, founded the Royal Exchange and was a noted philanthropist.

Sir Timothy. 'One that Treats every Body, and pays the Reckonings every where', B.E.: coll: late C.17–early 19. Prob. ex a noted 'treater'.

Sir Tristram's knot. A hangman's noose: coll: mid-C.16–early 17. Wm Bullein. Prob. ex some famous judge or magistrate.

Sir Walter Scott. A pot (of beer): rhyming s. (—1857); ob.

sirgarneo; all sirgarneo, see SIR GARNET.

sirrah may orig. (C.16) have been coll.

sirretch. A cherry; more properly, cherries: back s. (—1859). The 'logical' *seirrehc* is impossible, the former *e* is omitted, *hc* reversed, and *t* interpolated to make the *ch* sound unequivocal.

sirreverence; frequently *sir-reverence*. Human excrement; a lump thereof: late C.16–20: S.E. until ca 1820, then mainly (in C.20, nothing but) dial. In late C.18–

mid-19, a vulgarism. Ex *save* (via *sa'*) *reverence*, as an apology.

sis; often **siss.** Sister: coll: gen., term of address: orig. (—1859), U.S.; anglicized before 1887. cf.:

sissie, sissy; occ. **Cissy, cissy.** An effeminate boy or man; hence a passive homosexual: late C.19–20; ob. in latter sense. Ware declares it to have originated in 1890 as a Society term for an effeminate man in Society; the O.E.D. (Sup.) that it was orig. U.S. s. – but is this so? Ex *sissy*, sister, as form of address orig. (—1859) U.S. but anglicized before 1887: coll: cf. SIS.

sit. An engagement (for, in, work): general s.: 1888, Jacobi. Abbr. *situation.*

sit-down-upons. Trousers: 1840, J. T. Hewlett; ob. cf. SIT-UPON, 2.

sit-in-'ems. Trousers: jocular (—1887); ob. cf. SIT-DOWN-UPONS.

sit longer than a hen, see SITTING BREECHES.

sit-me-down. One's posterior: semi-nursery, semi-jocular: late C.19–20.

sit on or (rare in C.20) **upon.** To check; snub or rebuke: 1864. Often as *sat upon*, squashed, 'pulled up'.

sit up, make one. 'To make one bestir oneself, to set one thinking, to surprise or astonish one', Pettman, who wrongly regards it as esp. South African: coll (—1887).

sit up and beg. To have an erection: low: late C.19–20. Ex a dog's trick.

sit up and take notice. To take (a sudden) interest: coll orig. (1889), U.S.; anglicized by 1900.

sit upon. See SIT ON. 2. (Only in pl: *sit-upons.*) Trousers: 1841, J. T. Hewlett; ob. Suggested by SIT-DOWN-UPONS. 3. One's posterior: euphemistic: late C.19–20. cf. SIT-ME-DOWN.

sith-nom, sithnom. A month: back s. (—1859).

sitter. A sitting-room: Harrow (from ca 1890) >, by 1902, Oxford University undergraduates'. Charles Turley, *Godfrey Marten, Undergraduate*, 1904. The term has > gen. in *bed-sitter*. cf. BREKKER; RUGGER; SOCKER, 3; see 'Oxford-*er*,' p. 11. 2. In cricket a very easy catch: 1898, *Tit-Bits*, 25 June, 'Among recent neologisms of the cricket field is "sitter". So easy that it could be caught by a fieldsman sitting.' 3. An easy mark or task (1908). Ex shooting a sitting bird.

sitting(-)breeches on, have one's; in C.19, occ. **wear one's sitting breeches.** To stay long in company: coll: ca 1870–1910. From ca 1880, *sit longer than a hen*. cf. the Yorkshire *sit eggs*, to outstay one's welcome.

***sitting-pad.** Begging from a sitting position on the pavement: c. (—1859); ob. See PAD, n.

sitting-room. The posteriors: late C.19–20 jocular; slightly ob. (cf. SIT-ME-DOWN.) Prob. ex the smoke-room story of 'only a pair of blinds for her sitting-room' in connection with a pair of drawers. cf. the mid-C.16–early 18 *sitting-place*, the posterior, the rump.

situation. A 1st, 2nd, or 3rd place: 1871: racing coll >, ca 1905, S.E. 'Thormanby', *Men of the Turf*, ca 1887, 'The three worst horses, probably, that ever monopolized the Derby "situations"'.

siv(v)ey or **sivvy, 'pon my!** On my word of honour!: low: mid-C.19–20; slightly ob. J. Greenwood, 1883. Not *asseveration*, but prob. DAVY, corrupted, or, as Baumann implies, *soul.*

siwash. A mean and/or miserable seaman: Nova Scotian (and U.S.) nautical: mid-C.19–20. A corruption of Fr. *sauvage*, wild, savage.

six. A privy: Oxford University: ca 1870–1915. ?origin.

six-and-eightpence. 'The usual Fee given, to carry back the Body of the Executed Malefactor, to give it Christian Burial', B.E., who classes it as c.: more prob. coll: late C.17–mid-18. 2. A solicitor or attorney: coll: 1756, Foote. Because this was a usual fee. cf. GREEN-BAG.

six-and-tips. Whiskey and small beer: Anglo-Irish coll: ca 1780–1850. An elaboration of †*six*, six-shilling beer.

six feet and itches. Over six feet: lower classes' (—1909); ob. Ex *inches* written as *ichs.*

Six Mile Bridge assassin. (Gen. pl.) A soldier: Tipperary: late C.19–early 20. Ware, 'Once upon a time certain rioters were shot at this spot, not far from Mallow.'

six-monther. A third-term cadet in the old training-ship *Britannia*: naval coll: late C.19–early 20.

six-monthser. A very severe stipendiary magistrate: police coll (—1909). i.e. one 'who always gives, where he can, the full term (six months) allowed him by law'.

six of everything, with. Respectably married: work-people's coll (—1909). Applied only to the girl: her trousseau contains six of everything.

six-on-four, go. To be put on short

rations: naval: late C.19–20. Thus, a *six-on-four* is a supernumerary borne on a warship: Bowen, 'Supposed to have two-thirds rations'. cf. SIX UPON FOUR.

six-pounder. 'A servant maid, from the wages formerly given to maid servants, which was commonly six pounds [per annum, plus keep]', Grose, 1st ed.: coll: ca 1780–1850.

six quarter, get. To be dismissed from employment: commercial: ca 1860–1910. Origin?

six-quarter man; three-quarter man. A superior – an inferior – employee: cloth-drapers' (—1909). Ware, 'There are two widths of cloth – six quarter and three quarter.'

six upon four. Short rations: nautical coll: 1838, Glascock in *Land Sharks and Sea Gulls*; ob. Because the rations of four had to suffice for six. See also *go* SIX-ON-FOUR.

six-water grog. Grog in which water: grog ::1:6. Nautical coll: 1826, Glascock. In mid-C.19–20, often *six-water*.

***sixer.** Six months' hard labour: c. or low s.: 1869, 'Pomes' Marshall, 'I see what the upshot will be, | Dear me! | A sixer with H.A.R.D.' 2. A sixth imprisonment: 1872 (O.E.D.): low s. rather than c. 3. The six-ounce loaf served with dinner: prison c. (—1877). 4. Anything counting as six: orig. (1870) and mainly in cricket: coll. 5. A Christian girl: East End of London: late C.19–20. Ex Yiddish SHICKSTER.

sixes. Small hook-curls worn by men; composed of forehead hair, they are plastered to the forehead: military: ca 1879–90. Ex shape. If Manchon has not erred, the term app. > *number sixes* and an underworld term, still extant though ob.

sixpences, spit, see SPIT SIXPENCES.

sixpenny. A playing-field: 1864, *Eton School Days*: Eton College; ob. Ex the junior cricket club founded in 1830 and known as the Sixpenny Club, the subscription being sixpence; the name applied only in the summer. 2. The chocolate-coloured, white-ringed cap awarded as a 'colour' for junior cricket at Eton: mid-C.19–20.

sixpenny, adj. Inferior, cheap; worthless: coll: ca 1590–1630. Esp. *sixpenny striker*, a petty footpad (as in Shakespeare's *1 Henry IV*).

sixth-forming. A caning by the prefects assembled in the sixth-form room: Public Schools' coll: late C.19–20.

sixty, like. Very vigorously or rapidly: orig. (1848), U.S.; anglicized ca 1860. ?abbr. *like sixty to the minute* or *like sixty miles an hour*. cf. FORTY.

sixty per cent. A usurer: coll: 1853, Reade; slightly ob. cf. Fletcher, 1616, 'There are few gallants . . . that would receive such favours from the devil, though he appeared like a broker, and demanded sixty i' th' hundred.'

size, n. Jelly (to eat): London street s.: ca 1840–90. Augustus Mayhew, *Paved With Gold*, 1857.

size; gen. **size up.** To gauge, estimate; to regard carefully (in order to form an opinion of): coll: orig. (1847), U.S.; anglicized ca 1890. Marriott-Watson, 1891, *size*; Newnham Davis, 1896, *size up*. cf. the rare S.E. *size down*, v.t., to comprehend.

size of (a thing), **the.** What it amounts to: coll: from the middle 1880s. e.g. 'That's about the size of it.' Ex dial.

sizzler. An exceedingly fast ball, race-horse, etc.: coll: late C.19–20. cf. the familiar S.E. sense, a broiling hot day.

skalbanker, see SCOWBANKER. **skallewag,** see SCALAWAG.

skater. An N.C.O.'s chevron: Regular Army: late C.19–20; ob. Perhaps because its wearer 'skates on thin ice'.

***skates(-)lurk.** 'A begging impostor dressed as a sailor', H., 1st ed.: c.; †by 1903. Perhaps = *skate's* LURK, a fish's – hence a FISHY – trick!

skeary, skeery. Terrifying; (mostly U.S.) timorous: low coll: C.19–20. Blackmore.

skedaddle. A hasty flight; a scurry: coll: with article, 1870, Mortimer Collins; without, 1871, *Daily News*, 27 Jan. Ex:

skedaddle; occ. (though not in C.20) **skeedadle,** v.i. (Of soldiers) to flee: orig. (1861), U.S., anglicized ca 1864. H., 3rd ed., 'The American War has introduced a new and amusing word.' Prob. of fanciful origin, though H.'s 'The word is very fair Greek, the root being that of *σκεδάννῦμι* to disperse, to "retire tumultuously", and it was probably set afloat by some professor at Harvard' is not to be dismissed with contempt. 2. Hence, in gen. use, to run away, decamp, hastily depart: coll: 1862; Trollope, 1867. 3. Also ex sense 1, (of animals) to stampede or flee: 1879, F. Pollock.

skedaddler; skedaddling. One who 'skedaddles' (see the v.) (1864); the act (—1898).

skeery, see SKEARY.

skeeter. A mosquito: coll: orig. (1852), U.S.; then, ca 1870, Australian; then ca 1880, English – but it is still comparatively rare in Britain.

Skeffington's daughter, see SCAVENGER'S DAUGHTER.

skein of thread. Bed: rhyming s.: from ca 1870.

***skelder,** v.i. To beg, esp. as a wounded or demobilized soldier: c.: late C.16–mid-17, later use (esp. in Scott) being archaic. Ben Jonson. 2. v.t., to cheat, defraud (a person); obtain (money) by begging: c.: late C.16–mid-17. Ben Jonson. Perhaps Dutch *bedelen* perverted.

***skeldering,** vbl n. and ppl adj. of SKELDER: late C.16–mid-17 c. Ben Jonson, who, I surmise, introduced it from Holland; cf. SKELLUM.

skeleton army. Street-fighting or -brawling: London: late 1882–3. Ex the Skeleton Army 'formed to oppose the extreme vigour of the early Salvation Army' (Ware).

skel(l)um; scellum. A rascal, villain: perhaps orig. coll, but certainly very soon S.E. Coryat, D'Urfey. Ex Dutch or Ger. *schelum*.

skelter. A quick run, a rush, a scamper: dial. (—1900). Ex *helter-skelter*.

skerfer. A punch on the neck: boxing: from ca 1880; ob. Ex *scruff*, the nape of the neck.

***sket.** A skeleton key: c.: from ca 1870. By telescoping *skeleton*.

sketch. A person whose appearance offers a very odd sight (cf. SIGHT, 3): coll: from ca 1905. e.g. 'Lor, what a sketch she was!' 2. A small amount; a drop (of liquor): 1894 (O.E.D.); very ob. cf.:

sketchy. Unsubstantial (meal); flimsy (building, furniture); imperfect: coll: 1878, O.E.D.

skettling. Full-dressing: naval officers' (—1909). Perhaps a pun on *scuttling*.

Skevington's daughter, see SCAVENGER'S DAUGHTER.

***skew;** occ. **scew.** A cup or wooden dish: c. of ca 1560–1830. Ex Low L. *scutella*, a platter, a dish: cf. the Welsh Gypsy *skudela* in the same sense. 2. At Harrow School, from ca 1865, a hard passage for translation or exposition; also, an entrance examination at the end of term (that at the beginning of term is a *dab*). Ex v. 3. In back s. (—1859): see KEW.

skew, v.t. To fail in an examination: gen. as *be skewed*: 1859, Farrar in *Eric, or Little by Little*. 2. Also v.t., to do (very) badly, fail in (a lesson): likewise Harrow (—1899). Occ. v.i.: late C.19–20. Perhaps ex *skew at*, look at obliquely, esp. in a suspicious way.

skew-fisted. Ungainly, awkward: coll: late C.17–18.

skew-gee. Crooked; squinting: low coll: late C.19–20. Ex *on a*, or *the*, *skew*, slantwise (1881). cf. SKEWVOW.

skew-the-dew. A splay-footed person: low: late C.19–20; ob. cf. SKEWVOW.

skew-whiff, adj. and adv. Crooked(ly); askew: dial. and coll: 1754.

skewed, see SKEW, v., 1.

skewer. A pen: from ca 1880; ob. Ex shape. 2. An Aboriginal throwing-spear: Australian: since ca 1860. 3. A sword: ca 1840–1900. *Sinks*, 1848.

skewgy-newgy. A composition of caustic used to keep decks clean: yachtsmen's: 1886, *St James's Gazette*, 7 April, 'The mysterious name'. Very!: unless it be perchance a reduplicated perversion of *caustic*.

skewings. Perquisites: gilders', from ca 1850. Ex *skew*, to remove superfluous gold leaf. 'Analogous terms are *cabbage* (tailors'); *blue-pigeon* (plumbers'); *menavelings* (beggars'); *fluff* (railway clerks'); *pudding*, or *jam* (common)', F. & H. See those terms.

skewvow. Crooked: coll or s.: ca 1780–1880. An elaboration of *skew*, a slant, or possibly a jocular perversion of SKEW-WHIFF. Whence SKEW-GEE and SKEW-THE-DEW.

Ski, see SKY.

skid, n., see SKIV.

skid, put on the. To act, speak, cautiously: coll: 1885, *Punch*, 31 Jan. Ex *skid*, a chain or block retarding a wheel. Also *(s)he might put the skid on* is a coll semi-c.p. applied to a talkative person, occ. with the addition *with advantage to us*, *you*, *his listeners*: from ca 1870; ob.

skiddi(c)k, see SCUDDICK. **skiddoo,** see SKIDOO. **skie,** see SKY, v.

skidoo, skiddoo. To make off, to depart: 1907, Neil Munro. Ex SKEDADDLE.

skied; skyed. (Of a picture) hung on the upper line at the Exhibition of the Royal Academy: artistic coll >, ca 1900, S.E.: 1864, H., 3rd ed., at *skyed*. Opp. FLOORED, 3.

skiff. (Presumably) a leg: low s. of ca 1890–1910. *Morning Advertiser*, 6 April 1891, 'To drive an "old crock" with "skinny skiffs"'. ?origin: perhaps cognate is dial. *skiff*, to move lightly, skim along; ?cf. also †dial. *skife*, to kick up one's heels.

skiffle. A great hurry; among tailors, a job to be done in a hurry; low coll or s.: late C.19–20. With this thinning of *scuffle*, cf. that of BUMF in BIMPH; the word exists also in West Yorkshire dial.

skilamalink. Secret; SHADY: East London: late C.19–20; ob. Ware, 1909, remarks: 'If not brought in by Robson, it was re-introduced by him at the Olympic Theatre, and in a burlesque.' Origin?

skill. A goal kicked between posts: football: from ca 1890. This being the result of skill.

skillet. A ship's cook: nautical: from ca 1880; ob. Ex the cooking-utensil.

skilly. Gruel; oatmeal soup: 1839, Brandon: low s. >, ca 1890, coll. Abbr. *skilligolee*, perhaps on *skillet*, often, in dial., pronounced *skilly*. 2. Hence, a fount carrying its own lead: printers': ca 1870–1910. It was unpopular with compositors, for it lent itself to ill-paid piece-work. 3. Tea or coffee supplied to messes: *Conway* cadets': late C.19–20.

skilly and toke. Anything mild or insipid: proletarian: from ca 1860. See SKILLY, 1, and TOKE, n., 1.

skilly-pot. A teapot: H.M.S. *Conway*: late C.19–20. cf. SKILLY, 3.

***skim.** c.: 1869, *Daily News*, 29 July, 'They thought it contained his skim (money)'; ob. Perhaps the 'skim' of milk, i.e. cream.

skimmer. A broad-brimmed hat: Sedgeley Park School: ca 1800–65. One could send it skimming into the air.

***skin.** A purse: c. of ca 1810–80. Vaux, Haggart, Mayhew. Because made of skin. Hence, a QUEER *skin* is an empty one. 2. ?hence, and ?ca 1830–60, a sovereign. Perhaps partly by rhyming suggestion of 'sovrin'. 3. See SKINS. 4. A horse; a mule: military: from the late 1890s. 5. Foreskin: coll: mid-C.19–20.

skin, v.t. At cards, to win from a person all his money: 1812, Vaux. 2. Hence, to strip (of clothes, money); to fleece: 1851, Mayhew. In C.20, almost coll. cf. SKIN-GAME; SKIN THE LAMB. 3. To steal from: c. or low s.: 1891, *Morning Advertiser*, 21 March, 'Sergeant Hiscock . . . saw him skinning the sacks – that is, removing lumps [of coal] from the tops and placing them in an empty sack.' 4. To shadow, esp. just before arresting: c.: from ca 1880; ob. 5. In gaming, to PLANT (11) (a deck of cards): from ca 1880. 6. To lower (a price or value): 1859, H., 1st ed.; ob. 7. Also *skin alive*. To thrash: orig. (—1888), U.S.; anglicized ca 1895. Headon Hill, 1902, 'I'd have skinned the 'ussy if I'd caught her prying into my grounds.'

skin, go on the. To save money by rigid economy over a period: military, esp. in India: from ca 1885; ob. cf. SKIN, v., 1 and 2.

skin, in a bad. Angry: ill-humoured: late C.18–mid-19. Prob. suggested jocularly by S.E. *thin-skinned*.

skin, in his, her, etc. An evasive reply to a question as to a person's whereabouts: coll: C.18–20. Swift, *Polite Conversation*, Dialogue I. cf. THERE AND BACK.

skin a razor. To drive a hard bargain: coll: from ca 1870; ob.

skin a turd, he'd. He is parsimonious: low Canadian c.p.: late C.19–20.

skin alive, see SKIN, v., 7.

skin and blister. A sister: rhyming s.: late C.19–20.

skin-and-grief. A variant of *skin-and-bones*, (a) skinny (person): lower classes, (—1887); ob.

skin and whipcord, all. Extremely fit; with not a superfluous ounce of fat: coll: (U.S. and) Colonial: from ca 1880; slightly ob.

skin-coat. The female pudend. Esp. in *shake a skin-coat*, to coït: mid-C.17–18. 2. Skin. Only in *curry one's skin-coat*, to thrash a person: C.18–mid-19.

skin-disease. Fourpenny-ale: low: ca 1880–1914.

skin-game. A swindling game: 1882. Ex SKIN, v., 1, 2. cf.:

skin-house. A gambling den: from ca 1885; ob. Suggested by SKIN-GAME.

skin-merchant. A recruiting officer: coll: late C.18–mid-19. Burgoyne, 1792. A cynical reflection on the buying and selling of skins; cf. modern *gun-fodder*.

skin of one's teeth, by or (C.16–17) **with the.** Narrowly; difficultly: mid-C.16–20: S.E. until C.19, then coll. Orig. a lit. translation of the Hebrew.

skin of the creature. A bottle (containing liquor): Anglo-Irish: mid-C.19–20. See CREATURE.

skin the cat. 'To grasp the bar with both hands, raise the feet, and so draw the body, between the arms, over the bar', F. & H.: gymnastics: 1888.

skin the lamb. Lansquenet (the game of cards): 1864, H., 3rd ed.; ob. A perversion of *lansquenet*. 2. v. When an outsider wins a race, the bookmakers are said to 'skin the lamb': 1864, H., 3rd ed. Lit., fleece the public. Also, from ca 1870, *have a skinner*. 3. Hence, to concert and/or practise a swindle: from ca 1865. 4. Also, to mulct a person in, e.g. blackmail: from ca 1870.

skin the live rabbit. To retract the prepuce: low: late C.19–early 20.

skin-the-pizzle. The female pudend: low: mid-C.19–20. See PIZZLE.

skin-tight. A sausage: (lower classes') coll: from ca 1890; ob.

skinned rabbit. A very thin person: coll: from ca 1870; slightly ob.

skinner. Mayhew, 1856, '"Skinners", or women and boys who strip children of their clothes', in order to eye lustfully their nakedness: low s. verging on c.; ob. 2. *skinner, have a.* Here, *skinner* may be a punning corruption of *winner*; the whole phrase, however, is prob. a light-hearted perversion of SKIN THE LAMB (2), as H., 5th ed. (1874) suggests. Hence, a *skinner* has by 1893 > = a result very profitable to the bookies, as it had, in essence, been twenty years earlier. 3. A driver of horses: Canadian: late C.19–20. cf. SKIN, n., 4. 4. A hanger-on for profit at auctions: mid-C.19–20; ob.

skinners. Mental torture; terrible anxiety: low urban (—1909); slightly ob. Because it 'flays' one.

skins. A tanner: coll: ca 1780–1860.

skip. A dance: Anglo-Irish coll: late C.19–20. cf. HOP. 2. A skipper: Ned Ward, 1715.

skip, v. To make off (quickly): C.15–20: S.E. until ca 1830, then coll (mostly U.S.) with further sense, to abscond. Marryat, *King's Own*, 1830. 2. Hence, to die: late C.19–20. Often *skip out*. Savage, *Brought to Bay*, 1900.

skip-Jack. A dandy: s.: Ned Ward, 1703.

skip-kennel. A footman: coll: ca 1680–1840.

skip-louse. A tailor: coll: 1807, J. Beresford; ob. cf. PRICK-LOUSE.

skip the gutter! Houp la!; over she goes!: proletarian: ca 1865–1910.

***skipper**; in C.16–mid-17, often **skypper.** A barn: c.: mid-C.16–19; but after late C.19, only in SKIPPER-BIRD. As H. suggests, prob. ex the Welsh *ysgubor* (a barn), of which the *y* is silent, or, as O.E.D. proposes, ex Cornish *sciber* (the same). 2. Hence, a 'bed' out of doors: tramps' c.: late C.19–20. 3. The devil: C.19. ?ex *skipper*, a captain. 4. A master, a boss: coll: late C.19–20. Ex *skipper*, captain: cf. coll sense of CAPTAIN. 5. A military captain: naval: C.19–20: Alfred Burton, 1818. 6. One who is retreating (—1909): c. cf. SKIP, v., 1.

***skipper**; gen. **skipper it.** To sleep in a barn or hay-rick, hence under, e.g. a hedge: c.: mid-C.19–20. '*No. 747*', p. 413, valid for 1845; Mayhew, 1851, 'I skipper it – turn in under a hedge or anywhere.' Ex the n., 1. cf. HEDGE-SQUARE and:

***skipper-bird.** Mid-C.19–20 c., as in: Mayhew, 1851, 'The best places in England for skipper-birds (parties that never go to lodging-houses, but to barns or outhouses, sometimes without a blanket)'. Also KEY-HOLE-WHISTLER. Ex SKIPPER, n., 1, and v.

skipper's daughter. A crested wave: from ca 1888: coll.

skirry. A run or scurry: either coll or familiar S.E., as is the v.: resp. 1821, Haggart (who also has the v.) and 1781, George Parker. Ex *scurry*.

skirt. A woman: mid-C.16–20: S.E. until late C.19, then s. Hence, a *light skirt* is a loose woman: late C.19–20 (Manchon). 2. *the skirt*, women in gen.; women collectively: late C.19–20. Hyne, 1899. cf.:

skirt, v.i. To be a harlot: late C.19–20, ob. cf. SKIRT, FLUTTER A. 2. To skirt-dance: coll: mostly Cockney: from ca 1880.

skirt, a bit of. A woman, a girl: late C.19–20. Not necessarily pejorative. Hence:

skirt, do a bit of. To coït with a woman: late C.19–20. Ex preceding.

skirt, flutter a. To be a harlot: late C.19–20: coll. Ob.

***skirt-foist.** A female cheat: c. of ca 1650–1700. A. Wilson, ca 1650.

skirt-hunting. A search, 'watch-out', for either girls or harlots: coll: late C.19–20.

skit. Beer: military: from the 1890s. Ex S.E. *skit*, a small jet of water.

***skit.** (Gen. v.t.) To wheedle: c.: late C.18–mid-19. Prob. ex S.E. *skit*, to be skittish, to caper.

skite. A boaster; boasting: Australian: late C.19–20. Abbr. *blatherskite* (see BLETHERSKATE); or possibly ex Scottish and Northern dial., a person viewed with contempt; cf. also SKYTE.

***skitting-dealer.** A person feigning dumbness: C.18 c. Ex †*skit*, to be shy.

skittle. Chess played without 'the rigour of the game': coll: mid-C.19–20. 2. Also as v.i.: id.: id. 3. To knock down; to kill: mostly Australian: late C.19–20. Ex the game of skittles.

skittles. Nonsense: coll: 1864, *Orchestra*, 12 Nov., '*Le faire applaudir* is not "to make oneself applauded", and "joyous comedian" is simply skittles.' Perhaps ex *not all* BEER AND SKITTLES. 2. Hence, an interjection: coll: 1886, Kipling, '"Skittles!" said Pagett, M.P.'

skiv (1858, O.E.D.); **skid** (1859, H., 1st ed.). A sovereign (coin). 'Fashionable s.', says H. 2. A bookmaker's runner or tout: racing s., esp. at Epsom: late C.19–20.

skivvy; occ. **skivey.** A maid servant, esp. a rough GENERAL: from ca 1905. Ex SLAVEY.

skivvy! A naval asseveration or exclamation (—1909). Ex Japanese.

skoff, see SCOFF.

skookum. Satisfactory ('Everything's skookum'): Canadian West Coast: late C.19–20. Chinook jargon; lit., 'strong'.

skoot, see SCOOT. **skowbanker,** see SCOWBANKER. **skower,** see SCOUR. **skran,** see SCRAN. **skreigh,** see SCREIGH. **skrim(m)age,** see SCRIMMAGE.

skrimp, skrump or **scrump,** v.i. and v.t. To steal apples: dial. and provincial s.: late C.19–20. 2. Hence, to 'scrounge': Army: late C.19–20.

skrimshank, -er, see SCRIMSHANK, -ER.

skrip. A c. spelling of SCRIP.

skrouge, skrowdge, see SCROUGE, v.

skrump, see SKRIMP.

skrunt. A whore: Scots dial. >, by 1890, coll: mid-C.19–20.

skuddick, see SCUDDICK. **skug,** see SCUG.

skulker. 'A soldier who by feigned sickness, or other pretences evades his duty, a sailor who keeps below in time of danger; in the civil line, one who keeps out of the way, when any work is to be done', Grose, 1st ed.; 1748, Smollett, *Roderick Random*: coll till ca 1830, then S.E.

skull; skull-race, -thatcher, see SCULL, etc.

skullbanker, see SCOWBANKER.

skull's afly!, my. I'm awake, alert, shrewd!: C.19. cf. FLY, adj.

skunk. A mean, paltry, or contemptible wretch: coll: orig. (1841), U.S.; anglicized ca 1870. *Referee*, 1 June 1884, 'The bloodthirsty and cowardly skunks.' Ex the stink-emitting N. American animal.

skunk, v. To betray; leave in the lurch: London school-boys' (—1887). Ex preceding.

skute, see SCOOT.

Sky; occ. **Ski.** An outsider: Westminster School (—1869). Ex the *Volsci*, a tribe traditionally inimical to Rome; the Westminster boys being *Romans.* 2. Hence, though recorded earlier, 'a disagreeable person, an enemy' (H., 2nd ed.): ca 1860–1910.

***sky.** A pocket: c.: 1893, P. H. Emerson; Charles E. Leech. Abbr. SKY-ROCKET.

sky, v. To throw up into the air; esp. *sky a copper*, as in the earliest record: 1802, Maria Edgeworth. 2. Hence, with pun on BLUE (v., 2), to spend freely till one's money is gone: from ca 1885. 'Pomes' Marshall, 'With the takings safely skyed'. Ob. 3. To throw away; at football, to charge or knock down: Harrow: from ca 1890. F. & H., 1903; Vachell, 1905. Ex sense 1. 4. See SKIED.

sky-blue. Gin: perhaps orig. c.: 1755, *The Connoisseur*; †by 1859. 2. Thin or watery milk: late C.18–20: S.E. until ca 1850, then coll. Ob. cf. SIMPSON, n.; CHALKER.

sky-blue pink. Jocular c.p. for colour unknown or indeterminate: since ca 1885.

sky falls, – we shall catch larks, if or **when the.** A semi-proverbial c.p. retort on an extravagant hypothesis: late C.15–20; ob. cf. *if pigs had wings . . .*

***sky-farmer.** A beggar who, equipped with false passes and other papers, wanders about the country as though in distress from losses caused by fire, hurricane, or flood, or by disease among his cattle: c.: 1753, John Poulter. †by 1850. As Grose, 1st ed., suggests, either because he pretended to come from the Isle of Skye or because his farm was 'in the skies'.

sky-gazer. A sky-sail: nautical: from ca 1860; ob. On nautical *sky-scraper*.

sky-high. Very high indeed: coll: 1818 (Lady Morgan), adv.; 1840, adj.

sky-lantern. The moon: coll: ca 1840–70. Moncrieff, 1843.

sky-light; skylight. An eye: nautical: 1836, Michael Scott; ob.

sky-parlour. A garret: 1785, Grose: coll >, ca 1840, S.E. Also (in Baumann) *sky-lodging*: lower classes' coll (—1887); slightly ob.

sky-pilot. A clergyman, esp. if working among seamen: low (—1887; Baumann) > nautical s. (1888, Churchward) > by 1895 (W. Le Queux, in *The Temptress*) gen. s. Because he pilots men to a haven in the skies.

sky-rocket; occ. **skyrocket.** A pocket: rhyming s.: 1879, J. W. Horsley. cf. SKY, n.

sky-scraper; occ. **skyscraper.** A high-standing horse: coll: 1826, Hone; ob. Like the following senses, it derives ex the nautical *sky-scraper*, a sky-sail. 2. A cocked hat: nautical: ca 1830–90. 3. The penis: low: from ca 1840. 4. An unusually tall person (gen. of a man): coll: 1857, 'Ducange Anglicus'. 5. In cricket, a skied ball: coll: from ca 1890; slightly ob. 6. A rider on a PENNY-FARTHING bicycle: ca 1891–1900. *Daily News*, 7 March 1892, '... Often derisively styled "sky-scrapers"'.

sky the towel. To give in, yield: boxers' (from ca 1890).

sky-topper. A very high person or thing (e.g. house): coll: from ca 1880. A variant of SKY-SCRAPER.

skycer, see SHICER. **skyed**, see SKIED.

Skying a Copper. Hood's poem, *A Report from Below*, 'to which this title was popularly given until it absolutely dispossessed the true one' (Ware). 2. Hence, making a disturbance – upsetting the apple-cart: lower classes': ca 1830–50; Hood dying in 1845.

skylark, n. and v.; and derivatives **skylarker, skylarking.** Perhaps orig. s., as in *Sessions*, April 1803, but soon S.E.

***skylarker.** A housebreaker who, both as a blind and in order to spy out the land, works as a bricklayer: c.: from ca 1850; ob.

skylight. A 'daylight' or unliquored interval at top of one's drinking glass: 1816, Peacock; ob. by 1880. Suggested by *daylight*. 2. See SKY-LIGHT.

***skypper**, see SKIPPER, n., 1.

skyrocket, see SKY-ROCKET. **skyscraper,** see SKY-SCRAPER.

skyte. A dayboy: Shrewsbury School: from ca 1840. Pascoe, 1881. Gen. in pl: Desmond Coke, *The Bending of a Twig*, 1906, 'Are not the despised Day Boys called Skytes – "Scythians" or "outcasts"?' cf. the Westminster SKY. 2. A fool: Scottish Public Schools' coll: mid-C.19–20.

slab. A milestone: low: ca 1820–1910. Abbr. *slab of stone*. 2. A bricklayer's boy: ca 1840–90. Ex dialect. 3. A portion; a tall, awkward fellow: both Australian: late C.19–20.

slab-dab. A glover: s.: Ned Ward, 1703.

slabbering-bib. A parson's, lawyer's, neckband: late C.18–mid-19. Lit., a slobbering-bib.

slack. The seat (of a pair of trousers, gen. mentioned): coll: mid-C.19–20. Prob. ex SLACKS. 2. A severe or knock-down punch: boxing: C.19. Ex Jack Slack, a powerful hitter. Also *slack un*. cf. AUCTIONEER. 3. Impertinence, decided CHEEK: from ca 1810: s. >, ca 1910, coll. T. Hardy, 1876, 'Let's have none of your slack.' Abbr. *slack-jaw*. 4. A spell of inactivity or laziness: coll: 1851, Mayhew. Ex *slack period* or *spell*.

slack, v. To make water: late C.19–20. Ex relaxation. Also *slack off*.

slack, hold on the. To be lazy; avoid work: nautical (—1864); ob. Ex the loose or untautened part of a rope.

slack and slim. Slender and elegant: non-aristocratic (—1887); slightly ob.

slack in stays. Lazy: nautical coll: early C.19–20. Bowen, 'From the old description of a ship which is slow in going about'.

slack off, see SLACK, v. **slack un,** see SLACK, n., 2.

slacken your glib! Shut up!: low (—1887).

slacker. A shirker; a very lazy person: coll: 1898 (O.E.D.). cf. SLACKSTER.

slacks. Trousers (full length): 1824: coll >, ca 1905, S.E. Surtees. 2. Pilfered fruit: late C.19–20: greengrocers' s.

slackster. A SLACKER: ob. *Daily Chronicle*, 6 Nov. 1901, 'There are "slacksters", as the slang of the schools and universities has it, in all professions.'

slag. A coward; one unwilling to resent an affront: late C.18–early 19. Corruption of S.E. *slack(-mettled)*. 2. A (watch-)chain, whether of gold or of silver: c.: (—1857); ob. Perhaps a perversion of *slack* (hanging slack). 3. A rough: grafters': late C.19–20. Probably ex: 4. One who looks at the free attractions but avoids the paying shows: showmen's: since ca 1880.

***slagger.** A brothel-keeper: c. or low (—1909). Prob. a corruption of SLACKER: cf. SLAG, 1.

***slam.** A variant (—1887) of SLUM, n., 2, 4, 5.

slam, v. To brag; esp. among soldiers, to simulate tipsiness and brag of numerous drinks: from ca 1880. cf. SLUM, v. Perhaps ex: 2. To PATTER; talk fluently: itinerant showmen's: from ca 1870. Henley, 1884, 'You swatchel coves that pitch and slam'. According to H., 5th ed., ex 'a term in use among the birdsingers' – presumably dealers in singing birds – 'at the East-end [of London], by which they denote a certain style of note in chaffinches.'

slam-bang shop. A variant (Bee, 1823; †by 1910) of *slap-bang shop*: see SLAP-BANG.

slammer, slamming. (Anything) exceptional; a WHOPPER, WHOPPING: from ca 1890; ob.

***slaney.** A theatre: c.: from ca 1880. Ex SLUM (v., 8), to act.

slang. The special vocabulary (e.g. cant) of low, illiterate, or disreputable persons; low, illiterate language: 1756, Toldervy: c. >, ca 1780, s. >, ca 1820, coll >, ca 1850, S.E. Likewise, the senses 'jargon' (1802), 'illegitimate colloquial speech', i.e. what now we ordinarily understand by 'slang' (1818) and 'impertinence' or 'abuse' (1825), began as s. and > S.E. only ca 1860. The etymology is a puzzle: the O.E.D. hazards none; Bradley, Weekley, Wyld consider that cognates are afforded by Norwegian *slenja-keften*, to sling the jaw, to abuse, and by several other Norwegian forms in *-sleng*; that *slang* is ultimately from *sling* there can be little doubt – cf. SLANG THE MAULEYS; SLING LANGUAGE and SLING THE BAT; that it is an argotic perversion of Fr. *langue* is very improbable though not impossible. (See esp. the author's *Slang To-Day and Yesterday*, revised edition, 1935, at pp. 1–3.) All the following senses, except the last two, derive ultimately ex sense 1. 2. Nonsense; HUMBUG: ca 1760–90. Foote, 1762. 3. A line of work; a LAY (2) or LURK: c. of ca 1788–1800. 4. A warrant or a licence, esp. a hawker's: from ca 1810: c. >, ca 1850, s. 5. A travelling show: showmen's (—1859). Ob. 6. Hence, a performance or 'house' in a show, e.g. a circus: showmen's: 1861, Mayhew. cf. SLANG-COVE. 7. (Gen. in pl.) A short measure or weight: London, mostly costermongers': 1851, Mayhew. 8. (Ex Ger. c. *Schlange*, a watch-chain, or Dutch *slang*, a snake.) A watch-chain; any chain: c.: from ca 1810. 9. See SLANGS, 1.

***slang,** adj. Slangy: 1758: c. >, ca 1780, s. >, ca 1820, coll >, ca 1850, S.E. Ex the n., 1. 2. (Of persons or tone.) Rakish, impertinent: ca 1818–70: s. > coll. Ex sense 1. 3. (Of dress.) Loud; extravagant: coll: ca 1830–70. 4. (Of measures, weights.) Short, defective: costers': 1812, Vaux. 5. Hence, adv., as in Mayhew, 1851, 'He could always "work slang" with a true measure'; ob.

slang, v.i. To remain in debt: university s. of ca 1770–1800. See (?) Smeaton Oliphant (*à propos* of *tick*), *The New English*, at II, 180. 2. To exhibit at (e.g.) a fair: 1789, G. Parker; late-C.18–20. 3. v.i. and t., to cheat, swindle, defraud: 1812, Vaux. Also *slang it* (Mayhew, 1851). 4. To fetter: c. of ca 1810–50. Implied in SLANGED, and prob. ex SLANGS, 1. 5. v.i. to use slang; rail abusively: 1828, Lytton: s. > coll; slightly ob. 6. v.t. to abuse, scold, violently: 1844, Albert Smith. cf. SLANGING.

***slang, boy of the.** A C.19 variant of SLANG-BOY.

***slang, on or upon the.** At one's own line of work: c. of ca 1788–1850.

slang, out on the. Travelling with a hawker's licence: 1864, H., 3rd ed.

slang a dolly to the edge. 'To show and work a marionette on a small platform outside the booth' – as a means of attracting customers for the play shown inside: showmen's: from ca 1875. cf. SLANG, v., 2.

slang-and-pitcher shop. A cheapjack's van or stock-in-trade: mid-C.19–20. Ex SLANG (4), a hawker's licence, + *pitcher* (see PITCH, v., 2).

***slang-boy.** (Gen. pl.) A speaker of (underworld) cant: late C.18–mid-19. G. Parker, 1789. Also *boy of the slang*.

slang-cove, -cull. A showman: CULL, c. or showmen's s. of ca 1788–1850 (G. Parker, 1789); COVE, showmen's s. of mid-C.19–20 (Mayhew, 1851).

slang it. To use false weights: low: mid-C.19–20. cf. SLANG, n., 7 and v., 3.

slang the mauleys. To shake hands (lit., sling the mauleys): late C.18–20: low London. Of MAULEY, the hand, the dial. form is *mauler*. 2. See SLANGER OF ONE'S MAULEYS.

slang-tree. A stage; a trapeze: resp. itinerant actors' and showmen's: mid-C.19–20. Ex SLANG (n., 5), a travelling show. cf. SLANG-COVE and:

slang-tree, climb (up) the. To perform; make an exhibition of oneself: showmen's: resp. mid-C.19–20 and late C.19–20.

***slanged,** ppl adj. In fetters: c.: 1811, *Lex. Bal.* cf. SLANGS, 1, and SLANG, v., 4.

slanger of one's mauleys (or morleys). A boxer; one who excels with his fists: 1822, David Carey, *Life in Paris*; †by 1890.

slanging, vbl n. Exhibiting (e.g. a two-headed cow) at fair or market: showmen's s. verging on c.: late C.18–19. G. Parker, 1789. Ex SLANG, v., 1. 2. Abuse; violent scolding: mid-C.19–20: s. >, ca 1880, coll >, ca 1910, S.E. Lever, 1856. Ex SLANG, v., 6. 3. Singing: music halls': ca 1880–1900. Ware derives it ex 'the quantity of spoken slang between the verses'.

slanging-dues concerned, there has or have been. A low London c.p. uttered by one who suspects that he has been curtailed of his just portion or right: ca 1810–50.

slanging match. An altercation: since ca 1860: coll >, ca 1910, S.E.

***slangs.** Fetters; leg-irons: c.: from ca 1810; ob. Cognate with SLANG (8), a watch-chain or any chain whatsoever. cf. SLANGED. 2. *the slangs.* A collection of travelling shows; the travelling showman's world or profession: showmen's: prob. from ca 1850, though app. the first record occurs in T. Hood the Younger's *Comic Annual*, 1888 (p. 52). Ex SLANG (5), a travelling show.

slangular. Belonging to, characteristic of, slang (highly colloquial speech): jocular S.E. verging on coll: 1853, Dickens. On *angular*.

slangy. Flashy or pretentious (ca 1850–90), and (of dress) loud, vulgar (ca 1860–1900); may orig. have been coll. cf. SLANG, adj., 2, 3.

slant. A chance; an opportunity (e.g. of going somewhere): 1837, *Fraser's Magazine*, 'With the determination of playing them a slippery trick the very first slant I had'. Ex nautical *slant*, a slight breeze, a favourable wind, a period of windiness. 2. A plan designed to ensure a particular and favourable result (or scene of operations for that result): Australian: 1897, P. Warung; slightly ob. 3. An opportunity: Australian: since ca 1870.

***slant,** v. To run away: c.: from ca 1890. Ex dial. (Graham, 1896), to move away, itself ex *slant*, to move, travel, obliquely. 2. (v.i.) to exaggerate: from ca 1900; ob. Prob. ex *slant*, 'to diverge from a direct course'. 3. In racing, to lay a bet (v.i.): from ca 1901.

slantindicular (1855, Smedley); occ. **slanting-** (1840, J. T. Hewlett) or **slanten-** (1872, De Morgan). Slanting, oblique; neither perpendicular nor horizontal: jocular coll, orig. – 1832 – U.S. 2. Hence, fig.: from ca 1860. 3. Occ. as n. and adv. Ex *slanting* on *perpendicular*. cf.:

slantindicularly, etc. Slantingly, obliquely: 1834, De Quincey: jocular coll. Though recorded earlier than the adj., it must actually be later.

slaoc. Coals: back s. (—1859).

***slap.** Plunder, booty, SWAG (n., 3): c.: late C.18–early 19: mainly Anglo-Irish. ?ex *slap*, a blow. 2. Make-up: theatrical: 1860, H., 2nd ed.; ob. 'Pomes' Marshall, 1897, 'You could just distinguish faintly | That she favoured the judicious use of slap.' Perhaps ex the dial. version of *slop*; perhaps, however, as Ware suggests, ex 'its being liberally and literally slapped on'.

slap, v. Gen. *slap along*. To move, walk, quickly: from ca 1825: coll and (in C.20, nothing but) dial. ?ex *slap*, i.e. bang, *a door*.

slap, adj. Excellent; first-rate; in style: from ca 1850; ob. Mayhew, 1851, 'People's got proud now . . . and must have everything slap.' Abbr. SLAP-UP.

slap, adv. Quickly, suddenly, unexpectedly: coll: 1672, Villiers; Sterne. Also *slap off* (Reade, 1852, 'Finish . . . slap off') and †*slap down* (1865, Dickens). Lit., as if with a slap. 2. With vv. of motion: coll: 1676, Etherege (*slap down*); 1766, Mrs F. Sheridan; 1890, 'Rolf Boldrewood'. 3. With vv. of violent collision or impact: coll: 1825. Meredith, 1861, 'A punch slap into Old Tom's belt'. 4. Directly; straight: coll: 1829, Marryat, 'I . . . lay slap in the way'; Barham, 'Aimed slap at him'. 5. Precisely: coll: 1860, H., 2nd ed., '"Slap in the wind's eye," i.e. exactly to windward'.

slap at, have a. To engage in a fight with; to attempt: coll: late C.19–20.

slap-bang, whether adj., adv., or n. (except in its c. sense), is almost certainly S.E.; but *slap-bang shop*, which 'lived' ca 1780–1850, is prob. – until C.19, at least – coll, while its abbr., *slap-bang*, is c. In 1785, Grose, who gives a secondary sense that is indubitably coll or even s., defines it thus: '*Slap-bang shop*, a petty cook's shop where there is no credit given, but what is had must be paid down with the ready' – i.e. with cash – 'slap-bang, i.e. immediately. This is a common appellation for a night cellar frequented by thieves, and sometimes for a stage coach or caravan': with the latter, cf. the later, long †, *slap-bang coach*.

slap down and **slap off,** see SLAP, adv., 1 and (*s. d.* only) 2.

slap of the tongue. A reprimand; a sharp reply: Anglo-Irish: late C.19–20.

slap-up, adj. Excellent; superior, first-rate; grand: 1823, Bee, who says that it is Northern but does not distinguish between persons and things; 1827, *Sporting Magazine*, 'That slap-up work, *The Sporting Magazine*'; of persons, certainly in 1829, 'slap-up swell' (Thackeray, 1840, has 'slap-up acquaintances'): both, s. >, ca 1860, coll. On BANG-UP (2).

***slash.** An outside coat-pocket: c. (—1839). Abbr. *slash pocket*. Ex *slash*, a vertical slit for the exposition of the lining or an under garment of a contrasting or, at the least, different colour.

slash, in the. Fighting: tailors': from ca 1860.

slasher. Any person or thing exceptional, esp. if exceptionally severe: from ca 1820: coll. cf. RIPPER.

slashing. Exceptionally vigorous, expert, successful, brilliant, notable: from ca 1820: coll. Dickens, 'A slashing fortune', 1854. cf. SLASHER.

slashing, adv. Very; brilliantly: coll: from 1890s; slightly ob. F. & H., 1903, 'A slashing fine woman; a slashing good race; and so forth'. Ex the adj.

***slat.** A sheet: c.: a mid-C.17–mid-18 variant of SLATE, n., 1. 2. A half-crown: c.: a late C.18–early 19 variant of SLATE, n., 2.

***slate.** A sheet: c.: 1567, Harman; 1622, Fletcher; Grose, 1st ed.: †by 1840, and prob. ob. a century earlier. ?origin, unless a perversion of *flat* (even, level): cf. Ger. *Blatt*. cf. SLAT, 1. 2. A half-crown: c.: late C.17–18. ?origin. cf. SLAT, 2. 3. As in Andrew Lang, 1887 (earliest record), '"Slate" is a professional term for a severe criticism': book-world coll. 4. A quarrel: from ca 1880. Ex:

slate. To criticize severely: coll: 1848, Alaric Watts; Blackmore; Saintsbury; Kipling; Kernahan. Ex: 2. To abuse; reprimand or scold severely: 1840: s. (orig. political) >, ca 1870, coll. Ex: 3. To thrash; beat severely: ca 1825–70, then very rare: app. orig. Anglo-Irish. If this sense is earlier than the next but one, then it may well derive ex the Scottish and Northern *slate*, 'to bait, assail, or drive, with dogs', esp. since this hunting term was used fig. at least as early as 1755. 4. Hence, as a military coll, to punish (the enemy) severely: 1854, in the Crimea. 5. (Perhaps the originating sense: presumably ex covering a roof with slates.) To BONNET (2), knock his hat over the eyes of (a person): 1825, Westmacott. Ob. by 1890. As v.i. in form, FLY A TILE. 6. (Perhaps ex the military sense.) To bet heavily against (a horse, a human competitor): sporting: from early 1870s; slightly ob. 7. In medical s., gen. in the passive, to prophesy the death of (a patient): late C.19–20. Ex putting his name on a slate: see the author's *Slang*.

slate, on the. 'Written up against you': lower classes' coll: late C.19–20.

slate loose or **off, have a.** To be mentally deficient: s. >, ca 1900, coll: *loose*, 1860, H., 2nd ed.; *off*, 1867, Rhoda Broughton. The latter, ob. cf. SHINGLE SHORT; TILE LOOSE, and dial. *have a slate slipped*.

slated, ppl adj. See SLATE, v., esp. in senses 1, 2. cf. SLATING. **slated, be.** To be expected to die. See SLATE, v., 7.

slating, vbl n. See SLATE, v., esp. in senses 1, 2, 4. 2. adj., little used.

***slaughter-house.** A gaming-house where men are employed to pretend to be playing for high stakes: sharpers' c.: 1809 (O.E.D.); ob. 2. A shop where, at extremely low prices, goods are bought from small manufacturers (glad of a large turn-over even at a very small profit): 1851, Mayhew. One would, if it were not for the libel laws name several firms that buy thus. cf. SLAUGHTERER. 3. A factory paying miserable wages: operatives' (—1887). 4. The Surrey Sessions House: c. (—1909). 5. A particularly hard sailing ship with a brutal afterguard: nautical: late C.19–20; slightly ob. Bowen.

slaughterer. A vendor buying very cheaply from small manufacturers: 1851, Mayhew. cf. SLAUGHTER-HOUSE, 2. 2. A buyer for re-manufacture: as books for pulp, cloth for shoddy, &c.: late C.19–20 commercial.

slaughterman. A manufacturer paying very low wages: (esp. furniture) operatives' (—1887). cf. SLAUGHTER-HOUSE, 3.

slave-driver. A stern taskmaster or master: coll: from ca 1840.

slave one's life (coll) or **guts** (low coll). To work extremely hard: late C.19–20.

slavey. A male servant: coll: ca 1810–60. Thackeray. Ex *slave*. 2. A female servant: coll: ca 1810–70. 3. Esp. a hard-worked GENERAL: 1821, Egan; P. H. Emerson. cf. SKIVVY. 4. A servants' attic: London students' (—1887); ob.

***slaving gloak.** A servant: c.: C.19.

slawmineyeux. A Dutchman: nautical: ca 1860–1910. Ex Dutch *ja, mynheer* (yes, sir).

slay. At Shrewsbury School, from ca 1890, as in Desmond Coke, *The Bending of a Twig*, 1906, '"Slays" are spreads [feasts], ambitious beyond all imagining, ordered from the Shop.'

***sleek-and-slum shop.** 'A public house or tavern where single men and their wives resort', Bee: c. of ca 1820–90. See SLUM, a room.

***sleek wife.** A silk handkerchief: c. (—1823).

sleep black. To sleep unwashed: chimney-sweeps' coll: mid-C.19–20; ob.

sleep-drunk. Very drowsy; MUZZY (2): coll: from ca 1870; ob. Ex heavy awaking.

sleep on bones. (Of children) to sleep in the nurse's lap: coll: C.19–20; ob.

sleep the caller. To lose a shift by failing to hear the caller: miners' (esp. North Country) coll: late C.19–20. i.e. to *over-sleep (by failing to hear) the caller.*

sleep tight, mind the fleas don't bite. A children's bed-time c.p.: late C.19–20.

sleeping near a crack, (I, he, or you) must have been. A c.p. reply to an inquiry as to how a male has caught a cold: lower and lower-middle classes': late C.19–20. An innuendo in respect of the anatomical CRACK (2).

sleeping-partner. A bed-fellow: jocular coll: mid-C.19–20.

sleepless hat. A hat with the nap worn off: ca 1860–1905. cf.:

sleepy. Grose, 2nd ed., has this punning c.p.: *the cloth of your coat must be extremely sleepy; for it has not had a nap this long time*: late C.18–early 19. Whence SLEEP-LESS HAT.

sleepy-seeds. The mucus forming about the eyes in sleep: nursery: late C.19–20. Suggested by SANDMAN and *sleepy sickness.*

sleepy-walker. A sleep-walker: lower classes' coll (—1887).

sleeve-board. A word hard to pronounce: tailors': from ca 1870. Ex hardness.

sleever. An order taken by a COMMERCIAL (2) on a good day but held up for the next day, to preclude reporting a blank day to his employers: commercial travellers': late C.19–20. i.e. an order 'up one's sleeve'.

slender in the middle as a cow in the waist, as. Very fat: C.17–20 (ob.): coll till C.19, then dial. Burton, 1621; Fuller, 1732; Evans, *Leicestershire Words*, 1881.

slew. To defeat, baffle, outwit: late C.19–20.

slewed; occ. **slued.** Tipsy: coll: 1834, M. Scott (*slewed*); Dickens, 1844 (*slued*). Ob. Ex *slew*, to swing round. See SCREWED for short synonymy. 2. Hence, beaten, baffled: coll: late C.19–20.

slice, take a. 'To intrigue, particularly with a married woman, because a slice of [*sic*] a cut loaf is not missed', Grose, 2nd ed.: coll: mid-C.18–mid-19. Ex the C.17–20 proverbial *it is safe taking a shive* (in C.18–19, occ. *slice*) *of a cut loaf*, as in Shakespeare's *Titus Andronicus.*

***slice of fat.** A profitable robbery: c. (—1887).

slice off. To settle part of (an old score): military (—1909); very ob.

slick, v. To despatch rapidly, get done with: coll: 1860, H., 2nd ed.; ob. Ex *slick*, to polish: cf. *polish off.*

***slick-a-dee.** A pocket-book: Scots c. (—1839); ob. On DEE (2), the same.

'Slid! Coll abbr. *God's lid*, a late C.16–17 petty oath.

slide. (Esp. in the imperative.) To decamp: coll: U.S. (—1859), anglicized ca 1890. Whiteing, 1899, 'Cheese it, an' slide.' Occ. *slide out.* Ex *slide*, to move silently, stealthily.

slide up the board or **the straight, do a.** (Of a man) to coït: low: from ca 1870. cf. RUSH UP THE FRILLS or STRAIGHT.

sliders. A pair of drawers: coll: late C.17–mid-18. J. Dickenson, 1699.

'Slidikins. A petty oath: coll: late C.17–18. Ex 'SLID on '*Sbodikins.*

'Slife! God's life!: C.17–18 coll. Preserved only in period plays and Wardour Street novels. By abbr. cf. 'SLID, and:

'Slight! God's light!: a late C.16–17 oath: trivial coll.

slightly-tightly. Bemused (not drunk) with liquor: fast life: ca 1905–14. Perversion of *slightly* TIGHT (5).

sligo, tip (someone) **the.** To warn by winking; wink at: 1775, S. J. Pratt, 'I tips Slappim the sligo, and nudges the elbow of Trugge, as much as to say, . . . I have him in view.' Prob. on *sly*: *o* is a common s. suffix.

***slim.** Rum (the drink): c.: 1789, G. Parker; †by 1850. ?*rum* perverted.

slime, v.i. To CUT (3) games; to LOAF: Durham School: late C.19–20. Ex S.E. *slime*, to crawl slimily. 2. To sneak along: Felsted: late C.19–20. Whence *do a slime*, to take a mean or crafty advantage. cf. 3. To move, go, quietly, stealthily, or sneakingly: Harrow: late C.19–20. Howson & Warner, 1898, 'His house-beak slimed and twug him.'

slime, do a, see SLIME, 2.

sling. A draught of, pull at, a drink, bottle: 1788; †by 1903, prob. by 1860, perhaps by 1830. cf. GO, n., 2.

sling. To utter: coll: C.15–20. See SLING LANGUAGE and cf. sense 3. 2. To distribute or dispense: s. (—1860) >, ca 1890, coll. H., 2nd ed., '*Sling*, to pass from one person to another'. 3. Hence, to give (as in 'Sling us a tanner'): low (1887) >, by

1910, low coll. 4. To do easily: from ca 1864: s. >, ca 1900, coll. Mainly in SLING INK, etc. 5. To use (e.g. slang); relate (a story): from ca 1880: s. See SLING A YARN. 6. To abandon: mostly Australian. H. Lawson, 1902, 'Just you sling it [liquor] for a year.' 7. For c. usage, see SLING ONE'S HOOK, 2, and SLING THE SMASH. In c., moreover, *sling* = to throw away: late C.19–20. 8. See SLING A SNOT. 9. v.i. to sleep in a hammock: *Conway* cadets': late C.19–20. Abbr. *sling one's hammock*.

sling!, let her, see SLING YOURSELF!

sling a book, poem, an article. To write one: from ca 1870: s. >, 1900 coll. cf. SLING INK.

sling a cat. To vomit: low: mid-C.19–20; ob. cf. *shoot the* CAT.

sling a daddle. To shake hands: low: from ca 1870. cf. SLANG THE MAULEYS.

sling a foot. To dance: coll: from ca 1860; ob.

sling a hat. To wave one's hat in applause: coll: from 1830s; ob.

sling a nasty part. To act a part so well that it would be hard to rival it: orig. and mainly theatrical: from ca 1880. Ex:

sling (or jerk) a part. To undertake, to play, a role: theatrical: from ca 1880.

sling a pen, see SLING INK.

sling a pot. To drink (liquor): from ca 1870: coll rather than s.

sling a slobber. To give a kiss; hence, to kiss: low (—1909), Ex SLING, v., 3, and SLOBBER, which, very low s. for a kiss, dates from late C.19.

sling a snot. To blow one's nose with one's fingers: low: from ca 1860. Also, from ca 1870, simply *sling* (v.i.): ob.

sling a tinkler. To ring a bell: from ca 1870; ob.

sling a yarn. To tell a lie: s.: 1904, *Strand Magazine*, March.

sling about, v.i. To idle; to loaf: from ca 1870.

sling ink; occ. sling a pen. To write: from ca 1864: s. >, ca 1900, coll. Orig. U.S. and app. coined by Artemus Ward.

sling language or **words.** To talk: mid-C.19–20: s. >, ca 1900, coll. cf. SLING, v., 1; SLING A YARN; SLING THE BAT.

sling-next. The two cadets sleeping on either side of oneself: *Conway* cadets': late C.19–20.

sling off, v.i. To utter abuse or CHEEK or impertinence. 2. v.t. with *at* to give CHEEK to, to jeer at, to taunt. Both: late C.19–20.

sling (a person) **one in the eye.** To punch one in the eye, gen. with the implication of blackening it: 1899, Whiteing.

sling one's body. To dance vigorously: London lower classes' (—1909). i.e. sling it about.

sling one's bunk. To depart: ca 1860–1910. i.e. sling up one's hammock (and go).

sling one's Daniel; sling one's hook. To make off; decamp: *Daniel*, 1866, *Sessions*, Nov.; *hook*, 1873 or 1874 (H., 5th ed.). The origin of neither is clear; the latter may be nautical, though Ware derives it from mining-procedure. cf. SLING YOURSELF!

sling one's hammock. To get used to a new ship: naval coll: late C.19–20.

sling one's hook. See SLING ONE'S DANIEL. 2. In c., to pick pockets: from the 1870s. Anon., 1877, *Five Years' Penal Servitude*.

sling one's jelly or **juice.** To masturbate: low: from ca 1870.

sling over. 'To embrace emphatically': Society: ca 1905–14. Ex U.S., says Ware.

sling round on the loose. To act recklessly: from ca 1875. Possibly an elaboration of SLING ABOUT.

sling (a person) **slang.** To abuse, scold violently: from ca 1880: s. See SLING, v., 5.

sling tail. Pickled pork: low: ca 1825–90. *Sinks*, 1848.

sling the bat. To speak the vernacular (esp. of the foreign country, orig. India, where one happens to be): military: late C.19–20. Kipling, 1892. See BAT, 3.

sling the booze. To stand treat: low: from ca 1860. cf. SLING, v., 2.

sling the hatchet. To talk plausibly: military: late C.19–20. 2. See *sling the* HATCHET. 3. To tell a piteous tale: s.: 1893, P. H. Emerson.

sling the language. To swear fluently: lower classes' (—1903); ob.

***sling the smash.** To smuggle tobacco to prisoners: c.: from the 1870s. Anon., 1877, *Five Years' Penal Servitude*. cf. SLING, v., 2.

sling type. To set type: printers' s. (—1887) >, by 1910, coll; ob.

sling (esp. *it*) **up.** To abandon (job, country, talk, action, etc.): Australian: late C.19–20.

sling words, see SLING LANGUAGE.

sling yourself! or **let her sling!** Bestir yourself!; get a move on!: low: from ca

1880; the former is very ob. cf. SLING ONE'S DANIEL.

slinge. To play truant; to stay away from work: Newfoundland coll: C.19–20. Ex Irish and Sc. dial. *slinge*, to skulk.

slinger. (Gen. pl.) A piece of bread afloat in tea or coffee; a dumpling, a sausage: low (—1889). 2. **(Slinger.)** An inevitable nickname of all men surnamed Woods: naval and military: late C.19–20. cf. LACK(E)RY.

slink. A sneak, skulker, cheat: dial. (—1824) >, ca 1830, coll. *Examiner*, 1830, 'Such a d—d slink'. Ex *slink*, an abortive calf, etc.

slinky. Sneaky, mean, sly, furtive: dial. and coll: late C.19–20. Ex SLINK. 2. Hence, (of a person's gait) stealthy: late C.19–20.

slip. A counterfeit coin: ca 1590–1630: perhaps orig. c., as its use by Greene suggests. Origin doubtful. The derivative *nail up for a slip*, to try and find wanting (late C.16–early 17), may, orig. at least, have been coll. 2. A slash-pocket in the rearward skirt of a coat: ca 1810–40. 3. A slipper: domestic: since ca 1880. 4. Baked custard: middle-class: since ca 1860. Slippery stuff.

slip (her, him) **a length.** To coït with (a woman): low: late C.19–20. 2. Of a man, to have homosexual relations with: Australian low s.: late C.19–20.

slip at, let. To rush violently at a person and then assault him vigorously: coll (—1860). cf.:

slip into. To begin punching (a person) vigorously, gen. with the connotation that the person 'slipped into' receives a sound beating: low coll (—1860). cf. preceding entry. 2. To set about a thing, a task, with a will, vigorously: low coll (—1887). 3. To have sexual connection with: low: from ca 1870.

slip it. To decamp, make off: from ca 1880. J. W. Horsley, *Prisons and Prisoners*, 1898.

slip one's breath, cable, wind. To die: resp. 1819, Wolcot; 1751, Smollett, 'I told him [a doctor] as how I could slip my cable without direction or assistance'; 1772, Bridges. Orig. nautical s.; by mid-C.19, gen. coll.

slip oneself. To let oneself go; make the most of a thing or opportunity: Cockney coll: from ca 1890. Edwin Pugh's Cockney stories, *passim*.

slip-slop. Kissing: s.: Ned Ward, 1703.

slip-slops. Soft drinks: C.18. Ned Ward, *The Whole Pleasures of Matrimony*, 1714.

slip up. To swindle; to disappoint: Australian: 1890, *Melbourne Argus*, 9 Aug., 'I'd only be slipped up if I trusted to them.' Ex *slip*, to elude, evade, stealthily; give the slip to.

slipper. A sixpence: tailors' (—1909). Because it slips into corners and cracks. 2. A bed-pan: hospital coll: late C.19–20. Ex shape.

***slippery.** Soap: c. (—1839); slightly ob.

slippery, adj. Quick: coll: late C.19–20. Prob. ex:

slippy. Quick; spry, nimble: dial. (—1847) >, ca 1880, coll. Esp. *look slippy* (Runciman, 1885) and *be slippy* ('Rolf Boldrewood', 1889). Coulson Kernahan, 1902, 'We must look slippy about it . . . It's lucky I haven't far to go.' Ex *slippy* = *slippery* in its fig. as well as lit. senses.

slit. The female pudend; when not a euphemism it is a low coll: C.17–20.

slither, v.i. To hurry (away): low (—1889). Ex *slither*, to *slide*: cf. SLIDE. Imm. ex dial.

sloan. To hamper, obstruct, baulk: lower classes': 1899 only. Ex jockey Sloan's trick – learnt from Archer – of slanting his horse across the track and thus obstructing the other riders.

slobber. Ink badly distributed: printers' coll: from ca 1870. 2. A kiss: very low s.: from late C.19. Maugham, *Liza of Lambeth*, 1897.

slobber, v. To fail to grasp (the ball) cleanly in fielding: cricket coll: 1851, Pycroft; †by 1890. For semantics, cf. BUTTER in its cricketing sense (v., 5).

slobgollion. An oozy, stringy substance found in sperm oil: whalemen's: from ca 1880. Clarke Russell. Perhaps a perversion of SLUMGULLION on *slob*, mud, ooze.

slockdolager, see SOCKDOLAGER.

slog. (A period of) hard, steady work: coll: 1888. Ex v., 6. 2. A hard punch or blow; (at cricket) a hard hit: coll: 1867 (Lewis); as a SLOGGER (sense 3), it appears also in 1867 (ibid.), but is rare. Ex v., 1; cf. v., 4. 3. A large portion, esp. of cake: Public Schools': late C.19–20.

slog, v.t. To punch, hit, hard: coll: *Sessions*, Sept. 1824, 'One of them said, "Go back and slog him"'; v.i., not before 1888. cf. SLUG, v. 2. Hence, to thrash, chastise: 1859, H., 1st ed. 3. Hence, fig., attack violently: coll: 1891, *Spectator*, 10 Oct., 'They love snubbing their friends and slogging their enemies.' 4. (Ex sense 1.) To make runs at cricket by hard hitting: v.i. and v.t.: coll: resp. early 1860s and in 1867. 5. v.i., to walk heavily, perseveringly: coll: 1872, Calverley. Prob. ex sense 1. cf. FOOT-SLOGGER. 6. v.i. To work hard and steadily, often with *away*; v.t. with *at*: coll: 1888, *Daily News*, 22 May, 'I slogged at it, day in and day out.' Ex sense 1. 7. v.i., to steal fruit, esp. apples: schoolchildren's: from ca 1880. cf. SKRIMP.

slog on, have a. To work hard or hurriedly or both: 1888.

slogdollager, see SOCKDOLOGER.

slogger. (Gen. in pl.) A trial or 2nd-division rowing-race: Cambridge: ca 1852–80. In etymology, prob. cognate with ensuing senses; H., 1860, proposes *slow-goers*, but this seems unlikely. cf. the Oxford TOGGER. 2. A deliverer of heavy blows: coll: *Sinks*, 1848; 1857, T. Hughes, 'The Slogger pulls up at last . . . fairly blown.' Ex SLOG, v., 1. 3. At cricket, a hard hitter: coll (—1864). 4. A (hard) punch: pugilistic: *Boxiana*, IV, 1824; ob. Ex sense 2 reinforced by sense 3. 5. A slung shot (as a weapon): c.: 1892. 6. A quick worker: proletarian coll: from ca 1860.

slogging, vbl n. (cricket, 1860: Lewis) and ppl adj. See SLOG, v., various senses.

'Slood. A variant of 'SLUD.

sloop of war. A whore: rhyming s. (—1859).

sloosh. A wash, a sound of washing: from ca 1905. Ex *sluice*. 2. Hence, *sloosh* or *slooshy*, v.i. and v.t., to wash: 1907, W. De Morgan.

slop. A policeman: abbr. of back s. (—1859) ESCLOP (properly *ecilop*, police); ob. Already in the 2nd ed. (1860), H. writes 'At first back slang but now general'. 2. A tailor: from ca 1860; ob. 3. At Christ's Hospital, pejorative for a person: mid-C.19–20. cf. Nashe's 'slop of a ropehaler' (1599).

slop-feeder. A tea-spoon: low (?orig. c.): from ca 1810. Ex *slop(s)*, tea.

slop trade. Trade that is 'no class': tailors' coll: mid-C.19–20.

***slop-tubs.** Tea-things: c. >, ca 1870, low: from ca 1820; ob. cf. SLOP-FEEDER.

slope. A running-away, making-off; escape: coll: U.S. (—1859), anglicized ca 1880. Esp. *do a slope*: coll and dial.: from ca 1890. Ex:

slope, v. To make off; run away, decamp: coll: orig. (1839), U.S.; anglicized ca 1857. Song-writer Vance; 'Pomes' Marshall. Either ex *let's lope!* as H., 1st ed., proposes, or ex *slope*, to move obliquely. 2. With adv., esp. *off* (1844, Haliburton) and occ. *home(ward)*, the latter in Mayne Reid, 1851: coll: orig. U.S., anglicized by 1860. 3. (Ex sense 1.) To go loiteringly or saunteringly, 1851. 4. v.t., to leave (lodgings) without paying: 1908. Ex sense 1, influenced by dial. *slope*, to trick, cheat. 5. In c. of early C.17 (e.g., Rowlands, 1610), to lie down to sleep; to sleep. (cf. *slope*, v.t., to bend down.) It replaced COUCH A HOG'S HEAD.

slope, do a, see SLOPE, n.

slopper. A slop-basin: Leys School: late C.19–20. See 'Oxford-*er*', p. 11.

slopping-up. A drinking bout: low: from ca 1870; ob.

sloppy. Very sentimental: coll: late C.19–20. Ex *sloppy*, feeble, infirm.

slops, tea still in the chest, is to be considered either s. or low coll (—1859). Ex *slops*, (weak) tea as beverage.

slosh. Slush (liquid mud): dial. and Cockney coll (—1887). 2. A drink; drink in gen.: from the middle 1880s.

slosher. A school boarding-house assistant: Cheltenham College: late C.19–20. ?ex U.S. *slosh*, to move aimlessly about.

sloshiety paper. A gushing Society periodical: journalistic: 1883–ca 1890. Punning *society* + *sloshy*, slushy.

slouch at, no. Rather or very good at: U.S. (1874), partly anglicized in late 1890s. F. T. Bullen, 1898, 'He was no "slouch" at the business either.' Ex *slouch*, a lout, a clumsy fellow.

***slour.** To lock (up); fasten: c. (—1812); ob. by 1890. Vaux; Ainsworth; H., 3rd ed., classifies it as prison c. ?origin unless perchance a perversion of *lower*. 2. Also, to button (up) a garment: esp. in *sloured hoxter*, an inside pocket buttoned up: 1812, Vaux, *slour up*; the simple v. is unrecorded before 1834 in Ainsworth's *Rookwood*.

slow. Old-fashioned; behind the times: 1827, *Sporting Times*, 'Long courtships are . . . voted slow.' (The Winchester sense 'ignorant of Winchester notions', dating from ca 1880, is a variant.) 2. Hence, (of things) tedious, dull, boring: coll: 1841, Lever. 3. (Of persons) humdrum; dull, spiritless: 1841, Lever. 4. Hence, sexually timid: late C.19–20.

slow as a wet week, as. (Of persons) very slow; esp., unenterprising, mostly in sexual matters: late C.19–20.

slow as molasses in winter, see MOLASSES.

***slowed.** Imprisoned; in prison: c. (—1859); ob. by 1890. Ex *slow*, retard, but perhaps influenced by SLOUR, 1: cf. late C.19–20 *slower*, to check.

slows, troubled with the. Slow-moving: sporting: from ca 1870. Perhaps orig. U.S. and punning U.S. *slows*, milk-sickness.

slubberdegullion. A dirty and/or slobbering fellow; a sloven ne'er-do-well: from ca 1615; ob. Perhaps orig. coll, which it may have remained till C.19. On *slubber* (later *slobber*): cf. TATTERDEMALION.

'Slud! A C.17–18 oath: coll variant of 'SBLOOD! Jonson, Fielding.

slued, see SLEWED.

slug. An unascertained kind of strong liquor: 1756, Toldervy, 'Tape, glim, rush-light, white port, rasher of bacon, gunpowder; slug, wild-fire, knock-me-down, and strip me naked'; †by 1790. 2. ?hence, a dram, a drink: 1762, Smollett, '... That he might cast a slug into his bread-room.' (Since ca 1880, only U.S.) Hence, *fire a slug*, to take a drink of potent liquor: ca 1780–1840. 3. A set-back; a (great) disappointment: coll: late C.19–20. Ex dial. *slug*, a defeat. cf.:

slug, v.t. To strike heavily: dial. (—1862), soon > coll. *Echo*, 8 March 1869, 'He has several times been told by unionists on strike that he would be "slugged" if he went on as he was going.' Perhaps ex dial. *slug*, a heavy blow, recorded thirty years earlier. cf. SLOG, v., 1. and SLUG, n., 3.

slug, fire a, see SLUG, n., 2.

sluice. The female pudend: low coll: late C.17–20; ob. 'Facetious' Tom Brown. 2. The mouth: low: from ca 1830; ob. Prob. ex *sluice*, a channel, influenced by †*sluice*, a gap, but perhaps imm. ex:

sluice-house. The mouth: low: 1840, Egan; very ob. cf. SLUICE, 2.

sluice one's or the bolt, dominoes, gob, or **ivories.** To drink heartily: low: resp. mid-C.19–20, late C.18–20, and mid-C.19–20. All slightly ob. cf. SLUICE, 2, and:

sluicery. A public-house: low: ca 1820–90. Contrast SLUICE-HOUSE.

Sluker. An inhabitant, esp. a harlot, of the Parish of *St Luke*, London: Cockney (—1909). cf. ANGEL.

***slum.** A room: c.: ca 1810–50. ?origin, unless Bee is right in deriving it ex *slumber*. 2. Nonsense, GAMMON, BLARNEY: c.: ca 1820–1910. Egan's Grose cites, from *Randall's Diary*, 'And thus, without more slum, began'. Prob. ex sense 4. 3. Hence, Romany: c. of ca 1821–50. 'Jon Bee', 1823, 'The gipsey language, or cant, is slum.' 4. A trick or swindle: c.: 1812, Vaux; 1851, Mayhew. cf. SLUM, FAKE THE; SLUM, UP TO. 5. ?hence, a begging letter: c.: 1851, Mayhew, 'Of these documents there are two sorts, "slums" (letters) and "fakements" (petitions).' Ob. 6. Hence, any letter: prison c. (—1860). Ob. 7. (?ex *slum*, a begging letter.) An innuendo, a discreditable insinuation: c. (—1864). †by 1900. 8. A chest; a package (e.g. a roll of counterfeit notes): c. (—1859); ob. H., 1st ed., ' "He shook a slum of slops", stole a chest of tea.' Perhaps ex sense 4. 9. In the language of Punch and Judy showmen (partly c., partly Parlary), the call: from ca 1860. cf. SLUM-FAKE; SLUMMING, 2. 10. Sweetmeats for coughs: market-traders' (e.g. Petticoat Lane): C.20. 11. Abbr. (1908: O.E.D.) of SLUMGULLION. 12. The cheap jewellery, watches, etc., given as prizes: fair-grounds (carnivals): late C.19–20.

***slum.** To talk nonsense; speak cant: c. of ca 1820–80. cf. n., 2. 2. Hence, v.t., to trick, cheat, swindle: c. (—1859). H., 1st ed., in variant form, *slum the gorger*, 'to cheat on the sly, to be an eye servant', which is † – prob. since late C.19. 3. Hence, v.t., to hide; to pass to a confederate: c. (—1874). Implied in H., 5th ed., though already implied in SLUMMING, 1. 4. v.t., to do hurriedly and/or carelessly: coll (1865) >, ca 1900, S.E. Perhaps suggested by *to slam* (a door), influenced by *slum*, a poverty-stricken neighbourhood. 5. v.i., to enter, or haunt, slums for illegal or rather for illicit or immoral purposes: university s.: Oxford, ca 1860; Cambridge, ca 1864: ob. by 1910. 6. Hence, 'to keep to back streets in order to avoid observation', Barrère & Leland: university s. (—1897); ob. 7. Hence, from ca 1899, to keep in the background: gen. coll; ob. 8. v.i., to act: low theatrical: from ca 1870; ob. cf. SLUMMING, 2.

***slum, fake the.** To do the trick; effect a swindle: c.: mid-C.19–20.

***slum, up to.** Alert; knowing: c. (—1823). Ex SLUM, n., 4.

slum-fake. The coffin in a Punch and Judy show: showmen: from ca 1860. cf. SLUM (n., 9), the call, and SLUMMING, 2.

***slum-scribbler.** One who employs penmanship for illicit ends, e.g. for begging-letters: c. (—1861).

slum shop, sleek-and-, see SLEEK-AND-SLUM SHOP.

slumber in. Public Schools' s. of late C.19–20, as in P. G. Wodehouse, *Tales of St Austin's*, 1903, 'To slumber in is to stay in the house during school on a pretence of illness.'

slumgullion. 'Any cheap, nasty, washy beverage', H., 5th ed.: from ca 1870; ob. Perhaps a fantasy on *slub* (= *slob*) and the *gullion* of SLUBBERDEGULLION (cf. SLOBGOLLION); certainly fanciful.

slummery. Gibberish; 'ziph' (see *Slang*, p. 278): ca 1820–50: low s., perhaps orig. c. 'Jon Bee', 1823, 'Dutch Sam excelled in slummery – "Willus youvus givibus glasso ginibus".'

***slumming,** vbl n. Passing counterfeit money: c. (—1839); ob. Perhaps ex SLUM, v., 1. 2. Acting: low theatrical: from ca 1870; ob. Miss Braddon, 1872, 'The gorger's awfully coally on his own slumming, eh?' cf. SLUM, n., 9; SLUM-FAKE. 3. 'The secreting of type or sorts', Jacobi: printers' s. (—1888). Ex SLUM, v., 2.

slummy. A servant girl: low: late C.19–20. ?ex *slummy*, careless, influenced by *slummy*, from a slum neighbourhood. cf. SLAVEY. 2. One who lives in a slum: coll: late C.19–20.

slums, act in. To act in very small towns or in low plays: theatrical: ca 1865–1910.

slung. (Of a picture) rejected: artists' and art-students' (—1909). Prob. suggested by *hung*.

slung out on hands and knees. Dismissed: tailors': from ca 1870; ob.

slung sword, ship one's. To be promoted to warrant officer: naval: late C.19–20.

slur. A method of cheating at dice: ca 1640–1750: perhaps orig. s. or coll, but soon j. (therefore S.E.). Ex *slur*, to make a die leave the box without turning (Nashe, 1594).

slush. Food: nautical: late C.19–20. Ex nautical S.E. *slush*. cf. SLUSHY, n. 2. 'Coffee and [?or] tea served in a common coffee house': low urban (—1909).

slush-bucket. A foul feeder: coll: ca 1780–1850. (Extant in dial.)

slusher. A cook's assistant at shearing time on a station: Australian coll. *Melbourne Argus*, 20 Sept. 1890. cf. SLUSHY, 2.

slushy. A ship's cook: nautical coll (—1859). Ex *slush*, refuse fat of boiled meat. cf. SLUSH, 1. 2. Hence, influenced by SLUSHER, a cook's assistant at a shearing: Australian coll: 1896, A. B. Paterson, in *The Man from Snowy River*, 'The tarboy, the cook, and the slushy ... with the rest of the shearing horde'.

sly. Illegal, illicit: earliest and mainly in *sly grog*, Australian s., 1844 (O.E.D.) – *sly grog-selling*, *seller*, *shop*. Mayhew, 1851, 'sly trade'. Ex *sly*, secret, stealthy. cf. next two entries.

sly, on or **upon the.** Private(ly), secret(ly), illicit(ly): 1812, Vaux: coll >, ca 1870, S.E. Mayhew, 1851, 'Ladies that liked a drop on the sly'.

sly, run. To escape: low s. (?c.): late C.18–early 19. F. & H., whose quotation long anticipates the sporting sense: (of a dog) to run cunningly.

sly-boots; ca 1730–1830, occ. **sly-boot.** A sly or crafty person: coll: ca 1680, Lord Guildford was thus nicknamed (North, *Lives of the Norths*, p. 169). Esp. a person seemingly simple, actually subtle or shrewd. In C.19–20, often jocular and hardly if at all pejorative. cf. †*sly-cap*, a sly or a cunning man (Otway, 1681), and the much more gen. *smooth-boots*, late C.16–early 18.

sly grog, see SLY.

***smabble** or **snabble.** To despoil, knock down, half-skin; arrest: c. of ca 1720–1840. See SNABBLE.

smabbled or **snabbled.** Killed in battle: ca 1780–1840. Ex SMABBLE.

smack. A liking or fancy: tailors' coll: from ca 1870. 'He had a real smack for the old 'un,' F. & H. Cf. C.14–mid-17 S.E. *smack*, enjoyment, inclination (for a place). 2. A GO (8): coll: 1889, *Pall Mall Gazette*, 'I am longing to have a smack at these Matabeles.' 3. Hence, an attempt (*at*): coll: late C.19–20. Prob. ex dial. Hence:

smack, at one. At the first attempt; (all) at the one time: coll: late C.19–20. Ex senses 3, 2 of the preceding.

smack at, have a, see SMACK, n., 2.

smack calfskin. To kiss the Bible: low: C. 19.

smack(-)smooth. Perfectly even, level, smooth: 1755, Smollett: coll until late C. 19, then dial. Ex *smack*, vbl adv. 2. As complement, with semi-advl force: 'so as to leave a level surface': 1788, Dibdin. 3. Hence, adv.: smoothly; without hindrance: C.19–20: like sense 2, coll till C.20, then mainly dial. H. Martin, 1802, 'A tour ... went on smack smooth.'

smack-up. A fight: New Zealanders': from ca 1906.

smacker. A peso: South American English: late C.19–20.

smacker, (go down) with a. (To fall) 'smack': lower classes' coll (—1887).

***smacking-cove.** A coachman: c.: mid-C.17–early 19. Ex whip.

small, n., see SMALLS. **small, sing,** see SING SMALL.

small and early. (or hyphenated). An evening party, few-personed and early-departing: 1880, Lord Beaconsfield; coll. Adumbrated in Dickens, 1865, 'Mrs Podsnap added a small and early evening to the dinner.'

small beer of, think. (Gen. with *no.*) To have (or with *no*, not to have) a low opinion of (persons, mostly oneself): coll: 1825, Westmacott; Thackeray; Lytton. cf. 'Thinking no pale ale of himself' in Francis Francis, *Newton Dogvane*, 1859. Ex *small*, i.e. weak or inferior, beer. Also SMALL COALS.

small cap O. A second-in-command; an under overseer: printers': from ca 1870; ob. Lit., a *small capital letter O*, i.e. a capital in a word all of equal-sized capitals.

small cheque. A dram; a (small) drink: nautical: from ca 1880; ob. cf. *knock down a cheque*, spend all in drink.

small coals . . . A ca 1860–90 variant of SMALL BEER . . .

small cuts. A small pair of scissors: tailors': late C.19–20.

small-gang, v.t. To mob: low: mid-C.19–20; ob. Mayhew, 1851.

small jeff. A small employer: tailors': late C.19–20. cf. FLAT-IRON JEFF.

small pill. A diminutive football (used on runs): Leys School: late C.19–20.

small potatoes, see POTATOES.

smalls. 'Towns not boasting a regularly built and properly appointed theatre', *Ardrossan Herald*, 11 Sept. 1891: theatrical coll: from ca 1890. F. & H., however, in 1903 defines thus, implying a singular: 'A one-night performance in a small town or village by a minor company carrying its own "fit-up"'.

smarm, smalm, v.i. Coll (late C.19–20), to smooth down, as hair with pomade. The word prob. represents a blend: ?*sm*ear + *balm.*

smart. A very elegant young man about town: (London) Society: ca 1750–80.

smart, adj. Rather steep (ground): mid-C. 17–20: S.E. until late C.19, then coll (ob.) and dial.

smart as a carrot(, as). Gaily dressed: 1780: coll until mid-C.19, then dial. – which it had been since 1791 at least. Grose, 2nd ed., *as smart as a carrot new scraped.*

smart as threepence. Smartly dressed: lower classes' coll (—1887); ob.

smarty. A would-be clever, cunning, or witty person: U.S. (1880), anglicized – as a coll – ca 1905, chiefly as an impertinent person, and esp. in Australia and New Zealand.

smash. Lit. and fig., a heavy blow: coll and dial.: 1779. In 1780, it was used like SMACK, 2. 2. Mashed vegetables, esp. turnips: ca 1780–1830. Grose, 1st ed., 'Leg of mutton and smash, a leg of mutton and mashed turnips, (*sea term*)'. cf. modern *mash*, mashed potatoes. 3. Counterfeit coin: c.: late C.18–20; slightly ob. Potter, 1795. cf. v., 2, and SMASH-FEEDER. ?because it 'smashes' acceptors. 4. Loose change: c.: mid-C.19–20; rhyming s. on *cash.* 5. Tobacco: c.: from late 1880s. cf. SLING THE SMASH. ?because it breaks regulations.

***smash,** v. To kick down stairs: c.: late C.17–early 19. Prob. imitative. 2. To pass, occ. to utter (counterfeit money): c.: from ca 1810. *Lex. Bal.* – but see SMASHER, 4. cf. SMASHING, adj. 3. To give change for (a note, a coin): from ca 1810: either c. or low s.; ob. 4. To beat badly: pugilistic coll: from ca 1820. 5. v.i. to go bankrupt; be ruined: coll: 1839, Hood. Occ. *smash up*: not before 1870s; very rare in C.20. 6. Esp. *smash a brandy-peg*, to drink one: military: from ca 1880. Ware cites the *Daily News*, 7 May 1884.

smash!; smash me!; smash my eyes! A coll and dial. imprecation: ob. in C.20; resp. 1819 (mostly North Country dial.); 1894; 1833, Scott. H., 3rd ed., defines *smash-man-Geordie* as 'a pitman's oath' in Durham and Northumberland: cf. GEORDIE and SMASHER, 6.

smash, go (to). Variant of SMASH, v., 5: coll: mid-C.19–20.

***smash-feeder.** A silver or a Britannia-metal spoon: c.: resp. ca 1839–59 and ca 1859–1910. (The best imitation shillings were made from Britannia metal.) Ex SMASH, n., 3.

smash me!; smash my eyes! see SMASH!

smash the teapot. To break one's pledge of abstinence: urban lower classes' (—1909); ob. 2. To lose the privilege of tea: prison c.: from ca 1880.

smashed, adj. Reduced in rank: naval (—1909).

smashed(-)up. Penniless: low: ca 1830–1900. Mayhew, I, 1851. Suggested by BROKE.

smasher. Anything very large or unusually excellent: 1794. Ob. 2. Hence, a crushing reply, a very severe article or review: coll: 1828, *Blackwood's Magazine*, 'His reply . . . was a complete smasher.' Slightly ob. 3. Hence, a heavy fall (1875) or a damaging or settling blow (1897): coll. 4. A passer (1795, Potter) or, less gen., an utterer (1796, O.E.D.) of false money, whether coin or note: c.: late C.18–20. Ex SMASH, n., 3, or it may argue an existence for SMASH, v., 2, at least sixteen years before the app. earliest record. 5. Hence, a base coin or, says F. & H., forged note: c.: mid-C.19–20; very ob. Mayhew, 1851. 6. A North Country seaman: nautical (—1883). Clark Russell. Prob. ex SMASH. 7. 'A soft felt hat with a broad brim', Pettman: South African coll: from ca 1885.

***smashing.** The passing or uttering of false money: c. (—1812). Ex SMASH, v., 2.

***smashing**, adj. Counterfeit: c.: 1857, Borrow. 2. Engaged in 'smashing': c.: 1899, O.E.D. 3. Excellent; the adj. corresponding to SMASHER, 1: C.19–20.

smawm. A variant, mainly dial., of SMARM.

***smear.** A house-painter: c.: late C.17–mid-18. *Street Robberies Considered*, ca 1700. Ex the rough work of many painters. 2. Hence, a plasterer: ca 1720–1820: c. >, ca 1750, s.

***smear-gelt.** A bribe: ca 1780–1840: c. or low s. Prob. ex Yiddish *schmiergelt*.

***smeer.** An incorrect spelling of SMEAR.

smell. To make smelly; fill with offensive odour: coll: 1887.

smell, n. A boastful, conceited or otherwise objectionable boy; Sedgeley Park School (now Cotton College): ca 1800–65. Provost Husenbeth, *History of Sedgeley Park*, 1856. cf. STINKER.

smell a rat. ca 1780–1830, it was, to judge from Grose (all edd.), c.: not, however, that one lexicographer connotes irrefragable certainty.

smell at, get a. (Only in interrogative or negative.) To get a chance at; to approach: (low) coll (—1887). Ex olfactory inaccessibility.

smell my finger! A low male c.p. with an erotic implication: late C.19–20.

smell of bread and butter. To be tied to nursery ways: Public Schools' coll: late C.19–20.

smell of gunpowder, there's a. Someone has broken wind: Army: late C.19–20.

smell one's hat. To pray into one's hat on reaching one's pew in church: jocular coll (—1887).

smell-powder. A duellist: coll: ca 1820–60.

***smeller.** A garden: c.: early C.17. Rowlands. Prob. ex SMELLING CHEAT, 1. 2. The nose: late C.17–20: c. >, ca 1750, s. Walker, 1901, *In the Blood*, 'I tipped 'im one on the smeller as soon as 'e said it.' cf. SMELLERS, 1. 3. Hence, a blow on the nose: boxing: from early 1820s. cf. NOSER. 4. Hence, in late C.19–20, fig.: a grave set-back. 5. Anything exceptional in the way of violence, strength, etc.: coll: 1898, Kipling, 'Good old gales – regular smellers'. cf. SNORTER. 6. A sneaking spy; a Paul Pry: late C.19–20; slightly ob. 7. An objectionable fellow: New Zealand: late C.19–20. cf. SMELL and STINKER.

smeller, come a. To have a heavy fall (lit. or fig.): low: late C.19–20. cf. SMELLER, 3 and 4.

smellers. Nostrils: 1678, Cotton, 'For he on smellers, you must know, | Received a sad unlucky blow.' Prob. ex *smeller*, a feeler, e.g. of a fly. 2. As a cat's whiskers, it may orig. (1738) have been coll – Grose, 1st ed., clearly classifies it as coll or s. – but from ca 1850, at latest, it has certainly been S.E.

***smelling cheat** or **chete.** A garden; an orchard: c.: 1567, Harman; B.E.; Grose, 1st ed. †by 1830; ob. as early, prob., as 1700. Lit., a smelling, i.e. fragrant, thing. See CHEAT. 2. A nosegay: C.17–early 19 (prob. ob. by 1750): c. It seems likely that after C.16 the predominating sense of *smelling cheat* is nosegay, for in 1610 Rowlands writes, 'Smellar, a garden; not Smelling cheate, for thats a Nosegay'.

***smelt.** A half-guinea: c. of ca 1630–1830, but ob. as early, prob., as 1750. Shirley, 1635; Shadwell; Grose, 1st ed. Not impossibly an *s* perversion – *s* perversions are fairly common in English c. and s. (cf. the prefix-use of *s* in Italian) – of *melt* (v. as n.): the 'melt' or melting-down of a guinea. cf. SMISH for MISH.

smelts, westward for. (Esp. *go westward* . . .) *On the* SPREE: semi-proverbial coll: early C.17. Lit., in search of 'conies' (see CONY), male or female, a *smelt* being a simpleton.

smiff-box. The nose: pugilistic: ca 1860–90.

smifligate; smifligation. Ob. variants of SPIFLICATE, -ATION: 1839, Dickens.

***smiggins.** A barley soup, a (cold) meat hash: prison c.: ca 1820–80. Knapp & Baldwin, *Newgate Calendar*, vol. iii, 1825. A nickname, perhaps ex a warder named Higgins. (c. etymologies are heartbreaking.)

smile. A drink of liquor, esp. of whisky: U.S. (1850), anglicized ca 1870: s. till C.20, then coll. Jerome K. Jerome, 1889. cf.:

smile, v.i. To drink (liquor, esp. whisky): U.S. (1858), anglicized ca 1870.

smile!, I should. A lot I care!: c.p.: 1891.

smile like a brewer's horse. To smile delightedly or broadly: coll: C.17. Howell, 1659. A brewer's horse thrives on its food and the circumambient odour of hops.

smilence! Silence: non-aristocratic (—1909).

smiler. A kind of shandy-gaff: 1892, *Daily News*, 16 Nov.; ob.

smirk. 'A finical, spruce Fellow', B.E.: late C.17–early 19. Ex the S.E. v.

***smish.** A shirt: c.: from ca 1810; ob. Perversion of MISH, or via *s(e)miche* = *chemise*.

smit. In love: mid-C.19–20 coll, jocular on archaic past ppl.

smite. To obtain money from (a tutor): university: ca 1780–1830. ?ex *smite hip and thigh*. cf. RUSH and STING.

***smiter.** The arm: c.: ca 1670–1815.

Smith!, what an O. What a grim laugh!: non-aristocratic: ca 1835–50. Lit., 'what an "O. Smith"!' ex the cavernous laugh of one O. Smith, a popular actor of villains' parts.

smithereens; smithers. Small pieces or fragments: coll and dial., orig. Anglo-Irish: from ca 1840; the latter, only dial. after ca 1890. S. C. Hall, 1841, 'Harness ... broke into smithereens'; Halliwell, 1847, '*Smithers*, fragments, atoms'. Actually, *smithers*, of obscure etymology but perhaps cognate with *smite*, is the earlier, *-een* being (as in *colleen*) an Irish diminutive suffix. Esp. *go*, and *blow*, *to smithers*, and *blow*, *break*, *knock*, *split to* or *into smithereens*, and (rare in C.20) *go to smithereens*; cf. *all to smithereens*, all to smash.

Smithfield bargain. A bargain or deal in which the purchaser is taken in: coll: ca 1660–1830. 'Cheats' Wilson, 1662; Richardson, 1753. Adumbrated in Shakespeare's *2 Henry IV*, I, ii. Ex the horse and cattle (now the great meat) market. 2. Hence, ca 1770–1840, a marriage of convenience, with money the dominant factor: coll. cf. Breton, 1605, 'Fie on these market matches, where marriages are made without affection.'

smoak. C.17–18 spelling of SMOKE.

smock. Of all the numerous phrases in F. & H. and O.E.D. – 'usually suggestive of loose conduct or immorality in, or in relation to women', O.E.D. – only two are to be considered; these may possibly be coll and certainly the latter is not s.: *smock-alley* (Ned Ward), the female pudend; *smock-pensioner*, a male keep. cf. SKIRT.

smoke. A cigar, cigarette, or pipe. 1882: coll. 2. *Smoke, the*, 1864, H., 3rd ed.; *the big S.* (—1897); *the great S.* (—1874): London: tramps' s. >, ca 1900, gen. coll. cf. AULD REEKIE, Edinburgh. 3. (Also *smoke-on*: ex *have a smoke on.*) A blush: Scottish Public Schools': from ca 1885.

smoke, v. To ridicule, make fun of: late C.17–mid-19: coll >, ca 1800, S.E. Ned Ward, in *The London Spy*, 'We smoak'd the Beaus ... till they sneak'd off one by one'; Miss Burney; Keats. Perhaps ex *smoke*, to suspect (a person). 2. As a specific nuance of this: 'to affront a Stranger at his coming in', B.E.: late C.17–18. 3. To coït with (a woman); C.17–19. 4. v., to blush: Public Schools': from ca 1860. Farrar in *St Winifred's*, 1862. cf. the C.16 *smoke*, to fume, be very angry. 5. To decamp: low Australian: mid-C.19–20. Ex *smoke along*, to ride at great speed.

smoke, like. Rapidly: ca 1806, an Irish lady's maid writes of the Russian postillions that 'they drive like smoke up the hills' (*The Russian Journals of Maria and Katherine Wilmot, 1803–1808*, edited by J. H. M. Hide); 1833, M. Scott: coll till ca 1870, then S.E. Ex the manner in which smoke disperses in a high wind.

smoke, the great, see SMOKE, n., 2.

smoke and oakum, like. An early C.19 naval form of *like* SMOKE.

smoke-boat. A steamer: sailing-ships' pejorative: late C.19–20; ob.

smoke, gammon and spinach, – all, see ALL SMOKE ...

smoke-ho; -oh; smoko. A cessation from work in order nominally to smoke, certainly to rest: coll: 1897, Frank Bullen; H. Lawson, 1900.

smoke off. (Gen. in imperative.) To cease

blushing: Scottish Public Schools': from ca 1890.

smoke-on, see SMOKE, n., 3.

smoke-stack. A steamer: sailing-ship seamen's pejorative coll, as is their *steamboat man* for a sailor therein: from not later than 1885.

smoker. A chamber-pot: low: mid-C.19–20; ob. Ex steam arising therefrom in cold weather. 2. A voter: Preston s. or coll: ca 1800–32. Because every man who used the chimney of his cottage had a vote. 3. A steamer: coll: ca 1825–50. cf. PUFFER. 4. One who blushes: Public Schools': 1866. Ex SMOKE, v., 4. 5. A sultry day: low coll (—1887); slightly ob. cf. sense 1.

smoking, vbl n. of SMOKE, v., esp. 1, 3.

smoko, see SMOKE-HO.

smoky. Jealous: s. or coll: late C.17–mid-18. B.E., who is, I think, wrong in classifying it as c. Ex *smoky*, suspicious.

smole, n. and v. Smile; esp. in (*he*) *smoled a smile* (or *smole*): jocular >, by 1900, non-aristocratic (—1909); slightly ob. 'Invented' by F. C. Burnand, ca 1877, in *Punch*, says Ware. cf. SMILENCE!

smoocher. A gold-digger without a licence: Australian: ca 1851–1900.

smoodge, v.i. To flatter, wheedle, speak with deliberate amiability: Australian: late C.19–20. Ex *to smoothe.*

smoot, n. and v., see SMOUT. **smooth-boots,** see SLY-BOOTS.

***smooth white.** A shilling: c. and low: late C.19–20; ob.

'smorning. This morning: coll: late C.19–20.

smother. Trade s., mid-C.19–20, as in Mayhew, 1851, 'A "lick-up" is a boot or shoe re-lasted, and the bottom covered with a "smother" . . . obtained from the dust of the room.'

smother a parrot. To drink, neat, a glass of absinthe: Anglo-French: ca 1900–14. Like so many parrots, absinthe is green. cf. Fr. *étrangler un perroquet* – the same.

smother (or **s'm'other**) **evening!** A c.p. of cynical refusal: music-halls': 1884–5. Ex one of the great Arthur Roberts's songs; it was thus titled and themed.

smouch. 'Dried leaves of the ash tree, used by the smugglers for adulterating the black, or bohea teas', Grose, 1st ed.: ca 1780–1840: perhaps orig. c. or s. 2. See SMOUS.

Smouchy. A Jew: 1825, *The Universal Songster*, I, 172. Ex:

Smous, Smouse; Smouch, Smoutch. A Jew: *Smouse*, 1705 (Bosman); *Smous*, 1785 (Grose, who restricts it to a German Jew); *smouch*, 1765 (C. Johnston); *Smoutch*, 1785 (Cumberland). The *-s*, *-se*, forms are rare in C.19; both *-s(e)* and *-ch* forms are †by 1880, except as archaisms. Why the O.E.D. should treat *smou(t)ch* – an alteration of *smous(e)* – as S.E., and *smous(e)* as s., I cannot see: both, I believe, are s., *smous(e)* coming direct ex the Dutch *smous* (identical with German-Jewish *schmus*), patter, profit, Hebrew *schmuoss*, news, tales; Sewel, 1708, proposed derivation ex *Moses* – cf. IKEY. 2. Hence, in South Africa, an itinerant (esp. if Jewish) trader: coll: *smou(t)ch*, 1849; *smouse*, 1850, but anticipated fifty years before. Also *Smouser*: 1887 (Pettman); *smousing*, itinerant trading, from mid-1870s, is another South African coll.

smouse, v.i., corresponding to SMOUS, 2. **smousing,** see SMOUS, 2.

smout; smoot. A compositor seeking occasional work at various houses: printing (—1888). Jacobi. While *smoot* is in C.20, more gen., *smout* is recorded the earlier. Ex:

smout; smoot, v.i. To work on occasional jobs at various houses or even at one if it is not one's regular place of employment: printing: from ca 1680: in C.20, *smoot* (app. unrecorded before 1892) is the more gen. Moxon. In C.17–18, v.t. as *smout on* (a firm). Perhaps ex Dutch *smutte*, to slink: cf. dial. *smoot*, to creep, and *smoot after*, to court (a girl) furtively.

Smoutch, see SMOUS.

smug. A blacksmith: C.17–18: perhaps c. Rowlands, 1609; Ned Ward; Grose. Prob. ex C.16–17 *smuggy*, grimy, smutty, dirty. 2. Smuggling: Anglo-Chinese (—1864). cf. the v., 1, and SMUG-BOAT. 3. A (quiet and) hard-working student; esp. (at Oxford) one who takes no part in the social life of the place: university: 1882; ob. See quotation from Goschen at SAP, n., 2, and cf. SCRUBBER, 3. Ex *smug*, consciously respectable.

***smug,** v. To steal; run away with: 1825, T. Hook: c. rapidly > low s. Perhaps ex *smuggle*: cf. SMUG-BOAT; SMUGGING, 2. 2. To hush up: 1857, *Morning Chronicle*, 3 Oct., 'She wanted a guarantee the case should be smugged'; prob. orig. c.; by 1900, s. ?ex sense 1 or ex *smug*, to smarten up. 3. (?hence) to arrest, imprison: c.: from mid-1880s. J. W. Horsley, *Jottings from Jail*, 1887, 'Then two or three more coppers came up, and we got smugged, and got a sixer each.' 4. v.i., to copy; to crib: from ca 1860; ob. Perhaps ex sense 2. 5. To work hard: university: from ca 1890. Ex n., 2.

smug-boat. A boat carrying contraband; esp. an opium boat off the Chinese coast: nautical coll (—1867). Ex *smuggle*; cf. SMUG, v., 1, and:

***smug-lay.** The DODGE of selling (almost) worthless goods on the ground that they are valuable contraband: c. of ca 1810–50. Ex *smuggling*.

smugging. See SMUG, v. 2. (In pl) *smuggings!* Mine!: schoolboys' s. (—1859), shouted at the conclusion of a game, when (e.g. at top-spinning or marbles) it was lawful to purloin the plaything. In 1825, Hone notes that this practice is called *smugging*. Ex SMUG, v., 1.

smuggle, gen. v.t. To sharpen (a pencil) at both ends: schools' late C.19–20; ob. cf. the late C.17–18 *smuggle*, to caress.

smuggle the coal (or **cole**). 'To make people believe one has no Money when the Reckoning is to be paid', Miége, 1687; †by 1750. See COLE.

smuggler. A pencil sharpened at both ends: schools': see SMUGGLE. Esp. at Winchester.

***smuggling-ken.** A brothel: c. of ca 1720–1830. Punning *smuggle*, to caress, and *smuggle*, to 'contraband'.

***smut.** A furnace; a copper boiler: c. (—1811) >, ca 1840, low s.; †by 1890. As a furnace, app. †by 1859: witness H., 1st ed. Ex *smut*, soot.

smut!, ditto, brother, see BROTHER SMUT.

snab, see SNOB, 1.

***snabble.** To arrest: c.: 1724, Harper, 'But fileing of a rumbo ken, | My Boman is snabbled again'; †by 1790. Gen. as *snabbled*. 2. To rifle, plunder, steal; knock down, half-stun: c. of ca 1720–1840. Also SMABBLE; cf. SNAFFLE. 3. Hence, to kill, esp. in battle: c.: mid-C.18–early 19. cf. SMABBLED. 4. Gen. v.t., to copulate: low s.: late C.18–early 19.

snack. A racquets ball: Winchester: from ca 1860; ob. 2. It is possible that *snack*, a share, esp. in *go snacks*, be partners – cf. *go snicks* (see SNICK, n., 1) – may orig. have been c.: see B.E.

***snaffle.** 'A Highwayman that has got Booty', B.E.: c.: late C.17–18. Perhaps ex *snaffle*, a bridle-bit; but prob. allied with the v., 1. 2. Talk uninteresting or unintelligible to the others present: coll: from ca 1860; almost †. Perhaps because such conversation acts as a snaffle; more prob. ex East Anglian *snaffle*, to talk foolishly.

***snaffle.** To steal: 1724, Harper, 'From priggs that snaffle the prancers strong': c. >, ca 1840, dial. and low s. Cognate with SNABBLE. cf. the n., 1; SNAGGLE; SNAVEL. 2. To seize (a person); arrest: c. (—1860) >, ca 1890, low s. Ex *snaffle a horse*. 3. To appropriate, to seize a thing for oneself: mostly military: from the middle 1890s.

snaffle-biter. A horse-thief: s.: Ned Ward, 1709. cf.:

***snaffler.** A thief, only in *snaffler of prancers* (horses): from ca 1780: c. >, ca 1840, dial. and low s. Ex SNAFFLE, v., 1. 2. A highwayman: ca 1786–1840: c. cf. SNAFFLE, n., 1. 3. As = one who arrests, very rare: C.19.

***snaffling lay.** Highway robbery as a trade: c.: mid-C.18–early 19. Fielding, 1752, 'A clever fellow, and upon the snaffling lay at least'. Ex SNAFFLE, v., 1; cf. SNAFFLE, n., 1, and SNAFFLER, 2.

snag-catcher. A dentist: low: from ca 1880; very ob. Ex angling.

***snaggle,** v.i. and t. To angle for geese as a means of stealing them: either c. or low s.: from late 1830s; ob. Often as *snaggling*, vbl n. Prob. a corruption of *sniggle* (as in eel-fishing) and perhaps cognate with SNABBLE and SNAFFLE.

snaggle-tooth. A proletarian woman, esp. if a shrew, with an irregular set of teeth: urban lower classes' coll (—1909).

snags. False teeth: ?mostly naval: ca 1800–50. It occurs in W. N. Glascock, *Sailors and Saints* (I, 183), 1829.

snail(e)y. A bullock with horn slightly curled, like a snail's: Australian coll: from ca 1880. 'Rolf Boldrewood', 1884.

'Snails! God's nails!: a coll petty oath: late C.16–early 19.

snail's gallop, go a. To go very slowly indeed: semi-proverbial coll >, ca 1850, dial: from ca 1545. 'Proverbs' Heywood; Ray, 1670; N. Bailey, 1725; Colman, Jr, 1803; Combe, 1821; Brogden's *Lincolnshire Words*, 1866.

snaily, see SNAILEY.

snake. A skein of silk: tailors': from ca 1870; ob. Ex shape.

***snake.** To steal (something) warily: c.: from ca 1885. Ex dial.

snake, give (a person) **a.** To vex, annoy: low (—1887); ob.

snake-charmer. A bugler; a Highland piper: military: late C.19–20; ob. Ex music played to charm snakes.

snake in the grass. A looking-glass: rhyming s. (—1859).

snake-juice. Whisky: Australian: from ca 1890. Ex *see* SNAKES.

snake-tart. Eel-pie: mid-C.19–20; ob. cf. DOVE-TART.

snake the pool. To take the pool: billiards: from ca 1880.

snakes, a caution to. (Something) very surprising, odd, eccentric, or unusual: 1897, 'Pomes' Marshall, 'Her Sunday best was her week-day worst, | 'Twas simply a caution to snakes'; ob. cf. CAUTION, which, prob., it merely elaborates.

snakes!, great. A coll imprecation: 1897, F. T. Bullen; slightly ob. Orig. U.S. (*why in snakes* occurring in 1891 in *Scribner's Magazine*).

snakes, see. To have delirium tremens: U.S.; anglicized as coll ca 1900. Earlier form, *have* or *have got snakes in one's boots*, remained U.S.

***snakesman.** Only in LITTLE SNAKESMAN. cf. SNEAKSMAN.

***snam.** To steal; esp. to snatch (from the person): c.: from ca 1835. Origin?

***snam, (up)on the.** Thus engaged: c.: mid-C.19–20. cf. SNAM.

***snap.** A share: c.: from ca 1560; ob. Awdelay, 1561. Alsc *snaps*, as in *go snaps*, to go shares (cf. SNACK): late C.18–20: Pegge, ca 1800; H., 1st ed., spells it SNAPPS. cf. SNICK, n. 2. (A synonym of CLOYER.) A sharper, cheat, pilferer; esp. a thief claiming a share in booty (cf. sense 1): c.: late C.16–early 17 for 'cloyer' nuance; ca 1620–1720 for 'sharper' senses: former in Greene, latter in Fletcher and L'Estrange. In Ned Ward, 1731, *brother snap* is a sharking lawyer: C.18 s. 3. Affair, business; easy job: see SNAP, SOFT, and SNAP AWAY, GIVE THE. 4. Energy: U.S. (1872), anglicized ca 1890: coll >, ca 1910, S.E. Doyle, 1894, 'A young . . . man with plenty of snap about him'. cf. GO, n., 7; PEP; VIM. 5. An engagement (for work): theatrical: from ca 1890. cf. SNAPPS.

***snap,** v.i. To go shares with sharpers or thieves: early C.17 c. Field, 1609. cf. the n., 1 and 2; also: SNACK; SNICK (n.).

***snap, on the.** On the look-out for something to steal: c.: mid-C.19–20. cf. *snapper-up of unconsidered trifles* and SNAP, n., 2. 2. Hence, looking out for occasional work: from ca 1890: s.

snap, soft. An easy matter, business, project; a profitable affair; an easy job; occ. a pleasant time: s. >, ca 1910, coll: from ca 1885; orig. U.S. (1845).

snap away, give the. To blab; BLOW THE GAFF: low s.: from ca 1870.

***snap the glaze.** To break shop-windows or show-case glasses: c.: ca 1780–1840.

***snappage.** A share in booty: c.: early C. 17. Rowlands. cf. SNAP, 1; SNAPPING.

snapped, ppl adj. Abrupt, sudden, unexpected: coll: 1893, Leland.

***snapper.** An accomplice; a sharer (in booty): c.: ca 1530–50. cf. SNAP, n., 1. 2. A taker of snapshot photographs; the taker of the snapshot in question: from ca 1908: coll, now verging on S.E.

snapper-rigged. (Of a ship) poorly rigged and found; (of a man) poorly clothed: East Canadian (and U.S.) nautical: late C. 19–20.

***snapping.** A share in booty: c.: late C. 16–early 17. Greene, 1591. cf. SNAP, n., 1; SNAPPAGE; SNAPPER; and:

***snapps.** A variant of SNAP, n., 1. H., 1st ed., ' "Looking out for *snapps*", waiting for windfalls'; H., 2nd ed., 1860, adds 'or odd jobs'. cf. SNAP, 5.

snappy. Smartly intelligent; energetic; lively; pointed (story): coll: 1873. 2. Whence, smart (of dress); neatly elegant: coll: 1881; ob.

snare. 'To acquire; to seize; to win', C. J. Dennis: Australian: late C.19–20. Ex snaring animals.

snarl. An ill-tempered discussion; a quarrel: tailors': from ca 1860.

snatch. A hasty or illicit or mercenary copulation: coll: C.17–20. 'Melancholy' Burton, 'I could not abide marriage, but as a rambler I took a snatch when I could get it.' 2. Hence, ultimately, though imm. ex Yorkshire dial.: the female pudend: late C.19–20.

snatch-blatch. The female pudend: from ca 1890. On SNATCH, 2.

***snatch-cly.** A pickpocket, esp. one who snatches from women's pockets: c.: late C.18–19. See CLY.

***snatcher.** A young and inexperienced thief: c.: from ca 1860. 2. See RAG-AND-SNATCHER MAN.

snatchers. Handcuffs: Glasgow policemen's: since ca 1890. Ex-Inspector Elliot, *Tracking Glasgow Criminals*, 1904. cf. synonymous c. SNITCHER (3).

***snavel,** n. See RUNNING SNAVEL and cf. RUNNING SMOBBLE. 2. v., to steal, esp. by snatching or by pocket-picking: c.: from ca 1810. A corruption of SNABBLE or of SNAFFLE (v., 1), or perhaps a fusion of both. 3. To catch, to take: Australian: mid-C.19–20.

'Snayles! A C.16–17 variant of 'SNAILS!

***sneak;** in late C.18–19, gen. **the sneak.** The practice, or a specific act, of creeping in stealthily with a view to robbery; a theft thus effected: c.: late C.17–20; ob. Esp. in SNEAK, (UP)ON THE. 2. Partly hence, a stealthy departure or flight: c.: from ca 1810. 3. A pilferer, a stealthy enterer with a view to theft: from ca 1780: s. >, ca 1830, coll >, ca 1880, S.E. 4. See SNEAKS.

***sneak,** v.t. To steal from (a place) after stealthy entry: c.: from ca 1810; ob. Prob. ex SNEAK, GO UPON THE. cf. sense 4 and the n., 1. 2. To escape from (a person) by stealth: c.: from ca 1810; extremely ob. cf. the n., 2. 3. To walk about looking for something to steal or pilfer: c.: from ca 1820; ob. 4. To filch; steal furtively, stealthily: coll: 1883. Ex sense 1. 5. To tell tales (v.i.): schools': 1897, *Daily News*, 3 June, 'Sneaking, in the ethics of the public school boys, is the unpardonable sin.' Ex *sneak*, to be servile.

sneak, area, see AREA SNEAK. **sneak, evening,** see SNEAK, MORNING.

***sneak, give it to** (a person) **upon the,** see SNEAK, V., 2.

***sneak, go upon the.** To slip into houses whose doors are left open and there steal: c.: late C.18–20; ob. Ex SNEAK, UPON THE.

***sneak, morning.** The practice of 'going out early to rob private houses or shops by slipping in at the door unperceived', Vaux: c.: from ca 1810; ob. Ex: 2. In late C.18–20, the person doing this: c. Grose, 1st ed., where also *evening sneak*, one given to pilfering in the evening, also (in C.19–20) the doing of this.

***sneak, upon** or (in C.19–20) **on the.** Stealthily: c.: late C.17–20. Mainly in reference to robbery (see SNEAK, n., 1). 2. Prowling for booty: c.: from ca 1820. cf. SNEAK, V., 3.

***sneak, upright.** A thief preying on pot-boys, whom he robs of the pots as they are engaged in collecting them: c.: late C.18–20; ob.

***sneak on the lurk.** To prowl about for booty: c.: from ca 1820; ob. An elaboration of SNEAK, V., 3. See LURK.

sneaker. A large cup (or small basin) with a saucer and cover, esp. for drink; e.g. a *sneaker of punch*: from ca 1710: perhaps orig. s., soon > coll; by 1830, S.E.

***sneaking-budge.** A lone-hand thief or robber: c.: late C.17–early 19. cf. SNEAK, n., 1, and v., 1, and see BUDGE. 2. Fielding incorrectly uses it to mean pilfering or stealing, n. and adj.

***sneaks.** c. from ca 1870 as in James Greenwood's *In Strange Company*, 1873, 'Sneaks . . . are shoes with canvas tops and india-rubber soles.' Ex SNEAK, n., 2.

'Sneaks! God's neaks!, a coll petty oath: early C.17. Marston. Properly, *neaks* should be *neakes* or *neaques* = *nigs*. A variant of the oath occurs in Fletcher, 1619, 'I'll . . . goe up and downe drinking small beere and swearing 'odds neagues.' cf. 'SNIGS!

***sneaksman.** A stealthy thief, cowardly pilferer: c.: from ca 1810. Properly, one who goes *upon the* SNEAK. Ex SNEAK, n., 1, but perhaps influenced by LITTLE SNAKESMAN. 2. Hence, a shoplifter: c.: mid-C.19–20.

sneck up! snick up! Go hang!: late C.16–17 coll; extant in dial. 'Women of Abingdon' Porter, 1599; Shakespeare; dramatist Heywood. Lit., close the latch! cf. SHUT UP, and the Derbicism *put a sneck before one's snout*, to watch one's speech, to say little or nothing.

sneerg. Greens: back s. (—1859).

sneeze. The nose: from ca 1820; very ob. Ex SNEEZER, 2.

sneeze at. To underrate, disregard, scorn: coll: 1806, Surr; Combe, 1820, 'A . . . dame . . . who wish'd to change her name, | And . . . would not perhaps have sneezed at mine'. In C.20, mainly in *not to be* SNEEZED AT.

***sneeze-** or **snuff-lurker.** A thief that operates after disabling his victim with snuff, pepper, or any similar unpleasantness: c.: from ca 1859; ob. As = snuff, *sneeze*, once S.E., is now dial. cf. SNUFF, 1, and:

***sneeze-** or **snuff-racket, give it** (to a person) **on the.** To do this: from ca 1820; slightly ob. See SNEEZE-LURKER.

sneezed at, not to be. Not to be underrated, disregarded, despised: coll: 1813, Scott; 1891, Nat Gould. Ex SNEEZE AT.

***sneezer.** A snuff-box: c. of ca 1720–1880. *A New Canting Dict.*, 1725, '*Cog a Sneezer*, Beg a . . . Snuff-box'. Ex *sneeze*, snuff. 2. The nose: 1820. cf. SNORTER, 4. 3.

Hence, a pocket-handkerchief: low (—1857); ob. 4. A drink, esp. a dram of something strong: from ca 1820: dial. >, ca 1835, s. J. T. Hewlett, 1841, 'He knew he should get a sneezer of something short for his trouble'; Dickens. Lit., enough to make one sneeze. cf. SNIFTER, 1. 5. Something exceptionally good or bad, big or strong or violent, in some specified respect: s. >, in late C.19, coll: 1820, a blow (dial. >, ca 1840, s.); a gale, early C.19 (mainly nautical); a very well-bowled fast ball, late C.19–20 (cricket); in 1836, Haliburton speaks of 'a regular sneezer of a sinner'; a martinet (military s. of —1903). cf. preceding sense; SNORTER, 2; SNIFTER, 2. 6. A mouth-gag: c.: from ca 1890. Clarence Rook, *The Hooligan Nights*, 1899. Ex sense 3.

***sneezing-coffer.** A snuff-box: c. of ca 1810–50. cf. SNEEZER, 1.

Sneezy. The second month in the French Republican Calendar: late C.18–early 19. Ex (*le mois*) *brumaire*, the foggy month.

***snell.** A needle: c.; hawkers' s.: from ca 1845. Ex Scots *snell*, sharp. cf.:

***snell-fencer.** A needle-hawker: id.: id. Carew, *Autobiography of a Gipsy*.

***snib.** A petty thief: c.: ca 1605–1840. Dekker; Egan's Grose, where it is described as Scotch cant. ?cognate with *snib*, to check.

snib, v. To coït with (a woman): low Scots: from ca 1810. Prob. ex *snib*, to fasten (a door); cf. *snib a candle*, snuff it.

snibs! A term of derision or defiance: late C.19–20.

snick. A share: s. and dial.: from ca 1720. At Winchester, *go snicks* (—1891), to go shares. A variant of SNACK, 2. 2. Esp. in *for a snick*, for a certainty: proletarian: late C.19–20.

snick, v. To slip, cut, across or along (a road) suddenly or quickly: coll: 1883. Ex *snick*, v.i., to cut, snip, esp. crisply.

snick-fadge. A petty thief: c.: mid-C.19–20. Ex S.E. *snick off*.

snick up! see SNECK UP!

snicker. A glandered horse: late C.18–early 19. cf. SNITCHED.

***snicking.** A surreptitious obtaining: c. or low s.: ca 1670–1750. Head, 1673. See SNICK, n., and cf. SNACK; SNAP, v.; SNICKTOG.

***snickle,** v.i. To inform, peach: c.: mid-C.19–20: mostly U.S. Matsell. Prob. ex the now dial. *snickle*, to snare.

snicks, go, see SNICK, n.

***snicktog.** To go shares: c.: late C.19–20; ob. Perversion of SNICK, n. cf. SNACK (esp. as *go snacks*); SNAP, n., 1, and v.; SNICK (esp. *go snicks*); SNICKING.

***snid.** A sixpence: mainly Scots c. (—1839); ob. by 1900.

***sniddy,** see SNIDE, adj., and SNIDEY.

snide. An occ. form of SNID. 2. (Occ. *snyde.*) Anything spurious, esp. base coin or sham jewellery: c. (in C.20, low): implied in SNIDE-PITCHER, as early as 1862, but by itself unrecorded before ca 1885, except in H., 5th ed., 1874, 'Also . . . as a [n.], as, "He's a snide", though this seems but a contraction of *snide 'un*'; perhaps, however, the reference in '*No. 747*' at p. 416 is valid (as = base metal) for 1845. Origin obscure; see the adj. 3. Hence, a contemptible person: c. >, by 1890, low: see quotation from H. for sense 2.

***snide; snyde,** adj. Spurious, counterfeit, sham, bogus: c.: 1862, 'Snyde witnesses', O.E.D.; but the reference in Carew's *Autobiography of a Gipsy*, p. 418, points to 1845. 2. Hence, mean, contemptible: c.: from ca 1870. 'Pomes' Marshall, 'His pockets she tried, | Which is wifely, though snide.' Both senses also in forms *sniddy* and *snidey*: late C.19–20. Prob. ex S. German *aufschneiden* (to boast, show off, exaggerate) via Yiddish.

snide and shine (or S. and S.). A Jew, esp. of East London: East London Gentiles' (—1909). For *shine*, cf. SHEENY.

***snide lurk.** The passing of counterfeit money: c.: from ca 1845.

***snide-pitcher.** A passer of base money: c.: 1862 (O.E.D.). See SNIDE, n., 2.

***snide-pitching.** The passing of counterfeit money: c.: 1868, Temple Bar, 'Snyde-pitching is . . . a capital racket.' See SNIDE, n., 2; cf. last entry.

***snidesman.** A SNIDE-PITCHER: c.: 1897, Arthur Morrison.

***snidey.** Bad; unfavourable: c., and low: from ca 1870. Also *sniddy*. 2. Dirty: military: from ca 1875.

sniffer. The nose: pugilistic: ca 1840–90. Augustus Mayhew, *Paved With Gold*, 1857.

sniffy. Scornful, disdainful; occ. ill-tempered: coll and dial.: from ca 1870. Lit., apt to sniff in contempt. cf. SNEEZE AT.

snifter. A dram: low: from ca 1880; ob. Prob. ex U.S. *snifter* (1848), a small drink of spirits: cf. SNEEZER, 4. 2. Any thing or person excellent, or very big or strong:

late C.19–20. Ex dial. *snifter*, a strong breeze. cf. SNEEZER, 5; SNORTER, 2.

snifty-snidey. Supercilious, disdainful: Lancashire s. (—1904), not dial. cf. SNIFFY.

snig. To steal; pilfer: 1892, Kipling. Ex dial.

sniggered if (e.g. you will), **I'm.** A mild asseveration (—1860). Very ob. H., 2nd ed., 'Another form of this is JIGGERED.'

'Sniggers! A trivial oath: coll: ca 1630–1890. Rowley, Smollett, Haliburton. Whence perhaps SNIGGERED. cf.:

sniggle, v.i. To wriggle: creep stealthily: dial. (—1837) >, ca 1900, coll. Ex *snuggle*. 2. Whence, to get (something) *in* surreptitiously: dial. (—1881) >, ca 1900, coll.

'Snigs! *God's nigs*, a trivial oath: coll: ca 1640–90. More prob. a variant than an abbr. of 'SNIGGERS! cf. SNEAKS!

***snilch,** v.i.; rarely v.t. To see; to eye: c. of ca 1670–1850. ?origin. 2. Hence, to examine closely, to feel suspiciously: c.: mid-C.19–20; ob.

snip. A tailor; often as a nickname: late C.16–20: s. >, in C.18, coll. Jonson, Grose, Trollope. In late C.19–20, the inevitable naval and military nickname of all men surnamed Taylor or Parsons. Ex *to snip*, as in tailoring. 2. A swindle or cheat: low (—1725); †by 1840. cf. the v. 3. A good tip: racing: from ca 1890. 'Pomes' Marshall. 4. Hence, a bargain; a certainty; an easy win or acquisition: 1894. 5. See SNIPS.

snip, v.t. To cheat: low: ca 1720–1840. *A New Canting Dict.*, 1725. cf. the n., 2.

snip, go. To go shares: coll: mid-C.19–20.

snip-cabbage or **-louse.** A tailor: resp. C.18–early 19 (E. Ward, 1708); from ca 1820. Both are very ob. For former, cf. trade sense of CABBAGE.

snipe. A lawyer: from ca 1860. Prob. ex: 2. A long bill, esp. among lawyers, whose bills are often tragi-comic in their length: from ca 1855. Ex the long-billed bird. 3. See:

***snipes.** A pair of scissors: c.: from ca 1810.

snippet. The female pudend: Liverpool: late C.19–20.

snips. Handcuffs: low: from ca 1890. Ex *snip*, adv. denoting sound.

snish. Ammunition: military: from ca 1905. Ex Scots and Northern dial. *snish* (more gen. *sneesh*), snuff.

***snitch.** A fillip on the nose: c.: ca 1670–1750. Also *snitchel*: same status and period. 2. The nose: late C.17–20: c. >, ca 1830, dial. and low s. B.E. at *snite*. 3. Hence (cf. NOSE, n.), an informer, esp. by King's evidence: only (?first in *Lex. Bal.*) in SNITCH, TURN. 4. See SNITCHES.

***snitch,** v.i. To peach, turn King's evidence: c.: C.19–20. Vaux, Maginn. Prob. ex the n.; perhaps cognate with SNILCH. cf. NOSE, v. 2. v.t. To inform against: c.: C.19–20; rare, the gen. form being *snitch upon*. 3. To arrest (a person): c.: mid-C.19–20.

***snitch, turn.** To turn King's evidence: c.: from ca 1780. cf. NOSE, n.

snitched, ppl adj. Glandered: horse-dealers' s. (—1876). Hindley. cf. SNICKER,

***snitchel,** n. See SNITCH, n., 1. 2. v.t. To fillip on the nose: c.: late C.17–early 18.

***snitcher.** A member of a set of bloods: ca 1760–80. *The Annual Register*, 1761. ?origin. 2. One who peaches; an informer: c.: 1827. Ex SNITCH, v., 1. 3. In pl, handcuffs; or strings used therefor: c. (—1860).

***snitches.** Handcuffs: c.: from ca 1870. A corruption of SNITCHER, 3.

***snitching.** The art and practice of peaching; turning King's evidence: c. C.19–20:

***snitching-rascal.** A variant of SNITCHER, 2. (†by 1890.)

***snite his snitch.** 'Wipe his Nose, or give him a good Flap on the Face': resp. late C.17–20 (c. >, in C.19, low s.) and late C.17–early 19 (c.; Grose, 1785). By itself *snite* is S.E. > dial.

***sniv.** To hold one's tongue: c.: ca 1810–50. Ex *snib*, to fasten. 2. *sniv!* See BENDER! c. of ca 1810–40.

snivel, do a. To tell a pitiful tale: tailors': from ca 1865.

sniveller. A toadying seaman: nautical: late C.19–20.

snob. A shoemaker, cobbler, or an apprentice thereto: from ca 1780: s. >, ca 1800, coll and dial. In Scots coll, C.19–20, *snab*. ?etymology. cf. SNOBBER. 2. Hence in the Navy, a man earning extra money by repairing shipmates' boots in spare time: late C.19–20: coll. 3. A townsman: Cambridge University: ca 1795–1870. Perhaps ex sense 1. cf. the corresponding CAD. 4. Among workmen, a BLACK-LEG (3) or SCAB (2): coll: from ca 1859; very ob. Abbr. SNOBSTICK.

snob, v.i. and t. 'To sloven one's work', F. & H.: tailors': from ca 1870; ob.

snob-shop. The regimental boot repairer

or maker's workshop: military coll: late C.19–20. F. & Gibbons. See SNOB, n., 1.

snobber. A shoemaker, cobbler: coll: 1900. Ex SNOB, n., 1.

snobbery. Slovenly work; slack trade: tailors': from ca 1870; ob. cf. SNOB, v. Whence, *hide the snobbery*, to conceal bad workmanship, inferior material.

snobbing. Boot-repairing: coll: C.19–20. See SNOB, n., 1.

snob's boot. A sixpence: tailors': from ca 1870; ob. cf. SNOB'S DUCK.

snob's cat, full of piss and tantrums, – like a. A low c.p. applied to a person: ca 1820–50.

snob's duck. 'A leg of mutton, stuffed with sage and onions', F. & H.: tailors': from ca 1870; ob. See SNOB, n., 1, and cf. SNOB'S BOOT.

snobstick. A non-striker, a SCAB (2): workmen's coll (—1860); ob. Prob. a corruption of KNOBSTICK, as H., 2nd ed., suggests.

snoddy. A soldier: low: ca 1890–1914. A corruption of SWADDY.

snoodge, see SNOOZE. **snook,** see SNOOKS, COCK.

snook. To answer an examination paper throughout: to defeat (someone) in argument: Shrewsbury: late C.19–20. ?Ex *cock* SNOOKS. cf. SNORK.

snooker. A freshman at the Royal Military Academy: R.M.A.: 1872. Prob. ex *snook*, a variant of *snoke*, to sneak about (v.i.).

Snooks. 'The imaginary name of a practical joker; also a derisive retort on an idle question – *Snooks!*', F. & H.: from ca 1860; ob.

snooks, cock; occ. **cock a snook;** also **cut a snook, cut snooks.** To make the derisive gesture described at SIGHT, 5: coll: (resp.) —1903; 1904; 1879; —1903. Origin obscure. 'Cf. Fr. *faire un pied de nez*, Ger. *eine lange nase machen*. Perhaps name *Snook-s* felt as phonetically appropriate (cf. *Walker* W.).'

***snooze;** occ. **snoose** (ob.); in late C.18–early 19, occ. **snoodge.** A sleep; esp. a nap or doze: 1793 (O.E.D.): c. >, by 1820, s. >, ca 1840, coll: Ex the v. 2. Whence, a lodging; a bed: c.: from ca 1810; ob.

***snooze, v.;** occ. **snoose** (†in C.20) and **snoodge** (late C.18–20: Grose, 2nd ed.: since ca 1850, illiterate). To sleep: 1789, George Parker: c. >, ca 1810, s. >, ca 1840, coll. Grose, 1788, 'To snooze with a mort [wench] . . . *Cant*'. 2. Hence (in late C.19–20, the prevailing sense), to doze, take a nap: from ca 1840: coll. Thackeray, 'Snooze gently in thy arm-chair, thou easy bald-head.' Etymology problematic: the word may have been suggested by '*s*leep', '*n*ap', and 'd*oze*'.

***snooze-case.** A pillow-slip: low (—1864); slightly ob. Ex SNOOZE, n., 2.

***snooze-ken.** A variant of SNOOZING-KEN.

snoozem. Sleep; a sleep: low: 1838, Beckett, *Paradise Lost*; ob. by 1900. An elaboration of SNOOZE, n., 1.

snoozer. One who snoozes (see the v.): coll: O.E.D., 1878; prob. half a century earlier. 2. 'One of those thieves who take up their quarters at hotels for the purpose of robbery': c.: mid-C.19–20. Mayhew.

snoozing, n. and adj. See SNOOZE, v. From ca 1810. cf.:

***snoozing(-)ken.** A brothel: c. (—1811). See SNOOZE, v. Also, according to F. & H., a lodging-house, bed-room, bed. Occ. *snooze-ken*.

snoozle, v.i. To nestle and then sleep; to nuzzle: resp. ca 1830, 1850: coll and dial. Perhaps, as W. suggests, ex SNOOZE + *snuggle* + *nuzzle*. 2. Hence, v.t. to thrust affectionately, nuzzle: coll and dial.: 1847, Emily Brontë.

***snoozy.** A night-constable: c. of ca 1820–60. Ex SNOOZE, v., 1.

snoozy, adj. Sleepy: drowsy: coll: 1877. See SNOOZE, n., 1.

snoring-kennel. A bedroom: s.: Ned Ward, 1703.

snork. To surpass; cap (another) in argument, repartee; do the whole of (an examination paper): Shrewsbury School: late C.19–20. Perhaps ex: 2. A rebuff, a setback: id.: from ca 1880. Perhaps cf. dial. *snork*, a snort. 3. Whence, *snorks!*, a term of defiance: id.: from ca 1885.

snorter. A gale; a strong breeze: 1855 (O.E.D.): s. >, ca 1890, coll. cf. SNEEZER, 5. 2. Anything exceptional, esp. in size, severity, or strength: 1859, J. Lang, 'The Commander-in-Chief . . . certainly did put forth "a snorter of a General Order"': s. >, ca 1890, coll. cf. SNIFTER, 2. 3. A blow, punch on the nose: *Boxiana*, II, 1818. cf. SNEEZER, 5. 4. The nose: from ca 1880. cf. SNEEZER, 2. Baumann defines it as the mouth and classifies it as boxing s.: I do not know it in this sense, but he may well be right: he almost always is!

snorting. The ppl adj. corresponding to SNORTER, 2; esp., excellent: late C.19–20.

snorty. Irritable, irritated; peevish; captious: 1893, Kate Douglas Wiggin, 'She found Mr Gooch very snorty, very snorty indeed.' Ex *snort contemptuously*. cf. SNOTTY, adj., 2.

snossidge. A sausage: London's lower classes': ca 1890–1900.

snot. Nasal mucus: C.15–20: S.E. until C.19, when dial. and a vulgarism. Cognate with SNITE. 2. Hence, a term of contempt for a person: C.19–20: s. when not dial.; ob. except in dial. 3. A gentleman: Scots c. (—1839); ob.

snot, v.i., v.t., and v. reflexive. To blow the nose: late C.16–20: mostly dial.; in C. 19–20, also (though very ob.) a vulgarism. Ex the n., 1.

snot-box. The nose: low coll: mid-C.19–20; ob. Ex SNOT, n., 1.

snot-rag. A pocket-handkerchief: low: late C.19–20. cf. SNOT-BOX and SNOTTER.

snotted, ppl adj. Reprimanded: c.: late C.19–20; ob. Prob. a perversion of *snouted*, rooted up as with the snout; perhaps on SNOTTY, adj., 2.

snotter. A dirty, ragged handkerchief: low: from ca 1820; ob. Ex SNOT, mucus. 2. The nose: low: from ca 1830; very ob. 3. A handkerchief-thief: c.: mid-C.19–20; ob. 4. A midshipman: nautical (—1903). Perhaps influenced by nautical *snotter* (a short rope spliced at the ends). More gen. SNOTTY.

***snotter-hauling.** The thieving of handkerchiefs: c.: mid-C.19–20. Ex SNOTTER, 3.

snottie, see SNOTTY, n. **snotties' nurse,** see SNOTTY, n. **snottily,** adv. of SNOTTY, adj., 2.

snottinger. A handkerchief: low: from ca 1860; ob. Ex SNOT, n., 1, on MUCKENDER. cf. SNOT-RAG, and SNOTTER, 1.

snottle-box. The nose: low: mid-C.19–20; ob. cf. SNOT-BOX.

snotty; occ. **snottie.** A midshipman: nautical (—1899: *The Navy and Army Illustrated*, 23 Dec.). Prob. ex the adj., 2, not the adj., 1; 'Taffrail', however, derives it ex the buttons worn by midshipmen on their sleeves, whence arose the jest that the buttons were there to prevent them from wiping their noses on their sleeves. Hence, *snotties' nurse*, a naval officer detailed to look after the midshipmen: late C.19–20.

snotty, adj. Filthy; mean, contemptible: late C.17–20: S.E. until C.19, then dial. and s. Ex SNOT, n., 1. cf. S.E. *snotty-nosed*. 2. Angry, short-tempered; apt to take offence; very proud; proudly conceited: s.: *Sessions*, May 1847. Prob. ex sense 1.

***snout.** A hogshead: c. of ca 1720–1800. Ex a hog's nose. 2. Tobacco: c. (—1896: O.E.D.). 'Stuart Wood'. ?origin. 3. Among hawkers, a cigar: late C.19–20. Ex sense 2 and (?) shape.

snout-piece. The face: coll: C.17–19. 'Melancholy' Burton, 1621.

snouty. Overbearing; haughty; insolent: coll: 1858 (O.E.D.); somewhat ob. cf. SNIFFY.

Snow, see SNOWY, 2.

***snow.** Linen; esp. linen hung out to dry or bleach: c. (—1811). Ex whiteness. Also occ. SNOWY.

snow-broth. Cold tea: 1870, Judd; ob. Ex *snow-broth*: melted snow.

***snow-dropper** or **-gatherer.** A linen-thief: c.: from ca 1810, though *snow-dropper* is unrecorded before 1864, *-gatherer* before 1859. Ex SNOW, 1.

***snow-dropping.** Linen-thieving: c.: from ca 1810; recorded, 1839. cf. last entry.

snow-rupee. A genuine rupee: Southern Indian coll (—1886). Ex Telegu *tsanauvu*, authority, currency, by process of Hobson-Jobson.

snowball. A Negro: from ca 1780; ob. Ironic nickname.

'Snowns. A trivial oath: late C.16–early 17; coll abbr. *Od's nouns*.

***snowy.** Linen; esp. that hung out to dry: c. (—1877). Ex SNOW, 1. 2. (*Snowy.*) An inevitable nickname of men with flaxen or bleached hair: lower classes': late C.19–20. Also, in Australia, of Aboriginals: late C. 19–20. In the second and third nuances, often *Snow*.

snub-devil. A clergyman: ca 1780–1900.

***snudge.** One who, to steal later, hides himself in a house, esp. under a bed: c. (—1676); †by 1840. A special development ex *snudge*, to remain snugly quiet.

***snuff,** v.i. To blind (esp. a shopkeeper) with snuff and then, all being well, steal his goods: c.: from ca 1810; ob. 2. See SNUFF IT; SNUFF OUT.

snuff, beat to. To defeat utterly: coll: 1819; ob.

snuff, give (a person). To rebuke, reprimand, scold: coll: 1890, Anon., *Harry Fludyer*, 'He rather gave me snuff about my extravagance, but I was prepared for that.' 2. Hence, to punish: coll: 1896, Baden-Powell.

snuff, in high. In 'great form'; elated: coll: 1840, Dana; slightly ob.

snuff, up to. Alert; not easily tricked; shrewd: coll: 1811, Poole, 'He knew well enough | The game we're after: zooks, he's up to snuff.' Lit. of one who knows to what dangerous uses snuff can be put. Egan's Grose adds: 'Often rendered more emphatic by such adjuncts as "Up to snuff and twopenny", "Up to snuff, and a pinch above it".'

snuff and toddle. To die: boxing s.: ca 1810–60. cf. SNUFF IT and SNUFF OUT.

snuff-box. The nose: 1853, 'Cuthbert Bede'; ob.

snuff it. To die: s. (—1874) >, ca 1900, coll. H., 5th ed., 'Term very common among the lower orders of London ... Always to die from disease or accident'. Ex SNUFF OUT.

***snuff-lurker,** see SNEEZE-LURKER.

snuff out, v.i. To die: s. (—1864) >, ca 1900, S.E. Prob. ex snuffing out a candle. cf. SNUFF IT.

***snuff-racket.** See SNEEZE-RACKET and cf. SNEEZE-LURKER.

snuffers. The nostrils: ca 1650–1750: s. and dial. Cleveland.

snuffle. The nose: low: ca 1825–70. *Sinks*, 1848.

snuffler. An old debauchee: s.: Ned Ward, 1709.

snuffling community, the. Harlots: s.: Ned Ward, 1709.

snuffy. Drunk: low: from ca 1820; ob. Perhaps ex *snuffy*, apt to take offence, displeased, angry.

snug. A bar-parlour at inn or PUBLIC: from ca 1860: s. (ob.) and dial. Ex *snug*, comfortable; cf. S.E. *snuggery*.

snug, v. To coït with: C.19–20; ob. Ex *snug*, to make comfortable: cf. euphemistic *ease*. 2. Also v.i.: C.19–20; ob. Prob. ex *snug down*, to nestle.

snug, adj. Drunk: low: late C.19–20; very ob. cf. euphemistic *comfortable*.

***snug, all's.** All's quiet: c. of ca 1720–1840. cf. the †S.E. *snug*, secret, concealed, private. cf.:

snug as a bug in a rug. Very snug, cosy, comfortable: coll: from ca 1760. See quotation at MOPUS, 3.

snug as a duck in a ditch. The same: coll: C.18–19. (W. N. Glascock, 1825.)

snug as a pig in pease-straw. Very comfortable (-bly): coll: ca 1635–70. Davenport, 1639, 'He snores and sleeps as snug | As any pigge in pease-straw.' cf. SNUG AS A BUG IN A RUG.

snuggy. A public-house *snuggery*: from ca 1890. cf. SNUG, n.

snug's the word! Say nothing of this!: coll: C.18–19; ob. by 1860. Congreve, Maria Edgeworth, Lover. cf. SNUG, ALL'S.

snyde, see SNIDE.

snyder; snider. A tailor: coll: C.17–20; ob. F. & H., an early C.17 quotation. Ex Ger. *Schneider*, tailor; prob. imported by soldiers.

so. Tipsy: coll: from ca 1820. Ex SO-SO, 1. 2. Menstruating: women's euphemistic coll: mid-C.19–20. 3. Homosexual: from ca 1890. Thus 'a *so* man' is a homosexual, 'a *so* book' a Uranian novel, poem, etc. cf. the Venetian *così*.

so, ever, see EVER SO.

so and so; So and So. Senior Ordnance Store Officer: military: ca 1890–1914.

so fools say! A c.p. retort, esp. Cockney, to a person asserting that one is a fool; occ. elaborated with, *You ought to know – you work where they're made*: from ca 1890; ob. Edwin Pugh, *passim*.

so glad! A c.p. of ca 1847 (introduced by the French King) and of 1867–8 (from a song in W. Brough's *Field of the Cloth of Gold*): mostly London.

so is your old man! A c.p. from ca 1900; ob.

so long! *Au revoir!*: coll: 1865, F. H. Nixon. cf. Ger. *so lange*, but more prob., as W. suggests, the term is a corruption of *salaam*, though Ware's suggested derivation ex the Hebrew *Selah* (God be with you) is not to be wholly ignored.

so-so. Drunk: coll: 1809, Malkin. 2. Menstruating: women's euphemistic coll: mid-C.19–20.

so thin you can smell the shit through him. A low, mostly Cockney c.p., applied to an extremely thin man: from ca 1880.

so very human was, ca 1880–4, applied in so many ways that the *Daily News*, 27 Oct. 1884, could speak of it thus: 'In the slang of the day, "so very human".' Rather a c.p. than s.

soak. To ply with liquor: coll: 1822, Banim. Gen. in passive. Ex *soak*, to saturate. 2. To pawn: 1882, G. A. Sala, 'Soak my gems'. 3. v.i. gen. as *soak it*, to be lavish of bait: anglers' coll: late C.19–20. 4. (Also *soak it*.) Of the male: to linger over the sexual act; to delay withdrawal: low coll: C.19–20.

soak, in; come out of soak. Drunk; to

regain sobriety: low coll (—1887). Ex S.E. *soak*, a heavy drinking-bout.

soak, put in. To pawn: late C.19–20. cf. SOAK, v., 2.

soak one's clay or **face.** To drink; esp. to drink heavily: resp. C.19–20 (slightly ob.) and C.18. Barham, 1837. cf. SOAK, 1.

soaked. Tipsy; very drunk: see SOAK, 1. cf. *saturated.*

soap. Flattery: 1859, H., 1st ed.; ob. In C.20, gen. SOFT SOAP. Ex the v. 2. Cheese: Royal Military Academy (—1903); ob. 3. Girls collectively: ca 1883–1900. Ex the more gen. *bits of soap*, girls, esp. harlots and near-harlots.

soap, v.t. To flatter; address ingratiatingly: 1853, 'Cuthbert Bede'; ob. cf. SOFT-SOAP, V.

soap?, how are you off for. A c.p. senseless question: 1834, Marryat; 1886, Baring Gould. Origin obscure – but then the origin of almost every c.p. is obscure!

soap, soft, see SOFT SOAP, n. and v.

soap and bullion. Soup-and-bouilli: nautical (—1883); ob. Clark Russell. Partly a play on words and partly because of its nauseating smell. Also *hishee-hashee.*

soap and lather. Father: rhyming s.: late C.19–20.

soap and water. Daughter: rhyming s.: late C.19–20.

soap-crawler. A toady: ca 1860–1910. Ex SOAP, n., 1.

soap over, v.t. To HUMBUG: low (—1857); ob. cf. SOFT-SOAP.

soap-suds. 'Gin and water, hot, with lemon and lump sugar', Bee: low: ca 1820–70.

soapy. Unctuous; ingratiating; given to SOFT SOAP: 1865 (O.E.D.). 2. (Of fits) simulated, or caused by, chewing or eating soap: 1886, *Daily News*, 13 Dec.

soapy Isaac, see SUET(T)Y ISAAC.

sober-water. Soda-water: punning coll: from ca 1853; ob.

soc, Soc. A trades-union man: printers': ca 1870–1910. Ex *Society.*

soccer, see SOCKER, 3.

social E. A middle-class evasion of *social evil* (prostitution): coll: ca 1870–1905.

society. A workhouse: artisans' (—1909). Evasive.

Society-maddist. A person who, not born in Society, spends much time and money to get there: Society: ca 1881–95.

socius. A companion, a CHUM: Winchester: C.19–20; ob. Ex the school precept, *sociati omnes incedunto.* cf. the occ., cultured use, since mid-C.19, of *socius* as a comrade, itself perhaps ex the ecclesiastical term. 2. Whence, v.t., to accompany: ibid.: mid-C.19–20; ob.

sock. A pocket: c.: late C.17–mid-18. 2. As used by Shadwell in *The Squire of Alsatia*, 1688, in Act I, Sc. 1, it seems to = a small coin (cf. RAG): prob. c. 3. A blow, a beating: late C.17–20: c. >, ca 1850, low s.; † as a beating, except in *give* (one) *socks.* cf. the v., 1. 4. Eatables; esp., dainties: Sedgeley Park School, ca 1805–45; Eton: 1825, C. Westmacott. Perhaps ex *suckett*, dainty. 5. ?hence: credit: low (—1874).

sock, adv. Violently: (low) coll: late C.19–20. Charles Turley, *Godfrey Marten, Undergraduate*, 1904, 'One of you 'as 'it Susan sock in the eye.' Ex:

***sock.** To hit; strike hard; drub, thrash: late C.17–20: c. >, ca 1850, s. Kipling, 1890, 'We socks 'im with a stretcher-pole.' Origin obscure. 2. Hence, to 'give it' *to* a person: 1890, Kipling, ''Strewth, but it socked it them hard!' 3. v.i., to deliver blows: 1856. e.g. 'Sock him one on the jaw!' Ex sense 1. cf. SOCK INTO. 4. To treat one to SOCK (see the n., 4): Eton (—1850). 5. Hence, to give (one something): Eton (—1889). 6. cf. v.i. to buy, to eat, SOCK (see the n., 4): Eton: 1883, Brinsley Richards, 'We . . . socked prodigiously.' 7. ?hence v.i., to get credit: low: late C.19–20; ob. cf. the n., 5. 8. To win: Winchester College: late C.19–20. cf. the n., 3. 9. To tip (a schoolboy) with money: late C.19–20. Ex sense 4?

sock, give (one). To beat or thrash soundly; 1864, H., 3rd ed.; ob., the C.20 preferring *give* (one) *socks*, recorded by O.E.D. at 1897. Ex SOCK, n., 3. cf. SOCK, v., 1 and 2, and SOCK INTO.

sock, on. On TICK (2): see SOCK, n., 5.

sock into. To hit vigorously; pitch into: 1864. Ex SOCK, v., 3.

sock-shop. The tuck-shop: Eton: mid-C. 19–20. Ex SOCK, n., 4.

sockdologer (1830), **-ager** (—1848), rarely **-iger** (1842); occ. **sog-** (1869) or **slock-** (1838) or **slog-** (1862); also **stock-** (1864, H., 3rd ed.); occ. **-ll-.** A very heavy blow; a FINISHER: U.S., anglicized, to some extent, ca 1870; ob. A fanciful, assonantal elaboration of *sock*, a blow (see SOCK, n., 3, and cf. v. 1), influenced by *doxology*, 'regarded as final'. 2. Hence, anything exceptional: U.S. (1869), partly anglicized ca 1890; slightly ob. *Blackwood's Magazine*,

Feb. 1894, 'The pleasant remembrance of the capture of a real sockdologer' (large fish).

socker. A sloven, lout, simpleton, fool: coll: 1772, Bridges, 'The rabble then began to swear, | What the old socker said was fair'; ob. Also *sockie* (ob.) and *sockhead*, †. 2. A heavy blow: low: from ca 1870. Ex SOCK, v., 1. 3. Also *soccer*. Association football: from ca 1890: orig. Harrow School; by 1903, gen. The O.E.D. records *socker* at 1891, *soccer* at 1895; in C.20, usually *soccer*. By truncated *assoc.* + Oxford *-er*. cf. RUGGER.

socket, burnt to the. Dying: late C.17–18: coll >, ca 1700, S.E. Ray.

socket-money. 'Money demanded and spent upon marriage' B.E.: late C.17–18. Perhaps ex *socket*, the female pudend. 2. Hence, 'money paid for a treat, by a married man caught in an intrigue', Grose, 1st ed.: mid-C.18–mid-19. Bridges, 1772. cf. dial. *socket-brass*, hush-money. 3. Also, 'a whore's fee, or hire', Grose, 1st ed.: late C.18–mid-19. 4. Ex senses, 2, 3: hush-money: from ca 1860; ob. cf.:

socketer. A blackmailer: ca 1860–1910. Ex SOCKET, 4.

socketing. A variant (ca 1810–50) of BURNING SHAME, 2.

sockhead; sockie, see SOCKER, 1.

sod. A sodomist: low coll: early-C.19–20; ob. 2. Hence, a pejorative, orig. and gen. violent: early C.19–20. Often used in ignorance of its origin: cf. BUGGER. 3. Non-pejorative for 'chap, fellow' or even for 'girl, woman': English and Australian: late C.19–20.

sod about. To play the fool, indulge in horse-play; to potter about, to waste time: low: late C.19–20. cf. ARSE ABOUT.

sod it! Low coll expletive: since ca 1880.

sodduk, soddick. (Soft) bread; *Conway* cadets': from before 1880. Prob. a slurring of *soft* TACK.

sodger, see SOGER and SOLDIER, n., 1.

Sodom. London: literary coll: C.19. Ex *Sodom*, generic for any very corrupt place.

soft. A weakling; a very simple or a foolish person: dial. (—1854) >, by 1860, coll. George Eliot, 1859. cf. SOFTIE. 2. Bank-notes (as opp. to coin): c. (—1823). Also *soft-flimsy*, from ca 1870. cf. U.S. *soft*, adj. applied to paper money as early as ca 1830.

soft, adj. Half-witted: coll (and dial.): 1835, Marryat, 'A good sort of chap enough, but rather soft in the upperworks'; adumbrated by Miss Burney in 1775. Ex *soft*, 'more or less foolish, silly or simple.' 2. (?hence). Foolishly benevolent or kind; constantly helping others without thinking of one's own advantage or interests: coll: 1890, 'Rolf Boldrewood', 'He . . . did a soft thing in bringing those other chaps here.' Ex *soft*, compassionate. 3. Easy, idle, lazy: coll: 1889, *Daily News*, 12 Oct., 'People crowd into literature [*sic*], as into other "soft" professions, because it is genteel.' Ex *soft*, involving little effort or no work. 4. Broken in spirit: 1898, Sir G. Robertson: coll. Ex *soft*, physically weak, lacking in stamina.

soft, a bit of hard for a bit of. Copulation: low: mid-C.19–20.

***soft, do.** To utter counterfeit notes: c.: from ca 1870. See SOFT, n., 2.

soft?, hard (arse) or. Third class or first?: low coll: late C.19–20. cf.:

soft-arse. An arm-chair: Scottish Public Schools': late C.19–20.

soft as shit. Not physically nor morally tough; often applied by workmen to a man who can speak without filth and does occasionally think of something other than gambling, drinking, womanizing: low coll: late C.19–20.

soft ball. Lawn tennis: Royal Military Academy, Woolwich: late C.19–20 coll.

soft collar. A soft job; a very suitable locality; something easily obtained; something comfortable or agreeable: Australian coll: from ca 1860.

soft down on. In love with: low coll: from ca 1870. Elaboration of SOFT ON.

soft-flimsy, see SOFT, n., 2.

soft horn. A donkey, lit. or fig.: coll: from ca 1860; ob. Because an ass's ears, unlike horns, are soft.

soft is your horn. You've made a mistake: c.p.: ca 1820–50.

soft on or **upon.** In love with; sentimentally amorous for: 1840: S.E. >, ca 1880, coll. 'Rolf Boldrewood', 1888, 'I . . . thought she was rather soft on Jim.'

soft-roed. Tender-hearted: non-aristocratic London coll (—1887); slightly ob. Ex fish-roe.

soft sawder, n. See SAWDER. 2. v.t. and i. (gen. hyphenated): to flatter: coll: 1843, Haliburton; Hickie's *Aristophanes*, 1853. cf.:

soft sawder to order. An elaboration of *soft* SAWDER, n.: 1883, *Entr' Acte*, 7 April; ob. 2. Ware records the sense 'clothes made to order' and implies existence ca 1883–1900.

soft-sawderer. A flatterer: coll: mid-C. 19–20. Ex SOFT-SAWDER. cf.:

soft soap. Flattery; BLARNEY: U.S. (1830), anglicized ca 1860. T. Hughes, 1861, 'He and I are great chums, and a little soft soap will go a long way with him.' Ex *soft soap*, potash soap, on *soft* SAWDER.

soft-soap, v. To flatter: U.S. (1840), anglicized ca 1870. Ex the n.

soft-sop over is a variant (ca 1875–1910) of SOFT-SOAP, V.

soft sowder is a variant (e.g. in Carlyle) of *soft* SAWDER.

soft spot for (someone), **have a.** To be either sentimentally or affectionately attached to: coll: since ca 1880. cf. SOFT ON.

soft tack, see TACK.

soft thing, a. A very obliging simpleton: coll: mid-C.19–20. Ex SOFT, adj., 1. 2. A pleasant, an easy, task; an easy contest or win: coll: from ca 1890. Ex SOFT, adj., 3.

soft tommy. Bread, as opp. to biscuits: nautical coll: late C.18. 1878, W. S. Gilbert, 'I've treacle and toffee, and excellent coffee, | Soft tommy and succulent chops.' Also *soft* TACK (—1828), which has its corresponding HARD TACK. See TOMMY.

softie; properly **softy.** A silly, very simple, or weak-minded person: coll and dial.: 1863, Mrs Gaskell, '[Nancy] were but a softy after all.'

sog. A sovereign (coin): schools': late C. 19–20; very ob. Ex SOV.

soger, sojer; sodger. A soldier: coll and dial.: C.15–20. 2. If applied to a sailor, it constitutes a grave, disgracing pejorative, for it connotes shirking and malingering: nautical coll (—1829). R. H. Dana in *Before the Mast*; cf. Clark Russell in *Sailor's Language*, 1883. 3. See SOLDIER, n., 1. 4. Gen. *sodger*: a big cross made on an examination-paper to indicate a glaring error: Winchester (—1839). cf. PERCHER, 2.

soger; occ. **sodger or sojer.** To shirk and/or malinger; to pretend to work: mainly nautical (—1840); in C.20, coll. Also *soldier*.

soil. To tour in the country: theatrical: ca 1750–1800. (*Theatrical Biography*, vol. I, 1772.)

soixante-neuf, adopted from French, is a term diagrammatically descriptive (69) of a reciprocal sexual act: late C.19–20; orig., upper and middle classes'.

sold, ppl adj. Tricked: see SELL, v. cf.:

sold again and got the money! A costermonger's c.p. on having successfully 'done' someone in a bargain: ca 1850–80. Ex SELL, v. cf.:

sold like a bullock in Smithfield, ppl adj. Badly cheated or duped: almost a c.p.: ca 1810–50. cf. preceding entry.

sold out. Bankrupt: coll (—1859); ob. cf.:

sold out, be. To have sold all one's stock (*of* some article): coll: late C.19–20. Perhaps on the analogy of S.E. *be sold up*, to have had part or all of one's goods sold to pay one's creditors. cf. preceding entry.

soldier. A red herring: from ca 1810: sailors' and seaports'. Also *sodger, soger*. 2. A boiled lobster: ca 1820–1910. Both ex red uniform. 3. An inferior seaman: nautical coll: from ca 1835; ob. cf. SOGER, n., 2. 4. A forest kangaroo: Australian coll: from the late 1890s. 'Rolf Boldrewood'. 5. (Gen. *Soldier*.) The senior Royal Marine officer on board. *Young Soldier*, his subaltern: naval: late C.19–20. Bowen.

soldier, v. See SOGER, v.; but this form began by being coll, and in C.20 is S.E. 2. v.i., to clean one's equipment; doing routine work or fatigues: military: 1885: s. 3. v.t., to use temporarily (another man's horse): Australian (—1891); ob.

soldier, old. See OLD SOLDIER. 2. An empty bottle: ca 1880–1910. cf. DEAD MARINE. 3. *old soldier, come the*, see COME THE OLD SOLDIER.

soldier bold. A cold: rhyming s.: from ca 1860.

soldier-walking. Any operations by bluejackets on land: naval: late C.19–20. Bowen. cf. SOLDIER, n., 5.

soldiers!, oh. A proletarian exclamation: from ca 1880; ob. by 1909.

soldier's bite. A big bite: coll and dial.: C.19–20.

soldier's bottle. A large bottle: coll: late C.17–early 19.

soldier's breeze. A variant, dating from the early 1890s, of SOLDIER'S WIND: coll.

soldier's farewell, a. 'Go to bed!' with ribald additions and/or elaborations: military (—1909).

soldier's friend. A rifle: military coll: late C.19–20. cf. the Ger. *soldier's bride*.

soldier's joy. Masturbation: low coll: ca 1850–1910. 2. Pease pudding: nautical: C.19.

soldier's mast. A pole mast without sails, 'during the transition period from sail to steam in the Navy', Frank C. Bowen: nautical coll: mid-C.19.

***soldier's mawnd.** A sham sore or wound in the left arm: c.: late C.17–mid-18. cf. MASON'S MAUND. 2. Hence, 'a pretended soldier, begging with a counterfeit wound, which he pretends to have received at some famous siege or battle', Grose, 1st ed.: c.: mid-C.18–early 19.

soldier's pomatum. A piece of tallow candle: late C.18–mid-19.

soldier's supper. A drink of water and a smoke: coll: 1893 (O.E.D.). Ware, 'Nothing at all – tea being the final meal of the day'. cf. SUBALTERN'S LUNCHEON.

soldier's thigh. An empty pocket: dial. and s.: mid-C.19–20; ob.

soldier's wind. A fair wind either way, a beam wind: 1818, Alfred Burton: nautical coll >, ca 1890, j. Kingsley, Clark Russell.

sole-slogger. A shoemaker: lower classes' (—1887); ob. Baumann recalls Shakespeare's 'surgeon to old shoes'.

solemn; esp. in *give one's solemn*, 'to swear on oath', 'give one's word': ca 1890–1915.

solemnc(h)oly. Excessive seriousness: coll: from ca 1860. This blend of *solemn* + *melancholy* is an extension of the jocular S.E. adj. coined in America in 1772. A ludicrous perversion is LEMONCHOLY.

solfa. A parish clerk: late C.18–mid-19. Ex intoning responses.

solid. (Of time) complete, entire: C.18–20: S.E. until ca 1890, then coll. 'Rolf Boldrewood', 1890, 'I walked him up and down . . . for a solid hour.' 2. adv., solidly: low coll: mid-C.19–20.

solid dig. Copy that is to be set very close: printers': mid-C.19–20.

solitary. Solitary confinement: 1854, Dickens: prison s. >, by 1900, coll. 2. A whale cruising by himself, generally an outcast and savage bull: nautical coll: late C.19–20.

***sollomon,** see SOLOMON.

Solly. A Jew: coll: since ca 1870. Ex Solomon. cf. IKEY.

solo. A solitary walk (without a SOCIUS): Winchester: from ca 1870.

solo player. 'A miserable performer on any instrument, who always plays alone, because no one will stay in the room to hear him', Grose, 1st ed.: jocular coll of ca 1780–1850 punning the lit. sense.

***solomon.** A late C.17–early 19 variant of SALMON. 2. A job: navvies': ca 1860–1910.

solomon-gundy. A mid-C.18–19 coll form of *salmagundy*. cf. SALMON-GUNDY.

Solomon Isaac. A Jew: Canadian: from ca 1870.

sols and obs, see OB AND SOL.

some hopes! It is *most* unlikely: a c.p. from ca 1905.

some people (occ. parents) rear (occ. raise) awkward children. A c.p., dating since ca 1880 (?earlier) and directed at someone who has been (very) clumsy.

some say 'Good old sergeant!' A c.p. spoken or shouted by privates within the sergeant's hearing: gen. one added (often affectionately), *others say* 'Fuck *the* (*old*) *sergeant!*': military: from ca 1890.

some when, adv. Some time: Society c.p.: ca 1860–70.

something, adv. with adjj. An intensive, esp. with *cruel* (*s. cruel* = cruel or cruelly): dial. and low, in C.20 sol., coll: mid-C.19–20. e.g. ''E suffered something cruel' – or, frequently, 'some-think cruel'; 'the heat was something frightful'. 2. As in 'the something something' (the BLOODY BASTARD), 'the something horse' (the BLOODY horse): a coll euphemism: mid-C.19–20. 3. Hence as v. in past ppl, *somethinged* = DAMNED, etc.: 1859.

something damp, see DAMP.

something good. A good racing tip: s. (from ca 1890).

something short, see SHORT, SOMETHING. **somethinged,** see SOMETHING, 3.

somewheres. Somewhere; approximately: dial. and low coll: mid-C.19–20. 'It's somewheres along of fifty quid,' F. & H.; R. L. Stevenson, 1883, 'I know you've got that ship safe somewheres.'

son. Such phrases as *son of Apollo*, a scholar (late C.17–mid-19), *son of Mars*, a soldier (C.16–19), *son of Mercury*, a wit (id.), *son of parchment* (id.), *son of prattlement*, a barrister (C.18–mid-19), and *son of Venus*, a wencher (late C.17–mid-19) are – except for *son of Mars*, perhaps always S.E. – coll verging on, and in C.19 being, S.E.: *prattlement* is in *A New Canting Dict.*, 1725; the first, third, fourth, and sixth in B.E. 2. *son of wax*, a cobbler, C.19, is coll. 3. See SON OF A . . .

son, every mother's, see EVERY MAN JACK.

son of a bachelor. A bastard: coll bordering on S.E.: late C.17–20; ob. Ray.

son of a bitch or whore. (Lit., a bastard, hence) a pejorative for a man, a fellow: coll: C.18–20: the former in *The Triumph* *of Wit*, 1712, the latter, ca 1703, in 'Facetious' Tom Brown. 2. A moustache and imperial whiskers favoured by cattle-buyers and wool inspectors in the 1890s: Australian: ob.

son of a gun. 'A soldier's bastard', Bee, 1823; but, as gen. pejorative (increasingly less offensive), it dates from early C.18. cf. last entry.

son of a sea-cook, see SEA-COOK.

son of a sow or sow-gelder. A pejorative for a man, a fellow: coll verging on S.E.: C.17–mid-19. Chapman has *sow-gelder*.

son of the white hen. A lucky person (properly male): C.17–18: coll. Jonson, 1630; *Poor Robin's Almanach*, Feb. 1764. Ex Juvenal's *gallinae filius albae*.

song about, nothing to make a. Very unimportant: coll: mid-C.19–20. cf.:

song and dance. A fuss, a commotion: coll: late C.19–20.

song do not agree, his morning and evening. He soon tells another story for one told even recently: late C.18–19: coll >, ca 1830, S.E. An elaboration of *change one's*, or *sing another*, *song*.

sonkey. A lout: c. or perhaps only low (—1887). cf. SAWNEY and SUKEY (4) for both form and sense.

sonnie; properly **sonny.** A coll term of address to a boy or to a man younger than oneself, though not if the addressee is old or middle-aged: O.E.D. records at 1870, but prob. existing a decade earlier. In Australia, the *-on-* is occ. pronounced as in the preposition, as Morris remarked, citing A. B. Paterson's rhyme of *sonny* with *Johnnie*.

***sonny.** To catch sight of, to see, to notice: c.: 1845, in '*No. 747*'; app. †by 1900. cf. GRANNY, to understand.

soogun. A hay rope: Shelta: C.18–20.

sooer, see SOOR.

soogey. To scrub, to scour: naval: late C.19–20. A corruption of *squeeger*?

sook(e)y, see SUK'EY, 4.

sool. To set (a dog) on: Australian coll: from ca 1890. Prob. ex dial. *sowl*, to handle roughly, or *sowl into*, to attack fiercely. 2. Hence (as of a dog a cat), to worry: id.: 1896, Mrs Parker, ' "Sool 'em, sool 'em" ... the signal for the dogs to come out.'

soonish. Rather soon; quite soon; a little too soon: 1890 (E.D.D.): coll and dial.

sooper. A variant (—1909) of SUPER, n., 1–5.

soor; occ. **sooer.** An abusive term: Anglo-Indian (—1864) and Regular Army. Ex Hindustani for a pig.

soot-bag. A reticule: c. (—1839) >, by late 1850s, low s.

sootie or **-y.** A dealer in soot: coll: C.19–20. *Boxiana*, II, 1818.

so'p. Esp. in *so'p me bob!*, a variant of S'ELP ...: Cockney: 1898, W. Pett Ridge.

sop. A simpleton; a milk-sop: from ca 1620: S.E. until ca 1850, then coll; ob.

soph, Soph. A sophister: coll: mid-C.17–20; mainly Cambridge; ob. at Oxford by 1720, †by 1750. O.E.D. records at 1661; D'Urfey, 1719, 'I am a jolly soph.' Partly ex *sophomore*, which since C.18 is solely U.S. cf. HARRY-SOPH.

sopped through. Sopping-wet: lower classes' coll (—1887).

soppy boat. Gen. pl. Nickname for Folkestone fishing craft: nautical: mid-C. 19–early 20. Bowen. Ex their wetness.

sore, get. 'To become aggrieved', C. J. Dennis: coll (esp. Australian and U.S.): late C.19–20.

sore fist. A bad workman: tailors': from ca 1870; ob. ?ex *write a poor hand*, to sew badly, likewise tailorese.

sore-head. A curmudgeon: Australian: late C.19–20. C. J. Dennis.

sore leg. A German sausage: military: ca 1880–1915. 2. A plum pudding: low London: from ca 1880; ob. Prob. ex SPOTTED DOG.

sorra. Dial. and, to some extent, coll form of *sorrow*: C.19–20.

sorrow! Sorry!: late C.19–20: orig. and mainly jocular, and mostly Society. Ex *sorrow* as an imprecation (cf. *sorrow on* ...!). The O.E.D.'s C.15 instance of *sorrow* = *sorry* is inoperative; this use was prob. rare.

sorrowful tale. Three months in gaol: rhyming s. (—1859); ob.

sorry! I am sorry!: C.19–20: coll >, by 1850, S.E.

sort, a bad or **a good.** A bad, a good, fellow or girl, woman: coll: from ca 1880. In C.20, *bad sort* is rare except as *not a bad sort*. J. Sturgis, 1882, 'They cursed and said that Dick was a good sort'. cf. Fr. *espèce* (*de*).

sort!, that's your. A term of approbation, gen. of a specific action, method, occ. thing: 1792, Holcroft.

sort of; a sort of. In a way; to some extent; somehow; one might say: dial. (—1790) >, ca 1830, coll: *a sort of*, ob. by 1890; *sort of*, app. not before ca 1830.

Thackeray, 1859, ' "You were hurt by the betting just now?" "Well", replied the lad, "I am sort of hurt".' Orig. and mainly U.S. is *sorter* (1846), orig. *a sorter* (as in Marryat's *American Diary*, 1839). See also KIND OF.

sort of thing. A tag c.p. of late C.19–20.

sorts, all. Coll >, in late C.19, idiomatic S.E. is the phrase as used in these two examples from the O.E.D.: 1794, Mrs Radcliffe, 'There they were, all drinking Tuscany wine and all sorts'; 1839, Hood, 'There's a shop of all sorts, that sells everything.'

sorts, out of. Dispirited; slightly unwell: from ca 1620: S.E. until mid-C.19, then coll. In C.19, it received an unconventional impetus from printers.

sorty. Similar: coll: 1885; ob. 2. Mixed: coll: 1889, 'A "sorty" team.'

so's, see SO IS . . .

soss(-)brangle. A slatternly wench: low coll and dial.: late C.17–19. cf. *soss*, a slut (in mid-C.19–20, dial.).

sosseled, sossiled; sossled, see SOZZLED.

sot-weed. Tobacco: coll: C.18–early 19. T. Brown, 1702.

sou or souse, not a. Not a penny; penniless: coll: *not a sou* from ca 1820 (Byron); *not a souse*, ca 1675–1820, as in D'Urfey, 1676. Ex the French coin, orig. of considerably higher value than 5 centimes. In C.19 and occ. (though ob.) in C.20, *not a sous*: see SOUS.

soul, be a. To be a drunkard, esp. on brandy: coll or s.: late C.17–mid-18. B.E., '*He is a Soul*, or loves Brandy.' Ex *soul*, a person, + Fr. *soûl*, tipsy (as in Mathurin Régnier, d.1613). cf. SOUL IN SOAK.

soul!, bless my; 'pon my, etc. A mild asseveration: coll and dial.: the former, C.19–20; the latter, C.15–20, but S.E. till C.19.

soul, have no. To lack sensibility or gen. decency or emotional force: coll: 1704, Swift.

soul above, have a. To care not about, be indifferent or indifferently superior to (something): coll: 1899, G. B. Burgin.

soul-and-body lashing. 'Under sail, a piece of spun yarn tied round the waist and between the legs to prevent a man's oilskins blowing over his head when aloft': nautical: late C.19–20. Bowen. Because a matter of life and death.

soul-case. The body: late C.18–20; ob. by 1900.

soul-doctor, -driver. A clergyman: resp. late C.18–mid-19, late C.17–mid-19. On *soul-chaplain* or *-priest*. (In U.S., ca 1818–49, an Abolitionists' name for an overseer of slaves.)

soul-faker. A member of the Salvation Army: lower classes': 1883–ca 85. Ware, 'Before their value was recognized'.

soul in soak. Drunk: nautical: ca 1820–1910. Lit., soaking drunk: see *be a* SOUL and SOAK.

***sound.** Gen. *sound a cly*, to 'try' a pocket: c.: C.19. See CLOY.

sound as a bell, roach, trout. Perfectly sound or healthy: coll bordering on S.E.: resp. 1576 (1599, Shakespeare); 1655, T. Muffett, but in late C.19–20, † except in dial. from late C.13, also in Skelton, but in C.19 mainly, and in C.20 only, dial. (Dial., by the way, has also, from mid-C.19, *sound as an acorn*.)

sound card. A drinker, a boon companion: s. (—1650).

sound on, be. To have orthodox or well-grounded views concerning: coll: orig. U.S., anglicized ca 1890. 2. Hence, to be both intelligent on and reliable in (a given subject): coll: from ca 1900. e.g. 'He's very sound on the little-known subject of psychopaedics.'

soup. (Collective from 1856, simple from ca 1890.) Briefs, a brief, for prosecutions given to junior members of the Bar (esp. at Quarter Sessions) by the Clerk of the Peace or Arraigns, to defend such poor prisoners as have no choice, at two guineas a time: legal s. *Law Times*, 1856, 'But will soup so ladled out . . . support a barrister in the criminal courts?' 2. Hence (both collective and simple), the fee paid for such briefs or such a brief: 1889, B. C. Robinson: s. >, ca 1910, coll. 3. Bad ink: printers': from ca 1870. Ex its thickness or intrusive clots. 4. Melted plate: c.: late C.19–20; ob. If of silver, also *white soup*. 5. Nitro-glycerin: c. (—1905). Prob. orig. U.S. 6. Rare, though prob. to be considered coll, is *soup*, a picnic at which 'a great pot of soup is the principal feature', *Century Dict.*: from ca 1890; ob.

soup, in the. In a difficulty; in trouble: coll: orig. U.S. (1889), anglicized ca 1895. *Pall Mall Gazette*, Nov. 1898, 'Of course he knows we're in the soup – beastly ill luck.'

***soup, white,** see SOUP, 4.

***soup-shop.** A house (see FENCE, n., 2) for the disposal of stolen plate: c.: 1854

(O.E.D.). Punning the S.E. sense. F. & H., 'Melting-pots are kept going, no money passing from fence to thief until identification is impossible.'

***souper.** A SUPER (n., 6), i.e. a watch: c.: mid-C.19–20; ob. 2. A cadger of soup-tickets: coll: from ca 1875. Ex *souper*, a Roman Catholic converted to Protestantism by free soup or other charity. 3. See PEA-SOUPER.

soupy. Vomitingly drunk: low (—1909).

***sour.** Base silver money, gen. made of pewter: c.: 1883, J. Greenwood. cf.:

***sour, plant the.** To utter base silver coin: c.: from ca 1883. See SOUR.

sour ale (dial. only, milk) in summer, mend like. To get worse: (dial. and) coll: late C.17–early 19; extant in dial.

sour apple-tree, be tied to the. To be married to a bad-tempered husband: semi-proverbial coll: late C.17–18. Ray; Bailey. Via *crab-apple*.

sour cudgel, a. A severe beating: coll: C. 17. Withals, 1608.

sour on. To form a distaste or dislike to: U.S. (1862), anglicized as a coll ca 1895. *Daily News*, 13 Nov. 1900, 'Dan soured on Castlereagh boys . . . forthwith.' Ex *be sour towards*.

***sour-planter.** A passer of base silver coin: c.: from ca 1885. Ex *plant the* SOUR. cf. SHOVER, and see SNIDE, n. and adj.

***sours, swallow the.** To conceal counterfeit money: c. (—1887).

sous. As a sou in *not a sous*, it is a late C. 18–20 coll: ob. by 1880. W. quotes Barham, 'Not a sous had he got, not a guinea or note.'

souse, not a. See SOU, NOT A, and cf. SOUS.

souse, sell. To be sullen, surly; to frown: C.17 coll. Cotgrave.

souse-crown. A fool: coll: late C.17–early 19. Ex *souse*, a thump.

soused. Tipsy: coll: mid-C.19–20. Ex *soused*, soaked in liquor. cf. SOZZLED.

soush. A house: back s. (—1859). Additional *s*, euphonic.

south, put down. Lit., to put into one's pocket; hence, to put away safely, to bank, not to spend: late C.19–20. cf. TROUSER, v.

south jeopardy. The terrors of insolvency: Oxford University: ca 1820–40. Ex *jeopardy*, danger + some topical allusion.

***south sea or S. S.** Any strong distilled liquor: c. of ca 1720–50. *A New Canting Dict.* (1725), where also *south-sea mountain*, gin: c. of ca 1721–1830. Prob. ex the South Sea Bubble (1720).

South Spainer. A North Country ship in the Spanish trade; nautical coll: late C. 19–20. Bowen.

southerly buster, see BUSTER, 6.

sov. A sovereign: coll: 1850, *New Monthly Magazine*, 'As to the purse, there weren't above three or four sovs in it.'

sovereign's not in it, a. A nautical c.p. (—1909) applied to a person with jaundice. Ex the sufferer's dark yellow.

Sovereign's parade, the. The quarter-deck [officers'] of a man-of-war in C.18–early 19: naval. Bowen.

sow, as drunk as a. A C.19–20 (ob.) variant of DAVID'S SOW . . .

sow-belly. Salt pork: naval and military: from ca 1870; ob. In Canada, any pork.

sow in or on the arse, grease a fat, see GREASE A FAT . . .

sow potatoes (or scarlet-runners, etc.) on his neck, you could or might. A lower classes' c.p. (—1887; ob.) applied to a man with a dirty neck.

sower. An Indian cavalryman: Regular Army coll: late C.19–20. By the extension of a Hindustani word. Opp. SEPOY.

sowcar. A Regular Army term of abuse: late C.19–20. Ex Hindustani for a banker, esp. if miserly.

***sowr.** To beat severely: c.: ca 1720–50. ? = *sour*.

sow's-baby. A sucking pig: late C.17–20. 2. Sixpence: c. (—1859). Because smaller than a HOG (a shilling).

sow's ear, come sailing in a. A coll of ca 1670–1770 (Ray, Fuller). Apperson does not explain the phrase; ? = to prosper.

sozzled; occ. sossled; rarely sosseled (virtually † in C.20). Tipsy: late C.19–20. 'Pomes' Marshall, 1897, 'She was thick in the clear, | Fairly sosselled on beer.' Prob. ex dial. *sozzle*, to mix in a sloppy manner: cf. dial. *sozzly*, sloppy, wet, and, more significantly, U.S. *sozzle*, to render moist.

spadge. To walk: Christ's Hospital: from ca 1780. Ex L. *spatiare*. Whence *spadge*, an affected or mincing manner of walking: ibid.: from ca 1880.

spadger. A sparrow: dial. (recorded, 1862, as *spadger-pie*) >, ca 1880, coll (orig. provincial). Occ. adj. By dial. corruption rather than fanciful change.

spalpeen. A low fellow; a mean one; a scamp or rascal: Anglo-Irish coll >, ca 1905, S.E.: 1815, Maria Edgeworth, 'The spalpeen! turned into a buckeen, that would be a squireen, – but can't,' neatly illustrative of the Celtic diminutive suffix *-een* (properly, *in*); the radical is of uncertain meaning. The imm. source is S.E. *spalpeen*, a casual farm labourer. 2. Hence, a youngster, esp. a boy: coll: 1891, Bram Stoker.

spange, adj. and, occ., adv. New; dressy, smart: R.M.A., Woolwich: from ca 1880. 'A spange uniform', a new one; 'You look spange enough.' Perhaps ex Northern dial. *spanged*, variegated.

***spangle.** A seven-shilling piece: c. (—1811); †by 1903. Ex its brightness. 2. A sovereign: theatrical: ca 1860–1905.

spangle-guts, -shaker. A harlequin: theatrical: from ca 1870. Ex spangled costume. cf.:

spangles. Acrobats: circus s.: late C.19–20.

Spaniard. (Gen. pl.) 'Brighton fishing boats, from a colony of Spanish fishermen in that town' (Bowen): nautical: C.19.

Spanish (or. s.); gen. the S. Money; esp. ready money, and again esp., in coin: from ca 1786; ob. Barham, 1837, 'Bar its synonyms Spanish, blunt, stumpy and rowdy.' Elliptical for *Spanish coin* or *gold.* 2. Sack or canary wine: s. (—1650). 3. A large Spanish onion: lower class coll: mid-C.19–20.

Spanish, adj. As a pejorative, common in coll and s. ca 1570–1750 and by no means rare until well on into C.19. Ex commercial and naval rivalry (cf. DUTCH). See ensuing terms and, esp., 'Offensive Nationality' in my *Words!*

Spanish, walk, see CHALKS, WALK ONE'S.

Spanish coin. 'Fair words, and compliments', Grose, 1st ed.: ca 1780–1850. Ultimately ex Spanish courtesy derided; imm. ex SPANISH MONEY.

Spanish fag(g)ot. The sun: 1785, Grose; †by 1850. Ex heretic-burnings.

Spanish fly. Cantharides – an extremely potent aphrodisiac, taken in food or drink: C.19–20.

Spanish gout, needle, pox. Syphilis: coll: resp. late C.17–early 19; early C.19; C.17–early 19. *French, Italian,* similarly used.

Spanish guitar. A cigar: rhyming s.: late C. 19–20.

Spanish mare, ride the. To sit astride a beam, guys loosed, sea rough, as a punishment: nautical: ca 1840–80.

Spanish money. 'Fair Words and Compliments', B.E.: coll: late C.17–18. cf. SPANISH COIN.

Spanish padlock. 'A kind of girdle contrived by jealous husbands of that nation, to secure the chastity of their wives', Grose, 2nd ed.: C.16–19.

Spanish pike. A needle: coll: 1624, Ford, 'A French Gentleman that trayls a Spanish pike, a Tailor'; †by 1700.

Spanish plague. Building: dial. and coll: late C.17–mid-18. Ray.

Spanish pox, see SPANISH GOUT.

Spanish trumpeter; also *King of Spain's trumpeter.* An ass braying: ca 1780–1850. The clue is *Don Key.*

Spanish worm. A nail met in a board while sawing: carpenters' coll (—1785); †by 1860. Ex shape.

spank. A resounding blow, esp. with the open hand: coll and dial.: from ca 1780. In cricket, 1873. Ex the v., 1. 2. Hence, the sound so caused: coll and dial.: 1833, H. Scott. 3. A robbery effected by breaking a window-pane: c. of ca 1810–50. See the v., 4. 4. See SPANKS.

spank, v. To smack, slap, with the open hand: coll (—1727, N. Bailey) and dial. Echoic (cf. *spang*). 2. Hence, to crack (a whip): coll (rare and ob.): 1834, M. Scott. 3. To bring down, insert, slappingly: coll and dial., mainly the latter: 1880, Tennyson, "An 'e spanks 'is 'and into mine.' 4. To rob (a place) by breaking a window-pane (*spanking a* GLAZE is the c. term): c. (—1812). cf. the n., 3. 5. v.i., to fall, drop, with a smack: coll: 1800, Hurdis, 'The sullen shower ... on the ... pavement spanks'; slightly ob. 6. v.i., of a boat pounding the water as it sails along: coll (—1891). [The next group derives ultimately ex *spank*, to slap, to make a spanking sound, etc., influenced by dial. *spang.*] 7. To move quickly and briskly; to ride, drive, smartly or stylishly at a smart trot or a graceful canter: dial. (—1807) >, by 1811, coll. Thackeray, 1860, 'A gentleman in a natty gig, with a high-trotting horse, came spanking towards us.' Frequently with *along* (first, 1825, in dial.); and esp. of a ship bowling along. 8. Hence, v.t., to drive (horses) with stylish speed: coll: 1825, Westmacott; 1840, Thackeray, 'How knowingly did he spank the horses along.' Slightly ob.

spank, adv. With a smack: coll: 1810; rare, ob. Ex the v., 5.

spank, up the. At – or, to – the pawnbrokers': East Enders': from ca 1870.

Nevinson, 1895. Perhaps ex *up the* SPOUT on *bank*.

***spank, upon the.** By employing SPANK (n., 3): c.: C.19.

***spank a (or the) glaze,** see GLAZE, SPANK A, and cf. SPANK, v., 4.

spanker. A gold coin; gen. in pl as = ready money, coin: prob. c. (1663, Cowley) >, ca 1730, s.; †by 1830. Prob. ex †dial. *spank*, to sparkle. cf. SPANKS. 2. Any thing or person unusually fine, large, or excellent: coll and dial.: 1751, Smollett (concerning 'a buxom wench'), ''Sblood, ... to turn me adrift in the dark with such a spanker.' Ex SPANKING, adj., 1. 3. Hence, a resounding blow or slap: coll: 1772, Bridges; Meredith, 1894, 'A spanker on the nob'; in cricket, 1877. 4. A horse that travels with stylish speed: coll and dial.: 1814, Scott. Ex SPANK, v., 7.

spanking, n. A (good) beating, esp. with the open hand: coll and dial.: mid-C.19–20. Ex SPANK, v., 1.

spanking, ppl adj. Very large, fine, smart, showy; excellent: coll and dial.: from early Restoration days. Fanshawe, ca 1666; Bridges, 1772, 'A table ... a spanking dish'. Esp. of girls (—1707): cf. SPANKER, 2. 2. Hence, though influenced by the v. of motion, (of a horse) rapidly and smartly moving: coll and dial.: 1738. 3. Hence, (of persons) dashing: coll: C.19–20; ob. 4. (Of a breeze) brisk: coll: mid-C.19–20. 5. (Of pace) rapid; esp. smartly and vigorously rapid: coll: 1857, T. Hughes, 'The wheelers in a spanking trot, and leaders cantering.'

spanking, adv. Very: coll (—1887). Baumann, 'A spanking fine dinner'. Ex dial.

spankingly. Rapidly; esp. with smart rapidity: coll: C.19–20.

***spanks.** Coin (gold or silver): c.: ca 1720–1840. Ex SPANKER, 1.

spanky. Smart; showily smart: from ca 1870; slightly ob. Ex SPANKING, adj., 1.

spar. A dispute: coll: 1836 (O.E.D.). Ex *spar*, a boxing-match.

sparagrass, see SPARROW(-)GRASS.

spare a rub! Oblige me with some!; after you with it!: tailors' c.p.: from ca 1860.

spark. See SPARK, BRIGHT. 2. A diamond: c. (—1874). cf. SPARK-PROP. Ex S.E. *spark*, a small diamond, orig. *diamond spark*.

***spark,** v. To watch closely: Australian c. (—1901).

spark, bright. Ironic for a dull fellow: coll verging on S.E.: late C.19–20. cf. S.E. *gallant spark*; ex *spark*, a beau, via *gay spark*.

spark, have a. To be a youth, or man, of spirit: *Conway* cadets': from before 1890. Ex the cliché, *have no spark of courage*.

spark in one's throat, have a. To have a constant thirst: 1785, Grose; but adumbrated in Scots ca 1720. Ex the proverbial *the smith had always a spark in his throat* (Ray, 1678); cf. Spurgeon, 1880, 'He is not a blacksmith but he has a spark in his throat.'

***spark-prop.** A diamond breast-pin: c.: from the middle or late 1870s. Ex SPARK, n., 2.

sparkle up. To hasten; be quick: proletarian: from ca 1865; ob.

sparkler. A bright eye (gen. in pl): mid-C. 18–20: S.E. until 1850, then coll. In pugilistic s. of ca 1805–60, any sort of eye, as in *Boxiana*, III, 1821, 'One of his *sparklers* got a little *damaged*.' 2. A sparkling gem; esp. a diamond: from ca 1820: S.E. until mid-C.19, then coll; in C.20, virtually s.

sparm-fish. A sperm-whale: nautical coll (—1887).

sparrer. A boxer: coll: 1814, 'Rival sparrers', O.E.D. 2. Hence, from ca 1860, a sparring partner: coll. This is virtually the sense in Thackeray and Shaw. 3. A sol. form, C.19–20, of *sparrow*. 4. (Properly *sparrow*.) A find in a dust-bin, e.g. silver spoon or thimble: dustmen's (—1895).

***sparring bloke.** A pugilist: mid-C.19–20: c. >, ca 1880, low.

sparrow. Gen. in pl: beer, or beer-money, given to dustmen: 1879 (O.E.D.). Perhaps ex the colour of these birds and these men. 2. A milkman's secret customer (gen. in pl): milkmen's (—1901). Why? 3. See SPARRER, 4.

sparrow-catching, n. Walking the streets in search of men: low: from ca 1880.

sparrow(-)grass; sparagrass. Asparagus: mid-C.17–20: S.E. until early C.19, then dial. and coll; by 1870, low coll or, rather, sol. 'Cuthbert Bede', in 1865, 'I have heard the word sparrow-grass from the lips of a real Lady – but then she was in her seventies.'

spasm. The verse of a song, stanza of a poem: jocular coll: late C.19–20. Ex *stanza* + the agony caused by much amateur singing.

spatch(-)cock. A fowl killed, dressed and either grilled or broiled at short notice:

orig. (—1785) Anglo-Irish, but from ca 1850 mainly Anglo-Indian: coll >, ca 1860, S.E. R. F. Burton, *Goa*, 1851. Either abbr. *dispatch-cock*, or corrupted *spitchcock* (?*spit-cock*).

spatch(-)cock, v. To insert, interpolate: orig. military coll >, almost imm., gen. S.E.: 1901, General Redvers Buller, *The Times*, 11 Oct., 'I therefore spatchcocked into the middle of that telegram a sentence in which I suggested it would be necessary to surrender.' Ex the n. 2. Hence, to modify by interpolation: military coll >, by 1902, gen. S.E.

***speak, make a (gen. good or rum).** To make a (gen. good) haul, get a (good) SWAG (3): c. (—1811); †by 1860. Ex SPEAK TO.

speak, that would make a cat, see CAT SPEAK. . . .

speak at the mouth. To say one's say: ca 1870–1910. Ex North Country dial.

speak brown tomorrow. To get sun-burnt: Cockney: 1877–ca 1900. cf. TASTE THE SUN.

speak like a mouse in a cheese, see MOUSE IN A CHEESE.

***speak to.** To rob (person, place); to steal: c.: 1799; 1812, Vaux; †by 1860. A variant of SPEAK WITH. 2. See SPOKEN TO.

***speak with.** c. of ca 1720–1810, as in *A New Canting Dict.*, 1725, 'I will never speak with any thing but Wedge or Cloy, I'll never steal, or' – the basic sense – 'have to do with' – a nuance †by 1785 – 'any thing but Plate, or Money'; Grose, 1st ed. (to rob, steal). cf. SPEAK TO, 1.

***speak-softly shop.** A smuggler's house: c. or low (—1823); †by 1890.

***speaky.** Booty; capture of booty: c. (—1887). Ex *make a* SPEAK.

spec. A commercial venture: orig. (1794), U.S.; anglicized ca 1820 as s. >, ca 1890, coll. Abbr. *speculation*. cf. SPEC, ON. 2. Hence, 'a lottery, conducted on principles more or less honest, the prize to be awarded according to the performance of certain horses', J. Greenwood, 1869: racing (mostly London): ca 1850–65. 3. A good or enjoyable thing or a pleasant occasion: Winchester s. (—1891). Perhaps rather from *special* or from *speculation* influenced by *special*. cf. SPEC, ON, 2. 4. See SPECS.

spec, on. On chance; as, or at, a risk; esp. on the chance of getting something or of making a profit: 1832, Marryat: s. >, ca 1890, coll. See SPEC, 1. 2. At Winchester, on a pleasant occasion or outing: from before 1891.

speccing on one's fez. Expecting to obtain one's cap: Harrow: late C.19–20. cf. SPECK, V.

special, adv. In a special way; especially, particularly: C.14–20: S.E. until early C. 19, then coll. Helps, 1851, 'A case came on rather unexpectedly . . . and I was sent for "special" as we say.'

specimen. A person: from middle 1850s: derogatory, coll if with *bright*, *poor*, etc., s. if alone. Thoreau, 1854, 'There were some curious specimens among my visitors.' Ex such phrases as *specimens of the new spirit abroad*, via such as *strange specimen of the human race* (Dickens, 1837). cf. SPESS.

speck, v. To exult; to show oneself confident of a victory: at certain Public Schools, esp. at Shrewsbury: late C.19–20. 2. To search for gold after rain: Australian miners': late C.19–20. Rain erosion may uncover a lode, or specks of alluvial gold.

speck, n. A place; a position: Liverpool: late C.19–20. Ex S.E. *speck*, a spot.

***specked wiper.** A coloured handkerchief: c.: ca 1690–1890.

speckle-belly (or S.). A Nonconformist, a Dissenter: provincial s. (—1874); slightly ob. H., 5th ed., 'A term used in Worcester and the North, though the etymology seems unknown in either place.' Perhaps ex the tendency of the lower middle class to wear coloured waistcoats: cf. SPECKED WIPER.

speckled. Of a mixed nature, appearance, character, merit; motley: coll: 1845, S. Judd, 'It was a singularly . . . speckled group' (of persons).

speckled wipe. Variant, early C.19, of SPECKED WIPER.

specks. (App. never in singular.) Damaged oranges: costers' coll: 1851, Mayhew. Ex the markings caused by mildew, etc. 2. See:

specs; also **specks.** Spectacles for the sight: dial. (orig. and mainly *specks*; 1807, Hogg) >, ca 1820, coll (mainly *specs*). Barham, 1837, 'He wore green specs with a tortoise-shell rim'; R. D. Blackmore, 1882, 'Must have my thick specks.'

spectacles. Two scores of 0 by a batsman in the one match: cricket coll >, ca 1910, S.E.: 1865, Wanostrocht, 'The ominous "spectacles" have been worn by the best sighted men'; 1885, P. M. Thornton;

1898, Giffen. Abbr. *pair of spectacles*, same meaning: 1862. Lewis records the rare v., *be spectacled*, as early as 1854. Ex '0–0' in statistics.

spectacles-seat. The nose: 1895, Meredith, in *The Amazing Marriage* (O.E.D.); ob.

speech. 'A TIP [n., 2] or WRINKLE [n., 3] on any subject. On the turf a man will wait ... until he "gets the speech", as to whether [a horse] ... has a good chance. To "give the speech" is to communicate any special information of a private nature,' H., 5th ed.: mainly racing: from ca 1872.

speechless. Extremely drunk: coll: 1881, Besant & Rice.

***speel.** To decamp: Northern c. (—1839); ob. by 1910. Ex *speel* (Scottish and Northern dial.), v.i., to clamber, (of the sun) to mount. cf. SPEEL THE DRUM. 2. See SPIEL.

***speel-ken,** see SPELL-KEN.

***speel the drum.** To make off for, or to, the highway, esp. with stolen property: c. (—1859); very ob. Ex SPEEL, 1.

speeler, see SPIELER. **spefflicate,** see SPIFLICATE.

speg, adj. Smart: Winchester; †by 1903. Perhaps ex *spick and span*.

speiler, see SPIELER.

spell, n. An incorrect spelling: coll: C.18–20. 2. Hence, a mode of spelling a word: coll: C.19–20. *Monthly Magazine*, 1801, 'Why should this spell (as school children say ...) be authorised?' 3. A playhouse, a theatre: c. (—1812); ob. Also as adj. Both in Vaux, 1812. Abbr. SPELL-KEN.

***spell,** v. To advertise; put in print: c. (—1864). Esp. *spelt in the lear*, advertised-for in the newspaper, hence 'wanted'. Ob. 2. To be spelt: coll, esp. children's (—1877). Baumann, 'How does it spell?'

spell for. To long for: proletarian: mid-C. 19–20.

***spell-ken** or **spellken;** occ. **speel-ken** (—1860). A theatre: c. of ca 1800–90. Jackson, ca 1800, as quoted by Byron in *Don Juan*, note to xi, 19; Vaux. Ex Dutch *spel* (Ger. *spiel*), play; cf. SPIELER, and †S.E. *spill-house*, a gaming house.

spell-oh; occ. **spell-ho** or (in C.20) **spell-o.** A rest: *Conway* training-ship, and Australian, coll: early C.19–20. Henry Lawson, 1900, 'Bill ... was having a spell-oh under the cask when the white rooster crowed.' Ex *spell-oh*, a call to cease work or to rest. 2. Allotted-work: on the *Conway*: from before 1891.

***spelt in the lear,** see SPELL, v.

spencer. A small glass of gin: low London: 1804 (O.E.D.); †by 1880.

spend, (up)on the. Spending: late C.17–20: S.E. until late C.19 then coll (rarely *upon*). *Saturday Review*, 17 Dec. 1904, 'The Government is "on the spend".'

sperrib. A wife: London lower-middle classes' (—1909); slightly ob. Corruption of *spare rib*.

spess. A specimen: Felsted School: 1899, *The Felstedian*, July, 'Others ... calling out ... "frightful spesses", which word is specimens'. cf. SPECIMEN.

spew-alley. The female pudend: low: C. 19. 2. The throat: low coll: mid-C.19–20; ob. cf. GUTTER-LANE and RED LANE.

spew her caulking or **spew (the) oakum.** 'A ship spews oakum when the seams start,' F. & H.: nautical coll (from ca 1860) >, ca 1890, j.

***spice.** c. of ca 1800–50, thus: *a spice*, a footpad; *the spice*, footpad robbery. Vaux. ?ex *spice of adventure* or *danger*. See SPICE, HIGH TOBY.

***spice,** v.t. To rob: c. (—1811); †by 1850. *Lex. Bal.* cf. the n. 2. Gen. in full, *spice the soot*, to mix ashes and earth in with soot: chimney-sweepers' s.: 1798, O.E.D.; ob.

***spice, high toby.** Highway robbery: c.: late C.18–mid-19. Jackson, ca 1800, as quoted by Byron in his notes to *Don Juan*, xi, 'On the high toby spice flash the muzzle.' See SPICE, n.

***spice-gloak.** A footpad: c. of ca 1810–60. Ex SPICE, n.

spice island. The rectum; a privy: low: ca 1810–50. 2. Whence, applied to any filthy, stinking vicinity: low coll: ca 1810–70. Punning the Spice Islands.

***spicer.** A footpad: c.: ca 1820–60. Ex SPICE, v., 1.

spicy. Spirited; energetically lively: 1828 'A remarkably spicy team'. *Puck*, 1844, 'The milliners' hearts he did trepan, | My spicy, swell small college man.' Ob. Perhaps ex †Scottish *spicy*, proud, conceited. 2. Hence, smart-looking; neat: 1846, T. H. Huxley, 'The spicy oilcloth ... looks most respectable.' cf. the adv. 3. Hence, handsome: 1868, Whyte-Melville, (of a horse) 'What a spicy chestnut it is.' 4. Sexually luscious or attractive: low coll: from ca 1870. Ex *spicy*, highly flavoured.

spicy, adv. Smartly: low: 1859, Meredith, 'He've come to town dressed that spicy.' Ex the adj., 2.

spicy, cut it. To act the beau, the dandy: lower classes': from ca 1880. Ex SPICY, adj., 2.

***spider.** A wire pick-lock (of considerable utility): c.: 1845 in '*No. 747*'. 2. Claret and lemonade: ca 1890–1915. Ex: 3. A drink of brandy and lemonade: Australian: 1854, *Melbourne Argus*. 4. An inspector: navvies': from ca 1870.

spider, swallow a. To go bankrupt: coll: mid-C.17–18. Howell, 1659; Ray; Berthelson, 1754. Gen. *he has, you have*, etc., *swallowed a spider*.

spider-brusher. A domestic servant: 1833, T. Hook; ob. by 1890.

spider-catcher. A very thin man: late C. 17–mid-18. 2. A monkey: coll and dial.: ca 1820–70. Halliwell.

spider-claw, v.t. To grasp and stroke (the *testes*): low: late C.19–early 20.

spidereen. Nautical, ca 1860–1915: 'an imaginary vessel figuring in an unwilling reply: "What ship do you belong to?" "The *spidereen* frigate, with nine decks, and ne'er a bottom,' F. & H.

***spiel.** A grafter's patter: late C.19–20.

***spiel,** v. See SPEEL. 2. To talk glibly, plausibly; to patter: mostly Australian: from ca 1870. Perhaps a back-formation ex:

spieler; occ. **speeler** or **speiler.** A gambler, esp. a card-sharper; a professional swindler: Australia and New Zealand: 1886, *New Zealand Herald*, 1 June, 'A fresh gang of "speelers" are operating in the town.' Ex Ger. *spieler*, player, esp. at cards, a gamester. 2. Hence, a glib and crafty fellow: Australia: from ca 1905.

spierized, be. To have one's hair cut and shampooed: Oxford University: ca 1870–1910. Ex *Spiers*, a barber in 'the High'.

spif, see SPIFF, adj., 2.

spiff, n. See SPIFFS. 2. A SWELL: from ca 1873; ob. by 1910. Abbr. SPIFFY, but imm. ex the adj., 2.

spiff, v.t. Only in past ppl passive: see SPIFFED. 2. v.t., to pay, or allow, commission as to (say) half-a-crown on (a named article): trade: from ca 1890. *Ironmonger*, 19 Sept. 1891, 'A "job" chandelier . . . may be "spiffed", say 1*s*., but a more unsaleable one should bear a higher sum,' i.e. carry a higher commission. Ex SPIFFS. cf.:

spiff, adj. Esp. *s. stores*, one where SPIFFS are in force, and *spiff system* (recorded by O.E.D. at 1890), the procedure of paying commission to the assistants: from ca 1889. Ex SPIFFS. 2. (The form *spif* is almost wholly dial.) Smartly dressed; dandified; in good spirits or health; excellent, superior: dial. (—1862) >, ca 1870, s. >, ca 1890, coll; ob. F. & H. has: 'Awfully spiff,' 'How spiff you look,' '"How are you?" "Pretty spiff".' ?abbr. SPIFFY; cf. SPIFFING.

spiffed, ppl adj. Smartly dressed; 'tricked out'; very neat; spruce: 1877, W. S. Gilbert; ob. See SPIFF, v., 1, and cf. SPIFFING and SPIFFY. 2. Tipsy: mainly Scottish (—1860); ob. Perhaps ex *skew-whiff*, or even ex SQUIFFED. cf. SCREWED; SQUIFFY.

spiffing; occ. **spiffin.** (In dial., *spiving*.) First-rate, excellent; (of, or as to, dress) fine, smart, dandified, spruce: dial. and s. >, ca 1900, coll: 1872, 'The vulgar Pupkins said . . ., "It was spiffing?"'; G. Moore, 1884. Perhaps ex dial. (—1865) *spiffyn*, n., work well done: O.E.D., which relates RATTLE, V; RIPPING; TOPPING. cf. SPIFF, adj., 2, and SPIFFY, and the dial. *spiffer* (1882), anything exceptional or very large, fine, good. 2. Hence, adv.; ob.

spifflicate, etc., see SPIFLICATE, etc.

spiffs; occ. in the singular. Trade (esp. drapery) s. as in H., 1859: 'The percentage allowed . . . to [assistants] when they effect sale of old fashioned or undesirable stock'. (cf. SPIFF, v., 2, and adj., 1.) Prob. cognate with dial. *spiffyn*: see SPIFFING.

spiffy. Smart, in the fashion; fine (in appearance); spruce; first-rate, excellent: coll and dial.: 1860, H., 2nd ed. Recorded before SPIFF, adj., 2, but prob. ex this adj., which may have existed in dial. (where earliest in print) some years earlier than 1860. cf. also SPIFFING, for it is certain that SPIFF, n., 2, v., 1, adj., 2, SPIFFED, 1, and *spiffy* form a semantic and presumably a phonetic group, and I suspect that the trade group – SPIFF, n., 1, v., 2, adj., 1, SPIFFS, and dial. *spiffyn* (see SPIFFING etymology) – is cognate and ultimately ex the same radical; that root, prob., is either an echoic v. – cf. BIFF – with some such sense as to hit (hard), hence to startle or astonish, or an adv. of the *spang* kind – cf. its use in dial. *spiff and spack bran new*, quite new.

spiflicate (—1785); often **spifflicate** (1841 – in dial.) and, mainly Cornish dial., **spefflicate** (1871): s. that, ca 1870, > coll. 'To confound, silence, or dumbfound', Grose, 1st ed., 1785; hence, to handle roughly, treat severely, to thrash, O.E.D., 1796; hence, to crush, destroy, kill, as in Moore, 1818, 'Alas, alas, our ruin's fated; All done up, and spiflicated!'; hence, as in 'Jon Bee', 1823, to betray (a thief) to the intended victim or to the police – a very ob. sense; and, ex the first or the third nuance, to do something mysterious (and unpleasant) to, often as a vague threat to children – a sense dating from ca 1880 or at latest 1890, the author hearing it first, as a child, ca 1900. Etymology: O.E.D., 'Prob. a purely fanciful formation. cf. *smiflicate*, v.'; W., ?Fanciful formation on *suffocate*. cf. dial. *smothercate*,' which word blends, or perhaps, confuses *smother* and *suffocate*; H., 3rd ed., 'A corruption of ["stifle"], or of "suffocate"'; I diffidently suggest, 'Ex *spill*, to spoil by injury or damage, to render useless, to destroy the value of (a thing) . . . on the analogy of either *castigate*, the *f* being perhaps due to the influence of *stifle* or even of *smother* (in both of which the vowels are obviously inoperative on a problematic *spilligate*) or, more prob., merely arbitrarily intrusive as are so many elements of unconventional vocables; or, preferably, ex *spill*, as above, + *stiffle*, the dial. form of *stifle*, +, or with ending on the analogy of *castigate*, or ex *spill* + *stifle* + ending as in *fustigate*, to cudgel. Cf. the later SMIFLIGATE, and the (app. much later) dial. *tussicated*, intoxicated.'

spiflicating, ppl adj. Castigatory; crushing: coll: 1891, Meredith, 'You've got a spiflicating style of talk about you.' Rare and ob. cf.:

spiflication. The being 'spiflicated', the action of 'spiflicating'; severe punishment; complete destruction: (mostly jocular) coll: mid-C.19–20; slightly ob. Sir Richard Burton, 1855, 'Whose blood he vowed to drink – the Oriental form of threatening spiflication'. Ex SPIFLICATE.

spigot-sucker. A tippler: coll: C.17–18. Cotgrave. Ex the vent-hole peg of a cask. 2. A mouth-whore: low: C.19–20; ob. Ex physiological spigot.

***spike.** A casual ward: tramps' c.: 1866, *Temple Bar*, xvi, 184. Ex the hardness of beds, fare, and treatment. 2. Hence, the workhouse: (low) s.: 1894, D. C. Murray, 'To sleep in the workhouse is to go "on the spike".' cf. SPINNIKEN. 3. An Anglican High Church clergyman: ecclesiastical: late C.19–20. (The O.E.D. records it at 1902, but Mr R. Ellis Roberts clearly remembers it in the middle and late 1890s.) Ex SPIKY, 1. 4. A bayonet: military: late C.19–20. 5. *Spike*. The inevitable nickname of all (male) Sullivans: naval and military: late C.19–20. In areas where Irish potato-hoers were working, tramps used frequently to assume the name on entering the *spike* (sense 1).

spike, v. (Of an editor) to reject (a news-item, etc.): journalistic: 1908, A. S. M. Hutchinson, *Once Aboard the Lugger*.

spike, get the. To become annoyed or angry: low: 1895 (E.D.D.). cf. *cop the* NEEDLE.

Spike(-)Park. The grounds of a prison; hence, from ca 1860, the Queen's Bench Prison: 1837, Dickens; both †by 1890.

***spike-ranger.** A continual tramper from casual ward to casual ward: c.: from ca 1897.

spiker. (Usually pl.) A shark: nautical: late C.19–20.

spiky. Extreme and uncompromising in Anglo-Catholic belief or practice: orig. and mainly Church: 1881. Ex the stiffness and sharpness of opinions and attitude. cf. SPIKE, 3. 2. *Spiky*. A variant of SPIKE, 5. F. & Gibbons, 'From the celebrated prize fighter'.

spill. A small fee, gift or reward, of money: 1675, Crowne. †by ca 1840. Constructed with *of* (e.g. *a spill of money*). C.18–early 19. Prob. ex *to spill*; cf. *a splash*, a small quantity, of liquid. 2. A fall; a tumble, esp. from a horse: from ca 1840: coll >, ca 1890, S.E. Ex the v., 1. 3. A drink: ca 1890.

spill, v. To cause to fall from vehicle (from ca 1706 or 7) or from horse (—1785): coll: resp. Swift and Grose. 2. Hence, from a boat, a box, etc., etc.: coll: mid-C. 19–20.

spill and pelt. The practical fun at the end of each scene in the comic portion of a pantomime: theatrical: from ca 1830. Ware. Ex things deliberately spilt and hilariously thrown.

spill milk against posts. A phrase, says Ware, used in 'extreme condemnation of the habits of the man spoken of': lowest class (—1909).

Spillsbury, come home by. To have a 'spill', lit. or fig.: coll: late C.17–18. Hacket's *Life of Williams*, 1692. cf. CLAPHAM; PECKHAM.

spilt milk, cry over. To indulge vain regrets: 1836, Haliburton; 1860, Trollope; 1900, Dowling: coll >, ca 1900, S.E. In mid-C.19, *spilt water* offered a feeble rivalry.

spin. A brisk run or canter; a spurt: coll >, by 1890, S.E.: 1856 (O.E.D.); 1884, *Field*, 6 Dec., 'After a short undecided spin, Athos took a good lead.' Ex *to spin* (*along*). 2. A *spin*ster: Anglo-Indian coll: 1872, 'A most unhappy spin', O.E.D. Ware dates it from 70 years earlier.

spin, v.t. To fail in an examination: mostly military colleges (—1859) and esp. the R.M.A., Woolwich. Mostly in passive, as in Whyte-Melville, 1868, 'Don't you funk being spun?' Ex *spin*, to cause to whirl. 2. Hence, v.i., to be failed in an exam: 1869; rare. 3. To tell a story: naval: ca 1790–1850.

spin, get a. The same as SPIN, v., 2: same period.

spin a cuff. To bore a mess with a long, pointless story: naval (—1909). cf.:

spin a cuffer; spin a dippy. To tell an improbable story; a probable one: naval: late C.19–20. See CUFFER; the *dippy*, used only in this phrase, may possibly derive ex *dippy*, crazy.

spin a twist, see TWIST, SPIN A. **spin a yarn,** see YARN, n. **spin-house,** see SPINNING-HOUSE. **spin street-yarn,** see STREET-YARN. **spin-text,** see SPINTEXT.

spin the bat. To speak vigorously, very slangily: Indian Army: mid-C.19–early 20. Perhaps ex *spin a yarn* + SLING THE BAT.

spinach (occ. spelt spin(n)age), gammon and. Nonsense; HUMBUG: coll: 1850, Dickens, 'What a world of gammon and spinnage it is, though, ain't it!'; ob. The words *gammon and spinage* are part of the refrain to the song, 'A frog he would a-wooing go'. (Early C.19.) cf. GAMMON.

spindle. The penis: (low) coll: C.19–20; ob. cf. S.E. *spindle side*.

spindle-prick. Vocative to a man deficient in energy: low: late C.19–20. (Only mildly abusive.)

spindles, make or spin crooked. (Of a woman) so to act as to make her husband a cuckold: coll: late C.16–17.

***spiniken, -kin,** see SPINNIKEN.

spink. Milk: R.M.A., Woolwich: from ca 1890; slightly ob. ?origin if not a perversion of *drink* nor ex *spinked cattle* nor ex Fifeshire *spinkie*.

spinn-house. Incorrect for *spin-house* (see SPINNING-HOUSE). **spinnage,** see SPINACH.

***spinniken,** loosely **-kin.** A workhouse: c. (—1859). 2. *Spinniken, the.* St Giles's Workhouse: c. (—1864). cf. *the Lump*, that of Marylebone, and *the Pan*, that of St Pancras, both in H., 3rd ed.; note, however, that by 1874, these two terms were 'applied to all workhouses by tramps and costers', H., 5th ed. Ex KEN, a place, on *spin-house* (see SPINNING-HOUSE).

spinning. Rapid: coll: 1882, *Society*, 16 Dec., 'The Cambridgeshire enjoyed a spinning run.' Ex *spinning*, gyrating.

spinning-house; spin-house. Both ex *spin-house*, a house of correction for women, on the Continent (ex Dutch *spinnhuis*, cf. Ger. *spinnhaus*): the former, a house of labour and correction, esp. for harlots under university jurisdiction: Cambridge: C.19: perhaps always S.E., but prob. orig. coll; the latter, a workhouse: C.18–mid-19 coll, as in Brand's *History of Newcastle* (1702), where spelt *spinn-house*. cf. SPINNIKEN.

spinning-out. Loquacious: lower classes' coll (—1887). Baumann, 'A spinning-out sort of chap'.

spinsrap. A parsnip; parsnips: back s. (—1859). Also *spinsraps*.

spinster. A harlot: coll: ca 1620–1720. Fletcher, 1622; Fuller, 1662, 'Many would never be wretched spinsters were they spinsters in deed, nor come to so public and shameful punishment.' cf. *make* or *spin crooked* SPINDLES.

spintext; spin-text. A clergyman: late C.17–20: coll (in earliest examples, a nickname or an innuendo-surname) >, ca 1830, S.E.; very ob. Congreve, 1693, 'Spintext! Oh, the fanatick one-eyed parson!' Because he spins a long sermon from the text; cf. the spider-spinning lucubrations of medieval (and a few modern) philosophers. 2. Esp. a prosy one: C.18–20; ob. Vicesimus Knox, 1788, 'The race of formal spintexts, and solemn saygraces is nearly extinct.'

spirit, to kidnap (for export to the American plantations), ca 1665–1800, may orig. – to judge by B.E. and Grose – have been coll.

spiritual. A sacred song; a hymn: coll: 1870, "Negro Spirituals", T. W. Higginson, in *Army Life*. Abbr. *spiritual song*.

spiritual case. The lower-deck term, probably unintentional at first [i.e. orig. a sol.], for spherical case shot: naval: ca 1840–1900. Bowen.

spiritual flesh-broker. A parson: coll: late C.17–early 19.

spiritual whore. A woman infirm of faith;

esp. as a C.16 ecclesiastical c.p., *she is a spiritual whore* (Tyndale, 1528). cf. S.E. *go lusting* or *whoring after strange gods.*

spirity. Spirited; energetic; vivacious: from ca 1630: coll till C.19, then dial. 2. Ghostly: supernatural: jocular coll (—1887).

spiry. Very distinguished: 1825, T. Hook; ob. by 1890. Ex height.

spit; gen. **the very** or, in C.20, **the dead spit of.** A speaking likeness (of): 1825 (O.E.D.): coll >, ca 1890, S.E. – but still rather familiar. Mayhew, 1851, 'the very spit of the one I had for years; it's a real portrait'. Ex such forms as 'As like an urchin, as if they had been spit out of the mouths of them', Breton, 1602, and 'He's e'en as like thee as th' had'st spit him,' Cotton. cf. Fr. *c'est son père tout craché.*

spit, v. 'To foraminate a woman', F. & H.: v.t.: coll: C.18–20; ob. 2. To leave (visiting-cards), gen. *at* So-and-so's: coll: 1782, Mme D'Arblay; ob.

spit, put four quarters on the. To have sexual intercourse: low: C.19. cf. *make the* BEAST WITH TWO BACKS and SPIT, v., 1.

spit alley (or S.A.). The alleyway in which the junior officers' cabins are situated (in a man-of-war): naval: late C.19–20.

spit and a drag, a. A smoke on the sly: naval: late C.19–20. Ex *spit and drag,* a cigarette: rhyming s. (on FAG, n., 5): late C.19–20.

spit and a draw. A proletarian variant of the preceding. Prob. from the 1890s.

spit and a stride, a. A very short distance: Fletcher, 1621 (Apperson); 1676, Cotton, 'You are now ... within a spit, and a stride of the peak.' Coll till early C.19, then dial.

spit and polish. Furbishing; meticulous cleaning: naval and, esp., military: from ca 1860 or perhaps even earlier, though unrecorded before 1895: coll. cf. ELBOW-GREASE.

spit brown. To chew tobacco: nautical coll: late C.19–20.

spit-curl. A curl lying flat on the temple: U.S. (—1859); anglicized ca 1875 as a coll, chiefly among costers: cf. AGGERAWATORS.

spit o' my hand! A Cockney expletive, coll rather than s., dating from ca 1880; slightly ob.

spit one's death. To swear solemnly: Cockney: late C.19–20; ob. Perhaps on *may I die!* cf. the gesture of licking one's thumb and drawing it across one's throat; and cf. STRIKE ONE'S BREATH.

spit sixpences or **white broth.** To expectorate from a dry, though healthy, mouth: resp. coll (1772), Graves, 'Beginning to spit six-pences (as his saying is)' and s. (late C.19–early 20).

Spitalfield(s) breakfast. 'A tight necktie and a short pipe'; i.e. no breakfast at all: East End (—1864). Ex the poor district in East London. cf. *Irishman's dinner* and SOLDIER'S SUPPER, as well as *dine with* DUKE HUMPHREY, and the c.p. (—1874; ob.) *I'll go out and count the railings,* 'the park or area railings, mental instead of maxillary exercise', H., 5th ed.

spite Gabell. To cut off one's nose to spite one's face: Winchester: from ca 1820. Mansfield; Wrench. Ex the inadvisability of trying to get a rise out of Dr Henry Gabell (1764-1831), who was headmaster of the College from 1810 to 1823.

Spithead nightingale. A boatswain or his mate: nautical coll: late C.19–20; ob.

spiv. One who lives by his wits – within the law, for preference; esp. by the 'racing game'; c.: since ca 1890.

splash. Ostentation; a display thereof; a dash; a sensation: coll: esp. in *cut* (1806) or *make* (1824) *a splash.* cf. CUT A DASH. Ex noisy diving or swimming. 2. Hence, without article: coll: late C.19–20; rare-*Westminster Gazette,* 5 Dec. 1899, 'That last speech ... caused enough splash for some time to come.' 3. Face-powder: 1864, H., 3rd ed.; very ob. cf. SLAP, n., 2.

***splash,** adj. Fine, elegant, fashionable, distinguished: c. from ca 1830. Ex the n., 1.

splash-up, adj. and adv. (In) splendid (manner); TIP-TOP: lower classes' (—1887); ob. cf. BANG-UP.

splasher. A piece of oil-cloth protecting the wall against the splashing from a wash-hand bowl: domestic coll: late C.19–20.

splashing, n. Excessive or silly talk: proletarian: ca 1870–1910.

splashing, adj. and adv.; **splashy,** adj. Fine(ly); splendid(ly): ca 1885–1920. Baumann, 'A splashing (fine) feed'. cf. SPLASH, n., 1.

splatherer. A loquacious person; a braggart: tailors': from ca 1875; ob.

splathers!, hold your. Be silent!: tailors': from ca 1870; ob. Prob. ex Yorkshire *splather,* noisy talk. Whence:

splatterdash. A bustle; an uproar: late C.19–20; ob. ?ex *splutter* + *dash.*

splendacious, splendidious, splendidous,

splendiferous. Very splendid, remarkably fine, magnificent; excellent: resp. 1843, *Blackwood's*, 'Some splendacious pattern in blue and gold' O.E.D., which notes forms in *-aceous* (Thackeray, 1848) and *-atious*, all slightly ob. and all coll: C.15–20, being S.E. until C.19 (rare before 1880; now ob.), then coll; *splendidous*, S.E. in C.17, is rare in coll and now extremely ob.; *splendiferous* – loosely *-erus*, – S.E. in C.15–16 for 'abounding in splendour', was in C.17–early 19, like *splendidious*, 'subterranean' in usage, and, like *splendacious*, it arose again in 1843 (Haliburton's 'Splendiferous white hoss', O.E.D.), to be more gen. in U.S. than in Britain. All four are, in mid-C.19–20, jocular in tendency.

splice. A wife: ca 1820–1930. Ex *splice*, to marry. 2. Marriage; a wedding: 1830, Galt; 1876, Holland, 'I'm going to pay for the splice.'

splice, v. To join in matrimony (—1710): gen. in passive, as in 1751, Smollett, 'Trunnion! Trunnion! turn out and be spliced, or lie still and be damned.' Ex lit. nautical sense. 2. Hence. to coït: low: C.19–20. 3. At Winchester College (—1897), to throw or fling.

splice, sit on or **(upon) the.** To play a strictly defensive bat: cricket s.: from ca 1905. As if to sit on the shoulder of the bat.

splice the main-brace, see MAIN-BRACE, SPLICE THE.

spliced(, get). (To get) married: late C.18–20. Ainsworth, 1839. Ex SPLICE, V., 1.

spliced, with main-brace well. Drunk: orig. nautical. See MAIN-BRACE.

splicer. A sailor: lower classes' coll: late C.19–20. Ex the S.E. sense, one (gen. a sailor) who splices, or specializes in splicing ropes.

***split.** A detective, a police spy, an informer: c. (—1812). Ex the v., 2. cf. SPLIT ON. 2. See SPLITS. 3. A drink of two liquors mixed: coll: 1882, *Society*, 11 Nov., 'The "nips", the "stims", the "sherries and Angosturas", the "splits" of young Contango'. 4. A split soda: coll: 1884 (O.E.D.); but *a soda split* occurs in H., 5th ed., 1874. 5. Hence, a half-size bottle of mineral water, 1896. 6. A half-glass of spirits: coll (—1903). 7. A split bun or roll: coll (1905). 8. A split vote (1894). 9. A harlot's bully: c. (—1909). He splits her earnings with her. 10. Change (in money); small change: low: 1893, P. H. Emerson, *Signor Lippo*. 11. See SPLIT, LIKE.

split, v.i. To copulate: low: C.18–20. 2. To turn informer, give evidence to the police: c. (—1795) >, ca 1850, low s. 3. Hence, to betray confidence, give evidence injurious to others: 1840, Dickens, but prob. a decade earlier. See also SPLIT ABOUT and SPLIT ON. 4. Hence, v.t., to disclose, let out: 1850, Thackeray, 'Did I split anything?'; ob. 5. v.i., to act vigorously: coll: U.S. (ca 1848), anglicized ca 1870; ob. Prob. ex: 6. v.i., to move, esp. to run, walk, gallop, etc.: coll: 1790, R. Tyler, 'I was glad to take to my heels and split home, right off'; 1888, Adam Lindsay Gordon, *Poems*, 'We had run him for seven miles or more, | As hard as our nags could split.' Also *split along* and *go like split*.

split, (at) full. At full speed: coll: U.S. (middle 1830s), anglicized ca 1865. 'Rolf Boldrewood', 1890, 'In saddle and off full-split'. cf.:

split, like; esp. go like split. (To go) at full speed: coll: U.S. (ca 1848), partly anglicized ca 1870, but never so gen. as SPLIT, FULL.

split, make all. To cause, make, a commotion: coll: late C.16–17. Shakespeare.

split about. To divulge; esp. to the police: 1836, *Annual Register*.

split along. To move very fast: coll: C.19–20. See SPLIT, V., 6.

split-arse mechanic. A harlot: low: C.19. cf. SPLIT-MUTTON, 2.

split-arsed one. A female (esp., baby): low: late C.19–20.

split asunder. A costermonger: rhyming s. (—1859); ob.

split-cause. A lawyer: coll (—1785); ob. by 1870, †by 1910.

split chums. To break friendship: *Conway* cadets': from before 1891. cf. PART BRASS-RAGS.

split fair. To tell the truth: mid-C.19–20. See SPLIT, V., 2.

split-fig. A grocer: coll: late C.17–early 19; then dial. cf. NIP-CHEESE.

split-mutton. The penis: low: ?C.17–19. 2. Women in gen.; a woman as sex: low: ?C.18–20; ob. See MUTTON; cf. SPLIT-ARSE MECHANIC.

split my windpipe! 'A foolish kind of a Curse among the *Beaux*', B.E.: coll: late C.17–mid-18. Also *split me*: C.18–early 19 (Cibber, Thackeray).

***split on** or **upon.** To inform the police about (a person): c. (—1812) >, ca 1840, low s. >, ca 1870, gen. s. Vaux (*upon*; *on* app. unrecorded before 1875, O.E.D.). See SPLIT, v., 2, and cf. SPLIT ABOUT and SPLIT FAIR.

***split out.** v.i., to part company, to separate: c.: from ca 1875; ob.

split pea. Tea; rhyming s. (—1857). Rare; †by 1900.

split soda. 'A bottle of soda water divided between two guests. The "baby" soda is for one client': tavern coll: from ca 1860. Ware.

split the grain, enough to. Enough to make one drunk: coll: from ca 1880. Pugh (2): 'But . . . go easy with this. . . . Jest enough to screw you up, y'know, but not enough to split the grain.'

split-up. A lanky person: from ca 1875. Ex (*well*) *split-up*, long-limbed, itself (Baumann) s. from ca 1870, prob. suggested by SPLITS.

***split upon,** see SPLIT ON.

split with. To break off acquaintance with; to quarrel with: 1835, G. P. R. James (O.E.D.): s.

splits, the. In dancing or acrobatics, the act of separating one's legs and lowering oneself until, right-angled to the body, they extend flat along the ground: 1851, Mayhew (II, 569): coll >, ca 1890, S.E. Also, though rare and ob., in the singular, as in Mayhew, III, 1861. 2. The police: grafters'; late C.19–20. Ex SPLIT, n., 1.

splitter. A lawyer addicted to hair-splitting distinctions: ca 1660–1750. Richard Head, *Proteus Redivivus*, 1675. cf.:

splitter of causes. A lawyer: coll: late C. 17–18. cf. SPLIT-CAUSE.

splodger. A country lout: coll (—1860). 2. (esp. in address) CODGER: rhyming s.: 1856, H. Mayhew, *The Great World of London*. 3. A body-snatcher (?): ?ca 1840–80.

> 'I'm Happy Jack the Splodger.
> I'm as happy as I can be,
> 'Cos when I digs the bodies up,
> The worms crawl over me.'
> The 'saga' of *Happy Jack*

Perhaps ex English dial. *splodge*, to trudge through dirt or mire.

splodgy. Coarse-looking; (of complexion) pimply: proletarian coll: mid-C.19–20.

splosh. Money: low: 1893, Gus Elen, 'Since Jack Jones come into that little bit o' splosh'; ob. ?ex *splash*; prob. cognate with:

splosh, adv. Plump: coll: 1891, Anon., *Harry Fludyer*, 'Such larks when you heard the ball go splosh on a man's hat'. Echoic.

spoffish. Fussy, bustling, officious: 1836, Dickens. Very ob. Perhaps suggested by *officious* or *fussy*; obviously, however, derived ex or cognate with SPOFFLE; cf. SPOFFY.

spoffle, v.i. To fuss or bustle: from ca 1830; very ob. Ex East Anglian dial. *spuffle*, to fuss, bustle; be in a flurry or great haste (Forby's glossary, ca 1825). cf. SPOFFISH; SPOFFY.

spoffskins. A courtesan willing to pretend to (temporary) marriage: low: ca 1880–1910. Perhaps ex:

spoffy. The same as, and ex, SPOFFISH: 1860, H., 2nd ed.; ob. 2. Hence, n.

spogh, v.i. To show off, make a display; South African coll: 1871, Dugmore, *Reminiscences of an Albany Settler*. Ex Dutch *pochen*, to boast.

spoil, v. In boxing to damage, injure, seriously: sporting: 1811 (O.E.D.); very ob. Egan, 1821, has *spoil one's mouth*, to damage the face. 2. To prevent (a person) from succeeding, to render (a building, etc.) unsuitable for robbery: c. (—1812); ob. 3. Hence, in seashore-nautical s., as in R. C. Leslie, 1884, ' "Spoil a gent" is used . . . in the sense of disgusting him with the sea and so losing a good customer.'

spoil-bread. A baker: coll: from ca 1860; ob. cf.:

spoil-broth. A cook: same status and period. cf. next two entries.

spoil-iron. A smith: coll: from ca 1780; ob.

spoil-pudding. A long-winded preacher: ca 1785–1850.

spoil the shape of, see SHAPE, SPOIL A WOMAN'S.

spoiling salt water. A sea-cook's job: nautical coll: mid-C.19–early 20.

spoke. Spoken: in C.19–20, coll (latterly, low coll) when neither dial. nor jocular (e.g. 'English as she is spoke'). 2. See SPOKEN TO.

spoke-box. The mouth: jocular coll: 1874, Anon., *The Siliad*; ob.

***spoke to,** see SPEAK TO.

***spoken,** illiterately **spoke, to.** Robbed; stolen: see SPEAK TO. 2. In a bad way (gen. physically); dying: c. (—1812); ob. Lit., warned.

***spoke(n) to the crack, hoist, screw, sneak,** etc. Robbed or stolen in the manner indicated by the nn.: c.: C.19.

spondoolic(k)s, -ix; spondulacks; spondulicks (the most gen.), **-ics, ix.** Money; cash: U.S. (1857), anglicized ca 1885: resp. —1903, 1902; —1903; 1863, ca 1870, and 1857. Perhaps ex Gr. σπόνδυλικός, adj. of σπόνδυλος, a species of shell very popular in prehistoric and early historic commerce; cf. the use of cowrie shells as money in ancient Asia and in both ancient and modern Africa.

sponge, v.t. To throw up the sponge on behalf of (a defeated person or animal); gen. *to be sponged*, to have this happen to one: 1851, Mayhew; ob. cf.:

sponge, chuck or **throw up the.** To give in; submit: coll: resp. from ca 1875 and 1860. 'Rolf Boldrewood', 1889 (*chuck*); 'Captain Kettle' Hune, 1899. Ex boxing, where this action signifies defeat.

spoof. A nonsensically hoaxing game: 1889. The name and the game were invented by Arthur Roberts the comedian (1852–1933). 2. Hence, a card game in which certain cards, occurring together, are called 'spoof'; 1895. 3. Ex sense 1: HUMBUG; hoaxing: 1897; an instance of this (—1903). 4. A theatrical variation (ca 1896–1914) of OOF, money. 5. A confidence trick, a swindle: low (—1890); ob.

spoof, v.t. To hoax; HUMBUG: 1895, 'I "spoof" him – to use a latter-day term,' *Punch*, 28 Dec. Ex n., 1.

spoof, adj. Hoaxing; humbugging: 1895, A. Roberts, 'My "spoof French" has often been the subject of amusement.'

***spooferies, the.** A sporting club – or, generically, sporting clubs – of an inferior kind: ca 1889–1912. Ex SPOOF, n., 1.

spoon. A simpleton; a fool: 1799 (O.E.D.): s. >, ca 1850, coll; ob. Vaux, 1812, 'It is usual to call a very prating shallow fellow a *rank spoon.*' Ex its openness and shallowness, but imm. ex SPOONEY, n., 1. 2. A sentimental, esp. if silly, fondness: in pl, 1868; in singular, from ca 1880. Slightly ob. Ex *be* SPOONS ON. 3. Hence, a sweetheart: 1882 (O.E.D.); slightly ob.

spoon, v.i. To make love, esp. if very sentimentally and, in addition, rather sillily: 1831, Lady Granville. Prob. ex the n., 1. 2. Hence, to flirt: 1875, Trollope. 3. v.t. To court, to make love to, in a sentimental way: 1877, Mrs Forrester; ob. cf. SPOON ON. – All senses are frequent as vbl nn. in the same status; but derivatives not listed here are not much used and are rather S.E. than unconventional.

spoon, come the. To make ridiculous, too sentimental love: from ca 1890; ob.

spoon in one's mouth, born with a silver, see SILVER SPOON . . .

spoon in the wall, stick one's. To die: coll: mid-C.19–20.

spoon on. Same as SPOON, v., 3: from ca 1880; ob. Ex SPOON, v., 1.

spoon-victuals. (Of a batsman) getting under a ball: Cambridge cricketers': 1870s. An elaboration of *spoon* (in cricket j.).

spooney, spoony. A simpleton, a fool: 1795, Potter; ob. cf. SPOON, n., 1. 2. Hence (—1812), adj. 3. Sentimentally in love, foolishly amorous: 1836, Marryat; in 1828 with (*up*)*on* – 'I felt rather spoony upon that vixen.' Ex SPOON, v., 1. 4. Hence, one thus in love or thus amorous: 1857, 'C. Bede'. 5. An effeminate youth or man: ca 1825–80. Thackeray, *Vanity Fair*, 1848, 'Jim says he's remembered at Oxford as Miss Crawley still – the spooney.' Ex sense 1.

spoons, fill the mouth with empty. To go hungry: coll: late C.17–18. Ray.

spoons on (1863) or **with** (—1860; †by 1910), **be.** To be sentimentally, esp. if sillily, in love with (a girl; very rarely the converse). Prob. ex SPOON, n., 1. 2. Also (of a couple) *it's* (*a case of*) *spoons with them*, they are sentimentally in love: from ca 1863; ob.

spoony. See SPOONEY. 2. Adv., foolishly or sentimentally, esp. in *spoony drunk*, sentimentally drunk, as in the *Lex. Bal.*, 1811; ob.

spoony stuff. Weak, sentimental work, below contempt: London theatrical: ca 1882–1915. Ware.

sporran. The pubic hair: late C.19–20 low. Ex S.E. *sporran.*

sport, v. To read (a book, an author) for *sport*: ca 1690–1710. T. Brown, 'To divert the time with sporting an author'. 2. To stake (money), invest (it) riskily: ca 1705–1860: s. >, ca 1750, coll. 3. Hence, to lay (a bet): ca 1805–50. 4. Prob. ex senses 2, 3: to treat (a person) with food, etc.; to offer (a person) the hospitality of (wine, etc.): ?elsewhere than, 1828–30, in Lytton, as e.g. 'I doesn't care if I sports you a glass of port.' Cognate, however, is: to provide, as in *sport a dinner*, *a lunch*, etc.: from ca 1830. 5. Ex sense 2: v.i., to speculate or bet: ca 1760–1820. Chrysal, Johnston. 6. v.t. to spend (money) extravagantly or very freely or ostentatiously: 1859, H. Kingsley 'I took him for a flash overseer, sporting his salary.' 7. To exhibit, display, in company, in public, gen. showily or ostentatiously: from ca 1710 (esp. common ca 1770–1830): s. >, ca 1830, coll. Steele, 1712; J. H. Newman, 'A man . . . must sport an opinion when he really had none to give.' 8. Hence, to display on one's person; esp. to wear: s. (1778) >, ca 1890, coll. 'Pomes' Marshall, 'She sported her number one gloss on her hair | And her very best blush on her cheek.' 9. To go in for (smoking, riding, billiards, etc. etc.); to maintain (e.g., a house, a carriage): from ca 1805: s. >, ca 1900, coll. 10. To shut (a door), esp. to signify 'Engaged': orig. and mainly university. Ex *sport* OAK (3) or *timber*. cf. SPORT IN. 11. (Perhaps hence by metaphrasis:) to open (a door) violently, to force (it): ca 1805–20. 12. See vbl phrases here ensuing.

sport, old, see OLD SPORT.

sport a baulk, see BAULK.

sport a report. To publish it far and wide: mid-C.19–20; ob.

sport a right line, be unable to or **cannot.** To be drunk: ca 1770–1800. Oxford University. Because of inability to walk straight.

sport a toe. To dance: 1821, Pierce Egan, *Life in London*; app. †by 1870.

Sport and Win. Jim: rhyming s. (—1859); ob.

sport in. To shut (one) in by closing the door: 1825, Hone, 'Shutting my room door, as if I was "sported in" '; ob. cf. OAK, 3.

sport ivory or **one's ivory.** To grin: from ca 1785; ob.

sport literature. To write a book: 1853, Mrs Gaskell; ob. – very ob.!

sport oak, see OAK, 3.

sport off. To do easily, as if for sport: late C.19–20; ob. cf. SPORT, v., 1.

sport silk. To ride a race: the turf (coll): 1885, *Daily Chronicle*, 28 Dec. Ex the silk jacket worn by jockeys.

***sport the broom.** c., from ca 1875; as in Anon.'s *Five Years' Penal Servitude*, 1877, 'If a man wishes to see the governor, the doctor, or the chaplain, he is to "sport the broom", lay his little hairbroom on the floor at the door, directly the cell is opened in the morning.'

sport timber. The Inns of Court variation of *sport* OAK (3): from ca 1785; ob.

sported oak or **door.** Same as SPORTING DOOR: from ca 1870.

sporter. A wearer (of something showy, notable): coll: late C.19–20.

sportiness. Sporty characteristics or tendency: coll: 1896, *Daily Chronicle*, 31 Oct.

sporting action. At Winchester College, 'an affected manner, gesture or gait, or a betrayal of emotion', F. & H.: from ca 1870. cf. SPORT, v., 7.

sporting chance. A slight or a problematic chance: coll: from mid-1890s: sporting >, almost imm., gen. Mary Kingsley, 1897, 'One must diminish dead certainties to the level of sporting chances along here.'

sporting door. A door closed against intruders: university: from ca 1850; ob. Bristed, 1852. Also *the* OAK (3). See SPORT, v., in corresponding senses.

sportings. Clothes worn at the exeat: Charterhouse (—1900). Tod's *Charterhouse*, 1900.

sportsman is at certain Public Schools a synonym for CHAP, FELLOW, 'man': from ca 1890.

sportsman for liquor. 'A fine toper' (Ware): sporting: ca 1880–1910.

sportsmanlike. Straightforward; honourable: coll: 1899, E. Phillpotts.

sportsman's gap. The female pudend: low: C.19–20. (cf. S.E. *sporting house*, a brothel, and *sporting-piece*, a plaything.) Ex gaps in hedges.

sporty. Sportsmanlike; sporting; generous: 1889: s.

s'pose. Suppose, esp. in *s'pose so!*: coll: C.19–20.

spot. A drop of liquor: coll: 1885, D.C. Murray, 'A little spot of rum, William, with a squeeze of lemon in it.' In C.20 Anglo-Irish coll, it has a specific sense: a half-glass of whiskey. Ex *spot*, a small piece or quantity. cf. Fr. *larme*. 2. Hence, a small amount of. Gen. *a spot of . . .*, e.g. lunch, hence of rest, work, pleasure, music, etc.: s.: C.19–20. Wm Maginn's translation of *Memoirs of Vidocq*, 1829, 'He leads them to a *spot of work*' – a burglary. 3. A cake: low: from ca 1890; ob. See quotation at SCALDER, 2. 4. A person – usually a man – employed by an omnibus company to watch, secretly, its employees: 1894 (O.E.D.): coll >, ca 1910, j. Ex *spot* (v., 4), to detect.

***spot,** v. To note (a person) as criminal

or suspect: c.: 1718 (O.E.D.); 1851, Mayhew, 'At length he became spotted. The police got to know him, and he was apprehended, tried, and convicted.' Perhaps ex †*spot*, 'to stain with some accusation or reproach.' 2. Hence, to inform against (a person): c.: 1865, Dickens. 3. (Prob. ex sense 1:) to guess (a horse) beforehand as the winner in a race: orig. turf >, ca 1890, gen. coll: 1857, *Morning Chronicle*, 22 June, 'Having met with tolerable success in spotting the winners.' 4. Hence, to espy; mark, note; recognize, discover, detect: coll: 1860, O. W. Holmes. 5. Whence, prob.: to hit (a mark) in shooting: coll: 1882, Bret Harte. Although the earliest record of this, as of the preceding sense, is U.S., there is perhaps no need to postulate an American origin for either; cf., however, H., 1864, 'Orig. an Americanism, but now gen.' 6. (Ex spotting winners.) To gamble, v.t. and v.i.: low: from ca 1890; ob. 7. To pick out the best of (the land) for one's farm or station: New Zealand (—1898). cf. the Australian PEACOCK (v., 2).

spot, off the. Silly, imbecile: from ca 1880; ob. 2. See:

***spot, on the.** Alert; quite certain: 1887, Henley, 'Palm and be always on the spot': low, if not orig. c. Hence, *off the spot*: uncertain, not alert.

spot, soft. 'An easy, comfortable, or desirable berth, thing, or circumstance', F. & H.: late C.19–20; slightly ob. Ex Northern dial. *spot* (—1877), a place of employment, a job. 2. See SOFT SPOT.

spot, vacant; gen. **have a vacant spot.** To be half-witted: from ca 1890; slightly ob. cf. SHINGLE SHORT; TILE LOOSE.

spots off or **out of, knock,** see KNOCK INTO A . . . **spots, see,** see SEE STARS.

***spotted,** ppl adj. Known to the police: c. (—1791). Tufts. Ex SPOT, v., 1.

spotted Dick. A suet pudding made with currants or raisins: 1849, Soyer, *The Modern Housewife*: coll >, ca 1890, S.E. Ex the raisins that, on the surface, give the pudding a spotty appearance. cf. the next three entries.

spotted dog. The same as preceding entry: from ca 1865: coll. Prob. *dog* puns *dough*, as Ware suggests. 2. Among soldiers, a sausage or a saveloy: from ca 1885; very ob. Ex the legend. cf. SPOTTED MYSTERY.

spotted donkey; spotted leopard. The same as SPOTTED DICK: resp. schools' (—1887), ob.; low urban, from ca 1880.

spotted duff. A coll variant (from ca 1870) of SPOTTED DICK.

spotted mystery. Tinned beef: military: from ca 1880; ob. An elaboration on MYSTERY, a sausage, and on *potted* (*mystery*). cf. SPOTTED DOG, 2.

spousy. A spouse; gen., husband: jocular coll: ca 1795–1820. On HUBBY.

spout. A large mouth, esp. if mostly open: lower classes' coll (—1909). 2. A showman's palaver or PATTER (n., 2): showmen's: from ca 1880. 3. The penis: low: C.19–20.

***spout,** v. To pawn: c. (—1811). From ca 1850, (low) s.; in C.20, ob. Hughes, 1861, 'The dons are going to spout the college plate.' Ex *spout*, a pawnbroker's shoot.

spout, in great. In high spirits; noisy: late C.18–mid-19; then dial. Grose in his *Provincial Glossary*, 1787. Perhaps ex *spout*, to declaim.

spout, up the. In pawn: coll (—1812). See SPOUT, v. 2. Hence, imprisoned; in hospital: low (—1823); ob. 3. Hence, in a bad way (1853); bankrupt (—1854), this being mainly dial. 4. Pregnant with child: low: late C.19–20. Often in form, *to have been put up the spout*.

spout Billy. To make a living by reciting Shakespeare in tap-rooms: low coll (—1823); ob. by 1900. (Poor William!) Also *spout Bill*. cf. SWAN-SLINGER.

spout ink. To write books, etc.: coll: from ca 1880; ob. cf. SLING INK.

sprag. A dandy: s.: Ned Ward, 1709.

sprained one's ankle, to have, see ANKLE.

sprat. A sixpence: low s. (—1839) >, ca 1880, gen. s.; slightly ob. Prob. ex its smallness and that of the fish. 2. A sweetheart: low: from ca 1870; ob. cf. fig. use of BLOATER; DUCK, 3; PIPPIN.

sprat-weather. A dark winter's-day: fishermen's coll (—1887); ob. Such weather is suitable for the catching of sprats.

sprats. Personal effects; furniture: low: from ca 1880; ob. cf. STICKS, 2.

sprawne. A prawn: sol.; or, at best, illiterate coll: mid-C.17–mid-18.

***spread.** A saddle: c.: late C.18–mid-19. Tufts. cf. S.E. *spread*, a coverlet. 2. ?hence, a shawl: low (—1859); ob. 3. Butter: c. (—1811) >, ca 1840, low s.; slightly ob. H., 3rd ed., 'A term with workmen and schoolboys'. Because spread, but prob. influenced by *bread*. cf. SPREADER. 4. An umbrella: ca 1820–50. 5. A banquet; an excellent or a copious meal:

coll: from ca 1820. 'Pomes' Marshall, 1897, ''E didn't even give me an invite | To 'is New Year's spread.' 6. Hence, among sporting men, a dinner: from ca 1870. cf. the nuance 'any meal', as in *morning spread*, breakfast: *Spy*, II, 1826. 7. An option: Stock Exchange: late C.19–20; ob. Prob. suggested by *straddle*. 8. See DO A SPREAD. 9. 'A herbalist who sells a mixture of dried plants. He spreads these herbs out in front of him and lectures on the health-giving value of each'; *work the spread*, 'to graft as a herbalist': grafters': late C.19–20. 10. Jam, marmalade, or anything else spread on bread: Canadian: late C.19–20. Ex sense 3.

spread, do a, see DO A SPREAD.

spread oneself. To make every effort, esp. monetary; to do one's very best, 'damn the expense!': orig. (1832) U.S., in sense of making a display; anglicized ca 1890 as a coll.

spread-worker. A herbalist: showmen's: late C.19–20. See SPREAD, 9.

***spreader.** Butter: c.: early C.17. Rowlands. cf. SPREAD, 3.

***spreaders.** A burglar's large pliers: c.: from ca 1890. Pugh (2).

'Sprecious, Sprecious, S'pretious. A coll oath: C.17. Jonson. Abbr. *God's precious*.

spree. A boisterous frolic; a period of riotous enjoyment: Scots dial. >, by 1798, *Sessions*, coll. Origin problematic; but W.'s provisional identification, via early dial. variant *spray*, with *spreagh*, *spreath*, foray, cattle-raid, ex Gaelic *spréidh*, cattle, may well be correct. 2. Hence, a drinking bout, a tipsy carousal: coll: 1811, *Lex. Bal.* cf. SPREE, ON THE. 3. Hardly distinguishable from senses 1, 2: 'rough amusement, merrymaking, or sport; prolonged drinking or carousing; indulgence or participation in this', O.E.D.: Scots dial. (—1808) >, ca 1820, coll. Occ. without article, as in Frank Bullen, 1899, 'A steady course of spree'. 4. A conceited person: Winchester College: from ca 1870; ob. Pascoe, *Public Schools*, 1881. Ex adj.

spree, v.i. To carouse; have, take part in, a spree: coll: mid-C.19–20. Mrs Gaskell, 1855. Ex n., 1, 2. Whence *spreeing*, vbl n. and, occ., adj.

spree, adj. Befitting a Wykehamist; smart: Winchester: from ca 1860; ob. Perhaps ex SPREE-MESS. 2. Conceited: ibid.: from ca 1870. This sense is applied only to juniors; used of acts, it = 'permissible only to prefects, or those of senior standing', Wrench. Ex dial.; cognate with S.E. *spry* and *spruce*.

spree, on a. Enjoying oneself: coll: 1847. Ex SPREE, n., 1. cf.:

spree, on or **upon the.** e.g. *go on the spree*. Having a riotous time, esp. – and in C.20 almost solely – on a drinking bout: coll: 1851, Mayhew, who has the †*get on the spree*; H., 1st ed., '"Going on the spree", starting out with intent to have a frolic'. Ex SPREE, n., 1, 2, and cf. SPREE, ON A.

spree man, or as one word. A junior permitted to work hard: Winchester College: from ca 1870.

spree-mess. A feast, esp. in the form of a SPREAD at tea-time, raised by subscription or given by departing boys and always held at the end of the half-year: Winchester College: ca 1840–60. Mansfield. Ex SPREE, n., 1, 2, 3.

spreeish. Fond of or frequently sharing in sprees: coll: 1825, C. Westmacott. 2. Slightly intoxicated: coll: *Sessions*, April 1843. See SPREE, n., 2.

spress or **'spress.** Express; express train: sol.; or rather, low coll (—1887).

spring, v.i. To offer a higher price: 1832, *Sessions*; ob. by 1890. Whence SPRING TO. 2. To give; disburse; buy (a certain amount): coll: 1851, Mayhew, 'It's a feast at a poor country labourer's place when he springs sixpenn'orth of fresh herrings'; 1878, J. F. Sullivan, *The British Working Man*, 'Wot's 'e sprung?' (how much money has he given?). Ex *spring*, to cause to appear. Contrast RUSH, to charge extortionately. 3. Hence, to afford to buy: late C.19–20. cf. SPRING TO.

***spring a partridge.** To entice a person and then rob or swindle him: c.: late C. 17–mid-18. In *A New Canting Dict.*, 1725, collectively as *spring partridges*. Ex *spring partridges*, to cause them to rise.

spring a plant, see PLANT, SPRING A.

***spring-ankle warehouse.** 'Newgate, or any other gaol', Grose, 1st ed.: c. of ca 1780–1840: Anglo-Irish. A sprained ankle = disablement = imprisonment. But cf. ANKLE-SPRING WAREHOUSE.

spring at one's elbow, have a. To be a gamester: coll: latish C.17–mid-18. Ray, 1678. cf. *shake the* ELBOW.

spring fleet. N.E. coast collier brigs going into the Baltic trade in the slack coal season: nautical coll: late C.19–early 20.

spring-heeled Jack. A rocket-propelled torpedo: naval: very late C.19–very early 20.

spring like a ha'penny knife, with a. Floppy: with no resilience: lower classes' (—1909). Ex 'deadness' of such a knife.

spring to. To be able to pay or give; to afford: coll; 1901, Anon., *Troddles and Us*, 'It's seven pound fifteen, and we can spring to that between us.' Ex SPRING, 1. 2. Hence, to be able to accomplish: coll: 1903, F. & H.

springer-up. A tailor selling cheap, ready-made clothes: mid-C.19–20; ob. Mayhew, 1851; H., 1st ed., 'The clothes are said to be "sprung up", or "blown together".'

sprinkle. To christen: jocular coll: mid-C.19–20.

sprio. A sparrow: Sedgeley Park School: ca 1780–1870. *Sparrow* > *spro* >, by the principle of ease of pronunciation, *sprio*.

spruce up. To clean and dress oneself to go out or to go on parade: Regular Army coll: since ca 1895. i.e. make oneself *spruce* or smart.

sprung. Tipsy: low s. >, in C.20, coll: from ca 1825; ob. Often as in Judd, 1870, 'Ex-Corporal Whiston with his friends sallied from the store well-sprung.' Either ex *spring*, to moisten (in C.19–20, only in dial.), or, as the O.E.D.'s earliest quotation tends to show, ex *sprung*, split or cracked, *masts*.

sprung-up, adj., see SPRINGER-UP.

spud. A potato: dial. (—1840) >, by 1845, s. Possibly ex *Spuddy*, the nickname for a seller of bad potatoes (Mayhew, 1851), but prob. *spud* is the earlier. Perhaps an Anglo-Irish corruption of *potato* via MURPHY: cf. *Spud*, the inevitable nickname of any male Murphy and occ. of anyone with an Irish name. W., however, proposes a s. 'application of *spud*, weeding instrument', and pertinently compares the etymology of *parsnip*. Possible also is the *spud* adduced in the etymology of: 2. A baby's hand: dial. and nursery: mid-C.19–20; ob. Halliwell. ?a corruption of *pudsy*, pudgy, or simply a special application of *spud*, a stumpy person or thing.

spuddy. See SPUD, 1. 2. A seller of baked potatoes: costers': late C.19–20.

spug. A sparrow: Cotton College: since ca 1875. Adoption of dial. word.

spun-yarn trick. (Gen. pl.) An unfair trick: naval coll: late C.19–20. Ex the unfair use of spun yarn in competitive evolutions.

spunk. Mettle, spirit; PLUCK: 1773, Goldsmith, is preceded by Bridges, 1772, 'Whether quite sober or dead drunk, | I know, my dear, you've too much spunk'; Grose. App. coll >, ca 1800, S.E. >, ca 1850, coll >, ca 1890, s.: cf. the quotations and remarks in F. & H., O.E.D., and W., who derives it ex Gaelic *spong*, tinder. 2. Hence, the seminal fluid: coll: C.19–20. cf. METTLE. 3. A match: c. or low s. (—1839). Ex dial.

spunk-bound. (Of a man) lethargic; slow-witted: low: late C.19–20.

spunk-fencer. A match-seller: c. or low s. (—1839). Ex dial. *spunk*, a match.

spunky. Spirited; plucky: dial. (Burns 1786) >, ca 1800, coll. Lamb, 1805, 'Vittoria Corombona, a spunky Italian lady'; 1819, Moore, 'His spunkiest backers were forced to sing small.'

***spur.** To annoy: c.: from ca 1875; ob. Whence:

***spur, get the.** To be annoyed: c.: from ca 1880. cf. *cop the* NEEDLE.

spur in one's head, have got a. To be (slightly) drunk: ca 1770–1800: orig. and mainly jockeys'. *Gentleman's Magazine*, 1770.

spurt. A small quantity: s. (—1859) and dial. >, ca 1890, dial. only. Prob. ex *spurt*, a brief effort, a short run, etc.

Spy, Black; b.s., see BLACK SPY.

squab, n. A fat person: coll: Ned Ward, 1722.

squab, v.i. To squeeze by: King Edward School, Birmingham: late C.19–20. Prob. ex *squab*, to squeeze flat, influenced by sense of *squash*. 2. (Gen. as *squob*.) v.i. and v.t., to treat thus: 'With foot on wall or desk, and back against the victim who is similarly treated on the other side, or pressed against the opposite wall', F. & H.: ibid.: id.

squab up, v.i. and v.t. To push: ibid., id.

squabash. A crushing blow; to crush, defeat: resp. 1818, Prof. Wilson, and 1822: s. >, ca 1860, coll. A blend of *squash* + BASH. cf. Scottish *stramash*.

squabble. (Of type) to be or get mixed: printers' (—1887).

squad. A squadron: naval (—1887). (This is independent of the S.E. use in late C.17.)

squad, halt! Salt: military rhyming s.: late C.19–20.

squaddy. An occ. perversion of SWADDY: rare before C.20.

squaler. A weapon consisting of an 18-inch cane surmounted with a pear-shaped piece of lead used for killing squirrels and deer in Savernake Forest: Marlborough College: ca 1843–60. Either for *squirreller* or because it causes squirrels to *squeal.* But as *squailer* it is an archaeological technicality. The weapon is very old; by many archaeologists and ethnologists it is known as a *rabbit stick.*

squalino. To squeal: ca 1818–60. Ex *squall* + *squeal*; fanciful suffix.

***squall.** A voice: c. of ca 1720–60.

square, n. See the adj., which it merely substantivalizes. 2. Here, however, it may be noted that, in the underworld, all just and honest practices and actions are called *the square*, as opp. to *the* CROSS: from ca 1810. cf. fig. STRAIGHT. 3. A square dance: ball-room coll: ca 1890–1914. 4. A mortar-board: Cambridge: late C.19–20.

square, v. To settle (a matter) satisfactorily: coll: 1853, Dickens, 'I have squared it with the lad . . . and it's all right.' Ex *square*, to equalize, to balance (accounts). 2. Hence, to satisfy or win over, esp. by bribery or compensation; to get rid of thus: s. >, ca 1910, coll: 1859, Lever, 'The horses he had "nobbled", the jockeys squared, the owners "hocussed" '; 1879, T. H. Huxley. Specifically, *square his nibs* is to give a policeman money: H., 1st ed. 3. Hence, to get rid, or dispose, of by murder: 1888. 4. See SQUARE AT; SQUARE IT; SQUARE ROUND; SQUARE UP.

square, adj. Only in *(up)on the square.* (Predicatively.) Free from duplicity; just; straightforward, upright: from ca 1680: S.E. until ca 1830, then coll; by 1860. s. cf.:

square, adv. Justly; honestly; straightforwardly: late C.16–20: S.E. until ca 1840, then coll; in C.20, s. Mayhew, 1851, '. . . I wished to do the thing square and proper.' 2. Solidly, (almost) unanimously: coll: 1867; mostly U.S. 3. Correctly, duly: coll: 1889, 'Rolf Boldrewood', 'Here they were married, all square and regular, by the Scotch clergyman.'

square, be on the. To be a Mason: mid-C. 19–20.

square, on or upon the. See SQUARE, adj. 2. Engaged in squad-drill: military coll: late C.19–20. i.e. on the barracks-square.

square, run on the. To be honest or trustworthy: Society: from ca 1880; very ob.

square, straight down the crooked lane and all round the. A late C.19–early 20 c.p.: 'A humorous way of setting a man on his word', F. & H.

square, turn. To reform, and get one's living honestly: from ca 1850.

square affair. One's legitimate sweetheart (girl): Cockney and Australian: ca 1890–1914.

square at (1827, De Quincey; ob. by 1890); **square up to** (from ca 1850). To take up a boxing stance against (a person): coll till ca 1880, then S.E. Ex *squaring one's shoulders.*

square back-down. A palpable shuffling: sporting: from ca 1870. 2. See BACK-DOWN.

square clobber, square cove, square crib. Here, *square* = respectable, reputable: C. 19–20: coll (though CLOBBER and CRIB are not coll). A variation of *square*, honest, honourable, etc., applied to the implied activities.

square-face; squareface. Gin; schiedam: 1879 (O.E.D.). Mostly South African. Ex the square bottles in which it was retailed in all parts of South Africa; Pettman.

square-head; squarehead. A Scandinavian or a German: coll: late C.19–20. Ex shape of head. 2. Earlier, a free immigrant: Australia: ca 1870–90. 3. In c., an honest man: mid-C.19–20; ob.

square it. To act, esp. to live, honestly: 1873: coll.

square-mainsail coat. A frock coat: nautical, esp. naval: late C.19–20.

square off. To placate (a person): Australian: from ca 1905.

square-pusher. A decent girl: lower classes' (—1902). Lit., a SQUARE or respectable PUSHER or girl.

square-pushing. An instance, or the habit, of 'walking out' with a girl or young woman: military: from ca 1885. Ex the military practice of strolling with nursemaids and other maids round the square, or perhaps by back-formation ex the preceding. See also PUSHER, 2.

square round. To make room: Winchester coll: mid-C.19–20. Ex dial. sense, 'to sit so as to widen the circle and make room for others' (E.D.D.).

square-rigged. Well-dressed: from ca 1850 (ob.); coll, orig. and mainly nautical. Ex the lit. S.E. sense. cf. RIG-OUT.

square (the) yards. To settle a score, esp. to take vengeance: from ca 1835 (ob.): nautical. Dana, 'Many a delay and vexation . . . did he get to "square the yards with the bloody quill-driver".'

square-toes, see OLD SQUARE-TOES.

square up. To pay (a debt): coll: 1862, Mrs Henry Wood, 'I can square up some of my liabilities here.' Ex SQUARE, V., 1.

square up to, see SQUARE AT.

squaresel. A square-sail: nautical coll (—1887).

squarum. A lapstone: shoemakers': from ca 1860. i.e. *a square one.*

squash. A scrimmage or rough scrum: school football s.: from middle 1850s.

squash, v. To silence or snub (a person) crushingly: coll: from ca 1900.

squash ballad. A ballad 'prompting war and personal devotion': pacifists': 1896–1910. Ware. ?ex sentiment.

squashed fly or, gen., **flies.** A sandwich biscuit with currants: children's: late C.19–20.

squat. A seat: London lower classes' (—1909). Also *do a squat.*

squatter. A kind of bronze-wing pigeon: Australian coll nickname: from ca 1870.

squattez-vous! Sit down!: from late 1890s. Kipling's *Stalky*, 'Be quick, you ass! . . . Squattez-vous on the floor, then!' cf. TWIGGEZ-VOUS.

***squawl.** A variant of SQUALL.

***squeak,** n. A criminal that, apprehended, informs on his colleagues: c. (—1795); ob. by 1850, †by 1880. cf. the v., 1, and SQUEAL.

***squeak,** v. To turn informer: c.: C.18–20; ob. *A New Canting Dict.*, 1725; Ainsworth. cf. SQUEAL. Ex: 2. To confess (v.i.): s.: late C.17–20; ob. In C.19–20, rare except as in sense 1. Dryden, 1690, 'Put a civil question to him upon the rack, and he squeaks, I warrant him.'

***squeak beef.** To cry 'Stop thief!: c.: late C.17–early 19.

***squeak on.** The v.t. form of SQUEAK, v., 2.

squeak than wool, more, see WOOL, MORE SQUEAK THAN.

squeaker. A pot-boy: ca 1670–1830. 2. A child; esp. a bastard: from ca 1670. cf. SQUEALER, 2. 3. A youngster: nautical: mid-C.18–19. Bowen, who notes that in the training-ship *Conway* it designates a mizzen-top cadet (late C.19–20). John Masefield, however, in his history of the *Conway* (1933), defines it as 'a small, noisy cadet' – not that the definitions are mutually exclusive! Comparable is the late C.19–20 Public School sense, a boy in the lowest form. 4. A BLAB; an informer, esp. to the police: C.19–20. cf. SQUEAK, n. 5. A foxhound: sporting: 1828 (O.E.D.). 6. A pig, esp. if young: coll: from ca 1860. 7. A heavy blow: 1877: s. >, ca 1890, coll; ob. Ex effect. 8. See SQUEAKERS. 9. An Australian coll name applied to various birds from their cries: 1848, J. Gould, *The Birds of Australia.* 10. A cicada: South African coll (mostly juvenile): from the 1890s. Its 'cry' is hardly a squeak. 11. A tapioca pudding: nautical: late C.19–20.

squeaker, stifle the. To get rid of a bastard: late C.17–20; ob. 2. Hence, in C.19–20, to procure abortion. Both senses, low s.; almost c.

***squeakers.** Organ pipes: c.: late C.18–20; ob.

***squeal.** An informer: Scots c. (—1823); ob. cf. SQUEALER, 1. 2. Bacon: late C.19–20.

***squeal,** v.i.; v.t. with *on.* To turn informer: c., orig. (—1864), North Country; but in late C.19–20 mainly U.S. cf. SQUEAK, v., 1.

***squealer.** An informer: c. (—1864). Ex SQUEAL, v. 2. An illegitimate baby: low s. (—1864). cf. SQUEAKER, 2. 3. A noisy small boy: Wellington (the English public school): late C.19–20. cf. SQUEAKER, 3.

squeege. Squeeze (n. and v.): (in C.20, low) coll: late C.18–20.

squeegee, all. Very much askew: ca 1860–1910. Perhaps by corruption.

squeegee band. An improvised ship's band: nautical: 1896, *The Navy and Army Illustrated*, 3 Oct. Ex the sound made by the squeegee (a rubber deck-scraper) when vigorously used.

***squeeze.** The neck: c. (—1812); ob. Also *squeezer.* Ex squeezing by the gallows-rope. 2. Hence, the rope itself: c.: from ca 1830; ob. 3. Silk: c. (—1839). Also as adj. from ca 1870. Ex squeezeability into very small space. 4. Hence, a silk tie: c.: 1877 (O.E.D.). 5. Work, esp. in a crowd, e.g. stealing at a theatre: c. (—1864); ob. Perhaps ex: 6. A crowded assembly or (social) gathering: coll: 1799, Mrs Barbauld, 'There is a squeeze, a fuss, a drum, a rout, and lastly a hurricane, when the whole house is full from top to bottom.' 7. An escape, esp. if a narrow one: coll: 1875; ob. Ex *squeeze by* or *past.* 8. A strong commercial demand or money-market pressure: coll: 1890 (O.E.D.): trade and Stock Exchange. 9. An illegal exaction: Anglo-Chinese coll: from ca 1880. 10–12. Without date or quotation, F. & H. gives the following three s. senses: a hard bargain (from ca 1870); hence, a Hobson's choice (from ca 1880); a rise in salary (ca 1890–1910), this last because of the difficulty of obtaining it.

squeeze. To bring into trouble: 1804 (O.E.D.); ob. by 1890.

squeeze, at (1897) or **upon** (1892; ob.) **a.** At a pinch: coll.

squeeze-box. A ship's harmonium: naval (—1909). Ware, 'From the action of the feet'.

squeeze-crab. A morose or a peevish man: low (—1887).

squeeze-em-close. Sexual intercourse: coll: mid-C.19–20.

squeeze-wax. A surety: C.18–early 19. Ex sealing.

***squeezer.** The hangman's noose: c.: from ca 1830; ob. 'Father Prout' Mahoney. 2. Hence, the neck: c. of ca 1840–90. cf. SQUEEZE, n., 1. 3. (Gen. pl.) One of a set of cards with index values shown in the corners: from ca 1880.

squelcher. A heavy blow, crushing leading article, etc.: coll: 1854, 'Cuthbert Bede', 'There's a squelcher in the bread-basket.' 2. Fig., e.g. in argument: from ca 1890; ob.

squib. An apprentice PUFF, getting half the salary of a PUFF (one who, at a gaming-house, receives money with which, as a decoy, to play): ca 1730–1830: c. > s. > coll. 2. A gun: 1839, G. W. R. Reynolds; almost †. 3. A sweet in the form of a squib: coll: mid-C.19–20. Mayhew. 4. (Gen. pl.) A head of asparagus: London (mainly costers'): from ca 1850. Mayhew. Ex shape. 5. A paint-brush; gen. pl (—1864). 6. In Christ Church (Oxford) s., any member of the University not privileged to belong to 'the House': ca 1860–70.

squiffed. Tipsy: late C.19–20; ob. Prob. ex SQUIFFY.

squiffer. A concertina: rather low: prob. dating from ca 1890, for it was orig. a nautical term. Perhaps a perversion of *squeezer*: cf. dial. *squidge* for *squeeze*.

squiffy. Slightly drunk: from ca 1873. 2. Hence, drunk, in any degree: from ca 1880. Kipling, 1900, 'I never got squiffy but once . . . an' it made me horrid sick,' Prob. ex SKEW-WHIFF, perhaps on SWIPEY.

squilde. A 'term of street chaff': London proletariat: 1895–6. A blend of a Christian and a surname, i.e. *Oscar Wilde*.

squint, v. To lack (anything material): tailors': from ca 1870; ob.

squint-a-pipes. A squinting person: from ca 1786; †by 1870.

squinters. The eyes: boxers' and low: from ca 1860; ob. It may, however, have, orig., been Oxford University s. of ca 1760–1860. It occurs in the poem 'A Familiar Epistle' on p. 367 of *The Gentleman's Magazine*, May 1784.

squinting. Being without a necessity or a requisite (e.g. food): tailors': from ca 1860.

squire. A title prefixed to a country gentleman's surname and thus forming, very often, part of his appellation: mid-C. 17–20: S.E. until C.19, then coll. cf. SQUIRE, THE.

squire, stand. To stand treat: coll: ca 1780–1850. cf.:

squire, the. 'A Sir Timothy Treat-all', B.E.: late C.17–early 19. Sometimes amplified to *squire of the company*, as in Grose, 1st ed. cf. preceding entry. 2. A simpleton or a fool: late C.17–mid-18. B.E., who adds: '*A fat Squire*, a rich Fool'. cf., perhaps abbr. of *squire of* ALSATIA.

squire of Alsatia, see ALSATIA. **squire of the company,** see SQUIRE, THE, 1.

squire of the gimlet. A tapster: jocular coll: ca 1670–1800.

squire of the pad, see PAD.

squire of the placket. A pimp: jocular coll: ca 1630–1800. D'Avenant. With these *squire* terms, cf. the much larger KNIGHT group.

squirish. Of 'One that pretends to Pay all Reckonings, and is not strong enough in the Pocket', B.E.: late C.17–mid-18. Ex SQUIRE, THE, 1. 2. Foolish: same period. See SQUIRE, THE, 2.

squirl. A flourish in writing: dial. (ca 1840) >, before 1900, coll. Prob. ex *squiggle* and *twirl*.

squirm. A small objectionable boy: Public Schools: from ca 1880; ob. cf. SQUIRT.

squirrel. A harlot: late C.18–mid-19. Grose, 2nd ed., 'Because she, like that animal, covers her back with her tail. *Meretrix corpore corpus alit*.'

squirt. A paltry person; a contemptible person, esp. if mean or treacherous: coll: U.S. (—1848), anglicized ca 1875; common also in dial. cf. SQUIT. 2. Hence, at Public Schools, an obnoxious boy: from ca 1880. cf. SQUIRM. 3. A doctor; a dispensing chemist: from late 1850s; slightly ob. Ex *squirt*, a syringe. 4. Champagne: low: from ca 1870; ob. Ware, 'Suggested by its uppishness'. cf. FIZZ. 5. A water-pistol: mostly boys': from ca 1900.

squirt, v.i. To blab: low coll: C.19. Prob. ex excremental sense.

squirt, do a squeeze and a. (Of the male) to coït: low: C.19–20. Also *squirt one's juice*.

squish. Marmalade: university (—1874), hence Public Schools'. Ex *squishy*, soft and wet, or *squish*, v.i., to squirt out splashily or gushingly. 2. At Winchester, from ca 1880, also and mainly, it = weak tea.

squit. In the same sense as, and prob. cognate with, SQUIRT, n., 1: dial. (—1825), partly colloquialized ca 1880 (cf. Anstey, 1889, 'He's not half a bad little squit'). Esp. a small cadet (*Conway* s.: late C.19–20).

squitters. Diarrhoea: mid-C.17–20: S.E. till C.19, then dial.; in late C.19–20, also schoolboys' s. Cognate with *squirt*.

squivalens. Extras; perquisites: Australian: ca 1870–1910. Perhaps ex *equivalents*.

squiz. 'A brief glance', C. J. Dennis; a sly glance: (low) Australian. Ex *squint* + QUIZ. (cf. SWIZ.)

squo. Racquets played with a soft-ball: Charterhouse: from ca 1880. Also in *squo-ball* and *-court*. By a slurring of *squash*, that game. (A. H. Tod.)

squob; squob up, see SQUAB; SQUAB UP.

sres-wort; sreswort. Trousers: back s. (—1859).

sret-sio; sretsio. Oysters: back s. (—1874). H., 5th ed., where, of SPINSRAP; *sret-sio*; SRES-WORT; STARPS; STORRAC; STUN; STUNLAW, it is said that 'all these will take the *s*, which is now [i.e. there] initial, after them, if desired, and, as may be seen, some take it doubly.'

St, see SAINT.

stab, 'stab. Establishment, as in *on* (*the*) *stab*, in regular work at a fixed wage, as opp. to occasional piece-work: printers' (—1864).

stab, v.i. s. or coll (?orig. c.), ca 1670–1780, as in Cotton's *Complete Gamester*: 'Stabbing, . . . having a smooth box and small in the bottom, you drop in both your dice in such a manner as you would have them sticking therein . . . the dice lying one upon another; so that, turning up the box, the dice never tumble . . . by which means you have bottoms according to the tops you put in.'

stab in the thigh. To coït (with a woman): coll: C.19–20.

stab-rag. A (regimental) tailor: military: from ca 1840. *Punch*, 1841. Also RAG-STABBER: mid-C.19–20. cf. PRICK-LOUSE.

stab yourself and pass the bottle! Help yourself and pass the bottle: a theatrical c.p. (—1864); very ob. Ex dagger-and-poison melodrama.

stabber with a Bridport dagger, see BRIDPORT DAGGER.

stable Jack. A cavalryman: infantrymen's (—1909); ob.

stable-mind. Devotion to horses: Society (—1909); ob. By a pun.

stable-my-naggie, play at. To coït: C.19–20; ob.

Stable Yard, the. The Horse Guards, Whitehall: Londoners' and Army: ca 1810–60.

stack. To shuffle (a pack of cards) in a dishonest manner: C.20: coll. Ex U.S. (late C.19). 2. Hence, to take an unfair advantage: from ca 1905: coll.

stacks (of the ready). Plenty of money: coll: late C.19–20. In the singular, *stack*, a quantity, is S.E. (unrecorded before 1894: O.E.D.).

staff, the worse end of the. (Gen. preceded by *have*.) The disadvantage: coll: ca 1530–1890. One of the Coventry Plays, 1534; J. Wilson, *The Cheats*, 1664; North, 1740.

staff-breaker or **-climber.** A woman: low: C.19–20. Ex such literary euphemisms as *staff*, *staff of life*, and *staff of love*. cf. allusive S.E. *lance*.

staff naked. Gin: low (—1857). Perhaps a mere misprint for STARK-NAKED.

Stafford court, be tried or **have a trial in.** To be (severely) beaten, greatly ill-used: coll: early C.17. Cotgrave. (cf. the late C.14–early 15 *clad in Stafford blue*, blue-bruised by beating: either coll or merely jocular S.E.) Prob. ex:

Stafford law. 'Club' law; violence: coll: late C.16–mid-17. Occ., as in 'Water-Poet' Taylor, *Stafford's law*. Punning *staff*. cf. preceding entry.

***stag.** An informer: c. (—1725) >, ca 1820, low s.; virtually †. Ex the animal; cf. STAG, TURN. 2. A professional bailsman or alibi-provider: c. of ca 1820–90. Perhaps ironically on 'noble beast'. 3. Any such applicant for shares as intends to sell immediately at a profit or, if no profit quickly accrues, is ready to forfeit the deposit money: commercial: 1846, Thackeray. Perhaps ex sense 1. 4. Hence, an irregular outside dealer: commercial: 1854. 5. A shilling: low s. (—1857); ob. Henley, 1887. cf. HOG. 6. See STAG-DANCE, -MONTH, -PARTY, -WIDOW. 7.

See STAG, IN. 8. Sentry-go: military: late C.19–20. Prob. ex sense 1.

***stag,** v.t. To observe, watch, detect: late C.18–20: c. >, ca 1850, low s. (Also, from ca 1820, as v.i.) Ex the n., 1. 2. Hence, v.i., to turn informer (*against*): c.: from late 1830s. W. Carleton, 1839. cf. STAG, TURN. 3. To be severe towards (a person); to cripple (him) financially; refuse a loan to: from ca 1810. *Daily News*, 13 July 1870, 'A man refusing . . ., his line was . . . "stagged ", and when he went for an advance it was resolutely refused.' Ex sense 1. 4. v.i. and v.t., to beg (money); dun (a person): low s., perhaps orig. c. (—1860); ob. 5. v.i., to deal in shares as a STAG (see the n., 3 and 4): commercial: mid-C.19–20. Often *stag it*, as in Thackeray, 1845.

stag, in. Naked: C.17 coll. Dekker, 1602. ?ex a stag's colour.

stag, the. Ny*stag*mus (a succession of involuntary eyeball-twitchings): miners': late C.19–20.

***stag, turn.** To impeach one's accomplices: c. (—1785) >, ca 1840, low s. Grose, 1st ed., 'From a herd of deer who are said to turn their horns against any of their number who is hunted'.

stag-book. A book containing (gen. only) the names of bogus shareholders: commercial: 1854, *Household Words*. See STAG, n., 3.

stag-dance. A dance with only men present: U.S. (—1848), partly anglicized ca 1870. cf. BULL-DANCE; STAG-PARTY.

stag-mag. A stage-manager; to stage-manage: theatrical: from ca 1880.

stag-month. The month of a woman's lying-in: from ca 1870; ob. cf. the C.18 GANDER-MONTH; cf. also the next two entries.

stag-party. A party of men: U.S. (1856), anglicized ca 1870. cf. STAG-DANCE.

stag-widow. A man whose wife is lying in: from ca 1870. cf. STAG-MONTH.

stage-dooring. Hanging about the scenes, or about doors reserved for actors: theatrical coll: from ca 1870.

***stagger.** A spy; a look-out: c. (—1859) >, ca 1880, low s. Ex STAG, v., 1. 2. An attempt: dial. (—1880) >, ca 1890, s. Esp. in telegraphers' s. (—1895), 'a guess at an illegible word in a telegram', Funk & Wagnall.

staggering Bob. A calf: Canadian and Australian: mid-C.19–20. Ex Irish and North Country dial.; semantically cf. QUAKING CHEAT.

staggers, the. A drunken fit: coll: C.19–20. Ex *have the staggers*, to be unable to walk straight.

staggery. (Of an animal) affected with staggers (1778); (of a person) apt to stagger; unsteady (1837, Dickens). Coll.

stagging, vbl n.; ppl adj. See STAG, v., 5. Kingsley, 1849: both.

Staines, be at. To be in pecuniary difficulties: ca 1810–50. Also, *be at the Bush*, in reference to the Bush Inn at Staines.

stairs!, on the. A tailors' c.p. (from ca 1860) when a job is called for.

***stairs without a landing, the.** A treadmill: c.: ca 1880–1910. J. Greenwood, 1884, 'He's lodging now at Coldbath Fields – getting up the stairs without a landing.' cf. EVERLASTING STAIRCASE.

***stake.** A booty acquired by robbery, a SWAG (3); if large, *a prime* or *a heavy stake*: c. (—1812) >, ca 1850, low s.; ob. 2. Hence, same period, a valuable or desirable acquisition of any kind is a *stake*. 3. A (usually large) sum of money: Canadian coll: late C.19–20. 'He's made a stake in gold-mining.'

stake, v. To give, or to lend for a long while, something to (someone): coll: late C.19–20.

***stale.** A thief's or sharper's accomplice, gen. acting as a decoy: ca 1520–1650: S.E. >, ca 1590, c., as in Greene and 'Water-Poet' Taylor. Ex *stale*, a decoy-bird. An early form of STALL.

stale bear or **bull.** A BEAR having long been short of, a BULL having long held, stock: Stock Exchange coll: from ca 1890.

stale drunk, adj. Having been drunk at night and having taken too many spirit stimulants the next morning: from ca 1860.

stalk, the. The gallows in Punch and Judy: showmen's: mid-C.19–20.

stalk a judy. To follow (and accost) a woman: low: late C.19–20. cf.:

stalk the streets. (Of either sex) to look for sexual satisfaction: late C.19–20; ob.

stalky. Clever, cunning; cleverly or cunningly contrived: schoolboys': ca 1895–1900. Thus in Kipling's school-story. i.e. good at stalking.

***stall.** A pickpocket's helper, who distracts the victim's attention: c.: from ca 1590. Greene, 1591; Dekker. (Also *stallsman.*) Ex *stall*, a decoy-bird. cf. STALE. 2. Hence, the practice, or an act, of 'stalling', i.e. thus helping a pickpocket: c.: from ca 1810. Vaux, 'A violent pressure in a crowd, made by pickpockets'. 3. Hence, a pretext – or its means – for theft or imposition: from ca 1850: c. Mayhew. 4. Hence, any pretext or excuse; esp. a playing for time: from ca 1855. cf. STALL-OFF, n.

***stall,** v. To screen (a pickpocket or his thieving): c.: from ca 1590. Ex STALL, n., 1.: STALL OFF, and cf. STALL UP. 2. v.i., to make excuses, allege pretexts, play for time: from ca 1870. Ex the n., 3. 3. v.i., to play a role: theatrical: from ca 1860. Perhaps suggested by preceding sense. 4. v.i., to lodge, or to stay the night at, a public house: from ca 1855; slightly ob. Prob. ex dial. (in Shakespeare, S.E.) *stall*, to dwell. 5. v.i., to travel about: c.: ca 1840–90. '*No. 747*'. Perhaps the imm. origin of sense 4. 6. See STALL ONE'S MUG and STALL TO THE ROGUE. 7. v.i., to hang about: grafters': late C.19–20. Ex senses 2 and 4.

***stall, chuck** (one) **a.** The same as STALL, v., 1: c.: from ca 1880. J. Greenwood in the *Daily Telegraph*, 30 Dec. 1881, republished in 1884.

***stall, make a.** To effect a robbery as in STALL UP: c. (—1812).

stall, put up a, v.i. To mislead, to deceive, to hoodwink: lower classes' (late C.19–20) and military (C.20). Ex STALL, n., 4.

***stall-off.** An act of 'stalling off'; an evasive trick or story; a pretence, excuse, or prevarication: c. (—1812). Vaux; Mayhew. cf.:

***stall off,** v. See STALL, v., 1: c.: from ca 1810. 2. Hence, to avoid or get rid of evasively or plausibly: c. (—1812) >, ca 1850, s. 3. Hence, to extricate, free, get off (a person) by trickery or other artifice: c. (—1812) >, ca 1860, s.; ob. 4. Hence, or ex sense 2, to keep the mastery, maintain superiority, over (a competitor, be it horse, as orig., or man): sporting: 1883 (O.E.D.). Frequently *stall off the challenge of* (another horse in the race).

stall one's mug. To depart; esp. hurriedly: c.: mid-C.19–20; ob. Gen. *stall your mug!*, a sharp order. Prob. ex STALL OFF, v., 2.

stall-pot. (Gen. pl.) The occupant of a stall-seat: theatrical (—1909).

***stall to the rogue;** occ. **to the order of rogues.** To install (a beggar) in roguery, appoint him a member of the underworld: c.: ca 1565–1840, but archaic after C.17. By itself, *stall* is rare; Fletcher, 1622, has 'I . . . stall thee by the Salmon' – by the beggar's oath – '. . . To mand on the pad.'

***stall up.** To hustle, after surrounding, a person being robbed: c. (—1812). Vaux, who specifies the method whereby the victim's arms are forced up and kept in the air. cf. STALL, v., 1.

***stall-whimper.** A bastard: c. (—1676); †by 1840.

staller. A person constantly, or very good at, making excuses or playing for time: from ca 1870. Ex STALL, n., 3, via v., 2.

***staller-up.** One who acts as in STALL UP: c.: from ca 1810. 2. Hence, any accomplice of a pickpocket: c.: from ca 1820.

***stalling.** The 'ordination' and/or actual 'ordaining' of a beggar: c. (—1688); †by 1850. Randle Holme. See STALL TO THE ROGUE.

***stalling-ken.** Also, in C.16, *staulinge*, *stawling-*; in C.17, *stawling-*, *stuling-*. A house, office or room for the reception of stolen goods: c.: ca 1565–1840, but archaic after ca 1750. Here, *stalling* simply = placing.

stallion. A piebald horse: circusmen's: from ca 1860.

***stallsman;** incorrectly, **stalsman.** See STALL, n., 1.: c. (—1839); ob.

***stam flash.** To talk the s. of the underworld: c.: late C.17–early 19. See FLASH, n.; *stam*, unrecorded except in this phrase and ignored by the O.E.D., is prob. cognate with A.-S. *stemn*, a voice, via the *stefne* (*steven*) of M.E., which has occ. examples in *-m-* or *-mn-*; its imm. source is prob. either Ger. *stimmen*, to make one's voice heard, to sing (cf. the lit. meaning of *to cant*, particularly significant for our phrase), or the corresponding Dutch v., *stemmen*.

stammel. 'A brawny, lusty, strapping Wench', B.E.: late C.16–early 19. Deloney, 1597. Perhaps = 'wearer of a stammel' – coarse woollen – 'petticoat.' The form *strammel* does not occur before C.18 and is gen. applied to an animal.

***stammer.** An indictment: c. of ca 1820–60. Ex its effect.

stammer and stutter. Butter: theatrical rhyming s.: late C.19–20.

***stamp.** See STAMPS. 2. 'A particular manner of throwing the dice out of the box, by striking it with violence against the table', Grose, 2nd ed.: from ca 1770: dicing coll >, by 1830, j.; ob.

stamp-and-go. A shanty sung for a

straight pull along the deck: nautical: late C.19–20.

stamp-crab. A heavy walker: late C.19–early 20; ob. On BEETLE-CRUSHER.

***stamp-drawers.** Stockings: c.: C.17–early 19. See DRAWERS and STAMPS.

stamp-in-the-ashes. Some fancy drink: early C.16. cf. SWELL-NOSE.

***stamp one's drum.** To punch a hole in one's billy or kettle when it has become too old for further use; gen. as vbl n., *stamping* ...: tramps' c.: late C.19–20.

***stampers.** Shoes or boots: c.: from ca 1565; ob. Egan, 1828, 'My padders, my stampers, my buckets, otherwise my boots'. cf. STAMPS, 2. 2. Hence, feet: c.: ca 1650–90. cf. STAMPS, 1. 3. Carriers: c.: from ca 1670. *Sporting Magazine*, 1819, 'Costermongers, in all their gradations, down to the Stampers'; †by 1860. Hence in late C.17–18, *deuseaville stampers*, county or country carriers (see DAISYVILLE).

stamping-ground. A field, a park, a byway, notoriously frequented for amorous dalliance: British Empire: late C.19–20. Ex the stamping and covering by stallions.

***stamps.** Legs: c.: ca 1565–1840. Because with them one stamps. cf. STAMPERS, 2. 2. Hence, shoes: c. (—1812); ob. cf. STAMPERS, 1. 3. Types, esp. in *picking up stamps*, composing: printers' s. (—1875). cf. *stamp*, a die.

stand. A thief's assistant that keeps watch: c. of ca 1590–1640. Greene; 'Water-Poet' Taylor. Ex standing on watch: cf. STANDING. 2. An *erectio penis*: low coll: C.19–20. Ex the v. 3. A mouth-whore: low (?rather, c.): late C.19–20.

stand, v. To make a present of; to pay for: coll: from ca 1825: 1835, Dickens, '[He] "stood" considerable quantities of spirits-and-water.' 2. Hence, to pay for the drinks of (a person, or persons): coll: from ca 1840. 3. To make stand; set upright, leave standing; set firmly in a specified place, or position: 1837, Dickens: coll >, ca 1870, familiar S.E. e.g. 'stand a child in the corner'. 4. See STAND IN; STAND UP; STAND PAD: also see PATTER; RACKET; SAM; VELVET.

'stand always!', as the girl said. A c.p., mid-C.19–20 (ob.), with a punning reference to priapism. Ex the physiological S.E. sense of *stand*.

stand and freeze. Stand at ease: military jocular, rather than rhyming s.: from ca 1895.

stand at ease! Cheese: military rhyming s.: late C.19–20. 2. Fleas: rhyming s.: late C.19–20.

stand bluff or **buff.** To swear it is so; to stand firm; to take the consequences: late C.17–20; *bluff*, †by 1900; *buff*, ob. 'Hudibras' Butler; Fielding; Sheridan, 1777 (*bluff*: ?earliest record); Scott. See BUFF.

stand from under. Thunder: theatrical rhyming s.: late C.19–20.

stand (one) **in.** To cost (a person) so much, the sum gen. being stated: C.15–20: S.E. until ca 1850, then coll; in C.20, fashionable s. when not dial. Thackeray, 1848, 'It stands me in eight shillings a bottle.'

stand on one's hind legs. To show temper: coll: late C.19–20.

stand one's hand. To meet the bill (esp. for the company's refreshment or entertainment): coll: from ca 1880. H. Nisbet, 1892, 'I used to see her ... "standing her hand" liberally to all ... in the bar.' cf. STAND SHOT.

***stand pad** or (derivatively) **Paddy.** (Of a pedlar) to sell from a stationary position: tramps' c.: resp. C.18–20 and late C.19–20. Ex PAD, a road.

stand ready at the door. To be handy for use: coll: mid-C.19–20; ob. Ex spade, axe, saddle and bridle, whip, standing there.

stand right under! Clear out!: nautical coll (—1887). Ex nautical j. *stand from under!*

stand sam, see SAM, STAND.

stand shot; rarely **stand the shot.** Same as STAND ONE'S HAND: coll: from ca 1820. v.t. with *to*. cf. *stand* SAM and S.E. *stand treat*.

stand the bears. To suffer: s.: Ned Ward, 1703.

stand the patter, see PATTER, STAND THE.

stand to sense, see SENSE, IT STANDS TO.

stand-up. A dance: low coll: 1851, Mayhew, 'It was a penny a dance ..., and each stand-up took a quarter of an hour.' 2. A meal or a snack taken standing: coll (1884). cf. PERPENDICULAR, 1. 3. An act of copulation done standing: low coll: mid-C.19–20. Also a PERPENDICULAR (2) or KNEE-TREMBLER.

stand up, v.i. To shelter from the rain: coll and dial.: 1887, 'Mark Rutherford'.

stand up with. To dance with: coll: 1812, Jane Austen, 'If you want to dance, Fanny, I will stand up with you'; ob. 2. To act as bridesmaid or groomsman for: mid-C.19–20.

***stander.** A criminal's, esp. a thief's, sentinel: early C.17 c. Rowlands, 1610.

***standing.** A thieves' station: c.: 1548, Latimer; †by 1590.

standing, take. To accept composedly, endure patiently or without fuss: coll: 1901, *The Free Lance*, 27 April, 'Like a philosophical American, he took it standing, merely remarking . . .' Ex taking a high jump without a run up.

***standing budge.** A thief's or thieves' sentinel: c.: late C.17–early 19. B.E., 'The Thieves Scout or Perdu'; Grose. cf. *sneaking* BUDGE.

standing dish. Anyone who is constantly lunching, dining, or calling at a house': Society coll: from ca 1870; slightly ob. Ex the j. of cookery.

standing part. 'The original structure of anything that has since been embellished, even down to a much-patched pair of trousers' (Bowen): nautical coll: late C.19–20. Ex the nautical j. senses.

standing patterer. One of those men 'who take a stand on the curb of a public thoroughfare, and deliver prepared speeches to effect a sale of any articles they have to vend' (esp. broadsides), H., 1st ed.: London s. (from ca 1850), ob. by 1890, †by 1910; The Metropolitan Streets' Act, 1867, made it very difficult for them. Contrast FLYING STATIONER and cf. PAPER-WORKER.

standing prick has no conscience, a. A low c.p. (mid-C.19–20) that, from its verity and force, has >, virtually, a proverb. In Nathaniel Field's *Amends for Ladies*, 1618, there is this arresting adumbration: 'O man, what art thou when thy cock is up?'

standing room for (a man), **make.** To receive him sexually: low: late C.19–20. Whence *understandings*, a woman's conquests; ob.

standing ware. A variant of STAND, n., 2: mid-C.19–20.

stang(e)y. A tailor: low: late C.18–20; ob. (cf. PRICK-LOUSE.) Ex the needle: cf. *stang*, an eel-spear. 2. A person under petticoat government: rural (—1860). Ex the custom of *riding the stang*, where *stang* = a pole.

stap my vitals! A coll exclamation or asseveration: late C.17–20; ob. Ex Lord Foppington's pronunciation, in Vanbrugh's *The Relapse*, 1696, of *stop*. In late C.19–20, occ. affectedly, *stap me!*

***star.** A 'starring the glaze'; *the star*, this practice: c. (—1812); ob. Vaux, 'A person convicted of this offence, is . . . *done for a star*.' See STAR THE GLAZE. 2. One who 'shines' in society; a very distinguished person: mid-C.19–20: mostly coll. 3. Hence, in late C.19–20, a famous actor or actress, esp. the most prominent one in any given play or film: coll. Ex the v., 2. 4. 'An article introduced into a sale after the catalogue has been printed: marked in the official copy by a *star*', F. & H.: auctioneers': from ca 1880. 5. In reference to the badge worn by first offenders: prison s.: 1882 (O.E.D.). e.g. *star-class prisoners*.

star, v. See STAR THE GLAZE. 2. v.i., to act the leading part in a play: 1824 (O.E.D.): coll >, by 1860, S.E. Also, from 1825, *star it*: same status. 3. Hence, v.t., as in *star the provinces*, to tour there as the STAR (n., 3) of a dramatic company: 1850, Thackeray, 'She . . . had starred the provinces with great éclat': coll till ca 1870, then S.E.

***star, good on the.** (Esp. of a building) easy to open, i.e. burgle: c. (—1812). Also GOOD (1) ON THE CRACK (4).

star and garter!, my; gen pl. A coll expression of astonishment: 1850, R. G. Cumming, 'My stars and garters! what sort of man is this?' Ex honorific decorations, and cf. *my* STARS!

star company. A company with one star, and the rest mere nobodies: theatrical coll: ca 1884–1914.

star-gazer. A penis in erection: C.18–20; ob. 2. A hedge whore: from ca 1780; ob. 3. A horse that, in trotting, holds its head well up: late C.18–mid-19. 4. An imaginary sail: nautical: from ca 1865; ob. Smyth; Clark Russell. Prob. suggested by nautical *sky-scraper*.

star-gazing on one's back, go. (Of a woman) to coït: low: mid-C.19–20. Ex STAR-GAZER, 2.

star it, see STAR, v., 2.

***star-lay.** Robbery by breaking windows: c.: from ca 1810; ob. Ex STAR THE GLAZE.

***star-pitch.** A sleep(ing) in the open: tramps' c.: from ca 1870. cf. HEDGE-SQUARE.

star-queller. An actor whose imperfect acting mars that of better actors: theatrical: ca 1880–1910.

***star the glaze.** 'To break and rob a jeweller's show glass', Grose, 2nd ed.: c.: from ca 1786; ob. 2. Hence, to smash any window (or showcase) and steal the contents: c.: C.19–20; ob. Ex *star*, to mark or adorn with a star. cf. STAR, n., and STAR-LAY.

starboard fore-lift(, give a person a shake of one's). The right hand: nautical: mid-C. 19–early 20.

starbolic naked. A corruption of *stark-ballock naked*, utterly naked: low (esp. Australian): since ca 1870.

starbowlines. The starboard watch: nautical: mid-C.19–20; ob. cf. LARBOLIANS.

starch out of, take the. (Of a woman) to receive sexually: low: mid-C.19–20. Ex the S.E. sense, to abase or humiliate, with allusion to the *semen virile*.

starcher. A stiff white tie: late C.19–20; ob. Ex † *starcher* (starched cravat).

starchy. Drunk: from ca 1870; ob. (Not upperclass s.)

stare, as like as one can (or could). Very like in appearance: coll: 1714, Gay, 'A fine child, as like his dad as he could stare'; Jane Austen. Ob.

stare-cat. An inquisitive neighbour, esp. if a woman: women's: orig. U.S., anglicized ca 1902. cf. RUBBER-NECK.

stare like a dead (1694, Motteux) or **a stuck** (1720, Gay) **pig.** To gape and stare in utter astonishment or dismay: coll: the former, rare and †by 1800; the latter (G. Parker, 1789; Joseph Thomas, 1895), actively extant, but considered, in C.20, as slightly vulgar. Apperson, who cites the Cheshire *stare like a choked throstle* and *like a throttled cat* or *earwig*.

starers. Long-handled eye-glasses; a lorgnette: coll (Society >, by 1900, gen.): 1894, Anthony Hope, *The Dolly Dialogues*.

staring-quarter. An ox-cheek: late C.18–mid-19. In dial., a 'staring quarter' is a laughing-stock.

stark-ballock naked, see STARBOLIC NAKED.

stark-bol(l)ux. Stark-naked: Australian: since ca 1890. Ex preceding.

stark-naked. (Neat or raw) gin: low: 1820, J. H. Reynolds; almost †. cf. STRIP-ME-NAKED. 2. Occ. any unadulterated spirit: from late 1850s. 3. Hence, adj.: unadulterated: mid-C.19–20. All senses derive ex the notion of resultant poverty.

starling. See BROTHER STARLING. 2. A marked man: police: from ca 1890. Because 'spotted' or starred, marked with an asterisk for future reference.

starn, n. Stern: nautical coll (—1887). Ex dial.

starps. Sprats: back s. (—1859). See SRET-SIO.

starrer, see ANGLER.

stars!, my. Good heavens!: coll: 1728, Vanbrugh & Cibber, 'My stars! and you would really live in London half the year, to be sober in it?' 2. See STAR AND GARTER. cf.:

stars, see, see SEE STARS.

stars out! A *Conway* cadets' c.p. expressive of incredulity: ca 1900.

start. The brewer's procedure whereby he empties several barrels of liquor into a tub and thence conveys it, through a leather pipe, down to the butts in the cellar: late C.17–mid-18. 2. A prison: from ca 1820; ob. c. >, ca 1860, low s. Ex *the Start*, a C.18–19 nickname for Newgate Prison, either as starting-point of a personal 'epoch', or ex Romany *stardo*, imprisoned, and so cognate with STIR, prison. 3. A surprising incident or procedure: 1837, Dickens (QUEER START). Often RUM(MY) *start*: mid-C.19–20: cf. RUM GO. Ex the start of surprise.

start, v.t. To beat with a rope's end: naval: late C.18–19. 1825, W. N. Glascock. 2. 'To apply a smart word to an idle or forgetful person', *Gentleman's Magazine*, 1825. i.e. to make him jump by startling him. 3. To begin to complain, scold, boast, abuse or reminisce: coll: C.19–20.

start in, v.i.; v.t. with *on*. To begin work, one's job (on or at): coll: U.S. (—1892), anglicized ca 1900. e.g. 'I start in, Monday.'

start on. To tease, jest at, bully: coll: late C.19–20.

start tack or sheet, see TACK OR SHEET.

***starter.** A question: c.: late C.17–early 18. Because apt to make one start in surprise or dismay. cf. START, n., 3., and v. 2. A laxative. Its opposite is *stopper*, an astringent. These two terms, orig. undergraduates', date back to the 1890s. 3. One who frequently changes his occupation or his employer: ca 1810–80.

starting. A reprimand; a beating: proletarian: from ca 1820; ob. Ex START, v., 1 and 3.

starvation, adv. Gen. *starvation cheap*, as in Kipling, 1892 (the adv.'s first appearance in print): coll. Lit., so as to cause starvation: hence, excessively, extremely.

***stash.** To stop, desist from: c. (—1811) >, ca 1840, low s. >, ca 1870, s. *Lex. Bal.*, 1811, 'The cove tipped the prosecutor fifty quid to stash the business'; 1841, Leman Rede, 'Stash your patter' – SHUT

UP! – 'and come along.' Prob., as W. suggests, ex STOW + *squash*: cf. Vaux at *stash*. Perhaps, however, it blends *stop* + *squash*: Chignell. 2. Hence, to quit (a place): 1889, 'Rolf Boldrewood', 'The rest of us . . . stashed the camp and cleared out.' 3. See next three entries.

stash it. Specifically, 'to give over a lewd or intemperate course of life', H., 1859; ob. 2. *stash it!* Specifically, be quiet!: ibid. See STASH, 1.

***stash the glim.** To cease using the light; to extinguish it: c. (—1823) >, ca 1840, low s.; †by 1890. cf. *douse the* GLIM. Ex STASH, 1.

stash up. To terminate abruptly, as in the earliest record (H. G. Wells' *Tono Bungay*, 1909), 'She brought her [piano] playing to an end by – as schoolboys say – "stashing it up".' Ex STASH, 1.

state. A dreadful state, esp. of untidiness, confusion, dirtiness: coll: 1879, F. W. Robinson, 'Just look what a [dirty] state I am in!' 2. Agitation, anxiety, state of excitement: coll: 1837, Marryat.

state, lie in. To be 'in bed with three regular harlots', Grose, 1st ed.: ca 1780–1850.

state of elevation, in a. A coll >, in late C.19, S.E.; very ob. As in Smollett, 1749, 'We drank hard, and went home in a state of elevation, that is half-seas over.'

state tea. A 'tea at which every atom of the family plate is exhibited': Society: ca 1870–1914. Ware, 'Probably suggested by State ball'.

state-the-case-man. 'A pressed seaman whose protests were strong enough to bring an Admiralty order that he should be given a chance to state his case': naval coll: ca 1770–1840.

states can be saved without it. A political, hence cultured, c.p. expressive of ironic condemnation: ca 1880–90.

states of independency. The 'frontiers of extravagance', Egan's Grose: Oxford University, ca 1820–40.

station-jack. A meat pudding used on stations: Australian coll: 1853.

stationery. Free passes: theatrical: from ca 1880; ob. Ex synonymous PAPER, 2.

***staulinge-, stawling(e)-ken,** see STALLING-KEN.

stave-off. A scratch meal: coll: from ca 1880. Binstead.

stay. A cuckold: ca 1810–50. ?because he stays his hand.

stay. To lodge or reside regularly or permanently: standard Scots (C.18–20) >, in late C.19, Colonial, esp. South African, Australian, and New Zealand.

stay, come to. To become permanent, established, recognized, regularly used: coll: orig. (1863, Abraham Lincoln), U.S.; anglicized in late 1890s. *Athenaeum*, 13 April 1901, 'Lord Byron as a letter-writer has come to stay.'

stay and be hanged! A lower-middle class c.p. of C.19–early 20: 'Oh, all right!'

stay out. To stay in, esp. because on the sick list: Eton College (—1857). See esp. Brinsley Richards's and 'Mac' 's memoirs of Eton. By antiphrasis.

stay-tape. A tailor: coll: ca 1780–1850. Ex the frequency with which that article figured in tailors' bills. 2. A dry-goods clerk or salesman: trade: mid-C.19–20; ob.

stay-tape is scorched, one's. One is in bad health: tailors': late C.19–20.

staying. For a day, a week, etc., as in 'They have staying visitors': non-aristocratic coll (—1887).

staysel. A staysail: nautical coll (—1887).

'stead for **instead** is coll in late C.19–20.

steady. A steady admirer, wooer, of a girl (rarely vice versa): U.S. (ca 1899), anglicized by 1907.

steady the Buffs! A c.p. of adjuration or of self-admonition: mid C.19–20: military. Of anecdotal origin.

steal. A thieving; a theft; a thing stolen: Scots (—1825) >, ca 1890, coll. *Saturday Review*, 26 July 1890, 'This is an audacious steal from "In a Gondola"!'

steal a manchet or a roll out of the brewer's basket; gen. **have stolen . . .** To be tipsy: coll: ca 1670–1820. Ray, 1678, *manchet*; Fuller, 1732, *roll*.

stealers, the ten. The fingers: first half of C.17. Davenport, 1639. Ex Shakespeare's PICKERS AND STEALERS.

steam. A trip or excursion by steamer: coll: 1854, Kingsley (O.E.D.). Ex nautical usage as in *a few hours' steam away*. 2. A dish cooked by steaming: coll (orig. military): 1900 (O.E.D.).

steam, v.t. To convey on any steam-propelled vessel: coll: 1901 (O.E.D.).

steam, keep up the, see STEAMER.

steam ahead, away. To put on speed: coll: 1857, T. Hughes, 'Young Brooke . . . then steams away for the run in'; *ahead* not before late C.19. Ex the motion of a railway engine or of a steamer.

steam-engine. A potato-pie: Lancashire s.

(—1864); ob. Prob. ex the steam it emits when properly served at table.

steam-kettle. A steamer: sailing-ships' pejorative: mid-C.19–20; ob.

steam on the table, have. To have a boiled joint – generally steaming – on Sunday: workmen's: late C.18–20.

steam-packet. A jacket: rhyming s. (—1857).

steam-tugs. (Bed-)bugs: from ca 1890.

steamboat man, see SMOKE-STACK.

steamboating, n. Cutting simultaneously a pile of books which are as yet uncovered: book-binders' s. (—1875) >, by 1890, coll >, by 1910, j.

steamer. A tobacco-pipe. A SWELL *s.*, a long one: ca 1810–50. Bee, 1823, '"Keep up the steam or steamer," to smoke indefatigably'. 2. Stewed kangaroo, flavoured with pork: Australian: late C.19–20.

steamer ticket. A master mariner's certificate valid only on steamships: nautical coll: from ca 1880; ob.

steaming. A steamed pudding: military (—1897). cf. STEAM, n., 2.

Stedman, see PROMO.

***steel, the.** Any prison or lock-up: c. >, ca 1900, low s.: 1845, '*No. 747*', p. 413 (*steel*); 1889, Thor Fredur, 'He pitched into the policeman, was lugged off to the steel, . . . and got a month'; but adumbrated in *Lex. Bal.*, 1811. Ex *the Steel*, a nickname for Coldbath Fields prison, London, itself an abbr. of *Bastille*. cf. CHOKEY; LIMBO; QUOD; STIR. 3. A rare c. sense, viable only ca 1835–60, is that given by Brandon and 'Ducange Anglicus': the treadmill.

steel-bar driver or **flinger.** A tailor; esp. a journeyman tailor: resp. ca 1850–90; ca 1780–1890. Prob. *steel bar*, a needle, is also s. of same period.

steel-nose. Some kind of strong liquor: mid-C.17. Whitlock's *Zootomia*, 1654.

steel-pen coat. A dress coat: coll: 1873 (O.E.D.); ob. Ex the resemblance between the split nib and the divided coat-tail.

steep. Excessive, esp. of price, fine or damages, taxes, and figures; hard to believe, exaggerated, esp. of stories: U.S. (1856), anglicized ca 1880. Baumann, 'This sounds very steep'; *Westminster Gazette*, 22 April 1895, 'This is rather a steep statement.' cf. *stiff* (price) and *tall* (story).

steer. A piece of information; mostly *give a steer*: nautical: from ca 1870.

steer a trick. To take a turn at the wheel: nautical: mid-C.19–20.

steer small. To exercise care: from ca 1800: nautical coll >, by 1900, j. Ex S.E. sense, 'to steer well and within small compass' (Smyth).

steerage hammock. A long meat roly-poly (meat-pudding): nautical: late C.19–20.

steever, see STIVER.

***steevin.** A rare variant of STEPHEN. Bee, 1823.

stems. Legs: low: from ca 1860; ob.

step. Gen. *a good step* (Sterne, 1768) or *a tidy step* (Blackmore, 1894); occ. a *goodish step* (—1888). A walking distance: dial. and coll: mid-C.18–20. 2. A stepfather or stepmother: coll: late C.19–20.

step. To depart, make off, run away: coll: mid-C.19–20, though adumbrated as early as C.15. The variant *step it* occurs both in Mayhew, vol. III, and in H., 1st ed. 2. Hence, to desert: military: from ca 1870. 3. To clean one's own doorstep or others' doorsteps: coll: 1884; slightly ob. Ex *doorstep*.

step!, mind the. A c.p. 'look after yourself!' to a parting visitor: from ca 1880. Ex lit. admonition, perhaps orig. to a drunkard.

step below. To die: boxers' s.: ca 1810–60.

step out. To die: low: 1806, John Davis, *The Post-Captain*.

***stephen;** gen. **steven.** Money; esp. ready money: c. and low s.: ca 1810–50. *Lex. Bal.*, 'Stephen's at home; i.e. he has money'; Ainsworth. Perhaps suggested by *stever* = STIV(V)ER. 2. Esp. in *Stephen's at home*, the money's there or ready.

***stepper.** A treadmill: prison c.: mid-C. 19–20; ob. Mayhew. cf. EVERLASTING STAIRCASE. 2. See STEPPERS. 3. A doorstep-cleaner, esp. a step-girl: coll: 1884. Ex STEP, v., 3. 4. A trotting horse: Cockney: 1899, C. Rook, *The Hooligan Nights*.

steppers. The feet: 1853, *Household Words*. cf. STAMPERS, 2; STEPPER, 1.

***stepping-ken.** A dance-hall: late C.19–20: orig. c. and mostly U.S.

steps. Thick slices of bread and butter, overlaying each other on a plate: London lower classes': mid-C.19–20; ob. cf. DOORSTEP.

***steps, up the.** At the Old Bailey: c.: late C.19–20.

stereo. Stale news: printers' coll: from late 1880s. Ex *stereotype*.

stereo, adj. Stereoscopic: from ca 1875: coll.

sterics, the. Hysteria: a low coll abbr. of *hysterics*: 1765, Foote.

sterling. Persons born in Great Britain or Ireland: Australian coll: ca 1825–1910. Peter Cunningham, 1827. Gen. in juxtaposition to the complementary CURRENCY.

stern. The buttocks, esp. of persons: late C.16–20: mostly jocular, and since ca 1860 gen. considered a vulgarism. Furnivall, 1869, 'We don't want to ... fancy them cherubs without sterns.' 2. Also of hounds: hunting: mid-C.19–20.

stern, bring (a ship) down by the. To over-officer (a ship): nautical coll: from ca 1835. Dana. Officers slept towards the stern.

stern-chaser; -post. Resp. a sodomite, a penis: nautical: mid-C.19–20.

stern galley. Posteriors: *Conway* cadets': from before 1887.

steven, see STEPHEN. **stever,** see STIVER.

stew. (Great) alarm, anxiety, excitement: 1806, J. Beresford: coll >, ca 1905, S.E. In late C.19–20, esp. *be in an awful stew*. 2. A state of perspiration or overheating: coll: from ca 1890. Ex *stew*, to remain in a heated room (etc.). cf.:

stew, v.i. To study hard: orig. and mainly school s.: 1866, *Every Boy's Annual*, 'Cooper was stewing over his books.' See STEW, n., 2; cf.:

stew-pot. A hard-working student: gen. derisory: from ca 1880. Ex STEW, v.; the pun on the kitchen utensil was perhaps suggested by SWOT.

stewed. (Not very) drunk: s. (—1874; virtually †) synonym with CORNED.

stibber-gibber, adj. Given to telling lies: mid-C.16: ?c. Awdelay, 1561. ?origin.

stick. See STICKS. 2. A sermon: late 1750s–early 1760s. ?because wooden. 3. A dull, stupid, awkward, or (in the theatre) incompetent person: C.19–20: S.E. until mid-C.19, then coll. Via *wooden*. 4. Quasi-adverbially as an intensive of alliterative phrases; esp. in *stick, stark, staring* (*wild*, 1839, Hood; *mad*, 1909, W. J. Locke). 5. Gen. *the stick*, esp. *give* (a child) *the stick*; (in C.20) *get the stick*, to be caned. A beating with a stick: coll: 1856, Charlotte Yonge. 6. A crowbar or JEMMY: c.: from ca 1870. Horsley, *Jottings from Jail*. 7. A candle-stick; a candle: silversmiths': resp. coll and s.: late C.19–20. 8. A badly printed ink-roller: printers': from ca 1870. 9. A mast; a spar: nautical coll: C.19–20. 10. Gen. *the stick*. A venereal disease: low: from ca 1880. 11. A variant form of STICKER, 4: 1863; ob. 12. See BOARD, n., 2. 13. A ladder: builders': late C.19–20. Jocular. 14. A log: Australian saw-mills': late C.19–20. Ex sense 9. 15. Penis: (?) C.17–20. cf. archaic Fr. *verge*.

stick, v.t. (Of the man) to coït with: low: C.19–20. 2. v.t. (Mostly of persons) to continue long, remain persistently, in one place: C.19–20: coll until late C.19, then S.E. Of a cricketer, as early as 1832 (see STICKER, 4). 3. v.t., to put up with (things), tolerate (persons): 1899, 'He could not "stick" his mother-in-law,' *Daily News*, 26 Oct. Also *stick it*, to continue, without flinching, to do something: the phrase was used by soldiers in the Boer War (1899–1901), as J. Milne, *The Epistles of Atkins*, 1902, makes clear. 'Appears to be a ... variation on to *stand it*', W. 4. To bring to a stand(still): incapacitate from advance or retirement: coll: 1829, Scott, in the passive as in gen.; *Westminster Gazette*, 14 July 1902, 'The climber may easily find himself "stuck" on the face of a precipice.' 5. Hence, to nonplus; puzzle greatly: coll: 1884, *Literary Era*, 'You could not stick me on the hardest of them.' 6. To cheat (a person) out of money or in dealing; impose illicitly upon: 1699; slightly ob. *Blackwood's Magazine*, 1843, 'They think it ungentlemanly to cheat, or, as they call it, "stick" any of their own set.' Sometimes, esp. in the underworld, to desert: mid-C.19–20; esp. *stuck by a pal*. Also, *stick with*, to saddle (a person) with (anything unpleasant, sham, or worthless), e.g. with an inferior horse: 1900. 7. To settle (a matter); gen. *stick a point*: from ca 1890; ob. Lit., make it stick: cf. *stay put*. 8. To persuade to incur expense or loss; 'let in for': coll: 1895, J. G. Millais, '[He] publishes his work (at his own expense) and sticks his friends for a copy.' 9. See STICK IT IN; STICK OUT, etc. 10. See STUCK ON. 11. (cf. sense 2.) Of a horse: to refuse to start, to jib, to be obstinate: South African coll (—1891). cf. STICKS, 6.

stick, as close or full as (ever) it (he, they, etc.) can or could. This coll phrase expresses crowding or repletion: 1776, G. Semple, 'Piles ... driven in as close together as ever they can stick'; 1889, 'Rolf Boldrewood', 'She ... was ... as full of fun ... as she could stick.'

stick, be high up the. To be eminent in one's profession or at one's work: 'So high up the stick, they have no time ... to answer inquiries,' Sir C. Morgan, 1818; †by 1890.

stick, cut one's. A variant (Barham, Dickens, De Quincey, Thackeray, Kingsley, Boldrewood), ob. in C.20, of *cut one's sticks*: see CUT, v., 4.

stick, every, see STICKS, 2.

stick, fire a good. To be an excellent shot: shooting coll: from ca 1840. The *stick* is the gun or rifle; suggested by *play a good* STICK.

stick, get the. To be, as the most smartly turned out man, excused guard-duty and made the guard's orderly: Regular Army coll: late C.19–20.

stick, have the fiddle but not the. To have the means but not the sense to use them properly: coll: C.19. cf.:

stick, play a good. (Of a fiddler) to play well: 1748, Smollett; ob. Ex *stick*, a violin bow. 2. Hence, to perform, or play one's part, well at anything: coll: C.19–20.

stick, shoot for the. To shoot with a view to a good bag, not merely for pleasure: sporting coll: 1834 (O.E.D.). Ex a tally-stick.

stick, the wrong or right end of the; gen. preceded by *have* or *get*. To have the advantage or the disadvantage in a contest or a bargain: coll: 1890, 'Rolf Boldrewood'.

***stick a bust.** To commit a burglary: c. (—1899).

stick a pin there! Hold hard: coll: C.18. C. Hitchin, *The Regulator*, 1718.

stick and bangers. A billiard-cue and balls: sporting: late C.19–20.

stick and lift, v.i. To live from hand to mouth: low: from ca 1870; ob.

stick-and-string man. 'The old type of seaman, generally applied by a junior with a touch of envy' (Bowen): nautical: late C.19–20; ob.

stick-at-it. A persevering, conscientious person: coll: 1909, H. G. Wells.

stick away, v.i. To hide (an object); v.i., to go into hiding: South African coll: late C.19–20. Hicks, *The Cape as I Found It*, 1900. cf. S.E. *stick* (a thing) *out of the way*.

***stick-flams.** A pair of gloves: c.: late C. 17–19. Perhaps a corruption of *stick(-on-the)*-FAMS (lit., stick-on-the-hands).

stick for drinks. To win the toss to decide who shall pay for them: late C.19–20. An elaboration of STICK, v., 5; cf. ibid., 8.

stick-hopper. A hurdler: athletic coll: late C.19–20; ob. See STICKS, 5.

stick in it, with a. (Of a drink, esp. tea or coffee) with a dash of brandy: C.19–20. In late C.19–20, only Colonial and U.S. cf. Fr. *du café avec*.

stick-in-the-mud occurs as coll nickname as early as: *Sessions*, 7th session, 1733, 'James Baker, alias, *Stick-in-the-Mud*'.

stick-in-the-ribs. Thick soup (like glue): from ca 1870: not upper-class.

stick it. See STICK, v., 3, and cf. STICK IT OUT. 2. A contemptuous exclamation to a person; 'Oh, buzz off!': low: late C. 19–20. i.e. up your anus.

stick it in or **on,** v.i. To charge extortionately. v.t. *stick it into*, or, occ., *on to*: s. (—1821) >, ca 1880, coll: 1844, Dickens, 'We stick it into B. ... and make a devilish comfortable little property out of him.' See STICK, v., 5, and cf. RUSH.

stick it out. To endure and go on enduring: coll: 1901, 'Lucas Malet', 'It would be ridiculous to fly, so she must stick it out.' A variant of *stick it*: see STICK, v., 3.

stick it up. To cause a charge to be placed against one's name, orig. (1864) in a tavern-score, hence (also in 1864) in gen. – i.e. to obtain credit – as in *stick it up to me!*, put it on my account! Coll.

stick-jaw. A pudding or a sweetmeat that is very difficult to chew: coll: 1829, Caroline Southey. Occ. as adj.: late C.19–20: coll.

stick like shit to a blanket. To be very sticky: low coll: late C.19–20.

***stick man; stickman.** The accomplice of a pair of women engaged in robbing drunken men; to him they entrust their booty: c. (—1861); slightly ob.

stick on. See STICK IT IN.

stick on the price, to increase it: coll: mid-C.19–20. H., 1st ed., '*stick on*, to overcharge, or defraud'.

stick one's spoon in the wall, see SPOON IN THE WALL. **stick oneself up,** see STICK UP TO BE.

stick out. v.i., to be conspicuous; esp. too conspicuous: mid-C.17–20: S.E. until mid-C.19, then s. (mainly U.S.). *Daily Chronicle*, 3 Dec. 1902, ' "Of her" is all very well ... but when it occurs too often it "sticks out", as Mr Henry James would say.' Esp. *it sticks out a mile*, it's obvious: used absolutely or with *that*. 2. See STICK IT OUT. 3. To persist in demanding (e.g. money): coll: v.i., 1906; v.t. with *for*, 1902. 4. Hence, (v.t. with *that*) to persist in thinking: coll: 1904, R. Hichens, 'Do you stick out that Carey didn't love you?'

Also *stick* (a person) *out*, to maintain an opinion despite all his arguments: coll: from ca 1905.

***stick-slinger.** One who, gen. in company with harlots, robs or plunders with violence: c. (—1856). Mayhew. cf. BLUDGER.

stick to. To remain resolutely faithful to; or, despite all odds, attached to (a person or a party): C.16–20: S.E. until ca 1860; thereafter, coll; ca 1800–60, however, it was familiar S.E. 'Mrs Alexander' 1885, 'But I should have stuck to him through thick and thin.' 2. To refrain; hold (something) back: coll: 7 Feb. 1845, *Sessions*.

stick-up. A stand-up collar: from ca 1855 (ob.): coll >, by 1890, S.E. 'Ducange Anglicus', 1857.

stick up. See STICK UP FOR – TO – TO BE – STICK IT UP. 2. v.i., to stand firm in an argument: coll: 1858, Darwin, 'I admired the way you stuck up about deduction and induction.' 3. (v.t.) In Australia, to stop and rob (a person) on the road: 1846, J. L. Stokes: coll >, by 1880, S.E. Ex making the victim stick up his hands. 3*a*, Hence, to rob (a bank, etc.): 1888, Boldrewood: coll >, by 1890, S.E. 4. Hence, to demand money from (a person): 1890, Hornung: Australian coll >, by 1910, S.E. 5. To stop: 1863: Australian coll >, by 1890, 'standard'. 6. To pose or puzzle: 1896: Australian coll. 7. To increase (the price or, in games, the score): from ca 1875. C. Sheard, in his song, *I'm a Millionaire*, ca 1880, 'Though some stick it up, now I'll pay money down'; F. & H., 1903, '*To stick up tricks (points, runs, goals, &c.)* = to score'. 8. In cricket, to cause (a batsman) to play strictly on the defensive: coll: 1864, Pycroft: cf. STICK v., 4.

stick up for. To champion (a person); defend the character or cause of: coll: U.S. (1830s) >, almost imm., British. 1835, Anon., *A History of Van Diemen's Land*; Anstey, 1882, '"Why, you are sticking up for him now!" said Tom . . . astonished at this apparent change of front.' cf. STAND UP FOR.

stick up to. To oppose; esp. to continue offering resistance to: coll: from ca 1840: dial. till ca 1860, then coll. *Contemporary Review*, Feb. 1889, 'If there is no one who dare stick up to [the head boy], he soon becomes intolerable.'

stick up to be; occ. stick oneself up to be. To claim to be: coll: 1881, Blackmore, 'I never knew any good come of those fellows who stick up to be everything wonderful.'

stick wallah. A man scheming to *get the* STICK, esp. one who habitually aims at this: Regular Army: late C.19–20. Perhaps ex S.E. *button-stick*.

stick with, see STICK, v., 6.

sticker. A commodity hard to sell: coll: 1824, Dibdin. cf. SHOPKEEPER, and see STICKY, adj., 2. 2. Hence (—1887), a servant whom a registry office has difficulty in placing. G. R. Sims. 3. A lingering guest: coll (—1903). 4. A slow-scoring batsman hard to dislodge: cricket coll: 1832, Pierce Egan, in his *Book of Sports*; 1888, A. G. Steel; 1903, W. J. Ford. 5. 'A pointed question, an apt and startling comment or rejoinder, an embarrassing situation', F. & H.: coll: 1849, Thackeray. Ex STICK, v., 5. 6. A sticking knife, fishing spear, gaff: coll: 1896, Baring-Gould. 7. A *two-*, *three-*, *four-sticker* is a two (etc.)-masted ship, esp. a schooner on the Canadian and American coast: nautical coll: late C.19–20. 8. A butcher: proletarian coll from ca 1840. 9. A paper-hanger: builders': late C.19–20.

sticker-up. One who warmly or resolutely defends (always *for* something): coll: 1857, Borrow in *Romany Rye*. Ex STICK UP FOR. In Australia: 2. A rural method of cooking meat by roasting it on a spit: 1830, *The Hobart Town Almanack*: coll >, by 1870, S.E. And, 3, a bushranger: 1879, J. W. Barry: coll >, by 1890, S.E.; ob. Ex Australian *stick up*. cf. STICKING-UP.

sticking, or **dead stick.** A contretemps in which all the actors get muddled: theatrical: from ca 1860; the former, very ob.

sticking-up. The action of stopping (person or vehicle) on the road and robbing him or it: 1855, *Melbourne Argus*, 18 Jan.: coll >, by 1890, S.E. Ex Australian STICK UP (v.). cf. STICKER-UP, 3.

stickman, see STICK MAN.

***sticks.** (Rare in singular.) Pistols: from ca 1786: c. >, ca 1840, s.; ob. by 1859 (H., 1st ed.); †by 1914, except in still extant SHOOTING-STICK (1890). Whence, *stow your sticks!*, hide your pistols. Ex shape. 2. Household furniture: from ca 1810: s. until C.20, then coll. Abbr. *sticks of furniture*. The singular is rare and, in C.20, ob.: 1809, Malkin, *every stick*, app. the only form. 3. Legs: 1829, Glascock. 4. The stumps: cricket coll (in C.20, S.E.):

from ca 1840. 5. Hurdles: athletic coll: from mid-1890s. cf. STICK-HOPPER. 6. A horse that will not move; one that won't pull: South African coll (—1891). Bertram Mitford. Ex Cape Dutch *steeks*, used in the same way. 7. A drummer: military (—1909).

sticks, (as) cross as two. Very angry: coll: mid-C.19–20; ob.

sticks, beat (1820) – rarely **knock** (Thackeray, 1840) – **all to.** Utterly to overcome, clearly or completely to surpass: coll. Barham, 'They were beat all to sticks by the lovely Odille.'

sticks, cut one's. To make off: see CUT, v., 4. cf. *cut one's* STICK.

sticks, go to. To be ruined: coll: ca 1842, Carlyle. Emphatically, *go to sticks and staves*, as in *Susan Ferrier*, 1824. Kingsley, 1855, has the variant *go to noggin-staves.* Lit., be smashed.

sticks, in quick. Immediately; very quickly or rapidly: 1872, Besant & Rice, 'You won't pay her any more attentions, for you shall come out of this place in quick sticks.' Prob. a fusion of STICKS, legs, and *cut one's sticks*, see CUT, v., 4.

sticks, knock all to, see STICKS, BEAT ALL TO.

sticks and stones. One's household goods and possessions: proletarian coll: mid-C. 19–20.

stick(s) up. To set up a boat's mast: nautical s.: *stick*, 1845, rare in C.20; *sticks*, from not later than 1888 (Clark Russell). Occ. fig. Ex *stick*, a mast.

stick's end, keep (a person) **at the.** To treat with reserve: coll: 1886, Stevenson; ob. cf. *wouldn't touch* (*him*, *it*) *with a* BARGE-POLE.

sticks to, hold the; hold sticks with. To compete on equal terms with: resp., dial. (ca 1817) >, ca 1860, coll; and coll (1853, Reade). Perhaps ex single-stick.

sticky, n. (Not to be confused with S.E. *stické*, a game that, fusing racquets and lawn tennis, had a vogue ca 1903–13.) Lawn tennis in its first decade or perhaps its first three lustres: sporting and social. Ex *sphairistiké*, the game's original designation: invented, like its object, in 1874 by Major Wingfield. 2. Sealing-wax: from late 1850s. 3. Sticking-plaster: lower and lower-middle class coll: late C.19–20.

sticky, v. To render sticky: coll: 1865, Mrs Gaskell, 'I was sadly afraid of stickying my gloves.' Not a common word.

sticky, adj. (Of persons) wooden, dull; awkward: 1881, Mrs Lynn Linton. Ex STICK (3), a dull person. 2. (Of stock) not easy to sell: Stock Exchange: 1901, *The Times*, 24 Oct.: s. cf. STICKER, 1.

sticky-fingered. Thievish; covetous: proletarian: from ca 1870.

***stievel.** A fourpenny piece: old c., says Baumann. But this may be a confusion with STIVER.

***stiff.** Paper, a document; esp. a bill of exchange or a promissory note: c. (—1823). (In '*No. 747*' (a reference valid for 1845), an announcement-bill – a nuance app. †by 1900.) Hence, *give* (one) *the stiff*, to give (one) either of these documents; *take the*, or *do a bit of, stiff*, to accept a bill or a promissory note. 2. A forged bank-note: c.: late C.19–20; ob. 3. Ex sense 1, a clandestine letter: c.: late C.19–20. Griffiths, *Fast and Loose*, 1900. 4. A hawker's licence: London c. or low s.: from ca 1890. 5. A corpse: U.S. (—1859), anglicized ca 1880. Medical students' *carve a stiff* (dissection). Abbr. STIFF 'UN, 1. 6. ?hence, a horse certain not to run or, if running, not to win: the turf: from ca 1880. Abbr. STIFF 'UN, 2. 7. A wastrel; a penniless man: 1899, *Daily Chronicle*, 10 Aug. Perhaps orig. South African. Because cramped by lack of money. 8. Money: low: late C.19–20. 1897, 'Ouida', *The Massarenes*. Prob. ex sense 1.

stiff, adj. Closely packed: late C.17–20: S.E. until C.19, then coll, but only in *stiff with*, densely crowded with: 1907, 'There seemed ... more yachts than ever, and the water was "stiff" with masts and rigging.' 2. Certain to win: (esp. Australian) turf: late C.19–20. Prob. ex STIFF 'UN, 2, by antiphrasis.

stiff, bit of, see STIFF, n., 1.

stiff, bookmaker's. 'A horse nobbled at the public cost in the bookmakers' interest', F. & H.: the turf: from ca 1880. See STIFF, n., 6.

stiff, cut up. See CUT UP NASTY. Thackeray, ca 1885.

stiff and stout, the. A *penis erectus*: low: mid-C.17–20; ob. Urquhart.

stiff-arsed. Haughty; supercilious: low coll: mid-C.19–20. Ex *stiff-rumped*: cf. STIFF-RUMP; STIFF IN THE BACK.

stiff as a poker. (Gen. of posture) very stiff: coll: 1797, Colman, Jr.

stiff blade. A fellow-drinker: s.: from ca 1650.

***stiff-dealer.** A dealer in STIFF, n., 1.: c.: from ca 1820. 'Jon Bee'.

stiff-fencer. A hawker of writing paper: London low: from ca 1850. Ex STIFF, n., 1.

stiff in the back. Resolute; firm of character: coll: late C.19–20. 'Anthony Hope', 1897, 'Are you going to let him off? ... You never can be stiff in the back.'

stiff-lifter. A body-snatcher: Yorkshire s. (—1904), not dial. Ex STIFF, n., 5.

stiff one, see STIFF 'UN.

stiff or hard? By promissory note or in hard cash?: commercial: from ca 1860.

stiff-rump. A person haughty or supercilious; an obstinate one: coll: late C.17–early 19. Addison & Steele, 1709. cf. STIFF-ARSED; STIFF IN THE BACK.

stiff 'un; occ. **stiff one.** A corpse: 1823, Egan's Grose (*one*); 1831, *The Annual Register*. Also STIFFY. 2. A horse certain not to win: the turf: 1871, 'Hawk's-Eye', 'Safe uns, or stiff uns'. Also STIFF, n., 6; cf. DEAD 'UN; STUMER.

stiff upper lip, carry or **have** or **keep a.** To be firm, resolute; to show no, or only slight, signs of the distress one must be feeling: coll: resp. 1837, ob.; 1887, very ob.; and 1852. App. orig. U.S., for the earliest examples of *carry* and *keep* are American.

stiffen. To kill: 1888. 2. Hence to prevent (a horse) from doing its best: the turf: 1900, *Westminster Gazette*, 19 Dec.

stiffen it!, God. A low oath: late C.19–20. Eden Phillpotts, *Sons of the Morning*, 1900. Lit., render it useless, destroy it; but gen. as a vague and violent expletive. cf. STIFFEN.

stiffener. A blow that renders one unconscious: mid-C.19–20.

stiffy. A corpse: late C.19–20. See STIFF, n., 5, and STIFF 'UN, 1.

***stifler.** Always *the s.*: the gallows: c.: 1818, Scott; ob. Hence, NAB THE STIFLER, to be hanged; *queer the stifler*, to escape hanging. 2. A camouflet: military: 1836: s. 3. A dram of strong spirit: Anglo-Irish: C.19. It takes one's breath away.

still. A **still**-born infant: undertakers': from ca 1860.

still he is not happy! A c.p. applied to one whom nothing pleases, nothing satisfies: ca 1870–75. Ware quotes the *Daily Telegraph*, 28 July 1894, as attributing it to a phrase often spoken in a Gaiety burlesque of 1870.

still sow. 'A close, slie lurking knave', Florio: coll: late C.16–mid-17. Ex the proverb, *the still sow eats up all the draff.* 2. A harlot: s.: Ned Ward, 1709.

***stilting.** 'First-class pocket-picking', J. Greenwood, 1884: c. ?a perversion of *tilting*, or a pun on *stilting*, the action of stilt-walking.

Stilton, the. The correct thing: 1859, Hotten; virtually †. A polite variation of *the* CHEESE.

stim. A stimulant, gen. of liquor: Society: 1882.

stimulate, v.i. To drink alcoholic stimulants: C.19–20: S.E. until mid-1830s, then coll (mostly U.S.); except in U.S., †by 1930.

sting, n. Penis: lowish: late C.19–20. cf. PRICK, 3.

***sting.** To rob; to cheat: c. (—1812); †by 1903. 2. Hence, to demand or beg something, esp. money, from (a person); to get it thus: late C.19–20. 3. (Also ex sense 1.) To swindle, often in a very mild way and gen. in the passive voice: late C.19–20. 4. *Sting oneself*, to get stung, is coll and surprisingly old: 1663, Tuke, 'I've touch'd a nettle, and have stung my self.'

sting-bum. A niggard: late C.17–early 19.

stingareeing. 'The sport of catching *Stingrays*, or *Stingarees*': New Zealand coll: 1872, Hutton & Hector, *The Fishes of New Zealand*.

stinger. Anything that stings or smarts: late C.16–20: S.E. until C.19, then coll, in such senses as a sharp, heavy blow (1823, Bee) or the hand that deals it (1855, Browning) – something distressing, such as a very sharp frost (1853, Surtees) – a trenchant speech or a pungent (or crushing) argument, as in late C.19–20.

stinger, fetch a, see FETCH A STINGER.

stingo. Strong ale or beer: from ca 1630; ob. except in the trade name, *Watney's stingo nips*. Randolph, ca 1635; Ned Ward, 1703; Bridges, 1774; ca 1840, Barham (*styngo*); 1891, Nat Gould, 'Host Barnes had tapped a barrel of double stingo for the occasion.' Ex its 'bite' + Italianate *o*. cf. BINGO. 2. Hence, as adj. (C.19–20) and, 3, fig. energy, vigour (late C.19–20: coll).

stingy. (Of, esp. nettles) having a sting: coll: late C.19–20.

***stink.** A disagreeable exposure; considerable alarm: c. (—1812) >, ca 1850, low s. >, ca 1910, gen. s. 2. Hence, a ROW, or a fight: late C.19–20.

stink, kick up a, see PEN AND INK, 3; cf. STINK, 2.

stink-car. A motor-car: ca 1900–10.

Sporting Times, 27 April 1901. Prob. ex STINKER, 4, on the analogy of *stinkard*.

stink-finger, play at. To grope a woman: low: mid-C.19–20.

stink for a nosegay, take a. To err egregiously, be very gullible: coll: late C.18–mid-19. Malkin, *Gil Blas*, 1809.

stink-pot. See sense 3 of STINKER. 2. An objectionable fellow: late C.19–20. 3. A motor-car: ca 1898–1914.

stinker. A stinkard, or disgusting, contemptible person: C.17–20: a vulgarism. 2. A black eye: c. (—1823); †by 1910. cf. sense 5. 3. Any of the ill-smelling petrels, esp. the giant fulmar: nautical coll (—1896). Also *stink-pot* (—1865). 4. Anything with an offensive smell: a vulgarism: 1898, a motor-car; 1899, a rank cigar – former in O.E.D.; the latter in C. Rook, *The Hooligan Nights*. 5. A heavy blow: London, esp. boxing, s.: 1821, Pierce Egan, *Life in London*.

stinkibus. Bad liquor; esp. rank, adulterated spirits: C.18. Ned Ward, 1706; Smollett, 1771 (*stinkubus*). Spurious-Latin suffix on *stink*, cf. STINGO. 2. (Ex sense 1.) 'A cargo of spirits that had lain under water so long as to be spoiled', John Davidson, *Baptist Lake*, 1896: smugglers': C.19.

stinking. Disgusting; contemptible: C.13–20: S.E. until C.19, then a vulgarism. cf. STINKER, 1.

stinking, adv. A late C.19–20 Scots (somewhat uncouth) coll, as in *I'd be stinking fond*, i.e. foolish, *to do it*, I should never think of doing it, I'd certainly not do it.

stinkious. Gin: C.18. Perhaps ex STINKIBUS.

stinks. Chemistry: universities' and Public Schools': 1869 (O.E.D.). Ex the smells so desired by youth. 2. By 1902, also Natural Science: ibid. 3. In late C.19–20, a teacher of, lecturer on, chemistry: Public Schools'.

stinky. A farrier: military: from ca 1870. Ex burning of hair or hooves.

stipe. A stipendiary magistrate: rural: from ca 1859.

stir. An illiterate form of *sir* (in address): Scots: 1784, Burns; ob. cf. the slightly later Scottish *stirra*, sirrah. 2. A prison: mid-C.19–20: c. >, ca 1900, low s. Mayhew, 1851, 'I was in Brummagem, and was seven days in the new "stir"'; 1901, *Referee*, 28 April, 'Mr ... M'Hugh, M.P. ..., has gone to stir ... for a seditious libel.' Abbr. Romany *stariben*, *steripen*: cf. also Welsh Gypsy *star*, to be imprisoned, and *stardo*, imprisoned. (Much nonsense has been written about this word.) 3. A crowd: low: late C.19–early 20. Ex *stir*, bustle, animation: cf. PUSH. 4. Stew: military: late C.19–20. Ex the cooking-operation.

stir-shit. A sodomist: low: C.19–20.

stir on, have plenty of. To be wealthy: late C.19–early 20.

stir up. To visit on the spur of the moment: lower classes' (—1909). Ware.

Stir-Up Sunday. The last Sunday before Advent: dial. (—1825) >, ca 1860, coll. The appropriate collect begins 'Stir up, we beseech Thee, O Lord'; but, as the O.E.D. observes, 'the name is jocularly associated with the stirring of the Christmas mincemeat, which it was customary to begin making in that week.'

***stirabout.** A pottage of maize and oatmeal: prison c. (—1887). 2. Any pudding or porridge made by stirring the ingredients – generally oatmeal or wheat-flour – when cooking: lower classes' (—1909. Ware. Ex dial.

stirrup-oil. A beating, esp. with a strap: jocular coll (—1676) bordering on S.E.: ob. except in the All Fools' Day practical joke. Lexicographer Coles. Prob. suggested by *stirrup-leather*, an instrument of thrashing. cf. STRAP 'EM.

stirrups, up in the, see UP IN THE STIRRUPS.

stitch. A tailor: coll: from late C.17; very ob. cf. STITCH-LOUSE. 2. 'Also a term for lying with a woman', Grose, 1st ed.: low: late C.18–20; ob. 3. Elliptical for *stitch of canvas*: nautical, esp. naval, coll: since ca 1790; by 1850, S.E. W. N. Glascock, *Sketch-Book*, I, 1825, 'Standing out on a wind, with every stitch they could crack'.

stitch-back. Beer; strong liquor: ca 1690, B.E.; E. Ward, *History of the London Clubs*; †by 1800.

stitch-louse. A tailor: 1838, Beckett; ob. Ex STITCH on PRICK-LOUSE. cf.:

stitch off. To refrain from, have nothing to do with a thing; in the imperative, it = 'keep off it!': tailors': late C.19–20. Ex tailoring j.

stitches, or **S.** A sail-maker, esp. on board ship: nautical gen. as nickname: mid-C.19–20.

stitches, man of. The same as STITCH-LOUSE: mid-C.19–20 coll. cf. preceding two entries.

stiver. A small standard of value; esp. in *not a stiver*, not a penny: coll: mid-C.18–20. Ex *stiver*, a small Dutch coin. Other spellings: *stu(y)ver*, C.18; *stuiver*, C.19; *ste(e)ver*, late C.19–20, when the usual form; Yiddishly, *shtibbur*.

stiver-cramped. Needy: coll: ca 1780–1850.

stiver's worth of copper. A penny: East London: late C.19–20.

stizzle. To hurt: Tonbridge School: from ca 1880. 2. To cane (a boy): Tonbridge: since ca 1870. Marples, 'Origin obscure': ? a blend of *stick* + *sizzle*.

stoat. A virile person, esp. male, and mostly in FUCK *like a stoat*, frequently and athletically: low coll: since ca 1870.

stoater, see STOTER.

stock. A stock of impudence; esp. *a good stock*: coll: late C.18–mid-19. Also absolutely: CHEEK. 2. As in LIVESTOCK.

stock, v. To arrange (cards) fraudulently – i.e. to STACK them – may orig. (—1864) have been s. The O.E.D. classifies *stocking*, such manipulation, as s.: 1887.

***stock-buzzer.** A pickpocket of handkerchiefs: c. (—1861). Mayhew.

***stock-drawers.** Stockings: c.: mid-C.17–early 19. See DRAWERS.

stock in, take. Esp. *large*, etc., *stock in*, rarely *of*. To be interested in, have faith in, consider important: coll: 1878, Anon., 'Taking large stock in Natural Selection'.

stock-in-trade. The privities: coll: late C.19–20. Punning the lit. sense.

stock of, take. To scrutinize (gen. a person) with interest, curiosity, suspicion: coll (—1864). Ex S.E. sense, to evaluate, assess.

stockdol(l)ager, see SOCKDOLOGER.

stocking. A store of money: gen. *a fat* or *a long stocking*: dial. (—1873) >, ca 1875, coll. S. R. Whitehead, 1876, 'She had a "stocking" gathered to meet the wants of an evil day.' Ex a stocking used in preference to a bank. 2. See STOCK, v.

***stocking crib.** A hosier's shop: c.: ca 1810–60. Ex CRIB, n., 3.

stodge. Heavy eating; gorging: mostly schools': 1894, Norman Gale, concerning a bowler at cricket, 'Your non-success is due to Stodge.' Ex *stodge*, 'stiff farinaceous food', and see STODGING. 2. Hence, a heavy meal: mostly schools'. 3. The crumb of new bread (—1899). cf. sense 1. 4. Any food: s.: from ca 1880. Ex senses 1 and esp. 2.

stodge, v.t. To work steadily (*at* something, esp. if wearisome, dull, or heavy): coll: 1889 (S.O.D.). Prob. ex: 2. See STODGING. 3. To trudge through slush or mud; to walk heavily: dial. (—1854).

stodged, ppl adj. Crammed with food: dial. and coll: from ca 1870. cf. STODGING.

stodger. A gormandizer: s. or coll: late C.19–20. cf. STODGE, n., 1. 2. A dull and/or spiritless person: coll: from not later than 1904. 3. A penny bun: Charterhouse (—1900).

stodging, vbl n. and ppl adj. Gormandizing: coll: late C.19–20. Ex STODGE, v.t., to gorge (oneself or another) with food; often in passive: dial. (—1854) >, by 1860, coll; the O.E.D., which considers it to have been always S.E., records *stodge* as v.i. only in 1911 – but it occurs in Baumann (*sich satt essen*) in 1887. cf. STODGED.

stogy, a coarse cigar, may, orig. in England (ca 1890), have been coll. Ex *Conestoga*, U.S.A.

***stoll.** To understand (e.g. *stoll the* PATTER): North Country c.: from ca 1860. ?a corruption of *stall*, to place, used fig. 2. v.i., to tipple: low s.: from ca 1880; ob. Whence *stolled*, tipsy. ?origin: perhaps cognate with rare Norfolk *stole*, to drink, swallow.

Stolypin's necktie. 'The final halter': political: 1897–ca 1914. Ex a formerly well-known Russian functionary.

stomach, hot, see HOT A STOMACH.

stomach on one's chest, (have got) a. (To have) something lying heavy on one's stomach: jocular coll (—1887).

stomach thinks my throat is cut, my, see THROAT (IS) CUT ...

stomach-worm gnaws, the. I'm hungry: ca 1785–1850.

stomjack, or stom Jack. Stomach (n.): nursery sol. (—1887).

stone. See STONES cf. STONE-FRUIT. 2. *stone, kill two birds with one*. See BIRDS. 3. A diamond: South African s. (1887). 4. *the stone*. Diamonds: late C.19–20: gem-dealers' coll verging on j. A gem-trade proverb runs, 'When the stone goes well, all goes well.'

stone and a beating, give a. To beat easily: racing s. from ca 1850 >, by 1900, sporting coll. Ex racing and athletics j., *stone* being a stone-weight.

stone-brig, see STONE-DOUBLET.

stone-broke; ston(e)y-broke. (Almost) penniless; ruined: resp. from before 1887 (Baumann) and now rare; 1894, Astley. The link between the two forms is provided by R. C. Lehmann's *Harry Fludyer*, 1890, 'Pat said he was stoney or broke or something but he gave me a sov.'

stone(-)doublet, jug, pitcher, tavern; brig, frigate. A prison; orig. and esp. Newgate: *-doublet* – the exemplar – B.E.; Motteux, 1694; †by 1850; *-jug* – in C.19, the commonest, whence JUG – late C.18–19, Grose, 3rd ed., and Reade, 1856; *-pitcher*, ca 1810–60; *-tavern*, late C.18–mid-19, Grose, 3rd ed.; *-brig* and *-frigate* are both nautical (mainly naval), C.19, the latter recorded by Frank C. Bowen. Dial. has *stone-house* and, in 1799, U.S. has *stone jacket*.

stone-fence. A drink of whisky with nothing added: ca 1870–1910. B. & L., at *neat*; at *stone-fence*, however, it is defined as 'brandy and ale'.

stone-fruit. Children: low C.19–20; ob. Ex STONES; punning lit. sense.

stone-jug; stone-pitcher; stone-tavern, see STONE-DOUBLET.

stone the crows! An Australian expletive: coll: probably since mid-C.19.

stone under weight or **wanting, two.** Castrated: punning coll: 1785, Grose (*under weight*, the *wanting* form not before C.19); ob.

stone (up) in the ear, take a. To play the whore: late C.17–mid-18. Shadwell, 1691; 'Facetious' Tom Brown. cf. STONES.

stone-wall; stonewall. Parliamentary obstruction; a body of Parliamentary obstructionists: 1876: Australian >, by 1898, New Zealand political s. cf. the C.16–17 proverb, *it is evil running against a stone wall* and:

stone-wall; gen. stonewall. To play stolidly on the defensive: cricket s. (1889). Lit., to block everything as though one were a stone wall; but imm. ex S.E. *stonewall*, a cricketer doing this (1867). 2. In politics, v.i. and v.t., to obstruct (business) by lengthy speeches and other retarding tactics: Australian s. (from ca 1880) >, ca 1900, fairly gen. Ex the n.

stone(-)waller; stone(-)walling, n. and adj. One who stonewalls (in sport, ca 1890; in politics, ca 1885); the act or practice of doing this and the corresponding adj. (in cricket, ca 1895; in politics, 1880), see the v.

stone wanting, two, see STONE UNDER WEIGHT.

stones. Testicles: C.12–20: S.E. until ca 1850, then – except of a horse – a vulgarism. cf. STONE-FRUIT; *take a* STONE (UP) IN THE EAR. 2. Diamonds: South African s. (1887, *South African Sketches*, by Ellis).

stones, off the; on the stones. Outside London; in London: coll: ca 1830–80. Bulwer Lytton, 1841 (*off the stones*); Surtees, 1858, 'They now get upon the stones.' Ex the hardness of London streets.

stonewall, see STONE-WALL. **stoney,** see STONY. **stoney-broke,** see STONE-BROKE.

'stonish. To astonish: in C.19–20, gen. coll and mostly nursery.

stonnicky. A rope's end as an instrument for the inculcation of naval smartness: training-ships': ca 1860–1910. Perhaps cognate with *stunner*.

stony; less correctly, stoney. (Almost) penniless, ruined: from ca 1890. For earliest record, see STONE-BROKE. For semantics, cf. HARD-UP. cf.:

stony- (occ. stoney-)broke. The same: see STONE-BROKE.

stoob(s). Boots: back s. (—1859). See SRET-SIO.

***stook.** A pocket-handkerchief: c. (—1859). 1893 P. H. Emerson (*stoock*). Prob. ex Yiddish: cf. Ger. *Stück*. Hence, *stook-buzzer* or *-hauler*, a pickpocket specializing therein. 2. Gen. *in stook*, in trouble: London proletarian of late C. 19–20. From Yiddish, where it means difficulties and is pronounced *stooch*.

***stool-pigeon.** A card-sharper's decoy: c.: from ca 1880.

stool's foot in water, lay the. To prepare to receive a guest or guests: coll: ?C.18–mid-19.

***stoop.** Always *the stoop*. The pillory: c. of ca 1780–1840. Whence NAB (*nap*) *the stoop*, to be pilloried; *stoop-napper*, one in the pillory: both c.: same period. Ex the position therein enforced. 2. Catachrestic when used of a porch or a veranda: late C.18–20. Canada (and U.S.).

***stoop,** v.i. To become a victim to crook or criminal: c.: late C.16–early 17. Greene. 2. To set (a person) in the pillory: c. of ca 1810–40. Ex n., 1.

***stooping match.** 'The exhibition of one or more persons in the pillory', Vaux: c.: ca 1810–40.

***stop.** A police detective: c. (—1857); app. †by 1903. Ex action.

***stop, on the.** 'Picking pockets when the party is standing still': c.: mid-C.19–20. cf. STOP(-)LAY.

***Stop-Hole Abbey.** The chief rendezvous of the underworld: c.: late C.17–early 19. It was at some ruinous building in London.

***stop(-)lay, the.** Pocket-picking by two confederates, of whom one stops the victim and engages him in conversation and the other robs him: c.: mid-C.19–20.

stop my vitals! 'A silly Curse in use among the *Beaux*', B.E.: coll: late C.17–18. Often STAP MY VITALS!

stop off, v.t. To desist from, to cease doing or making: New Zealand: since ca 1880, 'Stop that row, Tommy . . . stop it off.' G. B. Lancaster, *Sons o' Men*, 1904.

***stop one's blubber.** *A New Canting Dict.*, 1725, '*I've stopt his Blubber* . . . I've done his Business. He'll tell no Tales, &c.': c.: C.18.

stop out, v.t. To cover (one's teeth) with black wax to render them invisible to the audience: theatrical coll: from ca 1870. Ex etching.

stop-out, n. A person given to stopping out late at night: coll: late C.19–20.

stop the show. To hold up the performance because of the loud, continuous applause for one's own acting: theatrical coll: late C.19–20.

stop thief. Beef: rhyming s. (1859, H.); orig. (—1857), stolen meat, as in 'Ducange Anglicus', but not after 1870 at latest.

stop up. To sit up instead of going to bed: coll: 1857, Mrs Gaskell.

stopper. Something that brings to a standstill or that terminates: s. (1825, W. N. Glascock) >, in late C.19, coll. Esp. in *clap a stopper on* ('that jaw of yours', Marryat, 1830), and in *put a* or *the stopper on*, to cause to cease (Dickens, 1841): both s. >, ca 1890, coll. 2. See STARTER, 2.

stopper, v.t. To stop: 1821, Scott, 'Stopper your jaw, Dick, will you?' cf. STOPPER, n., 1830 quotation. Ex lit. nautical sense.

stopping, hot, see HOT-STOPPING.

stopping oyster, see OYSTER, A CHOKING.

stops!, mind your. Be careful: coll: 1830, Marryat, 'Mind your stops . . . or I shall shy a biscuit at your head.' Ex an injunction to a child reading aloud.

store. 'A bullock, cow, or sheep bought to be fattened for the market: 1874: Australian coll >, by 1900, standard.

storey, upper, see UPPER STOREY.

storrac. Carrots: back s. (—1859).

story. A lie: a coll euphemism: ca 1697, Aubrey; Barham. Chiefly in *to tell stories* and *what a story!* 2. Whence, a STORY-TELLER: low coll and among children; esp. as *you story!*, you liar!: 1869. 3. See UPPER STOREY.

story-teller. A liar: euphemistic coll: 1748, Richardson, 'Wicked story-teller'.

***story with, do the.** To copulate with (a woman): prostitutes' c.: C.18. *Select Trials from 1720 to 1724*, pub. in 1734.

***stosh.** A variant of STASH.

***stoter;** occ. **stotor;** also **stoater** and **stouter.** A sharp, heavy blow: late C.17–early 19: c. >, ca 1800, low s.: Motteux, 1694, *stoater*; B.E., *stoter*; *stouter*, 1769. Only H. and F. & H. record *stotor*. Ex:

***stoter,** v. To fell heavily; hit hard: c.: 1690, D'Urfey; B.E., '*Stoter him*, or *tip him a Stoter*, settle him, give him a swinging Blow'; †by 1750. Ex Dutch *stooten*, to push or knock.

stotious. Drunk: s.: late C.19–20. An artificial word; cf. GALOPTIOUS.

***stoupe.** To give up (v.i.): c.: C.18–early 19. Halliwell. Ex *to stoop.*

stout, ca 1670–1700, was s. for strong beer. Swift; Johnson.

stout across the narrow. Corpulent: coll: C.20; ob. Anon., *Troddles*, 1901.

***stouter,** see STOTER.

stove-pipe (hat). A top hat, a CHIMNEY-POT: mid-C.19–20 (ob.); U.S. >, ca 1865, English. In late C.19–20, coll. Ex shape.

stove-pipes. Trousers: 1863.

***stow,** v.i. To cease talking, to SHUT UP: c. (—1567); ob. by 1820, †by 1850. Harman, 'Stow you, holde your peace'; B.E., '*Stow*, you have said enough'; Grose, 3rd ed., '*Stow you*, be silent.' 2. Hence, v.t., to desist from: c. (—1676) >, ca 1800, low s. >, ca 1850, gen. s. Coles, 1676, '*Stow your whids*, . . . speak warily'; *stow (one's) jabber*, 1806; *stow (one's) mag*, 1857; 'Ouida', 1882, '"Stow that, sir," cried Rake, vehemently.' Ob. Prob. ex S.E. *stow*, 'to place in a receptacle to be stored or kept in reserve'. cf. STASH, and:

***stow faking!; stow it!** Stop doing that!, gen. as a warning in the underworld: c.: resp. ca 1810–1900; C.19–20, ob. See STOW. cf.:

***stow magging and manging!** Be silent!; lit., stop talking!: c. of resp. ca 1810–80, ca 1820–80. See MAG, v., and MANG. Bee, 1823, has the variant *stowmarket!*

straddle, v.i. 'In Sports and Gaming, to play who shall pay the Reckoning', Dyche & Pardon, 1735; †by 1820.

straemash is a mainly dial. variant of STRAMASH.

stragger. A stranger: Oxford University undergraduates': late C.19–20. By 'the Oxford *-er*'.

straggling money. A sailor who overstays his furlough: nautical from ca 1800. Because he has money left.

straight, n. See the adj. and *in the* STRAIGHT.

straight, adj. (Of an utterance) outspoken; (of a statement) unreserved, certain: coll (—1887). Hence, *straight talk*, (a piece of) plain speaking: 1900. 2. Of persons or their conduct: honest, honourable; frank: coll: 1864 (O.E.D.). In C.16–mid-17, this sense was S.E., but 'the present use . . . is unconnected.' 3. Hence, (of any person) steady, (of a woman) chaste: coll: 1868, Lindsay Gordon, *keep* (one) *straight*, the chief usage. 4. (Of accounts) settled: coll: C.17–20. 5. See STRAIGHT FACE. 6. (Of spirits) undiluted, neat: Canadian coll: adopted, ca 1880, ex U.S.

straight! Honestly!; it's a fact!: low coll: 1890, Albert Chevalier; 1897, 'Pomes' Marshall, ' "If that isn't a good 'un," the bookie cried, "I'll forfeit a fiver, straight." '

straight, in the. A rare form of *straight, on the*, behaving reputably or like a good citizen: from late 1890s. Edgar Wallace, 1900, 'O the garden it is lovely – That's when Jerry's in the straight!' Ex lit. sense, along a straight line. 2. Near the end: racing coll > gen. (–1903). Ex coming up the straight of a racecourse and making a final effort.

straight, on the, see STRAIGHT, IN THE.

straight, out of the. Dishonest; illicit, illegal: late C.19–20.

straight arm, see MAKE A STRAIGHT ARM.

straight as a dog's hind leg. Crooked: jocular coll: late C.19–20. cf. Swift's 'Straight! Ay, straight as my leg, and that's crooked at knee.' Contrast:

straight as a loon's leg. Absolutely straight: nautical coll: late C.19–20.

straight as a pound of candles. Very straight: coll: 1748, Smollett, 'My hair hung down . . . as . . . straight as a pound of candles'; ob. cf. the (C.19) Cheshire *straight as a yard of pump water*, applied to a tall, thin man, and Ray's (C.17–18) *straight as the backbone of a herring*, which may have been coll before being proverbial S.E. 2. Hence, very honest: coll: C.19–20; extremely ob.

straight drinking. Drinking without sitting down – bar-drinking: London taverns': ca 1860–1905.

straight face; also **keep one's face straight.** (To do) this as a restraint from laughing: coll: 1897, *Spectator*, 25 Sept., 'An expressive vulgarism . . . "with a straight face".'

straight from the bog. A c.p. applied, in late C.19–20, to a crude Irishman.

straight from the horse's mouth. (Of information, news, etc.) genuine, authentic, correct: sporting s. (since ca 1830) >, by 1900, coll.

straight-hair. A convict: West Australian: ca 1840–70. 2. A West Australian: since ca 1870.

straight hooks. A butchers' joke, e.g., on April the First: from ca 1860.

***straight line, get on the.** To get on the right scent or track: c. (—1887).

***straight racket, on the.** Living honestly: c.: from ca 1885; ob.

straight tip, see TIP, STRAIGHT.

straight up and down the mast. (Of weather) calm: Irish nautical (—1909).

straighten up, v.i. To become honest or honourable: s. (ca 1906). Ex lit. sense, to assume an upright posture.

***Straights (occ. Streights), the.** Jonson, 1614: †by 1700: prob. c. Perhaps ex *straight*, adj., or *straits*, n. Gifford, 1816, 'These Streights consisted of a nest of obscure courts, alleys, and avenues, running between the bottom of St Martin's Lane, Half Moon, and Chandos Street'; they were 'frequented by bullies, knights of the post, and fencing masters'. cf. BERMUDAS.

strain hard. To tell a great or hearty lie: coll: late C.17–18.

strain one's taters. To make water: low: from ca 1880; ob. Ex the colour in which potatoes have been washed or strained.

***stram, the.** (Harlots') street-walking: c. >, ca 1900, low s.; ob.: 1887, Henley, 'You judes that clobber for the stram'. ?ex U.S. *stram*, to walk some distance (1869), influenced by STRUM, v., or *strumpet*.

stramash; also **straemash,** very rare outside of dial. A disturbance; a rough-and-tumble: dial. (—1821) >, ca 1835, coll. Barham, ca 1840, former sense; Henry Kingsley, 1855, 'I and three other . . . men . . . had a noble stramash on Folly Bridge. That is the last fighting I have seen.' Ex Northern and Scottish *stramash*, to break, crush, destroy, itself perhaps ex *stour* (a disturbance) + *smash*.

stram(m)el, see STAMMEL and STROMMEL.

strammer. Anything exceptional, esp. in size or intensity; this and *stramming*, huge, great, are dial. >, ca 1850, coll. Ex dial. *stram*, to bang or strike: it is therefore one of the numerous percussive intensives.

strange. Crazy; silly; stupid: Australian coll: late C.19–20.

stranger. A guinea: low (—1785). Ex rarity. 2. A sovereign: from ca 1830: low.

strangle-goose. A poulterer: ca 1780–1900.

strap. A barber: mid-C.19–20. Ex †*strap*, a strop, + (Hugh) *Strap*, a barber in Smollett's *Roderick Random*, 1748. 2. Credit: dial. (—1828) >, ca 1880, s. Esp. *on strap*, occ. *on the strap*. Slightly ob.

***strap,** v.i. To lie with a woman, esp. as vbl n. *strapping*: c.: late C.17–19. Prob. ex *strapping* (*wench, youth*, etc.). 2. To work, esp. if energetically, v.t., with *at*: from ca 1810; ob. Also with *away* (1849), and *to* (both v.i. and v.t.: mid-C.19–20). 3. v.t., to allow credit for (goods): dial. (—1862) >, ca 1890, s. Ex the n., 2.

strap-'em, oil of; strap-oil. Often preceded by *a dose of*. A thrashing with a strap: C. 19–20. Halliwell, 1847, 'It is a common joke on April 1st to send a lad for a pennyworth of strap-oil, which is generally ministered on his own person.' On STIRRUP-OIL.

strap(-)hanger. A passenger compelled, or occ. choosing, to hold on to a strap in omnibus, train, etc.: from ca 1904: s. *Punch*, 8 Nov. 1905.

strap-oil, see STRAP 'EM.

strapper. A very energetic or an unremitting worker: 1851, Mayhew, 'They are all picked men ... regular "strappers", and no mistake.' Ex STRAP, v., 2. 2. Penniless: English and Canadian: late C. 19–20. Probably ex rural *strap*, to strip (a cow), hence to draw (anything) dry, hence (London) to work to the limit.

***strapping,** vbl n. Lying with a woman: c.: late C.17–19.

straps. Sprats: a modified rhyming (or, perhaps, back) s. that is low urban (—1909).

straw, v.i. To do as in STRAWER, 1: London: mid-C.19–20; ob.

straw, one's eyes draw. Grose's variation of STRAWS, DRAW; *straw* is rare.

straw, pad in the, see PAD IN THE STRAW.

straw and t'other serves the thatcher, one eye draws. He (she, etc.) is half asleep: coll: late C.18–mid-19. An elaboration of STRAWS, DRAW.

straw-chipper. A barber: low: ca 1820–50. Moncrieff, 1823. cf. NOB-THATCHER.

straw-hat. A Billingsgate fishwife: s.: Ned Ward, 1703.

Straw House. The Sailors' Home, Dock Street, London: nautical: mid-C.19–20. Bowen, 1929, mentions that 'a century ago seamen were [there] given a sack of straw for their bed.'

straw-yard, see STRAWYARDS.

strawberry. A BRANDY-BLOSSOM or liquor-caused face-pimple: low (—1887).

strawer. London s. > coll (now almost †) of mid-C.19–20, as in Mayhew, 1851, 'The strawer offers to sell any passer by ... a straw and to give to the purchaser a paper which he dares not sell ... political, libellous, irreligious, or indecent.' Ex STRAW, V. 2. A straw hat: schools'. cf. STRAWYARD, 2.

strawing, vbl n., see STRAWER, 1.

straws, draw, gather, or **pick.** (Of the eyes, not the person) to show signs of sleep: late C.17–20 (ob.): coll >, by 1850, S.E. Motteux (*draw*), Swift (*draw*), Grose (*draw straw*), Wolcot (*pick*), J. Wilson (*gather*). Both *gather* and *pick* are virtually †. cf. STRAW AND...

strawyard. See STRAWYARDS. 2. A (man's) straw hat: coll: late C.19–20; ob.

strawyard bull, like a. A jocose reply (often amplified by *full of fuck and half starved*) to 'How do you feel?' or 'How are you?': low c.p.: from ca 1870; ob.

strawyarder. A longshoreman acting as a sailor: nautical: mid-C.19–20; slightly ob. 2. Esp. (—1903), a SCAB on shipboard duty during a strike.

strawyards, the. Night shelters (refuges, homes) for the destitute: the London poor: mid-C.19–20; ob. Mayhew, 1851.

streak; occ. **streek.** To go very fast: 1768, 'Helenore' Ross, '[She] forward on did streak.' Gen. *streak off* (*like greased lightning*: 1843, Carleton); occ. *streak away*, as in *Field*, 25 Sept. 1886. s. >, in late C.19, coll. Prob. ex flashes of lightning. The form *to streak it* is U.S.

streak, like a. With exceeding swiftness: late C.19–20. i.e. like a streak of lightning.

streak away, see STREAK.

streak down. To slip or slide down; to descend: s. (—1889): app. mostly South African. cf. STREAK, V.

streak of lightning. A glass, gen. of gin, occ. of other potent spirit: mid-C.19–20; very ob. Ex its sudden effect.

streak of misery. A tall, thin, miserable-looking person: coll: late C.19–20.

streaky. Bad-tempered, irritated; irritable: from late 1850s; ob. H., 2nd ed. Perhaps suggested by U.S. *streaked*, disconcerted, annoyed (1834: Thornton). 2. Changeable; variable: coll: 1898, Bartram (of courage, weather): 1899, A. C. Benson (of additions to a building).

stream, the. The fairway: an anchorage: nautical coll: late C.19–20.

Stream's Town; or **s.t.** The female pudend: low: ca 1820–90.

streek, see STREAK, V.

street, down or **up.** Towards or in the lower or the upper end of the street: low: coll: 1876, Miss Braddon.

Street, Grub, see GRUB STREET. **street, key of the,** see KEY. **street, man in the,** see MAN IN THE STREET.

street, not in the same (constructed with **be** and either **as** or **with**). (To be) far behind (lit. or fig.); much inferior to: s. >, ca 1910, coll: 1883, Mrs Kennard, comparing two race-horses.

street, not the length of a. A small interval: s. (1893, O.E.D.) that, like preceding entry, was orig. sporting; cf. STREETS AHEAD.

Street, Queer, see QUEER STREET.

street, up one's. What one can do well, what one knows all about: coll: late C.19–20.

***street-chanting.** The practice of singing in the streets for a living: c. (—1887).

***street-ganger.** A beggar: c.: late C.19–early 20.

street-knocker, grin like a. To *grin like a* CHESHIRE CAT: coll: from the 1830s. Prob. ex its brightness.

street-pitcher. A vendor or a mendicant taking a station (or PITCH) in the street: from late 1850s; slightly ob. H., 1st ed., who adds the specific sense (†by 1890) of the 'orator' advertising various activities (e.g. ballad-singing) and, where relevant, selling illustrative broadsheets or booklets.

street-yarn, spin. To walk about idly, gossiping from house to house: coll: mid-C.19–20; U.S., anglicized ca 1870; ob. cf. YARN.

street-yelp. A c.p. of the streets: lower classes': 1884; ob.

streets, be in the. A lower classes' coll variation (—1887) of *walk the streets*, to be a prostitute.

streets ahead (of) or **better (than), be.** To be far ahead (of) in a race: from ca 1895. 2. Hence, to be much superior (to): 1898 (O.E.D.). Both s.

Streights, the, see STRAIGHTS.

***stretch.** A yard (length): c. (—1811). Vaux, 'Five ... stretch signifies five ... yards.' 2. A year's imprisonment, esp. with hard labour: c.: from ca 1810. Vaux; Haggart, Horsley, Edgar Wallace. Ex sense 1 + *a long stretch*. Thus *one, two, three* (*four*, etc.) *stretch* = two (etc.) years' imprisonment, as in Haggart, 1821, and J. Greenwood, 1888. See also QUARTER STRETCH.

stretch, gen. v.i.; occ., in late C.19–20, *stretch it*. To exaggerate; tell lies: coll: from ca 1670. D'Urfey, Grose. cf. STRAIN HARD.

stretch leather, v., see LEATHER, n., 2, and cf. LEATHER-STRETCHER.

stretch off the land, a. A short sleep: nautical: late C.19–20. Ex a ship lying at anchor near land.

stretch one's legs according to the coverlet. To adapt oneself to (esp. one's financial) circumstances: late C.17–18: coll >, by 1750, S.E. Bailey, 1736. Ex the very old proverb, *whoso stretcheth his foot beyond the blanket shall stretch it in the straw*.

stretched, has had his breeches. (The boy) has received a thrashing: lower-class coll: mid-C.19–20.

stretched of one's mess, see MESS, LOSE THE NUMBER OF ONE'S.

stretcher. A university-*extension* student: university: late C.19–20; ob. 2. A layer-out of corpses: Anglo-Irish coll: late C.19–20. 3. A large *membrum virile*: low coll: 1749, John Cleland.

stretcher-fencer. A vendor of trouser-braces: low: mid-C.19–20. Ex:

stretchers. Trouser-braces: low: mid-C. 19–20. cf. preceding entry.

stretching. Helping oneself at table without the help of servants: coll: from ca 1895.

stretching-bee, -match. A hanging: low: resp. ca 1820–80 and ca 1820–1910.

stretchy. Stretchable, elastic: coll: 1854. 2. Hence, too easily stretched, too elastic: coll: from mid-1880s. 3. Inclined to stretch one's limbs or to stretch and yawn; sleepy: coll: from ca 1870. cf. the C.17 proverb, *stretching and yawning leadeth to bed*.

'Strewth! God's truth!: low coll when not deliberately jocular: 1892, Kipling, ''Strewth! but I socked it them 'ard.' Often pronounced drawlingly: *ster-ruth*.

strict Q.T., on the, see Q.T.

***stride-wide.** Ale: c.: ca 1570–1620. Harrison's *Description of England*, 1577.

strides. Trousers: theatrical (—1890). In which one strides; cf. STRIDE in C.19 tailoring j.

***strike.** A sovereign (coin) or its equivalent: c.: from ca 1700. 2. A *stike* or *stick*, a measure of quantity in small eels: incorrect: from ca 1670. 3. In curses: mid-C.19–20 coll. 4. A watch: c. (—1909). On the *lucus a non lucendo* principle.

***strike,** v.t. and v.i. To steal; to rob: c. of ca 1565–1750. Harman, Greene, B.E. 2. Hence, v.i., to borrow money: c.: C.17–early 19 (perhaps until late C.19). Mynshul, 1618. Esp. as vbl n., *striking*. 3. Hence, v.t. and v.i., to ask (a person) suddenly and/or pressingly *for* (a loan, etc.): low: mid-C.18–20; slightly ob. Fielding, 1751, '. . . Who in the vulgar language, had struck, or taken him in for a guinea'. cf. STING, v., 2. 4. v.i., to beg (also *strike it*): (low) Australian: from late 1890s; slightly ob. as *strike*. 5. Semantically ex sense 1: to open, as in *strike a* JIGGER, to pick a lock, to break open a door: c. (—1857). 6. As in Baumann's 'How warm you strike in here!', the connotation is a timely and most welcome arrival: lower classes' coll (—1887).

strike, make a. To be successful; lucky: coll: from ca 1860. Ex *strike*, the horizontal course of a stratum (of gold, etc.).

strike a bright. To have a bright idea: tailors' and lower classes' (—1909); ob. 2. To have a piece of good fortune: proletarian: from ca 1880; ob.

***strike a hand.** (Of a thief) to be successful on a given occasion: c.: late C.16–early 17. Greene, 1592. cf. STRIKE, v., 1.

***strike a jigger,** see STRIKE, v., 5.

strike a light. To run up a tavern score: see LIGHT. 2. *strike a light!* A mild expletive: coll: from ca 1880. cf. STRIKE ME BLIND!

strike all of a heap, see HEAP, STRIKE . . .

strike-fire. Gin: 1725, G. Smith on distilling.

strike-me-blind. Rice: nautical (—1890); slightly ob. Bowen, 'From the old superstition that its eating affected the eyesight'.

strike me blind! A (gen. proletarian) expletive: coll: 1704, Cibber. Also *strike me dumb!* (1696, Vanbrugh; †by 1890); . . . LUCKY! (1849, Cupples); . . . *silly!* (—1860; very ob.); . . . *pink!*, mid-C.19–20; and *strike me!*, late C.19–20. These imprecations may be constructed with *if* or *but*. cf. STRIKE A LIGHT, 2, and the Australian *strike me up a gum-tree!* (from ca 1870).

strike-me-dead. Small beer: naval: from early 1820s; ob. cf. STRIKE-FIRE. 2. Bread: military rhyming s.: from ca 1899.

strike me lucky! – pink! – silly! – up a gum-tree! see STRIKE ME BLIND! For the first, see also LUCKY!, STRIKE ME.

strike oil, see OIL, STRIKE.

strike one's breath or **spit one's death** = to 'cross one's heart' in assurance of one's truthfulness, 'often with the gesture of licking one's thumb and drawing it across one's throat: Australian coll: late C.19–20.

strike – or give me the bill! Mind what you're about: coll: ca 1660–1750. Walker, 1672. Ex injunction to man clumsy with this weapon.

***striking,** vbl n., see STRIKE, v., 1 and 2.

strill. A lie with intent to cheat: North Country c. (—1864); ob. Origin? 2. A piano: Parlary: late C.19–20. Hence, *strill* OMEE or *strill* POLONE, a pianist male or female. It app. derives ex Italian *strillo*, a shrill cry, a piercing note, etc.: cf. Italian *strillare*, to shriek, to scream.

string. A subject argued out; an argument (or logical résumé); a commodious set of syllogisms: Oxford University: C.18. Amherst, 1721; the O.E.D. records it also at 1780. Rarely in singular. Ex *string*, a continuous series. 2. A HOAX; a discredited story: printers': from ca 1890. Prob. ex STRING, ON A.

string, v., see STRING ON.

string, brother of the, see BROTHER . . .

string, feel like going to heaven in a. To feel utterly and confusedly happy: coll: C. (?18–19). Lit., so happy that one would willingly die a martyr; in late C.16–18, *go to heaven in a string* (applied orig. to Jesuits hanged *temp*. Elizabeth) meant, simply, to be hanged, as in Greene and Ned Ward.

string, go to heaven in a, see preceding entry.

string, on a. Esp. *have* or *have got* (one) *on a string*, to HOAX, befool: coll: from ca 1810. 'Pomes' Marshall, 'You can't kid me . . . they've been having you on a string.' Ex *lead in*, or *have in* or *on*, *a string*, to have completely under control. cf. STRING ON. 2. Hence, *have* (or *keep*) *on a string*, to keep a person in suspense for a long time: coll: late C.19–20. 3. *get* (one) *on a string* or *line*. See LINE, GET INTO.

string on. To befool, to 'lead up the garden path', as, e.g. 'You can't string *him* on!': from ca 1810. (Whence U.S. *string*, to HUMBUG.)

stringer. A ball difficult to play: cricket: from ca 1890. Perhaps ex STRING ON. 2. In pl, handcuffs: 1893, Kipling.

strings on, put the. To hold (a horse) back in a race, to ROPE him: turf: ca 1860–1900. *Fraser's Magazine*, Dec. 1863.

stringy-bark. Australian as in A. J. Vogan, *Black Police*, 1890, 'Stringy-bark, a curious combination of fuisl [*sic*] oil and turpentine, labelled "whisky"'. Ex the: 2. adj. Rough or uncultured; also (and orig.) rustic, belonging to the bush: Australian coll >, ca 1900. S.E. (slightly ob.): 1833, *New South Wales Magazine*, 1 Oct., concerning inferior workmanship, 'I am but, to use a colonial expression, "a stringy-bark carpenter".'

***strip.** To rob (a house or a person); esp. to steal everything in (a house); to swindle (a person) out of his money: late C.17–mid-18: c. B.E., whose phrases are of the '*strip the ken*, to gut the house' order, i.e. with direct object and no further construction. Ex *strip . . . of*, to plunder . . . of.

strip a peg. To buy ready-made, or second-hand clothes: 1908; slightly ob.

strip-bush. A fellow who steals clothes put out to dry after washing: either c. or low s. (—1864); ob.

strip-eel. A fishmonger: s.: Ned Ward, 1700.

strip-me-naked. Gin: from ca 1750. Toldervy, 1756. cf. STARK-NAKED.

strip (someone's) **masthead.** To thrash: nautical: ca 1760–1840. *Sessions*, 1786 (8th session).

stripes; old s. or **O.S.** A tiger: jocular coll: resp. 1909, 1885. 2. (Also *stripey.*) A sergeant of Marines: naval, esp. as a nickname: late C.19–20. Ex his badge of office.

stripped. (Of spirits) unadulterated, neat: mid-C.19–20; ob.

strippers. 'High cards cut wedge-shape, a little wider than the rest, so as to be easily drawn in a crooked game', F. & H.: gaming coll: from mid-1880s. See esp. Maskelyne, *Sharps and Flats*, 1894. Ex the manner of stacking, with a pun on impoverishment.

***stripping law.** The (jailers') art and/or practice of fleecing prisoners: c.: late C.16–early 17. Greene. cf. LAY, n., 2.

strive. To write with care: Christ's Hospital: from ca 1870. Ex L. *scribere*, to write, via *to* SCRIVE, on *strive*, to try very hard.

strode a pot, as good as ever, see PISSED, AS GOOD . . .

stroke, take a. (Of the male) to coït: low coll (—1785); ob.

***strolling mort.** A pretended-widow beggar roaming the country (often with a RUFFLER), making laces, tape, etc., and stealing as chance favours her: c. (—1673); †by 1830. In C.17, often *strowling m.*

***strommel** (ca 1565–1840); also **strummel** (C.16–19), very common; **stramel** (C.18) and **strammel** (C.18–19); **strommell** (C.17–18) and **stromell** (C.17); and **strumil** (C.18, rare). Straw: c. of ca 1565–1830. Harman, B.E., Grose (1st ed.), Scott. Perhaps via Anglo-Fr. ex Old Fr. *estramer*: cf. *stramage*, rushes strewn on a floor. 2. Hence, hair (prob. orig. of straw-coloured hair): c. (—1725); †by 1850, except in Norfolk. Ainsworth, 'With my strummel faked in the newest twig', done in the newest fashion. cf. STRUM, n., 1, and:

***strommel-** or **strummel-faker.** A barber: c. of ca 1810–40. Ex STROMMEL, 2.

***strommel-** or **strummel-patch.** A very contemptuous epithet for a person: late C. 16–early 17 c. Jonson, 1599, 'The horson strummell patch'. Ex STROMMEL, 1.

strong. (Of a charge or payment) heavy: coll: 1669; ob.

strong, be going. To be vigorous or prosperous: coll: 1898, *Punch*, 22 Oct., 'And though, just now, we're going strong, | The brandy cannot last for long.' Ex horse-racing.

strong, come it. See COME IT STRONG; cf. *go it* STRONG.

strong, come out. To speak or act vigorously or impressively; to 'launch out': coll: 1844, Dickens. cf. *be going* STRONG and:

strong, go it. To act recklessly or energetically: coll: from ca 1840. cf.:

strong, pitch it. To exaggerate; tell a TALL story: coll: 1841, Hood.

strong man, play the part of the. To be whipped at the cart's tail: low: ca 1780–1840. Grose, 1st ed., 'i.e. to push the cart and horses too'.

strong on. Laying great stress on: coll: 1883, 'Strong on the proprieties'.

strong on, go. To uphold or advocate energetically and/or emphatically: coll: 1844, Disraeli, '"We go strong on the Church?" said Mr Taper.'

strowling mort, see STROLLING MORT.

struck. Bewitched: dial. and coll: 1839, J. Keegan. In composition, *struck with*. cf. STRUCK SO.

struck comical, be. To be very astonished: low coll (—1828). cf. STRUCK.

struck on. (Low) coll form of *struck with*, charmed by (orig. a person – of the opposite – gen. female – sex): from early 1890s.

struck so. Struck motionless in a particular posture or grimace: from ca 1850: low coll. Mayhew. Ex STRUCK, bewitched.

struck with, see STRUCK.

strue. To con*strue* or translate: schools' coll: late C.19–20. 2. Hence, a 'construe': Shrewsbury School coll: from ca 1890.

struggle and strain. A train: rhyming s.: late C.19–20.

struggle-for-lifer. A struggler for life: s. or coll (—1895). Ex biological *struggle for life*, though imm. ex Daudet's *struggle-for-lifeur* (1889). 2. Hence, one who, thus struggling, is none too scrupulous in seeking success: 1899; ob.

struggle with, I (etc.) **could.** I could do with, I'd gladly take (e.g. a drink): lower classes' coll (—1887); ob.

***strum.** A wig: late C.17–early 19. Ex STROMMEL. A RUM STRUM is a long one. 2. A *strum*pet; a wench (if RUM, then handsome): c.: late C.17–early 19. 3. See STRAM.

strum, v.i. and v.t. To have intercourse (with a woman): low: from ca 1780; ob. Semantically, to play a rough tune (on her). Possibly suggested by a pun on the n., 2.

***strummel, s.-faker, s.-patch,** see STROMMEL, etc.

strunt. The male member: C.17. Middleton, in *Epigrams and Satyres*, 1608. Ex S.E. and dial. *strunt*, the fleshy part of an animal's tail.

strut like a crow in a gutter, see CROW IN A GUTTER.

'Struth! 'An emaciated oath', C. J. Dennis: low: late C.19–20. (*God's truth!*) Also 'STREWTH.

stub (or stubb). See STUBBS. 2. 'The lower part of a rainbow' (Bowen): nautical coll: mid-C.19–20; ob. An extension of the S.E. sense.

stub, v. To kick (a football) about: Felsted: late C.19–20. Ex *stub one's toe*.

stub-faced. Pitted with small-pox: late C.18–19. Grose, 2nd ed., where is the phrase *the devil run over his face with horse stubs* (horseshoe nails) *in his shoes*.

stubb, see STUB, n.

stubble. The female pubic hair: low: C.18–20. Whence, *shoot over the stubble* (or *in the bush*), to ejaculate before intromission, and *take a turn in the stubble*, to coït (both, C.19–20).

***stubble it!; stubble your whids!** Hold your tongue: c.: resp. late C.17–19 (B.E. and Lytton) and ca 1810–50 (Lytton). Prob. ex *stubble*, v.t., to clear of stubble.

Stubbs, put (a person) **through.** To inquire from a financial agency whether a person's credit is good: commercial coll: late C.19–20. The firm of Stubbs was founded in 1836.

***stubbs.** Nothing: c. of ca 1810–1900. Ex *stub*, the end (of, e.g., a cigar).

stubs in his shoes, see STUB-FACED.

stuck. See FLY-STUCK. 2. Adversely affected; left in an unenviable position; penniless; grossly deceived; utterly mistaken: from ca 1863. cf. STUCK IN.

stuck, dead. Utterly ruined or flabbergasted; wholly disappointed: low: from ca 1870.

stuck by. Deserted or grossly deceived or imposed on by (esp. one's pal): low: from ca 1880.

stuck for. Lacking; at a loss how to obtain: from ca 1870. Esp. *stuck for the ready*, penniless. cf. STUCK and *dead* STUCK.

stuck in (e.g. one's calculations). Mistaken; also, at a loss concerning: from ca 1870. Prob. an elaboration of STUCK, 2.

stuck in the mud. Cornered, baffled, nonplussed, stalemated: from ca 1880.

stuck on. Enamoured of (gen. a man of a woman): late C.19–20: rare among upper classes. Ex U.S. sense, captivated with (things).

stuck on one's lines. Having forgotten one's speech(es): theatrical coll: mid-C.19–20. Mayhew, III.

stuck pig, see STARE LIKE A DEAD PIG.

stuck-up. Unjustifiably 'superior'; offensively conceited or pretentious: coll: 1829. 2. See STICK UP, v., 8.

stuckuppishness. The n. of STUCK-UP: coll: 1853.

stud book, in the. Of ancient lineage; esp. in Burke or Debrett; upper class: late C. 19–20.

studding-sails on both sides, (with). With a girl on each arm: nautical: late C.19–20; ob.

studify, v.i. To study: illiterate coll: 1775, T. Bridges; †by 1850.

studnsel, stunsail or **-sel.** Nautical coll (—1887) for *studding-sail*.

study. To take care and thought for the convenience, desires, feelings of (a person);

esp. to humour (him): coll: mid-C.19–20. Dickens, 1852; Mrs Carlyle, 1858, 'With no husband to study, housekeeping is mere play'. Ex *study the advantage, convenience, feelings, wishes, of* (a person).

study up, v.t. To study for a special purpose: coll: from ca 1890.

stuff. Medicine: C.17–20: S.E. until mid-C.18, then coll. Moore, 1819, 'It isn't the stuff, but the patient that's shaken.' Also (ob. by 1890) *doctor's stuff*, recorded in 1779 (O.E.D.). Ex *stuff*, 'matter of an unspecified kind'. 2. Money, esp. cash: adumbrated by Bridges, 1772; definite in Sheridan, 1775, 'Has she got the stuff, Mr Fag? Is she rich, hey?'; Nat Gould, 1891. Slightly ob. Perhaps ex *stuff*, household goods, hence personal effects. 3. Whisky, always *the stuff* (Croker, 1825) or *good stuff* (1861, Meredith): coll. Prob. ex sense 1. 4. Stolen goods (*stuff* or *the stuff*): c. and low s.: 1865, *Daily Telegraph*, 5 Nov. 5. ?hence, 'contraband' smuggled into gaol: c.: late C.19–20. Esp. tobacco (—1904). 6. Men as fighting material: coll: 1883, *Manchester Examiner*, 24 Nov., 'The army of Ibrahim included a good deal of tougher stuff than the ordinary fellah of Egypt.' 7. Often employed as a coll (mid-C.19–20) to connote vagueness in the speaker's mind or intention, or to imply ignorance of the precise term or name. 'Does he suspect? Or is this chance and stuff?', R. L. Stevenson, *The Wrong Box*, 1889.

stuff, v.t.; **stuff up.** To HOAX, HUMBUG, befool (cf. CRAM): ?orig. (1844) U.S., in form *stuff up*; English by 1859 as *stuff*. Slightly ob. Prob. ex *stuff* (a person) *with*. 2. Hence, v.i., 'to make believe, to chaff, to tell false stories', H., 1st ed.; ob. by 1890, †by 1900. 3. v.i., to be or to live in a stuffy atmosphere or place; to be inside when one could be in the open air: late C.19–20. 4. (Of man) to copulate with: low: late (?mid-) C.19–20. Ex upholstery. Hence the defiant c.p., *go and get stuffed.*

stuff, – and. And such dull or useless matters: coll: late C.17–20. J. Lewis, ca 1697, 'You pretend to give the Duke notions of the mathematics, and stuff'; 1774, Goldsmith, 'Their Raphaels, Corregios [sic], and stuff'; 1852, Thackeray.

stuff, bit of, see BIT OF STUFF. **stuff, do one's,** see DO ONE'S STUFF. **stuff, good,** see STUFF, n., 3. **stuff, hot,** see HOT STUFF. **stuff, know one's,** see DO ONE'S STUFF.

stuff on the ball, put. To make the ball break: cricketers': ca 1880–1905. For *stuff* we now say *work* and for *put* we prefer *get*: S.E.

stuffed monkey. 'A very pleasant close almond biscuit': Jews' coll, mostly London: from ca 1890. Zangwill.

stuffing out of. See KNOCK THE BOTTOM ... But there are variants: *beat* ... (1887, very ob.) and *take* ... (1906, Lucas Malet): coll.

stuffy. Angry, irritable; sulky; obstinate, 'difficult': U.S., anglicized ca 1895 as a coll; authorized by Kipling, 1898 (*get stuffy*).

stug. Guts: back s.: late C.19–20.

stugging. The rolling motion of a ship that is stranded: nautical coll: mid-C.19–20. Cognate with *stog*, to walk heavily.

stuling-ken, see STALLING-KEN.

stumble, see TRUCKLE-BED.

stumer; occ., in C.20, **stumor;** rarely **stumour.** 'A horse against which money may be laid without risk', H., 5th ed., where spelt *shtumer*; racing s.: from ca 1873. This sense and this spelling were both ob. by 1904. In Glasgow sporting s., however, it is still applied to a horse that is losing. The word perhaps derives from Yiddish; but? cf. Swedish *stum*, dumb or mute. 2. Hence, a forged cheque or a worthless one (an 'R.D.'): 1890, *Blackwood's* (*stumer*). 3. Hence, or direct ex sense 1, a counterfeit banknote or a base coin: 1897, 'Pomes' Marshall (see quotation in next sense). 4. Hence (often as adj.), a sham; anything bogus or worthless: 1897, 'Pomes' Marshall, in a poem entitled *The Merry Stumer*, 'Stumer tricks ... stumer stake ... stumer note ... stumer cheque'.

stump. A leg: S.E. except in the pl, when (in C.19–20, at least) coll, esp. in *stir one's stumps*, to walk or dance briskly: C.17–mid-18, *bestir* ..., as in Jonson and B.E.; mid-C.17–20, *stir* ..., as in Anon., *Two Lancashire Lovers*, 1640; 1774, Bridges, 'Then cease your canting sobs and groans, And stir your stumps to save your bones'; 1809, Malkin; 1837, Lytton. 2. Money: low s.: ca 1820–50. Ex *stump*, a small piece. cf. STUMPY.

stump, v. To walk: from late 1850s. Gen. *stump it*, which in Lytton, 1841, means to decamp, a sense very ob and rare. Ex *stump*, to walk clumsily. 2. To beggar, ruin: dial. (—1828) >, by 1830, s. Esp. in passive, to be penniless, as in *Sessions*, Nov. 1834, and 'Pomes' Marshall, 1897,

'In the annals of the absolutely stumped'. Ex *stump*, to truncate, or perhaps (H., 1860) ex cricket. 3. See STUMP UP.

stump, pay on the. To disburse readily and/or promptly: coll: late C.19–20.

stump it, see STUMP, v., 1.

stump up, v.t. To pay down, disburse: 1821, Egan (see quotation at RUBBISH); 1881, Blackmore. Rare. Ex *stump up*, to dig up by the roots. cf. PLANK, v., 3. 2. Hence, v.i., to pay up; to disburse money, FORK OUT: 1835, Dickens, 'Why don't you ask your old governor to stump up?' 3. To exhaust (a horse) by strain: 1875, Reynardson: coll >, by 1900, S.E.

stumped, adj., see STUMP, v., 2.

stumper. Small cricket: Tonbridge School (—1904). At Harrow, *stumps*: coll. Ex *stump-cricket*.

stumps, see STUMP, n., 1. 2. See STUMPER. 3. *it's* (a case of) *stumps with* (*us*). (We) are lost, ruined: low (—1887), Ex STUMP, v. 2.

stumpy. Money: low: 1821, Moncrieff; 1835, Dickens. Ob. Ex STUMP, n., 2, which was perhaps suggested by *short of* BLUNT (money). 2. A stumpy person; gen. as nickname: coll and dial.: mid-C.19–20. Ex adj. 3. Whence, a Thames sailing barge without a topmast: nautical coll: from ca 1870.

stun. Nuts: back s. (—1859). See SRETSIO; cf. STUNLAW(S). 2. Stone (weight): sol. or, at best, low coll (—1887). cf. PUN, 2.

***stun,** v. To cheat, swindle, as in *stun out of the* REGULARS, to defraud or deprive (a man) of his rightful share of booty: c.: late C.19–20; ob. Ex lit. sense of *stun* and perhaps influenced by STING, v., 1.

stung, be, see STING.

stunlaw(s). Walnuts: back s. (—1859).

***stunned on skilly, be.** To be sent to prison and compelled to eat skilly: c. (—1859); †by 1900. cf. STUN, v.

stunner. An exceedingly attractive woman (Albert Smith, 1848) or thing (1848, Thackeray, of the performance of a play); a person excellent *at* doing something (Thackeray, 1855, of a cook) or a thing excellent in quality or remarkable in size (from ca 1875): coll. cf. STUNNING.

stunners on, put the. To astonish; confound: low (—1859). Ex STUNNER.

stunning. Excellent, first-rate; delightful; extremely attractive or handsome: coll: 1849, Dickens (of ale); 1851, Mayhew (of a ring); of a girl, from not later than 1856, F. E. Paget, 'The most stunning girl I ever set my eyes on'. Ex *stun*, to astound; cf. STUNNER and STUNNERS ON. cf. Fr. *épatant*, an exact semantic parallel. 2. Hence, clever, knowing: low coll (—1857); †by 1900.

stunning, adv. Exceedingly: coll: 1845, in 'The Stunning Meat Pie', in Labern's *Comic Songs*, was the line 'A stunning great meat pie'. See the adj.

stunning Joe Banks. 'Stunning' *par excellence*: low London: ca 1850–80. Ex STUNNING + Joe Banks, a noted public-house keeper and FENCE (fl. 1830–50), who, despite the lowness of his customers, was notoriously fair in his dealings with them.

stunningly. The adv. of STUNNING: coll: mid-C.19–20.

stunsail, stunsel, see STUDNSEL.

stunt. An item in an entertainment: coll: 1901, *Westminster Gazette*, 31 Jan., 'There will be many new "stunts" of a vaudeville nature.' Ob. Ex U.S. *stunt*, an athletic performance, any (daring) feat, 1895, itself perhaps ex Ger. *stunde*, an hour or, more prob., ex Dutch *stond*, a lesson. 2. Hence, an enterprise undertaken to gain an advantage or a reputation: coll: it occurs in a letter of 17 Feb. 1878 from Samuel ('Erewhon') Butler to Miss Savage, 'It was a stunt for advertising the books.'

stunt, adj. In the senses of the noun: coll.

stupe. A fool: 1762, Bickerstaffe, 'Was there ever such a poor stupe?'; Blackmore, 1876. Coll >, ca 1900, dial. Ex:

stupid. A stupid person: coll: 1712, Steele; 1860, George Eliot. Ex adj. 2. Bacon: Westmorland and Warwickshire s. (—1904), not dial.

stupid, adj. Very drunk: euphemistic, mostly Anglo-Irish, coll: C.19–20.

***sturaban** or **-bin.** A variant of STURIBEN.

***sturdy beggar.** A beggar who rather demands than asks, esp. – or rather, only – if of the 5th (in C.18, the 50th) Order of beggars: c.: C.16–18. An underworld application of the other world's gen. description.

***sturiben** or **-bin**; occ. **sturaban** or **-bin.** A prison: c.: ca 1855–1925, STIR being the usual C.20 word. A corruption of Romany *stariben* (*steripen*).

***stush.** A variant of STASH.

styx; Styx. A urinal: Leys School (—1904). Ex the gloomy river.

sub. A subordinate: coll: late C.17–20 (slightly ob.), but uncommon before

Herbert Spencer's use of it in 1840. 2. A subaltern (officer): coll: mid-C.18–20. Thackeray, 1862, 'When we were subs together in camp in 1803'. 3. A subject: coll: 1838, Beckett, 'No longer was he heard to sing, | Like loyal subs, "God save the King!"'; very ob. except in U.S. 4. A subscriber: coll: 1838, Hood. Rare and virtually †. 5. A substitute: cricketers' coll: 1864. 6. A subscription: coll (—1904). 7. An advance of money, esp. on wages: coll: 1855. Ex *subsist money* (1835). 8. A sub-lieutenant: naval: coll: late C.19–20; cf. sense 2. 9. All: Anglo-Indian (—1864). cf. SUBCHEESE.

sub, v.i. To pay, or receive, a SUB (n., 7): coll: from early 1870s. 2. From late 1890s, to pay (a workman) SUB. 3. v.i. and v.t., to sub-edit: coll, orig. and mainly journalistic: from ca 1890. 4. v.i., to act as a substitute (*for* somebody): coll: from late 1870s. 5. To subscribe: late C.19–20.

sub, do a. To borrow money: proletarian: from ca 1865; ob. Ex SUB, n., 7.

sub-beau. 'A wou'd-be-fine', B.E.: coll: late C.17–mid-18. Also *demi-beau.*

sub on one's contract. To raise a loan, using contract as a proof of ability to repay: theatrical: late C.19–20. See SUB, v., 1.

subaltern's luncheon. A glass of water and a tightening of one's belt: coll: late C.19–20; ob. cf. SOLDIER'S SUPPER.

subby. A sub-warden: Oxford undergraduates': from ca 1870. 2. A subaltern: military: ca 1860–1910.

subcheese or **sub-cheese.** Everything, all there is, *the whole* SHOOT: Indian Army: Forces in India: mid-C.19–20. Here, *cheese* is probably Hindustani *chiz*, thing: cf. CHEESE, THE.

sublime, when ironical, is coll: late C.19–20. e.g. 'sublime conceit'.

sublime rascal. A lawyer: ca 1820–80.

subsee. Vegetables: Regular Army: late C.19–20. Ex Hindustani.

substance, see SHADOW.

subtle. Drunk: s. (—1650).

subtle as a dead pig. Very ignorant or stupid: coll: ca 1670–1720. Walker, 1672; Robertson, *Phraseologia Generalis*, 1681.

such, adj. An intensive, the criterion being vague and/or ignored: coll: mid-C.16–20. Udall, ca 1553, 'Ye shall not . . . marry . . . Ye are such . . . an ass'; 1900, W. Glyn, '. . . Where we stayed the night at *such* an inn!'

such, as. Accordingly or consequently; thereupon: (rather illiterate) coll: 1721. W. Fowler, 1814, '[She] motioned for me to come to her Highness. As such she addressed me in the most pleasant manner possible.' Ex *as such*, in that capacity.

such a dawg! A theatrical c.p. (1888–ca 1914) applied to a tremendous MASHER.

such a few; such a many. So (very) few; so (very) many: coll: from ca 1840; ob. Thackeray, 1841, 'Such a many things in that time'.

such a reason my goose pissed or **pissed my goose.** A c.p. retort on anyone making an absurd excuse, giving an absurd reason: late C.18–mid-19.

such a thing as . . .!, there is. Look out for —!: a coll threat: late C.19–20. Ex the hint that since this thing exists it must be considered.

***suck.** Strong drink: c.: late C.17–early 19. Hence, RUM *suck*, excellent liquor. Ex *suck*, a small draught or drink. 2. A breast-pocket, says F. & H.; open to doubt. 3. A disappointing or deceptive incident, event, or result: U.S. (1856), anglicized ca 1890. Gen. *suck-in*, orig. U.S.; anglicized ca 1880. Ex SUCK IN, v. 4. A toady: university: from ca 1860; ob. Ex SUCKER. 5. See SUCKS.

suck. The fellator's v. (i. and t.) and occ. n.: low coll: C.19–20.

suck-and-swallow. The *pudendum muliebre*: low: C.19–20. cf. SUCKER, 3.

suck-bottle, -can, -pint, -pot, -spigot. A confirmed drunkard or tippler: coll verging on S.E.: resp. mid-C.17–mid-18 (Brome), C.19, C.17–19 (Cotgrave), C.19–20 (ob.), and late C.16–17.

suck-casa. A public-house: low: mid-C.19–20. Ex SUCK, n., 1 + CASA.

suck-egg. A silly person: dial. (—1851) > s. (—1890).

suck eggs, teach one's grandmother to, see GRANDMOTHER HOW TO . . .

suck-in, n. See SUCK, n., 3. 2. v., to deceive; to cheat: dial. (—1842) >, by 1850, s. (orig. U.S.; re-anglicized, as s., in late C.19). Ex *suck in*, to engulf in a whirlpool.

suck it and see! A derisive c.p. retort current in the 1890s.

suck off. A v. denoting the act of fellation: low coll: C.19–20.

suck one's face. To drink: low coll: late C.17–mid-18.

suck-pint, -pot, -spigot, see SUCK-BOTTLE. **suck the monkey,** see MONKEY SUCK THE.

suck the mop. To be the victim of an omnibus 'nursing' exploit: ca 1870–80. See NURSE, v. 2. 'To wait on the cab-rank for a job': cabmen's (—1889); ob. Ware.

suck the sugar-stick, see SUGAR-BASIN.

suck up to. To insinuate oneself into another's favour; to toady to: schoolboys' s. (—1860). Kipling, 1900, 'That little swine Manders . . . always suckin' up to King'.

sucked that out of his (or her or . . .) fingers, he (etc.) hasn't. He hasn't thought of that by himself – that's not *his* idea – he has authentic (or mysterious) information: c.p., mostly Cockney: late C.19–20.

sucker. A parasite or sponger: U.S. (1856); partly anglicized ca 1890. 2. A GREENHORN; a simpleton: coll: U.S. (1857), partly anglicized ca 1895. 3. The *membrum virile*: low: C.19–20; ?ob. 4. A baby: lower classes' coll: C.19–20. 5. (Gen. pl.) A sweet: dial. (—1823) >, by 1870, coll. cf. SUCKS. 6. A lesbian; fellatrix: low coll: C.19–20.

suckey, see SUCKY.

sucking Nelson. A midshipman: nautical coll: from ca 1820; ob. Lit., immature N.

sucks. Sweetmeats: coll: 1858, T. Hughes. (Lit., things to suck.) Also, collective singular, as in *a knob of suck* (1865). cf. SUCTION, 4.

sucks! An 'expression of derision': Bootham School: also, and from ca 1890, at other schools. Often *sucks to you.*

suckster, suckstress. A fellator, -trix: low coll: C.19–20; ob.

***sucky.** Rather drunk: late C.17–19: c. >, ca 1750, low s. Ex SUCK, n., 1.

suction. The drinking of (strong) liquor; drinking: 1817, Scott. 2. Hence (—1887; nautical, says Baumann), strong drink. 3. The phrases *power of suction*, capacity for BOOZE (Dickens, 1837); *live on suction*, to drink hard (—1904). 4. Sweetmeats: Winchester: late C.19–20. cf. SUCKS.

sudden death. A decision by one throw (not, e.g., by two out of three): 1834, Maginn. 2. A fowl served as a spatch-cock: Anglo-Indian: 1848. 3. A crumpet or a Sally Lunn: university (—1874); ob. 4. Coffee: Cockney: late C.19–20; ob.

suds, in the. In a difficulty; perplexed: from ca 1570: S.E. until C.18, then coll; in C.19–20, s.; very ob. Swift; Grose, 1st ed. 2. Fuddled; slightly drunk: ca 1765–80.

sued up, see SEWED UP.

***suet(t)y Isaac.** Suet pudding: c. (—1904); ob. Also *soapy Isaac*. Ex sallowness.

suff. Enough: New Zealand: from ca 1880. '"I've 'ad suff o' you, Tommy, I'm goin' 'ome"': G. B. Lancaster, *Sons o' Men*, 1904. Short for *sufficient*.

suffer much?, do you. A c.p. of mock pity: late C.19–20; ob.

sufferer. A tailor: low: from ca 1820; ob. ?ex patience. 2. A sovereign (coin): 1848, *Sinks*, †by 1900. cf.:

sufferin(g). A sovereign (coin): Cockney: mid-C.19–20.

suffering cats! An agonized c.p. directed at bad, or very shrill, singing: from ca 1870. Ex caterwauling.

***suffier.** A (seeming) drunkard taking part in VERSING LAW (swindling with false gold): c.: late C.16–early 17. Greene.

Suffolk bang. An inferior, excessively hard cheese: nautical coll: C.19.

Suffolk punch, see PUNCH, n.

Suffolk stiles. Ditches: coll: mid-C.17–early 18. Fuller, 1662. cf. ESSEX STILE.

sugar. Money: low: 1862, *Cornhill Magazine*, Nov., 'We have just touched for a rattling stake of sugar at Brum.' Ex SUGAR AND HONEY. 2. A grocer: lower classes' (—1909).

sugar! A cry of triumph, uttered as one stands upon one leg and shakes the other up and down: ca 1830–70. *Sinks*, 1848. Victory is sweet.

sugar, v.i. To shirk while pretending to row hard: Cambridge University rowing (—1890). 2. To tamper with (food); to fake (accounts); to give a specious appearance of prosperity to: from ca 1890. Prob. suggested by 'cooking' accounts and 'salting' mines (see COOK, SALT).

sugar and honey. Money: rhyming s. (—1859). cf. SUGAR, n.

sugar-baby. A child averse from going outside the house while it's raining: domestic: late C.19–20.

sugar bag. (A nest of) native honey; water sweetened with it: Australian rural coll: late C.19–20.

sugar-basin; sugar-stick. The female, the male, pudend: low: resp., mid-C.19–20; late C.18–20. Ob. Whence *suck the sugar-stick*, sexually to take a man.

sugar candy. Brandy: rhyming s. (—1859); ob.

sugar (for the bird), little bit of. A premium, a bonus; an unexpected benefit or acquisition: low: 1897–ca 1910.

sugar on, be. To be much in love with (a

person): non-aristocratic (—1887). Punning *be* SWEET ON.

sugar-shop. 'A head centre of bribery', electioneering (—1909); ob. Ex SUGAR, n., 1.

sugar-stick, see SUGAR-BASIN.

sugared!, I'm or **I'll be.** *I'm* DAMNED!; it connotes (profound) astonishment or (great) perplexity: from ca 1890. Anon., *Troddles*, 1901. Euphemistic for *buggered.*

suicide. Four horses driven in a line: Society and sporting: ca 1860–1900.

***suit.** 'Game', LAY (n., 2); method, trick; pretence; imposition: c. of ca 1810–50. 2. A watch and seals: c. of ca 1830–90. Ex S.E. *suit*, a complete set.

suit, birthday, see BIRTHDAY SUIT.

***suit, upon the.** In the (specified) manner: see SUIT, 1.

***suit and cloak.** A 'good store of Brandy or any other agreeable Liquor, let down Gutter-lane', B.E.: c.: late C.17–early 19.

suit of mourning. A pair of black eyes: ca 1820–80.

***suite,** see SUIT, 1.

sukey. A kettle: low (—1823); ob. ?origin: cf. Welsh Gypsy *šukar̦*, to hum, to whisper. ?hence, 2, a general servant or SLAVEY: from ca 1820; ob. Ex *Sukey*, a lower-class diminutive of *Susan*, a name frequent among servants. 3. Hence, *sukey-tawdry*, a slatternly woman in fine tawdry: ca 1820–50. 4. Perhaps hence, a simpleton: mid-C.19–20.

Sullivanize (or ise). To defeat thoroughly: sporting: late 1880s–90s. Ex John L. *Sullivan* (1858–1918), that American who dominated the heavy-weights from 1882, when he won fame, until 1892, when Jim Corbett ended his career. In Oct. 1887 he visited England, where he was received by the Prince of Wales and idolized by the crowd. He battered his opponents into unconsciousness, the police often having to interfere.

sulphur. Pungent or lurid talk: 1897: s. Slightly ob. Because sulphurous. cf. sense 2 of:

sultry. Indelicate: 1887, Kipling, 'Sultry stories': s. 2. Hence (of language), lurid: 1891, 'Sultry language', O.E.D.: s. cf. SULPHUR. 3. Uncomfortable, lively, HOT: 1899, Conan Doyle, 'I shall make it pretty sultry for you.'

sum. An arithmetical problem to solve to which one must apply a rule; such a problem solved: coll: C.19–20. Dickens, 1838 has 'Sums in simple interest'.

sum! Adsum!: Public Schools' coll: mid-C.19–20.

sumjao. To warn, correct, coerce: Anglo-Indian coll: 1826. Ex Hindustani.

summat. As 'somewhat', it is low coll (prob. ex the dial. use); as 'something', it is sol.: both, C.19–20.

summer-cabbage. An umbrella, a parasol: fast life: ca 1810–45. 2. A woman: F. & H.; but is this so? If correct, of ca 1850–1900.

summerhead. A sun-umbrella: Anglo-Indian coll: 1797. Corrupted *sombrero.*

sumpsy. An action of *assumpsit*: legal: from ca 1860.

sun, have been in the; have, or **have got, the sun in one's eyes.** To be drunk: resp. 1770 and 1840, Dickens, *have*; *have got* not before ca 1860. Also *have been standing too long in the sun* (1874). cf. SUNSHINE. Ex sun-dazzle or -drowsiness.

sun, taste the, see TASTE THE SUN.

sun-dodger. A heliographer: military: 1900, *Illustrated Bits*, 22 Dec. Via *sun-signalling.*

sun-dog. A mock sun: nautical coll verging on S.E.: from ca 1630.

sun over the foreyard, get the. To drink before noon: nautical (—1904). Bowen defines *sun over the foreyard* as 'the time by which a drink is permissible'; gen. *the sun is over the foreyard.* cf. *have been in the* SUN.

sun shines out of (someone's) **arse(-hole), think.** To regard almost with idolatry: low coll: late C.19–20, for certain; and perhaps since late C.16.

sunburnt. Having many (orig. and esp., male) children: late C.17–early 19. Punning *son.* 2. 'Clapped' (see CLAP, v., 1): ca 1720–1890. Punning BURNED.

Sunday. To spend Sunday (*with* a person): Society coll (—1909); ob.

Sunday, look both or **nine** or **two ways for,** see LOOK NINE . . .

Sunday-afternoon courting-dress. (Of servant-girls) best clothes: lower classes' coll (—1887).

Sunday clothes on, the old man has got his. A low c.p. indicating an *erectio penis.* In allusion to *starched.* From ca 1880.

Sunday face. The posteriors: low: from ca 1860; ob.

Sunday flash togs. (Of men) best clothes: low (—1880).

Sunday girl. A week-end mistress: ca 1890–1915.

Sunday-go-to-meeting clothes and **togs.**

Sunday clothes: resp. coll (C.20) and s. (1894, Baring-Gould). By jocular amplification of *Sunday clothes*. cf. SUNDAY-AFTERNOON COURTING-DRESS.

Sunday man. 'One who goes abroad on that day only, for fear of arrests', Grose, 1st ed.: from ca 1780; ob.: coll >, ca 1850, S.E. 2. A prostitute's bully: low: from ca 1880. Because he walks out with her on that day.

Sunday out(, one's). A domestic servant's monthly or alternate Sunday free: from late 1850s: coll. (Orig. a servants' term.)

Sunday promenader, see ONCE-A-WEEK MAN.

Sunday saint. One who, having been dissolute all the week, turns respectable and sanctimonious on Sunday: coll: from ca 1870. cf. Scottish *Sunday face*.

Sundayfied. Suitable to Sunday; in Sunday clothes: coll: 1899 (O.E.D.).

Sundayish. Rather like, or as on, Sunday: 1797: coll >, by C.20, S.E.

Sundays, see MONTH OF SUNDAYS.

Sundays come together or meet, when two. Never: semi-proverbial coll: from ca 1610; ob. except in dial. but cf. *when two Sundays come in a* WEEK: Haughton, 1616; Ray. cf. Shropshire *the first Sunday in the middle of the week* and *St* TIBB'S EVE.

Sunderland fitter. The Knave of Clubs: jocular North Country coll (—1847). Halliwell.

sundowner. A tramp habitually arriving at a station too late for work but in time to get a night's shelter and a ration: Australian coll >, by 1910, S.E.: 1875, Miss Bird. 2. A drink taken at or about sundown: India, Singapore, the East Indies, Australia: late C.19–20.

sundowning. This practice: Australian coll: from ca 1890. Kinglake.

sunk. Ruined: mid-C.19–20: coll.

sunny bank. A good fire in winter: coll: late C.17–early 19. Ex the warmth, with pun on *banking a fire*.

sunny south. The mouth: rhyming s.: 1887, *Referee*, 7 Nov.

sunshine, have been in the. To be drunk: 1857, George Eliot. As early as 1816 in dial. See SUN, HAVE BEEN IN THE.

sunspottery. The science of solar spots: astronomers' (—1887).

sup(e). A variant of SUPER, n., 1 (H., 1st ed.), 3 (1824, O.E.D.), 4 (—1904, F. & H.), and 6 (—1904, F. & H., esp *supe and* SLANG (n., 8), watch and chain).

super. A supernumerary: 1853, 'Cuthbert Bede': theatrical s. >, ca 1880, coll. 2. A supernumerary on a ship, i.e. a supercargo: nautical s. (1866), >, ca 1890, coll. 3. Ex senses 1 and 2, a supernumerary in gen.: coll: from ca 1880. 4. A superintendent of a station: Australian and New Zealand s.: from ca 1850, >, ca 1900, coll. 5. A police superintendent, esp. in address: coll: mid-C.19–20. 6. (Also *souper*). A watch: c.: from late 1850s. Ware derives it from *soup-plate*, hence SOUPER, hence *super*. cf. SUPER, BANG A; SUPER-SCREWING.

super, v. To be a SUPER, sense 1; often as vbl n., *supering*. 2. See SUPER LIST.

super, adj. Superficial (in measurement; gen. after the n.): trade coll: 1833, T. Hook, 'At so much per foot, super'. 2. Superfine: trade coll: from ca 1840. Bischoff, *Woollen Manufacture*, 1842.

***super, bang a.** To steal a watch by breaking the ring: c.: late C.19–20. See SUPER, n., 6.

super list, be on the. To be marked for supersession (Turley); more gen., *be supered*, to be superseded: at certain Public Schools: from the 1880s. Charles Turley, *Godfrey Marten, Schoolboy*, 1902, '"I have been in Lower Fourth exactly four terms," he went on, "and my people are getting sick, and Sandy says I shall be 'supered' in a term or two."'

***super-screwing.** Watch-stealing: c. (—1859). Ex twisting handles off. See SUPER, n., last sense, and *bang a* SUPER.

supered, be, see SUPER LIST.

supernacular. (Of liquor) excellent: 1848, Thackeray; ob. Ex:

supernaculum. A liquor to be drained to the last drop; excellent liquor; excellent anything: C.17–20; ob. W. King, 1704, 'Their jests were *Supernaculum*': Grose, 1st ed. ('Good liquor'). Ob. Ex the adv. cf. SUPERNACULAR. 2. Hence, a draught that utterly empties cup or glass: 1827, Disraeli. 3. A full glass: mid-C.19–20; like sense 2, ob.

supernaculum, adv.; occ., C.16, **-nagulum, -neg-**, and, C.17, **-nacullum, -nagullum.** To the last drop: late C.16–20; ob. Nashe, 1592, 'Drinking super nagulum, a devise of drinking new come out of France'. Ob. Ex the practice of placing one's upturned glass on the left thumb-nail, to show that not a drop has been left: a mock-L. translation of the Ger. *auf den Nagel (trinken)*. cf. Fr. *boire rubis sur l'ongle*. 2. Often elliptically, as in Cotton, 1664, and fig., as in Jonson, 1598, '[Cupid] plaies super nagulum with my liquor of life.'

supersnagative. First-rate; splendid; excellent: Australians' and New Zealanders': from ca 1890; ob. Perhaps ex *superfine* on SUPERNACULAR, but prob. fanciful on *superlative*.

superstitious pie. A minced or a Christmas pie: a Puritan or Precisian nickname: late C.17–mid-18. Because, by Puritans, made some weeks before Christmas.

***supouch.** An inn-hostess; a landlady: c.: late C.17–18. ?origin, unless ex *sup*, n. + (*to*) *pouch*.

supper, give the old man his; supper, warm the old man's. To confer the act of kind; to sit, skirts raised, before the fire. Low: late C.19–20.

supper, set one his. To perform a feat that another cannot imitate, let alone surpass: coll (—1891).

supple both ends of it. To abate a priapism: low Scots: late C.18–20.

suppose or I suppose. Nose: rhyming s. See I SUPPOSE.

suppose or **supposing**, introductory of a proposal or a suggestion, is coll: resp. 1779 and late C.19–20.

Surat. An adulterated or an inferior article: coll (mostly Lancashire): 1863, *The Times*, 8 May; ob. *Surat* cotton is inferior to American.

sure! Certainly!; with pleasure!; agreed!: coll: early C.18, in England, whence it fled to the U.S. Farquhar, in *The Beaux' Stratagem*, 1707.

sure!, be; I am sure!; you may be sure! At end of sentence, these phrases when asseverative are coll: 1830, N. Wheaton, 'To all my inquiries . . . I only received for answer – "I don't know, I'm sure".'

sure, for. As certain; for certain: indubitably: late C.16–20: S.E. until late C.19, then coll. Stevenson, 1883, 'Desperate blades, for sure'.

sure!, to be. Of course!: mid-C.17–20: S.E. until late C.19, then coll. 2. Often concessively: admitted!; indeed!: coll: mid-C.19–20.

sure!, – well, I'm; well, to be sure! I *am* surprised: coll: 1840, Thackeray, '"Well, I'm sure!" said Becky; and that was all she said'; *well, to be sure!*, app. not before late C.19.

sure and . . ., be. (Only in infinitive or imperative.) To be careful to; not to fail to: coll: from ca 1890. 'Be sure and look!'

sure as . . ., as. Very sure. Of these phrases prob. only those are coll of which the criterion-member or the gen. tone is familiar S.E. or coll. Thus, **(as) sure as the Creed** or **one's creed** is S.E., as is **(as) sure as fate** or **death**; but **(as) sure as a gun** (B. & Fletcher, 1622; Steele, 1703; Meredith, 1859) is coll, as are **sure as eggs** (Bridges, 1772), **sure as eggs is eggs** (Goldsmith), **sure as God made little apples** (late C.19–20; orig. dial.), **sure as the devil is in London** (mid-C.18), and the following in Ray, 1670, **as sure as check**, or **Exchequer pay** (ca 1570–1620), **as sure as a juggler's box** (ca 1650–1740), and **as sure as a louse in bosom** (late C.17–18), or, late C.17–mid-18, **in Pomfret.**

sure I don't know!, I'm. As asseverative tag, it is coll: mid-C.19–20.

surely me. A proletarian variation of *to be* SURE!, sense 1: from ca 1880.

surf. An actor or musician or scene-shifter who combines night-work at the theatre with some daily work outside: theatrical: from late 1850s. ?pun on *serf*. 2. Hence, a parasite, toady, sponger: low (—1887); ob.

surly as a butcher's dog, as. Extremely surly: coll: late C.17–20; ob. Ray: Spurgeon, 1869. Because the animal gets so much meat to eat. Apperson, who gives also the Cheshire *surly as a cow's husband*.

surly boots. A grumpy, morose fellow: coll, verging on S.E.: C.18–20; ob. e.g. Combe, 1812. cf.:

surly chops. A nautical variant of the preceding: coll (—1887).

surtout, see WOODEN SURTOUT.

surveyor of the highway(s). A person reeling drunk: late C.18–mid-19.

surveyor of the pavement. A person in the pillory: late C.18–mid-19.

sus. 'The remains of the Praefects' tea, passed on to their valets in college': Winchester College: late C.18–19. Wrench. Ex dial. *sus(s)* or *soss*, hog wash.

sus. per coll. Hanged by the neck: ca 1780–1850. Ex *suspensus per collum* (F. & H.; or *suspensio* . . ., W.; or *suspendatur* . . ., O.E.D.), the jailor's entry against a hanged man's name. cf.:

susancide. Self-murder: half-wits' jocular (—1909). Ex *Susan* + *suicide*.

suspence or suspense, in deadly. Hanged: ca 1780–1860.

suspicion. A very small quantity; a minute trace: 1809, Malkin: coll >, ca 1880, S.E. Trollope, 1867, 'He was engaged in brushing a suspicion of dust from his black gaiters.' Ex Fr. *soupçon*; cf. Fr. *larme* and SPOT, n., 1.

sut. Satisfactory; fortunate: tailors': from ca 1870. ?corruption of *sat(isfactory)*. 2. As an exclamation, it = 'good!' or 'serve you right!': late C.19–20.

***sutler.** 'He that Pockets up, Gloves, Knives, Handkerchiefs, Snuff and Tobacco-boxes, and all the lesser Moveables', B.E.: c. of late C.17–early 19. Ex military sense.

s'velp me. A Cockney variation of 'WELP.

swab. A naval officer's epaulette: nautical jocose or pejorative: since ca 1780: 1798, *Sporting Magazine*; Marryat. Ob. Ex the shape of a *swab*, anything for mopping up. 2. A surly or despicable fellow: s.: Ned Ward, 1709.

swabber, swobber. (Gen. pl.) In whist, the Ace of Hearts, Knave of Clubs, and the Ace and Deuce (2) of Trumps: late C.17–early 19: coll >, by 1750, S.E. First recorded in B.E. Prob. ex S.E. sense. 2. A drinker who spills his drink on the table: sailors' s. (—1650).

swack. A deception, whereas *swack-up* is a falsehood: mid-C.19–20. 2. Also v.t., *swack up*, to deceive. All; Christ's Hospital: from ca 1860. Perhaps cognate with Scottish *swack*, supple, smart, or *swack*, a whack.

***swad.** A soldier: dial., and c. >, mid-C. 19, s.: C.18–20; ob. in s. by 1910. *The Memoirs of John Hall*, 1708; Smyth, 1867, 'A newly raised soldier'. In late C.19–early 20, esp. a militiaman. Perhaps ex *swad*, a bumpkin, a lout. cf. SWADKIN; SWADDY, and:

swad-gill. A soldier: low s. (—1812) and dial.; † in s. by 1860. Vaux, who spells it *swod-gill*. Ex SWAD + GILL, a fellow.

***swadder.** A pedlar: c. of ca 1565–1750. In C.18, esp. of a pedlar given to robbery with violence. Perhaps cognate with *swad* as a term of abuse. cf. SWADDLER, 4.

swaddie, see SWADDY.

swaddle. To beat soundly; to cudgel: coll: ca 1570–1840. ca 1570, Anon., 'Thy bones will I swaddle, so have I blisse'; Dryden; B.E., 'I'll Swaddle your Hide'; Scott. Ex *swaddle*, to bandage.

swaddler. A Methodist: a coll (mainly Anglo-Irish) nickname from ca 1745. C. Wesley, *Journal*, 10 Sept. 1747, where the anecdotal origin is given; Grose; *Academy*, 11 May 1889. 2. Hence, a Methodist preacher, esp. in Ireland: coll: C.19. 3. Any Protestant: Anglo-Irish coll: from ca 1870. 4. (Often *swadler*.) A member of the 10th Order of the underworld: c. of late C.17–early 19. Grose, 1st ed., 'who not only rob, but beat and often murder passengers'. Ex SWADDLER, on SWADDLE.

swaddling, vbl n. See SWADDLE, v. 2. Methodism; conduct (supposed to be) characteristic of Methodists: coll: mid-C. 18–early 19. See SWADDLER, n., 1. 3. adj., Methodist: coll: mid-C.18–20; ob. In C.19–20, Protestant in gen.: likewise coll.

swaddy; swaddie, swoddy. A soldier: low >, ca 1860, naval and military s.: C.19–20. Vaux, 1812; Smyth, 1867, 'A discharged soldier', with which cf. Smyth on SWADKIN. Ex SWAD, n. Among soldiers, in late C.19–20, gen. of a private and esp. as a term of address. cf. U.S. *swatty*.

***swadkin.** A soldier: c. (1708, John Hall) >, ca 1850, dial. and naval s. (—1867); as latter, ob. Smyth, 'A newly raised soldier'. Diminutive of SWAD. cf. SWAD-GILL; SWADDY.

***swadler,** see SWADDLER, 4.

***swag.** A shop: c. (—1676); ob. ?origin. (cf. SWAG-SHOP.) Hence, a *rum swag* is a shop full of rich goods: †by 1850. 2. Imm. ex SWAG-SHOP: one who keeps a 'swag-shop'; s. (?low): 1851, Mayhew. 3. Any quantity of goods, esp. a pedlar's wares or a thief's booty, esp. as recently or prospectively obtained: c. (—1811) >, ca 1850, low s. >, by 1890, gen. s. in the wider sense, any unlawful gains or acquisition. *Lex. Bal.* Vaux, who, like the preceding glossarist, notes the nuance, 'wearing-apparel, linen, piece-goods, &c.' as, in a robbery, distinguished from 'plate, jewellery, or more portable articles' – †by 1900; Dickens, 1838, '"It's all arranged about bringing off the swag, is it?" asked the Jew. Sikes nodded'; 'Pomes' Marshall. Perhaps ex dial. *swag*, a large quantity; prob. ex the *swag* or bag in which the booty is carried. 4. Imm. ex, or the origin of, SWAG-SHOP and therefore ex sense 1: trade in small, trivial, or inferior articles: from ca 1850. Mostly in combination (see, e.g., SWAG-BARROW); when by itself, it is gen. attributive, as in Mayhew, 1851, 'The "penny apiece" or "swag" trade'. 5. A tramp's (hence, miners' and others') bundle of personal effects: 1852, Samuel Sidney, *The Three Colonies of Australia*, 'His leathern overalls, his fancy stick, and his swag done up in a mackintosh'; 1861, McCombie,

Australian Sketches; 1902, *Pall Mall Gazette*, 2 July, 'The unmarried shearer, roaming, swag on back, from station to station'. Coll >, ca 1880, S.E. Ex sense 3, which Cunningham notes as established in Australia before 1827. 6. Prizes offered at games of skill; showmen's: late C.19–20. Ex SWAG, n., 3. 7. A state, trend or tendency of the betting: sporting, esp. pugilistic: ca 1810–50. *Boxiana*, III, 1821, 'The scene was now changed – the Cockneys are alive: the swag is now for London.' Prob. ex sense 3.

swag, adj. Worthless; gen. *it's swag*: low: from ca 1860. Ex SWAG, n., 4.

swag, v.i. Gen. as SWAG IT. 2. v.t., to rob, plunder: c. (—1887). Ex n., 3.

swag-barrow. A coster's cart, esp. one carrying small or trashy articles (see SWAG, 4): low s.: from ca 1850. Also, *swag-barrowman*, a coster, or another, carrying on such trade. Both in Mayhew, 1851; ob.

***swag-chovey bloke.** A marine store dealer: c. (—1839) >, ca 1870, low s.: late C.19–20; ob. See SWAG, 4; CHOVEY is a shop.

swag it. To carry one's SWAG (5): 1861, McCombie: coll >, ca 1890, S.E.

swag-man; swagman. A man in the SWAG-TRADE or keeping a SWAG-SHOP: from ca 1850. Mayhew, 1851. Gen. *swag-man*. 2. A man travelling with a SWAG (5): Australian: 1883, Keighley: coll >, ca 1890, S.E. Gen. *swagman*. Also SWAGSMAN.

***swag of, a.** 'Emphatically a great deal', Vaux: c. of ca 1800–50. Ex SWAG, n., 3.

***swag-seller.** A pedlar: vagrants' c.: late C.19–20. Ex SWAG, n., 3.

swag-shop. A shop specializing in trivial or trashy articles, very cheap: mid-C.19–20: lower-class London. Mayhew, 1851. See SWAG, 1 and 4.

swag-straps, look for one's. To consider leaving one's job in search of another; New Zealand (mostly rural): late C.19–20. See SWAG, n., 5.

swag-trade. The trade in SWAG, 4: mid-C.19–20.

swagger. A SWAGGER-CANE or -STICK: military coll (—1887). i.e. a stick carried for swagger or show. 2. In Australia, hence in New Zealand, one who carries a SWAG (5): 1855, *Melbourne Argus*, 19 Jan.: coll >, ca 1880, S.E. cf. SWAG-MAN, 2; SWAGSMAN, and SWAGGIE.

swagger, adj. Smart, fashionable; SWELL; rather showy or ostentatious: (orig. Society) s.: 1879, *Cambridge Review*; 1897, 'Ouida', 'Lord, ma'am, they'll . . . take the matches away from their bedrooms, but, then, you see, ma'am, them as are swagger can do them things.' Ex S.E. *swagger*, superior and/or insolent behaviour.

swagger-cane or **-stick.** An officer's cane or stick for parade-ground appearance; a private's or non-com.'s walking-out stick or short cane: military coll: resp. 1889, 1887 (O.E.D.). Ex SWAGGER, adj.; cf., however, SWAGGER, n., 1.

swaggering, n. Tramping, esp. in the outback: Australian coll: late C.19–20.

swaggering Bob. An impudent buffoon: theatrical coll: mid-C.19–20; ob.

swaggery. A non-aristocratic variant (—1887; slightly ob.) of SWAGGER, adj.

swaggie, swaggy. A man carrying a SWAG (5) as a habit: Australian (gen. humorous) coll: 1892, E. W. Hornung; 1902, Henry Lawson. Ex SWAG-MAN, 2.

swagman, see SWAG-MAN.

swagsman. The same as SWAGGIE: 1879, J. Brunton Stephens: coll >, ca 1890, S.E. Ex SWAG-MAN, 2. 2. In c. (—1859), an accomplice who, after a burglary, carries the plunder. Ex SWAG, n., 3. Also a FENCE: c. (—1904). 3. An occ. variant of SWAG-MAN, 1.

swallow. Capacity (for food): late C.16–20: S.E. until ca 1850, then coll. 2. Esp. as a mouthful: from ca 1820: S.E. until ca 1890, then coll. These two senses are sometimes indistinguishable, as in the c.p., 'What a swallow!', which may refer to one act of swallowing or to appetite. Ex *swallow*, the throat or gullet.

swallow, v. To prepare (a part) hastily: theatrical: 1898 (O.E.D.). Ex SWALLOW THE CACKLE.

swallow a hair. To get drunk: s. (—1650).

swallow a gudgeon. To be gulled: coll: 1579, Lyly; Dekker & Webster, 1607; Fuller, 1732; Halliwell. †by 1900. Ex fig. *gudgeon*. Apperson.

swallow a sailor. To get drunk upon rum: ports' and harbours' (—1909). Ware.

swallow a spider, see SPIDER, 3, and SPIDER, SWALLOW A.

swallow a stake. See SWALLOWED A STAKE; the earlier *to have eaten a stake* is recorded by Palsgrave in 1530, but, app., was †by 1700.

swallow a tavern-token. To get drunk: coll: late C.16–18. Jonson, *Every Man in His Humour*, 'Drunk, sir! you hear not me say so: perhaps he swallowed a tavern token or some such device.' cf. TAVERN-FOX.

swallow (or swaller) and sigh. Collar and tie: theatrical rhyming s.: late C.19–20.

swallow bobby. 'Some of the first "nobs" in the colony [of New South Wales] used to "swallow bobby" (make false affidavits to an enormous extent)': A. Harris, *Settlers and Convicts*, 1847: Australian: ca 1810–90. cf. *swallow the* ANCHOR, and S'ELP ME BOB.

swallow my knife? – you say true, will you. I doubt it!: a c.p. applied esp. to an impossible story: from ca 1890 (ob.): not aristocratic.

swallow-tail. A dress-coat: coll: 1835, Frith, 'I should look a regular guy in a swallow-tail.'

swallow the anchor, see ANCHOR, SWALLOW THE.

swallow the cackle. To learn a part: theatrical (—1890).

swallowed a stake and cannot stoop, he (she) has. A c.p. applied to a very stiff, upright person: from ca 1660; ob. L'Estrange, 1667; Fuller, 1732. cf. at SWALLOW A STAKE.

swallowed a dictionary, he (she) has. He (she) uses very long words: coll: late C.19–20.

swan-slinger. A Shakespearian actor: theatrical (—1890); ob. Ex the phrase, *to sling the Swan of Avon* (late C.19–20; ob.). cf. SPOUT BILLY.

swank. Showy or conceited behaviour or speech; pretence: dial. (—1854) >, ca 1904, s. *Daily Chronicle*, 17 April 1905, 'What he said is quite true, barring the whisky – that is all swank'; Ware, 1909, records analogous senses, 'small talk, lying' as printers' s. Dates make it appear that the n. derives ex the v., but, dial. records being notoriously incomplete, the reverse may be true: in either case, *swank*, as Baumann suggests, derives prob. ex Ger. *Schwang* as in *in S. sein* (or *gehen*), to be in the fashion. 2. (Ex sense 1.) The tricks one plays; one's 'game': Cockney: from ca 1890. C. Rook, *The Hooligan Nights*, 1899. 3. Hence, flattery, BLARNEY: id.: id. ibid., 'I . . . calls 'im a rare toff an' a lot of old swank of that kind.'

swank, v. To behave showily or conceitedly; to swagger; to pretend (esp. to be better than, or superior to, what one is): dial. (—1809) >, ca 1870, s., though not gen. till ca 1901. H., 5th ed., '*Swank*, to boast or "gas" unduly'; A. McNeill, 1903, 'To see . . . your sons swanking about town with Hon. before their names'. For the most viable etymology, see the preceding entry: but one cannot ignore these possibilities: Perhaps ex *swing* (the body) via either Scottish *swank*, agile, or *swagger*; or simply a perversion of SWAGGER. 2. To work hard: Public and military school s. (—1890). Perhaps ex SWOT + *swank*.

swanker. One who behaves as in SWANK, v., 1 and 2: same period and status. cf. *swanking*, the vbl n.

***swank(e)y.** Inferior beer: c. (—1859). Prob. ex Ger. *schwank*, feeble. 2. A conceited or pretentious person: ca 1830–80. Ex SWANK, v., 1.

swank(e)y swipes. Table beer: 1848, *Sinks*. cf. SWANK(E)Y, 1.

swannery, keep a. To make out that all one's geese are swans: coll (—1785); ob. by 1890.

swap, swop. An exchanging; an exchange: coll >, ca 1850, s.: resp. ca 1625 (Purchas) and 1682 (Flatman). Ex *swap*, an act of striking (esp. the hands as a sign of a bargain made); or more imm. ex the v. cf. SWAP, HAVE THE.

swap, swop, v.t. To exchange (*for* something else, or a thing *with* somebody else): coll >, ca 1850, s.: resp. 1594, Lyly, 'Ile not swap my father for all this,' and 1624, Quarles, '. . . That for his belly swopt his heritage'. A 'low word', says Johnson; 'Irish cant', says Egan (1823). Orig. a horse-dealer's term ex *swap* (strike) *a bargain*. 2. See SWAP AWAY. 3. v.i., to make an exchange: coll >, ca 1850, s.: 1778, Miss Burney; 1885, Jerome K. Jerome, 'I am quite ready to swop.' Ex sense 1. 4. v.t., to dismiss from employment: 1862, *Macmillan's Magazine*. cf. SWAP, HAVE THE. 5. v.i., to change one's clothes: 1904, D. Sladen. Ex sense 1.

swap or **swop, have** or **get the.** To be dismissed from employment: from before 1890. Ex SWAP, v., 4.

swap away or **off,** v.t. To exchange: coll >, ca 1850, s.: resp. 1589, R. Harvey, 'He swapt away his silver for Copper retaile,' and from ca 1860; the latter, orig. and mainly U.S. Ex SWAP, v., 1.

swapper, swopper. One who exchanges: late C.17–20: coll >, ca 1850, s. Ex SWAP v., 1. 2. Gen. *swapper*. Anything very big, a WHOPPER (esp. of a lie): s. and dial.: from ca 1700. Ex *swap*, to strike.

swapping. An exchanging, an exchange;

barter: coll >, ca 1850, s.: 1695, J. Edwards. Ex SWAP, v., 1. cf. SWAPPER, 1; SWAP, n.

swapping, swopping, adj. Very big: coll >, ca 1850, s.: mid-C.15–20. Middleton, 1624, 'Swapping sins'. Ex *swap*, to strike; cf. SWAPPER, 2, and WHOPPING.

swarbout is an occ. C.16 variant of SWORBOTE.

swarry; occ. swarree, swarrey. A *soirée* or social evening: coll, in C.20 considered somewhat sol.: 1837, Dickens, 'A friendly swarry'; 1848, Thackeray (*swarrey*). 2. H., 5th ed., 'A boiled leg of mutton and trimmings': is this a mistake founded on the Dickens passage (and repeated by F. & H.), or, as H. says, a resultant therefrom?

swash-bucket. A slattern: proletarian coll: from ca 1870; ob. Ex *swash-bucket*, a receptacle for scullery refuse (ex *swash*, pig wash). In dial. as early as 1746 for 'a farmhouse slattern'.

swat. A (smart or heavy) blow: dial. (—1800) >, ca 1840, s. or coll, but never very gen. Ex next entry. 2, 3, 4. See SWOT.

swat, v. To strike smartly: dial. (—1796) >, before 1848 (Bartlett), U.S.; reimported into England before 1904 (witness F. & H.) as a coll. 2. See SWOT.

Swatchel. Punch, in Punch and Judy: showmen's (esp. and orig. P. & J. showmen): mid-C.19–20. Perhaps cognate with *swatch*, a sample or specimen, ex *swatch*, a sample piece of cloth; possibly, as the O.E.D. (Sup.) suggests, ex Ger. *schwätzeln*, frequentative of *schwatzen*, to tattle. Hence *swatchel* (occ. *schwassle*)*-box*, the Punch and Judy show or, more correctly, the booth; and *swatchel-cove*, a Punch and Judy man, or, esp., the patterer. Other terms, all from ca 1850, are: **buffer** (q.v.), the dog *Toby* (recorded in 1840), and **buffer-figure**, the dog's master; **crocodile**, the demon; **darkey** or **D.**, the Negro; **filio**, the baby; **(the) frame**, the street arrangement or PITCH, etc.; **(the) letter cloth**, the advertisement; **Mozzy** (q.v.), Judy; **nobbing slum** (q.v.), the bag for collected money; **peepsies** (q.v.), the pan-pipes; **(the) slum** (q.v., 9), the call; **(the) slum-fake**, the coffin; **the stalk** (q.v.) (occ. **prop.**), the gallows; **tambour** (q.v.), the drum; **vampire** (q.v.), the ghost; **vampo** or **V.** (q.v.), the clown. Despite its Italian origin, Punch and Judy vocabulary contains far more c. and/or low s. than Italian words.

sway (away on) all top-ropes, see TOP-ROPES.

swaying the main with an old mess-mate(, I've been). The bluejackets' c.p. explanation of a bibulous evening ashore: from ca 1860.

swear. A formal oath: mid-C.16–20: S.E. until ca 1870, then coll. Eden Phillpotts, 1899, 'We swore by a tremendous swear.' 2. Hence a profane oath, a SWEAR-WORD; a fit of swearing: coll: 1871, C. Gibbon, 'A good swear is a cure for the bile.' 3. A harsh noise made esp. by a cat, occ. by a bird: coll: 1895 (O.E.D.). Ex:

swear, v.i. (Of a canine or feline or, occ., a bird) to make a harsh and/or guttural sound: from late C.17: S.E. until C.19, then coll. The O.E.D. gives, at 1902, an example of a locomotive 'swearing'.

swear at. (Mostly of colours) to clash with: coll: 1884, *Daily News*, 10 Nov., 'Two tints that swear at each other'. Ex Fr. *jurer*.

swear by. To accept as authoritative, have (very) great confidence in: coll: 1815, Jane Austen; 1890, G. A. Henty, 'His fellows swear by him.' Ex *swear by*, to appeal to (a god).

swear by, enough to. A very small amount or slight degree: mid-C.18–20: coll >, in mid-C.19, s. On (*just*) *enough to mention.*

swear like a cutter (C.17–20; ob.), or **a lord** (C.16–17), or **a tinker** (C.17–20), or **a trooper** (1727). To swear profusely: coll soon > S.E.

swear off. To renounce: lower classes' s. (—1887) >, ca 1900, gen. s.

swear through an inch or a two-inch board; . . . a nine-inch plank; and see quotation in sense 2. To back up any lie: coll: resp. 1678, Ray; 1728, Earl of Ailesbury; from ca 1800, app. Nelson's variation of the other forms, according to Clark Russell in 1883. Dickens, in 1865, has 'That severe exertion which is known in legal circles as swearing your way through a stone wall'. cf. the Cheshire semi-proverbial 'Oo'd swear the cross off a jackass's back,' *oo* being 'she'. 2. These phrases are also indicative of vigorous bad language, as in R. Franck, 1658, 'It's thought they would have sworn through a double deal-board, they seem'd so enrag'd.'

swear-word. A profane oath or other word: coll; orig. U.S., anglicized ca 1880. cf. the U.S. *cuss-word.*

swearing-apartment. The street: taverns' (—1909). Ware. Prob. ex the barmaids' exclamatory question, 'If you want to swear, why don't you go out into the street?'

sweat. A long run taken in training: Public Schools': late C.19–20.

sweat. To lighten (a – gen. gold – coin) by friction or acid: coll (—1785) >, ca 1850, S.E. Ex *sweat*, to cause to perspire. 2. To deprive of: from ca 1784, as in Anon., *Ireland Sixty Years Ago*, 1847, '[In] 1784 . . . "sweating" him, i.e. making him give up all his fire-arms'. cf. S.E. *sweating*, a ruffianly practice of the MOHOCKS. 3. Esp. to fleece, to BLEED: from ca 1840: low s. Smyth, 1867 (see SWEAT THE PURSER). 4. v.i. and v.t., to squander (riches): from late 1850s. Ex *sweat*, to give off, get rid of, as by sweating. 5. Hence, v.t., to spend (money): from ca 1860. 6. Hence, to remove some of the contents of: 1867, in Conington's *Horace*, 'He'd find a bottle sweated and not rave.' 7. To unsolder (a tin box, etc.) by applying fire or a blow-pipe: c. (—1909). cf. senses 1, 6. 8. Perhaps ex sense 1: v.t., to pawn: low s. (orig., prob. Anglo-Irish): from ca 1800; †by ca 1880. 9. To force (a person) to do something: Winchester: mid-C.19–20. 10. Hence, v.i., to be engaged in compulsory work: ibid.: late C.19–20.

sweat, all of a. (Of a street, pavement, etc.) like a bog; slushy: coll, esp. London (—1887).

sweat, old, see OLD SWEAT.

sweat-box. A cell for prisoners waiting to go before the magistrate: low s.: from ca 1875, though unrecorded before 1888 (Churchward's *Blackbirding*).

sweat-gallery. (Coll for) fagging juniors: Winchester: from ca 1865; ob. Ex SWEATER, 2.

sweat one's guts out. To work extremely hard: (mostly lower class) coll: late C.19–20.

sweat-rag. A pocket-handkerchief: Australia: C.20. Lawson, 1902.

sweat the purser. To waste Government stores: naval: from ca 1840. In George Brewer's farce, *Bannian Day*, 1796, at I, iii, p. 8, and II, iii, p. 25, it seems to mean 'to take an illicit or, at the least, a sly drink at the expense of the ship's purser'.

sweater. An occupation or act causing one to sweat: coll: 1851, Mayhew, 'The business is a sweater, sir.' 2. A servant: Winchester: from ca 1860. cf. SWEAT-GALLERY. 3. A broker working for very small commissions, thus depriving others of business and himself of adequate profit: Stock Exchange coll: from ca 1870.

swede talk. Rural talk, countryman's talk: Cockney: late C.19–20.

sweep. A sweepstake: coll (1849) >, ca 1905, S.E. Kipling. 2. A scamp, a disreputable: from ca 1850. F. & H., 'You dirty sweep'. Ex (*chimney-*)*sweep*. 3. (Also BOGEY.) Mucus (esp. hardened mucus) that can easily be extracted from the nostrils: domestic and nurses', chiefly Scottish: late C.19–20. cf.:

sweep, v. To chimney-sweep for: low coll: 1848, Thackeray, 'The chimney-purifier, who has swep' the last three families'.

sweeper. A train that, following a through train, calls at all stations: Australian coll (—1908). Because it 'sweeps up' all passengers. 2. A sweepstake: Harrow and Oxford: late C.19–20. By the 'Oxford *-er*'.

sweeps and saints. Stockbrokers and their clientele: City of London: mid-C.19–20; ob. Ware, 'From the First of May (Sweeps' Day) and the First of November (All Saints' Day) being holidays on the Exchange'.

sweep's frill. 'Beard and whiskers worn round the chin, the rest of the face being clean shaven', F. & H.: 1892, *Tit Bits*, 19 March. cf.:

sweep's-trot. A loping amble: coll: 1842 Lover; ob.

***sweet.** Gullible; unsuspicious: c. (—1725) >, in late C.19, low s. 2. Clever, expert, dexterous: c. (—1725). cf. SWEET AS YOUR HAND. 3. In the speaker's opinion, attractive, very pleasant: coll: 1779. Fanny Burney, 1782, 'The sweetest caps! The most beautiful trimmings!' cf. NICE, and Fr. *mignon*.

sweet as a nut, adj. and adv. Advantageous(ly); with agreeable or consummate ease: coll: late C.19–20.

***sweet as (or 's) your hand.** 'Said of one dexterous at stealing', Grose, 1st ed.: c. (ob.) of C.18–20.

sweet-lips. A glutton; a gourmet: (low) coll: from ca 1870; ob.

sweet on, be. 'To coakse, wheedle, entice or allure', B.E.: late C.17–18. The O.E.D. considers it S.E.; B.E. classifies it as c.; prob. coll, as, I think, is the mid-C.18–20 sense, to be very fond of, enamoured with (one of the opposite sex).

sweet-pea. Whiskey: Anglo-Irish: ca 1810–70. 'A Real Paddy', *Life in Ireland*, 1822. Ex the colour of the resultant urine.

sweet-pea, do or plant a. (Of, and among,

women) to urinate, esp. in the open air: mid-C.19–20. Prob. suggested by *pluck a* ROSE, and, of course, punning on PEE.

sweetbread. A bribe; a timely reward of money: coll: ca 1670–90. Hacket, 1670, 'A few sweetbreads that I gave him out of my purse'.

***sweeten.** A beggar, says F. & H.: is this so? If correct, c.: presumably C.18.

***sweeten,** v. To decoy, draw in; swindle: c.: late C.17–early 19. 2. v.i., see SWEETENING, 1. 3. v.t., to allay the suspicions of (a victim): C.18: c. or low s. 4. To bribe; give alms to: late C.18–20: c. >, ca 1850, dial. and low s. Haggart, former nuance; Egan's Grose, latter. Prob. ex sense 1. 5. To contribute to (the pool), increase the stakes in (the pot, at poker): cards: from 1896. cf. SWEETENING. 6. v.i., to bid at an auction merely to run up the price: orig. and mainly auctioneers' (—1864). cf. SWEETENER.

sweeten and pinch. Occ. v., gen. n., ca 1670–1720, as in Anon., *Four for a Penny*, 1678: to get money, by politeness and considerateness, from a man about to be arrested. BUM-BAILIFFS' s.

***sweetener.** A decoy; a cheat or a swindler: c.: late C.17–early 19. Ex SWEETEN, v., 1. 2. A GUINEA-DROPPER: c.: same period. Ex SWEETENING, 1. 3. One who, at an auction, bids to run up the price: auctioneers' (—1864). 4. A temporary officer (gen. first mate) replacing his predecessor, who is in hiding: nautical, with esp. reference to the Atlantic clipper packets: ca 1850–1910. 5. See:

***sweeteners.** The lips: c. or low s.: from ca 1860. Esp. *fake the s.*, to kiss.

***sweetening.** Guinea-dropping, i.e. the dropping of a coin and consequent swindling of a gullible finder: c.: from ca 1670; †by 1870. *The Country Gentleman's Vade Mecum*, 1699. 2. The vbl n. – both the action and the concrete result – of SWEETEN, v., 5. 3. That of SWEETEN, v., 6. 4. That of SWEETEN, v., 4.

sweetheart. A tame rabbit: (sporting and dealers') coll: from late 1830s. Blaine's *Encyclopaedia of Rural Sports*, 1840. Ex winning ways of such rabbits.

sweetheart and bag-pudding. A c.p. applied to a girl got with child: C.17–early 18. Day, *Humour out of Breath*, 1608; Ray, 1670.

sweetie. A sweetmeat: dial. (—1758), and coll (from ca 1820) >, ca 1890, S.E. W. Havergal, 1824, 'Baby ... was satisfied with a bit of sweetie'; Thackeray, in 1860, has 'Bonbons or sweeties'; the pl is much the more gen.

sweetmeat; occ. **sweet-meat.** The male member. 2. A mere girl who is a kept mistress. Both senses are low and date from mid-C.19.

***sweetner.** See SWEETENER, 1, 2, of which it is a frequent variant.

swell. A fashionably or smartly dressed person (cf. HEAVY SWELL: 1819); hence, though rare before ca 1820, a (very) distinguished person, a lady or gentleman of the upper classes: s. (—1786) >, in late C. 19, coll. *Sessions*, Dec. 1786; Bee, 1823, of nob and swell, 'The latter makes a show of his finery; ... the nob, relying upon intrinsic worth, or bona-fide property, or intellectual ability, is clad in plainness.' Byron; Thackeray. Usually of men, and prob. ex SWELL, CUT A. 2. Hence, one who has done something notable or who is expert *at* something: s. >, in late C.19, coll: 1816, Moore, but not gen. before ca 1840; Barham, 'No! no! – The Abbey [Westminster] may do very well | For a feudal nob, or poetical "swell"'; the Eton usage. 3. See SWELLS.

swell, adj. Stylishly dressed: from ca 1812. Prob. ex n., 1. 2. Hence, from ca 1820, gentlemanly (Byron, 1823) or ladylike; of good social position (Disraeli, 1845). 3. (Of things) stylish, very distinguished: from ca 1811. 4. Hence, excellent, whether of things (e.g. *a swell time*) or of persons considered as to their ability (e.g. *a swell cricketer*): not before mid-C.19 and – except in U.S.A. – slightly ob. All four senses were orig. s. (1–3, indeed, were low s. for a decade or more); they > coll only in late C.19.

swell, v. To take a bath: Winchester: from ca 1860; ob. Ex SWILL, v. 2. See SWELL IT.

swell, cut a; do the swell. To swagger: resp. —1800–1840, as in *The Spirit of the Public Journals*, 1800, 'Our young lords and ... gentlemen "cutting a swell" as the fashionable phrase is', O.E.D.; and mid-C.19–20 (ob.), as in Baumann. (cf. SWELL, n., 1.) Ex *swell*, arrogant behaviour.

swell (or itch)?, does your nose. (Gen. completed by *at this* or *at that*.) Are you angry or annoyed?: coll: C.19.

swell, rank. 'A very "flashly" dressed person ... who ... apes a higher position than he actually occupies', H., 1st ed.; ob. by 1900. Ex SWELL, n., 1, first nuance.

swell fencer. A street vendor of needles: low London (—1859).

swell-head. A drunken man: low: late C. 19–20. Prob. ex U.S.

swell-headed. Conceited; puffed with pride: coll: 1817, Cobbett, 'The upstart, ... swell-headed farmer can bluster ... about Sinecures.'

swell hung in chains, a. A much-bejewelled person: low: mid-C.19–20; ob.

swell it. To play or ape the fine gentleman: low (—1887); ob. Ex SWELL, n., 1.

***swell mob.** That class of pickpockets who, to escape detection, dress and behave like respectable people: 1830, *Sessions*: c. >, by 1870, low s. Ex SWELL, adj., 1 and 2 + MOB.

***swell-mobsman.** One of the SWELL MOB: c. (—1851) >, by 1870, low s. Mayhew; Hotten, 3rd ed., 'Swell mobsmen, who pretend to be Dissenting preachers, and harangue in the open air for their confederates to rob'.

swell-nose. Strong ale: early C.16. Anon., *De Generibus Ebriosorum*, 1515.

swell's lush. Champagne: Australian: ca 1830–1900. In, e.g., *Sketches of Australian Life and Scenery* (by a Resident), 1876. See the two elements.

Swell Street, be (—1812) or **live** (—1904) **in.** To be a well-off family man of good social standing: low: from ca 1810; ob. By 1864 *Swell Street* had > the West End (London).

swelldom. The world of 'swells' (n., all senses): coll: 1855, Thackeray; ob.

swelled head. Excessive conceit, pride, or vanity: coll: 1891, Kipling. 2. Perhaps only one of Grose's jokes, and at most a piece of military punning s. of late C.18–early 19: 'A disorder to which horses are extremely liable ... Generally occasioned by remaining too long in one livery-stable or inn, and often rises to that height that it prevents their coming out of the stable door. The most certain cure is the *unguentum aureum* ... applied to the palm of the master of the inn or stable,' 2nd ed. cf. OAT-STEALER.

swelled nose, see SWELL?, DOES YOUR NOSE.

swellish. Dandified: 1820 (O.E.D.): s. >, in late C.19, coll. Ex SWELL, n., 1. 2. Gentlemanly; distinguished: from ca 1830: id.

swellishness. The n. of SWELLISH, 2: coll: late C.19–20.

swellism. The style (esp. in dress) or the social habits of a SWELL, in sense 1, rarely in other than the first nuance: 1840 (O.E.D.): s. >, by ca 1870, coll; ob. cf.:

swellness. The being a SWELL, esp. in sense 2 and never in the first nuance of sense 1: coll: 1894, T. H. Huxley, 'My swellness is an awful burden.' cf. SWELLISHNESS; SWELLISM.

swells. Occasions – e.g. Sunday church-services – on which surplices are worn: Winchester: from ca 1860. Ex SWELL, adj., 3.

swelp, s'welp. (God) so help: as in Whiteing, 1899, 'Swelp me lucky, I ain't tellin' yer no lie!' Also *swelp me!* (—1887); *swelp me* or *my bob!* (—1904); *swelp me davy* (—1887); *swelp my greens* or *taters!* (id.), with which cf. the (—1895) dial. *bless my taters!* and the earlier (1864) *s'elp my tater!* See also S'ELP ME BOB!, S'ELP MY GREENS! (1864); likewise *s'help!* Ex *so help* (*me, God!*).

swelter. Hot, hard work: lower classes' (—1887). cf.:

swelter, do a. To perspire profusely: 1884. Ex S.E. *swelter*, a state of perspiration.

Swensker. A Swede: nautical coll: mid-C. 19–20. Bowen, 'A corruption of Svenske'.

swi. A florin: low Australian: late C.19–20. Ex Ger. *zwei*, two.

swift. A fast-working compositor: printers' (—1841). Savage's *Dict. of Printing*.

swift, adj. Apt to take (sexual) liberties with, or to accept them from, the opposite sex: coll: late C.19–20. Suggested by FAST (2, 3).

swiftly flowing. Going: Australian rhyming s.: late C.19–20.

swig; in C.16, also **swyg.** Liquor: coll: mid-C.16–20; very ob. – has been so since early C.19. Udall, 1548. Etymology unknown: W. proposes Scandinavian *svik*, a tap. 2. Hence, a 'pull'; a (copious) draught: coll >, in late C.18, s.: from ca 1620. Middleton & Rowley, 'But one swig more, sweet madam'; Ned Ward; Marryat; Whiteing. Also, in C.17, *swigge*. 3. At Oxford University (orig. and esp. Jesus College), toast and (spiced) ale, or the bowl in which it is served: from ca 1825. Hence, *Swig Day*, the day (?St David's) it is ritualistically served.

swig; in C.18, occ. **swigg.** v.i. To drink deeply, eagerly, or much (esp. strong liquor): mid-C.17–20: coll >, in early C.19, s. Ex n., 1. 2. v.t., with either the liquor or its container as object: coll >, in early C.19, s.: resp. 1780, 'Slang Pastoral' Tomlinson, 'To swig porter all day', and 1682, in *Wit and Drollery*, 'I . . . swigg'd my horn'd barrel,' this latter nuance being ob.

swig, play at. To indulge in drink: coll: late C.17–18. Ex SWIG, n., 2.

Swig Day, see SWIG, n., 3.

swigged. Tipsy: mid-C.19–20: rather proletarian.

swigging, vbl n. (1723) and ppl adj. (1702). See SWIG, v., 1.

***swigman**; in C.16, also **swygman.** 'One of the 13th Rank of the Canting crew, carrying small Haberdashery-Wares about, pretending to sell them to colour their Roguery', B.E.; Awdelay, 1561, says that he 'goeth with a Peddlers pack'. c. of ca 1560–1800. Prob. ex SWAGMAN, despite the fact that *swag*, a bulgy bag, is recorded only in early C.14.

swiling, n. Sealing: Newfoundland nautical coll: late C.19–20. By corruption.

'Swill. A coll euphemism for (*by*) *God's will*: C.17. Marston.

swill. A bath: Shrewsbury School coll: mid-C.19–20.

swill, v.i. To wash at a conduit by throwing water over the body: Winchester College coll: C.19–20. cf. the Shrewsbury n. and:

swilled, get. To take a bath: Shrewsbury School coll: mid-C.19–20.

swim. A swimming, i.e. a dizzy, feeling: dial. and coll: 1829, Ebenezer Elliott. 2. A plan or enterprise, esp. a tortuous or a SHADY one: 1860, Sala; slightly ob.

swim, give one's dog a. To have the excuse of doing something or, esp., a reason for something to do: South African and Australian coll. An English approximation is *take one's dog for a walk*.

swim, how we apples, see APPLES SWIM . . .

swim, in the. Whereas *in the swim with*, in league with, has always, it seems, been S.E., *in the swim*, lucky, very fortunate, is coll and ob.: in 1869, *Macmillan's Magazine* (the earliest record, by the way) explained that it derives ex *swim*, a section of river much frequented by fish. By 1864, *in a good swim* = in luck, doing a good business; by 1874, *in the swim* = in the inner circle, movement or fashion; popular: a sense that, from coll, >, ca 1900, S.E. 2. In c. (—1860): a long time out of the hands of the police.

swim, out of the. The opp. to *in the* SWIM, except that it has no c. sense: 1869. Rare in C.20.

***swim for it, make (a man).** To cheat (a pal) out of his share of booty: c.: late C. 19–20.

swim in golden grease, lard, oil. To receive many bribes: C.17 coll. Jonson.

***swimmer.** A counterfeit (old) coin: c.: late C.17–early 19. Why? 2. A guardship: c. (—1811); †by 1860. cf. S.E. *swimmer*, an angler's float. 3. A half-push stroke: cricketers' (—1909).

***swimmer**, v. To cause (a man) to serve in the Navy instead of sending him to prison: c. (—1812); †by 1860. Gen. *be swimmered.* Ex the n., 2.

***swimmer, have a.** A variant of the preceding term: 1811, *Lex. Bal.*

swimming market. A (very) good market: Stock Exchange coll: from ca 1860.

swindge, swindging, see SWINGE, SWINGEING.

swindle. A lottery; a speculation; a toss for drinks: 1870, *Legal Reports*; slightly ob. Ex lit. S.E. sense. 2. Something other than it appears to be, a FRAUD: coll: 1866. cf. sense 1. 3. Any transaction in which money passes: from ca 1870, as in *what's the swindle?*, what's to pay?, which may orig. have been U.S., in *why don't you pay him his swindle?*, his price, and in *let's have a swindle!*, let's toss for it; all three phrases are ob., the third only slightly so.

swindle, v.i. To practise fraud: 1782 ed. of Bailey's Dict.: s. >, ca 1820, S.E. A back-formation ex SWINDLER. 2. Hence, v.t., esp. with *out of*: C.19–20: s. >, ca 1820, S.E. Sydney Smith, 1803.

***swindler.** A practiser of fraud or imposition for gain; a cheat: ca 1762: c. >, ca 1790, s. >, ca 1820, S.E. e.g. in Foote, 1776; Grose, 1st ed., but 'dictionaried' first in the 1782 ed. of Bailey. Ex Ger. *Schwindler*, a cheat; cf. *schwindeln*, to be extravagant or giddy. In England picked up from and applied orig. to German Jews in London; much used, too, by soldiers in the Seven Years' War.

swindling, n. and adj. ex SWINDLE, v., 1, date from late C.18; by 1820, S.E.

swine, go the complete (or entire). A London coll variation (—1887) of GO THE WHOLE HOG; ob.

swine, sing like a bird called the, see SING LIKE . . .

swine-up. A quarrel: lower classes': ca 1880–1915. Ware, 'Suspected to be of American origin'. Ex pigs' bad temper.

***swing, the.** The gallows: c. or low s.: ?late C.18–mid-19.

swing, v.i. To be hanged: s. >, in C.18, c. > s. >, in late C.19, coll: 1542, Udall, *swing in a halter*; *swing* by itself, app. not before C.18; Dickens in *Boz*, 'If I'm caught, I shall swing.' 2. Hence, v.t., to put to death by hanging: from ca 1815; ob. and, at all times, rare. 3. See next four entries. 4. To control (a market, a price, etc.): commercial coll: late C.19–20; slightly ob. cf. SWING IT.

swing for you if you don't (agree, do it, etc.)!, I'll. A c.p. threat: proletarian: ca 1820–90. See SWING, v., 1.

swing it. To wangle successfully, get something by trickery; to shirk or malinger esp. if successfully: from late 1890s. Prob. ex SWING, v., 4.

swing (a matter, business) **over one's head or shoulders.** To manage easily; find well within one's powers: commercial: from ca 1890. cf. S.E. *swing*, scope.

swing-tail. A hog: low: ca 1786–1860. Contrast SWISH-TAIL.

swing the monkey. To strike 'with knotted handkerchiefs a man who swings to a rope made fast aloft', Clark Russell: nautical coll: from ca 1880.

swinge; in C.16, occ. **swynge;** in C.16–18, **swindge.** To copulate with (a woman): ca 1620–1750. Fletcher, 1622; Dryden, 1668, 'And that baggage, Beatrix, how I would swinge her if I had her here.' Ex *swinge*, to castigate. 2. See all senses of:

swinge off. To toss off (a drink): ca 1525–1660. Also *s. up* (Skelton, 1529). ?cf. PUNISH. 2. To infect with (severe) gonorrhoea: late C.17–18. Gen. passive, *be swinged off*, as in B.E. Perhaps suggested by CLAP. 3. Occ. as variant of SWINGE: late C.17–early 18. Miège.

swingeing, swinging (pron. *swindjing*); in C.17–19, occ. **swindging.** Very effective, great, large, esp. of a lie: coll >, by 1700, s.: late C.16–20, but rare since mid-C.19. Greene, Motteux, Grose (2nd ed.), Dickens. 2. Hence, adv.: hugely: 1690, Dryden; 1872, C. D. Warner, 'A . . . swingeing cold night'. cf. S.E. *strapping*, adj. and adv.

swing(e)ingly. Very forcibly; hugely: coll >, by 1700, s.: 1672, Dryden, 'I have sinned swingingly, against my vow.' Archaic. Ex SWINGEING.

***swinger** (pron. *swindjer*). A rogue, a scoundrel: Scottish c. (? > low s.) of C.16–mid-18. Dunbar; A. Nicol, 1739. Prob. ex Flemish. 2. Something very effective or large (of a blow, not before 1830s): from 1590s, but rare since ca 1850: coll >, by 1700, s. Ex *swinge*, to beat. cf. WHOPPER. 3. Hence, esp. a bold or rank lie: ca 1670–1820. Eachard, 1670, 'Rap out . . . half a dozen swingers.' 4. A box on the ears: Charterhouse coll (—1890). 5. In pl, testicles: low: C.19–20. (Pron. as in *swing*.) 6. A lame leg: low: ca 1830–75.

swinging, adj., see SWINGEING.

swinging. A hanging: from late C.16: s. >, in late C.19, coll. Percivall, 1591, 'Swinging in a halter': R. L. Stevenson. Ex SWING, v., 1.

***swinging the stick;** or, **the bludgeon business.** A robbery committed with brutal violence and a life-preserver or bludgeon: c. (—1861). Mayhew.

swingingly, see SWINGEINGLY.

swinny. Drunk: low: late C.19–20. Ex dial. *swinny*, giddy, dizzy.

swipe; occ. **swype.** A heavy blow; in golf and cricket, a stroke made with the full swing of the arms: C.19–20: coll (?orig. dial.). Perhaps ex *sweep*; perhaps sibilated *wipe*, a blow. 2. Hence, one who does this: coll: 1825, Westmacott, 'A hard *swipe*, an active *field*, and a stout bowler'; †by 1900.

swipe, v.i. and t. 'To drink hastily and copiously; . . . at one gulp': low s. (—1823) and dial. (—1829) >, ca 1860, coll >, ca 1890, s.; in C.20, also of food. Often *swipe off*, ?ex *sweep off*. 2. The sporting v.i. (1857) is coll >, ca 1890, S.E. T. Hughes, 1857, 'The first ball of the over, Jack steps out and meets, swiping with all his force.' The v.t. not before ca 1851. 3. At Harrow: to birch (v.t.): from ca 1880. A sense-blend of *swish*, to birch, and *swipe*, v., 2. 4. To appropriate illicitly; steal; loot: U.S. (—1890), anglicized ca 1900, when used by Kipling.

swiper. A heavy drinker: 1836, F. Mahony: coll >, by 1890, s. Ex SWIPE, v., 1. 2. The cricketing sense dates from the early 1850s (e.g. in F. Gale, 1853): coll >, in late C.19, S.E. Ex SWIPE, v., 2.

swipes; occ. **swypes.** Small beer: from ca 1786: coll >, in late C.19, s. cf. SWIPE, v., 1, which it inconveniently precedes by thirty years or more. 2. Hence, any beer: from late C.18. Scott; Hood, 'Bread and cheese and swipes'. 3. A potman: ca 1810–50. Ex sense 1.

swipes, purser's. Small beer: nautical: ca 1786–1870. See SWIPES.

swipey. (Not very) tipsy: coll: from ca

1820. 1844, Dickens, 'He's only a little swipey, you know.' Never gen. and, by 1900, ob. Ex SWIPES. cf. SQUIFFY.

swiping is the vbl n. of SWIPE, v., 2; also *blind swiping*: coll: 1879, W. G. Grace. 2. A birching, esp. by a monitor: Shrewsbury School: from ca 1880. cf. SWIPE, v., 3.

swish-tail. A pheasant, 'so called by the persons who sell game for the poachers', Grose, 3rd ed.: ca 1790–1870. 2. A schoolmaster: late C.19–20; ob. On BUM-BRUSHER.

swished, ppl adj. Married: low (?orig. c.): ca 1810–80. cf. SWITCHED.

Swiss. A pheasant: Oxford: ca 1815–60.

Swiss admiral. A pretended naval officer: naval coll: from ca 1870; ob. Ex the Fr. *amiral suisse*, a naval officer employed ashore: cf. the allusive S.E. *Swiss navy*.

switch. A chimney-sweep's brush: chimney-sweeps' coll: C.19. (George Elson, 1900.)

switch, v. To copulate with (a woman): 1772, Bridges, 'Paris . . . longs to switch the gypsy'; ob. cf. SWINGE, v., 1: many old vv. of coïtion are sadistic. cf.:

switched, ppl adj. Married: low (—1864). Prob. suggested by SWISHED. Presumably cognate with SWITCH.

switchel, n. Cold tea: Newfoundland coll: late C.19–20. Ex U.S. *switchel*, molasses and water.

switchel, v. To have sexual intercourse: Restoration period. cf. SWITCH.

switching. A marriage: low: ca 1840–1900. Mary Carpenter, *Juvenile Delinquents*, 1853. Ex SWITCH.

swive, v.t. and i. To copulate (with a woman); hence *swiver*, *swiving*, and *the Queen of Swiveland* (Venus). Excellent S.E. that, dating from late C.14, >, early in C. 17, a vulgarism; †since ca 1800, except as a literary archaism and in several diall.

swivel-eye. A squinting eye: coll: 1864, H., 3rd ed.; 1865, Dickens; ob. Ex:

swivel-eyed. Squint-eyed: coll: 1757, Smollett. Perhaps suggested Sheridan's 'T'other [eye] turned on a swivel', 1775.

swivelly. Drunk: late C.19–20; very ob. Ex *swivel* on SQUIFFY.

swiver, see SWIVE. **Swiveland, Queen of,** ibid.

swiz; occ. **swizz.** A FRAUD; great disappointment: late C.19–20 schoolboys'. Prob. an abbr. of SWIZZLE, the longer form being perverted SWINDLE. 2. Abbr. of SWIZZLE, n., 1: mostly Cockney: from ca 1875; ob.

swizzle. Intoxicating drink, whether a specific cocktail or strong liquor in gen.: s. >, ca 1850, coll: from not later than 1791, for it appears in the 3rd ed. of Grose, where, moreover, it is said that at Ticonderoga, in North America, the 17th (English) Regiment had, ca 1760, a society named The Swizzle Club; 1813, Colonel Hawker, 'The boys . . . finished the evening with some . . . grub, swizzle, and singing.' Slightly ob. ?a corruption of SWIG or cognate with the U.S. *switchel*, which, however, is recorded later and may be ex swizzle; perhaps *swizzle* derives ex SWIG on *guzzle* or even on dial. *twizzle*, v.t., turn round quickly. 2. See SWIZ.

swizzle, v.i. To tipple: s. and dial. (—1847) >, ca 1880, coll: ob. Halliwell. Ex the n., 1. 2. v.t., to stir (drink) with a SWIZZLE-STICK: 1859, Trollope (O.E.D.): s. >, ca 1880, coll. Prob. ex sense 1 but strongly influenced by *twizzle* (see end of *swizzle*, n., 1). Whence the next entry.

swizzle-stick. A stick for stirring drink to a froth: coll: 1885 (O.E.D.).

swizzled. Tipsy: from ca 1850. Ex SWIZZLE, v., 1.

swizzy. A s. variant of SWIZZLE, **n., 1,** and v., 1.

swobbers, see SWABBER.

swob-gill, see SWAD-GILL. **swoddy,** see SWADDY.

Swolks! see 'SWOUNDS!

swollen head, have a. To be tipsy: coll: late C.19–20; ob.

swop, see SWAP.

swop me bob or **Bob!** A perversion of S'ELP (via SWELP) ME BOB!: 1890, P. H. Emerson.

sworbote (or S.)!, God. A coll corruption of *God's forbote!*: ca 1580–1620.

sword, ship one's slung, see SLUNG SWORD.

***sword-racket.** Enlisting in various regiments and deserting after getting the bounty: c. of ca 1810–50.

sworder. A ship engaged in catching *sword*-fish: nautical coll: late C.19–20.

sworn at Highgate, see HIGHGATE.

swot, swat. Mathematics: ca 1845–95: military. Also, a mathematician. (Rarely *swat*.) Perhaps ex a R.M.A. professor's pronunciation of *sweat* (v.). 2. Hence, (hard) study: Public Schools' (—1881) and universities'. Perhaps imm. ex v. 3. One who studies hard: 1866. Ex second nuance of sense 1.

swot; occ. **swat,** v.i. To study hard: from

ca 1859: Army >, ca 1870, gen. at the universities. Ex n., 1. Hence *swot* (*swat*) *up*, to work hard at, esp. for an examination; to MUG UP: rare before C.20.

swot, in a. In a rage: Shrewsbury (school): late C.19–20. Corruption of *sweat*.

'Swounds! A coll euphemism for *God's wounds!*: 1589, Nashe; †by 1650. cf. the very rare perversion of *'Swounds*: *Swolks!*, recorded by Swift in his *Polite Conversation.*

swret-sio. The earliest form (—1859) of SRET-SIO.

swyg, see SWIG, n. **swygman**, see SWIGMAN. **swynge**, see SWINGE. **swype**, see SWIPE. **swypes**, see SWIPES.

***sycher** and **zoucher.** A contemptible person: c., and low: from ca 1780; ob. B. & L.: ' "Sich" is provincial for a bad man.'

Sydney-bird, -duck, or **-sider.** A convict: Australian: ca 1850–90. Ex the convict settlement.

Sydney duck. Any one of the numerous – many of them disreputable – Australians who rushed to California in 1849 ff.: mid-C.19–20; in C.20, mostly historical. Orig. an Americanism, it was adopted, ca 1860, in Australia. They sailed from Sydney; *duck* is ironic.

Sydney harbour. A barber: Australian rhyming s.: late C.19–20.

Sydney or the bush, e.g. it's (either). A final choice or decision: Australian (esp. N.S.W.) c.p.: late C.19–20.

syebuck. A sixpence: low: ca 1780–1850. Ex SICE, six; the *buck* may be a mystifying suffix suggested by HOG, a shilling, but cf. BUCK, n., 6.

syntax. A schoolmaster: coll of 1780–1860. cf. William Combe's *Tour of Dr Syntax*, 1813. Ex grammar. cf. GERUND-GRINDER.

syph; incorrectly **siph. Syph**ilis: coll: late C.19–20. Contrast CLAP.

syrup. Money: dispensing chemists' (—1909). cf. BRADS.

T

T, marked with a. Known as a thief: coll: late C.18–mid-19. 'Formerly convicted thieves were branded with a "T" in the hand,' F. & H.

t. and o.; T. and O. Odds of two to one: sporting: from ca 1880; ob.

t.b. or **T.B.** Top boy: London schools' coll (—1887).

t.t.; occ. **tee-tee.** Teetotal; a teetotaller: late C.19–20.

t.w.k. Too well known: Army in India: mid-C.19–20.

ta!; rarely **taa!** Thanks!: coll, orig. and mainly nursery: 1772, Mrs Delany, 'You would not say "ta" to me for my congratulation.' Ex a young child's difficulty with *th* and *nks*. cf.:

ta-ta! Good-bye!; au revoir!: coll, orig. and chiefly nursery: 1837, Dickens, '"Tar, tar, Sammy," replied his father.' Perhaps suggested by Fr. *au 'voir*.

ta-ta's (or -tas), go; go for a ta-ta. (Of a child) to go for a walk: (proletarian) nursery coll: late C.19–20. Ex TA-TA!

tab. (Gen. pl.) An ear: tailors': from ca 1870. 2. An old maid; loosely, any oldish woman: theatrical (—1909). Abbr. TABBY, 1.

tab, drive. 'To go out on a party of pleasure with a wife and family', Grose, 1st ed.: ca 1780–1830. Perhaps ex:

tabby; occ. **tabbie.** An old maid: coll (in C.20, S.E.): 1761, G. Colman, 'I am not sorry for the coming in of these old tabbies, and am much obliged to her ladyship for leaving us to such an agreeable tête-à-tête'; Grose, 1st ed., 'Either from *Tabitha*, a formal antiquated name; or else from a tabby cat, old maids being often compared to cats'. 2. Hence, a spiteful tattler: coll: from ca 1840. cf. *cat*. 3. Loosely, any woman; mostly in *tabby-party*, a gathering of women: coll (—1874).

tabby party, see TABBY, 3.

table, on the, adj. and adv. On the operating table: medical coll: mid-C.19–20.

table-cloth, the. A white cloud topping Table Mountain: South African, esp. Cape Town coll >, ca 1880, S.E.: from mid-1830s.

table-end man. A husband whose desires are so urgent that he cannot wait to go upstairs: domestic: late C.19–20.

table-part. A role 'played only from the waist upwards, and therefore behind a table': theatrical coll: C.19–20.

tace is Latin for a candle! Be quiet; it'd be better for you to stop talking!: coll: 1688, Shadwell, 'I took him up with my old repartee; Peace, said I, *Tace* is *Latin* for a candle'; Swift; Fielding; Grose, 2nd ed.; Scott; then in dial., occ. *cat* for *candle*. The pun is double: L. *tace* = be silent!; a candle is snuffed or otherwise extinguished. cf. BRANDY IS LATIN FOR A GOOSE.

tach. A hat: back s. (—1859). Via *tah* aspirated.

tache on, keep one's. To remain unruffled; keep one's temper: Anglo-Indian: late C.19–20. Punning *thatch* (head of hair, see THATCHED) and Tatcho's hair-restorer.

tachs. A fad: Tonbridge School: from ca 1880. Ex *tache*, a trait, now dial.; cf. the Somersetshire *tetch*, a habit or gait.

tack. Foodstuff, esp. in *soft tack*, bread, and HARD TACK, ships' biscuit: orig. (ca 1830), nautical. Marryat, *soft tack*, 1833. cf. TACKLE (4), victuals, which is rather later. Prob. a sailor's pun on either *tackle*, cordage, or *tack*, a ship's (change of) direction, or ex dial. *tack*, cattle-pasture let on hire. The O.E.D. considers it S.E.; more prob., I think, nautical s. >, ca 1860, coll and then perhaps, in C.20, S.E. cf. TOMMY. 2. Hence, food (esp. cooked food) in gen.: coll: late C.19–20. Lyell, 'What a filthy looking restaurant! What ever [*sic*] sort of *tack* do they give you in this place?!' 3. A feast in one's study: Sherborne School: from ca 1870. 4. Gear (harness, etc.): hunting: late C.19–20.

tack, on the. Teetotal: military: late C.19–20. Ex TACK, 1. cf. TACK WALLAH.

tack-on. The act of adding something; the thing added: coll: 1905.

tack or sheet, will not start. Resolute; with mind firmly made up: nautical coll: C.19–20. Ex nautical j.

tack together. To marry: jocular coll: 1754, Foote; ob.

tack wallah. A teetotaller: military: late C.19–20. cf. TACK, ON THE.

tacked, have or have got (a person). From ca 1870. 'When a man has another vanquished, or for certain reasons bound to his service, he is said to have "got him tacked",' H., 5th ed.

tacking, n. Obtaining one's end by roundabout means: lower classes' (—1909). Ex nautical j., perhaps with a glance at *tact*.

***tackle.** A mistress: c.: 1688, Shadwell. †by 1830. Prob., like the next, ex *tackle*, instruments, equipment. 2. Clothes: c. >, ca 1840, nautical s.: late C.17–19. B.E., '*Rum-tackle*, ... very fine Cloth[e]s'. cf. RIGGING. 3. Orig. (Grose, 2nd ed.) *a man's tackle* = the male genitals: late C. 18–20; ob. 4. Victuals: s.: 1857, T. Hughes, 'Rare tackle that, sir, of a cold morning'; slightly ob. In dial., it dates from mid-C.18. Prob. suggested by TACK. 5. A watch-chain, a *red t.* being a gold chain: c.: from late 1870s. Ex *tackle*, cordage, and frequently in combination with TOY, a watch.

tackle, v. To lay hold of; encounter, attack, physically: coll: orig. (—1828), U.S., anglicized by 1840 at latest. Perhaps ex *tackle*, to harness a horse, influenced by *attack*. 2. Hence, to enter into a discussion, etc., with (a person), approach (a person on some subject): coll: 1840, Dickens; 1862, Thackeray, 'Tackle the lady, and speak your mind to her as best you can.' 3. Hence, to attempt to handle (a task, situation), or to understand or master (a subject); attack (a problem): coll: 1847, FitzGerald. 4. Hence, v.i., with *to* (1847, Trollope), to set to; or *with*, to grapple with (from late C.19 and mainly dial.). 5. v.t., ex senses 1 and 3: to fall upon (food), begin to eat, try to eat: coll: 1889, Jerome K. Jerome, 'We tackled the cold beef for lunch.'

tacks. An artist's paraphernalia: artists' (—1909). Ware. Ex *tackle*, equipment.

tact, go on the. To go *on the* WATER-WAGGON: military: from ca 1890; ob. Suggested by 'teetotal', perhaps; but imm. by corruption, ex *on the* TACK.

tadger. Penis: North Country, esp. Yorkshire: late C.19–20. Perhaps ex *tadpole*.

tadger, tadging, see TEAICH-GIR.

Tadpole. A party-hack: political: middle 1880s; ob. Gen. in the phrase *Tadpoles and Tapers*. Coined by Disraeli.

taepo, see TAIPO.

taf; taffy. Fat, adj.; fatty, n.: back s., 'near' back s.: from late 1850s.

taff. A potato: Christ's Hospital: from ca 1860. ?ex TATIE or TATER. 2. (*Taff*.) A C.19–20 abbr. (noted by Bowen) of:

Taffy. A Welshman: a coll nickname dating from ca 1680 though adumbrated in Harrison's *England*, where a Welshman is called a 'David'. Popularized by the old nursery-rhyme, 'Taffy was a Welshman, Taffy was a thief' (see interestingly the v. WELSH). Also an 'inevitable' nickname of anyone with a Welsh name or accent: lower classes': mid-C.19–20. Ex a (supposed) Welsh pronunciation of *Davy*. cf. PADDY; SAWNEY.

Taffy's Day. St David's Day (1 March): late C.17–20. See TAFFY.

tag. A lower servant, so called because he assists another (cf. S.E. *tag after*, to follow servilely): servants' s. (—1857) > coll. cf. corresponding PUG. 2. An off-side kick: Winchester: from ca 1840. Mansfield. 3. An actor: from ca 1860; virtually †by 1900, †by 1910. Ex tags of speeches. cf.: 4. The last line of a play, whether in prose or in verse: theatrical coll: late C.19–20. It is, Alfred Atkins tells me, considered unlucky to speak it at rehearsals.

taihoa! Wait a bit!: New Zealand coll: from ca 1840. Direct ex Maori.

tail. The posteriors; fundament: C.14–20: S.E. until ca 1750, then (dial. and) coll; in late C.19–20, low coll. 2. The penis; more gen., the female pudend: mid-C.14–20: S.E. until C.18, then coll; in C.19–20, low coll. 3. Hence, a harlot: ca 1780–1850; but extant in Glasgow. Grose, 1st ed. 'Mother, how many tails have you in your cab? how many girls have you in your nanny house?' Other derivatives – prob. not coll before late C.17 or early 18, all ob. except those marked †, and all drawn from F. & H. – are these: Penis, †*tail-pike*, *-pin*, *-pipe*, *-tackle*, *-trimmer*, and †*tenant-in-tail*, which also = a whore; pudend, *tail-gap*, *-gate*, *-hole*. Also *tail-feathers* pubic hair; †*tail-fence*, the hymen; †*tail-flowers*, the menses; †*tail-fruit*, children; *tail-juice* (or *-water*), urine or semen; *tail-trading*, harlotry; *tail-wagging* or *-work*, intercourse; cf. †TAIL, MAKE SETTLEMENT IN, *go tail-tickling* or *-twitching*, *play at up-tails all*, and, of women only, *turn up one's tail*, *get shot in the tail*; *hot* or †*light* or *warm in the tail*, (of a woman) wanton; but †*hot-tailed* or *with tail on fire* = venereally infected. These terms are not results of F. & H.'s imagination: most of them will be found in one or other of the following authors: Langland, Chaucer, Shakespeare, Rochester, Motteux, Ned Ward, Tom Brown, C.18 Stevens and

Grose. 4. The train or tail-like portion of a woman's dress: late C.13–20: S.E. until C.18, then coll. Bridges, 1774, 'Brimstones with their sweeping tails'. 5. A sword: c.: late C.17–early 19.

tail, v.i. To coït: C.18–20; ob. 2. v.t., to follow, as a detective a criminal: coll: late C.19–20. Perhaps ex Australian sense, *tail* (drive or tend) sheep or cattle.

tail, cow's. A rope's end frayed or badly knotted: nautical coll: from ca 1860. Whence *hanging in cow's* (or *cows'*) *tails*, of an ill-kept ship.

tail!, kiss my. A contemptuous retort: C.18–20; very ob.

tail, make settlement in, and **tenant-in-tail** (see TAIL, n., 2) constitute an indelicate pun on the legal S.E. *tail* (ex Fr. *taille*, assessment), limitation as to freehold or inheritance. K. W., 1661, has *tenure in tail.*

tail, she goes as if she cracked nuts with her. A semi-proverbial c.p. applied to a frisky woman: C.19–early 20.

tail, top over; tail over top. Head over heels: coll: C.14–20 (ob.): S.E. until mid-C.18, then coll. See TAIL, n., 1.

tail-block. A watch: nautical (—1864); ob. Ex lit. nautical sense.

tail-board. The back-flap of a (gen. female) child's breeches: low: from ca 1870. Ex the movable tail-board of a barrow, cart, van, etc.

***tail-buzzer.** A pickpocket: c. (—1859); ob. Ex TAIL, the breech, + BUZ, to steal. Orig., it would seem, of a thief specializing in removing articles from hip-pockets. cf.:

***tail-buzzing.** That kind of pickpocketry (see previous entry): c.: from ca 1845.

***tail-drawer.** A sword-stealer, esp. from gentlemen's sides: c.: late C.17–early 19. Ex TAIL, n., 5.

tail in the water, with. Thriving, prosperous: coll: ca 1850–1910.

tail is out, one's. One is angry: non-aristocratic: from ca 1860.

tail is up the turd is out, – as hasty as a sheep, as soon as the. A low, mostly rural, c.p. from ca 1860.

tail of the cart, the. (Plenty of) manure: farmers' coll: late C.19–20. Shovelled out freely, the cart-tail being down.

tail off. To run or go off; to retire, withdraw: coll: 1841, F. E. Paget, 'Mrs Spatterdash ... tailed off at last to a dissenting chapel,' O.E.D., which cites from Rider Haggard (1885) the occ. variant *tail out of it*. Ware, 'From the tails of birds and animals being last seen as they retreat'.

***tail-piece.** Three months' imprisonment: c.: ca 1850–1910. James Greenwood, 1869.

tail-pulling. 'The publication of books of little or no merit, the whole cost of which is paid by the author', F. & H.: publishers': from late 1890s; ob. In contradistinction to the honourable publication of books of considerable merit and – to say the least of it – inconsiderable saleability. The former is practised only by sharks and amateurs, the latter by all.

tail-tea. 'The afternoon tea following royal drawing-rooms, at which ladies who had been to court that afternoon, appeared in their trains': Society: 1880–1901. Ware.

tail-twisting. The act of twisting the British lion's tail: political: 1889 (O.E.D.). Whence the rare *tail-twist*, v.i., and *tail-twister*.

tail will catch the chin-cough, (e.g.) **his.** A c.p. applied to one sitting on the ground esp. if it is wet: ca 1670–1800. Ray, 1678.

tailer. An exclamation on falling, or sitting, unexpectedly on one's behind: late C.16–early 17. Shakespeare, *Midsummer Night*, II, i. Ex TAIL, n., 1, whence also: 2. Such a fall: C.19–20; very ob.

tailor, v.t. To shoot at (a bird) so as to miss or, gen., to damage: sporting: 1889, *Blackwood's Magazine*. Ex tailor's slashes. 2. v.i., to have dealings or run up bills with tailors: coll: 1861, T. Hughes; very ob. and never common.

tailor, the fag-end of a. A botcher: coll: late C.16–17.

tailoring, do a bit of. To SEW UP: from ca 1860; ob.

tailor's ragout. 'Bread sopt in the oil & vinegar in which cucumbers have been sliced', Grose, 3rd ed. (at *scratch platter*): ca 1790–1850. See CUCUMBER.

tails. A tail-coat, as opp. a jacket: coll. 1888.

tails, charity. A tail-coat worn by a Lower School boy taller than the average: Harrow School: from 1890s. Ex TAILS.

tails of the cat. A nautical coll variant (—1887; ob.) of CAT-O'-NINE-TAILS.

taipo; occ. **taepo.** A vicious horse; as name for a dog: New Zealand coll: mid-C. 19–20. Perhaps ex Maori: but see Morris. 2. Among Maoris, a s. term for a theodolite, 'because it is the "land-stealing devil"' (Morris). Ex *taepo*, Maori for a goblin.

taj. RIPPING; luscious: boys': ca 1900–12. Ex *Taj Mahal.*

take, v.i. To be taken: coll and dial.: 1674, †*took with child*; 1822, *took ill*, the gen. form; occ. as in 1890, *took studious*, jocular. Ex *be taken ill*, etc. 2. v.t., followed by *to do*: to require (a person or thing of a stated ability, capacity, or nature) to do something: coll: 1890, *Field*, 8 March, 'Any ignoramus can construct a straight line, but it takes an engineer to make a curve.' 3. v.i. To be a good (*well*) or bad (*badly*) subject for photographing: coll (orig. photographers'): 1889, B. Howard, 'The photographers . . . say a woman "takes" better standing.' 4. v.i., to hurt: Charterhouse: late C.19–20. Ex a disease or an injection *taking*, i.e. taking effect.

take a Burford bait. To get drunk: C.19 coll ex C.18–20 dial. Orig., to take a drink: coll: ca 1630–1780. 'Water-Poet' Taylor, 1636; Fuller, 1662; 1790, Grose in his *Provincial Glossary.*

take a carrot! I don't care!: a low c.p. (—1887); slightly ob.

take a dagger and drown yourself! A theatrical c.p. retort: ca 1860–1910. Ex old coll phrase = to say one thing and do another, as in Ray, 1678.

take a figure. To appeal to the ballot instead of to tossing: printers': from ca 1860.

take-a-fright. Night: rhyming s. (—1859); slightly ob.

take a pull on oneself, often shortened to *take a pull.* To take oneself in hand, to pull oneself together: Australian coll: since ca 1860.

take a stretch out of (esp. a horse). To exercise: Australian coll: late C.19–20. To cause to stretch its limbs.

take a trip. To give up a job: tradesmen's (—1909). Ware: 'Followed by movement searching for a new situation'.

take a tumble (to oneself), see TUMBLE, TAKE A, and TUMBLE TO, v., 2.

take an earth-bath, see EARTH-BATH.

take an oath. To take a drink: late C.19–early 20. cf. TAKING IT EASY.

take and give. To live, esp. as man and wife: rhyming s. (—1909).

***take beef.** To run away: c. (—1859); ob. cf. *cry* BEEF.

take (one's) **Bradlaugh.** To take one's oath: 1883–ca 85. Charles Bradlaugh was 'intimately associated with the Affirmation Bill' (Ware).

take care of. To arrest: police coll (—1909). By meiosis.

take care of Dowb. To look after one's self or one's own interests: political, ca 1855–60. The story goes that some high-placed person wished to look after an officer called Dowbiggin and sent to Lord Raglan in the Crimea the message 'Take care of Dowbiggin.' Communications broke down in the middle of the transmission of the message, so all that arrived was 'Take care of Dowb . . .' and the receiver surmised that Dowb was some part of the Russian force or position. When the true meaning came out 'Take care of Dowb' became current as a euphemism for jobbery of one sort or other.

take charge, see CHARGE, TAKE.

take down, v.t. To deceive grossly; to swindle: coll (orig. Australian): 1895, *Melbourne Argus*, 5 Dec., '[The defendant] accused him of having taken him down, stigmatised him as a thief and a robber.' 2. In Australian sporting s., 'to induce a man to bet, knowing that he must lose . . . To advise a man to bet, and then to "arrange" with an accomplice (a jockey, e.g.) for the bet to be lost . . . . To prove superior to a man in a game of skill', Morris: from ca 1895.

take gruel. To die: lower classes' (—1909). Ex gruel as staple food in long illness among the poor.

take gruel together, we or they. We or they live together as man and wife: 1884, *Referee*, 14 Dec.; †by 1890. Ex a euphemism in a police-court case late in 1884.

take-in. A (gross) deception, a swindle: 1778, Fanny Burney; H., 1st ed., 'Sometimes termed "a dead take in" '(†). Ex the v. 2. Hence, a person who, intentionally or not, deceives one: coll: 1818, *Blackwood's*, 'There are . . . at least twenty take-ins . . . for one true heiress.' 3. Hence, occ. as adj. = deceptive: late C.19–20. 4. A man who takes a woman in to dinner: coll: 1898.

take in. To deceive, impose on, swindle: coll: 1725, *A New Canting Dict.*; 1897, 'Pomes' Marshall, 'He was "dicky", She was tricky – | Took him in, and cleared him out.' On *draw in.* 2. To believe or accept as 'gospel': coll: 1864, 'The Undergraduates took it all in and cheered . . .'

take in a cargo. To get drunk: ca 1815–70. Egan, *Life in London.*

take in your washing! A nautical c.p. order to a careless boat's crew to bring fenders, rope's ends, etc., inboard: late C.19–20. Bowen.

take it, see TAKE THE BISCUIT.

take it out of that! Fight away!: London: ca 1820–60. Bee, 'Accompanied by showing the elbow, and patting it'.

take off. A mimic; a mimicking, caricature, burlesque: coll: from ca 1850. Ex:

take off. To mimic, parody; mock: coll: 1750, Chesterfield; 1766, Brooke, 'He . . . perfectly counterfeited or took off, as they call it, the real Christian.'

take off corner-pieces or **take corner-pieces off.** To beat or manhandle (esp. one's wife): low urban (—1909).

take on. To show emotion; grieve, distress oneself greatly: C.15–20: S.E. until early C.19, then coll and dial. Whyte-Melville, 1868, 'There's Missis walking about the drawing-room, taking-on awful': that it had, ca 1820, > a domestic servants' word appears from Scott, 1828, 'Her sister hurt her own cause by taking on, as the maid-servants call it, too vehemently.' 2. To become popular, CATCH ON: 1897, Ouida. 3. To welsh: turf: from ca 1860.

take (one) down a peg. To lower (a person's) pride: coll: mid-C.17–20. 'Hudibras' Butler.

take one's last drink, see LAST DRINK.

take one's teeth to. To begin eating (something) heartily: coll: late C.19–20.

take (e.g. energy) **out of** (a person) is S.E., but *take it out of* (him) is coll when = to tire or exhaust him (1887) and when = to exact satisfaction from, have revenge on him (1851, Mayhew).

take that fire-poker out of your spine and the (or **those**) **lazy-tongs out of your fish-hooks** (hands)! A nautical c.p. of adjuration to rid oneself of laziness: late C.19–20.

take the biscuit. To deserve a prize for excellence; to be supremely remarkable. cf. *take the* BUN, and *take the* CAKE. Recorded by 1890, but perhaps far older, for its original seems to be late Medieval and early modern Latin. Wilfred J. W. Blunt, in *Sebastiano* (p. 88), records that the inn-keeper's daughter at Bourgoin, a famous beauty, was present, in 1610, as a delegate at an International Innkeepers' Congress held at Rothenburg-am-Tauber. Against her name, the Secretary wrote, *Ista capit biscottum*, 'That one takes the biscuit.' ML possesses *biscottus* or *biscottum*, a biscuit. cf.:

take the bun. See last entry. A lower-classes' variant of ca 1900–14 is *take the kettle*.

take the cake, see CAKE, TAKE THE.

take the can back. To be reprimanded; see CARRY THE CAN: nautical and military: late C.19–20. Perhaps ex illicit usage of its contents.

take the count, see COUNT . . .

take the Huntley and Palmer, see HUNTLEY AND PALMER. **take the kettle**, see TAKE THE BUN.

take the marbles out of your mouth! Speak more distinctly: a non-cultured c.p.: late C.19–20.

take the number off the door. A c.p. of ca 1895–1915, applied to a house where the wife is a shrew. Ware, 'The removal of the number would make the cottage less discoverable.'

take the tiles off (the roof), enough (or **sufficient**) **to.** Extremely extravagant(ly): Society: ca 1878–1910.

take to one's land-tacks. To go ashore for a SPREE: nautical: late C.19–20.

take too much. To drink too much liquor; drink liquor very often indeed: coll verging on S.E.: late C.19–20. Perhaps orig. euphemistic.

take-up. A point at which a passenger gets in: coachmen's and cabmen's coll (—1887); ob.

take up one's bed. To leave the shop for good: tailor's: mid-C.19–20.

take your washing in, Ma; here come(s) the (name of unit). A military c.p. addressed, on the line of march, by one unit to another: late C.19–20.

taken short, be. 'To be pressed with the need of evacuation of faeces': coll (—1890). *Funk's Standard Dict.* Ex S.E. sense, 'to be taken by surprise'.

***taker** is a contemporaneous variant of TAKER-UP. Greene, 1591. (In BARNARD'S LAW.)

taker-in. The agent of TAKE IN, v., 1: coll (—1887).

***taker-up.** He who, in a gang of four swindlers, breaks the ice with, and 'butters up', the prospective victim: c. of ca 1590–1620. Greene, 1591.

taking. Attractive, charming, captivating: C.17–20: S.E. until early C.19, then coll. cf. TAKY.

taking any (occ. with object expressed), **not to be.** To be disinclined for: ca 1900–10. *Daily News*, 10 March 1900, 'In the language of the hour, "nobody was taking any".' Perhaps orig. of liquor. Now, and long, *not having* ANY.

taking it easy. Tipsy: ca 1880–1914. Perhaps ex *take one's ease in one's inn*, to enjoy oneself as if at home.

taky. TAKING: coll; in C.20, ob.: 1854, Wilkie Collins, 'Those two difficult and delicate operations in art technically described as "putting in taky touches, and bringing out bits of effect"'.

tale, pitch a. To spin a YARN: coll: late C.19–20.

tale!, tell that for a. A c.p. indicative of incredulity: from ca 1870.

tale-pitcher. A 'romancer': coll: from ca 1890. Ex *pitch a* TALE.

talent, the. Backers of horses as opp. the bookmakers: sporting coll >, ca 1910, j.: from the early 1880s. Clever because they make a horse a favourite.

talk. To talk about, discuss: late C.14–20: S.E. until ca 1850, then coll. 2. (Of a horse) to ROAR: stable s. (—1864) > coll. 3. See TALKING!

talk big or tall. To talk braggingly or turgidly: resp. coll, 1699, L'Estrange, and s. (—1888), orig. U.S. Coulson Kernahan, 1900, 'Public men who talk tall about the sacredness of labour.' cf. TALL, 1.

talk bullock. To use much – and picturesque – bad language: New Zealand coll: 1846, Charles R. Thatcher. Both bullock-drivers and their beasts have much to put up with.

talk by a bow. To quarrel: London lower classes': ca 1860–82.

talk it out, see TALKER, 2. **talk nineteen to the dozen,** see DOZEN, TALK ...

talk the hind leg off a bird (Apperson), **cow, dog, donkey** (Baumann), **horse** (mainly dial.), **jackass,** etc.; or **talk a bird's** (etc.) **hind leg off.** To wheedle, to charm; to talk excessively, often with implication of successful persuasion: coll: Cobbett, 1808 ('horse's hind leg'); Beckett, 1838, 'By George, you'd talk a dog's hind leg off.'

talk through one's hat, see HAT, TALK ...
talk through (the back of) one's neck, see NECK, TALK ...

talk to. To rebuke, scold: coll: 1878, W. S. Gilbert.

talkee-talkee house, the. Parliament: London jocular (—1887).

talker. A horse that ROARS: stable s.: from ca 1870. Ex TALK, v., 2. 2. From ca 1860, as in Howson & Warner, *Harrow School*, 1898, 'Then followed solos from those who could sing, and those who could not – it made no difference. The latter class were called talkers, and every boy was encouraged to stand up and talk it out.'

talking!, now you're. Now you're saying something arresting, important, amusing: coll: from ca 1880.

tall. (Of talk) grandiloquent, high-flown: coll: 1670, Eachard, 'Tall words and lofty notions'. 2. (Very) large or big or (of speed) great or (of time) long: U.S. (ca 1840); anglicized ca 1860. '"Very tall" scoring' (in cricket), 1864 (Lewis); 'Pomes' Marshall, 1897, 'Her cheek was fairly "tall".' Ex sense 1 or, more prob. (despite contradictoriness of earliest records), ex sense 2.

tall, talk, see TALK BIG.

***tall-men, tallmen.** Dice so loaded as to turn up 4, 5 or 6: c. of late C.16–early 17. Kyd, 1592. cf. HIGH-MEN.

tall 'un. A pint of coffee, half a pint being a short 'un: urban lower classes': late C.19–20.

tallow, piss one's, see PISS ONE'S TALLOW.

tallow-breeched. With fat behind: C.18–mid-19. cf.:

tallow-gutted. Pot-bellied: low coll: C.18–mid-19.

tally, v.t. To reckon (*that* ...): coll: 1860; ob. Ex *tally*, to count.

tally, live (rarely *on*). To live in concubinage: chiefly mining districts (—1864). Ex *tally*, a corresponding half or part of anything.

tally-ho, adj. and adv. In concubinage: low: late C.19–20. Ex preceding.

tally-husband or **-man.** A man living thus: from 1870s. On:

tally-wife or **-woman.** A woman living thus: resp. early 1860s and late 1880s. Like preceding, mostly Northern. See LIVE TALLY.

tallywag; occ. **tarriwag.** The penis: late C.18–20; ob., except in Derbyshire and Cheshire dial. 2. Gen. in pl, the testicles: resp. late C.18–20 and C.17–20 ('Water-Poet' Taylor; Grose; Beckett, 1838). ?origin, unless ex *tally*, the corresponding half, + (to) *wag*, v.i., an etymology that fits sense 1, since this sense derives ex sense 2.

talosk. Weather: Shelta: C.18-20.

tam; tammy. A tam-o'-shanter: from mid-1890s: coll >, by 1900, S.E.

tamarboo. A hackney coachman: ca 1840–60. *Sinks*, 1848. Ex a song thus entitled.

tamarinds. Money: dispensing chemists' (—1909). For semantics, cf. SYRUP.

tamaroo. Noisy: Anglo-Irish (—1909). cf. Erse *tormánać*, noisy.

tamasha. Anything entertaining or exciting; an entertainment, a display: Regular Army: late C.19–20. Ex Hindustani.

tambour. The drum in a Punch and Judy show: showmen's: mid-C.19–20. See SWATCHEL.

tame cat. 'A woman's fetch-and-carry'; coll: from ca 1870; ob. Ex S.E. sense.

***tame-cheater.** A cheater at cards: c.: C.19–20; ob.

tame jolly, see JOLLY, n., 2. **tammy,** see TAM.

***tamtart.** A girl: c.: 1845, in '*No. 747*'. A perversion of JAM-TART (2) or possibly its original.

tan; tan one's hide. To beat severely; to thrash: resp. s., mid-C.19–20 (H., 1859); and coll, mid-C.17–20. Mrs Henry Wood, 1862, 'The master couldn't tan him for not doing it.' Ex *hide*, human skin, + *tan*, to treat it.

tandem. 'A two wheeled chaise, buggy, or noddy, drawn by two horses, one before the other', Grose, 1st ed.: s. >, ca 1820, coll >, ca 1850, S.E. Prob. university wit, ex *tandem*, at length, so frequent in L. classical authors (esp. Cicero). 2. A pair of carriage horses thus harnessed: 1795, W. Felton: s. >, ca 1820, coll >, ca 1850, S.E. 3. Ex sense 1, influenced by sense 2, as adv.: one behind the other: 1795 (O.E.D.): same evolution of status. 4. As adj., long: Cambridge University: ca 1870–90. Ware, 'Used in speaking of a tall man'.

Tangier. 'A room in Newgate, where debtors were confined, hence called Tangerines', Grose, 3rd ed.: c. or low s. of ca 1785–1840.

tangle-foot. Whisky: U.S. (—1860), partly anglicized ca 1900. Ex effect.

tangle-monger. One 'who fogs and implies everything': Society: ca 1870–1905. Ware.

tank, v. To cane: King Edward's School, Birmingham: from ca 1870. Ex dial. *tank*, a blow.

tank, on the. Engaged in beer-drinking, often with implication 'heavy drinking': British Army: since ca 1890.

tankard, tears of the. Liquor-drippings on a waistcoat: coll: ca 1670–1830. Ray, 1678.

tanker. A steamer fitted for carrying tanks of oil: 1900: coll.

tanky. The foreman of the hold, 'which looks like a tank' (Ware): naval (—1909).

tanned, ppl adj. Beaten (severely), thrashed: perhaps as early as 1860. Ex TAN.

tanner. A sixpence: low (—1811) >, ca 1870, gen. s. Dickens, 1844. Etymology problematic: H., 1st ed., suggests Gypsy *tawno*, young, hence little; in 2nd ed., L. *tener*. But see the note at SIMON, 1. 2. Whence *tannercab*, a sixpenny cab (1908), and *tannergram*, a telegram (when, early in 1896, the minimum cost was reduced from 1s. to 6d.)

tanner and skin. Money: tanners': ca 1855–1900.

Tannhauser. Penis: cultured s. of ca 1861–90. Wagner's opera *Tannhäuser* was enlarged with new Venusberg music in 1860–61.

tanning. A thrashing: mid-C.19–20. Ex TAN. cf. TANNED.

tanny. A mid-C.19 variant of TEENY.

tantadlin, tantaublin, see TANTOBLIN.

tantarum, see TANTRUM.

Tantivy. A post-Restoration true-blue Tory or High Churchman: ca 1680–1740, but esp. ca 1681–9. G. Hickes, *The Spirit of Popery*, 1680–81; B.E., '... Or Latitudinarians, a lower sort of Flyers, like Batts, between Church-men and Dissenters'; Swift, 1730. Ex a caricature representing High Church clerics 'riding tantivy' to Rome, and partly a satire on the hunting parson and squire.

Tantivy-Boy; t.-b. Same as preceding: ca 1690–1710.

tantoblin; tantadlin (tart). A lump of excrement: s. and dial.: resp. 1654, Gayton: 1785, Grose (*t. tart*). †by ca 1840. Ex *tantablin*, etc., a tart or round pasty: extant in dial. In C.17 occ. *tantaublin*.

tantrems. 'Pranks, capers, or frolicking', H., 1st ed.: coll or s.: ca 1850–1910. Ex TANTRUMS, + the dial. senses of the same + the occ. dial. spelling *tantrim*. (H. thought *tantrem* distinct from:)

tantrum; occ., though in C.20 very ob., tantarum; in H., 1st ed., **tantrem.** (Gen. in pl) A display of petulance; a fit of anger: coll: 1748, Foote, 'I am glad here's a husband coming that will take you down in your tantrums'; Grose, 1st ed.; Reade. Possibly, as H., 2nd ed. (though actually of *tantrems*), suggests, ex the *tarantula* (1693, O.E.D.), properly *tarantella* (not till 1782?), a rapid, whirling Italian dance; but perhaps rather ex the cognate *tarantism*, that hysterical malady which expresses, or tends to express, itself in dancing frenziedly, for *tarantism*, recorded ca 1640, might easily be corrupted to *tant(a)rums*, the singular not appearing before C.19. Less prob. ex *trantran*, a tantara, for it does not occur in C.18. Much, much less prob. ex: 2. (Frequent in singular.) The penis: 1675, Cotton in *The Scoffer Scofft*; app. †by 1800. Possibly cognate with North Country *tantril* (a vagrant, a Gypsy), recorded as early as 1684 (E.D.D.). 3. See TANTREMS.

tanyard, the. The poor-house: Caithness s., not dial.: ca 1850–80. Pejorative, E.D.D., 'Very common for some years after the Poor Law Act, 1845. The paupers had the greatest aversion to indoor relief and called the Poorhouse by this name.'

tanyok. A halfpenny: Shelta: C.18–20.

taoc, toac; tog (not properly back s.). A coat: back s. (—1859). H., 1st ed., has also *toac-tisaw*, a waistcoat; F. & H., 1904, adds *taoc-ittep*, a petticoat. The correct form, *taoc*, app. appears first in H., 3rd ed., 1864; and H., 1874, notes that ' "Cool the *delo taoc*" means, "Look at the old coat," but is really intended to apply to the wearer as well.'

tap. A tap-house or -room: s. (—1725) >, early in C.19, coll. T. Hughes, 1857. 2. 'Liquor drawn from a particular tap': from ca 1620, though not certainly recorded before 1832; fig., however, used in 1623, 'A Gentleman of the first Tappe' (cf. *of the first water*).

tap, v.i. To spend, pay up, freely: ca 1712–20. Addison; Steele. Semantics, 'to "turn on the tap" of gifts'. 2. v.t., to broach, in these s. senses: *tap a guinea*, to change it (Grose, 2nd ed.), †by 1890; *tap a house*, to burgle it (late C.19–20, ob.); *tap a girl*, to deflower her – in C.19–20, often *tap a* JUDY; *tap one's* CLARET (1823, 'Jon Bee'), to make one's nose bleed, *tap* by itself occurring in Dickens, 1840, but ob. by 1900; *tap the* ADMIRAL. 3. To arrest; also *tap* (one) *on the shoulder* (implied in Grose, 1st ed., 'a tap on the shoulder, an arrest'): coll; resp. †by 1890, and ob.

tap, do the. To win at cards: military: late C.19–20. Prob. ex:

tap, get the. To obtain the mastery: tailors': from ca 1870.

tap-lash. A publican: coll: ca 1648–1750. Ex *t.-l.*, inferior beer.

tap of work, not to do a. To do no work: Australian coll: since ca 1890. Ex carpentry.

tap on the shoulder, n., and v., see TAP, v., 3. **tap one's claret,** see TAP, v., 2.

tap run dry? or tap-water run out? A showmen's c.p. addressed to a quack doctor unoccupied or idling while his fellows are working: from ca 1880. The implication being that most of his medicine consists of water.

tap the Admiral, he would. He'd do anything for a drink: naval: late C.19–20. Bowen, 'From the old naval myth that when Lord Nelson's body was being brought home seamen contrived to get at the rum in which it was preserved'. cf. TAP, v., 2. See also ADMIRAL.

***tape.** Strong liquor: c. (—1725) >, ca 1840, (low) s. 2. Occ. gin: from ca 1820; H., 1859, having '*tape*, gin, – term with female servants', and Egan's Grose quoting from Randall's *Scrap Book*. Gen., however, *white tape* (1725) is gin, as occ. is †*Holland tape* (1755) and rarely †*blue t.* (1785, Grose); *red tape* (1725) is brandy; loosely *red*, *white*, *blue t.*, any spirituous liquor. For semantics, cf. RIBBON. 3. Sending messages by TIC-TAC men: turf: ca 1885–1910.

tape-worm. An official collecting prices of stock for transmission on the *tape*: Stock Exchange: not before 1884. Punning the parasite. cf. *ticker*, an account.

taper, v.t. To give over gradually; v.i., to run short: from late 1850s. Ex:

taper, adj. (Of supplies, money) decreasing: 1851, Mayhew; ob. Lit., (becoming) slender (cf. *slender chance*). cf. also the later *thin* (*time*, etc.).

taper, run. (Esp. of money.) To run short: from before 1859; ob.

taper off, v.i. To leave off gradually; esp. to lessen gradually the amount and/or strength of one's drink: coll: from ca 1870; ob. Ex TAPER, V.

tapis, on the. Possible; rumoured: diplomatic coll (—1828) verging on S.E.

tapper (C.19); **shoulder-tapper** (ca 1780–1910). A bailiff; a policeman. Prob. on much earlier *shoulder-clapper*. Ex TAP, V., 3.

tappy, on the. Under consideration: mid-C.19–20: low coll. Ex Fr. *tapis*, carpet, imm., however, ex (*up*)*on the* TAPIS.

taps. The ears: ?mid-C.18–mid-19. Because they tap conversation.

tar. A sailor: coll: 1676, Wycherley, 'Dear tar, thy humble servant'; Dibdin in *Tom Bowling*, 1790; Macaulay, 1849. Abbr. TARPAULIN. cf. TARRY-BREEKS.

tar and maggots. Rice-pudding with treacle: girls' schools': late C.19–20.

tar-brush. A tarboosh: among wanderers, esp. in India (—1886). Ex Hindustani ex Persian *sarposh*, lit. head-cover.

tar-brush, a touch of the, see TOUCH OF THE...

tar out. To punish, SERVE OUT: coll: ca 1860–1910. cf. S.E. *tar on*, but perhaps suggested by *tar and feather*.

tar-tar. A rare † variant of TA-TA.

taradiddle, see TARRADIDDLE.

taradiddler. A fibber: 1880 (O.E.D.): s. >, by 1900, coll; ob. Ex preceding.

tardy. Late with, at, in doing; e.g. 'I was tardy task,' I was late with my work: Winchester College: mid-C.19–20. Also *tarde*.

tare an' ouns! An Anglo-Irish oath: C.19–20. Corruption of *tears and wounds* (*of Christ*).

tare and tret. 'City bon-ton for – a Rowland for an Oliver', Bee, i.e. tit for tat: ca 1820–50. Ex *t. and t.*, 'the two ordinary deductions in calculating the net weight of goods to be sold by retail', O.E.D.

taring. See TEARING. C.17–early 18.

tarnal. CONFOUNDED: dial. >, early in C.19, low coll; mostly U.S. Ex *eternal*.

tarnation, n., damnation; adj., adv., CONFOUNDED(ly): late C.18–20: rather illiterate coll and mostly U.S. Ex *damnation* (cf. DARN(ATION)), the adj. and adv. being influenced by TARNAL.

tarpaulin; occ., though not after ca 1850, **tarpawlin.** A sailor: coll: 1647, Cleveland; Bailey, 1725; Stevenson, 1893; Frank C. Bowen, 'A practical seaman, particularly applied when appointments went by favour rather than by merit.' In C.20, only archaic; ob., indeed, by 1870. Tar much used by sailors. cf. TAR and TARRY-BREEKS; also JACK TAR.

tarpaulin muster. A forecastle collection of money, esp. to buy liquor: nautical coll: late C.19–20. The money is thrown on to a tarpaulin.

tar(r)adiddle. A lie, esp. a petty one: from ca 1790: s. >, in mid-C.19, coll. On DIDDLE, the *tar(r)a-* being problematic: cf. *tarrywags* (at TALLYWAG) and *tara!*, an exclamation used by Dryden. Hence:

tar(r)adiddle, v.i. To HOAX, impose on, bewilder, by telling lies: s. >, by late C.19, coll; 1828, *The Examiner*, 'His enemies... squibbed ... and taradiddled him to death.' cf. the ob. dial. *taradiddled*, puzzled, bewildered.

tarriwag, see TALLYWAG.

tarry-breeks, -jacket, -John. A sailor: coll jocular nicknames: resp. orig. (1785, Forbes), Scottish; 1822, Scott; 1888, Stevenson (ib.). According to Bowen, 'a naval ranker officer' in C.17. cf. TAR; TARPAULIN.

tart. A girl or woman (but if old, always *old tart*): from early 1860s. Orig. endearingly and of chaste and unchaste alike; but by 1904 only of fast or immoral women – a tendency noted as early as 1884. H., 3rd ed. (1864), '*Tart*, a term of approval applied by the London lower orders to a young woman for whom some affection is felt'; *Morning Post*, 25 Jan. 1887; Baumann, 1887, 'My tart – *mein Schätzchen*'; in late 1880s, the occ. diminutive *tartlet* (Barrère & Leland); 'Pomes' Marshall, 1896; above all, F. & H.; B. & P. Ex the idea of sweetness in a woman and a JAM-TART (2): cf. *sweetness* as a term of address.

***tartar; T.** (Properly *Tatar*. 'The *r* was inserted in medieval times to suggest that the Asiatic hordes who occasioned such anxiety to Europe came from hell (Tartarus), and were the locusts of Revelation ix,' *The Century Dict.*) A thief, strolling vagabond, sharper: c.: 1598, Shakespeare, 'Here's a Bohemian Tartar'; †by 1780. Abbr. TARTARIAN. 2. An adept: from ca 1780; ob. Grose, 1st ed., 'He's is quite a tartar at cricket, or billiards.' Ex next. cf. HOT STUFF.

***Tartar, catch a.** 'Said, among the Canting Varlets, when a Rogue attacks one that he thinks a Passenger, but proves to be of [the 59th order of rogues], who, in his Turn, having overcome the Assailant, robs, plunders, and binds him', *A New Canting Dict.*, 1725: c.: C.18. Ex TARTAR, 1.

***Tartarian.** A strolling vagrant; a thief; a sharper or swindler: c.: though prob.from 1590s, not recorded before 1608, *The Merry Devil of Edmonton*; †by 1690. Nares. Ex *Tartarian*, a native of Central Asia, the home of a warlike race. See also TARTAR.

tartlet, see TART, 1.

tashi shingomai. To read the newspaper: Shelta: C.18–20.

tassel. An undergraduate: university s. of ca 1828–40. Because his cap has a tassel. cf. TUFT.

taste, a, adv. A little; slightly: coll: 1894, Hall Caine, 'Nancy will tidy the room a taste.' (cf. *a bit* used adverbially.) In Anglo-Irish, it dates from the 1820s.

taste of the creature, see CREATURE.

taste the sun. To enjoy the sunlight: Cockney: ca 1877–1900. cf. SEE THE BREEZE.

taster. 'A portion of ice-cream served in a [*taster* or] shallow glass': coll: from ca 1890. Ware.

tastey; properly **tasty.** Appetizing: from ca 1615: S.E. until mid-C.19, then coll. Buckle, ca 1862, 'A tasy pie'. 2. Hence, pleasant, attractive: from mid-1790s: S.E. until mid-C.19, then coll; ob. except where it merges with senses 1 and 4. 3. Elegant: from ca 1760: S.E. until ca 1870, then coll; rare in C.20. 4. Hence, of the best: late C.19–20: coll verging on s. 'Pomes' Marshall, 'He's fond of something tasty . . . me and him was spliced last Monday week.' 5. (Ex sense 1.) Sexually alluring, SPICY: from 1890s: s. rather than coll; slightly ob. Whiteing, 1899, 'Nice and tastey, observes my friend . . as he points to a leg that seems to fear nothing on earth . . . not even Lord Campbell's Act.'

tasty-looking. Appetizing: coll: from mid-1860s. Ex TASTY, 1.

***tat.** See TATS. 2. A rag; esp. an old rag: c.: 1839, Brandon; 1851, Mayhew. Hence, *milky tats*, white rags or linen. Ex *tatter*. 3. Abbr. *tattoo*, a pony (esp. for polo): Anglo-Indian coll (1840). Also *tatt*.

***tat,** v.i. To gather rags, be a rag-gatherer: c.: 1851, Mayhew. Prob. ex TAT, n., 2. 2. v.t., to thrash, flog: low s. (—1812); †by 1890. Ex dial. *tat*, to pat or tap.

***tat-box.** A dice-box: c. (—1859). Ex TATS. cf.:

***tat-monger; tatogey.** A sharper using loaded dice: c.: resp. late C.17–20, ob. (Shadwell, 1688); late C.19–20. Ex TATS; but what is the second element of *tatogey*? Perhaps *bogey*, or it may be F. & H.'s mistake.

***tat-shop.** A gambling-den: c. (—1823). See TATS.

tata, see TA-TA!; TA-TA'S, GO.

tater, 'tatur. A potato: dial. and low coll: C.19–20. cf. TATIE; TATTO.

tater (etc.), **on for a.** Fascinated; esp. of a man by a barmaid: lower classes' (—1909). i.e. ready for a *tête-à-tête*.

tater!, s'elp my. The earliest form (—1860) of, S'WELP *my taters!*. A variation is S'ELP MY GREENS! For hidden sense, see STRAIN ONE'S TATERS.

tater-and-point. A meal of potatoes: low coll: mid-C.19–20. See POINT.

tater-trap. The mouth: low: 1816, J. H. Lewis, *The Art of Writing*, 7th ed.; 1856, Mayhew. See TATER.

taters, settle one's. On, and equivalent to, *settle one's* HASH: low s. (and Shropshire dial.): late C.19–20; ob.

taters, strain one's, see STRAIN ONE'S TATERS. **taters!, s'welp my,** see TATER, S'ELP MY, and SWELP.

tatie, 'tato. A potato: dial. and low coll: C.19–20. cf. TATER.

taties in the mould. Cold (adj.): rhyming s.: late C.19–20.

***tatler,** see TATTLER. **'tato,** see TATIE.

tatol. A tutor in Commoners: Winchester College: from ca 1870. It looks like a corrupted-ending blend of '*tut*or' and '*Co*mmoners', perhaps punning (*a*) *tattle*.

***tats, tatts.** Dice; esp. false dice: c.: 1688, Shadwell; Henley, 1887, 'Rattle the tats, or mark the spot.' Perhaps ex *tat*, to touch lightly: cf. TAT, v., 2. 2. Teeth: low: late C.19–20.

***tats and all!** Same as BENDER!: c.: ca 1810–50. Ex preceding: cf. SOME HOPES!

***tat's-man; tatsman.** A dicer, esp. if sharping: c.: 1825, Westmacott. Ex TATS.

tatt, see TAT, n., 3. ***tatt-box, -monger, -shop,** see TAT-BOX, etc.

***tatter.** A rag-gatherer: c.: from ca 1860. Ex TAT, v., 1. Also *tatterer*; from the early 1890s.

***tatter,** v.i. To collect rags; be a rag-gatherer: c.: from ca 1860. ?ex TAT, n., 2. 2. As a variant of *totter*, it is incorrect – and rare. 3. v.t., in *tatter a* KIP, to wreck a brothel: 1766, Goldsmith; †by 1830.

***tatterdemal(l)ion.** 'A tatter'd Beggar, sometimes half Naked, with Design to move Charity, having better Cloaths at Home', *A New Canting Dict.*, 1725: c.: C.18. Ex lit. S.E. sense.

***tatterer,** see TATTER, n.

tattie. A potato: dial. and low coll, mostly Scots: C.19–20. cf. TATIE.

***tattle.** An occ. C.18–mid-19 variant of TATTLER.

tattle-basket. A chatterer: coll: Ned Ward, 1703.

tattle-water. A synonym of SCANDAL-BROTH, or *-water*, i.e. tea: ca 1865–1910.

***tattler;** occ. **tatler.** 'An Alarm, or Striking Watch, or (indeed) any', B.E.: c.: 1688, Shadwell; slightly ob. The origin is explained by B.E.'s definition. Hence, FLASH *a tattler*, to wear a watch (late C.18–20), and SPEAK *to a tattler* (1878) or

NIM *a t.* (—1859), to steal one. 2. A dog that barks: c.: C.19–20.

tatto. A potato: dial. and low coll, mostly Scots: C.19–20. cf. TATTIE.

***tattogey.** A player operating with loaded dice: c.: C.19. Ex *tattogey*, a dice-cloth.

***tatts,** see TATS. **tatty tog,** see TOG, n.

tatur, see TATER.

Taunton turkey. A herring: mid-C.19–20.

taut hand. A first-class working rating who gives no, or very little, trouble: naval: late C.19–20. Ex *t.h.*, a strict disciplinarian.

tavern-bitch has bit him in the head, the. He is drunk: C.17. Middleton, 1608. Prob. the first form of:

tavern-fox, hunt a. To get drunk: coll: 1630, 'Water Poet' Taylor; †by 1700. On SWALLOW A TAVERN-TOKEN, but ex TAVERN-BITCH ...

taw, I'll be one – or a marble – (up)on your. A threat (= 'I will pay you out!') derived ex the game of marbles, *taw* being the large and gen. superior marble with which one shoots: coll: resp. from late 1780s and early 1800s; †by 1890, except among schoolboys.

tax-collector. A highwayman: a ca 1860–90 variant of COLLECTOR.

tax-fencer. A disreputable shopkeeper: low London: 1878; ob. Ex avoidance of taxes.

tax-gatherer, see GATHER THE TAXES.

taxes, the. The tax-collector: coll: 1874, W. S. Gilbert.

***tayle; *tayle-drawer,** see TAIL, n., 5; TAIL-DRAWER.

tea. A spirituous liquor: from ca 1690. Sometimes defined: *cold tea*, brandy (1693); *Scotch tea*, whisky (1887). Ex the colour. 2. Urine: 1716, Gay; implied by Grose, 1st ed., in TEA-VOIDER; †by 1860.

tea, v.t. To supply with, or entertain at, tea: coll. 1812, Sir R. Wilson. 2. Hence, to drink tea, have one's tea: coll: 1823; Dickens, 1839, 'Father don't tea with us.'

tea and toast struggle. A Wesleyan tea meeting: lower classes' coll (—1909). On TEA-FIGHT.

tea and turn out. A proletarian c.p. of ca 1870–1905 applied to absence of supper.

tea-boardy. (Of a picture) inferior: studio s.: from ca 1870; ob. Ex old-fashioned lacquered tea-trays with landscapes on them.

tea-boat. A cup of tea: nautical: late C.19–20.

tea-bottle. An old maid: lower-middle classes' (—1909). Ex fondness for tea.

tea-cake or -cakes. A child's seat or fundament: Yorkshire s. (—1904), not dial.

tea-chop. A Chinese tea lighter (boat): nautical coll: ca 1860–1900. 2. pl, the Chinese watermen loading the tea clippers: id.: id.

tea-cup and saucer. A very respectable, middle-class play: theatrical: ca 1865–95. Contrast 'kitchen-sink' drama.

tea-fight. A tea-party: 1849, Albert Smith: s. >, ca 1880, coll.

tea in China, see CHINA, NOT FOR ALL THE TEA IN.

tea-kettle groom. A groom who has to work also in the kitchen, etc.: low (—1887).

tea-kettle purger. A total abstainer: London lower classes' (—1909). Punning *tee-totaller*. cf. TEA-POT.

***tea-leaf.** A thief: c.: from ca 1905 or earlier. cf.:

***tea-leafing.** Thieving; esp. 'the picking up of unconsidered trifles', as Clarence Rook defines it in *The Hooligan Nights*, 1899: c.: from ca 1890.

***tea-man, teaman.** A prisoner entitled to a pint of tea, instead of gruel, every evening: c.: from ca 1870; ob.

tea-pot. Same as TEA-KETTLE PURGER: same period and status. 2. A tea-party: universities': ca 1880–1900. 3. A Negro: ca 1830–60.

tea-pot lid(ding). To KID (pretend); 'kidding': rhyming s.: late C.19–20.

***tea-pot mended, have one's; or get it down the spout.** To be restored to the privilege of tea: prison c.: from ca 1880; ob. cf. SMASH THE TEA-POT.

***tea-pot sneaking,** n. Theft of tea-pots and plate: c. from ca 1860.

***tea-pot soak.** One who steals tea-pots: c.: from ca 1860. ?error for *tea-pot sneak*.

tea-shine. A TEA-FIGHT: coll. 1838, Mrs Carlyle; †by 1890.

tea-spoon. £5000: commercial: the 1860s and '70s.

tea squall. A tea party: ca 1810–50. *British Columbia Historical Quarterly* of April 1937 (p. 120) records it for 28 April 1820. cf. TEA-FIGHT.

tea-voider. A chamber-pot: ca 1780–1890. See TEA, n., 2.

tea-wag(g)on. An East Indiaman: nautical coll of ca 1835–90. Because these ships carried tea as a large part of their cargo.

tea with, take. To associate with: Australian: 1888, Boldrewood. 2. Hence, esp. to engage with, encounter, in a hostile way: 1896, Kipling, 'And some share our tucker with tigers, | And some with the gentle Masai (Dear boys!), | Take tea with the giddy Masai.'

teach-guy. A late, rare form of *teaich-guy* (see TEAICH-GENS).

teach iron to swim. To perform the impossible: coll verging on familiar S.E.: C.16–20; ob.

teach your grandmother to suck eggs, see GRANDMOTHER HOW TO . . . **teacher always a teacher, once a,** see POLICEMAN ALWAYS. . .

teaer, teaing. One who takes tea; the taking of tea, or the corresponding adj.: coll: resp. 1892, 1874, 1852 (Surtees). Ex TEA, v., 2. Often written *tea-er, tea-ing*, or *tea'er, tea'ing*.

Teague; in C.17, occ. **Teg,** in C.18 **Teigue.** An Irishman: coll nickname: 1661, *Merry Drollery* (*Teg*); Swift, 1733; 1900, Stanley Weyman; extremely ob., and since ca 1870 nearly archaic. An English 'transcription' of the Irish name *Tadhg*, pronounced (approximately) *tayg*. cf. PADDY; SAWNEY; TAFFY. 2. In Ulster, a Roman Catholic: coll (—1904).

Teagueland; Teaguelander. Ireland; an Irishman: coll: late C.17–19. TEAGUE.

teaich. Eight; eightpence: back s.: 1851, Mayhew. cf.:

teaich-gens. Eight shillings: back s. (—1859). Also *teaich-guy* (ib.), by perversion of *gens*, and *theg-gens* (id.), see GEN. Contrast:

teaich-gir (pronounced *tadger*). Right: back s. (—1874). Hence *tadging*, TIP-TOP, excellent, splendid: late C.19–20; ob.

teaing, see TEAER.

tear (pron. teer). Gonorrhoea: naval: late C.19–20.

tear, v.i. To move violently; rush (about): coll: 1599, Massinger; Dickens, 1843, 'And now two smaller Cratchits . . . came tearing in.' Perhaps ex *tearing through obstacles*.

tear, shed a, see SHED A TEAR.

tear and ages (1841, Lever) or **wounds,** occ. **'oun's** (1842, Lover). Anglo-Irish coll interjections of astonishment. cf. dial. *tear*, a passion; *ages* may = *aches*.

tear Christ's body; tear (the name of) God. To blaspheme: coll >, by 1550, S.E.: C.14–mid-17.

tear one's seat. To attempt too much: tailors': from ca 1870.

tear-pump, work the. To weep: late C.19–20; ob. On WATER-WORKS (2) *turn on the.* See also PUMPS, n.

tear-up. A stir, a commotion: coll: mid-C. 19–20. 2. Deliberate destruction (often nerve-caused) of clothes and/or furniture: prison c.: from ca 1870.

tearaway. A would-be rough, esp. in *ladies' tearaway*, a man specializing in snatching handbags from women: low, verging on c.: late C.19–20.

tearing. Violent; passionate; roistering; rollicking: coll: 1654, Gayton, 'Some tearing Tragedy full of Fights and Skirmishes'; 1869, J. R. Green, 'I am in such tearing spirits at the prospect of freedom'; ob. Hence, 2, grand; splendid, RIPPING: late C.17–20; rare since mid-C.19.

tears of the tankard, see TANKARD.

teary. Tearful: late C.14–20: S.E. until mid-C.19, then coll.

tease; teaze, very rare in C.20. One given to teasing; one playfully irritating another: coll: 1852, Dickens, 'What a teaze you are.' Ex the v.

***tease, teaze;** occ. **teize.** To whip, flog: c.: ca 1810–80. Ex:

***tease** (but gen. **teaze** or **teize**), **nab** or **nap the.** To be flogged; esp. to be whipped privately in gaol: c.: ca 1780–1840. Prob. ex *tease*, the act of teasing. cf. sense 4 of:

teaser; teazer, very rare in C.20. Something causing annoyance; a 'poser': coll: 1759, Franklin; of a difficult ball in cricket, 1856. 2. Hence, in boxing s. (1812), an opponent hard to beat. 3. 'An old horse belonging to a breeding-stud – "though devoid of *fun* himself, he is the cause of it in others",' Bee: turf: ca 1820–70. 4. A flogging or whipping: c. or low s.: from ca 1830. Ex TEASE, v. cf. TEASING. 5. A sixpence, ca 1835–80. *Sinks*, 1848. Ex sense 1.

***teasing.** A flogging: c. of ca 1820–80. Ex TEASE, v.; cf. TEASER, sense 4.

teasy. (Of persons) teasing; (of things) irritating: coll: from ca 1907. Rare. Ex dial.

***teaze,** see TEASE, n., v., and phrase, **teazer,** see TEASER.

teazle. The female pudend: low: C.19–20; ob. Ex *teasel*, a plant.

tec;'tec. A detective: *Sessions* June 1879; 1899, Whiteing. Occ. *teck*.

Teddy my godson. An address to a simpleton: Anglo-Irish coll: from ca 1780; ob.

tee-tee, see T.T.

teejay. A new boy: Winchester College: from ca 1870; ob. Abbr. *protégé*. Also *tejé*, 1st syllable as Eng. *tee*, 2nd as in Fr. 2. Hence, as v.

teek; tique. Mathema*tics*; arithme*tic*: Harrow: from ca 1880; ob. Ex a French master's pronunciation of the relevant syllable.

teeny; teeny-tiny; teeny-weeny. Tiny: resp., dial. (—1847) >, ca 1860, coll: coll, 1867, ob.; coll, 1894, Baring-Gould. Ex child's pronunciation.

teeth. See TOOTH for phrases, etc., not hereinunder. 2. (Only in pl.) A ship's guns: nautical: 1806, John Davis, *The Post-Captain*; slightly ob. ?ex *show one's teeth.*

teeth, draw, see DRAW TEETH.

teeth upwards, go to grass with. To be buried: late C.19–20; ob.

teeth well afloat, have one's or **the.** To be tipsy: from ca 1870; ob.

teethward (properly **teeth-ward), be clerk to the.** A coll of late C.16–early 17 as in Hollyband's, i.e. Claude Desainliens's, *Dictionarie French and English*, 1593, 'He is clarke to the teethward, he hath eaten his service book; spoken in mockage by [?of] such as maketh shew of learning and be not learned.'

***Teetotal Hotel(, the).** A prison: c.: from ca 1880; ob.

teetotically. Teetotally: non-aristocratic jocular: 1890s. A perversion, silly enough; but with a less foolish glance at *theoretically*.

teetottler. A teetotaller: jocular: ca 1885–1900.

Teg, Teigue, see TEAGUE. ***teize,** see TEASE, n., v., and phrase. **teje,** see TEEJAY.

***tekelite.** A defaulting debtor: ca 1830–50: c. of the Debtors' Prison in Whitecross Street, London. Ex Count Emeric Thokoly or Tokoly (1657–1705), spelt *Tekeli* (or *-ly*) or *Teckeli* (*-ly*) in England, where this great patriot, leader of insurrections against the Germanizing Habsburgs, 'was certainly the most talked-about, most praised and most abused Hungarian in 17th Century England.'

tekram. A market: back s.: from 1860s.

telegraph, v. To tattle to: Eton: 1825, *Spy*, 'I have never telegraphed the *big wigs* in my life': Oxford: ca 1815–60.

telescope. To silence (a person): Australian: ca 1890–1910. ?ex telescoped carriages.

teliman. A tailor: pidgin: mid-C.19–20.

tell, v. To say, esp. in such locutions as 'Tell him good night' and 'Tell her goodbye': Canadian (and U.S.) coll: mid-C.19–20.

tell, hear. To hear (something) spoken of; absolutely, as in 'So I've heard tell', so I've heard. C.13–20: S.E. until mid-C.19, then coll and dial. Stevenson, 1896, 'I asked him if he had ever heard tell of ... the house of Shaws.'

tell me!, don't; never tell me! I can hardly believe it!; don't be silly!: coll: resp. mid-C.18–20, slightly ob.; and C.17–20, extremely ob. Shakespeare in *Othello*; Foote (*don't...*).

tell one his own. To tell him frankly of his faults or mistakes: coll: C.16–20; ob. Horman, 1519. cf. *give a piece of one's mind.*

tell that to the marines! see MARINES.

tell you what, I'll; in C.19–20, often **I tell you what;** in mid-C.19–20, occ. **tell you what** (Baumann). I'll tell you something; this is how it is: coll. Shakespeare, Tennyson; Violet Hunt, 'I tell you what, Janet, we must have a man down who doesn't shoot – to amuse us!'

teller. A well-delivered blow: boxing s.: 1814, *Sporting Magazine*; 1834, Ainsworth, 'Ven luckily for Jem a teller | Vos planted right upon his smeller'. Ob. Lit., something that tells, makes a mark.

telling, that would be or **that's,** see TELLINGS. App. from ca 1830.

tellings, that's. A c.p. reply to a question that one should, or does, not wish to answer: from ca 1835; slightly ob. Marryat, 1837, '"Where is this ..., and when?" "That's tellings," replied the man.' A playful coll or perhaps, orig., a sol. for '*That's telling*' = *that would be telling*, phrases that are themselves – at first, though not now – somewhat trivially coll.

tempest. A confused or crowded throng or, esp., assembly: Society coll soon > S.E.: ca 1745–80. Smollett, 1746, in a note on *drum*, says: 'There are also drum-major, rout, tempest, and hurricane, differing only in degrees of multitude and uproar.'

temple. From ca 1860 at Winchester College, as in Pascoe, 1881, 'On the last night of term there is a bonfire in Ball Court, and all the temples or miniature architectural excavations in "Mead's" wall are lighted up with candle-ends.'

Temple of Bacchus. 'Merry-making after

getting a liceat', Egan's Grose: Oxford University: ca 1820–50.

temple of the low men, the female pudend, is a late C.19–20 jocular pun on the literary 'temple of *Hy*men'.

***temple-pickling.** The ducking, under a pump, of bailiffs, detectives, pickpockets, and other unwelcome persons: London c. or low s.: late C.17–18. Lit., a pickling within the limits of the Temple.

ten A matches. Non-safety matches: naval: late C.19–20. 'The only matches allowed in H.M. Ships are "safeties" and in the old days anyone found with any other kind was given "Ten A" (now number eleven) punishment,' Granville.

ten-bob squat. A (seat in a) stall: theatrical (—1909).

ten bones. (One person's) fingers and thumbs, esp. in a coll oath: C.15–19. cf.:

ten commandments. The ten fingers and thumbs, esp. of a wife: mid-C.15–20; ob. Heywood, ca 1540, 'Thy wives ten commandments may serch thy five wyttes'; Dekker & Webster, 1607; Scott; H., 3rd ed., 'A virago's fingers, or nails. Often heard in a female street disturbance.'

ten-pennyworth. The punishment designated '10A': naval: C.19.

ten-stroke. A complete victory: billiard-players' (—1909). Ten being the highest stroke.

ten-to-four gentleman or **toff.** A (superior) civil servant: jocular coll (—1887).

ten toes, see BAYARD OF TEN TOES.

ten (gen. **10**) **wedding.** A wedding at which (?and after) the wife = 1, the husband = 0: non-aristocratic (—1909); ob.

tena koe? How do you do?: coll, North Island of New Zealand: late C.19–20. Ex Maori (lit., 'that is you'). cf. TAIHOA!

tenant at will. 'One whose wife usually fetches him from the alehouse', Grose, 2nd ed.: ca 1786–1840. Orig., a legal pun. cf.:

tenant for life. A married man, because he is hers for life: ca 1810–1900.

tenant-in-tail, see TAIL, MAKE SETTLEMENT IN.

***tench.** A penitentiary: c.: mid-C.19–20; ob. Abbr. 'TENTIARY. cf. STEEL; STIR. 2. The female pudend: low s.: mid-C.19–20. ?ex sense 1, or a pun on the fish.

tenderfoot. A greenhorn; any raw, inexperienced person: U.S. coll (recorded ca 1880, but implied in 1861) >, ca 1890, Colonial coll >, ca 1905, S.E. Ex the tender feet characteristic of one unused to hardship.

tenement to let. A HOUSE TO LET: ca 1790–1850.

tenip. A pint: back s. (—1859). With *e* harmoniously intrusive.

tenner. A £10 note: coll: *Sessions*, March 1848. cf. FIVER. 2. (A sentence of) ten years' imprisonment: c. (1866, O.E.D.) >, ca 1890, s.

tennisy. Addicted to, fond of, lawn tennis: coll: 1890 (O.E.D.).

tenpence, up a tree for, see TREE.

tenpence to the shilling (only). Weak in the head: s. (—1860) >, ca 1900, coll. cf. S.E. *tenpenny*, cheap, hence inferior.

tent. An umbrella: Anglo-Irish (—1904).

tent(-)peg. An egg: late C.19–20: tramps' s.

'tentiary. A penitentiary: low coll: mid-C. 19–20.

tenting. 'This is the word now in use among circus people to describe their mode of doing business in the country,' *All the Year Round*, 16 Nov. 1861: coll >, by 1880, S.E. Thomas Frost, *Circus Life*, 1875, simply defines *tent* and the synonymous PITCH, V., 2, as 'to go on tour.'

'tention. Attention: Canadian (and U.S.) coll: late C.19–20.

tenuc. The female pudend: back s.: from ca 1860. 'Eased' *tnuc*.

tenure in tail, see TAIL, MAKE SETTLEMENT IN.

term-trotter. One who keeps the terms merely for form's sake: Oxford University: ca 1780–1820. Vicesimus Knox, 1782. cf. TROTTER, 2.

terms (with), on, often preceded by **get.** (To get) on an equal footing (with): sporting: 1887, Sir R. Roberts. Ex lit. sense, on friendly terms. 2. Hence, in cricket: (of a side) having made a score comparable with their opponents': 1897.

terra firma. (A) landed estate: jocular coll: late C.17–early 19.

terri. Coal: Shelta: C.18–20.

terrible as a mere intensive is coll; gen. = very large or great; excessive. From ca 1840. Dickens, 1844, 'She's a terrible one to laugh.' cf. AWFUL; FRIGHTFUL; TERRIFIC; TREMENDOUS. cf.:

terribly. A frequent intensive (= excessively, extremely, very, very greatly): mid-C. 19–20: coll. Trollope, Jowett. Ex *terribly*, very severely or painfully. cf. AWFULLY.

terrific; terrifically. Excessive, or very severe or great; extremely, excessively, frighteningly: coll: in 1809, J. W. Croker describes the extent of business as 'terrific', and in 1859 Darwin admits that the corrections in his *Origin of Species* are 'terrifically heavy'.

terror. A HOLY TERROR: coll: 1889.

terry. A heating-iron: Shelta: C.18–20.

testament. See BIBLE, 2.

tester. A sixpence: definitely in 1613 (O.E.D.), but prob. earlier by some twenty years: s. >, by 1700, coll; by 1850, ob., by 1890 †, except as an archaism. Farquhar, Swift, Grose (1st ed.), Lamb, H. Ex *tester*, a debased teston, and *teston*, orig. worth a shilling but by 1577, at latest, only sixpence.

testugger. A 'testamur' or certificate: Oxford undergraduates' (—1899). By 'the Oxford *-er*'.

***testy.** A c. form of TESTER (sixpence): C.19. See CAT ON TESTY DODGE. This form virtually proves the TESTER origin of TIZZY.

Tetbury portion. A CUNT and a CLAP: ca 1780–1850. cf. ROCHESTER PORTION; WHITECHAPEL P.; TIPPERARY FORTUNE.

tetra, additional, fine, 'splendid'; *go beyond the tetra*, to beat the record: Felsted School: from ca 1870. Farmer, *Public Schools' Word-Book*, 1900. Perversion of *extra*? or ex Greek *tetra*, combining-form of *tessera*, 'four' (cf. FOURSQUARE)?

***teviss.** A shilling: costers' s. and tramps' c. (—1859); ob. Perhaps *shilling* > *shill* 'backed' to *llihs* > *lihess* > *lehiss* > *teviss*.

texts. Various passages learnt by heart before breakfast by the Schoolroom forms: Bootham School coll, verging on j.: late C. 19–20.

Thames butter. Very bad butter: London's poorer classes': ca 1870–5. Ex a journalist's attack on a Frenchman who was making 'butter' out of Thames mudworms.

Thames on fire, set the. Earliest in Foote, ca 1770, as *set fire to the Thames*; in Wolcot, 1788, we find *burn the Thames*: both these forms were †by 1850. The present form arose ca 1786, being first recorded in Grose, 2nd ed. Gen. in negative: to do nothing wonderful; never to make one's mark: coll >, by 1860 at latest, S.E. A similar phrase has been applied to the Liffey and the Spree, and W. quotes Nigrinus, ca 1580, 'Er hat den Rhein und das meer angezündet,' he has set fire to the Rhine and the sea. The proposed derivation ex *temse*, a sieve, is unauthenticated; in any case, it is *prima facie* improbable.

thank the mussies! Thank the Lord!: lower classes': ca 1870–1914. Ex *mercy*.

thankee!; occ. **thanky.** Thank you!: illiterate coll verging on sol.: from ca 1820. Dickens, 1848, 'Thankee, my Lady.' Corruption of *thank ye!* cf.:

thanks! (I) thank you: coll: late C.16–20. Ex *my thanks to you*, etc. Likewise *many* or *best thanks*, rare before C.19, though Shakespeare has *great thanks*.

thanks!, no. You don't catch me!: Society c.p.: ca 1885–1905.

thanks be! (May) thanks be given to God: coll: late C.19–20. Also in Cornish dial.

thanky! see THANKEE!

***thary,** v.i. and v.t. To speak (to): tramps' c.; from ca 1845; ob. 'Gipsy' Carew, 1891, 'I grannied some of what you were a-tharyin' to your cousin.' App. ex Romany. cf. ROCKER.

that, at. (Estimated) at that rate or standard; even so; even so acting; in that respect; also; unexpectedly, or annoyingly, or indubitably; in addition; and, what's more; yet, however; in any case, anyway: U.S. s. (from 1840s), anglicized ca 1885; by 1900, coll. Keighley Goodchild, 1888, 'So we'll drain the flowing bowl, | 'Twill not jeopardise the soul, | For it's only tea, and weak at that.' Perhaps ex 'cheap, *or* dear, at that price'.

that!, come out of. Clear out!: late C.19–20. Lit., come out from inside or shelter.

that moan's soon made. That grief is easily consoled: Scots coll (—1885).

that won't pay the old woman her ninepence. A Bow Street Police Court c.p. (—1909; ob.) in condemnation of an evasive act.

thatch, see THATCHED, BE WELL.

thatch-gallows. A worthless fellow: coll: ca 1785–1850.

thatched, be well. To have a good head of hair: jocular coll verging on s. (—1874). Ex *thatch*, a head of hair, esp. if thick: itself coll: from ca 1630. cf. *Tatcho* hair-tonic punningly named by G. R. Sims ex the Romany for 'genuine'. See TACHE ...

Thatched Head. An Irishman: pejorative coll nickname: C.17. Beaumont & Fletcher.

thatched house under the hill, the. The female pudend: low coll or s.: ca 1770–1850. Used as a title by Stevens in 1772.

that's a cough-lozenge for him! He's

punished: a proletarian c.p. of ca 1850–90. Ex an advertisement for cough-lozenges.

that's all was, ca 1830–80, a much-used coll intensive, as, e.g., in 'When I'm in the army, won't I hate the French, that's all.'

'that's gone', as the girl said to the soldier in the park. A c.p. of ca 1890–1910. Binstead.

that's right! Yes!: low coll: late C.19–20. Ex S.E. formula of approval.

that's up against your shirt! That's a point against you!: lower classes' c.p. of ca 1900–14. Perhaps ex stains on a white shirt.

that's what I say. A much overdone conversational tag that verges on being a c.p.: late C.19–20.

that's where you spoil yourself! A non-aristocratic c.p. directed at a smart person overreaching himself: 1880–81.

***theatre.** A police court: c. (—1857); almost †. Because there the prospective prisoner assumes a part unnatural to him.

Theatre Royal, amen. A church: low (—1909). Why? Perhaps it was orig. theatrical; touring players perform frequently at Theatres Royal.

theatrical. (Gen. pl.) An actor or actress: stage coll (—1859). i.e. *theatrical person* or *people*.

thedi or **theddy; tedhi.** Fire: Shelta: C. 18–20.

theg. Eight, as in *theg* GEN, 8s., and *theg* YANNEPS, 8d. Rhyming s. (—1859). See also TEAICH.

then comes a pig to be killed! A c.p. expressive of disbelief: lower-middle and lower classes': ca 1900–14. Ware, 'Based upon the lines of Mrs Bond who would call to her poultry – "Come, chicks, come! Come to Mrs Bond and be killed." '

then the band began to play! then the band played! See BAND PLAYED.

then you woke up? A c.p. implying disbelief in a tall story: late C.19–20.

there, all. Shrewd; alert; smart. *Not all there*: mentally deficient. Coll: 1864, Mrs Gatty. The negative phrase sometimes = dishonest, or criminal, as in Anon., 1877, 'He stayed . . . doing the grand and sucking the flats till the folks began to smoke him as not all there.' Whence:

there, be. 'To be on the *qui vive*; alive; knowing; in one's element', F. & H.: coll (—1890).

there, get, see GET THERE.

there, have (a person). To 'pose' or 'stump' him: coll: late C.19–20.

there, that. That, as in Richardson, 1742, 'On leaving . . . Mrs B.'s . . . house, because of that there affair': dial. and illiterate coll. Occ. *that 'ere* (C.19–20); in U.S., *that 'air*.

there and back. A c.p. reply to an impertinent or unwelcome inquiry 'where are you going (to)?': late C.19–20.

there first. A thirst: rhyming s.: late C.19–20.

there is the door the carpenter made!; usually with *there* emphasized. You may go: lower-middle class c.p. of ca 1760–90. *Sessions*, 1767, trial of Rebecca Pearce.

there you ain't! A proletarian, esp. Cockney, c.p. imputing or declaring failure: ca 1880–1910.

there you are! A coll variation of the *there you go!* of surprise, disgust, or approval: app. not before C.20; app. unrecorded before 1907.

there's (h)air! There's a girl with a lot of hair!: London streets' c.p. of ca 1900–12. But also *there's 'air – like wire!*, which is self-explanatory.

they say, where **they** is indefinite and may refer to one person. It is said: coll verging on S.E.: C.17–20.

they're off, said the monkey. The race has started; or, applied to something that has come loose: c.p.: late C.19–20. Often enlarged thus: . . . *when he backed into the lawn-mower* (with a consequent loss of potency).

***thick.** A synonym of STIFF, n., 1, by which it was prob. suggested: c. of ca 1820–50. 2. A blockhead; a foolish person: coll, mostly schools'; also Anglo-Irish: late C.19–20. T. Hughes, 1857, 'What a thick I was to come!' Ex *thick*, stupid. 3. Cocoa: (mostly London) street s.: from ca 1870; ob. Ex the consistency of cocoa as usually made. 4. Porter, which is said to be 'a decoction of brewers' aprons': rather proletarian: from ca 1870; ob.

thick, adj. In close association; familiar; intimate: coll: ca 1756, Bishop Law '"Yes," said he, "we begin . . . without my seeking, to be pretty thick"'; Barham; G. Eliot. And see the *as* THICK AS . . . phrases. Ex *thick*, close. 2. Excessive in some unpleasant way; intolerable, unmanageable; unjust: from early 1880s, the O.E.D. recording it in 1884. '"It's a bit thick", he said indignantly, "when a man of my position is passed over for a beginner . . .",' Horace Wyndham, 1907. Perhaps ex S.E. *lay it on thick*, to exaggerate, to flatter fulsomely. 3. Hence, indelicate; esp. in *a bit thick*, rather indecent: from ca 1890; slightly ob. 4. Hence (?), noisy and/or bibulous, esp. the latter: from ca 1891. W. Pett Ridge, *Minor Dialogues*, 1895, ' "I was out at a smoker last night." "Thick?" "Thick isn't the word."' 5. See DEAD THICK.

thick, adv. Densely: coll: late C.19–20. 'The syrup runs thick,' O.E.D.

thick, got 'em. Very drunk: from ca 1890; slightly ob. 'Pomes' Marshall, 1897, 'I've got 'em thick, he said . . . And . . . went upstairs to bed.' The *'em* is generic: cf. GOT 'EM.

thick and thin. Unshakable devotion to a party or a principle: political: 1884, *Pall Mall Gazette*, 14 Feb., 'The hidebound partisans of thick and thin'. 2. Hence, gen. hyphenated, as adj. in same sense: 1886, J. Payn: political and journalistic. Both n. and adj. little used after ca 1901.

thick as . . ., as. Similes – all coll – elaborating THICK, adj., 1: *as glue*, C.19–20; *as inkle-weavers*, late C.17–20 (ob.), as in B.E., Cowper, Scott – ex their working so close together; as *peas in a shell*, late C.18–19 – cf. as *three in a bed*; *as thieves*, C.19–20, as in Theodore Hook, 1833, ex the confidential and secret manner of thieves conferring; *as three in a bed*, C.19–20, as in Scott, 1820, but since ca 1870 only in dial. – ex the close packed discomfort. Dial. has many synonyms, e.g. *thick as Darby and Joan, Dick and Laddy, Harry and Mary, herrings in a barrel, two dogs' heads*, and (also a C. 19–20 coll) *thick as thick*: see esp. E.D.D.

thick ear. (Gen. *give one a t.e.*) An ear swollen as the result of a blow: low coll: late C.19–20.

***thick one**; gen. **thick 'un.** A sovereign; a crown piece: both c. (—1859) >, almost imm., (low) s. 'House Scraps' Aitken; B. L. Farjeon. Hence, *smash a t. u.*, to change it. 2. (Always *thick 'un.*) A slice of bread and butter: Cockney: late C.19–20.

thick starch double blue. A 'rustling holiday dress for summer': middle classes': ca 1905–14. Ware. Ex its over-laundered state.

Thicker. Thucydides, as a text: Harrow: from ca 1890. See 'Oxford *-er*', p. 11.

thickest part of his thigh . . . see HUMDUDGEON.

Thicksides. Thucydides: Public Schools' and Oxford: from ca 1840. P. G. Wodehouse, *Tales of St Austin's*, 1903, 'I'm going to read Pickwick. Thicksides doesn't come within a mile of it.' cf. THICKER.

thief. A horse failing to run to form: racing: 1896 (O.E.D.).

thief and a murderer, you have killed a baboon and stole his face, – you are a. A c.p. of vulgar abuse: ca 1780–1830.

thief in a mill, safe as a, see SAFE AS.

thieves' cat. A CAT-O'-NINE-TAILS with knots: nautical (—1867); ob. Because it was used as a punishment for theft.

thieving hooks. Fingers: low (—1887).

thieving irons. Scissors: C.19. ?because used for cutting purses.

thilly. A makeweight: Shelta: C.18–20.

***thimble.** A watch: c. (—1811). 2. Hence *thimble twister*, a watch thief (—1859), as in H., and *t. and* SLANG (8), a watch and chain (—1901).

thimble, knight of the. A tailor: jocular coll: 1812 (O.E.D.). See KNIGHT.

***thimble-crib.** A watchmaker's shop: c.: ca 1810–60. Ex CRIB, n., 3.

thimble-rig. A sharping trick with three thimbles and a pea: s. (1825, Hone) >, ca 1850, coll >, before 1890, S.E. 2. Hence, from ca 1830, *thimble-rigger*, such a sharper. See RIG, n.

***thimble-twister.** See THIMBLE, 2. The vbl n. is *thimble-twisting* (—1845: '*No. 747*', *Autobiography of a Gipsy*).

***thimbled.** Owning or wearing a watch: c. (—1812). See THIMBLE. 2. Arrested; laid by the heels: c. of ca 1820–40. ?by a pun on THIMBLE = a watch = the watch = the police.

thin, n.; plural, *thin*. A thin slice of bread and butter: Cockneys': ca 1845–1910. Mayhew, I, 1851.

thin as a rasher of wind, see RASHER OF WIND.

thin-gut. A very thin person; a starveling: C.17–20: S.E. until C.19, then (low) coll; so ob. as to be virtually †.

thin 'un. A half sovereign: from ca 1860; almost †. On THICK ONE or 'UN.

thing. Penis; pudend: when used not euphemistically but carelessly (cf. AFFAIR, 2) or lightly, it is low coll: C.17–20. 2. See GOOD THING; OLD THING; KNOW A . . . 3. See THINGS and:

thing, the. (Always in predicate). That which is suitable, fitting, fashionable; the correct thing; (of a person) fit, in good form or condition: coll: 1762, Goldsmith, 'It is at once rich, tasty, and quite the thing'; 1775, Mme D'Arblay, 'Mr Bruce was quite the thing; he addressed himself with great gallantry to us all alternately'; 1781, Johnson (of a procedure), 'To use the vulgar phrase, not the thing'; 1864, Meredith (of health), 'You're not quite the thing to-day, sir.' 2. Hence, the requisite, special, or notable point: coll: 1850, Thackeray; M. Arnold, 1873, '[A state church] is in itself . . . unimportant. The thing is to re-cast religion.' 3. See THINGS, THE.

thing-a-merry, see THINGUMAJIG. **thingamobob,** see THINGUMBOB. **thingamy,** see THINGUMMY. **thing'em,** see THINGUM. **thing'em bob,** see THINGUMBOB. **thing-o-me(-my),** see THINGUMMY.

things. Personal effects carried with one at a given time; impedimenta: coll: C.17–20; e.g. in 1662, J. Davies, 'We . . . went to the Custom House to have our things search'd.' Ex *things*, possessions, goods. 2. Clothes: coll: from ca 1630, as in Sheridan, 1775, 'I suppose you don't mean to detain my apparel – I may have my things, I presume?' 3. Hence, esp. such garments, etc., as, in addition to her indoor dress, a woman dons for going out in: coll: 1833, T. Hook, 'Take off your things – and we will order . . . tea.' 4. Implements or utensils; equipment: if the kind is specified, then coll: C.18–20, 'The kitchen things' is recorded by O.E.D. at 1738. cf. sense 1. 5. Base coin: c. of mid C.19–20; ob. Ex contemptuous use of *things*.

things, . . . and. And other such things; *et cetera*: coll: 1596, Shakespeare, 'Ruffs and cuffs, and fardingales, and things'.

things, no great. (Predicatively.) Nothing much; mediocre; very ordinary: coll and dial.: 1816, 'Quiz', '"The Governor", – He's no great things . . ., Sir.'

***things, the.** Base coin: c. (—1839); virtually †.

things (will) happen (even) in the best-regulated families, these (occasionally **such**). An apologetic or an explanatory c.p., applied to a family quarrel or misfortune: domestic: late C.19–20.

thingstable. 'Mr Thingstable, Mr Constable, a ludicrous affection of delicacy in avoiding the . . . first syllable in the title of that officer, which in sound has some similarity to an indecent monosyllable,' Grose, 1st ed.; †by 1830. (cf. ROOSTER (5) for COCK.)

thingum; in C.19, occ. *thing'em.* THINGUMMY: coll: 1681, Flatman, 'The Thingum in the Old Bailey': from mid-C.19, only in dial. *Thing* + *um*, a meaningless suffix. Prob. earlier than:

thingum thangum. THINGUMMY: coll: 1680, Otway; †by 1800. Reduplicated THINGUM.

thingumajig (occ. **thingermajig, thingummijib** (or **-jig**), **thingymyjig,** etc.), often hyphened **thingum-a-jig; thingumary,** occ. **thingummarie,** also **thing-a-merry.** A THINGUMMY: coll: *-jig*, 1876, 'Lewis Carroll'; *-ary* (etc.), 1819; the rare *thing-a-merry*, occurring in 1827, is †by 1890. Elaborations of THINGUM. O.E.D. cf.:

thingumbob; occ. **thingamobob, thing'em bob, thing(-)em(-)bob, thingumebob, thingummybob.** A THINGUMMY: coll: resp. 1751, Smollett – cf. Grose, 1st ed., 'A vulgar address or nomination to any person whose name is unknown'; 1870; C.19–20; 1778, Miss Burney; 1832, Lytton; mid-C.19–20 and due to a confusion with THINGUMMY. Ex THINGUM + a senseless suffix. 2. In pl: see senses 3, 4, of:

thingummy; often **thingam(m)y;** rarely **thing-o-me** or **-o'-me** or **-o-my;** fairly often **thingummie** or **-umy.** A thing or, occ., a person one does not wish to, or cannot, specify, or the name of which one has forgotten: coll: resp. 1819; 1803; 1796, *thing-o'-me*, perhaps a nonce-use, as prob. also is *thing-o-me* in late 1790s; *thing-o-my*, rare, is of early C.19; *-ummie*, from ca 1820; *-umy*, H., 1864. Thackeray, 1862, 'What a bloated aristocrat Thingamy has become.' Ex THINGUM + diminutive *y* or (*ie*) or, less prob., ex *thing* + *of me* (= mine). cf. THINGUMAJIG; THINGUMBOB. 2. The penis or the pudend: euphemistic coll: C.19–20. 3. In pl, the testicles: *thingumbobs* in Grose, 1st ed.; *thingummies* (etc.) not till C.19; *thingumajigs* not before ca 1880, nor *thingumaries* before ca 1820. 4. (Also in pl.) Trousers: lower classes' (—1909).

think. An act or period of thinking: dial. (from ca 1830) >, ca 1840, coll. Ex v. 2. An opinion: coll: 1835, Lady Granville, 'My own private think is that he will . . .'

think!, I don't. This c.p. (which is rather s. than coll) reverses the ironical statement it follows: 1837, Dickens, '"Amiably disposed . . ., I don't think," resumed Mr Weller, in a tone of moral reproof.' In late C.19–20, it often elicits the dovetail, *you don't look as if you do* or *I didn't suppose you did.*

think!, only; think!, you can't. Phrases exclamatory and/or intensive of that which follows: 1782, Mme D'Arblay, 'You can't think how I'm encumbered . . .!'; 1864, Mrs Carlyle, 'Only think! I get . . .'

think?, what or who do you. Phrases, esp. if parenthetical, ushering in a surprising statement: coll: 1616, Jonson, ''Mongst these . . ., who do you think there was? Old Banks . . .'

think about breakfast, see BREAKFAST, THINK ABOUT.

think and thank. Thank you!; thanks, gratitude: Yiddish (—1909). Ware, 'Translated from the first words of the ordinary Hebrew morning prayer'.

think-box. The head: Australian: ca 1890–1910. *The Sydney Bulletin*, 18 Jan. 1902.

think small beer of, see SMALL BEER.

think up. To invent, or to compose, by taking thought; esp. by racking one's brains, to hit upon, to devise: U.S. coll (1885) anglicized ca 1900. e.g. 'Things look bad; I must think up some stunt.' Possibly, to bring up to the surface of one's mind by hard thinking.

thinker. An actor playing a THINKING PART: theatrical coll: 1886.

thinking part. A role in which one says very little or nothing: theatrical coll: 1898, *Daily News*, 12 March. Because in such a part, an actor has plenty of time for thought.

thinks he holds it, he. He's a vain conceited fellow: from ca 1870: a sporting c.p. > gen. ca 1875; ob. Presumably *it* is the prize.

thinks his shit doesn't stink, often preceded by *the sort of bloke who* or *he*. A c.p. applied to a conceited fellow: non-aristocratic, non-cultured: ca 1870. Often completed by *but it does, same as any other bugger's*.

thirsty. Causing thirst: late C.16–20: S.E. until C.19, then coll.

***thirteen clean shirts.** Three months' imprisonment: prison c.: late C.19–20; slightly ob. i.e. at the rate of one shirt a week.

thirteenth juryman. A judge who, in addressing a jury, shows leaning or prejudice: legal (—1895).

this child. I; myself: orig. (—1842), U.S., at first esp. among Negroes; partly anglicized, mostly in the Colonies, late in C.19.

this is *all* right! Everything is wrong!: non-aristocratic c.p.: of ca 1896–1905.

this is where you want it, accompanied by a tap on one's own forehead. You need brains: c.p. late C.19–20.

this savvy. This afternoon: Merseyside school-children's: late C.19–20. A slovening of 'this *after*noon'. Perhaps, rather, sol.

thistle-down. Children apt to wander, esp. on moor or heath: Anglo-Irish coll (—1909). cf. the Devonshire dial. *thistle-seed*, Gypsies.

thistle-whipper. A hare-hunter: hunting: 1801. Contemptuous.

thoke. A rest, esp. in or on one's bed; an idling: Winchester (—1891). Prob. ex THOKY, not as at Winchester but as in dial.

thoke, v. To lie late in bed; to idle: Winchester (—1891). Ex n.

thoke on or **upon.** To look forward to: ibid.; id. Elaboration of preceding.

thoker. A piece of bread soaked in water and toasted or baked in the ashes: Winchester College: mid-C.19–20. Wrench. Ex *toasted + soaked.*

thokester. An idler: ibid.; id. Ex THOKE, v.

thoky. Idle: Winchester College (—1891). Ex dial. *thoky*, earlier, *thokish*, sluggish, lazy.

Thomas, John; man Thomas. The penis: resp. C.19–20; C.17–mid-19, recorded in Grose, 1st ed., but implied in Fletcher's *Monsieur Thomas* in 1619. cf. DICK.

Thomond's cocks, all on one side, – like Lord. Applied ironically to a group of persons nominally in agreement, actually likely to quarrel: late C.18–early 19. Lord Thomond's cock-tender shut in one room a number of birds due to fight, the next day, against another 'team'; result, internecine warfare.

thomyok or **tomyok.** A magistrate: Shelta: C.18–20.

thornback. An old maid: late C.17–early 19. 'Facetious' Tom Brown. A pun on *maid*, the female young of the *thornback* (ray, skate).

thorough churchman. 'A person who goes in at one door of a church, and out at the other without stopping', Grose, 1st ed.: ca 1780–1850. A pun on †*thorough*, through.

thorough cough. A simultaneous cough and crepitation: late C.17–mid-19.

thorough-go-nimble. Diarrhoea: 1694, Motteux. Ob., except in dial. 2. Hence, inferior beer: ca 1820–60. Scott, 1822 (O.E.D.).

thorough good-natured wench. 'One who being asked to sit down, will lie down', Grose, 1st ed.: ca 1780–1880.

thorough passage. 'In at one Ear, and out at t'other', B.E.: late C.17–mid-19. cf. THOROUGH CHURCHMAN; THOROUGH-GO-NIMBLE.

thou. A thousand; esp. £1000: coll: 1869 (O.E.D.). Ware dates it from 1860. cf. SOV.

though. (As adv., gen. at end of phrase.) For all that; nevertheless; however, yet: C.19–20: S.E. until mid-C.19, then coll. Browning, 1872; Anstey, 1885, 'I've lost [the note]. She told me what was inside though.'

thought did!, you know what. A c.p. to 'I *think* . . .'; late C.19–20. If the other asks *What?*, one adds *Ran away with another man's wife*. A softening of the late C.18–mid-19 form recorded in Grose, 2nd ed.: '*What did thought do? Lay in bed and beshat himself, and thought he was up*; reproof to anyone who excuses himself for any breach of positive orders, by pleading that he thought to the contrary.'

thousand a year!, another (ten). A drinking pledge: coll: mid-C.19–20; very ob.

thousand pities; or **towns and cities.** A woman's breasts: rhyming s. (on *bubs and titties* – see BUB, 3; TITTY, 2): late C.19–20.

thousand strokes and a rolling suck(, a). A nautical c.p. applied to a leaky ship: from ca 1870. Her pumps require many strokes and suck – an indication that she is dry – only when the ship rolls.

thrash one's jacket or the life out of one. To thrash; to thrash severely: coll: resp. 1687 (T. Brown), in C.20 almost†; from ca 1870.

thread the needle. To coït with a woman: C.19–20; ob.

three. A Rugby three quarter: sporting coll: C.20. (O.E.D. record: 1905). 2. A third-term cadet in: the training-ship *Britannia*: late C.19–early 20.

three!, the cube of. An Oxford toast of 1705–6. Thomas Hearne in his *Reliquiae*, 'The great health now is . . ., . . . 27, . . . the number of the protesting lords.' In reference to a political incident of the day.

three acres and a cow. A satirical c.p. (1887–ca 89) directed at baseless or excessive optimism. An ironic reference to the slogan coined by Joseph Chamberlain's henchman, Jesse Collings, who proposed that every smallholder should possess them: he became known as *Three Acres and a Cow Collings*. The slogan may be derived from a popular song of the 1880s.

three and sixpenny thoughtful. A 'feminine theory novel': Society: ca 1890–8. Ware. Satirical of, e.g., Mrs Craigie and Mrs Humphry Ward.

three bags full (or three bagsful). Much: coll.: from ca 1890.

three balls, see UNCLE THREE BALLS.

three Bs. Brief, bright, brotherly: ecclesiastical (—1909). In reaction against the somnolence of so many services in Victorian days.

three cold Irish, see FENIAN.

three-cornered. (Of a horse) awkwardly shaped: coll: 1861, Whyte-Melville.

three-cornered constituency. A house where one person's 'vote' gives victory to either wife or husband: Society: ca 1870–1914. Ex boroughs in which one voted for two of the three members returned.

three-cornered pinch. A cocked hat, either a seaman's or resembling one: military: ca 1800–50. John L. Gardner, *The Military Sketch-Book*, 1827.

three-cornered scraper. A cocked hat: nautical: from ca 1810; †by 1900. *Saturday Evening Post*, 16 March 1822.

three-cornered tree, see THREE-LEGGED MARE.

three-decker. A pulpit. A pulpit in three tiers: coll nickname; 1874. 2. 'A sea pie or potato pie with three layers of meat and crust or potato': nautical coll: late C.19–20. Bowen. 3. A three-volume novel: book-world coll: ca 1840–1900, then historical.

three decks and no bottom. An ocean liner: sailing-ship men's c.p.: late C.19–20.

three draws and a spit. (Occ. hyphenated.) A cigarette: low: late C.19–20; ob.

three-er. Something counting for three, esp. in cricket: coll: from the early 1890s.

three Fs, the. FUCK, fun, and a foot-race: low: ca 1882–1914. Punning the three demands of the Irish Land League, Free Sale, Fixity of Tenure, and Fair Rent.

three-figure man. One whose arrest comports a reward of £100: policemen's: mid-C.19–20. John Lang, *The Forger's Wife*, 1855.

three ha'porth of Gorde(l)pus. A street ARAB: London (—1909); ob. Ex Cockney form of *God help us!*

three is an awkward number. A c.p. (1885–6) paraphrasing *two are company; three, not*. Ex Lord Durham's nullity-of-marriage law-suit (1885).

three-legged mare, stool. The gallows; in C.17–18, esp. that at Tyburn: resp. 1685, T. Brown, and Grose, 1st ed. – †by 1850;

and late C.17–mid-19, as in B.E. Also *three-cornered tree*, 1654, but †by 1800; *mare with the three legs*, Ainsworth, 1834, and rare; (*the*) *three trees*, late C.16–mid-17, as in Breton. Also (*the*) TRIPLE TREE, (*the*) TYBURN TREE. 'Formerly consisting of three posts, over which were laid three transverse beams', Grose, 1785. 2. *comb one's head with a three-legged* (or *a joint-*) *stool.* Gen. as threat, *I'll comb your head*, etc.: coll: late C.16–18, then in dial. Shakespeare (*noddle*).

three Ls. Look-out, lead, latitude: nautical coll: C.19.

three-man breeze. A stiff breeze: sailing-ships': late C.19–20. A pun on *catamaran*, from whose crew such a breeze sent several men out on to the weather outrigger.

three more and up goes the donkey! see DONKEY!, A PENNY . . .

three ones. 1 cwt, 1 qr, 1 lb: London warehousemen's: from ca 1870. Also Lord Nelson, cf.: 2. (With capitals) Trafalgar Square: London s.: from ca 1860. The reference is to Nelson's Column, Nelson having one arm, one eye, and one anus.

three-out. A glass holding the third of a quartern: coll: from ca 1836. Dickens in *Sketches by Boz*.

three-out brush. A drinking-glass shaped like an inverted cone and therefore rather like a painter's brush especially when dry: taverns' (—1909).

three-piece bamboo. A three-masted ship: pidgin and nautical: from ca 1870; slightly ob.

three planks. A coffin: lower classes' coll (—1909).

three-quarters of a peck, often abbr. *three-quarters* and by experts written '¾'. The neck: rhyming s. (—1857).

three-ride business. 'The crack way of running over hurdles, in which just three strides are taken mechanically between each hurdle': athletics: from ca 1870.

three sheets, short for *three* SHEETS IN THE WIND: *Sessions*, Nov. 1857, 'He said "A man will do anything when he is *tight*, or *three sheets*" – he had been drinking.'

three sixty-five; gen. written '365'. Eggs-and-bacon: commercial travellers': late C.19–20. Because eaten for breakfast every day of the year. On slates in commercial hotels may be seen the legend '7 (*or* 7). 365', which means 'Call me at 7 (*or* 7.30); eggs-and-bacon for breakfast.'

three skips of a louse; not three skips of a louse. (Of) no value; not at all: coll: 1633, Jonson, 'I care not, I, sir, not three skips of a louse'; †by 1850. Hence, *for three*, etc.: very easily, or with very little provocation, as in Murphy, 1769, 'I'd cudgel him back, breast and belly for three skips of a louse!'; †by 1850. cf. *for* TUPPENCE.

three slips for a tester(, give). (To give) the slip: coll: ca 1625–1700. F. Grove, 1627; Anon., ca 1685, '*How a Lass gave her Love Three Slips for a Tester* [part of a ballad title], and married another three weeks before Easter.' Lit., (to give) three counterfeit twopennies for a sixpence.

three Ss!, mind your. A naval c.p. rule for promotion: late C.19–20. i.e. be sober, silly [simple; not offensively intelligent], and civil.

three steps and overboard, see FISHERMAN'S WALK.

three-stride business. The taking of only three strides between hurdles, this being the CRACK style: athletics coll: late C.19–20.

three to one (and sure to lose), play. (Of a man) to coït: low: late C.18–20, ob. Physiological arithmetic.

three trees, see THREE-LEGGED MARE.

three (in late C.19–20, often two) turns round the long-boat and a pull at the scuttle characterizes, among sailors (—1867; ob.), the activities of an artful dodger, 'all jaw, and no good in him', Smyth. Also *Tom Cox's traverse*, 'up one hatchway and down another', Smyth; likewise ob. This *traverse* dates from (not later than) 1806, when John Davis used the phrase. Bowen makes the *two turns* phrase mean also: 'Under sail, killing time'.

three-up. A gambling game played with three coins: only if three heads or three tails fall is the toss operative: coll >, ca 1900, S.E.: 1851, Mayhew.

three vowels. An I.O.U.: from ca 1820. Scott, 1822. cf. VOWEL.

three-wheeler. A tricycle: sporting coll (—1887); ob.

threepence, smart as, see SMART AS THREEPENCE.

threepence more . . . see DONKEY!, A PENNY. . .

threepenny bit or upright. A coïtion with a whore, price 3d.: low: mid-C.19–20; late C.18–20. Grose, 2nd ed., applies it to the 'retailer of love'.

threepenny bits. The female breasts: rhyming s. (on *tits* – TIT, 6): late C.19–20.

threepenny masher. A young man 'of limited means and more or less superficial gentlemanly externals': non-aristocratic: ca 1883–90. Ware.

threepenny shot. A beef-steak pudding, globe-shaped: artisans' (—1909).

threepenny upright, see THREEPENNY BIT.

threp, thrip; *threp(p)s, thrups. Threepence; a threepenny bit: in C.17–18, c., but in C.19–20, (low) s.: resp. late C.19–20; id.; late C.17–mid-19; from late 1850s. B.E., *threpps*; H., 1st ed., *thrups*; *thrip* existed in U.S. as early as 1834 for a coin intermediate between a nickel and a dime. Ex popular pronunciation of *threepence*; the *s* arises ex the 'suffix' *-ence*. cf. THRUMBUSKIN.

thrill. A thriller, whether fiction or non-fiction: ca 1886–1905. Ex its effect. cf.:

thriller. A sensational play (1889) or, esp., novel (1896): s. cf. AWFUL, DREADFUL, as nn., and SHOCKER.

thrip, see THREP.

throat, have a. To have a sore throat: coll: late C.19–20.

throat a mile long and a palate at every inch of it, wish for a. Applied to a 'healthy' thirst: mid-C.19–20; slightly ob. 'A modern echo of Rabelais', F. & H.: see Motteux's *Rabelais*, V, xlii.

throat (is) cut, one's belly thinks one's. One is extremely hungry: 1540, Palsgrave: a semi-proverbial c.p.; in mid-C.19–20 mostly rural.

throats, cut one another's. To compete ruinously: coll: from 1880s. cf. *cut-throat.*

throttler. A punch on the throat: pugilistic: ca 1810–60. *Boxiana*, II, 1818. Ex S.E. *throttle*, jocular for throat.

***through, be.** To be acquitted: c. of ca 1810–50. Vaux, *be through it, through the piece.* Ex lit. S.E. sense.

through a side door, have come. To be illegitimate: coll: from ca 1860.

through a woman, go. To coït with her: low coll: C.19–20.

through-shot, adj. Spendthrift: coll: late C.19–20; ob. ?ex going through one's money much as a shot goes through paper.

through the piece, see THROUGH, BE.

throw. 'He threw me with a stone' = he threw a stone at me. This South African Midlands coll, of late C.19–20, shows Dutch influence; Pettman aligns Ger. *Er warf mir ein Loch in den Kopf*, he threw a stone at me and cut my head open. 2. To castrate (an animal): Australian: late C.19–20. Ex its being thrown to the ground for the operation

throw a chest, see CHEST, CHUCK OUT ONE'S.

throw a leg over. To coït with (the female): low coll: late C.18–20.

throw a levant. To make off: mid-C.19–20. Ex *levant*, to abscond.

throw at a dog, not a (this, that, or the other) **to.** Gen. preceded by *have*. No — at all: coll: from ca 1540, for it is implied in Heywood, 1546; 1600, Day, 'I have not a horse to cast at a dog'; Swift, ca 1706, 'Here's miss, has not a word to throw at a dog'; 1884, Stevenson & Henley. Slightly ob.

throw back. To revert to an ancestral type or character not present in recent generations: coll: 1879. Also fig., as indeed is the earliest recorded example. (The n. has always been considered S.E.)

throw down. A defeat: 1903. Ex *throw down*, a fall in wrestling.

throw-down, v. To be too much for, to FLOOR: 1891, Anon., *Harry Fludyer*, 'These blessed exams are getting awfully close now; but I think I shall floor mine, and Dick's sure to throw his examiners down.' Also of the exam itself and the papers constituting it. Perhaps ex throwing down a wicket at cricket.

throw it up against, at or to one. To reproach or upbraid one with: coll (*to*: low coll): from ca 1870. Ex vomiting, cf. THROW UP, 2.

throw me in the dirt. A shirt: rhyming s. (—1857); †by 1900. The modern form is DICKY DIRT: much C.20 rhyming s. retains something – actual word or semantic essence – of the discarded form: DAISY RECRUITS and GERMAN FLUTES, both = 'boots', afford a particularly interesting example.

throw mud at the clock. To despair much or utterly: lower classes' (—1909). Ware, 'Means defy time and die'.

***throw off.** To boast of booties of the past: c. of ca 1810–60. Vaux, who notes also: 2. To talk in a sarcastical strain, so as to convey offensive allusions under the mask of pleasantry, or innocent freedom: c. (—1812) >, by 1860, s. in sense, to be depreciative (*at* a person).

***throw over the bridge.** (Gen. ppl adj., *thrown . . .*) To swindle as in BRIDGE, v.

throw snot about. To weep: low: 1678, Ray; ob. See SNOT.

***throw the feet.** To hustle; to beg: tramps' c. and low s., orig. (—1900), U.S.

Ex a horse *throwing his feet*, lifting them well.

throw the hammer. To obtain money under false pretences: low military (—1909). Of erotic origin.

throw up. (Of the male) to experience the sexual orgasm: low: C.19–20. 2. To vomit: coll: late C.19–20. 'I wanted to throw up' whether lit. or fig. used.

throw up a maiden. To bowl a maiden over: cricketers': from ca 1880.

throw up one's accounts. To vomit: from ca 1760; ob. C. Johnston, 1763. A variant of *cast up one's* ACCOUNTS.

throw up the sponge, see SPONGE, CHUCK UP THE.

throw with, see THROW.

throwing up buckets; gen. preceded by **simply.** Very vexed: exceedingly disappointed: Australian: from ca 1875. On SICK.

thrum, n., see THRUMBUSKINS.

thrum, v.t. To thrash (a person): C.17–mid-19. Dekker. The vbl n. (a beating) is recorded in 1823. Ex strumming a musical instrument. 2. To coït with (a woman): C.17–early 19. Florio, 1610; Brydges, 1762.

***thrumbuskins, thrummop; thrum(m)s.** Threepence: c.: *thrum(m)s*, late C.17–19; the other two forms (Vaux, 1812) are elaborations and rare. B.E. has *thrumms*, Grose *thrums*; H. (all edd.) the latter. A corruption of *threepence*: cf. *thrups* (at THREP). Dial. has *thrum*, a commission of 3d. per stone on flax. cf.:

***thrummer.** A threepenny bit: c. or low s. (—1859); ex preceding.

***thrum(m)s,** see THRUMBUSKIN. **thruppenny bit,** see THREEPENNY BIT. **thrups,** see THREP.

thruster. One who, in the field, thrusts himself forward or rides very close to the hounds: hunting s.: from 1885. Ex usual sense. Also *thrusting*, n. and adj.

thumb. To drain (a glass) upon a thumbnail (see SUPERNACULUM): coll: ?C.18–mid-19. 2. To possess (a woman): C.18–19. In C.20, only in *well-thumbed* (*girl*), 'a foundered whore' (F. & H.). Ex *thumb*, to handle, paw, perhaps influenced by *tumble*.

thumb, as easy as kiss my. Exceedingly easy: coll: from ca 1890.

thumber. A sandwich; a slice of bread and meat eaten between finger and thumb: low (mostly London): late C.19–20; ob.

thumby; occ. **thummie, -y.** A little thumb; a pet-name for the thumb: coll: from ca 1810. Tennant, 1811.

thumby. Soiled by thumb-marks: coll: from late 1890s. 2. Clumsy: coll: 1909. Ex *all thumbs*.

thump. An occ. late C.19–20 variant of THUMPER, 2.

thump, v. To defeat; to lick, thrash (severely): coll: 1594, Shakespeare; 1827, Scott, 'We have thumped the Turks very well.' Ex *thump*, to strike violently. cf. THRUM, v., 1. 2. To coït with (a woman): s. or coll: C.17–20; ob. in C.19–20. Shakespeare in *Winter's Tale*, 'Delicate burthens of dildos and fadings, "jump her and thump her".' cf. THRUM, v., 2, KNOCK and proposed etymology of FUCK.

thump, – thatch, thistle, thunder and. 'Words to the Irish, like the Shibboleth of the Hebrews', Grose, 2nd ed.: Anglo-Irish of mid-C.18–mid-19. A cross between an (and esp. an) incantation and a c.p.

thump on the back with a stone, this is better than a. A c.p. 'said on giving any one a drink of good liquor on a cold morning', Grose, 2nd ed.: ca 1786–1850. cf. the mid-C.19–20 *it's better than a poke in the eye with a sharp stick*.

thumper. Anything unusually big: coll: 1660, Tatham punningly of a dragon's tail. cf. WHACKER; WHOPPER, the semantics being that it 'strikes' one. 2. Hence, esp. a notable lie: 1677, W. Hughes; Swift; J. R. Green, 1863.

thumpers. Dominoes (game): showmen's s.: mid-C.19–20. Ex noise made in falling.

thumping. Unusually large, heavy, or, of a lie, outrageous: coll: 1576, Fleming, 'He useth great and thumping words'; Grose, 2nd ed., 'A thumping boy'; of a lie, app. not before C.19, though applied to commendation as early as 1671. cf. THUMPER.

***thumpkin.** A hay-filled barn: c.: late C.19–20. ?etymology. cf. SKIPPER.

thunder!; by thunder!; (what, where, who, etc.) in thunder?; thunder and lightning!; thunder and turf! Imprecatively, exclamatorily, intensively used as s. (*thunder and turf*) or coll (the rest): resp. C.18–20 (Steele); C.19–20; mid-C.19–20; late C.19–20, ob.; and ca 1840–70 (Barham, Lover). cf. the German imprecations and U.S. *thunderation!*

thunder and lightning. See preceding. 2. Gin and bitters: C.19–20; ob. Also shrub and whisky: Anglo-Irish: C.19. Ex the effects. 3. Treacle and clotted cream; bread thus spread: s. and dial. (—1880).

Miss Braddon; E.D.D. The O.E.D. notes that sense 2 approximates to the dial. sense (brandy-sauce ignited); W. implies that sense 3 arises ex the colours, *black* (of thunder and treacle), *yellow* (of lightning and cream).

thunder-box. A commode: esp. in India: from ca 1870. cf.:

thunder-mug. A chamber-pot: low: C.18–mid-19. Ex noise therein caused.

Thunderbomb, the; or *H.M.S. Thunderbomb.* An imaginary ship of fabulous size: nautical coll: ca 1828, Buckstone in *Billy Taylor*, 'Straightway made her first lieutenant | Of the gallant Thunderbomb'.

thundering. Very forcible or violent: coll: adumbrated in Hall, 1597,' Graced with huff-cap terms and thundering threats'; 1618, T. Adams, 'He goes a thundering pace'; 1632, Lithgow, 'A thundering rage'. Ex the noise made thereby or in that manner. 2. Hence, as an intensive: very large or great; excessive: 1678, Cotton, 'A thundering meal'; of a lie, app. not before mid-C. 18. 3. Hence, as adv.: from not later than 1743 in Hervey's *Memoirs*, 'A thundering long sermon'; 1852, Dickens, 'A thundering bad son.' s. >, by 1900, coll. cf.:

thunderingly. Excessively: 1885, C. Gibbon, 'It's thunderingly annoying,' but prob. much earlier, for Thornton records it, for U.S., in 1839: s. >, by 1900, coll. Ex lit. S.E. sense, but not very gen. Ex THUNDERING, 2.

thunderstorm, like a dying duck (or pig) in a, see DYING DUCK . . .

thusly. Thus: U.S. (1889) >, by 1893, English: coll; mostly jocular. cf.:

thusness. The state or condition of being thus: jocular coll: U.S. (1867, Artemus Ward) > anglicized ca 1883. 2. Esp. *why this thusness?*, a pleonastic 'why?': 1888, Fergus Hume, 'Why all this thusness?', O.E.D. – which records the simpler form in the same year. Slightly ob. – thank Heaven!

thuzzy-muzzy. Enthusiasm: London lower classes': ca 1890–1912. Ex *enthusiasm* on MUZZY.

tib. A bit: back s. (—1851). Hence *tib fo* OCCABOT, a little tobacco. 2. A goose: c.: late C.18–early 19. Abbr.:

***tib o(f) the buttery.** A goose: c.: ca 1620–1830. Broome, 1641, 'Here's grunter and bleater with tib of the butt'ry, | And Margery Prater, all dress'd without slutt'ry.'

tib out, v.i. To break bounds: schools', mainly Public and esp. Charterhouse: 1840, J. T. Hewlett; 1855, Thackeray. Also *tibble*: late C.19–20. Etymology obscure: perhaps ex *tip* (*oneself*) *out*, to get out by giving a TIP (9).

Tibb's Eve (or Evening; properly Tib's), St. Never: coll, mainly Anglo-Irish (—1785); long ob., except in dial. cf. BLUE MOON; S.E. *Greek kalends*; *Queen* DICK.

tibby. A cat: late C.18–mid-19. Ex *tabby* + dial. *tib*(*by*)-*cat*, a female cat. 2. The head: low: from ca 1810; ob. Esp. in phrases signifying 'to take unawares', as in Vance, ca 1866, 'For to get me on the hop, or on my tibby drop, | You must wake up very early in the mornin'.' ?a corruption of Fr. *tête* mispronounced.

tibby drop. Hop: rhyming s.: late C.19–20.

Tib's, see TIBB'S EVE.

tic-tac; tick-tack. Gen. *t.-t. man* (1899), occ. *t.-t. telegraphy* (1905). n. and adj. (characteristic of, concerned with) the system of 'telegraphy'– actually, signalling with the arms – used by bookmakers communicating a change in the odds or some significant information to outside bookmakers: sporting. Occ. as v., to signal thus: 1907: likewise coll. Ex the onomatopaeia representing an alternating ticking (as of a clock), perhaps influenced by TAPE, n., 3. Hence, *tick-tacker*.

ticca, see TICKER, 3.

tice. A ball something between a half-volley and a Yorker; cricketers': from ca 1840; ob. i.e. an *enticer*.

'tice, v. To entice, decoy; gen. in passive: lower class coll: C.19–20. Mayhew, 1861. Also in dial.

tick. An objectionable or meanly contemptible person, though rarely of a female: C.17–20: S.E. until mid-C.19 or so; ?'submerged' for years; in C.20, s. e.g., 'That awful little tick!' Ex the insect parasite. 2. Credit, trust; reputed solvency: coll >, in C.19, s.: 1668, Sedley, 'I confess my tick is not good, and I never desire to game for more than I have about me'; 1901, *Sporting Times*, 17 Aug., 'During my late Oxford days, I got put up to at least twenty different ways of getting tick.' Ex (*up*)*on tick*, esp. TICK, RUN ON. 3. Hence, a score or reckoning, a debit account: coll >, ca 1800, s.: 1681, Prideaux (Dean of Norwich), 'The Mermaid Tavern [at Oxford] is lately broke, and our Christ Church men bear the blame of it, our ticks, as the noise of the town will have it, amounting to 1500*l*.'; Thackeray,

1862. 4. A watch: c. of ca 1780–1800. Parker, 1789. cf. TICKER, 2. Ex the sound. 5. A second, moment; properly and etymologically, the time elapsing between two ticks of the clock: coll: adumbrated by Browning in 1879, but not gen. before the late 1890s. Esp. *in a tick* or *in two ticks*, and *to the tick*, with meticulous punctuality.

tick, v.i. To buy, deal, on credit: coll >, ca 1800, s.: 1648, Winyard. Ex TICK, RUN ON. 2. Hence, to run into debt: 1742, Fielding; ob. 3. v.t., to have (an amount) entered against one: coll >, ca 1800, s.; ob.: 1674, S. Vincent; ca 1703, T. Brown, 'Pretty nymphs . . . forced to tick half a sice a-piece for their watering.' 4. v.i., to grant credit; supply goods, etc., on credit: coll >, ca 1800, s.; in C.20, rare: 1712, Arbuthnot, 'The money went to the lawyers; counsel won't tick.' 5. Hence (v.t.), to grant credit to (a person): 1842, 'Nimrod' Apperley, 'He never refused a tandem, and he ticked me for a terrier at once.' 6. See TICK UP.

tick, full as a, see FULL AS A TICK. **tick, go (up)on,** see TICK, RUN (UP)ON.

Tick, River. Oxford University, ca 1820–40, as in Egan's Grose (1823): 'Standing debts, which only discharge themselves at the end of three years by leaving the Lake of Credit, and meandering through the haunts of 100 creditors.'

tick, run (up)on, v.i. To buy on credit; run up a debt or into debt: 1642 (O.E.D.): coll >, ca 1800, s. A variant is *go on tick* (1672, Wycherley) or *go tick* (1861, Hughes). Thus *(up)on tick*, on credit – though, despite the dates, this prob. preceded *run on tick*, for we find *(up)on ticket* (on note of hand) a generation or so earlier: *ticket* being abbr. to *tick*. See TICK, n., 2.

tick being no go. No credit given: low (—1857). See TICK, n., 2.

tick-off, work the. A *tick-off* is a fortune-teller; gen. in *work the tick-off*, to practise fortune-telling: grafters': late C.19–20. Philip Allingham, *Cheapjack*, 1934, 'Dates from the time when grafters working this line sold cards on which were printed various . . . statements.'

tick-tack. Sexual intercourse: coll: mid-C.16–20. Weaver, *Lusty Juventus*, ca 1550. Ex the onomatopoeia. 2. See TIC-TAC.

tick-tack, done in a. Quickly done: low coll (—1887).

tick up, v.t. To put to account: late C.19–20. Ex TICK, v., 3. 2. v.i., to run into debt: late C.19–20; ob. Elaboration of TICK, v., 2.

***ticker.** A fraudulent debtor by profession: c. of mid-C.18. Recorded in title of Anon., *The Thief-Catcher*, 1753. Ex TICK, v., 1 and 2. 2. A watch: c. (1800, *The Oracle*) >, before 1864, 'street', i.e. low, s. >, by 1890, gen. s. Ex the noise: cf. Fr. *tocante* and TICK, n., 4. Rarely and (I consider) improperly, a clock: the O.E.D. records an instance in 1910. 3. Any person or thing engaged by the job, or on contract: Anglo-Indian coll (—1886). Properly *ticca* (ex Hindustani). 4. The heart: low (in U.S., c.): late C.19–20. Because it keeps the body's time.

ticket. A certificate: nautical s. (late 1890s). Chiefly *captain's* or *mate's ticket*. Ex *ticket*, a licence. 2. See TICKET, THE.

ticket, v. To sentence (someone) to imprisonment: low: from ca 1880. Fergus Hume, *Hagar of the Pawn Shop*, 1898.

ticket, get one's, see TICKET, WORK ONE'S.

ticket, have the run of the. To buy on credit, run up debts: late C.19–20; very ob. An elaboration of TICK, n., 2 and 3.

ticket, the. The requisite, needed, correct, or fashionable thing to do. Esp. *that's the ticket*: 1838, Haliburton; 1854, Thackeray, 'Very handsome and . . . finely dressed – only somehow she's not – she's not the ticket, you see.' (See also CHEESE, THE.) Perhaps ex *the winning ticket*. 2. Hence, the plan or procedure; the job, on (or in) hand: 1842, Marryat, 'What's the ticket, youngster – are you to go abroad with me?'

ticket?, what's the. What's the price?: late C.19–20; very ob.

ticket, work one's (occ. **the**). To obtain discharge from the Army by having oneself adjudged physically unfit: from late 1890s: s. >, ca 1910, coll. (The phrase *get one's ticket*, to be, in the ordinary way, discharged from the service, is military j.) Wyndham, *The Queen's Service*, 1899, 'It is a comparatively easy matter for a discontented man to work his ticket.'

ticket for soup!, that's the. You've got it – be off!: c.p. of ca 1859–1910. cf. TICKET, THE, sense 1, which it elaborates. H., 2nd ed., '[From] the card given to beggars for immediate relief at soup kitchens'.

ticket of leave. A holiday; an outing: lower classes': ca 1870–1900. Ex S.E. sense.

ticket-o(f)-leaver. A gen. term of abuse:

coll: ca 1855–1900. Surtees, *Ask Mamma,* 1858.

***ticketer.** One who hands out, or checks, cards in a casual ward: tramps' and beggars' c. (—1887).

tickey, tickie; tickey-nap, see TICKY; TICKY NAP.

ticking. The taking of goods on credit: mid-C.18–20. See TICK, v., 1, 2.

ticking, ppl adj. of TICK, v. 1673, Wycherley (sense 1).

tickle. To puzzle (a person): coll (—1874); ob. Ex dial. cf. TICKLER, 1.

tickle-pitcher. 'A Toss-pot, or Pot-companion', B.E.: coll: late C.17–early 19. 2. 'A lewd Man or Woman', *A New Canting Dict.*, 1725: low C.18. A pun on the fig. sense of PITCHER (1).

tickle (one's) sneezer. To punch, even to break, his nose: pugilistic: ca 1810–50. Anon., *Every Night Book*, 1827.

tickle-tail function. A harlot: s.: Ned Ward, 1703. cf.:

tickle-tail. A wanton; the penis: ?S.E. or low coll: C.17–20; ob. 2. A school-master; his rod: coll (—1785); ob. cf. TICKLE-TOBY.

tickle-text. A parson: from ca 1780; very ob.

tickle-Thomas. The female pudend: low: C.19–20. cf. *John* THOMAS.

tickle-toby. A rod or birch: coll: 1830, Bentham. 2. A wanton; the penis: ?C.17–19. cf. TICKLE-PITCHER, 2; TICKLE-TAIL.

tickle your tail!, I'll. A jocular coll threat of punishment: late C.19–20. Ex S.E. *tickle*, ironic for 'to chastise'.

tickled pink. Immensely pleased: late C. 19–20. 'I'll be tickled pink to accept the offer.' To the point of blushing with pleasure.

tickler. A thing (occ. person) hard to understand or deal with; a puzzler or TEASER: dial. (—1825) >, ca 1840, coll; ob. 2. A strong drink: low: late C.19–20. 3. The penis: low: C.19–20. 4. A short poker used to save an ornamental one: domestic: from ca 1870. 5. A whip: proletarian: from ca 1860.

***tickrum.** A licence: c.: ca 1670–1830. A corruption of *ticket.*

ticks. Debts, obligations: sporting (—1887); ob. Ex TICK, n., 2.

ticky, tickey, or **tickie**; occ. **tiki, tikki, tikkie.** A threepenny piece: South African coll: from ca 1850. Etymology obscure: perhaps ex a native attempt at *ticket* or at *threepenny*; perhaps – though much less likely – suggested by Romany *tikeno*, *tikno*, small, little; prob., however, as Pettman ably shows, ex Portuguese, hence Malayan, *pataca* (†Fr. *patac*).

ticky nap. A game of nap(oleon) with a TICKY stake for each trick: late C.19–20: South African.

tidd. A children's abbr. (late C.19–20) of TIDDLER, 1.

tiddipol. 'An overdressed fat young woman in humble life', Halliwell: provincial: C.19. cf.:

tiddivate, tidivate, see TITIVATE.

tiddle, v.i. To fidget, potter: S.E. until ca 1830, then dial. and coll: 1748, Richardson: slightly ob. 2. v.t., to advance slowly or by small movements (e.g. a ball, a wheelbarrow); *tiddle a girl,* to master her very gradually: coll: mid-C.19–20. Perhaps ex dial. *tiddle*, to tickle, possibly influenced by *diddle*; much more prob. by a development of sense ex S.E. (in C.19–20, dial. and coll) *tiddle*, to pamper, to fondle excessively.

tiddle-a-wink, see TIDDLYWINK. **tiddle-bat,** see TITTLEBAT.

tiddler. A stickleback: nursery coll: 1885 (O.E.D.). Ex TITTLEBAT, *tiddlebat*, the popular form. Hence: 2. Any small fish: Australian: late C.19–20.

tiddl(e)y, see TITLEY. **tiddlewinks, tiddley-wink,** see TIDDLYWINK.

tiddlies, run. To run over unsafe ice: provincial: mid-C.19–20.

tiddly, n. See TITLEY. 2. adj., drunk: late C.19–20: low. Ex TITLEY, n. 3. Little: dial. and nursery coll: C.19–20. 4. Hence (?), particularly smart: naval: late C.19–20.

tiddlywink; also **tid(d)leywink, tiddle-a-wink.** An unlicensed house (pawnbroker's, beer-shop, brothel, etc.): 1844, J. T. Hewlett. Perhaps ex TITLEY + *wink* (cf. *on the* SLY). Also KIDDLYWINK (3, 4). 2. pl only; with variant *tiddlewinks*: knick-knacks of food: 1893, J. A. Barry. Perhaps influenced by TIDDLY, 3. 3. A drink: rhyming s.: 1880, Barrett.

tiddlywink, v.i. To spend imprudently or with unsanctioned excess: Australian: 1888, Boldrewood, 'He's going too fast . . . I wonder what old Morgan would say to all this here tiddley-winkin', with steam engine, and wire fences'; ob. Ex the n.; rare except in the form of the vbl n.

tiddlywink, adj. Slim, puny: from ca 1863; ob. Not because *tiddlywinks* is considered a feeble, futile game, for it is recorded later, but ex TIDDLYWINK, n., 1. Occ. *tillywink*.

tiddlywinker. A cheat; a trifler: resp. 1893, ca 1895. Ultimately ex TIDDLYWINK, n., but imm., though nuance 2 is perhaps influenced by *tiddlywinks*, ex:

tiddlywinking, adj. Pottering; trifling: 1869. Ex TIDDLYWINK, n., 1.

tiddlywinks, see TIDDLYWINK, n., 2.

tiddy. Small, tiny: dial. (—1781) >, by 1860, coll, esp. nursery coll. Perhaps ex a confusion of *tiny + little*.

tiddy iddy. A reduplication of TIDDY: 1868, W. S. Gilbert.

tiddyvate, tidivate, see TITIVATE. **tidlywink,** see TIDDLYWINK.

tidemark. The dirty mark so many boys leave when they wash their necks: jocular: late C.19–20.

tidy. Fairly meritorious or satisfactory; (of a person) decent, nice: coll: 1844, Dickens, 'For a coastguardsman ... rather a tidy question'. Ex †S.E. *tidy*, excellent, worthy. 2. (In amount, degree) considerable: coll: 1838, Dickens, 'At a tidy pace'. Hence, *a tidy penny*, very fair earnings, etc. cf. sense 1, and the adv.

tidy, v.t., often with **up.** To make orderly, clean, etc.: from ca 1820: in serious contexts, familiar S.E.; in trivial, coll. Ex *tidy*, in good condition, clean. 2. Hence, v.i.: coll: 1853, Dickens, 'I have tidied over and over again, but it's useless.' 3. Also ex sense 1: *tidy away* or *up*, to stow away, clear up, for tidiness' sake: coll: 1867.

tidy, adv. Pretty well; a good deal; finely, comfortably: dial. and low coll: 1824 (O.E.D.); 1899, Whiteing, '"Was you knocked about much ...?" "Pretty tidy."'

***tie it up,** see TIE UP, v., 1.

tie one's hair or **wool.** To puzzle (a person): tailors': from ca 1870.

tie-mate. A particular friend: naval coll: mid-C.18–early 19.

tie-up. A knock-out blow, a SETTLER (3): boxing: 1818. Ex lit. sense (cf. cricket j.). 2. ?hence, a conclusion: 1829; rather ob. 3. An obstruction, stoppage, closure: from late 1880s: coll.

***tie up,** v. To forswear: c.: mid-C.19–20; ob. e.g. *tie up* PRIGGING, to live honestly. Ex the parallel s. sense, to desist, to desist from – a sense recorded by O.E.D. for 1760 (Foote). 2. To knock out: boxing: from ca 1810. cf. TIED-UP, 1. 3. To join in marriage: coll: 1894, Astley. 4. To get (a woman) with child: low: C.19–20; ob.

tie up your stocking! No heel-taps!: Oxford University: late C.19–20; ob.

tie with St Mary's knot, see ST MARY'S KNOT.

tied-up. Finished, settled: orig., boxing (—1859). 2. Costive: from ca 1870. 3. See TIE UP, v., 3.

tied with the tongue that cannot be untied with the teeth, a knot, see KNOT WITH THE TONGUE ...

tiers. Mountains; *tiersman*, one living in the mountains: Tasmanian: late C.19–20.

tiff. Liquor, esp. if thin or inferior: from ca 1630; ob. by 1870, †by 1930: coll >, ca 1750, s. Corbet, ca 1635; Fielding; Scott. Perhaps of echoic origin. 2. Hence, a small draught (rarely of other than diluted liquor, esp. punch): coll (—1727) >, ca 1750, s. Bailey; Scott. 3. A slight outburst of temper or ill-humour: coll (—1727). Bailey; Thackeray, 1840, 'Numerous tiffs and quarrels'; ob. Etymology problematic, but possibly ex (the effects implied by) sense 1; cf., however, echoic *huff* and *sniff*. 4. Hence, a slight quarrel, a briefly peevish disagreement: coll: 1754, Richardson. 5. Ex sense 1: a gust of laughter, etc.: coll: 1858, Carlyle. Rare and ob.

***tiff,** v.i., occ. t. (The rare form *tift* occurs only in sense 3.) To lie (with a woman): c.: late C.17–early 19. cf. the rare or 'nonce' *tiffity-taffety girls*, harlots (late C.16), and the C.15 (?later) *tiff*, to be idly employed. 2. v.t., to drink, esp. slowly or in sips: ca 1769–1850. Combe, 1811, 'He tiff'd his punch, and went to rest.' Ex the n., 2. 3. v.i., to have a tiff, be peevish or pettish: coll (—1727). Bailey; 1777, Sheridan, 'We tifted a little before going to church, and fairly quarrelled before the bells had done ringing'; slightly ob. Ex the n., 4. 4. To have, eat, lunch: Anglo-Indian coll (1803, Elphinstone) >, ca 1850, S.E. But much the earliest record I have seen is this, dated 23 Sept. 1712, from Bencoleen in Sumatra: 'At 12 I tiff, that is eat ... some good relishing bit, and drink a good draught': *The Letter Books of Joseph Collett*, ed. by H. H. Dodwell, 1933. Abbr. of the v. implicit in TIFFING.

tiffed. Annoyed; angry: coll: mid-C.18–20. *Sessions*, 31 May 1856. See TIFF, v., 3.

tiffin. A lunch, esp. if light: Anglo-Indian coll (1800) >, ca 1830, S.E. Ex TIFFING. 2. Hence, in New Zealand: a snack and a drink (gen. tea) at 10.30 or 11 a.m., as a rest from work: late C.19–20: rare coll.

tiffing. 'Eating, or drinking out of meal times', Grose, 1st ed.: ca 1780–1830. Ex TIFF, v., 2. Whence TIFFIN. It occurs in 1784 as *triffing.*

tiffish. Apt to take offence; peevish: coll (—1855). Rare. Ex TIFF, n., 3.

tiffity-taffety girls, see TIFF, v., 1.

tiffy. An engine-room ar*tifi*cer: nautical: from late 1890s. F. T. Bullen, 1899.

tiffy, adj. In a TIFF (n., 3): coll: 1810 (O.E.D.). 2. Hence, apt to take offence: coll (—1864). 3. Hence, faddy: from ca 1880; ob.

tift, see TIFF, v., 3.

tiger. A smart-liveried boy-groom: 1817 (O.E.D.); Lytton, '*Vulgo* Tiger'; ob. by 1880. Ex livery. 2. Hence, any boy acting as outdoor servant: from ca 1840; id. In Julia Byrne's *Red, White and Blue*, 1862, the term is applied to a soldier servant. 3. A vulgarly overdressed person: 1827, Scott; 1849, Thackeray. Ob. by 1860, †by 1890. Ex a tiger's bright colours. cf. sense 1. 4. Hence, a parasite, rake, SWELL-MOBSMAN: ca 1837–60. 5. Streaky bacon: navvies': from ca 1890. Ex the streaks. 6. A convict that tears to pieces another convict's yellowish suit: c.: from late 1890s. Ex the ferocity of the act + the colour of the suit. 7. Tough-crusted bread: schoolboys': ca 1870–1905. Ex its powers of resistance.

tiger, hot, see HOT TIGER.

tigerish. Flashy; loudly dressed: ca 1830–70. Lytton, 1853, 'Nothing could be more . . ., to use a slang word, *tigrish*, than his whole air.' Ex TIGER, 3. (The n., *tigerism*, may perhaps be considered s. or coll: in sense of TIGER, 1, mainly in 1840s; of TIGER, 3 and 4, rarely after 1830s.)

tiger's milk. Whisky: Army officers': from ca 1890. 2. Gin: 1850 (O.E.D.); †by 1890. 3. Brandy and water: G. R. Gleig, *The Subaltern's Log-Book,* 1828.

tiggy. A detective: Cockney: from ca 1890; very ob. E. Pugh, *The Spoilers*, 1906.

tight. Hard, severe, difficult: coll: 1764, Foote (O.E.D.); ob. except in *tight squeeze* (Haliburton, 1855; after U.S. *tight spot*), *place* (mentioned in 1856 as an Americanism), and *corner* (1891). cf. TIGHT FIT. 2. (Of a contest) close, (of a bargain) hard: U.S. coll (ca 1820) anglicized ca 1860. 3. (Of a person) close-fisted: coll (—1828). Mostly U.S. 4. (Of money) hard to come by; (of the money market) with little money circulating: 1846, *Daily News*, 21 Jan. 'In Paris money is "tight" also, and discounts difficult.' 5. Tipsy: 1843 in U.S.; 1853, Dickens's article in *Household Words*, 24 Sept.; Kipling. cf. SCREWED, (lit. screwed tight, hence) drunk. 6. Cramped; over-worked; meticulous: artists': from ca 1890. 7. (Of balls) in contact, (pockets) with small openings: billiards (—1909).

tight!, blow me. See BLOW, v., 3. (Ex blowing up bladders, balloons, etc.)

tight, sit. To sit close, stay under cover; not to budge: coll: from mid-1890s. 2. cf. the C.18 sense: to apply oneself closely *to*: 1738 (O.E.D.).

tight-arsed. (Of women) chaste: low coll: late C.19–20.

tight as a drum. Extremely drunk: 1908 A. S. M. Hutchinson, *Once Aboard the Lugger*.

tight boots, sit in. To be ill at ease with one's host: semi-proverbial coll (—1855).

tight cravat. The hangman's noose: coll: late C.18–mid-19.

tight cunts and easy boots! A male toast, current ca 1880–1914.

tight fit, a. Coll when used of things other than clothes: late C.19–20.

tight junior, see JUNIOR.

tighten, v.i. To tight-lace: (not aristocratic) coll: 1896 (O.E.D.); slightly ob.

tight(e)ner. A hearty meal; occ. a large amount (of liquor): low coll: 1851, Mayhew. Hence, *do a* or *the tightener*; the latter in J. E. Ritchie's *Night Side of London*, 1857.

tightness. Tipsiness: from some time in 1853–64. See TIGHT, 5.

tigress. A vulgarly overdressed woman: 1830s. On TIGER, 3.

tigser, n. 'A slang juvenile epithet used when a person is in quick motion . . . "Go it, tigser"': West Yorkshire s. (—1904), not dial. Prob. ex dial. *tig*, 'to run hither and thither when tormented by flies, &c.'.

tike, gen. **tyke; T.** A Yorkshireman: coll nickname: C.18–20. E. Ward, 1703 (Matthews). Ex YORKSHIRE TIKE. In Yorkshire, *tyke* or *tike* very gen. for a dog.

***tike (tyke)-lurking.** Dog-stealing: c. (—1859). Also BUFFER-LURKING.

tik(k)i, tikkie, see TICKY.

tilbury. (A) sixpence: ca 1790–1850. Grose, 3rd ed., 'From its formerly being the fare for crossing over from Gravesend to Tilbury fort'. cf. TIZZY.

Tilbury Docks. Socks: rhyming s.: late C.19–20.

tile. A hat: 1821, D. Haggart, *Life*. Esp. ca 1850–1900, a dress-hat; extant as *tile-hat*, esp. in Glasgow, where it is also called a *tum hat*. Ex *tile* as part of roof; cf. *be well* THATCHED, and PANTILE.

***tile-frisking,** n. Stealing hats from lobbies and halls; c. of ca 1823–80. cf. TILE.

tile-hat, see TILE.

tile loose, (have) a. (To be) slightly crazy: from mid-1840s. Ex tiles loose on roof; cf. SHINGLE SHORT.

tiled, adj. Hatted: 1792, *The Annual Register*. cf. TILE. 2. **To be tiled** is to be snug, comfortable: ca 1815–50. Charles Dibdin, *Life in London*, 1882. With a *tiled* roof over one's head. 3. Detained by the police; locked up: fast life: ca 1815–60. *Spy*, 1825, 'Safely *tiled* in'.

***tiled down.** Under cover: esp., out of the way, hidden: c.: 1845 in '*No. 747*'; app. †by 1900. Lit., under the tiles.

***tiler.** A shoplifter: c. of ca 1650–80. ?ex L. *tollere*.

tiles, (be or go) on the. (To be or go) on the loose; esp. a-drinking or on sexual adventure: low (—1857). Ex the procedure of cats.

till. The female pudend: low: C.19–20. Suggested by MONEY(-BOX).

***till-boy.** An assistant tampering with the cash in his master's till: c. (—1864). Perhaps on:

***till-sneak.** A thief specializing in shop-tills: c.: from ca 1860.

till the cows come home, see COWS COME . . .

tilladum. 'A slang word for to "weave" .... Hence *tilladumite* ... a handloom weaver', E.D.D.: Lancashire: from ca 1860. The former occurs in James Staton, *Rays fro' th' Loominary*, 1866; the latter in Staton's *Bobby Shuttle un his woife Sayroh*, 1873.

tiller soup. That rough treatment with a tiller by (the threat of) which a coxwain encourages his boat's crew: nautical: late C.19–20. cf. BELAYING-PIN SOUP.

till(e)y, easy as. Very easy: ?C.18–19. Lit., easy as saying:

till(e)y-vally; tully-valy, etc. Nonsense!: trivial coll of ca 1525–1890. Skelton, Scott. Vaguely onomatopoeic in origin.

tillywink, see TIDDLYWINK.

tilter. A sword or rapier: 1688, Shadwell; †by 1840. Ex *tilt*, to take part in a tourney or jousting.

timber. Wooden gates, fences, hurdles, etc.: hunting: 1791, 'G. Gambado'. 2. A wooden leg; hence, any leg: from late C.18. 3. The stocks: from ca 1850. Douglas Jerrold the First. cf. TIMBER-STAIRS. 4. A wicket, the wickets: cricket coll: 1861. cf. TIMBER-YARD. 5. See TIMBERS. 6. See TIMBER-MERCHANT. 7. (*Timber*.) A variant of LACKERY.

timber, bowl for, see BOWL FOR TIMBER.

timber, small. Lucifer matches: (mostly London) street s.: from ca 1859. cf. TIMBER-MERCHANT.

timber, sport, see SPORT TIMBER.

timber-jumper. A horse good at leaping gates and fences: hunting: 1847, Thackeray, 'I never put my leg over such a timber-jumper.'

timber-merchant. A street match-seller: (London) streets' (—1859) now verging on c. Ware, 1909, records *timber* (gen. pl), a lucifer match, as low s.

timber-stairs. The pillory: mid-C.18–early (?mid-)C.19. In Herd's collection of songs. cf. TIMBER, 3.

timber-toe. A wooden leg: from ca 1780; ob. Implied in Grose, 1st ed., where *timber-toe* is a person with a wooden leg, a sense reappearing in Hood. The variant *timber-toes* is C.19–20, and, from ca 1870 in the East End of London, it also = a person wearing clogs.

timber-toed. Having a wooden leg or legs: from ca 1810. See preceding.

timber-toes, see TIMBER-TOE.

timber-topper. The same as, and ex, TIMBER-JUMPER: hunting: 1883.

timber-tuned. With a heavy, *wooden* touch on a musical instrument; wooden in movement: late C.19–20; ob.

timber-yard. One's wickets; more precisely, the place where one's wickets stand: cricket: 1853, 'Cuthbert Bede', 'Verdant found that before he could get his hand in, the ball was got into his wicket . . . and . . . there was a row in his timber-yard'; virtually †.

timbered up to one's weight, not. Not in one's style: coll: mid-C.19–20; ob.

timbers. The wickets: cricketers' coll (—1877). Esp. in *shiver one's timbers*, to scatter the wickets and stumps. cf. TIMBER, 4; TIMBER-YARD; contrast BOWL FOR TIMBER. 2. Worked wood in gen., e.g. escritoires, cabinets, elaborate tables: artistic: ca 1880–1914.

timbers!, my; dash my t.!; shiver my t.! Nautical s. exclamations: resp. 1789, Dibdin, 'My timbers! what lingo he'd coil and belay'; mid-C.19–20, rare and hardly nautical; and 1835, Marryat.

time. In boxing sense; see TIME OF DAY, 5, and TIME, KNOCK OUT OF. 2. (The time spent in) a term of imprisonment: rare except in TIME, DO. 3. Among cab-drivers of ca 1863–1910, the hours are used to denote the amount of a fare. 'To express 9*s.* 9*d.* they say "it is a quarter to ten"; if 3*s.* 6*d.*, half-past three; if 11*s.* 9*d.*, a quarter to twelve,' H., 3rd ed. 4. See TIMES.

time for *by the time that* is coll and rather illiterate; it occurs mostly in Cockney speech: ?mid-C.19–20. C. Rook, *The Hooligan Nights*, 1899, 'An' time I'd got a 'ansom an' put 'im inside, the job was worked.'

***time, do.** To serve a term in prison: 1865: c. >, by 1890, s. H., 5th ed., 'Sometimes stir-time (imprisonment in the House of Correction) is distinguished from the more extended system of punishment . . . called "pinnel (penal) time" '; Nat Gould, 1898, 'If it had not been for me you would have been doing time before this.' Hence *timer*, a convict, in such combinations as *first, second, third timer*, a prisoner serving for a first, etc., stretch: c. (—1887).

time, hot, see HOT TIME.

time, in no; in less than no time. Very soon, immediately; (very) quickly: coll: resp. 1829, Glascock: 1875, Jowett – but prob. a decade or even two or three decades earlier.

time, knock out of. 'So to punish an opponent that he cannot come up to the call of time', F. & H.: boxing: from ca 1870; slightly ob.

time, on. Punctual(ly): coll, orig. (1878) U.S.; anglicized ca 1890.

time, short. A single act of copulation as opp. to 'a night of it': low, coll rather than s.: C.19–20. ?orig. a prostitutes' term.

time for, have no. 'To regard with impatient disfavour', C. J. Dennis: (?orig. Australian) coll: late C.19–20. i.e. 'have no time to spare for'. cf. the S.E. *have no use for*.

time of day. 'The time as shown by the clock' is S.E. but the derivative 'a point or stage in any course or period' is coll: 1687, T. Brown; 1699, Collier, 'The favour of a prince was not . . . unreputable at that time of day.' 2. Hence, *give one*, or *pass, the time of day*, to greet a person, to exchange greetings: resp. C.17–20, mid-C. 19–20: S.E. until late C.19, then coll and dial.; *give one . . .* is ob. as a coll. Whiteing, G. R. Sims. 3. The prevailing state of affairs; the present state of the case: coll: 1667, Poole; slightly ob. Ex sense 1. 4. Hence, WHAT'S WHAT; the right or most fashionable way of doing something; the latest DODGE: from ca 1815. 'Jon Bee', 1823, 'In the island (Wight) every good joke is "the time o' day" '; more clearly in Dickens, 1838, 'Pop that shawl away in my castor . . .; that's the time of day.' Esp. in *fly to the time of day*, FLY, alert, 'knowing' (1828, Maginn; ob.); *put one up to the time of day*, to initiate a person (1834, Ainsworth); *know the time of day* (adumbrated in Bunyan, 1682, but not at all gen. before ca 1895), to know 'what's what' – Ouida, 1897, ' "She knows the time o' day," said the other'; *that's your time of day!*, well done! (1860, H., 2nd ed.). 5. (*give one*) *the time of day*, (to administer) a knock-out blow: boxing: late C.19–20; slightly ob.

time on, mark, see MARK . . .

timer, see TIME, DO.

times, behind the. Old-fashioned; having only such knowledge (esp. of method) as is superannuated: mid-C.19–20: coll. cf.:

times go, as. As things are at present: coll: 1712, Steele.

Timmie. The gymnasium: certain schools': late C.19–20.

timmynoggy. A term for almost any time- or labour-saving device: naval: ca 1850–95. Ex dial. *timmynoggy*, 'a notched square piece of wood; used to support the lower end of the "vargood" ' or long spar serving as a bowline, itself ex dial. *timmy*, the stick or bat used in the game of rounders. cf. GADGET.

timothy. A brew, or a jorum, of liquor: Scottish: 1855, Strang. Ex the proper name (?of a brewer or a noted publican). 2. The penis, esp. a child's: either dial. or provincial s. (—1847). Halliwell. The personification of penis (DICK, 4; *man* or *John* THOMAS) and of pudend (FANNY) would make an interesting but unpublishable essay.

timp, see TYMP.

tin. Money, cash; orig. of small silver coins, so apt to wear thinly smooth and thus assume a tinny appearance: prob. from early C.19, but not recorded before 1836, in Smith's *The Individual*; 'Pomes' Marshall. cf. BRASS.

tin-chapel, adj. Nonconformist, esp. Methodist, depreciatory coll: late C.19–20.

tin gloves. A criss-cross of blisters methodically made by a bully on the back of a victim's hand: Winchester: ca 1840–60. Mansfield.

tin-hat, adj. Drunk: Anglo-Port Said (—1909). Often *tin hats* (F. & Gibbons).

tin-hatted. A nautical variant of TIN-HAT, adj.

tin-opener. A bayonet: dating from the Boer War (1899–1901): military. Ex its chief use.

tin-pot. An ironclad: naval: from ca 1880; ob. Contrast:

tin-potter. A malingerer: nautical (—1867); ob. Ex *tin-pot*, inferior.

tin-tab. The carpenter's shop: Dulwich College: late C.19–20. cf.:

tin tabernacle. An iron-built or tin-roofed church: 1898, William Le Queux, *Scribes and Pharisees*, V, 54: s. cf. DOLLY-SHOP and similar amenities.

tin tack. A sack: from ca 1870: rhyming s.

tin tank. A bank: from ca 1880: rhyming s.

tin-type!, not on your. Certainly not!: a c.p. of late C.19–20. Ex an old-fashioned type of photograph. Perhaps with a pun on *not on your* LIFE!, certainly not.

tin-wedding (day). The tenth anniversary of a wedding: coll: 1876. Punning *golden* and *silver* weddings.

'tina or tina. Concertina: mostly Cockney: from ca 1870. (Pugh.)

tinge. A commission allowed to assistants on the sale of outmoded stock: drapers' (—1860). cf. SUSPICION.

tink. A tinker; a disreputable vagabond: Scots coll: mid-C.19–20. E.D.D. By abbr.

tink-tinky, see TINKY.

***tinkard.** A begging tinker: c. of ca 1560–1620.

tinker. To batter: boxing: 1826, *Sporting Magazine*, 'Tom completely tinkered his opponent's upper-crust'; almost †. Ex *tinker*, v.t., mend tinker-wise.

tinker, swill like a. To tipple unstintedly: coll: late C.17–early 19.

tinker's budget or **news.** Stale news: coll and dial.: mid-C.19–20.

tinker's curse (or **cuss**) or **damn,** see CURSE.

tinkler. A bell: (low) coll: 1838, Dickens, 'Jerk the tinkler'.

tinkling box. A piano: South Lancashire s. (—1904), not dial.

tinky. A South African juvenile coll variant (—1899) of *tink-tinky*, itself orig. (the 1890s) coll for the bird properly known as *ting-ting*. Ex its cry, *tink, tink, tink.*

tinman. A rich man, esp. a millionaire: sporting: from ca 1880; ob. Ex TIN; cf. TINNY, adj.

***tinny; tinney** (Bee). A fire: c.: C.19. Hence *tinney-hunter* (ibid.), a thief working after fires.

tinny, adj. Rich: 1871, *Punch*, 14 Oct. Ex TIN.

tinter, see BARREL TINTER.

Tiny is an inevitable nickname of very big or tall men: lower classes': late C.19–20.

***tiny dodge.** Begging in the company of neatly dressed children (often borrowed for the purpose) and thus exciting sympathy: c.: from ca 1860.

***tip.** '*The tip* . . . money concerned in any dealings or contract . . .; synonymous with *the dues*', Vaux: c. of ca 1810–50. In *Boxiana* III, 1821, it means 'entrance money'. cf. v., 8, 9. 2. Special information conveyed by an expert, private knowledge, esp. as to investment in the money market and to racing; a hint for an examination: from ca 1840: s. >, by 1900, coll. *Quarterly Review*, 1886, 'It should be the first duty of consuls to keep the Foreign Office promptly supplied with every commercial tip that can be of use to British trade.' 3. Hence, something 'tipped' to win, to prosper; esp. a horse: 1873, Besant & Rice. 4. Hence, a special device, a WRINKLE (2): from the 1880s: s. 5. Hence, at Felsted School, from late 1880s, a false report; hence, ibid., from early 1890s, a foolish mistake in translating. *Felstedian*, 3 Feb. 1890, 'Some one ventured to suggest that it was all a beastly tip.' 6. See phrases. 7. A draught of liquor: c. (—1700) soon > s.; †by 1840. Prob. abbr. TIPPLE. 8. Drink in gen.: c. (—1700) soon > s.; †by 1830. Certainly ex TIPPLE.

tip, v. To render unsteady, esp. to intoxicate, mostly in the passive: C.17–early 18. Camden, 1605. Ex *tip*, to tilt or incline. 2. (Often *tip off*.) To drink off: late C.17–20: c. until mid-C.18, then s.; from mid-C.19, only in dial. Ex tipping the glass or bowl in order to drain it. 3. To die: rare except in C.19–20 dial. and in *tip off* (late C.17–20: c., as in B.E., > s. by 1730; in C.19–20, dial.), *tip over the perch* (1737, Ozell) or *tip the perch* (C.19–20, in the same sense). See PERCH. 4. To give; pass: C. 17–20: c. >, by 1730, s. Rowlands, 1610, 'Tip me that Cheate, Give me that thing.' Esp. of money. Perhaps ex *tip*, to touch lightly; the Romany *tipper*, to give, is a derivative. 5. Hence, to lend (esp. money): c.: late C.17–20. 6. Hence (of a person in the presence of others), to assume the character of: from ca 1740; ob. For its most frequent use, see TIP THE TRAVELLER. 7. Often almost synonymous with 'do' or 'make' (cf. FAKE): late C.17–20: c. >, early in C.18 though not in certain phrases, (low) s. See, e.g., TIP A NOD (1), STAVE, YARN; TIP THE GRAMPUS. 8. To earn: C.17–18: c. >, by 1730, (low) s. Rowlands, 1610; Bridges, ca 1770, 'This job will tip you one pound one.' Ex *tip*, to give, and cognate with: 9. To give a 'tip' or present of money to – whether to an inferior in recognition of a service or to a child or school-boy or -girl!: s. >, early in C.19, coll: 1706–7, Farquhar, 'Then I, Sir, tips me' – ethic dative – 'the verger with half a crown.' Ex sense 4. 10. Hence, v.i., in same sense: 1727, Gay, 'Did he tip handsomely?': s. >, early in C.19, coll. 11. To indicate by a secret wink: 1749, Fielding, 'I will tip you the proper person . . . as you do not know the town.' Ex TIP THE WINK. 12. To give private information, a friendly hint, about: from early 1880s: s. Esp. to indicate a horse as a probable winner, a stock as a profitable investment. Ex the n., 2; perhaps cognate with preceding sense of the v. 13. Hence, to supply (a person) with INSIDE information: from ca 1890: s. 14. Hence, v.i., to impart such information: s. (—1904).

tip, miss one's. To fall; fail at a jump: showmen's: from ca 1850. (In late C.19–20 circus s., to miss the word indicating that one is due to do something.) Dickens, 1854. 2. Hence, to fall, fail, in gen.: (—1860). 1869, H. J. Byron, 'Mr Topham Sawyer missed his own tip as well as his victim's, and came down a cropper on a convenient doorstep.' Lit., to fail in one's expertise: see TIP, n., 2.

tip, sling the. To give a hint; impart information: proletarian: from ca 1860.

***tip, stand the,** see TIP, TAKE THE.

tip, (gen. the) straight. Genuine or valuable (INSIDE) information, esp. and orig. as to a horse: s. >, by 1900, coll: from late 1860s, to judge by H., 5th ed. (1874); 1871, *Punch*, 26 Aug. Because direct from owner or trainer; influenced by STRAIGHT, honest. 2. Hence, the horse or the stock so recommended: from ca 1880: s. >, by 1905, coll.

***tip, take the.** c. of C.19–20, as in Vaux, 1812, '. . . To receive a bribe in any shape; and they say of a person who is known to be corruptible, that he will *stand the tip*.' Ex *tip*, a gratuity: a sense that the O.E.D. (rightly, I believe) classifies as S.E.

tip, that's the. That's the right thing: from ca 1860. Ex TIP, n., 1.

***tip a copper.** To SKY a coin: c. or low s.: mid-C.19–20.

***tip a (gen. one's) daddle, a (gen. one's) fin, the fives, the gripes in a tangle.** To shake hands; with *to* expressed or implied, to shake hands with or extend one's hand to be shaken: c. or low s.: resp. late C.18–20, mainly nautical (—1860), late C.18–20, late C.18–early 20. See DADDLE; the third and fourth occur in Anon., *Ireland Sixty Years Ago*, 1847; *tip the gripes* (grips) *in a tangle* is Anglo-Irish and rare.

***tip a mish.** 'To put on a shirt', F. & H.: c.: C.18–20; ob. The definition is suspect, for the normal sense is to give, lend it.

tip a moral. To give *the straight* TIP: racing: late C.19–20. See MORAL, 2 'moral' certainty.

tip a nod (to). To recognize (a person): low: mid-C.19–20. 2. The same as TIP THE WINK: 1861, Dickens.

tip a rise. To befool: low: from ca 1880. See RISE, 2.

tip-a-runner. The game of tip and run: coll: 1805; ob. Lewis.

tip a settler, a *sock. To land (a person) a knock-out blow, a heavy blow: low: resp. 1819 (Moore) and late C.17–20 (B.E.: c. > low s.).

tip a stave. To sing a song: nautical, ? esp. naval, in origin, and it goes back to ca 1790. It occurs in, e.g., W. N. Glascock *The Naval Sketch-Book*, 1825–6.

tip a yarn. To relate a story: low: from ca 1870.

tip all nine. To knock down all the skittles at once: from ca 1780. Perhaps ex *tip*, to touch; cf. TIP, v., 1.

tip-book. A literal translation; any other book likely to be especially useful in an examination: schools': 1845 (O.E.D.). See TIP, n., 4.

tip lark, the. A (racehorse) tipping business: the racing world: late C.19–20.

tip-merry. Slightly drunk: C.17. Ex TIP, n., last sense.

tip off. See TIP, v., 2. 2. To die: late C 17–20: c. until ca 1720, then (low) s.; in C.19–20, dial. cf. TIP, v., 3.

tip one's boom off. To depart hastily: nautical: from ca 1855; slightly ob.

***tip one's legs a gallop.** To make off; decamp hastily: c. (—1823); ob. cf.:

tip one's rags a gallop. A variant (W. T. Moncrieff, *Tom and Jerry*, 1821) of TIP THE RAGS . . .; †by 1870.

tip over the perch. See TIP, v., 3. (cf. C.19–20 dial. *tip over*, to swoon.)

Tip Street, be in. To be, at the time, generous with one's money: low: ca 1815–50. Pierce Egan, *Life in London*, 1821, 'Jerry is in *Tip Street* upon this occasion, and the Mollishers are all *nutty* upon him, putting it about, one to the other, that he is a well-breeched Swell.'

tip the double. To give the slip: low: 1838, Wright, *Morning at Bow Street*, 'In plain words he tipped them the double, he was vanished.' cf. TIP THE RAGS . . .

tip the grampus. To duck a man (for sleeping on watch): nautical: from ca 1860; ob. Also *blow the* GRAMPUS. Contrast:

tip the lion. To press a man's nose against his face and then either, as in Steele, 1712, bore out his eyes with one's fingers, or, as in Grose (1st ed.) and gen., 'at the same time to extend his mouth with the fingers, thereby giving him a sort of lionlike appearance'; †by 1850.

tip the little finger. To drink: Australian: late C.19–20; ob.

tip the long 'un. 'To foraminate a woman', F. & H.: late C.19–20: low.

tip the nines. (Of a sailing-ship carrying too much sail in dirty weather) to be 'driven right under' (Bowen): nautical: late C.19–20; ob.

tip the rags (occ. **legs) a gallop** or **the double.** To decamp: low: resp. C.19–20 and mid-C.19–20. cf. TIP THE DOUBLE,

tip the traveller. To exaggerate, to romance, as a traveller is apt to do: 1742, Fielding; Smollett; Grose. App. ob. by 1860. Variant of *play the traveller*. cf. the C.16–18 proverb, *a traveller may lie by authority*. 2. Hence (variant: *put the traveller*, C.19: Manchon), with *upon*, to impose upon; befool: implied in 1762 in Smollett; †in C.20.

tip the velvet, see VELVET.

tip the (occ. C.18–19, **a) wink.** To warn, signal to, with a wink: 1676, Etherege; Dryden; Pope; Grose. s. >, by 1850, coll. cf. TIP A NOD, 2.

tip-top. The very top; fig., the acme: coll: 1702, S. Parker. Ex *top* strengthened by *tip*, extremity, or, as O.E.D. suggests, reduplicated *top*. 2. Hence, occ. as collective singular, the SWELLS: coll: mid-C.18–mid-19. Thackeray, 1849, 'We go here to the best houses, the tiptops.'

tip-top, adj. At the very top; excellent; splendid, TOPPING: coll: before 1721, Vanbrugh, 'In tip-top spirits'; G. Eliot. Ex the n., 1.

tip-top, adv. Excellently; splendidly: from ca 1880. Ex preceding.

tip-topper. A SWELL: 1837, Thackeray; ob. Other forms (*tip-topping*, etc.) are too little used to qualify as unconventional: they're merely eccentric.

tip-toppedest, see TIPPEST-TOPPEST.

tip up. To hand over, FORK OUT, esp. money: low (—1859). 2. To hold out: low and nautical (—1887). Esp. as in Baumann, *tip up your fist* (or FIN), reach or give (me) your hand!, shake hands! cf. TIP A DADDLE.

tipper. One who gives a gratuity: 1877 (O.E.D.): coll >, by 1900, S.E. 2. A tipster: mostly racing: from ca 1890. cf. TIP, n., 2.

Tipperary fortune. Breasts, pudend, and anus: Anglo-Irish (—1785); ob. Grose, 1st ed., 'Two town lands, stream's town, and ballinocack, said of Irish women without fortune'. cf. at WIND-MILL; see ROCHESTER, TETBURY, WHITECHAPEL PORTION; also WHITECHAPEL FORTUNE.

Tipperary lawyer. A cudgel: Anglo-Irish: mid-C.19–20. cf. PLYMOUTH CLOAK.

tippery. Payment: non-aristocratic: ca 1830–1910. Ex TIP, n., 1 and v., 4.

tippest-toppest. Absolutely TIP-TOP: jocular (—1887); ob. Baumann (also *tip-toppedest*).

tippet; hempen t. (Marlowe); **St Johnstone's t.** (Scott); **Tyburn t.** (Latimer, 1549). A hangman's rope: mid-C.15–early 19: jocular coll verging on S.E.

tipping, n. See TIP, v. 2. adj. Excellent, 'topping': dial. (—1887) > school s. before 1904. Prob. ex TOPPING on RIPPING.

tipple. Liquor: late C.16–20: coll >, by 1700, s. Ex the v. Occ. of non-intoxicants: mid-C.19–20. 2. A drinking-bout: ?C.18–20.

tippling-ken. A tavern: low: C.18. Ned Ward, *A Vade Mecum for Maltworms*, 1715.

tipply. Unsteady: coll: 1906 (O.E.D.). Lit., apt to tipple over.

tippy. Extremely fashionable; SWELL: 1810, ob. by 1900. cf. the U.S. *tippy* (occ. *tippee*), an exquisite of 1804–5. Ex: 2. *the*

tippy. The height of fashion; the fashionable thing to do: ca 1784–1812. Ex *tip*, the very top. Either this or the previous sense, the context being neutral, appears in *The New Vocal Enchantress* (a song book), 1791. 3. Extremely ingenious; very neat, smart, effective: 1863, M. Dods, 'A tippy little bit of criticism'; ob. Perhaps ex TIP, n., 1. 4. Unsteady: coll: from mid-1880s. Lit., likely to tip over. cf. TIPPLY.

tipster. One who gives information, orig. in racing (1862) and by 1884 in gen.: coll >, by 1900, S.E. See TIP, n., 2.

tiptop, see TIP-TOP.

tique, see TEEK.

tire out, tire to death. To tire to exhaustion: coll: resp. mid-C.16–20, 1740.

tired, be born. To dislike work; occ. as 'an excuse for assumed apathy or genuine disinclination', F. & H.: from late 1890s. Whiteing, 1899. Occ. *be tired.*

tired, make (a person), see YOU MAKE ME TIRED.

tiresome. Troublesome, annoying, unpleasant: coll: 1798, Charlotte Smith, 'The tiresome custom you have got of never being ready'.

tirly-whirly. The female pudend: Scots: late C.18–20; ob. Burns. Reduplicated *whirly*. Lit., 'a whirled figure, ornament, or pattern': cf. lit. senses of *tirly*.

tirret, tirrit. A fit of temper, occ. fear; an 'upset': coll, orig. illiterate for *terror*, perhaps influenced by dial. *frit*, frightened: late C.16–20. Shakespeare.

tish. A par*titi*on; esp. a cubicle: Public Schools', universities': from the late 1880s.

tissey. An occ. variant of TIZZY; †by 1900.

tit. A girl or young woman (in mid-C.19–20, often in low s., of a harlot): from end of C.16: S.E. until C.18, then coll until C.19, then s.; from late C.19, low s. and possibly influenced by TITTER. T. Creevey, 1837, '[Lady Tavistock] thinks the Queen a resolute little tit.' Ex *tit*, a (small) horse: cf. FILLY. 2. The female pudend: low: C.18–20; ob. Abbr. *tit-bit*, *titmouse*, in same sense (C.17–18): the former occ. = the penis, as in Urquhart, 1653. 3. A sol. spelling and pronunciation of *teat*: prob. from C.17 or even earlier. 4. A student at Durham University: Durham townsmen's: late C.19–20. Also *'Varsity tit*. Ex *tit* applied to persons. 5. A horse: c.: 1834, Ainsworth; Charles E. Leach. Earlier in dial. 6. A female breast: Australian low coll: late C.19–20. Ex sense 3. 7. A fellow: s.: Ned Ward (1714) has *jolly tit* for pleasant fellow, boon companion. cf. sense 4. 8. A fool; cf.:

tit, look a(n absolute). To look very foolish, or SLOPPY and stupid: low: late C.19–20. By itself, *tit* = a foolish, ineffectual man.

tit-bit, see TIT, 2.

tit-fer (gen. titfer); tit-for-tat. A hat: the short form being an obvious abbr. (C.20) of the second, which is rhyming s. of late C.19–20.

tit willow. A pillow: from ca 1870.

titch. A flogging: Christ's Hospital: mid-C.19–20. ?ex *tight breeches* by blending, or ex dial. *titch*, touch. 2. Hence, occ. as a v.

titery, see TITTERY. **titfer,** see TIT-FER.

tith. Tight: coll and dial.: ca 1615–30. Rare except in dramatist Fletcher.

Titire-tu, see TITYRE-TU.

titivate, tittivate; occ. **tiddivate, tidi-, tiddyvate.** To put finishing or additional touches to (one's toilet, oneself): coll: resp. 1805, 1836, 1824, 1833, 1823. e.g. Dickens in *Boz*, 'Regular as clockwork – breakfast at nine – dress and tittivate a little', this quotation illustrating and affording the earliest example of the v.i. used as v. reflexive. Perhaps ex *tidy* with a quasi-Latin ending on *cultivate*: O.E.D. 'Or fanciful elaboraton of synonymous dial. *tiff*, Fr. *attifer*, "to decke, . . . adorne" (Cotgrave)': W. Also with †*off* or *up*.

titivated, -ating, -ation, -ator. Obvious derivatives ex TITIVATE: C.19–20. Coll.

title-page. The face: ca 1830–70. *Sinks*, 1848. cf. FRONTISPIECE. Hence, 2, a type-face: printers': since ca 1860.

titley; gen., and in C.20 almost always, **tiddly,** occ. **tiddley.** Intoxicating liquor: low (—1859). Prob. ex TIDDLYWINK, a public-house. 2. Hence, a drink: low: from ca 1870.

titley; tiddly. Drunk: low: app. unrecorded before C.20, though *on the tiddl(e)y*, intoxicated or in a fair way of becoming intoxicated, appears in *Punch* in 1895. If thus late, then ex the n., but if earlier than TIDDLYWINK, then perhaps a corruption (?orig. dial.) of *tipsy*.

titmouse. See TIT, n., 2. Ex *titmouse*, fig. = a small thing.

titotular bosh. Absolute nonsense: orig. and mainly music-halls': 1897–8. Punning *teetotal*.

***tit's back, as fine a fellow as ever crossed a.** A very fine fellow: either c. or low (—1887). See TIT 1.

***titter.** A girl or young woman: criminals' and tramps' c. (—1812) >, by 1900, low s. Henley, 1887, 'You flymy titters full of flam.' Either ex *titter*, a giggle, or ex Scots TITTY (1), a sister, or again, ex dial. TITTY (2), a breast: the third possibility is perhaps the likeliest, for *titty*, sister, is mainly a child's word unless we consider that dial. *titty*, a girl, has been influenced by *titty*, a breast.

tittery. Gin: C.18. Perhaps ex *titter*, to giggle: Bailey. Occ. *titery*, *tityre*.

Tittery-tu, see TITYRE-TU.

tittie, see TITTY. **tittivate,** see TITIVATE.

tittle. To whisper; to gossip: late C.14–20: S.E. until late C.18, then coll and dial.; in C.20, mainly dial. Prob. echoic.

tittle-tattle. Chatter, gossip: coll: C.18–20. Ned Ward, 1703. Ex TITTLE.

tittlebat. A somewhat illiterate, mainly London, coll form of *stickleback*: C.19–20. Also *tiddlebat*, *tittleback*. (Slovenliness generates many such popular corruptions.) cf. TIDDLER.

tittup; occ. **titup.** As n., eligible only in *the tit(t)up*, the thing: *that's the t.*, that's the thing; *the correct t.*, the correct thing: low: late C.19–20; ob. Ex *tit(t)up*, a horse's canter, itself echoic.

tit(t)uppy. Unsteady, shaky: coll: 1798, Jane Austen. Rarely of persons, and in C. 20 mainly dial. Ex *tit(t)up*, a horse's canter.

titty; occ. **tittie.** A sister; a girl or young woman: Scots coll (mostly among children as 'sister'): from ca 1720. Ramsay, Burns, Scott. Perhaps ex child's pronunciation of *sister*. cf. TITTER. 2. A or the breast, esp. the human mother's: nursery coll, and dial.: from ca 1740. (In dial., occ. *tetty*.) 3. A diminutive of *teat* (cf. TIT, 3): coll: C.19–20. 4. A kitten, a cat; also in address: nursery coll, and dial.: C.19–20. Clare, 1821. Ex child's pronunciation of *kitty*.

titty, drop of. A drink from the breast: nursery: C.19–20. See TITTY, 2.

titty and billy (or **-ie and -ie**). Sister and brother: Scots coll: C.19–20. Ex TITTY, 1. 2. Hence, *be titty-billy* (or *-ie*), to be intimate: Scots coll (—1825).

titty-oggy or **tittie-oggie.** Fellatio: low: late C.19–20.

titup, see TITTUP.

tityre, see TITTERY.

Tityre-tu; also **Titire-Tu, Tytere** (or **-ire**)**-tu, Tittery tu, tittyry.** A member of a band of rich and leisured roughs of ca 1620–60: a coll nickname > S.E. The O.E.D. records the name in 1623 (J. Chamberlain); 'Water-Poet' Taylor; Herrick. Ex the opening words of Virgil's *First Eclogue*.

tius. A suit (of clothes): back s. (—1909). Ware restricts it to East London.

tiv(v)y. The female pudend: low: C.19–20; ob. ?ex dial. *tiv(e)y*, activity.

tizzy; occ. **tizzey, tissey.** A sixpence: resp. 1804, 1809, and (†in C.20) 1829. Moncrieff, 1823, 'Hand us over three browns out of that 'ere tizzy.' Prob. a corruption of TESTER, via TILBURY. See also TESTY. cf. SWIZ for SWINDLE.

tizzy-poole. A fives ball: Winchester: from ca 1870. Because it used to cost 6d. and be sold by a head porter named Poole. cf. the Harrow *tizzy-tick*, 'an order on a tradesman to the extent of 6d. a day', F. & H.: mid-C.19–20.

to rights, see RIGHTS, BE TO. **toac,** see TAOC.

to the nines, *to the ruffian. To an extreme or superlative degree: for *to the nines*, see NINES; *to the ruffian* is c. of ca 1810–50.

toad. A piece of hot toast put into their beer by college men: Winchester: C.19. Wrench.

toad-in-the-hole. A sandwich-board: mostly London (—1864). Ex the meat dish so named. 2. Hence, occ., the man carrying it: late C.19–early 20.

toad is of feathers, as full of money as a. Penniless: coll: ca 1785–1900. Prob. suggested by:

toad of a side-pocket, as much need of it as a, see SIDE-POCKET.

toad on a chopping-block, (s)he sits like a. (S)he sits badly on a horse: coll (—1785). A picturesque simile as applied to a side-saddle. (In Lincolnshire dial.: . . . *on a shovel*.)

toast. A toper; (*old toast*) a lively old fellow fond of his liquor: ca 1668–1800, but ob. by 1730. Ex such phrases as *ale and toast*.

toast, (had) on. Swindled: from ca 1885. *St James's Gazette*, 6 Nov. 1886, refers to *had on toast* as 'a quaint and pleasing modern phrase'. 2. Hence, *on toast* = cornered: from early 1890s.

toast your blooming eye-brows! *Go to* BLAZES!: lower classes' c.p. of ca 1895–1915.

toasting-fork, -iron. A sword: jocular coll: 1596, Shakespeare, and Grose, 1st ed., have *t.-iron*, which is ob. by 1880; *t.-fork* dates from ca 1860 and occurs in *Tom Brown at Oxford*, 1861. cf. CHEESE-

TOASTER (and the †S.E. *toaster*), likewise derived ex its most gen. use.

toasty. Warmly tinted: artists': from mid-1890s. Lit., (burnt) brown.

tobacco, make dead men chew. To keep the names of dead men on the books: naval: late C.18–early 19. John Davis, *The Post Captain*, 1805.

tobacco chart. Gen. pl, 'the . . . inaccurate charts that could formerly be bought from any ship chandler at a low price': nautical: ca 1840–90. Bowen. Perhaps as sold at the price of an ounce of tobacco, or because they were tobacco-stained.

tobacco-pipe curls. Corkscrew curls worn by costers and Gypsies: (esp. London) lower classes' (—1887); ob. Ex the curve of such a pipe.

tobaccy. Tobacco: lower classes' coll: from the 1870s if not earlier. W. S. Gilbert, *H.M.S. Pinafore*, 'I've snuff and tobaccy and excellent jacky.'

tobby. A deck boy: nautical: late C.19–20: ?ex TOBY, n., 5: because always at hand.

***tober.** A road: tramps' c. and Romany, the former in 1845 in '*No. 747*'. See TOBY, 3.

tober omee (or **omey** or **homee** or **homey**). A toll-collector: grafters': late C.19–20.

toby. The buttocks: from ca 1675. Esp. in TICKLE *one's toby*, to beat him on the buttocks. Ex the proper name. 2. Hence, the female pudend, as in Cotton, ca 1678. ob. 3. (Always *the toby*). The highway: c. (—1811). *Lex. Bal.*, Lytton, Ainsworth, Hindley; ob., the gen. C.20 term being DRUM. Also, fig., robbery on the highway: 1812, Vaux. cf. TOBY MAN. Ex Shelta *tobar*, a road, itself perhaps a 'deliberate perversion of Irish *bothar*, road', W. Occ. *tober*. cf. the v. and the phrases. 4. Hence, a pitch: showmen's: from ca 1890. *Standard*, 29 Jan. 1893, 'We have to be out in the road early . . . to secure our "Toby".' 5. *Toby*, the dog in a Punch and Judy show: 1840: coll very soon > S.E.: see SWATCHEL. 'The dog in [The Book of] Tobit . . . is probably the eponym of "Dog Toby" of "Punch and Judy" ' (Sir Paul Harvey). 6. A lady's collar: Society coll: ca 1882–1918. Ex 'the wide frill worn round the neck by Mr Punch's dog' (Ware).

***toby,** v.t. To rob (a person) on the highway; hence, DONE FOR *a toby*, convicted for highway robbery: c. of ca 1810–50.

***toby, high** (or **main**). Highway robbery by a mounted person; that of footpads being *the low toby*. c. of ca 1810–50. See TOBY, n., 3. 2. Also (*high toby* only), the highway itself.

***toby, high spice; high toby spice.** The highway viewed as the locality for robbery: c. (—1812). Byron, 1812 (*h.t.s.*); Hindley, 1876 (*h.s.t.*). Ex TOBY, n., 3, and SPICE.

***toby, ply** or **ride the.** To practise highway robbery: c. of ca 1812–70. Ex TOBY, n., 3, and cf. TOBY, HIGH.

***toby concern** or **lay.** The practice of highway robbery: c.: 1811 (*lay*); †by 1880. 'Ducange Anglicus' and H., 1st ed., have *toby consarn*.

***toby gill; high toby gloak; toby man.** A highwayman: c.: from ca 1810; †by 1880. Vaux, 1812, has all three. (Romany: *tober kov*, COVE.) cf.:

***toby man, high** and **low.** A highwayman and a footpad: c.: ca 1810–80. Ex TOBY, n., 3, and cf. TOBY GILL.

toby spice, see TOBY, HIGH SPICE, and SPICE.

toco, toko. Chastisement; from ca 1820; ob. Bee, 1823, 'If . . . Blackee gets a whip about his back, why he has caught toco.' Hence, *to give* (a person) *toco*, to thrash him, as in Hughes, 1857, 'Administer toco to the wretched fags'. Perhaps ex (the dative or ablative of) Gr. τόκος, interest, as the O.E.D. suggests; or ex Hindustani *tokna*, to censure, via the imperative *toco*, as Yule & Burnell pertinently remarks; or, as I diffidently propose, ex some Negro or Polynesian word: cf. Maori *toko*, a rod (Edward Tregear's Dict., 1891), but see also TOKUS. cf.:

toco for yam, get or **nap.** To be punished; among sailors from ca 1860, to get paid out. Bee records this (the *get*), prob. the orig., form in 1823. On the analogy of a stone for a loaf of bread, and, presumably, at first a treatment meted out to slaves. See TOCO. 2. By 1874, *toco for yam* had come to mean 'a Roland for an Oliver'; ob.

Tod is the 'inevitable' nickname of any man surnamed Sloan (after the famous jockey) or Hunter (cf. the surname *Todhunter*): naval and military: late C.19–20.

tod, adj. Alone; esp. *be on one's tod*, to be, or to work, alone: grafters': from ca 1895. Ex a lost *Tod Sloan*, rhyming s. arising ca 1894: cf. TOD.

toddler. A walker – one who, on a given occasion, walks: coll: ca 1810–60. *Boxiana*, III, 1821. 2. See:

toddlers. Legs: ca 1835–80. *Sinks*, 1848. cf. preceding entry.

toddy, -ie. In address to a child of 1–3 years: coll: ?mid-C.19–20. Such a child toddles rather than walks; cf. dial. *toddy*, little, and familiar S.E. *toddles*, a toddling child.

toddy-blossom. A GROG-BLOSSOM: C.19–20; ob. Ex *toddy*, the beverage.

toddy-stick. A muddler: low: mid-C.19–20. On STICK (n., 3) used pejoratively.

todge. To smash (to a pulp): provincial: C.19–20. Ex dial. *todge*, stodge.

toe, v.t. To kick: low: from ca 1860: coll.

toe, have or **hold by the.** To hold securely: coll: mid-C.16–mid-17. Chronicler Hall and Bishop Hall. cf. *short* HAIRS.

toe, kiss the Pope's. Respectfully to set one's lips to the golden cross on the Pope's right sandal: 1768, the Earl Carlisle: s. >, ca 1890, coll.

toe, turn on the. To turn (a person) off the ladder in hanging: late C.16–early 17. Nashe, 1594.

toe a line. To form a rank or line: naval coll: mid-C.18–19, and perhaps rather earlier and rather later. W. N. Glascock, *The Naval Sketch-Book* (I, 237), 1825: 'The brigades of seamen embodied to act with our troops in America, as well as in the north coast of Spain, contrived to "*ship a bagnet*" [handle a bayonet] on a pinch, and to "toe" (for that was the phrase) "a tolerable line".'

toe-buster. An infantryman: cavalry-men's: ca 1880–1905.

toe-fit-ti(e). To tie a string to (a boy's) toe and haul him out of bed: Public Schools', esp. Winchester and Felsted: ca 1870–1900. *Felstedian*, Nov. 1881, '"To fit-ti", in reference to verbs of the third conjugation transferred from the similarity of sound to the schoolboy's toe.'

toe-fug. A footbath: Tonbridge: since ca 1870. Marples. Removal of smell.

toe-path. An infantry regiment: cavalry-men's: ca 1890–1914. Punning *tow-path*.

toe-rag. A beggar: provincial s. (—1909). Perhaps ex:

toe-ragger, -rigger. A term of opprobrium: Australia and New Zealand resp. as in *Truth* (the Sydney one), 12 Jan. 1896, '"A toe-ragger" is Maori. . . . The nastiest term of contempt was *tua rika rika*, or slave. The old whalers on the Maoriland coast in their anger called each other *toe-riggers*, and to-day the word in the form of *toe-ragger* has spread t[…] the whole of the South Seas.'

toes, claw one's. To indulge on[…] mid-C.15–early 16.

toes, cool one's. To have to wa[…] 1660–1700. Brathwait, 1665. cf[…] ONE'S HEELS.

toes, on old. Aged; in old age: […] cf. *old bones*.

toe's length, the. Almost no dis[…] from ca 1820; ob.

toes of, step or **tread on the.** T[…] umbrage to: coll: mid-C.19–[…] Browning, 1868. Ex lit. sense.

toes up. (Lying) dead: 1851[…] slightly ob. cf.:

toes up, turn one's. To die: 1[…] 'Several arbalestiers turned th[…]

toey. A SWELL: New South […] C.19–20; ob. ?corruption of: […]

toff. A SWELL; a NOB (sense[…] do person): proletarian: f[…] slightly ob. ca 1868, there was […] song entitled *The Shoredit*[…] Arthur Lloyd; Whiteing, 189[…] via TOFT. 2. Hence, a man […] and courage: late C.19–20; […] *Daily Telegraph*, 16 Sept. 19[…] out his wrists to be han[…] exclaimed, "Now I'll die like […] A BRICK, a person behaving […] 1898; slightly ob.

toff bundle-carrier. A gentle[…] panying a prosperous serio-co[…] to hall on her evening roun[…] ca 1870–1900. Ex TOFF, 1.

***toff-omee.** The superlative […] (—1909).

toff-shoving. Pushing abou[…] men in a crowd: London […] 1882–1900.

toffee, not for. Not at all; […] of means; not in any circu[…] cultured: late C.19–20.

toffer. A fashionable wh[…] 1860–1914. cf.:

tofficky. Showy; vulgarly d[…] 1860–1910. Ex TOFF, 1.

toffish; toffy. Stylish; SWE[…] ca 1873, when *toffishness* oc[…] wood's *Strange Company*; […] K. Jerome; *toffy*, ob., ex TO[…]

toft. A variant, prob. the i[…] TOFF, 1: ca 1850–1910. […] debased – and the dates se[…] this – then TUFT corrupted.[…]

***tog.** A coat: early C.18 […] 1820, low s. Tuft, 1798, '*Lo*[…]

Andrewes, 1809, '*Tatty tog*, a gaming cloth'; Vaux, 1812, '*Tog*, a coat'. Ex TOGE, or, less prob., TOGEMAN(S), a cloak. 2. See TOGE and TOGS. 3. See TAOC.

tog, v. First as past ppl *togged*, dressed, 1793, *to tog* being recorded not before 1812. Vaux, 'To *tog* is to . . . put on clothes; to *tog* a person, . . . to supply them with apparel.' Low s. verging on c. Ex TOGE.

tog, long; tog, tatty, see TOG, n.

tog, upper. An overcoat: c. of ca 1810–50. cf. TOGGER, 1. Ex TOG, n.

tog-bound. Having no good clothes: lower classes' (—1909).

tog-fencer. A tailor: London proletariat: ca 1870–1915.

tog it; t. out; t. up. v.i., to dress smartly: proletarian: resp. 1844, 1869, 1903. 2. As v.t., *tog out* occurs in 1820 in the *London Magazine* (I, 25), 'He was always togged out to the nines,' and *tog up* in 1894.

tog-maker. A low-class tailor: proletarian: late C.19–20. Prob. ex TOGS.

tog up, see TOG IT.

toga play. An Ancient-Classics drama: theatrical coll (—1909); ob. Ex the ancient Roman male garment.

***togamans,** see TOGEMAN(S).

***toge.** A coat: c.: late C.17–18. Ex TOGEMAN(S) on S.E. *toge* (= *toga*).

***togeman(s); togman.** A cloak; a (loose) coat; rarely, a gown: c. of ca 1565–1840, but ob. by 1800 if not indeed by 1750. Harman, 1567, all three forms; *togeman*, very rare after 1700, *togman* app. not later than 1700; Grose, 1st ed., *togmans*, 2nd ed., *togemans*; Bee, the rare *togamans*. Ex Roman *toga*, perhaps in its Fr. form (*toge*), + the c. suffix -MANS. cf. TOG; TOGE; TOGS.

togey. A knotted lanyard used disciplinarily or bullyingly: in the training-ship *Britannia*: late C.19–early 20. Prob. ex TOCO; cf. TOGY and *take* TOKO.

togged, togged out or **up; togged up to the nines,** see resp. TOG, v., and TOG IT.

togger. Perhaps only in *upper togger*, an overcoat: low s. of ca 1820–50. Egan, 1823, 'And with his upper togger gay, | Prepared to toddle swift away.' Ex TOG, n., 1. 2. A boat in the Torpids: Oxford University: from mid-1890s. Ex *Torpid*, via the Oxford *-er*', on Cambridge SLOGGER. 3. In pl, gen. *T.*, the Torpids, i.e. the races themselves, the competition as a whole: C.20. 4. At Harrow (also *Torpid*), a boy not yet two years in the School: from ca 1896.

toggery. Clothes: s. (1812, Vaux) >, ca 1890, coll. Moncrieff, 1823, 'This toggery will never fit – you must have a new rig-out.' 2. Hence, esp., official or vocational dress: from ca 1825; slightly ob. Marryat, 1837, has *long toggery*, landsmen's clothes: cf. *long* TOGS. 3. Hence, (a horse's) harness: from late 1850s; slightly ob. 4. Hence, loosely, one's 'gear' or belongings: from late 1850s; ob.

***toggy.** A cloak; a coat: c.: ca 1740–1910. Ex TOG, n., 1, on TOGGERY, or perhaps imm. ex †*toggy*, *tuggy*, an overcoat for the arctic regions.

togies, see TOGY. **togman,** see TOGEMAN(S).

***togs.** Clothes: c. (—1809) >, ca 1825, low s. >, ca 1860, gen. s.; in C.20, usually jocular coll. G. Andrewes's Dict.; Dickens; Blackmore. Ex TOG, n., 1. 2. In phrases – chiefly these two:

togs, long. Landsmen's clothes: nautical s. >, ca 1890, coll: 1830, Marryat, 'I retained a suit of "long togs", as we call them.' Prob. on *long clothes*. cf. at TOGGERY, 2, and the derivative:

togs, Sunday. One's best clothes: London and nautical s. (—1859) >, by 1904, gen. Ex TOGS; cf. TOGS, LONG.

togy. (Gen. pl.) A knotted rope's-end carried about hidden by elder boys to beat their fags with: Public Schools': from ca 1870; ob. Prob. ex TOCO. Also TOGEY.

toheno; occ. **tohereno.** Very nice: late C.19–20: costers'. Lit., *hot one* reversed.

***toke.** (Dry) bread: low s. (—1859) verging, orig., on c. Perhaps TUCK (food) or (*hard* and *soft*) TACK corrupted. 2. Hence, food in gen.: low s. and c.: from ca 1875. Anon., *Five Years' Penal Servitude*, 1877, 'What in prison slang is called his toke or chuck.' 3. A loaf of bread, esp. a small loaf of bread served in prison: (mostly prison) c.: late C.19–20. 4. (Prob. ex 1.) A piece, portion; lump: rare and low: from early 1870s; ob.

toke, v. To idle, LOAF: Leys School: late C.19–20. Ex THOKE, v.

token, Tom-fool's. Money: late C.17–mid-18. Contrast:

token, the. Venereal disease, esp. in *tip one* (gen. male) *the token*, to infect venereally: low: from ca 1780; very ob. Ex *token*, a blotch or discoloration indicative of disease, esp. the plague.

toko, see TOCO.

toko, take. 'To take four dozen lashes in

the old Navy without crying out' (Bowen): ca 1840–90. Ex TOCO FOR YAM.

tokus. A rare variant of TOCO. H. D. Miles, *Dick Turpin*, 1841. This form either shows the influence of or, more probably, comes straight from Yiddish *tokus*, the backside.

tol. A sword: c. of late C.17–18. Abbr. *Toledo*, a sword there made. Hence, RUM *tol*, a gold- or silver-hilted sword; QUEER *tol*, a brass- or steel-hilted one, i.e. an ordinary one. 2. A share; *a lot* (of . . .): back s. (—1851).

tol-lol. Intoxicated: Yorkshire and Nottinghamshire: from ca 1890. 2. See:

tol-lol(l); tol-lollish. Pretty good: resp. from middle 1790s and late 1850s; ob. Mrs A. M. Bennett, 1797; W. S. Gilbert, 'Lord Nelson, too, was pretty well – | That is, tol-lol-ish!' By the reduplication of the first syllable of *tolerable*. 2. As adv., tolerably: from late 1850s.

told, be. To obtain one's colours in a school team: Tonbridge: late C.19–20.

told out. Exhausted: coll: 1861, Whyte-Melville, of a horse. Lit., counted out.

tolerable. In fair health: coll: 1847, C. Brontë, 'We're tolerable, sir, I thank you.' 2. As adv. (= tolerably): from ca 1670: S.E. until late C.18, then coll and dial.

tolerably. (Predicatively, of health.) Pretty well: coll: 1778, Mme D'Arblay.

***tol(l)iban rig.** 'A species of cheat carried on by a woman, assuming the character of a deaf and dumb conjurer', Grose, 2nd ed.: c.: ca 1786–1850. Ex RIG (2), a trick, + TOLOBEN, *tol(l)iban*, the tongue.

tolly. A candle: Public Schools': mid-C. 19–20. (cf. the v.) Ex *tallow*. Hence, *the Tolly*, a tapering spire at the back of the Close of Rugby School: Rugby: late C.19–20. *Athenaeum*, 16 June 1900. 2. A flat instrument (e.g. a ruler) used in caning: Stonyhurst: late C.19–20. ?ex sense 1, or ex L. *tollere*. Esp. *get the tolly*. 3. A marble (as used in the game of marbles): children's: late C.19–20. cf. sense 2. 4. A cup or mug; a tin hip-bath: Marlborough College: since ca 1870.

tolly, gen. **tolly up.** To work by candlelight after the extinction of the other lights: Harrow School (—1889). Ex the n., 1.

tolly-shop. A prefect's room (where caning is done): Stonyhurst: late C.19–20. Ex TOLLY, n., 2. cf. *tolly-ticket*, a good-conduct card: ibid.: id. Because it ensured against caning, except for a particularly serious offence.

tolly up, see TOLLY, v.

toloben. The tongue: c.: late C.18–20. Hence, *toloben rig*, fortune-telling. cf. TOLLIBAN RIG. Also occ. spelt *tollibon* or *tullibon*. (I am, however, unconvinced about *toloben* being the tongue: it is vouched-for only by F. & H., and I think that there may be a confusion with Romany *tullopen* or *tullipen*, or *tulipen*, fat, lard, grease, a sense that, if extended to 'paint' for the face, might well explain *toloben-rig*, fortune-telling, and possibly also *tolliban-rig* as above.)

tom, v. (Of men) to coït with: North Country: late C.19–20. Ex a tomcat's sexual activities.

Tom. The big bell at Christ Church, S.E., but *after Tom*, after hours, is a Christ Church coll (—1874). 2. *Tom, long*, see LONG TOM. 3. *tom, old*. Gin: c. or low s. (—1823); ob. Occ. (—1887), merely *tom* or *Tom*. 4. Inevitable nickname of all men named King: naval and military: late C.19–20. Ex Tom King, the famous C.18 highwayman. 5. (Either *tom* or *Tom*.) 'A masculine woman of the town' (harlot): low London: mid-C.19–20. 6. A woman who does not care for the society of others than those of her own sex: Society: ca 1880–1914.

Tom-a-Styles or **-Stiles.** Anybody, esp. in law, with *John-a-Nokes* as his opponent: ca 1770–1830: coll >, by 1800, S.E. G. A. Stevens, 1772, 'From John o' Nokes to Tom o' Stiles, | What is it all but fooling?' Occ. *John-a-Stiles*. See *Words!*

Tom and funny. Money: rhyming s. (—1909); ob.

Tom-and-Jerry days. The Regency (1810–20); also, the reign of George IV: coll: ca 1825–60. Ex Tom and Jerry in Pierce Egan's *Life in London*, 1821, with a continuation in 1828. The v., *Tom-and-Jerry*, to behave riotously (1828), is rather S.E. than coll, but *Tom-and-Jerry* (—1864) or *T.-and-J. shop* (—1835), a low drinking-shop, is coll. The latter elaborates JERRY-SHOP, a low beerhouse, recorded in 1834. cf.:

Tom-and-Jerry gang. A noisy, riotous gang of fellows: ca 1810–40. In J. H. Lewis, *The Art of Writing*, 7th ed., 1816, it is applied to the House of Commons. cf. preceding entry.

Tom and Tib, see TOM, DICK, AND HARRY.

Tom Astoner. A dashing or devil-may-care fellow: nautical: from ca 1860; ob. Ex *to astonish* or perhaps abbr. *astonisher*;

Ned Ward, however, has, in 1706, *Tom Estenor*, which may pun a surname.

***Tom Bray's bilk.** 'Laying out ace and deuce at cribbage', Vaux, 1812: ca 1810–60: prob. orig. c. > (low) gaming s. ?ex noted sharper.

***Tom Brown.** 'Twelve in hand, in crib', Vaux: ca 1810–60: ?c. > s.

Tom Cony. A simpleton or very silly fellow: coll: late C.17–early 19.

Tom Cox. A shirker; one who talks much, does little: naval: mid-C.19–20. cf.:

Tom Cox's traverse. See THREE TURNS. cf. SOGER, V.

Tom, Dick, and Harry. The common run of men (and women): coll soon > S.E.: *T., D., and H.*, app. not before ca 1815, but Lindsay, in 1566, has *Jack and Tom, Tom and Tib* is frequent in C.17, *Jack, Tom, Will, and Dick* in 1604 (James I *loquitur*), *Tom, Jack and Dick* in 'Water-Poet' Taylor, 1622, *Tom and Dick* occurs in C.18, *Tom, Dick, and Francis* in Shakespeare (1596), *Dick, Tom, and Jack* in 1660 (A. Brome), *Jack, Tom, and Harry* ca 1693 (T. Brown), and *Tom, Jack, and Harry* in 1865. cf. TOM TILER.

Tom-doodle; rarely **-a-doodle.** A simpleton: popular coll: C.18–20; ob. Ned Ward, 1707, 'That . . . Tom-doodle of a son . . . talks of nothing but his mother.'

Tom Double. A double-dealer, a shuffler: coll: C.18–mid-19.

Tom Drum's entertainment. The (very) rough reception of a guest: coll: ca 1570–1640. Holinshed. Also *John* (Shakespeare), *Jack* ('Water-Poet' Taylor). Possibly ex an actual person's name; more prob., a pun on *drum*.

Tom Essence. A dandy: s.: Ned Ward, 1703.

Tom farthing (or F.). A fool: coll (1689, Shadwell) >, early in C.18, S.E. Pejorative *farthing*. cf. TOM-DOODLE.

Tom Fool than Tom Fool knows, more know. A semi-proverbial c.p. of C.18–20; ob. Defoe; F. & H., 'A sarcastic retort on failing to recognize, or professing to be unacquainted with, a person saluting'.

Tom Long. A person long a-coming or tiresomely long in telling a tale: coll (?> S.E.): from ca 1630; ob., except in dial., which in C.19–20 it mainly is. W. Foster, 1631, 'Surely this is Tom Long the carrier, who will never do his errand,' O.E.D., but this is preceded by 'Proverbs' Heywood, 1546, 'I will send it him by John Long the carrier,' i.e. at some vague date, and by Cotgrave, 1611, 'To stay' – in C.18–20, gen. *wait* – 'for John Long the Carrier; to tarry long for that which comes but slowly'. In his *Phraseologia Generalis*, 1681, W. Robertson has *Tom Long the carrier*; in late C.17, B.E. has *come by T. L. the c.*, 'of what is very late, or long a coming', and Grose, 1st ed., much the same phrase.

Tom-noddy. A stupid, a foolish, person: coll (—1828) >, by 1860, S.E.

***Tom o' Bedlam.** A madman, esp. if discharged from Bedlam and allowed to beg: c. and s.: C.17–early 19. cf. ABR(AH)-AM-COVE.

Tom Owen's stop. 'The left-hand open, scrawling over the antagonist's face, service with the right', Bee: pugilistic: ca 1820–40. Ex a boxer.

***Tom Pat.** A parson or hedge-priest: c.: late C.17–early 18. *Street Robberies Consider'd*. A RUM *Tom Pat* is a clerk in holy orders, i.e. a genuine cleric. App. *Pat* = PATRICO. 2. A shoe: c.: C.19–20; ob. (In Romany, a foot.)

Tom Pepper. A liar: nautical s. (—1818) >, by 1890, coll. In sailors' folk-lore, 'Tom Pepper was the seaman who was kicked out of Hell for lying' (Bowen).

Tom Right. Night: rhyming s. (—1857); ob.

tom-rot. A variant (—1887) of TOMMY-ROT.

Tom Sawyer. A lawyer: rhyming s.: late C.19–20.

Tom Tailor. A tailor in gen.: coll >, by 1890, S.E.: 1820, Scott.

Tom Tell-Troth (Truth). An honest man: coll: resp. C.17 and C.18–20 (ob.). *Tom True-Tongue*, C.14, is the generator; *Tom Truth*, mainly C.16 (e.g. Latimer), the imm. generator.

Tom Thacker. Tobacco: rhyming s. (on BACCA): late C.19–20.

Tom Thumb. Rum: rhyming s.: late C.19–20.

Tom Tiler or **Tyler.** Any ordinary man: coll: ca 1580–1640. Stonyhurst, 1582. cf. TOM, DICK, AND HARRY. 2. Hence, a henpecked husband: id.: early C.17.

tom-tit. To defecate: rhyming s. (late C.19–20) on SHIT. Also PONY AND TRAP (same period) on CRAP.

Tom Topper(s) or **Tug.** A ferryman; any river hand: low London: from ca 1860; ob. H., 3rd ed. ('*Topper* . . . From a popular song, entitled "*Overboard he vent*" '), for both; *Tug* presumably from that vessel, though perhaps imm. ex 'the small stage-play', H., 5th ed.

Tom Tripe. A pipe: rhyming s. (—1859); †by 1900. cf. TOMMY TRIPE.

Tom Tug. A fool: rhyming s. (—1874) on MUG (4). 2. See TOM TOPPER. 3. A bed-bug: rhyming s. (—1909). Contrast sense 1.

Tom Turdman. A nightman, a scavenger: low: from ca 1690; ob. E. Ward, 1703.

Tom Turd's field(s) or **Tom Turd's hole.** 'A place where the Nightmen lay their Soil', *Sessions*, 1733 (11th session): low: C.18.

Tom Tyler, see TOM TILER.

tomahawk. A policeman's baton: urban, esp. Cockney (—1909).

Tomasso di Rotto (or without caps). (An 'Italianizing' of) TOMMY-ROT: middle-class youths': ca 1905–14.

tomboy. Female genitals: C.17. Taylor the Water Poet, 'Playing the tomboy with her tomboy.'

tombstone. A pawn-ticket: low (—1864). 2. A projecting tooth, esp. if discoloured: from ca 1880.

tombstone-style. An advertisement (rarely of other matter) so 'displayed', i.e. composed, that it resembles a monumental inscription: printers' coll: from ca 1880.

tomfoolery. Jewellery: rhyming s.: late C. 19–20.

tomjohn; Tomjohn. A tonjon: Anglo-Indian (—1886). By Hobson-Jobson.

tommy, as applied to goods (mainly food) supplied to workmen in lieu of wages, is S.E.; so too, according to the O.E.D., it is as the soldiers' and, from ca 1860, the lower classes' word for (orig. brown) bread. The latter I hold to be s. in C.18–early 19, coll in mid-C.19–20, as are SOFT (or, 1811, *white*) TOMMY, bread as opp. to biscuit, and *brown tommy* (*Lex. Bal.*, but prob. much earlier); as used by workmen for food or provisions in gen., from ca 1860, it is coll. Perhaps by a pun: BROWN GEORGE suggesting *brown Tommy*, with alternative *Tommy Brown*, whence *Tommy*, whence *tommy*. But note that in Bedford (and elsewhere, *tommy* = loaves of bread distributed by charity on St *Thomas's* Day (21 December), for hundreds of years: this, which prob. explains the orig. of a puzzling word, I owe to Mr R. A. Parrott of Bedford. 2. A sham shirt-front: Dublin University (—1860); ob. Prob. on equivalent DICKEY (2) ex Gr. *τομή*, a section. 3. (Gen. in pl.) A tomato: low: from ca 1870. 4. *Tommy.* 'Tommy Atkins', a private British (specifically, non-Colonial) soldier: 1893, Kipling. *Tommy Atkins* occurs in Sala in 1883; coll >, by 1895, S.E. Ex *Thomas Atkins*, a specimen name for signature on attestation-forms and in pay-books since early C. 19. See *Words!* for further details. 5. A frequent term of address to a young boy whose name is unknown to the speaker: coll (—1887). cf. JACK (19) addressed to a man in these circumstances. 6. Penis: rather low: C.19–20. 7. *The* CURSE: feminine: late C.19–20. By personification.

tommy (or T.), v., see TOMMY TRIPE.

tommy or **Tommy, hell and.** An elaboration of *hell* in intensives or asseverations: from ca 1885. The *tommy* is perhaps ex TOMMY-ROT; the capital *T*, on ALL MY EYE AND BETTY MARTIN: ?cf. YO, TOMMY!

***tommy!, that's the.** That's right: c. (—1887). Prob. ex TOMMY, 1.

tommy and exes. Bread (see TOMMY, 1), beer, and tobacco: workmen's (—1909). Here *exes* = *extras*.

Tommy Atkins, see TOMMY, 4.

tommy-axe. A tomahawk: Australian coll: late C.19–20. Not certainly a corruption (by Hobson-Jobson) of *tomahawk*; perhaps on *tommy* as applied to a small tool or instrument, e.g. a spade – with which cf., in military j., *tommy bar*, 'a bentwire spanner used to unscrew the bases of Mills bombs'.

Tommy Cornstalk. An Australian soldier. 1899–1902 (during the Boer War): coll: Baker.

Tommy Dodd. In tossing coins, either the winner or the loser, by agreement; the mode of tossing: from ca 1863; ob.: rather proletarian. ca 1863 there was a music-hall song, 'Heads or tails are sure to win, Tommy Dodd, Tommy Dodd.' Rhyming on *odd*. 2. God: rhyming s.: late C.19–20. 3. A sodomite: since ca 1870. Rhyming on SOD. Since ca 1890, often abbr. to *Tommy*. 4. A small glass of beer: New Zealand and Australian: late C.19–20.

Tommy, get out and let your father in. Gin (the drink): navvies' rhyming s.: ca 1860–1900. (D. W. Barrett, *Navvies*, 1880.)

Tommy, make room for your uncle! A c.p. addressed to the younger man (men) in a group: from ca 1883. Ex a popular song.

Tommy o' Rann. Food: rhyming s. (—1859) on SCRAN, 2.

Tommy Pipes. Nickname for a boatswain – 'because he pipes or whistles all hands'. Naval: ca 1850–1910. Ware.

Tommy Rabbit (or r.). A pomegranate: rhyming s. (—1909).

Tommy Roller. A collar: rhyming s.: since ca 1880. (C. Bent, *Criminal Life*, 1891.)

Tommy Rollocks. Testicles: since ca 1870. Often abbr. to *rollocks*. Rhyming *ballocks*.

tommy-rot, also **tom-rot.** Nonsense; as exclamation, BOSH!: s. >, ca 1900, coll: 1884, George Moore, 'Bill . . . said it was all "Tommy rot".' Perhaps ex *tommy*, goods supplied instead of wages; though Manchon's theory that it is a euphemism (via the Tommies' former scarlet uniform) for *bloody* is not ridiculous; cf. *tommy* in *hell and* TOMMY. 2. Occ. as v.i., to fool about; v.t., to HUMBUG: rare: late C.19–20.

Tommy tit. 'A smart lively little fellow', Grose, 1st ed.: coll: mid-C.18–19.

Tommy-toes. (Little) toes: London children's (—1887).

Tommy Tripe. To observe, examine, watch: rhyming s. (—1874) on PIPE, v., 4. Occ. abbr. *Tommy* or *tommy*, as in 'Tommy his plates (of meat)', look at his feet!

Tommy Tucker. Supper: from ca 1860. Suggested by the nursery rhyme, 'Little Tommy Tucker sang for his supper.'

tommyrotic. Nonsensical: literary coll: from mid-1890s; ob. Whence, likewise ex TOMMY-ROT on *erotic*: *tommyrotics*, obscenity, esp. foolish obscenity: coll (—1904). For form, cf. HEROHOTIC.

ton. (Rare in singular.) Much; plenty: coll: from early 1890s. 2. Gen. *the ton*. The fashion; fashionable Society: from late 1760s: coll (mostly Society) until ca 1840, then S.E.; ca 1815–25, it verged on s. Ex Fr. *ton*.

ton for ton and man for man. The fair division of prizes between two ships sailing in company: naval c.p. verging on j.: C.19. Bowen.

ton of bricks, like a, see BRICK, LIKE A.

tone, t'one; tother, t'other. (Whether pronouns or adjj.) The one; the other: S.E. until C.18, then coll and dial.; in C.20, *t'one* as coll is slightly illiterate. Often in juxtaposition, *t'one . . . t'other*. N.B., *tother day* in †S.E. = the next day, occ. the preceding day; as = a few days ago, it arose in C.16 and was S.E. until C.18; then coll and dial.

toney, see TONY.

tongs. Forceps: dental and medical: from ca 1870.

tongs, pair of. A tall thin person: low: from ca 1880; ob. Ex the two thin 'legs'. 2. Whence, in sarcastic address or comment, *tongs!* 3. *touch with a pair of tongs*. See TOUCH WITH . . .

tongue, v.t. To talk (a person) down: low (—1860); ob. Ex the ob. S.E. sense, to attack with words, to reproach.

tongue, give (a lick with) the rough side of one's. To scold, abuse: coll: 1820, Scott; ob. cf. dial. *give a person the length of one's tongue*.

tongue, have a. To be sarcastic and/or ironic: non-aristocratic coll: from ca 1880. Charles Turley, *Godfrey Marten, Schoolboy*, 1902, '"He had a tongue", as servants say, and could be sarcastic.' Ex *have a sharp tongue*.

tongue, lose one's. To fall very, be long, silent: coll: 1870, Dickens.

tongue, and a little older than my teeth, – as old as my. A c.p. reply to *how old are you?*: late C.18–20; ob.

tongue enough for two sets of teeth(, with; to have). Applied to an exceedingly talkative person: ca 1786–1870. cf. TONGUE-PAD; TONGUE TOO LONG FOR ONE'S TEETH; TONGUED.

tongue in another's purse, put one's. To silence: ca 1540–1620. 'Proverbs' Heywood.

tongue is well hung, his (etc.). He is fluent, ready, glib of speech: coll: C.18, Swift; Berthelson's Dict., 1754. Apperson. cf. TONGUE-PAD. Perhaps also coll are the C.18 semi-proverbial *your tongue is made of very loose leather* ('Proverbs' Fuller, 1732) and the semi-proverbial C.16–17 *her (your*, etc.) *tongue runs on pattens* ('Proverbs' Heywood; Davies of Hereford), both recorded by Apperson, who notes the analogous *his* (etc.) *tongue runs on wheels* (mid-C.15–20; in mid-C.19–20, dial.) enshrined by Swift.

tongue of the trump, the. The best or most important thing or person: Scots coll: from ca 1870. In a Jew's harp, the tongue is the steel spring by which the sound is made.

tongue-pad. A talkative person, esp. if smooth and insinuating: late C.17–20: s. until late C.19, then dial. B.E.; Grose, in 1st ed., adds: 'A scold', a sense †by 1850. On FOOT-PAD. cf. the v. 2. A confidence trickster: s.: Ned Ward, 1703.

tongue-pad. To scold, v.t.; v.i., to chatter: resp. mid-C.17–20. C.19–20; both dial. in C.20. J. Stevens, 1707; Scott, the v.i. in 1825. Whence *tongue-padder* = *tongue-pad*, n., and vbl n., *t.-padding*, and see:

tongue-padder. A lawyer: s.: Ned Ward, 1703. 2. See TONGUE-PAD.

tongue runs nineteen to the dozen, one's, see DOZEN, TALK ... **tongue runs on pattens** or **wheels, one's,** see TONGUE IS WELL HUNG.

tongue to, call (a person) **everything one can lay one's.** To scold, abuse, violently: coll and dial.: late C.19–20. cf. TONGUE-PAD, n., 1, 2nd nuance.

tongue too long for one's teeth or **mouth.** Either *have a* ... or, more gen., as in Reade, 1859, 'Hum! Eve, wasn't your tongue a little too long for your teeth just now?' To be indiscreet or too ready to talk: mid-C.19–20; ob. Prob. ex TONGUE ENOUGH ...; cf. the C.17 proverb, *the tongue walks where the teeth speed not.*

tongued. Talkative: low (—1860); ob. cf. TONGUE ENOUGH ...

tonic. A halfpenny: ca 1820–50. ?origin: cf., however, TANNER. 2. A drink, esp. if taken as an appetizer: late C.19–20. cf. MEDICINE.

tonight's the night! A c.p. of late C.19–20; ob.

tonk. At cricket, to hit a ball into the air: Charterhouse and Durham (schools): late C.19–20. cf. TONKABOUT, the corresponding n. Ex the mainly Midland dial. *tank*, n., a blow; v., to strike.

tonkabout. The hitting of catches at cricket-practice: Charterhouse (—1900). A. H. Tod. Ex preceding term.

tony; in C.18, occ. **toney.** A fool, a simpleton: mid-C.17–early 19. Gayton, 1654; but it must be a few years earlier, for the rare v., *tony*, to befool or swindle, is recorded ca 1652. Ex ANT(H)ONY.

tony; loosely, **toney,** adj. Stylish, SWELL; high-toned: coll, orig. (—1886), U.S. >, in 1890s, Australian and New Zealand. H. Lawson, 1901. Ex *high tone*, or possibly ex ob. *ton-ish, tonish* (itself ex TON, 2, fashion).

too. Very; extremely: C.14–20: S.E. until early C.19, then coll – esp. as an emotional intensive among non-proletarian women. The O.E.D. has, at 1868, 'How too delightful your expeditions must have been.' cf.:

too, only. As mere intensive: coll: late C.19–20. ?ex preceding.

too all-but. A London society c.p. of 1881–2. Ware, 'Resulting out of *Punch*'s trouvaille "too-too"'.

too many cloths in the wind. Tipsy: late C.19–20. On *three* SHEETS IN THE WIND.

too many (gen. **too much**) **for.** Sufficient to overcome or quell; too able or strong, i.e. more than a match, for: coll: *much*, 1832; 1861, Dickens, 'Mr Jaggers was altogether too many for the Jury, and they gave in.' *Too many for* may be orig. U.S., for it occurs in *The Port Folio*, 14 Feb. 1801.

too mean to part with (his) shit. Excessively miserly or close-fisted: low: late C. 19–20.

too much!, this is. A c.p. retort or comment: from mid-1860s. F. & H. suggests that it echoes *Artemus Ward among the Shakers* (ca 1862).

too much of a good thing. Excessive; intolerable: coll: 1809, Sydney Smith, 'This (to use a very colloquial phrase) is surely too much of a good thing.' An elaboration of *too much*, but perhaps prompted by the literal sense, as in Shakespeare's *As You Like It*, IV, i, 'Why then, can one desire too much of a good thing?' cf. preceding entry.

too much with us. Excessively boring; an intolerable nuisance: Society c.p.: 1897–9. Ex the Wordsworthian *the world is too much with us.*

too numerous to mention. Angrily drunk: London: 1882–ca 90. Prob. *uttering curses too*, etc.

too short for Richard, too long for Dick. Yorkshire expression for 'no bloody good'; said to have reference to Richard III, the Hunchback: coll: C.19–20.

too-too (see TOO ALL-BUT) was in 1881 a Society c.p. cf. the derivative *too utterly too* (1883) and *too utterly utter* (late C.19–20; ob.): also Society c.pp.

too (effing or sanguinarily) **true.** A c.p. of emphatic agreement or endorsement or corroboration: late C.19–20.

tool. The penis: mid-C.16–20: S.E. until C.18, then coll; in C.19–20, s. unless the context definitely renders it archaic S.E. 2. A whip: ca 1820–90. Ex *tool*, to drive. 3. A small boy employed to creep through windows, etc., to effect entry: c.: ca 1840–1910. 1845 in '*No. 747*'. cf. the v., 4. 4. See TOOLS. 5. A run; to run: Charterhouse: late C.19–20. Ex the v., 3. 6. A brush: studio s.: from ca 1860. 7. A one-inch paint-brush: builders' and house-painters': late C.19–20.

tool, v.t. To drive: 1812, *Sporting Magazine*; 1849, Lytton, 'He could tool a coach'; 1899, Whiteing. Ex instrument for effect. 2. Hence, as in Jessop, 1881, 'The high-stepping mare that tools him along through the village street.' Rare. 3. (Ex sense 1.) v.i., to drive, to go or travel, esp. *along*: 1839. 4. Gen. v.i., to pick pockets: c. (—1859); slightly ob. Prob. ex the n., 3. 5. To murder (v.i.): Society: ca 1845–1900. Ex a metaphor by De Quincey. 6. See n., 5.

tool, dull or **poor.** An inferior workman: late C.17–20; in late C.19–20, dial. cf. *a poor* (occ. bad) *workman blames his tools.* 2. Hence, (*poor tool*) a shiftless person: C. 18–20; latterly dial.

tool, grind one's. (Of the male) to coït: low: mid-C.19–20.

tool off. To depart: 1881, *Punch*, 17 Dec.; ob. Ex TOOL, v., 3.

***tooler.** A burglar, a pickpocket: c. (—1859). See TOOL, n., 3, and v., 4. 2. Hence, MOLL-*tooler*, a female thief or pickpocket.

Tooley Street tailor. A conceitedly bumptious fellow: mostly London: ca 1870–80. H., 5th ed., 'The "three tailors of Tooley Street" are said to have immortalised themselves by preparing a petition for Parliament – and some say, presenting it – with only their own signatures thereto, which commenced, "We the people of England".' How *do* such yarns arise?

***tools.** The hands: c.: mid-C.19–20; ob. 2. Pistols: possibly c.: id. 3. As = housebreaking implements, merely a specific application of gen. S.E. sense. 4. Knives, forks and spoons: nautical: late C.19–20. Bowen.

***tools, fined for the.** Convicted for possessing a burglar's tools: c. of ca 1820–1910. cf. TOOL, v., 4, and TOBY, v.t. (analogous DONE FOR).

tooth. See TEETH, and the following compounds and phrases:

tooth, have an aching. To have a desire, a longing (*for*); coll: late C.16–20; in C.19–20, mostly dial. Lodge, 1590; North, 1742; 1887, Parish & Shaw, *Dict. of Kent Dialect.* 2. (*have . . . at* a person.) To be angry with: coll: C.18. N. Bailey, 1730.

tooth, have cut one's eye. To be 'knowing': a (—1860) variant of *have* CUT ONE'S EYE TEETH.

tooth, high in. Bombastic: low: from the 1870s; ob.

tooth, old or **up in the.** (Esp. of old maids) aged: from ca 1860. H., 2nd ed., '*Stable term* for aged horses which have lost the distinguishing mark in their teeth.'

tooth-carpenter. A dentist: low: from ca 1880. cf. TONGS.

tooth-drawer, like a. Thin: coll: mid-C. 17–18. Ray. Prob. ex, not *tooth-drawer*, a dentist, but †*tooth-drawer*, his instrument.

tooth-music. (The sound of) mastication: from ca 1786; ob.

toothache. A priapism: low: late C.19–20. Orig. IRISH TOOTHACHE. 2. A knife *has the toothache* if the blade is loose: schoolboys', mostly Colonial: id.

toothachy. Having, characteristic of, toothache: coll: 1838, Lady Granville.

toother. A punch on the mouth: boxing: from ca 1890; slightly ob.

toothpick. 'A large stick. An ironical expression', *Lex. Bal.*: London: ca 1810–50. In *Sinks*, 1848, an Irish watchman's shillelagh. 2. A very narrow fishing-boat with pointed prow: mainly nautical: 1897, Kipling. Ex shape. 3. A sword: military: ca 1790–1913. cf. CHEESE-TOASTER; TOASTING-FORK.

toothpick brigade, crutch and. Foppish 'men about town': London society: ca 1885–1905. Ex: 2. Hangers-on at stage doors, esp. at the Gaiety: London society: ca 1884–5. 'They affected, as the badge of their tribe, a crutch-handled stick and a toothpick,' F. & H.

toothy-peg. A tooth: nursery coll: 1828, Hood, 'Turn we to little Miss Kilmansegg, | Cutting her first little toothy-peg.' By itself, *toothy*, a child's tooth, is less common: lit., a little tooth.

tooting. Wind-music: s.: Ned Ward, 1703. 2. **(T.)** See:

Tooting Bec. Food: a meal, esp. supper, rhyming s. (on PECK): since ca 1880. Often abbr. to *Tooting.*

tootle. Twaddle; trashy verbiage: university: 1880s. Ex *tootle*, an act of tooting on a horn; cf., however, dial. *tootle*, silly gossip.

tootle-oo!; loosely, **toodle-oo!** Good-bye!: from ca 1905, according to Collinson; the O.E.D. (Sup.) records it at 1907. Probably a Cockney corruption of the French equivalent of '(I'll) see you soon': *à tout à l'heure.*

tootsie, tootsy; tootsie (or **-y)-wootsie.** A child's, a woman's small, foot: playful or affectionate coll: resp. 1854, Thackeray; ca 1890. The form *tootsicum* is a facetious 'literary' elaboration. On *foot*, but ex *toddle.*

top, n. In c., a dying speech: ca 1830–80. (Also known as a *croak.*) Ex the c. *top*, to behead (v., 4). 2. In earlier c., a cheating trick whereby one of the dice remained at the top of the box: gaming: ca 1705–50. *Tatler*, No. 68, 1709. Ex:

***top**, v.i. To cheat, esp. at cards: c >, by 1750, low s.: ca 1660–1820. v.t. with *on*, *upon*. 2. ?hence, v.i. and v.t. (the latter, gen. *top upon*), to insult: late C.17–early 19: c. >, by 1750, low s. 3. (Likewise ex sense 1.) To impose or foist (a thing) *on*: ca 1670–1750. 4. To behead, to hang: c.: C.18–20, in C.20 mostly in the passive. Implied in TOPPING CHEAT, T. COVE, and TOPMAN or TOPSMAN, though not separately recorded before 1811.

top, a little bit off the. Some of the best: coll: late C.19–20; ob. 2. Slightly crazy: from ca 1897; ob.

***top a clout** (a handkerchief) or other article is to draw a corner or an end to the top of the pocket in readiness for removal at a favourable moment: c. (—1812); slightly ob.

top ballocks. Female breasts: military: late C.19–20. e.g. 'a smashing pair of top ballocks' is a fine bust. cf.:

top buttocks. Female breasts: low: late C.19–20. cf. preceding entry.

top-diver. 'A Lover of Women. *An Old Top-diver*, one that has Lov'd *Old-hat* in his time', B.E.: low: late C.17–early 19. Grose.

top drawing-room. An attic or garret: London lower classes' jocular (—1909).

top-dressing. The hair: jocular coll: from ca 1870. James Brunton Stephens, 1874. An elaboration of *top* (as in the barber's 'You're getting a little bald on the top, sir'), with a pun on *t.-d.*, a fertilizing manure. 2. 'An introduction to a report: usually written by an experienced hand and set in larger type', F. & H.: journalistic: from ca 1870. cf. fig. use of WINDOW-DRESSING.

***top-fencer, -seller.** A seller of last dying speeches: ca 1830–70: resp. c. and (low) s. Ex TOP, n., 3.

***top-gob.** A pot-boy: c. (—1857); ob. Complete back s. is TOP-YOB.

top-hat. A tall or high hat (esp. as for formal occasions): coll: from ca 1810. *Saturday Evening Post*, 16 March 1822. Suggested by TOPPER, 2.

top-heavy. Drunk: coll: from ca 1675; ob. Ray, 1678; B.E.; Bailey, 1736; Grose; Hone, 1825.

top-hole, adj. Excellent; splendid, TOPPING: 1908, E. V. Lucas, 'A top-hole idea', but adumbrated by Conan Doyle, 1899, as *up to the top-hole*, though this may be considered a variant. On *top-notch*.

top-joint (pron. *jint*). A pint (of beer): rhyming s. (—1857); ob. cf. TOP-O'-REEB.

top-knot; topknot. The head: from 1820s. *Sessions*, April 1822. cf. TOP-PIECE.

top lights!, blast your. Blast your eyes: nautical: from ca 1790; ob.

top-lofty, toplofty; toploftical. Haughty; HIGH AND MIGHTY; HIGHFALUTIN: coll: resp. mid-C.19–20 and 1823; both slightly ob.

top-o'-reeb. A pot of beer: back s. (—1859).

top of Rome. (A) home: rhyming s. (—1857); ob.

top of the morning (to you)!, the. A cheery greeting: orig. and mainly Anglo-Irish: coll verging on S.E.: 1815, Scott.

top off or up. To finish off or up; to conclude: coll: both from ca 1835, Newman in 1836 having *up*, Dana *up* (printed 1840, known earlier). 2. To put the finishing touch to: coll: from ca 1870. Both senses derive ex *top* (or *top up*), to put the top on, to crown.

top (occ. top up) one's fruit, punnet, etc. To place the best fruit at the top of one's basket, punnet, etc.: garden-produce market: from mid-1880s. cf. TOPPERS, which prob. suggested it.

top-piece. The head: from 1830s: coll and dial. cf. TOP-KNOT.

top-ropes, sway away on all. To live extravagantly or riotously: nautical coll of ca 1810–1900. Ex fig. *sway* (incorrectly *swing*) *on all t.-r.*, to go to all lengths. Hence, 2. (*sway all top-ropes.*) To give oneself airs: nautical: late C.19–20; ob.

top-sawyer. A collar: tailors': from ca 1870; ob. 2. The sense, 'the best man; one in a superior position', may orig. (—1823) have been s. > coll >, by 1860, S.E. Ex the timber trade, where he 'who works the upper handle of a pit-saw' gets a much higher wage than those beneath him.

top-sawyer, play. To coït: mid-C.19–20; ob. cf. TOPS AND BOTTOMS.

top-seller, see TOP-FENCER.

top-shuffle. 'To shuffle the lower half of a pack over the upper half without disturbing it', F. & H.: gaming s. (—1904) > j.

top . . . tail, see TAIL, TOP . . .

top the officer. 'To arrogate superiority', Smyth: nautical: 1806, John Davis, *The Post-Captain*.

top up, see TOP ONE'S FRUIT and TOP OFF.

top upon, see TOP, v., 1, 2.

top-yob. A pot-boy: back s. (—1859); ob.

top your boom! Go away!: a nautical c.p. addressed to a man, esp. 'when he has forced his company where he was not invited': early C.19–20. Bowen.

topman. A hangman: C.17. (In C.19, TOPSMAN.) cf. TOP, v., 4.

topos. A variant of PROS, n.: English undergraduates' (—1884); ob. Ex Gr. *τόπος*, a place.

topper. A thing or person excellent or exceptionally good in his or its kind: coll: 1709, *The British Apollo*, of a bowl of punch compared with other drinks. Slightly ob. Lit., at the top. 2. A top-hat: s. (1820) >, by 1860, coll. 'Pomes' Marshall, 1897, 'A most successful raid | On a swell's discarded topper.' 3. A (violent) blow on the head (or 'top'): 1823, Bee; 1834, Ainsworth; ob. 4. See TOPPERS. 5. A cigar- or cigarette-end; a dottle: mostly London and mostly low (—1874). 6. A tall, thin person: low: from 1890s; ob.

topper, v. To knock on the head; to kill thus: from late 1860s; slightly ob. E. Farmer, 1869. Ex: 2. To punch: pugilistic: ca 1810–55. cf. TOPPER, n., 3.

topper-hunter. A scavenger (and seller) of 'toppers' (TOPPER, 5).

toppers. Large, fine fruit (esp. if strawberries) luring one from their display-point at basket- or punnet-top: 1839, Mogridge. Because they are at the top. cf. TOP ONE'S FRUIT.

topping, n. A hanging: late C.19–20. cf. TOP, v., 4.

topping, adj. In c., only in TOPPING CHEAT, TOPPING COVE. 2. Excellent in number, quantity, or quality; TIP-TOP: from ca 1820: coll >, ca 1890, s. Galt, 1822; Clough, 1860, 'Shady in Latin, said Lindsay, but topping in Plays and Aldrich.' Ex *topping*, eminent, and adumbrated in Ned Ward, 1703. 3. Hence, as an adv.: mid-C.19–20.

***topping(-)cheat.** A gallows (gen. *the t. c.*): c.: mid C.17–early 19. Ex CHEAT, *chete*, a thing; and cf. TOP, v., 4, and:

***topping cove** or **fellow.** A hangman: resp. c., mid-C.17–mid-19; (low) s., late C. 18–mid-19. The latter puns the lit. sense, a pre-eminent person. cf. TOPPING CHEAT; TOPSMAN.

topping man, as opp. *topping fellow* (in lit. sense), is a rich man: prob. the s. of a London social class or convivial set: ca 1788–1800.

toppy. Tipsy: coll: ca 1880–1915. cf. TOP-HEAVY. 2. Stylish; (too) showy: from ca 1890: coll. Perhaps suggested by TOPPING, 2.

tops and bottoms, play at. To copulate: mid-C.19–20; ob. Anatomical pun.

topsail, pay one's debts with the. (Of a sailor) to go to sea having left his debts unpaid: nautical: ca 1785–1850. Grose, 2nd ed., who adds, 'So soldiers are said to pay off their scores with the drum; that is, by marching away'; same period, but chiefly military.

topsel. A coll nautical variant (—1887) of *topsail*.

topside. Fig., on *top*; in control: coll: from late 1890s.

***topsman.** A hangman: from early 1820s: c. >, by 1860, low s. Ex TOP, v., 4, on *headsman*. cf. TOPPING-COVE; TOPMAN.

Topsy. A term of address to any little girl whose name is unknown to the speaker: non-aristocratic coll: mid-C.19–20.

topsy-boosy. Drunk: low: from ca 1890; ob. Reduplicated *boosy* (BOOZY). cf. TOPPY, 1.

tora-loorals. Feminine bust, esp. if somewhat exposed: theatrical (—1909); ob. Perhaps ex DAIRY via dial. *tooral-ooral* (merry with drink), itself ex *truly rural* used as a test for drunkenness.

torche-cul. Toilet-paper: coll: late C.17–mid-19. Direct ex the Fr. cf. BUM-FODDER, the English equivalent.

tormentor. (In a theatre) the first wing; a door therein: theatrical s. > coll: mid-C. 19–20, though not recorded before 1886 (O.E.D.). Because often a nuisance. 2. An instrument (cf. TICKLER) devised to annoy at fairs: coll: from ca 1890. 3. A flatterer: low: late C.19–20. Suggested by *back-scratcher*. 4. See TORMENTORS.

tormentor of catgut. A fiddler: coll (—1785); very ob. Because the violin-strings are made of catgut. Also CATGUT-SCRAPER.

tormentor of sheepskin. A drummer: from late C.18 to ca 1900. cf. preceding.

tormentors. Riding-spurs: 1844, C. J. R. Cook. cf. PERSUADER. 2. A cook's big forks: nautical (—1887). (Rather rare in singular.)

torn it!, that's. That has spoiled it, ruined, everything: s. (orig. low): 1909, 'Ian Hay'. Rare in other parts of the v. cf. the Northern proverbial *the swine's run through it*, of anything – orig. and esp. a marriage – ruined by bad luck, and TEAR ONE'S SEAT.

torrac. A carrot: back s. (—1859). Whence the indelicate c.p. retort (—1904), *ekat a torrac*: cf. *have a* BANANA!

torrid. Rather tipsy: ca 1780–1840. See MOPS AND BROOMS. Amorous drunk?

Tory. One of those who, in 1679–80, opposed the exclusion of James from the English crown: a nickname in use among the Exclusioners; rare after C.17. cf. TANTIVY and see esp. Roger North's *Examen*, II, v, §9. Ex *Tory,* a rapparee or outlaw and itself ex an Irish word = 'a pursuer'. cf. *whig*. 2. Hence, a Conservative: coll: from ca 1830, when *Conservative* superseded *Tory* as the official and formal name for a member of the traditionalist party. (The same holds of *Tory* used as an adj.)

Tory Rory. A London nickname given, ca 1780–1845, to 'those who wore their hats fiercely cocked' (Ware).

tosh. The penis: schoolboys': from 1870s. ?ex *tusk*; more prob. ex dial. *tosh*, 'a tusk; a projecting or unseemly tooth'. 2. A hat: modified back s.: ca 1875–1900. The correct *tah* > *ta-h*, *ta-aitch*, *tosh*. 3. (Also *tosh-can* or *-pan*.) A foot-pan, a bath: Public Schools' (—1881). Pascoe, *Life in Our Public Schools*. Perhaps a perversion of *wash*; possibly cognate is Romany *tov*, to wash. cf. the v. 4. Nonsense: 1892, *Oxford University Magazine*, 26 Oct., 'Frightful tosh'. Perhaps BOSH perverted; cf., however, dial. *toshy*, 'over-dressed; tawdry'. Often as an exclamation. 5. Hence, very easy bowling: cricketers': 1898. 6. A pocket: c.: C.19–20; ob. Ware, 'Prob. a corruption of French *poche*.'

tosh, v.t. To splash, throw water over: Public Schools': 1883, J. P. Groves. Ex the n., 3.

tosh-can, -pan, see TOSH, n., 3.

tosh-pond. The bathing pond: Royal Military Academy: from 1880s. Ex TOSH, n., 3.

tosh-room. A bathroom: Sandhurst: from ca 1860. Mockler-Ferryman.

tosh-soap. Cheese: Public Schools': from ca 1880. Ex TOSH, n., 3.

***tosher.** One who, in the Thames, steals copper from ships' bottoms: c. (—1859). For etymology, cf. TOSH, n., 3. Hence *toshing*, such theft: c. (—1867). Smyth. 2. A non-collegiate student at a university having residential colleges: undergraduates' (—1889); †by 1919. Ex *unattached*: see 'Oxford *-er*', p. 11. cf. BREKKER.

tosheroon. A variant of TUSHEROON.

toshy. Rubbishy: 1902, Belloc, 'Toshy novels.' Ex TOSH, n., 4.

toss-off. An act of masturbation: low coll (—1785). Presumably ex:

toss-off, v.i. and v. reflexive. (Gen. of the male.) To masturbate: low coll: from ca 1780.

toss-up. An even chance: coll: 1809, Malkin, 'It is a toss up who fails and who succeeds: the wit of to-day is the blockhead of to-morrow.' Ex *toss-up,* the 'skying' (see SKY) of a coin.

tossaroon, see TUSHEROON.

tossed. Drunk: C.19–20. Ex *tossed*, disordered, disturbed, but perhaps influenced by Scots *tosie*, *-y*, slightly intoxicated, occ. in form *tosy-mosy*.

tostificated. Drunk: late C.19–20; ob. Elaboration of dial. *tosticated* (i.e. corrupt *intoxicated*.).

tot. The sum-total of an addition, an addition sum: coll: from 1870s. Perhaps imm. ex TOT-UP, n.; ultimately ex *total*, less prob. ex L. *totum*, the whole. cf. *long* TOTS. 2. A very young or small child: dial. and coll: 1725, Ramsay. cf. Danish *tommel-tot,* Tom Thumb. Gen. *tiny* or *wee tot*, 3. ?hence, a (very) small drinking-vessel, esp. a child's mug or a tin mug: dial. (—1828) >, by 1840, coll. 4. (Perhaps ex sense 2; prob. ex sense 3.) A very small quantity, esp. of liquor: dial. (—1828) >, by 1850, coll, as in Whyte-Melville, 1868, 'He . . . often found himself pining for . . . the camp-fires, the fragrant fumes . . ., and the tot of rum.' 5. A bone; hence, anything worth taking from a dustbin or a refuse heap; but esp. a rag: dust-heap pickers', hence rag-and-bone men's: from early 1870s. Perhaps on *tat*, a rag, = the suggestion coming from the juxtaposition in *rag and bone*. Hence *tot-picker* (—1874) or *-raker* (—1904) or *-hunter* (—1909), and *totter* (—1891), such a scavenger, esp. if illicit, and *totting* (—1874), such scavenging. 6. See TOTE, n., 2.

tot, v.t. To add (orig. *together*) to ascertain the total of: coll: ca 1760, H. Brooke; slightly ob. Ex *total* or *tot* as abbr. *total* (or *totum*): cf. the n., 1. 2. Hence, *tot up*, to ascertain (esp. expeditiously) the total of: from mid 1830s. 3. Hence, vbl n. *totting-up*, *totting*: coll: resp. ca 1820, 1860. 4. Hence, v.i., to amount; often constructed with *to*. Coll: 1882, Besant, 'I . . . wondered how much it would tot up to.' 5. To drink drams: mid C.19–20. Ex the n., 4.

to't. To it: when not poetical, it is, in mid-C.19–20, coll.

tot-book. A book containing (long) addition sums to be worked out: coll: late C.19–20. cf. *long* TOTS. Ex TOT, n., 1.

tot-hunter, -picker or **-raker,** see TOT, n., 5.

Tot-hunting. 'Scouring the streets in search of pretty girls': low (—1909). Ware. cf. TOTTIE, 2.

tot-up. An adding up: coll: 1871. **2. v.:** see TOT, v., 2, 4.

tote; occ. **tot.** A hard drinker: ca 1870, a music-hall song entitled *Hasn't Got over It Yet*, 'As well we'd another old chum, | By all of his mates called the Tote, | So named on account of the rum | He constantly put down his throat.' Perhaps punning *tote*, total, and TOT, n., 4; perhaps ex: 2. (Occ. *tot.*) A *tot*al abstainer: low coll: prob. from late 1860s, but not irrefutably recorded before 1887. The music-hall song *Toper and Tote*, ca 1889, has: 'You'll always find the sober Tote | With a few pounds at command.' 3. A totalizator: from ca 1890: Australian coll >, ca 1901, gen. British coll. Kinglake, 1891.

***tote,** v.t. A variant of TOUT, v., 2: c. (—1887).

***toter.** A C.17 variant of TOUTER, a spy: c.: 1633, Jonson.

tother, t'other, see TONE, which cf.

tother, one with. Copulation: ?C.18–20; ob. Rather coll than s.

tother from which, tell. (Gen. in negative.) To distinguish between two persons or things: coll: late C.19–20. A jocular manipulation of *tell one from the other*.

tother school. One's former school; any school not a Public School: Winchester coll: mid C.19–20. cf. TOTHERUN. 2. As adj., unbecoming because alien to Winchester: id.: from ca 1860. cf. NON-LICET.

tother-sider, or as one word. A convict: coll of Victoria, Australia: ca 1860–1905. With reference to Sydney, where stood the earliest penal settlement: also *Sydney(-bird* or*)-sider*. The rivalry between Melbourne and Sydney, esp., now takes, and has long taken, the form of an exchange of *our 'Arbour!* and *stinking Yarra!* 2. One from the other side of Australia, esp. a Westralian: late C.19–20: Australian coll.

totherun. A preparatory school; a private school: Charterhouse: late C.19–20. i.e. *the other one* (one's former school). cf. TOTHER SCHOOL.

tots. Old clothes: street markets': since ca 1870. Ex TOT, n., 5.

tots, long. Very long addition sums: coll. late C.19–20. Ex TOT, n., 1.

totter, see TOT, n., 5.

totter-arse. A seesaw: provincial: from ca 1870. Ex dial. *t.-a.*, a person walking unsteadily.

Tottie; occ. **Totty.** A Hotten*tot*: coll: 1849, E. E. Napier. 2. *tottie*, rarely *totty*. A high-class whore: from ca 1880. Ex *Dot*, Dorothy, or ex *tottie*, *-y*, a little child: perhaps influenced by TITTY.

Tottie all-colours. A brightly dressed young woman (of the streets): low London (—1909).

Tottie one-lung. 'An asthmatic, or consumptive young person who, for good or bad, thinks herself somebody': low urban (—1909). Ware. See TOTTIE, 2.

totties. Potatoes: Regular Army: late C.19–20. Perversion of TATIE.

totting, see TOT, n., 5; TOT, v., 3.

totting, go. To collect (rags and) bones: low (—1887). See TOT, v.

Totty, see TOTTIE.

touch. Anything that will, at a stated price, interest customers at (about) that price: from ca 1710: coll >, in mid-C.19, s. Swift, 1712, 'I desire you to print in such a form, as in the booksellers' phrase will make a sixpenny touch'; Sir Erasmus Philipps, in his *Diary*, 22 Sept. 1720, 'At night went to the ball at the Angel. A guinea touch'; H., 3rd ed. (1864), 'Sometimes said of a woman to imply her worthlessness, as, "Only a half-crown touch."' Lit., something that will *touch*, appeal to. 2. At Eton (—1864), a present of money, a 'tip'. cf. sense 4. 3. A theft, esp. by pocket-picking: low s. bordering on c.: 1888, 'Rolf Boldrewood'. 4. Hence, the obtaining of money from a person, e.g. by a loan: from ca 1890.

touch, v. To receive (money), draw (it): mid-C.17–20: S.E. until C.19, then coll; in C.20, s. cf. Fr. *toucher de l'argent*. 2. ?hence, to steal: c.: late C.18–20. Holman, 1796, 'I could not go abroad without her, so I touch'd father's cash.' 3. To approach (a person) *for* money, to get from (a person) the money one asks (*for*): coll: 1760. C. Johnston, 1760, 'I am quite broke up; his grace has touched me for five hundred.' In late C.19–20, for things other than money. 4. To rob (a person: *for*, of the article concerned): c.: mid-C.19–20. 5. Hence, in Australian c. or low s. (—1904), to act unfairly towards, to cheat, to swindle. 6. The sense 'to arrest', ca 1780–1850, may, as the O.E.D. has it, be S.E.; or it may, as Grose, 1st ed. implies, be coll or s. 7. To rival, compare with, equal (in ability): coll: 1838, Dickens, 'Wasn't he always top-sawyer among you all? Is there any one of you that could touch him, or come near him?' Ex *touch*, to reach, get as far as.

touch, rum. An odd or eccentric fellow: 1804–6. T. Creevey. Perhaps *touch* here = a 'contact', a person whom one meets or deals with. 2. Hence, a very strange affair: from ca 1807; very ob. cf. *queer* START.

touch bone and whistle. 'Any one having broken wind backwards, according to the vulgar law, may be pinched by any of the company till he has touched bone (i.e. his teeth) and whistled,' Grose, 2nd ed. Often in the imperative. From late 1780s to mid-C.19.

touch bun for luck, see BUN. . .

***touch-crib.** A brothel: c. or low s.: C.19–20; ob. Ex euphemistic S.E. *touch*.

touch for, see TOUCH, v., 3, 4.

touch-hole. The pudend: low coll: C.17–20; ob. Punning a fire-arm's vent.

touch me. A shilling: from ca 1880; ob. Abbr. *touch me on the nob*, a BOB (2), rhyming s. of ca 1870–90. F. & H., 1904, has *touch-my-nob*, a bastard or composite form.

touch of the tar-brush, a. A pejorative c.p. applied to 'the naval officer who is primarily an efficient seaman': mid-C.19–20. Ex the constant use of tar on a ship. 2. A trace of 'black' blood is S.E. in C.20, but it was prob. s. at its origin (ca 1850) and coll from ca 1880 until the end of the century. Occ. *a dash of the* . . .

touch off (someone) **for.** A variant, mostly Colonial, of TOUCH, v., 3: late C. 19–20.

touch pot, touch penny. A semi-proverbial c.p. = No credit given: from ca 1650, ob. by 1880. Gayton, 1654; Graves, 1772; Scott, 1822. cf. Swift's 'He touch'd the pence when others touch'd the pot,' 1720.

touch-trap. The penis: low coll: opp. TOUCH-HOLE.

touch up. To caress intimately in order to inflame (a person to the sexual act): coll: C.18–20. 2. To coït with (a woman): late C.18–mid-19. 3. Reflexively, to masturbate: C.19–20. All senses ex *touch up*, to stimulate. 4. To borrow money from (someone): Feb. 1787, *Sessions*; by 1820, virtually superseded by TOUCH, v., 3.

touch with a pair of tongs, not to. (Gen. I, etc., would not.) To touch on no account: coll: from 1630s. Clarke, 1639; Fuller, 1732; 1876, Blackmore. cf. . . . *with a* BARGE-POLE.

touched, (slightly) insane, is, despite gen. opinion, S.E. It abbr. *touched in the head*, ex S.E. *touch*, to affect mentally, to taint. 2. (Of vegetables, fruit) beginning to go bad; defective: green-grocers' coll (—1887).

toucher. A(n instance of) close contact, a tight fit: dial. (—1828) >, by 1840, coll. Thus *to a toucher*, exactly. Hence, 2, as *near* or *nigh as a toucher*, almost, very nearly: 1840, J. T. Hewlett. Slightly ob. Orig. a coaching term, ex touching without disaster.

touching. Bribery; the obtaining of money esp. by theft or begging: resp. C.18–19 (C. D'Anvers, 1726); late C.19–20 (Arthur Morrison, 1896). Ex TOUCH, v., 2, 3.

touching-up. A caning: Public Schools': late C.19–20. 2, 3, 4. vbl n. of TOUCH UP.

touchy. 'Descriptive of a style in which points, broken lines, or touches are employed, as distinguished from firm unbroken line work', F. & H.: artistic s. (ca 1820) >, ca 1850, coll >, ca 1910, S.E. 2. adv., rather: Christ's Hospital: from ca 1840. e.g. *touchy a* LUX, rather a good thing. Ex *touch*, a small amount of, a SUSPICION.

tough, make it. To raise difficulties; take excessive pains: coll: late C.19–20; ob.

tough as a jockey's tail-end – as old Nick – as shoe-leather. Anglo-Irish phrases (the first, s.; the other two, coll) applied to a person who is a HARD CASE: resp. C.20, late C.19–20, and mid-C.19–20.

tough as an old lanyard knot. Exceedingly tough (whether meat or seaman): nautical coll: late C.19–20.

tough as tacker. Exceedingly tough: lower classes' coll (—1909). Ware. Perhaps S.W. dial. *tacker*, something insuperable.

tough 'un. A THUMPING lie; execrable pun: low (—1887).

***tough yarn.** 'A long story': c. (—1821); †by 1890, by when it meant a 'tall story': nautical.

toupee. The female pubic hair: mid-C.18–20; very ob. By ribald jest on lit. sense. 2. A merkin: mid-C.18–mid-19. Both, occ., *lady's low toupee*.

***tour;** also **toure, tower, towre.** To watch closely; spy on: c. of ca 1565–1650. Harman, 1567. Prob. unconnected with S.E. *twire* (v.i. only), to peer, peep. Possibly – as Grose (1st ed., at *touting*) suggests –

cognate with later c. TOUT, v.i. and t.; more prob. with *tower*, to fly up, as a hawk does, in order to (have the advantage of and then) swoop down on the prey.

tour of the Grand Dukes, the. A tour of the fashionable *demi-monde* of Paris: ca 1870–1914.

tousle. A whisker worn bushy: proletarian: from ca 1860; ob.

tout. (Also *toute*; *towte*, C.15–16.) The posteriors or rump: C.14–20: S.E. until C. 15, then †; revived by 'Thousand Nights' Payne as literary s. 2. A thieves' look-out man: c.: 1718, C. Hitching (*toute*, a C.18 variant); ob. Ex the v., 1. 3. Hence, 'a look out house, or eminence', Grose, 1st ed.: c. of ca 1780–1850. 4. As a solicitor of custom for tradesmen, etc., and 5, as a racing touter, *tout* is mid-C.19–20: both may orig. have been s. or coll, but the former was S.E. by 1880, the latter by 1910, at latest. 6. A watching or spying: c. (—1812); ob. Vaux, '*A strong tout*, is strict observation, or eye, upon any proceedings, or persons.' Esp. in *keep tout* (—1812) or, occ., *keep the tout* (1834, Ainsworth), to keep watch, esp. in an illicit activity. Ex sense 3.

***tout,** v.i. To be on the look-out, to watch very carefully: c. of mid C.17–mid-19, and in C.19 only in literary revival. Ex C.15–17 S.E. *tout*, to peep or peer. cf. TOUR. 2. v.t., to watch, spy on: mid-C.17–20: c. until C.19, then low s. until mid-C.19, then s. with esp. reference to a racing tout's activities. 3. The racing sense (from ca 1812) may orig. have been s., but is gen. considered as S.E.; the same applies to *tout*, v.i., to seek busily for trade (from ca 1730).

tout, keep (the) and **tout, strong,** see TOUT, n., 6. **toute,** see TOUT, n.

***touter.** A thieves' look-out man: c. or low s.: 1844, Dickens; ob. A rare variant of TOUT, n., 2.

***touting** (or **tooting)-ken.** A tavern, a beer-shop; a tavern-bar: c. (—1676); †by 1850. Ex *toot*, *tout*, to drink copiously.

touzery or **towzery gang, the.** Mock-auction swindlers: London low: from ca 1870; ob. 'They hire sale-rooms, usually in the suburbs, and advertise their ventures as ... "Important Sales of Bankrupts' Stock", etc.,' F. & H. Perhaps ex *touse* (*-ze*), horse-play, a ROW, or *touse* (*-ze*), to abuse or maltreat.

tow. (At hare and hounds) a long run-in: Shrewsbury School (—1881). Pascoe. Ex slow motion of towing a ship. 2. Money: low: from ca 1880; ob. Perhaps because, like tow, it 'burns' so quickly.

tow, v., see TOW OUT. **tow-line, get in a,** see LINE, GET IN A.

***tow out.** To decoy; to distract the attention of (a person) and thus assist a confederate in robbery: c. of ca 1810–50.

tow-row. A grenadier: military: ca 1780–1860. Ex 'With a tow-row, row-row, row-row, for the British Grenadiers'. cf. the adj. 2. A noise: dial. > (low) coll: from ca 1870. Reduplicated *row*, a disturbance. 3. As *tow-row!* it meant, among London crossing-sweepers of ca 1840–80, 'Be careful, a policeman is coming!' Mayhew, *Paved With Gold*, 1858.

tow-row, adj. Drunk (?and disorderly): C.18. Steele, 1709. On ROW, disturbance.

***tow-street.** To 'get (a person) in a line', i.e. to decoy him: c. (—1821); †by 1890.

towards you, I looks, see LOOKS TOWARDS.

towel (rare); **oaken towel.** (Esp. *rub one down with an oaken towel*, to cudgel or beat him.) A stick or cudgel: resp. 1756 (Toldervy) and 1739. Ob. Ex the v. 2. *lead* (rarely *leaden*) *towel.* A bullet: 1812, J. & H. Smith, 'Make Nunky surrender his dibs, | Rub his pate with a pair of lead towels'; ob. by 1900.

towel, v. To cudgel; to thrash: J. Dunton, 1705. For semantics, note the gen. ridiculed *dry-rub* etymology of *drub*.

towel, sky the, see SKY THE TOWEL.

towelling. A drubbing or thrashing: 1851, Mayhew, 'I got a towelling, but it did not do me much good.' Ex preceding. cf. TOWEL, n.

***tower.** Clipped money: c. of C.18–early 19. Ex, and gen. in, *they have been round the Tower with it*, 'that Piece of Money has been Clipt', B.E.: a late C.17–early 19 c.p. of the underworld. App. Tower Hill and, in fact, the whole neighbourhood of the Tower of London were rough, for cf. TOWER-HILL PLAY.

tower, towre, v., see TOUR.

Tower Hill, preach on. To be hanged: C. 16. Skelton in *Magnificence*. Tower Hill was long the place of execution in London. cf. TYBURN phrases.

***Tower-Hill play.** 'A slap on the Face and a kick on the Breech', B.E.: c.: late C.17–18. cf. TOWER, n., and:

Tower-Hill vinegar. The headsman's block: C.16–17. Ex TOWER HILL, PREACH ON.

Tower-rook. A guide to the Tower of London: Ned Ward, 1703.

town or **Town,** as in **go to, leave, t.** or **T.** London: coll: C.18–20. 2. (*town.*) A halfpenny: rhyming s. (—1909) on BROWN, n., 1.

town, in; town, out of, see IN TOWN; OUT OF TOWN.

town, on the. Engaged in crime: 1818, *The London Guide*; 1822, Pierce Egan, *The Life of Hayward*; †by 1900. 2. Applied to 'a man of the World. A person supposed to have a general knowledge of men and manners,' Pierce Egan, *Life in London*, 1821: coll: ca 1815–60.

town-bull, a wencher, is rather S.E. than coll or s., but perhaps *as lawless as a town-bull* (a notable wencher: late C.17–early 19) and *roar like a town-bull,* (to bellow: late C. 18–mid-19) are coll. cf. Ray, 1678, *then the town-bull is a bachelor*, i.e. 'as soon as such an one', Apperson: a c.p. †by 1850.

town-lout. A scholar living at home in the town; Rugby School: from ca 1860; ob. cf. TOWNEY.

town red, paint the, see RED, PAINT ...

***town shift.** A sharper; a scoundrel living by his wits: Londoners' c.: ca 1660–1730. Because he so often changed his lodgings, says Richard Head, *Proteus Redivivus*, 1675. 2. A sodomite: s.: Ned Ward, 1709.

town-stallion. A debauchee: s.: Ned Ward, 1703, cf. TOWN-BULL.

town tabby. 'A dowager of quality' (*Sinks*): ca 1830–80.

town-trap. A constable: s.: Ned Ward, 1709.

towner. A s. variant of S.E. *townee*: from ca 1885.

towney, towny. Alien to the school: Christ's Hospital: from ca 1860. Contrast HOUSEY, peculiar to the Hospital. 2. A fellow-townsman (or woman): in U.S., 1834; in England, 1865. cf. Fr. *mon pays(e)*. 3. A town-bred person, esp. a Londoner: coll: 1828, Peter Cunningham. 4. *towny*, adj. Townish: coll: 1837. 5. *towneys,* properly *townies.* Clothes more suitable to town wear than are the school's blue garments: Christ's Hospital: from ca 1860.

towns and cities, see THOUSAND PITIES.

towre, see TOWER. ***towre,** see TOUR.

towzery gang, see TOUZERY GANG.

tox. To in*tox*icate, gen. in ppl adjj., *toxed, toxing*: 1630s. Heywood.

toxy. In*toxi*cated: from ca 1905; very ob. Ex Scottish.

***toy.** A watch: c. (—1877); slightly ob. Horsley, *Jottings from Jail*, 1877. Hence, *toy-getter, -getting*, a watch-snatcher (Arthur Morrison, 1896: O.E.D.), watch-stealing; *toy and* TACKLE, a watch and chain; a *red toy* is a gold watch, while a *white toy* is a silver one.

toy-time. Evening preparation: Winchester: from ca 1860. Ex:

toys. A bureau, esp. in the form of desk and bookcase combined: Winchester: from ca 1860. Ironically ex *toy*, a trinket or knick-knack.

tra-la-la! Good-bye!: c.p. – slightly contemptuous and not too polite – of ca 1830–90. Ware, 'The phrase took its rise with a comic singer named Henri Clarke, whose speciality was imitating Parisians.' This being so, Clarke almost certainly knew the Fr. s. sense of *tra-la-la* (the posterior): cf., therefore, KISS MY —. 2. (Gen. pl.) One of the wealthiest and most extravagant class of dissipated men: mostly proletarian: ca 1889–1900.

trac. A Cockney variant of TRACK, n. It would seem to be also a c. term for threepence, esp. a threepenny piece: late C.19–20.

traces, kick over the, see KICK OVER ...

track. (Also *trag.*) A quart: back s. (—1859). Thus: *trauq* > *traq* > *trag* or *trak* > *track*.

track, inside. The truth: sporting s. > coll: from ca 1880; ob. cf. *have the inside running*, i.e. an advantage, and *inside information*, valuable 'tips' (see TIP, n., 2).

track up the dancers. To go, esp. if quickly, upstairs: c. (—1671); †by 1850. Ex †S.E. *track*, to go.

trade. An act of trading; an exchange; in politics, a private arrangement: U.S. s. (1829: Thornton), anglicized ca 1890 as coll. 2. *the trade* is prostitution: late C.18–19. cf. TRADER.

trade, v. To exchange, SWAP: U.S. coll anglicized ca 1885.

trade-mark. A scratch on the face; esp. in *draw, leave,* or *put one's trade-mark on one* or *one's face* or *down one's face*, to claw the face. Chiefly of women: (low) coll: from early 1870s. Anon. music-hall song, *Father, Take A Run!*, ca 1875.

trader. A harlot: ca 1680–1820. Radcliffe, 1682, *she-trader*, a variant. Also *trading dame*, as in Cotton, 1678. cf. TRADE, n., 2.

trading dame, see TRADER.

trading justices. Such low fellows as, 'smuggled into the commission of the peace', live 'by fomenting disputes, granting warrants and otherwise retailing justice, Grose, 3rd ed.: coll: ca 1785–1840.

trady. Belonging to, characteristic of, trade: coll: 1899 (O.E.D.).

traffic. A whore: c. of late C.16–early 17. Greene, 1591 (*traffique*). Ex the large amount of business she plies.

trag, see TRACK, n.

tragedy Jack. A heavy tragedian: pejorative theatrical: from ca 1875; ob.

trail. A befooling: rare coll: 1847, C. Brontë (see next entry); ob.

trail, v. To quiz or befool: coll: from ca 1845. C. Brontë, 1847, 'She was (what is vernacularly termed) trailing Mrs Dent; that is, playing on the ignorance; her trail might be clever, but . . . decidedly not good-natured'; Coulson Kernahan, 1900, 'To see the Ishmaelites "trail" a sufferer from "swelled head" is to undergo inoculation against that fell malady.' Ex *trail*, to draw (a person) out or on.

***trailer.** One who rides a horse away and sells him afar off: c.: late C.16–early 17. Greene, 1592. 2. A prowling cab-driver: London coll: ca 1870–1905.

traily. Slovenly; weak, languid: dial. (—1851) >, by 1860, coll.

train. To consort: coll: from ca 1880; slightly ob. cf. *tag about* (*with*) and the C.17 S.E. *train*, to walk in a notable's retinue. 2. (Also *train it*.) To travel by train: coll (—1887). Baumann (*train it*); 1888, *Pall Mall Gazette*, 2 April.

train-up, v.i. To hurry: proletarian: mid-C.19–20.

traipse, see TRAPES.

traitors at table, there are. A c.p. applied to a loaf of bread turned the wrong side upwards: mid-C.17–19. Ray, 1678, 'Are there traitors at the table that the loaf is turned wrong side upwards?'

tram. A tramway car: coll (1879). cf.:

tram. To travel by mining-district tram-road: coll: 1826. 2. Hence, by tram-car: likewise coll: from ca 1880 – see the n. Also *tram it* (1904, E. Nesbit). cf. TRAIN, 2.

tram-fare. Twopence: London streets': 1882–ca 95.

tramp. A journey on foot; a long, tiring, or arduous walk or march; a hike: coll: 1786, Burns; 1898, J. Hutchinson, 'Exhausted by a long tramp in hot weather'. Ex *tramp*, to walk, to walk steadily.

tramp, v. To go on a walking excursion, a hike: coll: mid-C.19–20. Also *tramp it*. 2. To proceed as a tramp: coll (—1891). 3. To drive out of or into some stated condition by *tramping*, vigorous walking: coll: 1853, Kane, 'Tramping the cold out of my joints'. 4. To make a voyage by tramp steamer: coll: 1899. 5. Hence, v.t., to run (such a steamer): coll: 1899, likewise in Cutcliffe Hyne.

***tramp-major.** A tramp who, in exchange for his keep at a casual ward, helps the porter: tramps' c.: late C.19–20.

tramping the ties. Trespassing on the railways: Canadian: late C.19–20. The *ties* are the sleepers of a railway track.

***trampler.** A lawyer or attorney: c. of ca 1605–50. Perhaps because he tramples on others; prob. ex †*trample*, to act as an intermediary.

trampolin. A double spring-board: circus: mid-C.19–20. Ex *trampolin*, performance on stilts.

tranklements or trollybobs. Entrails; intestines: proletarian: mid-C.19–20.

tranko. The elongated barrel which a performer manages with his feet, and keeps up in the air while lying on his back: circusmen's s. verging on j.: mid-C. 19–20. Origin?

trans. A translation: secondary schools': late C.19–20.

transfer. To steal: Society: ca 1895–1915. On CONVEY. cf.:

translate the truth. To lie evasively: Society c.p.: 1899. Ex a phrase used, by a Parisian newspaper, of Delcassé, the French cabinet-minister, in connection with the Muscat incident.

translated. Intoxicated; very drunk: Society: 1880s. Ware derives it ex Shakespeare's 'Bless thee, Bottom, thou art translated.'

translators. A pair of re-made boots and shoes: (low) London: mid-C.19–20; ob. Mayhew, 1851. Ex *translator*, a cobbler, esp. of old shoes.

transmogrify; occ. **transmografy, -aphy, -riphy; -migrafy; -mugrify.** To change, alter; esp. to metamorphose utterly or strangely: coll, humorous >, ca 1700, rather low: resp., 1700, but implied in 1661; 1656, 1688, 1671; 1725; 1786. Always v.t. and orig. of persons only. S. Holland, 1656; B.E. (*-mogrify*); *A New Canting Dict.*, 1725 (*-mogrify*, *-migrafy*); Burns (*-mugrify*); Barham; Mary Howitt, ca 1888. The Dictionary of 1725 asserts that *transmigrafy* is the correct form: if so, *transmigrate* prob. supplies, via illiterate corruption, the etymology. **2. The derivat-**

ives *transmogrification*, *transmogrifier*, are much less frequent: resp., K.W., 1661, 'To the botchers for transmogrification', and 1676.

***transnear.** To come up with (a person): c.: late C.17–early 19. Perhaps on C.17 S.E. *transpear*, the word prob. = to cross (e.g. a street) in order to approach.

trap. Trickery, a deceitful trick; fraud. Esp. in *understand trap*, to be wide-awake or, esp., alert to one's own interest. (Anon., 1679, *Counterfeits*, III, i, 'You're deceiv'd in old Gomez, he understands trap'; 1821, Scott: Apperson); *smell trap*, to suspect danger, as of a thief spotting a detective (J. Greenwood, 1869); and *be* UP TO TRAP (in dial. before 1828 – see Apperson; but recorded as coll in 1819 by O.E.D.; H., 1860). Low s.; very ob. except in the third phrase. cf. *the* TRAP IS DOWN. Ex lit. S.E. influenced by TRAPAN, TREPAN, a trick or stratagem. 2. A sheriff's officer, policeman (in Australia, ca 1860–90, a mounted one), detective: c. or low s.: 1703, Ned Ward; 1838, Dickens; 1895, Marriott-Watson. Slightly ob., except in South Africa, where it has, since the early 1880s, been esp. used both of an exciseman and of an I.D.B. (Illicit Diamond Buying) detective. Ex *trap*, to catch. 3. A smallish, sprung carriage; in Britain, esp. a gig, but in Australia and New Zealand a four-wheeled carriage: from ca 1805: coll >, by 1900, S.E. Perhaps ex *rattle trap*. 4. See TRAPS. 5. The mouth: low: from ca 1780 as POTATO-TRAP (-JAW), the simple form being of mid-C.19–20. 6. (Prob. ex sense 1.) A go-between employed by a pickpocket and a whore working together: c.: C.18. C. Hitching, in *The Regulator*, 1718, describes the procedure. 7. A guard-room: Army s.: late C.19–20.

trap is down!, the. The trick, or attempt to 'do' me, has failed; it's *no* GO!: a c.p. of ca 1870–1910. Ex TRAP, 1, with an allusion to the fallen door of a trap for birds, etc.

trap-stick. The penis: ca 1670–1900. Cotton; 'Burlesque' Bridges. Ex the lit. sense. 2. In pl, the legs; esp. thin legs: ca 1700–1850. Grose, 1st ed., 'From the sticks with which boys play at trap ball'.

***trapan; trepan** in these senses is rare and not earlier than ca 1680. 'He that draws in or wheedles a Cull, and Bites' – swindles – 'him', B.E.: c. of ca 1640–1830. Prob. ex (*to*) *trap*, with a c. disguise-suffix (cf. -MANS). 2. Hence, a deceitful or fraudulent trick or stratagem: (orig. low) s.: ca 1660–1830.

***trapan, trepan,** v. To ensnare, beguile, inveigle, swindle: c. or low s. (—1656) >, by 1750, (low) s.; ob. Ex the n., 1.

trapes; occ. **trapse;** often **traipse. A** slovenly or slatternly female: coll and (in late C.19–20, nothing but) dial.: ca 1673, Cotton, 'I had not car'd | If Pallas here had been preferr'd; | But to bestow it on that Trapes, | It mads me'; the other two forms, C.19–20, though *trapse* is almost †. Ex the v., 1. 2. (Same origin.) A going or wandering in listless or slovenly fashion; a wearisome or disagreeable tramp: coll and dial.: 1862, Mrs Henry Wood, 'It's such a toil and a trapes up them two pair of stairs.'

trapes; traipse. (In C.18–20, occ. *trapse*. Dial. has many variants, varying from *traaps* to *trapus* and *traipass*.) To walk untidily, listlessly, aimlessly; gad about: coll: 1593, Bilson implies it in 'This trapesing to and fro'. 1710–11, 2 March, Swift, 'I was traipsing to-day with your Mr Sterne,' ibid. Perhaps cognate with †*trape* (to walk idly to and fro), which prob. derives ex medieval Dutch *trappen*, to tread. 2. Hence, to trail, or hang, along or down: coll: from ca 1770; from late C.19, only in dial. 3. (Ex sense 1.) v.t., to tramp over, tread or tramp (e.g. the fields): 1885, Hall Caine.

trapesing, traipsing. n.: see TRAPES, v., **1.** 2. adj., 1760, Foote, *trapsing*: idem.

trapish. Slovenly; slatternly: coll: C.18. Rowe, 1705. Ex TRAPES, n., 1.

trapper. A horse used in a TRAP (3): coll: from early 1880s. cf. *vanner*, *busser*, *cabber*, etc., on the model of 'hunter', F. & H.

trappiness. The n. of TRAPPY: coll: 1885, *Field*, 26 Dec.

***trapping.** Blackmail: c.: late C.17–mid-18. Anon., *A Country Gentleman's Vade Mecum*. A special development from *trap*, to ensnare. cf. TRAPAN, n., 2.

trappy. Treacherous; trickily difficult; i.e. lit. or fig. containing a trap or traps: coll: 1882, *Daily Telegraph*, 13 Nov., 'The fences might have been increased in size, however, without being made trappy'; in cricket, of the ball: 1887.

traps. Personal effects; belongings; baggage: coll: 1813 (O.E.D.). Abbr. *trappings*. 2. Hence, in Australia, a SWAG (5): from late 1850s.

trapse, see TRAPES.

trash. (Contemptuously: cf. *dross*; FILTHY LUCRE.) Money: ca 1590–1830. Greene, ca 1591; 1809, Malkin. As the O.E.D. remarks, Shakespeare's 'Who steals my purse, steals trash' was prob. an operative factor.

trat. A pretty girl; an attractive harlot: proletarian: ca 1880–1905. Either a perversion or an anagram of TART.

trav. **Travelling money: Felsted School:** late C.19–20.

travel. To admit of, to bear, transportation: coll: (Dec.) 1852, Beck's *Florist*, 'Not . . . good plants for exhibition, as they travel badly', O.E.D. 2. To go, move, fast: coll: 1884, of a dog, 'How he travels.' By 1910 at latest, S.E.

travel in the market. Applied to the way or extent in or to which a horse is betted on or against: turf: ca 1870–1910.

travel on one's props. To leave luggage with the railway company as security against the travelling facilities granted, money lacking for the fares and freight, by the company: theatrical: late C.19–20.

travel out of the record. To wander from the point: coll: from mid-1850s; ob. Dickens in *Little Dorrit*. cf. *off the map*.

travel the road. To take to highway robbery: euphemistic coll: C.18–mid-19. Farquhar, in *The Beaux' Stratagem*, 1707. cf. sense 1 of:

traveller. A highwayman: coll: C.18–mid-19. cf. preceding. 2. A tramp: from ca 1760: coll till late C.19, then dial.; ca 1840–80, common among tramps, and often = an itinerant hawker. Goldsmith; Mayhew. 3. Esp. in Australia: 1869, 'Peripatetic Philosopher' Clarke: coll >, by 1900, S.E.; ob. 4. Also *traveller at His* or *Her Majesty's Expense*. A convict sent abroad: ca 1830–1910. 5. 'A thief who changes his quarry from town to town', F. & H.: c.: from ca 1830; ob. cf. senses 1, 2. 6. A Gypsy: low: ca 1865, in '*No. 747*'. 7. A sermon delivered, by the one preacher, on different occasions and in various places: coll: orig. (ca 1890) and mainly ecclesiastical, esp. among theological students.

traveller, tip the, see TIP THE TRAVELLER.

traveller's tale or **talent.** Exaggeration; romancing: ca 1820–50. Ex preceding.

travelling piquet. A coll name, ca 1785–1840, for 'a mode of amusing themselves, practised by two persons riding in a carriage, each reckoning towards his game' – app. 100 points – 'the persons or animals that pass by on the side next them, according to the following estimation', which ranges from 'a man or woman walking; 1' to 'a parson riding a grey horse, with blue furniture; game'. Grose, 3rd ed.

travelling scholarship (or **fellowship).** Rustication: jocular coll, Oxford and Cambridge University: from early 1790s to mid-C.19. *Gentleman's Magazine*, 1794, p. 1085, 'Soho, Jack! almost presented with a travelling scholarship? very nigh being sent to grass, hey?'

traverse, see THREE TURNS . . .

traverse the cart. To delay departure; be loath to depart: pedantic: ca 1845–70. Thackeray. 2. See *walk the* CART.

traviata, see COME THE TRAVIATA.

***tray, trey.** Three, whether as number or set: c. >, ca 1910, low s.: from mid-1890s. Ex *tray*, *trey*, the 3 at dice or cards. 2. Hence (also *tray-*, *trey-bit*), a threepenny piece: low: 1907 in O.E.D.; but prob. several years earlier. 3. *tray soddy mits*, threepence halfpenny: Parlary and low London: late C.19–20. Here, *soddy* = It. *soldi* (see SALTEE) and *mits* = It. *mezzo*, a half (see MADZA). 4. See TREE-MOON and TRAY OF MOONS.

tray of moons. A three-months' prison-sentence: ca 1870–1914. (Barry Pain, *The Memoirs of Constance Dix*, 1905.)

tray-bit, see TRAY, 2.

***tre-moon.** An occ. variant of TREE-MOON.

treacle. Thick, inferior port: from ca 1780. Ex thick sediment. 2. Love-making, as in *treacle moon*, a honeymoon: coll: 1815, Byron; ob. Ex sweetness.

treacle-factory. A training-ship: naval: late C.19–20. Ex the heavy 'incidence' of molasses.

***treacle-man.** A 'beautiful male decoy . . . pretended young man of the housemaid and the real forerunner of the burglar': c.: from ca 1880. Ex TREACLE, 2. 2. Hence, a COMMERCIAL (2) touting sewing-machines, etc., to women: commercial travellers': late C.19–20. 3. He who makes the smartest sales: drapers' assistants' (—1909).

tread, chuck a. (Of the male) to coït: low: from ca 1860. cf. TREADLE.

treader. (Gen. pl.) A shoe: low: from ca 1880; ob.

treadle, treddle. A whore: low: ca 1630–

1890. Ford, 1638; Halliwell. By a pun on the lever so named + *tread* (copulate with).

treason-monger. A dynamiter: political: 1885–6.

treasure. (Of a person) a GEM (3) or 'jewel': coll: 1810, Lady Granville. A certain lady calls all her maid-servants, irrespective of quality, 'treasures'.

treasury, the. The weekly payment: theatrical (—1874).

treat. Something very enjoyable or gratifying; the pleasure therefrom or the delight therein: coll: from late C.18. Rarely of a person (1825, Lady Granville). Esp. *a fair treat*. 2. Anything, anybody, objectionable or a great nuisance: low ironic coll: from 1890s. 3. *a treat*, adv.: most gratifyingly; very well indeed: low coll: 1899, *Daily News*, 8 May, 'This air makes yer liver work a treat.' All senses ultimately ex *treat*, entertainment offered by another person.

treat, a, see preceding, 3.

treble-seam. A three-seamed leather cricket ball: cricket s. (1897, *Globe*, 1 July).

treddle, see TREADLE.

***tree.** Only as in TREEWINS and TREE-MOON.

tree, v. To put in a difficulty; drive to the end of one's resources: orig. (1818: Thornton) U.S., anglicized in the 1850s as a coll >, by 1880, S.E. Henry Kingsley, 1859, 'It's no use . . . you are treed.' Ex treeing an animal. cf. TREE, UP A.

tree, bark up the wrong, see BARK . . .

tree, lame as a. Extremely lame: lower classes' coll (—1887). Perhaps ex the noisy walking of a man with a wooden leg.

tree, up a. Cornered; done for; in a serious difficulty; penniless: coll: U.S. (1825), anglicized ca 1840, Thackeray in 1839 having 'Up a tree, as the Americans say.' Ex a hunted animal taking refuge in a tree. Also *up the tree* and *up a tree for tenpence*.

***tree-moon.** Three months' imprisonment: c.: mid-C.19–20. '*No. 747*' (= year 1845). Also TRAY (or TREY) OF MOONS, often in C.20, abbr. to *tray* or *trey*.

Tree of Knowledge. 'The tree under which books, etc., are piled in the interval between morning school and [lunch],' F. & H.: Charterhouse: from ca 1860; ob. by 1900. Punning the lit. sense.

treer. 'A boy who avoids organised sports, but plays a private game with one or two friends. [Presumably because played at the trees by the side of the ground]', F. & H.: Durham School: ca 1850–90.

***treewins.** Threepence: c.: late C.17–20; ob. cf. TRESWINS. Ex WIN, n.

trek. To depart: from ca 1890: coll, orig. and mainly South African. Ex *trek*, to journey by ox-wagon, hence to migrate – itself ex Dutch.

tremble, (all) in a or **all of a; (up)on the tremble.** Trembling, esp. with emotion: coll: resp. 1719, ca 1760 (Henry Brooke); 1800 (Lamb).

tremblers. Stairs: Anglo-Irish: C.19. 'A Real Paddy', *Real Life in Ireland*, 1822.

trembly. Tremulous; quivering: coll: 1848, Dickens, 'So trembly and shaky'.

tremendous. As a mere hyperbole or intensive (= astounding; immense): coll: 1812, Southey, 'A tremendous change has been going on.' cf. AWFUL; TERRIBLE. 2. Extraordinary as regards some quality stated in the context: from ca 1830. George Eliot, 1866, 'A tremendous fellow at the classics'.

tremendously. Very greatly, extremely, excessively: coll: mid-C.19–20. Ex TREMENDOUS, 1.

trepan, see TRAPAN.

***treswins.** Threepence: c. (—1725); ob. cf. TREEWINS.

trey, see TRAY. **treyn(e), treyning-cheat,** see TRINE, v., 2.

triangles; gen. **the triangles.** Delirium tremens: low (—1864); very ob. A perversion of *tremens*, prob. on *the trembles* and perhaps also with an allusion to the percussive musical instrument; H., however, suggests that it is because, during 'd.ts', one sees everything 'out of the square'. cf. JIM-JAM (2).

triantelope; occ. **triantulope.** A tarantula: an Australian coll and popular corruption of that word: 1846, C. P. Hodgson, *Reminiscences of Australia*. On *antelope*.

***trib.** A prison: c.: late C.17–early 19. Abbr. *tribulation*, as remarked by B.E., who implies a more gen. sense in '*He is in Trib*, . . . he is layd by the Heels, or in a great deal of trouble.'

tribulation. The condition of being held in pawn; ca 1660–1780. Dryden.

trichi, -y; occ. **tritchie, -y.** A **Trichi**nopoli cigar: 1877, Sir Richard Burton.

***trick.** A watch: c. of late C.18–mid-19. Tufts, 1798. Ex *trick*, a small, esp. if cheap, toy or ornament, a trinket. 2. A person, esp. a child, who is alert and amusing:

Australian and New Zealand coll: late C. 19–20.

trick, do the. To effect one's purpose, do what is necessary or desirable: coll (—1812) >, by 1870 or so, S.E. 2. Hence (absolutely), to get a woman with child: low coll: from ca 1830.

trick and a half. 'A master-stroke of roguery', F. & H.: coll: C.19. A development ex *a trick worth two of that* (not coll but S.E.).

***trickar;** properly **tricker.** A device for opening a window: c.: late C.16–early 17. Greene, 1592. ?cf. JIGGER, 3.

trickett. A long drink of beer: New South Wales: ca 1895–1910. Ex Trickett, that champion sculler who knew that 'beer's best for an A1 nation.'

tricks, bag of, see BAG OF TRICKS.

tricks, been playing. Pregnant: euphemistic coll: C.19–20; ob.

trickum legis. A quirk or quibble in the law: jocular: ca 1790–1850. Lit., a trick of the law, *-um* pointing the jest at Law Latin.

tricky. Unexpectedly difficult, needing careful handling or cautious action; catchy, risky: coll: 1887, Saintsbury, 'One of the tricky things called echo sonnets.'

trier; tryer (try-er). A player who perseveres in the attempt to win: cricket s. (1891) >, ca 1905, gen. sporting coll.

trifa, see TRIPHA. **triffing,** see TIFFING.

***trig.** A piece of stick or paper left in the front door; if still there the next day, it practically shows that the house is unoccupied. The act is, *to trig the* JIGGER (door): c. (—1812). Ex *trig*, brake, a sprag. 2. A hurried walk, a tramp: from ca 1880: dial. and coll. cf. v., 1. 3. Trigonometry: coll, esp. schools' and universities': from not later than 1908 and prob. from mid-C.19.

trig, v. Grose, 2nd ed., '*To trig it*, to play truant': from late 1780s; slightly ob. Ex (S.E. > dial.) *trig*, to walk quickly: whence also the n., 2. 2. See the n., 1.

trig-hall. Open house; Liberty Hall: late C.18–20: dial. and (low) coll, the latter †by 1900. Ex North Country dial. *trig*, to stuff, to cram, to fill up (esp. the stomach).

trigging, lay a man. To knock him down: ca 1785–1850. Perhaps ex the v. *trig* of ninepins; or ex TRIG, V., 1.

trigry-mate; gen. **trigrymate.** 'An idle She-Companion', B.E.: late C.17–20: s. >, early in C.19, dial. Ex *trig*, to walk briskly. 2. Hence, an intimate friend: C. 19–20: coll > dial. Halliwell.

trike. A tricycle; to ride a tricycle: (low) coll: 1885; 1901, *Pall Mall Gazette*, 15 May, 'The commercial "trike" is, perhaps, the least supportable of the various tyrannies on wheels which it is the perambulating Londoners' lot to endure.' On BIKE; cf. Fr. and English *tri*. Hence, *triker*, the rider of one, and *triking*, such cycling: coll: from late 1880s.

trilby. A 'woman's exquisite foot': Society: 1894–ca 96. Ex Du Maurier's *Trilby*. 2. A trilby hat: coll: 1897, *Daily News*, 6 Feb. Same source.

Trilbys. Pig's feet or trotters: West Yorkshire s. (—1905), not dial. 2. Human feet: Australian: late C.19–20. Both ex TRILBY, 1.

trill. The anus: ?late C.17–mid-19. Halliwell. ?ex crepitation: cf. ARS MUSICA.

***trim.** To cheat; to fleece: C.17–20. Dekker; implied by B.E. in '*Trimming*, c. Cheating People of their Money': c. >, by 1720, s. Prob. ex *trim*, to thrash; cf.:

trim one's jacket. To thrash a person: coll: 1748, Smollett. An elaboration of S.E. *trim*, to thrash, with perhaps an allusion to *trim*, to decorate (a hat) or dress (hair: cf. DRESS (DOWN)).

trim the buff. (Absolutely.) To deflower, or merely to coït with, a woman: 1772, Bridges, 'And he . . . has liberty to take and trim | The buff of that bewitching brim,' i.e. harlot; ob. Ex BUFF, the human skin; and cf. TRIM ONE'S JACKET.

trim-tram. In *Lord Hervey and His Friends*, edited by the Earl of Ilchester and published in 1950, there occurs, in a letter dated 23 Oct. 1731, this passage: 'There was a most magnificent entertainment, and everything that depended on his servants was in perfection. Whether it was trim tram, I know not, but can give a shrewd guess,' the sense being either 'an absurdity' or 'absurd': upper-class: ?ca 1700–70. A reduplication on *trim*.

trimmer. A person who, a thing which, *trims* or thrashes, lit. or fig.: e.g. a stiff letter, article, review, a strict disciplinarian; a redoubtable competitor, fighter, runner (human or animal); a severe fight, blow, run, etc.; an especially well-delivered ball at cricket: coll: 1776, Foote, of a severe leading article; 1804, Nelson, of a letter – as, in 1816, Scott; 1827, *Sporting Magazine*, of a hound; 1832, P. E an, 'At last a trimmer Dick sent down.' cf. the adj. in:

***trimming,** n. See TRIM, v. 2. adj. Excellent, RIPPING; coll: 1778, the Earl of Carlisle, 'Such trimming gales as would make ... a landsman ... stare'; 1825, *Sporting Magazine*, of a run with hounds; slightly ob. cf. preceding entry.

trimmingly. To a notable extent; excellently: coll: 1789, A. C. Bowers, 'I had the gout trimmingly.' Ex TRIMMING, 2; cf. TRIMMER.

trimmings. Masked alcohol: tradesmen's: 1897, *Daily Telegraph*, 18 Jan.

trincum; gen. **trinkum;** occ. **trinkrum.** A trinket: from mid-1660s: S.E. until C.19, then coll (very ob.) and dial.: resp. C.18–20, C.17–20, late C.19–20. Merely *trinket* with 'Latin' *-um* for *-et*. 2. For reduplicated forms, see TRINKUM-TRANKUM.

***Trine.** Tyburn: c. of mid-C.17–18. Ex sense 2 of:

***trine.** To go: c. of C.17–mid-19. Fletcher, 1622; Scott. A survival from S.E. *trine*, to go, to march (C.14–16), itself of Scandinavian origin. 2. v.i. and t., to hang: c. of ca 1560–1840, but, like sense 1, ob. as early, prob., as mid-C.18. Also *tryne*, C.16–17, and *treyn*(*e*), C.17. Perhaps, as the O.E.D. observes, ex a shortening of *trine to the cheats*, to go to the gallows, to be hanged.

tringham trangham, tringum-trangum, see TRINKUM-TRANKUM.

***trining, treyning, tryning.** An execution by hanging: see TRINE, v., 2.

trinity (or **Trinity**) **kiss.** 'A triple kiss – generally given by daughters and very young sons, when going to bed, to father and mother': Society: ca 1870–80. Ware.

trinkerman. A Thames Estuary fisherman: nautical: mid-C.19–20.

trinkety; incorrectly **trinketty.** Of little importance or value: (rare) coll: 1817, Scott.

trinkum, see TRINCUM.

trinkum-trankum; also **tringham trangham, tringum-trangum.** A trinket (C.18–20); a whim or fancy (late C.17–early 19): s. >, early in C.19, mainly dial. B.E., *tringum-trangum*, 'a Whim, or Maggot'; 1702, Steele, *tringham trangham*, as adj.; 1718, Motteux, *trinkum-trankum*. Reduplicated *trinkum* (see at TRINCUM).

***trip.** A harlot; a thief's woman: c.: from mid-1870s; slightly ob. Horsley, *Jottings from Jail*, 1877. ?ex *tripping* motion.

trip up, see CARRY THE STICK.

tripe. Utter nonsense; very inferior writing, singing, acting, etc. etc.: from ca 1890: coll verging on S.E. Crockett, 1895, 'A song ... worth a shopful of such "tripe".' Ex the *tripe* as typical of inferior food, etc. 2. See TRIPES.

tripe, bag of. A term of opprobrium for a person: low coll or perhaps rather a vulgarism: C.19–20. Cobbett, 1822. Suggested by TRIPES. cf.:

tripe, blooming six feet of (or **six blooming feet of**). A tall, solid policeman: low urban: from ca 1880; ob.

Tripe, Mr Double. A (very) fat man: low: ca 1780–1850.

tripes; tripe. (Very rare, after C.18, in the singular.) The intestines; the paunch containing them: mid-C.15–20: S.E. until mid-C.18, then coll; in mid-C.19–20, low coll. Hood, 1834, 'I'm as marciful as any on 'em – and I'll stick my knife in his tripes as says otherwise.'

tripes and trillibubs or **trullibubs.** A jeering nickname for a fat man: ca 1780–1880. Lit. the entrails (of an animal). cf. *bag of* TRIPE and *Mr Double* TRIPE; see also TRIPES.

tripha or **trifa,** ritually unclean (opp. *kosher*), is Hebrew; it can be considered as s. only when it is loosely applied by Gentiles to things other than food.

***triple tree.** A gallows: c. of ca 1630–1750, then only archaically. Randolph, ca 1634; Brome, 1641; T. Brown, ca 1700. Ex the three parts. cf. THREE-LEGGED MARE.

Tripoly, come from. To vault, tumble; perform spiritedly: s. (—1847); †by 1890. Ex performances of Moorish dancers.

***tripos.** The intestines; the paunch: c. (—1887). On TRIPES.

tripos pup. An UNDERGRAD Cantab doing Honours: Cambridge undergraduates' (—1887); ob.

tripper. An excursionist: coll: 1813, 'Trippers to the seaside for a week'. Also *cheap tripper*, one who goes on a cheap trip: coll: 1872.

***tripper-up.** One who *trips* and then robs a person: c.: from mid-1880s. *Daily Chronicle*, 18 Nov. 1887.

***tripping-up.** The criminal practices in TRIPPER-UP.

trippist. A TRIPPER: coll: 1792.

Tristram's knot, Sir. A halter; esp. in *tie Sir Tristram's knot*, to hang: coll: ?C.17–19.

tritchie, -y; or T., see TRICHI. ***tritrace,** see TROLL.

triumph, ride. To go helter-skelter or full tilt: ca 1760–1850: coll bordering on S.E. Sterne, 1761. Presumably abbr. *ride in triumph.*

Trojan. A roisterer, boon companion, a dissolute: C.17–mid-18. Kemp, 1600; adumbrated in Shakespeare, 1588. Ex the fame of Troy. 2. Hence, a good fellow: coll: from ca 1660, though adumbrated in Kemp (as in 1); ob. Butler, 1663, 'True Trojans'; Scott, 1827, 'Trusty as a Trojan', *true* and *trusty* being the usual epithets: cf. *trusty* TROUT. 3. A brave, plucky, or energetic person (rarely of a woman); gen. in *like a Trojan*, very pluckily or energetically: coll: 1838 (in *Fraser's Magazine*; 1841, in book form), Thackeray, 'He bore . . . [the amputation] . . . like a Trojan': 1855, Dickens, 'He went on lying like a Trojan about the pony.' cf. *like a* TROOPER. 4. A professional gambler: buckish: ca 1805–40. J. J. Stockwell, *The Greeks*, 1817. Prob. ironic ex sense 2.

***troll** occurs in four phrases in Awdelay, 1561, as c. of ca 1550–80: *troll and troll by*, one who, esteemed by none, esteems nobody – perhaps ex C.14–17 *troll*, to saunter or ramble: *troll hazard of trace*, one who follows his master 'as far as he may see him' – cf. *trace* = *track*(*s*), n.; *t. h. of tritrace.*, 'he that goeth gaping after his master', in reference to *trey-trace*, of obscure origin but connected, allusively, with *try*-[*to*-]*trace*; and *troll with*, one who, a servant, is not to be known from his master.

trollybobs, see TRANKLEMENTS.

trollywags. Trousers: low: from ca 1870; very ob. ?on BAGS.

tromboning, go. To coït: low: from late 1880s. By anatomical analogy. cf. FLUTE, 2.

troop away, off, etc. To depart: coll: 1700, T. Brown, 'I thought 'twas time to troop off to an eating-house.'

***trooper.** A half-crown: c.: late C.17–early 19. (?a 'brave' coin, or because it frequently formed part of a trooper's pay.) 2. A prostitute: ca 1830–90. *Sinks*, 1848.

trooper, like a. Much; hard; vigorously: coll: 1727, *swear like a trooper*, the most frequent use; the O.E.D. records *eat like a trooper* in 1812, *lie* . . . in 1854; but in C. 20, anything but *swear* is ob. cf. TROJAN, 3, and see also SWEAR LIKE A CUTTER.

trooper's horse, you will die the death of a. A jocular c.p. = 'You will be hanged': ca 1780–1850. Grose, 1st ed., 'That is with your shoes on'.

trork. A quart: back s. (—1874). Variant of TRACK.

tros; tross. Sort: back s. (—1851 in form *trosseno*: Mayhew, I). Thus *trosseno*, lit. 'one sort', is used for a 'bad sort' (of day, coin, etc.), as also is DAB TROS, the more precise form of 'bad sort'.

trossy. Dirty; slatternly; slovenly: lower classes': late C.19–20. Perhaps ex preceding. 2. Hence, shoddy, inferior; spurious: late C.19–20.

trot. A child learning to run: coll: 1854, Thackeray, 'Ethel romped with the . . . rosy little trots.' (cf. TODDLES.) Hence, in late C.19–20, *trottie*, a toddling child. 2. Hence, a small and/or young animal: coll: from 1890s. 3. A walk; e.g. *do a trot*: from ca 1875: London lower classes' coll. 4. A succession of heads thrown at two-up: Australians' and New Zealanders': late C. 19–20. i.e. *trot* = a run. 5. See TROTS. 6. A synonym of TWAT, 1: low: C.18–20.

***trot.** To steal in broad daylight: c.: from ca 1860. 2. To walk with short, quick steps in a small area: coll: 1863, Mrs Cowden Clarke, 'She . . . will keep her husband trotting.' 3. See next entries.

trot, lie as fast as a dog can. To be a persistent liar: coll: C.19–20; ob.

trot, on the. Gadding about: Society coll: since ca 1880.

trot it out! Lit., show it: see next, sense 1. 2. Hence, speak!; confess!: from ca 1890.

trot out. To bring out (a person, hence an opinion, etc.) for inspection and/or approval; hence, to exhibit: coll: 1838, Lytton; 1888, Christie Murray, 'They would sit for hours solemnly trotting out for one another's admiration their commonplaces.' Ex the leading out of a horse to show his paces. 2. Hence, to spend, as in *trot out the pieces*: (low) coll: mid-C.19–20. 3. cf. *trot out a song*, to sing one: from ca 1870. This *trot* is generic for *do* and it occurs in such phrases as *trot out a speech*. Equivalent also is TROT IT OUT!, where the connection with sense 1 is obvious. 4. To walk out with (a woman), lover-wise: 1888, 'John Strange Winter'. Esp. *trot out a* JUDY: low s. cf. the analogous *trot round.* 5. *trot out one's pussy* (or *feed* it), to receive a man sexually: low: mid-C.19–20. See PUSS.

trot round, to. To escort or conduct round or to a place: from the middle 1890s. 'Seton Merriman', 1898, 'Perhaps you'll trot us round the works.' Prob. a development from TROT OUT, 4.

trot the udyju Pope o' Rome. To sidetrack or dismiss one's wife or other woman: low urban (mostly London): late C.19–20. In transposed s., *udyju* is JUDY (woman, girl), while POPE OF ROME is rhyming s. for *home*.

trot-town. A loafer, an idler: London coll (—1887); ob.

trot up. To bid against (a person), run up (a price): auctioneers' s. (—1864). cf. S.E. *trot*, to draw a person out, or on, in conversation in order to make him a butt.

trots. (Very rare in singular.) Feet: low London (—1909). Ex TROTTERS. 2. (Rare in singular.) Policeman: lower classes': mid-C.19–20; slightly ob. Because so much *on the* GO (4) OF TROT.

trotter. A tailor's assistant who touts for orders. Oxford and Cambridge (—1860). 2. One who goes, without residence, to Dublin for a degree: Dublin University: from ca 1880. 3. A day-student: Durham University: from ca 1890.

trotter-boxes, gen. **-cases.** Boots; shoes: low: mid-C.19–20; 1820, Hood, and Dickens in 1838 – *boxes* is vouched for by F. & H.; both are ob. Also *trotting-cases*: from late 1850s; ob.

trotters. The human feet: jocular coll verging on S.E.: late C.17–20. B.E. has *shake your trotters!*, be gone!; C.19–20 variants are *move your trotters!*, and, nautical, *box your trotters*, but the earliest remains gen. cf.:

trotters at B(e)ilby's ball, shake one's; sometimes with addition of **where the sheriff pays the fiddlers.** To be put in the stocks: low s. bordering on c.: ca 1780–1840. Grose, 1st ed., 'Perhaps the Bilboa's ball, i.e. the ball of fetters: fetters and stocks were anciently called the bilboes.' At BEILBY'S BALL, however, see another interpretation.

trottie, see TROTTY. **trotting-cases,** see TROTTER-BOXES.

trotty; occ. **trottie.** (adj.) Of small and dainty make or build: coll: 1891, 'Lucas Malet'. Ex TROT, n., 1.

trouble. Imprisonment; arrest. Mostly in *(be) in trouble*, (be) in gaol: coll in C.16, s. in C.19–20: recorded ca 1560 (in Cavendish's *Wolsey*), but app. then rare until C. 19. cf. *get into trouble*, to be fined, arrested, imprisoned, transported: from ca 1820. Prob. euphemistic. 2. As, certainly, is *trouble*, unmarried pregnancy: coll: 1891, Hardy. 3. Confinement (esp. of unmarried woman): euphemistic coll: mid-C. 19–20.

trouble. To trouble oneself; to worry: coll: 1880, Justin McCarthy; W. C. Smith, 1884, 'Do not trouble to bring back the boat.' Ex *trouble oneself*, to take the trouble.

trouble and strife. A wife: rhyming s.: late C.19–20. cf. the C.16 proverb, *he that hath a wife hath strife.*

troubled with corns, that horse is. i.e., foundered: c.p. C.19–20; ob.

troubled with the slows. (Of swimmer or boat) defeated: aquatics (—1909).

trouncer. A drink of strong liquor: (low) London: ca 1820–70. *Sessions*, Feb. 1838.

trouser, trowser. A Jack of all trades: East London: from ca 1895. Ex the 'comprehensiveness' of trousers.

trouser, v. To put (money) into one's trouser-pocket, hence to pocket (it): from ca 1890. 2. Hence, to earn: cabmen's (—1892). *Labour Commission Glossary*, 1892. cf. *put down* SOUTH, which *trouser*, 1, may have suggested.

trout. Orig. and gen. *trusty* (ca 1661) or *true* (1682) *trout*, a good fellow (cf. TROJAN, 2), a trusted servant or a confidential friend; Shadwell has *your humble trout*, your humble servant; Ned Ward (1709) applies *honest trout* to a respectable woman (?who is a 'good sort'). s. of ca 1660–1830. Contrast (*poor* and *queer*) FISH (2). Perhaps suggested by the alliteration of *true* TROJAN (later, *trusty Trojan*). 2. See OLD TROUT.

trouting, n. Catching trout: anglers' coll: 1898, *People*, 3 April.

trowser, see TROUSER, n.

truck. A hat: nautical (—1864); ob. H., 3rd ed., 'From the cap on the extremity of a mast', whence also, at least prob., is TRUCK-GUTTED.

***truck,** v.; frequent as vbl n., *trucking*. Of obscure meaning; I hazard the guess that it signifies: by legerdemain, to keep buying things with more or less the same coins; or, to steal certain more useful or valuable articles while getting change for the purchase of lesser articles. c. of mid-C.19–20. '*No. 747*'.

truck-gutted. Pot-bellied: nautical (—1860): slightly ob.

trucking, see TRUCK, v.

truckle (or trundle-) bed, stumble at the. To mistake the chambermaid's bed for one's wife's: semi-proverbial coll: ca 1670–1750. Ray, 1678.

trucks. Trousers: low (—1859); slightly ob. Prob. ex *truck*, (collective for) small, miscellaneous articles of little value and/or lowly use.

True. A member of the Whig Party: late C.17 coll nickname.

true as that the candle ate the cat or **as (that) the cat crew and the cock rocked the cradle.** i.e. untrue, false: a semi-proverbial coll or c.p.: mid-C.16–18: 1666, Torriano, the former; 1732, Fuller, the latter. Apperson, who also quotes *that's as true as* [*that*] *I am his uncle* (Ray, 1670).

true blue, see BLUE, TRUE.

true for you! An Anglo-Irish c.p. of assent to another's statement: from early 1830s. Direct ex Irish.

true inwardness. Reality; quintessence: literary j. verging on s.: from ca 1890; ob.

true till death. Breath: theatrical rhyming s.: late C.19–20.

truepenny, n. and adj. An honest fellow; true, genuine: coll: both from ca 1590; in C.19–20, ob., except in the earlier *old truepenny* (C.16–20), a hearty old fellow, a staunch friend, an honest man: dial. in C. 19–20. Ex a *true* or genuine coin of that denomination.

truff, v. To steal: North Country c. (—1864). Ex C.18 (?–mid-19) Scots *truff*, to obtain deceitfully, pilfer, steal.

***truff.** A purse: c.: C.18. C. Hitching, *The Regulator*, 1718. Perhaps by a pun on †S.E. *truff*, a truffle.

***trugging-house, -ken, -place.** A brothel: the first and third are c. or low s. of ca 1590–1620 – Greene has both; the second, c. of (?)C.17 – only F. & H. records it. Ex *trug*, a whore, esp. a dirty one. cf.:

trugmoldy. A harlot: s.: Ned Ward, 1703.

trull. A harlot: coll: Ned Ward, 1703.

truly, yours. I; myself: jocular coll bordering on and, in C.20, > S.E.: 1860, Sala; 1866, Wilkie Collins, 'Yours truly, sir, has an eye for a fine woman and a fine horse.' Contrast *your* NIBS.

trump. A very good fellow, a BRICK: coll: 1819; in Barham as a term of address (*my t.*), a usage †in C.20. Adumbrated by T. Brydges in 1762, 'I . . . Shall make him know I'm king of trumps.' Egan's Grose, 'One who displays courage on every suit'. 2. A breaking of wind: mid-C.19–20. Ex:

trump, v. To break wind: low coll: C.18–20; very ob. D'Urfey. Hence the vbl n., *trumping*, and *trumper*, the agential n.; the latter is rare.

trump, tongue of the, see TONGUE OF . . .

trumpery insanity. Temporary insanity: a c.p. directed at the frequency of this verdict in cases of suicide: ca 1880–1900.

trumpet-cleaning, gone. Dead: Regular Army: late C.19–20; ob. Perhaps ex a martial vision of a job in the heavenly orchestra.

trumpeter as an endearment = dear boy. (Low) coll of ca 1870–1900.

trumpeter, King of Spain's or **Spanish.** A braying ass: ca 1780–1850. Ex the pun, *Don Key*:: *donkey*. cf.:

trumpeter, for he smells strong, – he would make a good. A c.p. applied to one with fetid breath, *for he smells strong* being occ. omitted: ca 1785–1850. Grose, 2nd ed., where the second member is *for he has a strong breath*. Ex the pun, *strong breath*:: *good lungs*. cf. preceding.

trumpeter is dead, his (her, etc.). A c.p. applied to a person boasting or to a confirmed braggart: from ca 1725; ob. Franklin, 1729; Grose, 2nd ed., in the orig. form, *his . . . dead, he is therefore forced to sound his own trumpet*, which supplies the 'etymology'; but cf. also TRUMPETER, KING OF SPAIN'S.

trumpeters. Convicts' 'irons which connected the ordinary leg-chains with a brazil riveter round each leg immediately below the knees,' Price Warung, *Tales of the Early Days*, 1894, in ref. to Norfolk Island ca 1840; app. s. rather than c. They proclaimed the convict's presence if he so much as stirred.

trumpety. Trumpet-like; blaring: coll: 1822, *The Examiner*.

trumps, turn up. To turn out well, prove a success: coll: 1862, W. W. Collins. Ex games of cards. cf. TRUMP, n.

trun. To run: University of Oxford s. of ca 1760–1810. Short for S.E. *trundle*.

truncheon. Stomach: West Yorkshire s. (—1905), not dial. E.D.D., 'He filled his truncheon.'

trundle, the ob. coll n. (1869: Lewis) of:

trundle, v.t. and i. To bowl: cricket coll: 1849; cf. *trundler*, bowler, 1871, and *trundling*, n., bowling, 1861. 'Orig. the ball was trundled along the ground.' cf. WHEEL 'EM UP, contrast TRUNDLING BOWLER. 2. See LET 'EM TRUNDLE!

trundler. See preceding. 2. In pl, peas: c.: ca 1670–1830. Presumably because they roll along the ground. cf.:

trundling, see TRUNDLE, V.

trundling bowler. One who, bowling fast, makes the ball bound three or four times: cricketers' coll: 1851; †by 1890.

***trundling-cheat.** A wheeled vehicle, esp. cart or coach: 1630, Jonson; †by 1700. Ex *trundle*, v.i., to roll along, + CHEAT.

trunk. A nose: late C.17–20. Esp. in phrases (see next two entries).

trunk?, how fares your old. A c.p. jeer at a big-nosed man: ca 1690–1850. In allusion to an elephant's trunk.

trunk, shove a. 'To introduce oneself unasked into any place or company', Grose, 1st ed.: low: ca 1780–1890.

trunkmaker-like. With more noise than work: ca 1780–1840.

trunkmaker's daughter, – all round St Paul's, not forgetting the. A book-world c.p. applied to unsaleable books: late C. 18–early 19. *Globe*, 1 July 1890, 'By the trunkmaker was understood ... the depository for unsaleable books'; and St Paul's was then famed as a book-selling district.

trust him as far as I could throw him, I would not. A c.p. applied to an unreliable man: from ca 1870.

trusted alone, he may be. He is very experienced or shrewd: ca 1820–50. Rather sarcastic, the implication being that he may be so trusted to go anywhere without danger to himself.

trusty. An overcoat: Anglo-Irish coll: 1804, Maria Edgeworth. i.e. trustworthy garment.

trusty Trojan, see TROJAN, 2. **trusty trout,** see TROUT.

try. An attempt; an effort: coll verging on S.E.: from ca 1830.

try, v.i., with **across, after, in,** etc.; also v.t. To search (a place) to find (e.g. game): coll: v.i., 1810, *Sporting Magazine*, 'He bid the other defendants try across the Six Acres'; v.t., late C.19–20.

try back! A c.p. addressed to a person boasting: ca 1820–60.

try it on. To make an attempt (to outwit, to impose on a person): from ca 1810 both in this s. sense and in c., where it = to live by theft. Vaux. Both as v.i., the more gen., and as v.t. (Thackeray, 1849, 'No jokes ...; no trying it on me.' Hence, *coves that* or *who try it on*, professional thieves: c.: from ca 1812. 2. See next two entries.

try it on a, gen. **the, dog.** To experiment at the risk or expense of another, esp. a subordinate or a wife: from ca 1895: theatrical s. (as in the *Daily Telegraph*, 4 Feb. 1897) >, ca 1905, gen. coll. Ex MATINEE DOG, though ultimately ex experimenting with meat on a dog or with poisons on animals.

try it on with. The usual v.t. form of TRY IT ON in s. sense: from ca 1820. Esp. *try it on with a woman*, to attempt her chastity: 1823, 'Jon Bee'.

try-on. An attempt, orig. and gen., to BEST someone; e.g. an extortionate charge, a begging letter: from ca 1820. Ex TRY IT ON. 2. Whence *up to the try-on*: see UP TO THE CACKLE.

try some horse-muck in your shoes! Working-men's advice to undersized boys: c.p.: late C.19–20. As manure to make them grow.

tryer, see TRIER. **tryne,** see TRINE.

tu quoque. The female pudend: late C.18–early 19. Possibly suggested by *pu(dendum)* and TWAT; or a disguising of the latter.

tub. A pulpit: from ca 1640 (O.E.D. records it in 1643): coll >, ca 1850, S.E.; ob. Whence the coll (verging on s.) terms, *tub-drubber* (ca 1703, T. Brown; very ob.), *-man* (ca 1640–70), *-pounder* (rare; ca 1820–1910), *-preacher* (1643; very rare in C.19–20), and, the commonest, *-thumper* (from ca 1660; Grose, 1785, 'a Presbyterian parson'); also *tubster* (coll: ca 1680–1720). Likewise, *tub-thumping* (app. not before ca 1850), etc. Ex the tub from within which popular, and esp. Nonconformist, clergymen used, in the open air, to preach, but also, and in several instances, independently ex the humorous likening of a pulpit to a tub. 2. A bath; the practice of having a bath, esp. on rising: coll: 1849; 1886, *Field*, 20 Feb., 'A good tub and a hearty breakfast prepared us for the work of the day.' Ex *tub*, a bath-tub. 3. A seatless carriage on a railway train, an open truck: (low) coll: ca 1840–70. H. S. Brown, *Autobiography*, 1886. Ex sense 7. 4. 'A chest in Hall into which DISPARS not taken by the boys were put', F. & H.: ca 1840–70. Perhaps rather j. than s. or coll, as prob. also are *tub-mess* and *prefect of tub*: see Farmer's *Public School Word-Book*. 5. A (very) fat person: low coll: from mid-1890s. cf. TUBBY. 6. A cask or keg of spirit, holding about four gallons: smugglers' s. (—1835) >, by 1860, coll; ob. Ex *tub*, a varying measure of capacity. 7. A covered carriage of the sort called a *chariot*: s.: ca 1815–40.

tub, v.t. To wash, bathe, in a tub: coll:

1610, Jonson. 2. Hence, v.i., to bath in a tub, esp. on rising: coll: 1867. 3. To train (oarsmen) in a 'tub', i.e. a fool-proof practice boat: rowing s., orig. and esp. at the two older universities: 1883; the v.i., to practise rowing in a 'tub', dates from 1882. Whence *tubbing*, vbl n. to both v.t. and v.i. (from 1883) and *get tubbed*, to be thus coached. 4. (Of a tug) to make (a ship – esp. a big ship) fast to a buoy: nautical coll: late C.19–20.

tub, in the, see IN THE TUB.

tub-drubber,-man, see TUB, n., 1.

tub-men. Landsmen employed during the second, or secret, period of smuggling to receive the contraband from the luggers and carry it inland: ca 1830–80: s. >, by 1860, coll. See TUB, n., 6.

tub-mess, see TUB, n., 4.

tub-pair. A practice boat for two oarsmen: (orig. Oxford and Cambridge college) rowing s.: 1870 (O.E.D.). See TUB, v., 3 and 4.

tub-pounder, -preacher, -thumper, -thumping, see TUB, n., 1.

tubbichon. A non-cultured corruption of Fr. *tire-bouchon*, the lone corkscrew ringlet of back hair worn in front of the left shoulder (a fashion introduced by the Empress Eugénie): 1860s. cf. ZARNDER.

tubbing. See TUB, v., 3, 4. 2. Imprisonment: c.: late C.19–20; ob. Why?

tubby. Fat (person): as adj. (1835), S.E.; as nickname (mid-C.19–20), coll. 2. The latrine-attendant: Christ's Hospital: from ca 1870. Ex one so nicknamed.

tube. The tunnel in which runs an underground electric train: coll: from ca 1895. 2. Hence (often *the Tube*), abbr. *tube-railway*: coll: 1900.

tubs. A butter-man: low (—1864); ob. Ex butter in tubs.

tubster, see TUB, n., 1.

tuck. A hearty meal, esp. (orig. and mainly in schools) of delicacies: 1844, J. T. Hewlett. Also, in C.19 more gen., *tuck-out*, 1823; occ. in C.19, very often in C.20, *tuck-in*, 1859, H., 1st ed. (cf. TUCKER.) ?ex *tuck*, a fold or pleat: *tuck-out*, the earliest form, suggests a meal that removes a tuck or a crease from one's waistcoat or trousers-top; but prob. imm. ex the v., 2 and 3. 2. Hence, food; esp. delicacies (e.g. pastry, jam): orig. and mainly school s.: 1857, Hughes, 'The Slogger looks rather sodden, as if he . . . ate too much tuck.' 3. Appetite: dial. and provincial s.: from the 1830s. 4. The head: 1888, *The London Guide*; †by 1900. cf. sense 1 of the v.

***tuck,** v. To hang (a person): c. of late C. 17–19. But gen. *tuck up*: from mid-1730s: c. rapidly > (low) s. Richardson, 1740, 'The hangman asked the poor creature's pardon, and . . . then calmly tucked up the criminal.' Ex *tuck*, to put away in a safe place. 2. To eat, occ. to drink: v.t., 1784, Bage, 'We will . . . tuck up a bottle or two of claret'; hence, v.i., eat a lot or greedily, 1810; *tucking-in*, *tuck into* occurring in 1838 in Dickens. The simple v. is less frequent than the prepositional combinations. Etymology: prob. as in sense 1. 3. Ex 2, v.i. sense: to distend (another or oneself) with food: 1824, 'Comfortably tucked out'; †by 1900. Rare, esp. in simple form. 4. Prob. ex sense 1: to hang (a bell) high in the stock: 1860: bell-makers' and bell-ringers', perhaps coll rather than s. Abbr. *tuck high* (*in the stock*). Gen. *tuck up*.

***tuck-'em fair.** An execution: c. (—1700) >, in mid-C.18, low s. Parker, 1789, 'We went off at the fall of the leaf at Tuck'em Fair.' Ex TUCK, v., 1. Also *Tuck-up Fair*, s.v. TUCK UP, 4.

tuck-hunter. An assiduous feast-seeker: 1840, A. Bunn. Ex TUCK, n., 1.

tuck-in, tuck in; tuck-out, tuck out, n.; v. See TUCK, n., 1; v., 2.

tuck-man. A moneyed partner: commercial: from ca 1880; ob. Ex TUCK, n., 2.

tuck on (a price). To charge exorbitantly: non-aristocratic: from ca 1870; slightly ob.

tuck-parcel. A hamper from home: Charterhouse: ca 1860–1920; ob. by 1904 (F. & H.). See TUCK, n., 2, and cf.:

tuck-shop. A (mainly school) pastry-cook's shop: from mid-1850s. Hughes, 1857, 'Come . . . down to Sally Harrewell's . . . our schoolhouse tuck-shop.' Ex TUCK, n., 2.

tuck up. See TUCK, v., 1. 2. See TUCK, v., 2. 3. See TUCK, v., 4.

tuck-up fair or **T.-up F.** The gallows: c. (—1864); ob. On TUCK-'EM FAIR.

tucked-up. (Of dog or horse) thin-flanked from hunger or fatigue: from early 1840s: dial. and s. Ex *tuck*, a pleat. 2. Hence, exhausted: dial. >, by 1890, s. Kipling, 1891. cf. U.S. *tuckered out*. 3. Cramped, hindered, for lack of space or time: coll: 1887. Ex sense 1.

tucker. Rations, orig. of gold-diggers: Australian, hence from ca 1860, New Zealand: 1858, *Morning Chronicle*, 31 Aug., 'Diggers, who have great difficulty in making their tucker at digging'; slightly ob. 2. Hence, by ca 1870, food, as in Garnet Walch, 1874: Australian >, by 1875 or so, New Zealand. 3. Hence, *earn* (1883) or *make one's tucker*, to earn either merely or at least enough to pay for one's board and lodging: orig. Australian, then New Zealand. Ex TUCK, n., 2, or v., 2. cf. GRUB; SCOFF.

tucker, v. To eat one's tucker (see the n.), to eat a meal: Australian: late C.19–20.

tucking-in, vbl n., see TUCK, v., 2.

tuft. A titled undergraduate: 1755, in *tuft-hunter*, one who, at Oxford or Cambridge, toadies to the young noblemen; *t.-h.* > gen. and S.E. in mid-C.19; *tuft* is very ob. Ex the *tuft* or gold tassel worn on their caps by aristocratic students. Whence *tuft-hunting*: from 1780s; by 1850, S.E.

tug. A Colleger: Eton (—1881). Pascoe's *Life in Our Public Schools*, 1881. Ex the *toga* worn by Collegers to distinguish them from the rest of the school, says F. & H.; perhaps rather ex dial., where *tug* is to work hard, and (*a*) *tug*, arduous labour. 2. An uncouth person; esp. if dirty and/or none too scrupulous: late C.19–20. Perhaps ex the adj. 3. (*Tug.*) The inevitable nickname of all male Wilsons: naval and military: late C.19–20. Possibly ex adj., 1: at Winchester, *Tug* Wilson would be in contradistinction to, e.g., Sturt-Wilson. 4. (Gen. pl.) A tug-of-war match: Harrovian coll: late C.19–20.

tug, adj. Stale, vapid; common, ordinary: Winchester: from ca 1880. The origin is mysterious, unless perchance it is cognate with the dial. terms mentioned in the n., 1. 2. Whence *tug-clothes*, one's everyday clothes; *tug-jaw*, dull talk; and *tugs*, stale news.

tug-mutton. A whoremonger: C.17. 'Water-Poet' Taylor. Ex MUTTON. 2. A glutton: provincial s. (—1847); ob. The rhyming is prob. accidental.

Tug-Mutton Tuesday, see PAY-OFF WEDNESDAY.

tuggy. A fireplace cloth: chimney-sweeps': C.19. (G. Elson, *The Last of the Climbing Boys*, 1900.) cf. TOGGY.

tugger. A participator in a tug-of-war: 1909: coll. Ex *tug*, v.i., to pull.

tuggery. College at Eton; esp. in *try for tuggery*, to try to pass on to the foundation at Eton as a King's Scholar: Eton (—1883). Brinsley Richards, *Seven Years at Eton*, 1883. Ex TUG, n., 1.

tugs, see TUG, adj., 2 and n., 4.

tui. Tuition: Winchester: late C.19–20. On REMI.

tulip. A bishop's mitre, or the figure of one: from late 1870s. Ex the shape. 2. *my tulip*, my fine fellow, occurs mostly in *go it, my tulip!*, a London street c.p. of the 1840s–50s. F. & H.: 'An echo of the tulipomania of 1842'. Note, however, that *tulip* has since C.17 been used of a showy person. e.g. *Boxiana*, IV, 1824, 'A small number of Swells, Tulips, and Downey-coves'; ibid., 'Togged like a swelled tulip'.

tulip-sauce. Kissing; a kiss: cheaply jocular (—1904); very ob. Punning *two lips*.

tulips of the goes. 'Highest order of fashionables' (*Sinks*): ca 1835–55.

tullibon, see TOLOBEN.

tum (1868, W. S. Gilbert); **tum-tum** (—1904). Variants of TUMMY: coll, esp. nursery.

tum-hat, see TILE.

tum-tum. A dog-cart: Anglo-Indian: from ca 1860; ob. 2. See TUM.

tumbies. Ablutions: Oxford University: 1853, 'Cuthbert Bede'; ob. Ex *tubbing* (TUB, v., 1).

tumble, n., see TUMBLE, DO A and TAKE A.

tumble, v.i. To move stumblingly or hastily, rush, roll along: late C.16–20: S.E. until C.19, then coll. e.g. Lever, 1843, 'Tumble into bed, and go to sleep as fast as you can.' See also TUMBLE IN (v.) and TUMBLE UP. 2. To understand, perceive, something not obvious, something hidden; v.t. with *to*: low: from ca 1840. Mayhew, 1851, of long or highfalutin words, 'We can't tumble to that barrikin.' Either, as W. suggests, ex *under-stumble*, to understand, or perhaps, as the O.E.D. implies, ex *tumble on*, chance on (a thing). 3. (Always *tumble to.*) Hence, to assent to, agree with, form a liking for: from early 1860s. Mayhew. Rather rare. 4. (Of values, prices, stocks.) To fall rapidly in value: 1886: commercial s. Ex lit. sense ('fall to the ground').

tumble, do a. (Of a woman) to lie down to a man: low: C.19–20. cf. S.E. *tumble*, to handle with rough indelicacy.

tumble, take a. 'To comprehend suddenly', C. J. Dennis: Australian: late C.19–20. cf. TUMBLE, v., 2.

tumble-a-bed. A chambermaid; a harlot: coll (?C.18–) C.19. Ex v. phrase.

tumble along, see TUMBLE, v., 1.

tumble-down. Grog: Australian: ca 1815–

70. Peter Cunningham, *Two Years*, 1827. Proleptic. 2. Hence, alcoholic liquor: Australian: since ca 1870; ob.

tumble down the sink. A drink; to drink: rhyming s.: late C.19–20.

tumble-in. An act of copulation; to copulate: low: C.19–20. 2. Also, to go to bed: coll: from ca 1840. Ex *tumble into bed*: see quotation in TUMBLE, 1.

tumble to, v.i. To set-to vigorously: coll: mid-C.19–20; slightly ob. See TUMBLE, 1. 2. v.t., to understand: see TUMBLE, 2. 3. See TUMBLE, 3.

tumble to oneself, take a. To take oneself to task; to realize one's own faults: low (—1891). Ex TUMBLE, 2. 2. To go steady, be cautious: from ca 1905.

tumble to pieces. To be brought to bed with child and to be safely delivered of it: low: from ca 1870.

tumble up. To rise in the morning: coll: from ca 1840. Prob. ex: 2. To come up on deck: nautical coll: from late C.18. Ex TUMBLE, 1.

***tumbler.** A decoy for swindlers or card-sharpers: c.: C.17–early 19. Prob. ex *tumbler* (dog), a lurcher. 2. A cart: c.: ca 1670–1830. Esp. in SHOVE THE TUMBLER. Ex a cart's lumbering motion + *tumbril*. 3. One of a class or band of London street ruffians that set women on their heads: C.18: prob. s. > coll >, by 1800, archaic S.E. Steele, 1712. 4. A worthless horse: the turf (—1890). Because it tumbles about; cf. SCREW, n., 5.

tumbling down to grass, n. and adj. Breaking up, failing, going to the bad: non-aristocratic: 1884–ca 90. Ware, 'From the fact of land going out of cultivation, 1875–85'.

tumlet. A tumbler (glass): domestic Anglo-Indian 'pidgin' (—1886).

tummy. Stomach: coll: 1868, W. S. Gilbert. Prob., orig., a children's corruption of *stomach*. cf. TUM. 2. Hence, *tummy-tickling*, copulation, and *tummy-ache*: the former s.; the latter, coll.

tun. A tippler: low: mid-C.19–20; ob. Abbr. LUSHINGTON; but also punning *tun*, a large cask.

tund; tunder; tunding. To beat (a boy) with a stick, as punishment (1871); he who does this (1876); such a beating (1872): Winchester School: from ca 1870. *Punch*, ca 1890, Confession by a Wykehamist, 'I like to be tunded twice a day, | And swished three times a week.' Ex L. *tundere*, to beat.

tune; gen. tune up. To beat, thrash: from ca 1780; C.19–20. Both slightly ob. Grose, 2nd ed., 'His father tuned him delightfully: perhaps from fetching a tune out of the person beaten, or . . . the disagreeable sounds on instruments when tuning.'

tune the (old) cow died of, the. A grotesque or unpleasant noise: jocular coll: 1836, Marryat. Ex an old ballad. Apperson adduces Fuller's *that is the old tune upon the bag-pipe*, 1732. 2. Hence, advice or a homily instead of alms: from ca 1880; ob.

tuney; gen. tuny. Melodious: coll: 1885. Often pejorative.

tunker. A street preacher: ca 1850–1910. A corruption of *Dunker*, a German baptist.

***tunnel,** v.i.; **go tunnelling.** To catch partridges at night: poachers' c.: mid-C.19–20. '*No. 747*'.

tunnel-grunters. Potatoes: low: late C.19–20; ob. ?because so filling.

tup. *A stray tup on the loose*, a man questing for a woman: s. (—1890). 2. *Venison out of Tup Park*, mutton: late C.17–mid-18.

tup. Arrested; in gaol: low London, esp. in the Woolwich district (—1909). i.e. 'locked **up**'.

tuppence. Twopence: C.17–20: S.E. until C.19, then coll. So the adj. *tuppenny* (with which cf. TWOPENNY).

tuppence, for. Very easily: coll: late C.19–20.

tuppenny, see TWOPENNY.

Tupper. 'A commonplace honest bore': Society coll: ca 1842–90. Ware. Ex the *Proverbial Philosophy* (1838–42; revised and augmented up till 1867) of Martin Tupper (1810–89).

turd. A lump of excrement: C.11–20: S.E., but in mid-C.18–20 a vulgarism. Cuthbert Shaw, in his vigorous literary satire *The Race*, 1766, spells it *t—d*. Ex A.-S. *tord*, from a Germanic radical: cf. L. *tordere*.

turd, chuck a. To evacuate: low: C.19–20. See preceding.

turd, he will never shit a seaman's. He will never make a good seaman: nautical: from ca 1790; very ob.

turd, not worth a. Utterly worthless: C.13–20; in C.18–20, a vulgarism.

turd for you!, a. 'Go to hell and stay there,' F. & H.: low: mid-C.19–20. cf. the low *turd in your teeth* (Jonson, 1614; anticipated by Harman, 1567), and the late C.16 insult GOOD MAN (4) *turd*. See TURD.

turds for dinner, there were four; gen. amplified thus: **stir t., hold t., tread t.**, and **must-t.** 'To wit, a hog's face, feet, and chitterlings, with mustard', Grose, 3rd ed.: a low late C.18–early 19 rebus-c.p.

turf. The cricket pitch, the field being *long grass*: Winchester School: from ca 1860. 2. (Always with *a* or *the*.) The cricket field: Felsted School: from 1870s. *Felstedian*, Nov. 1881, 'There are (or were) six cricket pitches on turf.' 3. Prostitution: low: ca 1870–1905. Ware, 'From loose women being on parade'. Whence *turfer*, a harlot: low: ca 1875–1910. 4. A kick; to kick: Charterhouse: late C.19–20.

turf, v. To send (a boy) to bed at bed-time: Derby School: from ca 1880. 2. To chastise: Marlborough School: from ca 1880.

turf, on the. adj. and adv. applied, from ca 1860, to a harlot: low. Because, as a race-horse the turf, so she walks the streets.

turf it. To sleep on the ground with a tentlike canvas covering: 1883, James Greenwood, *Odd People*.

turfer, see TURF, n., 3.

turkey. A Royal Marine Light Infantry-man: naval: from ca 1870; ob. Ex the scarlet tunic.

turkey-buyer. A TOFF (1), a banker, an important person: Leadenhall Market: late C.19–20. Ware, 'Because it requires more than twopence to buy gobblers'.

turkey-cock, turn (or go) as red as a. To blush violently: coll, mostly provincial and Colonial: from ca 1860.

turkey-merchant. A driver of turkeys: late C.17–mid-18. A pun on *Turkey merchant*, one trading with Turkey (and/or the Levant). 2. Hence, a poulterer: mid-C.18–mid-19, though it survived till ca 1880 (see H., 1st–5th edd.). 3. Ex senses 1, 2: a chicken-thief: c.: 1837, Disraeli, in *Venetia*; ob. 4. A dealer in contraband silk: c. (—1839). cf. origin of sense 1. 5. An 'extensive financier in scrip – a City plunger': London-financial: from ca 1875; ob.

turkeys to market, be driving. To be unable to walk straight: semi-proverbial coll (—1869).

Turkish. Turkish tobacco: 1898. 2. Turkish delight: 1901, Fergus Hume. Both coll.

turn. A hanging from the gallows: rare coll: C.17–18. Shakespeare in *Measure for Measure*, IV, ii, 62; 'Hudibras' Butler. Abbr. *turn-off*. 2. A momentary nervous shock of fear or other emotion: coll: 1846, Dickens, 'What a hard-hearted monster you must be, John, not to have said so, at once, and saved me such a turn.' Ex *turn*, an attack of illness or faintness. 3. An act of copulation: low: C.19–20. (cf. C.17 S.E. *turn-up*, a whore.) 'Hence,' says F. & H., '*to take a turn* (or *to turn a woman up*) = to copulate [see RIDE]: also to *take a turn among the cabbages, up one's petticoats* (or *among one's frills*), *in Abraham's bosom, in Love Lane, Bushey Park, Cock Alley, Cupid's Alley, Cupid's corner, Hair Court, on Mount Pleasant, among the parsley, through the stubble*, or *a turn on one's back* (of women)'; the *Cupid* phrases may be literary euphemisms; *Bushey Park* and *Mount Pleasant* are confined to London.

turn, v., see below, up to TURNING-TREE.

turn a horse inside out. To school (a bucking horse) by 'slinging up one of [his] legs, and lunging him about severely in heavy ground': Australian coll: ca 1850–80. The Rev. J. D. Mereweather, 1859.

turn down. To toss off (a drink): coll: from ca 1760; very ob. Henry Brooke. Lit., turn it down one's throat. 2. To reject (an application); curtly say *no* to (a request, suggestion, invitation); refuse to accept (a suitor for one's hand): U.S. (from ca 1890), anglicized, esp. in the Dominions, ca 1900.

turn-in. A night's rest: coll: from ca 1830.

turn in. To go to bed: 1695, Congreve: coll, nautical till mid-C.19, then gen. Theodore Hook, 1837, 'Jack "turned in", as the sailors say.' Ex turning into one's hammock. cf. TURN OUT, v. 2. v.t. To abandon, to desist from doing: C.20. ?ex *turn* (i.e. hand) *in one's resignation*, where *turn in* may represent yet a third sense: coll and dating from late C.19. cf. TURN UP, v., 1.

turn it up, see TURN UP, v.

turn on. To put (a person) *to do* something: coll: from early 1890s.

turn-out. An interval: theatrical coll: 1851, Mayhew, 'The 'Delphi was better than it is. I've taken 3*s*. at the first turn-out!' 2. A fight with fists: *Sessions*, Dec. 1816.

turn out, v.i. To rise from bed: coll: 1805, W. Irving; R. H. Dana, 1840, 'No man can be a sailor . . . unless he has lived in the fo'castle with them, turned in and out with them.' Prob. suggested by TURN IN, 1. 2. v.t., as in *turn out one's hand*, to show it, esp. at cards: coll (—1904). Ex *turn out*, to empty (e.g. one's pockets). 3. To become a bushranger: Australian coll: ca 1830–90.

turn over. A book to dip into rather than read': journalistic coll: 1885, *Saturday Review*, 26 Dec.; but Ware dates it from 1880. 2. A transference of votes from one party to another: political: 1895. 3. v., see *be* TURNED OVER.

turn-round pudding. Porridge or a 'slop' pudding much stirred: lower classes' coll (—1909). cf. STIRABOUT.

turn the best side to London, see LONDON, PUT . . .

turn the tap on. To be ready with tears: lower class urban: 1883, *Daily Telegraph*, 8 Feb.

turn-up. A sudden departure: low: from late 1850s; ob. Prob. ex the v., 2. 2. 'An unexpected slice of luck', H., 5th ed.: racing coll: from ca 1870. Ex *to turn up lucky*. 3. An acquittal: c.: from ca 1820. Ex the v., 3.

turn up, v.t. To renounce, abandon (person or thing), cease dealing with (a tradesman), 'throw up' (a job): from ca 1620: S.E. until C.19, then s. Holten, 1859, 'I intend *turning it up*, i.e. leaving my present abode or altering my course of life.' Frequently *turn it up!* = 'oh!, stop that', 'stop doing that' or 'talking'. 2. Whence, v.i., to quit, to abscond, to run away: low (—1859). H., 1st ed., ' "Ned has *turned up*," i.e. run away.' Esp. to throw up one's job. (Gen. in passive.) 3. To acquit, discharge or release (an accused or imprisoned person): low s. or, more prob. (at first, anyway), c.: from ca 1810. Ex S.E. *turn up*, to turn (esp. a horse) loose. 4. To stop and search; to arrest (a criminal): c.: from ca 1850. (cf. TURNED OVER, 3.) Perhaps ironic ex preceding. 5. To chastise: Marlborough School: from ca 1880. Ex lit. sense, the punishment being on the posteriors. 6. See TURN, n., 3. 7. To hand out a share of stolen goods: c.: mid-C.19–20; ob.

turn up a trump. To have a piece of monetary luck: coll (—1812).

turn up crabs, see CRABS, COME OFF.

turn up one's toes or one's toes up, see TOES UP, TURN ONE'S.

turn up sweet. As in *to turn up a flat sweet*, to leave a PIGEON (4) in good humour after 'plucking' him: c.: from ca 1810.

***turned.** Converted to an honest life: (prison) c.: from ca 1870.

turned off. Married: Society: ca 1880–1914. 2. See *go up a ladder to* BED.

***turned over, be.** To be acquitted for lack of evidence: c.: from ca 1820. cf. TURN UP, V., 3. 2. Whence, to be remanded: c.: from ca 1830. 3. 'To be stopped by the police and searched', F. & H.: c.: from ca 1850. Horsley, *Jottings from Jail*, 1877, 'What catch would it be if you was to turn me over?' cf. TURN UP, V., 4. 4. Be transferred from one ship to another: naval coll: late C.18–mid (?late) 19.

***turner out.** A coiner of base money: c. (—1859). Ex *turn out*, to produce, to manufacture.

***turning-tree.** A gallows: either c. (F. & H.), s., or even coll: ca 1540–1660. Hall, in his chronicle of Henry VIII, ca 1548, 'She and her husband . . . were apprehended, arraigned, and hanged at the foresayd turnyng tree.' cf. later S.E. *turn off*, to hang.

turnip. An old-fashioned, thick, silver watch: W. N. Glascock, *Sailors and Saints*, 1829 (where, however, it is glossed simply as 'a watch'). Ex its resemblance to a small turnip.

turnip!, one's head to a. A fanciful bet: late C.17–19. Motteux's *Rabelais*, V, ii. cf. ALL LOMBARD STREET TO A CHINA ORANGE.

turnip, tickle one's. To thrash on the posteriors: late C.16–mid-17. There is a pun on *turn-up*. cf. *give one* TURNIPS.

turnip-pate, -pated. White- or very fair-haired: coll: late C.17–18; late C.18–20; ob. Ex colour.

***turnip-tops, cut.** To steal a watch with its chain and adjuncts: c. (—1887). Ex TURNIP.

***turnips, get or (k)nap; give turnips.** To abandon (a person), heartlessly or unscrupulously; to be thus abandoned: c. (—1812) >, ca 1830, low s.; extremely ob. Vaux (*give* and *nap*). Punning *turn-up* in its lit. sense: cf. TICKLE ONE'S TURNIP. 2. Whence *to get turnips*, to be jilted: from ca 1830. On Suffolk dial., *give*, or *get*, *cold turnips*, to jilt, be jilted.

turnpike-man. 'A parson, because the clergy collect their tolls at our entrance into and exit from the world,' Grose, 1st ed.: ca 1780–1850.

***turnpike-sailor.** A beggar pretending to be a distressed sailor: tramps' c.: ca 1835–1900. H., 5th ed., 'A sarcastic reference to the scene of their chief voyages'. 2. Hence, 'any lubberly seaman': nautical: from ca 1890; ob.

turpentine, talk. To discuss painting: coll: 1891, Kipling; slightly ob. Ex painters' use of oil of turpentine (catachrestically: *spirit of turpentine*: mid-C.17–20) in mixing colours.

turpin. A kettle: Yorkshire s. (—1847). ?ex *Dick Turpin.*

turps. Turpentine: from ca 1820: coll, workmen's and painters' >, ca 1880, gen. (e.g. photographers' and housewives'). By abbr.; *-s*, collective.

turtle. Turtle-soup: restaurant and hotel staffs' coll (—1887).

turtle doves. (A pair of) gloves: rhyming s. (—1857). Also *turtles.* P. H. Emerson, in *Signor Lippo Lippi*, 1893, 'A long-sleeve cadi on his napper, and a pair of turtles on his martins finished him.'

turtle-frolic. A feast of turtle: coll: 1787. Ob.; never gen.

turtle-soup. Sheep's-head broth: workmen's (—1909). cf. CITY SHERRY.

tush or **tosh.** Money: Cockney: late C.19–20. Ex:

tusheroon. A crown piece (5s.): low London (—1859). H., 1st ed. Also called a BULL (n., 2) or a *cartwheel*, ex its size. But H. errs, I believe: he should mean half-a-crown, for *tusheroon* and its C.20 variant *tossaroon* (2s. 6d.) are manifest corruptions of Lingua Franca MADZA CAROON.

***tuskin.** 'A country carter or ploughman', Grose, 1st ed.: either c. or provincial s.: ca 1780–1840. Cognate with, possibly ex, dial. *tush*, the broad part of a ploughshare, and *tush*, v.t., to drag or trail.

tussle. To argue (v.i.): coll (—1859) >, somewhere about 1890, S.E. Ex *tussle*, to struggle.

tussocker. A SUNDOWNER: New Zealand: from mid-1880s; slightly ob. V. Pyke, 1889, in *Wild Will Enderby*. Prob. because he loitered in the *tussocks*, till *dusk* (perhaps also operative).

***Tuttle; Tuttle Nask.** The bridewell in *Tuttle* Fields (London): resp. C.19, late C.17–19. See NASK, a prison. ('Closed in 1878', F. & H.)

tuz I. 'BAGS I!', 'FAIN I!': Felsted School: mid-C.19–20. Perhaps ex (*to*) *touse*, for cf. dial. *tuzel*, *tuzzle*, to tousle.

tuzzy-muzzy; occ. **tuzzi-muzzy** (or as one word). The female pudend: from ca 1710: (low) s. >, early in C.19, dial. Ned Ward, 1711. Ex *t.-m.*, a posy, nosegay, or garland.

twachel, -il, -ylle; twatchel. The pudend: mid-C.17–early 19. App. a diminutive of TWAT, influenced by *twachylle* = *twitchel*, a passage.

twack. To examine goods and buy nothing. Newfoundland coll: C.19–20. Ex East Anglian dial. *twack*, 'to turn quickly; to change one's mind'.

twaddle. (s. of ca 1783–5 for) 'perplexity, confusion, or anything else', Grose, 2nd ed.; earliest in Grose, 1st ed., in the Preface. Ex *twaddle*, prosy or gabbling nonsense – itself recorded only in 1782 and prob. ex *twattle*, idle talk. cf. BORE, n., which it for a while succeeded. 2. 'A diminutive person': ?ca 1820–80. F. & H., the sole authority. ?cognate with dial. *twaddle*, to walk feebly.

twaddle, v.i. To trifle: coll: ca 1770–1840. 'I have been twaddling enough to cut several slips from the most sacred *laurus*' (Earl of Mornington, letter of 15 Feb. 1791; in the Fortescue Manuscripts). Probably ex the n.

twaddy is a slang term fashionable in the 1780s: ?'characterized by twaddle'. In *The New Vocal Enchantress*, 1791, occurs on p. 32, a 'Song' beginning thus:

Hey for buckish words, for phrases we've a passion,
Immensely great and little once were all the fashion:
Hum'd, and then humbugg'd, twaddy, tippy, proz,
All have had their day, but now must yield to quoz.

twait, see TWAT.

***twang.** To coït with (a woman): c.: C.17–18.

twanger. Anything very fine or (e.g. a lie) large: dial. and s.: from ca 1870; very ob. as s. For semantics, cf. TWANGING entries.

twang(e)y. A tailor: North Country: ca 1780–1850. ?a musical pun, or a phonetic relative of STANG(E)Y.

twanging. Excellent: coll: 1609, Jonson; †by 1700. cf. TWANGER and:

twanging, go off. To go well: C.17 coll, as is *as good as ever twanged*, as good as may be: resp. Massinger and Ray. The latter phrase, with complementary *the worst that ever twanged*, arose, however, ca 1540. cf. *go off with a bang* of a great success.

twankey. Gin: from late 1890s: tea-trade. Ex *twankey*, green tea.

twat; in C.18, occ. **twait.** The female pudend: mid-C.17–20: perhaps always a vulgarism; certainly one in C.18–20; very far from being †. R. Fletcher, 1656; Tom Brown, ca 1704; Bailey; Browning, in *Pippa Passes*, by a hair-raising misapprehension – the literary world's worst 'brick'. Origin obscure, but cf. *twachylle* = *twitchel*, a passage, and dial. *twatch*, to mend a gap in a hedge, and see TWACHEL. 2. Also, as in *you silly twat!*, you fool!, and *that twat* in pejorative reference: late C.19–20.

twat-rug. 'The female pubic hair', F. & H.: low (—1904).

twat-scourer. A surgeon; a doctor: low s. (not a vulgarism, this): C.18. Bailey, 1727 (*t.-scowerer*). See TWAT, 1.

twatchel, see TWACHEL.

twattle; twattling, ppl adj. To sound; sounding: a vulgarism: C.17–18. Florio, 1611 (the adj.); Cotton, 1664 (the v.). Ex *twattle*, to talk idly, to babble. 2. Whence *twattling strings*, a vulgarism for the *sphincter ani*: mid-C.17–18. Implied in Cotton (as above).

tweak; tweake, C.17 only. A whore: C.17–18. Middleton, 1617. Ex *tweak*, a twitch, or the v. 2. A whoremonger: ?C.18–early 19. Halliwell. 3. An adept at sport: Shrewsbury School: from ca 1885.

tweak, v. To hit with a missile from a catapult: 1898, Kipling, 'Corkran ... "tweaked" a frisky heifer on the nose.' Ex:

tweaker; occ. **tweeker.** A catapult: from early 1880s. Ex S.E. (*to*) *tweak*.

twee. Dainty; chic; pleasing: coll: 1905; ob. Ex *tweet*, affected or childish *sweet*: coll: late C.19–20.

***tweedle.** 'A Brummagem ring of good appearance used for fraudulent purposes', F. & H.: c.: late C.19–20. ?ex *tweedledum and tweedledee*.

tweedledum sir. (Gen. pl.) A musical composer made baronet or knight: Society: ca 1860–90. cf. GALLIPOT BARONET.

tweeker, see TWEAKER.

tween(e)y, tweenie. A between-maid: coll: from 1880s. For semantics, cf. TWIXTER.

tweer, see TWIRE. **tweet,** see TWEE.

***twelve.** A shilling: c. (—1839); ob. cf. TWELVER.

twelve, after. adv. and advl n. From noon to 2 p.m.: Eton coll (—1861) > j.

twelve, more than, see SEVEN, BE MORE THAN.

twelve apostles; or **T.A.** The last twelve in the Mathematical Tripos: Cambridge University: from ca 1820; ob. 2. Hence, the first twelve students: Stonyhurst: from ca 1880.

***twelve godfathers.** A jury: c. (—1864) > low s.; ob. H., 3rd ed., 'Because they give a name to the crime ... Consequently it is a vulgar taunt to say, "You will be christened by *twelve godfathers* some day before long."'

twelve o'clock! It's time to be moving: artisans' c.p.: ca 1890–1914. Ex noon, break-off time.

twelve-pound actor. A healthy child born in 'the profession': theatrical (—1909).

twelver. A shilling: c. >, in C.19, low s.: late C.17–19. Ex the twelve pence.

twenty-in-the-pounder. One who, on liquidation, pays 20 shillings in the £: non-aristocratic coll (—1909).

twenty-two and twenty-two. Football: Winchester School coll: ca 1880–1910. This was the variety played with 22 a side.

twibby. Ingenious: London schools': ca 1875–95. Arbitrary formation: TWIGGEZ-VOUS?

***twibill.** A street ruffian: c.: C.17. Ex *twibill*, a two-edged axe, perhaps suggested by the obvious pun, 'doubly sharp'.

twice-laid. A hash-up of fish and potatoes: low (—1864); ob. except as nautical s. Bowen defines it as 'any sea dish that is cooked for the second time' and derives it ex 'the old name for rope made of the best yarns of an old rope'.

twicer. A printer working, or professing to work, at both press and case: printers' pejorative: from ca 1880. Jacobi, 1888. 2. One who goes to church twice on Sunday: late C.19–20. 3. Something doubly, hence very, forceful or valuable: low: 1857, Mayhew, 'He expressed his delight ... "Here's a start! a reg'lar twicer!"'; ob.

twicers. Twins: lower classes': mid-C.19–20.

twiddle-diddles. Human testicles: low: from ca 1786; ob. A reduplication of *twiddle* (v.) with a pun on DIDDLE (v.).

twiddle-poop. An effeminate-looking fellow: late C.18–mid-19. cf. preceding entry and see POOP.

twig. Style, fashion, method: low s. (—1806). Esp. *in twig*, handsome or stylish; cleverly (Vaux, 1812). Often *in good* or *prime twig*. Hence *out of twig*, disguised, esp. in *put* (*oneself* or *another*) *out of twig*; out of knowledge: low s. (—1812). ?etymology. Perhaps ex y.i. *twig*, to do anything vigorously. 2. Hence, condition; fettle, spirits: low s.: 1820, Randall's *Diary*, 'In search of lark, or some delicious gig, The mind delights on, when 'tis in prime twig'; ca 1840–70, very gen. in the boxing world. Both sets of senses were ob. by 1860, †by 1900. 3. The Headmaster: Marlborough: ca 1850–90. Ex *twig*, the rod or birch.

***twig,** v, To disengage; to sunder: c.: ca 1720–1840. *A New Canting Dict.*, 1725, has *twig the* DARBIES, to knock off the irons or handcuffs. Prob. cognate with *tweak*. 2. To watch; inspect: 1764, Foote, 'Now, twig him; now, mind him; mark how he hawls his muscles about'; slightly ob. Possibly suggested by *twig*, to beat, to reprove, but more prob., as W. suggests, cognate with dial. *twick*, to pinch (esp. in s. sense, to arrest), to nip (cf. S.E. *tweak*). 3. Hence, to see, recognize, perceive: 1796, Holman, 'He twigs me. He knows Dicky here.' 4. Hence, to understand: 1815, 'Zeluca' Moore, 'You twig me – eh?' 5. Hence, v.i., to comprehend: 1833, Michael Scott; 1853, Reade, 'If he is an old hand he will twig.' cf. TWIGGEZ-VOUS.

twig, hop the, see HOP. **twig, in and out of,** see TWIG, n., 1, 2.

twig, measure a. To act absurdly: coll: ca 1670–1750.

twig the fore (or the main). To look over the fore-mast (or main) to see that all the sails are furled and the yards properly squared: nautical: late C.19–20. Bowen. Ex TWIG, v., 2.

twigger. An unchaste, even a lascivious person; esp. a whore or near-whore: ca 1590–1720. Marlowe & Nashe in *Dido*, 1594; Motteux, 1694. Prob. ex *twigger*, (of a ewe) a prolific breeder, itself ex *twig*, to act vigorously. 2. Hence, a wencher: C.17, and much less gen.

twiggez-vous? Do you understand?: from ca 1892, when it occurs in a song of Marie Lloyd; virtually †. Kipling, in *Stalky & Co.*, '"Twiggez-vous?" "Nous twiggons."' (But *nous twiggons*, we understand, has not caught on.) Ex TWIG, v., 5, on Fr. *comprenez-vous*, do you understand. cf. SQUATTEZ-VOUS for form.

twilight. Toilet: Universities' and Public Schools': ca 1840–90.

***twine.** To give false change: c.: late C.19–20. Ex (S.E. > dial.) *twine*, to twist, wring, with a pun on *wring*.

***twinkler.** A light: c.: late C.19–20. cf. *twinkler*, a star.

twinkling, see BED-POST, IN THE . . .

twire. A glance; esp. a leer: 1676, Etherege, 'Amorous tweers', *tweer* only in C.17; 1719, D'Urfey; †by 1750. Ex v.i. *twire*, to peer, look round cautiously, peer. cf. TOUR.

***twirl.** A skeleton key: c.: from ca 1877. Horsley, *Jottings from Jail.* Because a burglar twirls it as he uses it.

***twirler.** A sharper with a *round-about* at a fair: c.: from ca 1870.

twiss. A chamber-pot: ca 1777–1830: Anglo-Irish. Richard *Twiss* (1747–1821) published in 1776 his *Tour in Ireland in 1775*, which, understandably, was very unpopular in Ireland: whereupon there were manufactured some of these utensils with his portrait at the bottom, which bore the rhyme, 'Let everyone — | On lying Dick Twiss.' (Earlier in the century, Sacheverell had been similarly execrated.)

twist. A drink of (gen.) two beverages mixed: late C.17–20; ob. In B.E., tea and coffee; by 1725, also brandy and eggs; by 1785, brandy, beer and eggs (Grose); by 1823, *gin-twist*, gin and hot water, with sugar and either lemon or orange juice ('Jon Bee'); in 1857, 'Ducange Anglicus' defines *twist* as brandy and gin; but from ca 1860, by far the commonest is *gin-twist*. Ex one thing twisted in with another. 2. An appetite, esp. a hearty one: from early 1780s; slightly ob. Ex the v., 1. 3. 'A stick spirally marked by a creeper having grown round it: also *twister*', F. & H.: Winchester School coll: from ca 1860. Perhaps ex a *twist* of tobacco. 4. *The twist* is the forcing of the arm up behind the back when a person is being arrested: coll: since ca 1860. (S. R. Crockett, *The Stickit Minister*, 1893.)

twist, v.i. and t. To eat; esp. to eat heartily: from ca 1690; ob. Also *twist down*, v.t., to eat heartily: from ca 1780. Perhaps ex twisting pieces off loaves, cakes, etc. cf. the n., 2. 2. In passive, to be hanged: from ca 1720; very ob. Ex twisting as one swings on the rope.

twist, spin a. A naval variation of, and suggested by, *spin a* YARN: from ca 1800 or perhaps 1790. In, e.g., W. N. Glascock, *Sketch-Book*, I (20 and 112), 1825. In Glascock's *Sailors and Saints* (I, 178), 1829, it has the variant *tip a twist*.

twist one's sleeve-lining. To change one's opinions or attitude: tailors': late C.19–20.

twister. A very hearty eater: 1694, Motteux; from mid-C.19, only in dial. Ex TWIST, v., 1. 2. Anything that puzzles or staggers one, a gross exaggeration, a lie: from ca 1870. 3. See TWIST, n., 3. 4. A sound thrashing; a grave anxiety, a TURN (2), as in 'It gave me a twister': low (—1887).

twistical. Rather twisted; fig., tortuous, devious: coll: 1815, D. Humphreys; ob. except in U.S. Ex *twist* on, e.g., *comical.*

twisting. A scolding; a thrashing: 1833, Marryat; ob.

twitchers. Tight boots: Lancashire coll (—1904). Ex the dial. sense, 'pincers'.

twitchet(t)y .... Nervous, fidgety: low coll (—1859). Ex *twitchy.*

***twittoc.** Two: c. (—1785); †by 1860. By perversion of *two.*

twixter. Either a lady-like young man, or a man-like young woman: low London (—1909); slightly ob. cf. TWEEN(E)Y. Ex *betwixt and between.*

twizzle, v.i. To spin (rapidly): dial. (—1825) >, ca 1880, coll. Prob. ex dial. *twistle,* v.t., to twirl. 2. Hence, v.t., to rotate; to shape by twisting: dial. (—1854) >, ca 1885, coll. 'My friends ... began twizzling up cigarettes,' C. Keene, 1887.

two. Two pennyworth (of spirits): 1894, G.A. Henty; ob.

two, adj. Only as in *two fools,* exceedingly foolish, is it coll. Donne's 'I am two fools, I know, | For loving, and for saying so | In whining poetry' is not an example – for he means that he is two different kinds of fool or a fool on two different counts – but it is relevant, for it supplies the semantic link. (Lit., doubly foolish.)

two and a kick, see KICK, n., 2.

two-and-from. A concertina: mostly Army: late C.19–20. Ole Luk-oie, *The Green Curve,* 1909.

two-acre back or **chest.** A massive woman wearing much heavy jewellery: jewellers': late C.19–20.

two-backed beast, the; do the ... Two persons *in coitu*; to coït: low coll: C.17–18. e.g. in *Othello,* I, i, 117; Urquhart's *Rabelais,* 1653.

two brothers alive and one married (i.e. as good as dead!). A music-halls' c.p. of 1897–8. Ware.

two buckle horses. Tuberculosis: stables' jocular (—1909); ob.

two ends and the bight of (a thing). The whole of (something): nautical coll: late C.19–20. cf.:

two ends and the middle of a bad lot. (Of a person) utterly objectionable: middle classes' (—1909); ob. Perhaps ex preceding.

two-eyed steak. A (Yarmouth) bloater: low: 1864. cf. GLASGOW MAGISTRATE. The O.E.D. has the rare variant (now †), *t.-e. beef-steak.*

two-fisted. Clumsy: coll and dial.: from late 1850s. cf. TWO-HANDED, 2. 2. Expert at fisticuffs: 1829, Glascock: a coll variant of *two-handed,* ambidextrous.

two-foot rule. A fool: rhyming s.: (—1859).

two Fs, the. A fringe (on the forehead) and a follower (or followers) worn by maidservants: middle classes': ca 1880–95.

two-handed. (Seldom of things.) Big; vigorous; strapping: coll: ca 1685–1910. Lamb, 1830. Prob. ex *t.-h.,* requiring or entailing the use of both hands. 2. Awkward, clumsy: ca 1860–1920. H., 3rd ed., 'A singular reversing of meaning'. Perhaps on TWO-FISTED.

two-handed put. 'The amorous congress', Grose, 2nd ed.: ca 1780–1840.

two (he)arts in a pond. Two bullocks' hearts in a two-sectioned dish: lower classes' (—1909).

two inches beyond upright. A non-aristocratic, non-cultured c.p. applied, ca 1900–14, to a hypocritical liar. Ware, 'Perversion of description of upright-standing man, who throws his head backwards beyond upright'.

two-legged calf. A gawky youth; a youthful country bumpkin as a wooer: rural: late C.19–20.

two-legged tree. The gallows: low: C.19.

two-legged tympany or **tympany with two heels,** a baby, is rare except in *have a t.-l. t.,* to be got with child, and *be cured of a tympany with two heels,* to be brought to child-bed: coll: ca 1579–1850. Tarlton, 1590; Ray. Ex *tympany,* a tumour.

two nick. A female baby: printers': from ca 1870. Anatomical wit. cf. ONE NICK.

***two poll one.** Swindled by two confederates: c. (—1812); †by 1850. Perhaps *poll* = *upon.*

two pun ten, see TWO UPON TEN.

two shoes (or **T.-S.**); gen. **little t.-s.** (Gen. in address to) a little girl: nursery coll: C. 19–20, though I find no earlier record than 1858, George Eliot in *Mr Gilfil's Love Story,* 'He delighted to tell the young shavers and two-shoes ...' Ex the heroine of *The History of Little Goody Two-Shoes,* 1766.

two slips for a tester, see THREE SLIPS ...

two-sticker. A two-master: nautical coll: 1884. Ex STICK (9), mast.

two Sundays come together, when, see SUNDAYS COME ...

two-ten. A shopkeepers' code c.p.: C.19–20. (George Seton, *A Budget of Anecdotes*, 1886.) 'Keep your *two* eyes upon his, or her, *ten* fingers.' cf. TWO UPON TEN.

two thieves beating a rogue. 'A man beating his hands against his sides to warm himself in cold weather; also called Beating the Booby, and Cuffing Jonas', Grose, 2nd ed.: coll: ca 1780–1850.

two-thirty. Dirty, grimy: rhyming s.: late C.19–20.

Two-to-One, Mr. A pawnbroker: low (—1823); †by 1890. cf. next two entries.

two to one against you. Very much against your getting your pledge back: lower classes' c.p. of ca 1890–1915. Ex the pawnbrokers' sign: two balls over one. cf.:

two-to-one shop. A pawnbroker's: ca 1780–1840. Grose, 1st ed., 'Alluding to the [arrangement of the] three blue balls, [in] the sign of that trade, or perhaps from its being two to one that the goods pledged are never redeemed.' cf. preceding two entries.

two-topmaster. A fishing schooner or coaster with both masts fitted with topmasts. As a rule the main top-mast only is carried (cf. BALD-HEADED): Canadian (and U.S.) nautical coll: late C.19–20.

two turns round the long-boat ..., see THREE TURNS ...

two twos, in. In a moment; immediately: s. (1838, Haliburton) >, ca 1890, coll. Lit., in the time taken to say *two* twice.

two-up. A form of gambling: s.: late C.19–20. Ex tossing up two coins or ex the 'heads' and 'tails' of one coin.

two-up school. A gambling den or group: (low) Australian: late C.19–20.

two upon ten, or two pun ten. Abbr. **two eyes upon ten fingers,** this is a trade c.p. dating from early 1860s or late 1850s. H., 3rd ed., 'When a supposed thief is present, one shopman asks the other if that *two pun*' (pound) *ten* matter was ever settled ... If it is not convenient to speak, a piece of paper is handed to the same assistant bearing the to him very significant amount of £2: 10: 0.' cf. JOHN AUDLEY. For etymology, see TWO-TEN, and HAS MR SHARP COME IN YET?

two-water rum. 'The real "grog". Two parts water to one rum' (Granville): naval coll: mid-C.19–20.

two white, two red, and (after you with the blacking-) brush!; hence, after you(, miss,) with the two two's and the two b's! A London streets' c.p. directed at the excessive use of cosmetics: 1860s. i.e. two dabs of red, two of white, and a brush to make up the eyebrows.

two with you! A c.p. 'suggesting a two-penny drink': taverns': ca 1885–1914.

twoer. Anything comprised by, or reckoned as, two: coll: (1) 1889, a hit for two runs at cricket; (2) a florin, as in Clarence Rook, *The Hooligan Nights*, 1899; (3) a hansom cab (ca 1895–1910); (4) a clay marble with two coloured rings painted on: from ca 1880.

twofer. A harlot: low: late C.19–20. Ex *two*.

twoops. (A) twopenny ale: ca 1752–60. The O.E.D. records it at 1729. Ex *two* + *p*(enny) + *-s*, the collective suffix as in TURPS.

twopence more ..., see DONKEY! **twopenn'orth of rope,** see TWOPENNY-ROPE.

twopenny; tuppenny. The head: low (—1859); ob. Rhyming s.; G. Orwell, 1933, explaining it thus: 'Head – loaf of bread – twopenny loaf – twopenny.' cf. LOAF OF BREAD, 2. 2. Hence, *tuck in your twopenny* (or *tuppenny*), at leap-frog, is used fig., stop!, or stop that!, as in the song *The Lord Mayor's Coachman*, ca 1888. 3. (*twopenny*). A professional pawner – one who acts as intermediary between pawnbroker and client: low London: ca 1870–1915. 'The usual fee being twopence', F. & H.

twopenny burster. A twopenny loaf of bread: 1821, W. T. Moncrieff, *Tom and Jerry*.

twopenny damn, not to care a. To care not at all: coll: ca 1820–90. cf. *not to care a* HOOT, a *tinker's* CURSE, etc.

twopenny hop. A cheap dance: coll: from ca 1850; ob. by 1904.

***twopenny-rope.** 'A [low] lodging-house: one in which the charge is (or was) twopence: sacking stretched on ropes served as a shakedown. *To have twopenn'orth of rope* = to "doss down" in such a place: Fr. *coucher à la corde*,' F. & H. (1904): from ca 1820. Dickens, *Pickwick*, ch. 16. Ob., if not indeed †.

twopenny upright. A C.19 variant of *threepenny upright* (see THREEPENNY BIT).

Twopenny Ward. ca 1600–40, part of one of the London prisons was thus named. Jonson, 1605, *Eastward Ho*, V, i, 'He lies in the twopenny ward.' Perhaps *twopenny* here, as it certainly did from 1560, =

'worthless'; or perhaps the initiation-fee was twopence.

twot, is a variant spelling, but the gen. pron., of TWAT.

twug. Harrow form of *twigged* (past ppl passive), caught. Ex TWIG, v., 3.

Twyford, my (his, etc.) name is. I know (he knows, etc.) nothing of the matter: a semi-proverbial c.p. of ca 1690–1830. The true origin of this c.p. is given in the *New Statesman & Nation*, 20 Feb. 1937: 'Josiah Twyford, 1640–1729, learned a secret process in the manufacture of a glaze by persistently feigning stupidity and was thus . . . able to lay the foundation of the famous firm of sanitary potters.'

Tyburn. The *Tyburn* phrases are on the borderline between coll and S.E.: the status of all such allusive topographical terms cannot be determined arbitrarily. The following are the chief. **Tyburn blossom,** a young thief, who will prob. ripen into a gallows-bird (ca 1785–1840: Grose, 2nd ed.); **T. check,** a halter (ca 1520–80: Skelton); **T. collar,** 'the fringe of beard worn under the chin', H., 2nd ed., 1860 (ca 1860–80. Synonymous with NEWGATE COLLAR or *fringe*. cf. *T. top*); **T. collop** (?: C.16); **T. face,** a hangdog look (Congreve, 1695); **T. fair (jig, show, stretch),** a hanging (mid-C.16–early 19); **T. tippet,** a halter (mid-C.16–mid-19: Latimer; Egan); **T. top** or **fore-top,** 'A wig with the foretop combed over the eyes in a knowing style', Grose, 2nd ed. (†by 1850), with variant *Tyburn-topped wig* (1774, Foote); **T. Tree,** the great Tyburn gallows (1727, Gay; †by 1850). Also **preach at T. cross,** to be hanged (1576, Gascoigne), with such variants as **dance the T. jig** (1698, Farquhar) or **a T. hornpipe on nothing** (late C.18–mid-19) – cf. *dance the* PADDINGTON FRISK – **fetch a T. stretch** (Tusser, 1573), **dangle in a T. string** (1882, J. Walker: 'literary'), **put on a T. piccadill** ('Water-Poet' Taylor) or **wear T. tiffany** (1612, Rowlands). Tyburn gallows, the place of execution for Middlesex from late C.12 till 1783, stood where the present Bayswater and Edgware Roads join with Oxford Street; from 1783 until 1903, the death penalty was exacted at Newgate Prison.

tye, v. See TIE UP. **tyke,** see TIKE.

tyker or **tiker.** A man who takes charge of dogs: from ca 1860.

Tykes, occ. **Tikes.** Australian Catholics' s. name for themselves: late C.19–20.

tyler, see TILER and ADAM, n., 2.

tymp; occ. **timp.** A tympanist, whether a drummer or a player of the tympan: musical: late C.19–20.

tympany, two-legged or **with two heels,** see TWO-LEGGED TYMPANY.

type-lifter or **-slinger.** An expert compositor: printers': from ca 1870. 2. Occ., a slovenly workman: printers' (—1904). cf. TYPO.

typhoid. A case of typhoid, a typhoid-patient: medical coll: 1890 (O.E.D.).

typo. A compositor: printers': orig. (1816), U.S.; anglicized ca 1860; slightly ob. Mayhew, 1861. Either abbr. *typographer* or imm. adopted from France. 2. A typographer, esp. if expert: printers' (—1887). 3. adj., typographic: 1891; comparatively rare.

tzing-tzing. Excellent; 'A1': low: ca 1880–1900. ?ex CHIN-CHIN!

U

U bet! A written jocularity (*Referee*, 14 Oct. 1883) for *you* BET!

U.P.; gen. **it's all U.P.** (It is) all UP, finished, remediless: 1823, Bee, '"'Tis all up" and "'tis U.P. with him," is said of a poor fellow who may not have a leg to stand upon'; Dickens, 1838, 'It's all U.P. there ... if she lasts a couple of hours, I shall be surprised.' The spelt pronunciation of *up*; perhaps suggested by:

U.P.K. spells (May) goslings. 'An expression used by boys at play to the losing party', *Gentleman's Magazine*, 1791 (I, 327). Here, *U.P.K.* is *up pick*, 'up with your pin or peg, the mark of the goal', Brand, 1813. At some time before 1854, the phrase had > *U.P. spells goslings*, indicative of completion or attainment, also of imminent death; from ca 1840, only in dial. Evans, *Leicestershire Words*, 1881, says: 'Meaning, as I always understood, "it is all up with him, and the goslings will soon feed on his grave."'

uck. To remove firmly, to heave, to hoist: naval (lower-deck): late C.19–20. For *huck*, a variant of dial. *hoick*, itself perhaps for *hoist*.

uckeye. All right, esp. exclamatorily: Regular Army: late C.19–20. F. & Gibbons, 'A perversion of the Hindustani word *uchcha.*' Perhaps also connected with the Scottish 'och aye!' and with O.K. (q.v.).

Uds! Alone or in combination (e.g. *Uds niggers!*), a trivial coll oath common in late C.16–17. A perversion of ODS.

udyju, see TROT THE UDYJU POPE O' ROME.

uff. A variant of OOF: *Sessions*, 30 July 1885.

Ugger, the. The Union: Oxford undergraduates' (—1899). By 'the Oxford *-er*'.

uglies, the. Delirium tremens: low: from ca 1870; ob. Perhaps on HORRORS.

ugly; Mr Ugly. As term of address: mid-C.19–20. Ex (an) *ugly* (person). 2. (*ugly.*) A bonnet-shade: Society: 1850s.

ugly, adj. Thick: lower-class coffee-houses': from ca 1860; ob.

ugly, come the. To threaten: from ca 1860. cf. S.E. *ugly customer*.

ugly, cut up, see CUT UP NASTY.

ugly as sin. Extremely ugly: coll: 1821, Scott: 1891, Stevenson. Apperson, who cites the prob. prototype, *ugly as the devil*, 1726, Defoe.

ugly customer. A vigorous boxer, not too scrupulous, but very difficult to knock out: pugilistic coll: since ca 1810. *Boxiana*, III, 1821. Ex S.E.

***ugly man; uglyman.** He who, in garrotting, actually perpetrates the outrage: c. (—1904). Suggested by the synonymous NASTY MAN.

ugly rush. Forcing a bill to prevent inquiry: Parliamentary (—1909).

ugmer, see HUGMER.

Uhlan. A tramp: tailors': ca 1870–1910. Ex Franco-Prussian War.

ullage(s). Dregs in glass or cask: from ca 1870. Lit., the wastage in a cask of liquor. 2. Whence (*ullage*) a useless thing or incompetent person: naval: late C.19–20.

ulster, see WOODEN SURTOUT.

ultramarine. BLUE in its s. senses: ca 1890–1914.

ultray. Very: coll corruption of *ultra*: from mid-C.19: Parlary. Mayhew assigns it specifically to Punch and Judy showmen.

ululation. 'First night condemnation by all the gallery and the back of the pit': journalistic: ca 1875–90. Ware.

um, 'um. Them: C.17–20: S.E. until ca 1720, then coll – increasingly low and increasingly rare – and dial. See WHAT-D'YE-CALL-'EM. 2. The: 'pidgin': C.19–20.

umble-cum-stumble. To understand (thoroughly): lower classes' (—1909). Ex UNDERCOMESTUMBLE.

umbrella. Very long or thick hair: jocular (—1887); ob. Baumann, 'He has a regular umbrella.'

umbrella, been measured for a new. Dressed badly; hence, embarked on a course of doubtful wisdom: c.p.: from ca 1895; ob. Only his umbrella fits.

umpire?, how's that. What do you say to that?; 'what price —?': coll: from ca 1880; ob. Ex the appeal at cricket.

unattached. (Of a member of the legislation) whose vote can never be counted on by any party: Parliamentary coll: mid-C. 19–20.

unbeknowns; -nst, adj. and adv. Unknown; without saying anything: resp., rare, mainly dial., mid-C.19–20; and coll and dial., mid-C.19–20. T. H. Huxley, 1854, 'I hate doing anything of the kind "unbeknownst" to people.' Ex *unbeknown* on the slightly earlier dial. *unknownst*.

***unbetty.** To unlock: c. (—1812). Ex BETTY, a picklock.

unboiled lobster, see LOBSTER, RAW.

unbounded assortment of gratuitous untruths. Extensive systematic lying: a Parliamentary c.p. of late 1885–mid-86. Ware, 'From speech (11th Nov., 1885) of Mr Gladstone's at Edinburgh'.

uncertainty. A girl baby: printers': from ca 1870. Opp. CERTAINTY, a boy baby. cf. also the complementary ONE-NICK and TWO-NICK.

uncle; gen. my, his, etc., uncle. A pawnbroker: 1756, Toldervy; Hood; Dickens. Hence, *uncle's*, a pawnbroker's shop. Prob. ex the legend of rich or present-giving uncles.

uncle, Dutch, see DUTCH UNCLE.

uncle, he has gone to visit his. A c.p. applied to 'one who leaves his wife soon after marriage', Grose, 1st ed.; †by 1900.

uncle, if my aunt had been a man she'd have been my. A c.p. addressed derisively to one who makes a ridiculous surmise: ca 1670–1850.

uncle, my, see UNCLE.

uncle, your. I; myself: non-aristocratic: late C.19–20; slightly ob. cf. *yours* TRULY, I, myself.

uncle (or U.) Antony to kill dead mice, helping. Wasting one's time; idling: coll C.20. C. Lee, *Our Little Town*, 1909.

Uncle Dick. Sick: rhyming s.: late C.19–20.

uncle Ned. Bed: rhyming s.: late C.19–20.

uncle over, come the. A variant of 'come the DUTCH UNCLE'.

Uncle Sam. The U.S. government or people: 'usually supposed to date back to the war of 1812' (F. & H.), this coll nickname has, in C.20, > S.E. Perhaps facetiously ex the letters *U.S.*

uncle Three Balls. A lower classes' variant (—1887) of UNCLE.

uncle's, mine or my. See UNCLE. 2. A privy or w.c.: ca 1780–1850, AUNT succeeding. cf. the Fr. *chez ma tante* (used also in sense 1).

uncommon. Uncommonly, very much: coll and dial.: from ca 1780.

under, down. In the Antipodes: 1889.

***under-dubber or -dubsman.** A warder other than the chief warder: c.: C.19. See DUB-COVE.

under-grounder. A bowled ball that does not rise: cricket coll: 1873; ob.

under hatches. Dead and buried: nautical coll: mid-C.19–20.

under one, do all. To do it all at one GO (n., 8): low (—1887).

under or over. 'Under the grass', dead, or 'over the grass', alive, but divorced or being divorced: Society, esp. Anglo-American: ca 1860–1914. (Applied to widows in reference to their husbands.)

under-petticoating, go. To go whoring or copulating: low: ca 1870–1920.

under-pinners. The legs: coll: from late 1850s; ob. cf. UNDERSTANDINGS.

under sailing orders. Dying: nautical coll: mid-C.19–20. cf. UNDER HATCHES.

***under-shell.** A waistcoat, as UPPER-SHELL is a coat: c.: C.19.

under the arm, see ARM, UNDER THE.

under the belt. In the stomach: coll: 1815, Scott.

***under the screw, be.** To be in prison: c. (—1864); ob.

under the sea. 'In sail, lying to in a heavy gale and making bad weather of it': nautical coll: late C.19–20. Bowen.

under the weather. Tipsy: nautical and Australian: mid-C.19–20. 2. Unwell: Canadian coll: late C.19–20.

undercome(-con- or -cum-)stumble; understumble. To understand: illiterate or jocularly perversive coll: resp. (low) coll and dial., mid-C.19–20, ex dial. *undercumstand*; ca 1550, Anon., *Misogonus*, 'You unde[r]stumble me well, sir, you have a good wit,' with *stumble* substituted for *stand*. cf. TUMBLE, v., 2; UMBLE-CUM-STUMBLE.

underdone. (Of complexion) pale or pasty: ca 1890–1915. It partly superseded DOUGHY.

undergrad. An undergraduate: coll: 1827. 2. Hence, a horse in training for steeple-chasing or hunting: the turf: late C.19–20; ob.

understandings. Boots, shoes: from ca 1820: coll >, by 1874, s.; ob. H., 5th ed., 'Men who wear exceptionally large or thick boots, are said to possess good understandings.' 2. Hence, legs; occ., feet: from ca 1800. cf. the pun in *Twelfth Night*, III, i, 90. 3. See STANDING ROOM.

undertake, v.i. To be a funeral-undertaker: coll (—1891).

undigested Ananias. A triumphant liar:

ca 1895–1914. Ware quotes the *Daily Telegraph*, 24 June 1896.

***undub.** To unlock, unfasten: c. of ca 1810–50. See DUB UP.

unearthly hour, time. A preposterously early hour or time: coll: 1865.

ungrateful man. A parson: ca 1780–1830. Grose, 1st ed. Because he 'at least once a week abuses his best benefactor, i.e. the devil'.

ungodly. Outrageous; (of noise) dreadful: coll: 1887, Stevenson. cf. INFERNAL; UNHOLY.

unguentum aureum. A bribe; a tip: ca 1780–1840. Lit., golden ointment: it cures surliness, reluctance, tardiness, and negligence.

unhintables, see UNMENTIONABLES.

unholy. Awful; outrageous: coll: 1865, Dickens. Whence, prob., UNGODLY.

unicorn. A carriage (or coach) drawn by three horses, two wheelers abreast and a leader: s. (—1785) >, by 1820, coll >, by 1850, S.E.; ob. Ex the unicorn's single horn compared with the leader out in front. 2. Hence, a horse-team thus arranged: from ca 1860: coll >, almost imm., S.E. 3. Hence, two men and a woman (or vice versa) criminally leagued: c.: from ca 1870; ob.

Union, the. The workhouse: lower classes' coll (—1887).

Union Jack. The Union Flag: coll (C.19–20).

United Kingdom of Sans Souci and Six Sous. 'Riddance of cares, and, ultimately, of sixpences', Egan's Grose: Oxford University: ca 1820–40.

***universal staircase.** The treadmill: c.: ca 1850–1910. Also EVERLASTING STAIRCASE.

unkinned. Unkind: Society: 1884–early 85. Ex Wilson Barrett's substitution, in *Hamlet*, of *unkin'd* for *unkind*.

unlocked, to have been sitting in the garden with the gate. To conceive (esp. a bastard) child: a virtual c.p.: late C.19–20; ob. With a pun on GARDEN. 2. To have caught a cold: ca 1890–1910.

unmentionables. Trousers: coll: U.S., anglicized, as a coll, by 1829 (Glascock); slightly ob. The chronology of these semi-euphemisms (all ob. in C.20) is: INEXPRESSIBLES, prob. 1790 or 1791; INDESCRIBABLES, 1794; *unexpressibles* and *unspeakables* (both, 1810; rare); INEFFABLES, 1823; *unmentionables*, 1830; *unexplicables*, 1836; *unwhisperables*, 1837; INNOMINABLES, ca 1840; INDISPENSABLES, 1841; *unutterables*, 1843; *unhintables* (—1904). Calverley satirized the group when, in his *Carmen Saeculare*, he described the garment as *crurum non enarrabile tegmen*, 'that leg-covering which cannot be told' (W.).

***unpalled.** Single-handed: c.: ca 1810–90. Lit., without a PAL. (But only of one who has been deprived of his pals.)

unparliamentary. Obscene: coll: from ca 1870.

unpaved. Rough; inflamed with drink: low: ca 1870–1910.

unrag. To undress: Yorkshire and Gloucestershire s. (—1905), not dial. Ex UNRIG, on *rags*, clothes.

unrelieved holocaust. A Society c.p. of 1883 applied to even a minor accident. Ex the phrase used by a writer in *The Times* to describe the destruction, in 1882 of the Ring Theatre in Vienna and of a circus at Berditscheff in Russia, both accompanied by a heavy loss of life.

unrig, to undress, is a coll verging on, prob. achieving the status of, S.E.: late C.16–20; in late C.19–20, dial. except where jocular.

unrove his life-line, he (has). He is dead, he died: nautical coll (—1883).

uns, see WE UNS and YOU UNS.

unshingling, n. Removing a man's hat and running away with it (and keeping it): Australian: ca 1840–90. Marcus Clarke, *Stories of Australia in the Early Days*, 1897. cf. TILE, 'a hat'.

***unslour.** To unlock, unfasten, unbutton: c.: ca 1810–50. See SLOUR and cf. UNBETTY and UNDUB.

unspit. To vomit: low (—1887).

unsweetened. Gin; properly, unsweetened gin: low: from ca 1860; ob.

***unthimble; unthimbled.** To rob of one's watch; thus robbed: c.: ca 1810–80. See THIMBLE.

untwisted, adj. Ruined, undone: coll: late C.17–early 19.

unutterables; unwhisperables, see UNMENTIONABLES.

up, v. To rise abruptly, approach, begin suddenly or boldly (to do something): coll and dial.: *Sessions*, 1830; Lover, 1831, 'The bishop ups and he tells him that ...' Gen. *up and* —, as in 'You have the ... insolence to up and stand for cap'n over me!' 2. See UP WITH. 3. To copulate with (a woman): low: mid-C.19–20. *Sessions*, 8 April 1874, 'The prisoner said, "I have *up*'d your old woman many a time, and I will up her again".'

up, adj. Occurring; amiss: as in 'What's up?', What's the matter?, or, when *up* is emphasized, What's wrong? Mid-C.19–20: coll rather than s. Albert Smith, 1849; Jeaffreson, 1863, 'I'll finish my cigar in the betting room and hear what's up.' Prob. ex *up to* (as in 'What are you up to now, you young rascal?'). 2. In the Services, *up* (as in *chai* – or CHAR – *up!*) = the tea, etc., is made (or cooked) and ready to be served; or, others than cooks speaking, '(More) tea, etc., is wanted': coll: mid-C.19–20.

up, adv. At or in school or college; on the school or college roll; in the capacity of pupil or student: coll: from mid-1840s. Gen. implies residence. Prob. abbr. *up there.* 2. On horseback: riding: 1856, H. Dixon.

up, preposition. In coïtion with (a woman): low: late (?mid-)C.19–20.

up-a-daisa, up-a-dais(e)y, see UPS-A-DAISY.

up a tree, see TREE. A proletarian intensive (mid-C.19–20; ob.) is *up a tree for tenpence*, penniless.

up against you!, that's. What do you say to that?: coll: late C.19–20.

up and —, see UP, V.

up-and-down job. An engineer's, a trimmer's job in a reciprocating-engined, as opposed to a turbine, steamer: nautical coll: from 1904.

up and down like a fiddler's elbow. Very restless: mostly lower-middle class: late C.19–20. Contrast the North Country dial. phrase, *like a fiddler's elbow*, crooked.

up and down like Tower-Bridge. A Cockney c.p. reply to 'How goes it?', with scabrous innuendo: late C.19–20.

up-and-down place. 'A shop where a cutter-out is expected to fill in his time sewing', F. & H.: tailors': from ca 1870; ob. Ex *up-and-down*, fluctuating, changeable.

up-and-downer. A violent quarrel: lower classes': late C.19–20. Ex changing positions of participants.

up at second school, be. 'To go to any one for work at 10 or 11 o'clock', F. & H.: Harrow School (—1904): coll > j.

up-foot. (To get or rise) to one's feet: low coll (—1887). Baumann, '[I] up-foot and told him.'

up in. Well informed on, clever at, practised in: coll: 1838, Dickens: 1885, Anstey, 'I did think Potter was better up in his work.'

up in one's hat. Tipsy: low: ca 1880–1910. cf. SCREWED.

up in the stirrups. Having plenty of money: low (—1812); ob. Vaux, '"In swell-street"' – see SWELL STREET. Ex riding.

up jib or the stacks or (the) stick(s). To be off; pack up and go: from ca 1860; ob. The first is nautical, the others non-aristocratic. H. Kingsley, 1865, 'I made them up stick and take me home.' cf.:

up killick. To run away: nautical: late C.19–20. Ex nautical j. *up killick*, to weigh anchor.

up on oneself, be. To be conceited: mostly Cockney: late C.19–20.

up one's sleeve, it is (was, etc.) six pots. He (etc.) is (was, etc.) drunk: mid-C.19–20; ob.

up or down. Heaven or hell: lower and lower-middle classes' euphemistic coll: mid-C.19–20.

up sticks, see UP JIB.

up-tails all, see UPTAILS ALL. **up the pole,** see POLE, UP THE. **up the spout,** see SPOUT, UP THE. **up the stacks,** see UP JIB. **up the tree,** see TREE, UP A. **up the weather, go,** see WEATHER, GO UP THE.

up to. Before, as in Trollope, 1862, 'She told me so, up to my face'; coll; ob. ?ex *looking up to.*

up to a thing or two, be. To 'know a thing or two': coll: 1816.

up to blue china, live. To spend all, or more than, one's income: ca 1880–1915. Ex *blue china* as a sign of gentility.

up to Dick, dictionary, see DICK, UP TO.

up to much, not. (Rather) incapable; (of things) inferior: (dial., from ca 1860; hence) coll: 1884, Sala, 'The shoes were not, to use a vulgarism, "up to much".'

up to slum, snuff, see SLUM, SNUFF, UP TO.

up to the or one's cackle, gossip, or try-on. Alert, shrewd, experienced: low: resp. C.19, late C.18–mid-19 (G. Parker, 1781), mid-C.19–20 (ob.). See also the nn. and cf. *up to* SNUFF.

up to the knocker; nines, see KNOCKER; NINES.

up to trap. Shrewd; alert: see TRAP, n., 1. It occurs in David Moir's *Mansie Wauch*, 1828.

up with. To raise (esp. one's arm); to lift or pick up: coll: 1760, Henry Brooke, 'She ups with her brawny arm.' cf. UP, V.

***uphills.** Dice so loaded as to turn up high

numbers: gaming c. (—1700) > s.; †by 1840. Opp. LOW MEN.

upon, see CROSS, ON THE; SAY-SO; SIVVY; SQUARE, n., 2; SUIT.

upper-and-downer. A wrestling-match: lower classes' (—1909). cf. UP-AND-DOWNER.

upper apartment. The head: ca 1810–50. (J. H. Lewis, *The Art of Writing*, 7th ed., 1816.)

***upper-ben or benjamin.** A great-coat: c. >, ca 1840, low s.: late C.18–20; ob. App., *upper ben* is C.19–20. The term BENJY, stated by H., 3rd ed., and by F. & H. to be a synonym, is also applied to a waistcoat. A great-coat was orig. termed a *joseph*, 'but, because of the preponderance of tailors named *Benjamin*, altered in deference to them', H., 5th ed. (Vaux, 1812, has also *upper* TOG.) 2. In pl, trousers: low: ca 1850–80.

upper-box Jackadandy, see BOX-LOBBY PUPPY.

upper-crust. The head: boxing: from ca 1810; ob. Ex *u.-c.*, the top crust of a loaf of bread. 2. Hence, a hat: ca 1850–1910. 3. The higher circles of society; the aristocracy: coll: orig. (mid-1830s), U.S.; anglicized ca 1890.

Upper Crust, Mr. 'He who lords it over others', Bee: low: ca 1820–40. Whence, perhaps, UPPER-CRUST, 3.

upper garret. Head, brains: Jan. 1790, *Sessions*. cf. UPPER STOREY.

upper lip, stiff, see STIFF UPPER LIP.

upper loft, see UPPER STOREY.

***upper shell.** A coat: c.: C.19. cf. UNDER-SHELL.

upper sixpenny. A playing field at the College: Eton: mid-(? early) C.19–20.

upper storey or **works.** The head; the brain: resp. 1788, Grose, ob., and from ca 1770, both Smollett and Foote using it in 1771–4. Occ., ca 1859–1910, *upper loft*. Keats in his letters has the variant *upper storeys*. All of architectural origin, *loft* prob. being suggested by BATS IN THE BELFRY: cf. *unfurnished in the upper storey* (or *the garret*), empty-headed, a nit-wit – a phrase given by Grose, 2nd ed., as *his upper storey is* or *garrets are unfurnished*; *wrong in his upper storey*, however, indicates lunacy. cf.:

upper storey, gone in the. Crazy; mad: mid-C.19–20. (T. Watters, at p. 79 of *China Review*, Sept.–Oct. 1876.)

upper ten, the. The upper classes; the aristocrats: coll: orig. U.S. and in the form *the upper ten thousand* (1844); in England the longer form (ob. in C.20) is recorded in 1861, the shorter a year earlier. 'Usually referred to N. P. Willis' – an American journalist well known in England – 'and orig. applied to the wealthy classes of New York as approximating that number', F. & H. cf. UPPER CRUST, 3. 2. Hence *upper-tendom*, the world of the upper classes: orig. (1855) and mainly U.S.: likewise coll. Also, 3, *upper-ten set*, servants employed by 'the upper ten': these servants' (—1909).

upper works. See UPPER STOREY. 2. Female breasts: low: from ca 1870.

uppers, (down) on one's. In (very) reduced, in poor, circumstances; occ., having a run of bad luck: U.S. (—1891) coll, anglicized ca 1900. Orig. *on one's uppers*; *down* being, app., unrecorded before 1904. Ex shoes so worn that one walks on the uppers.

uppish. Having, at the time, plenty of money: ca 1678–1720. The earliest sense of the word, which is otherwise, despite Swift's condemnation of the 'cock-a-hoop' sense, S.E.

uppy. (Of a stroke) uppish: cricketers' coll: 1851; †by 1900.

upright, n. A drink of beer strengthened with gin: 1796, *Sporting Magazine*; ob. 2. The sexual act performed standing, a PERPENDICULAR: late C.18–20. See THREEPENNY BIT.

***upright,** adj. Highest: c. (—1688); †by 1820. Randle Holme. Ex UPRIGHT MAN.

upright, go. A c.p. (late C.17–early 19) defined by B.E. as 'Said by Taylers and Shoemakers, to their Servants, when any Money is given to make them Drink and signifies, bring it all out in Drink, tho' the Donor intended less and expects Change or some return of Money'.

***upright man.** The leader of a band of criminals or beggars: c.: mid-C.16–early 19. Awdelay, 1561; Middleton; B.E., 'Having sole right to the first night's Lodging with the *Dells*' (s.v. DELL); Grose, 1st ed., 'The vilest stoutest rogue in the pack is generally chosen to this post.' Perhaps because he carries a short truncheon.

uproar. An opera: ca 1760–1830. G. A. Stevens, 1762, has it in the form *opperore*; Grose, 1st ed., *uproar*. cf. ROARATORIO, an oratorio.

ups-a-daisy!; upsi- or ups(e)y-daisy!; up-a-daisa, -daisy, -daisey, -dazy. A cry of encouragement to a child to rise, or as it is being raised, from a fall, or to overcome an obstacle, or when it is being 'baby-jumped': C.18–20: S.E. until mid-C.19, then coll. and dial. Resp., mid-C.19–20; id.; and mid-C.19–20, mid-C.18–20, id., and C.18. An elaboration on *up*, perhaps influenced (via *lackadaisy*) by *lack-a-day!*

upsee (occ. **upse, upsie, upsey, upzee,** but properly **upsy) Fre(e)ze,** i.e. **Friese;** hence **upsy Dutch;** hence **upsy English.** After the Frisian, Dutch, English fashion, orig. and esp. of modes of drinking: late C.16–17: perhaps orig. coll, but gen. considered S.E. Ex Dutch *op zijn*, on his, hence in his (sc. fashion).

upset the apple-cart, see APPLE-CART.

upsidaisy, see UPS-A-DAISY.

upshot. A riotous escapade, drunken frolic: ca 1810–40.

upsides with (a person), **be.** To be even or quits with; to be (more than) a match for: (orig. Scots; from mid-C.19, also English) dial. and coll: from the 1740s. 2. Hence, on a level with: coll: from ca 1880. Variant, *be upsides of*, to be alongside of: 1894.

upstairs. A special brand of spirits: London public-house: late C.19–20. Because usually kept on a shelf. The brand, etc., varies with the house. F. & H., 'A drop of upstairs'.

upstairs, kick (a person). To thrust (e.g. an unpopular statesman) into a higher office: political coll (—1887).

upstairs out of the world, go. To be hanged: jocular coll: late C.17–18. Congreve, 1695, 'By your looks you should go,' etc.

upsy-daisy, see UPS-A-DAISY.

uptails (up-tails) all, play at. To coït: ca 1640–1750: coll rather than s. Herrick. Ex the name of a song and its lively tune.

***uptucker.** A hangman: c. (—1864); ob. Ex TUCK, v., 1.

Urinal of the Planets, the. Ireland: literary coll: late C.17–mid-19. B.E., 'Because of its frequent and great Rains, as *Heidelberg* and *Cologne* in *Germany*, have the same Name on the same Account'.

urjee. A (humble) petition: Anglo-Indian coll (—1886). Corruption of *urz*(*ee*).

***use at** (a place). To frequent: c.: from mid-1870s. Horsley, *Jottings from Jail*, 1877, 'I got in company with some of the wildest people in London. They used to use at a pub. in Shoreditch.' Ex dial. *use about*, *round.*

use for, have no. To consider superfluous or tedious or objectionable: coll: orig. (1887), U.S.; anglicized ca 1900. cf. *have no* TIME FOR.

use up, see towards end of:

used up. Killed: military: mid-C.18–mid-19. Grose, 1st ed., 'Originating from a message sent by the late General [John] Guise, on the expedition' – ca 1740 – 'at Carthagena, when he desired the commander-in-chief, to order him some more grenadiers, for those he had were all used up'; actually, of the 1,200 attacking the castle of St Lazar, a half were, within a couple of hours, killed or wounded. 2. Hence, broken-hearted; utterly exhausted (1840); bankrupt: mid-C.19–20: the second nuance being coll bordering on S.E.; the other two, s.; all three nuances are ob. Calverley, 1871, 'But what is coffee but a noxious berry | Born to keep used-up Londoners awake?' The O.E.D. records *use up*, to tire out, as a coll at 1850: app. ex *used up*, utterly exhausted.

useless as tits on a bull (or a whore). Completely useless: Canadian low: late C.19–20.

***usher!** Yes!: c.: from 1870s; ob. Horsley, *Jottings from Jail*, 1877. Prob. ex Yiddish *user* (it is so), as F. & H. proposes; possibly suggested by *yessir!*, s.v. YES'M.

usher of the hall, the. The odd kitchen-man: Society: ca 1880–1910.

using the wee riddle. (vbl n.) Pilfering: Clydeside nautical: late C.19–20. Bowen, who gives an anecdotal explanation.

usual, as per. As usual: coll: 1874, W. S. Gilbert. Occ., later, *per usual*. Ex, and orig. jocular on, the commercial use of *per*, perhaps influenced by Fr. *comme par ordinaire*.

usual – his, her, my, our, their, your. His (etc.) usual state of health: coll: from mid-1880s. Annie S. Swan, 1887, 'Aunt Susan is in her usual.'

util. Only in *util actor*, that actor who can take almost any part: theatrical (—1909).

utility. (Gen. pl.) A minor part for a beginner: theatrical: from ca 1870; ob.

utter in affected use is S.E. except when it occurs in such a phrase as s. *the* BLOOMING *utter*, the utmost (Henley, 1887); even *utterly utter*, which the O.E.D. records at 1882, is S.E., but *quite too utterly utter* (F. & H., 1904) is coll.

V

V, make. To make horns (the first and second fingers being derisively forked out) as an implication of cuckoldry: coll: early C.17. Chapman.

V.C. Plucky: London: ca 1881–90. i.e. deserving the Victoria Cross.

V.R. Ve (i.e. we) are: a London, esp. Cockney, c.p. at the time of Queen Victoria's Diamond Jubilee (June 1897). Punning *V.R.*, Victoria Regina. cf. *Jubileeve it*. 2. In evasive reference to the prison van, which, in the reign of Victoria, bore these initials on each side: lower classes': ca 1850–1901. Ware. Also *vagabonds removed*: ibid.: id.

vac. A vacation: university and, though less, school coll: C.18–20. Often with capital initial. White, *West End*, 1900, 'Fork out . . . I'll pay you back in the Vac.'

vag, n. A vagabond: since ca 1690. Ned Ward, *The Wooden World Dissected*, 1707 (p. 2), 'It's the New-Bridewell of the Nation, where all the incorrigible Vaiges are sent, to wear out Ropes.' (Admittedly the quotation constitutes a probability, not a certainty.)

vag, v. To charge (someone) under the Vagrancy Act: Canadian (late C.19–20) and Australian (C.20). Adopted from U.S.

vag, on the. 'Under the provisions of the Vagrancy Act', C. J. Dennis: Australian and to some extent, English (and U.S.): late C.19–20. cf. VAG, v.

vagabonds removed, see V.R., 2.

vain, take one's name in. To mention a person's name: coll: C.18–20. Swift, 'Who's that takes my name in vain?'

vakeel. A barrister: Anglo-Indian coll: mid-C.19–20. Properly a representative. Ex Urdu *vakil*, Arabic *wakil*.

vainglorious man, see PISS MORE . . .

vally. A valet: illiterate coll: C.18 (?earlier)–20. cf. Scots *vallie*.

valve. The female pudend: low: C.19–20. Perhaps by confusion with *vulva*.

vamos, vamoss, vamoos, vamoose, vamoosh, vamose, vamous, varmoose. To depart, decamp, disappear: U.S. coll (ca 1840), anglicized as s.: 1844, Selby, in *London by Night*, 'Vamoose – scarper – fly!' The forms *vamoss*, *vamous* and *varmoose* are rare, while *vamoosh* or *vamosh* is illiterate and *vampose* or *vampoose* is incorrect – but rare after the 1850s. Ex Sp. *vamos*, let us go.

***vamp.** A robbery: c.: mid-C.19–20; ob. Perhaps ex the v., 1. 2. See VAMPS.

vamp, v. To pawn: late C.17–19: c. >, by 1780, low s. Ex *vamp*, to renovate.

***vamper.** A thief; esp. one of a gang frequenting public-houses and picking quarrels 'with the wearers of rings and watches, in hopes of getting up a fight, and so enabling their "pals" to steal the articles', H., 3rd ed., 1864. cf. VAMP, n., 1. 2. (Gen. in pl.) A stocking: c.: late C.17–early 19. 'Perhaps an error for *vampeis* or *vampeys*', O.E.D. cf. VAMPS.

vamping, n. and adj. of VAMP, v., 2.

vampire. The ghost in Punch and Judy: showmen's: mid-C.19–20. See SWATCHEL. cf. VAMPO. 2. A person insufferably boring or wearisome: from ca 1860; very ob. Ex lit. sense. (Occ. *vampyre*.)

vampo. The clown (see VAMPIRE, 1): id.: id.: ?ex Lingua Franca. See SWATCHEL.

vampo(o)se, see VAMOS.

vamps. Refooted stockings: London (—1859). Ex lit. S.E. sense.

Van, Madam, see MADAM VAN.

van John. A s. corruption of *vingt-et-un*: orig. and mainly university: 1853, 'Cuthbert Bede', '"Van John" was the favourite game'; ob.

Van Neck, Miss or **Mrs.** 'A large-breasted woman', Grose, 2nd ed.: low: late C.18–early 19. Because she is well to the fore.

vandemonianism. Rowdyism: Australian coll: ca 1860–90. Ex *Vandemonian*, an inhabitant of Van Diemen's Land (Tasmania), esp. as applied to a convict resident there in early C.19; suggested partly by *demon* and *pandemonium*.

vandook. A corruption of BUNDOOK: Regular Army: late C.19–20.

Vanity Fair. A chair: rhyming s.: since ca 1870.

vantage. Profitable work: printers' coll: late C.17–18. cf. FAT, n., 3.

vardi or **-ie,** see VARDY.

***vardo.** A waggon; *vardo-gill*, a waggoner: c. (—1812); †by 1900. Ex Romany *vardo* (or *wardo*), a cart. (Sampson's *verdo*.) 2. Hence, a caravan: grafters': from ca 1880.

vardo, v.t. To see, look at, observe: Parlary and low London (—1859). H., 1st ed., '*Vardo the cassey* [gen. CASA (2), *carsey*, *case*], look at the house'; H., 5th ed. (1874), 'This is by low Cockneys gen. pronounced *vardy*.' cf. DEKKO; perhaps ex Romany *varter*, v.t., to watch; note, too, that since in Romany *v* and *w* are nearly always interchangeable, there may be a connection with *ward* (esp. in *watch and ward*).

vardy, n. A verdict; an opinion: C.18–20 coll and (in C.20, nothing but) dial. Swift has *vardi*, an occ. C.18 form – and *vardie* occurs in C.18–20. Ex †*verdit*, verdict.

vardy, v. To swear upon oath: showmen's: since ca 1860. P. H. Emerson, *Signor Lippo*, 1893. 2. See VARDO, V.

varjus. Verjuice: Cockney (—1823); ob. cf. SARVICE.

varment, varmint. 'A sporting amateur with the knowledge or skill of a professional': mainly sporting: ca 1811–40. Byron, 1823, 'A thorough varmint, and a real *swell*, | Full flash, all fancy.' Perhaps ex dial. *varment*, a fox. 2. Hence, spruce, natty, dashing: ca 1811–80; extant in dial., though ob. even there. 3. Hence, *varment* (more gen. *varmint*) *man*, a SWELL: Oxford and Cambridge University: ca 1823–40. Anon., *Alma Mater*, 1827. 4. Vermin: low (—1823); ob.

varment, varmint, adj. See n., 2 and 3. 2. Knowing, cunning; clever: dial. (—1829) soon > s.; in C.20, only dial. Trelawny, 1831. Ex *varment*, a fox.

varmentish; varmentey. The adj. and n. of VARMENT, n., 1 and esp. 3: ca 1811–30. *Sporting Magazine*, 1819, 'Nothing under four horses would look "varmentish".'

varmint-man. See VARMENT, n., 3. 2. One who writes themes for idle undergraduates: university: ca 1840–1900. Perhaps ex sense 1.

varnish. Bad champagne: Society: ca 1860–1905.

***varnisher.** A coiner of counterfeit sovereigns: c. (—1864); ob. Because this finishing touch often gave an effect of varnish.

varsal; 'varsal. Uni*versal*, whole: mostly in *in the varsal world*: illiterate coll (1696, Farquhar) >, in C.19, dial. 2. Hence, single: ca 1760–1820, then dial.; rare and ob. Scott. 3. Hence, adv.: extremely: 1814, 'A varsal rich woman': rare coll and dial.; ob. cf. VERSAL.

varsity, V.; 'varsity, 'V. Orig. university coll, now gen. coll for *university*: from ca 1845. 2. As adj.: 1863 (O.E.D. Sup.); 1864, Tennyson. Whether as n. or adj., the term, in its wider sense, has not always been approved at the two older English universities. ca 1640–1700, *Versity*: likewise coll. 3. *varsity tit*, see TIT, 4.

vaseline. Butter: Royal Military Academy: late C.19–20. cf. GREASE, n., 5.

vast of, a. A great amount (e.g. of trouble) or number: dial. (1794: E.D.D.) > also, by 1900, proletarian coll.

vastly. Very: coll: C.18–early 19.

vatch. (To) have: back s., esp. butchers': late C.19–20.

vaulting-school. A coll or s. (?orig. c.) variation of *v.-house*, a brothel: ca 1605–1830. H. Parrot, 1606. 2. Hence, 'an Academy where Vaulting, and other Manly Exercises are Taught', B.E.: c. or s.: late C.17–early 19.

veal will be cheap, calves fall. A jeering c.p. addressed to a spindle-legged person from ca 1670; ob. Ray, 1678. cf. MUTTON DRESSED AS LAMB.

veg. Vegetable(s): eating-houses' coll: mid-C.19–20. e.g. 'Meat and two veg'. Ex abbr.

vegetable breakfast. A hanging: low jocular: late C.19–early 20. The meal consists of an artichoke (punning HEARTY CHOKE) and 'caper sauce'.

***velvet.** The tongue; 'especially the tongue of a MAGSMAN', H., 5th ed.: in gen., late C.17–20, c. >, by 1800, low s.; in particular sense, from ca 1870, low s. Ex its texture. See VELVET, TIP THE.

velvet, on. In an easy or advantageous position: 1769, Burke: S.E. rapidly > sporting coll, Grose, 1st ed., having '*to be upon velvet*, to have the best of a bet or match'; esp. as = sure to win. Hence the next two entries.

velvet, play on. To gamble with winnings: gaming s.: from ca 1880. Ex VELVET, ON; perhaps influenced by:

velvet, stand on. 'Men who have succeeded in their speculations, especially on the turf, are said to stand on velvet,' H. 5th ed., 1874.

***velvet, tip the.** 'To Tongue a Woman', B.E.: late C.17–20: c. >, by 1800, low s. See VELVET and TIP, v., 4, 6. 2. To scold: low: ca 1820–50.

velvet!, to the little gentleman in. This C.18 Anglo-Irish Tory and Roman Catholic toast verges on the coll, *the little . . . velvet* being that 'mole which threw up the mound causing Crop (King William [III]'s horse) to stumble'.

venerable monosyllable. The female pudend: ca 1785–1840. See MONOSYLLABLE.

vengeance, see WHIP-BELLY.

ventilator. A play, player, or management that empties a theatre: theatrical (—1904). F. & H. Neat wit on the lit. sense.

venture-girl. A poor young lady seeking a husband in India: Anglo-Indian: ca 1830–70.

venture it as Johnson did his wife, and she did well, – I'll. A semi-proverbial c.p. implying that it sometimes pays to take a risk: ca 1670–1800. Ray, 1678; Fuller, 1732.

verb-grinder. A (pedantic) schoolmaster: coll: 1809, Malkin; ob. On GERUND-GRINDER.

***verge.** A gold watch: c.: late C.19–20. Ex a *verge* (*watch*).

verites; V. At Charterhouse, a boarding-house: mid-C.19–20; ob. 'A corruption of *Oliverites*, after Dr Oliver Walford, 1838–55', F. & H.

vermilion. To besmear with blood: sporting: 1817 (O.E.D.); virtually †.

verneuk; verneuker; verneukerie. To swindle, cheat, deceive; one who does this; such behaviour: South African coll: resp. 1871, 1905, 1901. Direct ex Cape Dutch.

versal, 'versal. Universal, whole; gen. with *world*: illiterate coll: late C.16–19. Shakespeare; Sheridan. 2. Hence, single: id.: 1709, Mrs Manley, 'No versal thing'. cf. VARSAL.

verse, v., see:

***versing law.** Swindling with counterfeit gold: c. of ca 1590–1620. Greene. Ex: **verse*, v.i. and v.t., to practise fraud or imposition (on): id. ibid. cf.: **verser*. A member of a band of swindlers: c.: ca 1550–1620. ?ex *verse*, to overthrow, upset.

Versity, see VARSITY.

vert; 'vert. A pervert or convert to another religion (esp. Roman Catholicism): coll: 1864, *Union Review*, May. W., however, thinks that it may have originated, ca 1846, with Dean Stanley. 2. Occ. as v.i.: coll: 1888.

vertical. A plant living on the side of a perpendicular rock-face: gardening s. (—1902).

***vertical care-grinder.** A treadmill: c. (—1859); almost †. Known also as the EVERLASTING or UNIVERSAL STAIRCASE.

very famillionaire. Characteristic of the patronage shown by rich men: Society: 1870s. Ex *familiar* + *millionaire*.

very froncey. Very pronounced; vulgar: Society: ca 1870–1905. Ex *très français*, very French.

very well. An intensification of WELL, adj.

vessel. The nose: sporting: ca 1813–30. *Sporting Magazine*, LXI (1813), 'There, d–n your eyes, I've tapped your vessel.' cf. *tap one's* CLARET.

vest, lose one's. To get angry: low: ca 1890–1910. A mere elaboration of *get one's* SHIRT OUT; cf. SHIRTY.

vestal. 'Ironical for an incontinent person,' *The London Guide*, 1818: app. ca 1810–50. Short for *vestal virgin*.

vet. A veterinary surgeon: coll: 1864, H. Marryat. Whence:

vet, v. To cause (an animal) to be examined by a vet: coll: from ca 1890. 2. Hence, to examine, occ. to treat, (a person) medically: coll: 1898, Mrs Croker.

vex. (So much the) worse, as in *vex for you*: Christ's Hospital: from ca 1860. Perhaps ex L. *pejus* (pronounced – one may presume – *peddjus*), but more prob. simply an abbr. of *vexing* or *vexation*.

vic! CAVE!: Felsted School: from ca 1870. Hence, *keep vic*, to watch against official intrusion. Perhaps from L. *vicinus*, near, or even L. *vigil* or the imperative of *vigilare*, to watch.

Vicar of Bray. A tray; a 'trey' (the number 3): theatrical rhyming s.: late C. 19–20.

vicar of St Fools, the. (Implying) a fool: a semi-proverbial coll: mid-C.16–17. Heywood, 1562; Nashe, 1589; Howell, 1659, and Ray, 1670, omit the *Saint* (Apperson). Sc. *Church*; by punning 'topography'.

vice (or Vice), the. The Vice-Chancellor, -President, etc.: coll (—1887).

Vice-Chancellor's court. 'Creditor's last shift', Egan's Grose: Oxford University: ca 1820–50.

Vice-Chuggins, the. The Vice-Chancellor: Oxford undergraduates': late C.19–20.

victim. A person very much in love: Society: ca 1885–1914.

Victoria Monk. Semen: late C.19–20. Rhyming on SPUNK, 2. Ex a character famous in pornographic fiction. Strictly, that character was MARIA MONK and this, the original and still the commoner rhyming-s. form, became confused, in the popular mind, by the fame of *Victoria Monks* (with an *-s*), a very well-known music-hall singer, perhaps best remembered for her rendering of 'Won't you come home, Bill Bailey?'

victualler; victualling-house. A pander; a house of accommodation: late C.16–17: resp., Shakespeare, *2 Henry IV*, II, iv; and Webster, *A Cure for a Cuckold*. Because a tavern-keeper's trade often cloaked intrigue and bawdry.

victualling department or **office.** The stomach: boxing > gen. s.: resp. 1878 (O.E.D.) and 1751, Smollett; both are ob. By a pun on that Government office which victuals the Navy. cf. BREAD-BASKET; DUMPING-DEPOT.

***view the land.** To examine in advance the scene of a crime: c. (—1887).

viewy. Designed, or likely, to catch the eye; attractive: 1851, Mayhew; ob.

***vile, ville, vyle.** A city, a town: c.: in combination from 1560s; by itself, app. not before C.19. ROME VILLE, *-vyle*, *Rum-*, London: mid-C.16–20; *deuce-a-vile*, DEUSEAVILLE; DAISYVILLE, the country: mid-C.17–20. By itself, '*No. 747*' (valid for 1845); H., 1st ed., 1859, 'Pronounced *phial*, or *vial*.' Ex Fr. *ville*.

village blacksmith. A performer or actor not quite a failure, his engagements never lasting longer than a week: music-halls' and theatrical (—1909); ob. Ex Longfellow's poem, '*Week in, week out*, from morn till night . . .'

***village butler.** A petty thief; esp. an old thief 'that would rather steal a dishclout than discontinue the practice of thieving', Potter, 1795: c. of ca 1790–1850.

villain as ever scuttled a ship, I'm as mild a. A c.p. applied to oneself in jocular reproach: coll (—1904). Prob. on S.E. *I'm a bit of a villain myself, but —*

ville, see VILE.

vim. Force; energy: U.S. (adv., 1850, †; n., early 1870s), anglicized ca 1890: coll >, ca 1910, S.E. Either echoic or ex L. *vis* (accusative *vim*), energy, strength.

***vincent.** A dupe in a betting game: c.: ca 1590–1830; though prob. ob. in C.18–19. Etymology obscure: ?ironic ex L. *vincens*, (being) victorious. Whence:

***vincent's** (or **V.**) **law.** The art and practice of cheating at a betting game, esp. bowls or cards: c.: same period and history as preceding. Here, *law* = LAY (n., 2) = line of criminal activity.

***vinegar.** A cloak: c.: late C.17–early 19. Perhaps because it is worn in *sharp* weather. cf. the semantics presumably operative in: 2. 'The person, who with a whip in his hand, and a hat held before his eyes' – cf. the man who, in a public conveyance, pretends to sleep while women are strap-hanging – 'keeps the ring clear at boxing matches and cudgel playings', Grose, 1st ed.: sporting: ca 1720–1840.

vintage. Year of birth: U.S. (—1883) >, by 1890, English. Ex *vintage*(-year) of wines.

violently. Showily, 'loudly' (e.g. dressed): coll: 1782, Mme D'Arblay; ob.

violet; garden-violet. An onion; gen. in pl as = spring onions eaten as a salad. 2. pl, sage-and-onion stuffing. Both, proletarian-ironic: from ca 1870; slightly ob.

vir-gin, see MAN-TRAP.

virgins' bus, the. The last bus running from Piccadilly Corner westward: lower classes': ca 1870–1900. Its chief patronesses were prostitutes.

virtue. 'Smoking, drinking, whoring. When a man confesses to abstention from tobacco and intoxicating liquors he is perversely said to have no virtues,' F. & H.: non-aristocratic: ca 1880–1915.

virtue rewarded. A c.p. in reference to occupants of prison-vans (bearing *V.R.* on their sides): lower classes': ca 1870–1901. cf. V.R., 2.

vish. Angry; cross: Christ's Hospital: from ca 1890. Abbr. *vicious* in this sense. It superseded PASSY (abbr. *passionate*).

visitation. An over-long visit or protracted social call: coll: 1819. Ex the length of ecclesiastical visitations.

vitty. Fitty, i.e. fitting, suitable; neat: late C.16–20: S.E. until C.18, then s. (†by 1900) and dial.

viva. A viva-voce examination: university coll: from ca 1890. Whence:

viva, v.t. and, rarely, v.i. To subject, be subjected to, a 'viva': id.: 1893. Ex preceding.

voetsak! (To a dog) go away!: South African coll (—1877). Prob. ex Dutch *voort seg ek!*, away, I say! Sometimes *footsack!*

***voil.** A rare form (Egan's Grose, 1823) of VILE, n.

voker, v.t. To speak: tramps' c. and low s. (—1859); ob. This is a debased form of ROCKER. cf. L. *vocare*.

vote. To propose, suggest: coll: 1814, Scott. (O.E.D.) Only with *that* . . .

vote for the alderman, see ALDERMAN, VOTE FOR THE.

vouch. An assertion or formal statement: C.17–20: S.E. until C.19, then coll; ob.

***voucher.** One of those who 'put off False Money for Sham-coyners', B.E.: c. of ca 1670–1720. Head. (He 'vouches for' the counterfeit.)

voucher, force the. To elicit money from the betting public and then abscond: sporting (—1874).

voulez-vous squattez-vous? Will you sit down?: theatre GODS': from ca 1820. 'Started by Grimaldi', says Ware. cf. TWIGGEZ-VOUS.

vowel. To pay (a winner; indeed, any creditor) with an I.O.U.: C.18–19. Steele, 'I am vowelled by the Count, and cursedly out of humour.' Ex either spoken formula, or written statement of, 'I.O.U.'

vowel-mauler. An indistinct speaker: not upper classes': ca 1880–1910.

voyage, Hobbe's. An act of coïtion: late C.17–18. Vanbrugh, 1697, 'Matrimony's the spot . . . So now I am in for Hobbe's voyage; a great leap in the dark.' Ex some lost topical allusion, unless it be a jeer at HOB, a country bumpkin.

***voyage of discovery.** Going out stealing: c. (—1857).

***vrow-case.** A brothel: c.: (prob.) late C. 17–mid-19. F. & H., who app. deduce it, justifiably (I think), from B.E.'s *case-fro*, 'a Whore that Plies in a Bawdy-house'. Ex Dutch *vrouw*, a woman, + CASA (2), *case*, a house, shop, etc.

W

w. A w.c.: late C.19–20, non-aristocratic coll; ?orig. euphemistic. Always *the w.*

W.F.'s. Wild cattle: Tasmania: ca 1840–80. Fenton, *Bush Life in Tasmania Fifty Years Ago*, 1891, 'The brand on Mr William Field's wild cattle'.

w.h. or **W.H.** A whore: euphemistic coll (—1887); ob.

W.H.B., the. The 'Wandering Hand Brigade', those who are apt to take liberties with women: late C.19–20.

W.M.P. We accept the invitation: naval coll verging on j.: late C.19–20. i.e., with much pleasure.

W.P.; w.p. Abbr. (—1860) of WARMING-PAN, 3; ob.

wabbler. See FOOT-WABBLER and WOBBLER. **wack.** A mainly dial. form of WHACK.

wad. A gunner: naval: mid-C.19–20. Ware, 'A survival from the days of muzzle-loading cannon'. 2. Straw: proletarian: C.19.

waddle; orig. and gen. **waddle out;** often extended to **waddle out lame duck** or **w.o. of the Alley.** To become a defaulter on the Exchange: Stock Exchange: 1771, Garrick, 'The gaming fools are doves, the knaves are rooks, Change-Alley bankrupts waddle out lame ducks!'; 1860, Peacock (*waddle off*, rare); †by 1900. See LAME DUCK.

waddy. A walking-stick: Australian coll (—1898). Ex lit. Aboriginal sense, a club.

wade. A ford: coll: C.19–20. Ex *wade*, an act of wading.

wadge, wodge. A lumpy mass or bulgy bundle: dial. (—1860) >, ca 1880, coll. Ex *wad* on *wedge*. 2. Hence, late C.19–20, adj. *wodgy*.

wadmarel (C.19: nautical), **wadmus** (C. 18). Corruptions of *wadmal* (a woollen cloth).

wads. A gunner: naval, esp. as a nickname: from ca 1890. Ex the use he makes thereof.

waffle. Nonsense; gossip(ing); incessant or copious talk: printers' (—1888). Jacobi. Ex dial. *waffle*, a small dog's yelp or yap. cf. WAFFLES and:

waffle, v. To talk incessantly; printers': from ca 1890. Ex *waffle*, to yelp. 2. To talk nonsense: from ca 1890: Durham School >, by 1910 or so, gen. Perhaps ex sense 1; cf., however, the n. 3. See WOFFLE.

waffles. A loafer; a sauntering idler: low (—1904); ob. cf. WAFFLE.

wag, n. See WAG, HOP THE.

wag, v. To play truant; often *wag it*: mid-C.19–20. Dickens, 1848. Ex: 2. *wag*, to go, to depart: late C.16–20: S.E. until C. 19, then coll. 3. v.t., gen. in negative. To stir (e.g. a limb): late C.16–20: S.E. until mid-C.19, then coll. F. Harrison, 'I . . . declined to ask him . . . to wag a finger to get me there.' cf.: 4. v.i., to move one's limbs: C.13–20: S.E. until mid-C.19, then coll; ob. Whyte-Melville, 1860.

wag, hop the; play the wag; play the Charley-wag. To play truant: 1861, Mayhew, the first two; 1876, Hindley, the third, which is very ob. Ex WAG, v. – perhaps with a pun on lit. sense of *play the wag*, to be amusingly mischievous, to indulge constantly in jokes.

wag one's bottom. To be a harlot: mostly Cockney: late C.19–20.

wag-tail. A harlot: s.: Ned Ward, 1703.

wagabone, n. and adj. Vagabond: C.19. G. R. Sims, 'His wagabone ways'.

Wagga blanket. A rough bed-covering, used by tramps and made from sack or bag: Australian: late C.19–20. Derisive of the N.S.W. town of Wagga-Wagga, small and genuinely rural.

wagger. A truant: schools': from ca 1870. (E. Pugh, *A Street in Suburbia*, 1895.) cf. *hop the* WAG.

wagger-pagger-bagger. A waste-paper-basket: Oxford University: from ca 1905. See 'the Oxford *-er*', p. 11.

waggernery! O(h) agony!: lower Society: 1880s. The pun is specifically on *Wagner*, much ridiculed in that decade.

waggle. To overcome: low (—1904); ob. except in U.S.

waggley; gen. **waggly.** Unsteady; having frequent irregular curves: coll: 1894, E. Banks, 'Even in [the path's] most waggly parts'. Lit., waggling.

waggon. In the old guardships, the place where the supernumeraries slung their hammocks: nautical: ?ca 1840–90.

***waggon-hunter.** A brothel-keeper's tout visiting the inns at which the stage-coaches stopped: c.: 1760–1840.

***waggon-lay.** 'Waiting in the street to rob waggons going out or coming into town, both commonly happening in the dark', Grose, 3rd ed.: c.: late C.18–mid-19.

wagon, see WAGGON.

wahinë. A woman: New Zealand coll: late C.19–20. Direct ex Maori. cf. LUBRA.

waipiro. Intoxicating liquor: id.: id. Straight from Maori.

waistcoat. See WESKET. 2. *fetid waistcoat.* 'A waistcoat of a flaunting and vulgar pattern', F. & H.: ca 1859. So LOUD that it 'stinks to heaven'.

waistcoat piece. 'Breast and neck of mutton – from its resemblance to . . . half the front of a waistcoat not made up': tailors' (—1909). Ware.

wait. To postpone (a meal) for an expected person: coll: 1838, Dickens, 'It's a trying thing waiting supper for lovers.' cf. WAIT ABOUT. 2. To wait at; only in *wait table,* to wait at table: servants' coll (—1887).

wait about or around, v.i. To HANG ABOUT: coll: resp. 1879, Miss Braddon: 1895, orig. and mostly U.S.

wait till the clouds roll by! A c.p. inducive of optimism: 1884. Ware, 'From an American ballad'.

wait till (or until) you get it?, – will you have it now or. A c.p., addressed to someone either impatient or in a hurry: C.19–20. (Dickens, *The Pickwick Papers,* 1836–7, ch. 10.)

waler; orig. W. A (cavalry) horse imported from New South *Wales* into India: 1849 (O.E.D.): Anglo-Indian coll >, ca 1905, S.E. An advertisement in the *Madras Mail,* 25 June 1873: 'For sale. A brown waler gelding'. 2. Hence, a horse imported into India from any part of Australia: from early 1880s.

walk. To depart of necessity; to die: mid-C.19–20: resp. coll and s. Trollope, 1858 (latter sense). Ex *walk,* to go away. 2. v.t. To win easily: Public Schools' coll: from ca 1895. (P. G. Wodehouse, *A Prefect's Uncle,* 1903.) Abbr. *walk off with.*

walk, n. A postman's route or BEAT: Canadian coll: late C.19–20.

walk, the ghost doesn't, see GHOST WALKS.

walk around, gen. round. To beat easily: coll, U.S. (Haliburton, 1853) anglicized ca 1890. cf. the synonymous *run* RINGS ROUND.

walk down one's throat. To scold, abuse: late C.19–20. Ex *jump* . . .

walk into. To attack vigorously: coll: 1794, Lord Hood. 2. Hence, to scold or reprove strongly: coll: from 1850s. 3. To eat, drink, much or heartily of: 1837, Dickens; id., 1840, 'Little Jacob, walking . . . into a homemade plum cake, at a most surprising pace.' 4. To 'make a hole in' one's money: 1859, Henry Kingsley. 5. See:

walk into one's affections. To win a person's love or affection effortlessly and immediately: coll: 1858 (O.E.D.). 2. Jocularly for WALK INTO, 1 and 2: 1859, H., 1st ed.; also for WALK INTO, 3 (Baumann, 1887). 3. Hence ironically, to get into a person's debt: from ca 1860; ob.

walk it. To walk (as opp. to riding): coll: 1668, Pepys.

walk, knave, walk! A coll c.p. taught to parrots: mid-C.16–17. 'Proverbs' Heywood, 1546; Lyly; 'Hudibras' Butler; Roxburgh, *Ballads,* ca 1685.

walk one's chalks, see CHALKS, WALK ONE'S.

walk out with the bat. To achieve victory: Society: ca 1880–1900. Ex a cricketer 'carrying' his bat.

walk round. To prepare oneself to attack or be attacked: lower classes' (—1909). Ex dogs' circling. 2. See WALK AROUND.

walk Spanish, see CHALKS, WALK ONE'S.

***walk the barber.** To lead a girl astray: c. (—1851). (Anatomical.)

walk the chalk. To walk along a chalk line as a test of sobriety: military (—1823) >, by 1850, gen. See also *able to walk a* CHALK. 2. Hence, by 1845 at latest, to keep oneself up to the moral mark.

walk the hospitals. To study medicine: medical coll: from ca 1870.

walk the pegs. In cheating at cribbage, to move one's own pegs forward or one's opponent's back: 1803, low s. >, ca 1870, s. >, ca 1900, coll. Lit., to make walk.

walk the plank. An early variant of WALK THE CHALK. Naval: since ca 1810 or earlier. It occurs in W. N. Glascock, *Sailors and Saints,* 1829.

walk up (against) the wall, see WALL, CRAWL . . .

walk up Ladder Lane and down Hemp Street. To be hanged at the yard-arm: nautical: C.19. cf. HEMPEN . . .

walked out, the lamp (has). The lamp has gone out, went out: jocular (—1887); ob.

Walker! orig. and properly **Hook(e)y Walker!** 'Signifying that the story is not true, or that the thing will not occur', *Lex. Bal.*, 1811; *Walker* is recorded by Vaux in the following year. 2. Hence, be off!: late C.19–20. 3. As n., in, e.g., 'That is all (Hooky) Walker': late C.19–20. Ex sense 1, which derives perhaps ex 'some hook-nosed person named Walker', O.E.D.

walker. A postman: ca 1860–1910. Ex an old song entitled *Walker the Twopenny Postman.* 2. See WALKERS. 3. See preceding entry. 4. A coll abbr. of *shop-walker*: (—)1864.

Walker, my (or his, etc.) name's. I'm (he's, etc.) off: late C.19–20. Ex WALKER!, 2.

walkers. The feet: C.19. Pierce Egan, 1832. ?ex †*walkers*, legs.

walking cornet. An ensign of foot: military (—1785); †by 1890.

walking distiller, see DISTILLER.

walking-go. A walking-contest: coll: C. 19–20; very ob.

***walking mort.** A tramp's woman: c.: early C.19. On STROLLING MORT.

***walking poulterer.** One who hawks from door to door the fowls he steals: c. of ca 1785–1840.

walking stationer. 'A hawker of pamphlets, &c.', Grose, 2nd ed., 1788: (?orig. c. >) low s.; ob. by 1870, †by 1900.

walkist. A walker: sporting (esp. athletics) coll (—1887); ob.

wall, crawl or walk up the; in *Lex. Bal.*, 1811, also as *walk up against the wall.* 'To be scored up at a public house', Grose, 1st ed.: public-house (—1785); †by 1850. Ex the mounting bill written up, in chalk, on the wall.

wall, near the. Ill: Oxford University: ca 1820–50. *Spy*, 1825. Ex Dr Wall, a celebrated surgeon.

wall and it will not bite you!, look on the. A jeering c.p. addressed to one whose tongue has felt the bite of mustard: ca 1850–1910.

wall as anyone, see as far into a brick, see MILLSTONE.

wall-eyed. Inferior, careless (work); irregular (action): from the 1840s; ob. by 1890. Halliwell, 1847. Ex *wall-eyed*, squinting.

wall fruit. 'Kissing against a wall' (*Sinks*): ca 1830–80.

wallabies; W. Australians: coll: from ca 1908. Mostly in sporting circles and esp. of teams of Australians.

wallaby, on the. On tramp: Australian s. >, ca 1910, coll: 1869, Marcus Clarke. Abbr. *on the wallaby-track.* In the bush, often the only perceptible track.

wallah, in Anglo-Indian (hence in Army) compounds – e.g. COMPETITION WALLAH – is simply a chap, a fellow: late C.18–20. Only in certain (mostly, jocular) compounds (e.g. AMEN-WALLAH) is it eligible. Ex Hindustani *-wala*, connected with.

walled. (Of a picture) accepted by the Royal Academy: artists': 1882; ob.

wallflower. A second-hand coat, exposed for sale: low London: 1804; ob. For semantics, cf. next sense. 2. Orig. and gen., a lady keeping her seat by the wall because of her inability to attract partners: coll: 1820, Praed, 'The maiden wall-flowers of the room | Admire the freshness of his bloom.' 3. Hence, any person going to a ball but not dancing, whatever the reason: coll: from 1890s. *Free Lance*, 22 Nov. 1902, 'And male wall-flowers sitting out at dances | Will reckon up their matrimonial chances.'

wallop; occ. **wallup.** A clumsily ponderous, noisily brusque or violent movement of the body; a lurching: coll and dial.: 1820, Scott. Ex the v., 1. 2. A resounding, esp. if severe, blow: coll (—1823).

wallop, occ. **wallup,** v.i. To move with noisy and ponderous clumsiness; to lurch, flounder, or plunge: dial. (early C.18) >, ca 1815, coll (Scott, 1820: cf. n., 1). Ex *wallop*, to gallop; the word is echoic. 2. v.i., to dangle, to flap or flop about: recorded by O.E.D. in 1822, but prob. in fairly gen. coll use as early as 1780: see WALLOP IN A TETHER. 3. v.t., to belabour, thrash: dial. (—1825) >, in 1830s, coll. 4. Hence, fig., to get the better of: coll: from ca 1860. Meredith, 1865.

wallop, go (down). To fall noisily and heavily: coll and dial.: mid-C.19–20.

wallop (or wallup) in a tether or tow. To be hanged: Scots coll: from ca 1780; slightly ob. Burns, 1785: cf. WALLOP, v., 2.

walloper. One who belabours or drubs; that with which he does it – e.g. stick or cudgel: coll: from ca 1820. Ex WALLOP, v., 3. 2. A dancer: itinerant entertainers': late C.19–20. Perhaps influenced by It. *galoppo*, a lively dance, and *galoppare*, to gallop, and *galoppatore*, a galloper.

walloping, n. and adj., to WALLOP, v.: coll. cf. WALLOPER. 2. Also as adv., though it may be merely a reinforcing adj., as in Hyne, 1903, 'I came upon a walloping great stone.'

wallup, see WALLOP, **n. and v.**

wally (pron. *wolly*); **shock-a-lolly.** Cockney terms (quite distinct one from the other) for cucumber pickled in brine, the second term being rare: from ca 1880.

Wallyford. 'The usual run on a wet whole school-day' (about 3½ miles): Loretto coll: late C.19–20.

walnut, shoulder. To enlist as a soldier: coll: 1838, D. Jerrold; †by 1900. cf. BROWN BESS.

walnut-shell. A very light carriage: 1810 (O.E.D.): ob. cf. *cockle-shell* (boat).

Walter Joyce. Voice: rhyming s.: since ca 1880. (G. R. Sims used it in a Dagonet Ballad published in the *Referee* of 7 Nov. 1887.)

Waltham's calf, as wise as. Very foolish: coll: ca 1520–1830. Skelton. Perhaps suggested by *the wise men of Gotham*, who 'dragged the pond because the moon had fallen into it' (Charles Kingsley).

waltz; esp. **waltz hither and thither, (a)round** or **about.** To move in light or sprightly or nimble fashion; to buzz round or fuss about: from ca 1870: resp. coll and s.

waltz, do a (or the). To slide or skid: Cockney: late C.19–20.

walzing Matilda. Carrying one's swag: Australian: from ca 1890. A jocularity.

wamble; C.18–20, **womble.** A rolling, or a feeling of uneasiness or nausea, in the stomach: C.17–20: S.E. until mid-C.18, then coll and dial. As coll, ob. except in *the wombles*, a sensation of nausea. Ex *wamble*, to feel nausea. 2. Hence, milk fever: coll and dial.: C.18–20; ob. 3. A rolling or staggering movement or gait, esp. in *(up)on the wamble*, staggering, wobbly or wobbling: coll (ob.) and dial.: from ca 1820. Ex *wamble*, v.i. to roll about as one walks.

wamble- (or, C.18, **womble-)cropped** or **-stomached.** Sick at the stomach: resp. mid-C.16–20, but in C.19–20 only U.S. and until mid-C.18, S.E.; C.16–?, so prob. not late enough to be eligible. See WAMBLE, 1; cf.:

wamblety- (or **womblety-)cropped.** Suffering, in the stomach, the ill effects of a debauch: late C.17–early 19. A variant of preceding.

wames thegither, nail twa. To coït: Scots: C.17(?)–20. Lit., *wame*, belly.

wan-horse chaise. A one-horsed chaise: a Hyde Park Corner joke, ca 1820–30. Bee, 1823.

wander. To lead astray; fig., to confuse, bewilder: coll: from mid-1890s.

wander! Go away!: ca 1880–1905. Ware, who classifies it as street s.

wangle, v.t. To arrange to suit oneself; contrive or obtain with sly cunning, insidiously or illicitly; to manipulate, to FAKE: printers' s. (—1888). Possibly ex dial. *wangle*, to shake; perhaps ex *waggle*.

wank, see WHANK.

wanker. A bloater: Felsted School: 1892, *Felstedian*, Oct.; ibid., June 1897, 'He sniffs, 'eugh, wankers again.' Ex STINKER, 4 (via *stwanker*).

want an apron. To be out of work: workmen's (—1909); ob. Ware, 'The apron off'.

want doing, it will; it wants or **wanted doing.** It will, does, or did need doing: mid-C.16–20: S.E. until late C.19, then coll. 'Seton Merriman', 1898, 'Roden is a scoundrel . . . and wants thumping.'

want in; want out. To wish to enter; to wish to go out: from ca 1840: coll of Scotland, Northern Ireland, and U.S.

want to know all the ins and outs of a duck's bum. To be extremely inquisitive; esp. of one desirous of arriving at the underlying explanation: low: late C.19–20.

want to piss like a dressmaker. A Cockney figure of speech for urgent need, perhaps originating in sweated-labour days: late C. 19–20.

wanted. A wanted person (whether advertised for in the Situations Vacant, or sought by the police): coll: 1793, W. Roberts, 'I design to publish a list of Wanteds, solely for the use of your Paper.' In the police sense, the adj. app. arises ca 1810, the comparatively rare n., 1903.

***wap.** To copulate (gen. v.i.): c.: C.17–early 19. Ex *wap (down)*, to throw (down) violently: cf. KNOCK, to coït with (a woman). Whence, *wappened*, deflowered, wanton. cf. WAP-APACE. 2. See WHOP, v.

***wap-apace, mort.** A woman experienced in copulation: c.: late C.17–early 19. See WAP and cf. the c.p. *if she won't wap for a win, let her trine for a make*, 'If she won't Lie with a Man for a Penny, let her Hang for a Half-penny,' B.E.: same period.

wap-John. A gentleman's coachman: sporting: ca 1825–50.

wapper, see WHOPPER. **wapping,** see WHOPPING.

***wapping-dell, -mort.** A whore: c.: C.17–18.

war-caperer. A privateer: naval coll: (?) C.18–early 19.

war-cry. A mixture of *stout* and *mild* ale: taverns': 1882–ca 86. Ware derives it from the *War Cry*, the periodical of the Salvation Army, which 'spoke stoutly and ever [?] used mild terms'.

war-hat or **-pot.** A spiked helmet: military (—1904); ob. by 1915.

war-paint. One's best or official clothes, with jewels, decorations, etc.: coll: 1859, H. Kingsley, 'Old Lady E— in her war-paint and feathers'. Ex lit. sense. 2. Hence, make-up: theatrical: late C.19–20.

warbler. A singer who, for pay, liquor, or other benefit, goes to, and sings at meetings: low: from ca 1820; ob.

ware skins, quoth Grubber, when he flung the louse into the fire. A semi-proverbial c.p. of ca 1670–1770. Ray, 1678; Fuller, 1732 (*Grub* for *Grubber*, *shins* for *skins*).

warehouse. A fashionable pawn shop: Society (—1904); ob. Whence:

warehouse, v. To pawn (an article): Society (—1904); ob. cf. n. Perhaps ex: to put in prison: 1881, *Punch*, 12 Feb. cf. JUG, V.

warm. An act of warming, a becoming warm: mid-C.18–20: S.E. until mid-C.19, then coll. Esp. in *get* or *have a warm, give a warm.*

warm, v. To thrash: s. (—1811) and dial. (—1824) >, by 1850, coll. Also *warm one's jacket*: cf. DUST ONE'S JACKET. 2. Hence, to berate, *call over the* COALS: coll: from ca 1870. cf. the semi-c.p. *I'll warm yer*, a vague Cockney threat.

warm, adj. Rich: from ca 1570: S.E. until late C.18, then coll. Ex *warm*, comfortably established or settled. 2. Of an account or bill: exorbitant. Coll: from ca 1890; ob.

warm as they make them. Sexually loose: coll (—1909). cf.:

warm bit. Such a woman: low: 1880; slightly ob. cf.:

warm corner. 'A nook where birds are found in plenty', Ware, who by *birds* means harlots: sporting and Society (—1909). Punning S.E. sense.

warm flannel. Mixed spirits served hot: public-house (—1823); †by 1900. cf. HOT FLANNEL.

warm member or **'un.** A whore; a whoremonger: low: mid-C.19–20; ob. Ex *warm*, amorous, prone to sexual desire and practice. 2. (Only **w. m.**) A very energetic, pushful person: ca 1895, *Keep it Dark* (a music-hall song), 'Dr Kenealy, that popular bloke, | That extremely warm member, the member for Stoke.'

warm-sided. (A ship, a fort) mounting heavy batteries: naval coll (—1904). Because such a ship can supply a warm reception.

warm sun, out of God's blessing into the, see OUT OF . . .

warm the wax of one's ear. To box a person's ear: low: ca 1860–1915. An elaboration of *warm one's jacket* (see WARM, V.).

warm with, adj. and n. (Spirits) warmed with hot water and sweetened with sugar: coll: 1840, T. A. Trollope, the n.; 1836, Dickens, the adj. Contrast COLD WITHOUT.

warming-pan. A female bed-fellow: from the Restoration; ob. Esp. *a Scotch warming-pan.* 2. A large, old-fashioned watch, properly of gold (a silver one being a *frying-pan*): late C.17–20; very ob. Ex size: cf. TURNIP. 3. A locum tenens, esp. among the clergy: from mid-1840s; slightly ob. The abbr. *W.P.* is rare for any person other than 'a clergyman holding a living under a bond of resignation', F. & H.: clerical (—1864). Now only historical, the practice having been made illegal.

warming the bell. Having one's relief turned out early: nautical: late C.19–20. Bowen. (The bell that sounds the hours.)

***warp.** The criminal confederate who watches: c.: late C.16–early 17. Greene. ?*watch* corrupted.

warrab. A barrow: back s. (—1859).

warrant you, I or **I'll.** I'll be bound: coll: late C.18–20.

***warren.** A brothel; a boarding-school: c. > low s.: late C.17–early 19. Jocular. cf. CUNNY-WARREN. 2. 'He that is Security for Goods taken up, on Credit, by Extravagant young Gentlemen', B.E.: c.: C.17–18. Dekker. By sense-perversion – or perhaps merely, as the O.E.D. holds, by misapprehension, of *warren*, a variant of *warrant*.

warrigal. A worthless man: Australian bush-slang (—1898). Ex Aboriginal for 'wild' (orig. 'a dog'). 2. Hence the adj., wild: Australian: late C.19–20.

wars, have been in the. To show signs of injury, marks of ill or hard usage: coll: 1850, Scoresby. Ex a veteran soldier's scars.

wart. A youthful subaltern: 1894, 'J. S. Winter': s.

Warwicks. (At cards) sixes: Regular Army: late C.19–20. The Warwickshire Regiment used to be the 6th Foot.

wash. An act of 'washing': printers' (—1841). cf. v., 2. 2. A fictitious sale of securities (by simple transference, therefore to the brokers' profit): Stock Exchange (—1891). cf. v., 3. 3. School tea or coffee: Durham School (—1904). Because of its weakness. 4. Nonsense; drivelling sentiment: from ca 1905. Perhaps orig. Harrovian.

wash, v. To bear testing or investigation; prove to be genuine: coll: 1849, C. Brontë, 'That willn't wash, Miss.' 'As good fabrics and fast dyes stand the operation of washing', F. & H. 2. To punish, to RAG (a fellow workman for falsehood or misconduct) by banging type-cases on his desk, or (among tailors) by swearing and cursing loudly: printers' s. (—1841) >, by 1900, gen. craftsmen's. Savage's *Dict. of Printing*. Presumably ex the notion of purification. 3. To do or practise 'wash' as in n., 2: Stock Exchange: as v.t., app. unrecorded before 1895, but as v.i. implied in the vbl n. as in: 1870, Medbery, *Men and Mysteries of Wall Street*, 'Brokers had become fearful of forced quotations. Washing had become a constant trick before the panic, and bids were now closely scrutinised.' Perhaps ex *one hand washes the other*; perhaps ex *take in one another's washing*.

wash, it'll all come out in the. It will be discovered eventually; hence, never mind – it doesn't matter!: c.p. from ca 1902.

wash and brush-up tuppence. A c.p. uttered by the host when one was about to wash one's hands in a friend's house: ca 1885–1915.

wash-boards. White facings on the early uniforms: naval: early C.19–early 20.

wash one's face in an ale-clout. To take a glass of ale: coll: ca 1540–90. 'Proverbs' Heywood. Ex putting one's face far into the jug, etc.

wash one's or **the head without soap.** To scold a person: coll: ca 1580–1620. Barnaby Rich, 1581.

wash one's ivories or **neck.** To drink: low: 1823, Moncrieff (*ivories*); *neck* (—1904). On the †*wash one's brain, head*, etc., to drink wine; 'ivories' being teeth. cf. *sluice one's ivories* (*Punch*, 1882) and SLUICE ONE'S BOLT.

wash-out. A failure (thing or person); a disappointment or 'sell'; a cancellation: used in the Boer War (J. Milne, *The Epistles of Atkins*, 1902). Perhaps ex *w.-o.*, a gap or hole caused by violent erosion, but much more prob. ex: 2. In shooting, a shot right off the target: military: app. from ca 1850, if not earlier. Ex painting out of shots on the old iron targets by the application of paint or, gen., some kind of wash.

wash-pot. A hat: universities': ca 1880–1910. Ex the shape.

washer-dona. A washerwoman: low London: from ca 1860; ob.

washical. What do you call it?: illiterate: ca 1550–1600. Still, *Gammer Gurton's Needle*. Perhaps ex *what shall I call it?*

washing, n. Ex WASH, v., 2, 3: resp. 1825, 1870 (both earlier than v.).

***washman.** A beggar with sham sores: c. of ca 1550–80. Awdelay, 1561. Prob. because the sores will wash out.

wasp. A venereally diseased harlot: ca 1785–1850. Grose, 2nd ed., '... Who like a wasp carries a sting in her tail.'

waste, cut to. To apportion (time) wastefully: sporting: 1863; very ob. Ex tailoring sense, 'to cut (cloth) in a wasteful manner'.

waste, house of. 'A tavern or alehouse where idle people waste both their time and money', Grose, 1st ed.: literary coll: ca 1780–1850. cf.:

waste-butt. A publican: coll (—1823); †by 1890. 2. An eating-house: jocular c. of ca 1880–1915.

waste of ready. Esp. gambling: Oxford University: ca 1820–50. i.e. READY, cash.

Wat; occ. **wat.** A hare: late C.15–20: coll till C.19, then dial. A familiar use of the proper name: cf. NEDDY for a donkey.

***watch, his (her, my, etc.).** Himself, etc.: c.: ca 1530–1690. Copland, ca 1530; Harman; Dekker. cf. *his* NIBS; WATCH AND SEALS; and perhaps DIAL (face), for semantics.

watch, Paddy's, see PADDYWACK.

watch and seals. A sheep's head and pluck: low (—1860); ob. But earlier as *watch, chain and seals*: 1811, *Lex. Bal.*

watch-dropper. One who uses a cheap watch in a version of the ring-dropping game: Australian: late C.19–20.

watch my smoke! Just you watch me!; you won't see me for dust!: a nautical coll that is virtually a c.p.: late C.19–20. Ex the smoke of a departing steamer.

watch on – stop on. Watch-and-watch or

a double turn of duty (eight hours instead of four): naval coll: late C.19–20.

watch out, v.i. To be on one's guard; to look out: U.S. coll (1880s), anglicized ca 1905.

watcher. A person set to watch a *dress-lodger* (q.v.): low: from 1860s. Greenwood, *The Seven Curses of London*, 1869. 2. One spying for bribery: electioneering coll (—1909).

watchie or **-y.** A watchman: coll: ca 1810–40.

***watchmaker.** Gen. pl. 'The idle and dissolute, who live in Calmet's-buildings, Oxford-street': c. (—1839); †by 1880. cf.:

***watchmaker (in a crowd).** A thief who specializes in stealing watches: c.: mid-C. 19–20. Prob. ex preceding entry.

water. Boating, aquatics: Westminster School coll (—1881). Pascoe, *Our Public Schools.* 2. Additional nominal capital created by 'watering' (see the v., 2): U.S. coll (1883) anglicized ca 1885; by 1900, S.E. *St James's Gazette*, 14 June 1888.

water, v. To entertain freely, to 'treat': ca 1740–60. Water costing nothing. 2. To increase (the nominal capital of a company) by the creation of shares that, though they rank for interest, carry no corresponding capital: U.S. coll (1870) anglicized ca 1880; by 1900, S.E. Occ. *water up* (1899). i.e. weaken by dilution.

water, between wind and, see SHOOT BETWEEN WIND AND WATER. **water, hot,** see HOT WATER.

water, make a hole in the. To drown oneself suicidally: 1853, Dickens.

water, over the, see OVER THE WATER.

water, the malt's above the. He is drunk: semi-proverbial c.p.: ca 1670–1770. cf. the proverbial and equivalent *the malt is above wheat with him* (mid-C.16–early 19).

water-barrel, see WATER-BUTT.

water bewitched. Very thin beer: coll (—1678); ob. Ray. (Unholy influence at work.) 2. Hence, weak tea: coll: C.18–20. Swift; Grose; Dana. 3. Occ. of both (1699, T. Brown); †by 1800. 4. Occ. of punch (1785), occ. of coffee: dial. (—1825) and (as for broth) coll. In all four senses, occ. *water damaged*: C.19–20 coll; ob.

water-bobby. A water-policeman: lower classes' (—1887).

water bonse. A cry-baby: Cockney: late C.19–20; ob. J. W. Horsley, *I Remember*, 1912.

water-bottle. A total abstainer: lower class urban (—1909). Ware. cf. WATER-WAGGON.

water-box, -course, -gap, -gate. The female pudend: low: C.19–20. cf. WATER-ENGINE; WATERWORKS.

water-bruiser(, gen. rare old). A tough (and old, hard-working) shore-man: nautical (—1909).

water-butt, occ. **-barrel.** The stomach: lower classes': late C.19–20.

water-can, Jupiter Pluvius has got out (or **put,** or **turned, on) his.** A coll c.p. for 'It is raining'; applied mostly to a heavy shower. From ca 1870; ob.

water-colours, wife in, see WIFE IN ...

water-course, see WATER-BOX.

water-dog. A Norfolk dumpling: from ca 1860; ob.

water-dona. A washerwoman: low urban, esp. London (—1909). Also WASHER-DONA.

water-engine. 'The urinary organs male or female', F. & H.: low: late C.19–20.

water-funk. A person shy of water: schools': 1899, Kipling; now coll.

water-gap, -gate, see WATER-BOX.

water in one's shoes. A source of discomfort or annoyance: C.18 coll. North, ca 1740, 'They caressed his lordship ... and talked about a time to dine with him; all which (as they say) was "water in his shoes".' Abbr. *as welcome as water in one's shoes*, very unwelcome: mid-C.17–20: coll till late C.19, then dial. only. cf. S.E. *welcome as snow in harvest* and contrast *welcome as the eighteen trumpeters*, very welcome indeed: coll: ca 1610–40.

water-mill. The female pudend: low (—1811).

water of life. Gin: from early 1820s; ob. App. on Fr. *eau-de-vie* (brandy).

water one's nag, see NAG, WATER ONE'S.

water one's plants. To weep: jocular coll: ca 1540–1880; in C.19, dial. only. Udall; Lyly; Swift. On S.E. *water one's eyes*, to weep.

***water-pad.** A thief operating on the water, esp. on the Thames: c.: late C.17–early 19.

water-scriger. 'A doctor who prescribes from inspecting the water of his patients', Grose, 3rd ed.: late C.18–early 19. A *scriger* is presumably *scrier* (or *scryer*), one who (de)scries. cf. †S.E. *water-caster*.

***water-sneak, the.** 'Robbing ships ... on a ... river or canal, ... generally in the night': c. of ca 1810–90. Vaux. 2. Hence, *water-sneaksman*, such a thief: c. (—1823); †by 1900.

water the dragon, see DRAGON. **water up,** see WATER, v., 2.

water-waggon, on the. Teetotal for the time being: U.S. (—1904), anglicized by 1908.

Waterings, the 'Spital stands too nigh St Thomas à. Copious weeping sometimes produces an illness: proverbial c.p.: late C. 16–17. This place, near a brook used for watering horses, stood near London, and on the Canterbury road, and, as it was the Surrey execution-ground until the C.17, the name is often employed allusively in C.16–mid-17, as in Jonson, 1630, 'He may perhaps take a degree at Tyburn . . ., come to read a lecture | Upon Aquinas at St Thomas à Waterings, | And so go forth a laureat in hemp circle.'

waterloo (or W.). A halfpenny: London: ca 1830–75. Ex the former toll (a halfpenny) paid to cross Waterloo Bridge.

Waterloo day. Pay-day: military: from ca 1870; ob. cf. BALACLAVA DAY.

waterman; (not in 2) watersman. A blue silk handkerchief: c. or low (—1839); very ob. Because worn (light or dark) by friends of Cambridge and Oxford at the time of the boat-race. 2. An artist in water-colours: 1888: s.

waters. Paintings in water-colour: coll: 1909, *Daily Chronicle*, 4 June.

waters, watch one's. 'To keep a strict watch on any one's actions', Grose, 3rd ed.: coll: late C.18–early 19. Ex *urinospection.*

water's man, watersman, see WATERMAN, 1.

water's wet, the. A jocular c.p., addressed to someone trying the temperature of the water with his toes: late C.19–20.

waterworks. The urinary organs: low: mid-C.19–20; ob.

waterworks, turn on the. To weep: coll: mid-C.19–20. Ex jocular S.E. *waterworks*, tears. cf.:

watery-headed. 'Apt to shed tears', Grose, 1st ed.: ca 1780–1890.

waun(d)s! An illiterate form of WOUNDS!: C.17–18.

wave a flag of defiance. To be drunk: low: ca 1870–1915.

wavy in the syls. Imperfect in one's lines: theatrical (—1904); ob. Lit., unsteady in one's syllables.

wavy rule, make. To be rolling-drunk: printers': from ca 1880. Ex the rule or line that waves thus: ∼∼∼.

wax, n. A rage; esp. *be in a wax*: 1854, 'Cuthbert Bede', 'I used to rush out in a fearful state of wax.' ?ex *waxy* (s.v. WAXINESS), or, as W. suggests, 'evolved ex archaic to *wax wroth*'.

***wax, v.** To have one's eye on; to spy out: c.: from ca 1890. Clarence Rook, *The Hooligan Nights*, 1899, CRACKSMAN *loquitur*: 'There's a 'ouse I've 'ad waxed for about a week.'

wax, close as. Extremely mean or secretive: 1772, Cumberland: coll >, by 1850, S.E. Because impermeable to water and perhaps because sticky.

wax, lad or man of, see LAD O' WAX.

wax, my cock of. A shoemakers' term of address (—1823); ob.

wax, nose of; gen. **have a,** to be very impressionable: London (—1823); †by 1900.

wax (something) up. To mess up: low Cockney: 1899, C. Rook, *The Hooligan Nights*, '"Didn't I never tell you", he said, "how we waxed things up for that butcher . . . ?"'

waxed, be (well). To be (well-)known: tailors': from ca 1870. 'So-and-so has been well *waxed*, i.e. We know all about him,' F. & H.

waxiness; waxy. Angriness, proneness to rage; angry: resp. (—)1904 and 1853, Dickens. Although *waxy* is recorded earlier than *wax*, the latter may have arisen the earlier; yet, semantically, the transition from lit. *waxy* to fig. *waxy* is not difficult: cf. STICKY, adj. 2. *waxy* is also a nickname for a cobbler: 1851, Mayhew. Ex his frequent use of wax. 3. Short for:

waxy-homey. An actor who blacks up with burnt cork; a 'nigger-minstrel': theatrical: from ca 1880. The (cf. OMEE) *homey* = a man. 2. Any minstrel: partly Parlary: late C.19–20. Perhaps because he uses wax on the instrument he plays.

'way. Away: coll (U.S., 1866) anglicized late in C.19. Esp. in *'way back*.

way, be up her. To be *in coitu* with a woman: low: late C.19–20. Always in an innuendo: punning neighbourhood.

way, in a. In a state of vexation, anxiety, distress: dial. and coll: mid-C.19–20.

way, in a kind or **sort of.** A modifying tag: coll: mid-C.19–20.

way, in the (e.g. fish). Engaged in (e.g. the fish-trade): lower classes' coll: late C.19–20; slightly ob. 'He's in the grocery way.' Now, *way* is gen. replaced by *line*.

way, pretty Fanny's, see PRETTY FANNY'S WAY.

way, that; gen. **a little, or rather, that way.** 'Approximating to that condition': coll: mid-C.17–20. Dickens, 1837, '"I'm afraid you're wet." "Yes, I am a little that way."' cf.:

way, the other; gen. all, quite, very much the other way. Diverging from a stated condition: coll: mid-C.19–20. Trollope, 1858, 'They are patterns of excellence. I am all the other way.' cf. WAY, THAT.

way down, all the, see ALL . . .

***way for, be out of the.** To be in hiding from police wishing to arrest one for (such and such an offence): c. (—1812); ob.

way of (being, doing, etc.), by. In the habit of, giving oneself out as, having a reputation for, or making an attempt (esp. if persistent or habitual) at (being or doing something): coll: 1824, Miss Ferrier, 'The Colonel was by way of introducing him into the fashionable circles'; 1891, *Saturday Review*, 18 July, concerning *by way of being*, '. . . And this with an implied disclaimer of precise knowledge or warranty on the speaker's part'.

way of all flesh(, gone the). Dead: lower and lower middle classes' coll (—1909). Contrast with the S.E. sense as in 'Erewhon' Butler's novel.

way of life, the. Prostitution: low London: 1818, *The London Guide*.

ways about it (or that), no two. (There can be) no doubt of it: U.S. coll (1818: Thornton) anglicized ca 1840; by 1880, S.E.

ways for Sunday, look both or **nine** or **two,** see LOOK NINE . . .

we uns. We: low coll: late C.19–20. Orig. U.S.; cf. YOU UNS.

weak. Tea: coffee-stalls' and low coffee-houses': from ca 1860.

weak brother, sister. An unreliable person: religious s.: mid-C.19–20.

weak in the arm(, it's). A public-house c.p. (—1909; ob.) applied to a 'half-pint drawn in a pint pot'. Ware.

weanie, -y, see **weenie.**

weapon. Penis; esp. among workmen: late C.19–20. It has the best of precedents: see my *Shakespeare's Bawdy*.

wear a head. To be intelligent; to possess much sense: ca 1815–60. *Boxiana*, III, 1821.

wear a revolver-pocket. To carry a revolver: low: ca 1880–1914.

wear-arse. A one-horse chaise: ca 1785–1830. Ex jolting.

***wear it.** To be under 'the stigma of having turned a *nose*', Egan's Grose: c. of ca 1820–50. Ex:

***wear it upon.** To inform against, try to best (a person): c.: ca 1810–50. *It* is the nose: for semantics, cf. NOSE, a spy.

wear the bands. To be hungry: low s.: ca 1810–40.

***wear the broad arrow.** To be a convict: c. (—1909).

wear the head large. To have a headache from alcoholic excess: lower-middle class (—1909).

wear the leek. To be Welsh: lower and lower-middle classes' (—1909): coll rather than s.

weary. Drunk: proletarian: ca 1870–1920. cf. dial. *weary*, sickly, feeble. (Curiously enough, the Old High Ger. *wuorag*, drunk, is cognate with A.-S. *werig*.)

weasel, be bit by a barn. To be drunk: ca 1670–1700.

weather, go up the; go down the wind. To prosper; to fare ill, be unfortunate: coll: resp. early C.17 and C.17–20; in mid-C.19–20, dial. only. Breton, both; Pepys; Berthelson, 1754; Scott, 1827. Also, *go down the weather*, to become bankrupt: C.17.

weather-breeder. A fine, bright day: nautical (—1887).

weather-peeper. (One's) best eye; a good look-out: nautical (—1909).

weather-scupper. 'It is an old joke at sea', writes Clark Russell, in 1883, 'to advise a greenhorn to get a handspike and hold it down hard in the weather-scuppers to steady the ship's wild motions.' Coll; slightly ob.

weaver's bullock. A sprat: East-Londoners' (—1880); ob. cf. TWO-EYED STEAK.

***weaving.** 'A notorious card-sharping trick, done by keeping certain cards on the knee, or between the knee and the underside of the table, and using them when required by changing them for the cards held in the hand', H., 3rd ed.: 1803 (O.E.D.); prob. c. > gaming s.

weaving leather aprons. An evasive c.p. reply to an inquiry as to what one has been doing lately: low (—1864). H., 3rd ed., '*See* newspaper reports of the trial for the gold robberies on the South-Western Railway.' Similarly, to an inquiry as to one's vocation, *I'm a doll's-eye weaver*: low (—1874). Equivalent c.p. replies are *making a trundle for a goose's eye* or *a whim-wham to bridle a goose*: low (—1864).

web-foot. (pl. **web-foots.**) A dweller in the

Fens: coll nickname: from ca 1760; very ob.

wedding. The 'emptying a necessary house': London (—1785); †by 1850.

wedding, you have been to an Irish. A c.p. addressed to one who has a black eye: ca 1785–1850. Grose, 2nd ed., '... Where black eyes are given instead of favours'.

***wedge.** Silver, whether money or plate, but mostly the latter; hence, occ., money in general: c. (—1725). Grose, 2nd ed., '*Wedge*. Silver plate, because melted by the receivers of stolen goods into wedges'. 2. *the wedge*, the last student in the classical tripos list: Cambridge University (—1852): coll > j. Also the *wooden wedge*. On †WOODEN SPOON, the last man in the mathematical tripos, + T. H. *Wedgwood*, who, last in the classical tripos in 1824, was to be a famous etymologist. 3. A Jew: back s. (—1859). Lit., *wej*.

***wedge, flash the.** To FENCE the SWAG (3), to deposit stolen goods with a receiver: c.: mid-C.19–20. See WEDGE, 1.

***wedge-feeder.** A silver spoon: c. (—1812). See WEDGE, 1. cf.:

***wedge-hunter.** A thief specializing in silver plate and watches: c.: mid-C.19–20. See WEDGE, 1.

***wedge-lobb.** A silver snuff-box: c. (—1812). See WEDGE, 1. cf.:

***wedge-yack.** A silver watch: c.: mid-C. 19–20; slightly ob. Ex WEDGE, 1.

***wedges.** Cards cut narrower at one end than at the other, for the purpose of cheating: card-sharpers' c.: from ca 1880. (J. N. Maskelyne, *Sharps and Flats*, 1894.)

wee-jee; wejee. A chimney-pot: ca 1864–90. Etymology obscure; the word may be a perversion of WHEEZE, a GAG (n., 3, 4), though this origin fits only sense 3, which is perhaps the earliest. 2. Hence, a (chimney-pot) hat: late C.19–early 20: lower classes', as are senses 1 and 3. 3. Anything extremely good of its kind; esp. a clever invention: from ca 1860; ob. 4. Hence, a hand pump: N.E. Coast colliers': late C.19–20.

Wee-Wee, see WI-WI.

wee-wee. A urination; esp. *do a wee-wee*: nursery coll: late C.19–20. Perhaps ex *water* on PEE.

weed. A cigar, a cheroot: coll: 1847, Albert Smith. Ex *weed*, tobacco. 2. A hat-band: low (—1864); †by 1920. Perhaps ex the vague resemblance of its shape to that of a large cigar. 3. A leggy, ill-compacted, and otherwise inferior horse: 1845; Lever, 1859. Perhaps ex WEEDY, 1. 4. Hence, a thin, delicate, weak and soon-tiring person: 1869, A. L. Smith.

***weed,** v. To pilfer or steal part of, or a small amount from : c. (—1811); slightly ob. Hence, *weed a* LOB, steal small sums from a till; *weed a* SWAG (3), to abstract part of the spoils unknown to one's pals and before the division of that spoil. Ex *weed*, to remove the weeds from. Cf.:

***weeding dues are concerned.** An underworld c.p. (ca 1810–80) used when a process of 'weeding' (see WEED, v.) has been applied.

weedy. (Of horses, dogs) lank, leggy, loose-limbed, weak and spiritless: coll: 1800, *Sporting Magazine*; 1854, Surtees, 'He rode a weedy chestnut.' Lit., like a weed. 2. Hence (of persons), lanky and anaemic; weakly: coll: 1852, Surtees.

week, inside of a. From Monday to Saturday: coll: C.19–20.

week, knock into the middle of next. To knock out (lit. or fig.) completely: pugilistic s. (1821, Moncrieff) >, by 1900, gen. coll.

week, parson's, see PARSON'S WEEK.

week, when two Sundays come in a; also (in) the week of four Fridays. Never: coll: C.19–20; mid-C.18–early 19. H. Brooke, 1760. cf. SUNDAYS COME TOGETHER ...

week than a fortnight, rather keep you (for) a. A c.p. formula directed at a hearty eater: since ca 1870.

week-ender. A week-end mistress: from 1880s: coll. Ex lit. sense. 2. A week-end holiday: likewise low coll: from ca 1895. Oxford *-er*.

weekly-accompts. The small square white patches on the front, to right and left, of a middy's collar: ca 1805–70.

week's (or month's) end, an attack of the. Lack of funds, according as one is paid one's wages or salary every week or every month: jocular coll: ca 1890–1915.

weenie, weeny; weany (rare) **and weny** (C. 18 dial. only). Tiny: dial. (—1790) >, by 1830, coll. Ex *wee* on TEENY. 2. (Rarely other than *weenie!*) A telegraph clerks' warning that an inspector is coming: late C.19–20. ?ex *warning*.

weep and wail. A begging tale: rhyming s., often shortened to *weep*: from ca 1870.

weep Irish. To shed crocodile tears; feign sorrow: coll: late C.16–mid-18. Fuller, 1650; Mrs Centlivre. Ex the copious lamentations of the Irish at a keening.

weeper. (Gen. pl.) A long and flowing sidewhisker, such as was 'sported' by 'Lord Dundreary' in the play *Our Ameri-*

can Cousin: coll: from ca 1860; ob. Ex *Dundreary weepers* (1859), later PICCADILLY WEEPERS. E. A. Sothern played the leading part; in 1858, the piece was hardly a success; in 1859–60, it was the rage. 2. (Gen. pl.) An eye: late C.19–20. cf. PEEPER.

Weeping Cross (or weeping cross), return (home) or, more gen., **come home by.** To fail badly; be grievously disappointed: from early 1560s; ob. Bullein (1564), Gosson, Lyly, playwright Heywood, Grose, Spurgeon, William Morris (1884). Ex a place-name employed allusively.

weeping willow. A pillow: rhyming s.: mid-C.19–20.

weeze, see WHEEZE, n. **weezy,** see WHEEZY.

weigh, see WEIGHT, LET HIM . . .

weigh, under. Under way: erroneous: from ca 1780. Ex *weigh anchor*.

weigh forty, see WEIGHT, LET HIM . . .

weigh in. To start; in imperative, go ahead!: sporting: late C.19–20. (P. G. Wodehouse, *The Pothunters*, 1902.) cf.:

weigh in with. To produce (something additional), introduce (something extra or unexpected): coll: 1885, *Daily News*, Nov., 'The journal "weighs in" with a prismatic Christmas number.' Ex a jockey *weighing in*, being weighed after a race.

***weigh out.** To give in full (one's share): c.: late C.19–20. Ware cites the *People*, 6 Jan. 1895, and derives the term from 'the distribution of stolen plate melted down to avoid identification'.

weigh up. To appraise: coll: 1894 (O.E.D.). cf. *weigh*, to consider.

weighing the thumb, n. Cheating in weight by sticking down the scale with the thumb: low (—1896). Ware.

weight, let him alone till he weighs his. A police c.p. to the effect that a criminal is not yet worth arresting, for his offences are so small that no reward attaches to them, whereas a capital crime will produce a big reward: ca 1810–40. Vaux, who notes that *weigh forty* (of a criminal) is to carry a £40 reward for capture.

welch, welcher, welching. For these three terms see WELSH. **welcome, and,** see AND WELCOME. **welcome as water in one's shoes; w. as the eighteen trumpeters,** see WATER IN . . .

well, v. To pocket: low (—1860); virtually †. H., 5th ed., 'Any one of fair income and miserly habits is said to "*well it*".' Lit., to put as into a well: cf. *put down South*. But imm. ex: 2. c. *well*, to put (money) in the bank: 1845, in '*No. 747*'. Ex: 3. *well* = WELL, PUT IN THE: c.: from ca 1810; slightly ob. (In late C.19–20, low s.)

well, adj. Satisfactory, very good, capital: Society coll: ca 1860–1900.

***well, put (one) in the garden or the.** To defraud (an accomplice) of part of the booty forming his share: c. (—1812); ob. cf. WELL, v. A variant is *put* (one) *in a hole*. A person down a well is at a disadvantage. 2. Hence, to inconvenience or get the better of: mid-C.19–20; ob. (except . . . *hole*).

well-breeched. Rich: s.: ca 1810–60.

well down in the pickle. (Of a ship) heavily loaded: sailing ships' coll: late C. 19–20. The *pickle* is 'the briny'.

well firmed. 'Perfect in the "business" and words': theatrical: from ca 1870.

well fucked and far from home, see BARNEY'S BULL.

well-hung. (Of a man) large of genitals: low (—1823); ob.

well in. An Australian variant of *well off*, well to do: 1891, 'Rolf Boldrewood': coll.

well put-on. (Of a male person) well turned-out; well-dressed: lower-class Glasgow coll: from ca 1890.

well-sinking. Making money: Anglo-Indian: late C.18–20; ob. Ex excavating for treasure.

well to live, be. To be rather drunk: coll: ca 1610–1700; then dial. Ray, 1678. Ex *well to live* (*in the world*), prosperous.

well under. Drunk: Australian: from ca 1916. Prob. an abbr. of *well under water*.

'well, well,' quoth she, 'many wells, many buckets.' A proverb-c.p. of C.16 (Heywood, 1546).

welly. Almost: C.17–20: coll till C.18, then dial. Ex *well nigh*.

welsh, welsher, welshing; in C.19, often **-ch-.** To swindle (one) out of the money one has laid as a bet (orig. and properly at a race-course); he who does this; the doing: racing s. >, ca 1880, coll >, ca 1900, S.E.: resp. 1857, 1860, 1857. Perhaps ex the old nursery-rhyme, *Taffy was a Welshman, Taffy was a thief*: W.; my *Words!*

Welsh bait. A foodless, drinkless rest given a horse at the top of a hill: coll: C. 17–20; very ob. T. Powell, 1603. Ex *bait*, food. For pejorative *Welsh*, see *Words!* at 'Offensive Nationality'.

Welsh Camp. The late C.17–early 18 nickname for a field between Lamb's

Conduit and Gray's Inn Lane, where, late in C.17, 'the Mob got together in great numbers, doing great mischief,' B.E.

Welsh comb. The thumb and four fingers: coll or s.: ca 1785–1840. Contrast JEW'S HARP.

Welsh cricket. A louse: late C.16–early 17. Greene. 2. A tailor: ?C.17. Prob. via PRICK-LOUSE (a tailor).

Welsh ejectment. By unroofing the tenant's house: ca 1810–50.

Welsh fiddle. The itch: late C.17–early 19. Also SCOTCH FIDDLE. cf. the synonymous dial. *Welshman's hug*.

Welsh goat. A Welshman: nickname: mid-C.18–mid-19. Lord Hailes, 1770.

Welsh mile, long and narrow, – like a. Either thus or as *like ... mile*, applied to anything so shaped: coll: ca 1785–1850. Ex *Welsh mile*, a mile unconscionably long: cf. the equally S.E. *Welsh acre*.

Welsh parsley. Hemp; a halter: coll or s.: ca 1620–50. Fletcher.

Welsh rabbit. This dish, incorrectly spelt *W. rarebit* (Grose, 1785), is recorded by that eccentric poet John Byron in 1725: orig. coll, it had, by 1820, > S.E. Even in C.18 (see Grose) the Welsh were reputed to be fervid cheese-fanciers. For semantics, cf. BOMBAY DUCK.

Welshman's hose, turn (something) **like a; make a W. h. of; make like a W. h.** To suit the meaning of (a word, etc.) to one's purpose: coll: ca 1520–1600. Skelton.

welsher, see WELSH.

Welshie, -hy, Nickname for a Welsh person: coll: C.19–20. Ex adj.

***welt.** Only in B.E.'s '*rum-boozing-Welts*, bunches of Grapes': late C.17–18 c. The phrase, lit., = excellent drinking bunches (or, perhaps, grape-bunches). 2. A blow: coll: late C.19–20. Ex the S.E. *welt*, to flog.

welter. Anything unusually big or heavy of its kind: dial. (—1865) >, by ca 1890, coll. Kipling, 1899, 'He gave us eight cuts apiece – welters – for takin' unheard-of liberties with a new master.' Ex *welt*, to thrash.

wench, from Old English *wencel*, a child, is facetious and university-witted where once it was serious but used only in addressing an inferior (as in Shakespeare's *The Tempest*, 'Well demanded, wench') and where, orig., it means simply a girl: the facetious usage is coll, whereas the other two are S.E. A similar degradation of words is seen in *damsel* and the French *maîtresse*, *amie*, and *fille*.

were you born in a barn? A c.p., addressed to one who leaves a door open: mostly in Britain and in Canada, yet hardly rare in Australia and New Zealand: mid-C.19–20, and probably much earlier.

wesket, weskit. A waistcoat: coll bordering on sol.: C.19 (?earlier)–20.

west, go, see GO WEST.

west-central or **West Central. A** water-closet: London (—1860); ob. Ex *W.C.*, the London district, and *w.-c.*, a water-closet.

Westminster Abbey (often merely *Westminster*). Shabby: rhyming s.: from ca 1880.

Westminster brougham, see WHITECHAPEL BROUGHAM.

Westminster wedding. 'A Whore and a Rogue Married together', B.E.: low London: late C.17–early 19. Prob. ex the late C.16–early 19 proverb, *Who goes to Westminster for a wife, to Paul's for a man, or to Smithfield for a horse, may meet with a whore, a knave and a jade* (Apperson).

Westo. A Devon or Cornish ship or seaman: nautical coll: late C.19–20. Ex *West Country*.

Westphalia. The backside: trade (—1890); ob. Ex Westphalia hams.

westward for smelts, see SMELTS.

wet; occ. **whet** (Ned Ward). Liquor: late C.17–20. Ex HEAVY WET, or next sense. 2. A drink: coll: 1703, Steele; 1879, Brunlees Patterson, *Life in the Ranks*, 'Many are the ... devices ... to obtain a wet or reviver, first thing in the morning'. 3. A dull, stupid, futile or incompetent person: from late C.19–20: Public Schools'. See the adj., 7.

wet, v.t. See WET THE OTHER EYE and WHISTLE. 2. v.i., drink a glass of liquor: coll: ca 1780–1910.

wet, adj. Showing the influence, or characteristic, of drink; connected with liquor: coll: 1592, Nashe; 1805, *wet bargain*; 1848 Thackeray, 'A *wet night*', a frequent phrase. O.E.D.; F. & H., where also *wet goods*, liquor, and WET HAND or *wet 'un*, a toper – both of late C.19–20. 2. Hence, having drunk liquor; somewhat intoxicated: coll: 1704, Prior; 1834, Coleridge, 'Some men are like musical glasses; – to produce their finest tones, you must keep them wet.' Perhaps ex: 3. Prone to drink too much: coll: from 1690s. cf. the n., 2. 4. (Of a Quaker) not very strict: 1700, T. Brown. Hence, of other denominations: likewise coll: from ca 1830; ob. Perhaps suggested by Grose's (2nd ed.) *wet parson*, a parson given to liquor; indeed, this sense links with sense 3, for B.E. has '*Wet-Quaker*, a Drunkard of that Sect'. See WET QUAKER. 5. 'Of women when secreting letch-water': low coll: mid-C.18 (?earlier)–20. 'Burlesque Homer' Bridges, addressing cheap or inferior harlots, 'Or else in midnight cellars ply | For twopence wet and twopence dry'. cf. WET BOTTOM. 6. See WET 'UN. 7. SOFT silly, dull, stupid, DUD: late C.19–20: Public Schools'. Perhaps ex sense 2; perhaps ex WET GOOSE. (Rarely of things, occ. of occasions.)

wet, heavy, see HEAVY WET.

wet, twopenny. A drink costing twopence: C.19–early 20. See WET, n., 2.

wet all her self, to have. Of a Grand Banks fishing schooner 'when she has filled up with fish, used all the salt ... brought out, and turns for home': fishermen's coll: late C.19–20. Bowen.

wet arse and no fish, a. A fruitless quest or errand: coll: late C.19–20.

wet as a shag, see SHAG, WET AS A.

wet bob, see BOB.

wet bottom, get a; do a wet 'un; do, have or perform a bottom-wetter. (Of women) to have sexual intercourse: low coll, s., s.: C.19–20. cf.:

wet dream. An amorous dream accompanied by sexual emission: coll: C.19–20 – and prob. from at least a century earlier. 2. Hence, a dull, stupid person: Public Schools': late C.19–20.

wet goose. A poor simple fellow: rural: mid-C.19–20. cf. WET, adj., 6.

wet hand. A drunkard: coll (—1904). See WET, adj., 1.

wet ha'porth. A person entirely insignificant or physically weedy: North Country: late C.19–20.

wet one. A loose breaking of wind: proletarian: late C.19–20.

wet one's commission. Celebrate one's promotion alcoholically. Naval coll: from ca 1700. Shadwell, *The Fair Quaker of Deal*, 1710.

wet one's mouth, weasand, or, gen., **whistle,** see WHISTLE, n.

wet Quaker. 'A man who pretends to be religious, and is a dram drinker on the sly', H., 2nd ed.: ca 1860–1910. Ex WET, adj., 3, 4.

wet the baby's head. To celebrate a child's birth: since ca 1870.

wet the (or one's) neck. To be a drunkard: low: ca 1820–50. 2. To take a drink of liquor: *Boxiana* IV, 1824.

wet the other (1745) **or t'other** (1840) **eye.** To take one glass of liquor after another: s. >, by 1850, coll; ob.

wet-thee-through. Gin: low: ca 1820–60.

wet trance, in a. Bemused; abstracted: low: late C.19–20. Ex WET DREAM.

wet triangle, the. The North Sea: political coll: from ca 1905; ob.

wet 'un. See WET, adj., 1, and WET BOTTOM. 2. A diseased beast: slaughterers' (—1864). cf. WET, adj., 6, and WET GOOSE. 2. (Gen. pl.) A tear (*lacrima*): low: from ca 1870; ob.

Wetherall (or -ell) in command, General. A military c.p. applied to inclement weather's preventing a parade: from ca 1880; extremely ob.

wetter. A wetting, soaking, by rain: coll: 1884.

Wewi, see WI-WI.

whack; in C.19, occ. **wack.** A heavy, smart, resounding blow: from 1730s: dial. >, ca 1830, coll. Barham, Mayhew. Prob. echoic. 2. Hence, its sound: coll: mid-C.19–20. Thackeray. 3. A (full) share: c. (—1785) >, by 1800, s. >, by 1880, coll. Grose, 1st ed. Esp. in *take* (1830), *get* or *have one's whack*, and in *go whacks* (—1874). ?ex the sound of the physical division of booty. 4. Hence, fig.: mid-C.19–20. Walch, 1890, 'My word! he did more than his whack.' 5. See WHACK-UP, n. 6. See WHACK AT. 7. A pickpocket: Anglo-Irish c.: C.19.

whack, v. To strike with sharp, resounding vigour: coll and dial.: 1721, Ramsay. Also as v.i., esp. in *whack away* (mid-C.19–20), as in the *Daily Telegraph*, 21 Feb. 1886, 'The Flannigans and the Murphys paid no heed to him, but whacked away at each other with increasing vigour.' Prob. echoic; cf. the n., 1. 2. Hence, to defeat in a contest or rivalry: coll: from 1870s. 3. To bring, get, place, put, etc., esp. in a vigorous or violent manner: from C.17 'teens: dial. >, in late C.19, coll, as in Kipling, 1897, 'They whacked up a match.' Prob. ex sense 1. 4. To share or divide: c. (—1812) >, by 1860, s. >, by 1910, coll. Vaux, who spells it *wack*; J. Greenwood, 1888, *A Converted Burglar*, 'The sound, old-fashioned principle of "sharing the danger and whacking the swag".' Also *whack up*. Ex the n., 3. 5. See WHACK IT UP.

whack! An interjection politely = 'You lie!': printers': from ca 1870. Ex WHACKER.

whack, adv. With a 'whack' (n., 1): coll: 1812, H. and J. Smith. cf.:

whack at, have or take a. To attempt; to attack: coll: U.S (1891) >, before 1904, anglicized. Perhaps ex tree-felling.

whack it up, v.i. To coït: low: mid-C.19–20; ?ob. cf. WHACK, v., 1, 3, 4.

whack-up. A division of accounts: coll: 1885. Elaborating WHACK, n., 3.

whack up, v. See WHACK, v., 3 and 4: coll: from ca 1880. 2. See WHACK IT UP.

whacked; whacked to the wide (sc. *world*). Utterly exhausted: late C.19–20. Ex WHACK, v., 1.

whacker. Anything unusually large; esp. a THUMPING lie (cf. WHOPPER): coll and dial. (—1825). *Sporting Times,* in 1828, describes certain fences as whackers, as T. Hughes does caught fish in 1861. Ex WHACK, v., 1.

whacking. A thrashing: coll (—1859). Ex WHACK, v., 1. 2. Hence, a defeat in a contest: coll: late C.19–20. 3. A division or sharing: from ca 1850: (low) s.>, by 1900, coll. Ex WHACK, v., 4.

whacking, adj. Unusually big, large, fine, or strong: coll: 1806, Davis, *The Post-Captain.* Often *whacking great,* occ. *w. big.* Ex WHACK, v., 1; cf. WHACKER.

whacks, go, see WHACK, n., 3.

whacky. A person acting ridiculously or fooling about: tailors': from the 1880s. Ex Yorkshire dial. *whacky,* a dolt.

whale. A codfish: Cheltenham College: late C.19–20. Because a large fish. 2. A sardine: Royal Military Academy: from ca 1870. Because so small. 3. (Always in pl.) Anchovies on toast: rather proletarian: from ca 1880. cf. sense 2.

whale, go ahead like a. To forge ahead; act, speak, write vigorously: coll: from 1890s. Ex the majesty of a whale's movements.

whale, old, see OLD WHALE.

whale!, very like a. A c.p. applied to an improbability, esp. a preposterous assertion: from 1850s; ob. H., 1st ed.; in 2nd ed., *very like a whale in a tea-cup.* Ex Polonius's phrase when, in III, ii, 392–8, he is doing his best to approve Hamlet's similes.

whale on . . ., a. Greatly liking, having a great capacity for, expert at: coll: 1893, Justin McCarthy, 'He was not . . . a whale on geography'; rather ob. Ex the whale's large size. Also, occ., *whale at* and *for.*

whaler. A SUNDOWNER: Australian coll: ca 1890–1910. *Sydney Morning Herald,* 8 Aug. 1893, 'The nomad, the whaler, it is who will find the new order hostile to his vested interest of doing nothing.' (He didn't.) Ex his cruising about. He who travels up and down the banks of the Murrumbidgee River is a *Murrumbidgee whaler,* which some authorities consider to be the ironic original.

whales, see WHALE, 3.

whang. A 'whanging' sound or blow: dial. (—1824) and, from ca 1860, coll. Ex:

whang, v.t. To strike heavily and resoundingly: coll: C.19–20. Ex dial. (C.17–20). Echoic. 2. v.i. (of, e.g., a drum), to sound (as) under a blow: coll: 1875, Kinglake.

Whanger; Cod-Whanger. (Also in lower case.) A Newfoundland fish-curer: nautical: from ca 1810 or earlier. Precisely why?

whank; loosely **wank.** v.i., to masturbate: low: late C.19–20. Also *whank off.*

whanker (loosely **wanker**). A masturbator: low: late C.19–20. Ex WHANK.

whap, whapper, see WHOP; WHOPPER.

wharf-rat. A thief prowling about wharves: mid-C.19–20. Perhaps orig. U.S.

what! (more precisely **what?!**); occ. **eh what!** A questioning interjection or expletive, gen. at the end of a phrase or sentence: coll: 1785, Mme D'Arblay, '[George III] said, "What? what?" – meaning . . . "it is not possible. Do you think it is? – what?" '; not very gen. before mid-C.19. 2. Abbr. WHAT CHEER: Cockney: from ca 1880.

what, but. But that; that . . . not: coll: from ca 1560. Googe, 1563 (see quotation at WHAT'S WHAT); Arthur Murphy, 1753, 'There hardly arose an Incident, but what our Fellow-Traveller would repeat twenty or thirty Verses in a Breath.' Almost always with actual or implied negative; in late C.19–20, mostly *not but what.* 2. Except what; which (occ. who) . . . not: as in Charlotte Smith's 'Not one of these insinuations but what gathered something from malevolence', 1796.

what!, I('ll) tell you, as prefacing a proposal, is coll: mid-C.19–20. 'I'll tell you what, we'll row down,' 1872. Ex the same phrase as = let me tell you!

what?, or, used as a final, yet wholly indefinite, alternative in a disjunctive question: mid-C.19–20; mostly, and in conversation nearly always, coll. Edward FitzGerald, in a letter, 1842, 'Have you supposed me dead or what?'

what a life! A c.p. expressive of disgust: late C.19–20.

what a tail our cat's got! A lower classes' c.p. directed at a girl (or woman) flaunting in a new dress, the rear skirt of which she swings haughtily: mid-C.19–20; ob.

what about a (small) spot?; what is it?; what'll you have? see HOW WILL YOU HAVE IT?

what all, ... and I don't know. And various others unknown or unmentioned; in addition, all sorts of things: coll: mid-C. 19–20. Dickens, 1859, 'There's ... and ... and I dunno what all.' cf. WHO ALL.

what-call; what-call-ye-him. A variant (resp. early C.17, late C.15–early 17) of the *em* part of WHAT-D'YE-CALL-'EM (etc.).

what cheer! A coll greeting: C.18–20: lower classes'. James Isham, *Observations and Notes*, 1743.

what cheese. An occ. variant (ca 1890–1910) of HARD CHEESE.

what did Gladstone say in (e.g.) 1885? A political hecklers' c.p. of late C.19–20. For the most part, merely obstructive.

what do *you* think? 'What is your general opinion of things?': a middle-class c.p. introduced in 1882 by a comic singer. 2. See THINK, WHAT DO YOU?

what do you want? – I am on it. A military c.p. reproach to a constant grumbler: late C.19–20.

what-d'ye-call-'em (occ. um), her, him, it; less frequently **what-do-you-call-'em,** etc. A phrase connoting some thing or person forgotten, considered trivial or not to be named, or unknown by name: coll: C.17–20. Shakespeare, *As You Like It*, 'Good even, good Master What-ye-call't; how do you, sir' – a late C.16–17 variant; Ned Ward; Smollett; Dibdin; Dickens; etc., etc. The Shakespearian form has an alternative in *-you-* and a mid-C.19–20 variant: *what-you-may-call-it* (Dickens, 1848). cf. Cotton's satirical 'Where once your what shal's cal'ums – rot um! It makes me mad I have forgot um.'

what (e.g., do you do that) **for?; what for** (by itself)? Why: coll: mid-C.19–20.

what for, give one. To punish or hurt severely: from ca 1870. Du Maurier, 1894, 'Svengâli got "what for".' Ex *what for?*, why: 'to respond to [one's] remonstrant *what for?* by further assault', W. 2. Hence, to reprimand, reprove severely: from 1890s.

what ho! As greeting or expletive, it is (orig. low) coll: mid-C.19–20. Ballantyne, 1864, 'What ho! Coleman ... have you actually acquired the art of sleeping on a donkey?'; 1898, 'Pomes' Marshall, 'Where 'e let me in for drinks all round, and as I'd but a bob, I thought, "What ho! 'ow am *I* a-going on?" ' (cf. the semi-coll WHAT CHEER!) Orig., a S.E. formula to attract a person's attention.

what ho! she bumps. A satirical c.p. applied to 'any display of vigour – especially feminine': London (1899). Ware derives it from 'a boating adventure.... A popular song made this term more popular.'

what is there in it for me? What do I get out of it?: c.p.: late C.19–20.

what next, and next? A c.p. contemptuous of audacious assertion: ca 1820–1905.

what-o(h). A variant of WHAT HO!

what Paddy gave the drum. A sound thrashing: orig. (ca 1845), Irish military >, ca 1900, gen.; ob.

what price ...? see PRICE, WHAT.

what say? What do you think?; what do you say to the idea, plan, what not?: Cockney c.p.: from ca 1880. W. Pett Ridge, *Minor Dialogues*, 1895; Edwin Pugh, *Harry the Cockney*, 1912.

what the Connaught men shot at. Nothing: Anglo-Irish (—1883).

what the fucking hell! A very common lower-class expletive: mid-C.19–20.

what will you liq? What will you drink: middle-class c.p. of ca 1905–15. Ware. Ex *liquor*; punning LICK.

what-ye-call-it; what-you-may-call-it, see WHAT-D'YE-CALL-'EM.

what you can't carry you must drag! A nautical c.p. applied to clipper ships carrying too much canvas: late C.19–20; ob.

whatcher! A nautical variation of (S.E.) WHAT CHEER!

what's-his-name, -her-, -its-, -your-; whatse-name. Resp. for a man (or boy; loosely, thing), woman (or girl), thing, person addressed, or ambiguously for any of the first three of these, with name unknown, forgotten, to-be-avoided, or hardly worth mentioning: coll: resp. late C.17–20 (Dryden), C.19–20 (Scott), from 1830s (Dickens), mid-C.18–20 (Foote), and mid-C.19–20 (Reade); app. Marryat, in 1829, is the first to apply *what's-his-name* to a thing; *what's-their-names* (G. A. Stevens) is rare. cf. WHAT-D'YE-CALL-'EM.

what's-o'clock, know, see O'CLOCK.

what's-o-names. An exceedingly illiterate form (—1887) of WHAT'S-HIS-NAME.

what's the dynamite?; what's the lyddite? What's the ROW?: Society: resp. 1890–9 and 1899–1900. The former ex dynamiters' activities in the 1880s, the latter ex the Boer War.

what's the mat? What's the matter?: Public Schools': from ca 1880; ob.

what's the odds? What difference does it make?: coll: late C.19–20.

what's the time? A juvenile c.p., dating from the 1880s and directed, from cover, at a man whose feet are wide-spread as he walks. The posture is variously described as *ten to two* (o'clock), (*a*) *quarter to three* and (*a*) *quarter to one.*

what's this blown in? Whom have we here?: contemptuous c.p. from ca 1905.

what's what; orig. and gen. preceded by **know, tell w. w.** belonging to C.17–20, **understand w. w.** to C.18–20, and **guess, show** and **perceive w. w.** to C.19–20. 'To have [etc.] knowledge, taste, judgment, or experience; to be wide-awake . . ., equal to any emergency, FLY' F. & H.: coll: C.15–20. e.g. Barnaby Googe, 1563, 'Our wits be not so base, | But what we know as well as you | What's what in every case.' See also O'CLOCK and TIME OF DAY.

what's yer fighting weight; . . . Gladstone weight? I'm your man if you want to fight!: Cockney: ca 1883–1914; 1885–6 (ex politics).

what's-yer-name. An illiterate form (—1887) of WHAT'S-HIS-NAME. cf. WHAT'S-O-NAMES.

what's your poll today? How much have you earned today?: printers': from ca 1870. Ware, 'From numbers on a statement of wages'.

what's yours? see HOW WILL YOU HAVE IT?

whatsename, whatsiname; occ. **whatsername.** Slurred WHAT'S-HIS-NAME (etc.).

whatsomever. Whatever, whatsoever (adjj.): C.15–20: S.E. until C.19, then dial. and increasingly illiterate coll.

whatty; occ. **whaty.** A 'what-did-you-say': low: late C.18–mid-19. Ware derives it from an anecdote about George III, whose English was not perfect.

wheadle; wheedle. As a wheedler, prob. S.E. from the beginning, but as a sharper it is prob. c.: ca 1670–1830, but ob. by 1720. Wycherley, 1673; B.E. Whence, *cut a wheadle* (*wheedle*), 'to Decoy, by Fawning and Insinuation', B.E.: c. of ca 1690–1830. Ex:

wheadle, whed(d)le (C.17), **wheedle,** v. In its usual senses, it may, orig., have been s., ex Ger. *wedeln.* Blount records it in 1661. 2. WHIDDLE in its c. sense, of which it is a variant: c. of ca 1700–20.

wheedle the tire off a cart- (or cart's) wheel, can or be able to. To be extremely persuasive: non-aristocratic coll (—1887).

wheel. A 5-shilling piece: C.19. Extant in New Zealand, however, for the sum of five shillings. 2. A dollar: late C.18–early 19. Tufts. Both, however, mainly as CART-WHEEL.

wheel, v. To bicycle: coll: 1884. cf. WHEELER. 2. (Of the police) to convey (a DRUNK, 2) in a cab to the police station: low (—1909).

wheel, grease the. To coït: low: mid-C.19–20; ob.

wheel, keep a cart on the. To keep an affair alive: semi-proverbial coll (—1887); ob. In Yorkshire dial. it is *keep cart on wheels.*

wheel-band in the nick. 'Regular Drinking over the left Thumb', B.E.: drinking: late C.17–early 19. Contrast and cf. SUPERNACULUM.

wheel 'em up. To bowl: cricket coll: late C.19–20. cf. TRUNDLE.

wheel-man or **-woman**; or as one word. A cyclist: coll: 1874 (*-man*); ob. Also, for the former, KNIGHT OF THE *wheel*; very ob. coll. cf. WHEELER.

***wheel-of-life.** The treadmill: prison c.: ca 1870–1910. cf. EVERLASTING STAIRCASE.

wheelbarrow. A bullock waggon laden with supplies for convicts working in the bush or country: Australian: ca 1820–70.

wheelbarrow, as drunk as a. Exceedingly drunk: coll: ca 1670–1750. Cotton, 1675, where he gives the occ. variant . . . *as a drum* (not, as F. & H. has it, *as . . . the drum of a w.*).

wheelbarrow, go to heaven in a. To go to hell: coll: ca 1615–90. T. Adams, 1618. 'In the painted glass at Fairford, Gloucestershire, the devil is represented as wheeling off a scolding wife in a barrow,' F. & H.

wheelbarrows is a coll synonym of TRAVELLING PIQUET: mid-C.19–20.

wheeled, adj. or ppl. Conveyed in a cab: lower classes': late C.19–early 20.

wheeler. A cyclist: coll (—1887).

wheeling, n., see WHEEL, v. **wheelman,** see WHEEL-MAN.

wheels, grease the. To advance money for a particular purpose: coll. 1809, Malkin. Thus ensuring easier running.

wheeze. A theatrical GAG (4), esp. if frequently repeated: circus and theatrical s.: from early 1860s. Ex the act of wheezing: perhaps because clowns often affect a wheezy enunciation. In Lancashire dial., as early as 1873 is the sense, 'an amusing saying; a humorous anecdote'. 2. Hence, a catch phrase, esp. if often repeated; an 'antiquated fabrication' (W.): 1890, *Spectator*, 17 May. 3. Hence, a frequently employed trick or DODGE: from ca 1895. Like sense 2, s.

***wheeze,** v. To give information, to peach: c. (—1904). cf. n.

wheeze, crack a. 'To originate (or adapt) a smart saying at a "psychological" moment', F. & H.: from ca 1895; rather ob. See WHEEZE, n., 2.

wheezer. A phonograph: music-halls': 1897–8.

whelk. The female pudend: proletarian Cockney: from ca 1860. Anatomical. Whence the innuendo-c.p., comically threatening, *I'll have your whelk*: 1870s. 2. A sluggish fellow: Cockney: late C.19–20. cf. Fr. *mollusque*.

whelp. To be delivered of a child: low coll: late C.19–20; ob. cf. PUP (v.), which is far from being ob.

when. Lo!; see now!; then, mark you!: coll (—1887). Baumann, 'When up comes a chap with a basket on his shoulder'.

when!, say. Orig. a c.p. with 'dovetail' *Bob!* (or *bob!*). *Modern Society*, 6 June 1889, ' "Say when," said Bonko . . . commencing to pour out the spirit into my glass. "Bob!" replied I.'

when Adam was an oakum-boy in Chatham Dockyard. Indefinitely long ago: ca 1860–1900.

when hens make holy-water. Never: coll c.p.: C.17. See the quotation at NEVER-MASS.

where are you (a-)going to (– can't yer)?! Stop pushing!: low London: from ca 1880.

where did you get that hat? see HAT?, WHERE DID YOU GET THAT.

where did you get the Rossa? i.e. the borrowed plumes: 1885 only. Ex a New York police trial.

where Maggie wore the beads, see MAGGIE. . .

where the chicken got the axe, see CHICKEN . . .

where the monkey shoves (occ. puts) its nuts!, you can shove (occ. put) it or them. A c.p. retort to one who refuses to give a share or hand over something: low: late C.19–20. cf. STICK IT, 2, and:

where the sergeant put the pudding!, put it. 'You know what you can do with it': low c.p.: late C.19–20.

whereas, follow a. To become a bankrupt: commercial and legal: late C.18–mid-19. Grose, 2nd ed., where also the synonymous *march in the rear of a whereas*.

where's the war? A c.p. directed at a street wrangle: London streets': 1900–1901. Ex scattered fighting in Boer War.

wherewith; wherewithal. The NECESSARY (2), esp. money: resp. rare coll and dial.; coll, as first in Malkin, 1809, 'How the devil does she mean that I should get the wherewithal? . . . Does she take me for . . . treasurer to a charity?'

wherret. A blow: s.: 1703, Ned Ward.

wherry-go-nimble. Diarrhoea: lower class (—1904). If *wherry* is not a corruption of JERRY(-GO-NIMBLE), it is probably a Cockneyism for 'very'.

whet, see WET, n. **whet one's whistle,** see WHISTLE, n.

Whetstone(s) Park deer or **mutton.** A 'Whetstone whore': London fast life: ca 1670–1700. Ex *Whetstones Park*, 'a Lane betwixt Holborn and Lincolns-Inn-fields, fam'd for a Nest of Wenches, now depark'd', B.E.: the district was notorious at least as early as 1668. See esp. Grose, P.

whetting-corn(e). The female pudend: ?C. 17–mid-19. Lit., grindstone.

whew, the. Sir H. Maxwell, in *Notes and Queries*, 10 Dec. 1901, says that in C.15 the influenza was app. known as 'the Whew' just as, in C.20, it is known as 'the Flue'. (Mainly Scots) coll and gen. spelt *Quhew*.

whiblin. This C.17 word (unrecorded later than 1652) is explained by F. & H. as a eunuch and, in c., a sword; by the O.E.D. as perhaps THINGUMBOB. Perhaps ex *whibble* + *quiblin*.

***whid; whidd(e).** A word: c. (—1567); slightly ob. See phrases. Either ex A.-S. *cwide*, speech, as the O.E.D. suggests, or a perversion of *word*. 2. In pl, speech: c.: contemporaneous with 1. See phrases. 3. In singular, speech: c. (—1823) >, by 1860, low. Bee, ' "Hold your whid," is to stow magging'. 4. 'A word too much', H., 3rd ed.: mid-C.19–20; ob.: s.; closely linked with dial. *whid*, a lie, an exaggerated story. 5. Hence, in c. verging on low s., talk, PATTER, jocular speech, jest: likewise only in pl. Hindley, 1876, *The Life of a Cheap Jack*, 'The whids we used to crack over them.' 6. A broken-winded horse: horse-copers' c.: mid-C.19–20. '*No. 747*'. i.e. a ROARER.

***whid**, v.i. To talk cant: Scots c. (—1823). Ex n., 1, 2.

***whid, crack a**, see CRACK A WHID.

***whid, cut the** (Ainsworth); **cut whids.** To talk, speak: c.: resp. C.19 (rare) and mid-C.16–20. Mostly implied, as to *cut whids*, in *cut bene* WHIDS and *c. queer w.*

whidd, whidde, see WHID, n. and v.

***whiddle**; in C.18, occ. **wheadle (wheedle)**, q.v. at v., 2, and **whidel, whidle**, and **widdle**; see also **whittle.** v.i. and v.t. To tell; to peach, to impeach: from the Restoration; ob. The O.E.D. records it at 1661; not gen., I think, before the 1680s or 90s. Perhaps ex WHID, n., 1, 2. 2. Hence, to enter into a parley, esp. if nefarious: c. (—1725). 3. Hence, to 'hesitate with many words', H., 1st ed.: mid-C.19–20; ob. Either c. or low s.: cf. WHID, n., 3. 4. See OLIVER.

***whiddle beef.** To cry 'thief!': c.: late C. 17–mid-19. cf. *cry* BEEF.

***whiddler.** An informer to the police; a blabber of the gang's secrets: c.: late C.17–20; ob. Ex WHIDDLE, v., 1.

***whids, cut.** See WHID, CUT THE. Mostly in *cut bene* (or *bien*) *whids*, to speak fairly, kindly or courteously, and *cut queer whids*, to speak roughly or discourteously, or to use blasphemous or obscene language: c.: resp. (?only) C.19 and rare (1821, Scott; 1861, Reade, 'Thou cuttest whids'); and, both BENE and QUEER, mid-C.16–mid-19. See WHID, n., 1 and 2.

whiff, v.i. To smell unpleasantly: 1899, Kipling. Ex corresponding n.

whiffing, vbl n. Catching a mackerel with hooked line and a bright object: nautical: C.19. Perhaps ex *whiff*, a flat-fish, etc.

whifflegig. Trifling: coll: 1830, H. Lee, 'Whiffle-gig word-snappers'. Presumably ex (mainly dial.) *whiffle*, to talk idly. cf. WHIFFMAGIG.

whiffler. One who examines candidates for degrees: Oxford and Cambridge: ca 1785–1830. Ex the official sense.

whiffles. 'A relaxation of the scrotum', Grose, 1st ed.: ca 1780–1850.

whiffmagig. A trifler; a shifty or contemptible fellow: 1871, Meredith; ob. A variant of *whiffler* in these senses. cf. WHIFFLEGIG.

Whig. An irresolute person; a turncoat: middle classes': 1860–9. Ex the Whigs' temporizing at that period.

Whigland. Scotland: ca 1680–1830. Because the 'home' of Whigs. Whence *Whiglander* (gen. pl), a Scotsman: same period.

while, quite a. A considerable time: coll: C.20. Elinor Glyn, 1905.

whiles, when not deliberately archaic and 'literary', is, in late C.19–20, considered a somewhat illiterate coll for *while*.

whim; **whim-wham.** The female pudend: C.18; C.18–20, ob. Lit., fanciful object.

***whiners.** Prayers, esp. in CHOP *the whiners*, to pray: c.: C.18–20; ob. *A New Canting Dict.*, 1725; 1830, Bulwer Lytton. Ex *whine*, v.: lit., therefore, words that whine. 2. Whence, speech, GAB, esp. in CHOP *whiners*, to talk: low: mid-C.19–20; ob. *Punch*, 31 Jan. 1857.

whinn. An occ. C.19 spelling of WIN, n., 1.

whiny. Given to whining: New Zealand coll: late C.19–20.

whip. Money subscribed by a mess for additional wine: naval and military coll (—1864). Ex *whip*, now *whip-round* (1874), an appeal for money. 2. A compositor quick at his work: printing (—1890). cf. *whip*, a coachman.

whip, v. To drink quickly; gen. *whip off*; occ. in late C.17–18, *whip up*. C.17–20; slightly ob. Deloney. 2. Gen. *whip through.* To pierce with a sword, esp. in *whip through the lungs*: late C.17–mid-19. 3. To SWINDLE (v.t.): c.: late C.19–20; ob. cf. military FLOG (3) and *whip off.*

whip, drink or **lick on the.** To receive a thrashing: coll: C.15–16. Resp. Gascoigne and *The Towneley Mysteries.*

whip, old; gen. **the old whip.** One's ship; nautical (—1887). Perhaps rhyming.

whip-arse. A schoolmaster: coll: C.17. Cotgrave. cf. BUM-BRUSHER.

whip-belly; **w.-b. vengeance.** Thin weak liquor, esp. SWIPES: C.19–20; C.18–19. Swift; Grose, 2nd ed., with variant *pinch-gut vengeance*; Halliwell (*whip-belly*).

whip-cat. Drunken: s. or coll: late C.16–early 17. See WHIP THE CAT, 1. 2. n., a tailor, as in WHIP THE CAT, 4: 1851, Mayhew.

whip-handle. An insignificant little man: Scots: C.17. Urquhart.

whip-her-jenny, see WHIPPERGINNIE.

***whip-jack.** A beggar pretending to be a distressed, esp. a shipwrecked, sailor: c.: ca 1550–1880. Ponet, ca 1550. The semantics are not very clear. cf. TURNPIKE-SAILOR.

whip off. See WHIP, v., 1. B.E. gives *whip off*, to steal, as c.: but surely it is no worse than familiar S.E. cf. WHIP, v., 3.

whip-round, see WHIP, n., 1.

whip-the-cat. An itinerant tailor: mid-C.

19–20: Scots s. >, by 1900, coll. Ex sense 4 of:

whip the cat. To get intoxicated: ca 1580–1820. Implied by Stonyhurst in 1582; Cotgrave, 1611; 'Water-Poet' Taylor, 1630; *Gentleman's Magazine*, 1807. Synonymous with *jerk, shoot, the* CAT. 2. To play a practical joke: late C.17–early 19. 3. To be extremely mean: dial. (—1825) >, ca 1860, s.; ob. 4. To work as an itinerant tailor (hence, carpenter, etc.), by the day, at private houses: dial. (—1825) >, by 1840, s. or, rather, coll. 5. To vomit: low: mid-C.19–20. cf. 1. 6. To idle on Monday: workmen's (—1897). cf. *keep* ST MONDAY. Ex: 7. To idle at any time: workmen's (—1823); ob.

whip the devil or the old gentleman round the post. To achieve illicitly or surreptitiously what can be accomplished honourably or openly: coll: late C.18–20; ob.

whip through; whip up, see WHIP, v., 2 and 1 resp.

whipper-in. The horse that, at any moment of the race, is running last: racing s. (from ca 1890). Ex hunting. F. & H., 1904, gives *whipping-boy* in the same sense.

whipperginnie, or **whip her Ginny** or **whip-her-ginny.** Term of abuse for a woman: late C.16–early 17. One who merits 'whip her, Jinny!'

whipping-boy, see WHIPPER-IN.

whippy. In the game of hide-and-seek, the starting-out point: Australian, esp. children's: late C.19–20. Origin?

***whipster.** 'A sly, cunning fellow' (B. & L.): c.: C.19–early 20. A deviation ex †S.E. *whipster*, a mischievous fellow.

whirligigs; whirlygigs. Testicles: late C. 17–early 19. Ex lit. sense.

whishler. A ring-master: circus: mid-C.19–20. ?ex *whish!* (a warning).

whisk. A whipper-snapper; (often of a servant) 'a little inconsiderable impertinent Fellow', B.E.: ca 1625–1830. Perhaps ex *whisk*, a hair-like appendage.

whisker; in C.17–18, occ. **wisker.** Something excessive, great, very large; esp. a notable lie: 1668, Wilkins. In mid-C.19–20, mainly dial. Ex *whisk*, to move briskly.

whisker, the mother of that was a. A c.p. retort on an improbable story: ca 1850–1900. cf. *the dam of that was a whisker*, the mainly dial. synonym, applied, however, esp. to a big lie: see DAM OF . . .

whisker-bed. The face: 1853, 'Cuthbert Bede', 'His ivories rattled, his nozzle barked, his whisker-bed napped heavily.'

whisker-splitter; in C.18, occ. **wisker-.** A man given to sexual intrigue: ca 1785–1840. cf. the more gen. BEARD-SPLITTER.

whiskerando; occ. **-os.** A man heavily whiskered: jocular coll: from ca 1805; ob. Thackeray, 'The . . . whiskerando of a warrior'. Ex *Whiskerandos*, a character in Sheridan's comedy, *The Critic*, 1779. Hence *whiskerandoed*, (heavily) whiskered: 1838, Southey.

whiskers. A WHISKERANDO; often loosely of any man, as in the jocular greeting, 'Hallo, Whiskers!': mid-C.19–20.

whiskery. (Heavily) whiskered: coll: from ca 1860. Ex WHISKERS.

whiskey-, see WHISKY-.

whiskin. A pander: ca 1630–50. Brome, 1632. cf. PIMP-WHISK(IN).

whisking. (Of persons) briskly moving; lively; smart: coll: from ca 1610; ob. by 1860. Middleton & Dekker, 1611, 'What are your whisking gallants to our husbands'; Carlyle, 1824. Ex *whisk*, to move briskly. 2. Great, very big; excessive: s. (—1673) >, by 1750, coll >, by 1830, dial. cf. WHISKER.

whisky bottle. A Scotch drunkard: Scots (—1909). Ex the typically Scottish drink.

whisky-frisky. Flighty; lightly lively: rare coll: 1782, Miss Burney. cf. WHISKING, 1.

whisky jack; C.19–20, also **whiskey jack;** C.18, **whiskijack;** all three may be hyphenated. 'A popular name for the common grey jay of Canada': Canadian coll verging on S.E.: from ca 1770. Also *whisk(e)y john*, or, as for *whisky jack*, with capitals. The earlier is *whisky john*, a corruption of Red Indian *wiskatjan*. (In all the two-word forms, the second element may be capitalled.)

whisky-stall. (Gen. pl.) A stall-seat at, or near, the end of a row, enabling the occupant to go out for a drink without inconvenience to himself or his neighbours: journalistic: 1883–ca 1914.

whisper. A tip given in secret; esp. '*give the whisper*, . . . to give a quick tip to any one', H., 5th ed., where also *the whisper at the post*, an owner's final instructions to his jockey: racing: from early 1870s.

whisper, v.t. To borrow money from (a person); esp. borrow small sums: from ca 1870; ob. Ex the whisper with which such loans are usually begged.

whisper, angel's; gen. **the a. w.** The call to

defaulters' drill or extra fatigue duty; military: from 1890s. Wyndham, *The Queen's Service*, 1899.

whisper, (in a) pig's, see PIG'S WHISPER.

whisperer. A petty borrower: from ca 1870; ob. Ex WHISPER, V.

whispering syl-slinger. A prompter (*syl* = *syllable*): theatrical: late C.19–20; ob. cf. WAVY IN THE SYLS.

whister-clister, -snefet, -snivet. A cuff on the ear or the side of the head: resp. late C.18–mid-19, then dial.; C.16 (Udall); C. 16 (Palsgrave). Perhaps a reduplication of *whister*, that which 'whists' or puts to silence; even so, *-clister* may pun *clyster*, an enema, while *-snefet*, *-snivet* may be cognate with the vv. *snite*, *snivel*. Perhaps orig. dial., as the Palsgrave locus indicates; certainly dial. are the variants *whister-poop* (C.17–20), *whistersniff* (C.19–20), and *whister-twister* – which last (C.18–19) is certainly a punning reduplication.

whisticaster. A variant of the preceding: *The Night Watch* (II, 338), 1828.

whistle. The mouth or the throat: jocular coll: by itself, C.17–20. Ex *wet* (incorrectly *whet*: C.17–20) *one's whistle*, to take a drink: late C.14–20, likewise jocular coll. Chaucer, in *The Reeve's Tale*, 'So was hir joly whistle wel y-wet'; Walton; Burns; Marryat (*whet*). 2. A flute: late C.19–20. 3. Penis, esp. a child's: domestic: late C.19–20.

whistle and flute. A suit (of clothes): rhyming s.: late C.19–20.

whistle and ride. To work and talk: tailors' (—1890). Presumably ex a rider's whistling as he journeys.

whistle-belly vengeance. Inferior liquor, esp. bad beer: 1861, Hughes, 'Regular whistle-belly vengeance, and no mistake'. cf. WHIP-BELLY (*vengeance*), which prob. suggested *whistle-b. v.*

whistle-drunk. Exceedingly drunk: mid-C. 18. Fielding's *whistled-d.* is prob. a misprint.

whistle for. To expect, seek, try to get, in vain; to fail to obtain, go without; have a very slight chance of obtaining: coll: 1760, C. Johnston, '"Do you not desire to be free?" "Aye! . . . but I may whistle for that wind long enough, before it will blow," which indicates the origin, for sailors have for centuries whistled hopefully when becalmed. 2. Hence, *shall I whistle for it?*, a c.p. that is 'a jocular offer of aid to one long in commencing to urinate', F. & H.: late C.19–20; ob.

whistle in the cage, see SING OUT.

whistle off. To go off, to depart, lightly or, esp., suddenly: coll: from the 1680s (Shadwell); ob. by 1860.

whistle psalms to the taffrail. (Gen. as vbl n.) To give good advice unwanted and unheeded: jocular nautical: coll: late C.19–20.

whistlecup. A drinking-cup fitted with a whistle, the last toper capable of using it receiving it as a prize: public-house coll: from ca 1880. Also, a cup that, on becoming empty, warns the tapster: id.: id.

whistled drunk, see WHISTLE-DRUNK.

***whistler.** A bad farthing: c. of ca 1810–50. Ex the false ring it gives. 2. A ROARER or broken-winded horse: from early 1820s: coll >, by 1890, S.E. 3. An unlicensed vendor of spirits: 1821, Moncrieff; Dickens, 1837; very ob. Ex WHISTLING-SHOP. 4. A chance labourer at the docks: East Londoners': from ca 1880. Ware quotes the *Referee* of 29 March 1885. Ex whistling for work.

Whistler, adj. 'Misty, dreamy, milky, softly opalescent [in] atmosphere – from . . . pictures painted by [this] artist . . . Came to be applied to ethics, aesthetics, and even conversation, where the doctrines enunciated were foggy' (Ware): Society coll: 1880s.

whistling, adj. to WHISTLING-SHOP.

whistling-billy (or **Billy**). A locomotive: (children's) coll: from ca 1870; ob. cf. PUFFING-BILLY.

whistling-breeches. Corduroy trousers: unaristocratic: late C.19–20; ob. Ex the swishing sound that they are apt to make as one moves.

whistling psalms . . . see WHISTLE PSALMS . . .

whistling-shop. A room in the King's Bench Prison where spirits were sold secretly and illicitly: c. of ca 1785–1840. The signal indicative of 'open shop' was a whistle. 2. Hence, an unlicensed dram-shop: (low) s.: 1821, Moncrieff; Dickens, who, in 1837, also has 'whistling gentleman' (see WHISTLER, 3). Very ob.

whit(t), the. A prison: c.: ca 1670–1840. Anon., *A Warening for Housekeepers*, 1676, 'O then they rub us to the whitt'. Ex *Whit(t)*, a nickname for Newgate Prison, perhaps suggested by the *git* of *Newgate* as generally pronounced. 2. (*Whit*) Whitsuntide: coll: late C.19–20.

***white,** n., only in *large* (or *half-bull*) *white*, a half-crown, and *small white*, a shilling: counterfeiters' c. (—1823). 2. See WHITES. 3. A white waistcoat: coll: from ca 1860. *Sessions*, Sept. 1871.

white, adj. Honourable; fair dealing: U.S. s. (—1877), anglicized ca 1885. Ex the self-imputed characteristics of a white man. cf. WHITE MAN. 2. Hence as adv.: U.S. s. (—1900) anglicized ca 1905. e.g. *act white, use* (a person) *white*.

white-apron. A harlot: coll: ca 1590–1760. Satirist Hall; Pope. Ex dress.

white-ash breeze. The breeze caused by rowing: boating (—1904); slightly ob. F. & H., 'Oars are gen. made of white ash.' Imm. ex *white ash*, an oar: coll: mid-C.19–20.

white bottle. A bottle of medicine coloured white: coll among female surgery-habituées: late C.19–20.

white boy. A C.17 term of endearment-reference: coll: cf. WHITE-HEADED BOY.

White Brahmins. Excessively exclusive persons: among Europeans in India: from ca 1880; ob. Ex an extremely exclusive religious sect. Ware. 2. Also, among the educated Indians, the English: coll: from ca 1880; ob.

white broth, spit, see SPIT SIXPENCES.

white choker. A white tie: lower-class: from ca 1860; slightly ob. 2. Hence, a parson: id.: from ca 1890; ob.

white eye. Strong, inferior whisky: military (—1874); ob. Orig. U.S.; so named because 'its potency is believed to turn the eyes round in the sockets, leaving the whites only visible', H.

white face. Gin (the liquor): Australian: ca 1820–80. J. W., *Perils, Pastimes and Pleasures*, 1849.

white feather, show the, see FEATHER, SHOW THE WHITE.

white friar. A speck of white (froth, scum) floating on a (dark-coloured) liquid: from 1720s: coll >, in C.19, dial. Swift, 1729.

white Geordie. A shilling: Ayrshire: 1897, Ochiltree.

white-haired boy is an Australian and New Zealand variant of the next entry: late C.19–20.

white-headed boy; usually my, her (etc.) **w.-h. b.** Favourite; darling: 1820: coll; orig. Irish >, by 1890, fairly gen. Melmoth; Hall Caine. Ex the very fair hair of babies and young children. cf. SNOWY (2) and †S.E. *white* (i.e. favourite) *boy* and *son*.

white horse. (Indicative of) cowardice: Anglo-Irish coll: C.18–20; ob. Ware, 'From the tradition that James II fled from the battle of the Boyne on a white horse'.

white-horsed in, be. To obtain a job through influence: tailors' (—1890). Perhaps ex buying a 'boss' drinks at an inn, (a) white horse being a frequent sign, hence name, of an inn.

white jenny. A foreign-made silver watch: s.: from the 1880s.

white lace, see WHITE RIBBON.

white lapel. A lieutenant: naval: ?ca 1860–1910. Ex a feature of his uniform.

***white lot.** A silver watch and chain: c.: from ca 1860. Ex *white*, for centuries an epithet applied to silver. cf. WHITE WOOL.

white magic. Very beautiful fair women: Society: ca 1875–1905. Ex lit. S.E. sense. 2. The Roman Catholic ritual: Protestants' coll (—1909).

white man. An honourable man: U.S. s. (1865), anglicized ca 1887. Nat Gould, 1898, 'There goes a "white man" if ever there was one . . . That beard [is] the only black thing about him.' See WHITE, adj.; cf. SAHIB.

white man's hansom woman. A coloured mistress: West Indian: mid-C.19–20; ob. Clearly, there is a pun on *hansom cab* and *handsome*.

White Moor. Gen. pl. A Genoese: coll nickname: C.17. Ex a very uncomplimentary proverb recorded by Howell in 1642: too rough on the Moors.

white nigger. A term of contempt, for a white man: Sierra Leone Negroes' coll: from ca 1880. Ware quotes the *Daily News* of 20 June 1883. cf. the American Negroes' *poor white trash*.

white poodle. A rough woolly cloth: tailors': ca 1850–80. Ex poodle's coat.

white port. Some kind of strong liquor, prob. gin (cf. WHITE RIBBON . . .): ca 1750–90. Toldervy, 1756. See the quotation at SLUG, n., 1.

***white prop.** A diamond scarf-pin: c. (—1859). cf. WHITE LOT.

white rabbits! or simply **rabbits!** A South of England greeting on the first day of every month: late (?mid- or even earlier) C.19–20. 'Good luck!'

white ribbon, satin, tape, wine, wool; also **w. lace.** Gin: low: resp. C.19–20; C.19–20; from ca 1720 (*A New Canting Dict.*, 1725); 1820 (Randall's *Diary*); from ca 1780 (Grose, 1st ed.); mid-C.19–20 – occ. merely *lace* or its synonym DRIZ. H., 1st ed., describes *w. satin* and *w. tape* as women's terms, as, also, was *lace*. All are ob.; in fact, *white wine* and *w. wool* did not survive beyond C.19; *white satin* may well endure, however, because of the trade name, *White Satin Gin*. See also at RIBBON (4) and TAPE.

white sergeant. A 'breeches-wearing' wife, esp. and orig. as in the earliest record: Grose, 1st ed., 'A man fetched from the tavern . . . by his wife, is said to be arrested by the white sergeant.' †by 1890 or soon after. Ex the martial bearing of this hardly less formidable 'woman in white'.

***white sheep.** A c. term dating from ca 1880. Clarence Rook, *The Hooligan Nights*, 1899, 'The young man who walks out with [the servant], and takes a sympathetic interest in her employer's affairs, rarely takes a hand in the actual [burglary]. He is known as a "black cap" or a "white sheep" and is usually looked upon as useful in his way, but a bit too soft for the hard grind of the business.'

***white soup.** Silver plate melted down to avoid identification: c. (—1887).

white-stocking day. The days on which sailors' women-folk presented their half-pay notes to the owners: N.E. Coast: late C.19.

***white stuff.** Articles in silver: c.: late C.19–20. cf. RED STUFF.

white swelling, have a. To be big with child: late C.18–mid-19. Ex the medical *white swelling*, a watery tumour. cf. TYMPANY.

white tape, wine, or wool. Gin. See WHITE RIBBON.

***white 'un (or un).** A silver watch: c. (—1874).

white wine, see WHITE RIBBON.

***white wool.** Silver: c.: late C.17–mid-18. cf. WHITE LOT. 2. See WHITE RIBBON.

Whitechapel; w. An upper-cut: pugilistic (—1860); ob. 2. That procedure in tossing coins in which two out of three wins: London (—1864); ob. 3. The murder of a woman: (East) London: ca 1888–90. Ex numerous woman-murders in Whitechapel in 1888. 4. A lead from a single card: card-playing coll (—1899); slightly ob. Ex WHITECHAPEL PLAY.

Whitechapel beau. One who, as Grose (1st ed.) so neatly phrases it, 'dresses with a needle and thread, and undresses with a knife': ca 1780–1840. cf. the entries at WESTMINSTER, and WHITECHAPEL ONER.

Whitechapel breed, n. and adj. (A person) 'fat, ragged, and saucy', Grose, 1st ed.: low: ca 1780–1850.

Whitechapel brougham; also **Westminster b.** A costermonger's donkey-barrow: low London (—1860); ob. Occ. *Chapel cart*. On S.E. *Whitechapel cart*.

Whitechapel fortune. 'A clean gown and a pair of pattens': low London: 1845 in 'Gypsy' Carew, 1891 (i.e. '*No. 747*'). A euphemization of WHITECHAPEL PORTION.

Whitechapel oner. 'A leader of light and youth in the Aldgate district – chiefly in the high coster interests'; East London (—1909). Ware. cf. WHITECHAPEL BEAU.

Whitechapel play, n. and adj. Irregular or unskilful play, orig. and gen. at cards: coll: 1755, *The Connoisseur*. 2. Hence, in billiards (whence, in any game), unsportsmanlike methods: mid-C.19–20.

Whitechapel portion. 'Two torn Smocks, and what Nature gave': low (mostly London): late C.17–mid-19. cf. ROCHESTER or TETBURY PORTION, and TIPPERARY or WHITECHAPEL FORTUNE.

Whitechapel province. 'A club or brotherhood under the government of a praetor', Grose, 3rd ed. London club life: late C.18–early 19. Punning Roman provincial government: in C.18 (e.g. in D'Urfey 1719), *praetor* was occ. used of a mayor.

Whitechapel shave. 'Whitening judiciously applied to the jaws with the palm of the hand', Dickens, 1863, in *The Uncommercial Traveller*; ob. cf. WHITECHAPEL BEAU.

whitechokery. The upper classes: lower classes': ca 1870–1900. Ex the white CHOKER.

Whitehall, he's been to. He looks very cheerful: military c.p. of ca 1860–1905. Ex extension of leave obtained at Whitehall.

whiter. A white waistcoat: Harrow School. (—1904). Ex *white* by 'Oxford *-er*'.

***whites.** Silver money: c. (—1887). Ex WHITE, n.

whitewash. 'A glass of sherry as a finale, after drinking port and claret', H., 3rd ed.: from ca 1860; ob. Ex colour – and use. cf.:

whitewasher. A glass of white wine (e.g. sherry) taken at the end of a dinner: 1881, J. Grant. Ex WHITEWASH, n.

whither-go-ye. A wife: ca 1670–1830. Ray, 1678, has *how doth your whither-go-you?*, i.e. your wife. Ex this question so frequently asked by wives.

whither or no, Tom Collins, 'is a phrase among sailors, signifying, whether you will or not' (W. N. Glascock, *Sailors and Saints*, 1829, at II, 7). A variant – perhaps rather the original – is *Tom Collins, whether or no*, occurring in Alfred Burton, *Johnny Newcome*, 1818.

whitt, see WHIT.

***whittle.** To give information, to PEACH (v., 3); to confess at the gallows: from 1720s: c. >, by 1850, low s.; ob. Swift, 1727. A variant of WHIDDLE.

whiz, whizz. 'Buz, or noise, interruption of tongues': (low) London: ca 1820–90.

whiz!, hold your. Be quiet!; SHUT UP!: low (—1887); ob. Ex sibilant *whis*pering.

who all, and I don't know. And other persons unnamed: coll: from ca 1840; rare. cf. WHAT ALL. The *who all* may be owing to the influence of some such phrase as *and I don't know who else at all* or ... *what others, at all*, or to a confusion of both these phrases.

who *are* yer (you)? – who are *you*? An offensive inquiry and its truculent answer: c.pp. of London streets: from 1883.

who did yer (you) say? A c.p. 'levelled at a person of evident, or self-asserting importance, and uttered by one friend to another': London streets': 1890s.

who pawned her sister's ship? A Clare Market (London) c.p. of ca 1897–9, directed offensively at a woman. Ware proposes *shift* corrupted.

who shot the dog? A c.p. directed ill-naturedly at volunteers: London streets': 1860s.

who took it out of you? A c.p. connoting a dejected or washed-out look in the addressee: low London (—1909).

who wouldn't ... see SEA?, WHO ...

whoa-Ball; incorrectly **whow-ball.** A milkmaid: late C.17–early 19. Prob. = *whoa!* + *Ball*, a common name for a cow, as Grose suggests. cf. WHOBALL'S CHILDREN.

whoa, bust me! A low London exclamation of ca 1850–1910.

whoa, carry me out! see CARRY ME OUT.

whoa, Emma! An urban lower classes' c.p. directed at a woman 'of marked appearance or behaviour in the streets': ca 1880–1900. Ware, who gives it an anecdotal origin. 'Quotations' Benham has the form *whoa, Emma! mind the paint*. 2. Whence, a non-aristocratic warning to a person of either sex, to be careful: from ca 1900; ob.

whoa, Jameson! A c.p. constituting 'an admiring warning against plucky rashness': non-aristocratic, non-cultured: 1896–7. Ex the Jameson Raid.

Whoball's children, he is none of John. 'You cannot easily make him a fool,' Terence in English, 1598: a semi-proverbial c.p. of C.17. See WHOA-BALL.

whole boiling, shoot, see the nn.

whole-footed. (Of persons) unreserved, free and easy: from 1730s: s. >, ca 1760, coll >, ca 1820, dial. North, ca 1734. Ex *whole-footed*, 'treading with the whole foot on the ground, not lightly or on tip-toe', O.E.D.

whole hog, go the, see GO THE WHOLE HOG.

whole pile, go the. To put all one's money on a solitary chance: gamesters', anglicized ca 1885 ex U.S.

wholeskin brigade. A military unit that has not yet been in action: Boer War military.

whooper-up. A noisy, inferior singer: music-halls' and theatrical (—1909); ob. Ware.

whop; whap, C.19–20; **whapp,** C.15. A bump, heavy blow, resounding impact: coll: C.15–20. H. G. Wells, 1905, '... Explained the cyclist ... "I came rather a whop".' cf.:

whop, v., C.18–20; **whap,** C.16, 19–20; occ. **wap, wop,** C.19–20. To strike heavily, thrash, belabour: coll: mid-C.16–20. Dickens, 1837, '"Ain't nobody to be whopped for takin' this here liberty, sir?" said Mr Weller.' Ex *whop* (spelt *whapp*), to cast violently, take or put suddenly. 2. Hence, to defeat (utterly); to surpass, excel greatly: coll: from the 1830s. Thackeray, 'Where [his boys] might whop the French boys and learn all the modern languages.'

whop-straw; Johnny Whop-Straw. A clod-hopper, a rustic: (low) coll ex dial.: C.19–20. Clare, 1821.

whopper; whapper; wopper; wapper. Something, some animal or person, unusually large in its kind: coll: from ca 1780. Grose, 1st ed. (*whapper*); Marryat, 1829 (*whopper*); Surtees, 1854 (*wopper*); Walker, 1901, '"Blime, she's a whopper!" says Billy.' Ex WHOP, V. 2. Hence, a THUMPING lie: (low) coll: 1791, Nairne. 3. A person who 'whops': (low) coll: late C.19–20.

whopping. A severe beating, thrashing, defeat: (low) coll: C.19–20. Ex WHOP, V.

whopping, adj., C.19–20; **whapping,** C.18–20; **wapping,** C.17–20; **wopping,** mid-C.19–

20. Unusually large or great: coll. 2. Rarely, 'terribly' false (tales, etc.), 'terribly fine' (persons): id.; same period. Ex WHOP, v. cf. WHOPPER.

whore is, in mid-C.19–20, considered a vulgarism; *harlot* is considered preferable, but in C.20, archaic. 2. Hence, a term of opprobrium even for a man: coll: late C.19–20. Gen. pronounced *hoor* or *hoo'-er*.

whore-pipe. The penis: low (—1791); †by 1890.

whore's bird than a canary bird, he sings more like a. He has a strong, manly voice: c.p.: late C.18–early 19. A *whore's bird* is a debauchee.

whore's curse. 'A piece of gold coin value five shillings and threepence, frequently given to women of the town by such as professed always to give gold, and who before the introduction of those pieces, always gave half a guinea', Grose, 1st ed.: (mostly London) coll: mid-C.18.

whore's get. An indivisible phrase used mostly as a pejorative term of address: nautical (—1885); ob. Ex GET, n., 2, on *whore's son*.

who's robbing this coach? Mind your own business!: Australian c.p.: since ca 1880. In humorous allusion to bushranging. Hence, 'Let me get on with the job!': a jocular Australian c.p., dating since ca 1890.

who's smoking cabbage leaves? A c.p. to a person smoking a cigar, esp. if rank: mostly Londoners': late C.19–20. cf. CABBAGE, 4.

whow-ball, see WHOA-BALL.

whoy-oi! A 'cry used by coster-class upon sight of a gaily dressed girl passing near them. Also the cry of welcome amongst London costermongers' Ware, 1909. Whence HOY!

whuff, n. and v. A or to roar or bellow (e.g. like, or like that of, a rhinoceros): coll (—1887).

Whyms. Members of the Y.M.C.A.: clubmen's: ca 1882–1905. By telescoping of these initials.

Wi(-)Wi; occ. **Wee(-)Wee, or Wewi**; etymologizingly, **Oui-Oui.** Also, the singular form is often used as a pl. A Frenchman: New Zealand and hence, to some extent, Australia: 1842, R. G. Jameson; 1859, A. S. Thomson, 'The Wewis, as the French are now called'; 1881, Anon., *Percy Pomo* (*Weewees*). Ex the Frenchman's fondness for *oui! oui!* (and *non! non!*): cf. DEE-DONK.

wibble. Bad liquor; any thin, weak beverage: (?mainly provincial) s. or coll (—1785); ob., except in the provinces.

wibble-wobble. Unsteadily: coll (—1847). Halliwell. A 'reduplication of *wobble* (with vowel-variation symbolizing alternation of movement: cf. *zigzag*)', O.E.D. 2. Whence as v., to move unsteadily; to totter, oscillate, vibrate: from ca 1870 and likewise coll. Whence:

wibblety-wobblety. Unsteady: coll and dial.: from mid-1870s. Ex preceding.

wibling's witch, or **W. W.** The four of clubs: C.18–19. Grose, 1st ed., 'From one James Wibling, who in the reign of King James I, grew rich by private gaming, and who was commonly observed to have that card, and never to lose a game but when he had it not'.

***wicher-cully,** etc., see WITCHER.

wicked. Very bad, HORRID, BEASTLY: coll: C.17–20. T. Taylor, 1639, 'It is too well known what a wicked number of followers he hath had'; Horace Walpole, 'They talk wicked French.' 2. Hence, expensive: not upper class: late C.19–20.

wickedly. Very badly; horridly: coll: C.18–20. Sterne. Ex preceding.

***wicket.** A casement: c., or perhaps merely catachrestic: mid-C.17–early 19.

wicket-keep. A wicket-keeper: coll verging on S.E.: 1867. Abbr. *wicket-keeper*.

widda, widder, widdy. A widow: dial. and low coll: C.19–20. 2. Hence, *the widdy*. The gallows: Scots: ?C.19. cf. WIDOW, 3: ?pun on *widdy*, a halter.

widdle, see WHIDDLE. **widdy**, see WIDDA.

wide. Immoral; lax: mid-C.16–20: S.E. until late C.19, then coll. 2. Alert, well-informed, shrewd: 1877, Horsley, *Jottings from Jail*. Abbr. WIDE-AWAKE. It verges on c.

wide, go. To spend money freely: military: ca 1860–1905. i.e. to spread oneself.

wide at or **of the bow-hand** (i.e. the left). Wide of the mark: coll: late C.16–mid-17. Shakespeare, Dekker, Webster. Ex archery.

wide-awake. Sharp-witted; alert: s. (1833) >, ca 1860, coll. Dickens.

***wido**, n. A hooligan: Glasgow c. and low s.: late C.19–20. Prob. ex the adj.:

wido, adj. Wide-awake, alert: low (—1859); virtually †. cf. WIDE, 2.

widow. As title to the name: mid-C.16–20: S.E. until C.19, then mainly dial. and uncultured coll. 2. 'Fire expiring's call'd a widow,' *The British Apollo*, 1710: C.18–20; ob. cf. S.E. *widow's fire*. 3. (Always *the* *widow.*) The gallows: ?C.18–mid-19. Ex Fr. *la veuve*. 4. An additional hand dealt in certain card-games: late C.19–20: s. 5. A single word in the top line of a page: printers': late C.19–20. Printers think it unsightly. 6. (*the widow, the W.*) Champagne: 1899, Guy Boothby, 'A good luncheon and a glass of the Widow to wash it down'. Ware, however, states that it dates from forty years earlier. Ex *Veuve Clicquot*.

widow, grass, see GRASS WIDOW.

widow bewitched. A woman separated from her husband: coll (1725) >, in mid-C. 19, mainly dial. Bailey; Mrs Gaskell. cf. GRASS WIDOW, 2.

widow's mite. A light: rhyming s.: late C. 19–20.

***wife.** A leg-shackle: (mostly prison) c.: from ca 1810. Ex clinging. 2. A pimp's favourite harlot-mistress: white-slavers' c.: late C.19–20. 3. The passive member of a homosexual partnership: homosexuals': late C.19–20.

wife, all the world and his. Everybody: jocular coll: C.18–20. Swift. cf. the Fr. *tout le monde et son père*.

wife as a dog of a side-pocket, as much need of a, see SIDE-POCKET.

wife cries five loaves a penny, one's. She is in travail: a semi-proverbial c.p. of ca 1670–1758. Ray, 1678. i.e. she cries out, pain-racked.

wife in water-colours. A mistress or concubine: ca 1780–1840. Easily fading colours: bonds quickly dissolved. 2. Hence, in C.19, a morganatic wife.

wife out of Westminster. A wife of dubious morality: London coll: C.18–20; very ob., Ware in 1909 remarking: 'Sometimes still heard in the East of London'. Ex the proverb cited at WESTMINSTER WEDDING.

wifey, wifie, rarely **wif(e)y.** Endearment for a wife: coll: from ca 1820. Properly, little wife, but gen. used regardless of size.

wiffle-woffles, the. A stomach-ache; sorrow; melancholy, the dumps: mainly proletarian (—1859); ob. cf. COLLY-WOBBLES (sense), WIBBLE-WOBBLE (form).

wifflow gadget. The same as HOOK-ME-DINGHY: nautical: late C.19–20. See also GADGET.

wig. A severe scolding or reprimand: 1804, Sir J. Malcolm: s. >, by 1890, coll; slightly ob. cf. WIGGING, much more gen. in C.20. Perhaps ex a BIG WIG's rebuke. 2. Abbr. BIG WIG, a dignitary: coll (rare after ca 1870): 1828 (O.E.D.). 3. A penny: Ayrshire s. (—1905), not dial. Perhaps because it was the usual price of a *wig*, a bun or a tea-cake.

wig, v. To scold; rebuke, reprimand, reprove severely: s. (1828, G. R. Gleig) >, ca 1860, coll. Ex the n., 1, or WIGGING. cf. Fr. *laver la tête*. 2. To move off, go away: North Country c. (—1864). Whence? 3. (v.i.) To post a scout on the route of flight in a pigeon race with a hen pigeon, to attract the opponent's bird and retard his progress: pigeon-fanciers': from ca 1860.

wig!, dash my; my wig! see WIGS.

wig-block. The head: pugilistic s.: from ca 1840.

wig-faker. A hairdresser: low London: late C.18–19.

wig-wag, v., n. and adv. To wag lightly; such wagging: coll: late C.16–20. Reduplicated *wag*.

wigannowns. A man wearing a large wig: ca 1785–1830.

wigga-wagga. A flexible walking-cane: ca 1895–1912. Ex WIGGLE-WAGGLE.

wigging. A scolding; a severe rebuke, reproof, reprimand: s. (1813) >, by 1850, coll. Barham, 'If you wish to 'scape wigging, a dumb wife's handy.' Ex WIG, n., 1.

Wiggins, Mr. 'Any mannerist of small brains and showy feather.' Bee: London (—1823); †by 1900.

wiggle, v. To waggle, wriggle: C.13–20: S.E. till C.19, then coll. 2. Hence, the n.: coll: late C.19–20. 3. The same applies to simple derivatives.

wiggle-waggle, adj. (1778); hence v. and n., both from ca 1820. Vacillating; to move (v.i. and t.) in a wiggling, waggling way: coll.

wig(s)!, dash my; wig(s)!, my. Mild imprecations: coll: resp. 1797 (1812); 1891 (1871). Morris, 1891, 'I am writing a short narrative poem. My wig! but it is garrulous.' Perhaps ex dashing one's wig down in anger.

wigsby. A man wearing a wig: jocular coll: (—1785). Grose, 1st ed., has also *Mr Wigsby*; *wigster* occurs ca 1820. All three were ob. by 1880. cf. *rudesby*, a rude person, and WIGANNOWNS.

***wild.** A village: tramps' c. (—1839). Brandon; H., 2nd ed. cf. S.E. *vill*, c. VILE. 2. *the Wild.* The extreme Evangelical party in the Church of Scotland: nickname: from late 1820s.

wild-cat. A rash projector, risky investor

(1812); a risky or unsound business-undertaking (1839): U.S. coll, anglicized ca 1880; slightly ob. 2. Hence, adj., risky, unsound (business or business enterprise); hence, reckless or rash: coll, orig. (1838) U.S., anglicized ca 1880. Ex the American wild-cat; it 'dates from U.S. period of "frenzied finance" (1836)', W.

wild-catter, -catting. A person engaging in, an instance or the practice of, WILD-CAT business: coll: U.S. (1883), anglicized ca 1900.

***wild dell.** A DELL begotten and born under a hedge: c.: ?C.17–early 19.

wild-dog, v.i. To hunt dingoes: Australian coll: late C.19–20. Often shortened to *dog*.

wild-fire. Some strong liquor; perhaps brandy: ca 1750–80. See quotation at SLUG, n., 1.

wild goose. A recruit for the Irish Brigade in French service: military: mid-C.17–18. M. O'Conor, *Military History of the Irish Nation*, 1845. Ex *wild-goose chase*.

wild mare, ride the, see RIDE THE WILD MARE.

***wild rogue.** A born or thorough-paced thief: c.: late C.17–early 19.

wild squirt. Diarrhoea: low coll (—1785); ob.

wild train. A train not on the time-table, hence 'not entitled to the track' as is a regular train: railwaymen's (—1904).

wilderness. A windlass: nautical (not very gen.): late C.19–20.

wilds, the. Esp. in *give* (someone) *the wilds*, to make angry, to depress: Australian: from ca 1860. 'Tom Collins', *Such Is Life*, 1903.

wilful murder. The card-game known as 'blind hookey': from ca 1860; ob.

Wilhelm II much. A bit too much of the Kaiser!: Society: 1898. Ex his many activities.

will you shoot? Will you pay for a small drink of spirits?: Australian taverns' (—1909); ob.

William, an acceptance, occurs esp. in *meet sweet William*, to meet a bill on its presentation: commercial (—1864). Punning *bill*.

Willie, Willie!, o(h). A c.p. of 'satiric reproach addressed to a taradiddler rather than a flat liar': non-aristocratic: 1898–ca 1914. Ware. cf.:

Willie, Willie – wicked, wicked! This c.p. of ca 1900–14 constitutes a 'satiric street reproach addressed to a middle-aged woman talking to a youth'. Ware derives it ex a droll law-suit.

willin', willing. (Of persons) 'strenuous, hearty,' C. J. Dennis: Australian coll verging on S.E.: late C.19–20.

willock-eater. (Gen. pl.) An Eastbourne fishing-boat: nautical: late C.19–20. A willock is a guillemot, a not very edible bird.

willow. 'Poor, and of no Reputation', B.E.: late C.17–early 19. Lit., willowy.

Willy Arnot. Good whisky: Shetland Islands s. (1897), not dial. Perhaps ex a well-known landlord.

willy-willy. A whirlwind: Australian: late C.19–20. Thus: *whirlwind* > *whirl* > *wil* > *willie* (or *-y*) > *willy-willy*. Often shortened to *willy*. cf.:

willywaws. Squalls in the Straits of Magellan; but also light, variable winds elsewhere: nautical: late C.19–20. Perhaps ex *whirly-whirly*.

wilt. To run away, to BUNK: London: from ca 1880: ob. Ex *wilt*, (of flowers) to fade, to grow limp.

wimmeny-pimmeny. Dainty, elegant: lower classes' coll (—1887); slightly ob. Echoic.

***win, wing, winn, whin(n),** but gen. the first or the third. A penny: c. (—1567): resp. C.17–20, late C.19–20 (mostly in Ireland and hence U.S.), C.17–20, C.19–20. Harman, Dekker, B.E., Grose, Vaux (*Winchester*; †by 1900), 'Jon Bee' (who defines as a half-penny), H., Flynt (*wing*). Perhaps abbr. *Winchester*. 2. (*win*, and for senses 3, 4.) A victory: (sports and games) coll: from ca 1860. 3. A gain; gen. pl, (mostly monetary) gains: coll: from ca 1890. Perhaps abbr. *winning(s)*.

***win,** v. To steal: c.: from late C.17. cf. (*to*) MAKE, and, in Fr. c., the exactly synonymous *gagner*. The n. *winnings* may, as = 'plunder, goods, or money acquired by theft' (Grose, 2nd ed.), be c.: C.18–20.

win the button. To be the best: tailors': from ca 1860. Here, *button* = medal.

***Winchester,** see WIN, n., 1.

wind. The stomach: boxing: 1823. Dickens, 1853. A blow thereon 'takes away the breath by checking the action of the diaphragm'. 2. A strong liquor, prob. rum or gin: ca 1715–50. Anon., *The Quaker's Opera*, 1728. See the quotation at BUNTER'S TEA. Because it catches the breath.

wind, by the. Short of money: nautical: late C.19–20.

wind, carry the. To be mettlesome, or

high-spirited: sporting (—1904); ob. F. & H., 'Properly of horses tossing the nose as high as the ears.'

wind, go down the, see WEATHER, GO UP THE. **wind, in the,** see IN THE WIND. **wind, lagged for one's,** see WINDER, NAP A. **wind, slip one's,** see SLIP ONE'S BREATH. **wind, thin as a rasher of,** see RASHER OF WIND. **wind, three sheets in the,** see THREE SHEETS . . . **wind and water, shoot between,** see SHOOT BETWEEN.

wind-bag. A wind-jammer: nautical: late C.19–20.

wind-bagger. A deep-sea sailor: nautical: since ca 1880. Bart Kennedy, *London in Shadow*, 1902.

wind do twirl (or hyphenated). A girl: rhyming s. (—1859).

wind enough to last a Dutchman a week. More wind than enough: (orig. nautical) coll: from the 1830s; ob. cf. DUTCH.

wind-jammer. A sailing vessel: U.S. s. (1899) anglicized almost imm.; *The Athenaeum*, 8 Feb. 1902. 2. A player on a wind instrument: theatrical: from the 1870s. Perhaps influenced by U.S. *wind-iammer*, a talkative person.

wind-mill. The fundament: low (—1811); ob. *Lex. Bal.*, 'She has no fortune but her mills,' a low c.p.: i.e. 'wind-mill' and WATER-MILL.

wind one's cotton. To cause trouble: proletarian (—1860); ob.

wind-pudding. Air: low: from 1890s. Whence *live on w.p.*, go hungry.

***wind-stopper.** A garrotter: c.: late C.19–20. cf. UGLY MAN.

wind-sucker. A horse with the harness: stablemen's: from ca 1865.

wind up, v. To render (a race-horse) fit to run: racing: from ca 1870.

wind up, adj. Pinned up; hence, taut: rhyming s.: from ca 1870.

wind up the clock. To coït with a woman: educated: from ca 1760; ob. Perhaps ex a mildly pornographic passage in *Tristram Shandy*.

wind'ard of, get to. To get the better of (a person): nautical, esp. naval, coll: late C. 19–20. i.e. windward. 2. Also, to get on the right side of someone: naval: since ca 1900.

***winded-settled.** Transported for life: c. (—1859); ob. Ex pugilism.

winder. A knock-out blow (lit. or fig.), something that astounds one, an effort that takes one's breath away: coll: 1825, Westmacott. cf. next entry. 2. A window: sol. and dial.: C.19–20 – and prob. centuries earlier.

***winder, nap a.** To be transported for life: c. of ca 1810–60. Vaux, who has also *be lagged for one's wind.* 2. To be hanged: c. (—1859). See WINDER. 3. In boxing, to receive a blow that deprives one of breath: mid-C.19–20. 4. Hence, to receive a shock: a severe set-back: low: from ca 1860.

***winding-post, nap the.** To be transported: c. of ca 1820–60. cf. preceding.

windjammer, see WIND-JAMMER. **windmill,** see WIND-MILL.

windmill J. P. An ill-educated J.P.: New South Wales: ca 1850–80. Because presumed to indicate his name with a cross: on maps, X = a wind-mill.

windmills in the head. Empty projects: coll: late C.17–19. Ex the windmill-tilting of Don Quixote.

window. A monocle: lower classes': from ca 1860; slightly ob.

window, goldsmith's. A rich working in which the gold shows freely: gold-mining s. (orig. and mainly Australian). Boldrewood, 1891.

window-blind. A sanitary towel: low (—1904).

window-dressing. Manipulation of figures and accounts to show fictitious or exaggerated value: commercial coll. Ex lit. sense.

***window-fishing.** Entry through a window into a house: c.: late C.19–20.

window-peeper. An assessor and/or collector of the window-tax: coll: ca 1780–1860. This tax was removed in 1851.

windsel. A nautical variant of *windsail:* coll (—1887).

windward passage, one who navigates or uses the. A sodomite: low (—1785); ob.

windy. Conceited, over-proud: C.17–20: S.E. until mid-C.19, then Scots coll.

windy wallets. 'A noisy prater, vain boaster, romancing yarnster', F. & H.: C.19–20; ob. Ex dial.

wine. To drink wine, orig. and mainly at an undergraduates' wine-party: coll: 1829, C. Wordsworth. 2. Hence, to treat (a person) to wine: coll: from early 1860s. 3. Whence *dine and wine*, the entertainments being separate or combined: coll: 1867.

wine-bag. A toper specializing in wine: (low) coll: late C.19–20. cf.:

winey. Drunk; properly, drunk with wine: low (—1859).

***wing.** A quid of tobacco: prison c.: 1882, J. Greenwood, *Gaol Birds*. 2. See

WIN, n., 1. 3. (Gen. pl.) An arm: nautical: ca 1820–1910.

wing, v.t. 'To undertake (a part) at short notice and study it in the "wings" ', F. & H.: 1885, *Stage*, 31 Aug.

wing, hit under the. Tipsy: 1844, Albert Smith; ob. Lit., disabled as a bird shot there. cf.:

wing'd. Tipsy: ca 1840–90.

wingers. Long, flowing whiskers: military: ca 1900.

wingy. A man 'minus' a *wing* (arm): navvies' s.: D. W. Barrett, *Navvies*, 1881.

Winifred!, O(h). A c.p. expressive of disbelief: lower and lower-middle classes': 1890s. Ware, 'From St Winifred's Well, in Wales' and its reputedly marvellous cures.

wink, n., see WINKS. **wink, tip the,** see TIP, v.

wink in one's eye, have a. To feel sleepy: Australian coll of ca 1850–1910.

wink the other eye. Flippantly to ignore a speech, warning, etc.: coll: late C.19–20.

winkers. The eyes: from early 1730s: S.E. until C.19, then coll; by mid-C.19, s. cf. the dial. *winkers*, eye-lashes. 2. (Also, occ., *flanges*.) Long, wavy or flowing whiskers: ca 1865–80. Ex a horse's blinkers.

winkin(g), like. Very quickly or suddenly: coll: 1827, Hood, 'Both my legs began to bend like winkin'.' Lit., in the time it takes one to wink. 2. Hence, vigorously; 'like one o'clock' (s.v. LIKE A ...): coll: 1861, Dickens, 'Nod away at him, if you please, like winking.' cf. *like* WINKY.

winkle, n. Penis: children's; (young) schoolboys': late C.19–20.

winks. Periwinkles: streets' (mostly London): mid-C.19–20.

winks, forty, see FORTY.

winky, like. A variant of *like* WINKING (above): 1830, Lytton; 1902, Begbie.

winn, see WIN, n., 1. **winnings,** see WIN, v. **wins**, see WIN, n., 2.

winter-campaign. Riot(ing); a drunken ROW: 1884–5. Ex dynamiters' winter activities.

winter-cricket. A tailor: ca 1785–1890.

winter-hedge. A clothes-horse: proletarian (—1904); ob. Ex drying clothes, which in summer would be spread on hedges.

***winter-palace.** A prison: c. (—1887); slightly ob. A shelter for necessitous criminals.

winter's day, short and dirty, – he is like a. A late C.18–mid-19 c.p. cf. the dial. *winter Friday*, a cold, wretched-looking person.

wipe. An act of drinking: coll: late C.16–early 17. Rowlands. cf. SWIPE, v. 2. A handkerchief: low: 1789, George Parker; Henry Kingsley. cf. earlier WIPER. 3. A blow, hit, punch: low: from ca 1875.

wipe, v. To strike; to attack, with blows or taunts: C.16–20: S.E. until C.19, then s. and dial. cf. SWIPE, v.

wipe (a person) **down.** To flatter; to pacify: low (—1860).

wipe (a person's) **eye.** In shooting, to kill a bird that another has missed: sporting: from ca 1820. cf. sporting sense of next entry. 2. Hence, to get the better of: from late 1850s. 3. A variant of WIPE THE OTHER EYE. 4. To give him a black eye: 1874, R. H. Belcher, 'Cheeky! it's Sunday, or else I'd wipe your eye for you.'

wipe (a person's) **nose.** To cheat, defraud, swindle: C.15–mid-18. 2. The same as WIPE *a person's* EYE, 1: sporting: from ca 1840. Surtees.

***wipe-drawer.** A C.19 variant of WIPER-DRAWER.

***wipe-hauling.** The filching of handkerchiefs from owners' pockets: c.: 1845 in '*No. 747*'; ob. Ex WIPE, n., 2.

wipe round. To hit on: Cockney: 1895, E. Pugh, *A Street in Suburbia*, 'Garn! I'll woipe yer rarned the marth, talk ter me...'

wipe the other eye. To take another drink: from ca 1860. H., 3rd ed., in form *wipe one's eye*, to take, or to give, another drink: a public-house, esp. an old toper's, term.

wipe up. To steal: military: from ca 1908.

wipe your chin! A c.p. addressed to a person suspected of lying: Australian: from ca 1905. (To prevent the 'bulsh', the nonsense, getting into the beer he is probably drinking.)

***wiper.** A handkerchief: 1626, Jonson. In C.19–20, WIPE (n., 2). 2. A weapon; ?an assailant: C.17–20; ob. Conan Doyle. 3. A severe blow or reply (or taunt): s. > coll: from mid-1840s; slightly ob. cf. S.E. *wipe*, a blow, a sarcasm.

***wiper-drawer.** A handkerchief-stealer: c.: late C.17–18. See WIPER, 1.

wire. A telegram: coll: 1876. Ex *by wire*, recorded in 1859. cf. the v. 2. An expert pickpocket: c.: 1845, in '*No. 747*'; 1851, Mayhew. Ex the wire used in removing handkerchiefs from pockets. cf. WIRER.

wire, v.i. and t. To telegraph: coll: 1859, *Edinburgh Review*, April, 'Striving to debase the language by introducing the verb "to wire".' cf. n., 1. 2. Hence, to telegraph to (a person, a firm): coll: 1876

(O.E.D.). 3. v.i. and t., to pick pockets (of persons): c.: 1845, in '*No. 747*'. Ex the n., 2. 4. See phrasal vv. ensuing.

wire, pull one's, see PULL ONE'S WIRE.

wire away (1888) is rare for WIRE IN.

***wire-draw.** 'A Fetch or Trick to wheedle in *Bubbles*': c.: late C.17–mid-18. B.E. Ex the corresponding v., which is S.E.

wire in (—1864), rarely **wire away.** To set-to with a will. H., 5th ed., 'In its original form, "wire-in, and get your name up", it was very popular among London professional athletes,' but, at the very beginning, it derives perhaps ex wiring off one's claim or one's future farm. Whence WIRE INTO. cf.:

wire in and get your name up! Have a shot at it!: 1862–ca 1914. Ware, 'Originally very erotic'.

wire into (a meal, etc.). To set about eagerly, vigorously: 1887, Baumann. Ex WIRE IN.

wire-worm. A man who collects prices to WIRE to country clients: Stock Exchange: from ca 1890.

***wirer.** A pickpocket using a wire (see WIRE, n., 2): c. (—1857); ob.

wires, on. Jumpy: nervous: coll: late C.19–20. Prompted by S.E. *highly strung*.

wise as Waltham's calf, see WALTHAM'S CALF.

wish I may die! An asseverative tag: Cockney: mid-C.19–20.

wisker, see WHISKER. **wisker-splitter,** see WHISKER-SPLITTER.

wisty(-)castor or **wistycastor** (or **-er**). A blow; a punch: pugilistic: ca 1815–40. *Boxiana*, III, 1821, 'This round was all fighting, and the *wisty-castors* flew about till both went down.'

***Wit,** see WHIT.

wit as three folks, he has as much. Orig. and often self-explanatorily *he has . . . folks, two fools and a madman*: c.p. of late C.18–mid-19. cf. the C.17–18 proverb *he hath some wit but a fool hath the guidance of it*.

***witch-cove.** A wizard: c.: C.18–19.

***witcher;** occ. **wicher.** Silver: c.: mid-C.17–early 19. Coles, 1676. Hence, *witcher-bubber*, a silver bowl; *w.-cully*, a silversmith; and *w.-tilter*, a silver-hilted sword. Perhaps a corruption of *silver* influenced by *white*.

with, see THROW. **with and without,** see WARM WITH: COLD WITHOUT.

without any. Without liquor (for a stated period): lower classes' coll: from ca 1890.

***Witt, the,** see WHIT. **Wiwi,** see WI-WI.

wizzer or **wizzy.** Urination: Scottish children's: late C.19–20. Echoic.

wobble like a drunken tailor with two left legs. (Of a ship) to steer an erratic course: nautical c.p.: late C.19–20.

wobble-shop. A shop where liquor is sold unlicensed: c. or low (—1857); ob. cf. WHISTLER, 3, and WHISTLING-SHOP.

wobbler or **wabbler.** (See FOOT-WOBBLER.) Rare in simple form: military (—1874). 2. 'A boiled leg of mutton, alluding to the noise made in dressing it', Bee: ca 1820–50. 3. A horse that, in trotting, swerves from side to side: racing (—1897). 4. A pedestrian; a long-distance walker: sporting (—1909). cf. sense 1. 5. An egg: low Cockney: from ca 1880. Clarence Rook, *The Hooligan Nights*, 1899.

wodge, wodgy, see WADGE.

woe betide you (him, etc.). You'll be getting into trouble: coll: mid-C.19–20. Ex †S.E. sense.

woffle. To eat; drink: low (—1823) † by 1890. Perhaps cognate with Northamptonshire dial. *waffle*, to masticate and swallow with difficulty. 2. v.i. and t., 'To mask, evade, manipulate a note or even [a] difficult passage'; music-halls' and musicians' (—1909). Ware. Ex *waffle*, to yelp: cf. WAFFLE, V., 1.

wog (or **W.**). An Indian: an Arab: late C.19–20. Probably ex *golliwog*.

wolf, see a. (Of a woman) to be seduced: coll: C.19–20; ob. Ex the fig. sense, to lose one's voice.

***wolf in the breast.** An imposition consisting of complaints, by beggar women, of a gnawing pain in the breast: c.: mid-C.18–early 19. cf. medical *lupus* and:

wolf in the stomach, have a. To be famished: coll: late C.18–20; ob. cf. STOMACH-WORM. Ex the old proverb, *a growing youth has a wolf in his belly*.

Wolfland. Ireland: coll nickname: late C.17–early 18.

wollop, see WALLOP.

wolly. (Gen. pl.) An olive: East Londoners' (—1909). Ex the street cry, *Oh! olives!*

woman. In tossing, the Britannia side of the penny: from ca 1780.

woman and her husband, a. A c.p. applied to 'a married couple, where the woman is bigger than her husband', Grose, 2nd ed.: late C.18–mid-19.

woman of all work. 'A female servant, who

refuses none of her master's commands', Grose, 2nd ed.: ca 1785–1840.

woman of the world. A married woman: coll: ca 1580–1640. Shakespeare, *As You Like It* and *All's Well.*

woman-who-did or **-diddery.** A popular novel with sexual interest: book-world, resp. coll and s.: very late C.19–20; virtually †. Ex Grant Allen's *The Woman Who Did*, 1895.

womble, womblety, see WAMBLE, WAMBLETY.

wonder!, I. I doubt it, can't believe it, think it may be so: coll: 1858, *Punch*, 'What next, I wonder!'

wonder!, I shouldn't. I should not be surprised (*if*, etc.): coll: 1836, Dickens, ' "Do you think you could manage . . .?" "Shouldn't wonder," responded boots.'

wonder!, the. Coll abbr. of *in the name of wonder*: 1862 (O.E.D.).

won't have it, I (or **he**, etc.). I don't believe it; or, I won't admit it: coll: mid-C. 19–20.

won't run to it! see RUN TO IT!, WON'T.

won't you come home, Bill Bailey? A c.p. of the first decade. C.20. Ex the popular song.

wood. Money: London drinking s. (—1823); †by 1890. Ex liquor from the wood. 2. *wood, the.* The pulpit: 1854. Thackeray. Implicit in:

wood, look over the. To preach: late C.18–mid-19. Sc. *of the pulpit.*

wood, look through the. To stand in the pillory: id.

wood-and-water Joey. A parasite hanging about hotels: Australian: ca 1880–1910.

wood merchant. A seller of lucifer matches: London streets': ca 1875–1912.

wood-spoiler. A ship's carpenter: naval (—1909).

woodcock. A tailor presenting a long bill: from ca 1780; ob. cf. SNIPE, 2.

Woodcock's Cross, go crossless home by. To repent and be hanged. Without *crossless*, the phrase app. = to repent. (cf. WEEPING CROSS.) Coll: C.17.

woodcock's head. A tobacco-pipe: coll: 1599, Jonson; †by 1700. Early pipes were often made in the likeness of a woodcock's head.

wooden casement; w. cravat. A pillory: jocular: ca 1670–1720. Contrast *hempen cravat*, the gallows, the noose.

wooden doublet, see WOODEN SURTOUT.

wooden fit. A swoon: proletarian: late C.19–20.

wooden gods. The pieces on a draughts-board: London: ca 1820–1910.

wooden habeas. A coffin: ca 1780–1850. Grose, 1st ed., 'A man who dies in prison, is said to go out with a *wooden habeas.*' cf. WOODEN SURTOUT, contrast WOODEN CASEMENT, and see esp. Grose, P.; cf. also dial. *get a wooden suit*, to be buried.

wooden hill. The stairs: lower-middle and upper working classes': mid-C.19–20. cf. BEDFORDSHIRE.

wooden horse. A gallows: mid-C.16–17: s. soon > coll. D'Urfey. Whence, prob.:

wooden-legged mare. The gallows: ?C.18–mid-19. cf. THREE-LEGGED MARE.

wooden overcoat. A coffin: a variant (mostly mid-C.19) of WOODEN SURTOUT.

***wooden ruff.** Same as WOODEN CASEMENT: c.: late C.17–early 19.

wooden spoon. The person last on the Mathematical Tripos list: Cambridge University coll: C.19–20. Ex the spoon formerly presented to him. *Gradus ad Cantabrigiam*, 1803. 2. The Parliamentary usage mentioned in H., 3rd ed., is derivative: he whose name appears the least frequently in the division-lists. From ca 1860; ob. 3. A fool: Society: ca 1850–90. Ex sense 1.

wooden surtout. A coffin: from ca 1780. H. 3rd ed., 'Generally spoken of as a wooden surtout with nails for buttons'; ob. cf. WOODEN DOUBLET, W. HABEAS, W. OVERCOAT, or *w. ulster*, the earliest being *w. doublet* (1761), likewise the first to disappear; the latest is *w. ulster* (Ware, 1909).

wooden wedge. 'The last name in the classical honours list at Cambridge', H., 2nd ed.: Cambridge University coll (—1860). See WEDGE, 2. cf. WOODEN SPOON.

woodman. A carpenter: coll and dial.: late C.19–20. cf. CHIPS.

***woodpecker.** 'A Bystander that bets', B.E.: c.: C.17–early 19. Dekker, 1608, shows that he is an accomplice betting to encourage novices or fools.

***wool.** Courage, pluck: c. (—1860) >, ca 1870, pugilistic s.; slightly ob. H., 2nd ed., 'You are not half-*wooled*, term of reproach from one thief to another.' Prob. ex jocular S.E. *wool*, hair: see WOOL-TOPPED UN.

wool, v.t. To pull a person's hair: U.S., anglicized in late 1860s. 2. To BEST (a person): low (—1890). Ex *pull* (*the*) *wool over the eyes of.*

wool, more squeak than. More noise than

substance; much talk with little result; semi-proverbial coll: from ca 1730. On *great* (or *much*) *cry and little wool* (proverbial S.E.). See CRY AND . . .

***wool-bird.** A sheep: orig. (—1785), c. >, early in C.19, low s. H., 2nd ed., 'wing of a *woolbird*, a shoulder of lamb'. Also *woolly-bird*, c.: ca 1810–50.

wool-grower. The head: pugilistic: ca 1840–90.

***wool-hole.** A workhouse: tramps' c. (—1859); ob. H., 1st ed.; also in 'printing' Savage, 1841, where, further, one learns that the term was orig. printers' s. ex a lit. and technical sense.

wool on!, keep your. Don't get angry!: 1890. cf. WOOLLY, adj. Ex *keep your hair on.*

wool on the back. Money, wealth: commercial: 1909.

wool-topped un. A plucky fellow: boxing: ca. 1870–1900. H., 5th ed., where *a reg'lar woolled un,* a very plucky fellow. See WOOL, n.

woolbird, see WOOL-BIRD. ***woolled, see** WOOL, n.

woolly. A blanket: coll: from early 1860s; ob.

woolly, adj. In a bad temper: from early 1860s; ob. Perhaps the 'originator' of *keep your wool on.*

woolly bear. Any large, hairy caterpillar, but esp. the larva of the tiger-moth: coll, mainly children's: 1863, Wood; much earlier in dial. as *woolly boy.* Ex resemblance to the children's plaything.

woolly bird, see WOOL-BIRD.

woolly crown. 'A soft-headed fellow,' Grose, 1st ed.: ca 1690–1850.

woolly-headed boy. A favourite: tailors': from ca 1860. cf. WHITE-HEADED BOY.

Woolwich and Greenwich. Spinach: (mostly greengrocers') rhyming s.: late C. 19–20.

wooney or **woony.** Mother; darling: nursery and young children's: (?) mid-C. 19–20. Prob. a two-year-old's attempt at *mother*.

wooston. Very, as in 'A wooston jolly fellow': Christ's Hospital: late C.19–20. Ex *whoreson.*

wop, wopper, see WHOP, WHOPPER.

word!, my. Indicative of surprise or admiration: coll: 1857, Locker.

word, the. 'The right word for the right thing': hence, the thing to be done: coll. Shakespeare, Congreve, W. S. Gilbert.

word-grubber. A verbal critic; one who uses 'jaw-breakers' in ordinary conversation: late C.18–mid-19. cf. WORD-PECKER.

word of mouth, drink by. 'i.e. out of the bowl or bottle instead of a glass', Grose, 2nd ed.: drinkers': late C.18–mid-19. Extant in dial.

word-pecker. A punster: ca 1690–1840. Punning *woodpecker*.

words. A wordy dispute or quarrel: coll: late C.19–20.

work. (Esp. of a vendor or beggar) to go through or about (a place) in the course, and for the purposes, of one's business or affairs: 1834, Colonel Hawker, of a hound; 1851, Mayhew, of an itinerant vendor; 1859, H. Kingsley, of a parson. 2. To obtain or achieve, to get rid of, illicitly, deviously, or cunningly: 1839, Brandon, *Dict. of Flash*. Esp. 'Can you work it?' 'I think I can work it for you.' 3. Hence (of an itinerant vendor) to hawk: 1851, Mayhew. 4. To steal: c.: mid-C.18–20. Ex sense 2.

***work-bench.** A bedstead: c.: ca 1820–50.

***work back.** To recover (stolen property): c.: mid-C.19–20. '*No. 747*'.

work cut out, have (all) one's. To have enough, or all one can manage, to do: coll: 1879, H. C. Powell. Ex *cut out work for* (a person), which may, orig., have been a tailoring phrase.

work for a dead horse, see DEAD HORSE.

work off. To kill; esp. to hang: 1840, Dickens: slightly ob. Lit., to dispose of. 2. As *work oneself off*, to masturbate: low coll: perhaps since C.16; certainly old.

work one's fists. To be skilful in boxing: pugilistic (—1874); ob.

***work the bulls.** To get rid of false crown-pieces: c.: ca 1839–1910.

work the oracle. To achieve (esp. if illicitly or deviously) one's end in a skilful or cunning manner: orig. (—1859), low s. See WORK, 2.

work the pea. 'To swindle one's employer by skilfully appropriating small sums off the takings at the bar of a public-house, alluding to a conjuror's trick': barmen's: from ca 1860. B. & L.

***work the rattle.** (Gen. as vbl n. or as ppl adj.) To operate, as a professional thief, on the trains: c.: from ca 1890.

work things. To achieve something, not necessarily though usually dishonest or, at best, dubious: coll: late C.19–20. cf. WORK, 2, and WORK THE ORACLE.

work up. (Of men) to effect carnal union

with: low coll: late C.19–20. Variant: *work oneself up*.

worker. A draught bullock: Australian coll: since ca 1870.

***workman.** A professional gambler: gamblers' c.: ca 1800–50. J. J. Stockwell, *The Greeks*, 1817.

***works, the.** A convict establishment: prisoners' c.: from ca 1870.

workus. A workhouse: sol.: C.19–20. Usually *the workus*, generic. 2. A Methodist chapel: Anglicans': ca 1840–1914.

world. Knowledge of the fine world: Society: ca 1790–1820. John Trusler, *Life*, 1793, 'That . . . is a proof of your want of world. – No man of *Ton* ever goes to the Theatre, for the amusements of that Theatre.' Ex S.E. *the world*, fashionable society.

world and his wife, all the, see WIFE, ALL THE WORLD AND HIS.

world to a China orange, (all) the. An occ. variant (—1887) of ALL LOMBARD STREET TO A CHINA ORANGE.

worm. 'The latest slang term for a policeman', H., 1864; extremely ob.

worm, v.i. and t., esp. in *worming*, 'removing the beard of an oyster or muscle [*sic*]', H., 1st ed.: mostly lower-class London (—1859). Ex crustacean – or oyster's beard – likened to a worm.

worm-crusher. A foot-soldier: military: from 1890s; ob. cf. MUD-CRUSHER.

worm-eater. A skilful workman drilling minute holes in bogus-antique furniture to simulate worm-holes: cabinet-makers': from the 1880s.

worms. A line cut in the turf as a goal-line at football: Winchester College: from ca 1880. Wrench. Ex the worms so discovered.

Worms, be gone to the Diet of, see DIET OF . . .

worms, have one for the. To take a drink of liquor: since ca 1880. Ex jocular pretext of medicinal use. Compare Spanish *matar el gusano* – to kill the worm – applied to the first drink of the day, particularly if spirituous.

worrab. A barrow: back s.: from the 1860s.

worries the dog, see DOG, HE WORRIES THE.

worriment. Worry: lower classes' coll: late C.19–20.

worrit; occ. **-et.** Anxiety, mental distress, or a cause of these: (low) coll: 1838, Dickens. Ex next. 2. A person worrying himself or others: id.: 1848, Dickens.

worrit, v.t. To worry, distress, pester: (low) coll: 1818, Lamb. A corruption of *worry*, perhaps on dial. *wherrit*, to tease. 2. Hence v.i., to worry, to display uneasiness or impatience: id.: 1854, Wilkie Collins.

worriting, n. (1857) and adj. (1845) of WORRIT, V.

worse end, see STAFF, THE WORSE END OF THE.

worth . . ., not, see BEAN; CURSE; DAM; FIG; TURD, etc.

worth a plum, be. To be rich: coll: ca 1710–1800. G. Parker. Ex PLUM, £100,000.

worth it. (Predicatively.) Worth while: coll: late C.19–20.

wotchere(o). A proletarian slurring (from ca 1880; ob.) of WHAT CHEER!

wounds (e.g. by Christ's wounds!) occurs in oaths of mid-C.14–mid-18, and as a self-contained interjection (abbr. *God's wounds!*) of C.17–early 19; occ. in C.19, *wouns!*

wow-wow. A children's variant of BOW-WOW, a dog: coll (—1887).

wow-wow!; bow-wow! A Slade School c.p. of the late 1890s, as in R. Blaker, *Here Lies a Most Beautiful Lady*, 1935, '"Wow – wow-wow–" she gurgled; for "bow-wow" or "wow-wow" was currency in her circle at that time, to denote quiet contempt of an adversary's bombast.'

wowser. A person very puritanical in morals; a spoil-sport; one who neither swears, drinks (in especial), nor smokes: from ca 1895: Australian s. Perhaps ex *wow*, a bark of disapproval, + euphonic *s* + agential *er*; cf. the Yorkshire *wowsy*, 'an exclamation, esp. of surprise'.

wrap-rascal. A red cloak: C.18–early 19. 1738, *London Evening Post*. An extension of S.E. *w.-r.* (a loose overcoat or a surtout), perhaps influenced by *roquelaire*.

wrapped-up, esp. in *all nicely wrapped up*, in seemly language, and *not even wrapped-up*, crudely expressed: coll: late C.19–20. Ex *talk* PACK-THREAD.

wrapper. An overcoat, a top coat: fast life: ca 1810–45. P. Egan, *Finish*, 1828. cf. WRAP-RASCAL.

wrapt up in the tail of his mother's smock, he was. A c.p. applied to 'any one remarkable for his success with the ladies', Grose, 1st ed.: ca 1780–1850. (Female fondling of male children increases their latent sexuality: it didn't need Freud to tell us this: this has been folk-lore for centuries.) Ex *be wrapped in his mother's smock*, to be born lucky.

wrapt up in warm flannel. 'Drunk with spirituous liquors,' Grose, 1st ed.: ca 1780–1830. ?cf. the 'drapery' terms for gin (see WHITE RIBBON).

wrecking. The ruining, by 'shady' solicitors, of limited companies: financial coll: 1880–4.

wren. A harlot frequenting Curragh Camp: military: 1869, J. Greenwood, who adds, 'They do not live in houses or even huts, but build for themselves "nests" in the bush.'

***wrest; wrester.** A picklock (the thieves' tool): c.: late C.16–early 17. Greene, 1592. Ex S.E. *wrest*, v.

wriggle navels. To coït: C.18–20; ob. Prob. later than and suggested by WRIGGLING-POLE.

wriggle off. To depart: Londoners': ca 1860–90.

wriggling-pole. The penis: (late C.17 or early) C.18–20; very ob. D'Urfey.

***Wright, Mr.** A warder 'going between' a prisoner and his friends: prison c.: C.19–20; ob. Punning *wright*, an artificer, and *right*, adj. cf. RIGHT, MR.

***wring oneself.** To change one's clothes: c.: from ca 1860; ob. Ex *wring* (*out*) *one's clothes*.

***wrinkle.** A lie, a fib: c. (—1812); ob. 2. A cunning or adroit trick, device, expedient; a smart DODGE: orig. and often *put* (a person) *up to a wrinkle* (*or two*), as in Lady Granville, 1817: s. >, by 1860, coll. cf. the C.15–17 *wrinkle*, a tortuous action, a cunning device, a trick; the link is perhaps supplied by sense 1, or by such a repartee as occurs in Swift's *Polite Conversation*, I, or, most prob., by WRINKLE MORE ... 3. Hence, a helpful or valuable hint or piece of information: sporting s. (1818) >, by 1870, coll.

***wrinkle,** v. To tell a lie: c. (—1812); ob. Prob. ex the n., 1.

wrinkle-bellied. (Gen. of a harlot) having had many children: low coll: late C.18–20. Grose, 3rd ed., 'Child-bearing leaves wrinkles.' cf.:

wrinkle more in one's arse, have one (or a). To get one piece of knowledge more than one had, 'every fresh piece of knowledge being supposed by the vulgar naturalists to add a wrinkle to that part', Grose, 2nd ed.: low: ca 1786–1880. Here, perhaps, is the origin of WRINKLE, n., 2 and 3, previously considered so problematic. cf. preceding entry.

***wrinkler.** A person prone to telling lies: c. (—1812); ob. Ex WRINKLE, V.

wrist-watch. Contemptible: naval: ca 1900–13. Considered effeminate. 2. High-class; aristocratic: military: ca 1905–20. e.g. 'He talks pukka wrist-watch'; 'Oh, he's pukka wrist-watch, he is!'

writ-pusher. A lawyer's clerk: legal (—1909). cf. PROCESS-PUSHER.

write a poor hand, see SORE FIST. **write home about,** see NOTHING TO ...

write one's name across another's face. To strike him in the face: sporting: ca 1885–1912. cf.:

write one's name on (a joint). 'To have the first cut at anything; leaving sensible traces of one's presence on it', H., 2nd ed.: from late 1850s.

written, not enough. Insufficiently revised for style: authors' coll: from ca 1870; ob.

wrokin. A Dutch woman: ?C.17–19. Perhaps Dutch *vrouw* corrupted.

wrong end of the stick, the, see STICK, THE WRONG END ...

wrong in the upper storey. Crazy: mid-C. 19–20. cf. *wrong in the head*, itself coll (and dial.): from ca 1880 – perhaps rather earlier.

wrong side, get up (occ. out of bed) on the or the. To rise peevish or bad-tempered: coll: C.19–20. To do this, lit., is supposed to be unfortunate. Scott, 1824.

wrong side of the hedge, be or fall on the. To fall from a coach: coll: ca 1800–80.

wrong side of the hedge when the brains were given away, (he) was on the. He is brainless, or stupid, or at the least very dull: c.p.: ca 1810–80. In late C.19–20, the form is *on the wrong side of the door when* (*the*) *brains were handed out*.

wrong un (or 'un). A 'pulled' (s.v. PULL A HORSE'S ...) horse: racing s. (1889, *Sporting Times*, 29 June). 2. Hence, a welsher (s.v. WELSH, v.) or a whore, a base coin or a spurious note, etc.: from ca 1890: s. 3. (Perhaps suggested by 1.) A horse that has raced at a meeting unrecognized by the Jockey Club: racing s. (—1895). 4. The wrong sort of ball to hit: cricketers' s. (1897).

wroth of reses. A wreath of roses: theatrical: ca 1882–1914. Ware, 'Said of a male singer who vocalises too sentimentally.' A Spoonerism.

***wroughter.** In the three-card trick, he who plays the cards, the trickster being a

BROAD-PITCHER: c.: from (?late) 1860s. B. Hemying, 1870, in his *Out of the Ring*, includes these terms in 'The Welshers' Vocabulary'. ? because *wrought*-on: cf. *wrought-up*, excited.

wrux. A rotter: a HUMBUG: Public Schools': from ca 1875. Perhaps ex dial. (*w*)*rox*, n. and v., (to) decay, rot.

***wry mouth and a pissen (C.19 pissed) pair of breeches, a.** A hanging: ca 1780–1850: either c. or low s. cf.:

***wry-neck day.** A day on which a hanging occurs or is scheduled to occur: c.: ca 1786–1860. Prob. suggested by preceding.

Ws, between the two. Between wind and water: ca 1830–70. *Sinks*, 1848.

wuffler. A guinea-piece; a sovereign: late C.19–20; ob.

wushup, your (etc.). Your worship: C.19–20: orig. and gen. sol., but it may also be jocular s. Also *your washup*.

wusser. A canal boat: bargees': from the 1880s. ?*water* perverted.

wylo! Be off: Anglo-Chinese (—1864).

***wyn,** see WIN, n., 1.

X

X or ×. 'The sign of cheatery, or *Cross* [q.v.]', Bee, 1823. cf. X DIVISION.

X or letter X, take (a person). To secure (a violent prisoner), thus: 'Two constables firmly grasp the collar with one hand, the captive's arm being drawn down and the hand forced backwards over the holding arms; in this position the prisoner's arm is more easily broken than extricated,' F. & H.: c. and police s.: from early 1860s.

***X division.** Thieves, swindlers; criminals in gen.: c. (—1887). Ex X.

X-legs. Knock knees: coll verging on S.E.: mid-C.19–20. Ex shape when knocking.

X.Y.Z. A hack of all work: literary: ca 1887–1905. Ex an advertiser in *The Times* using this pseudonym and offering to do any sort of literary work at unprofessionally low prices.

Xmas. Christmas: low coll when uttered as *Exmas*, coll when (from ca 1750) written; earlier *X(s)tmas* was not pronounced. The *X* = *Christ* (cf. scholarly abbr. *Xianity*), or rather the *Ch* thereof – Gr. χ (khi).

Xs; more gen. as pronounced – **exes.** Expenses: 1894, Louise J. Miln. Perhaps orig. theatrical, as the earliest quotation suggests.

Y

yabber. Talk (1874); to talk (1885), v.i. esp. if unintelligibly: Australian 'pidgin'. Ex Aboriginal.

yabbie. A fresh-water crayfish: Australian coll: late C.19–20. Ex Aboriginal.

***yack**; rarely **yac.** A watch: c.: app. late C.18–very early 19 (Vaux, 1812, declaring it †) and revived ca 1835, for we find it in Brandon, 1839, and Mayhew, 1851, 'At last he was bowled out in the very act of nailing [stealing] a yack.' Perhaps a perversion, by a modified back s., of *watch*: cf. the process in YADNAB. Sampson, however, more convincingly derives it ex Welsh Gypsy *yakengeri*, a clock, lit. 'a thing of the eyes' (*yak*, an eye). (See also at CHRISTEN (2) and CHURCH.)

yacka, -er, see YAKKER.

yackum. Human excrement: low: late C. 19–20.

yad. A day; *yads*, days: back s. (—1859).

yadnab. Brandy: slightly modified back s. (—1859). The impossible *yd-* has > *yad-*.

***yaffle,** v.i. To eat: from ca 1786: c. >, ca 1820, low s. (†by 1850) and dial. Esp. as vbl n., *yaffling*. Perhaps cognate with dial. *yaffle*, to yelp, to mumble. v.t., to snatch, take illicitly, pilfer: low: late C.19–20. Perhaps a perversion of SNAFFLE.

yah! A proletarian cry of defiance: coll: C.17–20. Possibly implied in Swift's *Yahoos*.

yah-for-yes folk. Germans and Dutchmen: nautical coll: late C.19–20. Ex Ger. *ja*, yes.

yakker; occ. **yacka, yacker, yakka.** (Correctly **yakka.**) To work; work at: Australian 'pidgin': late C.19–20. Ex Aboriginal.

yam. Food: nautical (—1890). Presumably ex:

yam, v.i. and t. To eat; orig., to eat heartily: low and nautical: from ca 1720. William Hickey (1749–1809), in his *Memoirs*, 'Saying in the true Creolian language and style, "No! me can no yam more"'. H., 3rd ed., 'This word is used by the lowest class all over the world.' It is a native West African word (Senegalese *nyami*, to eat): W., after that extraordinary scholar, James Platt. The radical exists also in Malayan.

yam-stock (or Y,-S.). An inhabitant of St Helena: nickname: 1833, Theodore Hook.

yan. To go: Australian 'pidgin' (—1870). Ex Aboriginal. cf. YAKKA.

Yank. YANKEE (n. and adj.): coll: 1778 in orig. U.S. sense, C.19–20 for '(an) American'; the adj. *Yank* (of the U.S.), app. not before the 1830s, as in Hurrell Froude. Abbr.:

Yankee; occ. **Yank(e)y.** Orig. (early 1780s) among the English, this nickname for any inhabitant of the United States (other and earlier senses being U.S.) was coll. The theories as to its etymology are numerous (see, e.g., O.E.D. and W.'s *Romance of Words*): the two most convincing – and the latter (blessed by both W. and the O.E.D.) seems the better – are that *Yankee* derives ex U.S. Indian *Yangees* for *English*, and that it derives ex *Jankee*, Dutch for 'little John' (*Jan*), this *Jankee* being a pejorative nickname for a New England man, esp. for a New England sailor.

Yankee heaven; Yankee paradise. Paris: coll: resp. ca 1850–80; from 1880. cf. (?ex) the saying, 'All good Americans go to Paris when they die.'

Yankee main tack, lay (a person) **along like a.** (Gen. as a threat.) To knock a man down: naval: late C.19–early 20. A *Yankee main tack* is a direct line.

Yankee particular. A glass of spirits: Australian: ca 1820–80.

yap. A countryman: low s. verging on c.: and mostly U.S.: from 1890s. Perhaps ex dial. *yap*, a half-wit.

yap, v. To pay: back s. (—1859). H., 1st ed., where it occurs in the form *yap-poo*, to pay up; in H., 5th ed., it is *yap-pu*. cf. YAPPY. 2. To prate, talk volubly: coll: late C.19–20. Ex *yap*, to speak snappishly. 3. To retort angrily: Newfoundland coll: late C.19–20.

yappy. Foolishly generous; foolish, soft: from ca 1870. Ex YAP, v., 1. Or it may rather derive ex Yorkshire *yap*, a foolish person.

yapster. A dog: low (—1798); ob. Tufts. cf. S.E. *yapper*.

yaram, see YARRUM.

yard-arm, clear one's. To prove oneself innocent; to shelve responsibility as a precaution against anticipated trouble: nautical: late C.19–20.

yard of clay. A long clay pipe, a CHURCHWARDEN: from ca 1840: coll >, by 1880, S.E. *Punch*, 1842.

yard of pump-water. A tall, thin person: low: late C.19–20. 2. See PURSER'S GRIN.

yard of satin. A glass of gin: 1828, W. T. Moncrieff; ob. See SATIN.

yard of tin. A horn: jocular coaching and sporting coll: mid-C.19–20; ob. Reginald Herbert, *When Diamonds Were Trumps*, 1908.

yard of tripe. A pipe: rhyming: 1851, Mayhew, I; ob.

yardnarb. Brandy: from ca 1880. The back s. *ydnarb* > *yardnarb* for the sake of euphony. See also YADNAB.

yark. To cane: Durham School: mid-C. 19–20. A dial. form of *yerk*.

yarker. Ear: Cockney: late (?mid-)C. 19–20. Atkinson. i.e. *harker*, that with which one hearkens.

Yarmouth bee, see YARMOUTH CAPON.

Yarmouth bloater (or **B.**). A native of Yarmouth: coll: 1850, Dickens. Ex lit. sense, Yarmouth being famous for its herrings. cf.:

Yarmouth capon. A herring: jocular s. > coll: from ca 1660; ob. J. G. Nall, *Great Yarmouth*, 1886, 'In England a herring is popularly known as a Yarmouth capon.' Also, ca 1780–1850, a NORFOLK CAPON. cf. also GLASGOW MAGISTRATE. Occ. *Yarmouth bee*: mid-C.19–20; ob.

Yarmouth mittens. Bruised hands: nautical: from ca 1860; ob. Ex hardships of herring-fishing.

yarn, orig. (—1812) and often in **spin a yarn** (nautical s. >, ca 1860, gen. coll), to tell a – gen. long – story, hence from early 1830s to 'romance'. A story, gen. long, and often connoting the marvellous, indeed the incredible: nautical s. >, ca 1860, gen. coll. Reade. Ex the long process of yarn-spinning in the making of ropes and the tales with which sailors often accompany that task. Occ. *a sailor's yarn*. 2. Hence, a mere tale: coll: 1897, Hall Caine, 'Without motive a story is not a novel, but only a yarn.' cf. the journalistic sense of *a good yarn*, a story that is not necessarily true – indeed, better not.

yarn, v. To tell a story: nautical s. (—1812) >, by 1860, gen. coll. 1884, Clark Russell, 'Yarning and smoking and taking sailors' pleasure'. Ex preceding. Hence *yarning*, n. and adj.: from 1840s, and prob. earlier. 2. A C.19 Cockney pronunciation of *earn*. (But *yearn* is more gen.)

yarn a hammock. To make it fast with a slippery hitch so that the occupant will fall to the deck: naval: late C.19–20.

yarn-chopper, -slinger. A prosy talker; a fictional journalist: from ca 1880; ob.

yarn-spinner, -spinning. A story-teller; story-telling: coll: ca 1865. Ex YARN, n.

yarning, n. and adj., see YARN, V.

yarraman. A horse: Australian (—1875). Ex Aborigine.

***yarrum** (C.17–20); **yaram,** rare C.17 spelling; **yarum,** frequent C.16–18 spelling. Milk; esp. POPLAR(S) *of yar(r)um*, milk-porridge: c.: from 1560s. One of the small group of c. words in *-um* (or *-am*) – cf. PAN(N)AM or -UM – *yarrum* is of problematic origin; but I suspect that it is a corruption of *yellow* (illiterately *yallow*) – N.B. the colour of beastings – with *-um* substituted for *-ow*: cf. Italian waiters' *chirroff* for *chill off* and, possibly, Welsh Gypsy *yåro*, an egg (Sampson).

yaw-sighted. Squinting: nautical coll: 1751, Smollett. Ex *yaw*, a deviation from one's direct course, esp. if from unskilful steering.

Yaw-Yaw. A Dutchman: nautical (—1883). Clark Russell. Lit., yes, yes! 2. (*yaw-yaw.*) See HAW-HAW, of which it is an occ. variant.

yawner. A very wide brook: hunting: since ca 1830. (Rolf Boldrewood, *My Run Home*, 1897, at p. 360.)

yawn(e)y. A dolt: rare (—1904); ob. i.e. the adj. made n., on SAWNEY. (Much earlier in dial.)

ye gods and little fishes! A lower and lower-middle class c.p. indicative of contempt: ca 1884–1912. It then > a gen. derisive or jocular exclamation. Ware, 'Mocking the theatrical appeal to the gods'.

Yea-and-Nay man. A Quaker: coll verging on S.E.: late C.17–early 19. Ex Quakers' preference for plain answers. 2. Hence, 'a simple fellow, who can only answer yes and no', Grose, 1st ed.: ca 1780–1850. Contrast dial. *yea-nay*, irresolute. 3. Hence, a very poor, 'dumb' conversationalist: mid-C.19–20; ob.

year'd, 'tis. A semi-proverbial coll applied to 'a desperate debt', Ray: ca 1670–1750.

-yearer. A pupil in his first, second, etc. year: Public School coll: late C.19–20.

yearn, see YARN, V., 2.

Yeddan; Yeddican. Variants (ca 1880–1910) of YID.

yeh. Yes: Cockney: since when? i.e. *yes*? clipped form. 2. You: Cockney: C.19–20.

yeknod, see YERKNOD.

yell. Beer: 1848. *Sinks*, 'A pint of yell'; †by 1900. Short for its *yellow* colour.

yell-play. 'A farcical piece . . . where the laughter is required to be unceasing': theatrical coll (—1909). Ware.

yelling. The rolling of a ship: nautical coll: C.19. Ex the resultant noise.

yellow. A variant of YELLOW-HAMMER, 2: from ca 1870; ob. 2. See YELLOWS. 3. A punishment at Greenwich College: ca 1820–60. *Sessions*, 1831, where also *be yellowed*, to undergo punishment there.

yellow, v. To make a YELLOW ADMIRAL of: nautical coll: 1747; ob. 2. Hence, to retire (an officer): nautical coll: 1820, Lady Granville.

yellow, adj. *A New Canting Dict.*, 1725, asserts that *yellow*, jealous, was orig. a c. term: this is prob. correct.

yellow, baby's. (Mainly infantine) excrement: nursery coll: C.19–20.

yellow admiral. An officer too long ashore to be employed again at sea: naval: C.18–20.

Yellow Belly, or y.b. A native of the fens, orig. and esp. the Fens in Lincolnshire; 'also known in Romney Marshes, Kent' (E.D.D.): from the 1790s. Grose, *Provincial Glossary*, 1790; id., *Vulgar Tongue*, 2nd ed., 1788. Ex the frogs, which are yellow-bellied, or perhaps, as Grose holds, 'an allusion to the eels caught there'. 2. A half-caste: nautical (—1867). Esp. a Eurasian: Anglo-Indian: from ca 1860. 3. A knife-grinder: Yorkshire s. (—1905), not dial. Perhaps ex the yellowish leather apron.

yellow boy. A guinea or, in C.19–20, a sovereign: from the Restoration: c. >, in C.18, s. Wilson, *The Cheats*, 1662; Grose; Dickens. Ex its colour: cf. Welsh Gypsy *melano*, yellow, hence a sovereign.

Yellow Cat, the. The Golden Lion, 'a noted brothel in the Strand, so named by the ladies who frequented it', Grose, 1st ed.: low: ca 1750–80.

yellow fancy. A yellow silk handkerchief, white-spotted: pugilistic: from the 1830s.

yellow fever. Gold-fever: Australian jocular coll: 1861, M'Combie, *Australian Sketches*. 2. Drunkenness: Greenwich Hospital (—1867); ob. Sailors there punished for drunkenness used to wear a parti-coloured coat, in which yellow predominated.

***yellow gloak.** A jealous man, esp. a jealous husband: c. of ca 1810–70. cf. YELLOW HOSE; see GLOAK.

yellow-hammer. A gold coin: ca 1625–50. Middleton, Shirley. (cf. YELLOW BOY.) Ex the colour of the bird and the metal. 2. A charity boy in yellow breeches: C.19–20; slightly ob.

yellow hose or **stockings, he wears.** He is jealous: coll: C.17–18. Dekker; Bailey.

yellow jack (or J.). Yellow fever: nautical: 1834, W. N. Glascock, *Naval Sketch-Book*. Ex the yellow jack or flag displayed at naval hospitals, and from vessels in quarantine to indicate a contagious disease.

yellow-jacket. A wasp: Canadian coll: mid-C.19–20.

yellow-man. A yellow silk handkerchief (cf. YELLOW FANCY): pugilistic and sporting: ca 1820–80. *Sporting Magazine*, 1821.

yellow mould. A sovereign: tailors': from ca 1860; slightly ob.

yellow plaster. Alabaster: provincial coll: from ca 1870. ?suggested by rhyme.

yellow silk, n. Milk: rhyming s.: late C.19–20.

yellow-stocking. A charity boy: London: C.19–20.

***yellow stuff.** Gold: c.: mid-C.19–20.

yellows (or Y.). Pupils at the Blue Coat School: London (—1887). Ex YELLOW-STOCKING.

yelper. A town-crier: low: from early 1720s. 2. A wild beast: low: from ca 1820. 3. A whining fellow: coll: ca 1830–90. *Sinks*, 1848. 4. The Red-Necked Avocet: Australian: late C.19–20. Ex its distinctive call or note.

yelper, get the. To be discharged from employment; proletarian: ca 1870–1910.

yen(n)ep. A penny: back s. (—1859). Whence, e.g. *yenep-a-time*, a penny a time (a term in betting); *yenep-flatch*, 1½*d*.

yen(n)ork. A crown (-piece): back s. (—1859); ob. Also YNORK.

yeoman of the mouth. An officer attached to His (Her) Majesty's pantry: jocular nickname: late C.17–early 19.

yep! Yes!: 1897, Kipling: low coll ex dial. and U.S.

yerknod; properly **yeknod;** loosely, **jirknod.** A donkey: back s. (—1859).

yes – but in the right place. A FAST girl's c.p. rejoinder to 'You're cracked' or 'You must be cracked': late C.19–20.

yes, she gave me, see OUT?, DOES YOUR MOTHER . . .

yes'm; yessir! An illiterate 'collision' of *yes, ma'am!* and *yes, sir!* C.19–20.

yeute. No; not: Punch and Judy showmen's: mid-C.19–20.

Yid; loosely **Yit** (ob.). A Jew; orig. (—1874) and properly, a Jew speaking *Yid*dish. Also *Yiddisher*, recorded by Barrère & Leland, 1890: coll. *Yiddish* + agential *-er*.

Yiddisher; Yit, see YID.

yiesk. (A) fish: Shelta: C.18–20.

yiu. A street: Punch and Judy showmen's: mid-C.19–20. ?ex Fr. *rue*.

ynork. Mostly in FLATCH *ynork*, a half-crown: back s.: 1851, Mayhew, I. cf. YEN(N)ORK.

yo, Tommy! 'Exclamation of condemnation by the small actor [i.e. in minor theatres]. Amongst the lower classes it is a declaration of admiration addressed to the softer sex by the sterner,' Ware, 1909. Perhaps this *Tommy* is related to that in *hell and* TOMMY.

yob. A boy: back s. (—1859). 2. Hence, a youth: from ca 1890. 'Pomes' Marshall, ca 1897, 'And you bet that each gal, not to mention each yob, | Didn't care how much ooftish it cost 'em per nob.'

yob-gab. Boys' talk or 'ziph' (see p. 12): costers' s., and c.: mid-C.19–20.

yock. A fool; a simpleton: grafters' s., and c.: mid-C.19–20. 2. A man: Shelta: C.18–20.

yokuff. A large box, a chest: c. (—1812) >, ca 1850, low. Prob. a perversion of *coffer*.

yolly. A post-chaise: ca 1840–1900 at Winchester College. Ex *yellow*, a colour frequent in these vehicles: cf. †*yollow*, yellow.

yonker, see YOUNKER.

yonnie. A pebble, small stone: Australian: late C.19–20. Aboriginal?

york. 'A look, or observation', Vaux: c. or low: ca 1810–80. Ex:

***york,** v. To stare impertinently at: c. (—1812); †by 1880. Perhaps ex YORKSHIRE BITE, 1. 2. v.i. and t., to look (at), to examine: low: ca 1810–50.

***York Street is concerned; there is Y.S. concerned.** Someone is looking (hard): c. or low: ca 1810–60. cf. YORK, n. and v.

Yorkshire. Orig. implied boorishness, but the connotation of cunning, (business) sharpness, or trickery appears as early as 1650. Variations of the latter senses occur in certain of the ensuing phrases, all of which have, from coll, >, by late C.19, S.E. (See also NORTH, 1.)

Yorkshire, n. Sharp practice; cajolery: mid-C.19–20: coll (> S.E.) and dial. 2. Yorkshire pudding: coll: late C.19–20. Esp. in 'roast and Yorkshire'.

Yorkshire, v.t. To cheat, to take a person in, to prove too wide-awake for him: from ca 1870. Ex *come* (or *put*) *Yorkshire on* (or *over*) a person. F. & H.

Yorkshire bite. A very 'cute piece of overreaching: 1795. 2. Hence, a particularly sharp and/or overreaching person: 1801. See BITE, n., 6 and YORKSHIRE.

Yorkshire carrier, confident as a. Cocksure: C.18–20; ob. Ward, 1706. See YORKSHIRE.

Yorkshire compliment. 'A gift useless to the giver and not wanted by the receiver', F. & H.: mid-C.19–20; ob. See YORKSHIRE. Also, mainly dial., a NORTH-COUNTRY COMPLIMENT.

Yorkshire estate. Money in prospect, a 'castle in Spain'; esp. in *when I come into my Yorkshire estates*, when I have the means: mid-C.19–20; ob. See YORKSHIRE and cf. last entry.

Yorkshire hog. A fat wether: 1772, Bridges, 'A pastry-cook | That made good pigeon-pie of rook, | Cut venison from Yorkshire hogs | And made rare mutton-pies of dogs'; Grose, 1st ed.; extremely ob. cf. COTSWOLD LION and see YORKSHIRE.

Yorkshire on (upon), put, C.18–20; **come Yorkshire on** (C.19–20), more gen. **c. Y. over,** app. first recorded in Grose, 1785. To cheat, dupe, overreach, be too wide-awake for (a person). The antidote is to *be Yorkshire too*, which phrase, however, is rare outside of dial., though Wolcot has it in 1796. See YORKSHIRE and cf. YORKSHIRE, V.

Yorkshire reckoning. A reckoning, an entertainment, in which each person pays his share: mid-C.19–20. cf. dial. *go Yorkshire*, to do this. See YORKSHIRE.

Yorkshire tike or, gen., **tyke.** A Yorkshireman: coll nickname: mid-C.17–20. Howell, 1659. *Northern tike* (rare) occurs in Deloney ca 1600. See TIKE for improving status of this term.

Yorkshire too, be; Yorkshire upon . . ., see YORKSHIRE ON . . .

Yorkshire way-bit. A distance greater than a mile: coll: ca 1630–1830. Cleveland, 1640. In the earliest record, *Y. wea-bit*.

Yorky. A Yorkshireman (or -woman): coll: C.19–20. *Boxiana* II, 1818.

you and me. A flea, also tea: rhyming s.: from ca 1880.

you are another!; you're another! You also are a liar, thief, rogue, fool, or what you will: a c.p. retort (coll, not s.): C.16 (?earlier)–20. Udall; Fielding; Dickens, '"Sir," said Mr Tupman, "you're a fellow." "Sir," said Mr Pickwick, "you're another"'; Sir W. Harcourt, 1888, 'Little urchins in the street have a conclusive argument. They say "You're another".' A variant, late C.19–20 (?ob.), is *so's your father!* In mid-C.19–20, the orig. phrase is almost meaningless, though slightly contemptuous.

you bet, see BET!, YOU.

you can't think. You cannot imagine it; to an incredible degree: non-aristocratic, non-cultured c.p.: from ca 1890. W. Pett Ridge, *Minor Dialogues*, 1895, 'She took up such a 'igh and mighty attitude, you can't think.' This *you can't think*, coming at the end of a phrase or sentence, derives naturally ex that *you can't think!* (s.v. THINK!, ONLY) which precedes a sentence.

you don't look at the mantel-piece when (or while) you're poking the fire. A c.p. (verging on the proverbial) in reference to sexual intercourse: late C.19–20.

you fasten on! Go on!; proceed: non-aristocratic: from ca 1870; ob.

you know. This stop-gap, almost meaningless phrase ranks as coll and dates from at least as early as C.18.

you know what (? or !) An introductory c.p., a mere announcer of a phrase or of a statement: mid-C.19–20; perhaps going back to late C.17.

you know what thought did! see THOUGHT DID!

you'll be a long time dead! see DEAD, YOU'LL BE A LONG TIME.

you'll get yourself disliked. A satirical, proletarian c.p. addressed to anyone behaving objectionably: from ca 1878; now virtually S.E.

you'll wake up one of these mornings and find yourself dead. An Anglo-Irish c.p. of late C.19–20.

you make me tired! You bore me to tears: a c.p. introduced from U.S.A. in 1898 by the Duchess of Marlborough, 'a then leader of fashion' (Ware).

you may have broke your mother's heart – (but) you (bloody well) won't break mine! A military c.p., orig. and mostly drill-sergeants': from ca 1870, or earlier (?during the Napoleonic wars). cf. YOU SHAPE...

you must. A crust: rhyming s.: late C.19–20.

you never did. You never did hear the like of it; you've never heard anything so funny: Cockney coll: from ca 1870. A. Neil Lyons, *Matilda's Mabel*, 1903, 'My dearest Tilda. Such a go you never did! Mr Appleby proposed to me this afternoon!'

you never know! You never know what may come of it: c.p.: late C.19–20.

you pays your money and you takes your choice! You may choose what you like: c.p.: late C.19–20. Ex showmen's patter.

you shape like a whore at a christening! A lower classes' and military (esp. drill-sergeants') c.p. to a clumsy person: from the 1890s, if not indeed considerably earlier.

you should pay for them. A jocular c.p. addressed to one wearing squeaky boots or shoes: late C.19–20.

you talk like a halfpenny book. You talk foolishly: a Liverpool c.p.: late C.19–20.

you (or you'd) want to know all the ins-and-outs of a nag's arse! You're very inquisitive: Cockney: late C.19–20.

you'd only spend it. A c.p. reply to someone saying that he'd like to have a lot of money: late C.19–20.

you'd soon find it if there was hair round – or all around – it! A drill sergeants' c.p. to very new recruits learning their rifle drill and forbidden to look what they're doing: C.20, or prob. since ca 1870.

youlie, see YOWLIE.

you uns. You: low: late C.19–20. Ex U.S. cf. rarer WE UNS.

young. (Of inanimates) small, diminutive, not full-sized: mid-C.16–20: S.E. until, after virtually lapsing in C.17–early 19, it >, ca 1850, coll and jocular, as in Hornaday's 'Such a weapon is really a young cannon,' 1885.

young bear. A young midshipman very recently come to his first ship: Naval: ca 1810–60. *The Night Watch* (II, 71), 1828; *Dublin University Magazine*, Sept. 1834, p. 243.

young fellow (or feller) me lad. A semi-jocular term of address: coll: mid-C.19–20.

young gentleman, or man, lady or woman are coll when addressed in reproof or warning to persons of almost any age: from ca 1860. The first is also ironic coll for or to a midshipman from ca 1810.

young hopeful, see HOPEFUL.

young lady. A fiancée: low coll when not jocular: 1896, George Bernard Shaw. cf. YOUNG MAN and YOUNG WOMAN. 2. See YOUNG GENTLEMAN.

young man. A sweetheart or lover; a fiancé: coll (in C.19, always low; in C.20, often jocular): 1851, Mayhew, 'Treated to an ice by her young man – they seemed as if they were keeping company.' cf. YOUNG WOMAN. 2. See YOUNG GENTLEMAN.

young one or un (or 'un). A child; a youth (rarely a girl): low coll: C.19–20; *Lex. Bal.*, 1811, 'A familiar expression of contempt for another's ignorance, as "ah! I see you're a young one" '; this nuance is ob. As a young person, *young one* (or *'un*) may not precede the 1830s; the O.E.D. cites Egan at 1838. Opp. an *old un*, an old man, a father. 2. A truss of hay (as opposed to a rick): farmers': from ca 1830.

young shaver, see SHAVER.

Young Soldier, see SOLDIER, n., 5.

young thing. A youth 17–21 years old: masculine women's coll (—1909).

young 'un, see YOUNG ONE.

young woman. A sweetheart; a fiancée: coll: 1858 (O.E.D.). On YOUNG MAN. 2. See YOUNG GENTLEMAN.

youngster. A child, esp. a boy; a young person (gen. male) not of age: coll: 1732, Berkeley. By natural extension of orig. sense.

younker, earlier **yonker**, may always be S.E., though H., 2nd ed., '*younker*, in street language, a lad or a boy', causes one to doubt it.

your humble condumble. Your humble servant; I (myself): C.18. Scott, in letter of 30 Dec. 1808, 'Every assistance, that can be afforded by your humble condumble, as Swift says.' By rhyming reduplication. Recorded as early as Swift's *Polite Conversation*, 1738.

***your nabs; your nibs; *your watch**, see NABS; NIBS; WATCH, n.

your nose is bleeding. Your trouser-fly is undone: c.p.: from ca 1885; slightly ob.

you're a big lad for your age. A jocular c.p., addressed to an apprentice or other youthful worker: esp. in factories: late C. 19–20.

you're another! see YOU ARE ANOTHER!

you're off the grass! You haven't a chance: cricketers': ca 1900–14. i.e. outside the field.

you're so sharp you'll be cutting yourself! A late C.19–20 c.p., addressed to a 'smart' person.

yourn, see OURN.

yours and ours. Flowers: rhyming s.: late C.19–20.

yours to a cinder. A non-aristocratic c.p. ending to a letter: late C.19–20. Prob. orig. in the (coal-)mining centres.

yours truly, see TRULY, YOURS.

you've fixed it up nicely for me! No, you don't!; do you think I'm green?!: proletarian c.p.: ca 1880–1910.

you've got eyes in your head, haven't you? A disparaging c.p.: late C.19–20.

yowlie or -y. A member of the watch; a policeman: Edinburgh s.: C.19–20; ob. Jamieson, 'A low term' that prob. derives ex 'their youling or calling the hours'. Occ. *youlie.*

***yoxter.** 'A convict returned from transportation before his time', H., 3rd ed.: c. of ca 1860–90. Origin?

y'see. You see: coll (—1887).

yum. Yes: slovenly coll: mid-C.19–20.

yum-yum. Excellent; first rate: orig. (—1904) and mostly low. Ex *yum-yum!*, an exclamation of animal satisfaction (with, e.g., exquisite or delicious food). cf. YAM.

yus(s). Yes: Cockney: C.19–20.

Z

'Z. The *'S* of oaths: see 'S. cf. ZOOKS and 'ZOUNDS!

zack. Sixpence: New Zealand and Australian: since ca 1890. Perhaps a perversion of *six*; but cf. Dutch *zaakje*, 'small affair'.

zactly. Exactly: low coll (—1887).

zad; mere zad. A bandy-legged and/or crooked-backed person: ca 1720–1840. *A New Canting Dict.*, 1725. cf. *crooked as the letter* ZED. 2. Occ. of a thing: same period.

zanth. A chry*santh*emum: market-gardeners' coll: late C.19–20.

zarnder. The same as a TUBBICHON: London lower classes': ca 1863–70. Owing to its adoption by Princess (later Queen) Al*exandra*.

zarp; gen. **Zarp**. A policeman: the Transvaal: 1897, *Cape Argus*, weekly ed., 8 Dec.; ob. An anagram ex *Zuid Afrikaansche Republick Politie*, the South African Republic Police. Pettman.

zat? How's that?: cricketers' coll: late C.19–20.

'Zbloud; 'Zdeath, see 'SBLOOD, 'SDEATH.

zeb. Best: back s. (—1859). Modified *tseb*.

zed, crooked as the letter. Very crooked: coll (—1785) > ca 1840, dial. See also ZAD.

zed (gen. zedding) about. To zigzag, to diverge: Society: ca 1883–1900. Perhaps punning *gad(d)ing about*.

Zedland. The South-Western counties of England: s. or perhaps coll: from 1780s; very ob. There, dialectally, *s* is pronounced as *z*.

***ziff.** A young thief: c. (—1864). ?*thief* perverted.

zigzig, n. and v. Copulation; to copulate: Services': late C.19–20. A word known and used throughout the Near and Middle East, and in the Mediterranean. Ultimately, probably echoic. cf. JIG-A-JIG.

zip, n. An echoic word indicative of the noise made by (say) a bullet or a mosquito in its passage through the air: coll: 1875, Fogg.

zip, v.i. To make a *zip* sound: coll: from ca 1880.

Zlead(s), Zlid; 'Zlife. Minced oaths: coll: C.17–18. i.e. *God's lids, life.*

znees; zneesy. Frost; frosty or frozen: ca 1780–1840, but perhaps covering a period as great as C.18–mid-19. Perhaps as S.W. England coll; app. it is not dial. Perhaps ex *sneeze, sneezy*, which are, however, unrecorded in these senses. cf.:

znuz, a variant of ZNEES.

zoo. *Zoo*logical gardens (London, or elsewhere). Macauley, ca 1847, 'We treated the Clifton Zoo much too contemptuously.' The *zoo* has been telescoped to one syllable.

zooks. Sweets: schoolchildren's, esp. in West Country: late C.19–20. Ex dial. form of SUCKS = *suckers*, sweets.

Zooks!; Zookers!; Zoodikers! (rare); **'Zoonters!** Oaths and asseverations: coll: C.17–mid-19. See ODS.

zouch. A churl; an unmannerly fellow: C.18. *Street Robberies Consider'd*, 1728. Perhaps ex *ouch*, the exclamation.

zouch, see SYCHER.

'Zounds! An oath or asseveration: late C.16–20: coll until C.19, then archaic S.E. except when dial. Euphemistic abbr. *by God's wounds*. cf. ZOOKS!